Oxford Dictionary of
National Biography

Volume 3

Oxford Dictionary of National Biography

IN ASSOCIATION WITH

The British Academy

From the earliest times to the year 2000

Edited by

H. C. G. Matthew

and

Brian Harrison

Volume 3

Avranches–Barnewall

OXFORD
UNIVERSITY PRESS

OXFORD
UNIVERSITY PRESS

Great Clarendon Street, Oxford OX2 6DP

Oxford University Press is a department of the University of Oxford.
It furthers the University's objective of excellence in research, scholarship,
and education by publishing worldwide in

Oxford New York

Auckland Bangkok Buenos Aires Cape Town
Chennai Dar es Salaam Delhi Hong Kong Istanbul Karachi
Kolkata Kuala Lumpur Madrid Melbourne Mexico City Mumbai Nairobi
São Paulo Shanghai Taipei Tokyo Toronto

Oxford is a registered trade mark of Oxford University Press
in the UK and in certain other countries

Published in the United States
by Oxford University Press Inc., New York

First published 2004

British Library Cataloguing in Publication Data
Data available

Library of Congress Cataloging in Publication Data
Data available: for details see volume 1, p. iv

ISBN 0-19-861353-9 (this volume)
ISBN 0-19-861411-X (set of sixty volumes)

Text captured by Alliance Phototypesetters, Pondicherry
Illustrations reproduced and archived by
Alliance Graphics Ltd, UK
Typeset in OUP Swift by Interactive Sciences Limited, Gloucester
Printed in Great Britain on acid-free paper by
Butler and Tanner Ltd,
Frome, Somerset

LIST OF ABBREVIATIONS

1 *General abbreviations*

AB	bachelor of arts
ABC	Australian Broadcasting Corporation
ABC TV	ABC Television
act.	active
A$	Australian dollar
AD	*anno domini*
AFC	Air Force Cross
AIDS	acquired immune deficiency syndrome
AK	Alaska
AL	Alabama
A level	advanced level [examination]
ALS	associate of the Linnean Society
AM	master of arts
AMICE	associate member of the Institution of Civil Engineers
ANZAC	Australian and New Zealand Army Corps
appx *pl.* appxs	appendix(es)
AR	Arkansas
ARA	associate of the Royal Academy
ARCA	associate of the Royal College of Art
ARCM	associate of the Royal College of Music
ARCO	associate of the Royal College of Organists
ARIBA	associate of the Royal Institute of British Architects
ARP	air-raid precautions
ARRC	associate of the Royal Red Cross
ARSA	associate of the Royal Scottish Academy
art.	article / item
ASC	Army Service Corps
Asch	Austrian Schilling
ASDIC	Antisubmarine Detection Investigation Committee
ATS	Auxiliary Territorial Service
ATV	Associated Television
Aug	August
AZ	Arizona
b.	born
BA	bachelor of arts
BA (Admin.)	bachelor of arts (administration)
BAFTA	British Academy of Film and Television Arts
BAO	bachelor of arts in obstetrics
bap.	baptized
BBC	British Broadcasting Corporation / Company
BC	before Christ
BCE	before the common (*or* Christian) era
BCE	bachelor of civil engineering
BCG	bacillus of Calmette and Guérin [inoculation against tuberculosis]
BCh	bachelor of surgery
BChir	bachelor of surgery
BCL	bachelor of civil law
BCnL	bachelor of canon law
BCom	bachelor of commerce
BD	bachelor of divinity
BEd	bachelor of education
BEng	bachelor of engineering
bk *pl.* bks	book(s)
BL	bachelor of law / letters / literature
BLitt	bachelor of letters
BM	bachelor of medicine
BMus	bachelor of music
BP	before present
BP	British Petroleum
Bros.	Brothers
BS	(1) bachelor of science; (2) bachelor of surgery; (3) British standard
BSc	bachelor of science
BSc (Econ.)	bachelor of science (economics)
BSc (Eng.)	bachelor of science (engineering)
bt	baronet
BTh	bachelor of theology
bur.	buried
C.	command [identifier for published parliamentary papers]
c.	*circa*
c.	*capitulum pl. capitula*: chapter(s)
CA	California
Cantab.	Cantabrigiensis
cap.	*capitulum pl. capitula*: chapter(s)
CB	companion of the Bath
CBE	commander of the Order of the British Empire
CBS	Columbia Broadcasting System
cc	cubic centimetres
C$	Canadian dollar
CD	compact disc
Cd	command [identifier for published parliamentary papers]
CE	Common (*or* Christian) Era
cent.	century
cf.	compare
CH	Companion of Honour
chap.	chapter
ChB	bachelor of surgery
CI	Imperial Order of the Crown of India
CIA	Central Intelligence Agency
CID	Criminal Investigation Department
CIE	companion of the Order of the Indian Empire
Cie	Compagnie
CLit	companion of literature
CM	master of surgery
cm	centimetre(s)

Cmd	command [identifier for published parliamentary papers]
CMG	companion of the Order of St Michael and St George
Cmnd	command [identifier for published parliamentary papers]
CO	Colorado
Co.	company
co.	county
col. *pl.* cols.	column(s)
Corp.	corporation
CSE	certificate of secondary education
CSI	companion of the Order of the Star of India
CT	Connecticut
CVO	commander of the Royal Victorian Order
cwt	hundredweight
$	(American) dollar
d.	(1) penny (pence); (2) died
DBE	dame commander of the Order of the British Empire
DCH	diploma in child health
DCh	doctor of surgery
DCL	doctor of civil law
DCnL	doctor of canon law
DCVO	dame commander of the Royal Victorian Order
DD	doctor of divinity
DE	Delaware
Dec	December
dem.	demolished
DEng	doctor of engineering
des.	destroyed
DFC	Distinguished Flying Cross
DipEd	diploma in education
DipPsych	diploma in psychiatry
diss.	dissertation
DL	deputy lieutenant
DLitt	doctor of letters
DLittCelt	doctor of Celtic letters
DM	(1) Deutschmark; (2) doctor of medicine; (3) doctor of musical arts
DMus	doctor of music
DNA	dioxyribonucleic acid
doc.	document
DOL	doctor of oriental learning
DPH	diploma in public health
DPhil	doctor of philosophy
DPM	diploma in psychological medicine
DSC	Distinguished Service Cross
DSc	doctor of science
DSc (Econ.)	doctor of science (economics)
DSc (Eng.)	doctor of science (engineering)
DSM	Distinguished Service Medal
DSO	companion of the Distinguished Service Order
DSocSc	doctor of social science
DTech	doctor of technology
DTh	doctor of theology
DTM	diploma in tropical medicine
DTMH	diploma in tropical medicine and hygiene
DU	doctor of the university
DUniv	doctor of the university
dwt	pennyweight
EC	European Community
ed. *pl.* eds.	edited / edited by / editor(s)
Edin.	Edinburgh
edn	edition
EEC	European Economic Community
EFTA	European Free Trade Association
EICS	East India Company Service
EMI	Electrical and Musical Industries (Ltd)
Eng.	English
enl.	enlarged
ENSA	Entertainments National Service Association
ep. *pl.* epp.	*epistola(e)*
ESP	extra-sensory perception
esp.	especially
esq.	esquire
est.	estimate / estimated
EU	European Union
ex	sold by (*lit.* out of)
excl.	excludes / excluding
exh.	exhibited
exh. cat.	exhibition catalogue
f. *pl.* ff.	following [pages]
FA	Football Association
FACP	fellow of the American College of Physicians
facs.	facsimile
FANY	First Aid Nursing Yeomanry
FBA	fellow of the British Academy
FBI	Federation of British Industries
FCS	fellow of the Chemical Society
Feb	February
FEng	fellow of the Fellowship of Engineering
FFCM	fellow of the Faculty of Community Medicine
FGS	fellow of the Geological Society
fig.	figure
FIMechE	fellow of the Institution of Mechanical Engineers
FL	Florida
fl.	*floruit*
FLS	fellow of the Linnean Society
FM	frequency modulation
fol. *pl.* fols.	folio(s)
Fr	French francs
Fr.	French
FRAeS	fellow of the Royal Aeronautical Society
FRAI	fellow of the Royal Anthropological Institute
FRAM	fellow of the Royal Academy of Music
FRAS	(1) fellow of the Royal Asiatic Society; (2) fellow of the Royal Astronomical Society
FRCM	fellow of the Royal College of Music
FRCO	fellow of the Royal College of Organists
FRCOG	fellow of the Royal College of Obstetricians and Gynaecologists
FRCP(C)	fellow of the Royal College of Physicians of Canada
FRCP (Edin.)	fellow of the Royal College of Physicians of Edinburgh
FRCP (Lond.)	fellow of the Royal College of Physicians of London
FRCPath	fellow of the Royal College of Pathologists
FRCPsych	fellow of the Royal College of Psychiatrists
FRCS	fellow of the Royal College of Surgeons
FRGS	fellow of the Royal Geographical Society
FRIBA	fellow of the Royal Institute of British Architects
FRICS	fellow of the Royal Institute of Chartered Surveyors
FRS	fellow of the Royal Society
FRSA	fellow of the Royal Society of Arts

FRSCM	fellow of the Royal School of Church Music
FRSE	fellow of the Royal Society of Edinburgh
FRSL	fellow of the Royal Society of Literature
FSA	fellow of the Society of Antiquaries
ft	foot *pl.* feet
FTCL	fellow of Trinity College of Music, London
ft-lb per min.	foot-pounds per minute [unit of horsepower]
FZS	fellow of the Zoological Society
GA	Georgia
GBE	knight or dame grand cross of the Order of the British Empire
GCB	knight grand cross of the Order of the Bath
GCE	general certificate of education
GCH	knight grand cross of the Royal Guelphic Order
GCHQ	government communications headquarters
GCIE	knight grand commander of the Order of the Indian Empire
GCMG	knight or dame grand cross of the Order of St Michael and St George
GCSE	general certificate of secondary education
GCSI	knight grand commander of the Order of the Star of India
GCStJ	bailiff or dame grand cross of the order of St John of Jerusalem
GCVO	knight or dame grand cross of the Royal Victorian Order
GEC	General Electric Company
Ger.	German
GI	government (*or* general) issue
GMT	Greenwich mean time
GP	general practitioner
GPU	[Soviet special police unit]
GSO	general staff officer
Heb.	Hebrew
HEICS	Honourable East India Company Service
HI	Hawaii
HIV	human immunodeficiency virus
HK$	Hong Kong dollar
HM	his / her majesty('s)
HMAS	his / her majesty's Australian ship
HMNZS	his / her majesty's New Zealand ship
HMS	his / her majesty's ship
HMSO	His / Her Majesty's Stationery Office
HMV	His Master's Voice
Hon.	Honourable
hp	horsepower
hr	hour(s)
HRH	his / her royal highness
HTV	Harlech Television
IA	Iowa
ibid.	*ibidem*: in the same place
ICI	Imperial Chemical Industries (Ltd)
ID	Idaho
IL	Illinois
illus.	illustration
illustr.	illustrated
IN	Indiana
in.	inch(es)
Inc.	Incorporated
incl.	includes / including
IOU	I owe you
IQ	intelligence quotient
Ir£	Irish pound
IRA	Irish Republican Army
ISO	companion of the Imperial Service Order
It.	Italian
ITA	Independent Television Authority
ITV	Independent Television
Jan	January
JP	justice of the peace
jun.	junior
KB	knight of the Order of the Bath
KBE	knight commander of the Order of the British Empire
KC	king's counsel
kcal	kilocalorie
KCB	knight commander of the Order of the Bath
KCH	knight commander of the Royal Guelphic Order
KCIE	knight commander of the Order of the Indian Empire
KCMG	knight commander of the Order of St Michael and St George
KCSI	knight commander of the Order of the Star of India
KCVO	knight commander of the Royal Victorian Order
keV	kilo-electron-volt
KG	knight of the Order of the Garter
KGB	[Soviet committee of state security]
KH	knight of the Royal Guelphic Order
KLM	Koninklijke Luchtvaart Maatschappij (Royal Dutch Air Lines)
km	kilometre(s)
KP	knight of the Order of St Patrick
KS	Kansas
KT	knight of the Order of the Thistle
kt	knight
KY	Kentucky
£	pound(s) sterling
£E	Egyptian pound
L	lira *pl.* lire
l. *pl.* ll.	line(s)
LA	Lousiana
LAA	light anti-aircraft
LAH	licentiate of the Apothecaries' Hall, Dublin
Lat.	Latin
lb	pound(s), unit of weight
LDS	licence in dental surgery
lit.	literally
LittB	bachelor of letters
LittD	doctor of letters
LKQCPI	licentiate of the King and Queen's College of Physicians, Ireland
LLA	lady literate in arts
LLB	bachelor of laws
LLD	doctor of laws
LLM	master of laws
LM	licentiate in midwifery
LP	long-playing record
LRAM	licentiate of the Royal Academy of Music
LRCP	licentiate of the Royal College of Physicians
LRCPS (Glasgow)	licentiate of the Royal College of Physicians and Surgeons of Glasgow
LRCS	licentiate of the Royal College of Surgeons
LSA	licentiate of the Society of Apothecaries
LSD	lysergic acid diethylamide
LVO	lieutenant of the Royal Victorian Order
M. *pl.* MM.	Monsieur *pl.* Messieurs
m	metre(s)

m. *pl.* mm.	membrane(s)
MA	(1) Massachusetts; (2) master of arts
MAI	master of engineering
MB	bachelor of medicine
MBA	master of business administration
MBE	member of the Order of the British Empire
MC	Military Cross
MCC	Marylebone Cricket Club
MCh	master of surgery
MChir	master of surgery
MCom	master of commerce
MD	(1) doctor of medicine; (2) Maryland
MDMA	methylenedioxymethamphetamine
ME	Maine
MEd	master of education
MEng	master of engineering
MEP	member of the European parliament
MG	Morris Garages
MGM	Metro-Goldwyn-Mayer
Mgr	Monsignor
MI	(1) Michigan; (2) military intelligence
MI1c	[secret intelligence department]
MI5	[military intelligence department]
MI6	[secret intelligence department]
MI9	[secret escape service]
MICE	member of the Institution of Civil Engineers
MIEE	member of the Institution of Electrical Engineers
min.	minute(s)
Mk	mark
ML	(1) licentiate of medicine; (2) master of laws
MLitt	master of letters
Mlle	Mademoiselle
mm	millimetre(s)
Mme	Madame
MN	Minnesota
MO	Missouri
MOH	medical officer of health
MP	member of parliament
m.p.h.	miles per hour
MPhil	master of philosophy
MRCP	member of the Royal College of Physicians
MRCS	member of the Royal College of Surgeons
MRCVS	member of the Royal College of Veterinary Surgeons
MRIA	member of the Royal Irish Academy
MS	(1) master of science; (2) Mississippi
MS *pl.* MSS	manuscript(s)
MSc	master of science
MSc (Econ.)	master of science (economics)
MT	Montana
MusB	bachelor of music
MusBac	bachelor of music
MusD	doctor of music
MV	motor vessel
MVO	member of the Royal Victorian Order
n. *pl.* nn.	note(s)
NAAFI	Navy, Army, and Air Force Institutes
NASA	National Aeronautics and Space Administration
NATO	North Atlantic Treaty Organization
NBC	National Broadcasting Corporation
NC	North Carolina
NCO	non-commissioned officer
ND	North Dakota
n.d.	no date
NE	Nebraska
nem. con.	*nemine contradicente*: unanimously
new ser.	new series
NH	New Hampshire
NHS	National Health Service
NJ	New Jersey
NKVD	[Soviet people's commissariat for internal affairs]
NM	New Mexico
nm	nanometre(s)
no. *pl.* nos.	number(s)
Nov	November
n.p.	no place [of publication]
NS	new style
NV	Nevada
NY	New York
NZBS	New Zealand Broadcasting Service
OBE	officer of the Order of the British Empire
obit.	obituary
Oct	October
OCTU	officer cadets training unit
OECD	Organization for Economic Co-operation and Development
OEEC	Organization for European Economic Co-operation
OFM	order of Friars Minor [Franciscans]
OFMCap	Ordine Frati Minori Cappucini: member of the Capuchin order
OH	Ohio
OK	Oklahoma
O level	ordinary level [examination]
OM	Order of Merit
OP	order of Preachers [Dominicans]
op. *pl.* opp.	opus *pl.* opera
OPEC	Organization of Petroleum Exporting Countries
OR	Oregon
orig.	original
OS	old style
OSB	Order of St Benedict
OTC	Officers' Training Corps
OWS	Old Watercolour Society
Oxon.	Oxoniensis
p. *pl.* pp.	page(s)
PA	Pennsylvania
p.a.	per annum
para.	paragraph
PAYE	pay as you earn
pbk *pl.* pbks	paperback(s)
per.	[during the] period
PhD	doctor of philosophy
pl.	(1) plate(s); (2) plural
priv. coll.	private collection
pt *pl.* pts	part(s)
pubd	published
PVC	polyvinyl chloride
q. *pl.* qq.	(1) question(s); (2) quire(s)
QC	queen's counsel
R	rand
R.	Rex / Regina
r	recto
r.	reigned / ruled
RA	Royal Academy / Royal Academician

RAC	Royal Automobile Club
RAF	Royal Air Force
RAFVR	Royal Air Force Volunteer Reserve
RAM	[member of the] Royal Academy of Music
RAMC	Royal Army Medical Corps
RCA	Royal College of Art
RCNC	Royal Corps of Naval Constructors
RCOG	Royal College of Obstetricians and Gynaecologists
RDI	royal designer for industry
RE	Royal Engineers
repr. *pl.* reprs.	reprint(s) / reprinted
repro.	reproduced
rev.	revised / revised by / reviser / revision
Revd	Reverend
RHA	Royal Hibernian Academy
RI	(1) Rhode Island; (2) Royal Institute of Painters in Water-Colours
RIBA	Royal Institute of British Architects
RIN	Royal Indian Navy
RM	Reichsmark
RMS	Royal Mail steamer
RN	Royal Navy
RNA	ribonucleic acid
RNAS	Royal Naval Air Service
RNR	Royal Naval Reserve
RNVR	Royal Naval Volunteer Reserve
RO	Record Office
r.p.m.	revolutions per minute
RRS	royal research ship
Rs	rupees
RSA	(1) Royal Scottish Academician; (2) Royal Society of Arts
RSPCA	Royal Society for the Prevention of Cruelty to Animals
Rt Hon.	Right Honourable
Rt Revd	Right Reverend
RUC	Royal Ulster Constabulary
Russ.	Russian
RWS	Royal Watercolour Society
S4C	Sianel Pedwar Cymru
s.	shilling(s)
s.a.	*sub anno*: under the year
SABC	South African Broadcasting Corporation
SAS	Special Air Service
SC	South Carolina
ScD	doctor of science
S$	Singapore dollar
SD	South Dakota
sec.	second(s)
sel.	selected
sen.	senior
Sept	September
ser.	series
SHAPE	supreme headquarters allied powers, Europe
SIDRO	Société Internationale d'Énergie Hydro-Électrique
sig. *pl.* sigs.	signature(s)
sing.	singular
SIS	Secret Intelligence Service
SJ	Society of Jesus
Skr	Swedish krona
Span.	Spanish
SPCK	Society for Promoting Christian Knowledge
SS	(1) Santissimi; (2) Schutzstaffel; (3) steam ship
STB	bachelor of theology
STD	doctor of theology
STM	master of theology
STP	doctor of theology
supp.	supposedly
suppl. *pl.* suppls.	supplement(s)
s.v.	*sub verbo* / *sub voce*: under the word / heading
SY	steam yacht
TA	Territorial Army
TASS	[Soviet news agency]
TB	tuberculosis (*lit.* tubercle bacillus)
TD	(1) *teachtaí dála* (member of the Dáil); (2) territorial decoration
TN	Tennessee
TNT	trinitrotoluene
trans.	translated / translated by / translation / translator
TT	tourist trophy
TUC	Trades Union Congress
TX	Texas
U-boat	*Unterseeboot*: submarine
Ufa	Universum-Film AG
UMIST	University of Manchester Institute of Science and Technology
UN	United Nations
UNESCO	United Nations Educational, Scientific, and Cultural Organization
UNICEF	United Nations International Children's Emergency Fund
unpubd	unpublished
USS	United States ship
UT	Utah
v	verso
v.	versus
VA	Virginia
VAD	Voluntary Aid Detachment
VC	Victoria Cross
VE-day	victory in Europe day
Ven.	Venerable
VJ-day	victory over Japan day
vol. *pl.* vols.	volume(s)
VT	Vermont
WA	Washington [state]
WAAC	Women's Auxiliary Army Corps
WAAF	Women's Auxiliary Air Force
WEA	Workers' Educational Association
WHO	World Health Organization
WI	Wisconsin
WRAF	Women's Royal Air Force
WRNS	Women's Royal Naval Service
WV	West Virginia
WVS	Women's Voluntary Service
WY	Wyoming
¥	yen
YMCA	Young Men's Christian Association
YWCA	Young Women's Christian Association

2 *Institution abbreviations*

All Souls Oxf.	All Souls College, Oxford
AM Oxf.	Ashmolean Museum, Oxford
Balliol Oxf.	Balliol College, Oxford
BBC WAC	BBC Written Archives Centre, Reading
Beds. & Luton ARS	Bedfordshire and Luton Archives and Record Service, Bedford
Berks. RO	Berkshire Record Office, Reading
BFI	British Film Institute, London
BFI NFTVA	British Film Institute, London, National Film and Television Archive
BGS	British Geological Survey, Keyworth, Nottingham
Birm. CA	Birmingham Central Library, Birmingham City Archives
Birm. CL	Birmingham Central Library
BL	British Library, London
BL NSA	British Library, London, National Sound Archive
BL OIOC	British Library, London, Oriental and India Office Collections
BLPES	London School of Economics and Political Science, British Library of Political and Economic Science
BM	British Museum, London
Bodl. Oxf.	Bodleian Library, Oxford
Bodl. RH	Bodleian Library of Commonwealth and African Studies at Rhodes House, Oxford
Borth. Inst.	Borthwick Institute of Historical Research, University of York
Boston PL	Boston Public Library, Massachusetts
Bristol RO	Bristol Record Office
Bucks. RLSS	Buckinghamshire Records and Local Studies Service, Aylesbury
CAC Cam.	Churchill College, Cambridge, Churchill Archives Centre
Cambs. AS	Cambridgeshire Archive Service
CCC Cam.	Corpus Christi College, Cambridge
CCC Oxf.	Corpus Christi College, Oxford
Ches. & Chester ALSS	Cheshire and Chester Archives and Local Studies Service
Christ Church Oxf.	Christ Church, Oxford
Christies	Christies, London
City Westm. AC	City of Westminster Archives Centre, London
CKS	Centre for Kentish Studies, Maidstone
CLRO	Corporation of London Records Office
Coll. Arms	College of Arms, London
Col. U.	Columbia University, New York
Cornwall RO	Cornwall Record Office, Truro
Courtauld Inst.	Courtauld Institute of Art, London
CUL	Cambridge University Library
Cumbria AS	Cumbria Archive Service
Derbys. RO	Derbyshire Record Office, Matlock
Devon RO	Devon Record Office, Exeter
Dorset RO	Dorset Record Office, Dorchester
Duke U.	Duke University, Durham, North Carolina
Duke U., Perkins L.	Duke University, Durham, North Carolina, William R. Perkins Library
Durham Cath. CL	Durham Cathedral, chapter library
Durham RO	Durham Record Office
DWL	Dr Williams's Library, London
Essex RO	Essex Record Office
E. Sussex RO	East Sussex Record Office, Lewes
Eton	Eton College, Berkshire
FM Cam.	Fitzwilliam Museum, Cambridge
Folger	Folger Shakespeare Library, Washington, DC
Garr. Club	Garrick Club, London
Girton Cam.	Girton College, Cambridge
GL	Guildhall Library, London
Glos. RO	Gloucestershire Record Office, Gloucester
Gon. & Caius Cam.	Gonville and Caius College, Cambridge
Gov. Art Coll.	Government Art Collection
GS Lond.	Geological Society of London
Hants. RO	Hampshire Record Office, Winchester
Harris Man. Oxf.	Harris Manchester College, Oxford
Harvard TC	Harvard Theatre Collection, Harvard University, Cambridge, Massachusetts, Nathan Marsh Pusey Library
Harvard U.	Harvard University, Cambridge, Massachusetts
Harvard U., Houghton L.	Harvard University, Cambridge, Massachusetts, Houghton Library
Herefs. RO	Herefordshire Record Office, Hereford
Herts. ALS	Hertfordshire Archives and Local Studies, Hertford
Hist. Soc. Penn.	Historical Society of Pennsylvania, Philadelphia
HLRO	House of Lords Record Office, London
Hult. Arch.	Hulton Archive, London and New York
Hunt. L.	Huntington Library, San Marino, California
ICL	Imperial College, London
Inst. CE	Institution of Civil Engineers, London
Inst. EE	Institution of Electrical Engineers, London
IWM	Imperial War Museum, London
IWM FVA	Imperial War Museum, London, Film and Video Archive
IWM SA	Imperial War Museum, London, Sound Archive
JRL	John Rylands University Library of Manchester
King's AC Cam.	King's College Archives Centre, Cambridge
King's Cam.	King's College, Cambridge
King's Lond.	King's College, London
King's Lond., Liddell Hart C.	King's College, London, Liddell Hart Centre for Military Archives
Lancs. RO	Lancashire Record Office, Preston
L. Cong.	Library of Congress, Washington, DC
Leics. RO	Leicestershire, Leicester, and Rutland Record Office, Leicester
Lincs. Arch.	Lincolnshire Archives, Lincoln
Linn. Soc.	Linnean Society of London
LMA	London Metropolitan Archives
LPL	Lambeth Palace, London
Lpool RO	Liverpool Record Office and Local Studies Service
LUL	London University Library
Magd. Cam.	Magdalene College, Cambridge
Magd. Oxf.	Magdalen College, Oxford
Man. City Gall.	Manchester City Galleries
Man. CL	Manchester Central Library
Mass. Hist. Soc.	Massachusetts Historical Society, Boston
Merton Oxf.	Merton College, Oxford
MHS Oxf.	Museum of the History of Science, Oxford
Mitchell L., Glas.	Mitchell Library, Glasgow
Mitchell L., NSW	State Library of New South Wales, Sydney, Mitchell Library
Morgan L.	Pierpont Morgan Library, New York
NA Canada	National Archives of Canada, Ottawa
NA Ire.	National Archives of Ireland, Dublin
NAM	National Army Museum, London
NA Scot.	National Archives of Scotland, Edinburgh
News Int. RO	News International Record Office, London
NG Ire.	National Gallery of Ireland, Dublin

Lancashire and Cheshire Antiquarian Society, 1883–1943', *Transactions of the Lancashire and Cheshire Antiquarian Society*, 57 (1943–4), 1–17 • Manchester Literary Club papers • *Manchester Guardian* (28 Oct 1913) • J. R. Swann, *Lancashire authors* (1924) • *The Athenaeum* (17 Jan 1914) • *The Inquirer* (3 Jan 1914), 13 • *Lancashire Naturalist*, 6 (April 1913–March 1914), 383

Archives JRL, corresp. and papers • Man. CL, Manchester Archives and Local Studies, corresp. and papers relating to Manchester Town Hall • Man. CL, Manchester Archives and Local Studies, notes relating to Lancashire naturalists and mathematicians • Man. CL, Manchester Archives and Local Studies, local council corresp. and papers • Man. CL, Axoniana | Chetham's Library, Manchester, Phelps collection

Likenesses four photographs, repro. in *Vegetarian Messenger* • photograph, repro. in *Manchester Faces and Places* • photograph, repro. in *Temperance Star*, 2 (Feb 1890) • photograph, repro. in *Daily Mail* [northern edn] (28 Oct 1913) • photograph, repro. in Walmsley, 'Dr Axon—Manchester bookman'

Wealth at death £1354 13*s*. 9*d*.: probate, 30 Jan 1914, *CGPLA Eng. & Wales*

Axtell, Daniel (*bap.* 1622, *d.* 1660), parliamentarian army officer and regicide, was baptized on 26 May 1622 at Great Berkhamsted, Hertfordshire, probably the son of William Axtell (*d.* 1638), chief burgess of the town, and his wife, Dorothy Symons (*d.* 1629). He was apprenticed to a grocer in Watling Street, London, about 1638, and attended William Kiffin's Baptist congregation. He joined the parliamentarian forces during the first civil war, was captain in John Pickering's regiment of foot in April 1644, and major of the regiment, now commanded by John Hewson, in 1646, when he preached in Wallington church. He signed the regimental statement of soldiers' grievances in May 1647. In 1648 he suppressed disturbances in Kent and stormed Maidstone, and was given £100 for being 'extraordinary active and diligent' (Firth and Davies, 2.407) in his capture of Deal Castle. He was the lieutenant-colonel of Hewson's troops at Pride's Purge but in the army council voted for radical motions and against Hewson and Ireton. He commanded the soldiers at the trial of Charles I in January 1649, at which he was later accused of threatening to shoot Lady Fairfax (wife of the lord general) for her interruptions of proceedings, of beating soldiers to make them cry 'justice' and 'execution', and of insulting the king [*see also* Regicides]. In March 1649, on the command of the council of state, he arrested the Leveller leaders Richard Overton and Thomas Prince.

Cromwell's expedition for the reconquest of Ireland was launched in 1649 and Axtell accompanied Hewson's regiment, which suffered severe losses at the capture of Drogheda. He then helped Cromwell seize the headquarters of the confederate Catholics at Kilkenny, where he was appointed governor. Given command of a regiment, he marched from Kilkenny towards Athlone with 800 men, but was opposed by the marquess of Clanricarde, the royalist lord deputy. With reinforcements he then advanced to the peninsula of Meelick near Banagher, defended by 3000 Irish troops, and seized it in a hand-to-hand fight. Five hundred Irish were drowned in the Shannon, with only 300 escaping by swimming, and Clanricarde lost the castles he had recently captured. Axtell was suspended by Ireton, then in command in Ireland, and court-martialled for killing prisoners taken at Meelick after promise of quarter; he later justified the action on the grounds that God used him to suppress the Irish. Leaving Ireland, he was captured at sea and carried to the Isles of Scilly, then full of Irish soldiers who wished to kill him. Sir Richard Grenville's advisers, fearing retaliation, spared him, and he returned to Kilkenny as governor after Ireton's death.

With the rank of colonel Axtell sponsored the spread of the Baptist faith in Ireland by Christopher Blackwood and Thomas Patient. He was one of the representatives sent from Ireland to the first protectorate parliament in 1654. Following the rise to power of Henry Cromwell in Ireland, Axtell was among those who opposed his policies of accommodation and he resigned in November 1656 because 'the Godly were discouraged and wicked men countenanced' (Thurloe, *State papers*, 5.671). He retired to Berkhamsted Place, putting all his Irish lands on long leases, but returned to Ireland in 1658 on a mission to Henry Cromwell, who described him as 'well satisfied with the government' (ibid., 7.306–7). Axtell, whose wife's name was Elizabeth, sent his son William to Christ Church, Oxford, in 1658, and his son Daniel to Lincoln's Inn in 1659.

With the fall of the protectorate Axtell was reappointed a colonel in Ireland under Edmund Ludlow, but was soon sent back to England to suppress Booth's rising. As divisions emerged within the army leadership he deserted General Lambert and declared for Fleetwood, then retired again, but decided to support Lambert's stand against Monck in April 1660. Although he escaped after the fight at Daventry he was captured, exempted from the bill of indemnity, and arraigned for treason for his actions in the king's trial. He unsuccessfully pleaded that what he had done was by the authority of parliament and that he had played no part in the king's death. Before his execution he prayed for the conversion of Charles II to a godly way of life and said, 'If I had a thousand lives I could lay them all down for the cause' (*State trials*, 5.1289). He suffered the full penalties for treason at Tyburn on 19 October 1660 and his head was set up on Westminster Hall; he was survived by his wife.

Alan Thomson

Sources Greaves & Zaller, *BDBR* • *DNB* • *State trials*, vol. 5 • C. H. Firth and G. Davies, *The regimental history of Cromwell's army*, 2 vols. (1940) • *The memoirs of Edmund Ludlow*, ed. C. H. Firth, 2 vols. (1894) • I. Gentles, *The New Model Army in England, Ireland, and Scotland, 1645–1653* (1992) • Thurloe, *State papers*, vols. 3, 5–7 • 'Narrative of passages in Ireland, 1649–53, by Major William Meredith', *Eighth report*, 3 vols. in 5, HMC, 7 (1881–1910) [TCD MSS] • T. C. Barnard, *Cromwellian Ireland: English government and reform in Ireland, 1649–1660* (1975) • E. Ludlow, *A voyce from the watch tower*, ed. A. B. Worden, CS, 4th ser., 21 (1978) • B. Whitelocke, *Memorials of English affairs*, new edn, 4 vols. (1853) • W. Haller and G. Davies, eds., *The Leveller tracts, 1647–1653* (1944) • P. C. Birtchnell, 'Bitter records of Berkhamsted Place', *Hertfordshire Countryside*, 2/8 (1948), 101 • Beocham [P. C. Birtchnell], 'The American Axtells—into ye howling wilderness', *Berkhamsted St Peter Parochial Review*, 82/3 (1959) • P. B. Ellis, *Hell or Connaught: the Cromwellian colonization of Ireland, 1652–1660* (1975) • *The Clarke papers*, ed. C. H. Firth, 4 vols., CS, new ser., 49, 54, 61–2 (1891–1901) • B. Taft, 'Voting lists of the council of officers, December 1648', *BIHR*, 52 (1979), 138–54 • A. Woolrych, *Soldiers and*

statesmen: the general council of the army and its debates, 1647–1648 (1987) • parish register, Great Berkhamsted, Herts. ALS, D/P19/1/1
Archives Guildhall, London, commissary court of London MSS, GL MS 9168/20, fol. 32*v* • Herts. ALS, Great Berkhamsted parish register, D/P19/1/1 • PRO, State Papers Interregnum, SP28/25 pt 1, fols. 36, 60 • PRO, State Papers Interregnum, SP28/267 pt 2, fols. 87–101
Likenesses group portrait, line engraving, 1660 (*The regicides executed in 1660*), BM • etching (after line engraving, 1660, *The regicides executed in 1660*), NPG
Wealth at death estates confiscated as executed as traitor; held lands in Hertfordshire, Bedfordshire, and Ireland

Ayckbowm, Emily Harriet Elizabeth [*known as* Mother Emily] (**1836–1900**), Anglican nun, was born on 14 November 1836 in Heidelberg, Germany, the eldest surviving of the three children of the Revd Frederick (or Frederic) Ayckbowm (1793–1862) and his first wife, Mary Ann (or Anne) Hutchinson (1806–1842). She had a younger sister, Gertrude (*b*. 1838), and brother, Albert (*b*. 1840). Soon after the death of his wife her father remarried, and his second wife, Charlotte, became a devoted stepmother to the young family.

Emily Ayckbowm's birth had taken place during a visit to Germany by her parents, her father being of German extraction. Her childhood was spent in Chester, where her father was rector of Holy Trinity. It was a strict but happy home, both sisters being educated by a governess. In 1856 the sisters returned to England full of zeal after two years in Germany and Italy, and began work among the poor in their father's parish. Outraged by the system of pew rents, they began raising money for a new church with free seating. However, in August 1862 Frederick Ayckbowm died suddenly, and Gertrude, who had married on 2 March 1861, died of rapid consumption on 22 December 1861. Soon afterwards Holy Trinity was demolished and rebuilt retaining pew rents.

In 1864 Emily Ayckbowm founded a charitable society devoted to works of mercy, called the Church Extension Association. By 1867 it had over 200 subscribers who gave money, did church needlework and embroidery, and inscribed texts. After giving heroic assistance during the 1866 cholera outbreak in Chester, Emily took her terminally ill stepmother to London for treatment, where she died at the end of 1868. Emily decided to remain in London, and the idea of a sisterhood arising out of the Church Extension Association took shape. The new parish of St Augustine's, Kilburn, was being formed by the Revd R. C. Kirkpatrick who, in 1870, clothed Emily as the first novice of the Community of the Sisters of the Church. She was soon joined by others and the growth of the Community was rapid. Subsidizing the Church Extension Association, the Community undertook work among the poor, visiting convalescent homes, orphanages, sick dispensaries, schools, and destitute men. The work was centred in Kilburn, but spread across London and to other places in England; in time branches were established in Canada (1890), India (1892), Australia (1892), Burma (1894), New Zealand (1895), and South Africa (1903).

From the beginning, the Community was stamped with the strong personality of its founder: Mother Emily wrote the rule herself over a period of sixteen years, and also drew up the constitution. She wrote books of spiritual instruction for the sisters, dealing with the rule, the vows, silence, prayer, and the duties of superiors. She was a militant opposer of social injustice, and consequently the Community became more vocal than most about such issues. But this outspokenness was born from Emily Ayckbowm's deep spirituality and social conscience.

In the 1890s the Community faced attacks from the Charity Organization Society, a group of former Sisters of the Church, and some orphans dismissed for bad behaviour. Criticisms were made principally about caring for illegitimate children, and discipline in the orphanages. The situation was compounded by the lack of an episcopal visitor (which was not changed until 1903). Archbishop E. W. Benson was already a patron of the Church Extension Association, but his offer to mediate in these troubles was met by the Community's refusal to accept his terms, and its consequent removal of his and all other male patrons' names from the Community literature. Both Benson and Mother Emily were strong characters who deeply mistrusted one another, but such action may, with hindsight, be perceived as a damaging error of judgement by the Community.

The Community survived these problems, and the outbreak of the Second South African War saw sisters going to South Africa to nurse the wounded. In 1898 Emily Ayckbowm's health began to decline rapidly but she continued working on her spiritual writings. Early in 1900 several colds confined her to bed, followed by a severely ulcerated leg. After much suffering she died peacefully (of diabetes mellitus and gangrene) at Broadstairs on 5 June 1900 and was buried in the churchyard of St Peter's, Thanet, Broadstairs. VALERIE BONHAM

Sources *A valiant Victorian: the life and times of Mother Emily Ayckbowm, 1836–1900, of the Community of the Sisters of the Church* (1964) • A. M. Allchin, *The silent rebellion* (1958) • P. F. Anson, *The call of the cloister: religious communities and kindred bodies in the Anglican communion*, 4th edn (1964) • d. cert. • parish register, Chester, Holy Trinity, 17 Oct 1837 [baptism] • private information (2004) [archivist, Community of the Sisters of the Church]
Archives NRA, priv. coll., diary and papers • St Michael's Convent, Richmond, Surrey | Ches. & Chester ALSS, Holy Trinity, Chester MSS • LPL, Benson MSS
Likenesses photographs, *c*.1852–1868, St Michael's Convent • T. Blake Wigman, portrait, St Michael's Convent
Wealth at death contributed all worldly goods (a substantial sum) to the Community of the Sisters of the Church

Ayer, Sir Alfred Jules [Freddie] (**1910–1989**), philosopher, was born on 29 October 1910 at Neville Court, Abbey Road, north-west London, the only child of Jules Louis Cyprien Ayer, financier, later in the timber trade, who came from a Swiss Calvinist family, and his wife, Reine Citroën, who came from a Dutch Jewish family, associated with the Citroën car manufacturer. He had no religious upbringing, and his childhood years, which he described as solitary, were spent in London. At the age of seven he was sent to Ascham, at Eastbourne, and from there went on, first to

Sir Alfred Jules [Freddie] **Ayer** (**1910–1989**), by Humphrey Ocean, 1985

Eton College as a scholar, and then, in 1929, with an open scholarship in classics, to Christ Church, Oxford. Choosing not to read classical honour moderations, he obtained in 1932 a first in *literae humaniores*, which, so out of sympathy was he with the prevailing tone of Oxford philosophy, he owed entirely to his marks in ancient history.

On the advice of his tutor, Gilbert Ryle, who had already introduced him to the ideas of Bertrand Russell and Ludwig Wittgenstein—and to the latter personally—Ayer spent the winter of 1932–3 in Vienna, attending Moritz Schlick's lectures and the meetings of the Vienna circle, and then returned to a lectureship at Christ Church, to which he had been elected while still an undergraduate, and which he held until 1939.

In 1936 Ayer published his most famous book, *Language, Truth and Logic*, written at the age at which (as he liked to recall) David Hume had written his *Treatise of Human Nature* (1739). It was his version of Viennese logical positivism, though he also saw it as a recasting of the traditional theses of British empiricism into linguistic terms. The book is full of passionate iconoclasm, expressed in a fine cadenced prose. Its central thesis is the verification principle, which divided all statements into the verifiable or the unverifiable. Verifiable statements were either, like everyday beliefs or science, reducible to observation statements, or, like mathematics or logic, transformable by means of definitions into tautologies, and only they were meaningful. Unverifiable statements (metaphysics, ethics, religion) were literally nonsense. Difficulties found in formulating the principle were treated as comparatively insubstantial, though, when the book was reissued in 1946, the new thirty-six-page introduction, itself a model of philosophical frankness, gave them much greater weight.

Ayer's ideas scandalized established philosophy (notably H. W. B. Joseph, H. A. Prichard, and Harold Joachim), not least through their self-assurance, and they infiltrated pre-war Oxford mainly through a discussion group of younger dons who met in Isaiah Berlin's rooms in All Souls College. The young J. L. Austin was an early convert, but only briefly, and was then, for more than twenty-five years, Ayer's relentless critic. The more open-minded of the older philosophers, such as William Kneale and H. H. Price, regarded Ayer's impact on Oxford philosophy as salutary.

Ayer's next book, *The Foundations of Empirical Knowledge* (1940), philosophically his most refined work, supplemented the earlier attempt to set the limits of human knowledge with an account, based on sense-data, of how we attain this knowledge. By the time of its publication Ayer was in the army. He was commissioned in the Welsh Guards, but mostly served in the Special Operations Executive. He ended the war as a captain, attached to the British embassy in Paris.

In 1945 Ayer went to Wadham College, Oxford, as philosophy tutor, a post to which he had been elected in 1944, but in 1946 he obtained the Grote chair of the philosophy of mind and logic at University College, London. Here Ayer's charismatic powers as a teacher, enhanced by his swiftness in discussion, and his broad and growing fame as the author of *Language, Truth and Logic*, came into their own, and he converted a run-down department into the rival of Oxford and Cambridge. This was the happiest period of his career. In 1956 he published *The Problem of Knowledge*, in which, abandoning reductionism, he justified our everyday beliefs by their power to explain our sense-experience. This line of argument was developed in such later works as *The Origins of Pragmatism* (1968) and *Russell and Moore* (1971), in which the history of philosophy was deftly blended with philosophical argument, and *The Central Questions of Philosophy* (1973), which aimed at updating Russell's *The Problems of Philosophy* (1912).

In 1959 Ayer had accepted the Wykeham chair of logic at Oxford, which was held at New College, partly to continue his polemic with Austin, who died the following year. Ayer always held that philosophy, to be worthwhile, must aim at generality: Austin saw no reason to believe this. In *Sense and Sensibilia*, a very influential work in the late 1940s and 1950s, Austin had tried to show how Ayer's phenomenalism had grown out of a refusal to pay attention to the detail of the way in which we report our perceptual experience.

Though perhaps no longer at the epicentre of debate, Ayer fought with immense skill and undiminished speed and agility against such developments as ordinary-language philosophy, Wittgensteinianism, and the new essentialism. He liked philosophy to be high-spirited as well as serious. He remained a great and generous teacher, and a prolific writer, with twenty-six books to his name before his death (including two volumes of rather unrevelatory autobiography) and one after. He shone at international conferences. He retired in 1978 and was a fellow of Wolfson College, Oxford, from 1978 to 1983.

Like his friend and hero, Bertrand Russell, Ayer did not treat philosophy as a cloistered enterprise. In the post-war years he reached a wide audience through the BBC's *The Brains Trust*, and later was active against anti-homosexual legislation. Immediately after the war he helped to familiarize British readers with the leading ideas of such French philosophers as Jean-Paul Sartre, Maurice Merleau-Ponty, and Albert Camus. But it was their role in the world of letters, of which there was no equivalent in Britain, that appealed to him, and in due course what he saw as their indifference to clarity exasperated him.

Freddie, as Ayer was known, was highly gregarious, elegant, and an animated conversationalist. He was short, with large, dark brown eyes, and a sudden smile which irradiated his fine, somewhat pensive features. He spoke very fast, and to the accompaniment of quick, fluent gestures. His friends included writers, painters, politicians, and journalists. He hated religion, and followed competitive sport, particularly football, avidly. He loved the company of women, and was much loved in turn. Vanity was in his nature, but he combined this with great charm and total loyalty to his friends.

Ayer was made FBA in 1952, and a foreign honorary member of the American Academy of Arts and Sciences in 1963: he was knighted in 1970, and became a chevalier of the Légion d'honneur in 1977. He received honorary degrees from Brussels (1962), East Anglia (1972), London (1978), Trent, Canada (1980), Bard, USA (1983), and Durham (1986). He became an honorary fellow of New College, Oxford (1980).

Ayer was married four times: first, in 1932 to (Grace Isabel) Renée, daughter of Colonel Thomas Orde-Lees, explorer, of the Royal Marines; there was one son and one daughter. The marriage was dissolved in 1941 and in 1960 he married Alberta Constance (Dee), former wife of Alfred Wells, American diplomat, and daughter of John Chapman, business executive, from the local newspaper-owning family in Providence, Rhode Island: they had one son. The marriage was dissolved in 1983 and in the same year he married Vanessa Mary Addison, former wife of Nigel Lawson MP and daughter of Felix Salmon, businessman. She died in 1985 and in 1989 he married Alberta Ayer, who survived him. Ayer also had a daughter with Sheilah Graham, the Hollywood columnist (see W. W. Fairey, *One of the Family*, 1993). When Ayer died in University College Hospital, London, on 27 June 1989, the event received much publicity in the press, serious and popular, and it was seen as bringing to an end a long line of outspoken arbiters of liberal or secular opinion.

RICHARD WOLLHEIM

Sources A. J. Ayer, *Part of my life* (1977) • A. J. Ayer, *More of my life* (1984) • A. P. Griffiths, ed., *A. J. Ayer: memorial essays* (1992) • private information (2004) [friends] • personal knowledge (2004) • A. Quinton, 'Alfred James Ayer, 1910–1989', *PBA*, 94 (1997), 255–82
Archives McMaster University, Hamilton, Ontario, Russell archives, corresp. with Bertrand Russell • Rice University, Houston, Texas, Fondren Library, corresp. with Sir Julian Huxley | FILM BFI NFTVA, current affairs footage • BFI NFTVA, party political footage | SOUND BL NSA, *Bow dialogues*, 18 March 1969, C812/22 C2 • BL NSA, 'Describing life and work', 14 Jan 1980, C125/20 BD1 • BL NSA, 'Profile', NP4342 R BD1 • BL NSA, current affairs recordings • BL NSA, documentary recordings • BL NSA, oral history interview • BL NSA, performance recordings
Likenesses photographs, 1952, Hult. Arch. • H. Ocean, oils, 1985, NPG [*see illus.*] • S. Pyke, bromide print, 1988, NPG • photograph, repro. in Quinton, *PBA*, facing p. 255
Wealth at death £140,519: probate, 29 Sept 1989, *CGPLA Eng. & Wales*

Ayerst, William (1802–1883). *See under* Ayerst, William (1830–1904).

Ayerst, William (1830–1904), Church of England clergyman and missionary, was born on 16 March 1830 at Danzig. His father, **William Ayerst** (1802–1883), Church of England clergyman and missionary, attended St John's College, Cambridge, and became a fervent evangelical under the influence of Charles Simeon, who encouraged him to devote himself especially to the conversion of the Jews. He worked with the Revd R. S. Alexander in Danzig, Breslau, and Berlin between 1827 and 1837. In Berlin the mission became something of a focus for court interest; however, C. J. Blomfield's intervention brought the mission to an end. Ayerst then served in London as foreign secretary to the Jews' Society from 1841 to 1853, and from 1853 to his death was vicar of Egerton, Kent. His son was educated at King's College School, London (1847–9), and in 1849 became scholar and Lyon exhibitioner of Gonville and Caius College, Cambridge, graduating BA with a third class in the classical tripos and junior optime in 1853, and MA in 1856. Ordained deacon in 1853 and priest in 1854, he served the curacies successively of All Saints', Gordon Square (1853–5), St Paul's, Lisson Grove (1855–7), and St Giles-in-the-Fields (1857–9). While working as a curate he won the Hulsean prize at Cambridge in 1855 and the Norrisian prize in 1858. He also published *The Influence of Christianity on the Language of Modern Europe* (1856) and *The Pentateuch, its Own Witness* (1858).

On 28 September 1859 Ayerst married Helen Sarah Hough Drawbridge; they had ten children, of whom three sons and a daughter survived him. In the same year he went to India as rector of St Paul's School, Calcutta. In 1861 he was appointed to a chaplaincy on the Bengal ecclesiastical establishment; he served as senior chaplain with the Khyber field force from 1879 to 1881, and received the Afghan medal. After returning to London he was appointed by the London Society for Promoting Christianity Amongst the Jews as principal of its missionary college and minister of the Jews' Episcopal Chapel, Cambridge Heath. In 1882, however, he accepted the vicarage of Hungarton with Twyford and Thorpe Satchville, Leicestershire. In 1884 he opened at Cambridge, Ayerst Hostel, designed to aid men of modest means in obtaining a university degree and theological training. He resigned his living in 1886, but served as curate of Newton, Cambridgeshire, from 1888 to 1890, and continued his work at Ayerst Hostel until 1897. He was a well-known evangelical in the Cambridge tradition.

In 1885 members of the Church of England in Natal who

had stood by Bishop J. W. Colenso after his deposition from the see of Natal formally applied to the English archbishops through the church council of Natal for the consecration of a successor to Colenso. The request was refused. After some delay Ayerst accepted the offer of the bishopric, and again attempts were made to obtain consecration. This, in spite of Ayerst's persistency, was definitely refused by Archbishop E. W. Benson on 21 October 1891. In 1893 Ayerst married Annie Young Davidson. He passed his last years living quietly in London, and died on 6 April 1904 at his home, 146 Sinclair Road, Kensington, London.

Ayerst's first son by his first marriage, also **William Ayerst** (1860–1934), army officer, was born in Calcutta and educated at Tonbridge School and Ayerst Hostel, Cambridge. He joined the army in England, and in 1885 returned to India, serving on the Burma commission in 1886–91. He retired as lieutenant-colonel in 1910. Like his father and grandfather he was an energetic evangelical, being especially notable for his work in promoting the introduction of the Bible in Braille to India and Burma. His work subsequently developed into the Braille Missionary Union. A. R. Buckland, *rev.* H. C. G. Matthew

Sources *The Guardian* (13 April 1904) • A. C. Benson, *The life of Edward White Benson*, 2 vols. (1899) • C. F. Pascoe, *Two hundred years of the SPG*, rev. edn, 2 vols. (1901) • Venn, *Alum. Cant.* • *WWW* • *CGPLA Eng. & Wales* (1904)

Archives LPL, letters and papers relating to establishment of Ayerst

Wealth at death £2330 2*s.* 3*d.*: resworn probate, 28 May 1904, *CGPLA Eng. & Wales*

Ayerst, William (1860–1934). *See under* Ayerst, William (1830–1904).

Aylesbury, Sir Thomas, baronet (1579/80–1658), patron of mathematics, was born probably in early 1580, possibly in London, where some of his siblings were later baptized at St Andrew's, Holborn. He was the second son among at least eight children of William Aylesbury (*c.*1536–1620) and his first wife, Anne (*d.* 1596), daughter of John Poole and niece of Sir Henry Poole of Saperton. His father's occupation is unknown, though descent from the Warwickshire branch of the ancient Aylesbury family is certain. A queen's scholar at Westminster School in 1596, he matriculated at Christ Church, Oxford, in November 1598, aged eighteen, taking his BA in June 1602 and his MA on 19 June 1605. College records evidence his pursuit of mathematical and other studies at Christ Church until 1611, when he married, by licence issued on 3 October, Anne (1589–1661), daughter of Francis Denman, rector of West Retford, Nottinghamshire, and widow of William Darell (*d.* 1610). They had six known children, of whom William *Aylesbury (*bap.* 1612, *d.* 1656) died in Jamaica, Barbara died at Antwerp in 1652, and Frances (*bap.* 1617, *d.* 1667) married Edward *Hyde, later earl of Clarendon, in 1634 and became mother of *Anne, first wife of James II and mother of the two queens Mary and Anne. On their mutual offspring's marriage, Aylesbury wrote a warm letter to Hyde's father describing Frances as 'a child that none could have from me but a good man' (MS Clarendon 129).

After leaving Oxford, Aylesbury became secretary to Charles Howard, earl of Nottingham and lord high admiral of England. Aylesbury was a friend of Henry Percy, earl of Northumberland, and frequently visited him during his fourteen-year confinement in the Tower. His contemporary Richard Corbet admired his studious nature (Corbet, 54–7), noting his friendship with Thomas Harriot, pioneer of modern algebra and perhaps 'the greatest mathematician Oxford has produced' (Fauvel, Flood, and Wilson, 56), whose manuscripts were left to Aylesbury and Robert Sidney, Viscount Lisle, in 1621. Aylesbury was instrumental in the eventual publication of Harriot's *Artis analyticae praxis* (1631), engaging Walter Warner's work and the patronage of Algernon Percy, by then earl of Northumberland. Warner, with Harriot and Robert Hues, had enjoyed the hospitality and patronage of Henry Percy while he was imprisoned, and together they were known as his 'magi'. Aylesbury took significant part in Edmund Bolton's plans, frustrated by the king's death in 1625, for a royal academy.

Aylesbury continued as secretary to George Villiers, marquess of Buckingham, when he became lord high admiral, and in 1625 was appointed surveyor-general, being acknowledged six years later by King Charles for 'his good, faithful & acceptable service in the affair of the navy & other ways, before he was Surveyor & since' (Burton). Already a master of requests, Aylesbury was created baronet on 19 April 1627 and warden of Cranborne Chase, in Windsor Great Park. He usually spent the summer at Cranborne Lodge, welcoming men of science and giving, or finding, them patronage. Sadly, his accumulated collection of precious manuscripts and rare books was to be lost during the civil war. Aylesbury's involvement with the Northumberland circle and his Oxford connections, taken with his own employment and learning, combined to place him in a particularly significant position as a channel of communication between, and on behalf of, mathematicians of the period.

In 1631 Aylesbury was involved in trials of new machinery for improving the coinage by stamping rather than hammering. In 1632 he was granted a patent for life (renewed to him and his son William in 1637) for making and issuing weights and counterpoises for coinage. A small treatise by Aylesbury on the fineness of silver survives with some mathematical notes among Ussher's manuscripts (TCD, MS 794, fols. 51–61). Appointed as a commissioner of the mint in 1635, and later that year incorporated as MA by royal mandate at Cambridge, Aylesbury continued to work on improvements in the uniformity of the coinage. On 11 July 1640 he appears as a master of the mint in the warrant issued for a new standard coinage.

On 13 January 1643 Aylesbury was given leave to attend on the king as master of requests at Oxford, where his wife and family joined him a few months later. It seems likely that, as Burton conjectures, he took part in meetings while in Oxford which later led to the formation of the Royal Society. Having received on 26 June 1646 Fairfax's pass to leave Oxford with his family, Aylesbury petitioned the commission for compounding of delinquents to compound upon the articles for its surrender, being 'aged and sickly'. He held little property at the time: apart from Cranborne Lodge and another small cottage also in the forest of Windsor, together worth about £22 p.a., held for life and not compounded for, he had only a couple of decayed properties to compound for, together with goods and personal effects worth £80, and the lease of a house in Dean's Yard in Westminster. In December 1646 he was fined £59 and retired to Cranborne Lodge. Just before Aylesbury left England in 1649, he wrote a letter of encouragement to the young Christopher Wren.

Aylesbury moved first to Antwerp, and then in 1652, after his daughter, Barbara, was buried at Loosduyn, he settled in Breda, where he died on 29 June 1658 and was buried in the Great Church. Without surviving male issue, the baronetcy thus became extinct. The *rouwbord* (wooden memorial) erected in his honour at Breda by his son-in-law, Edward Hyde, was removed in 1798 but a transcript of the substantial Latin text survives (see Bakker). Wood (1.306) describes Aylesbury as: 'a learned man, and as great a lover and encourager of learning and learned men, especially of mathematicians, as any man in his time', and Burton notes that: 'in more than one instance, the publication of works of Science may justly be attributed to him, which but for his patronage & encouragement would probably never have appeared'. COLIN ALSBURY

Sources Venn, *Alum. Cant.* • GEC, *Peerage* • *DNB* • Foster, *Alum. Oxon.* • E. Burton, 'Sir Thomas Ailesbury', gaudy oration, 1818, Christ Church Oxf. • *CSP dom.*, *1620–60* • Bodl. Oxf., Clarendon MSS • *Report on the manuscripts of Lord De L'Isle and Dudley*, 6 vols., HMC, 77 (1925–66) • state papers colonial, East Indies, PRO • Bodl. Oxf., MSS Rawl. B. 73.19b, 20, B. 158, B. 153b, D. 766.40 • BL, Egerton charter 257 [1635] • C. Wren, *Parentalia, or, Memoirs of the family of Wrens* (1750) • M. Rogers, *William Dobson 1611–46* (1983) [exhibition catalogue, NPG, 21 Oct 1983–8 Jan 1984] • *Biographia Britannica, or, The lives of the most eminent persons who have flourished in Great Britain and Ireland*, 1 (1747) • Wood, *Ath. Oxon.: Fasti* (1815), 305 • T. D. Hardy, *Syllabus, in English, of the documents relating to England and other kingdoms contained in the collection known as 'Rymer's Foedera'*, 2, PRO, 76 (1873) • M. Feingold, *The mathematicians' apprenticeship: science, universities and society in England, 1560–1640* (1984) • J. Fauvel, R. Flood, and R. Wilson, eds., *Oxford figures* (1999) • C. D. Bakker, *Heraldische— en genealogische merkwaardigheden in de Groote—of O. L. Vr. Kerk te Breda* (1932) • R. Corbet, *Poems*, 3rd edn (1672)

Archives Bodl. Oxf., Clarendon MSS • PRO, state papers domestic • TCD, MS 794, fols. 51–61*r* • De Lisle and Dudley MSS

Likenesses portrait, *c*.1650; on loan to Plymouth Art Gallery • W. Dobson, oils, NPG • S. Harding, drawing (after picture at the Grove), AM Oxf.

Aylesbury, Thomas (*bap.* **1597**, *d.* **1660/61**), Church of England clergyman and religious writer, was baptized at St Martin's, Birmingham, on 17 July 1597, the eldest of eight children of William Aylesbury (*d.* in or after 1641) and his wife, Dorothy Walton (*bap.* 1570, *d.* in or after 1611). He was educated at King Edward's School, Birmingham, before matriculating as a pensioner in the Easter term of 1613 from Christ's College, Cambridge. Having graduated BA early in 1616, from 4 May 1618 he was vicar of Curdworth, Warwickshire. He probably proceeded MA the following year, and was incorporated MA at Oxford in July 1622.

By this time Aylesbury had gained important patrons. His *A Sermon Preached at Paules-Crosse* (1623), delivered on 2 June 1622, was dedicated to John Williams, bishop of Lincoln, and to 'my most worthy friend'. He was chosen to act as secretary to the conference held at Sir Humphrey Lynde's house on 27 June 1623 between the Jesuits led by John Fisher and the Church of England clergymen Daniel Featley and Francis White. His own anti-Catholicism was evident in *Paganisme and Papisme Parallel'd* (1624), an All Saints' day sermon delivered at the Temple Church in 1623 and dedicated to Henry Wriothesley, earl of Southampton. Critical alike of Roman Catholic eucharistic theology and of the separatist followers of men such as Robert Browne, Aylesbury affirmed in near Arminian tone in *Christus redivivus* (1624) that 'God tenders grace to all, if men joyne but to make it efficacious' (p. 17).

In June 1625 Aylesbury became rector of Berwick St Leonard, Wiltshire, although he was in London to deliver *The Passion Sermon at Pauls Crosse* (1626) on Good Friday, 1626. That year he proceeded BD. In 1631 he was granted the prebend of Horningsham and Tytherington in the diocese of Salisbury. By licence dated 11 September 1635 he married Joan Nosse or Moss, 'aged twenty-two', from Maiden Bradley. By 21 October 1639, when he wrote to Robert Long to ask him to insert fresh references in the text, Aylesbury had effectively completed his *A Treatise of the Confession of Sinne*, although it was not published until 1657. While denouncing the abuses associated with confession in the Catholic church, the work seeks to restore to its former integrity the practice of penitential confession, affirming the ministry of reconciliation, in confession and absolution, as integral to the role of a priest or minister.

In 1643 Aylesbury became rector of Kingston Deverill, Wiltshire; the combined value of his livings was about £200 or £300 a year, according to his son Thomas. In 1645 soldiers intruded on his conduct of a service at Horningsham and cut the prayer book to pieces with their swords. Aylesbury's conservative and royalist sympathies led to his involvement with the 'clubmen', a powerful, overtly neutralist movement in Somerset, Dorset, and Wiltshire. Despite his promises made before the county committee on 3 June 1645, witnesses related that on 25 July at Mere Beacon, Wiltshire, Aylesbury preached paralleling the rebellion of parliament with that of Absalom, and defending the use of the Book of Common Prayer. Taken to London, deprived of his livings, and imprisoned for some time, he eventually retired to a small property at Cloford, Somerset, worth less than £12 a year according to John Walker. There he, his wife, and eight children depended on the generosity of Sir George Horner and others. Their patronage allowed him to become vicar of Castle Cary in 1650. Two years after the anonymous publication of *A Treatise of the Confession of Sinne*, there appeared Aylesbury's *Diatribi de aeterno divini beneplaciti* (1659), dedicated by a 'presbytero Anglo' to his 'most holy mother Church'. It characterized John Calvin as 'too precise and rigid' (p. 87) and, writing of confession, esteemed them 'poor Reformers, that shall weed up both tares and wheat together'

(p. 112). His own annotations in a volume of Latin manuscript meditations on the life of Christ (Bodl. Oxf., MS Univ. 18), including 'Ave Maria, gratia plena', hint at his devotional life.

In poor health when his livings were restored to him in June 1660, Aylesbury died before 29 January 1661. His wife was still living in 1672. Of their sons, at least three survived to adulthood. Thomas (1647–1725) became rector of Corsley, Wiltshire, while William (*c.*1640–1698), already in 1672 the subject of court depositions on his scandalous behaviour, was ejected from his living of East Pennard, Somerset, in 1681. COLIN ALSBURY

Sources minute book of committee for plundered ministers, 1645–7, BL, Add. MS 15670, fol. 162 • book of county committee for Wiltshire giving compositions for delinquency by, and charges against, clergy of that county, 1645–6, BL, Add. MS 22084, fol. 144 • J. Potter, letter to J. Walker, 1706, Bodl. Oxf., MS J. Walker c.3, fol. 315 • will, 1641, Worcs. RO [William Aylesbury, brother] • parish registers, St Martin's, Birmingham, Birm. CL • letter from the Revd Thomas Aylesbury to Robert Long, 21 Oct 1639, PRO, SP 16/431, fol. 46 • *JHC*, 4 (1644–6), 493 • *The records of King Edward's School, Birmingham*, 6, ed. J. Izon, Dugdale Society, 30 (1974) • J. Peile, *Biographical register of Christ's College, 1505–1905, and of the earlier foundation, God's House, 1448–1505*, ed. [J. A. Venn], 1 (1910), 289 • Wood, *Ath. Oxon.*: *Fasti* (1815), 408, 427 • C. Alsbury, *And they 'cutt ye common prayer book to pieces with their swords'* (1997) • W. Dugdale, *The antiquities of Warwickshire illustrated* (1656), 681 • B. Williams, ed., *The subscription book of bishops Towson and Davenant, 1620–40*, Wilts RS, 32 (1976) • *Walker rev.*, 369

Archives PRO, letter to Robert Long, SP 16/431, fol. 46

Aylesbury, William (*bap.* **1612**, *d.* **1656**), translator and government official, was baptized at St Margaret, Lothbury, London, on 13 July 1612, the eldest son of Sir Thomas *Aylesbury, baronet (1579/80–1658), and his wife, Anne Darell, *née* Denman (1589–1661). On 18 July 1628 he matriculated from Christ Church, Oxford; he graduated BA on 27 April 1631. That year he was admitted to Lincoln's Inn; there is no record of his being called to the bar.

Although possessing a large fortune, Aylesbury soon afterwards became, at the invitation of Charles I, governor to the young duke of Buckingham and his brother, Lord Francis Villiers, and travelled with them through France and Italy. In 1640 Aylesbury was residing at Paris, and in his correspondence with his brother-in-law Sir Edward Hyde (Bodl. Oxf., Clarendon papers) bitterly lamented the course of English politics under the Long Parliament. In the middle of May 1641 he returned from Paris to London with the earl of Leicester, the English ambassador at the French court, with whom he had been apparently living in an official capacity for some months. Shortly afterwards he presented his former pupils to the king at Oxford, who promised him the next vacancy among the grooms of the chambers, but the promise was never fulfilled, and Aylesbury continued in the service of the duke of Buckingham, as his agent, until the final defeat of the royalists.

During his interview with Charles I, Aylesbury, who was well acquainted with Italian, was urged by the king to continue a translation into English of H. C. Davila's history of the French civil wars, which he had just begun, and during the following years he was mainly engaged in the work; but he was only in England at intervals, and witnessed his royal patron's disasters from the safe distance of Paris or Rome. He and his friend Sir Charles Cotterel, who provided substantial assistance, received, however, frequent encouragement from the king. In spite of his political troubles, Charles read through the whole of the manuscript before the book was printed. The translation was published with a dedication to the king in 1647.

On the fall of Charles I, Aylesbury sought refuge with his father, first at Amsterdam, and afterwards at Antwerp; and he took under his protection his sister, Lady Hyde. But his poverty, caused by the confiscation of the property of his family, forced him in 1650 to return to England; he retired to the neighbourhood of Oxford, where he lived on the charity of his more fortunate friends. Early in 1656, however, he obtained the office of secretary to Major-General Robert Sedgwick, who had just been appointed governor of Jamaica, and finally left England. Following Sedgwick's death on 24 May for three months he took an especially active part in the government of the island, but he too died on 24 August, in Jamaica, and was probably buried there. A letter reporting the news to John Thurloe, the secretary of state, describes him as 'a man well versed in the weighty affairs of state, who in his counsels and advice, both to army and fleet, was very useful, for the want of which we shall have more and more to grieve' (Thurloe, 5.374). SIDNEY LEE, *rev.* SEAN KELSEY

Sources Thurloe, *State papers*, 5.54–5, 170, 374 • A. Kippis and others, eds., *Biographia Britannica, or, The lives of the most eminent persons who have flourished in Great Britain and Ireland*, 2nd edn, 5 vols. (1778–93), vol. 1, p. 383 • Wood, *Ath. Oxon.*, new edn, 3.440 • R. Lockyer, *Buckingham: the life and political career of George Villiers, first duke of Buckingham, 1592–1628* (1981) • GEC, *Peerage* • Foster, *Alum. Oxon.* • W. P. Baildon, ed., *The records of the Honorable Society of Lincoln's Inn: admissions*, 1 (1896), 216

Archives Bodl. Oxf., Clarendon MSS

Likenesses oils, *c.*1649–1650, Bodl. Oxf., Clarendon collection; on loan to Plymouth City Museum and Art Gallery in 1979

Aylesford. For this title name *see* Finch, Heneage, first earl of Aylesford (1648/9–1719).

Aylestone. For this title name *see* Bowden, Herbert William, Baron Aylestone (1905–1994).

Aylett, Robert (*c.***1582–1655**), poet, was the son of Leonard Aylett and Anne Pater of Rivenhall, Essex. He attended Trinity Hall, Cambridge, where he graduated BA in 1605 and MA in 1608; he was incorporated MA at Oxford. Cambridge awarded him the degree of LLD in 1614, and in 1617 he was admitted as an advocate and began his professional career as an ecclesiastical lawyer.

In 1621 Aylett published his first known volume of poetry, *The Song of Songs which was Salomons, Metaphrased in English Heroiks by Way of Dialogue*. The volume also contained books 1 and 2 of *The Brides Ornaments*, and an elegy upon the death of John King, bishop of London, who seems to have been his patron. Book 1 of *The Brides Ornaments* is dedicated to John Argall: this, combined with the initials R.A. under which the work originally appeared, seems to account for Wood's mistaken attribution of the work to Richard *Argall. Each of the books of *The Brides Ornaments* takes five virtues, and offers an extended meditation—in effect, a doctrinal sermon in Spenserian stanzas—upon their qualities.

Further poetry quickly followed. In the next two years Aylett published numerous volumes of religious verse including the meditative *Peace with her Four Garders* (1622), and the narrative poems *Susanna* (1622) and *Joseph, or, Pharoahs Favourite* (1623).

Nothing is known of Aylett's first wife except what he wrote in his autobiographical eclogue on marriage *A Wife, not Ready Made, but Bespoke*, that she died soon after their marriage of a 'hectic fever'. He married his second wife, Judith Gaell (*bap.* 1594, *d.* 1623), on 23 January 1610. He eulogized her in *A Wife not Ready Made*, which was written ten years after her death (the poem was entered in the Stationers' register in 1633, although no edition is known until 1653). She was buried on 2 December 1623. On 1 June 1624 Aylett married Penelope, *née* Wiseman, the widow of John Stephens, a barrister.

The year 1625 saw the publication of books 3 and 4 of *The Brides Ornaments*, dedicated to King's successor George Montaigne, and to Richard Crakanthorpe, who died before its publication. They were published together with other poems, and dedicated to John Maynard. The volume included a long poetic reworking of Sylvester's translation of Du Bartas's *Urania*.

In 1628 Aylett was one of nine appointed by Laud to the court of high commission to push through Laud's reforms and to combat puritanism; he had special responsibility for his home county of Essex. He remained a loyal lieutenant of Laud throughout the years that followed, rising to the post of master in chancery in 1638, in which role he was responsible for legal advice to the House of Lords. Other of his poetical works belong to these years, including *David's Troubles Remembred*, a six-book sacred epic written in 3410 lines of rhymed couplets and published anonymously in 1638.

The fall of Laud had potentially serious implications for Aylett, who was named among Laud's followers in the articles of impeachment in February 1641. None the less, he retained his post as master in chancery, and in 1642 was appointed master of the faculties, continuing to work for the House of Lords until 1649.

In 1654 Aylett published *Divine and Moral Speculations in Metrical Numbers*, which represented, in effect, his collected works. The volume is dedicated to Henry, marquess of Dorchester, and bears an engraved portrait of Aylett himself. The volume reprints the four books of *The Brides Ornaments*, although the first two books were pruned from a combined total of 669 stanzas down to a more manageable 440. It also includes Aylett's autobiographical poem on marriage. His *Devotions* were published posthumously in 1655. Aylett's 'interminable output of uninspired verse' (Padelford, 'Supplement', 478) focuses almost exclusively on religious topics, and is heavily influenced by Spenser. Conservative in tone, it is often competent but rarely exciting.

Aylett died on 15 March 1655, at Feering, Essex, where he had lived for more than twenty years. He was buried five days later at Great Braxted church, Essex. His memorial in the church gave his age at death as seventy-three, and on a portrait of 1635 he is said to be fifty-two. His will includes benefactions to Penelope, his wife, and to many local Essex gentry. MATTHEW STEGGLE

Sources F. M. Padelford, 'Robert Aylett', *Huntington Library Bulletin*, 10 (1936), 1–48 • F. M. Padelford, 'Robert Aylett: a supplement', *Huntington Library Quarterly*, 2 (1938–9), 471–8 • J. H. Round, 'Robert Aylett and Richard Argall', *EngHR*, 38 (1923), 423–4 • R. Aylett, *Divine and moral speculations in metrical numbers* (1654)

Likenesses T. Cross, line print, 1635, BM, NPG; repro. in Aylett, *Divine and moral speculations* • pen-and-ink drawing (after engraving), NPG

Ayleward, Richard (1626–1669), composer and organist, was born at Winchester, the son of Richard Ayleward, a minor canon at the cathedral. He sang there as a chorister under Christopher Gibbons in 1638 and 1639. Nothing is known of his whereabouts during the interregnum. At the Restoration he was appointed organist and master of the choristers at Norwich Cathedral (12 March 1661).

Ayleward wrote at least three services (the one in D is complete with responses and litany) and twenty-five anthems, including 'The king shall rejoice' to mark the coronation of Charles II in 1661. All are preserved in a set of partbooks from Norwich Cathedral (now housed at King's College, Cambridge). Taken together they are remarkable, showing no obvious models in the music of the previous generation or similarities with that of his contemporaries—other than perhaps George Jeffreys and Matthew Locke. Some of the anthems are on a large scale and make considerable demands on resources. Thus, 'I was glad', for example, is for three trebles, three countertenors, two tenors, and four basses, and 'Blow up the trumpet'—in some respects recalling Monteverdi or Carissimi—would have taxed any cathedral choir in the land. Unusually, a number are set to poetic rather than biblical texts, and this suggests that they may have been written as devotional sacred music for some private household during the Commonwealth rather than the cathedral service after the Restoration. Among these is a cycle of four anthems, respectively for the nativity, circumcision, purification, and resurrection. Their metaphysical intensity suggests a poet such as Crashaw or Herbert; that on the circumcision ('Gently, o gently, father, do not bruise') is actually by William Cartwright.

For some reason Ayleward relinquished his position both as organist and as choirmaster between mid-1664 and 5 December 1665; a cryptic reference in one of the chapter books to 'sending for Mr Ayleward at the Assizes' in 1664 leaves one none the wiser. Following his reinstatement in 1665 he continued to serve until his death at Norwich on 15 October 1669. He was buried in the north aisle of Norwich Cathedral on 18 October. IAN SPINK

Sources H. W. Shaw, *The succession of organists of the Chapel Royal and the cathedrals of England and Wales from c.1538* (1991), 202–3 • I. Spink, *Restoration cathedral music, 1660–1714* (1995), 306–11

Ayliff, Mrs (*fl.* **1692–1696**), singer and actress, was a leading stage and concert soprano but her forename, age, and marital status are unknown. She appears to have made her début in the première of Purcell's *The Fairy Queen* at Dorset Garden Theatre in May 1692, singing as a fairy 'Sing while we trip it' and as a Chinese woman 'Thus happy and free', and then or later Mopsa in the duet 'Now the maids and the men'. In August that year Peter Motteux described her performance of Purcell's Italianate 'Ah me to many deaths decreed' in John Crowne's play *Regulus* as 'divinely sung' (*Gentleman's Journal*, August 1692, 26). She performed Purcell's music in numerous plays and in a revival of his opera *Dioclesian*. Mrs Ayliff is the only female singer named in manuscripts of Purcell's odes, having important solos in *Hail Bright Cecilia* (1692) and *Celebrate this Festival* (1693). Johann Franck wrote songs for her to perform in his London concerts and she also sang music by Raphael Courteville and John Eccles.

In spring 1695 Mrs Ayliff joined the theatre company led by Thomas Betterton at Lincoln's Inn Fields, where she undertook acting roles for the first time, creating Miss Prue, the 'silly awkard Country Girl' in Congreve's *Love for Love*, and the page Jocund in Thomas Dilke's *The Lover's Luck*. In November 1696, after singing music by Gottfried Finger and Eccles in *The Loves of Mars and Venus*, she disappears from stage records; Mary Delariviere Manley's *The Adventures of Rivella* (p. 91) implies that 'Mrs Alyfe' had been taken off the stage by a wealthy lover.

Olive Baldwin and Thelma Wilson

Sources W. Van Lennep and others, eds., *The London stage, 1660–1800*, pt 1: *1660–1700* (1965) • *Gentleman's Journal* (Aug 1692), 26–30 • *Gentleman's Journal* (May 1693), 169–76 • O. Baldwin and T. Wilson, 'Purcell's stage singers: a documentary list', *Performing the music of Henry Purcell* [Oxford 1993], ed. M. Burden (1996), 275–6 • C. L. Day and E. B. Murrie, *English song-books, 1651–1702: a bibliography with a first-line index of songs* (1940) • [M. D. Manley], *The adventures of Rivella, or, The history of the author of 'Atalantis'* (1714)

Ayliffe, John (**1676–1732**), lawyer and author, was born at Pember, Hampshire, the son of John Ayliffe. He was educated at Winchester College and New College, Oxford, where he matriculated in February 1696; he became BA (1699), MA (1703), LLB, and LLD (1710). He was a fellow of New College and, between 1704 and 1710, he practised as a proctor in the chancellor's court. In 1706–8 he fought off disciplinary actions, having been accused of professional misconduct. When the case came before the chancellor's court Ayliffe crossed swords with the chancellor's deputy and judge, Dr Thomas Wood. Asked to retract his words, Ayliffe refused and Wood gave an interlocutory sentence depriving him of his office as proctor (3 May 1706). The case came before the delegates of the university's congregation, who were divided, and went henceforth to the convocation house, where a majority of the delegates pronounced judgment in favour of Ayliffe. However, the proctor acting for the chancellor's office challenged that decision before the high court of delegates, who ordered that Ayliffe be reinstated as proctor. Ayliffe himself read out the delegates' judgment in the chancellor's court on 23 January 1708. During the following years and until 1710 he continued to appear regularly as proctor in the university's court. That year a letter to Dr John Irish, acting judge in the chancellor's court, cost him a reprimand for impertinence; also that year, he was being sued for debt in the same court. Whether any of these cases was related to Ayliffe's whig political opinions, or, as he himself put it, his 'adhering to the principles of the Revolution' (J. Ayliffe, *The Antient and Present State of the University of Oxford*, preface), is unknown. There is, however, little doubt that the proceedings, which, a few years later, cost him both his status in the university and his fellowship, were primarily politically motivated by those of a tory disposition.

In 1714 Ayliffe published a work on the University of Oxford and its colleges (*The Antient and Present State of the University of Oxford*, 2 vols.; reissued in 1723). The list of subscribers mentions some 300 names, 30 of whom were members of Ayliffe's own college. The book reflected a dual approach. Part of the work was historical and, as Ayliffe acknowledged, borrowed to a large extent from Anthony Wood's earlier work. The book was very much that of a lawyer: the chapters on the corporate status of the colleges and on the procedural law applied in the chancellor's court and other university bodies were some of the most comprehensive studies on the subject written by an English civil lawyer. On several aspects Ayliffe's expressed views were strongly polemical. As a recurrent theme, Ayliffe denounced the propensity of some heads of colleges and university officials, particularly in his own time, to act beyond their proper powers; that tendency would, in Ayliffe's account, correspond to the political inclination of those (in his own words) 'promoting Arbitrary Power in the Prince'. The argument no doubt had political merits, but may well also have been inspired by Ayliffe's personal grievances while researching his book, in particular when he tried to list the colleges' benefactions and their original purposes; on several occasions, he claimed, he had been denied access to the college archives. In some instances Ayliffe's attacks were more personal. In the last pages of his account he appears to refer to his own successful defence against the decision depriving him of his proctor's office and refers sharply to Thomas Wood. Nevertheless, Ayliffe's demotion from Oxford was provoked by more veiled attacks in his book.

In November 1714 Ayliffe was sued in the university court by both Dr Bernard Gardiner, at the time vice-chancellor, and Dr Thomas Braithwaite. Both actions were for injury and damage, and in Gardiner's case, the warrant for the defendant's arrest stated the value of the damage at £100. Both plaintiffs may have felt that they were the target of Ayliffe's accusations regarding the maladministration of Clarendon's benefaction. In addition Braithwaite may well have regarded Ayliffe's remarks on the 'supine negligence of a late warden' of New College as referring to himself, whereas the accusation that the keeper of the university archives had been denying access to the records to members of the university who had a legitimate interest clearly referred to Gardiner. This time Ayliffe's legal and procedural skills were no match for the determination of his adversaries. His own demeanour (including an escape from the bedel who had come to New College to serve him with the warrant of his arrest) did not help his cause. The chancellor's court pronounced a decree expelling Ayliffe from the university (7 September 1714/15). The following day the sentence was confirmed by the convocation house, which also pronounced Ayliffe's degradation.

About the same time Ayliffe's adversaries at New College moved to have him deprived of his fellowship. For several years the fellowship of New College had been divided on political lines. Braithwaite's election as warden in 1703 had been strongly contested by the college's whig minority; in 1712 another tory, Dr John Cobb, was elected as his successor. The charges brought against Ayliffe included his unauthorized absence from Oxford in December 1714 (while he was in London, seeking remedies against the proceedings in the university), persistent disobedience towards the college authorities, and an incident which ensured that the case became notorious, his threat, expressed during a conversation with another member of the college, that he might pistol the warden. Nevertheless, the proceedings failed to secure a majority in favour of his expulsion. The case was brought before the college visitor, the bishop of Winchester, who issued an order requiring Ayliffe to acknowledge that the charges were justified and to submit an apology to those directly concerned (26 July 1715). Ayliffe refused to submit and resigned. His detractors would claim that he had sold his fellowship.

Both the proceedings in the chancellor's court and in New College were discussed at length in a pamphlet published the following year, *The Case of Dr. Ayliffe, at Oxford* (1716). The pamphlet, probably written by Ayliffe himself, or at least directly inspired by him, emphasized the political background of the case and argued that the proceedings were marred by irregularities. Its publication provoked Gardiner and Braithwaite, or their supporters, to counter Ayliffe's accusations regarding the alleged malversations at the Clarendon printing house with *An Answer* (*c*.1716). Ayliffe failed to secure sufficient support either at Oxford or among whig journalists, and eventually abandoned his attempts to challenge the Oxford proceedings either through a writ of prohibition or an appeal to the high court of delegates.

Ayliffe was appointed a commissioner for licensing hawkers and pedlars, but did not give up his academic interests and ambitions. In 1726 he published a treatise on canon law (*Parergon juris canonici Anglicani, or, A commentary by way of supplement to the canons and constitutions of the Church of England*, 1726; 2nd edn, 1734). The *Parergon* was a traditional commonplace book on canon law and ecclesiastical discipline, alphabetically arranged by keywords. The introduction, based on a wide range of scholarship, outlined the history of the canon law and provided arguments for the general thesis that, subject to restrictions imposed by the common law, by customary and statute law, and by the prerogatives of the king, canon law was part of the law of the realm. Otherwise, the book was aimed at a practical level and tended to avoid arguments which might have involved the author in domestic political controversies. Ayliffe regularly referred to English authorities, both canonistic and lay (such as statutes and law reports); he occasionally drew comparisons with continental legal systems, especially the Netherlands, France, and the empire. He relied in the main, however, on highly traditional canon law and civil law authors, in particular late medieval canonists.

In 1732 a small publication on the Roman law of pledges was meant to attract sufficient public interest for a larger treatise on Roman law. The project failed to come to fruition in Ayliffe's time and it was only in 1734 that the first volume of his *New Pandect of Roman Civil Law* was published. The book followed to some extent the structure of the institutional system, but the subdivision in persons, things, and obligations was preceded by a historical introduction and a chapter on 'the law in general'. The book offered a systematic treatment of, mostly, private law, providing numerous references to parallels or differences in English law and in continental legal systems. For Ayliffe the Roman law's importance and authority were mainly founded in its rationality, which also explained why it had exercised a major influence in the law of nations. In a striking passage of the introduction Ayliffe played down the differences between common law and civil law:

> If there is that wide Difference between the *Common* and *Civil* Laws, in their Forms of Pleading, and Manner of Trial, this is only the Stile, Practice, and Course of the Courts: But there is a Mixture in the *Principles*, *Maxims*, and *Reasons* on these two Laws; and indeed, the Laws of all Countries are mixed with the *Civil* Law, which has arrived to any Degree of Perfection. 'Tis true, that the *Common* and *Civil* Laws had not the same Root and Stock; yet, by Inoculating and Grafting, the Body and Branches seem at this Day to be almost of a Piece.
> (J. Ayliffe, *A New Pandect of Roman Civil Law*, 1734, introduction, xlvii)

Throughout the work a large selection of major civilian authorities were quoted. However, as in the *Parergon*, the civil law authorities Ayliffe referred to were to a large extent typical late medieval and sixteenth-century authors, whom, by early eighteenth-century standards, it was no longer fashionable to quote directly. Thus, in spite of its intrinsic qualities as a modern treatise on Roman law, the book expressed an indebtedness to a scholarship which, already before Ayliffe's time, had largely become obsolete.

Ayliffe died at his residence in Crane Court, Fleet Street, London, on 5 November 1732, and was buried in St Dunstan's Church, Fleet Street. Ayliffe's influence on legal scholarship was limited. The English translation of Thomas Oughton's work on ecclesiastical procedure (1831) included, among various additions, extracts from the *Parergon*. The assessment of Ayliffe's work has varied. To some, it is 'dull, tedious and confused' (*DNB*), whereas others have referred to Ayliffe as 'the most learned [English] Romanist before Buckland' (Simpson, 25). A reappraisal has viewed Ayliffe as 'a symbol of … the renaissance of classical Roman law studies in British universities … a pioneer of serious modern Roman law studies in England' (Coquillette, 213). None of these assessments appears to be based on anything more than a cursory reading of Ayliffe's work, or a superficial acquaintance with civil law scholarship in his time.

ALAIN WIJFFELS

Sources *DNB* • Foster, *Alum. Oxon.* • J. Buxton and P. Williams, eds., *New College, Oxford, 1379–1979* (1979) • *Hist. U. Oxf.* 5: *18th-cent. Oxf.* • W. R. Ward, *Georgian Oxford: university politics in the eighteenth century* (1958) • C. Wordsworth, *Social life at the English universities in the eighteenth century* (1874) • D. R. Coquillette, *The civilian writers of Doctors' Commons, London* (1988) • A. W. B. Simpson, ed., *Biographical dictionary of the common law* (1984) • J. H. Baker, *Monuments of endlesse labours: English canonists and their work, 1300–1900* (1998) • will, PRO, PROB 11/659, fols. 3r–3v • [J. Ayliffe], *The case of Dr. Ayliffe, at Oxford* (1716) • *An answer to some passages in the case of Dr. Ayliffe at Oxford* [n.d., c.1716]

Archives Bodl. Oxf., chancellor's court • Bodl. Oxf., congregation • Bodl. Oxf., convocation house • Bodl. Oxf., MS Rawl. J, fol. 2

Aylmer, Brabazon (*bap.* 1645, *d.* in or after 1719), bookseller, was baptized on 7 December 1645 at St Mary's, Stoke Newington, Middlesex, the son of Anthony Aylmer (*d.* in or after 1661). His father was described as a gentleman of London in the apprentice records of the Stationers' Company when Brabazon was bound to Luke Fawne on 21 January 1661. He gained his freedom after the customary seven years' service in 1668, but only in 1671 did the first book with his imprint appear—Isaac Barrow's *The Duty and Reward of Bounty*—suggesting that he initially worked as a journeyman before setting himself up in his trade. Throughout his career Aylmer worked from a London address at the Three Pigeons against the Royal Exchange in Cornhill. According to his colleague and fellow bookseller John Dunton, he was:

> a very just and religious man … He is nicely exact in all his accompts, and is well acquainted with the mysteries of his Trade. [He] has been as often engaged in very honest and very useful designs as any other that can be named through the whole Trade. (Dunton, 1.206)

Aylmer's distinctive publishing programme saw his involvement with a number of prestigious authors and titles in the latitudinarian and episcopal traditions. He became the regular publisher of Isaac Barrow and John Tillotson (archbishop of Canterbury, 1691–4), and works by Edward Fowler, including *A Defence of the Resolution of this Case* (1684), appeared with his imprint. At the same time he handled numerous titles in the moderate nonconformist tradition, including William Bates's *The Danger of Prosperity* (1685), Thomas Manton's *Sermons* (1698), and works by John Howe. The usual publisher of George Keith's attacks upon the Quakers, Aylmer obtained the copyright for Milton's *Paradise Lost* in the early 1680s, though he soon sold on the right without publishing an edition. However, he published both Milton's *Epistolarum familiarum liber* (1674) and *Brief History of Muscovia* (1682), though he was refused a licence for Milton's letters of state. The fact that he confined himself to such works suggests a religious commitment of a recognizable type, encompassing the middle ground between moderate Anglicanism and moderate nonconformity. Moreover, his role as the publisher of major, large-scale titles, including three editions of Barrow's *Works*, and his work in partnership with William Rogers, Jonathan Robinson, and Thomas Parkhurst indicate a successful business operation and a secure place in the late seventeenth-century world of publishing.

Aylmer married his wife, Temperance (*fl.* 1682–1695), probably in 1682, but nothing more is known of her. The couple had at least six children. Aylmer's date of death is unknown. He was last heard of in July 1719 when he signed a deposition, referring to himself as the former apprentice of Luke Fawne and instructing Fawne's heirs in America that most of his former master's assets had been lost in the great fire.

Aylmer's eldest son, **Brabazon Aylmer** (*bap.* 1683), bookseller, was baptized on 24 May 1683 at St Faith's under St Paul's, London. He was bound as an apprentice to his father on 7 February 1698 and received his freedom from the Stationers' Company seven years later. From that date it becomes impossible to say whether titles were published by father or son. The term catalogues for 1707 contain some entries for Brabazon Aylmer senior and junior together, but later entries and imprints fail to distinguish between the two. No imprints with the name occur after 1714, suggesting the termination of the publishing business in that year. The date of his death is unknown.

MARJA SMOLENAARS

Sources H. R. Plomer and others, *A dictionary of the printers and booksellers who were at work in England, Scotland, and Ireland from 1668 to 1725* (1922) • N. H. Keeble, *The literary culture of nonconformity in later seventeenth-century England* (1987) • J. Dunton, *The life and errors of John Dunton, citizen of London*, 2 vols. (1705); repr. (1969) • J. L. Chester, ed., *The parish registers of St Michael, Cornhill, London*, Harleian Society, register section, 7 (1882) • F. A. Munby, *Publishing and bookselling* (1934) • D. F. McKenzie, ed., *Stationers' Company apprentices*, [2]: *1641–1700* (1974) • *IGI*

Aylmer, Brabazon (*bap.* 1683). *See under* Aylmer, Brabazon (*bap.* 1645, *d.* in or after 1719).

Aylmer, Charles (1786–1847), Jesuit, was born at Painstown, co. Kildare, on 29 August 1786; his brother became an officer of the Austrian cuirassiers, and was considered one of its best swordsmen. Aylmer was probably educated at Stonyhurst College, in Lancashire, where he entered the Society of Jesus; he was created DD in 1814 while at Palermo, where he was stationed for several years. With two fellow Jesuits, Paul Ferley and Bartholomew Esmonde, he compiled a short compendium of Catholic doctrine, *A Short Explanation of the Principal Articles of the Catholic Faith*, and a devotional manual, *The Devout Christian's Daily Companion, being a Selection of Pious Exercises for the Use of Catholics*, which were both published in 1812 by the royal printing office at Palermo for the use of English-speaking Catholics there. In 1816 he was made superior of the Jesuit residence in Dublin and in 1817 rector of Clongowes College. He made his final profession as a Jesuit on 16 January 1820, and again acted as superior of the Dublin house in 1822, 1829, and 1841. As well as carrying out the normal duties of a Jesuit priest, he helped to promote a society for the publication of Catholic books in Dublin, his permanent residence from about 1821. He died on 4 July 1847.

THOMPSON COOPER, *rev.* MARY HEIMANN

Sources 'Irish Jesuits since 1800', *Irish Monthly*, 18 (1890), 1–16 · L. McRedmond, *To the greater glory: a history of the Irish Jesuits* (1991)

Aylmer, Sir Felix [*real name* Felix Edward Aylmer Jones] (**1889–1979**), actor, was born on 21 February 1889 at Alexander House, Corsham, Wiltshire, the second child in the family of five sons (one of whom died as a child) and one daughter of Lieutenant-Colonel Thomas Edward Aylmer-Jones, Royal Engineers, and his wife, Lilian Cookworthy. He was educated at Magdalen College School and Exeter College, Oxford, where he took second classes in both mathematical moderations (1909) and physics (1911). After an undergraduate attachment to Oxford University Dramatic Society he decided to join the stage, to his parents' displeasure.

Aylmer began a course of stage training under the celebrated teacher Rosina Filippi. His first professional appearance was as a two-line Italian stooge with E. Seymour Hicks at the Coliseum in 1911, just after his twenty-second birthday. He then appeared in *Romeo and Juliet* at the New Theatre and in two memorable Shakespearian productions by Harley Granville-Barker in 1912 at the Savoy. In 1913 he joined the company of Barry Jackson at the Birmingham Repertory Theatre. This splendid training was interrupted by the First World War, in which Aylmer served in the Royal Naval Volunteer Reserve, hurrying back to the Birmingham stage and his wife as soon as hostilities had ceased. During the war he had married Barry Jackson's niece Cecily Minnie Jane (*d.* 1975), daughter of Robert Taaffe Byrne, managing director of the Leyland of Birmingham Rubber Company. They met when he played Prospero to her Miranda and after the war they appeared together again as Sir Peter and Lady Teazle. They had one daughter and two sons.

During the following years Aylmer was seen in many West End plays, including *The Doctor's Dilemma* by George Bernard Shaw (Kingsway, 1926) and *The Flashing Stream* (Lyric, 1938). He also appeared in plays in New York, such as *Loyalties* by John Galsworthy (Gaiety, 1922), produced by Basil Dean, and *The Last of Mrs Cheyney* by Frederick Lonsdale (Fulton, 1925). Some of his greatest successes were in the parts of members of the professions of law and diplomacy. For John Drinkwater in 1928 he played at the Royalty a king's counsel in the long-running comedy *Bird in Hand* by Drinkwater. This was followed by the role of a councillor of state in *Jew Süss* adapted from Lion Feuchtwanger's novel *Jud Süss* (Duke of York's, 1929), and then that of a crooked solicitor in the 1934 revival at the Sadler's Wells and the Shaftesbury of *The Voysey Inheritance* by Harley Granville-Barker. He was also the judge in Enid Bagnold's *The Chalk Garden* (Haymarket, 1956). Diplomats that he played included the foreign office official in the 1954 production of *The Spider's Web* by Agatha Christie.

Aylmer was not fond of Shakespeare. He once confided:

Sir Felix Aylmer (1889–1979), by Sir James Gunn, exh. RA 1962

> I am a bit of an anti-Shakespearian. I acknowledge his greatness, of course—but, you know, Shakespeare has done so much harm to actors. He has been responsible for so much work that is artificial and unreal that in my time he has seemed a machine for manufacturing ham actors who do not understand the psychological contents of the parts and the poetry. Everyone has to do Shakespeare if they want to make a reputation but it seems to me that they seldom do their best work in his plays. He stretches an actor's emotional range, of course—but then so do Ibsen and Strindberg. (private information)

Aylmer preferred G. B. Shaw, whom he first met very early in his career. He played in Shaw repeatedly and indeed appeared in three different parts in *Saint Joan* alone.

Not one to enthuse about the rapport normally enjoyed by stage actors with a live audience, Aylmer preferred the medium of the film. He claimed that the work the film actor had to do, under the close-up of the camera's pitiless eye, called for a greater skill than anything required on stage. He appeared in a number of supporting parts in large-scale films for American directors: Plautius, a Roman converted to Christianity, in *Quo vadis?* (1951); Isaak of York, the Jewish father of Elizabeth Taylor's Rebecca in *Ivanhoe* (1953); Merlin to Mel Ferrer's King Arthur in *Knights of the Round Table* (1953); and, in spite of his antipathy to Shakespeare, two memorable performances in productions by Laurence Olivier, namely Polonius in *Hamlet* (1948) and the Archbishop in *Henry V* (1944). Television too brought him fame: he appeared with Hugh Griffith in the popular comedy series entitled *The Walrus and the Carpenter*, and as Father Anselm with Derek Nimmo in *Oh Brother!*, a successful series about life in a monastery.

In 1959 he published a book, *Dickens incognito*, in which he outlined the controversial argument—now fully accepted—that Dickens had an affair with Nelly Ternan, a young actress. Although Graham Story conclusively rebutted its suggestion that they had a child who was given for adoption, Claire Tomalin has praised 'the originality and cleverness of the other part of Aylmer's detective work' (Tomalin, 302). The book created a sensation. However, the bubble burst within a week as other Dickens lovers pounced on a flaw in his argument and found gaps in his research. Contemporary criticism might have humiliated a lesser man but it was met by Aylmer with rueful amusement and perfect sang-froid. He was not deterred from writing a second book, *The Drood Case*, which was published in 1964.

Aylmer gave great service to his profession as an outstanding president of the British Actors' Equity Association from 1949 to 1969. In his official capacity, he criticized in 1963 the dirty and insanitary conditions still existing even in some West End theatres. He was also vice-president of the Royal Academy of Dramatic Art when the principal, John Fernald, resigned in 1965 after a disagreement on policy with the council. In 1950 Aylmer was appointed OBE for his services to the stage, and in 1965 he was knighted.

Having spent some time in Germany as a student, Aylmer later translated a number of plays from German. One of his favourite hobbies was composing limericks, clerihews, and verse for newspaper competitions. In this he vied with his son Ian, and together they won several prizes. His daughter, Jennifer, was for several years connected with the British Theatre Museum in London. A stroke precipitated Aylmer's retirement to his country house near Cobham, where he continued to live until shortly before he died, at a nursing home, Crann Mor, Pyrford, Surrey, on 2 September 1979.

Derek Nimmo, *rev.*

Sources *Daily Telegraph* (4 Sept 1979) • F. Gaye, ed., *Who's who in the theatre*, 14th edn (1967) • personal knowledge (1986) • private information (1986) • C. Tomalin, *The invisible woman: the story of Nelly Ternan and Charles Dickens*, new edn (1991) • *WWW* • *CGPLA Eng. & Wales* (1980) • b. cert. • d. cert. • d. cert. [Lady Aylmer]

Likenesses J. Gunn, portrait, exh. RA 1962, Garr. Club [*see illus.*]

Wealth at death £51,556: probate, 15 April 1980, *CGPLA Eng. & Wales*

Aylmer, Sir Gerald (*d.* **1559**), judge, was the younger son of Bartholomew Aylmer of Lyons, co. Kildare, and Margaret Cheevers. There is no record of his legal education, though it is likely that he attended the inns of court since most of his contemporaries on the bench had formal legal training. At an unknown date he married Alison, daughter of Gerald Fitzgerald of Athlone, and his sister married Sir Thomas Luttrell, chief justice of common pleas.

Aylmer was regarded as loyal to the Geraldine lord deputy, the earl of Kildare, when he served as sheriff of Limerick in the earlier 1520s. As a partisan of Kildare, he was made second justice of the court of common pleas on 19 December 1528. He was confirmed in that role on 23 August 1532, yet he was apparently acting as agent for disaffected councillors when he presented a critique of the Geraldine administration at the English court in 1533, along with John Alen. Aylmer was appointed chief baron of the exchequer on 25 June 1534, just before the Kildare rebellion, and when Sir Bartholomew Dillon died unexpectedly after only one year on the bench, Aylmer was named chief justice of king's bench (12 August 1535). Thereafter he was a principal agent of Cromwell and worked closely with John Alen, master of the rolls, in the defeat of the Geraldine revolt. They travelled to England in 1536 to receive the bill for suppression of the Irish monasteries, bringing the legislation to the Reformation Parliament of 1536–7. The act of St Wolstan's, introduced in September 1536 as a special commission of dissolution, assured Aylmer and his fellow chief justice and brother-in-law Thomas Luttrell an annual rent of £4 during the life of Sir Richard Weston, the last prior. Aylmer joined with Alen and others in the comprehensive commission to dissolve Irish monastic houses, gaining profitable estates in Meath. He conducted an inquisition at Limerick of ecclesiastical shrines in 1541, and he obtained the Franciscan friary at Drogheda by patent of 16 February 1543 for the price of £54 17*s.* 3*d.* His loyal service to the crown did not, however, conclusively demonstrate his commitment to the protestant faith.

The new lord deputy, Lord Leonard Grey, adopted a pro-Geraldine policy after the Kildare rebellion was quashed in 1536, and the wily Aylmer, along with John Alen, campaigned to undermine Grey's administration. Aylmer attended Sir Anthony St Leger to London in 1538, joining the commission of inquiry to bring charges against the viceroy. Yet he was knighted in 1539 and survived the downfall of both Grey and Cromwell in 1540 to serve under three sovereigns, being reappointed chief justice on 24 March 1547 and on 16 November 1553. In 1541 he was among the leading Irish lawyers who petitioned for a lease of Blackfriars monastery in Dublin to establish there an Irish inn of court. He was named lord justice along with Sir Thomas Cusake on 6 December 1552, an unusual honour for one of his position on the council. However, he was left off the council in 1556 when the new viceroy, Lord Fitzwalter, replaced the minions of his predecessor St Leger. Like most of his contemporaries, Aylmer was also an able military figure who was employed in the field against the Geraldines and the O'Neills, attending the lord deputy in expeditions against the O'Connors (1537) and the Kavanaghs (1538). He was knighted in the field after the battle of Bellahoe in 1539, and given a grant of Dollardstown, Meath. Near the end of his career the aged Aylmer came infrequently to the Irish council and Elizabeth wrote in 1559 that she wished to promote another Old English lawyer, John Plunkett, to the office of chief justice in his place.

Aylmer died in office in 1559, a tenacious survivor from the Cromwellian administration whose support of Lord Deputy St Leger demonstrated the kind of eclectic fidelity required of mid-Tudor administrators. His kinsman and namesake Sir Gerald Aylmer of co. Kildare, perhaps a son, was a leader of opposition to the cess among the pale élite in the 1580s. JON G. CRAWFORD

Sources F. E. Ball, *The judges in Ireland, 1221–1921*, 2 (1926) • B. Bradshaw, *The dissolution of the religious orders in Ireland under Henry VIII* (1974) • B. Bradshaw, *The Irish constitutional revolution of the sixteenth century* (1979) • C. Brady, *The chief governors: the rise and fall of reform government in Tudor Ireland, 1536–1588* (1994) • C. Brady, 'Court, castle and country: the framework of government in Tudor Ireland', *Natives and newcomers: essays on the making of Irish colonial society, 1534–1641*, ed. C. Brady and R. Gillespie (1986), 22–49, 217–19 • J. G. Crawford, *Anglicizing the government of Ireland: the Irish privy council and the expansion of Tudor rule, 1556–1578* (1993) • S. G. Ellis, *Reform and revival: English government in Ireland, 1470–1534*, Royal Historical Society Studies in History, 47 (1986) • S. G. Ellis, *Tudor Ireland: crown, community, and the conflict of cultures, 1470–1603* (1985) • J. L. J. Hughes, ed., *Patentee officers in Ireland, 1173–1826, including high sheriffs, 1661–1684 and 1761–1816*, IMC (1960) • C. Kenny, *King's Inns and the kingdom of Ireland* (1992) • C. Lennon, *The lords of Dublin in the age of the Reformation* (1989) • council book of the Irish privy council, 1556–71, Royal Irish Acad., MS 24 F. 17 • PRO, state papers, Ireland, SP 63
Archives PRO, letters, SP 63

Aylmer, Gerald Edward (1926–2000), historian, was born on 30 April 1926 at Stoke Court, Greete, Shropshire, the only child of Captain Edward Arthur Aylmer (1892–1974), naval officer, and his wife, (Gwladys) Phoebe, *née* Evans (1891–1968). On his father's side he was descended from a distinguished Anglo-Irish family with strong naval connections, and there were two admirals on his mother's side. He was educated at Beaudesert Park, Gloucestershire, and at Winchester College. After going up briefly to Balliol College, Oxford, in 1944 he entered the Royal Navy for war service. He spent his time there on the lower deck, probably because the service found itself at the end of the war with an unexpected surplus of officers. His naval career was later described by the jazz singer and art critic George Melly, who detected in Aylmer 'a kind of dogged nobility … an admirable probity', but also 'a love of gossip, a delight in alcoholic excess and a shared enthusiasm for many modern authors' (Melly, 127). Aylmer's own reminiscences, recorded much later on tape, confirm this colourful account.

In 1947 Aylmer returned to Balliol to read modern history. He secured a first in 1950 and, after a year in the USA during which he held a visiting fellowship at Princeton, he was elected to a junior research fellowship at Balliol and started work on a thesis on royal office-holders under Charles I; he received his doctorate in 1955. He was appointed to an assistant lectureship at the University of Manchester in 1954, and a full lectureship in 1957. In this rather conservative university he was regarded by some of his seniors as a trouble-maker. Within the university he campaigned for a greater attention to the needs of students, who were then taught largely by means of lectures, and against the domination of the professorial hierarchy. Outside it, he and his wife, Ursula, *née* Nixon (*b.* 1928)—whom he married on 6 August 1955, and with whom he had a son and a daughter—took active parts in the Campaign for Nuclear Disarmament. The principal concentration of his formidable energy was, however, upon his thesis. It was later rumoured that this was so large that it had to be delivered in a wheelbarrow and that the faculty of modern history in Oxford changed its regulations as a result to impose a word limit. Certainly the thesis was long, at about 350,000 words, and certainly the faculty imposed a word limit at about this time, though it is not clear whether Aylmer's thesis was the only cause of this. The wheelbarrow story is, however, sadly false. However that may be, the thesis was published as *The King's Servants: the Civil Service of Charles I* in 1961. The work won immediate praise.

In 1962 Aylmer was appointed head of the department of history in the newly created University of York. Reacting against professorial dominance and giving free rein to his own democratic instincts, he created a department in which every member of the teaching staff had a voice and was involved. He had a talent for selecting young men and women of ability, which made the history department one of the most distinguished and lively in the country. At the same time his devotion to research and writing continued, and in 1973 he published the second volume of what became a trilogy: *The State's Servants: the Civil Service of the English Republic, 1649–1660*.

In 1978 Aylmer was invited to accept the mastership of St Peter's College, Oxford, and he left York revered and loved by his colleagues. However, his experience at St Peter's was less happy, partly at least because the essential work of fund-raising was not congenial to him. Nevertheless he undertook it, securing endowments for three fellowships and extending the college's buildings. He retired two years early, in 1991, to give himself more time for research and writing. Yet he carried on teaching and supervising students, and he undertook many of the administrative tasks demanded of elder statesmen: he was, for example, president of the Royal Historical Society. Fortunately these posts did not distract him too far from his main task, and the final volume of the trilogy, *The Crown's Servants: Government and Civil Service under Charles II, 1660–1685*, was handed to the printer three days before he died.

Aylmer's claim to historical eminence rests principally upon that trilogy. In it he described the institutional structure of government over more than half a century and the men (almost all were men) who ran it. Unlike many works of institutional history these volumes were saved from dryness by constant reference to the political and social circumstances of the day and by the presence of hundreds of individuals in their pages. They showed how offices were acquired and how their holders were rewarded; what was the social composition of the civil service in the different periods; what—so far as it can be estimated—was the impact of government upon the general population. Aylmer's work was not confined to the bureaucracy. He wrote two excellent surveys, *The Struggle for the Constitution, 1603–1689* (1963) and *Rebellion or Revolution? England, 1640–1660* (1986). He edited several books, notably *The Levellers in the English Revolution* (1975), a collection of texts that appealed to his own radical sympathies. Rather surprisingly for an agnostic he also edited two very substantial and handsome works on English cathedrals: *A History of York Minster* (1977), with Reginald Cant, and *Hereford Cathedral: a History* (2000), with John Tiller. He received honorary doctorates from the universities of Exeter and Manchester, both in 1991, and was honoured by a Festschrift edited by John Morrill, Paul Slack, and Daniel Woolf, *Public Duty and Private Conscience in Seventeenth-Century England* (1993).

Aylmer's height—he was well over 6 feet—and his deep voice reinforced the natural authority of his character. He spoke with his head curiously angled and his eyes almost closed, perhaps reflecting an inner diffidence. His laughter, often at himself, was engaging. He was, above all, a man of principle and integrity. He died at the John Radcliffe Hospital, Oxford, on 17 December 2000, and was buried at Llangrove, near Ross-on-Wye, Herefordshire, on 6 January 2001. He was survived by his wife, Ursula, and their two children. PENRY WILLIAMS

Sources *Daily Telegraph* (29 Dec 2000) • *The Guardian* (29 Dec 2000) • *The Guardian* (4 Jan 2001) • *The Independent* (30 Dec 2000) • *The Independent* (9 Jan 2001) • *The Times* (10 Jan 2001) • *WWW* • C. Hill, 'Gerald Aylmer at Balliol', 1–8; G. Leff, 'Gerald Aylmer in Manchester and York', 9–18; A. Woolrych, 'Gerald Aylmer as a scholar', *Public duty and private conscience in seventeenth-century England: essays presented to G. E. Aylmer*, ed. J. Morrill, P. Slack, and D. Woolf (1993), 19–28 • G. Melly, *Rum, bum, and concertina* (1977) • personal knowledge (2004) • private information (2004)

Archives Bodl. Oxf., historical papers • priv. coll., personal papers

Likenesses M. D. Krakschnikoff, pastel drawing, 1929, priv. coll. • H. Mee, acrylic, *c*.1989, St Peter's College, Oxford • H. Mee, acrylic, priv. coll. • photograph, repro. in Morrill, Slack, and Woolf, *Public duty and private conscience*, frontispiece • photograph, repro. in *Daily Telegraph* • photograph, repro. in *The Guardian* (29 Dec 2000) • photograph, repro. in *The Independent* (30 Dec 2000) • photograph, repro. in *The Times*

Wealth at death £541,219, gross; £534,728, net: probate, 7 June 2001, *CGPLA Eng. & Wales*

Aylmer, John (1520/21–1594), bishop of London, was descended from the Norfolk branch of an ancient family long established in Tivetshall St Mary. The identities of his parents are unknown. He was born in 1520 or 1521, since his funeral inscription recorded his age at death as seventy-three. Before consecration he emphasized his putative Anglo-Saxon origins by signing himself 'Ælmer'. Otherwise his name is usually found in contemporary sources as 'Elmer'.

Thomas Fuller relates that as a schoolboy Aylmer attracted the notice of Henry Grey, third marquess of Dorset and later duke of Suffolk, who subsidized his studies at Cambridge. Although he probably became a fellow of Queens' nothing is definitely known about his university career except that he graduated BA in 1541, proceeding MA in 1545.

Early career and exile abroad, 1541–1559 Another of Aylmer's early patrons may have been Dr John Aylmer (*d.* 1550/1559?), presumably both a kinsman and the Cambridge graduate who proceeded BCL in 1514. He held a clutch of west country livings during the 1540s and was doubtless the John Aylmer who was prebendary of Wells from 1543. Although the future bishop has been credited with one or more of these promotions he seems until 1549 to have remained entirely within Dorset's household at Bradgate, Leicestershire, or else at court, as tutor to his daughters. Since Dorset was little interested in such matters Aylmer also apparently served as his 'corresponding secretary' with those leading evangelicals and reformers who took the trouble, for political reasons, to address him. Thus he was able to cultivate friendships with Martin Bucer and Heinrich Bullinger, encouraging Lady Jane Grey to write to them as her education progressed.

Thomas Becon encountered Aylmer at Bradgate in 1546–7—'a young man singularly well learned both in the Latin and Greek tongue' (Becon, 424)—and in 1550 Roger Ascham paid a celebrated visit. His account of his last meeting with Lady Jane purports to enshrine a conversation during which she contrasted the harsh treatment she received from her parents with the scholarly blandishments of Aylmer, who taught her 'so gently, so pleasantly, with such fair allurements to learning, that … when I am called from him I fall on weeping because, whatsoever I do else … is full of grief' (Ascham, 47). Ascham's encomium must be treated with caution, however. Even if he recorded these remarks verbatim they were not committed to cold print until 1570, when Aylmer was a candidate for the bishopric of London. Nor, surely, can he have overlooked (even if convention did not allow him to express) the obvious possibility that Jane had developed an adolescent crush on a young man who treated her with consideration and necessarily with deference.

Aylmer's earliest surviving letters, dating from May and December 1551 and both addressed to Bullinger, suggest a regime more austere than the romantic idyll conjured by later writers from Ascham's narrative. In the latter Aylmer asked that 'with the kindness we have so long experienced, you will instruct my pupil in your next letter as to what embellishment and adornment of person is becoming in young women professing godliness' (Robinson, *Original Letters*, 1.278).

As the Grey family moved closer to power under Edward VI Aylmer's services were rewarded. Although unordained he received ecclesiastical promotion. No institution records survive but he compounded for the first fruits of the rectory of Pimperne, Dorset, in December 1549; for those of Nailstone, Leicestershire, in July 1552; and, resigning Pimperne, for those of Bosworth, Leicestershire, in April 1553. On 15 June 1553, three weeks before Edward's death, he was installed archdeacon of Stow in Lincoln Cathedral, on the presentation of Thomas Ashton of Old Weston, Huntingdonshire.

Whilst Aylmer never seems to have recorded his reaction to Northumberland's attempt to place Lady Jane on the throne in July 1553 he grimly endured the consequences, appearing at the first convocation of Mary's reign in October to argue against transubstantiation. His loyalty to the Greys kept him in England for a while thereafter. Implicated in Wyatt's rebellion in January 1554 he was amongst those supporters of Suffolk who on 17 September were indicted for having raised rebellion at Leicester. He was by then in Strasbourg, having been deprived of all his preferments for marriage in March. The identity of his wife is unknown but she was presumably the mother of an (unnamed) daughter who during the 1570s married Adam Squire. She died before December 1561.

Like many leading exiles Aylmer is credited with a 'miraculous escape': according to Thomas Fuller, when those sent to apprehend Aylmer boarded the vessel in which he was to cross the channel he was hidden in a large wine-vat with a secret compartment.

Although John Strype asserted that it was Aylmer who in Strasbourg published a letter of Lady Jane Grey's it is more likely that its preserver and publisher was James Haddon, another of her tutors, who died there in 1556. Because Aylmer's name never occurs in the correspondence between the exiles of Frankfurt, Strasbourg, and Zürich the historian of the Marian exile wondered if his Grey connections 'made him think it advisable to remain hidden' (Garrett, 76). This was to overlook his own account of his travels abroad, sent years later to Thomas Cooper when Aylmer was stung into refuting the libels of Martin Marprelate. According to this he visited 'almost all Universities in *Italie* and *Germanie*, having great conference with the most and best learned men' and finally reaching Jena, Saxony, in 1558 (Cooper, 47). Here, but for the accession of Elizabeth, he would have taken up a lectureship in Hebrew. A testimonial from Johann Friedrich II, elector of Saxony, surviving amongst the state papers, seems to bear out the assertion.

During his wanderings Aylmer supported himself by taking pupils. One such was Robert Beale, who migrated with him from Strasbourg to Zürich in 1557 and later claimed that although he had acted as Aylmer's servant in lieu of fees Aylmer had nevertheless exacted payment for his studies and thereafter ignored him. On 10 December John Foxe, gathering material which would emerge into print in the first edition of his *Acts and Monuments* (1563), wrote to Aylmer from Basel requesting information about Lady Jane. In reply Aylmer assured him of a warm welcome in Zürich and promised help with his researches.

At the beginning of Elizabeth's reign Aylmer attempted to repair the damage inflicted by John Knox's disastrously timed *First Blast of the Trumpet*: his own *An harborowe for faithfull and trewe subjectes, against the late blowne blaste, concerning the government of women* was published anonymously, and ostensibly in Strasbourg. In fact it was issued in London by John Day in April 1559. As a defence of the queen's title it was scarcely felicitous, observing that women were 'weake in nature, feable in bodie, softe in courage, unskilfull in practise' (sig. B2*v*) and thereafter flat-footedly insisting upon Elizabeth's *personal* credentials as a ruler: here was no empty-headed, chattering gossip. The most scathing of Aylmer's later critics wittily took leave to doubt 'whether any man ever recommended himself to a woman by complimenting her at the expense of her sex' (Maitland, 214–15).

Elizabeth may also have taken note of the assertion that in England government by a woman could be tolerated because it would be less *her* government than government in her name and on her behalf. Yet probably more damaging to Aylmer's own immediate prospects was his demand for an end to episcopal lordliness and the equitable distribution of ecclesiastical revenues on behalf of educational projects and the provision of competent preachers throughout the realm. Whilst in choosing her leading advisers Elizabeth wisely overlooked the débâcle of Lady Jane she had no intention of making any fundamental alteration of the episcopal order. Aylmer quickly learned his lesson: when after his consecration opponents twitted him with his former iconoclasm he retorted that when he was a child he spake as a child.

'A misquared stone': 'exile' in England, 1559–1577 Back in England by March 1559 Aylmer was one of the delegates to the Westminster disputation, intended to discredit the Catholic resistance which was delaying a satisfactory religious settlement in parliament. Thereafter he remained in London with Lord John Grey, principal survivor of Mary's destruction of Lady Jane's family, to whom Elizabeth had restored their property in the Minories. A memorandum of late June or early July indicates that he was being considered by William Cecil for the episcopal bench, but he was passed over and from the Minories on 12 August applied to Lord Robert Dudley for help in recovering property in Norfolk which an 'unthrifty nephew' had illegally sold during the time of his 'grievous exile'; and also for the deanery of Winchester or else Durham 'for now as a misquared stone (I know not by what means) I serve her highness in no part of her building, which is no small grief to me' (BL, Add. MS 32091, fol. 172*r*).

No deanery was forthcoming. Aylmer therefore returned to Lincoln, where during the royal visitation he was restored to Nailstone, Bosworth, and the archdeaconry of Stow. At the beginning of 1560 he was back in London, where on 25 January he was finally ordained deacon by Edmund Grindal. Thereafter he was in some way embroiled in the 'foolish subject' of the crucifix remaining in the queen's chapel, an issue over which several of the newly appointed bishops threatened to resign or else submit to removal (Robinson, *Zurich Letters*, 1.67–9). Later that year he was ordained priest by Nicholas Bullingham, bishop of Lincoln.

On 20 November 1561 Aylmer was instituted rector of Cossington, Leicestershire, on the presentation of Thomas Burdett of Bramcote, Warwickshire, another survivor of Wyatt's rebellion. Next month he was one of eight married men suggested by Grindal for the provostship of Eton. The post went to one of the six unmarried candidates, William Day, who would survive to be considered as his successor in London. Thus Aylmer had by this point married his second wife, Judith Bures alias King of Suffolk, daughter of Robert King and widow of Nathaniel Treherne, with whom she appears to have had no children. Her funeral monument specifically states that she married Treherne in Mary's reign and Aylmer during Elizabeth's. They had eight sons and two daughters, the elder of whom, Judith, was born in September 1562.

On 20 April 1562 Aylmer received letters patent for the

archdeaconry of Lincoln and was installed on 6 November. Despite their future differences Aylmer always acknowledged that he was indebted to Cecil for this promotion. It represented a huge increase both in his workload and in his financial status: at almost £200 per annum it was worth more than three of the four Welsh bishoprics and henceforth his personal financial worries can have been few. The fragmentary evidence which survives for his tenure suggests an increasingly stern, conforming administrator—it is notable that he abstained from the debate on liturgical reform during the convocation of 1563—who had displeased his masters and was being kept at arm's length. In the account of himself submitted to Cooper he claimed that he had reformed Lincoln's chapter—'a neast of uncleane birdes'—and that, as both preacher and ecclesiastical commissioner, he had ensured that at his departure there was 'not one recusant … left in the countrey' (Cooper, 48). If this was special pleading he undoubtedly laboured tirelessly on behalf of Elizabeth's settlement, and whilst efforts to evangelize the city itself met with only partial success because of the poverty of its fourteen livings he was a leading light in the reorganization of its two grammar schools and their projected amalgamation during the 1560s.

With the archdeaconry of Lincoln came capitular duties. Bullingham collated Aylmer to the prebend of St Martin in December 1562. Installed in person on 6 September 1564, during which month he became a canon residentiary, he remained in residence thereafter. In September 1567 he exchanged St Martin for the prebend of Decem Librarum, retaining it until his consecration. Summoned to court to preach at Easter 1565, Aylmer renewed an old friendship with Sir Nicholas Throckmorton. Their meeting prompted his only personal letter to survive from the 1560s and it hints obscurely at a crisis in both their flagging careers. Convinced that Dudley (now earl of Leicester) was his only friend at court and that Cecil was blocking his advancement, Throckmorton seems to have warned Aylmer that his archdeaconry was as much as he could expect from Cecil: higher preferment depended on a new patron. At any rate, Aylmer asserted in reply that he believed that Leicester and Throckmorton were now his 'chiefest friends … in England as God knoweth' (PRO, SP 15/12/54). Throckmorton probably, if unintentionally, misled him: Leicester's 'friendship' never seems to have produced any tangible result.

Ascending the ladder In 1567 Matthew Parker, archbishop of Canterbury, asked Aylmer to locate manuscripts in Lincoln Cathedral Library and thereafter it was he who attempted to further Aylmer's career. Some months later he suggested to Leicester that if Grindal were promoted to York, Aylmer would prove 'a good, fast, earnest servitor' in London and 'fit for that busy governance, specially as these times be, when papists … have gotten such courage' (Bruce and Perowne, 350). Addressing Cecil thereafter Parker nevertheless doubted—perhaps on the basis of Leicester's reaction—whether Aylmer would be acceptable, and indeed London went to Edwin Sandys, bishop of Worcester, through the joint efforts of Cecil and Leicester.

Although Aylmer was destined for seven more years in the wilderness Parker had made his point. Aylmer's administrative abilities were increasingly recognized. At about this time he was appointed a JP for Lincolnshire and was perhaps as responsible as Bullingham for the form of clerical subscription introduced into Lincoln diocese in 1570: the articles foreshadow those which John Whitgift would attempt to enforce in 1583–4 on his elevation to Canterbury. In 1571 Aylmer was appointed to the quorum of the long-delayed commission responsible for putting the Acts of Uniformity and Supremacy into full execution in Lincoln and Peterborough dioceses. In 1572, when membership was increased from twenty-seven to seventy, he became an ecclesiastical commissioner.

Lincoln's affairs came under Parker's scrutiny during the brief vacancy that followed Bullingham's translation to Worcester in January 1571. One Richard Taylor had been presented to the valuable prebend of Corringham by virtue of a grant from Bullingham's predecessor and Parker duly admitted him on 3 February. The chapter, however, headed by its subdean, Michael Renniger, ignored his mandate to induct. Parker dispatched an angry missive threatening Renniger, Aylmer, and two other prebendaries with a summons for contempt of his jurisdiction.

Thomas Cooper's first act as bishop of Lincoln was to collate Aylmer to Corringham *pleno jure* (26 April). Despite a further archiepiscopal mandate for Taylor's induction on 2 May Renniger and the chapter inducted Aylmer three days later. Thereafter, in circumstances which remain obscure, resistance to Parker collapsed and in May 1573 Aylmer's bonds for Corringham's first fruits were cancelled on the grounds that Taylor was in possession. In the interim, in November 1571, Aylmer had resigned Nailstone.

It is difficult to divine whether Cooper was an accomplice in this peculiar episode or in some way the dupe of the chapter. In any event it was an odd baptism of fire and there followed a serious rift between Aylmer and Cooper over their relative jurisdiction within the archdeaconry. In mid-1572 they submitted their respective rights to the determination of Parker and Robert Horne, bishop of Winchester, who on 1 July proposed a judicious division of the spoils whereby Aylmer and Cooper should hold court jointly and so determine all causes except those which were indisputably the prerogative of the bishop. All fees and profits were to be divided except during episcopal visitations. Aylmer proceeded DTh at Cambridge this year and on 10 October 1573 was incorporated BTh and DTh at Oxford after twenty years' study.

Following Grindal's elevation to Canterbury in February 1576 Elizabeth's long-expressed distrust of 'prophesyings', clerical exercises designed to educate less able clergy, reached crisis point. Widely established throughout the southern province, they were broadly supported by bishops of the stamp of Sandys and Cooper. Although under pressure Cooper had virtually suppressed them in the south of his diocese they survived in Lincolnshire and Leicestershire and alarming reports about them began reaching court. Elizabeth confronted Grindal with an ultimatum: to convince her of their utility and orderliness or else to suppress them totally. Grindal rallied his forces, writing to his diocesans in mid-June for their opinions.

Cooper's reply voiced some dark suspicions. Elizabeth had apparently been informed that those under his aegis were 'riotous assemblies' where 'unlearned and base persons' were permitted to speak freely. If so he had:

> great cause to fear falsehood in fellowship, that information is made by some by whom in charity it ought not to be … I suspect there be some that seek to creep in favour, not only by their own well-doings but by the discrediting of others' well-doings, and so to suspect, I have greater cause than I can conveniently put in writing. (LPL, MS 2003, fols. 29*r*–30*r*)

Grindal evidently instructed Cooper to investigate further and report back. Evidence of the flurry of activity which followed survives in an unsolicited letter of Aylmer's—the only one Grindal apparently received on the subject that did not come from one of his diocesans. Dated from Cossington on 25 September it spoke of 'a rank of rangers and posting apostles that go from shire to shire, from exercise to exercise', naming Eusebius Paget and Anthony Gilby amongst others. As for Grindal's demand for a report on the exercises, Cooper had committed it 'to one Spark and Willock', who themselves refused the surplice and countenanced other liturgical irregularities: 'therefore your Grace had need take heed how you credit the certificate' (LPL, MS 3470, fol. 22*r*–*v*).

Quite apart from his contemptuous dismissal of John Willock, an old comrade-in-arms from Bradgate days, Aylmer was effectively accusing Cooper of dishonesty. Grindal must surely have surmised that it was Aylmer above all whom Cooper suspected of seeking to 'creep in favour' and that he now regarded himself as a bishop-in-waiting, effectively beyond Cooper's reach. It was widely rumoured that he had been marked out by Christopher Hatton for promotion, whilst only months later Edmund Spenser in his *Shepheardes Calender* characterized him as Morrell—a goatherd, not a true pastor—whose chief motivation was to reach the top of the greasy pole and whose motto was *In summo foelicitas*. Here he was contrasted with Grindal (Algrind), who preferred the 'lowe degree' but, having accepted the higher, was struck down by a glancing blow and now lay 'in lingring payne' (*Poetical Works*, 446).

The *de facto* primacy, 1577–1583 Whether or not Hatton abetted this apparently blatant attempt to sabotage Cooper's credibility it was undoubtedly Hatton's spectacular rise during the 1570s that provided Aylmer with what he had hitherto conspicuously lacked, a powerful patron. In the wake of Grindal's fatal letter to Elizabeth in December 1576, refusing to suppress the prophesyings, Aylmer's advancement was assured, and only two days after Sandys's confirmation to York on 8 March 1577 the chapter of St Paul's was instructed to elect Aylmer in his stead. He was consecrated by Grindal, Sandys, and John Piers of Rochester on 24 March.

Since his precipitate elevation meant that it would be impossible to grant him London's revenues retrospectively out of the *sede vacante* profits—standard procedure—Cecil (Lord Burghley since 1572) proposed that Sandys cede them to Aylmer from Michaelmas 1576 as he himself was to receive those of York from the same date. Sandys angrily refused. Aylmer conducted a personal investigation into Sandys's financial affairs, sending Burghley the result and tactlessly attempting to justify his claim to London's revenues on the grounds that otherwise he would be 'naked' and Sandys 'so well left' at York. Burghley—with malice aforethought?—passed the letter on to Sandys, whose fury knew no bounds. His rejoinder spoke of 'an envious heart covered with the coat of dissimulation … So soon as [I] had holpen him on with his rochet he was transformed and showed himself in his own nature' (PRO, SP 12/112/45).

Compromise, if not harmony, was effected: on 10 May Aylmer duly received the temporalities from Michaelmas 1576, but without favourable terms of composition. Required to compound strictly according to the terms of the Act for First Fruits and Tenths (1559) he had to produce five sureties. Since Hatton's other protégés, John Whitgift of Worcester and John Piers of Rochester, were similarly penalized at this time it is probable that their elevation had been steadily opposed by Burghley, whose own protégés (including Sandys) were not obliged to find sureties.

In May 1577 Elizabeth suspended Grindal from office for refusing to suppress the prophesyings. In a dramatic reversal of their fortunes the new bishop of London, as dean of the southern province, immediately assumed his functions, exercising a *de facto* primacy which in the event lasted until Grindal's death.

It imposed a huge, triple burden—Aylmer also became chief commissioner for ecclesiastical causes—and the strain soon began to tell. His naturally pugnacious temper, evidently soured by his years in the wilderness, quickly brought him into conflict with many whose support he could ill afford to forgo. Within weeks he had offended the earl of Lincoln and begun an acrimonious struggle with Sandys over dilapidations for London—a titanic battle which proved one of the most disreputable episodes of the reign. By 1578 he was in bad odour with Hatton and Elizabeth (who had instructed him to pay equal attention to Catholic recusants and protestant nonconformists) for what they regarded as his over-harsh dealings with the former. By early 1579 Burghley was prepared to listen to reports that Aylmer was despoiling his see by overmuch felling of timber and he was called before the privy council. Encountering dark hints of deprivation Aylmer dispatched a violently intemperate letter, accusing Burghley of deliberately seeking to undermine his authority.

Despite Burghley's tactful reply Aylmer's future clearly hung in the balance. By December it was rumoured that he was to be translated and he himself frequently requested removal. At first he proposed himself for Ely, which Richard Cox wished to resign, and in March 1580 applied for vacant Winchester. He continued to hanker after Ely following Cox's death in 1581, but in the event the see remained vacant until 1599. Even after Whitgift's elevation to Canterbury he continued to seek translation on the grounds that London needed a younger man.

The drive towards conformity Although during these years Aylmer's episcopal duties took third place to his other commitments he instantly made his mark on diocesan administration, appointing as vicar-general the able Edward Stanhope, later characterized by Marprelate as 'Tarquinius Superbus'. Others appointed to his diocesan establishment were William Cotton, future bishop of Exeter, William Hutchinson, and the bishop's own son-in-law Adam Squire, collated archdeacon of Middlesex in June 1577.

Aylmer conducted his primary visitation in late 1577. Although according to the diarist Thomas Earle he urged a form of subscription which a substantial minority of clergy refused, surviving evidence does not suggest a witch-hunt at this early juncture in the interests of conformity. Those granted preaching licences in the visitation's aftermath included a dozen or so 'moderate puritans' with whom he would clash over the next decade, including Edmund Chapman, George Gifford, Giles Whiting, and Arthur Dent.

His visitors' findings, however, undoubtedly alerted Aylmer to the circumstance that, as in Lincoln, the strict provisions of the prayer book were widely ignored and even openly flouted. If further proof were needed he soon discovered it at Rochford Hall, the Thames-side seat of Robert, second Lord Rich, Essex's most influential protestant patron. Encouraged by his bastard brother Richard, Lord Rich had been displaying increasing sympathy towards radical preachers, even to the point of promoting quasi-congregational exercises at Rochford. Aylmer later asserted that he had had 'many great storms at his hand for the staying of them' (BL, Lansdowne MS 33, fol. 48*r*), but to no avail.

Aylmer's response to the endemic radicalism of his vast diocese was to abandon the policy of *laissez-faire* towards nonconformist practices by means of which Elizabeth's first bench of bishops—innately sympathetic or else merely grateful for evangelical support—had sought to implement her settlement. In the summer of 1578 he took the draconian step of placing under an interdict the two radical city of London liberties, Holy Trinity Minories and St Anne Blackfriars, until their ministers and churchwardens should pledge themselves to observe the prayer book ceremonies. William Hutchinson's appointment as archdeacon of St Albans in July 1581 would likewise mark the beginning of the end of that ancient liberty's semi-independent status: ceded to London diocese in 1550 it had hitherto effectively remained a self-regulating outpost under archidiaconal control, its affairs seldom attracting the attention of the bishop.

Meanwhile Aylmer had struck decisively at the unbeneficed preachers and lecturers of the city, led by the single-minded John Field. Preachers were not obliged to wear the surplice in the pulpit but Aylmer's stipulation in January 1580 that all clergy must administer the sacraments four times a year presented them with a dilemma: either to accept the provisions of the prayer book by using the surplice at administration or to risk suspension. One direct consequence of this policy of divide-and-rule was that he alienated the city fathers, always more sympathetic towards radical than towards conformist courses. In March 1582 Aylmer dispatched a stinging rebuke to the incumbent lord mayor, Sir James Harvey, for indiscreet words used against himself and the late Bishop Horne, as well as for contemptuous behaviour towards conforming city clergy. Within months, he acidly observed, Harvey would be plain Sir James whilst he himself would still be John London.

Whilst the surviving evidence of his second visitation in 1580 suggests that Aylmer was still placing as much emphasis on recusancy as on protestant nonconformity, he had begun to cast a baleful eye on radical activities in and around Essex's two ancient boroughs, Colchester and Maldon. Colchester's poorly endowed, badly served parishes were subjected to tighter regulation whilst Timothy Fitzallen, vicar of nearby Dedham, was suspended in January 1581, thereafter resigning. A similar intervention in Maldon that year led to the resignation of Fabian Withers (although here Aylmer made what could be construed as a severe tactical blunder, agreeing to institute George Gifford in his place). Probably in equal and opposite reaction to these developments, clandestine clerical conferences were established (probably at Field's direct instigation) as a species of self-help and self-regulation. That which first met in 1582 under the leadership of Edmund Chapman, lecturer of Dedham, drew its membership from southern Suffolk as well as from the environs of Colchester. Another, centred on Braintree, was led by Gifford and Richard Rogers, lecturer of Wethersfield.

Despite these early skirmishes into radical strongholds it was as senior commissioner for ecclesiastical causes that Aylmer initially gained his reputation as the hammer of the puritans. Although R. G. Usher argued that it was not until the 1580s, under the guidance of Whitgift and Richard Bancroft, that the ecclesiastical commissioners' proceedings developed into a 'court of high commission', it was actually during Aylmer's *de facto* primacy that it emerged as a fully-fledged court of first instance. In 1580 Aylmer effectively widened its scope by procuring a privy council letter extending to the whole province his diocesan order that all clergy must regularly administer the sacraments. Robert Beale, now clerk of the council, claimed that Aylmer was guilty of sharp practice in securing signatures to the letter, which had never been fully debated, and then issued it under the commission's seal, which closely resembled the council's.

The high commission's encroaching powers were most forcefully challenged by the Riches, one of whose protégés was Robert Wright. After Lord Rich's death in February 1581 Wright briefly departed for Antwerp, where he was ordained according to a presbyterian rite. On his return Richard Rich and his nephew Robert, the 21-year-old third baron, personally solicited a preaching licence for him, bearding Aylmer in his study at Fulham in September. Aylmer refused to grant one unless fully informed of the nature of Wright's orders and assured that he would subscribe the Thirty-Nine Articles. At that point Richard Rich physically assaulted him. The affair led to the trial of Richard Rich and Wright before the high commission and the imprisonment of both in November.

Unfortunately for Aylmer, Lord Rich had just married Penelope Devereux, sister of Robert, earl of Essex, and could thus count on powerful support at court. In any case Burghley was unhappy on technical grounds with the conduct of the trial. It had turned finally on sworn depositions—accepted as proven evidence without the possibility of further defence—that Wright had denounced celebratory sermons on Elizabeth's accession day as tantamount to idolatry. All this, Burghley seems to have reasoned, was to have ridden roughshod over the basic principles of common law and also to have exceeded the commissioners' brief to take cognizance only of cases which specifically concerned breaches of the strict provisions of the Book of Common Prayer. By March 1582 Aylmer, under pressure from the council, released Richard Rich on bail. Elizabeth (who had sided firmly with the commissioners) was furious and Aylmer hastened to justify himself in what was perhaps, Grindal's act of epistolatory self-annihilation excepted, the most remarkable letter she ever received from one of her bishops. He informed her bluntly that there were limits to the commission's authority. 'Your highness thinketh that the Bishop of London may do what he will … wherein I beseech your Majesty to inform yourself better, and not to suppose my authority under you greater than it is' (Nicolas, 246). To instruct Elizabeth that she misunderstood the nature of the legal powers which she had delegated to him was a brave action but Aylmer subsequently assured Leicester that his letter had pacified her. The affair nevertheless dragged on until September when the council finally had the better of the argument: Rich and Wright were both released on promises of good behaviour.

A diocese in crisis Although Whitgift's accession to the primacy after Grindal's death on 6 July 1583 must have come as an immense relief Aylmer remained under intense personal pressure. On 2 November he wrote to Leicester of the 'unhappy paroxysm' which had soured relations between them (Nicolas, 348–9). Five days later, nervous about rumours that he was again to be called before the council, he solicited Burghley's unequivocal support: otherwise he must 'give over' sitting as a commissioner: 'I would to God my L. of Cant were in the commission, that I might have some ease for I am deadly weary' (BL, Lansdowne MS 38/86). A new commission, naming Whitgift as primate, was finally issued in January 1584.

Henceforth Aylmer had more time for diocesan affairs. He had conducted his third visitation in July 1583. The visitors, led by William Hutchinson, carefully scrutinized preaching licences and came down heavily upon those who omitted weekday services—a shorthand method of browbeating incumbents who placed more emphasis on preaching than upon the prayer book—and yet, considering what was to follow, the visitors took surprisingly little cognizance of nonconformist practices. Despite further regulation of Colchester's affairs its new town preacher, George Northey, absented himself and was not immediately penalized, whilst of Essex's many radical incumbents only four, including Gifford of Maldon, were called into consistory for refusing the surplice.

These diocesan measures were swiftly overtaken by national events. Aylmer proved to be Whitgift's principal coadjutor in his drive for conformity following his enthronement—was this the 'unhappy paroxysm' which had alienated Leicester?—and the archbishop's divisive articles, enshrining the proposition that the Book of Common Prayer contained nothing contrary to the word of God, were instantly introduced into London diocese. They first appear in the record in October 1583, when Aylmer made use of them in advance of their official promulgation to pounce on, and suspend, Northey of Colchester. Strenuous attempts by the Colchester authorities to have Northey restored included an appeal to Aylmer's old friend William Cole—their former town preacher and now president of Corpus Christi College, Oxford—to intercede with him on Northey's behalf. Cole found Aylmer inflexible and flatly advised that Northey should capitulate.

In early March 1584 Aylmer summoned eight leading Essex nonconformists—Gifford and Arthur Dent amongst them—to Fulham. All were shown the articles and asked if they were prepared to subscribe. Two unbeneficed men, Nicholas Ward and Thomas Carew, were immediately suspended upon refusal. The remainder were given time to deliberate.

If the subscription crisis of 1584 was not quite a storm in a teacup—it marked the beginning of the end of moderate puritan aspirations for the liberalization of Elizabeth's settlement—the evidence of John Field's papers argues that only thirteen other Essex incumbents were subsequently disciplined. The principal casualties proved to be Northey and George Gifford, deprived of his benefice in May or June. By September, however, Whitgift's campaign, steadily opposed by Burghley and the majority of the privy council, had collapsed and the case of Richard Rogers of Wethersfield was probably typical: Aylmer restored him after thirty weeks' suspension, apparently without demanding subscription.

Whilst they remained available as a cat-and-mouse tactic it must be doubted that Whitgift's articles were ever again fully implemented within the diocese of London. Compromise was probably effected by means of a form of limited subscription or else promises of good behaviour on the part of those whom Aylmer chose to pursue. Although never again beneficed Gifford was soon restored to his ministry in Maldon and remained there as town preacher until his death in 1600. Northey was released from suspension in late 1584, dying as Colchester's town preacher in 1593.

Altogether Aylmer's efforts to subdue his recalcitrant clergy during the 1580s were considerably less successful than was once supposed. John Field's papers, comprehensively quarried by early historians of nonconformity, appeared, for tactical reasons, to paint a picture of nonconformist defeat at every turn. It was one which John Strype, charting Aylmer's progress via his self-justifying letters to Burghley, was content broadly to endorse. Yet Strype failed to recognize that whenever Aylmer was forced to defend himself he had almost invariably lost the battle in advance, however long it may have taken Burghley to wear him down. Essentially Aylmer's efforts boil down to a persistent crusade against about thirty entrenched nonconformists—the members of the two clerical conferences and their close associates. Most remained in place until their deaths.

Despite strenuous attempts to alter the 1559 settlement in the parliament which met in November 1584 there appears to have been no sustained, constructive attempt to pursue the supporters of parliamentary puritanism in the rural parishes. During 1585 only half a dozen unbeneficed men—including Robert Wright, now preaching at Fryerning—continued under threat in the name of full subscription, and whilst a new tactic was introduced of indicting beneficed nonconformists at assize this policy seems to have been abandoned during 1586. The only other men to draw attention to themselves in these months were William Tunstall, vicar of Great Totham, summoned to answer charges in October 1585; Thomas Carew of Hatfield Peverel; Mark Wiersdale of Maldon; and William Dyke, suspended as preacher of St Albans in June 1586 despite the best efforts of Lady Bacon, Burghley's sister-in-law.

If 1585 provided a lull before a further storm it was perhaps because in mid-career Aylmer had made a serious political blunder: in April 1585 he fell foul of Elizabeth, Burghley, and Leicester by arresting Thomas Cartwright on his return to England and by August was again defending himself against charges of despoiling his see.

Aylmer conducted his 1586 visitation himself, narrowly escaping ridicule in Maldon when the authorities foiled a plot to snatch his cap and toss it around the crowd. Otherwise, with uncharacteristic restraint, he reported that 'disorders … were not so great as was feared (though more than is to be wished)' (BL, Lansdowne MS 50, fol. 88*r*). In London, Walter Travers, Thomas Barber, and Field were all suspended and in Essex no fewer than twenty-eight men, 'the painfullest ministers in Essex, whom the Bp. threatneth to deprive, sayinge we shalbe white with him or he wilbe black with us' (Peel, *Register*, 2.260–61). They included Gifford, Wiersdale, Tunstall, Carew, Rogers, and Dyke, as well as Northey of Colchester and several members of the Dedham conference, including Chapman.

Important also was the re-establishment at this visitation of clerical exercises for the supervision of the less able clergy, strictly under diocesan control: thus, at Whitgift's behest, the 'prophesyings' which had toppled Grindal were reintroduced in a modified form. Yet Aylmer soon discovered that there were those who had managed to obtain preaching licences in order to avoid attending them. This probably accounts for an obscure episode in October 1586, when George Withers was inhibited as archdeacon of Colchester for violating his privilege of granting licences.

Although a flurry of petitions to the privy council and to parliament followed the suspensions of 1586–7 Aylmer scored two decisive victories. Whilst no specific details of their cases are known, Tunstall of Great Totham, under threat since 1585, and Giles Whiting, rector of Panfield, were deprived by the high commission in May 1587. Later that year, however, Aylmer suffered another personal setback when his son-in-law Adam Squire, archdeacon of Middlesex, was discovered to be an adulterer.

Continuing as Whitgift's senior coadjutor on the high commission Aylmer took final responsibility for the deprivation that year of Robert Cawdrey, rector of Luffenham, Rutland. In this crucial test-case Cawdrey brought an action in queen's bench which in essence challenged the commission's competence under the strict provisions of the Act of Supremacy. His defeat 'in effect established the Court of High Commission as a proper and lawful court' (Elton, 221).

In March 1588 Aylmer again suspended Chapman of Dedham, this time for refusing to take part in an ordination at Fulham. On 6 July 1588 he ordered Stephen Egerton and his churchwardens in Blackfriars not to admit strangers to communion. He also suspended 'silver-tongued' Henry Smith, lecturer at St Clement Danes, inviting yet another head-on collision with Burghley, Smith's kinsman by marriage. Smith was restored. In 1591 Aylmer clashed with his dean, Alexander Nowell, who declined to induct the bishop's son Theophilus as archdeacon of London on the grounds that he was too young for such promotion. Instead Aylmer issued a special mandate to four senior prebendaries, headed by Lancelot Andrewes. Theophilus, only thirty-one at the time, was duly installed.

Meanwhile the puritan cause in parliament and the conference movement had alike collapsed. The death of Field, and then of Leicester, in 1588 shattered the cohesiveness of the moderate puritan party, and the appearance shortly afterwards of the Martin Marprelate tracts inadvertently tolled its death knell. The pursuit of Martinists and separatists thereafter by Whitgift and Richard Bancroft overwhelmed all organized opposition to their policies as long as Elizabeth lived. Yet the Marprelate tracts themselves bid fair to overwhelm Aylmer, principal butt of their relentless, satirical invective. He was characterized as Dumb John of London for his infrequent preaching and as Mar-elm for that tin-can always tied to his tail, his purported over-exploitation of his timber. Thus the visitation of 1589 took place in a strangely ambivalent atmosphere. The visitors do not appear to have wished to stir up any hornets' nests in the city. Of only three clergymen cited for failing to use the surplice, Stephen Egerton of Blackfriars was enjoined (rather than ordered) to do so but ignored the court's further monitions. Thomas Gataker later claimed that he had never received a summons to attend and ostentatiously left court without petitioning for release from excommunication. Neither seems to have been subsequently pursued.

In Essex the demise of the Dedham conference had left its members and supporters in disarray. Richard Parker, vicar of Dedham, had been exposed as an adulterer and resigned in 1590. William Tey of Peldon was now suspended by the high commission and Thomas Farrar of Langham threatened with sequestration. George Northey and Stephen Beamont of Easthorpe again came under pressure. Outside this Colchester circle Aylmer's principal target was Ezekiel Culverwell, preacher at Felsted and spiritual mentor to Lord Rich in succession to Robert Wright. Culverwell was now at loggerheads with the vicar of Felsted, William Rust, and accordingly fell victim to Aylmer's continuing feud with the Rich family. At St Albans William Dyke was again suspended.

All survived, but there is as much evidence of accommodation on both sides as of capitulation by the nonconformists. Edward Stanhope refused to turn the case against Culverwell into a witch-hunt and, mindful of his canonical duty, achieved an ostensible reconciliation between him and Rust. Richard Rogers of Wethersfield, whilst admitting that he had not administered the sacraments, was dismissed on production of a letter from Ambrose, earl of Warwick (whom he never once mentions in his diary), stating that Rogers was the earl's chaplain.

Last years, 1590–1594 With the death of Edmund Freake of Worcester in March 1591 the seventy-year-old Aylmer glimpsed a final prospect of escape from London. Within weeks Hatton informed Bancroft that Elizabeth had agreed to translate Aylmer to Worcester and to promote Bancroft in his place. Nothing came of the proposal but, according to Whitgift, Aylmer 'offred thrice, in two years' to resign in Bancroft's favour 'upon certain conditions, w[ch] he refused' (Peel, *Tracts*, xx).

In the summer of 1592 Aylmer conducted his final visitation. The act book of office does not survive but in the wake of recent events—eight nonconformist leaders, including Cartwright, had been tried in Star Chamber during the winter of 1590–91—there are signs that Aylmer may have been disposed to pour oil on troubled waters. In February 1592 Stanhope had granted a preaching licence to Richard Greenham without any form of subscription or obligation on his part because Thomas Fanshaw, queen's remembrancer, had promised that he would not preach contentiously. It is also instructive that, amongst the thirty-seven preachers described as *concionator notus*, there were some strange bedfellows: Bancroft and archdeacons Hutchinson and Theophilus Aylmer from amongst the hierarchs; long-lived Marian exiles such as Thomas Upcher and Robert Harrington; and nonconformists recently pursued by Aylmer, including Richard Rogers and Northey.

The 1592 call book also provides evidence of Aylmer's wider achievement in his efforts to promote an educated ministry. After the abuses of 1586 the granting of preaching licences had presumably been strictly monitored and some withdrawn. Yet by 1592 only 146 incumbents outside the city (including all 56 absentees) were not listed as holding one. Of the 90 men actually present 14 were ordered or invited to apply for a diocesan licence whilst only 29 remained 'tied to the exercises', most of them long-serving survivors from the first half of the reign. Many of the absentees can be added to the list of qualified preachers. Although the steady advance of a university-trained ministry was one of the hallmarks of Elizabeth's reign this represents a notable achievement. During his visitation in 1595 Aylmer's successor, Richard Fletcher, declared himself favourably impressed with the overall quality of the country clergy.

Yet until the end Aylmer remained *persona non grata* at court. In June 1592, suggesting candidates for the bishopric of Oxford, he sourly observed that he had seldom had any luck in recommending his friends for promotion. It appears to have been the last time he addressed Burghley in writing and his health may have suddenly collapsed, since the government thereafter took the unusual step of providing him with a coadjutor: on 12 November John Sterne was consecrated bishop of Colchester, the last of only three suffragans appointed under Elizabeth, and the last until 1870.

Aylmer died at Fulham Palace on 3 June 1594 and was buried at St Paul's Cathedral. According to Whitgift he 'signify'd the day before his death' his regret that he had not written to Elizabeth recommending Bancroft as his successor (Peel, *Tracts*, xx). Aylmer's dying voice would have cut little ice with Burghley, who espoused the claims of William Day, or with Essex, who successfully promoted those of Fletcher. 'Many a drye eye for the Byshopp of London', wrote Philip Gawdy to his brother, 'who is deade and buryed, and I feare me not ascended into heaven (saving my charity)'. He added that Aylmer had left £1500 a year to his children (*Seventh Report*, HMC, 524), an assessment which must have been close to the truth. In his will, dated 22 April 1594, his three eldest sons, Samuel, Theophilus, and John, received substantial property in Essex, Suffolk, and Lincolnshire respectively. Yet there were also large charitable bequests: £300 for the better maintenance of the Paul's Cross sermons; and to the poor of London (£100) and Fulham (£40).

Although Fletcher never mentioned the subject, Bancroft, finally consecrated to London in 1597 after Essex lent his support to Whitgift's long-waged campaign on Bancroft's behalf, penned a damning report on Aylmer's stewardship of the bishopric. Since 1576 he had purchased land to the value of £16,000 for his family's benefit whilst surveyors had set dilapidations of episcopal properties at £6500, of which £4000 needed to be spent on St Paul's Cathedral. Aylmer had also profited from timber during his time to the tune of £6000. Bancroft had begun a process against Samuel Aylmer in the court of arches for the recovery of £4210 only to discover that the late bishop had carefully disposed of his liquid assets before his death and that Samuel refused to part with what he naturally claimed was his patrimony. The result was a detailed exchequer inquiry into the relative liability of Samuel and of a corrupt sub-collector for these and other debts, to the tune of £1500. During the course of it Samuel found himself incarcerated in a debtors' prison.

Aylmer and the Elizabethan church John Aylmer was small of stature, compact, vigorous, and aggressive. With the understandable exception of John Strype (whose publisher, Brabazon Aylmer, was the bishop's direct descendant) historians have united in concluding that Aylmer's pugnacity made him ill-fitted for the second most politically sensitive post in the Church of England during the heart of Elizabeth's reign. Not for nothing did his funeral monument in St Paul's proclaim him 'bis pugil in causa religionis' ('twice a fighter in the cause of religion'). Vetting or omitting the nastier remarks in the letters which he paraphrased, Strype laboured to present a diligent, learned chief pastor whose only care was for the good of the church-state. Yet he could not conceal the fact that Aylmer had a genius for antagonizing supporters and opponents alike and was in many respects a typical bully: usually sycophantic to superiors, unmerciful with inferiors. Technically a formidable administrator, he never learned the true art of administration itself: that of handling those with whom he had to deal with a modicum of tact or consideration. As late as December 1592, bemoaning the decayed state of the Paul's Cross sermons to the privy council, he laid all the blame on his chaplain of twelve years' standing, William Cotton.

Although an able and respected scholar Aylmer exhibited no inclination to make a contribution to the major controversies of his time. George Orwell admired the *Harborowe* as a landmark in the history of political literature (it contains the striking marginal note 'God is English'), but when Walter Travers's *De disciplina* appeared in early 1574 to pump iron into presbyterian muscles, Aylmer refused Parker's request to answer it and failed to return the copy Parker had sent him. In 1581, pleading ill health, he declined to answer Edmund Campion.

Strype bent over backwards to emphasize those passages in his letters which spoke of his friendship with and dependence upon Burghley but they were largely drawn from those which show him at his most grovelling. There can be little doubt that in fact Burghley regarded his elevation as an unmitigated disaster, and his long-drawn game of cat-and-mouse with Aylmer must be accounted one of the least glorious strands in his career. It also involves a conundrum. Given Aylmer's divisiveness and his frequent requests for translation to a less burdensome diocese, why was Burghley unable or unwilling to engineer it?

BRETT USHER

Sources J. Strype, *Historical collections of the life and acts of … John Aylmer*, new edn (1821) • T. Becon, 'The jewel of joy', *The catechism of Thomas Becon … with other pieces written by him in the reign of King Edward the sixth*, ed. J. Ayre, 3, Parker Society, 17 (1844), 411–76 • H. Robinson, ed. and trans., *The Zurich letters, comprising the correspondence of several English bishops and others with some of the Helvetian reformers, during the early part of the reign of Queen Elizabeth*, 2 vols., Parker Society, 7–8 (1842–5) • H. Robinson, ed. and trans., *Original letters relative to the English Reformation*, 1 vol. in 2, Parker Society, [26] (1846–7) • Fuller, *Worthies* (1840) • T. Cooper, *An admonition to the people of England*, 1589, ed. E. Arber (1882) • R. Ascham, *The scholemaster*, ed. E. Arber, [new edn] (1870) • [J. Aylmer], *An harborowe for faithfull and trewe subjectes* [1559] • C. H. Garrett, *The Marian exiles: a study in the origins of Elizabethan puritanism* (1938) • P. Collinson, *The Elizabethan puritan movement* (1967) • P. Collinson, *The religion of protestants* (1982) • state papers foreign, Elizabeth I, PRO, SP 70/4, fol. 117 [letter from elector of Saxony to Elizabeth, 1559] • G. Orwell and R. Reynolds, eds., *British pamphleteers*, 1: *from the sixteenth century to the French Revolution* (1948), 28–33 [commentary and extracts from *Harborowe*] • J. F. Mozley, *John Foxe and his book* (1940) • W. Haller, *Foxe's 'Book of martyrs' and the elect nation* (1963) [*Harborowe*] • D. M. Loades, *Two Tudor conspiracies* (1965) [Wyatt's rebellion] • J. W. F. Hill, *Tudor and Stuart Lincoln* (1956) • C. W. Foster, ed., *Lincoln episcopal records, in the time of Thomas Cooper … bishop of Lincoln*, CYS, 11 (1913) • LPL, MS 3470, fol. 22 [Aylmer to Grindal on affairs in Lincoln, 1576] • LPL, MS 2003 • *Registrum Matthei Parker, diocesis Cantuariensis, AD 1559–1575*, ed. W. H. Frere and E. M. Thompson, 3 vols., CYS, 35–6, 39 (1928–33) [Corringham; dispute with Cooper] • W. P. M. Kennedy, ed., *Elizabethan episcopal administration*, 1–2, Alcuin Club, Collections, 25–6 (1924) • *Correspondence of Matthew Parker*, ed. J. Bruce and T. T. Perowne, Parker Society, 42 (1853) • N. H. Nicolas, *Memoirs of the life and times of Sir Christopher Hatton* (1847) [letters of Aylmer to Hatton and Elizabeth] • E. St J. Brooks, *Sir Christopher Hatton* (1946) • *Fasti Angl.*, 1541–1857, [Lincoln] • BL, Lansdowne MSS, esp. 33, 50 [letters to Burghley, 1577–92] • R. G. Usher, *The rise and fall of the high commission* (1913) • R. G. Usher, ed., *The presbyterian movement in the reign of Queen Elizabeth, as illustrated by the minute book of the Dedham classis, 1582–1589*, CS, 3rd ser., 8 (1905) • A. Peel, ed., *The seconde parte of a register*, 2 vols. (1915) • A. Peel, ed., *Tracts ascribed to Richard Bancroft* (1953) • R. O'Day, *The English clergy: the emergence and consolidation of a profession, 1558–1642* (1979) [diocesan exercises after 1586] • F. Heal, *Of prelates and princes: a study of the economic and social position of the Tudor episcopate* (1980) • B. Usher, 'Colchester and diocesan administration, 1539–1604' [study compiled to assist writers of Colchester volume of *VCH Essex*, 1993; copies at Essex RO as T/Z 440/1] • B. Usher, 'John Aylmer and the high commission', unpublished paper, priv. coll. • HoP, *Commons*, 1558–1603, 1.411–14 • *Two Elizabethan puritan diaries, by Richard Rogers and Samuel Ward*, ed. M. M. Knappen, SCH, 2 [1933] [diary of Richard Rogers] • GL, MSS 9531/13 [Aylmer's register] • call books of visitation, 1577–92, GL, MSS 9537/4–8 • G. R. Elton, *The Tudor constitution* (1960) • vicar-general's books, 1574–95, LMA, DL/C/333–5 • act books of office, LMA, DL/C/300, 301, 616 [1583–4; 1584–6; 1589–90] • S. R. Maitland, *Essays on subjects connected with the Reformation in England* (1849) • BL, Add. MS 32091 • state papers domestic, Elizabeth I, PRO, SP 12/112/45 • state papers domestic, Edward VI–James I, addenda, PRO, SP 15/12/54 • H. Chauncy, *The historical antiquities of Hertfordshire* (1700); repr. in 2 vols., 1 (1826), 318–19 • parish records of Cossington, Leicestershire [transcript at Society of Genealogists, London] • *Seventh report*, HMC, 6 (1879) • *The poetical works of Edmund Spenser*, ed. J. C. Smith and E. De Selincourt (1912)

Archives BL, Lansdowne MSS, letters to Burghley and privy council • BL, Add. MSS, letters to Christopher Hatton • GL, call books of visitation, MSS 9537/4–8 • GL, register, MSS 9531/13 • LMA, act books of office, DL/C/300, 301, 616 • LMA, vicar-general's books, DL/C/333–5

Likenesses R. White, engraving, repro. in J. Strype, *Life of Aylmer*, 2nd edn (1728), frontispiece • line engraving (after unknown artist), BM, NPG

Wealth at death considerable; property in Suffolk, Essex, and Lincolnshire; contemporary gossip stated he left children £1500 p.a.: will, Strype, *Historical collections*; *Seventh report*, HMC

Aylmer, Matthew, first Baron Aylmer of Balrath (*d.* **1720**), naval officer and politician, was the second son of Sir Christopher Aylmer (*c.*1615–1671), first baronet of Balrath, co. Meath, and his wife, Margaret, *née* Plunkett (*d.* 1671). In 1672 he entered the regiment of the duke of Buckingham, whose page he was—at least, according to tradition, which also claims that he subsequently raised troops in

Munster to fight for the Dutch against the French. In January 1677 he was appointed an ensign in the Tangier regiment and became a lieutenant in the earl of Inchiquin's regiment of foot at Tangier in August 1678. Aylmer began his naval career in the Mediterranean Fleet at much the same time, becoming a midshipman aboard the galley *Charles* in October 1677 and her lieutenant in April 1678; he served in her until 9 January 1679 when he was appointed captain of the double sloop *Chatham* by Arthur Herbert, the admiral on the station and Aylmer's patron. He subsequently held the commands of the prize *Date Tree* (1679) and the fireship *Castle* (1679–80) in the Mediterranean, and of the *Swan* on the Irish coast from July 1680 to 10 January 1682, when he was given command of the prize *Tiger* by 'his majesty's special command' (PRO, ADM 3/278, pt 2, p. 5), and returned to the Mediterranean to rejoin Herbert.

In 1682 Aylmer carried to England the news of Herbert's successful conclusion of a treaty with Algiers. Samuel Pepys encountered him in the Mediterranean in 1683–4, where he was still commanding the *Tiger*, and was distinctly unimpressed. Aylmer's carpenter told Pepys that his captain made 'good voyages' (transporting merchant goods in a warship for a commission) and had also 'made love to a young woman and lain both with her and her mother, and borrowed a great many hundred pounds of them' (Chappell, 137). Aylmer was described as one of Herbert's 'creatures' and one of 'the greatest libertines of the fleet', who regularly badgered his patron for 'good voyages' but was 'a very coward' who would 'stay in the Navy [no] longer than till he has got two or three thousand pounds in his pocket' (ibid., 186–7, 236). Pepys believed that Aylmer, a man of 'mean mind', 'deserved … to be hanged' for striking his flag to the Spanish at Cadiz on 5–6 July 1683, though he and his fellow captain Cloudesley Shovell had been heavily outnumbered (ibid., 167, 184). In the late 1670s or 1680s Aylmer married Sarah Ellis (*d.* 1710); they had at least four children.

Pepys's hostility (born of his hatred of Aylmer's patron, Herbert), and the groundless charge of being an Irish papist levelled against Aylmer in September 1680 during the Popish Plot crisis, had no discernible effect on his career. From 21 June to 14 July 1685 he commanded the *Mediterranean*, a hired vessel placed in the Severn estuary to search ships during the duke of Monmouth's rebellion, and on 27 September 1685 he was given command of the galley *Charles*. He held this position alongside a captaincy in the Queen Dowager's regiment of horse, to which he was commissioned on 1 June 1686. On 1 October 1688 Aylmer became captain of the *Swallow*, part of the fleet intended to repel William of Orange's invasion force. Aylmer quickly became one of the heads of the Orangist conspiracy in the fleet, having been recruited by the army officers Percy Kirke (an old Tangier colleague) and the second duke of Ormond. In turn Aylmer became an active recruiter for William among the captains of the fleet, and was described as one of eight who were prepared to defect with their ships to the prince's side. Aylmer smuggled William's letter to James II's admiral, Lord Dartmouth, into the admiral's toilet, and carried back to the prince Dartmouth's reply, effectively surrendering the fleet and praising Aylmer as a man 'entirely devoted to your highness' (Davies, 'Admirals', 86).

The success of the revolution made Aylmer's career. He was promoted to command the *Mary* on 22 December 1688 and was subsequently warmly recommended in particular by Herbert's rival, Edward Russell, who said of him in February 1690 that 'I am not biased with friendship to him though I love him extremely, but he is really a very useful man' (*Finch MSS*, 2.271). Aylmer commanded the *Mary* at the battle of Bantry Bay on 1 May 1689; she sustained severe damage to her rigging and sails, as well as taking fourteen shots in the hull, having three guns split, and losing one man dead and seven wounded. He subsequently moved to the *Suffolk* in Russell's division of the Blue squadron, and in 1690 commanded the *Royal Katherine* at the battle of Beachy Head. Over the winter of 1690–91 he took fourteen ships to the Mediterranean to confirm the treaties with the Barbary corsairs and to convoy English trade there. In September 1691, in command of the *Monck* in the North Sea, he took a large Dunkirk privateer off Scarborough. In spring 1692 he took command of the first-rate *London*, serving in her at the battle of Barfleur as second to Russell's flagship, the *Britannia*.

Aylmer became a rear-admiral on 8 February 1693 and a vice-admiral following Sir John Ashby's death in June; he was also a commissioner of the navy from 25 March 1694 to 16 July 1702. Throughout the 1690s Aylmer clearly relied heavily on the continuing patronage of Russell, whose whig politics he shared: in 1692 another admiral complained that 'Mr Russell has been tampering with [the earl of Portland] and others on the score of some favourite of his, and I believe it to be Mr Elmour [*sic*]' (*Finch MSS*, 4.192). In 1694 he was Russell's second-in-command in the Mediterranean, assuming acting command in September when the admiral was struck with dysentery. Following the peace of Ryswick, Aylmer was elected MP for Dover on 15 December 1697 in the interest of Russell's whig junto, and continued to serve as such, apart from an interruption in 1713–15, until his death; additionally, he became governor of Deal Castle in 1701.

In 1698–9 Aylmer went again to the Mediterranean to confirm the treaties, flying his flag in the *Boyne*, but his animosity towards George Churchill caused his retirement from active service in November 1699 following the latter's appointment to the Admiralty board. The death of the queen's husband, Prince George, in 1708 permitted Russell's return to the Admiralty, and Churchill's retirement in November 1709 allowed Aylmer to become commander-in-chief. However, a comparatively unsuccessful engagement with a French squadron in July 1710 (only one warship and one merchantman were taken) contributed to his displacement in January 1711. George I's accession, and the consequent return of the whigs to favour, led in 1714 to Aylmer's reappointment as commander-in-chief, in addition to appointments as governor of Greenwich Hospital (6 November 1714) and ranger of Greenwich Park. He was primarily responsible for the establishment of what was to become the Royal

Hospital school. He was appointed to the Admiralty board on 16 April 1717, resigning on 19 March 1718 following his appointment on the previous day as rear-admiral of Great Britain. On 1 May 1718 he was created Baron Aylmer of Balrath in the Irish peerage. Aylmer's and his wife's children included a son Henry, who succeeded to the title, and who, along with his son-in-law Sir John Norris and his nephew Sir Peter Warren, also became an admiral; their daughters were Elizabeth, Sarah, and Lucy, the last of whom received a portion of £4000 in Aylmer's will, dated 7 June 1720. A contemporary said of him that he had 'a very good head, indefatigable and designing; is very zealous for the liberties of the people; makes a good figure in the parliament, as well as the fleet; is handsome in his person, a brown man' (*Memoirs of the Secret Services*, 107). However, Jonathan Swift was as uncharitable as Pepys had once been, describing Aylmer as 'a virulent party man, born in Ireland' (*Prose Works*, 10.285). Aylmer's brother George was also a prominent naval captain and another of the leading lights in the Williamite conspiracy in the fleet in 1688: originally a page to the earl of Arlington, he became a captain in 1680, was described by Pepys as 'a swearing, idle fellow' (Chappell, 194–5), and was killed as captain of the *Portland* at the battle of Bantry Bay (1 May 1689). Matthew Aylmer died in the Queen's House at Greenwich on 18 August 1720 and was buried five days later in St Alfege's Church, Greenwich. J. D. Davies

Sources F. Aylmer, *The Aylmers of Ireland* (1931) • J. D. Davies, 'James II, William of Orange, and the admirals', *By force or by default? The revolution of 1688–1689*, ed. E. Cruickshanks (1989), 82–108 • PRO, ADM MSS 1/577, 5253; 2/169–75, 377–80, 1752–4; 3/277–8, 1–6; 6/424; 8/1–4, 106/341, 349, 374, 379–87 • Aylmer's order- and letter-books, BL, Add. MSS 28122–28124 • P. Le Fevre, 'Matthew Aylmer (*c*. 1650–1720)', *Mariner's Mirror*, 73 (1987), 206–8 • *The Tangier papers of Samuel Pepys*, ed. E. Chappell, Navy RS, 73 (1935) • *Memoirs of the secret services of John Macky*, ed. J. M. Grey, Roxburghe Club (1895), 107 • *Report on the manuscripts of Allan George Finch*, 5 vols., HMC, 71 (1913–2003), vols. 2–4 • *The manuscripts of the earl of Dartmouth*, 3 vols., HMC, 20 (1887–96), vols. 1, 3 • *Memoirs relating to the Lord Torrington*, ed. J. K. Laughton, CS, new ser., 46 (1889) • *The prose works of Jonathan Swift*, ed. T. Scott, 12 vols. (1897–1908), vol. 10, p. 285 • R. C. Anderson, 'English flag officers, 1688–1713', *Mariner's Mirror*, 35 (1949), 333–41 • R. R. Sedgwick, 'Aylmer, Matthew', HoP, *Commons, 1715–54* • GEC, *Peerage* • J. D. Davies, *Gentlemen and tarpaulins: the officers and men of the Restoration navy* (1991) • Magd. Cam., Pepys Library, MS 2855, fol. 220; MS 2859, fol. 37

Archives BL, naval order books, Add. MSS 28122–28124 | CKS, corresp. with Alexander Stanhope • PRO, Admiralty MSS

Likenesses J. Richardson, oils, *c*.1692–1693, NMM • oils (after P. Lely), NMM • oils (as a young man; after P. Lely), NMM

Wealth at death £4000 to daughter: PRO, PROB 11/575, fol. 318*v*

Ayloffe [Ayliffe], **John** (*c*.1645–1685), satirist and conspirator, was born in Foxley, Wiltshire, the younger son of John Ayliffe (*b*. 1611?). He matriculated at St Edmund Hall, Oxford, in July 1662 and was admitted to the Inner Temple in 1664. An unyielding opponent of the Stuart monarchy, he was 'one of the most consistently committed radicals of the century'—according to Sir Roger L'Estrange, there were few 'more daring men for a desperate exploit' (Greaves & Zaller, *BDBR*, 1.31). Ayloffe first became prominent in October 1673, when he placed a wooden shoe in the speaker's chair in the House of Commons, as a symbol of pernicious French influence. *Nostradamus's Prophecy*, a poem probably by Ayloffe and published in 1672, had referred to 'wooden shoes' as a sign of subservience to France, praised 'Venetian liberty', and attacked parliamentary corruption (Lord, *Poems on Affairs of State*, 185–9).

At the time of the Third Anglo-Dutch War, in 1671–3, Ayloffe was a leading member, along with his close friend and associate Andrew Marvell, in a clandestine organization headed by Peter Du Moulin, working in the interests of William of Orange against France. Ayloffe is probably the author, or co-author with Du Moulin, of the influential pamphlet *Englands Appeale from the Private Caballe at Whitehall* (1673), which in Haley's words 'did more than anything else to identify the French alliance in foreign affairs with the dangers of Popery at home' (Haley, 97–9). In 1677 he petitioned for pardon for 'printing *The Appeal* and *The Votes of Parliament* … for which he has suffered two years exile' (*Fourth Report*, HMC, 235). *The Votes of Parliament* may refer to a detailed satiric attack on parliamentary corruption circulated in 1677 under the title *A Seasonable Argument* (an earlier version, BL, Lansdowne MS 805, dates from 1672), on which Marvell and Ayloffe are likely to have collaborated (Chernaik, 97, 226).

During the Exclusion Bill crisis, Ayloffe was a trusted lieutenant of Shaftesbury—one of the two 'chief agents of the said Earl'—and an active member of the whig Green Ribbon Club (Lord, 'Satire and sedition', 260–61). He was involved in the Rye House plot in 1683, claiming that 'it was impossible England could ever be happy under such a government as we lived under, for the King designs to bring in arbitrary power', and, under a warrant of arrest for high treason, escaped to Holland; at this time his estates in Wiltshire were confiscated. In Holland, he continued to plot an insurrection against the hated Stuarts (on a secret mission to England to canvass support, he found that his reputation 'as an atheist' made him *persona non grata* with nonconformist ministers), and in 1685 he served as colonel of a regiment of foot in an unsuccessful invasion of Scotland led by the ninth earl of Argyll, a premature attempt to overthrow James II. After being captured and attempting suicide (stabbing himself with a penknife), he was executed as a traitor at the Temple gate on 30 October 1685, refusing to testify against his fellow conspirators and offering prayers on the scaffold 'to preserve the Protestant Religion' (ibid., 262–5; Greaves & Zaller, *BDBR*, 1.31).

Nearly all Ayloffe's extant poems are political and attest to his republican sympathies. 'Marvell's Ghost' (1678) imagines the poet returning from the dead to prophesy the downfall of the 'spurious race' of Stuarts, who have 'laid waste the commonweal' and have brought upon themselves 'those resentments … That drove the Tarquins out of Rome' (Lord, *Poems on Affairs of State*, 1.285–6). 'Britannia and Raleigh' (1674), one of a number of satires falsely attributed to Marvell in the early editions of *Poems on Affairs of State*, is generally accepted as Ayloffe's. Explicitly attacking monarchy as an institution, it lavishes praise on 'the sage Venetian state' as well as the two Brutuses, heroes of the republican pantheon, and ends with an open call to rebellion: 'No poisonous tyrant on thy ground shall live' (ibid., 1.228–36). An elegy on Sir Thomas Armstrong, executed in 1684 for his part in the Rye House plot, is attributed to Ayloffe in BL, Harley MS 7319: it is equally uncompromising in its attacks on monarchy, calling for the 'destruction' of the tyrannous Stuarts ('*Tarquin* and *Nero* were but types of thee') and praising Armstrong as 'a worthy Patriot' like '*Brutus* or just *Cato*'. Other poems probably by Ayloffe include two poems attributed to him in *Poems on Affairs of State* (1697), 'A Litany' (1681), a satire on high tory Anglican clergy, and 'Satyr' (1684?), attacking the duke of York as tyrant-in-waiting. More doubtful attributions to Ayloffe include 'Advice to a Painter to Draw the Duke by' (1673), an anti-Catholic satire on the duke of York, where the weight of evidence favours Henry Savile as author, and 'Oceana and Britannia' (1681).

WARREN CHERNAIK

Sources Greaves & Zaller, *BDBR*, 30–31 · G. Lord, 'Satire and sedition: the life and work of John Ayloffe', *Huntington Library Quarterly*, 29 (1965–6), 255–73 · G. de F. Lord and others, eds., *Poems on affairs of state: Augustan satirical verse, 1660–1714*, 7 vols. (1963–75), vol. 1 · 'The *Dictionary of National Biography*: Ayloffe, John', *BIHR*, 2 (1924–5), 93–4 · K. Haley, *William of Orange and the English opposition, 1672–4* (1953) · W. Chernaik, *The poet's time: politics and religion in the work of Andrew Marvell* (1983) · R. L. Greaves, *Secrets of the kingdom: British radicals from the Popish Plot to the revolution of 1688–89* (1992) · Foster, *Alum. Oxon.*, 1500–1714 [John Ayliffe] · *A true account of the proceedings against John Ayloffe* (1685) · *A collection of poems on affairs of state*, 3 vols. (1689) · *Poems on affairs of state … by the greatest wits of the age* (1697) · Bodl. Oxf., MS Eng. poet d. 49 · BL, Harley MSS 6845, 7315, 7319; Lansdowne MS 805; Add. MSS 27407, 23722 · *CSP dom.*, 1676–8; 1680–81; 1683–7 · *The poems and letters of Andrew Marvell*, ed. H. Margoliouth, rev. P. Legouis, 3rd edn, 2 vols. (1971) · J. E. Jackson, 'The Ayliffes of Grittenham', *Wiltshire Archaeological and Natural History Magazine*, 21 (1884), 194–210 · H. Weber, *Paper bullets: print and kingship under Charles II* (1996) · 'A seasonable argument (1677)', *English historical documents*, 8, ed. A. Browning (1953); repr. (1966) · G. Marshall, ed., *The visitation of Wiltshire, 1623* (1882) · *Fourth report*, HMC, 3 (1874)

Ayloffe, Sir Joseph, sixth baronet (1709/10–1781), antiquary, was the only son of Joseph Ayloffe (1662/3–1726), barrister, of Gray's Inn, London, and Mary Ayliffe (*d.* 1747), daughter of Brian Ayliffe, merchant of London. His father was said to have spent the last years of his life in Kirk Ireton, Derbyshire, in a most miserable state and died in 1726, aged sixty-three. Ayloffe was admitted to Westminster School in 1719 and Lincoln's Inn in 1724. He matriculated as a gentleman commoner at St John's College, Oxford, on 23 April 1726, aged sixteen, but left about 1728 without taking his degree and was called to the bar at Lincoln's Inn in 1730. Later the same year he succeeded to the baronetcy on the death of his unmarried cousin Sir John Ayloffe, fifth baronet. In January 1734 he married Margaret Railton (1704/5–1797), the daughter of Thomas Railton of Carlisle and the widow of Thomas Railton JP of Westminster. They had one son, Joseph, who died of smallpox in 1756, aged twenty-one.

Ayloffe was described by the Revd Mark Noble as having a better education than fortune, and for much of his life he had salaried employment. In 1736 he was appointed clerk to the commissioners for building Westminster Bridge at £200 p.a. He managed the commission's affairs efficiently and was discharged in 1750, when the bridge was completed. Confusion with Joseph Ayliffe has led to the mistaken claim that he was auditor-general of the Bridewell and Bethlem hospitals in 1750. Ayloffe launched a series of unsuccessful publishing schemes in 1751. His *Universal Librarian*, whose authorship was attributed anonymously 'to a Fellow of the Royal Society', was intended to review the most important new books published in Britain and abroad, but only volume 1, part 1 (1751), was published. He circulated proposals for printing the debates in parliament prior to the Restoration, but never published them. His plan to issue a translation of Diderot's *Encyclopédie* in parts, with additional articles on English subjects, was severely criticized in the *Gentleman's Magazine* after the first number was published in 1752, and the project was abandoned.

Ayloffe's chief interest was antiquarian research. He was elected fellow of the Royal Society in 1731 and of the Society of Antiquaries of London in 1732, and served as vice-president of both learned societies. Later in life he established himself as the unofficial legal adviser to the Society of Antiquaries and in 1776 drew up their petition to George III for accommodation in the new Somerset House. He was also a member of the Spalding Gentlemen's Society in 1739. In 1764 he found congenial employment with Andrew Ducarel and Thomas Astle as a commissioner for methodizing, regulating, and digesting the records in the state paper office in Whitehall. The salary was £100 p.a., and the following year the task was extended to cover some of the exchequer records for an additional £100 a year. Ayloffe continued this work until his death. The commissioners primarily arranged records rather than digesting or calendaring them, and twentieth-century archivists criticized their method for sorting without maintaining archival integrity.

In 1764 Ayloffe drew up proposals for a history of Suffolk, which he claimed to have been working on for many years, but according to John Nichols the project did not receive sufficient encouragement to proceed. All Ayloffe's antiquarian publications date from after his appointment at the state paper office. The most substantial were based on the work of others. In 1769 he revised John Thorpe's *Registrum Roffense* before publication, and in 1771 revised new editions of John Leland's *Collectanea* and Thomas Hearne's *Curious Discourses*. The work by which he is best known, *Calendars of the Ancient Charters … in the Tower of London*, was begun by Philip Morant but the 1774 edition is credited to Ayloffe. His friend Richard Gough called Ayloffe the Montfaucon of England for his work in publishing source materials for English history, which he believed was as important as the work of the French Benedictine monk Bernard de Montfaucon. Ayloffe read several papers at meetings of the Society of Antiquaries between 1766 and 1780, the most important of which were published in *Archaeologia* and separately. In 1769, with Lord Chancellor Hardwicke's encouragement and financial support, he proposed the engraving of the Tudor historical painting then at Windsor Castle, later moved to Hampton Court, *Henry VIII at the Field of the Cloth of Gold in 1520*, and read a paper on it in 1770. The painting was so large that to preserve the detail without joining plates James Basire engraved the largest copperplate and Whatman made the largest sheet of handmade paper (31 in. x 53 in.), known afterwards as antiquarian size. The print was finally distributed in 1775, and was followed by others described by Ayloffe and copied from Tudor historical paintings at Windsor Castle and Cowdray, Sussex. The latter were destroyed by fire in 1793 and the copies provide the only record. In 1772 Ayloffe superintended the opening of the tomb of Edward I in Westminster Abbey and gave an account of the discoveries.

Ayloffe was described by contemporaries as knowledgeable in history and antiquities, friendly, and sociable. He lived at various addresses in London: Carey Street, Lincoln's Inn, in 1739; Margaret Street, Cavendish Square, in 1762; and Kennington Lane, Lambeth, from at least 1766. He also had a house at Whartons, Framfield, Sussex, from about 1767. He died, aged seventy-one, at Kennington Lane on 19 April 1781, and was buried with his father and son in Hendon churchyard. Some prints and those of his manuscripts which had not been claimed by his friends were sold at Leigh and Sothebys auction sale from 25 February 1782. Ayloffe's widow died on 8 March 1797, aged ninety-two, and was also buried at Hendon.

BERNARD NURSE

Sources Nichols, *Lit. anecdotes* • *GM*, 1st ser., 22 (1752), 46–7 • *GM*, 1st ser., 51 (1781), 195–6 • J. Evans, *A history of the Society of Antiquaries* (1956) • M. Noble, 'Lives of the fellows of the Society of Antiquaries in London', 1, 1818, Getty Center, USA, MS CJPV87-A742 • R. J. B. Walker, *Old Westminster Bridge: the bridge of fools* (c.1979) • P. Morant, *The history and antiquities of the county of Essex*, 2 vols. (1768) • Foster, *Alum. Oxon.* • GEC, *Peerage* • *Old Westminsters*, vols. 1–2; suppl. 1 • W. P. Baildon, ed., *The records of the Honorable Society of Lincoln's Inn: admissions*, 1 (1896) • W. P. Baildon, ed., *The records of the Honorable Society of Lincoln's Inn: the black books*, 3 (1899) • H. Jenkinson, *Guide to the public records* (1949) • *Report of the Deputy Keeper of the Public Records*, 30 (1869), appx 7 • BL, Add. MSS 36608, fol. 370; 36609, fols. 29, 298, 301–4; 34650, fol. 4

Archives BL, corresp. and papers, Add. MSS 4300, 5701, 6402, 9051, 32702, 34650, 35608–35609, 35611–35613, 35615, 42560, 47013 • Bodl. Oxf., topographical notebooks and corresp. | Bodl. Oxf., corresp. with Richard Gough, Thomas Percy, and others

Ayloffe, William (*c*.1535–1584), judge, was the son of William Ayloffe of Hornchurch, Essex, and Anne, daughter of Sir Thomas Barnardiston of Ketton, Suffolk. His grandfather William (*d*. 1517) was a bencher of Lincoln's Inn and perhaps the first armigerous member of the family, having received a grant of arms in 1512; he had in 1507 married Audrey, daughter of alderman Sir John Shaa, the London goldsmith, and widow of John Wrytell. It was the grandfather who established the family seat at Brittons in Hornchurch, where William Ayloffe the judge lived. Ayloffe was himself admitted to Lincoln's Inn in 1553 and called to the bar in 1560. He was to be of great service to the inn in furthering the purchase of its freehold from his brother-in-law Edward Sulyard. In 1566 he was elected a bencher and in 1571 reader, serving as treasurer in 1573–4. He was created serjeant-at-law in 1577 with six others, and left an account of the elaborate creation ceremonies which was published in 1984.

On 3 February 1578, less than a year after receiving the coif, Ayloffe was appointed a justice of the queen's bench and continued in that office until his death. He accompanied Chief Justice Dyer three times on the midland circuit, but in 1579 changed to the Oxford, which he rode with Francis Wyndham for the rest of his life. In 1581 he and Wyndham were suspected of being too lenient with recusants on the circuit, but it is likely that the fault lay with the county administration. That he was hardly popular with the Roman Catholics is evident from an absurd legend invented in the same year by some English Catholics in Paris. The story was that, after the trial of Edmund Campion, Ayloffe remained on the bench to await the return of the jury, and on removing his glove found that his ring was covered with blood; however hard he tried to wipe it away, the blood continued to flow as a miraculous sign of the injustice that had polluted the seat of justice.

Ayloffe seems to have died suddenly on 17 November 1584, having made a short will on the day of his death. Although he appointed his wife as his executor, in 1593 the will was pronounced void, apparently on the grounds that 'my wief' was too imprecise. In fact he seems to have had only one wife, Jane, daughter of Eustace Sulyard, whom he had married by about 1560; they had three sons and at least one daughter. The eldest son, William (*d*. 1627), was admitted to Lincoln's Inn in 1577, knighted in 1603, and created a baronet in 1612; the baronetcy became extinct in 1787. A namesake admitted to the same inn in 1585 became the king's ancient serjeant-at-law, and as such leader of the English bar, in the later years of Charles I; he was also a great-grandson of the bencher who died in 1517 but by a different line.

J. H. BAKER

Sources Baker, *Serjeants*, 172–3, 305–11 • Sainty, *King's counsel*, 34 • Sainty, *Judges*, 30 • J. S. Cockburn, *A history of English assizes, 1558–1714* (1972), 209–10, 265–6 • Foss, *Judges*, 5.445–6 • will, PRO, PROB 11/67, sig. 38 • W. P. Baildon, ed., *The records of the Honorable Society of Lincoln's Inn: the black books*, 1 (1897) • W. C. Metcalfe, ed., *The visitations of Essex*, 1, Harleian Society, 13 (1878), 141 • J. W. Clay, ed., *The visitation of Cambridge … 1575 … 1619*, Harleian Society, 41 (1897), 129 • *LP Henry VIII*, 1, no. 266 • *CPR, 1494–1509*, 563, 565

Aylward, Gladys May (1902–1970), missionary, was born on 24 February 1902 in Edmonton, Middlesex, the eldest of the three children of Thomas John Aylward, postman, and his wife, Rosina Florence Whiskin, daughter of a surgical boot maker. After receiving an elementary education, at the age of fourteen she became a shop-girl, then a children's nanny, settling finally to be a parlourmaid. She was efficient and pleasant, liked frequent moves, and served in several well-known households in the West End of London.

Gladys Aylward's father, who had been vicar's warden of

St Aldhelm's Church, Edmonton, had joined a nearby gospel mission when she was nine; the Aylwards were brought up as active Christians, and in London a youth movement soon absorbed her free evenings to the exclusion of an earlier interest in the stage. In December 1929 she was accepted for missionary training by the China Inland Mission, which had been founded in 1865 partly to provide opportunity for men and women of strong faith but indifferent education; however, she was soon rejected as a willing yet hopeless student. Still intent on China, Gladys Aylward worked in the slums of Bristol and Swansea until she nearly died of double pneumonia. Back in Edmonton for convalescence, depressed by her failure to reach China, she went reluctantly with her mother to a Primitive Methodist meeting at Wood Green. Here she heard that a widowed Mrs Jeannie Lawson, an elderly member of a small independent mission in north China, needed a helper who must find her own way out.

Gladys Aylward returned home that evening a different woman. She became a parlourmaid again to save money for the cheapest fare, by the Trans-Siberian Railway. In an incident afterwards made famous on film, she sat in an attic room in the South Kensington home of the daughter of Sir Francis Younghusband and put her few coppers on the bed and prayed: 'Oh God! Here's me. Here's my Bible, here's my money! Use us, God! Use us!' (Burgess, rev. edn, 18).

On 15 October 1932 Gladys left Liverpool Street Station for China. She needed all her cockney wit and pluck to survive the passage through the Soviet Union, and reached north China via Japan to join Mrs Lawson, a prickly, unpredictable Scot, in the country town of Yangsheng, Shansi province.

They opened an inn for muleteers as a means of evangelism. There Gladys Aylward learned Chinese by ear rather than by book. After her patron's death the mandarin made her inspector of feet, in the campaign against female foot binding, a post which gave her openings everywhere. With her tiny size (she was but 5 feet tall) and very dark brown hair, her humour, and entire lack of colour or cultural prejudice, she became a greatly loved and masterly story-teller of simple Christianity: the Jesus of Gladys Aylward was real and alive, to be talked to and consulted at every turn.

Known as Ai Weh-te—the nearest the Chinese could get to Aylward and which meant, felicitously, 'the virtuous one'—Gladys became a Chinese citizen in 1936. Her best-known exploit, during the Japanese war, was in 1940 to lead 100 children through hardships and dangers to safety across the Yellow River. At Fufeng she fell dangerously ill, and on partial recovery worked as a Bible-woman and among lepers. In 1949 she was given passage money, and returned to England after seventeen years.

Gladys Aylward, whose adventures and achievements in China could be equalled by other missionaries, might have remained unknown had not her mother alerted Hugh Redwood, the celebrated religious journalist, who sent reporters to meet her. This led a BBC writer, Alan Burgess, to contact Gladys Aylward and dramatize her story on radio. In 1952 a publisher heard a repeat of the programme and suggested that Burgess should write a popular biography. His fictionalized *The Small Woman* (1957) became a best-seller and later a memorable and moving film, *The Inn of the Sixth Happiness* (1959). This she tried to stop and refused to see, because of the fictional love interest and her portrayal by a divorcee, Ingrid Bergman.

Book and film together made Gladys Aylward eminent, the archetype of the selfless, dedicated woman of faith, brushing away hardships and danger as she had once brushed crumbs from her employers' tables. Gladys Aylward, more than many of her generation, brought the Christian missionary ideal before the general public.

Gladys Aylward's last twelve years, apart from speaking tours, were spent in Taiwan. There her trusting nature made her the victim of embezzlement by the husband of an adopted daughter who helped her run an orphanage. She saved him from execution but attracted much unpopularity for putting temptation in his way. None the less, she lived it down, still the same uninhibited woman, intensely concerned about the poor and sinful, making Christianity vividly alive, with complete contempt for all she thought was wrong.

Gladys Aylward died in Taibei (Taipei) after a few hours' illness on 1 January 1970. The Chinese buried her in a marble tomb in the hilltop garden of Christ's College, Tamsui (Danshui), overlooking the estuary and facing mainland China. JOHN POLLOCK, *rev.*

Sources A. Burgess, *The small woman* (1957); abridged edn (1970) • P. Thompson, *A London sparrow* (1971) • *Gladys Aylward: her personal story, as told to Christine Hunter* (1970) • private information (1981) [family, Dr James Graham jun.] • *The Times* (5 Jan 1970) • C. M. Swift, *Gladys Aylward* (1984) • S. Howell, *Across the mountains* (1978) • *CGPLA Eng. & Wales* (1970)

Archives SOAS, letters and papers | SOUND BL NSA, performance recording

Likenesses photograph, Hult. Arch.

Wealth at death £912 in England: probate, 19 Jan 1970, *CGPLA Eng. & Wales*

Aylward, Margaret Louisa (1810–1889), philanthropist and Roman Catholic nun, was born on 23 November 1810 in Thomas Street, Waterford, the fifth child of William Aylward (*d.* 1840), merchant, and his wife, Ellen Mullowney, *née* Murphy (*c.*1781–*c.*1860). There were ten children born of the marriage, and a half-brother, from Ellen Murphy's first marriage, also lived with the family. The family's wealth was based on the provisions trade.

Aylward was educated at a local Quaker school and at the age of ten was sent as a boarder to the Ursuline convent in Thurles, co. Tipperary. She became fluent in French and a talented artist. When she returned to Waterford in 1830 she became involved in various charities around the city. Her sister Catherine joined the religious congregation, the Sisters of Charity, in Dublin in 1834 and Aylward followed her into that congregation. There she came under the influence of Eliza Bodenham, the mistress of novices, who in 1839 was dismissed from the congregation, an action that caused havoc in the community. Many of the novices subsequently left the community, believing that Bodenham had been harshly treated. Aylward was among those who left, and between 1839 and 1842 she continued to correspond with Bodenham, who had plans to begin a school for young ladies.

By 1845 Aylward was again considering joining a religious community and by the end of that year had become a novice in the Ursuline convent in Waterford. By January 1846, however, she had left the order. She moved to Dublin in 1848 and became involved in extensive philanthropic work: she worked with the lay charity the Ladies' Association for the Spiritual and Temporal Relief of the Sick Poor, known as the Ladies' Association. She organized a branch of this society in Marlborough Street in Dublin in 1851. The aim of the association was to relieve distress among the poor but also to catechize. Within five years it had 148 lady visitors and several branches around the city, and had formed St Mary's Industrial Institute, which attempted to find needlework for poor women.

Aylward worked closely with the Catholic clergy and was instrumental in bringing the French Daughters of Charity of St Vincent de Paul to Dublin in 1858 after eight years of negotiation. The visitations undertaken by Aylward and her co-workers in the Ladies' Association had alerted them to the extent of protestant missionary work among the poor in Dublin. She was particularly concerned with the work of the Irish Church Missions, which was an openly proselytizing organization and targeted the children of the very poor by educating and feeding them. Aylward and members of the Ladies' Association often stood outside the schools run by the Irish Church Missions and took down the names of the children attending. This led to acrimonious exchanges between the Ladies' Association and the agents of the Irish Church Missions. In order to counteract protestant proselytism Aylward founded an orphanage, St Brigid's, in 1856, which boarded out children to Catholic families. Aylward oversaw the running of the orphanage in all its details. In 1860 she failed to deliver up a child who had passed through the orphanage after the child's mother insisted on raising her daughter as a protestant, and, having claimed not to know of the child or her whereabouts, was imprisoned for six months on a contempt of court charge. The case was widely reported in the press of the period, and led to the disbandment of the Daughters of St Brigid, a group of six lay women, who formed the core of the Ladies' Association and the committee of the orphanage. Aylward's health was seriously affected by her imprisonment, but undaunted she established her first school in Dublin within five months of her release. With a reluctance perhaps born of her own failure to persevere in noviciates, she formed the religious congregation the Sisters of the Holy Faith, which was canonically approved in 1867. Organizing a religious congregation made her work appear respectable and allowed for permanency, particularly after her prison experience. The name of the new congregation echoed its mission against protestant proselytism. Aylward (who took the name Agatha on the founding of the congregation) remained independent in her actions; she did not, for example, wear a religious habit, and had numerous disagreements with clerics.

Aylward suffered much ill health in her later years. For the last two years of her life she was bedridden as a consequence of varicose ulcers. She was also affected by erysipelas for a great number of years. She died on 11 October 1889 and was buried in the convent cemetery at Glasnevin, Dublin. MARIA LUDDY

Sources J. Prunty, 'Margaret Louisa Aylward (1810–1889)', *Women, power and conciousness in 19th century Ireland*, ed. M. Cullen and M. Luddy (1995), 55–88 · M. Gibbons, *The life of Margaret Aylward* (1928) · J. Prunty, *Lady of charity, sister of faith: Margaret Aylward, 1810–1889* (1999)
Archives Holy Faith Convent, Glasnevin, Dublin | Dublin Diocesan Archives, Clonliffe, Dublin, Cullen MSS, letters
Wealth at death £131 12s. 11d.: probate, 14 April 1890, *CGPLA Ire.*

Aylward, Theodore (*bap.* 1731, *d.* 1801), musician, was baptized on 25 July 1731 at St Peter's, Chichester, the son of Henry Aylward, gentleman, and his wife, Ann. Of his education nothing is known, though when young he seems to have sung at Drury Lane Theatre; he later composed music for productions at Drury Lane, including *Harlequin's Invasion*, *Cymbeline* (both 1759), and *A Midsummer Night's Dream* (1763). He became a member of the Royal Society of Musicians on 3 July 1763 and was elected by a unanimous vote into the Madrigal Society on 15 November 1769. About 1760 he became organist of Oxford Chapel, London, and on 21 May 1762 was also appointed to St Lawrence Jewry. He resigned from Oxford Chapel in 1768 following his appointment to St Michael Cornhill on 29 April. On 5 June 1771 he was appointed professor of music at Gresham College. Aylward was an assistant director at the Handel commemorations of 1784, 1790, and 1791. He became a member of the Chichester Catch Club on 2 November 1787 and a founder member of the Glee Club (London) on 22 December of the same year. On 19 April 1781 he resigned from St Michael Cornhill in order to 'reside out of town' (Dawe, 75). In July 1787 he established his principal residence in South Street, Chichester, 'for the second time' (*John Marsh Journals*, 404). His London residence from at least 1782 was 9 Great Square, Gray's Inn. On 10 May 1788 Aylward was appointed organist of St George's Chapel, Windsor, whereupon he moved to a house in the castle. He was also private organist to Queen Charlotte, and taught at a school in Queen Square, London. On 19 and 21 November 1791 he took the accumulated degrees of BMus and DMus at Oxford, submitting the anthem 'I will cry unto God'. He is not believed to have married, but had a daughter by one Susan Small. He died on 27 February 1801 in either Windsor or London and was buried on 5 March in St George's Chapel. At his death his properties included a collection of musical instruments, which were sold to finance bequests of at least £2000. Aylward published a few songs and glees, a set of lessons for the harpsichord (op. 1, 1784), and six string quartets (op. 4, 1795?). Incomplete manuscript copies of two morning services and five anthems survive at St George's Chapel. Described as a 'stout Dutch-built man' (W. Ayrton, Royal College of Music, London, MS 2170), he was said by W. L. Bowles to have had 'considerable literary attainments' (G. Grove, *A Dictionary of Music and Musicians*, 1879). But Edward Taylor thought him 'not a musician by spirit' (*New Grove*).

W. B. SQUIRE, *rev.* DAVID BURCHELL

Sources H. W. Shaw, *The succession of organists of the Chapel Royal and the cathedrals of England and Wales from c.1538* (1991), 347–8 · Highfill, Burnim & Langhans, *BDA* · D. Dawe, *Organists of the City of London, 1666–1850* (1983) · Foster, *Alum. Oxon.* · *The John Marsh journals: the life and times of a gentleman composer*, ed. B. Robins (1998) · E. H. Fellowes, *Organists and masters of the choristers of St George's Chapel in Windsor Castle* (1939), 61–5 · C. E. Stephens, 'Notices of composers', *Bemrose's choir chant book*, ed. C. E. Stephens (1882) · *GM*, 1st ser., 58 (1788), 470 · *GM*, 1st ser., 71 (1801), 281, 478 · *GM*, 1st ser., 84/2 (1814), 44 · *New Grove* · R. L. Neighbarger, *An outward show: music for Shakespeare on the London stage, 1660–1830* (1992) · B. Matthews, ed., *The Royal Society of Musicians of Great Britain: list of members, 1738–1984* (1985) · [R. Hake], 'Catalogue of music belonging to the [Oxford] music school', 1854, Bodl. Oxf., MS Mus. A.86 · *IGI*

Wealth at death over £2000—total of bequests, incl. collection of musical instruments: Highfill, Burnim & Langhans, *BDA*

Aylworth [*alias* Harcourt], **William** (**1623–1679**), Jesuit, was born in Wales on 21 March 1623 and entered the Society of Jesus at Watten on 7 September 1641. He studied philosophy at Liège and continued his studies at Toulouse. His wish to serve on the mission in the Americas won the approval of his superiors and he transferred to Spain, studying theology at Alcalá, where he was ordained *c.*1650, while awaiting his departure to Peru or Paraguay. In the event he was unable to obtain permission to travel to South America and was recalled to the English province. He was professed of the four vows on 2 March 1659. He taught philosophy and theology at the province's college at Liège for eleven years, and served as a missioner in the Netherlands and England for a further nine years, apparently living at Holbeck Hall, Nottinghamshire, a home of the Pierrepoint family. He was the author of *Metaphysica scholastica*, published at Cologne in 1675 and dedicated to Gervase, later first Lord Pierrepoint. He seems to have been the Harcourt who was the subject of a number of Titus Oates's allegations during the Popish Plot crisis, which if true made him 'one of the most sought-after men in England' (Kenyon, 206). Neither Oates's information nor an order obtained by parliament in March 1679 that the library of the 'settled college of Jesuits' at Holbeck be seized resulted in his apprehension. By his own account he suffered a series of narrow escapes, including the discovery of his books and vestments, on one occasion avoiding arrest by crouching under a table for a seven-hour stretch. He eventually escaped to the Netherlands, reportedly accompanied by members of the Pierrepoint family, but with his health impaired he died at Haarlem on 10 September 1679. His account of his escapes was later published by Foley.

THOMPSON COOPER, *rev.* R. M. ARMSTRONG

Sources H. Foley, ed., *Records of the English province of the Society of Jesus*, 7 vols. in 8 (1875–83) · T. M. McCoog, *English and Welsh Jesuits, 1555–1650*, 2 vols., Catholic RS, 74–5 (1994–5) · Gillow, *Lit. biog. hist.* · J. Kenyon, *The Popish Plot* (1972) · T. G. Holt, '"A college of Jesuits" at Holbeck in Nottinghamshire', *Recusant History*, 19 (1988–9), 484–98

Archives Lancs. RO, newsletters to Sir T. Clifton, DDCl/1151–66

Aymer de Valence. *See* Valence, Aymer de, eleventh earl of Pembroke (*d.* 1324).

Ayreminne, Richard. *See* Airmyn, Richard (*c.*1290–1340).

Ayreminne, William. *See* Airmyn, William (*d.* 1336).

Ayres, John (*d.* **1704x9**), writing-master, according to early accounts began life in a humble way as a footman in the house of Sir William Ashurst, to whom he owed his education. His original teacher of writing was Thomas Topham, to whom he dedicated *The Accomplisht Clerk* of 1680. It is said that on marrying a fellow servant with £200, Ayres was able to set himself up as a teacher of handwriting and accounts in St Paul's Churchyard, where his industry and ability soon procured him so many pupils that his income from teaching alone was said to be £800 a year. Here, at the Hand and Pen near St Paul's School, he also produced a number of copybooks over the next twenty years. Samuel Pepys, who had five works by Ayres in his *Calligraphical Collection*, lists his work under the heading 'Maj.r Ayres', and contemporaries frequently referred to him as 'Major' or 'Colonel' Ayres. This title no doubt refers to his position in the City bands, and it also gives some indication of his social standing.

The interest taken in the work of Ayres by Pepys is a strong indication of the position he held in the field of contemporary calligraphy, of which Pepys was both collector and connoisseur. In a letter to John Bagford of 16 April 1697/8 Pepys wrote of 'having a particular reason' to know of Ayres's latest 'Copy-Book, whether it be yet finished or published or no', and, if the book be available, 'procure a very fair one and send it to me' (*Letters and the Second Diary*, 267). Pepys was not alone in his admiration of the work of Ayres, nor was Ayres himself unaware of his fellow penmen. In his preface to *A Tutor to Penmanship* of 1698, Ayres wrote of the 'different state of English & Forreign Pen-man-ship, at & since the coming-in of Printing' and praised the work of Van den Velde and Materot, as well as his English predecessors such as Richard Gething and Peter Gery in particular. In this regard it is worth noting that one of his own writing books was entitled *Materot redivivus* (1690). Towards his English contemporaries Ayres was less charitable. Most of the writing books of the period bubble with charges and counter-charges over the matter of style. The main controversy was whether 'owls, apes and monsters, and sprig'd letters' were allowable in serious works. These fanciful shapes, intended to show off the fluency of the writing-master and his command of penstrokes, were thought by some to entice unwilling pupils to better handwriting. Attacked by Charles Snell and others on this point, Ayres responded in kind with reflections on 'the malice and invincible ignorance' of his rivals. But although he did not despise the fanciful 'command of hand' exercises, it was his round hand which particularly impressed people, and which continued to influence later writing-masters, and therefore the development of English handwriting. Although Ayres himself looked back to the Italian masters, it is likely that the source of his own style was the Italian hand as transmuted through the work of northern calligraphers. While he was not against the occasional calligraphic flourish, Ayres was very scathing about the trick writing of contemporary shorthand masters, for the aim of shorthand, he said, 'is not to write much in a little room, but to write much in a little *time*' (A. Nicholas, preface, *Thoographia, or, A New Art of Short-Hand*, 1692).

There is considerable difficulty—and indeed diversity—in listing the major works of Ayres, for reasons that are common to many of the writing books of the period. They were for the most part issued with either a printed or an engraved title-page—sometimes with both—and usually included some pages of text in which the writing-master made clear his attitudes and aims. Popular works, such as those of Ayres, were frequently reissued. In these instances there would often be a new letterpress title-page, and possibly new text, but the original engraved plates which contained the calligraphic examples would remain unchanged. A detailed examination of several copies of a work is often required to decide on the original date and edition—and, not surprisingly in books intended for daily practical use, they have not always survived in sufficient numbers. The five works collected by Pepys (*The ala mode secretarie*, 1681; *The Accomplisht Clerk*, 1683; *The Penmans Daily Practise*, 1692; *A Tutor to Penmanship*, 1698; and *The Accomplish'd Clerk Regraved*, 1700) would make a more valuable contribution to the study of Ayres, and other penmen, if he had not preserved only the engraved plates and thrown out all printed matter—title-page, text, and, more importantly, often the date as well. Even the engraved titles have been found to differ on occasions from the original printed version, thus making the work of the bibliographer doubly difficult.

The date of Ayres's death is unknown, though it must have occurred between 1704 and 1709, since in 1704 he handed over his school to Robert More, and in 1709 his pupil John Rayner speaks of his master as dead. Bromley's *Catalogue of Engraved British Portraits* gives the date of his death as 1705. This is said to have taken place from apoplexy while he was regaling friends at Vauxhall Gardens.

JOYCE IRENE WHALLEY

Sources A. Heal, *The English writing-masters and their copy-books, 1570–1800* (1931) • W. Massey, *The origin and progress of letters … the second part …: a compendious account of the most celebrated English penmen* (1763) • J. I. Whalley, *English handwriting, 1540–1853* (1969) • R. McKitterick and J. I. Whalley, *Catalogue of the Pepys Library at Magdalene College, Cambridge*, 4: *Calligraphy* (1989) • R. Moore, *First invention of writing* (1716) • A. Chalmers, ed., *The general biographical dictionary*, new edn, 32 vols. (1812–17) • *Letters and the second diary of Samuel Pepys*, ed. R. G. Howarth (1932); repr. (1933)

Likenesses J. Sturt, line engraving, BM; repro. in J. Ayres, *A tutor to penmanship* (1698) • R. White, line engraving, BM, NPG; repro. in J. Ayres, *Arithmetick* (1693)

Ayres, Philip (1638–1712), poet and translator, was born at Cottingham, Northamptonshire, and educated at Westminster School under Richard Busby. He is said to have been a member of St John's College, Oxford, but there is no record of his having matriculated at that university. By January 1666 he was attached to Sir Richard Fanshawe's embassy to Spain and Portugal in the capacity of steward: he is listed by Lady Fanshawe in her *Memoirs* among those who accompanied Fanshawe on his journey from Madrid to Lisbon, but not among those who returned with her from Madrid after her husband's death in June 1666. His copy of Fanshawe's translation of Mendoza's *Querer por solo querer* (1670), now in the National Library of Scotland, bears the Spanish inscription 'Philip Ayres majordomo to his Excellency Sir Richard Fanshawe'.

Ayres began to learn Spanish on his travels and published, in 1670, *The Fortunate Fool*, a translation of *El necio bien afortunado* by A. G. de Salas Barbadillo, stating in the 'Epistle Dedicatory' that it was done '*à la volée* only for my Divertisment, at spare hours, and my practice in the *Spanish* tongue'. Ayres may have travelled to the Netherlands in the early 1670s. In the epistle to *The Hungarian Rebellion*, which he published in 1672, he claimed to be translating from a German text 'lately met with in *Holland*'. At some point in the 1670s Ayres obtained a post as tutor in the Drake family of Amersham. He was 'Dry Nurse', that is, tutor, to two Montagu Garrard Drakes, father and son, and he lived in the Drake household until his death in 1712.

Ayres's first publication was *A Short Account of the Life and Death of Pope Alexander the VII*, published in 1667, a translation of a text by Stefano Cavalli, published at Rome earlier in the same year. The preface to this pamphlet makes Ayres's own Anglican convictions clear, and singles Alexander VII out as an exceptional pontiff, free of what Ayres regards as Roman corruption. Nevertheless, Ayres hoped to see an end to the schism within western Christianity, a view not uncommon in the 1630s but comparatively rare later in the century. He returned to the subject ten years later, in his *Reuniting of Christianity, or, The manner how to rejoin all Christians under one sole confession of faith. Written in French by a learned protestant divine and now Englished* (1677). Despite the scepticism and hostility expressed in 'The translators animadversions on the foregoing discourses', Ayres translated, in 1680, a classic text of early modern hermeticism: Nicolas Pierre de Montfaucon de Villars's *Le comte de Gablis*. This is the text from which Pope drew his ironic supernatural 'machinery' in *The Rape of the Lock*.

The two literary works for which Ayres is chiefly remembered are the *Emblemata amatoria* (1683) and *Lyrick Poems* (1687). The former was the last of the English emblem books to achieve a popular success. Three-quarters of the copper plates are derived from the *Amorum emblemata* (Antwerp, 1608) of Otho Vaenius (Otto van Veen), and (in these cases) the Latin and Italian verses are from the same source. Almost all the remaining plates are from the *Thronus cupidinis* (Amsterdam, 1618). It is to be assumed that all the English verses and some of those in French, Latin, and Italian are Ayres's own compositions. Like Ayres's *Lyrick Poems*, this work looks to the modes and achievements of the first half of the seventeenth century. Despite this, the book was clearly popular: there were five English editions over the following thirty years.

The *Lyrick Poems* (1687) includes translations from the ancient Greek lyric poets, Petrarch, Tasso, Camões, Guarini, de la Vega, Quevedo, Gongora, and Marino, and most of the verses presented as original compositions are also translations. The collection also contains a Spanish poem by Ayres in which he styles himself 'Don Felipe Ayres'. The 'Preface' confirms the impression that Ayres was trying to fashion himself as a baroque poet on the continental model, referring to Fanshawe and Milton (poets closely involved with Spanish and Italian literature) as his models in English, as well as Spenser and Sidney. The volume also contains poems of friendship to John Dryden and Nahum Tate, as well as a surprisingly extravagant panegyric of James II.

Three further works require brief mention. An original conduct-book, homiletic in tone, *Vox clamantis, or, An essay for the honour, happiness and prosperity of the English gentry, and the whole nation* (1684), prescribes rules of élite behaviour in a context of divine-right royalism and high-church Anglicanism. In 1684 Ayres published *The voyages and adventures of Capt. Barth. Sharp and others ... journal of the same also Capt. Van Horn with his buccanieres surprizing of la Vera Cruz* (1684), a documentary work which anticipates Defoe's narratives of piracy. In 1689 he published an illustrated work, *Mythologica ethica, or, Three Centuries of Aesopian Fables*, a compendium drawn from various ancient and Renaissance sources owing at least its title to Freitag's *Mythologica ethica* (Antwerp, 1579). In its preface he is at pains to put forward a case for his dignity and status as a compiler, editor, and annotator.

In 1696 Ayres published *The Revengeful Mistress*, a set of interlocking prose narratives or 'novels', which set out to warn gentlemen travellers (and their guardians) of the dangers to be met with on the continent, the 'ill women' of Italy, and especially of Spain. He published no more, and died at Amersham on 1 December 1712. He was buried in St Mary's churchyard, Amersham, where a monumental inscription was erected to him.

PETER DAVIDSON and IAN WILLIAM MCLELLAN

Sources H. Thomas, 'The *Emblemata amatoria* of Philip Ayres', *The Library*, 3rd ser., 1 (1910), 90–95 • B. Westerweel, 'Philip Ayres and the love emblem tradition', *Anglo-Dutch relations in the field of the emblem*, ed. B. Westerweel (1997) • *The memoirs of Anne, Lady Halkett and Ann, Lady Fanshawe*, ed. J. Loftis (1979) • notice of Philip Ayres, Bodl. Oxf., MS Rawl. D. 1160, fol. 1 • autographs, Bodl. Oxf., MS Rawl. D. 1386, fols. 18–20 • gifts of books by Philip Ayres, Bodl. Oxf., MS Rawl. D. 878, fols. 4, 6, 17v, 25v, 26v, 29 • *Old Westminsters*, vol. 1

Ayres, Ruby Mildred (1881–1955), romantic novelist, was born on 28 January 1881 at Gresham Villa, St John's Road, Watford, the third daughter of Charles Pryor (or Prior) Ayres (1850–1914), architect, and his wife, Alice Whitford (1855–1903), daughter of William Griggs, surgeon, of Ramsgate, Kent. Charles Ayres had been articled to Edward Welby Pugin (1834–1875) and subsequently established a highly successful practice in Watford, designing a number of the public buildings there. Ruby Ayres was one of the most popular and prolific romantic novelists of the twentieth century. She began writing stories as a girl and claimed to have been expelled from school at the age of fifteen for writing 'an advanced love story'. Meanwhile 'she discovered from the appreciation of her schoolmates, that she could satisfy the feminine taste for romance' (*The Times*, 15 Nov 1955, 11). She entered a competition run by *Boy's Own Paper* for a school story, using a brother's name, and won the first prize of a guinea.

On 23 December 1909 Ayres married Reginald William Pocock (1880–1948), an insurance broker. The couple had no children and she continued to write, she said, to pass the time while her husband was at work. Shortly after her marriage her story 'The Professor and the Blue Stocking' was accepted by a magazine and she was soon commissioned to write serials for the *Daily Chronicle* and the *Daily Mirror*. She also contributed to women's magazines. In the 1950s she provided responses to readers' problems for *Home Companion*. Her first book, *Castles in Spain*, was published by Cassell in 1912. It is a bitter-sweet story, narrated in the form of a journal by an elderly bachelor, of love flowering too late and differs significantly from the rest of her work, published by Hodder and Stoughton, where the third-person narratives focus on young people and end in unions.

Ayres's relationship with Hodder and Stoughton began in 1916 and ended only at her death. She wrote some 136 novels for them, many of which were regularly reprinted and were issued in both quality and cheap/popular formats. Her immediate and continuing popularity can be gauged from the data available for *Richard Chatterton*, which was issued in 1916 with a print run of 8000 copies: in 1917 a further 25,000 copies were printed, in 1918 another 19,000, and in 1932 another 30,000. Meanwhile subsequent novels were published in initial print runs of 20,000 to 45,000 copies; these included *The Remembered Kiss* (1918), *The Romance of a Rogue* (1923), *Unofficial Wife* (1937), *The Constant Heart* (1941), and *Love without Wings* (1953).

In Ayres's fictional world the country is good, town life, especially that of London, often bad. Households, white middle-class if sometimes impoverished, regularly include a cook and a maid. Plots concentrate on the misunderstandings that keep potential lovers apart and the (strained) coincidences or crises that bring them together. A simple morality approves forgiveness, truth-telling, and kindness to animals. Ayres's heroes are always self-assured, decisive, morally sound, and financially secure, and older than the heroines. She claimed to admire 'the rough, tough, he-man type who can curse and swear a bit' (*Daily Mirror*, 15 Nov 1955, 11). Her heroines, who rarely need to seek paid employment, can be sweet, self-effacing, and loyal to a family which exploits them, or spoilt, wilful, and self-seeking, needing the stern attitude (and sometimes harsh words) of a man with a determined mouth and chin to unlock their better natures and to make them realize that the glamorous 'fast set' is not, after all, for them. 'Happiness', Ayres observed, 'lies in the simple things in life' (*Weekend Woman*, 1939, 102).

The attitude to money in Ayres's work is ambivalent: it is wrong to rank it above other values such as love and loyalty but a modicum of wealth is fundamental to the happy ending. However, she asserted that 'romance can be lively even when the strawberry season is over and there is only bread and cheese in the larder' (Vinson, 41). Deaths—often of rivals or other figures who threaten the perfect bliss of the central characters, or who provide useful legacies—occur with remarkable convenience, often in car or aeroplane crashes, and without distressing detail or mourning. A play, *Silver Wedding*, was produced in 1932.

Ayres was a good businesswoman. Her most frequently quoted remark was 'I write for money'. She normally negotiated directly with her publisher, dispensing with an agent except for her overseas interests. She once said: 'First I fix the price, then I fix the title, then I write the book' (*Daily Mail*, 15 Nov 1955, 3). She could write as many as 20,000 words a day. There is so little contextual information behind her plots that Ayres's novels do not become markedly dated and with only minor revision a number were issued in new editions many years after her death. Her books continue to be popular among library borrowers into the twenty-first century.

Ayres was a forthright but kindly person. Her pet dislikes were ballet and affected young men. In the 1920s she was a member of the Lyceum and Writers' clubs and in the 1930s and 1940s she belonged to the Ladies' Carlton Club. She died at Lulworth House, Ellesmere Road, Weybridge, Surrey, on 14 November 1955 of pneumonia and a cerebral thrombosis. She was cremated at Golders Green, Middlesex, on 18 November. C. M. P. Taylor

Sources R. Anderson, *The purple heart throbs* (1974) • J. Vinson, ed., *Twentieth-century romance and Gothic writers* (1982) • *Daily Telegraph* (15 Nov 1955), 8 • *Daily Mirror* (15 Nov 1955), 11 • *Daily Express* (15 Nov 1955), 1 • *Daily Mail* (15 Nov 1955), 3 • *The Times* (15–16 Nov 1955) • *WW* • Hodder and Stoughton, royalty ledgers, 16312–2 AYRES • m. cert. • d. cert. • parish register, Watford, St Andrew, 24 Feb 1881 [baptism]

Likenesses H. Coster, photographs, *c*.1935, NPG • photograph, repro. in *Daily Telegraph* • photograph, repro. in *Daily Mail*

Wealth at death £29,326 14*s*. 1*d*.: probate, 16 Feb 1956, *CGPLA Eng. & Wales*

Ayrton, Acton Smee (1816–1886), politician, born at Kew, London, was a son of Frederick Ayrton (student at Gray's Inn from 27 January 1802, barrister from *c*.1805, and afterwards in practice at Bombay) and Julia, only daughter of Lieutenant-Colonel Nugent. Acton Ayrton was educated at Ealing School. He went to India and practised as a solicitor at Bombay, returning about 1851 with a moderate fortune. On 30 April 1853 he was called to the bar at the Middle Temple, with the intention of devoting himself to a political career.

Ayrton was Liberal MP for Tower Hamlets, 1857–74, and was always a staunch reformer, supporting the ballot and franchise reform, though being cautious about the extreme effects of free trade. His long speech, on 24 April 1860, in support of the abortive bill for reforming the corporation of the City of London (*Hansard 3*, 1860, 69–85) attracted attention. Towards the end of his life he resumed his interest in that movement. He sat on the royal commissions on railway companies' charges, on the law courts, and on sanitary laws. In 1866, when addressing a meeting of working men in his constituency, he commented severely on the queen's retirement from public life owing to the death of the prince consort, and was rebuked by John Bright, who was present at the meeting. In the administration formed by Gladstone at the end of

Acton Smee Ayrton (1816–1886), by Ape (Carlo Pellegrini), pubd 1869

1868 Ayrton was nevertheless appointed parliamentary secretary to the Treasury, and held the post until 11 November 1869. From that date, when he was sworn of the privy council, to August 1873 he was first commissioner of works.

Ayrton's administration as commissioner of works was not popular; it was marked by zeal for economy in the public interest, as he saw it (described as 'scandalous parsimony' by his fellow radical, A. J. Mundella). He possessed great ability and varied knowledge, with notable independence of character, partly deriving from his membership of the commissions; but his manners were brusque, and he came into personal conflict with numerous prominent people with whom his official duties brought him into contact. He cut down the expenditure on the new Courts of Justice, and treated Alfred Stevens, the sculptor of the Wellington monument at St Paul's Cathedral, as a negligent contractor, and, but for the interposition of Robert Lowe, would have forced him to surrender his models (Martin, 2.379–80). He curtly dismissed Edward Middleton Barry as architect to the Palace of Westminster, and also had protracted differences with Sir J. D. Hooker, the director of Kew Gardens. Sir Algernon West, 'in some very complicated negotiations, made peace between them', and thought Ayrton the 'more reasonable man of the two' (West, 1.14). With two other members of the ministry (Gladstone and Lowe) Ayrton was caricatured at the Court Theatre in London in March 1873 in the burlesque *The Happy Land*, which was written by W. S. Gilbert and Gilbert à Beckett; the lord chancellor eventually required a softening of the satire.

In August 1873 Gladstone deemed it prudent to transfer Ayrton from the office of commissioner of works to that of judge-advocate-general. Ayrton resigned with the government in March 1874, and his political career came to a somewhat inglorious end. At the general election of 1874 he contested Tower Hamlets again, but was badly beaten, and after the redistribution of seats in 1885, in a contest for the Mile End division of Tower Hamlets, gained only 420 votes.

For the last few years of his life Ayrton was a daily frequenter of the Reform Club. He died, apparently unmarried, at the Mount Dore Hotel, Bournemouth, on 30 November 1886.

W. P. Courtney, *rev.* H. C. G. Matthew

Sources Boase, *Mod. Eng. biog.* • Gladstone, *Diaries* • *The letters of Queen Victoria*, ed. G. E. Buckle, 3 vols., 2nd ser. (1926–8), vols. 1–3 • M. H. Port, ed., *The Houses of Parliament* (1976) • M. H. Port, 'A contrast in styles at the office of works: Layard and Ayrton, aesthete and economist', *HJ*, 27 (1984), 151–76 • T. F. Gallagher, 'Ayrton, Acton Smee', *BDMBR*, vol. 2 • A. E. Street, *Memoir of George Edmund Street* (1888), 168–70 • *The Times* (2 Dec 1886) • A. Patchett Martin, *Life and letters of the Right Honourable Robert Lowe, Viscount Sherbrooke*, 2 vols. (1893) • A. West, *Recollections, 1832–1886*, 2 vols. (1899)

Archives BL, memoranda and corresp. with W. E. Gladstone, Add. MSS 44403–44784, *passim*

Likenesses Ape [C. Pellegrini], watercolour caricature, NPG; repro. in *VF* (23 Oct 1869) [*see illus.*] • Faustin, caricature, chromolithograph, NPG • G. A. W. Wilkie, marble bust, Gov. Art Coll. • wood-engraving (after photograph by Mayall), NPG; repro. in *ILN* (16 May 1857)

Wealth at death £31,455 18*s*. 1*d*.: resworn probate, Oct 1887, *CGPLA Eng. & Wales* (1886)

Ayrton, Edmund (1734–1808), composer and musician, was born on 21 October 1734 at Ripon, Yorkshire, the third of the four surviving children of Edward Ayrton (1698–1774), alderman and later mayor and magistrate of the borough of Ripon, and his wife, Catherine (1701?–1781), daughter of John Clough of Thirsk in the North Riding of Yorkshire. Educated at the free grammar school in Ripon, Ayrton 'was a contemporary of Beilby Porteus, afterwards Bishop of London' (*The Harmonicon*, 142), though Fétis suggests that he spent only five years at this establishment (Fétis, 1.177). His son William wrote that Ayrton was 'intended for the church … but his father, finding it prudent to indulge his son's natural inclination for music, placed him under the instruction of Dr [James] Nares, then organist of the cathedral of York' (*The Harmonicon*, 142), and it seems likely that this took place in 1744, Ayrton becoming a chorister and presumably also studying the organ. In 1755 he succeeded Samuel Wise as *rector chori* of the collegiate church of Southwell in Nottinghamshire—an establishment with an organ built by Bernard 'Father' Smith—where his duties included the posts of organist, auditor, and 'singingman' (possibly denominating the master of the choristers). On 22 April 1756 he went to London for three further months' instruction from Nares, whose appointment to the Chapel Royal had taken place only three months earlier. During his time at Southwell, Ayrton also taught music, and it was to a pupil, the 'only moderately well educated' (BL, Add. MS 52349, fol. 97) Ann Clay (1739–1800), that he was married in Southwell on 20 September 1762. On 1 January 1764 Ayrton left Southwell on being appointed a gentleman of the chapels royal in place of John Busswell, shortly after which he was installed as vicar-choral of St Paul's Cathedral (23 December 1767). He applied unsuccessfully for the post of organist at St Alban's Church, Wood Street, in April 1766, but joined the Royal Society of Musicians in June 1765 and became a freemason in the Somerset House lodge in January 1779. On 1 February 1772 he became a lay clerk at Westminster Abbey, and in 1780 master of the choristers of the Chapel Royal replacing James Nares, who, according to John Stafford Smith, Ayrton's successor as master of the boys, 'gave up the Membership of the boys to him' (ibid., fol. 7) after hearing his anthem 'Thy rightousness' (1778). This post also seems to have included a sinecure described as 'the post of Lutinist' (Baldwin, 246, 370–71).

By 1779 Ayrton was apparently also recruiting singers for Covent Garden; R. J. S. Stevens noted his participation in a type of choral audition at the Tilt Yard Coffee House in the presence of Antonio Sacchini, Johann Christian Bach, and Johann Christian Fischer at which Ayrton, as well as assembling the group, played the harpsichord. He was an assistant director at the first Handel commemoration in 1784, and at the commemorations in several subsequent years. On 29 April 1784 he was admitted to the degree of MusD at Trinity College, Cambridge. The anthem composed for the degree was dedicated to the honorary president and vice-presidents of the Royal Society of Musicians, and the published version contains an extensive list of subscribers. It was performed at St Paul's Cathedral on 29 July 1784 at the thanksgiving service held at the close of the War of American Independence. Ayrton is also said to have been admitted to the degree of 'Mus. Doc. Oxon, ad eundem 1788', but in the absence of any record, this ascription cannot be verified despite appearing on the title-pages of a number of his works.

Ayrton was the father of fourteen children, all from his marriage; six survived his death, the most famous of whom was William *Ayrton (1777–1858). Edmund Edward (1765–1811), the eldest son, was also a musician, noted by Doane as a tenor and organist living in Swansea in 1790. Benjamin (*b*. 1778, *d*. after 1808) became a doctor and went to sea on a South American merchant ship, marrying in Buenos Aires, where he died shortly afterwards, while Scrope Ayrton, the youngest son (1781–1811), was second in command of the brig *Bouncer* and died in combat at Verdun. The W. Ayrton listed by Burney and Doane was probably Ayrton's nephew William Francis Morrel (1778–1850);

the Morrel Ayrton (*fl.* 1790–1794) listed by Doane, while living at the same address as Edmund Ayrton, was almost certainly a great-nephew rather than a son, and is probably also identifiable with the 'Mr Ayrton, jun.' listed by Burney.

Ayrton's wife, Ann, died on 14 May 1800; however, he retained the post of master of children until his resignation, probably due to ill health, in 1805, despite an unpleasant episode in 1800 in which he was accused of starving the boys. Ayrton himself died on 22 May 1808, probably of tuberculosis, in the home that he had occupied at least since 1785, 24 James Street, Buckingham Gate, Westminster; it had the reputation of being haunted, allowing him to occupy it at a low rent. He was buried on 28 May 1808 in the north cloister of Westminster Abbey, near the graves of his wife and five of his children. On his death his estate was valued at £1470 before the sale of his household contents, which included an Amati violin dated 1641 and a violoncello by Duke and raised a further £215. Further instruments, including a family organ and harpsichords by Baker Harris and Tabel, were bequests to family members in his will, and a number of valuable manuscripts—including items by Hasse, Haydn, Porpora, Scarlatti, and Stradella—were later sold by Puttick and Simpson following the death of his son William. Portraits of Ayrton by John Hoppner and William Pether were also bequeathed.

Ayrton was mostly well respected among his colleagues—being, for example, a signatory to J. W. Callcott's doctoral certificate in 1800 and enthusiastically thanked by Archdeacon Robert Nares in the preface to the posthumous publication of his father's anthems in 1788—but Samuel Wesley described him as 'one of the most egregious blockheads under the sun' (Lightwood, 180). His extant compositions, the manuscripts of which are held by the British Library, are in the English ecclesiastical tradition following Maurice Greene, with strong Handelian influences, and include two complete morning and evening services in C and E♭, several anthems, and a number of chants and glees of lesser significance. His sister was married to Nicholas Thomas *Dall, the Danish painter, and his grandson John Ayrton *Paris was president of the Royal College of Physicians.

CLAIRE M. NELSON

Sources Venn, *Alum. Cant.* • Foster, *Alum. Oxon.* • E. Ayrton, *An anthem [Begin unto my God with timbrels] for voices and instruments in score … perform'd at … Cambridge, as an exercise previous to his being admitted to the degree of doctor in music … and afterwards at St Paul's Cathedral … on the 29th of July, 1784* [1788] • E. Ayrton, *Canon, five in two [Glory be to the Father]* [n.d., 1790?] • Dotted Crotchet, 'Southwell Minster', *MT*, 50 (1909), 501–10 • W. Ayrton, ed., 'The commemoration of Handel, in 1784', *Musical Library* (March–Dec 1834), 6–9 [Suppl. to *Musical Library*] • D. Baldwin, *The Chapel Royal ancient & modern* (1990) • J. D. Brown, *Biographical dictionary of musicians: with a bibliography of English writings on music* (1886); repr. (1970) • J. S. Bumpus, *A history of English cathedral music, 1549–1889*, 2 (1908) • J. L. Chester, ed., *The marriage, baptismal, and burial registers of the collegiate church or abbey of St Peter, Westminster*, Harleian Society, 10 (1876) • J. Coover, *Music at auction: Puttick and Simpson (of London), 1794–1971* (1988) • D. Dawe, *Organists of the City of London, 1666–1850* (1983) • J. Doane, *A musical directory for the year 1794*, facs. repr. (1993) • C. Burney, *An account of the musical performances … in commemoration of Handel* (1785) • *GM*, 1st ser., 70 (1800), 493 • *GM*, 1st ser., 78 (1808), 470 • E. L. Gerber, *Historisch-biographisches Lexikon der Tonkünstler* (1790–92) • *The Harmonicon*, 11 (1833), 141–2 • C. Humphries and W. C. Smith, *Music publishing in the British Isles*, 2nd edn (1970) • J. T. Lightwood, *Samuel Wesley, musician* (1937) • B. Matthews, ed., *The Royal Society of Musicians of Great Britain: list of members, 1738–1984* (1985) • S. McVeigh, 'Freemasonry and musical life in London in the late eighteenth century', *Music in eighteenth-century Britain*, ed. D. Wyn Jones (2000), 71–100 • [J. S. Sainsbury], ed., *A dictionary of musicians*, 2 vols. (1824) • H. W. Shaw, *The succession of organists of the Chapel Royal and the cathedrals of England and Wales from c.1538* (1991) • J. S. Smith, *A musical pilgrimage in Yorkshire* (1928) • R. J. S. Stevens, *Recollections of a musical life*, ed. M. Argent (1992) • J. E. West, *Cathedral organists past and present*, new edn (1921) • *DNB* • W. Shaw, 'Ayrton, Edmund', *New Grove*, 2nd edn • P. M. Young, 'Ayrton', *Die Musik in Geschichte und Gegenwart*, ed. F. Blume, 2nd edn (1944–) • F.-J. Fétis, *Biographie universelle des musiciens, et bibliographie générale de la musique*, 8 vols. (Brussels, 1835–44) • H. Mendel, *Musikalisches Conversations-Lexicon: eine Encyklopädie der gesammen musikalischen Wissenschaften für Gehildete aller Stände*, 12 vols. (1880–83) • Highfill, Burnim & Langhans, *BDA* • C. B. Hogan, ed., *The London stage, 1660–1800*, pt 5: *1776–1800* (1968) • *Catalogue of printed music to 1980*, BL • *International inventory of musical sciences* (1970–) • E. B. Schnapper, ed., *The British union-catalogue of early music printed before the year 1801*, 2 vols. (1957) • will, PRO, PROB 11/1480, sig. 448 • account of Ayrton's residuary estate, BL, Add. MS 52348, fols. 6–7v • biographical information, BL, Add. MS 52349 [incl. d. cert., fol. 98; catalogue of the sale of Ayrton's household goods, fols. 101–107v] • admission as a gentleman of his majesty's chapels royal, BL, Add. Ch. 75563 • lease for 24 James Street, BL, Add. Ch. 75863 • probate of will and two codicils, BL, Add. Ch. 75864 • 'Testamur' of MusD for J. W. Callcott, BL, Add. MS 27639 [signatories include 'Edmundus Ayrton Mus.D']

Archives BL, admission as a gentleman of his majesty's chapels royal, Add. Ch. 75563 • BL, biographical information, Add. MS 52349 • BL, lease for 24 James Street, Add. Ch. 75863 • BL, 'Testamur' of MusD for J. W. Callcott, signed by 'Edmundus Ayrton Mus.D', Add. MS 27639

Likenesses J. Hoppner, portrait, 1786, Leger Galleries Ltd, London; repro. in Baldwin, *Chapel Royal*, 307 • W. Pether, portrait

Wealth at death residuary estate valued at £1470 4*s.* 11*d.*; sale of household contents raised further £214 10*s.* 3*d.*: will, PRO, PROB 11/1480, sig. 448; BL, Add. MS 52348, fols. 6–7v; BL, Add. MS 52349, fols. 101–107v

Ayrton [*née* Walshe; *other married name* Balchin], **Elisabeth Evelyn** (**1910–1991**), novelist and cookery writer, was born on 2 February 1910 at Littlefield Farm, Worplesdon, Surrey, the eldest child of Douglas Thomas George Walshe (1880–1952) and his first wife, Phyllis Sydney, *née* Johnson (*c.*1882–1929). Both her parents were journalists; Douglas Walshe also wrote light-hearted and extremely popular romantic novels, allowing his family a comfortable life in the large house in Worplesdon, where Elisabeth grew up with her brother, William (1914–1981), and much younger sister, Veryan (*b.* 1921).

Elisabeth Walshe attended Sherborne School and Sutton high school, matriculating at seventeen and determined on university. In 1929 she entered Newnham College, Cambridge, reading English in part one and archaeology and anthropology in part two of her degree. She married fellow graduate Nigel Marlin *Balchin (1908–1970) on 21 January 1933 and taught English at an exclusive London school until the birth of her daughter Prudence in 1934. A second daughter, Penelope, followed in

1937. During the war she joined Maurice Buckmaster's Special Operations Executive, selecting and screening agents for undercover work in Europe.

A third daughter, Frejä, was born in December 1944, and in 1947 the family moved to a house near Canterbury, where Balchin, now a successful novelist, could write undisturbed. Elisabeth, too, was writing poetry and short stories, but he was dismissive, and she remained uncertain of their merit. Frustrated and isolated, her marriage effectively ended in 1948 when she fell in love with a friend of Balchin, the young painter Michael *Ayrton (1921–1975). They married on 28 November 1952, a year after her divorce. It was only then, in her early forties, that she began to take her writing seriously: encouraged by Ayrton, she sent stories to *Vogue* and *Harper's Bazaar*; her poetry was read on the BBC's Third Programme, and she made extensive contributions to *Woman's Hour*. She also wrote her first novel, *The Cook's Tale* (1957). A love story with recipes, it is set in the south of France, ranging in time from the mid-nineteenth century to the present. All the recipes were tested in her own kitchen.

Living with Ayrton, Elisabeth had become interested in cooking, from which came *Good Simple Cookery* (1958), a book for housewives suddenly cooking for themselves, and bewildered by the new diversity of ingredients. It became a classic, and remains among the best basic cookery books. Her next book was very different: a photographic volume, *Doric Temples* (1961), for which she provided a text informed by her archaeological interests. She and Ayrton travelled extensively in Greece from 1957, especially in Crete, the background for her second novel, *The Cretan* (1963), an atmospheric, sometimes brutal account of deafness, peasant life, and smuggled antiquities.

1967 brought another practical cookery book, *Time is of the Essence*, but it was her next books which united her various passions in a virtually new genre, the historical cookery book. *Royal Favourites* (1971) explored the origins of famous dishes from royal kitchens, with updated recipes, while *The Cookery of England* (1974) set concise, easy-to-follow recipes against a cultural background stretching from the fifteenth century to the present day, meticulously researched and engagingly presented.

In addition to work, there were many demands on Elisabeth's time. At Bradfields, the sprawling Essex farmhouse where the Ayrtons arrived in 1952, she played hostess to a wide circle of friends while managing and maintaining house, garden, and workaholic husband, and remaining in close contact with her daughters. Yet she never lost sight of her own need to write: she completed her third novel, *Two Years in my Afternoon*, in 1972, and an expedition to Kenya in 1973 left her planning a fourth.

Michael Ayrton's health, never robust, gradually deteriorated; his early death in November 1975 was a blow from which Elisabeth found it difficult to recover. She moved to Gloucestershire, where with her extended family she struggled to begin life again. Her Kenyan novel, *Day Eight* (1978), was followed by several cookery books, including *English Provincial Cooking* (1980) and an early response to the growing vegetarian movement, *The Pleasure of Vegetables* (1983). Her last book, *Traditional British Cooking* (1985), written with Theodora Fitzgibbon, continued the marriage of history and good food, celebrating British cooking during a period when its culinary traditions were generally despised. She created another splendid garden, and, with two of her daughters, ran a small antiques business, while also overseeing the continuing exhibitions of Michael Ayrton's work. Her appetite for travel remained prodigious, supported by health which remained good until almost the end of her life. Of middle height and build, fair-skinned with striking auburn hair, brown eyes, and a tendency to freckle which she deplored, Elisabeth Ayrton never looked her age. Her energy, common sense, and efficiency hid a shyness and lack of self-confidence which only those closest to her recognized. She could be alarmingly aloof on occasion, especially when inwardly intimidated; but when at ease she was warm, charming, and profoundly interested in people. She was an atheist and a lifelong socialist, with a firm belief that people should have what they needed; she was also unstintingly generous, and always preferred giving to receiving. She could, perhaps, have written more, but her diverse life, thoroughly enjoyed, enriched others as much as herself.

Elisabeth Ayrton died on 15 November 1991 at her home, the Maze House, Rockhampton, after a brief battle with cancer, and was buried with Michael Ayrton at St Botolph's Church, Hadstock, Essex, on 20 November. Her fifth novel, *The Echoing Voyage*, remained unfinished.

JUSTINE HOPKINS

Sources J. Hopkins, *Michael Ayrton: a biography* (1994) • *Newnham College Roll Letter* (1993), 91–3 • *The Times* (22 Nov 1991) • private information (2004) • b. cert. • d. cert.

Archives BBC WAC, corresp. and radio scripts • priv. coll., MSS | SOUND BL NSA

Likenesses M. Ayrton, oils, 1951 (*The chair*), priv. coll. • photograph, *c*.1972, repro. in E. Ayrton, *Good simple cookery*, rev. edn (1984), cover • photographs, priv. coll.

Wealth at death £182,026: probate, 28 Feb 1992, *CGPLA Eng. & Wales*

Ayrton [*née* Chaplin], **Matilda Charlotte** (1846–1883), physician, was born in Honfleur, France, the daughter of John Clarke Chaplin, a solicitor. Her early studies were in drawing and painting and she used her artistic talents throughout her subsequent career. But she began what was to prove a long struggle to qualify as a doctor about 1867. She attended classes at the Medical College for Women in London, opened in 1864 to train women in midwifery, and she passed the preliminary examination for the licence of the Society of Apothecaries just before the society closed its professional examinations to candidates who had not attended regular medical schools. At the time this move appeared to preclude women's obtaining any qualification that would entitle them to have their names entered on the General Medical Council's register. However, in 1869, Sophia Jex-Blake was pressing to be admitted to medical classes at Edinburgh University. The university court refused consent for mixed classes and was not prepared to make special arrangements for Jex-Blake alone, but conceded that special classes for a group of women might be possible. Jex-Blake advertised for women to join her and Matilda Chaplin was the second to do so. In October 1869 Chaplin, together with four other women, passed the matriculation examination for Edinburgh University, the first women to be fully enrolled at a modern British university.

These five with two others who joined them the following year were to become known as the *Edinburgh seven or 'septem contra Edinam' as over the next four years they battled in private and, in the later stages, in public for access to the full range of medical instruction and the right to graduate. This culminated in a lawsuit against the university. Chaplin was 'not individually in favour of such bellicose means being employed but she loyally worked with the little band of students, of whom she was so distinguished a member' (Orme, 345). In 1870–71 Chaplin took high honours in anatomy and surgery at the extramural examinations of the Royal College of Physicians and Surgeons of Edinburgh. She also wrote several articles for the *Medical Press and Circular* at this same time and in 1871 attended some medical classes in Paris.

In June 1873 the seven's legal battle for the right to graduate was finally lost. But in the meantime Chaplin had married her cousin, the physicist and engineer William Edward *Ayrton (1847–1908), on 21 December 1871. In 1873 her husband was appointed professor of physics and telegraphy at the new Imperial Engineering College in Tokyo and Mrs Ayrton went with him to Japan. Before leaving England she obtained a certificate in midwifery from the London Obstetrical Society and in Tokyo she started a school for Japanese midwives, lecturing there herself with the aid of an interpreter. She also continued with private medical studies and wrote and illustrated several newspaper articles about her travels.

In 1877 Mrs Ayrton became ill and she and her young daughter Edith Chaplin Ayrton (who later married the writer Israel Zangwill) returned to London. Here Ayrton recommenced her medical training at the London School of Medicine for Women; she obtained her MD in Paris in 1879 and in 1880 became a licentiate of the King and Queen's College of Physicians in Ireland, where she, the only female candidate, headed the pass lists in medicine and midwifery. She then began practice in Sloane Street, London, while studying diseases of the eye at the Royal Free Hospital. She was a founder member of a club for women students in Paris and of the Somerville Club in London, which provided rest, recreation, and assistance for women students. Through this club Ayrton was a much valued adviser to many young women. She continued to write articles on life in Japan and other topics and, in 1879, she published a book entitled *Child Life in Japan*, illustrated by her own sketches. But by 1880 her health was breaking down and the signs of tuberculosis were manifest. She was obliged to winter abroad, first in Algiers and then in Montpellier, continuing her medical studies in both places. Ayrton died of tuberculosis on 19 July 1883, aged thirty-seven, at her home, 68 Sloane Street, Chelsea, London, and was buried in Brompton cemetery on 24 July.

M. A. ELSTON

Sources *BMJ* (11 Aug 1883), 298 · E. Orme, 'Matilda Chaplin Ayrton', *Englishwoman's Review*, 14 (1883), 343–50 · S. Roberts, *Sophia Jex-Blake: a woman pioneer in nineteenth century medical reform* (1993) · M. A. Elston, 'Women doctors in the British health service: a sociological study of their careers and opportunities', PhD diss., U. Leeds, 1986 · G. Travers [M. Todd], *The life of Sophia Jex-Blake* (1918) · *DNB* · m. cert. · d. cert. · *CGPLA Eng. & Wales* (1883)

Archives priv. coll.

Wealth at death £737 15*s*. 1*d*.: resworn administration, 19 Dec 1883, *CGPLA Eng. & Wales*

Ayrton [*formerly* Ayrton Gould], **Michael** (1921–1975), artist and writer, was born at 3 Hamilton Terrace, St John's Wood, London, on 20 February 1921, the only child of Gerald Gould (1885–1936), poet and journalist, and his wife, Barbara Bodichon Ayrton *Gould (1886–1950), politician and sometime chairman of the Labour Party, and whose maiden name he adopted on becoming a practising artist. His early childhood was much influenced by his maternal grandmother, Sarah (Hertha) *Ayrton, and his uncle, the distinguished Jewish writer Israel Zangwill, whose son, the eminent psychologist Oliver Zangwill, had considerable influence on him.

Ayrton attended a co-educational private school but left at an early date. He was later educated at the Hall School in Hampstead, London (*c*.1927–1932), and The Beeches, a progressive boarding-school at Greater Felcourt in Sussex (*c*.1932–1935). At The Beeches, when aged fourteen, he had a brief affair with the French mistress, which resulted in her dismissal back to France and the traditional summons of the father by the headmaster. Gould was so relieved by the reason for his summons that he immediately removed his son from the school, terminated his formal education, and encouraged his artistic talents.

This early end to Ayrton's formal education undoubtedly contributed to his relentless autodidacticism which was to spur the massive erudition which made him such an effective broadcaster on the BBC's long-running and immensely successful programmes *The Brains Trust* and *Round Britain Quiz*. It also made him so formidable an opponent of academics in general and art historians in particular, who were foolish enough to patronize and underestimate the teenage school-leaver who never went to university. His first published work was a ferocious George Grosz-like anti-Nazi cartoon in *Labour*.

From 1936 to 1939 Ayrton studied painting informally in Vienna and Paris, working briefly under Pavel Tchelitchew, and he attended Heatherley's Art School and various other art schools in London. He travelled to Spain, saw some of the siege of Barcelona during the Spanish Civil War, and spent the summer of 1939 with fellow painters and friends Michael Middleton and John *Minton at Les Baux-de-Provence in France. After the outbreak of war he returned to London, had his first exhibition at the Zwemmer Gallery, and, with Minton, during leave from the RAF, executed the designs for John Gielgud's *Macbeth*, staged in 1942. Sir Hugh Walpole became an early patron, and, via Sir Kenneth Clark, Ayrton was given a modest job by the War Artists' Advisory Committee. He was invalided out of the RAF in 1942 and shared an exhibition with Minton at the Leicester Galleries in London.

Michael Ayrton (1921–1975), self-portrait, 1947

The relationship with Minton was of great intellectual value to both artists and was personally extremely close and intense, but it eventually became difficult, as the homosexual Minton probably fell in love with the heterosexual Ayrton who was unable to reciprocate Minton's feelings. For several years in the 1940s Ayrton shared a house in All Souls Place, London, behind Broadcasting House, with his lover, Joan Walsh (1919–1994), who changed her name by deed poll to Joan Ayrton, and the composer–conductor Constant Lambert, who became a close friend and collaborator. This ménage attracted, among others, John Arlott, Margot Fonteyn, Norman Douglas, William Walton, and Dylan Thomas. From 1942 onwards Ayrton's life was marred by ill health, borne with much stoical courage, and his career as an artist developed from a precocity noted by such distinguished elders as Wyndham Lewis (for whom Ayrton acted for some time as visual amanuensis) to a versatile fruition which never brought the honours, the critical acclaim, or the financial success enjoyed by many of his contemporaries.

In this respect, in a country and society which still regards amateurism as a professional advantage, Ayrton suffered from his relentless curiosity, his considerable eclecticism, and his formidable erudition, backed by a strong physical presence which many persons of weaker intellect or personality found intimidating. In fact, his handsome head with long, straight, swept-back hair and full beard, the powerful torso of the sculptor, and the mellifluous voice of a born teacher and conversationalist were compellingly attractive. What left him, at the height of his career, with a single honour—a doctorate from Exeter University (1975)—and no official recognition from the British 'art establishment' was the view, commonly held, that his exceptionally varied output was the sign of a jack of all trades. Possibly his lack of critical favour was accentuated by his youthful, undoubtedly intemperate but characteristically closely argued attack on Picasso and the received wisdom which surrounded Picasso's every doodle with adulation. In fairness, while Ayrton never recanted, he did, in two subsequent essays of equal brilliance, ameliorate his earlier views. All three essays—'The master of pastiche' (1944), 'A reply to myself' (1956), and 'The Midas minotaur' (1969)—are collected in his book *The Rudiments of Paradise* (1971).

For more than three decades Ayrton practised as a painter, sculptor, draughtsman, engraver, portraitist, stage designer, book illustrator, novelist, short-story writer, essayist, critic, art historian, radio and television broadcaster, and cinema and television film-maker. While inevitably in an *œuvre* so prodigious he occasionally let slip work that was not of the first rank, there was in fact none of these trades of which he was not the master.

Ayrton's principal exhibitions, other than regular dealers' selling shows in Britain, Europe, the USA, and Canada, were at Wakefield City Art Gallery (and subsequently on tour) in 1949, the Whitechapel Art Gallery in London in 1955 (a retrospective), the Philadelphia Museum of Art in 1963, the National Gallery of Canada in Ottawa (a regional tour) in 1965, Reading City Art Gallery in 1969, the Bruton Gallery, Bruton, Somerset, in 1971, the University of Sussex, Falmer, in 1972, Portsmouth City Art Gallery (and subsequently on tour) in 1973, and the University of Pennsylvania in Philadelphia in 1973.

The most important exhibition in Ayrton's lifetime, however, was 'Word and image'—a remarkably inventive show devoted to a comparison of the work of Ayrton and Wyndham Lewis, showing the interrelationship not only of the two artists and their styles but also of their writings as well as their visual work. This was held in 1971 at the National Book League, London, four years before Ayrton's death. The major retrospective exhibition which he should have had in his lifetime occurred only posthumously in 1977 at the City of Birmingham Museum and Art Gallery, and subsequently on tour; in 1981 there was a substantial touring exhibition which visited the Bruton Gallery in Somerset and the National Museum of Wales in Cardiff, among other places. Throughout the 1980s and 1990s a series of small exhibitions in various dealers' galleries and the publication of a definitive biography have in fact enhanced his reputation during a gradual favourable reassessment of the so-called neo-romantics of the 1940s and 1950s. Stylistically he was, in his occasionally spiky, distorted visions, a typical English neo-romantic—sharing a view of both landscape and the human figure with, among others, Minton, Graham Sutherland, Robert MacBryde, and Robert Colquhoun. His sense and use of distortion in and of the human body was most noticeable in his sculpture—particularly in the later work and especially in the minotaurs, who seemed to embody the disproportions and the pain of his own body as it slowly succumbed to progressive bone disease.

Ayrton's visual work, apart from his portraits, tended to be thematic, with certain ideas and images either obsessively recorded or constantly recurring. The discovery of Greek landscape and mythology was to haunt his work until he died. (He travelled extensively in Greece and the areas which were part of the Hellenistic world.) Daedalus and Icarus, Talos, and above all the Minotaur inspired much of his finest work, which ranged from pencil sketches to huge bronzes. For Armand Erpf, a benevolently eccentric American millionaire, he created in 1968 at Arkville in New York state a gigantic maze built of brick and stone, with a 7 foot bronze minotaur and a 7 foot bronze of Daedalus and Icarus in two central chambers.

Ayrton had several, beneficial, obsessions. One, present throughout his working life, was the mechanics of human and animal flight; hence his interests in Icarus, the bones of birds, and related matters. Hector Berlioz preoccupied him for years and inspired sculptures, paintings, a memorable short story, and a remarkable BBC television programme which he devised and narrated. Mirrors also fascinated him and, with their infinite variety of and capacity for reflections, dominated his later sculpture where he mingled bronze, polished metal sheet, and perspex to extraordinary effects. For the two years before his death he had been working on a major BBC television series on the multiple possibilities of mirrors and their imagery in life, art, mathematics, philosophy, and astronomy.

Ayrton's literary output was as varied as his visual work. He was a fine critic (he was art critic of *The Spectator* from 1944 to 1946) and published books on subjects ranging from *British Drawings* (1946) and *Hogarth's Drawings* (1948)—via several collections of distinguished essays, notably *Golden Sections* (1957) and *The Rudiments of Paradise* (1971)—to a pioneering scholarly monograph, *Giovanni Pisano, Sculptor* (1969), which had an introduction by Henry Moore.

As a poet Ayrton showed notable talent in the fragmentary *The Testament of Daedalus* (1962), which was a foretaste and forerunner of his subsequent novel, *The Maze Maker* (1967), and he published posthumously in 1977 *Archilochos*, a translation (with the assistance of Professor G. S. Kirk) of the seventh-century BC Greek poet who wrote in the Parian script. This book, containing Ayrton's last published words, was illustrated by his own characteristically spiky etchings done in the last eighteen months of his life.

Ayrton produced one collection of short stories, *Fabrications* (1972), influenced by Jorge Luis Borges in the tricks they played with time, history, and memory, but entirely Ayrtonian in their dry wit, originality of imagination, and a wholly beneficent solipsism deriving not from personal vanity but from the indubitable fact that his own experiences, serendipities, and ideas were genuinely of greater creative interest to himself and others than the notions and characters of most other people, Giovanni Pisano and Hector Berlioz excepted. Some of the ideas in *Fabrications* sprang from the memories and experiences of Ayrton's maternal grandfather, Professor William *Ayrton, an internationally renowned electrical engineer and gold medallist of the Royal Society. (His maternal grandmother, Hertha Ayrton, had herself received the Royal Society's Hughes medal in 1906.)

Ayrton's two novels, *The Maze Maker* and *The Midas Consequence* (1974), were both an integral part of his visual life. The former, a virtuoso account of the lives of Daedalus and Icarus, deals with mythology, Crete, the minotaur, the excitement of flight, and, above all, the genius of the *maker*, of the artist as master craftsman. *The Midas Consequence* is an equally virtuoso performance, dealing with the joys and pitfalls of being a prolific, omni-talented, and internationally revered modern artist. The hero, Capisco, is obviously—too obviously, for the unwary—based on Picasso. He is, of course, far more than that and he is, in part at least, Ayrton, but ultimately he is the paradigmatic artist and genius, enriched and pampered by society but, in the end, the property and prey of that same society.

Ayrton was a man who travelled widely throughout his life, was blessed by considerable domestic felicity, was a much loved member of the Savile Club, and had a large number of friends. He married, on 28 November 1952, Elisabeth Balchin [*see* Ayrton, Elisabeth Evelyn (1910–1991)], daughter of the writer Douglas Walshe, who had three daughters from her first marriage, to the writer Nigel Balchin (1908–1970). In the same year he moved with his wife, who was a distinguished authority on English cooking, a superb hostess, and herself a writer, to Bradfields, a beautiful sixteenth-century country house in Essex, formerly the property of the publisher and poet Sir Francis Meynell. Bradfields was Ayrton's principal home, social centre, and studio until his death in 1975. Michael and Elisabeth Ayrton had no children together but Ayrton was a devoted and loving stepfather.

Ayrton was massively industrious and prolific but, without being either self-conscious or boastful about it, divided his life—once he had established home, family, and studio at Bradfields—between work and play. While in the country he worked hard at his multifarious disciplines and then gave over the weekends to highly intellectual house parties with an endless supply of guests, who fed his prodigious appetite for knowledge and whom he entertained with his own dazzling near monologues, while Elisabeth provided sumptuous meals of genuine English *haute cuisine*. These were based almost entirely on poultry, game, joints of meat, and whole fish, as Ayrton could not abide stews, casseroles, or other dishes in which food was concealed in any way. He had to be able to *see* what he ate, a minor foible more than compensated for by his genuine craftsman's skill as a carver of meat as well as sculpture; and the sight and sound of Ayrton acting as host to Henry Moore or to George Steiner, for whom he created a magnificent chess set, is not lightly forgotten.

Ayrton was, while most happily married, no respecter of marriage as an institution and had indeed married Elisabeth by removing her from her husband. Immensely attractive to women, he had a considerable number of affairs both before and after his marriage, and he tended, after intense spells of work in the country, to travel alone to London for a few days in pursuit of both the intellectual stimulus of the capital and the pleasures of sexual adventure. It was a mark of his seductive personality and charm that no one much minded the way of life he deemed essential to his creativity. In the last years of his life he suffered increasingly from a highly debilitating form of ankylosing spondylitis which made it difficult for him to walk but did not prevent his sculpting in a sitting position and exploiting an exceptionally powerful torso, not entirely dissimilar to those of his minotaurs. After almost dying from an undiagnosed diabetic neuropathy, he made a virtually complete recovery and was planning a range of new work when, on 16 November 1975, he died of a sudden heart attack in his London flat. He was buried at the parish church at Hadstock, Essex. His wife survived him. Examples of Ayrton's work are to be found in the Tate collection; the National Portrait Gallery and Victoria and Albert Museum, London; the Art Gallery of New South Wales, Sydney, Australia; the Reading Museum and Art Gallery; the Portsmouth City Museum and Art Gallery; and the City Art Gallery, Southampton.

T. G. ROSENTHAL

Sources P. Cannon-Brookes, *Michael Ayrton: an illustrated commentary* (1978) • T. G. Rosenthal, 'Michael Ayrton: a memoir', *Encounter*, 46/6 (1976), 87–92 • J. Hopkins, *Michael Ayrton: a biography* (1994) • personal knowledge (2004) • private information (2004) • J. Hopkins, *The Independent* (3 Aug 1994) • J. E. Nyenhuis, *Myth and the creative process: Michael Ayrton and the myth of Daedalus, the maze maker* (2003)

Archives Tate collection, corresp. | FILM BBC TV Archives | SOUND BBC Sound Archives

Likenesses M. Ayrton, self-portrait, pen-and-ink and wash drawing, 1947, NPG [*see illus.*] • M. Ayrton, self-portrait, drawing, priv. coll.; repro. in M. Ayrton, *Fabrications* (1972), jacket • photograph, repro. in Hopkins, *Michael Ayrton*, following p. 210

Wealth at death £93,672: probate, 19 Feb 1976, *CGPLA Eng. & Wales*

Ayrton [*née* Marks], **(Phoebe) Sarah** [Hertha] **(1854–1923)**, electrical engineer and suffragist, was born Phoebe Sarah Marks on 28 April 1854 at 6 Queen Street, Portsea, near Portsmouth, third child of Alice Theresa (*d.* 1898), seamstress, daughter of Joseph Moss, glass merchant of Portsea, and Levi Marks (*d.* 1861), watchmaker and jeweller of Petworth, Sussex. Levi Marks, whose father was a Polish innkeeper, came to England to escape pogroms; he died as his impoverished family, with six boys, was expecting another child. When Sarah was nine her aunts Marion Hartog and Belle Leo, who ran a school in north-west London with Alphonse Hartog, invited her to live with them to be educated with her cousins. Her mother generously agreed. Sarah learned languages and music in this talented family; her cousin Marcus introduced her to science, and Numa (the first Jewish senior wrangler) to mathematics. Sarah and her family mostly became agnostic, though proud of their Jewish heritage. At sixteen she began teaching in London to support her mother. With Ottilie Blind, who called her Hertha after Swinburne (and the earth goddess Erda), she took the Cambridge University (local) examination for women. She was encouraged by her friends and patrons Barbara Bodichon, artist, women's activist, and co-founder of the new Girton College for women, and George Eliot. Marquis (Marky), as they called Sarah, with her curly black hair and grey-green eyes, was an exemplar for Mirah, heroine of *Daniel Deronda*, as Barbara Bodichon was for *Romola*.

Hertha read mathematics at Cambridge from 1877 to 1881, coached by Richard Glazebrook. While at Girton she constructed a sphygmomanometer (pulse recorder), led the choral society, founded the fire brigade, and with Charlotte Scott, Girton's first wrangler, formed a mathematical club. She published problems and solutions in *Mathematical Questions from the Educational Times* for almost two decades. After her return to London she earned money by teaching and embroidery. She ran a club for working girls and cared for her invalid sister. She invented a line divider, which was sold under her patent. In 1884 she went to Will Ayrton's evening classes in electricity at Finsbury Technical College.

Hertha and William Edward *Ayrton (1847–1908) were married in 1885 and their daughter, Barbara, was born in 1886. Will Ayrton was an electrical engineer and co-founder of the City and Guilds Institute. His first wife, his cousin Matilda Chaplin (1846–1883), was a pioneer woman doctor, with his encouragement; their daughter Edith, who married Israel Zangwill, wrote novels as Edith Ayrton Zangwill; the Zangwills' son, Oliver, was professor of experimental psychology at Cambridge.

Hertha Ayrton lectured to women on electricity and its domestic potentialities. She took over Ayrton's experiments on the electric arc at South Kensington while he was at the Chicago Electrical Congress in 1893. She traced the hissing, sputtering, and instability to oxidation of the positive carbon. Excluding air, she obtained a steady arc, and demonstrated a linear relationship between arc length, pressure, and potential difference, the Ayrton equation. Observing the image on a screen, she showed that cratering, as the carbon evaporates, determines the potential for a given current and arc length, and improved efficiency by reshaping the electrodes.

Her analysis and technical advances, described in twelve papers in *The Electrician* (1895–6), established her reputation, unique for a woman. She demonstrated her experiments at the Royal Society's Conversazione in 1899, and spoke on 'The hissing of the electric arc' at the Institution of Electrical Engineers. The institution elected her MIEE, the only woman member until 1958. Her lecture 'L'intensité lumineuse de l'arc à courants continus' at the International Electrical Congress in Paris in 1900 helped Marcus Hartog persuade the British Association to allow women on to their committees. John Perry gave her paper on 'The mechanism of the electric arc' at the Royal Society in 1901. Her book *The Electric Arc* (1902), which became a standard work, included the history from Davy's discovery in 1800 (and a dedication to Barbara Bodichon). She later patented anti-aircraft searchlights, developed for the Admiralty, and arc lamp technology.

From 1901, when Will Ayrton was convalescing at the seaside in Margate, Kent, she studied the formation of sand ripples and sand bars by wave motions of the water, conducting experiments in the landlady's zinc bath, with soap dishes and baking tins. Back home, in her attic, she produced stationary waves of different wavelengths by rocking glass vessels 4 to 44 inches wide, using permanganate, paint, or metal powder to show eddies and vortices. She reported her work to the Royal Society in 1904 (in person), in 1908, and 1911, and to the British Association and the Physical Society. The mathematical description gave difficulty: it is now known to involve complicated viscous effects and (chaotic) turbulence. After Will Ayrton died in 1908 she moved her laboratory down to the drawing room, as shown in the photograph 'Mrs Ayrton in her Laboratory' (Appleyard, 167–8). Her interest in vortices in water and air inspired the Ayrton fan, or flapper, used in the trenches in the First World War to dispel poison gas. She fought for its acceptance and organized its production, over 100,000 being used on the western front.

In 1902 John Perry, with distinguished co-signatories, proposed her candidature for the Royal Society, but lawyers pronounced that a married woman, having no standing in law, was ineligible. Such arguments were quashed by the Sex Disqualification Removal Act (1919), but no woman was proposed again until 1944. In 1906, however, she was awarded the society's Hughes medal for her work on the electric arc and on sand ripples. In 1998 she remained the only female recipient of this medal, awarded annually for original discovery in the physical sciences. Armstrong's obituary in *Nature* exemplifies the opposition to such work by a woman, and elicited a rebuttal.

Hertha Ayrton, despite recurrent ill health, supported by her extended family, was a stalwart of the women's movement. She chaired the physical science section of the International Congress of Women in London in 1899, and encouraged women in applied science. She supported the militant suffragists, as did her friend Marie Curie, who brought her daughters for summer holidays with her in 1912 and 1913. Hertha marched in all the suffrage processions: in 1911, with 800 women graduates in academic dress (which Cambridge women could not wear until 1948), she was in the science section. In 1912–13 Mrs Pankhurst and others recovering from hunger strike were nursed in Hertha's home, returning to prison when they recovered, under the 'Cat and Mouse Act' (the Prisoners' Temporary Discharge Act of 1913). Hertha was 'very proud' when her daughter Barbara Bodichon Ayrton *Gould (1886–1950) went to prison in 1912. Barbara became Labour member of parliament for Hendon North in 1945; her husband, Gerald Gould (*d.* 1936), was a poet and journalist; their son was the artist Michael *Ayrton (1921–1975).

Hertha Ayrton helped found the International Federation of University Women in 1919 and the National Union of Scientific Workers in 1920. She died of blood poisoning (resulting from an insect bite) on 26 August 1923 at New Cottage, North Lancing, Sussex. JOAN MASON

Sources *DNB* • E. Sharp, *Hertha Ayrton, 1854–1923: a memoir* (1926) • K. T. Butler and H. I. McMorran, eds., *Girton College register, 1869–1946* (1948), 8–9 • J. Mason, 'Hertha Ayrton and the admission of women to the Royal Society of London', *Notes and Records of the Royal Society*, 45 (1991), 201–20 • *Early days of the electrical industry, and other reminiscences of Alexander P. Trotter* (1948), 125–9 • R. Appleyard, *The history of the Institution of Electrical Engineers, 1871–1931* (1939), 167–8 • A. P. Trotter, 'Mrs. Ayrton's work on the electric arc', *Nature*, 113 (1924), 48–9 • H. Armstrong, *Nature*, 112 (1923), 800–01 • T. Mather, *Nature*, 112 (1923), 939 [rebuttal of Armstrong's obit.] • private information (2004) • b. cert. • d. cert.

Archives Museum of Jewish Life, Golders Green, London, Steinberg Centre, Edith Chaplin Ayrton diaries

Likenesses H. Darmesteter, portrait, Girton Cam. • photograph, repro. in Sharp, *Hertha Ayrton*, frontispiece • photograph, repro. in Appleyard, *History of the Institution of Electrical Engineers* • photographs, Girton Cam.

Wealth at death £8160 8*s.* 6*d.*: probate, 19 Oct 1923, *CGPLA Eng. & Wales*

Ayrton, William (1777–1858), impresario and writer, was born in London on 24 February 1777, one of the fourteen children of Edmund *Ayrton (1734–1808), composer, and his wife, Ann (1739–1800), daughter of Benjamin Clay. He was unsuccessful in winning the Gresham professorship of music in 1801; however, in 1807 he was elected a fellow of the Royal Society of Antiquaries, and in 1813 he became a founder member of the Philharmonic Society. In 1817 he was manager of the Italian opera at the King's Theatre, Haymarket. For this season, he went to Paris to engage some singers who were then little known, but whose reputations he helped to establish, including Camporese, Crivelli, and Pasta. With them, he introduced to England works by Paer and Cimarosa and, with particular success for twenty-three performances, Mozart's *Don Giovanni* (in Italian). A contentious lawsuit at the end of the season with the litigious lessee of the theatre, Edmund Waters, in which Ayrton sued for £1200, was settled in his favour for £700. His second season, in 1821 (by which time Waters was bankrupt), introduced Rossini's *La gazza ladra* to England (also in Italian). Ayrton contributed criticism to the *Morning Chronicle* (1813–26) and *The Examiner* (1837–51); but his most important journalistic work was as editor of *The Harmonicon* (1823–33), an invaluable record of the times that carried full, excellent reviews and included substantial music examples. He also edited *The Sacred Minstrelsy* (1834), a two-volume anthology of sacred music for domestic use, *Knight's Musical Library* (8 vols., 1834–7), and *The Madrigalian Feast* (1838). Among his songs are the popular vocal duets 'Fair and Fair' and 'Oh! Oh! Memory'. He became a fellow of the Royal Society in 1837. On 17 May 1803 he married Marianne, daughter of Samuel *Arnold; they had at least one son. He died at his home in Bridge Street, Westminster, London, on 8 May 1858.

JOHN WARRACK

Sources *New Grove* • J. Ebers, *Seven years of the King's Theatre* (1828) • E. Waters, *A statement of matters relating to the King's Theatre* (1818) • W. T. Parke, *Musical memoirs*, 2 vols. (1830) • *The Times* (12 Jan 1818) • *Annual Register* (1858) • A. Loewenberg, *Annals of opera* (March 1978) • *CGPLA Eng. & Wales* (1858) • d. cert.

Archives BL, corresp. and papers, Add. MSS 52334–52358, 60358–60381; Add. Ch 75963–75965 · Royal College of Music, London, commonplace book and newspaper cuttings
Wealth at death under £300: probate, 20 Nov 1858, *CGPLA Eng. & Wales*

Ayrton, William Edward (1847–1908), electrical engineer and physicist, was born in London on 14 September 1847 to the accomplished barrister and linguist Edward Nugent Ayrton (1815–1873), and his wife, thereby joining a family long connected with law and music, and traditionally supportive of women's rights. William's uncle was Acton Smee Ayrton, a notably unpopular minister in Gladstone's first administration. William early embraced the study of mathematics in response to unsuccessful paternal efforts to make him learn a different language every day of the week. He performed outstandingly at University College School from 1859, especially in geometry, but still endeavoured to win classical prizes to please his father. Enrolling as a student at University College, London, in 1864, he won Andrews scholarships in mathematics in 1865 and 1866; in the latter year Ayrton became engaged to his cousin and fellow London student, Matilda Charlotte Chaplin, (1846–1883) [*see* Ayrton, Matilda Charlotte], daughter of John Chaplin, a solicitor, and strongly encouraged her to train for the medical profession. In 1866–7 his talent was acknowledged by both George Carey Foster and Thomas Archer Hirst, whom he assisted in teaching experimental physics and mechanics respectively; Ayrton won praise too from Augustus De Morgan for his 'very scrutinizing turn' (Solomon and Mather, 65) in pure mathematics.

Service in India Ayrton's interest in the Indian government telegraph service developed when, as an undergraduate finalist, he was asked to prepare ten students for the service's examinations. He took such interest in this work that, though achieving only second-class BA honours, he excelled in the service's entrance examinations. The secretary of state for India rewarded him by financing a year's study of electrical theory and laboratory technique with Sir William Thomson at the department of natural philosophy, University of Glasgow, for 1867–8; Ayrton later described this experience as the inspiration of his life (Ayrton, 'Kelvin in the sixties', 268). In the second service examination, Ayrton won a scholarship for study in Europe, so he then took the opportunity to gain practical experience of Post Office telegraph operations under William Preece at Southampton, and also at the Telegraph Construction and Maintenance Company works in London.

As fourth grade assistant superintendent in the Indian telegraph service from 1 September 1868 Ayrton worked with the electrical superintendent, C. Louis Schwendler, to develop a speedy method for locating the prevalent faults in the overland telegraph lines that were severely impeding colonial communications. Their solution was so effective that it pre-empted emergency proposals to lay an alternative coastal submarine cable around the subcontinent, Ayrton accordingly receiving rapid promotion. He returned briefly on leave to London to marry Matilda

William Edward Ayrton (1847–1908), by W. & D. Downey, pubd 1893

Chaplin, on 21 December 1871 at St Matthew's parish church, Bayswater, London, she having been controversially ejected from her medical studies at Edinburgh University. Returning to India without Matilda, Ayrton deputized for Schwendler during the latter's illness and strove to improve the telegraph network in the Bombay and Calcutta districts. On leave in England in 1872 to study the signalling problems caused by dampness in porcelain line insulators, he was elected a member of the Society of Telegraph Engineers (STE). Up to mid-1873 he also assisted Sir William Thomson and Fleeming Jenkin in testing a new transatlantic cable for the Great Western Telegraph Company at Millwall and later at Mitcham.

Japanese telegraphs It was through the patronage of Thomson and W. J. M. Rankine at Glasgow University that Ayrton was offered a five-year contract as professor of physics and telegraphy at the Imperial College of Engineering in Tokyo, to commence in autumn 1873. Even for the dynamic young Ayrton, who characteristically embossed his notepaper with the motto 'Energy', the task set him by the Meiji government of turning samurai warriors into westernized English-speaking telegraph engineers proved daunting. According to family legend, after two suicides and one murder in his first term in Tokyo, Ayrton discouraged ritual sword wielding by discharging a large revolver into the ceiling of his small laboratory. He was not a gentle teacher, being quick to criticize passivity and slowness, but won over his students by employing them in collective class researches, and, in contrast to many European colleagues, in maintaining that the Japanese were indeed capable of independent scientific work. Soon Ayrton secured unprecedentedly lavish finance from the Meiji exchequer for a palatial new laboratory, although the execution of his designs brought him into considerable conflict with government officials and workmen. When it opened in 1877 its facilities and equipment compared favourably with contemporary laboratories in Britain and served as a model for several later institutions.

After the birth of their daughter, Edith, in 1874, Matilda Ayrton continued to teach midwifery to Japanese women, and to entertain her husband's students and colleagues. The next significant arrival for Ayrton was John Perry who, soon after taking up the chair of mechanical engineering in 1875, began a long series of joint researches with him, Ayrton experimenting day and night at fever-heat. Ayrton's activities became yet more intensive after Matilda, showing early signs of tuberculosis, departed with Edith in early 1877 to complete her medical doctorate at the Sorbonne. More than twenty papers by Ayrton and Perry from the Tokyo laboratory were published in British and Japanese journals between 1877 and 1880; these included the first ever determination of the dielectric constant of gases, and studies on the viscosity of dielectrics, Japanese magic mirrors, seismology, telegraphic tests, and contact electricity—a paper on the latter winning praise, if not agreement, from James Clerk Maxwell in 1879. As a later colleague, H. E. Armstrong, said of their Japanese period: 'In those days what Ayrton and Perry did not know or do or claim to have done was not worth knowing, doing or claiming' (Armstrong, 751).

Ayrton antagonized the Meiji administration by insisting that foreign supervision was necessary for the operation of its national telegraph system, and his contract at the Imperial College was not renewed. He nevertheless came to be venerated as the founder of electrical engineering in Japan, and 25 March is still acknowledged as 'Electricity day' to commemorate the occasion in 1878 on which he and his students opened the nation's first public electric lighting system at Tokyo's central telegraph station. Relinquishing to Perry his role as Japanese secretary for the STE, Ayrton became honorary editor of its *Proceedings* and chairman of its editorial committee for seven years after he returned to London in the autumn of 1878. Employed as an adviser to the telegraph company, Latimer, Clark, and Muirhead, he also soon took an interest in the newer technologies of electrical power and lighting. It was at the British Association meeting in Sheffield in 1879 that Ayrton first proposed alternate current transmission with step up and step down transformers as the safest and most economical means of distributing energy over long distances, a system almost universally adopted by the end of the twentieth century.

Teaching in London His reputation as an expert on both technical and educational matters won him the City and Guilds professorship of physics (later electrical engineering) at Finsbury in the autumn of 1879. Ayrton's teaching for this archetypal experiment of British technical education was initially undertaken in rooms borrowed from the Cowper Street School. Here dozens of day students and hundreds of evening students each year received a training in electrical measurement and construction techniques; indeed so broad was the constituency of Ayrton's uniquely practical course that, on at least one occasion in 1886, about three-quarters of the audience at STE meetings were Ayrton's former students. The popularity of his evening classes caused such overcrowding in 1881, however, that the laboratories often descended into chaos; the situation improved markedly with the opening of the purpose-built Finsbury Technical College in 1883 on an adjacent site.

Ayrton's fertile collaborations with Perry continued in London much as in Tokyo, particularly after Perry became a Finsbury colleague in 1881, the year in which Ayrton became a fellow of the Royal Society. Their researches, and now also patents, focused very much on the practical applications of electromagnetism, the restless Ayrton generally posing the practical problem, the less worldly Perry suggesting a solution which was then criticized and improved by Ayrton until both were satisfied. After experimenting, like many contemporaries in 1880–81, with televisual techniques of 'seeing at a distance', they soon devoted most of their energy to developing portable measuring instruments for lighting engineers. In 1881 they christened their first proportional reading devices for gauging current and potential difference as 'ammeters' and 'voltmeters' respectively. Dissatisfied, however, with the need for users to multiply readings by a contingent and unstable calibration value, they accomplished the first direct-reading instruments by late 1883. These radically new devices yielded numerical values at a glance, using a range of innovative techniques such as a proportional spiral spring; these were very widely adopted but were soon improved beyond recognition by others in the electrical industry. Ayrton and Perry's unparalleled instrumental output during the period 1881–4 also included dynamometers, wattmeters, dispersion photometers, and an ingenious ohmmeter for measuring resistance. Their clock-based domestic electricity meter would have made them a substantial fortune from royalties when such devices came into wide use in the 1890s if the pair had bothered to renew their 1882 patent.

Ayrton and Perry also undertook much work in developing electric motors and new forms of traction. In November 1882 Ayrton startled London traffic by driving the first ever electric tricycle at the illegal speed of 9 miles an hour through the City, thereby demonstrating the virtues of batteries made by the Fauré Accumulator Company (founded by Sir William Thomson and others) to which he and Perry were consultant engineers in 1882–3. Otherwise more sensitive to safety issues, the pair invented the block contact switching system in 1884 that automatically prevented two electric trains from travelling on the same stretch of track; on the grounds of safety and economy they also successfully campaigned for the introduction of insulated returns on electric railways. Ayrton and Perry assisted at trials of Fleeming Jenkin's telepherage system of telegraphing goods, later used in ski-lift (*téléférique*) systems round the world. Of their remarkably fruitful creative partnership at Finsbury, Perry later wrote: 'in that pioneering time, mere living was delightful' (Perry, *The Electrician*, 188).

Domestic life for Ayrton in London was rarely joyful, however, since Matilda's health steadily deteriorated from 1879; despite wintering in the Alps with Edith, she died from tuberculosis in July 1883. He had by then already met Phoebe Sarah (Hertha) Marks (1854–1923) [*see* Ayrton, (Phoebe) Sarah], a Cambridge-educated mathematician, at a party when taking an uncommon break from laboratory work in October 1882. She was the daughter of a jeweller, Levi Marks. About a year after Matilda's death, Hertha and 'Will' pursued their common interest in mathematics and electrical science, and she enrolled to study with him at Finsbury in October 1884. After a courtship that revolved around her critical proof-reading of his *Practical Electricity: a Laboratory and Lecture Course* (1887), the couple were married on 6 May 1885, Hertha having reconciled her orthodox Jewish mother to the union. Thereafter, the scientific careers of William and Hertha Ayrton were closely entwined yet complementary; he encouraged her scientific lecturing and research, while taking great care to establish the independence of her achievements. Their daughter, Barbara Bodichon Ayrton, was born on 3 April 1886; she married Gerald Gould in 1910, and as Barbara *Gould became a Labour MP in 1945.

In the autumn of 1885 Ayrton began teaching in the imposing City and Guilds Central Institution at South Kensington, on the design of which he had been consulted by the architect, Alfred Waterhouse, four years previously. Initially Ayrton was reluctant to take up the professorship of physics (later electrical engineering) at the Central since the terms of appointment prohibited commercial consultancy; he accepted the position in the spring of 1884 only after Oliver Lodge had declined it. Finding the Central building still incomplete in October, for the 1884–5 session Ayrton taught a handful of Central students, along with Hertha, alongside their juniors at Finsbury. Undeterred by accusations of failure at the small number of students initially enrolling at his and colleagues' courses in South Kensington in 1885, Ayrton implemented a wide-ranging scheme of advanced training in the theory and practice of applied physics, illustrated sympathetically by *Engineering* in November and December 1888. So dedicated did Ayrton's steadily growing small band of students become to the pursuit of high precision in physical experiments that it was not unusual to find them working with him in the laboratory at night to avoid disturbance from passing traffic.

Just as he had in Japan, Ayrton invited his third-year students to participate with him and his assistant, Thomas Mather, in collective research projects. Many of these involved developing and applying new techniques of electrical measurement, notably the secohmmeter for measuring self-induction (1886–7), alternating current frequency measurers (1889), and shunt devices (1894); the proposal made by Ayrton and his student, H. C. Haycraft, that ammeters and voltmeters be used to expedite laboratory measurements caused great controversy, however, among physicists in 1894. After Perry broke off his partnership about 1890, finding Ayrton too far away and undertaking the lion's share of the work anyway, Mather became Ayrton's chief research collaborator. Remote from the industrial districts of London, and barred from much commercial consultancy, Ayrton's activities with Mather generally concerned instruments for the physics laboratory, most notably the enduringly popular Ayrton–Mather galvanometer. Cognate with this move, Ayrton invited Hertha to take over his researches on the resistance of the electric arc light after she ascertained errors in the results he had intended to announce at the Chicago International Exhibition of 1893. Following his earlier work for the British Association for the Advancement of Science (BAAS) electrical standards committee (whose reassembly he had instigated in 1880), from 1896 Ayrton also collaborated with John Viriamu Jones on resistance standards and a high-precision form of Kelvin current balance in preparation for the opening of the National Physical Laboratory in 1902. Ayrton's individual contributions to research in physics and engineering were recognized in the award of royal medal by the Royal Society in 1901.

Thriving on disputation and possessing his father's analytical powers and legal acumen, Ayrton was long sought after as an expert witness, especially for patent work, although he accepted engagement only for cases that he considered just. Several times during the 1890s Ayrton used such skills to fend off plans to run an electric underground railway beneath Exhibition Road, collaborating with Arthur Rücker at the neighbouring Royal College of Science in 1890–91 to prove the magnitude of the electromagnetic threat thereby posed to their delicate laboratory researches. Ayrton prepared his many public speeches with the same rigour and meticulous accuracy as he conducted his laboratory work, and delivered them with considerable authority and panache. So popular, for example, was his lecture on 'The electric transmission of power' at the BAAS meeting at Bath in 1888, that by popular request he repeated it the following day. Similarly memorable was Ayrton's address as president of section A of the BAAS in 1898, his venture into the little charted territory of the physics of smell being inspired by the unusual olfactory sensitivities of the female Ayrtons.

Society activities Ayrton was highly active in London's science and engineering societies, attending nearly all meetings of the Physical Society of London (a forebear of the Institute of Physics), and was its president in 1890–92. Often in attendance when electrical papers were presented to the Institution of Civil Engineers (ICE), it was none the less the Institution of Electrical Engineers (IEE—as the STE was retitled in 1888), that was the mirror of Ayrton's life. He contributed to thirty-two papers read before its meetings in the ICE's rooms, and spoke in well over a hundred discussions, thereby publicizing the stream of novel techniques and devices emanating from his Finsbury and South Kensington laboratories. So devoted was Ayrton to advancing the interests of the IEE that, after his return from Japan, he served on its council continuously (in a variety of capacities) for the rest of his life, acting as president in 1892–3. Especially concerned to improve the IEE's often precarious finances, as honorary treasurer from 1897 to 1902 he presided over a £10,000 increase in the institution's fund to build its own premises.

In 1899 Ayrton helped Hertha secure an opportunity to be the first woman to read a paper to the IEE, although it was solely on the merits of her researches on the hissing of the electric arc that she was elected its first female member that year. After publishing *The Electric Arc* in 1902, she deferred further research to tend to Will after his health collapsed; he was suffering from high blood pressure and insomnia brought on by overwork. Returning to the Central again in 1903, he was commissioned by the Admiralty to solve the problems of roaring and wandering in its arc lit searchlights; these were solved only after Hertha Ayrton showed that these adverse phenomena were analogous to the hissing of smaller arc lights. Frustrated that the Admiralty overlooked her major contribution to the reports, and supportive of work by their friends the Pankhursts against cognate injustices, both became members of the Women's Social and Political Union (WSPU) in 1906. Strongly sympathetic to the militance of the suffragettes' campaign for women's enfranchisement, one of Ayrton's last public acts was to ride at the head of the WSPU's historic parade through Hyde Park in June 1908.

Despite recurrent ill health, Ayrton acted as dean of the City and Guilds College from 1904, overseeing its amalgamation into Imperial College in 1907, and somehow combined his college duties with several major trips abroad. In 1903 he participated in the Moseley commission to study education in the USA, and he went to southern Africa for the BAAS meeting in 1905, at which he was very critical of plans to install a hydroelectric plant at Victoria Falls to distribute power across the Cape. Such relentless activity further weakened his arterial system, however, and he died at home at 41 Norfolk Square, Hyde Park, London, on 8 November 1908. He was buried four days later at Brompton cemetery without religious rites, but with a choral service of sacred music, addresses being read by his son-in-law, Israel Zangwill, who had married his daughter Edith, and John Perry. A phenomenally energetic character, and often fearlessly critical—a quality some regarded rather as prickliness—the bearded and dashingly handsome Ayrton played a central role in the early history of electrical engineering, the development of the IEE, and in the promotion of women's rights. That he was far too busy—or latterly too ill—ever to write an autobiography might explain why so many of Ayrton's accomplishments that were recognized by his contemporaries have long been left undervalued by historians.

Graeme J. N. Gooday

Sources M. Soloman and T. Mather, 'William Edward Ayrton', *The Central* [City and Guilds College], 7 (1910), 65–91 · P. J. Hartog, 'Professor W. E. Ayrton: a biographical sketch', *Cassier's Magazine*, 22 (1902), 541–4 · *The Electrician* (5 Feb 1892), 346–7 · E. Sharp, *Hertha Ayrton, 1854–1923: a memoir* (1926) · J. P. [J. Perry], *PRS*, 85A (1911), i–viii · W. Mordey and J. Perry, '[Death of Professor W. E. Ayrton]', *Journal of the Institution of Electrical Engineers*, 42 (1908–9), 1–6 · J. Perry, 'Prof. William Edward Ayrton', *Nature*, 79 (1908–9), 74–5 · J. Perry, *The Electrician* (13 Nov 1908), 187–8 · W. E. Ayrton, 'Kelvin in the sixties', *Popular Science Monthly*, 27 (1908), 259–68 · 'A visit to Professor Ayrton's laboratory', *Japan Weekly Mail* (26 Oct 1878) · M. Ayrton, *Fabrications* (1972) · H. E. Armstrong, 'Prof. John Perry', *Nature*, 105 (1920), 751–2 · G. Gooday, 'The morals of energy metering', *The values of precision*, ed. M. N. Wise (1995), 239–82 · G. Gooday, 'Teaching telegraphy and electrotechnics in the physics laboratory', *History of Technology*, 13 (1991), 73–111 · Y. Takahashi, 'William Edward Ayrton at the Imperial College of Engineering in Tokyo', *IEEE Transactions on Education*, 33 (1990), 198–205 · E. S. Pankhurst, *The suffragette movement: an intimate account of persons and ideals* (1931) · W. H. Brock, 'The Japanese connexion', *British Journal for the History of Science*, 14 (1981), 227–43 · private information (2004) · d. cert. · *DNB* · priv. coll.

Archives Inst. EE, MS lectures | ICL, letters to S. P. Thompson · UCL, letters to Sir Francis Galton

Likenesses photograph, *c.*1867, repro. in Sharp, *Hertha Ayrton*, facing p. 114 · engraving, *c.*1892, repro. in *The Electrician*, facing p. 346 · W. & D. Downey, woodburytype photograph, NPG; repro. in W. Downey and D. Downey, *The cabinet portrait gallery*, 4 (1893) [*see illus.*] · photographs (with students), ICL

Wealth at death £43,590 2*s.* 2*d.*: probate, 5 Jan 1909, *CGPLA Eng. & Wales*

Ayscough, Francis (1701–1763), courtier and Church of England clergyman, was born in Surrey on 19 December 1701 and baptized on 25 December in St Olave's, Southwark, the second son of Gabriel Ayscough (*bap.* 1668) and his wife, Mary. He was educated at Abingdon School, Berkshire, and matriculated at Corpus Christi College, Oxford, on 28 March 1717, where he graduated BA on 12 December 1720 and proceeded MA on 24 March 1723. He was ordained deacon on 18 December 1726, elected a probationer fellow of Corpus Christi on 16 January 1727, and ordained priest on 16 June 1728. In January 1730 the fellows of Corpus Christi voted eight to four against appointing him to a full fellowship but he appealed successfully to the visitor, who awarded him reinstatement, his costs and arrears to be paid by the fellows personally. He proceeded BD on 22 February 1731 and DD in 1735.

While at Oxford, Ayscough acquired a reputation as 'a person well supported by zealous friends' (*The Proceedings of Corpus Christi College*, 38); certainly he was socially adept and moved easily in aristocratic circles. One of his Oxford pupils, between 1726 and 1728, was George Lyttelton, later first Baron Lyttelton, who considered him to be 'a gentleman of great learning, candour, and judgement' (Phillimore, 2.346). In 1730 Ayscough unsuccessfully proposed marriage to Ann Pitt, sister of Lyttelton's friend William Pitt. In 1732 he was introduced to Frederick, prince of

Wales, and at some time after that he was brought by Lyttelton into Frederick's circle. Meanwhile, Ayscough identified himself as a latitudinarian churchman by defending Benjamin Hoadly's views on the eucharist in *A Proper Answer to a Late Abusive Pamphlet Entitled 'The Winchester Converts'* (1735). In 1736, preaching before the House of Commons on the anniversary of the martyrdom of Charles I, he opposed 'enthusiasm' while defending liberty of speculation: 'are not men to think at all because mad men will think madley, and weak men will think weakly?' (Ayscough, *A Sermon*, 21). In August 1736 he was appointed chaplain and clerk of the closet to Frederick, in which role he assumed control of a substantial part of the prince's political patronage. Ayscough was active in election business, especially in the west country, throughout the later 1730s and 1740s. In 1741 he was nominated by Frederick to the living of Northchurch, Berkhamsted, Hertfordshire.

Ayscough was almost certainly the author of a political diary detailing the involvement of Frederick and his allies in the reconstruction of the government between January 1742 and November 1743, which is preserved in the Holland House manuscripts at the British Library. The diary, written by someone intimately involved with the prince's finances and his election patronage, is a useful source for the period immediately preceding and following the resignation of Sir Robert Walpole and for the political conduct of Frederick at this time. Ayscough acted as intermediary between Frederick and the Wilmington ministry on the one hand and his patron, Lyttelton, and Pitt on the other, during negotiations in late 1742 and early 1743 aimed at bringing Pitt and Lyttelton into the ministry. The paths of Ayscough and Lyttelton began to diverge at about this time. In 1744 Ayscough was appointed preceptor to Frederick's two eldest sons, George and Edward. On 21 January 1745 at St Martin-in-the-Fields, London, he fulfilled a longstanding arrangement and married Lyttelton's sister Anne (1714–1776), who brought with her an income of £6000 a year. However, his relations with Lyttelton were badly damaged by his management of the election at Okehampton in 1747, when on Frederick's behalf he unsuccessfully attempted to unseat Lyttelton, who had joined the Pelham administration, which Frederick opposed.

Ayscough remained close to the Pitt family and was particularly concerned in Frederick's lease of the borough of Old Sarum from Thomas Pitt, Ayscough's wife's brother-in-law, who by 1749 was deeply in debt. In June of that year Ayscough arranged that Frederick would pay Thomas Pitt £3000 per annum in return for the nomination 'of every M.P. that shall be at the borough of Old Sarum … without any further expense' (BL, Add. MS 59484, fol. 67). Other clerks to the royal closet had gone on to high preferments in the church, and Ayscough must have hoped for a bishopric on Frederick's accession to the throne. His portrait, painted in 1749 by Richard Wilson, in which he is seen presiding over the two young princes, suggests an ambitious as well as a masterful and evidently capable cleric. His hopes were dashed, however, by the death of the prince of Wales on 30 March 1751, which was immediately followed by Ayscough's replacement as tutor to the princes. Horace Walpole suggests that just before this event Ayscough had been instrumental in bringing about a renewed political understanding between the Lyttelton interest and Frederick's court at Leicester House. Walpole described Ayscough as 'an insolent man, unwelcome to the clergy on suspicions of heterodoxy, and of no fair reputation for integrity' (Walpole, 1.56) and suggested that under his care Prince George had failed to learn to write English—a slur that is contradicted by surviving letters from Prince George to his father. Politically inconvenient to the former allies of Prince Frederick, and too latitudinarian for most of the clergy, Ayscough did not receive further appointment until the veteran controversialist whom he had once defended, Benjamin Hoadly, appointed him a canon at Winchester in 1756. He had to wait for significant ecclesiastical promotion until the accession of one of his former pupils as King George III, after which he was given the deanery of Bristol in 1761.

Ayscough died in Bristol on 16 August 1763, and was buried in Bristol Cathedral on 19 August. He left £10,000 to his wife, who died in 1776. They had one son, George Edward *Ayscough, who died in 1779, after a life of debauchery.

M. St John Parker

Sources F. Ayscough, corresp. and papers, 1747–54, BL, Add. MS 59484 · *A vindication of the proceedings in the case of Mr. Ayscough, of Corpus Christi College, Oxon.* (1731) · *The proceedings of Corpus Christi College, Oxon, in the case of Mr. Ayscough, vindicated* (1730) · F. Ayscough, *A sermon preached before the … House of Commons on January 30 1736* (1736) [on Romans 12: 3] · [F. Ayscough], *A proper answer to a late abusive pamphlet entitled 'The Winchester converts', in a letter to the author [D. B. Tovey] by a member of the university* (1735) · *Memoirs and correspondence of George, Lord Lyttelton, from 1734 to 1773*, ed. R. Phillimore, 2 vols. (1845) · J. Bickersteth and R. W. Dunning, *Clerks to the closet in the royal household* (1991) · Nichols, *Lit. anecdotes*, 8.433 · biographical notices of Oxford writers, Bodl. Oxf., MS Rawl. J. 4°5, fol. 218v · *Fasti Angl., 1541–1857*, [Canterbury], 106 · *Fasti Angl., 1541–1857*, [Bristol], 18 · Foster, *Alum. Oxon., 1715–1886* · R. Harris, ed., 'A Leicester House political diary, 1742–3', *Camden miscellany, XXXI*, CS, 4th ser., 44 (1992), 375–411 · H. Walpole, *Memoirs of King George II*, ed. J. Brooke, 1 (1985), 55–6 · admissions register, CCC Oxf. · parish register, St Olave's, Southwark, 25 Dec 1701 [baptism] · parish register, Stepney, St Dunstan and All Saints, 4 June 1688 [baptism: G. Ayscough] · parish register, St Martin-in-the-Fields, 21 Jan 1745 [marriage] · Dropmore papers 2515C, BL, Add. MS 59484 [residential address] · parish register, Bristol Cathedral, 19 Aug 1763 [burial] · W. Musgrave, *Obituary prior to 1800*, ed. G. J. Armytage, 6 vols., Harleian Society, 44–9 (1899–1901), 1.75

Archives BL, corresp. and papers, Add. MS 59484 · BL, political diary, Add. MS 52234 A–E

Likenesses R. Wilson, group portrait, oils, 1749, NPG; on display at Beningbrough Hall and Gardens, Yorkshire

Wealth at death £10,000: George Lyttelton, letter to his brother William, 27 Sept 1763, in *Memoirs*, ed. Phillimore, 2.643 · left estate, real and personal, to wife

Ayscough, George Edward (*d.* 1779), soldier and author, was the son of Francis *Ayscough (1701–1763), dean of Bristol and sometime preceptor to Prince George, and his wife, Anne (1714–1776), daughter of Sir Thomas Lyttelton and sister of George, first Baron Lyttelton. Ayscough was commissioned in the 1st regiment of foot guards, from which he obtained leave in September 1769, perhaps on grounds of ill health, to tour the continent. An anonymous account of his travels entitled *Letters from an officer in the guards to his friend in England: containing some accounts of France and Italy* was published in 1778. Ayscough journeyed through France and Italy with 'a curiosity to see mankind in all situations' (Ayscough, 54). His itinerary took him to Lyons, Avignon, Provence, and Marseilles, from where he took ship for Genoa and went on to Pisa. In Italy he also visited Florence, Rome, and Venice (which greatly disappointed him), Padua, Verona, Milan, and Turin before crossing the Alps.

Ayscough's admission in his memoir that his 'way is always to speak [his] mind, right or wrong' signals a judgemental, bullish personality, whose outbursts appear comic to the modern reader. Of the French he writes:

> During this and several former expeditions to the Continent, I have studied the manners of the French nation, and I have found them volatile, even to a degree of childishness. To all *rules* there are, doubtless, exceptions; but a Frenchman is, in general, an unlettered prejudiced fop. (Ayscough, 23)

Reflecting on his experiences in Rome he writes:

> I felt a kind of enthusiastic delight at the first sight of Rome, but this was dampened by the recollection that this city, which was once inhabited by a nation of heroes and patriots, was now in the hands of the most effeminate and superstitious people in the universe. (ibid., 140)

Nevertheless he records, with evident satisfaction, having met Pope Clement XIV in Rome, and having received his benediction.

By June 1772 Ayscough seems to have been resident in St Anne's parish, Westminster. He was promoted to the Order of the Bath and made an application to the College of Arms to confirm his right to bear the arms of Ayscoughs, which can be traced to a branch of the family resident in Yorkshire in the fourteenth century. On 4 January 1774 he sold the manuscripts of his late uncle, Lord Lyttelton, and publishing rights, to James Dodsley for a down payment of £250 plus £150 payable within six months. Dodsley agreed to pay a further £200 if the miscellaneous *Works* of Lord Lyttelton, edited and published by Ayscough in the same year, were produced by him as a second edition. The surviving portion of a letter from James Bate to his sister dated 5 March 1774, put into a commonplace book kept by members of the Ayscough family during the eighteenth century, seems to indicate that Ayscough married—his wife's maiden name may have been Cockburn—and had a son. Bate refers to Ayscough having become 'unfortunate' which, in view of his transactions with Dodsley, may refer to financial difficulties.

In December 1776 Ayscough's version of Voltaire's tragedy *Sémiramis* (1748) was staged at Drury Lane. The play, dedicated to Ayscough's brother-in-law Sir James Cockburn and published by J. Dodsley, incorporated an epilogue by Richard Sheridan. The editor of the *London Review* dismissed the piece as 'not worth quarrelling about' (Kendrick and others, 466). Nevertheless, Ayscough's tragedy was performed eleven times, earning the author three crowded benefit nights. It appears that Ayscough recruited his brother officers to attend the first night of the play and he addressed them directly in his prologue, promising them '*(this great bus'ness ended) / He'll gladly re-assume the* Sash *once more*'. Ayscough died on 14 October 1779.

James William Kelly

Sources commonplace book, Bodl. Oxf., MS Eng. C.312 • BL, Add. MS 38729 [a copy of a document transferring ownership of George, Lord Lyttelton's manuscripts from George Edward Ayscough to James Dodsley, the original signed by both parties and dated 4 Jan 1774. The copy dated 13 August 1849] • [G. E. Ayscough], *Letters from an officer in the guards to his friend in England: containing some accounts of France and Italy* (1778) • W. Kendrick and others, *The London review of English and foreign literature*, 4 (1776), 463–7 • *The works of George Lord Lyttelton*, 2 vols. (1775) • D. E. Baker, *Biographia dramatica, or, A companion to the playhouse*, rev. I. Reed, new edn, rev. S. Jones, 3 vols. in 4 (1812) • Foster, *Alum. Oxon.* • T. Gilliland, *The dramatic mirror, containing the history of the stage from the earliest period, to the present time*, 1 (1808), 257–8 • C. H. Gray, *Theatrical criticism in London to 1795* (New York, 1931) • A. Nicoll, *A history of English drama, 1660–1900*, 6 vols. (1952–9), vol. 3 • Venn, *Alum. Cant.* • J. C. Walker, *The Ayscough family and their connections, being a paper read before the Spalding Gentleman's Society* (1896) • *WWW*

Archives Bodl. Oxf., commonplace book belonging to the Ayscough family, MS Eng. C.312

Likenesses S. Harding, stipple, pubd 1794 (after G. Dance), BM, NPG

Wealth at death 'unfortunate': Bodl. Oxf., MS Eng. C.312, fol. 3

Ayscough, Samuel (1745–1804), librarian and antiquary, was born in Nottingham and baptized at St Peter's, Nottingham, on 29 November 1745, the only son of George Ayscough (1721/2–1783), printer, and his second wife, Edith Wigley. His grandfather, William Ayscough, was a stationer and printer in Nottingham, and when he died on 2 March 1719 the business was run by his widow until George Ayscough was old enough to take it over. George continued the printing business until the year 1762, some thirty years after his mother's death. Although he enjoyed the esteem of his neighbours, he was not a good business man. He speculated unwisely, even to the extent of the alchemical folly of attempting to extract gold from the dross of coal. In 1762, having lost almost all his money, he took over a large farm at Great Wigston in Leicestershire, managing ultimately to lose the rest of his money and the patrimony of his children.

Samuel Ayscough was educated at the grammar school in Nottingham under Richard Johnson, author of *Noctes Nottinghamiae*. He helped his father in his various attempts to achieve some measure of business success, and when these failed took over the running of a mill. But even this was a failure, and it was owing to the timely help of an old schoolfellow and friend, John Eamer (later to be knighted and lord mayor of London), that he migrated to London about 1770 at Eamer's suggestion. There, newly clothed at Eamer's expense, he became overseer of street paviours, a position he also owed to Eamer's help. Before long, however, he found employment in some capacity with John Rivington, a prominent bookseller and publisher of London. Doubtless because of the experience he gained as an employee of Rivington, he progressed to a position as assistant to the principal librarian of the British Museum in the cataloguing department. Henceforth, his life was to revolve around that institution, one of his chief pleasures being to act as a guide to its treasures.

Samuel Ayscough (1745–1804), by James Basire, pubd 1804

With his salary from the British Museum, plus some income from arranging private libraries, and financial help from Eamer, Ayscough was in a position to send for and support his father until the latter's death on 18 November 1783. In 1782, with permission of the trustees of the museum, he published privately his catalogue of the undescribed manuscripts in the museum, a labour which took him some two years. He used 20,000 slips of paper in making the catalogue, having examined every manuscript, and employed two indexes for ease of reference. The first gives the manuscript numbers and the pages on which they are described; the second, all the names in the two volumes. The catalogue describes 5000 volumes and is still indispensable. He was not at that time a member of the permanent staff of the museum. When he did become a member about 1785 he had unsuccessfully applied for five earlier vacancies over a period of fifteen years. His first appointment was in the department of natural history, but in February 1791 he succeeded to the department of printed books. In 1787, with the help of Samuel Harper and Dr Paul Henry Maty, he produced a catalogue of the printed books in the museum entitled *Librorum impressorium qui in museo Britannico adservantur catalogus*, not entirely free from faults but of great immediate and subsequent value.

In addition to the catalogues of British Museum holdings, Ayscough earned his fame as the prince of index makers by compiling the index for the first seventy volumes of Ralph Griffiths's *Monthly Review* in 1786, with a continuation to volume 81 in 1796. His two-volume index to the first fifty-six volumes of the *Gentleman's Magazine* appeared in 1789. The index was divided into five parts: 'Essays', 'Poetry', 'Names', 'Books', and 'Plates and cuts', with the addition of an index to nine numbers of 'Miscellaneous correspondence'. In an unsigned two-page preface, Ayscough, adopting an editorial stance, wrote

> The Utility of a GENERAL INDEX, to so mixt a Work as the GENTLEMAN'S MAGAZINE, when by the Indulgence of the Publick it has increased to above Twenty Volumes, is too evident to be questioned; and we therefore hope that we are now making some return to our Friends, however unequal, for the Favours which we have received; for not to be able to find what we know to be in our possession, is a more vexatious circumstance than the mere want of what we have neglected to procure.

The index to the *Gentleman's Magazine* is not, however, without its limitations: the name Smith, for example, occurs in hundreds of entries bare of forenames. To accompany the third volume of an edition of Shakespeare's plays, Ayscough in 1790 published what is described on the title-page as an index to 'the remarkable words and passages made use of by Shakespeare', but is actually the first concordance of Shakespeare's plays. The publisher John Stockdale paid Ayscough 200 guineas for his index. Other indexes compiled by Ayscough were of the first twenty volumes of the *British Critic*, published in 1804; of John Bridges' *History and Antiquities of Northamptonshire* (1791); and of the first volume of Owen Manning's *History and Antiquities of the County of Surrey* (1804), the second and third volumes being published in 1809 and 1814, well after Ayscough's death. There is no evidence that he compiled the index to the *Annual Register* (1758–80) which has been ascribed to him. John Nichols, who knew him, ascribes to him the indexes to Dr Paul Henry Maty's *New Review* (1782–86). In 1802 he provided the indexes for, but did not edit, *Calendarium rotulorum patentium in Turri Londinensis*. The title-page names T. Astle as the editor; John Caley was the co-editor of this and other volumes of records. Ayscough is said to have claimed to have earned £1300 by his indexing.

Ayscough's single most extended literary effort was his *Remarks on the letters from an American farmer, or, A detection of the errors of Mr. J. Hector St. John, pointing out the pernicious tendency of those letters to Great Britain*, published in 1783, occasioned by the publication one year earlier of de Crevecoeur's *Letters of an American Farmer*. Ayscough claimed that the author was neither an American nor a farmer, and that his sole purpose was to urge Englishmen to migrate to America. The pamphlet was praised in reviews in the *Gentleman's Magazine* and in the *Monthly Review*. Ayscough contributed some forty pieces to the *Gentleman's Magazine*, the earliest in February 1781. His letters cover a number of topics—medical, agricultural, topographical, and architectural—and address miscellaneous matters such as impostures and the mortality of cats. His historical contributions include anecdotes of Cardinal Wolsey, Alexander Oldys, James Ralph, Bishop Wickham, and Archbishop Matthews, and a reprint of four letters by Ben Jonson. John Nichols was of the opinion that the pieces written by Ayscough for the *Gentleman's Magazine* were 'in a style which would not have discredited talents of which the world has a higher opinion' (Nichols, *Lit. anecdotes*, 9.56).

At some time between 1781 and 1785, but probably at the later date, Ayscough was ordained, something he had long desired. He was presented to the curacy of Normanton-on-Soar in Nottinghamshire, and afterwards was appointed assistant curate of the none too decorous parish of St Giles-in-the-Fields under the Revd Richard Southgate, a colleague at the British Museum. He so comported himself as to win the friendship of a number of eminent persons, including John Buckner, later bishop of Chichester. He was elected to the Society of Antiquaries on 12 March 1789. Eight years later, to the month and almost to the day, he communicated two items to *Archaeologia* (13, 1797): 'Copies of two manuscripts on the proper method of defence against invasion', and on 9 March 'Copy of a manuscript in the British Museum Harl. MSS. 6844, *fol.* 49'.

Ayscough delivered fifteen Fairchild lectures from 1790 to 1804. Thomas Fairchild, gardener, of Shoreditch, bequeathed a sum of money for a sermon each Whit Tuesday on the 'Wonderful works of God in the creation'. The sermons, intended for publication after Ayscough's death, never appeared. He had hoped unsuccessfully to find some 200 subscribers at about 2 guineas each to enable him to edit a collection of historical letters in the British Museum bequeathed by Thomas Birch. Another ambitious work remains in manuscript, a catalogue of the ancient rolls and charters in the British Museum, a work which occupied him for some five years from 1787 to 1792. His last effort in the museum was in arranging the books in classes and cataloguing the king's tracts.

About 1803 Ayscough was presented to the small vicarage of Cudham in Kent by Lord Chancellor Eldon. The vicarage was some 17 miles from London, but Ayscough travelled the distance every Saturday to fulfil his pastoral duties, returning on Monday. In a two-part letter to the *Gentleman's Magazine* (74, 1804, 830–33, 901–3), he gave a detailed account of his parish. He died in his apartments in the museum of what has been termed dropsy in the chest on 30 October 1804, and was buried in the cemetery of St George's, Bloomsbury. ARTHUR SHERBO

Sources *DNB* • Nichols, *Lit. anecdotes* • A. Sherbo, 'Samuel Ayscough of the British Museum (1745–1804), prince of index-makers', *Letters to Mr Urban of the Gentleman's Magazine* (1997) • P. R. Harris, *A history of the British Museum Library, 1753–1973* (1998) • *IGI* • *GM*, 1st ser., 74 (1804), 1094

Archives BL, catalogues of charters, rolls, and MSS in various libraries, Add. MSS 5015, 5017, 11257, 43500–43502; King's MS 387 • BL, annotated copy of Letsome's *Preacher's assistant* • Lincs. Arch., calendar of MSS relating to Lincolnshire in the British Museum

Likenesses J. Basire, line engraving, pubd 1804, BM, NPG [*see illus.*]

Ayscough, William. *See* Aiscough, William (*c.*1395–1450).

Ayscu [Ayscough], **Edward** (**1550–1616/17**), historian, was a native of Cotham or Nun Cotham, Lincolnshire. Several branches of the family were resident in Lincolnshire, and this has occasioned considerable confusion as to the identity of the historian, who was the son of Edward Ayscough (*d.* 1558), Henry VIII's cup-bearer, and his wife, Margaret Gibson (*d.* 1593), daughter of Thomas Gibson of Cotham. Anne Askew, the Henrician protestant martyr, was his father's sister. The elder Ayscough settled at Cotham some time before 1550, the year in which, in August, Edward the younger was born. Little is known about Ayscu's education or career, but he married Ursula, daughter of Henry Skipwith; she died in 1611. The couple had four sons, Henry, William, Edward, and John, and a daughter, Janet.

Ayscu the historian appears to have spent most of his time in Cotham, and it is from there that he dates his only known work, *A historie contayning the warres, treaties, marriages, and other occurrents betweene England and Scotland, from King William the Conqueror* (1607). One of a number of such histories written in the early years of the reign of James I, it was clearly inspired by the project to unite the kingdoms of Scotland and England. Dedicated to Henry, prince of Wales, it provides a history of the relations between the two kingdoms from Roman times to the accession of James to the English crown. Although presented largely in an English perspective, the *Historie* aspired to provide a balanced account that harmonized the conflicting narratives of Scottish and English chroniclers. Although Ayscu often takes Scottish historians to task on particular points, he is firm in his belief that the two countries, cohabiting the same island, were destined to unite both by common ethnic origins and by providence. He takes the side of Robert Bruce in recounting the Scottish wars of independence in the early fourteenth century, though he periodically slips into the habit of regarding the Scots as having 'rebelled' against an English overlordship whose legitimacy is presumed. Ayscu was well read in medieval chronicles and modern authorities such as William Camden. Although the *Historie* begins by stating that all European nations are descended from Noah's son Japheth (as was then commonly believed), its author shows a much greater degree of scepticism towards other ancient myths and legends, including that of Brutus the Trojan, than may be found in many contemporaneous works. A firm protestant who openly avows Anne Askew as his aunt, Ayscu makes frequent jibes against the papacy and Catholicism, while treading carefully around the queenship of James I's mother, Mary, queen of Scots.

Ayscu dated his will 31 August 1616, from Lincoln, but it was not proved until 17 March 1617, principally owing to the absence overseas of his eldest son and executor, Henry. In his will he describes himself as living in Lincoln, and it may have been there that he consulted the sources used in his *Historie*. Edward Ayscu the historian has in the past been confused with his cousin, **Sir Edward Ayscu** (1596–1654?) of South Kelsey, who was the great-great-grandson of his namesake's grandfather. The confusion probably stems from this second Edward Ayscu's antiquarian associations, above all with Sir Robert Cotton, with whom, and with Sir Henry Spelman, he served on a number of commissions between 1627 and 1630, for instance inquiring into the exactions of fees by crown officials since 1569. He was sheriff of Lincoln in 1632, having represented the city in parliament in 1628, and in 1640 he was a knight of the shire for Lincolnshire. Indicted for high treason at Grantham in 1643, he survived to draw up his will in November 1648, and probably lived longer, since it was not proved until 1 July 1654. Ayscu had married Frances Clifford while he was still a child, about 1606; she outlived her husband, dying in 1658 or 1659.

D. R. Woolf

Sources D. R. Woolf, *The idea of history in early Stuart England* (1990) • A. R. Maddison, ed., *Lincolnshire pedigrees*, 1, Harleian Society, 50 (1902) • *CSP dom.*, 1627–8 • BL, MS Cotton Julius C.III, fol. 9 • E. Stokes, ed., *Index of wills proved in the prerogative court of Canterbury*, 5: 1605–1619, British RS, 43 (1912) • Venn, *Alum. Cant.*

Wealth at death £600–£700—money and chattels: will, PRO, PROB 11/129, fols. 213–213v

Ayscu, Sir Edward (1596–1654?). *See under* Ayscu, Edward (1550–1616/17).

Ayscue, Sir George (*c.*1615–1672), naval officer, was the eldest son of William Ayscue (*d. c.*1632), originally of Lincoln, gentleman of the privy chamber to Charles I. The identity of his mother is uncertain. Ayscue was also a godson of George Abbot, archbishop of Canterbury, who bequeathed to him £10 and 'one of the summer nags I have running amongst my horses' (PRO, PROB 11/164, fol. 211). He leased Hamm Court, Weybridge, in 1634, and was knighted on 9 August 1641, perhaps one of the last to be elevated under the distraint of knighthood policy. He married, at some time between 1645 and 1651, Mary, daughter of Martin *Fotherby, bishop of Salisbury, and widow of John Boys (*d.* 1641).

There is no record of Ayscue serving in the navy before 1646 when he commanded the *Expedition* at the siege of Pendennis Castle, and he subsequently served as governor of the Isles of Scilly until January 1647. He was captain of the *Antelope* in 1647 and of the *Lion* in 1648. He was one of the leading opponents of the naval revolt in the latter year, when a substantial part of the fleet mutinied against Vice-Admiral Rainborough and joined the royalists, and served as rear-admiral of the force which went to Helvoetsluys to try to force the defectors to surrender. He was appointed admiral of the Irish seas in 1649, perhaps because of the influence of his kinsman by marriage, the leading politician Sir Henry Vane. He was thanked by parliament on 23 July 1649 for his part in keeping open the sea route to Dublin, then under siege by the marquess of Ormond. In 1650 he was appointed governor of Barbados and commander of the squadron intended to recapture that island, but before he could set out he was diverted to serve as Blake's second-in-command in the attack on the royalist garrison in Scilly (April to May 1651). Ayscue finally sailed for Barbados on 5 August 1651. Despite stiff resistance from the royalist governor, Lord Willoughby of Parham, which ruled out a direct assault, Ayscue eventually obtained the island's surrender on 11 January 1652.

Ayscue's fleet returned to Plymouth on 25 May 1652 to find the First Anglo-Dutch War had begun. On 12 June he engaged an outward-bound Dutch fleet off the Lizard, but this got away with only five losses. Early in July, acting on intelligence that a Dutch convoy of about forty ships was attempting to sail home up the channel, Ayscue intercepted them near Calais with nine ships, including his

Sir George Ayscue (*c.*1615–1672), by Sir Peter Lely, *c.*1665–6

flagship the *Rainbow*, and drove most of them ashore. However, on 8 July he learned that Tromp's Dutch fleet was approaching the Downs, and resolved to fight despite having only twenty ships against Tromp's sixty. Shore batteries were prepared at Deal and fireships fitted out at Dover to support Ayscue's precarious position. The Dutch moved towards him on 11 July but were hampered by light winds; when the wind freshened from the south-west, the Dutch moved away to pursue Blake's main fleet, which had gone north. As commander of the channel squadron with his flag now in the *George*, Ayscue escorted the homecoming East India ships into Plymouth at the end of July, where he learned that another Dutch fleet under De Ruyter was approaching. Ayscue caught up with him between Plymouth and Guernsey on 16 August. Each side overestimated the strength of the other, and the fighting was confused; Ayscue seems to have attacked the Dutch centre but was not supported by all the armed merchantmen in his fleet, and his remaining ships were badly damaged in close-quarter fighting. Despite losing no ships outright, the English withdrew to Plymouth hotly pursued by De Ruyter, who intended to attack them in their anchorage, but a change of wind forced him to withdraw. Nevertheless, he got his convoy through and kept the seas.

Shortly afterwards Ayscue retired from his command, receiving a pension of £800 p.a. from parliament (£300 of it in the form of lands in Ireland). Although there had been criticism of his conduct of the action, it was also true that he had been unwell in the summer, possibly of a fever contracted in the West Indies, and he was deeply concerned about his private affairs, especially the damage to his Hamm Court estate caused by projectors attempting to make the River Wey navigable. It is also possible that he was ideologically opposed to the war; the republican preacher Hugh Peters wrote to him at this time, decrying a war between two such kindred nations. Despite regular rumours that he would be re-employed, Ayscue lived in retirement at Hamm Court, entertaining the Swedish ambassador there in August 1656; the house was said to be:

> environed with ponds, moats and water, like a ship at sea: a fancy the fitter for the master's humour, who is himself so great a seaman. There, he said, he had cast anchor and intended to spend the rest of his life in a private retirement. (*Diary of Bulstrode Whitelocke*, 13 Aug 1656)

The Swedish connection led to Ayscue offering his services to Carl X in 1658, and on 26 August he was granted a commission as admiral, with a salary of 4000 riksdalers a year. Flying his flag in the *Victoria*, he sailed from Landstrom on 30 June 1659 to meet Edward Montagu's English fleet, which had been sent to support the Swedes, and the two admirals dined together on 8 July. It seems likely that by this time Ayscue had become a covert royalist—he was married to a member of one of the leading royalist families in Kent—but he seems to have taken no active part in the royalist attempts to win over Montagu and his fleet. Ayscue subsequently returned to Landstrom, staying there until 6 November, when he sailed to intercept a Dutch convoy; however, the target was too well protected. He returned to England in the summer of 1660, shortly before the expiry of his Swedish commission on 8 September. Over the next few years he renewed his contacts in the English navy, attending Trinity House dinners and visiting Chatham with Sir William Penn. He became captain of the *Henry* in October 1664, serving as vice-admiral to Montagu, now earl of Sandwich, throughout 1665, including at the battle of Lowestoft. Sandwich was implicated in the plundering of Dutch East Indiamen in September 1665, but Ayscue refused to have anything to do with it and openly attacked his conduct. Originally appointed admiral of the blue for the 1666 campaign, he became admiral of the white, flying his flag in the 92-gun *Prince*, when Prince Rupert's squadron was detached from the main fleet at the end of May. On the third day of the Four Days' Battle (3 June 1666) the *Prince* ran aground on the Galloper Sand. Cut off from any support from her own side and with Dutch fireships approaching, members of her crew panicked and struck her flag. Ayscue was paraded through The Hague—although stories of his being painted and having a tail pinned on him were propaganda—and interrogated by the Dutch (who were unable to comprehend his Lincolnshire accent) before being imprisoned in Loevestein Castle. He remained a prisoner until October 1667, well after the peace had been signed, and was received graciously by Charles II on 12 November, the blame for the *Prince's* loss being assigned to the crew rather than their commander. Ayscue commanded the *Triumph* briefly in May and June 1668, and in 1669 visited his Irish estates, which had been the source of protracted legal disputes with the bishop of Ossory in the preceding years. When the Third Anglo-Dutch War began, it was intended that Ayscue would be vice-admiral of the red, flying his flag in the *Saint Andrew* (to which he was appointed in January 1672). However, he died at his house in Westminster on 5 April 1672, and was buried at St Margaret's, Westminster, eight days later. He left his estate to his stepdaughter, Margaret Boys, his wife, Mary, and at least one son, George, having predeceased him.

Opinions of Ayscue varied. Clarendon called him 'a gentleman, but had kept ill company too long, which had blunted his understanding, if it had ever been sharp: he was of few words, yet spake to the purpose and to be easily understood' (*Life of … Clarendon*, 2.355). Pepys believed he did not have 'much of a seaman in him … by his discourse I find that he hath not minded anything in [his ship] at all' (Pepys, 5.317), but then Ayscue had just criticized the lack of organization of the Navy Board which Pepys served. On the other hand, Sir William Coventry found him 'a very honest, gallant man … he does not serve mercenarily, for he lives handsomely and honourably in the fleet, beyond his pay' (Coventry to Arlington, 22 April 1665, *CSP dom.*, 1664–5, 324). J. D. Davies

Sources P. Le Fevre, 'Sir George Ayscue, Commonwealth and Restoration admiral', *Mariner's Mirror*, 68 (1982), 189–201 · S. R. Gardiner and C. T. Atkinson, eds., *Letters and papers relating to the First Dutch War, 1652–1654*, 6 vols., Navy RS, 13, 17, 30, 37, 41, 66 (1898–1930) · B. Capp, *Cromwell's navy: the fleet and the English revolution, 1648–1660* (1989) · J. D. Davies, *Gentlemen and tarpaulins: the officers and men of the Restoration navy* (1991) · PRO, PROB 11/338, fol. 326 [will of George Ayscue] · J. R. Powell, 'Sir George Ayscue's capture of Barbados in 1651', *Mariner's Mirror*, 59 (1973), 281–90 · *The diary of Bulstrode Whitelocke, 1605–1675*, ed. R. Spalding, British Academy, Records of Social and Economic History, new ser., 13 (1990) · *The life of Edward, earl of Clarendon … written by himself*, new edn, 3 vols. (1827) · Pepys, *Diary* · F. L. Fox, *A distant storm: the Four Days battle of 1666* (1996) · PRO, PROB 11/164, fol. 211 [will of Archbishop George Abbot] · PRO, PROB 11/161, fols. 55–6 [will of William Ayscue] · A. R. Maddison, ed., *Lincolnshire pedigrees*, 1, Harleian Society, 50 (1902), 62

Archives Bodl. Oxf., corresp. with Pembroke, Willoughby, etc. · PRO, State Papers

Likenesses P. Lely, oils, *c.*1665–1666, NMM [*see illus.*]

Wealth at death see will, PRO, PROB 11/338, fol. 326

Ayton, John. *See* Aton, John (*d.* 1349).

Ayton, Richard (*bap.* **1786**, *d.* **1823**), playwright and writer, was baptized at St Stephen, Coleman Street, London, on 8 February 1786, the son of William Ayton (*d.* 1799) and his wife, Mary. His father, a son of William Ayton, banker in Lombard Street, moved some time afterwards to Macclesfield, Cheshire, and at the grammar school of that town young Ayton obtained a good elementary knowledge of Latin and Greek. In accordance with the wish of his father, that Ayton should be educated for the bar, he was sent to study law at Manchester and at the end of a year he became the pupil of a barrister in London; but, disliking the profession from the start, he never set himself seriously to prepare for it.

As soon as Ayton came of age, he retired to the coast of Sussex, resolved to limit his expenses to his comparatively small income, and there he amused himself with desultory reading and active outdoor exercise, boating being his special delight. In 1811 he returned to London and accepted a situation in a public office, but he relinquished it in 1813 to accompany William Daniell ARA in a voyage around Great Britain. An account of the voyage, with views drawn and engraved by Daniell, appeared in eight volumes between 1814 and 1825, but the letterpress of only the first two volumes is by Ayton. Disagreeing with Daniell about his plans for the future volumes, Ayton declined to proceed further with the account and began to write plays. Two of his farces, acted at Covent Garden, were total failures, but he adapted from the French several pieces for the English Opera House with some success.

During a voyage between Scarborough and London, Ayton was nearly shipwrecked and he received an injury to his ankle that confined him to bed for more than a year. In the spring of 1821 he was sufficiently recovered to go to the coast of Sussex, but his health continued to be uncertain and precarious. In July 1823 his illness assumed so serious a form that he went for medical advice to London, where he died shortly afterwards. During the last eighteen months of his life Ayton occupied himself in the composition of a number of essays, chiefly on pastimes and similar subjects, written in a genial and playful spirit and displaying considerable sprightliness and humour. These, with a short memoir prefixed, were published in 1825.

T. F. HENDERSON, *rev.* M. CLARE LOUGHLIN-CHOW

Sources 'Memoir', R. Ayton, *Essays and sketches of character* (1825) • Adams, *Drama* • *IGI*

Likenesses F. C. Lewis, stipple, 1825 (after R. Westall), BM, NPG; repro. in Ayton, *Essays*

Ayton, Sir Robert (1570–1638), poet and courtier, was born at the castle of Kinaldie, near St Andrews, Fife, the second of four sons, to Andrew Ayton (*d.* 1589), landowner, and his wife, Mariona London or Lundie, daughter of the laird of Balgonie. Through his father's mother, Marjorie Stewart, he could claim descent on the wrong side of the blanket from James II. A branch of the family of Ayton, originally established at Ayton ('the town on the river') in the Merse, Berwickshire, had been settled in Fife since the fifteenth century, when Andrew Ayton, '2d sone to the Laird of Aytone in the Merss', settled in Fife as sheriff-depute (17 October 1496), and was granted letters of take, or lease, to the west half of the lands of the town of Dunmure. In 1501 he was appointed keeper of Stirling Castle and sheriff of Stirlingshire, and further grants of lands followed. This Andrew Ayton, Robert Ayton's great-grandfather, was clearly a man of wealth and power, and he and his wife, Isobel Kincragy, produced three sons to divide the lands he had accumulated, and seven daughters who all married into well-known and landed Fife families.

Like his father, Ayton matriculated at St Leonard's College, St Andrews University, together with his elder brother, John, on 1 March 1584. He is listed in December that year as one of those who had subscribed the articles of religion, and he graduated BA in 1588 and MA probably in 1589, the year of his father's death. Ayton inherited £1000, but little is known of his life between leaving St Andrews and his appearance in London in 1603 after spending some years studying in Paris. Thomas Dempster,

Sir Robert Ayton (1570–1638), by Francesco Fanelli

historiographer royal to James VI and I (*Historia ecclesiastica gentis Scotorum*, 1627), records that 'diu in Galliis bonas artes excoluit', but what form of fine arts he studied is not known, and Dempster is an unreliable historian (though more reliable on his contemporaries). He also records that Ayton wrote poems in Latin, Greek, French, and Scots; no Greek or French specimens have survived. It was probably during this period that he wrote his earliest-known English poems, including 'Diophantus and Charidora', notable for being much more Scottish in orthography and grammar than most of his work.

That Ayton was established in London and close to the court by the end of 1603 is indicated by his poem 'To Queen Anne on a New Year's Day 1604'. Before leaving Paris he had written a long Latin panegyric to King James ('De foelici, et semper augusto, Jacobi VI, Scotiae insularumque adiacentium regis, imperio nunc recens florentissimis Angliae et Hiberniae sceptris amplificato',

1603) for presentation on his return, and the frequent poems addressed to the king thereafter were no doubt designed to secure royal favour. In 1608 he was appointed a groom of the privy chamber, a highly desirable post at £20 p.a. with generous livery. There were also Christmas and new year gifts (£100 was divided among the grooms and pages of the privy chamber at Christmas, and grooms got 40s. each at new year), immunity from prosecution, and other rich pickings.

In 1609 Ayton was one of the envoys appointed to deliver James's *Premonition to All Most Mighty Monarchs, Kings, Free Princes and States of Christendom*, his answer to the pope's response to his *Apologie for the Oath of Allegiance* (1607). Ayton's journey took him to Heidelberg, Wurtemberg, Hesse, Brunswick, Saxony, and Brandenburg, and his good offices were rewarded in 1611 with a life pension of £140 p.a. and a knighthood conferred at Rycot on 30 August 1612. Some time between this date and Prince Henry's funeral on 8 November 1612 he succeeded Sir William Fowler as secretary to Queen Anne, a post of power and privilege which ranked him fourth in order of precedence in the queen's household, which at this time also included Samuel Daniel and John Florio. On 26 February 1615 Ayton obtained a grant of denization (PRO, patent rolls, C66/1909/28) which made him a naturalized English citizen.

Queen Anne's death in 1619 did little to depress Ayton's career. In 1619 he secured the reversion of the mastership of the royal hospital and collegiate church of St Katharine by the Tower, though he was not to enjoy this until the death of the incumbent, Sir Julius Caesar, in 1636; also in 1619 he was granted a pension of £500, presumably in recognition of his services to the queen. In 1623, on the death of Thomas Murray of Tullibardine, provost of Eton, Ayton applied to succeed him, though, by his own account, his application was motivated by a desire to provide for Murray's widow and children as much as by personal ambition. There was keen competition for the post, which eventually went to Sir Henry Wotton. On the succession of Charles I in 1625 Ayton resumed his old post of secretary to the queen, which he retained until his death on 25 February 1638. He was buried three days later in the south aisle of the choir in Westminster Abbey.

Only Ayton's Latin poems were published in his lifetime, in Arthur Johnston's *Delitiae poetarum Scotorum* (1637). His English poems were collected by his nephew and executor, Sir John Ayton, second son of his elder brother, who helped himself to one or two for his own purposes in the process. In the introduction to this manuscript collection he explained that

> The author of these ensueing Poems did not affect the name of a Poet having neither publish't in print nor kept coppyes of anything he writ, either in lattin or English and which makes this small collection the more difficult and in many things imperfyte and uncorrect especially in the old Scotts peeces which were don in his younger days. (BL, Add. MS 10308)

The early poems are indeed the least rewarding of his output. Heavily influenced by the poets of the French *Pléiade*, whom he had encountered in Paris, and too often written in the uninspiring poulter's measure associated with 'diers' or laments, these pastoral love complaints make tedious reading today, as do his poems of compliment to James and his queen.

It was not until Ayton was settled in London that he found a lighter, more epigrammatic vein, and a gift for songwriting second to few among his contemporaries. Settings (mostly anonymous) of many of his poems have survived, and it is fairly clear that pieces such as 'Wrong not, sweete empress of my heart' (less plausibly attributed to Ralegh), 'Thou sent to mee a heart was crown'd', and 'There is none, noe none but I' were written to be sung. Elsewhere, in contrast to his earlier, passionate laments, he affected a light sententiousness and an amiably cynical approach to love, as befitted a middle-aged, cavalier poet in comfortable circumstances who never married:

> Yet have I been a lover by report,
> Yea, I have dyed for love as others doe,
> But, prais'd be God, it was in such a sort
> That I revived within an houre or two.
> ('On Love')

His authorship of 'I do confess thou'rt smooth and fair' has been challenged on behalf of a number of other poets, including Ralegh. The correct attribution of this and other poems is unlikely ever to be firmly established, but the style, the musicality, and the content are certainly close to Ayton's known work, and the possibility that it is indeed his cannot be lightly dismissed. Watson's failure to credit it explicitly to him in his *Choice Collection* means little, given the slapdash way in which the collection was compiled, and no other serious evidence has been adduced. His authorship of the very similar 'I lov'd the once, I'le love noe more' is unchallenged, and compares well with it.

HARRIET HARVEY WOOD

Sources *The English and Latin poems of Sir Robert Ayton*, ed. C. B. Gullans, STS, 4th ser., 1 (1963) · BL, Add. MSS 10308, 28622 · NL Scot., MS 19.3.6 · U. Edin. L., MS Laing III.436 · acta rectorum, vols. 2–3, and bursar's book, U. St Andr. L. · patent rolls, PRO, C 66 · *The poems of Sir Robert Aytoun*, ed. C. Rogers (1871) · *Thomae Dempsteri Historia ecclesiastica gentis Scotorum, sive, De scriptoribus Scotis*, ed. D. Irving, rev. edn, 2 vols., Bannatyne Club, 21 (1829) · A. Johnston, *Delitiae poetarum Scotorum* (1637) · H. M. Shire, *Song, dance and poetry at the court of Scotland under King James VI*, ed. K. Elliott (1969) · *James Watson's Choice collection of comic and serious Scots poems*, ed. H. H. Wood, 2 vols., STS, 4th ser., 10, 20 (1977–91) [incl. index; repr. of 1869 edn] · M. P. McDiarmid, 'Some versions of poems by Sir Robert Aytoun and Sir William Alexander', *N&Q*, 202 (1957), 32–5 · BL, Cotton MS Claudius C.iii · *DNB* · PRO, SP 16/457/10

Archives NL Scot., MS 19.3.6 | BL, Add. MSS 10308, 28622 · U. Edin. L., MS Laing III.436

Likenesses F. Fanelli, copper funerary bust, Westminster Abbey [*see illus.*]

Wealth at death see will, PRO, PROB 11/176, sig. 27

Ayton, William Alexander (1816–1909), Church of England clergyman and alchemist, was born on 28 April 1816 in the Bloomsbury district of London, the son of William Capon Ayton. He was educated at the Charterhouse School, London, and Trinity Hall, Cambridge, graduating BA in 1841. In the same year he took holy orders and he was ordained priest the following year. From 1850 to 1873 he held a series of rural livings in the midlands, and was then appointed vicar of Chacombe, Northamptonshire, where he remained until his retirement in 1894.

Ayton took up occult pursuits while at Cambridge but did not develop them extensively until the 1880s, when an unhappy involvement with the spurious Hermetic Brotherhood of Luxor in 1884 was followed by a significant role in the affairs of the Hermetic Order of the Golden Dawn, which he and his wife, Anne (*d.* 1898), joined in July 1888; he took as his motto within the order 'Virtute orta occidunt rarius' ('those that rise by virtue rarely fall'), and his wife's was 'Quam potera adjutato' ('I will help as much as I can'). In 1890 he conducted the marriage of Samuel Liddell Mathers (1854–1918), a founder of the order, and Mina Bergson at Chacombe, and following the collapse of the order in 1901 he acted as co-chief of its rump with A. E. Waite until his death.

Alchemy, however, was Ayton's great passion, his experiments being conducted largely in an alchemical laboratory that he had built in his cellar at Chacombe, 'where the Bishop cannot see it' (Yeats, 184). His letters reveal a profound knowledge of alchemical texts but he was very much a practising alchemist and claimed to have perfected the elixir of life, albeit fruitlessly: he told W. B. Yeats that he had 'put it away on a shelf … but when I got it down the other day it had all dried up' (ibid.). Ayton's final years, until his death at home at the age of ninety-two, on 1 January 1909, were spent at Grove Lodge, Saffron Walden, where he continued to warn of the dangers inherent in occultism while still encouraging others, such as Julius Kohn, the translator of many classical alchemical texts, in their own occult researches. R. A. GILBERT

Sources E. Howe, ed., *The alchemist of the Golden Dawn: the letters of the Revd W. A. Ayton to F. L. Gardner and others, 1886–1905* (1985) • R. A. Gilbert, *Revelations of the Golden Dawn* (1997) • W. B. Yeats, *Autobiographies* (1955) • J. Godwin, C. Chanel, and J. P. Deveney, *The Hermetic Brotherhood of Luxor* (1995) • Crockford (1908)

Archives NRA, priv. coll., Golden Dawn archives, incl. letters to G. D. Manual • Societas Rosicruciana in Anglia, London, high council library, Westcott MSS, incl. letters to G. D. Manual • Warburg Institute, London, Yorke collection, letters to F. L. Gardner

Aytoun, William Edmonstoune (1813–1865), poet, was born on 21 June 1813 in Edinburgh, the only son and youngest of the three children of Roger Aytoun (*d.* 1843), writer to the signet, and of Joan Keir (*d.* 1861). Through both father and mother he belonged to old Scottish families, his progenitors on the father's side being the Aytouns of Inchdairnie in Fife, and the Edmonstounes, formerly of Edmonstoune and Ednam, and afterwards of Corehouse in Lanarkshire, and on the mother's side the Keirs of Kinmouth and West Rhynd in Perthshire. He was also a descendant of the poet Sir Robert Ayton, member of the court of James VI, who had been friendly with Ben Jonson and Thomas Hobbes, and was the reputed author of the lines upon which Burns based 'Auld Lang Syne'. Both of Aytoun's parents were leading figures in Edinburgh society: his father was one of the founders of the Edinburgh Academy, where Aytoun studied between 1824 and 1828, and his mother was a good friend of Sir Walter Scott.

William Edmonstoune Aytoun (1813–1865), by David Octavius Hill and Robert Adamson

Owing to his mother's encouragement, Aytoun early on in life acquired an interest in writing ballad poetry, an interest which was to flourish in later years in his work for *Blackwood's Magazine*.

Aytoun studied law at Edinburgh University between 1828 and 1833, dabbling in verse poetry at the same time; his first publication was a small volume of poetry in 1832 entitled *Poland, Homer, and other Poems*, in which the qualities of his later style were already apparent. He thought of going to the English bar, but after a winter in London attending the courts of law he abandoned this intention. On graduating in 1833, Aytoun spent a year travelling and studying German literature. He returned to Edinburgh, and became a writer to the signet in 1835, but dedicated much time to literary work. The discipline of his legal practice was of great use in giving him a power of mastering the details of political and other questions which was of distinct service to him at a later period. In 1840 he was called to the Scottish bar, which had more attraction for him than the irksome monotony of a solicitor's practice, and made a fair position for himself there during the years in which he remained in active practice.

In 1836 Aytoun became a contributor to *Blackwood's Magazine*, a connection that was to last until his death in 1865. During this almost thirty-year connection he wrote over 200 poems, reviews, satires and short stories. Between 1836 and 1844 he worked together with Theodore Martin in the production of what are known as the

'Bon Gaultier Ballads', a series of parodies of contemporary verse, which acquired such great popularity that thirteen editions were published between 1855 and 1877. They were also associated at this time in writing many prose magazine articles of a humorous character, as well as a series of translations of Goethe's ballads and minor poems, which, after appearing in *Blackwood's Magazine*, were some years afterwards collected and published in a volume entitled *Poems and Ballads of Goethe* (1858). It was during this period that Aytoun began to write the series of ballads known as the 'Lays of the Scottish Cavaliers', eventually published in 1849. These ballad romances, originally featured in *Blackwood's Magazine*, were modelled on the works of Sir Walter Scott and Thomas Babington Macaulay, and were concerned with Scottish historical subjects and heroes. They became important texts in the romantic revival in mid-Victorian Scotland.

In 1844 Aytoun became one of the staff of *Blackwood's Magazine*, to which he continued until his death to contribute political and other articles on a great variety of subjects, including humorous tales such as 'My First Spec in the Biggleswades', and 'How We Got Up the Glenmutchkin Railway, and How We Got Out of It'.

In 1845 Aytoun was appointed professor of rhetoric and *belles-lettres* in the University of Edinburgh. Here he was in his element, and he made his lectures so attractive that he raised the number of students from 30 in 1846 to more than 1850 in 1864. On 11 April 1849 Aytoun married Jane Emily (*d.* 1859), daughter of the writer John *Wilson (Christopher North) (1785–1854). His professorial duties did not interfere with his position at the bar, and in 1852 when the tory party of Lord Derby came into power he was appointed the sheriff of Orkney and Shetland. In the following year Oxford conferred on him the honorary degree of DCL.

The duties of Aytoun's sheriffship and his work as professor, both conscientiously discharged, still left him leisure for literary work. In 1854 he produced the dramatic poem 'Firmilian', perhaps the most brilliant of his works, an extremely cutting parody of the so-called Spasmodic school of poetry, exemplified by Alexander Smith, J. W. Marston, and Sydney Dobell. Aytoun had been opposed to the aesthetic creed and productions of this group, who modelled themselves on the Romantic poets, but whose works he viewed as derivative and markedly inferior, characterized by verbosity, obscurity, and self-absorption. His parody began in May 1854 with a review for *Blackwood's Magazine* of the unpublished poetry of a fictitious young Spasmodic, T. Percy Jones. It was so effective as to lead to calls for the publication of Jones's work, and Aytoun, relishing the thought of further extending the burlesque, came out with *Firmilian, or, The Student of Badajoz: a Spasmodic Tragedy* in July 1854. The print run of 1048 copies sold out, and although its comic intelligence was generally recognized, it was still accepted by some as serious poetry, giving force to the remarks of reviewers such as that of *The Times*, who regarded *Firmilian* as 'the most perfect, as it is the most elaborate and the most legitimate, parody that has ever been written' (Weinstein, 151). The poem was influential in ending the vogue for the productions of the Spasmodic school, against whom the critical tide of opinion quickly turned.

Aytoun also produced serious poetry. In 1856 he published 'Bothwell', a poetical monologue, dealing with the relations between the hero and Mary, queen of Scots. It contained many fine passages, and three editions of it were published. In 1858 he published a collection, in two volumes, of the *Ballads of Scotland* carefully collated and annotated, of which four editions were published. In 1861 his novel *Norman Sinclair* appeared; it had already been serialized in *Blackwood's Magazine*, and is interesting for its pictures of society in early nineteenth-century Scotland, and for many passages which are, in fact, autobiographical. About this time Aytoun's health began to fail, and his spirits had sustained a shock from which he never wholly recovered in the death (15 April 1859) of his wife, to whom he had been devotedly attached. He sought relief in hard work, but life had thenceforth lost much of its zest for him. Being childless, his loneliness became intolerable, and on 24 December 1863 he married Fearne Jemima (*d.* 1904), daughter of James Kinnear. But by this time his health had seriously declined, and on 4 August 1865 he died at Blackhills, near Elgin where he had been living; he was buried at Edinburgh. A memoir of his life was published by Theodore Martin in 1867.

THEODORE MARTIN, *rev.* DAVID FINKELSTEIN

Sources T. Martin, *Memoir of W. E. Aytoun* (1867) • E. Feykman, *W. E. Aytoun: pioneer professor of English at Edinburgh* (1963) • M. A. Weinstein, *William Edmonstoune Aytoun and the Spasmodic controversy* (1968) • *Register of the Society of Writers to Her Majesty's Signet* (1983)

Archives NL Scot., corresp. and papers | Herts. ALS, corresp. with Lord Lytton • NA Scot., letters to Lady Mary Christopher Nisbet Hamilton and Robert Christopher Nisbet Hamilton • NL Scot., corresp. with Blackwoods • NL Scot., letters to Sir Theodore Martin

Likenesses B. Crombie, coloured etching, 1848, NPG; repro. in B. Crombie, *Modern Athenians* (1882) • P. Park, plaster bust, *c.*1851, NPG • J. Archer, pencil and watercolour drawing, 1855, Scot. NPG • D. O. Hill and R. Adamson, photograph, Scot. NPG [*see illus.*] • J. Rhind, marble bust (after P. Park), Scot. NPG • T. Rodger, two cartes-de-visite, NPG • wood-engraving, NPG; repro. in *ILN* (19 Aug 1865)

Ayub Khan, Mohammad (1907–1974), president of Pakistan, was born on 14 May 1907 at Rehana, in the Hazara district of the North-West Frontier Province of undivided British India. He was the fifth child of Mir Dad Khan, a retired Indian army junior officer. The family were comfortably off, but not wealthy members of the Tarin. They were 'lowland' Pushtuns whose native tongue was Hindko. Ayub was thus culturally isolated during his youth from the Pushtun nationalism of Abdul Ghaffar Khan's Khudai Khidmatgar movement. Ayub's later contribution to Pakistani nation-building was to lie not by the way of Pushtun nationalism, but by co-opting the Pushtun to the project of a centralized state.

His pious father had earmarked Ayub for religious training rather than a military career. These hopes were ended when the adolescent Ayub slapped the village *maulvi* (priest) when he chastised him. Ayub seemed far more interested in horse-riding than in studying, but Mir Dad

Mohammad Ayub Khan (1907–1974), by unknown photographer

Khan insisted that he be sent to the prestigious Muhammadan Anglo-Oriental College at Aligarh in the United Provinces. Here Ayub met Muslims from across northern India and gradually improved his Urdu pronunciation. He also imbibed the college's modernist approach to Islam which was to be a hallmark of the social and religious policy of his later rule.

Ayub sailed for England in July 1926 to take up a scholarship at the Royal Military College, Sandhurst, from where he was commissioned in 1928. He saw active service in Burma during the Second World War as the second in command of the 1st Assam regiment. In August 1947 he was appointed as an advisory officer to the ill-fated Punjab boundary force commanded by Major-General Rees. This force lamentably failed to prevent the massacres which accompanied the partition of the Punjab following independence. Ayub was later to date his distrust of politicians and his insistence on a strong army from this experience. These sentiments were reinforced during his posting as general officer commanding in East Pakistan from January 1948 onwards. He experienced the Bengali language riots and the turbulent student movement in Dacca at first hand. On 17 January 1951, shortly after his return to West Pakistan, he became the first Pakistani commander-in-chief, replacing the remaining British general, Douglas Gracey. From October 1954 to August 1955 Ayub also served as minister of defence. This was a period during which power was increasingly slipping from the politicians to the ailing, but authoritarian governor-general, Ghulam Muhammad. Ayub shared with Ghulam Muhammad and, later, with his successor Iskander Mirza, a distrust of the apparently chaotic democratic process. Ayub's main concern was to strengthen the Pakistan army, and to this end he was instrumental in forging closer security ties with the United States. The fear that these ties might be endangered if Bengali politicians from the more populous eastern wing of the country held power in the wake of Pakistan's first projected national elections precipitated the military coup of 8 October 1958. Some five months earlier Mirza and Ayub had separately conveyed their opinion to the US ambassador that 'only a dictatorship would work in Pakistan'. Following the coup President Mirza named Ayub as chief martial law administrator. But the Mirza–Ayub duumvirate lasted only until 27 October, when Mirza was deposed and shunted off to exile in London. Ayub Khan then became president of Pakistan, a post which he was to hold for over a decade.

Ayub sought to ensure political stability through a system of 'guided democracy'. This was to provide the platform for the modernization of the country. Its key components were land reform, and social reforms such as the Muslim family laws ordinance of 15 July 1961. Ayub also believed that rapid economic growth led by the private sector would assist the modernization process. Political parties were banned until July 1962, and the freedom of many individual politicians to take part in public life was restricted under the accountability process instituted by Ayub. These measures had an especially alienating impact in East Pakistan, where the Bengali élite had always looked to democratic politics rather than to influence in the bureaucracy and army to make its voice heard. The basic democracy scheme was introduced in 1959. This consisted of a five-tier structure of representation. Direct elections were held only at the lowest tier of union councils, and even here up to a third of the voting members could be nominated. The 1962 constitution created a powerful president who was to be elected by the 80,000 'basic democrats'. Although Ayub claimed that the system was to provide a training in citizenship, it was primarily intended to create a loyal support base for his regime. However, when Ayub's fortunes began to decline the basic democracy scheme proved a useless prop.

Ayub's social and economic reforms had a more lasting impact. The 1959 land reforms, with their high ceilings and generous compensation, were far from radical, but they did encourage the shift in parts of the Punjab from feudalism to capitalist farming, and the Muslim family laws ordinance formed the high-water mark of Islamic modernist influence with its establishment of arbitration in divorce cases and its discouragement of the contraction of polygamous marriages. The *ʿulamaʾ* (religious scholars), however, branded these reforms un-Islamic and were henceforth implacably opposed to Ayub's government.

Ayub Khan attached so much importance to economic advancement that he assumed the chairmanship of the planning commission in 1961. Compared with other developing countries, however, the key role in economic growth was given to the private sector. This reflected the preferences of the United States, which was Pakistan's major aid-giver. Rapid growth was achieved, including a rise in per capita income of 14 per cent during the period of the second five year plan (1960–65). But this growth-orientated strategy of directing resources to an entrepreneurial élite generated increasing social and regional tensions.

With the restoration of the political parties following the lifting of martial law and the introduction of a new constitution in 1962, discontent was increasingly channelled into opposition to the regime. Ayub was uncomfortable with his new political role (from December 1963) as head of the 'court party' Convention Muslim League. Although he won the tightly controlled 1965 presidential election contest against Fatima Jinnah, the sister of Pakistan's founder, the campaign revealed growing discontent. This was increasingly orchestrated by his former protégé and foreign minister, Zulfikar Ali Bhutto. Bhutto had split with Ayub after his alleged betrayal of Pakistan's interests in the 1966 Tashkent treaty. This had been brokered by the Soviet leader Kosygin in the wake of the 1965 Indo-Pakistan War, which had been caused in part by the infiltration of insurgents into the Indian state of Jammu and Kashmir. Ayub's acceptance of a ceasefire on 22 September 1965 had shocked a populace fed on a diet of victory reports by the state-controlled media.

Popular disturbances from November 1968, sparked by clashes between students and the police, lost Ayub the support of his former army colleagues. By March 1969 he was forced to step down in favour of General Agha Muhammad Yahya Khan. Ailing with heart problems, Ayub lived in quiet retirement in Islamabad, and died there on 20 April 1974. His son, Gohar Ayub, after an army career, rose to prominence in contemporary Pakistan politics.

Ayub Khan is remembered as a hard-headed administrator whose modernizing impulses foundered because his regime never acquired political legitimacy. Despite his best intentions, the 'golden decade' of development exacerbated class inequalities and Bengali grievances.

IAN TALBOT

Sources L. Ziring, *The Ayub era: politics in Pakistan, 1958–1969* (1971) • M. A. Khan, *Friends not masters: a political autobiography* (1967) • A. Gauhar, *Ayub Khan: Pakistan's first military ruler* (1996) • A. Gauhar, 'Pakistan: Ayub Khan's abdication', *Third World Quarterly*, 7/1 (1985), 102–31 • M. A. Khan, *Speeches and statements* (1961) • M. Musa, *My version: India-Pakistan war, 1965* (1983) • H. A. Rizvi, *The military and politics in Pakistan, 1947–86* (1988) • A. T. Rahman, *Basic democracies at the grass roots* (1962) • I. Talbot, *Pakistan: a modern history* (1999) • Lord Saint Brides [M. James], *Pakistan chronicle* (1993)

Archives George Washington University, Washington, DC, national security archives; Lyndon B. Johnson presidential files; country files, Pakistan • National Archives and Records Administration, College Park, Maryland, state department central files | FILM BFI NFTVA, current affairs footage • BFI NFTVA, news footage | SOUND BL NSA, news recording

Likenesses photograph, Pakistan High Commission, London [*see illus.*] • photographs, repro. in Gauhar, *Ayub Khan*

Azad, Abul Kalam (1888–1958), politician and author, was born on 11 November 1888 in Mecca, Arabia. His father, Sheikh Khairuddin Dehlavi (1831–1908), was an Islamic scholar and Sufi who had migrated to Mecca about the time of the 1857 revolt and there had married an Arab woman, the niece of the mufti of Medina. Azad, the youngest child, had one brother and three sisters. His name at birth was Muhiyuddin Ahmad, but he adopted Abul Kalam Azad ('free') as his pen-name in his teens, and that is the name by which he is known. The circumstances of his ancestry and birth meant that Azad was fluent in both Arabic and Urdu, which influenced his later thought and writing style.

In 1898 Khairuddin returned to India with his family and settled in Calcutta at the request of his many Sufi disciples in that city. Azad's mother died a year later, with the result that his father became the dominant figure in his upbringing. Azad was educated at home by his father in the traditional Indo-Islamic curriculum, which included Arabic, Persian, and Urdu languages, a thorough study of the Koran, the traditions of the prophet Muhammad (*hadith*), Islamic philosophy and theology, as well as mathematics. Contrary to some sources, he never studied at Cairo's al-Azhar, though he augmented his home-based religious education with insatiable reading, and his scholarly temperament and reputation for learning earned him the honorific *maulana*, indicating one who is trained in the Islamic religious sciences. He completed his education in his teens, and was married young. He and his elder brother, Abun Nasir, were married to sisters, the daughters of one of Khairuddin's disciples. Azad and his wife, Zulaikha (*d.* 1943), had one son, who died young.

Azad's intellectual precocity led him to revolt against his father's influence and against what he considered the rigidity of his education. His reading introduced him to the writings of Sir Saiyid Ahmad Khan, especially his commentary on the Koran, which opened up the world of Islamic modernism and the possibility of a reinterpretation of the scriptures. Given Azad's fluency in Arabic, he was able to read the works of Sheikh Muhammad Abduh and other Arab intellectuals, including Rashid Rida and the al-Manar group of Cairo, and thus learned of new religious and political ideas, including nationalism, in the Arab world. Further, Calcutta in the early twentieth century was a hotbed of Indian nationalist activity, with which he sympathized. His nationalism, consequently, derived from sources both Indian and Islamic; he saw no reason why the two should conflict.

Azad began to write for Urdu newspapers as a young man. In 1904 he started a journal, *Lisan us-Sidq*, in Calcutta. During the next few years he served as editor of *an-Nadwa* of Lucknow in 1905–6, and of *Vakil* of Amritsar. In Lucknow he worked with Maulana Shibli, another consummate Urdu stylist in both prose and poetry, who encouraged him to be true to his religious training through the medium of his writing. In Amritsar he reported on current affairs, with a concentration on events in the Muslim world. He also made at least one trip to the Middle East, in connection with the hadj. He then returned to Calcutta, where he was at the time of his father's death in 1908. He refused to succeed Khairuddin as a religious guide, but instead chose to guide the reading public religiously and politically through his journalism.

In July 1912 Azad began his most famous journalistic venture, the weekly *al-Hilal*. For the next four years, through *al-Hilal* and its successor, *al-Balagh*, Azad became known as an eloquent proponent of religious reform based almost exclusively on the Koran, and as an advocate of Muslim political activism. His elegant prose had some of the emotional content of verse, and his Urdu, replete with Persian and Arabic words, added to his learned reputation. He broke with the loyalist politics of the Muslim League and supported Indian nationalism, and he sympathized with Turkey during the Balkan wars of 1912–13. In the First World War, when Turkey and Britain were enemies, his pro-Turkish stance led to a forfeiture of *al-Hilal*'s security deposit. He then began *al-Balagh*, but that too was closed in 1916. He was interned by the British in Ranchi, Bihar, from 1916 until after the war, released only in January 1920. During his internment he wrote a lyrical autobiography, *Tazkirah*, and began a translation and commentary on the Koran, *Tarjuman al-Quran*.

Following his release Azad joined forces with Mahatma Gandhi and the Ali brothers in the combined Khilafat and non-co-operation movement against the British. This movement brought about a co-operation between Hindus and Muslims in Indian nationalist politics as never before, and featured the Gandhian technique of non-violent protest against British dominance. Muslim religious and political leaders, including Azad, were concerned about the punitive European treaty of peace with the Ottoman caliphate (*khilafat*) following the First World War, but they also saw the *khilafat* as an issue that could unite all Indian Muslims against the British. Gandhi saw the issue as a means of gaining a Muslim following for the Indian National Congress in its bid to represent all Indians in the movement for independence. Between 1920 and 1922 Azad became an accomplished orator and political figure. He was imprisoned in 1922, as were Gandhi and the movement's other leaders. Released in 1923, Azad was elected president of the special session of the National Congress held in Delhi to decide the future course of nationalist action. He called for Hindu–Muslim co-operation, but divisions over tactics persisted in the Congress through the 1920s. Gandhi again launched a nationwide civil disobedience movement in 1930, against the salt tax. Azad took part and was again imprisoned, but during the late 1920s and early 1930s he concentrated on his commentary on the Koran.

Azad became prominent in nationalist politics again after the 1937 legislative elections, the first held under the 1935 Government of India Act, which established provincial autonomy and expanded the legislatures. He was chosen as a member of the National Congress's parliamentary board to supervise its provincial ministries. In 1940 he was elected president of the Congress and held that office until 1946, an unusually long tenure resulting from the disruptions of wartime and the fact that the Congress leaders spent most of the war imprisoned. While a prisoner in Ahmadnagar Fort, he wrote *Ghubar-i-khatir*, an epistolary memoir that reveals more of his spiritual and intellectual odyssey than any of his other works.

As president of the Congress Azad played a pivotal role in the negotiations leading to India's independence, particularly during the Simla conference in 1945 and the cabinet mission of 1946. He remained adamantly opposed to partition, feeling that a division of India would do more harm to Indian Muslims than good. His disagreement with the politics of the Muslim League and with its leader, Muhammad Ali Jinnah, was fundamental. During the formation of the provisional government in 1946 Jinnah demanded for the League the right to name all Muslim members, while the Congress, with Azad in mind, maintained its right to name a Muslim. Azad, sensing that he was an obstacle to agreement, relinquished his presidency of the Congress to Nehru in July 1946 and stayed out of the provisional government when it was formed in September. He joined the government as education minister in January 1947 and remained in that office until his death.

Azad was a broken man after the 1947 partition, having lost the struggle to preserve India's unity. In the final decade of his life he presided over India's education policy, made many speeches on official occasions, and dictated a memoir of his political life, *India Wins Freedom* (1959; a complete version of the text was first published in 1988). In declining health as a result of a neglect of exercise and heavy smoking and drinking habits, he fell and broke his hip; he then suffered a stroke and died on 22 February 1958 in Delhi and was buried there in a tomb in front of Jama Masjid. He will be remembered for his intellectual integrity, his eloquent contributions to Urdu literature, and his courageous insistence that Muslim culture was an integral part of India's cultural life. GAIL MINAULT

Sources I. H. Douglas, *Abul Kalam Azad: an intellectual and religious biography*, ed. G. Minault and C. W. Troll (1988) • A. K. Azad, *India wins freedom*, complete edn (1988) • M. Hasan, ed., *Islam and Indian nationalism: reflections on Abul Kalam Azad* (1992) • G. Minault, *The Khilafat movement: religious symbolism and political motivation in India* (1982) • A. K. Azad, *Tazkirah*, rev. edn (1968) • A. R. Malehabadi, *Azad ki kahani khud Azad ki zabani* (1965) • N. Mansergh and others, eds., *The transfer of power, 1942–7*, 5–9 (1974–80)

Archives Indian Council for Cultural Relations, New Delhi • Nehru Memorial Library, New Delhi, newspapers | BL OIOC, transfer of power documents | FILM BFI NFTVA, news footage • Nehru Memorial Library, New Delhi

Likenesses S. Gujral, portrait, Delhi corporation • K. K. Hebbar, portrait, Indian Council for Cultural Relations, New Delhi • K. K. Hebbar, portrait, Indian parliament, Central Hall

Azariah, Vedanayagam Samuel (1874–1945), bishop of Dornakal, was born on 17 August 1874 in the church rectory of Vellalanvilai, a village located in the Madras presidency of south India. He was the younger of the two children of the Revd Thomas Vedanayagam (1821–1889), Anglican priest, and his second wife, Ellen. He became the first Indian bishop of an Anglican diocese and leader of agrarian depressed class and non-Brahman conversion movements to Christianity.

Azariah received his early education in schools established by the Church Missionary Society in Megnanapuram and Tinnevelly. From 1893 to 1896 he studied mathematics at Madras Christian College, where he was drawn into Christian missionary work through the inspiration of the Young Men's Christian Association (YMCA). He led spiritual meetings and evangelistic outreach for the YMCA in Madras during his college years and, in 1896, took a full-time position as a YMCA secretary, first in the Madura and then in the Tinnevelly districts. Azariah worked for the YMCA until 1909, attempting to revive

Vedanayagam Samuel Azariah (1874–1945), by Wiele & Klein

Christian life in rural south India by establishing a grass-roots network of YMCA branches in the towns and villages of his large districts.

Azariah's primary goal during his early career was to recruit Indian missionaries who would devote their lives to carrying the gospel to the unevangelized regions of India and beyond. He gradually extended his universe of activity and influence from his native Tinnevelly (where he established the first major indigenous Indian missionary society in 1903), to greater India (establishing the indigenous National Missionary Society in 1905), to wider Asia (touring Japan and China in 1907), and finally to the West, where Azariah burst upon the international missionary scene in 1910 with an impassioned speech to the Edinburgh World Missionary Conference against Western missionary paternalism toward 'native' Christians.

Although his work for the YMCA, the Indian Missionary Society (IMS), and the National Missionary Society (NMS) necessitated much travel during his early career, Azariah was always anchored at home by a strong and secure family life. He married Anbu Mariammal Samuel (1876–1950) on 29 June 1898 in a simple ceremony that, to his delight but to the bride's grandmother's distress, cost less than 40 rupees. During their long and harmonious marriage the couple had four sons and two daughters, in addition to at least one child who died in infancy.

Just as Azariah was gaining international recognition as an effective promoter of Indian missions he received what he interpreted as a divine call to conduct evangelism himself in a specific locality. In 1909 he resigned from the YMCA and the NMS to become superintending missionary for the IMS in Dornakal, located in a small railway depot in the rural Warangal district of south-eastern Hyderabad state. Here, within the favourite hunting grounds of the nizam of Hyderabad, Azariah became a missionary to the Telugu-speaking depressed and non-Brahman classes. He lived first in a tent and travelled through the villages by foot, bullock cart, and bicycle, with his food and Bible tracts hanging in a bag suspended from his handlebar.

Azariah's self-imposed obscurity in rural Dornakal did not last long. He was soon recruited into Anglican church leadership by Bishop Henry Whitehead of Madras (1853–1947), who persuaded his fellow bishops in India and civil authorities in Madras and London to constitute Dornakal as the centre of a new diocese with Azariah at its head. Azariah was consecrated as the first Indian Anglican bishop on Sunday 29 December 1912 in St Paul's Cathedral, Calcutta; and he remained the first and only Indian bishop of an Anglican diocese until his death.

During an age dominated by secular nationalism Azariah focused his energies mainly on sub-national local evangelism and transnational ecumenism. Azariah led grass-roots conversion movements of roughly 200,000 depressed class and non-Brahman Telugus into the church in his diocese; and he promoted education, temperance, and economic uplift in Andhra's villages. He also became the chief spokesman for non-Roman Catholic Indian Christians in key ecumenical fora: the National Christian Council, the Joint Committee on Union in south India, the Lambeth conferences of 1920 and 1930, the conferences on Faith and Order in Lausanne (1927) and Edinburgh (1937), and the International Missionary Council Conference at Tambaram (1938). Azariah was at least partly responsible for the first unification of episcopal and non-episcopal churches since the Reformation, which took place in south India two years after his death. The University of Cambridge awarded him the honorary degree of LLD in 1920.

As a man of faith in an age captivated by ideology Azariah rarely entered the political fray. One notable exception occurred in 1932, when he joined with Gandhi and other Indian nationalists to oppose the government's expanding policy of granting separate electorates along communal lines. Azariah's brief alliance with Gandhi in opposition to British policy was shattered later in the decade, however, because of a controversy over religious freedom in India. Azariah's advocacy of depressed class conversion movements to Christianity in this new age of mass, communally-based politics threatened Gandhi's bid to secure the allegiance of the untouchables within the political fold of his charismatically Hindu form of messianic nationalism. As a result, Gandhi considered Azariah to be his 'enemy number one' (private information).

Azariah rose to prominence in an age electrified by political nationalism, but he was neither very political nor very nationalistic. He was certainly influenced by Indian nationalism's desire for independence from Western control and, within the ecclesiastical arena, he helped the church to develop a more secure Indian identity and greater administrative independence from Western organizations. Azariah built both an Indian-style cathedral and an Indian-led clergy for his diocese. But he never advocated radical separation from either the Western church or the British empire. He worked to create an indigenous Indian form of Christianity, but never a Christianized form of Indian nationalism. His close association with Telugu depressed classes in the Dornakal diocese, who generally preferred British rule to the perceived threat of 'Hindu rule' or 'Brahman rule', made the bishop wary of Congressite plans for independence. Bishop Azariah's sympathy for Indian nationalism's broadest aspirations was always subdued and moderated by local and transnational concerns.

Azariah died in Dornakal on 1 January 1945 of complications from a malarial fever contracted during a trip to rural areas of his diocese. He was buried the next day at Dornakal Cathedral. His wife survived him. He was known throughout Dornakal as Thandrigaru, a Telugu term meaning 'honourable father', and he is remembered by Indian Christians today for his humble devotion to the needs of often neglected village congregations.

SUSAN BILLINGTON HARPER

Sources S. B. Harper, *In the shadow of the Mahatma: Bishop V. S. Azariah and the travails of Christianity in British India* (2000) • private information [K. Swaminathan, editor, *Collected works of Mahatma Gandhi*]

Archives BL OIOC • Indian Missionary Society of Tirunelveli archives, Palayamkottai, south India • LPL • National Missionary Society, Madras, India, archives • United Theological College, Bangalore, India, archives • Yale U., divinity school | Bishop's College, Calcutta, India, metropolitan archives of the church of India, Pakistan, Burma, and Ceylon • Bodl. RH, United Society for the Propagation of the Gospel archives • SOAS, joint archives of the International Missionary Council and the Conference of British Missionary Societies • U. Birm. L., Church Missionary Society archives

Likenesses L. C. Evetts, stained-glass window, Partnership House, 157 Waterloo Road, London, USPG archives • Wiele & Klein, photograph, NPG [*see illus.*]

Azikiwe, Nnamdi [*known as* Zik] (**1904–1996**), journalist and president of Nigeria, was born in Zungeru, Northern Nigeria, on 16 November 1904, the son of Obed-Edom Chukwuemeka Azikiwe (*c*.1854–1958), a civil servant attached to the Nigeria regiment of the Royal West African frontier force, and his wife, Nwannonaku Rachel Chinwe Ogbenyeanu (*c*.1884–1958), who was related to the royal family of Onitsha. He was baptized Benjamin Azikiwe. Though an Igbo he spent the first eight years of his life in Northern Nigeria. He was then educated in mission schools in Lagos, as well as in Onitsha and Calabar. He was from an early age aware of the other peoples of Nigeria, and the common interests of all Africans, and spoke all three of Nigeria's major languages. This was important in a career that was to emphasize the possibility of unity across ethnic groupings within Nigeria, and pan-Africanism without.

As a teenager Azikiwe conceived a desire to study in

Nnamdi Azikiwe [Zik] (**1904–1996**), by A. Harris

America, and he was roused by the black pride message of Garvey and Dubois, which he later sought to apply to Africa in his political and journalistic career. In 1921 he passed the civil service exams and became a Treasury department clerk, but his desire to study in America led him to stow away on a ship in 1924. However, he was put off at Accra. There he joined the Gold Coast police force. In 1925 his American dream was realized with the aid of sympathetic college presidents, and £300 from his father's savings. He went first to Storer College, West Virginia, followed by periods at Howard, Lincoln, Columbia, and Pennsylvania universities financed largely by his own exertions, including jobs as a miner, porter, dishwasher, and professional boxer. Gaining two master's degrees from Lincoln and Pennsylvania universities, from 1931 to 1934 he was an instructor in political science at Lincoln. Links with other future nationalist leaders were forged, and he also made connections with leading figures in British academic and colonial circles, including Margery Perham and Bronislaw Malinowski (through whom he later became a fellow of the Royal Anthropological Institute). While in America honing the political, intellectual, and journalistic skills upon which his career in west Africa was to be based, Azikiwe was often haunted by financial worries, leading to a suicide attempt in 1927.

In 1934 Azikiwe applied to compete, for Nigeria, as an athlete in the British empire games, but he was barred following protest from the South African team. As his own protest at this treatment he gave up the name Benjamin, replacing it legally with the name Nnamdi. Later the same year he returned to west Africa as editor of the *African Morning Post*, based in Accra, in the Gold Coast. In 1936 he married Flora Ogbenyeanu Ogoegbunam (*d.* 1983), daughter of the adazia of Onitsha; they had three sons and a daughter.

As editor of the *African Morning Post* (1934–7) Azikiwe introduced a new dynamism into politics through journalism, departing from the moderate approach of the educated élite common in the era of debating club politics. He demanded dominion status. His provocative style raised his newspaper's circulation from 2000 to 10,000 within two years. In 1937 he was charged with sedition, though the decision was reversed on appeal. Later that year he returned to Nigeria, where he became a hero of the nationalist movement. He started the Zik group of newspapers that was to play a prominent role in articulating nationalist demands. While editor-in-chief of the *West African Pilot* (1937–45) he also pursued an energetic political and commercial career, and founded the African Continental Bank.

Azikiwe's return to Nigeria helped stimulate the Nigerian Youth Movement, to which he brought Igbo support and his journalistic power. In 1944 he was one of the founders of the National Council of Nigeria and the Cameroons (NCNC); he acted as general secretary from 1944 to 1946, and president thereafter. The party called for independence and fostered a sense of nationhood. It was the first colony-wide political party with mass support, seeking independence as its goal. Nevertheless the British authorities now welcomed Azikiwe's activities, having identified him as a potential future leader with whom they could work, given his advocacy of a non-confrontational, constitutional path to political advancement within the Commonwealth. Azikiwe and his newspapers were loyal to the British cause during the Second World War, but kept up the assault upon colonial rule and clashed with the administration in the post-war years. His political message, expounded in speeches and writings such as *Renascent Africa* (1937), aimed at the mental emancipation of Africans as a precondition for throwing off the colonial yoke, and the creation of a Nigerian nation and pan-African unity. Many young Africans were already longing for a new Africa, and Azikiwe, with the prestige of foreign education behind him, was the embodiment of that idea. The message of 'Zik' inspired the formation of the Zikist movement, a radical youth base that buoyed the momentum of his political party, though which Azikiwe himself considered too radical by the late 1940s.

In the 1950s Azikiwe moved increasingly from journalism to politics. From 1951 to 1954 he was a member of the western house of assembly. In 1954 he became premier of the eastern region in the now federally structured colony, and he headed the Nigerian delegation at the four constitutional conferences with the British in the 1950s. He became president of the federal senate and was sworn a privy councillor in 1960. He gave up the active leadership of the NCNC later the same year when he became governor-general of the Federation of Nigeria (the first African to hold such a post) a month after independence, in October 1960. When Nigeria became a republic three years later he became the country's first president. He performed his duties as head of state with detachment, a sense of constitutional propriety, and a sympathy for the unity of Nigeria above its tribal fault lines. However, his record after independence was more equivocal than his contribution to the achievement of independence. He was ousted by a coup on 15 January 1966, though his absence from Nigeria at the time gave rise to the suspicion that he had co-operated with the Igbo officers who conducted it. During the Nigerian civil war which followed he was persuaded to support the Biafran cause and to use his enormous international prestige and contacts to further the secessionist claim. He then antagonized his erstwhile allies by his damaging defection to the one-Nigeria side.

After the Biafran war Azikiwe (who became the owelle of Onitsha, his home region, in 1973) faded into the political background, living in his adopted home town of Nsukku. It was a surprise when, in 1979, he was persuaded to come out of retirement to lead the Nigerian People's Party. He contested and lost the presidential elections, which were won by Alhaji Shehu Shagari, but he formed part of the new ruling coalition and sat on the council of state until 1983. In the latter year, having fallen out with Shagari, he again contested the presidential elections, but came a poor third. He was created grand commander of the Order of the Federal Republic of Nigeria in 1980.

Azikiwe was a prolific writer of scholarly, political, and journalistic speeches, articles, and books. These included *Liberia in World Politics* (1934) and an autobiography, *My Odyssey* (1970). Throughout his life he was keen on sport, with an interest in athletics, cricket, and boxing. He was the first chancellor of the University of Nigeria at Nsukku. He was a tall, scholarly figure with a loping stride, easily identifiable by his trademark spectacles, traditional west African robes, and cap. He died at Enugu, eastern Nigeria, on 11 May 1996. He was survived by his four children.

ASHLEY JACKSON

Sources N. Azikiwe, *My odyssey: an autobiography* (1970) • A. Igwe, *Nnamdi Azikiwe: the philosopher of our time* (1992) • V. Ikeotuonye, *Zik of new Africa* (1981) • M. S. O. Olisa and O. Ikejiani-Clark, eds., *Azikiwe and the African revolution* (1989) • A. Ikenga, *Nnamdi Azikiwe: tributes to an African legend* (Lagos, 1996) • K. A. B. Jones-Quartey, *A life of Azikiwe* (1965) • J. S. Coleman, *Nigeria: background to nationalism* (1958) • J. Flint, 'Managing nationalism: the colonial office and Nnamdi Azikiwe, 1932–43', *The statecraft of British imperialism: essays in honour of Wm. Roger Louis*, ed. R. King and R. Kilson (1999) • R. L. Sklar, *Nigerian political parties: power in an emergent African nation* (1963) • P. Zachernuk, 'Intellectual life in a colonial context: the Nigerian intelligentsia, 1860–1960', PhD diss., University of Toronto, 1991 • N. Azikiwe, *Zik: a selection of speeches* (1961)

Likenesses A. Harris, photograph, News International Syndication, London [*see illus.*] • photographs, Hult. Arch.

Baalun, John de. *See* Ballon, John de (*d.* 1235).

Baartman, Sara [*performing name* the Hottentot Venus] (1777x88–1815/16), celebrity and subject of scientific speculation, was born in the Cape of Good Hope and was a member of the Khoisan people, who were also called Hottentot. Altick claims she was a daughter of a drover who had been killed by Bushmen, though nothing more is known of her parents. Her original name is not known, but as a servant of the Dutch farmer Peter Cezar she was given the Afrikaans name Saartjie Baartman, which was subsequently Anglicized to Sara Baartman. In early 1810 Sara was brought to England by Henrick Cezar, the brother of Peter Cezar, and Alexander Dunlop, a ship's surgeon. While living at York Street, Piccadilly, London, she was exhibited by Cezar at public shows under the stage name of the Hottentot Venus. Contemporaries reported that Sara was treated like an animal, humiliated and intimidated by Cezar, while others claimed that standards of decency were being transgressed. Letters of protest appeared in newspapers, and the African Association petitioned for her release. Zachary Macaulay asked for a writ of habeas corpus to be issued against Alexander Dunlop and Henrick Cezar, in which Alexander Dunlop was called to prove that Sara had not been brought to England and exhibited against her will. The case was heard at the court of chancery on 24 November 1810. Dunlop produced a contract signed by himself and Sara dated 29 October 1810, which was to run from the preceding March for five years. This stated that she was his domestic servant and would allow herself to be exhibited in public in return for 12 guineas a year. Sara was questioned in Dutch and claimed she was not being held against her will. The case was dismissed.

Apart from Sara's baptism at the collegiate church, Manchester, on 1 December 1811, little is known about her life after the court case until she arrived in Paris in September 1814. Kirby reports that in Paris she claimed to have been married, and it is clear that she was exhibited in shows. She was reported as having died of an 'inflammatory ailment' (Gould, 294). However, the precise date of death and her age at death is not clear. Georges Cuvier gave the date 29 December 1815, but the Musée de l'Homme in Paris placed her death on 1 January 1816. In 1814 Sara claimed she was about twenty-six years old, but later estimates gave her age at death as thirty-eight.

Sara aroused intense interest: popular prints, songs, and shows appeared in both England and France, and she was sketched by scientists in Paris in 1814. After her death, Cuvier made a plaster cast of her body and wax casts were made of her genitals and anus. A partial dissection was made of her body, while her skeleton was preserved and mounted. It remained on display in the Musée de l'Homme until 1985. Reports of the dissection were published by Henri Ducrotay de Blainville in 1816 and by Cuvier in 1817. Sara was a focus of attention at the shows and by scientists partly because of her racial status: eighteenth-century 'racial science' envisaged the Hottentot as the lowest in a vertical model of humanity. This racial identity was inextricably linked to a sexual identity. Hottentots were believed to possess powerful sexual appetites, and this was supposedly manifest in the physical characteristics of the women. Khoisan women experience a condition called steatopygia, which produces large buttocks. Scientists such as Cuvier sought to discover whether they consisted of fat, muscle, or bone, and popular prints of Sara also emphasized enlarged buttocks. In addition, Khoisan women were thought to possess a veil of skin that hung in front of the genitals. Cuvier discovered that enlarged inner labia rather than an additional anatomical feature produced the effect of this so-called 'Hottentot apron'. The contemporary interest surrounding Sara Baartman—the Hottentot Venus—exemplified both the assumed racial inferiority and excessive sexuality often ascribed to black men and women at this time. In April 2002 the cast of Baartman's body, along with her skeleton and bottled organs, were returned by France to the South African government for burial, in August, on the banks of the Gamtoos River, Hankey, near Port Elizabeth. KAREN HARVEY

Sources P. R. Kirby, 'The Hottentot Venus', *Africana Notes and News*, 6/3 (1949), 55–62 • P. R. Kirby, 'More about the Hottentot Venus', *Africana Notes and News*, 10/4 (1953), 124–34 • S. J. Gould, 'The Hottentot Venus', *The flamingo's smile: reflections in natural history* (1985), 211–305 • S. L. Gilman, 'The Hottentot and the prostitute: toward an iconography of female sexuality', *Difference and pathology: stereotypes of sexuality, race, and madness* (1985), 76–108 • L. Schiebinger, *Nature's body: gender in the making of modern science* (1993) • R. D. Altick, *The shows of London* (1978) • P. Edwards and J. Walvin, 'Saartjie Baartman, the Hottentot Venus', *Black personalities in the era of the slave trade* (1983), 171–82

Likenesses two mezzotints, repro. in Kirby, 'The Hottentot Venus'

Babbage, Charles (1791–1871), mathematician and computer pioneer, was the first son born to Benjamin Babbage (*d.* 1827), a well-to-do London banker, and Elizabeth (Betsy, Betty) Plumleigh Teape (*d.* 1844). Confusion has surrounded both the year and place of Babbage's birth. This confusion is not an invention of modern historiography but dates back to the last century since when Babbage is variously cited as having been born in Totnes, Teignmouth, or London, in either 1791 or 1792. The date of birth has been consistently recorded as 26 December, and as the records of St Mary's Newington in London date his baptism as 6 January 1792, his year of birth was evidently 1791. The location of the church makes it likely that Charles was born at his father's house in Crosby Row, on what was to become Walworth Road in Southwark, London. Both parents were natives of Totnes and from well-known Devon families. Charles was one of four children: two brothers, born in 1794 and 1796, did not survive infancy; his sister, Mary Anne, was born in 1798 and outlived him.

Education Babbage's schooling was unsystematic and fractured by illness. After a violent fever at the age of about ten he was sent from London to Devon to recuperate. He was placed at a school in Alphington in the care of a clergyman who had instructions to administer a programme of tuition that would not tax the feeble boy, a mission, Babbage wryly recalled, which the clergyman 'faithfully accomplished' (Babbage, *Passages*, 1864, 10). When sufficiently recovered he was placed in a small school in Enfield for about three years. He was especially

Charles Babbage (1791–1871), by Antoine Claudet, *c.*1847–51

struck by a treatise on algebra, *Ward's Young Mathematician's Guide*, which he found in the school library. His interest in mathematics was already evident and he went so far as to institute early morning self-study sessions with a schoolfellow before formal classes began. He later passed into the care of a clergyman near Cambridge for a few years and finally, before going to Cambridge University, spent some time in Totnes, where he was instructed in classics by an Oxford tutor. 'Being passionately fond of algebra' (Babbage, *Passages*, 1864, 26) he spent his leisure reading what mathematical works came to hand. By the time he went to Cambridge he was already a moderately accomplished mathematician having studied Woodhouse's *Principles of Analytical Calculation* (1803), Lagrange's *Théorie des fonctions analytiques* (1797), *Analytical Institutions* (1748) by the Italian mathematician Marie Agnesi, and other works on fluxions.

Babbage entered Trinity College, Cambridge, in April 1810 and migrated to Peterhouse in 1812. He was a spirited undergraduate and relished the company of his friends. He played chess, participated in all-night sixpenny whist sessions, and missed lectures and chapel to go sailing on the river with his friends. He formed a close and enduring friendship with John *Herschel, son of the astronomer William Herschel, who had entered St John's College in 1809. Babbage espoused and advocated radical views: he admired Napoleonic France (with which Britain was still at war), decried the unquestioned acceptance of doctrine exemplified by the inflexible religious context of university life, and lamented the lack of receptivity to continental theories in mathematics. From his pre-university reading he was already conversant with the different notations used in differential calculus by Newton, Leibniz, and Lagrange, and looked forward, as a new undergraduate, to having his curiosity and mathematical puzzlements illuminated by his tutors. In this he was disappointed. Disaffected with the set curriculum he preferred instead a programme of study of his own which favoured the works of foreign mathematicians.

As a spoof on the dogmatism of Bible societies he produced rough proposals for a society for translating a work on calculus by the French mathematician Lacroix. The hypothetical society would promulgate the use of Leibniz's d-notation in preference to the orthodoxy of Newton's dot-notation favoured by the Cambridge dons. Edward Bromhead was shown an outline of the parodic scheme and this was converted into a serious proposal for the formation of a society for the promotion of analysis and the reform of mathematics. The Analytical Society was formed in 1811 and survived until 1817. Prominent among its leaders were Babbage, John Herschel, and George Peacock. The society published a mathematical work in 1813, *Memoirs of the Analytical Society*. The preface and first paper 'On continued products' were written by Babbage, and were followed by two papers by Herschel. The role of the Analytical Society in the incipient movement to reform Cambridge mathematics by ending its isolation from continental mathematics is undeniable, but success was not immediate and the extent of the society's impact on the analytical movement is still debated.

Babbage was Peterhouse's 'crack man' and he was expected to excel in the final Senate House mathematics examinations. However, he graduated without honours, receiving a 'poll' degree in 1814 and his MA in 1817. In the public disputations that were a part of the procedure to pre-classify candidates according to ability he attempted to defend the proposition that God was a material agent. The moderator regarded this thesis as blasphemous and dismissed Babbage out of hand. It is unclear whether this was the cause of Babbage not sitting the final examinations or whether he chose not to. Either way his failure to win honours put paid to any immediate hopes he may have had of a Cambridge fellowship and he left Cambridge in 1814. In later life Babbage recalled his student years with warmth devoid of rancour.

Family life Babbage married Georgiana Whitmore on 2 July 1814 in Teignmouth, Devon. After several temporary residences the couple made their home in London at 5 Devonshire Street, Portland Place, towards the end of 1815. Georgiana bore at least eight children of whom four survived childhood: Benjamin Herschel (named after Babbage's father and Babbage's friend John Herschel); Dugald Bromhead (named after Dugald Stewart, professor of moral philosophy at Edinburgh, and Edward Bromhead); Henry Prevost Babbage [*see below*]; and Georgiana (*d.* 1834). Babbage had no paying post and the couple lived for the most part on a modest but comfortable annual income of £450 of which £300 was an allowance from his father. In 1827 Babbage suffered a series of personal tragedies: his wife (in her mid-thirties), his father, and two of his children (his second son Charles and a newborn son) all died.

Taking Richard Wright, one of his workmen, as a travelling companion, Babbage embarked on a recuperative tour of the continent which lasted from October 1827 to November 1828. He travelled extensively, met prominent scientists, and visited workshops and craftsmen as part of his study of the techniques and machinery of manufacture. During this time the two younger children, Dugald and Henry, were cared for in the household of their late mother's sister, Harriet Isaac, near Worcester, while Herschel and Georgiana stayed in the family home in Devonshire Street cared for by Babbage's mother. Once returned to London, Babbage moved to 1 Dorset Street, Manchester Square, which remained his home until his death. His mother maintained a family base in nearby Devonshire Street and relieved him of the care of the children. His only daughter, Georgiana, died in 1834 in her teens. His mother, whom he adored, was a source of practical and moral support; his relationship with his father, whom on occasion he described as stern, intemperate, and critical, was less happy. On his father's death in February 1827 Babbage inherited a sizeable estate worth about £100,000. He did not remarry. His mother died on 5 December 1844 in her eighties.

Scientific work and reform Once settled in London, Babbage rapidly established himself on the scientific scene. He was energetic, polymathic, and inventive. He delivered a series of twelve general lectures on astronomy at the Royal Institution in 1815 and became a fellow of the Royal Society in 1816. He participated in the foundation of the Astronomical Society in 1820 serving as one of its first secretaries (1820–24), vice president (1824 and 1825), foreign secretary (1827–9), and member of council (1820–28 and 1830–33); he was presented with the society's gold medal in 1824 for his work on his calculating engine. Babbage was active in the British Association for the Advancement of Science (BAAS) and served as one of its trustees (1832–8). He successfully instituted a committee for statistical activities at the association's annual meeting in Cambridge in 1833. This was formalized into the statistical section of the BAAS in 1835 and also led to the foundation of the Statistical Society of London in 1834. His participation in the activities of scientific societies declined as the analytical engine increasingly dominated his attention from the mid-1830s. He was elected as Lucasian professor of mathematics at Cambridge in 1828 and occupied this coveted chair until 1839 though he gave no lectures and was rarely resident. In his seventies he wrote of the deep gratitude he still felt for the honour conferred on him by Cambridge, commenting, perhaps not without bitterness, that the Lucasian chair was the only honour he received in his own country. Babbage stood as a Liberal candidate for the two-member seat of Finsbury in the general election of 1832 and again in the by-election of 1834. He was defeated on both occasions—though doing well in 1832—and surrendered further political ambition.

Babbage's first publication ('On continued products', 1813) was the first of some dozen mathematical papers which dominated his published output until 1822. His writings on mathematics show a preoccupation with iterative procedures and the importance of appropriate notational representation to generalizing solutions. His major work was 'An essay towards the calculus of functions', which appeared in two parts in the *Philosophical Transactions of the Royal Society* in 1815 and 1816. Despite its originality this work was not pursued by others and he appears to have left no direct lasting mathematical legacy. In all Babbage was the author of at least eighty-three published papers and six full-length monographs between 1813 and 1868. His published scientific work is wide-ranging and includes writings on chess, barometric observation, calculating engines, the distribution of births between the two sexes, notation, geology, ciphers, machine tools, solar eclipses, lighthouses, submarines, occulting telegraphs, and statistics. Many of his miscellaneous scientific papers were short and sometimes insubstantial. However, the diversity of the topics is impressive even in an age in which polymathy was not unusual. Mathematical tables were a special interest. He was a connoisseur and collector of printed mathematical tables and a fastidious analyst of tabular errors. His own *Table of Logarithms* (1827) involved nine separate stages of checking and was generally considered the most reliable of his day. Babbage was an inveterate inventor and experimenter and delighted in instruments and mechanical contrivances. He constructed the first known ophthalmoscope in 1847 for examining the interior of the eye. He showed it to a well-known ophthalmic surgeon, Thomas Wharton Jones, who regarded it indifferently, an act subsequently regarded by a historian as a 'monumental folly'. Credit for the invention went to Hermann von Helmholtz four years later. In the late 1860s Babbage pioneered pressure die-casting techniques in the quest for a cheap means of producing repeatable parts for his calculating engines. Some of his cast parts date from at least as early as 1868, some twenty years before any other authenticated production.

Babbage's full-length works reflect his broader preoccupations with scientific and industrial life, political economy, and philosophy. His most successful work was *On the Economy of Machinery and Manufactures* first published in 1832. The book ran to four editions between 1832 and 1835 and was translated into six European languages. *Economy* was a product of a conscientious and detailed survey of factories and workshops in England and on the continent prompted by the demands for precision in the construction of his first calculating engine. The work is not a thesis on macroeconomic theory but an encyclopaedic record of craft, manufacturing, and industrial processes, as well as an analysis of the domestic organization of factories. He advocated the decimalization of currency, foresaw the role of tidal power as an energy source, and predicted the exhaustion of coal reserves, later commenting that if posterity failed to find a substitute for coal then it deserved to be frostbitten. *Economy* was a turning point in economic writing and firmly established Babbage as a leading authority of the industrial movement.

Babbage was a vociferous critic of the scientific establishment. His *Reflections on the Decline of Science in England*

(1830) was a scathing and sarcastic attack on the Royal Society and on the conduct of its officers, whose personal and professional probity he pointedly impugned. It was a broadside of outrage and insult and he argued more to protest than to persuade. Babbage's declinist views were shared by others though he was alone in the vehemence of their public expression. His friend Herschel, to whom he showed a draft, wrote that if he (Herschel) could do so with impunity he would give Babbage 'a good slap in the face' (Morrell and Thackray, 48). *Decline* gave a decisive boost to the movement to reform organized science though the nature and vigour of the assault was viewed by many of Babbage's contemporaries as ill considered. It also soured his relationship with the scientific establishment. He wrote to the duke of Somerset in 1835 flatly informing him that since its publication he had 'never attended the Royal Society nor even indirectly taken any part in its affairs' (Babbage to the seventh duke of Somerset, 3 Dec 1835, Bulstrode MSS, Bucks. RLSS).

The Ninth Bridgewater Treatise (1837), though fragmentary in parts, is Babbage's most philosophically rewarding work. Eight Bridgewater treatises were officially commissioned under the terms of the will of the eighth earl of Bridgewater. The purpose of the essays was to close the widening rift between rational science and natural theology. Babbage's *Ninth* was a supernumerary offering, not an official commission. In it he argued against William Whewell's assertion that scientific and religious modes of thought were incompatible and that mathematicians and mechanists were therefore disqualified from theological debate. This was anathema to Babbage, who set out to reconcile rational science with deism. One of Babbage's more intriguing arguments involved an explanation of miracles. He argued that just as programmed discontinuities in a sequence of numbers generated by his calculating engine were not a violation of computational rule, so, by analogy, miracles in nature were not a violation of natural law but a manifestation of a higher law—God's law, as yet undiscovered. In the pre-Darwinian decades there was major scientific opposition between uniformitarians who held that geological changes and by implication natural law were essentially gradual, and catastrophists who posited that extreme and comparatively sudden phenomena were responsible for geological discontinuities. Babbage visited the Temple of Serapis at Pozzuoli in 1828 and the geological speculations in his *Treatise* were based on observations he made there. His position was essentially allied to the views of the geologist Charles Lyell, a leading advocate of the uniformitarian doctrine.

The Great Exhibition of 1851 was the largest industrial manufacturing spectacular yet staged. Babbage's exclusion from the organization of the event was for him an incomprehensible affront to his self-perception as an elder statesman of the industrial movement. In *The Exposition of 1851, or, Views of the Industry, the Science and the Government of England* (1851) he vented his grievances by alleging weakness and incompetence on the part of the exhibition's commissioners. The book includes pitiful passages on solitude, and the despair to which his efforts, personal sacrifices, and lack of recognition had at times reduced him. The work is ungracious in its treatment of others. But it does provide a rare insight into the darker moments of Babbage's struggles and is, despite its title, emotionally more revealing than his overtly autobiographical work, *Passages from the Life of a Philosopher* (1864). *Passages* is a rambling, colourful, anecdotal account of Babbage's life and work. It is unusual by the conventions of autobiography in that it contains little introspection and few details of its author's personal life. Babbage's wife, Georgiana, is not mentioned and Babbage refers once and only obliquely to the blackest single year of his life, 1827, during which four members of his immediate family died. The chapter on the 'abominable nuisance' of street musicians is often cited in evidence of Babbage's reputation for eccentricity. He despaired at repeated interruption of his work by street disturbance and campaigned tirelessly for legal reforms, attracting, on occasions, public ridicule. His autopsy report, which came to light in 1983, raises the intriguing possibility that Babbage's acute sensitivity to noise was due to a medical condition involving cochlear degeneration caused by arterial disease. *Passages* remains a rewarding and entertaining volume, rich in mischief, self-parody, and false modesty. Babbage was offered the position of director and actuary of the fledgeling Protector Life Assurance Company with the prospect of an annual income of £2500, a substantial improvement on his father's grudging allowance. He spent several months studying the life assurance business and computed a new set of life tables. The venture was abandoned the day before its scheduled launch on 1 July 1824. Babbage used his actuarial knowledge as the basis for a small popular work, *A Comparative View of the Various Institutions for the Assurance of Lives* (1826). The book was not intended for the professional actuary but for the general populace unwary of the pitfalls of conveniently misrepresented benefits. It was, at least in part, a work of consumer protection with Babbage self-cast as champion of the exposé.

Calculating engines It is on the invention of automatic calculating engines that Babbage's posthumous fame largely rests. For all his other interests it is the engines, their design and construction, that dominated his working life. In later years he was reminded by a friend of the occasion of the first dawning of the idea to calculate mathematical tables by machine. The event supposedly occurred in 1812 or 1813 while Babbage was an undergraduate at Cambridge. The account is probably apocryphal. A more credible account of the genesis episode is that given closer to the event by Babbage himself. The occasion was a meeting in 1821 with Herschel during which they set about checking some newly computed astronomical tables. Dismayed by the errors Babbage exclaimed 'I wish to God these calculations had been executed by steam' (Buxton, 46). By May 1822 Babbage had completed a small experimental version of his difference engine, so called because of the mathematical principle on which it was based, the method of calculating finite differences. Following the favourable recommendation of the Royal Society in May 1823, and the advocacy of influential supporters, Babbage secured government financial backing for his proposal to construct a larger, fully engineered machine, Difference Engine no. 1. In June 1823 in a private interview with the chancellor, F. J. Robinson, he was granted £1500 from the Civil Contingency Fund to prosecute the venture. No written record appears to have been made of the meeting and the nature and extent of the government's commitment is obscure. For his part Babbage consistently maintained that he had been officially commissioned 'to complete and to bring to perfection an engine for the construction of numerical tables' (PRO, T 52/111, fol. 1) with the full expectation that requisite funds would be forthcoming.

Babbage engaged the engineer Joseph Clement and a period of concentrated work ensued. During Babbage's extended travels between 1827 and 1828 the project was entrusted to John Herschel. On his return the project was hindered by fitful funding difficulties. Repeated applications were made to the Treasury and the advice of the Royal Society was sought on two further occasions. Royal Society reports delivered in 1829 and 1831 were both favourable and the Treasury advanced further tranches of money. Babbage had Clement assemble a small section of the engine as a demonstration piece. The assembly, which worked impeccably, represented about one-seventh of the whole machine and was ready towards the end of 1832. This section of Difference Engine no. 1, transferred to the Science Museum, London, in 1862, is the first known automatic calculator and ranks among the most celebrated icons in the prehistory of computing. In March 1833 Clement halted work following an argument with Babbage over compensation for transferring the project from Clement's works near the Elephant and Castle to specially built fireproof workshops adjacent to Babbage's house. The physical construction of the engine was never resumed. At the time that Clement downed tools almost all the parts (about 12,000) for the calculating section of the engine were complete but unassembled. Some of these were later cut up or melted down by Babbage for reuse in the analytical engine, some were used by Henry Prevost, Babbage's youngest son, after his father's death, and the rest were consigned to the melting pot. An estimated 12,000 parts for automatically printing and stereotyping results remained unmade. After the last payment to Clement in August 1834 the government's outlay had totalled £17,478. The collapse of the project after a decade of design and development was the central trauma in Babbage's scientific life. He was never fully reconciled to the dismal outcome.

A desultory and unsatisfactory correspondence between Babbage and successive governments ensued. In 1842 he pressed for an interview with the politically beleaguered prime minister, Sir Robert Peel. By that time Babbage had invented the more sophisticated analytical engine and had conceived of a simpler difference engine. He had planned to propose to Peel a new financial basis for funding the construction of his new engine designs. The proposals were intended to allow the government to fulfil what Babbage regarded as its binding commitment to fund an engine to completion and at the same time relieve the Treasury of the full burden of so doing. The meeting with Peel, which took place on 11 November 1842, was unfortunate. They argued and Babbage stormed out ('if those are your views, I wish you good morning'; 11 Nov 1842, BL, Add. MS 37192, fol. 189), his new proposals undisclosed. Between 1847 and 1849 Babbage designed Difference Engine no. 2, an elegant and more efficient version of its predecessor. Plans were offered to the government in 1852 but with no result. (In a twentieth-century sequel, the calculating section of Difference Engine no. 2 was completed at the Science Museum, London, in 1991, the bicentennial anniversary of Babbage's birth.) Despite Babbage's impassioned advocacy for his engines, experts disagreed about the utility and cost benefits of producing mathematical tables by mechanical means. George Biddell Airy, astronomer royal from 1835 to 1881, *de facto* scientific adviser to government, and official arbiter of the utility of calculating engines, when consulted by the Treasury in 1842, pronounced Babbage's difference engine to be 'useless' (CUL, RGO 6/427, fol. 65).

Babbage's standing as the first pioneer of computing relies less on his difference engines than on his conception and design of the analytical engine. The most creatively active period of development occurred between 1834 and summer 1836, by which time the essential principles of the analytical engine had been established. He continued to work on improved designs until 1846 and then intermittently from the mid-1850s until his death. Unlike the difference engine, which was a fixed-function calculator, the analytical engine was conceived as a general-purpose machine capable of calculating virtually any mathematical function. It had a repertory of the four basic arithmetical functions (addition, subtraction, multiplication, and division) and was programmable—that is, it could be instructed to perform any of these operations in any sequence. The machine was to be programmed using punched cards, a technique borrowed from the Jacquard loom, where it was used to control the patterns of woven thread. The analytical engine could be instructed to repeat the same sequence of operations a specifiable number of times (a process later called looping or iteration) and was capable of choosing alternative actions depending on the value of a result (conditional branching). A landmark in the development of the design was the internal organization of the machine: Babbage separated the section which stored numbers (the 'store') from the section which processed numbers (the 'mill'). He made no serious attempt to construct a full-scale analytical engine until 1857 and his efforts were sporadic and inconclusive. Apart from a few small test assemblies, all that survived in mechanical form is an experimental section of the mill under construction at the time of his death.

Babbage published little on the conception and design of either of his engines. However, others did—notably Dionysius Lardner, who published in 1834 a long and sometimes bumptious article on Difference Engine no. 1, and Ada Augusta, countess of Lovelace, daughter of Lord Byron. Lovelace translated a paper on the analytical engine by the Italian engineer Luigi Menabrea (later prime minister of Italy) following a visit by Babbage to Turin in 1840. Working in close collaboration with Babbage she added copious notes of her own and her 'Sketch of the analytical engine' was published in 1843. While the originality of Lovelace's technical contribution to the 'Sketch' has been questioned it remains the most penetrating and articulate contemporary account of Babbage's most celebrated invention. Babbage, indebted to her for her expository role, addressed her in correspondence as 'my dear and much admired interpreter' (Babbage to Lovelace, 9 Sept 1843, transcript and facsimile in B. A. Toole, *Ada: the Enchantress of Numbers*, 1992, 236). The major record of Babbage's work on calculating engines was deposited in a substantial manuscript archive at the Science Museum, London. The archive includes some 500 large design drawings and twenty 'Scribbling books' which record, with little concessionary explanation, the evolution of his ideas.

Death and legacy Babbage died on 18 October 1871 at his house, 1 Dorset Street, Manchester Square, London, and was buried six days later in Kensal Green cemetery, London. His last days were disturbed by the din of organ grinders and street nuisances outside his house. A post-mortem examination conducted seventeen hours after death cited the evident cause of death as 'suppuration of the kidney'. The first published biography of Babbage referred to him in its title as the 'Irascible genius' (Moseley). The sharpness of this image remains unsoftened by subsequent scholarship.

Babbage bequeathed his workshop, drawings, and remaining engine parts to his youngest son, **Henry Prevost** [Henry Provost] **Babbage** (1824–1918), who continued to work on the engines; his efforts were conscientious but without the inventive inspiration of his father. Henry was born on 16 September 1824 and after attending Bruce Castle School, Tottenham, Middlesex, from 1831 to 1834 he entered University College School, in 1835, and University College, London, in 1840. He graduated in 1842. On his father's insistence Henry and his brother Dugald attended the workshop and drawing office at Dorset Street several times a week. It was here in his teens that Henry learned workshop skills and mechanical drawing from Babbage's workmen. The brothers also attended several of Babbage's celebrated Saturday soirées which were frequented by the social, scientific, and literary élite. Henry sailed for India as a military cadet in April 1843 and retired with the rank of major-general in 1874. He was married in India on 17 February 1852 to Mary (Min or Minnie) Bradshawe. He twice returned to England on furlough: the first lasted from May 1854 to November 1856 during which he involved himself in his father's engine pursuits; the second stretched from March 1871 to November 1873, during which time he was present at his father's death. He returned from India in 1875 to settle in Bromley, Kent, where he lived for ten years, moving to Cheltenham in 1885. In November 1854 he met Georg and Edvard Scheutz, the Swedish father and son who were in London to promote a difference engine of their own, the construction of which had been stimulated by Lardner's account of Babbage's machine published in 1834. Babbage had devised a mechanical notation, an elaborate system of notational symbols used to identify parts of his machines and describe their interrelated motions. After viewing the Scheutzes' difference engine, exhibited at Somerset House in April 1855, Henry produced the mechanical notations for the Swedish machine. These were exhibited, pasted on calico, at the British Association meeting in Glasgow in September that year, in Paris the following month, and at the Institution of Civil Engineers in May 1856. In later years Henry attempted to interest others in the notation but the technique was almost completely ignored. Henry sold the contents of his father's workshop in March 1872 but kept some tools, a few lathes, and a planing machine. He retained a workman called Wight and engaged another (Doncaster) to progress a large four-function calculator designed as part of the mill of the analytical engine. In retirement he worked sporadically on the mill, which he assembled in the workshop of R. W. Munro. In 1910 the device calculated and printed the first twenty-two multiples of pi to twenty-eight places though not without error. Henry compiled a large volume of papers, *Babbage's Calculating Engines*, published in 1889. This consists primarily of selections of his father's published work on the design and history of the machines and papers by others, as well as some material by Henry himself. He assembled five or six small demonstration pieces from unused parts of Difference Engine no. 1. These he sent to the universities of London, Cambridge, Manchester, and Harvard, USA. He died at Mayfield, Lansdown Place, Cheltenham, on 29 January 1918. In the late 1930s the Harvard model, offered in 1896, came to the attention of Howard Aiken, an early pioneer of electronic computing who drew attention to Babbage's work in the early years of the electronic age. Despite Henry's efforts to keep his father's work alive the direct influence of Babbage's work on the electronic computer is tenuous. Even so, the late twentieth century saw a significant revival of interest in this remarkable Victorian. DORON SWADE

Sources M. Campbell-Kelly, ed., *The works of Charles Babbage*, 11 vols. (1989) • C. Babbage, *Passages from the life of a philosopher* (1864); new edn with introduction, ed. M Campbell-Kelly (1994) • A. Hyman, *Charles Babbage: pioneer of the computer* (1982); repr. (1984) • B. Collier, *The little engines that could've: the calculating machines of Charles Babbage* (1990) • *Memoirs and correspondence of Major-General H. P. Babbage* (1910) • M. Moseley, *Irascible genius: a life of Charles Babbage, inventor* (1964) • H. W. Buxton, *Memoir of the life and labours of the late Charles Babbage*, ed. A. Hyman (1988) • J. M. Dubbey, *The mathematical work of Charles Babbage* (1978) • A. G. Bromley, 'The evolution of Babbage's calculating engines', *IEEE Annals of the History of Computing*, 9 (1987), 113–36 • H. W. Becher, 'Radicals, whigs and conservatives: the middle and lower classes in the analytical revolution at Cambridge in the age of aristocracy', *British Journal for the History of Science*, 28 (1995), 405–26 • *Babbage's calculating engines*, ed. [H. P. Babbage] (1889); repr. with introduction by A. G. Bromley (1982) • A. A. Lovelace, 'Sketch of the analytical engine', *Scientific Memoirs*, 3 (1843), 666–731 • D. Lardner, 'Babbage's calculating engine', *EdinR*, 59 (1834), 263–327 • M. Campbell-Kelly, 'Charles Babbage's table of logarithms', *IEEE Annals of the History of Computing*, 10 (1988), 159–69 • M. Lindgren, *Glory and failure*, trans. C. G. McKay (1987); [2nd edn] (Cambridge, MA, 1990) • D. Swade, *Charles Babbage and his calculating engines* (1991) • M. Campbell-Kelly,

'Charles Babbage and the assurance of lives', *IEEE Annals of the History of Computing*, 16 (1994), 5–14 • J. Morrell and A. Thackray, *Gentlemen of science: early years of the British Association for the Advancement of Science* (1981) • W. W. R. Ball, *A history of the study of mathematics at Cambridge* (1889) • H. Barton, 'Pressure diecasting in the eighteen-sixties: Charles Babbage's use of the technique on his "calculating engine"', *Diecasting and Metal Moulding* (May–June 1972), 14–15 • D. Swade, *The cogwheel brain: Charles Babbage and the quest to build the first computer* (2000) • d. cert. [Henry Prevost Babbage] • C. Babbage, letters to seventh duke of Somerset, Bucks. RLSS, Bulstrode papers • PRO, T 52/111 • CUL, R 606/427 • A. G. Bromley, 'Babbage's analytical engine plans 28 and 28a—the programmer's interface', *IEEE Annals of the History of Computing*, 22/4 (2000), 5–19

Archives BL, corresp. and papers, Add. MSS 37182–37205 • CUL, corresp., notebooks, and papers • MHS Oxf., papers • SML, papers, notebooks, and drawings; social diary and diplomas • U. Cam., scientific periodicals library, papers • Wanganui Regional Museum, New Zealand, literary MSS and papers | Birr Castle, Offaly, archives, letters to Lord Rose and Lady Rose • Bodl. Oxf., letters to William Somerville and Mary Somerville and papers • Bucks. RLSS, letters to duke of Somerset • Ransom HRC, corresp. with Sir John Herschel • RAS, letters to the Royal Astronomical Society • Royal Library of Belgium, Brussels, letters to A. Quetelet • RS, corresp. with Sir John Herschel • RS, letters to Sir John Lubbock • Scott Polar RI, letters to Sir John Franklin • U. St Andr. L., corresp. with James Forbes

Likenesses watercolour miniature, 1813 (paired with portrait of his fiancée, Georgiana), repro. in Swade, *Charles Babbage*; priv. coll. • J. Linnell, engraving, 1832, Sci. Mus. • J. Linnell, stipple, pubd 1833, BM, NPG • R. C. Roffe, engraving, 1833, Sci. Mus. • S. Laurence, drawing, *c*.1835–1837, repro. in Swade, *Charles Babbage*; priv. coll. • W. Brockedon, chalk drawing, 1840, NPG • S. Laurence, oils, *c*.1845, NPG • A. Claudet, daguerreotype, *c*.1847–1851, NPG [*see illus.*] • photograph, 1847–51, repro. in Swade, *Charles Babbage*; priv. coll. • H. Claudet, photograph, NPG

Wealth at death under £40,000: double probate, Dec 1872, *CGPLA Eng. & Wales* (1871)

Babbage, Henry Prevost (1824–1918). *See under* Babbage, Charles (1791–1871).

Babell, William (1689/90–1723), musical arranger and harpsichordist, was the son of a bassoonist in the Drury Lane Theatre orchestra, and was taught by his father, by John Christopher Pepusch, and possibly by Handel. A proficient violinist, harpsichordist, and organist, he was active in London's professional musical circles and apparently played in the private band of George I. For some years until his death he was organist at All Hallows, Bread Street.

Babell's fame as a harpsichordist derived from his arrangements of popular operatic arias for the instrument, a practice he originated and which won him an international reputation. Charles Burney criticized him for converting the music of Handel (among others) into:

> *showy* and brilliant lessons, which by mere rapidity of finger in playing single sounds, without the assistance of taste, expression, harmony, or modulation, enabled the performer to astonish ignorance, and acquire the reputation of a great player at a small expence.

Others regarded him more favourably; his published harpsichord works are considered to provide 'a valuable insight into early 18th-century practices of ornamentation and extemporization' (*New Grove*). He also wrote concertos for the violin and small flute.

Babell died at Canonbury, Islington, on 23 September 1723 at the age of thirty-three, his early death being attributed to his 'intemperate habits'. He was buried in All Hallows Church. J. A. F. MAITLAND, *rev.* K. D. REYNOLDS

Sources G. Gifford, 'Babell, William', *New Grove* • 'Babell, William', Grove, *Dict. mus.* (1927) • Burney, *Hist. mus.* • J. Hawkins, *A general history of the science and practice of music*, 5 vols. (1776)

Baber, Edward Colborne (1843–1890), orientalist and traveller, the son of Edward Baber and a great-nephew of Henry Hervey Baber, was born at Dulwich on 30 April 1843. He was educated at Rossall junior school where his father was headmaster, and from 1853 to 1862 at Christ's Hospital, going on from there with a scholarship to Magdalene College, Cambridge. He graduated BA in 1867. In 1866 he had gained through competitive examination a position as a Foreign Office student interpreter. He was appointed to Peking (Beijing) on 28 July 1866. Baber wrote to his father on 29 June 1867 of his studies of the Chinese language reporting how 'I have been working with small intermission between nine and twelve hours a day for six months, and yesterday evening I finished the colloquial course … the shortest time it has ever been done in' (*Proceedings*, 2nd ser., 5 July 1883, 469).

Baber passed quickly through the various grades of the service. He was promoted to third-class assistant on 18 November 1869, second-class assistant on 24 August 1871, and was acting vice-consul at Kiukiang (Jiujiang) from 1 September 1871 to 9 May 1872. He was acting vice-consul at Taipei (Tabei) in Taiwan from 6 June 1872 until 30 September 1873, and was appointed Chinese secretary of legation at Peking on 22 October 1879.

During this period, Baber made three very interesting journeys in the interior of China. The first of these was in 1876, when he accompanied Thomas Grosvenor across Yunnan to Bhamò, on the Burmese frontier, to investigate the murder of Augustus Raymond Margary. He prepared a map and narrative of the expedition, which formed the substance of the official blue book issued in 1877. He then journeyed to the Szechwan (Sichuan) highlands in 1877, during which he visited and studied the language of the Lolos tribe. A detailed account of this journey, with descriptions of Chinese customs and attitudes, was printed in 1886 under the title *Travels and Researches in Western China*. In 1878 he journeyed from Chungking (Chongqing) northward by a new route through mountain country, occupied by the Xifan tribes, to the great Lhasa Road, and wrote a monograph entitled *The Chinese Tea-Trade with Thibet* (1886). On 28 May 1883 he was presented with a Royal Geographical Society patron's medal.

From 23 October 1885 to 24 November 1886, Baber was acting consul-general in Korea. Soon afterwards he received the appointment of political resident at Bhamò on the upper Irawadi, where he died unmarried on 16 June 1890, at the age of forty-seven.

THOMAS SECCOMBE, *rev.* JANETTE RYAN

Sources *FO List* (1881) • *Proceedings* [Royal Geographical Society], 22 (1877–8), 326–7 • Venn, *Alum. Cant.* • *The Athenaeum* (28 June 1890), 831

Baber, Henry Hervey (*bap.* **1775**, *d.* **1869**), librarian, was baptized at Slingsby, Yorkshire, on 22 August 1775, the son of Thomas Baber, barrister, and grandson of Thomas Draper Baber, of Sunninghill, Berkshire. He entered St Paul's School, London, in 1786, and became a Bible clerk at All Souls, Oxford, in 1795, graduating BA in 1799 and proceeding MA in 1805. He was a sub-librarian of the Bodleian Library, curate of Ibstock, Leicestershire, in 1801, and vice-principal of St Mary's Hall, Oxford, in 1805 (and curate of St Mary the Virgin). In 1807 he was appointed assistant librarian of the department of printed books of the British Museum. In 1809 he married Ann (1785–1861), daughter of Harry Smith, a partner in Child's Bank; they had two sons and four daughters.

In 1812 Baber became under-librarian (keeper) of printed books. Between 1807 and 1819 he and Henry Ellis, his predecessor as keeper, produced a revised catalogue in seven volumes of the museum's printed books. With Charles Dietrich Eberhard König (keeper of natural history), Baber travelled to Munich in 1815 to select material to be purchased from the collections of Baron von Moll. He supervised the move of George III's library to the new museum building designed by Robert Smirke, planned a new edition of the catalogue of the department of printed books in the 1830s, and spoke for his department before the 1836 select committee of the House of Commons which investigated the museum.

Between 1816 and 1828 Baber published a three-volume edition of the Old Testament part of the Codex Alexandrinus (*Vetus Testamentum Graecum e codice MS. Alexandrino*), at a cost to the Treasury of £9000. In 1827 he was rewarded by the crown with the rectory of Stretham, Cambridgeshire (worth £900 per annum). When in 1837 the trustees of the museum decided that their staff should hold no other remunerative posts, Baber resigned. He spent the last thirty-two years of his life as rector of Stretham and died there at the rectory, 2 Front Street, on 28 March 1869. He was buried in Stretham churchyard on 3 April. P. R. HARRIS

Sources *The Times* (10 April 1869) • 'Select committee on … the British Museum', *Parl. papers* (1836), vol. 10, no. 440 • R. Cowtan, *Memories of the British Museum* (1872) • R. B. Gardiner, ed., *The admission registers of St Paul's School, from 1748 to 1876* (1884) • parish register (baptisms), Slingsby, Yorkshire, 22 Aug 1775 • parish register, Stretham, Cambridgeshire, Cambs. AS, 1809 [marriage] • parish register, Stretham, Cambridgeshire, Cambs. AS, 3 April 1869 [burial] • Foster, *Alum. Oxon.* • *CGPLA Eng. & Wales* (1869)

Archives BM • LPL, collations of his edition of *Codex Alexandrinus* | BL, letters to Sir Henry Ellis, Add. MS 6518

Likenesses portrait, *c*.1830, NPG • H. Corbould, lithograph, 1836, BM, department of prints and drawings • photograph (in old age), BM, department of prints and drawings

Wealth at death under £12,000: probate, 27 April 1869, *CGPLA Eng. & Wales*

Baber, Sir John (**1625–1704**), physician, the son of John Baber (1592–1646), recorder of Wells, Somerset, and Elizabeth, daughter of William Walrond of Isle Brewers, Somerset, was born in Wells on 18 April 1625. He was educated at Westminster School, and in 1642 was elected a student of Christ Church, Oxford. He was ejected from his studentship by the parliamentary visitors, but graduated bachelor of medicine on 3 December 1646, being admitted by virtue of the letters of Colonel John Lambert, governor of the garrison for Oxford. Travelling to the continent, Baber studied medicine at Leiden, and on 10 November 1648 took the degree of MD at Angers. On his return to England he was made DM at Oxford on 18 July 1650.

Baber was a candidate of the College of Physicians, London, on 4 July 1651, and became a fellow on 17 August 1657. He established a practice in London, where he lived in King Street, Covent Garden. During the protectorate he was involved in the affair of Don Pantalean Sa, the brother of the Portuguese ambassador, who was executed for his part in the murder of a man in 1653. Baber, who had harboured Sa after the murder, was pardoned by Cromwell on 9 August 1654 (*Writings and Speeches*, 3.397). Baber was a JP and involved in parish government.

After the Restoration, on the recommendation of a near neighbour, Thomas Manton, rector of St Paul's, Covent Garden, who, with other Presbyterian divines, had taken a prominent part in the return of Charles II, Baber was made physician to the king, and was knighted on 19 March 1661. In the same year his support for a local dissenting priest led him to be attacked as a 'Spye to all sides, a *Plague* to all his Neighbours, and a *Pestilence* to the whole Town' (Donne). Baber frequently acted as a messenger for Charles and Lord Arlington in negotiations in 1668 on comprehension and toleration with Manton and Richard Baxter. North, who describes him as 'well known for a Busy Body in such tricking affairs', states that he was 'in possession of the protectorship at court of dissenting preachers' (North, 362). In September 1669 Baber informed Manton of the king's intention to do his utmost to 'get them accepted within the establishment' (Harris, 7); but it would appear that Charles made use of him to inspire a false trust in his intentions. Baber was banished from court in 1681, along with other dissenters (Miller, 349–50).

Baber was three times married, first to Elizabeth (*d.* 1658), daughter of Sir John Richards of Yaverland, Isle of Wight; second to Anne, Viscountess Bayning (*d.* 1678), widow of Henry Murray, a groom of the chamber of Charles I, and daughter of Paul, Viscount Bayning, by licence (1 August 1674); third, on 15 February 1681, to Bridget (*d.* 1696), widow of Charles Needham, fourth Viscount Kilmorey, and of Sir John Shaw, and daughter of William Drury of Besthorpe, Norfolk. He had three sons, Francis, William, and John, from his first marriage, but no children from the other two marriages. Baber died in 1704 and was buried at St Paul's, Covent Garden, on 3 April of that year. Robert Wild's *The Grateful Nonconformist* (1665) was addressed to Baber.

T. F. HENDERSON, *rev.* PATRICK WALLIS

Sources *Old Westminsters*, vols. 1–2 • Foster, *Alum. Oxon.* • Munk, *Roll* • R. W. Innes Smith, *English-speaking students of medicine at the University of Leyden* (1932) • *Le Neve's Pedigrees of the knights*, ed. G. W. Marshall, Harleian Society, 8 (1873), 129–30 • J. Miller, *Charles II* (1991), 349–50 • *The writings and speeches of Oliver Cromwell*, ed. W. C.

Abbott and C. D. Crane, 3 (1945) • R. North, *Examen, or, An enquiry into the credit and veracity of a pretended complete history* (1740) • *Reliquiae Baxterianae, or, Mr Richard Baxter's narrative of the most memorable passages of his life and times*, ed. M. Sylvester, 1 vol. in 3 pts (1696) • J. Donne, *To the right honorable, the lord chancellor, the humble petition of Covent Garden* (1661) • W. Harris, *Some memoirs of the life and character of Thomas Manton* (1725) • *N&Q*, 12th ser., 12 (1923), 11, 452, 516

Babington, Anthony (1561–1586), conspirator, was born in October 1561 at Dethick, Derbyshire, the third child and eldest son of Henry Babington of Dethick and his second wife, Mary, daughter of George, Lord Darcy, and granddaughter of Thomas, Lord Darcy, who was beheaded for his role in the Pilgrimage of Grace. The family had been established in Derbyshire since the fifteenth century and had considerable property there and in adjoining counties. Henry Babington, who was said to be 'inclined to papistrie' (*DNB*), died in 1571, leaving Anthony as his heir under the guardianship of his mother, her second husband, Henry Foljambe, and Philip Draycot of Paynsley, Staffordshire, his future father-in-law. They were all probably inclined towards Catholicism. About 1579 Babington married Draycot's daughter Margery, and he appears to have spent some time at Lincoln's Inn the following year.

Babington won his place in history by his leadership of a Catholic conspiracy in 1586 to assassinate Queen Elizabeth and free Mary Stewart from imprisonment. This would, the conspirators hoped, be followed by an invasion by the forces of Philip II and the Catholic league in France, leading to the restoration of the Catholic religion. It was the first Catholic plot in which the murder of the queen was an integral part from the beginning. Babington's connection with Mary had begun about 1579 when he had served as a page in the household of the earl of Shrewsbury at Sheffield, where the earl had charge of the Scottish queen. In 1580 he had gone to Paris, where he met Thomas Morgan, one of the leaders of the Catholic secular clergy, and James Beaton, archbishop of Glasgow, Mary's ambassador to France. The suggestion put forward in older works, including the *Dictionary of National Biography*, that Babington joined a secret society of young men for the protection of Jesuit missionaries is not true: there was no such society. A few years later, probably in 1583–4 when he was back in England, he did carry some letters to Mary from Morgan but then, according to his own confession, dropped out of the business. This gave him, however, a contact with Mary which later proved fatal to them both.

The plotters In or about May 1586 Babington was visited by one of the key figures in the conspiracy, the Catholic priest John *Ballard (*d.* 1586), who had been in England since 1581. Ballard made a brief trip to Rome in 1584 in the company of Antony Tyrell, who was hatching his own plot against Elizabeth. Not long before visiting Babington, Ballard had been in touch with the Spanish ambassador in Paris, Bernardino de Mendoza, and had told him of a plot being raised in England to kill the queen and overthrow the protestant religion. He now informed Babington that the leaders of the Catholic league in France, the dukes of Guise and Mayenne, wished to take revenge upon Queen Elizabeth and had been appointed by the pope to lead an invasion force into England. Babington was at first sceptical: he objected that nothing could be done while Elizabeth was alive, that there was little support in England for an invasion, and that the French Catholic princes were unlikely to come.

To the first point Ballard replied that Elizabeth would be taken care of by another conspirator, **John Savage** (*d.* 1586). This man had served with Parma's army in the Netherlands. Returning home via Rheims, he had met Ballard and William Gifford, a leading secular priest, who entangled him in a plot to murder the queen. He was then brought into touch with Babington, who had by then acquired a small group of fellow plotters, all of them, according to the memoirs of the Jesuit William Weston, 'young men of his own rank, zealous and adventurous catholics, bold in danger, earnest for the protection of the catholic faith, or for any enterprise intended to promote the catholic cause' (Pollen, cvi). All were known to the government.

Thomas *Salisbury, or Salesbury (1561x4–1586), came from the important landed family of Salisbury of Lleweni, Denbighshire. His father had died when he was very young and he was brought up with his grandfather at Lleweni. On his grandfather's death in 1578 Thomas became the head of the family and ward of the earl of Leicester. He matriculated from Trinity College, Oxford, in 1580, where he seems to have moved in Catholic circles. He and Babington were said to have been 'bedfellows for a quarter of a year or more' (*CSP dom., 1581–90*, 346). **Edward Abington** (*c.*1553–1586) was the eldest son of John Abington, or Habington, of Hindlip, Worcestershire, and Catherine, daughter of John Wykes. John Abington was under-treasurer or cofferer to Queen Elizabeth. Edward was educated at Exeter College, Oxford, and took his BA in 1574. **Chidiock Tichborne** (*c.*1558–1586) was born in Southampton, the son of Peter Tichborne and his wife, Elizabeth, daughter of Henry Middleton. Like his father he was a known Catholic and was interrogated in 1583 about some 'popish relics' that he had brought back from abroad, where he had gone without leave; and in June 1586 accusations about 'popish practices' were laid against his family. **Charles Tilney** (1561–1586) was born on 23 September 1561, the son of Philip Tilney of Shelley Hall, Suffolk, and his wife, Anne, daughter of Francis Framlington of Crowshall, Debenham, Suffolk. He was cousin to Edmund *Tilney, master of the revels. Charles became a gentleman pensioner at court.

Two others, about whom little is known, were among this group of conspirators which met in London on 7 June 1586. Edward Windsor was the younger brother of Lord Windsor. He soon disappeared from the meetings of the plotters and was not present at the final trial. Robert Barnewell probably belonged to the prominent Irish pale family of that name. He used to attend court as a servant to the earl of Kildare and was apparently known by sight to Queen Elizabeth. One of Walsingham's agents left a brief physical description of him as tall, 'comely', white-faced, flaxen bearded, freckled, and disfigured with smallpox.

Five others joined the plot a little later. Edward Jones of Plas Cadwgan, Denbighshire, was the son of another Edward, tailor to Queen Mary, master of the wardrobe to Queen Elizabeth, and sheriff of Denbighshire in 1576. The father was a protégé of the earl of Leicester, to whom he recommended his son. Unhappily, the son turned to Catholicism under the influence of Thomas Salisbury, who involved him in the plot. They were deputed to set off a rising in north Wales. Henry Donne was a Londoner and a clerk of the first fruits office; he was probably an older relative of John Donne, the poet. Robert Gage came from Surrey, John Travers and John Charnock were both from Lancashire families; otherwise nothing is known of them. Sir Thomas Gerard, suspected by the government of involvement, was probably the Thomas Gerard of Bryn, Lancashire, MP for Lancashire in 1563. He was a known Catholic, the father of John Gerard, the Jesuit, and had been imprisoned in 1571 for plotting to free Mary Stewart. In 1586 his involvement was marginal and he escaped the main trial. He was, however, imprisoned in the Tower once again. Except for Savage, all those plotters about whom anything is known had links to the royal court. This was not a provincial conspiracy, but rather one hatched in London, mainly by young Catholic courtiers.

One man with a different background was deeply involved in the conspiracy. Gilbert *Gifford (1560–1590) was thought by Ballard, Babington, and the others to be one of themselves, but was in fact in the pay of the government. The son of a recusant family seated at Chillington, Staffordshire, Gifford had entered Douai College, by then at Rheims, in 1577 and transferred to the English College at Rome two years later. Here he seems to have made contact with one of Walsingham's agents. Whether for this or for some other reason, he was expelled from the English College. After a brief stay at Rheims, he went to Paris. By then he was probably in Walsingham's service. In December 1585 he returned to England with a letter of recommendation to Mary from her agent in Paris, Thomas Morgan. He was arrested on landing and taken to Walsingham, who employed him in carrying letters to and from Mary, then closely guarded by Sir Amias Paulet (or Poulet) at Chartley, without her knowing that all her correspondence was tampered with by the government. Walsingham's agents suborned a brewer from Burton upon Trent, known to Paulet and others as 'the honest man', who brought a regular supply of beer to Mary's household. The brewer placed letters to and from Mary in a small leather package inside the bunghole of the barrels as he delivered and collected them in the course of his business. Incoming and outgoing letters were received by Gifford and passed to Walsingham's cryptographer, Thomas Phelippes, for decoding. The originals were then resealed and sent to their intended recipients, while copies went to Walsingham. The government was thus kept fully informed of the entire progress of the plot, usually before the conspirators themselves.

The making of the plot Babington seems to have become the leader of the conspirators, perhaps *faute de mieux*. Weston described him as 'attractive in face and form, quick of intelligence, agreeable and facetious; he had a turn for literature unusual in men of the world' (Pollen, cvi). Perhaps he was not really a man of the world: he was certainly no leader. After their meeting on 7 June 1586 the conspirators settled down to discuss their position. Babington told them that:

> we seemed to stand in a dilemma ... On the one side lest by a massacre ... the magistrates here would take awaye our lives ... and on the other side lest the straunger shoulde invade and sacke our countrye, and bring it into servitude to foreigners. (ibid., 54)

He concluded that it would be best for them all to leave the realm and asked Robert Poley, whom he thought to be an accomplice but was actually in Walsingham's service, to get him a passport. Through Poley, Babington secured three interviews with Walsingham, who kept him waiting for his passport and tried, unsuccessfully, to persuade him to give up his enterprise and to reveal the names of his associates. Babington also had conversations with Poley in which he expressed his desire for the contemplative life. By the end of June a great deal of talking had been done—'thus we discoursed', recalled Babington in his confession (ibid., 55)—but active steps to raise support and set down plans were dragging. Extraordinarily, Babington spent some of the time arranging for the conspirators to have their portraits drawn. These have not survived, though they were at some stage shown to the queen, so that she might recognize them if any of the conspirators appeared at court.

Early in July Babington returned to London from the country and once more met Ballard, who urged action upon him. The other conspirators 'still cryed out of my delaye', he recalled in his confession (Pollen, 60); but now he acted. On 6 July he wrote a coded letter to Mary pledging his devotion to her cause. He had earlier, he said, despaired of the situation of the Catholics in England and had resolved to leave the country and live in solitude. But, he wrote, 'one Ballard, a man of vertue and learning', had come to him and told him of the preparations being made overseas by Christian princes to deliver England from its miserable state. He vowed 'either to prevaile in the churches behalf and your majesties, or fortunately to die for that honorable cause' (Pollen, 20). He himself with ten gentlemen and one hundred followers would deliver Mary from imprisonment. 'For the dispatch of the usurper [Elizabeth]' there were six gentlemen, 'all my private friends', who will undertake 'that tragical execution' (Pollen, 22). It was necessary to assure them that they or their posterity would be rewarded.

On 17 July Mary fatally replied. She expressed gratitude for Babington's letter and asked him to write frequently, commending his desire to frustrate the designs of 'our enemies'. She stressed that if remedy were not provided soon it would be too late. She followed this general exhortation with a practical and sensible agenda for preparing rebellion. They must assess what forces they could raise;

what towns and ports could be assured; what foreign forces they required and the means of paying them; what place of assembly should be appointed; what provision should be made of horses and armour. They must decide 'by what means do the six gentlemen deliberate to proceed' and the manner of 'my getting forth out of this hold'. They should give out to potential followers that these preparations were defensive, 'against the puritans of this realme' and against an attempt by Leicester's forces in the Netherlands to return and 'usurp the crown'. These statements would, she said, serve as a pretext for assembly 'without touching the crown'. Then 'set the six gentlemen to work', ensuring that as soon as they have accomplished their design—the murder of Elizabeth—Mary herself should be rescued. All must be ready before they acted. She proposed three possible means of rescue and concluded with the injunction: 'fail not to burn this present quickly'. She did not, of course, know that her letter would be read by Walsingham before Babington even received it. There was a postscript: 'I will be glad to know the names and qualities of the six gentlemen, which are to accomplish the designment [the murder of the queen]' (Pollen, 38–46). This was almost certainly added by Walsingham's agent Phelippes, with the object of luring Babington into giving away the names of the principal plotters. The stratagem failed, but Walsingham already had enough evidence on which to condemn Mary.

Arrest and trial On 2 August 1586, three days after Babington received Mary's letter, Phelippes asked Walsingham 'whether Babington is to be apprehended, or otherwise played with' (Pollen, cl). Walsingham evidently opted to give him a little more rope, in the hope of uncovering more details of the plot. He decided, however, to deal at once with Ballard, who was arrested two days later. Babington claimed in his confession that only then did he decide to put into effect the plan for assassinating the queen. He told Savage to go at once to court and kill the queen. Savage replied: 'I cannot go tomorrow for my apparel is not ready, and in this apparel shall I never come near the Queen' (Hargrave, 1.129). Babington gave him his ring and money for clothes and told him to act. Babington himself then went out to dinner with one of Walsingham's undercover agents, a man called Scudamore. Realizing in the course of the meal that Scudamore had received an order for his arrest, Babington went to the bar to pay the bill and fled, for once showing power of decision. He hid with some companions in St John's Wood, his face smeared with green walnut shells, and was eventually caught at the house of the Bellamy family in Harrow. The government of the city put on a show of public loyalty, witnessing 'her public joy by ringing of bells, making of bonfires, and singing of psalms' (Camden, 303).

All the conspirators were rigorously interrogated and each of them confessed fully, seemingly without the pains of torture, except perhaps in the case of Ballard. By the middle of September the crown had all the evidence it needed from their confessions. Seven defendants were arraigned before the judges on 13 and 14 September. Savage was dealt with first, since he had become involved separately from the others. He pleaded guilty to conspiracy, not guilty to assenting to kill the queen. However, since his confession stated clearly that he had sworn an oath to assassinate her, this plea could hardly be sustained and he changed it to guilty. Ballard, Babington, Barnewell, Donne, Salisbury, and Tichborne then all pleaded guilty to conspiring to free Mary and alter religion, not guilty to planning to kill the queen, Babington laying 'all the blame upon Ballard, for bringing him to his destruction' (Hargrave, 1.131). Told that they could not plead in different ways to separate charges, all except Tichborne changed their pleas to guilty. Tichborne claimed that he had intended to desert the conspirators and ride down to Hampshire, but had been prevented by lameness. He, too, then changed his plea. Counsel for the queen set out the evidence, in which the conspirators implicated one another in their confessions, and all were condemned to die traitors' deaths.

On 15 September the remaining seven were arraigned: Abington and Tilney of the original conspirators, and Jerome Bellamy, Charnock, Jones, Gage, and Travers of those who became involved later. All pleaded not guilty, Abington invoking the rule demanding two prosecution witnesses in treason trials. Their pleas were to no effect and all were predictably found guilty. Given the opportunity to speak for themselves, Bellamy, charged with harbouring Babington in Harrow, 'spoke very little for himself, only he seemed to be a very clownish, blunt, wilful and obstinate papist'; Abington said it was all the fault of Babington, 'that brainless youth'; Tilney and Jones begged that their debts be paid, Jones also asking that 'some consideration may be had of my posterity' (Hargrave, 1.140).

Execution Gallows were set up a week later near St Giles-in-the-Fields, where the plots had been laid, and the first seven conspirators, led by Ballard and Babington, were executed on 20 September 1586, 'not without some note of cruelty', according to Camden: that is to say, they were hanged only for a short time, cut down while they were still alive, and then castrated and disembowelled. Their statements on the gallows varied in import and effect. Babington cried '"*Parce mihi, domine Jesus*", that is "Spare me Lord Jesus"'. Tichborne made a long speech: 'I am a bad orator and my text is worse', he began. He blamed Babington, with whom he had lived in 'flourishing estate', for drawing him in. He acknowledged his fault 'and moved great pity among the multitude towards him, as in like manner did Tilney, a man of a modest spirit and goodly personage'. By contrast, 'Abington, being a man of a turbulent spirit, cast forth threats and terrors of blood to be spilt ere long in England' (Camden, 308).

The other seven were brought to the scaffold the next day and suffered the same death, 'but, more favourably, by the Queens commandment, who detested the former cruelty' (Camden, 308). They hung until they were dead and only then suffered the barbarity of castration and disembowelling. Salisbury, very penitently, warned Catholics not to attempt to restore religion by force of arms.

Jones condemned Babington's 'proud and headstrong mind'. Gage extolled the queen's bounty to his father and detested his own 'perfidious ingratitude'. The last to suffer was Jerome Bellamy, caught up in the business at the very end for hiding Babington and the others at his family's house in Harrow; his brother had strangled himself in prison (ibid., 309).

Aftermath The penalties for treason did not end with this brutality, for the lands and goods of convicted men were forfeit to the crown. In practice this severity was sometimes tempered. While the lands of Edward Jones seem all to have been forfeit, the entailed estates of his friend Thomas Salisbury passed to his brother John so that the Lleweni dynasty continued. Similarly, the entailed Babington lands passed successively to Anthony's brothers Francis and George, while other of his lands were forfeited and granted by the queen to Sir Walter Ralegh.

Reaction to the plot was predictably hostile. Two tracts were published in the following year: George Whetstone's *The Censure of a Loyal Subject* (1587) is a brief account in dialogue form of the executions, and W. Kempe's *A Dutiful Invective Against the Moste Haynous Treasons of Ballard and Babington* (1587) is a piece of clumsy doggerel covering the same unhappy ground. A more serious account of the matter was Bishop George Carleton's *A Thankfull Remembrance of God's Mercy* (4th edn, 1630), a description of various plots against monarchy and church, designed to demonstrate that both were protected by God's special mercy. The Roman Catholic church seems to have kept relative silence about the plotters, none of whom has ever been included in its lists of martyrs for the faith.

The significance of the Babington plot lay not in the capture and punishment of fourteen inept and unfortunate conspirators, but in the death of Mary Stewart, whose fate was bound up with theirs. She was the target at whom Walsingham had aimed all along. Throughout the entire course of the plot he had controlled events, knowing better than the conspirators what was going on. Did he create the plot as well as control it? The surviving evidence leaves much uncertain. It is hard to say when the plot originated and who began it. Gilbert Gifford may have been its begetter, but it is not certain that he was in Walsingham's pay at that point. Certainly Ballard, who recruited Babington, was not. However, without the provision of a system by which mail could be got to and from Mary, the plot would not have gone forward as it did; and that system was of Walsingham's devising. He could have stopped the plot well before he actually did, but he let it run on until he could be sure that he had the evidence against Mary. For how much of that evidence was he responsible? Probably for the forged postscript to Mary's fatal letter, just possibly for other sentences in it. But whatever the truth of that, Mary was undoubtedly aware of the plot and condoned it. One other point should be noted about these events: for all the efforts made by Ballard to raise support, the leading Catholics in England were loyal to the monarch and rebuffed his overtures. The real backing for the conspiracy lay abroad, with Mendoza in Paris and Philip II in the Escorial.

The poem called *Tichborne's Elegy* was written by Chidiock Tichborne in the Tower before his execution. Its final stanza may serve as an epitaph for all the conspirators:

I sought my death and found it in my womb,
I looked for life and saw it was a shade;
I trod the earth and knew it was my tomb,
And now I die, and now I was but made.
My glass is full, and now my glass is run,
And now I live, and now my life is done.

Penry Williams

Sources J. H. Pollen, *Mary queen of Scots and the Babington plot*, Scottish History Society, 3rd ser., 3 (1922) • C. Read, ed., *The Bardon papers: documents relating to the imprisonment and trial of Mary, queen of Scots*, CS, 3rd ser., 17 (1909) • C. Read, *Mr Secretary Walsingham and the policy of Queen Elizabeth*, 3 vols. (1925) • A. G. Smith, *The Babington plot* (1936) • W. Camden, *Annales, or, The historie of the most renowned and victorious Princesse Elizabeth*, trans. R. N. [R. Norton], 3rd edn (1635) • *CSP Scot.*, 1585–8 • *The letter-books of Sir Amias Poulet*, ed. J. Morris (1874) • *CSP for.*, 1586–8 • *CSP Spain*, 1580–86 • J. B. A. T. Teulet, ed., *Papiers d'état, pièces et documents inédits ou peu connus relatifs à l'histoire de l'Écosse au XVIème siècle*, 3 vols., Bannatyne Club, 107 (Paris, 1852–60), vol. 3 • G. Carleton, *A thankfull remembrance of God's mercy*, 4th edn (1630) • F. Hargrave, ed., *A complete collection of state-trials*, 4th edn, 11 vols. (1776–81) • A. Haynes, *Invisible power: the Elizabethan secret services* (1992) • A. Plowden, *The Elizabethan secret service* (1991) • G. Whetstone, *The censure of a loyal subject* (1587) • W. Kempe, *A dutiful invective against the moste haynous treasons of Ballard and Babington* (1587) • E. Jones, ed., *The new Oxford book of sixteenth-century verse* (1991) • *DNB*

Archives Queen's College, Oxford, petition to Queen Elizabeth • Yale U., Beinecke L., papers

Likenesses group portrait, engraving, 17th cent., repro. in Carleton, *Thankfull remembrance of God's mercy*

Babington, Benjamin Guy (1794–1866), physician and orientalist, the fourth son of the physician and mineralogist William *Babington (1756–1833) and his wife, Martha Elizabeth Babington, was born on 5 March 1794 in Guy's Hospital when his father was resident apothecary there. Educated at Charterhouse School from 1803 to 1807, he entered the navy as a midshipman and served at Walcheren and Copenhagen, but left the service early, and, having obtained a nomination for the Indian Civil Service, studied at the East India College, Haileybury; he was appointed to the Madras presidency in 1812. Babington possessed an aptitude for languages and soon became distinguished as an oriental scholar. He translated into English *A grammar of the high dialect of the Tamil language, termed Shen-Tamil: to which is added an introduction to Tamil poetry by the Reverend Father C. J. Beschi. Translated from the original Latin* (1822), and published other translations, including *The Vedàla Cadai, being the Tamul Version of a Collection of Ancient Tales in Sanscrit* (1831). His marriage in 1816 to Anna Maria, daughter of Benjamin Fayle, brought them three sons before her early death.

Babington's health suffered in India, and he returned to England in 1819 to study medicine at Guy's Hospital and Cambridge. After matriculating at Pembroke College, Cambridge, in 1820, at the age of twenty-five, and already a widower with a family, he became MB in 1825, ML in 1827, and MD in 1830. In 1831 he was elected fellow of the Royal College of Physicians, where he was censor and

Croonian lecturer in 1841. He became assistant physician to Guy's Hospital in 1837, and full physician in 1840. Babington was elected a fellow of the Royal Society in 1828 and in 1861 president of the Royal Medical and Chirurgical Society. He was the founder, and for some years the president, of the Epidemiological Society, and was appointed by the crown a member of the medical council of the General Board of Health. He was also physician to the Deaf and Dumb Hospital, and to other charities.

Babington was a man of remarkable intellectual power; proficient in several sciences, he was exact and thorough in all of them. In a lecture to the Hunterian Society on 18 March 1829 Babington demonstrated an ingenious instrument intended to allow the physician to examine the parts of the throat which were normally invisible. The instrument, which he proposed to call the glottiscope, consisted of an oblong piece of mirror fastened to a long piece of silver wire. With the patient's tongue held down by a spatula and the mirror placed against the palate, the epiglottis and upper part of the larynx became visible in the mirror. Babington's device, now known as the laryngoscope, was made public twenty-six years earlier than that of Manuel García, a Spanish singing teacher long credited with its invention.

Soon after his appointment at Guy's Hospital Babington studied animal chemistry, and assisted Astley Cooper, Richard Bright, and other colleagues in analysing morbid products. He also wrote in the *Medico-Chirurgical Transactions* two papers on the blood, in one of which he described the fat constantly present in the serum; in another he employed for the first time the term 'liquor sanguinis' to denote the fluid portion of the blood. He wrote some more strictly medical papers in *Guy's Hospital Reports*. He translated from the German J. F. C. Hecker's *Epidemics of the Middle Ages* (1844), and edited a translation of Ernst von Feuchtersleben's *Principles of Medical Psychology* for the Sydenham Society (1847).

Babington was highly regarded by his colleagues, but he hardly enjoyed the public reputation or gained the success which might have been expected. This was partly due to his retiring and unambitious character and partly, perhaps, to his having entered medicine somewhat late in life.

Babington resigned his appointments at Guy's Hospital in 1855, and died at his home, 31 George Street, Hanover Square, London, on 8 April 1866.

J. F. Payne, *rev.* Michael Bevan

Sources *Proceedings of the Royal Medical and Chirurgical Society*, 5 (1864–7), 249–50 · *The Lancet* (21 April 1866) · Venn, *Alum. Cant.* · *London and Provincial Medical Directory* (1848–69) · Munk, *Roll* · A. Evans, 'Let's not forget B. G. Babington', *The Lancet*, 356 (2000), 1870 · D. Harrison, 'Benjamin Guy Babington and his mirror', *Journal of Laryngology and Otology*, 112 (March 1998), 235–42

Likenesses C. A. Rivers, wax statuette, 1867 (after death mask), RCP Lond.

Wealth at death under £6000: probate, 29 June 1866, *CGPLA Eng. & Wales*

Babington, Brute (*d.* 1611), Church of Ireland bishop of Derry, came from Cheshire. He entered Christ's College, Cambridge, on 17 June 1572, graduated BA in 1576 (incorporating at Oxford on 15 July 1578), and MA in 1579 (as a member of St John's College). He was a fellow of Christ's in 1577–84, graduated BTh in 1586, and is later termed DTh. He was rector of Thurcaston, Leicestershire, from 1583 to 1610, prebendary of Bishopshill (Lichfield) from 1592 to 1601, and divinity lecturer at Lichfield. He also held the vicarage of Tettenhall (Staffordshire) in 1602, and the rectory of Cossington (Leicestershire) in 1605. Disappointed in his efforts to secure the deanery of Lichfield in 1603, he also lost his lectureship. In 1610 he turned to Ireland for preferment. On 11 August the king nominated him to the see of Derry, and he was appointed on 8 November 1610, being consecrated in Drogheda by Archbishop Henry Ussher.

Derry was a large see, strategically placed in the plantation of Ulster, which was then beginning to transform the province from a Gaelic stronghold into a major centre of English and Scottish settlement. According to his own account Babington's missionary efforts were successful. The leading Catholic priests were initially hostile, but by 'dealing with them lovingly and kindly', he persuaded well over half to submit and join the established church. By sitting in person in the new ecclesiastical courts and punishing offenders 'cum moderamine' ('with moderation') he confidently claimed 'I shall in short time bring this rude and uncivilized people to some good conformity' (*CSP Ire.*, *1611–14*, 3). Whether this optimism would have led to long-term success may be doubted—certainly other English bishops elsewhere in the plantation failed to win over large sections of the native clergy, though it could be argued that their methods were less sensitive and more coercive. The experiment was, in any case, cut short by his sudden demise in Derry on 10 September 1611 'being well at seven o'clock evening and dead at eight' (ibid., 103). As often happened in the case of unexplained sudden protestant deaths, later Catholic sources attributed his demise to providential judgment—in this case on his vain efforts to burn an image of the Virgin Mary in Coleraine Abbey.

Alan Ford

Sources Cooper, *Ath. Cantab.*, 3.44 · J. Peile, *Biographical register of Christ's College, 1505–1905, and of the earlier foundation, God's House, 1448–1505*, ed. [J. A. Venn], 1 (1910), 1.121 · H. Cotton, *Fasti ecclesiae Hibernicae*, 3 (1849), 316; 4 (1850), 254 · Venn, *Alum. Cant.* · Foster, *Alum. Oxon.* · *Calendar of the Irish patent rolls of James I* (before 1830); facs. edn as *Irish patent rolls of James I* (1966), 182–3 · *CSP Ire.*, *1611–14* · J. O'Heyne, *The Irish Dominicans of the seventeenth century* (1902), appx, p.10 · E. B. Fryde and others, eds., *Handbook of British chronology*, 3rd edn, Royal Historical Society Guides and Handbooks, 2 (1986)

Babington, (Charles) Cardale (1808–1895), botanist and archaeologist, was born on 23 November 1808, at Ludlow, Shropshire, the son of Joseph Babington (1768–1826), at that time a physician, and Catherine, daughter of John Whitter of Bradninch, Devon. The historian Lord Macaulay was his first cousin. His father having taken holy orders, Babington's early years were punctuated by frequent family moves, initially round the midlands and later in Wessex, moves reflected in frequent changes of school. A short, probably unhappy spell as a boarder at

Charterhouse School was succeeded by four years as a day boy at a school in Bath, whose good teaching, he later held, was responsible for equipping him for his university career. His father passed on to him his own fondness for field botany and fed that by introducing him to the chief works of identification then in vogue, and he spent much of his time in his teenage and undergraduate years exploring the local countryside for plants, an activity which was to culminate in a slender *Flora Bathoniensis*, written only after he had graduated and published later still, in 1834. At that period a parallel keenness for entomology had meanwhile developed into a passion for collecting and studying Coleoptera. These were to be the subject of more than half of his earliest published papers and so dominated his leisure hours at university as to earn him the nickname Beetles. After building up a collection of some 4000 specimens, however, he gradually lost that interest and after 1840 botany increasingly monopolized his scientific attention.

The year before Babington went up to Cambridge in 1826 John Stevens Henslow had been appointed professor of botany, a subject newly necessary for medical students, and his Easter term lectures, field excursions, and evening parties in his rooms were quickly winning a large and enthusiastic following among naturalists in the university. Henslow's college, moreover, was St John's, where Babington now followed his father and three of his father's brothers. He and Henslow soon became friends, and in time he became Henslow's *de facto* assistant and eventually deputy during the latter's absences after 1839 for much of each year tending his Suffolk parish. Although Babington could look forward to no university appointment in Cambridge until the chair of botany fell vacant, he had no need to train for a profession, his father having meanwhile died and left him financially independent. After graduating BA in 1830 and proceeding MA in 1833, he kept on his rooms in college and settled into a comfortable bachelor existence there. He was not elected a fellow until 1874 and his freedom from official duties enabled him to give all his time and energy to his personal research, such teaching as he did being purely informal and confined to sharpening the taxonomic acumen of undergraduates whose interest in botany was non-vocational. Many of those who came under his influence later produced county floras or otherwise rose to prominence as amateurs. That influence was exercised especially through the Ray Club, of which Babington served as secretary for fifty-five years and whose weekly meetings filled the role previously played by Henslow's parties. His particular protégés he sometimes took with him on the many tours of exploration he now embarked upon to almost every part of the British Isles. These early took in the Channel Islands, of which his impressively wide-ranging two seasons' fieldwork resulted in his second local flora, *Primitiae florae Sarnicae* (1839).

Increasingly, though, Babington's focus was more broadly national. The study of the higher plants of the British Isles had lapsed into shameful insularity, partly through the long isolation from the continent resulting from the Napoleonic wars, and there was a pressing need for a new, concise, scholarly handbook which brought British usage into line with that in France, Scandinavia, and especially Germany. Babington's *Manual of British Botany*, first published in 1843 after nine years in preparation, not only had all those assets but like its eighteenth-century predecessor, the Dillenian edition of Ray's *Synopsis*, was convenient for field use by being small enough for a pocket. Regularly revised in successive editions, of which eight appeared in his lifetime and two more after his death, it is credibly held to have revolutionized the situation in Britain.

By the 1840s Babington was acknowledged leader of taxonomic research on British higher plants, just as Hewett Cottrell Watson dominated research into their distribution and its causes. Pugnacious and agnostic where Babington was gentle and pious, Watson was temperamentally drawn to the radically inclined Botanical Society of London while Babington identified with its more academic counterpart in Edinburgh, each of them being engaged to overhaul their respective societies' large and chaotic herbaria (to the great benefit of their own personal collections). Babington's bond with Edinburgh was reinforced by election to its quasi-Masonic Brotherhood of the Friends of Truth and, in 1842, appointment as joint botanical editor of the *Annals and Magazine of Natural History*, then the most respected of the specialist journals in Britain and run from the Scottish capital. These moves led the ever-touchy Watson to suspect an emerging Cambridge–Edinburgh axis 'determined … to exclude all works which do not take up their species and names', as he grumbled in a letter to Sir William Hooker in May 1844 (Watson to Hooker, May 1844, RBG Kew, Hooker MSS). Dependent in his own work on checklists and on stable categories, he resented the steady rain of additions and amendments required by the finely discriminating researches of Babington in particular. There were species, there were subspecies and there were 'Bab-ies', he was once moved to quip. Nevertheless the two, while keeping their distance, respected each other and never became estranged.

Babington ventured outside the British Isles only once, to Iceland in 1846. The product was a magisterial paper in the *Journal of the Linnean Society* bringing together all information on the country's flora recorded up to that time. Usually, though, the challenges presented by British Isles plants were quite enough, and none of those teased him longer and more frustratingly than the blackberries. By no means the first to grapple with that perplexing group, Babington had the disadvantage of living in an area with minimal scope for prolonged familiarization with a wide range of the microspecies in the wild. Overdependent on dried examples, neglecting as a result the key characters offered by the floral organs, he was led to adopt much too broad an approach. Though *A Synopsis of the British Rubi* (1846) and his numerous subsequent publications, combined with his readiness to name specimens submitted (for he was always the most helpful and untiring of correspondents), made study of the group fashionable, the many years he devoted to it proved largely in vain. The path through the maze was to be discovered only after his death.

Babington's stature by mid-century was recognized by election as FRS in 1851 and president of the botany and zoology section of the British Association in 1853, 1858, and 1861. In 1860, exactly 200 years after Ray's pioneer Cambridge *Catalogus* had appeared, he filled the gap for a further century with an excellent new flora of the county. The next year, on Henslow's death, he at last succeeded to the chair of botany at Cambridge. His main achievement in that office was a new and larger building for the herbarium, for which he purchased the extensive and valuable collections of John Lindley and Gaston Genevier and donated the no less vast one formed by himself. The department's library also benefited from his personal generosity, for he regularly needed to supplement with his own funds the slender official budget. That budget, however, his younger colleagues would have much preferred spent instead on up-to-date laboratories, for by then experimental botany had come into general favour and left the professor isolated in his interests.

That Babington was almost equally devoted to antiquarian studies cannot have helped. It was said of him and his relation Churchill Babington, the university's Disney professor of archaeology, that each might fill the chair of the other, and to the publications of the Cambridge Antiquarian Society, of which he was one of the founders in 1840, he contributed over fifty papers. Through that body he also published in 1851 *Ancient Cambridgeshire*, an attempt to trace Roman and other early roads in the county, of which a much-enlarged edition was published in 1883. Another favourite was the Cambrian Archaeological Association, the committee of which he chaired for thirty years and whose president he became in 1881.

To his upbringing Babington also owed a lifelong interest in evangelical mission work, an interest that deepened after his late marriage, on 3 April 1866, to Anna Maria, daughter of John Walker of the Madras civil service. A wide range of bodies operating in that field received their strong support, while their commitment also found expression locally in the founding of a home for orphan girls in Cambridge.

Babington's last years were sad. Failing health had already compelled some shedding of activities when in 1891 an acute attack of pneumonia while in Scotland was succeeded by a rheumatic condition which confined him permanently to a wheelchair. This ended his botanical research and his visits to his beloved herbarium. A deputy professor, in the person of Francis Darwin, had to be appointed, to whom Babington voluntarily made over half his stipend, but his tenure of the chair terminated only with his death, at his home, 5 Brookside, Cambridge, on 22 July 1895. He was buried in the churchyard at Cherry Hinton, on the outskirts of Cambridge, on 26 July. His library of some 1600 volumes was bequeathed to the university, of which by the time of his death he had become the oldest resident member. His name is borne by three British plants, two of them, fittingly, blackberries, but *Babingtonia*, given to a genus of tropical members of the myrtle family by Lindley in 1842, has disappeared into synonymy. D. E. ALLEN

Sources A. M. B. [A. M. B. Babington], ed., *Memoirs, journal and botanical correspondence of Charles Cardale Babington* (1897) • J. Britten, *Journal of Botany, British and Foreign*, 33 (1895), 257–66 • S. M. Walters, *The shaping of Cambridge botany* (1981), 67–70 • D. E. Allen, *The botanists: a history of the Botanical Society of the British Isles through a hundred and fifty years*, St Paul's Bibliographies (1986), 9, 35, 183 • F. O. Bower, *Sixty years of botany in Britain (1875–1935)* (1938) • J. G. B. [J. G. Baker], *PRS*, 59 (1895–6), viii–x • private information (2004) • U. Cam., department of plant sciences, Babington MSS • *CGPLA Eng. & Wales* (1896)

Archives U. Cam., department of plant sciences, corresp. and papers • U. Cam., department of plant sciences, herbarium • U. Cam., Museum of Zoology, catalogue of insect collection | CUL, letters to Charles Darwin • CUL, letters to Sir George Stokes • NHM, letters to members of the Sowerby family • RBG Kew, letters to Sir William Hooker • Royal Literary and Scientific Institution, Bath, letters to Leonard Blomefield • Shetland Archives, Lerwick, corresp. with Thomas Edmonston

Likenesses I. Hoare, pencil sketch, 1825, repro. in A. M. B., ed., *Memoirs, journal and botanical correspondence* • Walker & Boutall, photograph, 1880–1889?, repro. in A. M. B., ed., *Memoirs, journal and botanical correspondence* • W. Vizard, oils, 1888, department of botany, Cambridge • W. Vizard, oils, 1896 (after photograph?), St John Cam. • E. Edwards, photograph, NPG; repro. in L. Reeve, ed., *Portraits of men of eminence in literature, science and art*, 3 (1865), 51 • Moull & Co., photograph, RS • photographs, RS

Wealth at death £36,731 16*s*. 4*d*.: resworn probate, Feb 1896, *CGPLA Eng. & Wales* (1895)

Babington, Churchill (1821–1889), scholar, was born at Roecliffe, Leicestershire, on 11 March 1821, the only son of Matthew Drake Babington (1788–1851), rector of Thringstone, and his wife, Hannah (*d*. 1873), daughter of Benjamin Fleetwood Churchill. He was connected with the Macaulay family, and slightly, on his mother's side, with that of the poet Charles *Churchill. Charles Cardale *Babington was a relation. He entered St John's College, Cambridge, in 1839. While he was still an undergraduate his youthful love of nature found expression in a contribution to T. R. Potter's *History and Antiquities of Charnwood Forest* (1842). He graduated BA in 1843, being the seventh in the classical tripos, and a senior optime in mathematics, and was president of the Cambridge Union in 1845. In 1846 he graduated MA, was elected a fellow of St John's College, and was ordained, having gained the Hulsean prize for an essay entitled 'Christianity in relation to the abolition of slavery'. From 1848 until 1861 he was perpetual curate of Horningsea, Cambridgeshire. In 1849 he published a defence of the English clergy and gentry of the seventeenth century against T. B. Macaulay's aspersions in the famous third chapter of his *History of England*. Gladstone, in reviewing G. O. Trevelyan's life of Macaulay in the *Quarterly Review* (1876), was strongly impressed with Babington's essays, and considered that he had convicted Macaulay at least of partiality.

In 1850 Babington was entrusted by the university with the task of editing the recently discovered fragments of *The Orations of Hyperides Against Demosthenes, and for Lycophron and for Euxenippus* from the papyri found at Thebes in Upper Egypt, and his edition was issued in two volumes

(1850 and 1853). In 1855 he brought out an edition of *The Benefits of Christ's Death*, supposed to be by the Italian reformer Aonio Paleario. In 1860 he edited for the Rolls series R. Pecock's *Repressor*, and in 1865, for the same series, the two first volumes of R. Higden's *Polychronicon*. In 1865 he was elected Disney professor of archaeology at Cambridge, and published his inaugural lecture. His contributions to the *Dictionary of Christian Antiquities* included the articles on medals, glass, gems, inscriptions, seals, rings, and tombs. He made numerous contributions to the journals of learned societies, such as the *Numismatic Chronicle*, Hooker's *Journal of Botany*, and the *Suffolk Institute Papers*.

Babington left Cambridge in 1866, relinquishing his chair and his fellowship, and accepted the rectory of Cockfield in Suffolk. In 1869 he married Matilda Whytt, daughter of Colonel John Alexander Wilson RA, but left no children. In Cockfield, Babington was able to concentrate his attention on ornithology, and the result was his very thorough monograph on *The Birds of Suffolk* (1886). During his last years he took up the study of conchology, and formed a fine collection both of British and exotic shells. He was an exemplary parish clergyman, and applied his archaeological knowledge in the restoration of Cockfield church, which took place during his incumbency and culminated in the erection of a new organ in 1887. Babington proceeded DD in 1879 and in the following year was elected an honorary fellow of St John's College, Cambridge. He died at Cockfield rectory on 12 January 1889, and was buried in the parish churchyard.

THOMAS SECCOMBE, *rev.* M. C. CURTHOYS

Sources *Bury and Norwich Post* (22 Jan 1889) • *West Suffolk Advertiser* (14 June 1890) • *Guardian* (15 Jan 1889) • Venn, *Alum. Cant.*

Wealth at death £4223 4*s*. 7*d*.: administration with will, 5 July 1889, *CGPLA Eng. & Wales*

Babington, Francis (*d*. 1569?), college head, was probably the third son of Humphry Babington of Rothley Temple in Leicestershire. He matriculated as a pensioner at Christ's College, Cambridge, in 1544, and proceeded BA in 1548–9. He became a fellow of St John's College, Cambridge, in 1551, proceeding MA in 1552. There is no evidence of his religious sympathies during the reign of Edward VI. However, he subscribed to the Roman Catholic articles of faith in 1555 prior to taking permanent leave of Cambridge for Oxford. He remained at Oxford for the rest of his academic career, taking in succession the degrees of MA (1554), BTh (1558), and DTh (1560). He was elected a proctor of the university on 18 April 1557, being already a fellow of All Souls.

Babington was ordained priest in London on 5 March 1557. He then began to accumulate church livings, being admitted first to the vicarage of Aldworth, Berkshire, on 6 November 1557, upon presentation by St John's College, Cambridge. On 27 November he received the rectory of Adstock, Buckinghamshire, then the rectory of Sherrington, Buckinghamshire. He subsequently resigned Adstock, and took in its stead that of Milton Keynes, Buckinghamshire. Upon the accession of Elizabeth I Babington professed himself to be a protestant, despite his prominence in enforcing Catholic orthodoxy at Oxford during the reign of Mary I. He also became chaplain to Lord Robert Dudley, then Elizabeth's master of horse. He preached the funeral sermon for Dudley's first wife, Amy Robsart (who was buried in St Mary's, Oxford, on 22 September 1560), an indication of the favour in which he was held. His conduct of the funeral, however, was marred by his repeated reference in the sermon to the 'lady so pitifully murdered' (Cooper, *Ath. Cantab.*, 1.557). Babington became master of Balliol College on 5 September 1559, and on 21 May 1560 was appointed vice-chancellor of the university, a post he held until 1562. With Dudley's support he was then appointed rector of Lincoln College in August 1560 (an appointment which lasted until 1563). He also held the benefice of Twyford, Buckinghamshire, in conjunction with the headship of Lincoln. He later came into possession of the rectories of Caythorpe, Lincolnshire (1560), and Holsworthy, Devon (1562).

Babington's career at Oxford reached its apogee with his appointments both to Lincoln College and to the post of Lady Margaret professor of divinity (made effective towards the end of 1560, and held until 1563). Though university statutes did not permit, he remained vice-chancellor while holding the professorship. In 1562 Babington was involved in forcing a protestant warden, John Man, upon Merton College, whose fellows were Roman Catholic in their sympathies. Nevertheless, it was suspicion of the sincerity of his adherence to protestantism that blocked his succession in early 1561 to the deanery of Christ Church, Oxford (the post went instead to Thomas Sampson), and which ultimately led to his downfall. Babington resigned the vice-chancellorship in Michaelmas term 1562. In 1563 he resigned as rector of Lincoln and then as Lady Margaret professor, and he was subsequently deprived of his church livings in 1564. He remained in Oxford for a year after his resignations, and then fled to continental Europe in 1565, where he apparently died in exile in December 1569.

Babington had a reputation for scholarship, and was known for his skill in philosophical and logical disputations. The contents of his personal library indicate a wide range of scholarly interest. He owned works of the church fathers (Origen, Clement of Alexandria, John Chrysostom, Augustine, and Gregory the Great) and of medieval theologians (Bede, Anselm, Bonaventura, Duns Scotus, and Hugo of St Cher), as well as works of his contemporaries, including Erasmus, and some mathematical works. He also collected manuscripts. Subsequent to his death, some of his books stayed at Lincoln. Others found their way to the library of the Jesuit College of the Immaculate Conception (in fact a nominal college, of no fixed location but embracing the counties of Derbyshire, Leicestershire, Nottinghamshire, and Rutland), where they remained during the seventeenth and eighteenth centuries. Most of these books are now at Stonyhurst College, Lancashire.

Babington's career reflects the difficulties faced by many English academics in the turbulent years of the mid-sixteenth century. Like a number (but by no means all) of his fellows, he sought to comply with the religious requirements of the successive regimes of Edward VI, Mary I, and Elizabeth I. Although a Roman Catholic, he was able for a time to dissemble his true confessional commitments after the accession of Elizabeth, and even joined in the persecution of Catholics resistant to changes at Oxford in the early 1560s. In the end Babington failed in this endeavour, and having lost the patronage of Dudley, he chose the path of exile taken by so many of his co-religionists. N. SCOTT AMOS

Sources Cooper, *Ath. Cantab.*, vol. 1 • Wood, *Ath. Oxon.: Fasti* (1815) • V. Green, *The commonwealth of Lincoln College, 1427–1977* (1979) • Venn, *Alum. Cant.* • P. Williams, 'Elizabethan Oxford: state, church and university', *Hist. U. Oxf.* 3: *Colleg. univ.*, 397–440 • N. R. Ker, 'The provision of books', *Hist. U. Oxf.* 3: *Colleg. univ.*, 441–77 • J. Peile, *Biographical register of Christ's College, 1505–1905, and of the earlier foundation, God's House, 1448–1505*, ed. [J. A. Venn], 1 (1910) • J. Jones, *Balliol College: a history, 1263–1939* (1988) • J. Venn and J. A. Venn, eds., *The book of matriculations and degrees … in the University of Cambridge from 1544 to 1659* (1913) • Foster, *Alum. Oxon.*, *1500–1714*, vol. 1 • H. W. C. Davis, *A history of Balliol College*, rev. R. H. C. Davis and R. Hunt (1963) • J. McConica, 'The Catholic experience in Tudor Oxford', *The reckoned expense: Edmund Campion and the early English Jesuits*, ed. T. M. McCoog (1996), 39–63 • E. Russell, 'Marian Oxford and the Counter-Reformation', *The church in pre-Reformation society: essays in honour of F. R. H. Du Boulay*, ed. C. M. Barron and C. Harper-Bill (1985), 212–27

Babington, Gervase (1549/50–1610), theologian and bishop of Worcester, was born in Nottinghamshire, as Sir John Harington noted, 'by birth … a gentleman of a verie good house' (Harington, 129). Claims that he was a native of Devon, made by John Prince in 1701 and repeated by Browne Willis, are incorrect. No record of his mother's family has been found, but his father, Bernard Babington of Puxley, was closely linked to the main branch of the family at Dethick in Derbyshire which was to gain notoriety in 1586 with the conspiracy of Anthony Babington. For his university education Gervase Babington was sent to Cambridge where he matriculated from Trinity College in Michaelmas term 1567. The master at Trinity was the recently appointed John Whitgift who was to become his mentor. He graduated BA in 1571, was admitted junior fellow of the college on 28 September 1573, and then two years later proceeded MA. Babington was also incorporated at Oxford on 15 July 1578 (and again in 1589). At this stage he was becoming known as a 'hard student' of theology, versed in Hebrew and Greek, recognized especially for a persuasive style of preaching, so that after his return to Cambridge he was selected preacher for the university in 1580.

Chaplain to the Herberts Of equal consequence for the advancement of Babington's career was his selection—after recommendation 'by the ancients and heads of the said university'—as domestic chaplain to Henry Herbert, second earl of Pembroke. He served as chaplain at Wilton House in 1581 and possibly during part of 1582, and maintained a close relationship with the Herberts for the rest of his life. Mary, countess of Pembroke and sister of Sir Philip Sidney, was notable for her learning and scholarship, a true bluestocking in the best sense of the word; it

Gervase Babington (1549/50–1610), by Renold Elstrack, pubd 1615

was she who made Wilton 'like a little Universitie … a more excellent nurcerie for learning and pietie' (Hannay, 132). Mary Herbert completed the metrical version of the Psalms that she and her brother had started, although opinion is mixed as to whether Harington was correct that she needed Babington's help because 'it was more then a womans skill, to expresse the sence so right as she hath done in her vearse' (Harington, 129). This supposition has been questioned, on the grounds that the finished translation can be explained by reliance on the Genevan Psalms and commentaries.

Babington benefited greatly from the court position and extensive patronage of Pembroke whose massive landholdings were concentrated in Wiltshire and Wales, and from the earl's concern to forward the protestant cause. In 1581 Babington was made warden of St Giles's Hospital, Wilton, which was followed by appointments to a set of livings, all in Wiltshire: vicar of Bulbridge (1585), and rector of both Ditchampton and Wilton St Mary (1585). Part of this accumulation is explained by the law (21 Hen. VIII c. 13), which permitted domestic chaplains to peers to purchase a dispensation to hold two benefices in plurality. During this period Babington began to publish the first of his theological and pastoral works, partly derived from his instruction to the Wilton household. In 1583 he dedicated to Pembroke *A Very Fruitfull Exposition of the Commaundements by Way of Questions and Answeres* which went through three further editions (1586, 1590, 1596). The following year he published and dedicated to the countess *A brief conference betwixt Mans frailtie and faith wherein is declared the true use and comfort of those blessings … in the fifth of Matthew … laide down in the plain order of dialogue* (1584; 5th edn, 1602). This commentary on the sermon on the mount clearly shows his advanced Calvinism especially in the prayers for the family. In morning prayer God is to be praised because he has 'chosen and elected us for thy children, when others as good as we by nature shall burn in hell eternally' (Hannay, 133). Babington's writings proved to be very popular, usually represented in a number of editions, often enlarged and revised. *A Profitable Exposition of the Lords Prayer, by Way of Questions and Answers for most Playnnes* was dated at Wilton 'the ii of May 1588', this time dedicated to both Herberts. His teachings were practical 'aswell for the terror of the dull and dead, as for the sweet comfort of the tender harted'. In the dedication he thanked his patrons for their great favours to 'me and mine'. Babington must have married in the early 1580s; only his wife's given name, Joan, is known from the later probate of his will. Their son, John Babington, who was to matriculate at Corpus Christi College, Oxford, on 23 July 1603 (aged eighteen), was also a student at the Inner Temple in 1606.

Ecclesiastical preferments Babington continued to add to his preferments. In 1588 he was installed in the prebend of Llandegla in the collegiate church of Brecon and also the prebend of Wellington in Hereford Cathedral. One of the requirements at Cambridge for the degree of DTh that he was granted in 1589 was the promise to preach at Paul's Cross within a year of his inception. He fulfilled this prescription with a sermon delivered on 11 October 1590 and printed the following year under the imprimatur of Archbishop Whitgift. The sermon unswervingly followed the Genevan line on predestination:

> All men [were] at the first before the Lord in his eternall counsell, to receive an end or use according to his will, to life or death … to heaven or hell. In which good pleasure of his … he hath disposed of some one way, of some another.

Indeed Babington's sermon, one commentator asserts, 'must rank among the harshest of Elizabethan statements on predestination' (Tyacke, 253). He was appointed treasurer of Llandaff, being collated on 28 January 1590, and under this title he preached before the court at Greenwich on 24 May 1591. Babington was a committed Calvinist, not a puritan in the sense of a nonconformist. His court sermon was a vigorous defence of Anglican *status quo*, of uniformity, and church discipline against those who would prefer 'open assemblies in this land, and … erect a forme according to [their] wils, in woods, in fields, in holes and corners' (McCullough, calendar). Thereafter he was appointed with some regularity as a court preacher, usually on the Lenten roster.

An important advancement came with his elevation to the see of Llandaff, probably through Pembroke's influence and the archbishop's backing. He was elected bishop on 7 August 1591, confirmed on the 27th, and then consecrated on 29 August in the parish church at Croydon by Whitgift. He held on to his lesser preferments as commendams because the diocese was impoverished, the stipend valued at the meagre annual sum of £154. His punning comment on Llandaff was that 'his true title should have bene Affe, for the land was gone' (Harington, 129). His cathedral was described in 1594 as in 'ruins and decayed state'—'more like a desolate and profane place than a house of Prayer' (Williams, 326). Babington fits Fincham's model of an 'evangelical' bishop whose primary role was always an active preacher and teacher. His activity as diocesan visitor and pastor is less distinct since there is no extant register or act book. However he was always a stickler for conformity, particularly against popish recusants. He was automatically a member of the council in the marches of Wales of which Pembroke was president and which had broad judicial and administrative powers especially against the suppression of recusancy.

Babington continued to write lengthy treatises even after he became bishop, and in 1592 published the first of his volumes on the Pentateuch, *Certaine Plaine, Briefe, and Comfortable Notes upon Everie Chapter of Genesis*. Its popularity is shown by the second 'enlarged' edition of 1596 which had, in fact, doubled in length. The sequel on Exodus and Leviticus did not appear until 1604, and by then he had been moved twice. He was elected to the see of Exeter on 4 February 1595 and enthroned on 22 March. There is a rare description of a confirmation at Barnstaple in August 1595 when on his first visitation he laid his hands on 'divers children' at the Castle Green. But on the following day such a crowd came in from the country that he withdrew to his lodgings and quietly left town, whereupon 'the people lamented that they had lost a fine harvest day' (Collinson, 52). The diocese was reckoned one of the poorest in England. Whether the low income or his ambition to push ahead explains his short tenure is open to question. The claim by Prince that Babington alienated the valuable manor of Crediton, one of the few remaining temporalities of the see which 'made Way for his translation', is a canard (Willis, 1.649). In truth the manor was procured during the vacancy of the see by William, Lord Burghley, and his son Robert Cecil for a relative under the terms of the Act of Exchange of 1559. Babington was nominated by the queen to Worcester on 30 August 1597, elected on 15 September, and confirmed on 4 October. In contrast the new diocese was one of the more affluent English sees. On his translation he relinquished his prebend at Hereford but added at the same time the rectorate of Stokeinteignhead, Devon.

Bishop of Worcester A clearer picture emerges of Babington as an energetic and influential administrator at Worcester. He was commended for his constant preaching by Miles Smith, bishop of Gloucester after 1612, who edited the literary works of his former patron in 1615, and this claim was seconded by an anonymous clergyman, not of his diocese, in a work of 1601 which praised Babington's 'painfull preaching' and scriptural commentaries (Fincham, 88). Robert Abbot, brother of the archbishop and of the same cut of theological cloth as Babington, also noted his forceful preaching. Babington continued to serve on the council for Wales, and played a very active role sitting as magistrate at the quarter sessions, while working with determination to obtain convictions of popish dissenters at assize hearings. He likewise employed both preaching and personal argument to persuade papists to recant, methods approved by one who heard his 'publike exhortations or private conferences' (Questier, 172, n. 20). Like many bishops Babington inherited a dispute between the cathedral close and the Worcester civic authorities. When the latter attempted to secure a new charter from the crown, extending their jurisdiction over the cathedral precinct, he appealed to the earl of Salisbury to block the request, protesting that they were 'very injuriously encroaching' upon his territory and the dean and chapters (*Salisbury MSS*, 18.460). The altercation, which dragged on from 1604 to 1607, was not settled until after the bishop's death.

Babington was regularly in his diocese, dividing his residence between the Worcester palace and Hartlebury Castle, with periodic appearances in London and at court to preach. His one foray into court politics ended almost disastrously. On 2 March 1600 Babington preached before the ageing queen at Whitehall in the Preaching Place, an outdoor pulpit open not just to courtiers but also to Londoners of lesser rank. The ill-fated second earl of Essex, even though under house arrest and in disgrace, still retained an enormous popularity with the masses. Chamberlain reported that the bishop 'made many profers and glaunces in his [Essex's] behalfe, as he was understoode by the whole auditorie, and by the Quene herself'. When Babington was carpeted for his impertinence, 'he flatly forswore that he had any such meaninge' (*Letters of John Chamberlain*, 1.92–3). Despite his protestations Babington's name disappeared from the court sermon roster until the new reign.

Last years and legacy Within a year of James I's accession Babington was one of nine bishops summoned to the Hampton Court conference to consider puritan demands for reform. Even though Stephen Egerton, one of the presenters of the Millenary Petition, in a letter before the conference identified him as one of three bishops who 'are turned Puritans', this characterization is highly doubtful (Tyacke, 17). Babington would probably have endorsed Whitgift's Lambeth articles but there is no evidence that he ever abetted nonconformity. In his Paul's Cross sermon of 1590 he pleaded for moderation between puritans and the establishment, reproving such sins as bitterness in church controversy. A better characterization would be as a Calvinist episcopalian. Even so Babington was not in agreement with Bishop Bancroft, the chief spokesman for the establishment at the conference, who upheld the legality of lay baptism in case of necessity, a point Babington strongly contested. Not long after the conference Whitgift was buried at Croydon; his old pupil Babington preached the funeral sermon on 27 March, using as his text 2 Chronicles 24: 15–16 and comparing the late archbishop to Jehoida who 'had done good in Israel in the service of God and of his house' (Fuller, 10.26–7). In April 1606 another confrontation between Babington and Bancroft took place in the House of Lords when Bancroft as primate tested opinion whether 'the papists might have a toleration for four years', and Babington retorted 'that it was pity they should be tolerated for seven days' (Questier, 141n.).

Babington died at Worcester on 17 May 1610, aged sixty, and was buried in his cathedral without a memorial. No will has been found but his public legacy was a large folio of five major works published in 1615. Included for the first time were his notes on Numbers and Deuteronomy, thereby completing his collection on the Pentateuch. Four editions, the last in 1637, show the influence of his writings. In 1624 Joseph Hall, a future bishop, opened the southern convocation with a sermon to his fellow clergy. 'I must say it,' he informed them, '*Stupor mundi clerus Britannicus*' ('The wonder of the world is the clergy of Britain'). Making his point Hall listed some twenty learned theologians and 'eloquent' preachers: named among his 'great lights' of the English church was Babington (Collinson, 92). JOHN S. MACAULEY

Sources *DNB* • Venn, *Alum. Cant.*, 1/1.62 • Foster, *Alum. Oxon.* • G. Babington, *Workes*, ed. M. Smith (1615) [memoir in preface contains life] • Wood, *Ath. Oxon.: Fasti* (1815), 211 • J. Harington, *A supplie or addicion to the catalogue of bishops to the yeare 1608*, ed. R. H. Miller (1979) • T. Fuller, *The church-history of Britain*, 11 pts in 1 (1655) • K. Fincham, *Prelate as pastor: the episcopate of James I* (1990) • N. Tyacke, *Anti-Calvinists: the rise of English Arminianism, c.1590–1640* (1987) • P. E. McCullough, *Sermons at court: politics and religion in Elizabethan and Jacobean preaching* (1998) [incl. CD-ROM] • B. Willis, *A survey of the cathedrals*, 2 vols. (1730), vol. 1 • *CSP dom.*, 1595–7; 1603–10 • *Calendar of the manuscripts of the most hon. the marquis of Salisbury*, 13, HMC, 9 (1915); 16–18 (1933–40); 24 (1976) • M. P. Hannay, *Philip's phoenix: Mary Sidney, countess of Pembroke* (1990) • P. Collinson, *The religion of protestants* (1982) • M. Maclure, *The Paul's Cross sermons, 1534–1642* (1958) • M. C. Questier, *Conversion, politics and religion in England, 1580–1625* (1996) • *Fasti Angl.*, 1541–1857, [Ely] • signet office and home office: docquet books and letters recommendatory, PRO, SO3/1, fols. 517v, 520 • G. Williams, *Recovery, reorientation and reformation: Wales, c.1415–1642*, History of Wales, 3 (1987) • J. Prince, *Danmonii orientales illustres, or, The worthies of Devon* (1701) • administration grant book, PRO, PROB 6/7, fol. 202 • *The letters of John Chamberlain*, ed. N. E. McClure, 2 vols. (1939)

Archives Devon RO, Exeter diocesan records, bishop's register • Worcs. RO, Worcester diocesan records, bishop's register

Likenesses R. Elstrack, line print, BM, NPG; repro. in Babington, *Works* (1615) [*see illus.*] • de Passe, line print, BM, NPG; repro. in H. Holland, *Herōologia Anglica* (1620) • portrait, repro. in G. Babington, *Workes* (1622)

Babington, Humphrey (*bap.* 1615, *d.* 1692), college administrator, was baptized on 5 November 1615 in the village of Cossington, Leicestershire, the younger of two sons of Adrian Babington, rector of that parish, and his wife, Margaret Cave. He entered Trinity College, Cambridge, as a sizar in 1634. He graduated BA in 1639, becoming a fellow of Trinity in 1640 and proceeding MA in 1642. He served as tutor at Trinity from 1642 to 1647. In 1650 he was ejected from his fellowship for refusing to take the engagement. He went on to become rector of the Nottinghamshire parishes of Keyworth in 1654 and Stanton on the Wolds in

1655, later serving as vicar of Easton Maudit in Northamptonshire, in 1657, and from the same year vicar of Grantham, Lincolnshire. After the Restoration he successfully petitioned the House of Lords to be restored to his fellowship at Trinity. In 1661 he became rector of Boothby Pagnell in Lincolnshire, succeeding Robert Sanderson after his elevation to the episcopate. He proceeded DD *per literas regias* in 1669.

Babington was an important figure in Trinity College throughout the Restoration, serving as senior dean in 1671–2 and also as senior bursar in 1674–8. He eventually became vice-master of the college in 1690. He appears on the roll of college benefactors, contributing funds for the development of Nevile's Court in the 1680s and building two sets of rooms for the use of the Babington family. Circumstantial evidence suggests that he was an important patron for Isaac Newton and possibly even the means by which Newton came to Trinity (Westfall, 70, 73–4). Babington died on 4 January 1692 after suffering a stroke, and was buried in the chapel of Trinity College. His extensive will indicated his substantial means. It also contained provisions for the founding of the Old Men's Hospital in Barrow, Leicestershire, which was established in 1694 in the memory of his uncle Theophilus Cave.

Babington's sole published work consists of a sermon, *Mercy and Judgement*, preached to the Lincoln assizes in July 1678. This was published a few months afterwards in Cambridge at the request of Thomas Harington, high sheriff of Lincoln. The sermon displays Babington's learning in Latin, Greek, and Hebrew and his political and religious views may be estimated by its assertion that 'Monarchy is the best safeguard against the great *furious Bulls* of Tyrannical *Popery*, and the lesser *giddy cattle* of Schismatical *Presbytery*' (Babington, 27).

JON PARKIN

Sources *Walker rev.*, 291 • Venn, *Alum. Cant.*, 1/1.62 • W. W. Rouse Ball and J. A. Venn, eds., *Admissions to Trinity College, Cambridge*, 1 (1916), 15, 32, 41, 56; 2 (1913), vi, vii, xii, 342 • R. S. Westfall, *Never at rest: a biography of Isaac Newton* (1980) • H. Babington, *Mercy and judgement: a sermon preached at the assizes held at Lincoln, July 15th 1678* (1678) • *The diary of Samuel Newton, alderman of Cambridge (1662–1717)*, ed. J. E. Foster, Cambridge Antiquarian RS, 23 (1890), 106 • *N&Q*, 2nd ser., 9 (1860), 152, 195 • *Seventh report*, HMC, 6 (1879), 87 • W. Kennett, *A register and chronicle ecclesiastical and civil* (1728), 357

Archives Bodl. Oxf., notice of death, Tanner MS 26, fol. 24 • LPL, admission to rectory of Keyworth, MS 998 (COMM III/6), fol. 6 • LPL, admission to rectory of Stanton on the Wolds, MS 997 (COMM III/3), fol. 115 • LPL, admission to vicarage of Eastern Mauditt, MS 96 (COMM III/4), fol. 128 • LPL, admission to vicarage of Grantham, MS 983 (COMM III/2), fol. 32 • Trinity Cam., list of maps donated to the college by Babington, MS 856, fol. 3 • Trinity Cam., mathematical MSS owned by Babington, MS 1311 | BL, letter to the bishop of St David's, Add. MS 5841, fol. 10 • Bodl. Oxf., corresp. with Herbert Astley, Tanner MS 285, fols. 91, 106, 109, 112, 114, 123 • Bodl. Oxf., letters to Herbert Astley, Tanner MS 46, fol. 27; MS 133, fol. 19 • Bodl. Oxf., corresp. with William Sancroft, Tanner MS 54, fols. 77, 124, 162 • Bodl. Oxf., letters to Sancroft, Tanner MS 290, fol. 157; MS 155, fol. 114

Babington, John (*bap.* **1604**, *d.* after **1635**), soldier and mathematician, was baptized on 21 August 1604 at St Nicholas Acon in the City of London, the son of John Babington and his wife, Dorothie Rosse. No details of his life are known beyond those disclosed in his book *Pyrotechnia, or, A Discourse of Artificiall Fireworks* (1635). Babington explains that he was, and had been for some years past, 'one of the inferiour gunners of his Majestie'. In the halcyon days of peace he had turned his attention from gunnery to fireworks, which were important both for military use and as popular civic entertainment. The major portion of his book sets out, clearly and with illustrations, how to make up the chemicals and structures for each type of firework display. Babington was a citizen of London and a member of the Salters' Company, which may have assisted his familiarity with these chemicals. This section was dedicated to the earl of Newport, master of the ordnance, and prefaced by verses in praise of the author, one of which was by John Bate, whom Taylor tentatively identifies with John Bate of Tower Hill, maker of gunnery and other mathematical instruments.

The second part of Babington's book, a 'Short treatise of geometrie', dedicated to Sir John Heyden, lieutenant of the ordnance, was intended for the use of young mathematical practitioners and gunners. A third section consists of logarithmetic tables, possibly the earliest to be published in England in this form. The circumstances of Babington's later life are unknown.

R. E. ANDERSON, *rev.* ANITA MCCONNELL

Sources E. G. R. Taylor, *The mathematical practitioners of Tudor and Stuart England* (1954); repr. (1970), 218 • J. Babington, *Pyrotechnia* (1635) • private information (2004)

Likenesses J. Moore, bronze medal, 1862, NPG • engraving (after J. Droeshout), repro. in Babington, *Pyrotechnia*, frontispiece

Babington, Sir William (*c.*1370–1454), justice, was from an ancient Northumberland family, whose members had, by the mid-fourteenth century, abandoned their interests there in favour first of Cambridgeshire and then of Nottinghamshire, where they had long held a manor at Rolleston near Newark. His father, John, married a Cambridgeshire bride but was buried in the Nottinghamshire church of East Bridgford. William's marriage to Margery, heir of the Martels of Chilwell, confirmed the shift of the family's interests, for she brought to the family the manors of Chilwell and Ruddington near Nottingham. Of age by 1395, William pursued a highly successful legal career, which enabled him to extend these landholdings greatly. By 1408 he was retained as an apprentice-at-law by the duchy of Lancaster; in January 1414 he was appointed king's attorney; and in June 1415 he became deputy chief steward of the northern parts of the duchy. In the following month he and others were called by the crown to take up the degree of serjeant-at-law. Their refusal, on grounds that are unclear, led to their appearance in parliament in November 1417, where they were obliged to accept the honour.

Thereafter Babington's promotion was rapid. A year's service as king's serjeant was followed, in November 1419, by appointment as chief baron of the exchequer, and, in June 1420, by elevation to a seat on the common bench. Three years later, in May 1423, he became the chief justice of that court, a position he held until his retirement in February 1436, and, at the dubbing of Henry VI on Whitsunday 1426, he received the further honour of the

Order of the Bath. He exploited his success not only to extend his estates through the purchase of several manors in Bedfordshire, Nottinghamshire, and Derbyshire, but also to find a remarkable series of wealthy brides for his sons and his younger brothers. The most noteworthy of these marriages was that of his son John to Maud, granddaughter of Eleanor, heir of the barony of St Amand, and hence, on the death of Maud's father, Gerard Braybrooke, in 1422, one of the three coheiresses of that barony. Only the couple's childless death prevented a further substantial addition to the Babington lands. The chief justice's influence probably also explains the marriage of his brother Thomas to one of the two daughters and coheirs of Robert Dethick of Dethick in Derbyshire. The Catholic conspirator, Sir Anthony Babington (*d.* 1586), was a direct descendant of this marriage in the male line.

On William's retirement from the bench in 1436, he was probably in his early sixties, and advanced age explains why little is known of him in the last years of his life. A comparison of the tax returns of 1436 and 1451 shows that, before the latter date, he had made over the bulk of his estates to his son and heir, William: in 1436 he was assessed on an annual income of £160 but by 1451 his assessment had fallen to £40 p.a., while that of his son had risen from £37 to £100 p.a. He drew up a short and uninformative will on 3 October 1454, directing burial in the newly built chapel of St Mary in the church of the monastery of Lenton, and died a few days later (his will was proved on 10 October but the jurors in his inquisition *post mortem* give his date of death as 13 October). His money and goods to the value of 600 marks were employed by his executors in the foundation of a chantry in the church of Flawford (demolished in 1773) in the parish of Ruddington. S. J. PAYLING

Sources S. J. Payling, *Political society in Lancastrian England* (1991) · G. T. C. [G. T. Clark], 'The pedigree of the family of Babington of Dethick and Kingston', *Collectanea Topographica et Genealogica*, 8 (1843) · Baker, *Serjeants* · G. T. C. [G. T. Clark], 'Inedited additions to the pedigree of Babington', *The topographer and genealogist*, ed. J. G. Nichols, 1 (1846), 131-41 · probate register, Borth. Inst., 2, fols. 301v–302 · Inquisition post mortem, PRO, C 139/157/23 · R. Somerville, *History of the duchy of Lancaster, 1265–1603* (1953) · *Chancery records*

Wealth at death £59 p.a.: PRO C 139/157/23 · £400 in money and goods: Borth. Inst., probate register 2, fols. 301v–302

Babington [Babyngton], **William** (*d.* 1453), abbot of Bury St Edmunds, derived his toponymic surname from Babington in east Somerset. He is chiefly known not for his rule at St Edmunds but as a distinguished canon lawyer and ecclesiastic. At the election of William Curteys to the abbacy of St Edmunds on 14 February 1429, Babington appears fifty-fifth in the list of the sixty-five monks present, and is denoted as a 'scholar': this indicates that he was one of the St Edmunds monks studying at Gloucester College, Oxford. Despite his junior status, he was among the proxies sent by the newly elected Curteys to the Roman curia to obtain papal confirmation and amplification of the abbey's privilege of exemption. The deputation's specific purpose was to prevent encroachment by William Alnwick, bishop of Norwich. The burden of the work seems to have fallen on Babington: he was successful, but only after remaining in Rome for nearly two years and after 'great labour and expense' (BL, Add. MS 14848, fol. 70).

By about 1442 Babington was well established at Oxford and a doctor of canon law. He was apparently a man of energy and public spirit. For instance, he struggled for the abolition of an abuse in the university, the charging of immoderate graduation fees. His endeavours involved him in a suit in the court of the chancellor's commissary against another canonist, Master John Scotbow. On 28 January 1443 the chancellor, Henry Sever, wrote to Archbishop Chichele asking him to arbitrate in the case, describing Babington as a 'weighty, learned and upright man' (Anstey, 1.230–31). Later that year Babington was himself one of six arbiters chosen to arbitrate a dispute, one between a university proctor, Master John Tristholme, and David Stephan and students of Trillock's Inn; he was one of the three arbiters chosen by Stephan's party. He remained at Oxford for the next three years, and from 1444–6 was principal of the school of canon law.

In the spring of 1446, on the death of Abbot William Curteys, Babington was elected abbot of Bury St Edmunds. He received his temporalities on 23 May. Little is known about his short abbatiate. On 28 November Henry VI granted him and the convent exemption from all taxes, in exchange for an annual payment of 40 marks, and also exemption from the obligation of acting as tax collectors. Then, on 23 December 1451, Henry pardoned him and the convent all their debts owed at the exchequer. Meanwhile, Babington's national importance was increasing. He was a trier of petitions at the parliament that met on 10 February 1447 in the abbey refectory at St Edmunds. (There is no known evidence implicating him or the monks in the fate during the parliament of Humphrey, duke of Gloucester.) Babington was again a trier of petitions in the Westminster parliament of 12 February 1449, and shortly afterwards, on 13 March, Henry appointed him his proctor at the papal curia. Henry renewed the appointment early in 1450, this time for five years. Late in 1450 Babington was in Cologne, perhaps on the way to or from Rome, travelling by the Rhine route, for on 9 November he was incorporated in the faculty of canon law at Cologne University.

By 1449 Babington held the office of president of the general chapter of the Benedictines in England. This appears in the letter of recommendation on his behalf addressed by Oxford University to Pope Nicholas V on 6 April 1449. It describes Babington as abbot of Bury, president of the general chapter, and the king's proctor at the curia, and dwells on his virtues but especially his pre-eminence in the school of canon law at Oxford. Babington's time in Rome coincided with the jubilee year of 1450, with which evidently his business there was mainly concerned. Possibly it was at his request that Pope Nicholas, on 1 January 1450, placed controls upon the application of Clement VI's statute which had come to be construed as allowing Benedictines to go to Rome for 'jubilee' indulgences without licence of their superiors: in future such licences were necessary. Nicholas also empowered

Babington to appoint priests to grant jubilee indulgences locally to Benedictines, their servants, and their tenants, in England and Wales, after confession, penance, and absolution. Since Babington, being in Rome, could not make the appointments personally, he was allowed to commission substitutes to do so. As king's proctor he is known at least once to have imprisoned a Benedictine, a Glastonbury monk, who had come to Rome for a jubilee indulgence, for alleged misdemeanour.

Babington died in the autumn of 1453. He left no register of his abbatiate, but two of his books are known to survive: a fifteenth-century copy of Peter of Blois's *Epistolae*, now Bodl. Oxf., MS Bodley 426, and a thirteenth-century copy of Guillaume d'Auxerre's *Summa aurea super quatuor libros sententiarum*, now Cambridge, Pembroke College, MS 4. The latter, which originally belonged to the monks' book collection, has Babington's signature on folio 74*v*.

Antonia Gransden

Sources BL, Add. MS 14848, fols. 23, 39*v*, 40*v*, 70, 78, 78*v*, 110*v*, 111 • H. Anstey, ed., *Epistolae academicae Oxon.*, 1, OHS, 35 (1898), 230–31, 271–3 • H. E. Salter, ed., *Registrum cancellarii Oxoniensis, 1434–1469*, 1, OHS, 93 (1932), 83–5, 104, 123, 133 • *CPR, 1441–6*, 435; *1446–52*, 233, 241, 267, 310, 519–20; *1452–61*, 147 • *Letters of Queen Margaret of Anjou and Bishop Beckington and others written in the reigns of Henry V and Henry VI*, ed. C. Monro, CS, 86 (1863), 59–60, no. 35 • *RotP*, 5.128–9, 141 • R. A. Griffiths, *The reign of King Henry VI: the exercise of royal authority, 1422–1461* (1981), 496–8 • H. Keussen, ed., *Die Matrikel der Universität Köln*, 1 (Bonn, 1928), 407 [art. 247, no. 45] • *CEPR letters*, 10.57–8, 530–31 • Dugdale, *Monasticon*, 3.115 • W. E. Lunt, *Papal revenues in the middle ages*, 2 vols. (1934); repr. (1965), vol. 1, pp. 121–5 • R. M. Thomson, *The archives of the abbey of Bury St Edmunds*, Suffolk RS, 21 (1980), 40

Archives BL, Add. MS 14848, fols. 23, 39*v*, 40*v*, 70, 78, 78*v*, 110*v*, 111 | Pembroke Cam., MS 4, fol. 74*v*

Babington, William (1756–1833), physician and mineralogist, the son of a clergyman, was born on 21 May 1756 at Port Glenone, near Coleraine, co. Antrim, Ireland. After being apprenticed to a practitioner at Londonderry, he completed his medical education at Guy's Hospital, London, but did not take a medical degree. In 1777 he was made assistant surgeon to the Haslar naval hospital in Portsmouth, and held this appointment for four years. He then became apothecary to Guy's Hospital, and also lectured on chemistry in the medical school attached to the hospital. He published *Syllabus of a Course of Lectures at Guy's Hospital* in 1789. William and Martha Elizabeth Babington were married before 1794, and had four sons and four daughters between 1794 and 1810. The family lived in Cornhill, London, until about 1796, in Basinghall Street until 1801, and then in a large house in Aldermanbury until 1830.

Babington resigned the post of apothecary, and, gaining his MD from the University of Aberdeen in 1795, was elected assistant physician to Guy's Hospital in the same year. He was elected to the post of full physician in 1802. In 1811 he and James Curry published *Outlines of a Course of Lectures on the Practice of Medicine as Delivered* [at Guy's]. Babington resigned from his post at Guy's in the same year because of the pressures of private practice; however, within a week the hospital governors persuaded him to serve once again as an assistant physician, which he did until 1813. He had also been admitted a licenciate of the College of Physicians in 1796 and he remained so until 1827, when he received the unusual honour of being elected fellow by special grace. In 1831 he was made honorary MD by the University of Dublin.

Babington was a very able and successful physician, whose skill and knowledge were confirmed by his contemporaries. He was a patron of the Royal Jennerian Society and a dominant figure in the Hunterian Society in the 1820s, being president of the latter in 1824 and orator in 1827. However, his chief interests were in chemistry and mineralogy, rather than in medicine. He lectured on chemistry at Guy's Hospital for many years, and published some memoirs in *Nicholson's Journal*. He was friendly with chemists such as Humphry Davy and Joseph Priestley, and he lectured on the application of science at the Chapter Coffee House Society in the 1790s. His interest in mineralogy was even greater, and he achieved more. While apothecary to Guy's Hospital he acquired the valuable collection of minerals which had belonged to John Stuart, earl of Bute. Babington made an elaborate catalogue of the collection, which served as the foundation of his *Systematic Arrangement of Minerals* (1795) and his *New System of Mineralogy* (1799). Babington was a member of the short-lived British Mineralogical Society (1799–1806), and joined the Askesian Society in 1801. He was elected a fellow of the Royal Society in 1805, being described as 'a gentleman eminently learned in chemistry and mineralogy' in the citation.

Babington did more by encouraging science than by his own work, and has some claim to be regarded as the founder of the Geological Society. The circumstances are recorded by G. B. Greenough:

> With a view to enable Count Bournon, of whom he had been a pupil, to publish his elaborate monograph on the carbonate of lime, Dr. Babington in 1807, invited to his house a number of gentlemen the most distinguished for their zeal in the prosecution of mineralogical knowledge. A subscription was opened and the necessary sum readily collected. The object having been accomplished, other meetings of the same gentlemen took place, for the joint purpose of friendly intercourse and mutual instruction. From such small beginnings sprang the Geological Society, and among the names of those by whose care and watchfulness it was supported during the early and most perilous crisis of its history, that of Dr. Babington must always stand conspicuous. (Greenough, 42–4)

Babington was president of the society in 1822, but he did not contribute to its *Transactions*. After this he took lessons in geology from Thomas Webster, and he attended the chemical lectures at London University in the year before his death. He was also appointed by the government to be one of the referees to put a price on the Greville collection of minerals, bought by the nation and preserved in the Natural History Museum.

Babington had acquired a large and lucrative medical practice, and continued with his medical and scientific work until within four days of his death, which occurred from influenza, at his home in Portland Place, London, on 29 April 1833. He was buried in the church of St Mary Aldermanbury. Four years after his death a monument was erected to him in St Paul's Cathedral by public subscription. He left a son, Benjamin Guy *Babington, also physician to Guy's Hospital, and a daughter, Martha, who married the physician Richard Bright.

J. F. PAYNE, *rev.* JOHN C. THACKRAY

Sources Munk, *Roll* • S. Wilks and G. T. Bettany, *A biographical history of Guy's Hospital* (1892) • G. L. Smyth, *The worthies of England*, 2 vols. (1850) • G. B. Greenough, 'President's address for 1834', *Proceedings of the Geological Society of London*, 2 (1833–8), 42–4 • R. G. Wills, 'The contribution of British medical men to the foundation of geology', *Proceedings of the Liverpool Geological Society*, 16 (1935), 200–19 • S. C. Lawrence, *Charitable knowledge: hospital pupils and practitioners in eighteenth-century London* (1996) • *IGI*

Likenesses J. Tannock, oils, 1820, GS Lond. • J. Towne, bust, 1834, Guy's Hospital, London • Behnes, statue on monument, 1837, St Paul's Cathedral, London • bust, 1839, RCP Lond. • N. Branwhite, group portrait, stipple, pubd 1881 (*Institutors of the Medical Society of London*; after S. Medley), BM • W. T. Fry, stipple (after J. Tannock), BM, NPG, Wellcome L. • S. Medley, portrait

Babion [Babyon]**, Peter** (*supp. fl.* **1150**), supposed religious writer, is the creation of the bibliographer John Bale (*d.* 1563). In his notebook, the *Index Britanniae scriptorum*, Bale conflated two entries in the *Catalogus* of Henry Kirkestede (*d.* in or after 1378) and two in the early fourteenth-century union catalogue of books on the British mainland compiled by the Oxford Franciscans, known as the *Registrum Anglie*. Kirkestede had listed an exposition of Matthew's gospel and numerous sermons under the name Babio. These were certainly by Geoffroi Babion de Loroux (*d.* 1158), archbishop of Bordeaux. Under the heading *Opera Petri Babilon*, the *Registrum* gives a treatise on the mass and a collection of sermons. The archbishop of Bordeaux may have written the former, though it has also been attributed to an otherwise unknown Peter, while the sermons are almost certainly those listed by Kirkestede. Bale noted that the two sets of sermons were the same, but failed to identify their author as Geoffroi Babion, and attributed all three works to a Petrus Babion (or Babylon).

The final item in Bale's list is the late twelfth-century comic play *Babio*, which he entered under Geoffroi Babion in his notebook, but under Peter Babion in his published work, known as the *Catalogus*. Earliest extant in Bodl. Oxf., MS Digby 53, written at the end of the twelfth century, *Babio* is anonymous, though it has tentatively been attributed to the late twelfth-century writer Nigel of Canterbury (also known as Nigel Wireker). This may be doubted, but it was certainly composed in England, which may explain why Bale thought that his Petrus Babion was British.

MARIOS COSTAMBEYS

Sources R. Sharpe, *A handlist of the Latin writers of Great Britain and Ireland before 1540* (1997) • R. H. Rouse and others, eds., *Registrum Anglie de libris doctorum et auctorum veterum* (1991) • Bale, *Index* • K. Bate, ed., *Three Latin comedies* (1976) [inc. *Babio*] • 'Gottfried Babion', *Lexikon des Mittelalters*, 10 vols. (1980–99) • Bale, *Cat.* • Tanner, *Bibl. Brit.-Hib.*

Archives Bodl. Oxf., MS Digby 53

Babthorpe family (*per. c.*1501–1635), gentry, in Yorkshire, could boast of an ancient pedigree which included a number of medieval knights who had been soldiers and courtiers. The family's principal seat was at Osgodby in the extensive East Riding parish of Hemingbrough, where they had been lords of the manor since about 1440. In addition they had residences at Babthorpe in the same parish and, from 1543, at Flotmanby in the parish of Folkton, near Filey. For many years they were involved in a dispute with the *Plumpton family over the descent of their ancestral estates. The issue was finally resolved in 1565 when an arbitration award left them in possession of the manors of Osgodby, Babthorpe, and Brackenholme and of other property in the East Riding.

The most notable of the Tudor Babthorpes was **Sir William Babthorpe** (*c.*1490–1555), son of William Babthorpe and Christina Sothill; succeeding his father aged eleven in 1501, he then became a ward of the crown. He was a lawyer who served as a legal member of the council in the north from 1525 until his death. He was a thrusting and ambitious man, and his steady accumulation of offices in the East Riding made him a powerful figure there. These covered a wide range of functions: commissioner for musters, justice of the peace, and *custos rotulorum*; steward of the lordship of Beverley; constable of Wressle Castle and steward and master forester of Wressle (offices in the gift of the earls of Northumberland who employed him as a legal adviser); and steward of Howden and Howdenshire. In April 1536 he was named as one of the commissioners for surveying the lands and goods of the dissolved religious foundations in the East Riding, but in October he joined the leaders of the Pilgrimage of Grace, a decision which owed much to the influence of his kinsman Robert Aske, and it was no doubt with his connivance that Wressle Castle became the rebels' headquarters. When it became clear that the uprising had failed, however, Babthorpe rapidly changed sides. In January 1537 he sought to prevent another uprising in the East Riding, and in May he was appointed as one of the special commissioners who were responsible for processing the indictments against his former associates. His initial stance did him no harm: he continued as a member of the council in the north and was able to purchase a considerable amount of monastic property, including the manor of Flotmanby, and to acquire leases of the rectories of Drax and Adlingfleet.

That Babthorpe was a politically important figure is demonstrated by his election to the parliaments of 1547 and April 1554 as one of the Yorkshire knights of the shire. At the coronation of Edward VI in 1547 he was made a knight of the Bath.

Babthorpe married Agnes, a daughter of Brian Palmes of Naburn, and they had two sons and two daughters. He died on 27 February 1555. His heir, **Sir William Babthorpe** (*c.*1529–1581), apparently received some part of his education at the Middle Temple in London and was knighted in 1560 by the duke of Norfolk at Berwick while serving in his expeditionary force. Sir William was married twice, first to Barbara, daughter of Sir Robert Constable of Everingham, and then, in 1564, to Frances, daughter of Sir Thomas Dawney of Sessay, and from these two marriages he had one son and four daughters.

In a report on the Yorkshire justices of the peace which was compiled in 1564 Sir William was described as a man who was no favourer of religion as established by the

Elizabethan settlement. In April 1565 Archbishop Young of York was in correspondence with Sir William Cecil about Babthorpe's unseemly talk, as he termed it, which was regarded as highly inflammatory. Cecil had already rebuked Babthorpe and his associates, and the archbishop assured him that they were now in great awe and obedience. When the northern rising broke out in 1569 Babthorpe demonstrated his loyalty by joining the royal army under the earl of Sussex.

As a suspected recusant Sir William came under pressure from the northern high commission. In 1580 he produced a certificate of conformity for himself and his family but admitted that his wife refused to go to church. A few months later he was entertaining Edmund Campion. In his will Babthorpe gave direction that he should be buried in the family chapel at Hemingbrough parish church. Although he was basically dependent on his estate revenue he had managed to buy some additional property, including the manor of Bowthorpe. He died in 1581.

Sir William was succeeded by his son, **Sir Ralph Babthorpe** (1561–1618), who had been admitted as a fellow commoner at Gonville and Caius College, Cambridge, in 1576. During his time there the younger Babthorpe consorted with other Roman Catholic undergraduates and was alleged to have worn a crucifix in bed. In 1579 he married Grace Birnand [**Grace Babthorpe** (*c*.1563–1635)], the daughter and sole heir of William Birnand of Knaresborough; they had four sons and three daughters. It was a marriage with major consequences in religious and ultimately in financial terms. Grace Babthorpe was a zealous Roman Catholic who later earned the praise of a Jesuit chaplain as 'the pillar of religion' in the East Riding. She had her children baptized at home by a Roman Catholic priest, took great pains over their religious upbringing, and kept them away from protestant services. In 1599 the Babthorpes were employing a Roman Catholic schoolmaster, William Boyes, who found himself in trouble for teaching without a licence.

Sir William Babthorpe (1580–1635), the eldest son, refused to go to church while a pupil at a clandestine school. In 1599 he was enrolled as a student at Gray's Inn in London. Not long afterwards he married Ursula Tyrwhitt, the daughter of a Roman Catholic squire seated in Lincolnshire, with whom he had six sons and four daughters. Of his three brothers Robert became a Benedictine monk, and Ralph and Thomas entered the Society of Jesus after studying at the English colleges at St Omer and Rome. His sister Barbara joined the Institution of the Blessed Virgin Mary which had been founded by her cousin Mary Ward (who had been brought up at Osgodby Hall) and eventually held the office of superioress-general.

During Elizabeth's reign Ralph Babthorpe thought it expedient as head of the family to hide his religious sympathies under the cloak of outward conformity. For some years the family was left in peace, but in 1592 Henry Hastings, third earl of Huntingdon, the lord president of the council in the north, launched a vigorous campaign against the recusant wives of well-to-do squires who were church papists. On 25 March the northern high commission under Huntingdon's chairmanship ordered Babthorpe to have daily prayers in his house as appointed in the Book of Common Prayer, and to allow no recusants under his roof. Subsequently, on 13 April, his wife was taken into custody and was sent to Sheriff Hutton Castle where, with other gentlewomen, she was kept a prisoner for almost two years.

Despite his wife's refusal to conform, Babthorpe appears to have emerged from this episode without any damage to his reputation; it is significant that in 1595, for example, he was serving as a deputy lieutenant. In 1603 he was one of many Yorkshire gentlemen knighted by James I on his journey south, and his son William probably received his knighthood at the same time.

Shortly before the accession of James I, Grace Babthorpe persuaded her husband to abandon his conformity by encouraging him to read two books which advanced the claims of the Roman Catholic church, to which he was consequently reconciled, though only gradually did his conversion become a matter of public knowledge. In a survey of Yorkshire Catholics carried out in 1604 it was noted that Sir Ralph and Sir William Babthorpe had recusant wives but that they themselves were only non-communicants. In 1607, however, the crown granted the benefits of Sir Ralph's recusancy to James, Lord Colville, who had to be bought off. Two years later Babthorpe managed to secure a lease of his estate at the modest rent of £62 12*s*. a year, which was subsequently reduced to £50. At the same time his new-found commitment had other consequences for him. From 1607 onwards he was frequently summoned to appear before the northern high commission, and on hearing that a warrant was on its way he took flight in order to escape the fine which would otherwise have been imposed. Sir William was then living in Lincolnshire, outside the jurisdiction of the commission, and after a while he was joined there by his father and the rest of the family.

The religious activities at Osgodby Hall were described by Father James Sharpe, a former chaplain, in an account written in 1610. According to this account all the servants were Roman Catholics and there were always two chaplains, one serving the household and the other looking after the spiritual needs of neighbouring families. On work days the normal schedule consisted of masses at 6 a.m. and 8 a.m., evensong, and matins, while on Sundays there were sermons and other additional features.

In 1612 the government decided that the leading recusants in each county should be called before the privy council and tendered the oath of allegiance which denounced the pope's deposing power. For anyone refusing the oath the statutory penalty was imprisonment for life and forfeiture of all property. The Babthorpe knights were both included in the Yorkshire list, but Sir Ralph had already departed for the continent and his son may also have taken avoiding action. Sir Ralph and his wife eventually settled at Louvain, where in 1618 he died of a stroke while engaged in spiritual exercises. Three years later Lady Babthorpe became a nun at the convent of St Monica in Louvain, where she died in 1635.

At the height of his prosperity Sir Ralph enjoyed a landed income of some £1300 a year and maintained an establishment of thirty servants or more. Although the manor of Bowthorpe had been sold in 1604 the estate was still largely intact at the time of his death. Within the next three years, however, Sir William disposed of virtually the whole of his patrimony. Such a financial catastrophe, which was without parallel among the recusant gentry of Yorkshire, can have been the product only of special factors. Probably the most important of these was an episode described in his mother's account of the family. She relates that when two priests were discovered in his house Sir William managed to hold off the pursuivants seeking to arrest them until they were safely away. As a result he was imprisoned for nearly a year and was forced to pay such a heavy fine that he was reduced to great poverty.

Having lost his houses at Osgodby and Babthorpe Sir William moved to his remaining property at Flotmanby, but in 1633 this too was sold. Now completely landless, he joined the Spanish army in the Netherlands and quickly attained the rank of captain. He was killed in 1635 while fighting against the French near Ardres in the Pas-de-Calais. J. T. CLIFFE

Sources J. Morris, ed., *The troubles of our Catholic forefathers related by themselves*, 1 (1872) [account of the Babthorpe family and Lady Babthorpe's recollections] • J. Morris, ed., *The troubles of our Catholic forefathers related by themselves*, 3 (1877) [Father James Sharpe's recollections of the Yorkshire mission] • *CSP dom.*, SP 1 (Henry VIII) • *CSP dom.*, SP 10 (Edward VI) • *CSP dom.*, SP 11 (Mary) • *CSP dom.*, SP 12 (Elizabeth) • high commission act books, Borth. Inst., vols. RVII/A/4 and RVII/AB/3, 4, 12, 15, 17–18 • PRO, chancery proceedings, ser. I, C.2 James I/B31/38 and S22/39 • PRO, chancery proceedings, six clerks' ser., C.5/589/2 and C.8/49/47 • BL, Lansdowne MS 153, fols. 52, 130, 301 • J. T. Cliffe, *The Yorkshire gentry from the Reformation to the civil war* (1969) • T. Burton, *The history and antiquities of the parish of Hemingborough in the county of York*, ed. J. Raine (1888) • HoP, *Commons, 1509–58*, 1.357–8 • A. Gooder, ed., *The parliamentary representation of the county of York, 1258–1832*, 2, Yorkshire Archaeological Society, 96 (1938), 8–11 • H. Aveling, *Post Reformation Catholicism in east Yorkshire, 1558–1790*, East Yorkshire Local History Society, 11 (1960) • state papers, domestic, Mary, PRO, SP 11

Babthorpe, Grace, Lady Babthorpe (*c*.1563–1635). *See under* Babthorpe family (*per. c*.1501–1635).

Babthorpe, Sir Ralph (1561–1618). *See under* Babthorpe family (*per. c*.1501–1635).

Babthorpe, Sir Robert (*d*. 1436), soldier and administrator, rose to prominence in the service of the Lancastrian dynasty. The family came from Babthorpe, in the parish of Hemingbrough, Yorkshire. Details of his parentage are not easy to establish, but he seems to have been the son of Robert Babthorpe and his wife, Margaret, who were in possession of the manor of Babthorpe in 1412. The lordship of Hemingbrough belonged to the priory of Durham, and Ralph Babthorpe, Sir Robert's grandfather, had been the prior's steward there.

It was in the service of Henry IV that Robert Babthorpe built his career. He was described as a king's esquire by 1403, though there is no record of him in Lancastrian service before the usurpation of 1399. It is possible that he owed his preferment to an association with John Waterton of Waterton, Lincolnshire, whose brother Sir Hugh and cousin Robert were leading figures in the new regime. Certainly, Babthorpe later married John Waterton's daughter and heir Eleanor, probably in 1409–10. After Eleanor's death he took as his second wife Bridget Pilkington, of the Lancashire family.

In 1406, after the death of the leading Lancastrian retainer Sir Thomas Rempston on 31 October, Babthorpe received his first appointment to major office. On 4 November he was granted the stewardships of the duchy of Lancaster's honour of Leicester in Leicestershire and Warwickshire, including Castle Donington and Kenilworth, and of the duchy's lands in Northamptonshire, including Higham Ferrers, all of which had previously been held by Rempston. These offices, which he held for life, formed the basis of his political influence, but under Henry V he was promoted further. He served on the Agincourt campaign, and it was probably at this point (certainly by March 1416) that he was knighted. He remained with the king in France for much of the rest of the decade, and was active at the siege of Rouen in 1418–19. He was controller of the king's household from 1416, and served as steward of the household from September 1421 to April 1424; by 1423 he was steward of Queen Catherine's Leicestershire estates. He was named an executor and administrator of Henry V's will. His brother William, a lawyer, was also promoted by Henry, becoming his attorney-general in 1419.

Babthorpe served as sheriff of Staffordshire in 1414–15; as an outsider in the shire he seems to have played a mediating role as part of Henry V's intervention to settle the disorder that had developed there in the latter years of the previous reign. It was not until the following decade that Babthorpe served as a JP, presumably because of his absences in France between 1415 and 1420. He was appointed to peace commissions in Leicestershire, Staffordshire, and Warwickshire in 1422, and served thereafter on the bench in Warwickshire and the East Riding of Yorkshire, as well as on a number of other commissions in Yorkshire.

On 1 March 1432 Babthorpe was reappointed as steward of Henry VI's household, a post he held until the summer of 1433, when he was replaced by the earl of Suffolk. He also seems to have served as a member of the king's council in 1433. The timing of Babthorpe's tenure of office suggests that his appointment formed part of the duke of Gloucester's attempt to take over control of government in 1432–3. Babthorpe's replacement as steward in 1433 therefore seems to be both an indication and a consequence of Gloucester's failure. Babthorpe was also replaced as steward of the duchy of Lancaster in Warwickshire in July 1433.

Babthorpe died in August 1436, and is said to have been buried in the church at Hemingbrough; seven years earlier, like his grandfather, he had been appointed the prior of Durham's steward there. His heir was his son Ralph, who was killed—together with his own son, another Ralph—fighting against the Yorkists at the first battle of St Albans in 1455. HELEN CASTOR

Sources R. Somerville, *History of the duchy of Lancaster, 1265–1603* (1953) · *Chancery records* · T. Burton, *The history and antiquities of the parish of Hemingborough in the county of York*, ed. J. Raine (1888) · W. Hardy, ed., 'Calendar of the Norman rolls, Henry V', *Report of the Deputy Keeper of the Public Records*, 41 (1880), appx I, pp. 671–810; 42 (1881), 313–472 · *The Plumpton letters and papers*, ed. J. Kirby, CS, 5th ser., 8 (1996) · M. J. Stanley Price, ed., *Yorkshire deeds*, 10, Yorkshire Archaeological Society, 120 (1955), 95 [deed 260] · J. L. Watts, *Henry VI and the politics of kingship* (1996) · E. Powell, *Kingship, law, and society: criminal justice in the reign of Henry V* (1989) · R. A. Griffiths, *The reign of King Henry VI: the exercise of royal authority, 1422–1461* (1981)

Babthorpe, Sir William (*c*.1490–1555). *See under* Babthorpe family (*per. c*.1501–1635).

Babthorpe, Sir William (*c*.1529–1581). *See under* Babthorpe family (*per. c*.1501–1635).

Babthorpe, Sir William (1580–1635). *See under* Babthorpe family (*per. c*.1501–1635).

Babyon, Peter. *See* Babion, Peter (*supp. fl.* 1150).

Bach, Edward (1886–1936), homoeopathic physician, was born at The Hollies, Alcester Road, Moseley, Birmingham, on 24 September 1886, the son of Walter Best Bach, a brass-founder, and his wife, Ada Brenda Tipper. He was educated at Winterloe School, Moseley, Birmingham, but left aged sixteen and worked in the foundry for three years in order to collect the money to pay for his medical education. However, when his father realized that his ambition was serious, he agreed to give him a sufficient allowance for him to enter Birmingham University. In 1912 he qualified in medicine at University College Hospital, London, after which he served there as casualty house surgeon. He then took up a similar appointment at the National Temperance Hospital, but ill health prevented him from completing his term there. On 14 January 1913 he married Gwendoline (*b*. 1888/9), daughter of Eouery Caiger, a consulting engineer. After her death he married on 2 May 1917 Kitty Emmeline Jane (*b*. 1889/90), daughter of James Light, a company secretary.

Bach became disillusioned by the way that conventional medicine concentrated on the curing of symptoms, and he came to believe that effective treatment depended upon knowledge of the causes of disease. Therefore, having been found unfit for military service, he returned to University College Hospital in 1915 as assistant bacteriologist, to develop his interest in immunology. He became well known as a bacteriologist among the orthodox profession, working in the field of intestinal toxaemia. In 1919 he moved to the London Homoeopathic Hospital. Here he demonstrated the presence of non-lactose-fermenting bacilli in the stools of many patients. These were similar to the typhoid bacillus but non-pathogenic. However, Bach believed that they caused toxins which could be absorbed into the bloodstream and produce ill health. He admired C. F. S. Hahnemann, the founder of homoeopathy, whom he considered had realized that disease originated above the physical plane. Bach regarded his own work in the laboratory as a natural sequel to homoeopathy and believed that he had demonstrated the validity of Hahnemann's theory of chronic disease.

Together with Dr Charles Wheeler, a physician at the hospital, Bach prepared vaccines from the bacteria he had discovered, for treatment in accordance with the received wisdom of the time. In 1925 they published *Chronic Disease, a Working Hypothesis*, an account of their work in which they claimed remarkable successes in 500 cases that had received no treatment other than the vaccines. Wheeler was the first doctor to prepare homoeopathic remedies from the polyvalent vaccines, and Dr Dishington of Glasgow used these clinically. On hearing of this work in 1927, Bach set about preparing a new stock of polyvalent vaccines suitable for potentizing. He had the remedies prepared at considerable personal expense. These were some of the bowel nosodes which John Paterson, the then bacteriologist at the hospital, later showed could be associated with other homoeopathic remedies. But Bach was already seeking a better method of treatment.

Because the load of routine work interfered with his research, Bach had left the London Homoeopathic Hospital in 1922. He continued his highly successful Harley Street practice and also treated the poor free of charge. In 1928 he is said to have realized at a dinner party that personalities could be classified into several distinct types, and he concluded that reactions to disease would also differ. That autumn he went to Wales and brought back two plants, *Mimulus* and *Impatiens*, from which he prepared remedies by a similar method to that used for the vaccines. He later added *Clematis* to his medicines. In 1930 he gave up his practice. He made another journey to Wales in search of more herbs. When walking through a dew-laden field he decided that a dewdrop, when warmed by the sun, could absorb the remedial properties of a plant. This led to his method of preparing remedies using only pure water. That year he wrote *Heal Thyself*, which was published in 1931 and has remained in print ever since. In it he summarized his theory that disease was due to soul and personality being in conflict.

From 1930 to 1934 Bach lived in Cromer, Norfolk, seeking and preparing further remedies with which he treated patients successfully. He did not charge for this treatment and his financial resources dwindled. He therefore moved to Mount Vernon, a small house in Oxfordshire. Here he wrote, lectured, sought further remedies, and trained assistants to carry on his work. His advertising, and use of medically unqualified assistants, brought him into conflict with the General Medical Council. He received two warnings, though formal proceedings were never instituted. Having produced thirty-seven flower remedies, and a mixture known as 'Rescue remedy', he was satisfied that his work was complete. He now had medicines available to treat all the negative factors that he believed caused disease.

Bach appears to have been a healer in the true sense and is reputed to have healed patients simply by touch. He had an intense unselfish desire to help others. He was a gentle man, an idealist yet practical. His tastes were simple; he loved the country, gardening, and carpentry. Nobody who knew him failed to admire him, however strongly they might disagree with his theories. Bach died as a result of cardiac failure and sarcoma on 27 November 1936 in the Ladygrave Nursing Home, Manor Road, Didcot, and was buried in St James's churchyard, Sotwell, Oxfordshire. The Edward Bach Centre was established at Mount Vernon in recognition of his work. BERNARD LEARY

Sources E. Bach, *Heal thyself* (1931) • J. Howard, *The work of Dr. Edward Bach* (1995) • private information (2004) [Judy Howard, Edward Bach Centre] • N. Weeks, *The medical discoveries of Dr. Edward Bach, physician* (1973) • *British Homoeopathic Journal*, 27/1 (1937), 78 • b. cert. • d. cert. • m. certs.
Archives Edward Bach Centre, Mount Vernon, Sotwell, Oxfordshire
Likenesses photograph, Edward Bach Centre, Mount Vernon, Sotwell, Oxfordshire

Bach, Johann Christian (1735–1782), composer, was born on 5 September 1735 in Leipzig, Saxony, the sixth and youngest son and the eleventh of the thirteen children of Johann Sebastian Bach (1685–1750), composer, and his second wife, Anna Magdalena (1701–1760), daughter of Johann Caspar Wilcke, court trumpeter. He was probably educated at the Thomasschule, Leipzig, where his father was responsible for his musical studies as *Kantor* at St Thomas's Church and civic director of music. After J. S. Bach's death in 1750, Johann Christian moved to Berlin, where his half-brother Carl Philipp Emanuel assumed responsibility for his welfare and education. His first surviving large-scale compositions, including at least five keyboard concertos, date from his years in Berlin, where he also gained renown as a harpsichordist.

In 1755 Bach made a decisive break with the inward-looking Lutheran traditions of his forebears by travelling to Italy, possibly in the company of an Italian lady singer, where he took counterpoint lessons with Padre Martini in Bologna, composed several Roman Catholic church works (he was received into the Roman Catholic church about 1760), and secured a Milanese patron, Count Agostino Litta, in whose house he lived from before 1757 and through whose efforts he became 'second organist' at Milan Cathedral in 1760. But it was in the opera house, not the organ loft, that he found his true métier. The success of his three operas for Italy, *Artaserse* (1760), *Catone in Utica* (1761), and *Alessandro nell' Indie* (1762), prompted an invitation to compose two works for the King's Theatre, London, and in 1762 Bach travelled to London, where he spent the remaining twenty years of his life as the dominant musical figure in the city, thereby earning the sobriquet 'the London Bach'.

By February 1764 Bach was music master to Queen Charlotte. His duties entailed accompanying the amateur music-making of the king and queen, teaching the harpsichord to the royal family, and organizing the queen's chamber music concerts. For the King's Theatre he composed five Italian operas, of which the first, *Orione* (1763), and the last, *La clemenza di Scipione* (1778), were perhaps the most successful, and an oratorio *Gioas, re di Giuda* (1770). Bach gave his first concert with his compatriot Carl Friedrich Abel in 1764 and in 1765 inaugurated the series of subscription concerts that eventually bore their names. Between 1765 and 1767 these were held at Carlisle House, Soho Square, and were organized by the impresario Teresa Cornelys. From January 1768 Bach and Abel managed the concerts themselves at Almack's assembly rooms in King Street, St James's. The Bach–Abel concerts moved in 1775 to the lavish Hanover Square rooms, specially built for the purpose with the financial assistance of Giovanni Gallini. At these concerts many of Bach's symphonies, concertos, cantatas, chamber works, and keyboard sonatas were given their first performances.

Johann Christian Bach (1735–1782), by Thomas Gainsborough, 1776 [replica]

As a composer and a soloist Bach did much to champion the pianoforte, an instrument then being developed in London by German immigrant craftsmen: the sonatas op. 5 are apparently the first works published in England to specify the piano on the title-page, and Bach is credited with performing the first solo on the instrument in public in London in 1768. The composer visited France, Germany, and Italy on a number of occasions, writing operas to be performed in Mannheim and Paris. He was acquainted with many great men of his age, including Sir Joshua Reynolds, John Zoffany, Thomas Gainsborough (who painted his portrait), Charles Burney, Denis Diderot, and Leopold and Wolfgang Amadeus Mozart. On the Mozarts' visit to London in 1764–5 Bach is reputed to have performed duets with the eight-year-old composer. This friendship with young Mozart, who was much influenced by Bach's music, was renewed at another meeting in Paris in 1778.

In the mid-1770s (the exact date is unknown) Bach married Cecilia Grassi, an Italian singer then past her prime. They had no children. Bach's last years were clouded by financial worries caused by declining receipts and heavy expenditure on the Hanover Square concerts. He died, leaving £4000 of debts, on 1 January 1782, presumably at the house in Paddington to which he had moved in November 1781, and was buried on 6 January 1782 in St Pancras's churchyard. STEPHEN ROE

Sources C. S. Terry, *John Christian Bach*, 2nd edn (1967) · H. Gärtner, *John Christian Bach: Mozart's friend and mentor*, trans. R. G. Pauly (1994) · S. Roe, 'Bach (12)', *New Grove*, 2nd edn · E. Warburton, 'Johann Christian Bach', *The New Grove Bach family*, ed. C. Wolff (1983)

Likenesses T. Gainsborough, oils, 1776, Civico Museo, Bologna, Bibliografico Musicale · T. Gainsborough, oils, replica, 1776, NPG [*see illus.*]

Bacharach, Alfred Louis (1891–1966), food scientist and musician, was born in Hampstead, London, on 11 August 1891, the son of Otto Leonhard Bacharach, a stockbroker, of Hampstead, and his wife, Alice Eva Wagner. He lived throughout his life in Hampstead. Bacharach was educated at St Paul's School, where he was a foundation scholar, and at Clare College, Cambridge (1910–13), where he read natural sciences. It was at Cambridge that the first of his interests, an intellectual commitment to left-wing political views, became apparent. He involved himself with the Independent Labour Party, joined the Fabian Society, and developed a concern that continued for nearly forty years with the affairs of the Working Men's College in north London. His commitment to socialist ideas was recognized during the tenure of the Labour government of 1924 by his appointment to the controlling bodies of a number of educational establishments including the Borough Polytechnic and Kynaston School.

Although Bacharach was deeply concerned with political theory and widely admired for his intellectual stature in this field, this was only one of his interests; many of those who came into contact with him in one sphere were only dimly aware of his other enthusiasms. His second great love was for music. He was an accomplished pianist and he gathered other musicians about him to play and talk. Out of this came the four books for which, as editor and author, his name became widely known. *The Musical Companion*, of which there was also a later edition, was first published in 1934, *Lives of the Great Composers* in 1935, *British Music of our Time* in 1946, and *The Music Masters* appeared in instalments between 1948 and 1954. These works helped to establish for Bacharach a considerable reputation as a connoisseur of music.

On leaving university in 1913 Bacharach worked for three years in the Wellcome Chemical Research Laboratories and then, for a further year, in the Wellcome Chemical Works. In 1920 he was employed by the firm of Joseph Nathan & Co. Ltd, later to become the Glaxo Laboratories, where he remained for thirty-five years. At that time there were problems with artificial baby foods: even when dried cows' milk, which was imported from New Zealand, was mixed with other ingredients in order to make it resemble human milk as closely as possible, it was not uniformly satisfactory as an artificial substitute. There was, for example, the danger of rickets, caused by a lack of vitamin D. Bacharach threw himself into the study of that vitamin, one form of which, as was demonstrated by research, could be manufactured by irradiation. Bacharach attacked the problem of measuring the amount of the vitamin present both in concentrated preparations and in the mixtures in which the concentrates were incorporated. At that time the only way to do this was to administer the test substance to young rachitic rats and examine the degree to which their condition was ameliorated. Bacharach was among the first to apply rigorous statistical techniques to improve the precision of such experiments. He also introduced, at least in British practice, the use of pure-bred rats in the tests.

Without being a profound scientific thinker, any more than he was a great musician or a major political figure, Bacharach was a keen observer of the passing scene and an expert commentator. His agile mind was at its most sparkling in discussion, suggestion, and debate. Whether it was on the council of the Royal Institute of Chemistry, of which he became a fellow and a vice-president, as chairman of the food group of the Society of Chemical Industry, as a member of the Chemical Council or of the council of the Society of Analytical Chemistry, or as president of the Nutrition Society, which he played a part in founding and of which he was the first honorary treasurer, Bacharach could be found debating and discussing, stimulating more pedestrian colleagues to delight, despair, admiration, or exasperation. He was invariably urbane, never dull, often the catalyst bringing about the collision of ideas from which something new emerged. In 1938 he published *Science and Nutrition*; in 1941, jointly with F. A. Robinson, he produced an English translation of László Zechmeister's *Principles and Practice of Chromatography*; and in 1946 he edited *The Nation's Food*.

There was yet a fourth strand to Bacharach's disparate interests—the complement to his virtuosity as a talker. This was his passion for grammatical exactitude. He held that scientific writers, as much as any others, might from time to time benefit if their attention was drawn to syntactical order; and so unflaggingly (and in violet ink) Bacharach dealt out deserved, and good-humoured, reproof. In his later years he would visit outlying branches of the learned scientific societies to which he belonged and deliver his lecture, 'Writing wrongs', the principles of which guided his actions, while meting out his judgments as a member of their publications committees. In 1950 he ceased to control the nutritional laboratories at Glaxo but, as head of the publicity services group, set about improving the standard of the company's literature.

There are some scientists who advance knowledge by working silently in their laboratories, there are others who found businesses or build machines. Bacharach was more than a man of science, he was an outstandingly eclectic man of his time. His major contribution was to make his contemporaries think.

On 13 March 1931 Bacharach married Elizabeth Owen (*b.* 1902/3) and they had two sons. He died on 16 July 1966 at 26 Willow Road, Hampstead, his home for many years.

MAGNUS PYKE, *rev.*

Sources *The Times* (18 July 1966), 12e · *The Times* (21 July 1966), 14g · *The Times* (29 July 1966), 14g · *Chemistry and Industry* (1 Oct 1966), 1651–3 · personal knowledge (1981) · m. cert. · d. cert. · C. Roth, ed., *Encyclopaedia Judaica*, 16 vols. (Jerusalem, 1971–2)
Likenesses photograph, repro. in *Chemistry and Industry*
Wealth at death £3140: probate, 11 Nov 1966, *CGPLA Eng. & Wales*

Bache, Constance (1846–1903). *See under* Bache, Walter (1842–1888).

Bache, Francis Edward (1833–1858), composer and organist, was born on 14 September 1833 at Birmingham, the eldest of the seven children of Samuel *Bache (1804–1876), a Unitarian minister, and his wife, Emily, *née* Higginson (*d.* 1855). From a very early age he showed extraordinary talent for music, learning the piano, organ, and violin. On the last instrument, which he studied with Alfred Mellon, he played in the orchestra at the Birmingham festivals of 1846 and 1847. Having decided to become a professional musician, he left school in the summer of 1849, and, after studying for a short time with the city organist of Birmingham, James Stimpson, went to London, and continued his studies with Sterndale Bennett. He became organist at All Saints' Church, Gordon Square, in October 1850, and in November his first overture was performed at the Adelphi Theatre.

From 1849 to 1853 Bache worked hard in London, teaching, studying, and, under contract to the publishing firm Addison, Hollier, and Lucas, composing numerous piano pieces. In October 1853 he went to study with Moritz Hauptmann in Leipzig, where he remained until the end of the following year; he returned to England in 1855 after short stays in Dresden and Paris. He then obtained an appointment as organist at Hackney, but was soon forced to give it up by illness. In 1856 he went to Algiers, where for a time the symptoms of his tuberculosis were alleviated. From Algiers he travelled through Paris en route to Leipzig, then, via Dresden and Vienna, to Rome, where he spent the winter. In June 1857 he returned to Britain, and passed the next winter at Torquay, but on his return to Birmingham in April 1858 his condition gradually worsened, and he died, at 44 Frederick Street, Edgbaston, on 24 August.

It is undeniable that Bache's potential was greater than his achievements; as a twentieth-century commentator remarked, 'Bache's early death deprived Victorian music of one of its most promising talents' (*New Grove*). But though much that he wrote was obviously the ephemeral and immature work of one whose powers were prevented from full development, some of his compositions show that he possessed considerable talent. His piano compositions evidence attractive spontaneity and polish in their essentially Mendelssohnian idiom; and similar traits, developed to a higher level, are encountered in his songs, especially those published as op. 16 (*c.*1850), which include settings of Uhland, Goethe, and Heine, and which constituted a significant contribution to the development of sensitive word-setting, on the German model, in nineteenth-century England.

W. B. SQUIRE, *rev.* CLIVE BROWN

Sources C. Bache, *Brother musicians: reminiscences of Edward and Walter Bache* (1901) [with a list of F. E. Bache's compositions] · N. Temperley, 'Bache, Francis Edward', *New Grove* · S. B., 'Francis Edward Bache', *Christian Reformer, or, Unitarian Magazine and Review*, new ser., 14 (1858), 713–19 · private information (1885) · d. cert.
Archives BL, letters to family, MS 54193

Bache, Samuel (1804–1876), Unitarian minister, was born on 24 December 1804 at Bridgnorth, Shropshire, to Joshua Tilt Bache, a grocer (*d.* 1837), and his wife, Margaret Silvester, of Newport, Shropshire. After his mother's death in 1808 he was raised by his father's sister, Mrs Maurice, at Stourbridge. He was educated by a Mr Beasley, of Nodland near Stourbridge, a cousin of the well-known Revd Ebenezer Beasley (1763–1824), dissenting minister at Uxbridge, and was for a time assistant in the school of the Revd Lant Carpenter (1780–1840) at Bristol. He was educated for the ministry at Manchester College, York, in 1826–9.

On 1 July 1829 Bache became minister at Dudley, and in 1832 moved to Birmingham as co-minister with John Kentish (1768–1853) at the New Meeting, Moor Street, once the congregation of Joseph Priestley (1733–1804); Kentish declined a salary after 1832 but continued to preach until 1844, after which Bache was in all but name sole pastor. During much of his pastorate, Bache also kept a school. In 1862 the chapel was sold to Roman Catholics, and the congregation moved to a handsome Gothic structure in Broad Street, called the church of the Messiah. In 1859 Bache took a leading part with the Revd John Cale Miller (1814–1880), the evangelical rector of St Martin's, in the establishment of Hospital Sunday, an institution begun in Birmingham.

Bache regularly attended the New Street Theatre in Birmingham; the only other minister to do so was the high-church clergyman at St Paul's. Shortly after his settlement Bache publicly defended theatre-going against evangelical denunciation, an action that brought him a gift of a case of port from an anonymous admirer. In 1840 he similarly defended the triennial music festivals against the criticism of the Quaker Joseph Sturge.

On his settlement in Birmingham in 1832 Bache married Emily (*d.* 1855), the second daughter of the Revd Edward Higginson (1781–1832) of Derby, whose eldest daughter, Helen, was the wife of the Revd James Martineau (1805–1900). Seven children were born, three of whom became prominent in the English musical world: Francis Edward *Bache (1833–1858), composer; Walter *Bache (1842–1888), pianist; and Constance *Bache (1846–1903), musical translator [*see under* Bache, Walter]. The youngest son, John Kentish Bache (1844–1916), became Unitarian minister at Moretonhampstead in 1868, and took Anglican orders, after his father's death, in 1876.

With a commanding, reserved presence, Bache was a compelling preacher and a dedicated teacher. His friend

Samuel Bache (1804–1876), by Joseph Moore, 1862

the Revd John Gordon (1807–1880) thought the very narrowness of his penetrating intellect was 'a condition of its exceptional power' (Gordon, 25). Among Unitarians Bache represented that section, deeply obligated to Priestley and aimed at carrying out the principles of John Locke's *Reasonableness of Christianity*, regarding Jesus Christ as the Messiah, the miraculously attested exponent of a pure morality and a simple theology, and the revealer, by his resurrection, of an eternal life; Bache's choice of the name for his new church in 1862 was thus a polemical statement at the height of a generational struggle within the denomination.

Such theologically conservative views had come under increasing attack from the 'new school', particularly identified with James Martineau and John James Tayler (1797–1869). Their abandonment of the gospel miracles led Bache to propose on 23 May 1866 that the British and Foreign Unitarian Association require as a condition of membership 'recognition of the special divine mission and authority, as a religious teacher, of Jesus Christ'. The motion, of which ample notice had been given, was severely attacked as an effort to impose a creed on a denomination that had steadily rejected human formularies, and its overwhelming defeat was widely hailed as a victory for religious liberty.

It was also a serious blow to Bache. His wife's death in 1855 had affected him deeply, and in 1868 failing health led him to resign his pulpit. Afflicted with 'softening of the brain', he lived the last two years of his life in a physician's house, Barnwood, in Gloucester, where he died on 7 January 1876. He was buried in Hockley cemetery on 13 January. ALEXANDER GORDON, *rev.* R. K. WEBB

Sources *The Inquirer* (22 Jan 1876) • J. Gordon, *The good and faithful servant: a sermon on the occasion of the death of the Rev. Samuel Bache* (1876) • *The Inquirer* (1865–6) • *Unitarian Herald* (1865–6) • S. Bache, *Miracles: the credentials of Christ* (1863) • d. cert. • letter, M. E. Bache to Alexander Gordon, 18 Oct 1885 • *Birmingham Daily Gazette* (13 Jan 1876)

Archives Harris Man. Oxf., lecture notes | JRL, letters to John Gordon

Likenesses J. Moore, bronze medal, 1862, NPG [*see illus.*]

Wealth at death under £6000: probate, 20 Jan 1876, *CGPLA Eng. & Wales*

Bache, Sarah (1771–1844), schoolmistress, was born at Bromsgrove, but was brought up in Worcester by close relatives named Laugher. With them, she attended the chapel of the Revd Thomas Belsham, a prominent Unitarian minister. She had many close connections within the Unitarian community: the Revd Thomas Laugher (*d.* 1769) was her uncle, and Joshua Tilt Bache (*d.* 1837), an important lay member of the sect, was her cousin. Some time after the death of her grandmother, Mrs Laugher, and before 1791, she moved to Birmingham, where she attended services led by Joseph Priestley. With the assistance of Phebe Penn, her half-sister, and A. Cameron, her niece, she for many years kept the Islington School, which, according to her obituary in the *Christian Reformer*, provided 'solid instruction and a truly parental instruction'. Another half-sister, Anna Penn, married the Revd Lant Carpenter; Sarah Bache contributed a hymn, 'See how he loved', to Carpenter's Exeter collection of 1812. She died at Hunter's Lane, Birmingham, on 23 July 1844.
ALEXANDER GORDON, *rev.* ROSEMARY MITCHELL

Sources *Christian Reformer, or, Unitarian Magazine and Review*, 11 (1844), 875–6 • *Birmingham Daily Gazette* (13 Jan 1876)

Likenesses T. Garner, line print (after F. Cruikshank), NPG

Bache, Walter (1842–1888), pianist, was born at Edgbaston, Birmingham, on 19 June 1842, the fourth of the seven children of Samuel *Bache (1804–1876), Unitarian minister, and his wife, Emily Higginson (*d.* 1855). He attended his father's proprietary school in Edgbaston, and took lessons with James Stimpson, city organist of Birmingham. In August 1858 he went to Leipzig, where he studied chiefly with Carl Reinecke and made friends with Arthur Sullivan, but moved on by way of Milan and Florence to seek out Liszt in Rome in June 1862. 'If I can spend some time with him and go through a good deal of music with him, I shall pick up at least a great deal of his ideas' (letter to his sister Constance, 25 July 1862; Bache, 157).

The three years Bache spent in Rome studying with Liszt, who treated him with great kindness, were indeed influential. He became an excellent pianist, and, back in London by 1865, he set about establishing Liszt's English reputation, beginning with a performance on two pianos of *Les préludes* on 4 July with Edward Dannreuther. For this he was regarded as 'dangerous' by the more conservative elements in English musical life, including *The Times* (whose critic, J. W. Davison, refused to meet him) and *The Athenaeum*, which thought the enterprise 'not worth the labour' (8 June). Two years later, together with Karl Klindworth, A. J. Hipkins, Frits Hartvigson, Dannreuther, and the painter Kümpel, he formed a private group which they called the Working Men's Society. This had the aim of promoting the music of Wagner and Liszt, initially by means of piano arrangements but from 1871 also with concerts introducing more and more of the so-called New German School, especially Liszt's major orchestral works. Bache spent much of his own money on them, regarding this as 'only an adequate return for the advantages he had derived from Liszt's tuition' (obituary, *MT*).

From 1869 until his retirement Bache gave an annual concert or recital devoted to Liszt, sometimes playing long programmes from memory (a preparatory concert for Liszt's London visit in 1886 included three concertos). Despite much critical hostility to Liszt (including from Bernard Shaw, who nevertheless respected Bache), he succeeded thereby in arousing first the interest and then the enthusiasm of the public. He visited Bayreuth for the first festival in 1876 and the second in 1882, making friendly contacts with Wagner. When Liszt, by then old and tired, visited England in the spring of 1886, Bache gave him a concert reception at the Grosvenor Gallery on 8 April, at which he persuaded London's leading musicians to give their services and a smart and influential audience to attend. He then joined Liszt in a series of concerts at which they appeared together. Liszt, who had referred to him as 'an artist of worth, intelligence and noble character' (letter to Malwine Tardieu, 9 Aug 1884; *Letters of Liszt*, 453), later wrote, 'Without Walter Bache and his long years of self-sacrificing efforts in the propaganda of my works, my visit to London were indeed not to be thought of' (letter to Bache, 17 Nov 1885; ibid., 478). On hearing of Liszt's death on 31 July 1886, Bache hurried to Bayreuth, arriving at the station just in time to join the funeral cortège. Bache was a popular piano teacher, and became a professor of piano at the Royal Academy of Music. He helped to found the Liszt scholarship there; after his death it was turned into the Liszt–Bache scholarship.

Bache's energies failed after Liszt's death, and he gave his last public recital on 22 October 1886. He died at his home, 17 Eastbourne Terrace, Hyde Park, London, on 26 March 1888, and was buried at Hampstead cemetery. In his memorial address, the principal of the Royal Academy of Music, Sir Alexander Mackenzie, spoke of Bache's 'unselfishness, honesty, truthfulness, tenderheartedness, generosity even to rashness', and called him 'a fine and sensitive artist, as well as a most noble man'. A vivid and affectionate account of Francis Edward *Bache and Walter Bache is given in *Brother Musicians* (1901) by their sister Constance. The youngest child of Samuel Bache, **Constance Bache** (1846–1903) was born in Birmingham on 11 March 1846 and studied the piano at the Munich conservatory and with Klindworth and Hartvigson. An accident to her right hand finished her public career, though she played occasionally in Birmingham before settling in London in 1883 as a teacher and writer. Her literary work included translations of Humperdinck's *Hänsel und Gretel*, Liszt's *St Elisabeth*, and the letters of Liszt and of Hans von Bülow. She also composed some songs. She died at Montreux, Switzerland, on 28 June 1903. JOHN WARRACK

Sources C. Bache, *Brother musicians: reminiscences of Edward and Walter Bache* (1901) · *New Grove* · Brown & Stratton, *Brit. mus.* · *MT*, 29 (1888), 229 · J. Bennett, *Forty years of music, 1865–1905* (1908) · *Letters of Franz Liszt*, ed. La Mara [I. M. Lipsius], trans. C. Bache, 2 vols. (1894) · *CGPLA Eng. & Wales* (1888) · *CGPLA Eng. & Wales* (1903) [Constance Bache]

Likenesses group portrait, photograph (with the Working Men's Society) · group portrait, photograph, repro. in Bache, *Brother musicians* · photograph (aged eighteen; taken in Leipzig) · portrait (as a child; after pencil sketch by Higginson)

Wealth at death £993 3*s*. 7*d*.: probate, 7 May 1888, *CGPLA Eng. & Wales* · £2330 2*s*. 6*d*.—Constance Bache: probate, 27 Nov 1903, *CGPLA Eng. & Wales*

Bacheler [Bachiler], **Daniel** (*bap.* **1572**, *d.* **1619**), lutenist and composer, was baptized on 16 March 1572 at Aston Clinton, Buckinghamshire, the fifth of the ten children of Richard Bacheler (1545–1583) and his wife, Elizabeth Cardell. On 13 November 1579 he was apprenticed to his mother's brother Thomas Cardell, a lutenist and dancing-master to Queen Elizabeth, with whom he went to live in King's Street in the parish of St Margaret's, Westminster. In June 1586 his apprenticeship was signed over to Sir Francis Walsingham, principal secretary of state.

For the Walsingham family Bacheler composed several pieces for the broken consort, the ultra-modern music for mixed instruments of which he was one of the originators. Eight of these have survived, one dated as early as 1588, when he would have been only sixteen; three of the Walsingham consort books, thought to be in his hand, are in Hull University Library. In Thomas Lant's illustration of the funeral procession of Walsingham's son-in-law Sir Philip Sidney, Bacheler is depicted sitting on Sidney's warhorse. After Walsingham's death in 1590 he joined the household of Robert Devereux, second earl of Essex, on his marriage to the widowed Frances Sidney. There he was paid £7 10*s*. a quarter and set to music Essex's poem 'To Plead my Faith'. This is his only surviving song. In August 1599 Bacheler was entrusted with letters from Queen Elizabeth to the earl, who was then fighting in Ireland.

When Lady Essex, by this time married to her third husband, the earl of Clanricarde, was invited to the court of Anne of Denmark, consort of James I, Bacheler accompanied her. Coming to the notice of the queen, in 1603 he was appointed the highest paid groom of her privy chamber, receiving £160 a year. Further rewards followed in return for such services as overseeing the maintenance of musical instruments at court and acting as a secretary, as when in 1606 he wrote on his mistress's behalf to the earl of Salisbury, thanking him for the present of a cup. In May 1604 Queen Anne granted to him and William Gomeldon 'a chest of arrows cast up as a wreck' in her manor of Portland (*CSP dom.*, 107); later he received the manor of Walton-cum-Trimley in Suffolk. In February 1607 he was granted a coat of arms bearing three dragons' heads, the dragon being the symbol of Denmark.

In his years at court Bacheler composed at least fifty pieces for the lute, the best known being 'Mounsiers Almaine'. While his earlier lute music exhibits a traditional style, with a complex contrapuntal structure and much use of imitation, later pieces found in Lord Herbert of Cherbury's lute book (Fitzwilliam Museum, Cambridge) reveal that he developed a simpler, chordal style. Throughout, the complexity and sheer technical difficulty of his music point to a superlative lutenist and a composer of enormous talent, second only to the great John Dowland, whose son Robert described Bacheler as 'right perfect'.

No record of a marriage has been found, but Cecily Bacheler of Twickenham, conveniently near Hampton Court, who died in 1610, was probably Bacheler's wife. In 1617 he witnessed the will of his uncle Thomas Cardell, who left him his chain of gold, but Bacheler died first, possibly of smallpox, which rampaged through the court in the winter of 1618–19. He was buried on 29 January 1619 in St Margaret's churchyard, Lee, Kent. He died intestate and without widow or children, and his brothers William and John disputed with his nephew Samuel over his considerable property. ANNE BATCHELOR

Sources A. Batchelor, *A Batchelor's delight* (1990), 37–63 · A. Ashbee, ed., *Records of English court music*, 9 vols. (1986–96) · A. Ashbee and D. Lasocki, eds., *A biographical dictionary of English court musicians, 1485–1714*, 1 (1998), 46–8 · D. Poulton, 'Bacheler, Daniel', *New Grove* · parish register (baptism), St Michael and All Angels, Aston Clinton · PRO, PROB 6/7, LH217; PROB 11/133, sentence 53, Parker/1619 · parish register (burial), St Margaret's, Lee
Likenesses T. Lant, engraving, 1587 (*Sequitur celebritas et pomposa funeris*), Penshurst Place, Kent
Wealth at death 'considerable property in several dioceses': will, PRO, PROB 11/133

Bachelor, Richard (*fl.* **1235**). *See under* Moneyers (*act.* *c.*1180–*c.*1500).

Bachhoffner, George Henry (**1810–1879**), scientific lecturer, was born in London on 13 April 1810. Nothing is known of his education, though in later life he was styled 'doctor of philosophy'. He was a well-known and popular lecturer on scientific subjects, publishing *Chemistry as Applied to the Fine Arts* (1837) and *A Popular Treatise on Voltaic Electricity and Electro-Magnetism* (1838). He was, with Sir George Cayley and others, one of the founders of the London Polytechnic Institution, Regent Street, which opened to the public in August 1838 as a place of popular instruction in science. He held the position of principal of the department of natural philosophy there from its foundation until August 1855. Among his many inventions was the Polytechnic gas fire, patented in 1850. He was briefly professor of natural philosophy at Elizabeth College, Guernsey. Appointed one of the district registrars of births, marriages, and deaths for Marylebone in 1837, he was superintendent registrar from 1853 to his death. He was lessee and manager of the Royal Colosseum, Regent's Park, from December 1856 until its final closure on 16 February 1864, delivering lecture courses similar to those that he had established at the Polytechnic Institution. Bachhoffner died at his home, 78 The Grove, Hammersmith, on 22 July 1879 leaving a widow, Caroline.

H. T. WOOD, *rev.* M. C. CURTHOYS

Sources Boase, *Mod. Eng. biog.* · private information (1885)
Wealth at death under £800: probate, 26 Sept 1879, *CGPLA Eng. & Wales*

Bachiler [Batchiler, Bachilor], **John** (*d.* **1674**), clergyman and ejected minister, of parents who are unknown, was admitted to Emmanuel College, Cambridge, in 1632 as coming from Oxfordshire. He graduated BA in 1636 and proceeded MA in 1639. In 1642 he was appointed by the House of Commons to give a weekly lecture at Lewisham, Kent, but was obstructed by the vicar and some of the local inhabitants. Other parishioners successfully petitioned the House of Lords in 1643 to confirm his appointment. Thomas Edwards later claimed that Bachiler was 'no Minister' (Edwards, 1.139).

Under the 1643 ordinance to control printing Bachiler was appointed one of the twelve divines empowered to license books of divinity. His licence appears at the beginning of a number of works. He did not restrict himself merely to giving his assent to publication, but added his comments, as, for example, on *Two Treatises … Concerning Infant Baptism* (1645) by John Tombes, where he acknowledged that the author was a godly man 'and of the Presbyterian judgement, though I am not of opinion with him' and he agreed to the publication of these treatises to encourage further contributions to the debate on infant baptism. Licensing *The Smoke in the Temple* (1645) by John Saltmarsh, a work advocating religious toleration, he described the book as 'this way of Peace and Reconciliation'. It was this which incensed presbyterians and led to complaints about him in the Westminster assembly. To Thomas Edwards, Bachiler was:

> Licenser-Generall of the Sectaries Books … who hath been a Man-midwife to bring forth more monsters begotten by the Divell, and borne of the Sectaries within this three last years then ever were brought into the light in England by all the former Licensers … for four score years. (Edwards, 3.102)

Bachiler was 'such a desperate Licenser' that:

> if the Devill himselfe should make a book, and give it the Title, A plea for liberty of conscience … he would license it, and … set before it the commendations of *A usefull Treatise*, of *A Sweet and Excellent Booke*, making for love and peace between brethren; or some such discourse. (Edwards, 3.104–5)

Several works licensed by Bachiler were attacks on Edwards himself, including two by William Walwyn and Thomas Webbe's *Mr Edwards Pen No Slander* (1646). The latter was one of the texts which, according to Edwards, Bachiler, 'an Independent', had tampered with to strengthen sectarian and Independent positions against the arguments of the presbyterians (Edwards, 2.138). Bachiler seems to have remained a licenser until 1647, when a new printing ordinance came into force. The following year he published a work of his own, *Golden Sands*, extolling the riches of free grace for the saints.

Between 1643 and 1645 Bachiler served in the parliamentarian army as chaplain to Colonel Valentine Walton, governor of King's Lynn. He then moved to Windsor as chaplain to Colonel Whichcote, governor of Windsor Castle. Here he encountered Charles I's young daughter Elizabeth, to whom he seems to have been some kind of chaplain and with whose virtues he was much taken. He stayed on as a civilian minister, preaching to both prisoners and garrison at Windsor, having in September 1647 become a fellow of Eton College. On 21 November 1648 he married Abigail Perwich (*bap.* 1631, *d.* 1674) at St John's, Hackney, Middlesex. In 1657 he was nominated an assistant to the Berkshire commission of ejectors. In 1658 he was appointed vicar of Datchet, Buckinghamshire, where the parishioners complained that he was an absentee, but he was exonerated by the trustees for the maintenance of preaching ministers. He lost all his positions in 1660.

After the Restoration, Bachiler took pains to dissociate himself from the religious radicals, subscribing both to a declaration against the Fifth Monarchist Thomas Venner in 1661, and in 1666 taking the Oxford oath, abhorring armed resistance to the king. At some point he moved to Hackney and became involved with the school kept by Mrs Perwich in the house of his father-in-law, Robert Perwich. He wrote a defence of the school and several volumes of religious queries, simple guides to religion, partly aimed against the Quakers, in the form of question and answer. He was buried in Hackney on 23 September 1674. By his will, made on 24 August and proved by his widow on 28 September, he left his estate to her, to be divided after her death (which occurred before the end of the year) between his nephews and nieces.

ANNE LAURENCE, *rev.*

Sources *Calamy rev.* • A. Laurence, *Parliamentary army chaplains, 1642–51* (1990) • T. Edwards, *Gangraena*, 3 pts (1646) • J. Batchiler, *The virgins pattern, in the exemplary life and lamented death of Mrs Susanna Perwich* (1661) • will, GL, London commissary court will register, 1673–6, fols. 152*v*–153*v* • W. B. Bannerman and A. W. Hughes Clarke, eds., *The registers of St Mary the Virgin, Aldermanbury, London*, 3 vols., Harleian Society, register section, 61–2, 65 (1931–5)

Back, Sir George (1796–1878), naval officer and explorer, was born on 6 November 1796 at Stockport, Cheshire, the second son of John Back and his wife, Ann. He entered the navy as midshipman of the *Arethusa* in 1808. He was present at the destruction of the batteries at Lequeitio, northern Spain, and, after being repeatedly under fire, in 1809, while on a cutting-out expedition with the *Arethusa*'s boats, he was taken prisoner by the French at Deba. The prisoners were sent to San Sebastian, and Back was small enough to be carried in one of the panniers of a sumpter mule across the Pyrenees. While a prisoner at Verdun, he studied mathematics, French, and drawing. In the winter of 1813–14 he travelled on foot through a large part of France, and on reaching England was appointed midshipman to the *Akbar*, in which he served against the French on the North American station. The *Akbar* was dismasted in a hurricane off Cape Hatteras, and nearly foundered. In 1816 she was paid off, and in 1817 Back was appointed Admiralty mate of the *Bulwark*.

In 1818 Back volunteered for service in the *Trent*, under Sir John Franklin, who was then entering on the first modern voyage of discovery in the Spitsbergen seas. On his return he rejoined the *Bulwark*, but in 1819 he set out with Franklin on his expedition by land to the Coppermine River, attempting to determine the latitude and longitude of the northern coast of North America, and the trend of the coast east of the Coppermine. In that terrible expedition it was largely owing to Back's dauntless determination that the party survived. At Fort Enterprise, Franklin sent him back to Fort Providence, and he was in imminent danger of starvation on the way. In five months he travelled 1204 miles on snow-shoes, with no other covering at

Sir George Back (1796–1878), by Maull & Polyblank

night in the woods but a blanket and a deerskin, frequently at −48 °F and once at 67 °F below zero, and sometimes without food for two or three days at a time. Later on, when Franklin was in dire straits, he again sent Back to get help from the Indians, and after incredible exertions and sufferings, and after seeing one of his companions die, he succeeded just in time to save Franklin's life. On returning to England he was made lieutenant on 1 January 1821.

In 1823 Back was appointed to the *Superb*, and sailed to the West Indies. In 1824, while at Lisbon, he was invited to join Franklin's expedition to the Mackenzie River, and hastened to do so, joining Franklin in London in December 1824. On that 1825–6 expedition he rendered Franklin notable service, especially in his dealings with the Inuit, and on coming home in 1827 he found that he had been promoted commander on 30 December 1825. His repeated applications for a ship met with no response, and he went to Italy to improve himself in the arts. At Naples in January 1832 he heard of the supposed loss of Captain Ross in the Arctic regions, and offered the Royal Geographical Society to go in search of him. He had been informed by Copper Indians on his previous journey of the existence of a river rising in the neighbourhood of the Great Slave Lake, and debouching on the Polar Sea, and by tracing this river to its mouth he hoped to make his way to Regent's

Inlet, where he thought Captain Ross might be. The council accepted his offer, and grants from government and Hudson's Bay Company, supplemented by a public subscription, financed the expedition, on which Back set out from Liverpool with only one companion of his own rank, Dr Richard King, as surgeon and naturalist, in February 1833.

Back's instructions were, in brief, firstly to make for the sea by the aforesaid river and, if possible, aid Captain Ross, and, secondly, to survey the coast as far as possible. The first winter he spent at Fort Reliance—a house that he constructed near the Great Slave Lake, when himself half-starved and amid starving Indians. In April he received news of Captain Ross's arrival in England, but he was ordered to push on to the river and survey the coast from there to Cape Turnagain. His first difficulty was to discover where the river lay, and to avoid embarking on the wrong one. The name of it was Thlew-ee-choh-deeseth, or Great Fish River (later known as the Back River). His journey down it is vividly recounted in his *Narrative of the Arctic Land Expedition to the Mouth of the Great Fish River, in 1834 and 1835* (1836), illustrated by his sketches. The ice prevented Back's proposed survey of the coast, and after again wintering at Fort Reliance he reached La Chêne, the Hudson Bay station where he had started over two years before, in August 1835, having travelled 7500 miles, including 1200 of discovery. Besides his discovery of a river over 440 miles long, he had made important observations of the Aurora Borealis, and had given the name of Montreal to an island afterwards sadly familiar in connection with the fate of Franklin.

In September 1835 Back reached England, and received a hero's welcome. He was awarded the Royal Geographical Society's gold medal, and was promoted by the Admiralty to the rank of captain on 30 September 1835, by order in council—an honour that no other officer in the navy had received except William IV. In February 1836 he was elected a fellow of the Royal Geographical Society. Also in 1836 he was, at his own proposal, appointed to the command of an expedition, the object of which was to complete the coast line between Regent's Inlet and Cape Turnagain. Back was given command of HMS *Terror* and the expedition set out in June 1836. The ship became trapped in ice; Back described the voyage in his *Narrative*, a book that captures much of the drama of Victorian Arctic exploration.

Few sailors ever survived more terrible perils and hardships than Back did on his expeditions. 'Arctic work', as Lord Brougham said of Franklin, 'had got into his blood', and he could not resist a challenge. Not surprisingly, his body reflected the demands made upon it, and after his last expedition he was for six years more or less an invalid, and never sailed again. In 1837 he received from the Royal Geographical Society both its medals. In March 1839 he was knighted; in 1844 he became president of the Raleigh Club (the Royal Geographical Society's exclusive dining club) and in January 1847 he was elected FRS. He also received the gold medal of the Société de Géographie de Paris (1835). He was employed by government to report on the harbour of Holyhead, but afterwards lived in retirement on half pay. On 13 October 1846 he married Theodosia Elizabeth (*d.* 1861), widow of Anthony Hammond of Savile Row, London. He was a vice-president and long on the council of the Royal Geographical Society, and contributed many reports. He continued an active interest in Arctic exploration, and served on the Arctic council which advised the Admiralty on the search expeditions for Franklin. Back and nearly all his fellow members of the council were wrong about the location of the missing men, so the Admiralty sent expeditions to the wrong places. With the end of the Franklin search, Back again withdrew into quiet retirement. He was made rear-admiral in March 1857, vice-admiral in September 1863, and admiral in October 1876, and in June 1854 he became DCL at the University of Oxford. Expeditions sometimes engender rivalry and recrimination. To his critics, Back was vain, dandyish, a womanizer, charming to persons from whom he hoped to gain, but 'intensely selfish, sly and sycophantic' (Holland, 27). However, to his admirers, who included the British public, he was in bravery, intelligence, and love of adventure the very model of an English sailor. He died at his home, 109 Gloucester Place, Portman Square, London, on 23 June 1878. His paintings, drawings, and sketches from his expeditions are an invaluable historical record. A. H. Beesly, *rev.* Andrew Lambert

Sources G. S. Ritchie, *The Admiralty chart: British naval hydrography in the nineteenth century* (1967) • A. Friendly, *Beaufort of the Admiralty* (1977) • *Navy List* • O'Byrne, *Naval biog. dict.* • C. A. Holland, 'Back, Sir George', *DCB*, vol. 10 • *Dod's Peerage* (1858) • private information (1885)

Archives McGill University, Montreal, McCord Museum, papers relating to Arctic expeditions • RGS • Scott Polar RI, corresp., journals, etc. | Bodl. Oxf., corresp. with Sir J. G. Wilkinson [some copies] • Derbys. RO, survey and sketchbooks, and corresp. with Franklin and Richardson • RGS, letters to Royal Geographical Society • Scott Polar RI, corresp. with John Richardson

Likenesses W. Drummond, lithograph, pubd 1828, BM; repro. in *Athenaeum portraits*, 50 • E. Finden, stipple, pubd 1828 (after R. Woodman), NPG • W. Brockedon, black and red chalk drawing, 1833, NPG • S. Pearce, group portrait, oils, 1851 (*The Arctic council planning a search for Sir John Franklin*), NPG • E. Edwards, photograph, NPG; repro. in L. Reeve, ed., *Men of eminence*, 3 (1865) • Maull & Polyblank, photograph, priv. coll. [*see illus.*] • engraving, repro. in *ILN*, 72 (1878), 4 • oils, McGill University, Montreal, McCord Museum

Wealth at death under £60,000: resworn probate, March 1879, *CGPLA Eng. & Wales* (1878)

Backhouse family (*per.* *c*.1770–1945), naturalists and horticulturists, came to prominence with James [i] Backhouse (1721–1798), who founded the Backhouse Bank in Darlington, co. Durham, in 1774 with his sons Jonathan (1747–1826) and James [ii] (1757–1804). It was Jonathan Backhouse who initiated the family's connection with horticulture, by following the mid-eighteenth-century fashion for large-scale tree planting on his estates at Weardale in co. Durham.

Descendants of Jonathan Backhouse (1747–1826) The tree planting of Jonathan Backhouse was an undertaking continued by three of his four sons: Jonathan *Backhouse (1779–1842), better known as a supporter of the Stockton

Robert Ormston Backhouse (1854–1940), by Vivian

and Darlington Railway; Edward (1781–1860), founder of the Backhouse Bank in Sunderland; and William [i]. All three brothers were awarded medals by the Royal Society of Arts for their enterprise. However, the youngest of the three, **William** [i] **Backhouse** (1779–1844), born at Darlington on 17 November 1779, was much more than a tree planter, and had a considerable reputation as a botanist in the north of England. He had close contact with the Newcastle botanist Nathaniel John Winch (1768–1838), with whom he corresponded from 1805 until 1831 and to whom he forwarded a list of rare Durham plants in February 1805. He was interested in British grasses and cultivated specimens sent to him by friends and correspondents who included James Janson (I'Anson) (1784–1821), Edward *Robson (1763–1813) (who was related by marriage to James [ii] Backhouse), William Brunton (1775–1806), the Revd James Dalton (1764–1843), and George Don (1764–1814). William [i] died suddenly on 9 June 1844 at the Quaker meeting-house in Darlington. His plant collection was considered of some significance; it was unfortunately destroyed by fire in 1865, when on loan to J. G. Baker.

William [i] Backhouse had married Mary Dixon (1783–1874) on 27 March 1806; they had two sons and three daughters. Their eldest son, **William** [ii] **Backhouse** (1807–1869), probably born in Darlington, continued the family interest in botany, became a competent entomologist, ornithologist, geologist, and meteorologist, and developed a number of new varieties of *Narcissus* (daffodils). Initially, however, William [ii] was employed in the family banking business; he worked in Newcastle following the opening of a branch of the Backhouse Bank there in 1825. While there his interests in natural history grew, and he became a founder member of the Natural History Society of Northumberland, Durham, and Newcastle upon Tyne in 1829. He was a competent entomologist, making extensive notes on Lepidoptera captured on the Backhouse estates in Durham. His interest in meteorology is revealed in diaries devoted to daily temperature and weather reports, and in requests from correspondents for readings from his 'weather gauge'. Watercolour drawings of local coastal sections, and extensive transcriptions, indicate a knowledge of geology. He formed a collection of stuffed birds and showed promise as an artist, producing watercolours, steel-engravings, and pencil drawings of a variety of subjects. After William [ii] returned to the Darlington bank he lived at St John's Hall, near Wolsingham, and there began his major horticultural work, the development of new varieties of *Narcissus*. In 1833 he married Amelia Flyer (*d.* 1837). In 1843 he married Katherine Aldam (1815–1868); they had four sons. William [ii] Backhouse died on 3 April 1869 at Chapeltown in Leeds. After his death his daffodil collection was purchased by Peter Barr and used in association with that of Edward Leeds (1802–1877) to establish a classification system for narcissi.

Three of William [ii] Backhouse's four sons from his second marriage, Charles James, Henry, and Robert Ormston, maintained the family interest in daffodils. Charles James (*b.* 1848) continued to live at St John's, while Henry (1849–1936) reared daffodils in Darlington between 1895 and 1907 and in Bournemouth from 1907 to 1925. **Robert Ormston Backhouse** (1854–1940) married Sarah Elizabeth Dodgson (1857–1921) in 1884, and two years later moved to Sutton Court, Sutton St Nicholas, Herefordshire. Furthering the Backhouse interest in narcissi, Sarah Elizabeth achieved national fame for her efforts and was awarded the Barr cup in 1916 for her hybridizing work. Together Sarah and Robert had begun to search for a pink-cupped daffodil, but it was not until 1923 (two years after his wife's death) that Robert astounded the horticultural world with the first pink-cupped, white-perianthed variety, which he named 'Mrs R. O. Backhouse'. He died at Sutton Court on 10 April 1940.

Robert and Sarah Backhouse's son, **William Ormston Backhouse** (1885–1962), was born on 20 February 1885 and educated at Bradfield College and at Trinity Hall, Cambridge. He worked for five years at the Cambridge Plant Breeding Station and the John Innes Institution, but left Britain to take up a post as an agricultural geneticist with the Argentine government. He established a number of wheat-breeding stations in Argentina, then moved to Patagonia, where on his estates he reared pigs, grew apples and other fruits, and started intensive honey production. He obtained narcissi from his parents, and in South America continued the family tradition set by his grandfather. He specialized in red-trumpeted daffodils, and on his return to England and Sutton Court in 1945 continued to develop these varieties. It was at Sutton Court that William Ormston Backhouse died on 7 August 1962.

Descendants of James [ii] Backhouse (1757–1804) James [ii] Backhouse, founder (together with his father and brother) of the Backhouse Bank, married Mary Dearman of Thorne, Yorkshire. Their sons were Nathan (1788–1805), Thomas (1792–1845), and **James** [iii] **Backhouse** (1794–1869). James [iii] Backhouse, who was born in Darlington on 8 July 1794, was encouraged to study plants by his elder brother. He was educated in Leeds but on his return to Darlington began to explore nearby Teesdale with the lead miner John Binks (1766–1817), who is credited with the discovery of many of the area's rare plants. Binks was undoubtedly a major influence on James [iii], as were his uncle Edward Robson, his cousin William [i] Backhouse, the Newcastle botanist Nathaniel John Winch, and William Hooker (1785–1865).

In 1815 James [iii] Backhouse, together with his brother Thomas, purchased the York nursery of John and George Telford, and by 1821 the business was flourishing. In 1822 James [iii] married Deborah Lowe (1793–1827) of Worcester. He began missionary work in York in 1824 and on 3 September 1831, having the previous year obtained the necessary documentation and in the company of George Washington Walker (1800–1859), he boarded the *Science*, bound for Australia. He stayed there until 1838, carrying out missionary duties and humanitarian work, but also collecting plants and seeds which he sent back to the York nursery and to Hooker in Glasgow. On the return journey he visited Mauritius *en route* for South Africa, where he continued his missionary duties until December 1840, finally arriving back in York on 21 February 1841. Backhouse described his travels in two books, his *Narrative of a Visit to the Australian Colonies* (1843) and *Narrative of a Visit to the Mauritius and South Africa* (1844), both illustrated with engravings by Edward Backhouse (1808–1879) of Sunderland, from original sketches by the author. Hooker and William Harvey (1811–1866) recognized the value of Backhouse's botanical observations, naming a myrtaceous shrub *Backhousia* in 1845.

Throughout his Australian journey James [iii] Backhouse had been in correspondence with his son, **James** [iv] **Backhouse** (1825–1890), and with his brother Thomas, the latter being responsible for the management and development of the nursery in James [iii]'s absence. James [iv] was born on 22 October 1825 in York. He inherited his father's love of botany, and from 1843 the two men explored upper Teesdale and other mountainous areas of Britain and Europe in search of alpine plants. Father and son jointly directed the growth of the York nursery from 1845 on the death of Thomas Backhouse, supervising its move to a 100 acre site at Holgate, York, in 1853. On 7 June 1855 James [iv] married Mary Robson of Dalton. He wrote a *Monograph of the British Hieracia* (1856) and in the pages of *The Phytologist* recorded his botanical discoveries in the upland areas of Teesdale and elsewhere in Britain. His son, **James** [v] **Backhouse** (1861–1945), was born on 14 April 1861 in York.

In addition, James [iv] was a keen archaeologist and geologist; he explored the caves of Teesdale in search of archaeological material and with his son James [v] formed an excellent personal museum. The Teesdale cave was excavated by the two men between 1878 and 1888; these explorations are described in James [v]'s *Upper Teesdale Past and Present* (1896). James [v] had close connections with the Yorkshire Museum, York, being an active member of the Yorkshire Philosophical Society and an honorary curator of zoology; the museum holds his collection of cave material and 4000 bird skins. However, he is best known as an ornithologist and as the author of the *Handbook of European Birds* (1890). On 15 May 1890 he married Mabel Grace Robson of Saffron Walden. The following year he formed a new company, Backhouse Nurseries (York) Ltd, which faced considerable competition from other plantsmen. Most of the land was sold in 1921 and the nursery finally ceased trading in 1955, ten years after James [v] died in 1945.

Descendants of Edward Backhouse (1781–1860) Edward *Backhouse (1808–1879), born in Darlington on 8 May 1808, was a son of Edward Backhouse (1781–1860), Jonathan Backhouse's son. A philanthropist, artist, pioneer photographer, and historian, he is best known for his *Early Church History* (with C. Taylor, 1884) and other religious works. A younger brother was Thomas James Backhouse (1810–1857), who married Margaret Richardson (1818–1854). Their son **Thomas William Backhouse** (1842–1920) was born on 14 August 1842. He lived at West Hendon House, Sunderland, and from the observatory he built there began the work which led to his being recognized as an outstanding meteorologist and astronomer. He began in 1858 to compile his *Astronomical Journal*, which eventually extended to thirty-six volumes, and published a series of fourteen maps of stars, accompanied by *A Catalogue of 9842 Stars Visible to the Naked Eye* (1911); the star maps were completed after his death. Thomas Backhouse's accurate meteorological observations were uninterrupted from 1857 until 1919; his contribution to the science was recognized by the Royal Meteorological Society, which appointed him as vice-president in 1918 and 1919. He died on 13 March 1920.

Lasting significance For almost 200 years members of the Backhouse family were actively involved in English horticulture, as tree planters, nurserymen, breeders, or botanists. Their name lives on in narcissi such as 'Mrs R. O. Backhouse' and 'Backhouse's Giant'. The remains of their York nursery (auctioned in 1955) later became a park run by York city council. The marriage between Jonathan Backhouse (1779–1842) and Hannah Chapman (coheir of Joseph Gurney, a private banker in Norwich) began a process which ended in 1896 with the Backhouse Bank's becoming a part of Barclay & Co. of Lombard Street (later to become Barclays, one of the 'big five' clearing banks).

PETER DAVIS

Sources P. Davis, 'The Backhouses and their scientific pursuits', *Quakers in natural history and medicine in Ireland and Britain* [Glasnevin 1994], ed. E. C. Nelson (1996), 37–54 • P. Davis, 'William Backhouse, 1807–1869, of St John's Hall, Wolsingham: entomologist, ornithologist and horticulturalist', *The Naturalist*, 112 (1987), 85–93 • P. Davis, 'James Backhouse of York, 1794–1869: missionary, traveller and botanist', *Archives of Natural History*, 16 (1989), 247–60 •

P. Davis, 'The Backhouses of Weardale, co. Durham, and Sutton Court, Hereford: their botanical and horticultural interests', *Garden History*, 18/1 (1990), 57–68 • Desmond, *Botanists*, rev. edn • J. Foster, *Descendants of John Backhouse* (1894) • Herefs. RO, Backhouse MSS [William [ii] Backhouse] • B. R. Hillard, 'Mr W. O. Backhouse—breeder of daffodils', *Gardeners' Chronicle*, 3rd ser., 152 (1962), 305 • M. B. Trott, 'Backhouse, James', *AusDB*, vol. 1 [James [iii] Backhouse] • *Annual Report and Transactions* [Yorkshire Philosophical Society] (1946) [James [v] Backhouse] • *CGPLA Eng. & Wales* (1869) [James [iii] Backhouse and William [ii] Backhouse] • *CGPLA Eng. & Wales* (1890) [James [iv] Backhouse] • *CGPLA Eng. & Wales* (1920) [Thomas William Backhouse] • *CGPLA Eng. & Wales* (1945) [James [v] Backhouse]

Archives Durham County Council, Durham • Herefs. RO • Linn. Soc. • NL Wales • priv. coll. • RBG Kew • Royal Horticultural Society, London • RS Friends, Lond. • University of Tasmania • Yorkshire Museum, York | Linn. Soc., Winch corresp.

Likenesses Vivian, photograph (Robert Ormston Backhouse), Royal Horticultural Society, Lindley Library [*see illus.*]

Wealth at death under £6000—James [iii] Backhouse: probate, 17 March 1869, *CGPLA Eng. & Wales* • £28,618 18*s*. 4*d*.—James [iv] Backhouse: resworn probate, July 1891, *CGPLA Eng. & Wales* • £1766 13*s*. 10*d*.—James [v] Backhouse: probate, 1945, *CGPLA Eng. & Wales* • £31,550 1*s*. 9*d*.—Robert Ormston Backhouse: probate, 3 May 1940, *CGPLA Eng. & Wales* • £85,479 4*s*. 10*d*.—Thomas William Backhouse: probate, 1920, *CGPLA Eng. & Wales* • under £3000—William [ii] Backhouse: probate, 10 June 1869, *CGPLA Eng. & Wales* • £119,184 6*s*. 0*d*.—William Ormston Backhouse: probate, 29 Oct 1962, *CGPLA Eng. & Wales*

Backhouse, Sir Edmund Trelawny, second baronet (1873–1944), Sinologist and fraudster, eldest of the four surviving sons of Jonathan Edmund Backhouse, first baronet (1849–1918), a banker, and Florence (1845–1902), youngest daughter of Sir John Salusbury Salusbury-*Trelawny, was born on 20 October 1873 at The Rookery, Middleton Tyas, Yorkshire. The naval officer Roger Roland Charles *Backhouse and the political activist Harriet Jane *Findlay were among his siblings. Educated at St George's School, Ascot (1882–6), and then at Winchester College, he entered Merton College, Oxford, as a 'postmaster' (foundation scholar) in 1892. At Oxford, Backhouse rebelled against his provincial, middle-class, Quaker origins, spending some £23,000 in three years on a cult of Ellen Terry, on jewellery, and on buying his way into a set of homosexual aesthetes. His studies—first classics, then English literature—were interrupted by a nervous breakdown in mid-1894. Although he had returned to Merton by the end of the year, he left Oxford in 1895 without taking a degree. His debts caught up with him shortly thereafter, and he seems to have fled abroad at the end of the year, at which point his affairs were wound up and bankruptcy proceedings initiated. Backhouse probably visited Greece, Russia, and the United States in this period, but next surfaced for certain in Cambridge, in July 1898, studying Chinese for three months with H. A. Giles. To China Backhouse went at the end of the same year, probably under family diktat: he was never to live in Britain again, but received an allowance from his father, and then, after the latter's death in 1918, from the estate, until his own death.

Failing to find a career in the Chinese customs service Backhouse worked unpaid from 1899 for G. E. Morrison, providing translations of Chinese documents for this influential correspondent of *The Times*, who acted as his patron and who also attempted, unsuccessfully, to repair Backhouse's relations with his father. Through Morrison he came to know J. O. P. Bland, secretary of the Shanghai municipal council and Shanghai correspondent for the paper. In 1909 Bland and Backhouse began their own collaboration on what was to become the most successful, and most disputed, contribution to modern Chinese history then published in Britain. *China under the Empress Dowager* (1910) consisted largely of documents translated by Backhouse, and polished by Bland, who constructed around them a vivid narrative of the latter days of the Qing dynasty and the Boxer uprising of 1900. The centrepiece of the volume was the purported diary of Jingshan, the Manchu official in whose house Backhouse was billeted in the aftermath of the rising. Backhouse claimed to have found the diary on entering the house, but is now known to have been, if not its forger, then certainly a close party to the forgery. He deposited the published sections in the British Museum in 1910, but his ineffective responses to challenges against the authenticity of the diary in the 1930s indicate that he knew full well that it was a fraud. Morrison, who knew Backhouse better than anyone at this point, always believed it to be so.

Backhouse's reputation as a Sinologist, however, was cemented by this work, and by a further volume with Bland, *Annals and Memoirs of the Court of Peking* (1914), and his collaboration with Sir Sydney Barton on a revision of Hillier's *Pocket Dictionary of Colloquial Chinese* (1918). On this basis he began fishing for an academic position in Britain. He was elected to the chair of Chinese at King's College, London, in December 1913 but never took it up, preferring to wait instead for the Oxford professorship, for which he appeared to be heir apparent. Backhouse had been smoothing his way back into Oxford with substantial donations of valuable Chinese books to the Bodleian Library in 1912 and 1914–15, but was to be disappointed in 1920 when W. E. Soothill was elected to the post. Thereafter his dealings with the Bodleian became more and more puzzling; he was advanced money to purchase books which never arrived in Oxford, or scrolls which turned out to be crude forgeries. The consequently strained relations between the Bodleian and Backhouse terminated in 1924—but not before his name was added to its benefactors' roll of honour, inscribed in stone.

Such strange activities had, in fact, become the singular feature of Backhouse's life. In Peking (Beijing) he had found employment in a variety of fields, using his language skills and contacts. He was a fixer and then an agent (1908–10) for the railway concession hunter Charles, sixth Lord ffrench, and an agent for the sale of battleships (1910–17) and of banknotes (1915–17). He was also trusted by Sir John Jordan at the British legation with a fantastic scheme to buy up surplus rifles in China for the British army in 1915. Backhouse's earliest activities on behalf of ffrench and the American Willard Straight appear to have been legitimate, and successful, but later he began to concoct contracts and contacts. Backhouse 'sold' six phantom battleships in 1916 for John Brown & Co. and 650 million imaginary banknotes that same year for the American Banknote Company of New York. In 1915 he assembled an imaginary flotilla of cargo ships, laden with rifles and machine-guns, whose progress down the Chinese coast from Shanghai to Canton (Guangzhou) is minutely recorded in the Foreign Office archives, but which never in fact existed. The complications created by these various plots, which unravelled at much the same time, caused him to flee China for Vancouver for a year in late 1917. He succeeded his father as baronet in 1918, but inherited nothing in the will, although his family footed much of the bill for his frauds on condition that he did not leave China.

In China, Backhouse's affairs became rather less ambitious in the 1920s and 1930s. He retreated further into the eccentric seclusion in Peking for which he was already well known—avoiding even accidental contact with Westerners, and dressing always in Chinese clothes. He seems to have been involved in various schemes, mostly shadowy or speculative, involving Chinese antiques and other articles, and to have been somewhat in thrall to his Chinese secretary. Backhouse was intermittently consulted as a scholar by the British legation but, while occasionally threatening writs against those who denied the authenticity of the Jingshan diary, he published nothing. His much vaunted projects, notably a new dictionary to trump Giles's standard work, were probably imaginary. His inactivity, and his reclusive behaviour, drew to him an air of scholar-gentlemanliness which impressed the small British colony in the 1930s, notably his first *Dictionary of National Biography* biographer, the painter Hope Danby.

The Sino-Japanese War after 1937 made life somewhat difficult for foreigners in Peking. Backhouse was forced to seek temporary refuge in the British legation in 1937, and in 1938 almost returned to Britain at the expense of his wearily loyal and worried family. He took final refuge in part of the unoccupied former Austrian legation in Peking's legation quarter in 1939, after the destruction of his house. There he drew to himself the admiring attention of the Swiss consul, Dr Richard Hoeppli, whom he regaled with tales of his lifelong, mostly homosexual, sexual adventures. Backhouse's notorious unpublished two volumes of memoirs, minutely detailing his intimacy with, among many others, Lord Rosebery and the Dowager Empress Cixi, were written at Hoeppli's request, and are largely constructed around imaginary interactions between himself and the blue-blooded and infamous. While vivid and pungent, the two books, 'Décadence Mandchoue' and 'The Dead Past', are drearily pornographic, enlivened only by splenetic outbursts against all those who had somehow conspired to suppress their author. These memoirs, fittingly, formed his last and posthumous contribution to the Bodleian.

Refusing (he claimed) repatriation in 1942, the by now sclerotically anti-British baronet stayed on in Japanese-occupied Peking. He converted to Catholicism in 1942, hoping that the church in Peking would provide him with money and shelter, as he was an enemy alien in distressed circumstances. This hope does not appear to have been realized. He died on 8 January 1944 in the Catholic Hôpital St Michel, Wangfujing, Peking, and was buried at the Chala Catholic cemetery at Pingzemen.

Backhouse developed a considerable reputation as a Sinologist, but hardly deserved it. He was certainly linguistically gifted, but his intellectual arrogance was considerable, and unfounded, while even his mastery of Chinese has not stood up to thorough examination. He was throughout his life hermitic, eccentric, evasive, litigious, profligate, and a gross snob; but he was also charmingly gentlemanly and persuasive. His fraudulent successes often owed as much to the ignorance and snobbery of those he duped as they did to his own skills. His Sinological successes owed much to the poor state of Chinese studies in Britain.

Backhouse's entry in the *Dictionary of National Biography* was the sole biographical note published about him until 1976, and much of the information recounted here was not at all widely known before then. His singular and lasting reputation is not as a Sinologist but as a fraud, fantasist, and forger, and to this fact he is indebted to his elegant biographer, Hugh Trevor-Roper. Backhouse may indeed in his memoirs have been the chronicler of, for example, male brothel life in late-imperial Peking, and there may be many small truths in those manuscripts that fill out the picture of his life, but we know now that not a word he ever said or wrote can be trusted.

ROBERT BICKERS

Sources H. Trevor-Roper, *A hidden life: the enigma of Sir Edmund Backhouse* (1976); repr. as *Hermit of Peking: the hidden life of Sir Edmund Backhouse* (1978) · Hui-min Lo, 'The Ching-shandiary: a clue to its forgery', *East Asian History*, 1 (1991), 98–124 · D. McMullen, '"Glorious veterans", "Sinologistes de chambre", and men of science: reflections on Professor Hugh Trevor-Roper's life of Sir Edmund Backhouse', *New Lugarno Review (Art International)*, 1 (1979), 78–83 · H. A. Giles, 'Autobiography', CUL, Add. MS 8964 · PRO, FO 228/3434 · *DNB* · E. T. Backhouse, memoirs, Bodl. Oxf., MSS Eng. misc. 1223–1226

Archives Bodl. Oxf., memoirs | Mitchell L., NSW, G. E. Morrison MSS · University of Toronto, Thomas Fisher Rare Book Library, J. O. P. Bland MSS

Likenesses photograph, *c.*1919, repro. in Trevor-Roper, *Hermit of Peking* · two photographs (one on deathbed, 1944), Bodl. Oxf.; repro. in Backhouse, memoirs

Backhouse, Edward (1808–1879), Quaker minister and historical writer, was born at Darlington on 8 May 1808, the son of Edward and Mary Backhouse. He lived from his youth at Sunderland, where he was partner in the collieries and the bank with which his family had been connected for many years, although he took no active part in the business. He was fond of travel, a good amateur painter, and a student of natural history. He devoted himself chiefly to the promotion of philanthropic and religious causes. He was a generous supporter of various institutions in Sunderland, including a mission hall which he founded in one of the poorer districts, and is said to have spent over £10,000 a year on charities. In politics he was an energetic Liberal, and especially interested in questions bearing directly upon morality. In later life he was a prominent opponent of the Contagious Diseases Acts, providing significant financial support to the Ladies' National

Association for their repeal. He was a devoted member of the Society of Friends, to which his family belonged. He began to preach in 1852, and two years later was recognized as a minister. In 1862 and 1863 he served as clerk to the yearly meeting of Friends in London. He married Katharine, daughter of Thomas and Mary Mounsey of Sunderland, in 1856. They had no children, but he always enjoyed the company of the young and the promotion of their happiness. From 1874 until his death he devoted himself to church history; his manuscript, edited by Charles Tylor, was published in 1884 as *Early Church History to the Death of Constantine*. The book, which makes no pretence to profound research, is interesting as an account of the early church from the Quaker point of view. Backhouse's health deteriorated in 1878; the following year he went to Hastings for a change of climate, and died there on 22 May 1879. LESLIE STEPHEN, *rev.* K. D. REYNOLDS

Sources *Biographical catalogue: being an account of the lives of Friends and others whose portraits are in the London Friends' Institute*, Society of Friends (1888) • E. Isichei, *Victorian Quakers* (1970) • J. R. Walkowitz, *Prostitution and Victorian society: women, class and the state* (1980) • *Annual Monitor* (1880), 20 • *Northern Echo* (24 May 1879) • *Sunderland Daily Echo* (23 May 1879) • *Sunderland Daily Echo* (28 May 1879)
Archives Durham RO, family papers, journals, sketchbooks
Likenesses photograph, 1888, London Friends' Institute
Wealth at death under £180,000: probate, 8 Nov 1879, *CGPLA Eng. & Wales*

Backhouse, James (1794–1869). *See under* Backhouse family (*per. c.*1770–1945).

Backhouse, James (1825–1890). *See under* Backhouse family (*per. c.*1770–1945).

Backhouse, James (1861–1945). *See under* Backhouse family (*per. c.*1770–1945).

Backhouse, John (1784–1845), civil servant, was born on 14 October 1784 at Wavertree, Lancashire, the son of John Backhouse, a Liverpool merchant. He was educated at the Carmel School, Westmorland, and the foundation school, Clitheroe, Lancashire. After becoming a partner in his father's business, he was sent in 1812 to be secretary of the firm's office in London. There his talents were soon recognized by George Canning, MP for Liverpool, who employed Backhouse as his private secretary, first at the Board of Control from 1816 and subsequently at the Foreign Office, first as private secretary and then as under-secretary while Canning was foreign secretary from September 1822 to January 1823. When Canning moved to the Foreign Office, he asked the prime minister to find Backhouse a vacancy which would pay £1000 a year and be 'not liable to the vicissitudes of ministerial arrangements' (Middleton, *Administration*, 128). This was achieved by his appointment as a commissioner of excise (January 1823–April 1827). When in April 1827 Backhouse succeeded Joseph Planta, who had been under-secretary at the Foreign Office since 1817, he was appointed to the office of receiver-general of excise, as his previous office as a commissioner was incompatible with the office of under-secretary. He received £1500 per annum from this office and £500 from the Foreign Office. After Canning's death Backhouse was not asked to resign, and by continuing to hold office irrespective of a change in ministry his subsequent career helped to define the position of the permanent under-secretary as the head of the Foreign Office.

From its inception in 1782 the Foreign Office had two under-secretaries by virtue of the amalgamation of the northern and southern departments. Both under-secretaries were political appointments, with equal rank and salary, and they shared equally the political business of the office along the lines of the old north–south division. The senior of the under-secretaries by virtue of experience came to be associated with questions relating to Turkey, Russia, and France, which were considered to be of enduring interest. By 1840 Backhouse had assumed responsibility for managing affairs relating to all the great foreign powers. He was also responsible for the personnel and administration of the Foreign Office and the management of the secret service fund. Palmerston described his two under-secretaries as being 'like the two figures in the weather house who rusticate and labour alternately' (Bourne, 417), but under Palmerston, Backhouse seems to have laboured more than he rusticated. A kindly, well-meaning man, he was overworked and overawed by Palmerston; in consequence his health was ruined and a mental collapse led to his retirement in April 1842.

Backhouse married in 1810 Catherine Nicholson of Stockport. They had four daughters and two sons, one of whom—George Canning Backhouse—was murdered in Havana on 31 August 1855 while on foreign service. Backhouse was a close friend of the publisher John Murray. He regularly contributed articles to popular periodicals and edited one book, the *Narrative of the American sailor Robert Adams' residence in the interior of Africa at Timbuctoo*. He died on 13 November 1845 at his residence in Hans Place, Chelsea, and was buried seven days later in Kensal Green cemetery. R. A. JONES

Sources R. Jones, *The nineteenth-century foreign office: an administrative history* (1971) • C. R. Middleton, *The administration of British foreign policy, 1782–1846* (1977) • C. R. Middleton, 'John Backhouse and the origins of the permanent under-secretaryship for foreign affairs, 1828–42', *Journal of British Studies*, 13/2 (1973–4), 24–45 • E. Jones-Parry, 'Under-secretaries of state for foreign affairs, 1782–1855', *EngHR*, 49 (1934), 308–20 • R. Bullen, ed., *The foreign office, 1782–1982* (1984) • K. Bourne, *Palmerston: the early years, 1784–1841* (1982) • E. Hertslet, *Recollections of the old foreign office* (1901) • *GM*, 2nd ser., 25 (1846), 95–7
Archives Duke U., Perkins L., corresp. and papers • PRO, corresp. and papers relating to mission to Don Carlos, FO 326/6 | All Souls Oxf., corresp. with Sir Charles Richard Vaughan • BL, corresp. with Lord Aberdeen, Add. MSS 43237–43242 • BL, letters to Lord Heytesbury, Add. MSS 41557–41563, *passim* • BL, corresp. with William Huskisson, Add. MSS 38742–38755, *passim* • NL Scot., letters to Lord Stuart de Rothesay • NRA Scotland, priv. coll., letters to James Fraser • PRO, corresp. with Stratford Canning, FO 352 • PRO, letters to Lord Granville, PRO 30/29 • St Deiniol's Library, Hawarden, letters to Sir John Gladstone • U. Southampton L., corresp. with Lord Palmerston; letters to duke of Wellington • W. Yorks. AS, Leeds, corresp. with A. G. Stapleton

Backhouse, Jonathan (1779–1842), banker and financier, was born in Darlington, co. Durham, the eldest son of Jonathan Backhouse (1747–1826), banker, and his wife,

Ann (*d.* 1826), the second daughter of Edward Pease of Darlington. Jonathan senior was the eldest of three sons of James Backhouse of Westmorland, a yarn and wool dealer, who had moved to Darlington during the 1750s to establish a flax-dressing and linen-manufacturing business [*see* Backhouse family (*per. c.*1770–1945)]. This was the precursor to the foundation, in 1774, of J. and J. Backhouse banking, a partnership shared by James, with his son Jonathan and later also with his nephew James junior. The family had earlier indicated its interest in wider commercial affairs by taking on the local agency of the Royal Exchange Assurance in 1759.

As private bankers, the Backhouses were not untypical of numerous entrepreneurs in the eighteenth-century economy who combined manufacturing ventures with the financing of trade generally. The Quaker Lloyds of Birmingham and the Gibbons family of Wolverhampton provide excellent illustrations in the metallurgical trades, while in mining there are several cases in the north-east of England. In textiles, the best-known example is provided by the Gurneys of Norwich, a Quaker family with a banking tradition going back to the later seventeenth century, but which also developed a thriving trade in woollen yarns in the first half of the eighteenth century. By integrating banking with manufacturing, these family concerns could both advance credit to customers and receive it from suppliers and so more easily sustain the expansion of business. Like the Gurneys, however, the Backhouses were to abandon manufacturing in favour of full banking, a move which had been accomplished by the end of the eighteenth century. At that time J. and J. Backhouse possessed an extensive agency network in co. Durham, underpinned by a considerable note issue payable at sight, and fourteen days after sight, in London.

In 1798, following the death of James senior, the title of the bank was changed to Jonathan Backhouse & Co. It was in this form that it became involved in the financing and projection of the pioneering Stockton and Darlington Railway, the first public railway to be empowered to use steam locomotives. The possibility of improving the transport infrastructure of south Durham and north-east Yorkshire had been discussed intermittently throughout the latter half of the eighteenth century, when attention was invariably focused on the construction of a canal linking the Auckland coalfield to the estuary of the River Tees. The capital cost, however, was viewed as prohibitive, and real progress had to await the development of a capital network spreading beyond the limited confines of co. Durham. In this respect, the Backhouses were well placed. As prosperous Quakers, they proved to be entirely typical of their religious sect in developing marital ties which facilitated substantial financial inflows from other parts of the country.

Of crucial importance was the marriage in 1811 of Jonathan Backhouse junior to Hannah Chapman (*d.* 1850), the elder daughter and coheir of Joseph Gurney, a private banker of Norwich; the couple had two daughters and a son. This dynastic alliance in itself transformed the prospects for transport improvement, especially when the Backhouses allied themselves with the Quaker Pease family of Darlington in the raising of capital. As woollen manufacturers and private bankers themselves, the Peases were related by marriage to the Backhouses, and developed their own ties with the Gurneys when Joseph Pease married Emma Gurney in 1826. It was thus the Backhouse–Pease alliance which emerged as the principal underwriters of the Stockton and Darlington Railway, authorized by parliament in 1821 and opened formally in September 1825. The early records of the company are illustrative of the strength of Quaker financial networks in mobilizing capital resources. This fact was reflected in Backhouse's appointment as first treasurer to the company, a position which he held until 1833, by which time the railway was well established as a conveyor of coal and other industrial raw materials along the lower Tees valley.

During the first three decades of the nineteenth century Backhouse proved to be the dominant partner in the bank, and he presided over a process of expansion which was to consolidate its position in the commercial infrastructure of co. Durham. In 1805 a branch was opened at Durham and in the following year at Sunderland. In the mid-1820s the network was extended to Newcastle upon Tyne, South Shields, and Stockton-on-Tees. In conformity with the evolution of the banking system in the country as a whole at this time, the north-east of England was afflicted periodically by phases of instability in response to the overextension of credit. Local banking crises occurred in the late 1790s, in 1803, 1815, 1819, 1823, and 1825. Jonathan Backhouse & Co. weathered all of these vicissitudes without difficulty.

The crisis of 1819 was particularly noteworthy insofar as it was the product of a crude attempt by the earl of Darlington to bankrupt the concern. At that time the Backhouses were busily projecting the Stockton and Darlington Railway with a proposed route to the Auckland coalfield through Lord Darlington's Raby estate. Incensed by the potential threat to his fox coverts, the earl attempted to accumulate the bank's paper notes to the point when their value exceeded the gold stock. The apocryphal-sounding but nevertheless true story is told that Backhouse became acquainted with Lord Darlington's plot and frustrated it by posting to London to obtain extra bullion stocks. His coach lost a wheel on the return journey, but the chaise was balanced by his placing the gold at an appropriate point over the rear axle.

Backhouse resigned as treasurer to the Stockton and Darlington Railway in 1833 in order to embark upon full-time ministry on behalf of the Society of Friends. He retained his partnership in the family bank, but bequeathed his authority to his son, Edmund (1824–1880). Jonathan Backhouse died at Darlington on 7 October 1842.

The family bank experienced mixed fortunes under later generations. Edmund Backhouse was followed as senior partner by his son, Jonathan Edmund (1849–1903). The latter was rewarded with a baronetcy in 1893 and presided over the merger in 1896 of the bank with Gurneys of

Norwich and Barclays of London to form Barclay & Co. of Lombard Street, destined to become one of the 'big five' clearing banks after the First World War. Sir Jonathan was appointed local director of the new company and was to prove instrumental in precipitating the absorption of the Pease family's private bank, J. and J. W. Pease, in 1902, but in circumstances which led to the financial ruin of the senior partner, Sir Joseph Whitwell Pease, and his sons Alfred and Joseph. M. W. KIRBY

Sources *Pease of Darlington* (privately printed, *c*.1902) • M. Phillips, *A history of banks, bankers and banking in Northumberland, Durham, and North Yorkshire* (1894) • P. W. Matthews, *History of Barclays Bank Limited*, ed. A. W. Tuke (1926) • A. Raistrick, *Quakers in science and industry* (1950); repr. (1968) • M. W. Kirby, *Men of business and politics: the rise and fall of the Quaker Pease dynasty of north-east England, 1700–1943* (1984) • M. W. Kirby, *The origins of railway enterprise: the Stockton and Darlington Railway, 1821–1863* (1993) • d. cert.

Archives Barclays Bank, Darlington • Durham RO, corresp. • U. Durham L., archives and special collections, corresp., family corresp., and papers

Backhouse [*née* Holden], **Margaret** (*bap.* **1818**, *d.* after **1885**), portrait and genre painter, one of several children of the Revd Henry Augustus Holden and his wife, Mary, was born at Summer Hill, near Birmingham, and baptized on 28 September 1818 at St Martin's, Birmingham. Her eldest brother was the Revd Henry *Holden (1814–1909) [*see under* Holden, Hubert Ashton], classical scholar and headmaster of the cathedral school, Durham. After a childhood passed at Woolstaston in Shropshire, and at Brighton, and instruction at a school in Calais, France, she went to Paris to study art under the watercolourist and miniature painter Jean-Baptiste Désiré Troivaux and a genre painter named Grenier. Following a period at Honfleur with her family, she returned to England. She lived for a year in Cheltenham, Gloucestershire, and subsequently spent nine or ten months at Sass's academy in London, probably in the early 1840s. Henry Sass took a personal interest in her work and encouraged more advanced study than was usually undertaken by women at that time. On 3 April 1845 she married the artist Henry Fleetwood Backhouse (*b.* 1818/19), the son of Thomas Backhouse, wine merchant. She took further instruction from William Mulready and the engraver Edward Goodall. She was an unsuccessful candidate for membership of the New Watercolour Society in 1850. After living at several addresses in north London in the late 1840s, by 1850 she had settled at 42 Richmond Road, Islington, London, where she remained until 1868 or 1869.

Most of Backhouse's *œuvre* consisted of privately commissioned portraits and subject compositions which did not appear in galleries. Her exhibited works, portraits and genre scenes depicting rural women and children, chiefly in watercolour, were shown at the Royal Academy (1846–82), the Society (later Royal Society) of British Artists (1848–75), the Liverpool Academy (1858), and notably the Society of Female Artists (SFA)—of which she was a member from 1873 to 1885—where she was represented by eighty works between 1857 and 1885. One of her first noticed works was *The Orphan* (exh. SFA, 1858). *A Little Gleaner* (exh. SFA, 1865) was praised as the most 'pictorially perfect' of her pictures (*Art Journal*, 1865, 68). In the 1860s and 1870s she often painted abroad—in Switzerland and Italy; her Italian subjects—*La bella Sorrentina*, exhibited at the Society of Lady Artists in 1875, is a typical title—are described by Ellen C. Clayton.

Backhouse's paintings were not highly priced, a maximum known figure being £52 10s. for *The Gypsy Poacher, or, Love versus Duty* (exh. SFA, 1865). According to Clayton, many of her pictures were issued as chromolithographs by Messrs Rowney. Her last known address was 2 Whitley Villas, 533 Caledonian Road, London, where she lived from 1871 until at least 1885. Her daughter, Mary, was also an artist. CHARLOTTE YELDHAM

Sources E. C. Clayton, *English female artists*, 2 (1876), 21–9 • Graves, *Artists* • J. Soden and C. Baile de Laperrière, eds., *The Society of Women Artists exhibitors, 1855–1996*, 4 vols. (1996) • Graves, *RA exhibitors* • J. Johnson, ed., *Works exhibited at the Royal Society of British Artists, 1824–1893, and the New English Art Club, 1888–1917*, 2 vols. (1975) • E. Morris and E. Roberts, *The Liverpool Academy and other exhibitions of contemporary art in Liverpool, 1774–1867* (1998) • Mallalieu, *Watercolour artists* • reviews, *Art Journal*, 20 (1858), 143; 21 (1859), 83–4; 22 (1860), 85; 23 (1861), 72; 24/1862, 72; 25 (1863), 95; 26 (1864), 97; 27 (1865), 68; 31 (1869), 82; 32 (1870), 89; 33 (1871), 90; 38 (1876), 125 • *IGI* • m. cert.

Backhouse, Robert Ormston (1854–1940). *See under* Backhouse family (*per. c*.1770–1945).

Backhouse, Sir Roger Roland Charles (1878–1939), naval officer, was born on 24 November 1878 at The Rookery, Middleton Tyas, Yorkshire, the fourth son (a twin with his brother Miles) of Sir Jonathan Edmund Backhouse, first baronet (1849–1918), and member of a well-known Quaker banking family, and his wife, Florence (1845–1902), youngest daughter of Sir John Salusbury Salusbury-*Trelawny, ninth baronet, and member of a famous and ancient Cornish family. The sinologist Edmund Trelawny *Backhouse and the political activist Harriet Jane *Findlay were among his siblings. At fourteen he entered the training ship *Britannia* at Dartmouth as a naval cadet. After passing out in 1894, he received his commission, and was appointed a midshipman in the battleship *Repulse* of the channel squadron. In 1895 he was transferred to a small cruiser in the Pacific squadron, HMS *Comus*. Backhouse remained in the Pacific until returning to Britain in 1898. After being promoted to the rank of sublieutenant in March 1898, he gained the maximum five first-class certificates and was promoted lieutenant in March 1899. There followed a year's service in the Mediterranean on board the battleship *Revenge*, where he began to make his name as a gunnery expert. He confirmed this early promise by winning the Egerton prize in 1902. After this achievement he was shuttled back and forth between serving on the staff of the gunnery school ship *Excellent* at Portsmouth and as gunnery officer on a number of battleships at sea, including service on board the new *Dreadnought*.

A man of great personal charm and integrity, Backhouse cut a rather imposing figure. Standing at 6 feet 4 inches tall, fit and lean, he was appreciated within the service for his drive, energy, and tenacity. In 1907, aged

Sir Roger Roland Charles Backhouse (1878–1939), by Walter Stoneman, 1932

twenty-nine, with his career advancing successfully in the Royal Navy, Backhouse, popularly known to all as RB, married Dora Louisa, the sixth daughter of John Ritchie Findlay, of Aberlour, Banffshire. This was in every way a successful marriage. Dora proved to be a very supportive partner and they had four daughters and two sons. Backhouse was promoted commander at the end of 1909, and in March 1911 began a period of nearly three and a half years at sea as flag commander to three successive Home Fleet commanders-in-chief: Sir F. C. B. Bridgeman, Sir G. A. Callaghan, and Sir John Jellicoe, in their flagships *Neptune* and *Iron Duke*. Promoted captain at the outbreak of war on 1 September 1914, Backhouse rejoined Admiral Jellicoe's staff and distinguished himself both as the gunnery expert and in compiling battle orders. The future first sea lord recommended that the quality of his work deserved a 'mention in dispatches'.

In November 1915, at the age of thirty-seven, Backhouse took command of the light cruiser *Conquest* and was attached to the Harwich force under Commodore Sir Reginald Yorke Tyrwhitt. It was a hectic time, and Backhouse and his ship were in the thick of a number of naval skirmishes. On 25 April 1916 he was caught up in the bombardment of the Suffolk port of Lowestoft by a force of German battle cruisers. Backhouse, supported by two other light cruisers and sixteen destroyers, was commanded by Tyrwhitt to intervene and draw off the enemy's fire. *Conquest* was hit and set on fire by a number of 12 inch shells, killing twenty-three of the crew and wounding sixteen others. Once the shellfire had ceased, Backhouse left the bridge and instantly took personal charge of the clean-up operation that did much to keep the *Conquest* afloat and enable it to limp back to port. Afterwards he received a commendation from the Board of Admiralty for the speed and effectiveness of his action, which had saved his ship and its company from foundering.

After Admiral Sir David Beatty assumed command of the Grand Fleet in November 1916, Backhouse joined Admiral Sir W. C. Pakenham, the newly appointed commander of the battle-cruiser squadron, as his flag captain and gunnery expert on board the *Lion*. A bout of ill health brought him ashore in the summer of 1918, but he had recovered sufficiently to take up a desk job at the Admiralty before the war ended on 11 November 1918. After the armistice he remained in Whitehall for several years, and was appointed director of naval ordnance in September 1920. He was sent to sea again in January 1923 in command of the battleship *Malaya*. After a twenty-month attachment in the Atlantic Fleet, Backhouse was brought home to attend a series of senior officers' courses at Portsmouth, during which he was promoted rear-admiral at the age of forty-six in April 1925. After achieving flag rank, Backhouse was sent to the *Iron Duke* in May 1926 to exercise command of the 3rd battle squadron of the Atlantic Fleet. A year later he returned home for a well-earned period of rest and recuperation on half pay.

Backhouse was appointed third sea lord and controller of the navy at the Admiralty in November 1928. He remained at his post throughout a crisis-strewn period in which financial and economic problems arose to batter both the Royal Navy and the governments of the day, causing significant 'casualties' on all sides. Promoted vice-admiral in October 1929, Backhouse had fought a long, hard battle with the Treasury mandarins over the Admiralty estimates. It was therefore with a profound sense of relief that he left the tortuous in-fighting of Whitehall to hoist his flag in the *Revenge* and take command in March 1932 of the 1st battle squadron, and become second in command of the Mediterranean Fleet under Admiral Sir Ernle Chatfield and subsequently Admiral Sir W. W. Fisher. Backhouse, who was knighted in 1933, remained in the Mediterranean until May 1934, and was promoted admiral while on station in February 1934, at the age of fifty-five. By this time he had made a name for himself as something of a tireless workaholic and an officer who pushed himself as hard as he drove his staff. Unwilling to accept sloppiness in either thought or deed, he did not suffer fools gladly, and could be quite withering with those who crossed him. Hardened by experience and confident in his own ability, Backhouse lavished immense care on all matters—great and small—that were passed to him for his scrutiny. Unfortunately, this attitude gained him the reputation of a micro-manager who found it almost pathologically difficult to delegate authority to others around him. Although this unflattering description of his working habits was rather exaggerated, it was not a totally erroneous picture of his performance in command, as his next appointment showed.

In August 1935 Backhouse was made the commander-in-chief, Home Fleet, with his flag in the battleship *Nelson*. He took as his chief of staff the 52-year-old Bertram Home Ramsay, an old friend from their days on the *Dreadnought* and a highly opinionated character who had made flag rank earlier in the year. Backhouse and Ramsay both liked their own way, and both relished making decisions and controlling events. They did not work well together. Within two months Backhouse was writing to Chatfield that Ramsay's appointment was not working out in the way that he had hoped, and that unless the younger man was prepared to rein in his own impetuous temperament he would have to go. Unwilling to change and accommodate his chief, Ramsay asked to be relieved of his post in December 1935. Supported by the Admiralty, Backhouse survived the Ramsay episode and prospered. He remained at the helm until April 1938, when it was announced that he would succeed Lord Chatfield as first sea lord and chief of naval staff later in the year. Before he took up his post at Admiralty House in August 1938, he was appointed first and principal aide-de-camp to George VI.

Backhouse could not have taken over as first sea lord at a more ominous time for the British government. Europe appeared to be on the verge of war over the *Sudetendeutsch* problem. Backhouse and the two other chiefs of staff—Air Chief Marshal Sir Cyril Newall and Lieutenant-General Viscount Gort—all thought the United Kingdom militarily so vulnerable as to require a political solution to the Czech problem; otherwise, the country might be drawn into a war with Germany, and possibly with the other members of the anti-Comintern pact (Italy and Japan) as well. Although Backhouse supported the Munich agreement on pragmatic grounds, his political chief, the cantankerous first lord—Alfred Duff Cooper—reacted angrily by denouncing appeasement and resigning from the government in protest. Duff Cooper's exit in early October allowed Chamberlain to appoint his friend the seventh earl of Stanhope as first lord. A more conciliatory fellow than his predecessor, Stanhope had little real knowledge of naval affairs, and came to rely heavily upon Backhouse's expertise in the few months that they worked together.

As first sea lord, Backhouse demonstrated repeatedly that he was not obsessed with detail and bureaucratic minutiae and that he was prepared to overhaul the administrative machinery of the Admiralty and cast aside some of the Royal Navy's inter-war strategic concepts. Overwhelmed by work during the recent Czech crisis, he was convinced that inefficiency prevailed within the Admiralty's administrative structure. By establishing the Binney committee to look into the organization of the naval staff and make recommendations for change, Backhouse was intent on delegating and decentralizing policy making as much as possible. He also sought to reform British strategic doctrine, which he considered had become hazardous because it still required the main fleet to go to Singapore if war broke out with Japan. As news filtering back from central Europe became gloomier, Backhouse became more adamant in his belief that the Mediterranean and the Middle East region were burgeoning theatres of military and economic importance to the United Kingdom, and that they should not be subordinated to the 'Singapore strategy'. Driven by the need to break the mould in strategic thinking, Backhouse brought the innovative Vice-Admiral Drax out of retirement, lodging him temporarily in the Admiralty, with instructions to devise a set of war plans that might leave the Royal Navy less exposed against the worldwide menace posed by the German, Italian, and Japanese fleets. What emerged from Drax's voluntary confinement in the Admiralty was a strategic plan that tossed aside the essential element of the Singapore strategy in favour of concentrating British naval and air power in the Mediterranean, north Africa, and Middle East at the outset of a future war. The aim would be to defeat the Italians, seen as the weakest among the United Kingdom's potential enemies. Even so, both Drax and Backhouse still envisaged a scaled-down version of a Far Eastern commitment—a 'flying squadron' of two capital ships, an aircraft-carrier, a cruiser squadron, and a destroyer flotilla—to deter the Japanese from interfering with or overrunning British possessions in the region. Although he did not live long enough to push these strategic concepts in Whitehall, the plans were consistent with Backhouse's view that the capital ship was still the most potent weapon in a fleet's arsenal. Although somewhat myopic about its vulnerability to aerial bombardment on the high seas, Backhouse was alive to the dangers posed by submarines to all naval craft, and urged his technical staff to design a new type of escort vessel with a strong anti-aircraft armament that would make it suitable for anti-submarine warfare as well as escort and patrol duties.

Hitler's seizure of the rump of Czechoslovakia in mid-March 1939 roughly coincided with the onset of Backhouse's fatal illness. What appeared to be a long and persistent bout of influenza was eventually diagnosed as a brain tumour: a terminal condition which forced him to retire in May and from which he died in London on 15 July 1939, shortly after being promoted admiral of the fleet. His wife survived him.

A man of consummate ability, who was scrupulous and fair and immensely liked by those who knew him well, Backhouse did not remain long enough as first lord to dispel the jaundiced impression—formed by some of his contemporaries at the time and by a host of naval historians subsequently—that he was a weak and indecisive leader who offered his staff little operational guidance. This unflattering assessment of his qualities is both exaggerated and unjust. Backhouse was not half-hearted about anything. An officer who expected no more and no less of his staff than he was prepared to give himself, Backhouse was not given to self-doubt, and was prepared to back his own judgement and not become a mere slave to tradition. Efficiency was his watchword, and this ensured that he could not do everything himself.

MALCOLM H. MURFETT

Sources M. H. Murfett, ed., *The first sea lords: from Fisher to Mountbatten* (1995) • M. H. Murfett, *Fool-proof relations: the search for Anglo-American naval co-operation during the Chamberlain years, 1937–1940* (1984) • *DNB* • first sea lords papers, PRO, ADM 205 • Board of the Admiralty: minutes and memos, PRO, ADM 167 • cases of the Admiralty and secretariat, PRO, ADM 116 • C.I.D. minutes and memos, PRO, CAB 2 • ad-hoc sub-committees of enquiry: proceedings and memos, PRO, CAB 16 • C. Barnett, *Engage the enemy more closely: the Royal Navy in the Second World War* (1991) • A. J. Marder, M. Jacobsen, and J. Horsfield, *Old friends, new enemies: the Royal Navy and the imperial Japanese navy*, 2 vols. (1981–90) • *CGPLA Eng. & Wales* (1939) • *WWW*, *1929–40*

Archives CAC Cam., John H. Godfrey MSS • NMM, Chatfield MSS | FILM BFI NFTVA, news footage

Likenesses W. Stoneman, photograph, 1932, NPG [*see illus.*] • Bassano, photograph, 1938, NPG

Wealth at death £8266 17*s.* 5*d.*: probate, 25 Oct 1939, *CGPLA Eng. & Wales*

Backhouse, Thomas William (1842–1920). *See under* Backhouse family (*per. c.*1770–1945).

Backhouse, William (1593–1662), alchemist and antiquary, was born on 17 January 1593, probably at Swallowfield, Berkshire, the youngest of the four sons of Samuel Backhouse (*d.* 1626), landowner, and his wife, Elisabeth (*d.* 1630), daughter of John Borlase of Little Marlow. Samuel had acquired Swallowfield in 1582. The family was of good standing in Berkshire and he was twice high sheriff (1598, 1601). In February 1611 William matriculated at Christ Church, Oxford, but he took no degree. About 1637 he married Anne (*d.* 1663), daughter of Brian Richards of Hartley Westfield, Hampshire. They had three children: Samuel (died young), John (*b.* 1640), and Flower (*b.* 1641). Backhouse's three brothers all predeceased him and in 1649, on the death of the eldest, John, he inherited Swallowfield. About this time he engaged William Lloyd, the future bishop of St Asaph, as tutor to his children.

Backhouse's life was outwardly obscure and uneventful but contemporaries testify that he was a respected figure in a network of people involved in occult and philosophical studies: 'a most renown'd chymist, Rosicrucian, and a great encourager of those that studied chymistry and astrology' (Wood). The most informative of Backhouse's contacts is Elias Ashmole, who acquired an estate near Swallowfield in 1649. Ashmole's first reference to Backhouse is dated 3 April 1651: 'Mr: Will: Backhouse of Swallowfeild in Com Berks, caused me to call him Father thence forward' (Bodl. Oxf., MS Ashmole 1136, fol. 24*v*). The relationship between Backhouse and his alchemical heir during the early 1650s is celebrated by Ashmole in an ode and in notes of various alchemical conversations; for example, on 13 May 1653:

> My father Backhouse lying sick in Fleetestreete over against St: Dunstans Church, & not knowing whether he should live or dye, about eleven a clock, told me in Silables the true Matter of the Philosophers Stone: which he bequeathed to me as a Legacy. (Bodl. Oxf., MS Ashmole 1136, fol. 29)

Both Backhouse's heraldic crest—an eagle holding in its claws a serpent—and his personal motto 'Scache cache' (archaic French, 'Know to conceal') were perfectly in tune with his character of secretive adept. He and his library of alchemical manuscripts greatly assisted Ashmole in the preparation of the latter's *Theatrum chemicum Britannicum* (1652).

Backhouse's learning extended to other fields. George Wharton, dedicating an almanac to Backhouse in 1653, refers to him as a master of astrology. His antiquarian interests are suggested both by the 'old deedes' that Ashmole recorded as being in his possession (7 Sept 1657; Bodl. Oxf., MS Ashmole 833, p. 443) and by Aubrey's observation of Backhouse's habit of a summer tour of antique buildings. In 1660 Samuel Hartlib noted in his 'Ephemerides' that Backhouse was 'a favourer of all manner of ingenuities', and that he possessed 'a long Gallery wherin are all manner of Inventions and Rarities' (Sheffield University, Hartlib MSS, Ephemerides, sect. 61, 3–4). Given this interest in scientific instruments, Anthony Wood's statement that Backhouse invented the waywiser (later called the odometer) is not inherently unlikely, though more probably he improved an already existing instrument for measuring distances travelled by means of a device for counting the revolutions of a wheel.

Backhouse's only undoubted original composition is an alchemical poem, 'The Magistery', in Ashmole's *Theatrum chemicum Britannicum* (342–3); it is signed W. B. (Ashmole expanded the initials in his own annotated copy of the *Theatrum*) and dated December 1633. Ashmole also explicitly ascribes two manuscript translations of alchemical texts to Backhouse: 'The pleasant founteine of knowledge … by John de la Founteine of Valencia in Henault' (Bodl. Oxf., MS Ashmole 58, fols. 1–23), a verse translation, dated 1644; and 'The golden fleece, or, The flower of treasures … by … Solomon Trismosin' (Bodl. Oxf., MS Ashmole 1395). Also in MS Ashmole 58, the verse translation of Jean de Meung's 'Planctus naturae: the complaint of nature against the erronious alchymist' (fols. 27–48*v*) is in the same hand as 'The founteine of knowledge', as is the closely associated 'The alchimysts answere to nature' (fols. 50–67); Anthony Wood ascribes the 'Planctus naturae' to Backhouse, so the 'Answere' is probably his too. The final translation in MS Ashmole 58, 'A treatise of the phillosophers stone … by Synesius the Greeke abbot' (fols. 72–88*v*), may also be Backhouse's work.

Backhouse's daughter, Flower, became sole heir to the Swallowfield estate when her brother John died childless in 1660. She married three times: first, in 1656, to William Bishop; next, in 1662 after his death, to her cousin Sir William Backhouse of London, who also left her a widow; and finally, in 1670, to Henry Hyde, who in 1674 became second earl of Clarendon. William Backhouse died of a wasting fever on 30 May 1662 and was buried on 17 June in Swallowfield church. JENNIFER SPEAKE

Sources C. H. Josten, 'William Backhouse of Swallowfield', *Ambix*, 4 (1949–51), 1–33 • Wood, *Ath. Oxon.* • *Elias Ashmole (1617–1692): his autobiographical and historical notes*, ed. C. H. Josten, 5 vols. (1966 [i.e. 1967]) • E. Ashmole, ed., *Theatrum chemicum Britannicum* (1652) • J. Aubrey, *Miscellanies* (1696), 100 • Bodl. Oxf., MS Ashmole 36, fols. 241b–242 • Bodl. Oxf., MS Ashmole 58 • Bodl. Oxf., MS Ashmole 332, fols. 12b, 48b • Bodl. Oxf., MS Ashmole 851, 20–21 • Bodl. Oxf., MS Ashmole 1136, fols. 24b, 27, 29 • Bodl. Oxf., MS Ashmole 1395 • University of Sheffield, Hartlib MSS

Archives Bodl. Oxf., MSS Ashmole

Backhouse, William (1779–1844). *See under* Backhouse family (*per. c.*1770–1945).

Backhouse, William (1807–1869). *See under* Backhouse family (*per. c.*1770–1945).

Backhouse, William Ormston (1885–1962). *See under* Backhouse family (*per. c.*1770–1945).

Backus, Isaac (1724–1806), Baptist minister and historian in America, was born on 9 January 1724 at Norwich, Connecticut, the fourth of eleven children of Samuel Backus (1694–1740), farmer and ironworks owner, and Elizabeth (1698–1769), daughter of John Tracy and Elizabeth Leffingwell. Both of Isaac's parents were members of founding families of Norwich. Isaac received seven years of schooling, but the death of his father when he was sixteen left him with responsibility for the farm. The family estate, which included land in the Delaware and Susquehanna purchases, provided an economic base for his extensive travels and activities. On 29 November 1749 he married Susanna Mason (1725–1800) of Rehoboth, Massachusetts, and they had nine children. Although he never attended college, his writings reveal a strong intellect. From 1765 to 1799 he served on the board of Rhode Island College and was awarded an honorary master of arts degree in 1797.

The Backus family, though well-to-do, had a tradition of religious dissent. Joseph Backus had opposed the Saybrook platform (1708), which reorganized Connecticut's Congregationalist churches along Presbyterian lines, and for this was expelled from the legislature. The revivalistic preaching of Eleazar Wheelock and Jedidiah Mills during the religious revival known as the great awakening led to Isaac's dramatic conversion on 24 August 1741. When the Connecticut legislature restricted itinerant preachers, Elizabeth and her son, with several others, withdrew from the Norwich church to organize a separatist (new light) congregation in 1746. Such action was a civil as well as a religious offence. In September of that year Isaac felt the call to preach, and for two years travelled throughout New England. A group of new lights in Titicut, a division of Middleborough and Bridgewater, Massachusetts, invited him to become their minister, and on 13 April 1748 he was ordained by this newly formed separatist congregation. His refusal to pay the parish tax to support the established Congregational church led to his arrest. Although he was numbered among the separatists for ten years, his arrest, combined with his acceptance of anti-paedobaptist beliefs and closed communion, led him to reorganize his separated congregation on 16 January 1756 as the First Baptist Church of Middleborough.

The arrest of Backus, an experience that also befell his mother, brother Samuel, and others who dissented from the established church, had a profound effect on his career. This persecution made him determined to address the issue and in so doing he developed a theory for separation of church and state. A member of the grievance committee of the Warren Association, created by Baptists in 1767, he collected affidavits, wrote reports, and petitioned government for relief. Supported by the Warren Association in 1774, he unsuccessfully appealed to the first continental congress for a declaration of full 'religious liberty'. By seeking material to reinforce his argument against 'oppression', religious and civil, he found the works of earlier dissenters, the theories of John Locke, and America's revolutionary rhetoric helpful. In Massachusetts his efforts to have the religious tax provision dropped from the new state constitution in 1780 failed. As a delegate to the constitutional convention in 1788, he voted for a new constitution for the United States because it prohibited any religious establishment.

On extensive travels, frequently for the Warren Association, Backus collected materials for his *A history of New England with particular reference to the denomination of Christians called Baptists* (1777–96). In this and all his publications he clearly distinguished between toleration and religious freedom. Theological and ecclesiastical differences with the Congregational church are represented in *Nature and Necessity of an Internal Call to Preach* (1754), *An Appeal to Public for Religious Liberty* (1773), and *The Liberal Support of Gospel Ministers* (1790). His activities and writings made him a principal protagonist for religious liberty in colonial America. Because the New England patriot leaders did not accept separation of church and state as a goal of the American War of Independence, unlike Thomas Jefferson and James Madison of Virginia, Massachusetts in 1833 became the last of the states to abandon religious taxation.

The acknowledged elder statesman of the Baptist cause, Backus played a major role in the increase of Baptist churches in New England from thirty-one in 1740 to 325 in 1795. The Warren Association of 1767 had become thirteen Baptist associations by 1804. His evangelical Calvinistic ministry reinforced his quest for religious liberty. Owing largely to his efforts a small dissenting sect of Baptists became the largest protestant denomination in the United States after 1800. His death occurred at home in Middleborough on 20 November 1806 following two strokes. He was buried in Titicut parish cemetery.

FREDERICK V. MILLS, SR.

Sources A. Hovey, *A memoir of the life and times of the Rev. Isaac Backus* (1972) • I. Backus, *A history of New England with particular reference to the Baptists* (1969) • *The diary of Isaac Backus*, ed. W. G. McLoughlin, 3 vols. (1979) • M. V. Backman, jun., 'Isaac Backus: a pioneer champion of religious liberty', PhD diss., University of Pennsylvania, 1959 • T. B. Maston, *Isaac Backus: pioneer of religious liberty* (1962) • W. G. McLoughlin, *Soul liberty: the Baptists' struggle in New England, 1630–1833* (1991) • S. Grenz, *Isaac Backus: puritan and Baptist* (1983) • W. G. McLoughlin, *Isaac Backus on church, state, and Calvinism: pamphlets, 1754–1789* (1968) • W. G. McLoughlin, *Isaac Backus and the American pietistic tradition* (1967)

Archives Brown University, Providence, Rhode Island, papers • Newton Center, Massachusetts, Andover Newton Theological School, papers

Likenesses A. H. Combe, granite monument in form of pulpit, 1892, Titicut parish cemetery, Middleborough, Massachusetts • portrait, Newton Center, Massachusetts, Andover Newton Theological School

Wealth at death modest means: will, 7 Nov 1805; *Diary*, ed. McLoughlin, appx 26

Backwell, Edward (*c.*1619–1683), goldsmith and banker, the son of Barnaby Backwell of Leighton Buzzard, Bedfordshire, a yeoman, was apprenticed in 1635 to Thomas Vyner, a leading goldsmith. He became free of the Goldsmiths' Company in 1651, of which he was to be prime warden in 1660.

Early financial dealings Like his master, Backwell was actively involved in credit finance during the time of the English republic. He also dealt in the former crown property that was put on the market; having bought the park at Hampton Court under the Commonwealth, he sold it back to the state at a profit under the protectorate. He was engaged in bullion transactions as early as 1650 and helped Vyner to handle captured Spanish plate in 1657. However, he was most active as treasurer for the Dunkirk garrison from the time of the town's capture and establishment as an English base on the continent in 1658, and this probably provided him with a natural transition from his role as a disbursing official and credit financier in the service of the republic to a similar position under the restored monarchy in 1660. He continued to manage the affairs of Dunkirk, although jointly with the more committed royalist financier Sir John Shaw, until after its sale to France in 1662, when he handled the bullion payments made by Louis XIV to Charles II. He also acted jointly with Sir Thomas Vyner in providing money for the supply of the royal household, and with the latter's nephew Sir Robert Vyner in handling bullion brought in for coinage at the Royal Mint, both Vyners having also already been involved in bringing over the French money received for Dunkirk.

Backwell was elected an alderman of the City shortly before the Restoration, early in 1660, but paid the customary large fine of £720 in the following year in order to be excused from continuing to serve. It is not clear whether this had any political or religious significance. It is indicative of Backwell's importance, or at least of his ceaseless activity, that he is mentioned more often than any other financier of the 1660s in Samuel Pepys's *Diary*. In January 1664 Pepys expressed himself strongly (in his famous naval white book, not in the diary) of the opinion that Backwell was profiteering at the crown's expense by asking 4*s.* and 7*d.* for each 'piece of eight' which he delivered, when the clerk of the acts had a merchant friend who would supply them at 4*s.* and 6½*d.* each. 'This is the unhappy posture of the King's credit. And the effect of making use but of one or two men', so Pepys reflected (*Samuel Pepys and the Second Dutch War*).

But all was not plain sailing for Backwell during these years. When he was on a confidential mission to Antwerp on the crown's behalf in the summer of 1665 his head clerk (who had been an under-officer in the exchequer with Pepys back in 1659–60) succumbed to the plague when in charge of the London office. In Backwell's absence this led to a temporary crisis of confidence in his creditworthiness and a run on his bank's resources, from which he had to be rescued by the crown largely with the help of Sir Robert Vyner, to whose assistance Backwell in turn rallied during another liquidity crisis in 1667–8. Both

Edward Backwell (*c.*1619–1683), by unknown engraver, pubd 1797

in his own capacity, by having advanced credit to the crown through numerous of its agents, and as the recipient of many reassigned Treasury orders for payment on future revenues, Backwell was inevitably one of those hardest hit by the stop of exchequer (December 1671–January 1672). As a result of this measure, taken to avert general bankruptcy, and to allow expenditure to continue in preparing for the Third Anglo-Dutch War, all hypothecated payments on incoming revenues were to be frozen for one year; this was later extended for a second year, by the end of which time the dates by which the hypothecated payments should have been made had all passed. When the crown reviewed its obligations to the bankers, initially in 1674, Backwell was reckoned to be owed a total of nearly £296,000 (principal, plus interest due since January 1672). This was less than the amount owed to Sir Robert Vyner (by then a baronet), whose uncle Sir Thomas, Backwell's old master, was not involved (having died in 1665), but it was more than that owed to any other goldsmith, and a very considerable sum, equivalent to about one-quarter of the crown's annual peacetime income; for this he was to receive a 6 per cent annuity, amounting to £17,759 13*s.* 8*d.*, in order to help him meet his obligations to his own creditors. The crown sought to give the letters patent, reissued in 1677, empowering the annuity payments to Backwell, Vyner, and the other goldsmith bankers, who had been the direct sufferers from the stop, the additional legal force of a statute; but a bill which had passed the Lords in 1678 failed in the Commons.

Crown agent Meanwhile the extent to which Backwell continued to act as a private banker after 1672 is doubtful;

he is not named in a 1676–7 pamphlet listing the bankers. He did, however, continue actively as a financial agent of the crown, and had already been rewarded early in 1671 by his appointment, jointly with his son John, as comptroller of customs in the port of London, the duties of which he performed by deputy. Along with Vyner he completed a four-year term as a commissioner of the customs and farmer of the customs revenues in 1671, so as comptroller he was not thereafter having to cross-check on his own activities as a farmer; he and Vyner were not members of the new syndicate, which offered to undertake the next and abortive farm, the failure of which led instead to the institution of direct management by salaried commissioners. While he was on a special mission to the Netherlands in 1674, trying to collect what the United Provinces and their allies owed Charles II, as the price of England abandoning their French ally and making a separate peace, Backwell made an ambitious, it might be said audacious, proposal to the lord treasurer, Lord Latimer, shortly to become earl of Danby. This was to the effect that he should 'buy' the first £5 million to be yielded by the new impost on wines and vinegar, due to be raised over the years 1674–8, for which he was to give £430,000, although of this he was actually to pay only £150,000 within the following ten months; the remaining £280,000 was to be written off as the debt which was owed him by the king (on which he offered to forgo further interest as from that midsummer). The correspondence is frustratingly one-sided, Danby's replies to Backwell not being known to have survived; but when, not surprisingly, the offer was not taken up, Backwell seems to have become convinced that the lord treasurer had turned against him, due to the promptings of some secret enemy, whom Backwell perhaps unwisely identified in a later letter as the merchant financier Sir John Banks, who had indeed prudently moved his own bank account away from Backwell and from Vyner to another goldsmiths' partnership before the 1672 financial crisis. Backwell did collect some of the money owing to the king by the Dutch, but his relations with the still dominant Danby may well have been damaged by this curious episode.

In 1676 an informer reported that Backwell had been seen calling on the duke of Buckingham, one of the leading opposition peers, at his house just outside London. By contrast with Vyner, who was eventually bankrupted by the actions of some of his private creditors against him, Backwell's bankruptcy in 1682 seems to have been precipitated by the crown's action against him in respect of money which he allegedly owed from his dealings with Sir George Carteret as treasurer of the navy many years earlier (1660–67), and following his death the next year payment of the 6 per cent annuity was stopped. Eventually a private act of parliament in favour of his creditors, and their heirs and executors, was passed in 1698, in the parliamentary session preceding the passage of a similar measure for Vyner's creditors. Under the terms of this act, a minority of one-third or less of the creditors, measured by their numbers and by the amounts which they were owed, was obliged to accept any agreement made with Backwell's own heirs and executors by a two-thirds majority, or else forfeit any claims whatever on his estate—statute thus being employed to prevent the possibility of any future legal actions. Some of his family did survive as Buckinghamshire landowners, albeit on a modest scale; one branch even added to their estates, although as absentees living in London. But the male lines all died out before the end of the eighteenth century, and Backwell's descendants in the female line finally sold up during the early twentieth century. Unlike the case with the Vyners, some of his family did continue as City financiers.

Banking activities Backwell's activities as a banker are very fully, yet also incompletely, documented. A series of large ledgers descended to one of his grandsons, who married into the Child family; these records then passed to Child's Bank, then to Glyn Mills, and subsequently into the possession of the Royal Bank of Scotland. They constitute the earliest known systematic archive of any British bank, antedating even those of Hoare and Child, and have therefore been of much interest to historians of banking and finance. The account books of the scriveners Robert Abbott, Robert Clayton, and John Morris, it is true, go back to an earlier date, in so far as these can be equated with bankers' cash ledgers. There is one general letter-book with entries running from the 1650s to the 1670s, sometimes misleadingly described as 'the Dunkirk ledger' because it begins with items about Backwell as paymaster for Dunkirk under the Cromwellian protectorate. It also contains a record of the full establishment for the garrison and ancillaries shortly after the Restoration, when the annual cost was calculated to be over £113,000, an absurdly large amount in relation to Charles II's total revenue at that time, and ample justification for the sale of Dunkirk to France the following year.

A less expected item to find is the full, lengthy text of the 1667 agreement made between all the incoming farmers of the hearth tax or chimney money, since Backwell was not one of them; however, Sir Robert Vyner, while notionally only one of the ten parties to this complex agreement, was clearly the power behind the whole undertaking, and Backwell may have felt it necessary to have the full facts about this partnership recorded because some of those involved, including of course Vyner himself, were currently banking with him. In general this volume illustrates his relations with the crown, both before and after the stop of the exchequer. The other nine surviving volumes are ledgers more properly so-called. They run from 1663 to 1672, with a gap in 1664 and another in 1665; it is clear from internal references, and from the alphabetical numbering of the volumes, that the series must have originated before 1663 (possibly even going back to the early 1650s), and must have continued after March 1672. They are basically records of debit and credit transactions with the system of internal balancing of the entries having been changed at some stage in 1665.

As with the other goldsmith bankers of the time, Backwell had among his clients many individuals who reassigned to him their orders guaranteed on future royal revenues after this system was implemented in 1665–6, although it is impossible to calculate what proportion such items constitute of the total private side of his business. Use has been made of the ledgers (chiefly of the continuous part of the series covering 1666–72) in order to calculate the scale of his advances to the crown, and the effect on his business of Sir George Downing's system of Treasury orders, devised to increase the crown's short-term credit, and their reassignability to third parties. More recently the use of computers has made it possible to construct day-to-day cashflow tables and diagrams for Backwell's relations with the other goldsmith bankers among his clients, and (separately) with Sir Robert Vyner. One or two special factors served to increase Backwell's potential vulnerability. Besides the crisis in his affairs, already noted, back in 1665, it has been suggested that the destruction of his City premises in the great fire of 1666 led him to abandon altogether his original trade as a goldsmith and to concentrate wholly on banking and government service. He lacked Vyner's continuing commitment to the craft through the latter's position as the king's goldsmith.

Although there is some disagreement as to how far Backwell was 'the bankers' banker' in the sense of providing clearing arrangements between others engaged in the business, he certainly had very active dealings with several, both individuals and partnerships; in the absence of comparable records for his contemporaries (except Vyner's fragmentary ledger of September–October 1666), we can only surmise or infer the extent to which he was unusual, or even unique, as a bankers' banker. For the general historian of the period, lacking the skills and application of the cliometrician, the transactions in his ledgers may be classified as follows: those with, first, other bankers, including his involvement in the foreign exchanges and the bullion market; second, royal office-holders, most notably receivers and paymasters, but also those serving abroad as diplomats; and, third, others ranging, if not from dustmen to dukes, at least from men and women of sub-gentry or plebeian status to royalty and the top ranks of the peerage. The largest numbers of individual entries are recorded with the other bankers, several of whom were also to be involved in the stop and its complicated aftermath. By contrast the largest total amounts of actual issues and receipts, and of obligations for future out-payments and in-payments due, relate to various branches of royal revenue and expenditure—for example, in 1663–4, the farm of the London excise, the customs farmers, and Stephen Fox as a disbursing official. However, the largest numbers of different individuals come from the third category, although these generally contain fewer entries per client, and are for amounts of smaller value. To complicate matters, some people appear in more than one capacity: thus Samuel Pepys had a private account with Backwell (as can be verified from his *Diary*), but also dealt with the banker in his capacity as treasurer for the garrison of Tangier. Fox too is represented in both capacities.

Domestic and political life Backwell was twice returned as MP for Wendover, Buckinghamshire, in 1673. On the first occasion the election was voided because the writ had been improperly issued; on the second he was again unseated after being accused of bribing the electors. He sat for the same constituency in all three of the Exclusion Parliaments of 1679–81, but is recorded as having taken an active part in only the first of these, serving on various committees and reportedly opposing the exclusion from the succession of James, duke of York. Nothing is known of him in the sittings of 1680 and 1681. It has been suggested that he used his privilege as an MP to protect himself against his creditors. He also served as a common councilman of London in 1676–81, which was unusual for someone who had been chosen as an alderman many years before. His eldest son sat in parliament for Wendover in James II's parliament of 1685 and after the revolution of 1688.

Backwell married his first wife, Sarah, the daughter of a London merchant called Brett, by 1653; they had one son, John, who was involved with his father in both banking and office-holding. He married, secondly, by 1662, Mary, the daughter of Richard Leigh or Lyse; she is the lady who appears in Pepys's *Diary*. By the time of her death in November 1669 they had three sons and two daughters; his son Leigh was apprenticed to his father in 1682, but disappears from the Goldsmiths' records after Backwell's death the following year. In January 1666 a warrant was drawn for him to be made a baronet, but this was never implemented. Either he declined the honour, or it was opposed, conceivably on account of either his humble origins or his Cromwellian past, though neither of these factors kept others from acquiring knighthoods, baronetcies, or even peerages under the restored monarchy.

Backwell died abroad in the Netherlands; his body was embalmed, and was buried in St Mary Woolnoth in the City on 13 June 1683, but exhumed on 20 October 1685 in order to be reburied at Tyringham in Buckinghamshire, where he had earlier gained control of the estate belonging to his son's father-in-law, Sir William Tyringham, an impoverished ex-cavalier. Although Backwell had made his will in 1679, it was not proved until after the passage of the act to satisfy his creditors in 1698. He left property in Buckinghamshire to his eldest son, in Huntingdonshire and the City to his second son, and further London properties to his third and fourth sons. Noting that everything left to the three younger ones was already mortgaged for the payment of his debts, he bequeathed to them jointly the large annuity granted by letters patent in 1677. His solitary bequest otherwise was a £40 annuity to a female relative. The will is unusual in lacking any religious prologue and in providing for no other legacies, either personal or philanthropic. Initially Backwell's brother and all four sons were made executors; a codicil of 1683 altered this to the second and fourth sons only. The only known visual representation of Backwell is a particularly fine life-size contemporary engraving in the possession of the

Goldsmiths' Company; the inscription is of a later date, but small details confirm the portrait's authenticity.

For the historian, Backwell is important as far and away the best documented banker of his time. The relationship of the goldsmiths of the 1660s and 1670s to the later development of banking and the new system of public credit established in the 1690s remains open to debate. As this brief account has sought to show, the history of banking after the Restoration is inseparable from that of public, alias royal, finance, which in turn cannot be separated from the general political history of the time.

G. E. AYLMER

Sources *CSP dom.* • J. M. S. Brooke and A. W. C. Hallen, eds., *The transcript of the registers of … St Mary Woolnoth and St Mary Woolnoth Haw … 1538 to 1760* (1886) • 'The Dunkirke affaire', *Three Banks Review*, 30 (1956), 40–50 • M. P. Ashley, *Financial and commercial policy under the Cromwellian protectorate* (1934) • A. B. Beaven, ed., *The aldermen of the City of London, temp. Henry III–[1912]*, 2 vols. (1908–13) • C. D. Chandaman, *The English public revenue, 1660–1688* (1975) • D. K. Clark, 'Edward Backwell as a royal agent', *Economic History Review*, 9 (1938–9), 45–55 • A. Heal, ed., *The London goldsmiths, 1200–1800: a record of the names and addresses of the craftsmen, their shop-signs and trade-cards* (1935) • HoP, *Commons* • J. K. Horsefield, 'The "stop of the exchequer" revisited', *Economic History Review*, 2nd ser., 35 (1982), 511–28 • Pepys, *Diary* • D. Mitchell, 'Innovation and the transfer of skill in the goldsmiths' trade in Restoration London', *Goldsmiths, silversmiths and bankers: innovation and the transfer of skill, 1550 to 1750* [London 1993], ed. D. Mitchell (1995), 5–22 • G. O. Nichols, 'English government borrowing, 1660–1688', *Journal of British Studies*, 10/2 (1970–71), 83–104 • F. G. Hilton Price, *A handbook of London bankers*, enl. edn (1890–91) • S. F. Quinn, 'Banking before the bank: London's unregulated goldsmith-bankers, 1660–1694', PhD diss., University of Illinois, 1994 • S. Quinn, 'Balances and goldsmith-bankers: the co-ordination and control of inter-banker clearing in seventeenth-century London', *Goldsmiths, silversmiths and bankers: innovation and the transfer of skill, 1550 to 1750* [London 1993], ed. D. Mitchell (1995), 53–76 • R. D. Richards, 'A pre-Bank of England English banker—Edward Backwell', *Economic History*, 1 (1926–9), 335–55 • R. D. Richards, *The early history of banking in England* (1929) • H. G. Roseveare, 'The advancement of the king's credit, 1660–1672: a study in economic, political and administrative history based mainly on the career of Sir George Downing, knight and baronet', PhD diss., U. Cam., 1962 • H. G. Roseveare, *Government, financial policy and the money markets in late 17th-century England* (1926); later pubn (Italy, 1981) • H. Roseveare, *The financial revolution, 1660–1760* (1991) • W. A. Shaw, ed., *Calendar of treasury books*, 1–9, PRO (1904–31) [incl. introductions by W. A. Shaw] • *VCH Buckinghamshire*, vol. 4 • J. R. Woodhead, *The rulers of London, 1660–1689* (1965) • *Samuel Pepys and the Second Dutch War: Pepys's navy white book and Brooke House papers*, ed. R. Latham, Navy RS, 133 (1995), 3 [transcribed by W. Matthews and C. Knighton]

Archives BL, letters, Add. MS 19402 • HLRO, Box 17, no. 628; 9–10 William III, no. 88 • PRO, exchequer of receipt, E.403/2510, 3034; E.406/20–1; E.407/33–4, 119 • Royal Bank of Scotland, London, group archives, ledgers, and papers | BL, Add. MSS • BL, Egerton MSS

Likenesses engraving, 1660?, Goldsmiths' Hall • stipple, pubd 1797 (after engraving), NPG • engraving, pubd 1797, BM [*see illus.*] • line print (on Dutch plate), BM, NPG

Wealth at death technically a bankrupt for about a year before he died; held estates in Buckinghamshire and elsewhere: will, PRO, PROB 11/448, sig. 246

Bacon, Alice Martha, Baroness Bacon (1909–1993), politician, was born on 10 September 1909 at 302 Castleford Road, Normanton, Yorkshire, the only child of Benjamin (Ben) Bacon (1882–1958), coalminer, and his wife, Charlotte (Lottie), *née* Handley (1888–1953). She was educated at elementary schools in Normanton and Altofts and at Normanton Girls' High School, and trained as a teacher at Stockwell College, Bromley, Kent, before taking up a post at an elementary school in Featherstone, Yorkshire, in 1929. She later moved to Queen Street elementary school, Normanton, from which she transferred, with the senior pupils, to Normanton modern school when it opened in 1937. There she taught mathematics and had responsibility for the girls' welfare. She was not averse to using the cane.

Alice Martha Bacon, Baroness Bacon (1909–1993), by Jorge Lewinski, 1969

Bacon was brought up in an atmosphere of politics and social concern: her father was secretary of the Whitwood branch of the National Union of Mineworkers, and an urban district and West Riding county councillor. She recalled the family's small terrace house being filled with footwear bought for the 'boots for bairns' campaign, and the local Miners' Welfare Institute being, especially in 1926, 'like a small national health service' (*A Labour of Love*). As a schoolgirl, she helped miners to complete forms for insurance claims. She joined the Labour Party when she was sixteen and shortly afterwards made her first political speech, at the Railwaymen's Institute in Normanton. She also joined the Labour League of Youth and swiftly came to national prominence. She joined the executive committee of Socialist Youth International and in 1935 she was the British delegate to its conference in Copenhagen. She was also active in the National Union of

Teachers, and in 1944 was elected president of its West Yorkshire county association. She gained a diploma in public administration as an external candidate at London University. In October 1938 she was chosen by Leeds Labour Party as its candidate for the north-east Leeds constituency and she was elected as its member of parliament in 1945; she represented that constituency until 1955, when the redistribution of seats took her to south-east Leeds, which she represented until 1970. One of her first parliamentary positions was as a member of the Home Office committee of inquiry into the closing hours of shops and the working conditions in mines and factories. When elected in 1941 she was the youngest woman ever to have joined the Labour Party's national executive committee; she remained a member until 1970, and in the 1950s and 1960s was in a key position as chairman of its publicity and political education subcommittee. She was the chairman of the Labour Party in 1950–51 and was 'among the committed socialist post-war innovators who helped to create the welfare state' (*Yorkshire Post*, 26 March 1993). She was made a CBE in 1953 in the coronation honours list.

Bacon's socialism was practical and she was mistrustful of ideology. Her main interests lay in education, housing, and pay and conditions in the workplace: she was an early advocate of comprehensive schools and an opponent of corporal punishment; she campaigned to rid the country of back-to-back housing and to compel landlords to effect repairs more quickly. In 1957 she introduced an unsuccessful bill against capital punishment. Her loyalties were always to the right of the party and especially to Herbert Morrison and to Hugh Gaitskell, her fellow Leeds MP, who, despite her habitual suspicion of middle-class intellectuals, succeeded him as her political mentor. She was a scourge of the left-wing Bevanites in the 1950s and later of the Trotskyites. She was surprised to be offered a position in Harold Wilson's Labour government; she was minister of state at the Home Office from 1964 to 1967 (where she was both capable and unhappy, feeling that she did not fit in with the ministerial team and finding it difficult to work with the home secretary, Roy Jenkins), and minister of state for education and science from 1967 to 1970 (where she felt wholly at home). She was sworn of the privy council in 1966. She was awarded a life peerage in Wilson's dissolution honours list in 1970. She once said, 'I have never been a part-time MP, or, come to that, a full-time MP. I have always been an overtime MP' (*Yorkshire Post*, 10 July 1985). She remained active after entering the House of Lords but increasingly spent her time in Yorkshire, where she was proud of her home and her garden, and where for twenty years she had cared for her aunt Sarah Handley. In 1972 she was awarded an honorary degree by Leeds University. In 1974 she was appointed a deputy lieutenant for West Yorkshire.

Bacon was an ordinary girl who made herself extraordinary opportunities. 'She never forgot her roots and would not allow anyone else to forget them either .... She was able to deal with world leaders and Leeds pensioners in the same honest, forthright manner' (*Wakefield Express*, 2 April 1993). 'There was no humbug in her, but she sensed it in others a mile off' (ibid., 30 April 1993). She understood the aspirations of working people and expressed them in political terms. She was down to earth, looked simple and homely, but was a strange mixture of the streetwise, the uncomplicated, and the naïve, and could be a shrewd political operator. She did not talk down to ordinary people but neither did she dress down to them: she took a pride in her appearance, dressing simply but smartly, and her neat blouses, jackets, and skirts were often couturier-made. At party conferences she spoke simply and directly and without oratorical tricks; there and on the floor of the House of Commons she addressed her audience rather as a good teacher addresses the school. Her voice was low-pitched but loud and grating, and she made no attempt to modify her Yorkshire vowels.

In later years Bacon suffered from rheumatoid arthritis. She died of bronchopneumonia on 24 March 1993 at Castleford and Normanton District General Hospital and was buried on 31 March in the graveyard of Normanton parish church. She never married. She left bequests of £80,000 and £40,000 for the benefit of the people of Leeds and Normanton. C. M. P. TAYLOR

Sources private information (2004) [Harold Bacon, Walter Harrison, Gerald Kaufman, Bill O'Brien, Lord Merlyn-Rees] • cuttings files, Yorkshire Post Newspapers Ltd, Leeds • *The Times* (30 March 1993) • *The Independent* (29 March 1993) • *Yorkshire Post* (26 March 1993) • *Wakefield Express* (2 April 1993) • *WWW* • D. Williamson and P. Ellis, eds., *Debrett's distinguished people of today* (1988) • T. Benn, *Out of the wilderness: diaries, 1963–67* (1987) • D. Healey, *The time of my life* (1988) • *The Castle diaries, 1964–1976*, abridged edn (1990) • *A labour of love: portrait of Alice Bacon*, 1980x89 [BBC radio programme] • school log book, Normanton senior (modern) school • admission register, Normanton council school • b. cert. • d. cert. • *CGPLA Eng. & Wales* (1993)

Archives priv. coll. | SOUND BBC WAC, 'A labour of love: portrait of Alice Bacon' • BL NSA, oral history interview

Likenesses J. Lewinski, photograph, 1969, NPG [*see illus.*] • photograph, repro. in *The Times* • photograph, repro. in *The Independent* • photographs, priv. coll.

Wealth at death under £125,000: probate, 8 July 1993, *CGPLA Eng. & Wales*

Bacon [*née* Cooke], **Anne, Lady Bacon** (*c.*1528–1610), gentlewoman and scholar, was probably born at Gidea Hall, Essex. She was third of the nine children of Sir Anthony *Cooke (1505/6–1576), one of the humanist educators who tutored Edward VI, and Anne (*d.* 1553), daughter of Sir William FitzWilliam and widow of Sir John Hawes of London, and second of the five Cooke sisters whose education by their father in the classical languages and the early church fathers made them, according to Thomas Fuller, 'all most eminent scholars, (the honour of their own and the shame of our sex)' (Fuller, *Worthies*, 1.328). In a Cambridge oration, Walter Haddon celebrated the Cooke household, where Anne came to excel in Greek, Latin, and Italian, as a 'small university', but one where 'the industry of the females was in full vigour' (Jardine and Stewart, 25). How fully the children of both sexes shared in educational opportunities is clear from Anne's inscription in a copy of *Moschopulus*: 'My father delivered this book to me and my brother Anthony, who was mine

Anne Bacon [Cooke], **Lady Bacon** (*c*.1528–1610), by unknown artist

elder brother and schoolfellow with me, to follow for writing of Greek' (Essex RO, Sage collection, 773). Under Sir Anthony's zealous protestant guidance, the rigorous intellectual training focused on advancing God's word, but there were playful occasions, as when she penned a spirited Latin letter exhorting a sister to marry Haddon. Anne's determination to put to significant use even her study of Italian, criticized by her mother as a potential distraction from godliness, bore fruit in her published translation of *Sermons* by Bernadino Ochino (*c*.1548).

In February 1553 Anne became the second wife of Sir Nicholas *Bacon (1510–1579), who would serve as Queen Elizabeth's lord keeper of the great seal. He celebrated in verse the 'fruits of mind' shared between them, their mutual profit from 'your Tully and my Seneck' (Jardine and Stewart, 27). Given her strong reformist convictions, it is surprising that Anne served Queen Mary as a gentlewoman of the privy chamber, but this role positioned her to help gain a pardon for her brother-in-law, William *Cecil. A presence at court to be reckoned with, she was described by the count of Feria as 'a tiresome bluestocking' (Hume, 1.18). After the deaths of two baby daughters, Anthony *Bacon was born in 1558 and Francis *Bacon in 1561. Lady Bacon helped to supervise their early education, and, when widowed in 1579, took up earnestly Sir Nicholas's charge of 'well bringing up' these 'poor orphans without a father' (Smith, Baker, and Kenny, 2.27).

In 1564, Anne Bacon made her mark on English religious prose with her translation from Latin of John Jewel's *Apologie of the Church of England*. The accuracy and stylistic distinction of her work received gratifying and immediate recognition when Archbishop Matthew Parker arranged publication of his manuscript copy, making her words the voice of the established church. In her widowhood, she took on a more activist role to advance 'right reformation', pressing Cecil, for example, to secure a fairer hearing for the nonconformist preachers deprived under Whitgift's articles of 1583. 'The Lord raise up many such matrons for the comfort of his poor afflicted church', wrote Nicholas Faunt in 1584, of her 'earnest care and travel for the restoring' of deprived preachers 'to their places' (Birch, 1.48), and Theodore Beza, John Walsall, and Thomas Wilcox celebrated her contributions in printed dedications to her. Even in her seventies, she kept radical puritanism alive in Hertfordshire, sheltering preachers at Gorhambury, securing them employment, and almost certainly supporting the major project to collect and disseminate a register of puritan documents. As a godly widow, she judged it her duty to admonish straying believers, and wrote like a minister to the earl of Essex in 1596 to exhort him against 'carnal dalliance' (Birch, 2.218).

Lady Bacon's formidable personality comes most vividly to life in over ninety surviving letters to her sons, most sent from Gorhambury to Anthony in London between 1592 and 1597. She counsels her adult sons about their bodily health, spiritual welfare, financial solvency, fit use for their talents, housing arrangements, and male companions, with a persistence only intensified by her frustration at the limited credit they give her advice. Her life as the female head of a godly household is richly illustrated—the daily business of transporting beer, catechizing servants, and negotiating with tenants, together with the sustained struggle of a strong-willed woman for authority: 'A man master would go nigh to break thy head for this speech' she tells a disrespectful manservant (LPL, MS 653.205). She impoverished herself to help with her sons' debts, signing bitterly regretted releases of her interest in family properties, until finally, after Anthony's death, she surrendered even Gorhambury to Francis in 1602.

Little is known of Anne's last years. On 27 August 1610, Sir Francis Bacon requested the company of his friend Sir Michael Hicks at her funeral, promising 'a good sermon' but no feast (Spedding, 4.218). His direction for his own burial adds the detail—'I desire it may be in St. Michael's church, near St. Alban's: there was my mother buried' (Spedding, 7.539). LYNNE MAGNUSSON

Sources M. K. McIntosh, 'Sir Anthony Cooke: Tudor humanist, educator, and religious reformer', *Proceedings of the American Philosophical Society*, 119 (1975), 233–50 · L. Jardine and A. Stewart, *Hostage to fortune: the troubled life of Francis Bacon, 1561–1626* (1998) · LPL, Anthony Bacon MSS, MSS 647–662 · *The letters and life of Francis Bacon*, ed. J. Spedding, 7 vols. (1861–74) · T. Birch, *Memoirs of the reign of Queen Elizabeth*, 2 vols. (1754) · *The papers of Nathaniel Bacon of Stiffkey*, ed. A. H. Smith, G. M. Baker, and R. W. Kenny, 1–3, Norfolk RS, 46, 49, 53 (1979–90) · A. Simpson, *The wealth of the gentry, 1540–1660: East Anglian studies* (1961) · W. Urwick, *Nonconformity in Hertfordshire* (1884) · P. Collinson, *The Elizabethan puritan movement* (1967) ·

M. A. S. Hume, ed., *Calendar of letters and state papers relating to English affairs, preserved principally in the archives of Simancas*, 4 vols., PRO (1892–9) • N. Bacon, *The recreations of his age* (1903) • *DNB* • Fuller, *Worthies* (1662) • Essex RO, Chelmsford, Sage collection, 773

Archives BL, Lansdowne MSS • CUL, Ii.5.37 • LPL, Anthony Bacon MSS

Likenesses terracotta bust, 1569, Gorhambury, Hertfordshire; repro. in D. du Maurier, *Golden lads: a study of Anthony Bacon, Francis and their friends* (1975), facing p. 16 • portrait, *c*.1576 (on the tomb of Sir Anthony Cooke), Romford Church, Essex; repro. in 'The Cookes of Gidea Hall', *Essex Review*, 21 (1912), facing p. 1 • attrib. G. Gower, oils, 1580, Gorhambury, Hertfordshire; repro. in Jardine and Stewart, *Hostage to fortune* • attrib. I. Oliver, watercolour miniature, *c*.1600, Walters Art Gallery, Baltimore • painted terracotta, priv. coll. [*see illus.*] • portrait (*Tree of Jesse showing the issue of the Lord Keeper Sir Nicholas Bacon by his two wives, Jane Fernley and Ann Cooke*), repro. in Jardine and Stewart, *Hostage to fortune*, facing p. 256; priv. coll.

Wealth at death possibly less than £300: comments about will, LPL, Anthony Bacon MSS, 653.175 (17 April 1593), 653.138, 653.110 • Hertfordshire properties surrendered to Sir Francis Bacon, 20 Nov 1602: Herts. ALS, IX.D.3 • was receiving £100 p.a. from stepson as half year's annuity out of manors of Ingham and Tymworth; final payment, 16 March 1610: *Papers of Sir Nicholas Bacon in the University of Chicago Library* (1989), 363

Bacon, Anthony (1558–1601), spy, was the fourth of five sons of Sir Nicholas *Bacon (1510–1579), administrator, of Gorhambury, Hertfordshire, and the first with his second wife, Anne, *née* Cooke (*c*.1528–1610) [*see* Bacon, Anne], daughter of Sir Anthony *Cooke of Gidea Hall, Essex, and his wife, Anne. Through the marriages of his mother's sisters he was nephew to Sir Henry Killigrew, Sir Thomas Hoby, and, most significantly, to Elizabeth I's secretary of state and later lord treasurer, William Cecil, Lord Burghley. He grew up with his younger brother, Sir Francis *Bacon, possibly with his half-brother Sir Edward *Bacon [*see under* Bacon, Sir Nathaniel], and with five sisters, at his parents' Hertfordshire estate of Gorhambury, tutored by John Walsall. Two other half-brothers were Sir Nathaniel *Bacon and Sir Nicholas *Bacon. From April 1573 Anthony and Francis studied for three years at Trinity College, Cambridge, under the master, John Whitgift, without graduating. From an early age, Anthony was prone to ill health: he recovered from a dangerous fever in 1560; Francis's earliest extant letter in 1574 attributes his brother's absence from Cambridge to his 'sore eyes', and Whitgift's accounts record moneys paid 'for Anthony being sick' (Jardine and Stewart, 37). These early illnesses were to become habitual and impact deeply on his career.

Anthony Bacon was admitted to Gray's Inn on 27 June 1576, studying under Richard Barker; his correspondence from the period shows an interest in the puritan Thomas Cartwright's writings against his erstwhile tutor Whitgift, an interest encouraged by his zealously nonconformist mother. Following his father's death in February 1579, and a bitter fight with his elder half-brothers, Bacon inherited estates worth £360 per annum, and the reversion of Gorhambury on his mother's death (she outlived him by nine years). An earlier attempt to marry him profitably had failed, and now at twenty-one, with personal assets that he could mortgage, he decided to go abroad. In December 1579, armed with letters of recommendation from Burghley and the French ambassador, Michel de Castelnau, seigneur de Mauvissière, he set off to Paris, where he began to provide intelligence reports for Burghley and Sir Francis Walsingham, principal secretary, and made a lifelong friend and correspondent in the latter's secretary, Nicholas Faunt. From Paris he moved on to Bourges, but, unable to reconcile himself to the strong Catholic faith of the city, he headed for the Calvinist republic of Geneva in the summer of 1581, lodging with Théodore Beza, who dedicated the French publication of his meditations on the penitential psalms to Bacon's mother 'for my sake' (LPL, MS 659, fol. 24).

Over the following years, Bacon frequently lost contact with England, citing illness; Walsingham rightly blamed his incapacity on an over-dependence on 'physic', and advised him, 'you shall find in time many incommodities, if you do not in time break it off' (LPL, MS 647, art. 52). Having spent time in Lyons, Montpellier, Toulouse, and Marseilles, in November 1583 Bacon travelled to Bordeaux, where he met the essayist Michel de Montaigne; there, at the request of Robert Dudley, earl of Leicester, he performed certain business for the queen: she welcomed 'so good a man as you to have and receive letters by' (LPL, MS 647, art. 75). At the same time, however, Bacon was fighting accusations that 'my lodging was charged to be the receptacle of all rebellious Huguenots', and was ill again with a persistent quartain ague. Moving on to Bearn, he was befriended by the theologian Lambert Daneau, who dedicated his commentary on the minor prophets to him. Elizabeth sanctioned his continued stay in France, using him as an unofficial contact with the Huguenot leader Henri of Navarre. By October 1584, Bacon was established in the Huguenot stronghold of Montauban, embraced by Navarre's court, including the poet Guillaume de Salluste Du Bartas. However, he gained an enemy in the wife of Henri's counsellor Philippe Duplessis Mornay when he refused to support her fight to wear wigs in church, and then rebuffed the prospect of marrying her daughter. His position deteriorated during 1585 and 1586, when Montauban was in desperate straits; in the heightened atmosphere of suspicion, Bacon and one of his pages were accused of sodomy, a capital offence. Details are sketchy: interrogations took place in August 1586 and November 1587, and Bacon may have been tried, because Navarre certainly intervened to commute a sentence against him, although this may have related to his debt problems. None of this was known in England, where Bacon's failure to return was regarded with increasing anger. One messenger, the Catholic Thomas Lawson, was jailed by Burghley; the next, Captain Francis Allen, was subjected to a tirade by Lady Bacon, who called her elder son 'a traitor to God and your country' (LPL, MS 647, art. 121).

In 1590 Bacon returned to Bordeaux, where he engaged in a merchants' controversy, renewed his acquaintance with Montaigne (sending one of the last known letters to the writer), and befriended the imprisoned Catholic double agent Anthony Standen. Hearing of this, Lady Bacon claimed that he was 'illegitimate and not to be born of her body' (LPL, MS 648, art. 51) and encouraged his brother to shun him. But when he finally returned home in February 1592 after a twelve-year absence, Francis welcomed him into his Gray's Inn lodgings. Anthony had hoped to profit from his long-standing intelligence service to his uncle Burghley, but soon found that path blocked, receiving instead only such fair words as:

> make fools fain, and yet even in these no offer or hopeful assurance of real kindness, which I thought I might justly expect at the Lord Treasurer's hands, who had inned my ten years' harvest into his own barn without any halfpenny charge. (LPL, MS 648, fols. 23*r*–26*v*)

Bacon's relations with Burghley and his cousin Sir Robert Cecil remained strained; an attempt in late 1596 by his aunt Lady Russell, wife of Sir John Russell of Blackfriars, London, to smooth matters over failed to help.

This rejection paved the way for Bacon's future life path. Francis Bacon introduced him to his own patron, Elizabeth's controversial favourite, Robert Devereux, second earl of Essex. Anthony Bacon soon enhanced Essex's remarkable secretariat by co-ordinating (unpaid) a massive foreign intelligence operation with contacts across Europe, including Thomas Bodley, Sir Thomas Chaloner, Dr Henry Hawkins, John Napier, Sir Anthony Sherley, and Standen. A good quantity of his correspondence is extant at Lambeth Palace Library and formed the basis of Thomas Birch's once standard history of Elizabeth's reign.

Bacon shuttled between Gray's Inn, the Bacon estates at Gorhambury and Redbourn, Hertfordshire, and his brother's estate at Twickenham, Middlesex, but he was increasingly incapacitated by the stone and gout (affecting his hands, ankles, and feet) which prevented him from ever attending on the queen. A final attempt in October 1593 to travel the few miles from Twickenham to the court at Windsor had to be abandoned at Eton. As Essex's nominee, he was returned as MP for Wallingford, Berkshire, in 1593 and Oxford, in 1597, but, even if he attended, he made no impact on either parliament. Bowing to Essex's desire to have him nearer at hand, in May 1594 he bought a London house in the disreputable Bishopsgate Street, much to his mother's concern: she complained that the presence of nearby Butt Inn with its 'continual interludes had even infected the inhabitants there with corrupt & lewd dispositions' (LPL, MS 650, art. 114). Her passions were similarly roused by Anthony's acquaintance with the urbane Spanish politician Antonio Pérez, who moved into Essex's circle and became a close friend: 'I would you were well rid of that old, dooted, polling papist. He will use discourses out of season to hinder your health, the want whereof is your great hindrance' (LPL, MS 653, art. 77). Worse was Bacon's decision in 1596 to move into the earl's residence, Essex House on the Strand. 'You have hitherto been esteemed as a worthy friend', she wrote, 'now shall be accounted his follower ... brought as it were into a kind of bondage' (LPL, MS 651, art. 210). Above all, Lady Bacon disapproved of what she considered her son's profligate spending: on his return to England, completely penniless, he had been forced to sell certain of his manors, and was to spend the rest of his life involved in complex debt arrangements.

In his final years, Bacon was almost certainly housebound but he maintained his powerful position at the heart of Essex's intelligence operations: Henry Wotton (a member of Essex's secretariat) described him as 'a gentleman of impotent feet, but a nimble head ... being of a provident nature ... and well knowing the advantage of a dangerous secret' (Wotton, 13). His intimacy and influence with Essex also aroused suspicions: Wotton alleged that Bacon extorted money from the earl by threatening to betray his secrets, a charge that is not repeated or supported elsewhere. Bacon's activities between 1597 and 1601, the turbulent period during which Essex fell from favour several times and controversially led English forces in Ireland, are difficult to reconstruct, since his papers from this period have been lost or, more likely, destroyed. While Essex was in Ireland in 1599, Bacon had a disagreement with his steward, Gelly Merrick; later, there was unsubstantiated gossip that the earl had given Essex House to Bacon in lieu of a cash sum owed to him. Certainly, Bacon remained in Essex House until Elizabeth ordered him and others to leave in March 1600; however, when Essex attempted his rebellion in February 1601, he was apparently not involved; he was not called to give evidence. By then, living on Crutched Friars in London, he was terminally ill: the date of his death is unknown, but he was buried on 17 May 1601 'in the chancel within the vault' in St Olave's, on nearby Hart Street (Bannerman, 132). On 23 June 1602 the administration of his estate was granted to Francis Bacon, but the newswriter John Chamberlain reported that he died 'so far in debt, that I think his brother is little the better by him' (*Letters of John Chamberlain*, 1.123). To ease this, on 20 November Lady Bacon freely surrendered her life interest in her manors, which she had insistently denied to Anthony, in favour of Francis.

Bacon's life has usually been treated by historians as an adjunct to that of his more famous brother, not least because Francis Bacon presented it to posterity in that way. As his health deteriorated, making public office impossible, Francis capitalized on his brother's connections in ways that ultimately erased Anthony's contribution. Dedicating the first edition of his *Essays* (1597) to him, for example, Francis Bacon declared that 'I sometimes wish your infirmities translated upon myself, that her Majesty mought have the service of so active and able a mind, and I mought be with excuse confined to these contemplations and studies for which I am fittest' (sig. A4*r*). In turn (and probably at Francis's urging) Anthony wrote to Essex, sub-dedicating the volume to him, praying 'leave to transfer my interest unto your Lordship' (*Works*, ed. Spedding, 6.521–2)—a manoeuvre that effectively wrote himself out of a transaction between Francis Bacon and Essex. In 1600, in an attempt to rehabilitate Essex with the queen, Francis Bacon confected a set of two letters, one from his brother to Essex and the other replying: both epistles, however, also served his interest by testifying generously to his talents. Later, he claimed intimate knowledge of his brother's affairs to forge links with his Scottish intelligence contacts, now useful figures in the new Jacobean regime, including David Foulis, Edward Bruce, and Sir Thomas Chaloner, citing:

> the infinite devotion and incessant endeavours (beyond the strength of his body and nature of the times) which appeared in my good brother towards your majesty's service … all which endeavours and duties for the most part were common to myself with him, though by design (as between brethren) dissembled. (*Letters*, ed. Spedding, 3.59)

The ploy worked: when James I granted Francis Bacon the office of learned counsel, and a life pension of £60 per annum in August 1604, the patent was awarded 'on account of the good, faithful and commendable service, until recently, of our beloved servant Anthony Bacon' (T. Rymer, ed., *Foedera, conventiones, literae*, 3rd edn, 1739–45, 7/2.121).

Viewed without the benefit of his brother's self-serving hindsight, however, another Anthony Bacon emerges. Early political compositions attributed by editors to Francis Bacon were probably in effect collaborative efforts—the latter writing up material provided by the former. Anthony Bacon was undeniably a highly capable intelligence gatherer, a literate, experienced, and informed man, with a formidable archive of useful secrets, whose talents—although divorced from flamboyant court life—were fully recognized by those players engaged in the complex negotiations of English and European politics during the last two decades of the sixteenth century, and whose meticulously kept correspondence provides an unparalleled insight into the period. ALAN STEWART

Sources L. Jardine and A. Stewart, *Hostage to fortune: the troubled life of Francis Bacon, 1561–1626* (1998) · LPL, Anthony Bacon papers, MSS 647–662 · T. Birch, *Memoirs of the reign of Queen Elizabeth*, 2 vols. (1754) · J. T. Freedman, 'Anthony Bacon and his world, 1558–1601', PhD diss., Temple University, 1979 · *DNB* · *The letters and life of Francis Bacon*, ed. J. Spedding, 7 vols. (1861–74) · HoP, *Commons, 1558–1603* · D. Du Maurier, *Golden lads: a study of Anthony Bacon, Francis and their friends* (1975) · State papers, domestic, Elizabeth, PRO, SP 12 · *CSP for.*, 1579–81, 1583–4, 1584–5 · *The papers of Nathaniel Bacon of Stiffkey*, ed. A. H. Smith, G. M. Baker, and R. W. Kenny, 1–3, Norfolk RS, 46, 49, 53 (1979–90) · P. E. J. Hammer, 'The uses of scholarship: the secretariat of Robert Devereux, 2nd earl of Essex, *c*.1585–1601', *EngHR*, 109 (1994), 26–51 · P. E. J. Hammer, *The polarisation of Elizabethan politics: the political career of Robert Devereux, 2nd earl of Essex, 1585–1597* (1999) · *The letters of John Chamberlain*, ed. N. E. McClure, 2 vols. (1939) · W. B. Bannerman, ed., *The registers of St Olave, Hart Street, London, 1563–1700* (1916) · F. Bacon, *Essayes, religious meditations, places of perswasion and disswasion* (1597) · H. Wotton, *Reliquiae Wottonianae* (1651) · *The works of Francis Bacon*, ed. J. Spedding, R. L. Ellis, and D. D. Heath, 14 vols. (1857–74)

Archives LPL, papers, MSS 647–662 · U. Edin., commonplace book | BL, Thomas Birch papers, Add. MS 4125 · U. Edin., Laing papers, III.193

Likenesses N. Hilliard?, portrait (Anthony Bacon?), Gorhambury collection · terracotta bust (Anthony or Francis Bacon?), Gorhambury collection

Bacon, Anthony (*bap.* **1717**, *d.* **1786**), merchant and ironmaster, the son of William Bacon and his wife, Elizabeth Richardson, was baptized at St Bees, Cumberland, on 24 January 1717. His father and grandfather Thomas were ships' captains in the coal trade between Whitehaven and Ireland, though his father also made several trading voyages to the Chesapeake. His mother died in 1725, when he was eight, and his father a few years later, and the boy was taken to Talbot county on the eastern shore of Maryland, where he was raised by his maternal uncles, Thomas (*d.* 1734) and Anthony (*d.* 1741) Richardson, who were merchants there. Young Anthony was trained by them as a merchant and as a mariner. He apparently made a good impression for, on coming of age, he was in 1738 made master of the *York*, a vessel in the Maryland tobacco trade owned by John Hanbury, the leading London tobacco importer.

After the death of his two uncles, Bacon found himself the guardian of his uncle Anthony's two young sons, Anthony and Thomas Richardson. He then moved to London, from where he operated as an itinerant merchant mariner during the period *c*.1742–1747 and as a resident merchant thereafter. In the 1740s he traded primarily with Maryland, but in the 1750s added Virginia and the Spanish wine trade. During the Seven Years' War he entered government contracting in collaboration with John Biggin, a native of Whitehaven and a large London coal merchant (who had been a major navy victualling contractor in the 1740s). Bacon was recognized as a specialist in shipping, and he provided vessels and carrying services to the Royal Navy. He was a major transporter of victuals in the Quebec campaign of 1759. In the later stages of the war he also branched out into army contracts, undertaking to victual and pay the troops stationed on the African coast at Fort Louis, Senegal, and at Goree. This transaction was in part an extension of his trade with the Canaries, source of both wine and coin for his African contracts.

His experiences in wartime contracting revealed new possibilities to Bacon. Although he continued to be active in North Carolina, he withdrew from the tobacco trade in 1764. Instead he sought to develop a strong presence—both trading and contracting—in Britain's new acquisitions in Africa (Senegambia) and the West Indies (the ceded islands—St Vincent, Tobago, Dominica, and Grenada). His agents and vessels in each area could handle both contracts and trade. His contracting business included providing pay and provisions to the army and navy and leasing slave labourers to the army in the ceded islands for fortification construction. In his own business he gave particular attention to obtaining slaves for sale in America and gum seneca, much in demand in England for use in dyeing cloth. To help with these complex schemes, he acquired new partners: in 1756, Gilbert Francklyn, a young gentleman from Maidstone; and in 1761 his own cousin and ward, Anthony Richardson, whom he had brought from Maryland in 1742.

This complex network of contracts required substantial advances from the crown. To attract the necessary ministerial understanding, Bacon obtained election to the House of Commons from 1764 to 1784 from the venal and costly borough of Aylesbury, previously represented by John Wilkes. In the house he played an important part in the passage of the Colonial Currency Act of 1764, a measure restricting the ability of colonial legislatures to issue paper money. Though the Board of Trade had originally favoured such a bill, the ministry hung back; but Bacon introduced the bill on his own, and, after mollifying some of the opponents by agreeing to restrict its scope, procured its passage with the support of the two members of the Board of Trade in the house. Bacon was personally interested in the bill inasmuch as he had substantial sums owing him in America, particularly in North Carolina. In parliament he consistently supported both the government of the day and parliament's full authority *vis-à-vis* the colonies. At the same time he advised ministers that it was inexpedient to tax the colonies, even though parliament had an undeniable right to do so.

As the American crisis developed, Bacon publicized his expediency argument in three pamphlets: *The true interest of Great Britain, with respect to her American colonies … by a merchant of London* (1766), *Considerations on the Present State of the North American Colonies* (1769), and *A short address to the government, the merchants, manufacturers and the colonists in America, and the sugar islands, on the present state of affairs, by a member of parliament* (1775), though the authorship of the first is not definite. Only twenty copies of the second were printed, as Bacon intended to restrict distribution to members of the government.

By the 1770s Bacon found his numerous contracts more trouble than they were worth, and gradually gave up those for Africa and the Antilles. At the outbreak of the American War of Independence, however, he returned to victual contracting, primarily in the British Isles, and also became heavily involved in the manufacture of cannon. He owned a coal mine in Workington, near Whitehaven, and was connected to families interested in iron furnaces and foundries thereabouts. Such links led to his acquaintance with the Cumberland ironmasters Isaac Wilkinson and his son John. It was probably through Isaac Wilkinson, then residing in Bristol, that Bacon was introduced to the iron-making potential of south Wales. In 1765 he leased lands and mining rights at Cyfarthfa, Glamorgan, where he and a cousin by marriage, Dr John Brownrigg, built a coke-using ironworks. The next year Bacon purchased a share in the nearby Plymouth works from Isaac Wilkinson and John Guest, its founders, and in 1780 he purchased the balance of Plymouth plus the nearby Hirwaun works. At that point Bacon owned three of the four significant coke iron furnaces in the Merthyr Tudful area. His interest in these works was heightened by the American war and by his association with John Wilkinson, who in 1773 had developed a new technique for manufacturing cannon by boring. Bacon, now John Wilkinson's partner, persuaded the Board of Ordnance of the superiority of the new method and obtained large orders for such cannon. These were at first manufactured by Wilkinson at Brosely, Shropshire, but, after Wilkinson's patent was declared void by the attorney-general, Bacon abandoned the partnership and started to make the cannon on his own in Wales. He moved his principal residence from London to Cyfarthfa to supervise his nearby furnaces and cannon foundry. The shifting of his interests from African and West Indian commerce to south Wales iron making is an extremely clear (if not necessarily common) example of the migration of capital from slave-based commerce to domestic industry.

Neither the date of marriage nor the precise identity of Bacon's wife, Elizabeth (*d.* 1799), is known. Their only child, Anthony Richardson Bacon, was born in 1757 but died in 1770. While his wife remained at the Cyfarthfa residence, Bacon, as a member of parliament, spent much time in the capital, where he kept a mistress, Mary Bushby, during the years *c.*1770 to 1786. At his death, in Cyfarthfa on 21 January 1786, Mary was left with their daughter, Elizabeth, and four sons, Anthony, Thomas, Robert, and William, of whom only the first two reached adulthood. Bacon was buried in London, at St Bartholomew by the Exchange. He made generous provision in his will for Mary Bushby and for the education of her children. He left his ironworks to his sons, but the two survivors, Anthony and Thomas, when they came of age, first leased and then sold their inherited undertakings and lived as rentiers. The Cyfarthfa works, which about 1807 were the largest ironworks in the world, were operated for over a century by the Crawshay family until absorbed into Guest, Keen, and Nettlefold in 1902. The Plymouth works were acquired by Richard Hill, an employee of Bacon who had married Mary Bushby's sister. His family controlled and managed the Plymouth Iron Company until the original works were closed about 1860.

JACOB M. PRICE

Sources L. B. Namier, 'Bacon, Anthony', HoP, *Commons* • L. B. Namier, 'Anthony Bacon, M.P.: an eighteenth century merchant', *Journal of Economic and Business History*, 2 (1929), 20–70 • W. Hutchinson, *The history of the county of Cumberland*, 2 vols. (1794) • *The registers of St Bees, Cumberland*, ed. H. B. Stout (1968), vol. 41 of Cumberland and Westmorland Antiquarian Society: parish register section [marriages] • J. W. Tyler, 'Foster Cunliffe and Sons', *Maryland Magazine of History*, 73 (1978), 251–2 • *The papers of George Washington*, ed. W. W. Abbot and others, [10 vols.] (1983–), vols. 1–2, 4 • R. C. Simmons and P. D. G. Thomas, eds., *Proceedings and debates of the British parliaments respecting North America, 1754–1783*, 6 vols. (1982–7) • A. Bacon, *The true interest of Great Britain… impartially considered* (1766) • A. Bacon, *Considerations on the present state of the North American colonies* (1769) • A. Bacon, *A short address to the government* (1775) • Buchanan and Simson letterbooks, NA Scot., C.S. 96/507 • will, PRO, PROB 11/1138, sig. 70 • will, PRO, PROB 11/1326, sig. 48 • parish register (burial), London, St Bartholomew by the Exchange, 1786

Archives Cumbria AS, Thomas Harrison MSS

Bacon, Sir Edmund Castell, thirteenth baronet and fourteenth baronet (1903–1982), landowner, was born on 18 March 1903 at 18 Cadogan Square, London, the only son and fifth of six children of Sir Nicholas Henry Bacon, twelfth and thirteenth baronet (1857–1947), of Raveningham Hall, Norfolk, and his wife, Constance Alice (*d.* 1962), younger daughter of Alexander Samuel Leslie-Melville, of Branston Hall, Lincolnshire. He was descended from Sir Nicholas Bacon, lord keeper to Queen Elizabeth I. Educated at Eton College and at Trinity College, Cambridge, he subsequently studied farming and estate management. In 1936 he married Priscilla Dora, daughter of Colonel Charles Edward Ponsonby, later baronet and MP for Sevenoaks. They had one son and four daughters.

During the Second World War, Bacon commanded the 55th (Suffolk yeomanry) anti-tank regiment of the Royal Artillery in Normandy and Belgium. He was mentioned in dispatches and appointed OBE in 1945. In 1947 his father died leaving him 4000 acres in Norfolk and 10,000 acres in Lincolnshire, a unique collection of English watercolours, and the collection of John Staniforth Beckett with its Dutch landscapes. Bacon also succeeded to his father's titles, becoming thirteenth baronet, of Redgrave (created in 1611), and fourteenth baronet, of Mildenhall (created in 1627). The family had a long tradition of public service, and in 1949 Bacon was appointed lord lieutenant of Norfolk, a post he held until 1978. His period of office ended with the successful silver jubilee appeal in 1977. Norfolk was one of the few counties which exceeded its target.

In 1953 the eastern counties of Britain suffered from the severest of weather and tidal surges, and Norfolk took the fullest brunt of them. Bacon energetically organized relief forces and headed a county relief appeal fund. No other county raised such a large sum in proportion to its population, and nowhere else were the funds so promptly distributed to the sufferers. It was this practical administrative ability which later enabled Bacon to spearhead the campaign for the crucial refurbishment of Norwich Cathedral after 1956; he was high steward at the cathedral from 1956 until 1979. His religious beliefs were deeply held but they were more a positive moral conviction than an exact allegiance to one particular doctrine of Christianity. When he was made an honorary freeman of Norwich, he said that nothing had given him so much satisfaction as the part he played safeguarding the structure of the cathedral for the next generation.

Bacon's interests in agricultural concerns were put to the test in the management of his own substantial estates. These enterprises and a family property company in London allowed him to develop a shrewd business sense, and led to appointments at both local and national level. He was president of Eastern Counties Farmers, the country's second largest agricultural co-operative, until 1973. As chairman of the British Sugar Corporation during an eleven-year period of rationalization (1957–68), he was able to introduce new company policy without causing the kind of conflicts within the labour force which became so prevalent in the next decade. His most demanding job was as chairman in 1966–71 of the agricultural National Economic Development Committee (Neddy), whose purpose was to stabilize agricultural markets. Towards the end of his life he was awarded the Royal Agricultural Society's gold medal for distinguished services to agriculture.

A director of Lloyds Bank, and president of the Norfolk branch of the Magistrates' Association for twenty-nine years, Bacon also played an active part in the founding of the University of East Anglia, where he was pro-chancellor from 1964 to 1973. He was awarded an honorary DCL there in 1969. Bacon proved to be a skilful chairman during the period of student unrest and demonstrations in the late 1960s, when he presided over critical meetings calmly and steadfastly. In 1969, following the unilateral declaration of independence in Rhodesia, Bacon provided much behind-the-scenes support for his friend, Sir Humphrey Gibbs, the governor.

Although Bacon lived and looked like a country squire (he was happiest dressed in baggy, very old cavalry-twill trousers), he was a versatile man with wide interests. Hugely built, with hunched shoulders and sharp blue eyes, he endeared himself to people by his simple charm. In 1965 he was appointed KBE and in 1970 he was among four new knights of the Garter, the first baronet ever to be so honoured by the queen. He died on 30 September 1982 at the County Hospital, Lincoln. He left estate valued at £855,542, and was succeeded in the baronetcies by his son, Nicholas Hickman Ponsonby Bacon (*b.* 1953).

NICHOLAS BACON, *rev.* ROBERT BROWN

Sources *The Times* (2 Oct 1982) · *Eastern Daily Press* (2 Oct 1982) · personal knowledge (1990) · private information (1990) · *WWW, 1981–90* · d. cert.
Archives CAC Cam., corresp. with Francis Bacon
Wealth at death £855,542: probate, 8 June 1983, *CGPLA Eng. & Wales*

Bacon, Edward (1548/9–1618). *See under* Bacon, Sir Nathaniel (1546?–1622).

Bacon, Francis, Viscount St Alban (1561–1626), lord chancellor, politician, and philosopher, was born on 22 January 1561 at York House in the Strand, London, the second of the two sons of Sir Nicholas *Bacon (1510–1579), lord keeper, and his second wife, Anne (*c.*1528–1610) [*see* Bacon, Anne], daughter of Sir Anthony *Cooke, tutor to Edward VI, and his wife, Anne, *née* Fitzwilliam. He was baptized in the local church of St Martin-in-the-Fields, but spent most of his childhood, together with his elder brother, Anthony *Bacon (1558–1601), at Gorhambury, near St Albans, Hertfordshire, which their father had purchased in 1557. In the 1560s Nicholas Bacon built a new house there, and this house (together with Verulam House, which Francis Bacon built nearby later in his life) became one of his three central emotional places (the other two being York House where he again lived, as lord keeper and lord chancellor later in his life, and Gray's Inn, where he lived for most of his life). The well-known story that Elizabeth I often referred to Francis as 'the young Lord-Keeper' is presumably no more than a legend.

Early years and education Bacon received his early education at home. Judging by their own experiences his parents must have set great store by education. In Nicholas Bacon's career from a sheep-reeve's son to lord keeper schooling had been crucial. His second wife's learning matched his own: her father, Sir Anthony Cooke, had inculcated classical erudition and protestant piety in his five daughters, and Anne Bacon was fluent in Greek and Latin as well as in Italian and French. Her erudition and piety were put to good use when, during Francis's infancy,

Francis Bacon, Viscount St Alban (1561–1626), attrib. Abraham van Blyenberch, *c.*1618

she translated John Jewel's *Apologia ecclesiae Anglicanae* into English.

The chaplains who served the Bacon household had strong leanings towards puritanism. One, John Walsall, a graduate of Christ Church, Oxford, acted as the sons' tutor from 1566 to at least 1569. By this time the Bacon brothers were joined in the schoolroom at Gorhambury by Sir Thomas Gresham's illegitimate daughter, who had just married their half-brother, Nathaniel *Bacon. When she returned home she wrote a letter of thanks to Anne, Lady Bacon, including regards for 'my brother Anthony and my good brother Frank' (R. Tittler, *Nicholas Bacon*, 1976, 156). Although there is no direct evidence there is little doubt that Bacon went through the whole of the normal primary and grammar school curriculum at home. His schooling not only included Christian teaching but also thorough training in the classics.

Having provided seven or eight years' education for his youngest sons at home Sir Nicholas Bacon sent them to university. All his sons went to Trinity College, Cambridge. Anthony and Francis (who had just turned twelve) went up to Cambridge on 5 April 1573 and matriculated on 10 June. They stayed there until December 1575, although their period of residence was twice interrupted when plague broke out in the Cambridge area. At Trinity the brothers, with their companion Edward Tyrell, one of Sir Nicholas's wards, were put under the personal tutelage of the master, Dr John Whitgift, the future archbishop of Canterbury. From these years at Cambridge dates Bacon's earliest extant letter. It is a request addressed on 3 July 1574 to his half-brother Nicholas Bacon, who had promised to send a deer for the graduation of Nicholas Sharpe, a fellow Trinity member.

According to the accounts kept by Whitgift he bought for the Bacon brothers' use the major classical texts and commentaries. These included the *Iliad*, Plato and Aristotle, 'tullies workes' (perhaps Cicero's philosophical works and letters), Cicero's rhetorical works, Demosthenes' *Orations*, Hermogenes' *Ars rhetorica* in a facing-page Greek and Latin edition, as well as the histories of Livy, Sallust, and Xenophon (P. Gaskell, 'Books bought by Whitgift's pupils in the 1570s', *Transactions of the Cambridge Bibliographical Society*, 7, 1979, 284–93).

Bacon's education was conducted largely in Latin and followed the medieval curriculum. But the impact of humanism had drastically changed the way in which this curriculum was taught. A particular emphasis was placed on practical problems at the expense of logical subtlety. As is evident from the books Bacon purchased in Cambridge there was a strong emphasis on philosophy, rhetoric, and history in his studies. This was a particularly typical feature of Renaissance humanism, whose main aim was to train youth for public life.

The next step for a gentleman intending a public career was entrance to the inns of court. Francis Bacon was entered at Gray's Inn on 27 June 1576 and was admitted in November. Meanwhile, however, he was sent to France to accompany Sir Amias Paulet, English ambassador to France. Originally both Francis and his half-brother Edward were to go, but in the end only Francis followed Paulet late in September 1576, whereas Edward travelled on his own, heading not only to protestant centres like Geneva and Strasbourg but also to Vienna, Venice, and Padua.

Travelling abroad was considered highly useful to a young gentleman's education—an opportunity for learning foreign languages and finding out about customs, politics, and institutions. But Bacon's stay in France (mostly in Paris, Poitiers, and Blois), which lasted almost exactly two and a half years, was not so much an educative grand tour. While he studied language, statecraft, and the civil law most of his time was presumably spent in performing routine diplomatic tasks.

When Bacon went to France he was only fifteen, and shared with Paulet's sons a tutor named Mr Duncumbe. When Duncumbe returned to England in October 1577 he was replaced by Jean Hotman, the son of the well-known Huguenot, François Hotman. In 1578 Bacon was placed in the household of a civil lawyer to acquire a deeper acquaintance with civil law, then very important in diplomacy. This early exposure to Roman law had presumably a profound influence on his legal thinking, and when later in life Bacon developed his ideas of legal reform the impact of the Roman civil law was especially marked.

During his stay in France, perhaps in autumn 1577, Bacon once visited England as the bearer of the diplomatic post, delivering letters to Walsingham, Burghley, and Leicester and to the queen herself. Fairly soon after his return to France he planned a trip to Italy but Paulet did not grant him permission, mainly on religious grounds (Jardine and Stewart, 61–3).

Bacon's stay in France came to an abrupt end a few months before it was scheduled when the news of his father's death in February 1579 reached him. The youngest son made haste and arrived in London within a month of this event. He also brought the diplomatic post from Paulet, which included a recommendation from Sir Amias to the queen: 'Mr. Francis Bacon, is of great hope, endowed with many good and singular parts; and if God give him life will prove a very able and sufficient subject to do your Highness good and acceptable service' (Jardine and Stewart, 66).

His father's sudden death was a serious setback for Francis Bacon. Sir Nicholas had settled estates for all of his other sons and was in the course of doing so for the youngest one when he died. Moreover, Sir Nicholas's two families contested his will, and although an agreement was eventually reached with the help of Lord Burghley the half-brothers were never again close. The situation was worst for the youngest son, who had neither land nor income nor even a position.

Aged eighteen Bacon resumed his studies in Gray's Inn. Sir Nicholas had been a central figure in Gray's Inn and all his sons had been admitted there, but Francis was the only one who took up law as a profession. As a law student he was expected to attend readings or series of formal lectures on a specific English statute, to participate in hypothetical legal situations and thereby to learn cases, and to argue in moot courts (to argue on both sides of a case). Whether it was due to his natural talents or the seriousness with which he pursued his studies Bacon made rapid progress. He was admitted to the bar as an utter barrister of Gray's Inn (the equivalent of graduation) in June 1582, became bencher in 1586 and in November 1587 was elected as a reader, delivering his first set of lectures on church advowsons in Lent 1588.

Early career While still pursuing his legal studies Bacon embarked on a public career. He sought the help of his uncle, William *Cecil, Lord Burghley, and his aunt, Lady Burghley [*see* Cecil, Mildred], in September 1580, commending his earlier suit, which Burghley had promised to forward to the queen, and calling Burghley 'my patron'. By October Burghley informed him of 'her Majesty's gracious opinion and meaning towards' him (*Works*, 8.13–14). When the duke of Alençon visited England in December 1580 Bacon was employed as a translator.

By the time the third and last session of the parliament, originally elected in 1572, met in January 1581 many by-elections had taken place. Among the new members was Francis Bacon, who had his twentieth birthday during the session. He sat for Bossiney, Cornwall, which was controlled by his godfather, the earl of Bedford. There is no evidence of Bacon's activities in this session. In the parliament of 1584 Lord Burghley won him a seat (Gatton, Surrey), but Bacon preferred the earl of Bedford's patronage, sitting for Weymouth and Melcombe Regis, Dorset. He was named to one committee and made his maiden speech on a bill concerning wards.

Bacon showed signs of sympathy to puritanism, not only attending the sermons of the puritan chaplain of Gray's Inn, but also accompanying his mother to the Temple chapel to hear the even more staunchly puritan sermons of Walter Travers. By 1584 Bacon, together with many key figures in the political nation, had become alarmed by both the perceived growing Catholic threat and the English church's suppression of the puritan clergy. He joined many others in critically reviewing in a tract this anti-puritan campaign led by his former tutor, recently appointed archbishop of Canterbury, John Whitgift, who demanded absolute submission to the church's discipline from the entire clergy.

Bacon's tract is his earliest extant longer writing and was obviously widely circulated. He strongly criticized the Catholics both within and without England and gave support for the puritan cause. But his argument was couched in strongly political terms. He appealed to 'all reason of state' and to the example 'of the most wise, most politic, and best governed estates'. For the danger within the queen should do everything possible to strengthen protestantism, mainly through promoting preaching and schooling, because all her 'force and strength and power' consisted in her protestant subjects. As for the problems without, the best remedy was a political alliance with the enemies of Spain, above all with Venice and the Netherlands (*Works*, 8.47–56).

In 1585 Bacon felt that his age (twenty-four) blocked the advancement of his career. He requested Burghley's help with his career at Gray's Inn, and asked Sir Christopher Hatton and Sir Francis Walsingham to advance his suit for a political office. Although no office was forthcoming various other employments kept him busy. Through Walsingham's patronage Bacon was soon employed to investigate English Catholics. In the parliament which met in winter 1586–7 Bacon (sitting for Taunton, Somerset) was more visible than before. He argued for the execution of Mary, queen of Scots, and was named to the committee appointed to draw up a petition for her execution. He also spoke in favour of the proposed subsidy and sat on three other committees. In September 1587 the privy council consulted the attorney-general, the solicitor-general, and Bacon on legal matters concerning examination reports of two Catholic prisoners. Bacon's first surviving legal works—'A brief discourse upon the commission of Bridewell' and another discourse in law French on crown prerogatives and ownership—were also written in this period. (There is however a near contemporary attribution of the former to William Fleetwood, recorder of London, GL, MS 9384.) In August 1588 Bacon was appointed to a government committee examining recusants in prison and a few months later, in December 1588, he was appointed to a committee of lawyers which was to review existing statutes. When a new parliament met in February 1589 he was busy throughout the session with committee work. In November 1589 he was granted a reversion of the clerkship of star chamber. Although he did not succeed to the post until 1608 the reversion demonstrated Bacon's growing importance and, since the post was worth £1600 per annum, it gave him a promise of economic security.

This steady advancement of Bacon's political and legal career is aptly reflected by the importance attached to a position paper he wrote on ecclesiastical politics. 'An advertisement touching the controversies of the Church of England' (written some time between 1589 and 1591) was Bacon's response to the conflict between the Church of England and the nonconformists, sparked off by the publication of the pamphlets said to be written by one Martin Marprelate. These tracts used scathing satire in heavily censuring the Church of England. Richard Bancroft, chaplain to Sir Christopher Hatton and a future bishop of London, hired such writers as John Lyly and Thomas Nashe to answer in a similar irreverent style.

Avoiding the mutual muckraking of both sides in the controversy Bacon emphasized his impartiality and called for a cessation to hostilities. According to him the puritans too easily imitated the government of foreign presbyterian churches. 'It may be', Bacon wrote in a remarkable passage, that 'in civil states, a republic is a better policy than a kingdom'. Yet, in church government hierarchy rather than 'the parity and equality of ministers' was to be sought (*Bacon*, ed. Vickers, 10). Nevertheless Bacon placed the main blame for the controversy at the bishops' door. 'The imperfections … of those which have chief place in the church have ever been principal causes and motives of schisms and divisions' (ibid., 6). Although his name was not mentioned in the tract Bancroft received Bacon's bitterest censure.

'An advertisement' was never printed in Bacon's lifetime, but several extant manuscript copies attest to its wide circulation. Both sides of the controversy—a presbyterian tract in 1591 and a treatise by Bancroft in 1593—invoked 'An advertisement' in their own defence (*Bacon*, ed. Vickers, 498). Bacon's famous comment on another occasion that 'her Majesty, not liking to make windows into men's hearts and secret thoughts', also indicates his middle path (*Works*, 8.98).

In 1592 Bacon was commissioned to write a response to the Jesuit Robert Parsons's anti-government tract *Responsio ad edictum reginae Angliae*, entitled 'Certain observations made upon a libel'. Just like Thomas Wilson and Thomas Norton in 1570, so Bacon in 1592 emphasized 'the resemblance between the two Philips, of Macedon and Spain', and thus identified England with republican Athens. English statesmen and counsellors were just like 'the Orators' in Athens, being 'sharpest sighted' and looking 'deepest into the projects and spreading' of the two Philips (*Works*, 8.182–3).

Bacon and Essex Bacon's life and career during the 1590s was dominated by his close friendship with Robert Devereux, the second earl of Essex. It is not clear when this relationship began and when it developed into an intimate friendship, but as early as summer 1588 there was at least a patronage relationship. In June 1588 Bacon wrote to the earl of Leicester asking his support for a suit which Essex was advancing on Bacon's behalf.

Quite suddenly in the early 1590s Bacon broached the entirely novel theme of natural philosophy that occupied him for the rest of his life. Early in 1592 he wrote to Lord Burghley. In one of his most famous letters, assuring his 'devotion' both as 'a good patriot' and 'an unworthy kinsman', Bacon expressed anxiety about his age: 'I wax now somewhat ancient; one and thirty years is a great deal of sand in the hour-glass'. But instead of merely putting forward a suit for office, he was, Bacon told his uncle, pursuing a place for a higher purpose. He wrote:

> I confess that I have as vast contemplative ends, as I have moderate civil ends; for I have taken all knowledge to be my province; and if I could purge it of two sorts of rovers, whereof the one with frivolous disputations, confutations, and verbosities, the other with blind experiments and auricular traditions and impostures, hath committed so many spoils, I hope I should bring in industrious observations, grounded conclusions, and profitable inventions and discoveries; the best state of that province. This, whether it be curiosity, or vain glory, or nature, or (if one take it favourably) *philanthropia*, is so fixed in my mind as it cannot be removed. And I do easily see, that place of any reasonable countenance doth bring commandment of more wits than of a man's own; which is the thing I greatly affect. (*Works*, 8.109)

In 1592 Bacon also produced a device entitled 'Of tribute, or, Giving that which is due'. There is no evidence that it was ever performed. The device consists of four speeches—the first arguing for 'the worthiest virtue' (fortitude), the second for 'the worthiest affection' (love), the third for 'the worthiest power' (knowledge), and the fourth for 'the worthiest person' (Queen Elizabeth). The one on knowledge enlarged on the plans and ambitions which Bacon outlined in his letter to Burghley. He excoriated extant natural philosophy both for its barren products and its futile methods, the main culprits being 'the Grecians' (scholasticism) and 'the alchemists' (Paracelsians). Bacon thus argued against the barrenness of scholastic natural philosophy and against the preposterous claims of alchemy. He hinted that he would form a new method which would replace both exploded schools, and produce not just words but works.

'Is truth ever barren?', Bacon asked and immediately provided the answer in another rhetorical question: 'Shall he not be able thereby to produce worthy effects, and to endow the life of man with infinite new commodities?' Moreover, he pointed to the mechanical artificers who had created printing, artillery, and the compass, as his forerunners. It is extremely significant that Bacon called knowledge 'the worthiest power', thus making as early as 1592 his novel link between natural philosophy and power (*Bacon*, ed. Vickers, 34–6).

When a new parliament met on 19 February 1593 Bacon sat as knight of the shire for Middlesex. This mirrored his enhanced importance. Nevertheless it was a catastrophic session for him. The queen had had two reasons to summon parliament: religious conformity and money. When the appeal for funds was made Bacon was among the first to speak, but curiously pleaded ignorance of war and did not speak about money but about the urgent need of a law reform. The appointed committee suggested the repetition of the exceptional grant of two subsidies made in the previous parliament. But in a conference of both houses Lord Burghley announced that the Lords would not assent to anything less than three subsidies, paid in three years (twice as quickly as usually), and that the assessments must be improved.

Burghley's son, Sir Robert Cecil, reported this message to the House of Commons. With Cecil seated Bacon, who had been a member of the committee of both houses, rose and, while assenting to three subsidies, opposed joining with the Lords in granting it. The Commons, Bacon insisted, should stand upon its privilege of first offering a subsidy. If his earlier speech had been rather irrelevant this one must have been a worse irritant for his uncle. But more was to come. After several days of work the Commons referred the matter to yet another committee. The councillors wanted three subsidies paid in three or four years. When the committee met again, on the morning of 8 March, Bacon rose and announced that he would assent to three subsidies 'but not to the payment under six years'. 'The gentlemen', he said, 'must sell their plate and the farmers their brass pots ere this will be paid. And as for us, we are here to search the wounds of the realm and not to skin them over'. He was convinced that a quick payment of three subsidies in three years would 'breed discontentment in the people' and make 'an ill precedent'. Moreover, history amply demonstrated that 'of all nations the English care not to be subject, base, taxable' (*Works*, 8.223). Bacon's heroic eloquence seems to have won no support. Walter Ralegh argued against him, as did Cecil, who refuted each of his cousin's arguments. The committee agreed to three subsidies payable in four years.

Many of those who had opposed the unprecedented demand for three subsidies in three years incurred the ire of the queen. Bacon's speeches, while ostensibly high principled, were scarcely prudent for a gentleman looking for a career in the service of the queen. He may have been reprimanded during the session, and certainly felt the queen's anger afterwards. The queen thought that Bacon was 'in more fault than any of the rest in Parliament' (*Works*, 8.254). As soon as Burghley had informed him of the queen's anger Bacon tried to excuse his speech. 'The manner of my speech', he told his uncle, 'did most evidently show that I spake simply and only to satisfy my conscience, and not with any advantage or policy to sway the cause'. In expressing his sincere opinions Bacon had simply endeavoured to signify his 'duty and zeal towards her Majesty and her service' (ibid., 8.234). 'There is', he later added, 'variety allowed in counsel, as a discord in music, to make it more perfect' (ibid., 8.362).

Such justifications failed to make amends. The disaster of Bacon's speeches was made much worse by the fact that immediately afterwards Essex launched a campaign on Bacon's behalf for the office of attorney-general. During the campaign Bacon gained some legal experience. In January and February 1594 he argued his first two cases in king's bench and one in the court of exchequer, which won him general applause. He was also involved in the treason trial of Roderigo Lopez, and prepared its official account. Yet by spring 1594 it was clear that Edward Coke was to become the next attorney-general. Bacon told Essex that he would 'retire myself with a couple of men to Cambridge, and there spend my life in my studies and contemplations, without looking back' (*Works*, 8.291).

No such retirement took place. In July 1594 the queen made Bacon one of her learned counsel and he was employed in several legal cases. One of them—obviously an investigation of the aftermath of Dr Lopez's conspiracy—required him to travel north. Due to an illness Bacon got no further than Huntingdon. He took this opportunity to visit Cambridge and take his MA degree.

Bacon wrote parts of the *Gesta Grayorum*, the Christmas festivities of 1594–5 at Gray's Inn. It was presented on 3 January 1595 in front of a formidable audience. Similar to the earlier device ('Of tribute'), it had six speakers arguing their choice of life. The first defended 'the Exercise of war', the second advised 'the Study of Philosophy', the third 'Eternizement and Fame by Buildings and Foundations', the fourth defended 'Absoluteness of State and Treasure', the fifth 'Virtue and a gracious Government', and the sixth 'Pastimes and Sports'. The second speech, pleading the cause of philosophy, urged 'the conquest of the works of nature', commending the erection of 'a most perfect and general library', 'a spacious, wonderful garden', 'a goodly huge cabinet', as well as 'a still-house [laboratory], so furnished with mills, instruments, furnaces, and vessels, as may be a palace fit for a philosopher's stone' (*Bacon*, ed. Vickers, 54–5). But the device was part of Christmas festivities, and the day was carried by the last counsellor who declared 'let other men's lives be as pilgrimages … but princes' lives are as progresses, dedicated only to variety and solace' (ibid., 60).

When Edward Coke was appointed attorney-general the solicitor-generalship became vacant. Essex pressed hard to secure it for Bacon, and if anything the suit became even more prolonged and exhaustive than the earlier one. Bacon even asked for a licence to travel abroad but the queen refused him. Venting his frustration to his brother Anthony, Bacon said that the queen had sworn that 'she will seek all England for a Solicitor rather than take me' (*Works*, 8.348). By July 1595 he could no longer contain himself but wrote to Lord Keeper Puckering: 'There hath nothing happened to me in the course of my business more contrary to my expectation, than your Lordship's failing me and crossing me now in the conclusion, when friends are best tried' (ibid., 8.364–5). Trying to atone Essex referred to Bacon's burst of anger as 'a natural freedom and plainness', which Bacon had also used with Essex as well as with other friends (ibid., 8.366).

Whatever Bacon's hopes, they were dashed early in November 1595 when the queen appointed Sir Thomas Fleming as solicitor-general. Most scholars agree that Bacon's opposition to the subsidy bill in 1593, which had offended the queen, and Essex's perseverance in pursuing the suit, which had annoyed her, account for Bacon's failure to obtain the post. Essex consoled Bacon by offering him a gift of land. Bacon responded that while he was 'more beholding to you than to any man', yet Essex could not purchase his loyalty, and that his first obligation was always to the queen and the public service (*Works*, 8.373). Afterwards, Bacon sold the land for £1800.

The painful experience of these suits led Bacon temporarily to entertain the idea of a purely scholarly career and 'not to follow the practice of the law … because it drinketh too much time, which I have dedicated to better purposes' (*Works*, 8.372). But when, in spring 1596, the office of master of the rolls fell vacant it gave him new hope that a place would also be vacated to which he could succeed, receiving strong support from Essex.

Intellectual and literary pursuits, most of them closely related to Essex and his circle, took up much of Bacon's time in the late 1590s. Essex had commissioned him to write a device for the Accession day celebration, presented at Essex House on 17 November 1595. Again Bacon's contribution consisted of three men defending their respective forms of life: a hermit defending contemplation, a soldier defending fame, and a statesman arguing for experience. These arguments were refuted by a squire who concluded by confirming his master's (representing Essex) dedication to the queen. In this, as in the earlier dramatic entertainments, Bacon could be seen as dramatizing his own choices between the active and contemplative modes of life.

In addition to literary devices Bacon used letters of advice to display his learning and intellectual abilities, and to put his ideas across. The first of these was a series of three letters addressed to the earl of Rutland (who travelled in Europe during 1595–7) perhaps late in 1595 or early in 1596, which Bacon wrote on Essex's behalf. Bacon strongly argued for the *vita activa*, which needed above all 'liberality or magnificence, and fortitude or magnanimity'. Underlying these virtues, however, was 'knowledge, which is not only the excellentest thing in man, but the very excellency of man'. Restricting his account to 'civil knowledge', Bacon emphasized that such a knowledge consisted of doing 'good unto others' and it therefore contrasted sharply with 'the study of *artes luxuriae*' (*Works*, 8.9–12).

Bacon wrote a somewhat different letter of advice to Essex himself in October 1596, after the latter's Cadiz expedition had weakened his position at court. Calling Essex 'a nature not to be ruled', Bacon advised him studiously to avoid giving such an impression. But he also counselled him to shun the impressions of 'a military dependance' and 'a popular reputation'. In both these, however, the earl should avoid the appearance but not the characteristic itself. He must abolish a military dependence 'in shows to the Queen' but retain it in practice. Similarly, in the queen's presence he must 'speak against popularity and popular courses vehemently; and tax it in all others: but nevertheless to go on in your honourable commonwealth courses as you do' (*Works*, 9.41–4).

Yet another intellectual pursuit to which Bacon devoted time in the 1590s was his idea of reforming the English law. In 1593 he had mentioned in parliament how in ancient Rome 'ten men' had been appointed 'to correct and recall all former laws' (*Works*, 8.214). In the Christmas festivities at Gray's Inn in 1594–5 he had the counsellor advising the prince in 'Virtue and a gracious Government' to advocate a similar project (*Bacon*, ed. Vickers, 59). In new year 1597 Bacon presented the queen with a work, 'Maxims of the law', which was meant as an example of how the English law should be restructured. It consists of twenty-five maxims in Latin each of which is followed by a fuller treatment.

Early in 1597 Bacon appeared in print for the first time. Some of his essays had already been circulated in manuscript (in 1597 he noted that 'they passed long agoe from my pen' (*Works*, 6.523)), and in 1596 one of them was plagiarized in Edward Monings's *The Langrave of Hessen his Princelie Receiving of her Majesties Embassador*, which borrowed a few passages from Bacon's essay 'Of studies'. On 24 January 1597 one Richard Serger entered in the Stationers' register 'a book entitled ESSAYES of M.F.B. *with prayers of his Sovereigne*' (*Bacon*, ed. Vickers, 546). In order to forestall this publication Bacon immediately assigned the rights to Humfrey Hooper. On 7 February 1597 the first edition of Bacon's *Essayes*, together with *Religious Meditations* and *Places of Perswasion and Disswasion*, was published. The ten essays treated personal and courtly issues and belong, too, to the literature of advice. They were written in a terse, aphoristic style (individual sentences were marked with a paragraph sign), which Bacon conceived as a genre setting down discrete observations on life, and aspiring to some kind of objective validity. The slim volume had considerable success and was reprinted in 1597, 1598, 1606, and 1612.

In 1597 Bacon tried his fortune with Lady Hatton, a young, rich widow (and the daughter of Burghley's eldest son)—but without success. To make matters worse she married Bacon's old rival Edward Coke in November 1598. One of the chief reasons for Bacon's suit was economic. His estate was 'weak and indebted', both because of the lack of inheritance and because he in his 'own industry' had 'rather referred and aspired to virtue than to gain' (*Works*, 9.61). When the marriage suit failed Bacon endeavoured to use his reversion of the star chamber clerkship to relieve his necessities. He would give it to the lord keeper Thomas Egerton's son if Egerton would give him the mastership of the rolls. Again the plan fell through, and in September 1598 Bacon was arrested for debt. Although his income increased considerably over time his economic situation was never secure, and he often had difficulties in settling his debts.

In the parliament which sat from October 1597 to February 1598 Bacon was an active member for Ipswich, serving in numerous committees. He delivered his speech in favour of three subsidies, payable in three years. He initiated the important social and economic legislative work of the session with a motion against enclosures and the depopulation of towns and houses of husbandry, and for the maintenance of tillage, which he had not written, he said, 'with polished pen but with a polished heart, free from affection and affectation'. He defended his initiative with a Machiavellian argument: 'in matters of policy ill is not to be thought ill which bringeth forth good' (*Works*, 9.82).

In September 1598 Bacon examined one John Stanley for being involved in Edward Squire's conspiracy to assassinate the queen. In 1599 he published a quasi-official account of the conspiracy entitled *Letter Written out of England to an English Gentleman in Padua*. From 1599 also comes a letter of advice to Fulke Greville on his studies ascribed to Bacon. The letter addressed the topic of employing research assistants, but it also criticized university learning and attacked the use of epitomes. Again, Bacon singled out Demosthenes and found 'his eloquence … more proper to a statesman than Cicero's'. While Livy and Thucydides were good historians Tacitus was 'simply the best' (*Bacon*, ed. Vickers, 105).

The situation in Ireland had been growing from bad to worse during the latter part of the 1590s. In 1598 Bacon had seen this as an exceptionally apposite opportunity for Essex 'to purchase honour' (*Works*, 9.95–6). After some deliberation Essex was appointed in March 1599 to suppress the Irish uprising. What did Bacon think about Essex continuing his military career? In 1604 Bacon wrote that he had been firmly against Essex 'going into Ireland'. 'I did not only dissuade', he wrote in 1604, 'but protest against his going', omitting 'no argument'. In particular, he said, he had cited the example of the ancient Romans, who, despite their overwhelming military strength, had had extreme difficulties against 'the ancient Gauls, or Britons, or Germans'. These people had 'placed their felicity only in liberty and the sharpness of their sword' and in 'the natural and elemental advantages of woods, and bogs, and hardness of bodies'. From such examples, Bacon claimed in 1604, he had 'concluded, that going over with such expectations as he did, and through the churlishness of the enterprise not like to answer it, would mightily diminish his reputation' (ibid., 10.146).

There is no contemporary evidence indicating that Bacon actually gave such advice. In a letter that appears to have been written by the time the earl had already decided to embark on this project, Bacon on the one hand pointed out the great merit and great peril of the enterprise which Essex was poised to undertake, and on the other found hopeful portents of its success. Moreover he cited exactly the same example of the ancient Romans as in 1604, but stressed the fact that triumphs against a 'barbarous' enemy did not 'extenuate the honour' (*Works*, 8.131), rather than the difficulty of the enterprise, as in 1604. It is impossible to say whether Bacon remembered in 1604 what he wanted, or whether he had first advised Essex against going to Ireland but, when the earl decided against such an advice, warned him about the great peril while trying to reassure him.

When Essex unexpectedly returned from Ireland in September 1599 Bacon worked hard to reconcile the earl to the queen, despite rumours to the contrary. When she came 'to dine at my lodge' he even presented her with 'a sonnet directly tending and alluding to draw on her Majesty's reconcilement to my Lord' (*Works*, 10.149). Although Bacon advised the queen to deal with Essex in private the case was heard in star chamber, where neither the earl nor Bacon was present. Finally, in June 1600 Essex was subjected to an informal trial at York House, where Bacon was involved as one of the queen's learned counsel. Essex was dismissed from all his offices of state and was to remain at Essex House.

In spring 1600 Bacon had been chosen double reader at Gray's Inn and gave his six-day series of lectures on the Statute of Uses. Double readers were senior barristers who had already given one reading. This statute was a common topic for readings and Bacon had appeared in an important case (*Dillon* v. *Freine* or *Chudleigh's case*) involving the statute in 1595. The Statute of Uses also offered means for discussing law reform.

As soon as Essex was fully freed in July 1600 Bacon wrote him a letter assuring him that he loved the earl more than anyone else. Yet he insisted even more strongly, just as in 1595, that he put 'the Queen's service' and 'the good of my country' before private friendship (*Works*, 9.191). Bacon still endeavoured to restore Essex to the queen's favour, composing letters on the earl's behalf. These did not have the desired effect, and in February 1601 Essex made his forlorn attempt at a rebellion.

At the trial that followed the queen made use of Bacon for the prosecution. When Essex accused Bacon of being an accomplice because he had written letters for Essex Bacon retorted: 'I have spent more time in vain in studying how to make the earl a good servant to the Queen, than I have done in anything else' (Jardine and Stewart, 244). Bacon was also commissioned to prosecute some of Essex's followers, and the queen called upon him to write the official account of the trial. Many of the accomplices paid large fines, most of which were given away as rewards. Bacon received £1200, although he had expected more.

The spring of 1601 was not a particularly happy period in Bacon's life. In addition to the Essex trial the antagonism between him and Edward Coke exploded in the exchequer in April. According to Bacon, Coke had told him: 'Mr. Bacon, if you have any tooth against me, pluck it out; for it will do you more hurt than all the teeth in your head will do you good'. To this Bacon had riposted: 'Mr. Attorney, I respect you: I fear you not: and the less you speak of your own greatness, the more I will think of it' (*Works*, 10.3). On top of all this his brother Anthony died in May.

In the last Elizabethan parliament, which met in October 1601, Bacon again sat for Ipswich. He was a particularly active member, speaking to most of the matters and sitting in most of the committees. He supported the subsidy bill of four subsidies and emphasized that the poor as well as the rich should contribute, a view which evoked a scathing comment from Walter Ralegh (Neale, 2.415). Bacon also insisted that parliament, as well as raising money, must enact laws. He brought in a bill 'against abuses in weights and measures' and spoke 'for repealing superfluous laws'. But he also noted that it was not enough to introduce bills; they should also be properly debated. It was 'unfitting', he said, 'to bandy bills like balls and to be silent, as if nobody were of counsel with the Commonwealth' (ibid., 2.417).

Bacon and Ralegh also argued against each other in a debate about the renewal of the Statute of Tillage. Bacon defended the bill, which enacted that land converted to pasture should be restored to tillage, noting that 'the husbandman', being 'a strong and hardy man', made the best soldier. Raleigh riposted that since 'all Nations abound with Corn' it was best 'to set it at Liberty, and leave every man Free, which is the Desire of a true Englishman'. Bacon's view, receiving support, for instance, from his cousin Robert Cecil, carried the day (H. Townshend, *Historical Collections*, 1680, 299–300). The most controversial issue of the session was the abuse of monopolies. Bacon's opinion was clear: 'For the prerogative royal of the Prince, for my own part I ever allowed of it: and it is such as I hope I shall never see discussed' (*Works*, 10.26).

In 1602 Bacon argued in *Slade's case*, although in the report of the case Coke completely ignored Bacon's argument. When the Irish problem became pressing in 1602 Bacon volunteered and offered his advice to Cecil. He strongly argued for a non-violent solution, emphasizing 'the recovery of the hearts of the people' (*Works*, 10.46). A letter of advice to Sir Henry Savile on the intellectual powers, which anticipated themes expounded in *The Advancement of Learning* and later editions of the *Essayes*, has also been dated to 1602.

Union of the kingdoms When James VI of Scotland succeeded Elizabeth I to the English throne Bacon, like so many others, made a serious effort to secure the new king's attention. Just before the death of Elizabeth I on 24 March 1603 Bacon began to recommend his services to those who were close to the new king. He also prepared a proclamation 'for cherising, entertaining, and preparing of men's affections' to the new king, but it was not used (*Works*, 10.67). Bacon's first impression of the new king was that he acted 'excellently well'; he was 'a prince the farthest from the appearance of vain-glory' (ibid., 10.73, 77). On 23 July 1603 James's bounty also reached Bacon. On that day he was knighted, though to his great disappointment so were 300 others, to mark the king's coronation. On 18 August 1604 Bacon was granted the office of learned counsel.

In 1603 Bacon also published a short treatise on the proposed union between England and Scotland entitled *A Brief Discourse Touching the Happy Union of the Kingdoms of England and Scotland*. It was clear to everybody that James was eagerly promoting a union between his two kingdoms. Bacon had his doubts, thinking that the king 'hastened to a mixture of both kingdoms and nations, faster perhaps than policy will conveniently bear' (*Works*, 10.77). But on the whole he fully supported the union. In his proclamation proposal in spring 1603 he had already spoken about uniting 'these two mighty and warlike nations of England and Scotland into one kingdom' (ibid., 10.68). In *Brief Discourse* he drew on an analogy between the principles of nature and policy. At the same time he revealed that he had been an attentive reader of Machiavelli, noting that 'so likewise the authority of Nicholas Machiavelli seemeth not to be contemned; who enquiring the causes of the growth of the Roman empire, doth give judgment, there was not one greater than this, that the state did so easily compound and incorporate with strangers' (ibid., 10.96).

Bacon also tried to capture James's attention with a treatise on ecclesiastical policy, written perhaps in August or September 1603. In *Certain Considerations Touching the Better Pacification and Edification of the Church of England* (1604) Bacon, again following Machiavelli, pointed out that, just like 'the civil state' 'the ecclesiastical state' requires to be constantly 'purged and restored'. The brunt of Bacon's critique was again directed against the hierarchy of the church and its government. Although 'the substance of doctrine is immutable' the 'policies and forms' of church government (just like those of civil government) 'are left free'. While he acknowledged that the government of bishops suited kingdoms better than 'parity of ministers and government by synods', he harshly criticized the bishops. Above all he censured their absolute power: 'the Bishop giveth orders alone; excommunicateth alone; judgeth alone' (*Works*, 10.107–9). Little wonder that the tract incurred the bishops' displeasure: it was suppressed by Richard Bancroft, bishop of London, and surviving copies of the printed version are incomplete.

Another tract which Bacon composed during the first months of the new reign was his *Apology in Certain Imputations Concerning the Late Earl of Essex* (May 1604); it enjoyed some success and was twice reprinted. In the tract Bacon defended his own conduct in the Essex affair by exactly the same line of argument which he had presented to Essex as early as in 1595. Bacon repeated that the queen and the public service had always had his first priority: 'whatsoever I did … was done in my duty and service to the Queen and the State' (*Works*, 10.141).

James's first parliament met in March 1604, and Bacon again sat for Ipswich. The parliament had five sessions between 1604 and 1610 and was finally dissolved in February 1611. Bacon was one of the most active members of the house, speaking in almost every debate and sitting in almost every important committee and often reporting from committees or conferences to the house. In the first session of 1604 he assumed a conciliatory role in the dispute over who was the member for the county of Buckingham and in debates on wardship, monopolies, and purveyance.

The union question dominated the first and third sessions, and Bacon was heavily involved in it. To avoid opposition James's plans for the union and its accomplishment were vague. Despite intensive committee work all that had been achieved by July when the parliament was prorogued was a joint Anglo-Scottish commission to prepare proposals for union. In autumn 1604 Bacon was busy with the work of the commission and wrote 'Certain articles or considerations touching the union of the kingdoms of England and Scotland', which argued that political and legal changes and innovations, while possible, were always difficult. Bacon also wrote a suggestion for a proclamation 'touching his Majesty's style', but it was not adopted when the proclamation was published in October 1604. In spring 1605 Bacon promoted the union by a new 'History of Britain' project, which would carry the union backwards in time. He did not proceed with this project but returned to it in 1610 when he wrote the beginning of 'The history of Great Britain' and sent it for comments to the king.

The second session of James's first parliament, between November 1605 and May 1606, concentrated on purveyance and matters of finance as well as the Gunpowder Plot, and Bacon kept a fairly low profile. As early as 1603 Bacon had mentioned that he had 'found out an alderman's daughter, an handsome maiden, to my liking' (*Works*, 10.80). Almost three years later, on 10 May 1606 he married her at Marylebone chapel. She was Alice (1592–1650), a daughter of Benedict *Barnham, a wealthy London alderman. Bacon was forty-five, she was barely fourteen.

The third session of James's first parliament, from November 1606 to July 1607, focused its attention on the Anglo-Scottish union. The commission had made three proposals: equal trading rights, repeal of expressedly hostile laws, and bestowal of a common nationality (naturalization). The first and third proposals aroused fierce opposition in the parliament, opposition which Bacon did his best to overcome. When, on 17 February 1607, Nicholas Fuller argued against the union by claiming that England would become overpopulated, Bacon arose to deliver a long speech, mustering all his eloquence in defence of the union in general and naturalization in particular. Just as fifteen years earlier in writing the official response to Robert Parsons's anti-government tract, now Bacon appealed to the examples of Demosthenes and the republican Athens. If an MP merely looked at the union from 'his particular vocation' he would perhaps oppose it, but putting his own private good before the common good would hardly enable him 'to give counsel or take counsel'. He told them that instead the MPs should 'raise their thoughts, and lay aside those considerations which their private vocations and degrees mought minister and present unto them, and would take upon them cogitations and minds agreeable to the dignity and honour of the estate'. Seeing beyond their own private good would prompt the MPs to lend their support to the union (*Works*, 10.307–8). Bacon's eloquence failed to pay off: a few days later the Commons decided against the naturalization of the *post nati*.

In so far as his particular vocation was concerned Bacon's efforts to promote the union brought him the long hoped for advancement to solicitor-general on 25 June 1607. In the same year Bacon wrote his most concrete work on the Anglo-Scottish union, 'Preparation for the union of laws'. He suggested that the English and Scottish laws should be organized in 'a book of two columns' which would make the comparison easy.

Although the House of Commons had decided in February 1607 against the naturalization of the *post nati*, their decision was reversed in 1608 by exchequer chamber, which ruled that the *post nati*, but not the *ante nati*, were naturalized. Bacon appeared as solicitor-general on behalf of the king's interest and argued for the winning side, and like the lord chancellor, Ellesmere, based his argument on the nature of kingship. But he did not, as Ellesmere did, draw an absolutist conclusion, arguing instead that the law limited the king's power.

Perhaps the most lasting effect of Bacon's close involvement in the Anglo-Scottish union project was his theory of civic greatness. From the very beginning of his public utterances concerning the union he linked it with the attainment of civic greatness. His strongest arguments to this effect were presented in his long speech in the House of Commons on 17 February 1607 and the closely related tract: 'Of the true greatness of the kingdom of Britain', which remained unfinished. He also treated it in an essay, 'Of the greatness of kingdoms', published in the second edition of the *Essayes* (1612). 'For greatness', he told his colleagues in the House of Commons:

> I think a man may speak it soberly and without bravery, that this kingdom of England, having Scotland united, Ireland reduced, the sea provinces of the Low Countries contracted, and shipping maintained, is one of the greatest monarchies, in forces truly esteemed, that hath been in the world. (*Works*, 10.323)

In his theory of civic greatness Bacon carefully followed Machiavelli's account and argued against more recent theories of civic greatness expounded by such theorists as Justus Lipsius and Giovanni Botero. While emphasizing the centrality of the army and military disposition Bacon concentrated on the morality underlying the army and questioned the importance of opulence, commerce, and victuals. He declared in the House of Commons, 'Neither is the authority of Machivel to be despised, who scorneth the proverb of estate taken first from a speech of Mucianus, that Moneys are the sinews of wars; and saith there are no sinews of wars but the very sinews of the arms of valiant men' (*Works*, 10.323–4).

Just as his notion of the politically active citizen was based on classical precedents, so it was the classical idea of the armed citizen which underlay Bacon's conception of civic greatness. The only way to pursue civic greatness successfully, much less to survive in the predatory world, was to attain a large population and to arm it. Walter Ralegh aptly summarized Bacon's argument:

> Certaine it is (as Sir Francis Bacon hath judiciously observed) That a State whose dimension or stemme is small, may aptly serve to be foundation of a great Monarchie: which chiefly comes to passe, where all regard of domesticall prosperitie is laid aside; and every mans care addressed to the benefit of his countrie. (W. Ralegh, *The Historie of the World*, 1614, 496)

In 1607–8 Bacon's career was at an important turning point. In June 1607 he had finally gained a crown office. On 16 July 1608 he became the clerk of star chamber, the reversion of which he had held since November 1589. Surviving notes of a review of his life that he made between 25 and 31 July 1608 offer an unusually personal insight into Bacon's life. He began with a detailed review of his economic situation. Although his marriage and the clerkship of star chamber had given him some financial security he still had a long list of possible lenders. He detailed his debts but also his property and income as well as the possible ways to increase them. Bacon then discussed how he could maintain access to the king. In particular he wanted to be 'affectionate and assured to the Scots' at the court. He considered the kind of advice he should offer, what legal cases he should prepare for, how to run his office better than his predecessor, and how to take advantage of the weakness of the attorney-general, Sir Henry Hobart. He also reminded himself of his political projects—'greatness of Britain', 'union in Parliament'—as well as of circulating his political and legal works—'my Argument of the postnati' and the speeches on naturalization and on union of laws (*Works*, 11.41–3).

Moreover Bacon listed his diet and medication. He also made extensive plans for improving his gardens at Gorhambury House and building a new house 'with an upper galery open upon the water, a tarace above that, and a supping roome open under that; a dynyng roome, a bedd chamber, a Cabanett, and a Roome for Musike' (*Works*, 11.765–7). These plans eventually became Verulam House, which was to cost him £9000 or £10,000 and which, forty years after Bacon's death, in a state of dereliction, was sold to two carpenters for £400.

Writings on natural philosophy, 1603–1613 As well as pondering his private life and political as well as legal projects in July 1608 Bacon reviewed his plans in natural philosophy, listing all those who he thought could help him with his project in general and with experiments in particular. Although political and legal work had started to pile up during the first decade of the new century Bacon had also devoted a considerable amount of time to natural philosophy. In October 1605 he published *The Twoo Bookes of Francis Bacon: of the Proficience and Advancement of Learning, Divine and Humane*. It was the product of his two enforced periods of leisure, first from March 1603 to March 1604 and then from December 1604 to October 1605. *The Advancement of Learning*, as it is commonly called, was Bacon's first published philosophical work and the only one which he published in English. All the other published philosophical works (and most of those which remained unpublished) were written in Latin—an indication of the international (rather than purely national) scope of his project. Initially Bacon planned to print *The Advancement of Learning* simultaneously in English and Latin, but haste prevented this and caused the first book of the volume to be printed before the second was finished. Bacon did not abandon the idea of a Latin edition, and in summer 1606 contacted Thomas Playfere, Lady Margaret professor of divinity at Cambridge, requesting him to translate *The Advancement of Learning* into Latin. Nothing came of this, but still in 1608 Bacon reminded himself of 'proceeding with the translation of my book of Advancment of learnyng' (*Works*, 11.64).

The Advancement of Learning was divided into two books. The first was an eloquent and powerful defence of the importance of learning to every field of life. It was therefore constructed according to the principles of epideictic oratory. The much longer and more important second book was a general survey of the contemporary state of human knowledge, identifying its deficiencies and supplying Bacon's broad suggestions for improvement. The book's real importance was not so much its encyclopaedic character but rather its professed aim of propagating the Baconian ideas of the advancement of learning and knowledge, and of the practical means of accomplishing it.

Bacon often referred to himself with studied moderation as a mere 'bell-ringer', whose only task was 'to ring a bell to call other wits together' (*Works*, 10.254, 300). Yet, by the first decade of the seventeenth century his calls for a new, productive natural philosophy began to emerge as a definite programme. The unpublished philosophical writings from this period are no less important than *The Advancement of Learning* for understanding how Bacon's great philosophical programme—ultimately entitled 'Instauratio magna' ('The great instauration')—was taking shape.

The earliest of these treatises, written in 1602–3 and called the 'Temporis partus masculus', continued Bacon's criticism of earlier philosophy, summoning all the schools of ancient and modern philosophy to the bar and heaping scorn on them. Its subtitle—'Instauratio magna imperii humani in universum'—contains the earliest mention of the great instauration. A similar criticism was repeated in the 'Cogitata et visa', written in 1607, and in 'Redargutio philosophiarum', written in 1608, where Aristotle and Plato were roundly criticized, and a more favourable account was given of Empedocles, Heraclitus, and Democritus.

'De interpretatione naturae proemium', composed in 1603, asserted Bacon's plans: 'Now among all the benefits that could be conferred upon mankind, I found none so great as the discovery of new arts, endowments, and commodities for the bettering of man's life' (*Works*, 10.84). In 'Scala intellectus, sive, Filum labyrinthi', a tract written in English, perhaps in 1607, he declared that his aim was to produce 'active and operative knowledge' (ibid., 3.503). A singular mistake in the dominant view of 'sciences' was that they had to be 'believed and accepted'. Bacon insisted, however, that they should 'be examined and further discovered'. It was, he added, 'natural to arts to be in perpetual agitation and growth' (ibid., 3.498, 502).

Bacon was convinced that the fulfilment of his programme required a wholesale change in the way in which men perceived knowledge and learning. But it also implied a new method of securing that knowledge. His first detailed methodological remarks occur in 'Valerius terminus of the interpretation of nature' in 1603. It also contains the earliest account of his doctrine of Idols, which were the systematic forms of error to which the human mind is subject: Idols of the Tribe, the Palace (later this was replaced by Market-place), the Cave, and the Theatre. In *The Advancement of Learning* Bacon also offered a devastating critique of current methodology, and by 1608 he reminded himself to finish his new method in natural philosophy under the title 'The key of interpretation' ('Clavis interpretationis'), entertaining the idea of publishing it in France.

From this period also comes the earliest evidence of

Bacon's conception of natural and experimental histories and their centrality to the new natural philosophy or science. In *The Advancement of Learning* Bacon discussed extant natural histories, their deficiencies and the ways to improve them, noting 'the use of History Mechanical is of all others the most radical and fundamental towards natural philosophy' (*Bacon*, ed. Vickers, 178). In 'Redargutio philosophiarum' (1608) he pointed out that true natural philosophy should draw its material from 'natural history and mechanical experiences' (*Works*, 3.583), and in a fragmentary piece entitled 'Cogitationes de scientia humana' (composed perhaps in 1604) he discussed this at greater length. The 'Cogitationes de rerum natura', perhaps also written in 1604, contains speculative discussions of bodies, the vacuum, and motion, defending Democritean atomism. In his private memoranda of 1608 Bacon listed various topics which urgently needed investigation. In the 'Phaenomena universi', written perhaps in 1611, he offered an introduction to and an example of natural history. He announced that an entirely new natural history was necessary before the 'instauration of the sciences' could take place (Bacon, *Philosophical Studies*, 7).

It was between 1607 and 1611 that Bacon started to conceive his entire philosophical plan as consisting of six books (or later six parts). But he not only charted such an extensive programme, at the same time he endeavoured to carry it out. At the beginning of the second book of *The Advancement of Learning* he made a bold attempt to invite James to begin a complete reform of the institutions of learning, including founding libraries and research institutes, raising the funding of universities and the salaries of professors, as well as initiating international scholarly co-operation.

In his private notes of 1608 Bacon listed the names of several men, including even the fourteen-year-old Prince Henry, whom he thought of as potential patrons of his programme, and he planned to enlist foreign support. He had clearly lost some confidence in the older generation and looked to the younger and even future generations to take up his call. In 1609 he wrote that 'my writings should not court the present time' but rather 'future ages' (*Works*, 11.135). He was also cognizant of the great labour needed in collecting natural histories. Although he criticized existing institutions in *The Advancement of Learning* three years later he listed several of them (the schools of Westminster, Eton, and Winchester, Trinity College and St John's College, Cambridge, and Magdalen College, Oxford) as potential places of support. But he also reminded himself of international co-operation and of founding a new college 'for Inventors' which would have the necessary equipment, including a library and a laboratory (ibid., 11.66).

By 1609 Bacon, corresponding with his closest friend Toby Matthew, confidently called his natural philosophical programme an '*Instauration*' and assured him that it 'sleeps not' (*Works*, 11.134–5). But he noted that religious controversies were a serious threat to his entire programme. In one of these letters to Matthew, written on 10 October 1609, Bacon famously referred to himself as:

> the miller of Huntingdon, that was wont to pray for peace amongst the willows; for while the winds blew, the wind-mills wrought, and the water-mill was less customed. So I see that controversies of religion must hinder the advancement of sciences. (ibid., 11.137–8)

Furthermore religion and philosophy should be kept separate for, as Bacon told Matthew, the world must not 'reject truth in philosophy, because the author dissenteth in religion' (ibid., 11.145).

There is some irony in the fact that these letters exist partly because of the heightened religious controversy which Bacon deplored. Matthew, son of the archbishop of York and a Catholic convert, was exiled for refusing to take the oath of allegiance imposed on Catholics in the aftermath of the Gunpowder Plot. Bacon and Matthew, unable to meet, were forced to correspond.

In 1609 Bacon published the *De sapientia veterum*, a collection of thirty-one ancient myths complete with his interpretations of their allegories. Although traditionally listed under literary works the *De sapientia veterum* treats various philosophical issues and has more recently been seen as an important contribution to both his natural and civil philosophy. In 1611 he wrote an unfinished tract 'De principiis atque originibus', which was designed to contain interpretations of the myths of the principles and origins of things, but in fact contains only the first. A short tract on tidal motion—'De fluxu et refluxu maris'—has also been dated to 1611.

In 1612 Bacon wrote an unfinished paper entitled 'Descriptio globi intellectualis', which was meant to be the beginning of the first book or part of the 'Instauratio'. It presented the classification or partition of sciences and was thus meant to survey the state of knowledge and learning—the intellectual globe. Bacon had, of course, done such a survey in the second book of *The Advancement of Learning*, but this had been written before he had any six-part plan. 'Descriptio' was thus meant to be a revision on Ramist lines of book two of *The Advancement of Learning*. 'Descriptio' was only a small fraction of the whole first part. Surveying all the branches of learning and their deficiencies with the same meticulousness as the extant fraction does would have produced a gigantic work.

Almost immediately after 'Descriptio' Bacon wrote a brief text entitled 'Thema coeli' on cosmology and astronomy. Since Bacon was convinced that the primary aim of philosophy was to bring great benefits for the whole of humankind, to improve its material conditions, and even to restore the prelapsarian state of felicity, the prolongation of life lay at the heart of his whole project. Indeed, as early as 1603 he had announced that 'immortality (if it were possible)' was among 'the true ends of knowledge' (*Works*, 3.222). Some time during the 1610s he also composed (and kept revising until he abandoned it unfinished) his earliest surviving treatise on the prolongation of life, entitled 'De viis mortis', which was discovered only in 1978.

During the decade from 1603 to 1613 Bacon thus pursued various parts of his natural philosophical project vigorously but in a somewhat eclectic manner and was not in a hurry to publish anything. As he told Lancelot Andrewes in 1609, 'I hasten not to publish' (*Works*, 11.141). Writing to Toby Matthew the following February Bacon explained his working habits: 'My great work goeth forward; and after my manner, I alter ever when I add. So that nothing is finished till all be finished' (ibid., 11.145).

The zenith of the political career In 1608 Bacon had only a little official business as solicitor-general, and it was a period of intense literary activity. In addition to the natural philosophical treatises mentioned above he produced a memorial of Queen Elizabeth entitled 'In felicem memoriam Reginae Elizabethae', which was composed according to the principles of demonstrative rhetoric. Towards the end of the year he wrote a treatise on Ireland entitled 'Certain considerations touching the plantation in Ireland', which he presented to James as a new year's gift. The main aim of Bacon's short treatise was to find means of inducing the best possible people to undertake the plantation project. The treatise was thus a piece in deliberative rhetoric which aimed at persuading people to a desired course of action (plantation), appealing to the classical deliberative *loci* of honour and profit.

In winter 1608–9 Bacon was involved in the case of the jurisdiction of the council of the marches, defending the council. As early as 1607 he had prepared a paper on the issue. It was in this debate that Bacon employed absolutist principles. It had been argued that the king's prerogatives were given to him by the common law, but Bacon replied with a staple absolutist argument that the king held some of his prerogatives 'mediately from the law, but immediately from God'. Some of his prerogatives were indeed of such nature that they could be disputed 'in his ordinary courts of Justice'. But 'his sovereign power' could not be censured by any judge. Because 'the end of all government' was the 'preservation of the public', it was 'necessary' that the king could flout the law. As soon as 'prerogatives are made envious or subject to the constructions of laws' a monarchy, Bacon argued, would degenerate into an aristocracy or oligarchy, and 'further way may be opened to Parliament or lawyers to dispute more liberties'. He warned that those who wanted to limit prerogatives by 'subjects' birthrights and laws' were perhaps opening 'a gap unto new Barons' wars'. A good king did indeed govern by the law. Had not James himself admitted that 'God forbid … that we should be governed by men's discretions and not by the law'? But this did not entail the limitation of the royal power by the law, for the king was accountable to God alone (*Works*, 10.371–2, 380).

In the last two sessions of James's first parliament, which sat in 1610, Bacon was a royal official for the first time. In the fierce debates about whether the king had the right of impositions Bacon defended the king not by absolutist arguments but by advocating a balanced constitution. 'The King's Sovereignty and the Liberty of Parliament are as the two elements and principles of this estate … [which] do not cross or destroy the one the other, but they strengthen and maintain the one the other' (*Works*, 11.177). By evoking such a view Bacon clearly tried to avoid getting involved in ideological disputes, but its reception was ambivalent. As Nicholas Fuller commented on Bacon's speech: 'though Mr. Solicitor's speech were full of rhetoric and art, yet it had some good substance in it' (Foster, 2.98).

Later Bacon gave another speech in which he defended the king's right of impositions, again insisting that the question was '*de vero et falso*, and not *de bono et malo*; of the legal point, and not of the inconvenience'. So the question was reduced 'whether the King have not such a prerogative by law' (*Works*, 11.191). The next speaker, Thomas Hedley, gave Bacon a lie direct: 'though it was said by one of the King's learned counsel that this question was not a question of *bonum et malum*, but of *vera et falsa*', yet it was 'a good and necessary argument to say, it is ill for the good of the commonwealth, ergo, no law' (Foster, 2.176). Whereas Bacon had defended the king's right of impositions by legal precedents Hedley countered by announcing that the whole excellence of the common law was precisely that it was constantly redefined in the light of new circumstances. If this were not the case, Hedley argued quoting Bacon's *Advancement of Learning*, judges would have been devoid of 'versatile *ingenium*' and 'subject to the reproof of *idem manebat neque idem decebat*' (ibid., 2.178). Hedley ended his long speech by appealing to 'the ancient freedom and liberty' of the Englishman, and made use of the speech which Bacon had delivered in the committee of grievances on 19 May. Finally he paraphrased lengthy passages from Bacon's speech of 17 February 1607 where Bacon had defended the Anglo-Scottish union by his theory of civic greatness. 'It is', Hedley declared:

> the sinews of men's arms then (namely a valiant, populous and military nation), as hath been well observed and collected by one of the worthies of this House, that there are the true sinews of war and hath made our nation so renowned through the world. (ibid., 2.195)

In August 1610 Bacon's mother, Anne, Lady Bacon, died. It was also about 1610 that Bacon returned to his essays. He was preparing another edition and planned to dedicate it to Prince Henry. The prince had made Bacon his own solicitor, and in 1611 he appointed him steward of King's Langley in the duchy of Lancaster. Bacon was hoping for the prince's support for some higher position, and the edition of essays was intended to demonstrate his abilities as a counsellor. Bacon had already written the dedication, but Prince Henry suddenly died in November 1612 just before the edition came out and Bacon rededicated it to his brother-in-law, Sir John Constable. The edition contained thirty-eight essays, many of which analyse civil business from a much broader perspective than the first edition. It sold even better than the first edition and was reprinted six times between 1612 and 1624.

Bacon had expressed hopes of preferment to the king early in 1611 and by the autumn had received a promise of the attorney-general's place. In May 1612 Bacon's cousin, the earl of Salisbury, died. This prompted Bacon to both censure Salisbury's competence as a politician and to recommend himself as an able successor. In all these suits for preferment Bacon consistently presented himself as the king's man. Writing to the king after Salisbury's death he stressed his 'little skill' in parliamentary business but hastened to add that he was 'a perfect and peremptory royalist' (*Works*, 11.280). Writing to the king's new favourite Robert Carr, Viscount Rochester, he noted that 'the Attorney and the Solicitor are as the King's champions for civil business'. In 1613 he recommended himself to the place of attorney-general on the grounds that he would be able 'to recover that strength to the King's prerogative which it hath had in times past, and which is due unto it' (ibid., 11.280, 342, 381).

After Salisbury's death Bacon acquired growing importance as a statesman and counsellor to James. Finally on 27 October 1613 he was appointed attorney-general. The years as solicitor and attorney became busier and busier with legal work. Among these in 1612 were the prosecutions of Lord Sanquhar for killing an English fencing master, and of James Whitelocke and Robert Mansell for slandering the king's commission of enquiry into the navy. As attorney-general, among Bacon's first tasks was to abolish duelling—a recent social habit which rapidly gained ground in the early 1610s. In autumn 1613 Bacon suggested that a proclamation should be published against duelling, proposing that the offenders should be prosecuted in star chamber. In January he brought a convenient case of two obscure persons before the court. Bacon's charge, together with the decree of the court, was soon published. The actual proclamation was published in February 1614 with a treatise, entitled *A Publication of His Majesties Edict, and Severe Censure against Private Combats and Combatants*. Some contemporaries attributed the treatise to Bacon, but it was composed by the earl of Northampton.

According to Northampton the best strategy for abolishing duelling was to replace it by a court of honour. Bacon, however, insisted that such a strategy merely served the contrary purpose. By accepting the notion of courtesy, honour, and insult of the duelling theory, the court of honour would encourage men to fight duels. The only way to eradicate duelling, Bacon believed, was to discredit the underlying theory.

More important issues at the beginning of Bacon's career as attorney were the king's finances and relations with parliament. Bacon had recommended calling a new parliament as early as 1612. In autumn that year he wrote to the king that 'your Majesty's recovery must be by the medicines of the Galenists and Arabians, and not of the Chemists or Paracelsians'. The recovery could not in other words be achieved 'by any one fine extract or strong water' but rather 'by a skilful compound of a number of ingredients' (*Works*, 11.312). Northampton, who was James's chief minister from Salisbury's death until his own death in June 1614, was against calling a new parliament. Bacon disagreed. In 1613 or very early 1614 Bacon again urged James to call a new parliament, arguing that 'parliament hath been the ordinary remedy to supply the King's wants'. He was convinced that the disappointing conflicts of the 1610 sessions could easily be avoided partly because Salisbury would no longer create envy and partly because 'the opposite party heretofore is now dissolved and broken' (ibid., 11.365).

Bacon wanted to give the impression that the failures in parliament were not based on deep ideological division, but could be explained by political intrigues and faction. He suggested that some course should be taken to avoid a packed house and 'to make men perceive that it is not safe [to] combine and make parties in Parliament, but that men be left to their consciences and free votes' (*Works*, 11.368). More important, the king 'should not descend below' himself; 'those tragical arguments and (as the schoolmen call them) ultimities of persuasions which were used last Parliament should for ever be abolished'. Instead, the king should act 'in a more familiar, but yet a more princely like manner' (ibid., 11.369, 371). James must not use 'the language of a Merchant … crying of his royalties to sale'. But neither should he act as 'a Tyrant', telling the MPs that 'he most set upon the tenters his laws and prerogatives, if they will not supply him' (ibid., 12.26). If the king should thus keep away from airing absolutist principles the MPs should no less forbear from using ideological arguments. Bacon seemed to believe that the grave problems which surfaced in parliament could be avoided as long as men set their ideological arguments aside.

The new parliament met in April 1614. Bacon was returned for St Albans and Ipswich as well as for Cambridge University, sitting eventually for Cambridge. Almost immediately the question was raised whether, as attorney-general, Bacon was eligible to sit in the Commons. Without a clear precedent Bacon was allowed to sit, but in future the attorney-general would be ineligible. James carefully followed Bacon's advice, telling the Commons several times that he 'would not deal with you like a merchant' or 'by way of a bargain'. He also distanced himself from absolutism, saying that he had never meant to 'stretch his prerogatives' (M. Jansson, *Proceedings in Parliament, 1614*, 1988, 44, 17, 141). None the less, without passing any legislation the parliament was dissolved after eight weeks. Bacon was unrepentant and insisted after the session to the king that he must rebut 'the opinion which is sometimes muttered, That his Majesty will call no more Parliaments' (*Works*, 12.85, 176).

In legal cases against Catholics, spawned by the oath of allegiance, Bacon also displayed reluctance to get involved in an ideological dispute. In January 1614, rather than developing a theoretical response, Bacon simply showered abuse on the Catholic resistance theorists. Their opinions, he argued in a similar case in king's bench in 1615, required rather 'detestation than contestation'. Those who wrote in favour of resistance or regicide deserved 'rather some holy league amongst all Christian Princes of either religion, Papists and Protestants, for the extirping and razing of this opinion and the authors thereof from the face of the earth, as the common enemies of mankind, than the stile of pen or speech' (*Works*, 12.165, 154).

During Christmas 1613 Bacon had been involved in preparing a masque to celebrate the marriage of the king's Scottish favourite Robert Carr, the earl of Somerset, to Frances Howard, whose marriage to the third earl of Essex had been annulled the previous September. *The Masque of*

Flowers was performed on twelfth night and printed soon afterwards with a dedication to Bacon. Somerset's position as James's principal favourite did not last long. By the end of 1615 his career was destroyed in a trial in star chamber, conducted by Bacon, for the murder of his former friend Sir Thomas Overbury. In May 1616, with Bacon acting as the chief prosecutor, both the earl and the countess of Somerset were tried, convicted, and sentenced to death, although this was commuted to imprisonment in the Tower.

The downfall of Somerset and the entire Howard faction coincided with the meteoric rise of George Villiers, the son of a minor Leicestershire gentleman, who was introduced to the king in late summer 1614. Just as his friendship with Essex had dominated a central period of Bacon's early career so his close relationship to Villiers (later earl, marquess, and duke of Buckingham) had a crucial impact on his later career. Bacon's earliest existing letter to Villiers dates from January 1616, by which time a familiar acquaintance had been formed between them. Bacon had always emphasized the central importance of public service to the earl of Essex; similarly, in August 1616, when George Villiers was created Viscount Villiers, Bacon reminded him that 'it is the life of an ox or beast always to eat, and never to exercise; but men are born (and specially christian men), not to cram in their fortunes, but to exercise their virtues'. Villiers should dedicate himself 'to the public' and 'countenance, and encourage, and advance able men and virtous men and meriting men' (*Works*, 13.6). There are also extant two different versions of a detailed advice letter which Bacon apparently wrote to Villiers at this time.

As attorney-general Bacon defended the king in numerous legal cases. In January 1616 he wrote to the king, noting that 'it pleased your Majesty to commit to my care and trust, for Westminster Hall matters, three particulars: that of the *Rege inconsulto* … that of the *Commendans* … and that of *Habeas Corpora*' (*Works*, 12.233). When Bacon gave his argument in king's bench concerning the first case he, according to his own account, 'lost not one auditor' and even Edward Coke had thought 'it was a famous argument' (ibid., 12.235). This case touched royal prerogatives, but it was the two other cases later in 1616 which brought the king and Edward Coke into collision. In June 1616 Coke was excluded from the privy council and was ordered to amend his reports. The result did not satisfy the king and in November 1616 Coke was removed from king's bench, and later from the privy council, and finally from office altogether. In 1613 Coke had been removed from the chief justiceship of common pleas to that of king's bench on Bacon's advice. This, Bacon had argued, had been 'a kind of discipline to him for opposing himself in the King's causes' (ibid., 11.382). Now, in 1616, Bacon played an equally prominent role in Coke's removal, and prepared its explanation. Coke had been, Bacon wrote, 'a perpetual turbulent carriage, first towards the liberties of his [the king's] church and the state ecclesiastical; then towards his prerogative royal, and the branches thereof; and likewise towards all the settled jurisdictions of his other courts' (ibid., 13.95).

The rapidly growing public and legal business which Bacon conducted reflected his growing importance. But Bacon also expected that it would reflect on his official position. In February 1616, when the lord chancellor, Ellesmere, fell ill, Bacon advertised himself as the fittest candidate to replace him. He especially warned James not to appoint Coke whom he called 'an over-ruling nature' (*Works*, 12.242). Bacon's expectations were somewhat premature, for Ellesmere recovered. Bacon immediately wrote to Villiers, suggesting that Villiers promote his suit for a place in the privy council, and he reminded Villiers of it at the end of May, pointing out that 'the time is … now or never' (ibid., 12.347). James made Bacon choose between a promise that he would succeed Ellesmere or a place on the privy council. Bacon chose the latter and was sworn a privy councillor on 9 June 1616.

This was an appropriate moment for Bacon to return to one of his lifelong projects: the reformation of the English laws. He had mentioned it to James in 1614 but now in 1616 he made a more comprehensive proposal 'touching the compiling and amendment of the laws of England'. Bacon explained his proposal by telling the king that 'the law is my profession' and that 'your Majesty hath set me in an eminent place' (*Works*, 13.62). The plan was not to alter the law's substance but rather to improve its organization. Bacon had to wait nine months before James accepted Ellesmere's resignation, and on 7 March 1617 Bacon took the office of lord keeper. Before being able to move to York House, the lord keeper's usual residence, he leased Dorset House for two terms from the earl of Dorset. In May 1617 Bacon took his seat in the court of chancery, declaring his programme for the office. He perceived that the defence of the king was his and other judges' 'lanthorn'. In his speech to Sir John Denham, who was sworn as a baron of exchequer in 1617, Bacon told him that 'above all you ought to maintain the King's prerogative, and to set down with yourself that the King's prerogative and the law are not two things; but the King's prerogative is law, and the principal part of the law' (ibid., 13.184, 203).

Only a week after Bacon's appointment in March the king and Villiers (who had been created earl of Buckingham) left London for Scotland. While this enhanced Bacon's status in London, it also brought difficulties. Ever since his dismissal Edward Coke had worked hard to regain his former position. Late in 1616 he had plans for his daughter Frances to marry Buckingham's brother Sir John Villiers. In June 1617 Coke renewed the marriage negotiations, but Coke's wife, Lady Hatton, opposed these plans, hid her daughter, and contacted Bacon for support (Bacon had of course competed with Coke for her hand twenty years earlier). When the mother of Buckingham and the intended groom applied to Bacon on Coke's behalf for a warrant to recover the bride, Bacon refused it, lending his support to Lady Hatton. As well as thwarting Coke's plans Bacon clearly believed that he was doing a favour to Buckingham. He wrote to Buckingham on 12 July 1617, claiming that 'Secretary Winwood hath officiously busied himself to make a match between your brother and Sir Edward Coke's daughter: and, as we hear, he doth it rather to make a faction, than out of any great affection to your Lordship'. The match, Bacon assured, would be 'very inconvenient both for your brother and yourself'. Buckingham himself would 'lose all such your friends as are adverse to Sir Edward Coke; (myself only except, who out of a pure love and thankfulness shall ever be firm to you)' (*Works*, 13.223–4).

On 25 July 1617 Bacon wrote to the king expressing his dislike of the proposed match. Describing the excellent present state of the kingdom in general and the rise of the king's 'prerogative and authority' in particular, Bacon warned the king that the proposed match would put all this in jeopardy:

> if there be but an opinion of his [Coke's] coming in with the strength of such an alliance, it will give a turn and relapse in men's minds unto the former state of things, hardly to be holpen; to the great weakening of your Majesty's service. (*Works*, 13.233)

There was an ominous silence. Soon, however, Bacon learned that both Buckingham and James were furious. Buckingham told him that 'you have carried yourself with much scorn and neglect both toward myself and friends' (*Works*, 13.237). The king's letter to Bacon is lost, but from Bacon's response is learned that it contained 'some matter of dislike, in which respect it hath grieved me more than any event which hath fallen out in my life' (ibid., 13.238). Bacon was ready to change his mind about the marriage, but could hardly make amends to the king, who wrote him a devastating letter in late August. In his reply Bacon could only hope for the speedy return of the king to London, 'expecting that that sun which when it went from us left us cold weather, and now it is returned towards us hath brought with it a blessed harvest' (ibid., 13.246). When James and Buckingham returned to London in mid-September Bacon received from Buckingham a reassurance of reconciliation and responded immediately: 'Your Lordship's pen or rather pencil hath pourtrayed towards me such magnanimity and nobleness and true kindness, as methinketh I see the image of some ancient virtue, and not any thing of these times' (ibid., 13.252).

In making an abject submission to Buckingham, Bacon clearly understood that being the favourite's friend meant being his faithful servant. Bacon played this role dutifully and also reaped the concomitant harvest. In August 1617 he had moved to York House, the residence of lord keeper, where he had been born. In October the death of the secretary, Sir Ralph Winwood, strengthened his position in government. James did not appoint a new secretary of state and Buckingham and Bacon were the two most powerful men under the king. The new year brought new honours: Bacon was made lord chancellor on 7 January 1618 and on 12 July he was raised to the peerage and created Baron Verulam of Verulam. Thereon he styled himself Francis, Lord Verulam—never Lord Bacon as subsequent generations have often styled him.

As the most eminent lawyer in the country Bacon was called upon to sit in judgment on notable men. In October 1618 he was among the six privy councillors who were on the commission to examine and ultimately to condemn Sir Walter Ralegh for his disastrous trip to search for a mine in Guiana. It was Bacon who delivered the death sentence to Ralegh on 22 October 1618. A year later he was involved in the star chamber case against the earl of Suffolk, who was accused of misappropriating money when he had been lord treasurer. After yet another year Bacon, in autumn 1620, prosecuted attorney-general Sir Henry Yelverton in star chamber.

But most of Bacon's days were filled with the routine of smaller cases in chancery. In many of these Buckingham contacted Bacon in favour of parties. By the end of January 1618 Buckingham wrote to Bacon:

> I have received your Lordship's letters, wherein I see the continuance of your love and respect to me in any thing I write to you of, for which I give your Lordship many thanks, desiring nothing for any man but what you shall find just and convenient to pass. (*Works*, 13.297)

By and large, however, Bacon's career in chancery was highly successful. He worked with exemplary efficiency and conscientiousness. He made the court sit mornings and afternoons and extended the term 'for the expediting and clearing of the causes of the court'. Within three months of his appointment Bacon had cleared the backlog. His rules for chancery (ordinances in chancery) emphasized expedition and fairness, limiting jurisdictional conflict and eliminating vexatious suits. The rules also sought to increase accuracy of record keeping and dealt with numerous specific abuses in detail. Bacon's career in chancery also resulted in the improvement in its relationship with the common law courts. For Bacon the equity jurisdiction was a complementary system of justice, not a rival to the common law.

Bacon's success is most evident in his concrete work in chancery. The court gained in popularity, the number of cases increasing during his term but dropping dramatically after his impeachment, and very few of his decisions were reversed, even then. There is ample evidence to suggest that despite his subsequent impeachment Bacon in fact frequently intervened to prevent even the appearance of improper influence or conflict of interest in chancery proceedings.

Bacon had always favoured the summoning of parliament. Even after the disastrous session of 1614 he had emphasized to the king its central importance. In 1617 he wrote to James that 'I was ever for a Parliament; which seemeth to me to be *cardo rerum* or *summa summarum* for the present occasions' (*Works*, 13.233). Bacon was thus enthusiastic when, early in October 1620, he was asked with other 'old Parliament-men' to advise the king how, 'without packing or degenerate arts, [to] prepare to a Parliament' (ibid., 14.114). He immediately set to work, thinking that 'the former grievances' and new potential problems needed to be carefully perused. It was important to consider 'what persons were fit to be of the House'. Equally crucial was 'the framing and having ready of some commonwealth bills, that may add respect to the King's government and acknowledgement of his care'. In all these it was of utmost importance to proceed with caution and secrecy. In particular, 'that which concerneth persons is not so fit to be communicated to the council-table'. Bacon realized that the king's finances would be the most pressing issue in the coming parliament; as he told Buckingham, 'the state of his Majesty's treasure still maketh me sad'. This must be reported to James 'faithfully and freely; for to flatter in this, were to betray his Majesty with a kiss' (ibid., 14.115–16).

By 18 October Bacon sent a proposed proclamation for the parliament. According to Bacon, although James was peace loving, the 'invasion of the Palatinate' had altered 'the balance of Christendom', and 'the reason of state' now demanded the king to take action. The king, Bacon's draft suggested, was therefore seeking 'the faithful advice and general assent of our loving subjects'. Even more important, 'moneys being the sinews of war', it was of utmost importance that the king receive 'some large and bountiful help of treasure from our people' (*Works*, 14.126). The king was, however, highly suspicious of revealing matters of state and the reasons for calling the parliament, 'whereof neither the people are capable, nor is it fit for his Majesty to open now unto them'. Bacon replied to Buckingham (who had passed on the king's opinion) that 'neither would I have thought of inserting matter of state for the vulgar, but that now-a-days there is no vulgar, but all statesmen' (ibid., 14.128–9).

Another matter which needed careful planning was grievances. Among these the committee had listed patents and monopolies and hoped that the king would revoke unpopular patents and monopolies before parliament gathered. The matter was debated in the council on 14 December where Bacon vigorously argued for revoking the most notorious patents, but was overruled by the majority.

The parliament assembled on 30 January 1621. Bacon was clearly at the pinnacle of his career. He had celebrated his sixtieth birthday with a lavish banquet at York House on 22 January 1621, and on 27 January he had been created Viscount St Alban.

'Instauratio magna' and *Novum organum* The turn of the year 1620–21 was also the climax of Bacon's philosophical work. While he had been extremely productive in his natural philosophical work between 1603 and 1612, after 1613, when he was appointed attorney-general, public business began to take a heavy toll and the periods when he could produce his 'vacation's fruits' became shorter and rarer. As lord keeper he made chancery sit mornings and afternoons and extended the term, reserving only 'the depth of the three long vacations … for studies, arts, and sciences' (*Works*, 13.190). Bacon must have dedicated most of these depths to preparing his major philosophical work, the *Novum organum*, which was published together with the preliminary material of his entire philosophical plan—the 'Instauratio magna'—in October 1620. The volume consisted of a preface, a plan of the whole work, the incomplete second part (*Novum organum*), and a preparative to the third part of natural and experimental histories, as well as a catalogue of particular histories.

In sending a copy of the book to the king Bacon explained his overall scheme and the particular intention of the *Novum organum*:

> The work, in what colours soever it may be set forth, is no more but a new logic, teaching to invent and judge by induction, (as finding syllogism incompetent for sciences of nature), and thereby to make philosophy and sciences both more true and more active. (*Works*, 14.119–20)

The ultimate goal, he told the king, was nothing less than 'to enlarge the bounds of Reason and to endow man's estate with new value' (ibid.). James thanked Bacon profusely for the volume and promised 'to read it thorough with care and attention, though I should steal some hours from my sleep', and then 'to use the liberty of a true friend, in not sparing to ask you the question in any point whereof I shall stand in doubt' (ibid., 14.122).

James's proposal raised serious doubts in Bacon's mind. It was one thing for Bacon to call James 'the wisest and most learned of kings'. It was quite another if the king took it upon himself to instruct Bacon in natural philosophy. The *Novum organum*, Bacon replied, 'doth disclaim to be tried by any thing but by experience, and the resultats of experience in a true way'. But he hastened to add that 'the sharpness and profoundness of your majesty's judgment ought to be an exception to this general rule; and your questions, observations, and admonishments, may do infinite good' (*Works*, 14.130). None of these questions, observations, and admonishments were forthcoming. In early February John Chamberlain revealed why: 'the King cannot forbeare somtimes in reading his last book [*Novum organum*] to say that yt is like the peace of God, that passeth all understanding' (*Letters of John Chamberlain*, 2.339).

The king was not the only person who received a copy of the *Novum organum*. Bacon sent three copies to the diplomat Henry Wotton in Vienna. Wotton acknowledged the receipt of them in December and told Bacon that he had presented one of them to the famous astronomer Johann Kepler. Modern scholarship has often argued that Bacon was intellectually a provincial, that he was only a well-educated English gentleman who, classical sources apart, made use of a fairly limited range of popular encyclopaedic works in his natural philosophical writings (Jardine, 6–7, 9). The fact that Kepler received a copy of the *Novum organum* within two months of its publication and that Wotton also fulfilled his earlier promise to Bacon of reporting '*Philosophical* experiments' suggests otherwise. Bacon actively participated in the vanguard of the philosophical discussions of the day. In 1616 Toby Matthew had informed Bacon of Galileo's defence of Copernican astronomy (Bacon, *The New Organon*, x). Three years later Matthew told Bacon that Galileo had written a response to Bacon's 'discourse concerning the flux and reflux of the sea' (*Works*, 14.36).

At the heart of Bacon's plan for the 'Instauratio magna'

lay a novel view of natural philosophy. He wanted to replace the Aristotelian image of science as a contemplation and organization of eternal truths long since discovered by a conception of science as a discovery of the unknown, and also to create a truly active or operative science, to be seen not so much as a contemplative *episteme* as part of the practical, active life. In his attempt to link human science (*scientia*) and human power (*potentia*) Bacon was making a novel claim which altered the function of science in human life.

In the plan of the work of the 'Instauratio magna' Bacon described the six-part division of this whole programme:

1. The Divisions of the Sciences.
2. The New Organon; or Directions for the Interpretation of Nature.
3. The Phenomena of the Universe; or a Natural and Experimental History for the Foundation of Philosophy.
4. The Ladder of the Intellect.
5. Forerunners, or Anticipations of Second Philosophy.
6. Second Philosophy; or Active Science.

The second part, the *Novum organum*, was further divided into two books. The first book is a short refutation of the impediments (idols) which hinder the acceptance of the new method. Its intention is to prepare the reader to embrace the new method presented in the much longer, though incomplete, second book.

According to Bacon, a crucial weakness in the old Aristotelian logic was that it jumped from empirical particulars to first principles (axioms), which formed the premises of deductive reasoning. But Bacon believed that the most general axioms should form the end rather than the beginning of scientific inference, and his own methodology was designed to avoid Aristotle's mistake. Natural histories (systematic accounts of natural phenomena) form the basis of all natural philosophy. For Bacon it was a serious mistake to assume (as Aristotle had done) that experience gives the human mind things as they are: our senses are unreliable—our mind is 'like an enchanted glass' (*Works*, 3.395). Rather than becoming a sceptic, however, Bacon took the sceptics' arguments in his stride, insisting that in order to yield reliable information human senses needed methodological assistance. Baconian logic proceeded along a strict hierarchy of increasing generality. A key role in it was intended for the induction of exclusion whereby all the wrong causes are eliminated or excluded, leaving only the true causes. The whole process is completed only when the fundamental laws of nature (the knowledge of forms) have been reached and, from there, new experiments or works have been derived by practical deduction.

An important role in Bacon's methodology, both in collecting natural histories and in the inductive process from this material to the forms, is assigned to observations and experiments. Thus Bacon endeavoured to follow the contemporary scientific experiments carried out in England and Europe, and he emphasized the centrality of technical scientific instruments which made possible an increasing variety of experiments. Bacon himself not only carried out numerous chemical and mechanical experiments, he reported many of them in the *Novum organum*.

Impeachment Bacon had not been wide of the mark in autumn 1620 when he predicted that patents and monopolies would be among the grievances presented in parliament. Attention was drawn to the issue of patents on the first full day of debate. Soon it was also asked who had sanctioned such grievances and had thus misled the king. When Sir Giles Mompesson's patent for inns came under scrutiny Buckingham, to whom Mompesson was related through marriage, became nervous and begged James to dissolve the parliament. The king refused, and the investigations continued. By the end of February another patent for gold and silver thread, whose profits had been divided among the king, Buckingham, and his brother, became a subject of enquiry. Soon it was revealed that Bacon, together with the lord treasurer, Montagu, had been a key figure as a legal referee certifying the original patents.

James visited the House of Lords on 10 March, expressing his hatred for 'projects and projectors' and speaking of his willingness to protect his people from monopolies. Whereas Buckingham was singled out for praise James was ready to offer up Bacon and Montagu: 'As for the thinges objected against the Chancelor and the Treasurer, I leave them to answere for themselves and to stand and fall as they acquitt them selves' (Lady de Villiers, ed., *The Hastings Journal of the Parliament of 1621*, *Camden Miscellany*, 20, 1953, 26–7).

Bacon defended himself by arguing that the referees could not be held responsible for the subsequent abuse of monopolies. Meanwhile allegations were brought before the parliamentary committee on courts of justice that he had accepted bribes. Bacon had taken gifts from two suitors whose trials had still been pending. He was shocked, and asked Buckingham to protect him. Bacon had never denied that he had taken these gifts; rather he insisted that they did not affect his decision, which had in fact gone against the suitors. Calling himself 'a good patriot born' he wrote to the king on 25 March: 'And for the briberies and gifts wherewith I am charged, when the books of hearts shall be opened, I hope I shall not be found to have the troubled fountain of a corrupt heart in a depraved habit of taking rewards to pervert justice; howsoever I may be frail, and partake of the abuse of the times' (*Works*, 14.226). It was during these troubled weeks that Bacon made his will. He bequeathed his 'compositions unpublished' to his brother-in-law Sir John Constable, who was advised to publish those which he might find fit. In particular Bacon advised that 'In felicem memoriam Reginae Elizabethae' should be published (ibid., 14.228).

In order to prosecute Bacon the parliament revived an obsolete procedure of impeachment: the Commons acted as accusers and the Lords as judges. Working hard the committee had managed to find some twenty-eight cases where Bacon or his servants were accused of improperly accepting gifts or loans. Although many of these charges were dubious Bacon decided to give up. On 21 April he once more appealed to the king. Bacon of course understood that he had been unable to 'move your Majesty, by your absolute power of pardon or otherwise, to take my cause into your hands'. Yet it was, he wrote to the king, 'the utmost of my desire' that 'your Majesty will graciously save me from a sentence with the good liking of the House'. This appeal was going to be 'the last suit I shall make to your Majesty in this business, prostrating myself at your mercy-seat, after fifteen years' service' (*Works*, 14.241).

Bacon obviously realized that it was futile to put up a defence. The king's willingness to permit the trial would virtually ensure conviction (Marwil, 56). On 22 April Bacon sent his 'humble submission and supplication' to the Lords, craving for 'a benign interpretation' (*Works*, 14.242). His final 'Confession and humble Submission' with responses to each charge was read to the Lords on 30 April. He confessed 'that I am guilty of corruption'. His only attempt at extenuation was that, on the one hand, he was not known to be 'an avaricious man' and, on the other, his 'estate' was 'so mean and poor, as my care is now chiefly to satisfy my debts' (ibid., 14.261). Bacon's punishment included a fine of £40,000 and imprisonment at the king's pleasure. He was also barred from any office or employment in the state and forbidden to sit in parliament or come within the verge (12 miles) of the court. The fine was never collected and his imprisonment in the Tower lasted only three days.

Although Bacon was impeached for taking bribes there is little doubt that underlying the whole impeachment was the attack against patents and monopolies. Bacon was thus a victim of a political campaign against the king's chief favourite, Buckingham. Neither James nor Buckingham did anything to help or protect Bacon. They abandoned him and thus made him the scapegoat for the grievances of monopolies. At the same time there is equally little doubt that there was a more personal factor in the impeachment. The whole attack against Bacon was to a considerable extent orchestrated by Edward Coke and Sir Lionel Cranfield, who were both his known enemies.

Last years and death As soon as Bacon had been released from the Tower he wrote to Buckingham not only thanking him 'for getting me out of prison' but also offering his services to the marquess and the king: 'now my body is out, my mind nevertheless will be still in prison, till I may be on my feet to do his Majesty and your Lordship faithful service' (*Works*, 14.281). Bacon's financial situation looked bleak. He was living 'upon the scraps of my former fortunes' but could not 'hold out longer'. He therefore humbly asked Buckingham to fulfil his 'loving promises … to settle my poor fortunes' (ibid., 14.297–8). He was given a generous pension of £1200 a year but its payment was withheld by the new lord treasurer, Cranfield. Bacon was also asking for release from the ban against coming within the verge of the court. Buckingham, who coveted Bacon's lease of York House, used these favours as a means of forcing Bacon to part with it. Extremely reluctant to do so Bacon even offered Gorhambury to make amends, but in the end he sold the lease to Cranfield in March 1622, from whom it passed to Buckingham. As Sir Edward Sackville advised Bacon, 'if York-house were gone, the town were yours' (ibid., 14.343). Indeed, as soon as Bacon consented to sell the lease Buckingham helped him obtain leave to come within the verge.

Early in June 1621 Bacon wrote to the Spanish ambassador, Count Gondomar, that he was 'to retire from the stage of civil action and betake myself to letters' (*Works*, 14.285). Comparing his fate with Demosthenes, Cicero, and Seneca, Bacon identified himself most closely with Seneca who, having been condemned, had 'abstained from intruding into matters of business' and had 'spent his time in writing books of excellent argument and use for all ages'. Yet Bacon also insisted that he could not 'altogether desert the civil person that I have borne' (ibid., 14.372–3). Thus his literary activities were not confined to natural philosophy but included forays into other fields as well.

In his last appeal for James's help during the impeachment trial on 21 April Bacon had mentioned that if time permitted he would 'present your Majesty with a good history of England, and a better digest of your laws' (*Works*, 14.242). In June he set himself to writing *The History of the Reign of King Henry VII*. He wrote with breathtaking speed, presenting the manuscript to the king early in October. The work was dedicated to Prince Charles and published in March 1622. It should be seen in the context of humanist historiography rather than as a precursor of its modern methods. Bacon was keenly interested in the conventional topics of virtue and fortune, but was unconventional in placing a much stronger emphasis on fortune than virtue. The central lesson of *The History of Henry VII* was that a ruler must remain open to accident and ready to seize the opportunities it offered.

Bacon planned to continue his career as a historian by writing a similar history of Henry VIII. He was sent material relating to the project, but, as he complained to Toby Matthew in 1623, Sir Robert Cotton had been 'somewhat dainty of his materials in this' (*Works*, 14.429).

Early in 1622 Bacon cherished hopes of an interview with the king. Among the topics he planned to discuss with James were 'the recompiling of laws' and a 'General Treatise *de Legibus et Justitia*' (*Works*, 14.351–2). The hopes of an interview were dashed, but in March Bacon fulfilled his second promise given in April 1621 by sending the king 'An offer of a digest to be made of the laws of England', arguing that the English laws 'are as mixt as our language, compounded of British, Roman, Saxon, Danish, Norman customs; and surely as our language is thereby so much the richer, so our laws are likewise by that mixture the more complete' (ibid., 14.362). He was also working hard on the more theoretical treatises on law and justice which exist in two different versions: a recently unearthed manuscript treatise entitled 'Aphorismi de jure gentium maiore sive de fontibus justiciae et juris', and another which appeared in the eighth book of *De augmentis* in October 1623 with the title 'Exemplum tractatus de justitia universali, sive de fontibus juris'.

Bacon argued that the remedy for the defects in contemporary law was to be sought from the Roman law, and he often related his own project of legal reform to Justinian's *Corpus juris civilis*. As his project developed the influence of the Roman law became more marked. Whereas in his early work 'Maxims of the law' he had sought to integrate Roman law concepts into a common law context, by the early 1620s he was assimilating his common law experience into a Roman law context. Nevertheless Bacon's strong Roman law bias did not involve replacing the English common law by the Roman civil law. Rather it served to emphasize the universal scope of his project. Although many of Bacon's ideas reflected his common law experience he sought to find the universal axioms of all different legal systems and focused on the methods of legal reasoning to remove uncertainty and ambiguity from the positive law.

When he sent his offer of a digest of English law to James, Bacon told him that he esteemed his '*Instauration*' as his 'great work' with which he still went on 'in silence' (*Works*, 14.358). Writing later in 1622 to Lancelot Andrewes he said he valued his '*Instauration*' most of all his work and explained how he was going to proceed. It was in this context that he put forward in 1623 a suit for the provostship of Eton.

The section of the 'Instauratio' that Bacon most urgently tried to accomplish was the natural histories of the third part. In November 1622 he published a volume entitled *Historia naturalis et experimentalis ad condendam philosophiam; sive phaenomena universi*. It contained the first instalment of his natural history project—a natural history of the winds, *Historia ventorum*—and a plan for five others to be published on a monthly basis. In January 1623 the second part of the project, *Historia vitae et mortis* ('History of life and death') appeared. A third natural history—'Historia densi et rari'—was well under way but other projects apparently intervened. Although the piece survives in two different versions Bacon never finished it.

Among the other projects was the translation into Latin of *The Advancement of Learning*, which was thereby going to take its place as the first part of the 'Instauratio'. It came out under the title *De dignitate et augmentis scientiarum libri IX* in October 1623. Twice as long as the original English edition, the original book two had grown into eight books. Bacon sent copies of the volume to James, Prince Charles, and Buckingham, and to Cambridge and Oxford. To Prince Charles he mentioned that the book translated into Latin could be 'a citizen of the world, as English books are not'. He also apologized that the history of Henry VIII had not progressed according to earlier promises (*Works*, 14.437).

Bacon also worked on the fourth and fifth divisions of the 'Instauratio', which were meant, respectively, to give examples of his method in action and provide some anticipatory results. The 'Abecedarium novum naturae', which was written in 1622, was originally to be included with the third part (the natural histories), but Bacon changed his mind. As it stands the 'Abecedarium', consisting mainly of a list of natural philosophical enquiries, was the introduction to the fourth part. At about the same time Bacon also wrote a short sketch for a study to be included in the fourth part entitled the 'Historia et inquisitio de animato et inanimato'. Two short tracts, 'Inquisitio de magnete' and 'Topica inquisitionis de luce et lumine', both dating from 1625, were similarly intended for the fourth part. A very short piece, which has been dated to the early 1620s, 'Prodromi sive anticipationes philosophia secundae' was the intended preface to part five of the 'Instauratio'.

In 1625 Bacon was also planning to finish the second part of the *Novum organum*, which, he said, he had already 'compassed and planned … out in my mind' (*Works*, 14.531). By this stage he hoped that someone else would take on the work on natural history, claiming that his published histories were not pure histories, but rather pieces which properly belonged to part four of the 'Instauratio'.

During his last years Bacon composed his utopia, the *New Atlantis*, and a natural historical work entitled *Sylva sylvarum*, meaning a collection of collections, a miscellany of subjects. It is a vast compilation of one thousand paragraphs consisting of extracts from many books and Bacon's own experiments and observations. The *New Atlantis* is a description of an island society and its scientific community: Salomon's House. In it Bacon developed ideas which he had outlined thirty years earlier in the early 1590s. The aim of the Salomon's House was nothing less than 'the knowledge of Causes, and secret motions of things; and the enlarging of the bounds of Human Empire, to the effecting of all things possible' (*Works*, 3.156). The actual description of the scientific community's work owes something to two contemporary scientists and craftsmen, the Dutchman Cornelis Drebbel, and the Frenchman Salomon de Caus, who both spent time in Jacobean England. The *Sylva sylvarum* and the *New Atlantis* were posthumously published in the same volume in 1626.

No matter how highly Bacon valued his natural philosophical project he never abandoned hope of a political comeback. *The History of Henry VII* was partly intended to show Bacon's abilities as a counsellor. In 1622 he planned to ask the king to employ him again 'publicly upon the stage' (*Works*, 14.349) and composed his '*Advertisement Touching an Holy Warre*', which alongside many contemporary eulogies for peace, and Anglo-Spanish grammars and dictionaries, testified to the rapprochement between Britain and Spain. Finally, in January 1623, 'the excellent Marquis brought' him 'to kiss the King's hands', which made Bacon think that he was 'in the state of grace' (ibid., 14.402). There were rumours that he would again be placed in high office (Jardine and Stewart, 490).

Prince Charles and Buckingham's hazardous trip to Madrid in 1623 inspired Bacon to wish he could participate fully in politics. Writing to Buckingham at Madrid in April, Bacon complained that 'I never felt my misfortunes so much as now' because he could not advise the marquess. 'But when I look abroad', he continued:

> and see the times so stirring, and so much dissimulation, falsehood, baseness and envy in the world, and so many idle clocks going in men's heads; then it grieveth me much, that I

> am not sometimes at your Lordship's elbow, that I mought give you some of the fruits of the careful advice, modest liberty, and true information.

He displayed no false modesty about his own political skill and experience. 'My good Lord', he went on, 'somewhat I have been, and much have I read; so that few things which concern states or greatness, are new cases unto me' (*Works*, 14.423–4).

As soon as Charles and Buckingham had returned from Madrid Bacon suggested that they could use his pen to capitalize upon the hazardous but futile trip. Sending a copy of the *De augmentis* to the prince a fortnight after their return to England, Bacon announced that he was ready to 'do your Highness's journey any honour with my pen' (*Works*, 14.437). Bacon also worked hard to offer Buckingham detailed advice concerning parliament, and even planned to declare his readiness to travel to the continent to negotiate a league with France. In January 1624 he petitioned to receive leave to sit in the coming parliament.

The return of Charles and Buckingham prompted a dramatic change from a peaceful to a more belligerent foreign policy in which Bacon fully participated. Early in 1624 he wrote to Prince Charles the 'Considerations touching a war with Spain' 'out of long-continued experience in business of estate, and much conversation in books of policy and history'. In it he reiterated his views on civic greatness. Referring directly to his earlier writings on the subject Bacon now declared that those who thought Spain too mighty a state for Great Britain made the crucial error of stressing such external factors as money and territorial size as opposed to the intrinsic virtues of the populace.

In December 1624 Bacon published the *Apophthegms New and Old* and *The Translation of Certaine Psalmes into English Verse*. Only a few months later, in April 1625, he published the third edition of *The Essayes or Counsels, Civill and Morall*. It was his most popular work during his own day and has remained so since—there were more than twenty editions in the seventeenth century. Bacon was aware of this, noting in 1622 that such writings as *The Essayes* would 'yield more lustre and reputation to my name' than those in natural philosophy (*Works*, 14.374). Whereas the first edition had contained ten and the 1612 edition thirty-eight, the third had fifty-eight essays, and can be read as his final comments on the contemporary world of politics. As the title announced, *The Essayes* treated the questions of public life and morality. Earlier scholarship tended to see them as his account of civil knowledge or science. Of late, however, this conclusion has been questioned. Despite his pronounced confidence in his own ability to offer sound counsel Bacon seems to have later become less sanguine, if not wholly sceptical, about the possibility of political science. The final edition of *The Essayes*, while treating the moral and political topics listed in *The Advancement of Learning* as demanding fuller treatment, stresses the contingency and instability of political affairs, which hardly conform to the requirements of a demonstrative science. Indeed, by 1622 Bacon counted his *Essayes* 'but as recreation of my other studies' (ibid.), and in 1625 he noted that his writings on ethics and politics (including *The Essayes*, *The History of Henry VII*, and the *De sapientia veterum*) formed no part of his 'Instauration' (ibid., 14.531).

In December 1625 Bacon composed his last will, at the end of which he suddenly stated: 'Whatsoever I have given, granted, confirmed, or appointed to my wife, in the former part of this will, I do now, for just and great causes, utterly revoke and make void, and leave her to her right only' (*Works*, 14.545). This decision is probably linked to the fact that Bacon's widow married his gentleman usher, John Underhill, less than a fortnight after Bacon's death. Bacon also intended to endow lectureships in Cambridge and Oxford 'for Natural Philosophy, and the sciences thereupon depending', but for want of funds this plan never materialized (ibid., 14.546). In March 1626 he endeavoured by a private bill to confiscate and sell his 'lands, leases, and chattels' for 'the payment of his debts' (Jardine and Stewart, 511).

Bacon died at Highgate on 9 April 1626. The only contemporary evidence of the circumstances is his last unfinished letter, which he obviously composed (without realizing it) on his deathbed. It was addressed to the earl of Arundel, in whose house Bacon had been forced to take refuge. In this letter, which has survived only in a printed version, he stated:

> I was likely to have had the fortune of Caius Plinius the elder, who lost his life by trying an experiment about the burning of the mountain Vesuvius. For I was also desirous to try an experiment or two, touching the conservation and induration of bodies. As for the experiment itself, it succeeded excellently well; but in the journey (between London and Highgate) I was taken with such a fit of casting, as I knew not whether it were the stone, or some surfeit, or cold, or indeed a touch of them all three. But when I came to your Lordship's house; I was not able to go back, and therefore was forced to take up my lodging here, where your house-keeper is very careful and diligent about me. (*Works*, 14.550)

According to the traditional story, in an unseasonably cold spring it had occurred to Bacon to test whether snow would preserve flesh from putrefaction, as salt does. In order to conduct the experiment, he obtained a hen and stuffed it with snow with his own hands, but also caught the chill from which he subsequently died in the earl of Arundel's house. Recently, however, it has been suggested that perhaps Bacon was using 'himself in some way as an experimental guinea-pig, in the hope of restoring his own failing health'. Maybe he had 'been inhaling remedial substances in London, in an attempt to alleviate the symptoms of ill-health and, he hopes, help prolong his life'. According to this conjecture 'Bacon died from an overdose of inhaled nitre or opiates' (Jardine and Stewart, 502–8). He was buried at St Michael's Church, St Albans.

Statesman and philosopher Throughout his life Bacon pursued both a political and a philosophical career. The relationship between these two pursuits has always been a central question in any biographical study of Bacon.

For a long time scholarship followed Bacon's own construction of his life and kept his two careers quite separate. His philosophical project was regarded as the more important and his quest for political power was often seen only as a means to promote his philosophical project. More recent commentators have put more emphasis on his political career and have argued that his natural philosophy and his political experience have something in common. This is most obvious in the centrality of the *vita activa* in both his political and natural philosophy. In his political career and thinking he always set a great store by the classical republican notion of the virtuous active citizen. Similarly he insisted that natural philosophy was not primarily contemplative *episteme* but rather a discovery of the unknown and part of the active life whose aim was 'the benefits and use of life' (*Works*, 4.21).

It has also been argued that Bacon's approach to natural philosophy was conditioned and shaped by his political experience and career (by Leary). There appear to be a number of similarities between his legal method and his natural philosophical method. According to the strongest claim the creation of 'an imperial monarchy' was Bacon's great project and his natural philosophy was merely 'a subordinate part of this programme' (Martin, 2–4, 68, 134, 175). Nevertheless there is little, if any, evidence to support this last view. Bacon of course sought patronage but never promised any short-sighted economic or military gains in return. Though he frequently failed to win patronage he never yielded to the temptation to put his vision of natural philosophy in the service of purely political state power. If Bacon had conceived science as merely serving an imperial state then surely it would have made sense to say so when, at the pinnacle of his political career, he dedicated the *Instauratio magna* to the king. Yet, far from doing so, he apologized for the precious time a statesman had spent on a project lacking any political relevance. The only way Bacon defended writing a philosophical treatise was in purely philosophical terms.

Furthermore Bacon never perceived his philosophical project in nationalistic terms. *The Advancement of Learning* apart he published his natural philosophical writings in Latin because he aimed them at an international audience. He always insisted that a reformed natural philosophy would serve, and bring benefits to, the whole of humankind—extend 'the power and dominion of the human race itself over the universe' (*Works*, 4.114). Therefore, in conducting natural philosophical work national boundaries must be ignored. Bacon was convinced that learning would make tremendous strides 'if there were more intelligence mutual between the universities of Europe than now there is'. Indeed, 'there may be many orders and foundations, which though they be divided under several sovereignties and territories, yet they take themselves to have a kind of contract, fraternity, and correspondence one with the other' (*Bacon*, ed. Vickers, 174).

In many respects Bacon's natural philosophical project stood in complete contrast with his theory of civic greatness (or 'imperial monarchy'). The former was an international enterprise requiring concomitant peace. He argued that one of the reasons why his own times were so conducive to learning was 'the present disposition of these times at this instant to peace' (*Bacon*, ed. Vickers, 288). In striking contrast Bacon always insisted in his writings on civic greatness that the most important quality of a truly great state was 'the valour and military disposition of the people' (*Works*, 7.48). He summarized his entire argument by emphasizing that 'no nation, which doth not directly professe Armes, may looke to have Greatnesse fall into their Mouths' (Bacon, *Essayes*, 95–6). Whereas natural philosophy was an international enterprise, progressing only in peace, civic greatness was its diametrical opposite: it was a purely national undertaking demanding not only a warlike disposition but continuous wars.

This contrast is most glaring when Bacon's writings on civic greatness are compared with the *New Atlantis*, which some commentators have seen not merely as a representation of the ideal society of Bacon's natural philosophy but also as an embodiment of his 'vision of an imperial monarchy sustained by natural philosophy' (Martin, 135). The society of New Atlantis, dominated by its natural philosophical knowledge, was completely devoid of the chief ingredient of civic greatness—war. Moreover the society of New Atlantis was organized as a self-contained unit which had as few contacts with other countries as possible—indeed it was described as being of 'solitary situation' 'divided by vast and unknown seas' from the rest of the world (*Bacon*, ed. Vickers, 463). Consequently strangers were rarely admitted to the island. This society, governed both by internal and external peace and tranquillity, was in marked contrast to the state which aimed at civic greatness, whose crucial quality was military spirit and warlike disposition, and which waged continuous wars to accomplish its desired end. Completely unlike New Atlantis a great state must be 'seated in no extreme angle, but commodiously in the midst of many regions' or 'in the very heart of the world' (*Works*, 7.63–4). Even more it had to have a large population and it therefore needed to be liberal in granting naturalization. New Atlantis's exclusion of itself from the rest of the world into peaceful perpetual existence was hardly compatible with the state which searched for civic greatness by martial enterprises.

Bacon's character and reputation Bacon's character and personality as well as his philosophical and political works have always provoked strongly contrasting interpretations. For many contemporaries Bacon was cold and arrogant, extravagant and pompous. In his letters John Chamberlain rarely had a good word for Bacon. He was especially critical of Bacon's ostentatious lifestyle and his indulgence in ceremonial. Similarly John Aubrey commented that when Bacon was at Gorhambury it seemed as if the court was there. The parliamentarian and diarist Simonds D'Ewes also depicted him in mostly negative terms. Commenting on Bacon's fall D'Ewes was convinced of his utter corruption, which was matched only by the prodigality that had eaten up his gains. Bacon could have been a good scholar and decent lawyer but, according to D'Ewes, he was immoderately ambitious and excessively proud, which necessitated his corrupt behaviour.

On top of these accusations D'Ewes also mentioned Bacon's 'most horrible and secret sin of sodomy' (Jardine and Stewart, 464). John Aubrey also noted that 'Bacon was a *paiderastos*' and such a view was often repeated in contemporary satirical verses (ibid.). A canon of St Paul's, embittered by Bacon's decision in a chancery case, is said by Chamberlain to have accused him of sodomy in a sermon in 1619, mentioning Bacon's 'Catamites' (*Letters of John Chamberlain*, 2.243). While there is no certainty about Bacon's sexual orientation or identity the likelihood that he may have been homosexual is undeniable.

The moral condemnations of Bacon have been repeated ever since the seventeenth century, but they were most vociferous during the nineteenth century when Lord Macaulay, above all, castigated Bacon's moral and professional character. Macaulay freely acknowledged Bacon's greatness as a philosopher but condemned outright his morality and his complete failure to maintain justice.

Nevertheless many of those contemporaries who knew Bacon more intimately depicted his personality and character in highly positive terms. William Rawley compiled and published a commemorative volume in Bacon's honour in 1626. The volume contained thirty-two Latin poems in his praise. These poems called Bacon 'the very nerve of genius' and 'the greatest philosopher since the fall of Greece' (Mathews, 7). But those who thought highly of Bacon admired his moral and personal traits as well as his intellectual powers. Ben Jonson called Bacon 'one of the greatest men and most worthy of admiration that hath been in many ages. In his adversity I ever prayed that God would give him strength … knowing no accident could do harm to virtue, but rather help to make it manifest' (ibid.). Similarly, Bacon's close friend Toby Matthew's praise, as he stated in his preface to the Italian edition of the *Essayes* in 1618, was 'not confined to the qualities of his intellect, but applies as well to those which are matters of the heart, the will and the moral virtue' (ibid., 13).

Two main strands can be distinguished in Bacon's impact on the Western philosophical tradition. First, his theory of scientific method in general, and induction in particular, was much commented on in subsequent epistemological debate. Second, and more important, Bacon's impact on Western philosophy is to be found in the ideological part of his philosophy—the active ethos with which he infused modern science.

The continental philosophers of the seventeenth century saw in Bacon an eloquent critic of scholasticism, but it was in England that he had his greatest impact. On the one hand Bacon's conviction that the advancement of science was an effective means to assuage humankind's sufferings and improve its state found eager response in republican England during the mid-seventeenth century. But his followers also focused their attention on the institutional aspects of his philosophy. The full translation of these ideas into action, in the founding of the Royal Society after the Restoration of 1660 represents Bacon's deification as a philosopher and the final victory of the Baconian project of collaboration, utility, and progress. Another high point in Bacon's fortune occurred in the eighteenth century, when the French *philosophes* revered him as the most important propagandist of science (although they largely ignored the more technical parts of his philosophy). Bacon's methodological precepts received an enthusiastic response from the English epistemologists of the early nineteenth century, but a reaction soon followed, and by the latter part of the century Bacon was ridiculed as an ignorant *Wunderdoktor*, as Justus von Liebig put it in the most extreme formulation.

Such negative assessments have continued in two contrasting forms. For some present-day epistemologists Bacon was a spokesman for a hopelessly naïve induction by enumeration, and had thus nothing to do with the development of modern science. In striking contrast the Frankfurt school criticized Bacon for being the very epitome of the modern scientific domination of nature and humankind.

Recent scholarship has, however, emphasized Bacon's central importance in early modern philosophy. His plan of scientific reform has been given a central place in historical accounts of the birth of the new science. Bacon declared that a new era in the history of humankind was at hand and that therefore traditional philosophy should be refuted. By replacing contemplative science, interested in words rather than works, with an active or operative science, humankind would have power to produce effects and thus to transform its conditions.

MARKKU PELTONEN

Sources *The works of Francis Bacon*, ed. J. Spedding, R. L. Ellis, and D. D. Heath, 14 vols. (1857–74) • *The Oxford authors: Francis Bacon*, ed. B. Vickers (1996) • F. Bacon, *Philosophical studies, c.1611–c.1619*, ed. G. Rees (1996), vol. 6 of *The Oxford Francis Bacon* • F. Bacon, *The essayes or counsels, civill and morall*, ed. M. Kiernan (1985) • F. Bacon, *The advancement of learning*, ed. M. Kiernan (2000), vol. 4 of *The Oxford Francis Bacon* • F. Bacon, *The* 'Instauratio magna': *last writings*, ed. G. Rees (2000), vol. 13 of *The Oxford Francis Bacon* • L. Jardine and A. Stewart, *Hostage to fortune: the troubled life of Francis Bacon, 1561–1626* (1998) • N. Mathews, *Francis Bacon: the history of a character assassination* (1996) • D. Coquillette, *Francis Bacon* (1992) • B. Vickers, *Francis Bacon and Renaissance prose* (1968) • B. Vickers, ed., *Essential articles for the study of Francis Bacon* (1968) • J. Marwil, *The trials of counsel: Francis Bacon in 1621* (1976) • M. Neustadt, 'The making of the instauration: science, politics, and law in the career of Francis Bacon', PhD diss., Johns Hopkins University, 1987 • M. Peltonen, ed., *The Cambridge companion to Bacon* (1996) • P. Zagorin, *Francis Bacon* (1998) • J. Martin, *Francis Bacon, the state, and the reform of natural philosophy* (1992) • J. Epstein, *Francis Bacon: a political biography* (1977) • J. Neale, *Elizabeth I and her parliaments*, 2 vols. (1953–7) • L. Jardine, *Francis Bacon: discovery and the art of discourse* (1974) • F. Bacon, *The new organon*, ed. L. Jardine and M. Silverthorne (2000) • S. Gaukroger, *Francis Bacon and the transformation of early-modern philosophy* (2001) • P. Rossi, *Francis Bacon: from magic to science* (1968) • J. Leary, *Francis Bacon and the politics of science* (1994) • E. Wolff, *Francis Bacon und seine Quellen*, 2 vols. (1910–13) • B. Wormald, *Francis Bacon: history, politics, and science, 1561–1626* (1993) • B. Vickers, 'The authenticity of Bacon's earliest writings', *Studies in Philology*, 94 (1997), 248–96 • P. Kocher, 'Francis Bacon and his father', *Huntington Library Quarterly*, 21 (1957–8), 133–58 • V. Heltzel, 'Young Francis Bacon's tutor', *Modern Language Notes*, 63 (1948), 483–5 • R. Johnson, 'Francis Bacon and Lionel Cranfield', *Huntington Library Quarterly*, 23 (1960), 301–20 • M. Peltonen, 'Francis Bacon, the earl of Northampton, and the Jacobean anti-duelling campaign', *HJ*, 44 (2001), 1–28 • A. Pérez-Ramos, *Francis Bacon's idea of science and the maker's knowledge tradition* (1988) • F. Anderson, *Francis Bacon: his career and his thought* (1962) • G. Rees, *Francis Bacon's natural philosophy: a new source* (1984) • D. Bergeron, 'Francis Bacon: an unpublished manuscript', *Papers of* *the Bibliographical Society of America*, 84 (1990), 397–404 • C. Bowen, *Francis Bacon: the temper of a man* (1963) • B. Farrington, *The philosophy of Francis Bacon: an essay on its development from 1603 to 1609* (1964) • J. Epstein, 'Francis Bacon and the issue of union, 1603–1608', *Huntington Library Quarterly*, 33 (1970), 121–32 • B. Farrington, 'Francis Bacon after his fall', *Studies in the Literary Imagination*, 4/1 (1971), 143–58 • M. Fattori, ed., *Francis Bacon, terminologia e fortuna nel XVII secolo* (1984) • D. Woolf, 'John Selden, John Borough and Francis Bacon's *History of Henry VII*, 1621', *Huntington Library Quarterly*, 47 (1984), 47–53 • E. Wood, 'Francis Bacon's "Cousin Sharpe"', *N&Q*, 196 (1951), 248–9 • V. Snow, 'Francis Bacon's advice to Fulke Greville on research techniques', *Huntington Library Quarterly*, 23 (1960), 369–78 • E. R. Foster, ed., *Proceedings in parliament, 1610*, 2 vols. (1966) • *The letters of John Chamberlain*, ed. N. E. McClure, 2 vols. (1939)

Archives BL, corresp. and papers, Add. MS 4106 • BL, memorandum book relating to public and private affairs, Add. MS 27278 • Bodl. Oxf., corresp. • Francis Bacon Library, Claremont, California, personal and family corresp. and papers • Hatfield House, Hertfordshire, letters and papers • Inner Temple, London, corresp. and papers • LPL, 'An advertisement touching the controversyes of the Church of England' • LPL, corresp. and papers • LPL, personal and family corresp. • Mirehouse, Keswick, papers and books • Queen's College, Oxford, letters • V&A NAL, confession of his faith | BL, speech on becoming Lord Keeper, copies of various works incl. essays, Harley MSS • BL, speeches and other compositions, Lansdowne MS 236 • BL, letters and speeches, Sloane MSS • CKS, corresp. with Lionel Cranfield

Likenesses coloured terracotta bust, *c*.1572, priv. coll. • N. Hilliard, miniature, 1578, Belvoir Castle, Leicestershire • attrib. W. Larkin, oils, type of *c*.1617, Trinity Cam.; version, Hardwick Hall, Derbyshire; version, LUL • attrib. A. Blyenberch, oils, *c*.1618, RS [*see illus.*] • effigy, 1630–39, St Michael's Church, St Albans • W. Marshall, line engraving, 1641 (after S. De Passe), BM, NPG; repro. in F. Bacon, *History of Henry VII* (1641) • J. Vanderbank, oils, 1731 (after A. Blyenberch, *c*.1618), NPG • J. Vanderbank, oils, 1731? (after unknown artist, *c*.1618), NPG • L. F. Roubiliac, marble bust, 1751, Trinity Cam. • W. H. Worthington, two line engravings, 1825 (after N. Hilliard), NPG • attrib. A. Blyenberch, oils, second version, NPG • S. De Passe, line engraving (after W. Larkin), BL, NPG; repro. in F. Bacon, *Sylva sylvarum* (1627) • engraving (after S. de Passe), repro. in F. Bacon, *Sylva sylvarum* (1627) • oils (after J. Vanderbank, 1731), NPG • two oil paintings, Trinity Cam.

Wealth at death c.£7000; debts £22,371 1*s*. 3*d*.; £19,658 4*s*. 4*d*.: *Works of Francis Bacon*, ed. Spedding, Ellis, and Heath, 14.352; Jardine and Stewart, *Hostage to fortune*, 513

Bacon, Sir Francis (*c*.1587–1657), judge, was the eldest of five sons and a daughter of John Bacon (*d*. 1618), of King's Lynn, and his wife, Elizabeth, daughter of Henry Paynell of Belaugh, Norfolk. He was a great-grandson of Thomas Bacon of Hessett in Suffolk. Although Hessett passed from Bury St Edmunds Abbey to the immediate ancestors of Lord Keeper Bacon, no firm links between his family and the Bacons of Hessett have been made, and their heraldry is distinct.

Bacon commenced his legal studies at Barnard's Inn, moved to Gray's Inn in February 1607, and was called to the bar in 1615. His first practice may have been either in chancery or in the provinces. About 1621 he married Elizabeth (1595–1651), daughter of William Robinson of Norwich; their eldest daughter, Barbara, was baptized at St Gregory's Church there in October 1622. The Bacons were firmly settled in the parish, paying towards the repair of the font and east window of the church, and their six sons and two daughters, all born in the 1620s, were eventually buried there, the last in 1710.

In 1634 Bacon was autumn reader at Gray's Inn; two years later the king granted him the office of drawing licences and pardons of alienations to the great seal for life, and in 1640 he was admitted serjeant-at-law. He became steward of Norwich in 1639 and recorder in 1642, the year he was appointed to the king's bench and knighted in October by the king at Bridgnorth. Parliament accepted his appointment, and, when demanding that the king dismiss several judges in February 1643, conceded 'that Mr Justice Bacon may be continued' (Clarendon, *Hist. rebellion*, 6.231). While Charles was at Oxford, Bacon was one of 'the sworn judges still at Westminster, of which there were three in number'. He presided alone in the king's bench, as his 'brothers' Reeve and Trevor did in the common pleas and exchequer (ibid., 7.317).

In 1645 Bacon was the only judge at the trial of Lord Macguire on the charge of high treason for his share in the Irish rising and massacre of 1641. Macguire had demanded to be tried by a jury of Irish peers, but 'Bacon delivered his judgment that a baron of Ireland was triable by a jury in this kingdom' (*State trials*, 4.665), and this judgment was formally approved of by both houses. When the prosecution desired 'speedy progress, this being a public case', Bacon said that 'a public case must have public justice on both sides. We must do that which the law doth allow' (ibid., 668). Bacon's impartiality was further shown when he committed James Symbal and others to prison 'for speaking of words against the king in time of war' (Whitelocke, 269). After the king's execution, new commissions were issued to the judges, requiring them to take the oath in the name of the people instead of in that of the king, and Bacon had the courage to resign. Five of his colleagues, after some hesitation, agreed to hold office, 'provided that by act of the commons the fundamental laws be not abolished' (ibid., 378).

Bacon retired to Norwich, where he soon lost his wife; she was buried at St Gregory's on 9 October 1651, aged fifty-six. He died on 22 August 1657, and was buried in the same place three days later. Their eldest son, Francis, commissioned a magnificent monument in the south-east chapel of St Thomas there. It has been wrongly stated that this Francis became reader in Gray's Inn in 1662, but in fact the Ipswich MP Francis Bacon (1600–1663) held that appointment. G. V. Benson, *rev.* J. M. Blatchly

Sources D. E. Davy's pedigree of Bacon of Lynn, BL, Add. MS 19116 • F. Blomefield, *History of Norwich* (1810), 2.272–9 • *IGI* • *State trials* • Clarendon, *Hist. rebellion*, vols. 6, 7 • B. Whitelocke, *Memorials of the English affairs* (1709)

Bacon, Francis (1600–1663), politician, was born on 30 January 1600, the fifth son of Edward *Bacon (1548/9–1618) [*see under* Bacon, Sir Nathaniel (1546?–1622)] of Shrubland Hall, Barham, Suffolk, and his wife, Helen (1564–1646), daughter and heir of Thomas Little of Bray, Berkshire. Always somewhat in the shadow of his brother Nathaniel *Bacon (*bap*. 1593, *d*. 1660), seven years his senior, Francis at least went up to a different Cambridge college, Queens', in 1617 as a fellow-commoner, but in the next year followed Nathaniel at Gray's Inn and was called to the bar eight years later. The brothers jointly presented their famous uncle Francis's works to the library of the inn in 1635, and Cave Beck dedicated his *Universal Character* to them jointly in 1657.

On 30 April 1633 Bacon married Katherine (*d.* 1660), daughter of Sir Thomas Wingfield of Letheringham, whose sister was married to William Bloyse, merchant of Ipswich, then newly established at Grundisburgh where the wedding took place. Bacon and Bloyse were lifelong colleagues; indeed Bacon bought Bloyse's house in St Nicholas's parish, Ipswich, about 1650.

The staunchly protestant Bacons of Shrubland were early supporters of the parliamentary cause. In a letter of April 1640 to John Winthrop, governor of Massachusetts, Bacon regrets having bought an estate from him, for 'if a good change come not by the Parliament I shall wish my money in my purse again and both it and myself with you' (*Winthrop Papers*, 4.228). Public life in Ipswich began for him when he was made town counsel and his brother recorder on the same day in 1642; next he became a Suffolk commissioner for assessment, for the sequestration of delinquents, and the levying of money for the war effort in 1643. Then came membership and the rotating chairmanship of the committee for the associated counties, and the hearing of evidence against scandalous ministers. When there were misgivings about the New Model Army in the seven counties, Bacon was a moderating influence.

In 1646 Bacon was first elected to parliament for Ipswich (Nathaniel representing Cambridge University), and was soon given committee responsibilities. In late 1647 he was one of those working for a peaceful settlement with the king. Secluded from the house at Pride's Purge, he was readmitted in June 1649, but did not sit with the Rump, returning to attend to Suffolk and Ipswich business. When in June 1652 the town invited the celebrated presbyterian preacher Stephen Marshall to take on its preachership, Bacon's entertainment helped secure his assent.

Nathaniel and Francis represented the town jointly from 1654 to 1660, William Bloyse sitting for the county, and Francis was a master of requests in 1656–9. Perhaps because his enthusiasm for the Commonwealth waned after Oliver Cromwell's death, he was listed as a possible member of a royalist uprising in Suffolk in 1658. Nothing came of this and in May 1660 it was the Bacons and the town clerk who were sent to Whitehall with gifts for the restored monarch; but in the 1660 Convention Francis, still pro-presbyterian, was given a manager, William Ellys.

Katherine Bacon bore her husband six sons and two daughters between 1634 and 1646, four of the sons dying young. She died at their Kensington house on 23 October 1660 and was buried at St Martin-in-the-Fields two days later. Bacon, already an ancient and bencher of his inn, was made a reader in 1662. He spent his last month at Grundisburgh where William Bloyse recorded his death on 23 September 1663; taken to London, his remains were interred next to his wife's on the 27th. He left property in Norfolk, Suffolk, and Staffordshire, and had shipping interests which possibly included trade with Danzig; his will provided mainly for his children Francis, Nathaniel, and Katherine. J. M. BLATCHLY

Sources private information (2004) [A. P. Barclay, History of Parliament Trust] · Ipswich Borough Archives · N. Bacon, *The annalls of Ipswche*, ed. W. H. Richardson (1884) · M. Candler's pedigrees of Bacon, CUL, Add. MS 6967 · parish registers, London, St Martin-in-the-Fields, City Westm. AC · parish registers, Barham, Suffolk, and Grundisburgh, Suffolk RO, Ipswich · will, PRO, PROB 11/312, sig. 117 · W. Bloyse's account book and diary, Suffolk RO, Ipswich, HA 30/787 · *The Winthrop papers*, ed. W. C. Ford and others, 4 (1944), 228

Wealth at death see will, PRO, PROB 11/312, sig. 117

Bacon, Francis (1909–1992), painter, was born on 28 October 1909 at 63 Lower Baggot Street, Dublin, the second of five children of English parents, Edward Anthony Mortimer Bacon, army officer, and his wife, Christina Winifred Firth. Bacon's father moved his family to Westbourne Terrace, London, during the First World War, when he worked in the ministry of war. After the war the family moved between England and Ireland and Bacon himself went to Dean Close School in Cheltenham, where he boarded from 1924 to 1926, frequently running away, before moving to London on an allowance provided by his mother.

Early influences In 1927 Bacon travelled to Berlin with a male friend of his father, who was entrusted with educating the young man. There Bacon was plunged into the decadent night-life of Weimar Germany, which after the puritanism of his Irish upbringing had a permanent impact. No less important were the subsequent months Bacon spent in Paris, where, in the summer of 1927, at the Galerie Pierre Rosenberg, he discovered Picasso's recent drawings. Picasso's depictions of figures on the beach at Dinard had a profound effect on Bacon.

In 1928 Bacon returned to London, where from 1929 to 1932 he lived in Queensberry Mews in South Kensington. There he worked designing modernist rugs and furniture, stylistically indebted to Le Corbusier and Eileen Gray. He rapidly established a reputation as a designer, being featured in a double-page spread in *Studio* in 1930 and receiving celebrated commissions including furniture for the kitchen of the politician R. A. Butler and a desk for the writer Patrick White. He also began to paint in oils for the first time, producing works that owed much to surrealism and cubism. Influenced by his friend and mentor, the Australian painter Roy de Maistre, in 1930 Bacon held an exhibition of five paintings and four rugs at his studio. Thereafter he turned increasingly to painting but it was another three years before his first significant paintings were exhibited, in two group shows at the Mayor Gallery, London, in 1933. One of these works, *Crucifixion* (1933; priv. coll.), was prestigiously illustrated in Herbert Read's *Art Now* (1933), opposite one of Picasso's paintings of a bather.

In February 1934 Bacon staged an unsuccessful exhibition of thirteen works in a cellar in Curzon Street in Mayfair. Visiting Paris again in 1935, Bacon purchased a book illustrated with colour plates entitled *Diseases of the Mouth*

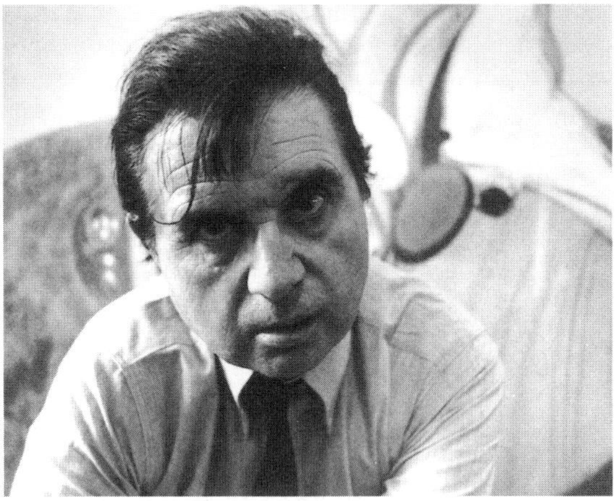

Francis Bacon (1909–1992), by John Hedgecoe, 1970

and this, together with seeing for the first time Sergei Eisenstein's film *Battleship Potemkin*, had a profound effect on him. Not only did he use stills from the film as source material but it also encouraged a tougher figurative dimension. Bacon's path was set and in the years that followed his painful vision of man and his predicament became one of the most recognizable, if horrific, bodies of work of the second half of the twentieth century.

Bacon's work was proposed for inclusion in the celebrated International Surrealist Exhibition, of 1936, being organized for London by Roland Penrose, Herbert Read, and André Breton, but he was famously judged by the Englishmen to be insufficiently surrealist. It was, however, a fortuitous rejection since subsequently it was Bacon's 'realism' that was at the centre of the claims made for him.

In January 1937 Thomas Agnew & Sons staged an exhibition, 'Young British Painters', which included a painting that Bacon had only just completed but which he subsequently destroyed. Entitled *Abstraction from the Human Form*, it depicted a semi-human figure and demonstrated that even before the Second World War Bacon had not only formulated but also was publicly exhibiting his tormented vision of the world. Already he was using photographs of contemporary events; drawing attention to the mouth; and presenting metonymic segments of the body, which is shown as bulbous and swollen.

Major works A chronic asthmatic from childhood, Bacon was declared unfit for military service, and spent the Second World War in London, where with the aid of his former nanny he held gambling parties. By 1942 Bacon was living in Cromwell Place, South Kensington, where he began to build on his pre-war imagery to produce his first major paintings, including a work that did more than any other to establish his reputation as one of the most powerful and horrifying painters of the twentieth century: *Three Studies for Figures at the Base of a Crucifixion* (1944; Tate collection). Against a fiery orange background three barely human figures provide a compendium of injuries: torsos are swollen and deformed, ribs scarred and dirtied, heads wounded and bandaged, and each mouth strains at the end of a taut spinal column. The exhibition of this triptych at a group show at the Lefevre Gallery in 1945 established Bacon's post-war reputation. Subsequently Bacon claimed this as his first mature work, even going so far as to destroy as much earlier work as he could. The result of this was to identify Bacon's work with the Second World War and to provide it with roots in the 1940s, not the 1930s. This had profound implications for readings of the artist's work, not as late flowering surrealism but as contemporary realism.

In November 1949 the Hanover Gallery, London, staged the first one-man exhibition of Francis Bacon. One of the seminal events in post-war British culture, this show was a revelation. The exhibition included full-length figures as well as a series of tormented heads culminating in one of Bacon's most confident early paintings, *Head VI* (1949; Arts Council collection, Hayward Gallery, London). A half-length portrait, this was the first painting in the most celebrated series that Bacon ever produced: a series from 1949 showing a boxed, screaming pope which established Bacon's international reputation. Bacon developed this theme during the early 1950s, taking as a starting point Velázquez's *Portrait of Pope Innocent X* (1650; Palazzo Doria Pamphilj, Rome). Bacon's pope, enthroned and enclosed by a box, drew attention to the discrepancy between the belief systems present at the time of Velázquez and modern discrediting of religious authority. Their contemporary resonance gained potency through the publication of photographs showing the Nuremberg trials of Nazi war criminals, boxed behind glass for their own protection. Although the origins of Bacon's vision lay with paintings of oppressors, including Nazi leaders, the subsequent status of these paintings depended on reading the tormented individuals as Everyman figures: a conflation of oppressor and victim.

Contemporary assessment of Bacon's work The first major essays on Francis Bacon established readings which remain largely in place. The two most important were by Robert Melville in the British publication *Horizon* in 1949 and Sam Hunter in the American *Magazine of Art* in 1952. The former became the basis for subsequent European responses to the artist, most pervasively that of David Sylvester, who became one of the artist's greatest champions, while the latter criticism was almost entirely neglected by all subsequent critics except Lawrence Alloway. Although both pioneering essays derived from conversations with Bacon, their emphasis was fundamentally different. Hunter provided an emphatically British context, including references to Wyndham Lewis, William Blake, Gainsborough, Turner, Sickert, and even Beardsley, and wrote of the importance of London to the artist. Melville, in contrast, developed a European context for Bacon's tormented vision through references to Dostoevsky and Kafka, to Dalí and Buñuel's film *Un chien andalou*, Picasso's 'air of extreme hazard', and Eisenstein's film *Battleship Potemkin*.

Both authors also emphasized the contemporary resonance of Bacon's work, a feature that helped him assume pre-eminence in the London art scene of the 1950s. However, while Hunter's text and accompanying photograph of Bacon's source material made a direct link between Bacon's paintings and his collecting of photographs of major international events and political leaders, including photographs of Goebbels and of Moscow at the time of the Russian Revolution, Melville instead gave a more elevated reading. This lacked such direct references and instead argued that 'Modern Painting has suddenly been humanised', proposing that '*Un Chien Andalou* has greater visual force and lucidity than anything achieved in the art of painting between the two wars ... only the recent paintings of Francis Bacon have discovered a comparable means of disclosing the human condition' (Melville).

In keeping with his belief that the image should act as an assault on the nervous system rather than a stimulus for the intellect, Bacon denied that he made preparatory studies for his paintings, preferring to emphasize the immediacy of chance to generate his images. This denial did much to discourage writers from pinning specific sources to his imagery and instead to stress a conflation of sources that extracts his work from being mere storytelling or illustration: a painting may be a portrait of an individual, but rarely is he, or occasionally she, identified. Only after his death were drawings by, and attributed to, Bacon publicized, published, and exhibited. Generally scrappy and weak, they were clearly personal notations that he did not consider worthy of exhibition but which none the less provide a revealing insight into his studio procedure and indicate a greater degree of planning than interviews with Bacon had suggested.

International reputation Bacon's international reputation grew dramatically. As early as 1948 the Museum of Modern Art in New York bought his important early work *Painting, 1946*. Then in 1953 he had his first one-man show at Durlacher Bros. in New York and in 1957 at the Galeries Rive Droite in Paris. In 1954 he also received major official recognition, representing Britain at the Venice Biennale together with Lucian Freud and Ben Nicholson.

Such events provided an international context for Bacon and consolidated existentialist readings of his work. Indeed, from as early as his first one-man show in 1949, he was associated with existentialism, as in a review by Nevile Wallis:

> Bacon's work is the most profoundly disquieting manifestation I have yet seen of that malaise, which since the last war, has inspired the philosophy of Sartre [There is] a literary parallel in Kafka's nightmares of frustration, which largely owed their inspiration to Kierkegaard's philosophy of despair. (N. Wallis, 'Nightmares', *The Observer*, 26 Nov 1949)

Sylvester, too, provided just such a context for Bacon. In 1952, in his first major essay on the artist, an article for *The Listener*, he referred to Bacon's enclosed spaces with direct reference to Sartre's *Huis clos*, quoting Garcin's 'Eh bien, continuons' and asserting that 'life is hell and we had better get used to the idea' (D. Sylvester, 'The paintings of Francis Bacon', *The Listener*, 47, 3 Jan 1952, 28–9).

In 1955 the Institute of Contemporary Arts in London held the first retrospective exhibition of Bacon's work, presenting thirteen paintings. In that same year an Arts Council retrospective of the work of Alberto Giacometti was also held in London. These two retrospectives did much to stimulate figurative art in Britain and to encourage supportive critics to discern an element of torment within their presentation of the human condition. Certainly Bacon paralleled Giacometti, in whose sculptures movement, whether potential or actual, suggests vulnerability and fear. Bacon's decisive, transitional group of paintings of a head that he began in 1948 has striking formal and conceptual links with Giacometti's caged nose, *The Nose* (Centre Pompidou, Paris) of the previous year. Both are concerned with movement: Giacometti allows actual movement while Bacon suggests twisting. Both use boxing to draw attention to the space in which the subject moves: Giacometti provides a box and Bacon an armature. Both emphasize a single element of the face as a metonym of the whole: Giacometti emphasizes the nose and mouth, Bacon simply the gaping mouth. Both, too, concentrated on the single figure and sought to deny narrative readings of their work.

Connecting directly 'with the nervous system' Bacon became notorious for his social life. An inveterate drinker and gambler, he loved chance, risk, and danger in his life. A focus in London was the Colony Room drinking club in Soho, which opened in 1949 and whose founder, Muriel Belcher, later one of the artist's subjects, employed Bacon to bring in people. Other regulars included a circle of Bacon's artist friends, among them the figurative painters Lucian Freud, Michael Andrews, and Frank Auerbach. Bacon's day began early and despite the incorporation of chance effects in his painting he followed a disciplined routine. Exhausting mornings of work in his small studio gave way to the release of life as a drinker and gambler in Soho when he mixed as freely with East End criminals as he did with the landed aristocracy. His extraordinary appearance—with his moon face and leather jacket—and his life of immense highs and lows contributed much to his status as the leading British artist of the last half-century: an extremist in both art and life.

Bacon was celebrated for the emotional impact of his work and for his desire to connect directly 'with the nervous system' rather than the intellect. He wanted, he explained, to show the effect, but not its cause, for example preferring to paint the anguished figures at the base of the crucifixion rather than the crucifixion itself. This allusiveness was praised for facilitating the metaphoric potential of his work as a revelation of the human condition, although this indirectness may also have had a more personal resonance that was fuelled by the artist's own anxiety. Indeed in one of Bacon's most powerful early works there is an intimation of why the painter's anxiety might have been so acute.

Two Figures (1953; priv. coll.) presents a darkened room in which two men, himself and Peter Lacey, make love on a bed. The vertical lines that run down the picture veil the figures and suggest a view glimpsed through a curtain, thereby placing the viewer outside the room, as if spying on the men. In this way the painting embodies the clandestine nature of an action at a time when homosexuality was still illegal in Britain. In *Two Figures* anxiety about the state monitoring and constraining the individual was expressed at a time of acute insecurity for homosexuals. A manifesto painting, *Two Figures* remained unexhibited until the Tate Gallery's retrospective exhibition of Bacon's work in 1962.

Dust and shadows Whereas in Bacon's pre-war and wartime paintings the range of colours had been wide, and paintings of the mid-1940s had used a strong, dominant orange, from the later 1940s until 1956–7 Bacon instead presented a dark realism of dust and shadows in which man is alone in a void.

Colour returned to Bacon's work in the Hanover Gallery's dramatic exhibition in 1957 of his recent paintings. However, this was a show that suggested a crisis of direction for the artist. While American abstract expressionism was resurgent in Europe, Bacon presented some of the least convincing and most uncharacteristic paintings of his career. The exhibition was dominated by a series of paintings based on a photographic reproduction of Van Gogh's *Painter on the Road to Tarascon*, which had been destroyed in the Second World War. The dark and dusty paintings upon which Bacon's reputation rested were replaced by heightened colour and the recent use of thin stained grounds and dusty smearings gave way to thick, free, allover painting. Despite their suggested movement, Bacon's earlier paintings had coherence; these latest pictures seemed uncomfortably hurried. The application of paint is slapdash rather than exhilarating, and the picture surface a dead end, not a space to be explored. Fortunately for his reputation, this moment was short-lived and Bacon subsequently derided most of these paintings. However, the lessons he learned about colour dramatically transformed his work through a series of paintings heralded by Bacon's triptych *Three Studies for a Crucifixion* (1962; Guggenheim Museum, New York), which formed the climax of his Tate Gallery retrospective in 1962.

By the time of this exhibition Bacon had moved from the Hanover Gallery to the Marlborough Gallery where he stayed from 1958 until his death. The devoted support and understanding he received there, above all from Valerie Beston, together with the Tate Gallery's retrospective, did much to consolidate Bacon's reputation.

Multi-figure compositions From the early 1960s Bacon created some of his most ambitious multi-figure compositions in which, for the first time, he placed at the centre of his efforts the exploration of his themes through the use of a large-scale triptych format, first used in 1944, to produce some of his most ambitious paintings. In 1961 he found a new studio at Reece Mews where he remained until his death. Although he had other studios, it was here that he did the majority of his paintings for the next thirty years. During the 1960s his range of colours widened and Bacon developed the interior settings that had previously been so stark, and introduced an ambiguous psychological dimension to his work. The possibilities of the triptych, using three canvases, each separately framed, allowed Bacon to show his figures to be at the same time related and separated. Several of these figures were based on Bacon's partner, George Dyer, with whom he became involved in 1963. Controversially, in one of the most powerful of all these triptychs, *Crucifixion* (1965; Staatsgalerie Moderner Kunst, Munich) one of the onlookers wears an armband bearing a swastika to suggest a more specific contemporary resonance than Bacon usually allowed. During 1965–6 he gave increasing attention to painting small triptychs of heads. He had painted the first of these, *Three Studies of the Human Head* (priv. coll.), in 1953, but now followed this early precedent in a memorable series of portraits of friends, including Isabel Rawsthorne, Muriel Belcher, and Lucian Freud. Reviewers likened this use of three views of the same subject to police mugshots of full-face and profile. This interpretation was encouraged by knowledge of Bacon's own use of public photo machines to provide him with source material.

By the late 1960s the settings of Bacon's paintings had become more sophisticated, with spatial distortion often turning rectangular boxes into spheres to suggest subjects trapped in a paperweight. Mirrors also began to play a central part in allowing Bacon to combine more than one view of the subject and to chart different forms of fragmentation and dissolution. An immensely cultured man, Bacon drew inspiration from multifarious sources, sometimes making these explicit through his use of titles, as in *Triptych Inspired by T. S. Eliot's Poem 'Sweeney Agonistes'* (1967; Hirshhorn Museum, Smithsonian Institution, Washington, DC) and *Triptych Inspired by the 'Oresteia' of Aeschylus* (1981; priv. coll.).

World acclaim In October 1971 the Grand Palais in Paris staged a major Francis Bacon retrospective that was dominated by his triptychs. Sadly the event, which should have been one of the triumphs of Bacon's life, was marred by tragedy: on the eve of the opening, Bacon's partner, George Dyer, committed suicide in their Paris hotel room. Bacon commemorated Dyer's death in ensuing paintings, including a triptych entitled *Triptych in Memory of George Dyer* (November–December 1971; Foundation Beyeler collection, Switzerland). From 1974 Bacon had an apartment in Paris, such was his love for the city and its culture. He did little work there but established deep friendships, and the leading French intellectual Michel Leiris became one of his most articulate champions. In 1974 Bacon met John Edwards, with whom he formed a close paternal relationship, and Edwards was later named as his sole heir.

The Metropolitan Museum of Art's exhibition 'Francis Bacon: Recent Paintings, 1968–74', in 1975, was the first time that works by a contemporary British artist had been shown by the museum. In the same year David Sylvester's interviews with Francis Bacon were published. Immensely revealing, the interviews provide insights not only into Bacon's art and times but also the art of the past.

By the 1980s Bacon received major accolades, exhibitions, and tributes. In 1983 a first retrospective of Bacon's work was held in Japan, travelling to Tokyo, Kyoto, and Nagoya. Two years later the Tate Gallery held its second Bacon retrospective, an exhibition that travelled to the Staatsgalerie in Stuttgart and the Nationalgalerie in Berlin. In 1988 even the Soviet Union staged a Bacon retrospective, an almost unprecedented honour for a Western artist that was balanced by transatlantic acclaim the following year, when a major exhibition was held in America, travelling to the Hirshhorn Museum in Washington, the Los Angeles County Museum, and the Museum of Modern Art in New York.

Later years By this time one of the striking features of Bacon's *œuvre* had become the consistency of his vision and the rigour with which he focused on his themes. He occasionally also made surprising, powerful statements on subjects that were otherwise peripheral to his concerns. In the 1950s Bacon had painted memorable depictions of animals, most movingly in paintings of 1952 and 1953 of a prowling dog, and in the early and mid-1950s of a caged chimpanzee. Although landscapes are virtually absent from his *œuvre*, Bacon did produce a turbulently evocative painting of dusty ground and windswept trees entitled *Landscape near Malabata, Tangier* (1963; priv. coll.). Two extraordinary paintings of the 1980s, both set in indeterminate indoor–outdoor spaces, provide a remarkable climax to this little pursued theme: the smudgy *Sand Dune* (1981; priv. coll.) and the ejaculatory *Jet of Water* (1988; Marlborough International Fine Art, London). Together these paintings not only demonstrated Bacon's brilliant handling of paint, but also provided a riposte to a Romantic vision of nature. His increasing use of the airbrush as a painting technique resulted in innovative textural effects. There were spectacular successes during this decade, especially his portraits of John Edwards of 1986–8, but there were also accusations that his work had become formulaic, less engaged, and lacking in tension. Bacon decided to paint a second, larger version of his seminal early painting *Three Studies for Figures at the Base of a Crucifixion*. This new version, *Second Version of Triptych, 1944* (1988; Tate collection) replaced the poignantly scruffy original with an altogether grander, more imperial version, something Bacon had long wished to do. The result was not without critics: they felt that the grander dimensions and slicker painting technique of this second version resulted in pastiche, which robbed the original of much of its charge. He nevertheless continued to provide new insights into existing themes through increasingly spare paintings in which he pared down the settings and concentrated on essential anatomical details. In *Triptych, 1991* (priv. coll.), Bacon's last triptych and his final statement of mortality, his general theme, there is a tremendous sense of desolation and loneliness. Much of each canvas is left bare and a defining feature is the dark square against which the figure is set: an engulfing void with intimations of death. A few months later, on 28 April 1992, Bacon died in Madrid where he had been visiting a friend. He was buried in Almudeña cemetery, Madrid. He was internationally the most acclaimed British painter of the twentieth century. JAMES HYMAN

Sources M. Leiris, *Francis Bacon: full face and in profile* (1983) · M. Leiris, *Francis Bacon* (1988) · D. Sylvester, *The brutality of fact: interviews with Francis Bacon*, 3rd edn (1987) · J. Russell, *Francis Bacon*, rev. edn (1993) · *Francis Bacon*, Centre Georges Pompidou, Paris (Paris, 1996) · M. Peppiatt, *Francis Bacon: anatomy of an enigma* (1996) · J. Hyman, *The battle for realism* (2001) · b. cert. · S. Hunter, 'Francis Bacon: the anatomy of horror', *Magazine of Art*, 45 (1952), 11–15 · R. Melville, 'Francis Bacon', *Horizon*, 20/120–21 (Dec 1949–Jan 1950), 419–23

Archives Tate collection, drawings and notes concerning his paintings | NRA, priv. coll., corresp. with Sir Robert Sainsbury and Lady Sainsbury, relating to exhibitions of his work · Tate collection, corresp. and papers of Ronald Alley | FILM BFI NFTVA, *The works*, BBC2, 7 May 1996 · BFI NFTVA, *Post mortem*, Channel 4, 25 Oct 1997 · BFI NFTVA, *Arthouse*, Channel 4, 2 Aug 1998 · BFI NFTVA, documentary footage

Likenesses photographs, 1960–85, Hult. Arch. · I. Penn, platinum palladium print, 1962, NPG · C. Barker, gilt-bronze mask, 1969, NPG · J. Hedgecoe, platinum print, 1970, NPG [*see illus.*] · A. Newman, bromide print, 1975, NPG · C. Shenstone, conté, *c*.1982, NPG · R. Spear, oils, 1984, NPG · L. Freud, portrait, Tate collection

Wealth at death £11,370,244: probate, 24 Nov 1992, *CGPLA Eng. & Wales*

Bacon, Francis Thomas [Tom] **(1904–1992)**, engineer and developer of the fuel cell, was born on 21 December 1904 at Ramsden Hall, Ramsden Crays, Billericay, Essex, the second of three sons of Thomas Walter Bacon (1863–1950), electrical engineer, and his wife, Edith Mary, *née* Leslie-Melville (1864–1950). On his father's side Bacon traced his ancestry to Sir Nicholas Bacon (1509–1579), lord keeper of the great seal in the time of Elizabeth I, and father (by his second marriage) of Sir Francis Bacon (1561–1626), the philosopher and lord chancellor of England. Tom Bacon, as he was universally called, devoted his life to the development of the fuel cell, which he always believed offered the possibility of power without the pollution associated with internal combustion engines. Fuel cells, which convert the chemical energy of a fuel directly into electricity, were discovered by Sir William Grove in 1839 but, despite high theoretical efficiencies, remained a scientific curiosity until Bacon, adopting the approach of a creative engineer, developed a viable power source which provided the electrical power for the Apollo spacecraft for man's first voyage to the moon.

Bacon was educated first at St Peter's Court preparatory school in Broadstairs, Kent, and then at Eton College from 1918 to 1922, gaining the school physics prize in 1922. From Eton he went to Trinity College, Cambridge, taking the mechanical sciences tripos in 1925. After Cambridge he became an apprentice with C. A. Parsons & Co. Ltd, in Newcastle. He was related to and strongly influenced by Sir Charles Parsons, who was described by Bacon as 'a marvellous man with the great quality of always keeping an open mind' (Williams, 3). After his apprenticeship in various departments he was responsible for the development and production of reflectors for searchlights and lights for the then fast growing film industry. During this period, on

Francis Thomas Bacon (1904–1992), by Lucinda Douglas-Menzies, 1987

4 August 1934, he married Barbara Winifred Papillon (1905/6–2000), daughter of Godfrey Keppel Papillon, estate agent, of the Manor House, Barrasford, Northumberland. They had two sons and one daughter.

Inspired by two articles in the periodical *Engineering* in 1932 Bacon began to contemplate the possibility of storing energy in the form of hydrogen and releasing it as electricity. Following Grove he first used platinum as catalyst and sulphuric acid as electrolyte. Hydrogen and oxygen were the two reacting gases. However, in order to reduce costs and improve power output, Bacon subsequently used nickel catalysts and potassium hydroxide as electrolyte. His original experiments were conducted clandestinely at Parsons but when he was discovered he was told either to stop them as not being relevant to the business or to leave; he left. Unlike many inventors he had independent means, his father having settled an appreciable portion of the family estate on him at an early age. This meant that throughout his life he was able to pursue his goal of power without pollution. In this aim the unwavering support of his wife, Barbara, was crucial. Also of great significance was Bacon's personal charm, which enabled him to gain support and finance from many quarters.

The first concrete support for Bacon's work came from Charles Merz, founder of the consulting engineers Merz and McClellan, who agreed to finance experiments at King's College, London, in Professor A. J. Allmand's laboratory. Many problems were encountered, and although initially it was hoped that fuel cells could be used to power submarines, by late 1941 it was clear that this was not likely to be viable in the short term. Bacon was then directed to research on ASDIC (underwater submarine detection) at Fairlie in Scotland.

After numerous rebuffs from industry, some of which were openly derisive, the Electrical Research Association agreed to sponsor fuel cell research, and in 1946 Bacon and his wife settled in a house in 19 acres in Little Shelford, Cambridgeshire, with their three children, Francis (the eldest, who died when twenty-three), Daphne, and Edward. Work was carried out successively in the departments of colloid science, metallurgy, and chemical engineering at Cambridge University from 1946 to 1956. Although a six-cell 150 watt unit was demonstrated at a London exhibition, no interest was shown by industry; the team disbanded and the apparatus was transferred to an outhouse on Bacon's estate. After an anxious six months of inactivity for Bacon, Lord Halsbury, the managing director of the National Research Development Corporation, agreed to finance further development of the Bacon fuel cell. Arthur Marshall, of Marshalls of Cambridge, provided the necessary facilities, and, with a very happy, competent team of engineers and chemists, under the scientific direction of Bacon, and not without overcoming many difficulties, developed a 6 kW system in 1959.

Although there was no interest in Britain the Leesona-Moos organization in the USA took out a licence which was then exploited by the Pratt and Whitney Division of United Aircraft to provide a highly efficient (75 per cent) power source for the Apollo moon project, the exhaust providing drinking water for the astronauts and humidification of the spacecraft atmosphere. After the success of the space mission Bacon was widely honoured, being invited to 10 Downing Street to meet the astronauts. On a visit Bacon made to the United States, President Nixon put his arm around his shoulders and said 'Without you Tom, we wouldn't have gotten to the Moon' (Williams, 13).

Bacon received many honours including being made OBE (civil division) in 1967 and a fellow of the Royal Society in 1973; he received the Churchill gold medal of the Society of Engineers in 1972. For the rest of his life he continued to promote the fuel cell with its potential for clean power. He died at his home, Trees, 34 High Street, Little Shelford, Cambridgeshire, of heart failure, on 24 May 1992. He was buried at All Saints' Church, Little Shelford, on 1 June. He was survived by his wife, Barbara, his daughter, Daphne, and his son Edward. His papers were deposited with the Archives Centre of Churchill College, Cambridge. KEITH R. WILLIAMS

Sources K. R. Williams, *Memoirs FRS*, 39 (1994), 3–18 · P. Farley, *Project X* (1970) · *The Times* (1 June 1992) · *The Independent* (3 June 1992) · *WWW*, 1991–5 · b. cert. · m. cert. · d. cert. · private information (2004) [family]

Archives CAC Cam., corresp. and papers

Likenesses C. Shenstone, conté-pencil drawing, *c*.1982, NPG · L. Douglas-Menzies, photograph, 1987, NPG [*see illus.*] · J. H. Hallett, oils, repro. in *Memoirs FRS*; priv. coll. · photograph, repro. in *Memoirs FRS* · photograph, repro. in *The Times* · photograph, repro. in *The Independent*

Wealth at death £495,852: probate, 19 Jan 1993, *CGPLA Eng. & Wales*

Bacon, George Washington (1829/30–1922), map publisher, was the son of George Washington Bacon and his wife, Sarah Anne, of London, and younger brother of Benjamin. Nothing is known of his education. He is reported to have started business in London in 1860 and is described as the 'American map publisher' who about 1862 traded from 48 Paternoster Row, London, publishing biographies of American presidents and political guides to the United States and acting as agent to the American atlas producer J. H. Coltton. In 1866 the firm was appointed agent for Ordnance Survey publications, but in 1867 Bacon and his partner, Francis Apperson, were declared bankrupt and their stock auctioned off. By 1868 Bacon was back in business at 337 Strand, publishing mainly British material. By 1870 his Strand Map Establishment, of 127 Strand, was selling mainly maps and atlases, but also domestic equipment such as sewing machines. The specialization in cartography was reinforced in October 1893 when he took over the important map business founded by James Wyld the elder. Bacon was elected fellow of the Royal Geographical Society in 1896. He retired as managing director in 1912, but remained a director until his death. In 1919 the firm moved to Norwich Street, London.

In 1869 Bacon acquired from Cassells maps which had appeared with the *Weekly Dispatch* from 1852 to 1862, and used them as the basis for numerous atlases and map series of Britain and the rest of the world published between 1869 and 1907 and presented as new and up to date. Equally out-of-date material was acquired from other publishers. Most remarkably the firm published from about 1885 until the 1920s maps printed from copper plates first used in 1792. Bacon also commonly plagiarized the maps of others and in 1900 was judged to have infringed copyright. It has been his town maps that have won widest praise, particularly those of London since they collectively constitute the finest record of the rapidly expanding capital. He also published thematic town maps (particularly of London), maps of military actions around the world, and comic cartographical interpretations of military and political events by Frederick Rose and others. He was quick to seize the publishing opportunities offered by the education boom of the late nineteenth century, issuing numerous school worksheets and materials covering geography and other subjects. In his lifetime Bacon was best known for his cycling, excursion, and touring maps, published in large numbers in a bewildering variety of attractive sizes, formats, and scales. He bought in all sorts of maps from other publishers, or simply plagiarized them to create touring maps which, although occasionally excellent, were generally of dubious reliability and poor quality. The maximum life was wrung from every product and the same maps were repackaged under different titles in attractively coloured pictorial covers. When the committee on the sale of Ordnance Survey maps called Bacon to give evidence on this genre of travelling map in 1896 it recognized his position as market leader. As well as publishing maps Bacon patented and marketed pseudo-medical cures and gadgets and wrote health guides.

Bacon died at his home, Woodlawn, Bacon Hill, Hindhead, Surrey, on 21 January 1922, at the age of ninety-two. With his wife, Ruth, he had a daughter, Alice Stanley Bacon, who survived him and was his sole executrix. He was an opportunist who exploited the map market to the full. His publications were rarely cartographically original, but frequently broke new ground in format and price and did much to make maps widely available and affordable. David Smith

Sources D. Smith, 'George Washington Bacon, 1862–*c*.1900', *Map Collector*, 65 (1993) • R. Hyde, *Printed maps of Victorian London, 1851–1900* (1975) • R. Hyde, *The A to Z of Victorian London* (1987) [introduction] • D. Smith, *Victorian maps of the British Isles* (1985) • *CGPLA Eng. & Wales* (1922) • *IGI* • private information (2004)

Wealth at death £113 3s: probate, 22 April 1922, *CGPLA Eng. & Wales*

Bacon, Sir James (1798–1895), judge, was born on 11 February 1798, the son of James Bacon and his wife, Catherine Day, of Manchester. His father was a certificated conveyancer between 1805 and 1825 and barrister of Middle Temple.

On 4 April 1822 Bacon joined Gray's Inn, and was called to the bar on 16 May 1827. He also joined Lincoln's Inn on 3 October 1833, and on 8 May 1845 became barrister there. On becoming queen's counsel he was elected bencher on 2 November 1846 and treasurer in 1869.

On 23 April 1827 Bacon married Laura Frances (*d.* 1859), daughter of William Cook of Clay Hill, Enfield, Middlesex; they had at least two sons.

Bacon practised on the home circuit and the Surrey sessions. He also reported and wrote for the press and was said to have been a sub-editor of *The Times*. Eventually he specialized in conveyancing, chancery, and bankruptcy business.

In 1859 Bacon was appointed under-secretary and secretary of causes to the master of the rolls, and on 7 September 1868 commissioner in bankruptcy for the London district, becoming chief judge under the Bankruptcy Act of 1869 until its repeal in 1883, and transfer of the bankruptcy jurisdiction to the Queen's Bench Division of the High Court of Justice. Having succeeded Sir William James as vice-chancellor on 2 July 1870, Bacon held the two offices until 1883. He was knighted on 14 January 1871.

The Judicature Acts of 1873 and 1875 allowed existing vice-chancellors to keep their titles for life, giving them the status of justices of the High Court, but provided that no more vice-chancellors would be appointed. Though considerably older, Bacon outlived his fellow vice-chancellors, Malins, Wickens, and Hall, and so became the last vice-chancellor, a post whose creation in 1813 he could remember.

Bacon continued as vice-chancellor after 1883. He was still in good health when he retired on 10 November 1886 at the age of eighty-eight. He was then sworn in as a member of the privy council (26 November 1886). Soon afterwards Bacon told one of the leaders of his court, Mr Miller, that if he had known how pleasant leisure was, he would have retired sooner. Bacon died of old age at his home, 1 Kensington Gardens Terrace, Hyde Park, London, on 1 June 1895.

Bacon's career spanned an era of incessant and unprecedented reform. It was perhaps no wonder that as vice-chancellor he showed some of the foibles of an old practitioner confronted with a new order or that many of his judgments were reversed or modified on appeal. Bacon was a courteous judge who liked to liven up court proceedings with humour and wit. He was a clever cartoonist and his illustrated trial notes were much appreciated by the lords justices of appeal. Lord Coleridge said: 'A man of keener intellect, of more vigorous health of mind and body, at 90, I never met.'

J. M. RIGG, *rev.* HUGH MOONEY

Sources *The Times* (3 June 1895) • J. Foster, *The peerage, baronetage, and knightage of the British empire for 1882*, 2 [1882] • *Annual Register* (1895), pt 2, p. 183 • *Law Times* (8 June 1894) • *Law Journal* (8 June 1895) • *Law Journal* (17 Feb 1894) • *Law Journal* (13 Nov 1886) • Burke, *Peerage* • J. Foster, *Men-at-the-bar: a biographical hand-list of the members of the various inns of court*, 2nd edn (1885) • *Law List* (1885) • *Law List* (1871) • *Law List* (1869) • *Law List* (1847) • *Clarke's New Law List* (1838) • *Clarke's New Law List* (1806–14) • W. Ballantine, *From the old world to the new* (1884), 209 • R. Palmer, first earl of Selborne, *Memorials*, ed. S. M. Palmer, 2 pts in 4 vols. (1896–8), vol. 1, p. 291; vol. 2, p. 64 • W. P. Baildon, ed., *The records of the Honorable Society of Lincoln's Inn* [incl. *Admissions*, 2 vols. (1896), and *Black books*, 6 vols. (1897–2001)] • J. Foster, *The register of admissions to Gray's Inn, 1521–1889, together with the register of marriages in Gray's Inn chapel, 1695–1754* (privately printed, London, 1889) • *Pump Court* (Feb 1895)

Archives LPL, letters to Lord Selborne

Likenesses J. E. Boehm, marble statue, 1879, Lincoln's Inn, London • London Stereoscopic Company, carte-de-visite, NPG • Spy [L. Ward], pencil drawing, NPG • photograph, NPG • wood-engraving, NPG; repro. in *ILN*, 57 (1870), 497

Wealth at death £136,465 8*s*. 6*d*.: probate, 20 June 1895, *CGPLA Eng. & Wales*

Bacon, Jane, Lady Bacon [*née* Jane Meautys; *other married name* Jane Cornwallis, Lady Cornwallis] (**1580/81–1659**), letter-writer, was the daughter of Hercules Meautys of West Ham, Essex, and Philippe, daughter of Richard Cooke of Gidea Hall, Essex. Her grandfather Sir Peter Meautys, who was descended from an ancient French family which had come from Normandy with Henry VII, was made ambassador to France by Henry VIII.

Jane is known mainly through a collection of correspondence written to her by family and friends in the period 1613–44 and lodged in the Braybrooke archives at Essex Record Office (D/DBy C11–27). 200 of these letters were transcribed and edited by Richard Neville, third Baron Braybrooke (1783–1858), and published anonymously in 1842 as *The Private Correspondence of Jane, Lady Cornwallis, 1613–1644*.

In 1608 Jane married, as his second wife, Sir William Cornwallis (*d*. 1611) of Brome, Suffolk, eldest son and heir of Sir Thomas *Cornwallis (*d*. 1604), sheriff of Norfolk and Suffolk. Sir William died in 1611, when Frederick, his and Jane's only child, was just one year and three days old, leaving Jane a substantial fortune and entitlement to the profits of the manors of Brome, Oakley, Stuston, Thrandeston, and Palgrave. Previously she had had settled upon her the manor of Wilton in the North Riding of Yorkshire, with lands in several adjoining parishes. Her husband's will, unusually for the time, stipulated that she alone would become legal guardian of their son and heir, with full responsibility for his upbringing, education, and training. Jane took on this role with serious and protective intent.

Being young and richly endowed Lady Cornwallis had several suitors, although she was in no particular hurry to remarry. In early 1613 negotiations began for a union with Nathaniel *Bacon (1585–1627), amateur painter and youngest son of twelve children of Sir Nicholas Bacon of Redgrave in Suffolk, premier baronet of England, and Anne Thornage; the courtship's delicate negotiations are recorded in Jane's published correspondence, which includes several letters from her future husband. Jane was evidently quite competent in managing her own affairs and showed herself an excellent woman of business. Her primary concern was to protect her son's inheritance but she also needed assurance that she was being sought for herself and not merely for her fortune. She insisted that Nathaniel both relinquish all claim to the Cornwallis estate and increase his own settlement, making proper provision for her in the event of his death. She seems to have driven a hard bargain for the Bacons finally agreed to settle the family estate at Culford in Suffolk, which by rights should have gone to the eldest son, Edmund.

The marriage took place quietly in the spring of 1614 and Jane's brother, Sir Thomas Meautys, wrote that he did not hear about it until the following winter, being with the forces of the prince of Orange in the Low Countries. Jane kept the Cornwallis name until her second husband was made knight of the Bath at the coronation of Charles I in 1626, after which time she is referred to in the letters as Lady Bacon.

Lady Bacon's preference was for the peaceful life of the country, and she only reluctantly visited London, much to the regret, as is revealed in the correspondence, of her friends in the city, who included Lucy Russell, countess of Bedford (1581–1627). The letters suggest that Lady Bacon must have been unwell in her confinements and was at times of a melancholic disposition. She was, however, exceedingly generous to her family and friends, and she particularly supported her brother and sister-in-law, whose pleading letters from abroad give some indication of the hardships endured at the time by soldiers' wives. Moreover she became guardian of her nephew as well as of her son Frederick's children.

There are few letters written by Lady Bacon herself but the reader gets to know her well through the letters she received, including those from King Charles and Queen Henrietta Maria. Altogether her correspondence provides not only a lively and informative insight into her family and social relations but also illuminates her more public concerns, such as the war in Europe and the conflict between king and parliament.

In addition to Frederick, Jane had three children from her second marriage: Anne, born 1615, Nicholas, born 1617, and Jane, who was born in February 1624 (she died at the age of three). About 1637 Anne married her mother's cousin, Thomas Meautys (*d.* 1649), the secretary and close confidant of Francis Bacon, Lord Verulam. Nicholas remained unmarried.

On the death of her husband in 1627 Lady Bacon inherited his estate; she subsequently arranged for the erection of his bust, in white marble within an oval, in the chancel of Culford church. She died on 8 May 1659, at the age of seventy-eight, and was buried in the chancel of Culford church, where her Cornwallis family monument, executed by Thomas Stanton, is to be found. She was succeeded by her eldest son, Frederick, whose portrait is in the picture gallery at Audley End, Essex, with those of his wife and his son Charles. A full-length portrait, formerly at Audley End and now in a private collection, is inscribed 'Jane, Lady Bacon' but might represent her mother-in-law, Anne, Lady Bacon. JOANNA MOODY

Sources Essex RO, Chelmsford, Braybrooke archives, Cornwallis-Bacon MSS, D/DBy C11–27 · *The private correspondence of Jane, Lady Cornwallis, 1613–1644*, ed. Lord Braybrooke (1842) · English Heritage, Photographic Library, A763/23 · *The letters of Lady Jane Bacon, 1613–44*, ed. J. Moody [forthcoming] · private information (2004) [G. Hughes; tenth Baron Braybrooke]
Archives Essex RO, Chelmsford, Braybrooke archives, Cornwallis-Bacon MSS, D/DBy C11–27
Likenesses oils (*Jane, Lady Bacon*), priv. coll.
Wealth at death Cornwallis / Bacon estate went to eldest son, Frederick, first Lord Cornwallis of Eye (1610–1662) and then to son Charles Cornwallis (1632–1673)

Bacon [Bacun], **John** (*c.*1250–*c.*1323), justice, was probably born in north-east Suffolk, near Great Yarmouth. He began his career as a junior clerk of the Westminster bench, *c.*1273. By 1280 he had entered the service of the more senior royal clerk, John Berewyk, and during the following decade assisted him in his duties both as keeper of writs and rolls on the southern eyre circuit and as treasurer to Queen Eleanor. In 1292, two years after the queen's death, Bacon was himself appointed keeper of writs and rolls of the common bench, with responsibility for the compilation of one of the court's subsidiary plea rolls, and for the interim custody of all original and judicial writs returned into the court, all final concords levied there, and all deeds produced in court whose authenticity was challenged. Contemporary law reports also show him playing a role in the adjudication of litigation. He was accused of serious official wrongdoing at the Lent parliament of 1305, but the two accusations against him were later withdrawn and he retained his post until 1313, when he was appointed one of the justices of the common bench. Bacon does not appear in any of the cases reported in the year-books during his period of office as a justice (1313–20). This is probably because the reporters recorded only cases heard in one of the two divisions of the court and he was sitting in the other division, dealing with more routine procedural matters. John Bacon probably died not long after his last known judicial appointment in October 1323.

John had at least four brothers. Adam, who was also a clerk, was in the service of John Salmon, bishop of Norwich, between 1309 and 1315 and was pardoned in 1318 for past adherence to the earl of Lancaster. Edmund, a knight, was in the king's service in Gascony from 1293 to 1297 and in Scotland in 1298 and 1303. He was constable of Wallingford during the first half of the reign of Edward II, and in the service of the king's half-brother Edmund of Kent from 1320. He was in Gascony again from 1324 and was captured near Bordeaux on his return from an embassy to Aragon in 1325. In 1330 he was a king's knight. A third brother, Henry, was also a knight; and a fourth, Robert, was a clerk. The Thomas Bacun who became a serjeant of the common bench in 1311, was a justice of the king's bench from 1332 to 1335, and died in 1336, was probably also a relative, possibly a brother.

John Bacon's earliest traceable property holdings were at Gorleston and Reston in north-east Suffolk, some held jointly with his mother, Sabina. He acquired further properties in the same area and had permission in 1293 to divert a highway to extend his house at Reston. By 1301 his mother had given him her holding at Ludham in south-east Norfolk, and he subsequently acquired other holdings in a number of neighbouring villages. He also made a series of property acquisitions at Widford and Mountnessing and surrounding villages in Essex, and at Ewelme in Oxfordshire. A clerk in major orders, John Bacon held a number of ecclesiastical livings, including those of Reston and Ewelme, and is known to have travelled to Rome on unspecified private business in 1306.

PAUL BRAND

Sources *Chancery records* · PRO, CP 25/1 · PRO, CP 40 · F. M. Maitland and others, eds., *Year books of Edward II*, 26 vols. in 28, SeldS (1903–69) · BL, Add. Charter 9915 · [W. Illingworth], ed., *Rotuli hundredorum temp. Hen. III et Edw. I*, RC, 2 (1818), 160–68, 185 · P. Brand, *The making of the common law* (1992) · PRO, Special Collection, Ancient Correspondence, SC 1/26 no. 72 · unpublished law reports

Bacon, John (1738–1816), ecclesiastical administrator, spent nearly the whole of his working life in the first fruits department of the office of Queen Anne's Bounty, where he rose from being junior clerk to become the receiver in 1782. He combined these offices with the duties of treasurer to the Corporation of the Sons of the Clergy. Elected FSA in 1774, in 1786 he published an edition of John Ecton's *Thesaurus rerum ecclesiasticarum*, a detailed account of the valuations of all ecclesiastical benefices which were charged with first fruits and tenths. He attracted severe criticism in the *Gentleman's Magazine* (1st ser., 56/2, 1786, 1027–8) for failing to acknowledge Ecton in his own preface and on the title-page.

Bacon was married and had two sons and a daughter, Maria, who married Sir William Johnston of Aberdeen. In 1783 he obtained the leasehold interest of the manor of Friern Barnet, from the dean and chapter of St Paul's. When the Land Tax Redemption Act authorized them to sell their landed property, he purchased in 1800 the reversion of the manor house and the whole estate. The house, formerly the priory of St John of Jerusalem, and its contents are described by Daniel Lysons in his *Environs of London*. Bacon died at his home, Friern House, Middlesex, on 26 February 1816, aged seventy-eight, and was buried in a small vault outside Friern Barnet church.

W. P. Courtney, *rev.* J. A. Marchand

Sources Nichols, *Lit. anecdotes*, 9.5–7 · *GM*, 1st ser., 56/2 (1786), 1027–8 · *GM*, 1st ser., 86/1 (1816), 276 · D. Lysons, *The environs of London*, 2 (1795), 22 · will, PRO, PROB 11/1578, sig. 123
Wealth at death see will, PRO, PROB 11/1578, sig. 123

Bacon, John (1740–1799), sculptor, was born on 24 November 1740 in Southwark, London, the son of Thomas Bacon, a clothworker. He was descended from an old family living in Wincanton in Somerset. In 1755 he was apprenticed to Nicholas Crispe, the owner of a porcelain factory in Vauxhall, with workshops in Bow churchyard and Lambeth. Crispe encouraged the young Bacon to exhibit with the Society of Arts. In 1759 Bacon's figure of *Peace* won him a premium, and over the next twenty years he was awarded eleven more premiums from the society, including their gold medal. Bacon worked for Crispe until 1764, when he began designing for the ceramic and metalwork industry. Among his clients were Daniel Pincot of Paternoster Row, Spitalfields; Josiah Wedgwood; William Duesbury of the Chelsea-Derby Porcelain Works; Sir William Chambers; Benjamin Vulliamy, the royal clockmaker, of Pall Mall; Matthew Boulton of Birmingham; James Tassie; and Neal & Co., of Hanley. Indeed, Bacon is considered to be the most important designer for British industry before John Flaxman. Bacon entered the Royal Academy Schools on 24 June 1769 and received the academy's first ever gold medal in sculpture for his relief *Aeneas Carrying his Father from Burning Troy* (1769). In 1770 he was elected an associate of the Royal Academy, and in 1771 he moved from Wardour Street to 17 Newman Street, Marylebone, where he established a large sculpture workshop that employed as many as twenty assistants, notably Henry Webber and Charles Peart. In that same year Bacon became chief designer and manager of the Coade Artificial Stone Company, a position he held until his death. In 1773 he married Elizabeth Wade, who died in February 1783 leaving him with five children—two sons, Thomas *Bacon (*b.* 1773) [*see under* Bacon, John] and John *Bacon the younger (1777–1859) and three daughters. In the autumn of 1783 he married Martha Holland, with whom he had three more sons.

The turning point in Bacon's career as a sculptor came with the exhibition of his life-size terracotta figure of *Mars* for the Society of Arts. The statue caught the attention of the archbishop of York, who commissioned a bust of George III. The sittings with the king proved to be highly advantageous to the sculptor. In 1778 Bacon was elected Royal Academician. His diploma piece, *Sickness*, served as the model for the sick man on the monument to Thomas Guy he sculpted for the chapel at Guy's Hospital. The memorial group to Guy has been praised as the finest British monument of its time. In 1778, when the competition was announced for the national monument to William Pitt the elder, earl of Chatham, the astute Bacon chose to show his model to the king, usurping the normal competition procedures of the Royal Academy. The sense of favouritism shown to Bacon with the awarding of the Chatham commission was the first of a series of such accusations and jealousies brought upon the sculptor. The memorial group to Chatham, some 30 feet high, established the scale for all future monuments in Westminster Abbey and brought praise from the king and Sir Joshua Reynolds, president of the Royal Academy. In 1784 Bacon won the competition held by the academy for a statue of Admiral Rodney for Spanish Town, Jamaica. The prestige of the Rodney figure, with its elegant relief panels, led to fifteen more commissions for funerary monuments for the island. In 1788 Bacon was selected to execute the marble statue of Dr Johnson, as well as that of John Howard, for St Paul's Cathedral, London. During the same period he was commissioned to execute the colossal figures of *Fame* and the *Genius of England*, together with *George III and the River Thames*, for Somerset House. His success at working in bronze caused him to be recognized as 'exceptional amongst British sculptors of the time' (Bryant, 25). In 1793 the court of directors of the East India Company commissioned Bacon to sculpt a series of works. The first of these was a marble portrait statue of Governor-General Cornwallis for their general court room, and the second the pediment decorations for East India House on Leadenhall Street.

In addition to the public and corporate commissions, the Bacon studio produced an array of funerary monuments, chimney-pieces, garden sculpture, and portrait busts. While his figures have neo-classical drapery, the elaborateness of their surfaces, like the illusionistic effects employed on some of the monuments, indicates his appreciation of the work of earlier sculptors such as Roubiliac. The productivity of the workshop was based first on Bacon's perfecting the use of a pointing machine that enabled his assistants to translate his models into full-scale works of sculpture. Second, he used a pattern book for clients to select a specific design for a monument. While these practices brought an extraordinary amount of work and prosperity to the studio, Bacon's entire career came under the critical eye of the fine-art establishment. In addition to the undue favouritism he received, his fellow artists, knowing that the sculptor had never studied in Italy, cited his natural inclination towards sentimentality as being out of date with the new neo-classical aesthetic. Despite these criticisms, which were often harsh, his work was much admired by his clients, who were powerful and influential both within Britain and abroad. Bacon was a staunch supporter of the British monarchy, an ardent Methodist, and a founding member of the Eclectic Society, later the Church Missionary Society.

Bacon died from an inflammation of the bowels at his home at 17 Newman Street on 7 August 1799 and was buried under the north gallery in Whitfield's Chapel, Tottenham Court Road. He left a substantial fortune, as well as many unfinished commissions, to his children. John Bacon the younger inherited his father's studio and remaining commissions, and Thomas, who had exhibited with the Royal Academy, assisted his brother for a brief time. MARY ANN STEGGLES

Sources A. Cunningham, *Lives of the British painters, sculptors and architects* (1830) · A. Cox-Johnson, *John Bacon* (1961) · A. Cox-Johnson, 'A gentleman's agreement', *Burlington Magazine*, 101 (1959), 236–42 · J. P. Pollard, 'Matthew Boulton and Conrad Heinrich Kuchler', *Numismatic Chronicle* (1970) · R. Cecil, *Memoirs of John Bacon, esq. with reflections drawn from a review of his moral and religious character* (1801) · M. Whinney, *Sculpture in Britain, 1530–1830* (1964) · T. Clifford, 'John Bacon [senior] and the manufacturers', *Apollo*, 122 (1985), 288–304 · M. Steggles, *Statues of the raj* (2001) · will, PRO, PROB 11/1328, sig. 565 · estate duties, PRO, IR 26/34, fol. 11v · J. Bryant, 'Bacon, John', *The dictionary of art*, ed. J. Turner (1996) · *GM*, 1st ser., 69 (1799), 808–10 · D. Solkin, 'Samaritan or Scrooge? The contested image of Thomas Guy in eighteenth century England', *Art Bulletin*, 78 (1996), 467–84

Likenesses W. Bate, miniature (after M. Chamberlain, 1785), NPG · W. Brockedon, sepia drawing (after bust by Bacon's son), BM · G. Dance, drawing, RA · J. Russell, pastel drawing, V&A · H. Singleton, group portrait, oils (*Royal Academicians, 1793*), RA · line engraving, BM, NPG; repro. in *European Magazine* (1790)

Wealth at death approx. £17,000 in 3 per cent consols; house and studio at 17 Newman Street: will, PRO, PROB 11/1328, sig. 565

Bacon, John (1777–1859), sculptor, was born on 13 March 1777 in his parents' house in Newman Street, London, the second son of the sculptor John *Bacon (1740–1799) and his wife, Elizabeth, *née* Wade (*d.* 1783). His elder brother, **Thomas Bacon** (*b.* 1773, *d.* after 1800), was also a sculptor who entered the Royal Academy Schools in 1788 and exhibited some religious works at the Royal Academy between 1793 and 1795. Until the age of twelve the younger John Bacon was under casual apprenticeship in his father's studio, and this enabled him to enter the Royal Academy Schools on 29 March 1790. He exhibited his first work in 1792, a statue entitled *Moses Striking the Rock*. From then on, his progress through the ranks was steady: he gained a silver medal in 1793 and a gold medal the following year for his study of the Greek prophet Cassandra. He continued to exhibit work at the Royal Academy until 1824, and he also exhibited at the British Institution in 1806 and 1807.

After his father's death the younger Bacon succeeded to his business and finished many of the works left in progress, including the popular statue of Lord Cornwallis, which led him to secure many important civic and imperial commissions. He was assisted in this by his brother Thomas, but soon after 1800 all trace of Thomas is lost. (The statue of William III in St James's Square, London, erected in 1808, was begun by the elder John Bacon and completed by Thomas.) The younger John Bacon's work, in a neo-classical style, was in such great demand by 1803 that he was encouraged to organize a public exhibition of his works, a largely unprecedented step at the time. He continued to receive numerous commissions: in 1806 his model of William Pitt the younger was unveiled in Cambridge; and 1809 was his *annus mirabilis*, during which he made statues of the Marquess Cornwallis for Calcutta, the Marquess Wellesley for Bombay, and George III for the Bank of Ireland. His statue in honour of Lord Lavington was unveiled in Antigua and featured a personified image of the island paying tribute to its imperial governor. Sadly, the statue did not fare well in its final colonial context—it was later destroyed by a hurricane. By 1814 the prestige of Bacon's work was so great that he was asked to restore the famous images *Madness* and *Melancholy* by the seventeenth-century sculptor Caius Gabriel Cibber, located at the Bethlem Hospital in London. His other works include portraits of various eminent late eighteenth- and early nineteenth-century dignitaries, including the bishop of Rochester, the archbishop of York, Richard Payne Knight (the art critic and theorist of the picturesque), captains Harvey, Hutt, and Cooke, and Admiral Totty.

In 1808 Bacon largely retired from public life, choosing to focus his attentions instead on ecclesiastic and architectural sculpture and monumental masonry. To this end, he formed a highly prolific partnership with Charles Manning (1776–1812), to whom he entrusted the design and execution of the majority of commissions while retaining the family name on the work. Manning's brother Samuel (1788–1842) succeeded him in the business, continuing its extensive production of monuments with Bacon as a sleeping partner until 1843. Bacon's work was treated with increasing disrespect in high aesthetic circles, since contemporaries felt that his later architectural masonry was mostly repetitive and dull, and he was blamed by later Victorian critics for the aesthetic and imaginative decline of mid-nineteenth-century British sculpture. Although his name was put forward, he did not receive sufficient votes to be elected ARA. Even though this has been attributed to his unusual business practices, it should also be noted that, in his diary, Joseph Farington recorded John Flaxman's views on 'the flimsiness of Bacon':

> Bacon he considered as scarcely to be taken up with a view of comparing his works with the pure standards of Sculpture. He had not made such his models, but worked *from notions of his own*, often showing much ingenuity, but void of greatness and simplicity. (Farington, *Diary*, 7, 2511)

More recently, however, Bacon's reputation has been reassessed more generously in the light of his earlier work, which has been, according to M. H. Grant, 'too little recorded or regarded' (*Dictionary of British Sculptors from the XIIIth Century to the XXth Century*, 25).

Bacon died at his home, 35 Bathwick Hill, Bath, Somerset, on 14 July 1859, leaving his two sons, John Bacon and Thomas Bacon, who were both clergymen, as executors of his ample estate. A comprehensive list of his works is included in *Allgemeines Künstler-lexikon: die bildenden Künstler aller Zeiten und Völker*. JASON EDWARDS

Sources *DNB* · R. Gunnis, *Dictionary of British sculptors, 1660–1851* (1953), 28–32 · A. Cunningham, *The lives of the most eminent British painters, sculptors, and architects*, 2 (1830) · Redgrave, *Artists* · S. C. Hutchison, 'The Royal Academy Schools, 1768–1830', *Walpole Society*, 38 (1960–62), 123–91 · J. Bryant, 'Bacon, John', *The dictionary of art*, ed. J. Turner (1996) · T. Clifford, 'John Bacon [senior] and the manufacturers', *Apollo*, 122 (1985), 288–304 · G. Meissner, ed., *Allgemeines Künstlerlexikon: die bildenden Künstler aller Zeiten und Völker*, [new edn, 34 vols.] (Leipzig and Munich, 1983–) · M. H. Grant, *A dictionary of British sculptors from the XIIIth century to the XXth century* (1953), 25 · *CGPLA Eng. & Wales* (1860) · *IGI*

Likenesses T. Blood, stipple (after J. Russell), BM, NPG; repro. in *European Magazine* (1815)

Wealth at death under £45,000: probate, 13 April 1860, *CGPLA Eng. & Wales*

Bacon, John Mackenzie (1846–1904), astronomer and aviator, born at Lambourn Woodlands, Berkshire, on 19 June 1846, was the fourth son of John Bacon (1809–1871), vicar of Lambourn Woodlands, a friend and neighbour of Charles Kingsley and Tom Hughes, and his wife, Mary Lousada, of Spanish ancestry. His great-grandfather was John Bacon RA, and his grandfather John *Bacon (1777–1859), sculptor. After education at home and at a coaching establishment at Old Charlton, near Woolwich, with a view to the army, he matriculated from Trinity College, Cambridge, in October 1865, and gained a foundation scholarship in 1869. Eye trouble compelled an *aegrotat* degree in the mathematical tripos of 1869. His close friends at Cambridge included William Kingdon Clifford, Francis Maitland Balfour, and Edward Henry Palmer, the orientalist.

From 1869 to 1875 Bacon worked with his eldest brother, Maunsell, at Cambridge as a pass 'coach'. On 11 April 1871 Bacon married Gertrude (1849–1894), youngest daughter of Charles John Myers, fellow of Trinity College, Cambridge, and vicar of Flintham, Nottingham; they had two sons and one daughter, Gertrude. After taking holy orders in 1870, he was unpaid curate of Harston, Cambridge, until 1876, when he settled at Coldash, Berkshire. His pastoral activities were limited by his own tubercular tendencies and his wife's nervous breakdown. He assisted in parochial work, was a poor-law guardian, initiated cottage shows, and encouraged handbell-ringing and agriculture.

Bacon acted as curate of Shaw, 4 miles from Coldash, from 1882 until 1889, when his *The Curse of Conventionalism: a Remonstrance by a Priest of the Church of England* boldly challenged the conventional clerical attitude to scientific questions, and brought on him the censure of the orthodox. Thereupon he abandoned clerical work and the clerical collar, and devoted himself to scientific study. Though still a believer, he declined to preach until 'I can have a lantern screen stretched across the chancel arch and a photograph of the Orion Nebula or some other glory of the heavens, to talk about' (G. Bacon, 173).

Astronomy and aeronautics had interested him from boyhood, and much of his life was devoted to stimulating public interest in these subjects. On 10 February 1888 he became a fellow of the Royal Astronomical Society, before which he read in 1898 a paper on 'Actinic qualities of light as affected by different conditions of atmosphere'. With the British Astronomical Association, which he joined in 1895 (and of which he became a member of council and of the eclipse committees), he witnessed at Vadsø, in the extreme north-east of Norway, the total eclipse of the sun on 9 August 1896. In December 1897 he led a party to Buxar in India for the solar eclipse of January 1898, and took the first animated photographs of the eclipse, but the films mysteriously disappeared on the voyage home. Of this eclipse Bacon gave an account in the *Journal* of the association (8.264). Bacon, as special correspondent to *The Times*, observed the solar eclipse of 28 May 1900 at Wadesborough, North Carolina, and made further experiments with the cinematograph.

From kite-flying Bacon early turned to ballooning and to the acoustic and meteorological researches for which it gave opportunity. His first balloon ascent was made from the Crystal Palace on 20 August 1888 with Captain Dale. He recorded enthusiastically, 'I left this world about 5.15 …' (G. Bacon, 151). Experiments in 1899 proved that sound travelled through the air less rapidly upwards than downwards. In August of that year he successfully experimented from his balloon with wireless telegraphy. In November 1902 Bacon crossed the sea from the Isle of Man to Galloway. On the voyage he proved the theory that the sea bottom was visible and could be photographed from a great height. Bacon photographed from his balloon, at a height of 600 feet, the beds of sand and rock 10 fathoms deep in the bottom of the Irish Sea; these photographs were exhibited at the Royal Society's soirée at Burlington House in the spring of 1903. With J. Nevil Maskelyne, Bacon began experiments in the inflation of balloons with hot air by the vaporization of petroleum, in place of coal gas, thereby greatly quickening the process and producing some very tense flights in craft potentially extremely explosive. Bacon also researched into the causes and cure of London fog, insisting on the need for stronger currents of air through the streets, by widening thoroughfares and increasing the number of open spaces.

Bacon became active and successful as a popular scientific lecturer and writer. He read before the Society of Arts papers on 'The balloon as an instrument of scientific research' (published in the *Journal of the Society of Arts*, 17 Feb 1899), and 'Scientific observations at high altitudes' (ibid., 24 Jan 1902). In a paper at the Cambridge meeting of the British Association on 'Upper air currents and their relation to the far travel of sound' (1904) he summarized his subsequent acoustic experiments in balloons. Bacon died of pleurisy at his home, Sunnyside, Coldash, on 26 December 1904, and was buried in Swallowfield churchyard, near Reading, four days later. Only the previous year (7 October 1903), he had married a second wife—Stella, youngest daughter of Captain T. B. H. Valintine of Goodwood—with whom he had a second daughter. His elder daughter, Gertrude, a frequent companion on his expeditions, wrote his biography.

W. B. Owen, *rev.* Julian Lock

Sources *The Times* (27 Dec 1904) • G. Bacon, *The record of an aeronaut: being the life of John M. Bacon* (1907) • J. M. Bacon, *The dominion of the air* (1902) • Venn, *Alum. Cant.* • *CGPLA Eng. & Wales* (1913)

Likenesses photographs, repro. in Bacon, *Record of an aeronaut*, frontispiece

Wealth at death £6652 14s. 8d.: resworn probate, Nov 1913, *CGPLA Eng. & Wales* (1905)

Bacon, Mathew (*b. c.*1700, *d.* in or before 1757), legal writer, was the second son of Edward Bacon of Rathkeny, co. Tipperary, Ireland. He was admitted to the Inner Temple on 27 May 1726, and to the Middle Temple on 21 June 1731. He was called to the bar on 24 November 1732. In 1731 he published anonymously the *Compleat Arbitrator, or, Law of Awards and Arbitraments*, which provided a straightforward and up-to-date account of the law of arbitration, and reached a third edition in 1770. In 1736 there appeared, also anonymously, the first two volumes of *A New Abridgment of the Law*, the third volume following in 1740. Only the first two thirds of the fourth volume were completed by Bacon before his death. The remainder of that volume, which appeared in 1759, and just over half of the fifth and final volume, which appeared in 1766, were written by Joseph Sayer, serjeant-at-law. The remaining portion of the fifth volume was completed by Owen Ruffhead. The work reached a seventh English edition, in eight volumes, in 1832. It was extremely popular in the United States of America, and was several times edited there by Bird Wilson, and by John Bouvier.

Unlike earlier abridgements, Bacon's work did not consist of notes of cases and statutes roughly put together under alphabetical heads, but rather foreshadowed modern legal encyclopaedias in containing a collection of scientific treatises on all branches of the law. Bacon's abridgement, which Charles Viner refused to regard as an abridgement at all, but just 'called so in order to make it more saleable', was in this way superior to Viner's, and attained a popularity which Viner's work was unable to match. Much, though not all, of Bacon's material was derived from the work of Jeffrey Gilbert, chief baron of the exchequer in Ireland from 1715 to 1722, and subsequently chief baron of the exchequer in England. There is a frequent resemblance between the text of Bacon's abridgement and Gilbert's published works *Devises* (1730), *Ejectments* (1734), and *Rents* (1758), though there is no such resemblance with certain other published works by Gilbert, and it is possible that Bacon obtained Gilbert's material not from his treatises but from a manuscript abridgement compiled by Gilbert. Bacon may also have used the works of Matthew Hale, William Hawkins, and Knightley D'Anvers. A section of Bacon's abridgement was published separately in 1798 as *Leases and Terms of Years*, with notes by Henry Gwillim. Bacon was probably also the author of another anonymous work, *A General Abridgment of Cases in Equity*, known as *Equity Cases Abridged*, part 1, the first equity digest, which was published in 1732 and reached a fifth edition in 1793. Bacon's will, leaving all his property to his brother John, was proved in London on 11 March 1757.

N. G. JONES

Sources H. A. C. Sturgess, ed., *Register of admissions to the Honourable Society of the Middle Temple, from the fifteenth century to the year 1944*, 1 (1949), 311 • Mathew Bacon's will, proved 11/3/1757, PRO, PROB 11/828/216 • J. D. Cowley, *A bibliography of abridgments, digests, dictionaries and indexes of English law to the year 1800* (1932), 56, 59–68 • W. H. Maxwell and L. F. Maxwell, eds., *English law to 1800*, 2nd edn (1955), vol. 1 of *A legal bibliography of the British Commonwealth of Nations* (1938–58), 16, 286, 479, 544 • P. R. G. [P. R. Glazebrook], 'Bacon, Matthew', *Biographical dictionary of the common law*, ed. A. W. B. Simpson (1984) • Holdsworth, *Eng. law*, 12.169–70, 393 • C. Viner, *A general abridgment of law and equity*, 18 (1743), preface

Wealth at death left all property to brother: will, PRO, PROB 11/828/216

Bacon, Montagu (1688–1749), Church of England clergyman and writer, was born in December 1688 at Coddenham, Suffolk (and baptized on 13 December), the second of the three sons of Nicholas Bacon of Shrubland Hall, Coddenham, and Lady Catherine Montagu (1660/61–1757), youngest daughter of Edward *Montagu, first earl of Sandwich, about whom in 1734 he wrote warmly to the public orator at Cambridge University, Philip Williams (in a letter reprinted in *GM*, 51, 1781). On his father's side Montagu was descended from Sir Nicholas Bacon, lord keeper of the great seal. He was educated at Westminster School and Trinity College, Cambridge, which he entered on 16 February 1705 but from where he did not graduate MA until 1734.

Prior to his graduation Bacon resided in Leicestershire where, as John Nichols surmises, he may have been curate of Newbold Verdun (Nichols, *Illustrations*, 4.243). Bacon referred to his residence there in letters to the dramatist George Jeffreys written from Quarles's coffee house, Cambridge, between October and December 1732. In the correspondence Bacon defended the reputation of the philosopher Malebranche, criticized Cambridge as a 'very dull place', and spoke of his weariness with college life. None the less it was the university which presented Bacon with the rectory of Newbold Verdun acquired from the duke of Norfolk. Bacon did not remain there long, however, being soon afflicted with mental illness. By this date Bacon had established himself as a learned and wide-ranging scholar of English poetry. After a spell at Duffield's madhouse in Little Chelsea, he moved to Manor Street, Chelsea, where he died on 7 April 1749. He was buried at Coddenham on 19 April.

Bacon's scholarship was collected by Zachary Gray in a single volume published posthumously as *Critical, Historical and Explanatory Notes upon Hudibras* (1752) to which was prefixed a dissertation on burlesque poetry.

ARTHUR H. GRANT, *rev.* PHILIP CARTER

Sources *GM*, 1st ser., 51 (1781) • Nichols, *Illustrations* • Nichols, *Lit. anecdotes* • Venn, *Alum. Cant.* • J. Duncombe, *Letters by several eminent persons deceased … with notes explanatory and historical*, 3 vols. (1772)

Archives Harrowby Manuscript Trust, Sandon Hall, Staffordshire, letters to James Montagu

Bacon, Sir Nathaniel (1546?–1622), local politician, was probably born at his father's house in Noble Street, London, the fifth of seven children of Sir Nicholas *Bacon (1510–1579), lord keeper, and his first wife, Jane (*d.* 1552), daughter of Thomas Ferneley, a merchant from West Creeting, Suffolk. His half-brothers included Anthony *Bacon (1558–1601) and Francis *Bacon (1561–1626), later Viscount St Alban. Educated under his father's watchful eye, he matriculated as a fellow-commoner at Trinity College, Cambridge, in 1561 and entered Gray's Inn in December 1562, becoming an ancient in November 1576. In July 1569 he married Anne (*d.* 1594), the illegitimate child of a liaison between his uncle Sir Thomas *Gresham and Anne Dutton. Their respective fathers endowed them with a fragmented estate of seven manors ranging from Stiffkey and Langham-cum-Morston in north Norfolk to Combs in east Suffolk. In the early 1590s these manors were yielding an annual income of about £2000, declining thereafter through the sale of Combs to finance dowries for his three heirs, Anne, Elizabeth, and Winefred.

In 1578 Bacon settled at Stiffkey Hall where, for over forty years, he devoted himself to the business of county government. Appointed JP in 1573, he remained on the bench until his death. Twice sheriff of Norfolk (1586–7 and 1599–1600), commissioner for musters (1596–1605), and deputy lieutenant (1605–22), he served variously as commissioner for the export of grain, for piracy, sewers, recusancy, subsidies, loans, and the impressment of mariners. Appointed deputy steward of the duchy of Lancaster estates in Norfolk in 1582, he succeeded to the stewardship in 1599, renting the valuable manor of Methwold where he became feodary, coroner, escheator, and clerk of the market in 1604. The unrivalled collection of records that these offices generated has been exploited by historians of Elizabethan and Jacobean government to exemplify an assiduous magistracy dedicated to the service of the state. Bacon's assiduity is not in doubt, but his dedication appears to have been directed more to implementing his own analysis of what best suited his 'country' (by which he usually meant north Norfolk) than to acting as the handmaid of central government.

Bacon epitomized a type of Elizabethan county magnate who, schooled in mid-Tudor common weal humanism, considered himself better placed than the state to decide what constituted good government in his locality. In Norfolk, which had two contrasting identities—the sheep and corn areas of the north and west and the wood-pasture of the centre and south—Bacon became spokesman for the former, where residence acquainted him with its economic and social problems. For their alleviation he advocated the repeal or amendment of a raft of government measures; some of these dealt with the export and marketing of grain. Others, particularly militia statutes, had introduced a rating system which fell inequitably on many parishes in his region. Such advocacy set him at loggerheads with his counterparts in south Norfolk where a different socio-economic structure pertained. Simultaneously he became involved in a bitter controversy as to whether county government, hitherto conducted by statutorily empowered magistrates and commissioners, should be buttressed by the intrusive activities of informers, deputy lieutenants, and patentees acting under the authority of the crown. In his view they were abusing the crown's power, acting arbitrarily and placing private gain before the public good; to thwart them he invoked legal and constitutional arguments and devices. Whatever the merits or success of his case, the discourse and debate he provoked began to transform the factions and affinities of mid-Tudor Norfolk into political groups that pursued particularist policies.

Although well connected at court through his family, Bacon rarely exploited the patronage network this offered. Instead he chose quarter sessions, the assizes, and parliament as the arenas in which he pursued the interests of his 'country'. Having served his parliamentary apprenticeship as burgess for Tavistock, Devon, in 1571 and 1572, he sat as second knight of the shire for Norfolk in 1584 and 1593, burgess for King's Lynn, Norfolk, in 1597, and first knight of the shire in 1604. Esteemed by his electoral supporters as 'a speciall phisytion that will put his best indevour to purge and cure those maladies' of his country (Smith, 315), he arrived at Westminster furnished with a sheaf of draft bills which embodied the nostrums of his neighbours. His frequent contributions to debates and his regular nomination to serve on committees (at least twenty-five) suggest that he earned their trust and undoubtedly articulated his own views on economic, social, and religious issues.

His puritan beliefs made Bacon an outspoken critic of church government, especially of the practices and procedures of the church courts. 'The office of bishops is to preach', he told the Commons during a debate on a Bill to Search for Recusants:

> for they and their officers beeing men utterly unacquaynted with theis proceedinges, or being no parte of their studie or exercise, it were not fit to use them in this cause, but to leave it to the justices of the peace and others of the laitie. (LPL, MS 2109)

A zealous favourer of moderate puritanism, he envisaged a society in which magistrates and ministers worked together to create a godly common weal. Such a view provided the imperative for his proactive magistracy, for the care he took to appoint preaching ministers, and for the institution of a weekly 'exercise' and conference led by local preachers, which continued for at least fifteen years at Wiveton, a coastal parish adjacent to his estate.

By the time Bacon was knighted in 1604 his reforming zeal had ebbed, although he remained deeply involved in local administration. Or perhaps the changing nature of puritanism, coupled with the years of peace under James I with their attendant amelioration of local rating demands, deprived him of his mission. His domestic life, clouded by the death of his first wife in 1594, was plunged into turmoil by his unhappy marriage on 21 July 1597 to Dorothy (*c*.1570–1629), daughter of Arthur Hopton and widow of William Smith of Burgh Castle, Suffolk. She failed to give him the heir he so badly wanted. Temperamentally incompatible, they quarrelled to the point where their servants talked openly of their 'great falling out'. Of his two stepsons, William Roberts, whom he planned to make his proxy heir by marriage to one of his granddaughters, and for whom he built Irmingland Hall, died aged sixteen, while Owen threatened to sue him for abusing his guardianship. Finally in 1620 the county rejected him as knight of the shire and even his heirs failed to inscribe his date of death, November 1622, on the tomb that he had commissioned in 1614.

Although he had inherited his father's industry and sense of responsibility, Bacon lacked his wit and wisdom. Self-righteous and plain-speaking to the point of tactlessness, an 'almost obsessive constitutionalist' who was dubbed 'Mr Lawier' by his sharp-tongued stepmother (MacCulloch, 260; *Papers of Nathaniel Bacon*, *Papers*, 3.20), and not given to sociability, he was referred to affectionately by his friends as 'honest Nathaniel' (*Letters of Philip Gawdy*, 65). Although he possessed a well-stocked library, he showed little interest in cultural pursuits, while his failure to complete the house and gardens that his father had designed suggests that he had no appreciation of the Renaissance features incorporated in their plan. He died at Stiffkey Hall and was buried at Stiffkey on 7 November 1622.

Sir Nicholas Bacon, first baronet (*c*.1543–1624), was the third child of Sir Nicholas Bacon and his wife Jane. Admitted fellow-commoner at Trinity College, Cambridge, in 1561, he entered Gray's Inn on 15 December 1562, becoming an ancient in 1576. About 1562 he married Anne (*d*. 1616), daughter and heir of Edmund Butts of Thornham, Norfolk, and Anne (*d*. 1609), daughter of Henry Bures of Acton, Suffolk. Through her he inherited substantial estates in north Norfolk and on the Suffolk–Essex border. From his father he received the mansion house at Redgrave, Suffolk, together with at least seven other manors. In 1586 he added by purchase the Culford Hall estate. It has been estimated that at death his annual income exceeded £4000. Such an inheritance, combined with the residual aura of his distinguished father, might be expected to have ensured his pre-eminence in a region that, after 1572, lacked a resident nobleman.

Bacon's political impact, however, never quite matched his socio-economic status since he lacked both the aspiration and the necessary application. He sat twice in parliament—for Beverley, Yorkshire, in 1563 and as first knight of the shire for Suffolk in 1572—'without once being mentioned in the records' (HoP, *Commons, 1558–1603*,). Despite this tardiness he was tireless in local administration. Sheriff of Suffolk in 1581–2, of Norfolk in 1597–8, and of Suffolk again in 1603–4, JP in Suffolk from 1573 and in Norfolk from 1578 almost continuously until 1624, he served on numerous special commissions and was steward of the honours of Eye and Clare. Knighted in 1578, he was appointed premier baronet of England in 1611.

Bacon's paramount concern was for good government within the liberty of St Edmund's, west Suffolk. When its landowners felt threatened during the 1590s by patentees' and lieutenancy exactions, he consorted with other justices within the liberty to flout what they deemed to be excessive demands by central government and its agents. A staunch patron of puritan ministers, he died on 22 November 1624, and was commemorated in Redgrave church by one of Nicholas Stone's monumental masterpieces.

Edward Bacon (1548/9–1618), the sixth child of Sir Nicholas Bacon, matriculated (according to Venn) at Trinity College, Cambridge, in 1561, aged twelve. In 1565 he entered Gray's Inn where he became ancient in 1576. His father set him up, as befitted a younger son, as a London-based agent complete with town house and a clerkship in chancery for licences and pardons of alienations (1571). A failed marriage suit in 1576 probably precipitated a two-year continental tour in which he reinforced his humanistic and radical protestant sympathies through studies under Johann Sturmius at Strasbourg and Lambert Danaeus at Geneva, while lodging in Beza's house.

About 1581 Edward Bacon married Helen, daughter and heir of Thomas Little of Bray, Berkshire, and Elizabeth, daughter of Sir Robert Lyton of Knebworth, Hertfordshire. Among their children were the politician and author Nathaniel *Bacon (*bap*. 1593, *d*. 1660) and the politician Francis *Bacon (1600–1663). Initially, presumably, he lived at Bray, since he served as a JP in Berkshire between 1583 and 1591. Elected burgess for Yarmouth in a by-election (1576), he sat for Tavistock, Devon, in 1584 and Weymouth and Melcombe Regis in 1586. By 1592 his wife had inherited Shrubland Hall, Barham, where he settled and lent support to both the puritan cause and county government in Suffolk. Although he is frequently confused with his nephew Edmund Bacon, the record clearly shows him as JP there between 1592 and 1609 and sheriff in 1600–01. Arguably he may also have sat as knight of the shire in 1593. He died at Shrubland Hall on 8 September 1618 and was buried in Barham church. A. Hassell Smith

Sources *The papers of Nathaniel Bacon of Stiffkey*, ed. A. H. Smith, G. M. Baker, and R. W. Kenny, 1–3, Norfolk RS, 46, 49, 53 (1979–90) • *The official papers of Sir Nathaniel Bacon of Stiffkey, Norfolk, … 1580–1620*, ed. H. W. Saunders, CS, 3rd ser., 26 (1915) • F. R. Brooks, ed., 'Supplementary Stiffkey papers', *Camden miscellany, XVI*, CS, 3rd ser., 52 (1936) • D. MacCulloch, *Suffolk and the Tudors: politics and religion in an English county, 1500–1600* (1986) • A. Hassell Smith, *County and court: government and politics in Norfolk, 1558–1603* (1974) • HoP, *Commons, 1558–1603* • 'The letters and will of Lady Dorothy Bacon, 1597–1629', ed. J. Key, *Miscellany*, Norfolk RS, 56 (1993) • A. Simpson, *The wealth of the gentry, 1540–1660: East Anglian studies* (1961) • *The ofspringe armes and matches of Syr Nicholas Bacon knight beholde heere in this table are represented to your sight*, (painting, 1577x9; priv. coll.) [photograph: Courtauld Inst., neg. B55/975] • *Letters of Philip Gawdy*, ed. I. H. Jeayes, Roxburghe Club, 148 (1906) • E. R. Sandeen, 'The correspondence of Sir Nicholas Bacon', MA diss., University of Chicago, 1955 • A. Fletcher and P. Roberts, eds., *Religion, culture and society in early modern Britain* (1994), esp. 155–60

Archives BL, corresp., Add. MSS 41306, 41655 • BL, corresp., Stowe MSS 150 • BL, corresp. and papers, Add. MS 41140 • BL, list of assessors of subsidy, Add. MS 38508 • BL, personal and family corresp. and papers, Add. MS 63081 • Folger, papers • Francis Bacon Library, Claremont, California, MSS • Norfolk RO, papers; further papers incl. relating to judiciary and militia • NRA, priv. coll., corresp. and papers • Raynham Hall, Norfolk, Raynham Hall muniments, papers • U. Reading L., accounts | Norfolk RO, Boxes IC 9, 126 X 6, 3 A 2, P 181 B and deposits by H. Bradfer-Lawrence, B. Cozens-Hardy, G. R. Martyn, Norfolk and Norwich Archaeological Society, P. C. Pearson [microfilm] • University of Chicago, Redgrave Hall muniments

Likenesses N. Stone, marble effigy on monument (Nicholas Bacon), Redgrave church, Suffolk • monument, Stiffkey church, Norfolk • portrait, priv. coll.; repro. in Smith, *County and court* • portrait (Nicholas Bacon), priv. coll. • portrait (Edward Bacon), priv. coll. • tomb chest (Edward Bacon), Barham church, Suffolk

Wealth at death approx. £2000 p.a. • over £4000 p.a.—Nicholas Bacon • £1800 p.a.—Edward Bacon

Bacon, Sir Nathaniel (1585–1627), painter, was born at Redgrave in Suffolk in August 1585, the grandson of Lord Keeper Bacon and the youngest son of Sir Nicholas *Bacon (*c*.1543–1624) [*see under* Bacon, Sir Nathaniel (1546?–1622)], subsequently the premier baronet of England, and his wife, Anne Butts (*c*.1547–1616). He was admitted to the Order of the Bath in February 1626 to mark Charles I's coronation. Raised at Redgrave Hall, Bacon acquired Brome

Sir Nathaniel Bacon (1585–1627), self-portrait, *c.*1618–20

Hall in Suffolk on his marriage, on 1 May 1614, to Jane, *née* Meautys (1580/81–1659) [*see* Bacon, Jane], widow of Sir William Cornwallis, and inherited Culford Hall, 4 miles north of Bury St Edmunds, from his parents.

Bacon has been described as 'The most accomplished [British] amateur painter of the [seventeenth] century' (Jackson-Stops, 150), although fewer than a dozen of his works survive, of which a number are self-portraits. The earliest documentary reference to specific pictures is in the inventory of Culford attached to his widow's will of 1659, which mentions 'Ten great peeces in wainscoate of fish and fowle &c done by Sr: Nath: Bacon'. The *Cookmaid with Still Life of Birds*, still in the possession of the artist's descendants, is thought to be one of these, as are the *Cookmaid with Still Life of Game*, acquired by the family in the 1950s, and the Tate collection's *Cookmaid with Still Life of Vegetables and Fruit*, all executed about 1620 to 1625. A tiny *Landscape*, painted on copper, bearing the conjoined monogram NB (Ashmolean Museum, Oxford), is thought to be the 'small Landskip drawn by Sir Nath. Bacon' listed in the Tradescant Collection in 1656 (*Musaeum Tradescantianum*, 1656, 40). If so it is the first known pure landscape by an English-born artist.

The main surviving source of personal information about Bacon is a group of letters to his wife, a considerable heiress and formerly an attendant of James I's queen, Anne of Denmark. These letters show Bacon as a devoted family man, much interested in his own health, and enthusiastic about horticulture. They also indicate that he travelled to the Low Countries and, judging from his artistic style and technique, it is extremely likely that he received some training there. No other British artist of the period painted still lifes, and indeed the cookmaid subject originated in the Low Countries. The Antwerp artist Frans Snijders was a major exponent of the genre, and Bacon visited that city in 1613.

A gentleman, Bacon did not need to paint for his living but his art was clearly significant to him. His funerary monument in St Mary's Church, Culford, bears two carved painter's palettes. He also included his palette and brushes in his great, full-length self-portrait (*c.*1620, priv. coll.). Contemporaries alluded to his skills as an artist. In 1622 Henry Peacham commended him as a well-born Englishman who could draw and paint, while Edward Norgate credited Bacon with inventing a particular 'Pinke' (that is to say, yellow) apparently used by other artists, such as Peter Oliver and John Hoskins. The antiquary George Vertue, who noted the Culford monument in 1739, stated that Bacon had visited Italy, but there is no corroborating evidence for this; Vertue also mentioned two mythological paintings, now lost.

Bacon died in June 1627 and was buried at St Mary's, Culford, on 1 July 1627. The record of his funeral states that he died of 'a lingering illness', and the letters indicate a decline in health from about 1622. Of his three children only Anne (*b.* 1615), who married, second, Sir Harbottle Grimston, had any children. Unusually wide-ranging in his work as a painter, perhaps as a result of his Netherlandish travels, Bacon explored genres not attempted by his British contemporaries, whose work was almost entirely confined to portraiture. KAREN HEARN

Sources *The private correspondence of Jane, Lady Cornwallis, 1613–1644*, ed. Lord Braybrooke (1842) • H. Peacham, *The gentleman's exercise* (1622), 126 • E. Norgate, *Miniatura, or, The art of limning*, ed. J. M. Muller and J. Murrell (1997) • K. Hearn, ed., *Dynasties: painting in Tudor and Jacobean England, 1530–1630* (1995), 166, 220–23 [exhibition catalogue, Tate Gallery, London, 12 Oct 1995 – 7 Jan 1996] • G. Jackson-Stops, ed., *The treasure houses of Britain: five hundred years of private patronage and art collecting* (1985), 150 [O. Millar; exhibition catalogue, National Gallery of Art, Washington, DC, 3 Nov 1985 – 16 March 1986] • Vertue, *Note books*, vol. 2 • G. Storey, *People and places* (1973) • B. Denvir, 'Sir Nathaniel Bacon', *The Connoisseur*, 137 (1956), 116–19 • C. H. C. Baker, *Lely and the Stuart portrait painters: a study of English portraiture before and after van Dyck*, 1 (1912), 71–3 • K. Hearn, R. Upstone, and G. Waterfield, *In celebration: the art of the country house* (1998), 26 [exhibition catalogue, Tate Gallery, London, 11 Nov 1998 – 28 Feb 1999] • K. Hearn, 'Sir Nathaniel Bacon I: horticulturist and artist', *British Art Journal*, 1/2 (2000), 13–15 • B. Juniper, 'Sir Nathaniel Bacon II: the vegetable world', *British Art Journal*, 1/2 (2000), 16–18 • [C. MacLeod], *Tudor and Jacobean portraits in the National Portrait Gallery collection at Montacute House* (1999), 25 • K. Hearn, 'Cookmaid with still life of vegetables and fruit', *NACF Review, 1995* (1996), 130 • funeral certificate, Coll. Arms • *DNB* • J. Bacon, will, 1659, Herts. ALS, Gorhambury MS

Archives Essex RO, Braybrooke MSS

Likenesses N. Bacon, self-portrait, oils, *c.*1618–1620, priv. coll. [*see illus.*] • N. Bacon, self-portrait, *c.*1620, repro. in Hearn, ed., *Dynasties*; priv. coll. • N. Bacon, self-portrait, oils, *c.*1625, NPG • N. Bacon, self-portrait, *c.*1626–1627, priv. coll. • attrib. N. Stone, monument, 1627–8, St Mary's Church, Culford • N. Bacon, self-portrait, repro. in Hearn, Upstone, and Waterfield, *In celebration*; priv. coll. • bust effigy, Culford church, Suffolk

Bacon, Nathaniel (*bap.* 1593, *d.* 1660), politician and author, was baptized on 12 December 1593 at Coddenham, Suffolk, a younger son of Sir Edward *Bacon (1548/9–1618) [*see under* Bacon, Sir Nathaniel], politician, and his wife, Helen, daughter and heir of Thomas Little, who owned Shrubland Hall, Suffolk. Francis *Bacon (1600–1663) was his brother. Born into a Suffolk family long influential in law and politics, his father, who was the son of Lord Keeper Sir Nicholas *Bacon and half-brother to Sir Francis *Bacon, came into possession of Shrubland Hall when he married. Nathaniel Bacon matriculated as a pensioner from Christ's College, Cambridge, in July 1606 and graduated BA in 1611. Admitted to Gray's Inn in August 1611, he was called to the bar in 1617 and became a bencher of Gray's in 1640. He lived for a time in Langham, Essex, where he served as a JP. After returning to Suffolk he served as recorder of Bury and in 1643 was elected recorder of Ipswich. He married in 1648 Susanna, daughter of Sir Nathaniel Barnardiston.

A staunch presbyterian—his father had studied with Beza in Geneva—Bacon was an early and determined opponent of Charles I. He was reported as refusing to pay the forced loan in 1628, and he worked diligently for the parliamentarian cause throughout the civil wars. In 1644 he became the chairman of the Cambridge committee of the eastern association, in which capacity he had extensive dealings with the earl of Manchester and probably with Oliver Cromwell, who had close ties to the association. In November 1645 Bacon was elected a recruiter MP for Cambridge University, and subscribed to the covenant. The lists of the *Commons Journals* show Bacon to have been an active member, serving on scores of committees that dealt with religious, legal, and military concerns. His most important committee duty came when he was appointed by the lower house to deal with the proposals for making accommodations with the king in 1648.

Excluded from parliament at Pride's Purge in December 1648, Bacon was admitted to the Rump Parliament in June 1649 and subscribed to the engagement. Although he took the post of admiralty judge in 1649, he did not support the Commonwealth as enthusiastically as he had supported the Long Parliament, sitting on only three committees from January to September 1649. Still, his presbyterian zeal made him a valuable member, and he is considered one of five religious 'experts' whose opinions carried special weight (Worden, 126). As one of the MPs for Ipswich during the protectorate, his staunch commitment to the Calvinist cause led him to support wholeheartedly the Commons' attack on the Quaker James Nayler, against whom Bacon railed vociferously and often during the second protectorate parliament. In 1657 he became a master of requests. He continued to hold this post in Richard Cromwell's government and also served in his parliament as well as in the restored Long Parliament of 1660.

But Bacon's greatest service to anti-Stuart causes came in the form of a political tract entitled *An Historical Discourse of the Uniformity of the Government of England*, which was probably written using notes collected by John Selden. Published in 1647 to justify the Long Parliament's war against Charles I, with a continuation appearing in 1651, the work has been referred to as 'the English *Francogallia*' (Burgess, 96). Contemporaries of various political leanings would have agreed. Indeed, according to Bacon's co-religionist and fellow anti-royalist Richard Baxter, *An Historical Discourse* was one of the four most influential tracts written in support of the parliamentarian cause, the other three being Henry Parker's *Observations upon some of his Majesties Late Answers and Expresses* (1642), Philip Hunton's *Treatise of Monarchie* (1643), and William Prynne's *Soveraigne Power of Parliaments and Kingdomes* (1643). But the reach of Bacon's treatise extended far beyond the civil wars and interregnum. Continually republished well into the eighteenth century, when it won the praise of the elder William Pitt, *An Historical Discourse* was secretly reprinted in 1672, in 1682 at the time of the exclusion crisis, in 1689 at the revolution, again in 1739, and by 1750 in a fifth edition. So fearful were the royalists of Bacon's message that Charles II's government attempted to suppress it by prosecuting the radical printer John Starkey, perhaps a member of the Green Ribbon Club, who dared to publish it. Although Starkey and his like-minded friends might want to 'pretend it is only an old book reprinted and an historical discourse of past times without any application to the present', the king's government knew better. In fact, Bacon's treatise, containing as it did 'numerous extracts to prove the anti-monarchical' agenda, was a 'dangerous book' that was 'dedicated to the service of rebellion' (*CSP dom., 1682*, 263, 608; *CSP dom., 1 March 1677–28 Feb 1678*, 406, 409).

Charles II and his advisers were right to be scared, for Bacon's *An Historical Discourse* argued with unrelenting force an anti-royalist ideology of enormous persuasive power. This was the radical ancient constitution which, according to modern scholarship, was first fully articulated during the civil wars by polemicists such as William Prynne and Bacon himself. Early a mainstay of the Long Parliament's cause, the ideology consisted of the following propositions: first, while government in general was from God, the particular form came from the people. In England the people in the remote past had made a contract with their ruler, a contract in which their obedience to him rested upon his governing according to the laws made by both king and community. The ruler who failed to act upon the bargain unkinged himself and left his subjects free to replace him with another. For proof of this theorizing, radical ancient constitutionalists such as Bacon turned to the *Modus tenendi parliamentum*, the *Mirror of Justices*, and the so-called laws of St Edward the Confessor. These three treatises, which claimed to date from the Saxon period but were in fact written in the early twelfth and early fourteenth centuries, described how institutions, especially the common law and a parliament that included the House of Commons, existed in Saxon England and had survived the Norman conquest intact. The continuity of Saxon institutions across the great divide of 1066 was assured when William I and all of his successors down to the Stuart period confirmed St Edward's laws in coronation charters, coronation oaths, and in documents such as Magna Carta. Stories supportive of this view of medieval history, which are now known to be wrong in important respects, could be read in the works of medieval chroniclers such as Matthew Paris and Henry Huntingdon and also in the more popular histories of Tudor and Stuart writers such as John Foxe, Raphael Holinshed, John Speed, and Richard Baker. By the 1640s, then, radical ancient constitutionalists could draw upon a large and substantial body of literature in support of their particular version of English history, law, and government.

In *An Historical Discourse* Bacon turned repeatedly to the medieval past, especially St Edward's laws and the *Mirror of Justices*, to justify the Long Parliament's right to make war against Charles Stuart and the duty of the English people to transfer allegiance to the Cromwellian regime. Bacon wrote to help those who needed guidance in such difficult times. In order to act justly and lawfully, he suggested, they must turn to their own national history, and in particular, to Saxon times. Then they would learn that the Saxon monarchy had been elective and the Saxons' relationship with their king contractual. And, Bacon would argue at length, what held for Saxon rulers held for the Stuarts.

Bacon found one part of St Edward's laws particularly apt for his polemical purposes. This was chapter 17, 'Of the Office of a King.' It read: 'The King … who is the vicar of the highest King, was established for this, that he rule and defend the kingdom and the people of the Lord and, above all, the Holy Church from wrongdoers'; but a king who failed in his duty 'loses the very name of king' (B. R. O'Brien, *God's Peace and King's Peace*, Philadelphia, 1999, 175–7). To Bacon, as to Prynne before him and radical ancient constitutionalists throughout the rest of the century, this meant that rulers who broke the terms of the contract with their people deposed themselves and freed their subjects from allegiance. No mere 'dead word', the people's right to make and unmake kings was frequently put into practice in Saxon times, when the nation 'made the monarchical crown in this land to walk circuit into all parts of the country to fit heads to wear itself until the Normans came'. This meant that 'a Saxon king was no other than a *primum mobile* set in a regular motion, by laws established by the whole body of the kingdom' (Bacon, 49–51, 53, 112ff.).

In addition to being ruled by a king of their own choosing, the Saxons were governed by a 'grand assembly' of '*king, baronibus, and populo*', that is, a parliament (Bacon, 59, 60). As for the relationship among the constituent parts, the two houses held the upper hand. So much was clear from the *Mirror of Justices*, which described parliament's ancient right to govern the kingdom. This task necessarily entailed sitting in judgment of the king, since rulers could not be judges in their own causes. 'To sum up all', Bacon concluded in the 1647 portion of his work:

> the Saxon commonweal was a building of greatest strength downward even to the foundation … It was a beautiful composure, mutually dependent in every part from the crown to the clown, the magistrates being all choice men, and the king the choisest of the chosen. (ibid., 111–12)

Nor was this situation altered by the arrival of the Normans, despite royalist claims to the contrary. Indeed, William I never shook 'off the clog of Saxon law' or 'raise[d] the title of conquest'. Instead he followed the Saxon coronation ceremony, making 'a solemn covenant to observe those laws which were *bone & approbate & antiquae leges Regni*', that is, St Edward's laws. So, too, did William govern with parliament, as the Saxons had done. In fact, William went so far as to confirm St Edward's laws in a parliamentary assembly of 1070, a confirmation that deserved, in Bacon's view, to 'be called the first Magna Carta in Norman times' (Bacon, *An Historical Discourse* 115–16, 118–19, 155ff., 160ff.). And so it went with William I's heirs and successors, each of whom promised in his turn to govern according to the ancient Saxon laws. This explained how the people of Stuart England came to be governed by the very same laws and institutions as their Saxon predecessors.

Writing a summation of his work in 1651, Bacon re-emphasized the continuity of an elective and contractual monarchy and a parliament which oversaw its proper functioning. With a salute to both past and present he wrote at the very end of his tract: 'as I found this nation a commonwealth, so I leave it, and so it may be forever' (Bacon). Since the 'commonwealth' of which he wrote referred not to a utopia but to the government established after the regicide, Bacon's ancient constitutionalism was indeed of the radical sort. Living in Gray's Inn in 1660 he was a man of some wealth, receiving an annual salary of £500 as master of requests and perhaps as much as £1500 for his anti-royalist services. He died in 1660 and was buried at Coddenham. His wife and seven children survived him—sons Philip and Francis and daughters Elizabeth, Katherine, Hanna, Ellen, and Susanna. The family were left land and property in Suffolk, including the family home at Ipswich, individual bequests of between £250 to £400, and Bacon's law, history, divinity, and philosophy books. JANELLE GREENBERG

Sources *JHC*, 4–6 (1644–51) · R. Baxter, *A holy commonwealth* (1659) · *Diary of Thomas Burton*, ed. J. T. Rutt, 4 vols. (1828) · *CSP dom.*, *1652–3*; *1655–8*; *1677–8*; *1682* · M. B. Rex, *University representation in England, 1604–1690* (1954) · C. Holmes, *The eastern association in the English civil war* (1974) · D. Underdown, *Pride's Purge: politics in the puritan revolution* (1971) · B. Worden, *The Rump Parliament, 1648–1653* (1974) · D. Brunton and D. H. Pennington, *Members of the Long Parliament* (1954) · G. Burgess, *The politics of the ancient constitution: an introduction to English political thought* (College Park, Pa., 1992) · J. Greenberg, *The radical face of the ancient constitution: St Edward's laws in early modern political thought* (2001) · J. G. A. Pocock, *The ancient constitution and the feudal law: a study of English historical thought in the seventeenth century. A reissue with a retrospect* (1987) · S. L. Kliger, *The Goths in England* (Cambridge, MA., 1952) · L. G. Schwoerer, *The declaration of rights, 1689* (1981) · R. L. Greaves, *Enemies under his feet: radicals and nonconformists in Britain, 1664–1677* (Stanford, CA., 1990) · C. Hill, 'The Norman Yoke', *Puritanism and revolution* (1958), 50–122 · J. P. Reid, 'The jurisprudence of liberty: the ancient constitution in the legal historiography of the seventeenth and eighteenth centuries', *The roots of liberty: Magna Carta, ancient constitution, and the Anglo-American tradition of rule of law*, ed. E. Sandoz (1993) · Venn, *Alum. Cant.* · G. M. Coles, 'Bacon, Edward', HoP, *Commons, 1558–1603*,

1.373–4 • N. Bacon, *An historical discourse of the uniformity of the government of England* (1647) • *DNB* • will, PRO, PROB 11/305, sig. 106
Archives Folger, papers | Suffolk RO, Ipswich, corresp. with the bailiffs of Ipswich about troop movements in civil war, etc., incl. a brief account of the battle of Naseby from eyewitnesses
Wealth at death see will, PRO, PROB 11/305, sig. 106

Bacon [*alias* Southwell], **Nathaniel** (1598–1676), Jesuit, was the son of John Bacon, gentleman, and Elizabeth Pannell (*d.* *c.*1606), his wife, and was the younger brother of Thomas *Bacon (*c.*1592–1637). He was born on 14 August 1598 in Norfolk, probably at Sculthorpe near Walsingham. His brother Thomas studied humanities in King's Lynn before moving on to the English Jesuit college in St Omer. Nathaniel may have followed the same programme before he arrived in St Omer about 1611. He was accepted at the English College, Rome, on 8 October 1617 under the alias of Southwell. Ordained priest on 21 December 1622, he was sent to England on 19 September 1624. On 8 March 1625 he entered the Jesuits. He spent his first year of probation at the noviciate near London then situated either in Edmonton or Camberwell. He moved to Watten for his second year, after which he returned to Rome as minister of the English College in 1627. He was professed of the four vows on 31 July 1634.

With the exception of a trip to Placentia (Italy) in November 1637 for reasons unexplained in the Jesuit catalogues Bacon remained in Rome for the rest of his life. He worked as minister, procurator, consultor, and confessor at the English College. By 1646 he had moved to the Gesù as secretary to father-general's assistant for Germany. In 1649 he was appointed first pro-secretary and then secretary of the society, a position he held under four successive father-generals until 1667. He later served as personal admonitor to Father-General Gian Paolo Oliva.

The latter years of Bacon's life were devoted to the compilation of the great biographical work, *Bibliotheca scriptorum Societatis Iesu* (Rome, 1676). Building on the solid foundations provided by earlier collections made by Pedro de Ribadeneira and Philippe Alegambe, he produced a volume noted for accuracy, elegance, research, and piety. He compiled a collection of Latin meditations in 1649, which apparently circulated in manuscript. Edward Mico SJ published an English translation, *A Journal of Meditations for every Day in the Year* (1669), with a considerable amount of new material added by the translator. He died at the Gesù on 2 December 1676 and was buried in Rome.

THOMPSON COOPER, *rev.* THOMAS M. MCCOOG

Sources T. M. McCoog, ed., *Monumenta Angliae*, 2: *English and Welsh Jesuits, catalogues, 1630–1640* (1992), 483–4 • T. M. McCoog, 'The creation of the first Jesuit communities in England', *Heythrop Journal*, 28 (1987), 40–56 • G. Holt, *St Omers and Bruges colleges, 1593–1773: a biographical dictionary*, Catholic RS, 69 (1979), 25 • W. Kelly, ed., *Liber ruber venerabilis collegii Anglorum de urbe*, 1, Catholic RS, 37 (1940), 185 • H. Foley, ed., *Records of the English province of the Society of Jesus*, 7/1 (1882), 26 • T. H. Clancy, *A literary history of the English Jesuits: a century of books, 1615–1714* (1996) • A. Kenny, ed., *The responsa scholarum of the English College, Rome*, 1, Catholic RS, 54 (1962), 239–40 • provincial catalogues, Archivum Romanum Societatis Iesu, Rome • T. M. McCoog, *English and Welsh Jesuits, 1555–1650*, 2, Catholic RS, 75 (1995), 299

Bacon, Nathaniel (1647–1676), politician in Virginia, was born on 2 January 1647, the son of Sir Thomas Bacon and his wife, Elizabeth Brooke, of Friston Hall, Suffolk. He attended St Catharine's College, Cambridge, for a while, toured the continent, spent time at Gray's Inn, and graduated MA from Cambridge in 1667. Then in 1670 he married Elizabeth Duke over the strong objections of her parents and his father, and as a result Sir Edward Duke disinherited his disobedient daughter. Bacon now had to scrabble for a livelihood, which involved him in fraudulent land dealings and protracted litigation. His father, fed up with his impish offspring, did what seventeenth-century English parents often did with their mischievous children. He gave Nathaniel £1800 and shipped him, Elizabeth, and their two daughters off to Virginia, where the couple could rely upon family connections as well as their grubstake. Bacon was related to Dame Frances Berkeley (*née* Culpeper), wife of the governor, Sir William Berkeley, while a cousin, also Nathaniel Bacon, sat on the council of state.

The Bacons landed in Virginia in 1674. Immediately Bacon purchased Curles Neck plantation in Henrico county, miles up the James River from Jamestown, where he fell to growing tobacco and trading with local Native Americans. Well situated, finely educated, bright, but of a gloomy, sometimes arrogant, temperament, and given to impetuousness, he soon gained the acceptance of his fellow planters. Indeed, his proximity to Berkeley brought a political rise that could only be accounted meteoric; on 3 March 1675 he won a seat on the council of state, which high office customarily went to men with records of long service in Virginia's local and provincial governments. Flying so high so fast went to the young councillor's head, and Bacon apparently presumed his new-found rank and nearness to the governor allowed him to question Berkeley's policies openly. That was one in a series of miscalculations that ended up with his becoming a rebel.

Bacon's rebellion exploded suddenly in 1676, following a protracted period of unsettled politics, economic dislocations, and a series of deadly skirmishes between frontier settlers and the Native Americans, which broke out in the summer of 1675. By early 1676 Berkeley's grip on the situation had weakened precipitously. Leading planters in the affected areas openly challenged his ability to lead the colony through its gravest crisis of the century. Bacon too questioned the governor's passive defensive strategies, which made him receptive to pleas that he lead a force of angry, terrorized militiamen against the Native American Indians. When Berkeley tartly refused his request for a commission in April 1676, Bacon took command anyway and attacked Native Americans without regard to who was friend or foe. Berkeley countered by declaring Bacon a rebel, removing him from his council seat, and calling an election for a new general assembly.

Bacon's neighbours promptly elected their hero to a seat in the house of burgesses. When Bacon went to Jamestown to take his place, he was captured, and brought before the council of state on 10 June, where he confessed his error, received Berkeley's pardon, regained his council place, and posted a bond for good behaviour. Several days later he slipped off to his plantation. Meanwhile, the general assembly continued its business of enacting defensive measures against the Native Americans and addressing constituents' complaints about abuses in local government. Its work neared completion on 23 June, when Bacon and a force of men suddenly seized control of the capital. Bacon extorted a commission as general and a pardon, which the terrified members of the assembly voted, but once he left Jamestown Berkeley again proclaimed him a rebel. From this point forward, what had started as a disagreement over Native American policy became a duel to the death between Bacon and Berkeley and their adherents. Throughout the ensuing summer and autumn each sought to gain the upper hand, and in the course of their struggle Berkeley seized Jamestown, only to have Bacon retake it and burn it to the ground. Bacon also promised freedom to servants and slaves who joined him, which cost him support among leading planters. He himself seemed to lack clear goals, and his situation grew more untenable as his men began sacking the estates of men loyal to Berkeley. The revolt came to an abrupt turning-point in October, when on the 26th Bacon unexpectedly died, probably from dysentery, and his followers buried him secretly. Bereft of its leader, the revolt soon collapsed. Berkeley regained control, but not before the crown dispatched a military expedition to smash Bacon and a commission to investigate the causes of the disturbance.

By leading the uprising that bears his name, Bacon became a central actor in colonial Virginia. Adherents adored him as their deliverer, whereas enemies despised him as a traitor. Reverberations of that partisanship echo still in the opinions of modern scholars, who have disagreed even over Bacon's nature and his impulses to rebellion, let alone his proper place in Anglo-Virginian history. Without portraits, diaries, or letters to depict him, only snippets of information remain, and, unfortunately, they are supple enough to form Bacon into variously a hater of Native Americans who destroyed the reputation of an ever popular governor, Sir William Berkeley, a patriot who struck the first blow for American independence, or someone else. Yet however one chooses to view him, his rebellion undoubtedly precipitated major changes for Virginia. The Native American nations nearest to the settlers suffered losses from which they never recovered. Berkeley was disgraced and dismissed. Virginia came under greater royal scrutiny and management after 1676, and the general assembly lost considerable autonomy, while the colony's social order stabilized.

WARREN M. BILLINGS

Sources C. M. Andrews, ed., *Narratives of the insurrections, 1675–1690* (1915) • W. M. Billings, J. E. Selby, and T. W. Tate, *Colonial Virginia: a history* (1986) • E. S. Morgan, *American slavery, American freedom: the ordeal of colonial Virginia* (1975) • J. T. Kneebone, J. J. Looney, B. Tarter, and S. G. Treadway, *Dictionary of Virginia biography* (1998) • W. L. Shea, *The Virginia militia in the seventeenth century* (1983) • W. E. Washburn, *The governor and the rebel: a history of Bacon's rebellion in Virginia* (1957) • S. S. Webb, *1676: the end of American independence* (1984) • T. J. Wertenbaker, *Torchbearer of the revolution: the story of Bacon's rebellion and its leader* (1940)

Wealth at death plantation in Henrico county, Virginia (bought for £500 in 1674), confiscated after rebellion

Bacon, Sir Nicholas (1510–1579), lawyer and administrator, was born on Childermas day (28 December) 1510, the second son and one of the five children of Robert Bacon (*d.* 1548), yeoman and sheep-reeve to the abbot of Bury St Edmunds, and his wife, Isabel (*d.* after 1548), daughter of John Cage, yeoman, of Pakenham, Suffolk. He seems most likely to have been born at his parents' home in Drinkstone, Suffolk. Both his brothers, Thomas (*d.* 1573 or later) and James (*d.* 1573), became prominent members of London livery companies, the Salters' and the Fishmongers' respectively. His sisters, Anne and Barbara, married within the lesser gentry of Suffolk, where the family had deep roots.

Marriages and family Bacon married Jane Ferneley (*d.* 1552), daughter of a Suffolk yeoman, on 5 April 1540 and with her had six surviving children, of whom only the second son, Nathaniel *Bacon, enjoyed a career of any note; the others were Elizabeth, Sir Nicholas *Bacon *see under* [Bacon, Nathaniel (1546?–1622)], Anne, Edward *Bacon *see under* [Bacon, Nathaniel (1546?–1622)], and a second Elizabeth. Jane's sister Anne married the London merchant and future royal financial agent Thomas Gresham (*c.*1518–1579), making Bacon and Gresham brothers-in-law.

Jane Bacon died late in 1552, and by February 1553 her husband had married Anne, daughter of the humanist and statesman Sir Anthony Cooke (1504–1576) of Gidea Hall, Essex, and a familiar figure at court in the days of Queen Katherine Parr. Bacon's children from this second marriage were the future courtier Anthony *Bacon and the future chancellor and philosopher Francis *Bacon. In addition to her formidable intellect, Anne *Bacon (*c.*1528–1610) brought with her an exceptionally important set of marital connections. Her four sisters married respectively: William Cecil (Mildred); the London goldsmith Ralph Rowlett (Margaret); the courtier-humanist Thomas Hoby and then John Russell, second earl of Bedford (Elizabeth); and the diplomat Henry Killigrew (Katherine).

Youth and education Bacon's career amply demonstrates the value of education to social mobility in his time. He progressed in 1523 from the abbey grammar school at Bury St Edmunds to Corpus Christi College, Cambridge. Both institutions were then known for progressive theological ideas. The tradition that Bacon's father intended him for the clergy but that the young Nicholas ran away when faced with the tonsure seems apocryphal: Bacon entered Corpus Christi, a college known for training clerics, on a Bible scholarship and must have accepted the idea of such a career. Entering a decade before the emergence of the 'Athenian tribe' which was such a fertile training ground for the generation of statesmen and intellectuals who served Elizabeth, Bacon nevertheless made connections at Cambridge which proved formative to both his intellectual development and his career. These included the future Archbishop Matthew Parker, the future protestant martyr Thomas Dusgate, and probably

Sir Nicholas Bacon (1510–1579), by unknown artist, 1579

other young reformers frequenting the White Horse inn and the parish church of St Mary the Great. Academically successful, Bacon came third among his year in 1527.

Bacon's early postgraduate years, 1527–32, are largely unrecorded, though it is obvious that thoughts of a clerical career proved ephemeral. It is likely that he followed his brothers to seek his fortune in London; he may have travelled abroad. Having perhaps first attended an inn of chancery, by 1532 he had entered Gray's Inn and quickly made his mark in legal studies. He became a barrister a year later, an ancient in 1536, a bencher in 1550, and treasurer in 1552, serving in the latter post at least into 1556 and thus through the extensive reconstruction of the inn's main hall in the reign of Mary.

Early career and estate In the study of the law Bacon found both his true métier and the first sure rungs to a career. By mid-1538 he had appeared on the payroll of the newly formed court of augmentations. His appointment indicates that he had the patronage of Thomas Cromwell, while the fact that Archbishop Thomas Cranmer described him in that year as 'of so good judgment touching Christ's religion', and recommended him (unsuccessfully) for the post of town clerk of Calais, shows that he was already committed to the reformist camp (HoP, *Commons, 1509–58*, 1.359). By 1539 Bacon was serving as deputy to the solicitor of the augmentations, Walter Henley, and by 1540 he had succeeded Henley as solicitor at £70 a year.

Throughout the 1540s Bacon began building a landed estate, purchasing properties (several of them former monastic) especially in and around the western half of his native Suffolk, and to a lesser extent in western Norfolk, Essex, London, and elsewhere. He bought the Suffolk manor of Redgrave in 1545, and began building his first country seat there almost at once. In 1560, with his well-established career in London and Westminster making it difficult to spend much time in Suffolk, he purchased the Hertfordshire manor of Gorhambury, outside St Albans, and built a substantial mansion there. The main construction of Gorhambury House took place from 1563 to 1568, with a long gallery added about 1574.

Bacon's work at the augmentations brought him further prominence as a loyal and effective official. No later than 1542 he had entered parliament, sitting as one of the knights of the shire for Westmorland, his selection being probably ultimately due to influence wielded at court, perhaps by the earl of Cumberland. He sat again in 1545, this time for Dartmouth, through the patronage either of his augmentations colleague Sir Thomas Arundel or that of his friend John, Lord Russell. Unusually, the townsmen paid Bacon for his services, suggesting that he was feed by them as their counsel, or even their recorder.

The next step in Bacon's rise came in September 1546, when he took over as attorney to the court of wards and liveries; his position was formalized in January 1547 and he held it until 1561. Although particular expertise was not then as necessary a qualification for office as it later became, Bacon would have been an obvious candidate under any circumstances. In addition to his obvious administrative skills and experience, his share in a report commissioned by Henry VIII on the state of the inns of court—what has come to be known from its authors as the 'Denton-Bacon-Carey report', written some time about 1538–40—exhibited his concerns for educating the sons of the well-to-do. This worthy but stillborn vision recommended the creation of a fifth inn, to be run as something of a humanist academy, in which young men could be trained in the arts of law and diplomacy.

Bacon worked diligently at the wards and frequently returned to the subject of education for the young. He eventually committed his views to paper in a manuscript of 1561 (BL, Add. MS 32379, fols. 26–33) entitled 'Articles devised for the bringing up … of the queen's majesty's wards'. In it he returned to the idea of a humanist academy which might not only educate the individual child in the broad sense, thus fulfilling the moral obligation of a guardian, but also prepare him for a career in government service.

Bacon matched his theoretical concerns for education with practical application. He provided fine educations for his five sons. To educate boys in communities with which he became associated he founded or refounded grammar schools at Redgrave, Bury St Edmunds, and St Albans, and wrote the governing statutes for each. To Cambridge he donated some seventy books in 1574, gave £200 in 1578 which he estimated (erroneously, as it happened) as sufficient to build the new chapel at Corpus Christi, and established six scholarships for boys from Redgrave School to attend that college. His statue stands across from Parker's at the entrance to the college chapel, rebuilt in the nineteenth century.

The death of Edward VI on 6 July 1553 and the subsequent scramble for the throne placed Bacon in a difficult position, both professionally and geographically. His close association with the Reformation, and with many who were prominent in advancing it, gave him reason to fear a Roman Catholic regime. Yet because his seat at Redgrave and the burgeoning political presence which went with it lay in precisely the East Anglian areas to which Mary Tudor fled, it was impossible for him to temporize in announcing his loyalties. Here his bride of five months, Anne Bacon, proved both her own mettle and her value to him. She had probably been recently in Mary's service, and now, between 9 and 12 or 13 June, she made her way to Kenninghall and there pledged her support to Mary. Her husband's movements are obscure, but thanks to Anne's prompt action he and Cecil were permitted to make their peace with Mary at Ipswich between 24 and 26 July; Robert Wingfield, in whose house the latter was staying, records that 'Bacon's wife, who had once been a waiting woman of Queen Mary's, was their chief aid in beseeching pardon for them' (MacCulloch, 270). Somewhat ironically in view of her strong protestant convictions, Anne became a gentlewoman of the new queen's privy chamber.

Notwithstanding that safe transition from Edward's regime to Mary's, the latter's reign proved awkward for Bacon. He retained his post at the wards, continued to be active at Gray's Inn, and kept his head down in other ways, neither advancing further nor losing his footing in royal service. At the same time, and along with his brother-in-law Sir William Cecil, he kept in close touch with his father-in-law, Sir Anthony Cooke, and other protestant exiles.

Lord keeper Elizabeth's accession found Bacon a strong candidate for high office. He had become known as broadly educated and particularly learned in the law; he had served long and well in the courts of augmentations and then wards; he had been linked with the Reformation and the rise of protestantism on the one hand but had demonstrated his moderation and ability to compromise on the other. Perhaps of equal importance to the rest, he could bring to the queen's service his strong links with several important circles. These included the extensive family connections wrought by both his marriages: those to Gresham and the world of London politics and finance; those to the Cooke sisters and their husbands and reform-minded associates. They also included his considerable political presence in East Anglia as well as important groups of friends and associates from his days at Cambridge, Gray's Inn, the augmentations, and the wards.

Within weeks of her accession Elizabeth called upon Bacon's advice in forming her government and his help in persuading the reluctant Parker to take the see of Canterbury. She knighted Bacon about 15 December 1558. A week later (too socially conservative to name a common-born lawyer lord chancellor) she made him a privy councillor and named him lord keeper of the great seal with all the perquisites and powers of the chancellorship. A statute confirming that arrangement, and perhaps reflecting his insecurity about it, followed later on: 5 Eliz. c. 18. As lord keeper Bacon presided *ex officio* over the House of Lords (the only non-peer to sit there), allowing him to exercise his renowned eloquence and wit as the queen's spokesman.

His appointment also honoured Bacon's extensive legal expertise by placing him at the head of the court of chancery. Although denied the full title of the office, Bacon served longer and arguably with greater impact than any lord chancellor of the century. He was greatly admired by his contemporaries, including Queen Elizabeth herself, who wept at his memory when appointing his successor. The latter was Sir Thomas Egerton, later Baron Ellesmere, who said of Bacon on this occasion that 'he was wiser than any that are ever like to succeed him' (Jones, 82), and whose reforms of chancery were largely an implementation of his predecessor's plans and policies. Bacon actively clarified that court's jurisdiction and issued specific orders to formalize several legal actions, including *supersedeas*, *certiorari*, and testimony *in perpetuam rei memoriam*. He regulated the duties of the six clerks and the clerks of the petty bag, insisted on rigorous standards of professionalism from the masters in chancery, and took particular pains to clarify the jurisdiction and advance the standing of the cursitors. In 1566 he issued ordinances regarding the latter's authority, saw to their incorporation as a professional body in 1573, and some time later negotiated the acquisition from Lincoln's Inn of a tract of land on Chancery Lane on which to build them an office building. On legal matters outside the purview of chancery as such, he proposed reform of the operation of JPs and of the printing and promulgation of statutes. Finally, his views on the nature of judicial leniency and on prerogative authority, expressed in several speeches and legal decisions rather than in any comprehensive treatise, considerably elucidated both concepts.

Religious policy As a privy councillor Bacon was involved in most of the activities of the queen's government. His first statements on religion came in his opening address to parliament in January 1559. Although his oft-quoted and notably eloquent speech could be taken more as a statement of Elizabeth's views than of his own, his call for moderation and tolerance seems to be essentially that of a man who was wholly committed to a reformist position, and anxious to foster its triumph as smoothly as possible against overt opposition. His leading role in that effort was nowhere more obvious than during the Easter recess, when he presided at the Westminster disputation between the Marian and the Elizabethan bishops over the nature of the church settlement then being debated. In an unusually heavy-handed display of support for the reformist position, Bacon bullied the Catholic bishops into submission and helped goad two of them into behaviour sufficiently offensive to justify their imprisonment. They remained incarcerated just long enough for the reconvened session to pass a more protestant version of the settlement, which scraped through the Lords by only three votes.

Bacon's position on religion in subsequent years was by no means as extreme as that of many of his contemporaries, and even some of his fellow privy councillors. Although not necessarily a radical puritan, Bacon unquestionably held strong reformist views. In his exercise of the ecclesiastical patronage which his keepership put at his disposal (he could expect to present to a substantial number of livings each year) he showed a perceptible sympathy with the aims of bishops and archdeacons who had been exiles under Mary. Indeed, to Catholics and conservatives both in England and abroad he came to symbolize the protestant cause. In 1568 the Spanish ambassador referred to him as 'one of the most pernicious heretics in Europe' (*CSP Spain*, 1568–79, 79). In 1572 he and Cecil were so sharply attacked for their views in an anonymous tract known as *A Treatise of Treasons againste Queen Elizabeth and the Crowne of England*, published abroad, that they were defended by name in the queen's proclamation ordering the destruction of seditious books of 28 September 1573. In subsequent years the value which Bacon placed on a *via media* kept him from espousing extreme positions in religion in the glare of court politics. Yet both he and his wife did their part in the cause of protestant reform whenever this could be done circumspectly. Together they sheltered and supported known puritans at Gorhambury and in other livings under their control. Bacon winked at the prophesyings which so distressed Elizabeth, furthered the influence of reformist gentry in East Anglia, and on several occasions even ran foul of his old friend Matthew Parker in encouraging the circumvention of the strict letter of the law in religious observance.

Another subtle expression of Bacon's perspective on religious issues is revealed by his views on foreign affairs. Again he generally thought along the same lines as Cecil, though there were exceptions to this. He was much slower than Cecil to counsel supporting the Scottish lords of the congregation in late 1559, and in May 1563 he drew a notably angry rebuke from Cecil when he urged the surrender of the plague-stricken English garrison at Newhaven (Le Havre) against the secretary's wishes. Nevertheless, the two shared an active vigilance against the Catholic forces of Europe, tempering it (Bacon perhaps more than Cecil) with a keen sensitivity to England's limited fiscal resources. Bacon offered Cecil valuable advice on how to handle the arrival of the duke of Alva's payships which were storm driven onto England's south coast in November 1568.

Standing at court In almost all respects Bacon proved surefooted in traversing the contentious political issues of Elizabeth's early years, but there was one exception. His apparent involvement in John Hales's efforts to build a case for the legitimacy of Katherine Seymour (Lady Jane Grey's sister) as Elizabeth's closest heir to the throne landed Bacon in hot water in summer 1563. Hales had circulated a pamphlet on the subject in the aftermath of Elizabeth's near-fatal bout of smallpox in October 1562, and after she reportedly designated Lord Robert Dudley as protector of the realm on what many took to be her deathbed. Once Hales's proposals came to light in the following spring, and the queen sought to probe the full extent of what she took to be a presumptuous and even treasonous intervention, it appeared that Bacon helped Hales gather information and legal opinions. Undoubtedly urged on by Dudley, who no doubt saw Bacon, with Cecil, as obstacles to his ambitions, Elizabeth vented her fury on her lord keeper. His influence dwindled rapidly in the latter months of 1563 until he was banished from the court and privy council altogether by the end of the year. His disgrace, and the 'disquietude of mind' and even ill health which came with it, lasted until spring 1565.

In the end, and with Cecil's help, Bacon regained his previous standing and even managed an eventual rapprochement with Dudley, now earl of Leicester. Yet the experience proved very painful and had lasting effects. It emphasized his dependence on the queen's favour, and on Cecil's continued support, for his career and very livelihood. It reconfirmed his inclinations to avoid behaviour which could be construed as extreme. It also took its toll on his health. Although this had not been especially robust beforehand, it now increasingly limited his activities and caused increasingly frequent, if short, absences from his official duties. Although most of his illnesses remain undefined, Bacon suffered from gout, a tendency towards kidney stones, and above all, the discomforts of substantial corpulence in his latter years.

Political involvements A full indication of Bacon's restoration to the queen's favour came following the flight to England of Mary, queen of Scots, in May 1568, and in the political challenges arising from that dramatic event. Acknowledging his reputation for legal acumen, eloquence, and integrity, Elizabeth chose Bacon to preside over the conference convened at Westminster later that year to determine the extent of Mary's responsibility for the murder of her husband, Lord Darnley. This was a tricky assignment in all sorts of ways, and Bacon excelled at giving the impression of a sensitive and fair-minded investigation while reaching a desirably indecisive conclusion.

The rising of the northern earls in 1569 gave another fillip to Bacon's fortunes at court. As Elizabeth well knew, the attempted coup was as much directed at Cecil and such of his close associates as Bacon as it was towards her. Its failure left those figures very much more in command of the scene than they had for some time been. She relied on both councillors to investigate the rising after its collapse.

The northern rising was also closely linked to the presence of Mary Stewart in England, and though the rising itself came to an abrupt end, Mary's presence continued to plague the queen and court. In her prolonged and agonizing indecision, Elizabeth chose Bacon in the following spring to preside over the York House conference which was at least to appear to hear from all sides on Mary's appropriate fate. Once again Bacon skilfully brought the meeting to the sort of impasse which the indecisive Elizabeth found appropriate. In the ensuing months, Bacon's urgings against the idea of freeing Mary earned him the reputation with the French ambassador Fenelon as 'chef de la partie contraire' (Teulet, 3.187), and earned him Elizabeth's mild disapproval as well. He then turned to support the idea of a royal match with the duc d'Anjou which had long been on the table, and which he and others preferred to a Marian succession.

In the end the Ridolfi Plot of 1572 did more to discredit Queen Mary than any machinations by Bacon or others at court. Bacon had but to preside, in the House of Lords, over the full expression of indignation which ensued. By that time he was not only fully restored in the queen's graces, but had realized the peak of his political influence. He would by no means disappear suddenly from the scene thereafter, but his declining health in subsequent years gradually diminished the force of his presence. To an increasing extent his involvement in current affairs came not directly in the council chamber, but through letters from Gorhambury or his house near Charing Cross in London.

In these latter years Bacon sustained his concern for the royal succession and for the nation's security from foreign entanglements or even attack. Yet he also retained his vivid awareness of England's modest resources in pursuing expensive and risky policies abroad. This made him more cautious than most of his fellow councillors on the question of open intervention in the Netherlands in 1575–6, and more willing than most to encourage the Dutch to come to terms with their Habsburg rulers or, when events made this increasingly implausible, to accept French support and even overlordship.

Throughout his career Bacon maintained a political presence away from court as well as at it. Even from his days at the augmentations, his prominence at Westminster made him a valuable high steward for numerous landholding interests, including the archdiocese of Canterbury and the dioceses of Ely, Gloucester, Bristol, Winchester, and Chester. The Elizabethan years brought him high stewardships for Trinity College, Cambridge; the honour of Clare, Suffolk; and the borough of St Albans. Those offices, added to the bulk of his landed estate and the extensive activity of his sons Nathaniel, Nicholas, and Edward, also gave him a key political presence in the counties of Suffolk and Norfolk, and particularly in urban centres like Norwich and Bury St Edmunds.

Right to the end, as much as his health permitted, Bacon remained engaged in the affairs of both the privy council and the chancery. A commission to investigate the operation of the mint in spring 1578, further plans to improve the cursitors' role in chancery, and the construction of a chapel for which he had left funds at his old Cambridge college, took up as much time in this period as his active correspondence and exchanges of news from court. These days brought recognition and honour as well. Elizabeth paid him the honour of a four-day visit to his home at Gorhambury in 1577, one which even an expenditure of nearly £600 could not tarnish. Months later the queen sent him a new year's gift of a silver bowl, crossing his gift to her *en route*.

Death and personality The end came on 20 February 1579, probably from pneumonia. As his son Francis later recalled, Bacon had several days earlier fallen asleep in his barber's chair and broken into a heavy sweat. Seeking to cool him, the barber opened the window onto a cold winter's day and thus gave Bacon a chill which led to his final illness. His body lay in state at his York House residence in London for nearly a fortnight, as tributes poured in from far and wide, before his burial in St Pauls Cathedral on 9 March. The tributes included a laudatory poem by George Whetstone, a verse from the Scottish humanist and royal tutor George Buchanan (who also wrote the inscription for Bacon's tomb, erected in the cathedral in 1576), and a touching letter from the puritan parliamentarian Thomas Norton which remarked at length upon Bacon's sensitivity towards his family.

Bacon was indeed a sensitive man, not only towards those with whom he dealt professionally, but also towards his wives and children. His poem to his wife, Anne, upon her illness in 1558, is but one of his written expressions of affection. His relatively few surviving family letters attest the same concern for her and for his children from both marriages: his was surely a companionate marriage.

Nor is it his only poem. Bacon was something of a bibliophile and a student of classical literature. He enjoyed reading poetry, or having Anne read it to him when he was ill. He also wrote a number of poems himself, evidently intended for his own pleasure rather than for publication. Although undated, they seem to have been composed after his marriage to Anne in 1553—many of them perhaps in the period of his disgrace from late 1563 to mid-1565—and were published only in 1919 by Samuel Daniel, under the title *The Recreations of his Age*. Most of them deal with weighty subjects in the classical mode, such as love, moral philosophy, and religion, and emphasize the stoic virtues (which were also Bacon's virtues) of hard work, education, reason over emotion, and the value of the mean estate. But some are lighter and anecdotal in nature. A few, including 'Of a Snowe Balle' and 'Of a Lover' draw clearly on Petrarchan conceits and show a playful inventiveness of imagery.

Despite his accomplishments and stature, and the high esteem of his contemporaries, there are indications that Bacon never forgot his origins, or felt entirely secure in the social and political circles to which he ascended. Although reasonably well off, his was very far from one of the great fortunes of the day. He must have felt the limits of his place every time he presided over the Lords, each and every one of whom held a rank which the conservative Elizabeth kept ever beyond his grasp. And before the queen paid him the honour of her first visit to Gorhambury in 1572, he wrote a confidential letter to Cecil asking how to bring the occasion off, pointing out how 'rawe' he was in such matters.

Cultural interests To support his literary and philosophical interests, Bacon assembled a library which was very substantial for its time. When in 1574 he gave some seventy volumes to Cambridge at Archbishop Parker's urging, he printed his own dated bookplate to mark the occasion:

allegedly the first Englishman to have such a device. It bears his arms, his motto (*Mediocria firma*—'Safety in moderation'), and a personal inscription marking the donation. In addition, he (and/or perhaps Anne) had stencilled a series of Latin *sententiae* on the walls at Gorhambury, largely Senecan (as was his motto) in substance and derivation. They show his deep humanist learning, his affinity for the works of Horace, Cicero, and Seneca in particular, and his essential humanity.

The eloquence and wit by which his contemporaries knew Bacon, and which they often quoted, undoubtedly owed something to these classical models. Most of his important parliamentary speeches have survived in manuscript copies which were made as much for the sake of their rhetorical content as for their political content. Contemporaries like George Puttenham, Thomas Nashe, and William Camden, and slightly later writers like Ben Jonson, who knew Bacon only by reputation, considered him among the most eloquent men of his time. Authors like these would perhaps have been especially attracted by the neo-classical tone of his speech and writings, but he could also turn a homely quip at will. When he first saw Cecil's house at Theobald's and found the privy too close to the larder and lodgings, he remarked that 'you had bene better to have offendyd yor yey outward than yor nose inward' (Tittler, 66). More famously, when Elizabeth made her first visit to Gorhambury and commented on how small it seemed, he covered his wounded pride with a witty allusion to his own expanding girth, 'Madame, my house is well, but it is you that have made me too great for my house' (ibid., 215). Her next stay allowed him to display a new long gallery 120 feet long, built in the hope of just such a return visit.

In addition to numerous protestant (and puritanically inclined) clerics and tutors, Bacon patronized several writers and scientists. The latter included Leonard Digges in his works on optics and Thomas Blundeville (who also served as a tutor in the Bacon household) in his mathematical investigations. His two country houses, Redgrave as well as the later Gorhambury, and the house at Stiffkey, Norfolk, which he built for his son Nathaniel, show him to have been an active builder. His accounts reveal his close supervision of their design and construction. The architectural vocabulary of these structures is for the most part that of the English Gothic tradition, but the porch which he added at Gorhambury is exceptional, and serves as another reminder of Bacon's humanistic inclinations. Evidently done by a master craftsman familiar with the artistically precocious circle of Protector Somerset, it represented one of the first truly Renaissance structures of its type in England.

The rewards of service Notwithstanding the expense of such building projects and his financial distance from the wealthiest men of the day, Bacon was certainly comfortably affluent at his death two years later. He had the satisfaction of having established his family, and especially the three sons of his first marriage, with estates and connections linking them to a wide circle of East Anglian gentry. He managed his properties and his professional income closely and well. For a man of his rank he lived in relative frugality, entertaining in the grand manner but rarely, and travelling little save from his London home at York House near Charing Cross to Redgrave, and later to Gorhambury. His worth in cash on hand and plate at his death came to some £4450, about equal to his annual income, to which his lands and other investments have to be added. His debts came to but £860. It may well be that he was poised to spend some of this cash to purchase an estate for young Francis, the only one of his five sons not yet thus provided for. His will nevertheless served them all handsomely, also containing bequests or gifts to twenty-five of his chancery associates, nine personal retainers, seventeen relatives, and a further nine friends and colleagues. His funeral alone cost some £900.

ROBERT TITTLER

Sources R. Tittler, *Nicholas Bacon: the making of a Tudor statesman* (1976) • *DNB* • W. J. Jones, *The Elizabethan court of chancery* (1967) • BL, Add MSS (esp. 32379, 33271); Harley MSS (esp. 398, 1877, 5176) • Folger, Bacon-Townshend papers • Hunt. L., Ellesmere papers • University of Chicago, Joseph Regenstein Library, Bacon MSS • HoP, *Commons*, 1509–58, 1.358–60 • A. Simpson, *The wealth of the gentry, 1540–1660: East Anglian studies* (1961) • E. R. Sandeen, 'The building activities of Sir Nicholas Bacon', PhD diss., University of Chicago, 1959 • W. C. Richardson, *History of the court of augmentations, 1536–1554* (1961) • P. Collinson, 'Sir Nicholas Bacon and the Elizabethan *via media*', *HJ*, 23 (1980), 255–73 • J. Hurstfield, *The queen's wards: wardship and marriage under Elizabeth* (1958) • N. Bacon, *The recreations of his age*, ed. S. Daniel (1919) • A. H. Smith, *County and court: government and politics in Norfolk, 1558–1603* (1974) • *The papers of Nathaniel Bacon of Stiffkey*, ed. A. H. Smith, G. M. Baker, and R. W. Kenny, 1: 1556–1577, Norfolk RS, 46 (1979) • E. McCutcheon, 'The great house *sententiae* of Sir Nicholas Bacon', *Proceedings of the Second International Congress of Neo-Latin Studies, Amsterdam, 1973* (1979), 747–57 • W. T. MacCaffrey, *The shaping of the Elizabethan regime: Elizabethan politics, 1558–1572* (1968) • W. T. MacCaffrey, *Queen Elizabeth and the making of policy, 1572–1588* (1981) • R. O'Day, *The English clergy: the emergence and consolidation of a profession, 1558–1642* (1979) • D. MacCulloch, 'The *Vita Mariae Angliae Reginae* of Robert Wingfield of Brantham', *Camden miscellany, XXVIII*, CS, 4th ser., 29 (1984), 181–301 • *CSP Spain, 1568–79* • *Correspondance diplomatique de Bertrand de Salignac de la Mothe Fénélon*, ed. A. Teulet, 7 vols., Bannatyne Club, 67 (1838–40) • *The works of Francis Bacon*, ed. J. Spedding, R. L. Ellis, and D. D. Heath, 14 vols. (1857–74) • J. Stow, *Chronicles of England* (1580)

Archives BL, papers, Add. MSS 5751, 5756, 5843, 6729 • BL, copies of speeches as lord keeper and papers, Harley MSS • CCC Cam. • Folger, Bacon–Townshend MSS • Herts. ALS, papers • LUL, papers • Raynham Hall, Norfolk • University of Chicago, Joseph Regenstein Library • University of Chicago Library, papers | BL, Add. MSS • BL, Harley MSS • BL, Lansdowne MSS • Hunt. L., Ellesmere MSS • Norfolk RO, Bradfer-Lawrence collection • PRO, chancery and state paper collections

Likenesses oils, 1562, CCC Cam. • oils, 1579, NPG; versions at Petworth House, West Sussex; Christ Church Oxf. [*see illus.*] • E. Passe, line engraving, 1620 (after oil portrait, 1579), BM, NPG; repro. in H. Holland, *Herōologia* (1620) • terracotta bust, Gorhambury, Hertfordshire

Wealth at death £4450; incl. £2000 in plate; debts of £860; lands est. to bring in over £4000: inventory, Simpson, *Wealth of the gentry*, chap. 2

Bacon, Sir Nicholas, first baronet (*c.*1543–1624). *See under* Bacon, Sir Nathaniel (1546?–1622).

Bacon, Phanuel (1700–1783), Church of England clergyman and writer, was born at Reading on 13 October 1700, the son of Phanuel Bacon (*b.* 1652), fellow of St John's College, Oxford, and his wife, Elizabeth Harrison. His father was also vicar of St Lawrence's, Reading, and author of *A Pastor's Admonition to his Parishioners* (1728). Bacon became a demy of Magdalen College, Oxford, and graduated BA on 12 June 1719, MA on 17 April 1722, BD on 29 April 1731, and DD on 9 December 1735. In 1734 he was presented to the rectory of Bramber in Sussex by Magdalen College. Later he was collated to the living of Marsh Baldon in Oxfordshire, which became his chief residence until his death in 1783.

In addition to carrying out his clerical duties Bacon established a reputation as a writer and dramatist. His first works of note were heroic ballads. In 1719 he published *The Kite*, an epic poem celebrating the foiling of the Jacobite plot. The poem was forgotten in subsequent years, and Bacon lived in relative obscurity for the next three decades. In 1756, however, *The Kite* was rediscovered and reprinted in the *Gentleman's Magazine*. It was an immediate sensation, but was republished anonymously because the editors of the magazine could not discover who had written it. When Bacon's authorship was established his fame grew. He subsequently published anonymously a number of new works, all of which were based on morality plays. Bacon's dramatic works were satirical and comical, but also had serious moral messages. Five separate works appeared in one collection, *Humorous Ethics, or, An Attempt to Cure the Vices and Follies of the Age by a Method Entirely New* (1757). The plays were *The Moral Quack*, *The Insignificants*, *The Tryal of the Time Killers*, *The Occulist*, and *The Taxes*. Bacon may have been spurred to write them by his own experiences: in the preface to *Humorous Ethics* he makes oblique reference to morally bankrupt people who had troubled him severely, and been prosecuted in the law courts. The characters he created included Sir Amorous Flutter, Sir Jeremy Tippler, Mr Cankerworth, Mr Saveall, Mr Cholerick, and Mr Saunter Dolittle. As well as portraying morally flawed and straying people getting their come-uppance, Bacon was prepared to indulge in political satire. In *The Taxes*, for example, he chided the government for the proliferation of tariffs levied on everything from malt and ale to chocolate, paper, and clothes. In 1757 the *Monthly Review* gave Bacon's book a decidedly lukewarm reception; and there is some question as to whether or not the plays were ever performed on stage, though the subtitle to the collection includes the line 'as they are now acting to the life at the great theatre by His Majesty's company of comedians'. His other works included *The Snipe* (1765), a popular ballad supposedly based on a true story, and *A Sermon on the Great and General Day of Judgment* (1731).

Bacon died on 10 January 1783 at Marsh Baldon, Oxfordshire. In his will he left significant properties and sums to Magdalen College, Oxford, as well as the Society for the Propagation of the Gospel and Queen Anne's Bounty. He was survived by his wife, Catherine. His gravestone contained a tribute to the modesty of his poetic wit:

> The soul of Ovid warbled on his tongue;
> And his gentle [?] Harp Aubereon strung.
> Athenian Wit reviv'd in all he spoke,
> Stript of indecent gibe, and cruel joke.
> His Mirth was moral, and without offense;
> T'was Wisdom, drest by Modesty and Sense.

J. S. Chamberlain

Sources BL, Add. MS 32326, vol. 5, fols. 54–55, 61–62 • will of Phanuel Bacon, PRO, PROB 11/1103 • *GM*, 1st ser., 53 (1783), 93, 406 • D. E. Baker, *Biographia dramatica, or, A companion to the playhouse*, rev. I. Reed, new edn, rev. S. Jones, 1 (1812), 14–15 • Genest, *Eng. stage*, 10.178–9 • Foster, *Alum. Oxon.*

Wealth at death approx. £3500: will, PRO, PROB 11/1103

Bacon, Philip (*d.* 1666), naval officer, was the second son of Nicholas Bacon of Shrubland Hall, Suffolk, and his wife, Martha, only child of Sir Richard Bingham of Bingham Melcombe, Dorset. Philip (who has sometimes wrongly been called Philemon) joined Charles II during his exile in Flanders, and by the favour of Sir Charles Berkeley obtained a place in the duke of York's troop. He was wounded at the battle of Mardyck (14 June 1658), one potentially lethal bullet being stopped by his hatband, whence it was plucked by the duke himself; soon afterwards Bacon was made a cornet of horse. After the Restoration he went as a reformado (volunteer officer) on Sir John Lawson's first expedition to Algiers, and was then (1661) made lieutenant of the *Assistance*. He served as lieutenant of the *Bonaventure* (1662) and the *St Andrew* (1663) in successive Mediterranean voyages, and returned in 1664 as lieutenant of Sir Thomas Allin's flagship *Plymouth*. While the fleet was at Algiers in November, Bacon replaced Nicholas Parker (left behind as consul) as captain of the *Nonsuch*. This ship was accidentally lost off Gibraltar on 2 December, and by the 29th, when Allin attacked the Dutch East India fleet, Bacon was back aboard the *Plymouth* as a supernumerary. A shot from the *King Solomon* struck him as he sat charging his gun, but again he was saved by his hat: 'had he stood up, he had gone' (*Journals of Sir Thomas Allin*, 1.192).

Bacon returned to England in March 1665, and by the 19th he was captain of the *Oxford*, which he would command at the battle of Lowestoft on 3 June. For his service there he was promoted to captain the 52-gun *Bristol*, in which he sailed once more for the Mediterranean in December. In his absence he was (16 March 1666) designated to command the *Assurance* in the summer's campaign, but on his return in May he remained with the *Bristol*. He was with Albemarle's part of the divided fleet, and on 28 May was instructed to cruise off the North Foreland in search of the enemy. It was his ship that, at 6 a.m. on 1 June, signalled the presence of the Dutch and the beginning of the Four Days' Fight. At 3 p.m. on the first afternoon Bacon received a fatal bullet wound to the thigh. His body was brought back to Harwich and thence to Coddenham church, Suffolk, for burial in the family vault. A marble monument records his achievements and the affection in which he was held. C. S. Knighton

Sources J. R. Tanner, ed., *A descriptive catalogue of the naval manuscripts in the Pepysian Library at Magdalene College, Cambridge*, 1, Navy RS, 26 (1903), 320 • *The journal of Edward Mountagu, first earl of Sandwich, admiral and general at sea, 1659–1665*, ed. R. C. Anderson, Navy RS, 64 (1929), 177, 272 • *The journals of Sir Thomas Allin, 1660–1678*, ed. R. C. Anderson, 2 vols., Navy RS, 79–80 (1939–40) • J. R. Powell and

E. K. Timings, eds., *The Rupert and Monck letter book, 1666*, Navy RS, 112 (1969), 16, 54–5, 198, 231, 233, 236, 244, 248 • D. Syrett and R. L. DiNardo, *The commissioned sea officers of the Royal Navy, 1660–1815*, rev. edn, Occasional Publications of the Navy RS, 1 (1994), 15 • J. Charnock, ed., *Biographia navalis*, 1 (1794) • Pepys, *Diary* • PRO, SP 29/158, nos. 5, 37, 38, 42 • monumental inscription, Coddenham church, Suffolk

Bacon, Sir Ranulph Robert Maunsell (1906–1988), police officer, was born on 6 August 1906 at 30 Ridgmount Gardens, Bloomsbury, London, the only son of Arthur Ranulph Bacon (1872–1949), electrical engineer, and his wife, Hester Mary Ayles. There was at least one sister, Joan Alice Mary (Mrs Bury). He was educated at Tonbridge School (1920–25) and Queens' College, Cambridge. His father, who was a nephew and collaborator of the astronomer and aviator John Mackenzie Bacon, had resolved that he should be an engineer, and was displeased when Bacon (attracted by the outdoor life) joined the Metropolitan Police after graduating in 1928. He was a large, cheerful, and powerful man who was nicknamed Rasher and for several years captained the police fifteen at rugby. His first arrest was of a brawling woman in Brompton Oratory. While on points duty in Brompton Road he met Alfreda Violet (1909–1984), the daughter of Alfred Annett, merchant, of 20 Ormonde Gate, Chelsea. They were married on 24 November 1932 at St George's, Hanover Square; their only child, a daughter, predeceased them.

After sixteen months on the beat in Chelsea and Fulham, Bacon was transferred to the fingerprint department at New Scotland Yard. His abilities impressed Lord Trenchard, the reforming commissioner of the Metropolitan Police, and after 1931 Bacon became a favourite among 'Trenchard's brats'. He was put in charge of the new map room at Scotland Yard, where crimes were flagged on maps of London so as to trace patterns of crime and pinpoint criminal localities. In 1934 he was accepted on the inaugural course at Hendon Police College, which Trenchard intended as a version of Sandhurst or Cranwell, training an élite of police officers. He was awarded the first baton of honour on graduating from Hendon in 1935. Afterwards he was inspector in charge of Paddington Green police station.

Bacon was eager to transfer to the armed forces on the outbreak of war, but was denied permission until 1940, when he was seconded to the army's provost service. He reached the ranks of lieutenant-colonel (1941) and deputy provost-marshal (1942) while serving in the Middle East. He proceeded to Ceylon in 1943 where he was initially police superintendent and afterwards inspector general of police (1944–7). Bacon returned to England in 1947 to become chief constable of Devon. He was awarded the king's police medal in 1953.

Convivial, energetic, and conservative minded, Bacon was reputedly one of the ablest policemen of his generation. In 1961 he returned to the Metropolitan Police as assistant commissioner in charge of administration and operations at Scotland Yard. Subsequently, in 1963, he was put in charge of the Criminal Investigation Department with a staff of 1800 officers whom he called his 'troops'. This department was under-manned, poorly managed, and ineffective. Less than one in six of London housebreakings were solved in 1963, and only 3.8 per cent of property stolen by burglars was recovered. Bacon swiftly launched a campaign against that 'violation of the Englishman's castle', housebreaking, believing that the psychological effect on householders, and especially their wives, 'of having their premises roamed by hostile strangers' was 'even worse' than the loss of valuables, 'and if such offences were to get out of hand could even affect the nation's morale' (*The Times*, 10 Dec 1963). He also sought to restore goodwill towards his officers. He felt that CID relations with journalists had 'sadly deteriorated since his days as a young constable' while the public had become estranged 'largely because so few police officers these days, because of the housing shortage in Central London, live near their work' (ibid.). During 1964 'Rasher of the Yard' attracted public attention by urging civilians to 'have a go' at criminals by pursuing and detaining them. He was promoted to deputy commissioner in April 1966, but having passed the age of sixty was obliged to retire in October of that year. He was created KBE (1966).

After leaving official service his expertise was sought by commercial security organizations. He sat on the board of Securicor Ltd (1966–81), and was successively a director (1970–81) and consultant (1981–6) of an American company, International Intelligence Inc. Having previously investigated the involvement of Italian American gangsters in gambling scandals in the Bahamas he became a member of the Gaming Board (1968–75), and was strenuous in monitoring the gambling clubs of London. When young he had represented his university in shooting competitions at Bisley; in retirement he accepted the presidency of the Gun Trade Association (1972–7) and the Shooting Sports Trust (1972–7). 'A shotgun is part of the adult Englishman's equipment', he told a public meeting (Massingberd, 69).

Bacon died of bronchopneumonia and heart disease on 30 March 1988 at the Avenue Clinic, 14 New Church Road, Hove, and was cremated on 6 April at the Downs crematorium, Brighton. RICHARD DAVENPORT-HINES

Sources H. Massingberd, ed., *The Daily Telegraph book of obituaries*, 1 (1995), 69–72 • *The Times* (10 Dec 1963), 8c • *The Times* (9 Dec 1965), 6g • *The Times* (1 Jan 1966), 5a • *The Times* (1 April 1988), 18f • b. cert. • m. cert. • d. cert. • *CGPLA Eng. & Wales* (1988) • C. H. Knott, *Register of Tonbridge School, 1900–1965* (1966), 113 • *The Times* (2 April 1988)

Wealth at death £237,092: probate, 13 Aug 1988, *CGPLA Eng. & Wales*

Bacon, Sir Reginald Hugh Spencer (1863–1947), naval officer, was born on 6 September 1863 at Wiggonholt rectory, Sussex, youngest of the eight children of the Revd Thomas Bacon and his wife, Emma Lavinia, daughter of George Shaw of Teignmouth. He entered the Royal Navy via the *Britannia* in January 1877. Rated midshipman on leaving, and already known to his peers as Porky, he was appointed (January 1879) to the *Alexandra*, flagship of Sir Geoffrey Hornby and then of Sir Beauchamp Seymour, 'the swell of the ocean', in the Mediterranean. After good results at Greenwich he was promoted lieutenant in

Sir Reginald Hugh Spencer Bacon (1863–1947), by Francis Dodd, 1917

August 1883 and went to sea in the sail training-ship *Cruiser* before specializing in torpedoes and qualifying at *Vernon*. He became torpedo officer in two flagships of the channel squadron, *Northumberland* and *Camperdown*. He returned to *Vernon* until promoted commander in June 1895, when he was appointed to the cruiser *Theseus* in the special service squadron which was suddenly withdrawn from the Mediterranean in January 1897 to reinforce the West African squadron under Sir Harry Rawson in dealing with the critical situation in Benin resulting from the massacre of an English party. Bacon accompanied the by now traditional naval brigade up country as intelligence officer, for which he was appointed to the DSO and mentioned in dispatches. Six months later, having written a spirited account of the expedition entitled *Benin, City of Blood* (1897), he was sent to the *Empress of India*, which took part in the queen's jubilee review before joining the Mediterranean Fleet. In 1898 she was ordered to Crete to join Admiral Sir Gerard Noel's punitive expedition after the massacre of the British vice-consul and his family. So far Bacon's had been the classical career of an enterprising officer of his day. The advent of Sir John Fisher as commander-in-chief, the Mediterranean Fleet, was to have a shattering effect on even so rhadamanthine an institution as the Royal Navy but it brought Bacon opportunities of which he took full advantage. Fisher welcomed ideas from junior officers; Bacon was quick to respond to his admiral's request for suggestions about the tactical deployment of torpedo boats. Fisher's approval of his proposals was instant and rewarding; on his recommendation Bacon was promoted captain in June 1900, only five years since he had been promoted commander.

Bacon's first appointment was to evaluate the technical aspects of the Paris Exhibition of that year; the next to attend one of the early war courses at the Royal Naval College, Greenwich. Thereafter he oversaw the introduction of submarine boats into the Royal Navy. G. J. Goschen's last act before he retired as first lord had been to order five Holland submersibles from America, to be built under licence by Vickers and by Maxim. Bacon was appointed inspecting captain of submarine boats, a post which he held until 1904 and which made him father of 'the trade', as the Submarine Service is affectionately known, supervising both the construction of its boats and the training of their crews.

Fisher became first sea lord on Trafalgar day, 1904, and at once recruited Bacon—said to be the cleverest officer in the Navy—to be his naval assistant. After working on the new designs committee with the specifications of the revolutionary *Dreadnought* and the new battle cruisers, and commanding the *Irresistible* in order to gain the sea time needed for further promotion, he was appointed in January 1906 to *Dreadnought* as her first captain. It was while he was in the Mediterranean that he obliged Fisher with private letters, ostensibly about the fleet in general and the seagoing reaction to board innovations and experiments, but occasionally commenting on individuals. However apart from a reference to certain admirals 'getting at the King', he was careful not to identify brother officers, doing so only once and that a junior; but the suspicion that he informed on a fellow officer stuck, an odium from which his standing never quite recovered. He lacked the gift of drawing loyalty or affection from his officers and men; and when the texts were almost inadvertently quoted by Fisher in his feud against Lord Charles Beresford in 1909, the effect may have contributed to Bacon's decision to retire from the service. He had served as flag captain and chief of staff to Sir Francis Bridgeman when he hoisted his flag in the *Dreadnought* as admiral in the Home (Reserves) Fleet; in 1907 he relieved Jellicoe as director of naval ordnance, in the middle of a controversy concerning the choice of a centralized fire-control system. Fisher and Jellicoe favoured Pollen's invention, but Jellicoe left the Admiralty for the fleet, and Bacon opted for the cheaper but less accurate system designed by Captain F. C. Dreyer. This was a controversial and, as events were to show, a mistaken decision, and though Bacon could scarcely have missed the flag list in July 1909, he was perhaps fortunate in being invited by McKenna to join the board as third sea lord and controller, again relieving Jellicoe. But he had been offered the post of managing director of the Coventry ordnance works and calculating that because of his short time at sea he would be unlikely to obtain any significant command afloat, he asked for his name to be transferred to the retired list that November.

By August 1914 Bacon had produced a new howitzer, of

which he took a detachment to Flanders in 1915, commanding the force in the rank of colonel 2nd commandant, Royal Marines. To the astonishment of many of his naval contemporaries and the fury of some, he was recalled to active naval service by Churchill, then first lord, and appointed to relieve Rear-Admiral Horace Hood in command of the Dover patrol and as senior naval officer, Dover. He was promoted vice-admiral late in 1916, and early in January 1917 proposed to Jellicoe, who had become first sea lord, a seaborne assault on the Belgian coast, using monitors to push floating piers ahead of them, and landing 14,000 men with artillery and transport over open beaches while Ostend and Zeebrugge were bombarded by other inshore craft. This promising scheme was never mounted because the army failed to co-ordinate its part of the plan. In 1918 the two ports were raided, but in accordance with plans amended significantly in the light of criticisms made by Bacon when the originals had been sent to him by mistake—they were being circulated in confidence to other officers while he was still in command at Dover.

Bacon's days there were numbered once Sir Eric Geddes became first lord in July 1917. Fortified by the appointments of Admiral Wemyss as deputy first sea lord and Rear-Admiral Roger Keyes as director of plans, Geddes set up a channel barrage committee under the latter on 13 November. This irked Bacon, whose conceit shone through in a series of petulant letters he sent to the first lord. These did not endear him to an equally self-confident man. But Bacon was the man in the job, and as such he was supported by Jellicoe, for too long for the latter's own good. Eventually their hands were forced. Bacon was cornered over the use of nets, mines, and searchlights and then over the disposition of his surface forces. Intelligence of numerous and safe transits of the Dover Strait by U-boats tipped the scales; Wemyss was adamant that he should go. Jellicoe was reluctant to relieve him. Wemyss contemplated resignation. A. J. Marder has argued that the primary cause of Jellicoe's dismissal was the impending sacking of Bacon, and it was indeed Jellicoe who was sacked by Geddes at Christmas time 1917 in a manner which still astonishes. Wemyss replaced Bacon with Keyes on new year's day 1918: an instant and significant increase in U-boat sinkings spoke for itself.

Bacon's considerable abilities were too valuable to lose, and again it was Churchill, now minister of munitions, who redeployed them, making him controller of the ministry inventions department. He was advanced to the rank of admiral in September 1918 and his name finally went onto the retired list on 31 March 1919. He moved to Hampshire and devoted himself to shooting and to chairing the Romsey bench, spending his summers at his house near Lerici in Italy. He also turned to writing, in a faintly pompous tone more reminiscent of Beresford than of Fisher. His autobiography needed two volumes, *A Naval Scrap Book, 1877–1900* (1925) and *From 1900 Onward* (1940); two more were devoted to the Dover patrol, and in 1923 he accepted Jellicoe's request to act as his literary representative when the official Jutland report was published. This led to Bacon writing *The Jutland Scandal* (1925), 'Dedicated to those two neglected goddesses, Justice and Truth, now worshipped in an obscure corner of the British Pantheon' (Bacon, *The Jutland Scandal*, dedication) which even Jellicoe thought was a shade too strong—'the criticism is obvious but he has overdone it … I am sorry that he rubbed it into Beatty so hard' (Winton, 292). To others it seemed able if trenchant; in the service there was some repugnance at the title. In 1929 he published the standard biography of Fisher, again in two volumes; sympathetic but not sycophantic, though now rather outdated. Seven years later he managed to deal with Jellicoe in one thick volume, an authorized work though he did not have access to all the admiral's papers, and refused to have the manuscript vetted by his literary executors.

Bacon married in 1894 Cicely Isabel (*d.* 1955), daughter of Henry Edward Surtees MP, of Redworth Hall, co. Durham. They had one daughter and two sons; the elder was killed at Loos and the younger died while a naval cadet. Edward VII had appointed Bacon CVO in 1907; he was promoted KCVO in 1916, and appointed KCB for his work at Dover. He enjoyed several foreign awards. Undeniably a man of brilliant professional attainments, with a most original mind and probably the cleverest of the many able young officers of his time, he justified Fisher's selection as a disciple in the promotion of many major reforms. He won early and accelerated promotion by merit, and his development of the submarine force alone would secure his fame. His work at Dover enhanced it. He was unfortunate in his manifestation of self-sufficiency and self-satisfaction. Bacon died at his home, Braishfield Lodge, near Romsey, on 9 June 1947, and was buried in Romsey.

A. B. Sainsbury

Sources *DNB* • S. W. Roskill, *Admiral of the fleet Earl Beatty: the last naval hero, an intimate biography* (1980) • A. T. Patterson, *Jellicoe: a biography* (1969) • *The Jellicoe papers*, ed. A. T. Patterson, 2, Navy RS, 111 (1968) • R. H. S. Bacon, *Life of John, Earl Jellicoe* (1936) • A. J. Marder, *From the Dreadnought to Scapa Flow: the Royal Navy in the Fisher era, 1904–1919*, 5 vols. (1961–70) • R. F. MacKay, *Fisher of Kilverstone* (1973) • J. Winton, *Jellicoe* (1981) • R. H. S. Bacon, *The Jutland scandal* (1925) • J. T. Sumida, *In defence of naval supremacy: finance, technology and British naval policy, 1889–1914* (1989) • *The Keyes papers*, ed. P. G. Halpern, 1, Navy RS, 117 (1972)

Archives BL, corresp. with Lord Jellicoe, Add. MS 49010 • BL, corresp. with Lord Keyes • CAC Cam., letters to A. Hurd | FILM IWM FVA, actuality footage • IWM FVA, documentary footage

Likenesses F. Dodd, charcoal and watercolour drawing, 1917, IWM [*see illus.*]

Wealth at death £10,816 2*s.* 8*d.*: probate, 13 Sept 1947, *CGPLA Eng. & Wales*

Bacon, Richard Mackenzie (1776–1844), newspaper editor and music critic, was born in Norwich on 1 May 1776, the only son of Richard Bacon (1745–1812), proprietor from 1794 of the *Norwich Mercury*, one of the leading provincial organs of liberal opinion. He was educated at the Norwich Free School, and on leaving joined the paper; he was manager of the printing department until 1804, when he became proprietor. He also had shares in the Theatre Royal from 1806, and from 1808 served in the Norwich rifle volunteers, rising to the rank of major. In 1813 he and Bryan Donkin obtained a patent for improvements in the apparatus employed in printing. The *Norwich Mercury* of 3 December 1814 published a prospectus of Bacon's printing machine, with an account of the progress it had then made, and it was highly praised by the author of the article 'Printing' in Rees's *Cyclopaedia* (1819). In 1816 he became editor of the *Mercury*. He published a number of pamphlets on social, political, and military matters.

Bacon also studied music in London with Samuel Arnold. Having published some music criticism, he founded in 1818 the *Quarterly Musical Magazine and Review*: this lasted for ten annual volumes. Written for the most part anonymously, but largely by Bacon himself and his daughters, the *Review* was one of the earliest musical journals in England and did much to encourage proper standards of critical discussion. Its interest centred on the education of professional musicians, but it also provided an account of musical events and a picture of early nineteenth-century musical thoughts and attitudes, which remain valuable. What appear to be Bacon's own discussions of new books and their subjects reflect a wide-ranging intellect and a probing mind well schooled in philosophical matters. The journal had considerable influence in its own day, and Bacon was widely respected. About 1822 he issued proposals for an encyclopaedia of music, to be printed by subscription, and to appear in 1823 under his editorship. Although he is said to have collected the materials for this project, it was never published. Bacon was largely responsible for founding the Norfolk and Norwich Triennial Musical Festival in 1824.

In 1797 Bacon had married Jane Louisa (1768–1808), only daughter of Augustine Noverre. Their eldest child, Richard Noverre Bacon (*d.* 1884), played the cello in the first Norwich Festival and edited the *Norwich Mercury* after his father's death. Bacon died at Cossey, Norfolk, on 27 November 1844. Besides Richard, Bacon was survived by five other children. His eldest daughter, Louisa Mary Bacon [*see* Barwell, Louisa Mary], had worked with her father on the *Quarterly* from its foundation, then, after her marriage to a Mr Barwell, wrote some books on children's musical education. Mary Anne Bacon (*c.*1806–1875) was a contributor to the *Quarterly* and to other journals, and edited a collection of manuscripts relating to her father. George Peter Bacon (*c.*1807–1878) was editor and proprietor of the *Sussex Advertiser*. Jane M. Bacon (*d.* 1870), a successful mezzo-soprano, studied music with William Horsley and singing with Manuel García, then settled and studied further in Paris before returning to London to complete her studies with Sir George Smart. A further daughter, Rose Bacon, also moved in musical circles.

John Warrack

Sources *New Grove* • *Quarterly Musical Magazine and Review*, 1–9 (1818–27) • J. F. Waller, ed., *The imperial dictionary of universal biography*, 3 vols. (1857–63) • *GM*, 2nd ser., 23 (1845), 109 • *Norwich Mercury* (7 Dec 1844) • *Norfolk Chronicle* (30 Nov 1844) • C. H. Timperley, *A dictionary of printers and printing* (1839) • W. Chappell, *Popular music of the olden time* (1859) • d. cert. • *DNB*
Archives CUL, corresp. and papers
Likenesses photograph (after painting), Central Public Library, Norwich • photograph (after painting), Central Public Library, Norwich • photograph (after portrait), Norfolk Studies Library, Gildengate House, Norwich

Bacon [Bacun], **Robert** (*d.* 1248), theologian, was born in the 1170s or 1180s, into a family of which nothing is known except that he had a sister Mabel, resident within the Forest of Savernake, Wiltshire. Bacon was to achieve distinction as a theologian and preacher; it is therefore frustrating that so little can be established about his early education. However, in 1948 Beryl Smalley demonstrated that the *tractatus* on the Psalms in Bodl. Oxf., MS Bodley 745, which is attributed to Brother R. Bacon, used as its basic text the commentary on the Psalms of the Parisian master Jean d'Abbeville; she deduced from this that Robert Bacon had been John's pupil in Paris about 1210. He is likely to have received considerable training in the arts before this. In a statement produced in the early 1240s to support the canonization of Edmund of Abingdon, Robert Bacon described himself as having been Edmund's pupil, auditor, and close companion. Although he provided no context for this relationship, C. H. Lawrence has suggested that it may have been formed in Oxford between about 1214 and 1219.

In 1219 Bacon, now described as master, received from the Benedictine abbey of Eynsham the presentation to the living of Lower Heyford, Oxfordshire. The abbey's propinquity to Oxford (and perhaps the presence of one of Edmund of Abingdon's brothers as a monk there) suggests that Bacon's promotion and his academic reputation were connected. It was a condition of the presentation that the incumbent should reside in his parish and fulfil the functions of parish priest. Bacon is likely therefore to have been ordained either before 1219 or shortly afterwards. By 1227, however, he had resigned the living, perhaps because he was already considering entering the Dominican order. The date of Bacon's profession is unknown, but Thomas 'of Eccleston', the Franciscan chronicler, alleged that it happened on the day of his entry into the order, and that he was dispensed from the usual probationary period. Jordan of Saxony, the provincial of the order, visited England in 1229, hoping to recruit a good haul of candidates; Bacon may have been among these.

Bacon then embarked upon the career that was to occupy him for the rest of his life, that of preaching and of teaching theology in Oxford. Here he worked on occasion with Robert Grosseteste (*d.* 1253), and he taught Richard Fishacre (*d.* 1248). It is also likely that he kept up his connection with Edmund of Abingdon, who became archbishop of Canterbury in 1233 amid the crisis that followed Henry III's dismissal in the previous year of his justiciar, Hubert de Burgh. In June 1233, according to Matthew Paris, Robert Bacon preached a sermon before the king at Oxford, warning him of the dangers to national peace posed by allowing Peter des Roches, bishop of Winchester, and his nephew Peter de Rivallis, to dominate royal counsels. Such blunt speaking did not apparently alienate Henry entirely; after the fall of the much disliked Poitevin counsellors in 1234, the king sometimes called on Bacon's services, usually to protect newly converted Jews, or to impose discipline on Oxford clerics, or on their prostitutes and concubines. But after 1238 Bacon seems to have evaded royal notice.

Robert Bacon may have performed commissions for Edmund of Abingdon until the archbishop's death in 1240. Much of his energy in the next few years went into promoting the canonization of his old friend. He featured prominently in the University of Oxford's appeal to the pope, he wrote an important *Veriloquium* on Edmund's sanctity, and in 1244 he was a member of the commission of three set up to investigate the facts. The bull of canonization of 1246 must have given him much satisfaction.

The rest of his time was spent in teaching and preaching. Smalley dated his commentary on the Psalms to the period 1230–48, and pointed out that he added much to Jean d'Abbeville's material, including some *quaestiones* and allusions to new Aristotelian material. The *tractatus* in the form in which it has been preserved was prepared, whether by Bacon himself or by an editor, as moralities for use in composing sermons. The attribution to him of the *Syncategoremata* in Oxford Bodl. Oxf., MS Digby 204, folios 88–100 is more doubtful. Bacon's sermons, famous in their day, have all disappeared except one for the first day of Rogation, in BL, Royal MS 7 A.ix, folio 70v. His high reputation among his contemporaries is best appreciated from the warmth of the tribute paid to him and to his pupil Richard Fishacre by Matthew Paris, in 1248, the year of their deaths. They were, he said, without equal in theological and other fields of knowledge; they taught with distinction for many years in the theology faculty of Oxford, while also preaching the word of God to the people. Bacon was buried in the church of the Blackfriars, Oxford. JEAN DUNBABIN

Sources B. Smalley, 'Robert Bacon and the early Dominican school at Oxford', *TRHS*, 4th ser., 30 (1948), 1–19 • Emden, *Oxf.*, 1.87 • W. A. Hinnebusch, *The early English Friars Preachers* (1951) • Paris, *Chron.*, 3.244–5; 5.16 • *Chancery records* • W. P. W. Phillimore and others, eds., *Rotuli Hugonis de Welles, episcopi Lincolniensis*, CYS, 1, 3 (1907–9) • A. B. Emden, *An Oxford hall in medieval times: being the early history of St Edmund Hall* (1927), 269 • N. Trevet, *Annales sex regum Angliae, 1135–1307*, ed. T. Hog, EHS, 6 (1845), 229 • *Fratris Thomae vulgo dicti de Eccleston tractatus de adventu Fratrum Minorum in Angliam*, ed. A. G. Little (1951), 81 • C. H. Lawrence, *St Edmund of Abingdon* (1960), 248–53 [other refs in text] • B. Smalley, *The study of the Bible in the middle ages*, 3rd edn (1983)

Archives BL, Royal MS 7 A.ix, fol. 70v • Bodl. Oxf., MS Bodley 745, pp. 193–497 • Bodl. Oxf., MS Digby 204, fols. 88–100

Bacon [Bakun], **Roger** (*c.***1214–1292**?), philosopher and Franciscan friar, is by inference from his later career usually assigned a birth date about 1214, and from early traditions it seems that he came from the south-west of England, perhaps near Ilchester in Somerset.

Early life and academic activities Bacon studied and probably lectured on arts in Oxford, and then lectured at Paris, where he was a pioneer in teaching Aristotle's natural philosophy. The assertion that he was in Paris by 1236 rests on the very dubious ascription to him of a work *De retardatione accidentium senectutum*, but he was certainly there by 1245. He was also there in 1251, but a question mark hangs over the intervening years. This arises largely from a reorientation of intellectual outlook which he himself fairly clearly dates at some twenty years earlier than works that he was writing *c.*1267. 'In the twenty years in which I have laboured specially at the study of wisdom, disregarding the crowd's approach, I have spent more than two thousand pounds on these matters' (*Opus tertium*, ed. Brewer, 59). In this view his early Aristotelian works deriving from his Paris lectures may be seen as representative of the 'crowd's approach', and, although early in date, they do not seem especially remarkable. His new approach may loosely be described as more 'scientifically' and technologically oriented, and was strongly influenced by Robert Grosseteste and the Franciscan school at Oxford, especially Adam Marsh, and to a lesser extent Thomas Wallensis, but a question remains as to how exactly he received this influence.

Grosseteste was lecturer to the Franciscans at Oxford from 1229 to 1235, when he became bishop of Lincoln, but for various reasons it is implausible to date much acquaintanceship to this period. Another possibility is to deny that Bacon knew Grosseteste at all, except perhaps for having heard the odd sermon. This may be a little extreme, and does not solve the problem of when he became acquainted with Adam Marsh (whom he certainly knew) and, possibly, Thomas Wallensis. Thomas was lecturer to the Oxford Franciscans from about 1240 to 1247, when he departed to become bishop of St David's, and was succeeded by Adam Marsh, who was also a regent master in theology from 1247 to 1250. Taking all these facts into consideration, there is much to be said for the hypothesis that Bacon returned to Oxford about 1247, in time to have come to know, albeit briefly, Thomas Wallensis, and to have attended Adam Marsh's theological lectures. Grosseteste was by that time bishop of Lincoln, but Oxford was in his diocese and he was friendly with Adam Marsh. It therefore seems quite likely that Bacon would at least have been introduced to him, although A. G. Little's suggestion that he became Grosseteste's assistant, and that one of Grosseteste's works was influenced by him, seems improbable.

It is often assumed that another important cause of Bacon's reorientation was the important pseudo-Aristotelian work, *Secretum secretorum*, which he believed to be by Aristotle himself. This takes the form of a long letter on kingship addressed to Aristotle's erstwhile pupil Alexander the Great, and has as a strong theme the extreme usefulness of philosophy, of various sciences (including those that would now be called pseudo-sciences), and of medicine. This theme was especially important to Bacon in his new orientation, and from at least 1267 he cites the work with great frequency. He also prepared an edition of it, which included an introductory treatise by himself together with a series of glosses. Since Robert Steele's edition (1920) it has been conventional to date the glosses to the 1250s and the introduction to about 1270. However, a study by S. P. Williams has made a strong case for dating both the introduction and the glosses to about 1270 or later. This weakens the case for its being an especially important factor in bringing about his 'conversion' to a new way of approaching knowledge, but at least it was to provide strong reinforcement.

Bacon as Franciscan; the works for the pope Another important event in Bacon's career that can only be dated tentatively is his entry into the Franciscan order; this has plausibly been put at 1257. Bacon's vocation is unexpected, for his likeness to St Francis was minimal: once again the influence of Adam Marsh and other Englishmen must be suspected. This in turn makes it probable that the event occurred in England, and renders less appealing J. Hackett's otherwise interesting conjecture that Bacon remained in Paris for most of the 1240s and 1250s. It may be accounted unfortunate for him that at roughly the same time Bonaventure became master-general of the order, a man who had a very different spirituality from Bacon's (with, for instance, far greater emphasis on prayer and contemplation). Whether or not it was from a truculent attitude which made it seem advisable to keep him under closer supervision, Bacon was soon back in Paris for a period of some ten years at least, during which time resentment against his superiors may well have induced hypochondria. Nevertheless he managed in this period to make contact with Guy Foulquois, who had formerly been a lawyer and military man, but by 1261 was a cardinal, and in 1264 became Pope Clement IV. Before this Guy had shown interest in Bacon's schemes and asked for his writings, a request that was repeated as a command after his elevation:

> Truly, in order that what you intend should be more evident to us, we will and command you as instructed by apostolic letters that, notwithstanding the contrary instruction of any prelate or any regulation of your order, you do not fail to send to us as quickly as possible and in a fair hand the work which, when we were established in a lesser position, we asked you to communicate to our beloved son Raymond de Laon, and that by your words you should make clear to us what remedies seem to you should be applied to those things that you have lately intimated as the occasion of such great danger, and that you do this without delay as secretly as possible. (*Opus tertium*, ed. Brewer, 1)

Because of constraints on writing that had been imposed on the Franciscan order to stop the spread of possibly heretical apocalyptic tracts, and perhaps for other reasons, Bacon had done relatively little writing over the past ten years, and, as he was later to protest to the pope, he had been speaking of works to be produced and not of those already written.

However, a papal command could not be ignored, and Bacon commenced a flurry of activity. The exact details have caused much dispute, and the following account must be to a degree conjectural. What is certain is that it brought about Bacon's most famous work, the *Opus maius*. This was divided into seven parts, and was aimed at promoting in summary form (albeit at some length) a wide expanse, although not the whole gamut, of natural knowledge. Part 1 treated the causes of human ignorance; part 2, the relation of the other sciences to theology; part 3, grammar and the power of languages; part 4, mathematics (including astronomy and astrology); part 5, optics (*perspectiva*); part 6, 'experimental science'; part 7, moral philosophy. It seems most likely that this was immediately dispatched to Rome, but then Bacon contracted three worries: the work could be lost in transit; it might be too long for a busy pope to read; some things had been omitted that should have been included. He accordingly started on another work, the *Opus minus*, to summarize and supplement the larger work. This, it may be surmised, was dispatched to the pope under the care of a special courier known simply as John. This young man, who came from a poor background, had been one of Bacon's favourite pupils, on whom he had tested his educational theories, and whom he had imbued with his own views as to the proper way to approach natural philosophy. It is not certain what happened to John in later life, but quite probably he remained in Rome for some time after this commission. A similar concern that had led Bacon to produce the *Opus minus* now led him to work on the considerably longer *Opus tertium*. This may never have been properly revised to Bacon's satisfaction, and was quite probably never sent to the pope, who died in 1268 without leaving any known record of how he reacted to Bacon's ideas. The editorial state of these three works, as of many others in the corpus, is unsatisfactory, but is steadily improving.

Later years Bacon did not give up writing with the death of Clement IV, but he seems to have become more and more disillusioned and infuriated with what he saw as the increasing corruption of knowledge. His efforts were directed mainly towards a great systematic treatise, in comparison with which the *Opus maius* had been (because of the shortness of time available) a mere summary. Scholars often refer to this projected writing as the *Scriptum principale*, but the evidence suggests that Bacon used this term generically rather than as the title of a specific work. More probably he saw the work as entitled *Compendium studii philosophiae* or *Compendium studii theologiae*. A fragment with the former title, which can be dated to 1272, was published in the nineteenth century by Brewer, and one with the latter title, datable to 1292, was published by Maloney in 1988. Other fragments, both published and unpublished, were clearly also intended as parts of the grand synthesis.

The evidence strongly suggests that Bacon was back in Oxford about 1270, and he may have spent much of the rest of his life in England. About 1278 there perhaps occurred one of the most controversial episodes in Bacon's career, for it is reported in the *Chronica XXIV generalium*, a work compiled some 100 years later, that in that year the master-general of the Franciscans, Girolamo da Ascoli, 'condemned and disapproved the teaching of Brother Roger Bacon, Englishman, Doctor of Sacred Theology, as containing certain suspect novelties, on account of which the said Roger was condemned to be imprisoned' (Crowley, 67). A somewhat earlier, but garbled, report says that for alchemical reasons Bacon was imprisoned and later released by Raimondo Gaufredi. Gaufredi did become master-general of the Franciscans in 1289, and did release many prisoners, especially in Italy and those of the spiritual or 'left wing' of the order, but notwithstanding many scholarly speculations, there is little evidence that Bacon belonged to this camp.

Because of the tenuous nature of the evidence some scholars have rejected the view that Bacon was imprisoned at all, but on the whole it seems reasonable to suppose that he was placed under some form of restraint, and this for two principal reasons. The first is that by his habitually expressed contempt for many intellectuals of his time, including prominent Dominicans and Franciscans, he was bound to have been highly unpopular in many quarters. The second is that in 1277 the bishop of Paris had produced a famous condemnation of 219 propositions that were not to be maintained (which was soon followed by a much shorter list from the Dominican archbishop of Canterbury, Robert Kilwardby). Bacon's supposed imprisonment was an internal Franciscan matter, but still these condemnations could have provided his superiors with a heaven-sent opportunity for indicting him. For instance, it would have been hard to defend him against the charge of maintaining 'That by diverse signs of the heaven are signified diverse conditions in men as regards both spiritual gifts and temporal things' (Denifle and Chatelain, 1.551). If he was released by the order of Raimondo Gaufredi, this could well have been about 1290, and his last datable writing can be assigned to 1292. Tradition avers that he died in June of that year, and that he was buried in Oxford.

Bacon's view of knowledge Bacon's intellectual schemes were heavily conditioned by his view of how knowledge had developed. Drawing on sources such as Josephus and Augustine, he held that the plenitude of philosophy had been revealed to the ancient patriarchs and prophets near the beginning of time. For various understandable reasons, its transmission to later ages was accompanied by notable deteriorations and corruptions, and reforms had continually been necessary, often by means of special divine illuminations. By his time there had been three particularly great restorers of knowledge, who significantly came from three distinct cultural and religious traditions: Solomon, Aristotle, Avicenna. The time was obviously ripe for a Christian renewal, and it seems fairly clear that Bacon saw himself as the potential provider of this, although, especially later in life, he emphasized the need for co-operative endeavours.

The ways to reform were manifold, but the means, as he stressed to the pope, were heavily dependent on financial resources, and his had become severely depleted, both (presumably) through his having become a Franciscan, and because of a severe reduction in his family's wealth as a result of their royalist allegiance in the recent troubles in England. One very important way towards the restoration of knowledge was the provision of more and better translations of ancient works, so as to be able to latch more reliably onto an earlier stage in the genealogy of knowledge. He made this point especially strongly with regard to Aristotle, who was one of his greatest heroes. Bacon's early works had typically taken a normal scholastic form of following through a particular Aristotelian text with a series of questions. In his later works he followed his own line of argument, but drew copiously on Aristotle to back up his views, and interestingly he seems often to have drawn not on Aristotle's own text but on a florilegium or florilegia, at least one of which was apparently a source for Johannes de Fonte's *Parvi flores* or *Auctoritates Aristotelis*. Aristotle was of course not infallible, but wherever possible Bacon attributed his apparent errors to bad translations.

Bacon's remarks on contemporary translators were scathing and his requirements stringent:

> While it is necessary that an interpreter should know excellently the science which he wishes to translate and the two languages from which and into which he translates, only Boethius the first interpreter knew fully the power of languages and only the Lord Robert called Great Head, lately bishop of Lincoln, knew the sciences. (*Opus maius*, ed. Bridges, 3.82)

Bacon himself tried to alleviate the situation by composing a Greek grammar and a fragmentary Hebrew one; his knowledge of Arabic probably remained at best minimal. On the more logical side of grammar he wrote considerably on the theory of linguistic signs, and regarded some logical doctrines, which it is tempting to call merely technical, as having profound philosophical and theological consequences. One such came from the theory of appellation, where Bacon insisted (in accord, as he saw it, with Aristotle) that a name could not univocally signify a being and a non-being, nor something past, present, and future, but only equivocally. (A point of reference here was the question of whether Christ was a man during the three days in the tomb.) Even in 1292 Bacon was fulminating against Richard of Cornwall for promoting the contrary opinion of the crowd back in 1250.

Another important way to restore knowledge was for Bacon that of experimental science (*scientia experimentalis*). Not surprisingly this phrase has for more than three centuries excited much interest as marking him out as an important, and for the thirteenth century possibly unique, precursor of modern science. Despite much well-reasoned scepticism from modern scholars, this view is not completely unjustified, but it does need to be augmented and modified. Both the Latin terms *experientia* and *experimentum*, just like early English 'experience' and 'experiment', covered a wide range of meanings, from active testing (perhaps in a legalistic sense), through experiences of a quasi-mystical kind, to the experience recognizable in such phrases as 'long experience'. All these meanings and more can be found in Bacon's discussions of experimental science. In some topics, such as that of the formation of rainbows and of haloes around the sun and moon, his procedures seem very similar to those of modern experimental science, while in others he is reminiscent of Francis Bacon and the compiling of histories (or accounts) of trades, with a view both to increasing knowledge and improving practice; moreover, he often approaches the borderlands of magic.

All this is particularly evident in Bacon's lavish praise of one of his contemporary heroes, Petrus Peregrinus, a man famous for his work on magnetism, but about whom little is known except that he may at times have acted as a military engineer:

> He investigated all works of founding metals, and all things that are worked with gold, silver, other metals and all minerals; and he knew all that pertained to warfare and arms and hunting; and he examined all that were for agriculture and the measurement of fields and rural works; also he considered the experiments, divinations and charms of old women and all magicians, and similarly the illusions and devices of all jugglers, so that nothing that should be known would be hidden from him, and he would know how far to reject them as false and magical. (*Opus tertium*, ed. Brewer, 47)

Bacon also moved easily from public to private experience, for he asserted that 'human and philosophical' experience was hardly sufficient for corporeal matters, let alone spiritual ones, and hence internal illuminations, arising from faith and from divine revelations, were necessary, and he even managed to cite from the non-Christian world the view found in the *Centiloquium* (erroneously ascribed to the astronomer Ptolemy) that 'The way of coming to the knowledge of things is twofold, one by the experience of philosophy, and the other by divine inspiration, which as he says, is much the better' (*Opus maius*, ed. Bridges, 2.169–70). This draws attention to the theme often found in pre-modern science of revelation as a proper source of scientific knowledge, which can seem less dated if the epithet 'divine' is shed from the term 'inspiration'.

Optics Many of Bacon's schemes remained purely programmatic, but he did make an exception in the case of optics:

> If the task is to set forth the individual natural sciences in their proper form, either I shall proceed to this, or others can be incited by my labours. But I do wish to compose a compendious treatise on optics [*de perspectiva*], because it is more beautiful than the other sciences, and without it nothing can be finely treated. (*Opera hactenus inedita*, 2.13)

Bacon's account of optics was indeed more systematic than that of other special sciences, and this was especially because he was able to draw heavily on the recently translated work of the great Arabic scientist Ibn al-Haytham, who flourished in Egypt in the early eleventh century, and became known in the West as Alhazen. Bacon seems to have been the first Latin writer to have assimilated his work with any thoroughness. A leading idea of Alhazen's treatise was that vision was effected by intromission, that is, by light and colour coming into the eye rather than visual rays being projected out of it. Bacon agreed with Alhazen on intromission, but also insisted that for vision to be completed there must be an action proceeding outwards from the eye. Although this may prima facie seem obscurantist, it was rooted in Bacon's more general doctrines of natural philosophy. Besides his major optical work Alhazen had also written on the theory and practice of constructing parabolic burning mirrors. This drew Bacon's attention especially because of the apparent use of the treatise by Petrus Peregrinus in his pioneering work in making such a mirror in France. Bacon followed his efforts assiduously, and later had several concave mirrors made for his own use.

Mathematics The optical work of Alhazen, like that of Ptolemy (another of Bacon's heroes), was highly mathematical, a point that greatly appealed to Bacon, and he spoke of geometry as being principally grounded in this science and in astronomy. But this by no means exhausted the range of mathematics' applicability, and Bacon waxed at length about its extreme utility and indeed necessity for a whole gamut of philosophical, theological, and human practical purposes. He himself had a certain, but in the technical sense not a high, level of competence in the subject. He frequently railed at the multiplication of 'useless' conclusions and demonstrations, and most modern mathematicians would look askance at his insistence that even geometrical theorems needed to be certified by the test of experience. Another strategic move that he made in pure mathematics is of some interest. Since at least the time of the Pythagoreans, there had been a tradition of treating arithmetic and geometry as two very distinct sciences: the former dealt with discrete quantity and the latter with continuous quantity, and there were various points (notably incommensurability) that resisted the assimilation of these disciplines. From the Renaissance onwards this divorce was increasingly seen as unsatisfactory, and there were frequent attempts to unite the two subjects under some form of universal mathematics. In antiquity also there had been some attempts at this, and Aristotle provided a few vague hints. Iamblichus, in a work no longer extant, apparently developed the idea further, and Proclus's commentary on Euclid contained a substantial (but still short) discussion of common mathematics. It is therefore of some interest to note that Bacon's first division of mathematics was into things common to the whole of mathematics and those proper to its specialized areas, and that the only completed section of the mathematical volume in his intended grand synthesis was that on the common mathematicals. His discussions are readily reminiscent of Proclus, but the latter's commentary on Euclid is not known to have been available in Latin in the middle ages, and it seems unlikely that Bacon consulted it in Greek. Accordingly the sources of Bacon's discussion remain problematic.

Multiplication of species Optics not only reinforced Bacon's faith in mathematics: it also suggested a generalization. Bacon's universe was a very active one, and he was extremely interested in how action was transferred from one body to another, especially when they were not in contact. A clear example was the transmission of lighting and heating action from the sun to things below, and Bacon proposed that other forms of action at a distance were of the same kind, whereby substances and qualities radiated species or likenesses of themselves in all directions, which were 'multiplied' through the medium in stages, with first one part of the medium being altered, which then altered another adjacent to it, and so on. It is sometimes tempting, but also historiographically hazardous, to compare Bacon's multiplication of species with the nineteenth-century incorporation of optics in a general theory of electromagnetic radiation. It would certainly be fanciful to claim an influence, and Bacon included many actions foreign to most modern conceptions. Prominent among these were astrological and psychic influences. For instance, Bacon had great faith in the power of words: when their utterance was backed up by the right psychological conditions, they were reinforced by corresponding mental species proceeding from the rational soul, and had great power for both good and ill, and this power could be further augmented by species proceeding from the appropriate configuration of the heavens.

Bacon's doctrine was certainly influenced by Grosseteste, but, it would appear, even more more strongly by the *De radiis* of al-Kindi. This work had the ominous alternative title *Theorica artium magicarum*, and, despite its short length, Bacon's contemporary Giles of Rome felt able to list eighteen serious errors contained in it. It is therefore not surprising that Bacon did not mention it in the works that he composed for the pope, but he cited it elsewhere, albeit in ambivalent terms. 'The book's author puts forward many excellent things about the multiplication of rays, which are philosophical and true, so that he may the better draw the readers' minds to the poison of falsity that is his principal intent' ('De laudibus mathematicae', BL, Royal MS 7 F.vii, fol. 72*v*). For Bacon, 'false mathematicians', a term that comprehended both magicians and a certain type of astrologer, had two main faults: they held that all things happen of necessity, and they called upon the action of demons. One of the main planks of Bacon's programme was to show that many effects that might vulgarly be accounted magical and dependent upon demons were in fact perfectly legitimate products of art and nature, and his doctrine of the multiplication of species was, by analogy with optics, particularly potent for providing such naturalistic explanations; to this extent al-Kindi's work was a great aid. Less acceptably the Arab philosopher proposed a naturalistic account of the efficacy of prayer, and was a rigorous astrological determinist. This could not be acceptable to Bacon, and determinist interpretations of astrology had for centuries been a principal reason for giving 'mathematicians' a bad name, an accusation to which Bacon was very sensitive, and did his utmost to repudiate. Hence al-Kindi was a dangerous friend.

Role of astrology Nevertheless Bacon was a fervent advocate of the power of astrology, and in this he was strongly backed up by his incorporation of celestial influences into the doctrine of multiplication of species. These influences could be particularly important in the context of Bacon's geographical investigations, for they were potent in explaining how peoples differed from each other in their customs. This gave Bacon visions of technological possibilities, and he was fond of quoting a supposed piece of advice that Aristotle gave to Alexander the Great:

> When Alexander found races having very bad customs and wrote to Aristotle about what to do concerning them, that prince of philosophers replied: If you can alter their air, let them live; if not kill them all. Oh what an occult reply this is!—but full of the power of wisdom. For he understood that by a change of the air that contains celestial virtues, men's customs are changed. (*Opus maius*, ed. Bridges, 1.393)

Bacon apparently thought that the required change of air could be brought about by mirrors deflecting the celestial virtues.

More routinely, astrological predictions could allow evasive action if danger seemed to be imminent, and more grandly Bacon following Albumasar (Abu Maʿshar) held that the rise of particular religions could be correlated with planetary conjunctions, although he naturally argued a special status for Christianity. Islam had been the latest moderately worthy candidate on the scene, but very soon there would arise the sect of Antichrist. This would be particularly dangerous, for he would be armed with the sort of technological weapons that Bacon himself wrote about: it was therefore imperative that Christians be likewise provided. Bacon's best-known recommendations were addressed to Pope Clement IV, but he continued similar themes with increased vehemence until the end of his life, which may well have contributed to his supposed confinement. It must, however, be noted that at least in his later years Bacon displayed reservations about the epistemological basis of astrology, and he stressed that not only should a good practitioner of the art be experienced in disciplines ranging from physiognomy through alchemy to agriculture, but that he should himself have been born under the right celestial configuration. The empirical orientation that justifiably recommended him to later ages of natural science is again evident.

Influence and reputation Roger Bacon's influence was vast but problematic, and at times it is tempting to suspect a conspiracy of silence. For instance, Thomas Bradwardine seems clearly to have used his edition of the *Secretum secretorum*, and to have been influenced by his views on the growth of knowledge, but in his writings he apparently never mentions his name. John Dumbleton, a younger contemporary of Bradwardine's at Merton College, Oxford, does refer to him in an optical context, but with the peculiarly grudging description as 'one who is called Bakun' (MS Vat. lat. 6750, fol. 194*v*). On the other hand, in alchemical circles he was sufficiently renowned to have attracted a wealth of pseudepigrapha to his name. Bacon himself did write on alchemy, and prized the science highly. He also showed a delight in the mystification of the subject, as when he told the pope that, although he had written separately four times to him about its secrets, he would still need a *viva voce* explanation for full understanding. However, Bacon's undoubtedly genuine writings on alchemy are small in volume, and it is hard to feel secure in accepting any of the later ascriptions.

Bacon also acquired a reputation as a magician, but this again has its problems. There seem no grounds for regarding him as the author of such works as a *De nigromantia* attributed to him, and apart from some stories retailed by a late fourteenth-century Franciscan chronicler, it is not until the sixteenth century that a full account of his supposed doings appears—in an anonymous romance, *The*

Famous Historie of Fryer Bacon, which formed the basis of Robert Greene's well-known play, *The Honorable Historie of Frier Bacon, and Frier Bungay.* (Bungay incidentally seems to have been a composite figure, formed from an innocent, and possibly dull, thirteenth-century Franciscan and a fifteenth-century friar with a definite reputation for magical practices.) The most famous legend is probably that of the talking brazen head. For England's greater protection Bacon and Bungay learned that they should construct such an object, but it was essential that they actually heard it speak. Enabling it to vocalize involved the advice of a devil and was extremely arduous. It thus turned out that the exhausted friars were asleep when it uttered its few enigmatic words 'Time is—Time was—Time is past': accordingly, as they were deaf to these, it disintegrated in a vast explosion and the project failed. Almost simultaneously with such legends there began the tradition of defending Bacon against charges of magic, and John Dee projected, and perhaps actually wrote, a treatise, 'Mirror of unity, or, Apologia for Friar Roger Bacon the Englishman, in which it is taught that he did nothing by the aid of demons, but was a most great philosopher, and performed naturally and in ways allowable to a Christian man, great things which the unlearned crowd is wont to ascribe to the action of demons' (*Dee on Astronomy*, 116).

The publishing history of Bacon's works was slow. The only one to appear in print before 1600 was the short but significant *Epistola de secretis operibus artis et naturae* (Paris, 1542). Some alchemical works (quite probably all spurious) were published in 1603 at Frankfurt under the title *Sanioris medicinae … de arte chymiae scripta*, and in the same place in 1614 Johann Combach brought out two volumes containing genuine mathematical and optical writings, largely drawn from the *Opus maius*. Thereafter, for over a century there were only trickles, despite the fact that members of the Royal Society of London in its early days, for whom Bacon had joined his namesake Francis as a hero of experimental science, were anxious to see more of his works in print. In 1733 there appeared in London a large folio volume, edited by Samuel Jebb, which contained most of the *Opus maius* and the *De multiplicatione specierum*, but it was only in the nineteenth century and more particularly the early twentieth century that serious editorial and scholarly work on Bacon really began to flourish. He was then often portrayed as a lone beacon of light in an age of darkness, and this understandably provoked a counter-reaction from many medievalists to bring his importance into perspective, and see him as a quite typical, although noisy, product of his own age, who perhaps suffered greatly from 'sour grapes' as a failed theologian. More recently emphasis has again been put on his individuality, originality, and influentiality, but now coupled with a determination to locate him much more precisely within the complex and vibrant web of medieval intellectual life. GEORGE MOLLAND

Sources T. Crowley, *Roger Bacon: the problem of the soul in his philosophical commentaries* (1950) • S. C. Easton, *Roger Bacon and his search for a universal science: a reconsideration of the life and work of Roger Bacon in the light of his own stated purposes* (1952) • A. G. Little, ed., *Roger Bacon: essays* (1914) • J. M. G. Hackett, ed., *Roger Bacon and the sciences: commemorative essays* (1997) • *The 'Opus maius' of Roger Bacon*, ed. J. H. Bridges, 3 vols. (1897–1900) • R. Bacon, *Moralis philosophia*, ed. E. Massa (1953) • *Fr. Rogeri Bacon opera quaedam hactenus inedita*, ed. J. S. Brewer, Rolls Series, 15 (1859) • *Part of the 'Opus tertium' of Roger Bacon, including a fragment now printed for the first time*, ed. A. G. Little (1912) • R. Bacon, *Opera hactenus inedita*, ed. R. Steele and others, 16 fasc. (1905–40) • F. A. Gasquet, 'An unpublished fragment of a work by Roger Bacon', *EngHR*, 12 (1897), 494–517 • R. Bacon, *Compendium of the study of theology*, ed. T. S. Maloney (1988) • D. C. Lindberg, *Roger Bacon's philosophy of nature: a critical edition, with English translation, introduction, and notes, of 'De multiplicatione specierum' and 'De speculis comburentibus'* (1983) • D. C. Lindberg, *Roger Bacon and the origins of 'Perspectiva' in the middle ages: a critical edition and English translation of Bacon's 'Perspectiva' with introduction and notes* (1996) • J. M. G. Hackett, 'The meaning of experimental science (*scientia experimentalis*) in the philosophy of Roger Bacon', PhD diss., University of Toronto, 1983 • C. Bérubé, *De la philosophie à la sagesse chez Saint Bonaventure et Roger Bacon* (1976) • A. C. Crombie, *Robert Grosseteste and the origins of experimental science, 1100–1700*, 2nd imp. (1961) • R. Carton, *L'expérience physique chez Roger Bacon: contribution à l'étude de la méthode et de la science expérimentales au XIII siècle* (1924) • A. G. Little, 'Roger Bacon: annual lecture on a master mind', *PBA*, 14 (1928), 265–96 • A. G. Molland, 'Roger Bacon as magician', *Traditio*, 30 (1974), 445–60 • A. G. Molland, 'Roger Bacon and the hermetic tradition in medieval science', *Vivarium*, 31 (1983), 140–60 • A. G. Molland, 'Roger Bacon's appropriation of past mathematics', *Tradition, transmission, transformation: proceedings of two conferences on premodern science*, ed. F. J Ragep, S. P. Ragep, and S. Livesey (1996), 347–65 • A. G. Molland, 'Roger Bacon's *De laudibus mathematicae*: a preliminary study', *Texts and contexts in ancient and medieval science: studies on the occasion of John E. Murdoch's seventieth birthday*, ed. E. Sylla and M. McVaugh (1997), 68–83 • W. R. Newman, 'The alchemy of Roger Bacon and the *Tres epistolae* attributed to him', *Comprendre et maîtriser la nature au moyen âge: mélanges d'histoire des sciences offerts à Guy Beaujouan* (Geneva, 1994), 461–79 • A. P. Bagliani, 'Ruggero Bacone, autore del *De retardatione accidentium senectutis*?', *Studi Medievali*, 3rd ser., 28 (1987), 707–28 • S. J. Williams, 'Roger Bacon and his edition of the pseudo-Aristotelian *Secretum secretorum*', *Speculum*, 69 (1994), 57–73 • A. de Libera, 'The Oxford and Paris traditions in logic', *The Cambridge history of later medieval philosophy: from the rediscovery of Aristotle to the disintegration of scholasticism, 1100–1600*, ed. N. Kretzmann, A. Kenny, and J. Pinborg (1982), 174–87 • J. Hamesse, 'Johannes de Fonte, compilateur des *Parvi flores*: le témoignage de plusieurs manuscripts de la Bibliothèque Vaticane', *Archivum Franciscanum Historicum*, 88 (1995), 515–31 • A. de Libera, 'Les *Summulae dialectices* de Roger Bacon [pts 1 and 2]', *Archives d'Histoire Doctrinale et Littéraire du Moyen Âge*, 53 (1986), 139–289 • A. de Libera, 'Les *Summulae dialectices* de Roger Bacon [pt 3]', *Archives d'Histoire Doctrinale et Littéraire du Moyen Âge*, 54 (1987), 171–278 • K. M. Fredborg, L. Nielsen, and J. Pinborg, 'An unedited part of Roger Bacon's *Opus maius*: *De signis*', *Traditio*, 34 (1978), 75–136 • F. Alessio, 'Un secolo di studi su Ruggero Bacone (1848–1957)', *Rivista Critica di Storia della Filosofia*, 14 (1959), 81–102 • J. M. G. Hackett and T. S. Maloney, 'A Roger Bacon bibliography 1957–85', *New Scholasticism*, 61 (1987), 184–207 • H. Denifle and A. Chatelain, eds., *Chartularium universitatis Parisiensis*, 4 vols. (Paris, 1889–97) • *John Dee on astronomy: 'Propaedeumata aphoristica' (1558 and 1568), Latin and English*, ed. and trans. W. Shumaker (1978) • BL, Royal MS 7 F.vii • Biblioteca Apostolica Vaticana, Vatican City, MS Vat. lat. • *Fratris Rogeri Bacon … Opus maius*, ed. S. Jebb (1733)

Archives BL, Royal MS 7 F.vii • Bodl. Oxf.

Likenesses drawing, Bodl. Oxf., MS Bodley 211, fol. 5 • etching, BM, NPG • portrait (of Roger Bacon?), repro. in O. Croll, *Basilica chymica* (1609), title-page • portrait (of Roger Bacon?), FM Cam., MS McLean 153, fol. aiiv

Bacon, Sir Thomas (*d.* 1336), justice, apparently came from Norfolk, where he held land at Burnham Deepdale.

His parentage is unknown, but he seems to have been connected in some way with Sir Edmund Bacon, who held the manor of Gresham; suggestions that he was lord of Baconsthorpe in the same county appear to result from confusion with a namesake. First recorded in November 1306, following his marriage to Denise, the widow of John de Boys (which brought him a life interest in lands and rents in Essex and Cambridgeshire), he had become a sergeant in the court of common pleas by Hilary term 1311, and appeared regularly in the central courts thereafter; at the London eyre of 1321, for instance, he is reported as acting as counsel in eighteen cases. If it was he, rather than his namesake, who was pardoned as an associate of Thomas, earl of Lancaster, in 1313, this might help to explain why his career was confined to the courts until 1327, and also why he advanced rapidly afterwards. His appointment as a justice of the common pleas on 30 December 1329 did not take effect, but that may have been the result of his heavy engagement in the Northamptonshire eyre of 1329–30, where he was one of the most active sergeants. But on 28 January 1332 he was appointed a justice of king's bench, and in the same year was made a knight-banneret, appropriate apparel being provided at the king's expense.

Bacon served in king's bench until Michaelmas 1335. At the same time he shouldered a substantial burden of judicial and administrative business, as a commissioner of oyer and terminer, and as a justice of assize and gaol delivery, mostly in East Anglia and the home counties. In the parliament of Hilary term 1332 he was a trier of petitions for Gascony, Ireland, and Wales, and later in that year he was an assessor of tallage in Norfolk and Suffolk. Two years later he was a commissioner to negotiate a lay subsidy in Kent, while in 1335 he was appointed to investigate the conduct of tax collectors in a number of counties in south-east England. Such employment continued after Bacon had left king's bench, his last commission being dated 10 October 1336. He was dead by 10 December following, and in October 1337 his executors—the prior and sub-prior of St Bartholomew's, Smithfield—were ordered to surrender his rolls into king's bench. Survived by his widow, who lived until 27 April 1349, Bacon is not known to have had any children. HENRY SUMMERSON

Sources *Chancery records* • *CIPM*, 7, 9, 10, 11 • Baker, *Serjeants*, 152, 498 • G. O. Sayles, ed., *Select cases in the court of king's bench*, 7 vols., SeldS, 55, 57–8, 74, 76, 82, 88 (1936–71), vols. 4–5 • Sainty, *Judges*, 24 • D. W. Sutherland, ed., *The eyre of Northamptonshire: 3–4 Edward III*, AD *1329–1330*, 1, SeldS, 97 (1983), li • *RotP*, 2.68 • P. Morant, *The history and antiquities of the county of Essex*, 2 (1768), 108

Bacon [*alias* Southwell], **Thomas** (*c.*1592–1637), Jesuit, was born at Sculthorpe, near Walsingham, Norfolk, the son of John Bacon, gentleman, and his wife, Elizabeth Pannell (*d. c.*1606); he was the elder brother of Nathaniel *Bacon, alias Southwell (1598–1676). He attended school at King's Lynn before going to the Jesuit college at St Omer, where he followed the humanity course. From there he went to the English College, Rome, where he was admitted on 2 October 1610 under the name of Southwell, the name of a well-known Norfolk recusant family. He entered the Society of Jesus in 1615, was ordained priest in July 1620, and was professed of the four vows on 19 April 1626. By that date he had transferred to the Jesuit college in Liège, where he was appointed professor of sacred scripture in 1621; from 1623, he was professor of theology there, and held the post until 1634. He published his *Regula viva, seu, Analysis fidei in Dei per ecclesiam*, a defence of the church's authority, at Antwerp in 1628, and embarked on a commentary (probably based on his own lectures) on the *Summa* of Thomas Aquinas, the first part of which was prepared for the press but remained unpublished. It was probably to Thomas that Sir Tobie Matthew was referring when, in a letter to Francis Bacon in 1621, he described him as 'The most prodigious wit that I ever knew of any nation and of this side of the sea' (*DNB*). Thomas died at the Jesuit house at Watten on 11 December 1637.

THOMPSON COOPER, *rev.* THOMAS H. CLANCY

Sources T. M. McCoog, *English and Welsh Jesuits, 1555–1650*, 2, Catholic RS, 75 (1995), 299–300 • H. Foley, ed., *Records of the English province of the Society of Jesus*, 5 (1879), 808 • A. F. Allison and D. M. Rogers, eds., *The contemporary printed literature of the English Counter-Reformation between 1558 and 1640*, 1 (1989) • *DNB*

Bacon, Thomas (1700?–1768), Church of England clergyman and musician, was probably born either in the Isle of Man or Cumberland. He had at least one brother. He is known to have been in charge of a coal depot in Dublin in 1737, the year in which he published *A Compleat System of the Revenue of Ireland*. In the same year he married a widow who kept a Dublin coffee house in Essex Street; this became known as 'Bacon's coffee house'.

In January 1742 Bacon established a newspaper, the *Dublin Mercury*, at the coffee house premises. Samuel Richardson's novel *Pamela* was first advertised in Ireland in this newspaper, and on 10 April 1742 it announced the first public performance of Handel's *Messiah*; the performance was reviewed in a later issue. In September 1742 Bacon received authorization to print the *Dublin Gazette*, the official newspaper of Ireland, but in July 1743 he ceased its publication without giving prior notice.

Soon after abandoning publishing Bacon studied for holy orders with Thomas Wilson, the bishop of Sodor and Man, his aim being to emigrate to Maryland, where his brother Anthony had prospered as a merchant. He was ordained deacon by Wilson on 23 September 1744 and as priest on 10 March 1745. Anthony Bacon returned to England in 1748, and traded successfully in London.

Accompanied by his wife and son John (Jacky), Thomas Bacon left the Isle of Man in June 1745 and arrived in Maryland in August or September. He took up residence in Talbot county, located on the eastern shore of Chesapeake Bay, and there served as curate of St Peter's parish until his appointment as rector in March 1746. It was there that he began to make a name for himself, not only as a clergyman, but also as a musician and composer. Bacon was an excellent violinist and cellist, and enjoyed visiting the homes of friends for dinner, discussion, and music. He often crossed Chesapeake Bay to visit Annapolis, the capital of Maryland, and the site of much social activity. He became an honorary member and chief musician of the Tuesday Club, a very exclusive group of men. Bacon composed several 'birthday odes' and occasional music for the club, and was dubbed 'Signior (*sic*) Lardini', a pun on his surname. He remained chief musician until 1754.

As a clergyman Bacon especially espoused social reform and was an advocate of education for poor children and slaves. At St Peter's parish he preached several sermons between 1749 and 1753 which were published and sold in aid of establishing a charity school. He even travelled to Williamsburg, the capital of Virginia, to solicit funds by preaching and performing. In May 1755 the building was completed, but the school never achieved success.

The mid-1750s proved to be a turning point for Bacon. His wife died in 1755; he was charged with rape later that year (eventually he was acquitted); and his son was killed in the local wars against the French and Indians. In 1757 he married Elizabeth Bozman (*d.* 21 July 1768), a parishioner from a nearby village. He had been the officiating priest at her marriage, only two years before, to the Revd Thomas Belchier, who was found to be a bigamist. However, Bacon married Elizabeth without previously publishing the banns of marriage and obtaining a marriage licence. He was indicted and fined, but the indictment was later dropped.

Along with his wife and three daughters Bacon left Talbot county in 1758 for All Saints' parish, Frederick county, where he was asked to serve as curate; he did not become rector there until 1762. All Saints' was the most desirable living in Maryland, worth almost £1000 a year, and while there Bacon sought permission from the general assembly of the provincial government to compile and publish a new edition and index of colonial laws. However, though his *Laws of Maryland* was completed in 1762, it was not printed until 1765. He made an unsuccessful attempt to commit the parish vestry to contributing to the establishment of a charity school in Frederick. By 1767 Bacon's health had declined badly; he died at Frederick, deeply in debt, on 26 May 1768. On that day John Cary wrote to Bacon's dear friend Walter Dulany that 'Our worthy, our good, and sincere friend, the Revd Mr. Bacon is now no more; he departed this life about ten minutes ago, sincerely lamented by all honest men here' (Dulany MS I, fol. 20). CAROLE LYNNE PRICE

Sources J. A. L. Lemay, *Men of letters in colonial Maryland* (Knoxville, Tenn., 1972) • S. A. Harrison and O. Tilghman, *History of Talbot county, Maryland*, 1 (1915) • L. C. Wroth, *A history of printing in colonial Maryland* (1922) • E. Allen, 'Rev. Thomas Bacon, 1745–1768, incumbent of St Peter's Talbot Co., and All Saints' Frederick Co., Maryland', *American Quarterly Church Review*, 17 (1865), 430–51 • J. B. Talley, 'Secular music in colonial Annapolis: the Tuesday Club, 1745–1756', DMA diss., Peabody Institute of the Johns Hopkins University, Peabody Conservatory of Music, 1983 • N. W. Rightmyer, *Maryland's established church* (1956) • W. E. Deibert, 'Thomas Bacon, colonial clergyman', *Maryland Historical Magazine*, 73 (1978), 79–85 • Archives of the Episcopal Diocese of Maryland, Baltimore, Maryland, USA, Callister MSS • Maryland Historical Society, Baltimore, Maryland, USA, Dulany MSS • The sermons of Thomas Bacon, Archives of the Episcopal Diocese of Maryland, USA • J. T. Walker, 'Reading interests of the professional classes in colonial Maryland, 1700–1776', *Maryland Historical Magazine*, 36 (1941), 184–201 • T. Bacon, *The laws of Maryland at large* (1765) • W. Hutchinson, *The history of the county of Cumberland*, 2 (1794), 41 n. • A. Hamilton, *History of the Tuesday Club* (1745–50) • administrative accounts, register of wills, Court House, Frederick county, Maryland, liber B2, fol. 72

Archives All Saints' Parish Archives, Frederick, Maryland • Archives of the Episcopal Diocese of Maryland, Baltimore • Johns Hopkins University, Baltimore, John Work Garrett Library | Maryland Historical Society, Baltimore, Dulany MSS

Likenesses pencil sketch, 1750, repro. in Hamilton, *History of the Tuesday Club*

Wealth at death £384 10*s.* 10*d.*; plus considerable library: administrative accounts, register of wills, liber B2, fol. 72

Bacon, Thomas (*b.* 1773, *d.* after **1800**). *See under* Bacon, John (1777–1859).

Baconthorpe [Baco], **John** (*c.*1290–1345x52), Carmelite friar and theologian, was born at Baconsthorpe, near South Erpingham in Norfolk. According to his younger contemporary John Trisse, Baconthorpe was 'tiny' (*minimus*), though 'very great in his wisdom and learning' (Xiberta, 206). Probably at a young age, he entered the Carmelite convent at Blakeney. He studied at Oxford, where he was taught by Robert Walsingham, regent master in 1312. Unlike most Carmelites of the English province, however, he went on to complete his studies in Paris, where he was taught by Guido Terreni. He lectured on the *Sentences* and the Bible, probably before 1318, but was still a bachelor in 1321, if (as seems likely) he is 'John the English Carmelite' who was present at Jean de Ponilly's ceremonial renunciation of his errors. He incepted very probably in 1323, and his regency may well have been prolonged beyond the required two years. In 1330, when he conducted his third quodlibetal disputation, he seems still to have been in Paris. He then returned to England and may have taught (as John Hornby, writing in 1374, testifies) at Cambridge, where there was a Carmelite house. In distinction 1, question 4 of his later 'canonical' questions on book 4 of the *Sentences*, Baconthorpe discusses Bradwardine's views on predestination in a way that suggests that he had disputed with him on the subject. Historians have seen this as evidence that Baconthorpe returned to teach at Oxford in the 1340s. But Bradwardine left Oxford in 1335. Perhaps Baconthorpe disputed with him there before then (Bradwardine had already begun to develop his own distinctive position); or perhaps later elsewhere. In addition to his teaching and writing, Baconthorpe was provincial of the English province, from 1326 or 1327 until 1333 at the earliest, but probably until 1336. He certainly died before 1352 and very probably after 1345.

As in the case of many fourteenth-century theologians, Baconthorpe's most important work is his *Quaestiones in quatuor libros sententiarum*, a commentary on the *Sentences*, an *ordinatio* (written up and revised version) of his lectures as a bachelor on the *Sentences*. A note in BL, Harley MS 1819, states that Baconthorpe completed book 1 of the commentary in March 1325. For books 1–3 there are two recensions: an earlier one, found in the one surviving manuscript, BL, Royal MS 11 C.vi, and a later one, found in all the editions (Paris, 1484; Milan, 1510; Venice, 1526; Cremona,

1618). Baconthorpe rewrote his questions on book 4, calling his earlier set the 'speculative questions'; the later set, the 'canonical questions', were written after 1336, since they use material from his commentary on St Matthew. Only some of the speculative questions survive, interspersed among the canonical questions in BL, Royal MS 9 C.vii (some of the former have been edited by Borchert, 1974). The other manuscripts (BL, Royal MS 11 B.xii; Paris, Bibliothèque Mazarine, MS 900; Vienna, Österreichische Nationalbibliothek, MS 1530) and the editions (Milan, Venice, and Cremona; the Paris edition has just books 1–3) have only the canonical questions. Three sets of quodlibetal questions by Baconthorpe are known (no surviving manuscript; editions: Venice, 1527; Cremona, 1618). According to the colophon in the first edition, the third of them was discussed by him 'in the school of the Carmelites at Paris in 1330'. The other two are probably earlier, since Baconthorpe refers to them, but not to the third set, in his *Sentences* commentary.

Part of Baconthorpe's work as a master of theology was to comment on the Bible. A commentary on St Matthew by him is preserved in Cambridge, Trinity College, MS 348 (after January 1336). A now lost manuscript contained his commentaries on the Pauline epistles, and commentaries on many other books of the Bible were attributed to him by John Bale. It has also been suggested that Baconthorpe wrote a commentary on Aristotle's *Metaphysics*; a commentary by him on the *De anima* is mentioned by Osbert Pickenham, a fellow English Carmelite, and by Richard Lavenham, and there is evidence that he commented on the *Nicomachean Ethics*. More unusually, Baconthorpe also commented on two works of Augustine, the *De trinitate* and the *De civitate Dei*, and on Anselm's *De incarnatione Verbi* and *Cur Deus homo* (Paris, Bibliothèque Nationale, MS 9540). He also wrote three short works on specifically Carmelite matters: a *Compendium historiarum et jurium pro defensione institutionis et confirmationis ordinis B. Mariae de Monte Carmeli*, a *Speculum de institutione ordinis ad venerationem virginis deiparae*, and a *Tractatus super regula ordinis Carmelitarum* (ed. in *Speculum ordinis fratrum Carmelitarum*, Venice, 1507, and in later collections); and there is evidence he wrote a short treatise on the immaculate conception.

Baconthorpe was one of the theologians who brought English philosophical and theological ideas to Paris in the 1310s and 1320s, and who, in his turn, was influenced by Parisian developments. He sometimes repeats the arguments of his teacher, Robert Walsingham and he is especially close to the secular master Thomas Wilton, from whom he takes his discussion of predestination in his commentary on the *Sentences* (bk 1, distinctions 40–41). He is usually opposed to the theories of Duns Scotus and those of Henri de Gand. Baconthorpe first lectured on the *Sentences* before he knew the work of the Parisian theologian, Pierre Aureole. But in his quodlibets and the written-up *Sentences* commentary (especially book 1), Aureole is his main adversary. Baconthorpe argues with him on a wide range of subjects, from Trinitarian relations and the object of theology to the nature of truth (Aureole holds that it is just in the intellect, Baconthorpe considers that it is also in things), and whether God knows each creature distinctly (as Baconthorpe maintains against Aureole). William Ockham's thought seems to have had almost no impact on him (probably because Ockham's work was not known in Paris when Baconthorpe studied and taught there). An unusual feature of the canonical questions on book 4 is their attempt to integrate theology with jurisprudence; although Baconthorpe was not a professional canonist, he shows himself a very able synthesist, far more at home in this field than most theologians.

The aspect of Baconthorpe's work which has most occupied historians is its relation to Averroism. Augusto Nifo judged him to be 'the chief [*princeps*] of the Averroists', a title that his early biographers were happy to repeat. More recently it has been questioned whether Baconthorpe should be considered an Averroist at all, since that description suggests that he upheld various doctrines incompatible with Christianity, whereas he was in fact very careful to avoid any unorthodoxy. His true position seems to have been more complex than either of these judgements represents. On many occasions Baconthorpe tended to interpret Averroes's own views in a way that diminished or removed their unacceptability to Christians. For instance, he accepted, like almost all his contemporaries, that according to Averroes there is only one *intellectus possibilis* ('possible intellect') for all men. But he devised the notion of a 'twofold conjunction' between the possible intellect and the individual man, which allowed him to attribute knowing to human individuals, not just to the single possible intellect; and he argued that in a certain way the possible intellect could be considered multiple. Where, however, there is no way of interpreting Averroes in a way acceptable to Christians, Baconthorpe is willing either to ignore him—as he does when discussing human freedom—or to set him aside. For example, he argues that Averroes's Aristotelian reasons for holding that the world must be eternal contradict the principles Averroes himself states elsewhere. None the less, he allows that God could (although he did not) have created the world not in time but eternally. This was Aquinas's position, but Baconthorpe has to justify it against the sophisticated arguments developed since the 1270s.

JOHN MARENBON

Sources B. M. Xiberta, *De scriptoribus scholasticis saeculi XIV ex ordine Carmelitarum* (Louvain, 1931), 167–240 • N. di S. Brocardo, 'Il profilo storico di Giovanni Baconthorp', *Ephemerides Carmeliticae*, 7 (1948), 431–543 • J. P. Etzwiler, 'John Baconthorpe, "prince of the Averroists"', *Franciscan Studies*, new ser., 36 (1976), 148–76 • J. P. Etzwiler, 'Baconthorpe and Latin Averroism: the doctrine of the unique intellect', *Carmelus*, 18 (1971), 235–92 • C. H. Lohr, 'Medieval Latin Aristotle commentaries', *Traditio*, 26 (1970), 135–216, esp. 154–5 • B. Smalley, 'John Baconthorp's postill on St Matthew', *Mediaeval and Renaissance Studies*, 4 (1958), 91–145 • H. A. Oberman, *Archbishop Thomas Bradwardine: a fourteenth-century Augustinian* (1957), 194–5 • Emden, *Oxf.*, 1.88–9 • Emden, *Cam.*, 669–70 • W. Ullmann, 'Baconthorp as a canonist', *Church and government in the middle ages*, ed. C. N. L. Brooke, D. E. Luscombe, G. H. Martin, and D. Owen (1970), 223–46 • A. Nifo, *De immortalitate animae* (1819) • E. Borchert, ed., *Die 'Quaestiones speculativae et canonicae' des Johannes Baconthorp* *über der sakramentalen Charakter*, Veröffentlichungen der Grabmann Instituts, new ser., 19 (1974) · B. de Cathaneis, ed., *Speculum ordinis fratrum Carmelitarum* (Venice, 1507)

Archives Österreichische Nationalbibliothek, Vienna, MS 1530 · Bibliothèque Mazarine, Paris, MS 900 · Bibliothèque Nationale, Paris, MS 9540 · BL, Harley MS 1819 · BL, Royal MS 9 C.vii; Royal MS 11 B.xii; Royal MS 11 C.vi · Trinity Cam., MS 348

Badby, John (*d.* 1410), Lollard heretic, was a craftsman (possibly a tailor or smith) of the diocese of Worcester, who achieved notoriety by his uninhibited denial of the doctrine of transubstantiation. Charged before his bishop, Thomas Peverell, on 2 January 1409, Badby insisted that the bread in the eucharist was not, and could not be, miraculously transformed into Christ's body. His acknowledgement of the influence of 'John Rakyer of Bristol' (a leading centre of Lollardy) represented a more general challenge to priestly power. Although Badby was adjudged a heretic, and so liable to the death penalty under the statute *De haeretico comburendo* enacted in 1401, recent precedents suggested that the church had no wish to make martyrs of insignificant men. However, circumstances arose in the following year in which Badby's case came to serve the highest affairs of state.

The coming to power of a 'ministry' led by Henry, prince of Wales (the future Henry V), emboldened the Commons to hope that he might endorse a Lollard solution to the crown's financial problems; the wholesale confiscation of the church's temporal possessions. This political misjudgement, perhaps inspired by the prince's friendship with allegedly 'Lollard' knights, provoked vigorous reactions from Henry IV and his ally Archbishop Arundel of Canterbury. The reassertion of orthodox authority, it seemed, might be furthered by making an example of a particularly obdurate Lollard. When on 1 March 1410 Badby was summoned before a convocation of the clergy, the hearing became a show trial of national importance. Badby remained impervious to persuasion, and was sentenced to be burnt at Smithfield on 5 March. As he was consigned to the flames, the prince—possibly seeking to embarrass political rivals by succeeding where they had failed—halted the execution and offered Badby a pension if he would recant. When Badby still refused, the prince's decision to return him to the fire sealed his own commitment to the cause of orthodoxy. Badby was the first layman to be executed as a consequence of anti-Lollard legislation; as his precursor William Sawtrey had been burnt in 1401 before the statute came into force, Badby was its first victim. PETER MCNIVEN

Sources P. McNiven, *Heresy and politics in the reign of Henry IV: the burning of John Badby* (1987), esp. 199–219 · D. Wilkins, ed., *Concilia Magnae Britanniae et Hiberniae*, 3 (1737), 325–8 · T. Walsingham, *The St Albans chronicle, 1406–1420*, ed. V. H. Galbraith (1937), 51–2 · *Thomae Walsingham, quondam monachi S. Albani, historia Anglicana*, ed. H. T. Riley, 2 vols., pt 1 of *Chronica monasterii S. Albani*, Rolls Series, 28 (1863–4), vol. 2, p. 282 · F. S. Haydon, ed., *Eulogium historiarum sive temporis*, 3 vols., Rolls Series, 9 (1858), vol. 3, pp. 416–17 · A. H. Thomas and I. D. Thornley, eds., *The great chronicle of London* (1938), 87–8 · 'William Gregory's chronicle of London', *The historical collections of a citizen of London in the fifteenth century*, ed. J. Gairdner, CS, new ser., 17 (1876), 55–239, esp. 105–6 · *The acts and monuments of John Foxe*, ed. J. Pratt, [new edn], 3 (1877), 235–9

Likenesses portrait, repro. in *Acts and monuments of John Foxe*, vol. 3, facing p. 238

Badby, William (*d.* 1380/81), Carmelite friar and preacher, was born in East Anglia, of unknown parents. He joined the Carmelite order and probably passed his early years in religious life at Norwich. He was sent for his studies to Oxford, where his ability was quickly recognized, and he became one of the leading Carmelite theologians there, incepting as DTh. John Bale, deriving his information from an obituary or notes in the lost register of the late fourteenth-century Carmelite provincial Robert Ivory, records that Badby was an eloquent preacher, frequently preaching at court before the nobility, and his reputation was such that crowds would flock to hear him as if going to a show. His fame brought him to the attention of John of Gaunt, duke of Lancaster, who appointed him one of his confessors and, on 4 July 1372, granted him an annuity of £10 a year. Bale claims that Badby was elected bishop of Worcester *c.*1380, but there was no vacancy in the Worcester diocese at this time, nor is there any trace of Badby's name in the episcopal records. The error must have arisen from Bale's misattribution to Badby (perhaps arising from a misreading of his own notes) of a work on penitence preserved in Oxford, Balliol College, MS 228 (6) and elsewhere, by Walter de Cantilupe, bishop of Worcester (*d.* 1266). Bale knew that this treatise was by a bishop of Worcester, and in his manuscript notes ascribes it to Cantilupe's predecessor, William de Blois (*d.* 1236). Badby died on 11 April in either 1380 or 1381. Bale gives titles of three more lost works—lectures on the Bible, a collection of sermons, and a set of 'diocesan constitutions'. RICHARD COPSEY

Sources J. Bale, Bodl. Oxf., MS Bodley 73 (SC 27635), fols. 42*v*, 119 · Bale, *Cat.*, 1.491 · *John of Gaunt's register*, ed. S. Armitage-Smith, 2 vols., CS, 3rd ser., 20–21 (1911), vol. 1, p. 175; vol. 2, pp. 92, 116 · R. Sharpe, *A handlist of the Latin writers of Great Britain and Ireland before 1540* (1997) · J. Goering and D. S. Taylor, 'The *summulae* of bishops Walter de Cantilupe (1240) and Peter Quinel (1287)', *Speculum*, 67 (1992), 576–94

Badcock, Sir Alexander Robert (1844–1907), army officer, born at Wheatleigh, Taunton, on 11 January 1844, was third son of Henry Badcock JP (*d.* 1888) of Wheatleigh, and Georgina *née* Jeffries. His father's family had long been connected with a bank in Taunton. Educated at Elstree School, Harrow School, and Addiscombe College, he was commissioned ensign on 1 October 1861, and promoted lieutenant on 1 October 1862 and captain on 1 October 1873. He married in 1865 Theophila Lowther, daughter of John Shore Dumergue of the Indian Civil Service, judge, of Aligarh. They had four sons, all of whom entered the army, and a daughter.

After a brief period of duty with the 38th regiment and then with the 29th Bengal native infantry, Badcock entered in 1864 the commissariat department, in which he remained until 1895, achieving notable success and rising to the post of commissary-general-in-chief in December 1890. In his three earliest campaigns, Bhutan (1864–5), the Black Mountain expedition (1868), and Perak (1875–6), he attracted notice for his organization, winning the thanks of government. He was principal commissariat officer under Sir Frederick Roberts in the Kurram field force (1878–9), taking part in the forcing of the Paiwar Pass and other actions. Returning from furlough when operations were resumed, he joined the Kabul field force, and owing to his careful preparations Roberts found in Sherpur, when it was invested, supplies for men stored for nearly four months and for animals for six weeks. Badcock also assisted in recovering the guns abandoned near Bhagwana. When the Kabul-Kandahar field force, consisting of 9986 men and eighteen guns with 8000 followers and 2300 horses and mules, started on 9 August 1880 he relieved Roberts's ‘greatest anxiety’, and the force reached Kandahar, 313 miles from Kabul, on 31 August with a margin of supplies. For these services he received the brevets of major and lieutenant-colonel, and the CB. Roberts reported to government that he knew of no officer so well qualified to be placed at the head of the commissariat in the field. He was promoted brevet colonel on 2 March 1885, major-general on 1 April 1897, and lieutenant-general on 3 April 1900.

In 1885 Badcock collected transport for the Sudan campaign, and in 1895 was created a CSI and received the thanks of government for his services in connection with the Chitral relief force. He was appointed quartermaster-general in India on 7 November 1895. He also acted as secretary in the military department (1890–91) and was president of a committee to consider the grant of compensation for the expense of provisions (October 1894). On his retirement at the expiration of his term of office as quartermaster-general in 1900, he took an active part in the organization of the imperial yeomanry for service in the Second South African War, and was appointed member of the Council of India, receiving on 26 June 1902 the KCB. He died at his home, 44 Grosvenor Road, Westminster, London, on 23 March 1907, while still holding that office, and was buried at Taunton.

[ANON.], *rev.* JAMES FALKNER

Sources *Army List* • *The Times* (25 March 1907) • Lord Roberts [F. S. Roberts], *Forty-one years in India*, 30th edn (1898) • H. B. Hanna, *The Second Afghan War*, 1 (1899) • *Hart's Army List* • *WWW* • Kelly, *Handbk*

Likenesses photograph, 1879, Royal Library, Album Second Afghan War [20]

Wealth at death £19,500 3*s*. 5*d*.: probate, 10 May 1907, *CGPLA Eng. & Wales*

Badcock, John [*pseuds.* Jon Bee, John Hinds] (*fl.* **1810–1830**), writer and journalist, is known only by his works and even the attribution of these is uncertain. He was the probable author of the pretentious introductory chapter to *Pancratia*, published in 1811. That year the *Lives of the Boxers* also appeared, arguments over the authorship of which contributed to a bitter rivalry between Badcock and Pierce Egan. Badcock's most sustained journalism was as Jon Bee in the 1820s, when he published thirteen volumes of the *Annals of Sporting and Fancy Gazette* between 1822 and 1828. Of his works on non-sporting subjects, the *Living Picture of London* was compiled as a guide to the city's condition in the year 1818, and a similar volume was produced in 1828. From a note in the *Fancy Gazette* (1.330), it appears that the volume entitled *Letters from London: Observations of a Russian during a Residence in England of Ten Months* (1816), which purported to be a translation from the original manuscript of ‘Oloff Napea, ex-officer of cavalry’, was also the production of Badcock. His last work under the signature of Jon Bee was an edition of the works of the playwright Samuel Foote (3 vols., 1830). There are indications here that Badcock was connected with Devon or Cornwall, a supposition supported by the fact that in the *Gentleman's Magazine* (1819, pt. i, 618–20, pt. ii, 326), Badcock had announced his intention of printing the lives of the celebrated natives of Devon. His later writings, as John Hinds, all concern horses and riding; they include *The Veterinary Surgeon*, issued in 1827 and 1829, and reissued at Philadelphia in 1848, and the preparation of new editions of W. Osmer's *Treatise on the Horse* and C. Thompson's *Rules for Bad Horsemen*, both of which appeared in 1830. This was the last year in which any work that can be attributed to Badcock was published. W. P. COURTNEY, *rev.* DENNIS BRAILSFORD

Sources *Pancratia* (1811) • J. C. Reid, *Bucks and bruisers: Pierce Egan and Regency England* (1971) • J. Ford, *Prizefighting: the age of Regency boximania* (1971)

Badcock, Samuel (**1747–1788**), theologian and writer on literature, was born at South Molton, Devon, on 23 February 1747, the son of a butcher. His mother's maiden name was Plake. His parents were dissenters and he was educated at a dissenting academy at Ottery St Mary. After training for the dissenting ministry, in 1768 he settled in Wimborne, Dorset, and was ordained on 23 August 1769. After three years there, he was appointed as minister in Barnstaple, where he remained until 1778. During this period, he contributed to the *Theological Repository* and thereby came to know Joseph Priestley.

In July 1779 Badcock wrote to Ralph Griffiths, editor of the *Monthly Review*, who had been making enquiries about him as a possible reviewer, to describe the scandal that caused him to sink ‘to the very Gates of Death’ and had forced him to leave Barnstaple. Badcock explained that three years earlier he had been connected with a family ‘in which there lived a Girl of most agreeable Person & of as lewd & vicious a Disposition’, who had almost succeeded in her attempt to seduce him—she came to his bedroom, but they were interrupted before what he called the ‘last act’. He never had anything to do with her again but when she became pregnant, after having been caught in bed with a footman, she blamed Badcock and tried to blackmail him. He confided in two friends who then spread the gossip throughout Barnstaple and his reputation was ruined. At this, he took to his bed in true eighteenth-century heroine style: ‘for two Months my life was dubious & frequently despaired of … I was reduced to a Skeleton’ (Bodl. Oxf., MS Add. C.90, fols. 8*r*–9*v*). He returned to his native town of South Molton to a congregation where he remained until 1786. His long-standing dissatisfaction with dissenting doctrine and what he described as ‘the shackles of a dissenting Minister among a low and illiteral people’ led him to join the Church of England in 1786 (ibid., fol. 115*r*). He was ordained deacon and priest within the same week in 1787 by Bishop Ross, of Exeter, and within a few months he became assistant to Dr Robert Gabriel at the Octagon Chapel in Bath.

Most of Badcock's contributions to literature appeared in periodicals. From 1744, when he sent to the *Westminster Magazine* a series of articles, until his death, he published widely in the *Gentleman's Magazine*, *London Magazine*, *London Review*, *General Evening Post*, and *St James's Chronicle*, but the most famous of his articles appeared in the *Monthly Review*. His authorship of the reviews of over 650 works between 1779 and 1787 should not have been known in his lifetime, as Ralph Griffiths maintained a strict policy of anonymity for all his reviewers and disapproved of Badcock's hints and disclosures. Alexander Chalmers described the *Monthly Review* as 'the great scene of his literary warfare' (*General Biographical Dictionary*, 1812, 3.292) and it is clear that Badcock greatly enjoyed his part in four important controversies. He reviewed at great length Martin Madan's infamous work on polygamy, *Thelypthora* (1780), and many responses to it; a number of works relating to Ossian and Chatterton between 1781 and 1785; and he engaged in furious combat with and about Joseph Priestley in 1783 and 1784. Although Badcock had been friendly with Priestley and had published in 1780 *A Slight Sketch of the Controversy between Dr Priestley and his Opponents*, he published a harshly critical review of Priestley's *History of the Corruptions of Christianity* in the *Monthly Review* for June 1783. This, and an article by him in the following year on Priestley's *Letters to Dr Horsley*, produced two answers from Priestley and pamphlets from J. E. Hamilton and Edward Harwood. Badcock then replied in *A Letter to Doctor Priestley: Occasioned by his Late Pamphlet*.

During his time in Barnstaple Badcock had become acquainted with the daughter of Samuel Wesley, master of Tiverton School and elder brother of John Wesley. The letters and anecdotes which he obtained from her were sent by him to the *Westminster Magazine* in 1774. A subsequent account, again based on her statements, of the Wesley family provoked a correspondence with John Wesley and was published in *Bibliotheca Topographica Britannica*, and reprinted in Nichols's *Literary Anecdotes*. Several of Wesley's letters were published by Priestley in 1791 under the title of *Original letters by Rev. John Wesley and his friends … communicated by the late Rev. S. Badcock*. Badcock's *Sermons preached at the Octagon Chapel, Bath, for the benefit of the general infirmary, 23 Dec. 1787* was printed for private distribution with its full text restored.

Badcock's published poetry included 'The Hermitage: Written at Castle-Hill, the Seat of Lord Fortescue', printed in January 1782 in the *London Magazine* (vol. 51, 41), 'An Author's Address to his Book', published in both the *London Magazine* (vol. 52, 192) and the *Gentleman's Magazine* (vol. 53, 389) in 1783, and 'To Eliza, on her Marriage', published in 1792 in the *Gentleman's Magazine* (vol. 62, 364) and in *Poems, Chiefly by Gentlemen of Devon and Cornwall*. His last work was a sermon preached at St Peter's, Exeter, at the Lent assizes, which was published in 1795. The papers which the topographer William Chapple had collected for an improved edition of Risdon's *Survey of Devon* were given to Badcock for arrangement and revision and he considered writing a new history of that county. Several letters on this matter were printed in Richard Polwhele's *Reminiscences*, but the work was stopped by Badcock's death.

By December 1787 Badcock was in bad health and circumstances but he looked forward to a prolonged stay in London with Sir John Chichester, one of his Devon patrons, at whose house in Queen Street, Mayfair, he died on 19 May 1788.

After his death, his friend Dr Robert Gabriel alleged that he was the virtual author of Dr Joseph White's Bampton lectures on the effects of Christianity and Islam, for which White had paid Badcock £500. A fierce war of words raged in the papers. Gabriel published *Facts Relating to the Rev. Dr White's Bampton Lectures* (1789), reprinting six letters from White to Badcock, and White rejoined with *A statement of Dr White's literary obligations to the late Rev. Mr Samuel Badcock and the Rev. Samuel Parr, LL.D.* (1790). These and other pamphlets relating to the controversy were very widely reviewed, achieving maximum exposure for both sides. White was criticized for failing to acknowledge the considerable assistance he had received, Badcock for exposing a private agreement.

As a reviewer, Badcock was remarkably well known during the eighteenth century. Although the *Gentleman's Magazine*'s obituary notice of the 'reverend, ingenious, and learned' Badcock had printed some biographical anecdotes about him, it was after the scandal of the Bampton lectures that both biographical notices and republications of some of his poems proliferated in periodicals in 1790–92. *The Peeper: a Collection of Essays* (1796) included as no. xxxiv a 'biographical sketch' of him and reprinted two of his poems.

W. P. Courtney, *rev.* Antonia Forster

Sources *GM*, 1st ser., 58 (1788), 469, 595–7, 691–3, 780–84, 869–70 · *GM*, 1st ser., 59 (1789), 713–14, 776–8, 871–2, 877–81 · *European Magazine and London Review*, 18 (1790), 163–5 · *European Magazine and London Review*, 19 (1791), 89–90 · *European Magazine and London Review*, 22 (1792), 182–4 · J. Watkins, *The peeper: a collection of essays, moral, biographical, and literary* (1796) · Nichols, *Lit. anecdotes*, vol. 5 · *Life and correspondence of Joseph Priestley*, ed. J. T. Rutt, 2 (1832) · B. C. Nangle, *The Monthly Review, first series, 1749–1789: indexes of contributors and articles* (1934) · W. Densham and J. Ogle, *The story of the Congregational churches of Dorset* (1899), 394 · R. Polwhele, *Reminiscences in prose and verse*, 1 (1836), 44–77 · R. Polwhele, *Traditions and recollections; domestic, clerical and literary*, 1 (1826), 184, 240–42 · Bodl. Oxf., Add. MS C. 90

Archives Bodl. Oxf., letters and MSS incl. letters to Ralph Griffiths, Add. MS C90

Wealth at death very little: Bodl. Oxf., Add. MS C90

Baddam, Benjamin (*c.*1693–1740?), printer and compiler of the *Memoirs* of the Royal Society, was the eldest of three children of Benjamin Baddam (1670–1700/01), free of the Glaziers' Company in 1692, who married Elizabeth Palmer (1672–1701x16), daughter of John Palmer, a dyer, at St Nicholas Cole Abbey in July 1692. Apprenticed (as Benjamin Maddam) on 1 May 1710 to Benjamin Harris, a well-known London printer and bookseller, he obtained his freedom as a citizen and Stationer of London on 4 August

1718, inheriting considerable London property from his grandfather John Baddam (*d.* 1717), a dyer, in Spitalfields and St Dunstan and All Saints, Stepney. By 1720 he was living in Blue Anchor Alley, Wellclose Square, where he insured his goods and merchandise against fire for £500. From this address Baddam printed two publications in 1720 (partnered in the first by Moses Carter): *Crambo's Elopement, or, The Austere Poetaster's Ramble*, in imitation of John Wilmot, second earl of Rochester; and *The Protestant Account of the Burning of London*, as an 'antidote' to a tract absolving papists from complicity in the great fire of London. In July 1723 Baddam purchased printed letters from the estate of John Matthews, and Samuel Negus listed him that year as a high-flying Fleet Street printer (Nichols, *Lit. anecdotes*, 1.304). However, in November the Stationers' Company filed a bill in chancery against Benjamin Baddam, of Ratcliff Highway, near Shadwell (and Wellclose Square, Stepney), for printing, publishing, or selling 'severall Thousands of Primmers and severall Thousands of the Psalms of David in English metre' (PRO, C11/2538/56), thereby flouting its royal monopoly. Despite an injunction against him, as the master reported to a meeting of the court of assistants at Stationers' Hall on 3 November 1723, Baddam intended to 'Controvert the Validity of the Companys Letters Patent' (court book of the Stationers' Company, 162). In February 1724 Baddam agreed to accept the company's terms, but refused to pay its legal costs; instead, and in return for an annual life allowance of £50, he proposed revealing 'a Method which if followed would put it out of the power of any person to clandestinely print any of the Companys copys for the future' (ibid., 166). Baddam's wife attended a court meeting on his behalf in October 1724. The outcome of the case is not clear.

During 1732 Baddam printed in Fleet Street a subscribed folio edition of Le Stourgeon's *Compleat Universal History of the Several Empire … throughout the Known World*, illustrated with maps by Henry Wilson and reprinted, with a new title-page, in 1738. Describing himself as a former pupil of J. T. Desaguliers, he publicized in the *Daily Advertiser* three courses of public lectures covering the full range of experimental philosophy which he gave at the London Coffee House in Ludgate Hill between 11 October and 30 December 1732, alternating with Abraham Chovet, a pioneering Huguenot anatomy lecturer who was appointed demonstrator to the Company of Barber-Surgeons in 1734. It was from Fleet Street, possibly in January 1733, that Baddam printed a trade advertisement for *Curiosities of all sorts, in pneumatics, hydrostatics, mechanics, &c., viz. air-pumps or pneumatical engines*, recently improved by Desaguliers and other natural philosophers, as well as barometers and thermometers recommended by the Royal Society, which were made and sold by Rees Williams in the Strand. From January to February 1733 he also worked briefly as a journeyman compositor in the famous Bowyer printing house.

Baddam's experience qualified him admirably for his most ambitious known project—an abridgement of the Royal Society's *Philosophical Transactions*. On 12 October 1738, as B. B. Philo Physiologiae, he issued proposals in the *Daily Advertiser* for subscriptions to this work, with details available from four well-established scientific instrument makers. It was then printed for him by Godfrey Smith in ten volumes, with 131 folding plates drawn by G. Smith and engraved by James Hulett, between 1738 and 1744, under the title *Memoirs of the Royal Society, being a new abridgment of the Philosophical Transactions for the years 1665 to 1735*. A second edition, extending to 1740, was published in 1745 for John Nourse (vols. 4–10 are reprinted from the original edition, with cancel title-pages). Previous abridgements of the *Philosophical Transactions* had been carried out on a piecemeal basis, whereas Baddam's version provided continuity and uniformity for the first time (Nichols, *Lit. anecdotes*, 1.482–3). The title of the *Memoirs* emphasized their 'general Use to the Publick, and worthy the Perusal of all Mathematicians, Artificers, Tradesmen, &c. for their Improvement, in various Branches of Business'. A supplementary volume of mathematical tracts, requested by the majority of the subscribers and announced at the end of the fourth volume, was never implemented. Baddam's preface, which explains his own approach, provides an informative 'short and succinct Narrative of the Royal Society and their Transactions'. A somewhat crudely drawn frontispiece depicts several scientific instruments, such as Boyle's air-pump and a Marshall-type microscope, as used by Robert Hooke, together with other objects from the Royal Society's collections. As Baddam indicates, the French were translating the *Philosophical Transactions* simultaneously (François de Brémond, and then Pierre Demours, for the period from 1731 to 1740). His own competent and useful abridgement served its purpose well for nearly seventy years.

Baddam's death—and his wife's—is obscure, but a Benjamin Baddam from Fetter Lane was buried at St Dunstan-in-the-West, Fleet Street, on 23 November 1740.

JOHN H. APPLEBY

Sources R. M. Wiles, *Serial publications in England before 1750* (1957) • R. V. Wallis and P. J. Wallis, eds., *Biobibliography of British mathematics and its applications*, 2 (1986) • court book H, Stationers' Hall, London, Stationers' Company Archives, pp. 162, 166, and 186–7 • orphans inventory, CLRO, ELJL 64/7; 368; box 47 (Matthews) • D. F. McKenzie, ed., *Stationers' Company apprentices*, [3]: *1701–1800* (1978) [indexed under Benjamin Maddam] • GL, MSS 11936/20, pp. 184, 315; 112160/2 and 10351, 5686 • PRO, PROB 11/558, sig. 128 [John Baddam]; C 11/2538/56 • Nichols, *Lit. anecdotes* • BM, department of prints and drawings, Heal 105/117 • G. Clifton, *Directory of British scientific instrument makers, 1550–1851*, ed. G. L'E. Turner (1995)

Archives GL, MSS 11936/20, pp. 184, 315; 10351, 5686; 112160/2, p. 92 | CLRO, ELJL 64/; 7 368; orphans inventory, box 47 (Matthews) • Stationers' Company, London, Stationers' Hall, court book, H, pp. 162, 166, 186–7

Baddeley, (Madeleine) Angela (1904–1976), actress, was born on 4 July 1904 at 64 Pretoria Road, West Ham, London, one of the four daughters of William Herman Clinton-Baddeley, journalist, and his wife, Louise Rosalie Bourdin. She was a descendant of Sir Henry Clinton, the

British general who captured New York during the American War of Independence. A first marriage, to Stephen Kerr Thomas, was short-lived, but produced a daughter. After a divorce she married on 8 July 1929 Glencairn Alexander Byam *Shaw (1904–1986), with whom she had a son and a daughter. Byam Shaw was an actor and theatrical producer known for his work with theatrical classics and in opera.

Angela Baddeley made her professional début in London in 1915 and by her early twenties had become one of the leading actresses on the West End stage. Her performance in *Richard III* was the first of many classical roles, but she played in many different kinds of production—as did her sister, Hermione *Baddeley (1906–1986)—and was known as a versatile actress. Some theatre critics wondered if she was almost too versatile, in that she never concentrated on one kind of role, but such a professional attitude served Baddeley well, as her career in live theatre lasted until her death. James Agate once favourably commented that she could be 'an ingénue without being a ninny', and Baddeley's versatility in performance came from what many viewed as a charming personality and depth of sensitivity. She was known to possess a 'subtle technique', which she developed throughout her long career. Her early theatre work included frequent stints as Jenny Diver in the long-running revival (1920–23) of John Gay's *The Beggar's Opera*, as well as roles in popular new plays such as J. M. Barrie's *Mary Rose*. She toured Australia with the theatrical producer Dion Boucicault and was as likely to be working in the West End as in one of the independent or more experimental theatres of the day, such as the Everyman at Hampstead or the 'Q' in Richmond. Notable performances were those in R. B. Sheridan's *School for Scandal* (as Lady Teazle in 1927) and as Florrie in W. Somerset Maugham's expressionistic play *Sheppey* (1933). During the 1930s she became well known for her work in productions of Emlyn Williams's plays, and was one of his favourite actresses.

Williams's work began to have a real impact on the West End theatre in the mid-1930s and Angela Baddeley played to great acclaim as Olivia Grayne in his macabre *Night Must Fall* in 1935. This role took her to her American stage début at the Barrymore Theater in New York in 1936. She worked a great deal with Williams during the 1930s and 1940s, often playing opposite him in lead roles, and became a founder member of what Richard Huggett claims can be loosely termed the Emlyn Williams repertory players. The connection with Williams also entangled her with Binkie Beaumont, one of the most powerful theatre producers of the day. Beaumont was notoriously camera-shy, despite, or perhaps because of, his immense power within the fairly closed London theatrical world of the mid-twentieth century, and Baddeley features, along with Williams, in one of the most famous first publicity shots of Beaumont printed in *The Tatler* in 1947. The photo, taken by the prolific and influential theatrical photographer of the day Angus McBean shows Beaumont as the 'puppet master' controlling the strings of the actors (Baddeley and Williams) in yet another of his West End hit productions, Terence Rattigan's *The Winslow Boy*. Baddeley's association with Beaumont and his production company from the 1930s to the 1950s led to significant roles in such plays as Dodie Smith's *Dear Octopus* (1938) and Williams's *The Light of Heart* (1939). She starred alongside such notable performers of the day as Michael Redgrave and Gladys Cooper. A notable performance was in Noël Coward's *Relative Values*, produced by Beaumont in 1950 as part of the Festival of Industry and the Arts.

Angela Baddeley was also acclaimed as a Shakespearian actor. She was a member of the Old Vic company in the late 1940s, and had major roles during numerous seasons at the Royal Memorial Theatre in Stratford upon Avon in the 1950s. Especially noteworthy were her appearances as the Nurse in *Romeo and Juliet*, and as Mrs Hardcastle in Oliver Goldsmith's *She Stoops to Conquer*. Her own favourite roles were as Cattrin in *The Light of Heart* by Emlyn Williams and Stella in J. B. Priestley's *Eden End*. In 1975 she was appointed CBE.

Unusually for a female actor, Baddeley sustained a career in live performance until her death, when she was appearing as Madame Armfeldt in *A Little Night Music* by Stephen Sondheim in the West End. But her most significant triumph in her later years was the immense popularity of her Mrs Bridges in the ITV television series *Upstairs Downstairs*, a chronicle of an upper-class Edwardian household. Baddeley played the feisty cook throughout the series, which lasted from 1971 to 1975, and there were even rumours of plans for a follow-on series which focused on the relationship between Mrs Bridges and the butler, Mr Hudson (played by Gordon Jackson), now married and running a seaside boarding-house. Such rumours were never borne out as Angela Baddeley died following a serious viral flu infection on 22 February 1976 at Grayshott Hall, Grayshott, Hampshire, near Haslemere. She was survived by her second husband. MAGGIE B. GALE

Sources V&A, Baddeley file · Mander and Mitchensen Theatre Collection, London, obituary cuttings file · R. Huggett, *Binkie Beaumont: éminence grise of the West End theatre, 1933–1973* (1989) · J. C. Trewin, *The turbulent thirties* (1960) · b. cert. · m. cert. [Glencairn Byam Shaw] · d. cert.

Wealth at death £56,781: probate, 1976, *CGPLA Eng. & Wales*

Baddeley, Hermione Youlanda Ruby Clinton (1906–1986), actress, was born on 13 November 1906 in Broseley, Shropshire, the youngest of four daughters (there were no sons) of William Herman Clinton-Baddeley, composer and journalist, and his wife, Louise Rosalie Bourdin. A descendant both of Sir Henry Clinton (1738?–1795), a British general in the American War of Independence, and of Robert Baddeley (1733–1794), the actor and pastry-cook who bequeathed the annual fruit cake to the cast playing at the Theatre Royal, Drury Lane, she combined aspects of both these ancestors in her long and eventful career. Her immediate senior sister, Angela *Baddeley (1904–1976), was also a successful actress. Their theatrical education was at the Margaret Morris School of Dancing in Chelsea,

Hermione Youlanda Ruby Clinton Baddeley (1906–1986), by Dudley Glanfield

London, where the pupils considered themselves vastly superior to the more competitive Italia Conti children.

Hermione Baddeley's first great success was in 1923, under Basil Dean's management, in Charles McEvoy's *The Likes of Her*, at the St Martin's Theatre, in which she played a badly behaved waif from the slums who had a famous plate-smashing scene. The next year Dean cast her as a murderous Arab urchin in *The Forest*, by John Galsworthy. Having established a career as a dramatic actress she switched to comedy in *The Punch Bowl* (1924), a revue at the Duke of York's, where she danced with Sonny Hale and credited her formidable comic technique to lessons learned from the comedian Alfred Lester. She joined The Co-optimists, at the Palace Theatre, in the same year. In *On with the Dance* (1925), Noël Coward's revue for Charles Cochran, she created (with Alice Delysia) Coward's topically satirical 'poor little rich girl'. This was the first of four productions for Cochran and then, among a number of undistinguished comedies, farces, and musicals, she played Sara in James Bridie's *Tobias and the Angel* (Westminster, 1932). She had a long run in *The Greeks Had a Word for It*, which transferred from Robert Newton's Shilling Theatre in Fulham, London, to the Duke of York's in 1934.

With *Floodlight* by Beverley Nichols (Saville, 1937) Hermione Baddeley began a long period as a queen of revue, having also plunged into an increasing social whirl with her husband, David Tennant, for whom she often performed in cabaret at his club, the Gargoyle. Herbert Farjeon's wit in *Nine Sharp* (subsequently *The Little Revue*, 1940) provided the perfect launching pad for her inspired clowning, bravura characterization, and skill at quick costume and make-up changes. Her most popular characters included an old girl at Torquay, a Windmill girl in *'Voilà Les Non-Stop Nudes'*, and her prototype funny ballerina, Madame Allover. When she was ill, five understudies barely kept the curtain up.

In her autobiography Baddeley suggests that she recruited Hermione Gingold to *Rise Above It* at the Comedy Theatre (1941). It was a legendary, explosive partnership, with Gingold's daunting control of laughter and Baddeley's penchant for wild improvisation. They were reunited less successfully in *Sky High* at the Phoenix the next year. Their final joint venture, Noël Coward's *Fallen Angels* at the Ambassador's in 1949, inspired the fury of the author at the liberties they took. He was mollified when the show became a fashionable success. Meanwhile, as a dramatic actress Hermione Baddeley's two outstanding successes were as Ida in Graham Greene's *Brighton Rock* (Garrick, 1943), which she repeated in the Boulting brothers' film (1947), and in *Grand National Night* (Apollo, 1946), by Dorothy and Campbell Christie. Her American début in *A Taste of Honey* (1961) led to an invitation from Tennessee Williams to create the role of Flora Goforth in *The Milk Train doesn't Stop here Anymore* at the Spoleto festival in Italy (1962) and on Broadway a year later. A newspaper strike killed the play but Williams greatly admired her performance.

In England, Hermione Baddeley played in many films from 1926 (*A Daughter in Revolt*)—most notably in *Kipps* (1941), *It always Rains on Sunday* (1947), *Quartet* (1948), *Passport to Pimlico* (1949), and *The Pickwick Papers* (1952). She was nominated for an Oscar in 1959 for *Room at the Top* (1958) and had a Hollywood success as the housekeeper, Ellen, in *Mary Poppins* (1964). For the last twenty years she lived mainly in Los Angeles and became a familiar face on television in situation comedies, especially *Bewitched* and *Maude*.

Always known as Totie, and originally a petite and delicate gamine, Hermione Baddeley grew into a still small but fuller figured beauty, and this lent authority to her later blowsier characterizations. In 1928 she married David Pax Tennant (*b.* 1902), son of Edward Priaulx Tennant, first Baron Glenconner and MP for Salisbury; they had a son and a daughter. The marriage was dissolved in 1937, and in 1941 she married Captain J. H. (Dozey) Willis MC, of the 12th lancers, the son of Major-General Edward Henry Willis, of the Royal Artillery. This marriage was also later dissolved. She enjoyed a stormy romance with the actor Laurence Harvey, but they did not marry. She died in Los Angeles at the Cedars Sinai Hospital on 19 August 1986.

Ned Sherrin, *rev.*

Sources H. Baddeley, *The unsinkable Hermione Baddeley* (1984) · *The Times* (22–7 Aug 1986) · *Contemporary Theatre, Film and Television*, 4 (1987) · P. Hartnoll, ed., *The Oxford companion to the theatre*, 4th edn

(1983) • E. Katz, *The international film encyclopedia* (1980) • D. Quinlan, *The illustrated directory of film character actors* (1985) • personal knowledge (1996)

Likenesses photographs, 1924–73, Hult. Arch. • D. Glanfield, photograph, NPG [*see illus.*]

Baddeley, Mountford John Byrde (1843–1906), compiler of guidebooks, born at Uttoxeter, Staffordshire, on 6 March 1843, was the second son of three children of Whieldon Baddeley, solicitor, of Rochester, Staffordshire, and his wife, Frances Blurton Webb. His elder brother, Richard Whieldon Baddeley (1840–1876), was the author of several novels and a volume of poems, *The Golden Lute* (1876), which was published posthumously. After education at King Edward VI's Grammar School, Birmingham, Baddeley obtained a classical scholarship at Clare College, Cambridge, and after matriculating in October 1864, graduated BA with a second class in the classical tripos in 1868. In 1869 he was appointed assistant master, and subsequently he became housemaster, at Somersetshire College, Bath. From 1880 to 1884 he was assistant master at Sheffield grammar school.

After retiring from teaching Baddeley settled at The Hollies, Windermere, and later moved to 2 Lake View Villas, Bowness-on-Windermere. Intimately acquainted with the Lake District and keenly interested in local affairs, he was chairman of the Bowness local board until its dissolution in 1894, and supported movements for preserving footpaths and for popularizing the area as a pleasure resort. On his initiative signposts were placed by the Lake District Association on mountain paths, and a flying squad of young members was organized to report periodically on the condition of the passes. The new road from Skelwith Bridge to Langdale, and the drive along the west side of Thirlmere, which was completed by the Manchester corporation in 1894, were largely due to Baddeley's active intervention. He was opposed to the multiplication of railways or of local industries, favouring legislation for the 'preservation of the scenery' (M. J. B. Baddeley, *English Lake District*, 1880, introduction).

From 1884 to 1906 Baddeley, who was an untiring walker through most parts of England and a close observer of nature, mainly occupied himself with preparing the Thorough Guide series of guidebooks for Great Britain and Ireland. The series opened with the *English Lake District* (1880; 21st edn, 1956), Baddeley's most popular work. The series soon extended to fifteen titles, covering Scotland, northern and western England, Wales, Ireland, and the Isle of Man. Baddeley's guides were accurate, concise, and practical. He had the gift not only of describing natural scenery but also of forming a comparative estimate of its beauty. He paid special attention to the needs of the walker; although an enthusiastic mountaineer he deprecated hazardous adventure.

In 1891 Baddeley married Millicent Satterthwaite, daughter of Robert Henry Machell Michaelson-Yeates of Olive Mount, Windermere. They had no children. Baddeley died on 19 November 1906, at his home, 2 Lake View Villas, Bowness, of pneumonia, which he contracted on a visit to Selby while revising one of his Yorkshire volumes; he was buried at Bowness. His wife survived him. In 1907 a clock tower was erected at Bowness in his memory by public subscription from friends and admirers in all parts of the British Isles. G. S. Woods, *rev.* Julian Lock

Sources *Lakes Chronicle* (28 Nov 1906) • *Sheffield Daily Telegraph* (24 Nov 1906) • Venn, *Alum. Cant.* • private information (1912) • *CGPLA Eng. & Wales* (1907)

Wealth at death £17,621 13*s*. 8*d*.: probate, 11 April 1907, *CGPLA Eng. & Wales*

Baddeley, Robert (1733–1794), actor, was born on 20 April 1733, perhaps in London. The identities of his parents are unknown; it is usually said that he was orphaned at an early age. He was brought up to be a cook. Among his early employers was the actor and manager Samuel Foote, who may have inspired him to follow a stage career. As a young man he spent three years as a valet on the grand tour, where he gained an insight into foreign customs as well as exposure to different languages and accents. It was his facility with these that later provided the basis for his most popular stage performances.

On his return to London, Baddeley rejoined Foote, this time as an actor at the Haymarket, where he made his début on 28 June 1760, as Sir William Wealthy in Foote's *The Minor*. He travelled with the play to Drury Lane, appearing there for the first time on 20 October 1760, and played several other roles at Drury Lane that season, including Gomez in Dryden's *The Spanish Fryar*—a part which was also included in his repertory in winter 1761 at the Smock Alley Theatre in Dublin. He became a full member of the Drury Lane company at the beginning of the 1762–3 season and remained there for the rest of his career, with the exception of a single appearance at Covent Garden as Polonius on 21 April 1772. He was most renowned for his comic foreigners, an early success (in addition to Gomez) being Canton, the Swiss valet in *The Clandestine Marriage*, by George Colman the elder and David Garrick.

In 1763 Baddeley eloped with Sophia Snow [*see* Baddeley, Sophia (1745?–1786)]. He supported his wife's acting career, introducing her into the Drury Lane company in 1764, but although the couple were successful on the stage they rapidly became estranged. By 1770 Baddeley was insisting his wife stop living with a Dr Hayes; Sophia consented on the condition that she receive her own salary from Garrick rather than have it paid to her husband. Baddeley agreed on condition that Sophia pay some of his debts. Hope of a settlement was frustrated when Garrick's brother and assistant manager George declared that he did not believe reports of Sophia's misconduct and challenged Baddeley to a duel. Baddeley was probably no stranger to duelling—Kelly recalled that he once challenged Foote to a duel while acting at the Haymarket—and assented. The parties met in Hyde Park on the morning of 17 March 1770. Baddeley fired first and missed; he was saved after Sophia stood between the combatants and implored George Garrick to spare her husband's life. A separation was subsequently agreed. Baddeley later lived with Catherine Sherry, and at the time of his death with Catherine Strickland.

Baddeley's separation did not harm his acting career. As well as continuing at Drury Lane he appeared at the Haymarket in some summer seasons and also experimented with other entertainments, such as 'The Modern Magic Lanthorn', which he presented at various locations in 1774 and 1775. On 8 May 1777 he made his first appearance as Moses in Sheridan's *The School for Scandal*, creating the role with which he would most be associated and which he perpetuated in at least two interludes written by himself.

Although he suffered an apoplectic fit on 30 May 1780, which prevented him from playing Catchpenny in *The Suicide* (by Colman the elder), Baddeley returned to the stage on 6 June and seems to have remained in good health until 19 November 1794, when he was taken ill while dressing for Moses in *The School for Scandal* at Drury Lane. He died the next morning, 20 November, at his home, 10 New Store Street, Bedford Square, and was buried beside Catherine Sherry, as he requested, in St Paul's, Covent Garden, on 27 November.

Baddeley was the last member of the Drury Lane company to wear the scarlet cloth and lace livery of a gentleman of the great chamber; ten actors of the company were meant to wear this livery as a badge of the company's royal protection. His commitment to Drury Lane and the theatrical profession had been demonstrated in 1774 by his place among the founders of the Society for the Relief of Indigent Persons Belonging to Drury Lane Theatre, usually called the 'theatrical fund'. His will, dated 23 April 1792 and proved on 18 December 1794, left his effects, his theatrical possessions, his 'Garrick's head' (probably his medallion as a member of the School of Garrick, a club established to honour Garrick's memory), and his houses at New Store Street and West Molesey, Surrey, to Catherine Strickland, 'Mrs Baddeley'. After her death the houses and £650 held in trust were to pass to the Drury Lane theatrical fund. The house at Molesey was to become Baddeley's Asylum, a home for theatrical folk who 'from accident or misfortune may have been prevented continuing their subscription long enough to entitle them to an annuity'. However, whether through legal problems regarding the bequest or insufficient money to support the property, the house was sold.

Baddeley also created a small trust whereby every 5 January the Drury Lane company, still in their costumes, receive a glass of punch and slice of cake, known as the 'Baddeley Cake'. This tradition was still being maintained at the close of the twentieth century.

FRANCESCA GREATOREX

Sources D. Cook, *Hours with the players*, 2 (1881) • M. Kelly, *Reminiscences*, 2nd edn, 2 vols. (1826); repr., R. Fiske, ed. (1975) • Genest, *Eng. stage* • *The thespian dictionary, or, Dramatic biography of the present age*, 2nd edn (1805) • T. Gilliland, *The dramatic mirror, containing the history of the stage from the earliest period, to the present time*, 2 vols. (1808) • H. Kelly, *Thespis* (1766) • W. J. Macqueen Pope, *Theatre Royal, Drury Lane* (1945) • Highfill, Burnim & Langhans, *BDA*

Likenesses J. Zoffany, oils, 1777, Lady Lever Art Gallery, Port Sunlight • S. De Wilde, oils (as Sir Harry Gubbin in *The tender husband*), Garr. Club • T. Parkinson, ink and watercolour drawing (as Trinculo in *The tempest*), BM • J. Zoffany, group portrait, oils (scene from *The clandestine marriage*), Garr. Club • miniature (as Anton in *The clandestine marriage*; after R. Cosway), Garr. Club • theatrical prints, BM, NPG

Wealth at death numerous effects and theatrical possessions; two freehold houses; £650 in trust: will, 18 Dec 1794

Baddeley [*née* Snow], **Sophia** (1745?–1786), actress and singer, was born, according to her friend and biographer Elizabeth Steele, in the parish of St Margaret, Westminster, in 1745, the daughter of the trumpeter Valentine Snow (*d.* 1770). Her baptism is not recorded in the register of St Margaret, unless she was Sophia Snow, daughter of John and Jane Snow, born on 16 April 1746, and was brought up by Valentine Snow and his wife, Mary, as their daughter. Snow was London's leading trumpeter, for whom Handel wrote virtuoso parts in his oratorios, including 'The trumpet shall sound' in *Messiah*. Sophia was taught music by her father, but finding his lessons 'a task of labour' (Steele, 1.3) she eloped with the actor Robert *Baddeley (1733–1794). They married with Valentine Snow as a witness on 24 January 1764, and that September she made her début at Drury Lane as Ophelia. Despite her beauty, her career developed slowly, and in January 1766 the prompter Hopkins found her performance of Ophelia 'very bad, all but the singing' (Stone, 2.1147). However, Thomas Snagg, who acted with her at Manchester in summer 1765, remembered her as the best and most beautiful Ophelia he ever saw, and David Garrick later described her in the role as an 'inspired idiot' (Wilson, 11). Following singing lessons from Thomas and Michael Arne and coaching from the actor Charles Holland she drew audiences to the theatre with her portrayal of tender heroines in comedies and musical pieces: 'One admired her person, another her voice, and a third her acting' (*Theatrical Biography*, 24). When she played Fanny in a command performance of *The Clandestine Marriage*, by George Colman and David Garrick, the royal family so admired her that they commissioned a portrait of her in the role from Johan Zoffany. She sang at Vauxhall and Ranelagh gardens and at Stratford upon Avon in September 1769 for Garrick's Shakespeare jubilee celebrations. There Boswell admired 'that beautiful insinuating creature' (Brady and Pottle, 299) as she sang 'Sweet Willy O!', a song in Shakespeare's praise which she was to make extraordinarily popular in London.

After about three years of marriage Sophia Baddeley became the mistress of a rich merchant and then of the actor Charles *Holland (1733–1769)—both affairs reputedly being condoned by her husband. Holland died of smallpox on 7 December 1769, and she was so distraught that she did not appear on stage for nearly a fortnight. George Garrick, Drury Lane's treasurer, agreed to pay her salary directly to her rather than to her husband, which led to a bloodless duel between the two men in March 1770. A legal separation was arranged, after which the Baddeleys spoke to each other only when in character on stage together. Dissolute aristocrats and wealthy men flocked around Mrs Baddeley, and success turned her head. She left Drury Lane at the beginning of the 1771–2 season after David Garrick refused her demands for special privileges and an increase of £3 a week and lived in

Sophia Baddeley (1745?–1786), by Johan Zoffany [as Fanny Sterling, with Robert Baddeley (right) as Canton and Thomas King (centre) as Lord Ogleby, in *The Clandestine Marriage* by George Coleman the elder and David Garrick]

great style under the protection of various lovers, of whom the chief appear to have been Captain John Hanger and Peniston Lamb, first Viscount Melbourne. When the Pantheon opened in 1772 the management attempted to exclude women of ill repute, but her aristocratic admirers insisted on her admission. She was generous, affectionate, and wildly extravagant. Her debts forced her to return to Drury Lane in 1774 and to act in Ireland and Liverpool in the summers of 1778 and 1779.

Mrs Baddeley made her last appearance at Drury Lane on 1 December 1780 in the title role of Arne's opera *Artaxerxes*. She continued to take lovers, progressively lower in the social scale, while her career and health degenerated. In winter and spring 1781–2 she sang at De Loutherbourg's scenic light-and-sound show, *Eidophusikon*, and wrote begging letters for help in supporting her young children, including a five-year-old son. To escape her creditors she fled from London and acted in Dublin (December 1782–January 1783) and then in Edinburgh. In May and June 1783 she appeared with Tate Wilkinson's company in York and Leeds, but at her York benefit she was 'so stupidly intoxicated with Laudanum, that it was with great difficulty she finished the performance' (Wilkinson, 2.151–2). She performed at Edinburgh in summer 1783 and from January 1785, but by April she was unable to continue. In her final illness she was kept from starvation by contributions from fellow performers and the Drury Lane Fund. She died at her lodgings in Shakespeare Square, Edinburgh, on 1 July 1786. Olive Baldwin and Thelma Wilson

Sources G. W. Stone, ed., *The London stage, 1660–1800*, pt 4: *1747–1776* (1962) • C. B. Hogan, ed., *The London stage, 1660–1800*, pt 5: *1776–1800* (1968) • E. Steele, *The memoirs of Mrs. Sophia Baddeley*, 3 vols. (1787) • 'A short history of duelling', *Town and Country Magazine*, 2 (1770), 157–8 • 'Memoirs of Captain H— and Mrs. B—y', *Town and Country Magazine*, 4 (1772), 233–6 • *The letters of David Garrick*, ed. D. M. Little and G. M. Kahrl, 3 vols. (1963) • *Morning Post* (14 July 1786) • *GM*, 1st ser., 56 (1786), 713–14 • *European Magazine and London Review*, 10 (1786), 140 • T. Snagg, *Recollections of occurrences* (1951) • C. H. Wilson, *The myrtle and vine*, 1 (1802) • T. Wilkinson, *The wandering patentee, or, A history of the Yorkshire theatres from 1770 to the present time*, 2 (1795) • *Theatrical biography, or, Memoirs of the principal performers of the three Theatre Royals*, 1 (1772) • *Boswell in search of a wife, 1766–1769*, ed. F. Brady and F. A. Pottle (1957), vol. 6 of *The Yale editions of the private papers of James Boswell*, trade edn (1950–89) • H. Kelly, *Thespis*, 1 (1766) • W. Hawkins, *Miscellanies in prose and verse, containing candid and impartial observations on the principal performers belonging to the two Theatres-Royal, from January 1773 to May 1775* (1775) • A. Pasquin [J. Williams], *The children of Thespis*, pt 2 (1787) • M. Sands, *Invitation to Ranelagh* (1946) • A. W. McDonald, *The Yorkshire stage, 1766–1803* (1989) • W. S. Clark, *The Irish stage in the county towns, 1720–1800* (1965) • J. C. Dibdin, *The annals of the Edinburgh stage* (1888) • R. J. Broadbent, *Annals of the Liverpool stage* (1908) • parish register, Westminster, St Margaret's [marriage]

Likenesses R. Earlom, print, 1772 (after J. Zoffany), BM, Harvard TC • R. Laurie, mezzotint, pubd 1772 (after J. Zoffany), BM, Harvard TC, NPG • E. Welsh, mezzotint, pubd 1772 (after Reynolds), BM • H. R. Cook, print, 1814 (after J. Zoffany), BM, Harvard TC • Davis, wood-engraving, repro. in 'A short history of duelling' • J. Taylor, print (as Mrs Strictland in *The suspicious husband*; after T. Parkinson), repro. in *New English theatre* (1776) • Thornthwaite, print (as Clarissa in *Lionel and Clarissa*; after J. Roberts), repro. in J. Bell, *Bell's British theatre*, 21 (1781) • J. Zoffany, triple portrait, oils (as Fanny in *The clandestine marriage*, with Thomas King as Lord Ogleby and Robert Baddeley as Canton), Garr. Club [*see illus.*] • print, repro. in *Town and Country Magazine* (May 1772) • print (as Joan in *I Henry VI*; after J. Roberts), repro. in J. Bell, ed., *Bell's edition of Shakespeare's plays*, 9 vols. (1773–4) • prints, BM, NPG

Wealth at death died in poverty: obituary notices

Baddeley, Thomas (1786/7–1823), Roman Catholic priest, is of unknown parentage. He was educated and later ordained at Oscott College. In 1815 he succeeded to the mission of Creswell, near Cheadle in Staffordshire, where the earl of Shrewsbury erected a Gothic chapel in the following year. Baddeley shortly afterwards established a seminary for ecclesiastical students. He was assiduous in the performance of his duties and, in 1819, Bishop Milner sent him an assistant. He was best known as the author of a controversial tract, *A Sure Way to Find out the True Religion* (1822). This consisted of six dialogues, which argued trenchantly against various protestant tenets, including justification by faith alone and the primacy of scriptural authority. The tract provoked several replies, including James Richardson's *Popery Unmasked* (1825). Even a reviewer in the *Catholic Miscellany* felt that Baddeley's arguments on the protestant churches' lack of apostolicity and manner of biblical interpretation were imprudently extreme. However, the critic commended his attempt to render his style 'easy and familiar' (*Catholic Miscellany*, 2/15, 118), an opinion which seems to be borne out by the longevity of the tract's appeal: it reached a seventh edition in 1847. Soon after its initial publication Baddeley died, apparently of overwork, on 18 February 1823, at Creswell, and was buried in the chapel. Rosemary Mitchell

Sources Gillow, *Lit. biog. hist.* • *Catholic Miscellany*, 2 (1823), 96, 117–24 • *DNB*

Badel, Alan Fernand (1923–1982), actor and theatre producer, was born in Rusholme, Manchester, on 11 September 1923, the son of Auguste Firman Joseph Badel (1891–1962), a shipping clerk and office manager of French birth, and his wife of Huguenot descent, Elizabeth Olive Till (*d.*

Alan Fernand Badel (1923–1982), by Vivienne, 1950s

1973). He had two brothers and a sister, as well as numerous cousins in Languedoc, where he spent holidays in his youth. Educated at Burnage high school, he gave his first public performance in a school production of James Bridie's *The Anatomist* in 1938, and in the following year, when barely sixteen, he entered the Royal Academy of Dramatic Art (RADA). There he soon distinguished himself, making his professional début in 1940, while still a student, as George in Bridie's 'moral play' *The Black Eye* at the Oxford Repertory Theatre, and winning the coveted Bancroft gold medal in 1941. On leaving RADA he had time for two engagements before his call-up for military service, as Pierrot in a revival at the Mercury Theatre in August 1941 of the mime-play *L'enfant prodigue* and as Lennox and First Murderer in *Macbeth* at the Piccadilly in July 1942. In the same year he married the actress (Marie) Yvonne Owen (1923–1990), who had been a contemporary at RADA and Pierrette to his Pierrot: their daughter Sarah (*b.* 1943) also became a successful actress.

Enlisted in the 6th airborne division, Badel served as a paratrooper until the Second World War's end, rising to the rank of sergeant and being wounded in action following the Normandy landings. Later he was attached to the army play unit, for which he played Othello to military audiences in Egypt and the Middle East. Before returning to the West End he was at the Farnham Repertory Theatre, where he took the lead in Emlyn Williams's *The Corn is Green* (April 1947), and was then cast as Stevie, the young resistance worker in Noël Coward's *Peace in our Time* (Lyric, Hammersmith, July 1947) and as Sandman in Peter Ustinov's *Frenzy* (St Martin's, March 1948). From February to July 1949 he was a member of the Birmingham Repertory company, playing the title role in Michael Brown's *The Modern Everyman*, the Fool in Henri Ghéon's *The Marvellous History of St Bernard*, the Scoundrel in Rodney Ackland's version of Aleksandr Nikolaevich Ostrovsky's *The Diary of a Scoundrel*, and a demonically driven Richard III, a performance which established his credentials as a Shakespearian actor.

Moving to the Stratford Memorial Theatre to play Ratty in a Christmas production of A. A. Milne's *Toad of Toad Hall*, Badel remained there for the 1950 festival season, appearing as Claudio in *Measure for Measure*, the Lord Chamberlain in *Henry VIII*, and Octavius in *Julius Caesar*; in *King Lear* he was much admired as a whey-faced, bird-like Fool, fearfully clutching a child's broken toy for a bauble. After playing the Prince in Nicholas Gray's *Beauty and the Beast* at the Westminster in December, he returned to Stratford in 1951 as Poins and Justice Shallow in *Henry IV, Parts 1 and 2*, the Dauphin in *Henry V*, and in *The Tempest* an Ariel at once lithe and statuesque, accounted by *The Times* 'a performance of flawless beauty' (27 June 1951). Engagements at the Old Vic in successive seasons broadened his Shakespearian range to include a fusspot Peter Quince in 1951–2 and in 1952–3 a lovesick Romeo, an unashamedly adolescent interpretation which, opposite Claire Bloom's touchingly childlike Juliet, thrilled its audiences, if not many critics, and served twice to prolong the play's run. After a brief appearance as Eilert Lovborg in Ibsen's *Hedda Gabler* at the Lyric, Hammersmith, in September 1954, he rejoined Anthony Quayle's Stratford company and opened the 1956 season with Hamlet, followed by Berowne in *Love's Labour's Lost* and, most tellingly, an affectedly Italianate Lucio in *Measure for Measure*.

The year 1957 witnessed a tentative reorientation of Badel's career. Having already directed the British première of Fritz Hochwälder's *The Public Prosecutor* (in which he also played the eponymous revolutionary magistrate) at the Arts Theatre in October, he formed a partnership with Viscount Furness, Furndel Productions Ltd, dedicated to presenting adventurous work unlikely to attract commercial managements. They gave the first British performance of an adaptation from James Joyce entitled *Ulysses in Nighttown* (Arts Theatre, May 1959), in which Badel was a haunting Stephen Dedalus, and mounted three further new plays at the Westminster: James Saunders's *The Ark* (September 1959), Gore Vidal's *Visit to a Small Planet* (February 1960), and Joseph Carole's *Roger the Sixth* (May 1960). Following the demise of Furndel, a progressive deafness, the legacy of wartime combat, exacerbated the strain of stage performance and impelled Badel increasingly towards cinema, television, and radio, though his intermittent theatrical appearances were no less accomplished: as Hero, the dissolute, self-loathing seducer of Jean Anouilh's *The Rehearsal* (Globe, April 1961), as a wittily polished John Tanner in George Bernard Shaw's *Man and Superman* (New Arts, November 1965), and as a perfectly cast, exhilaratingly romantic Edmund Kean in Jean-Paul

Sartre's *Kean*; the latter he enterprisingly played in repertory with one of the great tragedian's most famous roles, Othello, though, unlike Kean, without 'blacking up' (Oxford Playhouse, September–October 1970). His last performance was a reprise of a favourite role, Richard III, at St George's Theatre, Islington, in summer 1976. Offstage, unlike many actors, he remained happily married, and was an enthusiastic gardener and handyman, having mastered such unactorly skills as carpentry and bricklaying.

Despite making his screen début in *The Young Mr Pitt* as early as 1942, Badel was rarely well served by his subsequent films. The two starring roles which his theatrical reputation earned him in Hollywood, as John the Baptist in *Salome* (1953) and Richard Wagner in *Magic Fire* (1954), suffered from indifferent accompaniment, and thereafter he was restricted to prominent, but largely two-dimensional character parts, the most interesting of which were the rugby-promoting north-country industrialist in *This Sporting Life* (1963), the megalomaniac oil magnate in *Arabesque* (1966), the minister in *The Day of the Jackal* (1973), the sinister Dominican cardinal in *Luther* (1976), the KGB colonel in *Telefon* (1977), and the traitorous British naval officer in *The Riddle of the Sands* (1979). Television provided more rewarding opportunities, notably as Rawdon Crawley in *Vanity Fair* (1956), Mr Darcy in *Pride and Prejudice* (1957), Don Juan in Shaw's *Don Juan in Hell* (1962), the Cardinal in Bridget Boland's *The Prisoner* (1963), the Husband in Harold Pinter's *The Lover* (1963), Edmond Dantès in *The Count of Monte Cristo* (1964), Tom Simkins in Stan Barstow's *A Raging Calm* (1974), Edmund Gosse in Dennis Potter's *Where Adam Stood* (1976), Svengali in *Trilby* (1976), and Count Fosco in *The Woman in White* (1982), made in the last months of his life and screened posthumously. He died suddenly of a heart attack at his home, 1A St Martin's Square, Chichester, Sussex, on 19 March 1982.

Although the dazzling youthful promise, which had captivated no less a critic than Harold Hobson, was never entirely fulfilled, Badel remained an actor of magnetic stage presence and mesmerizing vocal command, from the suave to the spitfire, the elegiac to the barnstormingly heroic. Perceived as redolent of an outmoded romantic tradition, and thereby limiting the parts offered to him, his style of performance was none the less informed by an acute intelligence and an ironic view of character and situation, effectively undercutting all inflated emotion with a modern sensibility. Deplorably few openings came his way in work by post-war British playwrights, but arguably more regrettable still is that he never became a member of either the Royal Shakespeare Company or the National Theatre, where his distinctive gifts would have had greater scope to confront the classic roles of an international repertory. DONALD ROY

Sources *WWW*, 1981–90 • I. Herbert, ed., *Who's who in the theatre*, 1 (1981) • *The Times* (27 June 1951) • *The Times* (20 March 1982) • *The Guardian* (20 March 1982) • private information, 2004 [Sarah Badel] • W. Rigdon, ed., *The biographical encyclopaedia, and who's who of the American theatre* [1966] • M. Banham, ed., *The Cambridge guide to world theatre* (1988) • S. D'Amico, ed., *Enciclopedia dello spettacolo*, 1 (Rome, 1954) • J. Walker, ed., *Halliwell's filmgoer's companion*, 10th edn (1993) • E. Katz, *The international film encyclopaedia* (1980)

Likenesses Vivienne, photograph, 1950–59, NPG [*see illus.*] • Houston-Rogers, photograph, 1952, repro. in *Theatre World* (Nov 1952), 25 • photograph, 1956, repro. in *The Times* (11 April 1956), 3 • A. McBean, photograph, 1961, repro. in *Theatre World* (May 1961), 7 • A. McBean, photograph, 1961, repro. in *Plays and Players* (May 1961), cover • L. Morley, photograph, 1965, repro. in *The Times* (24 Nov 1965), 5 • L. Morley, photograph, 1965, repro. in *Plays and Players* (Jan 1966), 13 • Z. Dominic, photograph, 1970, repro. in *The Times* (9 Sept 1970), 7 • Z. Dominic, photograph, 1970, repro. in *Plays and Players* (March 1971), cover • photograph (in middle age), repro. in *The Times* (20 March 1982), 8 • photograph, repro. in *The Guardian*, 2

Wealth at death £30,114: administration, 16 July 1982, *CGPLA Eng. & Wales*

Badeley, Edward Lowth (1803/4–1868), ecclesiastical lawyer, was the younger son of John Badeley MD, of Leigh's Hall, near Chelmsford, and his wife, Charlotte Brackenbury. He matriculated at Brasenose College, Oxford, at the age of sixteen on 14 January 1820 and graduated BA in 1823, taking his MA degree in 1828. In January 1841 he was called to the bar as a member of the Inner Temple, and for a short time went on the home circuit, but his inclination was for the study of ecclesiastical law, and he was soon employed in solving its intricacies in the Tractarian cause. Like his friends and fellow lawyers J. R. Hope-Scott and Edward Bellasis he was a devoted follower of J. H. Newman, whom he first met in 1837. In 1848 he appeared before the queen's bench on behalf of the objectors to the appointment of R. D. Hampden as bishop of Hereford. A speech by him in support of the prohibition of marriage with a deceased wife's sister was submitted in 1849 by E. B. Pusey to the commission then sitting on the law of marriage. When Henry Phillpotts, bishop of Exeter, refused to admit the Revd G. C. Gorham to the vicarage of Brampford Speke on the ground of his unsound doctrine on the sacrament of baptism, Badeley argued the bishop's case before the judicial committee of the privy council in December 1849, and his speech on this occasion was published as a pamphlet. In the summer of 1850 Badeley and thirteen other churchmen, including H. E. Manning, signed a series of nine resolutions to the effect that the views of the privy council on baptism should be solemnly disowned by the national church. No such action was taken, and Badeley joined the Roman Catholic church in 1852.

Badeley acted as assistant counsel to Newman at the Achilli trial in 1852 and thereafter frequently advised him on legal matters. It was on his advice that Newman rejected as inadequate the partial retractation of the charges levelled against him by Charles Kingsley and consequently embarked upon the composition of his *Apologia*. In later life Badeley was frequently consulted on legal problems regarding the administration of ecclesiastical trusts and charities, and in 1865 he argued the legal validity of the seal of confession in the case of Constance Kent. He was deeply devoted to James Hope-Scott and his family, and his letters to Hope-Scott, written at intervals of two or three days over many years, offer a vivid commentary on contemporary legal and ecclesiastical matters. In January 1868 Newman gracefully dedicated to Badeley his *Verses on*

Various Occasions in gratitude for his staunch support at the time of the Achilli trial. Badeley died at his chambers at 3 Paper Buildings, the Inner Temple, on 29 March 1868.

W. P. COURTNEY, *rev.* G. MARTIN MURPHY

Sources *Memoirs of James Robert Hope-Scott, with selections from his correspondence*, ed. R. Ormsby, 2 vols. (1884) · *The letters and diaries of John Henry Newman*, ed. C. S. Dessain and others, [31 vols.] (1961–), vols. 6–24 · H. P. Liddon, *The life of Edward Bouverie Pusey*, ed. J. O. Johnston and others, 4 vols. (1893–7), vol. 3, pp. 165–6, 176–8 · H. Tristram, *Newman and his friends* (1933), 172–8 · Boase, *Mod. Eng. biog.* · Gillow, *Lit. biog. hist.* · *CGPLA Eng. & Wales* (1868)
Archives Birmingham Oratory, letters to John Henry Newman · BL, corresp. with W. E. Gladstone, Add. MS 44107 · CUL, letters to Lord Acton · NL Scot., corresp. with J. R. Hope-Scott
Wealth at death under £16,000: probate, 4 May 1868, *CGPLA Eng. & Wales*

Badeley, Henry John Fanshawe, Baron Badeley (1874–1951), civil servant and engraver, was born at Elswick, Newcastle upon Tyne, on 27 June 1874, the elder child and only son of Captain Henry Badeley (1842–1881), of Guy Harlings, Chelmsford, and his wife, Blanche (*d.* 1929), daughter of Christian Augustus Henry Allhusen of Elswick Hall and of Stoke Court, Stoke Poges. He was educated at Radley College and Trinity College, Oxford. A small energetic figure, he represented Oxford against Cambridge in athletics in the years 1895 to 1897, running in the quarter mile. He was also an accomplished oarsman, although golf remained his favourite form of relaxation. In 1902 he sold Guy Harlings, the family estate which he had inherited from his father.

In 1897 Badeley won first place in a civil service competition for a clerkship in the parliament office and left Oxford without taking a degree. His career was remarkable for its loyalty to, and affection for, the institution which he served. He developed an interest in matters parliamentary, legal, and heraldic. After studying under Frank Short at the Royal College of Art he was elected an associate of the Royal Society of Painter-Etchers and Engravers, and was almost at once appointed honorary secretary (1911–21). In 1914 he was elected a fellow and exhibited regularly until his death. His combined interest in heraldry and line engraving turned his talent for the latter towards the engraving of bookplates. His work in this field became widely known and he executed commissions for a large number of individuals and institutions, which included plates for the library of the House of Lords.

In 1919 Badeley became principal clerk of the judicial office and judicial taxing officer of the House of Lords. Here his energy and capacity for making personal contacts soon enabled him to break through formalities, and he became the adviser both of the lord chancellor of the day and of the law lords, as well as of all those members of the legal profession whose business brought them to the house.

The turning point of Badeley's career came in 1930 when he was appointed clerk assistant of the parliaments, while retaining the principal judicial clerkship. This was the first known promotion to the table of the House of Lords from the staff of the parliament office, and it opened for Badeley himself and for his successors an avenue to the top of their profession. Badeley reached this pinnacle in four years, becoming clerk of the parliaments in 1934. He was clearly suited for this office, although his qualifications differed somewhat from those of his predecessors. His strength lay in the force of his personality, coupled with a quick intelligence and a broad practical knowledge of parliamentary affairs.

Badeley was appointed KCB in 1935. He had also been made CBE in 1920 for his work as county director of auxiliary hospitals and voluntary aid detachments in the county of London (1917–19). From 1919 to 1923 he was president of the county of London branch of the British Red Cross Society.

On reaching the age of seventy in 1944 Badeley was due to retire, but he was granted by the crown an extension of five years. When this final term of service was completed he was created, in 1949, a member of the house he had served so well with the title of Baron Badeley of Badley in the county of Suffolk. Badeley took a devout interest in religious questions, and held pronounced Anglo-Catholic views. He was uncompromising in his attachment to his religious beliefs, and this formed a side of his character that was unsuspected by those who knew him on casual acquaintance only. In 1948 he was made an honorary fellow of Trinity College, Oxford. Badeley died at 35 Weymouth Street, London, on 27 September 1951. He was unmarried and the peerage became extinct.

VICTOR GOODMAN, *rev.* MARK POTTLE

Sources personal knowledge (1971) · private information (1971) · *The Times* (28 Sept 1951) · Burke, *Gen. GB* (1937)
Archives Bodl. Oxf., letters to Lord Ponsonby
Likenesses W. Stoneman, photograph, 1937, NPG
Wealth at death £9564 3*s.* 3*d.*: probate, 22 Jan 1952, *CGPLA Eng. & Wales*

Badenoch. For this title name *see* Comyn, John, lord of Badenoch (*d. c.*1277); Comyn, Sir John, lord of Badenoch (*d. c.*1302); Comyn, Sir John, lord of Badenoch (*d.* 1306).

Baden-Powell. For this title name *see* Powell, Robert Stephenson Smyth Baden-, first Baron Baden-Powell (1857–1941); Powell, Olave St Clair Baden-, Lady Baden-Powell (1889–1977).

Bader, Sir Douglas Robert Steuart (1910–1982), air force officer, was born at St John's Wood, London, on 21 February 1910, the younger child and younger son of Frederick Roberts Bader, a civil engineer working in India, and his wife, Jessie McKenzie. He was educated at St Edward's School, Oxford, where he was a scholar, and at the Royal Air Force College, Cranwell, where he was a prize cadet. He finished second in the contest for the sword of honour at Cranwell, and his confidential report described him as 'plucky, capable, headstrong'.

Bader was commissioned in August 1930 and was then posted as a pilot officer to 23 fighter squadron at the RAF station at Kenley. He was an exceptional pilot and was selected, with another officer from the squadron, to fly

Sir Douglas Robert Steuart Bader (1910–1982), by Paul Laib

the pair for the RAF at the Hendon air display in 1931 before a crowd of 175,000. As a young officer, he was good looking and charming. He was also determined and dogmatic, and could be thoroughly 'difficult'. He was, however, a natural leader, fearless and always eager for a challenge. While he could be brusque and impatient, he was socially at ease in any company. He was intensely loyal to the causes he cared about and to his friends.

Bader was twenty-one when on 14 December 1931 he crashed on Woodley airfield, near Reading. Both legs had to be amputated in the Royal Berkshire Hospital, where his life was saved. He was later transferred to the RAF Hospital at Uxbridge. Six months after his operations he was walking unaided on his artificial legs. 'I will never use a stick', he said.

He was discharged from the RAF in the spring of 1933. That summer he became a clerk in the Asiatic Petroleum Company (later Shell Petroleum) in the City, and on 5 October 1933, secretly at Hampstead register office, he married Olive Thelma Exley, the daughter of Lieutenant-Colonel Ivo Arthyr Exley Edwards RAF (retired), and Olive Maud Amy Addison, *née* Donaldson. Four years later, on 5 October 1937, the two were formally married at St Mary Abbots church, Kensington. There were no children of the marriage.

Bader was re-engaged by the RAF in November 1939, two months after the outbreak of the Second World War, and on 7 February 1940 he was posted to 19 fighter squadron at Duxford, near Cambridge, as a flying officer. Within six weeks he was appointed to command A flight in 222 squadron. As a flight lieutenant, he saw action with the squadron at Dunkirk. Promotion continued, and on 24 June 1940 he was posted to command 242 (Canadian) squadron at Coltishall, in Norfolk. He led the nearby Duxford wing with this unit with signal success throughout the battle of Britain; he was appointed to the DSO on 13 September and awarded the DFC a month later.

Bader's advocacy of his much misunderstood 'big wing' tactics served to fuel the controversy which existed between the air officers commanding nos. 11 and 12 groups of Fighter Command—Keith Park and Trafford Leigh-Mallory—and between the commander-in-chief, Sir Hugh Dowding, and the deputy chief of the air staff, Sholto Douglas. The controversy was further inflamed by Leigh-Mallory's decision to ask Bader to accompany him to the high-level tactical conference held at the Air Ministry on 17 October 1940 with Douglas in the chair. In March 1941 Bader became the first wing commander flying at Tangmere, in Sussex, and led his three Spitfire squadrons with notable success in the frequent offensive operations over northern France. His aggressive leadership was recognized with the award of a bar both to the DSO and the DFC. The French Croix de Guerre and the Légion d'honneur followed. There were three mentions in dispatches. With his official score of twenty-three enemy aircraft destroyed, Bader was shot down on 9 August 1941 near St Omer in the Pas-de-Calais and was a prisoner of war until he was released from Colditz in April 1945. He made repeated attempts to escape, refusing repatriation on the grounds that he expected to return to combat.

After the armistice the 'legless ace' was promoted to group captain and posted to command the North Weald sector in Essex. From here he led the victory fly-past over London on 15 September 1945. He retired from the RAF six months later and in July 1946 rejoined the Shell Company; eventually he was managing director of Shell Aircraft Ltd (1958–69). He flew himself to many parts of the world, often taking his wife with him. An outstanding games player before his accident, he played golf on his tin legs to a handicap of four.

Paul Brickhill's biography of Bader, *Reach for the Sky* (1954), was followed by the film bearing the same title with Kenneth More playing Bader (1956). This brought the battle of Britain pilot worldwide fame. Notwithstanding this, his unsung work for the disabled continued apace, and in 1956 he was appointed CBE.

Bader, who lived mainly in London, retired from Shell in 1969 and from 1972 to 1978 was a member of the Civil Aviation Authority. He accepted several non-executive directorships, maintained his long-established connections with Fleet Street, and continued with his numerous public speaking engagements. Latterly, his principal business base was as a consultant to Aircraft Equipment International at Ascot.

Bader's wife died in London on 24 January 1971 after a long illness. Two years later, on 3 January 1973, he married Mrs Joan Eileen Murray, the daughter of Horace Hipkiss, a steel mill owner. In the same year was published *Fight for the Sky*, Bader's story of the Hurricane and the Spitfire. Having been knighted in 1976 for service to the public and the disabled, he died in London on 4 September 1982, while being driven home through Chiswick after speaking at a dinner in Guildhall. He was FRAeS (1976), an honorary DSc of Queen's University, Belfast (1976), and deputy lieutenant of Greater London (1977). P. B. LUCAS, *rev.*

Sources P. B. Lucas, *Flying colours* (1981) • private information (1990) • personal knowledge (1990)
Archives Royal Air Force Museum, Hendon, department of research and information services, papers | FILM BFI NFTVA, *Secret lives*, Channel 4, 9 Dec 1996 • IWM FVA, actuality footage • IWM FVA, news footage | SOUND BL NSA, 'Paul Brickhill: reach for the sky — the story of Douglas Bader', 1991, 1CA0009932 • BL NSA, documentary footage • BL NSA, performance recording • IWM SA, 'British RAF officer and Hurricane pilot … discussion of the role of big wing during the battle of Britain', IWM Air Operations, 1982, 11716 • IWM SA, oral history interview
Likenesses C. Orde, drawing, 1941, IWM • P. Laib, photograph, NPG [*see illus.*] • photographs, Hult. Arch.
Wealth at death £38,023: probate, 17 March 1983, *CGPLA Eng. & Wales*

Bader, Ernest (1890–1982), chemical manufacturer and industrial reformer, was born in Regensdorf, Switzerland, on 24 November 1890, the youngest of thirteen children of a protestant farmer, Gottlieb Bader, and his wife, Barbara Meier. He was expelled from school at the age of twelve and went to work as a menial in a Zürich chemical factory, achieving white-collar status as a 'stocktaker's boy' in a silk factory at the age of fourteen. He studied commerce and languages at night school, and, at twenty-one, finally qualified as a clerk. After Swiss military service he emigrated to England in 1912, and found employment as a clerk for a silk merchant. He became naturalized in 1924. Active in the Swiss Baptist community of north London, Bader developed his own challenging religious and social beliefs, with the assistance of a supportive Englishwoman, (Annie Eliza) Dora Scott (*d.* 1979), a printer's daughter, whom he married in 1915. Their family life became the foundation for a highly successful family company, and eventually for an internationally renowned experiment in industrial democracy.

Deeply influenced by Christian socialism and the pacifist ideals of Reginald Sorensen, in 1914 Bader was torn between civic duty to neutral Switzerland and Christian love for warring mankind. He was conscripted in October 1914, but soon took the moral plunge as a deserter, and sought refuge with English pacifists; he joined Sorensen in the campaign against the war staged by the Fellowship of Reconciliation, and suffered particularly on account of his German accent. After spells as a handyman and a bank clerk, between 1917 and 1920 Bader worked on a smallholding adjoining Sorensen's farming community of conscientious objectors at Stanford-le-Hope, Essex. The Baders adopted three war orphans of different nationalities and backgrounds, before the births of their natural son, Godric, and a daughter.

In 1920 Bader deployed his wife's capital of £300 to start a London-based import agency for celluloid. This operation expanded into a specialist chemical manufacturing company, Scott Bader Ltd, making new products and synthetic resin; after 1940 the company was directed from Wollaston Hall, Wellingborough, and by 1950 it was worth perhaps £2 million or more. Bader combined marketing energy and individualistic leadership with a flair for spotting and applying new technology, and the company eventually became the leading innovator in plastics technology, in an industry generally dominated by capital-intensive giants. Futuristic faith in technology, personalized direction, a loyal (non-unionized) workforce, and a highly motivated management culture, financially underpinned by a policy of ploughing high rates of profit into new investment, produced an exceptional enterprise, which was welfare conscious yet consistently capable of shouldering high risks to achieve profitability.

Bader converted to the Quakers in 1945. Fired with post-war reconstruction ardour, workplace benevolence was not enough for him. He saw that authoritarian managements were less productive than participative systems, and that human dignity in the workplace and mutual service were industrial values that transcended the hierarchical work concepts promoted by private greed or remote nationalization. A wave of imitative experiments might, he conjectured, eventually implant self-government across industry, encouraging private manufacturers and state enterprise boards to devolve power gradually to employees, to share surpluses, rights, and duties, and to shoulder ethical responsibilities. Like the utopian socialist Robert Owen, Bader was prepared to sink his hard-won assets from capitalism into the moral quest for new and socially responsible industrial structures, based upon co-operation, with the aim of replacing the immoral crudities of power-conflict between a few owners and many employees. In 1946–7 he sought to put his ideas into practice through the Scott Bader Fellowship, a naïve experiment in management–staff relations outside unionization. This was followed in 1948 by an injurious strike over union recognition and bargaining rights, which taught Bader a sharp home truth: the quest for a new industrial order demanded more than Tolstoyean piety and joint consultation. Only common ownership and profit sharing would nurture a truly democratic model.

In 1951 Bader created the co-operative enterprise Scott Bader Commonwealth. While Gandhian principles of industrial trusteeship and co-operative ownership, expounded at home by Wilfred Wellock, were his inspiration, Robert Edwards, leader of the Chemical Workers' Union, gave unique practical guidance to this venture. At its launch Bader staged an epochal renunciation at Cambridge, in which the family donated 90 per cent of its shares in Scott Bader Ltd in favour of employee ownership; he remained managing director of the flourishing, worker-governed enterprise until his son, Godric, took over in 1957. An intrusive co-operative patriarch, Ernest stayed on as chairman until 1963, when he sold his remaining shares to the Commonwealth to provide resources for communal projects. As founder president from 1966 to 1971, Bader became a titular guardian of a new constitution which covenanted some 300 working co-partners, and enlisted as trustees Mary Stocks, Robert Edwards, and E. F. Schumacher. By 1970 the Commonwealth had profitably forged ahead in new polyesters, polymers, and plasticizers, taking a far-sighted market advantage in glass-fibre-reinforced plastics, and at one time producing more than half the British output of polyester resins.

In 1957 Bader founded, with the help of Canon Collins, the Association for the Democratic Integration of Industry, the national forerunner of ICOM (the Industrial Common Ownership Movement). The Common Ownership Act of 1976 finally acknowledged the success of Bader's pioneering activities. As a sage, however, he kept aloof from ICOM and the new Co-operative Development Agency, offering activists his purist Common Ownership Association (1976) based upon Gandhian principles of non-violence and altruism. Bader's wider sponsorship of 'third-world' projects brought him into touch with leaders of self-help development in Asia and Africa. He founded STRIVE (the Society for Training Rural Industries and Village Enterprises), eventually to merge with Schumacher's Intermediate Technology Group. In India he became deeply involved with the Vinoba Bhave movement and Jayaprakash Narayan's struggles to foster Gandhian-style socialism.

Like Gandhi, Bader accepted no honours, although, at the age of ninety, he received an honorary doctorate from Birmingham University. A contradictory, strong-willed, and often domineering industrialist, his ideas attracted strong admirers and detractors. By 1982, he had become a Quaker prophet, his experiment acclaimed as 'an island of industrial sanity' in a rising sea of social division and recession. His co-operative beliefs, longevity, personal conflicts, and ideological achievements uncannily resembled those of Robert Owen. When Bader died at his home, Wollaston Hall, Wollaston, Northamptonshire, on 5 February 1982, his insignificant private wealth accorded with his social testimony. He owned no private house, car, or personal business assets, nor had he made capital transfers or gifts before his death. He had been a 'paper millionaire' when he signed away his company ownership in 1951; the 10 per cent residual shares in the Commonwealth were relinquished to the co-operative in the 1970s.

JOHN G. CORINA

Sources Ernest Bader Archives, Scott Bader Commonwealth • private information (2004) • S. Hoe, *The man who gave his company away: a biography of Ernest Bader, founder of the Scott Bader Commonwealth* (1978) [foreword by E. F. Schumacher] • F. H. Blum, *Work and community: the Scott Bader Commonwealth and the quest for a new social order* (1968) • R. Hadley, 'Participation and common ownership: a study in employee participation in common ownership', PhD diss., U. Lond., 1971 • Lord R. Sorensen, 'A backbencher's pilgrimage', HLRO • *The Catalyst* [Scott Bader Limited] (1947–61) • *The Reactor* [Scott Bader house journal] (1961–7) • *The Times* (8 Feb 1982) • parish register (marriage), Edmonton district, Middlesex, 9 Oct 1915 • d. cert. • *The Friend* (26 Feb 1982)

Archives Wollaston Hall, Northamptonshire, Scott Bader Commonwealth archives, corresp. and papers

Likenesses aquatint (after H. Moore) • aquatint (after B. Hepworth) • bust; now destroyed • portraits, Wollaston Hall, Northamptonshire

Wealth at death £6848: probate, 1982, *CGPLA Eng. & Wales* • under £25,000: further grant, 4 July 1984, *CGPLA Eng. & Wales*

Badew, Richard (*d.* 1361), university principal and founder of University Hall, Cambridge, was born, towards the close of the thirteenth century, into an established knightly family which took its name from Great Baddow, near Chelmsford, Essex, where it had estates dispersed among several neighbouring villages. According to Philip Morant (*d.* 1770), the Essex historian, Richard was probably the third son of Richard Badew and his wife, Isabel, daughter of Peter Marshall, although the matter is not conclusive. Nothing definite is known of his early education. In view of his subsequent career, however, it is to be presumed that he acquired his university education at Cambridge. By 1316 Badew had attained the title of *magister*, and he was described as a deputy chancellor of Cambridge University in August and October 1320. Between 1316 and 1321 Richard Badew, together with Saer Ros, parson of Magna Samford, was involved in a lawsuit against Joan Mareschall, a Cambridge prostitute, who, after an earlier acquittal, had accused Badew, Ros, and Robert Branketre of bringing a false charge against her at Cambridge. The case ended in 1321 in favour of the defendants when Joan was declared to have been excommunicated and was thereby ineligible to plead. In 1322 Badew was one of six masters who, supported by twenty-two clerks, accused the mayor of Cambridge, his bailiffs, and some 250 prominent townsmen of perpetrating serious assaults on the masters and scholars and on their hostels.

In February 1325 Badew is recorded as chancellor of Cambridge University, and still held that office in 1326. During the latter year, while he was still chancellor, the university obtained a licence for the incorporation of University Hall, the predecessor of Clare College. University Hall had its origins in two houses acquired by the university in 1298, and it had probably been used as a hostel for graduates before 1326; it had attracted as benefactors Gilbert Rothbury (*d.* 1321), a royal justice, John Salmon (*d.* 1325), bishop of Norwich, and Thomas Cobham (*d.* 1327), bishop of Worcester. Badew probably did not have the means to give much in the way of endowment to University Hall, but he was regarded as its founder and patron. However, a worsening in his financial situation was paralleled by a growing realization that the endowment for University Hall was wholly inadequate. Badew's small properties were dispersed over Essex, Huntingdonshire, and Cambridgeshire, and between 1325 and 1343 he engaged in costly lawsuits with his bailiffs and rectors for default of payments. Moreover, he fought extensive litigation with university colleagues—in 1332 alone he was involved in eight separate lawsuits. Badew's straitened finances prevented him from aiding University Hall in a material sense; furthermore he was in dispute with at least two of its fellows, John Bokenham and William Thorpe.

By 1336 University Hall was in a parlous state, and the master of the hall, William Thaxted, appealed for assistance to Lady Elizabeth de Clare, widow of John de Burgh and youngest daughter of Gilbert, earl of Gloucester (*d.* 1295), and Joan of Acre, daughter of Edward I. Elizabeth responded by transferring the advowson of the church of Litlington, Cambridgeshire, to the master and fellows. But Badew was seemingly reluctant to relinquish his rights as founder and patron, and it was only by deeds of 6 April 1338 and 28 March 1346 that his complete extrication from University Hall was effected, leaving the way open to Lady Elizabeth to establish Clare College. In the meantime, as already indicated, the 1330s witnessed a series of disputes between the former chancellor Badew and members of the university. For instance, in 1331 the chancellor, John Langele, brought an action against Badew, demanding that he give an account of the money received by him when keeper of the university chest, and that he return nine charters that he had kept in his possession. The case led to a sentence of outlawry being passed on Badew in 1334. The sentence was revoked the following year, and the quarrelling parties seem to have reached a settlement in court. Badew held the rectorship of Braintree, Essex, from at least 1316 until 1333, and the rectorship of Somersham, Huntingdonshire, from 1335 until his death. He founded a chantry in Bicknacre Priory, Essex, in 1337, and a chantry in the church of Great Baddow, Essex, in 1361, the year of his death. ALAN B. COBBAN

Sources *Chancery records* • *Calendar of inquisitions miscellaneous (chancery)*, PRO, 2 (1916), 80 • P. Morant, *The history and antiquities of the county of Essex*, 2 (1768), 19 • T. Fuller, *The history of the University of Cambridge from the conquest to the year 1634*, ed. M. Prickett and T. Wright (1840), 83–4 • A. C. Chibnall, *Richard de Badew and the University of Cambridge, 1315–1340* (1963) • Emden, *Cam.* • W. J. Harrison, 'Clare College', *VCH Cambridgeshire and the Isle of Ely*, 3.340–50 • J. R. Wardale, *Clare College* (1899), 1–4

Badger, Charlotte (*b.* **1778?**, *d.* in or after **1816**), escaped convict, was one of the first European women to live in New Zealand. She may have been the child of Ann and Thomas Badger baptized on 31 July 1778 at the parish church of St John, Bromsgrove, Worcestershire. In July 1796 a Charlotte Badger was convicted at the Worcester assizes for housebreaking and theft in Bromsgrove. She was sentenced to seven years' transportation. After delays she arrived in 1801 at Port Jackson (Sydney), New South Wales, on the *Earl Cornwallis*. By 1806 she had two years of her sentence to serve and was an inmate of the women's prison at Parramatta, where she gave birth to a child. In April, with a friend, Catherine Hagerty, she was assigned as a servant to a settler in Tasmania. Later events suggest they shared the resentment of many convict women to enforced service.

On 29 April Charlotte Badger sailed for Hobart on the *Venus* with her child, Catherine Hagerty, and a crew including male convicts. During the following five weeks, while loading stores *en route*, the captain's authority was undermined. The captain later accused the crew and convicts of drunkenness, vandalism, and immorality. Badger's and Hagerty's behaviour was defiant. They threw property overboard and entertained the intoxicated crew with a dance.

On 17 June, at Port Dalrymple, Tasmania, the convicts seized control of the ship, assisted by crew members including the first mate, Benjamin Kelly. Accounts of Badger's part in the rebellion vary. One claims that, with Hagerty, she incited the men to mutiny. Another states she flogged the captain and, dressed as a man, armed herself with a pistol and raided another vessel for supplies and weapons. At the time she was described as very corpulent with thick lips and light hair. The captain acknowledged the influence of the women, but claimed Kelly was the ringleader. Judgement would have been harsh had he admitted losing his ship to a woman.

With a full cargo intended for Hobart, the mutineers sailed across the Tasman. During the voyage Badger is believed to have formed a liaison with John Lancashire, a fellow convict, and Hagerty with Kelly. On reaching New Zealand these four, and the child, settled in huts on the shore at Rangihoua in the Bay of Islands. The *Venus* left stores and sailed south. By April 1807 Hagerty was dead, and soon after Lancashire and Kelly appear to have left New Zealand.

There is no information on how Charlotte Badger and the child survived after her shipmates left and her supplies were exhausted. She may have been the convict woman reported living with a lesser chief at the Bay of Islands some years later. For a time she was accepted by the Maori of the area. On two occasions she is known to have been offered passage back to Port Jackson. She refused and in 1808 said she would rather die with the Maori.

Maori attitudes to Charlotte Badger changed, probably when it became known that Maori women kidnapped by the crew of the *Venus* had been killed by tribal enemies. Her freedom was threatened as contact with missionaries and other Europeans increased and Maori co-operated in the return of runaway convicts to New South Wales. The last sighting of her was in Tonga. About 1816 an English woman and a young girl landed there, and the woman said she was escaping from the Maori of New Zealand. Her description, a big stout woman, matched Badger's. Tonga was a port of call for ships crossing the Pacific, and one account of her life claims she finally found freedom in America. MARY LOUISE ORMSBY

Sources 'Piratical capture of the *Venus* colonial brig', *Sydney Gazette* (13 July 1806) • W. Jeffrey, *Century of our sea story* (1901) • G. W. Vennell, *The brown frontier* (1967) • R. A. A. Sherrin and J. H. Wallace, *Early history of New Zealand* (1890) • R. McNab, ed., *Historical records of New Zealand*, 2 vols. (1908–14) • M. de Vera, *An Australian woman's diary* (1982) • convict indent for *Earl Cornwallis*, 12 June 1801, Archives Office of New South Wales, Sydney, Australia, COD reel 138 • crown book, Worcestershire assizes summer circuit, PRO, ASSI 2/26 [RP 7837] • J. T. Bigge, Report, Appendix, Mitchell L., NSW, BT Box 23, 4568, 4583 • Mitchell L., NSW, Macarthur MSS, MS A2903, vol. 7 no. 1, 18–27, 58–9 • Governor King's letterbook, 1797–1806, Mitchell L., NSW, MS A2015, 525–6 • *Berrow's Worcester Journal* (14

July 1796) • F. M. Bladen, ed., *Historical records of New South Wales*, 5–6 (1897–8)

Badger, George Percy (1815–1888), Arabic scholar and missionary, was born on 6 April 1815 at Chelmsford, Essex, the son of Edward Badger, army sergeant, and his wife, Ann (*d.* 1844). He was brought up in Malta, where his father, a regimental schoolmaster, died during his childhood, leaving his education in a rudimentary state. His fluency in Maltese, however, laid the foundation of his later mastery of Arabic. From 1834 he worked successively for the Methodist, American protestant, and Anglican missions in Malta as teacher, Arabic typographer, and translator. At the American Board of Commissioners for Foreign Missions (ABCFM) press in Beirut in 1835–6 he improved his knowledge of Arabic. He travelled in Palestine, Syria, and Turkey. After returning to Malta he worked at the Church Missionary Society (CMS) press with Faris al-Shidyaq, preparing Arabic type founts and educational texts for publication; he also wrote an informative and popular guidebook, *Description of Malta and Gozo* (1838), which passed into several editions, and more controversial works on press freedom and education in Malta.

In 1840 Badger married Maria Christiana Wilcox (1818/19–1866), a missionary schoolmistress. In 1841 he went to London where, after a brief course of study at the CMS college in Islington, he was ordained priest in 1842, having abandoned evangelical protestantism in favour of Anglo-Catholicism under the influence of William Palmer. From 1842 to 1844 he served as an emissary of the bishop of London and the archbishop of Canterbury to the 'Nestorian' Church of the East in Kurdistan. He caused controversy there by his campaign against the American protestant mission. He was also accused of advising the patriarch to assert his independence from the local Kurdish ruler, advice which A. H. Layard and others blamed for the Kurdish massacre of Christians in 1843. It was partly to allay such criticism that Badger wrote *The Nestorians and their Rituals* (1852), after a return visit to the area in 1850. This is both an informative travelogue and a sourcebook for 'Nestorian' history, doctrine, and ritual. Badger was not, however, a Syriac scholar, and in this and later publications (1869 and 1875) he relied on Arabic renderings.

Between 1845 and 1862 Badger was a chaplain in the diocese of Bombay, serving mostly in Aden, where from 1854 he played a key role in British dealings with the local Arab tribes. He was there accompanied by Anna Henrietta Edwards [*see* Leonowens, Anna Harriette]. In 1856–7 he accompanied the campaign of General Sir James Outram in Persia, and in 1860 he served on the commission sent to Oman, which brought about the secession of Zanzibar. The Omani ruler Sayyid Thuwayni gave him the manuscript of Salil b. Raziq's chronicle, which he later translated and published as the *History of the Imâms and Seyyids of 'Omân* (1871); his notes in particular proved of lasting value. In 1861–2 he visited Egypt for Outram, and conducted a survey of military installations and of the Suez Canal works.

Two more diplomatic missions took Badger to Zanzibar, in 1872 and 1878, the latter apparently as a double agent for Lord Salisbury, who, probably fearing that commercial involvement in east Africa would precipitate entanglement of the British government in the affairs of the mainland, sought to undermine the efforts of British entrepreneurs to win concessions. Otherwise he devoted the rest of his life (from 1862 to 1888) mainly to scholarship. His major work, the *English–Arabic Lexicon* (1881), had been started with Faris al-Shidyaq in Malta some forty years earlier. It was reprinted in 1967 and is still sometimes used, despite its obsolescence. Other works include books and articles on Christianity and Islam (notably a defence of the Ottoman caliphate), a translation from Italian of Varthema's sixteenth-century *Travels* (1863) with notes drawing on Arabic sources, and a catalogue of the Islamic manuscripts of Fredrick Ayrton, as well as several reports in connection with his diplomatic and military activities. Badger was awarded the degree of DCL by the archbishop of Canterbury in 1873.

Badger's first wife died in 1866, and in 1871 he married Elizabeth Ann Talbot (1834–1897), his housekeeper. Her Somerset connections led to a friendship with the Allen family of West Bradley, and especially with Annie Allen (1858–1930s), forty-three years his junior, with whom he had an intense *amitié amoureuse*. He bequeathed to her a fine oil portrait, revealing a striking, handsome, full-bearded, and full-bodied gentleman, wearing his 1857 war medal and others awarded by the king of Italy (1873) and the sultan of Zanzibar (1880). Badger died on 21 February 1888 at 21 Leamington Road Villas, Westbourne Park, London, his residence for nearly twenty years. He was buried in Kensal Green cemetery on the 25th. G. J. Roper

Sources G. J. Roper, 'George Percy Badger (1815–1888)', *British Society for Middle Eastern Studies Bulletin*, 11 (1984), 140–55 • G. J. Roper, 'Arabic printing in Malta, 1825–1845', PhD diss., U. Durham, 1988 • W. Palmer, notebook, LPL, MS 2819 • M. Jackson, 'A late Victorian friendship', unpublished draft typescript, priv. coll. • J. F. Coakley, *The church of the East and the Church of England: a history of the archbishop of Canterbury's Assyrian mission* (1992) • J. S. Guest, *Survival among the Kurds* (1993) • R. J. Gavin, *Aden under British rule, 1839–1967* (1975) • R. Coupland, *The exploitation of east Africa, 1856–1890* (1939) • M. J. de Kiewiet, 'History of the Imperial British East Africa Company, 1876–1895', PhD diss., U. Lond., 1955 • *The Academy* (3 March 1888), 155 • *Journal of the Royal Asiatic Society of Great Britain and Ireland*, new ser., 20 (1888), 450 • *The Times* (23 Feb 1888) • J. B. Kelly, *Britain and the Persian Gulf, 1795–1880* (1968) • A. H. Layard, *Discoveries in the ruins of Nineveh and Babylon* (1853) • G. Waterfield, *Layard of Nineveh* (1963) • J. Outram, *Report on Egypt … supplement*, 1862, PRO, WO 106/6234 • H. J. Ross, *Letters from the East, 1837–1857* (1902) • private information (2004)

Archives BL OIOC, journal of service with the Persian expeditionary force, etc., MSS Eur. B 377 • CUL, chronicles of seyyids of Oman; corresp. and papers relating to Muscat–Zanzibar commission | BL, letters to Sir Austen Layard, Add. MSS 38991–39119, *passim* • LPL, corresp. with William Palmer • LPL, letters to A. C. Tait • U. Birm. L., Church Missionary Society archives

Likenesses group photograph, 1873, repro. in Coupland, *Exploitation of east Africa* • oils, priv. coll.

Wealth at death £15,982 2*s*. 7*d*.: probate, 1 May 1888, *CGPLA Eng. & Wales*

Badham, Charles (1780–1845), physician and classical scholar, was born in London on 17 April 1780, the son of David Badham. After receiving a sound classical education he entered Edinburgh University, where he graduated MD in 1802 with a dissertation entitled 'De urina et calculis'. Badham was admitted a licentiate of the Royal College of Physicians of London in 1803. On 8 May 1806 he matriculated from Pembroke College, Oxford, as a gentleman commoner. He graduated BA (1811), MA (1812), BM, and DM (1817). In March 1818 he was elected a fellow of the Royal Society, and in September of the same year he was admitted a fellow of the Royal College of Physicians. He was censor of the college in 1821, and wrote the Harveian oration in 1840, delivered in his place by Sir Henry Halford.

Badham began to practise in London in 1803, and before long he was appointed physician to the duke of Sussex. He also became physician to the Westminster General Dispensary, and in partnership with Dr Crichton of Clifford Street he delivered lectures in London on physic, chemistry, and the materia medica.

After the peace of 1815 was agreed, Badham decided to visit the continent, where he spent two years travelling; he visited the less-known parts of the kingdom of Naples and passed to the Ionian Islands and then to Albania, where he was consulted by Ali Pasha. He then crossed Mount Pindus, went through Thessaly, and by Thermopylae to Athens, and then, by the isthmus and gulf of Corinth, to the Neapolitan coast. Badham's fondness for travel, in which he spent nearly half his time, and his taste for classical literature, was indulged at the expense of greater professional fame and fortune in London. Badham was content to earn his living as a physician to travellers on the continent.

However, in 1808 Badham demonstrated his worth as a physician by the publication of *Observations on the Inflammatory Affections of the Mucous Membrane of the Bronchiae*, a second edition of which, corrected and enlarged, appeared in 1814 under the title of *An Essay on Bronchitis, with a Supplement Containing Remarks on Simple Pulmonary Abscess*. In this treatise bronchitis, acute and chronic, was for the first time separated from peripneumony and pleurisy and the other conditions with which it had previously been confused, and its history, differential diagnosis, and treatment were established.

In 1812 Badham published *Specimens of a New Translation of Juvenal*, which was followed by a version of *The Satires of Juvenal, Translated into English Verse* in 1814. These works were very severely criticized in the *Quarterly Review* by William Gifford, himself the author of a translation of the same satirist, who considered that in Badham's *Specimens* 'in no instance has he entered the authors mind: he sees not his object; he feels not his energy; he comprehends not his dignified sarcasm' (*QR*, 8.64).

In 1827 the chair of the practice of physic at Glasgow became vacant, and Badham was recommended by his friend Sir Henry Halford to the duke of Montrose for the post. Although the Scottish physicians were not pleased at seeing an Englishman preferred before them, Badham's lectures justified his appointment. At Glasgow he devoted himself almost exclusively to the duties of his chair. The vacations he spent in travel, mostly in the south of Europe. Badham was a contributor to *Blackwood's Magazine*. There appeared in April 1829 his 'Lines written at Warwick Castle', which had been printed with notes, for private circulation, in 1827. He also prepared 'An itinerary from Rome to Athens', but it was never published.

Badham was twice married: in early life to the beautiful Margaret Campbell, first cousin of the poet Thomas Campbell. Their four sons included the naturalist Charles David *Badham (1805–1857) and the classical scholar Charles *Badham (1813–1884). There were at least two daughters. About 1833 Badham married, secondly, Caroline, eldest daughter of Admiral Sir Edward *Foote (1767–1833). Badham died in London on 10 November 1845.

THOMPSON COOPER, *rev.* PATRICK WALLIS

Sources Munk, *Roll* • *St James's Chronicle* (15 Nov 1845) • review, *QR*, 8 (1812), 60–65 • review, *QR*, 11 (1814), 377–98 • *The Times* (26 June 1840), 6 • *GM*, 2nd ser., 25 (1846), 99 • [J. Watkins and F. Shoberl], *A biographical dictionary of the living authors of Great Britain and Ireland* (1816) • Foster, *Alum. Oxon.* • *Nomina eorum, qui gradum medicinae doctoris in academia Jacobi sexti Scotorum regis, quae Edinburgi est, adepti sunt, ab anno 1705 ad annum 1845*, University of Edinburgh (1846) • private information (1885)

Archives NL Scot., letters to Blackwoods

Badham, Charles (1813–1884), classical scholar and promoter of education, was born on 18 July 1813 at Ludlow, Shropshire, the fourth son of Charles *Badham (1780–1845), regius professor of medicine in the University of Glasgow from 1827 and amateur classicist, and his first wife, Margaret Campbell, a relation of Lewis *Campbell (1830–1908), Greek scholar and one of Badham's obituarists.

Because of his father's long periods in Europe as physician to English travellers, and his distrust of British schooling, Badham was educated first under Pestalozzi at Yverdun, where he became Pestalozzi's favourite pupil and began his mastery of both classical and modern languages. He was next a pupil in England of Dr Charles Mayo, formerly chaplain at Yverdun, and then at Eton of the famous classical teacher E. C. Hawtrey. In 1831 he entered Wadham College, Oxford, where he graduated BA in 1837 but with only third-class honours because, the family believed, the teaching did not suit his independent temperament; he took his MA in 1839.

The foundation and direction of Badham's Greek scholarship were formed during seven years of travel and study of manuscripts in European libraries, chiefly Italian; he began acquaintance with many scholars, especially the eminent Grecist G. C. Cobet of Leiden, who became a lifelong friend. In 1846 Badham returned to England and was incorporated MA at Peterhouse, Cambridge, where he went because of the Cambridge tradition of textual scholarship, and took holy orders (deacon 1846, priest 1848) to qualify himself for a college fellowship. He was always to be disappointed, however, and his marriage in January 1848 to Julia Matilda, daughter of John Smith of Dulwich Common, further prevented his election owing to the celibacy restrictions then in force. He failed also to gain preferment in the church, despite taking the degree of DD in 1852. His religious liberalism made him suspect, his friendship with F. D. Maurice in particular being held against him; his irascibility was also alleged. He achieved only headmasterships of minor schools, at Southampton (1851), Louth (1854), and Edgbaston proprietary school, Birmingham (1856), patronized largely by nonconformist parents. In Birmingham he won the esteem of the future Cardinal Newman. In 1857 after the death of his first wife, with whom he had a son and a daughter, Badham married his second wife, Georgiana Margaret Wilkinson, with whom he had four sons and four daughters.

Recognition of Badham's scholarship came more quickly on the continent than at home and in 1860 Cobet secured him an honorary DLitt at Leiden. In 1863, however, he was appointed to the prestigious post of external examiner in classics to the University of London, where the lexicographer Dr W. Smith was among his colleagues. Smith liked him personally and perceived his quality, describing him as 'the greatest of our living scholars' in an unsigned article, 'Dr. Badham and the Dutch school of critics', in the *Quarterly Review* (120, 1866, 324–55). In 1867 the University of Sydney, Australia, was looking deliberately in England for a new professor of classics and logic. Badham accepted appointment, with a panoply of testimonials from home and abroad (including Cobet, Newman, Smith, and W. H. Thompson, master of Trinity College, Cambridge; some are cited in the *Dictionary of National Biography*). Others' lack of judgement or their hostility denied Badham a comparable post in England, a wrong memorably expressed by A. E. Housman: 'the one English scholar of the mid-century whose reputation crossed the Channel … but at home was excluded from academical preferment, set to teach boys at Birmingham, and finally transported to the Antipodes' (*Manilius*, I, 1937, xlii).

Badham's excellence as a Greek scholar lay in acute textual conjecture, in the highest tradition of philology. He set out his principles in the introductions to his editions of Euripides' *Ion* and *Helen* (both 1851) and in prefatory letters to those of Plato's *Euthydemus and Laches* (1865), *Symposium* (1866), and *Philebus* (1878). He insisted on firmness towards texts demonstrably corrupt through scribal confusion, interference, or interpolation. Decrying vain conservatism, he advocated common sense as the foundation of critical method in general (*Criticism Applied to Shakespeare*, 1866, a pamphlet). Thompson wrote of him as 'a better emender than Porson, but lacking Porson's caution' (Badham and Campbell, 97). The 'Prefatory letters' contain illustrative emendations to both Greek dramatists and prose writers. Badham also published long series of papers on the text of Herodotus, Thucydides, and Plato (*Laws*) in the Dutch journal *Mnemosyne*, and on these and other authors in German periodicals, but very little in British journals.

In Australia, Badham and his family found the climate congenial and he responded immediately to a society without inbred hierarchies and to a young university without religious conformism. At home, the routines of schoolteaching had frustrated him; but now he had an academic position, there was paradoxically much less time for scholarship. Instead, there was endless opportunity for Badham's ideals and energy as promoter of education, and for powers of organization, advocacy, and influence hardly needed or perceived in England. For the rest of his life he worked selflessly to enhance the university's standing and funding. He crusaded for those disadvantaged for education through distance or poverty, persuading the New South Wales state government to provide bursaries and himself teaching by correspondence, and not only in classics. He urged opportunities for women students, and greater tolerance for non-Anglicans. For many years dean of arts and then of the new faculty of laws, and also principal, his last success in the university was to establish evening lectures for working people. He engaged forcefully in reform of the curriculum, examinations, and inspection in schools, arguing from direct experience of visits throughout the state. He put special weight on English language and literature, and developed proposals to encourage pupils towards 'either arts or science' according to their natural inclination and talent—ideas he had urged already in England (*Thoughts on Classical and Commercial Education*, 1864). His overriding ideal was to give all citizens 'together with a consciousness of being educated … a conscience'. His work on the Birmingham library committee from 1860 to 1867 qualified him as trustee and tireless chairman of the Sydney Free Public Library from its foundation in 1870 until his death. In all these activities he canvassed and cajoled, often at parliamentary level, wrote countless reports and papers, led by example, and exploited the influence of his offices in university and city. During a visit to Australia, Anthony Trollope captured his public image as 'the prince of professors and greatest of Grecians' (A. Trollope, *Australia*, 1873, chap. 2). The mixture in him of volatile temper, wit, eloquence, artistic taste, prodigious memory, and formidable intellect made him an exceptional personality. University, city, and state honoured him with a banquet on his seventieth birthday in 1883. His death on 27 February 1884 was announced by extraordinary public gazette, and government offices in Sydney closed to permit attendance at his funeral. He is buried under a simple stone in St Thomas's churchyard, north Sydney. His public speeches were admired and posthumously published.

CHRISTOPHER COLLARD

Sources H. Badham and L. Campbell, 'Charles Badham', *Biographisches Jahrbuch für Alterthumskunde*, 7 (1884), 92–8 • W. Radford, 'Charles Badham and his work for education in New South Wales', diss., University of Sydney, 1969 • W. Radford, 'Badham, Charles', *AusDB*, vol. 3 • T. J. Butler, 'Memoir of Professor Badham', in *Speeches and lectures delivered in Australia by the late Charles Badham*, ed. T. J. Butler (1890) • A. E. Piddington, *Worshipful masters* (1929), 3–15, 101–19 • A. E. Stephen, 'Numantia: a place of disillusioned aspirations', *Royal Australian Historical Society Journal and Proceedings*, 31 (1945), 249–76, esp. 257–61, 268–9 • [W. Smith], 'Dr. Badham and the Dutch school of critics', *QR*, 120 (1866), 324–55 [review] • C. Collard, 'Another "outsider": Charles Badham (1813–84)', *Tria lustra: essays and notes presented to John Pinsent*, ed. H. D. Jocelyn (1993), 340–41 • J. H. Heaton, *Australian dictionary of dates and men of the time* (1879)

Archives University of Leiden, autograph letters to G. C. Cobet | University of Sydney, senate minutes

Likenesses G. Anivitti, portrait, 1880?–1889, University of Sydney, New South Wales, Australia · photograph, repro. in Piddington, *Worshipful masters*, 4

Wealth at death £1000: administration with will, 5 Aug 1884, *CGPLA Eng. & Wales*

Badham, Charles David (1805–1857), naturalist, was born in London on 27 August 1805, the eldest son of Charles *Badham (1780–1845), classical scholar, and his first wife, Margaret Campbell, a first cousin of Thomas Campbell (1777–1844). He was educated at Westminster School, Emmanuel College, Cambridge, and Pembroke College, Oxford, from where he graduated MD in 1833. After taking his degree he was appointed a Radcliffe travelling fellow of the University of Oxford, residing for some time on the continent, especially at Rome and at Paris, where he practised medicine, having become a fellow of the College of Physicians in 1834. On returning to England in 1845 he was forced to give up medical practice for health reasons, choosing instead to enter the church. He was ordained deacon in Norwich on 31 January 1847 and priest the following year, becoming curate first of Wymondham and then of East Bergholt, Suffolk. He married Anna, daughter of James Deacon *Hume (1774–1842), on 8 April 1847.

As well as contributing to *Blackwood's Edinburgh Magazine* and *Fraser's Magazine*, Badham wrote several works of natural history, the first of which, *The Question Concerning the Sensibility … of Insects*, he published in Paris under the pseudonym Scarabaeus. His work on edible fungi, while being greeted with some derision, is said to have introduced many varieties of mushrooms to the English table. Badham died on 14 July 1857 in East Bergholt.

GILES HUDSON

Sources *Fraser's Magazine*, 56 (1857), 162–3 · Venn, *Alum. Cant.* · G. H. Brown, ed., *Lives of fellows of the Royal College of Physicians of London, 1826–1925* (1955) · *Old Westminsters*, vols. 1–2 · Desmond, *Botanists*, rev. edn · Munk, *Roll*

Archives NL Scot., letters to Blackwoods

Badiley, Richard (*c.*1616–1657), naval officer, was formerly a mariner, shipowner, and merchant. Though nothing is known of his origins, he was probably related to the John and Thomas Badiley who figure in Trinity House lists of shipmasters in the 1620s. Bred to the sea, Badiley first occurs in the records as master's mate of the *Increase*, at Cadiz in 1636, aged twenty and of Wapping. He was master of the *Advance* and *Peregrine* (which he part owned) on trading voyages to the eastern Mediterranean in the period 1637–45, fighting actions against Turkish corsairs in 1637, 1640, and 1644; in one his forty-four seamen successfully repelled an attack by over 500 'Turks'. He also traded with North America. By 1648 he was a younger brother of Trinity House, and in 1654 he was described as a freeman of the Fishmongers' Company. He later combined his commercial interests with his naval commitments, despite the inevitable difficulties; he also leased several merchant ships to the state. Though he appears to have taken no direct part in the civil war, he had strong puritan leanings and associations. Following the naval revolt in May 1648 he was one of a small group of Trinity House masters who rallied to the earl of Warwick and parliament, signing a declaration early in July which supported plans to pursue the rebel fleet and insisted that any treaty with the king must guarantee freedom and religious reform. The signatories included several men who, like Badiley, were to play leading roles in the Commonwealth navy, among them Robert Moulton, William Goodsonn, and Christopher Myngs (who later served with him in the Mediterranean). In August Badiley published *The Sea-Men Undeceived*, warning that the mutiny posed a grave threat to London's trade, though its tone was conciliatory and he stressed that he had taken the covenant and was still hoping for a settlement with the king.

Badiley was one of a number of experienced puritan shipmasters brought into the new republican navy to provide leadership. Early in 1649 he was appointed captain of the *Happy Entrance*, and commanded the fleet in the Downs, protecting merchant shipping in the channel. In June he won the council's permission to attack the *Antelope*, which had joined the royalists at Helvoetsluys in 1648, and a party under his lieutenant successfully fired the vessel. On 1 March 1650 he sailed for Portugal, as vice-admiral of Blake's expedition against Prince Rupert. At one point during the long blockade Badiley was dispatched with eight ships to revictual at Cadiz, and fought six French men-of-war he met at sea. He sailed for England on 14 October, convoying several rich Portuguese prizes. In the summer of 1651 he served as vice-admiral to Blake in the Downs, guarding against a possible attack to support the Scots' invasion. Following the Scots' defeat at Worcester, he assisted Blake with the reduction of Jersey before sailing in the *Paragon* in December, commanding a convoy to the straits, calling at Genoa, Leghorn, Zante, and Smyrna. When war broke out with the Dutch in 1652 he was still in the Mediterranean, along with another squadron under Henry Appleton, then at Leghorn. Badiley, convoying merchantmen from the Levant, hoped to be able to join forces before meeting the Dutch, but Appleton ignored an urgent plea for support and remained at Leghorn, leaving him with only four vessels to face a much larger Dutch force under Van Galen near Monte Cristo (south of Elba) on 27 August 1652. In a fierce action the next day, fought at close range and mainly hand-to-hand, Badiley's *Paragon* was badly damaged and a third of her crew killed or injured, while the *Phoenix* was captured. He retreated next day into Porto Longone (Elba), whose Spanish governor forbade the Dutch to attack him, and set about repairing his battered ships. He wrote to England begging for help and, rather to his embarrassment, his wife also lobbied in London for reinforcements to be sent. Plans for a relief force had to be abandoned following Blake's defeat by the Dutch on 30 November, however, and the two squadrons were left to their fate. Early in November Badiley received overall command of the English forces in the region, and promptly crossed to the mainland to assess the position at Leghorn. He had a poor opinion of Appleton's competence and commitment, and found morale and discipline low. Using his new authority, he pressed a number of merchant ships at Leghorn into the state's service, despite the reluctance of their masters, and arranged for others to be hired at Venice. He also set out to restore national honour by backing Captain Owen Cox's plan to recapture the *Phoenix*, which the Dutch were refitting there, overriding Appleton's strong opposition. Appleton had earlier tried to dismiss Cox, but Badiley reversed his order and on 20 November Cox carried out a successful night-time raid to board and seize the ship. This and other incidents led the grand duke of Tuscany on 18 February 1653 to order the English to leave the port, a decision also influenced by news of Blake's defeat, which led him to suppose that the Dutch would win the war. Badiley now attempted to rescue the English ships at Leghorn. His plan was to approach to lure out the Dutch warships, whereupon Appleton's ships would follow and the two small English squadrons would engage the Dutch fleet from both directions. The plan, sound in principle, ended in disaster. As the Dutch remained at anchor, Badiley ordered Appleton to slip out to sea during the night but, locked in disputes with his insubordinate captains, Appleton missed his chance. When the Dutch did sail out to confront Badiley, early next morning (4 March), Appleton followed so closely that they were able to turn back and destroy almost his entire force before Badiley was near enough to help. There was no point in Badiley, with a much smaller force and disaffected seamen, engaging the enemy alone, and he took his ships home to England, arriving in May. Appleton, freed by the Dutch, returned home overland and blamed Badiley for the disaster, accusing him of deliberately abandoning the Leghorn squadron to destruction and alleging malice, treachery, and cowardice. Rumours circulated that Badiley would be tried and hanged. In self-defence he published two vigorous pamphlets justifying his actions and making counter-accusations against Appleton and his associates. The matter was referred to a lengthy parliamentary inquiry, and ended with Badiley's total vindication. While Appleton was never employed again, Badiley was promoted to be rear-admiral of the fleet (7 December), and commanded the *Vanguard* for the last months of the war.

In October 1654 Badiley sailed in the *Andrew* as vice-admiral to Blake on his expedition to the Mediterranean, and took part in the hazardous attack on Porto Farino near Tunis in April 1655. He returned to England in the autumn. On 14 February 1656 he was appointed captain of the *Resolution* and vice-admiral commanding the fleet in the Downs, in the wake of Lawson's sudden resignation. Rumours that Badiley, too, was disaffected proved groundless and, despite his enemies' attempt to have him arrested for debt, he sailed with Blake's fleet to Spain on 15 March. After a largely fruitless summer blockading the Spanish coast, he sailed for England with Montagu late in September, bringing home the treasure captured by Stayner from the Plate ships. This was his last service at sea, though he was still consulted by the admiralty commissioners and continued his commercial activities.

Little is known of Badiley's private life. His first wife, Rebecca, died in 1641; his second wife corresponded with him during his enforced stay in Elba in 1652–3, and gave early warning of Appleton's campaign against him. One of Badiley's sisters was married to a business partner, the shipowner and master John Bennet, and another to Thomas Biggs, a naval surgeon. Badiley's writings reveal a strong puritan faith, and his first pamphlet mentions substantial religious compositions which remained unpublished. In 1653 he joined the gathered congregation, which contained several senior naval officers, at Stepney. In April 1657 he was living at Milk Yard, Wapping, in poor health, and he died there 'of an ulcer' on 7 or 11 August. He was buried on 14 August at St John-at-Wapping. Charles Longland, English agent at Leghorn and an old acquaintance, had earlier paid tribute to 'that honest man Capt. Badiley, who, like the silkworm, spun out his own bowels with the many cares and troubles that lay upon him day and night, yet ran through all with alacrity' (*CSP dom.*, 1653–4, 214).

Captain William Badiley, mariner, shipowner, and naval administrator, was probably Richard's elder brother. A younger brother of Trinity House by 1629, when he was trading with the Levant, he freighted ships for the Mediterranean and East Indies for the East India Company in the 1640s, and in 1649 was appointed one of the regulators to purge Trinity House and the navy. In 1652 he commanded the *Dolphin*, fighting courageously with Blake in two actions against the Dutch. He was appointed master attendant at Portsmouth in December 1653, in charge of the dockyard, and held the same position at Woolwich and Deptford from 1654 until his death in 1666, serving with great efficiency. He was the only Commonwealth elder brother of Trinity House to be reappointed at the Restoration. BERNARD CAPP

Sources T. A. Spalding, *A life of Richard Badiley* (1899) • B. Capp, *Cromwell's navy: the fleet and the English revolution, 1648–1660* (1989) • R. Badiley, *The sea-men undeceived* (1648) • R. Badiley, *Capt. Badiley's answer unto Capt. Appleton's remonstrance* (1653) • R. Badiley, *Capt. Badiley's reply to certaine declarations from Capt. Seamen* (1653) • *CSP dom.*, 1649–57 • PRO, HCA 13/52 • W. R. Chaplin, 'Nehemiah Bourne', *Publications of the Colonial Society of Massachusetts*, 42 (1952–6), 28–155 • 'A booke for church affaires att Stepney', Stepney Meeting-House, London

Badlesmere, Sir Bartholomew (*c*.1275–1322), soldier and administrator, was the son and heir of Guncelin of Badlesmere (*d.* 1301), of Badlesmere, Kent, and his wife, Joan, daughter of Ralph Fitzbernard of Kingsdown, Kent. Like his father, who was a royal banneret and justice of Chester from 1274 to 1281, Badlesmere made his way in the world through service to the crown. First summoned to serve in Gascony in 1294, he accompanied Edward I to Flanders in 1297, fought at Falkirk in 1298, and by 1299 was one of the king's household knights. His representing Kent in the Carlisle parliament of 1307 was a mark of corresponding importance in his own *pays*. Edward II's accession later that year accelerated his rise. He was made constable of Bristol Castle in August 1307, and began to receive numerous royal grants. Only in 1310–12, during the prolonged crisis caused by the opposition of the reforming ordainers to the king's favourite, Piers Gaveston, did his loyalties waver. He was among those barons who petitioned

Edward for reform in March 1310, and in 1312 he was ordered to surrender Bristol Castle, probably the sign of a more open opposition. But after Gaveston's execution in June 1312 he returned to a more comfortable position at the king's side.

By this time Badlesmere had a firm place in baronial society. His early connections had been with Henry de Lacy, fifth earl of Lincoln (*d.* 1311), whose retainer he was by October 1300, and with the northern magnate Robert Clifford, lord of Westmorland (*d.* 1314), with whom he served in Edward I's later Scottish campaigns. He had a closer association with Gilbert de Clare, eighth earl of Gloucester (*d.* 1314), perhaps resulting from his marriage, before 30 June 1308, to Gloucester's cousin, Margaret de Umfraville, *née* de Clare, the widow of the eldest son of the earl of Angus. As Gloucester's knight he earned an ignominious name at Bannockburn in 1314 when he left his lord to be killed in the mêlée.

Badlesmere was by now one of the king's chief councillors and lieutenants. Together with Aymer de Valence, earl of Pembroke (*d.* 1324), often his partner in these years, he led an expedition to the north in 1315; in 1316 he took a major role in the suppression of the Welsh rising of Llewelyn Bren (Llywelyn ap Rhys), and also of the disturbances that broke out in that year at Bristol, which constituted a revolt by the townsmen against Badlesmere himself. In the same year he was among the committee of bishops and magnates appointed to reform the royal household. In September 1316 Edward retained him for a very large fee in return for the promise of his service with a commensurately large retinue; and shortly afterwards he and Pembroke set off for the papal curia on a mission that had the repeal of the ordinances as one of its objectives.

All these activities point to Badlesmere's standing at Edward's court. He was, however, on the court's moderate wing. In 1317 he and Pembroke combined to restrain the most avaricious of the courtiers, Roger Damory (*d.* 1322), in order to placate the court's leading opponent, Thomas, earl of Lancaster (*d.* 1322); and he went on to play a part in the negotiations with Lancaster that culminated in the treaty of Leake in 1318. But his appointment as steward of the royal household in November 1318 was both a snub to Lancaster, who claimed the right of appointment, and a mark of his growing association with Hugh Despenser the younger (*d.* 1326), the chamberlain of the household and the rising star at court. He remained very close to Edward, particularly as the king's negotiator with the Scots, until June 1321, when, at Sherburn in Yorkshire, he deserted to the baronial party which was forming against the two Despensers. Resentment at the younger Despenser's dominance at court, and his own links with the marchers who formed the core of the opposition—his daughter Elizabeth married the son and heir of Roger (IV) Mortimer, lord of Wigmore (*d.* 1326), in 1316—may account for this dramatic change of sides. But although Badlesmere even engaged in forgery in his efforts to discredit the younger Despenser, the fabrication was detected and he achieved nothing. Lancaster, the opposition's leader, refused to receive him and Badlesmere returned to Kent. There his wife's exclusion of Queen Isabella from Leeds Castle in October 1321 inaugurated the short and violent civil war that ended with Lancaster's defeat at Boroughbridge on 16–17 March 1322. Badlesmere fought with the rebels at Boroughbridge, but escaped, only to be captured and subsequently hanged and decapitated in Canterbury on 14 April 1322.

Badlesmere left one son, Giles (1314–1338), and four daughters. Through the favour of the king and of the earl of Gloucester he had built up a large estate in Kent and elsewhere: a royal grant of 1315 enumerates lands in forty-six places spread through eight counties. To judge by his employment, he was an able man, who owed his promotion to both his diplomatic and military skills and his energetic acquisitiveness. That such a natural loyalist should have met a traitor's end reflects all Edward II's failings as a political manager. J. R. MADDICOTT, *rev.*

Sources J. C. Davies, *The baronial opposition to Edward II* (1918) • C. Moor, *Knights of Edward I*, 1 (1929) • J. R. Maddicott, *Thomas of Lancaster, 1307–1322: a study in the reign of Edward II* (1970) • J. R. S. Phillips, *Aymer de Valence, earl of Pembroke, 1307–1324: baronial politics in the reign of Edward II* (1972) • N. Fryde, *The tyranny and fall of Edward II, 1321–1326* (1979) • GEC, *Peerage*

Badley, John Haden (1865–1967), headmaster, was born on 21 February 1865 in Tower Street, Dudley, Worcestershire, the only son of James Payton Badley, surgeon, and his wife, Laura Elizabeth Best. He had three older sisters to whom he was always very close. The home atmosphere was restricted in some ways but very supportive and affectionate, and he enjoyed a happy childhood. Dr Badley seems to have been a rather remote figure to the children, but he gave his son every possible opportunity, and the money he accumulated—for he was a good man of business as well as a much respected doctor—provided the essential backing for his son's later schemes. Badley went to Rugby School at the age of fifteen and was head of his house for three years. He enjoyed his time there and won an exhibition as the best classic of his year, but he felt later that the Rugby training, with its heavy concentration on the classics, had been very narrow and bookish.

From Rugby, Badley went on in 1884 to Trinity College, Cambridge, where he gained a first class in part one of the classical tripos in 1887, and was elected to a college scholarship, staying on for a fourth year without taking any examination but reading widely. He wrote later that his Cambridge years, during which he was exposed to the ideas of Edward Carpenter and William Morris, had exerted a major influence on his later life. He met Amy Garrett (*d.* 1956), the sister of one of his Cambridge friends, whom he married in 1892. They had one son. He felt very uncertain about his future career until a friend, Goldsworthy Lowes Dickinson of King's College, put him in touch with Cecil Reddie. He joined Reddie's staff when the New School at Abbotsholme, Derbyshire, opened in October 1889, and was a master there until 1892. That short period determined the whole course of his professional life, for it was Reddie who helped him to discover what he wanted to do in education. He spoke later of having been apprenticed to a master craftsman.

Yet Badley's stay at Abbotsholme was to be brief. He disliked Reddie's autocratic system of management. He was anxious to marry, and he knew that there would be no role for his wife at Abbotsholme. In January 1893 he opened his own school at Bedales, near Haywards Heath in Sussex. Growth at first was slow, though the school soon became known in other countries through the writings of the French social theorist Edmond Demolins, who sent his own son to Bedales School. In 1898 a few girls were admitted, so that Badley could claim later that Bedales was the first boarding-school in the country to which boys and girls were admitted on a fully equal basis. The change would probably have occurred anyway since Badley himself was sympathetic and his wife was a supporter of the women's movement. Yet it happened in a curiously informal way when a mother who wished to send her daughters to the school offered to open a house for them. The number of boys and girls did not reach parity until the end of the First World War.

By 1900 the accommodation at old Bedales had become too small, and Badley bought a site and built a new school at Steep, near Petersfield in Hampshire. From then until his retirement in 1935 progress was steady. The school remained small; in 1935 there were 136 pupils, a decline from a high point of 194 in 1922. Badley believed in and practised democratic management, but there was no doubt that he was the leader—a quiet, rather withdrawn figure to many people, though not to the children. After the First World War a school council was set up, although its role was entirely advisory. Towards the end of his life he defined his objectives as three-fold: a healthy environment, a wide range of work with considerable emphasis on the arts and on manual training, and a community structured on family lines. Academic work was taken seriously, and Bedalians had a good record at the universities. There were experiments in the curriculum. During the 1920s there were extensive trials of the Dalton plan of assignment work, and the Montessori method was followed in the junior house. In 1920 the Bedales School Company had been set up to control the school.

Badley had abandoned traditional religious beliefs while he was at Cambridge, but he was deeply interested in the moral aspects of Christianity. He talked and wrote on religious subjects, and he published an edition of the Bible, re-arranged in historical sequence, *The Bible as Seen Today* (3 vols., 1965). His other major works include *Bedales: a Pioneer School* (1923), *A Schoolmaster's Testament* (1937), and an autobiography, *Memories and Reflections* (1955). Badley lived over thirty years after his retirement, dying on 6 March 1967 at the age of 102, at Fairhaven, Steep, Petersfield, Hampshire, a cottage on the school estate where he lived after his wife's death. He was cremated at Woking on 10 March 1967. He was the prophet of a new kind of school life, many of whose ideas have passed into the mainstream of English educational thinking.

JOHN ROACH

Sources J. H. Badley, *Bedales: a pioneer school* (1923) • J. H. Badley, *A schoolmaster's testament: forty years of educational experience* (1937) • J. H. Badley, *Memories and reflections* (1955) • R. Wake and P. Denton, *Bedales School: the first hundred years* (1993) • G. Brandreth and S. Henry, eds., *John Haden Badley 1865–1967: Bedales School and its founder* (1967) • J. L. Henderson, *Irregularly bold: a study of Bedales School* (1978) • W. A. C. Stewart, *The educational innovators*, 2: *Progressive schools, 1881–1967* (1968) • E. Demolins, *L'éducation nouvelle: l'école des Roches* (1898) • G. Crump, *Bedales since the war* (1936) • b. cert. • *CGPLA Eng. & Wales* (1967)

Archives Bedales School, Petersfield, Hampshire, Bedales School archive

Likenesses F. Yates, oils, 1921, Bedales School, Hampshire • photographs, repro. in Wake and Denton, *Bedales School* • photographs, repro. in Brandreth and Henry, eds., *John Haden Badley*

Wealth at death £5531: probate, 7 April 1967, *CGPLA Eng. & Wales*

Badmin, Stanley Roy (1906–1989), illustrator, painter, and printmaker, was born at 8A Niederwald Road, Sydenham, London, on 18 April 1906, the second child of Charles James Badmin, a schoolmaster, and his wife, Margaret (Madge) Raine, both of whom had come from Somerset. Important in his development into the essential illustrator of the English countryside were family holidays to Holcombe, in the Mendips, staying with his paternal grandfather, the village carpenter; these trips continued long after his grandfather's death, into adulthood and married life. Badmin was educated at Sydenham School, and continued to receive general private tuition on becoming an art student, for in 1922 he won a scholarship to Camberwell School of Arts and Crafts, and studied under Cosmo Clarke and Thomas Derrick. Then, in 1924, he won a studentship to the Royal College of Art, London (RCA), switching in his second year from painting to design; following the change he encountered such important teachers as Professor Tristram and Randolph Schwabe, the latter remaining a close friend. A precocious and conscientious student with a specialism in book illustration, he received his diploma in 1927.

In the following year Badmin prepared for an art teacher's diploma, taking a range of courses at the RCA and at Camberwell. Thus he could supplement his income early in his career by teaching at Richmond School of Art (1934) and St John's Wood School of Art (1936), experiences that sealed his friendship with colleague P. F. Millard. Nevertheless he quickly established himself, first as an illustrator and then as an etcher. He made his initial periodical contributions to *The Graphic* (1927) and *The Tatler* (1928), and had his inaugural solo show at the Twenty-One Gallery, London, in 1930. He married Margaret Georgina (Peggy) Colborne in the same year. Badmin had been introduced to the gallery in 1928 by Robert Sargent Austin, his etching tutor at the RCA. It published many of his masterly etchings during the few years until 1931, when the market in the medium slumped. He then transferred to the Fine Art Society and concentrated increasingly on watercolour while continuing to etch and maintaining an emphasis on rich, evocative topography. Election to the Royal Society of Painter-Etchers and Engravers (associate, 1931; member, 1935) was soon followed—and superseded—by election to the Royal Society of Painters in Water Colours (RWS; associate, 1932; member, 1939). A wider reputation was ensured in 1935, when Badmin received a major commission from *Fortune*, an American magazine, which asked him to depict various towns in the United States; the results were exhibited at MacDonald's Gallery, New York (1936). A growing international perspective also led to greater political awareness, the events of the Spanish Civil War encouraging him to join James Holland and others of the liberal left in the Artists' International Association. Maintaining his ideals beyond the Second World War, he became an active member of the Sydenham and Forest Hill Peace Group.

An important development in Badmin's illustrative style was marked by *Highways and Byways of Essex* (1938). Begun by F. L. M. Griggs, an artist revered for his prints and illustrations, it was completed by Badmin following Griggs's death. His meticulous use of pen and ink capitalized on his earlier etchings and offered lively anecdote in contrast to Griggs's sombre majesty. A unique eye for detail soon enabled him to make a mark as an important educational illustrator; his first Puffin picture book, *Village and Town* (1939), lithographed in colour, was followed by *Trees in Britain* (1942), through which Badmin's name became a byword for the accurate depiction of trees. He made a similarly distinctive contribution to a project aimed at adults, 'Recording Britain' (1940), in which artists were paid by the Pilgrim Trust to record threatened buildings and landscapes; fifteen of his drawings were included in the resulting three-volume publication, *Recording Britain* (1946–7). The Second World War emphasized the urgency of such an occupation, while also employing Badmin in other ways. He contributed drawings to exhibitions organized by the Ministry of Information and, following his call-up in 1942, worked on operational model-making at RAF Medmenham, near Henley-on-Thames. In its vision of a peaceful, profitable Britain, Badmin's art seemed to offer a perfect antidote to war and an ideal for the post-war generation. It received unparalleled popular exposure from 1948, when he joined the agency of Saxon Artists and took on frequent commercial commissions. He designed series of advertisements for Fisons and Bowater Paper, and produced posters for transport and travel companies. He was also patronized by Royle, one of the largest manufacturers of greetings cards and calendars. Equally in demand as an illustrator of books and periodicals, he published *Trees for Town and Country* (1947) and *British Countryside in Colour* (1951), and contributed to *Radio Times*. His constant professionalism and stamina became particularly useful from 24 March 1950, when, his first marriage having ended in divorce, he married Rosaline Elizabeth Wates Flew, *née* Downey, and took on the upbringing of her daughter, Elizabeth, along with that of his own two children, Patrick and Joanna; a fourth child, Galea, was born in 1951.

Only from the mid-1950s was Badmin able to paint two or three major pieces for each RWS exhibition and hold a show at the Leicester Galleries (1955). He also found time to embark on projects for Shell, perhaps the most important commercial patron of British art; his contribution to Geoffrey Grigson's *Shell Guide to Trees and Shrubs* (1958) and four volumes of Shell Guides to the counties greatly influenced and enhanced the house style.

In 1959 Badmin and his family moved to Bignor, near Pulborough, Sussex, from where he continued to paint and exhibit. He held a further show, at Worthing Art Gallery in 1967. In 1984 the RWS honoured his achievement by devoting a part of its autumn exhibition to his work. This was followed in 1985 by a major retrospective at Chris Beetles Gallery and an accompanying monograph. The overwhelming success of that show proved the artist's enduring appeal and value as an interpreter and chronicler of the native landscape. He died in his beloved Sussex, at St Richards Hospital, Chichester, on 28 April 1989.

CHRISTOPHER BEETLES

Sources C. Beetles, *S. R. Badmin and the English landscape* (1985) · private information (2004) [family] · b. cert. · m. cert. [Rosaline Flew] · d. cert.

Wealth at death under £70,000: probate, 23 June 1989, *CGPLA Eng. & Wales*

Baedeker, Fritz (1844–1925). *See under* Baedeker, Karl (1801–1859).

Baedeker, Karl (1801–1859), publisher, was born in Essen on 3 November 1801, the son of Gottschalk Diederich Baedeker (1788–1841), bookseller, and his wife, Marianne (1781–1847), daughter of bookseller Gehra of Neuwied. The family had a wide range of business activities connected to books, including publishing, bookselling, printing, and editing newspapers. After attending Heidelberg University and gaining experience in bookselling firms in Heidelberg and Berlin, Baedeker founded his own bookselling firm in Koblenz in 1827. The Romantic movement in Germany had given a new impetus to travel, which on the Rhine was particularly encouraged by the establishment in 1827 of regular steamboat excursions. In 1828 Baedeker bought the rights to J. A. Klein's *Rheinreise von Mainz bis Köln* and, after the death of the author, Baedeker himself revised and updated the work, recreating it for a new market. Using his own travel experiences he guided the tourist to the principal attractions in each place, saving travellers the expense of hiring their own guide. He thus created a new type of guidebook, which was widely copied throughout Europe and opened up tourism to a new class of visitor. The reliability of the information was ensured by annual journeys by Baedeker himself and by reference to respected published sources and expert scholars.

On 4 October 1829 Baedeker married Emilie (1808–1879), daughter of Heinrich Heintzmann, a civil servant of Essen, and his wife, Leopoldine von Paczenski und Tenczin. They had ten children. By the time of Baedeker's death in Koblenz on 4 October 1859 his firm had published guidebooks to several countries in continental Europe, and his sons, including **Fritz Baedeker** (1844–1925), took over a flourishing business. Fritz was born on 4 December 1844 in Koblenz and entered the family firm. Under his guidance the range of guidebooks continued to expand, and increasing emphasis was put on simultaneous French and English editions. These were not simply literal translations: each was adapted to the needs, preferences, and experiences of travellers from each country, but all had a strong emphasis on cultural sites, supplying accurate details of art galleries, cathedrals, and churches at a time when few individual guides were available. In 1872 the Baedeker firm with its cartographers H. Wagner and E. Debes, whose high-quality maps contributed considerably to the guides, moved to Leipzig, then the centre of the German book trade. On 18 June 1873 in Koblenz Baedeker married Florentine (Flöry; 1849–1916), daughter of Dietrich Wilhelm Landfermann, a civil servant.

The period 1870–1914 has been described as the firm's golden age, and it was in this period that Baedeker's impact on British tourism was most marked, marginalizing John Murray's Handbooks, hitherto the standard series for travel at home and abroad. For the serious tourist a Baedeker was indispensable, its tone, especially with respect to southern Europeans, assuring northerners of their superiority, and suggesting ways of avoiding dangers. When Lucy Honeychurch finds herself 'In Santa Croce with no Baedeker' in E. M. Forster's *A Room with a View* (1908) she is entirely lost. Like so many others, she relies on Baedeker to make the unfamiliar manageable, and to enable her to see foreign places while minimizing contact with foreigners. Her Baedeker tells her not only what she should see but also how she should respond to it. It was thus in the widest sense that the Baedeker family shaped the travel experiences of several generations of British tourists.

After 1914 the Baedeker firm laid particular emphasis on the British market. Fritz Baedeker died on 9 April 1925 in Leipzig, but the firm continued to prosper in family hands, with new ventures such as the publication of the first motoring guide in 1938. However, in 1943 Baedeker's archive and that of their cartographers were destroyed in a bombing raid, and after the war Leipzig was the wrong side of the iron curtain for a firm promoting international travel. The firm was refounded in 1948 in Hamburg, but its revised handbooks were more regional geographies than travel guides, with scant practical information. The firm never regained its pre-eminence in what had become a very competitive market, and certainly never regained its hold on the British imagination.

ELIZABETH BAIGENT

Sources H. Lulfing, 'Baedeker, Karl', in Otto, Graf zu Stolberg-Wernigerode, *Neue deutsche Biographie* (Berlin, 1953) • H. Baedeker, 'Verlag Karl Baedeker', *Leipziger Jahrbuch* (1940), 121–4

Baelz, Peter Richard (1923–2000), theologian and Church of England clergyman, was born on 27 July 1923 at Ivybank, Queen's Road, Forest Hill, London. His German Lutheran parents, Eberhard Friedrich Wolfgang Baelz, export merchant, and Adine Elsie Dora Focke, sent him to Dulwich College. A conscientious objector, he then read classics at Christ's College, Cambridge (1941–4), where he was a tennis blue. He trained for the Anglican ministry at Westcott House, Cambridge, was ordained deacon by the bishop of Birmingham, E. W. Barnes, in 1947, and served his curacy at Bournville. He contracted osteomyelitis, and was not priested until 1950. He married Anne Thelma Cleall-Harding, a student teacher, on 15 July 1950, and served a second curacy at Sherborne Abbey. He followed this with a brief spell as assistant chaplain at Ripon Hall, Oxford, before becoming vicar of Wishaw, Birmingham, in 1953. In 1956 he returned to Bournville as vicar. He became fellow and dean of Jesus College, Cambridge, in 1960, and was appointed a university lecturer in 1966. In 1972 he moved to Oxford, where he was canon of Christ Church and regius professor of moral and pastoral theology. His final appointment, in 1980, was as dean of Durham, and he retired in 1988. He was the Hulsean lecturer at Cambridge in 1965–6 and the Bampton lecturer at Oxford in 1974; he was created DD in 1979, and honorary DD at Durham in 1993. From 1993 to 1999 he was an honorary professor in the University of Wales, and from 1990 to 2000 an independent town councillor in Llandrindod Wells, Radnorshire. He was also treasurer of the Mid-Wales Mediation Group. He died in the Hospital Cefnllys, Llandrindod Wells, on 15 March 2000, and was buried in Llandrindod Wells on 23 March. His wife and three sons survived him.

Peter Baelz published widely in the philosophy of religion. His Hulsean lectures appeared as *Prayer and Providence* (1968), a work which was followed by *Christian Philosophy and Metaphysics* (1968). In 1975 the Bampton lectures, published as *The Forgotten Dream*, continued his philosophical explorations, and in 1977 he wrote *Ethics and Belief*. Two smaller works were *Does God Answer Prayer?* (1982) and a collection of essays on ministry, which he co-edited with William Jacob, called *Ministers of the Kingdom* (1985). He became regarded as one of the most prominent liberals in the Church of England, and the Festschrift presented to him in 1991 (edited by D. W. Hardy and Peter Sedgwick), entitled *The Weight of Glory*, was subtitled 'The future of liberal theology'. He chaired the deans' conference, steering through the general synod measures to reform cathedral statutes. He also spoke in the general synod on many ethical matters, and was for a number of years a member of the board for social responsibility. He was especially involved in the working parties on remarriage after divorce, homosexuality, assisted conception, and euthanasia. He chaired working parties on economics, vocation, and childlessness. He also spoke in the debate on nuclear disarmament in the general synod in 1982, and contributed articles on suicide, where he sought to bring a more pastoral approach to the previous thinking of the church.

Peter Baelz's ministry was distinctive because he never lost his pastoral way of relating to people—the result of being a parish priest until he was thirty-seven—allied to a sharp and probing intellect. He was deeply influenced by the master of Christ's College, Charles Raven, a noted scientist and theologian, and by the chaplain, Ian Ramsey, who became professor of the philosophy of religion at Oxford and later bishop of Durham in the 1960s. Peter Baelz continued the liberalism of these two theologians both in his writings and in his ministry. He welcomed the appointment of David Jenkins as bishop of Durham in

1984, and worked closely with him for the next four years until his retirement. His theological work was concerned with reconciling the religious dependence of human beings on God and their moral responsibility for their actions. In *Does God Answer Prayer?* he described prayer as 'creative participation in divine activity', and he continually emphasized the transformative effect of faith on human beings. His philosophical writings during his period as a university teacher were an attempt to communicate the nature of God to a contemporary audience. His description of himself as a liberal did not spring from the pressures of secularization, but rather arose from his deep understanding of the graciousness of a God who awaits the response of humanity. The philosophical climate of the day was something he met with cheerfulness, drawing out the ways in which contemporary questions about transcendence could be answered from within the Christian tradition.

Baelz gave many addresses on spirituality and was an excellent preacher, introducing his congregation to the mystery of God. Another channel through which he sought to communicate the Christian faith was the arts. He formed a close acquaintance at university with the abstract sculptor Anthony Caro, who remained a lifelong friend and went to Durham to lecture on several occasions. Baelz especially developed Durham Cathedral's links with the arts through his fostering of the arts and recreation chaplaincy. A modern window by Mark Angus was installed during his period as dean, as well as several pieces of sculpture in the cathedral and its surroundings.

PETER SEDGWICK

Sources *The Times* (20 March 2000) · *The Independent* (23 March 2000) · *Daily Telegraph* (22 March 2000) · *The Guardian* (31 March 2000) · P. R. Baelz, 'Penitent Catholic, impenitent liberal', *The weight of glory: a Festschrift for P. R. Baelz*, ed. P. Sedgwick and D. W. Hardy (1991) · b. cert. · m. cert. · d. cert. · personal knowledge (2004) · Crockford (1998–9)

Likenesses photograph, repro. in Sedgwick and Hardy, eds., *Weight of glory*, inside cover

Wealth at death £510,991—net: probate, 10 Aug 2000, *CGPLA Eng. & Wales*

Baen, Jacobus de (1673–1700). *See under* Baen, Jan de (1633–1702).

Baen, Jan de (1633–1702), portrait painter, was born on 20 February 1633 in Haarlem, Holland. Houbraken's life of de Baen, published within sixteen years of de Baen's death, would appear to be reliable because the artist painted a portrait of Dr Jacob Souburg of Dordrecht, Houbraken's father-in-law.

Both de Baen's parents died when he was three and he was brought up by his uncle, the painter Hinderk Pyman (*c.*1580–1647), in Emden. When Pyman died de Baen went to Amsterdam as apprentice to the portraitist Jacob Backer (1608–1651). On qualifying as a painter and etcher, de Baen deliberately chose to follow the style of Anthony Van Dyck, because it was marketable. His only etching is of the *Burning of Amsterdam Town Hall* (dated 1652).

At some point, according to Houbraken, Charles II invited de Baen to England, sending Thomas Killigrew

Jan de Baen (1633–1702), self-portrait [with his wife, Maria de Baen]

with the royal yacht to fetch him. This story is unproven. De Baen is said to have painted the king, Queen Catherine, and several courtiers, but in fact Charles II's principal painter, Peter Lely, was a jealous man, and de Baen made no headway at the English court. The known facts about his life are as follows. In December 1660 he was in The Hague. There, in 1665, he married Maria de Kinderen, and they had eight children, one of whom was the painter **Jacobus de Baen** (1673–1700). Jan was warden of the Confrerie Pictura in The Hague several times between 1666 and 1676. He took apprentices from 1672 onwards, and was governor of the Draughtsmen's Academy from 1699 to 1700. He was buried in The Hague on 8 March 1702.

Jan de Baen specialized in portraits of notable Dutch subjects: Admiral Tromp, Van Beverning, and Jan de Bisschop, the duke of Celle, and some court beauties were among his sitters, and also the grand duke of Tuscany to whom he presented his own self-portrait (Uffizi, Florence). He portrayed the young prince of Orange in antique dress (British Royal Collection) and he was patronized by the then current rulers of Holland, Johan and Cornelis De Witt. He painted an infamous *Apotheosis of Cornelis de Witt*, a huge horizontal picture showing Cornelis being crowned by trumpeting fames, nearly half of which depicts the burning of the English fleet in the Medway. It hung publicly in Dordrecht town hall. 'Filling their towns with abusive Pictures' was cited as one cause of the Third Anglo-Dutch War of 1672–8 (PRO, SP 29/311/101). After their fall later that year, portraits of the De Witts were ordered to be destroyed and de Baen's house was searched. Versions of the *Apotheosis* survived in private hands and can now be seen in Dordrecht Museum and the Rijksmuseum, Amsterdam. Perhaps to ingratiate himself with the newly empowered Orangists, de Baen cold-bloodedly painted the mutilated bodies of the De Witt brothers as they hung in the gallows after their executions.

When the French army captured Utrecht, Louis XIV tried to entice de Baen to paint his portrait, but the artist refused. Frederik-Willhelm, duke of Brandenburg, also invited him to Berlin in 1676, but de Baen sent his nephew and pupil, Jan van Sweel, instead. His wife is said to have prevented him from accepting these offers. He depicted William III as king of England several times, though none appears to be convincingly from the life. He was, according to Lionel Cust, 'a second-rate artist in spite of his success' (*DNB*).

Jan de Baen painted several large group portraits for public institutions: *The Regents of the House of Correction in Amsterdam* (Historical Museum, Amsterdam); *The Magistrates* (1682; Historical Museum, The Hague); *The Drapers of Leyden*, the owners of the East India Company (Hoorn Westfries Museum, Netherlands). These works, painted from life, are among his more powerful compositions. Another fine portrait is *Prince Johan-Maurits of Nassau-Siegen*, with the gardens of Cleves in the background (Mauritshuis, The Hague).

Jan taught his son Jacobus to paint. Jacobus came to England during William III's reign, in 1693, and subsequently travelled to Italy, France, and Germany. He led a dissolute life and died in 1700 aged twenty-seven in Vienna.

KATHARINE GIBSON

Sources A. Houbraken, *De groote schouburgh der Nederlantsche konstschilders en schilderessen*, 2 (Amsterdam, 1719), 303–15 • E. Buijsen, *Haagse schilders in de Gouden Eeuw: het Hoogsteder Lexicon van alle schilders werkzaam in Den Haag, 1600–1700* (The Hague, 1998) [exhibition catalogue, Haagse Historisch Museum, The Hague, 12 Dec 1998–7 Mar 1999] • *DNB* • 'Printed speech of his grace the duke of Lauderdale … at the opening of parliament', 12 June 1672, PRO, SP29/311/101, 10–11 • F. W. H. Hollstein, *Dutch and Flemish etchings, engravings and woodcuts, c.1450–1700*, 1 (1949), 64–5 • C. Wright, *Paintings in Dutch museums: an index of oil paintings in public collections in the Netherlands by artists born before 1870* (1980) • C. White, *The Dutch pictures in the collection of her majesty the queen* (1982), 16, cat. no. 12 • R. E. O. Ekkart, 'Baen, Jan de', *The dictionary of art*, ed. J. Turner (1996)

Likenesses J. de Baen, self-portrait, oils (with his wife), Museum Bredius, The Hague [*see illus.*]

Baeshe, Edward (*c*.1518–1587), naval administrator, is of obscure origins, though he was styled esquire in later life, and one of his benefactions is adorned with his coat of arms. His father's name was Alexander, and his mother's Alice Barley; but their status and residence are unknown. Edward seems to have been born in London, but nothing is known about his upbringing. On 30 November 1538 he married Thomasine in the church of St Dionis Backchurch. In the parish register her surname is given as Ager, without indication of status, but in a heraldic visitation of the following century, she is called Thomasine Baker and a coat of arms is ascribed to her family. It seems likely that family tradition had indulged in a little constructive embroidery, and that Baeshe and Thomasine both came from minor citizen families, on the same social level as the parish gentry.

By 1545 Baeshe was already a man of some substance, with connections in high places. In September of that year he acquired the manor of Lydencourt, Kent, jointly with Sir Richard Southwell, and in December he purchased two messuages in Shropshire (with one Richard Cutrice) for £231 8*s*. 0*d*. Other similar transactions indicate that he was acting as an agent or broker. In January 1546 he obtained the office of usher to the court of general surveyors, jointly with Richard Smyth, who is styled yeoman of the chamber—an indication of Baeshe's perceived status at that point. He seems to have begun acting as a London agent for the council of marine causes as soon as that body came into existence in 1545, and was certainly supplying victuals to the navy on a contract basis by 1548. In 1549 he began to receive grants jointly with Thomasine—first the rectory and advowson of Feltham, and then the manor of Cullynges in Hertfordshire—an indication that he intended to retain the benefits, rather than sell them on. In 1550, when he received the second grant, he was still described as 'of London', and held a garden in the parish of St Sepulchre.

In 1550 the office of general surveyor of victuals for the navy was created, and on 18 June Edward Baeshe was appointed to it, in recognition of services that he had already performed in that department. His fee was £50 a year, with 8*d*. a day for a clerk. This office he continued to hold, and discharge, for the rest of his life, although not on the same terms. After renewal by both Mary and Elizabeth, on 13 April 1565 he signed a contract to provide the same services, but in return for a fixed sum, calculated on a pro rata basis for the number of men in service. Baeshe was expected to provide the victuals, and take his profit, out of this global sum. Inflation necessitated two increases in the rate over the next twenty years, and Baeshe complained frequently to the council about his difficulties. However, he seems to have been both relatively honest and relatively effective, and there were few grumbles about what he provided. He also prospered. In November 1554 he received an annuity of £50, over and above his fee, and in December 1557 became constable of Portchester Castle, by no means a sinecure in time of war. He appears on the pardon roll of the first year of Elizabeth as 'of London, al. of Waltham, co. Hertford', and seems at this time to have moved out of the city. This probably coincided with the grant of the manor of Stansted Abbot, Hertfordshire, which he received in the same year, and where he seems thereafter to have resided.

Baeshe was still dealing in land, and in December 1559 paid, along with William Winter, a colleague on the navy board, the substantial sum of £2114 for lands in Dorset which he seems to have had no intention of occupying. In February 1562 he was appointed to the commissions of the peace for both Hertfordshire and Middlesex, which indicates not only his arrival among the county gentry, but also the fact that he was felt to be a reliable supporter of the new ecclesiastical settlement. At some point between 1560 and 1574 Thomasine died, and by the latter date Edward had married again, his second wife being Jane, the daughter of Sir Ralph *Sadler. In 1577 he built the north chapel at St James's Church, Stansted, and it is in a window there that his arms and motto appear. He had at least two sons but no recorded daughters. William, his second son, was a minor at the time of Baeshe's death on 20 May 1587, and is described in the visitation as 'drowned under London Bridge', an event that presumably occurred later. Baeshe was succeeded at Stansted by his elder son, Ralph, who died in his turn in 1598. Ralph seems to have been just eighteen in 1587, and the visitation ascribes both these sons to Jane, which makes it likely that Thomasine had died before 1570.

Edward Baeshe left lands at Writtle in Essex, and in the Forest of Dean, as well as the estate at Stansted and a house in London. He was buried at St James's Church, Stansted Abbot, where there is a tomb effigy. Although he was never knighted, he is a good example of those who prospered through service to the crown in the mid-sixteenth century. In addition to numerous lands and a great quantity of household goods, his will distributed at least 1000 ounces of plate among his wife, who was appointed sole executor, his two sons, and a number of trusted servants. After Ralph's death his wife, Frances Carey, married as her second husband George Manners, earl of Rutland. The Nicholas Baeshe who also appears in Hertfordshire at the same time (although not on the commission of the peace) was Edward Baeshe's cousin. He died in 1591. DAVID LOADES

Sources *LP Henry VIII* • *CPR*, 1547–84 • treasurer's accounts, PRO, E351 • *VCH Hertfordshire*, vols. 3–4 • W. C. Metcalfe, ed., *The visitations of Hertfordshire*, Harleian Society, 22 (1886) • J. L. Chester, ed., *The reiester booke of Saynte De'nis Backchurch parishe … begynnynge … 1538*, Harleian Society, register section, 3 (1878), 1 • M. Oppenheim, *A history of the administration of the Royal Navy* (1896) • D. M. Loades, *The Tudor navy* (1992) • will, PRO, PROB 11/71, fols. 182r–183r

Likenesses effigy, St James's Church, Stansted Abbot, Hertfordshire

Báetán mac Cairill (*d.* 581), king of Ulster, son of Cairell mac Muiredaig (*d.* *c.*540), king of Ulster, was a member of Dál Fiatach, a dynasty in modern co. Down. He became king of Ulster after the death of his brother Demmán in 572. According to Ulster genealogical material, he also achieved the kingship of Ireland, which was otherwise the almost exclusive prerogative of the Uí Néill dynasties (descendants of Níall Noígiallach) until the reign of Brian Bóruma (*d.* 1014). This claim does not find much acceptance elsewhere, although a list of kings in the Rawlinson genealogies doubtfully includes him: 'Let it be known that no king of any seed other than Níall's held Ireland after the arrival of Patrick except for two who ruled, Báetán and Brian. However, others do not count Báetán among the great kings' (*Corpus genealogiarum Hiberniae*, 1.124). The chronicles regard him at best as king of Ulster.

Báetán's supremacy in Ireland, if such it was, came during the two politically unclear decades which followed the death of Diarmait mac Cerbaill, high-king of Ireland, in 565. To add to the general uncertainty of this time, it is possible that Báetán's achievements may have been confused with those of two other Báetáns who flourished at about the same time and are found in lists of the kings of Ireland, namely Báetán mac Ninnedo of Cenél Conaill (*d.* 586), and Báetán mac Muirchertaich Meic Ercca of Cenél nÉogain (*d.* 572), both descendants of Níall.

Báetán mac Cairill features prominently in a list of seven great sovereigns of Ulster, which says that he was king of Scotland as well as Ireland, having won the submission of Áedán mac Gabráin who ruled the Gaelic-speaking settlement of Dál Riata in the west of Scotland. Báetán was supposed to have cleared the Isle of Man of 'foreigners' and to have taken the tribute of Skye and of the provinces of Munster and Connacht; a poem in *Senchas Síl Ír* describes the melancholy of the tribute-bearers who had to travel great distances to Báetán's Fort at 'Lethét', and who received little honour when they arrived. The dominion envisaged here would be more wide-ranging than that achieved by any other Irish king before or since. It is most unlikely that Munster and Connacht submitted to him. However, there is corroborating testimony for his activity in Man and conflict with Áedán mac Gabráin: an annal entry for 577 speaks of 'the first expedition by the Ulstermen to Man' (*Ann. Ulster*, s.a. 577). There is some evidence that the Ulstermen were expelled from the island by Áedán mac Gabráin shortly after Báetán's death. It has been suggested that the convention of Druim Cett, at which St Columba was present along with Áedán mac Gabráin and the Uí Néill potentate Áed mac Ainmerech, was an alliance between these two kings against Báetán. However, there is a strong case that the convention, placed in the chronicles at 575, was misdated, and in fact did not occur until after Báetán's death in 581. He had at least three sons, including Fiachna Crach (*d.* 608) and Dairchello, and was married to Cummíne Duibni ingen Fhurudráin of the Uí Thuirtri dynasty of the Airgialla.

PHILIP IRWIN

Sources M. E. Dobbs, ed. and trans., 'The history of the descendants of Ir', *Zeitschrift für Celtische Philologie*, 13 (1919–21), 308–59 • F. J. Byrne, *Irish kings and high-kings* (1973), 109–11 • D. Ó Cróinín, *Early medieval Ireland, 400–1200* (1995), 50–51 • *Ann. Ulster*, s.a. 577 • M. A. O'Brien, ed., *Corpus genealogiarum Hiberniae* (Dublin, 1962) • Adomnán of Iona, *Life of St Columba*, ed. and trans. R. Sharpe (1995), n. 204 • 'Rig ulad', *The Book of Leinster*, ed. O. J. Bergin and others, 1 (1954–83), 192–4, line 5789 • K. Meyer, ed., 'The Laud synchronisms', *Zeitschrift für Celtische Philologie*, 9 (1913), 471–85, esp. 484

Baffin, William (1584?–1621), Arctic explorer, was probably born in London, possibly in 1584. Neither his parents' names nor details of his early life are known. He certainly married, and may have been the William Baffin who married Susan Hodges at St Bride's, Fleet Street, on 24 January 1607. In 1612 he was chief pilot aboard the *Patience*, which led the navigator James Hall's fourth expedition to Greenland and sailed from Hull, accompanied by James Barker on the *Heartsease*, on 22 April. The voyage was largely financed by London merchants, who, if he was indeed a London man, may have insisted on Baffin's participation.

Baffin's narrative of the journey, first published in 1616 as *A Journall of the Voyage Made to Greenland*, described how the expedition reached 67° N on Greenland's west coast before turning south to trade with the indigenous inhabitants. On 9 July, at lat. 65°20′ N in Cockin Sound, Baffin made the first recorded observation of a measurement of longitude by an English navigator, although he noted that the complicated calculations had been made by 'some of the better sort' of mariners. He estimated his longitude using calculations derived from the sun's height when the moon reached a meridian line he had established. The calculation of 60°30′ was significantly further west than the real position of 52°50′, an error that can be attributed to the fact that the complex motions of the moon were not understood until detailed lunar tables became available two hundred years later. Baffin also described the death of Hall, mortally wounded by an arrow in an apparently unprovoked attack when trading for furs on 22 July. Despite the incident the expedition continued its search for a mine known from Danish sources, but found its minerals of no value. The expedition turned for home on 26 July when they also realized the indigenous inhabitants would not trade, and reached Hull on 17 September. Baffin's narrative provided a useful description of the fauna and flora of the area, the various seasonal habitations and boats, as well as the religious beliefs and funerary practices of the inhabitants. He was especially impressed with their small, one-person boats, covered with watertight sealskin and powered by a single paddle, which he described as having 'incredible speed' and great manoeuvrability.

In 1613 Baffin served with the Muscovy Company in their whaling expedition to the islands now known as Spitsbergen, employed in the *Tiger* as chief pilot to Captain Benjamin Joseph's fleet of seven vessels. The fleet left London on 30 May and found over a score of vessels from the chief ports of western Europe in the area. They managed to assert their company's charter rights over the foreign vessels and planted crosses asserting King James's claim to the islands. Baffin pioneered observations to measure the sun's refraction at high latitudes, calculating a variation of 26′ at 79° N. He also showed that the common sailing compass produced a critical error in latitude measurement of 5½° E. Hence it is clear that his work significantly improved the latitude calculations of mariners, especially in high latitudes. Between 16 April and 4 October 1614 Baffin was part of Joseph's next venture to the area in the *Tomasine*, which led a fleet of eleven ships. He set out with two small boats from the main expedition to explore and map a great deal of the previously unknown Spitsbergen coast.

However, it was the next two Arctic expeditions that established Baffin's real claim to distinction. On 15 March 1615 he sailed as pilot of the *Discovery*, commanded by Robert Bylot, the fourth venture by the Northwest Company of London to find the elusive passage to the south seas, following the previous expeditions of Hudson, Button, and Gibbons. With a small crew of sixteen men and two boys they left London on 16 April, reached Cape Farewell on 6 May, and crossed to Resolution Island at the entrance to Hudson Strait on 17 May. During this part of the journey Baffin described ice islands 240 feet high, speculating that they were seven times as deep; he was the first to record such measurements in feet rather than nautical terms. His narrative indicated he wanted to search for the elusive passage to the north, but Bylot insisted they try to penetrate the strait, although weather conditions meant they were unsuccessful for two weeks. On 8 June they landed on and named the Savage Islands, where they found evidence of a recently abandoned native camp, from which they took the skins they found, leaving knives and iron objects in return. Baffin also described finding a bag of carvings depicting human forms, including one of a woman with a child on her back, one of the first recorded examples of aboriginal art. Resuming their journey, they reached the vicinity of Salisbury Island by 22 June. Baffin noted that he had previously made a measurement of longitude at sea on 26 April using occultation of stars by the moon—the first recorded mention of such a measurement at sea by an English navigator. His new attempt near Salisbury Island used lunar observation and estimated the longitude to be 74°5′ W. (In 1821 William Edward Parry recalculated Baffin's measurement in the same place and found it to be less than a degree to the west.) By 8 July the expedition had penetrated into Foxe Channel, naming Mill Island on the way. Ice conditions hindered progress beyond 65°26′ N, and their discovery that the flood tide came from the south-east convinced them there was no passage. On 13 July they turned for home, and reached Plymouth on 8 September. Baffin's narrative clearly indicates that he did not believe there was a passage to the south seas in this vicinity, given the depth of tide and ice conditions, but he covered himself by suggesting that if one existed it could be only a small strait or creek. This was borne out by Parry's 1821 discovery of the Fury and Hecla Strait separating Melville peninsula from the land that Baffin had glimpsed, which Parry realized was an island and named in Baffin's honour. Baffin's journal and chart for this voyage survive (BL, MS 12206) and were first published by Thomas Rundall in 1849. It shows the exemplary nature of his daily recording system; longitude estimates were routinely made, as well as those for latitude, wind direction, and high tides, together with brief comments on the events of the day. Baffin also pioneered the modern notation of compass needle variation by recording the northern deflection, rather than the more typical use of the southern end by his contemporaries.

The most significant of Baffin's exploits was in 1616, again sailing under the command of Bylot in search of the north-west passage, when he succeeded in charting the basic outline of the area now known as Baffin Sea. They left Gravesend on 26 March, but were forced to shelter in ports in south-west England before sailing directly to the west coast of Greenland. Since their specific instructions were to try to reach 80° N before turning west and south-west to Japan, they coasted north past the area known as Hope Sanderson, the furthest point north that John Davis had reached on his third voyage in 1587. By 4 June they were at 74°4′, sailing with difficulty in a narrow channel only 7 or 8 leagues wide between the pack ice and the shore. On 1 July, at 75°40′ N, they found deep and open sea, leading to renewed hope that they would find a passage to the south seas since the land was trending north-west. The next day they discovered and named a large sound after

Wolstenholme, one of their major sponsors. By 5 July they were confronted by a great bank of ice and land to the west but had found two large inlets to the east and north. The large number of whales in the area led them to name the first Whale Sound and the other Thomas Smith Sound, after another company sponsor. This latter inlet was described as trending north beyond 78°. Baffin's measurements led him to claim that the area had the greatest compass variation ever known, which he measured at 56° W, and which cast doubt upon Gilbert's principle that compass variations varied directly with the size of neighbouring lands. Forced south and west by the ice, they subsequently found two major west trending passages, Jones Sound on 10 July and later Lancaster Sound on 12 July at 74°20′ N (again named after principal company shareholders), but were unable to penetrate them because of ice conditions. It is ironic that outside Lancaster Sound Baffin wrote 'here our hope of passage began to be lesse'. This sound would eventually prove to be the much sought-after passage through the Arctic islands in the nineteenth century. On 27 June at 65°40′ N they turned east to Cockin Sound in Greenland in search of fresh provisions for their sick crew members. They recovered after eating scurvy grass, so on 6 August sailed for home, and arrived in Dover on 30 August. Baffin concluded that the area north of Davis Strait was 'no other than a great bay. … I would hardly have believed to the contrary until mine eyes became witnesse of that I desired not to have found'. But the expedition was not a complete loss. Baffin advised the company that the northern part of the bay contained considerable whale and seal resources, but warned that ships could normally get into the area only in early July and would be able to stay for only about a month. He also provided convincing explanations for the origin of icebergs in the area.

Purchas's failure to include Baffin's map with the narrative of the 1616 expedition in his voluminous 1626 survey of exploration was made on grounds of cost and his belief that Baffin's work had shown there was no route to the Pacific via this route. Baffin's journal and maps were subsequently lost, so the utility of his exploratory work was often questioned until expeditions by Sir John Ross in 1818 and Parry in 1821–3 showed the accuracy of Baffin's work and immortalized his exploits by naming Baffin Island and bay after him. However, only Purchas suggested that Baffin 'would, if he might get employment, search the passage from Japan, by the coast of Asia' (Purchas, 411). If this was a true report of Baffin's opinion, then it was probably influenced by the disappointment of his own Arctic voyages and the standard view that Portuguese explorers had sailed eastwards from the Pacific through the passage. Whatever the truth of this opinion, it is clear that in 1617 Baffin sailed as master's mate on the *Anne Royal*, captained by Andrew Shilling, part of Martin Pring's East India Company fleet to India and Japan, which left Gravesend on 4 February and reached Surat in September. Some of the ships under Shilling's command were directed to the Red Sea, and reached Mocha on 13 April 1618. During the next four months Baffin surveyed and charted the area with his usual diligence and accuracy, following this up with similar activities during a visit to the Persian Gulf. He received a gratuity from the company for his comprehensive charts.

Baffin again sailed under Shilling's command for India in February 1620, with a fleet of four new ships led by the *London*. On hearing that Portuguese and Dutch ships had made common cause in the Persian Gulf to keep out British ships, they sailed to the area and attacked their rivals on 16 December. After two engagements the English drove off their rivals but Shilling had been mortally wounded in the engagement and command passed to Captain Blyth, who returned to Surat. In 1621 English officials in India were persuaded to help the shah of Persia's forces drive the Portuguese out of the historic trading entrepôt of Hormoz. The English began with an attack on the neighbouring strategic castle and Isle of Qeshm. Baffin was mortally wounded by a cannon ball on 23 January as he ventured too close to the castle walls when measuring their height to help range the English siege guns. The English attack was successful and the island was captured on 1 February but the castle at Hormoz did not fall until 23 April. Baffin's childless widow pressed a claim for compensation from the East India Company for her husband's work and untimely death and was finally awarded £500 in 1628. Baffin's recorded career may have been short, but his work provided very important additions to the science of navigation and to knowledge of Arctic regions.

WAYNE K. D. DAVIES

Sources C. R. Markham, ed., *The voyages of William Baffin, 1612–1622*, Hakluyt Society, 63 (1881) • S. Purchas, *Hakluytus posthumus, or, Purchas his pilgrimes*, bks 5, 10, 14 (1625); repr., Hakluyt Society, extra ser., 18, 23, 27 (1905–6) • T. Rundall, *Narratives of voyages to the north west in search of a passage to Cathay and India, 1496 to 1631* (1849) • *CSP col.*, 3.257 • *IGI* • J. Ross, *A voyage of discovery … for the purpose of exploring Baffin's Bay and … a north-west passage* (1819) • D. W. Waters, *The art of navigation in England in Elizabethan and early Stuart times* (1934) • M. Christy, ed., *The voyages of Captain Luke Fox of Hull, and Captain Thomas James of Bristol, in search of the north-west passage, in 1631–32*, 1, Hakluyt Society, 88 (1894) • W. E. Parry, *Journal of a second voyage for the discovery of a north-west passage from the Atlantic to the Pacific* (1824)

Archives BL, log and account, Add. MS 12206

Bagard, Thomas (*d.* 1544), civil lawyer and divine, was born in the diocese of Hereford, of unknown parentage. He was a scholar in civil law by March 1515 at Oxford University and was a member of New Inn. He was connected with the diocese of Worcester as early as 1520, having come to the attention of William More, prior of Worcester—Bagard received a small gift of 12*d.* from More at about this time. He had received the degree of BCL by 29 April 1521 and of DCL by 22 July 1528. He was nominated by Cardinal Thomas Wolsey as one of the first eighteen canons of the newly founded Cardinal College on 19 October 1526; Wolsey chose to call the fellows and scholars of the college 'canons' in order to maintain continuity with the suppressed Frideswide Priory. Bagard was still in this position in 1530.

Bagard was admitted to Doctors' Commons on 7 October 1528, having practised as a proctor in the consistory court of Worcester since 1527. He served as vicar-general to Geronimo de' Ghinucci, bishop of Worcester, from 1532, retaining the post until at least 1537. His ecclesiastical career was assisted by the patronage of de' Ghinucci, Edmund Bonner, and, especially, Sir Thomas Cromwell, principal secretary and vicegerent in spirituals. He was ordained by 1519, receiving the penny given to all who were in holy orders on 6 February. He had several benefices: he was rector of the free chapel of Parke, Herefordshire, from 1529 to 1538; vicar of Penbryn, Cardiganshire, in 1535; rector of Duntisbourne Abbots, Gloucestershire, from 1536; rector of Alvechurch, Worcestershire, from 1541; and rector of Rupple, Worcestershire, until 1542. He was rector of the parish church of Bredon, Worcestershire, from 1542 until his death. Bagard became chancellor of the diocese of Worcester through the intercession of the conservative Bonner and of Cromwell in 1532. Bagard seems to have held the position until at least 1535. He was replaced as chancellor by Dr Matthew Parker, who was appointed by the new bishop, Hugh Latimer. This may indicate Bagard's conservative religious views. With his appointment as canon and first prebendary of Worcester on 24 January 1542, he was one of the first to be endowed from the confiscated property of the dissolved priory of Worcester. Therefore, despite the dissolution of the monasteries he continued to prosper.

Whether or not Bagard was on good terms with Latimer may depend on how the latter reacted when the former allowed an inhibition (a disqualification from exercising any function of one's order) to be issued against the bishop in 1533. There may have been tension between them over religion. Bagard was sufficiently concerned about the matter to write to Cromwell, reminding him that he had made this decision only after seeking the vicegerent's counsel and with his express backing. This and other surviving letters indicate Bagard was careful to keep his relationship with Cromwell in good order at all times. Bonner attempted to assist him in this matter as well. However, in 1534 Cromwell suspected Bagard of disloyalty to the cause of the Reformation, prompting the latter to reply to the accusation in a long letter asserting his anxiety to serve Henry VIII. His final years were less active, although he continued to participate in the administration of the diocese. He died in 1544. JOHN F. JACKSON

Sources *LP Henry VIII*, 2/2; 5–6; 12/2 · Emden, *Oxf.*, 4.1501–40 · Foster, *Alum. Oxon.* · G. D. Squibb, *Doctors' Commons: a history of the College of Advocates and Doctors of Law* (1977), 44 · [C. Coote], *Sketches of the lives and characters of eminent English civilians, with an historical introduction relative to the College of Advocates* (1804) · D. MacCulloch, *Thomas Cranmer: a life* (1996), 9, 79 · J. Newman, 'Cardinal Wolsey's collegiate foundations', *Cardinal Wolsey: church, state and art*, ed. S. J. Gunn and P. G. Lindley (1991), 103–16 · D. Knowles [M. C. Knowles], *The religious orders in England*, 3 (1959), 123
Archives PRO

Bage, Charles Woolley (1751–1822), structural engineer, was probably born in Derby, the eldest of the three sons of Robert *Bage (1728?–1801), proprietor of a paper manufactory and later a novelist, and his wife, Elizabeth, *née* Woolley. Charles went to Shrewsbury as a young man and set up as a wine merchant on Pride Hill. From his arrival, he took a considerable interest in the town, and from 1784 to 1787 he was director of the House of Industry, an institution for supporting those poor people who were not in the workhouse. In 1789 he was admitted burgess of Shrewsbury, and in 1807 he held office as mayor.

Among his varied interests, Bage nurtured an interest in engineering—not surprising, given the exciting industrial developments in the area at this time. William Hazeldine's iron foundry was set up in Shrewsbury, and a short distance away at Coalbrookdale the first iron bridge had been erected in 1779. Bage was also interested in the manufacture of linen yarn, and counted among his close friends William Strutt of Derby, a noted builder of textile mills. He was also friendly with Hazeldine and Thomas Telford, then county surveyor for Shropshire. The introduction of steam-powered machinery had led to some disastrous fires in mills, and in 1792 Strutt had begun work on a mill which incorporated some iron columns, and encased the timber frame with brick and plaster, to minimize fire risk.

When John Marshall, a flax spinner, and the brothers Thomas and Benjamin Benyon, owners of a site at Castle Foregate, Ditherington, beside the Shrewsbury canal on the outskirts of the town, decided to build a new mill, Bage was appointed its designer and took a small share in the partnership. He took advice from Strutt, and modelled the building on those at Derby and Belper, but in order to render the structure more fire-resistant he decided to employ cast iron for the beams as well as the columns. (The building was not strictly fireproof, since the iron supports would have buckled under great heat.) By September 1796 he had prepared his design and outlined in a letter to Strutt the earliest known practical theory for the strength of cast-iron columns. Hazeldine cast the ironwork frame over the following year, and the Ditherington flax mill was operational by the end of 1797. The mill, which is Bage's most famous achievement, was a vast structure, 177 feet long, 39.6 feet wide, and five storeys high, giving a working floor area of 31,000 square feet.

Such was Bage's reputation as the first designer to make use of iron framing, in 1801 he was invited to give evidence to the London Bridge committee, which was considering Telford's proposal for a single-arch iron bridge across the Thames. In the following year he began carrying out tests on the strength of flanged beams, and developed a theory which he outlined to Strutt in August 1803. The theory was tested at Hazeldine's works, in 1803, where Bage carried out the first full-scale loading tests on iron roof-frames and probably the earliest tests on the torsional strength of iron. His findings were put into immediate effect by the erection of the Bage and Benyons flax mill in Meadow Lane, Leeds, and another, at Castle Fields, Shrewsbury, in 1804. Although other engineers had initial doubts over the suitability of cast iron for beams, it was soon adopted for all fire-resistant buildings until replaced by wrought iron in the mid-nineteenth century.

Bage had married in 1781 Margaret Boterall (*d.* 1806) of Shrewsbury; two years after her death he married Ann Harding (1787–1856). They had six children; their sons

Charles and Robert both went to Shrewsbury School in 1820. The absence of recorded marriages and baptisms suggests that Bage, like his father, may have been a Quaker.

Bage was responsible for other construction works in Shrewsbury, among them the Lancasterian School, built following the educationist Joseph Lancaster's visit to the town in 1811 and still in use almost two hundred years later. His last public service was to found the Gas Light Company in 1820, following the designs of the Derby Gas Light Company. Shrewsbury was lit by gas in 1821. By this time Bage was too ill to take part in the company's management. He died in Shrewsbury on 22 December 1822 and was buried at St Chad's churchyard, Shrewsbury.

Ditherington flax mill, the earliest multi-storey iron-framed building in the world, was still standing at the beginning of the twenty-first century. Bage, its designer, is now remembered as the pioneer of the construction method which made possible the twentieth-century skyscraper. ANITA MCCONNELL

Sources F. R. Gameson, 'The story of Charles Bage, wine merchant, who tried to put Shrewsbury on the industrial map', *Shropshire Magazine* (Jan 1954), 27–8 • H. R. Johnson and A. W. Skempton, 'William Strutt's cotton mills, 1793–1812', *Transactions of the Newcomen Society*, 30 (1955–7), 179–205 • A. W. Skempton and H. R. Johnson, 'The first iron frames', *ArchR*, 131 (1962), 175–86 • A. W. Skempton, 'Account of Bage's theory', *Proceedings of the VIII International Congress of the History of Science* [Florence] (1956), vol. 3, pp. 1029–39 • T. Swailes, 'Bage, Charles Woolley', *A biographical dictionary of civil engineers in Great Britain and Ireland*, ed. A. W. Skempton and others, 1 (2002) • 'Report from the select committee upon improvement of the Port of London', *Reports from Committees of the House of Commons*, 14 (1801), 631, no. 102 • will, PRO, PROB 11/1167, sig. 337 • B. Trinder, 'Ditherington flax mill, Shrewsbury—a re-evaluation', *Textile History*, 23 (1992), 189–223 • M. Watson, 'Matthew Murray and Broadford Works, Aberdeen: evidence for the earliest iron-framed flax mills', *Textile History*, 23/2 (1992), 225–42

Archives FILM 'House detectives at large: origins of the skyscraper: Ditherington Flax Mill, Shrewsbury', broadcast BBC TV 2, 6 April 2002

Bage, Robert (1728?–1801), businessman and novelist, was born at Darley, near Derby, on 29 February 1728, according to his lifelong friend William Hutton (W. Hutton, 478), although Bage wrote to Hutton on 11 March 1800 declaring, 'This day I am 70' (Bage correspondence, Birmingham Public Library). Bage's mother was the first among four wives of George (?) Bage, a paper maker, of Darley. She died soon after his birth and his father moved to Derby, where Bage was educated at a common school. Hutton recalled that by age seven Bage made 'such progress in letters, that he was the wonder of the neighbourhood', having mastered both Latin and the manual exercise, or drill in handling a musket (W. Hutton, 478). The later supposition that Bage was raised as a Quaker has been discredited (Sutherland, 32–3).

Business and family Bage's father trained him in paper making and at twenty-three, on 3 August 1751 at All Saints Church, Mackworth in Derby, Bage married Elizabeth Woolley. She was later described as 'a young woman who possessed beauty, good sense, good temper, and money', the last of which enabled him to enter business as a paper and cardboard manufacturer, at Elford, near Tamworth (C. Hutton, 'Memoir', xvii). There were three sons of the marriage: Charles *Bage (1751–1822), the eldest, a wine merchant and land surveyor at Shrewsbury, went into cotton manufacture, and died in 1822 aged seventy; a second son died in young manhood; Edward was an apothecary at Tamworth. Bage continued his self-education, setting aside three hours each afternoon for reading. In his thirties he taught himself French and Italian and travelled to Birmingham once a week to learn mathematics, which he picked up so quickly that within a month he was teaching his teacher. He later told William Godwin that he had relished poetry as a youth, but his study of mathematics, pursued for twelve years, supervened. Bage rarely travelled more than 50 miles from home, and never spent more than a week in London (*Godwin and Mary*, 101, 102; Paul, 1.262–3). According to Hutton, 'His person was of a smallish size, about five feet three inches, and of a spare habit, not robust, but his constitution good' (W. Hutton, 478–80).

In 1756 Bage proposed to the businessman William Hutton that he sell paper for him by wholesale purchase or on consignment. With this 'small hint' Hutton opened the 'Paper Warehouse' at Birmingham and subsequently 'acquired an ample fortune' (C. Hutton, *Life*, 97). The arrangement brought Bage about £500 a year for the rest of his life. Others asked Bage to supply them but he declined. Hutton indicated what kinds and quantities of paper and board he anticipated selling, and Bage manufactured accordingly. Bage's brother also supplied Hutton; perhaps this was Joseph Bage, a paper maker at Bridge, Chester, in the 1780s. Paper and board making were crafts, supply of raw materials was uncertain and irregular, and product quality could be uneven, causing occasional friendly disputes between Hutton and Bage. Bage obtained rags for paper from London and Germany. Later he had some interest in another paper factory at Shugborough, which also supplied Hutton.

Bage paid bills when tendered, and expected others to do likewise. In his witty, teasing notes to Hutton, written on invoices, he complained about Hutton's frequent requests for discounts, the inconsistency of excise tax on paper, the cost of rags, wet weather slowing paper's drying, his workmen's demands for higher wages, and the state of the country. He wrote to Hutton, 'God bless the king and thee But I wish you would both suck less vigorously' (Bage correspondence, Birmingham Public Library); none the less he usually complied with Hutton's requests and his workmen's and the excise officer's demands.

Bage had other business interests. In 1765 he engaged in a large ironworks with three partners, one of whom was Erasmus Darwin, a leading figure of the midlands Enlightenment and later described by his wife as Bage's 'very particular friend' (*Godwin and Mary*, 99). When the partnership was dissolved after fourteen years, Bage lost around £1500. According to Hutton, 'Fearing the distress of mind would overcome him, he took up the pen to turn the stream of sorrow into that of amusement; a scheme worthy a philosopher' (W. Hutton, 479). He later told William Godwin that he turned to novels 'for want of books to assist him in any other literary undertaking' (*Godwin and Mary*, 101). He published four novels, anonymously, from 1782 to 1788: *Mount Henneth* (2 vols., 1782; see Steeves, 27), *Barham Downs* (2 vols., 1784), *The Fair Syrian* (1787), and *James Wallace* (3 vols., 1788); two more novels followed in the 1790s. Perhaps thanks to his German business contacts, all but *James Wallace* were translated into German, and *Barham Downs* and *The Fair Syrian* were translated into French (Moran, 173–8).

The novels Bage is known to have subscribed to two works, *The Life of Miss Fanny Brown, a Clergyman's Daughter* (1760), a novel by John Alcock, music director at Lichfield Cathedral from 1749 to 1760 and organist at Tamworth parish church, and *An Inquiry into the Original State and Formation of the Earth* (1778) by John Whitehurst, a friend since youth and associate of the Derby Philosophical Society, to which Bage belonged. The society was founded in 1784 by Erasmus Darwin; it had links to the Lunar Society of Birmingham and the Manchester Literary and Philosophical Society, to the continental and Scottish Enlightenments, and to the English dissenting academies. It met regularly and united scientific research with commercial application. Some members' scientific interests appear in Bage's novels; more important, Bage fictionalizes ideas and values promoted by the society's members and others like them throughout Britain and Europe.

In order to do so, Bage uses plots of romantic comedy, set in contemporary middle-class and gentry society, in which a younger generation imbued with idealism, toleration, egalitarianism, entrepreneurship, and reform replaces an older generation still relying on hierarchy, legalism, and inherited authority. Characters are designed to individualize these diverse values and practices; they are also designed for social comprehensiveness, to represent various kinds of social and cultural difference found throughout Britain and its empire, from Indians to Scots, from peasants to aristocrats, emphasizing issues of class, gender, and ethnicity. In order to give voice to such characters and issues, Bage preferred the epistolary form in his earlier novels; in his later ones he includes many letters, and in all his works he includes numerous dialogues, debates, and inset biographies and autobiographies. There is much satire on the established order, for Bage addresses divisive issues from the American War of Independence through the Irish crisis of the 1780s to the French Revolution debate in the 1790s. The novels' import is that the values promoted in their pages can address and resolve these issues, working at the domestic and local level, through civil society rather than the state and its institutions, from the church through the legal system to armed force.

Bage maintained these politics through the local, national, and international conflicts of his time. On 1 August 1787, after another abrasive encounter with state officers, he wrote ruefully to Hutton,

> Oh how I wish thou wouldst bend all thy powers to write a history of Excise … with cases … Shewing the injustice the inequality of Clauses in acts … and the eternal direction every new one makes toward the oppression of the subject … It might be the most useful book extant. (Bage correspondence, Birmingham Public Library)

On 18 March 1789 Bage wrote teasing Hutton about the latter's news that he was writing a critique of the English judicial system, then held up by establishment supporters as the embodiment of British liberty:

> And hast thou dared to lift thy sacrilegious pen against Juries? Against the English palladium? Tremble then. I will hold thee up to public justice, in my next work. Send me thy book though when printed; that I may set about abusing it with a decent knowledge of its contents[.] I [am] not sure that every critic takes such pains. (ibid.)

A month later Bage wrote again,

> I received thy pamphlet; and am not certain whether I have not read it with more pleasure than any of thy former works. It is lively and the reasoning just. Only remember it is sometimes ag<st> the institution itself of Juries & County Courts that you have directed y<r> satire … which I think ought to be confined to the abuses of them. (ibid.)

A few months later, the outbreak of the French Revolution gave new hope for change in Britain to people like Bage and Hutton, though different degrees of enthusiasm for the revolution divided the Derby Philosophical Society and similar groups elsewhere. In July 1791 a mob supporting 'church and king' attacked the homes of leading religious dissenters, including Joseph Priestley and Hutton. Hutton and his family fled, penniless, but on identifying themselves at an inn as friends of Bage they received instant credit (W. Hutton, 479). Outraged at the mob violence, Bage wrote to his friend:

> Since the riots, in every company I have had the misfortune to go into, my ears have been insulted with the bigotry of 50 years <back> …, with, damn the presbyterians … <with> church and king <huzza> … and with true passive obedience & nonresistance … and may my house be burnt too, if I am not become as sick of my species and as desirous of keeping out of the way, as ever was true hermit? (Bage correspondence, Birmingham Public Library)

Bage supported Hutton's claims for compensation, and later kept him going when Hutton's business was undermined by the wartime economy, social instability, and possibly official persecution and unofficial boycott.

Bage himself soon contributed to the public debate on the revolution, advancing his earlier principles of toleration, egalitarianism, and reform in a new novel, *Man as he is* (4 vols., 1792). It narrates the rescue of a well-meaning young baronet from fashionable aristocratic vices by his love for a virtuous and independent woman, good friends, and his encounters in France with leaders of the earlier, moderate phase of the revolution. Perhaps prudentially, Bage did not identify himself on the title-page, even obliquely, as the author, and told Hutton, 'I have taken great pains, and sunk money to [William] Lane in the price, not to be known any more as a novel writer … The title of my last I even concealed from my sons'. Characteristically, he added, 'if thou hearest any thing said of it in Birm<m> … if good let me know … if bad … keep it to thyself. I can digest flattery but hate correction' (Bage correspondence, Birmingham Public Library).

In 1792 Bage moved to Tamworth after the death of his younger son left him 'solitary & melancholy', but walked to Elford three times a week (*Godwin and Mary*, 100). He was increasingly irritated by government suppression and local loyalist harassment of dissidents, writing to Hutton on 24 January 1793,

> No man's ear is open to anything but Church & king … and Damn the french … and damn the presbyterians. I abstain from all society, because respect for my moral principles is scarce sufficient to preserve me from insult on account of my political.

Bage himself may have encountered harassment by this time. In 1795 the excise unjustly seized a quantity of paper; Bage went to court and won, but heard the paper was to be reseized; similar measures were used by the government at that time to persecute or even bankrupt other dissidents. Nevertheless, Bage again had recourse to comic fiction to address the times, with *Hermsprong; or, Man as he is not* (1796), which directly attacks intolerance towards new ideas and proposals for sweeping reform. Though his anti-establishment satire is even sharper here than hitherto, the novel was well received and preferred to his earlier work by several generations of readers and critics. It was his last novel.

Final years and reputation William Godwin sought Bage out in June 1797 and heard him described as 'a short man, with white hair, snuff-coloured clothes, and a walking stick'. Godwin 'spent a most delightful day' with Bage and found him to be a materialist whose favourite book was Holbach's *Systême de la nature*, and who was 'uncommonly cheerful & placid, simple in his manners, & youthful in all his carriage' (*Godwin and Mary*, 100, 101). In March 1799 Bage thanked William Hayley for a copy of a new edition of the latter's *The Triumphs of Temper*; Bage heard through a friend that Hayley had read part of *The Fair Syrian* to his sister, drawing tears from her (Bodl. Oxf., MS Eng. lett. c. 19, fol. 38). Bage managed his paper business almost until his death on 1 September 1801. Four months later William Hutton eulogized him in the liberal *Monthly Magazine*:

> Trade, which is thought to corrupt the mind, made no such impression upon his. Though he laid no stress upon Revelation, his dealings were stamped with rectitude; he remarked to me, 'Fraud is beneath a man.' He had no other love for money than to use it, or he might have left a much larger property than he did. (W. Hutton, 478)

Hutton praised Bage's 'rich *talents* and rare endowments', but even more the fact that 'he was mild in the extreme; an enemy to no man, and, I believe, never had one himself'. 'His humanity will appear from his treatment of his servants, and even his horses, who all loved him, and whom he kept to old age.' Bage's novels were as well liked as he was; reviewers welcomed them from the first and continued to do so, the Godwin circle admired them, and despite increasing political intolerance in the 1790s only the rabid *Anti-Jacobin Review* (5, February 1800, 152) damned them. Barbauld's *British Novelists* included Bage (vol. 48, 1810, 1820), as did Scott's *Ballantyne's Novelist's Library* (vol. 9, 1824). Bage's novels were generally recognized as loose in construction but lively and engaging in style and narration and philosophical and moral in outlook, combining elements of Fielding, Smollett, Sterne, Voltaire, Le Sage, and Marivaux. Interest in his novels dwindled after the 1820s, to revive in the later twentieth century with the renewed attention to political and ideological aspects of literature. GARY KELLY

Sources R. Bage, letters to William Hutton, 1782–1801, Birmingham Public Library • A. L. Barbauld, 'Mr Bage', *The British novelists*, new edn, vol. 48, ed. A. L. Barbauld (1820), i–iii • *Godwin and Mary: letters of William Godwin and Mary Wollstonecraft*, ed. R. M. Wardle (1967) • [C. Hutton], 'Prefatory memoir to Robert Bage', *Ballantyne's novelist's library*, 9, ed. W. Scott (1824), xvi–xxxiv • C. Hutton, *The life of William Hutton* (1816) • W. Hutton, memoir, *Monthly Magazine*, 12 (Jan 1802), 478–80 • M. G. Moran, 'Robert Bage (1728–1801): a bibliography', *Bulletin of Bibliography*, 38 (Oct–Dec 1981), 173–8 • A. E. Musson and E. Robinson, 'Science and industry in the late eighteenth century', *Science and technology in the industrial revolution* (1969), 87–189 • E. A. Osborne, 'A preliminary survey for a bibliography of the novels of Robert Bage', *Book Handbook*, 1 (1947), 30–36 • C. Kegan Paul, *William Godwin: his friends and contemporaries*, 2 vols. (1876) • E. Robinson, 'The Derby philosophical society', in A. E. Musson and E. Robinson, *Science and technology in the industrial revolution* (1969), 190–99 • H. R. Steeves, 'The date of Bage's *Mount Henneth*', *N&Q*, 210 (1965), 27 • J. Sutherland, 'Bage's supposed Quaker upbringing', *N&Q*, 198 (1953), 32–3 • *IGI*
Archives Birm. CA, letters to William Hutton

Bagehot, Walter (1826–1877), political commentator, economist, and journalist, was born on 3 February 1826 at Langport, Somerset, the second son of Thomas Watson Bagehot (1795–1881), banker, and Edith Stuckey (1786–1870), a niece of Samuel Stuckey, founder in 1772 of Stuckey's Bank, which issued its own banknotes and enjoyed considerable prominence and respect in the west country. The first born, Watson Bagehot, died at age three; Walter's mother, by an earlier marriage to Joseph Estlin of Bristol, had three sons, of whom two had died and the third was mentally handicapped.

Family, education, and early career From an early age Bagehot's attention was directed to the world beyond Langport. His uncle, Vincent Stuckey, had ties to London politics, was acquainted with the politicians William Huskisson and Lord Althorp, and testified before parliamentary committees. Walter also was made acquainted with the republic of letters by his bookish father, who maintained a well-stocked and up-to-date library of French as well as English works on literature, philosophy, and history. He was thus exposed to the two kinds of activity that would occupy him during adult life—practical politics, including the making of economic policy, and reflective intellectual inquiry, especially about literature and history.

Bagehot's family life was distinguished by a warm, affectionate relationship with his mother, who possessed beauty, wit, vitality, and charm, but also a tendency to psychotic episodes, perhaps related to the fates suffered by the three sons of her first marriage and the first-born of her second. Her illness clouded Walter's otherwise bright temperament, but it also intensified his devotion. With his father he enjoyed companionship based on their shared intellectual interests.

Bagehot's education began with the appointment of a

Walter Bagehot (1826–1877), by Norman Hirst, pubd 1891 (after Adolphe Beau, 1864)

governess when he was five. At nine he became a day scholar at Langport grammar school, where he remained for four years. In 1839, when thirteen, he attended Bristol College and performed brilliantly in classics, mathematics, German, and Hebrew. In 1842, age sixteen, he began at university, which meant residing a considerable distance from Somerset for the first time. Since Oxford and Cambridge were objectionable to Walter's Unitarian father because of their doctrinal tests, he entered University College, London, where he enjoyed the stimulation provided by this young, vigorous institution and by the surrounding metropolis. His explorations in London included attendance at Anti-Corn Law League meetings, where he heard Cobden, Bright, and W. J. Fox. His studies emphasized classics, Roman history, mathematics, and poetry. He formed close friendships, particularly with Richard Holt Hutton (1826–1897) and William Caldwell Roscoe (1823–1859), and with them founded a debating society in which he took a leading part. After a one-year interruption caused by ill health, he took a first-class degree in classics in 1846; he stayed on for an additional two years studying political economy, metaphysics, and philosophy, earning the MA degree and a gold medal in philosophy in 1848.

It was time to choose a career. Bagehot considered law and banking, but also felt the lure of authorship. He began reading law in chambers with Charles Hall and Mr Quain, but without enthusiasm; persisting, however, he was called to the bar in 1852. Recognizing that his fluid, expansive mind was not suited to the law, he acknowledged his distaste for it and was happy to abandon it when his father suggested that he consider banking in Langport. This also was tempting because it allowed him to be near his ill mother. Thus barely weeks after qualifying he announced his determination to give up law 'utterly and forever'.

This decision was made easier for Bagehot by a transforming experience only a few months earlier. He was in Paris on vacation and witnessed Louis Napoleon's *coup d'état* in December 1851. Unsettled by the threat of anarchy on the Parisian streets, he concluded that the coup was justified, and he sent a measured defence of it to *The Inquirer*, a Unitarian journal with which his friends Hutton and Roscoe were connected. Although the editor disagreed with Bagehot's views, the article appeared; others followed, and altogether seven were published early in 1852. Many readers, including some of Bagehot's friends, were outraged, for liberal opinion tended to be critical of Louis Napoleon even if not sympathetic to the republicans. In defending Louis Napoleon, Bagehot anticipated themes in his subsequent work—that social order had to be defended against riot and convulsion; that French circumstances did not yet allow for constitutional liberty; and that liberty and representative government, valuable as they were, might be sacrificed to avoid revolution. He did not sympathize with Louis Napoleon's Caesarism, but he argued that French circumstances did not allow for the liberties he preferred. The articles gave Bagehot the gratification of confronting commonplace opinions with the conclusions of his independent mind—and he relished being provocative. He had gone to Paris deeply troubled about his uncertain future, but while there he discovered that he had a distinctive perspective, a voice of his own: the attractions of authorship were to become irresistible.

On leaving Paris Bagehot began working in the family bank, but with an eye on a career as a writer. Yet he continued work at Stuckey's Bank for the next nine years, at first in Langport and then in Bristol, but his heart was no more in banking than it had been in law. He disliked the need for precision, complaining that 'sums are matters of opinion' (Barrington, 213). The counting-house routine was dull, but at least it left time for reading and writing. Though in charge of the large Bristol branch from the late 1850s, the calling to which he devoted himself was literature. Thus, less than a year after returning from Paris and abandoning London and the law, he founded (with Hutton) the *National Review*. During the following nine years he served as co-editor and contributed twenty-nine articles, including 'The first Edinburgh reviewers', 'Parliamentary reform', and pieces on Shakespeare, Cowper, Shelley, Dickens, Gibbon, Scott, Macaulay, and Peel.

Marriage and *The Economist* A significant turning point came early in 1857 when, eager to contribute to *The Economist*, Bagehot was put in touch with the proprietor, James Wilson (1805–1860), formerly an organizer for the Anti-Corn Law League, and now member for Devonport, privy councillor, and financial secretary to the Treasury. Bagehot quickly gained Wilson's confidence and was engaged to write a series of letters on banking. His connection with Wilson, who had six daughters, soon became even closer. Walter, with high spirits and tall good looks, was much appreciated, especially by Elizabeth (Eliza), the eldest. After several extended visits, they were engaged on 7 November 1857, and marriage followed on 21 April 1858. After a wedding trip through Devon and Cornwall, they settled in the Somerset countryside, near Clevedon, close to Bristol and not too far from Langport.

Bagehot wrote for *The National* and *The Economist* while continuing in the family bank, but this soon changed. Wilson went to India in 1859 as financial member of the supreme council of India, but died less than a year later. He had made Walter a director of the paper, and, with Hutton as editor, Bagehot actively managed it. His responsibilities increased when Hutton resigned in 1861, and he became editor, a post he held until his death sixteen years later. During this period he wrote articles—one almost every week and sometimes more than one—on a wide variety of political and economic subjects. He had been travelling to work from Somerset, but at this time he moved from the Bristol branch of Stuckey's Bank to London, where he supervised the London office. However, this was subordinated to his journalism as he was drawn into the larger metropolitan world, where he became a 'literary lion in the world of political magnates' (Barrington, 272). He became acquainted with major figures, including Gladstone, was a member of Brooks's and Windham's, and took up residence in Belgravia.

As a close observer and analyst of public life, Bagehot wrote about all aspects of politics—the state of parties, the character of leaders, the fate of governments, the composition and reform of parliament, foreign policy, political events, leading figures, and crises in other countries. On whatever he wrote, however, his distinctive mode of analysis was to look beneath the surface to the underlying realities, where he identified problems and developments not noticed by conventional observers. He sought the 'living reality', which often was concealed by 'the paper description' or by myths or conventional wisdom. This made him aware of hardly visible changes that were disguised by 'outward sameness', and it led him to abandon old maxims that relied on what once might have been true but which were true no longer. Beneath the surface he discerned the 'practical machine' that produced the real outcomes.

The English Constitution and the analysis of political society
This approach was nowhere more evident than in Bagehot's most famous book, *The English Constitution* (1867), in which he analysed the major institutions of British government. It was initially published as nine essays in the *Fortnightly Review* between 15 May 1865 and 1 January 1867, a time of intense discussion of parliamentary reform, including an extension of the suffrage. Bagehot rejected the conventional account which held that the most important functions of government were performed by the legislative, executive, and judicial powers, and that each of these was separate from and checked the expansion of the others. A look at the realities, Bagehot argued, would show that the constitution consisted of two parts, the dignified and the efficient. The dignified part, mainly the monarchy, but including, in some respects, the House of Lords, was important, not because it governed, but because it attracted the attention and gained the reverence and obedience of the multitude, thus giving legitimacy to government. The dignified part sustained the authority of government but had little role in exercising that authority.

Real authority was located in parliament, especially the House of Commons, where executive and legislative functions were intricately combined. The House of Commons had many functions—to express the mind of the nation, to teach, to inform, and of course to legislate. Its most important function, however, was to appoint the cabinet, which Bagehot described as a committee of the legislature selected to perform the executive function. This reality was ignored by the traditional language of politics, in large part because the highly visible dignified part of the constitution disguised the realities of power located in the efficient part.

Bagehot is especially well-known for his interpretation of the monarchy. He emphasized the theatrical dimension of its activities. The uneducated multitude focused on its ceremonies, which were readily comprehended, and this left the cabinet and parliament to exercise authority without excessive intrusion from the uneducated populace. The monarchy also served other purposes: it headed the nation's morality—with the head of a family on the throne, sovereignty was made acceptable in a family-oriented nation—and it stifled rebellion, as even the discontented hesitated to rebel against a government of which a revered monarch was a part. But above all, the monarch generated reverence and thus strengthened government with something like the strength of religion. This understanding influenced interpretations of the monarchy well into the twentieth century. George V studied *The English Constitution* and believed himself to have been influenced by Bagehot's interpretation of the monarchy.

This interpretation was the occasion for Bagehot to introduce the concept of deference as a category of political analysis. It described the conduct of the multitude which made it possible for the efficient part of government—the executive—to exercise authority without being hampered by democratic pressures. Deference was given not to the real rulers but to the theatrical show of society with its display of wealth and enjoyment, headed by the monarch. 'The apparent rulers … are like the most imposing personages of a splendid procession: it is by them the mob are influenced; it is they whom the spectators cheer. The real rulers are secreted in second-rate carriages; no one … asks about them, but they are obeyed implicitly and unconsciously by reason of the splendour of those who eclipsed and preceded them' (*Collected Works*, 5.379–80). The spectacle overwhelmed the imagination of the populace, and it reflected a tacit agreement that the numerous, unwise part of the country would be ruled by the less numerous, wiser part. It was an abdication in favour of an élite which consisted of perhaps 10,000 persons—in effect, the educated part of the middle-class. This understanding reflected Bagehot's assumption that society was divided (but without the necessity for class conflict) between its tiny élite and the remainder of the populace, which without embarrassment he called uncultured, rude, narrow-minded, unintelligent, and incurious. His concept of deference reflected his insight into the relation of social structure to political institutions. It was still invoked in the mid-twentieth century to explain why substantial segments of the working-class electorate voted for tories.

Bagehot's interpretation of politics reflected his living in a pre-democratic age. Consequently, with increasing democratization and mass education, his interpretation has become implausible. Some critics, however, have denied that it was valid even when Bagehot wrote. His reliance on the concept of deference to explain political loyalties has been implicitly questioned by E. P. Thompson, whose hypothesis that in nineteenth-century England there was working-class consciousness, class enmity, and great potential for revolution made it necessary for him to deny a strong presence of deference among the working classes. Bagehot's interpretation of the monarchy has been disputed by historians with republican sympathies who regret the late nineteenth-century elaboration of the ceremonial role of the monarch and the great increase in the popularity of the monarchy during the century since Bagehot wrote. Some have even held Bagehot responsible for these developments, suggesting that he encouraged them to forestall the emergence of democratic forces and republican sentiment.

Bagehot disapproved of democracy on the grounds that it would give superiority to the uneducated; it would encourage demagogues who would mislead the poor, and thus he regarded it as pernicious. Yet he recognized a tendency in all modern societies to raise the average and lower those at the summit, and he understood that deference would disappear once democracy was established. He became pessimistic in the face of the difficulties of stemming the democratic tide. The only long-term remedy was to ensure that the working classes had education, morality, and comfort. Meanwhile concessions to democratic demands had to be made. The parliamentary reforms he was prepared to accept were modest: the influence of landed wealth was to be reduced; the more sensible representatives of new business wealth were to be incorporated into the ruling élite; and parliament was to be made more responsive to the needs of the working classes. His principle was to allow each person as much power and influence that could be exercised without reducing the power of those who were more fit to exercise it. In practice this meant he defended a property qualification, as he regarded property as an approximate indicator of political intelligence, education, and ability. He was prepared, however, to experiment with ways to increase representation for the working classes; reversing an earlier view, he came to the conclusion that women should be allowed to vote, subject to the same restrictions as men.

Bagehot's judgements of political figures, both contemporaries and those of an earlier generation, reflected his general political perspective. He greatly appreciated those, such as Sir Robert Peel, who worked effectively to make the efficient part of government run smoothly. These were the ones who engaged in politics as a profession—as 'political business'. He also approved of those, such as Edmund Burke, who shared his understanding of the need for the conciliation of discontents, but also for the preservation of liberty and stability. And he was critical of advocates of democracy, such as John Bright, who seemed indifferent to these considerations. Dullness he did not mind (provocatively, he called it stupidity), for it was essential for the preservation of liberty; its opposite, found in speculative minds, was dangerous, as it led to unnecessary political experiments. Thus he criticized intellectuals, the 'too clever by half' people, who were out of touch with public opinion.

In Bagehot's appreciative description of the English constitution he frequently pointed to contrasts with government in America, and this became a comparison of parliamentary and presidential types of government. The parliamentary type fixed ultimate power of decision in one place, in a newly elected House of Commons; it made government by discussion possible; it placed the choice of leaders among members of parliament, who were competent to judge the qualifications of the candidates; and it was capable of responding to a crisis. In contrast, the American constitution, by establishing checks and balances, divided power; it placed too much power in the hands of an incompetent populace and it was disabled in a crisis. Bagehot wrote many articles about the American Civil War, its origins, progress, and aftermath, and he often pointed to that calamity as a vindication of his preference for parliamentary government.

Giving political labels to Bagehot is difficult, for he sometimes leaned left, sometimes right, and never very far in either direction. Nominally he was a Liberal—when he stood for parliament it was as a Liberal, and his affiliation with *The Economist*, which had been linked with the free-trade movement, re-enforced this connection. This affiliation was combined, however, with conservative tendencies, evident in his criticisms of democracy and John Bright, in his concern about symptoms of instability, in his critique of intellectuals, whom he also called 'enthusiasts', and in his affinities with Burke's political outlook. He preferred middling governments, dominated by either liberal conservatives or conservative liberals. He is most appropriately labelled a centrist, for he saw dangers in the doctrinairism of the right which resisted change and of the left which was eager to accelerate it. Bagehot, always cautious, sought a balanced combination of tradition and innovation. In this he displayed a similarity to Macaulay. He has been called a crossbencher by nature, and he famously said he was 'between sizes in politics' (Barrington, 11).

Bagehot's appreciation of both conservative and liberal values was reflected in *Physics and Politics* (1872), in which he acknowledged the usefulness of custom, stability, and cohesion, while also recognizing that such things could be obstacles to discussion, progress, trade, and increased abundance. He put forward a hypothesis about social development which was based on historical study as well as writings about anthropology, and the book reflected the influence of Henry Sumner Maine, the jurist who emphasized the importance of historical study of legal concept, as well as Charles Darwin and other writers on evolution. Bagehot assumed a pre-political era, from which mankind emerged when it established nations with fixed rules—laws and a 'cake of custom'. The resulting society was unified but also stationary, isolated, status-ridden, hostile to trade, and unable to change—that is, to improve itself. With great difficulty and very slowly, and in very few places, this changed. Where discussion was allowed, variant customs were examined and natural selection took place; intelligence and originality were encouraged, human nature sprung forth, and the yoke of custom was thrown off. Thus a shift occurred from stationary conditions to an age of choice, trade, liberty, and economic growth. He was not recommending that custom be abandoned in pursuit of progress, but rather that a useful combination of features of both types of society be found. This was Bagehot's attempt to examine scientifically the political prerequisites of progress. His categories, historical claims, and assumptions later came to be regarded as obsolete, and this book has had less claim on the attention of posterity than some of his other works.

Although on three occasions Bagehot failed to win election to parliament (for Manchester, 1865; Bridgwater, 1866; University of London, 1867), he gained great influence by virtue of his forceful writing, his intimate knowledge of the City and Westminster, and his acknowledged authority as editor of a prestigious weekly. He realized that 'effective articles in great journals' could be decisive, especially in times of crisis, and though modesty prevented his claiming such influence, when writing these words he knew they described some of his own journalism. He confessed to his fiancée, 'I covet *power*, influence,' and he certainly achieved it (St John-Stevas, 'Walter Bagehot', 25).

Bagehot as economist and literary critic As an economist Bagehot is best known for *Lombard Street* (1873), which J. M. Keynes called 'an undying Classic' (Buchan, 242). It analysed the actual working of the banking system and was based on personal experiences and close observation. He focused on the role of the Bank of England, pointing out that since it served as a banker's bank, was the repository of monetary reserves for the entire nation, and had immense influence on the country's financial health, it ought to acknowledge that it functioned as a central bank. He proposed changes that would allow it to perform this role more effectively. To allow it to reduce the impact of trade cycles, he recommended that the bank increase gold reserves in prosperous times, and that in depressed periods, as a matter of policy, it advance a large amount of credit to sound businesses. The book had great influence and several of its recommendations ultimately were adopted; it was regarded as authoritative well into the twentieth century, and it made a significant contribution to the theory of central banking.

In *Lombard Street*, as in *The English Constitution*, Bagehot sought to describe and explain arrangements already in place which, while imperfect, served many useful purposes. He demonstrated great insight, but not the explanatory power claimed by classical economists with a universalistic perspective. This was in keeping with his belief (reflecting the influence of evolutionary theory) that political economy ought to recognize that different economies require different explanations, depending on the extent of their development and cultural circumstances. Consequently, when in the mid-1870s he set out to write a major treatise on political economy, he aimed to make his analysis concrete and empirical and to avoid claims to universal validity. By criticizing abstraction in economic theory, he anticipated behaviourist theories that explain economic events in terms of actual behaviour, including the motives, hopes, and fears of those whose conduct affects the economy. This work was not completed; the first part was published as *Postulates of Political Economy* (1876), and the remaining fragments were included in his posthumous *Economic Studies* (1880).

Bagehot's views also appeared weekly in *The Economist*, where he addressed many issues of economic and financial policy. He favoured free trade and competition, criticized protection and monopoly, and was sceptical about imperial expansion. On the whole he advocated *laissez-faire* policies, though without dogmatism, for he allowed many exceptions. He supported the income tax, favoured nationalization of the railways, and approved proposals for a universal coinage and decimalization. He recognized that the Factory Acts were beneficial, and while critical of organized labour he accepted that labour ought to have a right to organize. Always attentive to swings in the trade cycle, he often warned about overconfidence in the business community, reminding his readers, 'All people are most credulous when they are most happy' (W. Bagehot, *Lombard Street*, 1915, repr. 1931, 151). Bagehot's economic journalism was taken seriously in the City, by businessmen, and in Whitehall.

Bagehot's views have been criticized by twentieth-century economists, but the standing he once had is indicated by acknowledgements of his influence on central bankers in Britain and America in the 1920s. In his own time he testified before select committees and was elected to the Political Economy Club in 1864. He often was consulted by ministers and civil servants, and in response to a request from the chancellor of the exchequer (Sir Stafford Northcote) in 1876 for suggestions about how to raise short-term money, he invented the Treasury bill. Gladstone called him 'a sort of supplementary Chancellor of the Exchequer' (Buchan, 246).

As Gladstone's observation indicates, Bagehot was much more than a journalist, though in that capacity he stood out as one whose accounts of events provided a rich understanding of how political and economic developments unfolded in the world of practice. His quest for understanding of the underlying structure and principles that shaped surface reality led to his recognition of the importance of non-rational dimensions of political and economic conduct, and to his development of explanatory concepts, such as 'deferential community' and dignified and efficient parts of the constitution, which have been continuously useful to political analysts.

Bagehot also wrote about literature, both historical and contemporary, mainly British, and also about a few French writers. His interest in literature had begun early, and his enthusiasms and negative reactions were highly personal; they were reflected in his published criticisms, in his appreciation of Scott, for example, and in his doubts about Shelley and Dickens. While his essays were often illuminating, his judgements did not reflect a theoretical perspective, and his attempt to establish a typology has proved disappointing. As a result of this absence of a coherent theory about literature, he has no enduring place in the history of literary criticism. As René Wellek has concluded, 'Bagehot seems not very important today, though he is sane, representative, and symptomatic enough to deserve some attention' (Wellek, 4.180). At most, his discursive articles provide insights and arresting observations, as when he said Dickens 'describes London like a special correspondent for posterity' (*Collected Works*, 2.87).

Personal life Religion played a part in Bagehot's life, but its demands on him were not insistent. His parents were deeply religious but worshipped differently, his mother accepting the Church of England orthodoxy, while his father, like some of his ancestors, became Unitarian. Bagehot did not follow his father's example, though he was less than orthodox, as he had doubts about some historical claims of Christianity, which, however, did not prevent him from defending revelation. Although influenced by Darwinian ideas, he did not regard evolutionary theories as incompatible with belief in a deity. He was sufficiently interested in religious questions to take part in discussions at the Metaphysical Society, where leading representatives of all branches of Christianity, including Catholicism, as well as positivists, agnostics, and freethinkers, explored their differences. As in politics, Bagehot occupied a middling position. He rejected atheism and agnosticism, and while he admired J. H. Newman, he was not tempted by Catholicism. He was untroubled by religious diversity, and in the debating society he helped found while an undergraduate he spoke in opposition to government suppression of blasphemous publications. In papers read at the Metaphysical Society in 1870 and 1874, he revealed a suspicion that there was a widespread wish to persecute—sceptics by believers and believers by some sceptics—which he deplored.

Bagehot's physical appearance was striking: tall, slender, a mass of wavy black hair (and in a surviving portrait, a heavy black beard), a ruddy complexion, and fiery eyes—if not handsome, he was not easily ignored. In temperament he struck others as high-spirited, buoyant, vivacious, imaginative, and playful, but also as modest and self-deprecating. In his own description, he was cheerful but not sanguine, this perhaps reflecting what he called life's 'dark realities'—an allusion to his mother's illness. His conversation displayed acuity, liveliness, and whimsical humour, and was said to be racy. He impressed a sister-in-law as a man in whom 'life and thought and fancy abounded' (Barrington, 231). It was said that one seldom asked Bagehot a question without the answer making one think, or laugh, or both together. His lively mind was reflected in his original phrase making, for example, 'animated moderation', 'removable inequalities', 'blind money', and 'the cake of custom'. He was the first to use 'padding' as applied to writing.

Bagehot's interests and activities were varied. He loved the countryside, especially in Somerset. A dashing rider, he was fond in early life of hunting: 'There is as much variety of pluck in writing across a sheet as in riding across a country'. An avid reader, especially of literature, he greatly admired George Eliot and was a regular visitor at her Sunday at homes. Among his closest friends, in addition to Richard Holt Hutton and William Roscoe, were James Bryce (1838–1922), Lord Carnarvon (1831–1890), Matthew Arnold (1822–1888), and Arthur Hugh Clough (1819–1861). He was excellent at chess and often relaxed over a game with Hutton at the Athenaeum after sending *The Economist* to the printer; his election to membership at the Athenaeum in 1875 was an acknowledgement of intellectual eminence. He succeeded his father as vice-chairman of Stuckey's Bank and was continually occupied in managing the investments of his ageing father and the Wilson family. His last residence, at 8 Queen's Gate Place, was decorated and furnished by William Morris's firm, and Morris himself designed the drawing room. But for all the variety in his life (which did not include children of his own), work was all. He claimed there never was a week without doing some business, which meant some writing. 'As to holidays', he advised Hutton, 'it is one of the lessons of life to learn to be independent of them' (*Collected Works*, 13.673).

Bagehot's personal life was less than happy. His sadness about his mother's illness deepened in the mid-1860s when she became worse and needed continuous surveillance during the years before her death in 1870. From his marriage he may not have received much solace. Although it began with intense passion and evident happiness—Walter and Eliza's surviving love letters testify to it—after a few years some distance between them seems to have developed as Bagehot devoted long hours to his busy life away from home. His wife continually complained of many small symptoms and often retreated to her room with headaches. She became irascible and also withdrew from much of Bagehot's social life, leaving him to attend dinners and other events by himself or in the company of a sister-in-law. His wife was devoted to him but could not share his intellectual interests. On the other hand, he was not the easiest of husbands, as he was always working to a deadline. After his mother's death, his devotion to writing became even more frantic, leaving little time for domestic life. Financially, Bagehot was well off, and could have expected considerable wealth; had he lived longer, he would have inherited a substantial part of the family investments. These included the bank as well as fleets of barges and ocean-going ships. His wife could also have expected a considerable legacy from her father's estate.

Although quite vigorous and fond of exercise, Bagehot tended to get respiratory infections, which became especially frequent during the 1870s. He also had poor vision and a weak heart, and he suffered from migraine. In March 1877 in London he came down with a cold which turned into 'congestion of the lung'. Having promised his father he would visit over Easter, he travelled to Herd's Hill, Curry Rivell, near Landport, where he died, apparently of pneumonia, on 24 March 1877. He was buried in the family vault at All Saints' Church, Langport, Somerset. JOSEPH HAMBURGER

Sources *The collected works of Walter Bagehot*, ed. N. St John-Stevas, 15 vols. (1965–86) • Mrs R. Barrington [E. I. Barrington], *The works and life of Walter Bagehot*, 10 (1915) • A. Buchan, *The spare chancellor: the life of Walter Bagehot* (1959) • N. St John-Stevas, 'The political genius of Walter Bagehot', in *The collected works of Walter Bagehot*, ed. N. St John-Stevas, 5 (1974), 35–159 • N. St John-Stevas, 'Bagehot's religious views', in *The collected works of Walter Bagehot*, ed. N. St John-Stevas, 15 (1986), 245–302 • N. St John-Stevas, *Walter Bagehot: a study of his life and thought together with a selection from his political writings* (1959) • R. H. Hutton, 'Memoir of Walter Bagehot', in *The collected works of Walter Bagehot*, ed. N. St John-Stevas, 15 (1986), 83–127 • M. Westwater, *The Wilson sisters: a biographical study of upper middle-class Victorian life* (1984) • R. S. Sayers, 'Bagehot as an economist', in *The collected works of Walter Bagehot*, ed. N. St John-Stevas, 9 (1978), 27–43 • A. Briggs, 'Walter Bagehot', in P. Newman, *The new Palgrave: a dictionary of economics*, ed. J. Eatwell and M. Milgate (1987) • W. W. Rostow, 'Bagehot and the trade cycle', *The Economist: 1843–1943* (1943) • G. M. Young, 'The greatest Victorian', *Today and yesterday: collected essays and addresses* (1948) • W. Haley, 'Walter Bagehot: a literary appreciation', in *The collected works of Walter Bagehot*, ed. N. St John-Stevas, 1 (1965), 84–106 • R. Wellek, *A history of modern criticism, 1750–1950*, 4 (1965) • J. Burrow, 'Sense and circumstances: Bagehot and the nature of political understanding', *That noble science of politics*, ed. S. Collini, D. Winch, and J. Burrow (1983), 161–81 • W. M. Kuhn, *Democratic royalism* (1996)

Archives priv. coll. • UCL, lecture notebooks | BL, corresp. with W. E. Gladstone, Add. MSS 44392–44440, *passim* • U. Durham, letters to third Earl Grey • U. Hull, Brynmor Jones L., corresp. with Eliza Wilson

Likenesses A. Beau, photograph, 1864, probably priv. coll. • N. Hirst, mezzotint, pubd 1891 (after photograph by A. Beau, 1864) [*see illus.*] • mezzotint, pubd 1891 (after N. Hirst), NPG • E. Walker, engraving (after photograph by A. Beau, 1864)

Wealth at death under £40,000: probate, 5 May 1877, *CGPLA Eng. & Wales*

Bagenal [Bagnal], **Sir Henry** (*c.*1556–1598), soldier, was the son of Sir Nicholas *Bagenal (*d.* 1590/91), marshal of the army in Ireland, and Eleanor (*d.* 1573), daughter and coheir of Sir Edward Griffith of Penrhyn in north Wales. Named after his godfather Sir Henry Sidney, Bagenal probably matriculated from Jesus College, Oxford, in 1572 or 1573, aged sixteen, but left without a degree to serve in Ireland with his father, marshal of the army since 1566; Henry obtained a reversion of that post on 26 August 1583. The Bagenals had a vested interest in developing their Newry headquarters and sought extensive immunities from Sir Henry Sidney, the lord deputy. Sidney refused these but appointed Sir Nicholas as chief commissioner of Ulster and Henry as his assistant in May 1577. Henry was knighted the following year. It may have been the government's intention that this commission would lead to a lord presidency of Ulster similar to the presidencies set up in the provinces of Connaught and Munster. In reality this jurisdiction became restricted to those areas under the Bagenals' military control. Hugh O'Neill was asserting traditional claims of overlordship in the territories of Magennis and O'Hanlon, into which the Bagenals had encroached; he once famously told Bagenal to put his commission in his pocket.

Sir Henry became associated with a series of military disasters. In August 1580 he commanded the rear with Sir William Stanley when Lord Grey of Wilton led his forces, many of them raw recruits, into the Wicklow mountain passes; they were defeated by Feagh McHugh O'Byrne's and Viscount Baltinglass's men at Glenmalure on 25 August. As chief assistant to his father on the commission for Ulster, Henry was active in taking musters and surveying lands. He was also associated with the various divide-and-rule schemes of Lord Deputy Perrot in his efforts to contain the rival ambitions of New English and Gaelic lords. In 1584 Sir Henry was stationed as colonel of the garrison at Carrickfergus to contain and repulse the incursions of Sorley Boy MacDonald's Scots, but in September about 1300 of them landed on Rathlin Island under Angus MacDonald. Bagenal went on the attack but was ambushed in a narrow defile at Glenarm in the Glens of Antrim and had to make a precipitate retreat to Carrickfergus.

Bagenal was frequently in dispute with other English officials and military men. In February 1585, during a disagreement with Sir William Stanley, his brother Dudley Bagenal, then captain of a band in south Clandeboye, Antrim, came to blows with Stanley. The steward of Clandeboye, Nicholas Dawtrey, alleged it was Bagenal's ambitions that drove O'Neill into open warfare. In May 1586 Sir Nicholas sent Sir Henry to the court to report on the troubles in the Dublin council with Lord Deputy Perrot. He went equipped with references and petitions to Lord Burghley demanding changes in government policy on Ulster. One of these, *The Description and Present State of Ulster* (1586), is an edited extract from one of the many contemporary accounts of Ireland then in circulation. Possibly the source was Sir Edward Waterhouse, a friend of both the lord deputy and of the Bagenals. Bagenal's tract was much concerned to point out the crown's weakness in Ulster, where O'Neill was becoming more powerful and was bringing in Scottish mercenaries, and at a time when the Spanish Armada was more than a rhetorical threat. Bagenal recommended a division of O'Neill's lands in Tyrone, a restraint on O'Neill's control over the petty chiefs in co. Down, the enhancement of his own role as marshal, and a presidency for Ulster with a shire hall and a provincial gaol to dispense royal justice. Other proposals were more obviously self-interested, such as his application to develop Newry, and to tax local lords to build walls and a college where the sons of Ulster lords could be educated in civility and concurrently kept hostage. Finally, he wanted a similar commission to that held by Sir Richard Bingham in Connaught.

At first the queen endorsed many of Bagenal's demands including the grant of a commission similar to Bingham's, but her letter of April 1587 was never enrolled as a patent in the Irish chancery. Hostilities between the Bagenals and Perrot reached crisis point when the latter claimed he had been defamed by a letter purportedly from Turlough Luineach O'Neill to the queen, but actually forged 'by means of Sir Henry Bagenal and other of that Machiavellian device' (*CSP Ire.*, *1586–8*, 277). In the council chamber in Dublin Sir Nicholas demanded that Perrot clear his son's name of military incompetence—allegations made by Henry Wallop, the treasurer-at-war. They accused each other of being liars, drunkards, and cowards and came to blows. Nicholas Dawtrey, who had been commissioned by Burghley to evaluate plans for Ulster, also attacked Bagenal's covetousness and avowed that 'Mr Marshal hath neither agreed with English or Irish that hath had as much or more discretion in governing of Ulster than himself … [or with] … any commissioners that hath been employed in that province, except his sons' (PRO, SP 63/129/nos. 3, 20).

Sir Henry's visit to England was not a total failure. He wrote on 16 September 1586 to Edward Manners, third earl of Rutland, whose cousin Eleanor, daughter of Sir John Savage of Rock Savage, in the Wirral, Cheshire, he had married, inquiring if the earl had a parliamentary borough to spare; on 29 September he was returned at Grantham and in the event also returned for Anglesey, which he preferred. His marriage to Eleanor produced three sons: Arthur, mentally handicapped, became a ward of his uncle Sir Patrick Barnewell; Dudley, who founded the co. Carlow branch of the family (not to be confused with Henry's brother Dudley, killed by the Kavanaghs in May 1587); and Ambrose. Their six daughters married into the families of wealthy palesmen.

In September 1587 Bagenal went back to Ireland to deputize for his father, Sir Nicholas, and Perrot was commanded to allow him to do so 'without any trouble, molestation or impeachment' (*APC*, *1587–8*, 169–70, 226–7). With the active co-operation of the new lord deputy, Sir William Fitzwilliam, he led the invasion in 1588 against Sir Ross McMahon in Monaghan who, at O'Neill's behest, had refused to have a sheriff appointed there. In the final settlement of Monaghan, Bagenal received substantial termon (ecclesiastical) lands nominally outside the control of the McMahons. In October 1590 Sir Nicholas Bagenal formally resigned his office of marshal of the army provided his son succeeded him; Henry did so on 24 October and on the same day was sworn of the privy council. On 18 May 1591 he succeeded his father as chief commissioner for the government of Ulster, in effect an empty title. In the following year he wrote to Lord Burghley with a detailed analysis of his situation: 'The chiefest, or rather the only means to reduce these barbarous people to obedience is to so disunite them as all may be enforced to depend of the queen' (PRO, SP 63/163/no. 29). His proposals were little heeded; Burghley and the privy council had by then adopted a conciliatory attitude to Hugh O'Neill, even to the extent of exempting the earl's country from Bagenal's jurisdiction. Following the death of his second wife, Joanna O'Donnell, O'Neill asked Bagenal for the hand of his sister Mabel in marriage. This approach was repulsed with contempt; Sir Henry had Mabel removed to live with her sister Mary at Turvey, co. Dublin. Mabel's subsequent elopement and marriage to O'Neill so deepened the feud between the two men that she became 'the Helen of the Irish War' (Bagwell, 3.223). They were married in August 1591; Bagenal vainly attempted to prove that O'Neill was not properly divorced from his first wife and consistently refused to pay the £1000 dowry to O'Neill.

Bagenal kept a journal of the military campaign of the autumn of 1593. In September he led his soldiers into Monaghan again, attacking the McMahons *en route* for Fermanagh to repulse Hugh Maguire, whose forces had recently defeated Sir Richard Bingham. Maguire's defences at the Erne fords near Beleek were broken. Bagenal left troops under Captain Dowdall to consolidate his hold over Enniskillen, captured on 2 February 1594 after a nine-day siege. Bagenal and O'Neill gave conflicting accounts of their service against Maguire. A war of words preceded open hostilities; Bagenal reported to Dublin that O'Neill was in touch with Spain and was recruiting and arming his lordship, while O'Neill claimed that the real beneficiaries of his services to the crown were his enemies. The struggle for power in Ulster was personalized, and may have been overdramatized by historians. By May 1595 the relief of the Monaghan garrison had become crucial. Bagenal led out an army of 1750 men from Dundalk and Newry on 24 May; O'Neill had besieged the garrison and his forces attacked Bagenal at Clontibret near Monaghan, inflicting heavy losses. Bagenal's defeat, reported as a tactical withdrawal to Newry, was the first of O'Neill's victories. Bagenal had to be reinforced and revictualled at Newry by sea, sending back his wounded to Dublin by that route, because O'Neill had blocked the Moyry Pass—the famed Gap of the North. By July 1596 he had raided Bagenal's lands right to the gates of Newry.

In December 1596, and again in June 1597, Bagenal successfully revictualled the garrison at Armagh, but by 1598 the more northerly fort on the Blackwater was in dire straits. Bagenal went to relieve the fort. He knew the terrain well as far as Armagh and had good guides, but his army was stalked by ill luck and outmanoeuvred by O'Neill's forces. On 14 August 1598, on the field of battle at the Yellow Ford, Bagenal raised the visor of his helmet and was mortally wounded. Some dispatches say that his body fell into O'Neill's hands, others that it was brought off the field with those who sought refuge in Armagh Cathedral and was buried there, but in all probability it was buried in his father's church, St Patrick's in Newry. The Irish historian C. P. Meehan cites an almost contemporary character description of Bagenal:

> He was in sooth, a greedy adventurer, restless, rapacious, unscrupulous; in a word, one who deemed it no sin or shame to aid in any process by which the rightful owner might be

driven from his holding provided he got share of the spoil. (Meehan, 29–30)

Bagenal is also given a certain literary immortality in Sir Walter Scott's romantic ballad *Rokeby*.

J. J. N. McGurk

Sources *Reg. Oxf.*, 2/2.36 • *CSP Ire.*, 1586–8; 1592–7; 1598–9 • J. S. Brewer and W. Bullen, eds., *Calendar of the Carew manuscripts*, 2–3, PRO (1868–9) • *The Irish fiants of the Tudor sovereigns*, 4 vols. (1994) • *APC*, 1587–8, 1591–2 • *Calendar of the manuscripts of the most hon. the marquis of Salisbury*, 8, HMC, 9 (1899), 409–12 [Capt Cuny's dispatch to the earl of Essex on his action at the battle of the Yellow Ford] • E. Hogan, ed., *The description of Ireland … 1598* (1878) • L. Proudfoot and W. Nolan, eds., *Down history & society* (1997) • P. H. Bagenal, *Vicissitudes of an Anglo-Irish family, 1530–1800* (1925) • P. H. Bagenal, 'Sir Nicholas Bagenal, knight-marshal', *Journal of the Royal Society of Antiquaries of Ireland*, 6th ser., 5 (1915), 5–26 • S. G. Ellis, *Ireland in the age of the Tudors* (1998) • Burke, *Gen. Ire.* (1976) • P. O'Sullivan Beare, *Ireland under Elizabeth: chapters towards a history of Ireland in the reign of Elizabeth*, ed. and trans. M. J. Byrne (1903) • *AFM*, 2nd edn, vol. 6 • HoP, *Commons, 1558–1603* • G. A. Hayes-McCoy, *Irish battles* (1972), 106–31 • H. Morgan, *Tyrone's rebellion: the outbreak of the Nine Years' War in Tudor Ireland*, Royal Historical Society Studies in History, 67 (1993) • G. Hill, *An historical account of the MacDonnells of Antrim* (1873) • R. W. Dudley Edwards and M. O'Dowd, eds., *Sources for early modern Irish history, 1534–1641* (1985) • B. E. Howells, ed., *Calendar of letters relating to north Wales, 1533–circa 1700* (1967) • R. Bagwell, *Ireland under the Tudors*, 3 vols. (1885–90) • C. P. Meehan, *The rise and fall of the Irish Franciscan monasteries, and memoirs of the Irish hierarchy in the seventeenth century*, 2nd edn (1869) • *DNB*

Archives Hatfield House, Hertfordshire, Cecil papers, 'Plot for the government of Ulster', 163/48–49 • U. Wales, Bangor, Plas Newydd papers, ser. IV/8475; ser. V/1426–1461

Bagenal, (Philip) Hope Edward (1888–1979), architectural theorist and acoustician, was born on 11 February 1888 at 9 Mount Street, Dublin, the second of five children of Philip Henry Bagenal (1850–1927), civil servant and journalist, and his wife, Harriot Jocelyn Hore (1851/2–1942). He was always known by his second name, Hope. His parents were both Irish. The family settled in West Kensington in 1890, but later moved to Ipswich in 1896, to York in 1901, and to Harrogate in 1902. Hope attended Ipswich grammar school and St Peter's School, York, before being sent in 1902 to Uppingham School, where he found an influential mentor in the Revd Cuthbert Creighton. In 1905 Bagenal went to study engineering at Leeds University but he left without qualifying in 1909, disappointed by the intellectual narrowness and lack of stimulation. He found his true calling as an articled pupil in the architectural practice of Niven and Wigglesworth of High Holborn, London, and as a member of the Architectural Association, both of which he joined in 1909. The following year he met and secretly became engaged to Alison Mary Hogg (1892–1981).

In 1911 Bagenal was taken on as an assistant by Edwin Cooper and worked on site at the Port of London Authority building. His first book, *Clifford Manor*, and a technical paper, 'Robert Stevenson: a great architect engineer', were published in 1914. By March 1914 Bagenal had started a correspondence with Wallace Sabine, who was then completing his pioneering work on architectural acoustics at Harvard. Sabine explained the application of his landmark formula relating reverberation to absorption in auditorium design. Bagenal was well placed to recognize its significance to the architectural profession, and developed a ground-breaking career in acoustics consultancy.

Although Bagenal attended Quaker meetings, he never joined the Society of Friends. His ethical beliefs led him to volunteer for the Royal Army Medical Corps in September 1914. He married Alison Hogg in Hertingfordbury church, near Hertford, on 26 December that year before being dispatched to the front. Through two years in Belgium and in France he wrote a series of letters, articles, and poems which his father helped to get published. At the end of the war the best were anthologized in *Fields and Battlefields*, published in 1918 with the authorship credited to Bagenal's regimental number, 31540. He continued to write poetry between the wars, and published anthologies in 1932 and 1940. Having been seriously wounded at the Somme, where he won the DCM (he limped for the rest of his life), Bagenal was evacuated in August 1916 to convalesce at the Eastern General Hospital, Cambridge, where he met the physicist Alex Wood. With Wood he published *Planning for Good Acoustics* (1931), one of the earliest authoritative standard texts on the subject. The mathematics in the book were Wood's, but the style and clarity of exposition were characteristically Bagenal's.

In 1917 Bagenal resumed his architectural career by joining Smith and Brewer, a leading but small London practice, as an assistant. In 1918 he and his wife moved into Leaside, a cottage just outside Hertingfordbury, where they lived for the rest of their lives. In autumn 1919 he returned to the Architectural Association as librarian and editor of the *AA Journal*, and with dispensation to develop a private acoustics consultancy. He gave up the editorship about 1925 as his consultancy (the first in the UK) grew. His first major commission, in 1923, was as adviser to C. Cowles Voysey and Morgan on the design of the White Rocks Pavilion, Hastings. He went on to advise on most of the major concert hall, theatre, and civic hall projects of the inter-war era and post-war reconstruction. His overseas commissions included involvement in the New Delhi legislative chamber and in specifying the Sydney Opera House and New York Lincoln Center competition briefs.

As his work in acoustics developed, so did Bagenal's writing and teaching about architecture. He toured widely in the UK and abroad, drawing and photographing classical buildings, often with his friend Charles Holden, and won a scholarship to study in Italy and Greece in 1925 and 1926. He collaborated with Robert Atkinson in writing the *Theory and Elements of Architecture* (1926), a standard work on the foundations of classicism. He maintained a passionate interest in building materials and detailing, and always travelled with a geological map and studied how buildings weathered. As a theorist rather than a practitioner in architecture, he built only a few minor works, but his lectures at the Architectural Association, notably a 1937 critique of modernism (he was a committed classicist), impressed a generation of students.

In 1940 Bagenal moved his private office from the Architectural Association to Leaside and joined the Building Research Station as a temporary scientific officer; he remained there until the end of the war. In the post-war years Bagenal's consultancy work and invitations to lecture afforded him many opportunities to travel overseas. Among his most important acoustics projects were the Royal Festival Hall (1948–51), the Free Trade Hall, Manchester, and Fairfield Hall, Croydon. Hugh Creighton, the son of his Uppingham housemaster, joined him in the practice in the early 1950s. As consultant to the Building Research Station during the 1960s Bagenal investigated case studies of weathering of buildings in London. His prolific writings expanded into new areas, including topography, history, and theology.

In 1975 Bagenal was awarded an honorary fellowship of the Institute of Acoustics. He died at Leaside on 20 May 1979 and was buried at St Mary's churchyard, Hertingfordbury. His wife, Alison, survived him by two years. They were both survived by their eldest son, John, and their daughter Kate, whose twin brother, Philip, had been killed in action in 1943. Their second son, Beauchamp, died in 1959. Hope Bagenal could be intimidating and remote: physically tall and gaunt, difficult to know, intolerant of fools, yet generous and loyal in his friendship with those with whom he found an intellectual rapport. He was a natural prose writer, whether for publication or in private letters. The two major technical books to which he contributed remain classics in their genres.

DAVID TREVOR-JONES

Sources *The Times* (May 1979) • private information (2004) • Bagenal's letters [anthologized by John Bagenal] • P. H. Bagenal, 'Musical taste and concert hall design', *Proceedings of the Royal Musical Association*, 78 (1951–2), 11–29 • m. cert.

Archives Institute of Acoustics, St Albans, papers • RIBA BAL, personal corresp.

Likenesses photograph, repro. in D. Trevor-Jones, 'Hope Bagenal and the Royal Festival Hall', *Acoustics Bulletin*, 26/3 (May/June 2001); priv. coll. • photographs, priv. coll.

Wealth at death £16,421: probate, 13 Sept 1979, *CGPLA Eng. & Wales*

Bagenal [Bagnal], **Sir Nicholas** (*d.* 1590/91), soldier, was the second son of John Bagenal (*d.* 1558), a tailor by trade and mayor of Newcastle under Lyme on several occasions, and Elinor, daughter of Thomas Whittingham of Middlewich, Cheshire. Nothing is known about his early life until 1539 when Bagenal was responsible for the murder of a man in a brawl with 'certain light persons', and fled the law in England to the north of Ireland. There he came under the protection of the paramount chieftain of central Ulster, Conn O'Neill, who shortly thereafter made a compact with the crown under the 'surrender and regrant' programme. On 7 December 1542, after O'Neill's ennoblement as earl of Tyrone, the Irish council conveyed a petition to the court of Henry VIII for the pardon of Nicholas Bagenal for murder, at the earl's request. The pardon was granted in 1543.

In 1544 Bagenal requested and was granted permission from the Irish council to be sent to fight in the campaign of the English army in France. Returning to Ireland as a seasoned soldier, he was appointed by Edward VI as marshal of the army there in March 1547. In 1548 he campaigned in Leinster with the lord deputy, Sir Edward Bellingham, who was determined to pacify the midlands and southern highlands. Bagenal participated in the defeat of Cahir O'Connor and the slaughter of many of his kerne. In the early 1550s he was engaged primarily in martial activities in Ulster: he was sent in November 1551 by Lord Deputy Croft to expel the Scots from the Dufferin, and raided the lands of Shane O'Neill in Tyrone on behalf of Shane's half-brother Matthew O'Neill, baron of Dungannon, who represented the English interest in the region. Bagenal was knighted in the same year, and on 22 April 1552 was granted the lands of St Patrick's and St Mary's abbeys in Newry, the lordship of Mourne, and the manor of Carlingford.

On the accession of Queen Mary in 1553 Bagenal lost the office of marshal which was then conferred on Sir George Stanley. He does not appear to have offered any overt opposition to Mary's government, but he may have shared in the odium elicited by the radical protestant views of his elder brother who was also serving in Ireland. Sir Ralph Bagenal protested against the reconciliation with Rome and fled to France, where he was implicated in Henry Dudley's conspiracy. Nicholas, who had also left Ireland, was fearful of returning in the political climate of Mary's reign and was in 1556 bound over in a recognizance of £1000 to attend on the Irish councillors and assume responsibility for his bailiwick in Ulster. Meanwhile he maintained his connection with Staffordshire for which he was elected knight of the shire in 1559. He had about four years earlier married Eleanor (*d.* 1573), daughter of Sir Edward Griffith of Penrhyn; they had five sons, including Sir Henry *Bagenal (*c.*1556–1598), and six daughters.

Much to Bagenal's annoyance on his return to Ireland, Stanley was maintained as marshal by Queen Elizabeth while Sir Nicholas had to be content with a mere captaincy. On 23 April 1562 he wrote to the queen, complaining that his lands in Newry brought him in nothing owing to the depredations of Shane O'Neill, whereas while he was in office they were worth £1000 a year. When Sir Henry Sidney became deputy with the backing of the earl of Leicester (who had always been a patron of Bagenal) Sir Nicholas was reappointed as marshal in a patent dated 5 October 1565. Scarcely had he taken up the office when, early in 1566, he entered into an agreement to sell it and his lands to the adventurer Thomas Stucley for £3000. Sidney was supportive of this proposal, but the queen was justifiably suspicious of Stucley and Bagenal remained marshal.

In this capacity Bagenal continued to serve the crown in Ireland for a quarter of a century. His successful proprietorship of the town and vicinity of Newry made it a bastion of English civility in southern Ulster, and from there Bagenal exercised overlordship of some of the Gaelic rulers of the region. Sidney praised the marshal's settlement of Newry, with its new mansion house and church, as a model of Anglicization, and it was proposed that the town should become the seat of a presidency of Ulster in 1586. Already Bagenal had been appointed chief commissioner for Ulster in 1584, and in the following year he was elected to parliament to represent County Down.

Besides being active in the north, Bagenal was engaged in campaigns elsewhere under successive chief governors. His aggressive forays into southern Leinster exacerbated the cess controversy with the local gentry in 1576, but Bagenal was exonerated of any wrongdoing. His experience and knowledge of Ireland were respected by officials in Dublin and London, but in 1586 a bitter feud developed between Bagenal and Sir John Perrot which lasted until the lord deputy was recalled in 1588. The latter objected to the role of Bagenal and his sons as power-brokers in Ulster, while the marshal was a member of the faction of the Irish council that vehemently opposed the lord deputy's policies. On 15 July 1587 an affray occurred between the two men in Perrot's house as a result of which the aged marshal was knocked to the ground.

On 20 October 1590 Bagenal resigned the office of marshal on grounds of age and ill health, and on condition that it be conferred on his son Sir Henry. He died shortly thereafter, and was buried at Newry on 7 February 1591. Sir Henry succeeded to both the estates and the marshalship. COLM LENNON

Sources P. H. Bagenal, *Vicissitudes of an Anglo-Irish family, 1530–1800* (1925) · P. H. Bagenal, 'Sir Nicholas Bagenal, knight-marshal', *Journal of the Royal Society of Antiquaries of Ireland*, 6th ser., 5 (1915), 5–26 · 'Calendar of fiants, Henry VIII to Elizabeth', *Report of the Deputy Keeper of the Public Records in Ireland*, 7–22 (1875–90), appxs · *CSP Ire.*, *1509–88* · J. S. Brewer and W. Bullen, eds., *Calendar of the Carew manuscripts*, 2: *1575–1588*, PRO (1868) · J. L. J. Hughes, ed., *Patentee officers in Ireland, 1173–1826, including high sheriffs, 1661–1684 and 1761–1816*, IMC (1960) · H. Morgan, *Tyrone's rebellion: the outbreak of the Nine Years' War in Tudor Ireland*, Royal Historical Society Studies in History, 67 (1993) · 'Marshal Bagenal's description of Ulster, 1586', *Ulster Journal of Archaeology*, 2 (1854), 137–60 · C. Brady, *The chief governors: the rise and fall of reform government in Tudor Ireland, 1536–1588* (1994) · *DNB*

Likenesses portrait, repro. in Bagenal, *Vicissitudes of an Anglo-Irish family*, frontispiece; formerly in the possession of the Bagenal family of Mourne Abbey, co. Down, in 1925

Bagford, John (1650/51–1716), bookseller and antiquary, was born in Fetter Lane, London, the son of John Bagford. Very little is known about his early life and family background. He was trained and worked as a shoemaker and wrote a little tract about this trade (BL, Harley MS 5911), but beyond some schooling he did not receive any academic education. Bagford married his wife, Elizabeth, probably in the early 1670s; their son John was born in 1675. From 1686 Bagford was engaged in the book trade around Holborn, collecting and trading books for the great collectors of his day, such as Bishop John Moore of Ely, Robert and Edward Harley, Samuel Pepys, John Woodward, and Sir Hans Sloane. Bagford enjoyed a reputation as a knowledgeable and reliable book runner and formed important friendships with such scholars as Humfrey Wanley, Thomas Baker, and Thomas Hearne. Thus Bagford developed into one of the pioneer bibliographers of the early eighteenth century.

Bagford played a considerable part in a number of antiquarian pursuits of his day. He contributed, for example, to Edmund Gibson's edition of Camden's *Britannia* and John Strype's edition of John Stow's *Survey of London*. In 1707 Bagford was part of a group together with Wanley, William Stukeley, and others who attempted to refound the Society of Antiquaries. In those years Bagford met the antiquary Thomas Hearne at Oxford, and the two developed a close friendship and collaboration. Bagford also wrote antiquarian studies of his own, among them a well-received essay on London antiquities published by Hearne in his edition of Leland's *Collectanea* (1715). Bagford supplied Hearne with a considerable amount of material both for his publications and private collections. Both were involved in John Urry's edition of Chaucer (1721). In his *Robert of Gloucester* (1724), Hearne published a letter-essay he had written to Bagford earlier about Chaucer editions.

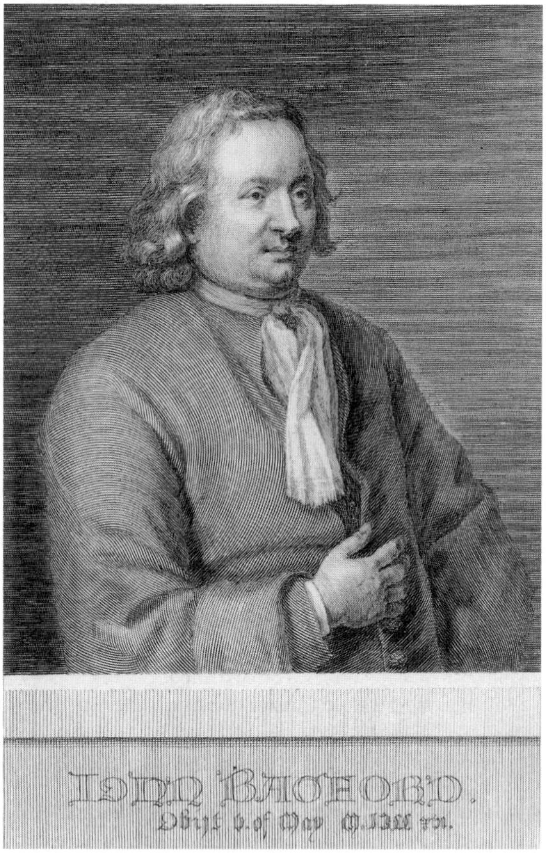

John Bagford (1650/51–1716), by George Vertue, 1728 (after Hugh Howard)

Bagford collected early printed books and ballads mainly for his planned history of printing and the printed book. In search of books, he made a number of trips to the Dutch towns of Haarlem, Leiden, and Amsterdam, where his friend and agent John Bullord had settled as a bookseller. In 1707 proposals for Bagford's work were published as was his essay on the invention of printing, which appeared in the *Philosophical Transactions* together with Wanley's account of Bagford's collections. Apparently the work itself did not attract enough subscribers and it was never completed. Not all his friends were confident that the autodidact Bagford could produce such a study.

Wanley, however, admired Bagford's skills in 'the different sorts of Ink, Illumination, Binding, Hands, parchment, Papers, or almost any sort of Workmanship' (Levine, 139). To Hearne

> there appeared in him such a plain, unaffected, honest simplicity, & at the same time such an unusual skill in the History of Printing & in our own History & Antiquities, that I immediately concluded him to be a valuable Man, as he most certainly is (*Remarks and Collections*, 5.74)

Hearne published an account of his friend in *Hemingi chartularium* (1723). Eventually Bagford's collections were consulted by Joseph Ames for his *Typographical Antiquities* (1749).

Today Bagford is known most as a collector of ballads. A great number of the ballads in the famous Roxburghe collection were originally gathered by Bagford for Robert Harley. The *Bagford Ballads*, finally edited and published by J. W. Ebsworth in 1878, represent Bagford's private collection of mainly Restoration ballads. His reputation was tarnished by later critics such as William Blades and T. F. Dibdin, who explained the presence in his collections of great amounts of title-pages, fragments, and scraps by accusing him of 'biblioclasm'. None of Bagford's contemporaries commented on Bagford tearing title-pages from books. Important work has been done since to rectify this image and to prove in more than one instance that Bagford preserved important fragments rather than mutilated books and manuscripts.

Bagford possibly remarried in 1703, but in his latter days he lived as a pensioner in the Charterhouse, where a place had been procured for him by Bishop Moore. He died in lodgings at Islington on 5 May 1716, the cause of his death unknown. He was buried on 7 May within the precincts of the Charterhouse. After his death, his collections were bought by Edward Harley and a small part of them came to Hearne. THEODOR HARMSEN

Sources Bodl. Oxf., MSS Rawlinson K (Hearne–Smith) • Bagford Collections, BL, Harley MSS • *Remarks and collections of Thomas Hearne*, ed. C. E. Doble and others, 11 vols., OHS, 2, 7, 13, 34, 42–3, 48, 50, 65, 67, 72 (1885–1921) • M. McC. Gatch, 'John Bagford, bookseller and antiquary', *British Library Journal*, 12 (1986), 150–71 • M. McC. Gatch, 'John Bagford as a collator and disseminator of manuscript fragments', *The Library*, 6th ser., 7 (1985), 95–114 • W. Y. Fletcher, 'John Bagford and his collections', *Transactions of the Bibliographical Society*, 4 (1896–8), 185–201 • T. A. Birrell, 'Anthony Wood, John Bagford and Thomas Hearne as bibliographers', *Pioneers in bibliography* (1988), 25–39 • C. Davenport, 'Bagford's notes on bookbindings', *Transactions of the Bibliographical Society*, 7 (1902–4), 123–59 • T. Hearne, 'A short discourse relating to the foregoing fragments', in *Hemingi chartularium ecclesiæ Wigorniensis*, ed. T. Hearne, 2 (1723), appx 9, pp. 652–74 • M. Nickson, 'Bagford and Sloane', *British Library Journal*, 9 (1983), 51–5 • *Letters of Humfrey Wanley: palaeographer, Anglo-Saxonist, librarian, 1672–1726*, ed. P. L. Heyworth (1989) • T. H. B. M. Harmsen, *Antiquarianism in the Augustan age: Thomas Hearne, 1678–1735* (2000) • C. E. Wright, *Fontes Harleiani: a study of the sources of the Harleian collection of manuscripts* (1972), 59 • T. F. Dibdin, *Bibliomania, or, Book madness: a bibliographical romance*, 2nd edn, [2 vols.] (1811), 430–37 • J. M. Levine, *Dr Woodward's shield: history, science, and satire in Augustan England* (1977), 139–42 • M. H. Wolf, ed., *Catalogue and indexes to the title-pages of English printed books preserved in the British Library's Bagford collection* (1974) • W. D. Macray, *Annals of the Bodleian Library, Oxford*, 2nd edn (1890); facs. edn (1984) • *Robert of Gloucester's chronicle*, ed. T. Hearne, 2 (1724), appx 4 • [J. Walker], ed., *Letters by eminent persons in the seventeenth and eighteenth centuries*, 2 vols. (1813), 2.21–3 • Nichols, *Lit. anecdotes*, 2.462–5 • A. Chalmers, ed., *The general biographical dictionary*, new edn, 3 (1812), 301–2 • W. L. Alderson and A. C. Henderson, *Chaucer and Augustan scholarship* (1970), 69–73 • W. Y. Fletcher, *English book collectors* (1902), 129–37 • S. De Ricci, *English collectors of books and manuscripts* (1930), 34 • R. Steele, 'John Bagford's own account of his collection of title-pages', *The Library*, new ser., 8 (1907), 223–4 • J. Evans, *A history of the Society of Antiquaries* (1956) • W. Blades, *The enemies of books* (1880) • J. W. Ebsworth, ed., *The Bagford ballads*, 5 vols. (1876–80)

Archives BL, 'The Bagford ballads', C. 40. m. 9–11 • BL, bibliographic collections, Lansdowne MS 808 • BL, commonplace books and collections relating to history of London, Sloane MSS 885, 893, 923, 1044, 1085–1086, 1106, 1378, 1435 • BL, corresp., papers, and collections relating to history of printing and London, Sloane MSS 4966, 5414, 5892–5954, 5966–5998 • BL, corresp. with Sloane and others, Sloane MSS 1435, 4039, 4040; Harley MS 4966 • Bodl. Oxf., collections and corresp., MSS Rawlinson K (Hearne–Smith) • Bodl. Oxf., corresp. Bagford–Hearne, and others, MSS Hearne Diaries, and MSS Rawlinson Letters 20, 21; MSS Rawlinson D. 1166, D. 1169, and D. 1188 • CUL, MS history of typography and account of first English impressions of the Bible • CUL, notes relating to printers | Bodl. Oxf., Hearne's corresp. with other scholars from Hearne's and Bagford's circle, esp. Thomas Baker, Richard Rawlinson, Browne Willis, Thomas Smith, MSS Rawlinson Letters

Likenesses G. Vertue, line engraving, 1728 (after oils by H. Howard), BM, NPG [*see illus.*] • H. Howard, oils, Bodl. Oxf.

Wealth at death see administration, PRO, PROB 6/92/239

Bagg, Sir James (*bap.* **1592**, *d.* **1638**), naval administrator, was baptized on 23 February 1592 at St Andrew's, Plymouth, the eldest of fourteen children of James Bagg (*d.* 1624), merchant and MP, and his second wife, Margaret, daughter of John Stone of Trevigo, Cornwall. He graduated from Leiden University in 1609 or 1611. By 1614, when their daughter Gertrude was baptized, he had married Grace, daughter of John Fortescue of Buckland Filleigh, Devon; they had one son and four daughters. In May 1614 he became comptroller of the customs at Plymouth and Fowey, his father having surrendered the office to him to evade condemnation for extortion. Six years later Bagg joined his father in the Virginia Company, being granted five shares. Elected to the 1621 parliament for Bodmin, presumably on the interest of his mother's family, he played no recorded part in its proceedings.

Bagg was ambitious for advancement and in October 1621, hearing of impending naval preparations, offered his services. The following year he pressed 190 seamen, and in April he victualled the ships assigned to convey Lord Digby as ambassador to Spain, earning Digby's written commendation. His diligence was rewarded by the lord admiral, the duke of Buckingham, who on 22 August appointed him vice-admiral of south Cornwall. In June 1623 Bagg wrote to Buckingham from Plymouth offering to become 'your servant in this place' (PRO, SP 14/147/3).

Returned for West Looe to the 1624 parliament, Bagg's Commons' service was interrupted by his father's death on 6 April. On the outbreak of war with Spain in 1625 he was elected for East Looe, but was prevented by his naval duties from taking his seat. He provided victuals at Plymouth and oversaw the pressing of seamen in the west country, although he was obstructed by Sir John Eliot, vice-admiral of Devon, who resented Bagg's intrusion into his jurisdiction. Bagg was knighted on 19 September. Following the disastrous Cadiz expedition, it was widely believed that Bagg's victuals had poisoned large numbers in the fleet, but he was held blameless by Buckingham, who received a steady stream of testimonies to his effectiveness. Granted the reversion to the captaincy of Plymouth Fort in February 1626 (to which he succeeded in June 1629), Bagg again served as member for East Looe in the 1626 parliament, where Eliot accused him, on 1 March, of having acted dishonestly in connection with money seized aboard the French ship the *St Peter* of Newhaven. Bagg himself endeavoured, on 21 April, to exonerate Buckingham from the charge of having connived in the employment of English warships against the Huguenots in 1625.

Following the parliament's dissolution Bagg determined to destroy Eliot, amassing evidence of irregularities in Eliot's vice-admiralty accounts and obtaining an inquiry after Eliot's officers bought a ship which Bagg believed properly belonged to Buckingham as prize. Buckingham was sympathetic to Bagg as Eliot, formerly his client, had now turned against him. On 25 October Eliot was suspended, and on 16 November Bagg and his cousin Sir John Drake were jointly appointed vice-admirals of Devon. In addition, in December Bagg and his servant Abraham Biggs were appointed joint collectors of new impositions in several ports. Bagg was now undisputed master of both admiralty and naval affairs in the west country, and also Buckingham's chief political agent there. Earlier in the year he had appraised the duke of his opponents' local activities, and when a forced loan was demanded that autumn Bagg, who heartily approved of this method of raising revenue, advised Buckingham on the composition of the relevant local commission, on which he himself naturally served.

Bagg provided victuals for Buckingham's ill-fated Île de Ré expedition in 1627, and in October he helped fit out the would-be relief force, putting himself more than £10,000 in debt. On the duke's return Buckingham authorized Bagg to sell some cargoes of salt to redeem his credit, whereupon Bagg sold the contents of the *Costly* of Dover, which were earmarked for the salting of provisions at Portsmouth. Buckingham, who had naturally not intended to impede naval preparations, instructed Bagg on 17 December to release this ship and her cargo, but either the letter arrived too late or Bagg disregarded the order, for by early January he had sold most of her contents. Buckingham refused to condemn him, but the navy's official victualler, Sir Allen Apsley, swore to have nothing more to do with Bagg, whose only interest, he alleged, was profit.

Bagg was returned to the 1628 parliament for Plympton Erle, and helped procure seats for several Buckingham clients. News of the episode involving the *Costly* spread, for on 2 April Sir Edward Seymour told the Commons that if they voted the king too much money 'all that we will give will be cast into a bottomless bag' (Russell, 288). Six days later Bagg came under direct attack when William Strode, the member for Bere Alston, alleged that Bagg had laid the cost of billeting the survivors of the Ré expedition on the country rather than use the money left for this purpose by the duke. However, as Bagg's letter to Buckingham of 22 November 1627 shows, the sum of £3500 to which Strode referred was provided for billeting the sick and wounded rather than healthy troops, the cost of whose accommodation was intended to be met locally. Nevertheless, Bagg was compelled to journey to Westminster to clear his name. Neither Buckingham nor the king doubted Bagg's probity, and on 18 May Charles instructed him to take charge of the preparations at Plymouth for the relief of La Rochelle.

Buckingham's assassination in August 1628 deprived Bagg of his patron and left his finances dangerously exposed, for he had used his initiative in supplying the navy, seldom waiting for a formal warrant. Buckingham had approved his methods but now Bagg was obliged, in 1629, to petition for repayment, which was granted in August 1630 by a grateful king. In 1632 Bagg missed high office on the death of the principal secretary of state, Viscount Dorchester, being passed over in favour of Sir Francis Windebanke. In November 1634 he was accused in Star Chamber by Sir Anthony Pell of refusing to repay £2000, given him to obtain from the crown repayment of a larger sum, and though he protested in April 1635 that he had paid this money to the late lord treasurer as required, the court narrowly found against him. However, the king ordered the judgment in the case to be set aside. Meanwhile, Bagg himself brought an action for slander in Star Chamber against his erstwhile ally John Mohun, first Baron Mohun, who said that Bagg had swindled the king of £80,000 during the war years. In reply Mohun framed his own bill, accusing Bagg of fraud on a grand scale. The two lawsuits, which proceeded in tandem, were finally concluded in June 1637, when the judges were so divided that, according to one observer, 'no man can well tell who proved the delinquent' (*De L'Isle and Dudley MSS*, 6.111). Both men were fined, and Mohun imprisoned; the king prevented imprisonment in Bagg's case but did not protect him from an investigation into his vice-admiralty accounts, and by 1634 part of his estate had been seized by the crown. In February 1636 it was claimed that he owed the king more than £29,253 but he maintained that, considering various allowances and a loan to the crown of £16,000, it was he who was actually owed nearly £7500. Bagg died intestate at his house in Queen Street, St Giles-in-the-Fields, Westminster, on 26 August 1638, and was buried the same day in the church of St Martin-in-the-Fields. His debts are said to have amounted to £60,000.

Andrew Thrush

Sources 'Bagg, James II', HoP, *Commons, 1604–29* [draft] · A. Thrush, 'The bottomless Bagg? Sir James Bagg and the navy, 1623–8', *The new maritime history of Devon*, ed. M. Duffy and others, 1 (1992) · BL, Add. MS 37816, fol. 183*v*; 37817 · PRO, HCA 30/820/10 · *The manuscripts of the Earl Cowper*, 3 vols., HMC, 23 (1888–9), vol. 1 · *CSP dom., 1611–39; addenda, 1625–49*, 112 · letter from John, Lord Digby, 10 April 1622, BL, Harley MS 1580, fol. 120v · letter from Charles I to Bagg, 18 May 1628, BL, Egerton MS 2552, fol. 30v · J. L. Vivian, ed., *The visitations of the county of Devon, comprising the herald's visitations of 1531, 1564, and 1620* (privately printed, Exeter, [1895]),

34 • E. Peacock, ed., *Index to English speaking students at Leyden University*, Index Library, 13 (1883), 5 • W. A. Shaw, *Knights of England*, 3 vols. (1906), vol. 2, p. 189 • S. M. Kingsbury, ed., *Records of the Virginia Company*, 4 vols. (1906–35), vol. 1, p. 383 • uncatalogued Coke MS, BL [formerly Derbyshire RO, Coke MS C95/33] • *JHC*, 1 (1547–1628), 828–9 • PRO, SO3/8 • C. Russell, *The crisis of parliaments* (1976), 288 • R. C. Johnson and others, eds., *Proceedings in parliament, 1628*, 6 vols. (1977–83) • PRO, AO1/1798/372 • Bodl. Oxf., MS Rawl. A. 210, fols. 11–27 • *Report on the manuscripts of Lord De L'Isle and Dudley*, 6, HMC, 77 (1966), 111 • PRO, SP14/147/3 • G. Radcliffe, *The earl of Strafforde's letters and dispatches, with an essay towards his life*, ed. W. Knowler, 1 (1739), 336–7, 423, 426, 489, 504 • M. A. E. Green, ed., *Calendar of the proceedings of the committee for compounding … 1643–1660*, 5 vols., PRO (1889–92), 1362 • parish register, St Martin-in-the-Fields, City Westm. AC, 26 Aug 1638 [burial]

Wealth at death debts of £60,000

Baggallay, Sir Richard (1816–1888), judge, was born in Stockwell, London, on 13 May 1816, the eldest son of Richard Baggallay (*d.* 1870), a merchant of Kingthorpe House, Upper Tooting, London, and his wife, Anne, daughter of Owen Marden. He was a contemporary of William Baliol Brett, Viscount Esher, at Gonville and Caius College, Cambridge, where he graduated BA (as fourteenth wrangler) in 1839 and MA in 1842. He was Frankland fellow of Caius College from 1845 until his marriage on 25 February 1847 to Marianne, youngest daughter of Henry Charles Lacy of Withdean Hall, Sussex, with whom he had six sons and six daughters. He was honorary fellow of Caius from 1880 until his death.

Baggallay joined Lincoln's Inn on 23 March 1837, was called to the bar on 14 June 1843, and elected bencher on 13 March 1861 and treasurer in 1875. He practised at the equity bar in the rolls court and became queen's counsel in 1861. He was counsel to Cambridge University from 1869 to 1875.

Baggallay was elected member of parliament for Hereford on 14 July 1865 as a Conservative reformer, and succeeded Sir W. B. Brett as solicitor-general on 16 September 1868. He was knighted on 14 December 1868 after the government went out of office. He had meanwhile lost his seat, and only re-entered parliament on 17 October 1870 when he was returned for Mid-Surrey. On the Conservative Party's return to power, he once again became solicitor-general (27 February 1874), becoming attorney-general two months later on 20 April on the early retirement of Sir John Karslake.

As attorney-general Baggallay piloted the Judicature Act of 1875 through committee, and by that act he was created in turn justice of appeal (29 October 1875) and later lord-justice of appeal, and joined the privy council.

Much of the burden of construing the Judicature Acts and determining procedure under the new system fell upon Baggallay. In the summer of 1882 his health broke down, and a prolonged rest failed to restore it. He retired from the bench in November 1885, but occasionally attended privy council meetings until shortly before his death from heart disease on 13 November 1888 at 10 Brunswick Square, Hove, Sussex, where he had gone to convalesce. J. M. Rigg, *rev.* Hugh Mooney

Sources *The Times* (14 Nov 1888) • *Law Journal* (17 Nov 1888), 592–3 • *Law Journal*, 17, 256 • *Law Journal* (1 Nov 1884), 655 • *Law Times* (24 Nov 1888) • *Law Times* (5 Dec 1885) • *Annual Register* (1868), 252, 254 • *Annual Register* (1888), 179 • *Solicitors' Journal*, 33 (1888–9), 46 • Burke, *Peerage* • J. Foster, *The peerage, baronetage, and knightage of the British empire for 1883*, 2 [1883] • *GM*, 2nd ser., 27 (1847), 543 • *Law List* (1843) • *Law List* (1876) • *Law List* (1875) • *Law List* (1862) • *Law List* (1861) • J. Foster, *Men-at-the-bar: a biographical hand-list of the members of the various inns of court*, 2nd edn (1885) • *Men of the time* (1884) • Venn, *Alum. Cant.* • grad. cert. • W. P. Baildon, ed., *The records of the Honorable Society of Lincoln's Inn* [incl. *Admissions*, 2 vols. (1896), and *Black books*, 6 vols. (1897–2001)] • *CGPLA Eng. & Wales* (1888)

Likenesses Lock & Whitfield, woodburytype, 1876, NPG; repro. in T. Cooper, *Men of mark: a gallery of contemporary portraits*, 1 (1876) • J. Sant, oils, exh. RA 1877, Merchant Taylors' Company, London • Ape [C. Pellegrini], chromolithograph, NPG; repro. in *VF* (11 Dec 1875) • Faustin, chromolithograph, NPG • Lock & Whitfield, carte-de-visite, NPG • photograph, NPG

Wealth at death £64,609 12*s.* 6*d.*: probate, 18 Dec 1888, *CGPLA Eng. & Wales*

Baggerley, Humphrey (*fl.* 1648–1654), army officer and supposed biographer, was among the troops who on 9 October 1648 surrendered at Appleby, Westmorland, to superior parliamentarian forces under Colonel Assheton. The royalist soldiers were granted very generous terms and, having been allowed his freedom, Baggerley probably travelled directly to the Isle of Man in the company of Sir Thomas Tyldesley. On 12 August 1651 he supervised the embarkation of the invasion force of James Stanley, seventh earl of Derby, from Castletown harbour, and—despite contrary winds—effected a landing on the Lancashire coast, at Preesall Sands, three days later. It seems more than likely that he fought at the disastrous battle of Wigan Lane on 25 August 1651, and that he was among the '4 Captains' taken there, following the royalist rout (Lilburne, 3). He was certainly held prisoner at Chester Castle but doubt arises as to whether he was the same gentleman who, on 13 October 1651, was given permission by the authorities to attend the earl after a court martial had passed a sentence of death upon him.

A detailed, highly partisan, and emotive account of the last three days of Derby's life exists, and is credited to the 'Rev. Humphrey Baggerley' (Seacome, 120–28). It is probable that the editor of these papers wrongly attributed them. However, it is just conceivable that there were two entirely different individuals who shared the same name; or that Baggerley was ordained after the Restoration (Draper, 217–18; Ormerod, 2.196, 316, 338). The author of the account was clearly closely connected to the Stanley household, knew the Manx clergy well, and provided the earl of Derby with companionship and spiritual solace on his journey to execution at the market square in Bolton on 15 October 1651. Before the axe fell he was entrusted with delivering the earl's last letter to his wife, who still held the Isle of Man for the king, and with returning his Order of the Garter to his son and heir. Nothing more is known of the 'Reverend' Humphrey Baggerley, but his military namesake was implicated in John Gerard's plot, of May 1654, to murder Oliver Cromwell.

The sudden decision of the lord protector, on Saturday 14 May, to abandon his normal routine and take a barge—instead of a coach—to his residence at Hampton Court caused the assassination attempt to be aborted and threw the plotters into confusion. Baggerley fled the City and went into hiding in Highgate village, but he was apprehended on 21 May 1654 and was escorted back to London under heavy guard. Charged with high treason, he was kept under especially 'close custody' in the Tower of London throughout the summer months. On 7 August 1654 he pleaded his innocence, complained that prison life was ruining his health, and urged that the authorities should quickly decide whether or not to try, acquit, or release him. His petition to the lord protector seems to have been heeded, for on 1 September 1654 he was banished from the land on giving his word that he would not 'act to the State's prejudice, nor return without leave' (*CSP dom.*, 1654, 353). Thereafter he disappears from the records and returns to the obscurity which shrouds both his actions as a royalist agent and the claims to his authorship of a significant work of cavalier hagiography.

JOHN CALLOW

Sources P. Draper, *The house of Stanley including the siege of Lathom House* (1864) • J. Seacome, *Memoirs containing a genealogical and historical account of the antient and honourable house of Stanley from the conquest, to the death of James, late earl of Derby, in the year 1735* (1741) • G. Ormerod, ed., *Tracts relating to military proceedings in Lancashire during the great civil war*, Chetham Society, 2 (1844) • *A description of the memorable sieges and battles in the north of England … chiefly contained in the memoirs of General Fairfax and James earl of Derby* (1785), 109–210 • *CSP dom.*, 1654, 273, 288–9, 353, 436 • F. R. Raines, ed., *Private devotions and miscellanies of James, seventh earl of Derby KG*, 3 vols., Chetham Society (1867) • S. Reid, *The finest knight in England, Sir Thomas Tyldesley, his regiments and the war in the north* (1987) • R. Lilburne, *Two letters from Col. Robert Lilburne … containing the particulars of the totall rout and overthrow of the earl of Derby, and the forces under his command in Lancashire on 25 of August 1651* (30 Aug 1651) • *A great victory … obtained by the parliaments forces against … the earl of Derby, on the 25 of August 1651 neer Wigon [sic] in Lancashire* (29 Aug 1651) • J. J. Bagley, *The earls of Derby 1485–1985* (1985) • E. Broxap, *The great civil war in Lancashire, 1642–1651*, 2nd edn (1973) • P. R. Newman, *The old service: royalist regimental colonels and the civil war, 1642–1646* (1993) • Madame Guizot de Witt, *The lady of Lathom* (1869), 177–8 • F. S. Hampson, *An interesting history of the execution of James Stanley seventh earl of Derby* (1914)

Baggs, Charles Michael (1806–1845), college head and vicar apostolic of the western district, was born at Belville, in co. Meath, Ireland, on 21 May 1806. He was the eldest son of a protestant barrister of Dublin, Charles Baggs, afterwards judge of the court of vice-admiralty in Demerara, and his wife, Eleanor, fourth daughter of John Howard Kyan, of Mount Howard and Ballymurtagh in the county of Wicklow. His father being a member of the established church of Ireland, Baggs's early education was at a protestant academy kept by a Mr King at Englefield Green in Surrey. Early in 1820 his father died suddenly at Demerara, three days after hearing of the death of a friend for whom he had become security for £60,000. Upon the news of this double calamity Charles Baggs was removed by his mother from Englefield Green to the Catholic school of Sedgley Park in Staffordshire, and from this time he was a member of the Roman Catholic church. He remained at Sedgley Park until June 1821, when, at the suggestion of William Poynter, vicar apostolic of the London district, he was transferred as an ecclesiastical student to St Edmund's College near Ware, Hertfordshire, where he remained for three years.

In the summer of 1824 Baggs was sent to the English College at Rome, which, from the date of his arrival on 9 June, became his home for nearly twenty years. His reputation as a student was always excellent. He took first prizes in Hebrew, mathematics, physics, and scripture, and was highly commended in theology. His remarkable ability was exhibited on 25 September 1830 when, in the presence of a distinguished audience presided over by Cardinal Zurla, he held his ground defending his theological theses in Latin. This display won for him his doctor's cap at the early age of twenty-four.

Baggs was ordained priest in December 1830. For several years he occupied the chair of professor of Hebrew at the English College. His knowledge of French and Italian in particular, as well as of Spanish and German, was remarkable. As a pulpit orator he soon became well known outside the walls of the college. His earliest published discourse was *On the Supremacy of the Roman Pontiffs*, delivered on 7 February 1836 in the fashionable church of Gesù e Maria in the via del Corso, and was issued from the press immediately afterwards, with an appendix in which he challenged some of the arguments of contemporary Anglican divines. The work was dedicated to Cardinal Weld. On 8 March 1836 his *Letter Addressed to the Rev. R. Burgess, Protestant Chaplain at Rome* appeared. This was a controversial piece, which in the same year was translated into Italian by Baggs himself.

His skill in languages, interest in controversy, and immersion in the Roman scene recall Wiseman's early career, and it is not surprising that in 1834 Wiseman made Baggs vice-rector of the college. Throughout the pontificate of Gregory XVI Baggs was 'cameriere d'onore', a member of the papal household. Upon him devolved the duty of presenting all the English visitors, both Catholic and protestant, who were admitted to a private audience with the pope. In this capacity Baggs enjoyed a high degree of popularity, not only among his co-religionists but among his compatriots generally.

Baggs's monograph entitled *The Papal Chapel Described and Illustrated from History and Antiquities* appeared at Rome in 1839, inscribed to Charles (later Cardinal) Acton. It was at one time popular as a handbook for English-speaking visitors, as was his larger work, *The Ceremonies of Holy Week at the Vatican and S. John Lateran's: Described and Illustrated from History and Antiquities*, published almost simultaneously. It was Baggs's practice to dedicate his publications to persons of influence in England or Rome and the last named was addressed to Hugh Charles, Lord Clifford of Chudleigh. It is dated 16 March 1839. During the following year Baggs published another work of ecclesiastical antiquarianism, *The Pontifical Mass sung at St Peter's Church on Easter Sunday, on the Festival of SS. Peter and Paul, and Christmas Day, with a Dissertation on Ecclesiastical Vestments*. This work was dedicated to Cardinal James Giustiniani, bishop of Albano and protector of the English College. These liturgical and antiquarian writings reflect the interests at this time of many catholics in England, where, following

Catholic emancipation, many new churches were being built. The great patron of A. W. Pugin and the Gothic revival was John, sixteenth earl of Shrewsbury; when his daughter Lady Gwendoline Talbot, the Princess Borghese, died in Rome it was Baggs who preached the funeral oration at San Carlo in the Corso on 23 December 1840. She was a cousin of Baggs and when the panegyric was printed he inscribed it to the father of the young princess.

Four months before this, Baggs became rector of the English College when his predecessor, Wiseman, was consecrated as bishop of Melipotamus on 8 June 1840. During the last ten years of his sojourn in Rome, Baggs continued to distinguish himself as a controversialist. On 30 June 1842 he read to the Accademia di Religione Cattolica his dissertation on the Puseyites. This was written in Italian to explain to a Roman audience the situation in the Church of England and the differences between the evangelicals, the high-church party, and the followers of Pusey. It is of special interest because it was composed before J. H. Newman joined the Church of Rome. Together with another treatise in Italian, *On the Present State of the Church of England*, it was subsequently published in the *Annali delle Scienze Religiose* (vol. 40, 1842, 60–92, and vol. 42, 1843, 94–117). It was during Baggs's rectorship that the English College was honoured by the visit of Pope Gregory XVI on 25 February 1843. His career at Rome was closed by his elevation to the episcopate. On 28 January 1844, in the church of San Gregorio on the Caelian Hill, he was consecrated bishop of Pella *in partibus infidelium* by Cardinal Fransoni, assisted by George Brown, then bishop of Tloa and afterwards of Liverpool, and by Dr Collier, the bishop of Port Louis in Mauritius.

In England the sudden death of Bishop Peter Augustine Baines had left vacant the office of vicar apostolic of the western district; Gregory XVI selected Baggs to fill it. He was the only secular priest to occupy that position in the 162 years of its existence. It was a surprise appointment and although Baggs's name had been put forward in 1840, he was not considered then to be a suitable candidate for the episcopate because of his lack of experience. On his departure from Rome the pope made him a present of books, while the students of the English College gave him a costly pectoral cross, and even the English protestants in Rome subscribed to buy him a crucifix. He formally took possession of his diocese on 30 May 1844, when he was welcomed by a large gathering of the clergy and laity at Prior Park near Bath. Here, two days afterwards, he held his first ordination. He visited his extensive diocese during the course of that summer, and reorganized it into four deaneries on 2 October. Shortly after taking up his residence at Prior Park, Baggs delivered a course of lectures on the supremacy of the pope in the church of St John the Evangelist at Bath. In August 1845 he suffered a nervous breakdown and spent some time convalescing at Lord Clifford's seaside residence. He returned to Prior Park, but died there on 16 October 1845 at the early age of thirty-nine. He was buried in the partially completed new church of Prior Park College on 23 October; his remains were removed a few years later to the nearby Midford Chapel and subsequently to Holy Souls cemetery, Arnos Vale, Bristol.

Some contemporaries attributed Baggs's early death to his inability to adapt to the English climate after so many years in Rome—'climate' being understood in more than a meteorological sense. Among the papers relating to the choice of his successor there is a submission from England to Rome that passes the following verdict on Baggs's brief episcopate:

> Never perhaps was there a man less fitted for the situation of vicar apostolic in England than Dr Baggs, and had it not pleased God to take him to himself he would in a short time have thrown the District into irremediable confusion. The chief cause of Dr Baggs' unfitness for the office of vicar apostolic arose from his being taken immediately from a College. He knew nothing of the duties of a missionary priest, he was quite ignorant of the peculiar difficulties of their situation and was always expecting everything to be done as if we were living in a catholic country. Dr Baggs having always been at College where everything, food, clothes etc were supplied him, had no idea of the value of money and consequently spent money most recklessly and imagined that his priests could do the same. In fact he never had been a missionary and a vicar apostolic in England will never be any good except he has been a missionary.
> (Archives of the Congregatio de Propaganda Fide, Rome, MS Anglia 10, fol. 845)

MICHAEL E. WILLIAMS

Sources *Catholic Directory* (1851) • W. M. Brady, *The episcopal succession in England, Scotland, and Ireland, AD 1400 to 1875*, 3 (1877), 330–33 • G. Oliver, *Collections illustrating the history of the Catholic religion in the counties of Cornwall, Devon, Dorset, Somerset, Wilts, and Gloucester* (1857), 230–33 • Gillow, *Lit. biog. hist.* • B. Plumb, *Arundel to Zabi: a biographical dictionary of the Catholic bishops of England and Wales (deceased), 1623–1987* (privately printed, Warrington, [1987]) • *Morning Post* (3 Nov 1845) • J. S. Roche, *A history of Prior Park College* (1931), 185–91 • Briggs correspondence, Leeds Diocesan Archives, nos. 647–8 • Archives of the Congregatio de Propaganda Fide, Rome, MS Anglia 10, fol. 845

Archives Bristol RO, Clifton diocesan records, corresp. and papers • English College, Rome, archives, corresp. and papers | Archives of the Congregatio de Propaganda Fide, Rome

Likenesses oils, Bishop's House, Leigh Woods, Clifton • portrait, repro. in *Catholic Directory* • portrait (after portrait), English College, Rome, Italy • stipple, BM

Bagnal, Sir Henry. *See* Bagenal, Sir Henry (*c*.1556–1598).

Bagnal, Sir Nicholas. *See* Bagenal, Sir Nicholas (*d*. 1590/91).

Bagnall, Gibbons (1719–1800), Church of England clergyman and poet, was the only son of Gibbons Bagnall (1688–1743) of Windsor, vintner, and his first wife, Elizabeth Harries. He was admitted to Balliol College, Oxford, on 12 July 1738, and gained his BA on 30 April 1741. He afterwards went to King's College, Cambridge, where he took his MA in 1760. After taking holy orders Bagnall became vicar of Holm Lacy in Herefordshire, and headmaster of the free school at Hereford. He had married Sarah Reeve of Windsor in 1757.

Bagnall was collated on 27 May 1760 to the prebend of Piona Parva in Hereford Cathedral, and on 1 August 1767 to the prebend of Barsham in the same cathedral establishment. He also held for some time the rectory of Upton Bishop, Herefordshire; and in 1783 he was presented to the nearby vicarage of Sellack. He died on 31 December 1800, in his eighty-second year.

Bagnall's most important published works were in verse. The first was *Education: an Essay* (1765). A more ambitious literary work was a verse translation, in two volumes, of F. de Salignac de La Mothe Fénelon's account of the adventures of Telemachus, son of Ulysses. However, this failed to capture the 'cadenced prose' of Fénelon, according to a contemporary critic (*A New Catalogue*, 1799). THOMPSON COOPER, *rev.* ROBERT BROWN

Sources Venn, *Alum. Cant.* • W. Hustler, ed., *Graduati Cantabrigienses* (1823) • *A new catalogue of living English authors: with complete lists of their publications, and biographical and critical memoirs* (1799) • *GM*, 1st ser., 70 (1800), 1300 • *Fasti Angl.* (Hardy) • private information (2004) [Society of Genealogists]

Bagnold, Enid Algerine [*married name* Enid Algerine Jones, Lady Jones] (**1889–1981**), novelist and playwright, was born at Borstal Cottage, Rochester, Kent, on 27 October 1889, the elder child and only daughter of Major (later Colonel) Arthur Henry Bagnold (1854–1943), a military engineer, and his wife, Ethel (1866–1931), daughter of William Henry Alger, who inherited a large chemical and fertilizer factory at Cattedown and became mayor of Plymouth. Her younger brother, with whom she was close, was Ralph Alger *Bagnold (1896–1990). Enid Bagnold spent three years of her childhood in Jamaica, where her father was posted, and then lived at Woolwich, before going to Prior's Field school, Godalming, run by the stimulating Mrs Leonard Huxley.

Enid Bagnold was a tomboyish, dramatic, outdoor, beautiful girl who soon escaped the conventionally respectable life of her parents by taking a flat in Chelsea, and for several years she studied art under Walter Sickert. She made friends easily among members of the marginally Bohemian set, including Henri Gaudier-Brzeska, who sculpted her. In 1912 she met James Thomas (Frank) *Harris (1856?–1931), then aged fifty-six, who employed her as a journalist on his magazine *Hearth and Home*, and with whom she had her first love affair.

In the First World War Bagnold worked as a nurse in a London hospital, and described her experiences in *A Diary without Dates* (1918, 2nd edn 1978), imagining herself writing to Antoine Bibesco, the Romanian diplomat whom she loved for many years with an unrequited passion. Within half an hour of the book's publication she was sacked by her matron for indiscipline, but it had an instantaneous success, H. G. Wells describing it in *The Dream* (1924) as one of the most human books written about the war.

Enid Bagnold thus achieved fame while still in her twenties, and her ambition never slackened. Her vitality, humour, audacity, and grace made her an exhilarating companion. She was ebulliently communicative, in talk as in writing, as lavish with words as a pianist is with notes, loving the inexhaustible variety of human experience as much as the language which expressed it. She was, however, too fond of the great and grand to be taken seriously by the literary establishment (apart from Sir C. O. Desmond MacCarthy, one of her closest friends), and in the view of one critic she remained 'a brilliantly erratic amateur'. Her literary strength lay in her gift for narrative, dialogue, and domestic scenes, for which she drew extensively on her own experience and the characters of her friends.

On 8 July 1920 Bagnold married Sir (George) Roderick *Jones (1877–1962), chairman and managing director of Reuters. 'Their partnership', wrote her biographer Anne Sebba, 'was marked by loyalty, not fidelity, respect but not passion', but for their children, three sons and a daughter, Enid's affection was unstinting. Her intimate friend Vita Sackville-West wrote of her in an unpublished poem:

> I never loved you, Enid, save as a friend,
> But as a friend I loved you nearly, dearly,
> You wild rash girl, so young, less flesh than bones,
> And then came Jones, and flesh succumbed to Jones
> And domesticity destroyed you in the end.
> (MS poem at Sissinghurst)

In London the Joneses entertained generously, and it was there, in a study designed for her by Sir Edwin Lutyens, and at their Sussex home, North End House, Rottingdean, that she wrote joyfully but intermittently, having no need to write for money.

Her first novel, *The Happy Foreigner* (1920), describing her experiences as a voluntary aid detachment nurse in France, was followed by *Serena Blandish* (1924), about a poor girl in search of a rich marriage. Then came a book for children, *Alice and Thomas and Jane* (1930), and in 1935 she published her best known book, *National Velvet*, the story of a butcher's daughter who wins a piebald horse in a raffle and, disguised as a boy, wins the Grand National. In 1944 it was made into a hugely successful film, with the youthful Elizabeth Taylor in the starring role. Her next novel, which she and many others considered her best, was *The Squire* (1938), a daringly outspoken description of the relationship between a mother (unmistakably herself) and the child to whom she gives birth.

In 1941 Bagnold wrote her first play, *Lottie Dundass*, about a stage-struck typist who dies of a heart attack after her first and only performance. It was an instant success in America and England, and Enid thereafter devoted her talent to the theatre, apart from one more novel, *The Loved and Envied* (1951), a story of high life clearly based on her friend Lady Diana Cooper, and her autobiography (1969). As a dramatist she had several failures, including *Gertie* (1952), *The Last Joke* (1960), and most disastrously, *Call me Jacky* (1967), but in compensation she enjoyed one major triumph with *The Chalk Garden* (1955), which ran in London for two years and was described by Kenneth Tynan as possibly the finest English comedy since those of William Congreve, and one critical success, particularly in America, with *The Chinese Prime Minister* (1964). She involved herself intensively (too intensively for many of the actors and directors) in the production of all her plays, and continued writing until late in her eighties, when she reworked *Call me Jacky* into *A Matter of Gravity* (1975). Her last published books were a selection of her poems (1978) and *Letters to Frank Harris and other Friends* (1980).

Enid Bagnold's husband died in 1962, and the last years of her life, despite the devotion of her children, became increasingly lonely. She needed regular injections to dull the pain of her arthritis, but she remained gallantly active, describing herself, characteristically and truthfully, as 'an old lady masking a sort of everlasting girl inside'. She was appointed CBE in 1976.

Enid Bagnold died of bronchopneumonia on 31 March 1981 at 17a Hamilton Terrace, London. Her ashes were buried at Rottingdean, Sussex, after her cremation at Golders Green. NIGEL NICOLSON

Sources *WWW*, vols. 4, 6, 8 · A. Sebba, *Enid Bagnold: a biography* (1986) · E. Bagnold, *Enid Bagnold's autobiography* (1969) · R. Jones, *A life in Reuters* (1951) · Sissinghurst Castle, Cranbrook, Kent, MSS
Archives priv. coll., family MS collections · Ransom HRC · Yale U., Beinecke L. | BL, corresp. with Sir Sydney Cockerell, Add. MS 52703 · NYPL, Berg collection · Rice University, Houston, Texas, Woodson Research Center, letters to Sir Julian Huxley · U. Sussex, corresp. with Leonard Woolf
Likenesses H. Gaudier-Brzeska, bronze bust, 1912, priv. coll. · photographs, priv. coll. · portraits, repro. in Sebba, *Enid Bagnold*
Wealth at death £72,034: probate, 2 Nov 1982, *CGPLA Eng. & Wales*

Bagnold, Ralph Alger (1896–1990), soldier and geomorphologist, was born on 3 April 1896 at the Manor House, Stoke, Devonport, the second of two children born to Major Arthur Henry Bagnold (1854–1943) of the Royal Engineers, and Ethel (1866–1931), the daughter of William Henry Alger, owner of a chemical and fertilizer factory, and his wife, Edith Elizabeth Wills. His elder sister, to whom he was very close, was Enid Algerine *Bagnold (1889–1981), the author.

Bagnold was educated at St Wilfrid's preparatory school in Bexhill (1904–9), Malvern College (1909–14), of which he was not excessively fond, and the Royal Military Academy, Woolwich (1914–15). In 1915 he joined the school of military engineering at Chatham as a second lieutenant in the Royal Engineers. In the same year he was posted to France as a member of the British expeditionary force, and developed an expertise in signals which was to remain with him for the rest of his military career. He fought at the Somme, Ypres, and Passchendaele, and was mentioned in dispatches. In 1919 he returned to England, and after he had held a temporary post in the War Office in London the army paid for him to go up to Gonville and Caius College, Cambridge. He took the engineering tripos course, which he found over-theoretical, but was awarded his degree and returned to the army in the summer of 1921. In 1926 he was posted to Egypt, and it was here that he developed his taste for desert exploration by motor car, using Model-T and Model-A Fords. In 1928 he served in India, and was mentioned in dispatches in Waziristan, but he then returned to the less exciting world of Catterick garrison in 1931. Finding life dull, he embarked on a 3700 mile expedition into the eastern Sahara, for which he was awarded the Royal Geographical Society's founder's medal in 1934. These travels are divertingly described in *Libyan Sands* (1935). Thereafter he served in the Far East, but was taken ill with 'tropical sprue' and was discharged from the army as a permanent invalid. The gloomy diagnosis of his condition proved to be unfounded, however, and he embarked with gusto on a career of scientific investigation at Imperial College, London, with the aim of understanding sand movement and dune development. To this end he conducted the first experiments with a wind tunnel and in 1938 undertook further journeys deep into the Libyan desert, visiting the Gilf Kebir, Jebel ʿUwaynat, and the Selima Sand Sea.

On the outbreak of war Bagnold was recalled to the army, where his experiences of desert travel and terrain trafficability proved to be uniquely valuable. He had the support of Wavell, set up the marauding long range desert group, became an acting lieutenant-colonel, and set off to harry the Italians and Rommel. He did this with success and became MBE in 1941.

Following the death of his father Bagnold was granted release from further military service and returned to England to find that he had been elected a fellow of the Royal Society—a remarkable tribute to a non-academic amateur. He married Dorothy Alice (Plankie; 1905/6–1989), secretary, daughter of Alfred Ernest Plank, civil servant, on 8 May 1946 at the parish church in Rottingdean, and together they raised a son, Stephen (*b.* 1947), and a daughter, Jane (*b.* 1948). He joined the Shell Refining and Marketing Company, from which he retired in 1949. From then on he maintained his interest in the flow of sediments, but moved from air to water, developing an important collaboration with Luna B. Leopold of the United States geological survey. His scientific reputation was recognized through the award of the Warren prize of the National Academy of Sciences (1969), the Penrose medal of the Geological Society of America (1970), the Wollaston medal of the Geological Society of London (1971), fellowship of Imperial College (1971), the Sorby medal of the International Association of Sedimentologists (1978), honorary DSc degrees from the universities of East Anglia (1972) and Aarhus (1978), and the David Linton award of the British Geomorphological Research Group (1981). Bagnold's last published paper, in the *Proceedings of the Royal Society*, appeared in 1986, when he was ninety years old. His autobiography, *Sand, Wind, and War* appeared in the year of his death (1990).

Bagnold's contributions were remarkable for their diversity and distinction. First, he was a professional soldier who reached the rank of brigadier and was mentioned in dispatches or decorated in both world wars. Second, he was a daring desert explorer who was one of the key pioneers of desert motoring in Egypt, Sudan, and Sinai. Third, he used his desert and administrative skills to establish a special army unit—the long range desert group—to commit 'piracy on the high desert' during the North African campaign. Fourth, he was an amateur scientist who pioneered the use of the wind tunnel in geomorphological and sedimentological research, wrote what is still the fundamental work on aeolian phenomena, *The Physics of Blown Sand and Desert Dunes* (1941), and established the physics of the interaction between fluids in motion and granular solids.

Bagnold, who in his latter years looked the epitome of a British brigadier, with a clipped moustache and a somewhat florid nose, died in the Hither Green Hospital, Hither

Green, London, on 28 May 1990. His scientific works are still widely cited more than half a century since they were first published. As a professional soldier and an amateur scientist, a field man and a theoretician, he was outstanding. ANDREW S. GOUDIE

Sources R. A. Bagnold, *Sand, wind, and war: memoirs of a desert explorer* (1990) • C. R. Thorne, R. C. MacArthur, and J. B. Bradley, eds., *The physics of sediment transport by wind and water* (1988) • A. Warren, 'Brigadier R. A. Bagnold, 1896–1990', *GJ*, 156 (1990), 353–4 • M. Haag, *The Independent* (30 May 1990) • *The Times* (30 May 1990) • D. M. McDowell, *The Independent* (11 June 1990) • *WW* • b. cert. • m. cert. • d. cert.

Archives CAC Cam., corresp. and papers, incl. operational reports, papers, etc., of the long-range desert group | FILM BFI NFTVA, 'Libyan desert — Bagnold', 1950

Likenesses photograph, repro. in Haag, *The Independent* (30 May 1990) • photograph, repro. in Thorne, MacArthur, and Bradley, eds., *Physics of sediment transport*, i • photographs (at various stages of his life), repro. in Bagnold, *Sand, wind, and war*

Wealth at death £359,190: probate, 17 Sept 1990, *CGPLA Eng. & Wales*

Bagot family (*per. c.*1490–1705), gentry, is one of the oldest in Staffordshire, as its motto 'Antiquum obtinens' ('Possessing Antiquity') implies. Its members trace their descent from the Bagod recorded in Domesday Book as holding Bramshall near Uttoxeter. A branch of the family was established at Bromley Bagot by the late twelfth century and became active in local affairs. Marriage to an heiress made Ralph Bagot lord of nearby Blithfield by 1362. Their son Sir John probably rebuilt the hall there, which became the family's home.

Sir Lewis Bagot (*c.*1461–1534) succeeded his father, also John, in 1490. Knighted at the marriage of Prince Arthur and Katherine of Aragon in 1501, he was sheriff of Staffordshire in 1506–7 and 1520–21 and was on the commission of the peace for much of his life from 1508. He was also one of the Staffordshire commissioners for the collection of the 1524 subsidy. He accompanied Henry VIII on his French expedition in 1513 and was summoned to attend him at the Field of Cloth of Gold in 1520. At his death he held the Staffordshire manors of Colton (near Blithfield) and Field (in Leigh parish near Bramshall) as well as those of Blithfield and Bromley Bagot. He married five times. His first wife was Lucy, daughter of John Kniveton of Underwood, Derbyshire; his second was named Emma; his third was Anne (*d.* 1514), daughter of Sir Nicholas Montgomery of Cubley, Derbyshire; his fourth was Margaret, daughter of Richard Vernon; the identity of his fifth wife, who survived him, is unknown. The effigies of Anne and another wife appear on either side of his own effigy on his tomb in Blithfield church, with the head of a third appearing behind. His heir was his second surviving son, Thomas, who died in 1541 and was buried under an incised table tomb in Blithfield church showing the figures of himself and his wife, Jane, daughter of Richard Astley of Patshull, Staffordshire.

Thomas's son **Richard Bagot** (*c.*1530–1597) succeeded as a minor. Blithfield being part of the duchy of Lancaster, his wardship and marriage were held by the crown, and they were sold in 1542 to John Jenyns, a gentleman of the privy chamber. In 1552 Richard, who may have been educated at Cambridge, married Mary (*d.* 1609), daughter of William Saunders of Welford, Northamptonshire. He became active in local affairs as sheriff (1569–70 and 1577–8), a JP, and a deputy lieutenant. He also served on various inquiries and commissions and was three times in charge of raising a loan for Elizabeth I. He was notably active in the enforcement of measures against Roman Catholics. In 1586 he was commended by the privy council on behalf of the queen for the help which he had given the two keepers of Mary, queen of Scots, during her imprisonment in Staffordshire in 1585 and 1586. In 1587, following his arrest of Nicholas Marwood, a priest who was considered dangerous, he was commended by the earl of Shrewsbury, the lord lieutenant, who also passed on the delight of the queen and the privy council. In 1585 Richard was involved in a revival of glassmaking on the Blithfield estate, where the industry had been long, though intermittently, established.

Richard Bagot was on friendly terms with the first two Devereux earls of Essex, William and his son Robert, who had a Staffordshire seat at Chartley, some 3½ miles from Blithfield. Richard's younger son Anthony was a member of Robert Devereux's household from 1579 and took part in the earl's rising of 1601, being pardoned in 1602. Richard Bagot's eldest daughter married another member of the Devereux household, William Trew, though against her father's wishes. Richard carried out extensive building work at Blithfield, remodelling the north range with its medieval great hall and the west range and probably rebuilding the south entrance front. He was pursuing the history of his family by 1576, and as a keen antiquary he was on good terms with Staffordshire's first county historian, Sampson Erdeswick of Sandon, despite Erdeswick's recusancy. Richard's tomb in Blithfield church bears effigies of himself and his wife.

Richard's heir was his son **Walter Bagot** (*bap.* 1557, *d.* 1623), who matriculated at Merton College, Oxford, in 1577. By 1586 he was married to Elizabeth (*d.* 1638), daughter of Roger Cave of Stanford, Northamptonshire, and Elizabeth Cecil, sister of Lord Burghley. Walter was elected one of the two MPs for Tamworth in 1586 and was appointed a JP in 1597, soon after he had succeeded his father. In 1598 he was appointed collector of the forced loan of 1596 in succession to his father. He was sheriff in 1599–1600 and 1603–4, commissioner for raising another loan in 1622, and a deputy lieutenant. William Trew told his wife in 1599 that the queen insisted on Walter's appointment as sheriff: 'she heard he was an honest man like his father and therefore was sorry she had spared him so long' (Folger Shakespeare Library, Washington, DC, Bagot papers, L.a. 912). Although in 1603 Walter sent a recusant arrested at Cannock to the privy council, he was more friendly towards Roman Catholics than his father had been. On one occasion when required to serve on a recusancy commission at Lichfield he declared that he had 'no mind to the business and would willingly have a cleanly shift to avoid it' (Petti, 84). He was involved in a further revival of glassmaking in 1607, but it was brought to an end by the royal ban on the use of wood in the industry in 1615. His monument in Blithfield church stresses the antiquity of the Bagot family.

Walter was succeeded by his son **Sir Hervey Bagot**, first baronet (1591–1660), who was created a baronet in 1627. He matriculated at Trinity College, Oxford, in 1608. By 1613 he had married Katherine, daughter of Humphrey Adderley of Weddington, Warwickshire. She died in 1623 and Hervey subsequently married Anne, daughter of Sir Clement Fisher of Great Packington, Warwickshire, and widow of Sir Thomas Dilke of Maxstoke Castle, also in Warwickshire, who was more than twenty years her second husband's senior. Hervey was living at Field Hall by 1620, having moved there from Trescott Grange, Staffordshire. He continued to make Field his home, giving Blithfield up to his son and heir, Edward, evidently on Edward's marriage in 1641. Hervey was appointed a JP in 1623 soon after succeeding his father, and he served as sheriff in 1626–7 and as royalist sheriff in 1642–3. He was one of the twenty-two commissioners appointed to collect Staffordshire's share of the 1642 subsidy. He was elected one of the county's MPs in 1628 and again at a by-election in 1641.

Sir Hervey Bagot was disabled from sitting in November 1642 after raising troops against parliament, and his property was sequestrated in 1643, although his wife secured possession of Field in 1644 for a payment of £70. Sir Hervey evidently settled in the close at Lichfield, where the royalist garrison was under the command of his third surviving son, Richard, and his second, Hervey, was in command of a regiment of foot. Both brothers fought with the king at Naseby in 1645 and after the defeat returned to Lichfield. Richard had been wounded, died soon afterwards, and was buried in the cathedral. His brother succeeded him as commander of the garrison until the beginning of 1646. Meantime Sir Hervey sat in the royalist parliament which assembled at Oxford in 1644, but he was living in the close again early in 1646. Through his eldest son he then approached the parliamentary governor of Stafford for protection and expressed his willingness to move to Stafford. He was evidently prevented from doing so when the parliamentarian siege of the close began in March, and he remained there until its surrender in July.

Sir Hervey Bagot returned to Field and petitioned parliament to be allowed to compound for his delinquencies. His estates, all in Staffordshire and consisting of the manors of Blithfield, Bromley Bagot, and Little Hay in Colton, one-third of the manor of Leigh, one-fifth of the manor of Newton adjoining Blithfield, and lands in Abbots Bromley, were valued at £334 18*s*. 8*d*., out of which he allowed his eldest son £200. In addition Lady Bagot had a jointure of £200. In 1647 Sir Hervey's fine was fixed at £1340, but in 1649 it was reduced on his petition to £1004 17*s*. At the time of the royalist rising in Cheshire in 1659 he was imprisoned in Stafford with a number of others but was released on bail of £2000. Described by Sir Simon Degge in 1656 as 'a very honest worthy gentleman' (Erdeswick, 263n.), he died at Field on 27 December 1660 and was buried in Blithfield church on 31 December between his two wives, Anne having died in 1656.

Sir Hervey's heir was his second son, **Sir Edward Bagot**, second baronet (1616–1673), who matriculated at Trinity College, Oxford, in 1635 and was a student of the Middle Temple in the same year. In 1641 he married Mary (*d*. 1686), daughter of William Lambard of Buckingham and widow of John Crawley of Someries, Bedfordshire, and they settled at Blithfield. Mary was sole heir to her father's property in Buckinghamshire, but that was sold to meet debts incurred during and after the civil war, including Sir Hervey's composition fine. Edward Bagot served as a JP in 1656–7 and was reappointed in 1660 shortly after the Restoration. He was one of the county MPs in the 1660 Convention Parliament. He served as a commissioner for assessment from 1660, a commissioner for corporations in 1662 and 1663, and a commissioner for loyal and indigent officers in 1662. He was appointed a deputy lieutenant in 1662. He died on 30 March 1673. His monument, with an inscription describing him as 'a true asserter of primitive episcopacy in the Church and hereditary monarchy in the State', entirely blocked the east window of Blithfield church until it was partially removed in 1823.

Sir Edward was succeeded by his third son, **Sir Walter Bagot**, third baronet (*bap*. 1645, *d*. 1705), who matriculated at Christ Church, Oxford, in 1662 and was a student of the Middle Temple in 1666. His marriage in 1670 to Jane (*d*. 1695), daughter and heir of Charles Salesbury of Bachymbyd in Denbighshire, brought extensive Welsh estates to the family. He was appointed a JP and a deputy lieutenant in 1677. He served as a commissioner for assessment for Staffordshire and Denbighshire from 1677 to 1680, for Staffordshire in 1689 and for Denbighshire in 1689 and 1690, and as a commissioner for inquiry into recusancy fines for Staffordshire in 1687 and for Cheshire in 1688. In 1679 he was elected one of the county MPs and as such sat in every parliament until 1695, though returned for that of 1690–95 at a by-election in 1693. His monument in Blithfield church, however, records that 'he was often disabled, by a complication of infirmities, from attending the service'; in 1688 he specified his infirmities as gout and stone. During the Popish Plot he supported the informer Stephen Dugdale against Lord Aston and Lord Stafford. Robert Plot, in his *Natural History of Staffordshire*, acknowledged him as 'one of the noblest promoters of this design' and dedicated a view of Blithfield Hall to him 'in memory of his beneficence' (Plot, 225).

The Bagots continued to hold one of the county seats as tories until 1780, when Sir William, the sixth baronet, was raised to the peerage as Baron Bagot of Bagot's Bromley. The family crest is a goat's head, and a herd of wild blackneck goats kept by the family until the later twentieth century was stated in 1710 to have been pastured in Bromley Wood adjoining Bagot's Park near Bagot's Bromley from time immemorial. Tradition claims that they were descended from goats presented to Sir John Bagot by Richard II in gratitude for hunting enjoyed by the king in the park. The crest appears on a seal used by Sir John in 1380, and if herd and crest are connected, the gift must have been made soon after the youthful Richard became king in 1377 rather than on one of his later visits to Staffordshire. M. W. Greenslade

Sources G. Wrottesley, 'A history of the Bagot family', *Collections for a history of Staffordshire*, William Salt Archaeological Society, new ser., 11 (1908), 1–224 · W. Bagot, *Memorials of the Bagot family*, privately printed, Blithfield (1824) · J. C. Wedgwood, 'The Staffordshire sheriffs (1086–1912), escheators (1247–1619), and keepers or justices of the peace (1263–1702)', *Collections for a history of Staffordshire*, William Salt Archaeological Society, 3rd ser. (1912), 272–344 · J. C. Wedgwood, 'Staffordshire parliamentary history [1]', *Collections for a history of Staffordshire*, William Salt Archaeological Society, 3rd ser. (1917 [i.e. 1919]) · J. C. Wedgwood, 'Staffordshire parliamentary history [2]', *Collections for a history of Staffordshire*, William Salt Archaeological Society, 3rd ser. (1920–22) · H. S. Grazebrook, ed., 'The heraldic visitations of Staffordshire … in 1614 and … 1663 and 1664', *Collections for a history of Staffordshire*, William Salt Archaeological Society, 5/2 (1884), 27 · HoP, *Commons, 1660–90*, 1.582–3 · Foster, *Alum. Oxon., 1500–1714*, 1.55 · W. A. Shaw, *The knights of England*, 2 (1906); repr. (1971), 33 · A. G. Petti, ed., *Roman Catholicism in Elizabethan and Jacobean Staffordshire: documents from the Bagot papers*, Staffordshire RS, 4th ser., 9 (1979) · E. S. Godfrey, *The development of English glassmaking, 1560–1640* (1975) · D. H. Pennington and I. A. Roots, eds., *The committee at Stafford, 1643–1645*, Staffordshire RS, 4th ser., 1 (1957) · H. Clayton, *Loyal and ancient city: Lichfield in the civil wars* [1987] · A. Oswald, 'Blithfield, Staffordshire, the home of Lord and Lady Bagot', *Country Life* (28 Oct 1954), 1488–92; (4 Nov 1954), 1576–9; (11 Nov 1954), 1664–7; (25 Nov 1954), 1862 · royalist composition papers (transcripts), William Salt Library, Stafford, S. MS. 339 (i), pp. 155–73 · Folger, Bagot papers, L.a.912 · Nancy, Lady Bagot, 'The history of the Bagot goats', William Salt Library, Stafford, Misc. 280 · statement on the Bagot goats by a jury sworn for the Abbots Bromley court leet, 6 Oct 1710, Staffs. RO, D. 4381/4 · S. Erdeswick, *A survey of Staffordshire* (1844) · R. Plot, *The natural history of Staffordshire* (1686) · Venn, *Alum. Cant.*, 1/1.68 · wills, Staffs. RO, D. 4038/I/1 and 2 [Lewis Bagot] · parish registers, Blithfield, Staffs. RO, D. 1386/1/1, D. 5192/1

Archives Folger, papers · priv. coll., corresp. and papers [Sir Hervey Bagot] · Staffs. RO, MSS, D. (W.) 1721/3; D. 3260; D. 4038; D. 4181 · Staffs. RO, notebook [Richard Bagot] | NL Scot., corresp. relating to captivity of Mary, queen of Scots [Richard Bagot]

Likenesses double portrait, 1626 (Hervey Bagot with his father, Henry Bagot), Blithfield Hall, Staffordshire · effigies on tombs (Sir Lewis Bagot and Richard Bagot), Blithfield church, Staffordshire

Bagot, Sir Charles (1781–1843), diplomatist and governor-in-chief of British North America, was born on 23 September 1781 at Blithfield Hall, Staffordshire, the second surviving son of William, first Baron Bagot (1728–1798), and Elizabeth Louisa (*d.* 1820), the eldest daughter of John St John, second Viscount Bolingbroke. William *Bagot and Richard *Bagot were his brothers. Bagot was educated at Rugby School and Christ Church, Oxford, and received his BA in 1801 and his MA in 1804. In November 1801 he entered Lincoln's Inn, but he abandoned his legal studies within a year. On 22 July 1806 he married Mary Charlotte Anne Wellesley-Pole (*d.* 1845), the daughter of William Wellesley-*Pole, the future third earl of Mornington, and a niece of the future duke of Wellington; they had four sons and six daughters.

In June 1807 Bagot entered the House of Commons for Castle Rising, a rotten borough in the gift of his uncle Richard Howard. In August 1807 he became under-secretary for foreign affairs, and formed a close friendship with his superior, George Canning. Later that year he abandoned his parliamentary seat in favour of a sinecure as steward of the Chiltern Hundreds. In October 1809 he followed Canning out of the Foreign Office but in 1814 briefly served as minister-plenipotentiary to France. On 31 July 1815 he became minister-plenipotentiary and special envoy to the United States and on 4 December was appointed to the privy council. In March 1816 he arrived in Washington, where, despite his youth and inexperience, he proved an able diplomat. He enjoyed neither Washington's climate nor its society, but he held his tongue and became popular and respected. He successfully resolved a number of the frictions arising out of the Anglo-American War of 1812–14. His greatest success was an agreement to limit naval forces on the Great Lakes, which was formalized in an exchange of diplomatic notes with the American secretary of state, Richard Rush, in April 1817, and became known as the Rush–Bagot agreement. Bagot was also involved in efforts to settle disputes over American access to the Atlantic fisheries and over the boundary from Lake of the Woods, in the far west of Upper Canada, to the Pacific, both of which were formally resolved by the convention of 1818 which was negotiated in London. Bagot thus helped to create what would eventually be the longest undefended border in the world.

Bagot returned to England in 1819. On 20 May 1820 he was created a GCB and on 23 May was made ambassador to Russia. He found St Petersburg more congenial than Washington, and formed a close and friendly relationship with the tsar, whom he sought to restrain from aggressive actions in Turkey. In 1821 he negotiated an end to Russian efforts to make the north Pacific a closed sea, and he began the negotiations which resulted in the Anglo-Russian treaty of 1825 defining the boundary between Alaska and British North America. In the autumn of 1824 Bagot persuaded Canning to transfer him to The Hague so that he could reduce the heavy expense of maintaining family homes in both London and St Petersburg. Until 1831 he served as ambassador to the Netherlands, and he played a minor part in the negotiations which established the independence of Belgium. In 1828 he declined appointment as governor-general of Bengal, but he was identified with the Conservatives, and the only diplomatic post he held after 1831 was a short mission to Vienna to congratulate Francis I on his accession in 1835.

When the Conservatives returned to power in 1841 Sir Robert Peel and Lord Stanley, the secretary of state for the colonies, persuaded Bagot to become governor-in-chief of British North America (27 September 1841). Bagot was selected partly because it was presumed his appointment would be welcomed in the United States, but also because the Conservatives were concerned to halt the trend towards responsible government in British North America. In the aftermath of the abortive rebellions of 1837, the whigs had accepted Lord Durham's recommendation that Upper and Lower Canada be amalgamated into the united province of Canada, thus placing the French Canadians in a minority, but they had also accepted Durham's recommendation that the colonial government must obtain the consent of the majority in the assembly, thus opening up the possibility that the French-Canadian party might have to be admitted to power on their own terms. Bagot's instructions were to continue the policies of his whig predecessor, Lord Sydenham, and to promote gradual assimilation of the French Canadians while governing through the non-party coalition which Sydenham had constructed in the assembly of the united province. Shortly after arriving at the capital in Kingston, Upper Canada, on 10 January 1842, and taking office two days later, Bagot realized that the non-party coalition was disintegrating and that he would have to conciliate the French-Canadian reformers led by Louis-Hippolyte LaFontaine. Bagot sought to win French-Canadian support by appointing to office a number of French Canadians, including Denis Benjamin Viger, who had been implicated in the rebellion of 1837 and whose appointment to the legislative council Stanley refused to confirm. To Stanley's horror Bagot also reported that many of the measures introduced by Sydenham to accelerate assimilation of the French Canadians were not working and ought to be abandoned and that the large civil list embodied in the Union Act of 1840 ought to be reduced. Bagot did persuade a moderate reformer, Francis Hincks, to join the executive council, and he opened negotiations with LaFontaine, but he was unable to break the solidarity of the French-Canadian bloc or to undermine their alliance with the English-Canadian reformers led by Robert Baldwin.

When the assembly of the united province met in September 1842 Bagot's conservative ministers could no longer command a majority. Bagot reluctantly accepted their resignations and negotiated an agreement which allowed the Baldwin–LaFontaine coalition to take office on 14 September 1842. He retained several executive councillors not directly identified with any party, but he gradually came to develop a healthy respect for LaFontaine and Baldwin, and, as his health deteriorated, the reformers dictated policy and controlled patronage. As Bagot admitted, the principle of responsible government which the British government had previously refused to acknowledge had in effect been conceded and the policy of assimilating the French Canadians abandoned. Bagot's actions not only earned him the animosity of Canadian Conservatives, but created consternation in London, where Peel, Stanley, and Prince Albert had all made clear their opposition to a surrender of the prerogative to the Canadian reformers whose loyalty to the crown and the imperial connection seemed suspect. When Bagot submitted his resignation late in 1842 because of poor health, the Conservatives enthusiastically accepted it and appointed as his successor Sir Charles Metcalfe in the hope that he could undo the harm they felt Bagot had done.

When Bagot died in Kingston on 19 May 1843, after having been replaced by Metcalfe as governor on 30 March that year, reformers throughout the united province of Canada mourned his death. His body was transferred to England for burial. It was his short Canadian administration which established his reputation: in fact, Bagot's actions may well have saved the imperial connection, for they helped to convince the reformers, particularly the French-Canadian reformers, that they could achieve their goals through constitutional means, and he had established the principle of responsible government so firmly that there was no going back. Bagot was not as able a politician as his predecessor in Canada, Lord Sydenham, nor as capable an administrator as his successor, Sir Charles Metcalfe. He owed the series of offices he held to his family connections and to influential friends, and he was deeply conservative, if not reactionary, in his political views. But he was a capable diplomat, who happened to be placed in Canada at precisely the moment when diplomatic skill was required. Bagot did not go to Canada to introduce a new political system. Initially he did everything he could to avoid surrendering power to the reformers. But in the end he was shrewd enough to make a virtue of necessity, thus earning a permanent place in the pantheon of great imperial statesmen. PHILLIP BUCKNER

Sources J. Monet, 'Bagot, Sir Charles', *DCB*, vol. 12 • G. P. de T. Glazebrook, *Sir Charles Bagot in Canada* (1929) • P. A. Buckner, *The transition to responsible government: British policy in British North America, 1815–1850* (1985) • J. Monet, *The last cannon shot* (1969) • J. M. S. Careless, *The union of the Canadas: the growth of Canadian institutions, 1841–1857* (1967) • C. R. Middleton, *The administration of British foreign policy, 1782–1846* (1977) • Foster, *Alum. Oxon.* • Burke, *Peerage* (1907)
Archives NA Canada • priv. coll., corresp. and papers • Staffs. RO | BL, corresp. with Peel, Rose, and Aberdeen, Add. MSS 40404–40526, 42793, 43217, 43086–43087, 43106–43107 • Keele University, Sneyd MSS • Lpool RO, Stanley MSS • PRO NIre., Stewart MSS • U. Southampton L., Temple MSS
Likenesses H. Pickersgill, portrait, exh. RA 1835, Christ Church Oxf.

Bagot, Sir Edward, second baronet (1616–1673). *See under* Bagot family (*per.* *c.*1490–1705).

Bagot, Sir Hervey, first baronet (1591–1660). *See under* Bagot family (*per.* *c.*1490–1705).

Bagot, Sir Lewis (*c.***1461–1534**). *See under* Bagot family (*per.* *c.*1490–1705).

Bagot, Lewis (1740–1802), bishop of Bristol, Norwich, and St Asaph, was born on 1 January 1740, the fifth son of Sir Walter Bagot, fifth baronet (1702–1768), of Blithfield, Staffordshire, and his wife, Lady Barbara Legge (*d.* 1765). He was a younger brother of William, first Baron Bagot. Educated at Westminster School, he matriculated at Christ Church, Oxford, on 8 March 1757. His verses on the death of George II and accession of George III were printed in the *Oxford Poems* in 1761. He graduated BA in 1760, but his education was interrupted by ill health, which obliged him to live in Lisbon until 1764, when he proceeded MA on 23 May. Bagot was subsequently appointed a canon of Christ Church in 1771 and in the same year married Mary Hay (*d.* 1799), daughter of the Hon. Edward Hay, niece of the earl of Kinnoul, and sister of his predecessor in the canonry of Christ Church. There were no children from the marriage. In 1772 he was made DCL and was also presented by Lord Northampton to the livings of Jevington and Rye in Sussex.

Bagot quickly gained a reputation as a high-churchman and a defender of the religious character of university

Lewis Bagot (1740–1802), by John Hoppner, 1794

education. In 1772 he wrote a tract claiming that a university education was inherently a process of religious instruction, and the following year he opposed any change to the subscription by Oxford graduates to the Thirty-Nine Articles. In 1777 Lewis Bagot was installed as dean of Christ Church. He continued his defence of the Anglican monopoly at Oxford by protesting that those who sought relief from the subscription would not give any guarantee that they only sought it for protestants. In this he was an ally of Sir Roger Newdigate.

On 23 February 1782 Bagot was consecrated bishop of Bristol, which he held together with the deanery of Christ Church, Oxford. He remained at Bristol for only fifteen months before translation to Norwich in May 1783. In 1790 he was translated to St Asaph, where he rebuilt the bishop's palace and declared his intention of spending most of his time in the diocese. His visitation queries asked detailed questions about the residence of clergy and the position of curates in the diocese. His later years were marked by ill health, and he was wasted almost to a skeleton when he died at London on 4 June 1802. He was buried at St Asaph Cathedral, which he regarded as his home.

Bagot's high-church views led him into disputes with dissenters, and in 1776 he published a tract entitled *The Dangerous Errors of the Anabaptists*. He was a staunch and intolerant anti-Unitarian, and the strength of his views brought him much vilification. His Warburton lecture on the 'prophecies' was published in 1780. His *Letter to the Revd William Bell*, published in 1781, advanced a high view of the eucharist akin to the views of bishops Atterbury and Horne. In the same year he gave fifty copies of Isaac Barrow's *Doctrine of the Sacraments*, which he had reprinted, to the Society for Promoting Christian Knowledge. An important ingredient in Bagot's thought was a strongly providential view of society, which rejected ideas that progress from savagery to civilization had been the work of human agency alone. But Bagot's social ideology offered no special place for the poor, though he advocated the expansion of church schools, and argued that people should willingly pay their rates to support the poor.

At the root of Bagot's ideas lay a strong conservatism; his 1784 visitation charge—described by Parson Woodforde as a very long but a very good charge—proposed church reform and censured neglect of duty in order to prevent greater social change. Bagot earned for himself a strong reputation as a bishop of 'thorough goodness' (Abbey). The poet William Cowper, who had been at Westminster School with Bagot, excoriated the English bench of bishops but concluded:

> ... Still [Providence] keeps a seat for worth and grace
> And therefore 'tis that though the sight be rare
> We sometimes see a Lowth or Bagot there.
> (Cowper, 282)

WILLIAM GIBSON

Sources Foster, *Alum. Oxon.* • *The diary of a country parson: the Reverend James Woodforde*, ed. J. Beresford, 5 vols. (1924–31) • L. Bagot, *Letter to the Revd William Bell* (1781) • L. Bagot, *A serious caution against the dangerous errors of the Anabaptists* (1776) • F. C. Mather, *High church prophet: Bishop Samuel Horsley (1733–1806) and the Caroline tradition in the later Georgian church* (1992) • R. A. Soloway, *Prelates and people: ecclesiastical social thought in England, 1783–1852* (1969) • W. R. Ward, *Georgian Oxford: university politics in the eighteenth century* (1958) • C. J. Abbey, *The English church and its bishops, 1700–1800*, 2 vols. (1887) • *IGI* • W. Cowper, 'Tirocinium, or, A review of schools', *The poems of William Cowper*, ed. J. D. Baird and C. Ryskamp, 3 vols. (1980–95), 2.282 • Burke, *Peerage* (1959) • *Old Westminsters*, 3.40

Archives NL Wales, St. Asaph visitation records | BL, letters to Charles Poyntz, (P38) • NL Wales, letters to W. D. Shipley • Warks. CRO, Newdigate MSS

Likenesses J. Hoppner, oils, 1794, Christ Church Oxf. [*see illus.*] • S. Reynolds, mezzotints, pubd 1819 (after J. Hoppner), BM, NPG • F. Chantrey, marble bust, 1829, Christ Church Oxf.

Bagot, Richard (*c*.1530–1597). *See under* Bagot family (*per. c*.1490–1705).

Bagot, Richard (1782–1854), bishop of Bath and Wells, was born at Blithfield, Staffordshire, on 22 November 1782, son of William, first Baron Bagot, and his wife, the Hon. Louisa St John, daughter of the second Viscount Bolingbroke. William *Bagot, second Baron Bagot, and Sir Charles *Bagot were his brothers. Richard was educated at Rugby School from January 1790 until 1799, when he matriculated at Christ Church, Oxford, graduating BA in 1803 and MA in 1806. He was awarded a DD (by diploma) in 1829. In 1803 Bagot was elected to an All Souls fellowship, which he resigned when he married Lady Harriet Villiers, daughter of George Bussey, fourth earl of Jersey, on 22 December 1806. They had eight sons and four daughters, all of whom survived their father. Ordained in 1806, Bagot

Richard Bagot (1782–1854), by Thomas Youngman Gooderson (after Sir Francis Grant, 1846)

was presented by his father to the rectory of Leigh, Staffordshire, and in 1807 to the rectory of Blithfield, the family seat. Family connections—his uncle Lewis *Bagot was bishop successively of Norwich and St Asaph—ensured further preferment. In 1812 he became a prebendary of Lichfield Cathedral, and in 1817 was elected to a canonry of Worcester. Bagot was appointed dean of Canterbury in 1827, and in 1829 he was elevated to the bishopric of Oxford, holding the deanery *in commendam*.

Bagot was of a modest, retiring, and nervous disposition; his nerves never recovered from an accident while dean of Canterbury in which he swallowed cotton wool used to stop a tooth. He utterly refused the bishopric of Oxford when it was first offered him by the duke of Wellington, and accepted it only on the assurance of William Howley that the diocese would 'never give him trouble' (Paget to Eden, 22 Jan 1879, Ollard MSS). It was Bagot's misfortune that the rise of the Oxford Movement and all its consequences proved Howley wrong, and exposed the bishop to a limelight which by nature he would have shunned.

The bishop of Oxford stood in an anomalous position in relation to the university: he was not ordinary within the colleges, though he ordained for some. Bagot's difficulties were compounded because, unlike his predecessor, Charles Lloyd, he lacked academic standing within the university and did not have a reputation for scholarship. The diffident bishop, nicknamed King Log on account of an undeserved reputation for lack of activity, seemed a most unlikely candidate for Tractarian reverence as an episcopal specimen successor of the apostles. Yet the Tractarians were to have few more genuine friends on the episcopal bench.

Bagot's birth and tory family background gave him the credentials of a moderate high-churchman of the old school; he attempted to tighten church discipline and episcopal authority in the diocese. In 1831 he deprived the Calvinist H. P. Bulteel from his curacy at St Aldates for preaching antinomianism, while in the last year of his episcopate, in 1845, Bagot took the Revd James Hawker Langley, perpetual curate of Wheatley, to the ecclesiastical courts for extempore preaching. His first episcopal charge in 1834 was distinctly high church in tone, and indeed his personal regard for Newman and Pusey was great. His forbearance, sympathy, and trust earned the respect of many Tractarians. In 1836 he took delight in Newman's new church at Littlemore, despite its supposedly 'papistical' features. In 1838 Newman dedicated his *Lectures on Justification* to the bishop. According to his private chaplain and nephew, Francis Paget, Bagot was able to retain a larger degree of personal influence with the Tractarian divines than an abler man might have attained.

Bagot consistently resisted intense low-church and evangelical pressure to act firmly against the Tractarian movement. The bishop's charge of 1838 restated the high-church themes of his earlier charge and vigorously denounced the ecclesiastical commission. In spite of some mild words of caution, which an over-sensitive Newman misinterpreted as evidence of coldness and rebuke, the tenor of the charge was broadly favourable to the authors of the Tracts for the Times, who were praised for recalling forgotten truths such as the authority and discipline of the church. Subsequently the bishop went out of his way to reassure Newman that he had not meant to censure the tracts. Bagot did not agree with the Tractarians *tout court*; his main concern was to check the rise of party division within the diocese, and he blamed opponents of the Tractarians primarily for fostering party spirit. When anti-Tractarians such as C. P. Golightly sought to establish a protestant martyrs' memorial in Oxford in 1838, partly as a deliberate hit at the Tractarians, Bagot attempted to defuse the situation by persuading Pusey to subscribe to the memorial, though he had no such success with Newman. On other occasions Newman's almost exaggerated respect for his diocesan as 'my pope' raised difficulties and caused the bishop embarrassment. Bagot privately pleaded with Newman to check the extravagances of his younger followers, because they tended 'to retard the progress of sound and high Church principles which you would inculcate' (*The Letters and Diaries of John Henry Newman*, ed. C. S. Dessain and others, 31 vols., 1–10, 2nd edn, 1978–, 7.190).

Tract 90 (1841) and the subsequent excesses of the movement put an increasing strain on Bagot's friendly relationship with the Tractarians. Always dependent on the counsel of Archbishop Howley, he was vulnerable to Lambeth pressure to take a somewhat firmer line with the Tractarians. The bishop's chaplain, Francis Paget, later likened

Bagot's position between 'Blomfield's on the one side, and Golightly and such like cattle on the other' as akin to that of 'a railway servant, caught and pressed … between the buffers of two engines' (Paget to Eden, 24 Jan 1879, Ollard MSS). In the period 1841–2, Bagot showed extreme deference to the advice of other bishops and clergy. He requested Newman to bring the series of Tracts for the Times to an immediate close and to state more clearly his view of the Thirty-Nine Articles. In a published letter to the bishop Newman appeared to comply with this request, having persuaded Bagot to yield from his original intention of getting Newman to 'suppress' Tract 90. While Bagot appeared satisfied and Howley congratulated him on his handling of the affair, others complained that the bishop had been 'hoodwinked': that Newman not only did not withdraw Tract 90 from circulation but, in opposition to the bishop's wishes, had a new edition printed. Low-church critics accused Bagot of 'swelling the sails of Puseyism' (Mead, 129).

Bagot struck a more critical note in his 1842 charge, which criticized theories by which 'the Articles may be made to mean anything or nothing', expressing fears and warnings for the disciples rather than leaders of the movement. In his later dealings with the Tractarians, over the poetry professorship contest in late 1841 and the controversy over the suspension of Pusey from preaching in 1843 for an unsound sermon on the eucharist, Bagot acted notably less sympathetically towards them. Although he could please neither side in the controversies, Bagot's careful line won the plaudits of high-church supporters of the movement such as William Palmer of Worcester, who dedicated his *Narrative of Events Connected with the Publication of the 'Tracts for the Times'* (1843) to the bishop.

Bagot's nervous character was a family trait, but whereas his elder brother gave way to nervous breakdowns, the bishop 'struggled to conceal the infirmity with all his power' (Ollard MSS). The strain of the Tractarian controversy, 'an ever present source of inward misery', finally took its toll. Bagot was for some years eager to be transferred from the Oxford diocese. The more candid among the Tractarians recognized that his going away would be perilous for them, and they hoped to avert it. By 1845, after pleading with the prime minister, Sir Robert Peel, and satisfying himself on the situation of the episcopal residence and the local climate, Bagot was translated to the see of Bath and Wells. He then suffered a complete nervous collapse. For a time his diocese was administered, in accordance with a special act of parliament, by the bishop of Gloucester and Bristol, Henry Monk. Bagot recovered, but the theological turmoil associated with the Oxford Movement pursued him to the last. In 1853–4 Bagot was caught up in the controversy involving one of his archdeacons, George Anthony Denison, whose teaching on the real presence in the eucharist was deemed inconsistent with Anglican formularies. Bagot differed from Denison in his interpretation of the church's eucharistic doctrine, but feared that low-church views of the sacrament would be sanctioned by any legal adjudication. Just before his death, the bishop put his hand to a quasi-censure or admonition of Denison; later, to the dismay of Bagot's family, Denison published his correspondence with Bagot, in which the bishop lamented Denison's speculations as to the eucharist. Latterly in failing health, Bagot died at Brighton on 15 May 1854, through 'a complication of disorders'. His wife survived him, and died on 18 October 1870. Newman offered a mass for the repose of her soul. PETER B. NOCKLES

Sources G. A. Solly, ed., *Rugby School register*, rev. edn, 1: *April 1675 – October 1857* (1933), 125 • Foster, *Alum. Oxon.* • Burke, *Peerage* • Pusey Oxf., Ollard papers • Pusey Oxf., Bagot papers, LBV 39, 71–2 • A. H. Mead, 'Richard Bagot, bishop of Oxford and the Oxford Movement, 1833–1845', DPhil diss., U. Oxf., 1965 • J. R. Garrard, 'William Howley (1766–1848): bishop of London, 1813–28, archbishop of Canterbury, 1828–48', DPhil diss., U. Oxf., 1992, esp. pp 320–35, 357, 410 • A. Burns, *The diocesan revival in the Church of England, c.1800–1870* (1999) • P. B. Nockles, 'Oxford, Tract 90 and the bishops', *John Henry Newman: reason, rhetoric and romanticism*, ed. D. Nicholls and F. Kerr (1991), 28–97

Archives Staffs. RO, corresp., family and institution papers | BL, corresp. with W. E. Gladstone, Add. MSS 44359–44372 • BL, corresp. with Sir Robert Peel, Add. MSS 40372–40584 • Keele University Library, Staffordshire, letters to Ralph Sneyd • Pusey Oxf., Denison MSS • Pusey Oxf., corresp. with Edward Pusey

Likenesses F. Grant, oils, 1846, Canterbury Cathedral, deanery • T. Y. Gooderson, portrait (after F. Grant, 1846), Canterbury Cathedral, deanery [*see illus.*] • H. W. Pickersgill, oils, All Souls Oxf. • oils, Blithfield Hall, Staffordshire

Bagot, Walter (*bap.* **1557**, *d.* **1623**). *See under* Bagot family (*per.* *c.*1490–1705).

Bagot, Sir Walter, third baronet (*bap.* **1645**, *d.* **1705**). *See under* Bagot family (*per.* *c.*1490–1705).

Bagot, Sir William (*d.* **1407**), administrator, came from a Staffordshire family, and was perhaps a younger brother of Sir John Bagot of Blithfield. He established himself as a landowner in Warwickshire by purchasing Baginton and two other manors in the 1380s, and by leasing Morehall from Stoneleigh Abbey. He also built up landed interests in Cheshire, in part by using a contrived pedigree. His wife, Margaret (*d.* 1417), was the sister and heir of Robert Whatton of Nottinghamshire, but she may not have come into her inheritance until after Bagot's death.

Bagot owed his early political rise and growing influence in Warwickshire largely to the patronage of Thomas Beauchamp, earl of Warwick (*d.* 1401), and in 1377 he was admitted with the earl to the confraternity of St Albans Abbey. However, he was also retained by John of Gaunt, duke of Lancaster (*d.* 1399), from before 1379, and when in 1384 he began a long dispute with one of Warwick's legal advisers, both Gaunt and Warwick arbitrated between them. While Gaunt was in Spain in 1386 Bagot became attached to his son, Henry Bolingbroke, earl of Derby (the future Henry IV), from whom he received livery. He had also formed a close relationship with the Mowbray earls of Nottingham. Before 1383 John (IV) Mowbray granted him for life the manor of Crick, Northamptonshire, worth £20 per annum, and he also enjoyed the lifelong confidence of Earl Thomas (*d.* 1399). Bagot was probably instrumental in persuading these young lords, Bolingbroke and Mowbray, to join the older lords appellant (Gloucester, Arundel, and

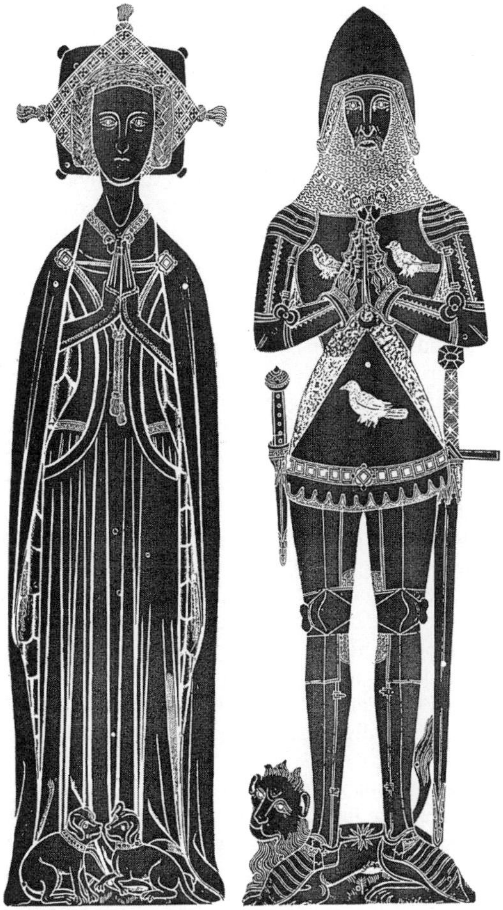

Sir William Bagot (*d.* 1407), memorial brass [with his wife, Margaret]

Warwick) in their attack on Richard II's favourites in December 1387, and the first of the eleven parliaments in which he represented Warwickshire was the Merciless Parliament of February 1388. Nevertheless, the king soon set about cultivating his support. He granted him the lordship of Middlewich, Cheshire, in 1389, and the keeping of Caernarfon Castle in 1390, and further signs of favour included valuable wardships and the stewardship of the manor of Cheylesmore, situated in the area of Warwickshire where Bagot was increasingly dominant.

A supreme opportunist, Bagot now allied himself more closely with the younger former appellants rather than with Warwick, who in 1391 brought a lawsuit against him for land at Walsall. He did not need to look to aristocratic influence to secure repeated election to parliament, and there were few who dared challenge his local interests. He emerged unscathed in 1395 when his disputes with the authorities at Coventry provoked an uprising, confounding an attempt to bring him to justice at the assizes at Warwick in 1396 by arrogantly riding into town at the head of his armed retainers. Indicted of several crimes, including homicide and maintenance, he was tried in king's bench but eventually acquitted. Bagot continued to serve Mowbray as his chief steward, general attorney, and lieutenant at the Marshalsea, and was named as his executor. Similarly, he preserved good relations with Bolingbroke, despite serious discrepancies in his accounts (for which he was temporarily imprisoned in Kenilworth Castle). He was still being paid as a member of Bolingbroke's entourage in June 1397.

In July 1397, when Gloucester, Arundel, and Warwick were arrested on Richard II's orders, Bagot was instructed to take possession of Warwick's goods, and in August the king granted him the substantial life annuity of £60. In the parliament assembled a month later he joined the speaker, Sir John Bussy (*d.* 1399), and Sir Henry Green, in formally requesting the annulment of the charters of pardon previously granted to the appellants, thus driving Richard's policies through the house. On 22 September, the day after Arundel's execution, he was appointed steward of the earl's confiscated lordships in the Welsh marches and constable of his castle at Holt. Furthermore, he was assigned a prominent place on the king's council to induce recalcitrants to pay fines. The subsequent quarrel between Mowbray and Bolingbroke cast doubt about where Bagot's loyalties lay. To dispel allegations of his involvement in a plot against Bolingbroke and his father, in March 1398 he entered bonds for £1000, payable in the event of his ever seeking to disinherit Gaunt or his progeny, and insisted that if he was ever proved party to the murder of one of them he should immediately be put to death without trial. In September Richard II lodged at Bagot's home, conveniently sited near Coventry where the duel between Mowbray and Bolingbroke was planned to take place, and in March 1399, following their exile, he retained Bagot as a councillor with a fee of £100 per annum.

When Richard II sailed for Ireland that spring Bagot was left behind with Bussy and Green to assist the duke of York in administering the kingdom. On receiving news of Bolingbroke's landing in Yorkshire they advised the removal of the government to St Albans, and safeguarded the queen at Wallingford Castle. Bagot raised 140 men to resist Bolingbroke, but retreated to Bristol at his approach, and although Bussy and Green were seized and executed he managed to escape by sea. Captured in Ireland, he was imprisoned in Knaresborough Castle and then in Newgate, before being sent on 16 October before the first parliament summoned by Henry IV. Bagot successfully defended himself against charges of plotting to kill Gaunt, and established through witnesses that during Henry's exile he had sent him intelligence about Richard II's plans, warning him of the confiscation of his Lancastrian inheritance. He staunchly defended Mowbray's reputation by exonerating him from any responsibility for the death of the duke of Gloucester. Henry showed leniency towards him by authorizing payment of an annuity of £100, although, wary of arousing popular feeling through any swift expression of clemency, he kept him incarcerated in the Tower of London for a year. Bagot was loosed from his chains in April 1400, and released seven months later. The Commons of February 1401 successfully petitioned for his restoration to law and property on the grounds that he had been falsely accused. Bagot again represented Warwickshire in parliament in 1402. He died on 6 September 1407 and was buried at Baginton church. The brass on his tomb showed him wearing the SS collar of Lancaster. About 1399 he had arranged the marriage of his only surviving child, Isabel, to Thomas Stafford, the nephew and heir of the chancellor, Edmund *Stafford, bishop of Exeter (*d.* 1419). When she failed to bear children his estates were sold. LINDA CLARK

Sources L. S. Woodger, 'Bagot, Sir William', HoP, *Commons* • C. L. Kingsford, ed., *Chronicles of London* (1905) • *RotP*, vol. 3 • N. H. Nicolas, ed., *Proceedings and ordinances of the privy council of England*, 7 vols., RC, 26 (1834–7), vol. 1 • W. Dugdale, *The antiquities of Warwickshire illustrated*, rev. W. Thomas, 2nd edn, 1 (1730), 231–2, 235 • *Thomae Walsingham, quondam monachi S. Albani, historia Anglicana*, ed. H. T. Riley, 2 vols., pt 1 of *Chronica monasterii S. Albani*, Rolls Series, 28 (1863–4), vol. 2, pp. 224, 232–3

Likenesses memorial brass, Church of St John the Baptist, Baginton, Warwickshire [*see illus.*]

Bagot, William, second Baron Bagot (1773–1856), antiquary, was the third son of William Bagot, first Baron Bagot (1728–1798), and Elizabeth Louisa St John (*d.* 1820), daughter of the second Viscount Bolingbroke. His brothers included Sir Charles *Bagot and Richard *Bagot. He was born in Bruton Street, London, on 11 September 1773. He was educated at Westminster School, and at Christ Church, Oxford, where he matriculated in 1791, but did not graduate. He received the honorary degree of DCL from the university in 1834. As the eldest surviving son, he succeeded to his father's title in 1798. Lord Bagot took an active interest in agriculture, natural history, and archaeology. He was a fellow of the Society of Antiquaries, and of the Linnean, Horticultural, and Zoological societies. In 1824 he published *Memorials of the Bagot Family*, containing a sketch of his ancestors, who had been Staffordshire landowners since the Norman conquest. He did not take an active part in politics, but gave consistent support to the tories, voting against reform in 1832. Lord Bagot was twice married. On 1 May 1799 he married the Hon. Emily Fitzroy, fourth daughter of Charles, first Baron Southampton. She died of consumption on 8 June 1800, having borne a daughter who died in infancy. On 17 February 1807 he married Lady Louisa Legge, eldest daughter of his cousin the third earl of Dartmouth; they had three sons and three daughters. After the death of his second wife, of typhus fever on 13 August 1816, Lord Bagot remained a widower until his death on 12 February 1856 at his home, Blithfield House, Abbots Bromley, Staffordshire.

T. F. HENDERSON, *rev.* K. D. REYNOLDS

Sources GEC, *Peerage* • *GM*, 2nd ser., 45 (1856), 422 • Foster, *Alum. Oxon.* • Boase, *Mod. Eng. biog.*

Archives Staffs. RO, corresp. and papers; family papers • William Salt Library, Stafford | Cumbria AS, O. R. Bagot MSS

Likenesses W. Bradley, pencil sketches, *c.*1838, Man. City Gall. • G. Clint, mezzotint (after J. Hoppner), BM • G. Hayter, group portrait, oils (*The trial of Queen Caroline, 1820*), NPG

Bagrit, Sir Leon (1902–1979), industrialist, was born on 13 March 1902 in Kiev, Ukraine, the younger son and second of three children of Manuel Bagrit, jewellery designer and jeweller, and his wife, Rachel Yousopovich. The family left Russia when he was a small child and arrived in London from Belgium in 1914. Bagrit knew no English then, but mastered it quickly, and soon gained a school prize for English literature at St Olave's School in Southwark, whose headmaster, W. G. Rushbrooke, took a close personal interest in the development of his many-sided gifts. These included music, and playing the violin in an orchestra helped him through the precarious early adult years.

After reading law at Birkbeck College, London University, Bagrit joined Messrs W. & T. Avery, manufacturers of weighing machines. He had no formal training in engineering but possessed an exceptional understanding of engineering and related matters which was vitally important to his subsequent career.

In 1926 he married Stella, daughter of Simon Feldman, businessman, and his wife, Rebecca. The couple had two daughters and seven grandchildren, to whom Bagrit was closely attached.

In 1927 Bagrit became general manager of a competitor, Herbert & Sons, leaving in 1935 to set up his own firm, B. & P. Swift, again in the weighing machine business, in order to exploit his own technical innovations. Its abilities were soon harnessed to the war effort, in aviation and other fields. In 1947 B. & P. Swift was acquired by Elliott Brothers (London) Ltd, of Lewisham, an old-established and substantially larger company, which had emerged from the war without a clear view of its future. Bagrit first became joint managing director, and not long afterwards sole managing director. At this point his undoubted flair for engineering was put to its greatest test, as he resolved to base the company's future on the introduction of automatic control as extensively as possible. He paid many visits to the United States, where important wartime developments had taken place and many of the basic ingredients of what subsequently became known as automation systems were already available.

If automation were to be introduced successfully over the widest possible field, a number of decisions of principle were vital in order to make the best use of financial and human resources. Particularly in the United States, licences were available to enable the firm's own large development effort to be concentrated elsewhere. Financial and organizational control over the multitude of facets involved in the business could be assured only by the creation of a large number of divisions or subsidiary companies under separate managements responsible for their success and controlled by a rigid system of budgets and monthly accounts—an approach which is commonplace today, but which Bagrit pioneered in Britain.

The company rapidly became successful, and in 1957 a merger with other, smaller, companies led to the establishment of Elliott-Automation Ltd, of which Bagrit was first deputy chairman and managing director, and from 1963 onwards chairman and managing director. He expanded the group's activities into Europe and other overseas territories. The company attracted investors in the United States and was one of the early UK stocks to be traded there in the ADR (American Depository Receipt) market. Bagrit's recognition in the City brought him part-time directorships, notably (in 1963) of the early technology-oriented investment trusts, Electronic Trust and Technology Investment Trust, which were later merged.

In 1967 Elliott-Automation, which by then employed about 24,000 people, was acquired by the English Electric Company, of which Bagrit became a deputy chairman. About a year later the English Electric Company was in turn acquired by the General Electric Company, and while Bagrit remained chairman of the company (later known as GEC–Elliott Automation Ltd) until 1973, he soon retired from an active role.

What distinguished Bagrit from other successful industrialists was his early recognition of the far-reaching problems in social and other fields which automation would bring about. He was confident that they could be solved, but not without active and detailed preparation. His thoughts were made public in 1964 through his Reith lectures entitled 'The age of automation', which were subsequently published as a book (1966). He had great breadth of vision and in business was more concerned with the broad sweep than with the detail, much of which he was happy to delegate to colleagues; however, there is no doubt of his ability to master detail when he considered it important. This approach left him time to pursue his many other interests. He was a director of the Royal Opera House, Covent Garden, from 1962 to 1970, and the founder of the Friends of Covent Garden, of which body he was chairman from 1962 to 1969. After his death Lady Bagrit created the Markova–Bagrit scholarship at the Royal Ballet School in London.

Bagrit was a notable collector in the field of visual arts. His close interest in the development of Israel centred particularly on the Haifa Technion (of whose British Friends he was president from 1962 to 1975), and on the Israel Museum. Lady Bagrit established a chair in his name for computer-aided design and scientific research development at Ben Gurion University.

Bagrit was knighted in 1962. He was a member of the Council for Scientific and Industrial Research from 1963 to 1965, and a member of the Advisory Council on Technology from 1964 to 1969. In 1965 the Royal Society of Arts awarded him the Albert medal for his work in the application of automation to industry. He received honorary doctorates from the universities of Surrey (1966) and Reading (1968). Bagrit died in London on 22 April 1979.

E. O. Herzfeld, *rev.*

Sources *The Times* (23 Nov 1979) • private information (1986) • personal knowledge (1986)

Wealth at death £2,276,444: administration with will, 19 March 1980, *CGPLA Eng. & Wales*

Bagshaw, Christopher (1552–1625?), Roman Catholic priest, was the son of George Bagshaw, a prosperous innkeeper in Lichfield, who came from a Derbyshire gentry family. His mother was Joanna, daughter of Richard Parsons. He seems to have matriculated at St John's College, Cambridge, in 1566, and then to have migrated to Balliol College, Oxford, where he became a probationer fellow in 1572, graduating BA in the same year and MA in 1575. While at Balliol he quarrelled with, and helped secure the ejection of, another fellow, Robert Persons, later the famous Jesuit. Balliol was noted for its Catholic tendencies, but Bagshaw was orthodox at this time and in 1579 he became principal 'or at least deputy for a time' (Wood, *Ath. Oxon.*, 2.390) of Gloucester Hall. He was also appointed a prebendary at Lichfield Cathedral, where his elder brother, a Church of England clergyman all his life, held a similar position. In 1582 Bagshaw left Oxford, travelling to the English College at Rheims, where in 1583 he was ordained as a Catholic priest. He was then sent to the English College at Rome, but was expelled from that institution in 1585. There is sufficient evidence that he was a difficult, irascible character who, being forced to live a collegial life in various places, found it almost impossible to do so without quarrelling with his fellows. It is fair to say, though, that much of the evidence for his love of faction and quarrels comes from his enemies, who seemed to be prepared to give as good as they got. He returned to Rheims from Rome, stopping briefly at Padua on the way, where he was awarded a doctorate of theology, presumably on the strength of his studies elsewhere.

Bagshaw then set out immediately in that same year of 1585 for England and was arrested within a very short time of his arrival in the country. He seems to have been carrying a letter to Scotland, sent by two agents of Mary, queen of Scots, in Paris, Charles Paget and the bishop of Ross. He was imprisoned in the Tower of London, where he stayed for about two years. He was a co-operative prisoner, and one of whom the government decided not to make an example. He was released, at least temporarily, in early 1588 and returned home to Lichfield. Then in March 1588 he was committed again to prison by the government, and sent to Wisbech Castle, Cambridgeshire, where he was to stay for the bulk of the next thirteen years. There were a number of Catholic priests interned at Wisbech, where they formed perforce a sort of college. At Wisbech there developed a quarrel between a group led by Bagshaw and one under another difficult character, the Jesuit William Weston. The 'Wisbech stirs' came to a head in 1595 and grew out of a series of disputes which had been brewing among English Catholics for at least fifteen years, and which were a matter of personalities, factions, strategy, and politics.

In 1598 Bagshaw became involved in the movement to overturn the appointment by the pope of the pro-Jesuit George Blackwell as archpriest. Bagshaw co-operated with the government to some degree in this, which may account for his being summoned to the Tower for a time in 1598, although it was also because he had been implicated in the Squire plot by an informant. Bagshaw was a leading figure among the opponents of Blackwell, who were known as appellants from their appeal to Rome against the appointment. He helped to concoct many of the memorials produced by the affair and composed or contributed to a number of the controversial pamphlets which the appellants published. His writings were characterized by extreme hatred of the Jesuits, especially of the leading English member of the society and erstwhile colleague of Bagshaw's at Oxford and Rome, Robert Persons.

Bagshaw was described in 1600 as being 'red-headed, gross and of low stature' (Anstruther). It was fitting that in 1601 he should be allowed by the government to be one of the party of four priests who set out to go to Rome on a second mission to appeal against Blackwell's appointment. Bagshaw got no further than Paris. Here he settled for the rest of his life, although there is a report that he was in Derbyshire in 1610. In 1612 he was involved in a public religious disputation with the English ambassador's chaplain in Paris, and, even according to the latter's report, gave a good account of himself. He is reported as having died in 1625. PETER HOLMES

Sources *DNB* • G. Anstruther, *The seminary priests*, 1 (1969) • Wood, *Ath. Oxon.*, new edn, 2.390, 675 • *The letters and memorials of William, Cardinal Allen (1532–1594)*, ed. T. F. Knox (1882), vol. 2 of *Records of the English Catholics under the penal laws* (1878–82), 205, 209, 378–80 • T. F. Knox and others, eds., *The first and second diaries of the English College, Douay* (1878) • T. G. Law, ed., *The archpriest controversy: documents relating to the dissensions of the Roman Catholic clergy, 1597–1602*, 2 vols., CS, new ser., 56, 58 (1896–8) • [C. Bagshaw], *A true relation of the faction begun at Wisbech* (1601) • P. Renold, ed., *The Wisbech stirs, 1595–1598*, Catholic RS, 51 (1958) • 'The memoirs of Father Persons', ed. J. H. Pollen, *Miscellanea, IV*, Catholic RS, 4 (1907), 1–161, 116–19 • L. Hicks, ed., *Letters and memorials of Father Robert Persons*, Catholic RS, 39 (1942), 200–01, 215–16 • *Letters of William Allen and Richard Barret, 1572–1598*, ed. P. Renold, Catholic RS, 58 (1967) • *Miscellanea, II*, Catholic RS, 2 (1906) • Gillow, *Lit. biog. hist.* • Venn, *Alum. Cant.* • C. Dodd [H. Tootell], *The church history of England, from the year 1500, to the year 1688*, 2 (1739), 67 • R. Tresswell and A. Vincent, *The visitation of Shropshire, taken in the year 1623*, ed. G. Grazebrook and J. P. Rylands, 1, Harleian Society, 28 (1889), 20 • R. Simms, ed., *Bibliotheca Staffordiensis* (1894), 38 • M. C. Questier, *Newsletters from the archpresbyterate of George Birkhead*, CS, 5th ser., 12 (1998)

Bagshaw, Edward (1589/90–1662), lawyer, was born in London, the second son of the London vintner Edward Bagshaw, whose family originated in Derbyshire, and his wife, probably named Mary Heming. Bagshaw's father died in 1597, and his mother then married the prominent Northamptonshire lawyer Augustine Nicholls. Although 1584 was traditionally given as his date of birth, Bagshaw was said to be fifteen in 1605 when he matriculated at Brasenose College, Oxford, where he was greatly influenced by his puritan tutor Robert Bolton. After proceeding BA in July 1608 Bagshaw was admitted to the Middle Temple and subsequently called to the bar in January 1616. His legal career prospered: in 1639 he was chosen a bencher of his inn, and that same year was appointed Lent reader. As his subject Bagshaw chose the medieval statute *Pro clero*, but his words attracted the attention of Archbishop Laud, who suspected a veiled attack upon the church. Despite Bagshaw's protestations, and his success in convincing Lord Keeper Finch of his sincerity, the readings were suspended after a threat of prosecution in the court of high commission.

Bagshaw sat for Southwark in the Long Parliament, in which he was a keen participant in ecclesiastical debates, condemning the canons of 1640 as *praemunire*, denouncing the *ex officio* oath, and complaining about the import of Catholic books. His eagerness to lard his speeches with details of ecclesiastical law and history was not always appreciated by his fellow MPs: D'Ewes described one as 'verie long, using discourse nothing pertinent to the matter in question' (*Journal*, ed. Notestein, 425). An orthodox Calvinist, Bagshaw rejected the defence of episcopacy *jure divino*, blaming the current problems upon certain bishops who had 'perverted the ways of godlinesse' (E. Bagshaw, *A Speech … Concerning the Triall of the Twelve Bishops*, 1642). Yet he defended true episcopacy, arguing that presbyterianism was incompatible with the common law. Already critical of the Scots, as the political crisis worsened Bagshaw moved towards the king's camp: in November 1641 he joined Hyde in speaking against the grand remonstrance and eventually he abandoned Westminster for Charles's parliament at Oxford. In June 1644, however, he was captured as a traitor and incarcerated in the king's bench prison, where he devoted his time to writing.

During the 1630s Bagshaw completed a biography of Robert Bolton and edited a number of his works, and he later published many of his own parliamentary speeches, together with a defence of his aborted Lent readings. Bagshaw set out his royalist political views in *The Rights of the Crown of England, as it is Established by Law* (1660), drafted in prison in 1644 but not published until the Restoration. In it he maintained that the crown's powers derived from God, but were assented to by the laws of England. No absolutist, Bagshaw reflected upon the experience of the 1640s and struggled to reconcile his high regard for the common law with the acknowledged powers of the king, 'inasmuch as the safety of the one, is the safety of the other' (pp. 116–17). In April 1645 he was released on bail, and soon thereafter returned to Northamptonshire, where he remained until his death in 1662 at Moreton Pinkney, where he was buried. Edward *Bagshaw (1629/30–1671), a prominent nonconformist minister, and Henry *Bagshaw, a Church of England clergyman, were his sons. P. R. N. CARTER

Sources C. Russell, *The fall of the British monarchies, 1637–1642* (1991) • J. P. Sommerville, *Politics and ideology in England, 1603–1640* (1986) • E. B. [E. Bagshaw], 'The life and death of the author', in *Mr Bolton's last and learned worke of the four last things*, ed. E. B. [E. Bagshaw], 3rd edn (1635) • C. Russell, *The causes of the English civil war* (1990) • *The journal of Sir Simonds D'Ewes from the beginning of the Long Parliament to the opening of the trial of the earl of Strafford*, ed. W. Notestein (1923) • C. H. Firth and R. S. Rait, eds., *Acts and ordinances of the interregnum, 1642–1660*, 3 vols. (1911) • W. R. Prest, *The rise of the barristers: a social history of the English bar, 1590–1640* (1986) • *CSP dom.*, 1635–45 • M. A. E. Green, ed., *Calendar of the proceedings of the committee for advance of money, 1642–1656*, 3 vols., PRO (1888) • Keeler, *Long Parliament*

Bagshaw, Edward (1629/30–1671), Independent minister and religious controversialist, was born at Broughton, Northamptonshire, the son of Edward *Bagshaw (*d.* 1662). After education at Westminster School, on 1 May 1646 he was elected to a studentship at Christ Church, Oxford, where he matriculated on 1 February 1647, aged seventeen. He graduated BA in 1649 and MA in 1651 (incorporated at Cambridge in 1654). Anthony Wood gives an account of his having been an unruly, intemperate, and provocative undergraduate, showing scant regard for authority or tradition, and of his having 'a turbulent and domineering' manner after graduation, addressing the vice-chancellor, John Owen, with his hat on (Wood, *Ath. Oxon.*, 3.944). Owen seems not to have taken offence, for through his good offices in 1656 Bagshaw was appointed second master at his old school, Westminster, under his old headmaster, Richard Busby. However, Bagshaw's habit of 'sitting with my Hat on at Church [i.e. in the abbey]' and his 'not overvaluing' Busby's Greek grammar (Bagshaw, 2) fuelled a quarrel with his superior over duties and responsibilities. Bagshaw was suspended by the governors, and finally expelled in May 1658. The episode prompted his apologetic *A True and Perfect Narrative of the Differences between Mr. Busby and Mr. Bagshawe* (1659).

After this disappointment Bagshaw returned to Oxford, 'propagating his Commonwealth Principles' according to Walter Pope, his 'Schoolfellow and intimate Friend', who describes Bagshaw as the ringleader of a move to abolish caps and hoods 'as Reliques of Popery' (Pope, 37, 40). On 25 August 1659 Bagshaw was presented to the vicarage of Ambrosden, Oxfordshire; on 3 November, rather surprisingly in the light of his later career, he was ordained by Ralph Brownrigg, bishop of Exeter. By 1661 Bagshaw had withdrawn from the established church and the living was vacant; in that year, too, he was deprived of his Christ Church studentship. In 1661 he became chaplain to Arthur Annesley, first earl of Anglesey, whom he accompanied to Ireland in July 1662. Prohibited from preaching by the archbishop of Dublin, James Margetson, and harassed for holding conventicles in his lodgings, he was released from Anglesey's service and returned to England in September 1662. In October he was reported as saying that 'the King only minded his mistresses', that 'popery was coming in', that London was 'much discontented' at the Bartholomew day ejections, that the Long Parliament was not lawfully dissolved, and that people would rather be governed by it than by the restored regime (*CSP dom.*, *1661–2*, 531–2). On 30 December a warrant was issued for him to be sent in custody to Secretary Henry Bennet. He was then living at Moreton Pinkney, Northamptonshire, presumably in the paternal home. Imprisoned first in the Gatehouse, Westminster, he was committed to the Tower for 'treasonable practices' on 16 January 1663, where, at the end of the month, a search of his room by the surveyor of the press, Roger L'Estrange, uncovered a manuscript in defence of a fellow prisoner named John Davis. This led to an interview with the king, 'who examined him of whom he had that Paper'. The boldness of Bagshaw's manner 'much offended' the king, 'whereupon he was sent back to the Tower, and laid in a deep, dark, dreadful dungeon' on 3 February 1664, whence, three days later, he was removed upon the intervention of his brother, the conformist minister Henry *Bagshaw (*Reliquiae Baxterianae*, 2.378). On 31 March 1664 a warrant was issued for his removal to Southsea Castle, Hampshire, 'an unwholesome place in the Sea by Portsmouth' (ibid.), where he arrived on 17 April. There his fellow prisoners included Vavasor Powell. In January 1666 it was reported that he refused to sue for pardon, but on 9 November 1667 a warrant was issued for his discharge. In 1669 a man of his name was reported to be preaching at Bicester in Oxfordshire, at Westbury in Buckinghamshire, at Wanlip in Leicestershire, and at Burton Dassett and Priors Marston in Warwickshire. In May 1671 he was sentenced at Middlesex sessions to detention in Newgate during the king's pleasure for refusing to take the oaths of allegiance and supremacy. He was still a prisoner, though not confined, when he died on 28 December 1671 at a house in Tuttle (Tothill) Street, Westminster. He was buried in Bunhill Fields; according to Wood, the inscription for his tombstone was composed by John Owen.

The intemperance which marked Bagshaw's encounters with superiors and with institutional authorities was a feature also of his literary career. He was a heated controversialist on behalf of nonconformist principles of an extreme congregational, even separatist, stamp. This brought him into conflict with Richard Baxter. In the tract which provoked the archbishop of Dublin to prohibit his preaching, *A Letter to a Person of Quality* (1662), Bagshaw had in fact intervened on Baxter's behalf in a controversy with Baxter's diocesan, George Morley, drawing upon himself the ire of Roger L'Estrange in *A Whipp, a Whipp for the Schismatical Animadverter* (1662); nevertheless, Bagshaw had none of Baxter's desire to minimize the nonconformists' separation from the established church nor his hope for eventual comprehension within the Church of England. On the contrary: Baxter's *The Cure of Church Divisions* (1670) drew from Bagshaw an *Antidote Against Mr. Baxters palliated Cure of Church Divisions* (1670) and, alternating with replies from Baxter, *A Defence of the Antidote* (1671) and *A Review and Conclusion of the Antidote* (1671), in which Bagshaw mocked what he took to be the inconsistencies of Baxter's 'middle way', rejected the legitimacy of parish churches, and refused to allow that occasional conformity to the episcopal church could be practised with integrity. In the *Review*, dated from Newgate 9 June 1671, he accused Baxter of having deserted 'the *Cause of Christ*, and *Non-conformity*' (E. Bagshaw, *A Review and Conclusion of the Antidote*, 1671, 4).

Theologically, Bagshaw was an extreme Calvinist with (though he denied this) antinomian tendencies and Fifth Monarchist sympathies. In such tracts as *A Practical Discourse Concerning Gods Decrees* (1659) and *The Doctrine of Free-Grace* (1662) he argued strenuously for double predestination and a limited atonement against the 'Arminian' doctrines of free will, conditional election, and universal redemption which he detected in such adversaries as Thomas Pierce. The *Practical Discourse* was dedicated to the regicide John Bradshaw, whereby, in the view of an episcopalian commentator, Bagshaw had 'unhappily nail'd himself down to a very harsh Doctrine, and to a very odious Patron' (Kennett, 603). Baxter described him as 'an Anabaptist, Fifth Monarchy man, and a Separatist, and a man of an extraordinary vehement spirit, who had been exasperated by many years hard and grievous imprisonment' (R. Baxter, *Apology for the Nonconformist Ministry*, 1681, 162). Though he could not approve that Bagshaw 'sided Tooth and Nail with the Fanatics', Walter Pope acknowledged Bagshaw's 'Natural and acquir'd parts' (Pope, 41). He had 'a great Reputation in the University as a Scholar', says Calamy (Calamy, *Abridgement*, 2.542), and he managed his controversial prose with pungency and forcefulness. At a date after 1665 Bagshaw had married Margaret (*d.* 1672), the blind second daughter of John Peacock, of Chawley, Cumnor, Berkshire, 'who fell in love with him for his preaching' (Pope, 41). There were no children.

N. H. KEEBLE

Sources E. Bagshaw, *A true and perfect narrative of the differences between Mr Busby and Mr Bagshawe* (1659) • *Reliquiae Baxterianae, or, Mr Richard Baxter's narrative of the most memorable passages of his life and times*, ed. M. Sylvester, 1 vol. in 3 pts (1696) • E. Calamy, ed., *An abridgement of Mr. Baxter's history of his life and times, with an account of the ministers, &c., who were ejected after the Restauration of King Charles II*, 2nd edn, 2 vols. (1713), vol. 2, pp. 542–3 • E. Calamy, *A continuation of the account of the ministers … who were ejected and silenced after the Restoration in 1660*, 2 vols. (1727), vol. 2, p. 719 • *CSP dom.*, 1661–2, 287, 531–2, 606; 1663–4, 2, 4, 8, 14, 461, 466, 469, 471, 536, 547; 1664–5, 545; 1665–6, 191; 1667, 475; 1667–8, 14 • *Calendar of the correspondence of Richard Baxter*, ed. N. H. Keeble and G. F. Nuttall, 2 vols. (1991) • *Calamy rev.* • W. Pope, *The life of the right reverend father in God, Seth, lord bishop of Salisbury* (1697); repr. as *The life of Seth, Lord Bishop of Salisbury*, ed. J. B. Bamborough (1961), 37–42 • G. L. Turner, ed., *Original records of early nonconformity under persecution and indulgence*, 3 vols. (1911–14), vol. 2, pp. 767, 797, 798, 832; vol. 3, p. 827 • Wood, *Ath. Oxon.*, new edn, 3.944–50 • Wood, *Ath. Oxon.: Fasti* (1820), 120, 165 • E. Bensly, 'Edward Bagshawe the younger', *N&Q*, 13th ser., 1 (1923), 96 • *Fourth report*, HMC, 3 (1874), 192 • *Seventh report*, HMC, 6 (1879), 104 • *The manuscripts of the duke of Leeds*, HMC, 22 (1888), 7 • W. Kennett, *A register and chronicle ecclesiastical and civil* (1728), 603, 609, 784–6 • J. Bridges, *The history and antiquities of Northamptonshire*, ed. P. Whalley, 2 (1791), 87–8 • Foster, *Alum. Oxon.*, 1500–1714 [Edward Bagshawe] • J. Sargeaunt, *Annals of Westminster School* (1898), 85–8

Bagshaw, Henry (1631x4–1709), Church of England clergyman, was born at Broughton, Northamptonshire, a younger son of the lawyer Edward *Bagshaw (1589/90–1662), an opponent of Laudianism who in the divisions which arose in the early 1640s became a defender of episcopacy and royalist. The noted Independent minister Edward *Bagshaw was an elder brother of Henry. The year of Henry's birth remains uncertain, as there is a contradiction between his reported ages at matriculation of seventeen in 1651 and at death of seventy-seven in 1709.

After attending Westminster School, Henry Bagshaw was elected a student of Christ Church, Oxford, in 1651, graduating BA in 1655 and proceeding MA in 1657. In 1663 he was appointed chaplain to Sir Richard Fanshawe, ambassador to Portugal and then Spain. Bagshaw preached the ambassador's funeral sermon in Madrid and returned to England in the retinue of his widow, Anne, Lady Fanshawe, and became chaplain to Richard Sterne, archbishop of York. He was collated in turn to the prebends of Barnby in York Minster in August 1667 and Fridaythorpe in May 1668, and resigned the latter in July 1670. Thanks to Sterne's influence he was also made a prebendary of Southwell Minster in 1668 and rector of Carlton in Lyndrick, Nottinghamshire. He was created BD in 1668 and DD in 1671.

In 1672 Bagshaw was made chaplain to Lord Treasurer Danby and rector of St Botolph without Bishopsgate, London. In April 1674 he married Mary Nicholls (*b.* 1647/8), the daughter of Sir Edward Nicholls, baronet, of Foxton, Northamptonshire. Two of his children were baptized at St Botolph without Bishopsgate, in 1676 and 1677. In the latter year he exchanged his London parish for Houghton-le-Spring, co. Durham, and in 1680 he was appointed a prebendary of Durham. Further children were baptized in Durham Cathedral (in 1684, 1688 and 1690), Houghton-le-Spring (1685), and (perhaps) St Andrew's, Holborn (in 1682). However, of the children known to have been born, nothing is known of the fate of the two or three daughters; only one of the four sons, Edward Bagshaw, seems to have survived.

Bagshaw was renowned for his pulpit oratory and published a number of sermons. In 1673 he preached before the lord mayor *The Excellency of Primitive Government*, which—suitably enough for a sermon upon the mayor's election—expounded the duty of the magistrate to create a faithful and righteous city. In 1676 he published *A Sermon Preached before the King at Whitehall* on Psalm 37, and in 1680 his *Diatribae, or, Discourses upon Select Texts*, in which he discussed what were in his view the 'two great enemies to Christianity, … the Papist and the Socinian' (epistle dedicatory). Bagshaw died at Houghton-le-Spring on 30 December 1709, and was buried in the chancel of the church.

T. F. HENDERSON, *rev.* CAROLINE L. LEACHMAN

Sources Wood, *Ath. Oxon.*, new edn, 4.631 • W. Hutchinson, *The history and antiquities of the county palatine of Durham*, 2 (1787), 206 • Foster, *Alum. Oxon.* • *IGI* • J. L. Chester and J. Foster, eds., *London marriage licences, 1521–1869* (1887) • J. Welch, *The list of the queen's scholars of St Peter's College, Westminster*, ed. [C. B. Phillimore], new edn (1852) • *Fasti Angl., 1541–1857*, [York]

Bagshawe [Bagshaw], **William** [*called* the Apostle of the Peak] (**1628–1702**), Presbyterian minister, was born on 17 January 1628 at Litton in the parish of Tideswell, Derbyshire, and baptized on 19 January at Tideswell, the eldest son of William Bagshawe (*d.* 1669), yeoman of Litton, and his first wife, Jane, daughter of Raphe Oldfield of Litton. Educated at a number of local schools, his religious development was greatly influenced by two local clergyman, John Rowlandson, vicar of Bakewell, and Immanuel Bourne, vicar of Ashover. By the age of fifteen Bagshawe believed that he had a call to the ministry. Although his father, who eventually became a wealthy landowner in the Peak and took the title of gentleman, had communicated his own puritan beliefs to his son, he sought to dissuade him from a clerical career. When the elder Bagshawe's efforts failed he partially disinherited his son. William matriculated in 1646 as a sizar from Corpus Christi College, Cambridge. In 1648 he preached his first sermon and served as a probationer at Wormhill, Tideswell, for several months. At the age of twenty-one he was appointed as an assistant minister to James Fisher at Sheffield and also served as a domestic chaplain to Colonel John Bright at nearby Attercliffe. Bagshawe was ordained at the Chesterfield classis on 1 January 1650 with his former spiritual mentor Bourne serving as temporary moderator. On 11 June 1650 he married Agnes (*d.* 1701), daughter of Peter Barker of Darley, Yorkshire, with whom he had two sons, John (*b.* 1654) and Samuel (*b.* 1656).

Admitted to the living at Glossop, Derbyshire, on 31 December 1651, Bagshawe was to remain in the parish for nearly twelve years. On 20 March 1654 he was voted assistant to the Classical Assembly, representing the hundred of Low Peak. During his ministry at Glossop he wrote at least three works, two of which are no longer extant. The most significant of these was probably his *Brief Directions for the Improvement of Infant Baptism* (1658), which contemporaries claimed showed that Bagshawe limited baptism to the children of believers and performed the ordinance in public worship, preceding it with a sermon. Edmund Calamy wrote of Bagshawe that 'His Administration of the Sacraments, especially that of the Lord's Supper was with great solemnity and care' (Calamy, *Abridgement*, 2.198). Over this period he also acquired a reputation locally for being a considerable theologian and conscientious pastor.

Unable to conform at the Restoration, Bagshawe was ejected from his living in 1662 and retired to his father's estate at Ford Hall, Chapel-en-le-Frith, Derbyshire. Though a committed presbyterian, he was also a partial conformist and for 'several years attended the Publick Worship in his Parish-Church, both parts of the Lord's Day' (Calamy, *Abridgement*, 2.199). At the same time he continued his preaching activities, often travelling over huge tracts of sparsely inhabited Pennine moorland to be present at conventicles, earning for himself the name the Apostle of the Peak. In 1669 Bagshawe's father died and although his inheritance had been considerably reduced on entering the ministry he did come into possession of the Ford Hall estate. From 1670 he enjoyed a greater degree of financial independence and Ford Hall became a focus for presbyterian activity in the Peak region. At the declaration of indulgence in 1672 Bagshawe took out a licence to preach as a presbyterian at any licensed building and regularly conducted worship at Glossop, Ashford, Malcoffe, Middleton, Bradwell, Chelmorton, Hucklow, and Ford Hall. During the late 1670s several warrants were issued against him, but he managed to avoid arrest and appeared to enjoy a degree of protection from sympathetic local magistrates.

Between 1672 and 1702 Bagshawe wrote a further sixteen works, although only eight of these were published during his lifetime and seven were never published. His literary output was considerable and at his death he left an enormous mass of manuscripts that amounted to fifty volumes, folio, quarto, and duodecimo. The most significant of his later publications were *De spiritualibus pecci* and his *Essays on Union to Christ*, which was published posthumously. The former provided an account of the development of protestantism in north Derbyshire, and gives an insight into Bagshawe's attitude towards his flock. While he praised the godly clergy and gentry of the Peak he also noted the 'scarcity paucity & scarceness' of his co-religionists among other groups, singling out the local lead miners for particular condemnation (Wood, 191). Nevertheless presbyterian strength in Derbyshire owed a great deal to his evangelistic endeavours. From the Act of Toleration (1689) until his death, he preached regularly to ten congregations. During this period Ford Hall was used over the summer months as a centre for study and prayer for Derbyshire presbyterians. Early in 1688 Bagshawe allowed the hall to be used as an academy for training presbyterian ministers and appointed Samuel Ogden to serve as a tutor alongside himself. When the better-equipped academy at Attercliffe became established, Bagshawe felt no qualms in closing down and sending his students there.

From 1698 Bagshawe's health began to deteriorate and his preaching activities became increasingly focused upon Ford Hall, though he continued to visit his congregations as often as he could. On 15 October 1701 he had his will drawn up and in November that year his wife, Agnes, died. Bagshawe died on Wednesday 1 April 1702 after a brief illness and was buried in the chancel of Chapel-en-le Frith parish church on 5 April. On his deathbed, hearing those around him lament that he could not preach to his congregation as usual he replied 'my silence is a sermon'. His nephew, the Revd John *Ashe of Ashford, who subsequently published a life and character of Bagshawe in 1704, preached his funeral sermon. This work is the main source of information about the Apostle of the Peak. In his will, Bagshawe made charitable bequests to four Derbyshire parishes. The inventory of his goods amounted to £268 8*s.*, of which his considerable library was valued at £152 10*s.* STUART B. JENNINGS

Sources J. Ashe, *A short account of the life and character of the Rev Mr William Bagshawe* (1704) • W. H. G. Bagshawe, *A memoir of William Bagshawe of Ford Hall* (1887) • *Calamy rev.* • will, 1702, Lichfield RO • E. Calamy, ed., *An abridgement of Mr. Baxter's history of his life and times, with an account of the ministers, &c., who were ejected after the Restauration of King Charles II*, 2nd edn, 2 vols. (1713) • J. M. Brentnall, *William Bagshawe, the Apostle of the Peak* (1970) • W. Braylesford Bunting, *Chapel-en-le-Frith: its history and its people* (1940) • J. Clegg, *The life of the Rev. John Ashe* (1736) • parish register, Tideswell, 19 Jan 1628, Derbys. RO [baptism] • A. Wood, *The politics of social conflict: the Peak country, 1520–1770* (1999) • *DNB* • Venn, *Alum. Cant.*
Archives JRL, muniments
Wealth at death £268 8*s.*: will, 1702, Lichfield RO

Bagster, Samuel, the elder (1772–1851), publisher and author, was born in Eagle Street, Red Lion Square, Holborn, London, on 26 December 1772, the second eldest of the five sons and two daughters of George Bagster (1739–1819), a businessman, and his wife, Mary, *née* Denton (1738–1823). He was educated from 1779 to 1783 at the Revd John Ryland's Northampton school, moving in 1783 to a day school at Hammersmith, run by Dr Morgan Jones. After three years he was apprenticed to William Otridge at 134 Strand.

Bagster was overjoyed when on 8 February 1794 his father bought the lease of a confectionery and pastry shop that was closing down at 81 Strand. He commenced business there as a general bookseller on 19 April 1794 and within an hour had sold a forty-five-volume set of Johnson's *Poets*. On 19 December 1797 he married Eunice Birch (1777–1877) whom he had met at a preaching rally led by William Romaine. They had nine sons, including Samuel *Bagster the younger, and three daughters; six of the children survived infancy.

Business at the Strand was brisk. In 1813 a humorous incident occurred with the publisher John Murray. Murray had contacted Bagster by letter, with a detailed proposition about some books. Bagster then called on Murray at Albemarle Street to explain why he would not be able to take on the venture. Murray was out, so Bagster left a note: 'Finding you out—I decline your offer, S.B.' A few hours later a distraught Murray rushed in to see Bagster, spluttering, 'Pray Sir! What have you found me out in doing?' After Bagster explained, the two laughed at the misunderstanding.

Bagster was determined to meet the need for inexpensive polyglot bibles. A Hebrew Bible and Septuagint, both in foolscap octavo, soon appeared, but the production of English bibles was a monopoly in the United Kingdom, confined to the king's printers in England, Scotland, and Ireland, and to the universities of Oxford and Cambridge. However, the patent did not apply to bibles with printed notes. In 1816 Bagster produced *The English Version of the Polyglot Bible* with a preface by T. Chevalier and over 60,000 parallel references, most selected and all verified by Bagster. He also attended to the minutest detail, even down to the choice of thread for sewing the sheets together.

In 1816 Bagster moved his premises to 16 Paternoster Row. The following year saw the issue of the *Biblia sacra polyglotta Bagsteriana*, which was completed in four volumes. It was a very thorough production and included the prolegomena of Dr Samuel Lee, the Hebrew Old Testament, the Samaritan Pentateuch, the Septuagint Greek version of the Old Testament, the Latin Vulgate, the authorized English 1611 version, the Greek *textus receptus* of the New Testament, and the Peshito or ancient Syriac version. Two other forms of the English Bible were issued, beginning the Facsimile Series. The publication of the polyglot was followed in 1821 by an octoglot edition of the liturgy of the Church of England; this Bagster presented to George IV in the year of its publication. In 1828 the archbishop of Canterbury, William Howley, presented Bagster to William IV.

A two-day fire destroyed the building at Paternoster Row on 1 and 2 March 1822. The stock, too, was all but ruined. Only the deeds and twenty-three copies of the New Testament were preserved. Inadequate insurance cover with the Sun Fire company raised £500 and a further £140 was gained by selling 20 tons in weight of ruined papers. To recover from the shock of the fire Bagster and his wife travelled around Europe in 1823, returning in September.

A friendship and working relationship with the self-taught orientalist William Greenfield began in 1822. In 1827 Bagster's *Comprehensive Bible*, edited by Greenfield, with 4000 illustrative notes, 500,000 marginal references, and a general introduction, was published. A number of other scholarly biblical works, all edited by Greenfield, were printed by Bagster. When Greenfield died Bagster wrote an account of his life in the *Imperial Magazine* (1834). The firm's motto, *Multae terricolis linguae, coelestibus una* ('Many tongues for those on earth, one for those in heaven'), believed to be by Greenfield, was inscribed in both Greek and Latin on Greenfield's tomb.

In 1837 Bagster encouraged Isaac Pitman (1813–1897) to invent a new shorthand system. *Stenographic Sound-Hand* was the result, and established Pitman's reputation. Other notable works published by Bagster include *The English Hexapla* (1841) containing six translations of the New Testament: those of Wyclif (1380), Tyndale (1534), and Cranmer (1539), and the Genevan (1557), the Anglo-Rhemish (1582), and the King James (1611) versions. They were arranged side by side for easy comparison and reference. Also included was a Greek version and an account of the English translations. This led to Bagster's publishing an account tracing the history of the English version of the scriptures from the Anglo-Saxon to the 1611 translation. His *Daily Light on the Daily Path, a Devotional Textbook* (1841) proved popular.

Samuel Bagster died at his home at Old Windsor, Berkshire, on 28 March 1851 and was buried in April in the family vault at Abney Park cemetery, Stoke Newington, Middlesex. His wife survived him by some twenty-six years, reaching the age of 100. Jonathan (1813–1872), his tenth child, followed him as senior member of the firm.

H. R. TEDDER, *rev.* J.-M. ALTER

Sources T. H. Horne, *An introduction to the critical study and knowledge of the holy scriptures* (1822) • W. T. Lowndes, *The bibliographer's manual of English literature*, ed. H. G. Bohn, [new edn], 6 vols. (1864) • *The Bookseller* (Feb 1880) • *GM*, 2nd ser., 35 (1851), 567 • J. Kitto, ed., *Journal of sacred literature*, 3rd ser., 3 (1856), 1,327 • S. Bagster, *Samuel Bagster of London, 1772–1851: an autobiography* (1972) • A. Baker, *The life of Sir Isaac Pitman* (1894) • T. H. Horne, *A manual of biblical bibliography* (1839) • d. cert. • *IGI*

Likenesses J. Linney, portrait, repro. in Bagster, *Samuel Bagster*

Bagster, Samuel, the younger (1800–1835), printer and author, was born in the Strand, London, on 19 October 1800, the eldest surviving son of Samuel *Bagster (1772–1851) and his wife, Eunice, *née* Birch (1777–1877). His two elder brothers died in infancy. He was educated at a school in Oxford, led by the Revd James Hinton, and was articled to his father's publishing business in 1815. He showed a keen interest in religion from an early age and in October 1822 became a member of Blackfriars Baptist Church. After acquiring technical training in his father's publishing house Bagster started his own printing business in Bartholomew Close in 1824. After a brief courtship he married Elizabeth Hunt (*d.* 1879) on 22 June 1825.

Bagster divided his time between printing, writing, social causes, and hobbies. He was a keen bee-keeper and poultry breeder. In 1831 he wrote and printed *The Management of Bees*, with forty wood-engravings. Published jointly by his father and William Pickering, the work was popular and highly thought of. Two further editions were published in 1838 and 1865. Bagster had been given the idea from a work by Samuel Purchas, son of the author of *Purchas, his Pilgrimes* (1624–5), entitled *A Theatre of Politicall Flying-Insects* (1657). Published in two parts, it described the history and management of bees and provided 'meditations and observations, theological and moral' upon the subject, which were reprinted by Bagster at the same time as his own work on bees.

Bagster contributed to his father's polyglot series *The Treasury of Scripture Knowledge* [*c*.1833/4]. This consisted of 'a rich and copious assemblage of more than 500,000 scripture references and parallel passages from Canne, Brown, Blayney, Scott, and others'. He also projected and planned to produce a series of questions on the gospels for Sunday school children, but the manuscript remained unfinished. Initially concerns about business worried Bagster, but within a few years he had established himself with many of the polyglot bibles and various other publications that came from his press.

Continued poor health induced Bagster to move to Aldine Cottage in the then rural Shepherd's Bush, where he continued his bee-keeping and poultry breeding. The Bagsters were active in the work of the local Baptist chapel. Bagster campaigned against the slave trade and for temperance, and wrote a number of pamphlets on the latter cause.

Bagster's health deteriorated during 1835; by early June he was extremely weak and was nursed by his wife at Aldine Cottage. Bagster sought to comfort his aged father with the words: 'I shall be in heaven before you'. On 1 July 1835, at the age of thirty-four, he died at his home; he left no children. He was buried at Tottenham Court Chapel, London.

In 1837 the Revd John Broad published a *Memoir of the Life and Christian Experience of Samuel Bagster, Junr.*

Bagster's remains were reinterred in 1843 in the family vault at Abney Park cemetery, Stoke Newington, Middlesex. H. R. TEDDER, *rev.* J.-M. ALTER

Sources J. Broad, *Memoir of the life and Christian experience of Samuel Bagster, junr.* (1837) • *Literary Gazette* (1834), 753 • S. Bagster, *Samuel Bagster of London, 1772–1851: an autobiography* (1972) • private information (1885) • *IGI*

Bagutti, Giovanni (*b.* **1681**, *d.* in or after **1731**). *See under* Artari, Giuseppe (1692/1700–1769).

Bagwell, Richard (**1840–1918**), historian, was born on 9 December 1840 in Marlfield House, Clonmel, co. Tipperary. He was the eldest son of John Bagwell, MP for Clonmel (1857–74), and his wife, Frances Eliza, *née* Prittie. He had one brother and four sisters. He was educated at Harrow School and Christ Church, Oxford, and was called to the bar at the Inner Temple in 1866. On 9 January 1873 he married Harriette Philippa Newton; they had one son and three daughters. He never practised as a lawyer but returned to live in Ireland, where he succeeded his father as owner of Marlfield House in 1883.

Bagwell believed in the positive contribution which resident Irish landlords made to Irish society and participated fully in local government in co. Tipperary. He was elected high sheriff of the county in 1869 and subsequently served as justice of the peace, magistrate, and foreman of the grand jury for co. Tipperary. In 1898 he was appointed a member of the Local Government Board, whose task was to supervise the implementation of the Local Government Act of that year. He was also a founding member of the Irish Loyal and Patriotic Union (ILPU), an organization of southern unionists formed in 1885 to resist home rule for Ireland and he remained a prominent member of the ILPU and the later Irish Unionist Alliance until his death in 1918. In the 1880s and 1890s he attended many public meetings in England, speaking in favour of the union, and he wrote pamphlets for the Irish Unionist Alliance, although most of these were published anonymously and none can now be attributed to him.

It was during the years before he took over the running of the Marlfield estate in 1883 that Bagwell did much of the research for *Ireland under the Tudors* (3 vols., 1885–90). He made use of the printed calendars of state papers in the first volume but the second volume required a considerable amount of research in the Public Record Office in London. Unionist business must have absorbed a great deal of his time in the 1880s and 1890s but he still continued his historical research. Research for the third volume was completed in between attending public meetings in England. His involvement in public affairs also helps to explain why *Ireland under the Stuarts* (3 vols., 1909–16) was not as satisfactory in terms of research as the Tudor volumes. Apart from his six volumes on Tudor and Stuart Ireland, his only other major historical work was to contribute entries on seventeenth-century Irish subjects to the *Dictionary of National Biography*.

From the first appearance of *Ireland under the Tudors* in 1885, Bagwell earned a reputation for objectivity and impartiality as a historian, a judgement which seems curiously at odds with his political commitment to unionism and landlord power in Ireland. A close analysis of his historical writings reveals, however, that he shared with W. E. H. Lecky a concern to refute James Anthony Froude's interpretation of Irish history. Froude's polemical views on Irish history, which he expressed first in his *History of England from the Fall of Wolsey to the Defeat of the Spanish Armada* (1856–70) and later in *The English in Ireland in the Eighteenth Century* (1881), had shocked many people in Ireland, particularly the intellectual élite within the Anglo-Irish community. Froude had made clear his contempt for the historical legacy of the Anglo-Irish, holding them and their ancestors responsible for what he perceived to be the chaotic state of nineteenth-century Ireland. W. E. H. Lecky, Bagwell, and G. H. Orpen all wrote their histories partly in response to Froude and all three endeavoured to restore the reputation of the Anglo-Irish as fair and responsible rulers whose presence assisted rather than hindered the development of law and order in Ireland.

Bagwell's support for the union as the most equitable system of government for Ireland never wavered. In 1917 he was prominent among those who opposed the compromise agreement of the southern unionist representatives at the Irish convention which allowed for a scheme for the government of Ireland. He died at Marlfield House on 4 December 1918 at the age of seventy-seven. In 1923 Marlfield House was burnt by republican forces in the Irish civil war. The fire destroyed both his library and his historical papers. MARY O'DOWD

Sources *WWW* • M. O'Dowd and C. Brady, 'Richard Bagwell' [unpub article] • Annual reports of the Irish Loyal and Patriotic Union, 1886–1920 • G. H. Bassett, *The book of county Tipperary* (1889) • P. Buckland, *Irish unionism*, 1: *The Anglo-Irish and the new Ireland* (1972) • W. P. Burke, *History of Clonmel* (1907); repr. (1983) • Burke, *Gen. Ire.* • J. Foster, *Men-at-the-bar: a biographical hand-list of the members of the various inns of court*, 2nd edn (1885) • A. Jackson, *The Ulster party: Irish unionists in the House of Commons, 1884–1911* (1989) • H. Robinson, *Memories, wise and otherwise* (1923) • S. Rosenbaum, ed., *Against home rule: the case for union* (1912)
Archives NL Ire. • Representative Church Body Library, Dublin | PRO NIre., Montgomery MSS
Likenesses Elliott & Fry, photograph, repro. in Rosenbaum, ed., *Against home rule* (1912)

Bagwell, William (*b. c.*1593, *d.* in or after **1664**), merchant and writer on astronomy, was, according to his own account, 'bred a merchant in good quality, skilfully furnished with knowledge in all things necessary, and having seen the world abroad' (Bagwell, *Mystery*, introduction). For several years he had carried on an extensive trade, when losses overseas led to his being sent to prison for debt. By 1654 he had been in and out of prison for twenty years. He relieved the tedium of imprisonment by writing 'An arithmetical description of the celestial and terrestrial globes' (BL, Sloane MSS 652, fols. 141–4), a treatise which he did not publish, believing it to be too abstruse for general use but nevertheless worthy to be placed in a university. After being set at liberty and found employment by some friends he published a simplified version of this treatise as *The Mystery of Astronomy Made Plain to the Meanest Capacity* (1655). This work is a natural philosophical text concerning geography, topography, and astronomy, which is mainly of interest in propounding the Aristotelian view of the universe at a relatively late date.

Bagwell was so affected by the discipline of his confinement that he published, in poetical form, *The Distressed Merchant, and Prisoner's Comfort* (1645); this was caricatured by the royalist Edmund Gayton in his *Wil Bagnal's ghost, or, The merry devill of Gadmunton in his perambulations of the prisons of London* (1655), and also in 'Wil Bagnalls Ballet' included in the collection entitled *Wit Restor'd* (1658). In 1660 Bagwell published another short poem, *An Affectionate Expostulation for the Pious Employment both of Wit and Wealth*. He is last heard of in 1664 when his collection of riddles and aphorisms entitled *Wit's Extraction* was published. This contains his portrait, engraved in 1659 and with an inscription giving his age as sixty-six.

Bagwell's name appears to be associated with *A concealement discovered for the publique advantage … the effect of a petition directed to the … Councell of State for the Common-wealth of England, by Will. Bagnell and John Brockendon, discoverers and plaintiffs in the behalf of the said Common-wealth* (1652), but it is possible that this William Bagnell was another person. T. F. HENDERSON, *rev.* H. K. HIGTON

Sources W. Bagwell, *The mystery of astronomy made plain* (1655) • W. Bagwell, *The distressed merchant and prisoner's comfort* (1645) • J. Granger, *A biographical history of England from Egbert the Great to the revolution*, 5th edn, 6 vols. (1824) • W. Bagwell, *Wit's extraction* (1664) • Burke, *Gen. Ire.*
Likenesses Gaywood, engraving, 1659, repro. in Bagwell, *Wit's extraction*

Baikie, William Balfour (**1825–1864**), traveller and surgeon, eldest son of Captain John Baikie RN, was born in Kirkwall, Orkney, on 27 August 1825 and educated privately and at the grammar school there. After taking his degree in medicine at Edinburgh, he entered the Royal Navy in 1848 as assistant surgeon. He served on the *Volage*, *Vanguard*, *Ceylon*, *Medusa*, and *Hibernia* in the Mediterranean, and then as assistant surgeon at the Haslar Hospital, Portsmouth, from 1851 to 1854. In 1852 he won the support of Sir Roderick Murchison for a South American expedition up New Granada's Magdalena River, which, however, never came to fruition. Murchison later procured for him the post of surgeon and naturalist to the Niger expedition of 1854, which tried to ascend the Niger in a purpose-built steamer, the *Pleiad*, and form a trading settlement in the interior. On the death of John Beecroft at Fernando Po, Baikie took command of the expedition. He demonstrated the navigability of the Niger and the value of quinine as a prophylactic against malaria. He clarified the topography of the area, providing information for a map by John Arrowsmith. His *Narrative of an Exploring Voyage up the … Niger and Isadda* (1856) gives a good account of his journey, but was criticized for understating the importance of the Royal Geographical Society in the expedition, an oversight which Baikie was careful to correct in his later publications.

The expedition returned to England in February 1855. Murchison and Baikie, who had returned to the Haslar Hospital, immediately began a successful campaign for a second expedition, which set off in 1857. Baikie had particular instructions to investigate the geology of the area for scientific and commercial ends. He went up the Niger in the iron steamer *Day Spring*, but was shipwrecked at the Bussa rapids. However, he bought land at Lokoja at the confluence of the Kwòra and Chàdda or Benué and soon had a considerable settlement there, which remained under his authority after the abandonment of a scheme to bring it under government control as part of a drive to secure cotton supplies. He explored the surrounding countryside and persuaded the king of Nupé, the next powerful sovereign to the sultan of Sakatù, to help the passage of traders by land and river to Lokoja. He opened up the navigation of the Niger, made roads, and established a regular market. The more ambitious schemes for exploiting the Niger came to nothing, however, and Baikie was called home for health reasons, but died *en route* at Sierra Leone on 12 December 1864. Baikie was far more scholarly than most African travellers, and his numerous books and articles in the journals of learned societies, published in his lifetime and posthumously, cover a wide range of topics; he wrote on the history and natural history of Orkney, and works on and in African languages, in which he had become interested on his second visit to the continent.

STANLEY LANE-POOLE, *rev.* ELIZABETH BAIGENT

Sources R. A. Stafford, *Scientist of empire: Sir Roderick Murchison, scientific exploration and Victorian imperialism* (1989) • R. Murchison, *Journal of the Royal Geographical Society*, 35 (1865), 122–4 • W. B. Baikie, 'Brief summary of an exploring trip up the rivers Kwòra and Chàdda (or Benué) in 1854', *Journal of the Royal Geographical Society*, 25 (1855), 108–21 • *DNB*
Archives BL, journals and papers, Add. MSS 32448–32449 • Foreign Office, London • RGS, maps | RGS, papers and letters to Royal Geographical Society
Likenesses memorial monument, St Magnus's Cathedral, Kirkwall • wood-engraving, NPG; repro. in *ILN* (28 Jan 1865)
Wealth at death under £2000: probate, 11 Oct 1865, *CGPLA Eng. & Wales*

Bailey. *See also* Baillie, Baily, Bayley, Bayly.

Bailey, Sir Abraham [Abe], **first baronet** (1864–1940), financier and politician in South Africa, was born at Cradock, Cape Colony, on 6 November 1864, the only son of Thomas Bailey (*d.* 1905) of Keighley, Yorkshire, a shopkeeper of Queenstown, which he represented in the Eastern Circle division for the Afrikaner Bond in the Cape legislative council. His mother was Ann Drummond (*d.* 1872), daughter of Peter McEwan of Muthill, Crieff, Perthshire. Bailey was educated in England at the Keighley trade and grammar School and at Clewer House, near Windsor.

After leaving school Bailey worked for a while in a textile firm. Returning to the Cape in 1881 he temporarily ran his father's business until he joined in the Barberton gold rush, arriving there in July 1886. He began dealing in shares with a capital of £100 which he lost. Borrowing £10 from a friend, he took out a broker's licence, and started dealing on the Barberton stock exchange. Leaving Barberton in March 1887, he went to the Witwatersrand goldfields where he became a foundation member of the Johannesburg stock exchange in January 1888. Soon Bailey started acquiring mining properties and extensive real estate operations.

Described as a 'freewheeling promoter' rather than a company developer, Bailey nevertheless played a significant role in the capitalization of the mining industry, particularly in the period immediately after the Second South African War. In 1897 he formed a company which, by Rand standards, was modest. This was the South African Gold Mines Company which had very substantial holdings of deep-level shares and properties by 1904. In 1905 he entered into a partnership with Julius Jeppe and founded what became the South African Townships, Mining and Finance Corporation, ranked among the 'big ten' which controlled Rand gold mining. Bailey was chairman of the latter as well as of the London and Rhodesian Mining and Land Company, one of the greatest holders of land and mining properties in Rhodesia, having taken a keen interest in the future of that country since the establishment of his friend Cecil Rhodes's British South Africa Company in 1889. He was a director of the influential London-based Central Mining and Investment Corporation Ltd and among the first shareholders in Rand Mines Ltd.

In 1894 Bailey married Caroline Mary (*d.* 1902), elder daughter of John Paddon, a Kimberley merchant. His second wife, whom he married on 5 September 1911, was Mary (1890–1960) [*see* Bailey, Dame Mary, Lady Bailey], only daughter of Derrick Warner William Westenra, fifth Baron Rossmore. Mary Bailey was well known as an airwoman in the early days of flying and in 1930 was created a dame of the British empire for her services to aviation. Bailey and his first wife had a son, John Milner (1900–1946), who succeeded him as second baronet, and one daughter. There were a further two sons and three daughters from his second marriage.

Known as the prince of the South African racing scene, Bailey became one of the largest breeders and owners of racehorses both in England and in South Africa, where he established a stud farm in Orange Free State and bred a fine line of winners. Bailey was an unusually successful gambler at the track as well as on the stock exchange. His most famous horse, Son-in-Law, which won the Cesarewitch and the Goodwood Cup, was also a great sire. Son-in-Law's son Foxlaw won the 1927 Gold Cup and Straitlace won the Oaks in 1924. Bailey's classic success was winning the Oaks in 1936 with Lovely Rose, and he was second in the Derby of 1935 with Robin Goodfellow. Bailey also took a keen interest in farming, and raised all kinds of livestock using scientific methods on his farm in the Colesberg district of the Cape.

Bailey began his public service on the Johannesburg health committee in the early 1890s. He was a member of the Reform Committee and for his part in the Jameson raid of 1895 was sentenced to two years' imprisonment, afterwards commuted to a fine of £2000. He served in the Second South African War as an intelligence officer in the 11th division and helped to raise an irregular corps. He rose to the rank of major, was twice mentioned in dispatches and received the king's and queen's medals and five clasps. During the war he formed a lasting friendship with the young British war correspondent Winston Leonard Spencer Churchill, later acting as his financial adviser. Churchill's daughter Diana married Bailey's eldest son, John, in 1932 but the union was short lived. In 1902 he entered the Cape legislative assembly as Progressive representative for Barkly West, Cecil Rhodes's old constituency, but resigned in 1905. After responsible government was granted to Transvaal in 1906, he represented Krugersdorp from 1907 to 1910 in the legislative assembly, becoming the opposition whip to the administration of General Louis Botha. He actively promoted the union of the four South African colonies, helping to finance *The State*, the organ of the Closer Union Society, which was founded to popularize the cause.

In 1915 Bailey was elected to the South African parliament as an independent member representing his old constituency, Krugersdorp, but sitting with General Botha's South African Party and not with the Unionists as was expected. He retained the seat until his defeat at the general election of 1924. During the 1914 rising and the

South-West Africa campaign Bailey had served under General Louis Botha with the rank of major, and was awarded the Croix de Guerre. He was similarly honoured by France in the First World War. He held strong views on political issues, especially on the Indian question, and in 1922 publicly expressed the wish that all the Indians should leave South Africa.

Through his South African Mails Syndicate and its two mouthpieces, the *Rand Daily Mail*, Transvaal's leading morning newspaper, and the *Sunday Times*, founded by him, as well as through his great wealth, Bailey was able to exercise considerable influence. From the early 1920s he divided his time between England and South Africa. He was famous for the hospitality which he dispensed at Rust-en-Vrede, his Muizenberg home near Cape Town, and at his London residence, 38 Bryanston Square. His skill and tact as a host made his homes places for the interchange of opinions and debate and at times neutral territory for the settlement of political differences. The critical meeting of 3 December 1916 which led to Lloyd George succeeding Herbert Asquith as prime minister was held at 38 Bryanston Square, and Bailey also urged Lloyd George to have Churchill in his new government. In March 1933 generals Smuts and Hertzog met at Rust-en-Vrede to form a coalition government for South Africa, although Bailey personally did not participate in these deliberations.

Bailey was an all-round sportsman whose great love for sport went back to 1894 when he captained the Transvaal team in the Currie cup cricket tournament at Newlands in the Cape. He also financed the visit of a South African cricket team to England in 1904. In his youth he had been a boxing enthusiast, trained by J. R. Couper whom he successfully backed in the famous fight against Wolf Bendorff (backed by B. Barnato), on 26 July 1889. Bailey was made a KCMG in 1911 for his services in promoting the unification of South Africa, and created a baronet in 1919 for services rendered during the First World War. He died at Rust-en-Vrede on 10 August 1940, having suffered the amputation of both legs, the first in July 1937 and the second in April 1938. He was buried five days later at Rust-en-Vrede. Under the terms of his will he left a quarter of his estate to the Abe Bailey Trust, which was to be established to further good relations between all white South Africans. His pictures at Bryanston Square were also put in trust for the nation. He bequeathed £100,000 or £5000 a year to the Royal Institute of International Affairs, for research. In 1925 he had purchased the valuable library of Charles Aiken Fairbridge, prominent Cape Town solicitor and book collector, and donated it to the South African Library, Cape Town. He also financed the addition of a wing to the library to house the collection.

MARYNA FRASER

Sources *DNB* · R. V. Kubicek, *Economic imperialism in theory and practice* (1979), 183 · P. H. Emden, *Randlords* (1935), 219–21 · J. Collings, *Gold under their hooves* (1987) · *DSAB*, vol. 2 · J. Mervis, *The fourth estate* (1989) · G. Wheatcroft, *The Randlords* (1985) · M. Bryant, *Taking stock* (1987) · E. Rosenthal, *On 'change through the years: a history of share dealing in South Africa* (1968) · J. B. Taylor, *A pioneer looks back* (1939) · Burke, *Peerage* · private information (2004) [son]

Archives National Archives of South Africa, Cape Town, MSS | Bodl. Oxf., corresp. with L. G. Curtis · Lpool RO, corresp. with seventeenth earl of Derby · NA Scot., corresp. with Lord Elibank · NA Scot., corresp. with Lord Lothian · National Library of South Africa, Cape Town, Merriman collection · University of Cape Town Libraries, corresp. with Patrick Duncan · University of Cape Town Libraries, letters to C. J. Sibbett

Likenesses P. A. de Laszlo, oils, 1916, Royal Institute of International Affairs, Chatham House, London · W. Stoneman, photograph, 1921, NPG · W. Orpen, oils, 1923 · O. Birley, oils, 1932, South African Library, Cape Town, South Africa, Fairbridge Wing · O. Birley, oils, 1932, Royal Institute of International Affairs, Chatham House, London · F. May, gouache drawing, 1936, NPG · Spy [L. Ward], caricature Hentschel-colourtype, NPG; repro. in *VF* (9 Sept 1908)

Wealth at death £10 million: private information

Bailey, Cyril (1871–1957), classical scholar, was born on 13 April 1871 in Kensington, London, the eldest child (of six) of Alfred Bailey, barrister and sometime Stowell law fellow of University College, Oxford, and his wife, Fanny Margaret, eldest daughter of George Coles, rubber merchant, of the firm of Warne & Co. He was cousin and godchild of Walter Leaf, editor of the *Iliad* and chairman of the Westminster Bank. Educated at St Paul's School (captain of the school in 1888–90), he went up to Balliol College, Oxford, as a scholar in 1890; he was to remain intimately connected with both institutions all his life. As an undergraduate he won the Hertford and Craven scholarships, but not the Ireland. Like many of his family, he was a good athlete—as cricketer, walker, cyclist, and mountaineer (member of the Alpine Club). He acted for the Oxford University Dramatic Society, and in later years he was active in producing Greek plays. He was of middle height, with a characteristic springy walk; his face is described as 'brown, lean, ascetic' (Lawrence Jones, *Balliol College Record*, 30). He aged slowly.

After taking a first in Greats (1894), Bailey was immediately offered a fellowship and tutorship at Exeter College; in 1902 he was able to return to Balliol as fellow and tutor; here he stayed for the rest of his career, retiring in 1939, but teaching again in the Second World War. Balliol was at that time the leading classical college in Oxford, and for twenty-five years Bailey shared with Arthur Pickard-Cambridge the tutoring of pupils of exceptional ability; some were known as 'Picker's boys', others as 'Cyril's boys'. Pickard-Cambridge went on from his college tutorship to become a vice-chancellor and a prominent figure in national higher education; Bailey took the other option and stayed on, combining the burdens of a conscientious college tutor not only with research and publication but also with a considerable load of administration.

He was a tutor of the old style, spending many hours with undergraduates, sitting and talking informally in his rooms in the evening, and on reading parties in England and in the Alps. He was a much loved tutor, who had the gift of sympathy, and many of his former pupils stayed in touch for decades; all those who knew him remark on his talent for friendship. He also found time to be a leading figure and trustee of the Balliol Boys' Club, a successful venture which brought together undergraduates and young men of the town. He wrote a short history of the club (1953). This activity was one expression of his concern for redressing the perceived injustices of society and spreading the benefits of education much more widely. His experience with the boys' club led to his becoming chairman of the Oxford Youth Advisory Committee; for his work in this area he was made CBE in 1939.

Bailey was a highly successful lecturer, though he used to comment wryly on the complete lack of instruction or help for novice lecturers. In the fashion of the time, much of his teaching took the form of 'composition', stylish translation from English into Greek and Latin prose and verse. Bailey was an elegant composer, and he had a fine presence and delivery; he was a natural choice as the university's public orator (1932–9). But he was not, like some Oxford and Cambridge dons of the time, content with this sort of scholarly activity. He had a lifelong interest, which issued in a number of substantial books, in the philosopher-poet Lucretius, one of the greatest of Latin poets, and in the Greek philosopher Epicurus, whose system Lucretius versified in his extraordinary poem *De rerum natura* ('On the nature of the world').

In 1898 Bailey published, at the age of twenty-seven, a text of Lucretius in the Oxford Classical Texts series. The series itself was new; not many British classical scholars at the time had any real mastery of the exacting techniques of editing a text, and those commissioning the first volumes made a number of mistakes. As Bailey observed later, it was 'much too early really, as I knew little about Lucretius and almost nothing about the principles of creating a text' (unpublished autobiography). Housman was characteristically severe: 'Some care, some judgment, and some independence are shown here, but not quite enough' (*The Classical Papers of A. E. Housman*, ed. J. Diggle and F. D. R. Goodyear, 1972, 523). A second edition appeared in 1922. Bailey produced in 1926 *Epicurus*, a collection of the fragments and the evidence for this important thinker. The book is useful, but it is not all-inclusive; it did not replace the more voluminous work, *Epicurea*, of Hermann Usener. In 1928 appeared *The Greek Atomists and Epicurus*, a study of the background of Epicurus's philosophy. It was well received, but in these books he avoided tackling the extremely difficult problems posed by the newly appearing papyrus fragments of Epicurus. That sort of abstruse and detailed philological work was not really to his taste.

The crown of Bailey's long Lucretian labours was his massive edition of *De rerum natura*, with translation and commentary, in three volumes, which appeared in 1947. All his work has the great merit of clarity of thought and elegance of expression; it is no surprise that he succeeded in the extremely difficult task of producing a skilful and readable English translation of Lucretius. Housman had criticized Bailey's Latin text of 1898 as too conservative; that of 1947 had become still more so. The commentary is rich in illustrative material, and the reader is in the presence of a guide who is fair-minded, judicious, and well informed. Critics were generally respectful, but some remarked on a comparative weakness in the editor's mastery of, or interest in, early Latin. Sometimes, too, one does not quite find the sort of sharply angled discussion which would illuminate particular problems; and Bailey does not respond very readily to a certain vertiginous quality in Lucretius' style, a sense of violence and extremity, so strangely at odds with the Epicurean philosophy of serenity and calm.

Bailey is the only tutorial fellow of an Oxford or Cambridge college to have been invited to the University of California to give the Sather lectures, the most prestigious set of lectures in the classical field. In 1932 he gave a set of eight lectures, which were published as *Phases in the Religion of Ancient Rome*. The book is very much in the spirit of Warde Fowler, of Lincoln College, Oxford, who had a great influence on him. The American trip made a great impression, and in his unpublished autobiography he makes interesting comments on a range of things that struck him, not all favourably—he records his shock at seeing a black professor being isolated at a separate table in a college refectory. Three years later appeared *Religion in Virgil*, a slightly disappointing production, in which the desire to set out the evidence in full and with fairness seems to have been indulged at the expense of exploring Virgil's thought or endeavouring to give answers to the questions raised.

Bailey had been convinced by Gilbert Murray of the vital importance for the classics of popularization. He edited a collection of essays, *The Legacy of Rome* (1923) to which H. H. Asquith contributed an introduction; the book was a great popular success. He also saw the importance of maintaining close links between classicists in universities and teachers of the subject in schools, and he was assiduous in visiting schools, a regular examiner in school certificate examinations, and for years the chairman of the annual joint conference affectionately known as 'Dons and beaks'. He was elected a governor of his old school, St Paul's, in 1901, and served for fifty years. He also served as a governor of Marlborough College. After his retirement, living in the village of East Hanney, he became a member of the governing body of the village school.

At that period Bailey also served on the parochial church council and the Wantage rural district council: he was the sort of man whom people wanted on their committees and similar bodies. He was president of the Old Pauline Club from 1921 to 1931, 'after which', he used to say, 'they reduced the maximum term to three years' (unpublished autobiography). He was a founder member of the Governing Bodies Association. Closer to his academic interests, he was a delegate of the Oxford University Press from 1921 to 1946, playing a central part in the decisions of the press in that difficult time. He devoted many hours and infinite tact to the long struggles and the bitter quarrels that plagued the early years of the project to produce an *Oxford Latin Dictionary* to replace that of Lewis and Short. Work on the book began in 1932, but the first fascicle was not published until 1968, eleven years after Bailey's death on 5 December 1957, at his home, The Mulberries, East Hanney. His contribution to the project, of which he was for some years senior co-editor, was very great.

Bailey was the best-loved Balliol figure of his time and

probably the most widely known, both to undergraduates and to old members. Many people expected him to be elected master of the college in 1924, in succession to A. L. Smith. When the college elected A. D. Lindsay, Bailey's response was both publicly and privately magnanimous. The charm of his personality was felt very widely. Eduard Fraenkel, a great émigré scholar, who was sometimes impatient with the amateurishness of British classicists, was asked which he put higher, Bailey or Pickard-Cambridge. The audience expected that preference would be given to the more technically irreproachable work of Pickard-Cambridge on the Attic theatre. After a short pause, Fraenkel replied with a line of Aristophanes (*Frogs*, 1413): 'One I think is clever, but the other is my delight'.

In January 1912 Bailey married Gemma Creighton (*d.* 1958), youngest daughter of Mandell *Creighton, historian of the papacy and bishop of London. She was Gilbert Murray's secretary, and they met at a class on Horace which Bailey was giving for women undergraduates at Oxford—both facts, in their different ways, being marks of his comparatively liberal attitudes. The marriage was unassailably happy. They had three daughters and one son. In 1923 she published a *Short History of Lady Margaret Hall*. That college was one of their shared interests: Bailey was chairman of the council of Lady Margaret Hall from 1921 to 1939, and was elected an honorary fellow. He was also an honorary fellow of Balliol, received honorary degrees from Oxford, Durham, Wales, Glasgow, and California, and—the honour which, he recorded, gave him most pleasure—was elected FBA in 1933.

Music played an important part in Bailey's life. He was among the moving spirits of the Oxford Subscription Concerts, and for years he was a devoted member of the Bach Choir ('one of the deepest joys of my life'; unpublished autobiography), becoming its president, although by his own account his singing was less than ravishing. He published a lively memoir of its controlling genius, Sir Hugh Allen. Bailey was a man of deep Christian faith, regular in his attendance at the college chapel. There is a drawing of him in chalk by Sir William Rothenstein and an etching by Andrew Freeth, both in Balliol. Those who knew the sitter regard the latter as the better likeness.

Bailey's career, like that of Russell Meiggs in the next generation at Balliol, is in a sense a period piece. For a certain time, roughly perhaps from 1840 to 1990, there were scholars of first-rate ability and international reputation who preferred not to seek promotion, titles, or even relief from the duties of teaching, and who were content with the position of tutor at an Oxford college, lavishing much of their time and energy on their pupils. They are not likely, in the present atmosphere of British academic life, to have many successors. JASPER GRIFFIN

Sources unpublished autobiography, Balliol Oxf. • W. Oakeshott, 'Cyril Bailey, 1871–1958', *PBA*, 46 (1960), 295–308 • *Balliol College Record* (1958), 28–32 • personal knowledge (2004) • *DNB* • private information (2004) • d. cert.

Archives Balliol Oxf., Jowett MSS • Balliol Oxf., Strachan-Davidson MSS • Bodl. Oxf., letters to William Clark • Bodl. Oxf., corresp. with Gilbert Murray • Rice University, Houston, Texas, Fondren Library, letters to Sir Julian Huxley

Likenesses W. Stoneman, two photographs, 1933–45, NPG • A. Freeth, drawing, priv. coll. • A. Freeth, etching, Balliol Oxf. • W. Rothenstein, chalk drawing, Balliol Oxf.

Wealth at death £21,174 18*s*. 10*d*.: probate, 13 March 1958, *CGPLA Eng. & Wales*

Bailey, Sir Donald Coleman (1901–1985), civil engineer, was born in Rotherham, Yorkshire, on 15 September 1901, the only child of Joseph Henry Bailey, commercial cashier, and his wife, Caroline Coleman. After attending Rotherham grammar school and the Leys School, Cambridge, Bailey went to Sheffield University, where he obtained a BEng in 1923. He was employed by Rowntree & Co. of York, the civil engineer's department at the London, Midland, and Scottish Railway, and the city engineer's department in Sheffield before joining the War Office in 1928 as civil engineering designer at the Military Engineering Experimental Establishment in Christchurch.

Among the unit's tasks was the development of improved transportable bridges for the increasingly mechanized army. In 1936 Bailey conceived the idea of a simple bridge structure based on standard rectangular trussed welded units (10 ft x 5 ft) bolted together in combinations to suit the job in hand. Each unit could be lifted by six men and fitted a standard 3 ton lorry. The panels were built up from small components, enabling work to be subcontracted to a large number of small engineering firms without disrupting heavy engineering production. The War Office displayed no interest, but Bailey persevered with detailed design in his own time. It was not until February 1941, after the tubular-girder design of Charles Inglis had failed under test (as predicted by Bailey), that he was ordered to design a new, all-purpose bridge. Bailey's private design work enabled the first prototype to be ready by 5 May, with production bridges reaching the army in December 1941. Lieutenant-General Sir Giffard Le Q. Martel declared that the Bailey bridge doubled the value of allied armoured and mechanized units. Over two thousand of the bridges were erected in north-west Europe between June 1944 and May 1945 and the design was also used extensively in Italy and the Far East. After the war both second-hand and new bridge panels found a ready civilian market and many Bailey bridges remained in use around the world.

Bailey was appointed OBE in 1944 and knighted in 1946. In 1946 he was promoted to senior principal scientific officer and became assistant director of the Military Engineering Experimental Establishment, subsequently becoming director. The Royal Commission on Awards to Inventors awarded him £12,000 in 1948 for his work on the bridge. He became deputy chief scientific officer, Ministry of Supply, in 1952. Bailey served on a number of technical committees, giving his name to the Bailey committee on house interiors (1952–3). He was appointed dean of the Royal Military College of Science at Shrivenham in 1962, and exerted a 'benign influence on the modern scientist-soldier' until his retirement in 1966. He was an honorary DEng (Sheffield, 1946), a commander of the order of Orange Nassau, a fellow of the Institution of Structural Engineers, a member of the Institution of Civil Engineers,

Sir Donald Coleman Bailey (1901–1985), by Walter Bird, 1962

and an honorary member of the Institution of Royal Engineers.

Bailey's quiet, unassuming exterior hid great determination and considerable inventive ability, which he applied not only to bridges but to a wide range of other technical equipment. It was a source of satisfaction to him that his bridges found as ready a use in the civilian market as they had in the military. In 1933 Bailey married Phyllis Amy (*d.* 1971), daughter of Charles Frederick Andrew, a retired farmer, of Wick, Bournemouth. They had one son, Richard Henry. In 1979 Bailey married Mildred Stacey (*b.* 1919/20), his housekeeper, a widow, the daughter of Herbert William Crees, licensed victualler. Bailey, whose home was at 9 Stour Way, Christchurch, died on 5 May 1985 at St Leonards Hospital near Bournemouth, survived by his second wife. A. P. MUNFORD, *rev.*

Sources *The Times* (6 May 1985) • G. Hartcup, *The challenge of war* (1970) • J. H. Joiner, *The Bailey story: a tribute to Sir Donald Bailey* (1987) • d. cert.
Likenesses W. Bird, photograph, 1962, NPG [*see illus.*] • G. Bell, portrait, 1982, repro. in Joiner, *The Bailey story*
Wealth at death £45,276: probate, 14 Aug 1985, *CGPLA Eng. & Wales*

Bailey, Sir Edward Battersby (1881–1965), geologist, was born in Marsden, Kent, on 1 July 1881, the third of six sons of James Battersby Bailey, medical practitioner, and his wife, Louise Florence, daughter of Isaac Carr, a Cumberland farmer. Bailey was educated at Kendal grammar school and went by open scholarship from there to Clare College, Cambridge. He gained first-class honours in both parts one (1901) and two (1902, geology and physics) of the natural sciences tripos and gained the Harkness scholarship (1902).

Bailey joined the geological survey as a field geologist in 1902. His studies of igneous rocks in the Scottish lowlands soon identified him as a skilled interpreter of the composition and history of ancient volcanoes. He enjoyed writing, and with Charles Thomas Clough and H. B. Maufe he described the geological mapping of Glencoe, demonstrating the relics of a large sunken volcano, called a 'cauldron-subsidence', surrounded by ring fractures, some occupied by igneous rocks later termed 'ring-dykes'. This fostered the recognition and study of ring-dykes elsewhere in the world. In 1910 came his revolutionary description of the general geological structure of the western Grampians as strata, some transported great distances, bent into recumbent folds of which the limbs were partly replaced by low-angled faults or slides. Bailey was uncertain of the depositional order of the strata within the folds but in 1930, after other workers had demonstrated the significance of current-bedding and graded bedding, he showed that the Ballachulish Slide was developed in the lower limb of a syncline. Later it was realized that the concept of recumbent folding applied to the whole of the Grampians.

In 1914 Bailey married Alice (*d.* 1956), daughter of David Meason of Kirkwall, and a sister of the wife of Sir John Flett; they later had a son and a daughter. The following year, Bailey's geological work was interrupted by the First World War; he served from 1915 to 1919 with the Royal Garrison Artillery. Wounded twice, losing his left eye and much use of his left arm, he was awarded the Military Cross and the French Croix de Guerre with palms. He was also made a chevalier of the Légion d'honneur and he retired from the army with the rank of lieutenant.

Bailey's fertile brain was unaffected by his war wounds and in 1919 he was given charge of west highland fieldwork and he saw through the press the complex geological map of Mull (1923) which he had helped to construct and which depicts the results of two great cauldron-subsidences and of gravitational differentiation of Tertiary magma; also there are crater lakes, pillow lavas, and ring-dykes. During the mapping, in 1922, Bailey studied a very pure white sandstone by Loch Aline, on the mainland opposite Mull; this, he inferred, formed the desert shores of the same sea that deposited the chalk of the English Downs. In the Second World War, when normal shipments of optical glass from overseas ceased, the purity of the Loch Aline sands was recalled and they were extensively mined and used.

In 1930 Bailey took up his appointment as professor of geology at Glasgow University. Some of his lectures to his Glasgow undergraduates were incorporated into his *Introduction to Geology* (1939), written with his colleagues J. Weir and W. J. McCallien. His book *Tectonic Essays, Mainly Alpine* (1935), also written during his years in Glasgow, still proves good reading. Among his researches were inferences concerning ancient submarine earthquakes and the accompanying tidal waves affecting sedimentation. These led other workers subsequently to develop the concept of turbidity-currents of high density and their effects on present-day ocean configuration.

Bailey's stay in Glasgow ended in 1937 when he was offered the directorship of the geological survey and its newly sited museum at South Kensington. The war, which occupied six of the eight years of his directorate, caused a change in his plans for the survey; these are outlined in his book *Geological Survey of Great Britain* (1952), as are the activities of his staff, diverted from regional geological mapping to successful work on minerals associated with the war effort. The museum was evacuated and became the headquarters of London region civil defence; from 1940 to 1942 Bailey was lieutenant commanding the geological survey and London region section of the Home Guard. In 1943 he visited Malta to advise on water resources there. He also worked extensively on the production of the two sheets of the 10-mile-to-1-inch geological map of Great Britain, which, however, was not published until 1948, whereas he retired in 1945, the year in which he was knighted.

Following his retirement, in collaboration with McCallien, Bailey then started researches into the origin of associated serpentine, pillow lava, and radiolarian chert in Scotland, Turkey, and Italy. He also prepared a second edition of the *Geology of Ben Nevis and Glen Coe* (1960) and he wrote biographies of Sir Charles Lyell (1962) and of James Hutton (1967). Bailey's first wife died in 1956, and in December 1962 he married Mary M. W. Young, who survived him.

Bailey was a tallish man of excellent physique; he had gained a freshman's heavyweight boxing medal at Cambridge. Always a keen walker, he had spartan habits and a strong personality. Dedicated to his work, he inspired others but at times he was over-enthusiastic or even intolerant, thus antagonizing some. Honorary doctorates were given to him by the universities of Belfast, Birmingham, Cambridge, Edinburgh, Glasgow, and Harvard. He was elected a fellow of the Royal Society in 1930 and awarded a royal medal in 1943. A foreign member of the national academies of Belgium, India, Norway, Switzerland, and the United States, he was also an honorary member of many geological societies and received several prestigious medals. One of the best-known and most colourful geologists of his time, he died in the Royal Free Hospital, London, on 19 March 1965 and was cremated at Golders Green.

C. JAMES STUBBLEFIELD, *rev.*

Sources C. J. Stubblefield, *Memoirs FRS*, 11 (1965), 1–21 • *Bulletin of the Geological Society of America*, 27 (1965) • personal knowledge (1981) • *WWW* • *CGPLA Eng. & Wales* (1965)

Archives BGS, drafts, notes, and papers | BGS, letters to Herbert Thomas

Likenesses photograph, repro. in Stubblefield, *Memoirs FRS*

Wealth at death £32,604: probate, 25 June 1965, *CGPLA Eng. & Wales*

Bailey, Frederick Marshman (1882–1967), explorer and naturalist, elder son of Major (later Lieutenant-Colonel) Frederick Bailey of the Royal Engineers, was born on 3 February 1882 at Lahore, where his father served in the Indian army for a few years. Later his father became head of the Indian forestry survey department and, on retirement from the army on health grounds, lecturer in forestry at Edinburgh University. His mother was Florence, daughter of John Clark Marshman, who had landed with his missionary parents in India in 1799. Marshman became the *Times* correspondent and was one of the founders of the newspaper the *Pioneer of India*.

F. M. Bailey was educated at Edinburgh Academy, where, to his disappointment, he spent only three years before going to Wellington College and then to the Royal Military College, Sandhurst. His first commissioned posting was in 1900 to the Middlesex regiment, which was then in the Nilgiri hills in India. There he became interested in birds, butterflies, and plants—an interest which he maintained throughout his travels, and which produced valuable material and many new species for museums in India and Britain. He transferred to the Durham light infantry, in which he developed proficiency in polo. His horsemanship, and the influence of Lord Roberts, a family friend, led to his posting to the 17th Bengal lancers. Hoping to see active service, in 1903 he asked to be transferred to the 32nd Sikh pioneers, whom he accompanied to Sikkim. This introduced him to Tibet, a country which intrigued him for the rest of his life and brought him a high reputation as an explorer.

Bailey was a member of the mission to Lhasa in 1903–4 led by Francis Younghusband to resolve the intransigence of the Tibetan government in implementing the Anglo-Chinese convention of 1890. On successfully completing this mission Bailey, now proficient in Tibetan, was given his first opportunity to explore when sent to report on the trade and trade routes between India and Gartok, in western Tibet. He travelled hundreds of miles, and lived for weeks at a time at a height of over 14,000 feet. Although only twenty-two, he gave a most detailed report on this assignment, which was published by the government of India (1905). In 1905 he applied to be transferred to the political department, and later that year went to Gyantse as trade agent to relieve the official due for leave. After the official's return, Bailey was for two years in the Chumbi valley, a wedge of Tibet which thrusts south of the Himalayas between Sikkim and Bhutan. It was a suitable area in which to pursue his interest in natural history. In 1911, accompanied by his young Tibetan servant, he embarked on an expedition to explore the Tsangpo River, discover its source from the Tibetan plateau, and find out whether, as previously reported, it had falls of some 150 feet in height. An approach from the south was barred by unfriendly hill people and was totally discouraged by the Indian government, so Bailey decided to enter in the east from China; he therefore obtained a passport in Peking (Beijing) which allowed him to travel through Szechwan (Sichuan) and Yunnan. He travelled to Ichang (Yichang) on the Yangtze (Yangzi) by steamer and from there hired a small boat to take him through the Yangtze gorges. He trekked through this most difficult mountainous area to Tatsienlu (Dajianlu) and eventually to Batang on the Tibetan frontier. He did not, however, manage to reach the Tsangpo, but returned to India through Mishmi country. In his book *China—Tibet—Assam* (1945) he gave a fine account of this journey.

Hoping to solve the mystery of the Tsangpo Gorge, Bailey set out in 1913 with Captain Henry Treise Morshead, Royal Engineers, who worked on the survey of India and, in defiance of official orders, they entered Tibet from Assam. Their three-and-a-half-month journey has been described as one of the longest and most remarkable journeys of exploration completed on foot in the twentieth century. It proved that the Tsangpo broke through the Himalayan range to emerge on the plains of India as the Brahmaputra. In Bailey's opinion the chief results of this expedition were to map some 380 miles of the Tsangpo, to discover the two portals of the Tsangpo Gorge, and the high mountains Gyala Peri and Namcha Barwa, and to recognize that the Subansiri was another river which had its source in Tibet and pierced the main Himalayan range. On this expedition he discovered the renowned blue poppy, and collected fragmentary flowering specimens on which the species *Meconopsis baileyi* was based. It was Kingdon Ward who introduced the plant to Britain in 1924 from seeds from the same locality. *No Passport to Tibet* (1957) was Bailey's account of the journey. As a result of his discoveries, Bailey was appointed CIE in 1915.

In 1915 Bailey was sent to France with the 31st Sikh pioneers. Wounded at Ypres, he returned to Britain. On recovery he was dispatched to Gallipoli with the Gurkhas, only to be wounded again by a bullet which passed through both his legs. Pronounced unfit for active service, he returned to the political department of the India Office. In 1916 he was posted to India, where he worked for two years as political officer in Kohat and then Charsada. In March 1917 he was sent as a political officer to Shustar, Persia. Early in 1918 he was ordered to Kashgar in Chinese Turkestan and then to Tashkent in Russian territory to report on the conditions in the region following the revolution of 1917 and the collapse of the eastern front under German pressure. Subversive movements seemed likely to affect the equilibrium on the north-west frontier of India; Bailey tried to establish good relations and influence the Tashkent authorities in favour of the allies. Because of the hostility of the Bolshevik government in Russian Turkestan, he had to go underground. Since he understood and could speak limited Russian, he could repeatedly change his identity. Despite having a price on his head, he got himself recruited into the Russian counter-espionage service, with the task, among other duties, of tracking a foreign agent named Bailey. He was thus able to reach Bukhara and finally Mashhad in Persia. His *Mission to Tashkent* (1946) tells the fascinating story of these dangerous adventures.

Bailey married on 7 April 1921 Irma, only child of William Hepburn, second Lord Cozens-Hardy, a barrister and secretary to his father, the first Lord Cozens-Hardy, when master of the rolls. There were no children. In the year of his marriage he was appointed political officer in Sikkim and, while living in Gangtok for seven years, he was able to travel into Tibet and Bhutan. He became a personal friend of the Dalai Lama, with whom he could converse freely. He next spent some months as a political officer in central India before going to Srinagar, Kashmir, as resident, and eventually to Nepal as British minister. He retired in 1938. After the outbreak of war in 1939 he joined the Home Guard and was in charge of the north Norfolk auxiliary units. For almost two years he was a king's messenger based at Miami and Washington.

Bailey was an unassuming man of handsome appearance and military bearing and spoke in a soft voice. He was modest and gentle-mannered, with immense charm and persuasiveness, and a fine sense of humour which earned him the nickname Hatter. Although he sometimes defied authority, his results usually justified his resolve. In 1912 the Royal Geographical Society granted him the Gill memorial award and in 1916 its gold medal. He also received in 1920 the premier award of the Royal Scottish Geographical Society, the Livingstone gold medal. In natural history his major interest was butterflies, which he collected in all his travels. His specimens were given to the British Museum (Natural History) and his cabinets of duplicates went to the Metropolitan Museum in New York. His fine collection of birds, mostly from Nepal, and his collection of mammals, were donated to the British Museum. He published a number of papers on many aspects of natural history. Bailey died at his home, Warborough House, Stiffkey, Norfolk, on 17 April 1967.

GEORGE TAYLOR, *rev.*

Sources *The Times* (19 April 1967) • A. Swinson, *Beyond the frontiers: the biography of Colonel F. M. Bailey, explorer and special agent* (1971) • personal knowledge (1981) • *CGPLA Eng. & Wales* (1967)

Archives BL OIOC, MSS, corresp., diaries, and papers, MS Eur. F 157 • BL OIOC, papers, incl. Russian diary, MSS Eur. C 162, D 658 • NHM, collecting diaries • RBG Kew, corresp. relating to Bhutan and walnuts | RGS, corresp. with Royal Geographical Society

Wealth at death £18,655: probate, 26 Sept 1967, *CGPLA Eng. & Wales*

Bailey, Sir George Edwin (1879–1965), electrical engineer and industrialist, was born in Loughborough on 19 October 1879, the tenth child of Thomas W. Bailey, master tailor, and his second wife, Ann Wilmot. He was educated at Loughborough grammar school, and entered the works of the Brush Electrical Engineering Company, Loughborough, as an apprentice, continuing his technical education at the University College, Nottingham. After a period as leading turbine draughtsman, he left the Brush Company in 1907 and joined the British Westinghouse Company at Trafford Park, Manchester, as a draughtsman in the engine department, rising to chief draughtsman in 1909. He married, in 1910, Margaret Fanny (*d.* 1971), daughter of Thomas Bolesworth, farmer, of Loughborough; they had one daughter. In 1913 Bailey became superintendent of the engine department, and was later responsible for manufacture; this determined his future career and interest in production and manufacture. During the First World War, British Westinghouse raised a body of defence volunteers at Trafford Park, captained by Bailey.

In 1919 British Westinghouse became the Metropolitan-Vickers Electrical Company, a name which was to become known throughout the world. Bailey was appointed as works manager, and in 1927 took a seat on the board, becoming director and general manager of manufacture.

In 1929 Metropolitan-Vickers was merged with the British Thomson-Houston Company and the Ediswan Electric Company to form Associated Electrical Industries Limited. Although the individual companies retained their own identities, Bailey was made responsible for the co-ordination of production in the group. In 1938 the company was involved with Robert Watson-Watt in producing the first radar sets, and George Bailey was proud to be involved with many technical developments in heavy-bomber production, with the first axial flow gas turbine to fly (the forerunner of the jet), and with much equipment for the navy and air force, including the first thousand radar sets ordered by the government. In what he regarded as 'the engineers' war', Bailey led the company through a great manufacturing programme. On 22 December 1940 the Trafford Park works was heavily bombed, but under Bailey's direction tools and materials were obtained from elsewhere and production resumed with little interruption. For his service during the war Bailey was knighted in 1944. The same year, he was appointed chairman of Metropolitan-Vickers Electrical Company.

In the following two years Bailey became managing director, and then deputy chairman, of Associated Electrical Industries. In 1951 Oliver Lyttelton (later Lord Chandos) entered the government as secretary of state for the colonies and Bailey took his place as chairman of the company until 1954, when Chandos returned, after which Bailey continued as director, retiring in 1957.

Bailey was a man of strong character, and it was undoubtedly his great energy and single-mindedness that caused him to be chosen for heavy responsibility in his early years. He was notable for his ability to handle men, and, despite his critical outlook and sometimes more than trenchant comments, he left no rancour. He was adept at devising various ways of maintaining good communications with his employees and his relations with the trade unions, although robust, were always sincere, and caused no ill feelings. The company boasted what was probably the first works committee in the country, anticipating the Whitley councils by nine months. Although Bailey regarded himself as a very hard man, he was far more sympathetic and sentimental about other people's misfortunes than he cared to admit, and often arranged for help to be given anonymously. He gave unremitting support for a wide range of extramural activities for the company's employees, such as choral singing, amateur dramatics, and boxing. He also assiduously encouraged an evening school, which offered tuition for women and girls in cookery, sewing, and dressmaking.

During the war Bailey served as a member of the engineering and industrial panel of the Ministry of Labour and National Service, and as a member of the committee which considered the position of skilled men in industry, led by Sir W. H. Beveridge, as well as serving on the industrial panel of the Ministry of Production. At various times he was president of the British Electrical and Allied Manufacturers' Association, the Engineering and Allied Employers' National Federation, the Manchester District Engineering Employers' Association, the Manchester Engineering Council, and the Institute of Production Engineers. His skill and wide experience were used to the full after the blitz on Manchester, in supervising the restoration of badly damaged factories in the district. His contribution to the Manchester Defence scheme earned him the appointment of CBE in 1941.

Despite his heavy responsibilities and the many calls on his time, Bailey never lost interest in golf, fishing, and gardening. Like his father before him, he was a good gardener and his chief interest was in the cultivation of carnations, in which he specialized. Bailey died at his home, Downside, Compton, Berkshire, on 14 October 1965.

H. WEST, *rev.* ANITA MCCONNELL

Sources private information (1981) • personal knowledge (1981) • *The Engineer* (22 Oct 1965), 669 • J. Dummelow, *1899–1949: Metropolitan-Vickers Electrical Co.* (1949) • *The Times* (15 Oct 1965), 23d • d. cert.

Likenesses many photographs, repro. in Dummelow, *1899–1849*

Wealth at death £39,746: probate, 10 March 1966, *CGPLA Eng. & Wales*

Bailey, Sir Harold Walter (1899–1996), Indo-Iranian scholar and philologist, was born on 16 December 1899 at 54 Northgate Street, Devizes, Wiltshire, one of three sons of Frederick Charles Bailey, labourer, and his wife, Emma Jane, *née* Richardt. When he was ten his parents moved to Australia to a farm, Glen Wood, Nangeenan, Western Australia, and it was in the unpromising conditions of the outback, which ruled out formal secondary education, that his interest in languages was first stimulated by a chance collection of books, later described by him to Arnold Toynbee as:

> a set of seven volumes of an encyclopaedia (eagerly devoured) and four other volumes with lessons in French, Latin, German, Greek, Italian, and Spanish. Later came Arabic and Persian, out of which Persian took the lead (joined later to Sanskrit). (Toynbee, 16)

Thus began the fascination with Iran which, nurtured by his study of Avestan grammar in the intervals of farm work, led him in 1922 to the University of Western Australia, Perth, to read classics (in the absence of any provision for oriental studies) and subsequently to write a thesis on Euripides, for which he was awarded an MA in 1927. In the latter year he won the Hackett studentship to Oxford University where, as a member of St Catherine's Society, he studied under F. W. Thomas and was awarded a first in oriental languages in 1929.

In 1929 Bailey was appointed as the first lecturer in Iranian studies (a post financed by the Parsi community of Bombay) at the School of Oriental Studies, London. At the same time, for his doctoral thesis, he embarked on the study of a major Zoroastrian text, the *Bundahišn* ('Primal creation'), a kind of encyclopaedia of Zoroastrianism written in Pahlavi, for which—although it was incomplete—he was awarded his Oxford DPhil in 1933. Learning that the Danish scholar Kaj Barr was working on the same

Sir Harold Walter Bailey (1899–1996), by Ronald Way, 1972

material and preparing to have it published, with characteristic generosity Bailey handed over his own materials to Barr (who died in 1970 without completing an edition); much later in his life Bailey returned to his edition of the *Bundahišn*, which was completed in 1989 but remains unpublished, partly because his insertion by hand of words in Pahlavi script into the copy intended for photographic reproduction rendered it partially illegible. His output in this period was already substantial: over twenty articles, mostly on Middle Iranian and Avestan problems, between 1930 and 1935.

In 1936 Bailey was elected to the chair of Sanskrit at Cambridge and became a fellow of Queens' College, living in the college until his retirement in 1967; he was not primarily a Sanskritist but the Cambridge chair gave him the freedom to pursue his Iranian studies. In the same year he delivered the Ratanbai Katrak lectures at Oxford, which were published as *Zoroastrian Problems in the Ninth-Century Books* (1943; 2nd edn, 1971) and which rank among his most important publications, helping to give the field of Old and Middle Iranian studies a new direction. By then he was already engaged in the study of Khotanese, the Middle Iranian language of Khotan in Chinese Turkestan, which was to occupy the major part of his immense scholastic energies over nearly half a century, resulting in the publication of five volumes of Khotanese texts in facsimile, two volumes of text, translation, and commentary, five volumes of text alone, and an etymological dictionary (*Dictionary of Khotan Saka*, 1979), as well as two further books and numerous articles. He was the pioneer in the study of this material, bringing to it great skill in reading the cursive script of the late Khotanese texts, unrivalled familiarity with the literatures of the region, and encyclopaedic knowledge of other Iranian and Indo-European languages (as well as knowledge of Chinese, Tibetan, and Turkish—over fifty languages in all). He started work on Khotanese in the hope that it would shed light on the *Bundahišn* (a hope not realized) but by publishing the entire Khotanese material, which had been acquired for the British Museum as a result of Sir Aurel Stein's central Asian expeditions, he inaugurated a whole new field within Iranian studies. He claimed not to be religious but his sympathy with the Zoroastrian and Buddhist texts that he studied was notable.

Though wedded to his Iranian studies and following a simple lifestyle (he was a vegetarian and near teetotaller), Bailey had other diversions in his life, enjoying until his mid-fifties walking or cycling holidays (his athleticism was revealed in his tall, slim figure), playing the violin in a chamber group which quite often met in his rooms at Queens' College, and later in life taking up gardening enthusiastically. His scholastic interests, too, extended widely, including for example the study of varieties of spoken Welsh in remote villages, a study pursued to such effect that Sir Ralph Turner, the director of the School of Oriental and African Studies, recorded how he was visited by Bailey while on holiday in Wales, and Bailey talked so knowledgeably about Welsh language and history that one of those present afterwards remarked that he did not know that Cambridge had a chair of Celtic (Sims-Williams and Hewitt, 113). Similarly, Bailey's enthusiasm for the languages and literatures of the Caucasus (in particular the Armenian, Georgian, and Ossetic epics) enabled him on a visit to the area in 1966 to astonish his audience by addressing them in both dialects of Ossetic; this resulted in his being presented with a full Osset costume, in which he was later painted for a portrait commissioned by his college from Ronald Way. His extraordinarily wide scholarly interests went hand in hand with an exceptional capacity to shut everything else out when he was busy writing.

Bailey's erudition received due recognition over the years. He became a fellow of the British Academy in 1944 and was subsequently a corresponding member of the Danish, Norwegian, and Swedish academies, the Australian Academy of the Humanities, the Institut de France, the Académie des Inscriptions et Belles-Lettres, and the Istituto Italiano per il Medio ed Estremo Oriente. He was knighted in 1960 for services to oriental studies, and received honorary degrees from Oxford, Manchester, Western Australia, and the Australian National University. He was president of the Philological Society (1948–52) and of the Royal Asiatic Society (1964–7), among others; a complimentary volume of the *Bulletin of the School of Oriental and African Studies* (33, 1970) included a bibliography of his 162 publications until then. He was a founder member of the Ancient India and Iran Trust in 1978, donating to it his vast library, and he helped to purchase Brooklands House in Cambridge as its base, living there himself and being active in the improvement of its garden. In his later years he suffered from failing eyesight, and active research became increasingly difficult; nevertheless, he was able to maintain contacts on a personal level—in part through the trust—with his many friends and colleagues, and clearly valued the opportunity to put his great store of knowledge at the service of others. He died on 11 January 1996 in Cambridge; a memorial service was held in Queens' College on 9 March 1996. He was unmarried. He was the most outstanding British Iranianist of the twentieth century; indeed, some have held that he was the greatest scholar of Queens' College since Erasmus.

J. L. BROCKINGTON

Sources N. Sims-Williams and G. Hewitt, *Bulletin of the School of Oriental and African Studies*, 60 (1997), 109–16 · A. D. H. Bivar, 'Professor Sir Harold Bailey, FBA', *Journal of the Royal Asiatic Society of Great Britain and Ireland*, 3rd ser., 6 (1996), 407–10 · A. Chaudhri and M. Szuppe, 'Sir Harold Bailey (1899–1996)', *Newsletter, Center for Iranian Studies*, 8/1 (spring 1996), 1–2 · E. Kahrs, 'In memoriam Sir Harold Walter Bailey', *Journal of the International Association of Buddhist Studies*, 20/2 (1998), 3–5 · R. E. Emmerick and D. M. Johnson, 'Writings of H. W. Bailey (books and articles)', *Bulletin of the School of Oriental and African Studies*, 33 (1970), ix–xiv · A. J. Toynbee, *A study of history*, 10 (1954) · *The Independent* (12 Jan 1996) · *The Times* (13 Jan 1996) · *The Guardian* (25 Jan 1996) · *WWW* [forthcoming] · Burke, *Peerage* · b. cert. · private information (2004)
Archives Ancient India and Iran Trust, Brooklands House, Cambridge, papers, etc. · Ancient India and Iran Trust, Brooklands House, Cambridge, personal library
Likenesses R. Way, oils, 1972, Queens' College, Cambridge; repro. in *The Independent* [*see illus.*] · photograph, repro. in *The Times*
Wealth at death £153,688: probate, 15 April 1996, *CGPLA Eng. & Wales*

Bailey, James (1791/2–1864), classical scholar, was the grandson of James Bailey, master of the village school at Gargrave, Yorkshire, and later headmaster of the free school at Guiseley. His place of birth and parentage are not known. Bailey is known to have been a boarder at Giggleswick School, from which he ran away, before being sent to Richmond grammar school under the headmastership of James Tate. To Tate he owed his love of classical scholarship. He was admitted to Trinity College, Cambridge, in 1808 as a sizar, gaining a scholarship in 1813. He obtained the university Browne medals for Greek ode and epigram, and the members' prizes in 1815 and 1816, the latter for an essay on hieroglyphics (reprinted in the *Classical Journal*, vols. 16 and 17). He graduated BA in 1814 and MA in 1823, but did not gain the fellowship for which his talents might have recommended him.

Bailey decided against entering the church, choosing instead to pursue literary ambitions, despite friendly warnings from Walter Scott, with whom he corresponded from 1812, and from whom he received encouragement and financial assistance, that letters provided an uncertain living. He seems to have remained in Cambridge, contributing in 1817 classical articles to John Ballantyne's *Sale Room*, and assisting John Richard Major in his new edition of J. Scapula's *Lexicon Graeco-Latinum* (1820). In the early 1820s he married and had a son. At the same time he was preparing his edition of Forcellini's Latin dictionary (2 vols., 1826), the work for which he was best known. In this he translated the Italian explanations into English, incorporated Forcellini's appendices within the main work, and added an extensive *auctarium* of his own.

In 1825 Bailey was appointed headmaster of the Perse Grammar School, Cambridge, at a salary of £125 a year; gradual increases to £400 a year testify to his effectiveness in raising the number of pupils. He resigned in 1833 owing to ill health, probably exacerbated by a chancery action brought by Cambridge townspeople challenging his policy of reducing the number of free places provided by the Perse trust from 100 to 16. Thereafter he lived on a pension of £100 and pursued his literary interests. Part 1 of his *Comicorum graecorum fragmenta*, with English translations by Francis Fawkes, Francis Wrangham, and Richard Cumberland, appeared in 1840, but there was no sequel. Troubled by debts—his books were sometimes in pawn—he moved in 1841 to Peckham, where the burden of supporting his son, who unsuccessfully claimed talents to poetry, increased his difficulties. On the recommendation of John Kaye, bishop of Lincoln, and Edward Maltby, bishop of Durham, both of whom were accomplished Cambridge-educated classicists, Bailey received a civil-list pension of £100 a year. He died, in poverty, of chronic bronchitis at 1 Isabella Cottages, Arthur Street, Old Kent Road, London, on 13 February 1864.

ALFRED GOODWIN, *rev.* M. C. CURTHOYS

Sources J. Gray, 'James Bailey, classical scholar', *Cambridge Review* (29 May 1965), 438–46 · Venn, *Alum. Cant.* · Boase, *Mod. Eng. biog.* · d. cert.
Archives FM Cam., corresp.
Wealth at death died in poverty

Bailey, James Richard Abe [Jim] (1919–2000), publisher and writer, was born on 23 October 1919 in London, the younger son and fourth of the five children of Sir Abraham (Abe) *Bailey, first baronet (1864–1940), a South African mining magnate, and his second wife, the Hon. Mary Westenra [*see* Bailey, Dame Mary (1890–1960)], daughter of the fifth Baron Rossmore. His father was prominent in political and financial circles; his mother won fame with a solo flight from Croydon to Cape Town in 1928. Jim Bailey attended Winchester College and entered Christ Church, Oxford, in 1938 to study politics, philosophy, and economics. A member of the Oxford University air squadron, he joined the Royal Air Force Volunteer Reserve as a fighter pilot on 2 September 1939 and served with 264 squadron during the battle of Britain. His outstanding record earned him the Distinguished Flying Cross in 1944, while the loss of so many comrades made Squadron Leader Bailey feel that he had experienced the vicissitudes of a lifetime in six years. The war inspired not only his memoir, *The Sky Suspended* (1965), but also numerous poems, published in *F as in Flight* (1961) and *The Poetry of a Fighter Pilot* (1993).

From 1946 to 1950 Bailey divided his time between England and South Africa. At Oxford he started a thesis on the history of the idea of progress, which became the book *National Ambitions* (1958). In Northern Cape he ran his inherited racing stud and sheep farm, and enjoyed the independence bestowed by wealth. Africa powerfully appealed to Bailey, a tall gangling man with a mop of fair hair, a slouching walk, and a rooted aversion to tidiness. Strong-willed and irreverent, sardonic yet romantic, he had a penchant for low life and hard drinking. His individualism unfitted him for party politics, but he was transparently a liberal whose cross-racial friendships defied the onset of apartheid.

At the bidding of Robert Crisp, Bailey gave financial backing to the *African Drum*, a monthly English-language magazine for black South Africans that first appeared in March 1951. Sales were poor, and Bailey saw why: black readers scorned the idealization by well-meaning white writers. In the autumn he bought out Crisp, moved the publication from Cape Town to Johannesburg, and hired untried staff from the townships. Out went kraals and folklore; in came jazz, boxing, and pin-up girls. The new *Drum*, with its title shortened, was written for urban black people largely by urban black people, such as Can Themba, Todd Matshikiza, 'Bloke' Modisane, and Casey Motsisi. Despite a string of white editors—Anthony Sampson, Sylvester Stein, and Tom Hopkinson—it grew into the most authentic manifestation of black culture in South African journalism. The courageous investigations of 'Mr Drum' (Henry Nxumalo) into the maltreatment of farm labourers and convicts were especially notable.

In 1958 Bailey married Gillian Mary Parker, but they divorced in 1963. Barbara Louise Taylor, *née* Epstein, a pianist, became his second wife on 16 April 1964. He brought up five children: Jonathan (*b.* 1959) from his first marriage, and Alaric (1965–1986) and Prospero (*b.* 1969) from his second, together with two stepchildren from Barbara Taylor's first marriage. *Drum* meanwhile spread throughout Anglophone Africa, and Bailey paid frequent visits to oversee local editions. Monthly sales peaked at about 450,000 in the 1960s, with a total readership in the region of 5 million, yet his pan-African vision proved over-ambitious. Newly independent black states were no more respectful of press freedom than was South Africa, where heightened censorship made meaningful political coverage impossible. The watchword had to be 'Publish and be banned!' (Stein, 61).

With his foghorn voice, baying laugh, and RAF slang, Bailey was at once extremely casual and rather grand. He could be stubborn and unpredictable; many editors and journalists fell out with him. Sex and sport were what sold *Drum*, he maintained, and his interest in stories about witch doctors and ritual murder upset black intellectuals. Nevertheless, most conceded that his flair and tenacity were as vital as his money to the periodical's survival. Even with the addition of *Golden City Post*, a Sunday newspaper, and *True Love*, a photo-story book, Drum Publications only broke even at best. Advertising revenues remained low, and Bailey would never share control with co-owners or an effective business manager. Controversially, he sold all three titles in April 1984 to the Afrikaner newspaper group Nasionale Pers.

'The bohemian billionaire', as Bailey was dubbed (with a degree of exaggeration), came to resemble an aged hippy. Historical speculation preoccupied him: in *The God-Kings and the Titans* (1973) and *Sailing to Paradise: the Discovery of the Americas by 7000 BC* (1994) he contended that mankind had comprised a single global civilization in the Bronze Age, and that America was the lost Atlantis. Ridicule from mainstream scholars in no way lessened his belief in the shared spiritual heritage of the new and old worlds. By the time he was appointed CBE in 1996, *Drum*'s heyday in the 1950s had become the stuff of literary legend in South Africa. Bailey died of cancer at Lanseria, north of Johannesburg, on 29 February 2000. His second wife, Barbara, survived him. JASON TOMES

Sources *The Guardian* (3 March 2000) • *Daily Telegraph* (3 March 2000) • *The Independent* (24 March 2000) • *The Times* (10 March 2000) • M. Nicol, *A good-looking corpse* (1991) • A. Sampson, *Drum: an African adventure—and afterwards* (1983) • S. Stein, *Who killed Mr Drum?* (1999) • T. Hopkinson, *In the fiery continent* (1962) • J. Bailey, *The sky suspended* (1965)

Archives Auckland Park, Johannesburg, Bailey's African history archives

Likenesses photograph, repro. in *The Times* • photograph, repro. in *Daily Telegraph* • photograph, repro. in *The Independent* • photograph, repro. in *The Guardian*

Bailey, John (1644–1697), nonconformist minister, was born on 24 February 1644, probably at Altham, near Blackburn, Lancashire, the son of Thomas Bailey (*d.* 1673). His father was notorious for his drunkenness and profligacy but the young Bailey acquired both his mother's piety and her strength of character. An Independent congregation led by the Revd Thomas Jolly met at Altham; its churchbook recorded in 1657 that Bailey was 'a wonderful child for a spirit of prayer, experimental discourse, and being the occasion of good to his father and a schoolfellow'. Cotton Mather reported independently that by this time the boy was already conducting family worship; either out of admiration or humiliation, Thomas Bailey abandoned his old habits and became a reformed character, and joined Jolly's congregation. John attended Blackburn grammar school, then under the mastership of Charles Sagar (1636–1698). Later he studied theology under Dr Thomas Harrison, a nonconformist minister at Chester.

John Bailey began his career as a lay preacher at the age of twenty-two. In February 1665 he was arrested with Thomas Jolly and imprisoned, perhaps not for the last time, in Lancaster gaol. He was released after three months, perhaps following intervention by the Houghton family of Houghton Cross; it seems, however, that he lost the favour of Sarah, Lady Houghton after criticizing the breach between herself and her husband, Sir Richard. In 1670 Bailey was 'formally set apart for the ministry', but later in the year he emigrated to Dublin, and there married his first wife, Lydia (*d.* 1690). In Dublin too, despite his own dislike of the ceremony, he appears to have undergone formal presbyterian ordination with the laying on of hands; as he later wrote to his congregation in Limerick: 'For you (tho it was a great act of self denial) I was ordained' (Bailey, *Man's Chief End*, 2nd pagination, 2). At Limerick there was among Bailey's auditory a relation of the duke of Ormond. When this came to the notice of the bishop he protested to the duke against the impunity

John Bailey (1644–1697), by unknown artist

which his connection thus encouraged among dissenters. Ormond's response was to invite Bailey to be his chaplain; but neither this, nor the offers of a deanery, or even the next vacant Irish bishopric, which reputedly followed, were sufficient to induce him to conform. Later Bailey's preaching activities led to his arraignment. It is reported that he protested before the judges of assize that:

> If I had been drinking, gaming and carousing at a tavern, with company, my lords, I presume that I would not have procured my being thus treated as an offender. Must prayers to God and preaching Christ with a company of Christians who are peaceable, inoffensive, and serviceable to his majesty and the government, as any of his subjects—must this be considered a greater crime?

to which the answer came that it was (Palmer, 1.331). He was imprisoned, and was released on promising to leave Ireland within a specified period without making further contact with his congregation, which he had by now served for twelve years.

Bailey emigrated to New England, probably in the spring of 1684, for it was surely not long after his arrival in Boston that he framed a letter, dated 8 May, to his congregation in Limerick. Nathaniel Mather thought Bailey had been encouraged to undertake the voyage by Samuel Willard, the minister at the Old South Church in Boston, and indeed the newcomer was soon appointed as his assistant; on 2 March 1685, Samuel Sewall recorded that Bailey 'preached from Amos 4.12 and Mr Willard from 2 Cor … both sermons and prayers excellent' (*Diary of Samuel Sewall*, 59). Soon after the Independent congregation at Watertown, Connecticut, invited Bailey to fill the vacancy caused by the death of its pastor, John Sherman; Bailey accepted, preaching his farewell sermon in Boston on 25 July 1686, and leaving the town in the same week. As he records, 'Upon the 6th October 1686 I was solemnly set apart for the pastoral work at Watertown without the imposition of hands' (Francis, 51). Sewall recorded that on 'Wednesday Oct 6: Mr Bayly is ordained at Watertown but not as congregational men are' (*Diary of Samuel Sewall*, 123). It seems clear that Bailey accepted the need to be 'set apart' to his new pastorate, but that he retained his dislike (shared by many Independents) of the ceremony to which he had reluctantly submitted in 1670.

Within a month or so of Bailey's ordination Thomas, his younger brother, was appointed as his assistant. It seems that John was already in poor health, for on 25 March 1686, before his departure for Watertown, Sewall recorded that 'Mr Willard exerciseth all day, Mr Bayly being constrained to keep house by reason of the gout' (*Diary of Samuel Sewall*, 101). Thomas Bailey died on 31 January 1689 aged only thirty-five; the church's anxiety to secure the services of a new assistant (Henry Gibbs) must surely reflect the continued ill health of their pastor. John Bailey's illness was compounded by bouts of depression, perhaps exacerbated by sadness at the death on 12 April 1690 of his wife, Lydia. Bailey for many years kept a diary, using it to keep an account of his lonely spiritual struggles. Later, Cotton Mather published extensive extracts, in which the demands of his conscience sometimes appear almost comically excessive—'I was too forgetful of God, and exceeding in tobacco. The Lord pardon that, and all other sins, and heal this nature, and humble this heart'—and in which the author occasionally approaches despair at his own weakness: 'I am oppressed unto death, and filled with the angry arrows of God: it ariseth not from any particular cause, but the sense of my woeful estate in general' (Mather, 234, 236).

In 1692 Bailey resigned his charge at Watertown and bid farewell to the town, its churches, and people:

> saints but sinners also, old but young also, all my children which grieved me most, friends and foes, the sweet singers of Israel, all widows and fatherless families, all moralized persons, all that heard me not now, the pulpit, pew seats and galleries (the cushion I left as a token of my love), all my administrations, him that digs the graves, neighbouring towns and churches. (Sprague, 1.203)

He returned to Boston, where in July 1693 he was accepted as an assistant to the pastor of the First Church. There on 26 December 1695 he married Susannah Wilkins (who on 28 December 1699, after Bailey's death, became the wife of the Revd Peter Thatcher). It was Burgess's practice to preach at the First Church once a month and at the Old South Church every other Sunday. But on Sunday 12 December 1697 'about 3 am just the time he should have stood up to preach for Mr Willard, Mr John Bayly dieth, after much pain and illness by the Gout and other distempers' (*Diary of Samuel Sewall*, 384). According to Francis, he 'was honourably interred on the 16th day in the tomb of Mr Thomas Deane' in Boston (Francis, 52). Cotton Mather preached his funeral sermon. An oil painting, representing his 'pensive and somewhat feminine face and long flowing hair' (*DNB*) is in the possession of the Massachusetts Historical Society. STEPHEN WRIGHT

Sources W. Sprague, *Annals of the American pulpit*, 1 (1857) · *The diary of Samuel Sewall, 1674–1729: newly edited from the manuscript at the Massachusetts Historical Society*, ed. M. H. Thomas, 2 vols. (1973) · W. Abram, *A history of Blackburn, town and parish* (1877) · C. Francis, *History of Watertown in Massachusetts* (1830) · *The note book of the Rev. Thomas Jolly, AD 1671–1693, extracts from the church book of Altham and Wymondhouses, AD 1649–1725, and an account of the Jolly family of Standish, Gorton, and Altham*, ed. H. Fishwick, Chetham Society, new ser., 33 (1894) · C. Mather, *Magnalia Christi Americana*, 7 bks in 1 vol. (1702) · J. Bailey, *Man's chief end to glorifie God, or, Some brief sermon-notes on I Cor 10. 31* (1689) · J. T. Cliffe, *The puritan gentry besieged, 1650–1700* (1993) · W. Emerson, *History of the First Church in Boston* (1812) · J. Farmer, *A genealogical register of the first settlers of New England* (1829); repr. (1964) · *The nonconformist's memorial … originally written by … Edmund Calamy*, ed. S. Palmer, [3rd edn], 1 (1802), 331

Likenesses oils, Mass. Hist. Soc. [*see illus.*]

Bailey, John (1750–1819), mathematician and land surveyor, was born at Blades Field, near Bowes, Yorkshire, the son of William Bailey. At an early age he showed strong artistic tendencies, and while employed as tutor to the children of his uncle, George Dixon of Cockfield, he devoted his spare time to engraving various pieces, which he afterwards published. Both in his artistic and mathematical studies he received valuable assistance from his uncle who was also versed in mineralogy, chemistry, hydraulics, pneumatics, and surveying. After completing the education of his uncle's children Bailey became mathematical teacher at Witton-le-Wear, and began work as a land surveyor, making surveys in Derbyshire, Leicestershire, Northumberland, Nottinghamshire, and Wiltshire. Shortly after his marriage, to the daughter of Nicholas Greenwell of Witton, he was appointed land agent to Lord Tankerville at Chillingham, a situation he retained until his death.

Bailey engraved several of the plates for the works of William Hutchinson, the topographer of Cumberland, Durham, and Northumberland. He also devoted much of his attention to the natural sciences, and his scientific acquirements were turned to practical use in promoting improvements in rural economy. In 1795 he published *Essay on the Construction of the Plough*, in which he employed mathematical calculations to demonstrate the advantages of the alterations he proposed. He was also the joint author of the reports on the counties of Cumberland and Northumberland, drawn up for the board of agriculture, and sole author for that on co. Durham. He died at Chillingham on 4 June 1819.

T. F. HENDERSON, *rev.* H. K. HIGTON

Sources F. W. Steer and others, *Dictionary of land surveyors and local cartographers of Great Britain and Ireland, 1550–1850*, ed. P. Eden, [4 vols.] (1975–9) · M. A. Richardson, ed., *The local historian's table book … historical division*, 5 vols. (1841–6), vol. 3, p. 197

Bailey, Sir John [Jack] (1898–1969), politician and co-operative movement activist, was born on 1 January 1898 in Miskin, Mountain Ash, Glamorgan, one of six children of John Bailey, miner, and his wife, Sarah Ann. Bailey attended Gwyn Ivor School, Miskin, until he was twelve. Working initially in a cobbler's shop, he entered the mines as a collier's boy. An accident in 1915 forced him to take a surface job, and in 1917 he enlisted in the South Wales Borderers and served in France.

Bailey returned to the mines in 1919. He studied economics through a correspondence course, administered at Ruskin College, Oxford, and joined the Independent Labour Party. Born into a Wesleyan Methodist family, Bailey considered entering the ministry. In 1921, however, he received a South Wales Miners' Federation scholarship to the Central Labour College in London. He unsuccessfully contested his first local government election, at Kensington, in 1922. Bailey also met Anne Glaser, whom he later married, in 1926; they had one son and two daughters. After returning home in 1923, Bailey was elected to Mountain Ash urban district council. In 1925 he was appointed as political secretary to the Co-operative Party in Bradford, Yorkshire. He served on Bradford city council (in 1928–31 and 1933–8), leading the juvenile employment and education committees.

Declining opportunities to stand for parliament, Bailey became a London-based national organizer for the Co-operative Party in 1936. In 1942 he succeeded S. F. Perry as the party's general secretary. Bailey was unsuccessful in recruiting candidates from among co-operative traders and initially the Co-operative Party hardly distinguished itself from its Labour parliamentary allies. However, post-war nationalization led co-operators, including Bailey, to question the apparent growth of centralized and bureaucratic state control, advocating instead democratic social ownership through co-operative and municipal enterprise. Tensions were heightened by the co-operative movement's defence of its own insurance society against Labour proposals of 1949 for nationalization of industrial insurance. Throughout the 1950s Labour policy was criticized as neglectful of consumer interests and of co-operation's potential role in economic and social regeneration. Bailey was instrumental in establishing the Co-operative Party's distinctive voice.

Bailey led negotiations concerning organizational relations between the Co-operative and Labour parties. In 1946 it was agreed that Co-operative parliamentarians would stand as 'Co-operative and Labour' candidates and, on election, join the Parliamentary Labour Party (PLP). However, while co-operators resented the lack of consultation on Labour policy development, other interested groups sought to curb Co-operative nomination of parliamentary candidates and impose greater discipline over Co-operative members of the PLP. Bailey actively opposed the 1956 proposal that individual co-operative societies affiliate directly to constituency Labour parties. In 1958, however, he conceded limits on the number of Co-operative parliamentary candidates.

Bailey wrote extensively, in Co-operative Party policy statements, as editor of the party's *Monthly Newsletter*, in other journals, and as author of a popular textbook, *The British Co-operative Movement* (1955, revised edn 1960). His interests embraced the global, including work for the

International Co-operative Alliance in eastern Europe and Africa, and the local, as secretary of Cheshunt and Waltham Cross Co-operative Party and vice-chairman of the East Hertfordshire Labour Party. He was also a director of the Enfield Highway Co-operative Society from 1952 and became president in 1968.

After retirement as Co-operative Party secretary in 1962 Bailey served on the national federation negotiating committee which considered amalgamation of national co-operative institutions to form a single focus for the movement. He presided at the Co-operative Congress of 1964 and was knighted in 1965. Bailey died in hospital at Enfield after a short illness on 18 January 1969. His funeral was held on 24 January at Enfield crematorium; Bailey was survived by his wife and children.

Self-discipline and hard work, combined with a belief in co-operative democracy as an economic and political philosophy, made Bailey a formidable political operator. Yet he also had 'some of the mystique (and occasional vagueness) of the visionary' (Carbery, 52). Bailey secured the constitutional relationship between the Labour and Co-operative parties and ensured a co-operative contribution to British politics. MARTIN PURVIS

Sources *Co-operative News* (25 Jan 1969) · *Co-operative Review* (Feb 1969) · T. F. Carbery, *Consumers in politics: a history and general review of the co-operative party* (1969) · *The Guardian* (20 Jan 1969) · *The Times* (20 Jan 1969) · *Daily Telegraph* (20 Jan 1969) · F. Beswick, 'In profile … Jack Bailey', *Co-operative News* (21 April 1962) · A. G. Peddie, 'Jack Bailey: a tribute', *Co-operative Review* (Dec 1962) · J. Bailey, *The British co-operative movement*, 2nd edn (1960) · J. Bailey, *Co-operators in politics* (1950) · J. Bellamy and J. Saville, 'Bailey, Sir John (Jack)', *DLB*, vol. 2 · d. cert.

Likenesses photograph, *c.*1962, Co-operative College, Manchester, National Co-operative Archive, Jack Bailey biographical file

Wealth at death £7863: probate, 23 July 1969, *CGPLA Eng. & Wales*

Bailey, John Cann (1864–1931), writer on literature, the third son of Elijah Crosier Bailey, solicitor and clerk of the peace for Norwich, and his wife, Jane Sarah, daughter of William Robert Cann, of Cavick House, Wymondham, Norfolk, was born at Cavick House on 10 January 1864. He was educated at Haileybury College and at New College, Oxford, where he obtained second classes in classical moderations (1884) and *literae humaniores* (1886); he was called to the bar by the Inner Temple in 1892. He moved to London with sufficient private means to enable him to stand for parliament (he unsuccessfully contested the Sowerby division of Yorkshire in the Conservative interest in 1895 and 1900), but with few social contacts other than those which he had formed at university. Bailey's easy, agreeable, and intelligent conversation gave him, however, a ready entrance into the metropolitan society of the 1890s. On 26 April 1900 he married Sarah Kathleen (*d.* 1941), the eldest daughter from his second marriage of G. W. *Lyttelton, fourth Baron Lyttelton. They had three daughters, the youngest of whom predeceased Bailey. Herself a spirited conversationalist, his wife gave him not only a very happy home life but the association of several important brothers-in-law, including Neville Gerald Lyttelton, army officer, Arthur Temple Lyttelton, suffragan bishop of Southampton, and Alfred Lyttelton, lawyer and statesman. He was a constant and valued member of the Literary (dining) Society, of which he eventually became president, and, as might be expected of so ardent a Johnsonian, was immensely gratified by his election to 'the Club'.

Bailey's intense pleasure in good talk may possibly have restricted his literary output, but his literary ambition was always circumscribed. He related that when people asked him to write a *magnum opus* he used to counter by enquiring: 'If I write it, will you buy it and will you read it?' It is arguable that his best work was, in fact, slight in compass. He himself may have rated highest his *Milton* (1915), a little book, but many of his contemporaries felt that *Dr Johnson and his Circle* (1913) gave his particular powers their fullest scope. Bailey's other publications include *Studies in some Famous Letters* (1899); an edition of the *Poems of William Cowper* (1905); *The Claims of French Poetry* (1907); *Some Political Ideas and Persons* (1921); *The Continuity of Letters* (1923); an edition of the *Diary of Lady Frederick Cavendish* (2 vols., 1927), the author being his sister-in-law; and *Shakespeare* (English Heritage series, 1929). Bailey was a constant contributor to the *Times Literary Supplement*, for which he did much important, though anonymous work; to the *Quarterly Review*, of which he was deputy editor in 1907–8 and again in 1909–10; to the *Edinburgh Review* and the *Fortnightly Review*; and to the *London Mercury*.

As chairman (1912–15) and president (1925–6) of the English Association, Bailey made a further contribution to the study of English letters; and as chairman (1923–31) of the executive committee of the National Trust, and also of the Fulham branch of the Charity Organization Society, he disclosed a practical interest in things of beauty and in matters of social welfare.

Never a strong man physically, Bailey was still actively involved in the literary world when he died, at his home, 4 Onslow Gardens, Kensington, London, on 29 June 1931. He was buried on 2 July in the churchyard of Wramplingham near Wymondham, as befitted one who valued both his connection with the county of Norfolk and his membership of the Church of England. His outlook had been that of a broad-churchman.

ALGERNON CECIL, *rev.* ANNETTE PEACH

Sources *John Bailey, 1864–1931: letters and diaries*, ed. S. Bailey (1935) · *The Times* (30 June 1931) · *Cox's county who's who series: Norfolk, Suffolk, and Cambridgeshire* (1912) · [A. Cecil], 'John Bailey', *TLS* (12 Sept 1935), 562 · personal knowledge (1949) · *CGPLA Eng. & Wales* (1931)

Archives Bodl. Oxf., corresp. with Geoffrey Dawson · NL Scot., letters to Blackwoods · U. St Andr. L., corresp. with Wilfred Ward and his wife

Likenesses photograph, repro. in Bailey, ed., *John Bailey*, frontispiece

Wealth at death £26,295 19*s.* 1*d.*: probate, 25 Sept 1931, *CGPLA Eng. & Wales*

Bailey, John Eglington (1840–1888), antiquary, born at Edgbaston, Birmingham, on 13 February 1840, was the son of Charles Bailey and his wife, Mary Elizabeth, daughter of John Eglington of Ashbourne. His parents moved during his childhood to Lancashire. Educated at Boteler's Grammar School, Warrington, he entered in his teens the counting-house of Ralli Brothers of Manchester, and continued there until 1886. He completed his education by attending evening classes at Owens College, and learned Pitman's shorthand. In 1866 he married Emma Mills, the second daughter of Samuel Mills of Ardwick. They had four children.

Bailey became interested at an early age in Thomas Fuller (1608–1661), the ecclesiastical historian, and delivered a lecture on him to the Manchester Phonographic Union, of which he was a founder member. This was printed in Henry Pitman's *Popular Lecturer* (new ser., 9, 1864). He devoted his holidays to visiting Fuller's various places of residence and in 1874, as the fruit of much research, Bailey published a life of Fuller, his most important work, and one which gained him admission into the Society of Antiquaries. He also became honorary secretary to the Chetham Society, Manchester, and was a contributor to the earliest volumes of the *Dictionary of National Biography*. A prolific writer, he published 420 articles and books on such diverse subjects as shorthand, local topography, and seventeenth-century divines. In 1881 he started a monthly antiquarian magazine, the *Palatine Note-Book*, which ran for just over four years. He collected many works on stenography with a view to writing a history of the subject, and he possessed a large library of antiquarian and general literature.

In 1886 illness put an end to Bailey's studies and projects. He died at Etchells, Stockport, Cheshire, on 23 August 1888, and was buried at Stretford church on 27 August. His collection of Fuller's sermons, completed and edited by W. E. A. Axon, was published in 1891.

J. G. ALGER, *rev.* ZOË LAWSON

Sources *Manchester Guardian* (24 Aug 1888) · W. E. A. Axon, 'List of the writings of John Eglington Bailey', *Transactions of the Lancashire and Cheshire Antiquarian Society*, 6 (1888), 129–50 · *N&Q*, 7th ser., 6 (1888), 180 · W. E. A. Axon, 'In memoriam J. E. Bailey F.S.A.', *Manchester Quarterly*, 28 (1888), 297–306 · W. E. A. Axon, *The Academy* (8 Sept 1888), 152–3 · H. Brierley, *Morgan Brierley: a memoir with a selection from his writings* (1900) · *CGPLA Eng. & Wales* (1889)

Archives Chetham's Library, Manchester, MS collection · NL Wales, corrected transcript of Flixton parish register | BL, letters to W. C. Hazlitt and S. G. Perceval, Add MSS 38901–38902, 41496 · Herts. ALS, letters to Lord Lytton · NL Wales, letters to William Beaumont

Likenesses photograph, repro. in H. T. Crofton, *History of the ancient chapel of Stretford in Manchester parish*, 1 (1899)

Wealth at death £5034 6*s.* 11*d.*: resworn probate, Nov 1889, *CGPLA Eng. & Wales*

Bailey, Kenneth (1909–1963), biochemist, was born on 18 August 1909 at Alsagers Bank, near Stoke upon Trent, the fourth child and elder son of Bertram Bailey, colliery clerk, and his wife, (Elizabeth) Florence Buckley. He received his early education at the Orme Boys' School, Newcastle under Lyme, on leaving which he enrolled at the University of Birmingham, where he achieved a BSc degree with first-class honours in 1931, and took his PhD in 1933. The award of a Beit fellowship in 1933 took him to the Royal College of Science, Imperial College, London. There he came under the influence of William Thomas Astbury, who visited the laboratory periodically to discuss the analysis and denaturation of proteins. This led to a scientific collaboration and the development of a friendship between the two very different men.

Bailey's work soon showed a remarkable understanding of the physical, chemical, and biological facets of protein structure and in 1939 the Rockefeller Foundation awarded him a travelling grant to join E. J. Cohn and J. T. Edsall at Harvard. In December 1939, however, he returned home, to work first at Porton and then at the Low Temperature Research Station in Cambridge. Later he joined a team investigating organo-phosphorous compounds in the university biochemical laboratory at Cambridge. He obtained a Cambridge PhD in 1944. After the war he was granted an ICI fellowship, which released him to do research on the chemistry of muscle and the coagulation of blood: both projects brought him once again into contact with Astbury. In 1948 he became an assistant director of research in the university and was elected a fellow of Trinity College. In 1953 he obtained a Cambridge ScD, was elected FRS, and spent a few months as visiting professor at Washington University, Seattle, where he finished editing, with Hans Neurath, *The Proteins* (1954), the first work to treat the subject comprehensively. In 1961 he became a reader in biochemistry.

Bailey made no attempt to build up a research school of his own: he firmly believed that worthwhile discoveries were made only by those who 'played about' at the bench. He never wanted more than one or two junior workers with him and refused offers of chairs at home and abroad. His researches were notable for their impact on the development of biological science. One was his clear demonstration in 1951 with F. R. Bettelheim, independently of the Leeds group under Lorand, of the nature of the action of thrombin on fibrinogen. This work led to the isolation of the fibrinopeptides and for the first time to an understanding of the molecular mechanisms involved in the formation of the fibrin clot.

Bailey's other great achievement was his discovery in 1946 of the protein tropomyosin, which, although originally isolated from skeletal muscle, was later shown to be present in most eucaryotic cells. He purified, crystallized, and characterized the protein in a way which could not be faulted even with the much more sophisticated methods of protein fractionation later available. Tropomyosin was the first fibrous protein to be crystallized and Bailey immediately recognized the uniqueness of the properties of this remarkable protein with 100 per cent α-helical content. It was not until after his death, however, that the importance of tropomyosin for the function of all contractile systems depending on actomyosin was appreciated. In vertebrate skeletal muscle, in association with the troponin complex, tropomyosin is concerned with the regulation of the interaction of actin with myosin and hence contraction itself.

Bailey also made another less direct but nevertheless important contribution, through his research student, B. B. Marsh, to the understanding of the regulation of contraction in muscle. Marsh's investigation, under Bailey's direction, of the changes which occur in post-mortem minced muscle tissue, resulted in the discovery of the Marsh factor, the further study of which by other investigators subsequently led to the discovery of the calcium pump of the sarcoplasmic reticulum.

Bailey was always somewhat reserved, and his gentle demeanour could often mask a deep intuitive understanding of people and affairs. He had, moreover, the rare gift of being able to express himself in lucid and, when needed, in vivid language. He was unmarried. His later years were marred by severe recurrent depressive illness and he committed suicide in Cambridge on 22 May 1963.

A. C. CHIBNALL, *rev.*

Sources R. Porter, *Nature*, 200 (1963), 520–21 • A. C. Chibnall, *Memoirs FRS*, 10 (1964), 1–13 • *The Times* (31 June 1963) • personal knowledge (1981) • private information (1981) • *CGPLA Eng. & Wales* (1963)
Archives CUL, corresp. and papers | U. Leeds, Brotherton L., corresp. with W. T. Astbury
Likenesses E. Blaine, photograph, 1953, Seattle • oils, RS
Wealth at death £13,996 0s. 11d.: probate, 30 Dec 1963, *CGPLA Eng. & Wales*

Bailey [*née* Westenra], **Dame Mary, Lady Bailey (1890–1960)**, aviator, was born in London on 1 December 1890, the only daughter and the eldest of three children of Derrick Warner William Westenra, fifth Baron Rossmore (1853–1921), and his wife, Mittie Naylor (*d.* 1953). On 5 September 1911 she married, as his second wife, Sir Abe *Bailey, first baronet (1864–1940), a South African mining magnate, financier, and politician. They had three daughters and two sons; the eldest son eventually succeeded his father as third baronet. Lady Bailey took an early interest in aviation and she trained as a pilot with the London aviation club at Stag Lane in 1926, gaining her Royal Aero Club certificate on 26 January 1927. Despite her inexperience, in July 1927 she broke the women's altitude record in a light aircraft by climbing to 17,283 feet in a D. H. Gipsy Moth, taking Mrs Geoffrey de Havilland as a passenger, and she was the first woman to fly across the Irish Sea. She also took a course in navigation. Her almost casual approach to flying showed the benefits of light aircraft for personal travel, and the increasing independence of women, even those with children, was highlighted by her exploits.

On 9 March 1928 she set off from Croydon for a solo flight to South Africa, using a de Havilland Cirrus Moth that had been fitted with additional fuel tanks. Her course lay via Malta, Tripoli, Cairo, and along the Nile to Khartoum, before heading for Tabora in Tanganyika. Unable to find Tabora, she landed to ask the way, and wrecked her machine beyond repair by attempting to leave in gusty conditions. She telegraphed her husband to order another aircraft, which was delivered to her by the South African Air Force twelve days later. She resumed her journey and arrived at Cape Town on 30 April 1928. Contrary to the hopes of her husband, she then decided to make the return flight. Her aircraft was again damaged, and her departure was delayed until 21 September. Her return route was to take her across the Sahara Desert, via Kano in Nigeria, and Dakar in French West Africa. The route had not previously been used, and the Sudanese government forbade women to fly solo, so for that leg of the journey she was accompanied by Captain Bentley of the South African Air Force, who had made a record flight from London to the Cape in 1927. Thick fog delayed her crossing of the channel from France, and she finally arrived back in England on 16 January 1929, a bitterly cold day. 'I have just gone to see my husband', she told reporters at Croydon (Cluett, 23). She had completed 18,000 miles in the air; for this, in 1930, she was awarded the Britannia trophy, presented for meritorious performance in the air. She was appointed DBE for services to aviation in the same year. Lady Bailey entered the king's cup air race in 1927, 1929, and 1930, and she flew in the international challenge competitions round Europe in 1929 and 1930. Lady Bailey continued to fly for many years, and she settled at Kenilworth, near Cape Town in South Africa after the death of her husband in 1940. She died there on 29 August 1960. A memorial service was held for her at St Clement Danes, Strand, London.

PETER G. COOKSLEY

Sources *The Times* (30 Aug 1960) • *The Times* (12 Oct 1960) • M. J. H. Taylor and D. Mondey, *Guinness aircraft: facts and feats* (1984) • A. J. Jackson, *De Havilland aircraft since 1915* [1962] • A. J. Jackson, *British civil aircraft* (1959) • D. Cluett, *The first, the fastest and the famous* (1985) • H. Coble and A. R. Payne, *Famous aircraft* (1937) • C. G. Burge, *Encyclopaedia of aviation* (1935) • I. Mackersey, *Jean Batten, Garbo of the skies* (1992) • *DNB* • W. Brown, *The sky's the limit* (1979) • Burke, *Peerage* (1939–99) • *CGPLA Eng. & Wales* (1961)
Archives FILM BFI NFTVA, a British Movietone clip | SOUND BL NSA, BBC recording
Likenesses photographs, *Aeroplane Monthly* Archive, London • photographs, Sci. Mus.
Wealth at death £37,666 8s. in England: South African probate sealed in England, 24 May 1961, *CGPLA Eng. & Wales*

Bailey, Nathan (*bap.* **1691**, *d.* **1742**), lexicographer and schoolmaster, was baptized on 7 October 1691 in Mill Yard church, a Seventh Day Baptist congregation in Whitechapel, Stepney, just east of the city of London. His church was opposed to infant baptism and Bailey signed a church document as early as 1692. In 1711 he was censured by the church for having indulged in:

> frequent light and low conversation with two single women, he being a single man and a high professor [that is, one who has openly professed his religion], and they in principle and practice being so unfit company for his diversion and pleasure. (Ball, 94)

He seems to have been dropped from the membership of the congregation by 1718. From as early as 1721 and until as late as 1736 he boarded and instructed youths in 'the *Latin*, *Greek*, and *Hebrew* Languages, *Writing*, *Accounts*, and other Parts of School Learning, in a Method more easy and expeditious than common … at his House in Stepney, near the Church' (N. Bailey, *Dictionarium Britannicum*, 1736). Whitley credits Bailey with an LLD degree—an honorary degree, according to *Transactions of the Baptist Historical Society*—but it is not known which institution awarded him this degree. The burial of his wife in 1738 is mentioned in the church records.

Bailey's first dictionary, *An universal etymological English dictionary: comprehending the derivations of the generality of words in the English tongue, either ancient or modern* (1721), was followed by what claimed to be a second volume in 1727, which included an 'orthographical dictionary, shewing both the orthography and orthoepia of the English tongue' (title-page). 'Volume II', as the 1727 volume is generally known, introduced accentuation markings for the first time in a general English dictionary—perhaps following the precedent of Thomas Dyche's *Spelling Dictionary* (1723)—to compensate for the presumed inexperience of the reader: 'forasmuch as many Persons of a small Share of Literature and not very conversant in Books, are frequently apt to accent Words wrong' (preface). The two octavos were soon succeeded by the folio *Dictionarium Britannicum* (1730; 2nd edn, 1736). Dozens of editions of the first octavo work were published during the eighteenth century and after; they formed the basis for a number of English–German dictionaries, which began to appear in Germany from 1736 onwards.

Bailey's English dictionaries gave a new prominence to etymology and to lexical comprehensiveness, including dialect terms, scientific terms, common words, and even vulgar ones; they also (in the second octavo volume and in the folios) made the first extensive use of pictorial illustration, inserting some 500 small woodcuts 'for the more easy and clear apprehending' of the terms defined according to the title-page of 'Volume II'. Most depicted heraldic elements and scientific and military equipment. Additional encyclopaedic materials included iconological and mythological information, and proverbs explained in homely English and paralleled in Greek, Latin, French, and Italian.

Samuel Johnson used the second edition of Bailey's folio as a basis for developing his own dictionary, which competed with Bailey's for decades. Though Johnson's dictionary achieved the prestige of literary authority, Bailey's long remained popular, especially among autodidacts. Even William Pitt, the first earl of Chatham, though schooled at Eton, honed his celebrated parliamentary rhetoric by reading one of Bailey's dictionaries 'twice … from beginning to end' (*N&Q*, 5th ser., 1, 1874, 448). Thomas Chatterton may have mined the antique diction for his forged Rowley poems from Bailey. Notable fictional devotees of Bailey include the inexperienced but confident Mrs Western in *Tom Jones*, the ten-year-old Lydgate in *Middlemarch*, and the carpenter hero of *Adam Bede*, who 'had read … a great deal of Bailey's Dictionary' (Eliot, 1.320). Abraham Lincoln is said to have used a copy of the fourteenth edition (1751) of Bailey's first octavo dictionary. On the title-page of the first edition Bailey had invited those readers who lacked a thorough literary education: 'the Ignorant, and … young Students, Artificers, Tradesmen and Foreigners' (here, as elsewhere, he followed the precedent and even the phrasing of John Kersey's *Dictionarium Anglo-Britannicum*, 1708). The success of Bailey's dictionaries contributed to the diffusion of literacy in the eighteenth century—even to the global diffusion of English, which, by virtue of its mixed lineage and lexical inheritances, Bailey reckoned to be 'the most Copious and Significant Language in Europe, if not in the World' (1721, preface).

Aside from another dictionary, the *Dictionarium domesticum* (1736)—actually an alphabetized farmhouse manual—and *The Antiquities of London and Westminster* (1722; 2nd edn, 1734), a duodecimo guidebook abridged from books 'voluminous and dear' to convey local knowledge to 'the Generality' (preface, 'To the reader'), Bailey wrote several textbooks for grammar schools; these appeared in numerous editions, and were apparently informed by his own experience as a schoolmaster. They include a translation of Erasmus's *Colloquies* (1725, reprinted occasionally until 1900), editions of selections from Ovid, Phaedrus, and Justin, an English spelling book, and an English translation of a Latin exercise book. The *Colloquies*, a collection of exemplary dialogues in Latin, had long been an obligatory school text; Bailey provided the student with a sinewy translation meant to ease his understanding of the Latin original. (He also shows sympathy with Erasmus's anti-clericalism.) Bailey's editions of selected classics resort to various devices to ease the student's task: these devices range from a numerical 'clavis' in the margin, signalling the grammatical order underlying the rhetorical order of a line of verse (apparently an innovation), to a fully articulated reordering of the Latin, to supplying an outright translation. In emphasizing grammatical order, Bailey tacitly adopted and extended a pedagogical approach that had been associated with John Brinsley and, before him, Martin Crusius. In emphasizing easiness for the student generally, even to the point of providing translations, Bailey professed himself a disciple of John Locke—'the great Mr. *Lock*', who had urged, 'If the *Latin* Tongue is to be learn'd, let it be done the easiest way' (N. Bailey, ed., *M. J. Justini ex Trogi Pompeii historiis externis*, 1732, iii). Bailey's English dictionaries gained much of their lasting popularity from a similar pragmatic expediency or concern for the reader.

Bailey died on 27 June 1742 and was buried on 4 July 1742 at Mill Yard church at the price rated for a member of the congregation. His death was noticed by the *Gentleman's Magazine*. An engraved head-and-shoulders portrait in three-quarters profile, captioned 'N. Bailey, *Philologos*' (which is how he was styled on several title-pages), appeared as the frontispiece to Bailey's *Introduction to the English Tongue* in 1726—the year in which his first octavo dictionary reached its third edition, and the year after his translation of Erasmus appeared. That portrait probably served as the model for a later frontispiece published in Germany, signed by the engraver Christoph Sysang (1736). In the original engraving Bailey looks well fed and amiable, if somewhat upstaged by his periwig, neck cloth, and what may be an academic gown; the Sysang engraving makes him look yet more august.

MICHAEL HANCHER

Sources De W. T. Starnes and G. E. Noyes, *The English dictionary from Cawdrey to Johnson, 1604–1755* (1946) • *DNB* • W. E. A. Axon, *English dialect words of the eighteenth century as shown in the 'Universal etymological dictionary' of Nathaniel Bailey* (1883) • *N&Q*, 5th ser., 1 (1874), 448, 514; 2 (1874), 156, 258, 514–15; 3 (1875), 175–6, 298, 509–

11; 4 (1875), 276; 7 (1877), 447; 8 (1877), 52–3, 178; 150 (1926), 400–02; 191 (1946), 185–9 • M. Hancher, 'Bailey and after: illustrating meaning', *Word and Image*, 8 (1992), 1–20 • D. E. Vancil, *Catalog of dictionaries, word-books, and philological texts, 1440–1900* (1993) • B. W. Ball, *The Seventh-day men: Sabbatarians and Sabbatarianism in England and Wales, 1600–1800* (1994) • A. H. Reddick, *The making of Johnson's dictionary, 1746–1773* (1990) • G. Eliot, *Adam Bede*, 2 vols. (1908) • *GM*, 1st ser., 12 (1742), 387 • *Transactions of the Baptist Historical Society*, 7 (1920–21), 185 • F. Watson, *The English grammar schools to 1660* (1908) • W. A. Whitley, *A Baptist bibliography* (1916) • J. A. Simpson, 'Nathaniel Bailey and the search for a lexicographical style', *Lexicographers and their works*, ed. G. James (1989) • private information (2004) [O. Burdick]

Archives DWL, photocopy of Mill Yard church minute book • Seventh Day Baptist Historical Society, Janesville, Mill Yard Church minute book [copy in DWL] • Southern Baptist Historical Society and Archives, Nashville, Mill Yard Church minute book [microfilm master]

Likenesses C. Sysang, engraving, repro. in N. Bailey, *Mr. Nathan Bailey's English dictionary*, trans. T. Arnold (1736), frontispiece • engraving, repro. in N. Bailey, *An introduction to the English tongue* (1726) • line engraving, BM, NPG

Bailey, Philip James (1816–1902), poet, was born in Nottingham on 22 April 1816, the only son of Thomas *Bailey (1785–1856), merchant, newspaper editor, and author, and his first wife, Marie-Anne, *née* Taylor (*c*.1791–*c*.1818). He showed an early interest in his father's poetical tastes, which his father stimulated by taking him to see Byron's lying-in-state at the Old Blackamoor's Head in Nottingham High Street, and by encouraging him to learn by heart the whole of *Childe Harold*. Educated in Nottingham, he was tutored in classics by Benjamin Carpenter, a Unitarian minister. In his sixteenth year Bailey matriculated at Glasgow University with a view to the Presbyterian ministry; but quickly renouncing this ambition, he began in 1833 to study law in a solicitor's office in London, and on 26 April 1834 he was entered a member of Lincoln's Inn. His legal studies were interrupted by his poetic pursuits, and in particular by the reading of Goethe's *Faust*. He felt compelled to produce his own version of the legend, and retired for that purpose in 1836 to the seclusion of his father's house at Old Basford, near Nottingham, where after three years he completed the original version of his poem *Festus*. It was printed in Manchester by W. H. Jones, and published at his father's cost without the author's name in London by William Pickering in 1839.

On the whole the reception of *Festus* was enthusiastic. If *The Athenaeum* (21 December 1839) pronounced the idea of the poem to be 'a mere plagiarism from the "Faust" of Goethe, with all its impiety and scarcely any of its poetry', Bulwer Lytton, R. H. Horne, and Mary Howitt joined with other leading figures in a chorus of praise, and some of these reviews are reprinted in the second edition.

Bailey married Anne Reed on 23 April 1840 at St Giles, Camberwell, and on 7 May of that year he was called to the bar, although he never practised. The couple had a daughter and a son (baptized Philip Festus James) but the marriage was not happy, in part because of the wife's intemperance. Anne Bailey lived off and on with her mother, and Bailey returned to Nottingham to help his father edit the *Nottingham Mercury*.

Philip James Bailey (1816–1902), by Henry John Whitlock

A second edition of *Festus* appeared in 1845. Bailey had made large additions, and when Tennyson wrote to Edward FitzGerald urging him to order it, he also cautioned 'You will most likely find it a great bore but there are really *very grand* things in Festus' (*Letters of Alfred Lord Tennyson*, 265). The second edition brought *Festus* its remarkable popularity in America; seventeen 'editions' of a version pirated in Boston were called for in the first nine years, and it was also reprinted numerous times in Philadelphia, Louisville, and New York. Bailey became something of a 'lion' for visiting Americans of the transcendental stamp. Nathaniel Hawthorne visited in the 1850s and described the poet as a 'dark, handsome, rather picturesque-looking man, with a grey beard, and dark hair. … there is a sadness glooming out of him, but no unkindness nor asperity' (N. Hawthorne, *English Note-Books*, 2 vols., 1856, 2.92). Unfortunately, the processes of addition and recasting went on in later editions until, in the eleventh or jubilee edition of 1889, the work reached more than 40,000 lines. That volume incorporated the greater part of three volumes of poetry, which Bailey had published separately. These were *The Angel World, and other Poems* (1850), which attracted the attention of the Pre-Raphaelites, and was noted by W. M. Rossetti for review in *The Germ*; *The Mystic, and other Poems* (1855); and *The Universal Hymn* (1867). Although the popularity of *Festus* fluctuated, it was alive at the end of the nineteenth century, and a *Festus Treasury* was edited by Albert Broadbent in 1901.

Bailey's poetic power was never so fresh and concentrated as in the first edition of *Festus*. His later additions turned the poem into a theological and metaphysical treatise, for which some critics claimed high philosophical merits, but beneath which the poetry was smothered. Theodore Watts claimed that the poem contained 'lovely oases of poetry' among 'wide tracts of ratiocinative writing' (*The Athenaeum*, 1 April 1876). Bailey was often regarded as the father of the 'spasmodic' school of poetry, and satirized as such along with Alexander Smith and Sydney Dobell by W. E. Aytoun in *Firmilian* (1854); but in his last year he denied the imputation in a long letter in which he restated, with a self-satisfied seriousness, the intention of his work.

Bailey wrote a play on the subject of Aurungzebe, admired by Talfourd but, despite an introduction to Macready, the play was not produced and was finally destroyed by Bailey in a fit of despondency. Besides the volumes afterwards incorporated in *Festus*, he published *The Age: a Colloquial Satire* (1858).

In 1856 Bailey received a civil-list pension of £100 in recognition of his literary work. After the death of his father in the same year, Bailey began an unsettled time of living in a number of seaside villages. His marriage became worse, and with the advent of the new divorce law escape was possible. The court for divorce ruled in his favour on 27 May 1862, after adultery with a Mr Shenton was proved; Bailey's son testified, though both he and the daughter were estranged from their father thereafter. On 24 February 1863 Bailey married Anne Sophia (*d.* 1896), daughter of Alderman George Carey of Nottingham. In 1864 they settled in Jersey, and from there paid frequent visits to Europe, including Rome and Naples, where Bailey witnessed the eruption of Vesuvius in 1872. In 1876 he returned to England, where he settled first at Lee near Ilfracombe, and in 1885 at Blackheath. Finally he retired to The Elms, 54 Ropewalk, in his native Nottingham. In 1901 Glasgow University conferred an honorary LLD degree on him in his absence. He died after an attack of influenza on 6 September 1902, and was buried in Nottingham cemetery on the 9th. RONALD BAYNE, *rev.* D. E. LATANÉ, JR.

Sources J. Ward, *Philip James Bailey: author of Festus* (1905) • 'Selections from the letters of Philip James Bailey', ed. M. Peckham, *Princeton Library Quarterly*, 9 (1948), 79–92 • '*Bailey v. Bailey and Shenton*', *The Times* (30 May 1862), 11 [divorce court report] • R. Birley, *Sunk without trace: some forgotten masterpieces reconsidered* (1962) • E. W. Gosse, *Portraits and sketches* (1912) • M. Peckham, 'English editions of Philip James Bailey's *Festus*', *Papers of the Bibliographical Society of America*, 44 (1950), 55–8 • J. Francis, 'Philip James Bailey', *N&Q*, 9th ser., 10 (1902), 242–3 • M. Brown, 'A Victorian poet's private papers', *Christian Science Monitor* (17 March 1919) • M. Brown, 'Philip James Bailey's letters', *Christian Science Monitor* (9 April 1919) • M. Brown, 'A poet in politics', *Christian Science Monitor* (29 April 1919) • M. Brown, 'A reformer of Nottingham', *Christian Science Monitor* (23 May 1919) • A. McKillop, 'A Victorian Faust', *Publications of the Modern Language Association of America*, 40 (1925), 743–68 • M. Peckham, 'Guilt and glory: a study of the 1839 *Festus*, a nineteenth-century poem of synthesis', PhD diss., University of Princeton, 1947 • *The Times* (8 Sept 1902), 8 • E. P. Whipple, *Essays and reviews*, 6th edn, 2 vols. (1873) • *The letters of Alfred Lord Tennyson*, ed. C. Y. Lang and E. F. Shannon, 1: *1821–1850* (1982)

Archives Notts. Arch., corresp. • Princeton University, New Jersey

Likenesses A. Toft, plaster/bronze bust, *c.*1840–1849, repro. in C. W. Moulton, ed., *The library of literary criticism of English and American authors*, 8 vols. (1901–5) • J. A. McBride, marble bust, *c.*1890, repro. in DLitB, 132; formerly at Scot. NPG • W. Morrison, photograph, *c.*1901, repro. in Ward, *Philip James Bailey* • G. Black, lithograph (after I. Broadhead), NPG • H. J. Whitlock, photograph, NPG [*see illus.*] • photograph (in old age), repro. in DLitB, 132

Wealth at death £407 5*s.* 6*d.*: probate, 22 Sept 1902, *CGPLA Eng. & Wales*

Bailey, Ruby Winifred. *See* Levick, Ruby Winifred (1871/2–1940).

Bailey, Samuel (*bap.* 1791, *d.* 1870), economist and philosopher, was baptized on 8 July 1791 at St Peter's Church (later the cathedral), Sheffield, the second son and fifth of the eleven children of Joseph Bailey, of Burngreave, and Mary Eaden. His father, originally an artisan, had become wealthy in the cutlery business (he was master cutler in 1801) and as a merchant. Samuel was educated in the free school at Sheffield, where his maternal grandfather was a master, and later at the Moravian school in Fulneck. A reserved boy, his only known recreation was that of riding on a schoolfellow's back.

Having left school, Samuel joined his father in the family firm, and he was one of the first Sheffield merchants to visit the United States, so as to establish business connections there. However, his real interest lay in writing and in public affairs. In 1821 he published *Essays on the Formation and Publication of Opinions and other Subjects*; a third edition appeared in 1831, the year in which he helped to found the Sheffield Banking Company, of which he was the first chairman. In his *Essays* Bailey argued that people were not responsible for their opinions because those are independent of the will; hence opinions should not be met with censure or punishment.

In his work on economics Bailey's main achievement was to take on the Ricardian establishment, in the years when David Ricardo's theories were at their most influential. In *A Critical Dissertation on the Nature, Measure and Causes of Value*, published in 1825, he challenged the basic assumption of Ricardo that value was determined by labour. To him, value was a relative concept, springing from subjective causes; the degree of 'esteem' or 'mental affection', much like the later utility, governed the intensity of demand. Supply conditions, such as output under constant or variable cost, could also affect relative values. Thus value could vary, especially from one period to another.

Bailey also exposed what he saw as the weaknesses of Ricardo's subsistence theory of wages, for example by means of applying the analysis of rent to wage differentials so as to reflect labour scarcity or variations in skill. Despite these perceptive insights, however, he did not go on to create an alternative and less rigid model of the economic system. Having immersed himself in too broad a range of intellectual interests, he had limited knowledge of the economic literature, and his work bore all the hallmarks of a self-taught and reclusive thinker. Not surprisingly, his writings provoked a range of conflicting reactions from economists. James Mill in 1826 (in an anonymous article in the *Westminster Review*, rebuffed that same year by Bailey), Malthus in 1827, and McCulloch in 1845 all claimed that he was playing with definitions rather than undermining the Ricardian edifice. He tended to receive more sympathetic treatment in the twentieth century. J. A. Schumpeter, in his idiosyncratic *History of Economic Analysis*, judged that Bailey's work of 1825 'must rank among the masterpieces of criticism in our field' and should 'suffice to secure to its author a place in or near front rank in the history of scientific economics' (Schumpeter, 486).

Bailey's other writings were mainly noted for their terseness and vigour of style. They included an extension of his work on opinions in 1829, and pamphlets on political representation and on the fluctuating value of money in the 1830s. The politics displayed in these works are those of a moderate utilitarian radical with a strong objection to state interference. His forays into philosophy clearly showed up his imperfect grasp of the subject. Thus his *Review of Berkeley's Theory of Vision* (1842) sought to demonstrate that Berkeley missed the point by assuming that space in a direct line from the eye was not directly visible. When taken to task by John Stuart Mill, Bailey's riposte was that people have a direct perception of external objects, which cannot be analysed into a complex operation. His *Theory of Reasoning* (1851) and three series of *Letters on the Philosophy of the Human Mind* (1855–63) caused less stir among fellow philosophers, being more fragmentary and discursive but with occasional flashes of insight. The latter sustains Bailey's criticism of Berkeley but also enlists Berkeley's nominalism in an attack on the theory of 'abstract ideas'. He criticizes German philosophers, especially Kant, and makes a defence of utilitarianism and determinism. His poetic works and two unscholarly volumes of textual amendments to Shakespeare's plays (1861–2) were soon forgotten, and his many manuscripts were not preserved.

In 1828 Bailey was elected one of the town trustees of Sheffield, and he later retired from his firm to embark on a political career. That was a total failure, as the voters of Sheffield had no time for his radical schemes of triennial parliaments, the secret ballot, and the abolition of tithes and taxes on knowledge; he came bottom of the poll in the general elections of 1831 and 1834 and never again entered the fray. He was several times president of the Sheffield Literary and Philosophical Society. Being unmarried, he adopted a lifestyle of quiet seclusion, admitting no intimate friends and few acquaintances, and of clockwork regularity. He attended board meetings of his bank with absolute punctuality to the last. His only break from routine was an annual visit to his sister-in-law at Cheltenham for a change of air. He died suddenly as he left his bath on 18 January 1870, at his home at Norbury, Sheffield. Of his £120,000 fortune, he left over £80,000 to the town trust.

T. A. B. Corley

Sources *DNB* • R. M. Rawner, 'Samuel Bailey', *The new Palgrave: a dictionary of economics*, ed. J. Eatwell, M. Milgate, and P. Newman (1987) • J. A. Schumpeter, *History of economic analysis*, ed. E. B. Schumpeter (1954) • E. Roll, *A history of economic thought*, 4th edn (1973) • E. R. A. Seligman, 'On some neglected British economists', *Economic Journal*, 13 (1903), 335–63, 511–35 • *IGI* • *CGPLA Eng. & Wales* (1870)
Archives U. Edin. L., special collections division, notebooks and literary papers
Likenesses W. Gordon, portrait, Sheffield Banking Co.
Wealth at death under £120,000: probate, 9 Feb 1870, *CGPLA Eng. & Wales*

Bailey, Thomas (1785–1856), newspaper editor and author, was born at Nottingham on 31 July 1785. His education was received partly in a day school in his native town, and partly in a boarding-school at Gilling, Yorkshire. Afterwards he was for some time engaged in his father's trade of silk hosier at Nottingham, and then as a wine merchant. A liberal in politics, though not a radical, he contested Nottingham, unsuccessfully, at the general election in 1830. From December 1835 to 1843 he was a member of the town council. In 1845–6 he became proprietor and editor of the *Nottingham Mercury*, but his opinions were too moderate for his readers, and the circulation of the paper declined. Bailey's leaders on the Ecclesiastical Titles Bill of 1851—he expected the bill to fail—caused further loss of circulation, and in 1852 the paper closed. Before this, in 1830, he had purchased a mansion at Basford, Nottingham, where he spent the later years of his life, writing and collecting books and engravings. Bailey published several collections of his poems, and *A Sermon on the Death of Byron* (1824). He wrote books about Nottinghamshire, of which *Annals of Nottinghamshire* (4 vols., 1852–5) is the most substantial. He also published *Village Reform: the Great Social Necessity of Britain* (1854), and *Records of Longevity; with an Introductory Discourse on Vital Statistics* (1857).

Bailey was an independent in religion, and was twice married. His first wife, who died about 1818, aged twenty-seven, was Marie-Anne, *née* Taylor. About 1825 he married Katherina, *née* Carver, of Broughton Astley, Leicestershire, who died in 1860. Philip James *Bailey was one of his four children from his first marriage. Bailey died from cancer of the stomach at Basford on 23 October 1856.

Thompson Cooper, *rev.* H. C. G. Matthew

Sources C. Brown, *Lives of Nottinghamshire worthies* (1882) • Boase, *Mod. Eng. biog.* • private information (2004) • J. T. Godfrey and C. B. Stevenson, eds., *Catalogue of engraved portraits, miniatures, etc., exhibited at the conversazione held at the Exchange Hall, Nottingham* (1900)
Archives NL Scot., collections
Likenesses R. Huskisson, oils, repro. in Godfrey and Stevenson, eds., *Catalogue of engraved portraits* • daguerreotype, coloured in oils, repro. in Godfrey and Stevenson, eds., *Catalogue of engraved portraits*

Bailey, William James (1888–1971), cyclist, was born on 6 April 1888, at 4 Grantham Place, Park Lane, Mayfair, London, the son of William Bailey, a domestic coachman, and his wife, Elizabeth Jane Butterfield. He trained as an engineer at the London Polytechnic engineering school, and it was as a member of the polytechnic cycling club that he won his first championships. He won the world amateur sprint cycle championship four times, in 1909,

1910, 1911, and 1913, and was only denied the chance of filling the gap in this sequence when the National Cyclists' Union was unable to raise the funds to send him to the United States for the 1912 event. He also won the Paris grand prix four years in succession from 1910 and held six national championships between 1909 and 1913 at distances from the quarter-mile to 5 miles.

Bailey turned professional in 1914 but the First World War was to rob him of his best years; when he resumed racing in 1920, after army service, he was thirty-two and past his best, yet he still managed to finish third in the world professional sprint final that year. He reached the quarter-final in 1927.

A physical fitness fanatic and always immaculately dressed, Bailey had a magnificent physique which, coupled with film-star good looks, attracted crowds of adoring followers wherever he appeared in his many tours of Europe, Australia, and the United States. In Paris he was known as Long Bill of the Rose because of the championship rose that seemed a permanent part of his wardrobe. His American victories came with such monotonous regularity that the hit song of the day was affectionately adapted by his fans at Madison Square Garden to: 'Won't You Go Home, Bill Bailey?'.

Bailey finally retired from competitive racing in 1930 but still maintained his involvement with the sport. In 1931 he used his training as an engineer to produce the Saxon Bailey, acclaimed as a classic lightweight racing bike. In 1933 he involved himself with the setting up of cycle races at the Brooklands motor racing circuit near Weybridge. This saw the beginning of the revival of road cycling.

Bailey was a founder director of *Bicycle* magazine, which was launched in 1936, and was regularly employed as track official or referee at the London six-day events throughout the 1930s. He held many administrative posts within the National Cyclists' Union and was British track team manager until his resignation in 1948, after which he continued to follow the sport as a spectator. He never fully recovered from a fall at his Chiswick flat, at the age of seventy-nine, in which he broke a hip. He died in St Luke's Hospital, Paddington, on 21 February 1971. The funeral was held at Mortlake crematorium. He had at least two sons. TONY RENNICK

Sources J. Wadley, *Cycling* (27 Feb 1971) • *Cycling* (6 March 1971) • P. Matthews and I. Buchanan, *The all-time greats of British and Irish sport* (1995) • F. Alderson, *Bicycling: a history* (1972) • b. cert. • d. cert. • *CGPLA Eng. & Wales* (1971)
Archives FILM BFI NFTVA, news footage
Wealth at death £12,851: probate, 11 June 1971, *CGPLA Eng. & Wales*

Bailhache, Sir Clement Meacher (1856–1924), judge, was born at Leeds on 2 November 1856, the eldest son of the Revd Clement Bailhache, a Baptist minister and secretary to the Baptist Missionary Society, and his wife, Emma, daughter of Edward Augustus Meacher, of Ivinghoe, Buckinghamshire. The Bailhaches were Huguenots who had settled in Jersey.

Bailhache was educated at the City of London School and at London University, where he graduated LLB in 1877. He practised as a solicitor at Newport, Monmouthshire. In 1881 he married Fanny Elizabeth, the daughter of Herman Liebstein, a member of the Chancery bar; they had a son and two daughters.

Bailhache's powers as an advocate led him to enrol at the Middle Temple and he was called to the bar in 1889. He was made a bencher in 1912. He joined the south Wales circuit, where he was already well known, and was an immediate success. Within ten years he was receiving briefs in important cases in London. He was expert in commercial law, and City firms using the newly established commercial court were quick to recognize his merits.

In 1908 Bailhache became king's counsel, when the favourite leaders of the commercial court were T. E. Scrutton (afterwards lord justice) and J. A. Hamilton (afterwards Viscount Sumner). Their speedy elevation to the bench gave Bailhache the lion's share of commercial work. He was so busy in the commercial court that he seldom appeared in cases which attracted publicity. But there was no one better at explaining a complicated set of facts and arguing for legal principle to be applied. His arguments and addresses were notoriously short, often limited to the single, best point. 'Few leaders at the bar have said so little or said it so well', was the judgement in his obituary in *The Times*.

In 1912 congestion in the common-law courts led Lord Haldane, who had just succeeded Lord Loreburn as lord chancellor, to promote Bailhache to the bench as an additional judge. The customary knighthood followed that year. As a judge, Bailhache usually presided in the commercial court where he was at his best. Quick to a fault, he got through a great quantity of work. It was said that he did not pay enough attention to the arguments of counsel, and his summary treatment of cases led to some successful appeals. His judgments were easily delivered and well expressed, and, however difficult the case, he preferred to deliver judgment at the end of proceedings.

Bailhache decided many important wartime cases in the commercial court including *Sanday* v. *British and Foreign Marine Insurance Company* (1915, constructive total loss by declaration of war) and *Becker Gray & Co.* v. *London Assurance Corporation* (1915, whether putting into port to avoid capture was a loss covered by insurance). Both judgments were affirmed in the Court of Appeal and in the House of Lords.

As a criminal judge Bailhache was less successful. He saw no reason why swift and businesslike methods should be confined to the commercial court and was known, for example, to ask counsel whether there was really any defence to the charge. His direction to the jury in *Director of Public Prosecutions* v. *Beard* (1920), on the effect of drunkenness upon criminal responsibility, led to an appeal to the House of Lords. Bailhache had said that if the accused was so drunk that he did not know what he was doing, or did not know that what he was doing was wrong, the defence of drunkenness succeeded to the extent of reducing the crime from murder to manslaughter. Their lordships held that he was wrong to apply the test of insanity to a case of drunkenness. The conviction for murder was upheld, with an intimation, however, that the death sentence would not be carried out.

Bailhache did no extra-judicial public work, apart from chairing a committee in 1916 to inquire into allegations about the aircraft supplied to the Royal Flying Corps and into reports on the administration and command of the RFC. He disliked all social occasions and pomp. A lifelong Baptist and teetotaller, he was addicted to smoking a pipe to and from court and even on such formal occasions as the Mansion House dinner for the judges. Bailhache died suddenly from a cerebral haemorrhage at Beach Cottage, Aldeburgh, Suffolk, on 8 September 1924.

THEOBALD MATHEW, *rev.* HUGH MOONEY

Sources *The Times* (9 Sept 1924) • *Law Journal* (13 Sept 1924), 581 • personal knowledge (1937) • *CGPLA Eng. & Wales* (1924)
Wealth at death £61,688 4*s*. 0*d*.: probate, 1 Oct 1924, *CGPLA Eng. & Wales*

Bailie, James Kennedy- (1793–1864), classical scholar, son of Nicholas Kennedy, a schoolmaster, was born in Ireland, and entered Trinity College, Dublin, as a pensioner in 1807, aged fourteen. He obtained a scholarship in 1810, graduated BA in 1812, was elected a junior fellow in 1817, and proceeded MA in 1819, BD in 1823, and DD in 1828. In 1823 Kennedy was appointed Donnelan lecturer in his university, and in Trinity College chapel delivered *Ten Lectures on the Philosophy of the Mosaic Record of Creation*, which he published in two volumes in 1827. He produced various classical works, including an edition of Homer's *Iliad* (1822) and a blank verse version of the *Agamemnon* (1823). He resigned his fellowship in 1830 on being presented to the college living of Ardtrea, co. Tyrone. In 1835 he assumed the additional surname of Bailie. In manner he was vain and pompous, and he is said to have claimed relationship with the marquess of Ailsa, which the latter declined to admit, although Kennedy offered to make him his heir on condition that the relationship was acknowledged. He died unmarried at Ardtrea on 18 January 1864, leaving his property to a nephew.

SIDNEY LEE, *rev.* RICHARD SMAIL

Sources Burtchaell & Sadleir, *Alum. Dubl.* • Boase, *Mod. Eng. biog.* • W. B. S. Taylor, *History of the University of Dublin* (1845)
Wealth at death under £5000: probate, 1864, *CGPLA Eng. & Wales*

Baillie. *See also* Bailey, Baily, Bayley, Bayly.

Baillie, Albert Victor (1864–1955), dean of Windsor, was born on 5 August 1864 at Karlsruhe, Baden, the third son of Evan Peter Montague Baillie (1824–1874) and his wife, Frances Anna Bruce (*d.* 1894), daughter of Thomas, seventh earl of Elgin. An aristocrat who could claim two popes among his forebears (one had been a widower before entering the priesthood) he was, as his Christian names bear witness, a godchild of Queen Victoria. His lineage and connections, of which he was unselfconsciously, unsnobbishly proud, did much to shape his career. He spent his early childhood in Karlsruhe, where his father was accredited as minister to the grand duchy of Baden (the dean was fond of pointing out that he was seven years older than the German Reich). In 1871, at the request of Queen Victoria's second daughter, Princess Alice, the wife of the grand duke of Hesse and by Rhine and herself a lifelong friend of the dean's mother, the minister exchanged Karlsruhe for Darmstadt. Evan Baillie's ill health and premature death terminated the German connection, but left his son with an affectionate understanding that the two great wars of his long life could not eradicate.

Proud as he was of being a Baillie of Dochfour, it was his mother and her sister that influenced Baillie's upbringing. His mother was lady-in-waiting to the duchess of Edinburgh, and his aunt Lady Augusta, having been lady-in-waiting to Queen Victoria's mother, the duchess of Kent, became lady of the bedchamber to the queen herself. In 1863 she had married Arthur Penrhyn Stanley, dean of Westminster, and it was in their hospitable household that Baillie as a young man met the literary and intellectual luminaries of the late Victorian age, Carlyle, Tennyson, Browning, Matthew Arnold, Lecky, Froude, and many others. On Lady Augusta's death Lady Frances came to the rescue and made the deanery her home.

After attending Marlborough College, which he hated, and Trinity College, Cambridge, which he loved (matriculated 1883; BA, 1886; honorary DD, 1918), Baillie prepared for holy orders under Bishop Lightfoot of Durham, the crowning experience in the development of a profound and profoundly charitable Christianity. His court connections brought him invitations to preach before Queen Victoria, with whom he enjoyed from the first the happiest of relations (he was said to have been her favourite godson). But poodledom was not to characterize his ministry. His first curacy was in the slums of Tyne Dock at South Shields, his second and third at Walworth and Plumstead—both, in the 1890s, rough, poverty-stricken districts of south-east London.

Before succeeding to the vicarage of Plumstead in 1895 Baillie had been for three years domestic chaplain to the future archbishop Randall Davidson, then bishop of Rochester. Davidson exemplified, not least in his relations with the queen, that undemanding yet compelling integrity that Baillie had all his life seen as the most profitable witness that a Christian minister could offer.

Success as rector of Rugby (1898–1912) and subdean of Coventry (1912–17) was followed by Baillie's appointment to Windsor in 1917. He was at home all his life in court circles, yet never enjoyed with either Edward VII or George V the sympathy that he had found with Queen Victoria and was to find again with Edward VIII and George VI. In his memoirs, charitable though they are, Baillie does not disguise the mischief made at Windsor by George V's old tutor, Canon J. N. Dalton, a character whom even Trollope would not have dared to invent.

Baillie's tenure of the deanery was notable for his raising, without any public appeal or state subvention, the enormous sums needed for the complete restoration of St George's Chapel (1920–27) and for initiating in 1936 the valuable series of monographs on the history of that remarkable foundation, *Fasti Wyndesorienses*. He was created CVO in 1921 and KCVO in 1932.

Baillie's leading characteristics were his approachableness and his readiness to enthuse and to encourage. Strikingly good-looking, and in his youth a fine horseman, he combined a superb public presence with a private tenderness and good nature that owed much to the standards of the Victorian aristocracy which he interestingly describes in his memoirs. Baillie's devotion to the theatre, issuing in many friendships with actors and actresses, was honoured shortly before his retirement with a special performance in the drawing room at the deanery by the Lunts of the play they were then giving in London. It is probable that this taste had displeased George V, who was said to have been incensed at rumours of the dean's opening a night club, wearing his mantle and Garter jewel.

Baillie was married on 9 August 1898 to Constance Elizabeth Hamilton-Russell, the third daughter of Gustavus, eighth Viscount Boyne. Her early death (27 September 1924), soon after the move to Windsor, and the loss of two of their three sons were heavy blows. He resigned the deanery in 1945 and retired to Baldock, where he died on 3 November 1955, survived only by his second son, Ean. He was a dignitary of a type long common in the English and most continental churches, but now virtually extinct.

RICHARD OLLARD

Sources A. V. Baillie, *My first eighty years* (1951) • S. L. Ollard, *Fasti Wyndesorienses: the deans and canons of Windsor* (privately printed, Windsor, 1950) • personal knowledge (2004) • private information (2004) • Burke, *Gen. GB* (1937) • Venn, *Alum. Cant.*

Archives St George's Chapel, Windsor, antiquarian notes, visitation report | FILM BFI NFTVA, news footage

Wealth at death £26,918 13*s*. 7*d*.: probate, 17 May 1956, *CGPLA Eng. & Wales*

Baillie, Alexander (*c*.1590–1655), abbot of Regensburg, of the family of Carnbroe, Lanarkshire, went to school in Scotland, then in August 1612 was enrolled at the protestant University of Helmstedt. Having become a Catholic he entered the Scots College, Rome, that same year. He is said to have also studied at Heidelberg and travelled in France and Italy.

On 25 November 1615 Baillie received the habit at the Scots Benedictine monastery in Regensburg and made his vows at the sister abbey in Würzburg on 30 November 1617. In 1622 he was prior there under Abbot William Ogilvie. He travelled to Scotland and, having returned, was in early 1623 made prior and cellarer at Regensburg. In 1628 he published at Würzburg a polemical work, *A True Information of the Unhallowed Offspring … of our Scottish-Calvinian Gospel*, which despite much tedious invective gives interesting glimpses of contemporary Scotland.

Invasion by the Swedish protestant forces in the 1630s caused immense disruption to the three Scots abbeys, scattering the monks and devastating their economy. Baillie escaped before Würzburg was captured in October 1631 and in January 1633 is found as cellarer at Regensburg. He again had to flee when that town was captured in November, then, returning after its recapture, was in December 1634 made administrator. On 13 November 1636 he was elected abbot of Erfurt but could not take possession because of enemy occupation and again administered the Regensburg abbey until finally, on 18 January 1646, he was elected its abbot.

Clearly a competent administrator Baillie restored its economy, though greatly hampered by a lack of monks and harassment from various quarters. In 1641 an attempt to oust the Scots was thwarted but in 1653, apparently worn out by poor health and troubles, he made an Irish monk his coadjutor and successor. This prospective takeover was, however, vetoed by Rome.

At Regensburg Baillie had a cartulary of the monastery compiled, personally checking the transcripts and adding his own chronicle; although the latter is somewhat subjective, both are valuable sources. Some historical work by him has survived in later compilations. He died at St Jakob, Regensburg, on 7 April 1655, having played a key role in preserving the three Scots monasteries.

MARK DILWORTH

Sources M. Dilworth, *The Scots in Franconia* (1974) • M. Dilworth, 'Two necrologies of Scottish Benedictine abbeys in Germany', *Innes Review*, 9 (1958), 173–203 • M. Ziegelbauer, *Historia rei literariae ordinis S. Benedicti*, 4 vols. (1754), 3.541, 4.129 • T. G. Law, *Catholic tractates of the sixteenth century, 1573–1600*, STS, 45 (1901), lx–lxi, 269–78 • J. H. Baxter, 'Scottish students at Helmstedt University', *SHR*, 24 (1926–7), 235–7, esp. 237 • P. J. Anderson, ed., *Records of the Scots colleges at Douai, Rome, Madrid, Valladolid and Ratisbon*, New Spalding Club, 30 (1906), 104

Archives Bayerisches Hauptstaatsarchiv, Munich, protocollum seu Codex Privilegiorum … (Baillie MS), KL St Jakob Regensburg, no. 1

Baillie, Alexander Dundas Ross Cochrane-Wishart-, first Baron Lamington (1816–1890), politician and author, was born on 24 November 1816, the younger of the two children of Admiral Sir Thomas John *Cochrane GCB (1789–1872) and his first wife, Matilda, daughter of Lieutenant-General Sir Charles Lockhart-Ross, seventh baronet, of Balnagowan, and his first wife, Matilda Theresa, Countess Lockhart Wishart of the Holy Roman empire; his mother, who died in 1819, took the married name Cochrane Wishart. Until 1880 his formal name was Alexander Dundas Wishart Ross Baillie-Cochrane, but on his elevation to the barony of Lamington he changed his surname to Cochrane-Wishart-Baillie. He is commonly referred to by historians as Cochrane-Baillie, the form of name used by his son and his descendants.

Cochrane (or Kok as he was nicknamed) was educated at Eton College and at Trinity College, Cambridge (BA 1837), where he was president of the union in his last year. By 1837 he had inherited the desolate estate of Lamington near Biggar in Lanarkshire, in direct descent through the female line. He greatly improved the estate and the welfare of its dependants, building sturdy, plain-Gothic cottages that outlived Lamington House itself.

On 4 December 1844, Cochrane married Annabella Mary Elizabeth Drummond (1824–1917), daughter of Andrew Drummond, of Cadlands, Hampshire, and his wife, Lady Elizabeth Drummond, Lord John Manners's sister; they had three daughters, Constance Mary Elizabeth, Amy Augusta Frederica Annabella, and Violet Marie Louise,

Alexander Dundas Ross Cochrane-Wishart-Baillie, first Baron Lamington (**1816–1890**), by Alfred, Count D'Orsay, 1846

and a son, Charles Wallace Alexander Napier Ross Cochrane-*Baillie, who succeeded his father as second baron.

By early 1841 Cochrane was a leading member, with Lord John Manners and G. S. Smythe, of what Disraeli by then was calling 'Young England'; in late January (according to Manners's journal) he went with a boisterous group to Canterbury to support Smythe's electoral bid. An incident in a public house resulted in his appearance before a magistrate. In the general election that summer, he stood unsuccessfully at Bridport as a Conservative, but was elected in September as a Liberal-Conservative. He made his maiden speech on 20 September of that year, opposing an increase in the grant for Maynooth College in Ireland. According to a letter from Cochrane's son in *The Times* of 25 February 1890, Peel offered him a post shortly after his election. Although Cochrane was less enthusiastic than the others about Disraeli, in October 1842 in Paris he and Smythe reached an informal agreement with him, and subsequently with Manners, that the Young England group would act together in parliament. Cochrane was not, however, a strong party man; he never wavered on matters such as Young England's opposition to the new poor law, but on other issues, especially protectionism, he vacillated. Having in November 1844 predicted that repeal of the corn laws would cause a revolution, on 9 February 1846 he declared himself in favour of repeal, and tried to appear consistent by arguing that he now favoured protection for all classes. In March 1846 he accepted the Chiltern Hundreds and stood for re-election at Bridport as a Peelite; he won by one vote, but on 27 April was unseated on petition. In the general election of 1847 he regained the seat, and held it until 1852.

In the 1852 general election Cochrane was defeated at Southampton, and shortly thereafter approached Disraeli, now chancellor of the exchequer, for 'any appointment in or under the government', citing his qualities of 'Earnestness, Zeal & Love of Labour'. Disraeli responded with 'expressions of good will', but the government fell before anything came of it (Disraeli, *Letters*, vol. 6, letter 2350 n1). In January 1853 he was again defeated at Southampton. On 5 January 1857 he was returned unopposed at a by-election for Lanarkshire, only to be defeated on 7 April in the general election. On 29 April 1859 he was elected at Honiton, and represented it until 1868. From 1864 to 1868, he was joint editor and writer for *The Owl*, a popular satirical weekly.

When the third Derby administration was formed in June 1866 Cochrane was again disappointed of place, although Disraeli told him he had given Derby a list with his name on it. In September 1867 Manners expressed concern to Disraeli that Cochrane was going to have his seat 'cut from under him by the Reform Bill'. Disraeli apparently offered him something, for in December Manners reported that Cochrane was grateful but reluctant to give up public life in England. A year later Disraeli offered him (possibly for the second time) the governorship of Cape Colony, but again the government fell before a decision was made. In the general election in November 1868 Cochrane was defeated in the Isle of Wight, but he was returned for that seat in 1870 and 1874. In September 1876 he was appointed a trustee of the National Portrait Gallery. He did not stand for re-election in 1880, and Disraeli (now Lord Beaconsfield), in his last days in office, recommended him for a peerage; on 3 May 1880 he was created Baron Lamington.

Cochrane published widely. His early *Poems* (privately printed 1838) were followed by *The Morea* (1840). He wrote four novels, *Ernest Vane* (1849), in which George Smythe figured as the character George Percy, *Lucille Belmont* (1849), *Florence the Beautiful* (1854), and, under the pseudonym of Leonard Holme, *A Young Artist's Life* (1864); several pamphlets, including *Exeter Hall* (1841), *Young Italy* (1850), *Who are the Liberals?* (1852), and *Justice to Scotland* (1854); and several historical works—*Historic Pictures* (2 vols., 1865), *Francis the First* (2 vols., 1870), *Historic Châteaux* (1876), and *The Théâtre Français in the Time of Louis XV* (1879). He contributed to *Blackwood's Edinburgh Magazine* between 1881 and 1890, the *Nineteenth Century* in 1883, the *National Review* in 1883 and 1884, and the *Fortnightly Review* in 1884; the last piece was an anonymous article, 'Forty years of parliament', by 'A Young England peer', blaming the decline of parliament on the 1867 Reform Act.

Lamington died on 15 February 1890, of influenza, at 26 Wilton Crescent, his London residence; on 20 February he was buried at Lamington in the episcopal chapel of the Holy Trinity which he himself had built. At the time, *Blackwood's Edinburgh Magazine* was running his reminiscences, 'In the days of the dandies' (reprinted as a book later in

1890), concluding in March with 'The Young England party'.

Cochrane is of importance primarily as a gifted member of Young England, the original of Buckhurst in Disraeli's *Coningsby* (1844), where he is portrayed as a 'most energetic … fiery and generous … reckless genius'. He was the eldest, the richest, and most Byronic of the group, with an impetuous, generous, self-assured, open nature, and an elegant and sophisticated manner. According to Richard Faber, Cochrane's writings show him to have been also the most heterosexual of the group. Independent by nature, he did not see himself as a central figure in the party, though he shared the group's belief in the need to address the 'condition of England question' by what in 1884 he called 'progressive Conservatism'. He admired Peel, and his political heroes were Canning and Castlereagh, but in the group his favourite was the mercurial Smythe (who in 1844 reciprocated by dallying in Koblenz with a woman he calls merely 'Cochrane's Green Gage'). He was prominent both in parliament and in society, especially in literary circles; he was highly regarded as an expert on Greece and Italy (he was knight of the Order of St Saviour of Greece), and after his death was fondly remembered as a 'kindly, cultivated country gentleman' (in 1883 his estates totalled 12,708 acres, worth nearly £12,000 a year). Although his life was full and productive, his career left a sense of failure, given the high expectations his talents aroused. M. G. WIEBE

Sources R. Faber, *Young England* (1987) • *Benjamin Disraeli letters*, ed. J. A. W. Gunn and others (1982–) • Bodl. Oxf., Dep. Hughenden • Gladstone Court Museum, Biggar, Lanarkshire, Grisell Annabella Hastings MSS • Rutland MSS, Belvoir Castle • A. Lamington, *In the days of the dandies* (1906) • Mrs Ware Scott, *Lamington, past and present* (1878) • A. Maccallum Scott, *Clydesdale* (1924), chap. 1 • *Wellesley index* • Burke, *Peerage* (1930) • GEC, *Peerage* • *The Times* (17 Feb 1890) • *The Times* (25 Feb 1890)

Archives Mitchell L., Glas., Glasgow City Archives, corresp., journals, and papers | BL, corresp. with Sir Robert Peel, Add. MSS 40532–40593 • Bodl. Oxf., letters to Benjamin Disraeli • Bodl. Oxf., letters to Mary Anne Disraeli • Flintshire RO, Hawarden, letters to W. E. Gladstone • Herts. ALS, corresp. with Lord Lytton • Lpool RO, letters to fourteenth earl of Derby • NA Scot., letters to Lady Ross • NL Scot., corresp. with Blackwoods • NL Scot., corresp. with Sir Thomas Cochrane • NRA, priv. coll., corresp. with Drummond family • Som. ARS, letters to Sir William Jolliffe • Trinity Cam., letters to Lord Houghton • UCL, letters to Lord Brougham

Likenesses Alfred, Count D'Orsay, lithograph, 1846, NPG [*see illus.*] • R. J. Lane, lithograph, 1846 (after A. D'Orsay), BM, NPG • lithograph, pubd 1871, BM, NPG • Alfred, Count D'Orsay, crayon, Lamington, Lanarkshire • De Boeuf, oils; formerly at Lamington, Lanarkshire • F. Grant, oils, Lamington, Lanarkshire • Swinton, crayon, Lamington, Lanarkshire • J. J. Tissot, chromolithograph caricature, NPG; repro. in *VF* (2 Dec 1871) • portrait, repro. in *ILN* (22 Feb 1890), 231

Wealth at death £17,694 13*s.* 11*d.*: confirmation, 10 Nov 1890, *CCI* • £4638 12*s.* 5*d.*: additional estate, 8 July 1891, *CCI* • £2264 8*s.*: additional estate, 26 Oct 1892, *CCI* • £36,100 1*s.* 10*d.*: additional estate, 27 July 1894, *CCI*

Baillie [Bailly], **Charles** (*c.*1541–1625), conspirator and informer, was probably born in the Low Countries of Scottish descent. He was a good linguist, and from about 1564 found employment in the household of Mary, queen of Scots. By 1571 he was in the service of John Leslie, bishop of Ross, who was the representative in London of the now imprisoned queen. Early in that year he was seized at Dover carrying a package of books and some letters, the latter tied close under his clothing against his back. It emerged that he had been sent by Leslie to the Spanish Netherlands, to pick up some copies of Leslie's seditious pamphlet *A Treatise Concerning Defence of the Honour of … Mary, Queen of Scotland*, which had been reprinted secretly at Liège, and that he had also carried abroad letters for various of the Catholic exiles there. When arrested he was returning from Brussels with a number of letters, including three highly dangerous ones from the Florentine banker and plotter Roberto Ridolfi, who was attempting to interest the duke of Alva in a plan to invade England, depose the queen, free Mary Stewart, and marry her to the duke of Norfolk. The three letters were addressed to Leslie, Norfolk, and Lord Lumley, and implicated them all in this plot.

The details of the events surrounding Baillie's arrest are controversial. Francis Edwards has argued that Lord Burghley knew in advance of this 'plot', and that Ridolfi was in the government's pay to entrap Norfolk and Queen Mary. The more straightforward and conventional interpretation (that of J. A. Froude and his successors) sees Ridolfi and Leslie as genuine, if foolish, conspirators, whose doings were uncovered first by Baillie's arrest, and then by some excellent detective work by Burghley. Initially Baillie's packet of letters was confiscated by Lord Cobham, lord warden of the Cinque Ports, who was minded to conceal this evidence which might harm his own brother and two important members of the nobility, and who passed the packet straight on to Leslie. Burghley set to work to discover the truth from Baillie, who was at first placed in the Marshalsea and then in the Tower. Burghley used well-tried techniques to break down the young Baillie, first by introducing informers into his prisons, one of whom set up lines of communication between Baillie and Leslie, which allowed Burghley to read all the letters between them. The rack was also employed, and confinement in Little Ease, a cell 4 feet square. As a result Baillie confessed as much as he knew, which was sufficient to see Leslie and Norfolk imprisoned, and which began the process that eventually led the latter to the block and threatened the life of Queen Mary. While he was in the Tower Baillie incised two inscriptions in the walls, signed with his name and dated 10 April and 10 September 1571 respectively. His use of the IHS monogram underlines his allegiance to Catholicism, while his use of French and Italian phrases points to his linguistic skills. Both graffiti moralize upon the predicament of their maker. In November 1572, however, Baillie was released, and was soon back in the Netherlands. He died at Hulpe, near Brussels, on 27 December 1625, in his eighty-fifth year, and was buried in the churchyard of Hulpe, where his gravestone was still visible in the nineteenth century, describing him as a secretary to the queen of Scots and a martyr for the Catholic faith. PETER HOLMES

Sources *DNB* • *A collection of state papers … left by William Cecill, Lord Burghley*, ed. W. Murdin, 2 (1759), 1–17 • *N&Q*, 2nd ser., 8 (1859), 267,

316 • *N&Q*, 3rd ser., 5 (1864), 284 • *CSP Scot. ser.*, 1589–1603, 574, 897, 898 • *Calendar of the manuscripts of the most hon. the marquis of Salisbury*, 24 vols., HMC, 9 (1883–1976), vol. 1, pp. 494–8, 523, 525–6, 533, 542; vol. 2, pp. 11–12 • F. Edwards, *The marvellous chance: Thomas Howard, fourth duke of Norfolk, and the Ridolphi plot, 1570–1572* (1968), chap. 1 • J. A. Froude, *History of England*, new edn, 12 vols. (1893), vol. 9, pp. 450–67 • J. Britton and E. W. Brayley, *Memoirs of the Tower of London* (1830), 320–22 • J. Bayley, *The history and antiquities of the Tower of London* (1821–5), 145–9, 176

Baillie, Charles, Lord Jerviswoode (1804–1879), lawyer and politician, was born at Mellerstain, Berwickshire, on 3 November 1804, the second son of George Baillie of Mellerstain, Berwickshire, and of Jerviswoode, Lanarkshire, and his wife, Mary, the youngest daughter of Sir James Pringle, baronet, of Stichill, Roxburghshire. He studied at St Andrews University, matriculating in 1823, and at Edinburgh University from 1826. Baillie married the Hon. Anne Hepburn Scott (*d.* 1880), daughter of the fourth Baron Polwarth, on 27 December 1831. They had a son and two daughters who survived to maturity.

Baillie was admitted as an advocate to the Scottish bar in 1830 and the influence of his family connections now helped secure his rapid rise in his chosen profession. One of his sisters was marchioness of Breadalbane, another was countess of Aberdeen, a third was Lady Polwarth, and a fourth was countess of Ashburton. Baillie was described as linked more completely to the Scottish nobility than any other lawyer of his generation.

Baillie was advocate-depute from 1844 to 1846, in Sir Robert Peel's second ministry, and again in 1852 in Lord Derby's short-lived first administration. He was appointed sheriff of Stirlingshire, on the recommendation of Lord Advocate James Moncreiff, a political opponent, on 2 March 1853, and he acted in that capacity until, on the re-accession of Lord Derby to power, he was made solicitor-general for Scotland in February 1858. Later, in July of that year, he was appointed lord advocate of Scotland in succession to John Inglis, who had been raised to the bench. This necessitated finding a seat in the House of Commons and Baillie was returned unopposed as Conservative member for Linlithgowshire in early February 1859. He had, however, represented this constituency for little more than two months when, in April 1859, he also was raised to the Scottish bench as a judge of the court of session. He held this position, under the courtesy title of Lord Jerviswoode, for the following fifteen years, from 1872 serving in the first division of the court. For twelve of these years he also sat in the supreme criminal court, having been appointed, in June 1862, a lord of justiciary.

As a counsel, Baillie had a fair but quiet practice. He was distinguished more for his deliberation than for his forensic ability, and he discouraged lengthy, contentious litigation. As a judge he had a reputation for courtesy, sagacity, patient and painstaking investigation, competent learning, and probity. He was held, however, to lack originality and to be so habitually laconic in his explanations that one commentator described him as 'deficient in the arts of expression'. In 1859 his elder brother, George, became tenth earl of Haddington. Together with his two younger brothers, Baillie was raised at the same time by royal warrant to the rank and precedence of an earl's son.

Jerviswoode officiated as convenor of the acting committee of the Wallace monument, a symbol of the mid-century revival of interest in Scottish national identity, erected on the Abbey Craig, Stirling. In 1861 he was elected assessor of the University of St Andrews. He was a trustee of the Board of Manufactures of Scotland. For a number of years he was the president of the Edinburgh Border Counties Association and in that capacity took an active part in the movements to celebrate the centenary of the birth of Sir Walter Scott.

Owing to ill health, in 1874 Jerviswoode retired with a pension from the bench and from public life to his country residence, Dryburgh House, near St Boswells, Roxburghshire. Here he lived in some seclusion until his death on 23 July 1879. His wife died the following summer.

Jerviswoode's more general significance as a political and judicial figure lies in his being one of a number of Scottish tories whose political careers were very much limited by the dominance of the Liberal Party in Scottish politics at this time, but who found an alternative prominence and influence on the Scottish bench. David Mure, whose career Jerviswoode's closely parallels, was another such figure, as were John Inglis and, from a slightly older generation, Duncan McNeill and John Hope.

GORDON F. MILLAR

Sources *The Scotsman* (24 July 1879) • *The Times* (26 July 1879) • *Law Times* (2 Aug 1879) • F. J. Grant, ed., *The Faculty of Advocates in Scotland, 1532–1943*, Scottish RS, 145 (1944), 8 • W. Anderson, *The Scottish nation* (1882), 174 • J. Foster, *Members of parliament, Scotland ... 1357–1882*, 2nd edn (privately printed, London, 1882), 19 • J. Foster, *The peerage, baronetage, and knightage of the British Empire for 1883*, 1 [1883], 334–5 • *Edinburgh Courant* (24 July 1879) • G. W. T. Omond, *The lord advocates of Scotland, second series, 1834–1880* (1914), 223–4 • H. J. Hanham, 'Mid-century Scottish nationalism: romantic and radical', *Ideas and institutions of Victorian Britain*, ed. R. Robson (1967), 173

Archives NA Scot., letters to Lord Polwarth • U. St Andr. L., corresp. with James Forbes

Wealth at death £29,795 2*s.* 10*d.*: probate, 23 Oct 1879, *CCI*

Baillie, Charles Wallace Alexander Napier Ross Cochrane-, second Baron Lamington (1860–1940), colonial governor, was born in London on 29 July 1860, the fourth child and only son of the politician and author Alexander Dundas Ross Cochrane-Wishart-*Baillie, first Baron Lamington (1816–1890), and his wife, Annabella Mary Elizabeth (*d.* 1917), elder daughter of Andrew Robert Drummond, of Cadlands, Hampshire. He was educated at Eton College and at Christ Church, Oxford (1877–81), graduating BA. In 1885 he became assistant private secretary to Lord Salisbury, and after an unsuccessful candidature at North St Pancras in the same year, he entered parliament as Conservative member for that constituency in 1886. He spent only four years in the House of Commons, succeeding his father as Baron Lamington in 1890.

Lamington was an enthusiastic sportsman and traveller, and after visiting Central America he undertook a lengthy expedition through Indo-China in 1890–91. Following the presentation of papers on this journey to the Royal Geographical Society of London, he was elected an honorary fellow of the society, and later appointed to its council (1908–12) and was vice-president from 1912 to 1915. On 13 June 1895 he married Mary Haughton Hozier (*d.* 1944), lady of the bedchamber to the princess of Wales and youngest daughter of the first Baron Newlands. They had two children. On 10 October 1895 Lamington was appointed governor of Queensland, arriving in the colony in 1896 and serving until 1901. In November 1899 Lamington called upon Andrew Dawson to form a short-lived administration, which became the first Labour government anywhere in the world. But in his dispatches Lamington demonstrated his clear dislike of the growing strength of socialism in Australia and he feared that the federation of the country could lead to its dominance. Queensland was at the time afflicted by a seven-year drought. To gain an understanding of the hardship this was causing, and also to investigate the condition of the indigenous peoples, Lamington travelled widely in Queensland and New Guinea.

In 1901 Lamington returned to his Lanarkshire estates, and two years later was appointed administrator of Bombay. There he took a keen interest in the conditions of the people and social reform. He resigned as governor in 1907 as a result of the serious illness of his wife.

Lamington was active in the territorial movement. He was lieutenant-colonel of the Lanarkshire yeomanry, and an honorary colonel of the 6th battalion of the Scottish Rifles (Cameronians). He was also captain of the Royal Company of Archers, the king's bodyguard for Scotland. During the First World War he vigorously encouraged recruiting, and in 1919 he went to Syria as commissioner of the British relief unit. Lamington retained an interest in movements supporting the welfare of subject peoples and minorities within the empire, and a greater mutual understanding between West and East. He was a member of a range of organizations working in this field.

On 13 March 1940 Lord Lamington was present at a meeting of the Royal Central Asian Society at Caxton Hall. At this meeting a man in the audience rose and fired several shots at the occupants of the platform, killing Sir Michael O'Dwyer and wounding others: Lamington was shot in the arm.

Described as 'tall and straight, with an erect and soldierly carriage' and as having a 'scientific mind and manner of thought' (*Queensland 1900*, 2), Lamington was appointed GCMG in 1900 and GCIE in 1903. He also had the singular honour of having a popular Australian dish named after him—a small, rectangular, plain sponge cake, dipped in chocolate and rolled in desiccated coconut—the 'lamington'. Lamington died at Lamington House, Lanarkshire, on 16 September 1940.

Alfred Cochrane, *rev.* Marc Brodie

Sources R. B. Joyce, 'Lamington, 2nd Baron', *AusDB*, 9.653 • Burke, *Peerage* • *Queensland 1900: a narrative of her past together with biographies of her leading men* (1900), pt 2 • *The Times* (18 Sept 1940) • P. M. Sykes, *Journal of the Royal Central Asian Society*, 27 (1940), 803 • R. Fitzgerald, *From the dreaming to 1915: a history of Queensland* (1982) • Foster, *Alum. Oxon.* • *WWBMP* • *GJ*, 96 (1940), 451 • *WW* • *WWW* • *The Times* (20 Feb 1917) • *The Times* (20 Jan 1944) • H. E. C. Stapylton, *Second series of Eton school lists … 1853–1892* (1900) • B. Kingston, *The Oxford history of Australia*, 3 (1988)
Archives BL OIOC, corresp., MS Eur. B 159 • Duke U., Perkins L., MSS as governor of Bombay • RGS, notebook of travel from Siam to Tonkin
Likenesses W. Stoneman, two photographs, 1917–28, NPG • photograph, repro. in *Queensland 1900*

Baillie, Charles William (1844–1899), inventor of the Baillie sounder and marine meteorologist, was born in Greenwich, Kent, of unknown parentage. He entered the Royal Navy in 1859, being promoted in 1870 to navigating lieutenant and first-class surveyor. He was serving on HMS *Sylvia* in the China seas when he devised the deep-sea sounder that was to bear his name. There were several types of such sounders employed for hydrography; in ideal conditions a weighted tube was sent down, the weight caused the tube to detach when the device reached the bottom, and the tube, containing a sample of the sea bed, was hauled in, but in practice the operation was often a failure. Baillie sent a model and drawings to the hydrographer of the navy; in June 1873 the first example was made at Chatham Dockyard, and others were then sent out to HMS *Challenger*, then on her circumnavigation. The Baillie sounder was far sturdier and heavier than its predecessors; it was able to function correctly in the deepest waters encountered by *Challenger*, and penetrated into soft sediments to capture a long core before slipping the iron weights and being hauled in.

In 1870 plans had been laid to establish a Japanese navy modelled on that of Britain. The following year a number of young Japanese officers went aboard *Sylvia* to learn about surveying, and in 1873 Baillie took employment at the Imperial Naval College, Hokei, being appointed naval director in 1877. Before leaving Britain he had married Helen Mary Sargent (*b.* 1848/9), born in Bermuda. Their eldest daughter was born in Brixham, their next three children were born in Japan, and a son was born in Greenwich after their return. Baillie retired from the Royal Navy in 1878 and resigned his college directorship in 1879.

During these years Baillie did not lose sight of his sounder, and in July 1874 he wrote to the hydrographer to ask about its performance. The department responded in August in its usual verbose style, 'The sounding machine known by Mr Baillie's name … has been very successfully used in the "Challenger" and therefore if their Lordships so approve, Mr Baillie's question might be answered in the affirmative' (PRO, HO, MB19, p. 72). Thus encouraged, Baillie wrote in October asking for a reward for his invention, which had not been patented. He was awarded 30 guineas, the hydrographer adding,

> Navigating Lt Baillie's invention is one of the most simple and efficient that has yet been made in connection with disengaging the sinker in deep sea sounding. It is the machine now used in all our surveying ships and throughout a three years' trial in the 'Challenger' it has not once been found wanting, and it has been selected by the German and Norwegian governments for deep sea exploration. (ibid., p. 521)

Baillie was back in England by July 1879 and was

recruited as an assistant in the marine department of the meteorological council, at an annual salary of £200. His first task was to continue and complete the study of sea temperatures and currents of the Pacific Ocean, as reported by ships' captains. In March 1888 he succeeded Henry Toynbee as marine superintendent, with a salary of £350. In February 1892 he was working on charts of the Red Sea and proposing a new method of depicting wind frequency, speed, and direction. He then dealt with similar charts of the Indian Ocean, and by June 1899 was submitting specimen charts of the south Atlantic.

In July 1899 Baillie's son Conyers Baillie wrote to the council to announce his father's sudden death at Albion Street, Broadstairs, on 24 June 1899. He was buried in the Royal Naval cemetery at Greenwich.

ANITA MCCONNELL

Sources *The Times* (1 July 1899), 12c • *Nature*, 60 (1899), 204 • *Monthly Notices of the Royal Astronomical Society*, 60 (1899–1900), 313–14 • minute books 18 and 19, Hydrographic Office Archives, Taunton • G. Fox, *Britain and Japan, 1858–1883* (1969), 265 • *Minutes of proceedings of the Meteorological Council, 1879–1899* • A. McConnell, *No sea too deep* (1982) • PRO, HO, MB19 • d. cert. • *CGPLA Eng. & Wales* (1899) • census returns, 1881

Wealth at death £280 11s.: probate, 13 July 1899, *CGPLA Eng. & Wales*

Baillie, Cuthbert (*d.* 1513), administrator, was a son of Sir William Baillie of Lamington. He was a determinant in the faculty of arts at the University of St Andrews in March 1490 and licentiate in 1491. Having held the benefice of Thankerton, by 1501 he was parson of Sanquhar, a prebend of Glasgow Cathedral. On 12 July 1512 Julius II received him as an apostolic notary. At that time he was involved in negotiations with Cardinal Dominico Grimani, whereby the cardinal would resign as commendator of Glenluce in Baillie's favour in return for a pension from the abbey. These must have been completed by March 1513, when Baillie brought an action before the council as commendator.

Baillie was chamberlain of Galloway from late 1498 to January 1500, while Sir Patrick Hume of Polwarth was comptroller, and was subsequently Hume's executor. Although he made several gifts of horses to James IV between 1505 and 1508, he did not re-enter royal service until 1511. In 1511–12 he seems to have had responsibility for the earl of Sutherland, who was under the king's wardship because of mental incapacity. He served as an auditor of exchequer (1511–12) and commissioner for leasing crown lands (1512–13). On 29 October 1512 James IV appointed him lord treasurer in succession to Andrew Stewart, bishop of Caithness. He was still acting in that capacity in September 1513, during the Flodden campaign, but Stewart was reappointed on 15 October 1513 and Baillie was certainly dead by the end of 1513.

Baillie's son Bernard, legitimated in 1529, is described as parson of Lamington and servant of David Beaton (*d.* 1546) between 1533 and 1541. Beaton later presented Bernard to the parsonage of Kirkbean, and he still held it when he died at the battle of Pinkie in 1547.

ATHOL MURRAY

Sources R. C. Reid, ed., *Wigtownshire charters*, Scottish History Society, 3rd ser., 51 (1960) • G. Burnett and others, eds., *The exchequer rolls of Scotland*, 11–14 (1888–93) • J. B. Paul, ed., *Compota thesaurariorum regum Scotorum / Accounts of the lord high treasurer of Scotland*, 3–4 (1901–2) • A. I. Dunlop, ed., *Acta facultatis artium universitatis Sanctiandree, 1413–1588*, St Andrews University Publications, 56 (1964) • G. Neilson and H. Paton, eds., *Acts of the lords of council in civil causes, 1496–1501*, 2 (1918) • J. W. Baillie, *Lives of the Baillies* (1872) • A. B. Calderwood, ed., *Acts of the lords of council, 1501–1503*, 3 (1993) • R. K. Hannay, ed., *Acts of the lords of council in public affairs, 1501–1554* (1932) • J. M. Thomson and others, eds., *Registrum magni sigilli regum Scotorum / The register of the great seal of Scotland*, 11 vols. (1882–1914), vol. 2 • *CEPR letters*, 18.117 • M. Livingstone, D. Hay Fleming, and others, eds., *Registrum secreti sigilli regum Scotorum / The register of the privy seal of Scotland*, 2–3 (1921–36) • *The letters of James V*, ed. R. K. Hannay and D. Hay (1954)

Baillie, Donald Macpherson (1887–1954), Church of Scotland minister and theologian, was born on 5 November 1887 in the Free Church manse at Gairloch, Ross-shire, the second son of the Revd John Baillie (1829–1891), Free Church minister of Gairloch, and his wife, Annie Macpherson (*d.* 1932). After her husband's death Annie Baillie almost single-handedly brought up her three boys, John, Donald, and Peter, in a rigidly Calvinist atmosphere, determined that all three were destined to be ministers. The youngest, Peter, was allowed to become a medical missionary but was drowned soon after his arrival in India. Donald and his brother, John *Baillie (1886–1960), learned from discussions with their mother around the family table to delight in rigorous thinking, but as they encountered a broader and more humane atmosphere in school and university they came increasingly to question scholastic Calvinism and sought a theology which was more open, vibrant, and engaged.

After education at Inverness Royal Academy, Donald took a first in philosophy at the University of Edinburgh, and then proceeded to study theology at New College, Edinburgh, and at Marburg and Heidelberg universities, where he studied under Wilhelm Herrmann, Adolph Jülicher, Ernst Troeltsch, and Johannes Weiss. He acted for three years as assistant to James Seth, the professor of moral philosophy in Edinburgh University, and was ordained in the United Free Church of Scotland in 1918. He held the charges of Bervie (1918–23), St John's, Cupar (1923–30), and St Columba's, Kilmacolm (1930–34), before being appointed in 1934 to a newly established chair in systematic theology at St Mary's College, University of St Andrews. He held this post until his death, and established a formidable reputation as an attractive teacher of great ability and a preacher of clarity, depth, and spirituality.

In addition to translations of F. D. E. Schleiermacher and various articles Baillie published only two books during his lifetime. His Kerr lectures, *Faith in God and its Christian Consummation* (1927; 2nd edn with introduction by John MacIntyre, 1964) was a fine example of the Kantian–Ritschlian tradition of protestant liberal theology, and also showed a singular openness to the new 'theology of crisis', particularly as represented by Emil Brunner, and to the concept of paradox, which was to play an important role in Baillie's later theology. His *God was in Christ: an Essay on Incarnation and Atonement* (1948) quickly became a theological classic and has had sustained influence on modern Christology in the English-speaking world, particularly with its suggestion that the 'paradox of grace'—'Not I, but Christ in me' illumines the incarnation. 'A toned down Christology', Baillie affirmed, 'is absurd. It must be all or nothing—all or nothing on both the divine and human side' (p. 132). His robust yet modest writing was characterized by great lucidity, honesty, and spiritual depth. Like his brother John he represented the best of the Scottish tradition of liberal evangelical theology, combining reverence with intellectual rigour and passion.

Baillie's posthumous publications—*The Theology of the Sacraments and other Papers* (1957), and two volumes of sermons, *To whom Shall we Go?* (1955) and *Out of Nazareth: a Selection of Sermons and Lectures* (1958)—served to consolidate his international reputation as a creative and constructive theologian.

Donald Baillie played a leading role in the ecumenical movement in Scotland, where he was convener of the Church of Scotland inter-church relations committee. He was prominent in the faith and order commission of the World Council of Churches, particularly at its Edinburgh 1937 and Lund 1952 conferences. He chaired the commission on intercommunion which reported to the 1952 World Conference on Faith and Order at Lund, and he was highly regarded as one of the most eirenic and constructive of ecumenical theologians.

A lifelong bachelor, with a wide and varied circle of friends, Donald Baillie suffered for most of his life from asthma, and died from emphysema on 31 October 1954, significantly, perhaps, the eve of All Saints' day, at Maryfield Hospital, Dundee. He was buried on 3 November at the western cemetery, St Andrews.

DUNCAN B. FORRESTER

Sources J. Baillie, 'Donald: a brother's impression', in D. Baillie, *The theology of the sacraments* (1957), 13–36 · J. Dow, 'Memoir', in D. M. Baillie, *To whom shall we go?* (1955), 1–19 · A. C. Cheyne, 'The Baillies and Scottish theology', *In divers manners: a St Mary's miscellany*, ed. D. W. D. Shaw (1990), 84–144 · J. MacIntyre, 'A tale of two exchanges: the Christology of D. M. Baillie', *In divers manners: a St Mary's miscellany*, ed. D. W. D. Shaw (1990) · J. A. Whyte, 'D. M. Baillie and the preaching of Christian doctrine', *In divers manners: a St Mary's miscellany*, ed. D. W. D. Shaw (1990) · D. Fergusson, ed., *Christ, church, and society: essays on John Baillie and Donald Baillie* (1993) · *WWW* · private information (2004) · *St Andrews Citizen* (6 Nov 1954)

Archives NRA Scotland, priv. coll., MSS · U. Edin., commonplace book, lecture notes · U. St Andr. L., corresp., diaries, papers · U. St Andr. L., MSS, MSS 37231–37236 | NL Scot., corresp. with T. & T. Clark, publishers

Likenesses photograph (in old age), U. St Andr., St Mary's College · photographs, repro. in Baillie, *To whom shall we go?*

Wealth at death £5525 9s. 9d.: confirmation, 29 Dec 1954, *CCI*

Baillie, George, of Jerviswood (1664–1738), landowner and politician, born on 16 March 1664 at Jerviswood Tower, Lanarkshire, was the eldest child of Robert *Baillie (*d.* 1684) and of his wife and cousin Rachel Johnston (*d.* 1697), daughter of the Presbyterian martyr Sir Archibald Johnston, Lord Wariston. 'Intended for the practice of the law' (Murray, 21), Baillie was studying in the Netherlands

George Baillie of Jerviswood (1664–1738), by William Aikman, 1717

when news reached him of his father's arrest on charges of high treason arising from the Rye House plot. He returned home to Scotland and witnessed Robert's execution in the Grassmarket of Edinburgh on 24 December 1684. The Jerviswood estates were subsequently confiscated and Baillie fled to the Netherlands, where he joined a band of stalwart Presbyterian exiles, including his father's friend Sir Patrick Hume, whose daughter Grisell (1665–1746) [*see* Baillie, Lady Grisell] he was later to marry (17 September 1691). With Hume's eldest son, Baillie served in the prince of Orange's horse guards 'till they were better provided for in the army, which they were before the Revolution' (Murray, 50). In 1689 he joined the prince's expedition to England, narrowly escaping shipwreck *en route*.

As a staunch supporter of the revolution's principles, Baillie expected and received preferment, though of a modest nature. He was restored to his estates and served as commissioner of supply for Berwickshire and Lanarkshire (1689) and as a commissioner of militia (1689). Tiresome months of solicitation at court proved more productive after his uncle, James Johnstone, became one of the Scottish secretaries of state in 1692; in the following year Baillie was appointed receiver-general (Scotland) at a salary of £300 p.a. He had been elected as a commissioner to the Scottish parliament in 1691 and represented Berwickshire until 1701; although he headed the poll for Berwickshire in 1702, he chose to represent Lanarkshire, for which he also had a commission (1702–7). Baillie had been politically aligned with Secretary James Johnstone's group from 1692 to 1696, but, on his uncle's dismissal from the secretaryship, became associated with the country party, voting against the government in 1701 on both the standing army and Darien questions. As the Jacobite George Lockhart of Carnwath remarked, Baillie gained a great reputation in King William's time 'by standing so stiffly by the interest of his country' (Lockhart, 95).

At the beginning of Queen Anne's reign Baillie remained part of the opposition and was, with the other members, bizarrely implicated by the duke of Queensberry, the leader of the Scottish administration, in the 'Scotch plot', an alleged Jacobite conspiracy. Early in 1704 the opposition sent him to London, in the company of the earls of Roxburghe and Rothes, to put its views before the queen and to urge the calling of a Scottish parliament. A change in the Scottish ministry shortly followed, with Baillie taking office as treasurer-depute and appointed a member of the Scottish privy council in an administration headed by the marquess of Tweeddale. This government of the 'new party', as the group became known, was not a happy one: Baillie and the rest were castigated as deserters of the country party (although, in fact, they still attempted, perhaps naïvely, to pursue country party principles in office), Tweeddale was widely considered incompetent, the powerful Scottish magnates were hostile, and the English government was unwilling to allow the new party the patronage powers which might have assured success. Baillie, diligent, principled (he was one of the few politicians brave enough, with the Edinburgh mob in full cry, to attend the meetings of the Scottish privy council during the deliberations on the *Worcester* affair), and perhaps more astute than most of his colleagues, shared their fate when the new party leaders were dismissed from office (June 1705). It was particularly galling for a man with Baillie's history that his successor as treasurer-depute, the earl of Glasgow, suggested that the main reason for the change in government was so that it would be 'thoroughly upon the Revolution bottom' (Hume Brown, 179).

The ousting of the new party, however, did not drive it to reunite with the opposition. Indeed, Andrew Fletcher of Saltoun's unsuccessful attempt to keep Baillie out of the 1705 parliament sprang entirely from spleen at what he regarded as Baillie's apostasy from the country party. The quarrel verged on farce when Baillie espoused John Law's land bank scheme. This was a project for remedying the dearth of money in Scotland which had much appeal for those who, like him, had, in 1696, backed the Company of Scotland (in which he had an investment of £1000 and of which he was a director) when it attempted to remedy a similar situation by issuing its own bills. Fletcher's insistence that the scheme was yet another plot to enslave the Scottish nation led to a duelling challenge between Fletcher and Lord Roxburghe: it was only with difficulty that Lord Charles Ker and Baillie, the respective seconds, succeeded in bringing about a reconciliation between the principals.

In refusing to rejoin the opposition, the new party hoped to hold the balance in the Scottish parliament. However, the *squadrone volante*, as it now became known, was ineluctably drawn in a court direction. Baillie's own, somewhat reluctant conversion to the necessity for Scotland's union with England, a court imperative by 1705, can be traced in his correspondence: union was first a potion which had to be drunk, then the lesser of two evils, and finally 'our onlie game' (*Correspondence*, 142, 144, 145). It was the votes of the *squadrone* which allowed the passage of the union treaty in 1706; the duke of Atholl reportedly asserted that they had 'acted like angels' and that the queen owed union to them (ibid., 174).

With the other *squadrone* leaders, Baillie now sought a role on the British stage. He represented Berwickshire in the first British parliament and, with the backing of the whigs, became a member of the Board of Trade, surviving several tory purges before being dismissed in 1712. He joined with other Scots in parliament in successfully urging the abolition of the Scottish privy council (1707) and in unsuccessfully resisting the extension of English treason penalties to Scotland (1709). It was thanks to a campaign organized by him and Lockhart that the imposition of new linen duties on Scotland was delayed for a year; he also opposed the malt tax (1713). As the effects of the Union became more apparent, Baillie came to resent the 'utmost contempt' with which the Scots were treated, even as he recognized that dissolving the Union (a bill was put forward in 1713) might have 'a worse effect and be more fatal to us' (*Polwarth MSS*, 1.12).

A convinced Hanoverian, Baillie welcomed the accession of George I, becoming one of the nine 'chief men in place' in the new House of Commons (*Letters and Works of Lady Mary Wortley Montagu*, ed. Lord Warncliffe, 3 vols., 1861, 1.136). He served as a lord of Admiralty (1714–17) and was appointed to the Treasury board formed on Robert Walpole's resignation in 1717. There he remained, retaining his post after Walpole's return to the Treasury in 1721, until 1725, when he was ousted (though with a pension equal to his salary) to satisfy the Argyll interest. He had broken with his long-time friend and *squadrone* ally the earl of Roxburghe in 1723, correctly observing that Roxburghe's performance as Scottish secretary had reduced Scotland to less weight in the management of affairs than any county in England, and in that year professed himself 'quite out of bussiness' and ready to depart public life were it not for his position as MP, from which he finally stepped down in 1734 (*Polwarth MSS*, 3.289, 282).

Although lacking the social clout which would have enabled him to scale the heights in Scottish or British politics, and impeded, particularly after the Union, by increasing deafness, Baillie possessed, as Lockhart admitted, a 'profound solid judgment' and was 'by far the most significant man of all his party, to whom he was a kind of dictator' (Lockhart, 95). He worked hard to keep the *squadrone* together, continually urging, though not always successfully, the necessity of acting in concert (*Correspondence*, 76, 163). No mere placeman, he was willing to vote against the court, as he did on the Spanish question in 1711, and determined always to act in ways which seemed right to him, in small matters as in large: when he was in the Admiralty he made his children return a present of a parrot from a gentleman who was soliciting something there (Murray, 8). At the time of the Jacobite rising of 1715 he urged mercy for the participants, despite the unpopularity of such a stance and the despoliation of his own Mellerstain lands. He also advised and assisted the relatives of the rebels. Lockhart thought him 'morose, proud, and severe' (Lockhart, 95), and, indeed, his own and his family's history had given him reason to be so. In private life, however, as Lady Murray's memoir indicates, he was very different, enjoying music, hawking, and hunting, and accompanying his offspring to balls and masquerades.

A devoted husband, Baillie wrote to Lady Grisell by every post during their long periods of separation; not until 1714 did his family move to London. He confided his political secrets only to her, he relied on her substantial managerial capabilities in looking after his Scottish interests, and he conscientiously filled requests for 'muslin with Indian flowers' and other items for her and the bairns. Three children were born of the marriage—a son, Robert (*b.* 1694), died in infancy; Grisell (1692–1759), who married Alexander Murray, son and heir of Sir David Murray of Stanhope, in 1710, with her father's reluctant consent: a legal separation was obtained in 1714; and Rachel (1696–1773), who in 1717 married Charles, Lord Binning (1697–1732), son and heir to the earl of Haddington. When Lord Binning became ill, Baillie accompanied the rest of the family to Naples (1731–3) in an unavailing attempt to improve his health.

Baillie devoted his retirement to his friends and his family, to his books and his prayers; he had for many years been representative elder for the parish of Earlston, in which lies Mellerstain, and he remained a devout Presbyterian to the end. This 'honest, serious, religious Man' (monument) died in Oxford on 6 August 1738, after a brief illness. He was buried in the mausoleum he had ordered to be built in the fields of Mellerstain; his estate passed in liferent to his wife and was eventually inherited by the second son of Lord and Lady Binning.

BARBARA C. MURISON

Sources *The household book of Lady Grisell Baillie, 1692–1733*, ed. R. Scott-Moncrieff, Scottish History Society, new ser., 1 (1911) • Lady Murray of Stanhope, *Memoirs of the lives and characters of the Right Honourable George Baillie of Jerviswood and of Lady Grisell Baillie* (1822) • *Correspondence of George Baillie of Jerviswood, 1702–1708*, ed. G. E. M. Kynynmond (1842) • M. D. Young, ed., *The parliaments of Scotland: burgh and shire commissioners*, 1 (1992) • *Report on the manuscripts of Lord Polwarth*, 1, HMC, 67 (1911); 3 (1931) • P. W. J. Riley, *The Union of England and Scotland* (1978) • P. W. J. Riley, *The English ministers and Scotland, 1707–1727* (1964) • P. W. J. Riley, *King William and the Scottish politicians* (1979) • G. Lockhart, *The Lockhart papers: containing memoirs and commentaries upon the affairs of Scotland from 1702 to 1715*, 2 vols. (1817) • *APS, 1689–1707, suppl.* • G. H. Rose, *A selection from the papers of the earls of Marchmont*, 3 vols. (1831) • J. Grant, ed., *Seafield correspondence from 1685–1708* (1912) • *Letters relating to Scotland in the reign of Queen Anne by James Ogilvy, first earl of Seafield and others*, ed. P. Hume Brown, Scottish History Society, 2nd ser., 11 (1915) • *The manuscripts of his grace the duke of Portland*, 10 vols., HMC, 29 (1891–1931), vol. 4 • G. S. Holmes, *British politics in the age of Anne* (1967) • J. M. Simpson, 'Baillie, George', HoP, *Commons, 1715–54*, 1.427–8 • NRA Scotland, 0104, 21

Archives NL Scot., letters • NRA, priv. coll., corresp. and papers | NA Scot., letters to Sir W. Bennet, incl. from Lady Grisell, GD205/box 33 • NA Scot., business letters to W. Hall, GD206/2/376 • NA Scot., letters to duke of Montrose

Likenesses J. Medina, oils, 1709, Mellerstain • W. Aikman, oils, 1717, Mellerstain [*see illus.*] • W. Aikman, double portrait, oils, 1725 (with granddaughter), Mellerstain

Wealth at death £37,724 in 1736: *Household book*, ed. R. Scott-Moncrieff, lxxviii

Baillie, Lady Grisell (1665–1746), heroine and business woman, was born on 25 December 1665 at Redbraes Castle, Berwickshire, the eldest survivor of the eighteen children of Sir Patrick *Hume (or Home) of Polwarth, later first earl of Marchmont (1641–1724), and Grisell Kerr (*d.* 1703), daughter of Sir Thomas Kerr of Cavers. The daughter of staunch Presbyterians, she occupies a prominent place in the martyrology of the covenanting movement. Her father's opposition to Lauderdale's policies led to his imprisonment in the 1670s; his close friend Robert Baillie of Jerviswood suffered similar treatment. In 1676 the young Grisell was entrusted by her father with the delivery of a letter to Baillie, at that time in custody in Edinburgh. She not only gained admittance to his cell, but also smuggled out a message. It was probably on this occasion, too, that she met the prisoner's son, George *Baillie (1664–1738), whom she was later to marry.

Grisell had shown intelligence, courage, and initiative, and thereafter her parents placed increasing reliance on her. In the early 1680s both Robert Baillie and Hume were caught up in the aftermath of the Rye House plot. Baillie was hanged for treason; Hume, fearing similar treatment, concealed himself in the family vault at Polwarth church. For a month Grisell kept him supplied with food and drink, putting food from her own plate at dinner into her lap in case the servants should suspect. When it was thought best to move Sir Patrick's place of concealment, it was Grisell who, with the assistance of a trusted servant, excavated a hiding place beneath the family house. It was actions of this sort that led Henry Grey Graham to bracket Grisell Baillie with Flora Macdonald in his pantheon of Scottish heroines.

Hume escaped to the continent and eventually, after a return to Scotland in the abortive Argyll rebellion, made his way to Utrecht, whence he sent for his ailing wife and ten surviving children. In the Netherlands Grisell displayed her burgeoning managerial abilities in organizing a large household bereft of servants except for 'a little girl to wash the dishes' and frequented by émigré Scots (including George Baillie) and other 'well-wishers to the Revolution' (Murray, 46–7). When the revolution came in 1688, Hume accompanied William of Orange's expedition; its success assured his family's prosperity. Grisell, who went over to England with the Princess Mary, was offered the post of maid of honour. However, this 'well made, clever … very handsome' person, with 'life and sweetness in her eyes … and great delicacy in all her features', with chestnut hair and 'the finest complexion' (ibid., 56), preferred to return home to Scotland and to marry, on 17 September 1691, her childhood love, George Baillie, now restored to the Jerviswood estates.

It was a long and happy marriage. Three children were born: a son, who died in infancy, and two daughters, Grisell (1692–1759), who married Sir Alexander Murray of Stanhope, and Rachel (1696–1773), who married Charles, Lord Binning. George Baillie followed a successful career, becoming a lord of the Treasury in 1717. His wife provided shrewd political assistance to him and to her father, lobbying for support on their behalf and keeping them apprised of the situation in Scotland when they were at court. The business skills acquired in Utrecht were now applied in a broader context. George Baillie gave her a free hand; the only question he ever asked was 'if his debt was paid' (Murray, 72). On hearing of the selection of a certain politician, of whom he disapproved, for a Treasury post, he suggested to the earl of Roxburghe, perhaps only half in jest, that the government should rather have 'put my Lady there' (*Correspondence*, 109). As her father aged, Grisell took over the management of his estates, once spending two months, working from five in the morning to twelve at night, sorting out the accounts. She also managed her brother's affairs while he was abroad and supervised the education of his children and of her own grandchildren, living some years at Oxford for the purpose.

Grisell's *Household Book* shows her hard at work. Servants were either diligent or dismissed; eight cooks came and went in 1715. She did not bear incompetence patiently, as when she noted the price paid for young trees by her gardener, 'which was a perfit cheat' (*Household Book*, 253). When the family removed temporarily to Italy for the sake of Lord Binning's health, Grisell learned Italian, the better to bargain with the tradespeople. As the inscription on her monument noted, 'unwearied application' and 'happy economy' went hand in hand in her management of affairs; she amassed an immense fortune. In her rare leisure moments she wrote poems and songs; the most famous is 'Werena my heart licht I wad dee'.

'Full of years and of good works' (monument), Grisell died in London on 6 December 1746, after a brief illness. On her deathbed she had asked for the last chapter of Proverbs to be read to her. It was an accurate description of this remarkable woman, who most certainly had never eaten 'the bread of idleness' (Proverbs 31: 27) and whose worth was indeed 'above rubies' (ibid., 31: 10). According to her own instructions she was buried (on 25 December 1746) beside her husband at Mellerstain, whose modest buildings were soon to be enlarged by the hand of Robert Adam and which came into the possession of her descendants the earls of Haddington. BARBARA C. MURISON

Sources Lady Murray [G. Baillie], *Memoirs of the lives and characters of the Right Honourable George Baillie of Jerviswood and of Lady Grisell Baillie*, 2nd edn (1824) • *The household book of Lady Grisell Baillie, 1692–1733*, ed. R. Scott-Moncrieff, Scottish History Society, new ser., 1 (1911) • [J. M. M. Warrender], *Marchmont and the Humes of Polwarth* (1894) • J. Anderson, *The ladies of the covenant* (1851) • HMC, 14 (1894) • H. Graham, *A group of Scottish women* (1908) • G. H. Rose, *A selection from the papers of the earls of Marchmont*, 3 vols. (1831) • R. Wodrow, *The history of the sufferings of the Church of Scotland from the Restoration to the revolution*, ed. R. Burns, 4 vols. (1828–30) • *Correspondence of George Baillie of Jerviswood, 1702–1708*, ed. G. E. M. Kynynmond (1842) • S. Tytler and J. L. Watson, *The songstresses of Scotland*, 1 (1871) • J. Baillie, *Metrical legends of exalted characters* (1821) • G. Crawfurd, *The lives and characters, of the officers of the crown, and of the state in Scotland* (1726) • monumental inscription, Mellerstain, Berwickshire

Archives NRA Scotland, priv. coll., corresp. • NRA Scotland, priv. coll., letters and papers | NA Scot., Ogilvy MSS, letters to Sir William Bennet • NA Scot., letters to William Hall and other family members

Likenesses J. Medina, oils, 1709, Mellerstain • W. Aikman, oils, 1717, priv. coll.; repro. in R. Marshall, *Women in Scotland, 1660–1780* (1979), 40 • M. Verelst, oils, 1725, Mellerstain; repro. in *Mellerstain, Gordon, Berwickshire: home of Lord and Lady Binning* (1985), 15 • L. F. Roubiliac, marble bust, Mellerstain

Wealth at death inherited husband's estate, valued at £37,724 in 1736; incl. lands of Jerviswood in Lanarkshire, and Mellerstain: *Household book of Lady Grisell Baillie*, ed. Scott-Moncrieff, xxix • Baillie had been a lord of the admiralty (£1000 p.a.) and a lord of the treasury (£1600 p.a.); 'the richest heiress in the Merse'; 'immense fortune' acquired under her 'attentive management': Lady Anne Purves, *Anecdotes of the family of Marchmont* (1784), appended to Warrender, *Marchmont and the Humes*, 147

Baillie, Lady Grisell (1822–1891), Church of Scotland deaconess, was born on 4 April 1822 at Mellerstain, near Kelso, the youngest of the eleven children of George Baillie (1763–1841) of Jerviswoode, MP for Berwickshire, and his wife, Mary, the youngest daughter of Sir James Pringle, bt, of Stichill. She had six brothers and four sisters. The Baillie family was well established in church life. George Baillie was descended from Robert Baillie the covenanter, whose great-grandfather was John Knox. Grisell was named after her great-great-grandmother, a heroine of the covenanting period.

After her father's death in 1841 the nineteen-year old Grisell Baillie was the only member of the family remaining at home with her widowed mother. In 1842 they moved from Mellerstain to Eildon Hall, and at the end of 1848 Grisell Baillie 'confessed Christ'. In 1849 her fourth brother, Major Robert Baillie, also underwent a religious conversion, and left the army to live with his mother and sister: he and his sister became increasingly close. In 1858 her eldest brother, George, inherited the title and estates of his cousin, Thomas Hamilton, earl of Haddington. Courtesy titles were bestowed on the family at this time by Queen Victoria.

Mary Baillie died on 13 August 1865, having been nursed faithfully by Lady Grisell. They had moved from Eildon Hall, firstly to Maxpoffle in 1859, and then to Dryburgh Abbey House in 1864 (not to be confused with nearby Dryburgh House, the residence of Lord Jerviswoode, Lady Grisell Baillie's second brother). Shortly before Mary Baillie's death, her fifth son, Admiral the Hon. Thomas Baillie, retired and came to live with them, sharing a life of prayer, Bible study, and philanthropy.

In 1854 Major Robert Baillie had become an elder at Bowden kirk, where the minister, Dr James Mackenzie Allardyce, was a great influence. Lady Grisell Baillie continued her philanthropic work, which included providing a water supply for the village of Newtown St Boswells and rebuilding the bridge over the Tweed at Mertoun, which had been badly damaged in a storm in 1840. She embraced the temperance movement, foreign missions, the YWCA, Sunday school, and young women's meetings. Both she

Lady Grisell Baillie (1822–1891), by David Octavius Hill and Robert Adamson, 1843–8

and the major were greatly loved, and were described as 'constant companions [who] walked with God and with each other in saintly lives of Christian service'. The major's death in August 1888, after a short illness, dealt a crushing blow to his sister.

This was a period of revival in the Church of Scotland, one of the leaders being Professor Archibald Hamilton Charteris. In 1869 he had proposed, and Major Baillie had seconded, a motion establishing the Christian Life and Work Committee. In 1885 Charteris put the question of women's work to the general assembly. While preparing for his 1887 Baird lectures Charteris visited the deaconess community at Kaiserwerth which had inspired the revival of women's work within the church in many countries. In 1887 he laid before the general assembly his plan for a women's guild, to consist of the guild itself, 'women workers' in the congregations, and an order of deaconesses. The middle grade came to nothing, but the guild and the deaconesses were sanctioned by the general assembly. Charteris favoured ordination, but others feared it would put the deaconess above the elder, and so in 1888 the general assembly resolved that deaconesses should simply be 'set apart' by the local kirk session.

Lady Grisell Baillie, the first deaconess of the Church of Scotland, was solemnly set apart in her sixty-seventh year on Sunday 9 December 1888 in Bowden kirk, in the presence of her brother, Admiral Baillie, and just over three months after the death of the major. The service was conducted by Dr Allardyce. The congregation of Bowden kirk viewed her new role as a continuation of that of her late brother. Admiral Baillie died on 31 July 1889, and in 1890 Lady Grisell Baillie moved across the Tweed to The Holmes, just south of Newtown St Boswells, but still on the Dryburgh estate. Her ministry continued in the same vein as hitherto—Sunday school teaching, prayer and Bible study groups, mothers' meetings, and philanthropy. In November 1891 the Women's Guild held its first conference in Edinburgh and Lady Grisell Baillie, as president, took the chair. She delivered the opening address (her first experience of public speaking), and her message was 'Go, work today in my vineyard'. A fortnight later she succumbed to influenza and died on 20 December at her home. She was buried in the family mausoleum on the Mellerstain estate on 24 December 1891. A memorial tablet to Major Robert and Lady Grisell Baillie was placed in Bowden kirk. In Edinburgh the Lady Grisell Baillie Memorial Deaconess Hospital was opened on 11 October 1894 to care for the sick poor and to train women as deaconesses and for other ministries.

VALERIE BONHAM

Sources D. P. Thomson, *Scotland's first deaconess: Lady Grisell Baillie* (1946), vol. 3 of *Women of the Scottish Church* • Countess of Ashburnham, *Lady Grisell Baillie: a sketch of her life* (1893) • A. Gordon, *The life of Archibald Hamilton Charteris* (1912) • A. L. Drummond and J. Bulloch, *The church in late Victorian Scotland* (1978) • M. S. Sherrard, ed., *Women of faith* (1993) • M. Levison, *Wrestling with the church* (1992) • Lady G. Baillie, *Recollections of a happy life: begun on earth, made perfect in the skies* • R. Reid, *The life of Lady Grisell Baillie, first deaconess of the Church of Scotland* (1989)

Archives Church of Scotland, Edinburgh, diaconate committee | NA Scot., letters to William Hall and his family • NRA Scotland

Likenesses D. O. Hill and R. Adamson, calotype, 1843–8, NPG [*see illus.*] • J. Swinton, pastels, 1844, Mellerstain House, Gordon, Berwickshire • group portrait (with Church of Scotland Woman's Guild), repro. in Sherrard, ed., *Women of faith* • portrait, repro. in Sherrard, ed., *Women of faith* • portrait (as a young woman), repro. in Thomson, *Scotland's first deaconess*

Wealth at death £28,346 14*s*. 5*d*.: confirmation, 14 May 1892, *CCI*

Baillie, Dame Isobel [*real name* Isabella Douglas Baillie] (**1895–1983**), singer, was born on 9 March 1895 in the border town of Hawick, Roxburghshire, Scotland, the youngest in a family of a son and three daughters of Martin Pott Baillie (*d.* 1903?), a master baker, and his wife, Isabella Douglas. She was baptized Isabella Douglas and known as Bella. The family moved to Newcastle upon Tyne when she was five. Not long afterwards they moved to Manchester, where Bella attended the board school in Princess Road. There her voice was noticed when she sang a verse of a hymn as a solo. She had always enjoyed singing at home but had received no tuition until her headmaster encouraged her. She won a scholarship to Manchester high school, where music was a low priority.

Bella left school at fifteen to work in a music shop in Fountain Street, Manchester, where she was put in charge of the piano roll department. After that she worked in the gas department of Manchester town hall. At this period the headmaster at the board school persuaded Bella's mother to let her study singing seriously. She went once a

Dame Isobel Baillie (1895–1983), by Lafayette, 1931

week to Jean Sadler-Fogg, a former pupil of Blanche Marchesi and the wife of the Hallé Orchestra's organist Charles Fogg and mother of the composer Eric Fogg. Mrs Sadler-Fogg took her pupil to sing to Marchesi, whose only remembered comment was 'That F could be better'. Bella was unable to pay Mrs Sadler-Fogg's fees, but paid her back when she began to get engagements. At fifteen she sang in her first performance of Handel's *Messiah* in a church in Stretford. Gradually she was invited to sing in churches and church halls throughout Lancashire and in parts of Yorkshire.

On 31 December 1917 Bella married Henry (Harry) Leonard Wrigley (1891–1957), a cotton trader, whom she had met before 1914 at a local concert where she sang and he recited *The Green Eye of the Little Yellow God*, the popular ballad by John Milton Hayes. At the time of their marriage he was on sick leave from France. Two days after the wedding he returned to the trenches, where he was wounded at Ypres. Their daughter Nancy was born in December 1918. Shortly afterwards Bella calculated that her earnings from singing exceeded her town hall salary, so she decided to devote all her time to singing. One of her first professional engagements in 1920 was in a popular ballad concert broadcast from Manchester's first local radio station in Trafford Park, before the BBC was founded. She also wrote, asking for an audition, to Hamilton Harty, who had in 1920 been appointed conductor of the Hallé Orchestra. Harty interviewed her, having already heard her sing in songs by Eric Fogg at a recital, and engaged her to sing the wordless soprano part in Alfredo Casella's symphonic suite *The Venetian Convent* at a Hallé concert in the Free Trade Hall, Manchester, on 17 November 1921. Harty then engaged her for Haydn's *The Creation* and for a performance of *Messiah*, the first time Handel's oratorio was broadcast. She became indelibly associated with *Messiah*. Baillie reckoned she had sung in it over a thousand times—on thirty-three occasions with the Royal Choral Society in London and nearly thirty times with the Hallé. Her 'I know that my redeemer liveth' was justly admired for its serenity and purity, but equally memorable were her declamation of the Christmas music and the crystalline clarity of her 'Rejoice greatly'. Only once, for John Tobin, did she add ornamentation to the vocal line, but she strongly disapproved of this later fashionable practice, considering that it detracted from both the flow of the vocal line and the devotional meaning of the text.

Harty advised her to sing as Isobel Baillie, saying that Bella Baillie led people to expect 'a music hall or musical comedy artist'. He also advised her to study in the summers of 1925 and 1926 with Guglielmo Sommer in Milan; but before that she had been engaged by Sir Henry Wood for six Promenade Concerts in the Queen's Hall in 1923, her London début. One of them was a Wagner night shared with Lauritz Melchior when he was still a baritone. Although she was principally associated with oratorio, to which her light silvery tone and superb clarity of enunciation were ideally suited, she also sang arias by Mozart and Micaela's arias from Bizet's *Carmen* and, with Wood conducting, sang Elsa in a concert performance of Wagner's *Lohengrin* in Leicester. Her participation in Wagner aroused the displeasure of Harty, who, in a letter written in 1928 after she had sung in the closing scene of *Götterdämmerung*, remonstrated with her that 'in music of this type you are quite out of the picture and merely a source of gratification to your enemies' (Baillie, 29). Nevertheless, he later engaged her for a Wagner concert in Bradford and to sing in the *Meistersinger* quintet. On 24 January 1938, on the insistence of Hyam Greenbaum, she sang Isolde, with Walter Widdop as Tristan, in two performances of act II that were televised (afternoon and evening) from Alexandra Palace. She wrote in her autobiography, 'I was far from being a natural Isolde but I enjoyed every minute of the adventure' (ibid., 115).

Isobel Baillie's only operatic appearance in Britain was at Covent Garden in the coronation season of 1937, when the 1774 Paris version of Gluck's *Orphée* was conducted by Fritz Reiner. But she did not step on the stage. She sang one aria during the ballet from the orchestra pit. She sang Marguerite in many concert performances of Gounod's *Faust* throughout Britain, but in 1940, on a tour of New Zealand, she sang the role on stage in sixteen performances. In 1929, with the tenor Francis Russell, she recorded the act I love duet from Puccini's *Madama Butterfly*.

The core of Isobel Baillie's career was in Britain between 1920 and 1974, the year she made her last recording to mark her forthcoming eightieth birthday. She first sang at the Three Choirs festival in 1929 at Worcester (*Messiah*) and performed at eighteen of these festivals thereafter, and sang under Elgar's baton in his *For the Fallen* at Worcester in 1932 and in *The Apostles* and *The Kingdom* elsewhere. On 6 September 1950 she sang in the first performance of Herbert Howells's *Hymnus paradisi* at Gloucester. Other British composers with whose music she was associated included Sir George Dyson, in the first performance of whose *The Canterbury Pilgrims* she sang the Wife of Bath on 19 March 1931, Gerald Finzi (whose *Dies natalis* was the only work she sang with Sir John Barbirolli's Hallé), and Harty. She frequently sang Harty's *Ode to a Nightingale*, and gave the first performance of his *The Children of Lir* in London on 1 March 1939. She was a regular soloist at the Leith Hill Festival at Dorking, conducted by Ralph Vaughan Williams, and sang in his works at the Three Choirs festival; she was also one of the sixteen soloists for whom he wrote his *Serenade to Music*, given in Sir Henry Wood's golden jubilee concert at the Royal Albert Hall on 5 October 1938. It was recorded a few days later, thereby preserving her marvellous ascent to top A on the words 'sweet harmony'. Her last major recording was in Vaughan Williams's *A Sea Symphony* in 1953, ending (apart from the 1974 disc) a career in the studios extending from a test recording made on 19 February 1924.

Isobel Baillie's repertory was wider than was often supposed, including many works by J. S. Bach, Berlioz, Brahms, Dvořák, Gurney, Kodály, Mendelssohn, Rakhmaninov (*The Bells* as well as songs), Schubert, Schumann, Strauss, Szymanowski, Tchaikovsky, and Wolf. In addition she sang a vast number of popular ballads. On 27 July 1933 she was the first British artist to sing at the Hollywood Bowl, in a concert conducted by Harty. This was her American début. In the autumn of 1937 she sang in London in Brahms's *German Requiem* and Beethoven's ninth symphony conducted by Arturo Toscanini.

During the Second World War Isobel Baillie sang for the Entertainments National Service Association in military bases, camps, and factory canteens. In December 1941 she performed with Kathleen Ferrier for the first time, in *Messiah* at Lytham St Anne's. She was the soprano in *Messiah* in Westminster Abbey in May 1943 when Ferrier made her legendary first London appearance. They became good friends and recorded duets by Purcell and Mendelssohn.

After the war Isobel Baillie went back to New Zealand in 1948 for recitals, returning home via Singapore, Kuala Lumpur, and Penang, in all of which she gave recitals. She sang in the cathedral at Washington, DC, in 1949 and toured South Africa (after flying there in the Comet) in 1953. After her virtual retirement in 1955 she gave lecture recitals and master classes throughout the world. She had begun to teach at the Royal College of Music in 1952 on the invitation of its director, Sir George Dyson; he then persuaded her to join the permanent teaching staff, of which she was a member from 1955 to 1957. In 1960–61 she was visiting professor of singing in the department of music at Cornell University, and on her return to England was asked by Sir Keith Falkner, with whom she had often sung and who was now director of the Royal College of Music, to rejoin the college staff; she remained for three years from 1961 to 1964. She also taught for many years at the Manchester School of Music in Albert Square, run by John Grierson, one of her regular accompanists. She returned to Cornell in 1980 at eighty-five to lecture with, it was said, 'very impressive vocal examples'. In 1982 she published her autobiography, *Never Sing Louder than Lovely*, valuable for its details about the singing of *Messiah* and for vivid pen-portraits of her colleagues. It ends with the words 'It has been a wonderful life and I would do it all again' (Baillie, 145). She attracted audiences not only by the beauty of her voice, with its secure technique and impeccable diction, but also by her friendly personality and her red-gold hair and lovely complexion. She personified the best in British oratorio singing. She was appointed CBE in 1951 and DBE in 1978.

After Isobel Baillie's husband retired from the cotton trade in 1945 the couple moved from their cottage in Silecroft, in the Breast of Blackcombe, above Barrow in Furness, to Trimmings, Gracious Street, Selborne, Hampshire. He died in 1957. Baillie later lived in St John's Wood, London, before returning to Manchester, where she died from heart failure at the Withington Hospital on 24 September 1983. MICHAEL KENNEDY

Sources I. Baillie, *Never sing louder than lovely* (1982) • *The Times* (26 Sept 1983) • personal knowledge (2004) • *CGPLA Eng. & Wales* (1984) • *DNB* • A. Blyth, 'Baillie, Dame Isobel', *New Grove*, 2.36 • m. cert. • d. cert.

Archives SOUND BL NSA, 'Never sing louder than lovely', BBC Radio 4, 26 Feb 1998, T6617W C1 • BL NSA, *Richard Baker compares notes*, H4972/4 • BL NSA, documentary recordings • BL NSA, performance recordings

Likenesses Lafayette, photograph, 1931, NPG [*see illus.*] • photograph, 1978, Hult. Arch. • watercolour, priv. coll.

Wealth at death under £40,000: probate, 4 Jan 1984, *CGPLA Eng. & Wales*

Baillie, James (*bap.* **1672**, *d.* **1744**), advocate, was baptized on 26 April 1672, the son of William Baillie of Glenlewin (*d.* 1714), advocate, and Eupham(ia) Watson (*d.* before 1682). His father's uncle was a Baillie of Lamington in Lanarkshire, which family had produced at least one judge, William Baillie, Lord Provand (*d.* 1593), and a number of soldiers during the political turbulence of the seventeenth century, including William Baillie (*d.* 1653) and Robert Baillie (*d.* 1684).

Little is known of James Baillie's early life and education; however, he passed advocate on 25 July 1702, having taken his public examination on a digest title *de servitudibus*. He was not active in the business and affairs of the Faculty of Advocates at the time, for his name does not feature regularly in the minute books of the faculty. It may thus be supposed that he was not in the front rank of pleaders before the court of session. Baillie married Jean Aytoun (1677–1774), daughter of Aytoun of Kinnaldie, on 29 April 1709. Thereafter little is recorded of Baillie until his edition of the sixteenth-century writer Thomas Craig's great polemic legal and political treatise *Jus feudale* was published at the press of Thomas and Walter Ruddiman in 1732. Regarded by D. M. Walker in his *Scottish Jurists* (1985) as the best, Baillie's edition was the third to be published. He included a short life of Craig, and rationalized the order of the text, adding short commentaries on the main subdivisions. He also added useful supplementary notes placing Craig's scholarship in a wider context. This work took up Baillie's energies for some time and at some cost, for the records of the Faculty of Advocates show that a subvention of £30 sterling was paid to him in January 1736, and members of faculty were strongly recommended to purchase their own copies. Baillie died on 17 November 1744. K. J. CAMPBELL

Sources D. M. Walker, *The Scottish jurists* (1985), 58 · J. M. Pinkerton, ed., *The minute book of the Faculty of Advocates*, 1: *1661–1712*, Stair Society, 29 (1976) · J. M. Pinkerton, ed., *The minute book of the Faculty of Advocates*, 2: *1713–1750*, Stair Society, 32 (1980) · F. H. Groome, ed., *Ordnance gazetteer of Scotland* (1885) · F. J. Grant, ed., *The Faculty of Advocates in Scotland, 1532–1943*, Scottish RS, 145 (1944) · *DNB* · private information (2004) [J. W. Cairns]

Baillie, Sir James Black (1872–1940), moral philosopher and academic administrator, was born on 24 October 1872 at West Mill, Cortachy, Forfarshire, the second son of William Baillie, forester, afterwards farmer, and his wife, Agnes Black. He was educated at Haddington School, the University of Edinburgh, and Trinity College, Cambridge (1897–1901), and continued his studies at Halle, Strasbourg, and Paris. In 1900 he was appointed lecturer in philosophy at University College, Dundee, and from 1902 to 1924 he was professor of moral philosophy at the University of Aberdeen. His first book, *The Origin and Significance of Hegel's Logic*, appeared in 1901; a further exposition of Hegel, *An Outline of the Idealistic Construction of Experience*, followed in 1906, and a translation of his *Phänomenologie des Geistes* (as *Phenomenology of Mind*), in 1910. On 31 March 1906 he married Helena May James (1865/6–1958), daughter of John Gwynne James, solicitor, of Hereford; there were no children of the marriage.

Baillie served from 1915 to 1917 in the intelligence division of the Admiralty, and from 1917 to 1919 as an arbitrator in industrial disputes for the Ministry of Labour, developing negotiating skills which were to stand him in good stead in his later career. He was made OBE in 1918. From 1920 to 1924 he was chairman of the trade boards for the flax and hemp, aerated waters, linen and cotton household goods, and jute industries. His last major philosophical work, *Studies in Human Nature*, appeared in 1921.

Baillie was appointed vice-chancellor of the University of Leeds in 1924, and there devoted considerable energy to the expansion and development of the university. He inaugurated an ambitious building scheme, and his term of office saw the completion of numerous new buildings for scientific and medical departments and of the Brotherton Library, and the commencement of the students' union and the main entrance block. Earlier attempts at fund-raising through general appeals had not been notably effective; Baillie preferred to make direct approaches to wealthy individuals, a tactic which proved highly successful. A meeting with Mussolini led to the Italian government's endowment of a lectureship in Italian, and to Baillie's becoming a knight commander of the *ordine della corona d'Italia*. He received a British knighthood in 1931.

Baillie had a commanding presence, and on public occasions displayed a gracious manner; unfortunately he did not see fit to deploy it in dealing with his colleagues at Leeds, where his abrasive and overbearing style aroused considerable ill feeling, and his abrupt volte-faces caused bewilderment. His private diaries teem with vitriolic abuse against his staff. Unswervingly convinced of his own rightness, he reacted with baffled rage to any opposition. It is unsurprising therefore that he failed to gain an extension of his term of office beyond the official retiring age. Baillie held the conventional prejudices of his day: he commented disparagingly on the supposed 'black blood' in Lord Harewood's family, and expressed distaste at the appointment of John Rothenstein, a Jew, as director of the Leeds Art Gallery. He combined a dour prudery with a taste for salacious gossip.

While vice-chancellor at Leeds, Baillie's work in the wider public sphere continued. He was a member of the royal commission on the civil service set up in 1929, chaired a court of enquiry into the Hull trawling industry in 1935, a government committee on wages and conditions in the road haulage industry in 1936, and an arbitration tribunal for the Trinidad oilfields in 1938; he was a member of the London conscientious objectors' tribunal.

On his retirement in 1938 Baillie moved to Weybridge, where he died of pulmonary embolism and prostate cancer on 9 June 1940. He was cremated at Golders Green, Middlesex, following a funeral service at Hersham parish church, Surrey, on 12 June. A selection from his religious commonplace book ('Privatissima') was published in 1952 as *Reflections on Life and Religion*, edited by Sir Walter Moberly and Oliver de Selincourt. Baillie is presented as Sir John Evans in Michael Innes's novel *The Weight of the Evidence* (1944). JOHN SMURTHWAITE

Sources P. H. J. H. Gosden and A. J. Taylor, eds., *Studies in the history of a university, 1874–1974: to commemorate the centenary of the University of Leeds* (1975) · A. N. Shimmin, *The University of Leeds: the first half-century* (1954) · J. Smurthwaite, *The life of John Alexander Symington* (1995) · *The Times* (11 June 1940) · *The Times* (13 June 1940) · *Yorkshire Post* (10 June 1940) · R. F. A. Hoernlé, 'Professor Baillie's "idealistic construction of experience"', *Mind*, new ser., 16 (1907), 549–71 · J. B. Baillie, journal, 1930–36, U. Leeds, Brotherton L., MS 671 · W. Yorks. AS, Leeds, Symington papers · b. cert. · m. cert. · d. cert.
Archives U. Leeds, Brotherton L., journal, MS 671 | W. Yorks. AS, Leeds, Symington MSS
Likenesses G. F. Watt, oils, *c*.1908, U. Leeds · G. F. Watt, oils, *c*.1924–1938, U. Leeds · W. Stoneman, photograph, 1931, NPG
Wealth at death £1571 15*s*. 8*d*.: confirmation, 6 Feb 1941, *CGPLA Eng. & Wales*

Baillie, Joanna (1762–1851), playwright and poet, was born in the manse of Bothwell, Lanarkshire, on 11 September 1762, the daughter of the Revd James Baillie (*c*.1722–1778), who had recently been appointed minister at Bothwell, and his wife, Dorothea Hunter (*c*.1721–1806). The Baillies traced their lineage back to the Scottish patriot William Wallace, and Joanna's mother was a sister of William and John Hunter, the celebrated physicians and anatomists. Joanna was the youngest of three children; she had had a twin sister, but this child had died unnamed a few hours after her birth.

Joanna Baillie (1762–1851), by Sir William John Newton

Childhood and education Joanna Baillie grew up in close companionship with her sister, Agnes (1760–1861), and brother, Matthew *Baillie (1761–1823). Her early years, which she recalled in an unpublished memoir written for her nephew, were marked by a passion for the outdoors: running in the garden, splashing in the River Clyde. Uninterested in books or in learning to read, she preferred staging impromptu amateur dramatics on a wagon in the schoolyard. She and her sister adored listening to ghost stories, sitting by the fire of a winter's evening enthralled by the sexton's supernatural tales and too frightened to go upstairs afterwards. Her own gift for narrative invention revealed itself early in stories told to her companions or acted out for her own pleasure. She was 'addicted to clambering on the roof of the house, to act over her scenes alone and in secret' (Le Breton, 9). In 1769 the Baillies moved from Bothwell to Hamilton, where Dr Baillie had been appointed to the collegiate church, and a few years later, at the age of ten, Joanna Baillie was sent to Miss McDonald's boarding-school in Glasgow. Her intellectual and artistic faculties were here stimulated, and the strength of her powers of reasoning and argument recognized. She had a talent for drawing, considerable musical ability, and a love of mathematics. Above all, however, was her facility in the writing and acting of plays. She visited the theatre for the first time:

> I had seen nothing of the kind before but a puppet show in a poor little outhouse when I was a mere child. But now I beheld a lighted up theatre with fine painted scenes and gay dressed Gentlemen and Ladies acting a story on the stage, like busy agitated people in their own dwellings, and my attention was rivetted with delight. (Baillie, 'Memoirs')

Her passion for theatre continued throughout her life.

In 1776 Joanna's father took up a post as professor of divinity at Glasgow University. In 1778 he died. Matthew Baillie went to Balliol College, Oxford, planning to follow in his uncles' footsteps and study medicine. With little inheritance, Mrs Baillie and her daughters retired to Long Calderwood, her family home, and lived the lives of quiet country gentlewomen. In 1783 Dr William Hunter died, leaving Matthew Baillie his house and museum collection in Windmill Street, London. The following year Joanna, Agnes, and their mother moved to Windmill Street to keep house for Matthew. In London, Joanna Baillie had access to literary society through her aunt Anne Hunter, the wife of Dr John Hunter, who was a poet of some renown and hosted a regular salon. Frances Burney, Elizabeth Carter, and Elizabeth Montagu were among those whom Agnes Baillie recalled meeting. Anne Hunter's example encouraged Joanna to write poetry. Her first poem, 'Winter Day', was evocative of the winter sights and sounds in the neighbourhood of Long Calderwood. Like her later tragedies it was written in blank verse:

> Thomson had written in blank verse, but I must confess I would much rather have written in rhime; only rhimes with me in those days were not easily found and I had not industry enough to toil for them. Ballads in rhime followed afterwards, and when I found I could write them with some degree of ease, I began to be proud of myself and to believe that I possessed some genius. (Baillie, 'Memoirs')

While at Windmill Street she also began seriously writing drama, 'following simply my own notions of real nature' and discovering that it was 'an occupation that suited me' (ibid.). She had a ready supply of books and studied the French authors Corneille, Racine, Molière, and Voltaire, as well as Shakespeare and the older English dramatists. She completed a tragedy, 'Arnold', which was never published, and 'a serious comedy' which was later burnt. *Rayner* was also written at this time, though it was heavily revised before it was published in *Miscellaneous Plays* (1804). Her first publication was a collection of poems, *Fugitive Verses*, which appeared anonymously in 1790 and of which, so far as is known, no copy survives.

Plays on the Passions In 1791 Matthew Baillie married Sophia Denman, and moved to Grosvenor Street. Mrs Baillie and her daughters settled, after two or three moves, in Colchester. There, Joanna Baillie conceived the idea of her *Plays on the Passions* and began by writing *Basil*, a tragedy on love, *The Tryal*, a comedy on love, and *De Monfort*, a tragedy on hatred. The scheme of the *Plays on the Passions*, as announced in volume 1, published anonymously in 1798, was ambitious: there were to be further volumes, a whole 'series of Plays; in which it is attempted to delineate the stronger passions of the mind, each passion being the subject of a tragedy and a comedy'. A long introductory discourse defended and explained this novel approach to the drama. The plays, the author explained, were part of an 'extensive design' and were a completely original concept. They arose from a particular view of human nature in which sympathetic curiosity and observation of the movement of feeling in others were paramount. Real passion, 'genuine and true to nature', was to be the subject;

each play was to focus on the growth of one master passion; while what was dramatized were the often hidden psychological processes giving rise to passionate action. This unusually analytic approach generated much discussion and controversy. The author's identity remained secret. In 1800 *De Monfort* was produced at Drury Lane with John Philip Kemble and Sarah Siddons in the leading parts. Splendidly staged, the play ran for eleven nights but was not a theatrical success. In 1802, a second volume of *Plays on the Passions* was published under Joanna Baillie's name, with a preface which acknowledged the reception given to volume one: 'praise mixed with a considerable portion of censure'. Volume 2 consisted of *The Election*, a comedy on hatred, *Ethwald*, a tragedy in two parts on ambition, and *The Second Marriage*, a comedy on ambition. Joanna Baillie considered that these plays, especially *Ethwald*, were written when she was at the height of her powers. Soon afterwards, in 1803, Francis Jeffrey published a long condemnatory review of the *Plays on the Passions* as a leading article in the *Edinburgh Review*. He attacked the theory, practice, and purpose of the plays; and though he also praised her 'pleasing and powerful genius' Joanna Baillie marked him down as her literary enemy and refused a personal introduction. It was not until 1820 that she agreed to meet him; characteristically, they then became warm friends.

By 1802 Joanna Baillie had moved from Colchester to Hampstead, where she was to live with her sister for the next half-century. In 1806 Mrs Baillie died. Neither sister married. They were sociable, hospitable, and much admired and visited, being on intimate terms of friendship with many eminent figures in the arts and sciences. Anna Barbauld and Lucy Aikin were neighbours and close friends, and Walter Scott was a regular correspondent with whom Joanna Baillie stayed in Scotland and who visited her whenever he was in London. In 1804 she published a volume entitled *Miscellaneous Plays*: the tragedies *Rayner* and *Constantine Paleologus*, and a comedy, *The Country Inn*. In a prefatory address to the reader she defended her plays as acting plays. Her ambition, she insisted, was to write plays that could be acted, 'to add a few pieces to the stock of what may be called our national or permanently acting plays'. The criticism that she had no understanding of practical stagecraft and that her plays were torpid and dull in performance rankled throughout her life, and she was always delighted to hear of a production being mounted, no matter how humble it might be. She believed that critics had unfairly labelled her a closet dramatist, partly because she was a woman and partly because they had failed to read her prefaces with care. She pointed also to the conventions of the theatre in her time, when lavish spectacle on huge stages was the order of the day. Her own plays, with their attention to psychological detail, worked best, she argued, in well-lit small theatres where facial expressions could clearly be seen. *Constantine Paleologus*, though written with John Kemble and Mrs Siddons in mind, was declined by Drury Lane. It was produced at the Surrey Theatre as a melodrama, *Constantine and Valeria*, and, in its original form, at Liverpool, Dublin, and Edinburgh. In 1810 Joanna Baillie took a Scottish theme for a new play, *The Family Legend*, which was performed at Edinburgh with a prologue by Walter Scott and an epilogue by Henry Mackenzie. This was a success and encouraged the managers of the Edinburgh theatre to revive *De Monfort*, which was also well received. *The Family Legend* was produced at Drury Lane in 1815 and *De Monfort* in 1821 with Edmund Kean in the title role.

In 1812 the third and final volume of Joanna Baillie's *Plays on the Passions* appeared. It consisted of two tragedies, *Orra* and *The Siege*, a comedy, *The Alienated Manor*, and a serious musical drama, *The Beacon*. One passion only was represented in the tragedies and comedy: Fear; and in the musical drama, Hope. Introducing what she described as 'probably the last volume of plays I shall ever publish' she went on to explain that it was her intention to complete her project by writing further dramas on the passions of Remorse, Jealousy, and Revenge, but she did not intend to publish them since publication had discouraged stage production. Her next published work did not appear until 1821, *Metrical Legends of Exalted Characters*, which told in verse the heroic stories of such historical figures as William Wallace, Christopher Columbus, and Lady Grisell Baillie. These were inspired in part by the huge popularity of Walter Scott's heroic ballads, her own enthusiasm for which had, she admitted, 'made the drama less interesting for a time' (Baillie, 'Memoirs'). In 1823 she edited and published by subscription a collection of poems by many of the leading writers of the day, in support of a widowed old school friend with a family of daughters to support. Financially secure herself, Joanna Baillie customarily gave half her earnings from her writings to charity, and engaged in many philanthropic activities. In the early 1820s she corresponded with the Sheffield campaigner James Montgomery in support of his efforts on behalf of chimney sweeps. She declined to send a poem, fearing that was 'just the very way to have the whole matter considered by the sober pot-boilers over the whole kingdom as a fanciful and visionary thing' whereas 'a plain statement of their miserable lot in prose, accompanied with a simple, reasonable plan for sweeping chimneys without them' was far better strategically. Better still was to win over the master bricklayers and get them to stop building crooked chimneys (letter, 5 Feb 1824, Wellcome L.).

Such pragmatism was regularly in evidence where literary matters were concerned. Joanna Baillie had a shrewd understanding of publishing as a trade marked by gender and class distinctions and driven by the profit motive. Authors down on their luck, women writers, and working-class poets like the shoemaker poet, John Struthers, applied to her for assistance. She took seriously the power her eminence gave her. She wrote letters, drew on all her contacts, and used her knowledge of the literary world either to advise or to further a less well-connected writer. She advised one aspiring author not to publish at his own expense because then publishers would not take the trouble to promote his book as they would if they were publishing at their own risk.

Later plays and reputation In 1823, Joanna Baillie's much-loved brother Matthew died. His children and grandchildren continued to display the affectionate closeness and pride in their aunt's achievements which had always marked the family. Religion had always been important to her. In 1826 she published *The Martyr*, a tragedy on religion, intended for reading only; and in 1831 she entered publicly into theological debate with a pamphlet, *A view of the general tenour of the New Testament regarding the nature and dignity of Jesus Christ*, in which she analysed the doctrines of the Trinitarians, the Arians, and the Socinians. In the years 1831–2 she experienced a period of unusual ill health which left her too weak to keep up her correspondence. However, she recovered and set about preparing three volumes of *Miscellaneous Plays* for the press. These included, along with nine other new plays, the continuation of *Plays on the Passions* promised earlier: a tragedy and comedy on jealousy and a tragedy on remorse. Their publication in 1836 created a furore. Critics were almost universally enthusiastic and welcoming. *Fraser's Magazine* declared: 'Had we heard that a MS play of Shakespeare's, or an early, but missing, novel of Scott's, had been discovered, and was already in the press, the information could not have been more welcome.' (*Fraser's Magazine*, 236) In 1840, urged on by her old friend the banker poet Samuel Rogers, she issued a new collection, *Fugitive Verses*, some of which were recently written. It was generally agreed that her popular songs, especially those in Scots dialect, would live on. In 1849 she published for private circulation the poem *Ahalya Baee*. She was anxious that all her works (with the exception of the theological pamphlet) be collected in a single volume, and had the satisfaction of seeing this 'great monster book' as she called it, which appeared in 1851, shortly before she died. Though no longer robust—'Ladies of four score and upwards cannot expect to be robust, and need not be gay. We sit by the fireside with our books' (Carhart, 62)—she had remained in good health until the end. She died on 23 February 1851 in Hampstead, having almost reached her ninetieth year. Her sister, Agnes, lived on to be 100. Both sisters were buried alongside their mother in Hampstead parish churchyard, and in 1899 a 16 foot high memorial was erected in Joanna Baillie's memory in the churchyard of her birthplace at Bothwell.

Few women writers have received such universal commendation for their personal qualities and literary powers as Joanna Baillie. Her intelligence and integrity were allied to a modest demeanour which made her, for many, the epitome of a Christian gentlewoman. She was also shrewd, observant of human nature, and persistent to the point of obstinacy in developing her own views and opinions. What Francis Jeffrey called her 'narrow and peculiar views of dramatic excellence' (*EdinR*, 261) remained essentially unchanged throughout her life, and she took pride in having carried out her major work, the *Plays on the Passions*, more or less in the form she had originally conceived. Her inventive faculties were widely remarked upon. She was on friendly terms with all the leading women writers of her time. Maria Edgeworth, recording a visit in 1818, summed up her appeal for many:

> Both Joanna and her sister have most agreeable and new conversation, not old, trumpery literature over again and reviews, but new circumstances worth telling, apropos to every subject that is touched upon; frank observations on character, without either ill-nature or the fear of committing themselves; no blue-stocking tittle-tattle, or habits of worshipping or being worshipped. (Hare, 268)

Joanna Baillie's contemporaries placed her above all women poets except Sappho. According to Harriet Martineau she had 'enjoyed a fame almost without parallel, and … been told every day for years, through every possible channel, that she was second only to Shakespeare' (H. Martineau, *Autobiography*, 1, 1983, 358). But even when Martineau met her, in the 1830s, that fame seemed to belong to a bygone era. There were no revivals of her plays in the nineteenth or twentieth centuries; and yet, as psychological studies, her tragedies would seem very suited to the intimacy of television or film. Twentieth-century scholars have recognized her importance as an innovator on the stage and as a dramatic theorist, and revisionary critics and literary historians of the Romantic period concerned to reassess the place of women writers are acknowledging her significance.

NORMA CLARKE

Sources *DNB* • M. Carhart, *The life and work of Joanna Baillie* (1923) • J. Baillie, 'Memoirs written to please my nephew' • J. Baillie, 'Memoir composed for Miss Berry', Royal College of Surgeons, Hunter-Baillie Collection • *Dramatic and poetical works of Joanna Baillie* (1851) • C. B. Burroughs, *Closet stages: Joanna Baillie and the theater theory of British Romantic women writers* (1997) • P. H. Le Breton, *Memoirs, miscellanies, and letters of the late Lucy Aikin* (1864) • *Fraser's Magazine*, 13 (1836), 236 • *EdinR*, 19 (1812), 261 • A. Hare, ed., *Life and letters of Maria Edgeworth*, 2 vols. (1894), vol. 1, pp. 253–4; vol. 2, pp. 49–54, 87–8 • letter, 5 Feb 1824, Wellcome L.

Archives Bodl. Oxf., corresp. • Holborn Library, Camden, London, Camden Local Studies and Archives Centre, letters • Hunt. L., letters and literary MSS • NL Scot., letters • RCS Eng., corresp. and papers • Swiss Cottage Library, London, memoir and corresp. • U. Glas. L., corresp. | BL, letters to G. Thomson, Add. MSS 35263–35265 • DWL, letters to H. C. Robinson • Harvard U., Houghton L., letters to Andrews Norton • Holborn Library, Camden, London, Camden Local Studies and Archives Centre, letters to William Beattie • Mitchell L., Glas., letters to Lady Davy and MS Song • NL Scot., letters to Anne Elliott • NL Scot., corresp. with J. G. Lockhart • NL Scot., corresp. with Anne Millar • NL Scot., corresp. with Sir Walter Scott • RA, corresp. with Sir Thomas Lawrence • RCS Eng., corresp. with Sir Walter Scott • RS, letters to Sir John Herschel • U. Nott. L., letters to countess of Charleville • UCL, letters to Samuel Rogers • Wellcome L., corresp. with Mary Berry

Likenesses J. C. D. Engleheart, miniature (after W. J. Newton), RCP Lond. • M. A. Knight, pencil drawing, watercolour, Scot. NPG • W. J. Newton, drawing, watercolour, BM [*see illus.*] • W. J. Newton, oils, BM • H. Robinson, engraving (after W. J. Newton), repro. in J. Baillie, *Dramatic and poetical works of Joanna Baillie* • H. Robinson, stipple, line engraving (after W. J. Newton), BM, NPG • H. R. Robinson, stipple (after J. J. Masquerier), NPG

Baillie, John (*d.* 1743), physician and writer, was employed as a doctor at St George's Hospital in London and in the English army. He accompanied the army to Flanders in the War of the Austrian Succession and died at Ghent of 'spotted fever' in December 1743. His only known works are a comedy, *The Married Coquet*, published after his death 'by subscription for the benefit of the widow' in 1746 (Baker, 1.15), and *An Essay on the Sublime*, published in 1747. The brief treatise on the sublime is probably the first systematic development of the topic in a psychological framework relying on the Lockean doctrine of the association of ideas. Baillie analyses the sublime in the arts as an imitation of the sublime in nature, which he regards as being grounded in the vastness of natural objects. Although following in many ways the earlier approaches by Addison and Shaftesbury, he surpasses them in discussing a wider range and variety of manifestations of the sublime in literature and the arts. Alexander Gerard sympathetically mentions Baillie's work in 1759 as a treatment very close to his own views on sublimity (Gerard, *An Essay on Taste*, 2nd edn, 1764, 11n.). ALEXANDER RUEGER

Sources D. E. Baker, *Biographia dramatica, or, A companion to the playhouse*, rev. I. Reed, new edn, rev. S. Jones, 3 vols. in 4 (1812) • [J. Mottley], *A compleat list of all the English dramatic poets*, pubd with T. Whincop, *Scanderbeg* (1747) • S. H. Monk, *The sublime: a study of critical theories in XVIII-century England* (1935) • S. H. Monk, 'Introduction', *John Baillie: an essay on the sublime*, ed. S. H. Monk, Augustan Reprint Society, 43 (1953), i–vi • A. Ashfield and P. de Bolla, eds., *The sublime: a reader in British eighteenth-century aesthetic theory* (1996)

Baillie, John (1741–1806), minister of the Secession church, was trained for the ministry by John Swanston of Kinross and became minister to the Carliol Street congregation in Newcastle upon Tyne about 1769. He was a popular preacher, but his convivial habits resulted in behaviour inappropriate for a minister and led eventually to his suspension in 1784. He drifted into debtor's prison but managed to escape to Scotland, where from 1786 to 1789 he was minister at the Crief Relief Presbyterian Chapel. He married about 1776, but nothing is known of his wife.

After clearing his debts and returning to Newcastle in 1789, Baillie for a short time assisted William Tinwell, the author of a treatise on arithmetic, in running a school in the Dog Bank. Afterwards he returned to preaching, first in a schoolroom in St Nicholas's churchyard at Newcastle, then at Malling's Rigg Chapel, Sunderland (1791–6), and from 1797 at the old Postern Chapel, Newcastle, which his friends had refurbished for his use.

During his second period in Newcastle, Baillie was obliged to supplement his ministerial income by writing and by assisting his daughter, Frances, who kept a school in Pilgrim Street, Newcastle, and later at Gateshead. Among his published works are several religious treatises and sermons, including one occasioned by the death of Frances in 1801. He also wrote several historical works, such as *An Impartial History of the Town and County of Newcastle-upon-Tyne* (1801) and *A History of the French Wars* (1802). He was considered to be a scholar of some ability and was a member of the prestigious Newcastle Literary and Philosophical Society. Baillie died at Gateshead on 12 December 1806 and was buried in the nonconformist necropolis at Ballast Hills, Newcastle.

THOMPSON COOPER, *rev.* M. J. MERCER

Sources C. Surman, index, DWL • R. Welford, *Men of mark 'twixt Tyne and Tweed*, 3 vols. (1895) • R. Small, *History of the congregations of the United Presbyterian church from 1733 to 1900*, 2 (1904) • *GM*, 1st ser., 76 (1806), 1182

Wealth at death often in debt; supplemented ministerial income by teaching and writing

Baillie, John (1772–1833), army officer in the East India Company and orientalist, younger son of George Baillie of Leys Castle, Inverness, and his wife, Anne (*née* Baillie), was born at Inverness on 10 May 1772, and entered the East India Company's service in 1790, arriving in India in 1791. He became ensign in 1793 and lieutenant in 1794, devoting his leisure largely to the study of oriental languages, with such success that on the foundation of the new college of Fort William, Calcutta, in 1800 he was appointed professor of Arabic and Persian languages and of Islamic law. In 1803, on the outbreak of the Second Anglo-Maratha War, he joined in the siege of Agra with the rank of captain, and soon after was appointed to the sensitive post of political agent at Bundelkhand. Disaffection was rife there, and the chiefs were forming threatening combinations. Baillie, however, succeeded in splitting their alliance and re-establishing control. For this service he was publicly thanked by the governor-general: he had transferred to the company a territory with a revenue of £225,000 a year. He resigned his professorship in 1807 for the position of resident at Lucknow, which he held until 1815.

In 1818 Baillie retired from East India Company service, and on his return to England was MP for the borough of Hedon from 1820 to 1831, and from 1832 until his death for the burghs of Inverness. He was a moderate whig, supporting Catholic emancipation but opposing the Reform Bill, and after 1832 a Conservative. He was elected a director of the East India Company on 28 May 1823. While at Fort William College, Baillie published highly regarded works on Arabic grammar. He also translated from Arabic part (relating to commercial transactions) of a digest of Islamic law in 1797, at the request of Sir John Shore (Lord Teignmouth) the governor-general. Baillie died at his home in Devonshire Place, London, on 20 April 1833. His collection of oriental works was presented by his heirs to Edinburgh University.

STANLEY LANE-POOLE, *rev.* JAMES FALKNER

Sources *Journal of the Bengal Asiatic Society* (1834) • *New Oriental Register and East India Directory* (1797–1802) • *East-India Register and Directory* (1803–25) • *East-India Register and Directory* (1833) • *WWBMP* • C. E. Buckland, *Dictionary of Indian biography* (1906) • *Annual Register* (1833) • V. C. P. Hodson, *List of officers of the Bengal army, 1758–1834*, 4 (1947)

Archives BL OIOC, corresp. relating to India, Home misc. series | BL OIOC, letters to Sir George Barlow, MS Eur. F 176

Likenesses J. Cochran, stipple, pubd 1823 (after A. Wivell), BM, NPG

Baillie, John (1886–1960), theologian and Church of Scotland minister, was born on 26 March 1886 in the Free Church manse at Gairloch, Scotland, the eldest of the three sons of John Baillie (1829–1891), Free Church of Scotland minister, and his wife, Annie Macpherson (1853–1932). John and his brother Donald *Baillie (1887–1954) were among the distinguished Scottish theologians of the modern era. Although Baillie later recalled 'a rigorously Calvinistic upbringing', mainly by his mother, who was soon widowed, there were also liberal strands in Free

Church culture and a huge respect for learning, which drove the brothers through brilliant academic careers at Inverness Royal Academy (where John studied between 1898 and 1904) and at the University of Edinburgh, both graduating with firsts in philosophy and distinction in divinity. Baillie spent the summer terms of 1909 and 1911 at the universities of Jena and Marburg, respectively. For a short time assistants in the philosophy department, the brothers spent time in the YMCA in France during the First World War.

In April 1919 Baillie married Florence Jewel Fowler and moved to Auburn Theological Seminary in New York state, and was ordained in the Presbyterian church there in 1920. Their only child, Ian Fowler Baillie, was born in 1921. *The Roots of Religion in the Human Soul* appeared in 1926 and *The Interpretation of Religion* in 1929. These books reflected wide cultural and theological experience from the manse in Gairloch to American society—the latter's poetry and politics, the polarization of church politics in the fundamentalist debate, as well as participation in conferences on the social gospel in the early 1920s. Baillie moved in 1927 to Emmanuel College, Toronto, in the newly formed United Church of Canada. His wife was suffering from tuberculosis during much of the 1920s, and was in sanatoria between 1923 and 1930. In 1930 he moved back to the Union Theological Seminary in New York, then arguably the world's greatest theological seminary. It provided a forum for theology where, along with Henry Sloane Coffin, Reinhold Niebuhr, and Pitney Van Dusen, he was to have a major impact on Western theology for the next two decades. Though Baillie returned to Edinburgh in 1934, the four exerted huge influence on the new World Council of Churches. They agreed on a *via media* between extreme liberalism on the one hand, and a narrow Barthianism on the other. Baillie was professor of divinity at Edinburgh University from 1934 to 1956. He also served as principal of New College, Edinburgh, and dean of the faculty of divinity (1950–56). A royal chaplain between 1947 and 1956, he was an extra chaplain to the queen in Scotland from 1956 to 1960.

The theme of the presence of God to faith was central to the three books that followed Baillie's first publications, *And the Life Everlasting* (1933), *Our Knowledge of God* (1939), and *Invitation to Pilgrimage* (1942). An emphasis on spirituality was manifested in *A Diary of Private Prayer* (1936), which sold tens of thousands of copies, a devotional work combining honest self-examination with concentration on God's reconciling grace. A wider social and political concern was demonstrated, during his moderatorial year in the Church of Scotland in 1943, with the preparation for the general assembly of the report of the special commission for the interpretation of God's will in the present crisis. The report, published in 1946 as *God's Will for Church and Nation*, combined critique of the Nazis with a programme for social reconstruction after the war, a programme echoed in the Beveridge reports. The report recognized the difficulty in applying Christian principles in society, and took the route of 'middle axioms', which should 'exhibit the relevance of the ruling principles to the particular field of action in which guidance is needed' (p. 45). It argued that 'Economic power must be made objectively responsible to the community as a whole' (ibid., 156). The report reflected awareness of the German church struggle, numerous Church of England and ecumenical gatherings, and also the work of the Moot, an influential forum that met in Oxford and London. As well as J. H. Oldham, its founder, participants included such influential writers and theologians as Eric Fenn, H. A. Hodges, Karl Mannheim, Walter Moberley and Alec Vidler, T. S. Eliot, H. H. Farmer, Donald Mackinnon, and John Middleton Murry. In 1952 Baillie became one of the presidents of the World Council of Churches.

Baillie's death precluded the delivery of his Gifford lectures, but they were published posthumously as *The Sense of the Presence of God* (1962). They provided a masterly synthesis of his life's work. In them he displayed a characteristic combination of an appeal to experience with an exploration of rational grounds for belief in God. Knowledge seems to imply certitude, he argued, but often does not go beyond probabilities. Our knowledge of the realities is primary, and our knowledge of truths concerning them secondary. Moral convictions are central to human life, and 'Our total experience of reality presents itself to us as a single experience' (p. 50). Baillie also discussed procedures for verification and falsification, and argued that 'A faith that is consistent with everything possible is not a faith in anything actual' (ibid., 71), stressing that the ultimate refutation of doubts was theological and incarnational. Faith was 'an awareness of the divine presence itself, however hidden behind the veils of sense' (ibid., 89). Baillie argued that 'In the widest sense of the term all language may be said to be symbolic' (ibid., 113); but admitted that not all theological statements were analogical. Despite being known in, with, and under other realities, there is a certain directness in apprehension of God. Love of God is always related to love of neighbour, and beyond this to a new humanity. Baillie thought that it was important not to confuse dogmas with the primary perceptions of faith, and also raised the wider issue of 'Faith and the Faiths'. What does it mean to speak of salvation in a name? he asked. While there was an awareness of God in 'the pagan religions', the way of Christ was decisive. In Baillie's view, scientific and religious accounts of the world complemented one another. What others may see as coincidence, Christians will read as providential. Furthermore, gratitude was 'not only the dominant note of Christian piety, but equally the dominant motive of Christian action in the world' (ibid., 236). Propositions were necessary but not sufficient, as faith depended on trust. We have to do with 'a God whose living and active presence among us can be perceived by faith in a large variety of human contexts and situations' (ibid., 61).

Baillie's theology, like that of his brother, remained resolutely liberal and evangelical. Sympathetic critics of each other's work and sensitive to theology in context, they could deploy arguments from various theological traditions when this seemed right. They deplored exclusivism and dogmatic narrowness. Baillie's 'strongly independent mind made him resistant to passing fashions, while his irenic spirit preferred to discover underlying unities rather than sharpen distinctions into conflicts' (*DSCHT*, 50). He has been characterized as steering a middle course between American fundamentalists and modernists. A Companion of Honour from 1957, Baillie received numerous honorary doctorates, and at his death was widely regarded as the doyen of Scottish theologians. He died on 29 September 1960 at 9 Whitehouse Terrace, Edinburgh, and was buried in the city. He was survived by his wife. GEORGE NEWLANDS

Sources G. Newlands, *John and Donald Baillie: transatlantic theology* (2002) • priv. coll., Baillie MSS • U. Edin., New Coll. L., Baillie MSS • D. Fergusson, ed., *Christ, church, and society: essays on John Baillie and Donald Baillie* (1993) • *WWW* • *DSCHT* • b. cert. • *CCI* (1961)
Archives NL Scot., corresp. with publishers • priv. coll. • U. Edin., New Coll. L., notebooks, sermons, and papers; further papers
Likenesses W. Hutchison, portrait, Edinburgh, New College • Russell, photograph, NPG
Wealth at death £64,266 2*s*. 0*d*.: confirmation, 11 Jan 1961, *CCI* • £66,202 18*s*. 0*d*.: corrective inventory, 17 Jan 1962, *CCI* (1961)

Baillie, Marianne (1795?–1831), travel writer and versifier, whose maiden name appears to have been Wathen, married before 1817 Alexander Baillie, who printed privately at Kingsbury her first known work, *Guy of Warwick, a Legende, and other Poems* (1817). This collection of undistinguished verse reached a second edition probably through the indulgence of friends. A period of financial difficulty appears to have followed soon after: in 1818 the Baillies went to live at Sion Cottage, Twickenham, possibly the property of Sophia Charlotte, Baroness Howe, whose second husband, Sir Wathen Waller, was probably a distant relative of Marianne Baillie. In the summer of 1818 the Baillies, accompanied by a male friend, set out on a tour through France, Italy, Austria, and Germany which Marianne Baillie described in her first travel book, *First Impressions of a Tour upon the Continent* (1819), one of the earliest accounts of the grand tour written by a woman. It was published by John Murray and dedicated to the Honourable John Hampden Trevor, the British diplomatic minister in Turin and, apparently, a family friend. *First Impressions* received a favourable, if condescending, review in the *London Literary Gazette*, where it was described as 'at once useful and agreeable' for travellers (*London Literary Gazette*, 17 July 1819, 453–4). The critic rightly noted Marianne Baillie's 'turn for observation': homely reflections on bed bugs and the inferior quality of French cutlery interrupt the often conventionally picturesque and romantic commentary on scenery and costumes. By January 1821 she had written another work, the subject of which is unknown, but Murray declined to publish it.

In June of that year the Baillies left for Portugal, accompanied by their first child, a son; they remained there until September 1823, living mainly in Lisbon. It appears probable that Trevor had secured a diplomatic appointment for Alexander Baillie. Marianne Baillie's letters to her mother during these years formed the substance for her best work, *Lisbon in the Years 1821, 1822, and 1823* (1824), published by Murray. In her letters the trials of the new constitutional government of Portugal and its eventual overthrow by the royalist party contend for space with descriptions of the beauties of rural Cintra, an account of a visit to a local convent, and praise for delicacies such as roasted chestnuts. She found the climate overpowering and the streets of Lisbon disgusting, but, despite constant nostalgic allusions to England, she was open-minded enough to appreciate the superiority of Portuguese courtesy and to be touched by the affectionate ways of her servants. Shortly after the birth of her second child, a daughter, in late 1822, she heard with relief that a post in London had been found for her husband; but she admitted to leaving Portugal 'almost with regret' (*Lisbon*, 2.250). Shortly after the publication of *Lisbon* a second edition was called for, which surprised even the author; in the same year the work received a favourable notice in the *Quarterly Review*. Her only other known work—a collection of old and new poems entitled *Trifles in Verse*—was printed privately in the same year. The Baillies do not appear to have travelled abroad again; in 1827 they were living in Stanley Cottage on Richmond Hill. By 1830 Marianne Baillie was in poor health, and she died in 1831. ROSEMARY MITCHELL

Sources *DNB* • M. Baillie, *Lisbon in the years 1821, 1822, and 1823* (1824) • M. Baillie, *First impressions of a tour upon the continent* (1819) • John Murray, London, archives • J. Robinson, ed., *Wayward women: a guide to women travellers* (1990), 275 • J. Martin, *Bibliographical catalogue of books privately printed*, 2nd edn (1854), 335
Archives John Murray, London, archives

Baillie, Matthew (1761–1823), morbid anatomist and physician, was born on 27 October 1761 at Shotts manse, Lanarkshire, the second but only surviving son of James Baillie (*c*.1722–1778) and his wife, Dorothea (*c*.1721–1806). They had an elder daughter, and also one younger, Joanna *Baillie the poet. James Baillie was successively minister of Shotts, Bothwell, and Hamilton; ultimately he was professor of divinity at the University of Glasgow. Dorothea Baillie's father was John Hunter of Long Calderwood, near East Kilbride, Lanarkshire; the anatomists William *Hunter and John *Hunter were her brothers.

Baillie was educated at the English school (1766–8) and the Latin school (1768–74) in Hamilton and at the University of Glasgow (1774–9), which nominated him to a Snell exhibition at Balliol College, Oxford, where he was also appointed to a Warner exhibition through the interest of his uncle William Hunter. He matriculated at Oxford in April 1779, and lived there full time for eighteen months reading classics and English history. Balliol was then at its nadir, but Baillie's tutor, Richard Prosser, later archdeacon of Durham, was a reformer for whom Baillie had great respect; Baillie and Prosser together were the college's elder statesmen as it rose to dominance forty years on. Late in 1780 Baillie went to live with William Hunter in London, thereafter keeping only minimal terms at Oxford, graduating BA in 1783 (MA, 1786). Hunter had established an anatomy school and museum in Great Windmill Street. Baillie attended dissections and lectures there, teaching in the dissecting room himself after one session. He also went to courses in chemistry, medicine, surgery, and obstetrics given by George Fordyce, William

Matthew Baillie (1761–1823), by Sir Thomas Lawrence, *c.*1806

Hunter's estranged younger brother John, Thomas Denman, and William Osborne. When William Hunter died in 1783 he left Baillie control of the anatomy school, the eventual freehold of the premises, thirty years use of the museum, and about £5000. The small Hunter family estate of Long Calderwood also passed to Baillie, but he renounced it in favour of John Hunter.

Baillie soon became an established anatomy lecturer, and continued in that role at Great Windmill Street, working in increasingly uneasy partnership with William Hunter's former partner William Cruikshank, until 1799. But he also completed his broader medical training as a pupil at St George's Hospital, where he was appointed physician in 1787. In mid-1788 he made a four-month tour of France, Germany, Switzerland, Belgium, and the Netherlands, visiting many hospitals and anatomy schools, recording critical observations on conditions in the former and techniques in the latter. He graduated BM at Oxford in 1786 (DM, 1789), and was elected FRCP (London) in 1790. William Hunter's posthumous *An Anatomical Description of the Human Gravid Uterus and its Contents* (1794) was edited for publication by Baillie. Two papers in *Philosophical Transactions* in 1788 and 1789 were followed by his election FRS in 1790 (FRSE, 1799); many medical societies gave him the professional accolade of honorary membership. He was Croonian lecturer of the Royal Society (1791), and of the Royal College of Physicians of London (1796–8), for whom he was also Goulstonian lecturer (1794); he gave the Harveian oration in 1798. In 1805 he was a founder member (and second president, 1808–10) of the Medical and Chirurgical Society of London, forerunner of the Royal Society of Medicine.

As trustee custodian of William Hunter's museum Baillie had free access to a collection containing many pathological specimens, and as physician to a large hospital he had frequent opportunities of examining diseased corpses. He became aware of the inadequacy of the existing literature of morbid anatomy, and, taking the view that the careful observation and description of diseased structures was an essential prerequisite for the understanding of diseases, wrote *The Morbid Anatomy of some of the most Important Parts of the Human Body* (1793). In the preface he acknowledged the stupendous work *De sedibus et causis morborum* ('On the sites and causes of disease'), of G. B. Morgagni (1761), which comprised large numbers of case histories and post-mortem investigations, but thought its bulk self-defeating; diseased structures were 'often described too generally' and issues were 'obscured, by taking notice of smaller collateral circumstances, which had no connection with them or the diseases from whence they arose'. Baillie's book was based on an organ by organ system of normal anatomy, giving terse but precise descriptions of disease-induced changes, with practically no reference to cases or speculation about causes, although it contained the first connection of cirrhosis of the liver with alcoholism. The work was limited to the thoracic and abdominal organs and the brain. Significant additions were made for the second (1797) edition, especially notes on symptoms corresponding to pathological change, including some of seminal importance for cardiology (the idea of rheumatism of the heart was introduced, for example, and hardening of the coronary arteries was linked to angina). The first text of its kind, it was very influential, appearing during the author's lifetime in five British and three American editions, two in French, four in German, and three in Italian; there were four later editions in English (1825–33), and one in Russian (1826). A series of superb drawings by William Clift, with commentaries by Baillie, was engraved to illustrate the *Morbid Anatomy*, and it was published in ten parts in 1799–1802. Baillie also wrote numerous journal papers in 1788–1820 (on, for example, pericardial absence, paraplegia, diabetes, and emphysema), which were collected and republished by James Wardrop (1825). In his will Baillie provided for the collection and printing, but not publication, of various writings which were circulated privately as *Lectures and Observations on Medicine* (1825).

Baillie's appointment as physician to St George's began a gradual buildup of his practice, and during the following decade it expanded considerably. When his very successful associate David Pitcairn fell ill in 1798 Baillie acquired his patients too, and in 1799 he gave up the teaching of anatomy and his St George's appointment in order to devote all his time to private practice. By 1810 his annual fee income had risen to £10,000, and he was so much in demand that he was regularly working sixteen hours a day. In the same year, following attendance on Princess Amelia, he was appointed physician-extraordinary to George III. He visited the deranged king at Windsor several hundred times during the regency, and was present at his death on 29 January 1820. As physician-in-ordinary to Princess Charlotte, the king's only legitimate grandchild, on whom hopes for the eventual succession were pinned, Baillie had overall responsibility for the management of her confinement in 1817, and was present throughout her fifty-hour labour. His brother-in-law, Sir Richard *Croft, sixth baronet (1762–1818), was principal accoucheur. It was a triple obstetric disaster. The child, an apparently healthy boy, was stillborn, the mother died a few hours afterwards, and Croft shot himself while depressed about it all three months later. Baillie's famous patients were not all royalty—he attended Lord Byron, Sir Walter Scott, and Edward Gibbon, and he examined Samuel Johnson's lungs post mortem.

Although London remained the base of his professional practice, in 1806 Baillie bought an estate at Duntisbourne Abbots in Gloucestershire, where he lived to an increasing extent in his later years, consulting by correspondence. In 1821 he made a melodramatic dash from there to Queen Caroline's deathbed at Hammersmith. Edward Jenner was a Gloucestershire neighbour and associate; Baillie was an early supporter of vaccination.

In 1791 Baillie married Sophia Denman (1771–1845), younger twin daughter of the obstetrician Thomas *Denman. They had a daughter and two sons. One of the sons died in infancy, but the other, William Hunter Baillie (1797–1894), survived his father as squire of Duntisbourne Abbots for more than sixty years. Baillie was of somewhat less than average height and build, with a round slightly plump face and prominent nose. Though direct and blunt in manner, and inclined to impatience with distractions and silly patients when overworked, he was of a generous disposition, sometimes waiving his fees. His relations with his family, medical colleagues, and patients were usually cordial. He enjoyed good health until early 1823, when a wasting decline, possibly tuberculosis, which was not arrested by a stay in Tunbridge Wells, set in. Baillie died at Duntisbourne Abbots on 23 September 1823, and was buried in Duntisbourne Abbots church a week later. He was commemorated with a bust and inscription in Westminster Abbey. Most of his estate, which was sworn at under £80,000, he left to his family, but his medical books and the copperplates for his *Morbid Anatomy* were left to the Royal College of Physicians of London. His anatomical specimens he had given to the college, with money for their upkeep, in 1818; they were transferred to the Royal College of Surgeons of England in 1938, but were destroyed by enemy action in 1941. Shortly after his death his widow gave the Royal College of Physicians of London a gold-headed cane which had belonged in turn to John Radcliffe, Richard Mead, Anthony Askew, William Pitcairn, David Pitcairn, and Baillie. It was engraved with all their arms—a symbol of fame and fortune in medicine which has become legendary. Baillie's arms—which were used without authority—were azure nine estoils (variously mullets), three three two and one or, impaling (for Sophia Denman) argent a chevron between three lion's heads erased gules. JOHN JONES

Sources F. Crainz, *The life and works of Matthew Baillie, MD, FRS L&E, FRCP, etc (1761–1823)* (1995) • A. E. Rodin, *The influence of Matthew Baillie's Morbid anatomy: biography, evaluation and reprint* (1973) • Munk, *Roll* • R. Palmer and J. Taylor, *The Hunterian Society: a catalogue of its records and collections relating to John Hunter and the Hunterian tradition with a history of the society*, ed. D. W. Findlay (1990) • J. Wardrop, *The works of Matthew Baillie, M.D., to which is prefixed an account of his life, collected from authentic sources* (1925), vol. 1 • V. G. Plarr, 'Matthew Baillie's diary of travel in 1788', *BMJ* (19 March 1927), 523–4 • W. Macmichael, *The gold-headed cane*, new edn (1953) • F. Crainz, *An obstetric tragedy: the case of her royal highness the Princess Charlotte Augusta. Some unpublished documents of 1817* (1977) • will, PRO, PROB 11/1102, sig. 180 [William Hunter]

Archives Balliol Oxf., biographical materials • LPL, letters and papers relating to George III • RCP Lond., papers • RCS Eng., travel journal and lecture notes • Wellcome L., family papers and notes on English history | Linn. Soc., corresp. with Sir James E. Smith • U. Glas., Wellcome Unit for the History of Medicine, Hunterian Society MSS

Likenesses E. Miles, miniature watercolour on ivory, *c*.1795, Sci. Mus. • attrib. T. Barber, oils, *c*.1806, RCP Lond. • T. Lawrence, oils, *c*.1806, RCP Lond. [*see illus.*] • J. Hoppner, oils, *c*.1809, RCP Lond. • C. Turner, mezzotint, pubd 1809 (after J. Hoppner), BM • J. Nollekens, marble bust, 1812, RCS Eng. • W. Owen, oils, *c*.1823, Balliol Oxf. • F. Chantrey, marble bust, 1824 (after Nollekens, 1812), RCP Lond. • F. Chantrey, marble bust, Westminster Abbey • T. Rowlandson, pencil caricature, RCS Eng. • oils, RCP Lond.

Wealth at death under £80,000: PRO; Crainz, *Life and works*

Baillie, Robert (1602–1662), Church of Scotland minister and author, son of James Baillie (*d*. before 1631), merchant burgess of Glasgow, and Helen Gibson (*d*. 1634), was born in Saltmarket Street, Glasgow, on 30 April 1602. He attended Glasgow high school and between 1617 and 1620 the University of Glasgow, graduating MA. At both school and university he was taught by Robert Blair, whom he later acknowledged as having been, after his parents, 'the first and principall instrument' of whatever piety, good letters, and moral virtue that he had. 'I have alwayes found my selfe more in your debt, than in any other man's on earth' (*Letters and Journals*, 1.xxiii).

Baillie's ambition was to spend his life as parish minister in a 'landwarrt kirk' (*Letters and Journals*, 1.xxiv), or country church, and from 1625 to 1631 he taught at Glasgow University as a regent while studying divinity in preparation for entering the ministry. In 1631 he was appointed minister of Kilwinning in Ayrshire by the earl of Eglinton, the father of one of his pupils, and now that he had a living he married, on 12 July 1632, in Glasgow, Lilias Fleming (*d*. 1653). Baillie had earned a reputation for outstanding academic ability, but he resisted a suggestion that he move to a more prestigious parish in Edinburgh in 1633 on the grounds that it would break his, and many of his parishioners' hearts if he left Kilwinning.

An additional motive for Baillie's remaining in rural obscurity was that, though he was willing to conform quietly to the innovations that Charles I was introducing to the Scottish church, he was at heart opposed to them. Moving to a high profile appointment in the capital would have brought him under pressure to declare open support for royal policy. As late as January 1637 he was ready to submit to the new prayer book which was being introduced, though he predicted that it would lead to 'the most pitiful schism that ever poor Kirk has felt' (*Letters and Journals*,

1.5). After disturbances provoked by the book broke out in July 1637 Baillie was instructed by the archbishop of Glasgow to preach in favour of it and the book of canons before the synod of Glasgow, but he begged to be excused, declaring that 'my mynde is no wayes satisfied', and that the books had caused him such 'grief, that I am scarce able to preach to my own flock' (*Letters and Journals*, 1.12). But, typically, when the order was renewed, Baillie was ready to obey, rather than 'cast my self in needless contests with a troublesome man' (ibid., 1.20), though a change of mind by the archbishop spared him from the ordeal.

In spite of his forebodings Baillie soon became involved in active opposition to the king's innovations, though he wrote in October 'I think our people possessed with a bloody devill, farr above anything that ever I could have imagined', so that he feared 'a bloudie Civill warr' (*Letters and Journals*, 1.23–5). When, in February 1638, the draft for the national covenant was produced, Baillie urged moderating the text at several points, and succeeded in getting an undertaking to abolish episcopacy removed. 'Bishopes I love', he had written before the troubles had begun, 'but pride, greid, luxurie, oppression, immersion in saicular affaires' would destroy them unless they were reformed (ibid., 1.2). In the Glasgow assembly at the end of 1638 Baillie again stood up for moderation, for though now willing to accept the abolition of episcopacy he argued that it should not be declared unlawful, and he opposed persecution of opponents.

Baillie was reluctant to accept the legitimacy of armed resistance to the king, but again was soon won over. He served as chaplain to Eglinton's regiment in the bishops' wars of 1639 and 1640, and he became an outstanding propagandist for the covenanting cause. *Laudensium autokatakrisis, the Canterburians self-conviction* was published in Edinburgh in 1640, and London and Amsterdam editions quickly followed. Moreover Baillie had for some years been writing about events in Scotland to his cousin, William Spang, minister to the Scottish congregation at Campvere in the Netherlands, and he now expanded these letters (which form the greater part of the published *Letters and Journals*) into detailed, though hasty and informal, narratives and analyses designed to provide Spang with material for justifying the covenanters abroad. From this material Spang published Latin apologias for the covenanters in 1640 and 1641.

Thus Baillie, in spite of his reservations and anxieties, became a well-known public figure, and in October he was summoned to the camp of the Scottish army occupying northern England. There, on 2 November 1640, he and three other ministers were ordered to go to London to support the Scots commissioners negotiating with the king (NL Scot., Adv. MS 33.4.6, 109–10). While in London he published a further three propaganda tracts, and he was given a leading part in working to secure the downfall of Archbishop Laud and the earl of Strafford, held to be the main authors of the religious and other grievances of both the Scots and the English puritans.

Pressures on Baillie to leave Kilwinning had by now been renewed. He refused an attempt to move him to the ministry in Glasgow in 1639, after pleading that he was already 'in a place eminent enough for any gifts I have' (*Letters and Journals*, 1.229), but in June 1642 he accepted an invitation to become joint professor of divinity (with David Dickson) in Glasgow. Late in 1642 the commission of the general assembly of the church resolved, in response to approaches from the English parliament in favour of religious union between the two countries, to send commissioners to England to help bring about reform there. Baillie was one of the delegates chosen, though it was not until 18 November 1643 that he and his colleagues reached London. They were admitted to the Westminster assembly of divines as observers, and in January 1645 Baillie returned to Scotland and reported optimistically to the general assembly on the progress being made. In spite of his protests that he wanted to return home, he was sent back to London in March, though he was delayed after his ship was blown off course to the Netherlands, and he recorded with pleasure visiting Spang and roaming the bookshops of Rotterdam. On 21 January 1647 Baillie again reported on the Westminster assembly to the commission of the general assembly in Edinburgh, presenting it with the confession of faith that had been approved.

Though Baillie, like the other Scots commissioners, had not been able to take a direct part in the debates of the Westminster assembly, he had been influential in discussions behind the scenes in the cause of uniformity, as well as preaching to the houses of Lords and Commons and supporting presbyterianism through further published tracts, including *An Historical Vindication of the Government of the Church of Scotland* (1646). However, initial triumph quickly turned sour. The English parliament, no longer in need of Scottish military help in its war against the king, showed little interest in enforcing uniformity, and in 1644 and 1645 royalists led by the marquess of Montrose won repeated victories over the covenanters' armies. In his letters Baillie expressed his bewilderment as to why God was allowing his people to be scattered—especially by a force that included so many Roman Catholics.

An outbreak of bubonic plague prevented Baillie from returning to Glasgow after reporting to the commission of the general assembly in 1647, but some of the classes of Glasgow University assembled at Kilwinning and he joined them and his family there. As plague approached the parish he retreated to Edinburgh, now plague free. Again he was perplexed, but concluded that plague was a gift—though a mysterious one—from God. Political events were also demoralizing. In 1648 most covenanters allied with moderate royalists in the engagement to help Charles I against the English parliament. The church opposed the scheme, and Baillie expressed naïve horror on finding that the state could defy the church, raise an army, and do what it liked.

The defeat of the engagers by Cromwell in England brought the kirk party regime, supported by the church, to power, and in March 1649 Baillie was one of a delegation it sent to The Hague to invite the young Charles II to Scotland. But Charles refused the terms offered, and Baillie soon became disillusioned with the kirk party because of its severe persecution of engagers and those who had not been active in opposing them. He bravely refused to vote to depose guilty ministers, and was especially active in support of his friend John Strang, the principal of Glasgow University. But finding that he was himself in danger of being classified as a malignant, Baillie soon retired to his university duties, as advised in July 1650 by his mentor Robert Blair: 'Get yow to your book and your work, and meddle not', for he was destroying his good name (*Letters and Journals*, 3.105).

When, in 1650–51, the church in Scotland tore itself apart over how to react to English invasion and the revival of royalist sentiment that it provoked, Baillie supported the majority resolutioners' party rather than the extremist remonstrants, though he was reluctant to involve himself in the bitter controversy: 'I loved not to appear in contradiction to some violent men' (*Letters and Journals*, 3.115). The remonstrants might be a minority party nationally, but in Glasgow they had a majority among ministers, and Baillie feared deposition from his professorship—his friend Strang was forced to resign as principal of the university in 1650. The remonstrant George Gillespie then became principal, while Baillie supported Strang's right to the post until the latter's death in 1654.

To professional problems was added personal grief, when on 7 June 1653 Baillie's wife, Lilias, his 'most gracious and vertuous companion', died of 'a languishing disease' (*Letters and Journals*, 3.219, 237). When in October 1656 Baillie remarried he chose as his new wife Helen (*d.* 1679), the widowed daughter of John Strang.

the restoration of the monarchy in 1660 led to Gillespie's deposition, and Baillie was offered promotion to the principalship by the earl of Lauderdale, Charles II's Scottish secretary, but he dithered. On the one hand the post was, 'no lesse than my due and just deserving', and he felt that acceptance would somehow avenge Strang's forced resignation, but he had always been 'farre averse from changes and advancement' and was ageing and ill (*Letters and Journals*, 3.418–19). None the less, he eventually accepted the appointment, which was made on 23 January 1661.

It was to prove an unhappy end to Baillie's career. He was already fearful of the king's intentions for the church, and expressed his opposition to the return of episcopacy, but before the end of the year appointment of bishops began. Baillie was demoralized, realizing that by accepting office as principal he had seemed to endorse this development. His last letter to Spang, in May 1662, reveals that he was ill, and scurvy had been diagnosed. What with physical pain and grief at the Restoration settlement 'It were a favour to me to be gone' (*Letters and Journals*, 3.483). Scotland had suffered so much for the covenants, and now all was lost and godly men were being persecuted. He met the new archbishop of Glasgow, but made clear that he was opposed to 'his way' and refused to use formal 'styles' in addressing him (ibid., 3.487). He longed to see his most ambitious academic work, a chronology of the world from the creation to Constantine the Great, published before his death, but he died in late August 1662 and his *Operis historicum et chronologicum* did not appear until 1663.

Baillie was a man who had felt his natural home was a country parish (he was still dreaming of returning to one in 1661) but whose talents and enthusiasm led to his half pushing himself, half being dragged, into more public roles in which he never felt entirely at home. He repeatedly expressed fears of the consequences of his actions and hesitated to speak out, but he recognized this vein of timidity in himself and sought to overcome it. He used his skills in favour of the dominant—and therefore relatively safe—covenanting cause in the 1640s, and once involved in the movement showed in his propaganda pamphlets and his letters that he could at times be virulent to the point of bloodthirstiness. More creditable were the occasions when he overcame his fears sufficiently to protest against the persecution of colleagues in the ministry. None the less, his protests, though brave, were muted, and it was pliancy, a willingness to be persuaded by prevailing opinion, that shaped his career. The man who was reluctant to accept the abolition of episcopacy in 1638 and 1639 soon became one of its most renowned opponents, but then accepted its reintroduction in 1661. Recognition of his tendency to accept the lead of others is clearly indicated in the judgement that this 'learned and modest man: though he published some very violent Writings' did so at 'the instigation of other persons' (Burnet, 23).

The distraction of public affairs limited Baillie's achievements as a scholar, but his reputation was high. It was claimed that he was a man of 'profound and universal learning', but the assertion that he understood twelve or thirteen languages (Wodrow, 1.288) is doubtless exaggerated. Only one personal description of Baillie survives. In 1657 Lauderdale referred to him as 'my old acquaintance, the some times litle monk of Kilwining' (Stephen, 2.38), words that conjure up the quiet, scholarly man rather than the strident covenanting propagandist.

DAVID STEVENSON

Sources F. N. McCoy, *Robert Baillie and the second Scots Reformation* (1974) • *DNB* • *Fasti Scot.*, new edn, vol. 7 • *The letters and journals of Robert Baillie*, ed. D. Laing, 3 vols. (1841–2) • D. Stevenson, 'Mere hasty babblements? Mr Robert Baillie', *King or covenant?* (1996), 17–39 • T. Carlyle, 'Baillie the covenanter', *Westminster Review*, 37 (1842); repr. in T. Carlyle, *Critical and miscellaneous essays*, 3rd edn, 4 vols. (1847) • G. Burnet, 'An appendix to the history of the Church of Scotland', *Memoirs of … James and William, dukes of Hamilton* (1677), 23 • R. Wodrow, *The history of the sufferings of the Church of Scotland from the Restoration to the revolution*, ed. R. Burns, 4 vols. (1828–30) • W. Stephen, ed., *Register of the consultations of the ministers of Edinburgh*, 2, Scottish History Society, 3rd ser., 16 (1930), 2.38 • NA Scot., CC9/7/26, fol. 442v

Archives NL Scot., corresp. and sermons • U. Edin. L., notebook, sermons, papers, La iii 109, 543 • U. Edin., New Coll. L., letters, journals, sermons [incl. copies] • U. Glas., letters and journals relating to affairs in Scotland [eighteenth-century transcripts] | NL Scot., corresp. with William Spang [copies]

Baillie, Robert, of Jerviswood (*d.* 1684), conspirator, was the son of George Baillie of St John's Kirk, Lanarkshire, of the Lamington Baillies, and the nephew of the covenanter leader, Archibald *Johnston of Wariston. Of presbyterian

Robert Baillie of Jerviswood (*d.* 1684), by unknown artist

principles, he was, according to his cousin, Gilbert *Burnet, 'a man of great piety and virtue, learned in the law, in mathematics, and in languages' (Burnet, 2.354). He married Wariston's daughter, Rachel Johnston, with whom he had nine children. He was first in trouble with the Scottish authorities in June 1676, when he was found guilty of riot for helping his brother-in-law, the presbyterian field preacher James *Kirkton, escape arrest. An informer named Captain William Carstairs had accosted Kirkton in the High Street in Edinburgh and requested that he go back to Carstairs's lodgings to visit a sick person who had asked to see him. Once Carstairs had Kirkton in his custody, however, he informed his victim he had a warrant against him which he would execute if he did not give him money. When Carstairs proved unable to produce the warrant a scuffle ensued, upon which Baillie and some others, who had heard about the minister's plight and had come to see if they could be of assistance, burst through the door and made Carstairs release his prisoner. The next day, however, Carstairs managed to procure a back-dated warrant, which he then produced when the case came before the council board. Baillie was fined £500 sterling and remanded in custody until payment was made. A review of his case led to his release in December and a remittal of the unpaid portion of the fine, although Carstairs had already managed to collect 3000 merks (£105) from Baillie as his informer's reward.

Baillie ran foul of the Scottish authorities again following his refusal to take the bond of 1677, requiring all landlords and masters to guarantee that their tenants and servants would not attend conventicles. He was subsequently charged with lawborrows (that is, required to take out a bond himself to keep the peace), and was put to the horn in March 1678 when he refused to comply. Charles II's decision to cancel the bond and lawborrows in April, however, meant that no further action was taken.

Concern for the security of the people's 'Laws, Liberties, and the Protestant Religion' (Sprat, 93) led to Baillie getting mixed up in the so-called Rye House plot of 1683, the alleged conspiracy involving malcontents in England, Scotland, and Ireland either to assassinate the king and the Catholic heir (the future James II) or to launch an insurrection to force Charles II to accede to their demands. Baillie was among a group of Scottish dissidents who went to London in April 1683, ostensibly to discuss setting up a Scottish colony in Carolina, but in reality to lay plans for co-ordinated uprisings in England and Scotland, to be led by the duke of Monmouth and the earl of Argyll respectively. Burnet recalls that Baillie told him that he believed 'the obligation between prince and subject was so equally mutual, that upon breach on the one side the other was free', and that the recent injustices in London, culminating in the *quo warranto* proceedings against the charter, were enough to set the people 'at liberty to look for themselves', although he supposedly 'confessed things were not ripe enough yet' (Burnet, 2.354). Nevertheless, he appears to have begun negotiating with the English dissidents for funding for Argyll's invasion force, asking initially for £30,000, though agreeing to the £10,000 which the English claimed was the most they could raise. In the end, no money materialized, and Baillie grew disillusioned by the foot-dragging of the English, exclaiming at a meeting with his fellow Scottish conspirators that they had 'too long been the dupes of a set of men who could do nothing but talk', but that this 'was no reason why the Scots should desist', adding that 'if they were successful, it would not be the first time that England owed its liberty to the imposition of the Scots' (M'Cormick, 14). The consensus of the meeting, however, was that they should tell the English that they would not act in concert with them unless they showed more vigour, and at the same time inform their friends in Scotland to stop any further steps being taken towards an insurrection.

Baillie was arrested in London on 26 June 1683, following Josiah Keeling's disclosure of the Rye House plot. When examined by the English authorities, Baillie protested his ignorance of any assassination plot, though he refused to answer questions about the insurrection. He was kept in irons in the Gatehouse and grew so physically incapacitated that he was barely able to move. His wife petitioned Charles II to allow him to be released on bail on account of ill health, though to no avail, and at the end of October the king ordered Baillie to be sent to Scotland, where he languished in prison for several more months. When Baillie at last received a citation to appear before the Scottish council in September 1684 to answer charges against him, he protested that he was too sick to be moved, so the clerk-register was sent with a list of questions to put to Baillie on oath in his prison cell. Baillie refused to answer on the grounds that 'he was not bound to accuse himselfe' (Roger Morrice ent'ring book, p. 441) and was fined £6000. As Baillie's health continued to deteriorate, the Scottish authorities deemed it desirable to establish his guilt before he died in custody, and so brought him to trial on 23 December on charges of treason. His conviction was secured only after a confession, which was wrought from William Carstares under torture and should therefore have been inadmissible as evidence, was read in court; the prosecution claimed the confession was read as an 'adminicle of proof', that is, not to serve as evidence against the accused, but merely to convince the jury that the testimony of the witnesses against the accused could be believed. Baillie was sentenced to be hanged, drawn, and quartered the following day, 24 December. Sir John Lauder of Fountainhall, one of the lawyers for the prosecution, recalled that Baillie 'carried all this with much calmenes and composure of mind', only complaining that 'the tyme they had given him to prepare himselfe for death was too short' and huffing a little that he should be thought 'guilty of any designe against the life of the King, or his Brother' or the monarchical government; he failed to purge himself, however, of that part of the indictment relating to the planned uprising, which 'looked like a tacit confession and acknowledgement theirof' (*Historical Notices*, 593). Baillie's estate, worth some 8000–9000 merks per year and unencumbered by any debts, was forfeited to the crown, but subsequently transferred by act of parliament in June 1686 to the duke of Gordon (whose predecessors had previously owned the lands in question). Baillie's son George *Baillie (1664–1738) fled to the Netherlands following his father's execution, only to return with William of Orange in 1688. He was restored to the family estates following the revolution. TIM HARRIS

Sources T. Sprat, *A true account and declaration of the horrid conspiracy against the late king* (1685) • *Bishop Burnet's History*, vol. 2 • *State trials*, 10.647–724 • [T. Sprat], *Copies of the informations and original papers relating to the proof of the horrid conspiracy against the late king, his present majesty and the government* (1685) • [G. Mackenzie], *A true and plain account of the discoveries made in Scotland, of the late conspiracies against his majesty and the government* (1685) • *Historical notices of Scotish affairs, selected from the manuscripts of Sir John Lauder of Fountainhall*, ed. D. Laing, 2 vols., Bannatyne Club, 87 (1848) • *The Lauderdale papers*, ed. O. Airy, 3, CS, new ser., 38 (1885) • *State papers and letters addressed to William Carstares*, ed. J. M'Cormick (1774) • *CSP dom.*, 1683–4 • *APS*, 1670–95 • R. Morrice, 'Ent'ring book', DWL • R. L. Greaves, *Secrets of the kingdom: British radicals from the Popish Plot to the revolution of 1688–89* (1992) • A. Lang, *Sir George Mackenzie, king's advocate, of Rosehaugh, his life and times 1636(?)–1691* (1909) • J. Willcock, *A Scots earl in covenanting times: being life and times of Archibald, 9th earl of Argyll (1629–1685)* (1907) • R. Wodrow, *Analecta, or, Materials for a history of remarkable providences, mostly relating to Scotch ministers and Christians*, ed. [M. Leishman], 3, Maitland Club, 60 (1843), 78–82

Archives NRA Scotland, priv. coll., Baillie-Hamilton archive, MSS and notebooks | NRA Scotland, priv. coll., Baillie-Hamilton archive, incl. account of Baillie's arrest, voyage from London to Leith, and imprisonment in the Tolbooth; also pamphlet accounts of trial

Likenesses pencil drawing, 1660? (after miniature, formerly priv. coll.), repro. in Anderson, *Scot. Nat.*; probably priv. coll. • J. Shury, line print and stipple (after pencil drawing?), BM, NPG; repro. in Chambers, *Scots.* (1875) • miniature, priv. coll. [*see illus.*] • painted miniature, Jerviswood, Lanarkshire

Wealth at death 8000–9000 merks p.a. in estate

Baillie, Thomas (*c*.1725–1802), naval officer, probably from Dublin, entered the navy about 1740, and became a lieutenant on 29 March 1745, in which rank he served in the *Mars*, *Gloucester*, *Scorpion*, *Culloden*, and, from 3 June 1752, the *Deptford* (50 guns), in which he was present at Byng's action near Minorca on 20 May 1756. He was subsequently one of the witnesses at Byng's trial.

Thomas Baillie (*c*.**1725–1802**), by Nathaniel Hone, 1779

Baillie was promoted to the command of the sloop *Alderney* on 10 November 1756, but soon joined the frigate *Tartar* (28 guns) as first lieutenant. With her captain, John Lockhart, ashore recovering from illness or wounds, Baillie took the *Tartar* out on a cruise, and captured a French privateer of 24 guns and 240 men, the *Victoire* of Le Havre, or possibly the *St Marie*; this ship was purchased into the service as the *Tartar's Prize*, and the command of her, with post rank, was given to Captain Baillie on 30 March 1757.

Having used his Dublin connections to recruit seamen for the *Tartar's Prize*, Baillie was present at the action off Lagos on 18 and 19 August 1759 under Admiral Boscawen. His days of command at sea, however, came to an end the following year when the *Tartar's Prize* 'sprang a plank' and was lost in the Mediterranean. In January 1761 he was appointed a captain of Greenwich Hospital, through the interest of the earl of Bute; in 1774 he became lieutenant-governor of the hospital.

In March 1778 Baillie published *The Case of the Royal Hospital for Seamen at Greenwich*, which sought to expose 'the several abuses that have been introduced into that great national establishment'. Baillie listed in his catalogue of errors the appointment of non-naval men to offices, profligate expenditure on official apartments, poor treatment of pensioners resident at the hospital, and the reappointment of fraudulent contractors.

These charges were not calculated to endear Baillie—who was basically an honest man—to his colleagues or to promote his career, and they resulted in his dismissal, and a libel action brought against him by 'the inferior officers' at Greenwich in November 1778. Magnificently defended by Thomas Erskine (who was later to become lord chancellor), Baillie won the case, but he was not reinstated, and a motion in the House of Lords to set up an inquiry into the management of Greenwich Hospital was defeated.

Sandwich, the first lord of the Admiralty, now seems less culpable in this affair than was once thought, and indeed had sided with Baillie against his colleagues in an earlier episode in 1771. But while he publicly declared that he knew nothing against Baillie's character as a naval officer, and also that he did not feel disposed to act vindictively against him, Sandwich was well aware that Baillie had exposed the way in which he had put his own Huntingdonshire voters into Greenwich Hospital in preference to seamen; and so, as a protégé of the earl of Bute, the public-spirited captain found himself aligned with Sandwich's enemies. Baillie's persistent applications to be reinstated at Greenwich or to be given a command at sea therefore proved fruitless, and he was left unemployed until, on the change of administration in 1782, the duke of Richmond, who became master-general of the Ordnance (and who had attempted to put Baillie's case in the Lords), appointed him to the lucrative office of clerk of the deliveries.

Baillie's fortunes further revived two years later, when he received a legacy of £500 from John Barnard, the son of a former lord mayor of London, who left him this money 'as a small token of my approbation of his worthy and disinterested, though ineffectual, endeavours to rescue that noble national charity [Greenwich Hospital] from the rapacious hands of the basest and most wicked of mankind' (Charnock, 6.215n). Baillie's old age was spent in the quiet enjoyment of his office under the Ordnance, which he held until his death on 15 December 1802.

Randolph Cock

Sources commission and warrant books, PRO, ADM 6/17, 18 • J. Charnock, ed., *Biographia navalis*, 6 vols. (1794–8) • *The private papers of John, earl of Sandwich*, ed. G. R. Barnes and J. H. Owen, 4 vols., Navy RS, 69, 71, 75, 78 (1932–8) • W. L. Clowes, *The Royal Navy: a history from the earliest times to the present*, 7 vols. (1897–1903) • N. A. M. Rodger, *The wooden world: an anatomy of the Georgian navy* (1986)

Archives PRO, ADM 6/17, 18 | NMM, letter to Sandwich, 10/6/1779, SAN/F/19/127

Likenesses N. Hone, oils, 1779, NMM [*see illus.*]

Baillie, William, of Provand (*d.* 1593), judge, was the son of Alexander Baillie of Carfin, Lanarkshire. No siblings are definitely known, though in his testament a legacy was left to James, son of the late Thomas Baillie, the latter having possibly been William's brother. William Baillie married Elizabeth Durham (*d.* 1585) and they had a daughter, Elizabeth. There is also mention of a son, William, who may have predeceased his father, as well as of an illegitimate son, John.

As a canon of Glasgow Cathedral before the Reformation, Baillie had the rich prebendal lands of Provand, which brought him considerable income, some of which he used to become feuar of valuable lands in north Ayrshire from the dean and chapter of Glasgow. By 15 November 1550 he had become a lord of session. He is recorded as one of twelve judges who were to 'deliver the billis & ressaif writingis in the utter tolbuyth' according to a schedule beginning on 21 January 1555 (NA Scot., CS1/1, fol. 67), and he was nominated to a major commission in 1566 to revise the laws. In May that year he replaced John Sinclair, bishop of Brechin, as lord president of the court of session even though he was by now unqualified, no longer being an ecclesiastic as required by law. This ground of objection caused Baillie to be removed from the presidency when Sir James Balfour of Pittendreich exchanged the office of clerk register for that of lord president on 6 December 1567, but he was recognized as presiding lord during any absence by Balfour. In 1571, after Balfour was forfeited and had absented himself from court, Baillie resumed the presidency on a *de facto* basis, until his legal disqualification was removed in 1579; thereafter he acted *de jure*. In 1577 he was granted a pension of £100. At his death, on 26 May 1593, he left an estate of £5118 Scots, of which £1300 was in ready money. Most of it went to his daughter, who had married Robert Hamilton of Newton.

John Finlay

Sources commissary court of Edinburgh, manuscript register of testaments, NA Scot., CC 8 • manuscript books of sederunt, NA Scot., C.S. 1 • manuscript acts of the lords of council, NA Scot., C.S. 5 • manuscript acts of the lords of council and session, NA Scot., C.S. 6 • manuscript register of acts and decrees, NA Scot., C.S. 7 • register of deeds, NA Scot., RD1 • register house charters, NA Scot., RH6 • *The practicks of Sir James Balfour of Pittendreich*, ed. P. G. B. McNeill, 2 vols., Stair Society, 21–2 (1962–3) • M. Livingstone and others, eds., *Registrum secreti sigilli regum Scotorum / The register of the privy seal of Scotland*, 4 (1952), no. 260; 7 (1966), no. 861 • J. M. Thomson and others, eds., *Registrum magni sigilli regum Scotorum / The register of the great seal of Scotland*, 11 vols. (1882–1914), vol. 4, no. 2601 • G. Brunton and D. Haig, *An historical account of the senators of the college of justice, from its institution in MDXXXII* (1832) • F. J. Grant, ed., *The Faculty of Advocates in Scotland, 1532–1943*, Scottish RS, 145 (1944) • R. K. Hannay, *The college of justice*, Stair Society, supplementary ser., 1 (1993)

Wealth at death £5118—in Scotland: NA Scot., CC 8/8/26, fols. 26*v*–28*v*

Baillie, William (*d.* 1653), army officer, was the son of Sir William Baillie of Lamington, an adherent of Mary, queen of Scots. His mother was a daughter of Sir Alexander Hume, lord provost of Edinburgh, and he was born illegitimate while his father's first wife, Margaret Maxwell, countess of Angus (widow of the sixth earl), was still alive. After her death in 1593 Sir William Baillie married his mistress, but the son was not thereby legitimized, and the estates were inherited by Margaret Baillie, the eldest daughter of the first marriage. In 1641 Baillie was to make an unsuccessful attempt to have the settlement of the Lamington estates reversed in his favour.

In early life, therefore, Baillie became a soldier. He has plausibly been suggested to be the Captain William Baily who went over to the Netherlands in 1625 in the earl of Essex's regiment and under whom the young Sydenham Poyntz served at the attempted relief of Breda. He must already have been a man of some military significance when early in 1629 he went to Sweden to serve under Gustavus Adolphus; his first commission was as lieutenant-colonel of Sir Alexander Hamilton's regiment of recruited infantry. In a 'list of Scottish officers that served his majesty of Sweden' at the time of the king's death in 1632, he is styled 'William Baily, colonel to a regiment of foote of Dutch' (*Letters and Journals of Robert Baillie*, 3.465). He left Swedish service at the end of 1633, presumably to return to Scotland. By October 1629, when his son and heir James was born, Baillie had married Janet Bruce, daughter of Sir William Bruce of Glenhouse and granddaughter of John Baillie of Letham, Stirlingshire.

Back in Scotland in 1638, Baillie was employed on many important services by the covenanters. In his army commission, ratified by parliament on 11 June 1640, he is designated 'William Baillie of Lethem, Stirlingshire', from the Letham estate which marriage had brought him. Under Alexander Leslie, earl of Leven, he was present with the army which in 1639 encamped on Duns Law, and the following year he took part as a major-general in the incursion into England. As lieutenant-general of foot he also distinguished himself under Leven at Marston Moor, the siege of York, and the capture of Newcastle. At the first he played a prominent role with Major-General Sir James Lumsden in rallying the Scottish foot. As a reward he received command of the Angus (Forfarshire) foot, whose colonel had died from his wounds.

In late November Baillie was appointed to command of an army, with Sir John Urry (or Hurry) as assistant general, intended to check the raids of Montrose and his highlanders in the north of Scotland. In March 1645 he confronted Montrose in Forfarshire. Following the latter's storming of Dundee on 4 April, Baillie mounted a speedy response which could have destroyed the royalist army had his subordinate Urry pursued the plunder-laden enemy aggressively. Despite his failure, Urry became a major-general of foot and horse, but he earned the covenanters a stunning defeat at Auldearn. Through the spring and early summer Baillie devastated royalist lands until he was defeated by Montrose at Alford on 2 July. Having lost a third of his 2000-man army, he retreated to Stirling. Attributing his defeat to the fact that his forces had been unnecessarily weakened by the drawing off of recruits, he resigned his commission; but after receiving from the authorities formal approbation of his conduct, he agreed to continue in command until an effective substitute could be found. The result fully justified his scruples. For the first half of August he protected Fife from Montrose's largest army, 5000 strong. On 15 August the opposing forces again came in sight of each other at Kilsyth. The committee of estates resolved to give battle, a determination so strongly disapproved of by Baillie that he declined to undertake the disposition of the troops, and consented to be present merely that he might lessen the disastrous results of a defeat which he felt to be inevitable. The covenanters lost 3000 men out of an army of 7000, and with that the last army in Scotland to oppose the royalists. So overwhelming was Montrose's victory that Scotland for a time was at his feet.

In a change from his military career, Baillie served as an MP for Lanarkshire in 1645–7 and 1648. For all his undoubted bravery and skill, he seemed fated to be thwarted by the incompetence and blunders of those whom he served. When the Scots, after the engagement with Charles I, resolved on an expedition into England to deliver the 'king from the power of sectaries', Baillie was appointed lieutenant-general of foot and colonel of Walter Scott's foot in the army raised by the duke of Hamilton. In July he argued successfully for the army to march through Lancashire. The loose order kept by the duke rendered the English royalist disaster at Preston on 17 August 1648 a foregone conclusion. In the grounds of Walton House, south of the town, Baillie mustered most of the Scottish infantry in case Cromwell tried to cross the Ribble. That night he led the council of war in deciding on a night march to join the engager cavalry under John Middleton. Baillie rallied his forces near Winwick, 3 miles from Warrington, 'maintaining the pass', according to Cromwell, 'with great resolution for many hours' (Cromwell, 1.637). On receiving an order from the earl of Callendar and Middleton to make as good conditions as he could, Baillie refused to surrender, but only 250 foot followed him to hold the bridge; the remaining men threw down their arms and fled to the moor. In despair, Baillie threatened suicide, before his officers persuaded him to surrender by promising to sign a document exonerating his conduct; he very reluctantly sent in a capitulation to Cromwell, which was accepted.

By 1651 Baillie had returned to Scotland. He satisfied the kirk over his repentance for his part in the engagement in June 1651. He died at Letham in 1653 and was survived by at least two sons. Both James and William (*b.* 1632) succeeded George Forrester, first Lord Forrester of Corstorphine, owing to that lord's resignation of 1650–51. A contemporary Scottish historian observed of Baillie that he was 'a wyse and vallient souldier, expert in militairie affaires, whereof he had given a good proofe, at home and abroad' (Gordon, 114). EDWARD M. FURGOL

Sources *The letters and journals of Robert Baillie*, ed. D. Laing, 3 vols., Bannatyne Club, 73 (1841–2) · *APS*, *1643–69* · J. Turner, *Memoirs of his own life and times, 1632–1670*, ed. T. Thomson, Bannatyne Club, 28 (1829) · P. Gordon, *A short abridgement of Britane's distemper*, ed. J. Dunn, Spalding Club, 10 (1844) · *Scots peerage* · G. Wishart, *The memoirs of James, marquis of Montrose, 1639–1650*, ed. and trans. A. D. Murdoch and H. F. M. Simpson (1893) · A. F. Mitchell and J. Christie, eds., *The records of the commissions of the general assemblies of the Church of Scotland*, 3 vols., Scottish History Society, 11, 25, 58 (1892–1909) · *A list of the severall regiments and chief officers of the Scottish army quartered neer Newcastle* (1644) · *Three letters concerning the surrender of many Scottish lords to the high sheriff of the county of Chester* (1648) · A. H. Woolrych, *Battles of the English civil war* (1966) · M. Napier, ed., *Memorials of Montrose and his times*, 2 vols., Maitland Club, 66 (1848–50) · GEC, *Peerage* · *The writings and speeches of Oliver Cromwell*, ed. W. C. Abbott and C. D. Crane, 1 (1937); facs. edn (1988) · A. T. S. Goodrick, ed., *The relation of Sydnam Poyntz, 1624–1636*, CS, 3rd ser., 14 (1908), 46 and n. · S. Murdoch and A. Grosjean, 'Scotland, Scandinavia and Northern Europe, 1580–1707', www.abdn.ac.uk/ssne/

Baillie, William (*d.* 1782), army officer in the East India Company, is of unknown origins. He entered the army of the East India Company on 18 October 1759 as an infantry lieutenant at Madras and subsequently attained the ranks of brevet-captain (5 September 1763), substantive captain (2 April 1764), major (12 April 1772), and lieutenant-colonel

(29 December 1775). Lieutenant-Colonel Mark Wilks, in *Historical Sketches of the South of India*, identified him with the Captain Baillie who did good service as commander of one of the three 'English' battalions in the pay of the company, employed under Colonel Joseph Smith, in the operations against Haidar Ali (*d.* 1782), the ruler of Mysore, in 1767–8. He commanded at Pondicherry during the demolition of the French fortifications there in 1779.

The government of the Madras presidency was notoriously corrupt and incompetent. Though knowing Haidar Ali's hostility, and warned that he intended war, it failed to prepare militarily, its forces being dispersed in different parts of the country. Haidar knew from his spies that the Madras government was unprepared for war. He, by contrast, much improved his army, with many of his infantry trained on European lines and commanded by European mercenaries; he also employed a force of French mercenaries under Lally *fils*. In July 1780 Haidar, with an army of about 100,000 fighting men, burst into the Carnatic through the Changama Pass. Baillie then commanded a detached brigade—two companies of European infantry, two artillery batteries, and five sepoy battalions—totalling about 2800 men, his first independent command in war, in the Guntor Circars. Baillie was ordered to unite his force with the army assembling near Madras under Lord Macleod, who was immediately afterwards succeeded by Sir Hector Munro (1726–1805), who was honest, but uninspiring and irresolute. Moving slowly with the huge camp-following then customary, hindered by heavy rain, and, some writers have alleged, with many needless delays, Baillie's force (with Baillie carried in a palanquin) marched southward, nearer to Madras. On 25 August he reached the Cortelar River and foolishly camped before crossing it. The river then rose, and was not crossed until 3 September. Hearing that Haidar was besieging Arcot, Munro set out for Conjeeveram (about 40 miles west of Madras on the road to Arcot) and ordered Baillie to meet him there. When Munro left Madras on 26 August, Baillie was only 25 miles away, and several officers suggested to Munro that it would be safest for him to join Baillie at Madras. However, Munro refused. Haidar, who knew the British movements, raised the siege of Arcot and led his army towards Munro's force; at the same time he detached his son Tipu with some 11,000 men to attack Baillie's contingent. On 6 September Baillie repulsed Tipu's attack near the village of Perambakam. From there he sent a message to Munro, who was camped at Conjeeveram, 14 miles away, that his losses prevented his further movement. Munro apparently feared leaving his supplies exposed at Conjeeveram, and, instead of bringing the help Baillie expected, merely sent a small reinforcement of highlanders and sepoys under Colonel Fletcher. Both commanders apparently lacked judgement and energy. Baillie, moving forward from the village of Polillur towards Conjeeveram, on the morning of 10 September 1780 was attacked by Haidar Ali's entire army: surrounded, outnumbered, and outgunned. In the battle the explosion of two ammunition tumbrils within the oblong into which Baillie had formed his troops nullified the artillery and was followed by a stampede of camp-followers through his ranks, producing irretrievable confusion. Despite the heroic efforts of their officers, the sepoys, panic-stricken, could not be rallied; but the Europeans, numbering about 500, formed a square under Baillie, who was wounded and on foot, and, on a rising bank of sand, fought with stubborn determination. They withstood the fierce charges of fresh bodies of Haidar's cavalry, supported by masses of infantry in the intervals, until all the officers were killed or wounded, and only sixteen soldiers remained unhurt. Baillie surrendered. It was the worst British defeat in south India, and part of one of the 'most discreditable campaigns in British military history' (Thornton, 66). The survivors, including those wounded thought worth removing, were taken prisoner. Among those seriously wounded was Baillie, whose personal courage in the battle and in the subsequent captivity was admitted alike by friends and foes. Reportedly he defiantly told Haidar the victory was due to British ill fortune, not Mysorean military prowess. Imprisoned at Seringapatam, and most of the time in heavy chains, the officers rejected Haidar's offers of high pay, horses, and women if they joined his service. They remained until 1784, when the survivors were returned to Madras. A few, like Captain David Baird, 73rd (afterwards 71st) highlanders, witnessed the long-deferred retribution when the British captured the fortress on 4 May 1799. However, Baillie was not of their number. Although ill, he was denied medical treatment, and, reportedly still in irons, died in captivity at Seringapatam, Mysore, on 13 November 1782.

H. M. Chichester, *rev.* Roger T. Stearn

Sources M. Wilks, *Historical sketches of the south of India, in an attempt to trace the history of Mysoor*, 3 vols. (1810–17) • Fort St George (Madras) army lists, 1759–82, BL OIOC • H. M. Vibart, *The military history of the Madras engineers and pioneers*, 2 vols. (1881–3), vol. 1 • *N&Q*, 2nd ser., 11 (1861), 83–6 • T. E. Hook, *The life of General, the Right Honourable Sir David Baird, bart. G.C.B., K.C.*, 1 (1832) • L. H. Thornton, *Light and shade in bygone India: a study of the soldier in India at the end of the eighteenth and beginning of the nineteeth centuries* (1927) • W. H. Wilkin, *The life of Sir David Baird* (1912) • P. Moon, *The British conquest and dominion of India* (1989) • H. H. Dodwell, ed., *British India, 1497–1858* (1929), vol. 4 of *The Cambridge history of the British empire* (1929–59) • C. A. Bayly, *Indian society and the making of the British empire* (1988), vol. 2/1 of *The new Cambridge history of India*, ed. G. Johnson • R. Callahan, *The East India Company and army reform, 1783–1798* (1972) • T. A. Heathcote, *The military in British India: the development of British land forces in south Asia, 1600–1947* (1995)

Baillie, William (1723–1810), art dealer and printmaker, was born on 5 June 1723 at Kilbride, co. Carlow, Ireland, the second son of Robert Baillie of Celbridge. He was educated in Dublin by Dr Thomas Sheridan, who kept a school at King's Mint House, Capel Street; he then went to London and entered the Middle Temple on 10 May 1742. Baillie soon exchanged his study of law for a commission in the army; he fought with the 13th foot at Culloden and in several engagements in Germany. In 1756 he was captain of grenadiers in the 51st foot at Minden. In 1761 he exchanged into the cavalry, but retired in 1761 with the rank of captain in the 18th light dragoons. In 1773 he was appointed a commissioner of stamps, probably a sinecure with light duties.

Both before and after leaving the army Baillie bought, sold, collected, and created art. With the Irish painter Nathaniel Hone he assisted in the formation of Lord Bute's collection and he himself owned a number of old-master paintings that were engraved by various artists, including himself. Baillie had made prints from at least 1753, when he etched his own painting of a grenadier, one of several military portraits and scenes, and he devoted more time to printmaking after leaving the army. In May 1769, when bound sets were advertised for sale, his output extended to forty-seven prints with three more in hand. Only thirty-five complete sets were available because the early plates had been destroyed after a small edition had been printed. The sets were bought by the printseller Walter Shropshire, who advertised in June a list of about thirty prints by Baillie that he had for sale singly. Baillie's specialization was the imitation of old-master drawings and prints, and through the intimate knowledge of the style and techniques of the masters that he proved in this way he acquired a reputation as a connoisseur. He employed a variety of printmaking techniques and, like other printmakers of the day, improvised when attempting to imitate drawings. He exhibited with the Society of Artists as an honorary exhibitor from 1762 until 1776, and was elected an honorary fellow, although his status as an amateur was not universally acknowledged. Both Horace Walpole and Richard Bull excluded his work from their collections of amateur productions because they considered him a professional, and it is true that when marketing his prints he missed very few tricks. He worked after a variety of Italian, Flemish, and Dutch masters but preferred Ostade, Douw, and especially the highly fashionable Rembrandt. One habit that he copied from Rembrandt was that master's trick of altering his plates each time that he retouched them so as to produce different effects. Baillie liked also to add a touch of drama so that his imitation of Rembrandt's *Three Trees*, only slightly caricatured in the first two versions, has a fork of lightning added to the stormy sky in the third and a second fork for good measure in the last. He even managed to acquire three of Rembrandt's original plates: *Cornelis Anslo, Preacher*, *Jan Uytenbogaert, Goldweigher*, and *The Hundred Guilder Print*. His most famous, or notorious, achievement was his 'improvement' of *The Hundred Guilder Print*, which he bought from the American auctioneer John Greenwood, who had acquired it in Holland. As Baillie demonstrated by exhibiting an impression that he had printed, the plate was so badly worn as to be a pale ghost of its former self. In 1775 Baillie reworked the print and then launched a subscription, proposing to sell impressions to subscribers for 4 guineas each, double what Thomas Worlidge had charged for his copy of the *Hundred Guilder Print* (1757) and the highest price yet asked in England for any new publication.

By 1803 Boydell was selling Baillie's complete works as 113 prints in two volumes, with impressions from the three Rembrandt plates thrown in. Opinions of Baillie's work varied dramatically. J. T. Smith, who considered Baillie and his friend Hone both 'swaggering fellows' (Smith, *Nollekens*, 2nd edn, 1.119), thought his *Hundred Guilder Print* 'execrable' and wrote that for years Baillie 'amused himself in what he called *etching*; but in what Rembrandt, as well as every true artist, would call scratching. He could not draw, nor had he an eye for effect' (Smith, *Book for a Rainy Day*, 115). This was harsh criticism, for much of Baillie's work was innovative and skilful and caught the spirit of the original, but it was stimulated by contemporary adulation for Baillie's work that was equally exaggerated. Baillie died at his home in Lisson Grove, Paddington, Middlesex, on 22 December 1810. His sizeable estate, with houses in London at Lisson Grove, Berkeley Street, the New Road, and Queen Anne Street East, was distributed among his wife, Elizabeth, and four children: George, Thomas, Phillippa, and Caroline. His own collections of pictures, engravings, drawings, and books were sold at Christies on 15–16 March 1811.

TIMOTHY CLAYTON and ANITA MCCONNELL

Sources W. G. Strickland, *A dictionary of Irish artists*, 1 (1913); repr. with introduction by T. J. Snoddy (1989), 17–18 · Thieme & Becker, *Allgemeines Lexikon*, 6.317 · G. K. Nagler, ed., *Neues allgemeines Künstler-Lexikon*, 22 vols. (Munich, 1835–52), vol. 1, pp. 227–8 · will, PRO, PROB 11/1518, sig. 3 · PRO, IR 26/167, no. 19 · H. Rossiter, 'Capt. William Baillie, 17th dragoons and John Greenwood, of Boston', *Bulletin of the Museum of Fine Arts*, 41 (1943) · C. White, D. Alexander, and E. D'Oench, *Rembrandt in eighteenth century England* (1983) [exhibition catalogue, Yale U. CBA] · N. Stogdon, 'Captain Baillie and "The hundred guilder print"', *Print Quarterly*, 13 (1996), 53–7 · [K. H. von Heinecken], *Dictionnaire des artistes dont nous avons des estampes*, 4 vols. (Leipzig, 1778–90), vol. 2, pp. 30–45 · Graves, *Soc. Artists* · J. T. Smith, *Nollekens and his times*, 2 vols. (1828) · J. T. Smith, *Nollekens and his times*, ed. W. Whitten, new edn, 2 vols. (1920) · J. T. Smith, *A book for a rainy day* (1905) · D. Alexander, *Amateurs and printmaking in England, 1750–1830* (1983) [exhibition catalogue, Wolfson College, Oxford, 13 June – 9 July 1983]

Likenesses W. Baillie, self-portrait, stipple (after N. Hone), BM, NPG · J. Gillray, caricatures (sketches for *Connoisseurs examining a collection of George Morland's*), V&A · portrait, repro. in Strickland, *Dictionary of Irish artists*

Wealth at death under £5000: PRO, death duty registers, IR 26/167, no. 19

Baillie, William, Lord Polkemmet (*c.*1736–1816), judge, was the eldest son of Thomas Baillie (*d.* 1785), writer to the signet, and his wife, Isobel Walker (*d.* 1777). Descended from an ancient Linlithgowshire family, he was educated for the bar and was admitted as an advocate in 1758. Baillie served as sheriff-depute of Linlithgowshire for more than twenty years. In 1793, as Lord Polkemmet, he was promoted to the bench and became a senator of the college of justice. He was said to have owed his preferment to Lord Braxfield.

A great favourite with Scottish lawyers, Baillie was liked for his good humour and use of Scottish dialect. After listening to an over-long speech by Henry Erskine he was said to have reserved his judgment to the following day, saying: 'I'll just mak'it play wimble-wamble in my wame o'er my toddy till the morrow' (Paterson). His remarkably long fingers also led to his being dubbed 'the judicial fugleman' (ibid.). Baillie was twice married. His first wife, with whom he had a large family, was a daughter of Sir

James Colquhoun of Luss. After her death he married Janet Sinclair (*d.* 1834), a sister of Sir John Sinclair; there were no children from the second marriage.

Although Lord Polkemmet was 'not considered as a first-rate lawyer, or at all fitted to solve difficult legal questions, he had a fund of good sense, which, in the great mass of cases enabled him to discharge his judicial duties with propriety' (Paterson). He died on 14 March 1816, aged about eighty; his second wife survived him. The baronetcy which was about to be conferred on him was given instead to his son Sir William Baillie (*d.* 1854).

ROBERT BROWN

Sources J. Paterson, *Kay's Edinburgh portraits: a series of anecdotal biographies chiefly of Scotchmen*, ed. J. Maidment, 2 vols. (1885) • *The Society of Writers to His Majesty's Signet with a list of the members* (1936) • Irving, *Scots.* • Boase, *Mod. Eng. biog.* • G. Brunton and D. Haig, *An historical account of the senators of the college of justice, from its institution in MDXXXII* (1832)

Likenesses J. Kay, caricature, etching, 1789, BM • J. Kay, caricature, etching, 1808, NPG

Baillieu, Clive Latham, first Baron Baillieu (1889–1967), businessman and mining financier, was born at Melbourne, Australia, on 24 September 1889, the eldest son of William Lawrence Baillieu (1859–1936) and his wife, Bertha Martha Latham (1865–1925). He was educated at Melbourne Church of England grammar school, Trinity College, Melbourne, and Magdalen College, Oxford, where he took a third in modern history (1913) and rowed for the Oxford crew which won the boat race in 1913. The following year he was called to the bar by the Inner Temple before returning to Australia in time to serve in the First World War with the Australian Imperial Force and the Royal Flying Corps from 1915 to 1918. He retired with the rank of major, having been mentioned in dispatches and having been appointed OBE in 1918. On 24 February 1915 he married Ruby Florence Evelyn (*d.* 1962), the daughter of his father's business associate William Clark.

Baillieu was born into the third generation of one of the most powerful business families in Australia, part of an interlocking élite that was in turn closely linked to imperial Britain. His father had made his name as an auctioneer during the Victorian land boom and successfully weathered the crash that followed, subsequently becoming involved in the Australian mining industry. This sector of the economy relied on the London money markets for capital, and members of the family spent much of their time shuttling between Australia and Britain.

Baillieu was quickly drawn into this dynamic world of imperial business. In 1923, after an interlude at the Melbourne bar, he returned to London to look after his father's mining interests and began working with William Sydney Robinson, the British representative of Broken Hill Smelters. He became closely involved with a number of lead and zinc mining and smelting enterprises, and in 1924 he joined the board of the Zinc Corporation, founded in 1911 to treat the tailing dumps from the Broken Hill mines in New South Wales. In 1936 he established (with Robinson) the New Broken Hill Consolidated mine. Although founded as a separate concern for financial reasons, the new enterprise was closely linked to the Zinc Corporation. From 1945 Baillieu was also chairman of the Central Mining and Investment Corporation. Between 1962 and 1965 he acted as deputy chairman of Rio Tinto Zinc Corporation, which had expanded to incorporate many of the mining companies with which he was involved.

Baillieu developed interests in a range of other businesses, including insurance and banking. He was on the board of the English, Scottish, and Australian Bank from 1929 and of the Midland Bank from 1944, and was linked to the New Zealand Loan and Mercantile Agency from 1923 (he later became joint president of its successor, the Dalgety and New Zealand Loan). His most significant business connection was with the Dunlop Rubber Company: he sat on the board from 1929, became deputy chairman in 1945, and acted as chairman from 1949 to 1957 and president thereafter. In addition he played a role in several mining, gas, and rubber industry organizations.

Although he did not have a parliamentary career, Baillieu played a long-running role in the public affairs of Britain and the empire. From 1929 to 1939 he sat on the imperial communications advisory committee, and between 1930 and 1947 he acted as Australian representative on the Imperial Economic Committee. Between the wars he became a friend of Churchill, and during the Second World War, like many other prominent businessmen, he was pressed into public service to help mobilize resources. He became a member of the Export Council and in 1941 travelled to Washington as director of the British purchasing commission in the USA. He also became a member of the British supply council in North America and from 1942 to 1943 headed the British raw materials mission in Washington and acted as British representative on the combined raw materials board. After returning to Britain, from 1943 to 1945 he acted as temporary chairman of the troubled Fairey Aviation Company at the request of the British government.

Baillieu's role in public affairs continued after the war. From 1945 to 1953 he sat on the National Production Advisory Council on Industry and from 1946 to 1948 on the National Investment Council. He was a member of the General Advisory Council of the British Broadcasting Corporation from 1947 to 1952 and in 1948 led a British trade mission to Argentina. He also helped to establish the British Institute of Management and subsequently sat on its council for five years, acted as its first president in 1959, and was made an honorary fellow in 1960. After 1958 Baillieu was a governor of the National Institute of Economic and Social Research.

Perhaps Baillieu's most significant public role in these years was as deputy president of the Federation of British Industries (FBI, a predecessor of the Confederation of British Industry) from 1944 to 1945 and president from 1945 to 1947. He was active in the FBI at a critical time, when British industry was wrestling not only with the need for post-war reconstruction or 'reconversion' but also with the Labour government's plans for the nationalization of key industries. Like other members of the federation, he was convinced of the need to dismantle wartime controls and engineer a full return to free enterprise, although he was also prepared to see some degree of co-operation between government and the private sector. It was said that the Labour government's obvious solution to its problems with nationalization would have been to nationalize Baillieu, a course of action precluded only by its potential cost and the difficulty of finding enough new chairmen to replace Baillieu on so many boards.

Baillieu's plans for reconstruction reflected his broader view of the post-war world order. He believed that a British industrial renaissance would bring domestic prosperity and allow the Commonwealth to be strengthened as a force for international co-operation, complemented by a closer relationship with the USA. An alliance of the English-speaking peoples, an idea also promoted by Churchill and Sir Robert Menzies, would ensure the effective operation of the United Nations and provide a continuing role for Britain as a world power. This was a perspective that, in the years before the Suez crisis, was shared by many politicians and civil servants. After 1951 Baillieu also pursued his vision through the position of chairman of the English Speaking Union. He was particularly proud of his role in raising funds for the American memorial chapel in St Paul's Cathedral. In 1965 he was the principal Commonwealth organizer of the various Winston Churchill memorial trusts.

Baillieu owed his business success to the combination of a congenial personality and a privileged upbringing. While his affable manner helped him through a number of difficult negotiating situations, his Oxford training meant that he fitted easily into the clubbable world of City finance—'a most delightful personality with a fine background' (Stanley Christopherson, chairman, Midland Bank, to Keith Mason, 25 May 1944, HSBC Group Archives, London, File 9/161).

Baillieu had an interest in aviation and a love of flying that presumably dated from his wartime service. A habitual traveller, his frequent trips to the USA and to various parts of the British empire often meant that he was absent from board meetings. Nevertheless, such visits made Baillieu one of the leading public figures for whom the British empire and Commonwealth was more than a symbol. He in turn helped to make real the idea of the Commonwealth as a global political, economic, and cultural entity. Although partly of French extraction, Baillieu was proud of his Britishness. At the annual dinner of the Melbourne Scots in 1956 he stressed:

> the underlying moral unity of the British race. Their natural tolerance, the spirit of give and take, the willingness to live and let live: the innate respect for law, and the determination to defend its processes. It is the abiding faith in those great charters of liberty, broadbased upon the people's will, which has moulded the political and judicial systems under which we live and move. All of which explains the continuing cohesion of the British section of the Commonwealth and our real message of hope to the world. (FBI records, MSS.200/F/3/D3/4/18, proposal of 'The toast of Scotland', 1 Dec 1956)

Baillieu's wider imperial identity sat easily with a sense of Australian patriotism. He was equally at home 'shooting on a northern moor or salmon fishing in Scottish rivers [or] walking in the hills round Mount Macedon, Victoria' ('Profile', *Concord: The News Bulletin of the English-Speaking Union of the Commonwealth*, 20, 1966). One contemporary described him as 'a great Anglo-Australian' (*3rd Annual Report and Accounts, 1964, Rio Tinto Zinc Corporation Ltd*). He could equally be seen as an inhabitant of a British world, one that remained a significant supra-national entity well into the post-war years.

Baillieu was appointed CMG in 1929 and KBE in 1938. In February 1953 he was created Baron Baillieu of Sefton (Australia) and Parkwood (Surrey), the first Australian hereditary peer with successors. He had one daughter and three sons, the eldest of whom, William Latham Baillieu, succeeded to the title. Predeceased by his wife in 1962, Baillieu died in Melbourne on 18 June 1967. At his funeral Sir Robert Menzies, the former Australian prime minister, gave an oration. A memorial service was also held at St Martin-in-the-Fields, London, on 11 July 1967.

SIMON J. POTTER

Sources *The Times* (19 June 1967) · *AusDB* · *The Magdalen College record, 1966* (1967) · *DBB* · U. Warwick Mod. RC, Federation of British Industries papers · English Speaking Union, Page Memorial Library, London · Rio Tinto plc Archive, London · HSBC Group Archives, London · Burke, *Peerage* (1967)

Archives University of Melbourne, papers | FILM University of Melbourne Archives, Australian Broadcasting Corporation (31 Jan 1965), TV interview with Lord Baillieu

Wealth at death £65,380 gross—in England: *DBB*

Baily, Charles (1815–1878), architect and archaeologist, was born at 71 Gracechurch Street, London, on 10 April 1815, the third son of William Baily, of Gracechurch Street, East Dulwich, and Standon, Dorking, Surrey, and his wife, Susanna. John Walker *Baily was one of his brothers. He was a pupil of William Adams Nicholson and then from 1843 to 1846 of Henry Goddard of Lincoln, with whom he remained as assistant. He subsequently assisted Robert Hesketh (1817–1880) and William John Donthorn and was for some years principal assistant to the city architect of London, William Mountague, in which capacity he took a leading part in constructing the new roofing of the Guildhall and in the building of the corporation library. His independent architectural work included the building of St John's Church, East Dulwich, and the restoration of Barnard's Inn Hall, and of Leigh church (with new tower), near Tunbridge Wells, Kent. He also worked on St George's Hall and the assize courts, Liverpool.

In January 1844 Baily was elected a fellow of the Society of Antiquaries, and he was also a prominent member of various archaeological societies. His 'Remarks on timber houses', illustrated with his own drawings, was published in *Surrey Archaeological Collections* (1862). He also assisted George Russell French, editor of *A Catalogue of the Antiquities and Works of Art Exhibited at Ironmongers' Hall, London, 1861* (2 vols., 1869), and was master of the Ironmongers' Company in 1874–5. After a violent illness of several weeks Baily committed suicide by jumping from an upper window only 14 inches wide, at his home, Eastleigh House, in Reigate, Surrey, on 2 October 1878. He left a widow, Frances.

GORDON GOODWIN, *rev.* ANNETTE PEACH

Sources *Dir. Brit. archs.* • *The Builder*, 36 (1878), 1072 • *IGI* • *Catalogue of the drawings collection of the Royal Institute of British Architects*, Royal Institute of British Architects, 20 vols. (1969–89) • Graves, *RA exhibitors* • *The architect's, engineer's, and building-trades' directory* (1868) • *CGPLA Eng. & Wales* (1878)

Wealth at death under £300: probate, 23 Dec 1878, *CGPLA Eng. & Wales*

Baily, Edward Hodges (1788–1867), sculptor and designer and modeller of silver, was born on 10 March 1788 at Bristol, the son of William Baily, a ship's carver, and his wife, Martha. After leaving school at the age of fourteen Baily was placed in a merchant's counting house where he remained for two years. He formed an acquaintance with a local artist called Weekes, a modeller of portraits in wax, and began himself to model likenesses in this medium. After seeing John Bacon's monument to Mrs Draper (Sterne's Eliza), Baily began to model in clay. He was recommended to John Flaxman by Dr Leigh of Bristol, for whom he had copied Flaxman's illustrations to *The Iliad*, and spent seven years in the sculptor's studio, where he was acknowledged as his favourite and most devoted pupil. Before leaving Bristol, Baily had married, on 21 April 1806, at the age of eighteen, Elizabeth Wadley, who later joined him in London. Their first son, Edward Hodges Baily, was baptized on 7 February 1824 at St Anne's, Soho, and a second son, Alfred, was baptized on 3 November 1825 in the Old Church, St Pancras. A daughter, Caroline, was baptized on 12 January 1812 in St Marylebone Church, Middlesex. They had another daughter, Aurelia.

Baily was admitted a student of the Royal Academy Schools on 8 March 1809, aged almost twenty-one, in which year he won the silver medal for models. Two years later he won the gold medal for sculpture. He was elected an associate of the Royal Academy on 3 November 1817, beating the painter John Constable after three ballots, and being the only sculptor elected that year. Election as Royal Academician came on the death of Sir Benjamin West when on 10 February 1821 he beat the engraver William Daniell in two ballots. While still a student at the Academy Schools, Baily had begun to work for the firm of Rundell, Bridge, and Rundell, goldsmiths to the royal family. He rose to become the firm's chief modeller and designer on Flaxman's death in 1826. He was also chief designer for the silversmith Paul Storr, and continued to work with him for the company which became Hunt and Roskell. The role of interpreter of artists' designs for 'art manufacture' continued throughout his career, often with the approbation of the queen and Prince Albert. Year after year the *Illustrated London News* and the *Art Journal* illustrated the silver and silver-gilt racing cups for Ascot, Doncaster, and Goodwood, and testimonials and presentation plate designed by Baily. In 1857, the year of his retirement, he designed the Turner gold medal for landscape painting for the Royal Academy.

While still working for Flaxman, Baily provided the models of the stone figures for the pediments of Nash's enlargement of Buckingham House in 1826. He also executed the statues, trophies, spandrels, and keystones for the archway (removed to Marble Arch, 1851) and the throne room frieze *Britannia Rewarding Arts and Science*. The statues *Britannia* and *Victory* now adorn facades of the National Gallery, London. In 1833 the *Literary Gazette* reported questions in the house as to the delays in payment of 'this eminent sculptor, whose productions do immortal honour to himself and country' (27 July 1833, no. 862, 477).

Major works by Baily include the seated figure of George O'Brien Wyndham, third earl of Egremont (1840; St Mary's, Petworth, Sussex), and numerous subject groups including *Maternal Affection* (Fitzwilliam Museum, Cambridge) and *Maternal Love* (Petworth House, Sussex). His *Eve at the Fountain* (1822; Bristol Museum and Art Gallery) was one of the most famous pieces of British sculpture in the nineteenth century. It was editioned in bronze by the French foundry Bardedienne as late as 1886. Baily executed numerous classicizing portrait busts of the leading scientists, politicians, poets, and painters of the day, creating excellent likenesses. Among them were Thomas Bewick, for the Literary and Philosophical Society of Newcastle upon Tyne (1825), a posthumous bust of the poet Lord Byron (1826; marble versions at Harrow School and Newstead Abbey, Nottinghamshire), Michael Faraday (1830; University Museum, Oxford), Sir John Herschel (1850; St John's College, Cambridge), and Richard Owen (1846; Royal College of Surgeons). In an age of public statuary, his output was prodigious: his *Charles, Second Earl Grey* (1838; Grey Street, Newcastle upon Tyne), *Sir Robert Peel* (1852; Market Place, Bury), and the colossal granite *Horatio, Viscount Nelson* (1843; Trafalgar Square, London), have become icons for their age. At the time, however, they elicited inevitable controversy. Following his award of second prize in the Nelson memorial competition in 1839 Baily was allocated the figure of Nelson which formed part of William Railton's design that won first prize. Baily had gained permission for the public 'to view this stupendous work' as announced in the *Standard* (25 Oct 1843), before Nelson was raised in two pieces to the top of William Railton's 150 foot column, on 6 November 1843. Among his private patrons were George O'Brien Wyndham, third earl of Egremont, the collector Elhanan Bicknell, whose gallery at Herne Hill, Surrey, included four subject groups, and Joseph Neeld MP of Grittleton House, Wiltshire, great-nephew of the jeweller Philip Rundell.

Baily, described by Lady Eastlake as 'a shrewd looking man of humour and sagacity' (E. Eastlake, *Journals and Correspondence*, 1895, 1.265), was held in high critical esteem by contemporaries for his powers of composition and for the exquisite finish of his work. His statue of Turner, exhibited at the Manchester Art Treasures Exhibition, was described as being 'from the chisel of the greatest of modern sculptors' (*Evening Star*, 13 May 1858). His influence on his numerous pupils, such as William Calder Marshall and John Henry Foley, was considerable. He was the acknowledged exponent of ideal or poetical sculpture, and his retirement coincided with a reaction against ideal and literary-inspired subjects, from which his reputation has never recovered. The obituarist of the *Art Journal* described Baily as 'one of the most successful and accomplished British sculptors of the nineteenth century' (*Art Journal*, 1 July 1867), a view which has remained unrefuted. Baily was elected a fellow of the Royal Society on 13 January 1842, and in 1858 he was elected to the Belgian Royal Academy of Fine Arts in Antwerp, both marks of the esteem in which he was held by contemporaries. Financial insecurity was a recurring theme throughout his life. His first declared bankruptcy in 1831 (*The Times*, 11 Nov 1831) coincided with his attempts to gain payment for the work commissioned for Buckingham House, and he was bankrupted again in 1838 (*The Times*, 3 March 1838). On both occasions he appealed to the Royal Academy for assistance, something he was to do again in 1858 and 1862. In 1857 Baily ceased to work for Hunt and Roskell and resigned as an active member of the Royal Academy in 1862. He spent his last years 'being in circumstances of much difficulty' on a pension of £200 p.a., as an honorary retired academician from 1863 (RA council minutes). He died at his home, 99 Devonshire Road, Holloway, London, on 22 May 1867 and was buried in Highgate cemetery. His wife predeceased him. His daughter Caroline married into the Papworth dynasty of architects and his grandson was the sculptor E. G. Papworth. A volume of Baily's designs for silversmiths is in the Victoria and Albert Museum, London; examples of his sculpture in marble and plaster are in Bristol City Museum and Art Gallery; the Fitzwilliam Museum, Cambridge; Manchester City Galleries; Petworth House, Sussex; and the Victoria and Albert Museum, London. KATHARINE EUSTACE

Sources council and general assembly minutes, RA • J. Riddel, 'Collections for the life of E. H. Baily', catalogue no. 19 (1911–1915), 1886, BL, Add. MS 38678 • S. C. Hutchison, 'The Royal Academy Schools, 1768–1830', *Walpole Society*, 38 (1960–62), 123–91, esp. 165 • *Art Journal* (1828–67) • *Art Journal*, 29 (1867), 170 • *ILN* • *Literary Gazette* • R. Gunnis, *Dictionary of British sculptors, 1660–1851* (1953); new edn (1968) • Graves, *RA exhibitors* • K. Eustace, 'Baily, Edward Hodges', *The dictionary of art*, ed. J. Turner (1996) • autograph letters, V&A NAL • J. Kenworthy-Browne, 'Marbles from a Victorian fantasy', *Country Life*, 140 (1966), 708–12 • C. Oman, 'A problem of artistic responsibility: the firm of Rundell, Bridge and Rundell', *Apollo*, 83 (1966), 174–83 • A. Radcliffe, 'Acquisitions of sculpture by the Royal Academy during its first century', *Apollo*, 89 (1969), 44–51 • R. Ormond, *Early Victorian portraits*, 2 vols. (1973) • N. B. Penny, 'English church monuments to women who died in childbed between 1780 and 1835', *Journal of the Warburg and Courtauld Institutes*, 38 (1975), 314–32 • N. Penny, *Church monuments in Romantic England* (1977) • B. Read, *Victorian sculpture* (1982) • D. Irwin, *John Flaxman, 1755–1826: sculptor illustrator designer* (1979) • D. Bindman, ed., *John Flaxman R.A.* (1979) [exhibition catalogue, RA] • A. Yarrington, *The commemoration of the hero, 1800–1864* (1988) • *CGPLA Eng. & Wales* (1867) • d. cert. • *IGI* • E. Knowles, '"The most brilliant genius that ever lived …"? Edward Hodges Baily, 1788–1867, R.A., F.R.S., member of the Royal Academy of the Arts, Antwerp', BA diss., Leicester University (1994) • *Men of the time* (1856)

Archives BL, collection for a biography, incl. corresp., Add. MS 38678

Likenesses watercolour, 1842 (*E. H. Baily completing the statue of Nelson in his studio*), RIBA • C. H. Lear, pencil and black chalk on paper, *c.*1846, NPG; repro. in Ormond, *Early Victorian portraits* • pencil drawing, *c.*1850 (with three pupils), NPG • J. Smyth, line engraving, BM, NPG; repro. in *Art Union* (1847) • Miss Turner, lithograph (after W. Beechey), BM, NPG • A. B. Wyon, bronze medallion, NPG • photographs, NPG • wood-engraving, NPG; repro. in *ILN* (8 June 1867), 569

Wealth at death under £50: administration with will, 21 June 1867, *CGPLA Eng. & Wales*

Baily, Francis (1774–1844), stockbroker and astronomer, was born at Newbury, Berkshire, on 28 April 1774, the third son of Richard Baily (1744–1814), a banker, and his wife, Sarah Head (1745–1823). At the age of fourteen, following his education at the old grammar school in Newbury, he embarked upon an apprenticeship in a mercantile house based in the City of London. When he was seventeen he became 'intimately acquainted' with the natural philosopher and radical dissenter Joseph Priestley, of whom 'he always continued a warm admirer' (Herschel, 3). Baily both appreciated Priestley's natural philosophy and sympathized with his political views. In 1796 he embarked on a journey to North America with the official aim of forming or extending the commercial interests of a mercantile house in England. However, he was also fuelled by his republican tendencies, and while *en route* he announced his intention to take up United States citizenship.

Baily kept a detailed account of his tour, which was published a few years after his death as *Journal of a Tour in Unsettled Parts of North America in 1796 and 1797* (1856). He admired the North American ideals of individualism, commercial spirit, liberty, and equal rights (Baily, 93–4). The journal also reveals his views on education and strong repulsion to slavery. He claimed, 'had they [negroes] the same advantages of education, they would equal white people in the improvement of their mental faculties' (Baily, 93). On returning to England in March 1798 he almost immediately began to make plans for another exploratory trip, and volunteered to travel in the service of the African Association, having formed a route of exploration to the Niger. However, the association was unable to raise the necessary funds, and soon afterwards Baily became a partner with one of his father's friends—'the eminent Mr. Whitmore of the Stock Exchange'.

Annuity practice During his long career on the stock exchange Baily became a powerful figure in defining financial practices—in particular those appropriate for annuities and assurance societies. In 1802 he published *Tables for the Purchasing and Renewing of Leases* (a second edition appeared in 1807 and a third in 1812), in which he attempted to standardize the calculating base for the rules deducing the true value of a property lease via demonstrable principles. His objective was to obtain the true sum for the purpose or renewal of a lease of such estate accordingly. This depended on finding the clear annual rent of the property via a set of rules and tables he gave for its calculation.

Baily's early works on annuity tables and assurance societies reveal that he drew strongly upon the eighteenth-

Francis Baily (1774–1844), by Thomas Goff Lupton (after Thomas Phillips, 1837)

century radical dissenter Richard Price. His work on life annuities and insurances attempted systematically to algebraize the subject and represent various cases of annuities and assurances by symbols. He was also one of the first not to rely on Price's Northampton mortality tables, since, he claimed, the duration of human life was in fact longer than these tables suggested. In 1808 he published his highly successful and authoritative *Doctrine of Interest and Annuities Analytically Investigated and Explained*. This was followed in 1810 by his sequel, *Doctrine of Life-Annuities and Assurances Analytically Investigated and Practically Explained*. The latter also contained a critical guide to the several life-assurance companies in London, which later that year was published separately as a very popular pamphlet.

Baily's overriding concern was to establish a system to facilitate the buying and selling of annuities and leases with the object of alleviating the state of the national debt. The prevailing funding system had begun well managed—the money required for the service of government was borrowed for only a short duration (five to seven years). However, as the exigencies of the state increased, the term of the loan was lengthened to a period of 99 years and finally to the prevailing system of borrowing money on perpetuities. For Baily each change was more disastrous than the former. Baily's solution to the national debt, drawing heavily on Price, was simply to exchange the perpetuities for terminable annuities. The difference would then be paid through the sinking fund—'the very purpose for which that fund was established'.

In 1806 Baily talked at length in his *The Rights of the Stock Brokers Defended Against the Attacks of the City of London* of the dangers of seemingly plausible projects devised to make money on the stock exchange during the eighteenth century. For Baily, speculative projects and theories had to be effectively expelled from the financial and intellectual market. This meant a careful policing of information. The question centred upon what information was acceptable and what was not. This is highlighted in his vigilance on the stock exchange, which culminated in his central role exposing the fraud of De Beranger in 1814. De Beranger had been employed to supply intelligence from the scene of the war abroad with the purpose of influencing the price of British funds. Baily epitomized sound, thorough, precise thinking: 'everything to which he turned his thoughts', wrote John Herschel, was 'reduced to number, weight, and measure' (Herschel, 8). Baily presented himself and indeed was represented by others as the perfect citizen, reliable and uncorrupted by interests.

Historical writing In 1812 Baily tried his hand at history and published *A New Chart of History*, accompanied by a *Description*—of which five editions were sold in three years. The work attempted to exhibit the chief revolutions of empire during the history of mankind. This was followed in 1813 by his popular two-volume work *An epitome of universal history, ancient and modern; from the earliest authentic records to the commencement of the present year*. Baily's approach was directly inspired by Priestley's *Chart of History*. He argued fiercely that, unless history was pursued systematically without the seemingly judgemental hand of human interests, 'the whole mass of historical records become confused; the transactions of various countries are divested of their two most essential qualities, *time* and *place*' (Baily, *An Epitome of Universal History*, 1813, 1.i–ii). History, like the position of the planets or information on the stock exchange, should be protected from deliberate or accidental distortion.

During the 1830s Baily applied his historical skills in an attempt to rejuvenate the reputation of John Flamsteed, the first astronomer royal, after his neighbour Edward Giles lent him a large collection of hitherto unknown correspondence between Flamsteed and Abraham Sharp, his assistant at the Royal Greenwich Observatory. Baily concluded that the letters implied that Flamsteed's adverse reputation was totally unjustified, and that he had been made the dupe of Isaac Newton and Edmond Halley. His sensational findings, *An account of the Rev. John Flamsteed, the first astronomer royal; compiled from his own manuscripts and other authentic documents, never before published*, were printed in 1835 at the public expense. For Baily the Flamsteed and Newton controversy provided a means to raise the profile and importance of methodical and practical work in the scientific labour process.

The Astronomical Society Baily was also concerned that British science was falling behind developments on the continent. The state-sponsored *Nautical Almanac*, prepared by the board of longitude superintended by Thomas Young, represented a good target for him to promote his case. In a devastating onslaught he condemned the board's almanac for not keeping pace with improvements in astronomy. His first offensive against the board was launched in 1819, and it was here that he deliberately first suggested the utility of forming an astronomical society, which he co-founded with several others, including Charles Babbage and Herschel in 1820. Baily's attack continued with greater fervour after the society was set up, and in 1822 he privately printed *Astronomical Tables and Remarks for the Year 1822*. The main thrust of his argument revolved around the necessity of a set of tables suitable for both the observatory astronomer and the navigator, coupled with itemizing the numerous mistakes he apparently detected in many of the *Nautical Almanac*'s calculations. By the close of the 1820s the credibility of the board of longitude had been successfully challenged, culminating in its closure, and the Admiralty had no choice but to turn to the Astronomical Society for advice on a new set of astronomical tables.

Baily laboured extremely hard to systematize mathematical tables in both assurance and astronomy. During the early 1820s he was very concerned with the need to remedy the prevailing confusion regarding the corrections for aberration, nutation, and refraction. In 1822, in collaboration with the actuary, mathematician, and stockbroker Benjamin Gompertz, he devised a means of simplifying their application. However, on learning that the Prussian astronomer Friedrich Bessel had devised and printed a similar scheme, he proceeded to publish and recommend Bessel's method instead. He accomplished this in the Astronomical Society's catalogue of 2881 stars (epoch 1 January 1830), which was accompanied by tables for reduction constructed on the new system. It was printed as an appendix to the second volume of the society's *Memoirs* in 1827, and Baily received the Astronomical Society's gold medal as a reward for his labours.

Baily relentlessly applied his tabular and calculating skills in revising former important star catalogues. His aim was to bridge the gap between the observations of past astronomers with those of the present: as Herschel put it, 'to ascertain *all* that *has really been* recorded of the stars, and to make that totality of knowledge the common property of astronomers' (Herschel, 41). Baily re-edited and published at his own expense the catalogues of Ptolemy, Ulugh Beigh, Tycho Brahe, Halley, Hevelius, Flamsteed, Lacaille, and Mayer in volume 13 of the *Memoirs* of the Royal Astronomical Society in 1843. He also produced most of the catalogue of the British Association for the Advancement of Science, which contained 8377 stars (reduced to 1 January 1850) of the sixth and higher magnitudes. The value of this catalogue, along with those he did for Lalande and Lacaille (the latter being reduced by Thomas Henderson), was greatly increased by the fact that he used a uniform system of reduction and nomenclature. Through Baily's labours the boundaries of the constellations were also revised and the stars composing them were arranged into a recognizable order. A paper on this subject was read to the Royal Astronomical Society on 12 May 1843 and was subsequently appended to the report of a committee (consisting of Herschel, William Whewell, and Baily) appointed by the British Association in 1840 to consider the subject.

Pendulum experiments In response to a proposed expedition by Captain Foster, Baily devised in 1828 a simplified kind of convertible pendulum of which two specimens, of iron and copper respectively, formed part of the scientific equipment of the *Chanticleer*. The accidental death of the ship's commander in February 1831 threw Baily into the role of completing the numerous observations in both hemispheres by swinging the pendulums in London. He produced a report for the Admiralty which was later published by the government. His results took up the entire seventh volume of the Royal Astronomical Society's *Memoirs*. The general result of 20,000 experiments gave $1/289.48$ for the ellipticity of the earth, showing a satisfactory agreement with Edward Sabine's result of $1/288.40$.

Baily had also independently set to work on determining the length of the seconds pendulum. Bessel had pointed out in 1828 that to date the resistance of the air had not been included as a factor of resistance in the measurement. Consequently, Baily had a vacuum apparatus erected in his house, and there carried out between 1831 and 1832 a series of experiments on eighty-six pendulums of every variety of form and material, of which the details were communicated to the Royal Society in May 1832. It appeared thence that the value of the new correction, while varying very sensibly with the shape and size of the pendulum, was in many cases more than double the old.

The subject of the length of the seconds pendulum led naturally to that of the national unit of length defined by statute (5 George IV), which now proved to be of an uncertain quantity. As a result, Baily obtained in 1833 from the Royal Astronomical Society authority to construct for them a tubular scale of 5 feet, the accuracy of which had been ascertained by repeated comparisons with the standard yard. The issue became particularly urgent with the burning of the houses of parliament in October 1834, and with it the destruction of the national standard. Thus a commission of seven, including Baily, was appointed in May 1838 to consider the best means of replacing it. It was decided in 1843 that Baily should be entrusted with the actual reconstruction of the standards of length. However, he died the following year before he was able to complete the task.

In 1835 a committee was appointed at the Royal Astronomical Society to repeat Henry Cavendish's experiment to measure the earth's density. However, nothing actually happened until, in 1837, Baily offered his services and was awarded a grant of £500 towards expenses. Between October 1838 and May 1842 he devoted his time to this task in the upper room of his house. He concluded that the earth was composed of materials on average 5.66 times as heavy as water, but an unknown error was detected in his results. The Scottish experimental philosopher James Forbes suggested that the anomalies in question might be due to the radiation of heat from the leaden masses employed to deflect the pendulum, and proposed gilding both them and the torsion box. The remedy was successful and Baily began the process afresh in January 1841. The printed observations published in the fourteenth volume of the *Memoirs of the Royal Astronomical Society* numbered 2153 (including a thousand observations deemed untrustworthy). The society awarded Baily his second gold medal in 1843 for his labours.

Baily also spent a great deal of time diffusing astronomical developments and methods of calculation into the sphere of the general public, with numerous of his articles appearing in the *Philosophical Magazine*. He is celebrated for his detection of a phenomenon known as 'Baily's beads'. While observing an annular eclipse in May 1836, he noted the breaking up of the fine solar crescent visible at the beginning and end of central eclipses into a row of lucid points, or beads, the intervals separating which at times appear to be drawn out, as the moon advances, into dark lines or belts—the whole being the combined effect of irradiation and the inequalities of the moon's edge.

As well as his work in founding and administering the Astronomical Society, Baily served on numerous scientific committees and held an array of positions in scientific societies. For example, from 1839 he was permanent trustee of the British Association, and on various occasions he was vice-president and treasurer of the Royal Society. He helped establish the Royal Geographical Society in 1830 and became its vice-president. He was also a fellow of the Linnean Society and the Society of Civil Engineers, was a corresponding member of the Institute of France and the academies of Berlin, Naples, and Palermo, and was enrolled on the lists of the American and Royal Irish academies.

Baily never married and lived for much of his life with his sister Elizabeth Baily, at 37 Tavistock Place, London. In June 1841 he was knocked senseless by a speeding rider while crossing Wellington Street, and was unconscious for a week. He died at home of kidney disease shortly after receiving an honorary degree from Oxford University, at the age of seventy, on 30 August 1844, and was buried at Thatcham church, Berkshire.

William J. Ashworth

Sources F. Baily, *Journal of a tour in unsettled parts of North America in 1796 and 1797* (1856) [incl. memoir by J. Herschel] • J. Herschel, 'Memoir of Francis Baily', *Memoirs of the Royal Astronomical Society*, 15 (1846) • L. G. H. Horton-Smith, *The Baily family of Thatcham and later of Spleen and of Newbury* (1951) • W. J. Ashworth, 'The calculating eye: Baily, Herschel, Babbage and the business of astronomy', *British Journal for the History of Science*, 27 (1994), 409–41 • W. J. Ashworth, '"Labour harder than thrashing": John Flamsteed, property and intellectual labour in nineteenth-century England', *Flamsteed's stars: new perspectives on the life and work of the first astronomer royal*, ed. F. Willmoth (1997), 199–216

Archives Bodl. Oxf., corresp. • CUL, papers • Institute of Actuaries, MSS • LUL, tables, etc., and letters received • RAS, corresp. and papers | BL, letters to Charles Babbage, Add. MSS 37182–37189 • CUL, letters to Sir George Airy • RAS, letters to Royal Astronomical Society • RS, letters to Sir John Herschel • RS, letters to Sir John Lubbock • RS, letters to S. P. Rigauld • RS, letters to Sir Edward Sabine • U. St Andr. L., corresp. with James Forbes

Likenesses T. Phillips, oils, 1838, RAS • T. Phillips, oils, exh. RA 1839, RAS • E. H. Baily, marble bust, 1848, RAS • E. H. Baily, marble bust, 1848, NMM • T. G. Lupton, engraving (after portrait by T. Phillips, 1837), NPG [*see illus.*] • J. F. Skill, J. Gilbert, W. and E. Walker, group portrait, pencil and wash (*Men of science living in 1807–08*), NPG

Wealth at death over £21,000: Horton-Smith, *The Baily family*

Baily, John Walker (1809–1873), collector of antiquities, was born on 9 January 1809 in Kent Road, London, the second son of William Baily, an ironmonger, of 71 Gracechurch Street, London, and his wife Susanna. He was educated at an academy in Walcot Place Road, Lambeth, and he succeeded his father in running the business. In 1862–3 he was master of the Ironmongers' Company. He married Marianne Marriot (*b. c.*1809) of Chertsey, Surrey, and had two sons, Walker and William Henry, and four daughters.

Baily shared his interest in collecting with both of his brothers (the younger, Charles *Baily, became an antiquary). In 1825 he purchased some archaeological finds from workmen excavating in Walworth Road, although from 1830 to 1840 he collected mostly arms and armour. In 1840 he built a Jacobean-style house in Camberwell named Champion Park, where he arranged his collection around the hall, stairs, and breakfast room. In May 1861 he loaned various items for the exhibition at Ironmongers' Hall, London, which he also helped to organize.

From 1863 Baily began collecting the Roman and medieval antiquities that were being unearthed on building sites and railway excavations in the City of London and Southwark. His principal acquisitions came from the Walbrook, from Roman cemeteries around the City perimeter, and from reclaimed land in Thames Street. Like his predecessor Charles Roach Smith, Baily made his purchases from touts who haunted the building sites, who always visited him first because he paid for seeing what they had to sell. Before long Champion Park was overcrowded with exhibits, for which Baily added a northern wing in 1869.

As well as pottery, coins, glass, and leatherwork, Baily's collection was remarkable for the weapons, which included a Roman trident, a Viking battleaxe, and a two-handed medieval sword. Among other notable acquisitions were a 'Tudor green' lobed cup decorated with a small clay model of a stag and a twelfth-century Romanesque hanging lamp (which Baily mistook for Roman). The collection's importance is enhanced by the beautiful manuscript catalogue that he prepared, which contains nearly 400 pages of accomplished watercolour drawings, together with the dimensions and find spot of every object.

Unlike Roach Smith's collection, Baily's did not acquire national significance, and at 2100 items was less than half the size. Baily also did not study his finds, although he regularly exhibited them to the London and Middlesex Archaeological Society and the British Archaeological Association. Some were published in records of exhibits and in articles by J. E. Price. Baily was elected to the British Archaeological Association in 1865 and to its council in 1869.

Towards the end of 1871 Baily contracted cancer of the rectum, and he died at 9 Champion Park on 4 March 1873. He was survived by his wife. His collections were sold by his executors in 1881. The arms and armour were purchased by Baron de Cosson, of Chertsey, and the collection of London antiquities was purchased by the corporation of London for £650—the same amount that Baily had paid. It became the foundation of the corporation's museum of City antiquities and is now incorporated within the Museum of London. MICHAEL RHODES

Sources *Journal of the British Archaeological Association*, 30 (1874), 349–51 · 'Catalogue of antiquities, Roman and medieval, drawn from his collection by John Walker Baily', 1872, GL, MS 17151/1 · J. Nicholl, *Some account of the Worshipful Company of Ironmongers*, 2nd edn (1866) · C. Welch, *Catalogue of the collection of London antiquities in the Guildhall Museum* (1903) · G. R. French, ed., *A catalogue of the antiquities and works of art, exhibited at Ironmongers Hall, London, in … May, 1861* (1869) [exhibition catalogue, Ironmongers Hall, London, May 1861] · J. E. Price, 'Note on Roman remains recently discovered in London and Middlesex', *Transactions of the London and Middlesex Archaeological Society*, 3 (1865–9), 195–222, 492–527 · J. E. Price, 'Notes on a Roman quern discovered in St Martin's-le-Grand', *Transactions of the London and Middlesex Archaeological Society*, 4 (1869–74), 124–30 · sale catalogue (1881) [Sothebys, 4 June 1881] · Museum of London Accession Register · census returns, 1871 · d. cert.
Archives GL
Wealth at death under £25,000: resworn probate, Nov 1875, *CGPLA Eng. & Wales* (1873)

Baily, Thomas (*c*.1527–1591), Roman Catholic priest and college head, was born in Yorkshire. On 3 June 1543, in his sixteenth year, he entered Clare College, Cambridge, as a scholar. He graduated BA in 1546. Wardale's *Clare College* says that the master and fellows of Clare resisted the king's wishes in 1549: 'In no college of the university can the flames of religious faction have blazed more fiercely than they did in Clare Hall.' John Maden, master 1549–53, was reconciled to the Roman Catholic church in 1555. It was during his mastership or just after that Baily was elected a fellow, on 16 December 1553; he became a proctor in 1554. At the beginning of Queen Mary's reign Baily was ordained a priest, and on 20 September 1557 he was elected master of the college. On Elizabeth's accession a change in the mastership took place in several Cambridge colleges and Baily was deprived of his mastership for refusing to comply with the royal injunctions. The last document he signed as master was dated 14 May 1560. His successor, Edward Leeds, signed the next extant document on 12 October 1560.

Baily fled, along with many other university men, to Louvain, where he became a doctor of divinity. At Louvain the exiles lived in two houses called Oxford and Cambridge. He remained until 30 January 1576, when he went to the English College, Douai, at the invitation of William Allen, the president of the college. Baily was vice-president and acted as president in Allen's absence. The college was administered by a triumvirate consisting of Allen, Baily, and Richard Bristow (one time fellow of Exeter College, Oxford). Baily was considered successful in carrying out his duties and commanded universal respect.

A Calvinist take-over in Douai led to the removal of the college to Rheims in 1578. On 17 January 1585 Baily visited Rome and returned in September the same year. In Rome there was a visitors' entry for Baily in the English Hospice pilgrims' book on 1 March 1585. On 27 January 1589 Baily left Rheims to return to Douai, where he spent the rest of his life with his fellow countrymen. He died at the English College, Douai, on 7 October 1591, 'much lamented by all the English' (Dodd, vol. 2, art. 4). He was buried in the chapel of St Nicholas in St James's Church, Douai, where some other English exiles were buried. ANTONY CHARLES RYAN

Sources J. R. Wardale, *Clare College* (1899) · C. Dodd [H. Tootell], *The church history of England, from the year 1500, to the year 1688*, 2 (1739), no. 4 · Gillow, *Lit. biog. hist.*, vol. 1 · Venn, *Alum. Cant.* · Cooper, *Ath. Cantab.*, vol. 2 · T. F. Knox and others, eds., *The first and second diaries of the English College, Douay* (1878) · *The letters and memorials of William, Cardinal Allen (1532–1594)*, ed. T. F. Knox (1882), vol. 2 of *Records of the English Catholics under the penal laws* (1878–82) · *Letters of William Allen and Richard Barret, 1572–1598*, ed. P. Renold, Catholic RS, 58 (1967) · BL, Add. MS 5863, fol. 135b

Bain, Alexander (1810–1877), clockmaker and inventor, was born in October 1810 at Houstry, in the parish of Watten, Caithness, the fifth of eleven children of John Bain, a crofter, and his wife, Isobel Waiter. After a basic education at the local village school, Bain was apprenticed to John Sellar, a watchmaker, of Wick. Subsequently, in 1837, he travelled to London, found employment as a journeyman clockmaker in Clerkenwell, and began to attend lectures, exhibitions, and demonstrations on the principles and practices of electrical science. In 1838 he began to consider how a clock could be driven by electricity. His original ideas led to five important patents, dating from 1841 to 1852, and containing a wealth of innovative principles. Bain was the first person, anywhere, to devise an electromagnetically maintained pendulum clock. For this priority, and for his other achievements, he has been called the 'father of electrical horology'. In 1843 Bain patented transmitting and receiving apparatus, based on the use of synchronized pendulums and scanning styli, which would enable 'copies of surfaces', such as drawings, to be sent electrically from one place to another. This patent was the first in the world in the field of picture telegraphy. In 1846 Bain opposed the formation of the Electric Telegraph Company, on the grounds that some of his patents would be infringed, and gave evidence to select committees of both houses of parliament. Following an agreement with the company's sponsors, he was awarded £7500.

Bain married Matilda Bowie, *née* Davis (*d*. 1856), a widow, on 15 May 1844. They had two sons and two daughters, and for a few years (from the late 1840s) the family lived in Beevor Lodge, a large house in Hammersmith.

At the Great Exhibition of 1851 Bain was awarded the exhibition medal, in class 10, for his clocks, and at about

Alexander Bain (1810–1877), by Campbell Harper?

this time he established a showroom and manufactory at 43 Old Bond Street, London.

Bain's ideas, patents, and inventions were numerous and varied. In addition to those relating to printing telegraphs, chemical telegraphs, and automatic telegraphs, and electric clocks, he contributed to the development of an electric log to record the speed of a ship underway; an electric alarm to give warning of fires in the holds of vessels; an apparatus to take soundings at sea; an electrical signalling instrument for use on railways; an effective (though incomplete) fire and police telegraph apparatus; an apparatus for communicating between the carriages of railway trains; another to enable the playing of musical instruments at a distance; a device for copying documents; apparatus for drawing off liquids; unspillable inkwells; propelling pencils; and repeating firearms. *The Times* (April 1844) described Bain as 'a most ingenious and meritorious inventor', and Schaffner wrote: 'He was not a commercial man but his inventive powers were most wonderful. He has given the world some invaluable inventions.'

For a short period, from 1850 to 1852, Bain's electrochemical telegraph system was operated by several companies in the USA, but litigation against Bain and others by Morse led to their closure. Bain lost his earlier fortune in court actions, and by 1872 was reduced to repairing clocks for a living. In 1873, through the good offices of William Thomson (Lord Kelvin), for whom he had done some repairs, Bain received a memorial of £80 per annum, and in the same year he was awarded a grant of £150 by the Royal Society.

About 1876 Bain was admitted, on Thomson's recommendation, to the Broomhill Home for Incurables, Kirkintilloch, and there he died on 2 January 1877. He was buried in Old Aisle cemetery, Kirkintilloch, Scotland.

R. W. Burns

Sources R. W. Burns, 'Alexander Bain', *Engineering Science and Education Journal*, 2/2 (April 1993), 85–93 • R. P. Gunn, *Alexander Bain of Watten*, Caithness Field Club (1976), 1–19 • J. Finlaison, *An account of some remarkable applications of the electric fluid to the useful arts by Mr Alexander Bain* (1843) • C. K. Aked, 'Electrifying time', *Journal of the Antiquarian Horological Society* (1977) • A. Bain, *A short history of electric clocks* (1852) • R. W. Burns, 'The electric telegraph and the development of picture telegraphy', *Papers presented at the 16th IEE weekend meeting on the history of electrical engineering* [Twickenham, Middx, 1988] (1988), 80–86 • A. Bain, *A treatise on numerous applications of electrical science to the useful arts* (1870) • Whitworth, special report, 'Electric telegraphs', chapter 11, *Lords Journal*, 78, 9 Vict., 10 Vict. • on the Bain–Morse interference, *US Patent Office Report* (1848), 1124–43 • Inst. EE • *The Times* (April 1844), 16a, 6d • T. P. Schaffner, *The telegraph manual: a complete history of the semaphoric, electric and magnetic telegraphs of Europe, Asia, Africa and America, ancient and modern* (1859) • d. cert.

Likenesses photograph, 1874, Inst. EE • C. Harper?, drawing, Sci. Mus. [*see illus.*]

Bain, Alexander (1818–1903), psychologist, was born on 11 June 1818, the second child of eight of George Bain, an impoverished Calvinist weaver of Aberdeen, and his wife, Margaret Paul. Bain left school at the age of eleven but, via evening classes at the mechanics' institute and adolescent autodidactic labours, he gained entrance to Marischal College, Aberdeen, in 1836, graduating joint top in 1840, his course comprising classics, mathematics, science, and philosophy. A lifelong religious scepticism dated from this period. Until 1845 he remained at Marischal College as assistant in moral philosophy (1841–4) and teacher of natural philosophy (1844–5), but applications for the chairs of natural philosophy and moral philosophy failed through objections to his religious views. A year as Andersonian professor of mathematics and natural philosophy at Anderson's University, Glasgow, followed (1845–6), but his progress was still hampered on religious grounds, and he moved to London to take up the post of assistant secretary under Edwin Chadwick at the metropolitan sanitary commission of the Board of Health. Drawn into London's radical intellectual circles, his horizons now broadened. This group included Herbert Spencer, G. H. Lewes, Thomas Carlyle, George and John Grote, Harriet Martineau, George Eliot, and J. S. Mill, whose influence was especially significant; Bain subsequently collaborated with J. S. Mill in editing his father's, James Mill's, *Analysis of the Phenomena of the Human Mind* (1873), and in 1882 he published *James Mill: a Biography* and *John Stuart Mill: a Criticism with Personal Recollections*. Bain began publishing articles in the *Westminster Review* in 1840 and contributed to various popular educational series issued by the Edinburgh publisher, Chambers. During these years of struggle up to 1860 there was little upon which Bain declined to write—the physical sciences, the Greeks, travel, and town water supplies being among the topics receiving his attention (though he rejected George Eliot's request for a review of Auguste Comte).

Alexander Bain (1818–1903), by Macmahon, 1892

In 1851 Bain resumed his academic career at the all-women Bedford College, London, where he lectured on moral science and geography until 1854. During 1854 he visited Paris, meeting Comte, with whom he was deeply unimpressed. By contrast, F. Longet's *Anatomie et physiologie* largely inspired Bain's final approach in *The Senses and the Intellect* (1855, a project initiated in 1848) and it was during this period that he prepared this and the companion, *The Emotions and the Will* (1859), which were his most influential works. In 1855 he married Frances Anne Wilkinson (*d.* 1892) and in 1856 spent the summer in Germany. He obtained an examinership in the University of London (1857–63) and became examiner in moral science for the Indian Civil Service (1858–70). In 1860 he finally obtained the chair of logic at the University of Aberdeen (following unification of the older King's and Marischal colleges); he was backed by the home secretary, Sir George Cornewall Lewis, against the wishes of the principal, Colin Campbell (who preferred James McCosh), and fellow cabinet member, the duke of Argyll. Bain's teaching duties included English grammar and rhetoric along with mental and moral philosophy.

Bain's reputation rests primarily on his being one of the founders of modern psychology, most crucially by virtue of *The Senses and the Intellect* and *The Emotions and the Will* (posterity's verdict on *The Study of Character with an Estimate of Phrenology*, 1861, being universally uncharitable). Revised editions of these continued in use as textbooks in both Britain and the USA into the 1890s. Alongside these, his founding, in 1876, and funding and editorship, until 1892, of the journal, *Mind*, was of considerable significance for psychology's emergence as a formal discipline, providing the primary English language forum for psychological papers until the appearance of more specialist journals in the USA in the 1890s (*Mind* becoming devoted to philosophy thereafter). Bain himself contributed numerous papers and notes until 1894 (many of which were later reprinted in the *Dissertations on Leading Philosophical Topics*, 1903).

Bain's psychological work was novel in several respects. Most obviously, his approach appeared to transform philosophical questions into empirical 'scientific' ones. While elements of the Scottish realist tradition of Thomas Reid, whom he 'read over again and again' (Bain, 234) in the early 1850s, and Dugald Stewart continued to lurk, under J. S. Mill's influence Bain substantially converted to the rival doctrine of associationism. Unlike Mill, however, he wished to found his account on the latest empirical scientific findings, emanating primarily from physiology. (An earlier interest in phrenology had been a harbinger of this orientation.) Essentially his method was to provide a systematic, natural history type of classification of mental states on the basis of the associative mechanisms by which they were lawfully generated. The works resulting from this fusion of associationist theory, physiology, and natural historical method thus bore a fundamentally scientific rather than philosophical character, linking associative mental processes with available knowledge of the nervous system and cerebral functioning. Thus, in learning, the establishment of habits was understood as involving the creation and progressive strengthening of relevant nerve pathways in the brain. Despite being associationist, Bain's account was less passive than those in earlier philosophical versions of this doctrine, the organism being understood as actively striving to make sense of the world, although he proposed nothing as distinct as an ego or self underlying this. Rather than simple, passive associations it was the capacity for active discrimination which constituted the core psychological process. The nervous system was spontaneously active, rather than merely reactive, and Bain's treatment of the role of spontaneous movements in facilitating the development of voluntary behaviour of an increasingly discriminative kind adumbrates modern notions of feedback loops. In adopting this perspective Bain was among the first major writers to incorporate the 'energy' concept fully into psychological theorizing and to insist on the firm physiological grounding of all psychological phenomena. While it is routine to credit pioneers with anticipating future developments in their fields, Bain managed this to a remarkable degree which only began to be appreciated from about 1980. Most classic theories of the child's cognitive development (including James Mark Baldwin's, Alfred Binet's, and Jean Piaget's) had important roots in Bain's analysis. His account of habit constituted the point of departure for William James's subsequent treatment of the topic and American learning theory generally (anticipating what E. B. Thorndike called the 'law of effect' for example, and introducing the notion of trial and error learning—although he used this rather more broadly than later learning theorists to cover rational as well as random learning). Moreover, C. S. Peirce, founder of the American philosophical school of pragmatism, took his lead from Bain's view of belief as 'that upon which a man is prepared to act'.

Bain always stressed psychology's practical importance, particularly for education (notably in *Education as a Science*, 1878), and continued publishing works attacking metaphysical idealism (for example, *Mind and Body: the Theories of their Relation*, 1872) and promoting the new discipline, most successfully in *Mental and Moral Science: a Compendium of Psychology and Ethics* (1868), as well as in *Logic* (1870). His educational concerns yielded the two-volume *English Composition and Rhetoric* (1867, enlarged 1887) and works on English grammar. His concern with social issues and the applicability of psychology resulted in a further set of anticipations of later disciplinary interests in social norms, occupational psychology, testing, and training, although he never ventured into quantitative psychometrics.

Although psychological rather than philosophical, Bain's system was transitional in two fundamental respects: first, while empirical and physiologically based it remained non-experimental, observational (often introspectionist), and descriptive (unlike contemporary developments in Germany initiated by W. Wundt and G. T. Fechner); second, Bain never fully assimilated the evolutionary vision which provided the unifying theoretical framework within which psychology first crystallized as a scientific discipline after 1870. Regarding the latter, this ironically helped the early success of his books *vis-à-vis* Herbert Spencer's rival *Principles of Psychology* (1855), the thoroughgoing evolutionism of which many initially found unacceptably radical. While he increasingly ascribed a role to heredity, his explanatory mode remained that of identifying the 'bottom-up' assembly of associative connections and discriminations rather than evolutionary functionalism.

Traditionally, historians of psychology located Bain firmly in the associationist camp, but this probably underestimates how far his thinking, especially in the 1850s and 1860s, continued to be influenced by his native Scottish realist philosophical background, and in 1860–61 he was still publishing papers sympathetic to phrenology in *Fraser's Magazine*. While abandoning Scottish realism's cruder 'faculty' analysis, his own fourfold classification of mental phenomena continued to bear a formal resemblance to this, as the very titles of his two major works indicate, even if he viewed them as dynamically interrelated segments of a single energy distribution process rather than distinct sets of powers.

Besides his own work Bain edited *The Moral Philosophy of Paley* (1852), G. Grote's *Aristotle* (1872), and G. Croom Robertson's philosophical remains (1894). He received an honorary LLD from the University of Edinburgh (1869) and a civil-list pension of £100 after 1895. The *Dictionary of National Biography* entry's assessment of his writings as 'lucid' would now receive little assent and if conceding his 'exceptional gift of methodical exposition' most would consider this a euphemistic way of putting it. Probably reflecting readers' reactions more accurately, E. Valentine, in the *Biographical Dictionary of Psychology*, describes his style as 'ponderous, verbose and lengthy'.

Bain's work was frostily received by pious Scottish academics and the equally pious American mental and moral philosophers who dominated psychology teaching in the USA until the late 1880s. Yale's president, Noah Porter, attacked his 'cerebral' approach vehemently in *The Sciences of Nature versus the Science of Man* of 1871 (although he was sympathetic to the German experimentalists who, as he saw it, eschewed Bain's physiological reductionism). In the intellectual context of American-Scottish mental and moral philosophy Bain's was a particularly irritating presence, not least since he was both a native and based in the heartland of that tradition—Thomas Reid himself having been a professor of philosophy at Aberdeen.

After retiring from his chair at Aberdeen in 1880 Bain remained active and was twice elected lord rector of the university, defeating Lord Randolph Churchill on the second occasion. In 1892 he presented a paper on the relationship between introspective and psychophysical experimental methods at the Second International Congress of Experimental Psychology in London. Following his wife's death that year, he married Barbara (*b.* 1858/9), daughter of John Forbes, sheriff clerk of Banffshire, and his wife, Eliza Young, in a civil ceremony on 14 April 1893. There were no children from either marriage. Bain's health failing, in 1895 he withdrew from the strenuous public life he had so long enjoyed. This had extended to widespread popular lecturing and support for causes such as public libraries and mechanics' institutes. Any image of Bain's personality is now dourly dominated by his daunting capacity for hard work, as a writer, scholar, editor, administrator, committee man, and propagandist for the cause of education. This edifice should not obscure the extent to which he was also a genuinely creative and doggedly independent thinker, and one held in much affection by his contemporaries, many of whom benefited directly from his support. In 1896 his health suffered a temporary breakdown, probably from influenza; however, he resumed work on recasting the curriculi of Aberdeen University and promoting the extension of Marischal College buildings. He had revisited Paris in 1876 (meeting Théodule Ribot) and Germany (1885), where he met Wundt, H. Helmholtz, H. Ebbinghaus, E. Haeckel, E. Du Bois-Reymond, and the young American psychologist James McKeen Cattell (who acted as interpreter in his encounter with Wundt). Bain died at his home, Ferryhill Lodge, Polmuir Road, Aberdeen, on 18 September 1903, survived by his second wife. He was buried in Aberdeen. His *Autobiography* appeared posthumously in 1904.

GRAHAM RICHARDS

Sources A. Bain, *Autobiography*, ed. [W. L. Davidson] (1904) • E. Valentine, 'Bain, Alexander', *Biographical dictionary of psychology*, ed. N. Sheehy, A. Chapman, and W. Conroy (1997) • A. P. Greenway, 'The incorporation of action into associationism: the psychology of A. Bain', *Journal of the History of the Behavioral Sciences*, 9 (1973), 42–

52 • M. H. Fisch, 'Alexander Bain and the genealogy of pragmatism', *Journal of the History of Ideas*, 15 (1954), 413–44 • D. G. Boyle, *Psychology: the Aberdeen connection* (1993) • J. A. Cardno, 'Bain and physiological psychology', *Australian Journal of Psychology*, 7 (1955), 108–20 • J. A. Cardno, 'Bain as a social psychologist', *Australian Journal of Psychology*, 8 (1956), 66–76 • W. I. Davidson, *Mind*, new ser., 13 (1904), 151–5 • R. Knight, 'A Bain centenary', *Aberdeen University Review*, 36 (1955–6), 160–63 • *DNB* • parish register (births and baptisms), Old Machal, Aberdeen, 11 June 1818 • m. cert. [for Barbara Forbes] • d. cert. • A. Still, 'Alexander Bain and the evolution of trial and error: a missed opportunity in the history of psychology', paper presented to British Psychological Society History and Philosophy Section, 8th Annual Conference, U. Aberdeen, 4–6 April 1995

Archives NL Scot., letters to Alexander Campbell Fraser • U. Aberdeen, King's College • UCL, corresp. with Edwin Chadwick, G. Grote, and G. C. Robertson

Likenesses A. Craig, oils, 1854, repro. in Bain, *Autobiography* • A. Clyne, chalk drawing, 1878, repro. in Bain, *Autobiography* • G. Reid, oils, 1882, U. Aberdeen; repro. in Bain, *Autobiography* • Macmahon, photograph, 1892, repro. in Bain, *Autobiography* [*see illus.*] • Synnberg Photo-gravure Co., photogravure, 1898, Wellcome L.

Wealth at death £2902 12*s.* 9*d.*: confirmation, 31 Dec 1903, *CCI*

Bain, Francis William (1863–1940), scholar and writer, the third son of Joseph Bain (1826–1911), archivist and antiquary, of Sweethope, Bothwell, Lanarkshire, and his wife, Charlotte, daughter of Edward Piper, of Alston, Cumberland, was born at Bothwell on 29 April 1863. He was elected an exhibitioner (1877) and a scholar (1878) on the foundation of Westminster School, becoming captain of the school in 1881. He went as a Westminster scholar to Christ Church, Oxford, in 1882. He obtained a second class in classical moderations (1884) and a first class in *literae humaniores* (1886), and was also a blue for association football for four years from 1883 to 1886, captaining the Oxford University team in his fourth year. In 1889 he was elected to a fellowship (which he held until 1897) at All Souls College; in 1890 he married Helen Margarita (*d.* 1931), daughter of Henry Blandford, of Blandford, Dorset.

In 1892, to the surprise of many of his friends, Bain took a post in the Indian educational service as professor of history and political economy at the Deccan College at Poona, where he remained until his retirement in 1919, after serving, in addition, as junior principal in 1908 and as senior principal in 1911. He was appointed CIE in 1918, and when he left Poona he received an address in a silver casket expressing the enthusiastic appreciation of many hundreds of former students not only for his teaching but for his deep sympathy with, and insight into, the higher elements in Indian life and thought; he was regarded 'not only as a professor but also as a prophet and a philosopher'.

After 1919 Bain lived quietly in London, paying frequent visits to All Souls, where, as in the years before 1914, he was always an eagerly awaited guest; but deeply affected by the death of his wife (1931) and of his only child, a daughter (1934), he retired into a self-imposed isolation, broken with difficulty even by his most intimate friends, which continued for the rest of his life. He died at 59 Bridge Avenue, Hammersmith, on 24 February 1940.

Bain, as an undergraduate, developed the views on life, philosophy, politics, and literature which he maintained with increasing tenacity to the end. Aristotle was for him 'the master of the wise'. In politics he was a tory with a creed based on his interpretation of Bolingbroke and Disraeli; for whigs, Liberals, and modern Conservatives he had a profound contempt. He freely discussed Indian political reform, and his biographer described him as a 'Tory who condemned dictatorial rule, an imperialist who wanted Indians to fight for self-rule' (Mutalik, 48). In modern physical and natural science he saw only a perversion of judgement and of the facts; the classical economists and most historians he regarded as ability corrupted by original sin; but into imaginative literature of all types he had a wonderful insight. He was remembered by students as an inspiring teacher and a lasting intellectual influence. He could expound with fascinating lucidity views which he was convinced were fundamentally wrong, and instruct his Indian students that 'this is what they must say' and then demonstrate its perversity and errors. Deep in Bain's mind was an inspiring mystical element which at Poona was richly nourished by his study of Indian life, religion, and the Sanskrit classics, which he learned to read after arriving in India. He also developed some proficiency in Marathi.

In his early years Bain published two or three volumes of fiction, philosophical pamphlets, and a remarkable essay, *The English Monarchy and its Revolutions* (1894), full of penetrating observations, all of which attracted no attention; but in 1899 he found the right scope for his genius when he published *A Digit of the Moon*, a Hindu love story, professing to be a translation from a Sanskrit manuscript. Even experts were at first taken in, but its quality both in imagination and style captured a large and critical public, which rightly hailed it as unique in English literature. It was followed by twelve other similar Hindu love stories, the last of which, *The Substance of a Dream* (1919), was as successful as its predecessors. The stories were reprinted between 1913 and 1920, and a few of them again in the 1950s. Translations appeared in several European and Indian languages. After 1919 Bain ceased to write.

Bain's personality was even more impressive than his best writing. Strikingly handsome, when stirred by his company he exercised almost a witchery over his friends; and in the common room at All Souls his conversation in that congenial atmosphere, discussing any and every topic, and soaring at times into flights of imaginative eloquence, was an experience impossible to describe, but thrilling to have shared. His loyalty to the college and to a limited circle of friends earned from all an affection as strong as was the admiration of his genius. Copies of most of Bain's writings are in the Codrington Library at All Souls. Besides those mentioned above, there may be noted his biographical study, *Queen Christina of Sweden* (1890), *On the Realisation of the Possible and the Spirit of Aristotle* (1899), and the essay *De vi physica et imbecillitate Darwiniana* (1903) which summarizes his homage to Aristotle and his views on 'modern science'. A list of the published writings is to be found in the biography of Bain by K. Mutalik.

C. G. Robertson, *rev.* J. B. Katz

Sources K. Mutalik, *Francis William Bain* (Bombay, 1963) • *The Times* (26 Feb 1940) • personal knowledge (1949) • *CGPLA Eng. & Wales* (1940)
Archives priv. coll. | All Souls Oxf., letters to W. R. Anson • BL, corresp. with Sir Sidney Cockerell, Add. MS 52704
Likenesses photograph (taken in Deccan College, Poona), repro. in Mutalik, *Francis William Bain*, 24
Wealth at death £425 4s. 11d.: administration with will (limited), 21 June 1940, *CGPLA Eng. & Wales*

Bain, Sir Frederick William (1889–1950), chemist and industrialist, was born on 22 March 1889 at Macduff, Banffshire, the son of James Bain, agent for the Macduff Commercial Company, and his wife, Isabella Strachan. Educated at the Banff Academy, he was only seventeen when the death of his father put an end to his hopes of a university career. He moved with his mother and younger sister to Aberdeen, where he worked for a company distributing fertilizers and in his spare time attended chemistry classes at the university. In 1915 he went to Flanders as company quartermaster sergeant in the 4th (territorial) battalion of Gordon Highlanders, which he had joined in 1908.

He soon received his commission, was mentioned in dispatches, and awarded the MC for gallantry, but on Christmas day 1915 he was severely wounded and lost his left arm in a bomb accident. Upon his recovery he entered the Ministry of Munitions, and soon became deputy director in the section of the trench warfare supply department which was responsible for the supply of materials for chemical warfare.

When the war ended Bain found himself without a job and handicapped by illness. By chance he met Christopher Clayton of the United Alkali Company and he went with him to Liverpool as his personal assistant. He was soon a director of the company and on the formation of Imperial Chemical Industries in 1926 he entered the new combine with enthusiasm, becoming vice-chairman, in 1931, and later chairman, of the general chemicals group. He became an executive manager of ICI in 1939, a director in 1940, and a deputy chairman in 1945, an appointment which he held until his death.

Between 1941 and 1944 Bain was seconded to the Ministry of Supply as chairman of the Chemical Control Board, and he was also chairman of the chemical planning committee of the Ministry of Production (1942–4). For these services he was knighted in 1945. After the war he was one of the most active presidents (1947–9) the Federation of British Industries has ever known. He was a member of innumerable committees and councils, including that of the Society of Chemical Industry, and one of his particular interests was the Association of British Chemical Manufacturers, of which he was for several years vice-chairman and of which he was made an honorary member and honorary vice-president shortly before he died.

Although Bain had studied chemistry he made no claim to be a chemist. The knowledge he had acquired was nevertheless invaluable to him in the career which he made for himself. With typical courage, undaunted by his small beginnings and his physical misfortune, he seized his slender opportunity and turned it to success. Hard work and natural ability played their part, but they were informed and vitalized by a tremendous zest for life, which enabled him to bring a cheerful enthusiasm to everything he undertook. He played as hard as he worked, for he had many gifts and wide interests. He loved plays and poetry, and good talk of an evening with his friends, when he could always prove himself the master in any argument over Burns, Milton, or Shakespeare. Those friends were many, for 'Freddy's' cheerful and generous personality was magnetic. Informal and eminently approachable, he had a remarkable memory for names and a gift for leadership, which was never more happily exercised than in his devoted work for Toc H, particularly in Lancashire where he was a pioneer of the movement. Social work, politics (he was always a staunch Liberal), and the repertory theatre also claimed his vigorous attention while he was in Liverpool. In later years he travelled widely on business and at the time of his death he was one of the joint chairmen of the Anglo-American Council of Productivity. He was everywhere welcome and respected, but he received no recognition which he valued more than the honorary LLD of the University of Aberdeen awarded in 1950.

On 4 October 1921 Bain married Isabel Margaret Adeline, daughter of J. G. *Adami, vice-chancellor of the University of Liverpool. They had one son, after whose birth his wife unfortunately suffered almost continuously from ill health until her death in 1945.

Bain died in Westminster Hospital, London, on 23 November 1950, as the result of a fall on 14 November, which might have been insignificant had he not lacked an arm to save himself. J. D. PRATT, *rev.*

Sources private information (1959) • personal knowledge (1959) • m. cert. • d. cert. • W. J. Reader, *Imperial Chemical Industries, a history*, 2 (1975) • *The Times* (16 Nov 1950), 8g • *The Times* (24 Nov 1950), 8g • *The Times* (25 Nov 1950), 4c • *The Times* (27 Nov 1950), 8e • *The Times* (29 Nov 1950), 6d • *The Times* (4 Dec 1950), 8e
Likenesses W. Stoneman, photograph, 1947, NPG • J. Gunn, drawing, 1947–9, Federation of British Industries, London
Wealth at death £31,381 8s. 5d.: administration with will, 17 Jan 1951, *CGPLA Eng. & Wales*

Bain [*née* Burn], **Louisa** (1803–1883), diarist, was born on 30 January 1803 at 37 Kirby Street, London, the tenth of the twelve children of English parents Thomas Burn (*b.* 1760), bookbinder, and his wife, Elizabeth Dyer (*d.* 1828). From the ages of seven to twelve she was educated at a school at Claybrook House, Fulham. On 15 September 1825 she entered into a very satisfying marriage to James Bain (1794–1866), a London bookseller. She bore eight children, all of whom were to survive her: Elizabeth (*b.* 1828), Sarah Louisa (*b.* 1828), James (*b.* 1829), William (*b.* 1831), Lucy Jane (*b.* 1833), Thomas George (*b.* 1835), Margaret (*b.* 1839), and Mary Elizabeth (*b.* 1842). The Bains first lived at 8 Panton Street, Haymarket, then occupied a building at 1 Haymarket. For seventy-eight years James Bain's business, Bain's of the Haymarket, operated successfully by himself and later his sons James and Thomas, was to occupy those premises. The expanding family itself in 1839 moved to Hampstead, then to Highgate, where the family attended the parish church of St Martin-in-the-Fields. After James Bain died of bronchitis on 10 December 1867, Louisa and the children moved to Broxbourne. There she died on 21 January 1883, just short of her eightieth birthday, after an illness reported in her diary as dropsy. She was buried at Broxbourne.

From August 1857 until 5 January 1883, without intermission, Louisa Bain kept a diary, filling twenty-two manuscript volumes, in which she recorded in detail mainly matters concerning her family and domestic events but also a great many contemporary disasters, deaths, and executions in the public world and some more mundane public events. The diary remains in the possession of her family, though a selection of excerpts was published by her grandson James S. Bain as *A Bookseller Looks Back* (1940). Louisa called her diary 'Dry facts, no feelings' (Bain, 39); largely a dispassionate record of events and bare of introspection, it none the less communicates some sense of her responses to the course of her adult life and reveals her to have been interested in the family business and deeply devoted to her marriage and her children and grandchildren. The entries suggest a strong-minded and conventional, but also generous-natured, personality. An anonymous photograph included with the excerpts shows an elderly woman with unremarkable but pleasant features. HARRIET BLODGETT

Sources J. S. Bain, *A bookseller looks back: the story of the Bains* (1940)
Archives priv. coll.
Likenesses photograph, repro. in Bain, *A bookseller looks back*, 39

Bain, Robert Nisbet (1854–1909), translator and historian, was born on 18 November 1854 in London, the eldest son of David Bain (*d.* after 1912), Cape and India merchant, and his wife, Elizabeth, daughter of Robert Cowan of Liverpool. After education at private schools, he spent some years as a shorthand writer in the office of Messrs Henry Kimber & Co., a firm of solicitors at 79 Lombard Street. From an early age Bain showed a talent for languages and an interest in literature. His aptitude for languages was useful when he entered the department of printed books in the British Museum as a second-class assistant in 1883; he easily headed the list of candidates in the entrance examination. In due course he was promoted to first-class assistant (the earlier designation of assistant keeper).

Besides his official duties at the British Museum, which mainly consisted of selecting and cataloguing books in the lesser-known languages of Europe (that is, Slavonic, Scandinavian, and Finno-Ugrian), Bain found the time for serious study of the history and literature of these countries. While on a visit to Germany in the early 1880s, he came across a novel. 'The unfamiliar name of the author attracted me, and when the obliging and erudite bookseller enlightened my ignorance … I pocketed the volume, curious to discover what a Magyar's idea of a good novel might be.' After reading Mór Jókai's novel in German he 'there and then determined to learn Hungarian' in order to be able to read Jókai's novels in the original (Bain, 137). Bain followed up his momentary decision with great fortitude and became the most prolific translator of Hungarian fiction in the nineteenth century. Between 1891 and 1904 he translated nine full-length novels by Jókai and a volume of short stories, thereby being chiefly instrumental in introducing Jókai to the English reading public; some of his translations were in print for nearly twenty years in many editions. It was also via Hungarian that Bain translated the original Turkish folk-tales collected by Dr Ignác Kunos (1896).

Bain also translated from other languages, including Finnish (short stories by Juhan Aho, 1893), Danish (stories by J. L. I. Lie, 1893, and a selection of Andersen's fairy tales, 1893, which he followed up by a sympathetic treatment of his life, *Hans Christian Andersen*, 1895), Russian (stories by Tolstoy and Maksim Gorky 1901 and 1902), and others.

As a translator, Bain admired colourful narrative and exotic background, hence his predilection for folk-tales and arch-Romantic novelists, like the Hungarian Jókai. He often took liberties with the original, abridging or condensing it freely, with the tacit approval, if not at the initiation, of his chief publisher, Messrs Jarrold. Contemporary critics were apt to notice this practice: 'The translation is fluent and at times, indeed, too free' declared *The Athenaeum* (20 February 1892) about his first rendering of Jókai into English.

Besides his literary work Bain's output of historical writing was also voluminous. Of this most is devoted to seventeenth- and eighteenth-century Russian and Scandinavian history. Overviews of *Scandinavia, 1513–1900* (1905) and of *Slavonic Europe, 1447–1796* (1908) were published in the Cambridge Historical Series. Bain produced a volume on the rise of modern Russia under Peter the Great (*The First Romanovs, 1613–1728*, 1905) and other monographs of the same period. He contributed several chapters to the *Cambridge Modern History* (vols. 3, 5, 6, 11) on east European and Scandinavian history. His entries in the tenth and eleventh editions of the *Encyclopaedia Britannica* on the same subjects, including well-written biographies of leading historical and literary figures, withstood the test of time for about half a century, most of them being rewritten or replaced only in the 1960 edition.

Bain was forty-two years old when on 29 July 1896 he married his cousin, Caroline Margaret Boswell Cowan (1862/3–1909), daughter of Charles Cowan. In his youth Bain was a fairly good gymnast and lightweight boxer. He was a zealous high-churchman and in his later life he was for some years a sidesman and a regular attendant at St Alban's Church, Holborn. He travelled in Europe on several occasions, the last time in 1908 when he visited Germany and Switzerland for a few weeks' respite from his failing health. According to his contemporaries it was the constant hard work which characterized his whole life that was ultimately responsible for his premature death at the age of fifty-four on 5 May 1909 at 7 Overstrand Mansions, Battersea Park, but the official cause of death was stated to be heart failure and malignant disease of the liver. His burial took place in Brookwood cemetery on 8 May. LÓRÁNT CZIGÁNY

Sources L. G. Czigány, 'The reception of Hungarian literature in Great Britain from Bowring's *Poetry of the Magyars* to the novels of Jókai', PhD diss., U. Lond., 1965, 453 • L. Czigány, *A magyar irodalom*

fogadtatása a viktoriánus Angliában (1976), 287 • L. Czigány, 'A magyar irodalom az Encyclopaedia Britannica tükrében', *Új Látóhatár* (1961), 369–74 • R. N. Bain, 'Maurus Jókai', *Monthly Review*, 4/2 (1901), 137–52 • *The Times* (11 May 1909) • *The Athenaeum* (15 May 1909), 588 • *BL cat.* • m. cert. • d. cert.

Archives NL Scot., letters to Blackwoods

Wealth at death £759 3*s.* 7*d.*: probate, 27 May 1909, *CGPLA Eng. & Wales*

Bainard [Baynard], **Fulk** (*b.* in or before **1167**, *d.* in or after **1243**), justice and administrator, was the elder son of Fulk Bainard and his wife, Christina. He had succeeded his father by 1189, holding most of his lands as a subtenant of the Bainard honour in Norfolk, Essex, and Lincolnshire, but also holding of the Bothal barony in Northumberland. With his wife, Petronilla, daughter of Robert Mantel, he acquired land in Suffolk.

Bainard first appears in the legal records in the 1200s, acting as an attorney in several pleas before the king's justices in Norfolk and Hertfordshire. He also litigated on his own account, notably in a long-running dispute over his wardship of the heir of Roger of Kerdeston, who must have been one of his vassals. As himself a vassal of Robert Fitzwalter (*d.* 1235), lord of the Bainard honour, he was bound also to become embroiled in the political crisis of John's reign. After the collapse of Fitzwalter's conspiracy to kill the king in 1212, Bainard was forced in 1213 to surrender his son Robert to John as a hostage. Whatever perils may have ensued for Robert, his father enlisted in the 'army of God and Holy Church' of which Fitzwalter was self-proclaimed 'marshal'.

In 1217 Bainard's confiscated lands were restored to him by the minority regime of Henry III, which he afterwards served in several capacities, as an assessor of tallages and of the fifteenth of 1225, as a keeper of the king's escheats in Norfolk, as a controller of shipping into and out of King's Lynn, and, most notably, as a justice. He was appointed to take assizes in Norfolk, Suffolk, and Lincolnshire, and in 1226 was commissioned to try, at Norwich, prisoners charged with homicide. In the same year he was granted a weekly market for his manor of Merton. Bainard almost disappears from the printed administrative records after 1233. He is last mentioned alive ten years later, by which date he must have been at least seventy-six. He was succeeded by his son Robert, an elder son, Fulk, having predeceased him without issue.

Fulk Bainard is not mentioned in any chronicle; almost nothing would be known of his life if it were not for the sudden proliferation of governmental records from the reigns of Richard I and John. These give, for the first time, an impression of how royal government impinged upon the life of a substantial subtenant, and of the extent to which he was drawn into its processes, and therefore into the political life of the kingdom. GEORGE GARNETT

Sources L. Landon, 'The Bainard family in Norfolk', *Norfolk Archaeology*, 22 (1924–6), 209–20 • *Pipe rolls* • H. C. M. Lyte and others, eds., *Liber feodorum: the book of fees*, 3 vols. (1920–31) • *Chancery records* (RC) • PRO

Bainbridge, Christopher (1462/3–1514), ambassador, archbishop of York, and cardinal, was born at Hilton, near Appleby, Westmorland, the eldest of six children of Reginald Bainbridge and Isobel Langton; he owed much in his education and early advancement to his maternal uncle Thomas *Langton, bishop of Winchester. In 1479 he held a papal dispensation to hold any benefice with or without cure on reaching the age of sixteen, and obtained another in 1482, where he is described as about twenty, to hold an additional benefice. He was rector of St Leonard Eastcheap, London, from 26 October 1478 and a canon of Salisbury from 1486. A 'magister' by 1486, probably of Oxford, he was soon afterwards at Ferrara, where he witnessed the degrees of two German students in May 1487 and May 1488 respectively, and at Bologna, where he was admitted DCL on 24 October 1492 (later he is also recorded as DCnL); he was in Rome in 1492–4, becoming in January 1493 a chamberlain of the English Hospice, from which he rented a house. Provost of Queen's College, Oxford (confirmed on 22 June 1496), he also served as a judge in the court of requests (1498–9) and as master of the rolls (from 13 November 1504); he was incorporated at Lincoln's Inn on 20 January 1505. A chaplain of Henry VII by 1497, he rose steadily in the ecclesiastical hierarchy; he was dean of York (21 December 1503) and of St George's Chapel, Windsor (28 November 1505) until provided to the see of Durham on 27 August 1507. He resigned Durham on being translated to York on 22 September 1508, where his archiepiscopal register survives. He was an executor of Henry VII's will and attended the coronation of Henry VIII.

Bainbridge's appointment on 24 September 1509 as Henry VIII's ambassador to Pope Julius II initiated the final and most significant stage of his career. His main job was to embolden the papacy against France and in favour of England; he remained inflexibly tied to this purpose, in spite of set-backs. When he arrived in Rome on 24 November 1509 the Venetian cardinals and ambassadors sought his support in persuading the pope to break up the League of Cambrai against Venice and to lift the interdict from that state; they found him over-cautious and suspected that his main purpose was to get the red hat, but by February 1510 they were appreciative of the help he had given. Julius II's change of policy and breach with the duke of Ferrara, an ally of Louis XII of France, was advantageous to Bainbridge, who accompanied the pope in August 1510 on his long military campaign against the duke in Romagna and on 17 March 1511 was raised to the cardinalate at Ravenna (with the title of San Pietro e Marcellino); the appointment expressed Julius II's own need to count upon Henry VIII's support against France. In November 1511 England joined the Holy League and by March 1512 a papal brief was drawn up transferring Louis XII's title as 'Most Christian King' to Henry VIII; this would be released to Bainbridge when Louis XII had been defeated, but that prospect became more remote in the summer when the English military expedition to Guyenne proved disastrous.

Bainbridge continued his belligerent policy after Leo X's election in March 1513; he strenuously opposed the readmission of the French and other cardinals who had called a council at Pisa against Julius II, and celebrated the Swiss victory against the French at Novara in June and Henry VIII's victories at Thérouanne in August and Flodden in October. Throughout the winter of 1513–14 he was counting on the formation of a decisive Anglo-imperial alliance against France, and the conferment of the French crown and titles upon Henry VIII; he hoped to accompany Maximilian to a summit meeting at Calais and then to return to England with legatine powers. All this came to nothing, thanks in part to the secret counter-diplomacy of Wolsey, Cardinal Adriano Castellesi, and Silvestro Gigli, bishop of Worcester, who had become ambassador of Henry VIII in Rome in 1512. Bainbridge was nevertheless acclaimed shortly after his death for his steadfastness, his exceptional loyalty, and his vehement defence of the king's interests, in a letter of Richard Pace to Henry VIII on 25 September 1514. As well as his energetic diplomacy, Bainbridge's duties in Rome on behalf of the English crown and clergy had also included taking charge of the English Hospice (from 1510 it was governed by his protégés, particularly his secretaries William Burbank and Pace), sponsoring in the papal consistory candidates for major benefices, and defending cases in the rota, the papal court of appeal. He also made some efforts to look after the affairs of his own diocese. Before he left England he had set up a commission to manage its administration, and subsequently reinforced its workings by instructions and favours sent from Rome, for instance granting an indulgence for contributions to the repair of St Wilfrid's Church, Ripon, on 1 June 1512.

As a curial cardinal Bainbridge had additional duties. He was immediately made legate to the papal army in the campaign against Ferrara, and on 22 March 1511 left Ravenna to join the forces assembling near Lugo with a plan of attack on a key fortress, the Bastia del Fossato Zaniolo. Because of bad weather and floods the campaign was abandoned at the end of April; Bainbridge then joined the army defending Bologna from the north. In mid-May he warned the city's administration of the worsening situation because of the army's lack of food and supplies; on 21 May Bologna fell, owing to an internal coup and the perfidy of Cardinal Alidosi, but this military failure was no fault of Bainbridge's. He received from Julius II the governorship of Vetralla, near Viterbo (15 October 1511), where a plaque survives bearing the papal and royal arms with those of Bainbridge; he was also given the presbyteral title church of Santa Prassede (22 December 1511) and the priory of Sant'Antonio, Reggio Emilia (19 June 1512). Bainbridge took part in the papal election in March 1513, receiving two votes in the first scrutiny and casting his own vote for Fabrizio del Carretto (not a member of the Sacred College); soon after being elected, Leo X conferred upon him the monastery of San Stefano, Bologna, and in July 1513 several benefices near Vicenza. He attended the first session of the Fifth Lateran Council (3 June 1513), being appointed to serve on two of its committees concerned with reform of the papal court. He was made protector of the Cistercian order (November 1513), in which capacity he tried to resolve a scandal at Sant'Ambrogio, Milan. In 1514 he was elected chamberlain (finance officer for one year) of the College of Cardinals.

In spite of living in the heyday of Renaissance Rome, Bainbridge appears to have been little interested in humanist scholarship or contemporary Italian art, though he was highly praised as a generous patron by his secretary and executor Richard Pace, who dedicated to him his translations of essays by Plutarch, and he took over the sponsorship of 'Pasquino' from 1512 to 1514, paying for the annual publication of topical verses attached to a battered antique statue outside his Roman residence (on the site of the later Palazzo Braschi, near piazza Navona). There is no evidence to support the anecdotal account of Bainbridge's violent cruelty by Girolamo Garimberto, accepted by later writers, although he may well have been a belligerent negotiator and over-forceful advocate. In his English will he made benefactions to Queen's College, Oxford, and there is evidence he planned to found a school partly from the revenues of San Stefano, Bologna; but the Roman will which he had papal permission to make has not been found. It is known that he possessed silver plate, rich vestments and tapestries, and a large sum in cash at his death (a fellow cardinal reported it to be about 9000 scudi), but his only surviving tangible items of property are an incomplete archiepiscopal service book according to English use, with musical notation (Cambridge University Library, MS ff.vi.1), and a pair of silver candle snuffers decorated with Henry VIII's arms and his own arms surmounted by the cardinal's hat (British Museum, MLA 1878, 112–30 633). Whether his death on 14 July 1514 was the direct result of poison, administered by a servant, Raimondo da Modena, at the instigation of Silvestro Gigli, has not been clearly established; there may have been other contributory causes, though Raimondo confessed his guilt under torture and later committed suicide. Bainbridge's funeral was celebrated lavishly on 31 July 1514 in the chapel of the English Hospice, now the English College at Rome, via Monserrato, where his marble tomb, with a recumbent effigy, remains. His career stands out as that of the only English prelate to become a resident cardinal of the curia, with an insider's understanding of its practices and acquaintance with many of its members, in the century and a half before the breach with Rome.

D. S. Chambers

Sources Emden, *Oxf.*, 1.91–3 • *LP Henry VIII*, vol. 1 • *CEPR letters*, vols. 12–14, 16 • D. S. Chambers, *Cardinal Bainbridge in the court of Rome, 1509 to 1514* (1965) [very full list of MS sources] • R. P. Brown, 'Thomas Langton and his tradition of learning', *Transactions of the Cumberland and Westmorland Antiquarian and Archaeological Society*, new ser., 26 (1925–6), 150–246 • B. Newns, 'The hospice of St Thomas and the English crown, 1474–1538', *The Venerabile*, 21 (1962) [sexcentenary issue: *The English hospice in Rome*] • *I diarii di Marino Sanuto*, ed. F. Stefani and others, 9–18 (Venice, 1883–7) • G. B. Parks, *The English traveler to Italy* (1954) • G. Garimberto, *La primaparte delle vite, overo fatti memorabili d'alcuni papi e di tutti i cardinali passati* (1565) • R. Cessi, *Dispacci degli ambasciatori Veneziani ala corte di Roma presso Giulio II* (1932) • C. Eubel and others, eds., *Hierarchia Catholica medii aevi*, 3, ed. W. van Gulik, C. Eubel, and L. Schmitz-Kallenberg (Münster, 1910)

Archives Österreichisches Staatsarchiv, Vienna, Haus-, Hof-, und Staatsarchiv, MS letters with autograph signature • Archivio di Stato, Bologna, MS letters with autograph signature • Archivio di Stato, Mantua, MS letters with autograph signature • Archivio di Stato, Milan, MS letters with autograph signature • BL, MS letters with autograph signature, Cotton MS Vitellius B.II • BM, pair of silver candle snuffers, MLA 1878, 112–30 633 • Borth. Inst., archepiscopal register • CUL, *Liber pontificalis* (service book) • PRO, MS letters with autograph signature, SP 1/4, SP 1/8

Likenesses Alinari, photograph (of tomb effigy), repro. in Parks, *English traveller to Italy*, pl. 11 • N. Parr, line engraving, NPG • marble effigy on tomb monument, chapel of the Venerable English College, via Monserrato, Rome • photograph (of tomb effigy), repro. in *The Venerabile*, 21 (1962), facing p. 202

Wealth at death est. 8000–9000 scudi: Chambers, *Cardinal Bainbridge*, 125–30

Bainbridge, Emerson Muschamp (1817–1892), department store owner, was born on 25 August 1817 in Eastgate, Weardale, co. Durham, the youngest child in the family of two sons and five daughters of Cuthbert Bainbridge (1772–1850), a farmer, and his wife, Mary Muschamp (1774–1850), the youngest child of Emerson Muschamp of Brotherlee, near Eastgate, bailiff to the bishop of Durham. His parents were devout Methodists.

Bainbridge was educated at Eastgate village school, and from 1830 to 1835 was apprenticed to Thomas Kidd, a draper, of The Side, Newcastle upon Tyne. After spending two years in London working for Lewis and Allenby, a famous silk and shawl warehouse in Regent Street, Bainbridge returned to Newcastle in 1838. There he joined W. Alder Dunn in setting up a woollen and linen drapery business at 12 and 14 Market Street, in the newly developed city centre, opposite Grainger Market. On 22 August 1839 he married Anne (Annie) Hudson (1821–1902), the second daughter of Thomas Hudson, a tanner, of Newcastle. They had fifteen children, ten of whom survived childhood.

From the outset the new drapery business was innovative. Dunn and Bainbridge marked their goods with fixed prices, which was less intimidating for the customer than was the old practice of individual bargaining, and they extended the range of goods, moving into 'novelties' such as gloves, stockings, and ribbons, and cords and tassels to go with their household fabrics. In 1841 the partnership was dissolved, with Dunn continuing to trade next door while Bainbridge operated from 12 Market Street, which he named Albert House. Bainbridge went into partnership with his cousin John Bell Muschamp, and the firm continued to expand the range of its merchandise, so that by 1845 their stock included mourning clothes, furs, and ready-made muslin dresses. In 1846 Bainbridge and Muschamp bought 11 Market Street and opened a 'French room', with goods imported from Paris. In an advertisement of 1846 they stated that 'Bainbridge and Muschamp are resolved that they will not be undersold by any House in the Kingdom'. By 1849 there were twenty-three separate departments, making Bainbridge's probably the first department store in the world, predating Au Bon Marché of Paris, which opened in 1852 and was the model for American stores in the 1860s.

The expansion continued in the 1850s. Bainbridge and Muschamp began to manufacture clothes on the premises, and in 1852 they bought two more adjoining shops and moved into men's ready-made clothing. The partnership with John Bell Muschamp ended in 1855, and from then on the business was called Bainbridge & Co. Bainbridge was successful partly because he was able to take advantage of the growth of the city centre and the expansion of the lower middle classes, who flocked into his store, eager to benefit from the lower prices, high quality, and wide range of drapery and haberdashery products. In 1865 he bought a 500 foot block of buildings behind Market Street, and a few years later he knocked them down and built a new store, four storeys high. He added a carpet-planning showroom in 1881 and a new building to house his carpet-beating machinery in 1884, and in 1885 he bought the Coach and Horses inn in Bigg Market, demolished it, and built a new furniture department. He extended the business to Leeds in 1883, when he bought a factory there to manufacture boys' and men's clothing, and in 1889 he moved his boot and shoe manufacturing business to the city, where by 1892 he employed a staff of nearly one thousand.

At the 1887 Jubilee Exhibition in Newcastle, Bainbridge & Co. set up a sumptuous house-furnishing exhibit. Bainbridge installed electric light in his store in 1890, and it was one of his employees who invented the 'Ariel messengers' to carry cash through the store by overhead tubes. By 1892 Bainbridge's employed a staff of 600 in Newcastle, and the store had 11,705 square yards of floor space. Shopping at Bainbridge's was seen as a pleasurable social activity, and the store offered not only a wide range of goods but also services such as funeral arrangements and house removals. Bainbridge had a paternalistic attitude towards his staff. He housed many of his workers in special accommodation, and before his death in 1892 he had established a benevolent society, offering sickness and holiday benefits, social activities, and sports teams.

Brought up in a Methodist household, Bainbridge became a Methodist lay preacher and a leading member of the Brunswick Place Methodist Chapel in Newcastle, and he was active in the temperance movement. He preferred to employ Methodists, often from the lead-mining districts of co. Durham. As his wealth increased he was able to build in the late 1860s a large family house in Newcastle, Leazes Villa, and to buy in 1877 a 1775 acre country estate, Eshott, near Fenton, Northumberland. Here, at Eshott Hall, he lived the life of a country gentleman. He made additions to the house, including a tower, improved the land, built labourers' cottages, erected a chapel, and started a library, and he enjoyed game shooting as a sport. At the same time he continued to be actively involved in the business, and his energy remained remarkable. Bainbridge was a director of the Consett Iron Company and of several collieries. He was a Liberal and served as a JP.

Bainbridge died at Eshott Hall on 21 February 1892 after suffering a stroke. Three of his four surviving sons, Thomas Hudson Bainbridge (1842–1912), George Bargate Bainbridge (1850–1944), and Arthur Emerson Bainbridge

(1862–1930), had joined the firm, and in his will Bainbridge left them each a third share in the business. Another son, Emerson Muschamp *Bainbridge (1845–1911), became a colliery manager and owner. The firm continued to prosper under the second and third generations of the family. George Bargate Bainbridge served as chairman until his death in 1944; and his son, (George) Aubrey Bainbridge (1881–1950), was managing director of Bainbridge & Co. until 1946. However, the firm ran into difficulties during the 1930s, and in 1938 Bainbridge's of Leeds went into liquidation.

The only member of the fourth generation of the family to enter the business was **George Vivian Muschamp Bainbridge** (1910–1976). Born on 15 November 1910 at Lough House, Benridge, Morpeth, Northumberland, he was the elder of the two sons of (George) Aubrey Bainbridge of Morpeth and his first wife, Mary, the daughter of Robert Atkinson Turnbull, a dentist, of Newcastle upon Tyne, and the great-grandson of Emerson Muschamp Bainbridge (1817–1892). Having read modern languages and psychology at Christ's College, Cambridge (*c.*1929–1932), he entered the business in 1932 and the following year was one of four new directors appointed to the board. On 8 February 1934 he married Pamela Ann Fenwick (*b.* 1913/14), the youngest daughter of Frederick Burnand *Fenwick of Newcastle upon Tyne, the son of John James *Fenwick, founder of Fenwick's department store [*see under* Fenwick family (*per.* 1882–1979)]. Bainbridge was in the Territorial Army and served with distinction in the Royal Artillery during the Second World War, reaching the rank of major. After the war he found time for voluntary work, serving as chairman of a number of organizations in the north-east, including the Murray House community centre and youth club, the Northumberland and Tyneside Council of Social Service, and the Byker community development project.

Bainbridge and his cousin Bill Sanderson became joint managing directors of the business in 1948 under the chairmanship of Sir Robert Burrows (who was married to the daughter of Arthur Emerson Bainbridge, the son of the founder of the firm); but without large amounts of capital it was impossible to revitalize the business, and in 1952 Bainbridge's was sold to the John Lewis Partnership. With the help of capital investment from John Lewis, Bainbridge later modernized the store and by the time of his retirement in 1974 he had built Bainbridge's up to be one of the leading department stores in the country. When new premises were opened in the Eldon Square shopping centre in Newcastle upon Tyne in 1976, Bainbridge's became the largest John Lewis store outside London. Bainbridge was appointed OBE in 1974. He died on 29 April 1976 and was buried on 4 May at the parish church at Corbridge, Northumberland. ANNE PIMLOTT BAKER

Sources A. Airey and J. Airey, *The Bainbridges of Newcastle: a family history, 1679–1976* (1979) · B. Lancaster, *The department store: a social history* (1995) · A. Airey, 'Bainbridge, Emerson Muschamp', *DBB* · J. Goodchild, 'Bainbridge, Emerson Muschamp', *DBB* · *The Journal* [Newcastle upon Tyne] (30 April 1976) · A. Adburgham, *Shops and shopping, 1800–1914: where, and in what manner the well-dressed Englishwoman bought her clothes*, 2nd edn (1981) · M. J. Winstanley, *The shopkeeper's world* (1983) · m. cert. · d. cert. · b. cert. [G. V. M. Bainbridge] · m. cert. [G. V. M. Bainbridge] · *Cambridge historical register*

Likenesses M. Rizzello, bronze bas relief; known to be at Bainbridge's, Eldon Way, Newcastle in 1976 · photograph (G. V. M. Bainbridge), repro. in Airey and Airey, *Bainbridges of Newcastle*, 189 · portrait, repro. in *DBB*, vol. 1, p. 102; priv. coll.

Wealth at death £407,715 0s. 7*d.*—E. M. Bainbridge: resworn probate, 1893, *CGPLA Eng. & Wales* · £29,760—G. V. M. Bainbridge: probate, 14 June 1976, *CGPLA Eng. & Wales*

Bainbridge, Emerson Muschamp (1845–1911), mining engineer and colliery owner, was born on 23 December 1845 in Portland Place, Newcastle upon Tyne, the third son and fourth child in the family of fifteen children (ten of whom survived childhood) of Emerson Muschamp *Bainbridge (1817–1892), founder of the department store Bainbridge & Co. in Newcastle, and his wife, Anne (Annie; 1821–1902), daughter of Thomas Hudson, tanner, of Newcastle. He was the only son not to join the family business. He was educated at Edenfield House, Doncaster, and Wesley College, Sheffield. He served an apprenticeship at the marquess of Londonderry's collieries in co. Durham while studying mathematics and mining engineering at the University of Durham. In 1867 Bainbridge was chosen to report to the North of England Institute of Mining Engineers on the haulage of coal, and in 1869 he was awarded a prize by the Institution of Civil Engineers for a paper on the feasibility of working coal at a depth of 4000 feet. He also won the Hermon prize in 1874 for a paper on the prevention of colliery explosions.

In 1870 Bainbridge was appointed manager of the duke of Norfolk's collieries in Sheffield and Tinsley. On 9 April 1874 he married Elizabeth Jefferson ('Jeffie'; *d.* 1892), daughter of G. J. Armstrong of Manchester, and sister of his late brother Cuthbert's widow. They had two sons and two daughters, but one son and one daughter died in childhood. Also in 1874 Bainbridge became managing director of the Nunnery Colliery Company Ltd, which belonged to the duke of Norfolk. Additionally he was appointed head of Bainbridge and Seymour, a firm of consulting mining engineers in London which collaborated in plans to build a ship canal to Sheffield. He founded Bolsover colliery, a limited company near Chesterfield mining pits in Derbyshire and Nottinghamshire, in 1889, and he was a director of several other collieries. He was a member of the royal commission on coal dust in mines in 1891, and a juror at the Brussels exposition in 1897. He was also involved in the development of the railways, and was chairman of the Lancashire, Derbyshire, and East Coast Railway. A Liberal and supporter of home rule, Bainbridge was elected MP for the Gainsborough division of Lincolnshire in 1895, and remained in the House of Commons until his defeat in the 1900 election.

Bainbridge, like his father, was a Methodist, and became chairman of the Federation of Free Churches. He was also a very rich man and devoted a considerable part of his wealth to charitable causes. He built a miners' orphanage in Bolsover in 1894, and established a model village there. At Seaford in Sussex he started a holiday home for factory women, and in Sheffield he founded a home for waifs and strays. He also supported the West London Mission, the YMCA, and the Salvation Army, and established a 'Start in Life' fund at the London Polytechnic. Bainbridge was a keen salmon fisherman, and rented a stretch of salmon river in Norway every year. He bought a Scottish estate, Auchnashellach, in Ross-shire, with a 40,000 acre deer forest.

Bainbridge's wife, Jeffie, died in 1892, and on 20 July 1898 he married his daughter's schoolfriend Norah Mossom (*b*. 1880?), daughter of J. Compton Merryweather of Whitehall Court, London. They had a son and a daughter. They built a villa at Roquebrune, near Menton, on the French riviera, and after Bainbridge's death Norah spent much time there, and with her second husband, Captain George Francis Warre, created a magnificent garden. Bainbridge died of double pneumonia at his London home, 47 Upper Grosvenor Street, on 12 May 1911. He was buried at Brookwood cemetery, Surrey, on 15 May 1911.

ANNE PIMLOTT BAKER

Sources A. Airey and J. Airey, *The Bainbridges of Newcastle: a family history, 1679–1976* (1979) • A. Airey, 'Bainbridge, Emerson Muschamp', *DBB* • *The Times* (13 May 1911) • *CGPLA Eng. & Wales* (1911) • *WWBMP* • m. certs. • b. cert.

Likenesses photographs, repro. in Airey and Airey, *The Bainbridges of Newcastle*, 97, 99

Wealth at death £461,769 4*s*. 7*d*.: resworn probate, June 1911, *CGPLA Eng. & Wales*

Bainbridge, Francis Arthur (1874–1921), physiologist, was born on 29 July 1874 at Stockton-on-Tees, co. Durham, the elder son of Robert Robinson Bainbridge, a chemist, and his wife, Mary Sanderson. Educated at the Leys School, Cambridge, where his contemporaries included Joseph Barcroft and Henry Dale, he gained an entrance scholarship to Trinity College, Cambridge, in 1893. He studied physiology and took a first class in both parts of the natural sciences tripos (1895 and 1897). He then entered St Bartholomew's Hospital, London, to complete his medical training, obtaining his Cambridge MB degree in 1901 and the MD in 1904.

At this period medicine did not appeal to Bainbridge, and seeing no permanent opening in pure physiology, he devoted himself for a time to pathology and bacteriology. In 1905 he became Gordon lecturer on pathology at Guy's Hospital, where he began studies on urine secretion by the frog kidney, to which he was to return later. In the same year he married Hilda Winifred, daughter of the Revd Edward Thornton Smith, of Bickley, Kent, with whom he had one daughter. In 1907 he went as assistant bacteriologist to the Lister Institute of Preventive Medicine, where his study and classification of paratyphoid and food-poisoning bacilli gained wide recognition, and formed the basis of his Milroy lectures at the Royal College of Physicians (1912). Throughout this period he had carried out research in the physiological laboratory at University College, encouraged particularly by Ernest Starling. In 1911 Bainbridge became professor of physiology at Durham University and was able to devote himself to physiology. Bainbridge joined the RAMC in 1914 and combined the duties of his chair with those of a medical officer at a local hospital. In 1915, when a chair of physiology was instituted at St Bartholomew's Hospital, he returned to London to fill the post, which he occupied until his premature death, at his home, 37 Clarence Gate Gardens, London, on 27 October 1921. He was elected FRS in 1919.

Bainbridge was of slight physique and had indifferent health. He was not regarded as an impressive teacher, though his lucidity of mind rendered him a very successful one. However, he was a brilliant experimenter, who gave careful thought beforehand to proposed research, and possessed both ingenuity in devising experiments and high technical skill in carrying them out. Thus his contributions to physiological science were of lasting value. Among these were his early work on the activity of lymph gland cells and the mechanism of lymph formation, on urinary secretion and the effect of partial removal of the kidneys, and on the physiology of the gall bladder, and his studies on the circulation. In this last work he established that an increase of pressure on the venous side of the heart acted as a stimulus, which through the nervous system accelerated the rate of the beat, a control mechanism he discovered to be partly due to depression of the vagus nerve, and partly due to the stimulation of the sympathetic supply to the heart. Apart from numerous scientific papers, Bainbridge produced a scholarly monograph on *The Physiology of Muscular Exercise* (1919), a masterly review of the subject, and with his former colleague from Durham, J. A. Menzies, wrote *Essentials of Physiology* (1914). F. W. ANDREWES, *rev*. E. M. TANSEY

Sources H. H. D. [H. Dale], *PRS*, 93B (1922), xxiv–xxvi • *The Lancet* (5 Nov 1921), 980–81 • C. S. Sherrington, *PRS*, 93B (1922), 5 [presidential address] • *The Times* (29 Oct 1921) • *WWW, 1916–28* • personal knowledge (1927) • W. J. O'Connor, *British physiologists, 1885–1914* (1991) • private information (1927)

Wealth at death £10,334 9*s*. 7*d*.: probate, 13 Dec 1921, *CGPLA Eng. & Wales*

Bainbridge, George Vivian Muschamp (1910–1976). *See under* Bainbridge, Emerson Muschamp (1817–1892).

Bainbridge, John (1582–1643), astronomer and physician, was born in Ashby-de-la-Zouch, Leicestershire, the son of Robert Bainbridge and his wife, Anne, daughter of Richard Everard. He was educated first at the grammar school there, and then at Emmanuel College, Cambridge, where he was admitted as a pensioner in the Lent term, 1600. His tutor is said to have been a distant relative, Joseph Hall. He proceeded BA in 1603–4 and MA in 1607. He received his MD in 1614. He returned to Ashby, where, for a while, he practised medicine, but eventually moved to London, near the church of All Hallows, London Wall, where he was licensed by the College of Physicians on 6 November 1618.

It is evident that Bainbridge had also been studying astronomy and some geometry, for the year after the great comet of 1618 there appeared his first book, *An Astronomicall Description of the Late Comet*, dedicated to King

James. This was a semi-popular work, Bainbridge leaving the technical details of his observations to his 'Latine cosmography', which was never published and does not survive. There are indications, in the sophistication of his work and correspondence immediately following publication of the former book, that by itself it does not do justice to the level of understanding he had already attained. Bainbridge had become acquainted with Henry Briggs and Henry Savile by late 1618, even before the book was published. Perhaps Briggs, already a noted mathematician, helped to bring Bainbridge to the notice of Savile, who had him appointed the first Savilian professor of astronomy at Oxford (and Briggs the first Savilian professor of geometry), in 1620; the two men went up to Merton College that year, and remained there until their deaths. Bainbridge became well established as a teacher and practitioner in his old profession as well, for, having been incorporated MD at Oxford in 1620, he was appointed junior, and then senior, reader of Linacre's lecture, in 1631 and 1635, and medical prescriptions survive among his later papers. It seems that he remained in Merton Street in Oxford for the remainder of his life, moving, on his marriage, from the college to lodgings across the street. His remaining publications, though small and few, reveal an acute intellect and deep learning.

His surviving work, in print and manuscript, provides evidence of Bainbridge's opinions on various matters: he clearly accepted the modern view that comets were supralunar, and condemned 'Those Philosophers, who still walke in the way of the Gentiles, are afraide to induce generation, or any other mutation into the heavens, rather choosing to follow their blinde guide [Aristotle]' (Bainbridge, 24); he was not a proponent of Ptolemy's geocentric universe; and he maintained an ambivalent view of astrology, for the early book contains certain 'Morall prognosticks of applications of the late comet or blazing-starre'. Yet he later also wrote 'Antiprognosticks, in which is briefly detected the vanity of Astrological predictions', which remained in manuscript.

At Oxford, Bainbridge prepared lectures in astronomy, as required by the Savilian statutes, and the surviving notes record his expressions of the latest developments in astronomy, including the theoretical work of Johannes Kepler. He prepared the *editio princeps* of (most of) Ptolemy's *Planetary Hypotheses*, published in 1620 in a volume that also contained Proclus's *Sphaira*. The textual reconstructions of the former have been highly praised by modern scholars. In the mid-1620s he took up the study of Arabic, with a view to the recovery, from medieval Arabic sources, of ancient astronomical observations. He made close and perceptive study of the contents of several Arabic astronomical books. This was not an isolated effort; he sought assistance from others, especially scholars in the Low Countries.

Applying his astronomical knowledge to chronology, a major field of scholarly endeavour in the period, Bainbridge made manifest numerous errors in Joseph Scaliger's explanation of the origins of the Julian calendar in the ancient Egyptian observations of the rising of Sirius, the dog star. His work on this subject was posthumously published, as *Canicularia* (1648), by his old student, colleague, and friend John Greaves, who succeeded him as Savilian professor of astronomy. The matrix of scholars that included Bainbridge, Briggs, and Savile also included Sir Christopher Heydon and James Ussher, archbishop of Armagh, with whom Bainbridge formed a close friendship and to whom, upon his death, he left his papers.

Bainbridge and his wife, Mary, had a son and a daughter who survived to maturity. He died at his home on 3 November 1643 and was buried in Merton College chapel. The college erected a large monument to him, with a long inscription composed by Greaves, who there memorialized Bainbridge's refutation of Scaliger. Mary Bainbridge had died, intestate, by 1646, in which year Greaves was deeply entangled in legal wrangling over the estate.

Bainbridge's character can be known only from his writings and the kind of life that he led. His legacy to a succeeding generation of astronomers lay in his skilful reconstruction of important astronomical texts from antiquity and his inspiring others, in particular Greaves, to extend his own efforts of recovery of astronomical texts from Arabic sources. An anecdote in Walter Pope's life of Seth Ward pokes fun at Bainbridge's command of Latin, but this, if true, evidently alludes to a mere slip of the pen in a lecture notice concerning Proclus's *Sphaira*. A. J. Apt

Sources Wood, *Ath. Oxon.* • G. J. Toomer, *Eastern wisedome and learning: the study of Arabic in seventeenth-century England* (1996), 72–5 • A. J. Apt, 'Kepler's astronomy in England', DPhil diss., U. Oxf., 1982, 188–99 • Venn, *Alum. Cant.* • A. Grafton, *Joseph Scaliger: a study in the history of classical scholarship*, 2 (1993), 207–8, 727 • J. Bainbridge, *An astronomical description of the late comet* (1619); facs. edn (1975) • A. Bott, *The monuments in Merton College chapel* (1964), 82–3 • M. Feingold, ed., *Before Newton: the life and times of Isaac Barrow* (1990), 294 • *The whole works of … James Ussher*, ed. C. R. Elrington and J. H. Todd, 17 vols. (1847–64), vol. 15, pp. 351–3 • 22 April 1646, PRO, ADMON, PROB 6/21, 46

Archives Bodl. Oxf. • TCD | Bodl. Oxf., letters to H. Baskerville and W. Snell

Bainbridge [Bainbrigg], **Thomas** (*bap.* **1574**, *d.* **1646**), college head, was the son of Edward Bainbrig (*c.*1508–1584), clothier of Hawkin Hall, Middleton, in Kirkby Lonsdale, Westmorland. Thomas, the younger son of his father's marriage to his second wife, Elizabeth Hodgson (*d.* 1590), was baptized on 18 February 1574 at Kirkby Lonsdale. Several members of the family attended Christ's, including Thomas's half-brother Christopher (fellow, 1574–84), who appears later to have bought out Thomas's share of their father's properties. Bainbridge matriculated pensioner from Christ's College in 1593; he graduated BA in 1597 and by Michaelmas 1599 was a fellow of his college. He proceeded MA in 1600, and he or a namesake incorporated at Oxford in 1603. His BD is not recorded, but he was made DD in 1617. From 1618 he was rector of Icklesham, Sussex, where he never lived. At Cambridge he attracted no attention save when in 1602 he was accused by two of his colleagues of immorality, a charge they were unable to substantiate. Despite, or because of, his unobtrusive character, he was elected master of Christ's on 26 May 1622;

there was apparently no contest, and his promotion may have been owed simply to his seniority. Nevertheless, on acquiring authority he developed a taste for its exercise, and would be reckoned a martinet for insisting on a rigorous performance by the fellows of their statutory duties.

Bainbridge has received most notice from the biographers of Milton, who was an undergraduate of Christ's during his mastership. Milton's rustication in Lent term 1626 would certainly have had the master's sanction, but the story that the delinquent was personally thrashed by the head of house is a fanciful elaboration, incompatible with the realities of discipline. Nor is there any evidence that Bainbridge directly impeded Milton's candidacy for a fellowship, thereby (as some have alleged) turning him against the Anglican establishment. But Bainbridge was certainly no friend of the radical young man, and on a later occasion was said to be ready to 'remove a couple of lawless persons' to find room in the college for young men of the better sort (Masson, 1.183n.). He also cultivated contacts at court. He had voted for the duke of Buckingham in the chancellorship election of 1626, and when the new chancellor duly went to Cambridge in March 1627 it was reported by Joseph Meade of Christ's that 'somebody' (presumed to be the master) 'will scarce worship any other God, as long as [the duke] is in town' (Williams, 1.202). In 1627/8 Bainbridge served as vice-chancellor, and so had the even more congenial duty of hosting the king himself on a visit in the Lent term. Later in 1628 he was involved in the controversy over the subversive lectures given, at the instigation of Lord Brooke, by Isaac Dorislaus.

Following Buckingham's assassination on 23 August 1628 Bainbridge wrote a personal letter to Charles I in which he described the university as 'so stownded' by the 'unexpressable disaster' that it would be a lifeless body until the king resurrected it with the nomination of a new chancellor (PRO, SP 16/114, no. 60). Despite seeming so well affected to the crown, Bainbridge was judged one of Cambridge's 'learned neutrals' in the 1640s, and was able to retain his place when most other heads of houses were ejected (Peile, *Christ's*, 131–2). His mastership was distinguished by the erection of the Fellows' Building and other works. He died in office, and was buried in the church of St Andrew the Great, opposite the college, on 9 September 1646.

Bainbridge's widow, Mary, lived until February 1671. He was also survived by sons Thomas and Edward (the latter an undergraduate at Christ's in his father's last years), and unmarried daughters Elizabeth, Mary, and Susan. He made careful arrangements to ensure that lands he held from the college in the Cambridgeshire villages of Bourn, Impington, and Cottenham would remain vested in his family, appointing the bishop of Exeter (Ralph Brownrigg), the masters of Corpus and Emmanuel (Richard Love and Richard Holdsworth), and Thomas Buick, one of the university bedells, as his feoffees. To the college itself, his 'best nurse and mother', he bequeathed £50, equivalent to the sum which had been spent on bringing a new cut of the river to the college grounds. His books were to be divided between his two sons. Other children died before he made his will, but the colourful story that he married at the age of sixty and then fathered an extensive family seems rather to attach to his father. C. S. Knighton

Sources Venn, *Alum. Cant.*, 1/1.69 • J. Peile, *Biographical register of Christ's College, 1505–1905, and of the earlier foundation, God's House, 1448–1505*, ed. [J. A. Venn], 1 (1910), 207 • *CSP dom.*, 1627–8, 189; 1631–3, 116 • PRO, SP 16/114, no. 60 • BL, Add. MS 5821, fols. 66v, 67 • T. Warton, *The life … of Ralph Bathurst* (1761), 153n. • D. Masson, *The life of John Milton*, 7 vols. (1859–94), vol. 1, pp. 122–3, 160, 167, 181, 183n., 187; vol. 3, p. 93 • W. R. Parker, *Milton: a biography*, 2 vols. (1968), vol. 1, pp. 25, 36, 39, 42; vol. 2, pp. 726 n.6, 729 n.20 • will, CUL, department of manuscripts and university archives, vice-chancellor's court will register III (1602–58), fols. 277–279v • J. B. Mullinger, *The University of Cambridge*, 3 (1911), 15, 57, 295 n.3, 302, 352 • J. Peile, *Christ's College* (1900), 131–3, 149, 152 • [T. Birch and R. F. Williams], eds., *The court and times of Charles the First*, 1 (1848), 202 • R. P. Brown, 'Bainbrig of Hawkin in Middleton, Westmorland', *Transactions of the Cumberland and Westmorland Antiquarian and Archaeological Society*, new ser., 24 (1923–4), 123–48

Archives PRO, letters to Edward Conway, secretary of state, to Charles I, to Viscount Dorchester, secretary of state, SP 16/64, no. 48; 16/114, no. 60; 16/197, no. 8

Wealth at death held lands in Bourne, Cottenham, and Impington, Cambridgeshire; pecuniary bequests in excess of £650, incl. £50 to college: CUL, department of manuscripts and university archives, vice-chancellor's court will register III, fols. 277–279v

Bainbrigg, Reginald (*c*.1489–1554). *See under* Bainbrigg, Reginald (1544/5–1612/13).

Bainbrigg, Reginald (1544/5–1612/13), schoolmaster and antiquary, born at Hilton, near Appleby, Westmorland, was probably a younger son of Christopher Bainbrigg (*c*.1505–1569), a member of a minor gentry family which had been at Hilton from the fifteenth century. Reginald Bainbrigg matriculated from Queen's College, Oxford, in 1572, and graduated BA in 1576 and MA in 1579.

In 1580 Bainbrigg was appointed headmaster of the grammar school at Appleby, founded by Robert Langton (*c*.1460–1524), his grandfather's cousin, and reconstituted by royal charter in 1574. There he combined his school work with antiquarian and archaeological research. He was one of the first to record the remains along Hadrian's Wall and has been described as 'the ablest of all the northern antiquaries' of his generation (Birley, 7). With considerable care and skill Bainbrigg recorded stones bearing ancient inscriptions from Cumberland, Westmorland, and neighbouring parts of Northumberland. He made two journeys, in 1599 and 1601, along Hadrian's Wall and into Tynedale and Redesdale, his notes being the earliest known record, and a key source, for several of the sites he visited. His antiquarian interests brought him into contact with William Camden and other contemporary scholars, such as John Denton of Cardew, who wrote the first historical account of Cumberland. Bainbrigg sent Camden copies of the inscriptions, which Camden printed in the 1607 edition of *Britannia*, acknowledging his indebtedness to him, but altering some of his readings in a cavalier fashion. Bainbrigg took some original Roman inscriptions back to Appleby, made copies of others, and added several *jeux d'esprit* of his own. In 1602 he built a small house in his garden for their preservation, carving an inscription stating that he had been teaching at

Appleby for twenty-two years and was fifty-seven years old. In 1722 twelve Roman stones remained at the school, but by 1911 only four Roman inscriptions survived, along with others of Bainbrigg's own devising.

Bainbrigg was a major benefactor to his school at Appleby. The existing school house proving too small, he purchased land nearby, on which he began to build. By his will, traditionally but perhaps erroneously dated 1606, he bequeathed almost all his possessions, including the building materials he had gathered, to his successors as masters of the grammar school, and a new school was completed after his death. Bainbrigg's personal library, which he also left to the school, was deposited in the library of the University of Newcastle upon Tyne in 1966. Of 295 volumes, 158 survive, providing a rare insight into the interests of an Elizabethan schoolmaster. In Appleby, Bainbrigg's reputation remained vivid in the later seventeenth century. He was remembered as a 'learn'd ingenious person', who was 'look'd upon as a Conjuror' who had cast spells to prevent the deciphering of the inscriptions in his collection (Machel MS, vol. 6, 189, 195–6). In his will Reginald Bainbrigg asked to be buried with his parents and siblings in St Michael's Church, Appleby. The absence of a record of his burial there suggests that his death, between April 1612 and September 1613, took place elsewhere.

Another **Reginald Bainbrigg** (*c.*1489–1554), probably an uncle or cousin of the schoolmaster and antiquary, was born at Middleton, Westmorland, the son of John Bainbrigg (*c.*1464–1542) and Margaret (*d.* 1551), his wife. He took the degree of BA at Cambridge in 1506, of MA in 1509, and of BTh in 1526. He was proctor of the university in 1517, a fellow of St Catharine's College, Cambridge, and master from 1529 to 1547. He held a succession of livings in Essex, being instituted to the rectory of Downham on 27 June 1525 and to that of Stambourne on 1 December 1526. He was made vicar of Bricklesea on 19 May 1530, of Steeple Bumpstead on 13 May 1532 (where he was living in 1554), and of Great Oakley on 11 January 1538. In 1537 he was appointed to a prebend stall at Wells. He appears to have died in November 1554. A third Reginald Bainbrigg (*d.* 1606), who matriculated at Peterhouse, Cambridge, in 1573, graduated BA in 1576–7, and was vicar of Steeple Bumpstead from 1582 to 1606, may have been a member of the same family. ANGUS J. L. WINCHESTER

Sources R. P. Brown, 'Thomas Langton and his tradition of learning', *Transactions of the Cumberland and Westmorland Antiquarian and Archaeological Society*, new ser., 26 (1925–6), 150–246 • F. Haverfield, 'Cotton Julius F. vi. Notes on Reginald Bainbrigg of Appleby, on William Camden and on some Roman inscriptions', *Transactions of the Cumberland and Westmorland Antiquarian and Archaeological Society*, new ser., 11 (1910–11), 343–78 • E. Hinchcliffe, *Appleby grammar school* (1974) • E. Birley, *Research on Hadrian's wall* (1961) • L. Buddon, 'Some notes on the history of Appleby grammar school', *Transactions of the Cumberland and Westmorland Antiquarian and Archaeological Society*, new ser., 39 (1938–9), 227–61 • Cumbria AS, Machel papers, vol. 6, pp. 189–99 • *DNB*

Archives BL, antiquarian notes, Cotton MSS Julius F. VI • BL, copy of account of tour to Hadrian's Wall, Lansdowne MS 121, fols. 160–64

Bainbrigg, Thomas. *See* Bainbridge, Thomas (*bap.* 1574, *d.* 1646).

Bainbrigg, Thomas (1636–1703), religious controversialist, was born in Cambridge on 26 June 1636, the son of Richard Bainbrigg and his wife, Rose (probably Rose Wilson, whom a Richard Bainbrigg married in 1631). Bainbrigg was admitted as a sizar to Trinity College, Cambridge, on 26 March 1651, was elected scholar in that year, and graduated BA in 1654–5 and became a fellow in 1656. He proceeded MA in 1661 by royal mandate. He was ordained deacon and priest in March 1664 and that year he became vicar of Barrington, Cambridgeshire. He was incorporated at Oxford in 1669. He served as proctor at Cambridge in 1678–9 and vicar of Chesterton near Cambridge in 1679. He was made DD by royal mandate in 1684.

The reign of James II saw Bainbrigg publish *An answer to a book entitled 'Reason and Authority', or, The motives of a late protestant's reconciliation to the Catholic church* (1687), which attacked a pamphlet by Joshua Basset, *Reason and Authority*, which was itself a reply to John Tillotson's discourse against transubstantiation. Several other tracts have been attributed to Bainbrigg, written in the early years of William III's reign in response to pamphlets by Abednego Seller concerning passive obedience. In 1700 Bainbrigg became vice-master of Trinity and rector of Orwell, Cambridgeshire. He died suddenly at Cambridge on 16 August 1703 and was buried in Trinity College chapel. His will was proved in the vice-chancellor's court of the university in 1703. STUART HANDLEY

Sources Venn, *Alum. Cant.* • Wood, *Ath. Oxon.*, new edn, vol. 4 • C. H. Cooper and J. W. Cooper, *Annals of Cambridge*, 5 vols. (1842–1908), vol. 4, p. 64 • T. Jones, ed., *A catalogue of the collection of tracts for and against popery*, 1, Chetham Society, 48 (1859) • E. Carter, *The history of the University of Cambridge* (1753) • *IGI* • J. Le Neve, *Monumenta Anglicana, 1700–1715* (1717), 58–9

Bainbrigge, Sir Philip (1786–1862), army officer, was descended from an ancient family long resident in Leicestershire and Derbyshire. He was the eldest son of Lieutenant-Colonel Philip Bainbrigge, of Ashbourne, Derbyshire, and Rachel, daughter of Peter Dobree of Beauregard, Guernsey, and was born in London. He entered the navy aged thirteen as a midshipman in the *Caesar*, under Admiral Sir James Saumarez, in 1799, but left because of ill health. His father, who served under the duke of York in the expedition to the Netherlands, was killed in the attack on Egmont op Zoom on 2 October 1799, and the next year the duke appointed young Bainbrigge to an ensigncy in the 20th regiment.

On 13 November 1800 Bainbrigge became a lieutenant, but being then only fourteen years of age, he obtained a year's leave, which he spent at Green's military academy at Deptford, and joined his regiment at Malta in 1801. At the peace of Amiens his regiment was reduced and he was placed on half pay, but was brought on full pay into the 7th fusiliers. After returning to England in 1803, he was employed in obtaining volunteers from the militia to form the 2nd battalion of the 7th, which when completed was moved to Colchester. Here the troops were reviewed by the duke of York, and Bainbrigge, who had come to notice by his zeal and diligence, was gazetted, on 17 October 1805, to a company in the 18th Royal Irish, and joined the 1st battalion in the West Indies. After the taking of Curaçao from the Dutch in 1807, he was appointed inspector of fortifications there, and made plans of the forts and defences, which subsequently recommended him to the authorities at the Horse Guards.

Bainbrigge transferred into the 93rd, and, on returning to England, laid his plans and surveys before the duke of York, who advised him to qualify himself for the staff by studying at the senior department of the Royal Military College at High Wycombe. He entered the college in 1809, and studied so diligently that in a year and a half he passed his examination with distinction. While there he invented a protracting pocket sextant, which was favourably noticed by the board of examiners, and enabled him to make surveys with remarkable accuracy and rapidity.

On leaving the college Bainbrigge was appointed deputy assistant quartermaster-general in the British army in Portugal. On arriving at Wellington's headquarters he was posted to the 4th division, commanded by Major-General Cole, and stationed near Torres Vedras. He was then brought to headquarters, where for some time he was employed in sketching ground and reporting on positions, thereby risking capture by the enemy who occupied the country. His aptitude was acknowledged, for in a letter to Marshal Beresford, dated Cartaxo, 4 January 1811, Wellington said he was appointed to the staff of the army because of the ability he showed at High Wycombe.

Bainbrigge was present at the sieges and storming of Ciudad Rodrigo and Badajoz. As soon as Badajoz was taken he was ordered to join the 6th division, under Sir Henry Clinton, at Albuera, and take charge of the quartermaster-general's department. On the advance of the army into Spain in 1812, Bainbrigge, who had examined the country which was to become the scene of operations, was brought to headquarters. He was present at the siege of the forts of Salamanca, at the actions of Costillegos and Costrejon, and at the crossing of the Guarena, his duties being to carry orders and make sketches of the country and positions, an important but risky role. On one occasion he was ordered to conduct a column of the army, at Pareda, through difficult country and in face of the enemy to Vallesa. He did so successfully, and brought the column in the middle of the night safely to its destination. On the day of the battle of Salamanca he was constantly with Wellington, and at a critical moment he carried the order for the advance of General Leith's division.

After this decisive victory Bainbrigge accompanied the army in the advance to Madrid, and from there to Valladolid and Burgos. He was present at part of the siege of Burgos, and soon after was appointed permanent assistant quartermaster-general with the rank of major. In the retreat from Burgos he rendered important services through his knowledge of the country, which was considered of so much value that Sir Henry Clinton asked for his return to the 6th division, but it was decided that he should remain at headquarters. Bainbrigge held the same position until the end of the war in 1814, and surveyed and sketched the country through which the army passed before entering France. He was present at the battles of Vitoria and Pyrenees, at the last siege of San Sebastian, and at the battles of Nive and Toulouse. He received no honours, and through some strange omission was not recommended for brevet rank, but on 21 January 1817 this was rectified, and he was promoted to the brevet rank of lieutenant-colonel.

In 1815 Bainbrigge applied for employment abroad, and joined the British army in its advance to Paris. He married in 1816 the eldest daughter of Joseph Fletcher; they had at least two sons. When he returned home after the peace, he continued to hold the appointment of permanent assistant quartermaster-general until 1841, when he was made deputy quartermaster-general in Dublin. Having attained the rank of major-general, 9 November 1846, he was appointed by Wellington to the command of the Belfast district. In 1852 the duke selected him to command the forces in Ceylon. There his exertions for the welfare of the troops under his command made him popular and widely respected, and his departure, when promoted lieutenant-general on 20 June 1854, was much regretted.

In 1838 Bainbrigge was made a CB, and subsequently received the 'grant for distinguished service'. On 31 March 1854 he was appointed colonel of the 26th regiment (Cameronians), and in May 1860 was created KCB.

In his military career Bainbrigge showed the advantage of scientific knowledge, and much of his success was a result of his diligent application of this knowledge in the field; he was greatly valued as an officer. He died at St Margaret's, near Titchfield, Hampshire, on 20 December 1862, at the age of seventy-six.

A. S. Bolton, *rev.* James Lunt

Sources *The Times* (29 Dec 1862) • *GM*, 3rd ser., 14 (1863), 230–36 • *Colburn's United Service Magazine*, 1 (1863), 271 • *Army List* (1801) • *Army List* (1804) • *Army List* (1806) • Boase, *Mod. Eng. biog.*

Archives BL, corresp. with Sir J. W. Gordon, Add. MSS 49506–49507

Wealth at death under £6000: probate, 8 Jan 1863, *CGPLA Eng. & Wales*

Baine, James (1710–1790), minister of the Relief church, was born at Bonhill, Dunbartonshire, the son of the Revd James Baine (1676–1755) and Grizel, *née* Semple (*d.* 1756). He was educated at the parish school, then at the grammar school in Dumbarton before studying at the universities of Glasgow and Edinburgh. He gained his MA at Glasgow on 4 May 1725. Baine was ordained to the ministry of Killearn parish church in 1732 and became involved in the evangelical awakening associated with the preaching of George Whitefield in 1742. On 22 May 1740 he married Margaret Potter, daughter of Michael Potter, professor of divinity at Glasgow University; they had three sons and three daughters. As an opponent of patronage in 1752 he opposed the deposition of Thomas Gillespie over his refusal to be involved in the induction of the new minister of Inverkeithing and identified himself with the popular party within the established church, 'one well known for his Ministerial Abilities and particularly eminent for his constant struggle for Christian and ministerial liberty' (South College Relief church minutes, NA Scot., CH3/433.1, fol. 10r).

In 1756 Baine was translated to the charge of first minister of the high kirk in Paisley, although by the 1760s he had become disenchanted with the established church. When he had come to Paisley a general kirk session administered the affairs of the high kirk as well as those of the Lairgh kirk parish where John Witherspoon was the minister. Baine asked the presbytery of Paisley to allow him to have a separate kirk session but they refused. Baine may have felt that his own position and prestige as a parish minister had been undermined. When Baine resigned his charge in Paisley he claimed that the major reason was that he was now 'advanced in life' and the 'high church' was 'commonly so crowded' and was 'much beyond his strength' (Dickson, 8).

Between August 1762 and August 1764 there was controversy within Edinburgh over the settlement of a minister of Lady Yester's Church. The moderate party within the Edinburgh presbytery believed that they had an opportunity to end the dominance which the popular party exercised over settlements within the city. When the moderates eventually triumphed Thomas Gillespie, founder of the Relief church, received a letter from a group who were determined to leave Lady Yester's Church and asked for Gillespie's advice. On 15 January 1765 a group of ninety-two subscribers indicated that they would form a Relief congregation and issued a call to Baine. Baine accepted their invitation and was inducted as the minister of the new Relief congregation by Thomas Gillespie in February 1766.

That his new church could seat up to 1200 and that he played an active part in its affairs gives the lie to his claim that he left his former position because of pressures of work. Although Baine left the Church of Scotland with feelings of resentment, he retained his commitment to Presbyterianism. His letter of resignation clearly stated that

> this change of my condition, and charge I have accepted, makes no change in my creed or Christian belief; none in my principles of Christian and ministerial communion; nay, none in my cordial regard to the constitution and interests of the Church of Scotland … at the same time, I abhor … that abuse of Church power of late, which to me appears … destructive of the ends of our office as ministers of Christ.

Baine denied that the presbytery of Relief had any separating principles because they 'dare not decline communion with any who have the knowledge, the visible uncorrupted profession of real Christianity' (Dickson, 9–10).

Baine was one of the ablest and most influential ministers within the early years of the Relief church. He championed the cause of congregations to call the minister of their own choice, even in the case of Blairlogie in 1769 when doubts were raised by Thomas Gillespie over the orthodoxy of Alexander Pirie. Gillespie believed that the only constraint to the free choice of any congregation was the suitability of the candidate, which the presbytery had the right to oversee. Baine believed that such a responsibility lay in the local congregation who should be able to exercise a free choice over the election of their minister. In the 1770s he became involved in two controversies, one in which he opposed the influence of James Cowan, minister of Colinsburgh, who held stricter views regarding the open communion than the founders of the Relief church, and the other in which he published a sermon against the theatre, *The Theatre Licentious and Perverted* (1770). Baine was especially critical of the portrayal by Samuel Foote of the preaching of George Whitefield and addressed further criticisms in his *Letter to Samuel Foote* published the following year. He died on 17 January 1790, aged eighty, maintaining to the end of his life his commitment to the principles of religious liberty and catholicity which characterized the Relief church from its earliest days. An earlier collection of sermons published in 1778 was followed by a posthumously published volume of *Select Sermons* (1850).

KENNETH B. E. ROXBURGH

Sources *DNB* • G. Struthers, *The history of the rise, progress, and principles of the Relief church* (1843) • K. B. E. Roxburgh, 'Thomas Gillespie and the origins of the Relief church in eighteenth-century Scotland', PhD diss., U. Edin., 1997 • W. Mackelvie, *Annals and statistics of the United Presbyterian church*, ed. W. Blair and D. Young (1873) • R. Small, *History of the congregations of the United Presbyterian church from 1733 to 1900*, 2 vols. (1904) • *Fasti Scot.*, new edn, 3.171 • J. Baine, *Memoirs of modern church reformation* (1766) • J. Dickson, *Centenary memorial: history of South College Street church* (1866) • South College Relief church minutes, NA Scot., CH3/433.1

Archives NL Scot., corresp. with John Campbell, fourth duke of Argyll

Likenesses J. Kay, caricature, etching, 1789, BM, NPG • oils, repro. in J. Baine, *Sermon on the presence of God the safety and comfort of his people* (1866)

Baines, Edward (1774–1848), newspaper proprietor, politician, and historian, was born at Walton-le-Dale, near Preston, Lancashire, on 5 February 1774, the second son of Richard Baines (*d.* 1811) and his wife, Jane (*née* Chew). Richard Baines, who was born near Ripon and came from a farming family, had moved to Preston and there married the daughter of a local merchant. He became a grocer, but Preston corporation took court proceedings against him as he was not a member of the Guild Merchant and so was not legally entitled to trade in the town. His son recorded that 'he resisted the vexatious interferences but was obliged to leave … and he removed to the village of Walton-le-Dale where he carried on his business' (Baines, *Life*, 14). This episode was said by Edward Baines to have been the last instance of the application of the medieval trading restrictions. Although that was not quite the case, it is clear that the symbolic significance of this demonstration of unreformed privilege helped to shape the markedly radical political views of the Baines family.

At the age of two Edward Baines was sent to live with his maternal uncle, Thomas Rigg, a slate merchant of Hawkshead in the southern Lake District, and for two years he attended the grammar school there. Wordsworth was a fellow pupil. When he was eight years old he returned to

Edward Baines (1774–1848), by John Cochran, pubd 1834 (after Thomas Hargreaves)

Preston to live with his family, and continued his education at the town's grammar school until the age of sixteen. He was then apprenticed to Thomas Walker, a printer and stationer of Church Street, Preston, who was also well known locally as a radical politician. His influence probably helped to develop further in Edward Baines the reformist political views which he already had in mind.

In 1795, with the approval of his parents and master, Baines moved to Leeds to complete his apprenticeship with Binns and Brown, printers and booksellers who were also proprietors of the *Leeds Mercury*. This was a crucial event in Baines's life, for although he remained a printer it was from this experience that he acquired his knowledge of, and taste for, journalism and newspapers. Two years later, in 1797, he set up in business as a printer at Briggate, Leeds, and on 2 July 1798 married Charlotte, daughter of Matthew Talbot, a prosperous Leeds currier. His printing business had not initially prospered—partly because of a partner who proved unsatisfactory—but by 1800 it enjoyed good fortunes, and Baines was financially more secure. This had been assisted by his marriage into a moneyed family, and the changed circumstances allowed him to contemplate an ambitious change of career. In 1801, with the help and encouragement of a group of reformist Liberals from the Leeds area, he bought the *Leeds Mercury*, with all its printing stock, from his erstwhile employers for £1552.

Baines then determinedly set about transforming what had become a semi-moribund venture, with a circulation of only 700–800 copies, into one of the most influential and respected provincial newspapers in the country. By the late 1820s the regular sale was in excess of 5000, and the *Leeds Mercury* had gained a wide reputation as a prominent mouthpiece for moderate and responsible social and political reform. The strongly held views of its owner-editor were directly reflected in its espousal of such causes as parliamentary reform, the abolition of the slave trade, Catholic emancipation, the extension of civil liberties, and the introduction of public education for all.

In his position as owner and editor of the town's most important newspaper, Baines inevitably began to play a significant role in the public affairs of Leeds. He promoted local improvements and encouraged and sponsored social projects such as the establishment of the Leeds Mechanics' Institution. His political views were expressed in his support for, and involvement in, the election of MPs for the West Riding, and in the late 1820s and early 1830s Baines was in regular correspondence with leading reformist politicians in London, informing them of opinion in Yorkshire.

While developing his newspaper Baines also engaged in historical research and writing. In 1815 he published his *History of the Wars of the French Revolution from 1792 to 1815*, which was later expanded to become a four-volume *History of the Reign of George III* (1823), while in 1822–3 appeared his important *History, Directory and Gazetteer of the County of York*. In 1824–5 the companion volumes, the *History, Directory and Gazetteer of the County Palatine of Lancaster*, were published, and the latter formed the basis of an ambitious four-volume *History of the County Palatine of Lancaster* (1836).

It is now known that most of the research and a sizeable proportion of the writing of these books was undertaken by others, notably the Oldham local historian Edwin Butterworth, and that therefore Baines's role was primarily that of enabler and publisher. However, the works have permanent value because of the quality of their research, the breadth of their scope, and their innovative style: as a liberal reformer of comparatively humble origins, interested in contemporary social and economic issues, Baines paid close attention to industrialization, recent history, and the local economic and social circumstances of Lancashire and Yorkshire. This was in very marked contrast to the backward-looking and élitist antiquarian approach which was so characteristic of most county histories at this time. That the Yorkshire and Lancashire topographical histories were published in revised and updated form later in the century, and that they were still highly valued and extensively used by local and regional historians at the end of the twentieth century, reflects the high and progressive standards which Baines set himself and those who worked for him.

Firmly established as an important reformist figure in local and, increasingly, in national political circles, Baines made the logical progression into parliamentary politics after the passing of the 1832 Reform Bill. At a by-election in February 1834 he was elected a whig MP for Leeds, and retained his seat in the 1835 and 1837 elections. In this period he gained a reputation at Westminster as a fluent speaker in the cause of continuing social reform, campaigning for legislation to regulate factory employment and conditions, for the abolition of tithes, and on behalf of the Anti-Corn Law Association. In Yorkshire he served as a JP for the West Riding of Yorkshire, and in this work, too, his reformist and liberal instincts were applied—he was a 'benevolent, just, and liberal-minded man' (*DNB*). In 1841, after seven years in parliament, he retired because his health was beginning to fail, and he spent his last few years in semi-retirement in Leeds, where he died on 3 August 1848, survived by his wife.

Edward and Charlotte Baines had eleven children, of whom several became significant public figures in their own right. His eldest son, Matthew Talbot *Baines, was a lawyer who went into politics, serving as MP for Kingston upon Hull, as president of the poor-law board, and eventually as chancellor of the duchy of Lancaster. Another son, Edward *Baines, succeeded his father as proprietor of the *Leeds Mercury* and maintained its place as one of the most important voices of liberal politics in the north of England. He was also the author of a biography of his father, and the important *History of the Cotton Manufacture*, to which his father contributed a chapter. Thomas *Baines, a younger son, became a newspaper proprietor in Liverpool and wrote a commercial history of Liverpool. The powerful moral, social, and entrepreneurial influence of their father is apparent in the careers of all three sons.

ALAN G. CROSBY

Sources E. Baines, *History, directory and gazetteer of the county palatine of Lancaster*, 1 (1824); facs. edn, with introduction by O. Ashmore, as *Baines's Lancashire: a new printing of the two volumes of History, directory and gazatteer (sic) of the county palatine of Lancaster* (1968) · *DNB* · C. Hardwick, *History of the borough of Preston and its environs* (1857), 652 · A. G. Crosby, *The history of the Preston Guild* (1991) · will, 1811, Lancs. RO, WRW A [Richard Baines] · D. Fraser, 'The life of Edward Baines: a filial biography of "the great liar of the north"', *Northern History*, 31 (1995), 208–22 · E. Baines, *Life of Edward Baines, late MP for the borough of Leeds* (1851)

Archives Lancs. RO, collections relating to history of Lancashire · W. Yorks. AS, Leeds, corresp., mainly with his son Edward

Likenesses J. Cochran, stipple, 1834 (after T. Hargraves), BM, NPG; repro. in W. Jerdan, *National portrait gallery of illustrious and eminent personages*, 5 (1834) [*see illus.*] · S. A. Duval, aquatint, pubd 1846 (after J. Stevenson), NPG · W. Behnes, stone statue, 1858, Leeds City Art Galleries

Baines, Sir Edward (1800–1890), journalist, politician, and educationist, was born in Leeds on 28 May 1800, the second son of Edward *Baines (1774–1848), editor of the *Leeds Mercury*, and his wife, Charlotte, daughter of Matthew Talbot, a Leeds currier. Matthew Talbot *Baines and Thomas *Baines were his brothers. Known until his father's death as Edward Baines junior, he was first educated at a private school in Leeds, then sent to New College, Manchester, a leading grammar school for protestant dissenters, where John Dalton, the eminent chemist, taught mathematics. There, aged fourteen, he started to teach in Independent (later Congregational) Sunday schools, which he continued to do until elected to parliament in 1859; his dissenting faith underpinned all his public actions. In 1815 he began to work for his father's newspaper, travelling widely as a reporter, and working as an editor from 1818. In 1827 his father took him into partnership, and in 1829 he married Martha (*d*. 1881), the only daughter of Thomas Blackburn of Liverpool. They had three sons and four daughters.

As a journalist, Baines covered the considerable unrest in the north after the end of the Napoleonic wars, exposing the government *agent-provocateur* Oliver the Spy—the first public example of his personal courage and sense of justice. They emerged again when he reported from the speakers' platform at the Peterloo massacre of 16 August 1819 in Manchester, taking the side of the peaceful demonstrators against local magistrates. For the rest of his life he played an ambivalent and frequently controversial role in popular demands for political reform; his more inflammatory writings often encouraged these demands among working-class groups, which pressure he used to foster middle-class radical programmes as a prophylactic against 'democracy'. For decades he trod an uneasy path between the various groups, excoriated as the mouthpiece of 'Bainesocracy' by working-class radicals and distrusted by other middle-class reformers, such as the leaders of the Manchester school of political and economic liberalism. As such he reinforced provincial divisions as well as serving as a major protester against a political world dominated by London and landed Anglicans; the tension was only partly abated when his elder brother, Matthew, who had become an Anglican, served as Palmerston's chancellor of the duchy of Lancaster from 1855 to 1858.

Baines's espousal of a limited extension of the franchise to those with a stake in property, and the creation of new industrial constituencies, underpinned his support for the 1832 Reform Act and the subsequent programme of Liberal reforms, although he was disappointed by their limited extent. He supported the new poor law of 1834 and then turned to attack protectionism in the form of the corn laws. In 1835 he published a *History of the Cotton Manufacture in Great Britain*. His attempts to seek compromise with the great Yorkshire landowners brought him into frequent conflict with the more radical Lancashire spokesmen, Cobden and Bright, but he gave support to Sir Robert Peel's dismantling of the corn laws in 1846. His advocacy of economic change also brought him into conflict with gentry and working-class leaders demanding factory reform and limited working hours in the Ten Hours Movement. This antipathy continued with the emergence of the more generalized demands of Chartism and mass demonstrations in Yorkshire. Baines deplored any state-imposed limits on individual economic freedom and began in his twenties to produce accounts of material progress, which made him one of the first 'scientific' polemicists of the industrial revolution and its rapidly growing towns. The collation of statistical trends remained a feature of his writings, most noticeably in *The Social, Educational and Religious State of the Manufacturing Districts* (1843). His approach left him open to criticism that he ignored present miseries, to which he argued always that the answer to these lay in economic progress and moral change rooted in individual responsibility.

This outworking of Baines's 'nonconformist conscience' was accompanied by a passionate belief in the need for widespread education. Characteristically, he avoided any suggestion of state involvement in this until he was in his late sixties. Instead, he became a leading proponent of educational voluntarism for learners of all ages. A founder member of the Leeds Literary and Philosophical Society for his own class, he turned his attention to working-class adult education after attending Dr George Birkbeck's first mechanics' institute in London in 1824. Baines was instrumental in founding several similar bodies in Yorkshire during the 1820s, bringing them together in 1837 in the West Riding (subsequently Yorkshire) Union of Mechanics' Institutes, of which he was president for forty-four years. Later, he was a leading figure in the setting up of the Yorkshire Village Library, which provided 27,000 volumes to some 144 villages. His concern to provide an educated workforce for the new industrial society extended eventually into schools, where his advocacy was much more controversial. Central to his beliefs was the assumption that people valued most that for which they paid and which they controlled. After a visit to the model factory system at New Lanark, although he disliked many of Robert Owen's views, Baines emphasized the duty of employers to support education for their workers' children. When limited state aid for schools, together with inspection, was introduced in the 1830s he opposed it on the grounds that it would remove individual responsibility for self-improvement and enhance the power of the Church of England—particularly of its high-church wing which he opposed vociferously as 'papist', despite his having supported Catholic emancipation in 1829. On this he differed sharply from some other nonconformist apologists but his editorials and prolific pamphleteering, with titles such as *An alarm to the nation, on the unjust, unconstitutional and dangerous measure of state education proposed by the government* (1847), served to sustain an extra-parliamentary voluntarist opposition which hindered repeated government attempts to extend publicly funded education. In the late 1860s he underwent a volte-face when his membership of the Taunton commission on endowed schools convinced him that, if the education of the middle classes was so inadequately served, then that of the working classes needed stronger support than voluntarism had so far provided. Thus he supported W. E. Forster's Elementary Education Act of 1870, but only because it was essentially permissive. After that he became instrumental in founding the Yorkshire College of Science, the forerunner of the University of Leeds, whose Victorian Gothic Baines wing is a memorial to his serving as chairman of its council from 1880 until 1887.

Baines followed in his father and elder brother's footsteps when he was elected MP for Leeds in 1859, after which he remained a firmly independent member of the Liberal groupings. From supporting Cobden's negotiation of a commercial treaty with France in 1860, an outcome of his free trade principles, he turned his attention to demanding an extended franchise. His view was that the growing respectability of many artisans justified an extension in the borough voting qualification from the £10 requirement of the 1832 act to £6. When the government refused to initiate legislation, he introduced private members' bills in 1861, 1864, and 1865. All were rejected but they served to feed the growing demand for reform. Even so, Disraeli's 'leap in the dark' Reform Act of 1867 went much further than Baines thought prudent. His ambivalent attitude to the new working-class electorate showed in his handling of his Leeds constituency and he was voted out of parliament in the 1874 election. W. E. Gladstone sent him an emollient letter of praise for his 'single-minded devotion, courage of purpose, perfect integrity and ability' in servicing the Liberal cause and it marked the effective end of his party political career (*DNB*). The remainder of his life was spent in local campaigns for sabbatarianism and teetotalism, which he had first espoused in 1837, in active journalism (which he only gave up in 1888), and as a continued champion of industrial Yorkshire's identity. In 1875 he provided a chapter on the history of the county's woollen trade for his brother Thomas's *Yorkshire Past and Present*, in which the first of the four volumes contained an engraving of a photograph of him.

Baines's own literary works included accounts of foreign travel, such as *A Visit to the Vaudois of Piedmont* (1855), and a biography of his father (1851), as well as numerous pamphlets on the causes he espoused so strongly. On his eightieth birthday a presentation was made to him in recognition of his service to the town in the Albert Hall in Leeds; he gave the £3000 raised to the Yorkshire College of Science. At various times he served as a justice of the peace and a deputy lieutenant for the West Riding of Yorkshire. In 1881 he was knighted. He died on 2 March 1890 at his house, St Ann's Hill, Burley, Yorkshire. In his will he left estate valued at £165,818 gross, including a controlling interest in the *Leeds Mercury*, to be divided among his children, with minor gifts to friends and servants. He was buried near Woodhouse Moor in the Leeds municipal cemetery, now a landscaped garden surrounded by the University of Leeds. J. R. Lowerson

Sources J. R. Lowerson, 'The political career of Sir Edward Baines, 1800–1890', MA diss., U. Leeds, 1965 • D. Fraser, 'Edward Baines', *Pressure from without in early Victorian England*, ed. P. Hollis (1974) • *The Times* (3 March 1890) • *The Times* (4 March 1890) • *The Times* (10 June 1890) • Boase, *Mod. Eng. biog.* • *DNB* • D. Fraser, 'The life of Edward Baines: a filial biography of "the great liar of the north"', *Northern History*, 31 (1995), 208–22

Archives Duke U., political corresp. • W. Yorks. AS, Leeds, corresp. and papers | BL, corresp. with Richard Cobden, Add. MS 43664 • BL, letters to Sir Austen Layard, Add. MSS 39101–39114, *passim* • Borth. Inst., letters to Lord Halifax • Man. CL, letter-books, Anti-Corn Law League • W. Sussex RO, corresp., mainly with Richard Cobden

Likenesses R. Waller, oils, 1874, Leeds corporation • W. Ouless, oils, 1884, Leeds City Art Gallery • B. R. Haydon, group portrait, oils (*The Anti-Slavery Society convention, 1840*), NPG • W. Holl, stipple (after photograph), NPG • D. J. Pound, stipple and line (after photograph by Mayall), BM, NPG; repro. in *Illustrated News of the World* • engraving (after photograph), repro. in T. Baines, *Yorkshire past and present*, 1 (1874)

Wealth at death £165,818 16*s*. 11*d*.: probate, 2 May 1890, *CGPLA Eng. & Wales*

Baines, Frederick Ebenezer (1832–1911), promoter of telegraphy, was born on 10 November 1832 and baptized at Chipping Barnet, Hertfordshire, on 19 January 1834. He was the younger son of Edward May Baines, surgeon, of Hendon and Chipping Barnet and his wife, Fanny.

Educated at private schools, Baines early showed interest in practical applications of electricity, and, helped by his uncle Edward Cowper, and an elder brother, G. L. Baines, mastered, when fourteen, the principles of telegraphy, constructing and manipulating telegraphic apparatus. Two years later, through the influence of Frederick Hill, an uncle by marriage, and Rowland Hill, he was put in charge of a small public telegraph office belonging to the Electric Telegraph Company, and situated within the post office at St Martin's-le-Grand, London, where he remained for three years.

In April 1855 Rowland Hill recommended Baines for the post of clerk in the correspondence branch of the General Post Office. After a few months Baines's knowledge of railways earned him a transfer to the home mails branch. His leisure was devoted to schemes for extending the telegraph network through submarine cables. He planned to avoid the necessity for lines to cross hostile lands. He devised one cable route to the Canary Islands and the West Indies, another crossing the south Atlantic and rounding the Cape of Good Hope to Australia. In a letter to *The Times* (14 September 1858) he further advocated the connection of the Atlantic and Pacific coasts by a line across Canada. His most important scheme, which he drew up in 1856, was for the government acquisition of existing telegraph systems. This was not the first such proposal, but it was the first to detail practical methods of organizing the transfer, and to list the expected benefits, supported by reliable figures. The government's permission to proceed came only in November 1867, and control of existing telegraph systems was transferred to the Post Office on 5 February 1870. Baines's knowledge of telegraphy was helpful in bringing the new public service into operation, including all the main features of his original scheme—free delivery within a mile, the creation of a legal monopoly, and a uniform sixpenny rate, irrespective of distance.

In 1875 Baines was made surveyor-general for telegraph business, and in 1878, with a view to decreasing the danger of invasion and increasing the efficiency of the coastguard service, he proposed the establishment of telegraphic communication around the coast of the British Isles, to be worked by the coastguard under the control and supervision of the Post Office. The proposal, renewed in 1881, and again in 1888, was adopted by the government in 1892.

In 1882 Baines was made inspector-general of mails, and assistant secretary in the Post Office under Sir Arthur Blackwood. He organized the parcel post service, introduced by Fawcett in 1883, and before leaving the Post Office had extended the service to the British colonies and most European countries. Different views and systems of postal administration on the continent made his task difficult. He became CB in 1885, and married, in 1887, Laura, eldest daughter of Walter Baily, barrister, of Hampstead. He retired through ill health on 1 August 1893.

Baines lived for the greater part of his life at 1 Wentworth Mansions, South End Road, Hampstead, where he took an active interest in parochial work. He assisted in the acquisition of Parliament Hill Fields for the public use, was a member of the Hampstead select vestry, and in 1890 edited *Records of Hampstead*. He was also an enthusiastic volunteer, serving as both a non-commissioned and a commissioned officer. His latter years he devoted to literature. His main work, *Forty Years at the Post-Office* (2 vols., 1895), reminiscences written in an agreeable style, contains valuable details of reforms at the Post Office both before and during Baines's connection with it. He also published *On the Track of the Mail Coach* (1896), and contributed an article on the Post Office to J. Samuelson's *The Civilisation of our Day* (1896).

Baines died on 4 July 1911 at his home in Hampstead, and was cremated at Golders Green. He was survived by his wife. S. E. FRYER, *rev.* ANITA MCCONNELL

Sources F. E. Baines, *Forty years at the Post-Office: a personal narrative*, 2 vols. (1895) · *The Times* (7 July 1911), 11f · review of *On the track of the mail coach*, *The Athenaeum* (25 Jan 1896), 110–11 · *The Athenaeum* (4 Feb 1895) · F. I. Scudamore, *Reports on the proposed government acquisition of telegraphs* (1866–8) · *St Martin's-le-Grand* [Post Office magazine], 3 (1893), 344–52 · *St Martin's-le-Grand* [Post Office magazine], 21 (1911), 417–19 · *CGPLA Eng. & Wales* (1911) · d. cert.

Likenesses Meisenbach, photograph, repro. in *St-Martin's-le-Grand*, 3 (1893), facing p. 344 · photograph, repro. in Baines, *Forty years at the Post-Office*, vol. 2, frontispiece

Wealth at death £2419 12*s.* 6*d.*: probate, 1 Sept 1911, *CGPLA Eng. & Wales*

Baines, John (1787–1838), mathematician, was born at Westfield Farm, Horbury, near Wakefield. He showed early a strong mathematical bias and became proficient also in natural science (especially botany), Latin, and Greek. His teaching career took him from Horbury Bridge (*c.*1810–1813) to Reading (*c.*1816) as a mathematics master, then to Nottingham (*c.*1818), Dewsbury (*c.*1819), and finally (*c.*1829) Thornhill, near Wakefield.

From 1810 at least, Baines sent mathematical contributions to periodicals, including the *Ladies' Diary*, the *Gentleman's Diary*, *The Enquirer*, and *York Miscellany*. He wrote to the *Northern Star* from Nottingham. The *Ladies' Diary* for 1833 carried a more substantial article on Cuvier's *Theory of the Earth*, written to prove its confirmation of the Mosaic account. Most of Baines's work shows considerable talent. He was an early friend of the mathematician T. S. Davies (1794–1851). Baines died at Thornhill on 1 May 1838, after nine years as master of the grammar school, and was buried at Horbury. R. E. ANDERSON, *rev.* RUTH WALLIS

Sources private information (1885) · T. T. Wilkinson, 'Mathematical repository', *Mechanics' Magazine*, 57 (1852), 292

Baines, Matthew Talbot (1799–1860), politician, the eldest son of Edward *Baines (1774–1848), journalist and politician, and his wife, Charlotte Talbot, was born on 17 February 1799. Sir Edward *Baines and Thomas *Baines were his younger brothers. He was educated at the Protestant Dissenters' and Richmond grammar schools and obtained a scholarship at Trinity College, Cambridge. He was president of the union in 1818, and graduated in 1820 as a senior optime, being converted to the Church of England. He was called to the bar in 1825, and, after practising with success on the northern circuit, was, in 1837, appointed recorder of Hull, and in 1841 became a queen's counsel. In 1847 he entered parliament as Liberal member for Hull, which he continued to represent until 1852, when he was chosen for Leeds. In Lord John Russell's administration he became, in 1849, president of the poor law board, and he held the same appointment in Lord Aberdeen's ministry. After Lord Palmerston acceded to power in 1855, he was appointed chancellor of the duchy of Lancaster, with a seat in the cabinet.

Though not a brilliant debater, Baines's solid talents won for him considerable respect, and his firmness, impartiality, and special knowledge of the forms of the house pointed him out as a probable occupant of the speaker's chair; he never achieved such an appointment, however, because ill health caused his retirement from public life in April 1859. He was married on 19 September 1833 to Anne, daughter of Lazarus Threlfall, with whom he had at least one child, a son. Baines died at his home, 13 Queen Square, Westminster, on 22 January 1860.

T. F. Henderson, *rev.* H. C. G. Matthew

Sources R. V. Taylor, ed., *The biographia Leodiensis, or, Biographical sketches of the worthies of Leeds* (1865) • Venn, *Alum. Cant.* • *GM*, 3rd ser., 8 (1860), 302

Archives W. Yorks. AS, Leeds, corresp. with father and brother

Likenesses W. Underwood, lithograph, pubd 1854 (after daguerreotype by Kilburn), NPG • D. J. Pound, stipple and line print (after photograph by Mayall), NPG; repro. in *ILN* • portrait, repro. in *ILN* (13 Oct 1855) • portrait, repro. in *ILN* (4 Feb 1860) • portrait, repro. in *ILN* (24 Nov 1860)

Wealth at death under £50,000: resworn probate, Dec 1860, *CGPLA Eng. & Wales* (1859)

Baines, Peter [*name in religion* Augustine] (**1786–1843**), vicar apostolic of the western district, was born on 25 June 1786 at Pear Tree Farm, Kirkby, near Liverpool, the elder son of James Baines, 'farmer and yeoman' (will, proved 1809, PRO), and his second wife, Catherine. He had a younger brother, Thomas. This Lancashire family was legendary for its steadfastness in the old faith (Baines file, Preston City Archives). At twelve years old Baines went on a scholarship as a boarder to the English Benedictine school at Lambspring in Hanover. After the suppression of the house by Prussia in April 1803, Baines and his schoolmates returned to England to join the sister Benedictine community of St Laurence, newly settled at Ampleforth in Yorkshire; there he was professed a monk in 1804, taking the name Augustine, and was ordained priest in 1810. He became a leading member of the small Ampleforth community, serving as procurator and then prefect of studies. In 1817 the president of the English Benedictine congregation appointed him chief missioner (parish priest) of the busy and fashionable city of Bath. A graphic picture of his

Peter Baines [Augustine] (**1786–1843**), by L. Thenweneti

daily round during the six years he spent there can be seen in his diary of 1817–19, which has been transcribed and published by the Catholic Record Society. He had by this time built a reputation he was never to lose as an outstanding and eloquent preacher.

At the general chapter of the English Benedictine congregation in 1822 Baines was elected first definitor of the regimen. His talents and his energy were recognized outside the congregation as well as within it, and in 1823 the vicar apostolic of the western district, Bishop Peter Bernardine Collingridge, chose (as was then the custom) Baines as his coadjutor with right of succession (the bishop for this extensive and poor district had traditionally been selected from the regular clergy).

Once consecrated, Baines began to prepare for the establishment of a seminary for the district. At first he looked to his Benedictine confrères to assist in this (Bishop Brown of Wales was to initiate a similar plan in 1850). In August 1826 Baines invited both the community of St Gregory, then at nearby Downside, which refused, and his own community of St Laurence at Ampleforth, from which he received an encouraging response. A measure of disagreement over these plans led him to put them aside until 1829, when he succeeded to the vicariate.

The intervening years were spent in Rome, whither Baines had travelled to recover from a serious illness. The experience was a formative one. As he later declared: 'In the Western District all that concerns the exterior of Religion is rigorously fashioned upon the Roman model … infinitely better suited for a country like England' (P. A.

Baines, *A History of the Pastoral*, 1841, 17–18). He made many friends and was especially favoured by Leo XII, who, according to many sources, intended to name him cardinal. He was appointed bishop assistant to the pontifical throne, and in that capacity attended the conclave electing Pius VIII in April 1829. This year, which had seen the death of Leo XII and of Bishop Collingridge, was also the year of the Catholic Emancipation Act in England. Baines was eager for the Roman Catholic church in England to move into the open, to build churches and schools which were now no longer illegal, and to take a place in public life.

Soon after his return to England, in December 1829, Baines bought the mansion of Prior Park, on one of the hills of Bath; he planned to make of it, like Oscott, a school, a seminary, and the bishop's residence. Using stone from the quarries at Combe Down above Prior Park, he adapted harmoniously the wings of the building to form the two colleges of St Peter (opened 1830) and St Paul (opened 1837). His most striking addition was the great flight after flight of steps leading from the Corinthian portico, with terraces laid out below. Finding an appropriate teaching faculty for these colleges caused headaches. For a while (1835–42) a small group of men from the newly formed Institute of Charity came from Italy, but their style proved unsuitable for an English school. In 1835 Nicholas Wiseman responded to Baines's proposal that he should become president of Prior Park. In the event Wiseman chose to settle in the midland district, at Oscott. Baines's original preference for his Benedictine confrères (he had hoped for a helpful reshuffle of personnel) had been disappointed. Dispute over this had involved, too, uncertainty about the canonical status of the Benedictine houses, and their consequent exemption—or otherwise—from the jurisdiction of the bishop while working on the district mission. The matter of episcopal jurisdiction exercised both Bishop Challoner (1691–1781) and Bishop Vaughan (1832–1903) and even the papal ruling secured by the latter, the bull *Romanos pontifices* (1881), did not finally clear up the matter of episcopal authority, based on edicts of the Council of Trent. The hostility engendered between the Benedictine factions was technically resolved by an official arbitration overseen by Bishop Scott of Glasgow in July 1835 in which all were cleared of blame. But the poor relations engendered grew into a legend.

All the same, despite such ups and downs, Prior Park blossomed, and St Peter's College 'in Bishop Baines's hands at once became the most advanced and progressive of the catholic schools' (C. Butler, *Downside Review*, 1931, 333). Another tribute was paid by a young monk of the community of St Gregory of that time (1811–32): W. P. Morris, later speaking as a bishop at the golden jubilee of Downside in 1864, called Baines 'the ornament and pride of the Benedictine body in modern times' (W. P. Morris to J. Bonomi, n.d., Clifton Diocesan Archives). Had Baines not died suddenly at a comparatively young age Prior Park would no doubt have financially secured itself. In 1840 the University of London presented a charter to St Paul's College warranting it to issue certificates to candidates for degrees.

The College of St Peter was run on original, creative, humane lines. Many records testify to Baines as far in advance of his time as an educator. His very individual views can be found in his book *A Course of Studies* (1838), in which he encouraged children 'to form their own ideas', and teachers to avoid 'teasings and scoldings', 'a cross and surly tone', and 'irksome drudgery' in lessons. 'The more children can learn whilst in motion and in the open air the better', he continued. The result was a style of practical involvement—a far cry from other schools of the period. This can be seen in the lengthy press reports of the yearly public examinations and exhibitions, and is evident too from the reminiscences of pupils such as Louis Guibara, who recalled not only the joys of fives in the Ball Place, skating and swimming at the Ponds, birdwatching, picnics, and 'building houses' in the Rainbow Wood and the Wilderness, but also the musical tradition at the school with the bishop watching rehearsals from a gallery: 'It is impossible to exaggerate the influence which that training had upon our lives.'

At Prior Park, T. J. Brindle, Baines's loyal vicar-general, later received into the church many of the most distinguished of the Oxford converts, including Ambrose St John, F. and J. M. Capes, and Robert Aston Coffin. J. H. Newman recommended Prior Park to his close friends the Bowdens as being likely to suit their son 'better than any other college' (*The Letters and Diaries of John Henry Newman*, ed. C. S. Dessain and others, 31 vols., 1–10, 2nd edn, 1978–, vol. 9). Records also testify to Baines's social conscience: from his letter to the *Bath and Cheltenham Gazette* in 1817, when he was chief missioner there, 'in favour of a poor black imprisoned for begging' to his last Lenten pastoral letter in 1843, in which he chided 'a great empire of which a large proportion are paupers in the midst of overflowing plenty; we are oppressors of the poor who have a claim in justice upon us' (*The Tablet*, 18 March 1843).

In 1839 Baines had had a census taken of his district, and his Lenten pastoral letter of February 1840 reflected on the subject of the civil position of Catholics in England and dwelt on the duty in charity of not provoking their 'separated brethren'—as he was criticized for calling the Anglican majority. The pastoral letter, and the twenty charges against it by anonymous 'converts', exemplify the changes which had taken place in Catholic life since the election of Gregory XVI in 1831. Baines was not happy either with the crusade for the conversion of England, initiated by Spencer, or with the Italianate devotional style and practices becoming popular: a contrast to the minimized tone and dry piety which English Catholics had hitherto preferred both by temperament and by precedent.

A Particular Sacred Congregation of eight cardinals in Rome considered the pastoral letter, together with Baines's written defence of it, to which lengthy comments were appended. There was no question of doctrinal error, but Baines was criticized for a 'caustic tone' (vol. 156, Anglia file, Archives of the Collegio di Propaganda Fide, Rome). During the months thus spent in Rome, Baines had several meetings with Gregory XVI (who as Cardinal Capellari, a Camaldolese monk and fellow regular, was a friend of ten years' standing). Required to clarify certain points, Baines stated 'I approve whatever the Church or its organ the Holy See approves.' He complained that not one of his accusers had come forward (*Letter to Sir Charles Wolseley*, 1841 [privately printed]). This lack of openness was alien to his own temperament, which was characteristically candid and ready to square up to a challenge. The petty intrigues continued, though his fellow bishops presented a loyally united front. Bishop John Briggs of the northern district wrote to Bishop Brown of Lancashire, then in Rome, about rumours that Baines might be superseded: 'How astonished and indignant would the catholic body throughout England be to find themselves dragged in the train of Phillipps's and Spencer's war of Enthusiasm' (to Bishop Brown, 15 Feb 1842, Clifton Diocesan Archives).

In March 1842 Baines suffered a stroke; he recovered, but on 6 July 1843 he died in his sleep. Portraits of Baines show a dark-haired man with a dignified bearing, a forceful countenance, and a smile of great felicity. Mary Russell Mitford, describing her one meeting with him, at Prior Park, gave her impression of his humour and intellect: 'The little tinct he retained from his rustic origin', as she recalled, gave him 'the finishing grace of truth'. While some had been at odds with him, Baines also inspired an ardent and stubborn loyalty. Bernard Ward described the reaction to his sudden death: 'The consternation was beyond description, and can only be imagined by recalling the enthusiastic devotion to his person which reigned among those who were nearest to him—a fact which should never be forgotten' (*Sequel to Catholic Emancipation*, 2.57). Within ten years Prior Park was closed and its contents sold. The body of Baines, which had been buried in accordance with his wishes in the chapel, was taken to Downside. William Clifford, a one-time pupil at Prior Park, on becoming bishop of Clifton in 1866, bought back the premises, and re-established a school. While he was missioner at Bath, Baines had become guardian of a young girl, Anna Mendoza y Rios. She married in 1829 Sir Patrick Bellew of Barmeath, later MP for co. Louth and the first Baron Bellew of the second creation. G. A. ELWES

Sources J. Bossy, *The English Catholic community, 1570–1850* (1975); repr. (1976), 388–90 • J. B. Dockery, *Collingridge: a Franciscan contribution to Catholic emancipation* [1954] • J. A. Williams, ed., *Post-Reformation Catholicism in Bath*, 1, Catholic RS, 65 (1975) • H. N. Birt, *Downside School* (1902) • C. Almond, *Ampleforth Abbey* (1903) • B. Ward, *The dawn of the Catholic revival in England, 1781–1803*, 2 vols. (1909) • B. N. Ward, *The eve of Catholic emancipation*, 3 vols. (1911–12) • B. Ward, *The sequel to Catholic emancipation*, 2 vols. (1915) • J. S. Roche, *Prior Park* (1931) • G. Oliver, *Collections illustrating the history of the Catholic religion in the counties of Cornwall, Devon, Dorset, Somerset, Wilts, and Gloucester* (1857) • *Memoir and letters of Lady Mary Arundell*, ed. J. Hirst (1894) • L. Guibara, 'Reminiscences of Mr James Kavanagh', 1888, Christian Brothers Archive, Woodeaves, Altrincham, Cheshire • B. Whelan, ed., *A series of lists relating to the English Benedictine congregation* (1933) • parish register, Gillmoss, Lancashire, St Swithin, 25 June 1786 [baptism] • will, 1809, PRO [J. Baines] • T. J. Brindle to Bishop Briggs, 6 July 1843, Leeds Roman Catholic Diocesan Archives • Baines file, Preston City Archives • Clifton Roman Catholic diocese, Bristol, archives

Archives Ampleforth Abbey, York, archives • Bristol RO, corresp. and papers • Christian Brothers Priory, Hale, Liverpool, archives • Clifton Roman Catholic diocese, Bristol, diary • Derryswood Archives, Bramley, Surrey • Downside Abbey, near Bath • Lancs. RO • St Antony's Friary, Forest Gate, London • St John's Presbytery, South Parade, Bath, diary | Leeds Roman Catholic Diocesan Archives, letters to Thomas Penswick • U. Hull, Brynmor Jones L., Everingham MSS

Likenesses miniature, 1829, St Ambrose, Leigh Woods, Clifton • L. Thenweneti, miniature; known to be in the collection of the bishop of Clifton in 1912 [*see illus.*] • oils, St Ambrose, Leigh Woods, Clifton • oils, Ampleforth Abbey, Yorkshire

Baines [*née* Hunt], **Sarah Jane** [Jennie] (**1866–1951**), suffragette and social reformer, was born on 30 November 1866 in Birmingham, the daughter of James Edward Hunt, gun maker, and his wife, Sarah Ann, *née* Hunt. She started work in a Birmingham small arms factory aged eleven and at fourteen was assisting her parents in Salvation Army activities, rising to the rank of lieutenant. At twenty she was assigned to caring for women charged in court and was appointed evangelist to an independent working men's mission in Bolton. These experiences involved her in the temperance movement and, eventually, the broader sphere of feminism.

On 26 September 1888, at Bolton, Jennie Hunt married George Baines, a bootmaker; they had five children, three of whom survived childhood. Motherhood and work as a sewing machinist delayed full-time public activities but confirmed her commitment to social reform. She joined the Independent Labour Party, the unemployed committee, and the feeding of school children committee and stood, unsuccessfully, for the board of guardians in Stockport.

In October 1905, on reading of the arrest of the militant suffragettes Christabel Pankhurst and Annie Kenney for assault, Jennie Baines joined their organization, the Women's Social and Political Union (WSPU), as a voluntary worker. Appointed a paid organizer in February 1908, she organized disruption of meetings, held open-air rallies, and established new branches in the midlands and north. Though slightly built, she possessed a 'deep, rich and powerful voice' that projected conviction (private information).

In November 1908 Jennie Baines was the first WSPU member to be tried by jury. Convicted of unlawful assembly outside the Coliseum in Leeds, she was sentenced to six weeks' imprisonment on refusing to be bound over because she did 'not recognise the laws of this Court administered by men' (*Votes for Women*, 26 Nov 1908). Her release occasioned an elaborate reception in Trafalgar Square. In July 1912, using the alias Lizzie Baker, she assisted Mary Leigh and Gladys Evans in their attempt to burn down the Theatre Royal in Dublin the night before the prime minister, H. H. Asquith, was scheduled to speak there. Sentenced to seven months' hard labour, she joined the others on hunger strike and was released after five days. On 8 July 1913, with her husband and son Wilfred, she allegedly attempted to bomb carriages in a Lancashire and Yorkshire Railway siding. Appearing at the assizes to deny involvement, Jennie was re-arrested under the 'Cat and Mouse Act' and consigned to Holloway prison, where she refused food and water and was released 'in a very serious condition' (*The Suffragette*, 15 Aug 1913). Though chorea had prevented force-feeding, WSPU leaders judged her health too frail to endure further imprisonment. Under the name Evans, Jennie and members of her family boarded the *Ballarat*, bound for Australia. George and Wilfred Baines were acquitted on 28 November and also embarked for Australia.

In Melbourne, the Baines joined the Victorian Socialist Party and the Labor Party but Jennie devoted her primary energies to the Women's Political Association and Women's Peace Army. With former suffragette Adela Pankhurst, she campaigned against conscription in 1916–17 and in August 1917 led a series of violent protests by women against the surging cost of living. Though sentenced to nine months' imprisonment, both women were freed on appeal. Jennie was gaoled again in March 1919 for flying the prohibited red flag. Faced with six months behind bars, she resorted to hunger striking, reputedly the first prisoner in Australia to do so, and was released on the attorney-general's advice.

Jennie Baines helped found the Victorian branch of the Communist Party in 1920 but was expelled in 1925 and rejoined the Labor Party. In 1928 she was appointed special magistrate to the South Melbourne children's court. She maintained her fiery eloquence on the hustings, abandoning the public platform only months before her death from cancer in Port Melbourne on 20 February 1951. She was cremated, survived by her husband and three children. Jennie Baines distilled her evangelical devotion to socialism in these words: 'To fight for that which is better and nobler in this world is to live in the highest sense, but to submit and tolerate the evils which exist is to merely vegetate in the sewers of iniquity' (*The Socialist*, 11 April 1919).

JUDITH SMART

Sources University of Queensland, Fryer Library, Baines MSS · E. G. Meyer, 'Jennie Baines: a life of commitment', BA diss., Monash University, 1989 · J. Smart, 'Feminists, food and the fair price: the cost of living demonstrations in Melbourne, August–September 1917', *Labour History*, 50 (May 1986), 113–31 · J. Smart, 'Jenny Baines: suffrage and an Australian connection', *Votes for women*, ed. J. Purvis and S. S. Holton (New York, 1999) · *Votes for Women* (1908–13) · *The Suffragette* (1913) · *Manchester Guardian* (1913) · *Woman Voter* [Melbourne: journal of Women's Political Association] (1914–19) · *The Socialist* [Melbourne: journal of Victorian Socialist Party] (1914–21) · *The Herald* [Melbourne] (March 1919) · *Pix* [popular magazine, Sydney] (13 March 1943) · private information (2004) [M. Stevenson; E. Baines] · *AusDB*

Archives University of Queensland, Brisbane, Fryer Library, MSS | National Archives of Australia, Melbourne, *Kiernan* v. *Walsh*, crown solicitor's file, CL 760 · National Archives of Australia, *Porter* v. *Adela Pankhurst et al.*, crown solicitor's file, CL 164

Likenesses photograph, 1909, repro. in D. Atkinson, *The suffragettes in pictures* (1996), 83 · photograph, repro. in E. Hill and O. Fenton Schafer, eds., *Great suffragists—and why: modern makers of history* (1909) · photograph (with Mrs Pethick Lawrence and Miss Drummond), repro. in *Votes for Women* (17 Dec 1908), 202

Baines, Sir Thomas (1622x4–1680). *See under* Finch, Sir John (1626–1682).

Baines, Thomas (1806–1881), journalist, newspaper proprietor, and local historian, was born in Leeds, the third son of Edward *Baines (1774–1848) and Charlotte Talbot, and younger brother of Matthew Talbot *Baines and Sir Edward *Baines. Both his father and brother represented Leeds in parliament, and Baines was a liberal in the family tradition, although he was no friend of advanced radicalism. On moving to Liverpool he acquired and transformed *Billinge's Advertiser* into the *Liverpool Times*, a paper he was to edit for nearly thirty years until 1858, when it finally fell victim to the competition of the new cheap daily press. Having married Fanny Higgins, daughter of councillor Vincent Higgins, Baines developed good local political connections: two of his daughters were to marry prominent members of the council, Edmund Knowles *Muspratt and Arthur Bower *Forwood. Encouraged by local support, Baines hoped to assume personal responsibility for the Liverpool office in London, an important channel of communication between the booming port and its MPs, proposing to run the office as an independent organization to which individuals, associations, and companies would subscribe. As it was, he was appointed to the vacant secretaryship of the office in 1858 as the paid servant of the corporation of Liverpool and the mercantile associations, and also found himself required to serve as personal secretary for the Liverpool MPs. No other municipality had a London office, a reflection of Liverpool's commercial pre-eminence in the mid-nineteenth century and its aspirations to the status of second metropolis, motifs which informed Baines's encyclopaedic studies *History of the Commerce and Town of Liverpool* (1852) and *Liverpool in 1859* (1859). Along with his other main works of local history, *Lancashire and Cheshire Past and Present* (1868–9) and *Yorkshire Past and Present* (1875), Baines's writings, as the *Liverpool Daily Courier* obituary notice aptly commented, were 'more marked by minuteness of research than for tact in compilation'. His liberalism is perhaps most apparent in his response to the flood of Irish immigration into Liverpool. Concern at the costly burden on local poor relief resources was balanced by sympathy for the destitute famine migrants. Irish landlords were taken to task in his study *Agricultural Resources of Great Britain, Ireland and the Colonies* (1847), which called for Irish poor-law reform and government assistance for overseas emigration. In journalism he had a particular aptitude for reporting military matters with both expert knowledge and clarity. The 'obliged friend and servant' of the corporation of Liverpool and the commercial associations of the port, Baines continued to work for the Liverpool office until his sudden death on 31 October 1881 at Seaforth Hall, near Liverpool, the residence of one of his daughters, Mrs E. K. Muspratt. He was survived by six of his seven children.

JOHN BELCHEM

Thomas Baines (1806–1881), by unknown engraver, pubd 1868

Sources *Daily Courier* [Liverpool] (1 Nov 1881) • C. D. Watkinson, 'The liberal party on Merseyside in the nineteenth century', PhD diss., U. Lpool, 1967 • W. O. Henderson, 'The Liverpool office in London', *Economica*, 13 (1933), 473–9
Likenesses line engraving, pubd 1868, NPG [*see illus.*] • T. Hargreaves, pencil drawing, repro. in J. A. Picton, *Memorials of Liverpool*, 4 (1873), 529
Wealth at death £250: probate, 4 Aug 1882, *CGPLA Eng. & Wales*

Baines, (John) Thomas (1820–1875), artist and explorer, was born on 27 November 1820 at King's Lynn, Norfolk, the second son and one of three surviving children of Mary Ann Watson and John Thomas Baines, a master mariner. His father and maternal grandfather were amateur artists, his brother Henry a professional. His mother strongly encouraged his artistic endeavours and was his chief publicist in his lifetime and after his death. After education at private schools in King's Lynn he was apprenticed to a painter of heraldic arms on coach panels, also in King's Lynn, but began sketching marine subjects. In 1842 he sailed for Cape Town, where he practised his trade until, in 1845, he became a marine and portrait painter. In 1846 he began his career as a traveller, using his writing and painting to finance his explorations. In the late 1840s he started to sketch the battlefield scenes which some regard as his most memorable work, and between 1851 and 1852 he was the official war artist to the British forces during the Cape Frontier War.

In 1853 Baines returned to England and worked for the Royal Geographical Society, on whose recommendation, in 1855, he joined Augustus Gregory's expedition to north-west Australia. Many fine paintings and sketches survive from his journey and the Baines River was named after him. His energy and judgement won him special thanks from the colonial government and the freedom of his native town. In 1858, again on the recommendation of the Royal Geographical Society of which he had been elected a fellow in 1857, he was appointed storekeeper and artist to David Livingstone's expedition to open up the Zambezi for trade. It was an unhappy expedition, from which Baines was unjustly dismissed for allegedly misappropriating stores after a disagreement with Livingstone's brother Charles. His paintings from the Zambezi were exhibited in London and Dublin and his manuscript map of the river (D. Middleton, 'The doctor who loved Africa', *Geographical Magazine*, 45/8, 1973, 596) lodged in the Royal Geographical Society. In 1861 he joined James Chapman on an expedition from the south-west coast of Africa to the Victoria Falls; he made a complete route survey, having been taught how to use surveying and astronomical instruments by Sir Thomas Maclear, astronomer royal at the Cape. He also collected scientific information and botanical specimens—the latter now at the Royal Botanic Gardens, Kew—and made many sketches and paintings, which were published as coloured lithographs in 1862. He returned to England to write and lecture before going back to southern Africa to lead an expedition which successfully secured concessions for a gold mining company, although the company failed to take advantage of his achievement. He mapped and wrote a valuable description of the route from the goldfields of the Tati to the capital of the Transvaal republic. In 1873 he was awarded a testimonial gold watch by the Royal Geographical Society. He continued to travel in southern Africa, surveying, drawing, and painting what he saw. On 8 May 1875 he died of dysentery at Durban and was buried in the old cemetery there.

Baines never married but his pleasant manner and faithful nature secured him many friends. He was energetic and active, despite his limp which resulted from the ill setting of a fractured femur and which earned him the nickname Cripple Thigh. Although largely self-taught and working under very difficult and, in the case of his war sketches, dangerous conditions, he produced technically accomplished and sympathetic sketches, watercolours, and oils, which were highly regarded in his own lifetime and were later much prized, especially in southern Africa and in Australia. ELIZABETH BAIGENT

Sources M. Diemont and J. Diemont, eds., *Brenthurst Baines: a selection of the works of Thomas Baines* (1975) • R. Braddon, *Thomas Baines and the north Australian expedition* (1986) • L. W. Bolze, *Thomas Baines centenary, 1875–1975: a tribute to southern Africa's renowned artist-explorer* (Johannesburg, 1975) • J. Carruthers, *Thomas Baines: eastern Cape sketches, 1848–1852* (1990) • J. P. R. Wallis, *Thomas Baines of King's Lynn: explorer and artist, 1820–1875* (1941); repr. (1982) • H. Luckett, *Thomas Baines, 1820–1875* (1975) • *Journal of the Royal Geographical Society*, 46 (1876), 141–4
Archives Brenthurst Library, Johannesburg, corresp., notebooks, diaries, and papers • Lynn Museum, King's Lynn, sketchbooks and paintings • National Archives of Zimbabwe, Harare, corresp. and papers • NHM, paintings and drawings • NL Aus., journal • RBG Kew, botanical specimens • RGS, papers and journals of African expedition | NL Scot., corresp. with Dr David

(John) Thomas Baines (1820–1875), by unknown photographer, 1860s

Livingstone [microfilm] · RGS, letters to Royal Geographical Society

Likenesses photograph, 1860–69, RGS [*see illus.*] · Bullawayo, portrait, 1975 · postage-stamp, 1975, Rhodesian General Post Office · J. T. Baines, self-portrait, Africana Museum, Johannesburg, South Africa · T. Wood, medallions · photograph, repro. in J. Britten and E. S. Boulger, *A biographical index of British and Irish botanists* (1893) · photograph, repro. in Wallis, *Thomas Baines*, frontispiece · wood-engraving, NPG; repro. in *ILN* (27 Feb 1858)

Bainham, James (*d.* 1532), lawyer and protestant martyr, was the youngest son of Sir Alexander Bainham and Elizabeth Langley, *née* Tracy, of Westbury-on-Severn in Gloucestershire, and nephew through his mother of Sir William Tracy, the evangelical landowner from Toddington in Gloucestershire whose will was refused probate in 1531 because of its heretical content. The source of his early education is unknown, but he probably attended a grammar school for he knew both Latin and Greek; later he was admitted to the inns of court and became a lawyer. However, he did not confine his energies to the law; he also espoused the evangelical faith articulated so eloquently in his uncle's will. Foxe describes him as 'an earnest reader of Scriptures, [and] a great maintainer of the godly' (*Acts and Monuments*, 4.697).

In 1531 Bainham was brought before Sir Thomas More, then lord chancellor, and accused of heresy. He had been linked to the evangelical cause after his marriage to Simon Fish's widow. Fish, a lawyer and evangelical pamphleteer, had previously come to More's attention following the publication of his pamphlet *The Supplication of Beggars*. He had been charged with heresy, but recanted before his death in 1531. A few months later Bainham married Fish's widow. According to Foxe, when Bainham first appeared before More, the chancellor attempted to persuade him to return to the traditional faith. Meeting with no success, More had him imprisoned in the Tower, where he was tortured. On 15 December 1531 he was brought before John Stokesley, bishop of London, and examined concerning his beliefs. Initially, he held to his evangelical beliefs, but after several re-examinations, he abjured these on 8 February 1532 and was released from prison.

Bainham soon regretted his decision, however, and publicly reasserted his evangelical beliefs. He was arrested as a result of this relapse and returned to the Tower, and on 19 April 1532 was brought back before the chancellor of the diocese of London. Reminded of his previous abjuration, Bainham rejected it, and went even further by explicitly denying the doctrine of transubstantiation, a clear and unequivocal indication of his heretical beliefs. Next day he was condemned to be burnt by the bishop's vicar-general, and was returned to the Tower, where he was apparently housed in a dark, dungeon-like space. According to Foxe, Hugh Latimer visited him there and found him 'syttyng upon a couche of straw with a boke and a waxe candell in his hand praying and readyng' (*Acts and Monuments*, 4.770). On this occasion Bainham asserted that the cause of his condemnation was his rejection of the doctrine of purgatory. On 30 April 1532, just ten days after his condemnation, he was burnt at Smithfield. As the flames consumed his limbs, Bainham allegedly declared, 'O ye papists! Behold … a miracle; for in this fire I feel no more pain than if I were in a bed of down: but it is to me as a bed of roses' (ibid., 4.705).

CAROLINE LITZENBERGER

Sources G. Burnet, *The history of the Reformation of the Church of England*, rev. N. Pocock, new edn, 1 (1865), 270 · *The acts and monuments of John Foxe*, new edn, ed. G. Townsend, 4 (1846) · A. C. Painter, 'Hugh Westwood', *Transactions of the Bristol and Gloucestershire Archaeological Society*, 54 (1932), 85–105 · will, PRO, PROB 11/22, sig. 26 [Elizabeth Bainham]

Archives Glos. RO · PRO

Bainton, Edgar Leslie (1880–1956), composer and conductor, was born on 14 February 1880 at 2 Florence Villas, De Beauvoir Square, Hackney, London, the second son among the three children of the Revd George Bainton, a Congregational minister, and his wife, Mary Cave, both Londoners by birth. They moved to Coventry shortly afterwards, where Bainton started learning the piano at the age of four and made his first public appearance as a pianist at nine. At eleven he was awarded a musical scholarship to King Henry VIII Grammar School in Coventry, and at sixteen an open scholarship to the Royal College of Music, London, to study the piano with Franklin Taylor. He was later awarded the Wilson scholarship to study composition with Sir Charles Villiers Stanford, and won the Hopkinson gold medal in 1900 and the Tagore medal in 1901.

In 1901 Bainton was appointed to the Newcastle upon Tyne Conservatoire of Music as a teacher of piano and composition. He worked there for the next thirty-two years, becoming principal in 1912. One of his students, Ethel Frances Eales (1885–1954), became his wife on 31 July 1905; their two daughters, Guendolen and Helen, were born in 1906 and 1909. During this time Bainton became increasingly important in the north-east of England, particularly as conductor of the Newcastle Philharmonic Orchestra and as pianist and annotator of programme notes for the Newcastle chamber music society. Works by Bainton such as *The Blessed Damozel*, a setting of D. G. Rossetti's poem, and *Prometheus* were performed at major local festivals in 1907 and 1909. Also during these years he came into regular contact with a group of Georgian poets, including Wilfrid Wilson Gibson, Gordon Bottomley, and Robert Trevelyan, who provided texts for his songs and operas.

In the summer of 1914 Bainton was intercepted in Germany *en route* for the Bayreuth Festival, which he visited yearly, and interned in a prison camp for British civilians in wartime Germany at Ruhleben, near Berlin. During the next four years he took charge of all the musical activities in the camp, from conducting orchestral concerts and supervising music examinations to writing music for productions of Shakespeare's *A Midsummer Night's Dream* and *Twelfth Night*. Early in 1918 he was invalided out to The Hague because of ill health, and on 8 December 1918, shortly after the armistice, he became the first British conductor to conduct the Concertgebouw Orchestra, in a concert of all British music.

During the 1920s Bainton's reputation as a composer continued to rise, with works such as *Three Pieces for Orchestra*, *Eclogue*, and the *Concerto fantasia* being performed at the Henry Wood Promenade Concerts and the Bournemouth Municipal Orchestra concerts. Commissions were completed for the Three Choirs Festival, and his orchestral rhapsody *Epithalamion* was featured by the BBC Symphony Orchestra in its festival of British music in 1931. He was also one of the first recipients of the Carnegie Trust's British music awards, for his choral symphony *Before Sunrise* in 1917 and for his *Concerto fantasia* in 1920. His work as a teacher, lecturer, adjudicator, and conductor was officially recognized with the award of a fellowship of the Royal College of Music and an honorary doctorate of music from Durham University, both in 1934.

In 1934 Bainton was appointed as director to the New South Wales Conservatorium of Music in Sydney, Australia, and he remained in that country until his death in 1956. In addition to fulfilling his duties as director, he was much in demand as a conductor of the recently founded ABC Sydney Symphony Orchestra and introduced much new British music to Australia. The climax of his career was the highly successful production of his opera *The Pearl Tree* by the conservatorium opera school in Sydney in 1944. After retirement in 1946 he continued in his career as conductor, teacher, and composer, even venturing into film music for a brief time.

It is as a composer that Bainton deserves primarily to be remembered. His music is characterized by richness of feeling, lyricism, and imagination inspired by literary sources. His orchestration in particular is noteworthy for its delicate clarity of expression, which reflects the composer's sensitivity and disciplined mind. His first symphony, *Before Sunrise*, for contralto, chorus, and orchestra, is a setting in four movements of poems by Algernon Swinburne dating from 1907. His second symphony of 1940 is more innovative, being cast in one extended movement in twelve sections. In his third symphony, completed in 1956, shortly before his death, Bainton reverted to a four-movement structure, but its character reflects the ruggedness of the Australian landscape that Bainton had come to know so well on his many walking tours.

Bainton's three extant chamber works are also of interest. His string quartet in A was completed in Ruhleben in 1915 as a work in three movements, of which the third returns to the theme and mood of the opening; in 1920 this work was heavily revised, and a finale added. The viola sonata of 1922 is one of Bainton's very finest works and also one of the great viola sonatas of its time. Written in three movements, it displays a dark and autumnal mood, with considerable harmonic flexibility and simultaneous use of contrasting metres in the second movement, which combines the functions of slow movement and scherzo, and in the finale, where the opening folksong-like theme of the second movement's unaccompanied viola melody floats above the military ostinato of the piano part, again with simultaneous contrasting metres, a most striking and original concept. The cello sonata of 1924, also in three movements, is less innovative but still striking in its lyricism and harmonic sensitivity; the second movement's final cadence is original.

Among Bainton's three large-scale operas, *Oithona* (after Ossian) was completed in 1905 and first performed at the 1915 Glastonbury Festival but was later withdrawn. His two most important operas were *The Crier by Night* (libretto by Gordon Bottomley) of 1912, broadcast from Australia in 1942, and *The Pearl Tree* (libretto by Robert Trevelyan) of 1925, premiered at the New South Wales Conservatorium opera school in 1944. Both works utilize the leitmotif method of composition familiar to Bainton from hearing Wagner's operas during his annual visits to the Bayreuth festivals. Bainton also composed several works for chorus and orchestra, inspired by the excellent standard of choral singing throughout Britain during the first half of the twentieth century. These are *The Blessed Damozel* of 1907, *Sunset at Sea* (Reginald Buckley) of 1910, *The Vindictive Staircase* (W. W. Gibson) of 1913, *A Song of Freedom and Joy* (Edward Carpenter) of 1920, *The Tower* (Robert Nichols) of 1924, *The Dancing Seal* (Gibson) of 1926, and *A Hymn to God the Father* (John Donne) of 1926.

Literary connections form an important feature of Bainton's shorter orchestral works, notably in *Pompilia* of 1903 and *Paracelsus* of 1904 (both inspired by Robert Browning), *The Golden River* of 1908 (John Ruskin), *Prometheus* of 1909 (Shelley), and *Epithalamion* of 1929 (Edmund Spenser). Bainton wrote over 100 each of songs and part-songs but only four church anthems, of which 'And I saw a new heaven', completed on 13 June 1928, remains his single most famous work. Edgar Bainton died while taking his regular swim at Point Piper Beach, Sydney, on 8 December 1956. MICHAEL JONES

Sources H. Bainton, *Remembered on waking* (Sydney, 1960) · M. Jones, 'E.B.—musical and spiritual traveller', *British Music*, 12 (1990) · D. Tunley, *Die Musik in Geschichte und Gegenwart* [entry on Bainton] · *New Grove* · www.musicweb.uk.net/bainton [Edgar Bainton Society], 12 July 2000, 1 March 2002 · b. cert. · m. cert.
Archives BL · Mitchell L., NSW, papers, letters, diaries, MSS, ML MSS 452 | Australian Music Centre, Sydney · New South Wales Conservatorium Library, Sydney · NL Aus. | FILM Screensound, Canberra | SOUND Screensound, Canberra
Likenesses double portrait, photograph, 1942 (with Helen Bainton) · A. Fleischmann, bust; formerly in New South Wales Conservatorium, 1944 · photograph, repro. in Bainton, *Remembered on waking*
Wealth at death £8899 6*s*. 3*d*.: 28 May 1957, supreme court of New South Wales (probate division), Australia

Baird, Andrew Wilson (1842–1908), tidal surveyor, was the eldest son in a family of five sons and four daughters born to Thomas Baird, of Woodlands, Cults, Aberdeen, and his wife, Catherine Imray. He was born in Aberdeen on 26 April 1842 and was educated in the town first at the grammar school and then at Marischal College. Baird entered the Military College of the East India Company at Addiscombe in June 1860 and was transferred to the Royal Military Academy at Woolwich in January 1861. He was commissioned lieutenant in the Royal Engineers on 18 December 1861 and, after instruction at Chatham, sailed for India on 1 March 1864. His first assignment was to help with harbour defence and reclamation work in Bombay. During 1868 he served as assistant field engineer to the Abyssinian expedition under Sir Robert Napier. For his work as traffic manager of the railway from the base he was mentioned in dispatches and received the war medal.

In December 1869 Baird became assistant superintendent of the trigonometrical survey of India and was employed on the triangulation in Kathiawar and Gujarat. His health suffered from the extreme heat and he went on furlough in the spring of 1870. While at home he married in Aberdeen on 14 March 1872 Margaret Elizabeth, only daughter of Charles Davidson, of Forrester Hill. In Britain he studied methods of tidal observations and their reduction by harmonic analysis using the method of Sir William Thomson, later Lord Kelvin. Tidal observations were initially undertaken for the survey of India only to determine the mean sea level for the trigonometrical survey, but, on his return to India in December 1871, Baird extended their scope to investigate changing sea level, setting up self-registering gauges, which he himself calibrated and adjusted, for long periods at three stations in the Gulf of Cutch.

In 1876 the governor-general in council commended Baird's work, which Baird described to the British Association at Glasgow that year. In 1877 it was decided to extend systematic tidal observations under the supervision of Baird, who had become deputy superintendent in the trigonometrical survey department. He organized a new department of the survey to cover the coast from Aden to Rangoon, with its centre at Poona. Over an area that included India, Burma, Ceylon, and the Andaman Islands, Baird began to record, collate, and process precise data on tides. In July 1881, while in Venice as one of the commissioners from India to the third International Congress of Geography, Baird exhibited the use of tidal and levelling apparatus in a canal and for this was awarded the gold medal of the first class. After some eighteen months on furlough in England, Baird resumed his tidal duties in March 1883. In August that year the wave which followed the volcanic eruption of Krakatoa, Java, was traced in all his tidal diagrams and Baird sent a paper on this subject to the Royal Society, of which he was elected fellow the following May.

From July 1885 to August 1897 Baird was master of the mint at Calcutta and Bombay and also assistant and deputy surveyor-general of India. On 12 August 1889 he became permanent mint-master at Calcutta. He reorganized the manufacturing department and successfully advocated the withdrawal of worn and dirt-encrusted coinage. He reached the rank of colonel on 9 April 1896 and retired on 20 April 1897. He was created CSI in June 1897. On his return to Britain he bought a small property at Palmers Cross, near Elgin. He died suddenly of heart failure in London on 2 April 1908 and was buried in Highgate cemetery. His wife, five daughters, and two sons survived him.

By the time of his death forty stations covered by Baird's department were regularly reporting tidal observations, a fact which speaks highly of his scientific and administrative skills. He had organized the first extensive tidal studies using harmonic analysis which, with his improvements, was subsequently widely adopted. He was the author of many papers on tidal observations and surveying.

ELIZABETH BAIGENT

Sources G. H. D. [G. H. Darwin], *PRS*, 82A (1909), xvii–xxi · *The Times* (10 April 1908) · War Office Records · BL OIOC · *PICE*, 172 (1907–8), 323 · *CGPLA Eng. & Wales* (1908) · *DNB*
Archives NRA, priv. coll., papers | CUL, corresp. with Lord Kelvin, Add. MSS 7342, 7656
Wealth at death no value given: sealed, 24 June 1908, *CGPLA Eng. & Wales*

Baird, Charles (1766–1843), engineer and manufacturer of steam-driven machinery, was born on 20 December 1766 at Westertown, near Carron, Stirlingshire, one of the ten children of Nicol Baird, superintendent of the Firth and Clyde Canal, and his wife, Christian. In 1782 he was apprenticed to the Carron Company, which was then the foremost ironworks in Scotland, and within three years he had been entrusted with the firm's production of cast-iron guns.

In the 1780s the quantity of the Carron Company's export of guns to Russia resulted in an invitation to the manager, Charles Gascoigne, to develop a gun factory there. Baird accompanied Gascoigne in 1786 and helped establish the Aleksandrovsk gun factory at Petrozavodsk, north-east of St Petersburg, and the Koncherzersky foundry. He remained for three years as Gascoigne's assistant.

In 1792 he entered into partnership with a St Petersburg mill owner, Francis Morgan, to establish an ironworks company which came to be known as the Baird Works. Its success was typical of the dominant role played by foreign entrepreneurs in early nineteenth-century Russian ironworks and machine industries. In June 1794 Baird married Sophia Morgan, the daughter of his business partner. They had three sons, of whom only one, Francis Baird (1802–1864), outlived his father.

The Baird Works specialized mainly in the manufacture of steam-driven machinery. It was responsible for the machinery for the imperial arsenal and the imperial glassworks, and by 1825 it was producing 130 steam engines of all kinds. In 1815 the factory built Russia's first steamship, the *Elizaveta*, which operated on the route from Kronstadt to St Petersburg. Baird's ten-year monopoly on that route enabled his steamships to dominate the waters around St Petersburg. Likewise, his development of a new method for purifying sugar, using non-animal substances, earned him a large share of the city's sugar supply.

The most lasting legacy of the Baird Works were structures in and around St Petersburg, for which the firm supplied the ironwork. One of the first of these was within the works: the Tallow Wharf Bridge (1805–6; demolished 1914), with a 63 foot span, built up from cast-iron segments. Twenty years later there followed a group of notable suspension bridges, designed by Georges Traitteur, including the Post Office Bridge over the Moika and two bridges over the Griboyedov Canal. In connection with these, Baird designed a hydraulic chain-testing machine. The firm was also associated with two of the St Petersburg projects of the French architect, Auguste Ricard de Montferrand: for his Alexander column (1832–4) it cast the reliefs on the base and the colossal angel on top of the column, and for St Isaac's Cathedral (1836–41) it supplied the ironwork of the dome of 130 foot diameter, Baird having contributed to the dome's structural design.

Baird was known for his business abilities as much as his technical expertise, in particular his assiduous cultivation of Russian officialdom. He was assisted by a number of talented engineers, including his nephew, William Handyside (1793–1850), and his son, Francis, who succeeded him as manager of the firm. His workforce included up to a hundred Russian serfs, for whom he paid a small fee to their masters. He received a number of Russian honours, including the order of St Anna (second class) and the order of St Vladimir (third class), and his achievements were recognized in Britain through his election to the Institution of Civil Engineers in 1841. He died on 10/22 December 1843 in St Petersburg and was buried in the Smolensk Lutheran cemetery there. ROBERT THORNE

Sources T. Tower, *Memoir of the late Charles Baird … and of his son, the late Francis Baird* (1867) • A. A. Polovtsov, ed., *Russkii biograficheskii slovar'* [Russian biographical dictionary], 2 (1900), 728 • J. G. Kohl, *Russia and the Russians in 1842*, 2 (1843) [Ger. orig. *Petersburg in Bildern und Skizzen* (1841)] • J. G. James, 'Russian iron bridges to 1850', *Transactions* [Newcomen Society], 54 (1982–3), 79–104 • W. L. Blackwell, *The beginnings of Russian industrialization, 1800–1860* (1968) • *Cemetery handbook* (1993) • S. G. Fedorov, *Wilhelm von Traitteur: ein badischer Baumeister als Neuerer in der russischen Architektur, 1814–1832* (Berlin, 2000)

Baird, Sir David, first baronet (1757–1829), army officer, was born on 26 December 1757 at Newbyth, Haddingtonshire, the fifth son of William Baird (*c.*1711–1766), merchant, and Alicia, *née* Johnstone, of Hiltown, Berwick (*d.* *c.*1787). Baird's siblings included five sisters, two older, two younger, and one close in age, and two younger brothers. Within years of his birth the family moved to Gordon House, near the top of Castle Hill, Edinburgh. After William Baird's death the family faced financial hardship and young David gave his mother some difficulty. The commission Baird obtained as an ensign in the 2nd regiment of foot on 14 December 1772 had been purchased by his mother for an older, more promising brother who died suddenly. Before sailing to Gibraltar to join his regiment in April 1773, Baird attended Lewis Lochée's military academy at Chelsea, where, as a 6 feet tall, athletic youth he enjoyed the emphasis on physical activity. He otherwise lacked education, being 'too volatile to attend closely to study' (Hook, 1.2), but proved a brave soldier and a good regimental officer who, over the course of three decades, saw active service on three continents. A comrade recalled him as 'a fine soldier-like man; with such a determined air, that you might draw the inference from his countenance, that he was ready, if ordered, to march into a fiery furnace' ('Recollections of the British army', 191).

India, 1780–1801 Having returned from Gibraltar with his regiment in 1776, Baird obtained a leave of absence and travelled to Elgin, where, on 26 December 1777, he became a captain in Lord Macleod's new regiment, the 73rd highlanders. The regiment was ordered to India and embarked for Portsmouth on 8 May 1778. They arrived fifteen days later, missing the India-bound fleet's departure, and were sent to the Channel Islands, then subject to French threat. After spending six months on Guernsey, they returned to Portsmouth in November, wintered nearby at Petersfield, departed for India on 7 March 1779, and reached Madras on 20 January 1780. In July 1780 Haidar Ali, ruler of Mysore, attacked Madras and the nawab of Arcot, a British ally. Baird accompanied the force sent to the relief of Arcot when, on 10 September 1780 at Perambaukum, they were surrounded and destroyed by Haidar and his son Tipu Sultan. Baird's corps 'fought with such determination and heroism, that many of them were seen loading their muskets after their legs had been shot away; almost all disdained to accept quarter' (Hildyard, 17). With sabre wounds to the head, a pike wound in the arm, and a ball in the thigh, Baird fell senseless to the ground. Nearly left for dead his pillaged body was found by two comrades; the trio were soon among Haidar's prisoners. Referring to her son's active disposition, a variously quoted apocryphal story credits Baird's mother, upon learning of her son's capture, with the statement 'God help the puir man that's chained to my Davy' ('Investigator', 5). Baird received rudimentary medical treatment before he was carried in a litter to Seringapatam, Mysore's

Sir David Baird, first baronet (1757–1829), by Thomas Hodgetts (after Sir Henry Raeburn, exh. RA 1814)

fortified capital, while the other 250 captives made the journey on foot. At Seringapatam the fifty officers were kept in 'small rooms, or rather dungeons' (Lindsay, 3.278), often with 9 lb irons shackled to each leg. The hungry and diseased prisoners manufactured clothing for themselves and, when not chained, grew food. On 11 March 1784, with the signing of the treaty of Mangalore, the survivors were released. After a brief convalescence Baird joined his regiment near Arcot. He became a major on 5 June 1787, obtained a leave of absence, and departed India in October 1787.

After three years in Britain he became a lieutenant-colonel on 8 December 1790 and returned to India in March 1791 to participate in the Third Anglo-Mysore War, a conflict precipitated in December 1789 by Tipu's attack on Travancore, a British ally. He arrived at Madras during the summer of 1791, and joined Governor-General Cornwallis's army near the recently captured town of Bangalore. Advancing slowly, Cornwallis reached Seringapatam on 5 February 1792, and the following evening attacked the force Tipu had assembled before his capital. During this action Baird successfully led his highland regiment and four Indian battalions against troops entrenched on Carrighaut Hill. Two weeks later peace was settled and Cornwallis's army dispersed. Baird was stationed at Madura when news arrived of the French declaration of war against Britain. He was ordered to Pondicherry and attended when the city surrendered without a fight on 22 August 1793. From Pondicherry Baird was dispatched to Tanjore to command the British force hired by the local raja. He worked against the plans of Lord Hobart, governor of Madras, to obtain greater control over the raja's military and fiscal affairs. Although Governor-General Sir John Shore blocked Hobart's venture, Baird was moved from Tanjore in September 1796. A year later he and his regiment were rotated home.

Baird sailed from Madras on 17 October 1797 and arrived at Cape Town in December, when Governor George Macartney asked him to remain and train the garrison. With thoughts of succeeding Macartney, he agreed. Promoted to major-general on 18 June 1798, in October he was ordered to lead 1800 men to Madras to counter the threat posed to British India by Napoleon Bonaparte's expedition to Egypt and the reception at Seringapatam of eighty-six French soldiers sent by the governor of Mauritius. Baird reached Madras on 7 January 1799 and on 1 February joined the army gathering at Vellore under General George Harris. Two days later, having determined that Tipu's reception of French soldiers constituted a *casus belli*, Governor-General Richard Wellesley, second earl of Mornington, ordered Harris to mobilize. When the army crossed into Mysore on 5 March, Baird knew 'Our object is Tippoo' (Baird to R. Baird, 13 Feb 1799, Baird MSS, M 1995.51.2). On 5 April Seringapatam was reached. A siege commenced, and once the walls were breached in early May, Harris decided to storm the city. Baird volunteered to lead the assault: he wanted, he said, to 'pay off old scores' (Hook, 1.205). The night before the assault he led men into the forward entrenchments located 1000 yards from the breach. At 1 p.m. on 4 May 1799 Baird rose from his trench yelling 'Come, my brave fellows, follow me, and prove yourselves worthy the name of British soldiers' (Beatson, 126) and in six minutes led 4000 men through heavy rocket and musket fire across the Cauvery River and into Seringapatam. They seized the ramparts and within hours had overcome all opposition. In the palace Baird took custody of royal prisoners and soon discovered Tipu:

> we found a man who being severely threatened said that the Sultan was killed in attempting to escape thru' the northern sally port and offered to conduct us to the body. We accordingly proceeded thither and under a slaughtered heap of several hundreds, many of whom were men of consequence in his service, had the pleasure to discover the body of the Sultan. He had been shot thru the head and body and was quite dead. (Baird to Harris, 6 May 1799, Baird MSS, M 1995.51, fol. 3)

The following morning Baird's breakfast was disrupted by Colonel Arthur Wellesley, the governor-general's brother and the future duke of Wellington, who arrived with orders to supersede Baird to the command of Seringapatam. Maladroitly relieved of his conquest by a junior officer, Baird left Tipu's palace without finishing his meal. Mutual antipathy lingered.

Egypt and Cape Town, 1800–1807 After the war Baird was stationed at Dinapore, Bengal, from where he wrote that he was 'a soldier whose greatest ambition ever has been and ever will be to endeavour to gain the approbation and applause of his King and Country', but who was 'now heartily sick of this country and wish to get home as soon as I can with propriety' (Baird to R. Baird, 13 June 1800, Baird MSS, M 1995.51, fol. 8). In 1801 he was instructed to lead an expedition to the Red Sea, co-operating with a larger force attacking Egypt from the Mediterranean. He sailed from Bombay in early April 1801 with 5000 men and reached Quseir on 8 June, from where he dispatched parties of engineers and sepoys 100 miles across the desert. After they had established a string of food and water depots between Quseir and the Nile, Baird, wanting to 'get forward' (S. Auchmuty to C. Beresford, 22 June 1801, Baird MSS, M 1995.44), sent the first of five columns to Keneh. The rest followed, and by 8 July all had reached the Nile. From Keneh, Baird floated 400 miles down the Nile, arriving at Alexandria in September, immediately after the French had capitulated to General John Hutchinson. The French removed from Egypt, Baird sailed from Suez in May 1802 and reached Calcutta in August. He left India for good in March 1803, after being superseded once more by Arthur Wellesley.

In July 1805 Baird, a popular hero due to his exploits in India and Egypt, went to Cork to prepare an army to attack the Cape Colony. A soldier who trained at Cork recalled that he appeared to have been 'bitten by a mad adjutant, or rather been inoculated with the pacing-stick drill' as he taught his men 'the mystery of standing on one leg … for two hours' ('Recollections of the British army', 192). On 31 August he left Ireland with 6000 troops. The force reached Table Bay on 4 January 1806 and landed two days later. On 8 January the Dutch made a stand near Cape Town. Baird described the battle of Blauberg:

> on approaching the Enemy our line was formed with much precision & expedition & the left or Highland Brigade advanced with utmost resolution & steadiness under a severe fire of round & grape-shot & musketry … a charge bore down all opposition. (Baird to the duke of York, 12 Jan 1806, Baird MSS, M 199.45, fol. 90)

Cape Town capitulated two days later. Hoping to obtain prize money, Baird, in spring 1806, agreed to lend troops to Admiral Sir Home Popham and Colonel Charles Beresford in an unsanctioned attack on Buenos Aires. Vast wealth never materialized, and Baird left Cape Town on 19 January 1807, recalled and censured by London. He was not in Britain long before sailing to the Baltic, where he led a division during the capture of Copenhagen in September 1807.

Later career, 1808–1809 In spring 1808 Baird spoke of 'rural felicity … [as] perhaps … the happiest state of any' (Baird to Young, 27 March 1808, Baird MSS, M 199.47.19) and was considering retiring when he agreed in April 1808 to train and lead an army to northern Spain, where General Sir John Moore was supporting the Seville-based junta opposed to Joseph Bonaparte's rule. He sailed from Cork with 10,000 men in September 1808 and reached Corunna on 13 October. Marching through the León mountains, he reached Astorga on 19 November. A week later, before his army had completed the mountain crossing, Moore instructed him to retreat, since the French had defeated the Spanish near Madrid. After re-entering the mountains Baird received countermanding instructions. He was told Madrid had risen against the French and that:

> If the flame catches elsewhere and becomes all general, the best results may be expected. If confined to Madrid, that town will be sacrificed, and it will be as bad, or worse than ever … I mean to proceed bridle in hand; for if the bubble bursts and Madrid falls, we shall have a run for it. (Moore to Baird, 6 Dec 1808, Sorrell, 35)

Baird turned his army around again and met Moore at Mayorga on 20 December, but the Madrid insurgency was broken, French armies approached, and they were compelled to retreat to Corunna. Morale became 'soured by fatigue and hunger' (*Diary of William Gavin*, xiii) and the rearguard actions Baird helped to organize were increasingly hampered by supply shortages, a breakdown in discipline, and the harsh Spanish winter. When the army reached the mountains, a 'march of death' began

> up Monte de Cabero … There was nothing to sustain our famished bodies, or shelter them from the rain or snow … The sick and wounded that we had been still enabled to drag with us in the waggons, were left to perish in the snow. The road was one line of bloody-footmarks, from the sore feet of men; and on its side lay the dead and dying. (Pococke, 75–6)

On 13 January 1809 Moore's army reached Corunna, and on 16 January the French attacked. Their weight centred on Baird's division, and early on grapeshot struck his left arm and torso. With his sash keeping his arm attached, he walked 2 miles to the harbour, where, on board a transport, his limb was amputated. The French were repulsed, but Moore was killed, leaving Baird commander. He relinquished his duties on 17 January and sailed home, reaching Portsmouth on 25 January 1809.

Final years, 1809–1829 Baird recuperated at Yardleybury, Hertfordshire, and after receiving a baronetcy on 13 April 1809, he journeyed to Scotland, declaring his intention to become 'a *great* and *good* farmer' (Baird to Young, 30 May 1809, Baird MSS, M 1995.47, fol. 22). On 4 August 1810 he married Ann Campbell Preston and moved to her house, Ferntower, near Crieff, Perthshire. A devoted husband, Baird jested 'I could command 10,000 men; yet I cannot command one woman' (Haley, 167). His torso remained painful, but he rode daily and claimed to be as good a shot with one arm as two. He was a member of the Melton Mowbray hunt, Leicestershire; it was said of Baird and a friend that except for them

> very few attempted to go strait. The fences were higher then, and no caps were worn, and both of them would have their clothes torn off their backs, and their flesh from their faces, rather then not go every inch of the way with the hounds.

Another Meltonian commented that if Baird 'did get a fall, and you thought he was out of the run, he would always pop up by your side' (Paget, 82). Promoted to general on 8 May 1814, he regularly sought patronage, including the Cape governorship, and perhaps needed money to fund Ferntower's ongoing improvements. In February 1820 he became Ireland's commander-in-chief, but after a riding accident in June 1822 left Dublin without the peerage he expected. Near Ferntower in the early autumn of 1828 he had another, more serious riding accident. He wintered in London and fell ill. At a royal levee in April he was appointed commander of Fort George, but he never reached the highlands. Suffering from fevers and headaches, he travelled to Ferntower and arrived home in debilitating pain on 20 July. Baird's condition deteriorated, and he died at home on 18 August 1829. He was succeeded in his baronetcy by his nephew David Baird.

As well as building an obelisk commemorating her husband on a summit overlooking the Strath and hiring T. E. Hook, a popular novelist, to write her husband's biography, Lady Baird commissioned David Wilkie to paint *General Sir David Baird Discovering the Body of the Sultaun Tippoo Sahib* and insisted that her husband be depicted wearing an impressive cape; the finished work was hung in the drawing room at Ferntower. In 1813 Baird reflected on his and Wellington's careers, indicating 'It is the highest pride of my life that anybody should ever have dreamed of my being put in the balance with him … I know both him and myself *now*' (Edgecumbe, 2.25). The duke meanwhile remembered Baird as 'a gallant, hard-headed, lion-hearted officer, but he had no talent, no *tact*' (Jennings, 102), yet at the Royal Academy exhibition in 1839, where Wilkie's grand canvas was the centrepiece, he proudly told his lady companion how well he had known Sir David. BRENDAN CARNDUFF

Sources *DNB* • National War Museum of Scotland, Baird MSS • T. E. Hook, *Life of General, the Right Honourable Sir David Baird, bart.*, 2 vols. (1832) • A. H. Haley, *Our Davy: General Sir David Baird, K. B., 1757–1829* (1989) • 'Investigator', *Letters commenting upon Mr. Theodore Hook's memoir of the life of Sir David Baird* (1834) • W. H. Wilkin, *The life of Sir David Captain Baird* (1913) • Lord Lindsay [A. W. C. Lindsay, earl of Crawford], *Lives of the Lindsays*, [new edn], 3 vols. (1849) • E. Longford [E. H. Pakenham, countess of Longford], *Wellington*, 1: *The years of the sword* (1969) • H. J. T. Hildyard, *Historical record of the 71st regiment highland light infantry* (1876) • A. Beatson, *A view of the origin and conduct of the war with Tippoo Sultaun* (1800) • A. Dirom, *A narrative of the campaign in India which terminated the war with Tippoo Sultan in 1792* (1793) • J. McGregor, *Medical sketches of the expedition to Egypt from India* (1804) • military journal of John Budgen, BL OIOC, MSS Eur. A 103 • P. Mackesy, *British victory in Egypt, 1801: the end of Napoleon's conquest* (1995) • 'Recollections of the British army in the early campaigns of the revolutionary war', *United Service Journal*, 1–3 (1836) • T. Pococke, *Journal of a soldier of the seventy-first, or Glasgow regiment highland light infantry, 1806–1815* (1819) • *The diary of William Gavin, ensign and quartermaster, 71st highland regiment, 1806–1815*, ed. C. Oman (1921) • T. S. Sorrell, *Notes on the campaign of 1808–1809 in the north of Spain* (1828) • G. Paget, *The Melton Mowbray of John Ferneley* (1931) • R. Edgecumbe, *The diary of Frances, Lady Shelly, 1787–1817* (1912) • *The Croker papers: the correspondence and diaries of … John Wilson Croker*, ed. L. J. Jennings, 3 vols. (1884)

Archives National War Museum of Scotland, Edinburgh, corresp. and papers • NL Scot., letter-book, MS 106 | BL, corresp. with Sir James Willoughby Gordon, Add. MS 49482, *passim* • BL, letters to Sir John Moore, Add. MS 57541 • BL, Aberdeen MSS, official corresp. as second-in-command in the Peninsula, Add. MS 43224 • BL OIOC, corresp. relating to India • PRO NIre., corresp. with Castlereagh, D3030

Likenesses T. Hickey, two charcoal and chalk sketches, 1799, Stratfield Saye, Hertfordshire • H. Singleton, oils, *c.*1800 (*The surrender of the two sons of Tipu Sahib, Sultan of Mysore, to David Baird*), Yale U. CBA • A. Cardon, stipple, pubd 1806 (after A. J. Oliver), BM, NPG • H. Raeburn, oils, exh. RA 1814, Lennoxlove, Lothian region, Scotland • attrib. J. Watson-Gordon, oils, *c.*1825, NPG • L. Macdonald, marble bust, *c.*1828, Scot. NPG • D. Wilkie, group portrait, oils, 1834–9 (*General Sir David Baird discovering the body of the Sultaun Tippoo Sahib*), NG Scot.; on loan to Edinburgh Castle • D. Wilkie, watercolour, 1836, NPG • D. Wilkie, group portrait, oils study, 1837–8 (*General Sir David Baird discovering the body of the Sultaun Tippoo Sahib*), Scot. NPG; various studies, AM Oxf.; BM; FM Cam.; Royal Scot. Acad.; V&A • F. Grant, oils, exh. RA 1839 (*The Melton Hunt*), Stratfield Saye, Hertfordshire • J. B. Philip, statue, 1870, Calcutta • A. W. Devis, oils (*The finding of the body of Tippoo Sahib by Major General Baird and others, 4 May 1799*) • T. Hodgetts, mezzotint (after H. Raeburn, exh. RA 1814), NPG [*see illus.*] • attrib. P. J. de Loutherbourg, watercolour, Scot. NPG

Baird, Sir Dugald (1899–1986), obstetrician, was born on 16 November 1899 in Beith, Ayrshire, the eldest in the family of three sons and one daughter of David Baird, head of the science department at Greenock Academy, and his wife, May, daughter of John Allan, farmer, of Alloway, Ayrshire. He was educated at Greenock Academy and then studied science and medicine at Glasgow University, graduating MB, ChB in 1922. He proceeded to MD with honours and was awarded the Bellahouston gold medal in 1934. He was elected a fellow of the Royal College of Obstetricians and Gynaecologists in 1935. After he qualified he worked in the Glasgow Royal Maternity and Women's Hospital and the Glasgow Royal Infirmary. In 1928 he married May Deans Tennent (*d.* 1983), daughter of Matthew Brown Tennent, grocer, of Newton, Lanarkshire. She was also a doctor and was involved in local and national politics. She was appointed CBE in 1962. There were two sons and two daughters of the marriage.

Baird's experiences as a medical student and junior doctor in Glasgow, where he attended home births, had a fundamental effect on his career. He was appalled at the conditions in which women had their confinements and the lack of concern about them among his senior colleagues. During his term as senior lecturer in the University of Glasgow (1931–7) he introduced sterilization for the many women who had had several children that he attended, and also, in some cases, he performed abortions for social reasons. He was shocked by the high maternal and infant mortality rates in the Glasgow Royal Maternity and Women's Hospital, where two mothers died each week from complications of childbirth. He became aware of the wide discrepancy in the health and reproductive efficiency of women in different socio-economic groups and quickly realized the importance of social factors in obstetrics.

When Baird moved to Aberdeen in 1937, as regius professor of midwifery, he saw opportunities for research in this field. Since the population was relatively stable and not too large, proper arrangements could be made for obstetric care and the keeping of statistics. He set up a records system based on good data and accurate measurements and introduced epidemiology into obstetric practice. Initially in Aberdeen he had conducted a thriving private practice in addition to his hospital work, but when the National Health Service was introduced in 1948 he gave up private practice to concentrate on his academic work and research.

Realizing that a multidisciplinary approach was most likely to succeed in improving obstetric care and reproductive performance, Baird persuaded the Medical Research Council to support this type of research. In 1955 the Obstetric Medicine Research Unit was established, with himself as the honorary director. It consisted of dietitians, sociologists, physiologists, endocrinologists, statisticians, and obstetricians, who worked together to elucidate the factors affecting reproduction in women. He was thus the instigator of social obstetrics, and much of what he pioneered later became commonly accepted practice.

Baird was also instrumental in altering the pattern of reproduction in Britain. He lectured on the fifth freedom—freedom from the tyranny of excessive fertility. In Aberdeen he introduced the first free family-planning clinic in Britain, and he offered abortion to Aberdeen women. This was very important in influencing the reform of the abortion law in 1967. He also encouraged women who had completed their family to be sterilized.

Baird was concerned with long-term effects in obstetrics. Because of the excellent record system at the Aberdeen Maternity Hospital he was able to study generations of women and the influence on daughters of their mothers' pregnancies. He saw deaths from cervical cancer as avoidable and instituted the first screening programme, the results of which showed that mortality could be reduced by this method.

Baird, who retired from his chair in 1965, sat on many local, national, and international committees and was a consultant to the World Health Authority. He was knighted in 1959 and received honorary degrees from Glasgow (1959), Manchester (1962), Aberdeen and Wales (both 1966), and Newcastle and Stirling (both 1974). In 1966, along with his wife, he was made a freeman of Aberdeen. He became an honorary FRCOG in 1986.

A big man with a strong physical presence, Baird had a quizzical face and the smile on his lips illustrated his marked sense of humour. In his earlier years he was a fine rugby football player and had a trial for the Scottish international team. In later life he played a good game of golf. Baird died in Edinburgh on 7 November 1986.

MALCOLM MACNAUGHTON, *rev.*

Sources personal knowledge (1996) • *WWW*
Archives SOUND priv. coll., conversation between Sir Dugald Baird and Malcolm Macnaughton, 1986
Wealth at death £211,188.07: confirmation, 5 Feb 1987, *CCI*

Baird, George Husband (1761–1840), Church of Scotland minister and university principal, was a native of the parish of Bo'ness on the Forth, Linlithgowshire, where his father, a landed gentleman of Stirlingshire, rented a farm from the duke of Hamilton. Born on 13 July 1761 at Inveravon, Bo'ness, Baird received his primary education at the parish school of Bo'ness, and, on the family's removal to a newly purchased property, named Manuel, in Linlithgowshire, at the parish school of Linlithgow. He was a plodding, persevering, and well-mannered, rather than a brilliant, schoolboy. In 1773, in his thirteenth year, he was entered as a student in humanity (Latin) and Greek at Edinburgh University. He speedily came under the favourable notice of Principal Robertson, the historian, and Professor Dalzel, and others, because of his devotion to his class-work and marked progress. Not content with the tasks of the university classes, he carried on simultaneously philological and philosophical researches, in which he was associated with James Finlayson, afterwards professor of logic at Edinburgh, and Josiah Walker, afterwards professor of humanity at Glasgow. As a result of these extra-collegiate studies he acquired an exceptionally varied and accurate knowledge of nearly all the living languages of Europe.

In 1784 Baird was recommended by Professor Dalzel as tutor in the family of Colonel Blair, of Blair. In 1786 he received licence as a preacher of the gospel from the presbytery of Linlithgow of the Church of Scotland. In 1787 he was presented to the parish of Dunkeld by the duke of Atholl, through influence brought to bear by his friend Finlayson. Before leaving for his parish he had encountered Robert Burns, and in his old age he delighted to tell of his having repeatedly met with the 'Ayrshire ploughman'; his name was among the subscribers to the poet's first volume, published at Kilmarnock in 1786. Baird was evangelical rather than with the Church of Scotland's 'moderates', but family ties threw him a good deal into the cultivated circle of the Robertsons and Blairs and their school. While he was parish clergyman at Dunkeld he was resident in the duke's family, and superintended the education of the duke's three sons. In 1789–90 he was presented to the large and important parish church of Edinburgh, known as 'Lady Yester's', but the ducal house of Atholl persuaded him to decline the call.

His marriage in August 1792 to Isabella, eldest daughter of Thomas *Elder, lord provost of Edinburgh, was a fortunate one. In November 1792 the town council presented him to New Greyfriars Church, Edinburgh, and also to the chair of Hebrew at Edinburgh University, which was in their gift. The senatus academicus conferred on him the honorary degree of DD in the same year. In 1793, though comparatively youthful and untried, he was elected by the town council principal of Edinburgh University, in succession to William Robertson. As principal he was called upon to punish a breach of the university's discipline committed by three students who subsequently attained to pre-eminent distinction. A challenge had been addressed to one of the professors, and the parties implicated in the misdemeanour were Lord Henry Petty (afterwards marquess of Lansdowne), Henry Brougham, and Francis Horner. These students were summoned before the senatus academicus. Only Brougham appeared, and the rebuke of the principal was so delivered and accepted that a warm friendship ensued, and lasted long after Brougham had entered public life.

In 1799 Principal Baird was translated to the New North Church. In 1801, on the death of Dr Blair, he was appointed his successor in the High Church, where he remained until his death. Towards the close of his life he vigorously promoted a scheme for the education of the poor in the highlands and islands of Scotland. He submitted his proposal to the general assembly of the Church of Scotland in May 1824, and it was sanctioned in the following year. In his sixty-seventh year, when enfeebled in health, he traversed the entire highlands of Argyll, the west of Inverness and Ross, and the western islands, from Lewis to Kintyre. In his sixty-eighth year he similarly visited the north highlands, and the Orkneys and Shetland. Through his influence Dr Andrew Bell, of Madras, bequeathed £5000 for education in the highlands of Scotland. Baird died on 14 January 1840 at Manuel.

A. B. GROSART, *rev.* M. C. CURTHOYS

Sources Anderson, *Scot. nat.* • *Fasti Scot.*, new edn, 1.68–9 • A. Grant, *The story of the University of Edinburgh during its first three hundred years*, 2 (1884), 270–71

Archives NL Scot., corresp. with George Combe • NL Scot., corresp. with John Lee • U. Edin., New Coll. L., letters to Thomas Chalmers

Likenesses J. Kay, caricature, etching, 1793 (with Thomas Elder), BM, NPG • W. Ward, mezzotint, pubd 1817 (after A. Geddes), BM • oils (after A. Geddes), U. Edin.

Baird, James (**1802–1876**), ironmaster and philanthropist, was born at Kirkwood in Lanarkshire on 5 December 1802, the fourth son of Alexander Baird (*d.* 1833), farmer, and Jean, the daughter of James Moffat. He attended the Old Monkland parish school, and may have attended classes at Anderson College in Glasgow. Alexander Baird was a man of considerable ambition and initiative. He enclosed many of the farms that had been in his family for generations, and seized the opportunity offered by the Napoleonic Wars to enlarge his landholdings and broaden his interests, taking over another 250 acres and building a mill. Wishing to provide for his growing family—by this time numbering seven sons and a daughter—he began to lease coalfields and to invest in the manufacture of iron. In 1809 he leased the coalworks at Woodside near Dalserf. In 1816 he added the Rochsolloch coalfield near Airdrie, and in 1822 the Merryston coalfield, to his operations. In 1826 James, together with his father and his brothers William and Alexander, leased the coalfields of Sunnyside, Hollandhirst, and New Gartsherrie. Two years later they leased the rights to mine ironstone at Cairnhill, adjoining Gartsherrie, and began to erect blast furnaces there. By 1842 they had sixteen furnaces operating at the Gartsherrie ironworks.

The Bairds' first furnace was put in blast on 4 May 1830. Alexander Baird retired that year, and four of his sons—William, Alexander, James, and George—formed a partnership, William Baird & Co., to continue the business, joined later by their brothers Robert and Douglas. James Baird was responsible for the management of the firm, and took a leading role in the development and improvement of plant. Building on the work of James Beaumont Neilson, the inventor and patentee of the hot-blast furnace, he organized the installation of the first circular furnace in Scotland in 1832, developed improved blast heaters, and introduced other innovations in order to improve efficiency and output. As a result of his endeavours, individual furnace production increased from 60 to 250 tons of iron per week. Attempts made in concert with other Scottish ironmasters to break Neilson's hot-blast patent met with less success—Bairds finally settled out of court, paying the patent holder over £106,000 in royalties and expenses.

William Baird & Co. expanded, acquiring coalfields and ironworks in other parts of Lanarkshire and in the counties of Ayr, Stirling, Dumbarton, and Cumberland. A subsidiary, the Eglinton Iron Company, added works at Eglinton in 1846, Blair in 1852, Muirkirk and Lugar in 1856, and Portland in 1864. It has been estimated that by the mid-1860s Bairds was responsible for 25 per cent of Scotland's output of pig iron, with a capacity to produce up to 300,000 tons per annum. It employed 10,000 men and boys, and recent historians agree with the contemporary view that Bairds was probably the largest single producer of pig iron in the world. James Baird practically retired from the business during the early 1860s, leaving its management in the hands of his nephews. His interest in industrial technology was undimmed, however, and he took out a number of patents for improvements to coal-cutting equipment.

Baird and his brothers were committed supporters of the Conservative Party. William Baird was MP for the Falkirk burghs in 1841–6, and James represented the same constituency in 1851–2 and 1852–7. He remained an active campaigner for the party in later years, and in 1873 chaired a meeting held to celebrate Benjamin Disraeli's being granted the freedom of the city of Glasgow, and his election as rector of the university. The Baird brothers built many churches to serve the communities in which their employees lived, and James Baird campaigned vigorously for the Church of Scotland to make greater efforts to serve the needs of the population in industrial areas. In 1873 he made a gift of £500,000 to the church, to 'assist in providing the means of meeting, or at least as far as possible promoting the mitigation of spiritual destitution among the population of Scotland'. The church set up the Baird Trust to administer the funds and carry out the wishes of the benefactor.

Baird's brothers all predeceased him, and on Robert's death in 1856 James succeeded to the estate of Auchmedden in Aberdeenshire. Already the owner of small estates in Ayrshire, he acquired Cambusdoon in Ayrshire in 1853, Knoydart in western Inverness-shire in 1857, and Muirkirk in Ayrshire in 1863. He served as a magistrate for Lanarkshire, and a deputy lieutenant for the counties of Ayr and Inverness.

In 1852 Baird married Charlotte, the daughter of Robert Lockhart of Castlehill, Lanarkshire. Two years after Charlotte's death in 1857, he married Isabella Agnew, daughter of Admiral James Hay of Belton, East Lothian, who survived him. He had no children. In 1876 he fell ill with bronchitis on a trip to London. He returned to Cambusdoon, but died two weeks later, on 20 June. He was buried beside his first wife at Alloway. The gross value of his estate in the United Kingdom was recorded as £1,190,868 14*s.* 5*d.* His obituary in the *Glasgow Herald* recorded that he was:

a man of great energy and force of character, [who] also possessed a Scotchman's prudence—not the prudence which never dares, but the fine spirit of caution which, first carefully counting the costs, goes boldly forward, and is seldom taken by surprise. (21 June 1876)

ARTHUR H. GRANT, *rev.* IAIN F. RUSSELL

Sources *DSBB* · A. McGeorge, *The Bairds of Gartsherrie* (1875) · *Glasgow Herald* (21 June 1876), 4 · *Glasgow Herald* (24 June 1876), 4 · J. MacLehose, *Memoirs and portraits of one hundred Glasgow men who have died during the last thirty years*, 1 (1886) · A. Miller, *The rise and progress of Coatbridge and surrounding neighbourhood* (1864) · inventory, NA Scot., SC6/44/153 · will, NA Scot., SC6/46/11 · parish register, Old Monkland parish, 5 Dec 1802

Archives U. Glas., William Baird & Co. Ltd papers, UGD 164 · University of Strathclyde, Glasgow, William Baird & Co. Ltd papers

Likenesses caricature, Mitchell L., Glas.; repro. in 'Men you know', *The Bailie*, no. 93 (29 July 1874) · photograph, repro. in *Memoirs and portraits*, following p. 16

Wealth at death £1,190,868 14*s*. 5*d*.: confirmation, 31 Aug 1876, *CCI*

Baird, Sir John, Lord Newbyth (*bap.* **1620**, *d.* **1698**), judge, was baptized in Edinburgh on 10 September 1620, the son of James Baird (*d.* 1655) of Little Fiddes and Byth, Aberdeenshire, advocate, and his wife, Bethia, daughter of John Dempster of Logiealton and Balbougie, advocate. He was admitted advocate on 3 June 1647. Probably about this time he married Margaret (*b.* after 1618, *d.* 1707), daughter of Sir William Hay of Linplum, because a son was born on 4 October 1648; the couple had two further sons and a daughter. By June 1653 Baird had been knighted.

Like his father, who died in August 1655, Baird was a covenanter, although he was quickly reconciled to the Restoration after 1660. He served as commissary of Edinburgh in 1661. He was excepted out of the Scottish Act of Indemnity in 1662, paying a fine of £2400. On 15 August 1663 he was appointed Lyon-depute. In November 1664 he was made a lord of session; since he had sold the Byth estate, he assumed the title of Lord Newbyth, based on lands he purchased in Haddingtonshire. Elected to the Scottish parliament in 1665 for Aberdeenshire, after taking the oaths on 8 August he was named to prepare a draft of a grant of taxation to the king. Returned again to the parliament in 1667, on 9 January he was appointed to the committee of supply.

On 9 August 1667 the king granted Baird the barony of Gilmertoun within the sheriffdom of Edinburgh; the grant was ratified by parliament on 23 December 1669. From September to November 1670 Baird was in London attending meetings as a Scottish commissioner for union with England. He was one of those left out of the new commission for lords of session on 1 November 1681, no doubt due to his political opposition to the harsh measures taken against opponents of the government. In 1685 he served as a commissioner of the cess and of supply in Edinburghshire.

Baird clearly welcomed the revolution of 1688 in Scotland. He was again appointed a commissioner of supply in Edinburghshire in 1689 and 1690. More difficulty seems to have occurred over his reappointment as a lord of session. In June 1689 he wrote to the Scottish secretary of state, the earl of Melville, of his surprise that 'I had not that common measure of justice allowed me, which was given to such of the lords of session who had suffered under the violence of the last government' (*Leven and Melville Papers*, 107–8). Evidently his plea for reinstatement was heeded, for on 22 October he was named in the new commission. He retained his place until his death in Edinburgh on 27 April 1698. He was succeeded by his son William, who had been created a baronet in 1680. His daughter apparently died in a coaching accident shortly before she was due to be married. In the Advocates' Library in Edinburgh there survive Lord Newbyth's collections of decisions from 1664 to 1667 and a collection of practiques for 1664 to 1681.

STUART HANDLEY

Sources F. J. Grant, ed., *The Faculty of Advocates in Scotland, 1532–1943*, Scottish RS, 145 (1944), 9 · M. D. Young, ed., *The parliaments of Scotland: burgh and shire commissioners*, 2 vols. (1992–3) · GEC, *Baronetage* · G. Brunton and D. Haig, *An historical account of the senators of the college of justice, from its institution in MDXXXII* (1832), 391 · W. Baird, *Dominus fecit: genealogical collections concerning the sir-name Baird* (1870) · *APS*, 1662–90 · C. S. Terry, *The Cromwellian Union*, Scottish History Society, 40 (1902) · W. H. L. Melville, ed., *Leven and Melville papers: letters and state papers chiefly addressed to George, earl of Melville … 1689–1691*, Bannatyne Club, 77 (1843) · *Correspondence of Sir Robert Kerr, first earl of Ancram*, 2 vols., Bannatyne Club (1815), vol. 2, p. 375 · *IGI*

Archives NL Scot., corresp. with first marquess of Tweeddale

Baird, John (*d.* **1804**), minister of the Presbyterian General Synod of Ulster and Church of Ireland clergyman, a native of Paisley, Renfrewshire, was educated at Edinburgh University, and in 1763 was ordained by the Edinburgh presbytery for a congregation in the Isle of Man. In 1766 he resigned this post and moved to Dublin. He was installed by the Dublin presbytery as minister of Capel Street (St Mary's Abbey) on 11 January 1767. Here he ministered for ten years, but not without considerable contention. In June 1769 the General Synod of Ulster suspended him for two weeks, following complaints from some members of his congregation and the local presbytery. Eight years later, in June 1777, synod was called upon to arbitrate between rival parties in the congregation. One group asked synod to dissolve the relation between the congregation and Baird. The other requested that synod interpose its influence to restore peace and continue Baird as minister. After a full debate synod decided *nem. con.* to dissolve the relation between Baird and the congregation, and declare the pulpit vacant. As a result of further investigation by a committee of synod, Baird was admonished by its moderator 'to act a part in future more suitable to his character as a man, & a Christian, and particularly as a Minister of the Gospel', and instructed not to preach or exercise the function of a minister within the bounds of the synod, unless by appointment of that body, and to vacate the manse within a month. Whereupon Baird 'renounced all subjection and dependence upon the General Synod and all its subordinate parts' (*Records*, 3, 5–6). The synod in 1778 reacted by declaring that Baird was deposed and deprived of the *regium donum* from 25 June 1777. To add to his tribulations, his wife died at the height of the controversy.

Shortly after his renunciation of the synod Baird brought out his first and only volume of a proposed series on the Old Testament, *Dissertations Chronological, Historical and Critical, of All the Books of the Old Testament*, based on Sunday evening lectures given at Capel Street. In the preface he gave his considered opinion of the members of his erstwhile congregation, when he stated that the lectures were 'delivered to a certain sort of people whose temper and behaviour in general, must, necessarily, render it very uncomfortable and dangerous to preside over them, in religious affairs'. On 12 November 1777 he dedicated the volume to James Traill, bishop of Down and Connor. Some time later (the actual date is unknown) he conformed and was ordained in the established Church of Ireland. The fact that he preached at an ordination in St Patrick's Cathedral, Dublin, held by the archbishop on 30 May 1779, indicates that his own ordination was prior to that date. On 7 September 1782 he was appointed by the crown rector of Cloghran, near Swords, co. Dublin, and instituted on 17 December. He memorialized the archbishop for permission to erect a glebe house in 1784, and received a grant of £100 for this purpose from the Board of First Fruits. He died in early 1804. W. D. Bailie

Sources J. Baird, 'Preface', *Dissertations chronological, historical and critical, of all the books of the Old Testament; through which is interspersed reflections, theological and moral arising from various subjects* (1778) • *Records of the General Synod of Ulster, from 1691 to 1820*, 3 vols. (1890–98) • J. McConnell and others, eds., *Fasti of the Irish Presbyterian church, 1613–1840*, rev. S. G. McConnell, 2 vols. in 12 pts (1935–51) • *DNB* • T. Witherow, *Historical and literary memorials of presbyterianism in Ireland, 1731–1800* (1880) • B. W. Adams, *History and description of Santry and Cloghran parishes, County Dublin* (1883) • C. H. Irwin, *A history of presbyterianism in Dublin and the south and west of Ireland* (1890)

Baird, John (1788–1820), radical, was, with **Andrew Hardie** (1792–1820) and **James Wilson** (1757–1820), one of the three 'Radical Martyrs' executed for their part in the Scottish insurrection of April 1820. Baird, born in Condorrat, Stirling, was the third son of a Condorrat weaver named James Baird (*b.* 1740) and Isobel Edmond. He had two brothers and two sisters. Baird joined the 2nd battalion of 95th regiment of foot (the Rifle brigade) on 13 September 1806 in Glasgow. Promoted to bugler, he went with his battalion in the expeditionary force commanded by General Whitelock to attack Napoleon's Spanish allies in Buenos Aires. His battalion was based at Colonia, in Uruguay. He returned on the transport *Osborne*, on which he became ill. Having recovered, he went with the 95th to Spain and saw action during the Peninsular campaign under Wellington. By 1812 he was stationed at Getafe outside Madrid. On 15 March 1813 Baird returned to Glasgow on furlough. He was due to report back to his unit on 22 May but obtained a certificate from the district surgeon, Glasgow, stating that he was ill. On 22 June 1813 he was posted as a deserter. There is no record that the army was able to arrest him. Like many others at this period he simply disappeared.

Baird eventually returned to Condorrat and joined his father and brothers in the weaving trade. He could read and write very well, began to devour radical literature, and joined his local circulating library, becoming a radical reformer seeking the universal franchise, annual parliaments, and the repeal of the Act of Union with England of 1707. He became a prominent figure among the Condorrat radicals.

Many Scottish radical leaders saw armed insurrection as the only way to achieve their ends. Conditions were right as the post-war depression and unemployment created great unrest in the industrial south of Scotland, particularly among weavers. Government agents, however, were at work among the radical leadership. John King of Anderston, sometimes calling himself John Andrews, appeared to be their chief agent. The Glasgow police commander, James Mitchell, reported to home secretary Lord Sidmouth in March 1820 that the radicals were preparing a general rising in Scotland. A few days later, on King's advice, Mitchell arrested the entire 28-man radical central committee in Gallowgate. He then wrote to Lord Sidmouth suggesting that the agents provocateurs take over and issue a call to the rank and file for the rising on, significantly, 1 April 1820 (All Fools' day). The idea, explained Mitchell, was 'to catch them abroad and undefended' so that the troops in Scotland could 'quench all thoughts of [Scottish] patriotic pride and Radical feeling among the disaffected' (Ellis and Mac a' Ghobhainn, 1989, 140). The 'Proclamation of the provisional government' (the authorship of which is clearly English) was duly issued (ibid., plate opposite p. 96). Some armed radicals answered the call, to be immediately arrested by the military.

On the evening of 4 April at about 11 p.m. King, the agent, had arrived at the house of John Baird's brother, Robert (baptized 8 April 1787 at Stirling), and his wife, where John Baird was lodging. Baird had been elected commander of the Condorrat insurgents. King told him that he had 'orders from the central committee'. Baird was to take his men and join with a larger contingent in an attack on the Carron Iron Works near Falkirk, which was the largest single ironworks in Europe, employing 2000 men and supplying all the main artillery pieces to both navy and army. There was, in fact, no larger contingent on the way, and a company of the 80th regiment were at the works waiting for the hapless radicals.

At 5 a.m. Baird was joined by Andrew Hardie with twenty-five men who had marched up from Glasgow on King's instructions. Baird and his ten men combined forces with them under his command. They set off towards the Glasgow and Edinburgh Canal. King was never seen again after this. Baird split his forces in case he missed the supposed main force, and he and Hardie took separate routes to a point about a mile and a half beyond Bonnybridge village. Here they rejoined forces.

A troop of the 10th hussars, commanded by Lieutenant Ellis Hodgson, and the Kilsyth troop of the Stirlingshire yeomanry, commanded by Lieutenant John James Davidson, a tory lawyer from Edinburgh, were converging on their position. Baird's men were resting on a hill in the area known as Bonnymuir. Hodgson and the 10th hussars led a sabre charge against them. Baird instructed his men to take defensive positions. Hardie wrote:

> Mr Baird defended himself in a most gallant manner; after discharging his piece he presented it at the officer [Hodgson] empty, and told him he would do for him if he did not stand off. The officer presented his pistol at him, but it flashed and did not go off. Mr Baird then took the butt end of his piece and struck a private on the left thigh, where upon the sergeant of Hussars [Sergeant Saxelby] fired at him. Baird then threw his musket from him and seized a pike, and while the sergeant was in the act of drawing his sword, wounded him in the right arm. (Ellis and Mac a' Ghobhainn, 1970, 172–3)

But with the reinforcement of yeomanry troops under Davidson, Hodgson called on the insurgents to surrender, and Baird, seeing the futility of a prolonged struggle, agreed. Several of the insurgents were sabred by yeomanry troops after their surrender. Significantly enough, Hodgson already knew the name of the insurgent's leader. King had done his work well.

The wounded were placed on a cart and the prisoners marched to Stirling Castle, where Baird told the commander, Major W. Preddie: 'Sir, if there is to be any severity exercised towards us, let it be on me. I am their leader, and have caused them being here. I hope that I alone may suffer' (Ellis and Mac a' Ghobhainn, 315). Preddie observed: 'Throughout he [Baird] never shrunk from the position he assumed' (ibid., 176). Baird wrote several letters from prison and appeared to have developed a friendship with Miss Isobella Condy of Stirling, who had nursed some of the prisoners.

The unrest was over within a week and numerous other radicals were arrested elsewhere in Scotland. There were to be eighty-eight charged with high treason. The trials started in July. To ensure convictions the lord president of the court of sessions, Charles Hope, accepted that all trials would be held under English law and not under Scottish law, contrary to the Act of Union of 1707. Sir William Rae, the lord advocate, prosecuted with the aid of a leading English lawyer, Mr Serjeant Hullock, who advised on English law. The trial of Baird and Hardie, with the Bonnymuir prisoners, began on 13 July at Stirling. Francis Jeffrey (1773–1850) led for the defence.

Baird was convicted on two of the four counts of high treason charged against him. On 4 August Baird, Hardie, and twenty others were sentenced to death. The twenty others had their sentences commuted, and a total of twenty-two were transported to the penal colonies for life. Throughout Scotland the other trials resulted in only one other death sentence. This was on 63-year-old James Wilson, a weaver of Strathaven.

On Friday 8 September 1820 Baird and Hardie were led to a public execution platform at Stirling Castle in front of a crowd of several thousand. Before his execution Baird told the crowd: 'What I have hitherto done, and which brought me here, was for the cause of truth and justice' (Ellis and Mac a' Ghobhainn, 279). The sympathy of the crowd caused the officer commanding to order his troops to present arms and a panic ensued. Sheriff Ranald MacDonald of Staffa refused to let the speeches continue. Both Baird and Hardie were hanged, their bodies cut down after half an hour, and their heads severed and held up with the cry: 'Behold the head of a traitor!'

When details of how the insurrection had been initiated by government spies and agents provocateurs were revealed by Peter Mackenzie in his *An Exposure of the Spy System Pursued in Glasgow* (1832) a protest movement forced the whig government of 1835 to ask William IV to grant absolute pardons to all the 1820 insurgents who had been transported for life. It was not until 1847 that the bodies of Baird and Hardie were exhumed from Stirling Castle and placed in Sighthill cemetery, Glasgow. Wilson was commemorated in his native Strathaven.

Peter Berresford Ellis

Sources P. B. Ellis and S. Mac A'Ghobhainn, *The Scottish insurrection of 1820* (1970); new edn (1989) · H. Cockburn, *An examination of the trials for sedition … in Scotland*, 2 vols. (1888) · [P. Mackenzie], ed., *An exposure of the spy system pursued in Glasgow during the years 1816–17–18–19 and 20 … edited … by a ten-pounder* (1832) · [P. Mackenzie], *The trial of James Wilson for high treason with an account of his execution in Glasgow, September 1820* (1832) · *A full account of the sentences of 22 radicals at Stirling for high treason* (1820) · W. C. MacDougall, *Wilson, Baird and Hardie* (1947) · trial record, PRO, KB8 · baptismal records, Stirling, 1 Sept 1790

Archives NA Scot. · NL Scot. | Devon RO, Sidmouth MSS · PRO, Home Office and War Office papers

Baird, John (1798–1859), architect, was born at Dalmuir, Old Kilpatrick. He was apprenticed to an architect relative, John Shepherd, in Glasgow in 1813, during which time the firm was apparently responsible for completing the west terrace of Peter Nicholson's Carlton Place. (Baird's future chief assistant, Alexander 'Greek' Thomson, was to marry Nicholson's granddaughter.) On his uncle's death in 1818, Baird took on the firm with his apprenticeship far from complete, and there are no identified projects for the next three years. Gildard implies that Baird may, simultaneously, have continued training in John Herbertson's office.

In 1821 Baird began the first of three Glasgow churches—Greyfriars United Presbyterian (1821), Wellington church (1823), and St John's Chapel (1823)—which were noted for their strong modelling and spare Grecian detail; Anderston parish church (1839) was perhaps the simplest example of this design approach, achieving grandeur with minimum effort. In all, he designed twelve churches, more than any other building type, which—outside Glasgow—were in fashionable but unconvincing Gothic; notable examples are the Congregational churches in Greenock and Dunfermline.

Baird is known to have worked on seven country houses or country house extensions—including possibly Garscube, Dunbartonshire (1827), Clober, Dunbartonshire (1833), Stonebyres, Lanarkshire (1844), and Urie, Aberdeenshire (1855)—mostly in the crisply decorative but architecturally unconvincing Jacobean of Cairnhill, Airdrie, Lanarkshire (1841). The office was much occupied at Woodlands Hill, Glasgow, preparing plans for the estate, for the simply classical Somerset Place (1840), for the grander, effulgently porticoed Claremont House, grandiose centrepiece of the later Claremont Terrace (1842–7), and for Woodlands Terrace (1849). Baird was the natural choice of designer for the relocation of Glasgow University to Woodlands Hill, and prepared three abortive schemes in 1846–9, in double-courtyard Jacobean style in homage to the original. In 1837 he had married Janet McKean from Bonhill. They had two daughters, Flora and Agnes.

Baird's principal buildings were commercial and innovative, helping to create the character of downtown Glasgow. They included the iron hammerbeam-roofed Argyle Arcade (1827), the austere Princes Square (1840), and vast warehouses or commercial buildings in West Nile Street (1851), in Buchanan Street and Ingram Street (both 1854), and in Argyle Street (1856). He was also responsible for the city block between South Hanover and Queen and Ingram streets (1854). Sir James Campbell's desire for an 'old Scottish' façade for Campbell's Warehouse (1854) was met—at Baird's suggestion—by an idiosyncratic and highly unScottish façade by R. W. Billings. The façade of the pioneering Gardner's Warehouse in Jamaica Street (1855), thought to be attributable to James Thomson, with a structure using Robert McConnell's patent iron beams, comprises plain structural columns, beams, and mullions only.

Taking over an architectural practice before one is fully trained often results in business taking higher priority than design, which depends instead upon the skills of assistants. Baird's early assistants are not known. In 1836 he was joined by Alexander Thomson, who was first his apprentice and then his assistant until 1849. In 1859 James Thomson became a partner in the firm, now called Baird and Thomson. Baird apparently never took part in architectural competitions, regarding them as 'a species of professional speculation—to use a mild epithet—which he consistently protested against to the last', although he had been prepared to act as judge with David Hamilton on the necropolis competition (*View of the Merchant's House of Glasgow*, 362, 382). Being 'a man not only of upright character and sound judgement but of also great experience in all that related to house property', he was extensively used as a building valuer and arbitrator, in recognition of which his business colleagues presented him with his portrait by Sir Daniel Macnee in 1857 (Honeyman, 1.23). Culturally, however, the office will be remembered for its contribution to early Victorian Glasgow. In John Honeyman's opinion, 'to the influence of such men we undoubtedly owe the excellence of our street architecture' (ibid., 1.24). One of the 'background' architects of early to mid-nineteenth century Glasgow, Baird was responsible for at least forty projects of consistently high quality. Gildard, fifty years later, referred to his 'large practice', second only in importance and public esteem to David Hamilton's; which, together with his substantial wealth and extensive list of creditors at his death, implies the existence of other building projects as yet unidentified. Baird died at his home, Westfield, Partickhill, Glasgow, on 18 December 1859, after which date the practice continued as Baird and Thomson. CHARLES MCKEAN

Sources Sheriff Court Inventory, Glasgow, NA Scot., 36/51/40, 175 · *Building Chronicle* (1854–7) · Colvin, *Archs.* · *Edinburgh*, Pevsner (1984) · A. Gomme and D. Walker, *Architecture of Glasgow* (1968) · J. Honeyman, 'John Baird', *Memoirs and portraits of one hundred Glasgow men who have died during the last thirty years*, ed. J. MacLehose, 1 (1886), 21–4 · T. Gildard, 'Recollections and reflections to the Glasgow Architectural Association', 1888, Mitchell L., Glas., MS B 214963, 20–22 · D. d'Angelo, 'The first John Baird', *Alexander Thomson Society Newsletter*, 24 (May 1999), 14–15 · [W. Papworth], ed., *The dictionary of architecture*, 11 vols. (1853–92) · R. McFadzean, *The life and work of Alexander Thomson* (1979) · T. Annan, J. O. Mitchell, and others, *The old country houses of the old Glasgow gentry* (1870) · G. Stamp and S. McKinstry, eds., *'Greek' Thomson* (1994) · *View of the Merchant's House of Glasgow* (1886), 362, 382 · F. A. Walker, 'Glasgow's new towns', *Glasgow: the forming of the city*, ed. P. Reed (1993), 24–41 · M. Glendinning, R. MacInnes, and A. MacKechnie, *A history of Scottish architecture* (1996) · C. McKean, ed., *Illustrated architectural guides to Scotland* (1982–)

Archives NA Scot. · U. Glas.

Likenesses D. Macnee, oils, Kelvingrove Art Gallery, Glasgow · photograph, repro. in Honeyman, 'John Baird'

Wealth at death £10,048 6*s.* 9½*d.*: SC 36/51/40

Baird, John (1799–1861), Church of Scotland minister, was born at Eccles, Berwickshire, on 17 February 1799, the eldest son of the Revd James Baird, who was successively minister of Legertwood, Eccles, and Swinton, all in Berwickshire. John Baird was educated at the grammar schools of Whitsome and Kelso, and proceeded to the University of Edinburgh. Here he founded the Plinian Society for the study of natural history in 1823, and was its first president. In 1825 he went to Ireland, where he served for some time as a preacher for the Irish Evangelical Society. In 1829 he was ordained minister of Yetholm in Roxburghshire. Four years later, on 11 June 1833, he married Margaret, the daughter of Robert Oliver of Blakelaw. They had two daughters before her early death in September 1837. His second wife, Elizabeth, whom he married on 14 November 1849, was the daughter of Nathaniel Hughes of Wexford; they had two sons and two daughters.

During his long ministry at Yetholm, Baird continued to pursue his botanical and geological interests. He was a founder member of the Berwickshire Naturalists' Club, of which he was president in 1837. Like many other Scottish ministers, he contributed a description of his parish to *The New Statistical Account of Scotland*; in 1822 he published *Geological Remarks on the Rock of Gibraltar*. However, he was better known for his evangelical work among the Gypsies of Kirk Yetholm, who were itinerant hawkers for eight months of the year and spent the winter at Kirk Yetholm, living in separation from the village community. Baird was keen to eradicate what he viewed as their particular vices—idleness, ignorance, poverty, and fierceness of temper—and to integrate them back into the God-fearing community. He aimed to persuade the parents to leave their children to be educated under his supervision when they went travelling. Baird was able to implement his ideas after the Society for the Reformation of the Gipsies of Scotland was founded in Edinburgh. In 1838–9 this organization raised sufficient finances to fund education, housing, and apprenticeships for the Gypsy children. Baird enjoyed some initial success, and his successor continued the work, although funds fell off after 1850. When George Smith of Coalville visited Kirk Yetholm in 1882, he found only one Gypsy who attended church, and concluded that the scheme had failed to produce any real improvement. Later opinion, while conceding that the decline of traditional Gypsy trades forced many to become more settled, considered that Baird's missionary activities may have contributed to the later nineteenth-century integration of the Gypsies into the village community. Baird died on 29 November 1861 at Yetholm. His wife survived him, dying in Hanover in April 1872.

ROSEMARY MITCHELL

Sources W. Baird, *Memoir of the late Rev. John Baird, minister of Yetholm* (1862) • *Fasti Scot.*, 2.96 • Boase, *Mod. Eng. biog.* • G. Smith, *I've been a-Gipsying* (1883), 330–31 • D. Mayall, *Gypsy-travellers in nineteenth-century society* (1988)

Wealth at death £2804 8*s.* 3*d.*: inventory, 27 March 1862, NA Scot., SC 62/44/35/7

Baird, John Logie (1888–1946), television engineer, was born on 13 August 1888 at The Lodge, West Argyle Street, Helensburgh, Dunbartonshire, Scotland, the youngest of the four children of the Revd John Baird, minister of the West Parish Church, Helensburgh, and his wife, Jessie Morrison Inglis. Baird was educated at three schools in Helensburgh, between 1893 and 1906 when he was admitted to an electrical engineering course at the Royal Technical College, Glasgow. In 1914 he was awarded an associateship of the college and, having been declared unfit for war service, he attended Glasgow University as a final year BSc degree student, but did not sit the examinations. He obtained a position as an assistant mains engineer with the Clyde Valley Electrical Power Company, but resigned in 1919 to follow, full time, various entrepreneurial business ventures.

Baird had a flair for marketing, and from 1917 to 1922 sold—at different periods in Glasgow, the West Indies, and London—medicated socks, boot polish, solid scent, jam, honey, fertilizer, coir fibre, and soap. His initiatives were mostly successful, even though he was dogged by the ill health which was a feature of his life. In 1922 he retired to Hastings to recuperate from a severe illness and, while there, began to study the problems of transmitting and receiving visual signals, namely, television. His resources were meagre: he lacked formal research training, he did not have access to workshop or laboratory facilities, and his financial position was precarious. Nevertheless, he rented an attic and began to assemble apparatus using what were, on the face of it, most unpromising materials. His investigations attracted some very modest support, and by April 1925 Baird was able to demonstrate, in public, at Selfridge's Oxford Street store, in London, the transmission of crude outlines of simple objects. Later, on 2 October 1925, he succeeded in reproducing an image of an object, which had tone gradation. A formal demonstration was given to about forty members of the Royal Institution on 26 January 1926. This was the world's first demonstration of television (albeit at a very rudimentary stage), which had been sought by many inventors since 1878, when the possibility of 'seeing at a distance' was first proposed. It was an outstanding achievement. Subsequently his basic television scheme was adopted by inventors and companies in France, Germany, the USA, and elsewhere.

John Logie Baird (1888–1946), by Howard Coster, 1935

An examination of Baird's *modus operandi* in the 1920s shows that he endeavoured to emulate the policies which, from 1896, had ensured success for Marconi and his companies. Baird and his supporters followed a plan which embraced publicity and the demonstration of 'firsts', the accumulation of patents, and company formation. Television Ltd was registered on 11 June 1925, Baird Television Development Company Ltd was established in April 1927, and Baird International Television Ltd was launched on 25 June 1928. Baird tried to anticipate every conceivable application of television and to safeguard by patent protection its practical implementation. He eventually held 178 patents: of these, eighty-eight were granted by the end of 1930. From 1926 to 1931 Baird demonstrated, sometimes for the first time ever, low-definition noctovision (in which subjects were illuminated by infra-red rays), daylight television, colour television, stereoscopic television, phonovision (the recording of sound and image on a gramophone disc), large-screen television, and zone television. Unfortunately, the exaggerated and premature claims made by Baird's business partners reflected adversely on Baird himself. However, a critical appraisal of his early work, to 1931, shows that his thoughts on television, and the realization of those thoughts, were entirely consonant with the television concepts of the well endowed Bell Telephone Laboratories, whose demonstrations in the same period were unsurpassed anywhere. On 30 September 1929 the BBC transmitted, using the Baird 30-line system, its first experimental television broadcast. Later, on 22 August 1932, the first public (in the UK), 30-line television service was inaugurated by the BBC; it remained in operation until 15 September 1935.

In November 1931, in New York, Baird married Margaret Cecilia (*d.* 1996), a concert pianist, daughter of the late Henry Albu, diamond merchant, of Johannesburg. They had one son, Malcolm, and one daughter, Diana.

Baird's 'blind spot' was to ignore for too long the inevitable move towards high-definition television, using very high frequencies and all-electronic means. When the London television station was opened by the BBC on 2 November 1936, two systems of television were employed, on an alternate basis. The ensuing trial highlighted the advantages of the 405-line, all-electronic system recommended by Isaac Shoenberg of EMI compared to Baird Television's 240-line system, which was based on mechanical scanning. The former was chosen for the new station, and the last BBC transmission using the Baird system was sent out on 30 January 1937.

Undaunted, Baird continued his work, concentrating on large-screen, colour, and stereoscopic television. He had his own private laboratory (set up in 1933) and he operated entirely independently from Baird Television Ltd. In December 1936 he demonstrated 120-line theatre television using a 2.4 x 2 metre screen; and in February 1938 he displayed large-screen (3.65 metres x 2.75 metres) colour television pictures. Both demonstrations were at the Dominion Theatre, London. 600-line colour television and stereoscopic colour television systems were shown in December 1940 and December 1941 respectively. Baird was the first person, anywhere, to design, construct, and exhibit (in 1944) a multi-gun colour television tube (the telechrome tube).

Despite poor health, Baird continued his endeavours until he died, from coronary thrombosis, at his rented home, Instow, 1 Station Road, at Bexhill, Sussex, on 14 June 1946. He was buried in Helensburgh cemetery.

R. W. BURNS

Sources R. W. Burns, *British television: the formative years* (1986) • J. L. Baird, *Sermons, soap and television* (1988) • M. Baird, *Television Baird* (1973) • S. Moseley, *John Baird* (1952) • R. W. Burns, 'J. L. Baird: success and failure', *Proceedings of the Institution of Electrical Engineers*, 126 (1979), 921–8 • archives, BBC WAC • archival material, Post Office Records Office, London • priv. coll. [patents, learned society papers, notes, letters etc.] • R. W. Burns, *Television: an international history of the formative years* (1998) • R. W. Burns, 'Bell Telephone Laboratories and the early development of television', *History of Technology*, 13 (1991), 181–213 • T. McArthur and P. Waddell, *The secret life of John Logie Baird* (1986) • A. Kamm and M. Baird, *John Logie Baird: a life* (2002) • *CGPLA Eng. & Wales* (1947) • d. cert. • private information (2004)

Archives University of Strathclyde, Glasgow, corresp., notebooks, papers, and photographs | BBC WAC, letters relating to the development of television • Post Office Records Office, London, letters relating to the development of television | FILM BBC, 'JLB—the man who saw the future' • Museum of the Moving Image, London [a phonovision disc recording of 30-line television, made in 1928]

Likenesses H. Coster, photograph, 1935 [*see illus.*] • D. Gilbert, statue, priv. coll. • J. Kerr-Lawson, pencil drawing, Scot. NPG • J. Kerr-Lawson, portrait, U. Glas. • photograph, repro. in Burns, *British television* • photograph, repro. in Baird, *Sermons, soap and television* • photograph, repro. in Baird, *Television Baird* • photograph, repro. in Moseley, *John Baird* • photograph, repro. in McArthur and Waddell, *Secret life of John Logie Baird* • photograph, Sci. Mus. • photograph, BFI • photograph, Popperfotos • photograph, Hult. Arch.

Wealth at death £7370: probate, 24 Jan 1947, *CGPLA Eng. & Wales*

Baird, William (1803–1872), zoologist and physician, was born at Eccles, Berwickshire, on 8 January 1803, a younger son of the Revd James Baird (*d.* 1814), then minister of Eccles, and his wife, Sarah. His older brother was the evangelical preacher John *Baird (1799–1861). He was educated at the high school, Edinburgh, and studied medicine at Edinburgh, Dublin, and Paris. In 1823, having already visited the West Indies and South America, Baird became a surgeon with the East India Company. While in that company's service he visited India and China five times, availing himself of every possibility to pursue his interest in natural history.

Baird was a zoologist of considerable ability, and communicated several papers to the Zoological and Linnean societies. In 1829, following his return to Britain, he helped to establish the Berwickshire Naturalists' Club, which served to extend the pursuit of natural science. After some years in private medical practice, in 1841 he accepted an appointment in the zoological department of the British Museum. There he had charge of the molluscan collection and, though he published little on the group, his curatorial efforts succeeded in making the collection available for study by others.

In 1850 Baird's important work on the natural history of British entomostraca was published by the Ray Society, and in 1858 he published his *Cyclopaedia of the Natural Sciences*. In 1862 he brought out a memoir of his brother, John, who died in the previous year. Baird was a contributor to a number of journals, including Loudon's *Magazine of Natural History*, *The Zoologist*, and the *Proceedings* of the Zoological Society, and he was elected FRS in 1867. He died on 27 January 1872 at his home, 38 Burlington Road, Westbourne Park, London. The Mary Baird (of the same address) who was executor of his will may have been his wife.

R. E. THOMPSON, *rev.* PETER OSBORNE

Sources *PRS*, 20 (1871–2), xxiii–xxiv • J. F. Waller, ed., *The imperial dictionary of universal biography*, 3 vols. (1857–63) • [T. T. Shore], ed., *Cassell's biographical dictionary* (1867–9) • Boase, *Mod. Eng. biog.* [John Baird] • bap. reg. Scot. • d. cert. • election certificate, RS • *CGPLA Eng. & Wales* (1872)

Archives Linn. Soc., drawings of entomostraca • Zoological Society of London, travel journals | Elgin Museum, letters to George Gordon

Wealth at death under £3000: probate, 28 Feb 1872, *CGPLA Eng. & Wales*

Bairnsfather, (Charles) Bruce (1887–1959), cartoonist and writer, was born at Strawberry Bank Cottage, Murree, Punjab, India, on 9 July 1887, the eldest son of Lieutenant (later Major) Thomas Henry (Tom) Bairnsfather (*d.* 1945), a Scottish officer in the Indian army, and Amelia Jane Eliza

(Charles) **Bruce Bairnsfather** (1887–1959), by unknown photographer, *c.*1914

(Janie) Every (*d.* 1959), daughter of a former deputy lieutenant of Derbyshire. Both of Bairnsfather's parents were descended from a common grandfather, Sir Edward Every, eighth baronet. His mother was a talented amateur painter, specializing in birds on silk, and his father also composed comic songs. He had two younger brothers: Malcolm Harvey Bairnsfather (1890–1891), who died of meningitis when a baby, and Thomas Duncan Bairnsfather (*b.* 1897), who died in the Second World War.

Bairnsfather was brought to England in 1895 and stayed with his mother's brother, the rector of Thornbury, near Bromyard, Worcestershire, before being enrolled at Rudyard Kipling's old school, the United Services College, Westward Ho!, Devon (1898–1904). Frequently caned for doodling in his books, he was a failure academically though he won a prize for drawing. His parents returned to England in 1899 and he was transferred to an army crammer, Trinity College, Stratford upon Avon, in 1904 while also attending evening classes in art at Stratford Technical College. At the age of seventeen he sold his first drawing, an advertisement for Player's navy mixture, for 2 guineas. Having chosen the army as a career, he failed the entrance exams to Sandhurst and Woolwich officer cadet schools but eventually managed to gain a commission as a second lieutenant in his father's old regiment, the Cheshires.

Disillusioned with military life, however, Bairnsfather resigned in 1907 to become an artist, studying under Charles van Havermaet and Dudley Hardy at the John Hassall School of Art in Earls Court, London. Unsuccessful as a professional poster artist, he returned to the family home at Bishopton, Warwickshire, and took a job as an electrical engineer at Spensers Ltd, Stratford, specialists in gas and electric country-house lighting. Beginning as a junior installing lighting at the Old Memorial Theatre, Stratford, he later travelled widely for the company. During this period he took part in a number of amateur theatrical productions, specializing in female impersonations, and was 'discovered' by Marie Corelli, the novelist, who lived locally and who arranged for him to audition for Sir Edward Moss's Empire music-hall group. (Bairnsfather backed out.) She also introduced him to the 'tea king', Sir Thomas Lipton, and he subsequently drew advertisements for Liptons, Player's cigarettes, Keene's mustard, and Beechams, and won a poster competition organized by an opera company.

In the First World War Bairnsfather served as machine-gun officer with the 1st battalion Royal 1st Warwickshires in France, eventually attaining the rank of captain. While stationed near Armentières he drew the first of his famous *Fragments from France* cartoons ('Where did that one go to?', *The Bystander*, January 1915) but did not see it published until he was hospitalized in April 1915 after suffering shell-shock and damage to the hearing in his left ear during the second battle of Ypres. Later, when posted to 34th division headquarters at Sutton Veney, Salisbury Plain, he drew his most celebrated cartoon, 'Well, if you knows of a better 'ole, go to it' (*The Bystander*, 24 Nov 1915), featuring two soldiers in a shell-hole during a bombardment. His best-known character, the pipe-smoking, walrus-moustached Midlands Tommy 'Old Bill' Busby—'dim, dull and honest' and usually wearing a scarf and balaclava helmet with his uniform—first appeared in 'When the 'ell is it going to be strawberry?' (*The Bystander*, 15 Sept 1915). Though very popular with the troops (*The Bystander*'s sales rocketed and in 1916 alone more than 250,000 copies were sold of *Fragments from France*, the first of eight collections of his drawings), the establishment objected strongly to 'these vulgar caricatures of our heroes' and questions were asked in parliament. None the less his works so improved morale that he was promoted officer-cartoonist and transferred to the intelligence department of the War Office to draw similar cartoons for the French, Italian, and American forces. In 1921 he married a 34-year-old Australian-born divorcee, the Hon. Mrs Cecilia Agnes (Ceal) Scott, *née* Bruton (1886/7–1966), the former wife of the Hon. Michael Scott OBE (fifth son of the third earl of Eldon) and sister of the stage writer Helen Jerome. They had one daughter, Barbara Bruce Bairnsfather (*b.* 1922), and he had a stepdaughter, Heather Scott (*b.* 1908).

The 'Old Bill' character, along with his younger friends Bert and Alf, was immensely popular both during and after the war, and Bairnsfather's celebrity continued to be such that he was the subject of one of the first talking motion pictures (1927), took part in the first experimental television transmissions from Alexandra Palace in north London (1936), and was invited to write, direct, and produce Canada's first major movie, *Carry on, Sergeant!* (1928). 'Old Bill' himself appeared in books, plays, musicals (including C. B. Cochran's *The Better 'Ole* in 1917, which gave Sybil Thorndike her first West End role), silent and talking films (including *The Better 'Ole* in 1926, featuring Charlie Chaplin's brother Syd, and Alexander Korda's *Old Bill and Son* in 1941, co-starring John Mills), and comic strips (*Daily Graphic*, *Passing Show*, *The Illustrated*, and *Judge*), and was reproduced on pottery, playing cards, jigsaw puzzles, postcards, and other merchandise. 'Old Bill' dolls were manufactured, a waxwork of the character appeared in Madame Tussaud's (1930), and a bus named after him became part of the collection of the Imperial War Museum in London (complete with 'Old Bill' radiator mascot). However, perhaps surprisingly, he was not used in government poster campaigns until the Second World War. Bairnsfather's characters also had considerable influence on the work of other cartoonists, notably (during the Second World War) the American Bill Mauldin ('Willie & Joe') and the Welshman W. J. P. Jones ('The Two Types'). Sir David Low's 'Colonel Blimp' (created in the 1930s) later attracted similar censure by the military and government authorities.

Although Bairnsfather repeatedly denied that 'Old Bill' was based on a single person—as he said, 'he was simply a hieroglyphic for a most prevalent type' (Bairnsfather, *Carry on, Sergeant!*, 54)—many suggestions have been made regarding his original model. Bairnsfather was not a good businessman (he was sued for bankruptcy in 1932) and benefited less than others from royalties on his work. However, he supplemented his earnings from cartoons by numerous lecture tours in Great Britain, the United States, and Canada; music-hall variety acts; illustrated journalism in, for example, *The Graphic*, *The Tatler*, *Life*, and *New Yorker*; scriptwriting; and by producing books of light-hearted memoirs. He also edited his own popular weekly magazine for the *Bystander* group, *Fragments* (1919–20).

When the Second World War broke out Bairnsfather was appointed official cartoonist to the American forces in Europe with the rank of captain and wore an American uniform. As well as contributing to *Stars and Stripes* and *Yank* he also drew cartoons at American bases and as nose art on aircraft. *Old Bill Does It Again!* was published in 1940, followed by *Old Bill & Son* (1940), *Jeeps and Jests* (1943), and *No Kiddin'* (1944). After the war he continued his lecture tours, talks, and other work but as an artist and performer never succeeded in breaking away from 'Old Bill' in his many incarnations.

In appearance Bairnsfather was clean-shaven, with brown eyes and prematurely thinning hair (he often wore a cap or trilby to hide this.) Also, unusually for one of his background, he had tattoos—a cobra on one arm and a butterfly on the other. He disliked describing his work as 'cartoons', preferring 'pictures' or 'drawings', and he once said that his religious beliefs were 'a mixture of The Sermon on the Mount, Kipling's "If", Omar Khayyam and Astronomy' (Holt and Holt, 39). Bruce Bairnsfather died on 29 September 1959 in the Royal Infirmary, Worcester, of acute renal failure after treatment for cancer of the bladder. He was survived by his wife. Cremated at Cheltenham crematorium, his memorial plaque mistakenly gives his age as seventy-one (he was seventy-two). In 1980 a blue plaque was erected to his memory at 1 Stirling Street, Kensington, London (one of his London studios).

MARK BRYANT

Sources T. Holt and V. Holt, *In search of the better 'ole* (1985) · B. Bairnsfather, *Wide canvas* (1939) · B. Bairnsfather, *Bullets and billets* (1916) · B. Bairnsfather, *From mud to mufti* (1919) · B. Bairnsfather, *Carry on, sergeant!* (1927) · V. Carter, *Bairnsfather: a few fragments from his life* (1918) · B. Bairnsfather and W. A. Mutch, *The Bairnsfather case* (1920) · M. Bryant, *Dictionary of twentieth-century British cartoonists and caricaturists* (2000) · M. Bryant and S. Heneage, eds., *Dictionary of British cartoonists and caricaturists, 1730–1980* (1994) · *DNB* · *WWW* · *Who's who in art* · M. Horn, ed., *The world encyclopedia of cartoons* (1980) · S. Houfe, *The dictionary of British book illustrators and caricaturists, 1800–1914* (1978) · A. Horne, *The dictionary of 20th century British book illustrators* (1994) · B. Peppin and L. Micklethwaite, *Dictionary of British book illustrators: the twentieth century* (1983) · P. V. Bradshaw, *They make us smile* (1942) · *CGPLA Eng. & Wales* (1959)

Archives FILM BFI, London · Canadian National Film Archive · L. Cong.

Likenesses photographs, *c.*1914–1940, Hult. Arch. [*see illus.*] · photograph, repro. in *The Bystander* (8 Nov 1916) · photograph, repro. in Bairnsfather, *Bullets and billets* · photograph, repro. in B. Bairnsfather, *Collected drawings of Bruce Bairnsfather* (1931) · photograph, repro. in Bairnsfather, *Wide canvas* · photograph, repro. in B. Bairnsfather, *No kiddin'* (1945) · photograph, repro. in B. Bairnsfather, *Fragments from France*, 8 vols. (1916–19) · photograph, repro. in Carter, *Bairnsfather* · photographs, repro. in Holt and Holt, *In search of the better 'ole*

Wealth at death £3154 8*s*. 8*d*.: probate, 14 Dec 1959, *CGPLA Eng. & Wales*

Bairstow, Sir Edward Cuthbert (1874–1946), musician, was born in Huddersfield on 22 August 1874, the eldest child and only son of James Oates Bairstow, wholesale clothier, and his wife, Elizabeth Adeline, *née* Watson. His father had a tenor voice and was a member of the Huddersfield Choral Society. Bairstow was educated at the high school, Nottingham, where his grandparents lived, until in 1889 his father retired and the family moved to London where he attended the Grocers' Company's School at Hackney Downs, and later had coaching from a private tutor. In Huddersfield he had been taught the organ by Henry Parratt (brother of Sir Walter Parratt), and in Nottingham by Arthur Page. Soon after arrival in London he had lessons from John Farmer, then organist of Balliol College, Oxford, and later (1892–9) he was articled to Sir Frederick Bridge, organist of Westminster Abbey. During this time he became organist of All Saints' Church, Norfolk Square, Paddington. In 1894 he obtained the degree of BMus at Durham University, proceeding to DMus in 1900. In 1899, on Bridge's recommendation, he was appointed organist of Wigan parish church and he conducted the Wigan Philharmonic Society (1901–6) and also the choral society at Blackburn. On 11 June 1902 he married Edith Harriet (*b.* 1875/6), daughter of John Thomas Hobson, a government inspector of alkali works. They had two sons and a daughter. In 1906 Bairstow was appointed to the more important post of organist at Leeds parish church. In addition to his church duties he had a busy life teaching, lecturing, performing, composing, and travelling each week to conduct the Blackburn St Cecilia Society (1903–13) and the Preston Choral Society (1907–13). At the Leeds triennial festival in 1907 he was official organist under the conductorship of Sir Charles Stanford.

Another chapter of Bairstow's life began in 1913 when he became organist and master of the choir at York Minster, where he remained until his death. The increased duties of his cathedral work made it impossible for him to continue conducting the choral societies in Lancashire but, now that his reputation as a choral trainer was established, he accepted the invitation to conduct the York Musical Society (1913–39), the Bradford Festival Chorus, and the Leeds Philharmonic Society. At York Minster, Bairstow's devoted work with the choir and music generally became well known and widely appreciated and perhaps reached the highest level of excellence during the 1300th celebrations in 1927. The Bairstows' home at 1 Minster Court, York, became well known for its hospitality towards other artists.

In the 1920s Bairstow became known as a judge at musical competition festivals in Britain, and in 1928 he also judged in Canada. His natural ability, teaching experience, and fearless judgements had a stimulating effect on the movement. He was much in demand, although he realized that he was not 'popular'; consequently he often remarked 'I have judged at every competition festival in the country—*once*.'

On the death of Joseph Cox Bridge in 1929, Bairstow accepted the chair of music at Durham University. The professorship at that time was non-resident and he was able to continue his work at York Minster. At Durham he set himself to raise the standard of the degree in music. In 1932 he was knighted, and he received the honorary degrees of LittD (1936) from Leeds and DMus (1945) from Oxford. For various periods he held office as president of musical bodies such as the Incorporated Society of Musicians and the Royal College of Organists; of the latter he was for many years an examiner and member of the council.

Probably Bairstow's chief influence was through his many pupils, who included the composer Gerald Finzi. He was a born teacher, although his strictness and insistence on regular, disciplined work did not endear him to all his pupils, Finzi among them. His success was due to his uncanny insight into the problems of teaching, to his sympathy, patience, perseverance, enthusiasm to stimulate the imagination of the pupil, appreciation of honest work done, and above all to his great love of music. His courage, forthright speech, and transparent sincerity made him greatly beloved by many, even though they were sometimes misunderstood by and embarrassing to a few.

Bairstow published two textbooks on music, *Counterpoint and Harmony* (1937) and *The Evolution of Musical Form* (1943), and one on singing, *Singing Learned from Speech* (1945), written in collaboration with his friend H. Plunket Greene. His published compositions, which reveal the influence of Brahms and Stanford, include church and organ music, songs, partsongs, and chamber music. For the coronation of George VI in 1937 he wrote the introit. His 1913 communion service in D was perhaps his most important work, while the austerely beautiful anthem 'Let all mortal flesh keep silence' became firmly established in the repertory of church music. Bairstow died in Purey Cust Nursing Home, York, on 1 May 1946.

ERNEST BULLOCK, *rev.* K. D. REYNOLDS

Sources *MT*, 87 (1946), 186–7 • *New Grove* • m. cert. • d. cert. • *WWW* • *CGPLA Eng. & Wales* (1946) • S. Banfield, *Gerald Finzi: an English composer* (1998)

Archives SOUND BL NSA, 'Edward Bairstow', M5129R C1 • BL NSA, oral history interview • BL NSA, performance recordings

Wealth at death £6142 16*s*. 8*d*.: probate, 31 July 1946, *CGPLA Eng. & Wales*

Bairstow, Sir Leonard (1880–1963), aeronautical engineer, was born on 25 June 1880 at Halifax in Yorkshire, the son of Uriah Bairstow, a commercial clerk, and his wife, Elizabeth Lister. He attended schools in Halifax, from where he went, in 1898, on a scholarship to the Royal College of Science, London. There he became a Whitworth scholar in 1902. In 1904 he entered the engineering department of the National Physical Laboratory (NPL) at Teddington, Middlesex, where he worked under T. E. Stanton on the problems of fatigue and of aerodynamics. In 1909 he moved to the new section of aerodynamics and became the principal in charge. There he carried out pioneer investigations into wind tunnel design, tested models, and measured the aerodynamic derivatives in the NPL wind tunnel. One of his assistants at the time was E. F. Relf.

In 1917 Bairstow was appointed to the Air Board where he worked for Sir David Henderson on aircraft design and aerodynamics research. As deputy to Alexander Ogilvie he co-ordinated the departmental work on structural strength, aerodynamics, performance, and airscrews. In 1920 he was appointed professor of aerodynamics at Imperial College, London, and in 1923 he became Zaharoff professor of aviation and head of the department of aeronautics.

Bairstow was a member of the advisory committee of aeronautics (later the Aeronautical Research Committee and during the Second World War expanded into the Aeronautical Research Council) from 1921 to 1955 and was its chairman from 1949 to 1952. He served on over fifty committees and had an unequalled record of service. In 1917 he was elected a fellow of the Royal Society and appointed CBE. He gave the seventh Wilbur Wright memorial lecture in 1919—an event well remembered for the subsequent controversy in which Bairstow's references to S. P. Langley's 'heavier than air' aircraft were ultimately justified. The first edition of his *Applied Aerodynamics* was published in 1920; it was the first, and for many years the only, comprehensive textbook in this field. He was chairman of the council of the Royal Aeronautical

Society in the year 1922–3. He married, first, Eleanor Mary Hamer (*d.* 1926); they had one son and one daughter. In 1930 he married Florence Katharine, the eldest daughter of D. J. Stephens, of Llandaff.

Bairstow was involved in two great controversies, whose outcome ultimately had considerable effect on the development of aeronautical research. Bairstow was a doughty fighter, always well equipped with extensive knowledge and powerful arguments, and it required considerable new experimental work and most careful theoretical exposition to convince him of his mistakes.

The first controversy arose over discrepancies between the measurements of aerodynamic derivatives made in an aeroplane in flight at the Royal Aircraft Establishment by W. S. Farren and G. P. Thomson and measurements made in wind tunnels at the NPL. Bairstow argued, with reason and conviction, that measurements made in a wind tunnel, by skilled observers, with accurate instruments, under ideal conditions, must be more reliable and were more reproducible than observations made by a pilot distracted by the problems of manoeuvring an aircraft. Tests on a standard aerofoil carried out in foreign laboratories failed to resolve the matter, which was eventually traced to a difference of turbulence between wind tunnels and the free air. Bairstow himself was finally convinced of the effects of turbulence in wind tunnels, and the long-running controversy ultimately led to important advances in the design of wind tunnels and the use of models.

The second controversy was over the theory of the 'boundary layer' of airflow round an aeroplane or wind tunnel model advanced by Ludwig Prandtl in 1904. Bairstow held that mathematical theory should encompass the whole surrounding air mass, rather than a thin layer, and he was inclined to reject Prandtl's argument. He was eventually persuaded to adopt it, whereupon he invented a rapid and precise method of solving the necessary equations. His criticism of Prandtl's theory was undoubtedly justified and it was not until M. J. Lighthill had developed the theory of differential equations with singular perturbations that an adequate theory could be constructed. Bairstow should be remembered not only for his part in these controversies but also for his considerable contributions to knowledge of the stability of aircraft.

Bairstow's main contributions to aeronautical science were in matters of stability, but he also dealt with solutions of equations of motion in perfect and viscous fluids, and in his early days at NPL he investigated some engineering problems of explosions and strength of materials. In the course of his investigations into stability, Bairstow made a number of small gliding models from mica sheets and aluminium foil. He also applied the model method to the design of wind tunnels, and in later papers he studied the stability of balloons and airships. His researches on the tail oscillations which occur in an aeroplane represent the first attempt to understand the important problem of flutter.

Bairstow's experience led to his appointment to two government committees which investigated the accidents to the airships R 38 and R 101. Unfortunately his earlier work, which would have permitted calculations of the structural stresses due to aerodynamic forces on the R 38, had not been consulted and it was not until after the accident that the accidents investigation subcommittee (in 1922) called attention to the dangerously low factor of safety.

In the case of the R 101 the airworthiness of airships panel, under the chairmanship of Bairstow, was intimately associated with the airship's design and construction and would have made the complete re-examination of the aerodynamic calculations necessitated by modifications to the original design, but unfortunately the refusal of a cabinet minister to postpone the date of the projected flight to India made this impossible. The immediate cause of the R 101's crash in 1930 was the stormy weather over northern France which caused a substantial loss of gas from the balloons, which fretted against the metal structure.

Bairstow retired from Imperial College in 1945. He was made an honorary fellow of the Royal Aeronautical Society the same year, and received its gold medal in 1946. He was knighted in 1952. He died at the county hospital in Winchester, Hampshire, on 8 September 1963, and was cremated at Southampton four days later. He was survived by his second wife.

G. Temple, *rev.* Anita McConnell

Sources G. Temple and others, *Memoirs FRS*, 11 (1965), 23–40 • J. L. Pritchard and J. L. Naylor, *Journal of the Royal Aeronautical Society*, 68 (1964) • *The Times* (13 Sept 1963), 14b

Likenesses W. Stoneman, photograph, 1921, NPG

Wealth at death £8925 16s.: probate, 21 Oct 1963, *CGPLA Eng. & Wales*

Baissac, Claude Marc Boucherville de (1907–1974), secret operations officer, was born on 28 February 1907 at Curepipe, Mauritius, the younger son and youngest of three children of Marie Louis Marc de Boucherville Baissac and his wife, Marie Louise Jeannette Dupont. His father was a British subject of French origin and represented the Sun Insurance Company of London. De Baissac attended school in Mauritius until he was sent as a boarder to the Lycée Henri IV in Paris where he finished his studies. He was physically strong, nearly 6 feet tall with brown hair and blue eyes, with an attractive personality, courage, resourcefulness, and a great zest for life.

Owing to a change in family circumstances de Baissac's father sent him to direct Mica Mine exploration in southern Madagascar in 1931, and he was the only European for miles around. In 1933 he returned to Paris and became publicity director for a film company. In 1937 he was appointed commercial director of Cie Simmons, a light metal company. He left Paris in early 1940, crossed the Pyrenees on foot, and headed for the British consulate in Barcelona. He was arrested by the Spanish in Barcelona, and imprisoned for seven months. After his release he reached Gibraltar from where he was shipped to Glasgow.

De Baissac joined the Special Operations Executive (SOE) in March 1942 and was dropped 'blind' on 30 July near Nîmes with Henri Peulevé as his wireless-telegraphy operator and assistant. Although both landed badly, Peulevé breaking a leg and de Baissac spraining an ankle, they reached their safe house in Cannes. When his ankle had recovered, de Baissac proceeded to Bordeaux in accordance with his brief to train and lead a network of Frenchmen willing to resist enemy occupation. His chief contact was Grandclément, son of Admiral Grandclément, in charge of région B of the Organisation Civile et Militaire, a grouping of men mainly with a military or naval background who were spread across occupied France. Région B extended from the Pyrenees to the Charente and was centred on Bordeaux, which was extremely important as a submarine base and port for the Far Eastern blockade-runners. De Baissac established contacts in the docks, and sent back vitally important information on the movement of ships and submarines, for which he was appointed to the DSO.

On 24 September 1942 de Baissac's sister, Lise Villameur, was dropped near Poitiers to establish another circuit and organize safe houses. On 1 November de Baissac received his new operator Major Roger Landes MC. In December Charles Hayes arrived as arms instructor and Mary Herbert as courier. De Baissac was flown back to London on 13 March 1943 to report; he returned to France on 14 April. In May a second operator, Marcel Defence, was sent to assist Landes in order to allow the latter to take a more active part in the organization, which had rapidly expanded to about 20,000 men under paramilitary training. In 134 parachute operations supplies had been received on ten different grounds. Sabotage attacks were made on aerodromes and railway lines, notably at Dax, Facture, Bayonne, and La Réole, and against the transformer station at Belin. The last of these operations stopped traffic between Bordeaux and the Spanish frontier for about three weeks at a time when the Germans were pressing Franco to co-operate.

Trouble started in July with the arrest of Grandclément's wife and there were fears for the safety of the whole circuit. De Baissac was recalled to London on 15 August. The circuit remained active during the rest of the war under Landes's direction. It engaged in intensive sabotage shortly before D-day, attacking all the enemy communication targets at the time of the landings.

De Baissac's next mission was to Normandy, in preparation for a possible allied landing. He was dropped near Chartres with his operator on 10 February 1944. He once again built up small groups, mainly in the Orne and Calvados, which he armed and trained for sabotage action designed to demoralize the Germans and delay their movements after the landings. He received his sister, Lise, as courier, four more agents and operators, and a group of SAS. He set up two sub-circuits to concentrate on intelligence work of value to allied army commanders, and himself crossed back and forth through enemy lines. When overrun by the Americans in mid-August, he was flown out to London and promptly briefed for a further mission, which was cancelled in view of the pace of the allied advance.

For his achievements in Normandy, de Baissac received a bar to his DSO. The French gave him the Croix de Guerre with palm and made him a chevalier of the Légion d'honneur. On 11 November 1944 in London, de Baissac married his former courier Mary Katherine, daughter of Brigadier-General Edmund Arthur Herbert; they had one daughter.

In May 1945 de Baissac left SOE and joined General Koenig's staff at Châlons-sur-Marne as liaison officer to the allied command. From November 1946 until he relinquished his commission in May 1947 he served with the Allied Control Commission in Wuppertal. He subsequently returned to mining and mineral interests in Africa and was later director of the Compagnie de Dépôt de Pétrolier in west Africa.

His first marriage having been dissolved in 1959 or 1960, on 9 November 1964 at the British consulate in Yaoundé, Cameroon, de Baissac married Colette Françoise, daughter of Marcel Frédéric Avril, a commercial director. They retired to Aix-en-Provence where de Baissac died on 22 December 1974. V. M. Atkins, *rev.*

Sources M. R. D. Foot, *SOE in France: an account of the work of the British Special Operations Executive in France, 1940–1944* (1966) • private information (1986) • personal knowledge (1986) • *The Times* (7 Jan 1975)

Baíthéne mac Brénainn (*d.* 598). *See under* Iona, abbots of (*act.* 563–927).

Bajpai, Sir Girja Shankar (1891–1954), administrator and politician in India, was born in Lucknow on 3 April 1891, the second of the three sons of Sir Seetla Prasad Bajpai, chief justice of Jaipur state, and his wife, Rukmini Shukla (*d.* 1945). Having won a science scholarship from Muir College, Allahabad, to Merton College, Oxford, Bajpai switched to history and in 1915 entered the Indian Civil Service. He was perhaps its most brilliant Indian member in the inter-war years, becoming the youngest secretary to the government of India, member of the legislative assembly, and member of the viceroy's executive council. He was also the first Indian in the British period to be officially involved in international affairs, as agent-general for India in the United States. Immensely industrious, persistent, and persuasive, fluent in French, Persian, and Bengali and a stylist in English, a good speaker, matching in repartee and debate men of the calibre of Bhulabhai Desai and M. A. Jinnah, he was a fine craftsman in all the fields he entered.

Chosen in 1922 for Lord Balfour's team for the Washington conference on naval disarmament, Bajpai went on to participate in the League of Nations in Geneva, in the second round-table conference in London, and in negotiations with other countries of the British empire and Commonwealth, notably South Africa, on the problems of Indian expatriates. In 1941 Whitehall allowed India to have its first representation in an independent country, and Bajpai was sent as agent-general to Washington, where he was to serve until 1946. He impressed not only Roosevelt and other Americans, but several international figures, such as the eminent French columnist Pertinax, who described him as 'un sort de Voltaire au sein de l'Empire Britannique' ('a sort of Voltaire at the heart of the British empire'). Bajpai was, however, to incur bitter criticism in his own country, where his name was associated with British propaganda against Gandhi and the Indian National Congress in the United States during the war.

In his legislative years Bajpai had developed friendly contacts with some of the Indian political leaders, such as Bhulabhai Desai, Satyamurti, K. M. Munshi, M. R. Jayakar, and Sir Tej Bahadur Sapru. His views on political freedom and how to secure it from Britain were very much like theirs. There is evidence that these Indian leaders also had misgivings about the policy of the Congress in the early 1940s. Bajpai had the unenviable duty of publicly defending in the United States the policies and actions of the government of India at a time of great nationalist upheaval when popular alienation from the raj was at its peak. The publication of American records has, however, revealed that he was not only urging the British government to abandon rigidity in its attitude on the constitutional issue, but also persuading the Americans to urge on the British government a more conciliatory policy towards India. Bajpai's deputy in Washington, Humphrey (later Lord) Trevelyan, wrote in his memoirs: 'Bajpai earned the respect of the British and Americans. He conducted himself with dignity and honesty tempered with adroitness. For this he was abused by his countrymen' (Trevelyan, 238).

Nehru's letter to Bajpai asking him to continue in service after the transfer of power was not exactly couched in a cordial tone, but it must be said to Nehru's credit that he did not take long to recognize Bajpai's talents and experience. He appointed him head of the department of external affairs as secretary-general. Bajpai influenced decisions of high policy until 1952, when ill health obliged him to retire. His outstanding career was crowned with his appointment as governor of Bombay state in 1952. He died there in harness on 5 December 1954 and was cremated on the same day, full of honours, a great Indian who also cared deeply for the British heritage. He was appointed CBE in 1922, CIE in 1926, KBE in 1935, and KCSI in 1943.

A strong supporter of the Commonwealth, Bajpai played a key role in drafting the final constitutional formula for enabling India to remain in it as a republic. His mastery of the Kashmir question briefly brought him back to diplomacy in 1953, when he led the Indian delegation in talks with Pakistan and the UN representative Frank Graham. He is, however, perhaps best remembered for his advice—which Nehru accepted before Bajpai left the foreign office, but which other influences later negated—to raise the boundary issue with China.

The chairman of the UN Kashmir commission, Josef Korbel, described Bajpai, as 'a small man with a shy smile, perfect manners and ivory cut hands, with the English of Shakespeare and himself the quintessence of ancient Indian culture and Oxford schooling' (Korbel, 123). Korbel added that Bajpai 'was a great diplomat of the English school', and his long interaction with the British certainly shaped him greatly, but he was unusual in his day for the broader influence deriving from his love and experience of Europe, especially France, supplemented by a deep understanding of the United States. Above all, he was quintessentially Indian, in personal commitment, no less than in his personal life. Outwardly a little austere, Bajpai had an air of detachment designed to ensure a privacy he prized, so that he could turn to reading and to things of beauty, particularly carpets, paintings, and flowers, and cultivating fine roses. With all his elegant manners and courtesy, he had a puckish streak, poking fun, yet willing to be its object. A devoted family man, Bajpai and his wife, Maharajdulari Misra (*d.* 1967), had four daughters and three sons. Nothing would have pleased him more than that his two surviving sons succeeded him as secretaries to the government of India, one of them as ambassador to the United States, providing the rare example of father and son occupying the same chair in Washington.

OLAF CAROE, *rev.* B. R. NANDA

Sources H. Trevelyan, *The India we left* (1972) · J. Korbel, *Danger in Kashmir*, rev. edn (1966) · *The foreign relations of the United States: diplomatic matters, 1941–1945* · *Selected works of Jawaharlal Nehru*, ed. S. Gopal and others, [2nd ser.], 28 vols. (1984–), vol. 1, pp. 549–50 · priv. coll., G. S. Bajpai MSS · private information (2004)

Archives BL OIOC, corresp. as agent-general for India in Washington, MS Eur. D 714 · NRA priv. coll., archive | BL OIOC, corresp. with Sir John Walton, MS Eur. D 545

Baker, Alexander (1582–1638), Jesuit, was born in Norfolk on 25 March 1582. He studied grammar and humanities for five years. Some time before 1600 or 1601 he left England for Spain, where he studied philosophy and theology at a Jesuit college in Seville. As he is not mentioned in Murphy's list of students at the English College in Seville, he may have been at another seminary there. In 1608 he was ordained subdeacon in Seville, deacon in Cadiz, and priest in Malaga. He entered the society at the English noviciate in Louvain on 23 April 1612, pronouncing his first vows on 23 April 1613. He was socius to the vice-prefect of the English mission in Brussels from 1614 to 1617. In Brussels in 1615 he reconciled William Coke (later ordained priest in Rome), a son of Sir Edward Coke, the famous lawyer, to the Catholic church. Baker then served as confessor at the Jesuit college in Douai (1617–18) and procurator and consultor at the English College in St Omer. He returned to Spain about 1621, first to Seville and then to the English College in Valladolid. By 1624 he was serving on the English mission as superior of the residence of Blessed Stanislaus (Devon) until 1626.

Some time after Baker's return to England, probably in 1625, he was arrested. Through the intercession of the French ambassador Baker and ten other Catholics were pardoned by Charles I on 12 July 1625 to the annoyance of a parliament eager to enforce penal laws against Catholic priests. Under Elizabeth, parliament contended, priests were pardoned only after conviction upon their banishment from a kingdom to which they were not to return under pain of death. On the contrary Baker had not yet been convicted and was not required to leave the kingdom 'and being now at liberty his conversation will be very dangerous to the perverting of many of his Majesty's subjects' (*JHL*, quoted in Foley, 1.154). There survives (PRO, SP 14/189/25, under date 1625) a manuscript by Baker in defence of the doctrine of regeneration by baptism as held by Catholics, showing its difference from the opinion of protestants.

After a year or two in the house of probation of St Ignatius (London), where he was professed of the four vows on 23 May 1627, Baker returned to Devon in 1629. Henry Foley's quasi-literal translation from the Latin 'Summaria mortuorum' (Rome, Archivum Romanum Societatis Iesu, Anglia 7, 267) that Baker twice journeyed to 'the remotest territories of the Indies' ('ad remotas Indorum terras'; Foley, 7/1.28) was transformed by the author of the *Dictionary of National Biography* article into the claim that he 'twice visited India as a missionary'. Baker travelled to North America, first to Newfoundland from approximately Easter to Christmas in 1629 and then to the recently founded colony in Maryland in 1634. With the exception of his eight months in Maryland, Baker worked in London throughout the 1630s until his death there on 24 August 1638. THOMAS M. McCOOG

Sources T. M. McCoog, *English and Welsh Jesuits, 1555–1650*, 1, Catholic RS, 74 (1994), 110 • T. M. McCoog, ed., *Monumenta Angliae*, 1: *English and Welsh Jesuits, catalogues, 1555–1629* (1992), 264–5; 2: *English and Welsh Jesuits, catalogues, 1630–1640* (1992), 219–20 • H. Foley, ed., *Records of the English province of the Society of Jesus*, 1 (1877), 153–4; 7/1 (1882), 28 • E. Henson, ed., *The registers of the English College at Valladolid, 1589–1862*, Catholic RS, 30 (1930), xxvi • H. More, *Historia missionis Anglicanae Societatis Iesu* (St Omer, 1660) • L. Codignola, *The coldest harbour of the land: Simon Stock and Lord Baltimore's colony in Newfoundland, 1621–1649*, trans. A. Weston (1988), 53–4 • M. Murphy, *St Gregory's College, Seville, 1592–1767*, Catholic RS, 73 (1992) • T. Hughes, *History of the Society of Jesus in North America*, 4 vols. (1907–17) • A. Kenny, ed., *The responsa scholarum of the English College, Rome*, 1, Catholic RS, 54 (1962)

Archives Archives of the British Province of the Society of Jesus, London • Archivum Romanum Societatis Iesu, Rome

Baker, (John Frederic) Allan (1903–1987), civil engineer, was born on 5 October 1903 at Eversleigh, Hounslow, the son of Harry James Baker, clerk to the district council, and his wife, Ethel Gertrude Fowler. He was educated at St Paul's School, London. On 2 February 1927 he married Nancy Elizabeth, daughter of William Wells, an inspector of taxes. They had a son (who died at an early age) and a daughter.

First employed by Middlesex county council in 1922, Baker qualified as a professional member of the Institution of Municipal Engineers, before in 1929 joining the Ministry of Transport's regional office in Exeter. After moving on to its offices in Bedford and Nottingham, he found the Ministry of War Transport's headquarters in 1945 planning a trunk road system of 3685 miles under the terms of the Trunk Roads Act (1936) and the Restriction of Ribbon Development Act (1935). In 1947 he became divisional road engineer for Wales and Monmouth and worked from Cardiff, where under the Special Roads Act (1949) he planned the Newport bypass and motorway standard approaches to a proposed Severn Bridge.

In 1953 Baker returned to London as deputy chief engineer (civil engineering) to lead the Ministry of Transport's plans for the first 1000 miles of motorway, and became chief engineer within a year. In 1956 Harold Watkinson, as minister of transport, announced the splayed 'H' pattern of M1 and M6 routes astride the M4 London to south Wales route, as well as the M50 and later the M5. Works included improving the A1 to motorway standard around Stevenage and new motorway bypasses for Preston and Lancaster, later combined as parts of the M6. At meetings held in 1962–4 with the Scottish development department, the County Surveyors' Society, and the Association of County Councils, Baker accommodated within his annual £60 million budgets Treasury concerns about the exchange rate and trade. These involved relative priority for motorway links for Southampton, Hull, Liverpool, and Glasgow, although as extensions beyond the first 1000 miles they could not expect Treasury approval for completion before 1975. In 1963 he was appointed director of highway engineering, an appointment that coincided with ministry approval for articulated lorries of 32 tons gross, given that they would primarily use the new motorways.

From 1954 until retirement on 1 May 1965 Baker was a member of the Road Research Board, which in 1960 published appraisals of the use of the London–Birmingham motorway, proving motorways the safest of road types. By his death in 1987 the proportion of the nation's traffic carried by the motorways which he had planned had grown to 38.3 per cent. Baker also served on the London roads committee in 1959 and on the revising national traffic signs committee from 1963 to 1964. From 1965 until 1969 he was highways and traffic engineering adviser to the Automobile Association.

Made an honorary member of the Institution of Highway Engineers in 1954, Baker was appointed CB in 1957. He received honorary fellowship of the Institution of Municipal Engineers in 1957 and served as a vice-chairman on the Public Works and Municipal Services Congress and Exhibition Council. He was elected to the Institution of Civil Engineers' council and served from 1956 to 1961. In 1967 the Worshipful Company of Carmen awarded him their Viva shield and gold award for pioneering Britain's motorway system. He served as vice-president of the international executive committee of the Permanent International Association of Road Congresses from 1960 to 1972, and as chairman of its British national committee. A member of the joint committee of the International Touring Alliance, Baker also organized biennial training weeks on traffic engineering for the International Road Federation. He served as chairman of the road engineering committee of the British Standards Institution and in 1976 helped to found the fellowship of engineering. A convivial man, he presented the Baker cup to the County Surveyors' Society in 1965 for the ladies' annual golf matches. He lived latterly at 36 Imber Close, Ember Lane, Esher, where he died on 20 July 1987.

PETER BALDWIN

Sources Archives of the Automobile Association, Basingstoke • Archives of the Institution of Highways and Transportation, London • A. Smith, *A history of the County Surveyors' Society, 1885–1985* (1985) • *CGPLA Eng. & Wales* (1988) • b. cert. • m. cert. • d. cert.

Wealth at death under £70,000: probate, 11 March 1988, *CGPLA Eng. & Wales*

Baker, Anne Elizabeth (1786–1861), philologist, was born at Northampton on 16 June 1786, and was baptized on 25 July at the Castle Hill Independent Church, the daughter of Richard Baker and his wife, Ann. She was the younger sister of George *Baker (1781–1851), the historian of Northamptonshire. Neither she nor her brother married, and for sixty years they shared a house and were constant companions. She was educated at home. Early on she showed an interest in antiquarian subjects, and it was her removal in 1812 of the whitewash from the chancel arch of St Peter's, Northampton, that led to the church's subsequent restoration. Between about 1815 and 1840 she travelled with her brother as he collected materials for his *History*, acting as his amanuensis, compiling the sections on geology and botany, and making drawings. Some of these she engraved for the published work. 'Provincialisms' which she collected while on these travels formed the basis of her *Glossary of Northamptonshire Words and Phrases, to which are Added, the Customs of the County* (2 vols., 1854), which was highly regarded by her contemporaries. Anne Elizabeth Baker died at Hazelrigg House, Gold Street, Northampton, on 22 April 1861.

THOMPSON COOPER, *rev.* PAUL STAMPER

Sources P. Stamper, 'Northamptonshire', *English county histories: a guide*, ed. C. R. J. Currie and C. P. Lewis (1994), 291–301 · *IGI* · *GM*, 3rd ser., 11 (1861), 208

Wealth at death £4000: probate, 19 June 1861, *CGPLA Eng. & Wales*

Baker, Sir Benjamin (1840–1907), civil engineer, was born at Keyford, Frome, Somerset, on 31 March 1840, the son of Benjamin Baker and Sarah Hollis. His father, a native of co. Carlow, Ireland, became principal assistant at ironworks at Tondu, Glamorgan. After being educated at Cheltenham grammar school, Baker was for four years (1856–60) apprentice at Price and Fox's Neath Abbey ironworks. At this time he had an affair with a young Welsh woman, with whom he had an illegitimate daughter. Her parents emigrated with their daughter to America, and Baker was ignorant of the birth for eight years.

Baker moved to London in 1860 to join the staff of William Wilson, a business associate of John Fowler, working on the construction of the Grosvenor Road railway bridge and Victoria Station. On completion of the work he joined Fowler's staff. Fowler persuaded Baker that his talents had a future in Britain when early in his career he contemplated emigrating to the colonies; he became Fowler's partner in 1875, and was associated with him until Fowler's death in 1898. As a consulting engineer Baker rapidly gained the highest reputation for skill and knowledge, and was consulted by the British and Egyptian governments, by colonial administrations, and by local and other authorities. The credit for the design and execution of the great civil engineering achievements with which Baker's name is associated was necessarily shared by him with Fowler and many other colleagues, but Baker's judgement and resource were highly important factors in the success of these undertakings.

London's underground railways In the 1860s Fowler was heavily involved with the underground railway system of London. As assistant in Fowler's office, Baker was employed on the construction of the Metropolitan Railway, its St John's Wood extension. In 1869 he became Fowler's chief assistant in the construction of the Metropolitan District Railway from Westminster to Mansion House. In his 1881 paper, 'The actual lateral pressure of earthwork', he discussed some fruits of this experience (*PICE*, 65, 1880–81, 140–241), and described the work itself in 1885 (B. Baker, 'The Metropolitan and Metropolitan District railways', *PICE*, 81, 1884–5, 1–33). Subsequently Fowler and Baker acted as consulting engineers for the first 'tube' railway the City and South London Line, opened in 1890 (later part of the Northern Line), and with J. H. Greathead were the joint engineers for the Central London Railway, opened in 1900. In the construction of this line Baker carried out the plan suggested by him in 1874, of making the line dip down between the stations in order to reduce the required tractive effort. This subsequently became standard practice on tube railways. After Greathead's death in 1896 Baker also acted as joint engineer with W. R. Galbraith for the Baker Street and Waterloo (Bakerloo) Railway . Almost his last act before his death was to attend the opening of the Euston–Angel extension of the City and South London Railway; Basil Mott and David Hay were his partners in work on this project.

The Forth Bridge In the early years of his career Baker began to study structural theory and the strength of materials. For *Engineering* he wrote a series of articles on long span bridges in 1867, and another, on the strength of beams, columns, and arches, in 1868. Both series were published in book form, as was his paper on the lateral pressure of earthwork. A third series, on the strength of brickwork, was written in 1872. These publications established Baker's international reputation, and were extensively abstracted and translated. In the work on long span bridges, published at a time when Fowler's practice was actively considering a major crossing of the Severn, Baker concluded that the longest span could be achieved using cantilevers supporting an independent girder. This system was finally adopted for the Forth railway bridge. To his early training in the Neath Abbey ironworks he owed the foundation of his thorough knowledge of the properties and strength of metals, on which he wrote many papers. Baker's technical writings displayed a rare ability to illustrate engineering principles in a way which even a lay audience could understand. This was seen, for example, in his illustration of the cantilever principle by a human model in his lectures on the Forth railway bridge. This specialist knowledge enabled him to play a principal part in association with Fowler in the design of the Forth Bridge. This, the longest span bridge in the world at the time, was begun in 1883 and completed in 1890. Baker worked almost continuously on site, carrying out numerous tests on the steelwork and research into wind pressure. His services were rewarded by the honour of KCMG (17 April 1890) and the prix Poncelet of the Institut de

France. The success of the bridge paved the way for the widespread use of structural steel.

Egypt and the Aswan Dam From 1869 Baker was also associated with Fowler in investigating and advising upon engineering projects in Egypt. One of these was for a railway between Wadi Halfa and Shendi and a ship incline at Aswan, and another was a project for a sweet-water canal between Alexandria and Cairo, which was never built.

For the remainder of his life Baker played a prominent part in the engineering work which distinguished British involvement in Egypt in the late nineteenth and early twentieth centuries. He was consulted by the Egyptian government on various occasions on the repair of the Nile delta barrage and when, after several years' investigation, schemes were prepared by Sir William Willcocks in 1894 for the storage of the waters of the Nile for irrigation purposes, Baker was appointed to the commission which approved the project for a reservoir at Aswan and chose a site for the dam. To meet objections to the partial submergence by this plan of the temples at Philae, the height of the proposed dam was reduced from 85 to 65 feet. The work, for which Baker was consulting engineer, was begun in 1898 and was completed in 1902, when Baker was made KCB and was appointed to the order of the Mejidiye. The dam was 6400 feet in length, pierced by 180 sluice openings at different levels. Baker was also consulting engineer for a subsidiary dam which was built at the same time at Asyut, below Aswan. When the contractors, John Aird & Sons, had this work well in hand, with a large part of their contract time to run, Baker, realizing the advantages of early completion of the dam, advised the Egyptian government to cancel the contract and to instruct the contractors to finish the work at the earliest possible moment, regardless of cost, leaving the question of contractors' profit to be settled by him. His advice was followed, the work was completed a year early, and the value of the extra year's supply of water was estimated to be £600,000. The Aswan Reservoir was from the first found to be inadequate to meet demand and as no suitable site could be found for another reservoir above the site, it was decided to raise the dam there to about the height originally proposed by Willcocks. Baker solved the difficult problem of uniting new to old masonry so as to form a solid structure by building the upper portion of the dam as an independent structure which could be united to the lower by grouting with cement when it had ceased to settle and contract. Just before his death he went to Egypt to settle the plans for this work (completed in 1912), as well as preliminary plans for a bridge across the Nile at Bulaq.

Other works Smaller but important works which Baker also undertook included: the vessel which he designed with John Dixon in 1877 to transport Cleopatra's Needle from Egypt to England, a project which first brought his name to the notice of the general public ('Cleopatra's Needle', *PICE*, 61.233); the Chignecto Rhip Railway, for which Fowler and Baker were consulting engineers, commenced in 1888 and abandoned in 1891 owing to financial difficulties; the Avonmouth docks (in association with Sir John Wolfe Barry, 1902–8); the Rosslare and Waterford Railway; the widening of the Buccleuch Dock entrance at Barrow; and the construction of the bascule bridges at Walney (Barrow in Furness) and across the Swale near Queenborough.

Baker gave much professional advice on structures at home and abroad. He advised on three important works of Thomas Telford—the Menai Bridge, Buildwas Bridge, and Over Bridge at Gloucester—doing much to ensure their survival. He acted as consultant with Allan Duncan Stewart (1831–1894), who had earlier assisted in the Forth railway bridge design, on the Wembley Tower project, conceived as the tallest structure in the world but soon abandoned. When the roof of Charing Cross railway station collapsed on 5 December 1905 he at once examined it, at some personal danger, and gave useful advice. He had earlier been consulted by Captain J. B. Eads in connection with the design of the St Louis Bridge across the Mississippi (1868) and in regard to the first Hudson river tunnel when the latter faced failure, he designed a pneumatic shield which enabled the work to be completed (1888–91). His fame as a bridge engineer led to him acting jointly with Fowler as consultant to Schneider and Hersent's scheme for a cross-channel railway bridge. Nowhere were his abilities appreciated more highly than in Canada and the United States. He was an honorary member of both the Canadian and the American Societies of Civil Engineers and of the American Society of Mechanical Engineers.

Government service Baker served from 1888 until his death on the ordnance committee, of which he became the senior civil member on the death of Sir Frederick Bramwell in 1903. He was active in many government inquiries and regularly gave evidence on parliamentary bills. He was a member of the committee on light railways in 1895, and of the committee appointed by the Board of Trade in 1900 to inquire into the loss of strength in steel rails. To the London county council he reported in 1891, with Alexander Binnie, on the main drainage of London, and in 1897, with George Frederick Deacon, on the supply of water to London from Wales. On Fowler's death in 1898 he retained many of Sir John's consultancies, maintaining the office at 2 Queen Square Place, Westminster, under the name of Baker and Hurtzig. His partner, Arthur Dameron Hurtzig, continued the practice after Baker's death. In addition Baker had a partnership with Frederick Shelford, acting as consultants to the crown agents.

Baker was elected an associate of the Institution of Civil Engineers in 1867, a member in 1877, a member of council in 1882, and president in 1895, remaining on the council until his death. During his presidency the council was enlarged to give the membership overseas and outside London better representation and the system of election was modified. Baker was a major influence on the foundation of the Engineering Standards Committee, forerunner of the British Standards Institution, by ICE and the other leading engineering institutions. He helped draft the first British standards relating to bridges and building construction. He became a fellow of the Royal Society in

1890 and a member of its council in 1892–3, and was one of its vice-presidents from 1896 until his death.

Baker was president of the mechanical science section of the British Association at Aberdeen in 1885. He was also active in the Royal Institution, in the Institution of Mechanical Engineers (on the council of which he sat from 1899 until death), in the Society of Arts, and in the Iron and Steel Institute. He was an associate of the Institution of Naval Architects and an honorary associate of the Royal Institute of British Architects. Honorary degrees were conferred upon him by the universities of Cambridge (DSc, 1900), Edinburgh (LLD, 1890), and Dublin (MEng, 1892).

Baker died suddenly from syncope at his home, Bowden Green, Pangbourne, on 19 May 1907, and was buried at Idbury, near Chipping Norton. He was unmarried and left the bulk of his estate to his sister, Mrs Fanny Maria Kemp, and her family.

A memorial window, designed by J. N. Comper, was unveiled by the earl of Cromer on 3 October 1909 in the north aisle of the nave of Westminster Abbey.

W. F. Spear, *rev.* Mike Chrimes

Sources *Engineering*, 83 (24 May 1907), 685–6 • *PICE*, 170 (1906–7), 377–83 • *The Engineer*, 103 (24 May 1907), 524 • L. T. C. Rolt, *Great engineers* (1962) • S. B. Hamilton, 'Sir Benjamin Baker, with particular reference to his contribution to the study of earth pressures', *Géotechnique*, 8 (1958), 105–12 • R. A. Paxton, ed., *100 years of the Forth Bridge* (1990) • A. W. Skempton, 'Landmarks in early soil mechanics', *The measurement, selection, and use of design parameters in geotechnical engineering: Seventh European Conference on Soil Mechanics and Foundation Engineering* [Brighton 1979], 5 (1981), 1–26 • W. Westhofen, *The Forth Bridge* (1890) • *The Times* (20 May 1907)

Archives ICL • Inst. CE, Baker and Hurtzig records; papers and drawings • NA Scot. • PRO | ICL, Unwin MS, letters to W. C. Unwin • Mott MacDonald Consulting Engineers, London, MSS

Likenesses Bassano, photographs • T. Fall, photograph, repro. in *PICE*, 117 (1893–4) • T. Fall, photograph, repro. in *Engineering* • J. C. Michie, portrait, ICL, Department of Civil Engineering; replica, Inst. CE • engraving, Inst. CE • pastel drawing, Museum of London Transport

Wealth at death £170,513 9*s*. 4*d*.: probate, 19 June 1907, *CGPLA Eng. & Wales*

Baker, Charles. *See* Lewis, David (1617–1679).

Baker, Charles (1803–1874), teacher of deaf people, was born on 31 July 1803, the second son of Thomas Baker, a pawnbroker, of Birmingham and his wife, Charlotte Eldred. His elder brother was Franklin *Baker (1800–1867); his younger brothers included Sir Thomas Baker (1810–1886), a solicitor in Manchester, and Alfred Baker (1815–1893), a surgeon in Birmingham. While a youth he was for a short time an assistant at the Deaf and Dumb Institution at Edgbaston, near Birmingham, a pioneering provincial school for deaf children. He then tried other employment, but his services were again sought by the committee of the institution in 1826, when a difficulty arose because of the failure of the master, who was a Swiss, to control the pupils. Baker had never contemplated teaching as a profession, but without much thought for the future he entered upon his work. He at once gained the affections of the children and he remained at the institution. Three years later he was invited to help in the establishment, at Doncaster, of a deaf and dumb institution for the county of York. The plan had originated with the Revd William Fenton, rector of Cowthorpe, in company with whom he visited all the large towns of the county, and obtained sufficient support to warrant carrying out the scheme.

Baker then faced a lack of suitable books, for although institutions for the deaf and dumb had existed for forty years, no attempt had been made to provide a suitable course of instruction. He therefore set himself to supply this want. He wrote a graded reading and comprehension course, the *Circle of Knowledge*, consisting of consecutive lessons, with accompanying material for teachers, a graded series of books about Bible characters, events, and history, and many other works of special relevance to the teaching of deaf and deaf mute people. The *Circle of Knowledge*, which sold over 400,000 copies, was used in the education of the royal children, and of the grandchildren of King Louis-Philippe, and was widely used in the colonies and in Russia. The first gradation was translated into Chinese by the London Missionary Society, and was used in the schools of China and Japan. Baker produced many textbooks for Bible classes. He also contributed to the *Penny Cyclopædia*, the *Journal of Education*, the *Polytechnic Journal*, and the publications of the Central Society of Education, and translated J. C. Amman's *Dissertatio de loquela* (as *Dissertation on Speech*, 1873).

Baker was an active worker in connection with the local institutions of Doncaster, and was a member of the committee for the establishment of a free public library for the town. He was held in high regard by teachers of deaf people in England and in America, by whom he was acknowledged to be the leader of the older school of thought, which emphasized written methods of instruction. In June 1870 the Columbian Institution of the Deaf and Dumb conferred on him the degree of doctor of philosophy, an honour which he appreciated, but he never assumed the title. He died at Doncaster on 27 May 1874, leaving a widow, Mary Baker. His will named five daughters and one son. His old pupils erected a mural tablet to his memory in the institution where he had laboured so long.

C. W. Sutton, *rev.* M. C. Curthoys

Sources private information (1885) • *American Annals of the Deaf and Dumb*, 20 (1875), 201 • Boase, *Mod. Eng. biog.* • M. G. McLoughlin, *A history of the education of the deaf in England* (1987)

Archives NL Scot., corresp. with George Combe

Likenesses portrait, repro. in *American Annals of the Deaf and Dumb*

Wealth at death under £12,000: probate, 10 Aug 1874, *CGPLA Eng. & Wales*

Baker, Charles Henry Collins (1880–1959), art historian and painter, was born on 24 January 1880 at Bay Hill, Ilminster, Somerset, the son of John Collins Baker, solicitor, and his wife, Fanny Henrietta Remmett. He was educated at Berkhamsted before attending the Royal Academy Schools. On 9 July 1903 he married Muriel Isabella (1874/5–1956), daughter of H. R. T. Alexander, taxing master of the Supreme Court: they had one daughter, Phyllis. Collins Baker began his career as a landscape painter, signing his works C. H. C. B. He exhibited in 1907 at the Royal Academy and in 1909–16 at the New English Art Club, also serving as the club's honorary secretary from 1921 to 1925. His paintings are now held by Manchester City Galleries, Leeds City Art Gallery, and Huddersfield Art Gallery. In 1911 he began to figure as an art critic, contributing articles to *The Outlook* and to the *Saturday Review*; he also accepted an appointment as private assistant to Sir Charles Holroyd, director of the National Gallery, rising to the rank of keeper in 1914. Early in his career at the National Gallery he wrote his most important book, *Lely and the Stuart Portrait Painters* (2 vols., 1912), which is a pioneering work in the study of British art. He continued as keeper under Holroyd's successor, Charles John Holmes, who was director from 1916 to 1928.

While continuing his work as keeper, Collins Baker in 1928 accepted the position of surveyor of the king's pictures, publishing *A Catalogue of the Pictures at Hampton Court* in 1929. Ellis Waterhouse, who worked for him at the National Gallery, wrote on 16 January 1976 that 'CHCB was certainly not happy as surveyor … [he] was very unassuming and unsuspicious and totally unsnobbish and miraculously unsuited to having anything to do with a world of royal servants' (Archives of the Royal Collection). However, Collins Baker retained the position until he resigned in 1934, and was made CVO in the same year. He also accepted the offer in 1930 to prepare a catalogue (published in 1936) of the British paintings in the Henry E. Huntington Library and Art Gallery in San Marino, California. Increasing friction with the board of trustees at the National Gallery, in particular with the chairman, Lord Lee, encouraged him in the autumn of 1931 to explore with Max Farrand, the director of the Huntington, the possibility of a professional connection. On 2 February 1932 he accepted the post of senior research associate in British art at the Huntington and in March resigned from the National Gallery. For a while he remained in England, continuing his work as surveyor of the Royal Collection; this led to the publication in 1937 of a catalogue of the pictures at Windsor. After moving to California in late 1933 he pursued a variety of projects, principally a study of the papers at the Huntington of James Brydges, first duke of Chandos, which he published with his wife, Muriel, in 1949. In that year he retired and returned to England, where he spent the remainder of his life. Although incapacitated by arthritis in his last years, he continued work on a projected book on minor Georgian portrait painters. He died on 3 July 1959 at his home, 8 Holyoake Walk, Finchley, Middlesex.

Waterhouse wrote of Collins Baker, in his obituary in the *Burlington Magazine*, that he belonged to:

> the last great age of the self-taught scholar in England, before it was permissible to call oneself an art historian, and *Lely and the Stuart Portrait Painters* (1912), achieved with no greater mechanical aid than a bicycle, is the last great scholarly monument of that generation. It seems to me almost the foundation stone of the serious study of our native paintings … [He was] a man as warm-hearted as he was undemonstrative. His influence on those who worked with him was not only on their studies, it was much more pervasively strengthening, and his absolute integrity was a shining example. (Waterhouse, 354)

Significantly, it was to Collins Baker that Waterhouse dedicated his own pioneering and influential book *Painting in Britain, 1530–1790* (1953). SHELLEY M. BENNETT

Sources D. Cast, 'Baker, Charles Henry Collins', *The dictionary of art*, ed. J. Turner (1996) • E. Waterhouse, *Burlington Magazine*, 101 (1959), 354 • *The Times* (6 July 1959) • *New York Times* (6 July 1959) • b. cert. • m. cert. • d. cert. • C. J. Holmes, *Self and partners* (1936) • O. Millar, 'Caring for the queen's pictures: surveyors past and present', in C. Lloyd, *The queen's pictures: royal collectors through the centuries* (1991), 14–18 [exhibition catalogue, National Gallery, London, 1992] • O. Millar, *The queen's pictures* (1977), 209 • B. Dolman, ed., *A dictionary of contemporary British artists, 1929*, 2nd edn (1981), 20 • J. Johnson, ed., *Works exhibited at the Royal Society of British Artists, 1824–1893, and the New English Art Club, 1888–1917*, 2 vols. (1975); repr. (1981), 548 • *WWW, 1951–60* • A. Jarman and others, eds., *Royal Academy exhibitors, 1905–1970: a dictionary of artists and their work in the summer exhibition of the Royal Academy of Arts*, 1 (1973), 73 • Royal Collection, archives

Archives Courtauld Inst., Witt Library • Hunt. L. • National Gallery, London, MSS • NPG, Heinz Archive and Library, notebooks and papers | U. Glas. L., letters to D. S. MacColl

Likenesses F. Dodd, chalk drawing, 1932, NPG • photographs, NPG

Wealth at death £7070 19*s*. 4*d*.: probate, 28 Oct 1959, *CGPLA Eng. & Wales*

Baker, David [*name in religion* Augustine] (**1575–1641**), Benedictine monk and mystical writer, was born in Abergavenny, Monmouthshire, on 9 December 1575, the thirteenth and youngest child of William Baker (*d.* 1606), receiver-general of the barony of Abergavenny and recorder of the borough—two positions which at this time were virtually hereditary in the Baker family—and his wife, Maud Lewis, daughter of the vicar of Abergavenny and sister to David Lewis, judge of the admiralty and first principal of Jesus College, Oxford. The Bakers, on their part, claimed direct descent from Owain Glyn Dŵr and were distant cousins of the earl of Salisbury through the Welsh origins of the Cecil family. Although Monmouthshire was second only to Lancashire as a hotbed of recusancy, the Bakers conformed to the established church while retaining a benevolent attitude towards Catholicism. After some years at the local grammar school David Baker was sent in February 1587 to Christ's Hospital, London, partly in order that this Welsh-speaking boy should acquire fluency in English. On 20 May 1590 he matriculated as a commoner at Broadgates Hall, Oxford, where, although he was under the tutelage of a relative, William Prichard, student of Christ Church, he fell into dissolute company; his father summoned him home in May 1592 without his taking a degree. Two plans of his father for settling his feckless son—one an advantageous marriage, the other a local church benefice—came to naught, and he was put to studying law under his brother's guidance until, in November 1596, he was ready to go to London again to become a member first, very briefly, of Clifford's Inn, then of the Inner Temple. Law proved to be a world which captured his enthusiasm: even if he went to the theatre he took a law manual with him in

David Baker (1575–1641), after William Faithorne the elder?

case there were any *longueurs* in the performance. He retained a lifelong affection for the gardens of the inns of court, and several leading lawyers later testified that he could have reached the summit of their profession. But on 7 October 1598 his brother died and his father recalled him to Abergavenny, procuring for him the recordership, but also counting on his help with the many far-flung courts he was obliged to hold as steward of the barony.

It was in the course of this business that Baker found his road to Damascus. In 1600, riding home at nightfall, he had what he was convinced was a miraculous escape from drowning while negotiating a narrow bridge across the torrential River Monnow. Previously totally without any faith he now began to reflect upon his religious position and, as always, worked it out by reading many books. He was reconciled to the Roman Catholic church by Father Richard Floyd in May 1603. In January 1605 he took the familiar road to London to seek out some Englishmen who, he heard, were Benedictines, belonging to the Italian reformed congregation of St Justina in Padua, where he entered the noviciate on 27 May, taking the name of Augustine. The superiors treated him with great kindness, even providing him with twenty wines to sample and choose which suited him best, but his health broke down and, though remaining a monk, he returned to England in June 1606 just in time to attend to his dying father, who now also embraced the Catholic religion.

In 1607 in England Baker was professed as a Benedictine, at first belonging to his Italian congregation. But on 21 November its two leading English members, Vincent Sadler and Edward Maihew, having made contact with the blind and long imprisoned nonagenarian Father Sigebert Buckley, who had been a monk of the Marian refoundation at Westminster Abbey and was the last surviving representative in good standing of the pre-Reformation English Benedictine congregation, were aggregated to that congregation by him, as was also Baker shortly afterwards. This whole episode is rather obscure and scholars dispute whether it was masterminded by Baker whose legal instincts had led him to see the advantages that would accrue to the new wave of Benedictine monks arising in the early seventeenth century if they could claim membership of the same historic corporation as had existed in England since its conversion, as well as the legal right to its properties and privileges in the event of a Catholic restoration. This was a live issue at this time of high hopes for England's conversion under the Stuarts, when Robert Persons was asserting the claims of the Jesuits, as the religious order most attuned to the needs of the times, to some share of the former monastic patrimony. It seems unlikely that Baker himself took the initiative in devising this adroit manoeuvre—he was hardly in a position to do so—but he undoubtedly placed his legal expertise at its service. Here is shown the high value he always set on continuity, though he may have been unconsciously straining the evidence in assuming that the former English Benedictine congregation was a legal corporation and a tightly knit entity like the more centralized congregations of his own age.

In 1608, after some time as a poor man's lawyer, Baker embarked on a life of retirement and prayer at Sir Nicholas Fortescue's house at Cook Hill in Worcestershire. Here he claims to have been granted for a short time the grace of passive contemplation. He also read widely in the mystical writers of Spain, the Rhineland, and fourteenth-century England. In 1610 he was in London again, where he gave legal tuition to Philip Powell, the future Benedictine martyr, also from Abergavenny, and subsequently financed his education at Louvain. In 1613 Baker was ordained priest at Rheims, not out of any missionary or pastoral zeal, but, as he says, to confirm him in his prayerful ways. He does not appear to have received any formal theological training. On 23 August 1619 the three independent groupings of Benedictine Englishmen—those attached to Italian monasteries, those who had joined monasteries in Spain, and those like Baker who belonged to the revived English congregation—after many false starts and protracted negotiations, were united into a single body by a papal brief, *Ex incumbenti*, of Paul V. Baker was the first of the monks to accept this union and now affiliated himself to one of its monasteries, the priory of

St Lawrence at Dieulouard in Lorraine (later at Ampleforth), though there is no evidence that he ever resided there.

There remained, however, a coterie of English monks who did not accept this union. One of them, the eccentric John Barnes, attacked the validity of its historical claims in his *Examen trophaeorum congregationis praetensae Anglicanae ordinis sancti Benedicti* (Rheims, 1622), in which he contended that the only fully formed congregation existing in England before the Reformation was that of Cluny. Baker was commissioned by the president of his congregation, Rudesind Barlow, to collect materials for a refutation of Barnes and embarked on a *voyage littéraire* of the principal English libraries, particularly that of Sir Robert Cotton, and consulted all the leading antiquaries: Camden, Selden, Spelman, and Bishop Godwin, being readily accepted as one of their circle. These researches, now embodied in four folio volumes in Jesus College, Oxford, provided the historical basis for Clement Reyner's *Apostolatus Benedictinorum in Anglia* (Douai, 1626). An ecclesiastical history of England was also projected, but never realized.

In 1624 the negotiations for the royal Spanish marriage broke down, and fearing renewed persecution of Catholics Baker returned to the continent where he was asked to undertake the spiritual formation of a group of young Englishwomen who had just begun a Benedictine nunnery at Cambrai, the ancestor of the modern Stanbrook in Worcestershire. They included four descendants of Sir Thomas More, one of whom, Gertrude More, was to be Baker's most receptive disciple. He took infinite pains over instructing these nuns in the life of prayer, especially as this had to be done more from books than from contact with a living tradition. He translated and copied out for their use whole treatises by the contemplative masters which he borrowed either from Sir Robert Cotton or from the exiled English Carthusians and Bridgettines. Thus he rescued from oblivion the medieval English spiritual tradition represented by Walter Hilton, Richard Rolle, Julian of Norwich, and the *Cloud of Unknowing*, another instance of his zeal for continuity. He also composed many treatises of his own, forty of which would be drawn upon by Serenus Cressy to compile a systematic digest of his teaching, the *Sancta sophia*, in 1657. The distinctive notes of his doctrine were interior freedom and responsiveness to the promptings of the spirit. He discouraged dependence on spiritual directors and stood loosely to external observances. This ran counter to prevalent axioms of spiritual practice and aroused suspicions of illuminism in Father Francis Hull who had come to be chaplain to the nuns in 1629. The controversy was brought before the general chapter of the English congregation on 1 August 1633. The commission there appointed to examine Baker's manuscripts gave unstinted approval to his teaching, but for the sake of harmony removed both protagonists from their posts at Cambrai. Baker thereupon took up residence at St Gregory's Priory, Douai (later Downside), where the prior was Rudesind Barlow.

Here events repeated themselves. For a man much given to solitariness, who kept to his room and would not join the community even for the choir offices, Baker nevertheless had a talent for attracting a following, not only among the younger monks, but also from many in the seminaries and religious orders of the town. At this time when the English Benedictines were only beginning to find their bearings there were tensions between those who saw the *raison d'être* of their life as the mission to England, and those, led by Rudesind Barlow, who gave priority to the establishment of a full monastic observance. Baker had written a treatise on the English mission whose first draft suggested that he was inclined to support the conventual party. But he was annoyed when these began to make partisan use of his writings because he felt that their rigid attachment to external forms was as harmful to spiritual progress as total absorption in the apostolate. He therefore composed a second edition of his treatise in which he held up as a cautionary tale a description of an activist conventual easily recognizable as a portrait of Rudesind Barlow. At first Barlow took the rebuke very edifyingly, thinking it was a private admonition, but he was outraged when he discovered it was being publicly circulated. This was a grave lapse of judgement on Baker's part and revealed a man who, although his writings show him to have a very fine intuition into human psychology, had little sense of what made for community living, especially in a house where he was a guest.

In 1638 the president was induced to order Baker, aged and infirm as he was, to leave Douai for the English mission. He gently submitted to this harsh decision in spite of the outcry by his followers, and passed the last three years of his life near the inns of court, saved from pursuivants only by the rumour that the plague infested his lodgings. He had to change his lodgings four times and died of a fever on 9 August 1641, while being cared for by Mrs Watson, mother of one of the Cambrai nuns. He was buried in St Andrew's churchyard, Holborn. His teaching on prayer, although written in a crabbed and parenthetical style often attributed to his legal background, has remained a central element in the English Benedictine spiritual patrimony, but it has also attained a far wider audience including the Cambridge Platonists, the Quakers, the nonjurors, German pietists, and the Scottish mystics. So experienced an authority as Evelyn Underhill has rated him 'one of the most lucid and orderly of guides to the contemplative life' (E. Underhill, *Mysticism*, 13th edn, 1960, 559).

DAVID DANIEL REES

Sources J. McCann and H. Connolly, eds., *Memorials of Father Augustine Baker and other documents relating to the English Benedictines*, Catholic RS, 33 (1933) • P. Salvin and S. Cressy, *The life of Father Augustine Baker*, ed. D. J. McCann (1933) • B. Weld-Blundell, ed., *The inner life and the writings of Dame Gertrude More*, 2 vols. (1910–11) • *The confessions of Venerable Father Augustine Baker*, ed. J. McCann (1922) • D. Lunn, *The English Benedictines, 1540–1688* (1980) • A. Low, *Augustine Baker* (1970) • J. Gaffney, *Augustine Baker's inner light: a study in English recusant spirituality* (1989) • R. Baker Gabb, *The families of Baker, of Bailey Baker and Baker Gabb, Abergavenny* (1903) • J. A. Bradney, *A history of Monmouthshire*, 1/2 (1906) • T. P. Ellis, *The Welsh Benedictines of the terror* (privately printed, Newtown, 1936)

Archives Ampleforth Abbey, York, archives, papers • Bibliothèque Mazarine, Paris • Colwich Abbey, near Stafford • Downside

Abbey, near Bath, Downside Abbey Archives, MSS • Jesus College, Oxford • Stanbrook Abbey, Callow End, near Worcester, archives, MSS • Yale U., Beinecke L., MSS of devotional treatises | Archives Départementales, Lille
Likenesses W. Holl, stipple, pubd 1835, BM, NPG • engraving, repro. in *Sancta sophia* (1657) • engraving (after W. Faithorne the elder?), NPG [*see illus.*]

Baker, David Bristow (1803–1852), religious writer, was born in Newington, Surrey, second son of David Bristow Baker, a merchant in Blackfriars. In 1824 (the same year in which he was admitted to the Middle Temple) he went up to St John's College, Cambridge, where he graduated BA in 1829 and MA in 1832. From 1841 until his death he was incumbent of Claygate, Surrey. His works include *A Treatise of the Nature of Doubt … in Religious Questions* and *Discourses and Sacramental Addresses to a Village Congregation*, which ran to a second edition within a year of its publication in 1832. He died in Parliament Street, Westminster, on 24 July 1852. A. H. Bullen, *rev.* Sarah Brolly

Sources Venn, *Alum. Cant.* • Allibone, *Dict.* • Boase, *Mod. Eng. biog.* • J. Hutchinson, ed., *A catalogue of notable Middle Templars: with brief biographical notices* (1902)

Baker, David Lionel Erskine (1730–1767?), theatre historian, was born in the parish of St Dunstan in the West, London, on 30 January 1730, the elder son of Henry *Baker (1698–1774), a scientific writer, and his wife, Sophia (1701–1762), who was the youngest daughter of the journalist and novelist Daniel *Defoe (1660?–1731). Henry *Baker, a minor author, was his brother. He was named after his godfather, the ninth earl of Buchan. A studious youth, he was placed by the duke of Montague in the drawing room of the Tower of London to become a royal engineer. In 1747 his proud father gave a lengthy account of his intellectual achievements to the nonconformist minister Philip Doddridge:

> At twelve years old he had translated the whole twenty-four books of *Telemachus* from the French; before he was fifteen he translated from the Italian, and published, a treatise of physic of Dr Cocchi of Florence concerning the diet and doctrines of Pythagoras, and last year, before he was seventeen, he likewise published a treatise of Sir Isaac Newton's *Metaphysics* compared with those of Dr Leibnitz, from the French of M. Voltaire. (*Correspondence and Diary*, 5.29)

He was, moreover, praised for his mastery of Latin, Greek, and mathematics, and was knowledgeable in natural history. Communications from Baker were published in the *Transactions of the Royal Society*. But his promise for a scientific career was not to be fulfilled.

Despite family opposition, Baker repeatedly joined companies of strolling players. (Isaac Reed asserted that he was adopted by an uncle and succeeded to his business as a silk throwster in Spitalfields, but failed in that line; this may have been an attempt by his family to wean him from the stage.) He possibly played in Belfast and Drogheda with Sheriffe's company in the spring of 1758, but it is difficult positively to identify his appearances on the stage as there were several actors named Baker. Before 6 October 1762 Baker married Elizabeth Clendon (*d.* 1778), an actress, who on that date made her début at Covent Garden (as Roxana in Nathaniel Lee's *The Rival Queens*). Baker too might have appeared at that theatre between 1762 and 1765. Afterwards, Elizabeth Baker was closely identified with the Edinburgh stage.

In 1764 Baker published *The Companion to the Play House* in two volumes, containing notices on plays, authors, and actors. A revised version, edited by Isaac Reed, appeared as *Biographia dramatica* in 1782, and a third edition, by Stephen Jones, appeared in 1812. Baker's work was indebted to that of his predecessor Gerard Langbaine, and adds little concerning early dramatists, but has remained a useful reference work for the history of the early eighteenth-century stage. He wrote a small dramatic piece, *The Muse of Ossian* (1763), and translated a two-act Italian comedy as *The Maid and the Mistress* (*La serva padrona*), which was put on in Edinburgh and published in 1763. It is unlikely that he was the 'Mr Baker' who in 1745 wrote a preface to the translation of *The Continuation of Don Quixote*.

Baker's later life is obscure. His death is variously recorded as taking place in Edinburgh in 1770, in 1780, and, according to John Nichols's *Literary Anecdotes of the Eighteenth Century* (5.277), on 16 February 1767. His wife retired from the stage in 1774 and became a fashionable teacher of elocution in Edinburgh.

A. H. Bullen, *rev.* K. D. Reynolds

Sources Highfill, Burnim & Langhans, *BDA* • *The correspondence and diary of Philip Doddridge*, ed. J. D. Humphreys, 5 vols. (1829–31) • Nichols, *Lit. anecdotes* • *N&Q*, 2nd ser., 8 (1859), 94 • *N&Q*, 2nd ser., 12 (1861), 129 • D. E. Baker, *Biographia dramatica, or, A companion to the playhouse*, rev. I. Reed, new edn, 2 vols. (1782) • D. E. Baker, *Biographia dramatica, or, A companion to the playhouse*, rev. I. Reed, new edn, rev. S. Jones, 3 vols. in 4 (1812)
Likenesses H. R. Cook, stipple, 1810 (after portrait by S. Harding), BM, NPG; repro. in Highfill, Burnim & Langhans, *BDA*

Baker [*née* von Sass], **Florence Barbara Maria**, Lady **Baker** (1841–1916), traveller in Africa, was born on 6 August 1841, probably in a German-speaking region of Hungary. She was the sole survivor of an attack on her home in which the rest of her family died during the disturbances of 1848. Nothing more is known of her antecedents or early life. She is next recorded in January 1859 in the Turkish town of Widden, later in Bulgaria, being offered for sale in the slave market; at that time she was using the name Finnian. Samuel White *Baker (1821–1893), who was in Widden on a hunting excursion, offered the highest bid and made off with his prize. He told no one of Florence's existence, and, rather than return to England, took her off with him on his quest for the source of the Nile. He later hinted that they had been married abroad, but it seems certain that they were not married until 4 November 1865, soon after they arrived in England, at St James's Church, Piccadilly, London. Despite Samuel Baker's attempts to keep the story of their meeting and subsequent relationship secret, rumours spread sufficiently for Queen Victoria to refuse to receive his wife at court.

Despite its inauspicious beginning, theirs was to be a very happy partnership. As her husband was later to

Florence Barbara Maria Baker, Lady Baker (1841–1916), by unknown photographer

write, Florence Baker possessed 'a share of sang-froid admirably suited to African travel' and particularly 'was not a *screamer*' (Baker, *Albert Ny'anza*, 67). She was slight and small and, in spite of her long golden hair, was often mistaken for a boy, since she dressed in blouse, breeches, and gaiters. She was as active physically as she was mentally alert and coped with African exploration as well as did her husband, a man renowned for his strength. The first lap of their journey, exploring the Abyssinian tributaries, was easy going, allowing her time to decorate their camps with 'many charms and indescribable comforts that could only be provided with a lady's hand' (Baker, *Nile Tributaries*, 251). She also learned enough Arabic to be an effective partner in their joint enterprise. The hard work began at Gondokoro, the navigable head of the Nile, where traders in slaves and ivory made strangers unwelcome. A mutiny among the porters was quelled by Florence Baker's appeal to the men for loyalty and to her husband for clemency. The dramatic appearance of Speke and Grant dashed Baker's hopes of being the first at the source of the Nile, but they urged him to find his way to a second lake said to be linked to the Victoria. Speke and Grant were surprised and rather shocked to meet Florence and neither mentioned her in his account of their travels. The Bakers left Gondokoro and after a gruelling journey lasting a year, in which both suffered from fever and Florence nearly died from sunstroke, they reached the lake (which they called Albert), the first travellers from the outside to do so.

On their arrival in England in 1865 Florence Baker was to need all her composure to face Victorian society and the Baker clan, which included her husband's four daughters by his first marriage, the eldest of whom was only six years her junior. However, she was soon at home in Hedenham Hall, Norfolk, and on good terms with the Baker family. Her husband was knighted in 1866, and, although she did not welcome his appointment in 1869 as commander of the khedive of Egypt's expedition into the country south of Gondokoro to annex territory to Egypt and abolish the slave trade, she went with him. She maintained high domestic standards on the houseboat from where the mission was directed, took charge of the health of the party, did what she could for the victims of the slave hunt, and found time to keep a meteorological record. When her husband's attempt to raise the Egyptian flag over Bunyoro brought fierce opposition and they were driven out under a rain of spears, Lady Baker marched 'close to [Samuel] with some ammunition for a large rifle … two bottles of brandy, two drinking cups, and two umbrellas and my pistol in my belt' (letter to Agnes Baker, quoted in A. Baker, 157, 160). They reached safety in one of their old camps where they were welcomed and Lady Baker was given the name Myadu or Morning Star.

On their return to England in 1873 Sir Samuel bought the small estate of Sandford Orleigh, at Newton Abbot in Devon, where Florence proved as good a chatelaine as in their African camps. Here in October 1883 she effectively vetoed Gordon's suggestion that her husband go out to the Sudan to restore order, broken down by the Mahdist uprising: she would not return to Egypt and he had promised not to go without her. After Sir Samuel's death in 1893 she was at first inconsolable, but she mustered her courage to live on cheerfully until her death at Sandford Orleigh on 11 March 1916. She was buried with her husband in the family vault at Grimley, near Worcester.

DOROTHY MIDDLETON

Sources S. W. Baker, *Albert Ny'anza, great basin of the Nile* (1872) • S. W. Baker, *The Nile tributaries of Abyssinia* (1867) • S. W. Baker, *Ismailïa*, 2 vols. (1876) • R. Hall, *Lovers on the Nile* (1980) • T. D. Murray and A. Silva White, *Sir Samuel Baker: a memoir* (1895) • *Morning Star: Florence Baker's diary of the expedition to put down the slave trade on the Nile, 1870–1873*, ed. A. Baker (1972)

Archives RGS

Likenesses photograph, NPG [*see illus.*]

Wealth at death £11,748 1s. 5d.: resworn probate, May 1916, *CGPLA Eng. & Wales*

Baker, Franklin (1800–1867), Unitarian minister, was born in Birmingham, on 27 August 1800, the eldest son and third of ten children of Thomas Baker, a pawnbroker, and his wife, Charlotte Eldred. Several of the children attained unusual distinction. In addition to Franklin Baker, they included Charles *Baker (1803–1874), famous as an instructor of deaf people; Sir Thomas Baker (1810–1886), Unitarian minister at Sidmouth in 1833–4 and later a solicitor in Manchester where he was active in municipal affairs, lord mayor, and historian of the Unitarian congregation in Cross Street; Alfred Baker (1815–1893), an eminent Birmingham surgeon; and Harriet (1805–1850), who married Edward White Benson (1800–1843) and became mother of a second Edward White Benson (1829–1896), archbishop of Canterbury in 1882–96.

Encouraged by the Revd John Kentish (1768–1853), minister of New Meeting, the Unitarian congregation attended by the Bakers, Franklin Baker became a schoolmaster in Dudley. There he studied with the Revd James Hews Bransby (1783–1847), entering the University of Glasgow on Dr Williams's foundation in 1820, and graduating MA in 1822.

Baker accepted the pulpit at Bank Street Chapel, Bolton, and was ordained on 23 September 1824. Circumstances were not auspicious. When the Revd John Holland (1766–1826) had retired in 1820, one faction of the congregation carried the appointment of the Revd Noah Jones (1801–1861) of Walmsley, a recent convert from Congregationalism; the other faction withdrew to establish a new congregation in Moor Lane, where the Revd George Harris (1794–1859), from Renshaw Street, Liverpool, abundantly satisfied the seceders' desire for aggressive Unitarian preaching, and drew in audiences that quickly overshadowed the older congregation.

The growth did not survive Harris's departure for Glasgow in 1825, and in 1843 Moor Lane reunited with Bank Street, where Baker had steadily rebuilt the congregation; it was further reinforced by amalgamation with a Christian Brethren congregation, influenced by Joseph Barker (1806–1875), in 1855. The next year, a new Gothic church was opened; Baker had commemorated the closing of the old chapel at the end of 1853 by four lectures which, published the next year as *The History of the Rise and Progress of Nonconformity in Bolton*, are a useful contribution to local and denominational history. An initiative in 1862 for an additional Sunday school resulted in the formation of a new congregation, Unity Church, first in Commission Street and after 1893 in Deane Road. Baker gained an impressive reputation as a preacher. He was active in charitable work, notably during the cotton famine of 1862–4, and in liberal politics; but he rejected as inappropriate an invitation to become a justice of the peace.

On 30 September 1835 Baker had married Mary Crook (1802–1879), daughter of Jeremiah Crook, a Liverpool merchant formerly of Bolton, another of whose daughters married Baker's brother Thomas; there were no children. After retiring in 1864, Baker lived for three years at Caton, near Lancaster. From about 1860 he was troubled by an enlarged prostate gland, and a fall during the removal to Caton hastened his decline. He died on 25 May 1867, from consequences of the prostate condition, at 59 Hagley Road, Edgbaston, where he had gone a few weeks earlier to be cared for by his brother; he was buried in Birmingham on 31 May. R. K. Webb

Sources *The Inquirer* (8 June 1867) · *The Inquirer* (24 April 1886) · *Bi-centenary commemoration, 1696–1896* (Bank Street Chapel, Bolton, 1896) · Registers, New Meeting, Birmingham · F. Baker, *The history of the rise and progress of nonconformity in Bolton* (1854) · The services at the ordination of the Rev. Franklin Baker, M.A., September 23, 1824, 1825 · d. cert.

Wealth at death under £6000: probate, 21 Sept 1867, *CGPLA Eng. & Wales*

Baker, Geoffrey le (*fl.* 1326–1358), chronicler, was born in Swinbrook in Oxfordshire. He is noteworthy as the author of two chronicles. The smaller of these, the *Chroniculum*, begins *in primordio temporis* and ends on 20 July 1347, with a colophon revealing Baker's name and Osney as the place where he concluded the lesser work. Stow thought that he was a canon regular, but Baker terms himself *clericus*, so he was probably an unbeneficed clerk, untraced as yet in ordination lists. He is identifiable as the 'Geoffrey Pachon of Swynebrook, chaplain', one of the malefactors pardoned by Edward II in 1326 on condition that they aided him against the incursion of his queen, Isabella. Baker states that he wrote at the behest of Thomas de la More, knight, who also features in the larger chronicle. Significantly, in view of Baker's political views, the *Chroniculum* is objective, with no derogatory comments about Bishop Adam Orleton or Isabella, *nobilissima regina Anglie*.

The larger (anonymous) *Chronicon* extends from 1303 until 1356, its final words indicating that the author remained alive in 1358. The structure is based on Adam Murimuth's recension of 1341, but whereas the latter is laconic and circumspect, Baker is expansive and opinionated. The basis of E. M. Thompson's edition is provided by items 10 and 11 in the late fourteenth-century Bodl. Oxf., MS Bodley 761, folios 99*r*–145*v*, 149*r*–156*v*, a miscellany which belonged to Thomas Walmesford, or to someone else close to the Bohun family, lords of Chadlington hundred in which Swinbrook lay. Thompson considered that the chronicles were not Baker's autograph but the work of an uncritical copyist using an unrevised text. There are, for instance, two consecutive versions of the early years of Edward III's reign, the second of which appears in the charred BL, Cotton MS Appendix lii—also late fourteenth-century—the vestige of a copy of the *Chronicon* confined to that reign. Elizabethan transcripts of the *Vita et mors Edwardi secundi*—that part of Baker's chronicle covering Edward II's reign—fostered the belief that behind the Latin text lay a French original by Sir Thomas de la More, an idea countenanced by Stubbs. But Thompson concluded that More was responsible merely for a specific passage, his eyewitness account of the renunciation of homage to Edward II at Kenilworth.

In the *Chronicon* before 1328 Baker interpolates into Murimuth's narrative passages designed to place the responsibility for Edward II's abdication and death upon Orleton, Bishop Henry Burghersh of Lincoln (*d.* 1340), and, under their tutelage, the queen. He regards Isabella's journey to France in 1325, the dispatch of her son to perform homage to Charles IV of France, her invasion, and Edward's murder as elements in a preconceived plan of which Orleton is the principal architect. John Stratford, More's kinsman, who was then bishop of Winchester and later became archbishop of Canterbury, escapes criticism, and Murimuth's subsequent account of the crisis of 1341 is omitted. Mortimer attracts no opprobrium until the Scottish treaty of 1328, while Earl Humphrey (VII) de

Bohun is lauded, despite being a rebel who died ignominiously at Boroughbridge in 1322. Edward himself is *generosus dominus* and *amicicie cultor fidelissimus*. His queen exhibited 'feminine characteristics' of *rapidissima ira* and *avaricia insaciabilis vis-à-vis* the Despensers, and acted towards her imprisoned husband as an iron lady (*ferrea virago*). In short, this part of the chronicle apportions blame for Edward II's fate. It has affinities with the attack on Orleton at the time of his promotion to Winchester in 1333, reading like a counterblast to Robert Reading's virulent condemnation of Edward's rule—a *pièce justificative* for that of Isabella and Mortimer.

The editor of Orleton's Hereford register sought to interpret 'de la More's *Vita et mors*' as a riposte to the *Libellus famosus* of 1341—a tract directed against Stratford and attributed by some to Orleton. The content of the *Libellus* militates against this. Baker himself claims that the circumstances of Edward's captivity were revealed to him by William Bishop after the black death (1348–9) and Thompson believed that the chronicle (as it has survived) was not begun until after 1341, the concluding date of Murimuth's text. But this would not preclude the possibility that Baker incorporated material he had prepared earlier. William Bishop is not identifiable with certainty, although there was a king's serjeant of that name, also a man in Mortimer's retinue pardoned in 1321 for attacking the Despenser lands. In view of More's authenticity, the attribution cannot be readily dismissed. At the same time it is clear that Baker's 'passion of Edward of Caernarfon'—the former king's mistreatment in captivity—owes much to his inventiveness, as, probably, does the deathbed scene in Berkeley Castle, while Orleton's responsibility for ordering Edward's killing is a gratuitous invention.

Baker's account of Bannockburn (1314), derived from a Carmelite source, is particularly informative, but popular jingoism impairs his treatment of the Scottish treaty of 1328. Following Edward III's assumption of personal rule in 1330, the chronicler, saving a final barb against Orleton, rarely betrays political animus. Indeed, with certain notable exceptions, such as the black death and the inauguration of the Order of the Garter, he has comparatively little to say about domestic events. The Scottish conflict is well reported and there is an independent description of the battle of Halidon Hill (1333). Predominant, however, is his treatment of the Hundred Years' War, about which he is remarkably well informed, despite occasional confusion of dates and a penchant for anti-French gossip. Clearly he had access to eyewitness reports, newsletters, and official documents. The naval engagement of Sluys (1340) is detailed, even to the names of the recaptured English ships. There is a lengthy description of Edward's campaign of 1346–7, concluding with the battle of Crécy and the capture of Calais, while the text of the truce that followed in 1347 is methodically itemized. Baker names the bishops of London and Norwich, Ralph Stratford and John (*recte* William) Bateman, as royal candidates for the cardinalate in 1350, emphasizing papal partiality in the elevation of eleven Frenchmen. The *chevauchée* of Edward, the Black Prince, from Bordeaux to Narbonne is reliably plotted between 5 October and 2 December 1355, and Baker's description of the prince's subsequent campaign, culminating in the battle of Poitiers (1356), which concludes the chronicle, is indispensable and preferable to that of Froissart. Despite Thompson's excellent notes, the value of the *Chronicon* for the period 1330–56 continues to be underestimated. Stow translated lengthy passages for his *Annales* (1601, 1605), thus first introducing Baker to a wider audience. ROY MARTIN HAINES

Sources Bodl. Oxf., MS Bodley 761 · BL, Cotton MS Appendix lii · *Chancery records* · *Chronicon Galfridi le Baker de Swynebroke*, ed. E. M. Thompson (1889) · W. Stubbs, ed., *Chronicles of the reigns of Edward I and Edward II*, 2 vols., Rolls Series, 76 (1882–3) · A. T. Bannister, ed., *The register of Adam de Orleton, bishop of Hereford* (AD 1317–1327), Cantilupe Society (1907) · A. Gransden, *Historical writing in England*, 2 (1982) · R. M. Haines, *The church and politics in fourteenth-century England: the career of Adam Orleton, c. 1275–1345*, Cambridge Studies in Medieval Life and Thought, 3rd ser., 10 (1978) · R. M. Haines, *Archbishop John Stratford: political revolutionary and champion of the liberties of the English church*, Pontifical Institute of Medieval Studies: Texts and Studies, 76 (1986) · *Adae Murimuth continuatio chronicarum. Robertus de Avesbury de gestis mirabilibus regis Edwardi tertii*, ed. E. M. Thompson, Rolls Series, 93 (1889)
Archives BL, Cotton MS Appendix lii · Bodl. Oxf., MS Bodley 761

Baker, Sir Geoffrey Harding (1912–1980), army officer, was born at Murree, India, on 20 June 1912, the only son and youngest of the five children of Colonel Cecil Norris Baker CIE (1869–1934) and his wife, Ella Mary Hutchinson. His father was in the Northamptonshire regiment but bad health restricted his later career to staff appointments. He had been chief paymaster in China during the Boxer uprising. Baker was educated at Wellington College, Berkshire, and the Royal Military Academy, Woolwich, where he was senior under-officer and won the sword of honour. Tall and fair-haired, he was called George the Swede by his friends: thereafter he was George.

Commissioned into the Royal Artillery in 1932, Baker went with the 11th field brigade from Aldershot to Meerut in 1935. In 1937 he was given his 'jacket' in F (Sphinx) battery, Royal Horse Artillery (RHA), at Risalpur. As part of the 4th regiment RHA the battery went to Egypt on mobilization. After attending the Middle East Staff College Baker became brigade-major Royal Artillery, 4th Indian division, which fought against the Italians in Eritrea. He was at the battle of Keren and won the MC (1941) for his services in the field. After instructing at the Staff College he was promoted lieutenant-colonel GSO1 at the headquarters of the Eighth Army. He was heard to criticize the failure to concentrate artillery for maximum fire effect, and welcomed the change of policy at El Alamein. He remained on the staff until the Sicilian campaign when he commanded the 127th field regiment, 51st Highland division.

Baker was posted home in 1944 to headquarters, Twenty-First Army group, as brigadier general staff, and remained in this demanding post until the end of the war. In 1946 he married Valerie Stirling Hamilton, army officer, daughter of Major John Leonard (Ian) Lockhart, of the Royal Hampshire regiment; they had two sons and a daughter. After commanding the third RHA at Münsterlager in the British army of the Rhine (1950–52), he was

Sir Geoffrey Harding Baker (1912–1980), by Bassano, 1946

promoted director of administrative planning in the War Office. When Field Marshal Sir A. F. Harding became governor of Cyprus in 1955 he selected Baker to be chief of staff and director of operations against the dissident organization EOKA. Baker had to operate at many levels, including general headquarters, Middle East, and as well as working with Foreign and Colonial Office staffs oversaw subordinate district security committees which co-ordinated the work of all agencies. Baker showed flair for getting a variety of people to work together on agreed priorities and for evolving sound plans. Although his task was complicated by the Suez operation in 1956 Baker's contribution to pacifying Cyprus, involving twelve major army units, was considerable.

While serving as major-general, chief of staff, southern command, in 1961 Baker was selected for the new post of chief of staff contingencies (Liveoak) at Supreme Headquarters, Allied Powers in Europe (SHAPE). Liveoak was set up to deal with the four-power confrontation in Berlin; there the Russians supported, by a surprise show of force, East German measures to restrict emigration to the West. Baker's task was complex and internationally delicate, for stakes being played for over Berlin in 1961–3 were high.

Baker returned to the War Office in 1963 as vice-chief of the Imperial General Staff and lieutenant-general, and his tour was prolonged owing to the abolition of separate service ministries in 1964. He helped to evolve new staff procedures in the Ministry of Defence. After a brief respite as general officer commanding-in-chief, southern command (1966–8), Baker was appointed chief of the general staff in 1968. By then, general retrenchment in defence was following the financial crisis of 1967, and garrisons overseas were being reduced. Baker proved an excellent choice. Trusted and liked, he commanded complete loyalty in the army. In the higher councils of defence he helped to heal the divisions between the Royal Navy and Royal Air Force over the carrier controversy. His sound advice was given in the best way. He was a complete master of committee procedure. Modest, always approachable and courteous to subordinates with problems, he radiated confidence through the sound and sensible advice he gave. Otherwise he let his staff get on with their work without interference.

When the army was committed in Ulster in August 1969, Baker's experience in Cyprus gave him a sure touch. His advice to politicians was sound and he guided commanders on the ground in a constructive way. His visits to Ulster did much to sustain morale and support the troops in carrying out often distasteful duties in the glare of television publicity. Baker was the first of a new type of senior officer, expert in his own field, and enjoying the respect of civil servant, diplomat, politician, and journalist alike. Always calm and capable of sound compromise, he was a man for the time, bringing the army through a period of change yet preserving the best of the past.

On retirement in March 1971 Baker was made field marshal, having been master gunner, St James's Park, since 1970 and colonel commandant Royal Artillery since 1964. He had been appointed OBE (1943), CBE (1946), CB (1955), CMG (1957), KCB (1964), and GCB (1968). He became constable of the Tower in 1975 and was a freeman of the City of London. He was a governor of Wellington and Radley colleges. Baker died at Wellington College on 8 May 1980.

R. H. WHITWORTH, *rev.*

Sources *The Times* (10 May 1980) · *The Times* (4 June 1980) · *Journal of the Royal Artillery*, 107 (1980) · personal knowledge (1986) · private information (1986) · *WWW* · *CGPLA Eng. & Wales* (1980)
Archives Bodl. RH, report on the Cyprus emergency | FILM IWM FVA, actuality footage
Likenesses Bassano, photograph, 1946, NPG [*see illus.*] · I. J. Bilton, portrait, Woolwich · stained glass window, Sandhurst
Wealth at death £28,871: probate, 30 June 1980, *CGPLA Eng. & Wales*

Baker, George (1540–1612), surgeon, was the second son of Christopher Baker of Tenterden, Kent. His grandfather was John Baker of Tenterden and his great-grandfather Simon Baker of Faversham, Kent. He had an elder brother, Peter, who was admiral of the Blue squadron and died a prisoner of war in Spain, and a younger brother William. Baker married twice: first to Anne, daughter of William Swayne of Hacking, Middlesex, with whom he had four children, Alexander, Frances, Dowglas, and Ann; second to Anne, daughter or possibly widow of Paul French, a prebend of Windsor, with whom he had three children, George, Grace, and Elizabeth. His first-born son, Alexander, was a justice of the peace, master of the Barber–Surgeons' Company (1622), and surgeon to James I. He died in 1635 and was buried in Westminster Abbey.

Baker was admitted to the Company of the Barber-Surgeons in the 1560s about the time he took up his career as professional surgeon in London. He had a considerable practice in his 'house in Bartholmewe lane beside the Royall exchange' (Baker, *The Newe Iewell of Health*, Address to the reader). On 10 May 1573 the College of Arms granted confirmation of his right to bear arms and crest, this right including his father and posterity. A new grant was made on 1 April 1579 'with slight alterations to Crest' (Foster and Rylands). In the college record the new grant is dated May 1579. Before 1574 he entered the service of the young Edward de Vere, earl of Oxford, of whose bounty he 'had experience since it pleased your honor to entertain me … for my profession in the art of Chirurgiry since the which time I haue accounted bothe my self and all my labours whatsoeuer, to be due vnto your honor' (Baker, *Composition*, Dedication).

Baker reaped the rewards of his professional virtues in the 1590s. Robert Balthorp, master of the company (1565 and 1573), died on 9 December 1591 bequeathing to Baker, 'her maiesties Chirurgion', his 'Syringe of silver gilted and three pypes of silver gilted' (Young, 530). On 4 February 1592 he was appointed sergeant-surgeon to the queen and on the following day was 'liberate on the grant for payment of £40 a year' (private information). In August 1597 he was elected master of the company; on 20 July 1607 he was appointed one of the examiners of surgeons, and on 4 March 1610 he secured a grant, with survivorship, to himself and his eldest son, Alexander, of the office of the king's surgeon on surrender of a former patent. Baker was also a man of property. On 20 April 1597 he and his colleague William Goodrouse were granted a forty-year lease in reversion, without proviso for tenants, of Nunnington Mansion House and divers lands, tenements, and woods in Northfleet, Gravesend, and Milton. They received £63 13*s*. 6½*d*. in respect of their service as the queen's surgeons.

Baker was quick-tempered and violent. Thus he fell out with his colleague William Clowes, who had been admitted to the Barber-Surgeons' Company on 8 November 1569, and challenged him to a duel. It is on record in the minutes of the court of assistants that on 25 March 1577 there was at 'this Corte … a greate contention and stryffe spoken of and ended betwene George Baker and William Clowes for that they bothe contrary to order and to the good and holesome rules of this howse misused eche other and fought in the Felds together'. The master, wardens, and assistants intervened and, wishing that the two hotspurs 'might be and continewe loving brothers', they 'pardoned this greate offence in hope of amendment' (Young, 428). The two did comply with the company's wish, making up for their gross misdemeanour by each editing a work of the other in 1579.

Baker considered himself a Galenist who thought it opportune to warn against the harm done by empirics and Paracelsians, but he none the less kept an open mind about chemical medicine. His first publication, entitled *The Composition or Making of the Moste Excellent and Pretious Oil called Oleum magistrale* (1574) and dedicated to the earl of Oxford, was a translation made through a French intermediary from Aparicio de Zubia's pamphlet on the *oleum magistrale*. However, the formula of the medicinal oil as revealed by the convert Morisco empiric at his death in 1566 covers only folios 1 to 6. The publication contains *Also the Third Book of Galen* (fols. 7–11), which Baker translated from the French epitome of Martin Grégoire (1574), 'wherein', as he put it in the address to the reader signed 'From my house in London the XV. of Marche 1574', Galen 'bothe learned & abundantly … teacheth the curing of these wounds'.

Baker recommended distilled medicaments as exceeding all others in virtue in *The Newe Iewell of Health*, which he dedicated from his house in Bartholomew Lane to Anne Cecil, countess of Oxford, in February 1576. This was a revamped translation of Conrad Gesner's *Thesaurus Euonymi Philiatri de remediis secretis* (1552). Baker drew on Peter Morwyng's version of Gesner's popular handbook *The Treasure of Euonymus* (1559, 1565) and probably on Thomas Hill's translation of the augmented edition (1569). In 1599 Baker's text was reprinted by Peter Short under the new significant title *The Practise of the New and Old Phisicke*. Baker renewed his advocacy of chemical cures in his treatise on *The Nature and Property of Quicksilver*, which William Clowes edited in his treatise on syphilis (1579). Baker responded to his colleague's favour, editing, in his turn, Clowes's *Antidotary of Select Medicines*, which marked Clowes's own shift towards chemical therapy, in his (Baker's) miscellany *Guydos Questions, Newly Corrected* (1579). It also contained Galen's third and fourth book. With the exception of the *Antidotary*, this was another of those compilations of traditional works taken from the medieval surgeon Guy de Chauliac and from Galen.

In his last publication Baker again revamped a translation which B. Traheron, in 1543, had made from the medieval surgeon Giovanni de Vigo and brought it out as *The Whole Worke of the Famous Chirurgion Maister Iohn Vigo: Newly Corrected* (1586). But remaining faithful to his policy of selecting authors who advocated the use of chemical therapy, he added Thomas Gale's volume on surgery which had already appeared in 1563. Gale, who served under Philip II at the siege of St Quentin, is likely to have met there the Morisco practitioner Aparicio de Zubia. In editing the works of Galen and Guy de Chauliac, Baker gave ample evidence that he did not envisage a break with traditional medicine. Yet despite his commitment to the past his new orientation towards chemical medicine seems to have incurred the disapproval of the College of Physicians. He was denounced, together with his colleague John Banister, as a surgeon guilty of illegal medicine. The annals of the College of Physicians for 5 July 1588 record that Baker had been summoned to appear in the college that day but had refused 'because he was in the Queen's house and did not have sufficient leisure to enable him to come easily'. And, even if he had, he would still refuse to obey, saying that 'he marvailed muche how the President dirst be so saucie as to send for him to the College'.

As newly elected master of the Barber-Surgeons' Company (1597) Baker wrote an eloquent and learned preface to John Gerard's *The Herball, or, Generall Historie of Plantes* (1597), calling himself 'one of hir Maiesties chiefe Chirurgions in ordinarie'. Gerard, who was appointed junior warden of the Barber-Surgeons' Company in 1597, advocated in his pioneer work the use of the medicinal properties of English herbs for chemical medicine.

On his death Baker left behind an unpublished translation, *The Apologie and Treatise, Containing the Voyages Made into Divers Places*, which he had rendered from the text of the French surgeon Ambroise Paré. The botanist Thomas Johnson published Baker's translation as book 29 in *The Workes of the Famous Chirurgion Ambroise Parey* (1634), 1133–73. In his address to the reader Johnson states that 'George Baker, a Surgeon of this City, since that time, as I heare, [is] dead beyond the Seas'. Baker made his will on 25 August 1607; it was proved in London on 1 December 1612.

GUSTAV UNGERER

Sources S. Young, *The annals of the Barber-Surgeons of London: compiled from their records and other sources* (1890) • C. Webster, 'Alchemical and Paracelsian medicine', *Health, medicine and mortality in the sixteenth century*, ed. C. Webster (1979), 301–31 • G. Ungerer, 'George Baker: translator of Aparicio de Zubia's pamphlet on the "oleum magistrale"', *Medical History*, 30 (1986), 203–11 • H. J. Webb, 'English military surgery during the age of Elizabeth', *Bulletin of the History of Medicine*, 15 (1944), 261–75 • 'Confirmation of arms and crest to George Baker of London', *The Genealogist*, new ser., 6 (1889–90), 242 • *STC, 1475–1640* • J. Foster and W. H. Rylands, eds., *Grantees of arms named in docquets and patents to the end of the seventeenth century*, Harleian Society, 66 (1915) • *CSP dom.*, 1595–7; 1603–10 • G. Baker, *The newe iewell of health, wherein is contayned the most excellent secretes of phisicke and philosophie* (1576) • G. Baker, *The composition or making of the moste excellent and pretious oil called oleum magistrale* (1574) • private information (2004) [Jessie Dobson, archivist of the Worshipful Company of Barbers]

Archives Coll. Arms, record R 21.84

Likenesses several woodcuts (with medical scenes), NPG • woodcut, NPG; repro. in G. Baker, *The practise of the new and old phisicke*, 4 vols. (1599)

Baker, Sir George, first baronet (*bap.* **1723**, *d.* **1809**), physician, was born at Modbury, Devon, and baptized there on 8 February 1723, the son of George Baker, vicar of Modbury, and his wife, Bridget (*d.* 1734), daughter of Stephen *Weston, bishop of Exeter, and his wife, Lucy. He was educated at Eton College and King's College, Cambridge, where he became a fellow and graduated BA in 1744 and MA in 1749. He proceeded MD in 1756 and in the following year was elected a fellow of the College of Physicians. He began to practise at Stamford, Lincolnshire, but settled in London in 1761; among his patients was Sir Joshua Reynolds. He became a fellow of the Royal Society, was four times censor for the College of Physicians, was appointed Harveian orator for 1761, and was physician to George III and Queen Charlotte. In this last capacity he was in attendance on the king during the whole time of his mental illness from 1788, and he recommended a visit to Cheltenham to take the waters in the early stages of the affliction. Created a baronet in 1776, he was elected president of the College of Physicians nine times between 1785 and 1795. Baker married Jane Morris (*d.* 1813), daughter of Roger Morris; they had a son and a daughter. Widely

Sir George Baker, first baronet (*bap.* **1723**, *d.* **1809**), by Ozias Humphry, 1794

famed for his deep medical knowledge, Baker was also well known for his graceful Latin prose and amusing epigrams. There was a tradition that Gray dedicated his 'Elegy Written in a Country Churchyard' to him, but the earliest extant editions bear no dedication.

Baker's most important discovery related to the Devonshire colic and *colica Pictonum* of Poitou. Awareness of the colic was heightened during the great expansion of the cider industry in the eighteenth century, but the cause of it was unknown. John Huxham's earlier theory that excessive acidity caused the colic was disproved by Baker, who showed that it was a form of lead poisoning. As a Devon man, Baker was familiar with the disease, and noticed that while colic was most common in his own county it was almost unknown in Herefordshire, where cider was also produced locally. He inquired into the process of manufacture, and found that in the structure of the Devon presses and vats large pieces of lead were used, whereas in Herefordshire stone, wood, and iron formed all the apparatus. Baker carried out a series of simple but brilliant experiments which demonstrated the presence of lead in Devon cider, and showed that there was none in that of Herefordshire. His findings were published in *An Essay Concerning the Cause of the Endemical Colic of Devonshire* (1767). This provoked a great storm of protest. Many pamphlets were printed, by Francis Geach and the Revd Thomas Alcock among others, to ridicule Baker's findings and revive Huxham's earlier speculations (*Some observations on Dr Baker's essay on the endemical colic of Devonshire, by Francis Geach, surgeon at Plymouth and F.R.S: in which are added some remarks on the same subject by the Rev. Mr. Alcock*, 1767). However, by extending and repeating his experiments, Baker eventually succeeded in convincing his contemporaries, and from that time lead vessels were no longer used, after which colic ceased to be endemic in Devon. In other essays Baker traced further unsuspected ways in which lead poisoning might arise—for example, from lead water-pipes, from tinned linings of iron vessels, from the glaze of earthenware, and from large doses of medicinal preparations of lead. He examined the subsequent symptoms in detail, corresponding with Benjamin Franklin of Philadelphia, among others, and drew general attention to the wider implications of lead contaminants in food manufacture and water supplies.

Baker has been fairly characterized as 'a pioneer in the use of chemical analysis to solve an epidemical problem' (McConaghey, 359–60). His other works include *De catarro et de dysenteria Londinensi epidemicis utrisque an M.DCC.LXII, libellus* (1764), and the preface to the *Pharmacopeia Londinensis* of 1788; in English he wrote *An Inquiry into the Merits of a Method of Inoculating the Smallpox* (1766) and *Medical Tracts, Read at the College of Physicians between the Years 1767 and 1785*, collected and republished by his son, Sir Frederick Francis Baker, in 1818. Baker retired from active practice in 1798, and died on 15 June 1809. He was buried at St James's Church, Piccadilly, where a tablet was erected to his memory. NORMAN MOORE, *rev.* RICHARD ADAIR

Sources R. McConaghey, 'Sir George Baker and the Devonshire colic', *Medical History*, 11 (1967), 345–60 • M. Epps, 'An essay concerning the discovery of the cause of the endemical colic of Devonshire', BSc diss., WI, 1994 • Burke, *Peerage* • parish register (baptism), Modbury, Devon • I. Macalpine and R. Hunter, *George III and the mad-business* (1969) • Venn, *Alum. Cant.* • *DNB*

Archives Wellcome L., lecture notes | Linn. Soc., corresp. with Richard Pulteney • NA Scot., papers relating to dismissal of George Ernst from the service of the king

Likenesses O. Humphry, oils, 1794, RCP Lond. [*see illus.*]

Baker, George (1773?–1847), organist, was born in Exeter, the son of John Baker. At the time of his matriculation at Oxford in 1797 he stated his age to be twenty-four, thus dating his birth at 1773. His first music lessons were from his mother's sister, and he was proficient on the harpsichord at the age of seven. His next teachers were William Jackson, organist of Exeter Cathedral, and Hugh Bond, also of Exeter. He was taught the violin by Ward. At the age of seventeen Baker went to London under the patronage of the earl of Uxbridge, and through his patron became a pupil of J. B. Cramer and J. L. Dussek. While in London he performed his celebrated piece 'The Storm' at the Hanover Square Rooms, meeting with the approval of Dr Burney.

In 1794 or 1795 Baker was appointed organist of St Mary's Church, Stafford, a new organ by Geib having been purchased five years before. He matriculated in 1797 and took the degree of BMus at St Edmund Hall, Oxford, but he appears not to have taken his doctor's degree while at Stafford, for in the town's corporation books he is called 'Mr Baker'. On 5 March 1795 there is an entry to the effect 'that the organist be placed under restrictions as to the use of the organ, and that the mayor have a master key to prevent him having access thereto', and on 16 July 1795 'it is ordered that Mr George Baker be in future prohibited from playing the piece of music called "The Storm"'. During the following years several entries show that Baker habitually neglected his duties, and on 19 May 1800 the record is 'Resignation of Baker'. In the previous year he had married the eldest daughter of the Revd E. Knight of Milwich.

In 1810 Baker was appointed to the post of organist at All Saints', Derby, and finally, in 1824, he accepted a position at Rugeley, but from 1839 his duties were undertaken by a deputy. He produced a large number of compositions, including organ voluntaries, piano sonatas, anthems, glees, and violin solos, which were quickly forgotten. He is said to have been very handsome, with a fair complexion. He died on 19 February 1847 at Rugeley.

J. A. F. MAITLAND, *rev.* ANNE PIMLOTT BAKER

Sources Brown & Stratton, *Brit. mus.* • J. D. Brown, *Biographical dictionary of musicians: with a bibliography of English writings on music* (1886) • Grove, *Dict. mus.* • [J. S. Sainsbury], ed., *A dictionary of musicians*, 2 vols. (1824) • *Musical World* (17 April 1847), 246–7 • Corporation Books, Stafford, 1885 • Foster, *Alum. Oxon.*

Baker, George (1781–1851), county historian, the son of Richard Baker and his wife, Ann, was born in Northampton and lived there all his life. As a thirteen-year-old schoolboy at Mr Comfield's establishment in Horsemarket, Northampton, he wrote a manuscript history of Northampton and a life of Dr John Hinchcliffe (*d.* 1794), bishop of Peterborough. After leaving school he became a wool-stapler and pursued antiquarian interests in his spare time, notably by assisting John Britton with the Northamptonshire section of *The Beauties of England and Wales*. That appeared in 1810, as did Baker's first published work, *A Catalogue of Books, Poems, Tracts, and Small Detached Pieces*; only twenty copies of this work appeared, privately published on the Strawberry Hill Press. Baker's proposals for *The History and Antiquities of the County of Northampton* were issued in 1815. Correspondence suggests it was conceived originally as a partnership between himself, Britton, and the leading topographical publisher John Bowyer Nichols. The final terms of agreement are unknown, but it was Nichols who published the five parts of Baker's *History* which appeared in 1822–41.

The first volume, published in three parts between 1822 and 1830, contained the hundreds of Spelhoe, Newbottle Grove, Fawsley, Chipping Warden, and Kings Sutton. Based on extensive documentary work, excavations, questionnaires, and parochial visits, considerable assistance during the last being provided by Baker's sister and constant companion of sixty years Anne Elizabeth *Baker (1786–1861), the volume was well received. Nevertheless, from early as 1822 the exacting standards that Baker set himself had given rise to misgivings about the likelihood of the enterprise being completed. Volume two, intended to complete the southern third of the county, began to appear in 1836 with a part containing Norton and Cleley; a second, in 1841, covered Towcester. By then, however, Baker's health and will were broken and 220 of his subscribers, 400 strong at the outset, had died or resigned. He had also run through most of his fortune, and in 1842 his antiquities, library, and manuscript collections were dispersed in a six-day sale. The last were acquired by Sir Thomas Phillipps and are now part of the Phillipps collection in the Bodleian Library. A place index was published in 1868.

Baker, who was a Unitarian, took a deep interest in various local institutions, and was a magistrate for the borough of Northampton. He died unmarried at his home, Hazelrigg House, in Gold Street, Northampton, on 12 October 1851, and was buried in the Independent chapel in King Street. PAUL STAMPER

Sources P. Stamper, 'Northamptonshire', *English county histories: a guide*, ed. C. R. J. Currie and C. P. Lewis (1994), 291–301 • *GM*, 2nd ser., 36 (1851), 551–2, 629 • *Northampton Mercury* (18 Oct 1851) • *Northampton Herald* (18 Oct 1851) • A. Mee, *Northamptonshire: a county of spires and stately homes* (1945), 225

Archives BL, corresp., Add. MSS 24864, 34570, 36527, 38794, Egerton MSS 2838, 2841, 2248 • Bodl. Oxf., Northamptonshire collections • Northampton Library, Northamptonshire studies collection • Northants. RO, Northamptonshire collections, corresp. | Birm. CL, William Hamper MSS • Bodl. Oxf., corresp.

Likenesses Turner, lithograph (after N. C. Branwhite), BM, NPG • pencil drawing, Northampton Library, Northamptonshire studies collection; repro. in Stamper, 'Northamptonshire', 296

Wealth at death left all to sister: will, Northants. RO, X6169

Baker, Sir George Gillespie (1910–1984), judge, was born in Stirling on 25 April 1910, the only child of Captain John Kilgour Baker, of Stirling, and his wife, Jane Gillespie. Baker's mother, whom he did not remember, died in 1914. His father, a captain in the Cameron Highlanders, was killed in 1918. He had remarried shortly before his death. Baker's upbringing thus became the task of relatives who, though devoted, were unable to afford him the advantages of normal family life. His childhood was lonely. This gave him a lasting sensitivity to the needs of children, a quality which served him well in later years when it became his lot to deal with the child casualties of broken marriages. He was in due course sent to Glasgow Academy and thence to Strathallan School in Perthshire. For his further education he moved south to Oxford, but he retained throughout his life a gentle Scottish accent which led to his nickname of Scottie. He became a senior Hulme scholar at Brasenose College and a pupil of the redoubtable W. T. S. Stallybrass, later principal of Brasenose. He obtained a first class in jurisprudence (1930) and a second class in the BCL (1931). He attempted but failed to obtain a fellowship at All Souls.

Baker had always wanted a career at the bar. He joined the Middle Temple, of which he was elected a Harmsworth scholar, and was called to the bar in 1932. His resources other than his own abilities were limited. Work in London was then scarce. He joined the Oxford circuit and there sought and gradually acquired a small, good general practice.

But, as with those of almost all his generation, Baker's prospects of steady professional advancement were shattered in 1939 by the outbreak of war. Baker, though by this time married and a father, at once volunteered and joined the Royal West Kent regiment as a private. He was later commissioned into the Cameronians. He served successively in Africa, Italy, and Germany, his services winning him a military OBE in 1945. After an unsuccessful foray into politics as Conservative candidate for Southall in the 1945 election and a short spell of service at Nuremberg on the British War Crimes Executive, he returned to the uncertainties of post-war practice at the bar, by this time the father of three sons. His determination never faltered. His work returned and indeed increased so rapidly, again largely on circuit, that he was well justified in taking silk in 1952. Two small recorderships had already come his way: Bridgnorth and Smethwick. Then in 1952 he became recorder of Wolverhampton, an important appointment.

In 1954 Baker was elected leader of the Oxford circuit, a post which he greatly valued, discharged with great tact and skill, and held until his appointment to the High Court bench in 1961, when he was knighted. By that time his judicial qualities had manifested themselves not only in his recorderships but in his chairmanships of successive government committees between 1956 and 1961. His practice had lain mainly in the fields of criminal and general common-law work. He had done some but not a great deal of divorce work. His appointment to the High Court bench came as no surprise, but his assignment to the Probate, Divorce, and Admiralty Division did. His qualities, thus already manifested, soon justified the appointment. He was patient, courteous, sensitive, and above all decisive. But, as with many of his judicial contemporaries in that division, he found the state of the law cruel and the hard-fought, bitter, defended divorce cases of the time exceedingly unattractive. He welcomed the changes in the law of divorce in 1969, especially the abolition of the concept of matrimonial offence. He also welcomed the changes made in 1970 regarding the redistribution of matrimonial property on divorce. Little did he then realize that it would fall to him as president of the newly created Family Division to secure the smooth transition from the old law to the new.

Baker's appointment to that post in 1971 came more as a surprise to him than to his friends, though there were other contenders. At the same time he was sworn of the privy council. He proved a superb administrator and with the support of a younger generation of judges soon welded the new division into an effective and efficient unit. Though technically he had no control over divorce work done in the county courts, the deep respect which he commanded enabled him to improve their efficiency. He, like others, was disappointed in his ambition to see the creation of a unified family court and also by the bitterness with which disputes over custody, access, and the division of matrimonial property continued to be conducted.

Baker retired in 1979, giving tiredness as his reason. That this was true was not surprising. He in fact retired to nurse his wife, Jessie Raphael McCall, whom he had married on 30 August 1935, and to whom he showed lasting devotion. She was the daughter of Thomas Scott Findlay, nurseryman, of Glasgow. The marriage was one of great happiness and produced three sons (one of whom became a High Court judge). Baker was deeply devoted to his children and grandchildren. The breakdown in his wife's health some years before his retirement laid a great and continuous burden on him until her death in 1983. Thereafter he sought to mitigate his loneliness by accepting a government invitation to investigate the operation of the emergency laws in Northern Ireland, a task not without danger to himself but which he discharged with characteristic thoroughness, courageously criticizing some aspects of that policy.

Baker's deep personal integrity was founded on his staunch Presbyterian faith. He sometimes seemed shy and diffident, but was a profoundly kind man. Amid all his activities he found time for innumerable interests outside the law, especially in the field of education. His college made him an honorary fellow in 1966. He became a governor of Strathallan School, of Epsom College, and of Wycombe Abbey. He was an active bencher (1961) of the Middle Temple and was appointed treasurer in 1976. His recreations included golf and latterly fishing. But the heavy burdens he had carried for so long eventually took their toll. Early in June 1984 he suffered a stroke and he died on 13 June 1984 at Mount Vernon Hospital, Northwood, Middlesex. ROSKILL, *rev.*

Sources *The Times* (14 June 1984) · private information (1990) · personal knowledge (1990) · Burke, *Peerage* (1967)

Wealth at death £415,780: probate, 31 July 1984

Baker, Henry (*d.* 1689), army officer, was a lieutenant in the Irish army during the reign of Charles II. He was one of the protestant officers purged by the earl of Tyrconnell in 1686, after which he returned to his land at Dunmahon, co. Louth. After the English revolution of 1688 he left his family, swore allegiance to William III, and was promoted to the rank of major by the rebel 'consult'. He was joint commander of the abortive raid on Carrickfergus (21 February 1689), when he led a thousand men on a night march from Belfast for a surprise attack at dawn. The weather was so bad that they did not reach their destination until the next day, and were kept out by musket fire from the walls.

Tyrconnell sent Richard Hamilton with an army to crush the rebellion in the north. The rebels attempted to block Hamilton's advance at Dromore, co. Down, which Baker occupied with four ill-armed companies of foot on the night of 13 March. The next day two troops of Irish horsemen were reported to be approaching Dromore, and Baker formed his men up to block the entrance to the town. The horsemen supporting him sallied out to find that they were facing Hamilton's army. In the rout that followed, 'the Break of Dromore', Baker's men fled to Hillsborough and beyond.

On 15 March Baker reached Coleraine, where he took part in the unsuccessful defence of the Bann (7 April), when Hamilton's men crossed in boats at Portglenone. With the remnants of the rebel anti-Jacobite forces, now leaderless, Baker fled to Londonderry. He arrived in mid-April to find the leadership of the city in crisis. Adam Murray had raised a mob against the governor, Robert Lundy, who was suspected of planning to surrender. On 19 April 1689 Baker was elected joint governor of Londonderry with George Walker, and commander of all the forces in the city, positions he held throughout the worst fighting of the siege. He was attainted of high treason by the Dublin parliament.

Baker's relationship with John Michelburne, who had also put himself forward as a candidate for the governorship, became strained. On 15 May he and Michelburne drew swords on each other following an argument over the allocation of the tobacco ration. In the fight that followed Baker wounded Michelburne in the leg and had him arrested and confined to his quarters.

Baker fell ill with a cold in early June and by 21 June was confined to bed. He appointed Michelburne as his deputy 'saying he was the fittest person to fill that station' (Ash, 79). He returned to duty and stayed up directing his men throughout the night of 28 June when fresh troops led by Lord Clancarty attacked the butcher's gate. Weakened through fever and exhaustion, he died on 30 June 1689.

> He was a great loss to the garrison, greatly beloved and very well qualified for the government, being endured with great patience and moderation; free from envy or malice as may be seen in the affair betwixt him and Mitchelburn. (Ash, 82)

Michelburne, Walker, and four others acted as his pallbearers. He was buried in St Columb's Cathedral in the city. Ann Baker, his widow, survived him with their four children, who were compensated by the crown with a forfeited estate. PIERS WAUCHOPE

Sources C. Dalton, ed., *Irish army lists, 1661–1685* (privately printed, London, 1907) · C. D. Milligan, *History of the siege of Londonderry, 1689* (1951) · J. Hempton, ed., *The siege and history of Londonderry* (1861) · *The case of John Baker (a minor) eldest son of Colonel Henry Baker deceased (and of his brother and sisters) late governor of Londonderry* (1695) · P. Wauchope, 'Colonel John Michelburne', *Irish Sword*, 20 (1996–7), 137–44 · T. Ash, 'A circumstantial journal of the siege of Londonderry', *Two diaries of Derry in 1689*, ed. T. Witherow (1888)

Baker, Henry (1698–1774), natural philosopher and teacher of deaf people, was born on 8 May 1698 in Quality Court, Chancery Lane, London, to William Baker, a clerk in chancery, and his wife, Mary, the daughter of Aaron Pengry, comptroller of the petty bag office. His father died when he was very young, and he himself recorded that he was brought up by his paternal grandmother. At the age of fifteen he was apprenticed to a bookseller of Pall Mall, John Parker, whose business was later bought by Robert Dodsley, who printed Baker's books on microscopy. In 1720, having completed his apprenticeship, Baker went to Enfield on a visit to John Forster, an attorney and a relative, whose eight-year-old daughter had been born deaf, and was consequently dumb. He undertook the task of teaching this child, as well as her sister and younger brother, also born deaf, to speak and read, with such success that this became his chosen career. He achieved both reputation and a considerable fortune in the teaching of

Henry Baker (1698–1774), by William Nutter, pubd 1812 (after W. B. Thomson)

deaf people and those with speech defects, and had many aristocratic clients.

Baker was certainly aware of the theories of speech training of Dr John Wallis, fellow of the Royal Society and Savilian professor of geometry, whose treatise of speech, *De loquela*, Baker paraphrased into English as *A Short Essay on Speech* (1723). Wallis had written that for each sound the organ producing it and the position in which it is produced must be minutely studied; for, 'by such Organs, in such Positions, the Breath issuing from the lungs, will form such Sounds, whether the Person do or do not hear himself speak' ('Autobiography', 41). It is likely that Baker applied this laborious process of teaching the production of each individual sound, though he kept his actual methods a close secret. His success is attested by a witness, Louis Dutens, who 'was astonished at the facility with which they [Baker's pupils] understood what I said by observing the motion of my lips; they also answered me, but their voice wanted modulation and so was disagreeable' (Dutens, 101–2).

Baker's unusual gift led to a meeting with Daniel *Defoe, whose early novel, *The History of the Life and Adventures of Mr Duncan Campbell* (1720), concerned a deaf conjuror. For this book Defoe had studied Wallis's method of teaching deaf people, which accounted for his initial interest in Baker. Their acquaintance led to the joint establishment in 1728 of a publication, *The Universal Spectator and Weekly Journal*. Baker wrote for it, using the pseudonym Henry Stonecastle, until 1733, and it continued to exist for a further thirteen years. The association had a more personal result for Baker married, in April 1729, Defoe's youngest daughter, Sophia (1701–1762). They had two sons: the elder, David Lionel Erskine *Baker (1730–1767?), continued in the literary tradition of his father and maternal grandfather; the younger, Henry *Baker (1734–1766), a lawyer, attempted the same but with less distinction.

Baker's involvement with a literary journal was in no way surprising for, like his father-in-law, he had strong literary interests. In his youth he produced several volumes of verse, both original and translated, and achieved success with a poem published in 1727 entitled *The Universe: a Philosophical Poem Intended to Restrain the Pride of Man*. This reached a posthumous third edition in 1805, and contained a short eulogy of the author. The work revealed Baker to be a typical natural philosopher of his time, keenly interested in the wonders of nature, as manifesting the power of the creator. From 1740 Baker's literary skills were used in prose, embodying his scientific discoveries. He became a fellow of the Society of Antiquaries in that year, and in 1741, a fellow of the Royal Society, to whose *Philosophical Transactions* he was a frequent contributor. The book that established his name as a scientific writer was *The Microscope Made Easy*, which appeared in 1742, and achieved five editions in the author's lifetime, as well as translation into Dutch and French. Written for the novice, it was divided into two parts, the first describing various types of microscope, how best to use each, and how to prepare specimens, while the second part was concerned with the examination of various natural objects, such as the flea, hairs, and pollen. The particular microscopes that he described and illustrated were all made by John Cuff, who did much business as a result. Eleven years after the publication of what proved to be a best-seller, Baker published a second microscopical work, *Employment for the Microscope* (1753) that repeated the success of its predecessor. Also written for a popular audience, *Employment* described Baker's own microscopical discoveries, which had been presented to the Royal Society.

Baker's most important scientific study, for which he received the Copley medal of the Royal Society in 1744, concerned his observation under the microscope of crystal morphology. For this work, using crystals from solution, he found the then current design of the compound microscope awkward, and had Cuff make him one of completely new design. Baker made this study the first part of *Employment for the Microscope*. His other main microscopical research involved repeating the experiments on freshwater polyps (*Hydra viridis*) of Abraham Trembley. Trembley's discoveries, reported to the Royal Society in January 1743, caused a sensation, since the polyps, when cut in two, grew into two complete specimens, a plant-like property strangely combined with the animal-like ability to move and ingest worms. Baker, in association with Martin Folkes, examined the creatures with the microscope, and, with due acknowledgement to Trembley, published in November 1743 *An Attempt towards a Natural History of the Polype*. He also examined, and made measurements on the twenty-six bead microscopes bequeathed to the Royal Society by the Dutch microscopical pioneer Antoni van Leeuwenhoek. Baker's account of these unique instruments is a valuable historical document.

A well-known popularizer of science in Britain, Baker also corresponded regularly with members of philosophical societies all over Europe. An important result of these contacts was that he introduced into England two new plants, the alpine strawberry, for which the seeds were sent to him by a correspondent in Turin, and, more importantly, *Rheum palmatum*, a variety of rhubarb with wide-ranging medicinal uses, which was sent from Russia. Baker's interest in the practical applications of scientific knowledge led to his being one of the founders of the Society for the Encouragement of Arts, Manufactures, and Commerce, established formally in 1755.

Henry Baker died at lodgings in the Strand on 25 November 1774 and is said to have been buried at St Mary-le-Strand. His two sons predeceased him and he left most of his estate to his grandson, William Baker, a clergyman. In addition he bequeathed to the Royal Society £100 to establish a lecture bearing his name. Among famous Bakerian lecturers in the fifty years following his death were Humphry Davy and Michael Faraday. Baker had amassed a considerable collection of antiquities and natural specimens that was sold at auction during nine days beginning on 13 March 1775. G. L'E. TURNER

Sources G. L'E. Turner, 'Henry Baker, FRS, founder of the Bakerian lecture', *Notes and Records of the Royal Society*, 29 (1974–5), 53–79 • H. Baker, 'Memoranda, principally relating to pecuniary affairs, interspersed with anecdotes of himself and family', MHS Oxf., Baker papers, Royal Microscopical Society archives • 'Defoe, Daniel', *DNB* • 'The autobiography of John Wallis, FRS', ed. C. J. Scriba, *Notes and Records of the Royal Society*, 25 (1970), 17–46 • L. Dutens, *Memoirs of a traveller, now in retirement*, 1 (1806) • Nichols, *Lit. anecdotes*, vol. 5 • H. Baker, autobiographical memoranda, V&A NAL, Forster Library

Archives JRL, corresp. and papers • RS, lectures • V&A NAL, autobiographical memoranda • Yale U., Beinecke L., letter-books | BL, Egerton MS 738 • BL, corresp. with Emmanuel Mendaz da Costa, Add. MS 28534 • Bodl. Oxf., Montague MSS • RSA, letters to the Royal Society of Arts and related papers • V&A NAL, corresp. with William Anderson

Likenesses Thomson, stipple, pubd 1812 (after W. Nutter), NPG • photograph, *c*.1993 (after W. B. Thomson), RS • Brightwen [H. S. Turner], lithograph (after W. Shipley), BM • W. Nutter, stipple (after W. B. Thomson), BM, NPG; repro. in Nichols, *Lit. anecdotes*, vol. 5, facing p. 272 [*see illus.*] • W. Shipley, pencil miniature • W. B. Thomson, portrait, oils; sold at auction, Godalming, 1993 • Turner, lithograph, BM, NPG • photograph (after W. Nutter), RS

Wealth at death wealthy: will

Baker, Henry (1734–1766), author, was born on 10 February 1734 at Enfield, Middlesex, the second son of Henry *Baker FRS (1698–1774), teacher of deaf people, and Sophia Defoe (1701–1762), the youngest and favourite daughter of Daniel *Defoe. The obscurity surrounding Baker's career suggests how little he matched his uncle, father, and brother, David Lionel Erskine *Baker (1730–1767?), who is said to have inherited his father's literary talent (Turner, 55).

His paternal grandfather having been a clerk in chancery, Baker followed family tradition in becoming a lawyer, but, according to John Nichols, 'in no creditable line' (Nichols, *Bowyer*, 416). John Robert Moore states that Baker had a 'brief career as a shabby attorney', his sole claim to fame being that from him descended 'the English family of Defoe Bakers' (Moore, 330–31). Baker's career was not fruitless; he readied for the press 'The clerk to the commission', a collection of statutes about bankruptcy with cases and precedents. This work, which according to George Chalmers was published under another title in 1768 and is possibly not extant, must have addressed topics about the treatment of debtors which Defoe's writings long explored.

His father's literary pretensions may not have given Baker a sure model. The manuscript of his father's courtship conveys a sentimentality barely concealing mercenary motives. To Chalmers, the elder Henry Baker was 'a person more respectable as a philosopher than a poet' (Chalmers, 63), and George Potter shows that, if he worked briefly with Defoe on the *Universal Spectator*, his poem 'The Universe' is not original because it postdated the first epistle of Alexander Pope's *Essay on Man* and borrowed from James Thomson's 'Spring' (Potter, 303–4).

About the younger Henry Baker's authorship, Nichols says that he wrote occasional poetry and essays for periodicals, and he attributes to him *Essays Pastoral and Elegiac*, an anonymous publication of 1756 in two octavo volumes (Nichols, *Lit. anecdotes*, 5.277–8). The wording of the title page, 'Essays pastoral and elegiac; containing, Morning, or, The complaint; Noon, or, The contest; Evening, or, The exclamation; Night, or, The wanderer; addressed to the Right Hon. the earl of Chesterfield', voices conventional pretensions in its deference to Philip Stanhope and allusions to poetic modes favoured by Edward Young.

Baker's only son, William Baker, was born on 17 February 1763. Baker died on 24 August 1766 and was buried near his mother in the churchyard of St Mary-le-Strand, London. To Nichols, Baker's father, 'an intelligent, upright, and benevolent man', was 'unhappy in his children'. His grandson William, his only heir, was a consolation. Not having known his father beyond the age of three, William inherited in 1774 his grandfather's property and papers, including his great-grandfather Defoe's manuscript of *The Compleat English Gentleman*. He entered the church as rector of Lyndon and South Luffenham, Rutland, and effected the lineal descent of the Defoe Bakers.

T. F. HENDERSON, *rev.* ROBERT JAMES MERRETT

Sources J. Nichols, *Biographical and literary anecdotes of William Bowyer, printer, FSA, and of many of his learned friends* (privately printed, London, 1782) • Nichols, *Lit. anecdotes*, vol. 5 • G. L'E. Turner, 'Henry Baker, FRS, founder of the Bakerian lecture', *Notes and Records of the Royal Society*, 29 (1974–5), 53–79 • G. R. Potter, 'Henry Baker, F. R. S. (1698–1774)', *Modern Philology*, 29 (1931–2), 301–21 • *N&Q*, 2nd ser., 8 (1859), 51, 94, 197, 299 • G. Chalmers, *The life of Daniel Defoe* (1790) • J. R. Moore, *Daniel Defoe: citizen of the modern world* (1958)

Archives L. Cong., MSS

Baker, Henry Aaron (1753–1836), architect, came from an unknown background. Between 1777 and 1779 he was a student at the Dublin Society's School of Architectural Drawing under Thomas Ivory (*d*. 1786); he also served a regular apprenticeship to Ivory, whom he assisted in the school. In 1787 he succeeded Ivory as master of the school, a post which he retained for nearly fifty years. The new premises for the society's three drawing schools, which were opened in Hawkins Street in 1796, were built to his design, and he was much later to be responsible for the drawing school and bust gallery (1823–7) adjoining Leinster House.

By the end of 1786 Baker had also worked 'sometime' in the office of James Gandon. This association lasted until the end of Gandon's active career: Baker acted as assistant on Gandon's last major commission, a library and hall for the King's Inns in Dublin. Gandon resigned from the undertaking about 1808, leaving Baker in charge of completing the unfinished building. In Dublin Baker also prepared several designs for the wide streets commissioners between 1799 and 1816, including schemes for Westmoreland and D'Olier streets, executed from 1800 onwards; he was architect to the Dublin prisons from 1815. Yet despite his long career and his participation in several major architectural competitions, relatively few surviving buildings by him have been identified. Works outside Dublin include the Bishop's Gate at Londonderry (1789), the Pillar of Lloyd near Kells, co. Meath (1791), the market house at Castlecomer, co. Kilkenny (1809), and the Spring-Rice Column in Pery Square, Limerick (1826–31). His neo-classical architectural style combined a liking for bold forms with an insistence on shallow planar recessions, delicate stone detail, and the tripartite and segment-headed openings characteristic of advanced ideas around 1800.

Baker was a founder member of the Royal Hibernian Academy in 1823. He served as secretary in 1826–7 and as professor of architecture from 1827 until 1831. He died on 4 June 1836 and was buried in the graveyard of St Thomas's Church, Dublin. A. M. ROWAN

Sources [W. Papworth], ed., *The dictionary of architecture*, 11 vols. (1853–92) · J. Turpin, *A school of art in Dublin since the eighteenth century: a history of the National College of Art and Design* (1995), 21, 48, 51–2, 63, 105 · E. McParland, *James Gandon: Vitruvius Hibernicus* (1985), 174, 199n. · E. McParland, 'The wide streets commissioners', *Quarterly Bulletin of the Irish Georgian Society*, 15 (1972), 18–26 · W. G. Strickland, *A dictionary of Irish artists*, 2 (1913), 622 · *Freeman's Journal* [Dublin] (7 June 1836)

Archives RIBA | City Archives, Dublin, wide streets commissioners MSS · Irish Architectural Archive, Dublin, Murray collection · Representative Church Body, Dublin

Baker, Henry Frederick (1866–1956), mathematician, was born at 1 Clement Court, Cambridge, on 3 July 1866, the son of Henry Baker, a domestic butler, and his wife, Sarah Ann Baker, *née* Britham. After attending various small schools he entered the Perse School, Cambridge. He was awarded a sizarship at St John's College, Cambridge, in the summer of 1883, but remained at school in order to prepare for the entrance scholarship examination to be held in the following December. He was elected to a foundation scholarship and began residence in October 1884. In 1887 he was bracketed senior wrangler with three others, and in the following year he was placed in the first division of the first class in part one of the mathematical tripos. He was elected into a fellowship of St John's College in 1888 and remained a fellow for nearly sixty-eight years. In 1889 he was awarded a Smith's prize.

In 1893 Baker married Lily Isabella Homfeld Klopp (1871–1903), daughter of Otto Charles Klopp, a merchant,

Henry Frederick Baker (1866–1956), by Walter Stoneman, 1926

of Homfeld House, Putney, and originally from Leer, Germany. They had two sons. He spent the whole of his working life in Cambridge, first as a college lecturer, then as a university lecturer (1895–1914), holding the special Cayley lectureship (1903–14), and finally as Lowndean professor of astronomy and geometry (1914–36). He was elected FRS in 1898 and received the Sylvester medal in 1910. He was awarded the De Morgan medal of the London Mathematical Society in 1905 and was president of the society in 1910 and 1911. In 1913 Baker married again, his first wife having died prematurely (aged thirty-two) in 1903. His second wife was Muriel Irene Woodyard (1885–1956), daughter of Henry Walter Woodyard, an engineer. She was eighteen years his junior. They had one daughter.

Baker's whole life was devoted to the service of mathematics, through research, and by his power to communicate his enthusiasm to his pupils. His researches covered a wide range of subjects, but chronologically they fall into two distinct periods. In the earlier period, which lasted until about 1911 or 1912, Baker's main interest was in the theory of algebraic functions and related topics, although his work on this often had a bearing on other branches of pure mathematics, to which he made useful contributions from time to time. Subjects on which he wrote included invariant theory, differential equations, and Lie groups; moreover, his work on algebraic functions led him, after the turn of the century, to consider wider problems in the theory of functions, especially functions of several complex variables. While many of Baker's papers were noteworthy in their day, it was his two books, *Abel's Theorem and the Allied Theory, Including Theta Functions* (1897) and *An Introduction to the Theory of Multiply Periodic Functions*

(1907), which were his most lasting contributions to mathematics during this first period.

Some of the problems which Baker was considering when he wrote *Multiply Periodic Functions* led him to take an interest in geometry; on the one hand he came to read T. Reye's *Geometrie der Lage*, and on the other he came in contact with the work of the Italian school of geometers on the theory of complex algebraic surfaces. Their work, and the closely related analytic theory of Émile Picard, achieved the difficult generalization of Riemann's ideas from one complex variable to two. These subjects fascinated him, and he soon began to write on them. He made the work of the Italian geometers the subject of his presidential address to the London Mathematical Society in 1911 which became one of the classic surveys of the subject, and he was soon recognized as a leader of British geometers. On the death of the Lowndean professor, Sir Robert Ball, in November 1913, Baker was the obvious choice of those electors to the chair who wished to appoint a geometer. It was, however, contested by other electors who wished to continue the astronomical traditions of the chair. The deadlock was only broken when, quite exceptionally, the appointment was passed to the chancellor, who selected Baker. Baker had no intention, however, of neglecting that part of his responsibilities which related to astronomy, and for many years he lectured with considerable success on gravitational astronomy and wrote some useful papers on this subject. He was among the first in Britain to understand Poincaré's novel reformulation of celestial mechanics. For the rest of his life, however, his real love was geometry; for over twenty years he taught and wrote on it, and it is for the work done as a professor that he will best be remembered. His own contributions are summed up in a treatise of six volumes, entitled *Principles of Geometry* (1922–33). He continued working on geometry after his retirement and published his last paper when he was eighty-six.

Baker's standing as a mathematician has to be judged against the background of the mathematical traditions in the university. He early came under the influence of Arthur Cayley and from him derived his concern with algebraic manipulations. But Cayley was an old man and pure mathematics in Cambridge had little in common with the exciting things which were going on in the subject on the continent. A. R. Forsyth, who succeeded Cayley as professor in 1895, strove hard to bring the continental ideas into Cambridge, but was not himself able to assimilate the continental standards of rigour. Baker, who learned much during visits paid to Klein at Göttingen, picked up these standards by reading the works of Leopold Kronecker and Karl Theodor Wilhelm Weierstrass as a young man. He was a better mathematician than Forsyth, and presented the advanced theory of complex functions in a much more comprehensive, comprehensible, and therefore influential way. His early training, however, led him to prefer the objectives of the older Cambridge mathematicians, using the new ideas primarily as tools. The result was that in his fifties he was little affected by the revolution brought about among the Cambridge mathematical analysts by G. H. Hardy in the first decade of the twentieth century. During this period Baker's position was essentially that of one of the leaders of the older generation.

When he changed his interests to geometry, Baker again came to the subject at an awkward stage. In spite of the great advances which the Italians had achieved in the theory of surfaces, it was already apparent that their methods were not proving adequate, and indeed the proofs of a number of the most important theorems had already been shown to be faulty. Baker did not invent any new methods and his work was largely devoted to examining the difficulties, and to using algebraic methods of the type used years before by Cayley to examine special cases. This he did extremely well, but his work served to make it still clearer that radical changes in approach were necessary before real progress could be made. This was not the case in projective geometry. In that field there were no structural problems, and each individual problem was an end in itself. It was here that Baker was at his best, for at heart he believed that the object of mathematics was to solve special problems completely, basic principles and general theories being of less interest to him. The fact that Baker did not achieve any major breakthrough was to a large degree due to his native modesty; he had an admiration amounting to veneration for the great masters of mathematics, and he could not imagine that he could ever take his place beside them.

While Baker's original contributions to mathematics were considerable, his forte lay in expounding the work of others and in inspiring the younger generation of geometers. In this last he was conspicuously successful. Between 1920 and 1936 he attracted around him a large following of young and enthusiastic geometers, many of whom won Smith's prizes and subsequently achieved high positions. An important feature of the school he founded was his Saturday afternoon seminar or 'tea party', one of the earliest seminars held in Cambridge. This was the focus of the great activity in geometry which he stirred up, and was the essential key to his success.

In appearance Baker was a heavily built man, with a thick moustache. This made him rather formidable to strangers and as he was also very shy some found him difficult to approach at first. But once the barriers were broken down his pupils found him less awe-inspiring, although they always treated him with great respect. The protocol at his tea parties was strict, and a pupil could not stay away without an acceptable excuse, but provided the rules were obeyed the atmosphere was extremely friendly. Baker died at his home, 3 Storeys Way, Cambridge, on 17 March 1956, and his widow survived him by only a few months. W. V. D. Hodge, *rev.* J. J. Gray

Sources W. V. D. Hodge, *Memoirs FRS*, 2 (1956), 49–68 • private information (1956) • personal knowledge (1956) • *The Times* (19 March 1956) • J. J. Gray, 'Mathematics in Cambridge and beyond', *Cambridge minds*, ed. R. Mason (1994), 86–99 • J. J. Gray, 'Algebraic geometry in the late nineteenth century', *The history of modern*

mathematics, ed. D. E. Rowe and J. McCleary, 1: *Ideas and their reception* (1989), 361–85 • b. cert. • d. cert. • *CGPLA Eng. & Wales* (1956)
Archives St John Cam., letters to Sir F. Larmor
Likenesses W. Stoneman, photograph, 1926, NPG [*see illus.*] • Maull & Fox, photograph, RS • Russell & Sons, photograph, RS
Wealth at death £14,376 4*s.* 11*d.*: probate, 13 July 1956, *CGPLA Eng. & Wales*

Baker, Sir Henry Williams, third baronet (1821–1877), hymn writer, was born in London on 27 May 1821, the eldest of the two sons and five daughters of Vice-Admiral Sir Henry Loraine Baker, second baronet (1787–1859), and his wife, Louisa Anne (*d.* 1861), only daughter of William Williams of Castle Hall, Dorset, sometime MP for Weymouth. His grandfather was Sir Robert Baker of Dunstable House, Surrey, and of Nicholashayne, Culmstock, Devon, on whom a baronetcy was conferred in 1796; his father served with distinction in a naval career of more than fifty years.

After completing his university education at Trinity College, Cambridge, Baker took his BA degree in 1844, was ordained in 1846, and proceeded MA in 1847. In 1851 he was presented to the vicarage of Monkland near Leominster. On the death of his father, on 2 November 1859, he succeeded him as third baronet. While at Monkland, Sir Henry wrote two devotional books—*Daily Prayers for the Use of Those who have to Work Hard* and *A Daily Textbook* (1854), for a similar readership—and, more importantly, began his hymn-writing career. His greatest accomplishment was the extraordinarily successful *Hymns Ancient and Modern*, first published in 1860. One of its instigators, he became chair of the proprietors, and it was to his zeal and business sense that the project owed its success. The original edition was strongly influenced by Tractarianism, and intermittently suspected of 'popery', but an appendix in 1868 and a complete revision in 1875 made it a widely acceptable, and even best-selling, hymnal.

It was Sir Henry's initiative which recruited contributors from different church parties, won over potential competitors, and exploited every opportunity to promote the cause of church music in general, and the sales of *Ancient and Modern* in particular. For the 1861 music edition, in which a tune was printed for every text, he put up a considerable share of the capital and recruited W. H. Monk as editor. Many ineradicable associations of hymn and tune can be traced to this and subsequent editions. Sir Henry was also largely responsible for an important change in hymn publishing: he insisted that the proprietors claim copyright and exercise it to protect and promote their work.

Sometimes an irascible and even high-handed man of business, Sir Henry was also a writer of devotional hymns, unflowery translations, and sensitive paraphrases and adaptations. When he died *Hymns Ancient and Modern* contained more than thirty of his own texts and two melodies, as well as traces of his editing throughout. His chief enduring hymns include 'O praise ye the Lord!', 'We love the place' (with William Bullock), 'Praise, O praise our God and king' (drawing upon Milton), 'O God of love, O king of peace', and 'The king of love my shepherd is'. He died unmarried on 12 February 1877, at the vicarage of Monkland, Horkesley House, and was buried in the parish churchyard. Stained-glass windows were put up to his memory in his own church and in All Saints', Notting Hill. SUSAN DRAIN

Sources J. Julian, ed., *A dictionary of hymnology*, rev. edn (1907) • M. Frost, ed., *Historical companion to 'Hymns ancient and modern'* (1962) • W. K. L. Clarke, *One hundred years of 'Hymns ancient and modern'* (1960) • *'Hymns ancient and modern' … historical edition*, ed. W. H. Frere (1909) • S. Drain, *The Anglican church in nineteenth century Britain: hymns ancient and modern* (1989) • J. Miller, *Singers and songs of the church*, 2nd edn (1869) • Allibone, *Dict.* • *Pall Mall Gazette* (13 Feb 1877) • *Church Times* (16 Feb 1877) • *Church Times* (23 Feb 1877) • *Literary Churchman* (24 Feb 1877) • *Manchester Guardian* (14 Feb 1877) • *Manchester Guardian* (21 Feb 1877) • Burke, *Peerage* • *GM*, 1st ser., 66 (1796) • *GM*, 3rd ser., 7 (1859)
Archives Canterbury Press, Norwich, Hymns Ancient and Modern Ltd
Wealth at death under £10,000—effects

Baker, Sir Herbert (1862–1946), architect and author, was born on 9 June 1862 at Owletts, Cobham, Kent, the fourth of the eleven children of Thomas Henry Baker (1824–1904), gentleman farmer and JP, and his wife, Frances Georgina (*d.* 1916), daughter of William Davis of Rochester. After a rural childhood at Owletts and a public school education, Baker trained as an architect in London before embarking on one of the great imperial careers in British architecture. He designed major government buildings in South Africa, India, Rhodesia, and Kenya, as well as imperial works in London and Oxford. Baker was also an accomplished domestic architect, the designer of several war memorials, and the rebuilder of the Bank of England. A literary man, Baker produced grand-manner classicism at the core and on the periphery of the British empire during the sunset decades of that architectural tradition and political era.

Education and architectural training Baker briefly attended Haileybury College, then in 1873 entered Tonbridge School, where he excelled in mathematics and captained both the cricket and football teams. At this point he decided upon a career in architecture, largely because his parents thought him skilled in drawing. A cousin in London, Arthur Baker (1841–1896), was an architect and young Herbert went to him about 1880 for his first professional training. After a three-year pupillage Baker joined the more established firm of Ernest George and Peto, where he rose to become the partners' leading assistant. Baker also pursued studies at the Royal Academy School of Design and took sketching trips across Britain and northern Europe, often in the company of his younger office-mate Edwin Lutyens. He won the Royal Institute of British Architects' Ashpitel prize (1889) for the highest score in the associate examination before opening his own office in Gravesend in 1891. One year later he set out to seek his fortune in South Africa.

Career in South Africa Baker travelled to the Cape Colony in 1892, ostensibly to assist in the nascent fruit farm operation of his brother Lionel. A chance meeting with Cecil

Sir Herbert Baker (1862–1946), by Elliott & Fry

Rhodes led to the commission for the prime minister's Cape Town residence, Groote Schuur (completed in 1896). Baker developed his so-called Cape Dutch style from careful study of early Dutch and Huguenot homesteads, favouring simple massings of whitewashed walls and random-laid stone, generous verandas, broad tiled roofs, high gables and chimneys, and wood-beam interior ceilings. Altogether, Baker designed some 300 South African houses, including The Woolsack (Cape Town, 1900) for Rudyard Kipling and the Big House (1902–5) for the duke of Westminster. Before the Second South African War (1899–1902) Baker worked in the British Cape Colony. Afterwards, he was invited by the British high commissioner, Alfred, Lord Milner, to help reconstruct and integrate into the British system the defeated Transvaal and Orange Free State. Shifting his post-war practice northward, the architect moved to Johannesburg in 1902, building his home, Stonehouse, which he shared for a while with several of Milner's young, Oxford-educated colonial administrators.

During the Second South African War, Baker's patron Rhodes had sent the architect on a Mediterranean study trip in 1899–1900. When the empire-builder died two years later, Baker designed a stoa-like memorial, composed of a U-shaped, open Doric colonnade, on the side of Table Mountain above Groote Schuur (1905–8). When South Africa's four colonies formally united in 1910, Baker's political connections with the general and politician Jan Smuts secured him the commission for the main government office complex in Pretoria. Drawing inspiration from Greek hillside sanctuaries, Baker's Union Buildings (1910–13) sprawl across their own acropolis-like site on the slope of Meintjes Kop, with two massive office blocks linked by a semicircular colonnade embracing an outdoor amphitheatre designed for large public gatherings. A pair of tall towers symbolized the 'two races of South Africa' (British and Dutch). From elevated corner offices ministers could look out from columnar loggias to 'gather inspiration and visions of greatness' (Baker, 60).

Altogether Baker spent some twenty years in South Africa, having been given, as he said, 'the opportunity for an architecture which establishes a nation' (Baker, 48). Besides mansions and official complexes, he built cathedrals in Pretoria and Johannesburg, Pretoria's rail station, a Johannesburg medical institute, commercial offices, colleges, and also mineworkers' villages on the Witwatersrand. Baker's partners in South Africa were Ernest Willmott Sloper (1871–1916), Francis Fleming (1875–1950), Franklin Kendall (1870–1948), and Francis Masey (1861–1912).

Career in India In 1904 the architect returned briefly to England, where he renewed a boyhood acquaintance with a distant cousin, Florence Edmeades (1878–1965) of Nurstead Court, Kent, daughter of Major-General Henry Edmeades and his wife, Mary Elizabeth Collings. They married on 21 June 1904, when Baker was aged forty-two, and together had four children: Ann, Henry, Allaire, and Alfred.

Despite great success in South Africa during the prime of his life, Baker recognized the limits of a career located on one imperial fringe. In 1912 he welcomed the opportunity to collaborate with his old friend Lutyens in the designing of a vast new government complex at New Delhi. The fifty-year-old Baker left South Africa, moved his family and practice back home to England, and travelled out to India as needed over the next decade and a half.

In India, Baker successfully argued for the positioning of Lutyens's Viceroy House and his secretariat buildings at the same level on either side of the crest of Raisina Hill. This created an acropolis-like platform and symbolized to Baker the equality of the colonial bureaucracy and executive. Baker's pair of quarter-mile-long, matching secretariat buildings (1912–27) flanked the ceremonial King's Way up to the viceroy's house. The secretariat buildings themselves were composed of thick, dark-stone basements surmounted by lighter-coloured office storeys, projecting loggias as at Pretoria, plus skyline towers, turrets, and high central domes. The overall massing bore reminiscences of Greenwich Hospital (begun in 1696).

Off the King's Way to the north-east, Baker also constructed a new legislative building (1917–29). This was a circular structure at Lutyens's insistence, three storeys high and 570 feet in diameter. Behind its sweeping colonnade lay a central domed hall symbolizing a united India, plus three semicircular halls for the council of state, the legislative assembly, and the chamber of princes, the last of which Baker emblazoned with specially invented heraldic escutcheons.

Baker's purpose was to 'graft' the 'ordered beauty' of a Wren-inspired English classical composition—which the architect thought symbolized 'good government' and the 'idea of law and order'—with selected features of an otherwise unruly Indian architecture: for example, wide overhanging *chajjas* to block the rain and sun, pierced window screen *jaalis* for shade and ventilation, and open columnar *chattris* for skyline interest and guard shelters (Baker, 63 and 219–21). Along with their warm wall colours, generous interior courtyards, and small recessed windows, Baker's hybrid buildings functionally adapted European classicism to a tropical climate. At the same time they deliberately symbolized the larger imperial project, in which Indians could politically elevate themselves only by grafting their own culture onto British constitutional structures.

Practice in Britain Back in his home near Westminster Abbey (first at 14 Barton Street and then 2 Smith Square), Baker in the 1920s and 1930s established with his partner Alexander T. Scott (1887–1962) a flourishing practice in his native country. He designed a series of church renovations, City banks, and a Thames bridge at Mortlake, as well as the imperial India House (1928–30), South Africa House (1930–35), Royal Empire Society (1938), and London House, a Commonwealth students' hostel for the University of London (1936–8). Here Baker transposed his grand-manner classical style evolved on the imperial periphery back to the metropolitan core: broad wall surfaces, pitched tile roofs, discrete ornamental flourishes, and large, loose-jointed geometrical massings.

Baker also possessed a more informal public manner which confirmed his early loyalties to the arts and crafts movement. This was evidenced in the brick, stone, and flint Church House (1935–40; bombed and rebuilt), built as the administrative headquarters for the Church of England, and emblazoned with carefully researched saints' arms and emblems. At Rhodes House in Oxford (1929), for his late patron's scholarship students, Baker's rough stone exteriors, tile roofs, and interior oak ceilings and whitewashed walls synthesized classical grandeur with Cotswold vernacularism in an attempt to be, as Baker explained, 'as styleless and elementary as possible' (Baker, 136).

Baker served, too, as one of the architects for the Imperial War Graves Commission from 1917 to 1928. Advocating the symbolism of the cross and the atmosphere of the English churchyard, and utilizing a sombre classical palette, he supervised the construction of over 100 cemeteries in France and himself designed the memorial cemeteries for the South African missing at Delville Wood and for the Indian missing at Neuve Chapelle. At home he produced several schools' war memorials, including what is often considered his greatest masterpiece, the war memorial cloister at Winchester College (1922–4), a simple four-square block beneath a solid pitched roof, 'a work after my own heart', wrote Baker, 'building in a manner which I loved in the architecture of my native country, flint and stone, oak roof-trees, all made living in expression with symbols, heraldry, and sculpture' (Baker, 97).

The Bank of England Baker's last great public commission occurred in the heart of the City of London. Here Baker rebuilt the Bank of England (1921–42), razing the entire pre-existing 3 acre complex, except for the early nineteenth-century perimeter walls erected by John Soane. In stages Baker erected a steel-framed, stone-clad office building, seven storeys at its highest, with a ring of vaulted, top-lit, Soanean bank halls along the lower perimeter base. Always attentive to symbolism, Baker tried to embody the Bank of England's 'tradition of the private house' and 'that invisible thing, Trust' (Baker, 123–4). He created a domiciliary executive core and lavishly embellished the building with allegorical sculptures, marble mosaics of historic coins, Greek inscriptions, and wall paintings depicting contemporary bank staff at work. At the bank Baker employed a whole host of artistic collaborators, notably the sculptor Charles Wheeler and the artist D. Y. Cameron. Today Baker's mixed reputation rests largely on the perceived failures of this his most prominent English building. The Bank of England's stacked superstructure rests uncomfortably on the low base, and critics continue to resent the loss of the earlier building, conveniently ignoring Soane's wilful destruction of his own predecessors' work as well as the existential perils faced by any capitalist architecture.

Private life: friends, ideals, interests In his personal as well as professional life, Baker lived amid Britain's leading imperial protagonists. He numbered among his friends and acquaintances Rhodes, Kipling, Smuts, Milner, T. E. Lawrence—who wrote *The Seven Pillars of Wisdom* (1926–35) while living upstairs from Baker in Barton Street—and of course that other great imperial architect Lutyens, with whom Baker's fortune and fame has been inextricably linked.

After their early London friendship, Lutyens had visited Baker in South Africa, and in 1908 the two briefly discussed joining formally as partners. In India after 1912, antagonisms arose over aesthetic and administrative matters, which were only much later soothed, when in the 1920s and 1930s the two became rival bank headquarters builders in the City of London. Historians have judged Baker the lesser of the two architecturally and Baker frankly credited his friend's superior handling of 'abstract and geometrical qualities' and the 'Shakespearean quality' of Lutyens's architecture, 'with its wit, fun, vitality, and rare beauty' (Baker, 67 and 208). Baker, on the other hand, concentrated on legible symbols, messages, sentiments, and significations. 'Content in art, national and human sentiment, and their expression in architecture, seem to me to be of the greatest importance' (Baker, 68). Towards this end, Baker's public buildings were usually composed with symbolic meaning and festooned with appropriate heraldry, sculpture, painting, and inscriptions. Modernist eyes have favoured Lutyens's inventive handling of classicism's broad masses and surfaces, above the more literary approach of Baker, the less naturally assured artist.

On a personal level, Baker's friends knew him as a British patriot and pious Anglican, reserved, idealistic, and with an underlying gentleness. 'I like the look of that young man', Rhodes reportedly remarked after their first meeting, 'he doesn't talk too much' (*The Times*, 6 Feb 1946, 7e). Outside architecture, literature was Baker's chief intellectual interest. He translated French verse, was a member of the Literary Society Dining Club, and besides the biography *Cecil Rhodes by his Architect* (1934) also wrote texts explaining several of his buildings' decorative programmes, including *The Church House: its Art and Symbolism* (1940). Baker's own autobiography, *Architecture and Personalities* (1944), is chock full of quotations and allusions and is perhaps the most literary memoir ever penned by an architect.

In physical appearance, the well-built architect possessed a high, broad forehead and strong, prominent features, with eyes sloping down seriously at the ends. From Baker's schooldays athletics was a passion, and he continued playing cricket in South Africa. While in India he rode regularly in the mornings and was known to run the 3 miles back and forth between his home and office. When Baker returned to live in England he was active in Kent county cricket, designed a new grandstand at Lord's, and hosted rustic cricket parties for his colleagues at the family home, Owletts.

Owletts Throughout Baker's life Owletts and the Kent countryside remained touchstones of his personality and inspired his love of local materials and fine craftsmanship. The four-square, red-brick Owletts, with its high tiled roof and massive pair of chimneys, had been built in 1683 and came into Baker's family in 1796. Baker spent his boyhood there and lived at Owletts as much as in London when he returned from South Africa. In his memoir Baker described 'the life of the country' as 'the deeper part … of my being', and himself as 'one born and bred in an English home and amongst English fields' (Baker, 210 and 215). He enjoyed working in the Owletts garden, with its bird-bath made of salvaged Bank of England Corinthian capitals, and he donated the house to the National Trust in 1937. At the beginning of the war, physically disabled from a stroke suffered some years earlier, Baker retired to Owletts, where he died after a short illness on 4 February 1946. His wife survived him. An old cherry tree from the orchard provided wood for a casket, handmade by Baker's three sons to hold their father's ashes, which was interred in Westminster Abbey on 12 February 1946.

Conclusion The end of Baker's life marked also nearly the end of Britain's overseas empire and the grand-manner classical style with which his career was so strongly connected. After going out to South Africa to seek his fortune, Baker became that emerging nation's most significant architect, before returning in middle age to the heart of empire to fashion, in Lutyens's shadow, great public buildings for New Delhi and the metropolis itself.

For his efforts and talents Baker was elected a fellow of the Royal Institute of British Architects (1900) and a member of the Royal Academy (1932). He was knighted in 1926 and created KCIE in 1930. He was awarded the royal gold medal for architecture (1927) and honorary doctorates at the universities of Witwatersrand (LLD, 1934) and Oxford (DCL, 1937). Baker himself in 1912 endowed a travelling scholarship for young South African architects to the British School at Rome, and out of a bequest of £60,221 left £5000 to the Royal Academy of Art for advanced students from Great Britain, Northern Ireland, and the Commonwealth. An architectural firm bearing Baker's name continued to operate until the early 1970s.

DANIEL M. ABRAMSON

Sources H. Baker, *Architecture and personalities* (1944) • M. Keath, *Herbert Baker: architecture and idealism, 1892–1913, the South African years* (1992) • *The Times* (12 Feb 1946) • *The Times* (13 Feb 1946) • *The Times* (1 Aug 1946) • *The Builder*, 170 (1946), 158–9 • A. E. Richardson, 'Sir Herbert Baker', *RIBA Journal*, 53 (1945–6), 189–90 • *DNB* • R. G. Irving, *Indian summer: Lutyens, Baker, and imperial Delhi* (1981) • D. E. Greig, *Herbert Baker in South Africa* (1970) • R. S. Sayers, *The Bank of England, 1891–1944*, 3 vols. (1976) • R. McNab, *The story of South Africa House* (1983) • D. Radford, 'Mining villages of Herbert Baker: an investigation of their form and layout', *South African Journal of Art and Architectural History*, 1/2 (May 1990), 53–62 • D. Radford, 'The architecture of Herbert Baker's mining housing', *South African Journal of Art and Architectural History*, 1/3 (Sept 1990), 89–97 • 'Presentation of the royal gold medal to Sir Herbert Baker', *RIBA Journal*, 34 (1926–7), 591–4 • W. Wendland, 'Architectural drawings and records of Sir Herbert Baker's firm', *South African Architectural Record*, 52 (Nov 1967), 21–2 • m. cert. • d. cert.

Archives Johannesburg Public Library, South Africa, Harold Strange collection, Herbert Baker and Frank Fleming MSS • priv. coll., diary, MSS, and drawings • RIBA, MSS and drawings; corresp. and papers; sketchbooks • University of Cape Town Library, Sir Herbert Baker and Partners correspondence, building specifications, photographs, and newspaper clippings | BL, corresp. with Lord Gladstone, Add. MSS 46072–46111 • Bodl. Oxf., corresp. with L. G. Curtis • Bodl. Oxf., corresp. relating to Round Table • Bodl. Oxf., corresp. with countess of Selborne • NA Scot., corresp. with Lord Lothian • NL Wales, corresp. with Thomas Jones • RIBA BAL, corresp. with W. W. Begley • University of Cape Town Library, corresp. with Patrick Duncan • University of Cape Town Library, corresp. relating to Rhodes memorial and St George's Cathedral, Cape Town • University of Cape Town Library, corresp. with C. J. Sibbett

Likenesses W. Rothenstein, chalk drawing, 1925, NPG • C. Wheeler, bronze head, *c.*1932–1937, South Africa House, London • A. K. Lawrence, oils, *c.*1936, Bank of England, London • C. Wheeler, marble bust, 1944, Bank of England, London • Elliott & Fry, photograph, NPG [*see illus.*] • J. M. Solomon, graphite drawing, repro. in Greig, *Herbert Baker* • C. H. Thompson, oils, South Africa National Gallery, Cape Town, South Africa

Wealth at death £60,221 3*s.* 5*d.*: probate, 25 July 1946, *CGPLA Eng. & Wales*

Baker, Herbert Brereton (1862–1935), chemist, was born at Livesey, near Blackburn, on 25 June 1862, the second son of John Baker, curate in charge of Livesey, afterwards vicar of St John's Church, Blackburn, and his wife, Caroline Slater. Ill health kept him indoors; he could read before he was four years old and at ten he had read most of his father's library. He was educated first at Blackburn grammar school and then at Manchester grammar school, where, changing from the classical to the science side, he came under the influence of Francis Jones, often referred to by him as 'the best of all teachers'. A Brackenbury scholarship at Balliol College and a school Brackenbury award enabled Baker to go to Oxford where, with Harold Baily Dixon as his tutor, he in 1883 obtained a first class in natural science. From 1883 to 1885 he was demonstrator in chemistry at Balliol and private assistant to Dixon, who communicated to Baker his own enthusiasm for investigation and led him into that field of research to which later he contributed so notably—the influence of moisture on chemical change.

In 1886 Baker went as chemistry master and head of the science side to Dulwich College. Here he built up a most successful science side; the excellence of his teaching and his own interest in research were an inspiration to many of his pupils. During his time at Dulwich, Baker attained an eminence rare for a schoolmaster; some of his most remarkable results were obtained while he was there, and he was elected FRS in 1902. In the same year he was appointed headmaster of Alleyn's School, Dulwich, but in 1904 he returned to Oxford as Lee's reader in chemistry at Christ Church, of which he was elected a student and tutor. Here he was responsible for the teaching of inorganic chemistry in the university and his experimentally illustrated lectures were highly popular. On 21 March 1905 he married Muriel (*b.* 1875/6), only child of Harry James Powell, partner in the Whitefriars glassworks. She too was a trained chemist and collaborated with her husband in a number of his researches. They had one son, who predeceased his father, and one daughter.

In 1912 Baker accepted the chief professorship of chemistry at the Imperial College of Science and Technology, South Kensington, in succession to Sir T. E. Thorpe; he held this post until his retirement in 1932. In April 1915 he was called upon by the rector of the Imperial College, Sir Alfred Keogh, then director of medical services at the War Office, to advise on the steps to be taken against German gas attacks. For his valuable services in this and other scientific duties undertaken for the war departments he was appointed CBE in 1917.

Baker's claim to fame rests on his achievements as an experimentalist rather than as a theoretical chemist. A competent glass-worker, his exceptional skill in the preparation and manipulation of intensively dried substances enabled him to achieve results which others, with less mastery of the technique, were sometimes at first unable to repeat. Perhaps his most outstanding achievements in this field were the demonstration that dried ammonium chloride does not dissociate when volatilized by heat; that hydrogen and oxygen prepared by the electrolysis of pure barium hydroxide do not combine on heating when carefully dried; and that while very dry nitrogen trioxide does not break up on vaporization, the slightest trace of moisture causes the gas to dissociate completely into nitric oxide and nitrogen peroxide. He demonstrated the slowing down or complete stoppage of chemical action in numerous other instances and his remarkable success in demonstrating this effect led chemists to refer to the relative dryness of things as dry, very dry, or 'Baker dry'.

In 1923 Baker was awarded the Davy medal of the Royal Society, and in 1912 the Longstaff medal of the Chemical Society, of which he was elected president in 1926. In 1926 the University of Aberdeen conferred upon him the honorary degree of LLD. Active in the laboratory until his final days, Baker died at his home, Latchmoor House, Gerrards Cross, on 27 April 1935. His wife survived him.

B. M. Jones, *rev.*

Sources J. F. Thorpe, *Obits. FRS*, 1 (1932–5), 523–6 · J. C. P., *Nature*, 135 (1935), 901–2 · J. C. Philip, *JCS* (1935), 1893–6 · personal knowledge (1949) · m. cert. · *CGPLA Eng. & Wales* (1935)
Archives RIBA BAL · University of Cape Town Library | BL, corresp. with Lord Gladstone, Add. MSS 46072–46111 · Bodl. Oxf., Palmer and Curtis MSS · Bodl. RH, corresp. with Patrick Duncan · NA Scot., Kerr MSS · NL Wales, Jones MSS · RIBA BAL, Begley MSS · University of Cape Town Library, corresp. with Patrick Duncan and C. J. Sibbett
Likenesses W. Stoneman, photograph, 1917, NPG; repro. in Thorpe, *Obits. FRS*
Wealth at death £15,919 7*s.* 0*d.*: resworn probate, 15 July 1935, *CGPLA Eng. & Wales*

Baker, Humphrey (*fl.* **1557–1574**), writer on astrology and arithmetic, whose origins are unknown, was living in London when his almanac was published in 1557. A small volume, printed in black letter, it was entitled *The rules and right ample documentes, touchinge the use and practise of the common almanackes, which are named ephemerides: a briefe … introduction upon the iudicall astrologie … with a treatise … touching the coniunction of the planets … the hole faithfully and clerely translated into Englysche by Humprey Baker BL*; its lengthy title reproduced that of the French original by Oronce Fine, *Les canons & documens très amples, touchant l'usage et practique des communs almanachz* (1556).

Baker's enthusiasm for arithmetic pervades his small primer on that subject, likewise printed in black letter. *The Wellspring of Sciences* (1562) went through many editions, with varying titles. That of 1574 was enlarged as *The well springe of sciences, which teacheth the perfect works and practice of arithmeticke … augmented and amended … certaine tables of the agreement of measures, and waightes, of divers places in Europe, the one with another, etc*, and dedicated 'to the Governor, Consuls, Asistentes, &c. of the Company of Merchentes Adventurers'. In this dedication Baker excused himself for not entering fully into the merits of arithmetic, on the grounds that 'where good wine is to sell, there need no garlande be hanged out'. The tables of weights and measures were those employed in the main European centres of trade. This style continued up to the edition of 1602; Baker was surely dead by the time that Henry Phillippes issued it as *Baker's arithmetic … newly corrected and enlarged, and made more plain and easie* (1646). This Baker should not be confused with his contemporary, Humphrey Baker (*d.* 1603), eminent in the Joiners' Company.

Anita McConnell

Sources O. Fine, *The rules and right ample documentes*, trans. H. Baker (1557)

Baker [*married name* Pearson], **Hylda** (**1905–1986**), comedian, was born on 14 February 1905 at Farnworth, Bolton, Lancashire, the eldest of the seven children (three boys, four girls) of Harold (Chukky) Baker (1884–1966), comedian, and Margaret Halliwell, seamstress, both of Farnworth. She was chiefly educated at St Hillary's boarding-school, Eastbourne, in 1911–14. She married Benjamin Pearson of Doncaster on 12 January 1929 at Doncaster register office, but they were estranged after four years and the marriage was later dissolved. She had three failed pregnancies but no children.

Hylda Baker made her stage début, aged ten, in 1915 at the Opera House, Tunbridge Wells, and toured as a singer-cum-dancer-cum-instrumentalist. Aged fourteen, but passing herself off as eighteen, she was leading lady in the touring revue *Jingles* in 1919. Through the inter-war years she sang and danced, including male impersonation, in variety, battling to find a successful niche. She also developed her comic talent, and during the 1940s was one of the first female 'proprietors' of revues such as the wartime *Meet the Girls* and the post-1945 *Bearskins and Blushes*, with its mix of low comedy and stationary nudes. The early 1950s were the springboard for her late-flowering stardom. In 1952 she was signed by the Lew and Leslie Grade organization and began to top the bill at the 'number one' theatres, for example, playing Widow Twankey at the Empire Theatre, Sunderland, in 1952; she was an overnight television success on *The Good Old Days* in 1955. During this time she created her most effective routine, her one-sided conversation piece with the tall, silent Cynthia, a character played by many actors over the years.

Now aged fifty, Baker was to enjoy a decade or so of prosperity. She made her West End star début in 1956 in a showcase revue at the Prince of Wales Theatre and, ever one to cherish more serious roles, she undertook telling cameo parts in films, for instance as Aunt Ada in *Saturday Night and Sunday Morning* (1960) and Mrs Sowerberry in *Oliver!* (1968). Of her varied television work by far the most popular was the Granada TV series *Nearest and Dearest* (also made into a film in 1972), which ran from 1968 to 1972; as Nellie Pledge she ran a pickle factory with her brother, Eli, played by Jimmy Jewell. In 1967 she made her legitimate West End début at the Vaudeville Theatre as the clumsy usherette in Charles Wood's play *Fill the Stage with Happy Hours*. Her later years were marred by disappointments and, eventually, debilitating illness. She died on 1 May 1986 at Horton Hospital, Epsom, Surrey, of bronchial pneumonia, and was cremated at Twickenham.

The Edwardian convention of comedic glamour, associated with Marie Lloyd, migrated with the end of music hall to the USA, where its inheritors included Mae West and Marilyn Monroe. Henceforward, from about 1918, British female comedy concentrated more on the eccentric, the hard-done-by, and the woebegone, after the manner of Nellie Wallace, or on 'char-lady' types such as Suzette Tarri, and Elsie and Doris Waters. Hylda Baker fed off that tradition. Crucially, like them, she played dame, not principal boy, in pantomime. Indeed, she stood close to the grand school of 'dame' gossips as exemplified by Norman Evans as Fanny 'Over the garden wall' Fairbottom, or Rex Jameson's Mrs Shufflewick, or, later, by Les Dawson in matronly mode. Under 5 feet in height, she presented a feisty, beady-eyed atom of Lancastrian grit, her harsh, robust voice struggling to find elements of strangulated 'poshness'. This indomitable straining after respectability was thus charged with clanking malapropisms—'the condescension was running down the walls'; 'no one has dallied with my afflictions and I say that without fear of contraception'. With her ill-fitting check suit, ankle-strapped shoes, commodious handbag, flat bonnet, and constantly uncurling feather boa, she sustained a bossy, vehement commentary on the vagaries of human nature with the speechless but somehow comprehending Cynthia. Her continuingly famous catch-phrase—and it is no bad criterion of comic genius to have one's memory so preserved—was a judgement on the unspoken sagacity of the lofty Cynthia: 'she knows, y'know'. Writing in the *Sunday Mirror* (19 October 1969), Gordon McGill concluded, 'hers is an old humour, dredged out of the damp, dirty gutters of her native Lancashire'.

Hurled into a highly competitive trade as a child, Hylda Baker's private and semi-public life was a combative, prickly, often lonely affair, strewn with abrasive relationships—her rasping feud with Jimmy Jewell formed the stuff of showbiz-tabloid lore—and a fearful litany of accidents and ailments, not least the desperate flaw of a feeble memory. Her insistence on her own theatrical rights came close to self-parody and, despite occasional shows of generosity, she was granted the unremitting admiration, but seldom the warm affection, of her stage colleagues. Only a handful of people attended her funeral; rather it is her stage persona that has justly survived, a shrewdly-observed portrait of dogged northern womanhood.

ERIC MIDWINTER

Sources J. Ferguson, *'She knows you know': the remarkable story of Hylda Baker* (1997) • J. Fisher, *Funny way to be a hero* (1973)

Archives Lancs. RO, corresp. and papers | SOUND BBC WAC • BL NSA, documentary recordings • BL NSA, performance recordings

Likenesses C. Ware, photograph, 1963 (with Tommy Cooper), Hult. Arch. • portrait, Theatre Museum, Covent Garden, London • portrait, Jerwood Library of the Performing Arts, London, Mander and Mitchenson theatre collection

Wealth at death under £40,000: probate, 23 July 1986, *CGPLA Eng. & Wales*

Baker, James (*fl.* 1538–1547). *See under* Baker, Matthew (1529/30–1613).

Baker, James Franklin Bethune- (1861–1951), theologian, was born on 23 August 1861 in Birmingham, the third son of Alfred Baker, surgeon, and his wife, Emmeline Bethune, daughter of George Armitage. Charles Baker (1803–1874), an instructor of deaf people, and Franklin Baker (1800–1867), a Unitarian minister, were his uncles; his aunt was the mother of Archbishop E. W. Benson. In 1884 he assumed the additional name of Bethune.

Bethune-Baker was educated at King Edward's School, Birmingham, and gained a classical scholarship at Pembroke College, Cambridge. In 1884 he took a first class in part one, in 1885 a third class in part two of the classical tripos; in 1886 a first class in part two of the theological tripos. In 1886 he won the George Williams prize and submitted an unsuccessful (and so unpublished) essay for the Burney prize in which his later modernist theology is clearly foreshadowed; in 1887 he submitted a successful essay entitled 'The influence of Christianity on war', and in the following year won the Norrisian prize. In 1886 he returned to teach at King Edward's School; and in 1888, although an anxious request for reassurance of his orthodoxy came from the dean of Pembroke, E. J. Heriz Smith, he was ordained deacon, accepting a title at St George's, Edgbaston. He was ordained priest in the next year and in 1891 was elected to a fellowship at Pembroke, which he retained until his death. He was also made dean, an office to which in 1906 he was not reappointed in consequence of complaints concerning his attitude to biblical criticism. Thereafter, although continuing to attend college chapel regularly, he never again felt confident to preach there, except on the occasion of a memorial service for his friend A. J. Mason, master of Pembroke College and canon of Canterbury. Bethune-Baker married in 1891 Ethel (*d.* 1949), the daughter of Furneaux Jordan, a surgeon, of Birmingham, and they had one son, who died as a schoolboy at Marlborough.

Bethune-Baker proceeded BD in 1901 and DD in 1912. His scholarly reputation was established by *The Meaning of Homoousios in the Constantinopolitan Creed* (1901) and his *Introduction to the Early History of Christian Doctrine* (1903), which became a standard textbook. Through the Archbishop's Mission to Assyrian Christians a copy of a Syriac manuscript containing the *Bazaar of Heraclides* by Nestorius came into his hands; with the aid of a translation by Dom Richard Hugh Connolly (whose name did not appear on account of the papal anti-modernist decrees of 1907) he wrote *Nestorius and his Teaching* (1908), claiming that Nestorius did not hold the doctrines attributed to him and was wrongly condemned by the ecumenical council of Ephesus in 431. In 1911 he succeeded W. R. Inge as Lady Margaret professor. Except for his time-absorbing work as editor of the *Journal of Theological Studies* (1903–35), by which he guided and maintained the standards of British theology for a generation, his interest now turned from personal contributions to learning and was more devoted to teaching in Cambridge and to the advancement of liberal Christianity. In 1913–14 he became involved in the controversy concerning clerical orthodoxy in the Church of England. His open letter to Charles Gore, *The Miracle of Christianity* (1914), pleads for the logical consequences of the liberal view of the Bible adopted by Gore himself in *Lux mundi* (1889). This avowal of sympathy with the 'critical school' led his friend Bishop J. R. Harmer of Rochester to request his resignation from the office of examining chaplain, which he had held since 1905; believing that hope lay only in the coexistence of conservative and modernist views he refused, and Harmer (who did not share this belief) relieved him of his post. The claim that the Anglican principle of comprehensiveness extended not only to the unity of Catholic and protestant but also to that of conservative and modernist he later expounded in *Unity and Truth in the Church of England* (1934). His dogmatic beliefs are best seen in *The Faith of the Apostles' Creed* (1918) and in a collection of essays, published at the suggestion of S. C. Roberts, *The Way of Modernism* (1927). He advocated an evolutionary, immanentist approach to the incarnation and free enquiry in historical criticism, rejecting as irreligious the view that the virgin birth and the resurrection are truths to be accepted on supernatural authority by all believers. He lacked the philosophical equipment to make these writings wholly successful, but their subject-matter was his deepest concern. He was examining chaplain (1924–35) to Bishop E. W. Barnes, of whose *Rise of Christianity* (1947) he disapproved. He was elected FBA in 1924 and resigned his professorship in 1935. He took part in college meetings almost until the end of his life and still drove his car in his eighty-ninth year.

In the teaching of theology at Cambridge, Bethune-Baker played a leading part, encouraging in his pupils an attitude of detachment and impartiality. In 1922 he founded the Cambridge D Society for the discussion of philosophical and systematic theology. He had a keenly critical mind, a strong, sometimes obstinate personality, and a satirical tongue which enjoyed opposition and in some induced alarm. He had also a capacity for deep and generous friendship, and above all a profound concern for the presentation of the faith in a form tenable to the modern mind.

Bethune-Baker died in Addenbrooke's Hospital, Cambridge, on 13 January 1951. HENRY CHADWICK, *rev.*

Sources H. E. Wynn, 'James Franklin Bethune-Baker, 1861–1951', *PBA*, 39 (1953), 355–62 • *The Times* (15 Jan 1951) • *Cambridge Review* (5 May 1951) • W. N. Pittenger, 'The Christian apologetic of James Franklin Bethune-Baker', *Anglican Theological Review*, 37 (1955), 260–77 • *CGPLA Eng. & Wales* (1951)

Likenesses R. Schwabe, pencil drawing, 1935, Cambridge University Divinity School • photograph, repro. in Wynn, *PBA*, 355

Wealth at death £32,427 17*s.* 4*d.*: probate, 16 May 1951, *CGPLA Eng. & Wales*

Baker, Sir John (*c.*1489–1558), judge and administrator, was born *c.*1489, being about sixty-two in 1551, the eldest of four sons of Richard Baker (*d.* 1504), landowner, of Cranbrook, Kent, and his wife, Joan (*d.* in or after 1504). He was bequeathed property in 1496 by his grandfather Thomas Baker of Cranbrook. However, in 1504 his father revoked this legacy and substituted it for an annuity of £10 until the age of twenty-four, in order to have his son educated in the law.

Baker was in chambers at the Inner Temple by June 1506, and became a bencher in 1517. He somehow managed to contribute to the cost of some chambers under the library in which he was given a perpetual interest in 1506. A series of offices at the inn followed, including frequent service as governor, and he gave his first reading in 1522 and his second in 1530. In the meantime he was subsidy commissioner in Kent in 1514, and JP for the county from 1515 to 1558. By 1547, although the longest-serving JP, he was less active, despite appointment as *custos rotulorum*, because of his commitments in central government. The rising lawyer served as counsel in the court of requests in 1519, and in the following year secured appointment as under-sheriff of London. This led, in 1526, to the post of recorder of London, the principal legal office in the city. In the same year Baker began a career-long relationship with the duchy of Lancaster, being retained of counsel. His first wife was probably called Katherine (*d.* before 1530), and was the daughter of Richard Sackville of Withyham, Sussex. They had no children. By 1530 he had married Elizabeth (*d.* in or before 1558), daughter and heir of Thomas Dingeley of Stanford Dingley, Berkshire, and Middle Aston, Oxfordshire, and widow of his close friend George Barrett of Aveley, Essex. The couple had two sons, Sir Richard Baker (*b.* in or before 1530, *d.* 1594), and John Baker (*b.* in or before 1531, *d.* 1604x6), father of Sir Richard *Baker (*c.*1568–1645), the religious writer and historian, and three daughters. In 1535 Baker surrendered the recordership upon appointment as attorney-general of the duchy of Lancaster on 13 May. However, he only held office for a year, being named attorney-general in 1536, which he remained until 1540. There followed a succession of high offices of state: chancellor of the court of first fruits and tenths (1540–54); chancellor of the exchequer (1540–58); and under-treasurer of England (1543–58). Baker was the first to hold simultaneously the offices of chancellor and under-treasurer, thus beginning a process leading to the eventual rise of the chancellorship. He was a privy councillor from 1540 to 1558. Baker was knighted by 18 June 1540. His parliamentary career was long, active, and distinguished, beginning with representation of London in the Reformation Parliament of 1529, and concluding with service as knight for the shire of Kent in four parliaments (April and November 1554, 1555, 1558). Baker was MP for an unknown constituency in 1536, for Guildford, Surrey, in 1542, Lancaster in 1545, Huntingdonshire in 1547, and Bramber, Sussex, in October 1553. He was one of the most eminent speakers of the House of Commons, filling the post in 1545 and 1547.

Baker's success can be attributed to a shrewd legal mind, a capacity for hard work, and the ability to form enduring friendships among the prominent and influential men of his day. His legal expertise was much sought after, and he sat on innumerable committees and commissions, keeping in close touch with Kent, the civic authorities in London, and the royal administration. He was on the quorum of the peace in Kent and Middlesex from 1547. Baker's offices were staffed with a growing retinue of dependants, many from the vicinity of Cranbrook, and several were highly capable. His friendships, of which there were many, were drawn exclusively from the religious conservatives of the period, both ecclesiastical and lay. Baker's closest friends and associates were Sir John Gage, of West Firle, Sussex, William Fitzwilliam, earl of Southampton, and Sir William Petre, of Ingatestone, Essex. He was also close to the Sackville family of Sussex. From the affair surrounding Elizabeth Barton (the Holy Maid of Kent), to the Marian martyrdoms he was active in religious affairs. While he demonstrated a remarkable ability to work with those of opposing viewpoints, Baker was, nevertheless, a purposeful politician: he was one of the leading voices on the privy council for religious conservatism in the final years of Henry VIII's reign, and he was one of the first to oppose Edward Seymour, duke of Somerset, lord protector to Edward VI.

Baker's continued service under Henry, Edward, and Mary I is remarkable, especially given that he signed the engagement for the alteration of the succession to Lady Jane Grey, despite his reluctance, and provided legal advice on the subject on 11 June and signed the letters patent for the limitation of the crown on 21 June 1553. He demurred over the whole proceedings. Under Mary, however, he earned an unsavoury reputation for undue zeal in the suppression of heresy, in his capacity as a commissioner for the diocese of Canterbury, and received from John Foxe the unpleasant sobriquet 'Butcher Baker'. In that connection Sir Robert Brooke reported him as having given the opinion in 1555 that a writ *de haeretico comburendo* was not necessary for the sheriff to burn a heretic if present at the conviction. Like Sir Thomas More, who in the previous generation was equally fond of burning heretics, his ferocity towards those of different beliefs may be contrasted with a generally cultivated character. The Catholic writer Robert Wingfield of Brantham, Suffolk, at any rate, described him as gravely serious and deeply learned in the law. He seems to have been a bibliophile and left to the Inner Temple a unique manuscript year-book, described by John Selden, which contained civilian glosses. It has not been noticed since the seventeenth century; but another manuscript year-book of his is now in the British Library (Harley MS 452). Mary held him in particularly high regard for his services to Katherine of Aragon and, when he retired as chancellor of the court of first fruits and tenths in 1554, he was granted a generous annuity of £233.

Baker's other talent lay in family aggrandizement. He inherited but a single tenement; at his death he possessed one of the largest estates in the Weald of Kent. He began investing in property well before the dissolution of the monasteries. Planning for the long term, he purchased reversionary interests for relatively modest amounts, and skilfully built up an estate around his residence at Sissinghurst, Kent. By 1547 his annual income from land and fees was £420, making him one of the richer gentlemen in Kent. With talent, resources, and connections, he was ideally suited to benefit from the dissolutions of the monasteries and chantries, and the state confiscations that marked the political turmoil of the mid-sixteenth century. In the parliament of 1539 Baker had his estates disgravelled, the principal beneficiary being his heir. He made his will on 16 October 1555. He died on 23 December 1558 in London and was buried the following month under a monument in Cranbrook church beside his second wife. J. D. Alsop

Sources HoP, *Commons, 1509–58*, 1.366–71 • *LP Henry VIII* • *CPR, 1547–58* • *APC, 1542–58* • state papers, domestic, PRO, SP 10–11 • will, PRO, PROB 11/11, fols. 132*r*–133*r* [Thomas Baker, 1496, grandfather] • will, PRO, PROB 11/14, fols. 159*r*–160*v* [Richard Baker, 1504, father] • will, PRO, PROB 11/42 A, fols. 183*r*–191*v* • M. Zell, *Industry in the countryside: Wealden society in the sixteenth century* (1996) • M. L. Zell, 'Church and gentry in Reformation Kent, 1533–

1553', PhD diss., U. Cal., Los Angeles, 1974 • F. V. Baker, 'Notes on the life of Sir John Baker of Sissinghurst, Kent', *Archaeologia Cantiana*, 38 (1926), 5–27 • *The acts and monuments of John Foxe*, ed. S. R. Cattley, 8 vols. (1837–41), vol. 7, pp. 287–306 • *The diary of Henry Machyn, citizen and merchant-taylor of London, from AD 1550 to AD 1563*, ed. J. G. Nichols, CS, 42 (1848)

Archives BL, Harley MS 452 | PRO, state papers, corresp., SP 1, 10, 11 • PRO, Exchequer, corresp.

Likenesses G. P. Harding, watercolour copy (after lost portrait by John Baker?), NPG; repro. in I. A. Dasent, *The speakers of the House of Commons* (1911), facing p. 130

Baker, John (1660–1716), naval officer and politician, was a son of James Baker (*d.* before 1666), a mariner of Deal, and his wife, Elizabeth (*d.* after 1715). He was appointed second lieutenant of the *Woolwich* on 14 November 1688, became captain of the *Mary Galley* on 12 October 1691, and was noted in the following year as a client of Henry Priestman, a commissioner of the Admiralty. During the remainder of the Nine Years' War (1689–97) he successively commanded the *Boyne*, *Newcastle*, *Resolution*, and *Falmouth*, usually in the Mediterranean, and was captain of the *Medway* in peacetime, from 1697 to 1700. He commanded the *Pembroke* in 1701–2 and then the *Monmouth* from March 1702 to January 1707, fighting in her at Vigo (1702), Gibraltar and Malaga (1704), Barcelona (1705), and Toulon (1707).

Promoted rear-admiral of the white on 26 January 1708, Baker flew his flag in the *Monmouth* as second-in-command to Sir George Byng during that year's operations, convoying troops from Dunkirk and then patrolling off Scotland as part of the counter-measures to the attempted Franco-Jacobite invasion. He then carried the new queen of Portugal, the Holy Roman emperor's daughter, from the Netherlands to Spithead, before taking her on to Lisbon in company with Byng. In 1709 he hoisted his flag in the *Stirling Castle* for an expedition to North America, but after this was cancelled his force was switched to the Mediterranean, where he arrived in October. In November he was detached to Lisbon, flying his flag in the *Somerset*, to protect incoming Portuguese trade from the Indies. Baker remained in the Mediterranean throughout 1711 and 1712, and returned to England at the peace, when he became MP for Weymouth and Melcombe Regis. Despite being unseated on petition in 1714 he was re-elected in the following year. Politically he was closely associated with his naval patron, Byng, and thereby with the whigs and the earl of Orford's Admiralty administration.

In May 1715 Baker sailed for the Mediterranean once more with orders to check the activities of the North African corsairs. He negotiated treaties with Tripoli and Tunis, and was also involved in building up the infrastructure of the newly acquired naval base at Port Mahon, Minorca. In April 1716 the Jacobite duke of Leeds, whose flag-captain Baker had been, suggested offering him an earldom, £200,000, an admiral's flag, and the position of commander-in-chief, if he would bring his squadron over to James Francis Edward Stuart, the Pretender, but Baker's squadron was recalled before the offer could be made.

Having only just been relieved, Baker died at Port Mahon on 10 November 1716. He was buried at Westminster Abbey, where his monument describes him as 'a brave, judicious and experienced officer, a sincere friend, and a true lover of his country'. On several occasions during his career he expressed genuine concern for the well-being of his men, and in his will he bequeathed £2000 for the relief of his poor relatives. The diamond rings given him by the queen of Portugal and the Holy Roman empress were bequeathed to Orford and Byng respectively. Having never married, Baker made over all his lands to his nephew Hercules Baker, a captain under him in 1715, MP for Hythe from 1722 to 1744, and treasurer of Greenwich Hospital from 1736 to 1744. J. D. DAVIES

Sources *DNB* • letter-book, 1708–12, NMM, MS LBK/44 • journal, 1709–11, NMM, MS JOD/22 • PRO, Admiralty MSS, ADM 1/376 • PRO, Admiralty MSS, ADM 6/424 • PRO, Admiralty MSS, ADM 8 • *The Byng papers: selected from the letters and papers of Admiral Sir George Byng, first Viscount Torrington, and of his son, Admiral the Hon. John Byng*, ed. B. Tunstall, 3 vols., Navy RS, 67–8, 70 (1930–32) • PRO, PROB 11/555, fols. 95–7 • *Calendar of the Stuart papers belonging to his majesty the king, preserved at Windsor Castle*, 7 vols., HMC, 56 (1902–23), vol. 2, pp. 51–5, 146 • NMM, Sergison MSS, SER/136 • J. Baker, letters to the earl of Sunderland, BL, Add. MS 61859, fols. 34, 36, 41, 50, 54, 58 • corresp. with George Bubb Dodington, envoy in Spain, BL, Egerton MS 2170, fols. 118, 152, 189, 295 • R. R. Sedgwick, 'Baker, John', HoP, *Commons*, *1715–54*

Archives NMM, journal and letter-book • TCD, corresp., journal | BL, corresp. with George Bubb Dodington, Egerton MS 2170, fols. 118, 152, 189, 295 • PRO, ADM 1/376

Likenesses G. White, mezzotint (after T. Gibson), BM, NPG

Wealth at death annuities of £50 to mother, and £40 to brother and two sisters; nephews and nieces £100 apiece; £2000 to be administered for relief of his poor relatives: will, PRO, PROB 11/555, fols. 95–7

Baker, John (1677/8–1745), Church of England clergyman and college administrator, was born in Burley, Rutland, the son of John Baker. He was admitted to Westminster School, on the foundation, in 1691, and thence elected to Trinity College, Cambridge, in 1695, aged seventeen. Having matriculated in 1696 he graduated BA in 1699 and proceeded MA (1702), BD (1709), and DD *comitiis regiis* (1717). He was elected a minor fellow of Trinity on 2 October 1701 and a major fellow on 17 April 1702; in 1722 he was appointed vice-master of the college. He was made vicar of St Mary's in Cambridge in 1725, and in 1731 rector of Dickleburgh in Norfolk. He was a steadfast supporter of the master of Trinity, Richard Bentley, in all his battles both within the college and in the university. His subservience to Bentley is ridiculed in the anonymously published 'Trinity College triumph':

> But Baker alone to the lodge was admitted
> Where he bow'd and he cring'd, and he smil'd and he
> prated.

Baker fell heavily into debt and had to relinquish the vice-mastership; his living of Dickleburgh was sequestrated for the payment of his debts. 'He had been a great beau', wrote William Cole, the Cambridge antiquary, 'but latterly was as much the reverse of it, wearing four or five nightcaps under his wig and square cap, and a black cloak over his cloath gown and cassock, under which were various waistcoats, in the hottest weather' (BL, Add. MS 5804, fol. 81). Baker died in Neville's Court, Trinity College, on 30

October 1745 and was buried in All Saints' Church, Cambridge, according to instructions given a few days before his death. THOMPSON COOPER, *rev.* S. J. SKEDD

Sources Venn, *Alum. Cant.* • J. H. Monk, *The life of Richard Bentley* (1830), 401, 403 • F. Blomefield and C. Parkin, *An essay towards a topographical history of the county of Norfolk*, [2nd edn], 11 vols. (1805–10), 1.196 • *GM*, 1st ser., 49 (1779), 640
Archives BL, letters to B. Fairfax, Add. MS 62709

Baker, John (1736–1771), flower painter, of whose family background or early life nothing is known, was apprenticed to the coach-painter Thomas Maxfield of London, and first practised in that line. However, he subsequently specialized in flower painting. According to Edward Edwards 'his productions had considerable merit, although they were too much marked by that sharpness of touch, which is peculiar to all those who have been bred coach-painters' (Edwards, 38). He exhibited pictures with the Society of Artists from 1762 to 1768 and he was a founder member of the Royal Academy (1768), where he also exhibited works. With his wife, Elizabeth, Baker had a daughter, Sally, and a son, John, whom he took as an apprentice, and who also trained as a painter at the Royal Academy Schools. The apprenticeship binding of John Baker junior records his father's address as Denmark Street, in the parish of St Giles-in-the-Fields. John Baker died in London on 30 April 1771, and soon after an example of his work, *Still Life with Flowers*, was presented to the academy by Charles Catton (Royal Academy). The academy provided charitable financial support for his widow, and helped to pay for her funeral in 1804.

MARTIN MYRONE

Sources E. Edwards, *Anecdotes of painters* (1808); facs. edn (1970) • W. Sandby, *The history of the Royal Academy of Arts*, 2 vols. (1862) • Farington, *Diary* • GL, Painter–Stainers' Company MSS • RA • Waterhouse, *18c painters* • *IGI*

Baker, John Fleetwood, Baron Baker (1901–1985), civil engineer, was born on 19 March 1901 at Liscard, Cheshire, the younger child and only son of Joseph William Baker (1872–1958), etcher and watercolour painter, and his wife, Emily Carole Fleetwood (1874–1952). Baker was educated at Rossall School, Lancashire, from 1915 to 1920, and from there he won an open mathematical scholarship to Clare College, Cambridge, where he read mechanical sciences. He was placed in the first class in the tripos (1923). In January 1924 he found employment as an assistant to Professor A. J. Sutton Pippard in an investigation into the structural problems of airships. The work went well, and a year later Baker transferred to the Royal Aircraft Works, Cardington, as a technical assistant in the design department; he resigned in 1926 to join Pippard as an assistant lecturer at University College, Cardiff, but he continued to spend time at Cardington. The work was concerned essentially with the determination of elastic stresses in the main transverse space frames of airships, and Baker's publications from this period show the great complexity of the investigation, and the drudgery it involved. These few years may be viewed as an apprenticeship served by Baker.

Baker married, in 1928, Fiona Mary MacAlister (*d.* 1979), the daughter of John Walker, cotton broker in Liverpool. There were two daughters. The next eight years, 1928–36, saw Baker make a first start in his life's work, although it was, as it turned out, a false one. The steel industry set up the steel structures research committee in the late 1920s to try to bring some order into the multitude of conflicting regulations governing the design of steel-framed buildings. The committee had many eminent members from industry, government, and academe, and Baker was appointed as technical officer to the committee, although he was prevented by a severe illness (probably tuberculosis) from taking up his post until January 1930. Three volumes (1931, 1934, and 1936) record the theoretical and experimental findings of the committee, and many of the papers in them were written by Baker. His contributions were recognized immediately, and he was awarded the Telford gold medal of the Institution of Civil Engineers in 1932, and appointed to the professorship of civil engineering at Bristol in 1933.

However, at the end of this work Baker realized that the elastic method of structural analysis could never serve as the basis of a rational design method for steel structures. The actual elastic state of a structure is extremely sensitive to accidental imperfections, and cannot, in any real sense, be predicted. What can be predicted with great accuracy, however, is the collapse load of a ductile structure, and Baker's work was directed from 1936 onwards to the development of the plastic method of design. (When a ductile structure is, hypothetically, overloaded, it suffers large but controlled deflections resulting from the plastic deformation of the material.) In only twelve years the appropriate British standard was altered (in 1948) to permit design by plastic collapse methods. A spectacular application of the new ideas had been made in the meantime to the design of the Morrison air-raid shelter (for which Baker received official acknowledgement from the Royal Commission on Awards to Inventors); Baker was scientific adviser to the Ministry of Home Security from 1939, and was concerned with many aspects of air-raid precautions, as he described in his *Enterprise versus Bureaucracy* (1978).

In 1943 Baker moved to Cambridge University as a fellow of Clare College and professor of mechanical sciences and head of the engineering department, where he built up a substantial research team working on problems of structural design. At the same time he completely revised the educational programme of the department, succeeding in constructing new buildings, doubling the teaching staff, and greatly expanding research activity in all fields of engineering (including management studies). He served on several university committees, the council of the Institution of Civil Engineers, the University Grants Committee, and other national bodies. He wrote a two-volume account of elastic and plastic methods of design, *The Steel Skeleton* (1954, 1956), and, later, a two-volume text, *Plastic Design of Frames* (1969, 1971). He retired from his chair in 1968.

Before and after his retirement Baker's advice was constantly sought on senior university appointments, both in the UK and in the Commonwealth. His advice was also sought by industry, particularly on practical design problems of steel structures, and he was at various times a director of four industrial companies, including one heavy engineering firm and a large firm of structural engineers. He took part in an inquiry for the Ministry of Transport into the feasibility of adding a road above the rail track of the old Forth Bridge, and in another inquiry for the Central Electricity Generating Board into the cause of the collapse of the Tyne crossing towers.

Baker's pioneering work on the plastic theory of structures was recognized academically by the award of eight medals (including the royal medal of the Royal Society in 1970), by twelve honorary degrees, by election as FRS in 1956 and as a founder FEng in 1976, by honorary fellowship of the Institution of Mechanical Engineers, and by honorary membership of the Royal Institute of British Architects. He was a fellow and vice-president of the Institution of Civil Engineers and fellow of the Institute of Welding. He was appointed OBE in 1941, knighted in 1961, and made a life peer in 1977. Baker died in Cambridge on 9 September 1985, and was buried there.

JACQUES HEYMAN

Sources J. Heyman, *Memoirs FRS*, 33 (1987), 1–20 • T. J. N. Hilken, *Engineering at Cambridge University, 1783–1965* (1967) • private information (2004) • personal knowledge (2004) • *CGPLA Eng. & Wales* (1986)

Archives CAC Cam., corresp. and papers • CAC Cam. • CUL, consultancy papers | CAC Cam., corresp. with Francis Bacon • ICL, corresp. with Lord Jackson • U. Glas., Archives and Business Records Centre, corresp. with Sir E. C. Bullard

Likenesses E. Kennington, oils, 1953, U. Cam., department of engineering • E. Nisbet, photograph, 1958, repro. in Heyman, *Memoirs FRS*, facing p. 1

Wealth at death £219,708: probate, 3 April 1986, *CGPLA Eng. & Wales*

Baker, John Gilbert (1834–1920), botanist, was born on 13 January 1834 at Guisborough, Yorkshire, the son of John Baker, draper and grocer, and his wife, Mary Gilbert. In August 1834 his parents moved to Thirsk, Yorkshire, and opened a shop. In 1843 he became a pupil at the Quaker school in Ackworth, Yorkshire, and then in 1846 at the Quaker school at Bootham in York, whose pupils were encouraged to study natural history. His schooling ended late in 1847, after which he helped his father in the family business until 1864. He married Hannah Unthank (*d.* 1902) in August 1860. Their son Edmund Gilbert (1864–1949) was also a botanist and eventually became assistant keeper at the Natural History Museum, London.

Baker began collecting plants when he was only twelve and he briefly had charge of the school herbarium at Bootham. When he was fifteen the *Phytologist* published his note on the occurrence in a rather boggy wood in north-east Yorkshire of a sedge he identified as being *Carex persoonii* (now *Carex curta*). His intimate knowledge of the local flora encouraged him to collaborate with John Nowell in issuing a supplement to H. Baines's *Flora of Yorkshire* (1840) in 1854. The following year he read a paper at the annual meeting at Glasgow of the British Association, on British flowering plants and ferns, which he declared was an attempt to classify them according to their 'geognostic relations'.

When the scheme for the national exchange of plant specimens was suspended by the Botanical Society of London, Baker suggested that the Thirsk Natural History Society might take over the service. His proposal was approved and in 1859 he became curator and secretary of the Thirsk Botanical Exchange Club under the aegis of the Thirsk Natural History Society. It was largely through his efficient management of this exchange of plant specimens that Thirsk became an important centre for field botany in Britain. His first major work, *North Yorkshire: Studies of its Botany, Geology, Climate and Physical Geography* (1863) was a pioneering ecological survey of over 1100 species of flowering plants and ferns. Unfortunately most of the copies were lost in a fire which devastated the family business in 1864. The Yorkshire Naturalists' Union began reprinting the work in its *Transactions* in 1888, and an enlarged edition was published in 1906. It is a measure of the esteem in which Baker was held that donations from fellow botanists enabled him to replace the library he had lost in the fire.

On 20 November 1865 Joseph Hooker, recently appointed director at the Royal Botanic Gardens at Kew, wrote to Baker that he anticipated 'soon to be in need of a person of *careful, neat, accurate* and *industrious* habits, who has made some progress in Systematic Botany and is really fond of the pursuit' (Hooker to Baker, 20 Nov 1865, RBG Kew, Baker MSS). Shortly afterwards Baker took up an appointment as an assistant in the Kew herbarium in January 1866. The work of the Thirsk Botanical Exchange Club was then taken over by the newly formed London Botanical Exchange Club with Baker as joint curator. His first task at Kew was the completion of the late Sir William Hooker's *Synopsis filicum*, which was published in 1868. In addition to taxonomic work, he lectured on botany at the London Hospital medical school, 1869–81, at Kew to student gardeners, 1874–1904, and at the Chelsea Physic Garden, 1882–96. He was elected a fellow of the Royal Society in 1878. He became principal assistant to the keeper of the Kew herbarium in 1884 and its keeper in 1890.

Baker contributed substantially to the colonial floras prepared at Kew during his quarter of a century in the herbarium. *Flora of Mauritius and Seychelles* (1877) was entirely his own work; so, too, was volume 6 of the *Flora Capensis* (1896–7); he described species in the *Flora of British India* and *Flora of Tropical Africa*. The *Journal of the Linnean Society* published his enumeration of the plants of Madagascar. It has been calculated that he wrote about 400 papers which appeared mainly in the *Journal of Botany*, *Journal of the Linnean Society*, and *Kew Bulletin*.

Baker was a regular contributor to the *Gardeners' Chronicle* between 1869 and 1899 on monocotyledons of interest to gardeners. These articles formed the basis of his handbooks on Amaryllidaceae (1887), Bromeliaceae (1889), and Iridaceae (1892). His research on roses which began with a paper on British species in the *Naturalist* (1864) culminated with the text to Alfred Parson's plates in the *Genus Rosa* (1910–14). Ferns remained an abiding interest. He revised

Sir William Hooker's *Synopsis filicum* in 1874; contributed the volume on ferns to C. F. P. von Martius's *Flora Brasiliensis*; described 100 new or rare ferns in volume 17 of *Icones plantarum* (1886–7); and wrote a *Handbook of the Fern-Allies* (1887). He never abandoned his interest in British plants, as *A Flora of the English Lake District* (1885) testified.

It has been said that Baker's output was so impressive because he chose to study plant families that did not require microscopic examination. It is more likely, however, that his wholehearted dedication to the task in hand is the explanation. Joseph Forster's portrait of him depicts him completely absorbed in his work, plants and herbarium sheets around him on his desk. A kind and considerate man, he had a number of interests, in particular poetry, but botany was always his chief concern. The Linnean Society honoured him with its gold medal in 1899, and the Royal Horticultural Society with the Victoria medal of honour in 1897 and the Veitch memorial medal in 1907. The plant genera *Bakerella* (a genus in Loranthaceae, native to Madagascar, *Bakeria* (now *Bakerantha*, a South American Bromeliad), and *Neobakeria* (a South African genus belonging to Liciaceae) were named in his honour.

Baker retired in 1899. His wife died in 1902 and he died at his home, 3 Cumberland Road, Kew, on 16 August 1920. He was buried at the Quaker burial-ground, Isleworth, on 19 August. RAY DESMOND

Sources D. P. [D. Prain], *PRS*, 92B (1921), xxiv–xxx • *Report of the Botanical Society and Exchange Club of the British Isles*, 6 (1920–22), 93–100 • *Journal of Botany, British and Foreign*, 58 (1920), 233–8 • *Proceedings of the Linnean Society of London*, 133rd session (1920–21), 41–4 • *Bulletin of Miscellaneous Information* [RBG Kew] (1907), appx, 96–103 • F. A. Stafleu and E. A. Mennega, *Taxonomic literature: a selective guide*, suppl. 1, Regnum Vegetabile, 125 (1992), 277–82 • RBG Kew, Baker MSS • *CGPLA Eng. & Wales* (1920)

Archives Carlisle Library, MS flora of Lake District • NHM, notes on plant records • RBG Kew, corresp.; plant catalogues

Likenesses J. W. Forster, oils, exh. RA 1893, RBG Kew • photograph, repro. in *Garden* (9 Nov 1901), 315 • photograph, repro. in D. E. Allen, *The botanists* (1986), 70 • photograph, repro. in E. Nelmes and W. Cuthbertson, *Curtis's Botanical Magazine dedications, 1827–1927* (1931), 210 • photographs, RBG Kew

Wealth at death £12,960 4*s*. 1*d*.: probate, 9 Nov 1920, *CGPLA Eng. & Wales*

Baker, John Norman Leonard (1893–1971), geographer, was born on 12 December 1893 at 33 Beaumont Street, St Clements, Liverpool, the first son of the Revd John William Baker, Church of England clergyman, and his wife, Louisa (1858–1945). From Liverpool College (1911–13) he went up to Jesus College, Oxford, as an exhibitioner in 1913. Apart from military service, and a brief period as lecturer at Bedford College, London (1922–3), he retained an association with Jesus College for the rest of his life.

Baker's undergraduate career, when he read modern history, was interrupted by the First World War. Wounded on the Somme, he was required to convalesce, and during this period he married Phyllis Marguerite Hancock (1892–1981) on 8 November 1917. There followed two years in the Indian army, which were important in awakening his interest in geography; he later published several papers on India. After completing his history degree in 1920, Baker turned to geography, obtaining the diploma in geography with distinction in 1921, and gaining the Herbertson memorial prize. In 1923 he joined the small staff of the Oxford school of geography when he was appointed assistant to the reader and librarian. He was subsequently university lecturer from 1927, reader from 1933, and reader in historical geography from 1935. In these capacities he was heavily involved in teaching, first for the diploma and then, from 1932, for the new honour school of geography, the planning and arrangements for which owed much to his influence. He was active in geographical organizations outside Oxford: he was a fellow and council member of the Royal Geographical Society, but had more influence on other societies where he was not in the shadow of Kenneth Mason; as founder member of the Institute of British Geographers (a group of academic geographers who felt that the RGS with its continuing emphasis on exploration could not fully meet their professional aspirations), of which he was president in 1946; and in section E (Geography) of the British Association for the Advancement of Science of which he was section president in 1955.

Baker's scholarly research was concerned principally with the history of geography, exploration, and discovery. He was painstaking in his collection of factual material and had little time for modish theory. He published numerous papers on the great explorers and his book, *A History of Geographical Discovery and Exploration* (1931) became the standard work on the subject. In 1963, six of his former pupils—all on the staff of the school of geography—edited and presented to him a selection of his writings under the title of *The History of Geography*. In 1964 he was awarded the prestigious Victoria medal of the Royal Geographical Society 'for contributions to the history of geography'. He was also an active member of the Hakluyt Society from 1924 onwards, and he served as its president between 1955 and 1960.

In 1939 Baker was elected to an official fellowship of Jesus College on his appointment as senior bursar, a position he held until 1962. During the Second World War he was engaged in intelligence work, but thereafter his college duties occupied an increasing proportion of his time and he resigned his readership in 1947, though he continued to give tutorials to his college students and to those in the department who studied his option on exploration. His withdrawal to his college probably reflected his disappointment that he was not appointed professor of geography at Oxford in 1932 and perhaps his lack of sympathy with the appointee, Kenneth Mason: it certainly reflects his intense college loyalty and love of tradition. As bursar he guided his college through its period of wartime growth and also published articles on its history in the college magazine, and a 150-page history, *Jesus College, Oxford, 1571–1971* (1971).

Baker was elected a university member of Oxford city council in 1945 by the constituency of college heads and bursars. From then on, he gave generously of his time to civic affairs, drawing on his bursarial skills on behalf of the finance and estates committees, and on his geographical knowledge to the benefit of city planning, including the vexed issue of Oxford roads. He was alderman in 1963 and lord mayor, 1964–5, the first university member to hold the latter office. He continued to serve the council until 1967. Baker died in Oxford on 16 December 1971 and was cremated on 21 December 1971 at the Oxford crematorium.

Baker, or J. N. L. B. as he was always known, made a significant contribution to the early study of exploration and the history of geographical ideas from the earliest times to the early twentieth century, and although post-war developments in the subject left him somewhat intellectually isolated, his writings remain a valuable basis of reference. He combined broad scholarship with administrative skills backed up by down-to-earth common sense. These qualities were evident in his contribution both to learned societies and to the day-to-day running of his Oxford college. He was held in great affection by his pupils and his wider interest in people and their welfare is evident in his contribution to civic life in Oxford. This sense of public responsibility was a legacy he passed on to his two daughters, the elder of whom, Janet Young (Baroness Young) played an active role in Oxford and national politics. IAN SCARGILL

Sources R. W. Steel, 'John Norman Leonard Baker, 1893–1971', *Geographers' Bibliographical Studies*, 16 (1995), 1–11 [includes full bibliography] · R. W. Steel, 'John Norman Leonard Baker', *GJ*, 138 (1972), 276–7 · C. F. W. R. Gullick and others, 'An appreciation', in *The history of geography: papers by J. N. L. Baker* (1963) · 'Mr J. N. L. Baker: geography at Oxford', *The Times* (18 Dec 1971) · D. Peters, 'With camera and pen', *Oxford Times* (30 Jan 1959) · L. B. Cross, 'J. N. L. Baker, 1893–1971', *Jesus College Record* (1971), 20–21 · R. W. Steel, 'J. N. L. Baker: a personal view', *Jesus College Record* (1992–3), 22–7 · E. C. Thompson, 'J. N. L. Baker: a memoir', Jesus College, Oxford · *CGPLA Eng. & Wales* (1972)

Archives Jesus College, Oxford · U. Oxf., school of geography and the environment

Likenesses H. A. Freeth, charcoal drawing, priv. coll. · H. A. Freeth, pen-and-ink drawing, Jesus College, Oxford · Halland, oils, priv. coll.

Wealth at death £25,330: probate, 7 Feb 1972, *CGPLA Eng. & Wales*

Baker, John Wynn (*c.*1730–1775), agricultural improver and writer, emigrated from England, possibly from Worcester, to Ireland in 1761 after the collapse of a business scheme to convey brine from salt pits to the River Severn by a system of pipes. He published his first experimental treatise in Dublin, *Some Hints for the Better Improvement of Husbandry*, in 1762. In this work Baker proposed that the Dublin Society should establish an experimental farm. The society agreed and voted him £100 to set up the farm and a further £200 to conduct experiments. Baker hired a 354 acre property in Laughlinstown, co. Kildare (9 miles outside Dublin), and published annual reports of his experimental programme from 1764 until 1773. He established a factory for manufacturing agricultural implements in 1765 (again with the financial assistance of the Dublin Society). The factory enjoyed considerable success until it was destroyed by fire two years later. During the 1760s and early 1770s Baker contributed articles to the journal *Museum Rusticum et Commerciale*, and produced pamphlets on agriculture and related matters. The pamphlets include *A Plan for Instructing Youths in the Knowledge of Husbandry* (1765), in which Baker proposed the establishment of an academy to teach boys to farm scientifically, and *Considerations upon the Exportation of Corn* (1771), in which he advocated statutory regulation of the price of corn in Ireland. He published a more substantial treatise in 1771, *Practical Agriculture Epitomised, and Adapted to the Tenantry of Ireland*, which contained an extended account of agricultural innovations in France. Baker was elected a fellow of the Royal Society on 14 February 1771 in recognition, as his certificate declares, of his contribution 'to polite and philosophical literature'. Despite his considerable reputation Baker suffered in his final years from financial difficulties exacerbated by an increasingly fractious relationship with his sponsors, the Dublin Society. Baker is known to have married and had children. He died at Wynnsfield, co. Kildare, on 5 August 1775, and was buried at Celbridge, co. Kildare. Arthur Young wrote warmly of Baker's publications in a biographical article in *Annals of Agriculture* (1787), though he also complained of Baker's unsystematic approach to experimentation.

SEBASTIAN MITCHELL

Sources G. E. Fussell, 'John Wynn Baker: an "improver" in eighteenth-century Ireland', *Agricultural History*, 5 (1831), 151–6 · A. Young, 'Some particulars relative to the late John Whyn Baker', *Annals of agriculture and other useful arts*, ed. A. Young, 8 (1787), 125–35 · A. Young, *A tour in Ireland*, 2 vols. (1780) · G. E. Fussell, *More old English farming books, … 1731–1793* (1950), vol. 2 of *The old English farming books* (1947–91) · A. Young, *The farmer's letter to the people of England* (1767) · J. Donaldson, *Agricultural biography* (1854) · J. W. Baker, *Some hints for the better improvement of husbandry* (1762) · J. W. Baker, *A short description and list, with the prices of the instruments of husbandry made in the factory at Laughlinstown* (1767) · election certificate, RS · M. Peters, *Winter riches, or, A miscellany of rudiments, directions and observations necessary for the laborious farmer* (1771)

Baker, Kenneth [Kenny] (**1921–1999**), jazz trumpeter, was born at 73 Queen Street in the east Yorkshire town of Withernsea on 1 March 1921. Both parents were musical: Kenny's father, Herman Baker, a boot- and shoemaker, played the clarinet and saxophone, while his mother, Charlotte Gray, sang and played the piano and the violin. At his mother's insistence he studied the piano, commencing at the age of ten. But none of his parents' instruments appealed to him, and in his early teens he joined a local brass band. He was given the tenor horn to play but exchanged it for a cornet after a few months. After he moved with his parents to Hull at the age of fifteen he began working with local dance bands but continued his academic musical studies with his mother, who wanted him to become an orchestral player.

Baker worked in a Hull music shop during the day and became the solo cornet player with the West Hull Silver Prize Band as well as forming a small group to play at dances and local hotels. By now his interest was turning to jazz, for he had heard such players as Louis Armstrong, Duke Ellington, and Jimmie Lunceford on record. In 1939 he answered an advertisement to join the travelling show of the comedian Sandy Powell, which ended its tour with

Kenneth Baker (1921–1999), by unknown photographer

a season at the London Coliseum. With the outbreak of the Second World War Baker joined the pit orchestra at the Cambridge Theatre, London, under the leadership of Lew Stone for the show *Under your Hat*, featuring Jack Hulbert and Cicely Courtnedge. It was his introduction to the West End and led to much similar work with the band leaders Van Philips, Bert Ambrose, Maurice Winnick, and Sid Millward.

The move to London also gave Baker many opportunities to play jazz at late-night clubs, where he first met such players as George Chisholm and George Shearing. With the clarinettist Harry Parry he made broadcasts on the BBC's *Radio Rhythm Club* programmes before joining the RAF in February 1942. He then became a member of the RAF Fighter Command band. Stationed at RAF Hendon, he was given a 'living-out' pass which allowed him to retain his flat in central London. The exigencies of the service were such that he was able to play with civilian bands in the evenings. His final months in uniform were with the RAF regiment in Lincolnshire.

Released from the RAF in 1945, Baker joined the new band formed by the trombonist Ted Heath and remained with it until December 1948, working as lead and solo trumpet player as well as providing arrangements. He had by now achieved a reputation for musical excellence and became a member of the élite coterie of London-based musicians who were constantly in demand by radio and recording producers. Baker spent much of his working life during the latter half of the century helping to provide all manner of music for film and television productions in addition to gramophone and radio employment. Perhaps one of his most famous trumpet solos was one apparently played on screen by the actress Kay Kendall in 1953, when she mimed to Baker's exuberant music in the film *Genevieve*. Despite these studio commitments Kenny continued to play jazz whenever the opportunity arose. He formed his own octet in March 1952 and employed the young Tubby Hayes and Stan Tracey in the early days of their professional careers. Also in 1952, he commenced a long-running weekly series for the BBC under the title *Let's Settle for Music* using an *ad hoc* unit which he named Kenny Baker's Dozen. This immensely popular series used some of Britain's finest jazz musicians playing Baker's own arrangements of jazz pieces and songs from shows and films. The series ran until the end of 1958.

Throughout his career Kenny worked successfully in a number of different musical environments simultaneously. During the fifties he produced dozens of *Let's Settle for Music* programmes for the BBC while also appearing on stage in variety at locations such as Blackpool, as well as continuing with his studio work. As a variety artiste he appealed to non-specialist audiences with gallery-fetching pieces such as *Carnival of Venice*, and in 1966 he joined a new band formed by Jack Parnell at Elstree studios for television work which included backing such artistes as Barbra Streisand, Liberace, and Tony Bennett. For five years (1976–81) he was an integral part of the popular television series *The Muppet Show*, which brought him into contact with many visiting American musicians and singers.

Baker's reputation as a world-class player was international, and when the band leader Harry James died in 1983 he was asked to take over the leadership of James's band, as he was probably one of the few people capable of playing Harry's solos. He declined the offer, saying he preferred living in his native Britain to living in the United States. Nevertheless he worked with a number of visiting Americans during their European tours, including Benny Goodman and Gerry Mulligan.

In the mid-nineties Kenny worked regularly with the trombonist Don Lusher in a small group called the Best of British Jazz and also made several appearances with the Ted Heath Orchestra (following Heath's death) under Lusher's leadership. He also re-formed his Baker's Dozen for specific engagements including recording dates. He continued working up to within a few weeks of his death, in St Richard's Hospital, Chichester, Sussex, on 7 December 1999 at the age of seventy-eight. He was married three times and was survived by his third wife, Susan Mary, and their daughter. During his long career in music he was a source of inspiration to many and was always prepared to offer encouragement and assistance to younger players.

ALUN MORGAN

Sources *The Times* (10 Dec 1999) · *The Independent* (11 Dec 1999) · *The Guardian* (9 Dec 1999) · *Daily Telegraph* (10 Dec 1999) · b. cert. · d. cert.

Archives SOUND BL NSA, performance recordings

Likenesses photograph, News International Syndication, London [*see illus.*] · photograph, repro. in *The Guardian* · photograph, repro. in *The Independent* · photograph, repro. in *Daily Telegraph*

Baker [*née* Willcocks], **Mary** [*alias* Princess Caraboo] (*bap.* **1791**, *d.* **1864**), impostor, enjoyed a brief period of celebrity beginning when, on Good Friday 1817, a young woman wearing a black turban and speaking an unknown language was found wandering in Almondsbury, north-east of Bristol. Her black hair was long and thick, she had large brown eyes, full lips, and very white teeth, and she aroused the sympathy of the American-born Elizabeth Worrall, wife of the town clerk of Bristol, who had rented the local manor house, Knole Park. The girl became excited when she was shown pictures of China, and when she was offered a bed for the night at The Bowl inn she identified a drawing of a pineapple with the word 'ananas'. Mrs Worrall's husband, Samuel, known as 'Devil' Worrall and a notorious drunkard, then intervened, declaring that the young woman was a beggar and must be taken to Bristol and tried for vagrancy. It was during her brief imprisonment there that she was identified by a Portuguese sailor, Manuel Enes, who claimed to understand her language: she came from an island called Javasu, had been kidnapped by pirates, and had managed to jump overboard in the Bristol Channel. She was a princess, and her name was Caraboo.

There followed a triumphant summer at Knole. Surrounded by admirers, Caraboo provided examples of the written language of Javasu, performed an exotic war dance involving a gong, showed great skill in archery, cooked a chicken curry, and swam naked in the lake. She had to contend with a Greek manservant who believed her to be a fraud, and was once woken in the middle of the night by shouts of 'Fire!' She betrayed no sign of alarm. Her authenticity was proved beyond question by Dr Wilkinson, a polymath from Bath who gave subscription lectures on everything from electricity to washable wallpaper. He considered that incisions on the back of her head could have been made only by oriental surgeons. By showing her Edmund Fry's *Pantographia*, a manual of languages, he identified her native dialect as Rejang, spoken in Sumatra. Samuel Worrall, keen to inspire confidence in his private Tolzey Bank, welcomed the presence of a royal visitor, and authorized Wilkinson to publish his findings in the newspapers, asking for any further information about the princess.

Information was provided almost immediately by a Mrs Neale, who ran a boarding-house in Bristol. The 'Princess Caraboo' was in fact Mary Willcocks, the daughter of Thomas Willcocks, a cobbler from Witheridge in Devon. For a short time she was internationally famous, and there was much merriment at the expense of Dr Wilkinson, Mrs Worrall, and her husband, whose bank shortly afterwards collapsed.

Mary Willcocks had been baptized in Witheridge church on 23 November 1791 and had suffered as a child from rheumatic fever. Since then, according to her father, she had 'never been right in the head'. Always a tomboy, she had left the village when she was nineteen, lived rough on the road, and arrived in London very ill. After a crude cupping operation in a poorhouse hospital that left the scars found by Dr Wilkinson, she had worked as a nursemaid for a family in Clapham, telling the children wonderful stories. She had become fascinated by Hebrew prayers and by the Jewish family next door, and was sacked for attending a Jewish wedding without her employers' permission. Thereafter she succeeded in getting herself admitted to a Magdalen hospital, a home for fallen women, having admired the uniform brown dresses and straw hats of the inmates; when her innocence was discovered, she was expelled. She drifted north across the river to jobs in Smithfield and Islington, and may, as she claimed, have travelled to France: she certainly spoke a smattering of French. She became pregnant, and hired a cab from the Bay Tree in Tottenham Court Road, where she was working, to a secret address where the child was born. After a short time in the workhouse, she took it to the foundling hospital, claiming first that the father was an Exeter bricklayer named John Edward Baker, and then a Frenchman that she had met in a bookshop. The child died, and she again took to the road, travelling with Gypsies, whose language and rituals are recognizable in Princess Caraboo's performance at Knole. Her appearance at Almondsbury followed a period of begging in Bristol. Seeing the success of Breton girls in their traditional head-dresses, she made herself a turban and pretended to be French. Taken to the French consul, she claimed to be Spanish. Invited to meet a Spanish cook, she had been reduced to talking what she called her 'lingo'.

After Caraboo's exposure, Mrs Worrall paid Mary Willcocks's passage to America under the supervision of two Moravian sisters. She arrived in Philadelphia to find herself famous, and was persuaded by a showman called Sanders to appear at the Washington Hall as 'Princess Carraboo', dancing and speaking her language. The show was not a success, and in her last letter to Mrs Worrall, written in November 1817, she was in New York, complaining of the horrors of celebrity. She appears to have remained in Philadelphia until 1824, when she returned to London and exhibited herself in New Bond Street as Princess Caraboo, again without much success. She may then have visited the south of France and Spain, but was back in Bedminster, south of the river in Bristol, in 1828, where she was married. She used her cousin's name, Burgess, and described herself as a widow. Her husband, oddly enough, was called Richard Baker, and they had one daughter born the following year. For the next thirty years she supplied leeches to the Bristol Infirmary, respectable, genteel, and apparently embarrassed (as when children ran after her calling 'Caraboo!') by her earlier notoriety. She fell dead in Mill Street, Bedminster, on Christmas eve 1864, and was buried in Hebron Road burial-ground. Her daughter, Mary, carried on the business, living alone in Bedminster in a house full of cats until her death in a fire in February 1900. JOHN WELLS

Sources J. M. Gutch, *Caraboo: a narrative of a singular imposition* (1817) • J. Wells, *Caraboo: her true story* (1994) • Bristol Library, Collection of Newspapers • City Museum and Art Gallery, Bristol • Bristol Royal Infirmary archives • *N&Q*, 3rd ser. (1865) • private information (2004)

Likenesses E. Bird, portrait, 1817, City Museum and Art Gallery, Bristol • N. Branwhite, engraving, repro. in Gutch, *Caraboo* • N. Branwhite, pencil sketches, City Museum and Art Gallery, Bristol • T. Lawrence, pencil drawing; lost since 1925

Baker, Matthew (1529/30–1613), shipwright, was the son of James Baker [*see below*], shipwright to Henry VIII. In 1550 Baker sailed to the Levant in the bark *Aucher* commanded by Roger Bodenham. Though only a young man, his was an inquisitive role during the voyage, and he acquired valuable knowledge of Venetian boat-building techniques. Following his return to England he appears to have continued to work with his father. He received letters patent as master shipwright in the royal dockyards in August 1572, with an allowance of 1s. per day. Though retained as one of the queen's officers, charged with the maintenance of the fabric of her ships, Baker was free to undertake private commissions. In 1576 he and his fellow shipwright James Addye built the bark *Gabriel*, of 25–30 tons, for the adventurers who financed Martin Frobisher's three expeditions to Baffin Island. The *Gabriel*, Frobisher's flagship in the first (1576) expedition, was the only vessel utilized in the enterprise to complete all three transatlantic passages. Baker was also the builder of the *Judith*, purchased from William Borough by the Frobisher adventurers, which sailed in the latter two voyages.

Upon the occasion of John Hawkins's more famous 'first bargain' of October 1579 Baker and the shipwright Peter Pett also entered into an agreement with the queen to ground and grave the same twenty-five royal ships that Hawkins was to furnish, and to repair their faulty spars and masts. Their recompense under the agreement was £1000 per year, from which they would meet the costs of materials and their storage. The history and aftermath of this contract illustrate perfectly the backstabbing and betrayal endemic in the Elizabethan naval establishment. Disagreements regarding the demarcation of responsibilities under the respective contracts of treasurer and shipwrights led to accusations of dishonesty against Hawkins by Baker and Pett. Though there was probably some justice to their charges, a commission established to investigate this and other complaints resulted in the cancellation of the bargains of 1579, and the conclusion of a new one—the 'second bargain'—in 1585 with Hawkins alone. Baker and Pett subsequently drew up a critical report on Hawkins's performance of this; in the meantime, following a brief reconciliation between Hawkins and Pett, the former had criticized Baker in turn to Lord Burghley: 'Peter Pett and I have found fault with the idle expense in those quarters of Mathew Bakers, whereof at large I can inform your lordship, he hath laboured with the rest of that idle company to return to their old vomit' (PRO, SP 12/178, 12; Williamson, 358). Baker's personal antipathy towards Hawkins was buttressed by that of his long-time ally Sir William Winter, surveyor of the ships and master of the ordnance, who himself had been stabbed by Hawkins's report of 1578 on the state of the ships. William Borough, clerk of the ships from 1580, also appears to have been an ally, praising Baker's honesty in an otherwise wounding report upon the cost to the queen of the contracts of 1579.

When internecine feuding did not obstruct the work of the shipyards, Baker was far more than an adept marine architect. He was the first English shipwright to replace the old geometrical foundation of boat measurement with mathematical techniques, and his calculation, using a ship's dimensions to establish her burden and deadweight tonnage, became a standard for almost half a century following its statement in 1582. In 1627 it was referred to as 'Mr Baker's Old Way' (PRO, SP 12/152, 19; Oppenheim, 132, 266). He was also the architect of the *Galleon Oughtred* (later *Galleon Leicester*), Edward Fenton's flagship in the ill-starred Moluccas voyage of 1582. It has been suggested that the *Galleon* may be notable for being the first English vessel to be constructed entirely from blueprints. Baker appears also to have had much responsibility for the gradual replacement of the older, 'high-charged' style of English galleon with a shallower, race-built design (Sir John Hawkins's much credited role in this achievement was largely an administrative one). In the early 1570s he was the architect of the queen's ships *Dreadnought* and *Foresight*, two of the first of this new breed, and he experimented further with his designs in subsequent commissions. Though the precise extent of his innovations and their influence upon his contemporaries cannot be determined, he himself accused at least one man—the author William Bourne—of poaching his work. During the Armada campaign, in addition to his habitual duties in making ready the queen's ships, Baker helped to design and construct land fortifications hurriedly raised at Gravesend and Tilbury.

Baker never retired, though in later years he was in receipt of a pension of £40 per year in addition to his master shipwright's perquisites. He died on 31 August 1613, aged eighty-three, still supervising repairs in the dockyards—in this case to the ship *Merhonour*, one of his own designs of 1590. By the time of his death, and in no small part as a result of his efforts, the master shipwright's role and responsibilities had become some of the most important in the embryonic naval establishment.

Baker is regarded as the author of the first and largest section of a collection of handwritten papers, later catalogued as 'Fragments of ancient English shipwrightry' by Samuel Pepys (Cambridge, Magdalene College, Pepys Library, MS 2820). This is a document of huge significance: a set of schematics of ships and related material, containing the earliest technical drawings of English vessels, with formulae—many of them of Baker's own devising—for laying out their dimensions and proportions. One non-technical image therein, of the master shipwright and his assistant at work in their drawing office, may be a self-portrait.

Though of a somewhat adversarial nature (a common characteristic within his jealous profession) Baker was probably the most gifted English shipwright of his age. His former apprentice Phineas Pett, who had good reason to resent him, wrote in 1603: 'your ever memorable works I set before me as a notable precedent and pattern to direct me in any work that I do' (Pepys Library, MS 2878, p. 353). In his *Seaman's Secrets* of 1607 the navigator John Davis recommended him 'for his skill and surpassing grounded knowledge for the building of Ships advantageable to all purpose, [he] hath not in any nation his equall' (Oppenheim, 152). William Borough regarded his skills as superior to those of Richard Chapman—with Peter (and, later, Phineas) Pett, the other member of the triumvirate of famous Elizabethan shipbuilders.

Of Matthew's father, **James Baker** (*fl.* 1538–1547), less is known. Extant records do not provide the names of those who built the ships of Henry VIII's navy, though Baker is thought to have been responsible, among other commissions, for the ship *Bull*, built in 1546 and rebuilt by his son in 1570. He was the first shipwright of the period known to have received a retainer—of 4*d*. per day (1538), later raised to 8*d*. (1544)—to maintain the king's ships. He was reported as being 'skilful in ships' in an order in council of 21 August 1545 which dispatched him to Portsmouth to carry out emergency repairs upon a royal ship there (*APC*, 1.233). He was examined in the following year for possessing proscribed protestant texts, but the king sent word to his examiners: 'you shall find him a very simple man, and therefore wold that without putting him in any great fear you should search of him as much as you may' (Oppenheim, 73–4). He seems to have been absolved of these charges; in 1547 he was given a licence to export 200 cloths. His date of death is not known, but the appointment of his son as master shipwright in 1572 may have been made to fill that particular vacancy in the naval establishment.

JAMES MCDERMOTT

Sources M. Oppenheim, *A history of the administration of the Royal Navy* (1896) • 'Fragments of ancient English shipwrightry', Magd. Cam., Pepys Library, Pepys MS 2820 • Magd. Cam., Pepys Library, Pepys MS 2878 • J. A. Williamson, *Sir John Hawkins: the time and the man* (1927) • R. Barker, 'Fragments from the Pepysian Library', *Revista da Universidade de Coimbra*, 32 (1986), 161–78 • D. M. Loades, *The Tudor navy* (1992) • J. S. Corbett, ed., *Papers relating to the navy during the Spanish war, 1585–1587*, Navy RS, 11 (1898) • N. A. M. Rodger, *The safeguard of the sea: a naval history of Britain*, 1: 660–1649 (1997) • BL, Lansdowne MS 43/113 • financial accounts relating to Martin Frobisher's northwest voyages, PRO, EKR E164/35 • PRO, SP12/178, 12 • T. Glasgow, 'The shape of the ships that defeated the Spanish Armada', *Mariner's Mirror*, 50 (1964), 177–88 • R. Hakluyt, *The principal navigations, voyages, traffiques and discoveries of the English nation*, 5, Hakluyt Society, extra ser., 5 (1904), 5 • C. S. L. Davies, 'The administration of the Royal Navy under Henry VIII: the origins of the navy board', *EngHR*, 80 (1965), 268–86 • *The voyages and works of John Davis*, ed. A. H. Markham, Hakluyt Society, 59 (1880) • S. Bellabarba, 'The ancient methods of designing hulls', *Mariner's Mirror*, 79 (1993), 274–92 • *APC*, 1542–7 • *LP Henry VIII*, vol. 21

Likenesses M. Baker?, self-portrait?, Magd. Cam., Pepys Library, Pepys MS 2820

Baker, Pacificus (1695–1774), Franciscan friar, was brought up as a protestant, but later converted. He studied at Douai in the Southern Netherlands, and was there professed a Franciscan. After ordination he was sent to the English mission and was attached to the Sardinian chapel in Lincoln's Inn Fields. Baker is known to have attended the execution of Simon, Lord Lovat, on 9 April 1747. During his lifetime he discharged with credit the offices of procurator and definitor of his order, and was twice elected provincial of the English province, first in 1761 and second in 1770.

An 'eminent spiritualist' (Oliver, 543), with the reputation of being a good preacher, Baker was described as 'my particular acquaintance' by the Revd William Cole, as well as 'a very honest and worthy man' (Gillow, *Lit. biog. hist.*, 1.117). He was the author of numerous devotional works including *The Devout Christian's Companion for Holy Days* (1757), as well as guides to the mass (1768), and a Lenten guide for Holy Week (1769). Other works included *The Christian Advent* (1782), and a book about keeping Sundays holy, as well as essays on the Cord of St Francis and the Lord's prayer. According to one authority, these works were without much originality and were 'remarkable for unction, solidity, and moderation; but we wish the style was less diffuse and redundant of words' (Oliver, 543).

Baker died in London on 16 March 1774.

THOMPSON COOPER, *rev.* ROBERT BROWN

Sources G. Oliver, *Collections illustrating the history of the Catholic religion in the counties of Cornwall, Devon, Dorset, Somerset, Wilts, and Gloucester* (1857) • Gillow, *Lit. biog. hist.* • F. Blom and others, *English Catholic books, 1701–1800: a bibliography* (1996)

Likenesses W. Holl, engraving, repro. in *Laity's Directory* (1836)

Baker, Philip (1522/3–1590?), college head, was born in Barnstaple, Devon, of a gentry family, and educated at Eton College. Admitted to King's College, Cambridge, in 1540, aged seventeen, he was a fellow in 1543–56, graduated BA in 1544–5, MA in 1548, BTh in 1554, and DTh in 1562. He was a proctor of the university in 1549–50, was appointed provost of King's College by Elizabeth I in 1558, and was vice-chancellor in 1561–2. He was ordained deacon in 1553 and was appointed as rector of Ringwood, Hampshire (1554), rector of St Andrew by the Wardrobe, London (1559–62), prebendary of Stretton, Salisbury (1559), prebendary of Putston Minor, Hereford (1560), rector of Elsworth, Cambridgeshire (1559–70), and possibly rector of Winwick, Lancashire. In 1564 Queen Elizabeth visited Cambridge and stayed in the provost's lodge for five days: Baker was one of those who made a formal speech in her presence.

The following year, 1565, eleven fellows of King's complained that Baker favoured 'papists' and administered the affairs of the college badly. His opinions must have been widely known, as he had been deprived of the living of St Andrew by the Wardrobe in 1562 for his refusal to subscribe to a confession of faith. The bishop of Lincoln made a visitation in response to the complaints of the fellows and Baker was required to suppress 'popish' ceremonies and ornaments in the college. In 1567 the college granted him leave of absence for two years. In 1569 a Mr Colpots made a further protest to the chancellor, William Cecil, on behalf of the college; Baker 'still kept a great heap of Popish pelf … he never preached, neither at home, nor abroad, weltring in idleness, and wholly serving Mammon … *Pistori quam Pastori similior*: i.e. more like a baker than a shepherd' (Strype, 144). Baker does indeed seem to have been absent from the college a great deal during his period in office. Detailed charges were also made that he had appropriated college funds.

As a result of these accusations a new visitation was commissioned, led by the bishop of Ely; Baker did not wait to face it but fled abroad. In 1570 he was formally deprived of the provostship and his other preferments. Although one of the charges levelled against him had been that he dishonestly used college resources, Fuller went out of his way to praise the way in which Baker on his departure meticulously returned all college property. He may have returned to England: although Willis states that 'he retired to Louvain, and died there beyond the seas' (Willis,

2.600), two somewhat contradictory pieces of evidence indicate otherwise. Sterry states that it was Philip Baker, the former provost, who made a will in 1585, died in London in 1590, and was buried in St Margaret Moyses on 12 August; the will was certainly made by a former Catholic priest who left a few small bequests, but it makes no reference to Cambridge. However, in Cambridge University Library there is a four-volume collection of commentaries on St Thomas Aquinas by Gregory of Valentia (1549–1603), a Jesuit theologian, in an edition printed in Venice between 1598 and 1601; an inscription records that it was a gift to the university from Philip Baker, formerly provost of King's College. Baker's arms were argent on a saltire engrailed sable, five escallops of the field on a chief of the second a lion passant of the first.

MARGARET LUCILLE KEKEWICH

Sources J. Strype, *The history of the life and acts of … Edmund Grindal* (1710) • Venn, *Alum. Cant.* • T. Fuller, *The history of the University of Cambridge from the conquest to the year 1634*, ed. M. Prickett and T. Wright (1840) • B. Willis, *A survey of the cathedrals*, 3 vols. (1742), vol. 2 • W. Sterry, ed., *The Eton College register, 1441–1698* (1943) • E. B. G., 'Dr Philip Baker', *N&Q*, 199 (1954), 224 • J. C. Smith, 'Philip Baker, provost of King's College', *N&Q*, 151 (1926), 314 • H. R. P. Baker, 'Philip Baker, provost of King's College, 1558–70', *N&Q*, 151 (1926), 353–4 • A. C. F. Beales, *Education under penalty* (1963), 31 • M. H. Curtis, *Oxford and Cambridge in transition, 1558–1642* (1959), 286 n. J • Cooper, *Ath. Cantab.*, vol. 2 • W. B. Bannerman, ed., *The registers of St Mildred, Bread Street, and of St Margaret Moses, Friday Street, London*, Harleian Society, register section, 42 (1912), 70 • will, PRO, PROB 11/76, sig. 57 • 'Liber protocoll: Collegii Regalis, 1500–78', King's Cam., 89, 110 • A. Allen, 'Skeleton Collegii Regalis Cantab.', King's Cam., vol. 2

Baker, Philip John Noel-, Baron Noel-Baker (1889–1982), politician and Nobel prizewinner, was born at Woodstock, Brondesbury Park, London, on 1 November 1889, the sixth and penultimate child of (Joseph) Allen Baker (1852–1918) and his wife, Elizabeth Balmer Moscrip. His father had moved to Britain from New Brunswick, Canada, in 1876; his mother was from the Scottish borders. Allen Baker developed a successful engineering business and became a Progressive member of the London county council. From 1905 until his death in 1918 he was Liberal MP for East Finsbury and, as a member of the Society of Friends, a prominent peace campaigner.

Philip Baker had a Quaker education at Bootham School, York, followed by Haverford College in Pennsylvania, USA. He entered King's College, Cambridge, in 1908 and took a second in part one of the history tripos (1910) and a first in the second part of the economics tripos (1912). He was president of the Cambridge Union in 1912 and of the university athletic club (1910–12). During his glittering undergraduate career he was selected for the 1500 metres at the 1912 Stockholm Olympics. A finalist at his first Olympics, eight years later at Antwerp he came second to another Briton, Albert Hill, in the same event. After graduating, he held a senior Whewell scholarship in international law at Cambridge (1912) and was elected a fellow of King's College in 1915.

Baker's political ideas were influenced heavily by his father; in 1911, during a visit to the United States, he was attracted by the progressivism of Theodore Roosevelt. His

Philip John Noel-Baker, Baron Noel-Baker (1889–1982), by Howard Coster, 1946

political sentiments were evident in his appointment as vice-principal of Ruskin College, Oxford, in 1914. During the First World War he served with the Friends' Ambulance Unit in France and in Italy. He was awarded the Mons star and silver medal for valour (1917) and the *croce di guerra* (1918). He also met Irene Noel (*b*. 1879/80), a friend of Virginia Woolf, and the daughter of Francis Edward Noel, the British owner of a Greek estate, Achmetaga. She was working as a nurse; they were married on 12 June 1915. On his marriage he adopted the additional surname Noel (he began to hyphenate his surname in the early 1940s).

Noel Baker's political background and wartime experiences produced a strong commitment to international co-operation and disarmament. He was a member of the British delegation to the Paris peace conference and then worked with the League of Nations secretariat until 1922. From 1923 to 1924 he was secretary to the British delegation to the League of Nations, working closely with Edgar Cecil. Subsequently he was private secretary to Charles Alfred Cripps, the minister responsible for League of Nations affairs in the Labour government of 1924. In that year's general election Noel Baker stood unsuccessfully as Labour candidate for Birmingham Handsworth, a safe Conservative seat. From 1924 until 1929 he was Cassel professor of international relations at the University of London, an appointment secured without previous academic experience. His specialist credentials were confirmed in 1926 with the publication of *Disarmament*. However, he was increasingly committed to a political career and in May 1929 became the Labour MP for Coventry. Like many liberal internationalists he saw the Labour Party as the best available instrument for his ideals.

Arthur Henderson, the foreign secretary in the Labour government of 1929, appointed Noel Baker his parliamentary private secretary. Thus the newly elected MP had some involvement in one of the increasingly beleaguered government's few successful fields. On economic issues he could be critical of the administration and felt some sympathy for the arguments developed by Sir Oswald Mosley in spring 1930. Essentially, however, he was a party loyalist and his rapport with Henderson was close. Following the loss of his Coventry seat at the 1931 election, Noel Baker went to Geneva as Henderson's principal assistant, during the latter's presidency of the disarmament conference of 1932–3. Noel Baker was optimistic about the prospects for agreement, and the failure of the conference marked the first of a series of disappointments that culminated in the outbreak of the Second World War. As the international situation deteriorated he continued to campaign for collective security and armaments reduction. His book *The Private Manufacture of Armaments* (1936) was a critical analysis of the private arms trade.

Noel Baker unsuccessfully contested Coventry in the 1935 election but was victorious in a by-election at Derby in July 1936. He remained an MP for the town (his seat became Derby South at the 1950 election) until he retired from the House of Commons in 1970. During the late 1930s he stood in the second tier of Labour parliamentarians. He had an acknowledged expertise but his political experience was limited. Following the reform of the national executive committee in 1937, he was elected to that body's constituency section. He clearly had a significant standing among party activists. His reputation among Labour MPs secured his election to the parliamentary committee.

Yet Noel-Baker's talents did not guarantee him easy access to office in the Churchill coalition. Attlee was unsympathetic to his claims—'too unbalanced in his judgements' (*War Diary of Hugh Dalton*, 12–13, 18 May 1940). Eventually in February 1942 he was appointed joint parliamentary secretary at the Ministry of War Transport, where he performed competently until the termination of the coalition. Within the Labour Party he used his position on the national executive committee to criticize proposals for the severe post-war treatment of Germany.

Labour's electoral victory in 1945 brought Noel-Baker back to the Foreign Office as minister of state under Ernest Bevin. There was no repeat of the rapport with Henderson. Noel-Baker would not have been Bevin's choice, and the foreign secretary was relieved when Noel-Baker was replaced in October 1946. The differences were stylistic and not substantive. Noel-Baker's liberalism and support for collective security combined readily to produce a critical view of Soviet foreign policy. Thus early in 1940 he had gone to Finland as a member of a labour mission to investigate the Soviet–Finnish conflict, and had returned a strong supporter of the Finns (Dalton, *Fateful Years*, 293). On his return to the Foreign Office he was comfortable with Bevin's foreign policy and gave conventional justifications for restoring European colonialism in south-east Asia (Saville, 197–8).

Noel-Baker left the Foreign Office for the Air Ministry and then in 1947 joined the cabinet as secretary of state for the Commonwealth. The image of him as the academic in politics proved damaging: 'You'll have to try to keep Noel-Baker practical', was Herbert Morrison's advice to his junior minister (*Gordon Walker: Political Diaries*, 168, 6 Oct 1947). Noel-Baker's relationship with his permanent under-secretary Percivale Liesching was poor, and Attlee felt that he was a lightweight in cabinet. Following the 1950 election he was shifted to the Ministry of Fuel and Power and dropped from the cabinet. Faced with the threat of coal and power shortages, his last ministerial post was not a happy one. Hugh Gaitskell, a previous incumbent, felt that he should be replaced, but 'he is a very nice man and deserves better things' (*Diary of Hugh Gaitskell*, 226, 10 Jan 1951).

Noel-Baker's stock also declined in the wider party. He chaired the Labour Party conference in 1947, but was voted off the national executive the following year in favour of a young back-bencher, Michael Foot. Back in opposition from 1951 he remained on the parliamentary committee until November 1959. He opposed the Bevanite left and favoured withdrawing the whip from Bevan in 1955. Strongly multilateralist on disarmament, he opposed proposals that the Labour Party should shift to a unilateralist policy on nuclear weapons. In his final term in the Commons he opposed the Wilson government's policy towards Biafra. Characteristically, his most significant achievement in these later years lay outside party politics. The publication of his book *The Arms Race: a Programme for World Disarmament* in 1958 was the prelude to the award of the Nobel peace prize the following year. The proceeds were used in support of the disarmament cause. Made a life peer in July 1977, he was active into the 1980s both on disarmament and on international sports bodies, including the International Council for Sport and Physical Recreation, which he founded.

Noel-Baker's marriage produced a son, Francis Edward (*b.* 1920), who became a Labour MP (1945–50; 1955–68), but his relationship with Irene was not a success. She spent much time in Greece; Philip was absorbed in his campaigns. He began a relationship with Megan Lloyd *George (1902–1966), probably in 1936. This lasted for twenty years, with a hiatus during and after the war. It ended paradoxically with the death of Irene Noel-Baker. For those few who knew of this complex and often painful situation it was hard to reconcile the Philip Noel-Baker revealed here with the public figure.

Philip Noel-Baker was charming, talented, and intellectually serious. Athletic and convivial, he nevertheless bore a puritan legacy. 'Phil Baker shd do half what he does, and should drink wine' was Virginia Woolf's verdict (*Diary of Virginia Woolf*, 34, 17 Nov 1936). Several politicians felt that his positive qualities were subverted by a lack of judgement; this sentiment undoubtedly limited his ministerial opportunities. Yet the paradox was that his espousal of principle was typically accompanied by conventional positions on immediate issues. He died at his home, 16 South Eaton Place, Westminster, London, on 8 October 1982. DAVID HOWELL

Sources D. J. Whittaker, *Fighter for peace: Philip Noel-Baker, 1889–1982* (1989) • M. Jones, *A radical life: the biography of Megan Lloyd George, 1902–1966* (1991) • *The political diary of Hugh Dalton, 1918–1940, 1945–1960*, ed. B. Pimlott (1986) • *The Second World War diary of Hugh Dalton, 1940–1945*, ed. B. Pimlott (1986) • H. Dalton, *The fateful years: memoirs, 1931–1945* (1957) • H. Dalton, *High tide and after: memoirs, 1945–1960* (1962) • *The diary of Hugh Gaitskell, 1945–1956*, ed. P. M. Williams (1983) • *Patrick Gordon Walker: political diaries, 1932–1971*, ed. R. Pearce (1991) • *The diary of Virginia Woolf*, ed. A. O. Bell and A. McNeillie, 5 (1984) • S. Brooke, *Labour's war: the labour party during the Second World War* (1992) • A. Glees, *Exile politics during the Second World War: the German social democrats in Britain* (1982) • *Labour party conference report* (1947) • E. B. Baker and P. J. Noel Baker, *J. Allen Baker: a memoir* (1927) • J. Saville, *The politics of continuity: British foreign policy and the labour government, 1945–46* (1993) • *DNB* • *The Labour who's who* (1927) • *WW* • d. cert. • J. J. Withers, *A register of admissions to King's College, Cambridge, 1797–1925* (1929) • b. cert. • m. cert.

Archives Bodl. RH, corresp. relating to colonial questions • CAC Cam., corresp. and papers • PRO, papers relating to the League of Nations, FO 800/249 | BL, corresp. with Lord Cecil, Add. MSS 51106–51109 • BLPES, Dalton MSS • Bodl. Oxf., corresp. with C. Attlee; corresp. with Lord Monckton; corresp. with G. Murray • CAC Cam., corresp. with A. V. Hill • Georgetown University, Washington, DC, letters to B. Jackson • HLRO, letters to D. Lloyd George • JRL, letters to the *Manchester Guardian* • King's Lond., Liddell Hart C., corresp. with B. H. Liddell Hart • McMaster University, Hamilton, Ontario, corresp. with B. Russell • NAM, corresp. with Sir R. Bucher • NL Wales, letters to M. Lloyd George • People's History Museum, Manchester, labour party national executive committee minutes • St Ant. Oxf., Middle East Centre, corresp. with C. Edmonds • U. Sussex, corresp. with L. Woolf

Likenesses H. Coster, photographs, 1930–46, NPG [*see illus.*] • W. Stoneman, photograph, 1947, NPG • W. Bird, photograph, 1963, NPG

Wealth at death under £25,000: probate, 29 Oct 1982, *CGPLA Eng. & Wales*

Baker, Sir Richard (*c.*1568–1645), religious writer and historian, was born at Sissinghurst, Kent, the elder son of John Baker (*b.* in or before 1531, *d.* 1604x6), MP in 1554–5 and lawyer, and Catherine, daughter of Reginald Scott, of Scots Hall, Ashford, Kent. His father was the younger son of Sir John *Baker (*c.*1489–1558), of Sissinghurst, by his second marriage, to Elizabeth (*d.* in or before 1558), daughter of Thomas Dingley of Stanford Dingley, Berkshire, and Middle Aston, Oxfordshire. Sir Richard Baker has to be distinguished from his uncle Richard (*b.* in or before 1530, *d.* 1594), also a knight, who was Sir John's elder son and heir. The historian's father, John Baker, had moved to London, where he was a member of the Inner Temple, and in Michaelmas term 1584 Richard Baker, described as a gentleman, of Kent, matriculated at Oxford from Hart Hall. Contemporaries there included John Donne, and Baker shared a room with Henry Wotton, the diplomat, who was then a commoner of New College. Like Donne, Baker left the hall without graduating, and after studying law in London he travelled on the continent, acquiring languages and journeying as far east as Poland; after his return he was granted the degree of MA by decree, in 1594.

Baker sat in the Commons as member for Arundel in 1593 and East Grinstead in 1597, probably as a nominee of Thomas, Lord Buckhurst, his uncle by marriage. He served and reported on a Commons committee on the weaving trade in 1597. In 1603, when he was knighted by James I at Theobalds, he was living in Highgate in north London. He was a JP for Middlesex, and he also had lands in Essex, Gloucestershire, Kent, and Oxfordshire, where he had inherited the manor of Middle Aston. He served as high sheriff of Oxfordshire in 1620–21. Shortly afterwards he married Margaret (*b.* *c.*1600), daughter of Sir George Mainwaring of Ightfield, Shropshire. They had at least five children—two sons and three daughters survived them—but the alliance proved even more ill-starred than John Aubrey's unlucky contract with Joan Sumner, another paradigm of the age. To the entire ruin of his fortune, Baker gave security for his father-in-law's debts. By 1625 he was a crown debtor, and his Oxfordshire estate was impounded. Within ten years his other lands had followed, and he was reduced to living in the Fleet prison in London for the rest of his life.

With his lands and offices gone, Baker turned, as his friend Thomas Fuller observed, to the consolations of scholarship. He seems to have kept his books, or some of them, with him in the Fleet, and he manifestly had access to printers. His first published work was an essay in popular moralism: *Cato variegatus, or, Catoes Morall Distichs, Translated and Paraphrased with Variations of Expressing in English Verse*, which appeared in 1636. He followed it with *Meditations on the Lord's Prayer* in 1637, and a translation of the letters of J.-L. Guez de Balzac (1597–1654) in 1638. The renderings and variations of Cato's themes were only moderately inspired, but Baker's religious writings struck a popular response. He produced a series of meditations on the penitential psalms, beginning with *Meditations and Disquisitions on the Seven Psalmes of David*, published in 1639 and dedicated to Mary, countess of Dorset, with an additional study of Psalms 102, 130, and 143 dedicated to Henry Montagu, earl of Manchester. A further study of Psalm 23 followed in 1640, and *An Apologie for Laymen's Writing in Divinity, with a Short Meditation upon the Fall of Lucifer* in 1641. The *Apologie* was dedicated to his cousin Sir John Baker of Sissinghurst (*d.* 1661), and *Motives for Prayer upon the Seaven Dayes of the Weeke* (1642), a meditative work on the creation of the world, to Sir John's wife, Elizabeth. Sir John Baker's adherence to the king in the early years of the civil war began the final decline in the family's fortunes.

Richard Baker also wrote a rebuttal of Prynne's *Histrio-Mastix* which remained in manuscript until 1662, when it was published posthumously under the title *Theatrum redivivum, or, The Theatre Vindicated*. It was characterized by much common sense, and contained notices of Alleyn, Burbage, and Tarlton. It was reprinted in 1670 as *Theatrum triumphans*. The meditations on the psalms, some of which were reprinted at Leipzig in 1688, were collected and edited by Alexander Balloch Grosart in 1882.

While his pious and occasional works were appearing in print, Baker was also reflecting on history. He translated a study of Tacitus by Vergilio, marchese di Malvezzi, probably on a commission from Richard and Thomas Whittaker, printers and booksellers, who published it as *Discourses upon Cornelius Tacitus* in 1642. By that time Baker had almost completed his principal work, *A Chronicle of the Kings of England from the Time of the Romans' Government unto the Death of King James*, which was published in 1643. It was dedicated to Charles, prince of Wales, and contained a commendatory letter from Sir Henry Wotton. In his preface Baker refers to the distinction between histories, which were literary exercises reflecting upon matters of state, and chronicles, which could touch on 'meaner accidents'—the prosaic detail of everyday life. He made a robust defence of his labours and listed more than ninety authors and texts which he had consulted. His narrative is lively, often but not excessively anecdotal, and he took notice of what would later be called literary, social, and even economic affairs.

The *Chronicle* was reprinted posthumously with some revisions in 1653, and a third edition was published in 1660 with a continuation to the end of 1658 by Edward Phillips, John Milton's nephew. Five more editions, with extended continuations, appeared from 1665 to 1684, when an abridgement was also published. The ninth edition was printed in 1696. The later editors were anonymous, though the account of Charles II's restoration, which first appeared in 1665, was attributed to General Monck's brother-in-law, Sir Thomas Clarges. The last edition of the work, extended to the end of the reign of George I, appeared in 1730 and was reprinted in 1733.

Baker's *Chronicle* was translated into Dutch as early as 1649, and republished in Amsterdam in 1681. There was evidently a steady demand for it in England, though it was sharply criticized by Thomas Blount, in *Animadversions upon Sir Richard Baker's Chronicle and its Continuation* (1672). Blount was learned, and given to publishing animadversions. Some of his strictures were merely captious, but Baker's frankly engaging narrative was perhaps already at odds with the emergent historical scholarship evident in the works of Rymer and Madox. Thomas Hearne commented in 1721 that the *Chronicle* was a slight work but that it had become rare and expensive; he lived to see its tenth edition nine years later. Daines Barrington subsequently observed that Addison had done Baker a disservice by noting that Sir Roger de Coverley thought highly of the *Chronicle* and kept it close to hand. No doubt it had an old-fashioned air before the middle of the eighteenth century, but even so James Boswell turned to it in 1785 for the epigraph of his *Journal of a Tour to the Hebrides*.

Both the *Chronicle* and its critics have to be seen in a historical context. Baker intended his narrative to be readable, and so it proved. It was vigorous enough to survive successive extensions, and for three-quarters of a century it was effectively unrivalled on its own ground. More specialized studies aside, a new era began only in 1725, with Nicholas Tindal's translation of Rapin's *History*; it continued from 1752 onwards with Hume's work. In some respects, Baker was closer to his older sources than to the world of his readers. On the one hand he had read law in Elizabeth's London and had spoken in her parliaments. On the other he cites without elaboration a story of Froissart about a knight who knew instantaneously of events occurring at a great distance. He was thoroughly a man of his own time, who wrote in unpromising circumstances, keeping his good humour and wide sympathies, and his work proved surprisingly durable.

Baker died in the Fleet on 18 February 1645 and was buried in St Bride's Church. His daughters married London tradesmen, one of whom is said to have burned an autograph manuscript of Baker's life, a loss which was regretted by Isaac D'Israeli. Baker's printed books, or a substantial number of them, were acquired by Archbishop John Williams, who gave them to the chapter library of Westminster Abbey as one of his many benefactions there.

G. H. MARTIN

Sources *DNB* • Wood, *Ath. Oxon.*, new edn, vols. 2–4 • Foster, *Alum. Oxon.* • J. E. Mousley, 'Baker, Richard', HoP, *Commons, 1558–1603* • N. Nicolson, *Sissinghurst Castle: an illustrated history* (1967) • J. H. Lloyd, *History of Highgate* (1888) • Fuller, *Worthies* (1811) • L. E. Tanner, *Westminster Abbey … the library and muniment room* (1933) • *STC, 1475–1640* • Wing, *STC*

Likenesses W. Marshall, line engraving, repro. in R. Baker, *A chronicle of the kings of England*, 2nd edn (1653)

Baker, Richard (*bap.* **1741**, *d.* **1818**), writer on theology, was baptized on 24 February 1741 in Great Yarmouth, son and heir of Richard Baker (1702–1774), mayor of that town in 1754 and 1769, and collector of the customs, and his wife, Sarah Laws (*d.* 1772). He matriculated on 7 March 1758 at Pembroke College, Cambridge, where he was a fellow from 1763 and held various college offices. He took the degrees of BA as seventh senior optime in 1762, MA in 1765, and DD in 1788. He was the friend of Thomas Gray, the poet, at Pembroke, one of three college fellows who witnessed the signing of his will on 2 July 1770. In 1797 he presented the college chapel with a painting formerly belonging to Sir Joshua Reynolds, *The Entombment* after Barocci.

After his marriage to Elizabeth Harrison (1747/8–1814) in 1772, Baker, who had been ordained priest in the London diocese on 19 February 1769, moved out of college to become rector of Great Poringland, Norfolk, in 1772, on the presentation of the bishop of Norwich, a post he held until 1779. He was also instituted on 6 April 1772 to the lucrative Pembroke living of Cawston, in the same county, where he remained incumbent until his death. He was a diligent parish priest, took pains 'with a neglected & abandoned people', and had a Sunday school with 100 children by the 1790s (R. Baker to W. W. Bulwer, 23 June 1790, Norfolk RO, BUL 4/118/9). His seniority in the deanery enabled him on occasion to act on behalf of the archdeacon of Norfolk, as during the visitations of 1784 and 1790. His eldest son, Richard, also took holy orders. In 1799 Parson Woodforde was relieved not to appoint this young man his curate at Weston Longueville, 'as of late I heard that Dr. Baker and whole Family are very Violent Democrats indeed' (*Diary*, 5.195, 26 May 1799). Baker's second son, John Harrison Baker, major of the 34th regiment, was killed at the battle of Toulouse on 11 April 1814, aged thirty-two.

Baker's main work was *The Harmony, or Agreement, of the Four Evangelists, in their Several Relations of the Life and Death of Jesus the Christ* (4 pts, 1783–7), in which he juxtaposed extracts from the gospels with the aim of demonstrating their essential consistency. He aimed at a cheap, plain production, 'To make the Scriptures more level to every capacity, and to put such an explanation within reach of the Poor' (preface). He also published a sermon on John 7: 17, *How the Knowledge of Salvation is Attainable*, dated 1782. In 1811 he completed his output with *The Psalms of David Evangelized*, a characteristic attempt on his part to make the Psalms immediately appealing to the ordinary churchgoer. His 'amiable and pious' (memorial inscription, Cawston church) wife died on 13 August 1814, in her sixty-seventh year, and was buried on 17 August in Cawston church. Baker himself died on 6 April 1818, and was buried in the chancel of the same church on 12 April.

NIGEL ASTON

Sources *GM*, 1st ser., 88/1 (1818), 646 • Venn, *Alum. Cant.* • C. J. Palmer, *The history of Great Yarmouth* (1856), 315, 317 • C. J. Palmer, *The perlustration of Great Yarmouth*, 2 (1874), 187 • *Correspondence of Thomas Gray*, ed. P. Toynbee and L. Whibley, 3 (1935), 1134 • D. Turner, *List of Norfolk benefices* (1847), 13, 34 • W. Rye, *An account of the church and parish of Cawston, in the county of Norfolk* (1898) • D. P. Mortlock, *All Saints, Poringland: a guide to the church* (1973) • *The diary of a country parson: the Reverend James Woodforde*, ed. J. Beresford, 2 (1926), 154, 186, 190; 3 (1927), 222; 4 (1929), 123–4, 300, 310; 5 (1931), 144–5, 180, 189 • *DNB* • *Transcript of Great Yarmouth baptism register, 1721–54* (1949) • parish register (burial), Cawston, Norfolk, 1813–53 • Pembroke Cam., archives

Archives BL, 'Graduati Cantabrigiensis', Add. MS 19209, fol. 36 • Pembroke Cam., archives | Norfolk RO, Bulwer of Heydon collection, corresp. with W. W. Bulwer, BUL 4/118, 606 x 6

Baker, Richard Edward St Barbe (1889–1982), conservationist, was born on 9 October 1889 at West End, near Southampton, the eldest of five children of John Richard St Barbe Baker, horticulturist, and his wife, Charlotte, *née* Purrott. His father grew trees for a living on his own land and from his earliest days Baker was surrounded by and dedicated to woods and trees. After early schooling locally, at the age of thirteen he was sent to Dean Close School, Cheltenham. Four years later, on discovering that his father was having to sell off land to pay for his education, Baker resolved to leave school and fulfil an early ambition of going to Canada. There, at Saskatoon, he became one of the early students of Saskatchewan University, where he read arts and sciences. In the three and a half years he spent in Canada he gained much experience of working in the forests and it was from this that he decided he should qualify as a forester. He also held deep religious beliefs and on returning to England in 1913 he went to Cambridge to study divinity. At the outbreak of the First World War he volunteered for service overseas and was commissioned in the Royal Horse and Field Artillery. Severely wounded three times in the course of his war service (and awarded the Military Cross), he was finally invalided out in April 1918. After a period of convalescence he returned to Cambridge, to Gonville and Caius College, and took a diploma in forestry. His first application to become assistant conservator of forests in Kenya was turned down on medical grounds as he was still recuperating from the injuries he had suffered, but the post was granted in November 1920 and a public career that was to lead to world renown began.

In Kenya, Baker saw at once the pressing need for widespread reafforestation to stem the erosion and desiccation of the land caused by unremitting felling of the forests. No funding was available for this, but with the collaboration of Chief Josiah Njonjo a team of volunteers—*Watu wa Miti* (Men of the Trees)—was formed, a dedicated group of fifty warriors being sworn in on 22 July 1922 at the first dance of the trees. Over the years millions of trees were planted. On his return to England in 1924 Baker founded the Men of the Trees Society (renamed the International Tree Foundation in 1992), the activities of which led within his lifetime to the planting of billions of trees throughout the world. Between 1924 and 1929 he was conservator of forests in Nigeria and from then until the Second World War he travelled throughout the world to establish tree planting and conservation programmes. Of special concern to him was the saving of the giant redwoods of California, and he returned there year after year to pursue this. A discussion with Franklin D. Roosevelt in 1932 resulted in the formation of the Civilian Conservation Camps Corps, which contributed massive labour to forest conservation over a nine-year period.

In the years following the war until the very end of his life Baker continued to travel the world, campaigning vigorously for the preservation and restoration of forests and the reclamation of desert areas (the Sahara being seen as a particular challenge), lecturing widely, participating in international conferences and symposia, and tirelessly spreading his expertise. His (ever modest) autobiographical writings gave a hint of the great range of his benevolent achievements over the course of a long career. He married first, on 23 January 1946, Doreen Whitworth Long (*b.* 1919/20), daughter of George Henry William Long, farmer, of Puncknowle, Dorset. They had a son and a daughter. The marriage was dissolved in 1953 and in 1959 Baker married Catriona Burnett of Mount Cook, New Zealand, and took up residence there. In 1971 he was made an honorary LLD of the University of Saskatchewan and he was appointed OBE in 1978. In June 1982, in his ninety-third year, he returned to Saskatoon, where, on 5 June, in celebration of World Environment day, he planted what proved to be his last tree. He died there peacefully four days later and following a Baha'i funeral service (a faith he had held since 1922) was buried in the Woodlawn cemetery in Saskatoon.

Although he made no claims to being a writer as such, in the period from 1940 to the late 1970s Baker published some twenty-five seminal books about trees and the challenges he had undertaken, many being illustrated with his own very accomplished photographs. He also wrote many specialist articles. St Barbe, as he was affectionately known to many, was a practical man of exceptional vitality, motivated by an unwavering belief in the need to reverse the destruction that had been wrought from the earliest times upon the forests of this planet. The combination of his ideals, backed by his religious convictions and blended with his agreeable personality, his ability to relate constructively to everyone he encountered, and his tireless energy, culminated in the vast contribution he made to pioneering the saving of the world's forests. He was always the first to declare that what had been achieved was the outcome of teamwork, but there can be no doubt that he was the indispensable catalyst.

RICHARD BURLEIGH

Sources R. St B. Baker, *My life my trees*, 2nd edn (1985) • R. St B. Baker, *I planted trees* (1944) • R. St B. Baker, *Green glory: the story of the forests of the world* (1948) • R. St B. Baker, *Dance of the trees: the adventures of a forester* (1956) • R. St B. Baker, *Among the trees*, 2 vols. (1935–41) • R. St B. Baker, *Trees: a book of the seasons*, 2nd edn (1948) • *The Times* (12 June 1982) • *WWW*, 1981–90 • m. cert. [Doreen Whitworth Long]

Likenesses H. Coster, photograph, *c*.1932, NPG • H. Coster, photograph, *c*.1940, repro. in Baker, *I planted trees*, frontispiece • E. Cardell, photograph, 1953, repro. in Baker, *Dance of the trees*, facing p. 48 • photograph, 1953 ('Reunion in Kikuyuland'), repro. in Baker, *My life my trees*, following p. 78 • R. Moody, wooden head, 1955, NPG

Baker, Robert (*fl. c*.1563), mariner and poet, is known only through his one published writing. Possibly a relative of the Bakers of Sissinghurst who had connections with the London overseas trading community, Robert Baker composed a poem about two English voyages to Guinea, undertaken in the early 1560s, on which he had served as a factor or commercial agent. The poem may have been published when licensed in 1568, but if so, no copy seems to be extant. It eventually appeared, perhaps not in its original entirety, in the first (1589) edition of Hakluyt's *Voiages* (Hakluyt, 130–42), but was omitted from the second, better-known edition, leading to its being for long overlooked in studies of the period. The poem, in 1384 lines as published, is thin on facts identifying the precise voyages, and certain details in the title and side-notes may have been added by Hakluyt. Nevertheless, it undoubtedly refers to two actual voyages, although these are semi-imaginatively related. It concentrates on adventures—or rather misadventures—while trading on the coast of Guinea, on the first voyage an affray with local Africans, on the second voyage the separation of a boat from the mother ship and a desperate journey along the coast, avoiding a Portuguese fort, before Baker and his companions find refuge ashore with an African group. Three survivors are finally rescued by a French ship, and Baker claims to be writing the poem in a prison in France, awaiting ransom. In the poem he sets the misadventures within an extensive but clumsy overall framework of classical mythology, rival gods assisting or otherwise harming the English voyagers.

Baker's poem, although providing only limited evidence on voyages which were among the earliest to far continents by Englishmen, does throw some light on English attitudes of the period. In particular, his general lack of sympathy with things African, most probably engendered by his unhappy misadventures, extends to a jaundiced view of Africans which has been latterly interpreted as an early manifestation of typical 'racist' disparagement of non-European peoples by the English. Considered as literature, the poem, albeit composed in somewhat clip-clop verse, is not without occasional felicities, while its subject matter and form give it a notable place in English and even European literary history. Among writings in English other than the entirely factual, it is almost the first, in either prose or verse, to take as its theme long-distance sea travel and cultural encounter in distant lands, a theme within the genre of travel literature to which English readers later became much attached. Further, its mythological framework places it firmly within a common style of contemporary European literature, if only as a small leaf on a broad stream. Yet the combination of mythology with an account of genuine distant voyaging gives this minor poem a measure of significant resemblance to a more considerable and subtle work, a masterpiece of European literature of the period, the epic *Os Lusiadas*. Each of these works sprang out of novel overseas experience, that of a maritime nation and that of an intercontinental traveller, and each celebrated access to worlds new to Europe, while lamenting occasional marine disaster. Camoens published in 1572; Baker wrote a decade earlier.

P. E. H. HAIR

Sources R. Hakluyt, *The principall navigations, voiages and discoveries of the English nation* (1589) • P. E. H. Hair, ed., *Robert Baker: the travails in Guinea of an unknown Tudor poet in verse* (1990) • Arber, *Regs. Stationers* • B. Penrose, *Robert Baker: an ancient mariner of 1565* (1942) • P. E. H. Hair and J. D. Alsop, *English seamen and traders in Guinea, 1553–1565: the new evidence of their wills* (1992)

Baker, Robert (1803–1880), surgeon and factory inspector, was born on 15 August 1803 in York, the second son of John Baker, druggist, of High Ousegate, York, and his wife, Hannah. His career shows many parallels with that of the better-known Charles Turner Thackrah, but evidence of association is lacking. In March 1818 Baker was apprenticed to William Pearson for five years, Pearson being surgeon to the Hull General (later Royal) Infirmary. Baker's medical education was continued at Guy's Hospital, London. He passed the Society of Apothecaries' qualifying examination in 1823, apparently while under age, and then gained membership of the Royal College of Surgeons. He appears on the college registers only from 1828 to 1843.

Baker's first appointment was in Leeds, as a poor-law surgeon, which he later described as 'an ordeal all the medical men of the town go through as the high road to better practice'. The direction of Baker's career was determined by the cholera epidemic of 1831–2. Baker's sanitary reports on the cholera in Tyneside, and on housing and environmental conditions in Leeds, included a use of maps which brought him to wider notice. On his own account he abandoned medical practice for factory work as a result of contracting cholera in the course of his poor-law duties. In the early 1830s he was employed as factory surgeon to the mill of Hindes and Derham and later claimed credit for the half-time education system for child factory workers whose health appeared precarious.

On 22 October 1834 Baker was appointed a 'superintendent' (equivalent to sub-inspector) according to the Factory Act of 1833. By 1837 he had ceased acting as a certifying surgeon, which involved some conflict of interest. He was still the only factory inspector with medical qualifications at the time of the famous sanitary report of 1842 by Edwin Chadwick, to which Baker was a contributor. In spite of local support he was not promoted until 15 June 1858. In 1861 he became, with his younger colleague Alexander Redgrave, one of two inspectors covering the British Isles following the retirement of John Kincaid. Baker supervised the north-west, the midlands, the west country, Wales, and northern Ireland. In this capacity he submitted biannual reports and advised on legislation, which was elaborated and then codified by the Factories Act of 1878. He retired in the same year and was appointed CB.

Baker's publications were occasional. He was most consistent in his concern for working children and in his advocacy of some form of comprehensive medical supervision of all factories. In his later career he was hardworking and respected, especially by those in whose interests he was acting, but not innovative, as he had been during the heroic period of sanitary reform. The medical qualifications which at first gave him distinction tended later to restrict his outlook on what might be achieved in the field of occupational health.

Baker had a wife, Maria, who died in 1903. They had a numerous family, of whom four sons and four daughters were living in 1878. Baker died at home at Milverton Hill near Leamington Spa on 6 February 1880.

MARGARET PELLING, *rev.*

Sources *BMJ* (6 March 1880), 383 • W. R. Lee, 'Robert Baker: the first doctor in the factory department', *British Journal of Industrial Medicine*, 21 (1964), 85–93, 167–79 • E. Chadwick, *Report on the sanitary condition of the labouring population … 1842*, ed. M. Flinn (1965) • will, proved, Birmingham, 17 Sept 1880 • private information (1993) [P. W. J. Bartrip]

Wealth at death under £4000: probate, 17 Sept 1880, *CGPLA Eng. & Wales*

Baker, Sir Rowland (1908–1983), naval architect, was born on 3 June 1908 at Upchurch, Sittingbourne, Kent, the eldest son of Isaac Baker, a sailing bargee, and his wife, Lizzie Palmer. He had a brother and three sisters. Always top of the class in school and successful at sports, he became an apprentice at Chatham Dockyard, where, after four years of dockyard school, he won a place as a constructor cadet at the Royal Naval College, Greenwich, graduating in 1931 and completing his sea training in 1932. He was married on 28 November 1931 to Frances Edna Cornish (*b.* 1912); they had two girls and a boy.

As an assistant constructor Baker held a number of appointments in both the Whitehall design office and in dockyards. On promotion to constructor in 1938 he took charge of sloop design, for which his principal task was the structural design of the *Seagull*, the first all-welded ship for the Royal Navy. It was a brilliant design, well ahead of its time with longitudinal framing and flush butt joints. No commercial shipyard would build it so it was built in Devonport Dockyard, showing considerable savings in both time and cost over a riveted half-sister on an adjoining slip. He then designed the very cheap *Bangor*-class mine-sweepers followed by the *Algerines*, both built in large numbers. He was also responsible for the highly successful improved *Black Swan*-class sloops.

Baker continued to make an important contribution to naval design during the Second World War. After the fall of France, the need was felt for large numbers of ships and craft to carry men and vehicles for a beach landing. The majority of landing ships and craft for both the Royal Navy and United States Navy were conceived by Baker, working for Earl Mountbatten. The combination of light weight for shallow draught, simplicity of construction, and seaworthiness made their design very difficult. A particular feature was his conviction that bow doors would always leak and, unlike modern ferries, his vessels would float upright with the vehicle deck flooded. In November 1941 he was granted a special pay allowance in recognition of his unusual responsibilities. Late in 1941 he spent some time in the USA initiating the design of the LST(2), the backbone of the allied invasion fleet, for which he was awarded the American medal of freedom after the war. In 1947 Baker described the design of landing ships and craft in two papers to the Institution of Naval Architects. After the war he was lent to the Canadian navy as constructor commodore, designing a successful icebreaker, the novel *St Laurent*-class frigates, and other vessels—and making many new friends.

On return from Canada in 1956 Baker was put in charge of the nuclear submarine programme as technical chief executive, *Dreadnought* project, again under Mountbatten. It was a strange organization with many staff having dual line of authority but Baker transmitted his own enthusiasm and the project was completed at cost and on time, very rare among defence projects of that day. Baker had proved that his managerial skill was as great as his design skill. *Dreadnought* used American machinery in order to get her into service quickly but while she was being built the first British nuclear submarine machinery was installed for test at Dounreay and *Valiant*, the first all-British nuclear submarine, was being built, all under Baker's direction. Even before *Dreadnought* was completed he was put in charge of the Polaris submarine project, which was also completed within time and cost budgets.

Baker was appointed KB in the new year's honours of 1968, an unusual honour for a civil servant of his rank, and he retired in November of that year. He was persuaded to return to sort out problems with the Mk 24 torpedo; later he tried, unsuccessfully, to develop a plant for the offshore oil industry.

Baker was an unforgettable man for whom to work. His command of the English language, learned on a working Thames barge, was unusual for a senior civil servant and very disconcerting to those unfamiliar with his ways. His staff worshipped him in classical mode: his thunderbolts were as effective as those of Zeus—he would often throw files at his staff. On the other hand, his kind and valuable support was there when the going was tough. One junior officer (the author of this memoir) received a note reading 'Cor mate, you aint 'arf sticking your neck out! Don't worry, I'll back you if it goes wrong.'

Baker's design skills were shown in the advanced longitudinal structure of *Seagull*, the safety of his flimsy landing craft, and the many novelties in the Canadian *St Laurent*-class frigates, further developed in later classes. He very strongly believed that a new design of ship should be 25 per cent novel and 75 per cent well-tried practice in order to be both up to date and reliable. In the submarine projects he pushed the use of network scheduling used in *Dreadnought*, a technique then unfamiliar in the UK, and then the more advanced PERT (programme evaluation and review technique) system for Polaris. It was no coincidence that both held to budget. Following a divorce, he married on 15 March 1972 Barbara Mary Comley (*b.* 1921), who survived him. Baker off duty was full of fun and his ribald performance at the annual submarine dinner was unforgettable. He died at the Royal United Hospital, Bath, on 25 November 1983. DAVID K. BROWN

Sources *WWW* • private information (2004) • D. K. Brown, *A century of naval construction: the history of the Royal Corps of Naval Constructors, 1883–1983* (1983) • NMM, royal corps of naval constructors centenary MSS • *CGPLA Eng. & Wales* (1984) • b. cert. • m. cert. • d. cert. • D. K. Brown, *Sir Rowland Baker RCNC* (1995)

Archives NMM, royal corps of naval constructors centenary MSS

Wealth at death £23,334: probate, 28 Feb 1984, *CGPLA Eng. & Wales*

Baker, Samuel (*d.* 1658), Church of England clergyman, matriculated from Christ's College, Cambridge, in July 1612 and graduated BA in 1616. Ordained priest on 14 November 1618 in the diocese of Norwich he proceeded MA the following year. In January 1626 he was presented to the rectory of St Margaret Pattens, London, and in 1627 he proceeded BD. It is possible that he married at St James's, Duke's Place, on 22 May 1632, but the bride's name is unknown. If true it is also possible that the marriage was not to Joan, recorded as his wife in the 1640s, and that it did not last long, for in 1633 Baker was appointed household chaplain to William Juxon, bishop of London. One of his duties in this capacity was to license books for the press, and it was later alleged that a number of theological books licensed by Baker, including William Jones's *Commentary upon the Epistles to Philemon and to the Hebrewes* (1635) and Richard Clerke's *Sermons* (1637), had been heavily censored to make them appear less anti-Catholic. The clerical convert Richard Carpenter, who had defected to the Church of Rome but subsequently returned to the Church of England, complained that Baker had permitted him to preach at Paul's Cross only on condition that he did not speak 'revengefully and ungratefully against the church of Rome, as having had my breeding from them', and that he attributed his conversion to 'the sight and love of the orders and ceremonies newly begun in the church of England, a thing which (the Lord knowes) had not entred into my thoughts before this admonishment' (Kent Archives Office, U350 C2/53). Carpenter also complained that when he submitted his sermon for licensing, 'Mr Baker answered by noe meanes, and gave this reason, because now the Church of Rome and we were in a faire and quiet way, and it was not fitt to multiply Controversies' (Kent Archives Office, U350 Q5).

Baker was generously rewarded with ecclesiastical preferment. In June 1636 he became minister of St Christopher-le-Stocks, London, in October he was collated to a prebendal stall in St Paul's, London, and in July 1637 he resigned St Margaret Pattens to become rector of St Mary-at-Hill. In August 1638 he was appointed a canon of Windsor, resigning in May 1639 to become a canon of Canterbury; that year he proceeded DD. He may have been the Samuel Baker who married Joan Bray at Canterbury on 25 June 1642. On 15 January 1640 he had been appointed a chaplain-in-ordinary to the king. In April he resigned St Christopher-le-Stocks to become rector of South Weald, Essex. He kept St Mary-at-Hill, but in June his dispensation to hold it in plurality was found to be legally invalid. However, he was unanimously reappointed to St Mary by the trustees (acting on behalf of the parishioners), and remained in possession of both until the civil war. None the less, his rapid promotion provoked some adverse comment: one hostile account later claimed that 'Baker, the Bishop of London's chaplaine, being one morning desired to present a Petition from a Minister to his Lord for a Prebend's place, carried the matter so craftily, that he had it for himselfe'. According to the same account 'this Baker was so over-joyed with the death of some good Divines, and the going away of others, that he made verses of them, and the same day hee made them hee broke his legge' (*The Scots Scouts Discoveries*, E1v). While the reliability of these stories is dubious it is clear that Baker was widely regarded as an enemy of the puritan clergy and a loyal servant of the Laudian regime. Sir Edward Dering remarked in his *Discourse of Proper Sacrifice* (1644) that he had always regarded Baker as more extreme in his views than his fellow licenser William Bray.

On 24 April 1643 the House of Commons ordered Baker to be sequestrated from the living of South Weald on the grounds that 'he hath indeavoured to corrupt his People at such times as he hath preached there with the leaven of Popish doctrine'; that 'he beleeved not the Pope to be Anti-Christ, because his Mother the Church whom he would not outrun had not yet revealed it'; that he had licensed 'divers Popish Bookes pleading for Auricular Confession and other points of Popery'; that he had bowed to the altar when administering the sacrament, and had knelt down on the altar steps 'with his hands lift up'; and that he had 'expressed ill affection to the Parliament' (HLRO, Main MSS). On 16 May the House of Lords confirmed the order of the Commons, despite a personal appearance by Baker to confess that he had two livings and two prebendaries and 'hath had some Misfortune in licensing Books, which he is sorry for'. On 26 May the committee for sequestrations ordered the seizure of Baker's house and goods, valued at £80 12*s*., and on 27 July the Commons ordered Baker to be sequestrated from the living of St Mary-at-Hill, although his wife, Joan, was later granted one-fifth of the living by the committee for plundered ministers.

Baker is said to have assisted Brian Walton in the preparation of the polyglot Bible; and when Walton borrowed the Codex Alexandrinus in 1653, Baker was one of the five persons who stood surety for its safe return. On 16 March 1658 the vestry of St Mary-at-Hill granted Baker £10 out of the parish funds 'for his releefe in his great necessitie and sicknes', and he must have died before 25 May 1658, when the vestry minutes recorded that the living was vacant (Guildhall Library, MS 1240/1). ARNOLD HUNT

Sources Venn, *Alum. Cant.* • *Walker rev.* • G. Hennessy, *Novum repertorium ecclesiasticum parochiale Londinense, or, London diocesan clergy succession from the earliest time to the year 1898* (1898) • *Fasti Angl., 1541–1857*, [St Paul's, London] • *Fasti Angl., 1541–1857*, [Canterbury] • *JHL* • *JHC* • *The Scots scouts discoveries* (1642) • E. Dering, *Discourse of proper sacrifice* (1644) • W. Prynne, *Canterburies doome* (1644) • W. W. Greg, *Licensers for the press, &c. to 1640* (1962) • vestry minutes of the parish of St Mary-at-Hill, London, 1609–1752, GL, MS 1240/1 • CKS, Dering papers, U 350 • HLRO, Main papers collection, HL

Baker, Sir Samuel White (1821–1893), traveller and explorer in Africa, was born on 8 June 1821 in London, the second of the eight children of Samuel Baker (*d.* 1862) of Lypiatt Park, Gloucestershire, and his first wife, Mary, daughter of Thomas Dobson of Enfield, Middlesex. His father was a wealthy shipowner who had sugar plantations in Mauritius and Jamaica and had served as a director of the Great Western Railway and chairman of the Gloucester Bank. His elder brother died in childhood and Baker eventually inherited his father's wealth.

Education, youthful hunting, and first marriage Baker, who had a fair complexion, light hair, and piercing blue eyes, lived most of his early years in Enfield. When he was twelve his family rented a house from Sir John Guise, at Highnam Court, about 2 miles from Gloucester. He first studied in a private school at Rottingdean, and from 1833 to 1835 he attended College School, Gloucester. He benefited little from these schools, possibly because he refused to accept the discipline and conformity required by the public school system. In 1838, however, his attitude towards learning changed: the Revd Henry Peter Dunster, a private tutor in Tottenham, accepted Baker as a pupil and interested him in history, geography, and the classics. In 1840 Baker departed for Germany to finish his education. Although he attended lectures and learned the German language, he devoted most of his eighteen months in Germany to hunting. He also perfected his knowledge of the rifle and devised a massive charge of 16 drams of powder for use against larger game.

After returning to England, Baker and his brother John, in a double ceremony on 3 August 1843, married sisters, Henrietta Biddulph (*d.* 1855) and Elizabeth, daughters of Charles Martin, rector of Maisemore. After a brief, unsuccessful, stint in his father's London office in Fenchurch Street, Baker travelled to Mauritius in early 1845, where he and John managed Fairfund, the family estate on the island. However, he spent only a few months on the island, which he found too restricting and utterly boring.

Sir Samuel White Baker (1821–1893), by Maull & Co., 1860s

Planting and hunting in Ceylon In late 1845 Baker relocated to Ceylon, ostensibly to establish a coffee plantation and an English colony at Nuwera Eliya, a station 6000 feet above sea level and 115 miles from Colombo by road. It was a sad reunion when his wife joined him the following year. His son Charles had died in Mauritius, and in September 1846 his daughter Jane succumbed to fever at sea off the Maldive Islands. Despite these tragedies, Baker continued with his colonization scheme. He purchased land from the government and persuaded his brothers John and Valentine *Baker (1827–1887) to join the enterprise. In September 1848 the *Earl of Hardwicke* set sail from London with a party of eighteen adults and a cargo of stock, machinery, seeds, and hounds. Initially the struggling colony suffered as poor soil conditions restricted farming and wild animals often ate the crops. Eventually, however, the settlers overcame these difficulties and established a relatively prosperous estate which remained in the Baker family throughout the century.

In his nine years in Ceylon, Baker explored much of the island and established an impressive reputation as a big game hunter. During his many elephant- and stag-hunting expeditions, he experimented with new rifles, stalking methods, and ballistic techniques. He recounted his experiences in *The Rifle and Hound in Ceylon* (1853), and in *Eight Years' Wanderings in Ceylon*, which appeared two years later. In 1855 a fever-stricken Baker returned with his family to England. After the unexpected death of his wife from typhus fever on 29 December 1855 at Bagnères-de-Bigorre, France, Baker sought consolation and solace by volunteering for the Crimean War; unfortunately, he arrived at the front just as Britain and Russia had concluded a peace agreement. Baker then spent time hunting in the Balkans. Afterwards, he contemplated becoming an unofficial spy to report on Russian military designs against India. After returning to England, Baker also considered entering the service of the Anglican church.

Travels in eastern Europe and Asia Minor: acquisition of Florence Finally, in November 1858, Baker decided to resolve his personal problems by embarking on a hunting trip down the Danube River with Maharaja Duleep Singh, the hereditary ruler of the Punjab, who had been living in England since his dispossession. After the boat in which they were travelling collided with an ice floe, Baker and the maharaja abandoned the vessel and took refuge in the Danube town of Widden. While in the town they attended a slave auction where Baker unexpectedly bought a young woman named Florence Barbara Maria Finnian von Sass (1841–1916) [*see* Baker, Florence Barbara Maria]. Shortly thereafter they travelled to Bucharest and eventually both ended up in the Black Sea port of Constanza. In March 1859 Baker accepted a position as manager-general with the Danube and Black Sea Railway which planned to build a line from Constanza to the Danube east of Bucharest. After this project was completed in October 1860, Baker and Florence journeyed through Asia Minor, spending several months hunting in the Sapanca region.

During his time in eastern Europe and Asia Minor, Baker became increasingly intrigued by the prospect of exploring Africa. After John Hanning Speke and James Augustus Grant departed from Bagamoyo for Lake Victoria and the White Nile on 2 October 1860, Baker decided to launch his own expedition to discover the sources of the Nile River. He then planned to link up with Speke and Grant. The journey, which ultimately would take four and a half years, would bring him fame and fortune. More importantly, the expedition enabled Baker and Florence, who were not married, to escape the harsh moral strictures of Victorian England.

The Nile expedition, 1861–1865 On 15 April 1861 Baker and Florence left Cairo in a *dahabia*—a vessel similar to a dhow—for a twenty-six-day trip up the Nile to Korosko. The couple then went by camel caravan from Kassala to the Sudanese–Abyssinian border to explore the eastern tributaries of the Nile. Baker—who established his headquarters at Sofi, a village along the banks of the Atbara River—spent five months exploring the Setit River, a tributary of the Atbara, and hunting big game, often with the Hamran Arabs. He also explored other tributaries of the Atbara, including the Bahr Salamat and the Angareb, and then travelled along the Rehad to its confluence with the Blue Nile. After completing this phase of the expedition, Baker and Florence marched to Khartoum, where they arrived on 11 June 1862. The results of this fourteen-month journey, while not overly significant, were nevertheless impressive. Sir Roderick Murchison, president of the Royal Geographical Society, acknowledged the importance of Baker's explorations and his discovery that the Nile sediment was due to the Abyssinian tributaries. Additionally, Baker gained experience as an African explorer, mastered Arabic, and learned to use the astronomical instruments which were vital for determining geographical locations.

For the next six months Baker remained in Khartoum, waiting for the end of the rainy season and preparing for the next phase of his expedition. On 18 December 1862 he started up the Nile with a *dahabia*, two sailing barges (known as *nuggars*), twenty-nine transport animals, and a party of ninety-six, including forty-five armed men and forty sailors. On 2 February 1863 this expedition reached Gondokoro, an important headquarters for the Arab slave trade. Baker immediately clashed with Arab slave traders and the local Bari people, both of whom considered him a spy of the British government. Additionally, the Arabs feared that the Englishman would try to end the lucrative slave trade. Consequently, they encouraged two mutinies among Baker's men, the second of which resulted in several desertions. On 15 February 1863 Speke and Grant arrived in Gondokoro, after more than two years of exploration work in east Africa. Baker provided them with his surplus supplies and three vessels for the trip down the Nile. In return, Speke informed Baker of a second unexplored lake, the Luta N'zigé, west of Bunyoro, and urged him to complete the discovery of the Nile source. Speke also gave him his own maps. Lastly, the two explorers promised to keep Baker's relationship with Florence a secret after they reached England.

Preparing for the next phase of his trip, Baker had to contend with Arab slave traders who were determined to prevent him from travelling to the south. To break free of Gondokoro, Baker, who experienced difficulty getting provisions and persuading porters to march through hostile territory, attached his small party to a large ivory- and slave-trading caravan commanded by Khurshid Agha. He hoped to make his own way after he reached Faloro. Therefore, on 26 March 1863, Baker and Florence left Gondokoro on the first leg of what proved to be an arduous two-year journey through some of east Africa's more remote areas.

After reaching the country of the Latuka and neighbouring Madi, east of Gondokoro, there was a delay of eleven months because of the onset of the rainy season and the refusal of local slave traders to give Baker the provisions necessary for him to continue his southward march. During this period he visited Latomé, where he suppressed a mutiny by his porters, and Tirangolé, the capital of Lutuka country. By the end of 1863 Baker and Florence had not moved beyond Obbo, which was only about 150 miles from Gondokoro. Finally, on 3 January 1864, they persuaded Ibrahim, a freebooter who worked for Khurshid Agha, to turn the caravan southwards to Bunyoro. Baker arrived at the White Nile on 22 January 1864, marched east to Karuma Falls the following day, and then crossed into the kingdom of Bunyoro.

Once again further travel became difficult as Kamrasi, the king (*omukama*) of Bunyoro, kept his visitors in the capital, Kisuna, for several weeks under virtual house arrest. After depleting Baker's caravan of numerous 'gifts', the king announced that he wanted to exchange several of his wives for Florence. Baker responded to this outrage by threatening to shoot him if he persisted in making advances toward her. Shortly afterwards Kamrasi grudgingly gave his permission for the couple to leave his kingdom. In late February 1864 they left with a 300-man escort provided by Kamrasi and made their way along the right bank of the Kafa River. The march was especially demanding as Florence was in a coma caused by sunstroke. Nevertheless, on 14 March 1864, the determined couple reached Mbakovia, a village on the south-eastern shore of Luta N'zigé. For the next thirteen days they travelled in a north-easterly direction along the lake's shore before reaching Magungo, the entrance of the Victoria Nile. Owing to unsettled conditions in Madi and Koshi districts, Baker cancelled plans to travel by boat from Fashoro northwards to trace the White Nile; instead, he went east along the Victoria Nile until he came upon the falls which he named after his friend Sir Roderick Murchison. He also gave Luta N'zigé the appellation Albert Nyanza, after Prince Albert, Victoria's consort. Baker remained for two months at Patooan Island, suffering from fever. King Kamrasi, who was being threatened by a neighbour, Chief Rionga, eventually arranged for fifty of his men to transport Baker and Florence to Kisuna. For the next few months the king detained the couple, repeatedly asking for more gifts and help against Rionga. On 17 November 1864 Baker finally started his return journey north, arriving in Gondokoro on 15 March 1865 and in Khartoum on 5 May 1865. After spending almost two months in the Sudanese capital he left for England on 1 July 1865, via Berber, Suakin, Cairo, Alexandria, Marseilles, and Paris. On arrival in England on 14 October 1865 Baker finalized arrangements for his marriage to Florence, which took place on 4 November 1865.

Recognition and rewards The discovery of the Albert Nyanza marked the pinnacle of Baker's career as an African explorer in so far as it helped to resolve the mystery of the source of the Nile. Soon after his return to England in 1865 he learned that he had been awarded the Royal Geographical Society's prestigious gold medal for his work in Africa. Numerous other awards soon followed. In August 1866 Baker received a knighthood; in the same year he became an honorary MA of Cambridge, and also published his account of the expedition, entitled *The Albert Ny'anza, Great Basin of the Nile, and Explorations of the Nile Sources*. The work, which went through several editions, remains one of the most important narratives of African exploration during the Victorian era. In 1867 the Paris Geographical Society conferred on him its *grande médaille d'or*, and on 3 June 1869 he was elected FRS. He also became an honorary member of the geographical societies of Paris, Berlin, Italy, and the United States.

For the next few years Baker and his wife lived at Hedenham Hall, Norfolk. It was at this manor house that he wrote *The Nile Tributaries of Abyssinia, and the Sword Hunters of the Hamran Arabs*, and a boys' adventure story, *Cast up by the Sea*, which were published in 1867 and 1868 respectively.

Governing the Nile basin, 1869–1873 In 1869 the prince of Wales invited Baker to accompany him on his visit to Egypt and journey up the Nile, despite the disapproval of Queen Victoria. The same year, on 1 April, the Khedive Isma'il appointed Baker to a four-year term as governor-general of the equatorial Nile basin, with the rank of pasha and major-general in the Ottoman army. It was the most senior post a European ever received under an Egyptian administration. According to the khedive's firman, Baker's duties included annexing the equatorial Nile basin, establishing Egyptian authority over the region south of Gondokoro, suppressing the slave trade, introducing cotton cultivation, organizing a network of trading stations throughout the annexed territories, and opening the great lakes near the equator to navigation. To carry out the mission, the khedive provided Baker with a flotilla of ten steamers and fifty-five sailing ships, and about 1700 officers and men. On 5 December 1869 he and Lady Baker departed Cairo for Suakin; a month later they were in Khartoum. However, because of unfavourable conditions on the Nile and an inability to penetrate the sudd it was not until April 1871 that the party arrived in Gondokoro. On 26 May 1871 Baker annexed Gondokoro—which he renamed Isma'iliyyah—and the surrounding country in the name of the khedive. The local Bari people, however, refused to recognize Egyptian authority. After seizing some of their cattle to feed his men, Baker had to defend his expedition against attacks by the Bari. On 22 January 1872 Baker left a garrison of troops at Gondokoro to prevent a resurgence of Bari hostility and started on a southward journey with 212 officers and men. When he reached Fatick, a village north of the Victoria Nile and the Bunyoro frontier, Baker had to contend with yet another crisis. The local Arab community opposed his efforts to establish Egyptian authority and to end the slave trade. However, unlike the situation in Gondokoro, where the Bari had formed an alliance with the Arab traders, the Acholi looked upon the Fatick Arabs as enemies. As a result, they welcomed Baker's expedition and placed themselves under its protection. On 14 May 1872 while at Masindi—which became the Bunyoro capital after the death of Kamrasi Baker declared that the kingdom was under Egyptian protection. This development forced the hand of Abou Saood, a local slave and ivory trader. He perceived Baker's action as a threat to his commercial interests and therefore encouraged the Bunyoro king, Kabarega, to attack Baker's men. On 14 June 1872 Baker withdrew to Fatick, where he clashed with Abou Saood's irregulars. He easily defeated the slave trader's retainers, many of whom subsequently deserted and joined Baker's entourage. With their help Baker built a fort at Fatick which represented the southernmost outpost of Egyptian influence in eastern Africa. The expedition produced mixed results. Although he had suppressed the slave trade in some areas and had extended the khedive's authority to Gondokoro and Fatick, he had failed to pacify the lawless region between these two places. Moreover, he was unable to annex the wealthy kingdoms of Bunyoro and Buganda. Despite Baker's dubious performance, the khedive bestowed on him the imperial order of the Osmanieh, second class.

Retirement and reputation Baker received a hero's welcome on his return to England. Apart from various glowing newspaper accounts of his travels, the prince of Wales met him to learn first hand of his experiences in Africa. On 8 December 1873 he received an enthusiastic reception at the Royal Geographical Society, and the following year he published a two-volume account of his expedition entitled *Ismailïa: a narrative of the expedition to central Africa for the suppression of the slave trade*, which further enhanced his popularity.

Baker and his wife eventually moved into Sandford Orleigh, Highweek, a forty-room mansion in south Devon, near Newton Abbot. This estate remained Baker's home for the rest of his life. He regularly wrote books and newspaper and magazine articles about a variety of political and sporting subjects. Additionally, he was elected president of the Devonshire Association, and served as a town councillor in Newton Abbot. Every autumn he undertook a hunting expedition to Scotland, or travelled abroad: in 1879, for example, Baker spent nearly a year in Cyprus; between 1879 and 1892 he visited India seven times, killing a total of twenty-two tigers. There were other hunting expeditions to Japan, to the Rocky Mountains, and to virtually every European country. The Bakers also visited Egypt regularly and, in the late 1870s, made a protracted round-the-world voyage. Baker died of a heart attack at Sandford Orleigh on 30 December 1893. His body was cremated and his ashes buried at Grimley, near Worcester, on 5 January 1894. He was survived by his second wife, and by three daughters of the seven children of his first marriage.

Sir Samuel Baker was typical of many Victorian explorers and adventurers in as much as he was a strong-willed, unconventional, intolerant, and self-reliant individual, often insensitive to social norms and to those around him. Post-colonial scholars have emphasized Baker's deep-seated contempt for non-European peoples and cultures, a facet of his personality and career that has been profoundly unattractive to posterity. But it is important not to see Baker as exceptional in this regard: in his own time, the idealization of British civilization and the refusal to acknowledge any worth in non-European societies were commonplace. Moreover, this emphasis tends to overlook Baker's genuine concerns for the welfare of the people of Africa as evinced in his suppression of the slave trade along the White Nile. Despite his personal shortcomings, Baker's reputation as one of the most important British explorers of the nineteenth century is assured.

THOMAS PAUL OFCANSKY

Sources S. W. Baker, *The Albert N'yanza: great basin of the Nile*, 2 vols. (1866) • S. W. Baker, *Ismailïa*, 2 vols. (1874) • D. Middleton, *Baker of the Nile* (1949) • R. Hall, *Lovers on the Nile* (1980) • T. D. Murray and A. Silva White, *Sir Samuel Baker: a memoir* (1895) • R. O. Collins, 'Samuel White Baker: Prospero in purgatory', *Africa and its explorers*, ed. R. I. Rotberg (1970), 139–73 • S. W. Baker, *Wild beasts and their ways*, ed. J. A. Casada, new edn (1988) [with a new foreword by J. A. Casada, ix–xv] • *Morning Star: Florence Baker's diary of the expedition to put down the slave trade on the Nile, 1870–1873*, ed. A. Baker (1972) • J. B. Baker, 'Samuel Baker's route to the Albert Nyanza', *GJ*, 131 (1965), 13–20 • J. Gray, 'Ismail Pasha and Sir Samuel Baker', *Uganda Journal*, 25 (1961), 199–213 • S. W. Baker, *Eight years' wanderings in Ceylon* (1855) • A. M. Moorehead, *The White Nile*, rev. edn (1971) • A. Moorehead, *The Blue Nile*, rev. edn (1972) • J. A. Casada, 'British exploration in east Africa: a bibliography with commentary', *Africana Journal*, 5 (1974), 195–239 • C. Hibbert, *Africa explored: Europeans in the dark continent, 1769–1899* (1982)

Archives Bodl. Oxf., letters • Bodl. RH • PRO, FO 78, 84, 633 • RGS, diaries and papers relating to Nile expeditions; letters to Royal Geographical Society • Wellcome L., letters | BL, letters to Gordon, Add. MS 51305 • BL, letters to Lord Morley, Add. MS 48266, fols. 132–1476 • Bodl. Oxf., letters to Douglas Murray • NL Scot., letters to J. A. Grant • RGS, letters to Sir George Back • RGS, Speke MSS • Sheff. Arch., Montagu-Stuart MSS, letters to Earl of Wharncliffe • U. Reading L., letters to Macmillan & Co. Ltd

Likenesses Maull & Co., photograph, 1860–69, NPG [*see illus.*] • C. H. Jeens, line engraving, BM, NPG; repro. in S. W. Baker, *The Albert N'yanza* • C. H. Jeens, line engraving, BM, NPG; repro. in S. W. Baker, *Ismailïa* • Lock & Whitfield, woodburytype, NPG; repro. in T. Cooper, *Men of mark* (1880) • cartes-de-visite, NPG • photograph, repro. in Murray and White, *Sir Samuel Baker* • photograph, repro. in Middleton, *Baker of the Nile* • photographs, RGS; repro. in A. Hugon, *The exploration of Africa: from Cairo to the Cape* (1993) • photographs, repro. in Hall, *Lovers on the Nile*

Wealth at death £61,066 15*s*. 9*d*.: probate, 22 Feb 1894, *CGPLA Eng. & Wales*

Baker [*née* Wakelin], **Sarah** (**1736/7–1816**), actress and theatre manager, was born in London, the daughter of Ann Wakelin, *née* Clark (*d*. 1787), an acrobatic dancer and troupe manager at Sadler's Wells, and James Wakelin (*fl*. 1749–1779), a minor actor. With her sister Mary, she performed as a dancer in her mother's company at Sadler's Wells and on tour in Norwich, Yarmouth, and Bristol. Sarah was also a puppeteer, and Mrs Wakelin's company was regularly fined at Stourbridge fair, Cambridge, between 1762 and 1777, for offering rope-dancing, slack wire, puppet shows, and pantomime. Some time before 1761 Sarah married a Mr Baker, an acrobat in the Wakelin troupe, who may have been the famous clown-tumbler Polander. She had three children, Ann, Henry, and Sarah, before her husband's death about 1769.

Sarah assumed the management of the Sadler's Wells company, first noted at Canterbury, with rope-dancing, tumbling, musical interludes, burlettas, and all the clothes, scenery, and machinery 'entirely new' (*Kentish Gazette*, 19 Nov 1772). The values of the fairground and family touring group were thoroughly instilled in Sarah:

> When Mrs. Baker (who had many years previously only employed actors and actresses of cherry-wood, holly, oak, or ebony, and dressed and undressed both the ladies and gentlemen herself), first engaged a living company, she not only used to beat the drum behind the scenes, in Richard, and other martial plays, but was occasionally her own prompter. (Dibdin, 1.96–7)

Mrs Baker's touring circuit took in Dover, Canterbury, Rochester, Faversham, and Tunbridge Wells, as well as occasional visits to Folkestone, Deal, Sandwich, Lewes, and Sittingbourne. The acting company included many family members: her mother, until her retirement in 1777, her sister Mary, her own children, Ann, Henry, and Sarah, and her cousins the Irelands, some of whom were musicians for the company. She also employed many successful popular entertainers, such as the clown Lewy Owen. A playbill for the 1770s at Bartholomew fair advertises Mrs Baker's company at the Greyhound Yard Theatre, performing Charles Dibdin's ballad opera *The Waterman*, with Rugg as Waterman, Connell as Bundle, Lewy Owen as Robin, Miss Heydon as Mrs Bundle and Miss Wakelin as Wilhelmina. The afterpiece was *Harlequin's Whim, or, The Mery Medly*, with Douglas as Harlequin, Rugg as Lover, and Mrs Baker herself as Columbine.

After her mother's retirement, in 1778, Sarah started to offer plays, both comedy and tragedy, as well as fairground or variety entertainment. Her acting company gave a start to performers like William *Dowton (1764–1851), who joined in 1791 and married her daughter Sarah (1768–1817) in 1794, and was an early employer of Thomas Dibdin and Edmund Kean. Part of the attraction, as Dibdin recalled, was the offer of a regular salary, 'not a joint-stock concern' (Dibdin, 1.91–2), as many other touring managements were. As the company's reputation for serious drama became more established, Sarah and her actor-cum-stage manager Jem Gardner, and later her prompter, Bony Long, tempted such leading London performers as Charles Incledon, George F. Cooke, Dorothy Jordan, and Joseph Grimaldi into occasional, lucrative engagements.

The repertory Sarah offered included several Shakespeare plays; *Hamlet*, *Macbeth*, *Richard III*, *As You Like It*, and *The Merchant of Venice* were offered at least once a week during the 1780s, in addition to comic opera and topical interludes, often with local comment, as in Thomas Dibdin's afterpiece *The Merry Hop-Pickers, or, Kentish Frolicks*. Other favourites were Cumberland's *The West Indian* and *The Brother* and Mrs Inchbald's *œuvre*. By 1795 the Baker company's repertory was very considerable, and Sarah was advertising pieces direct from London and 'diversity of nouvelle matter' (Hodgson, 76). The success of her policy of celebrity recruitment and an up-to-date repertory maximizing the taste of her provincial audiences was indicated by the returns Joseph Grimaldi recorded for playing Scaramouche in *Don Juan* for a couple of nights in Maidstone and Canterbury in March 1802. Sarah split the house takings with Grimaldi, after charges, and he netted a very healthy £311 6*s*. 6*d*. for four days' work.

Successful touring managements like Sarah Baker's were often responsible for building permanent provincial theatres in the major towns on their circuits. Her will lists her theatres in the five main circuit towns and small theatres in Folkestone and in Ore, near Hastings. In Canterbury she built her 'great grand theatre' (Hodgson, 70) in 1789 at a cost of £3000 after she had seen off the challenge of a rival manager, Hurst, whose disastrous management dissipated his initial success. However, rivals were not always so easily defeated. At Margate Sarah ran into considerable difficulties with the company run by Charles Mate. Mate had already failed in his attempts to oust her at Dover and Rochester, as he complained in a letter to Winston: 'Mrs Beaker … who had got possession of some of my Inland Towns enved me my little Margate Retret' (ibid., 69). Baker had rented a converted stable from a local banker and magistrate, Mr Cobb. In 1784 Baker wanted to build a better theatre in Margate, but Cobb refused:

> whereupon the gentle fair one entered a remonstrance, and declared her right to murder Shakespear equally with Mate; and told him, for all he was a Justice, she would build in spite of him. Accordingly the following year produced a Baker's company, who exercised their calling near the church, and instituted a theatrical warfare. (Winston, 12)

Cobb and Mate then hatched a plan to establish a patent at Margate, which project garnered support from the local freemasons and nobility and passed, at great expense, through both houses of parliament. With fewer resources than Cobb and Mate, Sarah conceded defeat. She struck her temporary wooden theatre and moved it wholesale to Faversham. However, she learned a valuable lesson, and in Rochester, where she had occupied her newly built Theatre Royal, Star Hill, since 1791, she herself applied in 1798 for a royal patent in order to force the local JPs to grant her a licence after rioting by nearby Chatham sailors had caused her existing licence to be cancelled. In Tunbridge Wells her aspirations to have a permanent house brought her into conflict with Glassington's company at Hunt's Warehouse. But here she had the support of significant local patrons, and she erected a new theatre 'at the request of several of her friends … securing it by lease' (ibid., 16), where she remained unmolested until she upgraded the theatre to a £60 capacity, at a cost of £1600, in 1802. All of the new theatres were simple, rectangular buildings, with pit, boxes, and an upper gallery, and similar dimensions to allow scenery to be directly transferred. The theatres had only one entrance, past the box office, where Sarah herself took money for all the seats. In the larger towns she also built dwelling houses connected to the theatres, which were let out of season.

Sarah's management style was combative. Dibdin noted her 'usual rapidity of utterance' (Dibdin, 1.102) and, when provoked, her use of 'lingual expression more idiomatic of Peckham-fair technicals than the elegance to be expected from a directress of the British drama' (ibid., 1.94). Her hard-headed financial sense was tempered towards her company members, who record regular payment in full and guaranteed accommodation at reasonable rates. 'She owned an excellent heart, with much of the appearance and manners of a gentlewoman' (ibid., 1.94), and she occasionally bartered toys for tickets with local children. Sarah passed over the management of the highly successful company to William Dowton in June 1815. She died in Rochester, Kent, on 20 February 1816 and was buried in Rochester Cathedral churchyard. Her will left approximately £16,000 in investment and property, in carefully secured trust funds. As Dibdin's epitaph on her gravestone records:

> If industry have claim to moral worth;
> … then she, whose frame
> Decays beneath, with humble hope may aim
> At happiness to come. Alone, untaught,
> And self-assisted, (save by Heaven) she sought

To render each his own, and fairly save
What might help others when she found a grave.

J. MILLING

Sources N. Hodgson, 'Sarah Baker (1736/7–1816), governess-general of the Kentish drama', *Studies in English Theatre History* (1952), 65–83 • J. Winston, *The theatric tourist* (1805) • T. Dibdin, *The reminiscences of Thomas Dibdin*, 2 vols. (1827) • S. Rosenfeld, *Theatre of the London fairs* (1960) • S. Rosenfeld, 'The players in Cambridge, 1662–1800', *Studies in English Theatre History* (1952), 24–37 • J. Bratton, 'Sarah Baker: the making of a "character"', *Scenes from provincial stages*, ed. R. Foulkes (1994), 43–54 • A. Matthews, *Anecdotes of actors* (1844) • Highfill, Burnim & Langhans, *BDA* • C. Dickens, *Memoirs of Joseph Grimaldi*, ed. R. Findlater, rev. edn (1968)
Archives Harvard TC | Birm. CL, Winston MSS
Wealth at death approx. £16,000 in investments and seven theatre buildings: will, Hodgson, 'Sarah Baker', 73

Baker, Shirley Waldemar (1836–1903), missionary and prime minister of Tonga, was born in Camden Town, London. He was the son of George Baker and his wife, Jane Woolmer, daughter of a Methodist minister, who married 'below her station'. He grew up in drab circumstances and in 1852 stowed away to Australia, where he acquired a knowledge of pharmacy and some experience as a schoolteacher, and studied for the Wesleyan ministry. He married Elizabeth Powell in 1859; they had one son and four daughters. In 1860 Baker was sent as a missionary to the island of Tonga in the south Pacific where, despite his lack of formal training, he soon acquired a reputation as a skilled medical practitioner. Combined with his personal ambition and evident sympathy for indigenous interests, this soon earned him considerable influence, especially with the king, whose wife he regularly attended.

For some time before the cession of Fiji to Britain in 1874 the Tongans, wary of colonial encroachments, had been concerned for the preservation of their own independence. To this end Baker, at the request of King George of Tonga, negotiated treaties with Germany and Britain recognizing Tonga as an autonomous kingdom, and drew up a new constitution and legal code which were promulgated in 1875. The policy of remaining Tongan by appearing Western was successful, but the changes wrought by Baker and the personal power he had acquired antagonized his rivals for influence in Tonga. He was suspected of disloyalty to both Wesleyan and British interests. In 1879, therefore, the Wesleyan conference in Sydney, at the request of Sir Arthur Gordon (afterwards Lord Stanmore), British high commissioner for the Western Pacific, appointed a commission to inquire into charges made against Baker by the British vice-consul in connection with his aggressively competitive method of collecting money from the Tongans, even though it was for church purposes. Baker was recalled to Australia, but he returned independently to Tonga in 1880, whereupon the king appointed him prime minister. In 1881 he resigned from the Wesleyan ministry.

Under Baker's guidance the Tongan constitution was revised, giving the little kingdom of 20,000 people a cabinet, a privy council, and a parliament. Also its land laws were simplified, a state education system was introduced, and Tongan law was applied to European settlers. In 1885 the Free Wesleyan Church of Tonga was set up independently of the conference in Sydney. These changes aroused much opposition among traders, traditional Wesleyans, and various Tongan title-holders whose position as king's advisers Baker had usurped. In January 1887 their discontent, encouraged by a visiting British official, Basil Thomson, culminated in an attempt on Baker's life, in which his son and daughter were injured. Six Tongans were executed and others given lesser sentences for this assault. None the less, opposition remained strong and further disorder likely. Besides, Sir John Thurston, high commissioner for the Western Pacific, was resentful that Baker did not do more to promote British interests yet had accepted an award from the German government, so in 1890 he exiled him to New Zealand.

Although Baker had secured Tonga's political and ecclesiastical independence, when he returned to Tonga in 1897 his influence was at an end, King George having died in 1893. Disappointed in his hope of preferment among Free Wesleyan adherents, he introduced the Church of England to Tonga. He died at Ha'apai on 30 November 1903. Baker had many faults of character but he deserved to be more sympathetically memorialized than he came to be in the well-known writings of his opponent Basil Thomson, who ridiculed him as an uncouth upstart. He was self-seeking but he was also the king's loyal and capable servant. 'Tonga for the Tongans' was not just his slogan; it became his enduring achievement.

HUGH LARACY

Sources N. Rutherford, *Shirley Baker and the king of Tonga* (1971) • N. Rutherford, 'Baker, Shirley Waldemar', *AusDB*, vol. 3

Baker, Sir (William) Stanley (1928–1976), actor and film producer, was born at 32 Albany Street in Ferndale, a village in the Rhondda valley in south Wales, on 28 February 1928, the third of the three children of John Henry Baker and his wife, Elizabeth Louisa, *née* Lock. His father had lost a leg in a mining accident in 1917, and found it hard to gain full-time employment, and the family lived in poverty. As a child, Stanley resented the charity on which they depended, earned money from part-time jobs when he could, and acquired the playground bully image which became his trade mark as an actor. He was educated at Ferndale secondary school, where his English teacher was Glynne Morse, who wrote school plays for his pupils. Morse was struck by his 'satanic' stage presence as a child and took him to Cardiff to audition at the age of thirteen for the film producer Sir Michael Balcon, who cast him as the boy patriot Peter for the Ealing Studios war film *Under Cover* (1942).

Baker began his professional stage career by understudying Richard Burton, who became his lifelong friend, in Emlyn Williams's play *The Druid's Rest* (1943). Burton came from a similar background in the mining valleys and had a similarly dedicated teacher. With the Houstons, Glyn and Donald, they provided a Welsh contrast, virile and rugby-loving, to the English stars, polite and addicted to cricket, in post-war British cinema. In 1944 Morse took Baker to audition for Sir Barry Jackson at the Birmingham

Sir (William) Stanley Baker (1928–1976), by Cornel Lucas, 1955

Repertory, thought to be the finest training ground for actors in the country, where he stayed for two years before undertaking his military service (1946–8) in the army. Among his roles was that of Hector Malone in the young Peter Brook's production of Shaw's *Man and Superman* (1945), in which a then unknown Paul Scofield played John Tanner.

Baker's first major stage success came when he played Corporal Joe Adams in Christopher Fry's poetic drama, *A Sleep of Prisoners* (1951). After the army, he had appeared in several popular films, such as *Captain Horatio Hornblower RN* (1951, with Gregory Peck) without exactly starring; but as Adams, he was able to prove that his talents had a wider range than mere bravado. He was chosen for the part of Bennett, the bullying first lieutenant, in *The Cruel Sea* (1953), an epic war film, also made at Ealing Studios, the first of several major action movies in which he starred as a hard-bitten hero or as a resolute villain. These included *The Red Beret* (1953), *Hell below Zero* (1954), *The Good Die Young* (1954), *A Hill in Korea* (1956), *Campbell's Kingdom* (1957), *Violent Playground* (1958), *The Angry Hills* (1959), and the most successful war film of its time, *The Guns of Navarone* (1961), again with Gregory Peck. With his beetle brows and face (in Burton's phrase) 'like a clenched fist', Baker became known as the British Humphrey Bogart and played similar tough-guy parts in imitation of the Hollywood *films noirs*; but he also appeared as Henry Tudor in Laurence Olivier's film of *Richard III* (1956) and in several forgettable costume dramas, such as Sir Mordred in *Knights of the Round Table* (1954).

During the 1950s Baker made more than thirty films and left the poverty of his childhood for the affluence of his early middle age, when he was among the most highly paid of British stars. Burton introduced him to a young actress, Ellen Rose Martin (*b*. 1925/6), whom he married on 21 October 1950. They had four children, Glyn, Sally, Martin, and Adam, in a partnership which lasted to the end of his life. In 1959 the American film director Joseph Losey, blacklisted in Hollywood by McCarthy's House Un-American Activities Committee, came to live in Britain and cast Baker as Inspector Morgan in what seemed a minor detective story, *Blind Date* (1959), although the script demanded a subtle sense of danger which had previously eluded Baker. Losey made three other films with him, each of which extended his range as an actor, although in *The Criminal* (1960) he still played a tough guy, Johnny Bannion. In *Eve* (1962) and *Accident* (1967) Losey cast Baker against type as a bogus writer and a university don, with startling success. In *Accident* he proved his ability to develop the nuances of Harold Pinter's spare dialogue in a menacing performance which alone would have established his reputation as a major screen actor.

Losey and the writer-director Cy Endfield, also a refugee from McCarthy's Hollywood, brought out another side to Baker's character, his socialist instincts. In the early 1960s, he went into partnership with Endfield to co-produce a film, *Zulu* (1964). The true-life story of the defence of Rorke's Drift in 1879 by the South Wales Borderers, in which Baker played the tough commanding officer of the besieged garrison, Lieutenant Chard, with Michael Caine as more cavalier second-in-command, Lieutenant Bromhead, was a spectacular epic, reputed to have grossed more than $12 million through its sales worldwide, eight times its original investment. Baker became a successful film producer overnight, with his own company, Diamond Films, although other movies which he produced, including *Sands of the Kalahari* (1965), lacked the box-office appeal of *Zulu*. In *Dingaka* (1965) he cast black actors in the leading roles against the wishes of the South African government, and suffered the consequences, while in *Robbery* (1967), a taut thriller, he starred as the criminal mastermind of a train robbery.

With this experience, Baker was invited to become with Burton and Sir Geraint Evans a director of the newly formed independent television company Harlech Television (HTV) in 1968. Throughout his career he had acted on television, memorably as Rochester in *Jane Eyre* (1957); and in his last three years, some of his best performances were reserved for the small screen, notably as the drunken psychiatrist in HTV's *Graceless I Go* and as the father in Richard Llewellyn's novel, *How Green was my Valley* (1975), adapted into a six-part BBC television serial, basing his performance on the memory of his own father, whom he loved and admired. He was politically active, making party political broadcasts for the prime minister, Harold Wilson, who included his name in his resignation honours list in 1976. Baker, who endured an operation for cancer earlier in the year, was knighted a few weeks before his death at Residencia Sanitaria Carlos Haya, a hospital in Malaga, Spain, close to his second home in Marbella, on 28 June 1976. JOHN ELSOM

Sources A. Storey, *Stanley Baker: portrait of an actor* (1977) · D. Berry, *Wales and cinema* (1994) · *The Times* (29 June 1976) · *WWW* · L. Halliwell, *Halliwell's film guide*, 6th edn (1988) · J. Walker, ed., *Halliwell's filmgoer's companion*, 11th edn (1995) · J. C. Trewin, *The Birmingham Repertory Theatre, 1913–1963* (1963) · b. cert. · m. cert. · d. cert.

Archives FILM BFI NFTVA, performance footage

Likenesses photographs, 1953–76, Hult. Arch. • C. Lucas, photograph, 1955, NPG [*see illus.*]
Wealth at death £421,823: probate, 29 April 1977, *CGPLA Eng. & Wales*

Baker, Thomas (*bap.* **1623**, *d.* **1689**), mathematician, son of James Baker of Ilton, Somerset, steward to the Strangeways family, was baptized there on 21 December 1623. He matriculated at Magdalen Hall, Oxford, in 1640, became a scholar at Wadham College in 1645, and graduated BA in 1647. According to Wood, Baker, though educated on puritanical lines, performed some small service for the royalist garrison at Oxford, through which he became in 1660 minister, and in 1681 vicar, of Bishop's Nympton, in Devon.

Outside his curatorial and family duties, Baker occupied himself with mathematical studies. His *Geometrical Key, or, Gate of Equations Unlocked* came to the notice of the Royal Society who in 1682 discussed and approved its publication, but dallied, until Robert Clavell FRS and publisher, saw it into print in 1684. Baker was elected to the Royal Society in November 1684, but was never admitted in person. The *Key* was a polyglot Latin and English work which attempted to do without arithmetic in the solution of equations by means of construction. Baker's other mathematical works were noted by the Royal Society but remained unpublished. They did, however, send him various mathematical questions, to which he gave such satisfactory answers that the society awarded him an engraved medal, which his son James preserved. Nothing is known of Baker's wife but he had at least one son and several married daughters. His son James and daughter Joane inherited at his death in May 1689. He was buried at Bishop's Nympton on 22 May.

F. Y. EDGEWORTH, *rev.* ANITA MCCONNELL

Sources M. Hunter, *The Royal Society and its fellows, 1660–1700: the morphology of an early scientific institution* (1982) • T. Birch, *The history of the Royal Society of London*, 4 vols. (1756–7); repr. with introduction by A. R. Hall (1968), vol. 4 • D. E. Smith, *Rara arithmetica* (1908); repr. (1976), 629 • Wood, *Ath. Oxon.* • S. P. Rigaud and S. J. Rigaud, eds., *Correspondence of scientific men of the seventeenth century*, 2 (1841); repr. (1965), 1–32

Baker, Thomas (**1656–1740**), nonjuring Church of England clergyman and antiquary, was born at Crook Hall, Lanchester, co. Durham, on 14 September 1656, the second of the six children of George Baker (*d.* 1677), of Crook, and his wife, Margaret Forster, of Edderstone. He was educated at the free school in Durham under the Revd Thomas Battersby, and in June 1674, at the age of seventeen, he went up to St John's College, Cambridge, which, but for a three-year period in the north-east in the late 1680s, was to be his home for the rest of his life. He graduated BA in 1678 and proceeded MA in 1681, and in 1680 he was elected Ashton fellow. Early in 1685, like Joshua Barnes and Matthew Prior, he contributed to a collection of poems by members of the University of Cambridge on the occasion of the death of Charles II and the accession of James II, *Moestissimae ac laetissimae academiae Cantabrigiensis*. Ordained deacon on 20 December 1685, he was ordained priest on 9 December 1686. In June 1687 he was appointed rector of Long Newton in the diocese of Durham by Bishop Nathaniel Crewe, a living he had to relinquish on 1 August 1690 because he refused to take the oaths to the new king, holding that his oath to James II was sacred and demanded unconditional loyalty. However, while at Long Newton he had resented what he felt to be Bishop Crewe's opportunism, and had strongly disapproved of James's attempts at Catholicizing England; although a nonjuror he continued to hold communion with the established church and was certainly not a Jacobite.

As he had acquired his BD degree in 1688, just before the revolution, Baker did not simultaneously lose his fellowship. He lived on as a full and regular member of the college, but the prospect of a career in the church was over. Apart from being personally disappointed, over the next decade Baker came to be increasingly alarmed at the growth of latitudinarianism and deism, clearly connected with the developments in science and philosophy. He was a conservative Anglican clergyman who felt that this dangerous spirit of modernity of the post-revolution era had to be opposed. To this end he thoroughly prepared himself to write a book that would bring out the essential inadequacy of human knowledge and the fatal consequences of an overvaluing of human reason, emphasizing instead the need for a humble and reverent belief in revelation as our only certainty. He was a well-informed amateur, not a scientist or a philosopher, and his *Reflections upon Learning* (1699), while evidently touching a chord with the general reader—it went through eight editions before 1760—met with severe criticism from specialists. Although the book was published anonymously Baker became involved in an acrimonious controversy over it with the geologist and physician John Woodward, and this unpleasant experience clearly played a part in his decision to turn his attention to more congenial subjects.

In the first decade of the eighteenth century Baker began a thorough study of the past, especially that of his college and of his university. For a nonjuror and antiquarian scholar at that period Cambridge was not the most congenial environment, yet Baker came to be one of the best informed historical and antiquarian scholars of his day. Not only was he the expert on St John's College, he was also familiar with the holdings of the other college libraries and the university library. He was sent material by scholars and friends from all over England, and he had access to books and manuscripts from some of the best collections in the country, including those of Harley, Thomas and Richard Rawlinson, John Bagford, John Strype, Thomas Hearne, White Kennett, Francis Peck, Humfrey Wanley, and the library of Bishop John Moore of Ely, which came to Cambridge in 1715. In the course of the years he transcribed many original documents, printed and manuscript, which he saw as an indispensable research tool for his work. Although he had completed the first draft of a history of St John's College by the end of 1705, he refrained from publishing it, fearful of adverse reactions in his own circle. Similarly in the early 1730s he abandoned the 'Athenae Cantabrigienses', a comprehensive history of Cambridge University like Anthony Wood's work on Oxford, because, cautious and perfectionist as he was, he had become daunted by the extent and the difficulty of the task. None the less, he continued to collect material, and ultimately there were forty-two volumes of transcripts. He also accumulated a valuable library of some 5000 printed books and manuscripts. Apart from works by and about St John's and Cambridge men, and an impressive number of bibliographical reference works, emphases in his library were early printed books, and the history of the church and the state, especially in the sixteenth century. Baker was a bibliophile, but a utilitarian one. He spent much time carefully correcting, repairing, and supplementing the defective and incomplete books and manuscripts that he, as a book collector of modest means, often had to be contented with. His letters, the preliminary pages and margins of his books and manuscripts, and his interleaved copy of Andrew Maunsell's 1595 catalogue abundantly illustrate his expertise as a bibliographer.

Baker's extensive correspondence makes clear that he was at the centre of a network of some forty scholars and book collectors from many different backgrounds, and that in this way he played a very important role in the world of historical and antiquarian scholarship. Eirenical and undogmatic, unlike his fellow nonjuror and Oxford friend Thomas Hearne, he was naturally moderate and had a gift for nuance unusual in the ideologically polarized climate of the time. In his communications with other scholars Baker was a public-spirited man with a lofty ideal of serving the cause of learning, alongside the practical consideration of obtaining information for his own work. He had a deep reverence for the past and he came to idealize certain parts of it. Yet as a historian he also had a great respect for facts. Hence the openness and fairness in his accounts of such—for most nonjurors—'suspect' figures as William Prynne and Gilbert Burnet and hence also his constant insistence on the need for original documents as the basis of history writing. He hated frivolousness, inaccuracy, and speculation in a historian, and for that reason he dismissed such foreign writers as Gregorio Leti and the historical writings of such English authors as Francis Bacon and Sir William Temple as insufficiently based on authentic material.

Baker's only publication as a historical and antiquarian scholar, a reprint of Bishop John Fisher's *Funeral Sermon of Margaret Countess of Richmond and Derby*, appeared in 1708, with a long and interesting preface. Both here and in his college history, his treatment of the founders and early benefactors of the college reveals his admiration for their orthodoxy, firmness, and integrity, and there is a clear element of identification on his part with these heroes of a glorious past, and also of justification of his own nonjuring position. Baker himself was a benefactor of the college. After the death of his eldest brother, George, in 1699 he had become actively involved in the management of the leasehold collieries of the Baker family in the Durham area, and mainly with the proceeds from this family business he founded the six Baker exhibitions at St John's in 1710.

On 21 January 1717 Baker was officially deprived of his fellowship because he refused to take the oath of abjuration. Baker, for whom loyalty to the college had always been a major driving force and who was by now sixty, experienced this as a disgrace, and the event had a traumatic effect on him. Between 1717 and his death in 1740 he went through all his books and manuscripts and branded them with the words 'Thomas Baker Collegii Johannis Socius Ejectus'. Although in practical terms the change was not so great, as he was allowed to keep his rooms in the college, he was so bitter and disillusioned that he seriously considered leaving St John's and Cambridge for good. However, both had become too much part of his life for him to be able to take that drastic step. He had not been away from Cambridge very often, in spite of pressing invitations from several of his friends to visit them in London, Oxford, or elsewhere. There had been the necessary business visits to the north-east, which he always tried to combine with work among the Durham collections. In 1709 he had spent some time transcribing material in the state paper office in London, and occasionally he went over to Ely to search the episcopal registers there, but from 1717 onward he led a more and more retired life, spending his days among his books and manuscripts, copying material from the collections of others, and writing letters to his many friends and acquaintances. As more of his Cambridge friends dropped away he kept to his rooms, going out only sporadically for a walk in the garden or a visit to the coffee house. On 2 July 1740 he died of a stroke, at St John's, at the age of eighty-three, and three days later he was buried in the ante-chapel of St John's College next to the tomb of Hugh Ashton, one of the earliest benefactors of the college; he had never married. His library, preserved at St John's and at Cambridge University Library, stands as an impressive monument to the piety and learning of this modest and conscientious scholar.

FRANS KORSTEN

Sources Bodl. Oxf., MS Eng. hist. D. 1; MSS Rawl. 30, 42; MSS Rawl. A, B, C, D; MSS Rawl. letters 22, 23, 27[B], 30, 42, 107, 112, 114[X]; MSS Smith 47, 56; MSS Tanner 314, 342; MSS Willis 35, 37, 39, 45 · BL, Add. MSS 4275, 5485, 5820, 5831, 5853–5854, 6209, 6396, 22190; MSS Harley 3777, 7028–7050; MSS Lansdowne 988, 990, 1035; MSS Loan 29/63, 29/251; MS Stowe 749 · CUL, Add. MSS 2, 10, 7647, 8286; MSS Mm.1.35–53, 2.22–25 · St John Cam., MS 15.40; MSS H 26, 27, 42; N 27; O 54, 55 · U. Durham L., archives and special collections, Baker MSS · Christ Church Oxf., MS Arch W Epist. 11 · *Remarks and collections of Thomas Hearne*, ed. C. E. Doble and others, 11 vols., OHS, 2, 7, 13, 34, 42–3, 48, 50, 65, 67, 72 (1885–1921) · R. Masters, *Memoirs of the life and writings of the late Rev. Thomas Baker B. D.* (1784) · T. Baker, *History of the college of St John the Evangelist, Cambridge*, ed. J. E. B. Mayor, 2 vols. (1869) · F. Korsten, *A catalogue of the library of Thomas Baker* (1990) · *DNB* · F. Korsten, 'Thomas Baker's *Reflections upon learning*', *Studies in seventeenth century English literature, history and bibliography*, ed. G. A. M. Janssens and F. G. A. M. Aarts (1984), 133–48 · R. Surtees, *The history and antiquities of the county palatine of Durham*, 3 (1823), 353–8

Archives BL, corresp. and papers, Add. MSS 5820–5850 · CUL, papers · St John Cam., collection of MSS · U. Durham L., archives and special collections, corresp. and papers · Yale U., Farmington,

Lewis Walpole Library, biographical papers | BL, letters to Lord Oxford, Add. MS 70422 · Bodl. Oxf., letters to Thomas Hearne · Bodl. Oxf., letters to Richard Rawlinson · Bodl. Oxf., letters to Thomas Smith · Bodl. Oxf., letters to Browne Willis · Bodl. Oxf., papers

Likenesses attrib. C. Bridges, oils (after G. Vertue), St John Cam.; copies: Bodl. Oxf.; S. Antiquaries, Lond.; St John's College, Oxford · J. Simon, mezzotint (after C. Bridges), BM · G. Vertue, drawing, probably USA · photograph (after G. Vertue), NPG

Baker, Thomas (*b*. 1680/81), playwright and journalist, was said to have been 'the Son of an eminent Attorney in *King-street*, near *Guildhall*, in the City of *London*' (Mottley, 166). His comedy *The Humour of the Age* was premièred at Drury Lane on 1 March 1701 and in his dedicatory letter the young author owned himself 'oblig'd to the Town for the extraordinary Reception this Rough Draught met with'. In February 1702 the Drury Lane actors were prosecuted for immoral expressions in three plays, including Baker's, but were acquitted. Baker's very successful *Tunbridge-Walks, or, The Yeoman of Kent*, was premièred in January 1703. It received regular performances throughout the first half of the century and was revived by Kitty Clive for her benefit in 1764. *Biographia dramatica* claimed that Baker, realizing that he had acquired effeminate mannerisms, wrote the part of the fop Maiden (played by William Bullock) to parody himself and then reformed his behaviour.

Baker was apparently working as a lawyer by November 1703, when the prologue to Mary Pix's *The Different Widows* refers to his attending a judge at Westminster Hall. This was a period of puritan attacks on theatrical immorality and Baker's next play, the racy *An Act at Oxford*, was banned. The dedicatory letter of the 1704 text speaks of the 'favourable Reception and happy agreeable Conversation' Baker had had at Oxford, but it is not clear whether he was ever a student there. The play was reworked as *Hampstead Heath*, which seems to have achieved only three performances, at Drury Lane in autumn 1705. In the 'Long Vacation Prologue', spoken by Richard Estcourt at Drury Lane in September 1708, Baker deplored the union of London's two theatre companies, which had taken place that January and reduced opportunities for actors and playwrights. Baker claimed that his last play, *The Fine Lady's Airs* (premièred on 14 December 1708), was well received, but it proved too satirical for the taste of the time, as did Thomas D'Urfey's *The Modern Prophets* a few months later. Baker referred to the failure of D'Urfey's play in the prologue he wrote for Susanna Centlivre's *The Busybody* (first performed on 12 May 1709) and D'Urfey responded with a full-scale attack, in which he claimed *The Fine Lady's Airs* had been 'deservedly hist' (D'Urfey, 'Preface' to *The Modern Prophets*, 1709). Baker was by now disenchanted with the business of playwrighting and was considering abandoning it for 'something which may prove more serviceable to the Publick, and beneficial to my self' (Baker, 'Dedication', *The Fine Lady's Airs*).

Baker turned to journalism and on 8 July 1709, writing under the pseudonym of Phoebe Crackenthorpe, 'a Lady that knows every thing', inaugurated the *Female Tatler*. This entertaining tri-weekly periodical, with its satirical portraits, theatrical gossip, and mock advertisements, was published first by Benjamin Bragge and from number 19 by Anne Baldwin. The *Female Tatler* aroused the wrath of a rival journal, the *British Apollo*, which repeatedly attacked the supposed Mrs Crackenthorpe:

> this wise Undertaker,
> By Trade's an *At—ney*, by Name is a *B—r*.
> (14 Sept 1709)

It wrote (more than once) of the thrashing 'B—r' received for his satirical attack on a city deputy, of the damning of his play, of his poverty, and of his being cast off by his nearest relations. In number 51 of the *Female Tatler* (2 November 1709) Mrs Crackenthorpe announced that 'she' was resigning in favour of 'a Society of Modest Ladies' and Baker's connection with the journal ceased. According to Mottley, Baker left London for Worcestershire, 'being under Disgrace with his Father, who allow'd him but a very scanty Income' and died there 'the Death of the great *Sylla*, the *Roman* Dictator, of that loathsome distemper the *Morbus Pediculosus*' (Mottley, 167).

OLIVE BALDWIN and THELMA WILSON

Sources E. L. Avery, ed., *The London stage, 1660–1800*, pt 2: *1700–1729* (1960) · [G. Jacob], *The poetical register, or, The lives and characters of the English dramatick poets*, [1] (1719) · [J. Mottley], *A compleat list of all the English dramatic poets*, pubd with T. Whincop, *Scanderbeg* (1747) · D. E. Baker, *Biographia dramatica, or, A companion to the playhouse*, rev. I. Reed, new edn, rev. S. Jones, 3 vols. in 4 (1812) · *British Apollo* (31 Aug–26 Oct 1709) · *Female Tatler* (8 July–17 Aug 1709) [pubd by B. Bragge] · *Female Tatler* (19 Aug–2 Nov 1709) [pubd by A. Baldwin] · P. Danchin, ed., *The prologues and epilogues of the eighteenth century: a complete edition* (1990–), vol. 1 · J. H. Smith, 'Thomas Baker and the *Female Tatler*', *Modern Philology*, 49 (1951–2), 182–8 · W. Graham, 'Thomas Baker, Mrs. Manley and the *Female Tatler*', *Modern Philology*, 34 (1936–7), 267–72 · J. Milhous and R. D. Hume, eds., *A register of English theatrical documents, 1660–1737*, 2 vols. (1991)

Baker, Sir Thomas (1771?–1845), naval officer, of an old Kentish family, was a descendant, direct or collateral, of Vice-Admiral John *Baker (1660–1716). He entered the navy in August 1781 on the storeship *Dromedary* and was on her books until 1785. He was then three years in the East India Company service, but in 1788 he returned to the navy. After serving on the home, Halifax, and East India stations, he was promoted lieutenant on 13 October 1792. In 1793 he commanded the cutter *Lion*, in 1794 the lugger *Valiant*, and on 24 November 1795 he was promoted commander for good service in carrying dispatches to the West Indies. In 1796–7 he commanded the sloop *Fairy* in the North Sea, and on 13 June 1797 he reached captain's rank, commanding the *Princess Royal*.

In January 1799 Baker was appointed to the 28-gun frigate *Nemesis* in which, on 25 July 1800, when in command of a small squadron off Ostend, he met a number of Danish merchant vessels under convoy of the frigate *Freya*. Neutral powers argued that the convoy of a ship of war was a guarantee that none of the vessels carried contraband, and that they were therefore exempt from search. This the British government had never admitted, and in accordance with his instructions Baker insisted on searching the Danish ships. The *Freya* resisted but was quickly overpowered, and together with her convoy was brought into the Downs. After some negotiations the affair seemed to be amicably arranged, and the *Freya* and her convoy were restored; but the tsar of Russia made it a pretext for renewing the 'armed neutrality', which he induced Denmark to join. This led to the dispatch of the fleet under Sir Hyde Parker, and the battle of Copenhagen. Baker's conduct was approved by the Admiralty, and in January 1801 he was appointed to the 36-gun frigate *Phoebe*, which he commanded on the Irish station until the peace of Amiens in October 1801.

On the renewal of the war in 1803 Baker commissioned the *Phoenix* (42 guns), attached to the Channel Fleet under William Cornwallis off Ushant and in the Bay of Biscay. On 10 August 1805, being then to the north-west of Cape Finisterre, he fell in with and, after a brilliant and well-fought action of rather more than three hours' duration, captured the French 46-gun frigate *Didon*. The *Didon* had been sent off from Ferrol on the 6th with important dispatches from Villeneuve to Admiral Allemand, who was on his way to join him with five sail of the line. In consequence of this capture, Allemand never joined Villeneuve, and his ships had no further part in the campaign. On 14 August the *Phoenix* with her prize joined the British 74-gun *Dragon*, and the next day the three ships were sighted by Villeneuve, who took for granted that they were a part of the British fleet under Cornwallis looking for him. Not caring to risk an encounter, he turned south to Cadiz, and the fate that befell him off Cape Trafalgar. Baker in the meantime took his prize to Plymouth and, returning to his former station, on 2 November sighted the French squadron of four ships of the line under Dumanoir, escaping from Trafalgar. Knowing that Sir Richard John Strachan was off Ferrol, he at once sailed thither, and the same night joined Strachan, to whom he gave the news which directly led to the capture of the four French ships on 4 November, the *Phoenix* with the other frigates having an important part in the action. In the space of four months Baker had the opportunity, and ability, to exercise a major influence on the naval campaign of 1805. His performance was exemplary.

A fortnight later Baker was appointed to the *Didon* from which, in May 1806, he was moved to the *Tribune*, which he commanded for the next two years in the Bay of Biscay with distinguished success. In May 1808 he joined the *Vanguard* as flag-captain to Rear-Admiral Thomas Bertie in the Baltic. On leaving her in 1811, he spent some time in Sweden, where he married the daughter of Count Routh, a Swedish noble; they had several children. From 1812 to 1815 he commanded the 74-gun *Cumberland* in the West Indies, in the North Sea, and in charge of a convoy of East Indiamen to the Cape. In 1814 the prince of Orange conferred on him the order of William of the Netherlands, and on 4 June 1815 he was made a CB. He was appointed colonel of marines on 12 August 1819, was promoted rear-admiral on 19 July 1821, and was commander-in-chief on the coast of South America from 1829 to 1833. He was nominated KCB on 8 January 1831, became vice-admiral on 10 January 1837, and was awarded a good-service pension of £300 a year on 19 February 1842. He died at his residence, The Shrubbery, Walmer, Kent, on 26 February 1845. His second son, Horace Mann Baker, died a lieutenant, RN, in 1848. J. K. LAUGHTON, *rev.* ANDREW LAMBERT

Sources O. Feldbaek, *Denmark and the armed neutrality of 1800–1801* (1980) • J. S. Corbett, *The campaign of Trafalgar* (1910) • O'Byrne, *Naval biog. dict.* • *GM*, 2nd ser., 23 (1845), 436–7 • W. James, *The naval history of Great Britain, from the declaration of war by France, in February 1793, to the accession of George IV, in January 1820*, [2nd edn], 6 vols. (1826)

Baker, Thomas Barwick Lloyd (1807–1886), promoter of reformatory schools, was born at the family seat, Hardwicke Court, the only son of Thomas John Lloyd Baker and his wife, Mary, daughter of William Sharp of Fulham. Like his father, Baker went to Eton College and Christ Church, Oxford, where he matriculated in 1826 but did not graduate. He entered Lincoln's Inn in 1828 and in 1833 became a magistrate for Gloucestershire, where Hardwicke Court was located. Shortly afterwards he became a visiting magistrate at the county gaol and house of correction at Gloucester. In 1841, on the death of his father, a noted innovator in local poor-law administration, Baker inherited Hardwicke Court. A high-church Anglican, Baker contributed substantially to the restoration of Hardwicke, Uley, and other churches, and urged the different skeins of Anglicanism to rejoice in diversity and tolerance of one another. He was a staunch tory all his life, and was president of the Gloucestershire chamber of commerce, a captain in the county yeomanry cavalry, a deputy lieutenant of Gloucestershire, and high sheriff of Gloucester in 1847–8. Baker was well known locally as an ornithologist and, indeed, his first published work in 1835 was an index of birds. On 10 March 1840 he married Mary, daughter of Nicholas Lewis Fenwick of Besford Court, Worcestershire; they had two sons, Granville Edwin Lloyd Baker (*b.* 1841), high sheriff of Gloucestershire in 1898, and Henry Orde Lloyd Baker (*b.* 1842).

Baker became internationally known for two things: his pioneering work in reformatory schools and his writings on crime and punishment. He first encountered reformatories for young offenders in London in 1837 and was also in close touch with the well-known pioneer of these institutions, the Revd Sydney Turner. Following a large conference on the subject at Birmingham in 1851 attended by Turner and the other doyen of the movement, Mary Carpenter, Baker knocked two farm cottages in the grounds of Hardwicke Court into one and opened Hardwicke Reformatory. A close associate and co-manager at the beginning of the project was George Henry Bengough (1829–1865), a local landowner and theorist about crime and punishment who, for the first two years, spent long periods living and teaching at the reformatory. With a permanent staff of four and an average of forty young males up to 1870, the institution was certified under the 1854

Reformatory Schools Act, which regulated and encouraged the spread of these institutions; after 1870 the number of inmates rose to an average of seventy.

Baker was leader of one of two schools of thought about reformatories. On one side, Mary Carpenter and her supporters propounded a model for reformatories in which staff were viewed as substitute parents and agents of holistic personal transformation of the individual offender, and in which individualized treatment and long periods of education and patient, careful nurturing characterized by disciplined but warm engagement between staff and inmates would serve to rescue the young offenders from the delinquency formerly fostered by their corrupting social environment. Baker took the reverse view: reformatories were to be reserved only for recidivistic youth and should deter further delinquency by severity. At Hardwicke, therefore, the inmates were compelled to carry out heavy spade work on the clay soil of the farm and were punished by beating or confinement in cells for any disobedience. Baker was sure that hard labour in the countryside away from the corruption of cities would condition minds and bodies to habitual labour, induce mental tranquillity, and (incidentally) roughen and callous hands deliberately kept tender and nimble for pickpocketing or till raiding. There were night classes in reading, writing, and arithmetic, but classroom education took second place to labour, and the inmates slept in hammocks in dormitories. Baker kept the young offenders for much shorter periods than reformatories run on the nurturing/interactive model, only two years on average, and always released them on licence, often to work for local farmers. The regime depended on a marks system, whereby compliance earned amelioration of severity; it was this model, of deterrent, rigidly routinized, total institutions, which prevailed in the reformatories that spread across Britain following these pioneering projects, rather than that of Mary Carpenter. Baker was convinced that his severe model hugely reduced crime by general deterrence and the habituation of the inmates themselves to labour and obedience.

Baker wrote about 200 journal and newspaper articles (in both the local and the national press) on crime and punishment. In all his writings he advanced the view that an effective system of criminal justice administration rested on the double foundations of the criminal's cognition of punishment and of motivation for good behaviour. He believed that to deter crime there must be very widespread knowledge of the punishment for criminal behaviour, and that this punishment should operate not on the basis of maximum retributive severity to all offenders, nor yet on what he viewed as unsuccessful individualized reformatory programmes, but on the basis of an accumulation of punishment in accordance with the known convictions and proven antecedent behaviour of the offender. A first conviction for the majority of offenders would carry a very short prison sentence to achieve the maximum shock; each subsequent conviction would carry a higher penalty until the fourth, which would automatically carry a sentence of life imprisonment to secure the maximum incapacitation from crime of the individual offender and the maximum of deterrence to others.

Allied to this 'cumulative system' of deterrence, Baker demanded a prison system which enlisted the offender's motivation and energy in his own reformation. The initial regime would be extremely severe but, as the prisoner demonstrated compliance and commitment to the programmes of the institution, would progressively allow greater freedom and comfort until eventually the prisoner would secure conditional release on licence supervised by the police. In 1871 a version of this system was introduced by Baker in Gloucestershire following work on similar lines pioneered by Sir Walter Crofton in Ireland.

Baker also designed a system, known as 'The Berkshire system', to test the veracity of those claiming relief at workhouses on the basis that they were travelling to a place of employment. This was experimentally tried in Gloucestershire from 1868 onwards. Baker was regularly cited by internationally known theorists of crime and punishment of his time, such as the fourth earl of Carnarvon, William Tallack, E. C. Wines, and Professor Von Holtzendorff. He was also a founder of the highly influential National Association for the Promotion of Social Science. A selection of his writings was published by Herbert Philips and Edmund Verney in 1889 as *War with Crime*.

Baker suffered ill health from 1882 onwards and thereafter took a lesser part in local public affairs, although he continued to publish up to 1885. He died at Hardwicke Court on 10 December 1886, and was buried at Hardwicke church. BILL FORSYTHE

Sources *Annual reports of the inspector of reformatories and industrial schools* (1853–90) · J. Manton, *Mary Carpenter and the children of the streets* (1976) · T. B. L. Baker, *'War with crime': being a selection of reprinted papers*, ed. H. Philips and E. Verney (1889) · L. Radzinowicz and R. Hood, *A history of English criminal law and its administration from 1750*, rev. edn, 5: *The emergence of penal policy in Victorian and Edwardian England* (1990) · M. Carpenter, *Reformatory schools for the children of the perishing and dangerous classes* (1851) · *The Times* (13 Dec 1886) · *The Times* (14 Dec 1886) · *The Times* (16 Dec 1886) · *National union catalog*, Library of Congress · 'Royal commission on reformatories and industrial schools', *Parl. papers* (1884), 45.1, C. 3876; 45.89, C. 3876-I · m. cert.

Archives Glos. RO, personal corresp. and papers | Bodl. Oxf., corresp. with Sir Thomas Phillipps · Glos. RO, letters to H. C. Clifford

Likenesses G. Richmond, portrait, repro. in Baker, *War with crime*

Wealth at death £8171 4*s*.: probate, June 1887, *CGPLA Eng. & Wales*

Baker, Sir Thomas Durand (1837–1893), army officer, was born on 23 March 1837, son of John Durand Baker, vicar of Bishop's Tawton, north Devon. He was educated at Cheltenham. Baker was commissioned an ensign in the 18th (Royal Irish) regiment on 18 August 1854, served with his regiment at the siege of Sevastopol from 30 December 1854, and was mentioned in dispatches for gallantry on 18 June 1855 during the attack on the Redan redoubt. He was promoted lieutenant on 12 January 1855. He was present when the fortress fell on 8 September, and returned to England in July 1856. For his success during the war he received the campaign medal with clasp and the Turkish and Sardinian medals. In November 1857 he embarked with his regiment for India, to help suppress the Indian mutiny which had begun in May 1857. He served during 1858 with the field force operating in central India in pursuit of Tantia Topi. Baker was promoted captain on 26 October 1858, and successfully obtained admission to the Staff College at Camberley, from which he passed out in 1862.

In 1863 Baker accompanied the 2nd battalion, Royal Irish regiment to New Zealand; there he served as deputy assistant adjutant-general to the forces between 20 March 1864 and 31 March 1866, and then as assistant adjutant-general until the end of April 1867. He served as assistant military secretary to Lieutenant-General Sir Duncan Cameron in the engagement at Rangiriri on 20 November 1863, and participated in the Waikato and Wanganui campaigns in 1864–6. Baker was a staff officer with Major-General Carey's force during the unsuccessful assault on Orakau on 31 March 1864 when he led one of the assault columns, and was also present when it was finally captured on 2 April. For his bravery, untiring energy, and zeal in New Zealand he was mentioned in dispatches and received the campaign medal, and on 21 March 1865 was given a brevet majority.

On 2 October 1873 Baker was appointed assistant adjutant and quartermaster-general of the Asante expedition, and accompanied Sir Garnet Wolseley to the Gold Coast. He served throughout the campaign, participated in the engagement at Esaman (14 October), the relief of Abrakampa (5 and 6 November), the battle of Amoaful (31 January 1874), and the battle of Ordahsu and the capture of Kumasi (4 February). In addition to his duties as quartermaster-general, from 14 October 1873 to 17 December 1874 he also performed those of chief of staff. For his services in the Asante kingdom he was mentioned in dispatches by Wolseley, who attributed to Baker's untiring energy much of the success that had attended the operations, and expressed the view that he possessed 'every quality that is valuable to a staff officer'. Baker was promoted brevet lieutenant-colonel on 1 April 1874, received the medal with clasp, and was made a CB.

Following his return from the Gold Coast, on 22 May 1874 Baker was appointed a deputy assistant quartermaster-general on the headquarters staff in London, and on 10 November 1875 an assistant adjutant-general. On 21 April 1877 he was made an aide-de-camp to the queen, with rank of colonel in the army. During the 1877 Russo-Turkish War he was attached to the Russian army, and was present at the principal operations in the Balkans. In November 1878 he accompanied Lord Lytton, the new viceroy, to India, as his military secretary. Baker was serving as a member of the army reform commission—appointed to examine reductions in the Indian army without impairing its efficiency—when, in September 1879, news of the murder at Kabul of Sir Louis Cavagnari reached Simla. When Sir Frederick Roberts was ordered to advance on Kabul to seek retribution he requested that Baker should command the 2nd infantry brigade.

Baker accompanied Roberts when he rejoined his division in the Kurram valley and on 19 September was present when Afghan troops attacked entrenchments occupied by his brigade at the Shutar Gardan Pass. By 1 October 1879 the whole of the Kabul field force was concentrated in the Logar valley in Afghanistan. On 6 October Baker commanded his brigade during the successful battle of Charasia and was present when Kabul was reoccupied three days later. In November Baker led a force to Maidan, on the Kabul–Ghazni Road, where he repulsed an Afghan attack before returning to Kabul. On 8 November he commanded a force co-operating with other columns, between Arghandeh and Maidan, attempting to destroy a large gathering of Afghans. However, on hearing news of the failure of Massey's column he returned to Kabul. Baker attacked an Afghan force occupying the Takht-i-Shah Hill on 13 December and the following day attacked the Asmai heights, although on this occasion he was forced by superior numbers to withdraw. On 23 December Baker took part in the complete defeat and dispersion of the Afghan force which had attacked the Sherpur entrenchments. Shortly afterwards he commanded an expedition which advanced into Kohistan and destroyed a fortified post. He commanded an infantry brigade of the force with which Roberts left Kabul for Kandahar on 9 August 1880, following the arrival of Sir Donald Stewart and news of the defeat of Maiwand, to relieve the beleaguered garrison. Following a three-week march Baker took a prominent part during the battle of Kandahar on 1 September, after which the city was relieved. He then returned to England. For his services in Afghanistan he was mentioned in dispatches, received the campaign medal with three clasps and a bronze star, and on 22 February 1881 was promoted KCB.

On 30 March 1881 Baker was appointed a brigadier-general under Sir Frederick Roberts, to command the base and line of communications in Natal in operations being planned against the Boers of the Transvaal following the earlier disastrous defeat at Majuba Hill. However, an armistice was concluded and Baker returned home the following September without having seen any active service. On 1 April 1882 he was promoted lieutenant-colonel, appointed deputy quartermaster-general in Ireland, and, on 3 September, deputy adjutant-general in Ireland.

Baker returned to India on 10 October 1884 when he was nominated adjutant-general in the East Indies, with the local rank of major-general. He served during the 1886–7 Burmese expedition and was mentioned in dispatches. He was promoted major-general on 1 September 1866 and then held command of a division of the Bengal army until 1890. He then returned to England, and was appointed quartermaster-general to the forces at the Horse Guards on 1 October 1890. On 29 April 1891 he was made a temporary lieutenant-general and on 15 June 1892 was awarded a good-service pension. While on leave of absence from his duties at the War Office, Baker died of dropsy at the Hotel de France, Pau, France, on 9 February 1893, after a brief illness. He was buried on 18 February in Bishop's Tawton churchyard. T. R. MOREMAN

Sources *The Times* (10 Feb 1893) · B. Robson, *The road to Kabul: the Second Afghan War, 1878–1881* (1986) · *DNB* · T. A. Heathcote, *The military in British India: the development of British land forces in south Asia, 1600–1947* (1995) · J. Belich, *The New Zealand wars and the Victorian interpretation of racial conflict* (1986) · H. Brackenbury, *The Ashanti war*, 2 vols. (1874) · Lord Roberts [F. S. Roberts], *Forty-one years in India*, 2 vols. (1897) · *Army List* · *CGPLA Eng. & Wales* (1893)

Archives BL OIOC, MSS · BL OIOC, papers relating to Second Afghan War, MS Eur. D 567 · NAM, papers relating to Second Afghan War | NAM, letters to Lord Roberts

Likenesses photograph, BL OIOC

Wealth at death £5283 19*s*. 1*d*.: administration, 8 March 1893, *CGPLA Eng. & Wales*

Baker, Valentine [*called* Baker Pasha] (**1827–1887**), army officer, was born on 1 April 1827 at Enfield, the third son of Samuel Baker (*d*. 1862), later of Lypiatt Park, Stroud, Gloucestershire, and his first wife, Mary, daughter of Thomas Dobson of Enfield. The family's wealth had been established by the first Valentine Baker, a privateer during the American War of Independence and owner of sugar plantations in Jamaica and Mauritius. Samuel Baker inherited the plantations and was also a successful businessman, shipowner, director of the Great Western Railway, and chairman of the Gloucester Bank. He was unusual in his regard for education, and his close-knit family of seven surviving children attended local schools, including the College School, Gloucester, were tutored at home, and studied abroad.

Valentine Baker [Baker Pasha] (**1827–1887**), by unknown engraver, pubd 1884

Early military career Baker was intended for the army, with a commission purchased in the 10th hussars. He went first in 1848 to Ceylon, where his eldest brother, the explorer Samuel White *Baker (1821–1893), had purchased land, intending, with family and settlers, to create an English colony, at the same time indulging the brothers' passion for big-game hunting. In 1848 Baker joined, as ensign, the Ceylon rifles, and in April 1851 went to India to join the 10th hussars.

In 1852 Baker transferred to the 12th lancers in order to participate in the Basuto War in South Africa, distinguishing himself by his gallantry in action at the Berea in December 1852. Promoted lieutenant without purchase in July 1853, he served in India. He was still with the 12th lancers when the regiment was sent to the Crimea, reaching Balaklava in April 1855, and was present at the battle of Chernaya and the fall of Sevastopol. His active service showed him faults of the British cavalry which he later tried to reform.

In 1856, when the 12th lancers returned to India, Baker rejoined the 10th hussars, an expensive regiment with the highest social position in the cavalry of the line, as captain (by purchase). He obtained his majority (by purchase) in 1859 and, taking command of the regiment in 1860, remained as its colonel (by purchase, full colonel 1865) until 1873. As a peace-time soldier Baker established his reputation as a brilliant cavalry officer, a perfectionist devoted to his troops, and a theorist. In 1858 he produced *The British Cavalry*, an extension of Lewis Nolan's work: his practical recommendations on equipment, uniform, and stud farms were later in part adopted. In 1860 he wrote *Our National Defences*, expounding his conviction that France's aggressive preparations were directed at Britain and proposing defence changes including linked battalions and a 'national guard'. In 1869 he set out proposals in *Army Reform*, recommending changes in regimental administration, and submitted comments to the royal commission on military education, condemning the 'cramming' system. As background to his studies he travelled in Europe, inspecting military establishments, and was present as an observer during the Austro-Prussian and Franco-Prussian wars. In his writing Baker expressed himself clearly and incisively, 'always jolting the establishment, questioning the status quo or challenging the fashionable' (Anglesey, 3.117).

As colonel of the 10th hussars Baker made his regiment smart, efficient, and dynamic, and won the devotion of his officers and men. He was prepared to make changes and experiment, and he had the gift of communicating his ideas and enthusiasms. He was the first to experiment with railway transport of troops (July 1860), and his regiment was among the first to learn the new system of signalling.

Friendship with the prince of Wales, and marriage In 1863, when the prince of Wales (later Edward VII) became colonel-in-chief, Baker had additional support for his innovations, and the relationship between the two developed into friendship. From 1863 to 1867, while the 10th hussars were stationed in Ireland, Baker was able, at relative distance from the War Office, to work on various reforms, including his new 'non-pivot drill'. The 10th was used in support of the civil power and against the Fenians. During the 1867 Fenian uprising Baker commanded the Thurles flying column, for which he was commended by the commander-in-chief, Ireland.

Back in England regimental highlights were ceremonial occasions, with the prince and the colonel leading the parades and the regiment presenting its disciplined best and its superior horses (Baker's policy was to invest in blood horses with staying power). When the 10th hussars were posted to India at the end of 1872, Baker resigned.

The years of his command were also successful for Baker personally. On 13 December 1865 he married Fanny (*d.* 1885), only child of Frank Wormald of Potterton Hall, Aberford, Yorkshire; they had two daughters. His friendship with the prince of Wales led to membership of the Marlborough Club, London, a social centre for the prince's friends. He became a friend of Frederick Burnaby (1842–1885) of the Royal Horse Guards, and won the approval of the duke of Cambridge, the commander-in-chief of the British army.

Baker in central Asia In April 1873, while awaiting a new appointment, Baker set out with two military companions on a journey to northern Persia, Turkestan, and the borders of Afghanistan. It was a private expedition, a grand hunting party, but also an exploratory venture prompted by Russian advances through central Asia.

Baker kept a daily journal in which, as well as sporting descriptions, he reported on political discussions and military possibilities. The journey was full of incident and endurance: Baker fell seriously ill, and suffered frustration because his expedition lacked official approval. In his detailed account, published in 1876 as *Clouds in the East*, he provided an evaluation of Russian advances towards India, criticized British foreign policy, urged military preparedness and a 'bolder policy' against Russia in Asia, and proposed a nine-point plan of action (the basis of his lecture to the Royal United Service Institution in May 1874).

Baker and Miss Dickinson: imprisoned and cashiered In September 1874 Valentine Baker was appointed assistant quartermaster-general at Aldershot, with his first major responsibility the organization of a grand army review to take place in August 1875. It was a period of consolidation in his career: he was expected to be an established general by the 1880s. Instead an incident took place on a train and Baker's career in the British army was ended.

On 17 June 1875 Baker travelled to London with an appointment to dine with the duke of Cambridge. In a first-class compartment he talked with a young lady, Miss Dickinson, the sister of a Royal Engineers officer, and, it was alleged, tried to rape her. He was arrested; evidence against him was given by two gentlemen in the next compartment in addition to the detailed account of Miss Dickinson. There was public outcry against him, much moral indignation, and crowds gathered at the trial, which began on 30 July at Croydon assizes. The judge, Mr Justice Brett, spoke of the incident as 'a sudden outbreak of wickedness' and hoped that at some future time Baker might redeem himself 'by some brilliant service' (*The Times*, 3 Aug 1875, 10). On 2 August he was acquitted of attempted rape, convicted on the lesser charge of indecent assault, fined £500, and sentenced to a year's imprisonment.

Baker was cashiered, 'Her Majesty having no further occasion for his services' (*Annual Register*, 1875, 55). This was the queen's decision. She thought his brother Samuel Baker unprincipled, and was convinced that Valentine was like him, and a disgrace to the British army. Baker's wife, family, and friends, including the prince of Wales, stood by him. They, and his regiment, and most of the army believed, and continued to believe, that there had been mitigating circumstances, evidence not revealed, and that it had not been a fair trial.

The Eastern question On release from prison Baker left for Constantinople in September 1876, taking up an appointment, through the intervention of the prince, with the Turkish government. He was to organize a new system of civil gendarmerie, and was to advise the Turkish army on strengthening the fortifications around Constantinople.

War between Russia and Turkey broke out in April 1877, and in August Baker took up a command as general available for special services (henceforth he was known as Baker Pasha) and set out for the front at Shumla in Bulgaria. With him at his camp were his gendarmerie officers and an assortment of doctors, newspaper correspondents, MPs, and army officers come to observe the war. Among these was Herbert Kitchener, who was to become a friend and champion of Baker. Also there arrived unexpectedly Fred Burnaby.

The Russian armies crossed the Danube, but the Turkish armies stopped their advance. It was not until the fortress of Plevna fell on 10 December 1877 that the Russians began to cross the mountains. Baker commanded the centre division of the army at Kamarli, and, recognizing the importance of the pass of Tashkesan, he made an offer to the Turkish commander, guaranteeing that he would hold it to the last. This his division did, in a battle that lasted more than ten hours against vastly superior Russian forces. No reinforcements came, and the losses were severe. Just before nightfall another Russian attack was repulsed, and Baker's troops knew the day was won. That rear-guard action allowed the Turkish army to make an organized retreat: there was a telegram from the sultan and Baker was promoted lieutenant-general.

Baker, with Burnaby as his companion and support, joined the main body of the army in its retreat across Bulgaria. He was consulted by the Turkish army about defences for Constantinople, and asked to take on the command of the existing fortifications. Before he could take up the new post, the Turkish government had yielded to Russian demands in the treaty of San Stefano, and Baker, disgusted at the humiliation that would now be served upon the army—and his opinion of and love for his Turkish soldiers were great—asked for leave of absence.

Baker was acclaimed by the British public as a hero. The newspapers were enthusiastic in describing his military achievements, and Tashkesan was applauded as one of the most brilliant rear-guard actions of all time. He was re-elected to the Marlborough Club in March 1878 (and in 1881 to the Army and Navy Club). His *War in Bulgaria* (2 vols., 1879) revealed the enthusiastic soldier and the disappointed general, and his disillusionment with the Turkish high command; but it argued for continued support of Turkey against Russian advances on India. From the war he drew military lessons for Britain. Like others, he emphasized the lethality of rifle firepower and the necessity of entrenching, loose formations, and flank attacks, but claimed that cavalry could still be effective in battle.

Baker stayed on in Turkey with a new army position. His standing was high with the Turkish government and he was in favour with the sultan. His major tasks were to carry out army reforms; by 1879 his plans were sufficiently advanced for him to include chapters on the reorganization of the Turkish army in *War in Bulgaria*.

Organizing the Egyptian army In 1882 came an invitation from the khedive to organize and command a new Egyptian army. As a consequence of the British occupation of Egypt, Lord Dufferin, ambassador at Constantinople, had been authorized to draw up plans for a reformed Egyptian administration. High priority was given to a new army under the command of a British general with British officers in all supporting ranks.

Baker, consulting Dufferin, was assured that his appointment would be supported by the British cabinet. By October 1882 he was in Cairo with his plans for the army and his list of British officers willing to serve under him approved by the khedive. Two months later he was relieved of his post: the queen would not accept his appointment. The cabinet denied that it had given its approval, claiming that it was not possible for British officers to serve under a general who was not himself a serving British general. Baker was offered a command, as inspector-general, of a new gendarmerie and police force, a post to which the queen had no objections. Baker accepted, handing over his army plans and list to Sir Evelyn Wood.

In the new force Baker planned to use semi-military mounted troops in rural Egypt and civilian police in the towns; he was able to choose as officers a number of those who had served with him in Turkey. Administratively, the gendarmerie became the responsibility of the ministry of the interior. The calibre of the recruited men was low, but in mid-1883, when cholera swept Cairo, the new service showed its value in manning the cordons. Administrative difficulties followed with the British cabinet's appointment of Clifford Lloyd to undertake reforms in the ministry. Lloyd, with little knowledge of Egypt, took exception to Baker's gendarmerie, and by the end of 1883 had decided upon its abolition.

The British gave no support to the Egyptian government in its actions in the Sudan, but interfered. In February 1883 the khedive, on Baker's recommendation, appointed General Williams Hicks Pasha to retrain the army and overcome the Mahdist rebels. Hicks was assured of the support of a Sudan committee, with Baker as its executive officer. But the British objected to the committee and obstructed communications between Baker (ministry of interior) and Hicks (ministry of war). Hicks was not informed of the administrative changes, and became increasingly isolated. In November 1883 his army was annihilated by Mahdist forces and another Egyptian army was defeated. Military action was required immediately to relieve garrisons in eastern Sudan. The British government refused to allow the new Egyptian army to go to the Sudan (because its officers were also serving British officers), nor would it send the British army of occupation. The only force available was the gendarmerie, and the khedive made a personal appeal to Baker. By December 1883 the gendarmerie, unwilling, ill-prepared, undisciplined, was on its way.

At Suakin on the Red Sea, Baker tried to carry out the contradictory instructions received from the khedive and Sir Evelyn Baring, the British consul-general—to pacify the country, but not to embark on military action—while training his troops. The promised support from Cairo—ships, supplies, more troops—was delayed. The Sudanese reinforcements arrived without their promised leader, Zobehr Pasha, because of British objections to his background as a slave dealer. When the telegraph was installed, an official message arrived that the Egyptian government, under pressure from the British, was abandoning all activities in the Sudan. Baker and his force were left isolated. On 4 February 1884, with nearly 4000 men, he marched out of Trinkitat to cross the desert to relieve the garrison at Tokar: accompanying him was his friend Burnaby, who had arrived in response to a telegram from Baker's wife. The Mahdist rebels were waiting, Baker's force was attacked and panicked: more than 2300 men were killed at al-Teb, many speared in the back. Among those who died were gendarmerie officers who had been with Baker in Bulgaria.

Rear-Admiral Sir William Hewett, stationed with his five ships in Suakin harbour, took over. The remnants of Baker's force were shipped back to Cairo, the officers to find that their posts had been abolished. There was consternation in London, and on 14 February the British government agreed to immediate military action. Major-General Sir Gerald Graham was in Suakin by 22 February, commanding a British force which included a troopship with men of the 10th hussars (who welcomed Baker enthusiastically). At the second battle of al-Teb on 29 February the Mahdists were defeated. Baker, acting as chief intelligence officer, was severely wounded in the face, and received special commendation in Graham's dispatches. Baker's friends and the public appealed once more for his reinstatement: again the queen refused.

Lloyd resigned in May 1884, his reforms were set aside, and Baker began rebuilding his force. Still believing in the need for semi-military troops, he concentrated on the gendarmerie, allowing the traditional policing system to remain. In January 1885 Baker, sharing in the public grief over the death of Gordon at Khartoum, also suffered personal losses. Burnaby was killed at Abu Klea. Baker's elder daughter, Hermione, died, aged eighteen, later that month, and his wife, Fanny, in February, both from typhoid: their deaths 'seemed to have crushed his spirit' (*Annual Register*, 1887, 161). He stayed on in Cairo, continuing as inspector-general of the gendarmerie.

Death and reputation In June 1887, the year of her jubilee, the queen wrote to the prince of Wales proposing that Baker be reinstated. There was no immediate announcement, instead administrative delays. Following an attack of fever, on 17 November 1887 Baker died of a heart attack aboard the steam-launch *Vigilant* on the Sweetwater Canal at Tell al-Kebir. A telegram from the War Office gave instructions from the duke of Cambridge that he was to be buried with full military honours. A union flag was draped on his coffin and on 19 November the procession set out for the English cemetery in Cairo from the house of Sir Frederick Stephenson, commander of the British army in Egypt, who spoke of Baker as the bravest soldier England had ever had. Sir Evelyn Baring wrote to the prime minister about Baker with warmth and understanding, and also to Samuel Baker of his close friendship with Baker; Lord Salisbury, in responding to Baring, was equally generous.

The Times obituary commented, 'his career … might have been among the most brilliant in our service'; and wrote of 'the error which deprived his country of his services', and 'the splendid atonement which he sought to make' (*The Times*, 18 Nov 1887, 7). A memorial plaque in honour of 'Lieutenant General Valentine Baker Pasha' was erected in the Anglican cathedral, Cairo, by the British army.

Baker was strongly built, high-coloured, and walrus-moustached, with piercing dark eyes. He was an exceptional soldier, 'one of the most remarkable cavalrymen of the age' (Anglesey, 3.116), and he had once been a member of the social circle around the prince of Wales. But he was essentially a quiet, serious man, courageous in action and in word, a companion to his fellow officers, generous to his men, considerate to those of different race and religion; private, more interested in family than society, he was without bravado. He was liked and held in high respect by his peers, by Sir Evelyn Baring, Sir Frederick Stephenson, Admiral Hewett, and General Graham. He also enjoyed the continuing loyal regard of the officers and men of the 10th hussars and the long-standing friendship of their colonel-in-chief, the prince of Wales. If Baker had been responsible for the incident on the train, and many believed otherwise, it had been an aberration.

DOROTHY ANDERSON

Sources V. Baker, *Clouds in the East: travels and adventures on the Perso-Turkoman frontier* (1876) • V. Baker, *War in Bulgaria: a narrative of personal experiences*, 2 vols. (1879) • D. Anderson, *Baker Pasha: misconduct and mischance* (1999) • A. Baker, *A question of honour: the life of Lieutenant General Baker Pasha* (1996) • E. Sartorius, *Three months in the Soudan* (1885) • T. D. Murray and A. Silva White, *Sir Samuel Baker: a memoir* (1895) • Marquess of Anglesey [G. C. H. V. Paget], *A history of the British cavalry, 1816 to 1919*, 2 (1975) • Marquess of Anglesey [G. C. H. V. Paget], *A history of the British cavalry, 1816 to 1919*, 3 (1982) • E. Baring, *Modern Egypt*, 2 vols. (1908) • R. S. Liddell, *The memoirs of the tenth royal hussars (prince of Wales's own), historical and social* (1891) • *The Times* (3 Aug 1875) • *The Times* (18 Nov 1887) • P. Magnus, *King Edward the Seventh* (1964) • A. Milner, *England in Egypt*, 4th edn (1893) • E. Ollier, *Cassell's illustrated history of the Russo-Turkish war*, 2 vols. (1877–9) • C. Royle, *The Egyptian campaigns, 1882 to 1885*, rev. edn (1900) • M. Alexander, *The true blue: the life and adventures of Colonel Fred Burnaby, 1842–85* (1957) • M. Brander, *The 10th royal hussars (prince of Wales's own)* (1969) • *The Standard* (19 Nov 1887)

Archives priv. coll. | BL, corresp. with Sir Austen Layard, Add. MSS 39013–39036, 39130–39134, *passim* • PRO, corresp. with E. Baring, FO 633

Likenesses engraving, pubd 1884, NPG [*see illus.*] • Ape [C. Pellegrini], chromolithograph caricature, NPG; repro. in *VF* (9 March 1878) • photograph, NPG • photograph (as a young man), repro. in Baker, *Question of honour*, pl. 2

Wealth at death £6568 11*s*. 10*d*.: resworn probate, April 1889, *CGPLA Eng. & Wales*

Baker, William (1668–1732), bishop of Norwich, was born on 20 December 1668 at Ilton, Somerset, the second, but first surviving, son of William Baker, vicar of Ilton (*d*. 1708), and his wife, Mary, *née* Baker (*fl*. 1666–1683). He was educated first at Crewkerne School, and entered Wadham College, Oxford, in 1686. Baker is said to have 'lived freely in his youth and spoilt a good natural constitution' (*Diaries of Thomas Wilson*, 83). He was made fellow of Wadham in 1693, and was granted his DD in 1707 despite an attempt, possibly by Thomas Hearne, to block the degree (*Remarks*, 2.26). In 1719 he was elected warden of Wadham College; the election caused a stir, with stories of bribery and the spectacular contrition, and then madness, of John Leaves, the fellow whose vote turned the election.

Baker was successively rector of St Ebbe's in Oxford, Padworth in Berkshire, and, from 1712 to 1715, Bladon in Oxfordshire—all three in the Oxford diocese. In 1715 he was collated to the archdeaconry of Oxford; during the same year he was made rector of St Giles-in-the-Fields, London, an incumbency which he held until his death. In September 1715 Baker had become a chaplain-in-ordinary to George I; he was deprived of a journey with the king to Hanover in 1722, but was made bishop of Bangor in 1723, and translated to Norwich in 1727. During his brief tenure of the see of Bangor he managed to make his only brother, Nicholas, treasurer of the church there; and his two nephews, John Baker and William Baker, were provided for by being made joint registrars of the diocese of Norwich.

Four of Baker's sermons were published, all demonstrating his strong whig principles, for which he earned the opprobrium of several tories. Dr William King included Baker in his list of whig churchmen 'who preach up Comprehension, Moderation … Occasional Conformity, Resistance … and all the detestable doctrines of Forty-one' (King, *Works*, 2.217); the earl of Oxford, in 1732, thought him 'a most worthless wretch' (*Portland MSS*, 6.156). Thomas Hearne, his erstwhile Oxford opponent, although allowing that he was 'a very personable man', and had been a 'great Tutor' at Wadham College, called him a 'stinking Whigg', and 'a man of but little learning' who, 'tho' a great drinker, was grown so miserably covetous and sordid at the last, as not to allow himself hardly necessaries' (*Remarks*, 7.11; 11.137, 139). Baker died, unmarried, at Bath on 4 December 1732 and was buried in the abbey there.

IAN ATHERTON

Sources R. B. Gardiner, ed., *The registers of Wadham College, Oxford*, 1 (1889) • F. Blomefield and C. Parkin, *An essay towards a topographical history of the county of Norfolk*, [2nd edn], 11 vols. (1805–10) • *Remarks and collections of Thomas Hearne*, ed. C. E. Doble and others, 11 vols., OHS, 2, 7, 13, 34, 42–3, 48, 50, 65, 67, 72 (1885–1921) • Ilton parish register, 1642–1742, Som. ARS, D/P/ilt 2/1/1 • *Fasti Angl.* (Hardy) • *Fasti Angl., 1541–1857*, [Ely] • *The manuscripts of his grace the duke of Portland*, 10 vols., HMC, 29 (1891–1931), vols. 5–6 • *The diaries of Thomas Wilson*, ed. C. L. S. Linnell (1964) • W. King, 'A vindication of the reverend Dr Henry Sacheverell', *The original works of William*

King (1776), 186–257 · *ESTC* · order to admit Baker as chaplain-in-ordinary to the king, 7 Sept 1715, PRO, LC 3/63, 115 · N. Sykes, *William Wake, archbishop of Canterbury*, 2 vols. (1957) · G. Hennessy, *Novum repertorium ecclesiasticum parochiale Londinense, or, London diocesan clergy succession from the earliest time to the year 1898* (1898) · *GM*, 1st ser., 2 (1732), 1125

Likenesses J. Mollinson, engraving (after portrait), Wadham College, Oxford · oils, Wadham College, Oxford

Baker, William (*bap.* **1742**, *d.* **1785**), printer and classical scholar, was baptized on 5 April 1742 at St Mary, Reading, the son of William Baker, a schoolmaster, and his wife, Jane, *née* Cox. His father had hoped for a career in the church for him, encouraged in this by Dr Robert Bolton, dean of Carlisle, who had virtually assured the young William a university place. When Bolton was unable to fulfil his promise, Baker was apprenticed to Mr Kippax, printer of Cullum Street, London. He was not only diligent in Kippax's employ, often working overtime, but he also used his free hours to good purpose, buying books and studying. He eventually made himself proficient in Greek and Latin, as well as in Italian and French, and attained some knowledge of Hebrew. He tended to overt-exert himself, however, and before he was twenty-one he suffered a severe illness. While there is no sale catalogue of his library, there is evidence in his two major publications that he acquired a respectable library of classical and other works. When Kippax died, Baker took over the business, later moving to Ingram Court, Fenchurch Street, in the City of London and forming a partnership with John William Galabin.

Baker's *Peregrinations of the Mind* (1770) is a series of twenty-three essays on such various topics as war, the stage, matrimony, in defence of theatrical humour. Each is headed by a motto from Greek, Latin, and English authors; Baker translated the classical mottoes, including the originals in an appendix. There are also many footnotes in various languages. In 1783 Baker printed his *Theses Graecae et Latinae selectae*, a compendium of his notes compiled over years of reading the works of classical writers. He made many friends among antiquaries and scholars of his day, including Oliver Goldsmith, Dr Edmund Barker, James Merrick, Hugh Farmer, and Caesar de Missy.

Baker again suffered from his tendency to over-exert himself, this time from walking, in December 1784. Following a nine-month illness he died in London of an enlargement of the omentum on 29 September 1785.

William Baker was buried in the vault of St Dionis Backchurch, Lime Street and Fenchurch Street, London. A Latin inscription to his memory was placed on a family tomb in St Mary Church, Reading. His library became the property of the physician and philanthropist Dr J. C. Lettsom (1744–1815). H. R. TEDDER, *rev.* ARTHUR SHERBO

Sources *BL cat.* · *GM*, 1st ser., 55 (1785) · *IGI* · Nichols, *Illustrations*, 2.666; 4.498, 609 · Nichols, *Lit. anecdotes*, 3.715–16 · *Chambers's biographical dictionary* · C. Coates, *History of Reading* (1802)

Baker, William [*name in religion* Anselm] (**1833–1885**), heraldic artist and mural painter, was born in Birmingham on 23 January 1833, the son of Thomas Baker, a coach painter. He appears to have worked as a gun-stocker, and he learned to paint and draw at the Hardmans' studios in Birmingham. He became a Cistercian monk at Mount St Bernard's Abbey, near Coalville, Leicestershire, in 1857. The leading heraldic artist in England, nicknamed the Herald Monk, he drew two-thirds of the coats of arms in Joseph Foster's *Peerage of the British Empire* (1880), signing his work F. A. (Frater Anselmus).

Anselm also painted the murals in the chapel of St Scholastica's Priory, Atherstone, Warwickshire, in St Winifred's, Sheepshed, in the Temple in Garendon Park, and in the lady and infirmary chapels at Mount St Bernard's Abbey: all show the influence of Fra Angelico. He illustrated editions of the liturgical works *Hortus animæ* and *Horæ diurnæ*, published in London, and several works published in Malines and Tournai. His *Liber vitæ*, a record of the benefactors of St Bernard's Abbey, is magnificently illustrated with pictures of the arms and patron saints of the benefactors. 'The armorial bearings of English cardinals' and 'The arms of the Cistercian houses of England' were never published. Anselm died at Mount St Bernard's Abbey on 11 February 1885 and was buried there two days later. THOMPSON COOPER, *rev.* ANNE PIMLOTT BAKER

Sources *The Tablet* (21 Feb 1885) · *The Academy* (21 Feb 1885), 133 · *The Athenaeum* (21 Feb 1885), 256 · Boase, *Mod. Eng. biog.* · *Men of the time* (1885)

Archives Mount St Bernard Abbey, Leicestershire, heraldic MSS

Baker, Sir William Erskine (**1808–1881**), army officer and engineer, was the fourth son of Captain Joseph Baker RN, and was born on 29 November 1808 at Leith. He was educated at Ludlow and at Addiscombe College (1825–6), and after attending an extended engineering course while a cadet he went out to India as a lieutenant in the Bengal Engineers in 1828. On 29 June 1837 he married, at Karnal, Frances Gertrude, third daughter of Major-General A. Duncan; she survived her husband.

Baker was promoted captain in 1840, and saw service in the First Anglo-Sikh War. He led one of the attacking columns to the entrenchments at the battle of Sobraon, for which he was thanked in the dispatch and promoted major. He was afterwards almost exclusively employed in the public works department, and was successively superintendent of the Delhi canals, superintendent of canals and forests in Sind, director of the Ganges Canal project, consulting engineer to the government of India for railways, and secretary to the government of India in the public works department. His services as a civil engineer were considerable, and he was widely regarded as the greatest authority of his time on irrigation. His military promotion continued during his civil employment, and he became lieutenant-colonel in 1854 and colonel in 1857.

In 1858 Baker returned to England, and was appointed military secretary to the India Office. But his expertise was rather that of an engineer than a soldier, and in 1861 he became a member of the Council of India, and as such was chief adviser to the home government on Indian civil engineering. He was promoted major-general in 1865, colonel-commandant of the Royal (formerly Bengal) Engineers in 1871, and lieutenant-general in 1874; he was made a KCB in 1870. Retiring from public life in 1875, he was appointed general in 1877, and died at his home at Castle Banwell, Somerset, on 16 December 1881. Sir William Erskine Baker's work in Sind was memorable; the great irrigation works which he carried out there remained as a monument to his energy and organizational skill. H. M. STEPHENS, *rev.* JAMES FALKNER

Sources *The Times* (20 Dec 1881) • *Army List* • W. Porter, *History of the corps of royal engineers*, 2 (1889) • *East-India Register* • C. E. Buckland, *Dictionary of Indian biography* (1906) • Boase, *Mod. Eng. biog.* • Kelly, *Handbk* • V. C. P. Hodson, *List of officers of the Bengal army, 1758–1834*, 4 (1947) • *CGPLA Eng. & Wales* (1882)

Archives BL, letters to Sir Stafford Northcote, Add. MS 50030 • CUL, corresp. with Lord Mayo

Wealth at death £38,503 1*s.* 4*d.*: probate, 28 Jan 1882, *CGPLA Eng. & Wales*

Baker, William Garrard (*bap.* **1815**, *d.* **1902**), manufacturing chemist, baptized at Chelmsford, was the eldest of five sons (there were also two daughters) of William Baker, a chemist and druggist in Chelmsford. Baker's early life and education remain obscure and it seems likely that he was educated locally before being, as he himself recalled, apprenticed to his father. When he was qualified, he went to London, occupying himself in managing 'a business in London for my father, waiting for something to turn up' (*Chemist and Druggist*, 30 Jan 1897).

In 1839 the opportunity for which Baker had been waiting appeared, when Thomas Grimwade retired from the chemical manufacturing business he and John *May (1809–1893) (together with Joseph Pickett who had died in 1835) had established in Battersea. May needed a new partner and he and Baker quickly came to terms, signing a partnership agreement in 1840. Since 1834 the factory had been on rented land but in 1841 the partners were able to buy the piece of land known as Garden Wharf, thereby securing for themselves a more permanent position in Battersea, then very much an industrial area. In the event the business stayed there until 1934, well after the time of both May and Baker.

For the first two or three decades Baker took charge of the manufacturing, and the prize medals awarded to May and Baker's products—acids and metallic salts—at the Great Exhibition of 1851 and the Paris Exhibition of 1855 suggest that he was skilled and able at doing so. May took responsibility for the marketing of their products and both men became members of the Pharmaceutical Society, formed in 1841 to protect the interests of chemists and druggists. In the 1860s the partners took on a young man, Thomas Tyrer, as an apprentice and he stayed with the firm after he completed his apprenticeship, gradually taking over more responsibility for the manufacturing side of the business.

In 1876 John May retired, selling his interest (two-thirds as opposed to Baker's one-third) in the firm to Richard Heath, a solicitor in Warwick, who was eager to invest in a chemical business which would provide employment for one of his two stepsons, William Blenkinsop. Although Baker was, by virtue of his age and experience, the senior partner in the new partnership with Heath, it was Tyrer, now admitted as a junior partner, who supervised the training of Blenkinsop and who, to all intents and purposes, as the surviving correspondence makes clear, was running the business. In the 1870s Baker's health was poor, with rheumatic gout and neuralgia troubling him, but he refused to leave the business. Both Tyrer and Blenkinsop expressed their doubts as to his ability to make any contribution to the firm, Tyrer suggesting that he came into the office only to criticize and that his tendency had been always to wait, like Mr Micawber, for something to turn up. In 1883 Blenkinsop told his stepfather that Baker, now in his late sixties, did little except 'appear on 'Change' for the firm; the purchase of raw materials, particularly expensive ones such as quicksilver (used to make the mercurial compounds which were then the only remedy for venereal disease) was a delicate business—one which according to Blenkinsop, Baker did not handle particularly well.

In 1890 Heath proposed to end the partnership and incorporate the business, suggesting that both Baker and Tyrer should retire. Lengthy and by no means amicable negotiations followed resulting in the incorporation of May and Baker Ltd and the departure of Tyrer. However, despite his age, Baker refused to go and was made a director of the new company; also a director from 1891 until his death in 1893 was John May, a recognition that the names of the two men who had built up the company carried considerable weight in the industry.

It was not until 1897, at the age of eighty-two, that Baker finally retired and went to live in Brighton. From there he still travelled up to Battersea for board meetings, a journey attended with considerable ceremony. He travelled with his invalid chair on the train from Brighton to Clapham Junction; there two May and Baker employees met him and lifted him into a brougham for the short journey to Battersea where he was carried into the office at Garden Wharf. His refusal to sever his connection with the business seems to have been driven as much by a need for remuneration—Tyrer suggested that Baker had an expensive family and was himself a spendthrift—as by his fondness for the company he had helped to create.

Baker died at his home, 9 Compton Avenue, Brighton, on 16 May 1902. May and Baker passed first into the hands of the Blenkinsop family and then, in the 1920s, into the ownership of the French chemical company Rhône-Poulenc. Its discovery and development of the sulphonamide drug M & B 693 in the late 1930s gave the company a considerable place in the history of the pharmaceutical industry. JUDY SLINN

Sources J. Slinn, *A history of May & Baker, 1834–1984* (1984) • *Chemist and Druggist* (30 Jan 1897), 162–3 • *Chemist and Druggist* (24 May 1902), 821 • *CGPLA Eng. & Wales* (1902)

Archives Rhône-Poulenc Roversite, Dagenham, Essex, May and Baker archives

Likenesses portrait (the company)

Wealth at death £871 6*s.* 7*d.*: probate, 19 June 1902, *CGPLA Eng. & Wales*

Bakewell, Robert (**1725–1795**), stock breeder and farmer, was born at Dishley Grange, Dishley (otherwise Dixley),

Robert Bakewell (1725–1795), by John Boultbee, *c.*1788–91

near Loughborough, Leicestershire, on 23 May 1725. His father, also a farmer, had been born at the same place and rented a farm there of 440 acres. About 1755 Robert Bakewell, having qualified himself for experiments in husbandry and cattle breeding by visiting farms in the west of England and other parts of the country, took charge of the farm on the failure of his father's health; he succeeded to the entire management of it on his father's death in 1760.

As a stock breeder Bakewell aimed at obtaining a better breed of sheep and cattle, and he succeeded in producing the new Leicester breed of sheep—small-boned, barrel-shaped animals which fattened rapidly and were highly profitable, having a high proportion of meat to the less valuable parts of the carcass. Bakewell also produced the Dishley cattle, called the new Leicestershire longhorn, 'a small, clean-boned, round, short-carcased, kindly-looking cattle, inclined to be fat' (Culley, 26); and he produced a breed of black horses, remarkable for their strength in harness on the farm, and for their utility in the army. He was the first to carry on the trade of hiring out rams and bulls on a large scale, and he established a club, the Dishley Society, for the express object of ensuring purity of breed. By 1770 his rams fetched 25 guineas, and a few years later he was making £3000 a year by their hire, deriving in one year from one particular ram, known as Two-pounder, as much as 1200 guineas. Many of the present humane notions regarding animals were anticipated by Bakewell, his stock being treated with marked kindness; even his bulls were remarkable for their obedience and docility.

In Bakewell's experiments on feeding and housing stock he was as bold as in breeding. He stood first in the kingdom 'as an improver of grass-land by watering' (Marshall, 284 ff.); he flooded his meadows, making a canal of a mile and a quarter in length, and was able by means of irrigation to cut grass four times a year. By means of double floors to his stalls, he collected farm refuse and diluted it for liquid manure. On these accounts Bakewell received many distinguished visitors. All were shown the boats in which he carried some of his crops; his wharf for these boats; his plan of conveying his turnips about the farm by water; his teams of cows instead of oxen; his own design of plough; and his collection of animal skeletons, and carcasses (in pickle), for testing where breeds varied in bone and flesh.

Bakewell's achievements as a pioneer of selective breeding were not quite so extraordinary as has been supposed. For centuries attempts had been made to improve stock by crossing it with animals that had the desired characteristics, and before Bakewell the emphasis in sheep breeding had already moved towards a concern with the carcass. Another midland breeder, Joseph Allom, had already made some progress, and in Bakewell's time there were a score of well-known breeders in the midlands alone who were engaged in the improvement of sheep. Similarly, Bakewell's experiments with cattle were based on Lancashires; this breed had already been improved by Webster of Canley, near Coventry.

Bakewell's fame owed something to his farm and his horses and pigs; he received publicity from two of the leading agricultural writers of the day, Arthur Young and William Marshall, and he had an extensive correspondence and travelled widely, visiting other leading breeders and farmers. He was as lavish with his hospitality to visitors as he was niggardly in explaining his methods. (It is generally believed that the new Leicester sheep were derived from a cross between the Lincoln and Ryeland breeds.)

The advantages of Bakewell's sheep were partially offset by an inferior fleece and a propensity to put on fat if not slaughtered at two years old. Consequently their mutton was 'too fat for genteel tables' and not inviting 'to weak appetites', being better suited to the needs of working people (Culley, 108). Further, the new breed was not prolific, and was unsuited to exposed terrain. Bakewell's new longhorn cattle were even more defective, putting on masses of fat but failing to yield the good milk and exhibit the fecundity of the original stock. They became obsolete within a generation, after Bakewell's death, being superseded by Charles Colling's Durham shorthorns. Even in his own county, Bakewell's sheep gave way to Lincoln and Leicester cross-breeds, which had an even greater aptitude for early fattening and less of the undesirable characteristics of the new Leicesters. However, although it disappeared as a separate breed, the new Leicester did play a major part in the improvement of British and overseas breeds of longwool sheep. Bakewell helped to lay the foundations of an important industry producing pedigree stock for home and overseas markets, and his principle of breeding 'in and in' had an early influence in the development of the ideas of Charles Darwin.

In appearance, Bakewell resembled the popular idea of the English yeoman: 'a tall, broad-shouldered, stout man of brown-red complexion, clad in a brown coat, scarlet waistcoat, leather breeches and top-boots' (Prothero, 184). He died at home, unmarried, on 1 October 1795, aged seventy, and was buried at Dishley. His nephew succeeded to his farm, which maintained its reputation for some years. JENNETT HUMPHREYS, *rev.* G. E. MINGAY

Sources J. Thirsk, ed., *The agrarian history of England and Wales*, 6, ed. G. E. Mingay (1989), 317–18, 338–43, 352 • J. Thirsk, ed., *The*

agrarian history of England and Wales, 5/1 (1984), 100, 109, 321 • J. Thirsk, ed., *The agrarian history of England and Wales*, 5/2 (1985), 578 • R. Trow-Smith, *A history of British livestock husbandry, 1700–1900*, 2 (1959), 26–9, 36, 54–64 • R. Trow-Smith, *English husbandry* (1951), 156, 164–6, 170 • R. E. Prothero, *English farming past and present*, ed. D. Hall, 6th edn (1961), 184–8 • H. C. Pawson, *Robert Bakewell* (1957) • G. Culley, *Observations on live stock*, 4th edn (1807), 26, 108 • W. Marshall, *The rural economy of the midland counties*, 1 (1790), 270, 284–5, 292–493 • A. Young, *The farmer's tour through the east of England*, 1 (1771), 102–35 • A. Young, *On the husbandry of three celebrated British farmers, Messrs. Bakewell, Arbuthnot and Ducket* (1811) • A. Young, ed., *Annals of agriculture and other useful arts*, 6 (1786), 466–98 • *GM*, 1st ser., 63 (1793), 792 • *GM*, 1st ser., 65 (1795), 969–70 • J. Monk, *General view of the agriculture of Leicestershire* (1794) • W. Youatt, *On cattle* (1834), 192, 196, 208

Archives E. Sussex RO, letters to first earl of Sheffield • U. Newcastle, Robertson Library, letters to George Culley

Likenesses J. Boultbee, oils, *c.*1788–1791, NPG [*see illus.*] • F. Engleheart, line print, pubd 1842, NPG • J. Boultbee, oils, Leicester Museum and Art Gallery • oils, Offices of Royal Agricultural Society of England, London

Bakewell, Robert (1767–1843), geologist, was born on 10 March 1767 in Nottingham, the youngest son of Robert Bakewell (1729–1768), a Quaker wool-stapler, and his wife, Mary (1740–1811), daughter of George Mason, farmer and Quaker preacher of Kirkbymoorside, Yorkshire, and later America. He was distantly related to Robert Bakewell (1725–1795), the noted farmer and stockbreeder. Following his father's early death Bakewell was sent to the school for well-to-do Friends at Hartshill, Warwickshire, where he proved to be a precocious child, constructing telescopes and writing his first paper, on water spouts, which was published in 1786. By 1789 Bakewell had moved to Wakefield as a wool-stapler. The following year, on 24 September, he married Apphia (*d.* 1820), daughter of Thomas Simpson. The Simpsons were Unitarian and Bakewell had joined this church by September 1791. The couple had six children, the last baptized in 1800.

Bakewell's activities as wool-stapler were interspersed with travel. His interest in natural history was revealed by a visit to north Wales about 1801. From 1801 Bakewell, dependent on foreign trade, was also highly active in the national peace movement, corresponding with the whig politician Samuel Whitbread (1764–1815) in 1807. The following year Bakewell's first book, *Observations on the Influence of Soil and Climate upon Wool*, was published. However, in July 1810, unable to meet his creditors at a time of national financial difficulty, Bakewell assigned all his estates to them and fled to London, where he became a geological consultant, building on his knowledge of soils, charging 'one hundred pounds for any time not exceeding one month and twenty pounds for travelling expenses' (Banks MSS). His first advertisement for the services of Robert Bakewell & Sons, in the *Mineralogical and Statistical Survey of Estates*, was issued by August 1810. Bakewell was elected annual subscriber to the Royal Institution late the same year—clearly he was in search of patrons. In 1811 he published descriptions of the cobalt mine on Alderley Edge and on the application of mineralogical and chemical science to the selection of building stone. In the autumn of that year his first known geological consulting took him to Shropshire and Radnorshire, and the following year he was in Charnwood Forest, acting as consultant to the earl of Moira.

In 1811 Bakewell began to give public lectures on geology throughout Britain, with courses in Derby, Liverpool, and Manchester in 1811; London in 1812; Newcastle, Leeds, and London in 1813; Exeter and Bath in 1815; and Cornwall, Cheltenham, and Gloucester in 1816. His last were in Bristol and London in 1817. Probably the first such lectures to be given throughout Britain, they particularly directed the attention of landed proprietors to the neglected mineral treasures of their estates, as well as offering Bakewell chances to make field observations all over Britain. Those on the geology of Manchester were published in 1814, on Northumberland and Durham in 1815 (amid charges of plagiarism), and on the south coast in 1816.

Lecturing soon revealed to Bakewell the need for an introductory textbook on geology and inspired his *An Introduction to Geology*, for which he is best remembered. It was first published in June 1813, partly at his own expense. In the early 1900s the historian of the Geological Society recorded that Bakewell's was 'undoubtedly the best of the early text-books' (H. B. Woodward, *History of the Geological Society of London*, 1907, 84). It went through five English editions and three American. The first edition already distinguished bedding from slaty cleavage and correctly identified the feeder origin of the basalt on Titterstone Clee Hill.

Introduction was motivated by the need to use geology in the practical exploration of the valuable mineral treasures of the British Isles, but it deprecated the excessive foreign influence on British geology, which many other working geologists also felt was too dominant. Bakewell noted how 'the term "well educated Geognost" … denotes a perfect disciple of Werner, who has lost the use of his own eyes by constantly looking through the eyes of his master' and called Werner's theory of mineral veins 'demonstrably repugnant to facts'. Such views were not well received by the Wernerian-dominated Geological Society and Bakewell was forced to decline membership about 1813, the year in which he also unsuccessfully applied for the post of professor of mineralogy to the Dublin Society.

John Farey met Bakewell in May 1812 and they engaged in stimulating discussions, both before and after the publication of Bakewell's first edition. Farey advised Bakewell how the book could be improved and the second edition contained additional notes on the work of William Smith (1769–1839) and Farey. It was this edition, also translated into German, which inspired Charles Lyell to take his first interest in geology. Adam Sedgwick also regarded himself as a pupil, because of the influence Bakewell's book had on him.

In 1819 Bakewell contributed to Abraham Rees's influential *Cyclopaedia*, on both wool and geology. Bakewell's popularizing attempt at *An Introduction to Mineralogy* appeared the same year. This was sufficiently successful for an unknown rival to issue a volume with the same title in 1829 under the carefully chosen pseudonym of J. R. Bakewell. In 1820 Bakewell produced his mocking, and highly political, *Geological Primer in Verse*, which for many years was wrongly credited to John Scafe. The *Primer* caused a new rift with members of the Geological Society, who found it 'an offence of such overwhelming magnitude that there are no purifying waters in Oxford or London to efface it' (Bakewell to Sedgwick, 10 Dec 1830, Sedgwick MSS).

Bakewell's first wife had died in March 1820 and on 31 August that year he married Esther (*c*.1770–1851), daughter of Dr Henry Hinckley (*c*.1724–1779) of Guy's Hospital, former treasurer of the Royal College of Physicians. The marriage brought Bakewell financial independence and late in 1820 the couple set off on a long tour to the Tarentaise and to Switzerland. Bakewell's two-volume *Travels in the Tarentaise … 1820* [*to*] *1822* appeared in 1823. Because of his battles with the Geological Society there were few reviews. He considered the *Literary Gazette*'s review particularly unfair; it might have contributed to his now abandoning geology for three or four years. The work contained an early description in English of the volcanic geology of the Auvergne and insights into the ages of alpine rocks based on fossils.

However, Bakewell had never been totally convinced of the importance of dating rocks from fossils, and wrote in 1834 how 'the importance attached to [fossil] shells is a ridiculous fallacy' (Bakewell to Mantell, 7 Dec 1834, Mantell MSS).

In 1825 the Bakewells settled in a cottage on Downshire Hill, Hampstead, Middlesex. In 1828 Bakewell issued the third edition of his textbook which was soon taken up by Benjamin Silliman (1779–1864) at Yale as his course text; a first American edition appeared in 1829. Eight hundred copies of the second American edition were sold in New England in the spring of 1835 and Silliman noted that the book was 'conspicuous for attractiveness, … of a style generally vigorous and correct, often eloquent and beautiful and of an independence of spirit' (4th edn, 1833, preface). In 1833 Bakewell resumed occasional geological lecturing. He also wrote the sections on geology for J. R. Macculloch's *Statistical Account of the British Empire* (1837).

Bakewell, who could be caustic in his criticisms, was long a victim of gout. He died on 15 August 1843 at home in Hampstead. His geological collections were sold at auction in May 1844. His wife's 'earnest wish [was] that there should not be any Memoir or Obituary of him in any of the Periodicals … since there were no circumstances connected with his early years … of sufficient interest to be brought before the public' (Esther Bakewell to Mantell, 16 Aug 1843, Mantell MSS). She must have feared Bakewell's early radical politics and financial problems might be revealed. As a result the only notice that appeared was that of Silliman in America, unaware of her embargo.

Bakewell's son Robert (1792–1875) moved in 1828 to America to teach drawing at Yale. His youngest son, Frederick Collier (1800–1869), after a career as a newspaper proprietor, became a scientific writer and inventor. His most important invention was the facsimile machine patented in 1848.

H. S. Torrens

Sources B. G. Bakewell, *The family book of Bakewell, Page, Campbell* … (1898) • I. Trentham-Edgar, 'Bakewell', *N&Q*, 167 (1934), 455–6 • B. Silliman, 'Death of Mr Bakewell', *American Journal of Science*, 145 (1843), 403–4 • R. Bakewell, 'Singular water spout near Nottingham', *GM*, 1st ser., 56 (1786), 111–12 • bankruptcy assignment, 1810, W. Yorks. AS, Wakefield • J. E. Cookson, *The friends of peace* (1982) • H. S. Torrens, 'Joseph Harrison Fryer, 1777–1855', in S. Figueirôa and M. Lopes, *Geological sciences in Latin America* (1994), 29–46 • N. B. Harte, 'On Rees's *Cyclopaedia* as a source', *Textile History*, 5 (1974), 119–27 • H. F. Berry, *A history of the Royal Dublin Society* (1915) • R. Bakewell, *The Times* (13 May 1833) [letter] • J. Farey, 'Notes and observations on Bakewell's *Introduction to geology*', *Philosophical Magazine*, 1st ser., 42–3 (1813–14) • G. P. Fisher, *Life of Benjamin Silliman M.D., LL.D.*, 2 vols. (1866) • Sutro Library, San Francisco, Banks MSS • CUL, Sedgwick MSS • NL NZ, Turnbull L., Mantell MSS

Archives CUL, Sedgwick MSS • NL NZ, Turnbull L., letters to Gideon Algernon Mantell • Norwich Castle Museum, Woodward MSS • Yale U., Silliman MSS

Bakewell, Thomas (1761–1835), mad-doctor and poet, was born on 1 June 1761 at Kingstone, near Uttoxeter, in Staffordshire. He was raised by his maternal grandfather, John Chadwick, who kept a private mad-house at Grindon in the Peak District. Chadwick moved to Ashbourne in Derbyshire, where Bakewell received a limited education at the school of a Mr Richards. He was profoundly influenced by his experiences in his grandfather's mad-house. He received no formal medical training. After Chadwick's death, the management of the mad-house passed to his son John Chadwick, Thomas Bakewell's uncle. After assisting Chadwick for three years, Bakewell was apprenticed in 1774 as a tape weaver. He progressed eventually to become foreman over 300 men.

Bakewell resumed work with the insane about 1793, taking over the house from his dying uncle. Business difficulties led him to emigrate to North America two or three years later. He returned about 1802 and set up practice as a mad-doctor in the Staffordshire town of Cheadle. In 1805, Bakewell published *The Domestic Guide in Cases of Insanity*. This provided practical advice to people managing insane relatives at home. He considered mental illness to emanate from a diseased state of the brain. Social factors, like alcohol abuse, religious excess, or relationship difficulties might be precipitants which acted on the physical predisposition. Bakewell's approach to the management of patients emphasized humanity along with the imposition of firm authority. Treatment comprised methods in general usage, including warm and cold bathing and emetic and purgative medicines. The book achieved some critical approval and enhanced Bakewell's local reputation.

Bakewell opened his own private mad-house in 1808 at Spring Vale, near Stone, in Staffordshire. His intention was to put into practice the system of management and treatment learned from his relatives. In its early years Spring Vale was not commercially successful. Bakewell attributed this to his ability to cure patients; admissions were not frequent enough to replace discharges. His financial difficulties were partly alleviated by his third marriage, to Sarah Glover, who both invested money and took on the role of matron. By 1820 Spring Vale was flourishing, and within a few years was catering for up to forty patients. The treatment methods there embodied what Bakewell liked to call his 'system of cure'. This comprised a regime of fresh air, vigorous exercise, and a nourishing diet, supplemented by active medical intervention which centred around achieving efficient digestive and bowel action. 'Moral treatment' was also employed, concentrating on the promotion of rational and sensible behaviour. Bakewell sought to foster a supportive milieu that resembled a large family, with recreational activities, occupation, and religious observance, intended to divert thoughts away from the irrational. He claimed a cure rate of nine out of ten patients referred at an early stage of their disorder.

Bakewell became an active campaigner for his principles of treatment. He was galvanized by the passage of the County Asylums Act 1808, which encouraged county justices to provide asylums for pauper lunatics. His conviction was that large public asylums would become 'mighty prisons', in which confinement would take precedence over curative treatment. He lobbied leading politicians and was called as a witness before the select committee on mad-houses in 1815. After his appearance in 1815, Bakewell published *A Letter to the Select Committee on Madhouses*, in which he developed his argument against public asylums and detailed his alternative treatment methods. There were two other publications: in 1807 he had published *The Moorland Bard*, a book of poetry; in 1820 he issued *Remarks on a Publication by James Loch*, a strident polemic against the highland clearances, and in particular the part played in them by the marquess of Stafford, against whom Bakewell had a personal grievance resulting from a land dispute. Between 1815 and 1830, while building up his business at Spring Vale, Bakewell continued to campaign for a better public understanding of the needs of the insane. He delivered lectures in towns around the midlands and north. He became a frequent contributor to literary journals, first the *Monthly Magazine* and then the *Imperial Magazine*. In his articles he outlined the origins and causes of mental disorder and expanded his ideas on treatment. Many columns were devoted to his critique of public asylums, and his perception of their inevitable therapeutic failure. He called for a nationally regulated system in which the lunatic would be regarded as the 'child of the state' and a series of small curative asylums would be built around the country. Through his writings Bakewell attained some celebrity as a prototype popular psychiatrist.

Bakewell led a fairly colourful life. He married three times and produced twenty-four children, nine with his first wife, four with his second, and eleven with his third, Sarah. He became a well-known local character in Staffordshire, contributing on a range of issues, political, social, agricultural, and industrial, to the county press. He died on 6 September 1835 at Spring Vale, and was buried in St Michael's Church, Stone. After his death, the asylum at Spring Vale was taken over by his wife together with his son, Samuel Bakewell; it was subsequently relocated a few miles away at Oulton, and later moved to Church Stretton, Shropshire. LEONARD D. SMITH

Sources R. Porter, *Mind forg'd manacles: a history of madness in England from the Restoration to the Regency* (1987) • W. L. Parry-Jones, *The trade in lunacy: a study of private madhouses in England in the eighteenth and nineteenth centuries* (1972) • BL, Add. MSS 38257, fol. 9*b*; 38739, fols. 298–9, 312–15 • *Staffordshire Advertiser* (12 Sept 1835) • *Stone and Eccleshall Advertiser* (27 Jan 1894) • 'Memoir of Mr Thomas Bakewell, keeper of Spring Vale Asylum, near Stone, Staffordshire', *Imperial Magazine*, 8 (1826), 401–15, 513–19 • *Stone Newsletter* (17 Jan 1986)

Likenesses Thomson, engraving (after original painting), repro. in 'Memoir'

Balam, Richard (*fl.* 1653), mathematician, is known only as the author of *Algebra, or, The Doctrine of Composing, Inferring, and Resolving an Equation* (1653). There seems to be nothing original in this work but a multitude of terms which have perished with their inventor.

F. Y. EDGEWORTH, *rev.* ANITA MCCONNELL

Sources R. Balam, *Algebra, or, The doctrine of composing, inferring, and resolving an equation* (1653)

Balatine, Alan (*supp. fl.* 1520–1560), supposed historian, appears in Thomas Dempster's *Historia ecclesiastica gentis Scotorum* as one of the distinguished writers of the Scots. According to Dempster, Balatine was born in Scotland but spent most of his life as a writer and teacher in Germany, where he died some time after 1560. Dempster claims that Balatine was the author of at least three works, 'De astrolabio', 'De terra mensura', and 'Chronicon universalis'. The last of these may have been used as a source by Edward Hall in his *Chronicle* of 1542, as he lists one 'Balantyne' among his 'Englishe Writers' (Hall, 4), 'Englishe' referring to the language of the text rather than the nationality of the writer. However, it is probable that this Balantyne is in fact John *Bellenden, whose translation of Hector Boece's *Scotorum historia* was printed about 1540, and which seems to have been widely available in England. Other writers offer slightly different interpretations: John Pits, in his *Relationum historicarum de rebus Anglicis* (1619) claims Balatine (without a first name) as English, while Thomas Tanner (*Bibliotheca Britannico-Hibernica*, 1748) simply repeats what his predecessors have said. There is, therefore, no conclusive proof that Balatine had an existence independent of that of John Bellenden, though it is possible that his works, which would give some proof, simply have not survived.

NICOLA ROYAN

Sources *Thomae Dempsteri Historia ecclesiastica gentis Scotorum, sive, De scriptoribus Scotis*, ed. D. Irving, rev. edn, 1, Bannatyne Club, 21 (1829), 100 • *Hall's chronicle*, ed. H. Ellis (1809) • J. Pits, *Relationum historicarum de rebus Anglicis*, ed. [W. Bishop] (Paris, 1619), 825 • Tanner, *Bibl. Brit.-Hib.* • R. Sharpe, *Hand-list of Latin writers of Great Britain and Ireland before 1540* (1997)

Balcanquhall, Walter (1548/9–1616), Church of Scotland minister, was associated with the place name of Balcanquhal in the parish of Strathmiglo, Fife. Although Archbishop Patrick Adamson of St Andrews accused him in 1584 of 'small educatioun in learning' (Calderwood, 4.84), Balcanquhall was educated at St Andrews University, where he matriculated at St Leonard's College in 1566 and graduated in 1569. By 1570 he had entered the ministry of the reformed church in the subordinate capacity of exhorter at Auchtertool in Fife. Thereafter he served as minister in 1571 at Bothans and Barro in Lothian before moving to Edinburgh. On Whit Sunday 1574 he entered St Giles's as minister in Edinburgh, and along with his colleagues James Lawson and John Durie became an enthusiastic supporter of the presbyterian cause within the church.

With the downfall of the earl of Morton in 1578 and the growing ascendancy of Esmé Stewart, amid heightened fears of a popish plot and of French influence at court, Balcanquhall was summoned before the privy council in December 1580 to answer for his sermon condemning the influx of Roman Catholics to Edinburgh and French courtiers who 'polluted' the king's ear. He attended Morton before his execution on 2 June 1581 and offended the king by criticizing Stewart's activities, for which he was called before the privy council in 1581. He then declined the council's jurisdiction in matters spiritual, arguing that the general assembly was the appropriate body 'to whom the judgement of his doctrine sould apperteane' (Calderwood, 3.584). The assembly, for its part, found nothing in his sermon 'that conteinit either errour, slander or just offence, bot solid, good and true doctrine' (Thomson, *Acts*, 2.543). Balcanquhall also opposed the crown's appointment of Robert Montgomery, minister of Stirling, to the archbishopric of Glasgow, and in 1582, despite threats of violence, he intimated from the pulpit of Edinburgh Montgomery's excommunication for accepting the archbishopric in defiance of the general assembly's wishes.

On 15 May 1584 James Stewart, earl of Arran, became chancellor at the head of an anti-presbyterian regime. Balcanquhall was outspoken in his condemnation of the 'black acts', issued that month, which asserted the king's supremacy over the church, reaffirmed the role of bishops, proscribed presbyteries, and prohibited meetings of other church courts without the king's express consent. At that point, too, he used the pulpit of Edinburgh 'to sound mightelie in the praise' of Andrew Melville, who had escaped prosecution for opposing the 'black acts' by fleeing to England (*Autobiography and Diary of … Melvill*, 145). He also preached against 'godlesse start-ups' (Calderwood, 4.20), and before long he and Lawson were obliged to seek safety in England. From Berwick they wrote to their congregation of Edinburgh in June 1584 condemning Arran's hostility to the church:

> Ye see the whole discipline violentlie plucked out of the hands of them to whome Christ Jesus has committed the spirituall government, and givin into the hands of them who have their calling in the world of men, and not of God; Assembleis discharged and excommunicatioun made null by them who have no power to bind and loose. (Calderwood, 4.74)

Balcanquhall was married to Margaret Marjoribanks, daughter of an Edinburgh merchant. During his absence in England his wife, who had remained in Edinburgh together with Lawson's wife, conducted a spirited defence of the presbyterian exiles and launched a scathing attack on Adamson as archbishop.

Having arrived in London by 23 June, with other presbyterian exiles, Balcanquhall had meetings with Sir Francis Walsingham and 'talked with the godly and zealous brethren' there (*CSP Scot., 1584–5*, no. 195). He also attended Lawson's funeral in London in October 1584 and was a witness to his testament. While in London he preached several sermons until prevented from doing so again. In January 1585 he was summoned before Bishop John Aylmer of London, who explained that a command for the exiled Scots ministers to cease preaching had been issued on the privy council's initiative. With the fall of Arran's government in November 1585, however, following the palace revolution effected by the leaders of the Ruthven raid, now returned from exile, Balcanquhall journeyed home in the company of Andrew Melville and resumed his ministry in Edinburgh. He preached before the king in St Giles's in January 1586, claiming that ministers had as great authority as bishops, but James rebuked him, undertaking to 'prove there sould be bishops and spirituall magistrats endued with authoritie over the ministrie' (Calderwood, 4.491). Balcanquhall was appointed to attend the coronation of Queen Anne in 1590, but in 1591 he irritated the king by defending Knox's reputation, and in 1592 James was again offended by one of his sermons. Balcanquhall continued to preach against Arran, who was received at court in 1592, by recounting 'what mischeefe he had done before' and how Lennox had been 'the cheefe worker of his bringing in' (Calderwood, 5.187). After the riot in Edinburgh in December 1596 Balcanquhall was denounced for not compearing before the privy council, but he escaped imprisonment by fleeing to Yorkshire and in a joint letter with Robert Bruce maintained his innocence.

With the division of Edinburgh into separate parishes, in 1598 Balcanquhall was appointed minister of Trinity Church for the north-east quarter of the burgh. In 1600 he again incurred the king's wrath for declining to acknowledge James's version of the Gowrie conspiracy and was ordered to be translated from Edinburgh; however, he re-entered his ministry there on the king's birthday (19 June 1601). In 1606 he protested at the harsh treatment accorded those convicted of treason for holding a general assembly at Aberdeen in defiance of the king's wishes. He also condemned the assembly's decision in 1610 to acquiesce in the king's revival of episcopacy. By 19 July 1616 Balcanquhall had ceased preaching, and he died on 4 August following, in his sixty-eighth year. He was buried the following day. He had three sons: Walter *Balcanquhall, dean first of Rochester and then of Durham; Robert, minister of Tranent; and Samuel; and six daughters: Katherine, Rachel, Sarah, Margaret, Libra, and Anna.

James Kirk

Sources D. Calderwood, *The history of the Kirk of Scotland*, ed. T. Thomson and D. Laing, 8 vols., Wodrow Society, 7 (1842–9) • J. Spottiswoode, *History of the Church of Scotland*, ed. M. Napier and M. Russell, 3 vols., Spottiswoode Society, 6 (1847–51) • *The autobiography and diary of Mr James Melvill*, ed. R. Pitcairn, Wodrow Society (1842) • J. Row, *The history of the Kirk of Scotland, from the year 1558 to August 1637*, ed. D. Laing, Wodrow Society, 4 (1842) • T. Thomson, ed., *Acts and proceedings of the general assemblies of the Kirk of Scotland*, 3 pts, Bannatyne Club, 81 (1839–45) • *Reg. PCS*, 1st ser. • J. M. Anderson, ed., *Early records of the University of St Andrews*, Scottish History Society, 3rd ser., 8 (1926) • A. I. Dunlop, ed., *Acta facultatis artium* *universitatis Sanctiandree, 1413–1588*, 2 vols., Scottish History Society, 3rd ser., 54–5 (1964) • [T. Thomson], ed., *The historie and life of King James the Sext*, Bannatyne Club, 13 (1825) • J. Kirk, ed., *The records of the synod of Lothian and Tweeddale, 1589–1596, 1640–1649*, Stair Society, 30 (1977) • D. Laing, ed., *The miscellany of the Wodrow Society*, Wodrow Society, [9] (1844), vol. 1 • G. Donaldson, ed., *Accounts of the collectors of thirds of benefices, 1561–1572*, Scottish History Society, 3rd ser., 42 (1949) • A. I. Cameron, ed., *The Warrender papers*, Scottish History Society, 3rd ser., 19 (1932), vol. 2 • G. Donaldson, *Scottish church history* (1985) • J. Kirk, *Patterns of reform: continuity and change in the Reformation kirk* (1989) • J. Gray, *Register of ministers, exhorters and readers*, ed. A. Macdonald, Maitland Club, 5 (1830)

Balcanquhall, Walter (*c*.1586–1645), dean of Rochester, was born in Edinburgh, one of three sons of Walter *Balcanquhall (1548/9–1616), Church of Scotland minister, and his wife, Margaret Marjoribanks. He was educated at Edinburgh University, graduating MA on 27 July 1609. Admitted to Pembroke College, Cambridge, in 1610, he became a fellow the following year and proceeded BD in 1616. Now a convinced episcopalian, he was instituted to a series of livings, becoming vicar of Harston in 1615 and of Waterbeach, Cambridgeshire, in 1617. He was appointed a chaplain to the king, and on 16 December 1617 was made master of the Savoy Hospital in the Strand, but early the following year he gave up this post (becoming instead a clerk of the closet) in order to represent the Church of Scotland at the Synod of Dort. In his lively letters home, preserved in the *Golden Remains* of John Hales, Balcanquhall endorsed the synod's condemnation of the remonstrants, but distanced himself from militant counter-remonstrants like Gomarus and their doctrines of supralapsarianism and limited atonement.

In 1621 Balcanquhall was restored as master of the Savoy and proceeded DD. He married at Bishopsbourne on 21 September 1624 Elizabeth, daughter of Anthony Aucher and widow of Sir William Hamilton. In March 1625 he became dean of Rochester and the same year vicar of Goudhurst, Kent. He acted as one of George Heriot's executors, compiling the statutes for Heriot's Hospital in Edinburgh in 1627. Having become rector of Kingstone, Kent, in 1632 he also acquired a living at Adisham, 'the house whairof' according to the marquess of Hamilton, 'hee built himselfe from the ground, and wch he hath made the best parsonage house in Kent' (*Letters … Baillie*, 1.478). In *The Honour of Christian Churches* (1633), a sermon preached before Charles I, he denounced puritans 'who think that all religion consisteth in preaching and hearing of sermons', and defended the Laudian beautification of English churches and worship.

Balcanquhall's sympathy for the Laudian agenda won him a key role as an intelligence gatherer for the king during the Scottish crisis of the late 1630s. He used his Scottish connections to acquire information about the activities of the covenanters from informants (or 'busie fleas', as Baillie called them) such as William Wilkie, regent at Glasgow University. The marquess of Hamilton told Laud that

> his Matie hath no chaplain can doe him lyke service, especially in the point of intelligence; for he hath gotten a great hand with that part of the Covenanting clergie, whom he hath made resent the tyrannie of some of the rest of the ministrie, and especially of the laitie and lay elders, even to a verie high discontentment, I hope ere long to an open breach; by these men he cometh to knowe all the secrets of that partie, wch is of singular wse to his Maties service and me. (*Letters … Baillie*, 1.478–9)

Balcanquhall advised the king on the perils and advantages of allowing the covenanters to hold a general assembly, and he was an observer at the Glasgow assembly in November and December 1638, speaking in defence of the bishops. He was commissioned by the king to write a historical narrative of the Scottish crisis. *A Large Declaration* was published in 1639 under the king's name, though Baillie believed it was written 'at Canterburie's direction' and penned by Balcanquhall with help from the bishop of Ross and the archbishop of St Andrews. Baillie confessed that 'this booke put us to the extreame lyne of desperation' since it showed that Charles had no regard for the covenanters' grievances (*Letters … Baillie*, 1.208–9). Baillie confessed,

> We have been much mistaken with that man: we esteemed him ever a Dordracenist, and opposed to Canterburie in that cause; bot now we see he hes made the king in his Manifesto print as much for Arminians as the heart of Canterburie could wish. (*Letters … Baillie*, 1.140)

In recognition of his services to the monarch Balcanquhall was appointed dean of Durham, and installed on 14 May 1639. In 1640 he became vicar of Boxley, Kent. The covenanters denounced him in *Ane Information*, and at the end of the year Baillie reported from London that many Englishmen thought Balcanquhall 'a vile man' (*Letters … Baillie*, 1.286). In 1641 the Scottish parliament condemned him as an incendiary. Soon after the civil war began he was deprived of his mastership of the Savoy by the English parliamentarians; by 1644 he had been sequestered and had fled to Oxford. According to Anthony Wood, he 'did afterwards shift from place to place for security. At length flying for the safety of his life to Chirk Castle in Denbighshire' (Wood, *Ath. Oxon.*, 1.384), where he died during a cold winter on Christmas day 1645. He was buried in the parish church at Chirk, and some years later a monument was erected there in his honour by Sir Thomas Middleton of Chirk Castle. His widow, Elizabeth, had by 1650 become Lady Hammond. JOHN COFFEY

Sources *The letters and journals of Robert Baillie*, ed. D. Laing, 3 vols. (1841–2) • Venn, *Alum. Cant.* • Wood, *Ath. Oxon.*, new edn, 1.384; 3.180, 839 • *Walker rev.*, 42 • J. Hales, *Golden remains of the ever memorable Mr John Hales of Eton College* (1659) • J. Spalding, *The history of the troubles and memorable transactions in Scotland and England, from 1624 to 1645*, ed. J. Skene, 2 vols., Bannatyne Club, 25 (1828–9), vol. 1, pp. 191–2, 331, 334; vol. 2, pp. 8, 40, 284 • M. A. E. Green, ed., *Calendar of the proceedings of the committee for compounding … 1643–1660*, 1, PRO (1889), 7, 91, 504, 516, 520, 528, 547; 3 (1891), 2076 • N. W. S. Cranfield, 'Chaplains in ordinary at the early Stuart court: the purple road', *Patronage and recruitment in the Tudor and early Stuart church*, ed. C. Cross (1996), 120–47 • *CSP dom.*, *1611–35*; *1638–43* • Foster, *Alum. Oxon.* • PRO, PROB 6/24, fol. 44*r*

Wealth at death in debt: M. A. E. Green, ed., *Calendar of … the committee for compounding*, 3.2076

Balcarres. For this title name *see* Lindsay, Alexander, first earl of Balcarres (1618–1659); Mackenzie, Anna, countess of Balcarres and countess of Argyll (*c*.1621–1707); Lindsay,

Colin, third earl of Balcarres (1652–1721); Lindsay, Alexander, sixth earl of Balcarres and *de jure* twenty-third earl of Crawford (1752–1825); Lindsay, Alexander William Crawford, twenty-fifth earl of Crawford and eighth earl of Balcarres (1812–1880); Lindsay, James Ludovic, twenty-sixth earl of Crawford and ninth earl of Balcarres (1847–1913); Lindsay, David Alexander Edward, twenty-seventh earl of Crawford and tenth earl of Balcarres (1871–1940); Lindsay, David Alexander Robert, twenty-eighth earl of Crawford and eleventh earl of Balcarres (1900–1975).

Balchen, Sir John (1670–1744), naval officer, was born on 2 February 1670 at Godalming, Surrey, the fourth and only surviving child of John Balchin and Ann Edsur. His paternal forebears were yeoman landholders of long standing in the vicinity. (Although the name is commonly spelt Balchin, the admiral always wrote Balchen, as did most of his correspondents.) He went off to the navy at fifteen and for much of the 1690s was in the West Indies, where he was made lieutenant in 1692. In a memorial to the Admiralty requesting employment, dated 12 June 1699, he related his early history:

> I have served in the navy for fourteen years past in several stations, and was lieutenant of the *Dragon* and *Cambridge* almost five years, then had the honour of a commission from Admiral [John] Neville in the West Indies to command the *Virgin*'s prize, which bears date from 25 July 1697, and was confirmed by my lords of the admiralty on our arrival in England. I continued in command of the *Virgin* till September 1698, then being paid off, and never at any time have committed any misdemeanour which might occasion my being called to a court martial, to be turned out or suspended.

The death rate of officers in Neville's squadron was phenomenal; Balchen was a survivor and thus, though he lacked influential connections, made post aged twenty-seven. In 1701 he was appointed to command the fireship *Firebrand*. During the period ashore he had married, about 1699, Susannah, daughter of Colonel Apreece of Washingly, Huntingdonshire; they had six children.

In December 1701 Balchen moved to the fireship *Vulcan* and was attached to the main fleet under Sir George Rooke on the coast of Spain. Whether he took part in the attack on French and Spanish ships at Vigo (12 October 1702) is not certain, but near there he captured the *Modéré* (56 guns) and was given command of her; in February 1703 he was appointed to the *Adventure* (44 guns), in which he continued for the next two years, cruising in the North Sea and channel. On 19 March 1705 he was transferred to the *Chester* (54 guns) and was sent out to the west African coast (1705–6). Having survived that, he saw service in home waters where in autumn 1707 he was part of a small squadron escorting the Virginia and Portugal convoys to open sea. They were intercepted, however, by a dozen French warships, the conjoined squadrons of Forbin and Duguay-Trouin. Nearly all the merchant ships and transports escaped while the British escorts were being severely mauled. After rebuffing multiple attacks (10 October), the *Chester* at length succumbed to boarding when she was slowed and hemmed in by two enemy ships. A year later Balchen, back in England on parole, was fully exonerated

Sir John Balchen (1670–1744), by Jonathan Richardson the elder, *c.*1695

by the court martial which tried him for loss of his ship on 27 September 1708. He was not formally exchanged until 1709; in August of that year he was given command of the *Gloucester*, a new ship of 60 guns. Leaving Spithead with cruising orders in late October, he had scarcely cleared land before encountering Duguay-Trouin and was again forced to surrender his ship (26 October). At the court martial (14 December 1709) the evidence showed that the *Gloucester* was engaged for above two hours with Duguay-Trouin's own ship, the *Lis* (74 guns), while another ship was also firing at her and three other ships were standing by, ready to board. Greatly damaged aloft, she could not carry head-sails. The court found no fault in Balchen or his ship's company and he was soon appointed to the *Colchester* (54 guns). On 9 November 1710 while *en route* from Plymouth to Portsmouth he encountered a 20-gun French privateer, 'chace'd him Large with a very strong Gale of wind', and secured his prize (PRO, ADM 1/1470).

During 1712 and 1713 the *Colchester* was in the Mediterranean with Sir John Jennings. After coming home in December 1713 Balchen had a quiet year before being appointed to the *Diamond* (40 guns) in February 1715 for a voyage to the West Indies and the suppression of piracy. He returned in May 1716. Immediately on paying off the *Diamond* Balchen was appointed to the guardship *Orford* in the Medway; he continued in her until February 1718, when he commissioned the *Shrewsbury* (80 guns), in which he accompanied Sir George Byng to the Mediterranean. On arrival Vice-Admiral Charles Cornwall, until then the commander-in-chief, hoisted his flag on the *Shrewsbury*, and was second in command in the battle off Cape Passaro on 31 July. The ship returned to England in December, and the following May Balchen was appointed to the *Monmouth* (70 guns), in which he accompanied Admiral Sir John Norris to the Baltic in the three successive summers of 1719, 1720, and 1721. Between 1722 and 1725 he commanded the guardship *Ipswich* at Spithead, and in February 1726 he was again appointed to the *Monmouth*, which cruised in the Baltic, in 1726 with Sir Charles Wager, and in 1727 with Norris. He was afterwards, in October 1727, sent out as part of a reinforcement to Wager at Gibraltar, thought to be still under Spanish siege, though in reality a cessation of arms had been arranged. On 19 July 1728 Balchen was promoted rear-admiral. After moving his flag from the *Dreadnought* (60 guns) to the *Princess Amelia* (80 guns) in 1731 he went out to the Mediterranean as second in command under Wager. The mission was designed to solidify peace with Spain by exhibiting a strong force alongside the Spanish navy to ensure a quiet landing of a Spanish garrison at Leghorn. After this was successfully done the British fleet returned home in December. In February 1734 Balchen was advanced to the rank of vice-admiral.

During the later 1730s and early 1740s Balchen generally served as flag-officer in charge of the ships at Plymouth. War with Spain in 1739 led to his being ordered to cruise off Ferrol to inhibit movements of Spanish warships and transports; on 9 April 1740 he left Plymouth with four ships of the line and was joined by three others. The mission was decided upon too late; the Cadiz and Ferrol squadrons had already come together and Balchen's force was outnumbered 14 to 7. When this was learned in London (28 April) there was great anxiety. Sir Charles Wager, the first lord, insisted that Balchen should be either recalled or reinforced. In May news came from France that Balchen had been beaten and taken (PRO, SP 42/81, fols. 323, 330), but the report was false. Balchen had learned that the Spanish forces had joined and therefore withdrew to 46° N to await further orders. Throughout the rest of 1740 he was kept in constant readiness because neutral France's mobilization of the Brest squadron meant that a powerful squadron would be needed to escort the planned expeditions (Lord Cathcart's assault force for the West Indies and Commodore George Anson's adventure to the Pacific) 150 leagues to sea, and Balchen was to command it.

In fact, however, Balchen was seldom ordered to sea, and then only to guard convoys. In June 1741 he confided to an old friend, Admiral Nicholas Haddock, stationed in the Mediterranean, his sense of missing out on fame and fortune:

> [We] have Nobody spoke of Now but Mr. Virnon [*sic*]; he has all the Glory, and success pursues him. The West Indie people will be so Rich there wont be Roome for them to purchase Lands; whilst I am forced to drudge from place to place for Nothing. (BL, Egerton MS 2529, fol. 220)

At long last he was a flag-officer in time of war yet he saw no prospects. At this same time Philip Vanbrugh, naval commissioner at Plymouth, wrote to a friend, 'Vice Admiral Balchen is here, but no flag hoisted, nor much to do, which gives him much trouble; whereas ease and quiet is most agreeable to me' (Matcham, 159). Seniority advanced Balchen to the rank of admiral on 11 August 1743. Retirement came the following April; he was made governor of Greenwich Hospital and given a handsome pension of £600 per annum. A knighthood was added in May.

Almost immediately, however, on 1 June, he was called back to active duty. A senior admiral was needed to command a large combined fleet of seventeen British and eight Dutch warships to counter the Brest squadron, which, it was soon learned, had gone to the Tagus and was blockading a fleet of desperately needed storeships and victuallers for the Mediterranean. At the start of the voyage some rich prizes finally came Balchen's way, as six large merchant ships from St Domingue fell to his squadron. In early September he escorted the replenishment ships to Gibraltar, safely past the French force which had withdrawn to Cadiz. Ideally he would have remained, as ordered, to seal that squadron in Cadiz harbour and look out for the incoming treasure ships from Havana, but the Dutch warships were destitute of provisions and though the British supplied them there was only enough to see the fleet home.

On 3 October, in the Channel approaches, the ships were caught in a ferocious storm and dispersed. Most were dismasted or seriously leaking when they got into Plymouth or Spithead, but Balchen's flagship, the *Victory* (100 guns), last seen on 4 October, was not among them. Frigates were sent to search, and Captain Thomas Grenville of the *Falkland* called at Guernsey, where he heard that wreckage had also washed up on Jersey and Alderney. On Guernsey's western and northern shores he saw masts and spars with 'VICT' carved on them, and countless other fragments and furnishings that were unmistakably hers. He did not report seeing bodies. From the evidence and complete absence of survivors—over 1100 men were aboard—it appeared that the ship may have overturned, but it was practically certain that it had also been broken upon rocks, possibly on the Caskets (PRO, ADM 1/1830, Grenville, 18 Oct 1744).

Balchen died at the age of seventy-five after fifty-eight years of naval service. He was a hard-working, thoroughgoing professional, recognized for his readiness to accept duty whenever and wherever required. When the Admiralty sent a notice in August 1740 stipulating that officers resigning their new appointments (almost always on a claim of ill health) must apply through the admiral in command, he responded, 'I believe I shall have but few Applications for that purpose, for they know I am no favourer of Quitting; they must be bad if I write for them' (Baugh, *British Naval Administration*, 117). Yet he was sympathetic when it came to issues affecting lower-deck morale. In 1729 he asked the Admiralty to allow volunteer recruits to go with the captains they had chosen if the captain happened to be re-assigned, and in 1741 he strongly recommended that trustworthy volunteers should be allowed ashore. His practical knowledge respecting ships and seamanship may be seen in plain-spoken letters of January

1735 concerning the *Princess Amelia*'s frightening instability (Baugh, *Naval Administration*, 212–16). It was an absurd twist of fate that he became best known to history by a shipwreck.

Balchen's unexpected death in the line of duty having terminated his pension, the crown immediately settled £500 per annum on his widow. Four of Balchen's six children predeceased him. His youngest and only surviving son, George, who was promoted lieutenant by Nicholas Haddock in 1735 as a favour to the father (BL, Egerton MS, 2528, fol. 22), did not survive him long, dying of illness at Barbados in December 1745, aged twenty-eight, while captain of the *Pembroke*. The monument to the admiral in Westminster Abbey was erected by his wife. Its inscription (fully quoted in some older naval histories and biographies) mentions George Balchen's death and ends with the comment that he 'imitated the virtues and bravery of his good, but unfortunate father'. A surviving daughter, Frances, married Captain Temple West.

Daniel A. Baugh

Sources *DNB* • W. G. V. Balchin, 'Admiral Sir John Balchin (1669–1744)', *Mariner's Mirror*, 80 (1994), 332–5 • H. W. Richmond, *The navy in the war of 1739–48*, 3 vols. (1920) • J. H. Owen, *War at sea under Queen Anne, 1702–1708* (1938) • BL, Egerton MSS, 2528 fol. 22; 2529 fol. 220 • D. A. Baugh, ed., *Naval administration, 1715–1750*, Navy RS, 120 (1977) • (captain's letters), Grenville, 18 Oct 1744, PRO, ADM 1/1830 • D. A. Baugh, *British naval administration in the age of Walpole* (1965) • PRO, SP 42/81, fols. 323, 330 • PRO, ADM 8 series (ships, officers, and stations) • T. Lediard, *The naval history of England*, 2 vols. (1735) • M. E. Matcham, *A forgotten John Russell* (1905) • PRO, ADM 1/1470 • monument inscription, Westminster Abbey, London

Archives PRO | BL, Egerton MSS • Hunt. L., letters to Sir George Pocock • Surrey HC, letters to Philip Vanbrugh

Likenesses J. Richardson the elder, portrait, *c.*1695, NMM [*see illus.*] • G. Kneller, portrait, 1743–1744?, NMM

Balchin, Nigel Marlin (1908–1970), writer, was born on 3 December 1908 at Butts Potterne, Wiltshire, the third of the three children of William Edwin Balchin (1872–1958), grocer and master baker, and his wife, Ada Elizabeth Curtis (1870–1939). Balchin was educated at Dauntsey's School, West Lavington, near Devizes in Wiltshire, and then as an exhibitioner and prizeman at Peterhouse, Cambridge, graduating in 1930 with a first in natural sciences. At Cambridge he wrote short stories which were influenced by his scientific studies. After graduation he joined the National Institute of Psychology and became a consultant to J. S. Rowntree & Son, the chocolate manufacturers in York. Here he pioneered a study of the psychology of the workplace to increase efficiency (he also claimed to be largely responsible for the marketing success of the Aero and Kit Kat chocolate bars).

On 21 January 1933 Balchin married Elisabeth Evelyn Walshe (1910–1991) [*see* Ayrton, Elisabeth Evelyn], whom he had met in Cambridge where she was a student; she was the daughter of the writer Douglas Walshe, and was later a writer herself. The couple had three daughters, including Penelope Leach, the developmental child psychologist. In the mid-1930s Balchin developed a second career as a writer and became a regular contributor to *Punch*. Several articles for that journal were republished in book form as *How to Run a Bassoon Factory* (1934) and *Business for Pleasure* (1935) under the pseudonym Mark Spade; both were satires on efficiency in the workplace, and drew on his work at Rowntrees. He also wrote three novels under his own name—*No Sky* (1934), *Simple Life* (1935), and *Lightbody on Liberty* (1936), all critically and commercially successful—and several stage plays.

Balchin joined the War Office as a psychologist in its personnel section in 1941 and went on to become deputy scientific adviser to the army council, attaining the rank of brigadier. His experience of the cynical machinations of government departments in wartime, and the internecine rivalries and skulduggery of civil service mandarins, were graphically portrayed in his fourth and fifth novels, *Darkness Falls from the Skies* (1942) and *The Small Back Room* (1943). The latter was made into a film by Michael Powell and Emric Pressburger in 1949. They were riveting stories, with steadily mounting tension and drama, but they also acquired instant status as contemporary social documents. In detached, terse, unsentimental prose, bitterness and humour being deployed in equal measure, Balchin captured the authentic atmosphere of London during the blitz, especially from the viewpoint of those working in Whitehall. He interwove private lives and emotions with depictions of life in government offices; the frustration of those in the lower ranks, desperate to get things moving but fated to see fresh initiatives stifled, were contrasted with the Machiavellian manoeuvres of complacent senior civil servants and their masters, intent on maintaining their own positions. With the publication of these two books Balchin attained some prominence as a novelist. He was also popularly credited, in later years, with having coined the terms 'back room boy' and 'boffin'.

With the ending of the war Balchin moved from London to Kent, and decided to become a full-time writer. He consolidated his success with *Mine Own Executioner* (1945), a cleverly developed tale of a psychologist who, inspired initially with zeal and dedication, becomes disillusioned and goes sadly adrift in failing to prevent a steadily developing catastrophe. During the next ten years Balchin produced a novel on average every eighteen months, but these later works, while well crafted and usually quite absorbing, were not in the same league as their immediate predecessors. His output also included a number of short stories and some non-fiction work, and he continued to write plays.

By the late 1940s Balchin's marriage was over. A cordial ménage with the artist Michael Ayrton and his partner Joan, with whom Balchin was having an affair, ended when Elisabeth and Ayrton fell in love (they married in 1952). Balchin's novel *A Way through the Wood* (1951) draws on this experience. Divorced from his first wife in 1951, Balchin married Yovanka Zorana Tomich (*b.* 1930), a Yugoslav refugee, on 5 February 1953; they had a son and a daughter. From 1952 until 1963 he devoted most of his attention to writing screenplays, at first in England and later in Hollywood. He received a BAFTA award for *The Man Who Never Was* (1955) and did some preliminary work on

Cleopatra (1963), but life in Hollywood soon palled owing to his growing reliance on alcohol. During the 1960s he wrote three more novels, including *Seen Dimly before Dawn* (1962), and some television plays.

In appearance Balchin was a tall, sparse man, with penetrating blue eyes and an erudite expression. In later life he grew a beard. He interested himself in a wide range of activities, including music, gardening, wood-carving, and all types of sport (polo excepted). He died from a coronary thrombosis and pneumonia in the Greenaway Nursing Home, Fellowes Road, Hampstead, London, on 17 May 1970. He was cremated at Hampstead cemetery three days later. His wife survived him. PETER ROWLAND

Sources 'The Balchin Family Society', www.balchin-family.org.uk, Jan 2001 • private information (2004) [Prue Hopkins, daughter; Dauntsey's School Foundation; Cambridge University Library] • H. Jordan, 'Nigel Balchin', *Book and Magazine Collector* (Oct 1994) • *WWW*, 1961–70 • *WW* (1945–70) • S. J. Kunitz and V. Colby, eds., *Twentieth-century authors: a biographical dictionary of modern literature, first supplement* (1955) • *The Times* (18 May 1970) • *The new Cambridge bibliography of English literature*, [2nd edn], 4, ed. I. R. Willison (1972) • D. C. Browning, ed., *Everyman's dictionary of literary biography* (1979) • b. cert. • m. certs. • d. cert.

Archives Borth. Inst. • J. S. Rowntree & Sons, York, archives
Likenesses M. Gerson, photograph, 1952, repro. in *The Times*
Wealth at death £41,891: probate, 1970, *CGPLA Eng. & Wales*

Balcon, Sir Michael Elias (1896–1977), film producer, was born on 19 May 1896 at 116 Summer Lane, Edgbaston, Birmingham, the youngest son and fourth of five children of Louis Balcon (*c*.1858–1946) and his wife, Laura Greenberg (*c*.1863–1934). His parents, Jewish immigrants from eastern Europe, had met in England. Louis Balcon described himself as a tailor, but seems rarely to have practised his trade. He preferred to travel, especially to South Africa, where his brother-in-law had settled, leaving his wife to bring up the children as best she might. Michael Balcon's childhood, in his own words, was 'respectable but impoverished' (Balcon, 2). Despite poverty, all the children were given a good education. Balcon himself won a scholarship in 1907 to George Dixon Grammar School in Birmingham, where his scholastic career, so he later claimed, was 'undistinguished' (Balcon, 5). Even so, he hoped to follow his elder brothers to university, but to his disappointment the family's financial needs obliged him to leave school in 1913 and work as apprentice to a jeweller. When war broke out he volunteered for service, but was turned down owing to defective eyesight. In 1915 he joined the Dunlop Rubber Company's huge plant at Aston Cross, known as Fort Dunlop, and he rose to become personal assistant to the managing director.

After the war a friend, Victor Saville, whose family was in show business, invited Balcon to join him in setting up a film distribution company. Together they formed Victory Motion Pictures; the chairman, and financial backer, was Oscar Deutsch, a rich scrap-metal dealer who later founded the Odeon cinema chain. In 1921 Saville and Balcon moved to London, opening an office in Soho, and in 1923, with backing from Deutsch and a prominent London distributor, C. M. Woolf, they produced their first feature film, a melodrama called *Woman to Woman* (1923). It

Sir Michael Elias Balcon (1896–1977), by Howard Coster, 1936

starred a then popular Hollywood actress, Betty Compson, and was directed at Islington Studios by a leading British director of the period, Graham Cutts. The film was a screen hit. On the strength of it, Balcon and Cutts took a lease on Islington Studios and formed Gainsborough Pictures. The studio, recently vacated by the Hollywood company Famous Players–Lasky (later to become Paramount), was small but well equipped and fully staffed. The staff included an ambitious, highly versatile young man called Alfred Hitchcock.

That same year, 1924, Balcon married on 10 April Aileen Freda Leatherman (1904–1988), daughter of Beatrice Leatherman, born in Middlesex, but brought up in Johannesburg. In 1946 she was appointed MBE for her war work. Their marriage was happy and lasted until Balcon's death. They had two children: Jill, born 1925, and Jonathan, born 1931. Jill Balcon, who became an actress, married future poet laureate Cecil Day-Lewis; their son, Daniel Day-Lewis, also became an actor.

Under Balcon's leadership Gainsborough earned a reputation for high-quality films, often with cosmopolitan themes. Several of them were shot at the giant Ufa Studios in Berlin, where Balcon established a good working relationship with the great producer Erich Pommer. In 1925 Balcon gave Hitchcock his first chance to direct with *The Pleasure Garden*, filmed in Germany and Italy. Gainsborough often featured matinée idol Ivor Novello in such films as *The Rat* (1925), directed by Graham Cutts, and *The Lodger* (1926), directed by Hitchcock.

In 1928 Gainsborough was relaunched as a public company. On the board, along with Balcon and C. M. Woolf, was Maurice Ostrer, one of the Ostrer brothers who controlled Gaumont-British, which was fast becoming Britain's largest film company. Gainsborough was now in effect an outpost of the Gaumont empire, and Balcon found his independence steadily eroded. In 1931 he was appointed head of production at Gaumont's Lime Grove Studios in Shepherd's Bush, while still overseeing production at Islington. In both capacities he reported to the Ostrers. It may have been the ambiguity of his status, as much as the pressures of running two studios, that contributed to a nervous breakdown late in 1931.

Over the next five years Gaumont and Gainsborough,

under Balcon's guidance, produced some of the most popular British films of the period in a wide range of genres. Hitchcock, enticed away from Gainsborough a few years earlier, now rejoined his old boss and hit his stride with such classics as *The Man Who Knew Too Much* (1934), *The 39 Steps* (1935), and *Sabotage* (1936). There were musicals with Jessie Matthews, including *Evergreen* (1934) and *First a Girl* (1935); Ben Travers's Aldwych farces and the comedies of Jack Hulbert and Cicely Courtneidge; historical biopics starring the actorly George Arliss; stylish thrillers (*Rome Express*, 1932); romantic comedies (*The Good Companions*, 1933); horror vehicles for Boris Karloff, temporarily lured from Hollywood (*The Ghoul*, 1933); big-budget science-fiction spectaculars (*The Tunnel*, 1935); war movies (*I was a Spy*, 1933); and ambitious costume dramas such as *Jew Süss* (1934) and *Tudor Rose* (1936). *Jew Süss*, a project especially dear to Balcon's heart, represented a rare attempt to circumvent the stifling British censorship and denounce, under a historical guise, the antisemitic policies of Nazi Germany.

Many technicians and actors who were fleeing Nazi oppression found refuge at Gaumont-British, with Balcon's active encouragement. Among them were the brilliant, autocratic art director Alfred Junge, and the cinematographers Günther Krampf and Mutz Greenbaum, as well as director Berthold Viertel and the producer Hermann Fellner. The actor Conrad Veidt, under pressure from the Nazis to make films for the Reich, only escaped from Germany thanks to Balcon's direct intervention.

In the teeth of scepticism from the Gaumont board, Balcon backed the documentary pioneer Robert J. Flaherty to make *Man of Aran* (1934), although Flaherty's maverick working methods left the studio with little control over the production. The shoot, remote and uncontactable off the west coast of Ireland, went wildly over-schedule and over-budget, and the film never recouped its cost. According to the director Michael Powell, when faced with Flaherty 'Mickey Balcon, protesting feebly, was as helpless as the Wedding Guest with the Ancient Mariner' (Powell, 237). In the trade, *Man of Aran* became known as 'Balcon's folly', but Balcon always remained proud of having backed the film.

Though Gaumont and Gainsborough productions generally did well in Britain, they rarely found much favour in the USA. The Ostrers, noting the flashier successes of Alexander Korda, became obsessed with the perennial mirage that haunts British film producers—the dream of cracking the American market. In 1936 Balcon was sent to Hollywood for several months to scout talent and forge links with the big studios. Never at ease in the movie capital, he returned home with relief, only to find the Gaumont empire near collapse. The Ostrers' erratic financial policies and ambitious export drive had led to a financial crisis. The Lime Grove Studios were closed down, staff were laid off, and in November Balcon left to join MGM, who were setting up their British operation at Denham.

The eighteen months Balcon spent at MGM were probably the unhappiest of his career. He clashed with the autocratic Louis B. Mayer, and during his stint at Denham as nominal head of production he produced only one film: *A Yank at Oxford* (1938), an inanely Hollywoodized view of British university life. Luckily at this juncture his old friend Reginald Baker, an accountant who had helped him raise the money to lease Islington, invited Balcon to produce films at Ealing Studios. Baker and his colleagues on the board of Associated Talking Pictures, who owned Ealing, were dissatisfied with the studio's production head, the theatrical impresario Basil Dean, and were looking for a replacement. Balcon was offered the job, and he readily accepted.

At Ealing, a small, almost cottage-like studio, Balcon found his spiritual home. Under his benevolently paternalistic rule it developed into the nearest the British film industry ever came to a studio after the classic Hollywood pattern. Like, for example, Warner Brothers in the 1930s, Ealing had its roster of personnel—directors, writers, and technicians—on permanent salary, its pool of actors, its recurrent thematic preoccupations, and from all these there was derived a very recognizable house style of film-making that was to a large degree Balcon's own personal creation. Despite its tiny capacity—even at its most productive, the studio never managed to turn out more than six feature films a year—Ealing became the most famous British film studio in the world.

Balcon, who always liked to surround himself with a trusted team of associates, brought to Ealing several former colleagues from Gainsborough and Gaumont. Among them were his elder brother Chandos, who acted as his right-hand man, the technical expert Baynham Honri, the script editor Angus MacPhail, the screenwriter Sidney Gilliat, and the director Robert Stevenson. There was also a promising young assistant director, Penrose Tennyson, whom Balcon soon allowed to direct his first film. Regrettably, Tennyson died in a flying accident in 1941, having directed only three films.

With characteristic caution, Balcon initially produced a spread of films broadly similar to those made under Basil Dean. Among them were the studio's biggest money-spinners, the George Formby comedies, though Balcon himself liked neither the films nor their star. But with the outbreak of war the character of Ealing began to change. Balcon brought in several of the film-makers who had worked with John Grierson in the British documentary movement of the 1930s, most notably Alberto Cavalcanti and Harry Watt. Under their influence Ealing's war films took on a downbeat, even truculent tone, devoid of flag-waving bombast and sceptical of the competence of the top brass. *The Next of Kin* (1942), a vivid dramatization of the slogan 'Careless talk costs lives', angered Churchill, but was released at the insistence of the War Office. Others in the same vein included *The Foreman Went to France* (1942), *Went the Day Well?* (1942), *Nine Men* (1943), and *San Demetrio London* (1944).

During the war Balcon himself adopted an embattled stance, tilting with unconcealed relish at the obstructive red tape of government ministries and fighting his corner against the ambitions of rival film companies. A frequent target for his barbs was the encroaching Rank Organisation, headed by flour millionaire J. Arthur Rank, which had grown in a few years to become the dominant force in the British film industry, swallowing among others Gaumont-British and the Odeon cinema chain. But Ealing, lacking distribution muscle, was too small to stand alone. In 1944 Balcon and Baker (who acted as the studio's financial head) performed a deft volte-face and struck a financing and distribution deal with Rank.

Backed by Rank's ample resources, Ealing entered into its finest period. Balcon expressly set out to make films 'reflecting Britain and the British character'. There was the occasional venture into national epic (*Scott of the Antarctic*, 1948), classic adaptation (*Nicholas Nickleby*, 1947), romantic costume drama (*Saraband for Dead Lovers*, 1949), and even once, brilliantly, the supernatural (*Dead of Night*, 1945). The studio also explored distant territory. The footloose Harry Watt shot *The Overlanders* (1946) in Australia and *Where No Vultures Fly* (1951) in east Africa. But Ealing, and Balcon himself, always seemed more at home with small-scale, realist films that followed the documentary-influenced tradition of the war years, such as the East End domestic drama *It Always Rains on Sunday* (1947); the archetypal police procedural, *The Blue Lamp* (1950), which first introduced the reassuring figure of Dixon of Dock Green; or *Mandy* (1952), a sensitive, unsentimental study of a deaf child and her parents.

In 1948, with Ealing at the peak of its creativity, Balcon was awarded a knighthood for his services to British cinema. From this period, too, date the films for which he and his studio will always be best remembered: the classic Ealing comedies. Starting with *Hue and Cry* (1947), in which a gang of boys hunt down crooks across the bomb-sites of post-war London, these films present a vision of controlled anarchy, often benevolent, as in *Passport to Pimlico* (1949) and *The Lavender Hill Mob* (1951). But from time to time a darker note tinged the humour, as in Robert Hamer's elegantly ruthless *Kind Hearts and Coronets* (1949), or Alexander Mackendrick's sharp political satire *The Man in the White Suit* (1951) and his Gothic black comedy *The Ladykillers* (1955).

Hamer and Mackendrick were two of those who benefited from Balcon's policy of fostering young talent; others were the directors Charles Frend, Charles Crichton, Seth Holt, the screenwriter T. E. B. Clarke, and the cinematographer Douglas Slocombe. Throughout his career he believed in nurturing and encouraging promising young men (rarely women), giving them generous opportunities and leaving them free to develop their abilities within a supportive environment. Monja Danischewsky, Ealing's witty and gregarious publicity officer, referred to Ealing as 'Mr Balcon's Academy for Young Gentlemen' (Danischewsky, *White Russian*, 133). Production decisions were reached at the 'round table' conferences, attended by all the senior personnel with Balcon presiding benignly. He often let himself be overruled by majority opinion, with the standing joke, 'Well, if you fellows feel so strongly, on my head be it' (Fluegel, 7).

There were limits to his tolerance, though. Jokes about sex or religion, or any radical criticism of British institutions, were rarely allowed to creep into Ealing's films. In this, they reflected Balcon's own character. In many ways he cut an anomalous figure as a prominent film producer: an essentially shy man, he retained a strangely unworldly innocence in many matters (especially regarding sex), and a personal modesty almost unique in his profession. His politics were moderately left-wing, and though he enjoyed comfort, his lifestyle was anything but ostentatious. As he pointed out, 'I have never owned a yacht, a racehorse or even a swimming-pool. Neither do I smoke cigars' (Balcon, 220).

In the late 1940s J. Arthur Rank began to withdraw from the day-to-day running of his organization, handing over to his managing director, the far less sympathetic John Davis. The relationship between Ealing and Rank became strained, and in 1955 the connection was severed. Ealing Studios were sold to the BBC, and Balcon led his depleted team to a corner of the MGM studio at Borehamwood, where for a few years they lived out a shadowy afterlife as Ealing Films. The last Ealing film appeared in 1959.

Balcon's involvement with the British film industry was not yet over. In 1959 he became chairman of the newly formed Bryanston production company, and in 1964 of British Lion. Always open to new ideas, he was proud to be associated with the British new wave in such films as *Saturday Night and Sunday Morning* (1960). But in neither company was he able to exercise the same hands-on control of production that he had enjoyed at Ealing, and at British Lion in particular he sometimes felt himself to be little more than a figurehead. In 1966 he resigned, and became chairman of the British Film Institute production board, funding low-budget experimental work. He remained in this post well past his seventy-fifth birthday, continuing his lifelong practice of helping and encouraging young film-makers.

In his private life, Balcon was an avid theatre- and opera-goer and he enjoyed travel, especially to Italy. He had a wide circle of friends, and loved to dispense hospitality at Upper Parrock, the fifteenth-century house set on a Sussex hilltop near the Kent border where he and his wife had lived since the Second World War. It was there that he died peacefully at the age of eighty-one on 17 October 1977. He was cremated and his ashes were buried at Upper Parrock. PHILIP KEMP

Sources M. Balcon, *A lifetime of films* (1969) • BFI, Michael Balcon collection • M. Danischewsky, *White Russian, red face* (1966) • M. Danischewsky, ed., *Michael Balcon's 25 years in films* (1948) • J. Fluegel, ed., *Michael Balcon: the pursuit of British cinema* (1984) • C. Barr, *Ealing Studios* (1977) • M. Powell, *A life in films* (1986) • private information (2004) [family, friends, colleagues] • b. cert. • m. cert. • d. cert.

Archives BFI, collection | BFI, corresp. incl. memos with Ivor Montague • University of Stirling, corresp. with John Grierson | FILM BFI NFTVA, 'Speaking personally', 27 Oct 1951 • BFI NFTVA, film profile, 12 Sept 1961 • BFI NFTVA, 'Sir Michael Balcon—film maker', 12 June 1969 • BFI NFTVA, documentary footage | SOUND BL NSA, oral history interview

Likenesses J. Epstein, bronze bust, 1933, NPG • H. Coster, photographs, *c.*1936, NPG [*see illus.*] • W. Stoneman, photograph, 1948,

NPG · W. Bird, photograph, 1961, NPG · G. Argent, photograph, 1970, NPG
Wealth at death £272,880: probate, 3 May 1978, *CGPLA Eng. & Wales*

Bald (*fl. c.*900), supposed physician and medical writer, was the owner and probable author of a work titled *Læceboc* (leechbook), a compilation in Old English of medical recipes and treatments. All that is known of Bald is to be found in the Latin verse colophon to the *Læceboc*, as found in the British Library manuscript (BL, Royal MS 12 D.xvii) and written about 950, most probably at Winchester. The colophon begins: 'Bald owns this book, which he ordered Cild to write'. It also states that the *Læceboc* is the dearest of all Bald's books. Everything else that can be said about Bald is inference from these statements and from the internal evidence of the work itself.

The manuscript appears to be a copy of an exemplar written some fifty years earlier, hence the suggestion that Bald may have been active about 900, that is, in the very last years of the reign of Alfred the Great. The work is in two books dealing respectively with externally and internally manifested ailments. It draws on the standard works of early medieval Mediterranean medicine as well as on native material and is distinguished by its high level of organization. It is impossible to know whether Bald or Cild selected and arranged the materials, because the word *componere* (write) could mean either 'write down' or 'compose' in medieval Latin. It may be conjectured that Bald was a physician and a layman able to read English (and probably medical Latin) living in the late ninth century, probably in the vicinity of Winchester, who had available to him several books on medicine in Latin and English, from which he (or Cild) selected, modified, and arranged medical materials into the two parts of the *Læceboc*. It is tempting to think that its composition may have owed something to the stimulus of Alfred's revival of learning. At any rate, Bald, whether or not he was author of his *Læceboc*, has left to posterity an example of vernacular medical material of the greatest value for assessing the medical competence of Anglo-Saxon practitioners. If his book had not survived it would not be known that such practitioners were familiar with the standard works in Latin containing the best of Greek and Roman medicine, and integrated them into an English tradition to produce prescriptions that were 'about as good as anything prescribed before the mid-twentieth century' (Cameron, 117).

M. L. CAMERON

Sources BL, Royal MS 12 D.xvii · *Bald's leechbook: British Museum Royal Manuscript, 12.D.17*, ed. C. E. Wright (1955) · O. Cockayne, ed., *Leechdoms, wortcunning, and starcraft of early England* (1865), vol. 2 · N. R. Ker, ed., *Catalogue of manuscripts containing Anglo-Saxon* (1957) · M. L. Cameron, *Anglo-Saxon medicine* (1993)
Archives BL, Royal MS 12 D.xvii

Bald, Alexander (1783–1859), poet, was born at Alloa, Clackmannanshire, on 9 June 1783, the son of Alexander Bald (*d.* 1823) and his wife, Jane, *née* Christie. His father was the superintendent at a local coal works and author of *The Farmer and Corn Dealer's Assistant* (1790), for many years an indispensable book for tenant farmers in Scotland. His elder brother, Robert *Bald (1776–1861), later became an eminent mining engineer. Alexander was from an early age trained for commerce, and for more than fifty years conducted business at Alloa as a timber merchant and brick manufacturer. On 15 September 1809, he married Ann, *née* Geddes, at Alloa. Throughout his life he devoted much of his leisure to literature, and was the friend and patron of many literary men in Scotland including John Grieve and James Hogg, whose talents he was among the first to recognize. He established a Shakespeare Club in his native town, and attracted eminent literary figures to its annual celebrations. Bald regularly contributed poems to the *Scots Magazine*, including 'The Lily of the Vale', which has been erroneously attributed to Allan Ramsay. Bald died at his home, Craigward Cottage, Alloa, on 21 October 1859. He was survived by his wife.

SIDNEY LEE, *rev.* SARAH COUPER

Sources C. Rogers, *A century of Scottish life*, 2nd edn (1872), 119 · C. Rogers, *The modern Scottish minstrel, or, The songs of Scotland of the past half-century*, 5 (1857), 34 · NA Scot., SC 64/42/11/9–28 · NA Scot., SC 64/42/11/98–105 · *IGI*
Wealth at death £2982 12*s.* 11½*d.*: confirmation, 3 March 1860, NA Scot., SC 64/42/11/9–28 · £10: additional inventory, 2 June 1860, NA Scot., SC 64/42/11/98–105

Bald, Robert (1776–1861), mining engineer, was born at Culross, Perthshire, one of two sons of Alexander Bald (*d.* 1823) and his wife, Jane Christie. Alexander *Bald (1783–1859) was his younger brother. The father was then colliery manager for the earl of Dundonald, and from about 1777 until his death he was employed in a similar capacity by the earl of Mar at his collieries in and around Alloa, Clackmannanshire, one of a number of rapidly growing coal-producing districts in central Scotland.

Bald served an apprenticeship in colliery management under his father, enhancing his surveying and engineering skills under the guidance of Thomas Telford, civil engineer, whom he accompanied to Sweden to assist in surveying the route of the proposed Gotha Canal. He succeeded his father as manager of the Mar collieries in 1824. Sharing responsibility with Robert Jameson, factor for the Mar estate, and initially encouraged by Francis Miller Erskine, twenty-fifth earl of Mar (*b.* 1795), Bald embarked on an expansionary strategy for the mines he managed. This involved productivity improvements, to be achieved both by the introduction of new technology and also by more efficient labour management. Convinced that the dissipated habits of the colliers were adversely affecting labour productivity, Bald instituted a vigorous programme of social reform, which included the improvement of the colliers' accommodation. Moral reform too was attempted, with the introduction in the main mining communities of prayer meetings, which were run on lines similar to the Scottish kirk sessions, and based on the communal 'colliery court' established on the Mar estate in the mid-eighteenth century; among other duties the 'brethren' were responsible for chastising those who were drunk or profane. A paternalistic employer with radical inclinations, Bald was also heavily involved in the campaign for parliamentary reform in 1831–2.

Labour disputes and the financial costs of Bald's programme apparently led to a breach between Bald and the trustees of the Mar estate in 1835, even though a year earlier it had been reported that under Bald's management the coal workers at Alloa colliery were 'the most orderly and well disposed class of men in Scotland' (NA Scot., GD 124/11/592/3). Similar problems led to the premature ending of a partnership Bald had joined as a lessee of collieries at Collyland, Woodlands, and Devonside. Freed of some of those ties, Bald then established himself as a full-time consultant mining engineer, based in Edinburgh from 1835, although he had been called as an expert witness during legal actions concerning coal rights as early as 1805.

Bald was Scotland's most respected mining engineer and coal 'viewer' in the first half of the nineteenth century, and surveyed and reported on most of the country's major colliery enterprises, including those of the Bairds, the Dixons, and the Dunlops in the west of Scotland. He had an intimate knowledge of the coal industry, based on first-hand experience, and a considerable reputation, which extended to mainland Europe in both coalmining and land surveying. He was elected a fellow of the Royal Society of Edinburgh in 1817, and was also an honorary member of the Institution of Civil Engineers, as well as of the Geological Society of London.

Less well known is Bald's concern about female coal 'bearers', whose employment underground was a striking feature of the coal industry in the east of Scotland. He first drew attention to their condition in his invaluable *General View of the Coal Trade in Scotland* (1808), the most accessible account of the coal industry in Scotland for this period; and he is credited with assisting in the campaign to reform employment abuses in coalmines promoted by Lord Ashley, later seventh earl of Shaftesbury. The employment of women and young children underground at Alloa colliery ceased some time before the legislation of 1842 which abolished the practice. Bald is not known to have married; he died, aged eighty-six, at his home in Alloa, on 28 December 1861.

CHRISTOPHER A. WHATLEY

Sources J. L. Carvel, *One hundred years in coal: the history of the Alloa Coal Company* (1944) • B. F. Duckham, *History of the Scottish coal industry, 1700–1815* (1970), vol. 1 of *History of the Scottish coal industry* • R. Bald, *A general view of the coal trade in Scotland* (1808) • Report on books of the Alloa colliery, 23 Dec 1834, NA Scot., Mar and Kellie MSS, GD 124/11/592/3 • *The Scotsman* (30 Dec 1861) • Boase, *Mod. Eng. biog.* • *Quarterly Journal of the Geological Society*, 19 (1863)

Archives NA Scot., survey reports, GD27 | NA Scot., Mar and Kellie MSS, GD124

Likenesses portrait, Clackmannan District Council Offices, Greenfield House, Tullibody Road, Alloa, Clackmannanshire

Wealth at death £1054 4*s.* 7*d.*: confirmation, 4 April 1862, NA Scot., SC 64/42/11/770

Bald, William (1789/90–1857), surveyor and civil engineer, was born in Burntisland, Fife, and educated at Burntisland and in Edinburgh before becoming apprenticed to the eminent Scottish land surveyor, John Ainslie. From 1803 onwards he was employed on very extensive estate surveys throughout Scotland, and his maps were used by Aaron Arrowsmith for his own map of Scotland. While still in his teens, and with an audacity that marked his whole career, he made himself known to the officers conducting the Ordnance Survey of Great Britain, who recommended him to an MP for co. Mayo, Ireland, as capable of providing the Mayo grand jury with an accurate county map. (Grand juries were the principal road-making authorities and were empowered to commission such county surveys.) Bald started work in 1809 and soon secured other appointments in Mayo, first as one of the engineers employed by the government to survey and map the bogs of Ireland, and later as a road engineer. His survey of the county, completed in 1817 and published in 1830, was the most ambitious of all the Irish grand jury maps, paying special attention to trigonometrical accuracy and to the correct representation of relief and altitude. Bald planned to follow it with other county surveys of similar quality, but this ambition was frustrated when the Ordnance Survey was directed to produce its own map of Ireland in 1824, and henceforth he devoted his energies to civil engineering, a profession for which he further equipped himself by a period of renewed study and visits to places of scientific interest abroad.

After 1832 Bald's career becomes a catalogue of the roads, harbours, river navigations, canals, and railways designed by himself or with his advice. His first and most spectacular project in this period was the new Antrim coast road of 1832–7, which involved much blasting and tunnelling in the cliffs between Larne and Ballycastle. Another road design of the same period, which included Ireland's first suspension bridge, was from Kenmare to Bantry, in the south-west. In less difficult country, such as the Irish midlands, he was an advocate of railways, and later reproached the government's commission on this subject with the inadequacy of the network it proposed for Ireland. His interest in tidal rivers began with work on the River Boyne and culminated in 1839 with re-employment in his native country as engineer to the Clyde River Trust, a post from which he was dismissed six years later after criticizing the trustees in a Glasgow newspaper. This experience does not seem to have damaged his career, and his last recorded assignment was in the same area, reporting in 1854 on the navigational implications of the Glasgow Waterworks Bill.

Bald was a prolific and articulate writer and speaker on scientific topics, the way in which science might promote economic development, and the training of civil engineers. Although he was never honoured by the government, he was elected to several learned societies, including the Royal Geological Society, the Royal Irish Academy, the Royal Society of Edinburgh, and the Société de Géographie de Paris, to the last of which he had exhibited his Mayo map while living in Paris in the late 1820s. He was thrice married (his third wife's name was Margaret) and had nine children, one of whom, Charles (*b.* 1812/13), worked as a surveyor on his father's projects, as did William Bald, junior, probably also a son. He died on 26 March 1857 at 14 Werrington Street, Oakley Square, St Pancras, London, and was buried in Highgate cemetery.

J. H. ANDREWS, *rev.* ELIZABETH BAIGENT

Sources M. C. Storrie, 'William Bald, FRSE, *c.*1789–1857: surveyor, cartographer and civil engineer', *Transactions of the Institute of British Geographers*, 47 (1969), 205–31

Archives Admiralty Library, Taunton, Hydrographic Office • BL • Clyde Port Authority • NA Scot. • NL Ire. • RGS

Baldock, Ralph (*d.* **1313**), administrator and bishop of London, was first recorded in February 1275, when he was admitted as rector of Little Woolstone in Buckinghamshire. In St Paul's he held, probably successively, the prebendal stalls of Holborn and Newington and is also found as prebendary of Islington. He first occurs as archdeacon of Middlesex in June 1278, became dean of St Paul's in 1294, and was elected bishop of London on 23 or 24 February 1304. Three canons, who had been deprived by the archbishop during the vacancy of the see, appealed to the pope to declare the election void owing to their exclusion, but the bishop-elect prevailed, and was consecrated at Lyons on 30 January 1306.

Later that year Baldock was commissioned by Pope Clement V (*r.* 1305–14) to conduct an inquiry at Hereford into the miracles attributed to Thomas de Cantilupe (*d.* 1282). At the Carlisle parliament in January 1307 he was sworn a member of the king's council. Edward I promoted him to chancellor in April, but his tenure of this office lasted only until the king's death in July. His presence at the Stamford parliament in August 1309 denotes loyalty to Edward II. Baldock was one of five bishops appointed as *lords ordainer in March 1310. In late 1311 he attended the Council of Vienne. He provided for the resumption of theological lectures in his cathedral by appropriating the church of Ealing to the chancellorship of St Paul's, and wrote a history of England, which existed in the sixteenth century but is now lost. The extent of his intellectual interests is shown by the list of 126 *libri scolastici* made after his death; mostly devoted to theology and canon law, they also include works of natural science, medicine, and history. Baldock's codification of the customs and statutes of St Paul's, made while he was dean, was unparalleled among medieval English cathedral codes for its comprehensiveness and logical arrangement.

St Paul's Cathedral was at this time being rebuilt and enlarged, and its new lady chapel was built by Baldock. He began it while he was still dean, continued it as bishop, bequeathed money for its completion and, after his death at Stepney on 24 July 1313, was buried there, under a handsome monument which was destroyed in the mid-sixteenth century. Master Robert *Baldock, chancellor of England from 1323 to 1326, probably his nephew, was one of the bishop's executors. Robert's brother Richard, described as a king's clerk in 1325, became a canon of Salisbury and York.

H. A. TIPPING, *rev.* M. C. BUCK

Sources R. C. Fowler, ed., *Registrum Radulphi Baldock, Gilberti Segrave, Ricardi Newport, et Stephani Gravesend*, CYS, 7 (1911) • *Fasti Angl.*, *1066–1300*, [St Paul's, London] • *Fasti Angl.*, *1300–1541*, [St Paul's, London] • *Chancery records* (RC) • Emden, *Oxf.* • W. S. Simpson, ed., *Documents illustrating the history of St Paul's Cathedral*, CS, new ser., 26 (1880) • W. Dugdale, *The history of St Paul's Cathedral in London*, new edn, ed. H. Ellis (1818) • H. R. Luard, ed., *Flores historiarum*, 3 vols., Rolls Series, 95 (1890) • W. Stubbs, ed., *Chronicles of the reigns of Edward I and Edward II*, 2 vols., Rolls Series, 76 (1882–3) • F. M. Powicke and C. R. Cheney, eds., *Councils and synods with other documents relating to the English church, 1205–1313*, 2 vols. (1964) • J. H. Denton, *Robert Winchelsey and the crown, 1294–1313: a study in the defence of ecclesiastical liberty*, Cambridge Studies in Medieval Life and Thought, 3rd ser., 14 (1980) • *Ann. mon.*, vol. 4 • K. Edwards, *The English secular cathedrals in the middle ages: a constitutional study with special reference to the fourteenth century*, 2nd edn (1967) • W. S. Simpson, ed., *Registrum statutorum et consuetudinum ecclesiae cathedralis Sancti Pauli Londinensis* (1873) • exchequer, king's remembrances, memoranda roll, PRO, E. 159/97, m.38 • G. Hennessy, *Novum repertorium ecclesiasticum parochiale Londinense, or, London diocesan clergy succession from the earliest time to the year 1898* (1898)

Archives GL, MS 9531/1

Likenesses brass on marble monument (destroyed in the reign of Edward VI)

Wealth at death books at manor of Stepney in Middlesex: St Paul's Cathedral, London, deanery, cited Emden, *Oxf.*, iii, 2147–9

Baldock, Robert (*d.* **1327**), administrator, was of obscure origins, but was probably born in Baldock in Hertfordshire. He was an executor, and almost certainly a relative, of Ralph *Baldock (*d.* 1313), bishop of London (1306–13) whose family name, the Pauline annalist suggests, was Catel. His brother Richard was a royal clerk. He was educated at Oxford, where he was BCL by 1294, and also entered royal service. Named king's clerk in 1316, he embarked upon a number of diplomatic missions in France and Scotland, before in January 1320 assuming custody of the privy seal. He remained keeper until 7 July 1323, being the first holder of the office to take an important role in a wider political and administrative sphere. This arose from the confidence placed in him by Edward II—he is occasionally described as his secretary—and by the younger Hugh Despenser, whose protégé he seems to have been. He reunited the office of keeper with that of controller of the wardrobe, thereby circumventing an intention of the ordinances of 1311. Other activities often prevented Baldock from discharging all the responsibilities of these dual offices in person. Thus he was scheduled to accompany the king abroad in the spring of 1320 and in anticipation located his household at Wissant. He did go to the continent in June when he left behind a 'small seal of absence'. In September of the same year he was appointed to treat with Robert I of Scotland and on 3 December received safe conduct for attending to royal affairs in various parts of the realm.

The Bridlington chronicler cited as a grievance of the lords assembled at Sherburn in Elmet (28 June 1321) the fact that the keeper and other officers had been appointed contrary to the ordinances and were the source of novelties, evils, and oppressions. In July of that year Baldock was named first among the evil and false councillors whom the younger Despenser had allegedly appointed for the disinheritance and destruction of magnates and people. But his rise continued. He succeeded Bishop Salmon as chancellor on 20 August 1323 and in November of the following year was a commissioner for negotiating peace with the Scots. He retained the chancellorship until 26 October 1326, by which time the king was a fugitive.

Despite Edward's efforts Baldock was the only chancellor of the reign who was not supported by the resources of a bishopric. This may be attributed in part to the deliberate policy of Pope John XXII, and in part to the opportunism of other potential candidates, coupled with Baldock's unpopularity at the curia. And so the king's attempts to secure for him the sees of Coventry and Lichfield, Winchester, and Norwich, in 1321, 1323, and 1325 respectively, all came to nothing. He did secure a number of canonries and the archdeaconry of Middlesex, but this and most of the canonries were for varying periods subject to litigation. The king's attempt to give him the Lincoln prebend of Aylesbury in 1322 led to an acrimonious conflict at Avignon which lasted for the remainder of the reign. He was summoned to the curia, and in 1324 excommunicated.

His close association with their regime meant that Baldock shared the intense unpopularity of Edward II and the Despensers; in particular he was held responsible for the measures against bishops Stratford, Orleton, Burghersh, Hotham, and Droxford. He stayed by the king in his retreat from London in October 1326 and was captured with him and the younger Despenser in the neighbourhood of Neath Abbey on 16 November. At Hereford he was claimed as a clerk by Bishop Orleton, who allegedly took him to London to answer in convocation for his misdeeds. A mob, claiming infringement of the city's liberties, dragged Baldock from Orleton's house, Monthalt, and lodged him in Newgate gaol where, miserably abused, he died on 28 May 1327. He was buried in the cemetery of the canons, St Paul's, London. ROY MARTIN HAINES

Sources Norfolk RO, Reg /1/2 • *Chronicon Galfridi le Baker de Swynebroke*, ed. E. M. Thompson (1889) • W. Stubbs, ed., *Chronicles of the reigns of Edward I and Edward II*, 2 vols., Rolls Series, 76 (1882–3) • N. Denholm-Young, ed. and trans., *The life of Edward II by the so-called monk of Malmesbury* (1957) • Rymer, *Foedera* • *Chancery records* • Tout, *Admin. hist.*, vols. 2–6 • J. C. Davies, *The baronial opposition to Edward II* (1918) • W. E. L. Smith, *Episcopal appointments and patronage in the reign of Edward II*, SCH, 3 (1938) • R. M. Haines, *Archbishop John Stratford: political revolutionary and champion of the liberties of the English church*, Pontifical Institute of Medieval Studies: Texts and Studies, 76 (1986) • R. M. Haines, *The church and politics in fourteenth-century England: the career of Adam Orleton, c. 1275–1345*, Cambridge Studies in Medieval Life and Thought, 3rd ser., 10 (1978) • Emden, *Oxf.*, 1.96–8; 3.xii–xiii • *Fasti Angl., 1300–1541*, [Lincoln; Salisbury; Mon. cath (SP); St. Paul's, London; Bath and Wells; Coventry; Introduction]

Archives Norfolk RO, Reg /1/2

Baldock, Sir Robert (1624/5–1691), judge, was born at Stanway, Essex, the son and heir of Samuel Baldock (*b. c.*1599), rector of Stanway. He was admitted a sizar of Pembroke College, Cambridge, on 29 October 1640, aged fifteen. Baldock entered Gray's Inn in July 1644, was called to the bar on 11 February 1651, and earned the degree of ancient on 18 May 1667. A decade later he gave the last of more than 400 recorded readings at Gray's Inn. Initiated over 250 years earlier, these readings had been held regularly until 1642 and quickly died out afterwards. Readers were selected from among the company to interpret cycles of statute law for the instruction of the students. The readings encompassed ten to twelve days spaced over three to four weeks (Baker, 31–7). In the same year (1677) he took the degree of serjeant.

Baldock married Mary, daughter of Bacqueville Bacon, coheir of her brother Henry, and the couple settled at Great Hocham in Norfolk. Mary died in 1662 and Baldock later remarried; however, the name of his second spouse is not recorded. He and Mary had two children: Robert, who died in a naval battle in 1673, and Mary, his surviving heir, who married George, son of Thomas Townshend of West Wretham, Norfolk, in 1675.

Early references to Baldock's legal career beyond Gray's Inn are scattered. He served as a justice of the peace for Norfolk after the Restoration. Robert Doughty reported in July 1664, 'I was at Norwich general quarter sessions, where Mr Bacon had the cushion, as Mr Long had before him & Mr Corey & Mr Baldock were to have after him' (Rosenheim, 38). In the only case in which he is specifically mentioned, Baldock ordered a verdict of not guilty returned in a dispute over the theft of 50*s*. In 1671, while recorder at Great Yarmouth, Baldock was knighted by Charles II during the latter's visit there. Two other references concerning his legal duties are extant for the period before Baldock became a serjeant in 1685. In the first, Edward L'Estrange was ordered to meet with him 'or in his absence, with Mr Norris about the validity of unexecuted warrants issued during the last Lieutenancy' (Cozens-Hardy, 40). Baldock was not available and Norris held that the warrants were still valid. Roger North, describing the fraudulent conveyance in a case involving Sir William Doyly, observed that Baldock possessed the 'wit and will' to prepare one (North, 2.124). Contemporary views of his legal abilities seem somewhat mixed; nevertheless, he became a serjeant under James II.

In this capacity Baldock gained notoriety in June 1688, when he served as one of the prosecutors in the trial of the seven bishops. The case centred on the refusal of William Sancroft, archbishop of Canterbury, and six others to read the king's declaration of indulgence. When the bishops met with James and presented their petition of protest, they were arrested and charged with seditious libel. During the ensuing trial, in June 1688, Baldock followed the opening arguments of Sir Thomas Powis for the crown and Lord Somers for the bishops with a 'feeble speech: admitting the right of the subject to petition the King, but objecting to the manner in which the Bishops had petitioned' (Phillipps, 2.316). His statement adds to the conclusion that none of the prosecutors 'made any significant contribution' to the case (Landon, 210). After a lengthy debate regarding the right of the bishops to petition, Baldock concluded, 'I cannot deny, nor shall not, but that the subject has a right to petition; but I shall affirm it also, he has a duty to obey' (*State trials*, 12.417). Throughout the proceedings, though he did not speak frequently and played a distinctly subordinate role to the principal prosecutors, William Williams and Powis, Baldock consistently defended the royal prerogative to suspend and dispense with laws enacted by parliament. After the bishops were acquitted, an angry King James dismissed two of the justices who heard the case, replacing one with Sir Robert Baldock.

The appointment to the king's bench on 6 July 1688 marks the high point of Baldock's legal career; yet it also illustrates the lack of outstanding legal talent willing to serve the monarch: the consequence of long-term efforts to politicize the bench. Under Charles and James generally undistinguished justices served the state and their tenure grew less secure. Sir Robert Baldock had little opportunity to justify the king's confidence or prove his own ability, as James fled to exile by the year's end and William never seriously considered him for a judicial appointment in the new administration. Baldock retired to Great Hocham and died there on 4 October 1691. He was buried in Great Hocham, where there is a monument to him in the local church. MICHAEL J. GALGANO

Sources Foss, *Judges* • J. H. Baker, 'Readings in Gray's Inn, their decline and disappearance', *The legal profession and the common law: historical essays* (1986), 31–9 • R. J. Fletcher, ed., *The pension book of Gray's Inn*, 2 (1910) • J. M. Rosenheim, ed., *The notebook of Robert Doughty, 1662–1665*, Norfolk RS, 54 (1989) • R. North, *The life of the Right Honourable Francis North, baron of Guilford*, 3rd edn, 2 vols. (1819) • *The autobiography of Sir John Bramston*, ed. [Lord Braybrooke], CS, 32 (1845) • S. M. Phillipps, *State trials, or, A collection of the most interesting trials, prior to the revolution of 1688, reviewed and illustrated, by Samuel March Phillipps*, 2 (1826) • M. Landon, *The triumph of the lawyers: their role in English politics, 1678–1689* (1970) • *State trials* • B. Cozens-Hardy, ed., *Norfolk lieutenancy journal, 1676–1701*, Norfolk RS, 30 (1961) • A. W. Hughes Clarke and A. Campling, eds., *The visitation of Norfolk … 1664, made by Sir Edward Bysshe*, 2, Harleian Society, 86 (1934) • A. F. Havinghurst, 'The judiciary and politics in the reign of Charles II [2 pts]', *Law Quarterly Review*, 66 (1950), 62–78, 229–52 • A. Strickland and [E. Strickland], *The lives of the seven bishops committed to the Tower in 1688* (1866) • H. Nenner, *By colour of law: legal culture and constitutional politics in England, 1660–1689* (1977) • Evelyn, *Diary*, vol. 4 • Venn, *Alum. Cant.*

Baldred. *See* Balthere (*d.* 756).

Baldred (*d.* **608?**). *See under* Balthere (*d.* 756).

Baldred (*fl.* *c.***823–827**), king of Kent, is a very obscure figure. In 823 the Mercian king Ceolwulf, who had ruled Kent as part of the Mercian kingdom, was deposed and replaced by Beornwulf (*d.* 826?). At about this time the moneyers of the Canterbury mint began to issue coins in the name of a certain Baldred, 'king of Kent'. It is not clear whether Baldred was an independent ruler, or whether he was an under-king who had been established by Beornwulf and who acknowledged his overlordship. The Canterbury moneyers do not seem to have struck any coins for Beornwulf; on the other hand, an archiepiscopal charter of 826 suggests that Beornwulf's authority was recognized in Kent. Earlier, the Mercian king Cenwulf had briefly set up his brother as under-king of Kent, and it is possible that Baldred was similarly a kinsman of Beornwulf; the alliterating initial letter of their names may point to such a relationship. Baldred's brief reign ended when a West Saxon army, acting on the orders of Ecgberht (*d.* 839), king of Wessex, invaded Kent and drove him north across the Thames; this probably took place in 826 or 827. In the course of his flight Baldred granted an estate

Baldred (*fl.* *c.***823–827**), coin

to Archbishop Wulfred of Canterbury, but this attempt to enlist the support of God and a powerful local figure did not save him; he is not heard of again. There are no surviving charters in his name. William of Malmesbury incorrectly treats him as the successor of King Cuthred (*d.* 807) and gives him a reign of eighteen years. S. E. KELLY

Sources *ASC*, s.a. 825 [texts A, E] • *AS chart.*, S 1267, 1438 • N. Brooks, *The early history of the church of Canterbury: Christ Church from 597 to 1066* (1984) • P. Grierson and M. Blackburn, *Medieval European coinage: with a catalogue of the coins in the Fitzwilliam Museum, Cambridge*, 1: *The early middle ages (5th–10th centuries)* (1986), 283, 285–6, 288–9 • S. Keynes, 'The control of Kent in the ninth century', *Early Medieval Europe*, 2 (1993), 111–32, esp. 119–20 • *Willelmi Malmesbiriensis monachi de gestis regum Anglorum*, ed. W. Stubbs, 2 vols., Rolls Series (1887–9), vol. 1, p. 18

Likenesses coin, BM [*see illus.*]

Baldrey, Joshua Kirby (**1754–1828**), draughtsman and engraver, was the eldest son of Andrew Baldrey (*d.* 1802), of Ipswich, and his wife, Mary (1728–1806). Andrew, the illegitimate son of Andrew Rankin and Elizabeth Baldrey, was successively apprentice, partner, and successor in the general painting business of Joshua's godfather Joshua Kirby, and trained his own sons Joshua and Robert. Joshua in turn took as pupils Robert Clamp, stipple portrait engraver, and his own son John Baldrey, by his first marriage.

For over twenty years Joshua Baldrey worked in London or Cambridge, never settling permanently in either. His first imprints as engraver and printseller were issued from Mr Dibbs's at Green Street, Grosvenor Square, in 1780, but he was in Trumpington Street in Cambridge in 1785, and back at Doughty & Co. in Holborn three years later, producing a series of satires against Hastings, Thurlow, and Pitt. He exhibited portraits at the Royal Academy in 1793 and 1794. Among his best works are *The Finding of Moses*, after Salvator Rosa (1785); *Diana in a Landscape*, after Carlo Maratta; *Lady Rawdon*, after Reynolds (1783); and *Atalanta*, after Henry Bunbury (1790). Baldrey worked after

George Morland in soft-ground etching and after Bunbury in stipple. From about 1800 he and his son John, whose satires and portraits are in stipple and line, were together in Trinity Street, Cambridge. In 1811 Baldrey described himself as a miniature painter there, but in May 1809 he had published at 5 guineas a two-sheet reproduction of the east window of King's College chapel, Cambridge, which he had drawn, engraved, and, for an extra guinea, coloured by hand. His eight-page *Dissertation on the Windows of King's College Chapel, Cambridge* (1818) was to advertise the remaining stock of the prints and to solicit orders for a projected engraving of one of the south windows. His *Dissertation* concludes sadly: 'All these works have been executed by a man with a large increasing family, experiencing much sickness; and from the unpropitious state of the times, struggling with great difficulties' (p. 19). A large engraving of the Nollekens statue of Pitt in the Senate House, published in London in 1815, while competent, is heavy and lifeless.

Baldrey must have been a widower when on 12 June 1808 he married Mary Jane Copsey by licence at Great St Mary's in Cambridge; a daughter, Sarah, was witness. When he died in poverty at Hatfield Woodside, Hertfordshire, on 6 December 1828 it was reported that he left a large family.

J. M. Blatchly

Sources Redgrave, *Artists* • I. Maxted, *The London book trades, 1775–1800: a preliminary checklist of members* (1977) • parish registers, Ipswich and Framlingham, Suffolk RO, Ipswich • parish registers, Great St Mary, Cambridge, Cambs. AS • J. Pendred, *The London and country printers, booksellers and stationers vade mecum* (1785); repr. with introduction and appx by G. Pollard as *The earliest directory of the book trade* (1955) • *Holden's London and country directory for the year 1811*, facs. edn (1996), vol. 2, 'Cambridge' • Graves, *RA exhibitors* • private information (2004) [curator, Gainsborough's House, Sudbury] • Anderton catalogues, vol. 7, no. 1576; vol. 8, no. 1897 [exhibition catalogues, Society of Artists, BM, print room] • *DNB*

Baldwin [Baldwin de Meulles] (*d.* **1086x90**), magnate, is usually described in contemporary sources as son of Count Gilbert, brother of Richard son of Count Gilbert, or as Baldwin the Sheriff (of Devon) or Baldwin of Exeter. He was the second son of Gilbert, count of Eu and possibly also of Brionne. The latter was a son of Godefroy, an illegitimate son of Richard (I), duke of Normandy. One of the guardians of the young duke (the future king, William I), Gilbert was murdered either late in 1040 or in January 1041. His sons Baldwin and Richard escaped to Flanders, returning thence after the marriage of Duke William to Matilda of Flanders. William gave to Baldwin the lordships of Meulles and Le Sap. Baldwin's wife was a kinswoman of the duke. At a later date, in the chronicle of Forde Abbey, she is named as Albreda, but in a ducal charter of 1066 and in Domesday Book as Emma. The Forde tradition may thus be an error, but the possibility that Baldwin married twice cannot be discounted. It has been suggested that Emma may have been a daughter of Richard Goz, vicomte of the Avranchin (Keats-Rohan, 50).

Orderic Vitalis included Baldwin and his brother Richard de *Clare, ancestor of the Clare family, in his list of notable laymen at Duke William's court in 1066. His presence at the battle of Hastings is not attested, though, like that of his brother Richard, it is probable. In 1068 King William travelled to south-west England to deal with resistance there spearheaded by Gytha, mother of Harold Godwineson, and he ordered a castle to be built at Exeter, which he committed to Baldwin. The latter is found soon afterwards as sheriff of Devon, an office he evidently still held at the time of the Domesday Survey, and possibly retained until his death not long afterwards. In 1086 he was the major lay landholder in the county. His estates were concentrated round Exeter and Okehampton, where a castle is referred to in Domesday Book, and they extended along the valley of the River Torre towards the north coast of Devon. They had been acquired from various pre-conquest landholders; this, together with a heavy obligation to knight service of more than 90 fees, suggests that military considerations had been very much to the forefront in the creation of what came to be known as the barony of Okehampton. Moreover, the fact that Baldwin's English estates were concentrated in the south-west, unlike those of many others of the greatest landholders, points to his having been most active at an early stage of the conquest, but not participating in the takeover of the midlands and the north; nor were his lands overall as valuable as those acquired by his brother Richard. His presence at the royal court is attested occasionally in the witness lists of royal documents.

The precise date of Baldwin's death is not known, but in Orderic's account of a terrifying vision of spectres of the dead experienced by a priest of Lisieux on 1 January 1091 there figured Baldwin and Richard his brother, who had died 'recently' (Ordericus Vitalis, *Eccl. hist.*, 4.236–50). Baldwin's estates were divided between two sons: Robert succeeded to Le Sap and Meulles, and William fitz Baldwin to the lands in south-west England. There was a third son, Richard, and at least two daughters. An illegitimate son, Wiger, became a monk of Bec, a house with which Baldwin had strong family connections. His father, Count Gilbert, had been the overlord of Herluin, founder of the abbey, and Baldwin himself gave land to the abbey from his estates in Normandy and in England.

Judith A. Green

Sources *The Gesta Normannorum ducum of William of Jumièges, Orderic Vitalis, and Robert of Torigni*, ed. and trans. E. M. C. van Houts, 1, OMT (1992), 130–31; 2, OMT (1995), 270–71 • Ordericus Vitalis, *Eccl. hist.*, 2.140, 214; 4.208–12, 236–50 • *Reg. RAN*, 1.58–9, 76, 90, 125, 135, 147, 150, 206, 220 • A. Farley, ed., *Domesday Book*, 2 vols. (1783), 1.81, 93, 105b–108b; 4.307 • *Les actes de Guillaume le Conquérant et de la reine Mathilde pour les abbayes caennaises*, ed. L. Musset (Caen, 1967), no. 2 • Dugdale, *Monasticon*, new edn, 5.377 • K. S. B. Keats-Rohan, 'The Bretons and Normans of England, 1066–1154: the family, the fief and the feudal monarchy', *Nottingham Medieval Studies*, 36 (1992), 42–78 • J. C. Ward, 'Fashions in monastic endowment: the foundations of the Clare family, 1066–1314', *Journal of Ecclesiastical History*, 32 (1981), 427–51 • J. C. Ward, 'Royal service and reward: the Clare family and the crown, 1066–1154', *Anglo-Norman Studies*, 11 (1988), 261–78

Wealth at death £342 19*s.* 10*d.*—English estates: Farley, ed., *Domesday book*

Baldwin (*d.* **1097**), abbot of Bury St Edmunds, was born in Chartres and became a Benedictine monk at St Denis, Paris, before serving as the prior of one of the abbey's daughter houses at Leberaw in Alsace. He came to England as Edward the Confessor's physician, and he received the church of Deerhurst in Gloucestershire and the manor of Taynton in Oxfordshire from the king, which he held as a dependency of St Denis. His royal and continental connections made him the ideal successor to Leofstan, abbot of Bury St Edmunds, in 1065.

With the appointment of Lanfranc as archbishop of Canterbury in 1070, the ecclesiastical landscape changed dramatically as he wished to implement the plans of the reforming papacy, which called for sees to be located in the major towns and for abbots to be subject to diocesan control. To protect Bury from this threat Baldwin travelled to Rome in 1071 where he secured a privilege which placed his abbey under the protection of the papacy. Neither letters of criticism from Lanfranc nor the testimony of jurors from nine counties persuaded Herfast, the bishop of Thetford, to abandon his claim to Bury. According to the *Liber de miraculis sancti Eadmundi*, when Herfast damaged his eyes in a riding accident, Baldwin agreed to save his sight only if he agreed to give up his claim. Orders from Rome, oral memory, and oaths made under duress did not, however, resolve the dispute, and at Easter 1081 the rival parties assembled in front of the king and the royal council in London. Baldwin defeated his opponent by producing four spurious charters in which English kings forbade the bishop of East Anglia from interfering with Bury Abbey in any way. Subsequent attempts to move the see to Bury were easily disposed of, as Baldwin not only kept the writ which enforced this decision but also had the foresight to forge a diploma in which William I expressly forbade Herfast and his successors from seeking to revive their claim to Bury. Baldwin's actions ensured that Bury was not chosen as the new ecclesiastical capital of East Anglia, and the documents which he collated guaranteed the monastery's independence until the dissolution.

One of the problems which many abbots faced during the Norman conquest was the hostility of Norman lords towards their founding saints, which was often the prelude to seizing these houses' wealth. As late as 1095 the nobles of William II's court recommended that the king should seize the wealth from Edmund's shrine as they argued that the saint was buried elsewhere. Baldwin responded with a programme of hagiography which quashed these dangerous rumours and justified the Bury version of events. Scribes interpolated Ælfric's life of St Edmund to establish that Edmund was buried at Bury. Baldwin also commissioned Hermann, the archdeacon, to write the *Liber de miraculis sancti Eadmundi*. In this work it was claimed that the saint had made himself 'as heavy as a mountain' in order to avoid being buried elsewhere, and that Abbot Leofstan had conclusively proved during Edward the Confessor's reign that Edmund was buried in the abbey's shrine. Baldwin worked with English monks and continental scholars to establish a new past in order to protect the abbey from episcopal and baronial aggression.

Norman barons also posed a threat to abbeys by occupying the latter's estates and seeking to exercise lordship over their men. At some time between 1066 and 1070, Baldwin received two writs which ruled out such enterprise. The first guaranteed his right to retain the lands which had formerly been leased out to his subtenants who had died while fighting against William I, and the second excluded royal tax collectors from the eight and a half hundreds in western Suffolk, confirming the fiscal privileges which the abbey had received *c.*1043–1044. The best means by which land could be transferred to Norman barons, namely through forfeiture for treason and failure to pay the geld, were expressly ruled out by these privileges. Baldwin also commissioned the feudal book which, by listing all the abbey's human and arable capital, made it extremely difficult for other lords to exploit the ambiguities between soke, commendation, and tenure in order to gain control of the monastery's property. This inventory drew upon the accounting techniques introduced by his predecessor, Abbot Leofstan, and was used until the late twelfth century by the Bury monks.

Baldwin continued to have connections with the region of his birthplace, as many of the post-1066 tenants in the eight and a half hundreds came from the Chartres region. In the town of Bury St Edmunds, Baldwin cleared arable land to make way for 342 new houses, and it is possible that some of the burgesses who abandoned 328 dwellings in Ipswich about that time may have moved to Bury, attracted by the extremely low rents offered by Baldwin. The *Liber de miraculis* records that Abbot Baldwin sat in silence for three days as he pondered how to pay for the building of a new abbey church, and he actively encouraged both English and French to settle on the abbey's estates. The abbey choir was built in the new Gothic style and, with its splendid carved vaulting, was thought by contemporaries to rival the temple of Solomon. When it was completed in 1095, St Edmund was translated to the new shrine. Baldwin died in January 1097 and was buried at Bury St Edmunds. He defended his abbey's rights against the ideals of a reforming episcopate and the avariciousness of the Norman aristocracy by drawing upon his medical knowledge, the skills of his monks, and connections with both the royal and papal courts. Contemporaries observed that Baldwin 'renewed everything within and without' (*De gestis pontificum*, 156) and that 'he was the true father and the illustrious restorer of his house' (Hermann, 58).

A. F. WAREHAM

Sources Hermann the Archdeacon, 'De miraculis Sancti Eadmundi', *Memorials of St Edmund's Abbey*, ed. T. Arnold, 1, Rolls Series, 96 (1890), 26–92 • A. Gransden, 'Baldwin, abbot of Bury St Edmunds, 1065–1097', *Anglo-Norman Studies*, 4 (1981), 65–76 • D. C. Douglas, ed., *Feudal documents from the abbey of Bury St Edmunds*, British Academy, Records of Social and Economic History, 8 (1932) • *The letters of Lanfranc, archbishop of Canterbury*, ed. and trans. H. Clover and M. Gibson, OMT (1979) • *Willelmi Malmesbiriensis monachi de gestis pontificum Anglorum libri quinque*, ed. N. E. S. A. Hamilton, Rolls Series, 52 (1870), 156 • F. E. Harmer, ed., *Anglo-Saxon writs* (1952) • S. Keynes, ed., *Facsimiles of Anglo-Saxon charters*, Anglo-Saxon Charters, suppl. ser., 1 (1991), 7–8 [facs. 21]

Baldwin [Baldwin of Forde] (*c.***1125–1190**), archbishop of Canterbury, was born in Exeter, probably the son of Hugh d'Eu, archdeacon of Totnes, and a woman of unknown

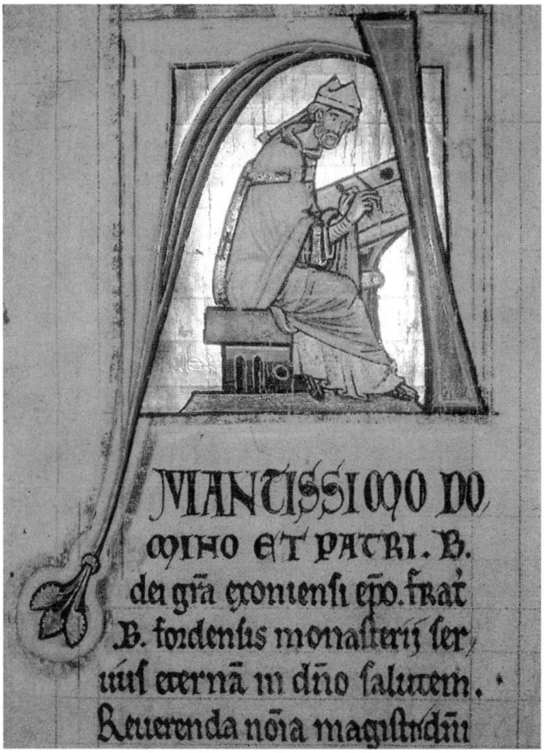

Baldwin [of Forde] (*c.***1125–1190**), illuminated initial

name. This parentage is suggested by Baldwin's having succeeded to the archdeaconry of Totnes on Hugh's death and by his being called Master Baldwin fitz Hugh in a charter. Gervase of Canterbury's claim that Baldwin was born of people of no account expressed the contempt of an aristocratic community. His mother became a nun and must have been literate, since Roger, a monk at Forde, asked for a copy to be made for her in readable letters of the *Visions* of Elisabeth of Schönau.

Monk and religious writer The decade of Baldwin's birth is deduced from the fact that Eugenius III appointed him to be tutor to his nephew in 1150 or 1151: it is likely that he was then in his mid-twenties. Before that he studied law in Bologna under the future Urban III, and his writings suggest that he had followed theology in the schools, perhaps at Laon. Exeter probably provided his earlier education. By 1155 he was back home as a clerk serving the bishop of Exeter, Robert of Chichester. This is the most likely time that he himself taught; the monk Roger mentioned above recalled that Baldwin had read his boyish verses and suggested subjects to him.

Bishop Bartholomew made Baldwin archdeacon of Totnes—after his father's death—on 23 May 1162, in which post he was active until about 1170 when he became a Cistercian at Forde Abbey. His decision reflects the pressures on the bishop and his clerks from the increasingly bitter disagreement between Henry II and Thomas Becket. Bartholomew on the whole stuck by Becket: his clerks numbered relatives of John of Salisbury, Thomas's confidential clerk and companion in exile. At this stage John wrote warmly of Baldwin's loyalty and integrity.

An abbey had existed at Forde only since 1141. It must have been attracting other recruits besides Baldwin since in 1172 it was able to found a daughter house. Within a short time the new and able monk became abbot at Forde. Exactly when is unknown, but by 1173 Baldwin was at the general chapter at Cîteaux where he had 'secret matters' to discuss with the abbot of Cîteaux, who had been asked by the pope that year to try to make peace between Henry II and his sons (Baldwin, *De commendatione fidei*, preface, section 4, 344; cf.xxix–xxx). Baldwin's years as abbot saw the pope put Baldwin's legal training to use, appointing him judge-delegate in a number of cases, when he often worked with bishops and gained a reputation as a man with a future. His writings show other sides of his character.

The longest of Baldwin's writings, *De sacramento altaris*, was dedicated to Bartholomew. Twelve manuscripts survive showing that it continued to be read into the fifteenth century, getting attention well beyond his own order, though not much outside England. It explores the biblical account of the institution of the eucharist and its forerunner, the passover. The influence of Augustine is very strong. Baldwin's twenty-two sermons, on the other hand, most of which started as addresses to his community, echo Bernard of Clairvaux, and the biblical book which that saint loved best, the Song of Solomon. Here too twelve manuscripts from England and northern France survive, the latest from the late fifteenth century. Two sermons were printed at Cambridge in 1521. Another work, on faith, survives in two English manuscripts, though at least five others are known to have existed before the dissolution.

Bishop and archbishop Not surprisingly, in 1178 Baldwin attracted the notice of a cardinal visiting England, Peter of St Agatha, who recommended him to Alexander III as a possible cardinal since he was 'held in very high esteem by the whole Cistercian order, because of his very broad culture, his worthiness and his piety.' (Glorieux). Perhaps these very qualities, as well as the political role he had played in 1173, induced Henry II to support his election to Worcester in 1180. He was consecrated bishop on 10 August. In this new role he continued to act as judge-delegate, an activity reflected in the notable Worcester collection of decretals, possibly put together by Master Silvester, a clerk whom Baldwin had inherited from his predecessor, Bishop Roger, and whom he was to take with him to Canterbury.

Although Walter Map, scarcely a friend of Cistercians, praised Baldwin's determination to continue to write after he had become a bishop, the only piece definitely linked to the Worcester years is a sermon on the cross written for the lately reformed canons of Waltham.

On Sunday 22 July 1184 Baldwin intervened to delay the hanging outside the city of a seducer and thief who had been condemned before the king. His foolhardiness, inspired by respect for the day, the feast of St Mary Magdalen, instead of bringing down royal wrath, seems to have increased the king's opinion of him, for Henry began to move him higher, to Canterbury, vacant since February. Negotiations to secure the agreement of both the bishops of the province and of the monks who served the cathedral took until the middle of December. Baldwin's enthronement occurred on 19 May 1185, by which time his pallium had arrived from Rome.

Baldwin's Canterbury *acta* show that he had an active concern for his diocese and province. There is little specifically Cistercian in them, except for a moving letter to the abbots' meeting at Cîteaux asking for their prayers, and pleading that the duties of his new office prevented him from being with them. A very positive achievement was his assertion of Canterbury's claims over Wales. Urban III created him legate on 17 or 18 December 1185, but it was not until June 1187 that Baldwin travelled towards the Welsh border, and then crossed briefly over to 'visit' it formally. In the next year, from early March to the middle of April, he travelled more widely through the principality than probably any archbishop, everywhere preaching the crusade. His route can be reconstructed thanks to the lively account written by one of his companions, the testy and witty Gerald of Wales. Gerald provides the only good description of what the archbishop looked like: 'swarthy … with an honest, venerable face, only moderately tall, of good physique and inclined to be thin rather than corpulent' (Gerald of Wales, *Journey*, 205). In each cathedral Baldwin celebrated mass, symbolizing his superior position as legate and archbishop. For a sixty-year-old he showed impressive stamina, even urging his companions to dismount and walk up a valley to make them fit for the journey to Jerusalem.

Baldwin had taken the cross in March 1185, when bad relations within the royal family and between Henry and Philip Augustus made any expedition very unlikely. In 1188 Angevin–Capetian relations were better, and circumstances for a crusade more propitious. Although Baldwin's sermons often had to be translated into Welsh, Gerald claimed that 3000 took the cross. No sooner was Baldwin back in England than he set out for Normandy to try to make peace between the old king and his restless sons. He only returned to England at the end of July 1189, by when Henry was dead (6 July).

The Hackington dispute By that time Baldwin's quarrel at Canterbury had reached its nadir, the monks having been virtually imprisoned in their monastery since January 1188. It is hardly surprising that the Canterbury historian Gervase thought that Baldwin's keenness to preach in Wales was caused chiefly by the desire to put a distance between himself and the community. The whole story goes back to December 1185, a year after Baldwin's election, when he began to try to regain control of some property and revenues that his predecessor had let slip into the hands of the monks. His full purpose emerged in 1186, when Urban III gave him permission to build and endow a new collegiate church at Hackington, just outside Canterbury. He claimed to be fulfilling an intention of his two great predecessors, Anselm and Becket, and that he would dedicate it to the latter, whom he said lacked churches in his honour. To the monks the scheme was totally unacceptable, especially when they realized that Baldwin had got authority to divert up to half of the offerings in the cathedral, most of which were given at the martyr's shrine. It seemed to them that the saint upon whom they depended was to be hijacked on behalf of an institution which they foresaw as the beginning of the end for their wealth and privileges. Massive documentation survives from the struggle: a narrative account by Gervase, and a dossier of over 550 letters, compiled by another monk, Reginald. This last reveals that the Canterbury Benedictines bombarded everyone they could think of—the German emperor, the king of France, cardinals, bishops, and abbots, these last including even Baldwin's Cistercian colleagues, the abbots of Cîteaux and Clairvaux, and the general chapter of the order.

The monks posed as the heirs and protectors of Becket, and Gervase records how one young monk dreamed that Thomas put Baldwin to flight with a burning sword. His prior interpreted the fact that the sword was inscribed 'The sword of blessed Peter' as a sure sign that Rome would ultimately quash Baldwin's plans. Now it is clear that Rome was in no very good position to settle anything quickly, since no fewer than four men served as pope between 1185 and the end of the struggle in 1189. The claim that Thomas and the monks were one now seems odd, since, as Barlow has shown, 'His lasting unpopularity with the monks is undoubted' (F. Barlow, *Thomas Becket* 1986, 271). Symptomatic of that is the fact that the candidates whom the monks would have preferred in 1172 and 1184 (and later in 1191), Odo of Canterbury, abbot of Battle, and Reginald fitz Jocelin, had both opposed Becket when he was alive. It is also clear that Baldwin was not the first, or last, archbishop to have difficulties with Christ Church. It was a rich and touchy body with which an austere Cistercian might well have found it hard to establish friendly relations, but it may well have been crucial that in the early days of his primacy Baldwin spent little time at Canterbury. Certainly his high ideals about the corporate life of a religious community, as expressed in one of his Forde sermons, never stood a chance of taking shape at Christ Church once he had embarked upon the Hackington scheme.

Baldwin's persistence can look like mere stubbornness, but it seems more likely that his previous experience as well as a real need had more to do with it. His promotion probably rested principally upon his training as a canon lawyer, which must have predisposed him to believe that if he had a pope on his side, as well as the king, he would triumph. But he never had any pope for very long. As archbishop of a church served by monks he lacked any canonries and lesser posts in his cathedral with which to reward loyal clerks. At Hackington he would have many—the monks reckoned he planned on sixty or seventy—and so he stood his ground. But the monks did all they could to frustrate him, deploying people and money at Rome to good effect, so that Baldwin was forced to temporize over papal mandates ordering him to desist while leaning more heavily on what the king might do by threats. Finally it was the new king, Richard I, who in November 1189 oversaw the patching up of a compromise. The monks were pleased that Baldwin had to give up the Hackington plan but dismayed that he got permission to try something similar at Lambeth. His successor, Hubert Walter, attempted this, but eventually the monks forced him to desist.

Crusade and death Richard's motive in making peace at Canterbury was his determination to go on crusade. Baldwin left England in March 1190 with an advance party, never to return. He travelled with Hubert Walter, the bishop of Salisbury, his own nephew Joseph, a poet, and his old companion at Forde, Abbot Robert. The party made their way steadily south through France, reaching Marseilles at the beginning of August. The voyage to Tyre took about five weeks, and by 12 October they were at Acre. It was there that Baldwin died on 19 November, sickened perhaps by the army's dissolute behaviour. He made Hubert Walter his executor, and the latter saw to the pay of some twenty knights and fifty serjeants. Baldwin also left some of his vestments to the community at Canterbury, a generous gesture which did not soften the picture that they kept of him.

Baldwin's whole career reveals a deeply spiritual person, and it is striking that now his writings probably circulate more widely and in more languages than those of any other medieval archbishop of Canterbury, with the one exception of Anselm. This spirituality was recognized by Urban III, who commented that whereas Becket when he dismounted went straight to the hall and Richard of Dover went to the barn, Baldwin went to the church. Yet in a now lost letter the same pope is supposed to have addressed him as 'the most fervent monk, warm abbot, lukewarm bishop, negligent archbishop' (Gerald of Wales, *Speculum* in *Opera*, 4.76). Although Baldwin was capable of serious errors of judgement, like the promotion of the worthless Roger Norreys (*d.* 1223), first to be prior of Christ Church, Canterbury, and then to be abbot of Evesham, Urban's comment still seems too hard. But it is easy now to see that the archbishop's decision to create a collegiate church made an unbreakable rod for his own back, forcing him into excessive dependence on royal support.

CHRISTOPHER HOLDSWORTH

Sources F. Barlow, ed., *Exeter, 1046–1184*, English Episcopal Acta, 11 (1995) • *Balduini de Forda opera*, ed. D. N. Bell (Tournai, 1991) • Baldwin of Forde, *Spiritual tractates*, trans. D. N. Bell, 2 vols., Cistercian fathers, 38, 39 (1986) • C. R. Cheney and B. E. A. Jones, eds., *Canterbury, 1162–1190*, English Episcopal Acta, 2 (1986) • *The historical works of Gervase of Canterbury*, ed. W. Stubbs, 2: *The minor works comprising the Gesta regum with its continuation, the Actus pontificum and the Mappa mundi*, Rolls Series, 73 (1880) • W. Stubbs, ed., *Chronicles and memorials of the reign of Richard I*, 2: *Epistolae Cantuarienses*, Rolls Series, 38 (1865) • Gerald of Wales, *'The journey through Wales' and 'The description of Wales'*, trans. L. Thorpe (1978) • *Gir. Camb. opera*, vol. 4 • *Gir. Camb. opera*, vol. 7 • W. Stubbs, ed., *Chronicles and memorials of the reign of Richard I*, 1: *Itinerarium peregrinorum et gesta regis Ricardi*, Rolls Series, 38 (1864) • C. Holdsworth, 'Baldwin of Forde, Cistercian and archbishop of Canterbury', *Annual Report* [Friends of Lambeth Palace Library] (1989), 13–31 • D. Knowles, C. N. L. Brooke, and V. C. M. London, eds., *The heads of religious houses, England and Wales*, 1: 940–1216 (1972) • *Fasti Angl., 1066–1300*, [Monastic cathedrals] • R. R. Darlington, ed., *The cartulary of Worcester Cathedral Priory (register I)*, PRSoc., 76, new ser., 38 (1968) • M. G. Cheney, *Roger, bishop of Worcester, 1164–1179* (1980) • W. H. Hale, ed., *Registrum, sive, Liber irrotularius et consuetudinaris prioratus Beatae Mariae Wigorniensis*, CS, 91 (1865) • C. Tyerman, *England and the crusades, 1095–1588* (1988) • P. Glorieux, 'Candidats pour la pourpre en 1178', *Mélanges de Science Réligieuse*, 2 (1954), 17–19

Likenesses illuminated initial, CCC Cam., MS 200, fol. 1r [*see illus.*] • seal (as archbishop), repro. in Cheney and Jones, eds., *Canterbury*, nos. 270, 298; 229–31, 253–4

Baldwin family (*per. c.*1760–1857), newspaper proprietors, came to prominence with **Henry Baldwin** (1734–1813). Born on 26 December 1734 in London, he was the second son, in the family of three sons and four daughters, of Robert Baldwin, apothecary, of Faringdon, Berkshire, and his wife, Jane. Baldwin was apprenticed on 5 September 1749 as a printer to Edward Say, newspaper publisher, and admitted to the livery at the Stationers' Company on 27 December 1756. His first known venture as printer was the *London Packet*, but on 4 March 1761 he launched the *St James's Chronicle* from Whitefriars as a thrice-weekly evening newspaper.

Shortly before its début, Baldwin purchased from fellow printer William Rayner the *London Spy*, *Read's Weekly Journal*, and the *St James's Evening Post, or, British Gazette*. The *Spy* and the *Journal* were merged to form a Saturday paper, and the *St James's Evening Post* became the *St James's Chronicle*. To secure financial support, Baldwin formed a joint-stock company; the other proprietors included George Colman, David Garrick, and Bonnell Thornton. The meetings of the proprietors of the *St James's Chronicle* were to span more than fifty years and its minute books are the most detailed of any eighteenth-century newspaper.

Within a few months of the paper's launch, Baldwin was joined as editor by Nathaniel Thomas, fresh from Oxford University. And with writers of the calibre of Colman, William Cowper, Oliver Goldsmith, and Thornton involved, the early days of the paper were indeed heady, as John Nichols was to describe in his *Literary Anecdotes* (1812): 'Baldwin with the aid of a phalanx of first-rate wits brought it to a height of literary eminence till then unobtainable in any journal' (Griffiths, *Encyclopedia*, 87).

Under Baldwin, the *Chronicle* was also to be an outspoken critic of the government; and on 21 May 1765, with Charles Say and Henry Woodfall, he was summoned to the House of Lords because of an article published three days earlier describing a mass meeting of impoverished weavers. Four years later, on 21 December 1769, he reprinted the Junius letter from the *Public Advertiser* attacking the king and the government. As a result, Baldwin, with others, was charged—and acquitted. One consequence of the Junius trial was that parliamentary debates were now reported increasingly and with great accuracy, leading the government, on 5 February 1771, to reaffirm that they should not be published. Notwithstanding, the debate was immediately published by Baldwin. As a consequence, with Wright, another publisher, he was made to kneel in penance before the speaker, the last ever to do so, and after being reprimanded was discharged on paying his fees. Baldwin rose in silence, ostentatiously brushed his knees, and in an audible aside remarked: 'What a damned dirty House' (Griffiths, *Encyclopedia*, 87).

The following year, Baldwin, increasingly successful, moved to new premises at 108 Fleet Street. His marriage to Eleanor, *née* Graham, produced three sons, Robert, George, and Charles [*see below*], and three daughters. His remaining time as chief proprietor was to be less eventful, and in 1792 he served as master of the Stationers' Company. Henry Baldwin died on 21 February 1813, and the *St James's Chronicle* of 20–22 February noted:

> Upwards of 40 years a Proprietor and Printer of this Paper: but who had long retired from business. … The firm rectitude of his mind, the real tenderness of his heart, and the sincerity of his attachments were best known in his domestic circle and to his chosen friends. (*St James's Chronicle*, 20–22 Feb 1813)

Henry Baldwin was succeeded as proprietor of the *St James's Chronicle* by his son **Charles Baldwin** (1774–1869), who was bound to his father as an apprentice compositor on 7 July 1789. 'So quickly did he attain the knowledge of the business that at 18 Mr Baldwin senior confided in him the entire superintendence of the working part of his establishment' (Griffiths, *Encyclopedia*, 87). In 1801, at the age of twenty-seven, Charles saw his efforts rewarded when his father changed the firm's name to Henry Baldwin & Son and later relinquished his two shares. He married Elizabeth Ann Laurents of Jersey. They had fifteen children, one of whom, Edward [*see below*], later took over the business. By 1808, through gift, exchange, and purchase, Charles Baldwin owned seven of the eight shares in the company and with the death of Christopher Moody, the other shareholder, seven years later he became sole owner.

In 1809 Charles Baldwin bought the rival *London Evening-Post*, and then in 1819 purchased the *London Chronicle* for £300 from its owner, Colonel Robert Torrens, and absorbed it into the *St James's Chronicle*. That same year, Baldwin and his new editor, Dr Stanley Lees Giffard, were loud in their condemnation of the crowds at the Peterloo massacre on 16 August:

> What has long been desired by every friend of order has at length taken place. The strong arm of the law has been put forth to put, we trust, a final stop to the assemblage of the ignorant and the seditious. (Griffiths, *Encyclopedia*, 86)

With the appointment of George Canning as prime minister in April 1827, the old tories sought to start a newspaper in opposition and approached Baldwin. After long discussions he agreed, and on 21 May 1827 *The Standard* was launched, carrying Baldwin's declaration:

> I was not willing to risk the continuance of my old and valued journal [the *St James's Chronicle*]; I preferred the heavier risk of establishing at my own expense and hazard, a Daily Evening Paper to be conducted on the same principles and by the same editor [Giffard]. I also engaged the assistance of Dr Maginn and other celebrated writers.

For Baldwin and his editor, there were to be three unshakeable principles: total opposition to Catholic emancipation, to parliamentary reform, and to repeal of the corn laws—and for the next twenty years they were to fight hard in the struggle to defend these. Initially, the sales of the paper were barely 700, but within five years the circulation had risen to more than 1500; and with his other papers Baldwin was 'said to be worth upwards of £100,000'. Profits on *The Standard* alone were estimated to be between £7000 and £8000 per year; and, apart from *The Standard* and the *St James's Chronicle*, he was also owner of the *London Packet*, which came out twice weekly, and the *London Journal*, a weekly—'all got up with scarcely any expense out of *The Standard*' (Griffiths, *Encyclopedia*, 86). It was believed that his total income from newspapers was more than £15,000 a year.

In 1844, having reached the age of seventy, Charles Baldwin decided to retire. He continued, however, to attend the Stationers' Hall, having twice been master of the company, in 1842 and 1843, and the Literary Society, of which he was a founder member in 1799. He unsuccessfully contested the constituency of Lambeth in 1837 and 1841. He died aged ninety-five at his daughter's house, 27 Sussex Gardens, Hyde Park, London, on 18 February 1869, and to the very end it was said that 'his genial disposition, amiable manners and lively conversation endeared him to a large circle of younger friends' (Griffiths, *Encyclopedia*, 86). However, his passing was totally ignored by *The Standard*.

Since Baldwin's retirement in 1844, the papers had been run by his son **Edward Baldwin** (1803–1890). He had been educated at St John's College, Oxford (BA 1824, MA 1827), and one of his first acts on assuming control was to develop the *Morning Herald*, which he had recently purchased from the Thwaites family. In writing of the transaction, James Grant described Edward Baldwin as a thoroughly enterprising and enlightened trader in journalism, 'who, two decades after Dudley's death, bought the *Morning Herald* from the little group of fifth-rate capitalists to which it had gone' (Griffiths, *Encyclopedia*, 86). He immediately entered on a course of spirited rivalry with *The Times*, which set all its resources in motion to crush the new competitor. With Giffard acting as editor in addition to his *Standard* role, Edward's first task was to engage the best journalists and increase the honorarium paid for leading articles from 3 guineas to 5 guineas.

After an initial loss, the railway mania of 1845 meant that, through the huge increase in advertising extolling new railway companies, the *Herald* was running a twenty-page paper and making big profits. However, later that year, on 17 November, *The Times* exposed the competing railway companies, showing that there were more than 1200 projected railways seeking to raise some £500 million. The bubble burst immediately, but Baldwin, still intent on overtaking *The Times*, continued to pay high wages. The average circulation dropped, however, from 6400 in 1845 to 3700 by 1854.

It was a state of affairs that could not last, and in March 1857 there appeared a short notice in *The Times* announcing the bankruptcy proceedings of Edward Baldwin—and with it the end of almost 100 years of his family's involvement in the London newspaper world. Edward Baldwin himself moved to Streatham Green, London, where he died on 31 January 1890. His wife's identity is unknown, but at least two sons survived him. In his obituary it was noted that 'his connexion with the Press belongs to a past generation, but in his time he played a prominent part in the newspaper world and was an ardent supporter of the early policy of Lord Derby and Mr Disraeli' (Griffiths, *Encyclopedia*, 86). D. M. GRIFFITHS

Sources D. Griffiths, *Plant here the standard* (1945) • D. Griffiths, ed., *The encyclopedia of the British press, 1422–1992* (1992) • *St James's Chronicle* (20–22 Feb 1813) • R. Rosenberg, *English rights and liberties* (1965) • A. Aspinall, *Politics and the press, c.1780–1850* (1949) • apprentices' register, Stationers' Company, London • R. P. Bond and M. N. Bond, 'The minute books of the *St James's Chronicle*', *Studies in Bibliography*, 28 (1975), 17–40 • Boase, *Mod. Eng. biog.* • *CGPLA Eng. & Wales* (1869) • *CGPLA Eng. & Wales* (1890) • C. Y. Ferdinand, 'Richard Baldwin junior, bookseller', *Studies in Bibliography*, 42 (1989), 254–64 • *IGI* • Foster, *Alum. Oxon.*

Archives University of North Carolina, Chapel Hill, minute books of the *St James's Chronicle*

Likenesses oils (Edward Baldwin), repro. in Griffiths, *Plant here the standard*

Wealth at death under £1000—Charles Baldwin: probate, 5 July 1869, *CGPLA Eng. & Wales* • £399 5s. 11d.—Edward Baldwin: probate, 2 April 1890, *CGPLA Eng. & Wales*

Baldwin fitz Gilbert. *See* Clare, Baldwin de (*fl.* 1130–1154).

Baldwin, Abigail (*bap.* 1658, *d.* 1713). *See under* Baldwin, Richard (*c.*1653–1698).

Baldwin, Alfred (1841–1908), industrialist and politician, was born at Stourport, Worcestershire, on 4 June 1841, the youngest of twelve children of George Pearce Baldwin (1789–1840), a small-scale iron founder and businessman, and his second wife, Sarah Chalkley Stanley (1801–1874), the eldest daughter of the Revd Jacob Stanley, a distinguished Wesleyan Methodist minister who was president of the Methodist conference in 1845. Alfred's father died eight months prior to his birth, and he was brought up by his mother.

After being educated at the Wesleyan Collegiate Institution at Taunton, Baldwin, at the age of sixteen, became a partner in the main family firm, Baldwin, Son & Co. of Stourport. By the 1860s this was a relatively big firm, making ironwork of all kinds, and there were worsted spinning mills at Stourport, a carpet manufactory at Bridgnorth, and a tin-plate works at Wolverhampton. On 9 August 1866, at Wolverhampton parish church, Baldwin married Louisa Macdonald (1845–1925) [*see* Baldwin, Louisa, *under* Macdonald sisters (*act.* 1837–1925)], one of the famous daughters of the Revd George Browne Macdonald, a Wesleyan minister, and his second wife, Hannah, *née* Jones. Louisa's eldest sister Alice was the mother of Rudyard Kipling; the second, Georgiana, married Edward Burne-Jones, and the next, Agnes, married Edward Poynter. The Baldwins had only one child, Stanley *Baldwin, who succeeded his father as MP for Bewdley and later became prime minister. A devout woman obsessed with death, Louisa Baldwin developed during her pregnancy a prolonged and never fully diagnosed illness; over the next sixteen years she spent much time at continental spas. Alfred Baldwin bought Lower Park, Bewdley, as his family residence.

Alfred Baldwin (1841–1908), by Sir Benjamin Stone, 1897

In the 1860s the family business was split, with Baldwin assisting in running the operations of E. P. and W. Baldwin Ltd at the Wilden forge. Following a financial crisis and the death of certain members of the family in the late 1860s, Alfred bought out the remaining partners and secured control in September 1870. He moved to Wilden House overlooking the forge. Responsible for a rapid growth of the firm, he soon established a reputation as a benevolent employer and as a patriarch of the Wilden district. On the former count, by 1890 he had introduced a works medical service, a friendly society, a scheme for the encouragement of the education of workers' children, and the maintenance of high standards of safety and cleanliness, and on the latter he was responsible for the building of a school, a church (with stained glass by Burne-Jones), and a vicarage at Wilden.

During the 1870s and 1880s Baldwin's horizons began to expand. In 1873 the Swindon tin-plate works near Dudley was acquired and in 1886 a separate company, Alfred Baldwin & Co. Ltd, was established to erect and operate a tin-plate works near Pontypool, Monmouthshire. Further developments in the Pontypool region followed in 1892, when the Pont-y-moel tin-plate works was restarted in conjunction with Wright, Butler & Co. The links with this concern, and the business relationship between Baldwin and Colonel Roper Wright, led to a fusion of their business interests.

On 7 April 1902 the various interests of the two parties were brought together under unified control through the formation of Baldwins Ltd. Baldwin became chairman and his only son, Stanley, and Colonel Wright were among the original directors of the company. Following Baldwin's death in 1908, Colonel Wright succeeded him as chairman and Stanley became second in command. At the time of its formation Baldwins took over five concerns: E. P. and W. Baldwin Ltd; Wright, Butler & Co.; the Bryn Navigation Colliery Ltd; Alfred Baldwin & Co. Ltd; and the Blackwall Galvanised Iron Company Ltd. Baldwins Ltd was to become one of the giants of the British steel industry in the first half of the twentieth century, particularly following the acquisition and re-opening of the Port Talbot steel works, Glamorgan, in 1906.

Although his business interests were concentrated on iron, steel, and tin-plate manufacture, Baldwin also played a much wider role through directorships of a number of other concerns. Most notable among these were those of the Great Western Railway and the Metropolitan Bank (of England and Wales). At the former he was unanimously elected chairman in March 1905 following the resignation of F. A. V. Campbell, third earl of Cawdor (1847–1911), on taking up the post of first lord of the Admiralty, while at the latter, under his chairmanship from 1896, the bank was transformed from a local Birmingham bank into a successful national one.

While the centre of Baldwin's business interests gradually moved away from the midlands, most notably into south Wales, at the time of his death he could still be described as ranking as 'one of the commercial kings of the Metropolis of the Midlands' (*Western Mail*). As befitted somebody with a strong yeoman background, and living for much of his married life at Wilden House, Baldwin also played a significant role in local affairs. By the end of the nineteenth century he had been made a JP for both Staffordshire and Worcestershire, and a deputy lieutenant for Worcestershire.

Although having been raised as a Wesleyan, Baldwin had become a high Anglican by his mid-twenties. A widely and deeply read man, he was an ardent believer in the strenuous life and devoted himself wholly to commerce and politics. In 1892 he entered parliament, unopposed, as the Unionist member for Bewdley (West Worcestershire). He was re-elected, again unopposed, in 1895 and 1900, and represented the constituency until his death. Although he rarely spoke in parliament, he was an ardent supporter of Joseph Chamberlain's tariff reform policy, and an equally vehement opponent of home rule for Ireland, of the disestablishment of the Church of England, and of local option in abolishing public houses. While his responsibilities as an MP meant spending time in London, he disliked the vulgarity of life in the capital. Alfred Baldwin died suddenly of cardiac failure on 13 February 1908, having returned home to Kensington Palace Mansions, De Vere Gardens, London, after a board meeting of the Great Western Railway. TREVOR BOYNS

Sources C. Baber and T. Boyns, 'Baldwin, Alfred', *DBB* • K. Middlemas and J. Barnes, *Baldwin: a biography* (1969) • P. Williamson, *Stanley Baldwin: conservative leadership and national values* (1999) • *Western Mail* [Cardiff] (14 Feb 1908) • *Dod's Parliamentary Companion*

Archives British Steel Corporation, Spencer Works, Llan-wern, Newport, Monmouthshire, archives • priv. coll., letters, etc. • Worcs. RO, diaries and corresp. | Worcs. RO, letters to W. H. Cory
Likenesses B. Stone, photograph, 1897, NPG [*see illus.*]
Wealth at death £199,376 7s. 3d.: resworn probate, 21 March 1908, *CGPLA Eng. & Wales*

Baldwin, Charles (1774–1869). *See under* Baldwin family (*per. c.*1760–1857).

Baldwin, Edward (1803–1890). *See under* Baldwin family (*per. c.*1760–1857).

Baldwin, Emily (1807–1880), headmistress, was born on 18 September 1807 at 47 Paternoster Row, London, one of seven children of Robert Baldwin (1780–1858), publisher, and his wife, Maria, daughter of Henry Baldwin, a leading City publisher and printer. Both her parents were members of the large Baldwin family, whose activities in publishing dated back to the seventeenth century. Her father started the *London Magazine* in 1820, and her uncle Charles Baldwin was founder of *The Standard*, a conservative newspaper. Her home background was cultured and literary and she benefited from a scholarly mother. But nothing is known of Emily Baldwin's education or indeed what led her into a career in teaching. She is known to have run a school at Leamington, and for fourteen years, immediately prior to her appointment at Howell's School, she was head of a highly successful school at Notting Hill.

Emily Baldwin was already fifty-three years of age and an experienced headmistress when she was appointed as 'chief matron' of Howell's School, Llandaff, an Anglican school closely associated with the cathedral. Her own religious sympathies were high-church Anglican. The school was a new foundation, one of two boarding-schools for the education of female orphans erected in Wales, the other being at Denbigh, by the Drapers' Company of the City of London. Thomas Howell, a Monmouthshire draper, who died in 1540, had left a sum of money in his will to provide dowries for female orphans. By the nineteenth century, when the legacy was providing an income of some £2000 per annum, a long legal wrangle had arisen over the Drapers' administration of the charity and, following rulings by the court of chancery and an act of parliament (1852), the schools, the first endowed schools for girls in Wales, were built. Emily Baldwin was appointed by the court of chancery in London.

A small, well-built woman with a strong nose and determined chin, wearing her hair in out-dated ringlets and attired in the beribboned cap and voluminous petticoats of an earlier decade, Miss Baldwin made her mark on the school at Llandaff. She brought diplomacy, cheerfulness, and perseverance, as well as a commitment to high standards of academic achievement, to her role as headmistress. She was to need all these qualities in dealing with the all-male board of governors, including the influential Alfred Ollivant, bishop of Llandaff, and the Drapers' Company, which controlled the expenditure of the school.

Emily Baldwin's achievement during the years of her headship (1860–72) was to transform the image of the school at Llandaff from a charity foundation into a highly regarded girls' school. From the outset the school took paying boarders, and within a few years also took day girls, as well as orphans. The first intakes of girls, both orphans and paying pupils, were drawn from the class of small traders, clerks, and farmers, but by the early 1870s the school catered largely for the middle class, attracting the daughters of professional men, the clergy, and army officers. While most girls' charity residential schools provided only a basic elementary education, the curriculum at Llandaff covered 'the principles of the Christian Religion, Reading, Writing, Arithmetic, English Grammar, Geography, Biography, History, the Elements of Astronomy, Garden Botany, Music, French, Drawing and such subjects as the Governors may direct' (Letter books 1859–64). In the course of the 1860s it was further expanded to include geometry, Italian, and Latin. Miss Baldwin made constant demands on the Drapers' Company to buy books, lists of which she drew up herself, and to provide well-qualified teachers. While her academic aspirations for her pupils are clear, the traditional female accomplishments, such as music and drawing, were also taught, and the original scheme for the school had laid down that all girls should be taught needlework.

Emily Baldwin ran the school efficiently and with authority. Her regime, however, unlike that of many of her contemporaries, was characterized by kindliness and common sense. She ensured that the food was appetizing, that there were novels and story books in the library as well as academic texts, and that the younger girls had shuttlecocks and hoops. She taught the children herself, gave rewards for achievement, and encouraged pupils with problems to come to her personally. Under Miss Baldwin there was no corporal punishment at Llandaff, and as one member of staff recorded: 'I never saw Miss Baldwin strike a child' (McCann, 93). Her obituary in the *Western Mail* (6 December 1880) singled out not only her ability and assiduity but her 'affection for the pupils which characterized her administration and won for her, not only the esteem of the governors but the affectionate regard of all those who were under her charge'.

There is no evidence that Emily Baldwin had any connection with the feminist movement in education. The historian of the school, Jean McCann, noting that Miss Buss had founded North London Collegiate School in 1850 and Miss Beale had become headmistress of Cheltenham Ladies' College in 1857, states, 'it would appear not a ripple reached Llandaff'. Ill health forced Emily to retire, aged sixty-five, in 1872 on a meagre pension from the Drapers' Company, the insolvency of her father's publishing business having left the family in straitened circumstances. She returned to London, living at times with her spinster sisters and at times alone in a series of lodgings. Emily Baldwin died on 2 December 1880 at 34 Coleherne Road, South Kensington, London. DEIRDRE BEDDOE

Sources J. E. McCann, *Thomas Howell and the school at Llandaff* (1972) · W. G. Evans, *Education and female emancipation: the Welsh experience, 1847–1914* (1990), 62–72 · *Western Mail* [Cardiff] (6 Dec 1880) · will of Emily Baldwin, 26 May 1873 · Howell's School, Llandaff, Governors' minute books, ladies' committee book, letter books, 1859–64; 1864–70 · d. cert.

Likenesses photograph, *c.*1860, Howell's School, Llandaff, Cardiff · photograph, 1860–61 (with her first orphans), Howell's School, Llandaff, Cardiff

Wealth at death under £500: probate, 15 Dec 1880, *CGPLA Eng. & Wales*

Baldwin, Ernest Hubert Francis (1909–1969), biochemist, was born on 29 March 1909 at 167 Tredworth Road, Gloucester, the eldest son of Hubert Charles Baldwin, organist and music teacher, and of his wife, Nellie Victoria Baldwin, *née* Hailes. He was educated at the Crypt Grammar School, Gloucester, and St John's College, Cambridge (1928–30), where he was a prize and open exhibitioner. He obtained a first in both parts of the natural sciences tripos, including part two in biochemistry. After this he obtained various scholarships, including being a senior student of the Royal Commission for the Exhibition of 1851 (1933–5), which enabled him to remain in the Cambridge department of biochemistry. In 1933 he married Pauline Mary Edwards, daughter of Walter Bushby Edwards, with whom he had one daughter, Nicola, and one son, Nigel St John. Baldwin was a fellow of St John's (1936–41). From 1936 to 1943 he was university demonstrator and subsequently he became lecturer in biochemistry (1943–50).

During his time in Cambridge Baldwin was influenced by Sir Frederick Gowland Hopkins's wide approach to biochemistry and applied himself to the comparative aspects of the subject, in particular, to the study of nitrogen metabolism and the phosphagens. He collaborated with such eminent biochemists as Joseph Needham and Dorothy Needham, and published a number of papers jointly with them. In 1937 he published a small book, *Comparative Biochemistry*, which became a classic introduction to the subject and went into four editions. During his time at Cambridge he acquired wide recognition as a gifted teacher; he had a sense of the modern and was a stimulating lecturer. During the Second World War much of the burden of the teaching of biochemistry in Cambridge fell on him. One result was the publication in 1947 of his *Dynamic Aspects of Biochemistry*, which in many respects was the first textbook of modern biochemistry. It gave a new and lucid interpretation of the metabolic interactions within the body and helped to take biochemistry from the thrall of natural-product chemistry on the one hand and physiological chemistry on the other, giving it a status of its own. The book received worldwide acclaim and over the years was translated into many languages and ran into five editions. The second edition (1952) was awarded the Cortina Ulisse prize.

In 1950 Baldwin was appointed to the chair of biochemistry at University College, London, where he developed the new first-degree course in biochemistry, an innovation for the University of London, and helped to oversee the move of his department into new, purpose-built accommodation. Baldwin continued his work on comparative biochemistry and, with collaborators, added much to our knowledge of nitrogen metabolism and the relation between ureotelic metabolism and water shortage. In this work he was as much or more regarded abroad than at home, as witnessed by his appointment as visiting professor at the University of California (1956–7), and as Rose Morgan professor in the University of Kansas (1965). In 1962 he published a slim volume, *The Nature of Biochemistry*, intended to give senior-school pupils a feel for biochemistry. It went into two editions and was translated into a number of languages. His memoir of Gowland Hopkins was published in the same year. During his time in Cambridge and London Baldwin also published numerous scientific papers, most of them on aspects of comparative biochemistry.

Baldwin was a tall, slightly stooped figure, bearded, and with a quizzical expression. He was an accomplished pianist and, with his family, an able presenter of theatrical puppets. Always amiable, he was fond of giving sherry parties for his staff and students alike. He suffered from the genetic condition myotonic muscular dystrophy and his later years were dogged by frequent bouts of illness. He died suddenly of congestive heart failure at his home, 8 Crofters Road, Moor Park, Northwood, Middlesex, on 7 December 1969; his body was cremated at the Breakspear crematorium, Rickmansworth. He was survived by his wife. S. P. DATTA

Sources *WWW*, *1961–70* · *Nature*, 225 (1970), 569–70 · G. A. Kerkut, 'Ernest Baldwin, 1909–1969', *Comparative Biochemistry and Physiology*, 34 (1970), 1–2 · personal knowledge (2004) · b. cert. · d. cert.
Archives UCL, corresp. and papers
Wealth at death £16,699: probate, 13 Aug 1970, *CGPLA Eng. & Wales*

Baldwin, George (1744–1826), diplomatist and writer, son of William Baldwin, hop merchant, was born, in the Borough, near London, in May 1744 according to his own account, though others give 1743 as the date. In 1760 he went to Cyprus (where his brother was consul) and in 1763 to Acre. Increasingly aware of the political structure and commercial potential of the area, he returned to England in 1768 to obtain leave to explore possible connections between India and Egypt by way of the Red Sea, a route in theory blocked to non-Muslims to protect the holy cities and trade through Jiddah but in fact open to them provided enough profit accrued to the beys. Baldwin returned to Cyprus to settle his late brother's affairs and acted as consul there. In 1773, in Cairo, Mehemed Bey promised him 'if you bring the India ships to Suez, I will lay an aqueduct from the Nile to Suez, and you shall drink of the Nile water' (Baldwin, *Political Recollections*, 3–4). He was favourably received too in Constantinople by Britain's ambassador.

In 1774 Baldwin returned to Cairo with the holy caravan from Mecca, and thence to England. Learning that John Shaw had successfully reached Suez up the Red Sea from Bengal, he offered his services to the East India Company, whose ships were to come up the Red Sea to Suez for transshipment. His offer was accepted. Back in Egypt in 1775, as the only English merchant, and a fluent Arabic speaker, he set up commerce with England, and began linking this trade to Suez and India, organizing schedules and quick

George Baldwin (1744–1826), by J. Bouvier, 1780

turnarounds. Between 1776 and 1778, with ships arriving both at Alexandria and Suez, Baldwin reputedly drank prosperity to England with the combined waters of the Nile, Thames, and Ganges atop the pyramid. The success of his business competed with the trade of the Porte and the East India Company's trade around the Cape; the sultan issued a prohibitory firman, and threatened reprisals. In May 1779 a caravan from Suez to Cairo was attacked; some merchants died, others were imprisoned. In July Baldwin became a hostage or 'prisoner at large' to secure their release. In November he escaped and reached Izmir. There he married Jane (1763–1839), the strikingly beautiful daughter of his agent, William Maltass.

Baldwin set out for India, hoping to restore his fortunes, but was robbed and wounded and quickly returned. He then set off, with his wife, for Europe in 1780, where she drew much attention from rich and powerful men. In Vienna, the sculptor Cerroschi executed her bust for the emperor, and her full-length portrait was painted for Count Kaunitz, the foreign minister. In London, Joshua Reynolds, William Pyne, and Richard Cosway all painted her. Cosway's portrait entitled *A Grecian Lady* (1782) was engraved by Bartolozzi. The Baldwins' marriage was tempestuous and unhappy. She died in 1839 leaving a daughter.

Baldwin was welcomed into London society as an exotic newcomer. He was described by Wright as 'lolling on oriental cushions, amid strange hangings' (T. Wright, *Life of William Blake*, 1929, 2.31) and had some interesting pictures to share. Baldwin became intrigued by Cosway's keen interest in the therapeutic powers of magnetism as expounded by John de Mainauduc. Baldwin's presence was noted in William Blake's lines:

> Cosway, Frazer and Baldwin of Egypt's lake,
> Fear to associate with Blake,
> This life is a warfare against evils,
> They heal the sick, he [Blake] casts out devils.
> (ibid.)

Baldwin presented the India board with his *Narrative of Facts Relating to the Plunder of the English Merchants by the Arabs … in 1779* (1780) and at the board's request prepared the memorial 'Speculations on the resources of Egypt' (written between 1773 and 1785 but published in 1801 in his *Political Recollections*), in which he pointed to Egypt's pivotal position and trading potential ('She is the resort of all traders of the world'), and the instability of the government. He advised that, with no English presence, Mediterranean trade would go to France, and English trade should be supported by political means. Very few senior officials in London, however, found his argument about the strategic importance of Egypt convincing.

In 1785 an envoy signed agreements for safe French transit through Egypt and the Red Sea. To counter-balance this influence, in June 1786 Baldwin was appointed to Egypt as consul-general with a brief to obtain a similar agreement for Britain, to discover 'the motions of the French' and keep the English in India advised (PRO, FO 78, 24/1). In 1790 he published *A Memorial Relating to the Slave Trade in Egypt* at the request of the privy council. In 1792 he sent news to India of the declaration of war on France, enabling British forces to expel the French from Pondicherry. In 1796 another agent came 'to inveigle the Beys of Egypt into the designs of the French', and to obtain consent to pass an army through Egypt to annihilate British dominion in India (Baldwin, *Political Recollections*, 30).

While in Egypt, Baldwin's interest in magnetism continued; he believed the cures effected to be 'many and marvellous'. He created a special room in the form of a temple at his consulary mansion at Alexandria. Here, between 1795 and 1797 he held more than fifty sessions with an itinerant Italian poet who sank easily into a 'magnetic sleep' and responded in verse. Baldwin collected these responses and published them privately as *Investigation into Principles* (1801) and *La prima musa* (1802). He also conducted research on the powers of sweet olive oil to combat plague, described in 'An essay on the plague', written in 1791 and published in his *Political Recollections* (1801).

In 1793 Britain, dissatisfied with Baldwin's progress with a treaty, abolished his post. The letter dismissing him did not arrive until 1796 and he continued to act as consul-general until that date. In 1794 he agreed a commercial treaty with the beys which acknowledged the right of the British to navigate all ports of the Ottoman empire. In March 1798, ill and disillusioned, he left Cairo. That May Napoleon sailed for Egypt, took Alexandria and marched south, vindicating Baldwin's repeated insistence on the region's strategic importance.

Baldwin moved around war-torn Europe, but after the battle of Marengo in June 1800 left Florence, and eventually reached Naples. There, in December 1800, he was asked to join the British expedition at Malta to advise them on Egypt. He recommended they land on the Red Sea, make a direct assault on Alexandria, or land at Abu Qir. Attached to Admiral Lord Keith, he also advised the military commander, Sir Ralph Abercromby. In his *Political Recollections* Baldwin provides eyewitness accounts of the preparations for and landing at Abu Qir on 8 March 1801, and of Abercromby's last hours. He used his local knowledge to set up supplies for the army. By May he was back in London reporting on the invasion.

Baldwin's interest in magnetism was now 'cried down' and its supporters 'held up to derision' (Baldwin, *Legacy*, xxxix), and he did not publish on the subject again until 1811, when the privately printed *Legacy to his Daughter* commented on, among other matters, the present and past state of magnetism as he saw it and repeated his records of the sessions with the Italian poet.

Baldwin died in Earls Court, Brompton, London, on 19 February 1826. His collection of classical cameos and busts, illustrated in his privately printed, undated collection of sixty lithographs (BL), was sold at Christies in London on 8 and 9 May 1828.

JAMES MEW, *rev.* DEBORAH MANLEY

Sources G. Baldwin, *Political recollections relative to Egypt* (1801) • G. Baldwin, *Narrative of facts relating to the plunder of the English merchants by the Arabs … in 1779* (1780) • G. Baldwin, *A memorial relating to the slave trade in Egypt* (1790) • R. S. Zahlan, 'George Baldwin: soldier of fortune', *Travellers in Egypt*, ed. P. Starkey and J. Starkey (1998), 24–38 • *GM*, 1st ser., 96/1 (1826), 203 • *GM*, 2nd ser., 12 (1839), 656 • E. M. Goulburn, *John William Burgon, late dean of Chichester: a biography*, 2 vols. (1892) • H. Dodwell, *The founder of modern Egypt: a study of Muhammad 'Ali* (1931) • W. R. Dawson and E. P. Uphill, *Who was who in Egyptology*, 3rd edn, rev. M. L. Bierbrier (1995) • G. Baldwin, *Mr Baldwin's legacy to his daughter, or, The divinity of truth* (1811) [privately printed] • G. Baldwin, *La prima musa* (1802) [privately printed] • G. Baldwin, *Investigation into principles* (1801) [privately printed] • P. Fara, 'An attractive therapy: animal magnetism in eighteenth-century England', *History of Science*, 33 (1995), 127–77, esp. 142–67 • 60 lithographs of gems by T. Bouvier with lithographic letterpress, BL, Baldwin's museum [privately printed 1810?]

Archives PRO, MSS FO 78/1, FO 24/1, FO 78/7 | NL Scot., corresp. with Robert Liston

Likenesses J. Bouvier, lithograph, 1780, NPG [*see illus.*] • engraving (after drawing by J. Bouvier, 1780), NPG

Baldwin, Henry (1734–1813). *See under* Baldwin family (*per.* c.1760–1857).

Baldwin, Sir John (*bap.* before **1470**, *d.* **1545**), judge, was born shortly before 1470, a younger son of William Baldwin (*d.* 1479?) of Aylesbury, Buckinghamshire, and Agnes, daughter of William Dormer of Wycombe in the same county. William's brother, John Baldwin (*d.* 1469), was a bencher of Gray's Inn and common serjeant of the city of London. The Aylesbury estates had been left to William by the common serjeant, and were inherited by the younger John from his brother Richard in 1484. John joined the Inner Temple, but the details of his career there suggest that he cannot have been admitted much before 1500, and it is not clear how he spent his earlier years. The identity of his first wife is also uncertain, but she was probably called

Agnes and was the mother of his only son and three daughters. She died before 1518, when he married Anne, daughter of Sir William Norris MP (*d.* 1506) of Yattendon, Berkshire, and widow of William Wroughton. Anne, however, became insane before her husband's death.

John Baldwin is mentioned as counsel in the court of requests in 1506, and by 1510 was a justice of the peace for Buckinghamshire. Thereafter his rise was steady. He gave his first reading in the Inner Temple in 1516, and served as its treasurer from 1521 to 1523, in which latter year the subsidy commissioners rated him as being worth £133 in goods. In 1529 he was elected member of parliament for Hindon, Wiltshire, and the following year became attorney-general for Wales and the duchy of Cornwall. When he was nominated for the coif in 1531, he delivered a third reading in the Inner Temple, on the statute *De prisonam frangentibus*, a text of which survives in BL, Harley MS 1691. Upon his creation he was appointed a king's serjeant, together with his brother bencher Thomas Audley, and three years later was knighted, an honour that Spelman noted as unprecedented for a serjeant. Following the death of Robert Norwich he was selected (presumably by Audley) to be chief justice of the common pleas, and was appointed on 19 April 1535.

The printed year-books come to an end in 1535, and what little is known of Baldwin's judicial career is mostly derived from Dyer's reports. Dyer was not wholly complimentary, noting of a case in 1538 that neither he nor anyone else understood Baldwin's dissenting opinion. Spelman reports that Baldwin was given the task of passing sentence on the Carthusian priors in June 1535 for treason, the other judges not bothering to await the verdict. Baldwin went the Norfolk circuit until 1541, and then the home. At Bury assizes in 1538 he was an innocent party to a tragic miscarriage of justice. After a man had been tried before him and executed for murder on the evidence of his small son, it was discovered that the supposed victim was still alive and that the boy had been suborned; the case was the subject of a thorough investigation by the king's council.

Baldwin retained the family seat at Aylesbury, a town where he was the principal inhabitant and rebuilt the sessions house in 1538. In his later years he made numerous further land purchases in the same vicinity and elsewhere, including in 1536 an estate in Little Marlow, which provided a country home, and in 1540 the site of the Greyfriars in Aylesbury. He died in office on 24 October 1545, probably at Marlow, and was buried in Aylesbury church. His daughter Alice (the last abbess of Burnham), who died a few months later, directed her executor to erect a marble tomb with pictures of her parents and their children, and 'such epitaff or scripture as he shall thinke convyent'; but it is not known whether this was done. Baldwin's son William was admitted to the Inner Temple in 1525 but died in 1538, and so after the death of Alice the inheritance was shared between his two remaining daughters, Agnes and Pernel. The Aylesbury estate descended to Sir Thomas Pakington (*d.* 1571), son of Agnes and Robert Pakington MP (assassinated in 1536), and the Little Marlow estate to John Burlace MP (*d.* 1593), son of Pernel and Edward Burlace (*d.* 1544). It was to Burlace that the chief justice left all his law books.

J. H. Baker

Sources HoP, *Commons, 1509–58*, 1.372–3, 456; 3.48 · will, PRO, PROB 11/30, sig. 39 · inquisition post mortem, PRO, C 142/73/7 · Baker, *Serjeants*, 498 · Sainty, *King's counsel*, 14 · PRO, CP 40/1085(2), m.1 · F. A. Inderwick and R. A. Roberts, eds., *A calendar of the Inner Temple records*, 1 (1896) · *The reports of Sir John Spelman*, ed. J. H. Baker, 1, SeldS, 93 (1977), 39, 57, 208, 209 · will, PRO, PROB 11/31, sig. 5 [Alice Baldwin's will] · HoP, *Commons, 1558–1603*, 1.456 · BL, Harley MS 1691, fol. 187 · PRO, REQ 1/3–5

Wealth at death £133—goods in 1523 · left estates around Aylesbury: will, PRO, PROB 11/30, sig. 39

Baldwin, John (*d.* 1615), music copyist and composer, is of unknown origins and parentage. According to Ernest Brennecke, Baldwin was admitted a lay clerk of St George's Chapel, Windsor, in 1575; he cites no documentary evidence in support of this claim and none exists today, though subsequent repair work on the Windsor records may have obscured it. Baldwin is first mentioned there in 1586–7, when he received his stipendiary £10 p.a. plus 22*s*. livery money. He supplemented this income by acting as the chapel's music copyist, and additional payments of 20*s*. were made to him 'pro scriptione sacrarum Cantionum' ('for the copying of sacred songs', that is, services and anthems for the chapel liturgy) in every year for which accounts survive. On 3 February 1594 the lord chamberlain commanded the subdean of the Chapel Royal 'that John Bauldwyne of the College of Wynsor shoulde be placed next in ordynarye in Her Majesties Chapple', and on 23 March 1595 it was ordered that Baldwin be sworn 'gentleman in ordinarie (without pay) … until a tenor's place be voyde, and then he to have and be sworne into wages for the firste and nexte tenor that shalbe admitted' (Rimbault, 35–6). On 28 March 1596 Baldwin witnessed a promise of good behaviour by another of the Windsor clerks. He finally gained his Chapel Royal position on 20 August 1598, following the death of Robert Tallentire. Baldwin sang at the funeral of Queen Elizabeth, the coronation of James I, and the funeral of Prince Henry. On 9 September 1613 he married Elizabeth Jonson in the church of St George the Martyr, Southwark.

Baldwin is one of the most important and versatile of late Elizabethan music scribes. He was wholly responsible for at least three collections: Oxford, Christ Church, MSS 979–983, a set of partbooks probably started in the late 1570s which contains over 170 pieces, most of them vocal and sacred; his so-called commonplace book (BL, RM 24.d.2), compiled over a period of roughly twenty-five years from *c.*1581 to *c.*1606; and My Ladye Nevells Booke, an important source of William Byrd's keyboard music, which was finished on 11 September 1591 and is now in the possession of the marquess of Abergavenny. Baldwin also repaired and completed the Forrest–Heyther collection of masses (Bodl. Oxf., MSS mus. sch. e.376–381), which passed into his hands about 1581. In addition he copied two pieces into Robert Dow's partbooks (Oxford, Christ Church, MSS 984–988) at the instigation of their then owner, Giles Thompson, who was dean of Windsor from

1603. Baldwin's work is always elegant and usually accurate, though he was occasionally guilty of modernizing the Latin sacred music of earlier generations by filling out its melismatic passages with additional text underlay.

Baldwin's commonplace book includes eighteen of his own compositions, the best-known being his setting of Nicholas Breton's 'In the merry month of May', which was probably sung before Queen Elizabeth at Elvetham House, Hampshire, on 22 September 1591. According to a contemporary account:

> three excellent Musicians … disguised in auncient countrey attire, did greet her with a pleasant song of Coridon and Phyllida, made in three parts of purpose. The song, as well for the worth of the dittie, as for the aptnes of the note thereto applied, it pleaseth her Highnesse, after it had been once sung, to command it againe, and highly to grace it with her chearefull acceptance and commendation. (Nichols, 3.116)

Many of Baldwin's textless compositions appear to have had a didactic purpose and incorporate complex proportional changes and contrapuntal devices, as in his 'upon the plainesong' and In nomine in five parts. There are also two four-part motets, *Redime me* and *Pater noster*, in Christ Church, MSS 979–983.

Baldwin died in Southwark on 28 August 1615, possibly of plague, and was buried the following day in the parish of St George the Martyr. Letters of administration were granted to his wife on 7 September. Their son was born some three months later and was baptized John on 1 December. DAVID MATEER

Sources treasurer's rolls, St George's Chapel, Windsor: 1586–7, XV.59.13; 1591–2, XV.59.15; 1592–3, XV.59.16; 1593–4, XV.59.17 • A. Ashbee and D. Lasocki, eds., *A biographical dictionary of English court musicians, 1485–1714*, 2 vols. (1998) • D. Mateer, 'John Baldwin and changing concepts of text underlay', *English choral practice, c.1400–c.1650*, ed. J. G. Morehen (1995), 143–60 • H. Gaskin, 'Music copyists in late sixteenth-century England, with particular reference to the manuscripts of John Baldwin', PhD diss., U. Cam., 1985 • H. Gaskin, 'Baldwin and the Nevell hand', *Byrd studies*, ed. A. Brown and R. Turbet (1992), 159–73 • R. Bray, 'John Baldwin', *Music and Letters*, 56 (1975), 55–9 • R. Bray, 'British Library, R. M. 24 d 2, John Baldwin's commonplace book: an index and commentary', *Royal Musical Association Research Chronicle*, 12 (1974), 137–51 • R. Bray, 'The part-books Oxford, Christ Church, MSS 979–983: an index and commentary', *Musica Disciplina*, 25 (1971), 179–97 • A. Brown, '"My Lady Nevell's Book" as a source of Byrd's keyboard music', *Proceedings of the Royal Musical Association*, 95 (1968–9), 29–39 • E. Brennecke, 'A singing man of Windsor', *Music and Letters*, 33 (1952), 33–40 • A. Ashbee, ed., *Records of English court music*, 9 vols. (1986–96) • E. F. Rimbault, ed., *The old cheque book, or book of remembrance of the Chapel Royal, from 1561 to 1744*, CS, 3rd ser., 3 (1872); 2nd repr. (New York, 1966) • J. Nichols, *The progresses and public processions of Queen Elizabeth*, new edn, 3 vols. (1823) • S. Bond, ed., *The chapter acts of the dean and canons of Windsor: 1430, 1523–1672* (1966) • E. Crownfield, 'British Library MS R.M. 24.d.2 and Oxford, Christ Church Library MSS 979–83; two Elizabethan musical sources copied by John Baldwin', MA diss., New York University, 1985 • J. D. Bergsagel, 'The date and provenance of the Forrest–Heyther collection of Tudor masses', *Music and Letters*, 44 (1963), 240–48 • parish register, Southwark, St George the Martyr, 29 Aug 1615 [burial] • parish register, Southwark, St George the Martyr, 9 Sept 1613 [marriage]

Archives BL, commonplace book, MS RM 24.d.2 [copied by John Baldwin] • Christ Church Oxf., John Baldwin's part-books, MSS 979–983 [copied by John Baldwin] • priv. coll., 'My Ladye Nevells Booke' [copied by John Baldwin] | Bodl. Oxf., Forrest–Heyther part-books, MSS Mus. Sch. e.376–381 [partly copied by John Baldwin] • Christ Church Oxf., Dow part-books, MSS 984–988 [partly copied by John Baldwin]

Baldwin, Louisa (1845–1925). *See under* Macdonald sisters (*act.* 1837–1925).

Baldwin, Lucy, Countess Baldwin of Bewdley (1869–1945). *See under* Baldwin, Stanley, first Earl Baldwin of Bewdley (1867–1947).

Baldwin, Richard (*c.*1653–1698), publisher, was probably born in Wycombe, Buckinghamshire, the son of Thomas Baldwin, a hemp-dresser. No further information survives about his family and education. On 5 August 1668 Baldwin was apprenticed to George Eversden, a bookseller then working in St John's Lane, London; he was made free of the Stationers' Company on 25 August 1675.

Baldwin lived in London for the next six years, and apparently began his professional career as a bookbinder. On 7 December 1676 he married Abigail Mulford [**Abigail Baldwin** (*bap.* 1658, *d.* 1713)] in St Botolph, Aldersgate; the couple had at least one child, Mary. Erroneously named Anne in some sources, Abigail was baptized in St James's, Clerkenwell, in October 1658. Until Richard's death in 1698, her publishing career was inextricable from that of her husband.

Baldwin, it seems, was still working as a bookbinder when he opened his premises in Ball Court, near the Black Bull, Great Old Bailey, some time before 1681. He rapidly expanded his trade, however, by diversifying into the publication of whig broadsides and pamphlets. As early as 1676 Baldwin was bound over to the Hereford sessions in connection with a certain 'infamous paper' (*CSP dom.*, *1 March 1676–28 Feb 1677*, 50); nevertheless, his first imprint did not appear until 1680. In 1681 he emerged suddenly as a major whig publisher, heading a second generation of opposition stationers precisely as the fortunes of their predecessors, including Francis Smith, declined.

The political crisis of 1681–3 was a defining point for Baldwin. He was instrumental in the whig propaganda machine: in addition to incendiary tracts by Thomas Hunt and pamphlets supporting the earl of Shaftesbury, he also published a number of outspoken but short-lived opposition newspapers, including the *London Mercury* and the *Protestant Courant*. Baldwin quickly became identified as one of a small new breed of stationers—'publishers' rather than 'booksellers'—who specialized in publishing and distributing works for others (Treadwell, 114–15). This professional development is reflected in the exceptional number of imprints to which the Baldwins lent their names over the next three decades.

While Baldwin was not directly responsible for many of the works bearing his imprint, he was nevertheless subject, as a dedicated whig publisher, to surveillance and prosecution. In October 1681 he was summoned before the privy council for publishing seditious pamphlets. The following spring he was in constant trouble on account of his newspaper the *Protestant Courant*. Repeatedly libellous comments in this publication provoked a search of his premises by the Stationers' Company. Having refused to co-operate, Baldwin was fined £10; he remained estranged from the Stationers' Company for many years. In May 1682 he was prosecuted for the same newspaper's misrepresention of a case against the earl of Shaftesbury. In addition to allegedly 'base and scandalous Reflections' upon the prosecution and its witnesses, the article cast doubt upon the very integrity of the court's proceedings (*Loyal Protestant*, no. 155). At Baldwin's ensuing trial before the lord chief justice, he suffered an extended character assassination by Jeffreys, who was determined that Baldwin 'might be made an Example of' at all costs (*London Mercury*, no. 13). Having refused to divulge the identity of the author of the libel, Baldwin was remanded to the king's bench prison; upon producing a number of recognizances, he was released on a bond of good behaviour a week later.

Prosecuted again in the autumn of 1682, Baldwin nevertheless continued to publish undeterred, and Thomas Hunt's *Defence of the Charter and Municipal Rights of the City of London* appeared in January 1683. This publication provoked the outrage of Roger L'Estrange, surveyor of the press, at the failure of both his agents and the Stationers' Company to monitor Baldwin adequately; it was common knowledge that Baldwin's publishing operation ensured the anonymity of those whose works he published and distributed. Baldwin's activities continued to be monitored closely throughout 1683, by which time the successful tory reappropriation of power had splintered an unofficial alliance of opposition stationers into a disparate number of mutually suspicious individuals. That summer Baldwin—isolated, unbeholden to his fellow stationers, and under the pressures of close surveillance—appeared, despite his whig convictions, as a government witness against opposition authors and stationers, including the family of Francis Smith. In July 1683 the attorney-general nevertheless decreed that warrants for searching Baldwin's premises might be granted upon the merest suspicion; the following month he was again investigated, as the publisher of a seditious work by Hunt.

There is little evidence of activity on Baldwin's part throughout the reign of James II; he certainly lent his imprint to relatively few works in the aftermath of the tory reaction. This situation changed dramatically with the accession of William III, which he greeted with enthusiasm, publishing several works championing the cause of the revolution of 1688. He continued to publish whig tracts on a large scale until his death in 1698. Nevertheless, he was frequently questioned in connection with his work, and in 1690 a warrant committed him to Newgate prison for high treason upon publishing *A Modest Enquiry into the Causes of the Present Disasters in England*. Despite the gravity of this charge, he appears, unusually, to have secured release on bail. In the same year the Baldwins moved to the Oxford Arms, Warwick Lane. Baldwin was summoned before the House of Commons the following year, when some blunt criticisms of parliament's prosecution of the French war were published, together with incendiary remarks about the king of France, in *Mercurius Reformatus*. He finally entered into the livery of the Stationers' Company in 1692. In addition to his core business in political and satirical pamphlets and newspapers, his expanding stock included dramatic, scientific, and historical works; he also published a number of periodicals, including the *Gentleman's Journal* and *Miscellaneous Letters*. After a brief and acrimonious merger with the *Post Boy*, a rival publication, Baldwin's longest-lived newspaper appeared independently, as the *Post Man*, in 1695. In this organ, as with innumerable titles in his pamphlet stock, Baldwin's anti-papist and, more specifically, anti-French sentiments were undisguised. The *Post Man* incurred the censure of state authorities when it carried further libellous comments on the French king and the duke of Burgundy in October 1697. Nevertheless, despite the arrest of the author and printer of the offending article, Baldwin himself appears to have escaped prosecution.

Baldwin died in 1698, probably at his home, and, according to Dunton, was buried at his Buckinghamshire birthplace; he was said to have been forty-five years old. Dunton describes him as a man of 'Generous Temper', with a purse and heart 'open to all Men, that he thought were Honest', and whose 'Conversation was very diverting' (Dunton, 342). After her husband's death Abigail Baldwin continued to run their flourishing business in Warwick Lane, publishing and distributing a wide range of pamphlets and periodicals under the imprint 'A. Baldwin'. In addition to treatises on issues such as social welfare and the standing army, she published pamphlets by whig authors, including Defoe, and periodicals which ranged from the economic journal the *British Merchant of Commerce Preserved* to the notorious *Female Tatler*. A formidable businesswoman in her own right, Abigail Baldwin was remembered by Dunton for her remarkable bookkeeping skills. She died on or after 14 November 1713, and was buried in St Martin Ludgate on the 29th of that month. In addition to a flourishing business, which she bequeathed to her son-in-law, the printer James Roberts, Abigail Baldwin left some tenanted property in Parkers Lane, Middlesex, and a significant amount of money, silver, and jewellery. The business continued under Roberts for a further forty-one years.

Richard and Abigail Baldwin are key figures in the history of publishing. Responding to the political pressures of their time, their business evolved pragmatically and influentially beyond the mandate of traditional 'bookselling'. Perhaps most renowned as agents of whig propaganda, they also influenced the developing role of newspapers and periodicals within the popular literary culture of the early eighteenth century. BETH LYNCH

Sources M. Treadwell, 'London trade publishers, 1675–1750', *The Library*, 6th ser., 4 (1982), 99–134 • D. F. McKenzie, ed., *Stationers' Company apprentices*, [2]: *1641–1700* (1974) • T. J. Crist, 'Francis Smith and the opposition press in England, 1660–1688', PhD diss., U. Cam., 1977 • L. Rostenberg, 'Richard and Anne Baldwin, whig patriot publishers', *Literary, political, scientific, religious, and legal publishing, printing, and bookselling in England, 1551–1700: twelve studies*, 2 (1965), 369–415 • Wing, *STC* • *CSP dom.*, *1676–7*; *1682–3*; *1690–91*; *1697*; *1700–02* • E. Howe, *A list of London bookbinders, 1648–1815* (1950) • C. Nelson and M. Seccombe, eds., *British newspapers and periodicals,*

1641–1700: a short-title catalogue of serials printed in England, Scotland, Ireland, and British America (1987) • J. Dunton, *The life and errors of John Dunton … written by himself* (1705) • P. G. Morrison, *Index of printers, publishers and booksellers in Donald Wing's 'Short-title catalogue of books … 1641–1700'* (1955) • *London Mercury* (15–18 May 1682) • *Loyal Protestant, and True Domestick Intelligence*, 155 (16 May 1682) • *Loyal Protestant, and True Domestick Intelligence*, 158 (23 May 1682) • *Loyal Protestant, and True Domestick Intelligence*, 169 (17 June 1682) • H. R. Plomer and others, *A dictionary of the printers and booksellers who were at work in England, Scotland, and Ireland from 1668 to 1725* (1922) • H. R. Plomer and others, *A dictionary of the booksellers and printers who were at work in England, Scotland, and Ireland from 1641 to 1667* (1907) • N. Luttrell, *A brief historical relation of state affairs from September 1678 to April 1714*, 4 (1857) • G. E. B. Eyre, ed., *A transcript of the registers of the Worshipful Company of Stationers from 1640 to 1708*, 3 vols. (1913–14) • E. Arber, ed., *The term catalogues, 1668–1709*, 3 vols. (privately printed, London, 1903–6) • will, GL, MS 9171/56/55 [Abigail Baldwin]

Wealth at death £750; property in Parkers Lane, Middlesex; also silver, jewellery, and linen; publishing business; specific gifts bequeathed; Abigail Baldwin: will, GL, MS 9171/56/55, proved 3 Dec 1713

Baldwin, Richard (*c*.1666–1758), college head, is of uncertain origins. The matriculation register of Trinity College, Dublin, recorded that he entered the college on 29 April 1684, at the age of seventeen, had been born in Athy, in co. Carlow (though Athy is in co. Kildare), the son of Richard Baldwin of Athy, and that he had attended Kilkenny College under the care of the Revd Dr Edward Hinton. Much to the puzzlement of his colleagues Baldwin never discussed his background. Dr John Lawson, professor of oratory and history at the college, who gave the oration at Baldwin's funeral, enlightened those in attendance by stating that Baldwin had in fact been born in England and brought to Ireland in his infancy. Lawson's revelation was supported by an account in a local history of Colne, Lancashire:

> Richard Baldwen the son of James Baldwen, of Parke Hill, near Colne, born AD 1672, and educated at the grammar school of that place, where he is said to have given a mortal blow to a school fellow, upon which he fled to Ireland, and was admitted to Trinity College, Dublin, where in 1717 he became provost. (Whitaker, 2.519)

A more detailed retelling of this account, by a Mr Adamson, which was prepared in connection with a subsequent legal challenge to Baldwin's will, was included in Taylor's *History of the University of Dublin*. The baptismal register of St Bartholomew's in Colne records that Richard Baldwen, son of James Baldwen of Park Hill, Barrowford, Colne, was baptized on 14 April 1672, but the dates are inconsistent, since if this was the record of Baldwin's birth he would have been only twelve on entry to Trinity. Another variation of Baldwin's background appeared in a letter to the *Daily Express* in July 1892 from J. R. Baldwin, who claimed that Baldwin had been the son of a James Baldwin from Ingthorpe Grange, Skipton, Yorkshire, and that the incident in which he supposedly killed a fellow pupil had occurred at Sedbergh School and had involved a cricket ball.

The real circumstances behind Baldwin's arrival in Ireland remain unclear, but his attendance at Kilkenny College can be confirmed by the college register, which records that he left the school to enter Trinity College in 1685. His entry into Kilkenny College was not recorded, since he arrived before the granting of a charter and statutes to the college by James, first duke of Ormond, in March 1685, which required that a register be taken when boys were 'admitted into the said School … as also the time of their departure' (Macalister, item 18). Although Baldwin is recorded as having matriculated a year earlier than when he was supposed to have left Kilkenny the date noted for matriculation was not always the date from which attendance at university began. The dramatist William Congreve was also a pupil at Kilkenny during this time. Baldwin was elected as a scholar of Trinity College in 1686 and commenced with a BA in early 1689.

Richard Baldwin (*c*.**1666–1758**), by Francis Bindon, 1745

After the Jacobite occupation of Trinity in 1689 Baldwin fled to England and possibly took up a teaching position in Chester. His experiences during this time made a deep impression and contributed to his becoming an avowed whig and constant opponent of the tories within and without the college for the rest of his life. Samuel Burdy's biography of the Revd Philip Skelton, of 1792, contained a number of anecdotes concerning Baldwin's battle with Jacobite sympathizers, including his supposed comment about his tory antithesis, Jonathan Swift, whom he judged 'remarkable for nothing else while a student than his skill in kindling a good fire' (Burdy, 33). Baldwin was elected fellow of Trinity in 1693, became senior fellow in 1697, vice-provost in 1713, and provost in 1717. The speed of his elevation to high office has caused some historians to speculate that whig forces outside the college led to Baldwin's 'being preferred to men more highly gifted' (Taylor, 250) than himself; this is supported by the fact that his selection as provost coincided with the Hanoverian succession. His manner of leadership has been described as autocratic and he himself 'a forerunner of the more severe type of Victorian head-master, with sound but unimaginative scholarship and an insistence on hard work and the observance of a strict disciplinary code', but behind Dublin's Georgian façade was a culture of 'riots and drunken brawls among half-educated would-be gentlemen' (McDowell and Webb, 38) to which students were easily attracted. Baldwin made significant progress in improving student behaviour, however; Swift, in a letter to the earl of Peterborough in April 1726, described Trinity as a place where 'youths are instructed with much stricter discipline than either Oxford or Cambridge' (Williams, 3.133). Two of the college's finest buildings, the printing house (1734) and the library (1732), were completed during his provostship.

Baldwin died in Trinity on 30 September 1758, reputedly at the age of ninety-two, having completed forty-one years as provost, the longest tenure of any before or since; he was buried in the college chapel on 4 October. He left the college his entire fortune of £24,000 and 200,000 acres in real estate located in several counties in Ireland. His will was disputed by certain persons in England who claimed to be his relatives citing the evidence that suggested that Baldwin had been born in Colne. Litigation continued intermittently for sixty-two years before the case was decided in favour of the college in 1820. There is a large, sculpted monument to Baldwin by Christopher Hewetson in the public theatre of the college. H. T. WELCH

Sources R. B. McDowell and D. A. Webb, *Trinity College, Dublin, 1592–1952: an academic history* (1982) • C. Maxwell, *A history of Trinity College Dublin, 1591–1892* (1946) • J. W. Stubbs, *The history of the University of Dublin, from its foundation to the end of the eighteenth century* (1889) • J. V. Luce, *Trinity College Dublin: the first 400 years* (1992) • T. D. Whitaker, *An history of the original parish of Whalley and honor of Clitheroe … To which is subjoined an account of the parish of Cartmell … The third edition, revised and enlarged. With additional engravings. Fourth edition, revised and enlarged by J. G. Nichols … and … P. A. Lyons*, 2 vols. (1872–6) • parish register, St Bartholomew, Colne, 14 April 1672 [baptism: Richard Baldwen] • A. Crookshank and D. Webb, *Paintings and sculptures in Trinity College, Dublin* (1990) • entrance and leaving book of Kilkenny College, TCD, MS 2019, fol. 50 • Burtchaell & Sadleir, *Alum. Dubl.*, 2nd edn • R. A. S. Macalister, 'The charter and statutes of Kilkenny College', *Journal of the Royal Society of Antiquaries of Ireland*, 40/1 (March 1910), 32–7 • *Daily Express* (July 1892) • S. Burdy, *The life of Philip Skelton* (1792); repr. (1914) • *The correspondence of Jonathan Swift*, ed. H. Williams, 3 (1963) • W. B. S. Taylor, *History of the University of Dublin* (1845) • *DNB*

Archives TCD, corresp. with W. King

Likenesses F. Bindon, oils, 1745, TCD [*see illus.*] • S. Vierpyl, marble bust, 1761, TCD • C. Hewetson, sculpture on monument, 1781, TCD • R. Howe, oils, 1783, TCD • Bindon?, oils, TCD • portraits, repro. in Crookshank and Webb, *Painting and sculptures*

Wealth at death £24,000; plus 200,000 acres of land in co. Wicklow, King's county, co. Kildare, Meath, and Down: Stubbs, *History of the University*; *DNB* • land worth £50,000

Baldwin, Robert (1804–1858), lawyer and politician in Canada, was born on 12 May 1804 at York, Upper Canada, the eldest of the five sons of **William Warren Baldwin** (1775–1844), also a lawyer and politician in Canada, and his wife, (Margaret) Phoebe Willcocks (1771–1851). Robert Baldwin's grandfather, also Robert Baldwin (1741–1816), was a member of a moderately prosperous Anglo-Irish family. In 1799 he left Ireland as a widower to settle some 40 miles east of York (later Toronto), the capital of Upper Canada, with two sons and four daughters. William Warren was the fifth of the sixteen children born to him and Barbara Spread (1748–1791). Born at Knockmore, co. Cork, on 25 April 1775, he studied medicine at the University of Edinburgh (*c.*1794–7), and in 1802 he left the family home to go to York to practise medicine. On 31 May 1803 he married Phoebe, the daughter of his influential landlord, William Willcocks, formerly mayor of Cork. He had already been admitted to the bar, and had been licensed to practise law in the previous month. Shrewd, hard-working, and well placed, William prospered; his wife inherited her father's property in 1813 and additional property in 1822.

Entry into politics Although neither William nor his father had trouble securing government appointments, William identified more with the 'outs' than the 'ins'. Anxious about the prospects of his family, he felt that a Scots clique discriminated against all others. Indeed, several friends and acquaintances had already fallen foul of officialdom. His father had sought parliamentary reform in Ireland: William found similar reason to agitate for reform in Upper Canada. Although the province had an assembly, it had an appointed lieutenant-governor and two appointed councils, one legislative, the other executive. This structure invited abuses. In 1820 William stood successfully for the assembly, and soon gravitated to the side of the government's critics. In the country tradition of British politics, he was for limited government and the independence of its constituent parts. He proposed a bill in 1822 to free the assembly from the control of the legislative council (the latter emasculated the legislation). In 1824 he failed in a bid for re-election, but he was soon joined in his political and legal enterprises by his son Robert.

Robert, who had earlier attended the district grammar school in York, had begun studying law in 1819; he became a clerk in his father's law office in 1820 and was called to the bar in 1825. On 31 May 1827 he married a first cousin, Augusta Elizabeth Sullivan (1811–1836), to whom he was devoted and with whom he had two sons and two daughters. In 1828 he stood unsuccessfully for the assembly but had the satisfaction of seeing his father triumphant. Both Baldwins were identified with the nascent reform movement, whose members prized their status as gentlemen because it helped make reform respectable. None the less, both men lost in the elections of 1830. Neither stood four years later when reformers won a majority of seats. This angered the fiery William Lyon Mackenzie, who felt that they had failed their colleagues.

Robert Baldwin (1804–1858), by Thomas Waterman Wood, 1855

The struggle for responsible government The Baldwins distrusted Mackenzie and other radicals, who they felt were inclined to take the reformers in an American, republican direction. They desired British forms and solutions. In a reform petition of 5 July 1828 to the British government William complained of the irresponsibility of officials, arguing that responsibility had already been granted constitutionally. He informed the prime minister, Wellington, that Upper Canada needed 'a provincial ministry … responsible to the provincial parliament' (Careless, 105). Increasingly the Baldwins, especially Robert, came to see responsible government as the great panacea. The governor should choose his executive councillors from the party that had control of the assembly and should hear their advice on all matters. If unable to accept that advice, he should dissolve the assembly and call an election.

The conception that the ministers of the crown should be responsible to parliament for the conduct of the executive arm of government was well established in Britain. In both Canadas, notably Lower Canada, notions of responsibility had been raised before the Anglo-American War (1812–14). It was the Baldwins' genius that they (especially Robert) came to promote responsible government which, as William explained to Joseph Hume in 1830, 'would, of itself, indirectly lead to the removal of all our present grievances and prevent the recurrence of any such for the future' (Wilson, 22). The issue of responsible government was to become heated after the arrival of a new governor in January 1836.

Sir Francis Bond Head had the reputation of a tried reformer. He decided to bring Robert Baldwin into the executive council. Baldwin accepted the offer, albeit reluctantly, being desolate after the recent death of his beloved wife. Joining Baldwin and the three tories on the council were two reformers, John Rolph and J. H. Dunn. On 3–4 March 1836 the entire council drafted and adopted a memorandum arguing that the constitution demanded the establishment of responsible government. Head denied that he needed to consult the council on all matters. Four of the councillors, but not Baldwin and Rolph, were prepared to yield. When the penitents failed to secure the agreement of the recalcitrants, all resigned. Head appointed a new council, including two relatives of the Baldwins, one being William's brother Augustus. The assembly stopped the supplies in protest. Head refused assent to all money bills, dissolved the assembly, and called an election.

William Baldwin, who headed both the newly formed Constitutional Reform Society of Upper Canada and the Toronto Political Union, was one of those Head purged from office, being dismissed as a judge. Neither Baldwin stood in the election that summer, but Robert took his concerns, and those of the reformers generally, to England. A dispatch from Head beseeched Glenelg, the colonial secretary, not to see him. Glenelg, who certainly felt that the old councillors had been wrong to argue that the governor must always consult them, obliged. Consequently, Baldwin set out his understanding of responsible government for the colonial secretary in a missive of 13 July. He did talk to other influential politicians, Lord John Russell, J. A. Roebuck, and Joseph Hume among them, before going to Ireland, and arrived back in Upper Canada in February 1837.

That December Mackenzie and a small group of radicals, dismayed at the smashing victory of the tories in the election of 1836, and spurred on by a revolt in Lower Canada, led a rebellion at Toronto. The Baldwins were not involved, though Head used Robert's good offices to offer the rebels an amnesty. He revoked the offer when reinforcements arrived, leaving Baldwin feeling that his trust had been abused. The insurgents were soon put to flight. Although he was not sympathetic to the rebels, Baldwin later defended several accused insurgents in court.

The British dispatched Lord Durham to investigate the causes of the rebellions in the Canadas and to make recommendations. Reflecting the fact that rebellion, exacerbated by national tensions between French and 'English', had been more serious in Lower Canada, Durham spent most of his time there, but while in Toronto he met both Baldwins, and asked them to put their views in writing. William produced a rather prolix document, enumerating varied grievances and making several recommendations, including the establishment of both an aristocracy and a responsible executive council. Robert sent a copy of his missive to Glenelg of 13 July 1836. Durham's landmark report of January 1839, in which he recommended the establishment of responsible government, echoed the phrases of Robert's letter. However, Durham elaborated on the proposal therein by arguing that the provinces should have control of internal affairs while the imperial government should manage external ones. The report fuelled a widespread reform campaign for responsible government in which both Baldwins were active.

The British government dispatched Charles Poulett Thomson, a prominent whig, to preside over Durham's proposed union of the two Canadas. He arrived in October 1839 and trumpeted the idea of 'harmony', that men of goodwill could make the existing political system work. In February 1840 Robert Baldwin agreed to become solicitor-general of Upper Canada. He declared publicly, but opaquely, that 'in accepting the office I consider myself to have given a public pledge that I have reasonably well-grounded confidence that the government of my country is to be carried on in accordance with the principle of responsible government' (Wilson, 93). It is likely that his decision had been influenced by colonial secretary Lord John Russell's dispatch of 16 October 1839 which declared that the holding of public office was no longer contingent only on good behaviour: officials could be asked to relinquish their posts for reasons of public policy. William Warren Baldwin also chose to view the Russell dispatch as a grant of responsible government.

The Canadian union was proclaimed in February 1841; an election followed. Like many Reformers in Lower Canada, but unlike most in Upper Canada, Robert Baldwin was successful. In June he told the governor-in-chief, who had been elevated to the peerage as Baron Sydenham, that representatives of the French-Canadian Reformers must be added to the council. Sydenham chose to regard Baldwin's insistence as a resignation. The episode left the tories delighted and Sydenham convinced, if his dispatches to Britain can be believed, that Baldwin was an unprincipled scoundrel. The latter worked to forge a province-wide Reform alliance. He had won two seats in the election, and, after choosing one, suggested that Louis-Hippolyte LaFontaine, the leader of the French-Canadian Reformers who had been defeated in his riding by chicanery, run in the by-election for the other. LaFontaine agreed, and won the ensuing contest. Sydenham's system was threatened, though he did not live to see it crumble, since he died on 19 September 1841.

Sydenham's replacement, Sir Charles Bagot, a career diplomat, arrived in January 1842. Bagot had been told by the new tory colonial secretary, Lord Stanley, to bring the ablest men into his council. Although Bagot was not anxious to see 'radicals' like Robert Baldwin or the French Reformers in office, he recognized reality and brought both LaFontaine and Baldwin into his ministry that September. The new ministers had to face by-elections. Baldwin was defeated—by a cousin. Bagot was not displeased. LaFontaine, however, obligingly found a seat for Baldwin in Lower Canada, which, though he was unable to speak French, he won by acclamation in another by-election. Bagot told Stanley that responsible government now existed in practice, but he persisted in making various appointments personally. LaFontaine persuaded Baldwin not to protest because Bagot was increasingly ill. His deteriorating condition eventually removed him from day-to-day affairs, making Baldwin and LaFontaine, in a practical sense, the first prime ministers of the province.

Death of William Baldwin and the final battles for responsible government In March a new governor, Charles Metcalfe, arrived, carrying instructions from Stanley not to feel himself obliged to accept his ministers' advice in every particular and to control the use of patronage. Baldwin fell out with Metcalfe over the crucial question of patronage as well as the governor's reservation of a bill aimed at the Orange order. On 26 November 1843 all but one of the ministers resigned. Some weeks after, at Toronto on 8 January 1844, William Warren Baldwin died, and was buried in the family cemetery at their country home, Spadina, leaving his son Robert, who pined still for his wife, even more bereft. He was to miss the advice of his father, whom he regarded 'as one of the kindest of parents and best of men' (Wilson, 198). William's strong personality had helped offset the rather drab and wooden public persona of his son. That prop was now taken from Robert, though William had convinced his son that he was destined to bring the country responsible government. A devout Anglican, William felt that God had foreordained it.

The political battle was joined in earnest. Loyal addresses poured in on Metcalfe, as did assurances from Lord Stanley and others that he had been right not to compromise the governor's authority. Nevertheless, Metcalfe's political position became ever more difficult. He was obliged to let his chief minister, William Henry Draper, have free use of patronage to maintain his slim parliamentary majority. The election in November was marred by vitriolic campaigning and violence at the polls; the government maintained a slim majority and Baldwin and LaFontaine were both returned in opposition. Baldwin went on the offensive, endlessly lecturing his opponents on responsible government and on the necessity of Canadians managing their own affairs.

Since he was dying from cancer, Metcalfe returned to Britain in October 1845. Lord Cathcart, commander of the forces in British North America, was appointed, first administrator, then governor-general. Interested in military matters, he let his councillors have a free hand, and once again the government, with Draper still at the head, acted as a responsible party government. Earl Grey, the colonial secretary, suggested to Lieutenant-Governor Harvey of Nova Scotia in a dispatch of 3 November 1846 that the members of his council could expect him to accept their advice. Grey sent Lord Elgin to Canada as governor-in-chief, intimating that he should allow a responsible executive to dispense patronage.

The 'Great Ministry' The new governor-in-chief arrived in Montreal, the capital of the Canadas, in January 1847. Despite the reconstitution of the ministry that spring, he felt it no longer reflected the will of the people, and he dissolved the assembly on 6 December 1847. The ensuing election saw the Reformers win a majority in both sections of the Canadas, with Baldwin again elected. The Baldwin–LaFontaine government, which came to be known as the 'Great Ministry', took office on 11 March 1848, with Baldwin as attorney-general for Upper Canada. Baldwin and LaFontaine formed the first truly responsible ministry in that they took office and exercised complete authority over internal affairs as a matter of course. Other responsible ministries had existed, but only on sufferance. The establishment of responsible government was inextricably bound up with its recognition.

Baldwin always insisted that the new ministry was LaFontaine's, but he was, in fact, co-premier. The government was exceedingly active legislatively and carried two measures with which Baldwin is particularly identified: a bill providing for the secularization of the University of Toronto, and the Municipal Corporations Act, which went some distance towards introducing responsible local government to the western half of the province. More controversial was the Rebellion Losses Bill, which promised to compensate those in Lower Canada who had suffered property losses in the troubles of 1837–8. Opponents of the measure worried that traitors would be rewarded. The bill passed the assembly, with Baldwin speaking briefly on its behalf. Despite his personal doubts, Elgin gave it royal assent on 25 April 1849, signifying for all to see that responsible government was in place, that the ministers, not the crown, controlled policy and legislation. A tory mob roamed Montreal for days, burning the parliament buildings and searching for LaFontaine, Baldwin, and other perceived traitors.

The bill helped persuade the tories of Montreal that they had been deserted by the British government. On 13 October they published a manifesto advocating annexation to the United States. Annexationist sympathy existed too among a group of ultra-Reformers known as the Clear Grits, who sought the introduction of American democratic devices. Baldwin, who, unlike his father, believed that Canada's ties to Britain must be permanent, battled annexationists of whatever stripe, helping extirpate them from office. He annoyed the radicals further when he proved hard to draw out on the vexed clergy reserves issue, which raised the question of state support for organized religion. His retreat on school reform provoked them yet again. On the other hand, he disagreed with Francis Hincks, the inspector-general, who favoured railroads and government involvement in their financing. And he quarrelled with other Reformers such as George Brown of the Toronto *Globe*, who took an increasingly intolerant stance with respect to French and Catholic rights. A devout Anglican but no religious bigot, Baldwin had struggled hard to forge a bi-'racial' Reform Party. Symbolically, he had had his four children educated in Catholic, francophone schools in Quebec. Increasingly tired, ill, and disillusioned, he announced, on 30 June 1851, his retirement as minister after an old adversary, William Lyon Mackenzie, had proposed abolition of the court of chancery, which Baldwin had reformed in 1849. Although it was defeated, Mackenzie's motion had won a majority of votes from Upper Canada. LaFontaine soon followed Baldwin's lead. Baldwin did stand in the ensuing election, but, seen as yesterday's man and harried by Mackenzie, suffered a humiliating defeat.

Death and reputation Reclusive and plagued by ill health, Baldwin lived out his days at the estate he had inherited from his parents, obliging his elder daughter to forsake her happiness and look after him. He refused several prime appointments. A weak heart and lung congestion carried him off at Toronto on 9 December 1858. Uxorious to a fault, he had been melancholy and unhappy since the loss of his wife in 1836. He joined her in death, with his coffin chained to hers and his body mutilated in imitation of the scars she bore from her tragic last birth. He was buried initially in the family cemetery at Spadina, on 13 December, but in 1874 was reinterred at St James's cemetery, Toronto.

A cold, reserved public man, Baldwin had not inspired great love or affection. Although he was somewhat taller than average, his hunched posture, paunch, rather lifeless grey eyes, and increasingly bald pate made him physically unprepossessing in later life. This evidently clouded some judgements. The anonymous author of an obituary in the *Upper Canada Law Journal* (January 1859, 1) paid him a most modest compliment. Of but moderate talents, he had been 'an able and honest politician'. He had been that—and much more. Possibly driven by a desire to measure up to the father he so respected, he rarely stooped and seldom pandered. He knew his objective—responsible government. His genius was that he recognized its efficacy in conferring legitimacy on colonial government and in ensuring the maintenance of the imperial tie. His contribution was that he persevered through much political turmoil and personal anguish. COLIN FREDERICK READ

Sources G. E. Wilson, *The life of Robert Baldwin: a study in the struggle for responsible government* (1933) • S. Leacock, *Baldwin, LaFontaine, Hincks: responsible government* (1910) • J. M. S. Careless, 'Robert Baldwin', *The pre-confederation premiers: Ontario government leaders, 1841–1867*, ed. J. M. S. Careless (1980), 89–147 • M. S. Cross and R. L. Fraser, 'Baldwin, Robert', *DCB*, vol. 8 • R. L. Fraser, 'Baldwin, William Warren', *DCB*, vol. 7 • R. M. Baldwin and J. Baldwin, *The Baldwins and the great experiment* (1969) • Metropolitan Toronto Public Library, Baldwin MSS • P. A. Buckner, *The transition to responsible government: British policy in British North America, 1815–1850* (1985) • Surrogate Court Records, Toronto, Public Archives of Ontario, Toronto, MS 638 • W. L. Mackenzie correspondence, Public Archives of Ontario, Toronto, Mackenzie–Lindsey MSS, F37 • Public Archives of Ontario, Toronto, Baldwin MS 88 • A. S. Thompson, *Spadina: a story of old Toronto* (1975) • H. Scadding, *Toronto of old*, ed. F. H. Armstrong (1966) • W. D. Reid, *Death notices of Ontario* (1980)

Archives Metropolitan Toronto Public Library • NA Canada, Baldwin-Ross MSS, MG24 B11 • priv. coll. • Public Archives of Ontario, Toronto | Metropolitan Toronto Public Library, Laurent Quetton de St George MSS • National Library of Quebec, Quebec City, Lafontaine collection, MS 101 • Public Archives of Ontario, Toronto, Mackenzie–Lindsey MSS, W. L. Mackenzie corresp. • St Sulpice Library, Montreal, Lafontaine collection

Likenesses T. Hamel, oils, 1840–49, Musée du Seminaire de Québec, Québec, Canada • T. Hamel, oils, 1840–49 (after his oil painting?), probably priv. coll. • H. F. Meyer, lithograph, 1845, Metropolitan Toronto Public Library • H. F. Meyer, stipple and line on wove paper, 1846, Metropolitan Toronto Public Library • T. Hamel, lithograph, 1850 (after oil painting by T. Hamel, 1840–49), Metropolitan Toronto Public Library • T. W. Wood, oils on paper, 1855, NPG [*see illus.*] • E. J. Palmer, photograph, tin type, 1856?, Metropolitan

Toronto Public Library • G. T. Berthon, oils, 1859, Osgoode Hall, Toronto • J. W. L. Forster, oils, 1906 (after oil painting by G. T. Berthon, 1859), Ontario Legislature, Toronto • monument, *c*.1922 (with Lafontaine), Ottawa • E. J. Palmer, albumen print (after his photograph), Metropolitan Toronto Public Library • lithograph (after T. Hamel), Royal Ontario Museum, Toronto, Sigmund Samuel Gallery • marble bust, Assembly Chamber, Ottawa

Wealth at death £1104 17*s*. 6*d*.—goods and chattels: inventory, Surrogate Court, Toronto, MS 638 • £8865 4*s*. 7*d*.—rights and credits: inventory, Surrogate Court, Toronto, MS 638 • considerable real estate

Baldwin, Stanley, first Earl Baldwin of Bewdley (1867–1947), prime minister, was born at Lower Park House, Bewdley, Worcestershire, on 3 August 1867, the only child of Alfred *Baldwin (1841–1908) and his wife, Louisa Macdonald (1845–1925) [*see* Baldwin, Louisa, *under* Macdonald sisters].

The Baldwin family The Baldwin family had been yeomen and tenant farmers in Corvedale, Shropshire, since at least the early sixteenth century. They made no mark beyond local affairs, apart from one ancestor implicated in a plot to free Mary, queen of Scots, in 1585 and imprisoned in the Tower until he escaped four years later. In the second half of the seventeenth century a branch of the family developed iron forges, and in 1788 the descendant of one of these moved from Shrewsbury down the River Severn to Stourport in Worcestershire, a more promising location on the emerging canal system. This was Thomas Baldwin (1751–1823), Stanley's great-grandfather, and the successful iron foundry which he established there was expanded by his sons George Pearce Baldwin (1789–1840) and Enoch Baldwin (1793–1857). The former had a large family; his second wife was Sarah, daughter of the Revd Jacob Stanley, a Methodist minister in Northumberland, and president of the Methodist conference in 1845, and their youngest son, born after his death, was Alfred Baldwin.

After George Pearce's death his brother Enoch formed E. P. and W. Baldwin in partnership with his two eldest nephews, Pearce (1813–1851) and William (1817–1863). The business came to concentrate on the wrought iron and tin plate works at nearby Wilden, which they acquired in 1854. Following the founders' deaths the company passed to the control of Alfred Baldwin and his two surviving older brothers, George (1826–1881) and Stanley (1828–1907). However, the latter's bad management and drinking, combined with a trade depression, brought the firm close to bankruptcy in the late 1860s. Matters improved only after 1870, when Alfred Baldwin raised £20,000 and bought out his brothers to take sole control of the business. He moved into Wilden House, opposite the works, with his wife and young son, who had been born at the family's previous residence. The child was baptized Stanley, probably after his grandmother's maiden name; within the family this was always shortened to Stan.

Baldwin's mother's family was originally from Skye but settled in Ulster at Enniskillen after the Jacobite rising of 1745, and later converted to Methodism. The Revd James Macdonald (1761–1833) was ordained by John Wesley, and moved to England to preach. His son the Revd George Browne Macdonald (1805–1868) was Methodist minister in Wolverhampton, where he became friendly with Alfred Baldwin's elder brothers. His five daughters were a remarkable group of engaging and artistically gifted women who moved in the high-minded circles of William Morris and Rossetti; one was the mother of Rudyard Kipling, and two others married the artists Edward Burne-Jones and Edward Poynter. The latter occasion was a double wedding with Louisa's marriage to Alfred Baldwin, in Wolverhampton on 9 August 1866. Their relationship was close and loving: so much so that the parents feared that their son might feel excluded. Stanley was their only child. Not long after his birth Louisa developed a recurrent illness which made walking difficult and required long periods of rest in darkened rooms, and which lasted until a sudden recovery when Stanley was aged sixteen. She published poetry, children's books, and four novels, and encouraged Stanley's love of English language and literature.

Stanley Baldwin, first Earl Baldwin of Bewdley (1867–1947), by Vandyk, 1927

The making of a politician, 1867–1916 Stanley's childhood was not lonely as there were nearby relatives and frequent visits to and from his cousins. However, he had to entertain himself for much of the time at Wilden, and so developed his two lifelong recreations of country walks and reading. He spent much time in his father's library and became absorbed in history and literature, his favourite authors being Scott and Dickens. The ironworks at Wilden were in a rural setting, and as the young Stanley roamed the surrounding district he acquired an abiding love of the English countryside. These two activities came together in his vision of England, its history and the virtues of its people: fairness, moderation, civility, and common sense.

At ten Baldwin went in May 1878 to Hawtrey's Preparatory School at Slough, where he was active in sports and won eighteen prizes, coming top of the school. However, he tended not to do himself justice in examinations, and when thirteen he failed to win a scholarship to Harrow. He went there instead as an ordinary pupil in September 1881, and during his first four years won form prizes for history and mathematics, and competed in football, cricket, and squash. In June 1883 his father was summoned by a telegram from the headmaster, Dr Montagu Butler, owing to an item of juvenile pornography which Stanley had written and—compounding the offence—sent to his cousin Ambrose Poynter at Eton. Alfred Baldwin told his wife that the affair was 'much exaggerated and far more folly than anything else' (A. W. Baldwin, 44), but the incident soured Stanley's relationship with the headmaster. He felt that it was held against him when he was not made a prefect, and in the sixth form his work deteriorated as he assumed an attitude of detachment and laziness. In the autumn of 1885 he went up to Trinity College, Cambridge, where he read for the historical tripos and graduated with a third class in 1888. Baldwin later felt that he had not made the most of his opportunities at Cambridge. However, he does not seem to have disappointed his parents, and his father's letter a few weeks later on his twenty-first birthday was one of loving encouragement and confidence. One sentence in it, 'You ought to be a first-class man, and it is entirely in your own hands' (ibid., 53), may have been mistakenly recalled in Baldwin's comment of 1935 that his father had written, 'I hope you won't have a "Third" in life' (Jones, *Diary with Letters*, 155).

At Cambridge, Stanley was influenced by the works of J. R. Seeley and Sir Henry Maine—although in later life he humorously suggested otherwise—and was in close contact with the economic historian and college chaplain William Cunningham. He spent one Easter holiday at the Trinity College mission in the London slums and considered entering the Anglican ministry, but after graduating he returned home and joined his father's business in July 1888. Alfred Baldwin's ability and effort had not only saved the firm but led to substantial growth despite the economic difficulties of the period, and he played an increasingly prominent role in the London trade from the 1880s. Responsive to new techniques, he expanded his activities to south Wales, founding Alfred Baldwin & Co. as sheet metal manufacturers in Monmouthshire in 1886. The various companies were amalgamated into Baldwins Ltd in 1902, together with other steelworks and collieries in south Wales. This created an efficient and integrated business with assets of £1 million, employing about 4000 workers in several regions, and quoted on the London stock exchange. Stanley spent a quarter of a century in these concerns, and made his own contribution to their progress. After the first few months he adapted to the demands of business life; it engaged his interest, and he worked both hard and effectively. He took a metallurgy course, and was aware of technical developments. He made business tours of the United States and Canada in 1890, and of Germany and Austria-Hungary in 1897–8. After 1892 his father lived mainly in London and Stanley managed the several works; he had become a partner in 1890 and in 1902 became a managing director of Baldwins Ltd. He had sole responsibility for its midland division, which accounted for about a quarter of the company. The patriarchal relationship which his father had established with the Wilden workforce shaped his views and style of management. Stanley knew his workers and was at ease with them; his record of good labour relations was a source of pride and a model on which he later drew.

By 1906 Stanley had established himself as an experienced and capable businessman. On his father's death in 1908 he was invited to succeed him on the boards of the Great Western Railway and Metropolitan Bank, and he became vice-chairman of Baldwins Ltd. He remained engaged in business until appointed to ministerial office in 1917, and continued into the mid-1920s to talk of returning to commerce. The years in business had several important effects. They gave him self-confidence, the patience to wait for the timely moment, breadth of outlook, and experience of the wider world; he was never restricted to a narrow party view. Baldwin did not regard himself as a professional politician, but rather as a practical businessman 'called to special work' at a time when his experience of industry and labour was providentially valuable (S. Baldwin, *On England*, 1926, 19). Nor did he see himself as rich, although he inherited nearly £200,000 from his father and became wealthier before and during the First World War. His repeated assertions that he was an 'ordinary' or 'plain' man were sincere, and derived from his unostentatious upbringing across the road from the Wilden forges. After 1920 the economic problems of the iron and steel industries dramatically reduced his income; in common with similar businesses the value of Baldwins Ltd's shares collapsed and for many years they paid no dividend. Baldwin had to run down his capital and sell his London house, becoming more reliant on his ministerial salary and official residences.

This was in the future, and it was as a young businessman rising in the family firm that Baldwin married and began a family in the 1890s. While he was staying with his Burne-Jones cousins at Rottingdean, near Brighton, his eye was caught by Lucy Ridsdale [*see below*]. Previously rather shy with young women, Baldwin was attracted by her 'absolute innocence and unworldliness' (Baldwin to his mother, April 1892, Hyde, 27). They were married on 12 September 1892 in Rottingdean parish church, and had seven children. Their first was a still-born son in January 1894; the six surviving children were Diana (1895–1982), Leonora, known as Lorna (1896–1989), (Pamela) Margaret, known as Margot (1897–1976), Oliver (1899–1958), Esther, known as Betty (1902–1981), and (Arthur) Windham (1904–1976). Baldwin's chosen biographer, G. M. Young, later gave deep offence to the family by asserting that 'there was not much passion in their mating' (G. M. Young, 23). He misread their comfortable partnership, for as well as the many children there was enduring love, mutual confidence, and almost uncritical support, despite some differences in their temperaments and interests. Their elder son, Oliver, was affected by his experiences when serving in Armenia after the end of the First World War and became estranged from his parents in the 1920s, although there was some reconciliation after his election as a Labour MP in 1929. The family lived at Dunley Hall, 2 miles from Stourport, from 1892 to 1902, when Baldwin rented Astley Hall, which was more suitable for his growing family and status, but still not far from the Wilden works. He bought Astley in 1912 and it remained his home thereafter, although between 1923 and 1937 he was there only briefly at Christmas and in the summer. His London address was 27 Queen's Gate, South Kensington, from 1908 to 1912, when he acquired the lease of 93 Eaton Square. This was sold in 1925, and when out of office in 1929–31 it was only through the generosity of the duke of Westminster that Baldwin found an affordable London residence, at 10 Upper Brook Street, and so was able to remain in politics.

Baldwin's involvement in public life began in support of his father, who sat as Conservative MP for Bewdley (West Worcestershire) from 1892 to 1908. Although it was a safe seat, regular speaking and canvassing were expected, and Stanley became known throughout the division; he also took part in local government and societies, and became a magistrate in 1897. Like his father and many other Conservative industrialists, he supported Joseph Chamberlain's 'tariff reform' policy after 1903. He began to seek a constituency in the area, and in 1906 stood unsuccessfully at Kidderminster. He was more disheartened not to be selected as candidate for the Worcester City by-election in 1907, and considered that his chance had passed. However, the sudden death of his father from a heart attack on 13 February 1908 created a vacancy at Bewdley. He was unanimously invited to stand as Conservative candidate for his late father's seat, and after an unopposed return was introduced into the House of Commons on 3 March 1908. His maiden speech was delivered on 22 June 1908 in opposition to a Liberal measure for an eight-hour day in the coal industry. Quietly delivered to a largely empty House, and making little impact at the time, it demonstrates that key features of Baldwin's approach were present from the start. It was already well judged in tone, with self-deprecatory touches of humour which enhanced rather than obscured his message. It exposed his opponents' inconsistencies in a gently reproving manner, but was strikingly non-partisan and ascribed honesty of purpose to those on both sides of the issue. Most of all, it was related directly to his own expertise and model of good industrial relations.

After this Baldwin kept a low profile, but the handful of similar short speeches which he made before 1914 were well received for their moderation and sincerity. He was one of twelve Conservative MPs who voted for the second reading of the Old Age Pensions Act in 1908, and he approved the principle of the National Insurance Act. He played a minor part in the Unionist Social Reform Committee, an unofficial body devising a more active social agenda. He said little during the bitter struggle over Irish home rule, and favoured a moderate compromise. When war broke out he found little that he could do, although from June 1915 he worked many hours on a judicial committee reviewing the cases of internees. He was a member of the Unionist Business Committee, a back-bench 'ginger group', and hosted meetings of Conservative MPs concerned over Lloyd George's move to the War Office in July 1916. By the end of 1916 he had lost confidence in Asquith and became convinced that a change was needed, a conclusion which he found shared by his cousin Rudyard Kipling. Frustrated that he was contributing little to the war effort at Westminster, he considered giving up his seat to concentrate on local work but was persuaded by Lucy to remain. By December 1916 he was an inconspicuous but respected back-bencher who would have been on nobody's list of possible future prime ministers, least of all his own.

The rise to the premiership, 1916–1923 The First World War had a crucial impact on Baldwin's outlook and political career. Too old to fight himself, his feelings of duty and service were powerfully engaged. He felt humble in comparison to those risking their lives, and convinced that political leadership after the war must live up to the sacrifice of the dead. The wartime atmosphere of national unity and class co-operation reinforced his values and beliefs, and his focus moved from business to government and politics. At the same time the absence of many Conservative MPs on war service opened the way to his advance.

In December 1916 the leader of the Conservative Party, Andrew Bonar Law, who had joined Lloyd George's coalition as chancellor of the exchequer, needed a parliamentary private secretary. The post was at the most junior level, but discretion and reliability were vital. Baldwin's name was suggested by the chief whip, Lord Edmund Talbot, and endorsed by Law's youthful private secretary, J. C. C. Davidson, and he was offered the unpaid position. Its lowly status appealed to Baldwin, and his appointment was announced on 22 December 1916. Baldwin would also answer questions in the Commons on behalf of the new financial secretary to the treasury, (Samuel) Hardman Lever, who was not an MP and would be working in the United States. On 29 January 1917 Baldwin was appointed a junior lord of the Treasury; as this was normally a whip's position, it was stated that he was assisting the chancellor of the exchequer. His success in this role led to a close working relationship and friendship with Law, and on 18 June 1917 the position was regularized when he became financial secretary jointly with Lever; when the latter retired in May 1919, the post reverted to Baldwin alone.

This was the most prominent of all of the junior ministerships; in prestige it was equalled by the under-secretary at the Foreign Office, but the responsibilities of the Treasury were wider and involved more work in the House. In addition, Law's position as second figure in the government and a member of the five-man war cabinet meant that Baldwin's responsibilities were much greater than normal. There was a heavy workload, particularly in answering questions and speaking in the Commons, where he sometimes also deputized for Law as leader of the House. Baldwin continued to work well with Austen Chamberlain when the latter became chancellor after the general election of 1918, although the personal relationship was not as close. As financial secretary, Baldwin acquired a wide range of administrative experience and made many contacts among the junior ministers and back-benchers. His competent handling of the post enhanced his reputation, without marking him out as a rising star. In May 1920 Law offered him the governor-generalships of South Africa or Australia, which were customarily drawn from solid and dependable middle-rank figures, but was not surprised when he declined. Baldwin's courteous manner in the House and the high regard in which he was widely held also led to his being mentioned as a possible speaker at this time, but he remained where he was and in June 1920 was made a privy councillor.

In March 1921 Law retired owing to illness, and Austen Chamberlain became Conservative leader. In the ensuing reshuffle Baldwin was promoted to Lloyd George's cabinet as president of the Board of Trade on 1 April. He was recommended for the post by Law, and his appointment was intended to reassure opinion on the Conservative benches, where doubts about the coalition were beginning to emerge. It was also important to retain an orthodox Conservative in this key economic post, especially as it had charge of the most controversial measure of the session. The Safeguarding of Industries Bill gave tariff protection to specific industries, but there were many pitfalls and sensitivities along the way. Baldwin handled them effectively, although he was exhausted by the time of its third reading on 12 August 1921. In the following session he was responsible for another significant measure with protectionist aspects, the Merchandise Marks Act, which required a product to show its country of origin. His steady reputation with backbench Conservative MPs led Austen Chamberlain to ask him to take a leading part in securing the passage of the Anglo-Irish treaty in December 1921.

Throughout this period Baldwin was a mainly silent observer in Lloyd George's cabinet, becoming increasingly alienated by the combination of expediency and manoeuvre with which matters were tackled. Invited by the prime minister to comment on a financial issue at one meeting, he responded that he felt like 'the director of a fraudulent company engaged in cooking the balance sheet' (G. M. Young, 29). He was in sympathy with Conservative Party opposition to the possibility of an early and rushed renewal of the coalition's mandate in the general election scare of January 1922, and commented privately on the atmosphere of intrigue that pervaded the government. His unhappiness was crystallized by the Chanak crisis in September 1922, which led to a breach with Lloyd George and the senior Conservative ministers who supported him. Holidaying at Aix-les-Bains in the French Alps, Baldwin became aware from the newspapers that the government was risking a war in Turkey. On returning on 1 October, he found that the crisis was being used to precipitate an election and continue the coalition in its present form. He was almost alone in the cabinet in objecting to this, and decided that he would resign. With all the party's senior figures ranged against him, he expected to be on the losing side and that it would be the end of his political career. Instead, and unexpectedly, the political convulsion of October 1922 swept away the existing Conservative leadership and catapulted Baldwin to the political heights.

Although supported by only one even less prominent cabinet minister (Sir Arthur Griffith-Boscawen), Baldwin's hostility to the coalition was shared by key figures among Conservative Party managers, many of the junior ministers, and a large majority of back-benchers, and constituency opinion. He also played a part in persuading Law to come out of retirement and provide the vital element of a credible alternative leader. This was the crucial factor in the fall of the coalition, but Baldwin also spoke to telling effect in the decisive meeting of Conservative MPs at the Carlton Club on 19 October. He articulated the fear that Lloyd George would divide and destroy the Conservative Party as he had the Liberals, and underlined the danger of his methods: 'A dynamic force is a very terrible thing; it may crush you, but it is not necessarily right' (Carlton Club speech, Middlemas and Barnes, 123). Deep hostility to Lloyd George and rumours that his allies among the Conservative leadership were plotting to restore the coalition particularly influenced Baldwin and his inner circle during the next ten years. There were several instances of this antagonism, including Baldwin's invented 'Afghan' proverb, alluding to Lloyd George's nickname: 'He who lives in the bosom of the goat spends his remaining years plucking out the fleas.' However, the defaced picture of Lloyd George which Thomas Jones found at Astley Hall has been given exaggerated significance; it was in a scrapbook prepared some years earlier by Baldwin's mother for his children, and was most likely the result of some juvenile scribbling by one of them from before 1914.

After the Carlton Club vote overwhelmingly rejected the coalition, Law became Conservative Party leader and prime minister. He offered the Treasury to Baldwin, the most senior and experienced anti-coalitionist in the Commons. At first Baldwin demurred and suggested Reginald McKenna, the former Liberal chancellor, but when the latter declined Baldwin accepted the post on 24 October 1922. In January 1923 Baldwin visited the United States and negotiated terms for the repayment of Britain's war debt which were stiff but in his view the best available. This opinion became public when he spoke unguardedly to reporters on his return on 29 January, precipitating a cabinet crisis. Law was vehemently opposed to the terms and almost resigned, but was persuaded by the cabinet to accept them; after this his relations with Baldwin were strained. On 16 February 1923 Baldwin's speech on the address displayed a power of language, sincerity, and idealism which made a deep impression on both the Commons and the country, closing with the affirmation that 'salvation for this country and the whole world' was to be found in four simple words: 'Faith, Hope, Love, and Work.' He presented only one budget as chancellor, and on 16 April 1923 in a comparatively short and lively speech used the unexpected revenue surplus of £100 million mainly to redeem debt, and also reduced income tax by 6*d.* and beer duty by a penny.

First term as prime minister 1923–1924 In May 1923 Law's illness forced his retirement, and a new prime minister had to be found from within the present cabinet. The choice lay between Baldwin, the novice chancellor, and Lord Curzon, who was an experienced foreign secretary but a difficult colleague. Law declined to advise the king, who chose Baldwin for several reasons: he had the support of key figures in the cabinet, and was thought more likely to be able to reunite the Conservative Party and thereby strengthen the government. Above all, a prime minister in the House of Lords, where the Labour Party—now the official opposition—had no official representation, would have been a constitutional problem and have emphasized divisive issues of class privilege. Baldwin seemed more suited to the new democratic age, and so these twists of fortune brought him unexpectedly to the premiership on 22 May 1923. He was elected leader of the Conservative Party on 28 May, and also continued as chancellor until 27 August 1923, when—McKenna having again declined—he appointed Neville Chamberlain. The new prime minister felt the office had come too soon and that he lacked experience; naïvety certainly appeared to many to be the hallmark of his brief first government. He mishandled an approach to Austen Chamberlain, and the leading Conservative former coalitionists remained aloof and critical. On 19 September Baldwin met Poincaré in Paris and assumed too readily that he had resolved the Ruhr crisis, although the meeting began the process which led to the Dawes plan of 1924.

Defects of judgement seemed even more evident during the following weeks, as Baldwin propelled his party into an unnecessary general election. In fact, although the parliament still had four and a half years to run, the problems facing the government were mounting. Unemployment was rising and the Labour Party advancing, but the government seemed to be drifting. Agriculture was in crisis and, still disunited, Conservative morale was slipping. However, Baldwin's attempt to break this downward spiral led to disarray and defeat, and nearly ended his career. Like most Conservatives he believed that protectionist tariffs would revive industry and employment; this was his primary motive, rather than tactical concerns of reuniting his party or pre-empting Lloyd George. After mulling over the problem while holidaying at Aix and then hosting the Imperial Economic Conference on his return in October, he resolved to declare his belief in protection. However, Law had pledged in 1922 that there would be no move to tariffs in the present parliament. For this reason, as soon as Baldwin declared his hand at the Conservative conference at Plymouth on 25 October 1923, a pre-election atmosphere was created. Baldwin succeeded in keeping his cabinet together and in avoiding the resignation of its anti-tariff minority, even though he decided that the election could not be delayed and secured a dissolution from the king on 12 November.

The election campaign raised Baldwin's standing, and he was recognized as his party's best electoral asset, but the Conservatives were unprepared, and their proposals were vague and contradictory. Although Central Office projected victory, the outcome in December 1923 was a net loss of eighty-eight seats; the Conservatives had lost their majority, although they remained the largest single party in the House of Commons. Baldwin's first reaction was that he should resign as prime minister immediately, but after reflecting at Chequers over the weekend of 8–9 December he decided to stay in office and meet parliament. Resignation would open the way to revived coalitionism and efforts to deny Labour the chance of office, while there were tactical advantages in making the Liberals side openly with Labour. After the Christmas recess the government was defeated on 21 January 1924; Baldwin resigned the next day and the first Labour government was formed. Despite the election defeat Baldwin survived as Conservative leader because the alternative was a humiliating return to coalitionism, which most of the party disliked even more. After a period of fruitless intrigue during the recess, the Conservative former coalitionists accepted that no alternative leader would win sufficient support. The outcome was the reunion of the party under Baldwin's continued leadership, which was confirmed by a party meeting on 11 February 1924. The recovery of unity was welcome, but it was not the motive for Baldwin's misguided tariff venture; there had been no hidden plan, and certainly no riding for a fall.

Character, outlook, and image By 1924 Baldwin had established his position as a national figure with a distinctive message shaped by his character and beliefs. Among Conservative leaders only Disraeli and Margaret Thatcher have conveyed their own personal vision with similar impact and influence. Baldwin often attributed his imagination and gift with words to his mother's Celtic background, although his personality and mannerisms had many similarities with his father's temperament. According to one of his ministers, Baldwin was 'emotional, impulsive, secretive, and intensely personal in [his] likes, dislikes, and moral judgements' (Amery, *My Political Life*, 505). Baldwin's outwardly stolid manner concealed a nervous disposition. One of his daughters recalled that he 'abhorred noise and shouting' and 'had a horror of being asked questions'. He was uncomfortable at larger social events 'and always tried to keep near the wall in case the floor gave way!' (Margaret Huntington-Whiteley, in Hyde, 43). He had a number of distracting nervous mannerisms and facial twitches, was prone to fidgeting, and had a habit when sitting in the Commons of sniffing or licking at the edges of his order papers. In times of stress he would compulsively pace up and down the room, pouring out a flow of conversation as he rehearsed events or debated a decision. He often felt sick with tension before delivering a speech and drained afterwards, although once under way was steadier and at times uplifted.

Baldwin was of medium height, and his fairly slim figure of 1923 became considerably more rounded during the 1930s. He had blue eyes and his bushy eyebrows and hair, which was parted in the centre and smoothed back, were originally a sandy colour. He was a regular smoker, and the pipe which he used from the First World War onwards became a public hallmark; it gave him something to occupy his hands, and he would spend much time on the rituals of cleaning and lighting it. Baldwin had a robust sense of humour and could both charm and fascinate, but there were also times when he seemed self-absorbed and unappreciative. He was sometimes awkward in personal relations with colleagues, but managed his cabinets in a relaxed style. He sought consensus, and was proud of the fact that only one, relatively minor, figure had resigned from his 1924–9 cabinet because of disagreement on policy. Baldwin was not an interventionist by nature: 'he never moves of his own motion' was the jaundiced view of Austen Chamberlain (Austen Chamberlain to Ida Chamberlain, 2 July 1931, Birmingham University Library, Austen Chamberlain MSS, AC/5/1/545). He had learned the merits of delegation during his business career, and this was his customary style of management. In his view the prime minister should give advice and support, rather than meddle or dictate. He preferred to trust his chosen colleagues to tackle the problems in their domains, with inter-departmental frictions resolved in informal meetings and difficult decisions debated in cabinet under his adjudicatory chairmanship. However, the willingness to wait for consensus could give the impression that Baldwin had no clear agenda and tended to drift, following opinion rather than leading it. He could take some time before reaching a decision, a process which he called 'rumination'. This could appear to be procrastination, but once he had formed a conclusion he usually adhered to it and acted with firmness, and he could be dogged and stubborn once convinced that his course was right. He did not always reveal his inner thoughts or explain his actions fully to his colleagues, and the result could be incomprehension and the assumption that he was acting impulsively. Baldwin's concerns and timing were not primarily shaped by considerations of parliamentary tactics or partisan opportunities, and this further tended to confuse his colleagues and disappoint his supporters.

Baldwin was sometimes criticized for focusing too much on generalities, and detail had no fascination for him. While there was a suggestion of intellectual laziness, he was not—despite some self-deprecatory remarks—an indolent man. His periods of nervous and physical exhaustion were the product of responsibility combined with consistent hard work. When parliament was sitting he regularly worked up to fourteen hours on weekdays, and felt himself to be 'at the beck and call of everyone' (letter to his mother, 1923, in Hyde, 163). He spent much of this time in the Palace of Westminster, sitting on the front bench or working in his room near the chamber. He was not very fond of 10 Downing Street, but loved the country estate of Chequers and stayed there every available weekend during his periods of office. Here he could quietly read and walk, relaxing in the company of the family and a few friends. Baldwin had a lifelong enjoyment of reading, and often turned a conversation towards books. He loved music and played the piano, visited the theatre, and regularly attended cricket matches; in May 1938 he was elected president of the MCC. His main form of exercise and physical relaxation was walking in the countryside, rambling for miles. This was also his restorative during his summer holiday, which usually lasted for at least a month; from 1921 this was taken at Aix-les-Bains. The countryside was a haven, a source of peace and tranquillity: 'life in the country makes you see things whole', Baldwin remarked in 1935 (Butler, *Art of the Possible*, 30).

Baldwin greatly preferred oral to written communication: 'my tongue, not my pen, is my instrument' (Jones, *Diary with Letters*, 540). His private correspondence was mainly personal, and he was the master of the short friendly note of congratulations or condolence. To spread the burden of crafting the many speeches which he gave, Baldwin innovated in using his aides and advisers as speech-writers. He drew on several people, but most of all on Thomas Jones, who served Baldwin as deputy secretary of the cabinet in his first two ministries and continued to assist after retiring from the civil service in 1930. Even so, their drafts reflected Baldwin's guidance and views, and many of the most important passages or entire speeches were entirely his own. Baldwin relied for support and an audience on an inner circle in which the most important figures were the Davidsons, Jones, and Geoffrey Dawson, the editor of *The Times*. The close bond with J. C. C. Davidson was forged when Baldwin first assisted Law at the Treasury, and continued when Davidson transferred to work for Baldwin during Law's first retirement. Baldwin appointed him chancellor of the duchy of Lancaster in 1923–4 and in the 1930s (a non-departmental post in which he effectively acted as chief of staff) and—with less success—as Conservative Party chairman in 1926–30. Equally important was Baldwin's avuncular relationship with Davidson's wife, Joan (known as Mimi), a friend of one of Baldwin's daughters. She was both bracing and supportive to him, and his favourite companion on long country walks.

Baldwin's sincere religious faith was based on the certainty of divine judgment and providence, and belief in a purpose in life. The concepts of service and duty were central to his personality and conduct: Thomas Jones considered that 'he felt things deeply, and his conscience was more active than his intellect' (Jones, *Diary with Letters*, xxx). Baldwin's religion was practical, concerned with good works and Christian conduct, and derived from the King James Bible and the Book of Common Prayer. His outlook was a simple and implicitly democratic protestantism, believing 'from my heart the words of Browning, "All service ranks the same with God"' (S. Baldwin, *On England*,

1926, 19). He was comfortable with a low-church and evangelical frame of mind, and proud of the nonconformist elements in his ancestry. As prime minister, he was invited to address the most important nonconformist bodies, and spoke in a moral language which resonated with them. Baldwin and his wife began each day by kneeling together in prayer, a routine which did not change when he was prime minister. They believed that they were working 'for the country and for God's sake' (Jones, *Diary with Letters*, xxxiv).

Baldwin considered that 'the political career properly viewed is really a kind of ministry' (S. Baldwin, *On England*, 1926, 197), and spoke with sincere conviction of offering the 'service of our lives' (S. Baldwin, *Service of our Lives*, 1937, 144). He wrote privately after the defeat of 1923 that his motive for continuing in politics was 'the longing to help the bewildered multitude of common folk' which 'only comes from love and pity' (Baldwin to Joan Davidson, 24 Dec 1923, *Memoirs of a Conservative*, 193). He put much emphasis on the responsibility of those in more fortunate positions to raise not only the standard of living but also the 'standard of ideals' (speech to the Primrose League, *The Times*, 3 May 1924). Duties rather than rights were the path to progress; betterment could not be imposed by law but grew from the moral sense of society. This in turn was shaped by the conduct of leading men, a belief which sustained Baldwin's antipathy towards Lloyd George and the press barons. He saw his mission as cleaning up public life after it had been tainted during the coalition, which had come to represent every negative force. When under pressure Baldwin would raise these moral boundaries, and tended to portray himself as a lone crusader—'every crook in the country is out for my scalp', he wrote at the height of the party crisis in 1930 (Baldwin to Irwin, 16 Oct 1930, BL OIOC, Halifax MSS, Eur. C.152/19/1/147).

The sacrifice of the First World War deepened Baldwin's sense of duty and obligation, and he tried to set an example by anonymously giving up much of his fortune to reduce the national debt. His conscience was troubled by the large profits which Baldwins Ltd had made, and he sought to return these. Calculating his wealth at £580,000, he realized one-fifth of this and presented £120,000 of war loan stock to the Treasury for cancellation. In the hope that others would follow, he explained his action in an anonymous letter in *The Times* on 24 June 1919 (this was signed 'F. S. T.', which stood for 'financial secretary to the Treasury'). The story became known after he became prime minister, further adding to his reputation for integrity and modesty. It was important to him that the service he gave required sacrifices, and hence his comments about the unpleasantness of political life and his desire to retire to country life and obscurity. He discerned the working of providence in his unexpected elevation: 'I knew that I had been chosen as God's instrument for the work of the healing of the nation' (A. W. Baldwin, 328).

The early years at Wilden shaped Baldwin's outlook; the local roots, framework of stability and tradition, and communal feeling between employer and worker were the inspirations and examples on which he later drew, although he was aware that it was a world which was passing. He recognized the disruptions which had taken place because of the war, and considered the post-war world to be unstable and in need of careful handling. Baldwin shared the general Conservative apprehension about the vast new electorate created in 1918, and saw it as a race against time to educate 'democracy', which 'can rise to great heights [but] can also sink to great depths' (S. Baldwin, *On England*, 1926, 71). Baldwin refused to believe that there was anything to fear as far as the British working class was concerned, provided it was treated fairly and with respect. His focus on industrial relations directly addressed the social and economic concerns of the day, and placed responsibilities on owners and managers as much as unions and workers. Baldwin wanted a stable capitalist system with a human heart, economic freedom with social duty. He believed in individual responsibility and moral choice, and opposed the soulless uniformity of state control or dictatorship. For these reasons Baldwin was always more concerned with the general atmosphere than with the details of policy and legislation. His concern was with public attitudes, and it was these which he sought to reach and shape.

Baldwin's principal means of doing so was through his speeches. He paid particular attention to non-political bodies and neutral audiences, and these provided the venues for many of his most influential speeches. Together with their content, this elevated Baldwin to a unique position of appearing to be almost 'above politics'. His hallmarks were a positive message and an emphasis on honesty rather than party dogma. He was noted for his generous treatment of opponents and avoided making personal attacks. Baldwin evoked simple images which interlocked with the values and traditions of British political culture: the rural heritage, the Christian virtues of charity and patience, tolerance based upon mutual respect, a generosity of spirit which accepted elements of merit in other points of view, an appeal to co-operation based upon goodwill, and a desire to seek common ground. Baldwin used the rhetoric of the missionary rather than the politician, talking of 'preaching' a 'gospel' and evoking prayer in phrases such as 'give peace in our time, O Lord'. His language transcended party boundaries, and he could convincingly claim that 'the twin ideals of social justice and individual freedom' were Conservative aims (S. Baldwin, *An Interpreter of England*, 1939, 111–12). His style of Conservatism was inclusive, moderate, and based on a moral agenda—a positive creed of civic values and virtue. Delivered in this way, it had a powerful appeal to three key electoral groups of the inter-war era: former Liberals (contributing further to that party's disintegration), women (who were often repelled by tones of harshness and confrontation), and the uncommitted new generation of voters (who were frequently impatient with pre-war controversies).

Baldwin was convinced that the Labour Party's idealistic appeal could be countered only from the moral high ground. He presented an open attitude and generous tone, acknowledging the sincerity and idealism of Labour's 'best elements'. He feared that more dangerous forces lay beneath the Labour Party: direct-action syndicalism, Bolshevism, confiscatory socialism, class hatred, and envy. To contain these, he sought to encourage Labour towards constitutionalism. He treated Labour as a conventional political party; he was not frightened by its aspirations to government, but welcomed them as a move towards responsibility. He was determined to show 'fair play' to Labour after his defeats in the general elections of 1923 and 1929, and he encouraged Conservative MPs and ministers to avoid provocative styles or shows of superiority. Baldwin's strategy combined encouraging the moderate and parliamentary sides of the labour movement with firm resistance to extremism and unconstitutional pressure. At the same time Conservative electoral success was partly based on arousing fear of socialism. In election campaigns Baldwin would raise concerns that Labour's moderates were not really in control, thus mobilizing support to contain Labour without having to condemn or alienate it. He suggested that a gulf existed between the common sense of the British worker and the foreign influences of 'German Socialism and Russian Communism and French Syndicalism' (S. Baldwin, *On England*, 1926, 153), to which Italian Fascism was added later. Baldwin disliked arrogance and dogma, remarking that 'intelligentsia' was 'a very ugly word for a very ugly thing' (S. Baldwin, *Our Inheritance*, 1928, 123–4). As dictatorships challenged democracy in the 1930s, Baldwin saw Britain as a beacon to other countries, keeping alive the 'torch of freedom'.

The image of Baldwin as a 'countryman' was an important part of his appeal, especially in establishing his identity in 1923–4. His appearance reinforced this: the baggy suits and pipe-smoking which were fixed upon by cartoonists were not contrived, but they synchronized with the popular view of an ordinary and trustworthy man. Although rural England was not a constant theme, it was the subject of some of Baldwin's most vivid and affecting passages. Later criticism of this as inappropriate to the problems of an urban and industrial society misses the point that these images were the means and not the ends. Baldwin was not trying to turn the clock back, but to graft the rootless modern experience on to the solid oak of the past: 'the country represents the eternal values and the eternal traditions from which we must never allow ourselves to be separated' (S. Baldwin, *This Torch of Freedom*, 1935, 120). His language resonated with the urban masses and suburban classes, many of whom shared the view that 'England is the country, and the country is England' (S. Baldwin, *On England*, 1926, 6). Even so, perhaps the most central of Baldwin's speeches was not the 'On England' speech of 1924 but those on 'Service' in March 1925 and his Glasgow University rectorial address 'Freedom and discipline' in January 1930.

Baldwin's rapport with the public was founded on his personality and message, which sprang from the heart. His religious faith and gift of language—his cousin Kipling described him as the true poet in the family—enabled him to put his finger on the national pulse. Baldwin made a powerful appeal to the public mood of inter-war Britain, crossing class and party boundaries, and his sincerity and goodwill earned the respect of many opponents. The time and attention that he gave to the House of Commons established a fund of benevolence that enabled him to surmount some blunders with little damage. His experience and sensitivity to the mood of the House were the basis for his most effective speeches, and he was acknowledged even by his critics to possess the power to raise a debate to a higher level. However, there were also uninspired orations which fell flat and periods when he did not speak much in the House or seem to offer the lead that his colleagues and party were looking for. These partly coincided with periods of uncertainty and the absence of a theme of principle and importance—in 1928 and 1936—or periods in opposition, when he did not want to commit himself too soon or specifically. The pressure of work, the need to keep some distance, and the changed and greatly increased parliamentary Conservative Party made him a more remote figure to many MPs after 1931.

Baldwin was not technically skilled as an orator, and it was sincerity and clarity which made his best speeches effective. His usual stance was to hold his jacket lapels or thrust his hands deep into the pockets, from which they emerged at intervals to smooth back his hair. A member of his first cabinet described his speaking as 'not in the least oratorical, but intensely human', with a delivery that was 'slow, steady, uneloquent but convincing' (*Real Old Tory Politics*, 18 March 1925). He had a sense of timing, catching the moment and the mood. The tone was low-key, taking the audience into his confidence and going to the heart of the issue. There were no distracting rhetorical flourishes, as the use of plain language was his great skill. There was concern, not confrontation; responsiveness, not dismissal; reasonableness, not prejudice; explanation, not invective; and humour, without humiliation or sarcasm. Through it all ran the 'human touch' and an empathy with the 'ordinary man': middle-class, middle-aged, middle-brow in culture, middle of the road in politics. Baldwin reached a mass audience far beyond any previous politician. His speeches were collected in books which sold thousands of copies, and the only figure to have exceeded him in this was Winston Churchill. He exploited the cinema newsreels and made masterly use of the new medium of radio, employing a conversational style as if addressing each listener individually. His public image of the pipe-smoking Englishman, honest but not clever, was both reassuring and popular. He became a trusted figure, familiar to the public at large in a way in which no previous prime minister had ever been.

The first Labour government, 1924 Baldwin's public identity became firmly established between 1924 and 1926, as his influence and authority grew. In February 1924, at the Conservative Party meeting which confirmed his leadership and the dropping of the tariff policy, he spoke of the 'perfectly genuine and altruistic feeling' of wanting to improve society which inspired Labour's supporters, and declared, 'it is a spirit which can only be beaten by a similar spirit in our Party' (*The Times*, 12 Feb 1924, 17). In a series of major public speeches during the following months Baldwin set out what came to be termed the 'new conservatism'. This did not change the party's fundamental principles, but expressed them through an ethos and language which was Baldwin's own. Principled, distinctive, moderate, and unprovocative, it helped the Conservative Party to capture the inter-war middle ground. The period in opposition also saw improvements in party organization and work on future policy. Baldwin established a series of parliamentary policy committees, each chaired by the relevant former minister, and their conclusions were published in the pamphlet *Looking Ahead* on 20 June 1924. Another innovation was a secretariat to support these committees and the shadow cabinet; although this lapsed when the party returned to office, the parliamentary committees continued under back-bench chairmanship and became a permanent and important feature of the Conservative parliamentary party.

Baldwin made two other striking public statements during these months. He gave one of his most admired non-political addresses, 'On England', to the Royal Society of St George on 6 May. The other was typical in a different way, and more controversial. An interview published in *The People* on 18 May 1924 concluded with unexpectedly sharp attacks on some of his critics, including Churchill and Birkenhead, while Rothermere and Beaverbrook were dismissed as 'men I would not have in my house' (Hyde, 211). Whether Baldwin expected this part of the conversation to be published is unclear, but in embarrassment he had to retreat behind denials and apologies. This incident, and the problems caused by Churchill's candidature in the Westminster Abbey by-election, revealed that tensions over coalitionism were still strong. However, these were echoes of the past rather than portents of the future. During the period of the first Labour government, the Conservative Party united behind Baldwin's political strategy. This looked to a realignment around the main parties of Conservative and Labour, and the disappearance of the Liberal Party, which would no longer have a role. With the minority Labour government getting into difficulties and the Liberals in disarray, Conservative confidence increased and the party looked forward to an election.

When the MacDonald ministry was defeated on 8 October 1924, Baldwin ruled out any arrangement with the Liberals and supported Labour's claim for a dissolution. The Conservatives were strongly placed for the election, and their mobilization of an anti-socialist vote was helped by Liberal disorganization and financial weakness. Baldwin maintained a restrained and moderate tone which was particularly effective in his radio broadcast, a new feature in this election. Aware that the radio audience listened at home, he spoke as if he was chatting by the fireside; this was far more effective than the speeches at mass meetings which the other party leaders used. Speaking of the left-wing dogma of class hostility, he affirmed that 'no gospel founded on hate will ever be the gospel of our people' (Middlemas and Barnes, 275). The 'Zinoviev letter', which appeared in confused circumstances near the end of the campaign, was not the cause of Conservative victory but reinforced some of their themes. Baldwin's moral tone and message of harmony made a particular appeal to former Liberal voters, and thus the Liberal collapse resulted in unexpectedly large Conservative gains. The 412 MPs returned were more than the totals of the Liberals in 1906 or Labour in 1945, and gave Baldwin a huge overall majority.

The search for stability: second term as prime minister, 1924–1929 Now truly prime minister in his own right, Baldwin began his second term on 4 November 1924. He was fifty-seven, at the height of his powers, acknowledged to possess a unique rapport with the public, and securely in control of his party. Baldwin used the strength of his position to reunite the Conservative leadership with appointments which were generous, but clearly of his own making. Curzon was displaced from the Foreign Office to make way for Austen Chamberlain and Birkenhead was given the India Office, but Baldwin adroitly excluded Horne, whom he disliked. The boldest and most unexpected move was the offer of the Treasury to Winston Churchill, who had recently been making his way back to the Conservative Party. These appointments put the most influential and effective former coalitionists in prestigious posts, but ones where they would be fully occupied by their departmental responsibilities. The choice of Churchill as chancellor took everyone by surprise, but his presence there underlined Baldwin's pledge not to move to protectionism, while the need for economies in public spending would give full scope to his ingenuity. Neville Chamberlain, who had the strongest claim on the exchequer, preferred instead to go to the Ministry of Health, where he embarked on a major programme of reform in local government, factory legislation, housing, and the poor law. With other posts filled by the most successful ministers of the 1922–4 government, the result was a powerful and balanced cabinet team. Baldwin allowed wide-ranging discussion and chaired the cabinet in a relaxed and adjudicatory style, but where his views were definite his interventions were decisive. Although there was some friction at the start, it became a cohesive team. The cabinet was notable for the continuity of its membership; even in its later period, when several ministers were ill or ineffectual, Baldwin decided against reshuffling his pack.

Baldwin avoided any appearance of triumphalism after his victory, which he presented as an opportunity for service, with much hard work ahead. His aim was to restore stability and good government, which would lead to the recovery of confidence, revival of trade, and reduction of unemployment. The return to the gold standard in Churchill's first budget of April 1925 was part of this; most financial and economic opinion endorsed it, but the pound was over-valued and it compounded Britain's trade problems. Baldwin's government had solid achievements on several fronts, although most of these were in its first eighteen months in office. At home there was the granting of pensions to widows and orphans, local government and poor-law reform, measures for transport and education, and the creation of a national electricity generating authority, something which Baldwin particularly supported. The vexed issue of the Northern Ireland boundary was laid to rest in December 1925, with Baldwin's relaxed personal style during a weekend meeting at Chequers playing an important part. In foreign affairs the Locarno treaty seemed to herald a new era of peace and the government sought further disarmament, although by the end of its life this had led to friction with the United States over the differing needs of their navies. The government encouraged rationalization in the cotton and steel industries, but gave only limited extensions of the safeguarding duties and refused to include major sectors of the economy.

Industrial peace was Baldwin's key theme from 1923 to 1927, as he sought to bring both employers and workers to embrace a spirit of 'partnership in industry'. He wished to discourage reliance on the state to solve industrial problems, which he regarded as a dangerous legacy of the Lloyd George era. He wanted a more self-reliant approach in which industries worked out their own problems, with the government aiding as adjudicator. Baldwin personally shaped and controlled his government's policy in this key area, and imposed a moderate course on the more hard-line and anti-trade union elements in the cabinet and party. The first instance arose over a bill introduced by a Conservative back-bencher, F. A. Macquisten, on the contentious issue of the trade union political levy. Union members had to take the awkward step of 'contracting out' of the levy, and changing the law to make those who wished to pay 'contract in' had widespread Conservative support. However, Baldwin considered that this would be seen as a provocative and partisan use of the government's majority, and told a stunned cabinet that he would intervene against passing the bill. Baldwin's speech on 6 March 1925 established him as the most powerful parliamentary speaker of the era, and was perhaps his greatest triumph. He acknowledged that the principle of the bill was right, but asked his party to hold their hand as a gesture towards creating 'a new atmosphere in a new parliament for a new age, in which people can come together'. Speaking with quiet sincerity in a packed and hushed chamber, he evoked a spirit of goodwill and closed with the moving affirmation that 'there are many in all ranks and all parties who will re-echo my prayer, "Give peace in our time, O Lord"' (*Hansard 5C*, 181, 6 March 1925, 840–41). The speech elevated the debate to a different moral plane, and had a tremendous impact. The bill was dropped, and Baldwin's authority over his cabinet and party was complete. He also touched a chord with many of the public; when the speech was printed in the booklet *Peace and Goodwill in Industry*, half a million copies were sold in three months.

Baldwin's second conciliatory gesture averted a potential general strike by granting a subsidy to the troubled coal industry on 30 July 1925. The trade unions celebrated 'Red Friday' as a victory and many Conservatives were uneasy, but Baldwin was aware that both the government's emergency organization and public opinion were not ready to face a general strike. He appointed a royal commission under Sir Herbert Samuel to produce a plan acceptable to both owners and miners, but stubbornness on both sides of the coal dispute thwarted this hope and the government's many other attempts to find a negotiated solution. No common ground had been found when the nine-month subsidy expired on 30 April 1926, and the owners sought to impose their terms with a lock-out from 1 May. The government's negotiations with the TUC failed to avert a national stoppage in support of the miners, which began on 3 May. Baldwin showed his greatest strengths in handling the unprecedented dangers of the general strike, and the combination of calmness and firmness which he displayed created a reassuring atmosphere and avoided reactions of provocation or panic. The government was now prepared and able to keep essential supplies moving; this was important at the outset, as the TUC leadership had no desire for a long struggle. Baldwin's most important move was to shift the issue from an industrial dispute to a threat to the constitution, in which the TUC were the anti-democratic force seeking to dictate to the legitimate government. This was the line which he took in his first speech in the Commons on 3 May, in the message to the public printed in the *British Gazette* on 6 May, and in the crucial broadcasts which he made on 8 and 12 May (the day the strike was called off). His tone throughout was one of sorrow not anger, and the strikers were depicted as misled rather than dangerous. Baldwin appealed for calm and fortitude, for support for the elected government, and for trust in himself. When the strike was abandoned he maintained the same conciliatory tone, calling for no reprisals and offering further government negotiations and help in the coal dispute. However, despite many hours of wearisome effort, the latter dragged on for another nine months.

Baldwin's public standing was at its height in the wake of the general strike, but he did not use this for any immediate purpose. Long hours of work and stress had left him physically and mentally drained, and he was also suffering from lumbago in the summer of 1926. He recovered during his holiday at Aix in September, but returned to a heavy workload and by April 1927 was again exhausted. His illness and tiredness, and the tiredness of some of his ministers, contributed to the sense that the government was drifting and lacked a strong lead. The middle and later phases of the ministry were preoccupied with a range of problems, for most of which there were no clear or immediate solutions. The hope for a new atmosphere in industry bore little fruit owing to the continuing economic stagnation and the bitterness of the coal strike. Legislation on trade union matters was inevitable in the wake of the general strike, and the Trade Disputes and Trade Union Act of 1927 was a generally moderate response. However, it included 'contracting in' for the political levy and aroused bitter opposition from the labour movement in parliament and the country, further souring the mood and denting Baldwin's conciliatory image. In August 1927 he became the first serving prime minister to visit an overseas dominion when he accompanied the prince of Wales on a nineteen-day tour across Canada, during which he delivered twenty-six speeches.

Baldwin maintained a moderate course to the end of the government. In keeping with the spirit of confidence in the good sense of democracy, in 1928 the franchise was equalized for both sexes at the age of twenty-one, and proposals to strengthen the powers of the House of Lords were dropped. In these and other areas Baldwin disappointed not only the right wing of the Conservative Party but also much of its mainstream. There were mutterings on the back benches and in the constituencies that the government was 'semi-socialist', and a spread of apathy and discontent. With unemployment stuck around the 1 million mark, there was strong pressure for the extension of safeguarding duties, especially to the depressed iron and steel industry. However, in 1928 Baldwin ruled this out owing to the pledge against protection which had been made at the 1924 election. Agriculture was in an even worse condition, and here again the government could offer little assistance without reopening the dangerous tariff issue. The House of Commons had a steady diet of worthy but dull measures, and it is this which explains the gap between the solid record of legislation on the one hand and the widespread impression of drift and lack of inspiration on the other. The government's last major measure, the Derating Bill, was too late to affect employment and too complex to be an effective election platform. After its passage Baldwin decided to hold the election in the spring and polling was fixed for 30 May 1929. The Conservatives entered the campaign with few positive cards other than the appeal of Baldwin himself, and their strategy was founded upon this. The slogans of 'Safety first' and 'Trust in Baldwin' were intended to contrast with the poor reputation of Lloyd George, whose effort to revitalize the Liberal Party posed the greatest danger to the seats that the Conservatives had won in 1924. Baldwin toured the country and was considered to have performed well, but his and Central Office's expectations of victory were dashed. Almost all the gains of 1924 were swept away, and only 260 Conservative MPs remained. Labour was for the first time the largest party in the Commons, although still lacking an overall majority. To show that he accepted the electoral verdict with good grace and preclude any coalitionist intrigues with Lloyd George, who held the parliamentary balance, Baldwin decided against meeting parliament and resigned as prime minister on 4 June.

Leader of the opposition, 1929–1931 The period in opposition during the second Labour government of 1929–31 was difficult for Baldwin. His moderate line had failed to keep the Conservatives in office, and the results had shifted the balance in the parliamentary party towards the safer and southern constituencies. Soon after the defeat pressures began to build for a change in policy—at least a major extension of the safeguarding duties, and preferably a full tariff programme, including duties on food imports. This left Baldwin in a difficult position, attempting to straddle the divide as party and public opinion diverged. His strategy during 1929–30 was based on the need to recover the lost seats in the urban midlands and north, which were essential if the Conservatives were to regain a majority. Any suggestion of 'food taxes' was still an electoral liability in these areas, and so Baldwin resisted the pressure for tariffs. This ran counter to the mood in the party's strongholds, and led to the internal crisis which seriously threatened his position in the summer and autumn of 1930. The balancing act on which Baldwin was engaged made it difficult to sound a strong lead, and this further disappointed his followers. Labour still seemed to be popular during 1929–30, and Baldwin did not want to precipitate an election too soon. This dictated a mild and cautious approach in parliament which combined with some lacklustre Commons performances to erode confidence in his leadership.

The main danger which Baldwin faced was the rising discontent of his followers, but extra pressure was added by the campaign of the press lords, led by Beaverbrook with Rothermere's support. The 'empire crusade' sought to push the Conservative Party towards a full tariff reform programme, including food taxes, and was dangerous because its vigour and policy had a powerful appeal in the tory heartlands. It was this which enabled it to apply pressure to back-bench MPs and to secure a worrying share of Conservative votes when it ran candidates in by-elections. Baldwin intensely disliked the idea of compromise with the press lords, but the support which they were mobilizing could not be ignored. From November 1929 to March 1931 there were periods of negotiation and uneasy co-operation, as well as open conflict. Baldwin was pushed into advances in party policy, but these seemed reluctant and minimal. Tensions rose in the summer of 1930, and Baldwin had to accept the departure of the unpopular Davidson from the party chairmanship. He was replaced by Neville Chamberlain, and tactical mistakes by the press lords enabled Baldwin to counter-attack. He summoned a party meeting at Caxton Hall on 24 June 1930, and swung the audience behind him in outrage at dictatorial demands made by Rothermere. Changing the issue from policy to the constitutional threat of dictation by the press was Baldwin's trump card throughout the crisis, and was played again in October 1930 and March 1931. The most serious phase of the party crisis came in September 1930, and Baldwin's colleagues began to consider his position hopeless. However, the impact of the slump and rising unemployment was changing the mood in the industrial regions, and on 9 October Baldwin announced that he would ask for a 'free hand' to introduce tariffs at the next election. Almost all of the party now rallied behind him, and his leadership was endorsed by a large margin at a second party meeting on 30 October 1930.

Renewed attacks by Beaverbrook in February and March 1931 were less dangerous, but they coincided with unease over Baldwin's moderate policy on India and a decline in confidence among his front-bench colleagues. Neville Chamberlain presented him with a critical memo written by the senior official at Central Office, Robert Topping, on 1 March 1931, and Baldwin decided to retire. This low mood lasted for only a few hours and, rallied by his friends and wife, he decided to fight back. His position was actually much stronger than in the previous year, and a powerful and effective speech in the House on India on 12 March and a frank discussion with the shadow cabinet restored his authority. Beaverbrook gave up after his last throw in the Westminster St George's by-election was defeated, during which Baldwin made his most famous denunciation of the press lords as seeking 'power without responsibility—the prerogative of the harlot throughout the ages' (Middlemas and Barnes, 600) in a speech at Queen's Hall on 17 March.

From the spring of 1931 the Conservative Party was united behind Baldwin, and by-elections pointed to them winning a large majority at the next election. As the depression worsened, Baldwin concentrated on attacking the tottering Labour government. The costs of unemployment payments had unbalanced the budget, and Conservatives were determined that this must be dealt with by reductions in spending and not increases in taxation. The need for 'economy' and preserving the 'free hand' on tariffs were Baldwin's priorities in the financial crisis which overwhelmed the Labour government in August 1931. He wanted Labour to meet its responsibilities and produce effective proposals to balance the budget or, failing that, to leave office having exposed its unfitness for government. Baldwin sought to avoid saving Labour from unpopularity or becoming entangled in a coalition, and tried to preserve a distance and continue his holiday in France. However, the collapse of the pound and the paralysis of the government forced him to return to London on 22 August, and two days later he reluctantly agreed to join an all-party 'national' emergency cabinet. The severity of the crisis and pressure of time left no better option, and at least this outcome avoided the greater danger of a purely Conservative government implementing spending and welfare cuts that might be very unpopular. Neville Chamberlain had represented the Conservatives in meetings with the other parties' leaders during Baldwin's absence, and also had some influence in pressing this solution on him. Even so, when Baldwin went to Buckingham Palace for the crucial meeting on 24 August he expected to become the prime minister of a mainly Conservative ministry with some Liberal support. Instead, the king pressed him that it was his patriotic duty to sacrifice personal and party claims and serve under MacDonald, who had agreed to remain as prime minister until the crisis was resolved. Baldwin could hardly refuse, but he insisted that it was a temporary and emergency arrangement, and that once the currency had been stabilized there would be an election in which the Conservatives would seek a mandate for the 'free hand'. In fact, the temporary National Government went on to win two elections and hold power from 1931 to 1940. Having made his name in the downfall of one coalition, Baldwin spent the rest of his political career as the central figure in another.

Although it was forced to abandon the gold standard on 21 September 1931, the National Government's very existence became a key factor in restoring stability and maintaining foreign confidence. The need to secure a mandate became imperative, and Baldwin and his party were willing to support a national appeal under MacDonald, provided that this did not restrict them from seeking the 'free hand' on tariffs. After a struggle with the free-traders in the cabinet, Baldwin secured the best position for the Conservatives under the circumstances: each party would campaign under its own manifesto, and the government as a whole would simply ask for 'a doctor's mandate' to implement whatever remedies it felt necessary. In fact, as the Conservatives provided most of its parliamentary support, this effectively meant the introduction of tariffs. The election which swiftly followed at the end of October was an unprecedented landslide; the government won 554 seats, of which 470 were Conservative. With the unity of the government preserved by an agreement that ministers could vote as they wished on this issue, the Import Duties Bill was passed in January 1932. Baldwin led the British delegation to the Imperial Conference at Ottawa in July and August, and successfully negotiated preferential arrangements with the dominions. While implementing these caused Snowden and the Samuelite Liberals to leave the government in September 1932, sufficient Labour and Liberal elements remained for its national status to be credible and there was greater harmony in the cabinet. Baldwin had reversed his defeat of 1923, and secured the abandonment of free trade which the bulk of his party had been seeking for nearly three decades. This was a significant achievement, although in the circumstances there was no triumphalism and it was not to bring the hoped-for prosperity or closer unity of the empire.

The National Government: lord president of the council, 1931–1935 From 25 August 1931 to 7 June 1935 Baldwin was the second figure in the National Government, occupying the prestigious non-departmental post of lord president of the council (he was also lord privy seal from 29 September 1932 to 31 December 1933). This was symbolized by his move into 11 Downing Street after the general election of 1931, which helped his strained personal finances. He chaired the cabinet in MacDonald's absences and deputized for him in the Commons, acting effectively as leader of the House. Baldwin was kept very busy and worked long hours, having a heavy load of committee work and giving much time and attention to the House of Commons. The position suited his strengths of co-ordination and communication, and the lesser responsibility meant that he did not suffer nervous exhaustion similar to that of 1926–7 and 1936. Baldwin had a good personal relationship with MacDonald and saw the value in retaining him as prime minister. He did much to hold the government together, supporting MacDonald and assuaging his fears of being seen as a Conservative puppet. Baldwin had the trust of the other non-Conservative ministers, and his non-partisan image made it easier for them to serve without loss of dignity; he was willing to allow them a generous share of cabinet posts and to follow policies that had clearly bipartisan aspects, as in agriculture, housing, education, and India. He was the guarantee that the right-wing Conservatives would not call the tune, while at the same time soothing his followers' fears that too many concessions were being made.

It is hard to assess Baldwin's contribution, other than in the National Government's overall performance. Its cohesion was good, with friendly co-operation in cabinet and little faction or dissent in parliament, apart from on the issue of India. It achieved consensus on domestic and overseas policy, surmounted the crises which it faced, and saw a slow recovery in the economy and employment. There were periods of anxiety, but it was never seriously in danger. Baldwin worked in effective partnership with the other key Conservative figure of Neville Chamberlain, the chancellor of the exchequer, and provided the atmosphere and public appeal which complemented Chamberlain's administrative drive and command of policy. There were two key areas where Baldwin had a particularly significant role. The first of these was India, over which he had been in conflict with the 'die-hards' of the Conservative right since his endorsement of the Irwin declaration's promise of eventual dominion status in October 1929. Baldwin wanted to maintain Britain's role in India, but accepted that a partnership with elements of Indian opinion would be required. He recognized the commitments which previous governments had given, and—in similar vein to his view of democracy at home—concluded that the only stable way forward was constructive progress in a generous spirit, which would encourage moderation. He was strongly influenced by the precedent of the Irish question, and was determined to maintain a bipartisan line and prevent India from becoming a party issue. Although placing emphasis on the safeguards to reassure Conservative opinion, he regarded Churchill's vehement opposition as dangerously negative. Baldwin risked his leadership over India late in 1929 and early in 1931, and had to exert his authority at key moments during Churchill's campaign to capture the Conservative rank and file in 1933–4. India took up much of Baldwin's time at the House of Commons; it was the subject of some of his most impressive speeches, and the Government of India Act was passed successfully in 1935.

The second and most controversial area was rearmament, and especially the key aspect of air policy. With the air minister in the Lords, Baldwin made the significant statements in the Commons, including the pledge of 8 March 1934 that Britain would not be inferior to any country within striking distance. Baldwin did not lack experience in foreign and defence matters, having been prime minister and chairman of the committee of imperial defence, and he chaired the cabinet disarmament committee during the Geneva conference of 1932–4. He understood the impact of new technology, and his warning in the Commons on 10 November 1932 that 'the bomber will always get through' (*Hansard 5C*, 270, 10 Nov 1932, 632) was strategically correct at the time. Another striking speech on 30 July 1934 warned that Britain's defensive frontier was no longer the white cliffs of Dover, but lay on the Rhine (ibid., 292, 30 July 1934, 2339). This led to the problem of how to gauge and respond to the threat from Germany, as Hitler's new regime offered a kaleidoscope of promises and threats after 1933. There were some more helpful developments, principally the conclusion of the Anglo-German naval agreement in June 1935, which severely limited the size of the German fleet and avoided the fear of another naval race. Baldwin bore much of the blame after 1939 for supposed failures of judgement on appeasement and rearmament, especially in the early stages of 1933–6. He was certainly concerned about the economic strain and aware of public hopes for disarmament and fear of another war, but German moves led him to press for increased spending on air defence in 1933–4. On 19 July 1934 he announced a substantial expansion of the RAF, which was followed by further increases to keep pace with Germany in May 1935, February 1936, and, in one of Baldwin's last acts, February 1937. However, German propaganda boasts of having reached air parity misled Baldwin into apologizing to the House on 22 May 1935 for having failed to maintain the margin promised in March 1934. This damaged Baldwin's reputation, and contributed to the later view that he and the government had been negligent and dilatory. In fact, between 1933 and 1935 the international dangers were less apparent than the benefit of hindsight later made them, and the government's measures seemed to be prudent and sufficient. During this time Baldwin's speeches contributed to the development of public opinion from the negative atmosphere of 1933 to a general acceptance of the need for more substantial rearmament.

Final term as prime minister, 1935–1937 On 7 June 1935 Baldwin exchanged posts with MacDonald, and at sixty-seven began his third and final term as prime minister. There was a cabinet reshuffle, including the promotion of Samuel Hoare as foreign secretary, but the character of the National Government was unchanged. Baldwin was now comfortable with the arrangement, considering that it provided valuable stability in troubled times. He was conscious of problems in Europe and the spread of totalitarian regimes, and sought to strengthen Britain morally as well as militarily, so that it would continue to uphold the 'torch of freedom' and the heritage of toleration and constitutional government. Baldwin was not a mirror simply reflecting public opinion; he sought to shape it, but by working with the grain rather than sounding sudden alarms. He used the general election to secure a mandate for increased rearmament, presenting this as doing 'what is necessary to repair the gaps in our defences' (Middlemas and Barnes, 866). Although this and the promise that 'there will be no great armaments' (Hyde, 398) were designed to underline the defensive nature of the government's intentions, Baldwin was firm about the need for action. In his first election broadcast, on 25 October 1935, he stated, 'I will not be responsible for the conduct of any Government in this country at the present time, if I am not given power to remedy the deficiencies which have accrued in our defences since the War' (*The Times*, 26 Oct 1935, 17), having used almost identical words in the House of Commons two days earlier (*Hansard 5C*, 305, 24 Oct 1935, 152). Given the fall in unemployment, the recent problems of the Labour leadership, and the unsettled international situation, it was unlikely that this would cause the rejection of the National Government. However, even if Baldwin was not risking everything, it was certainly far from the 'putting party before country' of the later crude Churchillian condemnation of his conduct in 1933–5. The economic picture had continued to improve, and the general election which Baldwin called in November 1935 returned the National Government with a comfortable majority, having 429 MPs (of whom 387 were Conservatives) to Labour's 154.

Baldwin's final ministry had achievements in domestic reform, including raising the school-leaving age to fifteen in 1936 and major programmes of slum clearance, but this has been overshadowed by criticism of its foreign and defence policies. The first international crisis was Italy's attack on Abyssinia in 1935, to which Baldwin's response was constrained by awareness that British public opinion and the French government were unwilling to risk war. A plan to buy off Italy was devised by Hoare in conjunction with the French foreign minister, Laval, but it was leaked to the press before it could be put to either the cabinet or Mussolini. The generous reward which it offered to the aggressor aroused a storm of criticism in Britain, shaking the National Government and damaging Baldwin's reputation. In particular, the plan seemed a cynical betrayal of the commitment to the League of Nations which the government had strongly emphasized in the election campaign only a few weeks before. Hoare was forced to resign, and Baldwin's speech in the debate on 10 December 1935 was unconvincing, taking refuge behind the suggestion that he could not disclose the full facts—'my lips are not yet unsealed' (*Hansard 5C*, 307, 10 Dec 1935, 856)—and appealing for trust. The government's supporters did not want it to founder, and rallied behind Baldwin after a misjudged attack on his honour by the Labour leader, Clement Attlee. This traumatic experience damaged confidence in Baldwin, although his moving broadcast tribute on the death of the king on 20 January 1936 partly restored his public position. Baldwin appointed the untarnished and youthful Anthony Eden as foreign secretary, but was aware that Hoare had been treated poorly and felt an obligation to bring him back to the cabinet as soon as possible.

The next crisis was caused by Hitler's remilitarization of the Rhineland in March 1936. Baldwin recognized that this aspect of the discredited Versailles treaty no longer enjoyed public support, and told the cabinet that a military response would be out of proportion. When the new French foreign minister, Flandin, came to London and proposed full sanctions against Germany, Baldwin was concerned that the crisis would escalate and rejected the plan on the ground that Britain was militarily unready for war. The government had been considering remilitarization as part of a general arms limitation agreement, and although Hitler had acted unilaterally in the reoccupation, he also now offered to enter such negotiations. Baldwin chaired the cabinet foreign policy committee, but left the execution of policy to Eden. He gave only general guidance, urging the improvement of relations with Germany and expressing concern over the French alliance with Russia, which could drag the Western powers into a Nazi–Communist struggle. The strains of the foreign situation and the responsibilities and workload of the premiership overcame Baldwin in the middle of 1936, and he suffered his most severe period of nervous exhaustion. He was required to rest, and during these months the government seemed to lose direction. In the uncertain period following the outbreak of the Spanish Civil War Baldwin decided against holidaying at Aix and stayed at a series of English country houses, before returning reinvigorated to Downing Street on 12 October 1936. On 12 November, replying to Churchill's criticism of the pace of air rearmament, Baldwin declared with 'appalling frankness' (*Hansard 5C*, 317, 12 Nov 1936, 1144) that no public mandate for rearmament could have been secured in 1933. This was misunderstood or misrepresented by his critics, especially in Churchill's war memoirs, to refer to the general election of 1935, and was taken as an admission that Baldwin had put party concerns before national security.

The major event of Baldwin's final months as prime minister was the crisis over the new king's wish to marry Mrs Simpson, an American whose second divorce was impending. The problem was not the monarch's private morality but his public role, for a divorcee would not be acceptable as queen. Controversy over this divided the nation in a dangerous international period and potentially threatened the unity of the empire, for since the Statute of Westminster the monarch was the symbolic link with the dominions. At first Baldwin was reluctant to broach the subject, but in a strained conversation on 20 October 1936 he warned the king that the public reaction would be hostile. Baldwin tried to dissuade Edward, but the monarch was determined upon the marriage and at their next meeting on 16 November raised the possibility of abdication. The king's proposal of a morganatic marriage was rejected by the dominions and the cabinet, and Australia and Canada warned that they would not recognize Mrs Simpson as queen. When the British press broke their silence on 2 December, Baldwin informed the king that the only options remaining were renunciation of Mrs Simpson or abdication, still hoping that he would choose the former. The crisis assumed a political dimension when Beaverbrook and Churchill tried to rally support for the king, but the mood in the Commons was strongly against them and the Labour opposition indicated that they would refuse to form a ministry if Baldwin had to resign. Once again Baldwin successfully neutralized a political crisis by presenting it as a constitutional issue, thus discounting any party implications.

Although sometimes stilted, Baldwin's meetings with the king were conducted politely, showing goodwill and a fatherly concern. However, he was firm in rejecting on 4 December the king's wish to put his case before the public in a radio broadcast; the nation would be divided into opposing camps, and it would be unconstitutional if the monarch acted independently of the advice of his ministers. Baldwin sought to appeal to Edward's sense of duty, but was appalled at the king's lack of responsibility or moral struggle. On the final visit to Fort Belvedere on the evening of 7 December Baldwin was prepared to strive all night with the king's conscience but found that Edward had resolved to abdicate, and the instrument was signed on 10 December. Baldwin conducted the abdication crisis with discretion, informing only a few close colleagues and consulting the full cabinet only when necessary. He was praised on all sides for the tact, patience, and sympathy with which he had resolved a potentially corrosive situation, and was restored to the height of public esteem. His success was capped by masterly performances in his broadcast to the nation and speech in the Commons after the abdication; the latter was a moment of great theatre in a packed House, in which Baldwin's plain statement was all the more effective. In the lobby afterwards he confided to a back-bench MP: 'I had a success, my dear Nicolson, at the moment I most needed it. Now is the time to go' (*Harold Nicolson: Diaries and Letters*, 107–8).

In fact, Baldwin had decided during his period of breakdown earlier in 1936 that he would retire at the time of the coronation in May 1937. The premiership was passed to Neville Chamberlain, who had been waiting with some impatience. Baldwin's last ministerial action was to announce the first increase in MPs' salaries since their introduction in 1912 and the establishment of a salary for the leader of the opposition. This was a typical gesture, for the changes were of most value to Labour MPs, and 'was done with Baldwin's usual consummate good taste. No man has ever left in such a blaze of affection' (*Harold Nicolson: Diaries and Letters*, 113). He resigned the next day, 28 May 1937, and was created a knight of the Garter.

Peerage and last years Baldwin underlined his withdrawal from active politics by leaving the House of Commons, but he accepted a peerage and on 8 June was created Earl Baldwin of Bewdley. He was much interested in his family's pedigree and their roots in Corvedale in Shropshire, and chose Viscount Corvedale as accompanying junior title. During his political career he had received many honours: fourteen universities conferred honorary doctorates upon him; he was lord rector of the universities of Edinburgh (1923–6) and Glasgow (1928–31) and was chancellor of the universities of St Andrews, from 1929, and Cambridge, from 1930, until his death.

Retirement was followed by a nervous collapse in July 1937, and arthritis prevented Baldwin's usual walks at Aix. In 1937 he founded the Imperial Relations Trust to improve contacts among the dominions. He was also chairman of the Rhodes Trust and, from 1930, the Pilgrim Trust. Baldwin was concerned by the resignation of Eden in February 1938 and had reservations about Chamberlain's conduct of affairs but, on 4 October 1938, in his only speech in the House of Lords, gave general support to the Munich settlement. He was also concerned about the victims of oppression, and in December 1938 an appeal broadcast in Britain and North America raised £500,000 for the Lord Baldwin Fund for Refugees. He delivered a series of lectures on his familiar themes of the English character and democracy in Canada in April 1939, and in August 1939 he spoke in New York; these events attracted much attention and were broadcast across the continent. However, the outbreak of war reduced his activities, and the Baldwins retired to live quietly at Astley.

Baldwin's last years were saddened by his own and his wife's declining strength, by financial worries which left them with almost no staff to assist them, and by the cold blast of public disapproval after Dunkirk. He was condemned as principal among the 'guilty men' responsible for the misjudgments of appeasement and the inadequacies of rearmament, and even local tradesmen showed hostility. There were hurtful attacks in the press, particularly when the wrought-iron gates at Astley, which had been presented on his retirement, were requisitioned for salvage. He visited London regularly in 1941–3 and was cheered by a friendly lunch with Churchill in February 1943, but his physical decline continued in the later years of the war. After the shock of Lucy's sudden death in 1945, he was often depressed and suffered increasing lameness and deafness. He died quietly in his sleep at Astley Hall on 13 December 1947; his remains were cremated in Birmingham on 17 December, and he and Lucy were interred together in Worcester Cathedral. His son Oliver succeeded him as second Earl Baldwin; on Oliver's death in 1958 the title passed to his younger brother, Windham.

Assessments and significance Baldwin was one of the few prime ministers to retire at the time of his own choosing, and almost unique in departing at the height of his popularity and prestige. However, the outbreak and problems of the war led to a rapid reversal, and his reputation slumped to the lowest depths within his own lifetime. Baldwin refused to write his memoirs, but agreed that the Oxford historian G. M. Young be commissioned to write a biography. Unfortunately Young was influenced by the hostile view of Baldwin which was pervasive by the late 1940s, and became so disenchanted with his subject that he sought to be excused from his contract. When the publishers insisted, the slim volume which appeared in 1952 further damaged Baldwin's reputation, giving authority to the charges against him and explaining them in relation to weaknesses in his character and capacity. It confirmed the prevailing view of Baldwin as lazy and indecisive, a second-rate figure who took the line of least resistance. Young's tone and methods upset the family and moved Baldwin's younger son Windham to publish a reply, *My Father: the True Story*, in 1955. This drew on family papers for Baldwin's early years, and made effective use of Hansard and published official sources to counter the criticism of his conduct in the 1930s. This was the first step in restoring Baldwin's reputation, although the hostile Churchillian view was dominant until the 1970s and remained influential thereafter.

The opening of state and private archives produced the first historical assessment, a lengthy biography by Keith Middlemas and John Barnes, in 1969. This was a revisionist work which sought to rehabilitate Baldwin, and particularly tackle the question of rearmament. During the remainder of the century a fuller and more sophisticated understanding was developed by a range of works from H. M. Hyde's narrative life in 1973 to the analytical study by Philip Williamson in 1999. The latter took a distinctive approach, focusing on Baldwin's background, purposes, and methods, and in particular his public speeches. From this Baldwin emerged as a more complex and subtle figure in character and political conduct, with concerns and methods which reflected his era. Since the 1970s there has been greater emphasis on Baldwin's domestic statecraft, and in particular his role in the dominance of the Conservatives between the wars and the related aspects of his public image and use of new media. The pendulum has swung almost completely towards a positive view, although the problems which Britain faced in economic strength and military readiness in the 1930s still leave some awkwardness. Baldwin is now seen as having done more than most and perhaps as much as was possible in the context, but the fact remains that it was not enough to deter the aggressors or ensure their defeat. Less equivocal was his rediscovery as a moderate and inclusive Conservative for the modern age, part of a 'one nation' tradition. Baldwin was little mentioned by the Conservative Party in the early post-war decades, when he was still an embarrassment. During the Thatcher years his brand of Conservatism was derided as 'wet' and based on weakness and concession. However, by the early 1990s it had become acceptable to cite Baldwin as an inspiration or model, and John Major deliberately echoed him when seeking to project a unifying style of Conservatism.

Whether critical or favourable, assessments of Baldwin have agreed on his importance and influence in the inter-war years, and he is often seen as the defining figure of the age. He was its outstanding public speaker, and his radio broadcasts and parliamentary speeches frequently combined to great effect his command of language, sensitivity to atmosphere and unifying moral purpose. His political role was that of a mediator and his aim was to create a spirit of harmony and unity, not just in the government but in the nation as a whole. Baldwin's effectiveness and his legacy need to be judged in this light, rather than by legislative achievements. His priorities were restoring standards in public life, educating democracy, encouraging moderation within the labour movement, promoting national unity across class divisions, and maintaining the constitution as the guarantor of both liberty and property. Baldwin's major battles related to these themes, from rejecting the cynicism of the Lloyd George coalition to the abdication crisis. 'Safety first' is the least appropriate slogan for his career: Baldwin did not play safe over the coalition in 1922, tariffs in 1923, the political levy and coal subsidy in 1925, the general strike threat in 1926, the press lords in 1929–30, India from 1929 to 1935, or in joining the National Government in 1931. He combined goodwill and firmness in preserving a popular constitutional monarchy in 1936 and in seeking a stable and developing India at the heart of the empire.

Baldwin's promotion of social harmony and industrial reconciliation played a significant role in soothing tensions in the 1920s. In 1926 the challenge of direct action was defeated in an atmosphere of calmness and confidence, and fears of social upheaval faded. Other possible Conservative leaders would not have been able to match Baldwin's remarkable ability to project an idealistic appeal to the new democracy, suffused with 'a breadth of outlook, a tolerance and a warm humanity' (Amery, *My Political Life*, 398). His relations with the Labour Party were cordial and constructive, and he refused to consider manoeuvres to prevent them from taking office in 1924 or 1929. The tone set by Baldwin in the 1920s enabled leading figures from the three parties to work together in the National Governments of the 1930s with remarkably little friction. Baldwin's co-ordinating role in 1931–5 contributed much to the cohesion and stability of the National Government. With the tariff secured, most Conservatives were comfortable with this cautiously reformist ministry, especially as its cross-party appeal brought public support and large electoral majorities. By the time of his retirement in 1937 prosperity had returned to much of the country, and new initiatives were being developed in the areas still gripped by depression.

Baldwin's leadership was an essential factor in the electoral success which the Conservative Party won between the wars. He enjoyed widespread popularity with uncommitted, Liberal and even Labour voters, and was acknowledged to be the Conservatives' greatest electoral asset. However, his most significant achievement was to ensure the security and confidence of the Conservative elements in British society as they adjusted to the coming of democracy. In 1922–4 Baldwin preserved the independence of the Conservative Party and provided it with a distinct and attractive identity at a time of political confusion and uncertainty. At the same time, he left no fertile opening to the right and was principally responsible for confining fascism to the margins of British politics. Apart from the miscalculation of the general election in 1923 he successfully aligned his party with the outlook and aspirations of much of the British people. Rather than allowing it to be seen as a class-defined, reactionary, and divisive force, Baldwin projected a democratic and inclusive Conservatism which combined preservation of continuity with the past with acceptance of modern economic and imperial realities. The openness and adaptability of his approach contributed to Conservative resilience and recovery after the defeat of 1945, even if its originator was too unpopular to acknowledge. By the time of his retirement he had recast the party in his own image and shaped the outlook of the next generation of Conservative leaders, in particular Eden, Butler, and Macmillan.

Against these achievements can be set Baldwin's weaknesses and failures. He was not absorbed or engaged in some areas, and could delegate too much or hold back from intervening when more direction and urgency was needed. At the same time the stress of work and responsibility built up to periods of nervous exhaustion, during which there was a lack of control. His parliamentary performances could sometimes be poor, and he tended to personalize political issues—particularly in his hostility to Lloyd George and the press lords. He made a number of less than successful cabinet appointments, such as Steel-Maitland and Joynson-Hicks in 1924 and Inskip in 1936. It can be argued that he accepted too readily the limitations imposed by public opinion, particularly over tariffs in the 1920s and foreign policy in the 1930s. Criticism of Baldwin's record focuses most on the area which he left mainly to others: foreign affairs. The failure to check the ambitions of the dictators is a complex matter, but without the support of other powers Britain was overstretched in meeting challenges from Japan, Italy, and Germany. In the aftermath of the horrors of the western front and with fear of destruction from the air, it was commonly accepted that a new basis of peace and understanding was required. The Anglo-German naval agreement of 1935 was intended as a first step and can be claimed as a partial success, for during the Second World War the German surface fleet was never a serious danger. Baldwin's approach was more limited and sceptical than that of his successor; rightly or wrongly, he would not have flown to Munich. Rearmament was certainly constrained by financial and political anxieties, but a programme was initiated in 1934—when the threat was far from definite—and had grown massively by the time Baldwin retired in 1937. The initial expansion of the RAF in 1934–5 was concentrated upon a deterrent bomber force, and much of the military equipment had to be abandoned in France in 1940. The state of the country's defences as it faced invasion after Dunkirk did not fully reflect the National Government's rearmament efforts, but this was the image which sank into popular mythology. Even so, in unexpectedly adverse and isolated circumstances, Britain had sufficient naval and air resources—in particular through the development of radar and modern fighter aircraft—to make invasion too hazardous to risk.

It can never be known if another approach or another prime minister would have achieved more in deterring the aggressive powers or carrying the country for earlier and larger rearmament. In the political and economic circumstances of 1930s Britain it is likely that they would not, and they might have left a divided country no more able to withstand adversity than was France in 1940. It would take time for Britain to match the rearmament of Nazi Germany, and Baldwin can be criticized for the vulnerabilities and deficiencies that were exposed from the Rhineland crisis to Dunkirk. At the same time, his constructive legacy must also be acknowledged: the consensus built around the non-provocative defence and foreign policy of the 1930s was what sustained public unity and the will to victory after 1940. Churchill may have provided the words and been an unsullied symbol, but all that he built rested on the strong and enduring foundations laid down by Baldwin.

Baldwin's wife, **Lucy Baldwin** [*née* Ridsdale], Countess Baldwin of Bewdley (1869–1945), campaigner for maternity care, was born on 19 January 1869 in Bayswater, London. She was the eldest daughter of Edward Lucas Jenks Ridsdale (1833–1901), a scientist and master of the Royal Mint, and his wife, Esther Lucy Thacker (*d.* 1909). Always known as Cissie, she was brought up with her sister and three brothers in the village of Rottingdean on the Sussex coast. The Ridsdales were a sociable and lively family, and Lucy became an enthusiastic cricketer, playing for the pioneering women's team, the White Heather club. Hers and Stanley's was a loving, supportive, and enduring partnership; Lucy was the more extrovert, but they shared a strong and certain Christian faith and had similar moral values. A sadness was that her first child, in 1894, was stillborn, but in the following ten years Lucy bore two sons and four daughters who survived. All of her labours were difficult, lengthy, and painful, and this influenced her later charitable work.

Lucy enjoyed entertaining, preferred London to the country, and did not share her husband's love of walking. One of her daughters commented, 'two people could not have been more unlike', but that 'should they ever differ, it was always done quietly and politely' (Margaret Huntington-Whiteley, in Hyde, 43). She was a little below average in height and of homely appearance, and normally wore her hair in a bun. She had little concern for fashionable clothes or colours, which made her seem a slightly drab figure, and she retained a fondness for large hats. Her humour was 'of a magisterial kind', and 'her outspokenness sometimes blunt and direct' (*The Times*, 26 June 1945). Lucy accompanied her husband on his journeys and on the public platform, and was herself an 'excellent speaker' (ibid., 19 June 1945). She behaved conventionally in the role of a statesman's wife and was not caught up in the world of politics, but their shared moral outlook meant that her support and encouragement gave him vital sustenance. This was particularly important at two key moments: the decision to break with the coalition in October 1922 and not to resign the leadership in March 1931. Lucy's private name for Stanley was Tiger Baldwin, and she was the more ambitious of the two; it was said that 'she had more influence upon him than he on her' (ibid., 26 June 1945).

Lucy Baldwin's other significant public role was in the campaign for improved maternity care. In 1928 she became vice-chair of a new body, the National Birthday Trust Fund. She was concerned generally to reduce the dangers and mortality level of childbirth, but differed from some of her fellow campaigners in placing special emphasis on the need for proper pain relief during labour. The cost limited its use to the wealthy few, and in 1929 Lucy Baldwin established the Anaesthetics Fund as a subsidiary body to campaign for provision for all women who needed it. She raised funds which were used to develop cheaper forms of analgesia which could be safely administered by midwives at the mother's home. She also sought to educate public opinion and her work contributed to the passage of the Midwives Act of 1936, which created the system of a national salaried service. During the Second World War she lived quietly in retirement with her husband at their home, Astley Hall, near Stourport, where conditions were difficult because of concern over money and lack of staff. She died at Astley, quite suddenly, from a heart attack on 17 June 1945, and was later interred with her husband in Worcester Cathedral. STUART BALL

Sources P. Williamson, *Stanley Baldwin* (1999) • H. M. Hyde, *Baldwin* (1973) • A. W. Baldwin, *My father: the true story* (1955) • K. Middlemas and J. Barnes, *Baldwin* (1969) • T. Jones, *A diary with letters, 1931–1950* (1954) • *Memoirs of a Conservative: J. C. C. Davidson's memoirs and papers, 1910–37*, ed. R. R. James (1969) • T. Jones, *Whitehall diary*, ed. K. Middlemas, 1–2 (1969) • J. Ramsden, *The age of Balfour and Baldwin, 1902–1940* (1978) • S. Ball, *Baldwin and the Conservative Party: the crisis of 1929–1931* (1988) • Baldwin MSS, CUL • U. Birm. L., Austen and Neville Chamberlain MSS • BL OIOC, Halifax MSS • HLRO, Davidson papers • Trinity Cam., Butler MSS • Lpool RO, Derby papers • A. S. Williams, *Ladies of influence: women of the élite in interwar Britain* (2000) • G. M. Young, *Stanley Baldwin* (1952) • L. S. Amery, *My political life*, 2 (1953) • Lord Butler, *The art of the possible* (1971) • *Harold Nicolson: diaries and letters, 1930–1964*, ed. S. Olson (1980) • *The Leo Amery diaries*, ed. J. Barnes and D. Nicholson, 1 (1980) • *The modernisation of conservative politics: the diaries and letters of William Bridgeman, 1904–1935*, ed. P. Williamson (1988) • *Parliament and politics in the age of Baldwin and MacDonald: the Headlam diaries, 1923–1935*, ed. S. Ball (1992) • *Real old tory politics: the political diaries of Sir Robert Sanders, Lord Bayford, 1910–1935*, ed. J. Ramsden (1984) • *The Reith diaries*, ed. C. Stuart (1975) • M. Gilbert, ed., *Winston S. Churchill*, companion vol. 5 (1979–82) • Lord Templewood, *Nine troubled years* (1954) • Lord Percy of Newcastle, *Some memories* (1958) • *Stanley Baldwin*, British Universities Film and Video Council, [n.d.] [VHS video] • D. Cannadine, 'Politics, propaganda and art: the case of two "Worcestershire lads"', *Midland History*, 4 (1977), 97–122 • J. Ramsden, 'Baldwin and film', *Politics, propaganda and film, 1918–1945*, ed. N. Pronay and D. W. Spring (1982), 126–43 • S. Nicholas, 'The construction of a national identity: Stanley Baldwin, "Englishness" and the mass media in inter-war Britain', *The Conservatives and British society, 1880–1990*, ed. M. Francis and I. Zweiniger-Bargielowska (1996), 127–46 • R. Self, 'Conservative reunion and the general election of 1923', *20th-Century British History*, 3 (1992), 249–73 • P. Williamson, '"Safety first": Baldwin, the Conservative Party, and the 1929 general election', *HJ*, 25 (1982), 385–409 • J. Campbell, 'Stanley Baldwin', *British prime ministers in the twentieth century*, ed. J. P. Mackintosh, 1: *Balfour to Chamberlain* (1977), 188–218 • R. Blake, 'Baldwin and the right', *The Baldwin age*, ed. J. T. Raymond (1960), 25–65 • K. Young, *Baldwin* (1976) • d. cert.

Archives CUL, political corresp. and papers • NRA, personal corresp. and papers • priv. coll., family MSS • Worcs. RO, MSS | BL, corresp. with A. J. Balfour, Add. MS 49694, *passim* • BL, corresp. with Lord Cecil, Add. MS 51080 • BL, corresp. with Sir Sydney Cockerell, Add. MS 52704 • BL, corresp. with J. A. Spender, Add. MS 46388 • BL OIOC, Halifax MSS • Bodl. Oxf., letters to Herbert Asquith • Bodl. Oxf., letters to Margot Asquith • Bodl. Oxf., corresp. with Geoffrey Dawson • Bodl. Oxf., letters to H. A. L. Fisher • Bodl. Oxf., corresp. with H. A. Gwynne • Bodl. Oxf., corresp. with Gilbert Murray • Bodl. Oxf., corresp. with Lord Simon • Borth Inst., letters to earl of Halifax • CAC Cam., corresp. with Lord Croft • CAC Cam., corresp. with Sir Edward Spears • CKS, letters to Lord Stanhope • CUL, letters to second Earl Baldwin and John Boyle • CUL, letters to Oliver Baldwin • CUL, corresp. with Sir Samuel Hoare • CUL, letters to Lord and Lady Kennet • Devon RO, letters to Sibyl Heeley • Flintshire RO, Hawarden, letters to Sir J. H. Morris-Jones • Herts. ALS, letters to Lady Desborough • HLRO, Davidson MSS • HLRO, corresp. with Lord Beaverbrook • HLRO, corresp. with David Lloyd George • HLRO, corresp. with Herbert Samuel • HLRO, corresp. with John St Loe Strachey • Lpool RO, corresp. with seventeenth earl of Derby • NA Scot., corresp. with A. J. Balfour • NA Scot., letters to Sir Henry Craik • NA Scot., corresp. with Lord Elibank • NA Scot., corresp. with Lord Lothian • NL Aus., corresp. with first Viscount Stonehaven • NL Wales, corresp. with Thomas Jones • PRO NIre., letters to Lady Londonderry • Shrops. RRC, letters to first Viscount Bridgeman • Trinity Cam., corresp. with Sir Joseph John Thomson • U. Birm. L., corresp. with Austen Chamberlain • U. Birm. L., corresp. with Francis Brett Young • U. Glas., Archives and Business Records Centre, corresp. with first Viscount Weir • U. Newcastle, Robinson L., corresp. with Walter Runciman • U. Warwick Mod. RC, corresp. with Sir Leslie Scott • University of Cape Town Library, corresp. with C. J. Sibbett • University of Sheffield Library, corresp. with W. A. S. Hewins • Worcs. RO, letters to W. H. Cory | FILM BFI NFTVA, *Men of our time*, 27 May 1964 • BFI NFTVA, 'Stanley Baldwin', 4 Jan 1975 • BFI NFTVA, documentary footage • BFI NFTVA, news footage • BFI NFTVA, other footage (speech) • BFI NFTVA, propaganda footage • IWM FVA, news footage • IWM FVA, actuality footage • IWM FVA, documentary footage | SOUND BL NSA, 'The announcement in parliament of the abdication', T8840R • 'Man with the pipe', M894WC1

Likenesses B. Stone, photograph, 1909, NPG • W. Stoneman, two photographs, 1920–38, NPG • M. Beerbohm, chalk caricature, 1924 (*The old and young self*), Athenaeum Club, London • photographs, 1924, Hult. Arch. • Lady Kennet, bust, *c*.1925, Bewdley town hall, Worcestershire • O. Birley, oils, 1926, Goldsmiths' Hall, London • G. Philpot, oils, 1926, Carlton Club, London • N. Trent, bronze bust, 1927, Harrow School, Middlesex • Vandyk, two photographs, 1927, NPG [*see illus.*] • W. Rothenstein, chalk sketch, 1928, NPG • statuette, 1928, priv. coll. • W. C. Dongworth, miniature, *c*.1930, NPG • H. Coster, photographs, 1930–39, NPG • R. G. Eves, oils, *c*.1933, NPG • W. T. Monnington, oils, 1933, Trinity Cam. • O. Birley, oils, 1938, Carlton Club, London • bust, 1940, Stourport Library, Worcestershire • F. Dodd, oils, 1943, Bodl. RH; chalk study sketch, 1942, NPG • T. Cottrell, cigarette card, NPG • F. Dodd, pencil drawing, NPG • D. Low, caricature, sketch (*Mister Baldwin*), repro. in *New Statesman* (Nov 1933) • B. Partridge, ink caricature, NPG; repro. in *Punch* (7 Nov 1923) • B. Partridge, ink caricature, NPG; repro. in *Punch* (19 Nov 1924) • B. Partridge, ink caricature, NPG; repro. in *Punch* (1 Nov 1926) • A. P. F. Ritchie, cigarette card, NPG • cigarette card, NPG • photograph (after drawing by F. Dodd), NPG

Wealth at death £280,971 3*s*. 1*d*.: probate, 18 March 1948, *CGPLA Eng. & Wales* • £32,846 1*s*. 3*d*.—Lucy Baldwin, Countess Baldwin: probate, 14 Sept 1945, *CGPLA Eng. & Wales*

Baldwin, Thomas (*d*. 1693), clergyman and ejected minister, came from Middlesex. Nothing certain is known of his parentage or date of birth. He was admitted pensioner at Queens' College, Cambridge, on 29 May 1645, matriculating in 1646, graduating BA in 1649, and proceeding MA in 1654. When, in 1649, Richard Vines, master of Pembroke College, was asked by his friend Richard Baxter to find him a master for Kidderminster School, Vines eventually recommended Baldwin. Baxter later referred to him as 'our Schoolmaster at Kidderminster, sent to me by Mr. Vines from Cambridge' (*Reliquiae Baxterianae*, 3.92). Baldwin was ordained by Bradford North classis in Shropshire on 22 February 1653, and became one of Baxter's assistants, living for a time in his house (*Reliquiae Baxterianae*, 1.1.114). During that time he transcribed out of Baxter's shorthand notes the sermons which would become his *Treatise of Conversion* (1657).

In 1654 he became vicar of Wolverley, near Kidderminster, in succession to Laus Deo Mawlden. In 1656 he became vicar of Chaddesley Corbett, Worcestershire, a place also very close to Kidderminster. In December 1657 Baxter told Abraham Pinchbecke that Baldwin 'hath had a very long sicknes, which hath left him distempered though he Preach againe, and I hope will overgrow it' (Keeble and Nuttall, 1.281). In November 1658 Baldwin was wanted by the people of St Ann Blackfriars in London as their minister, but in the end stayed at Chaddesley. The decision lay, according to a letter of 20 November 1658 from Blackfriars, with Baxter and the neighbouring ministers. Baldwin was ejected from Chaddesley in 1662.

Baldwin's house was, under the declaration of indulgence, licensed in 1672 for presbyterian worship. Once Baxter left Kidderminster in 1661, Baldwin became the leader of the town's nonconformists, a group of about 600 people: 'I desired, when I was driven from Kidderminster, that the People would be ruled by [Baldwin] and Mr Sergeant' (*Reliquiae Baxterianae*, 3.92). With, however, 'the imprisonment of the most Religious and blameless of the Flock' (ibid.) Baldwin became embittered and, to Baxter's sorrow, was turning towards a separatist position, so alienated was he 'from Prelacy and Conformity, and the People with him' (ibid.). The result was that, particularly in the years 1668–70, Baxter was at variance both with Baldwin and with his former 'Flock'. The death of George Dance, the vicar of Kidderminster, in 1670, and the ministry of his successors Samuel Hiron and, from 1677, Richard White (both men who sought to 'build bridges' with the nonconformists) greatly eased the situation in the town. In 1681 (Keeble and Nuttall, no. 1064) Baxter could write to his Kidderminster friends: 'God hath given you an able and pious man [Richard White]. Take him and Mr. Baldwin and Mr. Serjeant [Richard Sergeant] conjunct for your teachers and Guides' (Keeble and Nuttall, 2.224).

In the new climate of feeling which followed the Act of Toleration of 1689 the Kidderminster nonconformists raised funds for the building of a meeting-house. Baldwin would certainly have been its first minister but for his death at Kidderminster in January 1693 (he was buried there on 1 February 1693). A commemorative sermon, published as *The Reward of Christian Patience*, was preached by his friend Richard White, who referred to Baldwin's 'afflictions', kidney stone and gout. He reported that his friend had asked for 'a healer' of divisions to be chosen as his successor.

Baldwin married first, on 24 May 1660 at Kidderminster, Elizabeth Soley; and second, on 29 December 1677 at Kidderminster, Eleanor or Ellen Bennett. She survived him, dying in 1714. Baldwin's will was made on 14 January 1693. It mentions 'my dear wife Ellen', his sons Thomas and John, his daughter Hannah, and several grandchildren. John was bequeathed most of his library (PRO, PROB 11/414/48). 'A good Scholar, a sober, calm, grave, moderate, peaceable Minister .... An extraordinary Preacher' (*Reliquiae Baxterianae*, 3.92) is Baxter's verdict on the man who was perhaps his most valued assistant.

C. D. GILBERT

Sources *Calendar of the correspondence of Richard Baxter*, ed. N. H. Keeble and G. F. Nuttall, 2 vols. (1991) • *Reliquiae Baxterianae, or, Mr Richard Baxter's narrative of the most memorable passages of his life and times*, ed. M. Sylvester, 1 vol. in 3 pts (1696), pt 2, pp. 374, 376; pt 3, p. 92 • *Calamy rev.* • R. White, *The reward of Christian patience* (1693) [title-page says preached for Thomas Badland, but it is of Baldwin] • will, PRO, PROB 11/414, sig. 48 • C. D. Gilbert, *A history of King Charles I Grammar School, Kidderminster* (1980) • parish register, Kidderminster, St Mary's • archives, Baxter Church, Kidderminster • triers' registers, 1654–9, LPL, Comm. III/3–7 • A. Gordon, ed., *Freedom after ejection: a review (1690–1692) of presbyterian and congregational nonconformity in England and Wales* (1917), 126 • Venn, *Alum. Cant.*

Archives DWL, Baxter letters • LPL, triers' admission registers

Wealth at death will, PRO, PROB 11/414, sig. 48 • estate and contributions: Gordon, ed., *Freedom after ejection*, 126

Baldwin, Thomas (*c.*1750–1820), architect and property developer, of unknown parentage, was mainly active in Bath, although not born there. He married Elizabeth, daughter of John Chapman, alderman of the city, on 15 September 1779, at St James's Church. They had at least one daughter and one son. He began his career as clerk to the Palladian local architect Thomas Warr Atwood, who brought him into the firm as someone familiar with London fashion, able to handle Robert Adam's refined but shallow surface detail. In 1775 Atwood was awarded the contract to build the city's new guildhall, but his sudden death in November that year did not interrupt his clerk's assimilation into the Bath building scene. Over the next eleven months Baldwin's designs, first for the east front, then for the west or entrance front, and finally for a suite of banquet room and council chamber in a style indistinguishable from that of the Adam brothers, were accepted by the council. In the same year, 1776, Baldwin was appointed city architect and surveyor. From this base he mounted a successful practice, executing public works and speculative building on the grandest scale, only halted by his dismissal from his official positions for false accounting and his subsequent bankruptcy in 1796.

Baldwin was master of two related styles. His public buildings were conceived in a robust stylar Palladian, but display the refined ornaments of neo-classicism and command the city centre with both authority and elegance. In 1786 he built the Cross Bath with a north façade of subtle serpentine curves and refined neo-classical forms. This confirmed his connection with the city's hot springs: he was made inspector of the baths in 1787 and in 1790 he was ordered to begin the west front of the Great Pump Room with its exquisitely ornamented twin colonnades.

For his speculative housing Baldwin devised shallow elevations which gave an impression of expensive surface detail but were relatively cheap to construct: Northumberland Buildings (*c.*1788) was his first experiment in this style. After 1788 Baldwin took over the development of the Bathwick estate, a project conceived on the most ambitious scale: Great Pulteney Street alone is 1100 feet long and 100 feet wide, although the thin pilasters and applied pediments of Bathwick's terraces prevent them from ranking alongside the Royal Crescent and the King's Circus as works of European significance. Bath Street, which he was building in the old centre after 1791, is probably his finest work, with sweeping quadrant arms and a covered promenade of Ionic columns. Unfortunately, its creation opened up an unsatisfactory vista to the almost blank east wall of Baldwin's earlier Cross Bath. At the same time suspicions were growing over his handling of council funds. Before his disgrace and dismissal, he had prepared designs for the north front of the Pump Room, overlooking the abbey churchyard. This was to have had a projecting Corinthian portico, but John Palmer who succeeded him, completed the north front with an engaged portico. Palmer also rebuilt the Cross Bath, re-siting the serpentine north façade to face east down the new Bath Street.

Baldwin continued to work after his bankruptcy, rebuilding Hafod in Cardiganshire for Thomas Johnes in 1807 and designing the town hall in Devizes, Wiltshire (1806–8). He died at 3 Harington Place, Bath, on 7 March 1820, and was buried in St Michael's Church there.

TIMOTHY MOWL

Sources Colvin, *Archs.* • W. Ison, *The Georgian buildings of Bath*, rev. edn (1980) • J. Root, 'Thomas Baldwin: his public career in Bath', *Bath History*, 5 (1994), 80–103 • J. Manco, 'The Cross Bath', *Bath History*, 2 (1988), 49–84 • Bath city council minutes, 1776–92, Bath RO, Bath • parish register, St James's, Bath, 15 Sept 1779 [marriage]

Baldwin, Sir Timothy (*bap.* **1619**, *d.* **1696**), lawyer, was baptized at Burwarton, Shropshire, on 28 September 1619, the second son of Charles Baldwin (1598–1675) of Elsich, Shropshire, and his wife, Mary (*d.* 1669), daughter and coheir of Francis Holland of Burwarton and widow of Robert Lutley. He matriculated at Balliol College, Oxford, on 6 March 1635, graduating BA on 17 October 1638. He was elected a fellow of All Souls College the following year and retained his fellowship until 1661. He gained a BCL on 26 June 1641, and in 1647 he was appointed sinecure rector of Llandrillo in Rhos. After initially losing his fellowship during the parliamentary visitation of the university in 1648, he retained it by dint, according to Wood, of paying judicious attention to Thomas Kelsey, deputy governor of the city of Oxford, and plying his wife with presents. He gained a DCL on 6 December 1652.

In 1654 Baldwin published *The privileges of an ambassador, written by way of a letter to a friend who desired his opinion concerning the Portugal ambassador*, which deals with the manslaughter charge against Don Pantaleone, the brother of the Portuguese ambassador. In 1655 he was reported by Wood to be one of a number of royalists who were encouraging an Oxford apothecary to sell coffee publicly near to All Souls. In 1656 he translated into Latin and published Lord Herbert of Cherbury's *History of the Expedition to Rhé in 1627*. On 24 January 1660 Baldwin was admitted to Doctors' Commons and on 21 June 1660 he became principal of Hart Hall, Oxford. On 31 July 1660 he was named one of the royal commissioners to visit the university. In 1663 he edited and published Richard Zouch's *The Jurisdiction of the Admiralty of England*. Baldwin resigned his principal's office in 1663, the same year he was appointed chancellor of the diocese of Hereford and Worcester. In 1667 he became high steward of Leominster. At some point in or after 1668 he married Ellen, daughter of Sir William Owen of Condover, Shropshire, the widow of Sir George Norton (*d.* 1668) of Abbotsleigh, Somerset. On 29 June 1670 he was made a master in chancery, and knighted on 10 July following.

Baldwin resigned his mastership in 1682. This may have been because of ill health, for he made his will, 'languishing and weak in body' (will, PRO, PROB 11/436, sig. 24), on 1 May 1685. By the time he came to make his will he had married again, his second wife being Mary (1630–1702), daughter of Gerard Skrymsher of Aqualate, Staffordshire, the widow of Nicholas Acton (*d.* 1664) of Bockleton, Worcestershire. In 1685 he was replaced as steward of Leominster, but returned to the post in 1688. Although he may have relinquished it to his nephew Charles Baldwin in 1691, Luttrell thought Baldwin was in possession of it until his death, mentioning his successor in an entry dated 4 August 1696. The main recipient of his will was his nephew Charles Baldwin (son of his brother, Sir Samuel), who had married Elizabeth, the daughter of his second wife, Mary, and her first husband, Nicholas Acton.

STUART HANDLEY

Sources Foster, *Alum. Oxon.* • E. H. Martin, 'History of several families connected with Diddlebury, I: the Baldwyns', *Transactions of the Shropshire Archaeological and Natural History Society*, 4th ser., 2 (1912), 135, 327–41 • Keeler, *Long Parliament*, 94–5 • *Le Neve's Pedigrees of the knights*, ed. G. W. Marshall, Harleian Society, 8 (1873), 238–9 • G. D. Squibb, *Doctors' Commons: a history of the College of Advocates and Doctors of Law* (1977), 178 • M. Burrows, *Worthies of All Souls* (1874), 196, 216 • will, PRO, PROB 11/436, sig. 24 • N. Luttrell, *A brief historical relation of state affairs from September 1678 to April 1714*, 4 (1857), 93 • A. M. Burke, ed., *Memorials of St Margaret's Church, Westminster* (1914), 133

Baldwin, William (*d.* in or before **1563**), author and printer, has left few biographical traces, although uncorroborated evidence—including claims that he himself lodged in the 1587 edition of *Mirror for Magistrates*—suggests that he was from Wales. Records survive concerning a Shropshireman named William Baldwin, whose service in the household of Mary I may correspond with Baldwin's involvement in the production of court revels. Baldwin may have supplicated the regents of Oxford University in 1533 for a degree and entered service as a schoolmaster but this too cannot be confirmed.

Nothing certain is known about Baldwin's life until 1547, when he entered into employment with Edward Whitchurch, a London printer with protestant leanings, whom he served as corrector. Whitchurch published Baldwin's *Treatise of Moral Philosophy* (1547) and *Canticles or Balades of Salomon* (1549). A collection of classical and humanistic adages and sententiae, the former text is tinged with Erasmianism. It attempts on the one hand to introduce classical learning to a readership dedicated to self-education, and on the other to harmonize classical philosophy with Christian belief. A very popular text, the *Treatise* underwent frequent revision and expansion by the compiler and others; it had been reissued twenty-four times by 1620. Baldwin's *Canticles*, dedicated to the young Edward VI, is a metrical translation of the Song of Solomon. In Solomon's wise aphorisms Baldwin found a Christian analogue to classical philosophy considered in the *Treatise*, further strengthening his humanist project by popularizing an important collection of scriptural poetry.

Anti-papal propaganda infuses Baldwin's translation of *Wonderful News of the Death of Paul III* (1552), from a Latin original by Matthias Flacius Illyricus. It exploits the scriptural figure of spiritual fornication, familiar from Hosea and other prophetic texts, to satirize the alleged depravity of Roman Catholicism. The pamphlet purports to report on the damnation of the late pope, whose infractions, which include sodomy, incest, and poisoning, are inscribed on stone pillars in hell. The translation qualifies eirenic humanistic concerns with a vitriolic protestant attack on the structure and teachings of the Church of Rome.

By late 1552 Baldwin had composed his *Marvelous History Entitled Beware the Cat, Concerning Diverse Wonderful and Incredible Matters* but it was not published until 1570, after the accession of Queen Elizabeth. Baldwin's 'Argument' sets the story within the context of the Christmas revels of 1552, when the author assisted George Ferrers, master of the revels, with the annual festivities at the royal court. The work is structured as a dialogue among Ferrers, his 'astronomer' (Master Wilmot), 'divine' (Streamer), Baldwin's rather naïve narrative persona, and others concerning whether or not animals are capable of speech and rationality in the manner of human beings.

In the manner of humanistic satires the work constitutes a virtuoso array of diverse literary forms: beast fable and dream vision coexist with medical treatise, proverb, and hymn. Through Streamer's outrageous insistence that animals can reason, superstitions of all kinds are held up for examination and ridicule. But if the didactic purpose of *Beware the Cat* betrays the influence of Erasmian humanism, parodic inversion and scepticism concerning human rationality are reminiscent of carnivalesque tradition in England and in Europe. In the manner of satires attributed to Luke Shepherd, Thomas More's *Utopia*, and François Rabelais's *Gargantua and Pantagruel*, Baldwin's satire dramatizes a topsy-turvy travesty of sanctioned forms of social order that highlights the arbitrariness and transitory nature of norms that govern everyday life.

Baldwin's next literary endeavour, his edition of *A Mirror for Magistrates*, continues in the vein of anti-Catholic polemic. For that reason the first edition (*c*.1554) appears to have been suppressed during the reign of Mary I, and it survives only in the form of two duplicate leaves from the tale of Owen Glendower and five title-pages. The text remained unpublished until Thomas Marsh printed it in 1559, soon after Elizabeth's accession. A collection of visionary poems by Baldwin, Ferrers, Thomas Churchyard, Thomas Phaer, Thomas Chaloner, and Thomas Sackville, the *Mirror for Magistrates* exemplifies misconduct by public officials and warns them of vices to be avoided. Enjoying great popularity, the text went through seven more editions by 1610. It influenced tragedies composed by Christopher Marlowe, William Shakespeare, and others. Baldwin's only other extant literary effort is *The Funerals of King Edward the Sixth*, a funeral elegy on the late monarch printed in 1560, again by Marsh.

During his literary career Baldwin continued to work at Whitchurch's printing shop and played an occasional role in the production of revels at the royal court. Accounts and correspondence of the master of the revels, Thomas Cawarden, indicate that Baldwin may have had a hand in 'a comedy concerning the way of life' and perhaps in a morality play but this cannot be confirmed.

Baldwin wrote in the 1563 *Mirror* that he had been 'called to an other trade of lyfe' in 1559, and he is probably the William Baldwin who was ordained deacon by Archbishop Grindal in that year; Thomas Churchyard describes him as a minister in the 1587 *Mirror*, and Wood noted that he gave up printing for the church. Baldwin was appointed vicar of Tortington, Sussex, in 1559–60 and rector of St Michael-le-Querne, London, in 1561; he died some time before 1 November 1563. Stowe's *Historical Memoranda* gives an account of a Baldwin preaching at Paul's Cross in September 1563, who died a week later of the plague. This was probably the writer.

Baldwin is remembered not only as an anti-Catholic satirist but also as a literary innovator whose works influenced writers as historically distant and as thematically diverse as Thomas Nashe, Edmund Spenser, and Alexander Pope. JOHN N. KING

Sources N. A. Gutierrez, 'Baldwin, William', *Sixteenth-century British nondramatic writers: first series*, ed. D. A. Richardson, DLitB, 132 (1993), 19–26 • N. A. Gutierrez, 'Beware the cat: mimesis in a skin of oratory', *Style*, 23 (1989), 49–69 • J. N. King, *English Reformation literature: the Tudor origins of the protestant tradition* (1982) • M. D. Bristol, *Carnival and theatre* (1985) • *STC, 1475–1640* • *DNB* • Wood, *Ath. Oxon.*, new edn, vol. 1 • D. S. Kastan, 'The death of William Baldwin', *N&Q*, 226 (1981), 516–17

Baldwin [Bawden], **William** [*alias* Octaviano Fuscincelli] (**1562–1632**), Jesuit, was born on 10 November 1562 in Cornwall, perhaps near Bodmin, birthplace of John Cornelius, with whom, according to Henry More SJ, Baldwin made his rudimentary studies. He entered Exeter College, Oxford, on 20 December 1577. Presumably he was reconciled to the Roman church some time in 1582 before his departure for the English College in Rheims, where he arrived on 31 December 1582. He was sent to Rome on 13 August 1583. Richard Barret, prefect of studies in Rheims, held Baldwin in high esteem, describing him as 'most obedient' and as a 'disciple of Cornelius' in a letter to Alfonso Agazzari, rector of the English College, Rome, on 11 August 1583 (*Diaries of the English College*, 331). Baldwin enrolled at the English College on 1 October. He was ordained in Rome on 16 April 1588 and entered the Society of Jesus there on 2 February 1590. He remained in Rome as English confessor at St Peter's for a year after his noviceship. On 12 January 1593 he was sent to the Spanish Netherlands, where he lectured on theology in Louvain for a year.

Summoned to Spain by Robert Parsons in late 1594, Baldwin, disguised as a Neapolitan merchant, Octaviano Fuscincelli, escorted six boys to the English College in Seville. The boys did not know that the merchant, who consistently spoke Latin and Italian, was an English Jesuit. Their vessel was intercepted at Calais by an English man-of-war. Taken to England, the boys were entrusted to John Whitgift, archbishop of Canterbury, and Baldwin was jailed in Bridewell. He got word to Henry Garnet, the Jesuit superior, but the speed with which Catholics sought to ransom Baldwin aroused suspicions. To quell them he suggested that officials ask John Gerard if he knew a merchant named Fuscincelli. Since that was Baldwin's official Jesuit alias, Gerard recognized it and replied yes. Cleared of suspicion Baldwin was ransomed in exchange for an English prisoner named Hawkins. He remained in England, living with Richard Cotton at Warblington, Hampshire, until late 1595, when he went to Rome to serve as minister of the English College under Father Rector Muzio Vitelleschi, future general of the society. In April of 1598 he was sent to Brussels as William Holt's successor as vice-prefect of the English mission, supervising English affairs at the court of Isabella and Albert in Brussels and relaying communications between Rome and England, a position he held until 1610. In Antwerp on 10 February 1602 he was professed of the four vows.

In 1605 Sir Thomas Edmonds, English ambassador, demanded that Baldwin, proclaimed a traitor because of alleged conspiracies with Ambrogio Spinola, commander of Spanish forces in Flanders for an invasion of England at the time of the Gunpowder Plot, be returned to England for trial. Archduke Albert refused. Recognized by letters he carried, despite his disguise, Baldwin was apprehended near Speyer in 1610 by soldiers of the elector palatine. Chained and imprisoned he was eventually turned over to Edward Cecil, brother of Robert Cecil, earl of Salisbury, who treated him with respect and kindness. By November he was in the Tower of London. King James replied to the archduke's demand for Baldwin's immediate release by promising that he would be free to return to the Spanish Netherlands once his innocence of any involvement in the Gunpowder Plot was established. But no legal proceedings were initiated and he remained in the Tower until 15 June 1618 when he and eleven other Jesuits were banished from the realm through the intercession of the count of Gondomar, Spanish ambassador. His stay in Brussels was brief: he hastened to Rome to explain and defend the unique status of the beleaguered English mission to Vitelleschi, now father-general. On 16 January 1619 he left Rome for Spain where he visited the English colleges on his journey back to Flanders. On 22 January 1621 he was named rector of the English College in Louvain and in early 1622 was transferred to the English College in St Omer. On 12 November 1622 he became, with the support and approval of the Infanta Isabella, the first Englishman to be rector of the college. He died at St Omer on 28 September 1632. THOMAS M. MCCOOG

Sources T. M. McCoog, *English and Welsh Jesuits, 1555–1650*, 2 vols., Catholic RS, 74–5 (1994–5), 110 • T. M. McCoog, ed., *Monumenta Angliae*, 2: *English and Welsh Jesuits, catalogues, 1630–1640* (1992), 220 • W. Kelly, ed., *Liber ruber venerabilis collegii Anglorum de urbe*, 1, Catholic RS, 37 (1940), 42 • Foster, *Alum. Oxon.* • T. F. Knox and others, eds., *The first and second diaries of the English College, Douay* (1878), 69, 192, 197 • H. Foley, ed., *Records of the English province of the Society of Jesus*, 3 (1878), 510–11; 7/1 (1882), 42; 7/2 (1883), 888 • H. More, *Historia missionis Anglicanae Societatis Iesu* (St Omer, 1660), 374
Archives Archives of the British Province of the Society of Jesus, London • Archivum Romanum Societatis Iesu, Rome • Stonyhurst College, Lancashire

Baldwin, William Warren (1775–1844). *See under* Baldwin, Robert (1804–1858).

Baldwulf. *See* Beadwulf (*fl.* 791–795).

Baldwyn, Edward (*bap.* 1745, *d.* 1817), schoolmaster and pamphleteer, was baptized on 21 August 1745 in the parish of St Lawrence, Ludlow, Shropshire, the son of William Baldwyn and his wife, Ann. He matriculated from St John's College, Oxford, on 25 June 1762, aged sixteen, and graduated BA in 1767 and MA in 1784. He became a fellow of the college while still an undergraduate, vacating the fellowship only on his marriage in Ludlow on 9 July 1772 to Mary Nash, with whom he had four sons. Baldwyn is described as being of average height, with a light, fresh complexion, bright blue eyes, and sandy hair, with a very upright and sprightly walk but delicate health (Claridge, 146).

In 1784 Baldwyn was appointed as master of Bradford grammar school. Under his leadership the school flourished. The number of pupils rose to fifty and the school began to make a net profit of about £225 per year. To increase the number of scholars still further, Baldwyn added a modern side to the curriculum. French and geography were introduced as well as writing and accounts, to be taught by a newly appointed master, the students paying extra for the classes. His commercialization of education emulated the developments already seen at Bingley and Leeds grammar schools. Baldwyn's salary was increased to 100 guineas in 1791 and a 'proper house', worth £25 per year, was built for him.

Baldwyn's time in Bradford was, however, dominated by his quarrel with the vicar of Bradford, John Crosse, and with the Sunday lecturer at the parish church, William Atkinson. Since 1703, the master of Bradford grammar school had, save for four years, also held the post of lecturer. Baldwyn regarded the post as a perquisite, but Crosse, who became vicar in the same year that Baldwyn took over the school, appointed Atkinson instead. Baldwyn attributed this to a grudge, for Crosse had also been a candidate for the job as master of Bradford grammar school, but there were also theological differences. Crosse, like Atkinson, was an evangelical, with sympathies for Methodism. Baldwyn was more orthodox.

When Atkinson published a volume of 'Poetical Essays' in 1786, Baldwyn could not resist the opportunity to attack. Under the pseudonym Trim he published *A Critique on the Poetical Essays of the Rev. William Atkinson* (1787) criticizing both Atkinson's writing and morality. He followed this up with *Remarks on Two of the most Singular Characters of the Age* (1788?, 2nd edn 1790), accusing Crosse of simony and embezzling money from the parish. Atkinson's printed replies (and perhaps also a physical skirmish) provoked Trim to write four more pamphlets sarcastically attacking Crosse, Atkinson, and Atkinson's brother Johnson Atkinson Busfeild, one of the grammar school's governors. Busfeild had accused Baldwyn of mismanaging the school and drinking on Sundays, charges which were soon dropped. After a lull from 1791, the hostilities reopened in 1797, perhaps for political reasons. Busfeild was captain of the volunteers, while Baldwyn opposed Pitt and the war with revolutionary France. He was blackballed from the Bradford Coffee Room for his political views by a Major Sturges, and in response published *A Letter to Major Sturges on the Injustice and Illiberality of his Late Conduct* (1797), an anti-Pittite pamphlet. Sturges responded by getting up a petition levelling fifteen specific charges of pedagogical misconduct at Baldwyn (he was accused *inter alia* of leaving school during school hours, of cruelty to the boys, of not taking the boys to church). Since two other governors of the school, in addition to Crosse and Busfeild, had signed the petition, Baldwyn's position was in jeopardy, but his denials and counter-assertions, published in a sixty-eight-page document (now lost) seem to have quieted the opposition and he remained in his post for another five years. Baldwyn is also credited with entering a number of other literary squabbles with several anonymous short pamphlets, perhaps including *A Letter to Richard Hill, Esq. Member for the County of Salop* (1782) by 'a burgess of Ludlow'. He was not, as is sometimes claimed, the author of those works for children written under the name Edward Baldwin. This was a pseudonym used by William Godwin.

In 1802 Baldwyn returned to Shropshire where he was rector of Abdon and perpetual curate of Clee St Margaret's. He planned to produce an edition of Catullus, writing to Wilkes for advice, but the project was never completed. He died in Kentish Town, London, on 11 February 1817 and was buried in St Pancras churchyard. M. O. GRENBY

Sources W. Claridge, 'Incidents in the life of the Rev. Edward Baldwyn, MA, head master of Bradford grammar school, 1784–1802', *Bradford Antiquary*, 1 (1881–8), 146–53 • A. E. Busby, *History of Bradford grammar school* (1969), 59–62 • *GM*, 1st ser., 87/1 (1817), 279 • C. E. C. Smyth, *Bradford grammar school: past and present* (1912) • F. T. Cansick, *A collection of curious and interesting epitaphs*, 2 (1872), 98 • *A new catalogue of living English authors: with complete lists of their publications, and biographical and critical memoirs* (1799) • Foster, *Alum. Oxon.* • BL, Add. MS 30873, fol. 139

Bale, John (1495–1563), bishop of Ossory, evangelical polemicist, and historian, was born to parents of humble means at the village of Cove, near Dunwich in Suffolk, on 21 November 1495.

Early career and marriage Throughout his life, despite wide travels, Bale continually proclaimed his identity as a Suffolk man. He began his formal education at the Carmelite convent at Norwich at twelve years of age and went to Jesus College, Cambridge, about 1514 in order to continue his schooling. Despite the intellectual ferment at Cambridge University, instigated by clerics like Hugh Latimer and Miles Coverdale who had been influenced by Lutheran ideas, Bale remained at this time a friar loyal to the old religion. After study at Cambridge and abroad, at Louvain and Toulouse, he was awarded the degree of BTh at Cambridge in 1529 and the DTh about two years later. In 1530 he became prior of the white friars' convent in the port town of Maldon in Essex. In 1533 he was promoted to the Carmelite convent at Ipswich, and he had become prior at Doncaster by July 1534.

At the time of England's separation from the Church of Rome during the early 1530s, Bale fell under the influence of Thomas, first Baron Wentworth of Nettlestead, to whom he attributed his conversion to protestantism. Bale enjoyed the patronage of Wentworth, an important East Anglian peer who used his influence at court in order to further the protestant cause. He began to come under suspicion himself, and about 1534 was charged with heresy before Archbishop Lee of York, but escaped conviction. In 1536, immediately before his final break with the Carmelite order, Bale left his priorate at Doncaster for the post of a stipendiary priest at Thorndon in Suffolk.

Although Bale's desire to marry was probably one reason for his leaving the Carmelites, he never made this explicit in his writings. Nevertheless by 1536 he had renounced clerical vows, laid aside monastic attire, and married a woman named Dorothy. Virtually nothing is known about her besides her name, but she must have been a widow when Bale married her because she had a son of apprentice age. Bale's silence about her, even though she accompanied him during two periods of exile and his intervening service as a bishop in Ireland, is noteworthy. For example, she receives only a passing comment in *The Vocacyon of Johan Bale to the Bishoprick of Ossorie in Ireland* (1553), when he mentions that he set sail for Ireland with 'my wyfe & one servaunt' (*Vocacyon*, 51). Bale's commitment to marriage is in keeping with his obsessive attack on clerical celibacy, which resounds throughout his polemical writings. He sees the mandatory vow of celibacy as an invitation to all forms of sexual transgression, including fornication, adultery, paedophilia, and homosexuality. Thus the *Vocacyon* attacks an Irish priest for fathering bastards in order to increase the size of church offerings, and his writings repeatedly allege that the papacy established 'stews of both kinds in Rome' (that is, heterosexual and homosexual brothels) for the patronage of unmarried clergy. It may be that Bale's boyhood experience at a Carmelite convent shaped his views on clerical sexuality.

Protestant playwright Bale and other reformers soon became dissatisfied with the conservative nature of religious reformation in the later years of Henry VIII's reign. In 1537, while he was serving as a priest at Thorndon, Bale was arrested for preaching heresy in a sermon that denounced 'papistry'. He was subsequently freed, thanks in part to the intercession of John Leland, the king's antiquarian, who was a strong supporter of Bale and his writings, and to whom Bale dedicated his 'Anglorum Heliades' of *c*.1539–1540, a historical and bibliographical account of the Carmelite order in England. This work has the additional interest of showing that Bale had not yet completed his transition from Catholic to protestant theology. Bale also enjoyed the support of Thomas Cromwell, the king's principal minister and vicegerent for religious affairs, and would later acknowledge that Cromwell had arranged his release from prison as a reward for his polemical comedies. The minister supported a troupe of actors led by Bale, who staged allegorical morality plays which promoted protestant ideas and satirized Catholic beliefs by personifying the two sides as Virtues and Vices respectively.

Of twenty-four plays known to have been written by Bale, only five are still extant. His first composition, and the one most widely read today, *King John*, was staged at Archbishop Cranmer's house during Christmastide at the end of 1538. Based upon historical material in William Tyndale's *Obedience of a Christian Man*, the play flatters Henry VIII as the successor to King John who attacks papal tyranny and completes England's schism from the Church of Rome. Despite assistance from Nobility, Clergy, and Civil Order, the medieval king's attempts at religious reform are blocked by a variety of stage Vices who include Usurped Power (as Pope Innocent III), Private Wealth (as Cardinal Pandulphus), Dissimulation (as Raymundus, a papal legate, and Simon, monk of Swinset), and Sedition (as Stephen Langton). Poisoned by Usurped Power, King John dies before he can complete the task of ecclesiastical reform. After John's death, the play moves triumphantly to Bale's own age when Imperial Majesty (a dramatic type for Henry VIII) defends 'Christian faith' and 'the authority of God's holy word' against continuing papal aggression.

Printed in 1548 but probably composed much earlier, Bale's *Comedy Concerning Three Laws* depicts the downfall of the personified virtues Natural Law, Mosaic Law, and Christian Law. Allegorical costuming presents the victorious Vices and manifestations of Roman Catholic 'error': Sodomy is presented as a monk, Avarice as a common lawyer, Covetousness as a bishop, False Doctrine as a popish doctor, and Hypocrisy as a Franciscan friar. Appearing as an old witch, Idolatry is identified with the Whore of Babylon, herself a symbol of papal Rome. Along with Infidelity, many of these figures possess the attributes of the medieval Vice, whose comic aspect included vulgar blasphemy and obscene jesting. Modelled on the book of Revelation, the last two acts of the drama culminate in the expulsion of Infidelity by Divine Vengeance. The consequent restoration of the three laws in preparation for the marriage of the Bridegroom and the Spouse at the descent of the New Jerusalem provides an optimistic allegory of the completion of the protestant reformation.

Bale's three remaining plays, composed in 1538 under Cromwell's patronage, adopt themes, conventions, and devices from the medieval mystery and morality plays to protestant purposes. *The Chief Promises of God*, *John the Baptist's Preaching*, and *The Temptation of Jesus Christ* reverse the emphases of the cycles of biblical mystery plays popular during Bale's lifetime. (Derek van der Straten printed them at Wesel, in the county of Cleves, in 1547, during Bale's first exile from England.) Thus *The Chief Promises of God* consists of dialogue between Pater Coelestis (the Heavenly Father) and Adam, Noah, Abraham, Moses, David, Isaiah, and John the Baptist, and represents divine covenants as precursors of the protestant reformation.

The first exile and its fruits The passage of the Act of Six Articles in 1539 marked a major shift in religious policy by reimposing strict orthodoxy and banning protestant tracts, and presaged the downfall of Cromwell, who was executed in the following year. After this reversal of Henry VIII's commitment to ecclesiastical reform Bale fled to the continent, where he continued to produce outspoken controversial writings, including a number of anti-Roman Catholic martyrologies: *A Brief Chronicle Concerning the Examination and Death of Sir John Oldcastle* (1544), *The Examination of William Thorpe*, and *The Examinations of Anne Askew* (1547). These works provided models for John Foxe's highly influential *Actes and Monuments*, known popularly as the book of martyrs (1563). While in Germany, Bale also compiled *Acts of English Votaries* (1546), an exposé of alleged monastic corruption, as well as *Yet another Course at the Romish Foxes* (1543), which denounces Stephen Gardiner, bishop of Winchester, for persecuting English protestants. (Foxe's *Actes and Monuments* records Gardiner's counter-attack on Bale's propagandist tracts.) The most influential product of Bale's first exile, however, was *The Image of both Churches* (1545), which provided the first complete commentary on the book of Revelation to be printed in English. This work views Christian history as a continuing struggle between the 'true' church, based on Jesus's teachings in the gospels, and the 'false' Church of Rome, whose leadership by the pope results from its subversion by Antichrist and the misinterpretation of scriptural texts.

During this exile Bale also wrote and edited numerous tracts including the *Apocalypsis goliae*, an anticlerical satire attributed to Walter Map and reissued by Bale as *Rhythmi vetustissimi de corrupto ecclesiae statu* (1546); an eyewitness account of the death of Martin Luther by Justus Jonas; and Princess Elizabeth's translation of a devotional text by Marguerite de Navarre entitled *Godly Meditations of the Christian Soul* (1548). These works, with many others like them, generally denounce the papacy, the ritualism of the Roman liturgy, belief in transubstantiation and the mass, the veneration of saints, and the cult of the Virgin Mary. In their place Bale advocates protestant practices designed to nurture individual faith: gospel preaching, lay education in the vernacular Bible, and a service of holy communion that commemorates Christ's sacrifice rather than re-enacting it. Owing to tighter restraints on publication in the later years of Henry VIII's reign, Bale arranged for the printing of his polemical works in Antwerp and, after the imperial authorities also imposed tighter restrictions on protestant publication, in Wesel. He courted death in arranging for the smuggling of his tracts into England, where they went on sale surreptitiously under the pseudonyms of James Harrison and Henry Stalbridge.

Bale also compiled his *Illustrium Maioris Britannie scriptorum … summarium*, which was printed in Wesel in 1548. He more than once expresses indignation and dismay at the destruction of libraries resulting from the dissolution of the monasteries—'To destroye all without consyderacyon, is and wyll be unto Englande for ever, a moste horryble infamy amonge the grave senyours of other nacyons' (Aston, 327)—and in this book he continued John Leland's antiquarian project of preserving and cataloguing their manuscript holdings, in an arrangement along the lines of his own apocalyptic periodization of history in the *Image of both Churches*. The book was distributed from Wesel for a learned continental readership, and from Ipswich for English readers literate in Latin. In this and his other writings at this time, Bale was trying to capitalize on the major shift in religious policy that followed Henry VIII's death in 1547 and the accession of his nine-year-old son, Edward VI, as successive governments countenanced a thorough programme of protestant reform of a kind prevented during the late king's reign. Bale's dedication of his *Summarium* appeals to Edward VI for patronage, but he failed to secure assistance from the crown until Protector Somerset's downfall in 1549 and the installation of John Dudley in his place. In certain respects, Bale's *Index Britanniae scriptorum*, an untitled manuscript that remained unpublished until the twentieth century (Bodl. Oxf., MS Selden supra 64), is a more useful bibliographical tool than his *Summarium* (or its printed successor). Mostly compiled between about 1548 and 1552, entries in this private notebook document Bale's monumental effort to record the title, opening lines, and location of every extant learned book composed by a British author.

Ireland and the *Vocacyon* Edward's accession enabled Bale and other reformers to return to England. In 1548 he and John Foxe are recorded as living in the duchess of Richmond's house in London. He was collated rector of Bishopstoke, Hampshire, on 26 June 1551 by John Ponet, bishop of Winchester, and in the same year was made vicar of Swaffham. Then on 15 August 1552 he met Edward VI at Southampton and was promised the Irish bishopric of Ossory; formal nomination followed on 22 October. His appointment, typical of the increasingly radical religious climate that followed Somerset's removal from office, was intended to contribute to Dudley's efforts to convert the Irish to protestantism.

Late in 1552 Bale travelled to Ireland, where he was consecrated at Dublin on 2 February 1553. Residing at Kilkenny, he took up his diocesan duties. Even before his installation Bale's ardent upholding of protestant doctrine had created controversy. The Irish church had not yet accepted the official 'Form of consecrating bishops' enacted by parliament, but retained a Catholic ordination ceremony to which Bale refused to subscribe. He succeeded in his protest, but not without the disapproval and formal complaint of the dean of Dublin Cathedral.

The Vocacyon of Johan Bale provides a detailed account of Bale's uncompromising activity as an evangelical prelate in a remote see beyond the pale. Although the Irish bishops formally accepted the royal supremacy, they resisted changes in religion. The refusal of the conservative archbishop of Armagh, George Dowdall, to implement ecclesiastical reforms meant that traditional ceremonies remained in place. Other bishops either barely conformed or resigned their sees. Bale added to his own difficulties by trying to enforce the use of the 1552 revision of the Book of Common Prayer, even though it was effectively unknown in Ireland, where the 1549 version was reprinted in 1551, a year after it had ceased to be published in England. None the less, in spite of unco-operative clergy and a generally hostile populace, his powerful sermons had made a number of converts by the time of Edward VI's death in 1553.

Bale's *Vocacyon*, one of the earliest known autobiographical writings in English, is largely a record of conflict between the bishop and his flock. Among the events recounted in this lively work are the poisoning of Bale's superior, Archbishop Goodacre, by a group of priests, and the murder of Bale's own servants for following his orders by working on a Catholic feast day. The text fashions Bale's identity as an uncompromising reformist bishop pitted against recalcitrant Irish clerics who, he alleges, broke their religious vows but continued to observe Catholic practices. When Mary I succeeded to the throne of England, Bale's position became precarious. Nevertheless, he stirred up further contention by the staging of his own polemical plays at the market cross in Kilkenny.

In the face of their bishop's opposition and continued preaching, the Irish clergy restored the mass and other prohibited religious practices. Fleeing from priests who he feared were plotting to murder him, Bale withdrew to Dublin in September 1553 and then set sail for the Netherlands. *En route* he was taken prisoner by a Flemish man-of-war, which was then forced into port at St Ives in Cornwall by bad weather. Arrested on suspicion of treason, he was released to continue his voyage, only to be arrested for a second time at Dover and held there for several weeks. Eventually, being 'by that time so full of lyce as I coulde swarme' (*Vocacyon*, 77), a payment of £30 secured his passage to the Low Countries.

Bale reassures the readership of his *Vocacyon* that the persecution of English protestants under Queen Mary is only the latest bout of suffering in a cycle that will eventually lead to providential deliverance. Offering his own experience as an example of how the persecuted faithful will undergo this deliverance, Bale styles himself a martyr, not in the sense of one who dies for his faith, but as one who openly testifies to the point of death if necessary. He stresses the typological relationship between his own experiences and those of various New Testament figures, notably St Paul. Although the book's colophon bears the impudent joke that it was 'Imprinted at Rome before the sign of St Peter in December anno domini 1553', it seems likely that Hugh Singleton and Joos Lambrecht printed it at a later date in Wesel, the place of Bale's earlier exile. The false colophon helped to protect the publishers of the volume from reprisals.

Second exile, return, and death Following his landing in the Netherlands, Bale made his way to Frankfurt am Main, where in September 1554 he took part in the disputes among the English protestant exiles over liturgy and church government, eventually siding with Richard Cox and the Book of Common Prayer. He was still in Frankfurt in July 1555, when his former patron John Ponet wrote to him urging him to continue with his polemical writings: 'blow therfor boldly the trumnpet of Gods treuth, and play the bushop amonge your companions ther, as thoughe ye were among your flok in Yerland' (Baskerville, 443). By the end of that year he was living in Basel, where he channelled his energy into the completion of his massive bibliographical project, a revision of his *Summarium*. He laboured on this while residing at the home of the master printer Joannes Oporinus, along with his friend and fellow exile John Foxe. Under the title of *Scriptorum illustrium Maioris Brytannie … catalogus*, Oporinus published the fruit of decades of bibliographical toil in two weighty folio volumes (1557–9). Like its predecessor, the *Catalogus* is divided into 'Centuries'—groupings of 100 authors. Although Bale enumerates texts regardless of their theological content, he places great emphasis on documenting the continuity of the 'true' church from early Christian times until his generation. To this end he devotes great effort to recording the works of proto-protestant writers, notably English Lollards who looked to John Wyclif for their inspiration. Bale interspersed the entries in this catalogue of manuscripts and printed books with historical summaries that supply an apocalyptic context for texts by British authors. In 1558 Oporinus published related anti-papal material in another work by Bale, his *Acta Romanorum pontificum*.

Following the accession of Elizabeth, Bale returned to England, and on 10 January 1560 was appointed by the crown as canon of the eleventh prebend in Canterbury Cathedral. In the previous year Queen Elizabeth had ordered Warham and Robert St Leger, the son and brother respectively of Sir Anthony St Leger, lord deputy of Ireland, to return to Bale books and manuscripts which he had been forced to leave behind in 1553. The St Legers denied all knowledge of them, and their fate remains uncertain. None the less, Bale continued to complain to Archbishop Matthew Parker that he had not received his property. The queen had spoken for Bale on the grounds that the return of his manuscripts and continuation of his historical research was needed 'for the illustration and settyng forth of the storye of this our realme, by him, the said Bale' (McKisack, 18). The aged scholar was unable, however, to undertake the work envisioned by the queen. Writing nothing of great significance toward the end of his life, he did praise Elizabeth in a revised ending to *King John*. In May 1560 he was reported to be staging a play satirizing the friars in a private house in Canterbury, with a cast of schoolboys from the city's grammar school. In the following year he published his *Declaration of Edmonde Bonners Articles*, originally written in 1554, which attacks the Catholic bishop of London for persecuting protestants under Mary. He attended the convocation of 1563, but had died before 26 November that year, and was buried at Canterbury. Eight years later the fervently protestant preacher Robert Pownall asked in his will to be buried next to Bale, whose widow had in the meantime been granted a generous pension by the cathedral authorities.

Bale's influence Extensive holdings of Bale's papers are preserved in the British Library, London, the Bodleian Library, Oxford, Cambridge University Library, and the Henry E. Huntington Library in California. A number of his works were collected in *The Select Works of John Bale*, published by the Parker Society in 1849. More recently, his *Index Britanniae scriptorum*, first published in 1902, was reissued in 1990, the same year in which the Renaissance English Text Society published a scholarly edition of his *Vocacyon*. Bale's edition of Anne Askew's *Examinations*, with his own commentary, was published in 1996 as part of Oxford University Press's Women Writers in English series. Biographical studies include works by H. McCusker (1942), L. P. Fairfield (1976), and P. Happé (1996). The importance of the apocalyptic in Bale's thinking has been investigated by John N. King.

Bale's writings are indeed notable for a consistent historiographical vision which is expressed most fully in his *Image of both Churches*, but is also vital to the polemical plays, propaganda tracts, and works of scholarship written from the 1530s onwards. Above all, his interpretation of Revelation affords an apocalyptic paradigm for virtually everything that he wrote. In his eyes, a proper understanding of Revelation should enable believers to trace the historical trajectory of the conflict between 'true' and 'false' churches through the seven ages prophesied by the blowing of seven trumpets, the opening of the seven seals, and the pouring of the seven vials. These ages proceed from an initial period of apostolic purity to the sixth age, which encompasses the persecution of the faithful from the time of John Wyclif until Bale's own lifetime. Wyclif and William Tyndale are leading representatives of the 'true' religion which had been brought directly to England by Joseph of Arimathea, one which remained uncorrupted by fraudulent apostolic succession of Roman pontiffs who act as agents of Antichrist. Present history looks forward to the final age, when the world as it is known will come to an end.

Bale was an outstanding radical reformer of the first generation of English protestants. Surviving many of his colleagues who were burnt at the stake as heretics or died in exile, he enjoyed a literary career noteworthy for his mastery of an ensemble of polemical forms, the intensity of his invective, his satirical flair, and his breadth of learning. His unparalleled acerbity earned for him the epithet (coined by Thomas Fuller) of 'Bilious Bale'. As the standards of Elizabethan literary taste became more decorous, a process signalled by the poetic treatises of Sir Philip Sidney and George Puttenham, Bale's recourse to invective, scatological humour, and sexual innuendo alienated many English readers, and his works soon fell out of print. His apocalyptic ideas, however, exerted a continuing influence on works as diverse as John Foxe's *Actes and Monuments* (1563), book 1 of Edmund Spenser's *Faerie Queene* (1590), and Thomas Dekker's *Whore of Babylon* (1607), while the antiquarian learning contained within his comprehensive bibliographies continues to influence scholars. JOHN N. KING

Sources J. N. King, 'John Bale', *Sixteenth-century British nondramatic writers: first series*, ed. D. A. Richardson, DLitB, 132 (1993), 27–35 • J. N. King, *English reformation literature: the Tudor origins of the protestant tradition* (1982) • *STC, 1475–1640* • *The vocacyon of John Bale*, ed. P. Happé and J. N. King, Renaissance English Text Society, 7th ser., 14 (1990) • *The complete plays of John Bale*, ed. P. Happé, 2 vols. (1985–6) • P. Beal, *Index of English literary manuscripts*, ed. P. J. Croft and others, 1/1–2 (1980) • Bale, *Index* • S. G. Ellis, *Ireland in the age of the Tudors* (1998) • H. McCusker, *John Bale, dramatist and antiquary* (1942) • L. P. Fairfield, *John Bale: mythmaker for the English Reformation* (1976) • P. Happé, *John Bale* (1996) • M. McKisack, *Medieval history in the Tudor age* (1971) • M. Aston, *Lollards and reformers* (1984) • P. Collinson, N. Ramsay, and M. Sparks, eds., *A history of Canterbury Cathedral* (1995) • *Fasti Angl., 1541–1857*, [Canterbury] • E. J. Baskerville,

'John Ponet in exile: a Ponet letter to John Bale', *Journal of Ecclesiastical History*, 37 (1986), 442–7

Archives BL, *Illustrium Maioris Britannie* with MS annotations and additions • BL, religious collections, incl. many papers relating to Carmelite order, transcripts of some of his notes and papers, Add. MSS 5141, 6116, 6261, Cl MS Tit DX101, Hl MSS 1819, 3838, 7031 • Bodl. Oxf., collections relating to Carmelites and bibliographical studies, his MS additions to a volume relating to John Wycliffe and the Lollards • LPL, papers, annotations to other MSS • NRA, further papers and annotations to other MSS • U. Edin. L., *Illustrium Maioris Britannie* with his MS notes and additions | Trinity Cam., epitome of John Leland's work with notes on papal history

Likenesses Passe, line engraving, BM; repro. in H. Holland, *Herōologia* (1620) • engravings, repro. in *Complete plays of John Bale*, ed. Happé, frontispieces

Bale, Robert (*b. c.*1410, *d.* in or after 1473), chronicler, was, according to John Bale (*d.* 1563), a lawyer, public notary, and judge in civil cases in London, as well as being a chronicler of London affairs. He was probably the Robert Bale identified by Kingsford as a scrivener who married Agnes Haunsard before 1438 and had several children with her. A wedding gift of £100 from Agnes's uncle, Thomas Haunsard, was invested in houses and tenements at Southwark. A man of some means, Bale the scrivener was involved in legal disputes concerning debt and deceit in 1457 and 1465–70 and is last referred to in a further legal action in 1473.

By 1509, according to the great chronicle, the name Bale was associated with the authorship of a long book. That book was probably the chronicle later attributed to Robert Bale. In his attribution John Bale is making specific reference to the London chronicle found in Trinity College, Dublin, MS 509, with the last entry written into TCD, MS 604. A second copy of this text, down to 1437, exists in Hatfield House, Cecil MS 281, but this text has never been associated with Bale; after 1437 the Cecil text varies from that in TCD, MSS 509 and 604. Bale's chronicle, as preserved in TCD, MSS 509 and 604, commences in 1189 and concludes in 1461, dating by mayoral years. The later years are recorded contemporaneously with the events they describe, and include an extensive eyewitness account of Cade's uprising (1450), one of the best surviving records of this event. It may be the material from 1438–1461, in particular, which should be considered to be the work of Robert Bale.

According to John Bale, Robert Bale wrote *Londinensis urbis chronicon*, *Instrumenta libertatum Londini*, *Gesta regis Edwardi tertii*, *Alphabetum sanctorum Angliae*, and *De praefectis et consulibus Londini*. Only the London chronicle is extant. M-R. McLaren

Sources Bale, *Cat.*, 2.65 • C. L. Kingsford, 'Robert Bale, the London chronicler', *EngHR*, 31 (1916), 126–8 • M.-R. McLaren, 'The London chronicles of the fifteenth century: the manuscripts, their authors and their aims', PhD diss., University of Melbourne, 1990, 54–62; 183–6; 286–97 • A. H. Thomas and I. D. Thornley, eds., *The great chronicle of London* (1938); repr. (1983) • R. Flenley, ed., *Six town chronicles of England* (1911) [incl. Bale's chronicle, 114–53] • M.-R. McLaren, 'The textual transmission of the London chronicles', *English Manuscript Studies, 1100–1700*, 3 (1992), 39–72 • M.-R. McLaren, *The London chronicles of the fifteenth century: a revolution in English writing* (2002)

Archives TCD, MS 509 • TCD, MS 604 | Hatfield House, Hertfordshire, Cecil MS 281

Bale, Robert (*d.* 1503), prior of Burnham Norton and historian, was born 3 miles from Walsingham, Norfolk, and joined the Carmelites at their house at Burnham Norton in the same county. He was a great lover of the liturgy and history of his order, which is reflected in his three known works. He composed a short chronicle of the Carmelites (Bodl. Oxf., MS Selden supra 72, fols. 5–11*v*) and a liturgical office to the prophet Elijah (CUL, MS Ff.6.28, fols. 34–42*v*) which has been published by B. Zimmerman, *Ordinaire de l'ordre de Notre-Dame du Mont-Carmel* (1910), though the lessons of matins are omitted. An office of St Simon Stock, now lost, was probably a text used in the English province. John Bale (no relation) noted a few years later that, although not an eloquent preacher, he impressed with his learning and his ability to resolve legal problems. Bale adds that his works were 'unpolished and dull' and certainly there is little in them to support the assertion that Robert Bale spent part of each year studying at Oxford and Cambridge. His title of lector was an award from the order itself. He was prior for some years in Burnham Norton and died there on 11 November 1503. He bequeathed his collection of books to his convent. Richard Copsey

Sources J. Bale, Bodl. Oxf., MS Bodley 73 (SC 27635), fols. 2, 135*v* • J. Bale, BL, Harley MS 3838, fols. 109–109*v* • Bale, *Cat.*, 2.65 • Emden, *Oxf.* • Emden, *Cam.* • J. Bale, *Illustrium Maioris Britannie scriptorum … summarium* (1548), fols. 252–252*v*

Archives Bodl. Oxf., MS Selden supra 72 (SC 3460), fols. 5–11*v* [copy] • CUL, MS Ff 6.28, fols. 34–42*v* [copy]

Bales, Christopher (1564–1590), Roman Catholic priest, was born (or baptized) on 12 March 1564 in Coniscliffe, co. Durham, a son of John and Katherine Bales; he had a brother, John, a tailor. He was brought up a protestant, but on 10 June 1581 he entered the English College, then at Rheims, and on 13 August 1583 he was among a large party who left for the English College in Rome, which he entered on 1 October that year. However, a year later he returned to Rheims on account of ill health and continued his studies there until his priestly ordination at Laon on 28 March 1587, for which he seems to have obtained a dispensation because he was under the canonical age. He was sent back to England on 2 November 1588 and probably served in and around London, lodging in the Gray's Inn area and using the aliases Evers, Mallett, and Rivers. He was arrested and tortured by Richard Topcliffe in Bridewell before being moved to the Gatehouse. Bales was tried under the act of 27 Elizabeth proclaiming seminary priests in England to be guilty of treason. He was convicted and put to death in Fleet Street on 4 March 1590. On the same day two laymen accused of harbouring him were hanged, Nicholas Horner in Smithfield and Alexander Blake in Gray's Inn Lane. J. T. Rhodes

Sources G. Anstruther, *The seminary priests*, 1 (1969) • J. H. Pollen, ed., *Unpublished documents relating to the English martyrs*, 1, Catholic RS, 5 (1908) • R. Challoner, *Memoirs of missionary priests*, ed. J. H. Pollen, rev. edn (1924) • J. H. Pollen, ed., *Acts of English martyrs* (1891) • Gillow, *Lit. biog. hist.* • *DNB* • J. A. Myerscough, *The martyrs of Durham and the north-east* (1956) • W. Kelly, ed., *Liber ruber venerabilis collegii Anglorum de urbe*, 1, Catholic RS, 37 (1940), 44–5

Bales, Peter (*bap.* 1547, *d.* 1610?), writing-master and calligrapher, was baptized at St Michael Cornhill, London, on 15 June 1547. Parish records show that he was the eldest child of Thomas Bales of Birchin Lane, a draper and a citizen of London, and his wife, Elizabeth. According to the preface of Joseph Champion's *The Parallel* (1750), Bales had already begun to practise his art by 1559, when he was only twelve years old. Wood's *Athenae Oxonienses* provides information about the next stage of his career, linking his name to Gloucester Hall, Oxford, where it is most likely that he was a writing-master rather than a student. On 10 March 1575 his penmanship was brought to the attention of the court when he presented Queen Elizabeth with a gold and crystal ring, set with a specimen of his 'micrographical performance, in which the writing was so wonderfully small, yet so very legible, that it surprized all who saw it' (Kippis, 1.536). This virtuoso piece, which included, among other devotional texts, minute transcriptions of the Credo, the Lord's prayer, and the ten commandments, much impressed the queen, who is said to have worn the ring on many occasions.

While such marvellous calligraphic feats suggest a natural inclination towards flamboyance and self-promotion, the mainstay of Bales's career was in the rather more prosaic dissemination of 'swift', 'true', and 'fair' writing. To this end, by 1590 he had set up a school near the sign of the Dolphin at the upper end of the Old Bailey, London, where some of the leading citizens sent their children. In an age before the wide-scale availability of printed texts Bales also offered his services as a scribe and a copyist in an advertisement that promised: 'you may have anything faire written in any kind of hand, usuall, and bookes of copies faire as you shall bespeake' (Heal, 9). He was evidently successful in this enterprise: in the 1580s and 1590s he was regularly commissioned to transcribe public documents into book form in his even, 'type-like lettering' (ibid.). According to the extensive memoir in the *Biographia Britannica* (1778), his connection with courtly circles also led him to become involved in Elizabethan espionage. Working alongside one Thomas Phillips—whose job was to decipher the letters in code which were intercepted by Arthur Gregory, who could '*unseal* a letter, and so dextrously *close* it again … that no eye could discern its having been opened' (Kippis, 1.536)—Bales was employed either to transcribe their contents or to forge new letters and additional paragraphs to send on in their place. In a bid to secure himself a permanent position, Bales next attempted to gain a place at court; although he was unsuccessful in his efforts, it was around this time that he was appointed to the chancery as a clerk, a fact which is attested at the foot of another of his celebrated micrographical performances: a complete, hand-written Bible small enough to fit into a walnut shell.

Several events in Bales's life suggest that he was an innovative, rapacious, and competitive man. In 1590 he published *The Writing Schoolemaster*, one of the first engraved copybooks. Owing to an error by John Evelyn in his *Numismata* (1697), it has long been considered as the first work to present a system of ciphers as a form of shorthand. In fact, it was neither the first treatise on shorthand (that honour can be awarded to Timothy Bright for his *Characterie: an Art of Short Swift, and Secret Writing, by Character*, 1588) nor a full exposition on a new system of ciphers, as it was dependent on reducing full words into abbreviated longhand characters. Nevertheless, Bales was determined to profit from this publication, and his underhand dealings led to a lawsuit between the author and his publisher, Thomas Orwin, in which the former was found guilty of undercutting the publisher for his personal gain. His showmanship and competitiveness can be witnessed again in 1595, when, at the age of forty-eight, he challenged Daniel Johnson, a rival penman whose youthfulness assured him greater steadiness of hand, to a writing match for the prestigious prize of a golden pen valued at £20. It was conducted in public at the 'Black Fryers within Conduit Yard', and the jury consisted of William Seager, a herald at arms; Anthony Dew and John Gwilliams, both clerks in the high court of chancery; William Pank, a penman in the court of London; and George Chapman, a gentleman. Under their judgement Bales and Johnson matched their talents for, as Bales put it, 'best and fairest writing of all kinde of handes … for Secretarie and Clerklike writing … [and] for best teachinge' (Heal, 9). Evidently Bales's hand was still steady, and his experience was pre-eminent; despite Johnson's publication of vociferous accusations of Bales's corruption in packing the jury with his friends, the golden pen was awarded to the older penman. By posting public placards returning Johnson's slur upon him, Bales proudly capitalized on his victory: in addition to renaming his premises 'the Hand and Golden Pen', he also wrote his own account of this public spectacle in a piece of penmanship entitled 'The original cause' (1596/7, now Harl. MS 675, held in the British Library, London).

Bales's leading patrons at court in the 1570s and 1580s seem to have been Sir Francis Walsingham and Sir Christopher Hatton; their deaths in 1590 and 1591 respectively led him to concentrate his attention on Lord Burghley (*d.* 1598), who either then or earlier had made Bales his writing-master and penman. The last known facts of his life are remarkably eventful. During the later part of his career he was 'innocently engaged' in the employment of John Danyell of Deresburie. This gentleman, one of the retinue of the earl of Essex, sought to improve his own fortunes by trying to sell some revealing letters, forged by Bales, to the earl's enemies. On being brought to trial at the Star Chamber for this crime Danyell was convicted on Bales's evidence, forced to pay damages totalling £3000, sentenced to sit in pillory, and then imprisoned for life. Although Bales had also been incarcerated, during the trial he was eventually absolved of all guilt in Danyell's scheme to destroy the earl of Essex.

That Bales weathered the Danyell débâcle is clear from his advancement to the position of 'tutor to the late noble Prince Henry' (Heal, 9), which must have taken place early in the new reign. Although no research has been undertaken to support this conclusion, it seems possible that he owed both his survival and his promotion to Burghley's son, Robert Cecil, first earl of Salisbury, who served as principal minister in the last years of Elizabeth's reign and the beginning of James I's. With the premature death of Henry, prince of Wales, Bales's career is difficult to trace. In his *The Origins and Progress of Letters* (1763), William Massey assumed that he died before 1614; indeed no mention of Bales's name is known after 1610, when the writing-master John Davies of Hereford made a scathing reference to his rival with his 'golden Pen' in a satiric verse entitled *The Scourge of Folly*. His reputation survived intact, however: by the late seventeenth century, his flamboyant character and idiosyncratic experiences had become a touchstone of virtuosity for later writing-masters, who often drew comparisons between themselves and this celebrated figure. LUCY PELTZ

Sources J. Champion, *The parallel* (1750) • J. Evelyn, *Numismata: a discourse of medals, antient and modern* (1697) • A. Heal, *The English writing-masters and their copy-books, 1570–1800* (1931) • I. D'Israeli, *Curiosities of literature*, 14th edn, 3 vols. (1849) • A. Kippis and others, eds., *Biographia Britannica, or, The lives of the most eminent persons who have flourished in Great Britain and Ireland*, 2nd edn, 5 vols. (1778–93) • W. Massey, *The origin and progress of letters: an essay in two parts* (1763) • Wood, *Ath. Oxon.*, new edn

Archives BL, account of his winning the golden pen, Harley MS 6 75/1 • BL, 'curious' miniature Bible written by Peter Bales, Harley MS 5305 • BL, desires to be retained in Lord Burghley's service, Harley MS XCIX 102 • BL, petition against commercial abuses, Harley MS 306/26 • BL, petition to be presented to an office of arms, Harley MS XCIX 59 • BL, 'The original cause', Harley MS 675 • LPL, MS with verse in praise of John Aylmer and John Whitgift | LPL, letters to John Whitgift

Balfe, Michael William (1808–1870), composer, the third child of William Balfe and his wife, Kate, *née* Ryan, was born at 10 Pitt Street, Dublin, on 15 May 1808. The family moved to Wexford when he was two years old. Balfe received his first musical instruction from his father, a competent violinist and dancing-master, and continued to study violin with Joseph Halliday, the bandmaster of the Cavan militia. In 1814 his teachers included a bandmaster named Meadows, who apparently directed a performance of a polacca by Balfe before the boy was seven years old. He continued his studies in Dublin under William O'Rourke (Rooke), demonstrating his precocity by his first public performance as a violinist on 20 June 1817 and by the composition in the same year of the ballad 'Young Fanny', sung under the title 'The Lover's Mistake' by Madame Vestris. After O'Rourke went to London about 1820, Balfe studied with James Barton and Alexander Lee, and was just beginning his professional career as a violinist when, on 6 January 1823, his father died. Having refused an offer of adoption from a rich relative of his mother's, who wished him to join him in the West Indies, Balfe approached Charles Edward Horn, then on a concert tour to Ireland with the request that he become his articled pupil. Impressed by Balfe's talent, Horn agreed. In London, Balfe also studied composition with Horn's father, Carl Friedrich Horn, an enthusiast for J. S. Bach and an accomplished musician. At the same time he tried his luck as a singer: he appeared without success at the oratorio concerts on 19 March 1823, and then made an equally unsuccessful stage début in Norwich as Caspar in a version of Weber's *Der Freischütz*.

Michael William Balfe (1808–1870), by Herbert Watkins, late 1850s

In 1825 Balfe attracted the attention of Count Mazzara, who invited him to accompany him to Italy. On the journey through Paris he met Cherubini, on whom he made a very favourable impression. In Rome, maintained at the count's expense, he took lessons in composition with Ferdinando Paer, and when Mazzara returned to England in 1826 he sent Balfe to Milan to study singing with Fillipo Galli and counterpoint with Vincenzo Federici. In the autumn of 1826 Balfe's first theatrical composition, a *ballo pantomimo serio* entitled *Il naufragio di La Pérouse* was staged in Milan at the Teatro alla Cannobiana. Unable to obtain an engagement in Milan as a singer, however, he returned to Paris. There Cherubini introduced him to Rossini, who, impressed by his singing, undertook to recommend him to the Théâtre des Italiens if he would study with Bordogni for a year. Supported in his studies by Cherubini, he made excellent progress and duly appeared in 1827 as Figaro in Rossini's *Il barbiere di Siviglia* with notable success. A three-year engagement on advantageous terms followed, but after only two seasons Balfe returned to Italy, apparently because of ill health. He soon obtained an engagement at the Teatro Carolino in Palermo, where, on 1 January 1830, he appeared as Valdeburgo in Bellini's *La straniera*.

During his time in Paris, Balfe had composed insertions for a revival of Zingarelli's *Romeo e Giulietta* and had begun an opera on Chateaubriand's *Atala*, and in Italy he continued to compose. A dispute between manager and chorus at Palermo during the carnival of 1829–30 led to a commission to write a short opera without chorus, *I rivali di se stessi*, which, composed in some twenty days, became his first staged opera. After completing his engagement at Palermo, Balfe appeared at Piacenza and at Bergamo, where he met and shortly afterwards married the Hungarian singer Lina Roser (*d.* 1888), with whom he had two daughters—one of whom predeceased him, while the other, Victoire *Balfe, began a successful singing career in 1857 and was married successively to Sir John Crampton and the duke of Frías. At Pavia in 1831 Balfe wrote *Un avvertimento ai gelosi*, a *farsa giocosa*, for the Teatro Fraschini. The next two years were spent in Milan, where his third opera, *Enrico Quatro al passo del Marno*, was produced at the Teatro Carcano on 19 February 1833, with himself and his wife singing principal parts. Through Maria Malibran's influence he was engaged to sing at La Scala, but at her suggestion returned to England in 1834.

In London, Balfe decisively established himself as a composer with the success of *The Siege of Rochelle*, the first of a number of works to librettos by the highly experienced purveyor of English opera Edward Fitzball. After opening at Drury Lane on 29 October 1835, it achieved seventy-three performances in its first season. For Malibran, Balfe then wrote *The Maid of Artois*, given its première at Drury Lane on 27 May 1836, which set the seal on his success; his librettist this time was the manager of the theatre, Alfred Bunn, who was to provide Balfe with several more librettos. Three further operas (*Catherine Grey*, *Joan of Arc*, and *Diadeste*), and incidental music to Planché's *Caractacus*, followed at Drury Lane during the next two seasons. *Diadeste* received particular acclaim and later that year, on 19 July 1838, Balfe enjoyed the honour, unique among his generation of English composers, of having an opera, *Falstaff*, commissioned for the Italian Opera and performed with a distinguished cast at Her Majesty's Theatre. Balfe took more than usual care over this work, which contains some of his most finished music.

At the same time Balfe continued his singing career, his roles including Papageno in the first English production of *The Magic Flute* at Drury Lane on 10 March 1838. For the next two seasons he composed little, but toured in Ireland and England, producing several of his operas with success. He then determined to form his own English opera company and opened a season at the Lyceum with his latest work, *Keolanthe*, on 9 March 1841, in which his wife made her London début. But the venture collapsed in little more than two months, and Balfe decided to pursue his career in Paris. His nearly completed opera *Elfrida*, designed for the Théâtre des Italiens, had to be abandoned because of the pregnancy of its intended leading lady, Giulia Grisi, but he was soon offered a libretto by Scribe. The resulting opera, *Les puits d'amour*, created a sensation at its première at the Opéra-Comique on 20 April 1843, and Balfe was offered alluring inducements to retain him in Paris; however, he returned to London to mount the opera in an English version, as *Geraldine, or, The Lovers' Well* at the Princess's Theatre in August 1843. Then, at Drury Lane on 27 November 1843, he presented *The Bohemian Girl*, on which he and Bunn had been working for some time. This was to be Balfe's greatest success. Despite some harsh reviews, it ran for more than a hundred nights and soon became the only nineteenth-century English opera to enjoy a genuinely international reputation; it was translated into Italian, French, and German, and was performed throughout Europe and America.

During the next two years Balfe produced four more operas, two for Paris (*Les quatre fils d'Aymon* and *L'étoile de Séville*) and two for London (*The Daughter of St Mark* and *The Enchantress*). Of these *Les quatre fils d'Aymon*, produced at the Opéra-Comique on 15 July 1844, was especially successful; as *The Castle of Aymon* it was given in London the same year, and, as *Die vier Haimonskinder*, was directed by Balfe at Vienna in 1846, along with *The Bohemian Girl* (*Die Zigeunerin*). In the same year Balfe accepted the direction of the Italian Opera at Her Majesty's Theatre in succession to Michael Costa. Two more operas, *The Bondman* and *The Maid of Honour*, followed at Drury Lane in 1846 and 1847, and Balfe also directed a season of opera at the Theatre Royal in Manchester in 1848–9. For the 1849–50 season he was in Berlin, where, among other works, he produced *The Bondman* as *Der Mulatte*. Back in London he took over the direction of the Grand National Concerts, and in 1851 provided Italian recitatives for Beethoven's *Fidelio*, for its performance at the Royal Italian Opera; at the same time he published *Indispensable Studies for a Bass Voice* and *Indispensable Studies for a Soprano Voice*. The following year he launched his two newest operas, *The Sicilian Bride* at Drury Lane and *The Devil's in it* at the Surrey. After the closure of Her Majesty's Theatre he began a series of travels that took him to St Petersburg, Vienna, and Italy. In Italy he wrote the opera *Pittore e duca*, performed at Trieste in 1854, and began, but did not complete, another (*Lo scudiero*). He returned to England in 1857, and in that year published *A New Universal Method of Singing*. Stimulated by the establishment of the Pyne–Harrison Opera Company he wrote six more operas between 1857 and 1863 (*The Rose of Castille*, *Satanella*, *Bianca*, *The Puritan's Daughter*, *Blanche de Nevers*, and *The Armourer of Nantes*) and an operetta, *The Sleeping Queen*, which, together with the cantata *Mazeppa* (1862), brought his active career in London music to a close.

In 1864 Balfe purchased a small estate, Rowney Abbey, in Hertfordshire and relinquished the house in Seymour Street where he had lived for several years. Leading the life of a gentleman farmer, he worked slowly and painstakingly on his last opera, *The Knight of the Leopard*, based on Sir Walter Scott's *The Talisman*, which remained incomplete at his death. (Balfe declined an invitation to produce the opera in Paris, and, completed by Costa, it was given its première in London in 1874.) It was probably also during these last years that Balfe wrote his two tuneful but superficial chamber works, the A major piano trio and the A♭ major cello sonata, published after his death. In 1869 he supervised an acclaimed French five-act version of *The Bohemian Girl* (*La bohémienne*) in Paris. He returned to Rowney in the spring of 1870, where his long-standing bronchial condition worsened, leading to his death on 20 October 1870. He was buried in London at Kensal Green cemetery, and in 1878 a memorial tablet was erected in Westminster Abbey.

Although Balfe admitted to William Harrison (the first Thaddeus in *The Bohemian Girl*) that he specially admired and even borrowed from Beethoven, his music owed little to nineteenth-century German models. His aim was generally to give the public precisely what it wanted with as little useless expenditure of time as possible. G. B. Shaw shrewdly observed: 'Balfe, whose ballads are better than Tchaikowsky's, never, as far as I know, wrote a whole scene well' (G. B. Shaw, *Music in London*, 1932). This ignores the fact that Balfe's ephemeral *Catherine Grey* (1837) was one of the first English Romantic operas with continuous music rather than spoken dialogue, though it rightly identifies the ballads as the key to Balfe's success. It was these ballads, raised by their inspired tunefulness to the level of genuine art, which Balfe made the centrepiece of his operas, introducing the melodies at various points in the work so that they made their fullest impact, ensuring the success of the opera and the subsequent sales of the favourite number. The most famous of many was 'I dreamt that I dwelt in marble halls', from *The Bohemian Girl*. For French and Italian stages he modified his approach somewhat, following more closely the examples of Auber and Rossini, and occasionally imitating the sensationalism of Meyerbeer, though the role of the ballad remained central. *The Knight of the Leopard* suggests his familiarity with Verdi. In addition to his operas, Balfe wrote about thirty-five songs, among the most well known being 'By Killarney's Lakes', 'Come into the garden, Maud', and 'Excelsior'. His *Seven Poems by Longfellow* (*c.*1855) contain some of the best English art songs of the period. Although Balfe was criticized by contemporary English adherents of German music trained at the Royal Academy for not being like Spohr, Weber, and Mendelssohn, and in the late nineteenth century for his failure to anticipate Wagner, his most popular work, *The Bohemian Girl*, nevertheless remained a repertory piece until the 1930s, and was revived, in a bowdlerized version, by Sir Thomas Beecham as late as 1951; it lasted even longer in Irish theatres. CLIVE BROWN

Sources C. L. Kenney, *A memoir of Michael William Balfe* (1875) · W. A. Barrett, *Balfe: his life and work* (1882) · A. Bunn, *The stage: both before and behind the curtain*, 3 vols. (1840) · *DNB* · M. Maretzek, *Sharps and flats* (1870), 71ff. · C. Harrison, *Stray records* (1892), 1.95ff. · *Neue Berliner Musikzeitung*, 4 (1850), 35–6 · *The Harmonicon*, 1 (1823), 59 · N. Temperley, 'The English Romantic opera', *Victorian Studies*, 9 (1965–6), 293–302 · B. Carr, 'The first all-sung English 19th-century opera', *MT*, 115 (1974), 125–6 · E. F. Rimbault, 'Balfe, Michael William', Grove, *Dict. mus.* (1927) · N. Temperley, 'Balfe, Michael William', *New Grove* · N. Burton, 'Balfe', *The new Grove dictionary of opera*, ed. S. Sadie, 1 (1992) · N. Burton, 'Siege of Rochelle', *The new Grove dictionary of opera*, ed. S. Sadie, 4 (1992) · N. Burton, 'Bohemian Girl', *The new Grove dictionary of opera*, ed. S. Sadie, 1 (1992)

Archives BL, music collections, corresp., compositions, and musical papers, Add. MSS 29325–29364, 32669–32672, 33535–33536 · BL, music collections, musical MSS, Egerton MSS 2736, 2740–2741

Likenesses attrib. R. Rothwell, oils, *c.*1840, NPG · D. Maclise, pencil and wash drawing, 1843, NG Ire. · C. Grey, etching, pubd 1851, NG Ire. · H. Watkins, albumen print photograph, 1856–9, NPG [*see illus.*] · H. Watkins, carte-de-visite, 1860–69, NPG · Mayer, carte-de-visite, 1861, NPG · L. A. Malempré, marble statue, exh. RA 1874, Drury Lane Theatre, London · T. Farrell, marble bust, 1878, NG Ire. · Russell & Sons, cabinet photograph, *c.*1882 (after photograph, 1840–49), NPG · Ballantine, memorial window, St Patrick's Cathedral, Dublin · L. A. Malempré, marble medallion, Irish Academy of Music, Dublin · R. Rothwell, oils, Irish Academy of Music, Dublin · J. Wood, red chalk and charcoal drawing, NG Ire. · engraving, repro. in Kenney, *Memoir of Michael Balfe*, frontispiece · lithographs and woodcuts, BM, NPG, Harvard TC · medallion, Westminster Abbey, London

Wealth at death under £6000: probate, 5 Nov 1870, *CGPLA Eng. & Wales*

Balfe, Victoire [Victoria; *married names* Victoire Crampton; Victoire Fernández de Velasco, duchess of Frías in the Spanish nobility] (**1837–1871**), singer, the second daughter of the composer Michael William *Balfe (1808–1870) and his wife, the singer Lina Roser, was born in the rue de la Victoire, Paris, on 1 September 1837. She was trained as a singer by her father, and as a pianist at the Paris Conservatoire; she later studied in London, with Sterndale Bennett and Manuel García, and in Italy. She made a successful first appearance in London under Frederick Gye's management at the Lyceum Theatre on 28 May 1857, as Amina in *La sonnambula*. According to J. E. Cox, her high soprano voice was well schooled and she promised well, but she was 'too well received … it turned her head, and made her … vain and presuming' (Cox, 2.314). After appearances in Dublin and Birmingham she sang at the Teatro Regio, Turin, in February–March 1859, again as Amina and as Zerlina in *Don Giovanni*, but a leading critic judged her disappointing—beautiful but with 'uncertain intonation' and an 'incorrect' technique (Regli)—a judgement confirmed when she returned to the London opera stage on 25 April 1859 for a season under the management of E. T. Smith at Drury Lane, where she added to her old parts that of Arline in her father's *The Bohemian Girl* (*La Zingara*) for his benefit in July 1859. On 31 March 1860, while appearing in St Petersburg, she was married to Sir John Fiennes Twisleton *Crampton, second baronet, the British minister to Russia, but this marriage was annulled on her petition on 20 November 1863 on grounds of impotence (*The Times*, 21 Nov 1863). She married secondly, in 1864, José Bernardin Fernández de Velasco, duke of Frías, a grandee of Spain. She died at Madrid on 22 January 1871, and was buried in Burgos Cathedral. She left three children. G. C. BOASE, *rev.* JOHN ROSSELLI

Sources C. L. Kenney, *A memoir of Michael William Balfe* (1875), 249–50, 259–62 · *The Times* (21 Nov 1863), 11b · J. E. Cox, *Musical recollections of the last half-century*, 2 (1872), 314 · F. Regli, ed., *Dizionario biografico dei più celebri poeti ed artisti … che fiorirono in Italia dal 1800 al 1860* (Turin, 1860) · H. Chorley, *Thirty years' musical recollections*, 1 (1862), 306 · M. T. de la Peña and P. León Tello, eds., *Archivo de los duques de Frías*, 3 vols. (1955), 1.513 · Archivo Histórico Nacional, *Catálogo alfabético … títulos del reino y grandezas de España*, 3 vols. (1951–4) · A. Basso, ed., *Storia del Teatro Regio di Torino*, 5 vols. (1976–88), vol. 5

Likenesses D. J. Pound, stipple and line engraving (after photograph), NPG; repro. in D. J. Pound, *Drawing room portrait gallery of eminent personages* (1860), pl. 36 · engraving (after photograph), repro. in *ILN* (1 Aug 1857), p. 116 · engraving (after photograph), repro. in *Ballou's Pictorial Drawing Room Magazine*, 13 (1857), p. 224 · portraits (after photograph), repro. in *Illustrated News of the World*

(28 May 1859), pp. 323, 328 • two prints (after photograph), Harvard U.

Balfour. For this title name *see* individual entries under Balfour; *see also* Bruce, Alexander Hugh, sixth Lord Balfour of Burleigh (1849–1921).

Balfour, Alexander (1767–1829), novelist, was born in the parish of Monikie, Forfarshire, Scotland, and was baptized on 1 March 1767 which was possibly also the date of his birth. He was the son of William Balfour and his wife, Ann, *née* Honyman. Being a twin, and physically weak, he was cared for by a relative. His education was scanty, and he was early apprenticed to a weaver. Nevertheless, Balfour started writing poetry when he was twelve and was published in the 'poets' corner' of local newspapers. Later he taught in a school in his native parish, where his rough and ready but successful teaching was much appreciated.

In 1793 Balfour became one of the clerks of a merchant manufacturer in Arbroath, and in 1794 he married. His writing career continued with poems published in the *British Chronicle* newspaper and Anderson's *Bee*. In 1793 he was one of the writers in the *Dundee Repository* and in 1796 in the *Aberdeen Magazine*. In 1797 he changed his employment, but in 1799, on the death of his first employer, he carried on the business in partnership with his widow. On her retirement in 1800 he took another partner, and, having succeeded in obtaining a government contract to supply the navy with canvas, in a few years he possessed considerable property. During the war with France, he published patriotic poems and songs in the *Dundee Advertiser*, which were reprinted in London. He also contributed poems and songs to the *Northern Minstrel* of Newcastle upon Tyne, and to the Montrose *Literary Mirror*, wrote an account of Arbroath for Brewster's *Encyclopaedia*, and produced several papers for Tilloch's *Philosophical Journal*. In 1814 he moved to Trottick, near Dundee, as manager of a branch of a London house. In the following year it became bankrupt, and Balfour was again thrown on the world. He found inferior employment as manager of a manufacturing establishment at Balgonie, Fife, from 1815 to 1818 and turned to literature as a source of income. *Campbell, or, The Scottish Probationer* (1819) was very successful. In the same year, he also edited his friend Richard Gall's *Poems* with a memoir.

In October 1818, for the sake of his children's education, Balfour moved to Edinburgh, to work as a clerk in Blackwood's publishing house. Unhappily in the course of a few months he was struck down by paralysis, and in June 1819 was obliged to relinquish his employment. He recovered so far that he could be wheeled about in a specially prepared chair. His intellect was untouched, and he devoted himself to literature. In 1820 he published *Contemplation, and other Poems*, in 1822 came his second novel, *Farmer's Three Daughters*; and in 1823 *The Foundling of Glenthorn, or, The Smuggler's Cave, a Romance*. Though written for the popular press, his novels are characterized by penetrating insight and skilful depiction of character. In 1825 he republished from Constable's *Edinburgh Magazine Characters Omitted in Crabbe's Parish Register*, and his *Highland Mary* appeared in 1827. In that year, too, he received a Treasury grant of £100 from Canning. In his last two years he was a voluminous contributor to the *Saturday Evening Post*, under the pseudonym of Penseroso, as well as to other periodicals. Many of these articles were posthumously published as *Weeds and Wildflowers* (1830).

Balfour died on 12 September 1829 at Lauriston Place, Edinburgh, and was buried on 15 September at the West Church. He was survived by his wife, two sons, and three daughters. A. B. GROSART, *rev.* SAYONI BASU

Sources D. M. Moir, 'Memoir', in A. Balfour, *Weeds and wildflowers* (1830) • C. Rogers, *The modern Scottish minstrel, or, The songs of Scotland of the past half-century*, 2 (1856) • bap. reg. Scot.

Archives NL Scot., letters to D. M. Moir • University of Toronto, letters to David Macbeth Moir

Balfour, Alexander (1824–1886), merchant, was born on 2 September 1824 at Levenbank, Leven, Fife, Scotland, the eldest son of Henry Balfour, a foundry owner, and his wife, Agnes, *née* Bisset. The family had a business background. Alexander was educated locally at Leven parish school, then at Dundee Academy and St Andrews University, and gained his first commercial experience with an uncle in Dundee. His career flourished when he moved to Liverpool, the great centre of nineteenth-century international trade, where he first became a clerk in a small firm which shipped goods to and from Mexico; later he took a job with the partnership of Graham, Kelly & Co. By 1850 he had decided to go into business for himself, and in February 1851 he formed a partnership with two other young clerks from Fife, Stephen Williamson and David Duncan, who were also working for Liverpool merchant houses. The new firm did not have sufficient funds or reputation to trade immediately on its own account, but instead, using borrowed capital from one of Williamson's uncles, the partners shipped manufactures to Chile on consignment or joint account, generally for principals in the United Kingdom. This was a familiar nineteenth-century commercial pattern, which minimized risk (since the partners did not own the goods they shipped) but limited profit, since the firm would earn only a commission income.

Balfour Williamson, as the new firm was styled, was thus typical of many that sprang up in Liverpool to handle the growing volume of British and world trade. The firm was exceptional in the way that it flourished during the next three or four decades, despite a close call in 1857, when a financial crisis threatened its solvency. The partners soon diversified their business. Even when the firm shipped British manufactures on its own account, rather than merely on a commission basis, it was obvious that, given limited purchasing power on the west coast of South America, such a business would never yield a good living. Accordingly, the partners developed a return trade in local primary products. Soon Balfour Williamson owned land on the west coast, received in settlement of debt or purchased as a substitute for holding cash at a time of currency depreciation. The firm also contributed to the diversification and modernization of the Chilean economy. The partners managed local mines, arranged agencies, and floated companies to work concessions in high-risk/high-return infrastructural projects. Balfour Williamson promoted Chilean industrialization by processing primary products, especially in the grain trade, and filled gaps in the local market for complementary business services by investing in warehouses, shipping, and insurance agencies. By 1876 it was one of the largest shipowners on the west coast of South America, with a fleet of more than twenty vessels. Eventually, like many British trading houses, Balfour Williamson entered the world of financial services and merchant banking, supplying mortgages, banking facilities, and loans. The house also diversified geographically along the Pacific coast, developing business interests in Peru and California.

Balfour's contribution to the commercial success of the partnership derived from his prudence and a capacity for hard work typical of Victorian businessmen. His great strengths were attention to detail and careful consideration of issues. Of central importance, too, were his Victorian virtues of integrity and trust which underpinned the firm's reputation for fair dealing. But Balfour was not without his faults. Though he mellowed in later life, he had a hasty temper which frequently got the better of him, contributing in no small way to the dispute with Duncan which subsequently split the partnership. Duncan accused Balfour of mismanagement and left the firm in 1863 to join what became Duncan Fox, one of Balfour Williamson's main rivals in Chile. Williamson was also a scathing critic of his partner's business acumen. Balfour was unsuited to Chile, where flexibility and imagination were needed. He visited that country only on tours of duty between 1860 and 1868 and he left much of the overseas business to the more daring Williamson. Nevertheless, Williamson, increasingly regarded as the head of the firm, recognized his partner's solid qualities, since it was he who, in 1863, made the crucial choice between Balfour and Duncan—in Balfour's favour.

Outside business Balfour used his accumulated wealth and reputation as a devout Christian and committed philanthropist to support the temperance cause, the welfare of children, and improved conditions for seamen. In 1864 he married Mary Jessie (*d.* 1923), the third daughter of the Revd Roxburgh, with whom he had at least four children. During the 1870s he represented St Peter's ward on Liverpool city council and served as a JP for Denbighshire but, unlike his partner, Williamson, would not stand for parliament. He bought a country estate, Mount Alyn, at Rossett—south of Chester, but close enough for contact with Liverpool, since he did not retire—and there he indulged his taste for painting and music. However, ill health, the untimely death of his eldest son, and depression seem to have troubled his later years, and he died at Mount Alyn on 16 April 1886, shortly after an unsuccessful operation to remove a cancerous growth.

Robert G. Greenhill

Sources R. Greenhill, 'Balfour, Alexander', *DBB* • W. Hunt, *Heirs of great adventure: the history of Balfour Williamson & Co.*, 2 vols. (1951–60) • Lord Forres [S. K. G. Williamson], ed., *Balfour, Williamson and Company and allied firms: memoirs of a merchant house* (1929) • R. H. Lundie, *Alexander Balfour: a memoir*, 2nd edn (1889) • *Liverpool Daily Post* (17 April 1886) • *The Times* (22 April 1886)

Archives UCL | Merseyside Archives, Bryson MSS

Wealth at death £132,148 17s. 3d.: probate, 6 Jan 1887, *CGPLA Eng. & Wales*

Balfour, Sir Andrew, first baronet (1630–1694), botanist and antiquary, was born at Balfour Castle, Denmiln, Fife, on 18 January 1630, the fifth and youngest son in the large family of Sir Michael Balfour and his wife, Jane or Joanna (*d.* 1640), daughter of Sir James Durham of Pitkerro. His eldest brother was Sir James *Balfour, first baronet (1603/4–1657), the antiquary. Andrew Balfour was brought up at Balfour Castle, the family seat. After an early education at the parish school of Abdie he studied philosophy under Thomas Gleig at St Andrews University and graduated MA about 1650. Encouraged by his brother James to be a keen collector of literary, antiquarian, and natural history objects, and by then an aspiring medical student, he probably visited Oxford and London before travelling to France in 1657, primarily to see the gardens of the duc d'Orléans at Blois. These beautiful gardens were superintended by Robert Morison with whom Balfour struck up a friendship. He then lived for several years in Paris, undertaking the most advanced medical education available in Europe; he went on to Montpellier, and then graduated MD at Caen on 20 September 1661.

Arriving afterwards in London, Balfour became acquainted with many famous physicians of the day, including Harvey, Glisson, Charleton, and Wedderburn, the king's physician, and was presented to Charles II. The king recognized Balfour as an exceptionally cultivated man and acquired for him a position as tutor to the wayward young earl of Rochester, John Wilmot, whom he accompanied on a grand tour from 1661 to 1664. Balfour made good use of his time abroad, especially in Padua and Bologna, and gathered a magnificent collection of medical and natural history books, curiosities, medals, instruments, pictures, and busts. His taste and varied interests are well shown in letters to Patrick Murray, laird of Livingstone, which were collected by Balfour's son for anonymous publication as *Letters Written to a Friend* (1700).

In 1667 Balfour went to live in St Andrews where he practised as a physician, collected local plants, experimented in science and medicine, and made anatomical dissections (*Scots Magazine*, 1803, 752). But he soon got bored with St Andrews and moved in 1670 to Edinburgh where he built up another medical practice. At this point he is reputed to have experimented on blood transfusions in dogs. In Edinburgh he started a small botanical garden in which he grew a number of exotic species, enhanced by Murray's collection and by seeds from European botanists and from Morison, now at Oxford. It is not clear if this is the same garden he indubitably took on with Robert Sibbald, a distant cousin, in 1670 at St Anne's Yards, near Holyrood Abbey. Balfour appointed John Sutherland as first curator, and bore the cost of the salary until he persuaded the university to take the garden over as an adjunct to the medical school. In 1675 a larger plot next to Trinity Church and Hospital (now underneath Waverley

Station) was acquired, to which Balfour transferred many of his plants. Sutherland's catalogue of 1684 reveals that there were some 2000 non-indigenous species growing in the garden. Balfour continued to act as patron to the garden.

Balfour played a prominent role in Edinburgh's learned society, and opened his remarkable private museum, gallery, and library to scholars. He was also active in establishing professorial chairs in Edinburgh University (making sure to place his own candidate, James Gregory, in mathematics) and in founding the Royal College of Physicians of Edinburgh. He became its third president in 1685. He improved the infirmary and arranged publication of the first *Edinburgh Pharmacopoeia* (1685), in which he wrote the parts on materia medica. He was created baronet (at an unknown date) and physician-in-ordinary to Charles II. Balfour's old age was uncomfortable with gout and other disorders, and he died on 9 or 10 January 1694, suddenly while walking in the street. His wife, about whom little is known, apparently predeceased him; there was certainly one son. Balfour was buried in Greyfriars kirkyard, Edinburgh.

Most of Balfour's collections were broken up after his death. The library was sold, and its contents are listed in *Bibliotheca Balfouriana* (1695). The Royal College of Physicians of Edinburgh holds only a manuscript list of 'Plants I have seen'. He left his valuable collection of medical and scientific manuscripts to Robert Sibbald; this is also presumed sold. The medical and natural history specimens (listed in *Auctarium musaei Balfouriani*, 1697) were purchased by the city for Edinburgh University although hardly any items survive. Sibbald produced an authoritative account of Balfour's life, much of which is repeated in translation in John Walker's *Essays on Natural History* and in various biographical dictionaries. JANET BROWNE

Sources R. Sibbald, *Memoria Balfouriana* (1699) • R. Pulteney, *Historical and biographical sketches of the progress of botany in England*, 2 (1790), 3–4 • J. Walker, *Essays on natural history and rural economy* (1812), 347–69 • 'Sketch of the life, travels, studies, and character of Sir Andrew Balfour', *Scots Magazine*, 65 (1803), 747–60 • R. Sibbald, *Auctarium musaei Balfouriani e musaeo Sibbaldiano* (1697) • Anderson, *Scot. nat.* • M. F. Conolly, *Biographical dictionary of eminent men of Fife* (1866) • A. D. C. Simpson, 'Sir Robert Sibbald—the founder of the college', *Proceedings of the Royal College of Physicians of Edinburgh tercentenary congress* [Edinburgh 1981], ed. R. Passmore (1981), 59–86
Archives Royal College of Physicians of Edinburgh, botanical catalogue • U. Edin. L., MS catalogue of natural history collection
Likenesses portrait (said to have been done during the grand tour)

Balfour, Sir Andrew (1873–1931), expert in tropical medicine and novelist, was born in Edinburgh on 21 March 1873, the eldest son of Thomas Alexander Goldie Balfour MD, of Edinburgh, and his wife, Margaret, daughter of Peter Christall, of Elgin. He was educated at George Watson's College and at the University of Edinburgh, graduating MB CM in 1894, and MD in 1898 with a thesis on the toxicity of dyestuffs and river pollution, for which he received a gold medal. After a short period of private practice with his father he entered Gonville and Caius College, Cambridge, as an advanced student, in 1895. He graduated DPH there in 1897, and BSc in public health at Edinburgh in 1900.

During the Second South African War, Balfour served in 1900–01 as a civil surgeon and gained the queen's medal with three clasps. In 1901 the advice and friendship of Patrick Manson awakened in him an interest in tropical medicine, which was to make his reputation. The following year he became director of the Wellcome Tropical Research Laboratories at Khartoum and local medical officer of health. His knowledge of Arabic, his popularity with the Sudanese, and his untiring energy resulted in the eradication of malaria in Khartoum. His work there earned the support and approval of the three British administrators, Lord Cromer, Lord Kitchener, and Sir Reginald Wingate, to whom he strongly advocated the care and health of the indigenous population as essential features of modern imperial rule. Also in 1902 Balfour married Grace, third daughter of George Nutter, of Sidcup, Kent; they had two sons.

In addition to the duties of organization Balfour made several important discoveries in protozoology. These resulted from his work on spirochaetosis in birds and in man, the study of the life history of spirochaete bacteria in the tick, and the identification of a leishmanoid disease of the skin. In order to study protozoa he explored the upper reaches of the White Nile in a floating laboratory. All his scientific work was published in four reports of the Wellcome Research Laboratories between 1904 and 1911. In 1913 he returned to England and became the founder of the Wellcome Bureau of Scientific Research.

During the First World War Balfour was given the rank of lieutenant-colonel and rendered conspicuous service in the army medical corps. First as president of the medical advisory committee of the Mediterranean expeditionary force in Mudros, Salonika, Egypt, and Mesopotamia, and then as scientific adviser in east Africa, he organized sanitary reforms throughout these theatres of war. Subsequently he was asked to reorganize the health service of Egypt, and later, in 1918, at the request of General Sir Edmund Allenby, he reported on anti-malarial measures in Palestine.

When the war ended Balfour resumed his scientific research at the Wellcome Bureau, but he was soon called away from his laboratory. In 1921 and 1923 he visited Mauritius and Bermuda to advise the Colonial Office on health reform in these islands. In 1923 he was appointed director of the London School of Hygiene and Tropical Medicine and for seven years worked with boundless energy towards the perfecting of the school. The predominant place which the school achieved in the teaching of and research into preventive medicine owed much to Balfour's initial administration. In the course of his work Balfour contributed extensively to medical literature, writing on the prevention of tropical diseases and sanitary reform. His writings include *Public Health and Preventive Medicine* (with C. J. Lewis, 1902); *Memoranda on Medical Diseases in Tropical and Sub-Tropical Areas* (1916); *War Against Tropical Disease* (1920); *Reports to the Health Committee of the*

League of Nations on Tuberculosis and Sleeping Sickness in Equatorial Africa (1923); and *Health Problems of the Empire* (with H. H. Scott, 1924).

Early in his career Balfour also achieved fame as a novelist. His novels of historical adventure, 'wild tales' as he called them, show the influence of R. L. Stevenson and G. A. Henty, but he had a distinctive and vigorous style of his own. He wrote *By Stroke of Sword* (1897), *To Arms* (1898), *Vengeance is Mine* (1899), *Cashiered and other War Stories* (1902), and *The Golden Kingdom* (1903).

Balfour was appointed CMG in 1912, CB in 1918, and KCMG in 1930. Honorary degrees were conferred on him by the University of Edinburgh and by the universities of Johns Hopkins and Rochester, USA. He was elected FRCP (London and Edinburgh). In 1920 he was awarded the Mary Kingsley medal of the Liverpool School of Tropical Medicine and from 1925 to 1927 he was president of the Royal Society of Tropical Medicine and Hygiene.

Balfour was endowed with qualities which brought him distinction in various paths of life. He was a fine athlete, and played rugby for both Edinburgh and Cambridge, obtaining his 'blue' at the latter university; he was also capped twice for Scotland. He was a noted boxer, a keen fisherman, and a big-game shot. He was of a kindly and modest disposition, and his conversation and speeches were adorned with wit and humour. His work in tropical medicine and public health was of outstanding merit. Sadly Balfour's health broke down in 1929 under the strain of overwork and he died by his own hand at Penshurst, near Tonbridge, Kent, on 30 January 1931. He was buried at Grange cemetery, Edinburgh, on 5 February.

A. S. MacNalty, *rev.* Mary E. Gibson

Sources C. M. Wenyon, 'Sir Andrew Balfour', *Transactions of the Royal Society of Tropical Medicine and Hygiene*, 24 (1930), 655–9 · P. H. Manson-Bahr, *History of the School of Tropical Medicine in London, 1899–1949* (1956), 167–73 · P. H. Manson-Bahr, 'Sir Andrew Balfour', *BMJ* (7 Feb 1931), 245–6 · *The Lancet* (7 Feb 1931), 325–7 · C. M. Wenyon, 'Sir Andrew Balfour', *Nature*, 127 (1931), 279–81 · private information (1949) · personal knowledge (1949) · *The Times* (30 May 1931)

Archives London School of Hygiene and Tropical Medicine, papers · U. Durham L., archives and special collections, letters relating to the Sudan · Wellcome L., MS bibliography of current work in tropical medicine | London School of Hygiene and Tropical Medicine, Ross MSS · U. Durham L., archives and special collections, corresp. with Sir Reginald Wingate

Likenesses A. Howes, relief portrait on bronze tablet, 1832, London School of Hygiene and Tropical Medicine · W. Stoneman, photographs, NPG · photograph, Royal Society of Tropical Medicine and Hygiene, London · portrait, repro. in Manson-Bahr, 'Sir Andrew Balfour', 245

Wealth at death £7340: *The Times*

Balfour, Arthur, first Baron Riverdale (1873–1957), steel maker and industrialist, was, by his own account, born in London on 9 January 1873. For some years his parentage was a mystery. He went to Sheffield in 1882 as an 'orphan' with Mary Fraser (1847–1906), the daughter of a Scottish banker. Only in 1906 did he discover that she was in fact his mother. However, he never discovered the identity of his father. In later years, he stated that his father was Herbert Balfour, but this was a fiction concocted to ease the formalities of his peerage. He finished his education in

Arthur Balfour, first Baron Riverdale (1873–1957), by Harold Knight, 1936

1887–9 at Ashville College, Harrogate, and was afterwards employed in the office of Seebohm and Dieckstahl, a Sheffield crucible steel firm founded by German interests. His mother married Robert Schott, the head of the business, at about the same time.

Balfour went to the United States for a few years to enlarge his experience, and did well at a foundry in Buffalo, New York, where he rose from the shop floor to be manager. He thus began early the interest in overseas trade for which he and his firm became famous. (By the end of his career he had made seventy-three journeys by sea to America.) He returned to Sheffield in 1897, and in 1899, when the firm became a limited company with a capital of £150,000, he was appointed Schott's successor as managing director, taking over also the post of local vice-consul for Denmark. In the same year Balfour married Frances Josephine (*d.* 1960), daughter of Charles Henry Bingham, a partner in the local silver and electroplate firm of Walker and Hall. He chose a world tour for his honeymoon, opening new branches for his firm. The couple had two sons and three daughters.

Seebohm and Dieckstahl was a typical Sheffield small-scale tool steel maker, with a mainly European and American trade, and with a product-line that included rifle steels, and engineering steels and tools. Largely because of Balfour's awareness of American developments, his firm was one of the first two in Sheffield to develop high-speed steel in 1901. The company prospered, establishing a research laboratory in 1905 and selling in the United States considerable quantities of tool steels. The engineers' tool department established in 1910 became the most considerable of the company's activities. The name of the firm was changed in 1915 to Arthur Balfour & Co. Ltd, reflecting Balfour's place at its head and also his sensitivity to its old German name.

From 1911 when he was the master cutler (one of the youngest holders of the office), honours and interests came to Balfour yearly. He chaired a committee to deal with the new national insurance in Sheffield in 1912; he was a member of the royal commission on railways in 1913, and in 1914 became a member of the advisory committee on war munitions and of the industry advisory committee to the Treasury, on which he served until 1918. While his company stepped up its output of tool steels for the war effort, Balfour played a leading part in 1915 in establishing High Speed Steel Alloys Ltd in Widnes, a consortium which aimed to make the Sheffield steel industry independent of Germany for its supplies of tungsten powder. In 1915 he was also made consul for Belgium, and undertook much work for the 9000 Belgians who were given asylum in his district. He was a member of the manpower committee, the Advisory Council for Scientific and Industrial Research (of which he was chairman in 1937–46), the engineering industries committee, and the committee on commercial and industrial policy after the war under Lord Balfour of Burleigh. On a visit to Italy he had a long talk on the prospect of her entry into the war with the prime minister, Salandra, who thought his country unable to stand a long war.

The era of steadily rising profits and expansion for Arthur Balfour & Co. came to an end in the inter-war period. The US market became too competitive and was restricted by the Fordney McCumber Tariff of 1921. Arthur Balfour and leading representatives of the Sheffield high-speed steel trade travelled to Washington to protest, Balfour himself testifying before the US senate in 1921, but this proved unavailing. New initiatives were needed and Balfour reacted to the increasing self-sufficiency of the USA and Europe by opening new accounts in China, Japan, India, and South America, and the firm's business in the important Australian market was further extended. Although the early 1930s slump proved to be a difficult time for the company—its losses between 1930 and 1932 totalled nearly £50,000 and the company was heavily overdrawn at the bank—it had broadly maintained its place as one of the leading producers of high-quality steel and tools. The recovery of the export position at Balfours represented a considerable achievement for such a family firm, and the indefatigable travels and salesmanship of Arthur Balfour (alongside the efforts of his brother Bertram, and Bertram's son, Gerald) played a large part.

During the period of reconstruction after the war Balfour served on the coal industry commission (1919) and the therm charges committee (1922–3), and on the advisory councils of the Post Office, the Board of Trade, and the department of overseas trade, as well as on the safeguarding of industries permanent panel. In 1923 he was British delegate to the international conference on customs and other formalities, and also a member of the government committee appointed to draw up the agenda for the Imperial Conference.

Perhaps Balfour's most important industrial appointment was as chairman of the committee on industry and trade between 1924 and 1928. The final report, which appeared in 1929 in six volumes, contained a searching examination of the country's industrial competitiveness and made recommendations concerning the UK's future ability to compete in overseas markets. It was one of the ironies of Balfour's career that his own company (and other Sheffield tool steel firms, some of which were called to give evidence) epitomized many of the problems that the committee had so extensively documented—particularly in its small-scale structure, wide product range, and lack of selling organization overseas.

Balfour was a British delegate at the League of Nations economic conference of 1927; and in October 1930, as a member of the Economic Advisory Council, he wrote to the prime minister prophesying the severity of the approaching slump. A shrewd, if orthodox, economist, he had a staunch faith in retrenchment and a wholesome hatred of inflation. He continued to serve, often as chairman, on committees and advisory bodies right up to the threshold of war, and he led the commission which went to Canada in 1939 to negotiate the scheme for training Royal Air Force pilots there. Knighted in 1923, he was raised to the baronetcy in 1929, and became Baron Riverdale of Sheffield in 1935, the first Sheffield industrialist to receive this honour. He took the title from his home, Riverdale Grange, on the wooded slopes of western Sheffield. Besides his leadership of Arthur Balfour & Co. and its subsidiaries, Balfour was a director of six other companies. He also served on several Sheffield trade bodies, as a JP, and, for a short time, on the city council. The University of Sheffield conferred on him the honorary degree of LLD in 1934.

Riverdale was an influential figure, who successfully promoted overseas trade, both in his own business and as a national policy. Yet the reason for his great reputation is not readily apparent. He left few papers and is rarely mentioned in reminiscences. In his prime, a tall, robust man of 15 stone, he seemed to thrive on being ever busy and active. Riverdale's son Robin [*see below*], in a candid portrayal of his father, stated:

> If my father had any failings, they were that all his interests were in the same field, related to business; and, like so many Sheffield steelmasters, he carried on working too long … [and] … towards the end of the [Second World War], by which time he was in his early seventies, the pressures of a lifetime's constant labour of body and mind caught up with him. ('Lord Riverdale remembers', *Quality*, Sept–Oct 1984, 33)

Riverdale had a serious breakdown and was never the same again, though he remained chairman of the company until his death. After a period of steady physical and mental decline, he died at his home in Sheffield on 7 July 1957, and was cremated.

Riverdale was succeeded by his elder son, **Robert Arthur** [Robin] **Balfour**, second Baron Riverdale (1901–1998), steel maker and industrialist, who was born on 1

September 1901 in Sheffield and was educated at Aysgarth School and Oundle School, which he left in 1918 to join his father's firm. He became a director in 1924. His greatest interest was in the scientific and technical aspects of steel making. His obituarist in *The Times* described him and his father as 'a near-perfect team. Balfour senior was a natural businessman who was happiest drumming up orders overseas and in this country, while Robin took care of the technology at home' (*The Times*, 3 July 1998). During the Second World War he served as an officer in the Royal Naval Volunteer Reserve, seeing action in *Ark Royal* off Dakar in the operation to sink warships of Vichy France. After the war he returned to the family business, becoming managing director in 1949 and chairman after his father's death in 1957. Following the amalgamation of Arthur Balfour & Co. Ltd with its fellow Sheffield steel firm Darwins to form Balfour Darwins, he was chairman of the latter (1961–9) and then president (1967–75).

Riverdale was a director of numerous companies, including Yorkshire Television and the National Provincial Bank. Active in many committees and organizations both locally and nationally, he was master cutler in 1946, president of the Sheffield chamber of commerce in 1950 (and a member of the executive council of the Association of British Chambers of Commerce thereafter), and for more than fifty years Belgian consul for the Sheffield area. A keen yachtsman, he was known as 'Twin Keel Balfour' for his design of a twin-keeled yacht. He was also a motoring enthusiast, and lovingly restored a Sheffield Simplex car (built at Tinsley, though discovered in Australia), which he drove from Land's End to John O'Groats. In his *Who's Who* entry he described himself as 'a Churchman and a Conservative'. He married on 1 September 1926 Nancy Marguerite Rundle (*d.* 1928), daughter of Rear-Admiral Mark Rundle. They had one son, Mark (1927–1995), who succeeded his father as managing director of Balfour Darwins and was chairman of Sheffield Rolling Mills Ltd. Following his first wife's death Robin Balfour married, on 9 February 1933, Christian Mary (*d.* 1991), daughter of Major Rowland Hill, an army officer. They had a son, David (*b.* 1938), and a daughter, Frances (*b.* 1946). In retirement Riverdale wrote three books, *Squeeze the Trigger Gently* (1990), about deer-stalking, *A Life, a Sail, a Changing Sea* (1996), about yachting, and his autobiography, published posthumously in 1998, *Nine Lives in One*. He died on 26 June 1998, and was succeeded as third baron by his grandson Anthony Robert Balfour (*b.* 1960). By this time the steel firm had passed out of family control, having gone through several further mergers.

MARY WALTON, *rev.* GEOFFREY TWEEDALE

Sources R. A. Balfour, second Baron Riverdale, 'Lord Riverdale remembers', *Quality* (May–Dec 1984) • Arthur Balfour & Co. Ltd, *A centenary: 1865–1965* (1967) • *DNB* • private information (1971) • Lord Riverdale, 'Sheffield steel: memories of fifty years', *Quality*, 7 (May 1936) • G. Tweedale, 'Balfour, Arthur', *DBB* • G. Tweedale, *Sheffield steel and America: a century of commercial and technological interdependence, 1830–1930* (1987) • G. Tweedale, *Steel city: entrepreneurship, strategy, and technology in Sheffield, 1743–1993* (1995) • *Histories of famous firms* (1957) • *Iron, steel, and allied trades, Sheffield, 1905: industries of Sheffield and district* [1905] • *The Times* (8 July 1957) • *Sheffield Telegraph* (8 July 1957) • R. A. Balfour, second Baron Riverdale, *Nine lives in one* (1998) • *Daily Telegraph* (29 June 1998) • *The Times* (3 July 1998) • Burke, *Peerage*

Archives Sheff. Arch., personal papers

Likenesses H. Knight, oils, 1936, NPG [*see illus.*] • oils, priv. coll. • oils, Cutler's Hall, Sheffield • oils; formerly at Arthur Balfour & Co. [presented by Belgian war refugees] • oils; formerly at Arthur Balfour & Co. [given by the directors of the Telegraph Construction Company] • photograph (with Sir Austen Chamberlain and Sir Enoch Hill, 1936), repro. in O. R. Hobson, *A hundred years of the Halifax* (1953)

Wealth at death £87,226 4*s*. 0*d*.: probate, 30 Aug 1957, *CGPLA Eng. & Wales*

Balfour, Arthur James, first earl of Balfour (1848–1930), prime minister and philosopher, was born on 25 July 1848 at Whittingehame House, East Lothian, the third of eight children and eldest son of James Maitland Balfour (1820–1856), landowner (and MP, 1841–7), and his wife, Lady Blanche Mary Harriet (*d.* 1872, aged forty-seven), second daughter of the second marquess of Salisbury and sister of Robert *Cecil, later third marquess of Salisbury and prime minister. Arthur had four brothers and three sisters. The intellectual vigour of Lady Blanche was markedly imparted not only to Arthur but also to her eldest child, Eleanor Mildred (Nora; 1845–1936) [*see* Sidgwick, Eleanor Mildred], who became a leader in women's education; also to her sixth child, Francis Maitland (Frank) *Balfour (1851–1882), who was already, at thirty, professor of animal morphology at Cambridge and a fellow of the Royal Society when he died in a mountaineering accident; and to her seventh child, Gerald William *Balfour (1853–1945), fellow of Trinity College, Cambridge, from 1878, and a cabinet minister from 1895 to 1905. Arthur Balfour was deeply but not simplistically influenced by his mother's religious certainties; she was the chief influence in his upbringing after his father's death from tuberculosis when he was eight.

Education In 1859, aged ten, Balfour went to the Revd C. G. Chittenden's Hoddesdon Grange preparatory school in Hertfordshire, where his short-sightedness and apparently delicate health proved a handicap. However, like his brothers, he would grow to stand 6 feet tall, and as an adult he acquired an enduring love of tennis and golf, and gave proof of considerable physical stamina. Yet his first headmaster noted enduring characteristics when he found the boy lacking in 'vital energy' and 'always pondering' (Dugdale, 1.21).

From 1861 until 1866 Balfour coasted imperturbably through Eton College, where he was in Mr Birch's house (succeeded in 1864 by Mr Thackeray). There he was, in the name of manliness, denied the spectacles that could have corrected his myopia. He made no great impact at Eton, but impressed William Johnson Cory. At Trinity College, Cambridge (1866–9), he soon adopted spectacles and became addicted to court tennis. Otherwise his intense interest in the philosophical basis of scientific knowledge led him to Henry *Sidgwick (1838–1900) as his tutor. In view of his later reputation as a philosopher it occasions surprise to find that Balfour achieved only a second class in his final moral sciences tripos. However, a Cambridge

Arthur James Balfour, first earl of Balfour (1848–1930), by John Singer Sargent, 1908

friend later explained to his youngest sister, Alice (1850–1936), that her brother 'was considered in those days very indolent, as indolent in fact as clever'. He was not thought 'to be a great reader, but to have a wonderful capacity for picking the brains of other people' (Mackay, *Balfour*, 6). According to Sidgwick, at the time, his examination answers were somewhat lacking in weight. For this the likely explanation is Balfour's lifelong antipathy to the physical process of handwriting. He may also have spent too much time cogitating about his projected philosophical book. He had, his friend and contemporary John *Strutt recalled, 'a mind which could ill submit to the bondage of following a prescribed course of study' (Rayleigh, 11).

Balfour's aversion to driving a pen led him to develop a remarkable ability to dictate lucid memoranda on complicated subjects. These required little subsequent amendment. Once the typewriter came into use, he would read over the double-spaced product and use a pen to insert or substitute an occasional word.

Balfour left Cambridge in the year in which he came of age and inherited a comfortable fortune, together with Whittingehame and the Strathconan estate in Ross-shire; in 1870 he acquired a house in London at 4 Carlton Gardens—conveniently close, as it transpired, to the houses of parliament and close to the Gladstones at no. 11, of which family he became almost a member in the 1870s. He entertained Gladstone (then prime minister) at Strathconan, who found him 'a person of great charm' (Gladstone, *Diaries*, 7 Oct 1872); Gladstone's chaotic departure provided a story on which Balfour dined out for the rest of his life (see A. J. Balfour, *Chapters of Autobiography*, ed. B. E. C. Dugdale, 1930, chap. 6).

Philosophy, society, and the Souls Balfour's intellectualism owed less to his formal education than to the habit of rationalistic discussion and debate that prevailed within his family circle. His mother, until her death in 1872, and his eldest sister, Nora, accustomed him to female participation in these activities. Music and games such as croquet and, by the late 1870s, lawn tennis also prevailed at Whittingehame; and by the mid-1880s Balfour was devoting every September to golf, a game he continued to play competently well into the 1920s. He built a small private course at Whittingehame and was one of those who made golf a society sport. Balfour, who had a handicap of eight when he was prime minister, won the Parliamentary Handicap in 1894, 1897, and 1910 (aged sixty-two). He was captain of the Royal and Ancient Club at St Andrews in 1894 and of the new Rye Club in 1895. He especially enjoyed playing in the many courses in East Lothian near Whittingehame, and when he was prime minister the London–Edinburgh express made a special stop to allow him and his guests to alight near his house.

In 1876 Nora married Henry Sidgwick, who remained an important influence on Balfour (all three, over many years, played a leading role in the Society for Psychical Research, Balfour giving the society's presidential address in 1894). Whether at Whittingehame or in Cambridge, the family discussions would be invigorated by the atheism of Sidgwick and the scepticism of Frank and Gerald, while Arthur would argue from a theistic standpoint. Meanwhile in 1871 the family had been extended to the benefit of Balfour's scientific interests by the marriage of his second sister, Evelyn, to his Cambridge friend John Strutt, who, as Lord Rayleigh, won a Nobel prize for physics in 1904. While presiding over Balfourian familial debates as undisputed chief, Balfour would encourage every participant to have his or her say. It was the family group, self-sufficient but ramifying by degrees into other like-minded coteries, that was the proving ground both of Balfour's philosophical ideas and of his capacity for political debate. But until 1873 Balfour's interest in politics remained academic.

Indeed, until as late as 1879 when his first book was published, Balfour's chief preoccupation was with philosophy. While sharing the interest of his uncle, the third marquess of Salisbury, and of his brother Frank in science—and becoming a fellow of the Royal Society in 1888—he was mainly concerned to show that theism could remain intellectually respectable despite the Darwinian challenge. Towards the end of his life Balfour told his niece and future biographer Mrs Blanche *Dugdale (the eldest daughter of his youngest brother, Eustace):

> I took *Defence of Philosophical Doubt* very seriously. I thought I was making a contribution to religious thought of an original kind, and whatever may be its merits it *was* the solid background of twenty years of my life. In my youth it was my great safeguard against the *feeling* of frivolity. This is much more important now—biographically—than the book itself. (Dugdale, 1.49)

Neither in *A Defence of Philosophic Doubt* (1879; republished, 1920), instalments of which had appeared in 1878 in *Mind* and in John Morley's *Fortnightly Review*, nor in his *Foundations of Belief* did Balfour carry the theory of knowledge beyond that offered by David Hume. Originally, he preferred 'scepticism' to 'doubt' in the title, but Salisbury persuaded him otherwise. However *The Foundations*, published in 1895, developed in a more positive and popular form the findings of the first book and received much more attention and praise, reaching an eighth edition in 1901. Essentially his argument was always that only in a theistic system can life be held to possess meaning. The intellectual foundations of science were, he argued, as much open to doubt as were those of theology; yet there were reasonable grounds for believing in both kinds of system. In *Theism and Humanism* (1915) he concluded that God was 'the condition of scientific knowledge'. Balfour's *Essays and Addresses* was published in 1893.

While the Balfours took much pleasure in their own company, they also developed strong social links and attachments. In the summer of 1870 Spencer Lyttelton, a Cambridge contemporary, took Balfour to his home at Hagley Hall in Worcestershire. Balfour thus penetrated the cousinhood of twelve Lytteltons, the children of the fourth Baron Lyttelton, and seven Gladstones, the progeny of William Ewart Gladstone, who was linked with Lord Lyttelton by marriage. Balfour visited the Gladstones at Hawarden several times in the 1870s and the former prime minister stayed at Whittingehame for a week in November 1874. Something of a Gladstone–Balfour attachment developed, though politically it came to nothing. 'Del miglior luto' ('more than common clay') was Gladstone's comment on him (Gladstone, *Diaries*, 20 Nov 1874), and he moved briefly into Balfour's London house when selling his own. Balfour became attracted to May Lyttelton and hoped to marry her. In 1875, however, she died from typhoid fever at the age of twenty-four. Balfour was passionately distressed. His serious intention to marry was not renewed. While there are no indications that Balfour was homosexual, his heterosexual drive was evidently not potent. His household was maintained by his sister Alice, who also remained unmarried.

Balfour had a talent for friendship with women as much as with men, but always on a highly civilized plane. He was capable of deep emotion, but his manner was cool and detached. Quick of wit, he was endlessly curious. In his younger days, especially, he was impatient of slower intellects, but his ceaseless cogitations could hamper his own ability to reach a decision.

Based on the country-house coteries was the aesthetically oriented group known as the Souls. Younger members with a political future were George Nathaniel Curzon and George Wyndham, with whose sister Mary (from 1883 the wife of Hugh Elcho) Balfour began about 1880 a platonic friendship maintained from 1886 by regular correspondence (see *The Letters of Arthur Balfour and Lady Elcho*, ed. J. Ridley and C. Percy, 1992). By the mid-1880s, when the group reached its zenith, Balfour, with his graceful charm, was its chief adornment. But the steel underlying his languid demeanour would soon become manifest in the House of Commons. In 1887 the Irish nationalists derided his appointment as Irish secretary; but it was not long before Balfour revealed that it was not with 'Pretty Fanny' (a Cambridge sobriquet) that they had to deal, nor was it with 'Clara', 'Niminy-Pimminy', 'Tiger Lily', 'Daddy Long Legs', or 'Lisping Hawthorn Bird'. Instead they found it more appropriate to settle for 'Bloody Balfour'.

Back-bench politician, 1874–1885 Balfour found personal contact with his uncle Lord Robert Cecil more than congenial. He long remembered as magical a visit which his uncle paid to him at Eton. At the time Balfour was aged seventeen and Salisbury thirty-five. They were instantly at one on the miseries of life at the college. Salisbury's five sons—born between 1861 and 1869—were, like their Balfour cousins, brought up in a highly intellectual, self-sufficient family group. Balfour's political career would stem from Salisbury's, and Salisbury's eldest son, Lord James Cecil, later the fourth marquess, would serve usefully in Balfour's cabinet from 1903 to 1905. The third son, Lord Robert Cecil, would be Balfour's deputy at the Foreign Office in 1918–19. From an early stage, Balfour was a manager of his coterie of ministerial relatives that became known as the 'Hotel Cecil'.

Since his time at Cambridge, Balfour had considered going into politics, but Scottish seats seemed usually to go to radicals. In 1873 Salisbury happened to suggest that the borough of Hertford, being subject to his influence, might provide Balfour with useful occupation. The prospect of debating in the House of Commons appealed to Balfour.

Balfour was elected unopposed in February 1874 as Conservative member for Hertford and held the seat in 1880, attending the Congress of Berlin as his uncle's secretary. However, he took some years to make an impression in the house. His association with the Gladstones and the Salisburys made quick preferment from Disraeli unlikely. In 1877 he tentatively proposed the award of university degrees to women—an objective dear to the Sidgwicks—but it was not until 1879 that he made a fleeting impact by arguing for a liberal solution to the problem of burials in Anglican churchyards. Balfour was, from his schooldays onwards, a communicant member of both the Church of England and the Church of Scotland, and religious subjects were always likely to rouse him. But until the early 1880s he presented the Commons with little but a spectacle of picturesque repose.

In 1882 Balfour came briefly to the fore by attributing

'infamy' to Gladstone's 'Kilmainham treaty' with Charles Stuart Parnell. In retrospect his stinging attack on an old family friend, who was astonished by 'the almost raving licence of an unbridled tongue' (Gladstone, *Diaries*, 17 May 1882), emphasizes his identity of view with his uncle on the Irish question and its potential advantages to the Conservative Party—and thus his potential for becoming a Conservative and Unionist leader. The episode marked the end of close contacts with the Gladstones.

Meanwhile it was characteristic of Balfour, as a backbencher, to associate himself with the self-styled 'Fourth Party'. Sir Henry Drummond Wolff, Lord Randolph Churchill, and John Eldon Gorst staged in 1880 a series of protests against the freethinking Charles Bradlaugh's being allowed to take the parliamentary oath. This was just the kind of issue likely to catch Balfour's interest. Moreover, apart from the religious aspect, it allowed him to develop his debating skills at a time when the Conservative opposition to Gladstone in the Commons was lacking in bite and inspiration. As Henry Lucy remarked in his parliamentary diary for 20 August 1880:

> He is not without desire to say hard things of the adversary opposite, and sometimes yields to the temptation. But it is ever done with such sweet and gentle grace, and is smoothed over by such earnest protestations of innocent intention, that the adversary rather likes it than otherwise. (Lucy, *Diary of Two Parliaments*, 2.85)

However, in so far as Churchill could be seen as a rival to Lord Salisbury for the leadership of the Conservative Party, there was no doubt where Balfour's ultimate loyalty lay; and by 1884 his adherence to the Fourth Party had much diminished. Salisbury appreciated the help which he received from Balfour in establishing control of the Conservative Party machine, and when in June 1885 he was asked by the queen to form a caretaker government, he consulted his nephew on its composition. Balfour does not seem to have proposed himself for a post, but his closeness to his uncle is strikingly evident in the following note of 26 June: 'My dear Arthur, I entirely forgot to ask you tonight, who I was to make Scotch Law Officers. Is Macdonald to be Lord Advocate—& who is to be Solicitor General? Yours ever aff^ly, Salisbury' (*Salisbury–Balfour Correspondence*, 122).

Two early portfolios, 1885–1887 From June 1885 to January 1886 Balfour was president of the Local Government Board (being sworn of the privy council on 24 June 1885). Although he displayed little overt enthusiasm for this post, which was outside the cabinet, he contributed to the preparation of what became the County Councils Act of 1888. In November 1885 Balfour moved to the new seat of Manchester East, where he was comfortably elected; he held the seat until 1906. In December 1886 Gladstone approached Balfour while the latter was staying at Eaton Hall asking him to contact Lord Salisbury about a bipartisan solution to Irish home rule, with the Conservatives staying in government to propose a bill; Balfour treated the initiative as a mere tactical gambit and the moment passed. He later commented: 'I did not at the time realise the full significance of the episode' (A. J. Balfour, *Chapters of Autobiography*, ed. B. E. C. Dugdale, 1930, 212). On returning to power in July 1886 Salisbury, thoroughly assured of Balfour's hostility to the Land League in Ireland, appointed him, from 4 August, as secretary of state for Scotland to deal energetically with the Land League in Scotland. This he duly did, and in November Salisbury was able to promote him to cabinet rank without discernible murmurings of nepotism. While Balfour would never show much positive enthusiasm for the actual work of administration, he was, at the age of thirty-eight, reaching a stage where a major issue, such as the Irish question, could enlist his serious involvement.

Chief secretary for Ireland, 1887–1891 In October 1887 the war of attrition between Irish tenants and their landlords took the new form of the Plan of Campaign, a demand for the abatement of rent within the constitutional campaign for home rule. When a landlord demurred, he was paid the rent minus the abatement. The abatement was paid into a tenants' trust fund, thus giving the campaign some appearance of legality.

At Westminster in January 1887 the Irish home-rulers returned in jubilant mood. Churchill had resigned from the exchequer and the Irish scented government weakness. They mounted seventeen nights of obstruction against the proposals of Sir Michael Hicks Beach, the Irish secretary, for strengthening the law against the Plan of Campaign. When the usually formidable Hicks Beach, afflicted with eye troubles, resigned from the Irish Office, there was a sense of crisis. Salisbury reiterated his belief that the future of the British empire was at stake in the Irish struggle. To ride the political whirlwind, he chose a man for long seen by parliamentarians as (according to Lucy) 'a sort of fragile ornamentation', namely his nephew Arthur Balfour. On 5 March 1887 Balfour was examined by the physician Sir William Jenner and pronounced 'a sound man' and 'a first-class life'; he became secretary of state on 8 March. His secretaryship was to prove one of the most controversial of all the periods of controversial office in that island.

Despite 'occasional lapses due to physical lassitude and exhausted patience', Balfour proceeded to quell the Irish members at Westminster and restore respect for the law in Ireland. He introduced a new sense that unionism could consist of more than opposition to home rule. He offered a policy of energetic coercion, in the form of the Criminal Law Amendment Act 1887, combined with a variety of forms of constructive social relief—ironically, in effect a return to Gladstone's policy in his pre-home-rule years, though Balfour made much more of the moral and political importance of coercion. He took on, and faced down, Irish opposition in the Commons: the Parnellites 'cannot make much of Balfour who foils them by his skill and coolness and indeed leaves no just opening for their rancour', Cranbrook told Salisbury (1 Sept 1887, Curtis, 215). Balfour was deliberately antagonistic to the constitutional Parnellites, for he regarded them as worse than Fenians. He turned their tactics against them and had considerable success in breaking up the National League. He treated with cool contempt the outcry which followed the violence which occurred at Mitchelstown on 9 September 1887—it was from this incident that he became known as Bloody Balfour. His approach gave heart to the Unionists, though it had little long-term effect in diminishing support for home rule in Ireland, Balfour's ultimate objective.

In 1888 Balfour was a party to the decision to prosecute Parnell and other Irish nationalists before a special commission of English judges: 'few governments have ever committed an error of such magnitude' (Curtis, 277). What was, at its root, an attempt to discredit home rule boomeranged when it became clear that the case was based on forgeries and when Richard *Pigott killed himself in melodramatic circumstances; Balfour became cautious about the commission, but too late. *The Times* was certainly discredited and the government seemed a party to the newspaper's folly. Balfour needed all his now considerable debating skills in the censure debate in February 1890, the twelfth vote of censure during his secretaryship. In October 1890 he toured co. Mayo and co. Galway with his sister Alice.

While Balfour's coercive measures blended well with his uncle's ideas, he made skilful use in his constructive programme of ideas offered by the great anti-home-rule radical Joseph Chamberlain. He thus contributed to the gradual emergence of a composite Conservative and Unionist Party. When W. H. Smith died in 1891, there was little doubt that Balfour would replace him as leader of the House of Commons. Looking back on his career, Balfour would see Edward Carson, who served him in Ireland as chief prosecutor, as of special significance for his own rise towards the Conservative leadership—something to which he never enthusiastically aspired. In the late 1920s he told Mrs Dugdale: 'I made Carson, and Carson made me.' But this was to understate his own Irish record. It was Balfour with his tenacious, wide-ranging, and receptive mind who implemented a variety of intelligent palliatives to leaven coercion with hope. He passed two Land Purchase Acts (1887, 1891) and a Light Railway Act (1889), and established a congested districts board (1891), which incorporated ideas offered in 1888 by Chamberlain. Salisbury agreed that even a Conservative government should, in such critical circumstances, gamble on these radical constructive policies despite their cost to the taxpayer.

Balfour was at one with Salisbury in believing that home rule could not solve the Irish problem. It would, they thought, merely stoke the fires of a distinctive Catholic nationalism in Ireland. In persisting for years to come with his policies of reconciliation within the Union, Balfour was, however, sustained by a touch of optimism. This stood in contrast to his uncle's deep underlying pessimism.

Leading in the Commons, 1891–1902 In October 1891 Balfour became first lord of the Treasury and leader of the House of Commons. Apart from the intervening Liberal governments of Gladstone and Lord Rosebery, in 1892–5, Balfour continued in this role until 1902, when he became prime minister. Having made an extraordinary effort as Irish secretary, he did not easily come to terms with the routine of patient attendance required of the leader of the Commons. After the Liberal victory at the elections of July 1892, he was noticed at Westminster 'beaming like a boy about to have a long-deferred holiday' (G. P. Gooch, *The Life of Lord Courtney*, 1920, 296).

However, once installed in the Commons as opposition leader in 1892, Balfour blossomed. He presented an attractive contrast to his likely future parliamentary rival on the Liberal front bench, H. H. Asquith, the home secretary. Although Asquith was some four years younger, he seemed prosaic compared with Balfour, whose 'sunny nature' and 'light-hearted humour' were, in Lucy's opinion, of 'inestimable value' to a party leader in the Commons.

In 1893 Balfour duly fought Gladstone's second Home Rule Bill clause by clause, as did Chamberlain. The rejection of the bill by the House of Lords in September 1893 would provide Balfour with a contentious precedent when, as Unionist leader, he again found himself in opposition after his electoral defeat of 1906.

When, in June 1895, Salisbury returned to office, Balfour again became first lord of the Treasury and leader of the House of Commons. Chamberlain and the Liberal Unionists, seventy-one in number, now sat on the government benches with the 340 Conservatives as members of a Unionist coalition. Chamberlain became colonial secretary and, by dint of his more forceful personality and more powerful platform oratory, could be mistaken as a serious rival to Balfour for the succession to Salisbury. Balfour also tended to muff set speeches through lack of preparation, but after Gladstone's retirement there was no one in the Commons to match him for finesse and resourcefulness in debate. Moreover, Conservatives continued to value the aristocratic and Anglican Balfour precisely because they saw him as an irremovable obstacle to the Unitarian manufacturer's hopes of becoming Unionist leader.

Constructive work, 1891–1892 and 1895–1902 The main areas of Balfour's constructive work before succeeding to the premiership in 1902 were to do with Ireland, education, and Britain's imperial position.

Balfour was fully aware of the importance of open markets for British industry and thus of national prosperity, but, despite his work in Ireland, shared his uncle's deep distrust of government enterprise. They both believed that this meant waste and higher taxation, thus handing an electoral advantage to the Liberals, who also stood for government economy. But they agreed on persistence with constructive work in Ireland to save the Union. In November 1895 Balfour wrote to Chamberlain:

> Though I was the Minister principally responsible for the great expenditure in Ireland, I yet confess to have looked in alarm at any great extension of the system. It has led abroad to some of the worst kinds of parliamentary corruption, and has cast upon foreign exchequers some of the heaviest burdens by which they are overweighted. (Mackay, *Balfour*, 58–9)

From 1895 to 1900 Gerald Balfour (an MP since 1885) was chief secretary for Ireland. In 1896, with parliamentary help from his elder brother, he was able to pass a Land Law Bill which further eased the purchase of land by Irish tenants; and in 1898 he followed this with an important Irish Local Government Act.

Meanwhile, Balfour's interest in foreign affairs and, increasingly, in defence policy is readily traceable back to 1878. In that year, as Salisbury's private secretary, he went to the Congress of Berlin, and he also contributed to debates on relations with Turkey and Afghanistan. He showed that he was already concerned about the Russian advance towards India. British naval supremacy also, which Balfour consistently saw as fundamental, was increasingly challenged by the emergence of various industrializing states as naval powers. By the early 1890s it was the military combination of France and Russia which seemed the principal threat to the British empire. Moreover, Britain's small volunteer army seemed almost insignificant compared with the large conscript armies maintained by the leading continental states.

Soon after the Unionist coalition took office in June 1895, Balfour made a serious effort to innovate a much needed scheme for the co-ordination of defence policy. But Salisbury's marked incapacity in this sphere was inextricably linked with his inborn horror of warfare. Consequently Balfour tolerated the appointment of an ineffective cabinet committee which, contrary to his own recommendation, did not provide for the attendance of the professional service chiefs.

Taking a long view, the question of state education was doubtless of even greater importance for British economic and defensive strength than was the long overdue reform of the War Office or the co-ordination of defence policy. Yet, even if Balfour is deservedly remembered for the Education Act of 1902 above any of his other constructive achievements, it cannot be said that it arose from a wholehearted enthusiasm for such a reform. He was not an eager reformer, especially where an increased burden of central taxation might be entailed. As far as the elementary schools were concerned, Conservatives and Liberals alike preferred to place the burden on the rates. However, since 1870 only the patchwork of locally elected school boards, fiercely undenominational for the most part, had been entitled to do this. The Liberal Party backed the school boards which sought to raise standards—and therefore the rates. The denominational schools, with their Conservative links, had no rate support. To compete with the board schools they had to raise subscriptions or plead for government grants.

When the Unionist coalition came to power in 1895 some of its formerly Liberal component, led by Chamberlain, continued to back the school boards. However, the Anglican majority of Unionists wished to save the denominational (otherwise called voluntary) schools. Balfour certainly agreed, not least because of the strong support given by Anglican voters to the Conservatives in the recent elections.

Sir John Gorst, of Fourth Party antecedents, was the minister (without cabinet rank) in charge of the bill of 1896. This resembled the Education Bill eventually passed by Balfour, but it was largely restricted to primary education. It proposed a national system of education committees for all of England and Wales, appointed by the county and borough councils, to replace the existing patchwork. Balfour intimated: 'I shall be content if we succeed in saving the Voluntary Schools: I shall *not* be content if we fail in this object' (Mackay, *Balfour*, 73). He wanted no complications, yet such were the resentments aroused by the bill that Balfour's parliamentary skills were overborne. The bill was swamped at the committee stage with hundreds of amendments regarding the arrangements for religious instruction.

Balfour consequently harboured no desire to be further involved in the question of state schools. However, in 1901 the attempts of the school boards to provide some education beyond the elementary level were shown to be illegal. A major bill to provide for a national system of primary and secondary education could no longer be easily avoided, whatever the political pitfalls entailed. The duke of Devonshire, as lord president of the council, had the chief ministerial responsibility, but it was clear that only the reluctant Balfour was capable of piloting it through the House of Commons. (In 1899 he had demonstrated his outstanding parliamentary and drafting skills in getting the London Government Act passed.) While preparing the Education Bill finally presented in March 1902, both Devonshire and Balfour derived invaluable assistance from R. L. *Morant, a civil servant who had been Gorst's private secretary.

By February 1902 Balfour was reminding cabinet ministers of their fundamental predicament, namely their 'great reluctance to compel the local authority to support the denominational schools' despite their 'great anxiety to prevent these schools from being squeezed out of existence' through lack of rate aid (Mackay, *Balfour*, 100). Devonshire supplied a tactically successful, but administratively deplorable, solution in the form of an adoptive clause. This allowed the local authorities to opt out of the system if they so wished. However, on 7 July, at the committee stage of the bill, Chamberlain happened to have a disabling cab accident; and on the 9th Henry Hobhouse, a Liberal Unionist squire, duly moved deletion of the adoptive clause. Balfour promptly allowed a free vote. The chaos threatened by the option had become sufficiently manifest. Crucially for the effectiveness of the bill, the amendment was passed by a large majority.

However, Balfour knew that there would be an electoral price to pay. According to the diary of his sister Evelyn, he said on 10 July at a family dinner at 10 Downing Street 'that owing to the debate on the education bill he was beginning to hate both education and religion'. His mood was not lightened by Chamberlain's subsequent congratulations on his 'surprising patience and resource' in handling the bill, even if the Hobhouse amendment had 'brought all the fighting Nonconformists into the field' (Mackay, *Balfour*, 102).

During the autumn Balfour (prime minister since 12

July) fended off Chamberlain's pleas for concessions to the nonconformists, and in October at Manchester he appealed to the country at large. Why, people had asked, had the government chosen to disturb 'the social peace' with this measure? 'The answer is this, that the existing educational system of this country is chaotic, is ineffectual, is utterly behind the age, makes us the laughing stock of every advanced nation in Europe and America'; and it was 'not consistent with the duty of an English government—of a British government—to allow that state of things longer to continue' (*The Times*, 15 Oct 1902, 5).

In December 1902 the bill became law and provided the basis of a badly needed improvement. However, apart from overcoming some of the more immediate difficulties, such as those orchestrated among Welsh nonconformists by David Lloyd George, it has to be said that Balfour showed little subsequent interest in the development of state schools. On the other hand, it was remarkable that a minister of his supra-departmental status took personal charge of an educational reform of such difficulty and magnitude.

Continuous interest in university education combined with political prominence to make Balfour chancellor of Edinburgh University in 1891, an office he held until his death (on his eightieth birthday the university sent a special letter of thanks for his active chancellorship, during which the size and scope of university activities greatly expanded). As with defence problems, he rose above party in dealing with the fragmentation of London University. As early as 1887 he discussed the matter with the Liberal lawyer and educationist Richard Burdon Haldane. By an act of 1898, London University became a unified teaching entity; and in May 1902, despite his heavy involvement with the Education Bill, Balfour accepted Haldane's invitation to serve on a committee to set up the Imperial College of Science and Technology. Having become prime minister in July, he set up and served on a privy council committee which granted charters to the universities at Manchester and Liverpool in 1903 and subsequently to those at Leeds (1904), Sheffield (1905), and Bristol (1909). However, government provision in the scientific and technological fields continued to lag behind that given in Germany.

In the later 1890s foreign affairs and defence received increasing attention from Balfour. Germany's advance in industrial power was by then causing some alarm in Britain, and the German navy law of 1898 was received with misgiving. However Balfour did not for some years regard the German navy as a primary threat. Until 1908 he continued to see Russia—the military ally of France—as the main threat to the British empire. Deputizing for his ailing uncle at the Foreign Office in the spring of 1898, Balfour was inclined to support Chamberlain's optimistic bid for a German alliance, despite the latter's failure to secure prior cabinet assent. Later in the same year, when again acting as foreign secretary, Balfour signed an agreement with Germany about a German loan to Portugal on the security of the Portuguese colonies in Africa. He thereby went further to conciliate Germany than Chamberlain, or indeed Salisbury, would probably have done. Balfour continued to hope for an acceptable alliance with Germany until the Anglo-Japanese alliance was signed in January 1902.

In March 1901 George Curzon, now viceroy of India, informed Balfour: 'As long as we rule India we are the greatest power in the world.' In December, Balfour wrote to Lord Lansdowne, the foreign secretary, in less sanguine terms:

> The weakest spot in the Empire is probably the Indian frontier … A quarrel with Russia anywhere, about anything, means the invasion of India and, if England were with allies, I doubt whether it would be possible for the French to resist joining in the fray. (Mackay, *Balfour*, 124)

Balfour preferred, if possible, to join the triple alliance rather than to seek an ally in Japan—a less civilized alternative, he thought.

Meanwhile in October 1899 the government had drifted into the Second South African War, where Balfour's scepticism did not extend to significant criticism of the enthusiastic ambitions of Joseph Chamberlain and Alfred Milner. Staggered by reports of a series of early defeats, the public tended to complain of a lack of patriotic ginger in some of Balfour's speeches. But J. S. Sandars, his long-serving private secretary, noted his 'nerve and promptitude' in getting Lord Roberts appointed in place of the discredited General Buller; and Almeric FitzRoy, secretary to the privy council, wrote in December 1899: 'Certainly anything that brings me into contact with [Balfour] is a matter of congratulation. There is a freshness, a serenity, almost a buoyancy about him which is as attractive as it is inspiring' (Mackay, *Balfour*, 81–2). Cabinets of varied complexion would, especially in stressful times, find Balfour's presence a reassuring source of unconfused enlightenment for many years yet to come. At the general election in the autumn of 1900 Balfour was returned for Manchester East with a comfortable majority. Balfour was by now often tired—'fagged out' in Lord Balcarres's view (J. Vincent, ed., *The Crawford Papers*, 1984, 64), and his uncle's lassitude left him carrying much of the work of co-ordinating the government as the victories of 1900 turned to the concentration camp scandals of 1901–2 and the war proved, in proportion to the size of the enemy, one of the most expensive ever fought. By 1902 it was clear that Salisbury's health would not long delay Balfour's succession to the premiership.

Prime minister On 11 July 1902 Lord Salisbury, with what Julian Amery called 'characteristic insouciance', surrendered his seals of office to the king, without telling his colleagues (J. L. Garvin and J. Amery, 4.452). That afternoon the king sent for Balfour, who accepted his invitation to form a government, having first taken care to consult Joseph Chamberlain (in bed after his serious cab accident) and the duke of Devonshire. Though neither Joe nor the duke seriously expected the premiership for himself, Salisbury's handling of his resignation did not ease Balfour's start. He kissed hands on 12 July. As he was already first lord of the Treasury, there was no change of office and consequently no by-election. Balfour recognized the oddity of the situation by arranging that his successor as prime minister should be officially recognized as such.

Balfour's inheritance from his uncle was inauspicious. The large parliamentary majority achieved by the 'khaki election' of 1900 was felt to have been based on a cheat, as jingoism turned to frustration. The Unionists faced major difficulties of finance, imperial organization, and a host of domestic social questions. Salisbury and the 'Hotel Cecil' were increasingly felt to exemplify the problem of archaic aristocratic power which prevented Britain from adequately confronting the new century; and Arthur Balfour was a chief inmate of that hotel. As far as the new prime minister was concerned, this view was in part misleading. Balfour was interested in modernization—'national efficiency' as the contemporary term had it—and he had a wide range of contacts which included many Liberal Imperialists and the Webbs; in some respects, it is not fanciful to see him as a likely leader of coalition government. But his pessimism and his debts to his aristocratic Conservative associates prevented him from moving much beyond their camp.

Balfour formed his government with no programme of constructive reform, but in view of his continuing involvement with the Education Bill and his post-war quest for retrenchment, this is unsurprising. His large majority was to be used defensively. His search for economies is implied by his asking Hicks Beach to remain at the exchequer. Hicks Beach stipulated that his stay should be brief and that Chamberlain's proposals for a scheme of colonial preference should be left in abeyance. Balfour then appointed C. T. Ritchie, a resolute free-trader, as chancellor, an appointment which did not square with Balfour's subsequent actions.

Balfour had for long studied the question of tariffs. In a world which, with the single exception of Britain, had been protectionist since the 1880s, he thought it obvious that Britain should be able to retaliate in kind against countries imposing tariffs on goods imported from her. Therefore he felt some sympathy with Chamberlain's contentious nostrum of an array of tariffs on British imports which could be lowered on goods coming from the colonies. But until May 1903, when Chamberlain publicly broached the idea of tariff reform, Balfour was left with something of a breathing space.

Defence policy in the Balfour government In August 1902 Balfour was surprised by a question in the Commons as to when action on the co-ordination of defence policy might be expected. However, because he had given much previous thought to the subject, he was able at once to reply at some length. In view of the exceptionally complex problems involved in defending so great a colonial empire, he agreed that they could not 'leave this matter to one Department, or to two Departments acting separately' (Mackay, *Balfour*, 116). But despite long consideration, he had not yet settled on a remedy. In October H. O. Arnold-Forster, financial secretary of the Admiralty, made detailed suggestions. A month later, two of the several personal friends included in Balfour's cabinet, namely Lord Selborne, the first lord of the Admiralty, and St John Brodrick, the war secretary, urgently pressed Balfour for a decision. In the wake of the Second South African War, Brodrick envisaged a striking force of 120,000 men for use abroad and a like number of auxiliary troops for home defence; but he felt threatened by the prevalent 'blue water' philosophy. Balfour wanted a body which would assess the various strategic needs of Britain and her empire. He sought to contain defence expenditure while providing for the defence of India and taking account of Selborne's naval concerns.

In December 1902 Balfour inaugurated the committee of imperial defence. At the first meeting on the 18th, the two service ministers and, crucially, their chief professional advisers were confirmed as permanent members. Initially, Balfour was content to let the duke of Devonshire (of the Hartington commission of 1890) take the chair, but, as this was a recipe for inaction, he was himself from the outset assiduous in his attendance. Whenever in office—and sometimes when out of it—he would, from 1903 until as late as 1928, contribute a series of unfailingly lucid, balanced, and knowledgeable memoranda on strategic and policy matters, and he would much enhance the value of the meetings by his active participation. As prime minister, Balfour lent crucial support to the radical naval reforms initiated by Admiral Sir John Fisher. These reforms increased fighting efficiency at a lower cost to the taxpayer. Fisher also had aggressive views on reform of the War Office.

In August 1902 Balfour had added his old acquaintance Lord Esher to the royal commission on the earlier conduct of the Second South African War (a commission which Balfour had required his reluctant uncle, Lord Salisbury, to appoint). When it reported in July 1903, an illuminating note was appended by Esher. Clearly the reform of the War Office could no longer be delayed. Esher, however, declined to be the secretary of state for war, so Balfour turned to Arnold-Forster. But to tackle the problem of the War Office itself Balfour set up a special committee consisting of Esher, Fisher, and Sir George Clark. When the Esher committee issued its reports in February and March 1904, Balfour gave it his indispensable backing. The dual system of secretary of state and commander-in-chief was at last abolished; an army council was established; a general staff was initiated; and the committee of imperial defence was provided with a secretariat. From December 1916 this body served Lloyd George's war cabinet, and from 1919 it provided a secretariat for the peacetime cabinet.

During the Russo-Japanese War (1904–5) Balfour, by now formally presiding at the committee, was mainly concerned to avoid being drawn into war with Russia and her military ally, France. He saw the Anglo-French entente of April 1904 as a welcome diplomatic development, but nothing more. The defence of India and the maintenance of naval supremacy remained the chief objectives of his defence policy.

Chamberlain, tariff reform, and the Unionist débâcle Meanwhile, in March 1903, George Wyndham, who had been Balfour's private secretary in 1887–9, was presenting to the cabinet a major land purchase measure. Although the Irish Land Act of 1903 crowned Balfour's efforts to establish a class of peasant proprietors in Ireland and helped to produce a more stable society, it could not eradicate Irish nationalism: home rule was no more 'killed by kindness' than it had ever been. Moreover, Chamberlain disliked the compensation given to landlords; and, now that he was convinced of German enmity to Britain, he was ready to embark on a crusade for a system of imperial preference. On 15 May 1903 his campaign was launched at Birmingham.

For Balfour, Chamberlain's move proved disastrous. Because tariff reform entailed the imposition of food taxes, it antagonized the working classes. It made headway only among Unionists, while failing to convert many of the Unionist free-traders. At Westminster, Balfour faced defeat by either the more extreme tariff reformers or the most uncompromising free-traders finding common ground with the opposition. His party was as comprehensively split as any party has been, short of actual defeat. This Balfour avoided by skilfully preventing a vote being taken in the Commons on the tariff question. Balfour worked consistently to unite the party on his own policy of retaliation. This, he argued, would tend to promote worldwide free trade to Britain's advantage while avoiding deliberate protection of British industries. On this precarious footing, he contrived to hold on to power for another two and a half years. As Henry Lucy commented in August 1905:

> The most striking thing about the session is that it should have closed today. There are few members among the crowd who met in February who would have put their money on the duration of the session to such a date … That what is deemed impossible should have happened is due directly and solely to the stubborn will of one man. None but Mr Arthur Balfour would have carried the Government through. … He has answered at question time, made speeches in successive debates, and never committed himself by an embarrassing admission. That may not be the highest form of statesmanship. As an intellectual feat it is unparalleled. (Lucy, *Balfourian Parliament*, 408–11)

Even so, the government had thoroughly alienated the nonconformist middle class and encouraged it into vigorous political action.

Balfour's cabinet was never harmonious, its political differences being accentuated by cliques which Balfour's handling of his colleagues encouraged. Lord George Hamilton later told Beatrice Webb that, whereas Lord Salisbury in cabinet addressed colleagues by their offices, 'when Balfour took his place, cabinets degenerated into cliquey conversations between "Arthur" and "Bob" and "George"—sometimes almost unintelligible in their intimate allusions, to the outer circle of the Cabinet' (Egremont, 167). In a cabinet memorandum of 1 August 1903 Balfour had carefully spelt out his views on the fiscal issue, published on 16 September 1903 as a booklet entitled *Economic Notes on Insular Free Trade*. He asserted Britain's right to impose retaliatory tariffs against countries erecting protective barriers against British exports. Chamberlain on 9 September sent what was in effect an offer of resignation, and Balfour—unbeknown to his colleagues—had it in his pocket at the critical cabinet on 14 September 1903. At the start of this cabinet, however, Ritchie, the chancellor, who had written a counter-memorandum supporting free trade, and Lord Balfour of Burleigh were dismissed by Balfour. Chamberlain then also indicated his intention to resign so as to be free to crusade in the country for imperial preference. Following the cabinet the free-traders in it—Ritchie, Lord George Hamilton, the duke of Devonshire, and Lord Balfour of Burleigh—met and, without realizing that Chamberlain's resignation was being accepted (for they thought Balfour was favourable to Chamberlain), all decided on resignation save Devonshire. By the end of next day the resignations of all save Devonshire, and including Chamberlain, were accepted. Devonshire resigned a few weeks later. This was by any standards a spectacular débâcle, and it remains hard to identify Balfour's game. Gollin has seen it as a crafty negotiation to purge the government and establish a Balfour–Devonshire axis. Balfour certainly baffled his colleagues, most of whom thought they had been in some way cheated by the premier, as did the king, who complained bitterly that resignations had been accepted and made public without his having been consulted. The resignations weakened the reputation of an already semi-discredited government; the ministry lost all the twenty-two by-elections held during Balfour's premiership except one (three months after he became prime minister). When even Oswestry was lost in July 1904 it was clear that a general election defeat of some magnitude was in the offing.

The end of Balfour's premiership Balfour hoped to play the patriotic and the Irish cards. As late as August 1905 he believed that his government's record could impress the electorate, but he needed to rally the dissident semi-faithful at the Conservative Party conference to be held in November. He put it to Sandars that success could be claimed in 'Ireland, Foreign Affairs, Colonial Policy, Education, National Defence' and even 'Social Reform'. Moreover, he could attach importance to the recent renewal of the Japanese alliance. Fisher had followed redistribution of the fleets with construction of the revolutionary *Dreadnought*—thus pre-empting the Germans. By way of social reform, Balfour had personally addressed the shortcomings of the licensing laws. Here again he had demonstrated his outstanding ability to overcome drafting difficulties, and the Licensing Act of 1904 worked well over many years. He looked seriously at the problem of unemployment, but the increasingly fashionable view that philanthropy and self-help were no longer sufficient safeguards held little appeal for him. However, by June 1905 the cabinet was selecting prospective members of the royal commission on the poor laws (1905–9), including Beatrice Webb. But, lacking in common touch and in flair for party organization, Balfour had lost the centrist position which the 'national efficiency' campaign of the early 1900s had given him, and the ground of social reform had been increasingly captured, though not systematically occupied, by the Liberals, who in turn looked over their shoulders at the Labour Representation Committee.

Balfour was, in fact, heading for a crushing electoral defeat. The tories offered less to their working-class voters than at almost any election in their history, and working-class voters probably felt less attracted to the tories than at almost any time in their history. Balfour was unable or unwilling to offer the trade unionists any recompense for the confusion caused by the Taff Vale judgment of 1901. Chamberlain, the former 'tribune of the people', was deemed to have promised pensions and given war. His proffered food taxes combined with a general reaction against imperialism to mark him out as a leader of the plutocrats rather than the common people. Balfour, though aristocratic, had avoided commitment to food taxes, but his Licensing Act could make him seem to be the brewers' friend. The importation of Chinese labour into South Africa confirmed working-class resentment of the Unionists. In November 1903 Balfour had accepted the arguments deployed in favour of the policy by Lord Milner; but by September 1905 he thought that Milner's 'inexplicable illegality' in permitting corporal punishment of the Chinese had made the issue the 'worst rock ahead from a purely electioneering point of view' (Mackay, *Balfour*, 216–17).

Even so, Balfour, like many others, had little appreciation of the full strength of the factors which, in remarkable combination, were about to overwhelm him and his party. He and Chamberlain tried to focus attention on the home-rule issue at a time when Ulstermen were bickering and the Union was not under immediate threat. The party organizations of the Liberals and the incipient Labour groups were lively and cohesive compared with those led respectively by Balfour and Chamberlain. Further immediate difficulties occurred in 1905; on 2 March George Wyndham resigned the Irish secretaryship after a prolonged public row about the terms of appointment of Sir Antony MacDonnell, a keen devolutionist, to Dublin Castle. Wyndham's nerves finally gave way and Balfour paid the penalty of having close family friends and relatives in his cabinet, for his explanations were inevitably circumscribed, and it was felt that Balfour had allowed, as his first biographer put it, 'the principle of Unionism to be tampered with' (Dugdale, 1.420). After an equally prolonged dispute over the partition of Bengal and the role of the commander-in-chief of the Indian army, Lord Curzon resigned on 28 August 1905 as viceroy of India, the only viceroy to resign on a question of policy. The Souls proved difficult to retain in office. In November 1905, at the Conservative conference, Balfour's own amendment to a Chamberlainite resolution was overwhelmingly rejected. Even the bulk of Conservatives had run out of patience with Balfour and his endless mastery of the parliamentary game. Balfour hoped that political disputes would resolve themselves by delay; in his case, delay compounded rather than solved his difficulties.

On 1 December 1905 Edward VII accepted Balfour's resignation as prime minister. He was the last premier to cede power to the leader of the opposition without having first been defeated in a general election, and, indeed, his government had never suffered a serious defeat in the House of Commons (the usual reason for such a resignation). Balfour later explained that his party had come to lack the 'unanimous vigour' (Dugdale, 1.424) needed to pass a redistribution bill. In fact, Balfour hoped that Sir Henry Campbell-Bannerman's attempt to form a Liberal cabinet would founder on the reef of Ireland. Instead, Balfour handed over to his opponents the initiative of deciding on the dates and dictating the circumstances of the general election. As in September 1903, he baffled his party and the electorate by his over-scheming.

Unionist leader in opposition, 1906–1911 As a result of the electoral landslide of January 1906 the Liberals, with 377 seats, found themselves in command of the House of Commons without depending on either the Irish nationalists (83) or Labour (53); the Unionists had 157 seats, as opposed to 334 in 1900. Balfour, having at the outset of the polling heavily lost the seat at Manchester East which he had held since 1885, was quick to draw a long-term consolation from the early results. On 17 January he suggested to Austen Chamberlain that 'the new Labour issue' marked the beginning of a new era in British politics which would, he thought, end 'in the break-up of the Liberal party' (Mackay, *Balfour*, 227).

By 27 February 1906 a safe seat had been found for Balfour in the City of London, where A. G. H. Gibbs rather reluctantly made way, but his fortunes seemed at a low ebb. After a bout of influenza he reappeared in the Commons on 12 March. When he resumed his subtle evasions on the tariff question, he was derided in a house of dramatically new complexion. In the diminished Unionist Party the tariff reformers were now in the majority. Joseph Chamberlain's position seemed strong. By the 'Valentine letters' of February 1906 Balfour accepted Chamberlain's case for imperial preference; fiscal reform, Balfour agreed against his better judgement, 'is, and must remain, the first constructive work of the Unionist Party' (Ramsden, 25). However, in July Chamberlain was abruptly removed by a paralytic stroke from all prospect of the Unionist leadership.

Meanwhile Balfour, with characteristic resilience, was already preparing a strategy to defend the established order against what he portrayed as incipient social revolution and a radical government untrustworthy on imperial and constitutional questions. In a notorious statement shortly after his party had been routed in the election, he declared: 'The great Unionist Party should still control, whether in power or in opposition, the destinies of this great Empire' (speech of 15 Jan 1906, Zebel, 151). In April 1906 he had taken up and refined a suggestion emanating from Lord Lansdowne. Selected Liberal measures would be stiffly opposed in the Commons and subsequently amended or rejected by the solid Unionist majority in the House of Lords.

In the Commons it did not take long for Balfour to restore much of his former eminence as a debater; and by May 1908 his recognized expertise in defence matters was such that, notwithstanding his obduracy as leader of the opposition, he was invited to attend a meeting of the committee of imperial defence on the question of a possible invasion of the British Isles. Esher, whom Balfour had made a permanent member of the committee in December 1905, reported to the king that the Liberal ministers (now headed by Asquith) had been astonished by Balfour's 'statement, lasting about an hour, quite perfect in form and language, and most closely reasoned' (Mackay, *Balfour*, 172). Yet, as his anachronistic use of the House of Lords had already shown, Balfour remained above all a party leader and a party man.

In 1907 five out of nine government measures had been blocked, and in the previous year an Education Bill of nonconformist stamp had been abandoned, while a Plural Voting Bill had been rejected outright by the Lords. It was on 28 June 1907 that Lloyd George quipped during a debate on the Lords' veto powers that the upper house was not so much a 'trusty mastiff' defending the public interest but 'Mr Balfour's poodle'. But Balfour and Lansdowne knew that electoral prospects would be harmed if the Lords blocked government bills enjoying widespread popular support. Therefore the Trades Disputes Bill of 1906, which sheltered the funds of the unions from law suits, had been allowed to pass; and in 1908 the Old Age Pensions Bill promoted by Lloyd George, who was now chancellor, was likewise enacted. In that year six other government measures passed while five failed. In 1907 Balfour opposed a move by Unionist peers to reform the composition of their house: he did so on the grounds—described as 'disingenuous' in the official history of the Conservative Party (Ramsden, 32)—that this would weaken the Commons. This was a difficult position to sustain, when Balfour's policy was to use the unelected chamber to decide which items of government legislation should reach the statute book. He met the objection—though not very energetically—by supporting in 1907 the idea of life peers. Balfour, as David Nicholls has shown, emphasized functionality rather than legalism in analysing institutions: 'from the point of view of politics, Function is more important than Structure' (BL, Add. MS 49962, fol. 40, Nicholls, 34), and the Lords, he believed, represented a functionally useful aspect of the constitution: 'it is only bad theory that asks for anything more' (Dugdale, 2.34).

Meanwhile, with Joseph Chamberlain out of the active running Balfour remained fairly secure, if not popular, in the Unionist leadership. He was felt to be remote, supercilious, and vacillating. Balfour, for his part, disdained his critics: 'I am certainly not going to condescend to go about the country explaining that I am "honest and industrious" like a second coachman out of place!' he told Lord Dalkeith in July 1907 (Egremont, 213). He had little to contribute to the restructuring of party organization in the wake of defeat. At the level of policy, in the interests of party unity he moved closer to the tariff reformers and they moved closer to him, though Balfour felt personally embarrassed by the distance this placed between him and his Cecil relatives, several of whom were prominent 'free fooders'. Appreciating that social reforms must be offered to the electorate, he sought to finance them by indirect rather than by direct taxation. In the face of some growth of support in the country for confiscatory socialism, Balfour was at last able to reunite the Unionists on a strategy not so much of imperial preference as of defending private property at home.

By June 1908, however, the mounting strength of the German naval challenge was causing Balfour 'profound anxiety' and he encouraged the government, despite its programme of social reform, to build more ships. But the outcome was disconcerting. By the spring of 1909, the government found that it needed to find extra revenue not only to build more battleships but also to cover the true cost of old-age pensions. Thus was set in motion a sequence of events that proved dire for Balfour.

In 1908 Balfour's tactics, aided by economic depression, seemed to be achieving something of a Unionist electoral recovery, the government losing all its by-elections, but Lloyd George's revolutionary budget of 1909 transformed the situation. Balfour and Lansdowne were initially, if reluctantly, inclined to let it pass; but on 30 July Lloyd George assailed the upper classes in the Limehouse speech. He ridiculed the rich, and especially the dukes, for demanding more warships and then expecting ordinary working people to pay for them. However, Balfour was now ready to offer a fiscal alternative to Lloyd George's redistributory proposals. If the Lords rejected the budget and a general election followed, the united Unionists could offer tariff reform, including some protection for British manufacturers and thus jobs. Balfour made it clear that he would resign the party leadership if the Lords did not reject the budget; Lloyd George's rather Balfourian tactic of attaching to the budget several items which, Balfour argued, were not strictly financial genuinely angered the Unionist leader. Balfour had launched the Lords on a course ultimately fatal to his own leadership of the party.

The budget was duly rejected by the House of Lords on 30 November 1909 and parliament was dissolved on 3 December. At the general election in January 1910 the Unionists drew nearly level with the Liberals. However, with support from the Irish nationalists and the Labour Party, Asquith could continue to govern. The Lords now permitted the budget to pass but the Irish, with home rule now clearly in view, demanded removal of the Lords' powers of veto. From June to November Balfour was engaged in fruitless inter-party negotiations on the House of Lords and also on Lloyd George's imaginative proposal of a coalition. The election campaign of November and December 1910 saw Balfour trying to divert attention away from class cleavage to the enhanced danger of home rule. Only a few days before polling began on 3 December, he accepted advice from the Unionist press and Lansdowne to offer a referendum on tariff reform if the Unionists returned to power, hoping thus to allay working-class fears of food taxes. However the results of December 1910 gave the Unionists only 271 seats to the Liberals' 272, and the latter could also draw on the Irish home-rulers and the Labour Party. The prospects of the Parliament Bill, and therefore of home rule, were greatly improved. At the same time the resentment of many tariff reformers at Balfour's referendum offer weakened his hold on the party.

From February to May 1911 the Parliament Bill progressed through the Commons, thanks to rigorous use of the closure, and by early July it lay radically amended in the House of Lords. Balfour took the erroneous view that the king could be won over to the Unionist position and he had 'intrigues with the palace to give him [Edward VII] unconstitutional advice' (Ramsden, 38). There was, however, never much doubt that the Lords would not be allowed total intransigence, and that the direction in which Balfour had encouraged them could not, in fact, be sustained. On 7 July Balfour was informed that Asquith had, in the previous November, obtained from George V a pledge to create peers in sufficient number to secure the passage of the bill. On 21 July 1911 the shadow cabinet voted narrowly for compromise, and on 25 July Balfour announced that the Lords would be advised to pass the Parliament Bill. He regarded the 'policy which its advocates call "fighting to the last" as essentially theatrical, though not on that account necessarily wrong' (Dugdale, 2.70), a view whose fuller and earlier transmission might have saved some time in British politics. Lord Halsbury's last-ditch stand, supported by many peers and by several in the shadow cabinet including Austen Chamberlain, was thus a significant snub to Balfour, who left for Germany before the vital vote in the Lords on 10 August. Balfour's position as party leader was clearly becoming untenable. While in Germany he decided to resign, telling the chief whip and the party chairman in September, and his leading colleagues and the king in early November, and making his resignation public on 8 November 1911. From his party's point of view, Balfour had been as disastrous an opposition leader as he had been a prime minister. He left, moreover, no obvious successor.

Philosophical intermission Balfour was sixty-three years old when he resigned as Unionist leader. Though he remained a member of the shadow cabinet it might have been expected that his political career was over. His first inclination was to turn back to philosophy. During his years as opposition leader he had served on the council of the Royal Society, in 1907–8, and was again on it in 1912–14. An invitation to give the Gifford lectures at Glasgow University allowed him to develop further his intellectual justification of a theistic philosophy. Despite some major distractions he was able to deliver, by the winter of 1914, ten closely reasoned lectures from his customary brief list of headings. The content was published in 1915 in *Theism and Humanism*; from its fees attractive iron gates at Whittingehame were erected.

Balfour's extended family, in which he took great pleasure, now included three nephews and eight nieces—the children of his brothers Gerald and Eustace—most of whom had grown up. Much as in the past, Balfour aired his lines of philosophical thought and discussed them with these young people who often stayed at Whittingehame. In her biography (published in 1936) Blanche Dugdale describes this as a particularly happy time in Balfour's life. The usual activities, especially lawn tennis, continued, as did the family's devotion to him.

But meanwhile intimations of war were soon attracting Balfour's attention. From 1912 he was involved at the committee of imperial defence, where Maurice Hankey had begun his long career as secretary. Balfour tried without success to get Winston Churchill, the first lord of the Admiralty, to appreciate that submarines were essentially the weapon of the weaker naval power; and in correspondence with Admiral Lord Fisher it was Balfour who pointed out that, if war should come, U-boats would probably sink British and other merchant shipping without restraint—'for a submarine could not capture' (20 May 1913).

Balfour did not attempt to guide the proceedings of Andrew Bonar Law, his successor as Unionist leader, but he became involved as the home-rule issue moved into its final and most dangerous pre-war phase. For Roman Catholic Ireland Balfour continued, as a last resort, to prefer a grant of independence rather than home rule. At the same time, he strongly supported the Ulster protestants in their demand for independence of Dublin. In 1913, when Asquith invited Bonar Law to secret talks at Cherkley on the question of Ulster exclusion, Balfour was alarmed that Asquith might find a solution and thereby spoil the chances of a Unionist victory at a general election; his speech at Aberdeen on 3 November 1913 was a strong waving of the Orange flag. Balfour's policy at this time recalled the policy of himself and Salisbury in 1885–6, when they had seen the especial advantages to the Conservatives of Liberal difficulties over Ireland. As Horace Plunkett noted, 'sometimes he plays the game when he ought not' (C. B. Shannon, 286). Balfour perhaps underestimated the political will of the Ulster Unionists and their willingness to take up arms, and he perhaps overplayed the party card. Even so, some, such as Hankey, saw him as a possible means of achieving an agreed settlement. This was an unrealistic reading of his mood. Asquith, for his part (and more accurately), in mid-July 1914 told the king that he would not have Balfour at the all-party conference because, on the home-rule question, he was 'a real wrecker' (R. Jenkins, *Asquith*, 1964, 320).

First lord of the Admiralty, 1915–1916 After the outbreak of war with Germany in August 1914, the Government of Ireland Act was set aside for the duration. Balfour did not question the rightness of the British decision to defend Belgium. Asquith appointed him a full member of the committee of imperial defence and in November he became a member of Asquith's war council. He was the only member of the shadow cabinet thus appointed, and he soon showed qualities of imagination and foresight. Balfour proved as shrewd a policy maker under others as he had been a disappointing party leader. He advised on home defence and wrote an important paper on the effect of high army recruitment on the economy ('Limits of enlistment', 1 January 1915, proposing non-enlistment for certain categories of key workers); and soon he became the leading spokesman, at the top political level, for the view that wastage of lives in France endangered Britain's long-term strength. In the new year he argued persuasively in favour of Churchill's proposal to attack the Dardanelles with ships alone. At the decisive meeting of the war council on 28 January 1915, it seemed that troops would not be available. However, it also appeared that the ships could be easily withdrawn if the bombardment failed, and in Balfour's view the alluring strategic possibilities made the venture well worth the likely cost.

In May Churchill, at the time of his break with Fisher at the Admiralty, suggested that Balfour should replace Lord Kitchener at the War Office. Bonar Law, for his part, went to Lloyd George, who was still chancellor, to demand a new prime minister: Balfour, Grey, or Lloyd George himself. In the ensuing coalition Balfour, on 25 May 1915, became first lord of the Admiralty, the most important of the six cabinet posts offered to the Unionists. His status in the new cabinet was second only to that of Asquith himself.

Fisher declined to serve under Balfour, blaming him even more than Churchill for the Dardanelles disaster. But with the scientifically inclined but undynamic Admiral Sir Henry Jackson—a fellow of the Royal Society, like Balfour himself—as first sea lord, Balfour restored professional opinion to pre-Churchillian shares of responsibility. In the North Sea the sound, unadventurous policy followed by Admiral Jellicoe in the early days of the war was maintained. Balfour remained, perhaps, unduly optimistic about the Dardanelles campaign, despite the military set-backs. Meanwhile, having for long admired Lloyd George as a political opponent, he was much impressed by his work, from May 1915, at the Ministry of Munitions. Balfour, however, differed from Lloyd George by opposing conscription; and in December and January he argued against further great offensives being mounted on the western front before the British forces had reached their peak. But he could not prevail against the military policies which culminated in July at the battle of the Somme.

A little earlier, on 2 June 1916, Balfour took it on himself to draft a public communiqué based on Jellicoe's report of ships known to have been lost on either side at Jutland. After discussion, Balfour characteristically decided to publish the disappointing tally without reassuring comment, for example on Britain's unshaken command of the North Sea. This was, his niece wrote, 'a supreme example of Balfour's faulty understanding of the psychology of the common man' (Dugdale, 2.113–14).

Towards the end of 1916, the U-boat problem was assuming very serious proportions. Already convoys were used for the protection of troop ships and cross-channel traffic, but Jackson and his advisers believed that a general system of convoys was obviated by a number of considerations. Of these one carried special weight, the lack of a sufficient number of escorts. On this, as on all naval matters, Balfour remained open to suggestion and plied his professional advisers with searching questions.

In the summer of 1916 Balfour supported the solution proposed by Lloyd George, on Asquith's prompting, of immediate home rule for the south of Ireland, with Ulster deferred for the duration. He was, however, unable to persuade his Unionist colleagues and the proposed settlement collapsed, leaving the way clear for Sinn Féin. Balfour was ready enough to accept the Free State, for he always favoured independence for Ireland rather than home rule as long as Ulster was exempt. 'What was the Ireland the Free State took over? It was the Ireland that we made', he told his prospective biographer in 1928 (C. B. Shannon, 281).

Balfour always opposed proposals for a negotiated peace in Europe, notably when Lord Lansdowne, his erstwhile colleague, presented his 'peace memorandum' to Asquith in November 1916, an initiative partly responsible for triggering the political crisis of the coalition. By December 1916 Balfour agreed with those who thought that a more quickly decisive prime minister was required, despite the fact that Asquith was determined to keep him as first lord. Realizing that Lloyd George, as part of his move to take over the running of the war, wanted a change at the Admiralty, and rather than see Lloyd George resign, Balfour pressed, from his sickbed, his own resignation on Asquith on 5 December. Asquith asked him to reconsider. When Asquith declined to serve in a cabinet led by Bonar Law, Balfour, in turn, asked Asquith to reconsider. On 6 December Balfour attended a meeting at Buckingham Palace and was unsuccessful in requesting Asquith to serve under Bonar Law. The upshot was the Lloyd George coalition. Many high-ranking sailors were sorry to see Balfour leave the Admiralty, admirals Jellicoe and Beatty included. Carson, Balfour's replacement, proved himself in major respects less capable, though he supplied a Balfourian deficiency by making regular visits to the naval bases and the Grand Fleet.

Foreign secretary, 1916–1919 Outstanding among Balfour's wartime services was his part—rated by Bonar Law 'the biggest'—in the resolution of the cabinet crisis ending with the formation of Lloyd George's coalition in December 1916. Although politics was Balfour's enduring passion and, at the time of the crisis, he remained in the ministerial first rank, he not only accepted Lloyd George's wish that he should leave the Admiralty but also supported the installation of his pre-war political adversary as prime minister. This selfless conduct—not emulated by Asquith—was entirely in the interest of a more energetic and decisive running of the war. Lloyd George, for his part, wanted a greater show of energy at the head of the Admiralty, but he deemed Balfour ideally suited to the Foreign Office, and had suggested him as a temporary substitute for Grey as early as March 1915 (Zebel, 202). This not unfamiliar employment Balfour accepted. In his memoirs Lloyd George later paid fitting tribute to the quality of Balfour's whole wartime contribution: 'his unfailing courage' which 'steadied faltering spirits in hours of doubt and dread' (Lloyd George, 2.1014). Indeed, Balfour never swerved from insistence on the military defeat of Germany.

However, the fact remains that Balfour's role had been somewhat diminished. While, uniquely, he had unrestricted access to Lloyd George's small war cabinet, he was not a member of it. Even so, given the erosion of his political base within his own party, his continuance in one of the great offices of state testifies to Lloyd George's confidence in him, and perhaps to the latter's desire to keep the Foreign Office from the Liberals and from the Bonar Law Unionists.

The first memorable episode of Balfour's term at the Foreign Office occurred in April 1917 when, at the age of sixty-eight and hating sea voyages, he went at the head of a mission to Washington. Balfour had for long attached much importance to Anglo-American friendship and, now that the American declaration of war on Germany was imminent, the war cabinet decided that 'someone of the highest status' in Britain 'who would have the entrée to all circles, should proceed to Washington' (Mackay, *Balfour*, 313). Balfour 'very sportingly' (thought Hankey) agreed to go: he sought to establish a good rapport with President Wilson and smooth the way for American co-operation, especially in resisting the unrestricted onslaught of the U-boats against shipping, now at its height. Balfour did all that was asked of him. He was well received in the house of representatives when he addressed it, even by its Irish Catholic members (ironically, the previous MP to address it was Parnell in 1880). From the USA Balfour went to Canada, where he was also enthusiastically received when he visited Ottawa, Toronto, and Quebec.

The Balfour declaration, 1917 The question of Britain's role in the Middle East as the Ottoman empire disintegrated exercised the government from the start of the war. Balfour was much less enthusiastic about an extension of British responsibilities in the Middle East than some of his colleagues. By the time that he became foreign secretary the de Bunsen committee had reported, recommending a British sphere of influence in Palestine to the exclusion of France, and Mark *Sykes had made his notorious agreement with Picot (May 1916) partitioning the area post-war, with Britain getting Palestine. Initially British policy was shaped by traditional strategic concerns, but as the war progressed the support of Jews in the USA and Russia became important. Balfour, like Lloyd George, was sympathetic to Zionism. When prime minister, he had supported Joseph Chamberlain's plans for Jewish resettlement in east Africa, and in the aftermath of those plans he had met Chaim *Weizmann on 9 January 1906, in Manchester during the election campaign, who strongly impressed him. In his house in Carlton Gardens, he again met Weizmann in December 1914; Weizmann reported:

> Our talk lasted an hour and a half. Balfour remembered everything we had discussed eight years ago. … He said that, in his opinion, the [Jewish] question would not be solved until either the Jews became completely assimilated here or a normal Jewish society came into existence in Palestine. (Zebel, 241)

Further conversations followed in 1916 and 1917, and while in the USA Balfour also met influential Zionists, impressing Justice L. D. Brandeis with his 'quietly emphatic remark: "I am a Zionist"' (ibid., 244). In the summer of 1917 strategic and Zionist concerns coincided to encourage the Foreign Office, Balfour, Lloyd George, and, from 3 September 1917, the war cabinet to contemplate a public statement. A delay occurred through the strong opposition from Edwin Montagu, representing an important section of British Jewry, who argued that a Jewish national home would be disadvantageous to the position of Jews in their present countries, and from Curzon, who drew attention to the problems that a 'national home' would cause with and for the existing Islamic population in and around Palestine. On 5 October Balfour consulted the American government on a draft more cautious than the original. He gained the Americans' agreement (on condition that they were not publicly associated with the declaration), and on 2 November 1917 what was at once known as the Balfour declaration was published in the form of a letter from Balfour to Lord Rothschild; it stated that the British government favoured 'the establishment in Palestine of a national home for the Jewish people' on the clear understanding that there should be no disadvantage to 'the civil and religious rights of existing non-Jewish communities in Palestine, or the rights and political status enjoyed by Jews in any other country' (facsimile in Stein, frontispiece). Of the many initiatives of the British government in the First World War, it perhaps cast the longest shadow. Balfour told the cabinet that it implied a 'British, American, or other protectorate' and not the early establishment of an independent Jewish state (cabinet minutes, Zebel, 247). Balfour pressed for the acceptance and publication of the declaration with unwonted energy and uncharacteristic personal commitment, hard to explain in terms of his background and other beliefs.

The end of the First World War Just after the publication of the Balfour declaration and following the revolution in Russia, Lord Lansdowne published in the *Daily Telegraph* (29 November 1917) his plan for a negotiated peace; a muddle arising from a discussion in the street led Lansdowne initially to think that the letter had the foreign secretary's approval, a curious misjudgement on the writer's part. Arguing against Churchill and others, Balfour declined to see a priority interest in defeating Bolshevism and he hoped the Bolsheviks could be kept in tow, but the maintenance of an active eastern front was his determining priority; he therefore opposed aid to the White Russians, but also supported British intervention to prop up the war effort in north Russia and Siberia, a position which led to muddle and acrimony (Young, 402). Even after the end of hostilities, and with the need to keep the Russians active against the Germans and Austrians gone, Balfour remained hostile to intervention against Bolshevism: 'If Russia chose to be Bolshevik, we should not gainsay it', he wrote in a memorandum on 29 November 1918 (Tomes, 229). Balfour's efforts were focused on attempting to maintain freedom for the Baltic states from both Russia and Germany. In 1920 Balfour stated that he hoped Britain would never formally recognize the Bolshevik regime, but it was not until the 1924 general election that Balfour, for reasons of domestic political advantage, played the anti-Bolshevik card (ibid., 233–4).

As the war ended, Balfour and the Foreign Office prepared a British approach to the peace. Balfour had always hoped the German and Austrian empires could survive defeat, and initially stated: 'I don't want to trample her [Germany] in the mud' (Zebel, 255), though he later modified this view. He supported the maintenance of the coalition led by Lloyd George to oversee the peace and the aftermath of war, announcing his views in an exchange with Bonar Law in November 1918. In the 'coupon' election in December 1918, Balfour was again returned for the City of London. At the Paris peace conference of 1919 Balfour inevitably played second fiddle to Lloyd George (they both had apartments at 23 rue Nitot). However, early on, during the temporary absence of the national leaders, Balfour did valuable work in expediting preparations for their return. Hankey, who was now the secretary of the peacetime cabinet, commented on 'Balfour's extraordinary aptitude', despite some recent ill health and his seventy years, 'for rising to the occasion'; and Robert Vansittart, a member of Balfour's diplomatic team in Paris, aptly conveys in his memoirs the respect and affection which Balfour—as in days gone by—inspired in his subordinates: 'It was hopeless to avoid devotion to AJB, and I never tried.' Even so, Balfour's reputation during the negotiations was that of a man withdrawn, even somnolent, allowing others to set the pace (Tomes, 163). Balfour may have simply been tired during the exhausting sessions in Paris, but his absence of intervention may also have been conditioned by a recognition that the conference must make rapid progress with its vast agenda if it was to retain legitimacy, and above all that the Europeans must not estrange by prevarication the attachment of the USA to the settlement.

Balfour remained less hostile to the Germans than some of the British delegation. He accepted the need for reparations but recommended the easing of the blockade. When asked if the German foreign minister had not behaved insultingly when remaining seated on receiving the allies' peace terms, Balfour remarked: 'I did not notice. I do not stare at a gentleman in distress' (Zebel, 260). The German treaty having been signed in June, Balfour remained as leader of the British delegation until the Austrian treaty was concluded in September. Minority treaties were negotiated with the many successor states. Ironically, Balfour negotiated for eastern Europe a settlement based on just the recognition of nationalities which his political career at home had been dedicated—in the case of the Irish—to preventing. As Lloyd George's foreign secretary, he had performed his tasks with admirable patience, good humour, and undiminished ability.

Lord president of the council, 1919–1922, and Unionist politics
On 23 October 1919 Balfour, exhausted by continuous major office since 1915 and now in his seventy-second year, exchanged offices with George, Earl Curzon, but this did not mean the end of his prominent role in foreign affairs (nor did he, as many expected, take a peerage). While lord president he represented Britain on the council of the League of Nations. He was under no illusions about the likely potential of that body without the United States, but he recognized that it had its uses. Therefore, despite some ill health and disinclination to travel to Geneva, he led the British delegation there each autumn during 1920–22. According to Gilbert Murray, who was a delegate to the league from 1921 to 1923:

> AJB dominates the Assembly, easily and without effort. … It is partly mere charm and unassuming dignity, partly his great prestige, partly a real diplomatic power of making almost anyone do what he wants. … He makes no effort and is irresistible. (Mackay, *Balfour*, 328)

Balfour's flexibility with respect to the league was marked. Its idealism would seem far from Balfourian scepticism of temperament, but he had been honorary president of the League of Nations Union from 1918, and, though equivocal about the league's likely efficacy and though, as foreign secretary, leaving the details of the negotiations about its formation to his cousin, Lord Robert Cecil, Balfour's presence and support were of importance in establishing the status of the league as a body with wider support than that of its enthusiasts. He was sceptical about each of the tenets of the league, but he none the less thought it worth a try.

In 1920 the committee of imperial defence was revived with Hankey again as its secretary, while remaining also secretary of the cabinet; and soon Balfour, too, was back in a prominent role. By 1921, when an important international conference was in prospect at Washington to deal with naval limitation and related Asiatic questions, Lloyd George, who was preoccupied with Irish matters, had no doubt that Balfour was the man to send. Although the relevant treaty marked the formal end of British naval superiority, American willingness to accept parity with Britain was, in the light of superior American shipbuilding capability, a great boon. On his return to Britain in March 1922, Balfour was acclaimed as a statesman of international renown. The king made him a knight of the Garter and pressed an earldom upon him. On 5 May, with some reluctance, he was created earl of Balfour and Viscount Traprain and ended his long association with the Commons. Curzon was ill for much of the summer of 1922 and Balfour was acting foreign secretary. As such he issued the 'Balfour note' of 1 August 1922 advocating the cancellation of all war debts but, failing that, stating Britain's need to exercise her own claims to the extent needed to pay her own debts to the USA—a generally poorly received, if forward-looking, initiative.

Balfour had consistently supported the Lloyd George coalition from its inception, believing that it offered the best available counterweight to socialism in Britain. But when, in March 1921, the Coalition Liberals rejected fusion with the Conservatives, the outlook for national reconstruction under Lloyd George was bleak. Balfour was furious at the hostility of Bonar Law and Curzon to the coalition. At the famous meeting at the Carlton Club on 19 October 1922 he spoke for the continuance of the coalition, an appeal rejected by 188 to 88 votes. Lloyd George and his ministers at once left office.

Balfour did not go over to the new prime minister, Bonar Law, and indeed was in effect again a party leader, though without a party. He was pessimistic about Conservative chances. However, though unwilling to join the government, he again became British representative at the league in Geneva, resigning in February 1923. In March 1923 he played a part in an extensive inquiry into defence policy, in spite of suffering from a protracted, though not very serious, breakdown of health.

In May 1923 the king sounded Balfour's opinion as to whether Lord Curzon should succeed Bonar Law as prime minister; Balfour advised against. Balfour felt himself qualified to answer the subsequent enquiry whether 'dear George' would be chosen. His reply was: 'No, dear George will not' (Churchill, 287).

Non-political life in the 1920s However, Balfour's high public standing was no longer reflected in his private financial status. He and his brother Gerald had invested heavily, before the war, with what his second biographer describes as manic intensity (Young, 321), in an enterprise aiming to produce a supply of industrial fuel from processed peat. Unfortunately they both persisted with this loss-making venture after the war by financing a company called Peco, which went bankrupt. By 1922 Balfour, who had never had to worry about money, was having overdraft problems; and in 1928 he was working on his *Chapters of Autobiography* (not completed; published posthumously in 1930, edited by Mrs Dugdale) with an eye to the royalties. But he never freed himself from debt and his family could not, as he had hoped, live at Whittingehame House after him.

In the 1920s Balfour maintained an energetic level of non-political activities. He had been made a member of the Order of Merit in 1916. In 1919 he became chancellor of the University of Cambridge, an office he held until his death. He was an active chancellor, playing a part in the raising of money from Rockefeller for the new university library in 1928 (on the death of H. M. Butler in 1918, there was some suggestion that he might become master of Trinity College, but nothing came of this). One of the founding fellows of the British Academy, he was its president from 1921 until 1928, the longest tenure of the office in its history—'a strangely inactive' period, according to Mortimer Wheeler, during which Balfour 'lent the majesty of his name for no less than seven years without imperilling it by the utterance of an annual address' (M. Wheeler, *The British Academy*, 1970). While president, however, Balfour gave his second series of Gifford lectures, and in 1923 the published version of these appeared as *Theism and Thought*. It was to the academy that he delivered his final reflections on philosophy, 'Familiar beliefs and transcendent reason', in 1925. He declined the presidency of the Royal Society in 1920, thus turning down what would have been a unique double. He wrote an introduction to *Science, Religion and Reality*, edited by the young Joseph Needham in 1925.

Again lord president, 1925–1929 In May 1923 Bonar Law was succeeded as prime minister by Stanley Baldwin. Although Balfour gave him public support, Baldwin did not at once offer him a cabinet post. However, when Curzon died in April 1925 it was Balfour who filled his place. By then Baldwin was more securely in the saddle and Balfour, as a peer and increasingly deaf at the age of seventy-six, could at last no longer be seen as a possible prime minister.

But Balfour continued to illuminate the proceedings of the committee of imperial defence as he had done when out of office in 1923. In that year, as a member of the Salisbury committee on co-ordination of defence and chairman of its special subcommittee on relations between the navy and the air force, he decided to back the RAF in its wish to continue to train and administer the Fleet Air Arm. This arrangement was not reversed until 1937, unfortunately. But in 1923 the RAF's existence as an independent service was under threat and Balfour saw its survival as the main priority.

It was at a meeting of the main Salisbury committee on 10 May 1923 that Balfour, when discussing the outlook for peace, said that he had been gradually driven to conclude 'that nothing, not the League of Nations or anything else' would ensure peace except 'the certainty of every civilized man, woman and child that everybody will be destroyed if there is war' (Mackay, *Balfour*, 346). Research, he believed, might produce this ultimate solution.

In the opening months of 1925 Balfour toured the Middle East, attending in his robes as chancellor of the University of Cambridge the opening of the Hebrew University in Jerusalem and being entertained by Chaim Weizmann. Arab protests required him to cut short his tour. While in Palestine, Balfour was invited by Baldwin to replace the deceased Curzon as lord president; he took office on 29 April. His chief achievement during this last period of office was the chairing (as a result of Baldwin's lumbago) of the inter-imperial relations committee at the Imperial Conference in 1926, from whose unanimous report derived the Statute of Westminster (1931), defining the relations of dominions (of European settlement) within the empire.

At the committee of imperial defence in 1926 Churchill's proposed Ministry of Defence met with Balfour's usual scepticism on this subject. But despite a severe set-back to his health in March 1928 Balfour, on his final appearance in July, showed good judgement in condemning as 'dangerous' and 'wholly impracticable' Churchill's move, as an economizing chancellor, to place his ten-year rule on a daily forward-moving basis. He also wanted additional spending on naval anti-aircraft weapons ahead of cruisers.

As lord president Balfour continued to take a close interest in scientific and technological developments, especially within the bodies for which he was responsible, namely the Department of Scientific and Industrial Research and the Medical Research Council; during both his periods as lord president he was an assiduous attender at their meetings. It was said that the 'Lord Presidency used to be considered a general utility office. He [Balfour] converted it into a Ministry of Research' (Sir Frank Heath, quoted in Rayleigh, 46). Always concerned about the future of the British economy, he instituted a committee of civil research which, with the prime minister sometimes in the chair, reported on fourteen important subjects (such as overseas loans, the safeguarding of the iron and steel industry, and unemployment) before ill health in the autumn of 1928 finally removed him from active work. Out of courtesy and respect, Baldwin insisted on his retaining his office until the end of the government in May 1929.

Meanwhile, on 25 July 1928, his eightieth birthday, Balfour was presented at Westminster with a well-chosen tribute from both houses of parliament—a Rolls-Royce. He had for long been a motoring enthusiast. Mrs Dugdale noticed how Balfour, in responding, addressed his earlier remarks 'almost personally to Lloyd George' (Dugdale, 2.397).

Death Apart from a number of colds and occasional influenza, Balfour had enjoyed good health until the year 1928. He remained until then a regular tennis player. At the end of that year most of his teeth had to be removed and he began to suffer from the unremitting circulatory trouble which ended his life. Late in January 1929 Balfour was conveyed from Whittingehame to Fisher's Hill, his brother Gerald's home near Woking, Surrey. In the past he had suffered from occasional bouts of phlebitis and by the autumn of 1929 he was immobilized by it. Finally, soon after receiving a visit from Weizmann, Balfour died at Fisher's Hill on 19 March 1930. At his own request a public funeral was declined and he was buried on 22 March beside members of his family at Whittingehame. Despite the snowy weather, attenders came from far and wide. By special remainder, the title passed to his brother Gerald.

Balfour's image Balfour's lack of popular rapport was reflected in rather rapid public discounting of his memory, but he was in his day a fertile source for artists and cartoonists. His features, which seemed both hard and languid, were perhaps best caught in the oil sketch by Sir James Guthrie (*c*.1925, NPG), and his character was brilliantly satirized by Max Beerbohm, for whom Balfour became something of an obsession, and by Francis Carruthers Gould, whose daily cartoons in the *Westminster Gazette* in the 1900s amicably depicted the disintegration of Balfour's government.

Assessment As an intellectual statesman, Balfour achieved rare distinction, especially during the later years of his long career. Before he became prime minister, his wholehearted identification with the main strands of his uncle's Conservatism provided the political basis of his increasing mastery of the parliamentary game. Less eminent in the Commons after the watershed elections of 1906, his inexhaustible skill as a debater nevertheless remained a feature of life in the house until he retired from the Unionist leadership in 1911. Among his increasingly rare subsequent appearances in the Commons was his memorable rebuttal, on 8 March 1916, of Churchill's attack on his regime at the Admiralty. This brought Churchill to admit that Balfour was 'a master of parliamentary sword-play and of every dialectical art' (Mackay, *Balfour*, 291).

In addition to his parliamentary roles Balfour undertook a remarkable amount of supra-departmental constructive work. While never an eager reformer, he established over the years a reputation for sagacity which was recognized across the party-political spectrum, initially in the foreign and defence areas of policy and latterly on a broad international plane as well.

Historical interpretations of Balfour's life have not changed radically. While there has been a journalistic tendency to sense undiscovered mysteries in a man of such intelligence and achievement wrapped in so languid an exterior, this bafflement has not been experienced by his biographers; and the emphasis already placed by Sir Robert Ensor, in *England* (1936), on Balfour's constructive achievements as prime minister remains valid, despite the many refinements and amplifications flowing from subsequent research. His life was recorded in two volumes (1936) by his niece, Blanche Elizabeth Campbell Dugdale, which while interesting on the personal side was no more than a competent memoir. Balfour's political papers were given to the British Library, though a significant deposit remained at Whittingehame together with several family memoirs. Material from both deposits was used to good effect in Kenneth Young's biography (1963); it, with Sydney H. Zebel's political biography (1973), Max Egremont's life (1980), and Ruddock Mackay's study (1985), are the chief works of research, though many aspects of Balfour's long career have their own studies, notably Perry Curtis's *Coercion and Conciliation in Ireland, 1880–1892* (1963).

Balfour was never a nostalgic Conservative, acid though his comments on change often were. The intellectual tone of the twentieth century was more welcome to him than the religiosity of Victorian society in his youth. He adapted well to political change once it had happened. Though he had what his second biographer calls 'a certain touch of almost feminine wilfulness' (Young, 322), he was able to abandon intellectual positions without regret once they had become impracticable. His niece recalled that 'he was never shaken in his belief that the younger generation was better than the one before' (Balfour, 655), and this was reflected in his general approach to life and public affairs. Essentially melancholy at heart and in important respects pessimistic, Balfour was, even so, 'capable at times of a soaring imagination' which allowed him to change a generation as the passing of time required (ibid., 656). Indeed, it was once he had shed the Cecil entanglements of his youth that his most constructive years in public life began.

Balfour believed that his main constructive achievements were in Ireland and Palestine. In a longer perspective, however, his Education Act can be seen as more substantially beneficial. Although arising from political exigencies rather than reforming zeal, it stands out in tribute to Balfour's tenacity and intellect, and to his ability to produce out of strong parliamentary cross-currents a workable major bill. In the sphere of defence, he amply repaired the lamentable effects of Salisbury's antipathy to the subject. During the First World War he put aside party advantage to an extent which his earlier partisanship would not have suggested, and he played a significant role as an elder statesman—the only former prime minister involved in the crisis—in the appointment of Lloyd George to the premiership in December 1916. If he lacked the rapport with the general public possessed by the greatest prime ministers, his counsel proved its special value at the highest political level throughout the exceptional number of twenty-seven years that he served as a member of the cabinet.

RUDDOCK MACKAY and H. C. G. MATTHEW

Sources *DNB* • *The letters of Arthur Balfour and Lady Elcho, 1885–1917*, ed. J. Ridley and C. Percy (1992) • *Salisbury–Balfour correspondence: letters exchanged between the third marquess of Salisbury and his nephew Arthur James Balfour, 1869–1892*, ed. R. H. Williams (1988) • B. E. C. Dugdale, *Arthur James Balfour, first earl of Balfour*, 2 vols. (1936) • K. Young, *Arthur James Balfour* (1963) • S. H. Zebel, *Balfour* (1973) • M. Egremont, *Balfour* (1980) • R. F. Mackay, *Balfour: intellectual statesman* (1985) • J. Tomes, *Balfour and foreign policy: the international thought of a conservative statesman* (1997) • E. Balfour, 'My uncle—A. J. Balfour', *The Listener* (25 Oct 1956), 655–6 • W. M. Short, *The mind of Arthur James Balfour* (1918) • Lord Rayleigh [J. Strutt], *Lord Balfour in his relation to science* (1930) • D. Nicholls, 'Few are chosen: some reflections on the politics of A. J. Balfour', *Review of Politics*, 30 (1968), 33–42 • P. Harris, *Life in a Scottish country house: the story of A. J. Balfour and Whittingehame House* (1989) • R. Quinault, 'Golf and Edwardian politics', in N. Harte and R. Quinault, *Land and society in Britain, 1700–1914* (1996), 191–210 • A. M. Gollin, *Balfour's burden: Arthur Balfour and imperial preference* (1965) • R. A. Rempel, *Unionists divided: Arthur Balfour, Joseph Chamberlain and the unionist free traders* (1972) • J. L. Garvin and J. Amery, *The life of Joseph Chamberlain*, 6 vols. (1932–69) • A. Sykes, *Tariff reform in British politics, 1903–1913* (1979) • P. Fraser, 'The unionist debacle of 1911 and Mr Balfour's retirement', *Journal of Modern History*, 35 (1963), 354–65 • R. Jenkins, *Mr Balfour's poodle* (1954) • R. F. Mackay, *Fisher of Kilverstone* (1974) • L. Stein, *The Balfour declaration* (1961) • M. Vereté, 'The Balfour declaration and its makers', *Middle Eastern Studies*, 6 (Jan 1970), 48–75 • J. Ramsden, *The age of Balfour and Baldwin, 1902–1940* (1978) • R. T. Shannon, *The age of Salisbury, 1881–1902: unionism and empire* (1996) • L. P. Curtis, *Coercion and conciliation in Ireland* (1963) • C. B. Shannon, *Arthur J. Balfour and Ireland, 1874–1922* (1988) • P. T. Marsh, *The discipline of popular government: Lord Salisbury's statecraft, 1881–1902* (1978) • Gladstone, *Diaries* • Lord Beaverbrook, *Politicians and the war*, 2 vols. (1928–30) • D. Lloyd George, *War memoirs*, new edn, 2 vols. (1938) • W. S. Churchill, *Great contemporaries* (1937) • C. Hazlehurst, *Politicians at war, July 1914 to May 1915* (1971) • Lord Hankey [M. Hankey], *The supreme command, 1914–1918*, 2 vols. (1961) • J. Turner, *British politics and the Great War: coalition and conflict, 1915–1918* (1992) • R. H. Ullman, *Anglo-Soviet relations, 1917–1921*, 3 vols. (1961–72) • B. K. Murray, *The people's budget, 1909/10* (1980) • *University of Edinburgh Journal*, 2 (1927–8), 148–9 • R. Williams, *Defending the empire: the conservative party and British defence policy, 1899–1915* (1991) • H. Lucy, *A diary of two parliaments, 1885–6*, 2 vols. (1886) • H. Lucy, *A diary of the Salisbury parliament, 1886–1892* (1892) • H. Lucy, *The Balfourian parliament, 1900–1905* (1906)

Archives BL, corresp. and papers, Add. MS 49683–49962 • Bodl. Oxf., corresp. • Bodl. Oxf., letters and papers, MSS Eng. hist. c. 713–773 • JRL, corresp. • NA Scot., corresp. and papers • PRO, corresp. and papers, FO 800/199–217 • PRO, Irish Papers, PRO 30/60/1–13 • Whittingehame House, East Lothian | Beds. & Luton ARS, Halsbury MSS • BL, corresp. with H. O. Arnold-Forster, Add. MSS 50276–50352 • BL, corresp. with Lord Bertie, Add. MSS 63043–63049 • BL, corresp. with William Brodrick, Add. MS 50072 • BL, letters to Sir Henry Campbell-Bannerman, Add. MSS 41217–41238, *passim* • BL, corresp. with Lord Cecil, Add. MS 51071 • BL, corresp. with Sir Charles Dilke, Add. MS 43877 • BL, Gladstone MSS, Add. MSS 45986, 46238, 44444–44785, *passim* • BL, letters to Lord Halsbury, Add. MS 56372, fols. 196–219*v* • BL, corresp. with Lord Long, Add. MS 62403 • BL, corresp. with Lord Northcliffe, Add. MS 62153 • BL, corresp. with Sir R. S. Paget, Add. MS 51252 • BL, corresp. with Lord Ritchie, Add. MS 53780 • BL OIOC, corresp. with Lord Curzon, MSS Eur. F 111–112 • BL OIOC, letters to Lord Reading, MSS Eur. E 238, F 118 • Bodl. Oxf., letters to Lord Ampthill; corresp. with H. H. Asquith; letters to M. Asquith [copies]; corresp. with Sir Henry Burdett; letters to H. A. L. Fischer; corresp. with H. A. Gwynne; letters to Philip Kerr; corresp. with Gilbert Murray; corresp. with Lord Selborne • Bodl. Oxf., letters to W. H. Dickinson; letters to Edward VII; letters to Lord Goschen; corresp. with Viscount Hanworth; corresp. with Lewis Harcourt; corresp. with Lord Milner; letters to Hastings Rashdall; corresp. with Lord Selborne • Bodl. Oxf., Goschen MSS • CAC Cam., corresp. with Lord Randolph Churchill; corresp. with Sir Henry Page Croft; corresp. with Lord Fisher; corresp. with Alfred Lyttelton; letters to Edith Lyttelton • CAC Cam., letters to W. T. Stead • Cardiff Central Library, letters to Sir Hugh Owen • Chatsworth House, Derbyshire, letters to duke of Devonshire • CKS, letters to Aretas Akers-Douglas • CKS, letters to Edward Stanhope • CUL, letters to Stanley Baldwin; letters to Samuel Hoare • CUL, corresp. with Lord Hardinge • Edinburgh City Archives, letters to Edinburgh Philosophical Institution • Glos. RO, corresp. with Sir Michael Hicks Beach • Helmingham Hall, Stowmarket, letters to Sir Joseph Ridgeway • Herts. ALS, corresp. with Lady Desborough • HLRO, letters to Lord Ashbourne; corresp. with Andrew Bonar Law; corresp. with David Lloyd George; corresp. with Herbert Samuel; corresp. with John St Loe Strachey • IWM, corresp. with Sir Henry Wilson • Keele University Library, LePlay Collection, corresp. with Victor Veracis Branford • King's AC Cam., letters to Oscar Browning • L. Cong., corresp. with Moreton Frewen • LPL, corresp. with E. W. Benson; corresp. with Randall Thomas Davidson • Lpool RO, corresp. with Lord Derby • Man. CL, Manchester Archives and Local Studies, letters to T. C. Horsfall • Mitchell L., Glas., Glasgow City Archives, letters to James Parker Smith • Morgan L., W. E. Henley MSS • NAM, letters to Lord Roberts • NL Scot., letters to Sir Henry Craik; letters to Sir Charles Dalrymple; letters to A. C. Fraser; letters to Sir George Henschel; corresp. with Lord Lothian; letters to Alexander Murray • NL Scot., corresp. with Arthur Elliott; corresp. with Lord Haldane • NL Scot., corresp. with Lord Rosebery and some papers relating to Donald Macleod • NL Wales, corresp. with Thomas Jones • NRA Scotland, priv. coll., corresp. with Lord Balfour of Burleigh • NRA Scotland, priv. coll., corresp. with Sir John Ewart • Plunkett Foundation, Long Hanborough, Oxfordshire, corresp. with Sir Horace Plunkett • PRO, corresp. with A. Anderson, PRO 30/68/10–15 • PRO, corresp. with Lord Kitchener, PRO 30/57; WO 159 • PRO, corresp. with Lord Midleton, PRO 30/67 • PRO NIre., letters to duke of Abercorn; corresp. with Edward Carson • Surrey HC, corresp. with Lord Onslow • Trinity Cam., corresp. with Sir Joseph John Thomson • U. Birm. L., corresp. with Austen Chamberlain and Joseph Chamberlain • U. Birm. L., letters to Oliver Lodge • U. Edin. L., letters to Sir Charles Pearson; letters to Charles Sarolea • U. Leeds, Brotherton L., letters to Sir Edmund Gosse • U. Newcastle, corresp. with Walter Runciman • U. Reading L., letters to Lady Astor • U. St Andr. L., letters to Sir James Donaldson • U. St Andr. L., corresp. with Wilfred Ward • UCL, corresp. with Sir Edwin Chadwick • University of Bristol Library, letters to Alfred Austin • University of Sheffield Library, corresp. with W. A. S. Hewins • W. Sussex RO, letters to L. J. Maxse • Wilts. & Swindon RO, corresp. with Lord Long; corresp. with Lord Pembroke • Yale U., Sterling Memorial Library, corresp. with Edward House | FILM BFI NFTVA, documentary footage • BFI NFTVA, news footage • BFI NFTVA, propaganda footage (Hepworth Manufacturing Company) • IWM FVA, actuality footage

Likenesses G. Richmond, chalk drawing, 1877, NPG • Russell & Sons, photograph, 1887, NPG; repro. in *Our conservative and unionist statesmen*, 2 vols. (1896–7), pt 3 • Violet, duchess of Rutland, lithograph, 1888, NPG • E. O. Ford, plaster bust, *c.*1892, Scot. NPG • S. Hodges, oils, *c.*1894, Constitutional Club, London • C. M. Hardie, group portrait, 1899 (*Curling at Carsebreck*), Scot. NPG • B. Stone, photograph, 1899, NPG • M. Beerbohm, caricatures, drawings,

1900, U. Cal., Los Angeles, William Andrews Clark Memorial Library • G. Reid, oils, *c*.1900, U. Edin. • G. C. Beresford, negative, 1902, NPG • London Stereoscopic Co., cabinet photograph, 1902, NPG • S. P. Hall, double portrait, oils, *c*.1902–1903 (with Joseph Chamberlain), NPG • J. S. Sargent, oils, 1908, NPG [*see illus.*] • M. Beerbohm, caricatures, drawings, 1909, AM Oxf. • M. Beerbohm, caricatures, drawings, 1912, Merton Oxf. • O. Edis, autochrome photograph, 1914, NPG • M. Beerbohm, caricature, drawing, 1920, National Gallery of Victoria, Melbourne, Australia • W. Stoneman, photograph, 1921, NPG • J. Guthrie, group portrait, oils, 1921–30 (*Statesmen of World War I, 1914–18*), NPG • C. Simms, group portrait, oils, 1923 (*The introduction of Lady Astor to the House of Commons, 1st December 1919*), Palace of Westminster, London • J. Guthrie, oils sketch, *c*.1925, NPG • L. Alma-Tadema, oils, NPG • M. Beerbohm, caricatures, drawings, Indiana University, Bloomington, Lilly Library • W. & D. Downey, various photographs, NPG • O. Edis, various photographs, NPG • H. Furniss, caricatures, ink drawings, NPG • F. C. Gould, caricatures, ink drawings, NPG • S. P. Hall, pencil drawing, NPG • P. A. de Laszlo, oils, NPG • P. A. de Laszlo, oils, Trinity Cam. • London Stereoscopic Co., photograph, NPG; repro. in *Our conservative and unionist statesmen*, 2 vols. (1896–7), pt 3 • London Stereoscopic Co., various photographs, NPG • W. Orpen, group portrait, oils (*A peace conference at the Quai d'Orsay*), IWM • W. Orpen, group portrait, oils (*The signing of peace in the Hall of Mirrors, Versailles, 28th June 1919*), IWM • B. Partridge, two caricatures, drawings, NPG; repro. in *Punch* (6 May–16 Sept 1903) • C. Sims, oils, Scot. NPG • B. Stone, photograph, NPG • J. Tenniel, pencil caricature (*April showers, or a spoilt Easter holiday*), FM Cam.; repro. in *Punch* (23 April 1892) • G. F. Watt, oils, Eton • Xit, caricature, Hentschel-colourtype, NPG; repro. in *VF* (27 Jan 1910) • bronze medal, Scot. NPG

Wealth at death £76,433 5*s*. 2*d*.: confirmation, 27 Aug 1930, *CCI*

Balfour, Blanche Elizabeth Campbell. *See* Dugdale, Blanche Elizabeth Campbell (1880–1948).

Balfour, Clara Lucas [*née* Clara Lucas] **(1808–1878)**, advocate of women's advancement and temperance activist, was born in the New Forest, Hampshire, on 21 December 1808. She was the only child of John Lydell Lucas (*c*.1767–1818), a butcher and cattle dealer from Gosport, and Sarah (*d*. 1834, maiden name unknown), both of whom were relatively well educated. By the age of four Clara could already read exceptionally well. At a very young age she was removed from her mother's care and went to live with her father and his family on the Isle of Wight. Family oral history has it that 'a great wrong' had been done to Sarah, having been 'deceived by a form of marriage she later discovered to be bigamous' (Cunliffe-Jones, 10). This may help explain why Clara was baptized only at the age of nine after her father's death in 1818, and why there is no evidence of Clara's parents living together during her childhood. In 1818 Clara and her mother moved to London, where for several years they lived close to poverty, supporting themselves by needlework. However, between 1819 and 1822 enough money was scraped together to send Clara to a boarding-school in Woodford.

On 29 September 1824 Clara married James Balfour (1796–1884), who was nearly twenty-eight. Clara was not yet sixteen. For the first two decades of their married life the Balfours lived 'at the bottom of the wheel of Fortune' (Dunlop, 153) with no reliable income. Between 1825 and 1843 they had seven children, four of whom, including Jabez Spencer *Balfour, survived into adulthood. During the first thirteen years of their marriage Clara Lucas Balfour's already harsh life was further burdened by her husband's excessive drinking. Her firsthand experience of the physical and psychological consequences of alcoholism is vividly and accurately portrayed in her later temperance writing. However, in spite of the hardship of their early married life, she still somehow found time to continue her self-education, and at some point in the mid-1830s she began to write.

A key event in the lives of the Balfours occurred in 1837 when they became aware of the still young temperance movement. After hearing a temperance address on 9 October 1837 James signed 'the pledge'. Clara then signed on 16 October 1837. From this point onwards, both the Balfours remained dedicated to the cause of temperance.

At this period, some time between 1837 and 1840, Clara Lucas Balfour wrote *Common Sense versus Socialism*, an attack on a local Owenite group, which brought her to the attention of the Carlyles, Jane (1801–1866) and Thomas (1795–1881), who quickly became key patrons and friends of the Balfours. In 1838 she began writing for the temperance cause, publishing *The Triumph of Teetotalism over Quackery* and *King Alcohol's Walk*. Although she herself had been christened, and had christened her own children, in the Church of England, in 1840 Clara Lucas Balfour wrote to Jabez Burns (1805–1876), temperance campaigner, writer, and minister of the Baptist chapel, Church Street, Edgeware, asking to be rebaptized. Having converted, she then remained an active and central figure in the Baptist community throughout her life.

Also in 1840 the Balfours met John Dunlop (1789–1868), pioneering temperance campaigner and author of *Artificial and Compulsory Drinking Usages in Great Britain and Ireland* (1839). Dunlop encouraged Clara Lucas Balfour to expand her temperance work, arranging for her to have a salary of £25 for co-editing the *Temperance Journal* in May of 1841, and then encouraging her to lecture. She began by speaking on temperance at ladies' 'drawing room' meetings, but in October 1841 gave her first public lecture. Almost immediately she branched out from the subject of temperance and began lecturing on a wide variety of topics, including literature, biography, and history, but most notably on such subjects as 'Capacities of women' and 'The idea of education as applied to woman'. Clara Lucas Balfour's unusual and pioneering career as a professional woman lecturer was in full swing by the end of 1842, with her lectures no longer limited to speaking to groups of ladies in the London area. For the next thirty years she maintained a gruelling schedule, speaking to large audiences of working men at mechanics' institutes and to other single- and mixed-sex public forums as far afield as Sheffield and Plymouth.

At the same time as her lecturing career began, Clara Lucas Balfour's first collection of temperance poems and tales, *A Garland of Waterflowers*, was published in 1841. From this point on she wrote as prolifically as she lectured. She contributed almost weekly to a number of temperance journals, such as *British Workman*, *Band of Hope Review*, and the *Temperance Journal*. She wrote over thirty temperance works, including *Morning Dewdrops* (1853), prefaced by Harriet Beecher Stowe (1811–1896) and still being reprinted in the 1890s, *The Victim* (1860), *Confessions of a Decanter* (1862), and *Our 'Old October'* (1868). In 1850 she edited and republished Margaret G. Derenzy's *A Whisper to a Newly Married Pair from a Widowed Wife* (1824, hitherto mistakenly attributed to her); and then, building on her love of reading and literature, *Sketches of English Literature from the Fourteenth to the Present Century* was written for Longman in 1852.

Clara Lucas Balfour's other non-temperance writing focused on issues of social and moral reform, and on women's role in society and history. In works such as *The Women of Scripture* (1847), *Working Women of the Last Half Century: the Lessons of their Lives* (1854), *The Bible Patterns of a Good Woman* (1867), and *Women Worth Emulating* (1877), she manipulated Victorian 'domestic ideology', which situated women exclusively in the private sphere. Arguing for a drastic improvement in women's education in order that they would then be better prepared to carry out their duty as society's moral and spiritual guardians, she has been interpreted as merely reinforcing patriarchal notions of the ideal Victorian woman. However, Clara Lucas Balfour also consistently argued that the women who strove to live up to this notion of 'ideal womanhood' were not in any way feeble-minded or inadequate in relation to men. For her, woman was 'emphatically called the "help-meet" of man, not help-less, not inadequate, and therefore not inferior' (*The Women of Scripture*, 12). Whereas she has previously been regarded almost exclusively in the light of her temperance work, a century later feminist historians can view her 'separate spheres feminism' as a necessary precursor to the late nineteenth-century women's movement. Through the example of her own life, and through her use of biography and history in her writing and lectures, Clara Lucas Balfour provided her contemporaries with much needed examples of women 'doing, as well as suffering; thinking as well as feeling; directing, as well as obeying' (*Working Women of the Last Half Century*, 3).

In 1876, after almost forty years of temperance campaigning and lecturing on 'the woman question', Clara Lucas Balfour was a key motivator in the creation of the British Women's Temperance Association, which over the next two decades would be closely involved in the social purity movement and in the fight for women's suffrage. She was elected its president in May 1877. Clara Lucas Balfour died of cancer of the uterus at 88 London Road, Croydon, on 3 July 1878, and was buried in Paddington cemetery. KRISTIN G. DOERN

Sources J. Cunliffe-Jones, 'Clara Lucas Balfour, 1808–1878: lecturer, writer and pioneer of women's studies', MEd diss., U. Lpool, 1988 • C. Burns, *Memorial leaves: a selection from the papers of Cecil Burns (Mrs. Dawson Burns), with a biographical sketch* (1898) • J. Dunlop, *Autobiography of John Dunlop* (privately printed, London, 1932) • C. L. Balfour, *Our 'Old October': being a true sketch of a temperance meeting in the earliest days of the temperance reformation* (1868) • D. Burns, *The late Mrs. Clara Lucas Balfour: a memorial discourse* (1878) • J. Inwards, *Memorials of temperance workers: containing brief sketches of nearly one hundred deceased and worthy labourers* (1879) • *Memories of old friends, being extracts from the journals and letters of Caroline Fox, from 1835–1871*, ed. H. M. Pym, 2 vols. (1882) • P. T. Winskill, *The temperance movement and its workers*, 4 vols. (1891–2) • D. Burns, *Temperance history: a consecutive narrative of the rise, development, and extensions of the temperance reform* (1889–91) • *DNB* • d. cert. • m. cert. • parish register (baptism), Portsea, Southampton, 26 April 1818

Likenesses woodcut, NPG

Balfour, Edward Green (1813–1889), surgeon and naturalist, was born on 6 September 1813 in Montrose, the second son of Captain George Balfour of the East India Company marine service, and Susan Hume, a sister of Joseph *Hume MP. After studying at the Montrose Academy, Balfour went to Edinburgh where he studied surgery at the university. He was admitted to the Royal College of Surgeons of Edinburgh in 1833 and a year later set sail for India, where a family friend had arranged for a commission as an assistant surgeon in the Madras medical service. Balfour's voyage to India was delayed by a visit to the island of Mauritius, where he was able to observe at first hand the ecological destruction about which French naturalists had written. This kindled in him a lifelong interest in what he believed was a direct relationship between deforestation, climatic change, and environmental degradation.

India On arrival in India Balfour was attached to a European regiment. However, rapid progress first in Hindustani and later in Persian brought him to the attention of his superiors and he was soon transferred to a regiment of sepoy infantry. Sepoy regiments, unlike European ones, moved frequently between stations and were more likely to be posted to the smaller cantonments, and Balfour accordingly spent most of the next ten years travelling about southern India. His interest in environmental change and its relationship to human societies was further provoked and he was able to collect a great body of information which would serve as the basis for a string of articles and books on health and the environment in India. These writings brought him to the attention of the government. His article entitled 'On the influence exercised by trees on the climate of a country' (1849), in which he argued that tree felling in southern India lay behind recent climatic change, was employed by the government of Madras in its efforts to persuade the East India Company to allow it to impose a stricter conservation regime in its territories. This work also made an impact upon the newly arrived governor-general of India, Lord Dalhousie, who was persuaded of the need for tighter forestry controls.

In 1848 Balfour returned to the presidency capital where he was given medical charge of the governor's bodyguard. While this was a prestigious appointment, it did not entail much regimental duty and Balfour could devote a substantial amount of his time to his writings and his other interests. The reduced medical demands also enabled him to take up an appointment as agent to the court of the nawab of the Carnatic, which eventually culminated in his serving from 1858 to 1861 on a commission called to look into the nawab's debts. He also served briefly in 1850 as assistant assay master at the Madras mint.

Even when faced with these extensive outside commitments Balfour continued to keep up his medical career, and in 1852 he was promoted to the rank of full surgeon. This year also saw his marriage on 24 May to Marion Matilda Agnes Gilchrist, the daughter of a fellow surgeon on the Madras establishment. Their first and apparently only child, Edith, was born on 28 June 1861. Following his promotion Balfour filled a number of staff positions in Madras, Mysore, Burma, and Hyderabad, and in 1871 his talents and lengthy service were rewarded when he was promoted to the highest ranking medical post in the presidency, that of surgeon-general. He held this position until his departure from India in 1876.

Environment and society Balfour was clearly a polymath whose writings spanned topics as diverse as forestry, Persian poetry, cholera, and indigenous medical knowledge. Nevertheless, certain patterns can be discerned in his work. Most significant perhaps is the connection he identified between forests, climatic change, famine, and the outbreak of diseases. The importance he attached to this relationship stemmed partly from his medical training in Edinburgh where the impact of environmental factors on human health had been stressed, partly from his readings of French physiocrats as well as the works of Alexander von Humboldt and Joseph Priestley, and partly from his firsthand observations in Mauritius and in India. Balfour's major work on forestry was *The timber trees, timber and fancy woods, as also the forests of India and of eastern and southern Asia*, which was first published in 1858. In 1863 the government of India had set up a timber-purchasing agency in Burma, largely on the recommendation of the military finance department, which coincidentally had been headed by Balfour's brother George [*see below*] until 1862. The government's expanded presence in commercial forestry led it to pressurize Balfour to bring out a second edition, which provided a more comprehensive listing of the types of trees to be found in India and their possible commercial use. A third edition appeared in 1870. Balfour's insistence that the state should take on a greater role in policing and preserving India's forests was instrumental in pushing the British administration in India into taking up a more proactive conservationist role, and hence we can conclude that Balfour was one of the most important figures in nineteenth-century environmentalism.

Balfour's environmental efforts cannot, however, be separated from his views of society, and here again Balfour shared many characteristics with the French physiocrats. In particular he accepted that the state had a major role to play in engineering necessary or desirable social change. Like many of his contemporaries, Balfour held fairly fixed views as to what denoted proper social organization and productive economic activity, and again like many of his contemporaries he believed that statistics were a crucial tool in determining benchmarks and in guiding policy. In the case of forest conservation, Balfour not only singled out agriculturists, landowners, and timber merchants as contributing to deforestation, he also emphasized what he saw as the destructiveness of India's tribal population. He insisted that their 'slash and burn' style of agriculture was responsible for the destruction of large stands of timber. Hitherto tribal communities had been stereotyped as unproductive; Balfour and his readers could now argue on the basis of what was presented as scientific evidence that tribal societies were inherently destructive. This helped to justify demands that tribal societies be disciplined and reformed.

Balfour also employed statistics to make judgements on how best to preserve the health of Europeans in India. In works such as 'Statistical data for forming troops and maintaining them in health in different climates and localities' (*Quarterly Journal of the Statistical Society of London*, 8, 1845, 192–209), *Statistics of Cholera* (1849), and 'Remarks on the abstract tables of the men discharged from the military' (*Quarterly Journal of the Statistical Society of London*, 14, 1851, 348–56), which was read by his uncle, Joseph Hume, to the Statistical Society of London, Balfour spoke out against the common belief in 'seasoning', the idea that given enough time humans will adjust to new climates. He believed instead that different races had different tolerances for climates and diseases. The statistics he accumulated suggested that Europeans fared better at higher altitudes and he accordingly became a champion of locating asylums and cantonments in the hills of India. Balfour also chaired a committee which in 1853 published the *Barometrical Survey of India*.

Arguably, Balfour's most influential work was his *Cyclopaedia of India and Southern Asia*, which was first published in Madras in 1857. It had been compiled from the notes he had taken when organizing exhibitions of local items for display at London's Great Exhibition. His accumulation of further information led him to release a second edition in Madras in 1871. The second edition, which was largely self-funded, had almost triple the number of entries. Sales were good and he managed to recoup his investment within a few years. The third edition was again larger and this time it was published in Britain where it was favourably reviewed. It was a mammoth undertaking, containing entries on historical and mythological figures, the flora and fauna of India, castes, historical battles, soil types, diseases, minerals, major texts, marriage customs, and towns and villages. It also provided definitions of some of the more common words from the major vernaculars. There is even a lengthy entry on himself as well as one for his brother George.

Advocate of museums; Indian language and literature Edward Balfour's commitment to collecting and organizing information on India led to his appointment as secretary to the committees called to prepare Madras's contributions to the Great Exhibition of 1851, the Paris exhibitions of 1855 and 1868, the Universal Exhibition of London in 1862, and the Vienna Exhibition of 1873. In addition, much of the material he collected was used to stock the government central museum in Madras, which had been founded in 1850 with Balfour as superintendent. He held this post until 1859. Balfour passionately believed that museums were an ideal medium through which useful information could be communicated to the people of India. He had initially envisaged a network of museums across southern India. The plan was for six satellite museums to be located in various regions of the presidency with the main museum in Madras serving as a central repository. However, the outlying museums quickly faltered and by 1861 there remained only one at Rajahmundry and it had been turned over to district authorities. Despite these setbacks the museum in Madras became one of the most popular museums in India, particularly through such innovations as setting aside special days when only women would be admitted. By 1879 the museum was attracting just under 180,000 people per year and by 1886 this figure had risen to 230,000. Balfour was particularly pleased at the number of visitors who were apparently illiterate, for this confirmed his faith in the museum as a means for public instruction. At the outset the museum had an unmistakably utilitarian purpose—most of the collection consisted of items of commercial value. In one surviving document of 1851 it was described as a museum of practical and economic geology. To these collections Balfour added samples of all the woods of India which he had been able to acquire. Only later were archaeological and ethnological items added. Balfour's enthusiasm for collecting can also be glimpsed in the Madras Zoological Gardens, which he helped to found in 1856. Also, in 1866, he had a hand in establishing a museum in Mysore.

While Balfour is best-known for his work in scientific disciplines, he did maintain an interest in Indian languages and literature. In 1850 he published *Gul-Dastah, or, The Bunch of Roses*, which consisted of his translations of a number of works by Indian and Persian poets. Credit for the erection of the Muhammadan Public Library in Madras can also be assigned in part to Balfour. He translated several English works on astronomy into Hindustani and a statistical map of the world into Hindustani, Tamil, and Telugu. Yet despite his knowledge of Hindustani and Persian, which was sufficiently advanced that he continued to serve as interpreter to the government on many occasions, Balfour was very sceptical of the state of indigenous scientific knowledge. In the preface to the first edition of the *Cyclopaedia*, he insisted that indigenous people are so close to subsistence level that they do not have the means or the freedom to reflect accurately upon their surroundings.

Balfour's final years in India were marked by a number of initiatives he took in an effort to make Western medicine more accessible to the peoples of India. He personally translated an English midwifery manual into Hindustani and arranged for it to appear in Tamil, Telugu, and Kannada, and in 1871 he urged (unsuccessfully) the Madras government to establish five vernacular medical schools: two in Telugu-speaking areas, two in Tamil-speaking areas, and one in the Malayalam-speaking region. He also published a description of medical discoveries and recent lessons that was entitled *Medical Hints to the People of India*. He intended that this book would inspire Indians studying Western medicine as well as win over practitioners of traditional medicine (*vaids* and *hakims*) to Western medical practices. Balfour's other great initiative was to try to open up medical opportunities for European women in India. He had long recognized that their maleness prevented European doctors from penetrating into the domestic spaces of Indian society. In contrast, European women would be able to move more freely within a large segment of Indian society. His lobbying of the government and the medical establishment in Madras began in 1872 and his first success came in 1875 when Mary Scharlieb was admitted to the Madras Medical College as its first woman applicant. Scharlieb, the wife of a barrister in Madras, had been trained as a midwife but found midwifery too constraining. Her entry into the Madras Medical College cleared the way for other women applicants.

Balfour continued to write about India following his retirement and return to England in 1876. The outbreak of the Deccan famine of 1877–9 and its horrific death toll prompted him to return to the subject of deforestation and climatic change. This resulted in his book *Indian Forestry*, which appeared in 1885. He also brought out revised editions of some of his earlier works, notably his *Cyclopaedia*, and a book on agricultural pests. Balfour died on 8 December 1889 at 107 Gloucester Terrace, London. He was survived by his wife. Balfour was a major figure in Britain's scientific encounter with India, and his researches into a number of areas, including botany and public health, became standard reading for several generations of scholars, surgeons, and administrators. However, he never received the attention many felt he merited. There was no knighthood, nor was he the subject of a biography. D. G. Crawford, the historian of the Indian Medical Service, was sensitive to this slight, and argued that had Balfour been stationed in India at a later date, when India featured more prominently in British public life, he would not have been so overlooked.

Edward Balfour's elder brother **Sir George Balfour** (1809–1894), army officer and politician, was born in Montrose, and studied at the Montrose Academy and the East India Company's Addiscombe College. He entered the Madras artillery in 1825. He transferred to the Royal Artillery in the following year but continued to serve in India where he first saw action with the Malacca field force in 1832–3. Promotion to captain came in 1844, major and lieutenant-colonel in 1854, colonel in 1855, major-general in 1865, lieutenant-general in 1874, and general in 1877. His administrative skills and particularly his detailed knowledge of military accounts led to his appointment as a staff officer with the Madras force during the war with China in 1840–42. The commander of that expedition, Henry Pottinger, was so impressed with Balfour's handling of the indemnity levied against the defeated Chinese that Balfour was appointed to serve as British consul at Shanghai; he served from 1843 to 1846. Shanghai was one of the treaty ports which the Chinese had reluctantly agreed to open under the terms of the treaty of Nanking (Nanjing). Balfour proved to be quite successful in negotiating with the Chinese. While he was thought to be of insufficient rank to merit an audience with the provincial governor, he did meet frequently with the highest-ranking official in Shanghai, the *taotai* or intendant, with whom he established excellent working relations. Balfour's military rank no doubt helped, for it invested him with greater stature than would have accrued had he been simply a merchant as was the case with other consuls in India. Balfour reinforced this impression by emphasizing diplomatic relations and protocol, even at the expense of commercial transactions. It was during Balfour's time in Shanghai that the area of international settlement was laid down. It began initially with his purchase of land amounting to 150 acres. This was done without the prior approval of the government and was partly funded by his own money. Balfour was, however, convinced of the long-term importance of Shanghai as a point of entry into the vast interior markets of China.

British relations with Chinese officials during his time in Shanghai were also facilitated by Balfour's willingness to take a hard line on the opium trade. Opium was a banned product in China, and while consuls could do little about opium trading occurring outside their jurisdiction, many would also turn a blind eye to that being carried out under their noses. Balfour co-operated with Chinese authorities in seeking to interdict the trade. On one occasion he used British sailors to board a British merchant vessel; once aboard they discovered several bales of opium, which were thrown over the side, and those in charge of the ship were fined. He also sought to prevent conflict by limiting European movement outside the city to journeys of no more than one day's ride. He left Shanghai in 1846 after a disagreement with his superiors as to whether he was entitled to maintain his position in the army lists. A furlough in Britain resulted in his marriage in 1848 to his cousin Charlotte Isabella Hume, the third daughter of Joseph Hume. It is not clear whether they had children.

In late 1848 Balfour returned to Madras, where he served in a number of administrative positions. These included a spell on the military board from 1849 to 1857 which brought him to the attention of the governor-general. He was consequently appointed to the military finance commission, which had been formed to look into India-wide economies in the aftermath of the revolt. He gained a reputation for 'obstinate ability' (*The Times*, 15 March 1894), though his 'largely generous nature' prevented him from lapsing into complete 'obstinacy'. His command over detail led to his appointment as chief of the military finance department from 1860 to 1862. He returned to England where he served on the royal commission on recruiting in 1866 and in 1868–70, and in 1868 he was appointed assistant to the controller-in-chief, war department, a post he held until 1871.

Balfour then turned to politics and sat as the Liberal MP for Kincardineshire from December 1872 until 1892. His parliamentary career was, however, far from distinguished. While in principle an advocate of Irish land reforms and home rule, he spoke rarely in parliament and generally failed to attract much attention: significantly, he only merited one entry in Gladstone's diary and that was in 1866, six years before his election as a Liberal MP. He made a somewhat greater impact outside parliament. In letters to *The Times*, which were later collected together and printed as *Trade and Salt in India Free* (1875), Balfour argued for the abolition of duties on most goods imported into India as well as the abolition of taxes on the production and selling of salt. He reasoned that not only did these taxes hamper economic growth, they antagonized the population of India which might ultimately weaken British rule from within, should British India ever be threatened from without. Four years earlier he had written to *The Times* to criticize some of their correspondent's facts on Indian budgetary affairs. Balfour was also convinced by the deforestation arguments of his brother, and in 1866 he took exception to several papers delivered to the Royal Geographical Society which were critical of Edward's work in this area. George Balfour was made CB in 1874 and KCB in 1870. He died in London on 12 March 1894. DOUGLAS M. PEERS

Sources R. H. Grove, *Green imperialism: colonial expansion, tropical island Edens, and the origins of environmentalism, 1600–1860* (1995) • *The Times* (11 Dec 1889) • *The Times* (13 March 1894) [Sir George Balfour] • *The Times* (15 March 1894) [Sir George Balfour] • S. Jex-Blake, 'Medical women', *Nineteenth Century*, 22 (1887), 692–707 • I. H. Burkill, *Chapters on the history of botany in India* (Calcutta, 1965) • L. C. Johnson, *Shanghai: from market town to treaty port, 1074–1858* (1995) • D. G. Crawford, *A history of the Indian medical service, 1600–1913*, 2 vols. (1914) • D. G. Crawford, ed., *Roll of the Indian Medical Service, 1615–1930* (1930) • S. F. Markham and H. Hargreaves, eds., *The museums of India* (1936) • *WWBMP*, vol. 2 • M. Harrison, *Public health in British India: Anglo-Indian preventive medicine, 1859–1914* (1994) • M. Rangarajan, 'Imperial agendas and India's forests: the early history of Indian forestry, 1800–1878', *Indian Economic and Social History Review*, 31 (1994), 147–67 • P. D. Curtin, *Death by migration: Europe's encounter with the tropical world in the nineteenth century* (1989) • J. K. Fairbank, *Trade and diplomacy on the China coast: the opening of the treaty ports, 1842–1854*, 2 vols. (1953) • J. H. Leslie, *A list of the officers who have served in the Madras artillery from its formation in 1748 down to 1861* (1900) • G. Prakash, 'Science "gone native" in colonial India', *Representations*, 40 (1992), 153–78 • W. C. Costin, *Great Britain and China, 1833–1860* (1937) • J. Y. Wong, *Anglo-Chinese relations, 1839–1860: a calendar of Chinese documents in the British foreign office records* (1983) • *CGPLA Eng. & Wales* (1889) • *DNB*

Archives BL, corresp. with Lord Ripon, Add. MSS 43622, 43624 [Sir George Balfour] • PRO, letters to Sir Henry Pottinger, FO 705 [Sir George Balfour] • UCL, letters to Sir Edwin Chadwick [Sir George Balfour]

Likenesses oils, Government Museum, Madras, India

Wealth at death £16,087 13*s*. 10*d*.: resworn probate, Feb 1890, *CGPLA Eng. & Wales* (1889) • £8491 9*s*. 5*d*.—Sir George Balfour: resworn probate, 1895, *CGPLA Eng. & Wales* (1894)

Balfour [*née* Lytton], **Elizabeth Edith** [Betty], **countess of Balfour (1867–1942)**, social hostess and biographer, was born on 12 June 1867 at Hyde Park Gate, London, the eldest of the five surviving children of Edward Robert Bulwer-*Lytton, first earl of Lytton (1831–1891), viceroy, diplomat, and poet, and his wife, Edith (*d.* 1936), daughter of the Hon. Edward Villiers. Always known as Betty, she was educated by governesses wherever her father was posted, including India when he became viceroy. They returned to Knebworth, the family home in Hertfordshire, in 1880. Her father was a strong influence. 'He would take for granted', she wrote, 'that his children shared all his interests, whether in matters literary or political or domestic, and no direct instruction could have been so stimulating' (*Letters of … Lytton*, 2.257).

On 21 December 1887 Betty married Gerald William *Balfour (1853–1945), the clever, strikingly good-looking MP and younger brother of Arthur Balfour; they had a son and five daughters, including Lady Evelyn Barbara (Eve) *Balfour. Through her husband, she entered the world of the Souls, the group whose central figure was Arthur Balfour. Although Lady Betty Balfour never emulated the Souls' great worldly hostesses like Lady Desborough, her London house in Addison Road was nevertheless known for its good talk and for its musical parties. Betty shared with Arthur Balfour a love of music (especially for Handel). Although she was undoubtedly attractive, her contemporaries remarked more on her charm and her social gifts as a talker and even more as a listener than as a beauty. In 1895 Gerald Balfour was made chief secretary for Ireland, and in Dublin his wife's gifts as a hostess with wide-ranging tastes became apparent. The chief secretary's house became a centre not only for politicians but also, at that time of great artistic vitality in Ireland, for the arts as well: visitors included the poets W. B. Yeats and George William Russell (AE).

On their return to England in 1900 the Balfours commissioned Betty's brother-in-law Edwin Lutyens to build them a country house. This was Fisher's Hill, near Woking, where musicians such as Ethel Smythe and politicians of all parties would meet, including the marquess of Salisbury, as well as Sidney and Beatrice Webb. The latter counted Betty as her only real friend in society, and thought her 'a woman of quite unusual delightfulness, good to look at, sweet to listen to, original in purpose' (*Diary*, 3.50). Lord Balcarres, another friend, explained why he enjoyed her company:

> She is to begin with a well of humour: then her reading has been extensive and prudently chosen. For years past she has lived among men who rule this country and help to rule the greater world: and this has quickened her critical faculties which gives acumen and breadth to her talk on everyday matters. There is moreover an unerring logic together with the warmest of hearts: what a combination! (Vincent, 44)

By 1910 Lady Betty Balfour had become an active supporter of the suffrage movement, but she never participated in violent protest actions. Instead, her suffragist sister-in-law Frances Balfour described her as taking on the hardest of all tasks: attacking and trying to convince one by one the Conservative leaders. She was ahead of her time in her attitude towards female education, encouraging Ruth, her eldest daughter, to train as a doctor, and a younger daughter, Eve, to read agriculture at Reading University. Eve went on to become secretary of the Soil Association, and a founder of the organic movement.

Lady Betty Balfour edited her father's official papers and letters as viceroy. *The History of Lord Lytton's Indian Administration, 1876–1880* appeared in 1899. In addition she published a selection of his poems (1894) and edited *The Personal and Literary Letters of Robert, First Earl of Lytton* (1906). In the latter volume, more biographer than editor, she described her father's character, his passionate desire to be a poet; and explained his difficult relationship with his father, Bulwer Lytton, the novelist. In an edition of the letters of her sister Constance Lytton (1925), she produced a perceptive portrait of the great suffragette.

On Arthur Balfour's death in 1930 Gerald Balfour succeeded as earl of Balfour and Lady Betty became countess. She died of a perforated duodenal ulcer at Fisher's Hill Cottage on 28 March 1942. Her husband survived her, dying in 1945. CLAYRE PERCY

Sources private information (2004) • Burke, *Peerage* (1959) • *Personal and literary letters of Robert, first earl of Lytton*, ed. E. E. Balfour, 2 vols. (1906) • *The diary of Beatrice Webb*, ed. N. MacKenzie and J. MacKenzie, 4 vols. (1982–5), vols. 3–4 • *The Crawford papers: the journals of David Lindsay, twenty-seventh earl of Crawford … 1892–1940*, ed. J. Vincent (1984) • E. M. M. Fingall, *Seventy years young* (1937) • F. Balfour, *Ne obliviscaris: dinna forget*, 2 [1930] • *Lady Gregory's diaries, 1892–1902*, ed. J. Pethica (1996) • *Letters of Constance Lytton*, ed. E. E. Balfour (1925) • *The letters of Edwin Lutyens to his wife Lady Emily*, ed. C. Percy and J. Ridley (1985) • *The letters of Arthur Balfour and Lady Elcho, 1885–1917*, ed. J. Ridley and C. Percy (1992) • *CGPLA Eng. & Wales* (1942)

Archives BL, corresp. with Arthur James Balfour, Add. MS 49831, *passim* • BL OIOC, letters to Sir Alfred Lyall • Bodl. Oxf., letters to Margot Asquith • Bodl. Oxf., letters to countess of Selborne • Herts. ALS, letters to Lady Desborough • Knebworth House, Hertfordshire, corresp. with Lord Lytton • Plunkett Foundation for Co-operative Studies, Long Hanborough, letters to Sir Horace Plunkett

Likenesses oils, *c*.1920, priv. coll. • photograph, *c*.1920, priv. coll.

Wealth at death £4899 7*s*. 1*d*.: probate, 9 June 1942, *CGPLA Eng. & Wales*

Balfour, Lady Evelyn Barbara [Eve] (**1898–1990**), promoter of organic farming and a founder of the Soil Association, was born on 16 July 1898 in Dublin, the fourth child of Gerald William *Balfour, second earl of Balfour (1853–1945), and Lady Elizabeth Edith *Balfour (1867–1942). Her father was Conservative MP for Leeds Central, chief secretary for Ireland (1895–1900), president of the Board of Trade (1900–05), and president of the Local Government Board (1905); her mother was the eldest daughter of the first earl of Lytton, poet and viceroy of India. Lady Frances *Balfour (1858–1931), her aunt, was a leading Scottish suffragist, churchwoman, and author, who voiced her opinions on many social issues. Educated privately, Eve Balfour's later childhood was spent at her parents' house in Fisher's Hill, near Woking, and Whittingehame in East Lothian, the Scottish constituency of her bachelor uncle, Arthur James *Balfour, who was prime minister from 1902 to 1905.

In 1915 Eve Balfour went to Reading University to study for a diploma in agriculture. In 1918, claiming to be twenty-five, she secured her first job working for the Women's War Agricultural Committee, running a small farm in Monmouthshire. She managed a team of land girls, ploughing the land with horses and milking the cows by hand. In the following year, in conjunction with her elder sister, Mary Edith Balfour, she purchased New Bells Farm, Haughley, near Stowmarket, Suffolk. During this period she played an important role mobilizing local opposition to the unpopular tithe tax levied on agriculture by the church and presented evidence to the royal

Lady Evelyn Barbara Balfour (1898–1990), by Elliott & Fry, 1943

commission. In addition to running the farm she pursued a wide variety of activities, including playing the saxophone in a dance band formed initially for her and her sister's own amusement. The band provided an extra source of income when it played at Saturday night dances in a nearby Ipswich hotel. She gained a pilot's licence in 1931 and crewed for her brother on his annual sailing trips to Scandinavia. She wrote three detective novels with Beryl Hearnden (under the pseudonym Hearnden Balfour), the most successful of which, *The Paper Chase* (1928), was translated into several languages.

During the 1930s Lady Eve, as she was commonly known, became critical of orthodox farming methods, being particularly influenced by Lord Portsmouth's text *Famine in England* (1938), which raised doubts about their sustainability. His book inspired her to contact Sir Robert McCarrison, whose research into the Hunza tribesmen of India's north-west frontier had shown a positive relationship between their impressive health and stamina and methods of soil cultivation. Her interest in organic farming can also be traced to her contacts with Sir Albert Howard, a British scientist who developed the Indore process of composting based on eastern methods.

By this time Eve Balfour was also the tenant farmer of the neighbouring holding, Walnut Tree Farm. Following discussions with the owner, Miss Alice Debenham, they inaugurated the Haughley experiment into organic farming on the land. Miss Debenham registered the gift of her farm to Haughley Research Farms Ltd shortly before she died in 1940. Miss Debenham's sister Agnes was acquainted with one of the directors of the publishers Faber and Faber, through whom Lady Eve contacted Richard De la Mere, editor of their agricultural list. As a result, Eve Balfour's book *The Living Soil* was published by Faber in 1943. Reprinted nine times it became a classic text for the organic movement providing an influential synthesis of existing knowledge. It gave a persuasive account based on experiments in agriculture, botany, nutrition, and preventative medicine, and had far-reaching conclusions for agriculture and social policy. Coinciding with an era of unease about the future of British agriculture, it nevertheless received praise from Donald P. Hopkins, who was an ardent supporter of artificial fertilizers. In 1946 Lady Eve became the co-founder and first president of the Soil Association which aimed to co-ordinate the collection and distribution of information on organic methods of production. Lady Eve had hoped that the government would provide support and funding for organic production, but the 1947 Agriculture Act committed Britain to a system of highly mechanized, intensive methods. The association's membership increased to 3000 by 1952, partly as a result of the publication of its journal *Mother Earth* (subsequently renamed *Living Earth*) and partly due to the commitment of a small band of individuals including Lady Eve. During this period she embarked on a number of lecture tours abroad. The association was frequently in financial crisis because of the cost of the Haughley experiment. In 1963 she moved to Theberton, near the Suffolk coast, but made regular trips back to Haughley. Growing debts incurred by this centre precipitated the sale of the farms in 1970. The results of the investigation were published in 1975 as an addendum to a reprint of *The Living Soil*.

Lady Eve officially retired from the Soil Association in 1984 at the age of eighty-five. She continued to cultivate a large garden before having a stroke in 1989 from which she died, at Belhaven Hospital, Dunbar, on 14 January 1990. She had been made OBE a few weeks before her death, while the very next day Margaret Thatcher's Conservative government announced the first ever British grant enabling farmers to convert to organic methods. This marked a fitting, if rather belated, tribute to an individual who had striven to popularize organic farming at a time when its supporters were commonly regarded as eccentrics.

John Martin

Sources 'Lady Eve Balfour, British pioneer of organic farming', *Annual Obituary* (1990), 3–6 · *The Times* (17 Jan 1990) · *East Anglian Daily Times* (15 Jan 1990) · *Living Earth*, 199 (1998), 23–5 · *Living Earth*, 191 (1996), 16–17 · E. B. Balfour, *The living soil and the Haughley experiment*, rev. edn (1975) · P. Conford, *The organic tradition* (1988) · Lord Portsmouth [G. V. Wallop], *Famine in England* (1938) · A. Howard, *An agricultural testament* (1940) · Lord Northbourne [W. E. C. James], *Look to the land* (1940) · K. E. Barlow, *The discipline of peace* (1942) · Burke, *Peerage* (1980) · P. Conford, 'A forum for organic husbandry: the *New English Weekly* and agricultural policy, 1939–49', *Agricultural History Review*, 46 (1998), 197–210

Archives NRA, priv. coll., family MSS · PRO, family MSS, PRO 30/60 · Soil Association, Bristol | FILM East Anglian Film Archive, 'The tithe war', 1972

Likenesses Elliott & Fry, photograph, 1943, NPG [*see illus.*] · photograph (after portrait by M. Eastman), repro. in Conford, *The organic tradition* · portrait, repro. in *Living Earth*, 191, cover · portrait, repro. in *Living Earth*, 199 (July–Sept 1998), 1 · portrait, repro. in *East Anglian Daily Times* · portrait, repro. in *East Anglian Daily Times* (19 Sept 1988)

Wealth at death under £100,000: probate, 25 April 1990, *CGPLA Eng. & Wales*

Balfour [*née* Campbell], **Lady Frances** (**1858–1931**), suffragist leader and churchwoman, was born at Argyll Lodge, Kensington, London, on 22 February 1858, the fifth daughter and tenth of twelve children of George Douglas *Campbell, eighth duke of Argyll (1823–1900), and his first wife, Lady Elizabeth Georgiana Leveson-Gower (1824–1878), the eldest daughter of the second duke of Sutherland. Lady Frances's youth was spent at the three Campbell residences: Inveraray Castle, the ancestral home in Argyllshire; Rosneath Castle in Dunbartonshire; and Argyll Lodge in London. Her formal education was provided by an English governess. However, the main method by which she learned throughout her life was by listening to and participating in the conversations, particularly at the dinner table, of her parents, in-laws, and male acquaintances, especially ministers and politicians, whose company and friendship she preferred. Lady Frances had a congenital hip dislocation, which left her with one leg shorter than the other and necessitated her wearing a built-up shoe on her right foot. Restless and energetic, she attributed her hot temper to the bedrest which she was forced to endure throughout her childhood for the pelvic disability from which she suffered all her life.

On 12 May 1879 Lady Frances Campbell married Eustace James Anthony Balfour (1854–1911), youngest brother of Arthur James Balfour, later prime minister. Their five children were reared in their home at 32 Addison Road, Kensington. A fellow of the Royal Institute of British Architects, Eustace was a partner in the London architectural firm of Balfour and Turner Ltd. He also served as surveyor and architect of the duke of Westminster's London estate from 1890 to his retirement in 1910. In addition, he was active in the London Scottish Volunteers, in which he rose to the rank of lieutenant-colonel. In 1903 he was appointed an aide-de-camp to Edward VII. Since Lady Frances destroyed all Eustace's letters to her, it is difficult to discern much about their marriage. Frances's mercurial temperament, Eustace's alcoholism, his extended holidays on the continent away from his family, and his preference for the military life seem to suggest that the marriage was not particularly congenial to him. While Eustace may not have provided her with the intellectual companionship she sought, Lady Frances had great love and affection for her husband; this love and loyalty motivated her support for Eustace in his disputes with his sister Alice Balfour, concerning his excessive drinking, and explain Lady Frances's refusal to accept alcoholism as acceptable grounds for divorce when she sat as a member of the divorce commission. Frances and Eustace were opposites in temperament and interests, and thus were concerned with different spheres of activity. While Eustace turned to the volunteer movement, Lady Frances found intellectual companionship with politicians and clerics, especially her brothers-in-law Arthur and Gerald Balfour, as well as Sir Robert Finlay, Robert H. Story, Archibald Fleming, Alexander Macrae, and A. J. Milne.

Lady Frances Balfour (**1858–1931**), by Bassano, 1919

With one exception, Frances's relations with the Balfour family were close. Her sister-in-law, Lady Betty Balfour, Gerald's wife, was her closest friend, feminist ally, and literary executor; as such, she edited and preserved Lady Frances's papers. However, relations between Lady Frances and Alice Balfour, the unmarried sister who managed Arthur Balfour's households, were often strained, not least because of their competition for Arthur's favour and approval. Lady Frances had little appreciation of the difficulties which Alice encountered in managing Arthur's very active households, and found Alice tedious and petty, while Alice had difficulty accepting Frances's candour and insensitivity to the feelings of others, especially those in her own family.

Like many of her generation Lady Frances first found opportunities for social service through the 'social purity' campaigns. Thus, in 1885 she became president of the Travellers' Aid Society, which provided temporary lodging to protect young country women seeking work in the cities from the snares of white slavery procurers, and she remained president until her death in 1931.

In 1889 Lady Frances began her political work when she joined the campaign to secure the enfranchisement of British women. Indeed, she was one of the highest ranking members of the aristocracy to assume a leadership role in the women's suffrage movement. One of the few women of her class to agitate for votes for women from the 1880s onwards, she became a leader of the constitutional suffragists. Her feminism, like much of the rest of her political philosophy, derived from her personal experiences. In her youth and adolescence she heard the arguments against slavery advanced by members of her family (her mother and grandmother, Harriet, duchess of Sutherland, were ardent abolitionists). As a young woman she was thwarted in her desire to become a nurse and frustrated because she could observe, but not aspire to a seat in, parliament. Thus, as a feminist, Lady Frances espoused equal rights for women and was absolutely convinced that women should be permitted to study and train for careers in all the professions on the same terms as men: she eloquently supported her niece Ruth Balfour's decision to study and practise medicine. But Lady Frances wanted no part in the sex war into which the suffragettes led by the Women's Social and Political Union ventured, and deplored the tactics of the militants. While she did not believe women should be exalted on pedestals, she believed that advocates of women's rights were wrong in viewing men as 'enemies' in order to achieve their objective of complete equality for women. Her feminism, as Olive Banks has observed, was 'rooted in nineteenth century concepts of freedom and democracy' (Banks, 12). In a lengthy obituary, the *New York Times* (26 February 1931, 28) noted that, '[s]ince the attainment of the vote for women [Lady Frances Balfour] had sought to obtain equality of legislation relating to divorce and other matters involving both sexes, in addition to laboring for the liberty of women in various phases of industry and society'.

Lady Frances was involved in almost every aspect of the suffragists' work. As Norman Maclean, a personal friend, noted, 'She had a personal magnetism and a gift of making friends no less remarkable than her courage and her crusading spirit' (*DNB*). Her contributions to the suffragist movement included marching, speaking, and writing for the cause. She helped lead the 'Mud March' of February 1907 and was a popular speaker, averaging approximately three speeches a week to suffragist meetings from Inverness to Plymouth during 1910–12. Lady Frances was, as Maclean observed, 'A mistress of invective, … [who] wielded the dagger of sarcastic wit with the same zest as her ancestors had wielded the broadsword'.

Lady Frances served on the executive committee of the National Union for Women's Suffrage Society from its inception in 1897 until 1918, when British women over the age of thirty were accorded the vote. In addition, she was president of the London Society for Women's Suffrage, the largest women's suffrage society in Britain, from 1896 to 1918 and an active member of the editorial board of the *Englishwoman's Review*.

However, Lady Frances's most effective work for women was her less publicized personal efforts to influence British politicians and members of parliament on behalf of the 'cause'. She was in many ways the real political heir of her father, the eighth duke of Argyll, a whig-Liberal government minister for more than twenty years and a renowned orator. Through marriage her relatives included the Princess Louise, the fourth daughter of Queen Victoria, who married Frances's eldest brother, John Douglas Sutherland *Campbell, later ninth duke of Argyll, and Lord Salisbury, the prime minister, and uncle of the Balfours. While Lady Frances was constrained to observe parliament from behind the grille in the ladies' gallery, at tea time and in the hallways of parliament she lobbied members on behalf of her special cause. Her vast range of contacts in the Liberal, Conservative, and Unionist parties made her one of the most valuable participants in the suffrage fight. After her father broke with Gladstone in 1881, Lady Frances followed the duke into the ranks of the Liberal Unionists, a move which proved a workable compromise for one married into a staunchly Conservative family.

After the vote had been secured for women, Lady Frances's work for women's rights and equality continued through the National Council of Women of Great Britain and Ireland. She became a member of the executive committee in 1917 and in 1921 was elevated to the presidency. Following her retirement as president in 1923, she served as one of the organization's vice-presidents until her death in 1931. In recognition of her services to women's rights, Lady Frances was named one of two female members of the royal commission on divorce and matrimonial causes which sat from 1910 to 1912. She was, in addition, the first chairman of the Lyceum Club, and a member of the executive committee of the Women's Municipal Party, which encouraged women of all parties to stand for election to councils. Honorary degrees from the University of Durham (DLitt 1919) and the University of Edinburgh (LLD 1921) provided further recognition of her service and talents.

Keenly interested in the religious establishment, Lady Frances included among her close acquaintances many prominent clerics. Her major religious endeavours were made on behalf of the interests of the Church of Scotland, where she was a staunch defender of tradition. Although she usually rejected and denounced such innovations as closing hymns with three Amens, she supported all church efforts to provide equal opportunities for women. Her work for women's enfranchisement within the church included serving as the only president of the Scottish Churches' League for Woman's Suffrage, an organization which she helped to establish in 1912. From 1893 until 1930 she was one of the few women who regularly attended the annual meeting of the general assembly of the Church of Scotland, becoming a familiar 'fixture' in the Throne Gallery. Frail and infirm, she made one of her last trips to the general assembly in May 1929 to see the Church of Scotland reunited.

Lady Frances's most significant work on behalf of her church was undertaken from 1905 to 1909, when she effected the rebuilding of Crown Court Church in London's Covent Garden. Besides serving as the only woman on the rebuilding committee, she personally raised almost all the money to finance the project, and secured as its architect her husband Eustace and as its treasurer her brother Lord George Campbell. Lady Frances succeeded to the presidency of the Crown Court Church's Woman's Guild following the death of her sister, Lady Victoria *Campbell, in 1910 and served in this capacity until her death.

Lady Frances published numerous articles and letters in British periodicals and the daily press. After her husband's death in 1911 she wrote her first book-length publications, mainly to supplement her limited income. In addition to a two-volume autobiography in 1930, *Ne obliviscaris: Dinna Forget* (a reference to the Campbell motto), she wrote five biographies: *Lady Victoria Campbell* (1911), *The Life and Letters of the Reverend James MacGregor* (1912), *Dr Elsie Inglis* (1918), *The Life of George, Fourth Earl of Aberdeen* (2 vols., 1923), and *A Memoir of Lord Balfour of Burleigh* (1925).

Lady Frances Balfour died at her London home, 32 Addison Road, Kensington, on 25 February 1931 from pneumonia and heart failure. She was buried at Whittingehame, the Balfour family home in East Lothian.

JOAN B. HUFFMAN

Sources NA Scot., Balfour MSS • F. Balfour, *Ne obliviscaris: dinna forget*, 2 vols. [1930] • F. Balfour, *Lady Victoria Campbell* (1911) • O. Banks, *The biographical dictionary of British feminists*, 1 (1985) • Women's Library, London, Women's suffrage collection • *New York Times* (26 Feb 1931) • Women's Library, London, Travellers' Aid Society collection • *DNB* • B. E. C. Dugdale, *Family homespun* (1940) • private information • P. Jalland, *Women, marriage and politics, 1860–1914* (1986) • d. cert. • m. cert. • d. cert. (Eustace Balfour) • LMA, National Council of Women MSS

Archives NA Scot., diaries, personal and family corresp. • National Council of Women, London, MSS • priv. coll. | BL, corresp. with Arthur James Balfour, Add. MSS 49831, *passim* • Bodl. Oxf., letters to Margot Asquith • Hatfield House, Hertfordshire, Cecil/Salisbury MSS • Inveraray Castle, Campbell MSS • Women's Library, London, Women's suffrage collection | SOUND BBC WAC

Likenesses Princess Louise, portrait, 1871–8, priv. coll. • E. Burne-Jones, portrait, 1880, Musée des Beaux-Arts, Nantes, France • R. Luxmoore, portrait, exh. RA 1894 • Bassano, photograph, 1919, NPG [*see illus.*] • E. Shaw, portrait, 1919 • J. Y. Hunter, portrait, 1925, priv. coll. • stained-glass window, 1990, Crown Court Church, London

Wealth at death £8458 1s. 4d.: administration, 29 April 1931, *CGPLA Eng. & Wales*

Balfour, Francis (*d.* in or after **1816**), surgeon and orientalist, was born in Edinburgh and took his MD degree there in 1767. He entered the East India Company's service in Bengal as assistant surgeon on 3 July 1769, and was appointed full surgeon on 10 August 1777.

Balfour was a close acquaintance of Warren Hastings and dedicated a book—*The Forms of Herkern*—to him in 1781. In 1783, while at Benares, he corresponded frequently with Hastings in an abortive attempt to disclose a plot between the resident of Benares, Francis Fowke, and Raja Cheyte Sing, which he claimed to have discovered.

Balfour devoted much time to oriental studies. *The Forms of Herkern*, translated into English by Balfour, was published in Calcutta in 1781 and in London in 1804. The work comprised the endeavours of a state letter-writer in Persian; a vocabulary is given by Balfour at the end and the book is by far the most valuable of his publications. Balfour was one of the earliest members of the Bengal Asiatic Society, founded in 1784, and he contributed two papers to its *Transactions* (in 1790 and 1805) on oriental languages and literature, and a third (in 1795) on the barometer. Of his medical works one of the most remarkable was *A Treatise on Sol-Lunar Influence in Fevers* (1784), which went to several editions and saw a German translation. In it Balfour expounded his favourite theory, that fevers are under the direct influence of the moon, and reach their critical stage with the full moon, a theme he returned to in a paper of 1805. Contemporaries regarded his views as rather extreme.

Balfour retired from the East India Company's service on 16 September 1807 and returned to Edinburgh. He is thought to have died in or after 1816.

SIDNEY LEE, *rev.* ELIZABETH BAIGENT

Sources BL, Add. MSS 29159–29160 • Dodwell [E. Dodwell] and Miles [J. S. Miles], eds., *Alphabetical list of the Honourable East India Company's Bengal civil servants, from the year 1780 to the year 1838* (1839) • H. J. Rose, *A new general biographical dictionary*, ed. H. J. Rose and T. Wright, 12 vols. (1853) • *Nomina eorum, qui gradum medicinae doctoris in academia Jacobi sexti Scotorum regis, quae Edinburgi est, adepti sunt, ab anno 1705 ad annum 1845*, University of Edinburgh (1846)

Archives BL, corresp. with Warren Hastings, Add. MSS 29151–29160

Balfour, Francis Maitland (1851–1882), comparative embryologist and morphologist, was born on 10 November 1851 at Queen Street, Edinburgh, the fifth of the eight children (and third son) of James Maitland Balfour (1820–1856), landowner and MP, and Lady Blanche Gascoyne-Cecil (1825–1872), second daughter of James Gascoyne-Cecil, second marquess of Salisbury, and his wife, Frances Mary. Arthur James *Balfour (1848–1930), Conservative prime minister, was an elder brother; his sister Nora married Henry Sidgwick (1838–1900), the philosopher.

Raised at Whittingehame in East Lothian, Frank, as he was known, showed an early aptitude for natural history. After two years at The Grange, a private boarding-school at Hoddesdon, Hertfordshire, in 1866 he went to Harrow School. There his abilities in natural history were honed by George Griffith, the school's first science master. Although he was considered by some to be awkward and uncoordinated, Balfour's forceful personality was already obvious, and it led many to believe he would soon make his mark. Indeed, a geological essay written for the Harrow Scientific Society in 1868 brought him to the attention of Thomas Huxley, whose influence was to be lifelong.

Balfour entered Trinity College, Cambridge, in October 1870, and won a natural science scholarship the following spring (Huxley was an examiner). Michael Foster, praelector in physiology, encouraged him to undertake original research on the nature of the primitive streak in chick embryos and its possible relationship to the amphibian blastopore. Thus began Balfour's pursuit of homologies between embryos of different organisms, which led to his first three papers in embryology and *The Elements of Embryology* (1874), co-authored with Foster. Balfour graduated in December 1873, though the time spent on his investigations 'diminished somewhat the brilliancy of his degree, for he was placed second instead of first, as had been expected, in the Natural Sciences Tripos' (Clark, 284).

In February 1874 Balfour was one of the first two British naturalists to work at Anton Dohrn's Stazione Zoologica in Naples, where shark and dogfish embryology was the subject of his investigations. Embryology was considered the best means to establish evolutionary relationships, and elasmobranchs, as primitive vertebrates, were thought likely to illuminate vertebrate ancestry. This initial work, presented in August to the British Association for the Advancement of Science (BAAS), brought Balfour to the attention of the British scientific community. On 17 October he was elected natural sciences fellow of Trinity College; Huxley, the examiner, gave more weight to research than to examination results.

As part of his efforts to establish physiology, histology, and embryology at Cambridge, Foster gave responsibility for embryology and morphology to Balfour. The latter's first lectures in embryology in July 1875 were only a modest success, and an inadequate forecast of his enormously popular lectures as lecturer in animal morphology from October 1876. During this period Balfour also continued his research work at Naples. His *Monograph on the Development of Elasmobranch Fishes* (4 vols., 1878) enhanced his reputation as a leading evolutionary embryologist, and led to his election as FRS at the age of twenty-six in June 1878.

Under Balfour's direction the Cambridge Morphological Laboratory became the world centre for comparative and evolutionary embryology. Students such as Adam Sedgwick, William Bateson, D'Arcy Thompson, William Weldon, and Henry Osborn were attracted to work with Balfour, as much for his personality as for his growing scientific reputation. The awkward, uncompromising youth had grown into a tall man who, though brilliant and admired by all, retained an endearing shyness.

Although most of the research was left to his students, Balfour was not idle. He ran the laboratory, assisted by Adam Sedgwick, who succeeded him as director. He threw himself energetically into college and university committees, and in 1880 was vice-president of section D of the BAAS. In four years of intensive labour he synthesized all available embryological knowledge into the comprehensive and highly acclaimed *Treatise on Comparative Embryology* (2 vols., 1880–81). While he accepted a recapitulation of evolution in development, he avoided the doctrinaire excesses of Ernst Haeckel. From his very first paper he sought to separate primary features from secondary embryonic or larval adaptations, and sought evidence for natural selection during ontogeny, as he documented the links between embryology and evolution. Balfour's law relates yolk concentration to the rate of cell division in the early embryo.

Balfour's work brought him much acclaim, especially after publication of the *Treatise*. A Royal Society medal, appointment as the youngest member of the society's council, and an honorary LLD degree from Glasgow University all came his way in 1881 and it seemed that an illustrious career lay ahead. However, despite these accolades, and the growth of animal morphology at Cambridge, the brightest new star in the biological sky, who Darwin thought would 'one day be the first of English Biologists' (Dugdale, 1.70), held no appointment at the university. Oxford sought him as Linacre professor of human and comparative anatomy, and Edinburgh as regius professor of natural history. Balfour was tempted by Edinburgh, which was less than 30 miles from Whittingehame, the family seat. In January 1882, however, Foster spearheaded a petition to the Cambridge senate seeking a university position for Balfour. Just weeks later, in Capri, while nursing a student, William Caldwell, back to health, Balfour contracted typhoid. It was thought he would not live. Cambridge was finally moved to act and appointed him to a 'Professorship of Animal Morphology terminable with the tenure of the first Professor' (Clark, 288).

By July 1882 Balfour had recuperated sufficiently to travel to Switzerland for his favourite relaxation, alpine climbing. After testing his condition on some easy climbs, he and a guide set out on 18 July to scale Mont Blanc. Both men died on the glacier of Treyney, Courmayeur, Italy, on 19 July. Balfour was buried at Whittingehame on 5 August. Reactions to his death indicate the depth of loss felt by friends and the scientific and university communities. For Huxley the deaths of Darwin and Balfour in the same year meant the loss of 'the best of the old and the best of the young' (Huxley, 2.38). Cambridge established a library and a studentship in Balfour's name. The first studentship went to William Caldwell, whose discovery 'monotremes oviparous, ovum meroblastic', cabled to the BAAS meeting in Montreal in 1884, was a dramatic demonstration of the evolutionary embryology espoused by Balfour.

BRIAN K. HALL

Sources M. Foster, 'Introductory biographical note', *The works of Francis Maitland Balfour*, ed. M. Foster and A. Sedgwick (1885), 1.1–24 · T. E. Alexander, 'Francis Maitland Balfour's contributions to embryology', PhD diss., U. Cal., Los Angeles, 1969 · F. B. Churchill, 'Balfour, Francis Maitland', *DSB* · G. L. Geison, *Michael Foster and the Cambridge school of physiology: the scientific enterprise in late Victorian society* (1978) · H. F. Osborn, *Impressions of great naturalists* (1924) · J. W. Clark, *Old friends at Cambridge and elsewhere* (1900) · M. Ridley, 'Embryology and classical zoology in Great Britain', *A history of embryology*, ed. T. J. Horder, J. A. Witkowski, and C. C. Wylie (1986), 35–68 · M. Foster, *Nature*, 26 (1882), 313–14, 405–10 · M. Foster, *BMJ* (29 July 1882), 195–6 · M. F. [M. Foster], *PRS*, 35 (1883), xx–xxvii · W. Leaf, *The Times* (11 Aug 1882) · W. Leaf, 'In memoriam: Francis Maitland Balfour', *Alpine Journal*, 11 (1882–4), 101–3 · H. F. Osborn, *Science*, 2 (1883), 299–301 · T. J. Parker, *New Zealand Journal of Science*, 1 (1882–3), 265–6 · W. Waldeyer, *Archiv für Mikroskopische Anatomie*, 21 (1882), 828–35 · B. K. Hall, 'Germ layers and the germ-layer theory revisited: primary and secondary germ layers, neural crest as a fourth germ layer, homology, demise of the germ-layer theory', *Evolutionary Biology*, 30 (1998), 121–86 · B. K. Hall, *Evolutionary developmental biology*, 2nd edn (1998) · F. Balfour, *Ne obliviscaris: dinna forget*, 2 vols. [1930] · L. Huxley, *Life and letters of Thomas Henry Huxley*, 2 vols. (1900) · K. E. Roe and R. G. Frederick, *Dictionary of theoretical concepts in biology* (1981) · *DNB* · *CGPLA Eng. & Wales* (1882) · B. E. C. Dugdale, *Arthur James Balfour, first earl of Balfour*, 2 vols. (1936)

Archives CUL, letters • NA Scot., corresp. | American Museum of Natural History, New York, H. F. Osborn's notes from Balfour's lectures • Stazione Zoologica, Naples, letters to Anton Dohrn

Likenesses photograph, *c.*1875, Stazione Zoologica, Naples • J. Collier, oils, 1882, Trinity Cam. • A. von Hildebrand, bronze bust, 1882 (after J. Collier), U. Cam., Zoology Department; version, Trinity Cam. • A. G. Dew-Smith, portrait, Trinity Cam. • E. Wilson, engraving, repro. in Foster and Sedgwick, eds., *The works of Francis Maitland Balfour*, vol. 1, frontispiece • portrait, Johns Hopkins University, Baltimore, Maryland • wood-engraving, NPG; repro. in *ILN* (19 Aug 1882)

Wealth at death £30,025 8*s.* 3*d.*: probate, 23 Sept 1882, *CGPLA Eng. & Wales*

Balfour, Sir George (1809–1894). *See under* Balfour, Edward Green (1813–1889).

Balfour, George William (1823–1903), physician and cardiologist, was born at the manse, Sorn, Ayrshire, on 2 June 1823, the eighth of the thirteen children of Lewis Balfour DD and Henrietta Scott Balfour, third daughter of George Smith DD, the minister of Galston who was satirized by Robert Burns in 'The Holy Fair'. Balfour had an academic pedigree: his father was the grandson of James Balfour (1705–1795), professor of moral philosophy and of public law at Edinburgh, and his mother was the granddaughter of Robert Whytt (1714–1766), physiologist, and professor of medicine at Edinburgh from 1747 to 1766.

After being educated at the local school in his father's Colinton parish on the outskirts of Edinburgh, Balfour decided to emigrate to Australia, and to that end he obtained a diploma in veterinary surgery in 1841. However, after completing his studies he abandoned his emigration plans and decided to join the medical profession. He continued his education in Edinburgh where he was a student of anatomy under Robert Knox of Burke and Hare fame. By using his veterinary studies to gain exemptions he graduated MD at St Andrews in 1845—when he also became a licentiate of the Royal College of Surgeons of Edinburgh. In 1846, after acting as resident medical officer in Edinburgh's maternity hospital, Balfour went to Vienna where he studied the clinical methods of J. Skoda, the pathological researches of C. L. Sigmund, and the homoeopathic treatment of W. Fleischmann. On his return from Austria he started a successful career as a medical author by enterprisingly publishing papers summarizing his Viennese teachers' current work.

Balfour began his medical work by establishing himself as a general practitioner in the countryside around Edinburgh; he spent a year in Corstorphine before moving to Cramond, where he practised until his return to the capital in 1857. The good reputation he gained in Cramond allowed him to earn a living in Edinburgh's competitive medical market place, and his efforts to build a practice were further helped in 1861 when he became a fellow of the Royal College of Physicians of Edinburgh. In 1866 he was appointed physician to the city's Royal Hospital for Sick Children and he also became a physician at the Royal Public Dispensary. He was elected a physician to the Royal Infirmary in 1867 and was made consulting physician there in 1882 on the expiry of his term of office. Balfour won some recognition at the infirmary as a clinical

George William Balfour (1823–1903), by Reginald Henry Campbell

teacher, though contemporaries were more apt to praise his bedside teaching than his formal lecture-theatre presentations. Nevertheless, Sophia Jex-Blake and other women medical students did praise his teaching; Balfour was an early supporter of women's medical education and at the infirmary he conducted three special ward rounds for women students each week. He continued to support Jex-Blake throughout her career and he was on the executive committee of the School of Medicine for Women.

During his professional advancement Balfour did not neglect his writing career. A paper on haematophobia published in 1858 questioned the routine use of bloodletting. In 1865 he published *An Introduction to the Study of Medicine*. In 1868, following a suggestion of his father-in-law, James Craig of Ratho, he wrote two able papers on the treatment of aneurysm by iodide of potassium, and from then on he specialized in cardiology. Balfour's book *Lectures on Diseases of the Heart and Aorta* (1876) greatly enhanced his reputation (it includes Balfour's test to ascertain whether the heart is still active in cases of apparent death); the work also features in J. M. Norman's *Morton's Medical Bibliography* (1991). Another book by Balfour, *The Senile Heart* (1894), was of equal quality and established him as Scotland's premier cardiologist. Indeed with Sir William Tennant Gairdner in Glasgow and Charles Hilton Fagge in London, Balfour made the most important contributions of his generation to the clinical study of disorders of the circulation.

Balfour, who was interested in bibliography, was librarian to the Royal College of Physicians of Edinburgh from

1873 to 1882 and from 1887 to 1899. He was president of the college from 1882 to 1884 and was a member of the university court of St Andrews for many years. He received the honorary degree of LLD at Edinburgh in 1884, and at St Andrews in 1896. He was appointed physician-in-ordinary to Queen Victoria in 1900 and honorary physician to Edward VII in 1901.

Balfour was married three times: to Agnes (*d.* 1851), daughter of George Thomson, in 1848, with whom he had one son, Lewis; to Margaret Bethune (*d.* 1879), eldest daughter of James Craig, of Ratho, in 1854, with whom he had eight sons and three daughters; and in 1881 to Henrietta, daughter of John Usher, who survived him. His eldest brother, John Balfour (*d.* 1887), was a surgeon to the East India Company and served throughout the Second Anglo-Burmese War and during the Indian mutiny before returning to Britain, where he practised at Leven, Fife. Another brother, Mackintosh, spent his life in India, where he was manager of the Agra Bank. Robert Louis Stevenson (1850–1894) was the son of Balfour's sister, Margaret Isabella. Balfour took a close interest in his nephew's health, and Stevenson called him 'that wise youth my uncle' (*Letters*, 140); Balfour was the first to learn (by cable) of Stevenson's death in Samoa. He later wrote a short introduction to Margaret Stevenson's *From Saranac to Marquesas and Beyond* (1903). It is suggested that although Balfour could appear to be somewhat forbidding, he charmed his friends with his quaint humour and culture. In 1899 Balfour retired from Edinburgh to Colinton, the home of his youth, where he died at his home, Westfield, after a long illness, on 9 August 1903. He was buried in Ratho churchyard.

G. A. Gibson, *rev.* Iain Milne

Sources *The Lancet* (22 Aug 1903), 570 · *BMJ* (22 Aug 1903), 439–40 · *Edinburgh Medical Journal*, new ser., 14 (1903), 286–8; 296–7 · W. S. Craig, *History of the Royal College of Physicians of Edinburgh* (1976), 649 · *Scottish Medical and Surgical Journal*, 13 (1903), 237–43 · R. Thin, *Royal College of Physicians portraits* (1927) · B. Balfour-Melville, *The Balfours of Pilrig* (1907) · G. W. Balfour, *Letter of application for the chair of practice of physic in the University of Edinburgh* (1876) [incl. testimonials] · *The letters of Robert Louis Stevenson*, ed. B. A. Booth and E. Mehew, 1 (1994) · *CGPLA Eng. & Wales* (1903) · J. M. Norman, *Morton's medical bibliography*, 5th edn (1991)

Archives Royal College of Physicians of Edinburgh

Likenesses J. Bowie, oils, 1904 (after photograph), Royal College of Physicians of Edinburgh · R. H. Campbell, portrait, Royal College of Physicians of Edinburgh [*see illus.*] · photograph, repro. in *Scottish Medical and Surgical Journal*, 238

Wealth at death £5306 8*s*. 9*d*.: confirmation, 7 Nov 1903, *CCI*

Balfour, Gerald William, second earl of Balfour (1853–1945), politician and psychical researcher, was born on 9 April 1853, in Edinburgh, the seventh of eight children of James Maitland Balfour (1820–1856), MP, sportsman, and country gentleman, and his wife, Lady Blanche Mary Harriet Gascoyne-Cecil (1825–1872), daughter of the second marquess of Salisbury. Among his three sisters and four brothers were Eleanor *Sidgwick and Arthur James *Balfour, first earl of Balfour. After their father's early death from tuberculosis, the children were raised by Lady Blanche, whose deep evangelical faith and sense of duty to humanity influenced them profoundly. In due course Balfour became a communicant in both the Church of England and the Church of Scotland. When not attending school, he spent most of his youth at the family estate of Whittingehame in East Lothian. During the Christmas holiday of 1863 he nearly died of diphtheria, but was nursed through the crisis by his mother and Sir James Simpson, summoned from Edinburgh for the purpose.

Balfour was educated at Eton College, where he came under the influence of Oscar Browning, and in 1871 entered Trinity College, Cambridge. His striking intelligence and attractive personality won him election to the Cambridge Conversazione Society, better known as the Apostles, and in 1875 he came fifth in the classical tripos. In 1872, on his mother's death from heart failure, he had inherited some £21,000, which enabled him to postpone decisions about his future. Initially, an academic career at Cambridge attracted him. In 1878 he became a fellow of Trinity and lecturer in classics. Already, however, he was drawn to philosophical studies, and by autumn 1881, he had abandoned Cambridge for a life of metaphysical speculation in Florence. Settled at the Villa Capponi, Balfour pondered his 'system of ultimate categories of thought', as Walter Leaf recalled (C. M. Leaf, *Walter Leaf, 1852–1927*, 1932, 89). Another visitor, his brother-in-law Henry Sidgwick, reported in 1883 that Balfour's 'system is still in a germinal state', and it never advanced much further. Balfour's Florentine idyll was tragically interrupted in the summer of 1882 when he accompanied to England the body of his brother Francis Maitland *Balfour, killed in an alpine accident.

Back in England permanently by the mid-1880s, Balfour was drawn into the heady London social circle of the Souls and fell under the spell of the flirtatious Laura Tennant, who rejected his marriage proposal in 1884 (Jalland, 106–7). In 1887 he embarked on a long and successful marriage to Lady Elizabeth Lytton [*see* Balfour, Elizabeth Edith, countess of Balfour (1867–1942)], eldest daughter of Edward Robert Bulwer-*Lytton, the first earl of Lytton. By then Balfour had succumbed to the family penchant for politics, having been elected Conservative member for Central Leeds in 1885. He retained his seat through four subsequent general elections, until the Conservative débâcle of January 1906, when he was defeated and retired permanently from politics.

On first entering parliament Balfour briefly served as private secretary to his brother Arthur, president of the Local Government Board. Thereafter, from 1886 to 1895, he played no major part in the Commons, although he was a member of the royal commission on labour, appointed in 1891. In 1895 he was named chief secretary for Ireland in Lord Salisbury's third administration and pursued the goal of rendering Irish nationalism irrelevant: he shepherded through parliament the Land Purchase Act of 1896 and the Local Government (Ireland) Act of 1898, while also promoting progressive policies for Irish economic development. In 1900 he was sworn of the privy council and accepted the presidency of the Board of Trade. In that capacity he endorsed the export tax of 1*s*. per ton on coal and bore responsibility for the Port of London Bill as well as the Sugar Convention Act. He cautiously leant towards imperial preference in the great debate over tariff reform that rocked Arthur Balfour's premiership of 1902–5. In March 1905, Gerald Balfour transferred to the presidency of the Local Government Board, where he remained until the Conservatives resigned from office in December.

Balfour's was a respectable, though hardly distinguished, parliamentary career, and historians have subsequently shown little interest in it. In politics he was always eclipsed by his brother, whose repertory of debating skills included an incisive wit which Gerald altogether lacked. Indeed, the latter's style on the floor of the house inclined to donnishness. His qualities of thoroughness, detachment, accuracy, and discernment made him, however, a valued colleague, and, as prime minister, Arthur Balfour often turned, in confidence, to 'Gerry' for advice.

After leaving politics Balfour pursued a variety of public and private interests. He was chairman of the royal commission on lighthouse administration in 1906–8 and, in 1919–22, chaired the Cambridge committee of the Asquith royal commission on Oxford and Cambridge universities, for which service he received the honorary LLD. Together with Arthur Balfour he invested heavily in schemes to convert peat into commercial fuel, and by the 1920s had lost substantial sums of money on these unsuccessful ventures.

The interest that absorbed Balfour most from 1906 until the end of his life was psychical research. Although he had joined the Society for Psychical Research in 1883, shortly after its establishment, and became a council member in 1890, he was inactive until he became the society's president in 1906. Several members of his family were also involved in psychical research, but it was Eleanor Sidgwick who worked most closely with him in exploring the mental phenomena of mediumship. They both became convinced of the possibility of telepathy, and Balfour was eventually persuaded that discarnate intelligences could communicate telepathically with the living. He also suggested that the human organism is polypsychic—that is, that each self is composed of numerous psychic centres that might be able to communicate with one another telepathically.

Balfour's main contribution to psychical research was the collation and interpretation of what became known as the 'Palm Sunday' scripts, some 3000 pieces of automatic writing collected primarily from four automatists during the first thirty years of the twentieth century. Sifting through the documents, while comparing their terms of reference and classical allusions as these emerged over the decades, Balfour concluded that they demonstrated a coherent and sustained attempt to communicate with the living by numerous deceased relatives and friends, especially May Lyttelton, whose death on Palm Sunday 1875 had terminated her budding romance with Arthur Balfour. In 'The ear of Dionysius' (1917) and 'A study of the psychological aspects of Mrs Willett's mediumship' (1935)—Gerald Balfour's major papers in the *Proceedings* of the Society for Psychical Research—he focused on the work of one of the automatists, Mrs Winifred Coombe-Tennant, who used the pseudonym Mrs Willett. The long-sustained inquiry into these scripts, which prompted his only significant excursions into print, left Balfour confident that individual consciousness survives bodily death. The conviction afforded him personal reassurance and comfort, although it did not convert many sceptics.

In private life, Balfour and Lady Betty, an advocate of women's suffrage, enjoyed a close companionship that ended only with her death in 1942. They had six children, one son and five daughters, among them the first president of the Soil Association, Lady Evelyn Barbara *Balfour (1898–1990). Balfour's unworldly serenity, devotion to family, and high standards of integrity earned him deep personal esteem and affection from those who knew him well, although those who did not tended to find him aloof and humourless. Beatrice Webb described him as a 'medieval and saintly knight', while Lady Jebb recalled that his fellow Trinity undergraduates had dubbed him 'the BVM' for his 'divinely beautiful face' (M. R. Bobbitt, ed., *With Dearest Love to All: the Life and Letters of Lady Jebb*, 1960, 175). Throughout his life, he retained his classical good looks, and, standing 6 feet tall, he cut a handsome figure even in extreme old age. While his children were young, he and Lady Betty spent half the year at Whittingehame, the site of extended family gatherings. After the First World War, however, their own home at Fisher's Hill, near Woking, Surrey, increasingly became the centre of Balfour reunions. Eleanor Sidgwick had become a permanent resident there during the war, as did Arthur Balfour in 1929, a year before his death.

In 1930, by special remainder, Gerald Balfour succeeded to the earldom bestowed on his brother in 1922, but the last years of the second earl's life were overshadowed by the family's reduced economic position. The main house at Whittingehame had to be vacated, and Balfour depended on his salary from various company directorships. At his death on 14 January 1945, aged ninety-one, he was living in Lady Eleanor's Cottage on the Whittingehame estate, where he was buried. His son, Robert Arthur Lytton, Viscount Traprain, succeeded him.

JANET OPPENHEIM

Sources *The Times* (15 Jan 1945) • *The Times* (19 Jan 1945) • *The Times* (6 Feb 1945) • *WWW* • B. E. C. Dugdale, *Arthur James Balfour, first earl of Balfour*, 2 vols. (1936) • B. E. C. Dugdale, 'Obituary: the earl of Balfour', *Proceedings of the Society for Psychical Research*, 47 (1942–6), 249–58 • private information (2004) • P. Harris, *Life in a Scottish country house: the story of A. J. Balfour and Whittinghame House* (1989) • *Salisbury–Balfour correspondence: letters exchanged between the third marquess of Salisbury and his nephew Arthur James Balfour, 1869–1892*, ed. R. H. Williams (1988) • *The diary of Beatrice Webb*, ed. N. MacKenzie and J. MacKenzie, 4 vols. (1982–5), vol. 3, pp. 50–52; vol. 4, pp. 189, 341–2, 479–80 • J. Balfour, 'The "Palm Sunday" case: new light on an old love story', *Proceedings of the Society for Psychical Research*, 52 (1958–60), 79–267 • F. Nicol, 'The founders of the SPR', *Proceedings of the Society for Psychical Research*, 55 (1966–72), 341–67 • E. Sidgwick, 'Some things I remember about my mother', 1922, NA Scot., Earl of Balfour muniments, GD 433/2/145 • E. Sidgwick, 'A short history of my mother', 1933, NA Scot., Earl of Balfour muniments, GD 433/2/220 • letter from H. Sidgwick to F. W. H. Myers, 12 March 1883, Trinity Cam., Add. MS C.100, fol. 164 • P. Jalland, *Women, marriage and politics, 1860–1914*, pbk edn (1988) • J. Oppenheim, *The other world: spiritualism and psychical research in England, 1850–1914* (1985)

Archives NA Scot., corresp. and papers • PRO, semi-official papers, PRO 30/60 | BL, corresp. with Arthur James Balfour, Add. MS 49831, *passim* • Bodl. Oxf., corresp. with Herbert Asquith • CAC Cam., corresp. with Sir Cecil Spring-Rice • CUL, Society for Psychical Research archives, corresp. with Sir Oliver Lodge • Hatfield House, Hertfordshire, Salisbury MSS • HLRO, corresp. with fifth Earl Cadogan • ICL, corresp. and papers relating to Imperial College • King's AC Cam., letters to Oscar Browning • U. Birm. L., corresp. with Joseph Chamberlain

Likenesses B. Stone, photograph, 1897, NPG • G. F. Watts, oils, 1899, Watts Gallery, Compton, Surrey • W. Stoneman, photograph, 1921, NPG • A. C. Hoskins, photograph, NPG; repro. in *Our conservative and unionist statesmen* (1896–9), vol. 3 • Spy [L. Ward], caricature, chromolithograph, NPG; repro. in *VF* (10 Dec 1896) • G. F. Watts, portrait, The Tower, Whittingehame • marble bust, priv. coll. • portraits, priv. coll.

Wealth at death £23,369 15*s*. 5*d*.: probate, 22 May 1945, *CGPLA Eng. & Wales*

Balfour, Sir (Thomas) Graham (1858–1929), author and educationist, born in Chelsea on 2 December 1858, was the only child of Surgeon-General Thomas Graham *Balfour and his wife, Georgina, daughter of George Prentice of Armagh. On his father's side he was closely connected, through the Balfours of Pilrig, with Robert Louis Stevenson. He was educated at Marlborough College and at Worcester College, Oxford. His school life was partly impaired by ill health; at the university he obtained a first class in classical moderations (1880) and a second class in *literae humaniores* (1882), and won distinction as a rifle shot.

In 1885 Balfour was called to the bar by the Inner Temple, but he found the practice of advocacy uncongenial, and his chief piece of work was his contribution (the chapter on Battersea) to Charles Booth's *Life and Labour of the People in London* (1891–1903). For a time he travelled extensively, and in 1891, after the death of his parents, he accepted Stevenson's invitation to make his home at Vailima, Samoa. On Stevenson's death in 1894 Balfour returned to England. In 1896 he married Rhoda, daughter of Leonard Dobbin Brooke of Birkenhead; they had two sons. The Balfours settled at Oxford, where he wrote his two principal works. His *Educational Systems of Great Britain and Ireland* appeared in 1898 and rapidly became a standard authority; his *Life of Robert Louis Stevenson*, written at the request of Stevenson's family for the Edinburgh edition of his works, followed in 1901, and established Balfour's reputation as a biographer.

During Balfour's residence in Oxford he served the delegacy of local examinations, first as examiner, then as assistant secretary. In 1902 he was appointed director of technical education, and in 1903 general director of education, to the county of Staffordshire. His appointment came at a critical time following the Education Act of 1902 which had remodelled the educational administration of England. The organization of resources and provision now replaced religion as the central issue in elementary education, and Balfour has been accounted highly successful in dealing with the changed priorities. His task was to build up the local education service serving a population of 600,000 and to co-ordinate the existing authorities which comprised five county boroughs, nine boroughs and urban districts with powers over elementary education, and twenty-nine school boards. His administration of education in Staffordshire became an example to the country at large. In his first ten years forty-nine new council schools were built. Although the product of a classical education, with no experience of industry or commerce, he successfully promoted technical education, extending the pottery school at Stoke, and establishing the technical colleges at Wednesbury and Wolverhampton and the mining college on Cannock Chase. He was a pioneer both of school gardens and of school libraries. In his report, *Ten Years of Staffordshire Education, 1903–1913* (1913), he described how the new county education committee had sought to administer rather than to control, and had tried to leave as much initiative as possible to school managers and teachers. The addresses on educational administration that he gave to the University of Birmingham in 1921 were considered to be models of their kind.

In 1907 Balfour received the honorary degree of MA from Cambridge University and in 1924 that of LLD from the University of Birmingham. He was knighted in 1917. He served as chairman of the association of directors and secretaries of education (1908), and as a member of the reconstruction committee on adult education (1917–19), the committee on the position of science in education (1916–18), and the consultative committee of the Board of Education (1926–9). During the last year of the European war (1918–19) he served as director of education in France (lines of communication) for the YMCA.

Balfour retired in 1926 and returned to Oxford, where he became a member of the city education committee, the delegacy for extramural studies, and the council of Barnett House. He died at 4 Blackhall Road, Oxford, on 26 October 1929. W. H. HADOW, *rev.* M. C. CURTHOYS

Sources *The Times* (28 Oct 1929) • private information (1937) • *WWW* • A. Crombie, '"A free hand and ready help"? The supervision and control of elementary education in Staffordshire, *c*.1902–1914', *Oxford Review of Education*, 28 (2002), 173–86

Archives NL Scot., corresp. and papers relating to R. L. Stevenson

Wealth at death £2465 3*s*. 9*d*.: probate, 13 Dec 1929, *CGPLA Eng. & Wales*

Balfour, Harold Harington, first Baron Balfour of Inchrye (1897–1988), airman, businessman, and politician, was born on 1 November 1897 in Farnham, Surrey, the younger son and second of the three children of Colonel Nigel Harington Balfour OBE, a serving officer, of Belton, Camberley, Surrey, and his wife, Grace Annette Marie, youngest daughter of Henry Robarts Madocks and granddaughter of Field Marshal Baron Napier of Magdala. His elder brother was killed in January 1941 when his ship, HMS *Southampton*, was sunk in the Mediterranean. Balfour was educated at Chilverton Elms, Dover, Kent, and the Royal Naval College, Osborne. Soon after the outbreak of the First World War in 1914, he volunteered for service with the 60th rifles, but his urge to fly encouraged him to transfer to the Royal Flying Corps when a chance was offered the next year. There then began a distinguished, yet hazardous spell as a fighter pilot on the western front, which culminated in his promotion, in 1917, to command a flight in the famous 43 fighter squadron, in which he had served earlier under the command of Major William Sholto Douglas. Once wounded in action and, by temperament, by no means fitted for war, he was awarded the MC and bar for gallantry. He remained with the newly formed Royal Air Force until 1923. In 1921 he married Diana Blanche Harvey (*d.* 1982), daughter of Sir Robert Grenville Harvey, second baronet; they had one son. The marriage was dissolved in 1946.

Faced with a continuing need to earn a living, Balfour became, initially, a news reporter on the *Daily Mail* before joining Whitehall Securities in the Pearson group in 1925, when the organization was entering the field of commercial aviation. He was also attracted by politics; he stood unsuccessfully as the Conservative candidate for the Stratford division of West Ham, London, in 1924 and was elected in 1929 as member for the Isle of Thanet, Kent, which he represented until 1945, when he was created Baron Balfour of Inchrye, of Shefford in the county of Berkshire.

In 1938, as the Royal Air Force was rearming for war, Balfour accepted Neville Chamberlain's invitation to join the government as parliamentary under-secretary of state for air, first, under Sir H. Kingsley Wood, and later, in Winston Churchill's national government, under Sir Archibald Sinclair. It was an inspired appointment in which he served with signal ability until 1944, often flying himself about in a Spitfire and forming a first-hand judgement of Fighter Command's 'big wing' controversy in the battle of Britain.

Balfour adorned the office which he was to hold for six and a half years. His achievements at the Air Ministry were many. Outstanding among them was the establishment, in the spring of 1940, of the great empire air training scheme of which he was a prime instigator and which, in the next five years, was responsible for training more than 130,000 aircrew in countries of the Commonwealth and empire. Its contribution to victory was undoubted. Moreover, his relationship with the Royal Air Force's senior officers, from the chief of the air staff, Sir Charles Portal, and the air staff, to the heads of operational commands, was both effective and forthright, not least because they respected his knowledge of aviation and his own service record in the First World War.

Eventually Churchill, having earlier failed to persuade Balfour to accept, first, the office of financial secretary to the Treasury, and later, a civil department of state (Balfour refused each to remain loyal to the Royal Air Force), in 1944 appointed him resident minister in west Africa; he resigned with the Conservatives in 1945. A senior privy councillor (sworn on 5 August 1941), he remained active in politics for much of his life, speaking frequently for tory friends in the country and often intervening in House of Lords debates. This he combined with his business interests, which included a directorship of British European Airways (BEA) from 1955 to 1966 and chairmanship of BEA Helicopters Ltd in 1964–6. He also held the presidency of the Chambers of Commerce of the British Empire from 1946 to 1949 and of the Commonwealth and Empire Industries Association from 1956 to 1960. His autobiography, *Wings over Westminster* (1973), one of his three published works, was well received, reflecting his early training as a Fleet Street journalist and his feeling for words. He wrote touching little stanzas and verses on the back of old envelopes. In 1947 he married his second wife, Mary Ainslie, daughter of Albert Peter Anthony Profumo, barrister; they had one daughter.

An upstanding and attractive man, who was intensely loyal, Balfour was a persuasive speaker on a public platform, his sensitivity and humour enabling him quickly to catch the mood of an audience. His all-round judgement was acute. Although he lived happily in London at End House, St Mary Abbot's Place, Kensington, with his family often around him, his love of fishing and shooting took him regularly to Scotland. There, in his contented twilight years, he once confided in a member of his family: 'You know, I would sooner be stone deaf on a grouse moor than able to hear a pin drop in a bath chair.' Balfour died on 21 September 1988 at the King Edward VII Hospital in London. He was succeeded in the barony by his son, Ian (*b.* 1924). P. B. LUCAS, *rev.*

Sources H. Balfour, *Wings over Westminster* (1973) • personal knowledge (1996) • *WWW* • private information (1996)
Archives CAC Cam. • HLRO, corresp. and papers • IWM, Moscow diary [copy] | HLRO, corresp. with Lord Beaverbrook | FILM BFI NFTVA, documentary footage | SOUND BL NSA, documentary recording
Wealth at death £852,882: probate, 25 Nov 1988, *CGPLA Eng. & Wales*

Balfour, Henry (1863–1939), museum curator, was born at 6 Bedford Villas, Dingwall Road, Croydon, on 11 April 1863, the son of Lewis Balfour (1833–1885), silk broker of Croydon, and Sarah Walker Comber (1836?–1916). Educated at Charterhouse School and Trinity College, Oxford, Balfour obtained a second class in natural science (biology) in 1885. As a result of the influence of H. N. Moseley and E. B. Tylor, Balfour became interested in anthropology: even before he took his degree he and W. B. Spencer were helping Tylor and Moseley to arrange Pitt Rivers's collections, which had been given to the University of Oxford in 1883. After taking his degree Balfour continued working at the Pitt Rivers Museum. In 1887 he married Edith Marie Louise (*d.* 1938), only daughter of Robert Francis Wilkins of Kingswear, south Devon; she shared his many interests, his work, and, until her health began to suffer, his travels. They had one son. He was appointed curator of the museum in 1891, a post which he held until his death. He became a research fellow of Exeter College in 1904 and was re-elected in 1919.

Balfour taught technology and prehistoric archaeology for the Oxford diploma course in anthropology which began in 1907. Later he also taught for the Sudan, tropical African, Malay, and Burmese civil service courses. Balfour always lectured in the museum using the objects on display as his examples, and he learned many of the techniques employed in their manufacture and use to demonstrate to his students. Teaching gave him contact with

Henry Balfour (1863–1939), by Walter Stoneman, 1926

undergraduates and with a long succession of colonial civil service probationers and of officers on leave from service overseas. In turn it led to a series of lifelong friendships which considerably enriched the collections both in numbers of objects and in the quality of documentation.

Throughout his life Balfour enjoyed travelling. In the earliest days his travels were connected with his continuing interest in zoology, as is to be seen in the drawings and observations in his diaries. Five times between 1905 and 1909 Balfour travelled to Norway where he studied the habits of whales and whalers. He also made a collection of artefacts for the museum. Each of his journeys was driven by the quest for knowledge and by the wish to add to the series of objects contained in the Pitt Rivers Museum. His honeymoon was spent in Lapland. In southern Africa he became the first to detect palaeolithic implements in the gravels of the Zambezi rivers and to correlate them to prehistoric European types. His visits to southern Africa were used to help him to direct knowledge of other parts of that continent. In Assam he travelled widely on foot through the Naga Hills. His most wide-ranging journey was to Australia and New Zealand and islands in Indonesia and the Pacific with a return via Japan and the USA. When he was confined to England as a result of arthritis, a voluminous correspondence with scholars worldwide enabled him to enhance the collections beyond the expected colonial heritage typical of most anthropological collections.

Balfour was a man of great energy and many interests. As an undergraduate he had a great reputation as oarsman and as a talented fencer, and as a lecturer, it is said, his demonstrations of boomerang throwing in the university parks led to a prohibitionary statute after he accidentally hit a nanny pushing a pram. He was a natural draughtsman; his drawings, still to be seen in the Pitt Rivers Museum displays, also enrich his travel diaries, and his command of caricature is seen in the illustrations he provided for the illustrated programmes for the Oxford University fencing club. An active member of many learned societies, Balfour became president of the Royal Anthropological Institute in 1904 and of the Museums Association in 1909; he was president of the Folklore Society in 1923–4, of the Royal Geographical Society from 1936 to 1938, and of the Prehistoric Society of East Anglia (later the Prehistoric Society). He was elected to a fellowship of the Royal Society in 1924.

Throughout his life Balfour remained first and foremost a curator. He was renowned for his 'austere dedication' to his work; left in comfortable financial circumstances after the death of his parents, he supplemented the meagre university staff allowance from his own funds. This single-mindedness was tempered by a talent for friendship, his considerable charm, and a lively sense of humour. His energy and determination gave him the strength to battle on behalf of the museum against plagues of rats, leaking roofs, and the threatened takeover by the Royal Flying Corps in the First World War. One anecdote especially serves to illustrate his dedication to the furtherance of knowledge. While cataloguing alone late one night, he accidentally cut himself with an arrow tipped with the poison curare. Knowing that there was no available antidote, and believing that his death was therefore imminent and unavoidable, he resolved to keep notes of the progressive effects of the poison for the elucidation of others. Fortunately it had degraded or otherwise lost its effectiveness, and he lived to tell the tale.

Balfour's powers of observation were acute, refined by his training as a zoologist, and he became an admirable collector as well as a naturalist. He was perhaps the first to demonstrate that the drumming or bleating of snipe is caused by the vibration of the outer tail-feathers, and this same analytical eye is shown in his observations made in his travel diaries. A trained scientist, he was admirably suited to curate a museum based on a system of classification. The museum owes much of its present plan of displays to Balfour. It owes its tradition of teaching to him also, together with its rich documentation of the objects in the collection.

The Pitt Rivers Museum absorbed Balfour's energies: collecting and documenting the objects, and then arranging and labelling them (his handwritten labels are still a much-loved feature of the museum). With the exception of *The Evolution of Decorative Art* (1893) he did not write books, but was a prolific writer of short articles on many topics, notably musical instruments, archery, anthropology, and archaeology. These articles encouraged others to send him information, all of which he added to the documentation which underpins the Pitt Rivers's collection. He was a catalyst, his articles often seminal, and many remain standard works today—some of his firsthand observations remain the only accounts of practices long since discontinued. For him the museum was an important vehicle for disseminating knowledge, to his own students in the lectures he gave there, to scholars studying the collection or for the school teachers, and to children whose visits he encouraged. He saw his educational philosophy as being more widely applicable, telling the Royal Anthropological Institute in his presidential address of 1904:

> Few people have any idea of the great wealth of human interest there is buried in the data accumulated in the journals of our societies, or illustrated by the specimens locked up in the cases and drawers of our museums. It is this practically unexploited wealth of interest and information that we should endeavour to disseminate.

The Pitt Rivers Museum remains as much a monument to Balfour's scholarship as to its founder's.

In 1935 the University of Oxford conferred on him the title of professor. In later years Balfour suffered from arthritis, and kept a Rolls-Royce and chauffeur to permit him to stay mobile in a degree of comfort. He died at his home, Langley Lodge, Headington, on 9 February 1939. His bequests made him one of the Pitt Rivers's major donors: he not only gave an important collection of objects but also bequeathed his library of several thousand books, which formed the founding collection of the Balfour Library. HÉLÈNE LA RUE

Sources J. H. Hutton, *Obits. FRS*, 3 (1939–41) · J. H. Hutton, *Man* (May 1939) · annual reports of the Pitt Rivers Museum, Oxford, 1888–1940 · *DNB*

Archives U. Oxf., Pitt Rivers Museum, collections of musical instruments and other items · U. Oxf., Pitt Rivers Museum, diaries

Likenesses W. Stoneman, photograph, 1926, NPG [*see illus.*] · photograph, U. Oxf., Pitt Rivers Museum · photographs, Bodl. Oxf.

Wealth at death £42,893 8*s*. 4*d*.: probate, 3 May 1939, *CGPLA Eng. & Wales*

Balfour, Sir Isaac Bayley (1853–1922), botanist, was born at 27 Inverleith Row, Edinburgh, on 31 March 1853, the third child and second son of John Hutton *Balfour (1808–1884), professor of botany in the University of Edinburgh, and his wife, Marion, daughter of Isaac Bayley, of Edinburgh, an attorney. As though predestined to repeat his father's career, Balfour spent much time in boyhood roaming the Royal Botanic Garden, where he won an early grounding in plantsmanship at the hands of the curator and staff. His formal education was at Edinburgh Academy and Edinburgh University, where he specialized in botany, graduating BSc in 1873. He later studied under Julius von Sachs at Würzburg and with Anton de Bary at Strasbourg. From 1875 to 1878 he acted as lecturer in botany to the Royal Veterinary College; for this he was required to obtain a medical qualification and so became assistant to Charles Wyville Thomson, professor of natural history at Edinburgh, for two years, working with T. H. Huxley, Thomson's substitute during his absence on the *Challenger* voyage. He graduated MB in 1877 and MD in 1883.

In 1874 Balfour had served as botanist-cum-geologist on an expedition sent to Rodriguez Island in the Indian Ocean to observe the transit of Venus. His report on the island's flora, published in the Royal Society's *Philosophical Transactions* in 1879, established him as a plant taxonomist and gained him a DSc. That same year Balfour spent seven weeks on another Indian Ocean island, Socotra, investigating its flora and geology. Working up the rich collections he made there occupied his spare time over the next eight years and his *Botany of Socotra* (1888), including descriptions of some three hundred new species, was to be his most substantial published work.

Balfour crowned that golden year of 1879 by obtaining the regius chair of botany at Glasgow. However, his stay in that post proved short, for in 1884 he secured the Sherardian chair of botany at Oxford, combined with a fellowship of Magdalen College. In that year he married Agnes Boyd, daughter of Robert Balloch, merchant, of Glasgow. They had one son and one daughter.

During his tenure at Oxford Balfour established relations with the Clarendon Press, inducing it to found, in 1887, the *Annals of Botany*, a quarterly journal intended to publish results from experimental botanical research. Under his editorship, the press also produced a series of translations of continental textbooks. In 1888 Balfour returned to his native Edinburgh on his appointment as professor of botany in the university, queen's botanist in Scotland, and regius keeper of the Royal Botanic Garden, three positions earlier held by his father and which he was to hold for a third of a century, until shortly before his death.

Balfour's main interest was in rhododendrons and primulas, on which he was recognized as the foremost authority; he also did valuable work on the propagation of plants and the germination of seeds. But his influence was greatest as an administrator, in which role he displayed exceptional ability. In each of the universities which he served he found a department needing reorganization: in Glasgow he saved the herbarium and secured rebuilding of the plant houses, in his few years at Oxford, where he found botany in a sorry state, he did the same, and in both he reorganized the teaching on modern lines. But he did most at Edinburgh: there he reconstituted the botanical garden, rebuilt its plant houses, enlarged the laboratories, and created a new rock-garden, no less renowned than his father's. For a quarter of a century Balfour was the most effective all-round botanist in Britain.

Balfour was elected a fellow of the Royal Society in 1884 and created KBE in 1920. The University of Edinburgh conferred on him an honorary LLD in 1921. The next year ill health prevented his assuming the presidency of the British Association and realizing his intention of writing a history of the Edinburgh botanic garden, and his death followed, at Court Hill, Haslemere, on 30 November 1922. F. O. BOWER, *rev.* D. E. ALLEN

Sources [D. Prain], *PRS*, 96B (1924), i–xvii · J. B. F. [J. B. Farmer], *Annals of Botany*, 37 (1923), 335–9 · *Gardeners' Chronicle*, 3rd ser., 71 (1922), 161 [unsigned, untitled biography] · H. R. Fletcher and W. H. Brown, *The Royal Botanic Garden, Edinburgh, 1670–1970* (1970), 195–

232 · F. O. Bower, *Sixty years of botany in Britain (1875–1935)* (1938), 57–9 · A. D. Boney, *The Linnean*, 17 (2001), 38
Archives NHM, letters to A. C. L. G. Gunther · RBG Kew · Royal Botanic Garden, Edinburgh, corresp. and papers; corresp. relating to George Don; Socotra · U. Edin. L., lecture notes and papers | Oxf. U. Mus. NH, letters to Sir E. B. Poulton · U. Glas., Archives and Business Records Centre, corresp. with F. O. Bower
Likenesses Maull & Fox, photograph, RS · lithograph, repro. in *Gardeners' Chronicle*, 2 (1891), 275 · photograph, repro. in Fletcher and Brown, *The Royal Botanic Garden Edinburgh*, facing p. 193 · photograph, repro. in J. B. F., *Annals of Botany* · photograph, repro. in D. P., *PRS*
Wealth at death £3828 16*s*. 11*d*.: confirmation, 10 Feb 1923, *CCI*

Balfour, Jabez Spencer (1843–1916), company promoter and politician, was born in Marylebone, Middlesex, on 4 September 1843, the younger son of James Balfour (1796–1884) and Clara Lucas *Balfour (1808–1878), who were prominent workers in the mid-Victorian temperance movement. Balfour's career is best understood in the context of the increasingly prominent part played by militant middle-class nonconformists in the business world, in the Liberal Party generally, and in the anti-drink campaign in particular, during the later nineteenth century. After some years working as a parliamentary agent at Westminster, Balfour embarked in the late 1860s on an ambitious, spectacular, but ultimately disastrous course as promoter and director of a number of interlocking public companies involved in large-scale property development in London and the provinces. The continuous growth of the Balfour group of companies in the 1870s and 1880s rested on two simple but erroneous assumptions: first, that the judicious acquisition of suitable land and its development by speculative builders offered an infallible opportunity for profitable investment; and second, that the combined resources of many small savers represented a hitherto untapped but potentially unlimited source of capital which might be applied to this purpose. The Liberator Building Society (1868) was the key to Balfour's operations. Thanks to skilful publicity, an attractive rate of interest, and the effective use of contacts in the worlds of temperance and nonconformity the Liberator had become the country's largest building society by the end of the 1870s, with a nationwide network of local agents and thousands of depositors.

Balfour's growing eminence in the City was paralleled and reinforced by a career in radical politics. After his marriage in 1866 to Ellen Mead, he and his wife moved in 1869 to Croydon, where he was elected to the local school board in 1874 and served as first mayor of the borough in 1883–4. He became Liberal MP for Tamworth in 1880, but following the borough's disfranchisement he was without a seat until 1889, when he was returned unopposed in a by-election at Burnley. An assiduous constituency man and a plausible public speaker, Balfour was said to have been disappointed at not being given office by Gladstone in 1892.

At the end of the 1880s Balfour gave every appearance of being a highly successful and prosperous public figure. Energetic, genial, and generous, he had acquired a country house at Burcot in Oxfordshire, and he and his wife had a son and a daughter. Balfour at this time boasted an impressive string of company directorships, but the subsequent economic recession revealed the speculative and unsound nature of his building schemes. From September 1892, when his London and General Bank (which had provided banking facilities for the Balfour group) suspended payment, his companies followed one another in quick succession into the bankruptcy courts. The demise of the Liberator caused a particular furore because many thrifty but misguided small investors lost their life savings. Investigations by the official receiver uncovered a sorry tale of misleading statements, false accounting, and petty fraud by Balfour and his fellow directors over many years. Faced with the likelihood of prosecution, Balfour resigned his seat in parliament and fled to Argentina in December 1892. His dramatic disappearance was immediately taken as an admission of guilt, and for many years afterwards his name was a byword for financial skulduggery and sanctimonious humbug. Eventually extradited in 1895, he was tried and sentenced to fourteen years' imprisonment. After his release in 1906, with maximum remission for good conduct, Balfour lived quietly in London and supported himself as a consulting engineer. He was travelling by train to take up a new appointment at Morriston colliery in south Wales when he died on 23 February 1916.

DUNCAN BYTHELL

Sources *The Times* (Sept–Dec 1892) · *The Times* (March–July 1893) · *The Times* (March 1895) · *The Times* (Nov 1895), 25–6 · *The Times* (25 Feb 1916) · *The Times* (26 Feb 1916) · *Burnley Gazette* (1889–92) · 'The story of the Liberator crash', *Westminster Popular*, 5 (1894) · J. S. Balfour, *My prison life* (1907) · E. J. Cleary, 'Balfour, Jabez Spencer', *DBB* · E. J. Cleary, *The building society movement* (1965) · H. O. O'Hagan, *Leaves from my life*, 2 vols. (1929)
Likenesses Spy [L. Ward], caricature, watercolour study, NPG; repro. in *VF* (19 March 1892)

Balfour, Sir James, of Pittendreich (*c*.1525–1583), politician and legal writer, was the eldest son of Sir Michael Balfour (*d*. 1577) of Mountquhanie in Fife, and Joneta Boswell. He may have been educated at St Andrews in 1539 or 1540, when he would have been about fifteen years old, and was at Wittenberg in 1544. In 1546, with his father and his brothers David and Gilbert, he entered St Andrews Castle and joined those who on 29 May had slain Cardinal David Beaton and were holding out against the earl of Arran, the governor of Scotland. Balfour had at some point taken priest's orders, but was now a fanatical Calvinist. After the castle surrendered, on 31 July 1547, Balfour and the evangelical preacher John Knox were among those impressed into the French service as galley slaves. About 1549 the Balfour brothers were released, and by 1553 James Balfour had become official of Lothian, a high ecclesiastical judge, while by 1555 he was vicar of Kilmany, Fife. After the 'uproar for religion' which broke out at Perth in May 1559 Balfour became a propagandist for the queen regent, Mary of Guise, and he also joined the reformers in order to bring dissension among them and to spy on their activities. In 1560 he became rector of Flisk, Fife. After the young Queen Mary's return from France, on 14 August 1561, Balfour was made an extraordinary (and unpaid) lord of the court of session on the spiritual side (12 November 1561), and on 15 November 1563 he was promoted to an ordinary (permanent and paid) place on the bench.

When the new commissary courts were organized at the beginning of 1564 to replace the pre-Reformation church courts, Balfour, as a former official of Lothian, was chosen as chief of the four commissaries of Edinburgh, with a salary of 400 merks. He held the office until October 1565. By 1565 he was a privy councillor, at first (in July) as one of the *extraordinarii*, and from September onwards as a regular councillor. In the spring of 1566 he was appointed to the valuable office of clerk register; he was also knighted, with the style of Sir James Balfour of Pittendreich, Fife. At this time he claimed to be a Lutheran. In the same year he was appointed to a parliamentary commission to revise the laws. The result of the commission's labours was the collection of the acts of the Scottish parliament from 1424 to 1566, published at Edinburgh in the latter year and known as the Black Acts because the typeface used was English black letter. Balfour's work is commended in the preface to this compilation.

By October 1566 Balfour was active in support of James Hepburn, fourth earl of Bothwell, who regarded King Henry (formerly Lord Darnley) as an obstacle to his ambitions. When the king was murdered on 10 February 1567, Balfour was widely regarded as the principal counsellor and deviser of the deed, and as a result he was arrested by the earl of Moray and warded in Edinburgh Castle. But his confinement was brief, and he was soon made captain of the castle. He appeared at the parliament of April and served on the committee dealing with the manner of holding the sessions. A fortnight after Mary's marriage to Bothwell (15 May 1567), Balfour joined with the opposition lords in a band to free the queen from Bothwell's control. When Mary marched to defeat and capture at Carberry Hill, on 15 June, Balfour did nothing to support her. At Bothwell's request, he gave out a casket of letters to a servant of Bothwell, but at the same time he informed the opposition lords, who intercepted the papers, and he also gave them artillery from the castle.

After Mary's abdication the new regent, the earl of Moray, agreed that Balfour, as the person most strongly implicated in King Henry's assassination, was to use his good offices to pursue the murderers. In exchange for the captaincy of Edinburgh Castle Balfour received a remission for any crimes and was granted the priory of Pittenweem, Fife; he also received a pension out of the priory of St Andrews for his son, and was given a lump sum of £5000. In addition, he exchanged the office of clerk register for that of lord president of the court of session (6 December 1567). In the same month he appeared in parliament and among the lords of the articles as prior of Pittenweem. However, at the insistence of the earl of Lennox, father of the murdered king, and after acrimonious debate in the council, the government decided to prosecute William Maitland of Lethington and Balfour. The latter was warded in Stirling and almost immediately placed in free ward in St Andrews on caution of £20,000 not to practise with England. But when Lennox became regent in July 1570, after Moray's murder, Balfour joined the Marians, and for two years was the most extreme partisan of the queen in the ensuing civil war. Forfeited in August 1571, Balfour received a remission in November 1572 for crimes of which he declared himself innocent: his forfeiture was reduced, and he made profession of the true religion. He assisted in the pacification of Perth (23 February 1573) between the parties to the civil war, and took his place in parliament as prior of Pittenweem and served on committees to revise the law and consider church policy. In May 1579, however, the earl of Morton (formerly regent, and still in control of the person of the young James VI) began proceedings against Balfour and the Hamiltons, and on 24 November the forfeiture of 1571 was extended to disinherit Balfour's heirs. Balfour, who was probably now over fifty, joined the Hamilton exiles in Paris. After he had left Scotland, he corresponded with the captive Queen Mary, and about August was present at a meeting of the chief conspirators against Morton. He was now regarded as a Catholic and a Spanish agent.

Balfour spent most of his brief exile in France. In 1580 he went to Dieppe, and then returned to Scotland, reaching the Isle of May in the Forth, with, it was said, a 'messe' of French crowns, on 17 December. He had been engaged in searching for evidence to incriminate Morton in King Henry's death. Since he was still under sentence of forfeiture, Balfour was conveyed secretly to Edinburgh, where on 31 December Morton was arrested as an accessory in the late king's murder; he was executed six months later, an interval which suggests that Balfour had failed to discover any truly damaging evidence to support the accusation. Queen Elizabeth marvelled at Balfour's presence in Scotland and wanted his arrest. Almost immediately after Morton's execution Balfour was granted a remission or respite for three years, on condition of his standing trial for King Henry's death, and was thereby enabled to continue the work of codifying the laws which had been begun under Morton. King James made a declaration of protection in his favour, but was twice compelled to declare that the protection did not wipe out the previous forfeiture, and that it did not decide the question of Balfour's guilt. In June 1582 Balfour appeared as an elder at the general assembly of the church and he regained possession of his lands, for in 1582 and 1583 he directed the transcription of ancient chronicles at Burleigh.

Balfour died in 1583, some time after 31 July, and was survived by his wife, Dame Margaret Balfour, heir of Burleigh, and by six sons and three daughters. The family subsequently benefited from further restoration of Sir James's properties. His eldest son, Michael, was created Lord Balfour of Burleigh by James VI in 1607, and that line continued uninterrupted until the forfeiture of the fifth lord after the 1715 rising.

There is no doubt that Balfour was a most able man, of undisputed legal talents. These are apparent from his contribution to the Black Acts, and still more from his *Practicks* (1754; new edn, 1962–3). The latter, effectively a legal encyclopaedia compiled from all available sources—statutes, decisions, and the 'auld lawes'—was unique in respect of its great bulk. The pre-eminent written record of Scots law for over a century, the *Practicks* must have satisfied a pressing need for a compendium of this kind. About twenty manuscript copies survive from between the sixteenth and the eighteenth centuries. As late as 1861 Lord President Inglis referred to it as a work of undoubted authority. Besides its intrinsic worth, it is valuable as a source of judicial records no longer extant. The opinion of contemporaries (including Mary, queen of Scots, and John Knox) was that Balfour was a repeated religious and political turncoat; and he had some involvement in the deaths of many of the public figures of his time—particularly King Henry. Richard Bannatyne, John Knox's secretary, reported in 1573 that it was said of Balfour that he would 'tak the way that myght mak him advancement, howbeit that the same were to the destructione of all honest and godlie men, and of his native cuntrie also' (Bannatyne, 41). Walter Goodall, in his preface to the 1754 edition of the *Practicks*, attempted a limited rehabilitation, but subsequent historians have found no reason to question these opinions. PETER G. B. MCNEILL

Sources *The 'Practicks' of Sir James Balfour of Pittendreich*, ed. P. G. B. McNeill, 2, Stair Society, 22 (1963), 670–73 · *John Knox's History of the Reformation in Scotland*, ed. W. C. Dickinson, 2 vols. (1949) · *APS*, 1424–1592 · *Reg. PCS*, 1st ser., vol. 3 · *CSP Scot.*, 1571–81 · J. M. Thomson and others, eds., *Registrum magni sigilli regum Scotorum / The register of the great seal of Scotland*, 11 vols. (1882–1914), vols. 3, 5 · J. Balfour, *Practicks, or, A system of the more ancient laws of Scotland*, ed. W. Goodall (1754) · R. Bannatyne, *Journal of the transactions in Scotland, during the contest between the adherents of Queen Mary, and those of her son*, ed. J. G. Dalyell (1806) · *Scots peerage*, 1.533–7 · G. Donaldson, *Scotland: James V to James VII* (1965), vol. 3 of *The Edinburgh history of Scotland* (1965–75) · G. R. Hewitt, *Scotland under Morton, 1572–80* (1982) · A. I. Dunlop, ed., *Acta facultatis artium universitatis Sanctiandree, 1413–1588*, 2, Scottish History Society, 3rd ser., 55 (1964), 396, 399

Wealth at death technically under forfeiture: *APS*, vol. 3, p. 319; *Register of the secret seal of Scotland*, HMSO 8, no. 1674; Burton and Masson, eds., *Register of the privy council*, vol. 3, p. 625

Balfour, Sir James, of Denmiln and Kinnaird, first baronet (1603/4–1657), antiquary and herald, was probably born at Denmiln, Fife, the son of Sir Michael Balfour of Denmiln (*c.*1580–1652), later MP for Fife and comptroller of the household to Charles I, and his wife, Jane or Joanna (*d.* 1640), daughter of Sir James Durham of Pitkerro. He was educated at home, and then sent to travel on the continent as a young man, for an unknown period of time.

On his return some time before 1626 Balfour began to interest himself in literary pursuits. His first interest was poetry, and he translated the *Panthea* of Johannes Leochaeus, or John Leech, into Scots verse. However, the age was one in which many Scots undertook research into the national past, and Balfour soon turned to the study of Scottish history and antiquities. He was particularly interested in heraldry, and to further his knowledge of this subject he went to London in 1628. Here he attached himself to Sir William Segar, Garter king at arms, and became acquainted with antiquarians Roger Dodsworth and Sir William Dugdale. He later contributed a short account of Scottish religious houses entitled 'Coenobia Scotica' to Dugdale's *Monasticum Anglicanum*. His chief patron was

Sir James Balfour of Denmiln and Kinnaird, first baronet (1603/4–1657), by unknown artist

George Hay, earl of Kinnoul and chancellor of Scotland, by whose influence Balfour was created Lyon king at arms by Charles I as replacement to Sir Jerome Lyndsay of Annatland; he was crowned as Lyon by Kinnoul on 15 June 1630. He also received other marks of favour from King Charles. He was knighted on 7 May 1630, and on 9 January 1631 he was granted the lands and barony of Kinnaird in Fife by royal charter. He seems, however, to have been in possession of these lands before the grant, because some Latin verses addressed to him by Leech in 1626 already refer to him as *Kinardius*. He was created a baronet by the king on 22 December 1633, and granted 16,000 acres of land in Nova Scotia, of which, however, he appears never to have taken possession.

Although a staunch presbyterian, Balfour was a firm supporter of King Charles, and was frequently at court while the king still held effective power. When the civil war began, he was naturally regarded with suspicion by the party hostile to the king, and to avoid being embroiled in conflict he retired to his Scottish estates, to which he had succeeded on his father's death on 14 February 1652. Here he pursued his antiquarian studies, mostly at Kinnaird. He continued to perform the duties of Lyon king at arms until he was deprived of the office by Cromwell in 1654.

Balfour was four times married. His first wife was Anne, daughter of Sir John Ayton of Ayton, whom he married on 21 October 1630. She died on 26 August 1644. He next married Jean, daughter of Sir James Durham of Pitkerro, who died shortly after the marriage, on 19 July 1645. His third wife was Margaret, daughter of Sir James Arnot of Ferney, who died on 15 December 1653, aged only twenty-five. His fourth and last marriage was to Janet, daughter of Sir William Auchinleck of Balmano, in June 1654. She may have outlived him. By these marriages Balfour had six sons and twelve daughters, many of whom died young.

In the pursuit of his antiquarian interests, Balfour maintained a literary correspondence with Dugdale and Dodsworth, as well as other leading figures in the field, including David Buchanan, Sir Robert Gordon of Straloch, Robert Maule, Henry Maule of Melgum, and William Drummond of Hawthornden. He produced a number of original works, only one of which, the *Annals of the History of Scotland from Malcolm III to Charles II*, has ever been published. This was compiled with great care with regard to proper names, titles, and offices, taken from original manuscripts, and a painstaking consideration for the accuracy of dates. As the title implies, however, it is not a history proper, but a chronological list of historical events, with no sustained narrative, and may have been a collection of materials made for the composition of a full history of Scotland. Some of Balfour's manuscript treatises are still preserved in the Advocates' Library in the National Library of Scotland, but many others were dispersed among his friends, and some were destroyed during the English capture of Perth, where he had sent them. The subjects of his treatises were mainly heraldic, but he also wrote on Scottish officers of state, princely revenues, the archbishops of St Andrews, gemstones, the coronation of Charles I, funeral ceremonies, the genealogy of Scottish earls to 1647, and the geography of the Fife coastline.

Balfour was also a diligent collector of manuscripts and related materials, and it is due to him that much material was preserved which might have been lost in the dispersion of Scotland's monastic libraries. These included many chronicles, registers of Scottish religious houses and bishoprics, the cartularies of Dunfermline, Dryburgh, Arbroath, and Aberdeen, and the registers of the priory of St Andrews and the monastery of Cupar. He amassed, at great expense, a large and valuable library of books dealing with Scottish history, antiquities, and heraldry, which at his death passed to his brother David. This library was, however, dispersed by auction after David Balfour's death.

Balfour died in Fife on 14 February 1657, and was buried in Abdie church in Fife. He was succeeded in the baronetcy by Robert Balfour, his eldest surviving son and heir by his third marriage. ALEXANDER DU TOIT

Sources GEC, *Baronetage*, 2.395–6 • J. Haig, preface, in *The historical works of Sir James Balfour*, ed. J. Haig, 1 (1824), xi–xxxiii • R. Sibbald, *Memoria Balfouriana* (1699) • D. Allan, *Virtue, bearing and the Scottish enlightenment: ideas of scholarship in early modern history* (1993), 87, 114, 158 • L. R. Timperley, ed., *A directory of landownership in Scotland, c.1770*, Scottish RS, new ser., 5 (1976), 137

Archives NL Scot., Advocates' Library, historical MSS, memoirs, etc. | U. Edin., Laing collection, list of Scottish officers of state

Likenesses oils, Scot. NPG [*see illus.*]

Wealth at death estates of Kinnaird (£930 in 1771) and Denmiln (£1015 3*s*. 1*d*. in 1771): Timperly, ed. *A directory of landownership*

Balfour, James, of Pilrig (1705–1795), moral philosopher, was born at Pilrig, near Edinburgh, the eldest child of James Balfour (1681–1737), businessman, and his wife, Louisa, *née* Hamilton (1686–1750), of Airdrie. His brother John *Balfour (1715–1795) became a prominent Edinburgh bookseller and papermaker. James was sent by his father to study at Leiden in 1729. Having returned later that year, he was called to the Scottish bar and was made advocate on 17 September 1730. In August 1737 he married Cecilia Elphinstone (1705–1780), and having served as treasurer to the Faculty of Advocates, he became sheriff-substitute of the county of Edinburghshire in 1748.

In 1754, on the death of William Cleghorn, Balfour was appointed professor of moral philosophy at the University of Edinburgh, despite Cleghorn's reported recommendation that the post go to Adam Ferguson. Balfour's timely attack on David Hume in his anonymously published work *A Delineation of the Nature and Obligation of Morality with Reflexions upon Mr. Hume's Book Entitled 'An Inquiry Concerning the Principles of Morals'* (1753) much improved his chances of election. However, Balfour proved a far from accomplished teacher, and the moral philosophy class at Edinburgh 'dwindled to nothing', prompting efforts to replace him (Sher, *Church and University*, 107). In June 1759 there was an unsuccessful proposal to give the chair to Ferguson. In 1761 Lord Provost George Lind tried again to remove Balfour, asking Lord Milton to suggest that the professor be made commissary clerk in exchange for his resignation from the university. Two years later Principal William Robertson proposed to make Balfour sheriff-depute in exchange for his vacation of the chair. Finally, in 1764 Adam Ferguson was able to take tenure as Balfour accepted transfer to the professorship of the law of nature and nations.

Balfour was the author of three philosophical studies. In his *Delineation of the Nature and Obligation of Morality* he sought to establish principles through which the good of individuals may be made to coincide with the 'general good'. Private happiness was posited as the chief end of each person, while it was the good of others that was supposed to constitute the greatest happiness. Moral obligation was based on the will of God. Balfour adopted Francis Hutcheson's notion of a 'moral sense' as the basis of moral judgements emphasizing the beauty of the virtuous character in a manner close to the third earl of Shaftesbury, and attempted to subvert Hume's 'anatomical' portrait of human individuals motivated by pride and self-interest. Selfish motives and pride, in particular, were judged inimical to the general good of society, with Hume's refusal to condemn such motives being seen as an abandonment of the moral philosopher's duty to cultivate selfless motives and humility in his audience. Balfour accepted that 'a general sentiment of humanity' did not naturally arise and therefore believed it imperative that the moral philosopher encourage such passions in society. His attempt to do so involved liberal citation of classical examples and the use of Christian language and argument. Hume's response, a politely engaging letter to the author via the publishers, was met with a reply from Balfour, which is printed in the family history (Balfour-Melville, 113–16).

In 1768 Balfour's *Philosophical Essays* (also published anonymously) presented reflections on 'academical philosophy', 'active power', and 'liberty and necessity'. His views were critical of Lord Kames as well as Hume. The *Philosophical Dissertations* (1782) contained essays on matter and motion, liberty and necessity, the foundation of moral obligation, and evidence for the truth of revealed religion. Balfour's eldest sister, Helen, married the Edinburgh bookseller and publisher Gavin Hamilton; their eldest son, Balfour's nephew, was Robert *Hamilton (1743–1829), professor of mathematics in Marischal College, Aberdeen, and author of a treatise on the national debt. The character David Balfour in *Kidnapped* was modelled on Balfour's cousin, who was a great-great-grandfather of Robert Louis Stevenson. James Balfour died at his home, Pilrig House, near Edinburgh, on 6 March 1795. CHRISTOPHER J. FINLAY

Sources *DNB* · B. Balfour-Melville, *The Balfours of Pilrig* (1907) · R. B. Sher, *Church and university in the Scottish Enlightenment: the moderate literati of Edinburgh* (1985) · R. B. Sher, 'Professors of virtue: a social history of the chair of moral philosophy at Edinburgh', *Studies in the philosophy of the Scottish Enlightenment*, ed. M. A. Stewart (1990), 87–126 · J. V. Price, 'Balfour, James', *The dictionary of eighteenth-century British philosophers*, ed. J. W. Yolton, J. V. Price, and J. Stephens (1999)

Likenesses Stavely, portrait, 1790, repro. in Balfour-Melville, *Balfours of Pilrig* · portrait, repro. in Balfour-Melville, *Balfours of Pilrig*

Balfour, John, third Lord Balfour of Burleigh (*d.* 1696/7), nobleman, was the son and heir of Robert *Balfour (formerly Arnot), second Lord Balfour of Burleigh (*d.* 1663), and Margaret Balfour, Lady Balfour (*d.* 1639), who married in 1606. After being sent to France to complete his education and to avoid the dangers of civil war, he managed to embroil himself in a quarrel with another nobleman and subsequently fought a duel in defence of his honour, in which he was badly wounded. Whether on account of this affray, or as a response to the deteriorating political situation of the French crown, he determined to travel back home to Scotland early in 1649. His journey took him to London, where he met and hastily married his kinswoman Isabel, the daughter of Sir William *Balfour of Pitcullo (*d.* 1660), lieutenant of the Tower of London. However, his father had not been informed of the match, and when the couple returned to his estates in March 1649 he attempted to have their union annulled, purely on the grounds that he had not given his permission for it. Greatly angered, Lord Balfour brought the case before the general assembly of the Church of Scotland, but received no answer to his petition. The matter was sidelined and quickly forgotten by the assembly, and John and his bride went on to raise a family of three sons and six daughters in quiet obscurity. John inherited the title of Lord Balfour of Burleigh from his father in August 1663, and died between 10 December 1696 and 27 February 1697. However, he gained a posthumous and entirely undeserved notoriety, as a covenanter rebel, through the confusion of his identity with that of John *Balfour of Kinloch (*fl.* 1663–1683), who had been nicknamed 'Burley' purely on account of his appearance. JOHN CALLOW

Sources Anderson, *Scot. nat.*, vol. 1 · *Scots peerage* · GEC, *Peerage* · B. Balfour, *Melville of Pilrig: the Balfours of Pilrig* (1907) · F. Balfour, *A memoir of Lord Balfour of Burleigh* (*c.*1925) · Lord Balfour of Burleigh, *The rise and development of presbyterianism in Scotland* (1911) · M. Grant, *No king but Christ: the story of Donald Cargill* (1988) · G. G. Simpson, ed., *The Scottish soldier abroad, 1247–1967* (1992) · *Reg. PCS*, 3rd ser., vols. 2, 6

Balfour, John, of Kinloch (*fl.* 1663–1683), covenanter, was the son of John Balfour (*d.* *c.*1652), portioner of Kinloch, in the parish of Collessie, and his wife, Grissel Hay (*d.* *c.*1653). Served heir to his grandfather Robert Balfour on 26 February 1663, he was described as a 'broad man' with 'farid dusk brown hair' (NA Scot., JC2/15, fol. 224*r*). He married Barbara Hackston, sister of David Hackston of Rathillet, and they had a son, perhaps named David. In July 1672 and 1676 Balfour was called before the privy council for attending conventicles, but refused to appear, leaving him open to arrest. In January 1678 he is listed as not having signed the bond for public peace and in the same year he is among those heritors in the parish of Collessie who had not signed the bond against conventicles and disorderly walking. In March 1678 between sixty and eighty armed men met at his house and attacked a troop of horse under Captain Carstares sent by the privy council to capture conventiclers. Balfour participated in the murder of Archbishop Sharp on Magnus Muir (Moor) on 3 May 1679, at which his brother-in-law Hackston was present. He escaped to the west of Scotland and was involved in the declaration of Rutherglen on 29 May 1679, which condemned past violations of the covenants and the reintroduction of episcopacy, and which preceded a covenanter rising. He was one of the officers of the covenanting army at the battle of Drumclog on 1 June 1679 under the name of Captain Burghlie. On 22 June 1679 he took part in the covenanter defeat at the battle of Bothwell Bridge and was among those proclaimed traitors on 26 June. On 14 August 1679 a reward of 10,000 merks and indemnity was offered for Balfour and Hackston for participation in Sharp's murder. Balfour fled to Holland about October 1679 and a process of treason was raised against him about January 1683. On 2 April 1683 the lords of justiciary deemed him a traitor and his goods were pronounced forfeit. His later career is unclear, 'and nothing certain is known of his last deeds and days' (Hewison, 2.512). ALISON G. MUIR

Sources *Reg. PCS*, 3rd ser., vols. 3, 5–6, 8, 10 · J. K. Hewison, *The covenanters: a history of the church in Scotland from the Reformation to the revolution*, 2 (1908) · trial of Balfour of Kinloch, 2 April 1683, NA Scot., MS justiciary records, books of adjournal, JC2/16 · trial of Hackston of Rathillet, 30 July 1680, NA Scot., MS justiciary records, books of adjournal, JC2/15, fols. 214*r*–26*v* · *CSP dom.*, *1679–80*; *1683–4* · services of heirs, NA Scot., CC22/27, CC22/42

Archives NA Scot., trial of Balfour of Kinloch, 2 April 1683, MS justiciary records, books of adjournal, JC2/16 · NA Scot., trial of Hackston of Rathillet, 30 July 1680, MS justiciary records, books of adjournal, JC2/15, fols. 214*r*–26*v*

Likenesses C. Sweet (after A. Pithie), repro. in Hewison, *The covenanters*, vol. 2, p. 252 · portrait, repro. in Hewison, *The covenanters*, vol. 2, p. 298

Balfour, John (1715–1795), bookseller and printer, was born in South Leith, Edinburghshire, on 1 December 1715, the ninth among the sixteen children of the manufacturer and shipbuilder James Balfour (1681–1737) and Louisa Hamilton (1686–1750). When he was three the family moved to the Pilrig estate on the boundary of Edinburgh. His generation of an influential family included his eldest brother, James *Balfour of Pilrig, and brothers-in-law Robert *Whytt, William *Leechman, and Gavin *Hamilton, who was also his cousin. Balfour had a presbyterian upbringing and memorized one of the first books he encountered, *The Shorter Catechism*, to respond to his father's regular examination. He was educated at Edinburgh University from 1728 (matriculating in the humanity class in 1729–30) and privately; his father paid for writing classes, a Greek Testament in 1730, and mathematics classes for two years. About 1733 Balfour was taken on as a clerk in the bookselling shop of Gavin Hamilton, who had married his sister Helen. After surviving illness in 1736, he managed the business while Hamilton and other magistrates were in London in 1737 testifying about the murder of Captain John Porteous. Balfour became Hamilton's partner aged twenty-four, after inheriting £300 from his father's estate. His fiery nature caused his sister to warn her husband that their temperaments were not compatible: this was true, yet combined they were outstanding booksellers.

On 4 January 1747 Balfour married Catherine (*d.* 1802), daughter of Ludovick Cant of Thurston, with whom he had six children. During the 1740s Hamilton and Balfour were prominent among the Scottish defenders in a series of copyright prosecutions brought before the Scottish courts by London booksellers. The reprinting opportunities that arose, and their ambitions for Scottish book publishing, led them to form an Edinburgh printing partnership in 1750 with Patrick Neill as Hamilton, Balfour, and Neill. In 1754 Balfour helped bring about Hamilton and Balfour's appointment as printer to Edinburgh University, for the life of the surviving partner, persuading the Ruddiman family to stand aside by pledging not to print a thrice-weekly newspaper to rival their *Caledonian Mercury* (a promise broken with the *Edinburgh Chronicle* in 1759). He also lobbied from his seat on the Edinburgh town council, where a politician commented on his strong-headedness: 'John Balfour sometimes had an opportunity to give us a vote without hurting his beloved schemes, but his zeal had eat up his understanding' (Rochead to Drummond, 28 Sept 1754).

With Neill as their printer, Hamilton and Balfour ran a worthy academic press, producing student texts and fine editions of the classics, including Sallust and Virgil in 1755, Phaedrus in 1757, and an edition of Terence in 1758 by a clever young printer they were nurturing, William Smellie. The firm also reprinted English classics by authors such as Jonathan Swift and participated in the first Scottish edition of Shakespeare's works. They produced original work in science, medicine, history, and poetry by Scottish authors such as Francis Home, John Home, David Hume, Robert Wallace, Robert Whytt, and William Wilkie, as well as multiple volumes of *Essays and Observations, Physical and Literary* by the Edinburgh Philosophical Society, James Macpherson's *Fragments of Ancient Poetry* (which started the Ossian craze), the original *Edinburgh Review* of 1755–6, and French work in the original and in translation, including Montesquieu and Voltaire. Balfour was in charge of the firm's European book trade, as well as its exports to America, selling books to David Hall of Philadelphia on the suggestion of William Strahan, and corresponding with Benjamin Franklin over debts in New York and Antigua. On an early visit to learned circles in London, he was introduced by the principal of Edinburgh University as a man who would be useful in the republic of letters (William Wishart to John Ward, 3 July 1751, BL, Add. MS 6211, fol. 181). Balfour enjoyed auctioning books at the New Exchange. At the shop on the High Street he greeted the literati, promoted titles and publishing ideas, and negotiated with authors. His unfailing tact and politeness with customers did not extend to his relations with Hamilton, who broke up the firm in August 1762, remarking how uncivil Balfour had been throughout their contract. At this time Balfour was raging publicly against Alexander Donaldson, who he believed had obtained a printing discount falsely; Donaldson, now an enemy, claimed that the incident was due to Balfour's 'troublesome temper' (NA Scot., Currie Mack. Misc. 1/20, *Balfour* v. *Donaldson*, 'Answers for Mr Alexander Donaldson, 1763', 2).

Hamilton kept the paper mill at Bogsmill and the nearby Millbank House, and Balfour continued the reprinting of English literature with a 1764 edition of Alexander Pope's works in the face of a cheaper version and sarcastic advertising by Donaldson. From 1764 Balfour was the leading importer of French books in Scotland, advertising thousands of titles in his sale catalogues and selling at cheaper prices than those available in London; he travelled in France and was familiar with the trade there, corresponding with Charles Joseph Panckoucke of Paris. He became printer to the Faculty of Advocates in 1772. In 1773, encouraged by Strahan, he bought the lease of Bogsmill, now Redhall Paper Mill, from Hamilton's son, Robert. Millbank became the family's summer home, and there Balfour oversaw the making of Bank of Scotland notes and entertained bank officials. In 1783, after the laird sued to prevent his unauthorized expansion of Millbank, he began building up the larger Kate's Mill (named after his wife) into a considerable paper producer.

From 1767 to 1771 Balfour had a printing partnership with Smellie and William Auld; the firm's output included 10,000 copies of the first Gaelic New Testament in 1767 and the first edition of William Buchan's *Domestic Medicine* in 1769. He continued in partnership with Smellie, who printed Edinburgh University theses in Latin, from 1772 to 1783; thereafter, although not taking an active role as Edinburgh University printer, he kept the position until 1794 while Smellie continued printing medical theses under their joint imprint. In 1777 Balfour brought his sons Elphingston (*b.* 1754) and John (*b.* 1756), and his clerk, John Drysdale, into partnership of his book and paper business as John Balfour & Co. The Balfour tradition of litigation continued. In 1782 Elphingston stood surety in an appeal by 'John Balfour Bookseller', either the father or the son, and two relatives against a fine for damages caused by 'the burning of a Popish chapel' in Edinburgh, an accusation stoutly denied (NA Scot., CS 271/23, 646, 'Bond of caution for John Balfour and others').

In 1754 Hamilton had purchased the copyright of the first volume of David Hume's *History of Great Britain* but had failed to penetrate the London market. Balfour, uneasy in this affair, saw Edinburgh and London co-operation as a way to publish Scottish literary figures successfully, and in 1769 he joined William Strahan and Thomas Cadell in paying William Robertson £4000 for the copyright of *The History of the Reign of Charles V*. They also collaborated with William Creech in publishing subsequent editions of Buchan's *Domestic Medicine*. Now a substantial literary proprietor, Balfour tried to stop the Irish smuggling trade, warning Scottish customs in 1777 that the consortium was apprehensive of a pirated edition of Robertson's *History of America*; the piracy was not found, but his letter caused increased scrutiny at the western ports, and book smugglers became more covert. Balfour also traded with John Nourse and John Murray of London, and at Edinburgh published with Alexander Kincaid and Creech *The British Poets* in forty-four volumes in 1773–6 (over which he and Creech fought at the court of session in 1781–2). He took part, along with Cadell, in ventures with Charles Elliot, including the Edinburgh–London edition of the Justamond translation of Raynal's *East and West Indies* in 1776.

In the 1770s Balfour was an esteemed figure in Edinburgh bookselling, but in the 1780s, with paper making his primary interest, his desire for bookselling privileges brought him into conflict with the rising generation. He stirred up a paper war in 1781 in a futile attempt to have Elphingston replace Creech as bookseller to the new Society of Antiquaries, and in 1790 he saw off a bid by Creech to become university printer. He tried to thwart a 1787 reprint of *Decisions of the Court of Session, 1752–56* by Elliot, who compared him to 'the Dog in the Fable that could not eat the bone himself yet would not let another take it' (Elliot to Balfour, 22 Nov 1786, Elliot letter 3901, Elliot letter-books, archives of John Murray, London). He continued book auctioning, now at Writers' Court, where 'he used to place at his right hand a well-filled punch-bowl, with a large spoon and glasses, with which he occasionally regaled himself and his best customers' (Constable, 3.537).

In their old age Balfour and his wife had their portraits painted by Henry Raeburn. Balfour died on 16 October 1795, aged seventy-nine, at Millbank House, where Gavin Hamilton had died twenty-eight years earlier, and was buried in Greyfriars churchyard, Edinburgh. He 'left his family very well provided for' (Balfour-Melville, 134), with John junior carrying on the paper making and Elphingston the bookselling business.

WARREN MCDOUGALL

Sources W. McDougall, 'Gavin Hamilton, John Balfour and Patrick Neill: a study of publishing in Edinburgh in the 18th century', PhD diss., U. Edin., 1974 • E. Balfour-Melville, *The Balfours of Pilrig* (1907) • Balfour of Pilrig household and estate accounts, 1716–97, NA Scot., GD 69/284 • Balfour of Pilrig ledger, 1704–32, NA Scot., GD 1/8, vol. 31 • acknowledgement of father's bond of provision, 1741, NA Scot., GD 69/184 • correspondence with James Anderson, 1737, U. Edin. L., La.II.511/1 • [E. Hamilton], *Short memoir of Gavin Hamilton, publisher and bookseller in Edinburgh* (1840) • W. McDougall, 'Hamilton, Balfour, and Neill and *The Edinburgh Chronicle*', *Scottish Book Collector*, 2/11 (1991), 1–13 • A. Turnbull, 'Academiae typographus', *University of Edinburgh Gazette*, 25 (Oct 1959), 34–42 • application by J. Dickson, E. Balfour, J. Paterson, and W. Creech for appointment as printers to Edinburgh University, 17 May 1795; John Balfour's resignation, 1794, Edinburgh City Archives, McLeod's Bundle 184, bay D, no. 42 • J. Rochhead to G. Drummond, 28 Sept 1754, NA Scot., Fletcher of Saltoun papers • J. Balfour and G. Wallace, contract and correspondence, 1759–79, U. Edin. L., La.II.694 • *John Balfour* v. *Alexander Donaldson*, 1761–4, NA Scot., Currie Mack. Misc. 1/20 • *Balfour* vs. *Donaldson*, three printed papers, 1761–4, Signet Library, Edinburgh, session papers vol. 90(2) • John Balfour v. George Inglis regarding Bogsmill paper mill, 19–27 Nov 1777, NA Scot., bill chamber process no. 43809 • W. McDougall, 'Copyright litigation in the court of session, 1738–49, and the rise of the Scottish book trade', *Edinburgh Bibliographical Society Transactions*, 5/5 (1988), 2–31 • W. McDougall, 'Scottish books for America in the mid-18th century', and 'A catalogue of Hamilton, Balfour and Neill publications, 1750–1762', *Spreading the word: the distribution networks of print, 1550–1850*, ed. R. Myers and M. Harris (1998), 21–46, 187–232 • W. McDougall, 'Smugglers, reprinters and hot pursuers: the Irish–Scottish book trade and copyright prosecutions in the late eighteenth century', *The Stationers' Company and the book trade, 1550–1990*, ed. R. Myers and M. Harris, St Paul's Bibliographies (1997), 151–83 • W. Zachs, *The first John Murray and the late eighteenth-century London book trade* (1998) • T. Constable, *Archibald Constable and his literary correspondents*, 3 vols. (1873) • R. Kerr, *Memoirs of the life, writings, and correspondence of William Smellie*, ed. R. Sher (1996) • bap. reg. Scot., South Leith baptismal register, 1711–56 • *Scots Magazine*, 57 (Oct 1795), 683

Archives American Philosophical Society, Philadelphia, David Hall, out-letter books and account book • BL, Strahan papers • Edinburgh City Archives, resignation as university printer, 1794, with the application of E. Balfour and others [James Dickson, E. Balfour, John Paterson, W. Creech], 1795, McLeod's bundle 184, bay D, no. 42 • John Murray, London, archives, Charles Elliot letter-books and ledgers, and accounts • John Murray, London, archives, John Murray papers, letters and accounts • Maryland Historical Society, Baltimore, letters to the Hamilton family • NA Scot., Balfour of Pilrig household and estate accounts, GD 69/284 • NA Scot., bond with James Balfour of Pilrig and Dr Robert Whytt, GD 69/191 • NA Scot., *Balfour* v. *Donaldson*, twenty papers in Currie Mack. Misc. 1/20 • NA Scot., inventory of process *Balfour* v. *William Creech* (over *British poets*), CS 238/B6/18 • NA Scot., decreets for John Balfour sen. and jun. against Gavin Alston, general minute book of the court of session, 2.265, 3.149 • NA Scot., decreet for John Balfour paper makers against W. Creech, general minute book of the court of session, 1.57 • NA Scot., letters to Sir John Clerk of Penicuik, GD 18/5478/1–2 • NA Scot., letters to Sir Hew Dalrymple of North Berwick, GD 110/1025/1–3 • NA Scot., letters to the earl of Findlater, GD 248/982/1 • NA Scot., dispute with George Inglis of Redhall over Bogsmill paper mill, bill chamber process no. 43809 • NA Scot., bond of caution regarding the burning down of a popish chapel, CS 271/1/23,646 • NA Scot., holograph acknowledgement of his father's bond of provision, GD 69/184 • NA Scot., ledger, GD 1/8, vol. 31 • NA Scot., petition to suspend a warrant against Balfour for refusing to pay a special town tax, bill chamber process no. 53,728 • NL Scot., letters to Richard Gough, Adv. MS 29.5.7, vol. 1 • U. Edin. L., corresp. with James Anderson, Hawick, La.II.511/1 • U. Edin. L., DA papers—Library, accounts for Dr William Robertson • U. Edin. L., letters, contract, and costs of publishing, to

George Wallace, La.II.694/6 • U. Edin. L., note to Revd Robert Wallace enclosing letter by W. Strahan, La.II.511 • U. Edin. L., signature in Adam Watt's humanity class, Edinburgh University, 1729 and 1730, MS college matriculation roll, I, 73 and 76
Likenesses H. Raeburn, portrait, after 1787

Balfour, John Blair, **first Baron Kinross** (1837–1905), advocate and politician, born at Clackmannan on 11 July 1837, was the second son (in a family of two sons and a daughter) of Peter Balfour (1794–1862), parish minister of that place, and his wife, Jane Ramsay (*d.* 1871), daughter of Peter Blair of Perth. Educated at Edinburgh Academy, of which he was 'dux' (leading scholar), he passed to the University of Edinburgh, where he had a distinguished career, but did not graduate. Passing to the Scottish bar on 26 November 1861, he rose with almost unexampled rapidity to be the foremost advocate in Scotland, his only rival being Alexander Asher. On 4 August 1869 he married Lilias Oswald, daughter of Donald Mackenzie, Lord Mackenzie, judge of the supreme court of Scotland. She died on 19 June 1872, having had one son. On 6 April 1877 he married Marianne Elizabeth (*d.* 25 Sept 1913), daughter of James *Moncreiff, first Baron Moncreiff, lord justice-clerk of Scotland. They had four sons and one daughter.

Balfour first engaged prominently in politics at the general election of April 1880, when he contested North Ayrshire, as a Liberal, against Robert William Cochran-Patrick, afterwards permanent under-secretary for Scotland. Balfour was defeated by fifty-five votes, but was returned unopposed for Clackmannan and Kinross on 1 December 1880 on the appointment of W. P. Adam, the sitting member, as governor of Madras. Appointed immediately solicitor-general for Scotland in Gladstone's second ministry, he in 1881 succeeded John McLaren as lord advocate. He was made honorary LLD of the University of Edinburgh in 1882, and became a privy councillor in 1883. He remained in office until the Liberals lost power in 1885. For nearly 150 years before 1885 the lord advocates had been practically ministers for Scotland; but during Lord Salisbury's short-lived administration of 1885–6 the ancient office of secretary of state for Scotland, which had been abolished at the close of the Jacobite rising of 1745–6, was revived. Balfour was thus the last of the old line of lord advocates, and, though he was always stronger as a lawyer than as a politician, managed the affairs of Scotland with ability in the face of considerable difficulties caused by the crofter question and the movement in favour of home rule for Scotland. In 1886 he was again lord advocate, but left office when the Gladstone government was defeated in June that year on the Irish question. In 1885–6 and again in 1889–92 he was dean of the faculty of advocates. From 1892 to 1895 he was once more lord advocate under Gladstone and Lord Rosebery, and, during that period, took a prominent part in carrying through the House of Commons the Local Government Act for Scotland (1894), by which parish councils, framed on the model of the English act, were established.

The defeat of the Rosebery government in June 1895 was the end of Balfour's official career; but at the ensuing general election he was again returned by his old constituency, and remained in parliament until 1899. In that year the lord president of the Court of Session, James Patrick Bannerman Robertson, became a lord of appeal, on the death of William Watson (Lord Watson), and so high was the estimation in which Balfour was held that the Conservative government bestowed on him the vacant office. 'I have never in my life known an appointment which gave such universal pleasure', Lord Rosebery said at a banquet given by the Scottish Liberal Club in honour of Balfour's appointment. On 15 July 1902 Balfour was raised to the peerage as Baron Kinross of Glasclune. His health, which had begun to fail before he left the bar, broke down rapidly after he became a judge. Balfour died on 22 January 1905 at 6 Rothesay Terrace, Edinburgh, and was buried in the Dean cemetery there.

G. W. T. Omond, *rev.* H. C. G. Matthew

Sources *The Scotsman* (23 Jan 1905) • *The Times* (23 Jan 1905) • Roll of the faculty of advocates, Edinburgh • *Records of the Juridical Society* (1859–63) • [W. M. Watson], ed., *The history of the Speculative Society, 1764–1904* (1905) • Burke, *Peerage* • Gladstone, *Diaries*
Archives NL Scot., corresp. and papers | BL, corresp. with W. E. Gladstone, Add. MSS 44463–44789 • Bodl. Oxf., corresp. and papers relating to crofters • NL Scot., corresp. mainly with Lord Rosebery
Likenesses B. Stone, photographs, 1898, NPG • J. C. Horsley, portrait, 1912, priv. coll. • G. Reid, oils, Scot. NPG • G. Reid, portrait, priv. coll. • Spy [L. Ward], lithograph, repro. in *VF* (1 May 1886), 489 • drawing, repro. in *ILN* (1892), 260
Wealth at death £157,490 19*s*.: confirmation, 3 March 1905, *CCI*

Balfour, John Hutton (1808–1884), botanist, was born in Edinburgh on 15 September 1808, the eldest son of Andrew Balfour, an army surgeon who later settled in that city as a printer and publisher, and Magdalene, daughter of the Revd George Goldie, an Edinburgh minister. James Hutton the geologist was a first cousin of his grandfather. Balfour was a brilliant student and was able to resist his mother's determination that he follow her father into the church. After a thorough grounding in classics at Edinburgh high school and Edinburgh University, he was initially sent at sixteen to study theology at St Andrews, but he had acquired his father's fondness for botany and both he and his teachers there saw he was better suited to a medical career. His parents reluctantly permitted him to attend Professor Robert Graham's botany class at Edinburgh, on the condition that he completed his divinity studies. In 1827 they finally gave way, and Balfour was apprenticed to the professor of military surgery, Sir George Ballingall, apparently with the aim of following his father into that branch of the subject. He graduated MD in 1832 and, after qualifying MRCS and FRCS Edinburgh, extended his surgical studies in Paris before returning to Edinburgh in 1834 to take up private practice. The next year he was elected a fellow of the Royal Society of Edinburgh, of which he was later to be an active secretary for more than ten years.

Botany now increasingly took over. In 1836 the Botanical Society of Edinburgh, the first specialist body in that subject in Britain of national standing, had its inaugural meeting in Balfour's house, and in 1838 he was equally to the fore in the founding of the Edinburgh Botanical Club.

John Hutton Balfour (1808–1884), by Maull & Polyblank, 1855

In 1840 he began lecturing on botany in the Edinburgh Extra Academical School of Medicine, and equipped by that he successfully competed the next year for the chair at Glasgow University vacated by Sir William Hooker, which at last enabled him to give up medical practice. His Glasgow stay, however, proved brief, for in 1845, on the death of Graham, he returned to Edinburgh as professor of medicine and botany, regius keeper of the Royal Botanic Garden, and queen's botanist for Scotland. Soon after, with his future now on a settled course, he married Marion Spottiswood Bayley, the daughter of Isaac Bayley, a writer to the signet. Among their children was the botanist Sir Isaac Bayley *Balfour.

Though Balfour served the Edinburgh medical faculty as dean for nearly thirty years, he took no regular part in the clinical teaching and was otherwise free to devote all his considerable energies to botany. His induction into botany occurred before microscopical work had been largely developed, and before the advent of later concerns with plant morphology and physiology, so he was, almost of necessity, for the most part a systematist. His original work was not extensive and it was as a teacher and writer of textbooks that he was distinguished academically. His teaching was painstaking and conscientious, earnest and impressive, and characterized by a wealth of illustration and a gift for imparting his own enthusiasm.

That enthusiasm was most of all in evidence in the lively tradition of Saturday student excursions that Balfour inherited from his predecessor. On the longer of these trips, undeterred by the frequently rough going and primitive conditions, leading botanical 'outsiders' would often join the party, augmenting with taxonomic expertise the professor's discourses on the local vegetation and geological features. No one was more tireless than the wiry Balfour, his geniality contagious, his jokes and puns keeping everyone in good spirits as they toiled up some long ascent. Not for nothing was he known to generations of students by the nickname 'Woody Fibre'. On one occasion, in the Isle of Arran, the party became lost in the hills in deep mist, and in the account subsequently published by him of that shaking experience the deeply religious strain in his character is strikingly apparent. He resembled an Old Testament prophet in appearance, and his youthful immersion in theology had left its mark so that the intricacy of nature was always for him indubitable testimony to a great designing mind. Among the many books he wrote were several linking botany with religion, one of them, *Phyto-Theology* (1851), winning a wide enough readership to achieve a third edition.

Amid all this activity the Royal Botanic Garden was in no way neglected. Under Balfour's care and in co-operation with the successive principal gardeners, the very able McNabs, father and son, the garden was much enlarged and improved, and a fine new palm house, an arboretum, a good museum, and excellent teaching accommodation provided. Latterly as many as 354 students a year were attending Balfour's botanical lectures there. A final accomplishment was the construction and planting of the great rock-garden.

Severe illness brought about Balfour's retirement in 1879, when each of the three universities with which he had been connected marked the occasion by conferring on him an honorary LLD. He had been elected a fellow of the Royal Society in 1856, and was also a member of a wide range of other scientific bodies. He died at Inverleith House, Edinburgh, on 11 February 1884. He is commemorated in the genus *Balfourodendron*; two British plants long bore his name as well, but *Poa balfourii*, a grass which he collected on Ben Voirlich in 1842, is now considered a mere variant of a more widespread species, and *Rubus balfourianus*, a name given in his honour by Babington to a blackberry, after a century disappeared into synonymy.

D. E. Allen

Sources I. B. Balfour, 'A sketch of the professors of botany in Edinburgh from 1670 until 1887', *Makers of British botany: a collection of biographies by living botanists*, ed. F. W. Oliver (1913), 280–301, esp. 293–300 • *PRS*, 96B (1924), i–xvii [obit. of Sir I. B. Balfour] • *Transactions of the Botanical Society* [Edinburgh], 16 (1886), 187–9 • *Nature*, 29 (1883–4), 385–7 • *Scottish Naturalist*, new ser., 1 (1883–4), 160–62 • *History of the Berwickshire naturalists' club*, 11 (1885), 218–26 • H. R. Fletcher and W. H. Brown, *The Royal Botanic Garden, Edinburgh, 1670–1970* (1970), 126–48 • C. Roger, *Botanizing excursions in high and low lands* (1877) • Alisma, *Reminiscences of a student's life at Edinburgh in the seventies* (1918) • *DNB*

Archives Museum and Art Gallery, Perth, British herbarium • NA Scot., corresp. • Royal Botanic Garden, Edinburgh, corresp. and papers • Wellcome L., lecture notes | NA Scot., Horrox MSS • U. Newcastle, letters to Sir Walter Trevelyan • U. St Andr., corresp. with James Forbes

Likenesses Maull & Polyblank, photograph, 1855, NPG [*see illus.*] • J. Horsburgh, oils, 1878, Scot. NPG • D. MacNee, oils, exh. RA 1878, U. Edin. • L. Ghémar, lithograph, NPG • W. Hole, etching, NPG; repro. in W. Hole, *Quasi cursores* (1884) • Maull & Co., photograph,

RS • J. Moffat, photograph, RS • photograph, repro. in L. Reeve, ed., *Portraits of men of eminence* (1855) • photograph, Royal Botanic Garden, Edinburgh • portrait, U. Edin., botany department

Balfour, Nancy (1911–1997), journalist and arts administrator, was born near San Francisco, California, USA, on 17 May 1911, the daughter of Alexander Balfour and his wife, Ruth Macfarland. Brought up in England, she was educated at High Wycombe School, and Lady Margaret Hall, Oxford, where she read philosophy, politics, and economics: she later gave significant works of modern British art to her Oxford college. She worked at the research department of the Foreign Office during the war, and subsequently at the North American desk of the BBC until 1948. But the majority of her professional career as a journalist and editor was devoted to *The Economist*, where she was to become assistant editor in charge of the American survey, and was nicknamed Colonel Balfour; she was abrasive, frank, and hectoring, and particularly enjoyed a good argument with no holds barred. Although not a gourmet, she entertained extensively: small dinner parties and larger cocktail gatherings; a guest, apologizing the day after a discussion at one of her gatherings had seemed to get out of hand, was reassured by Nancy that the noisy argument had been immensely enjoyable, and just what she liked. Surprisingly, for all her frankness in private she was often muted in public, and could quite calmly sit silent through an entire committee meeting, returning to the fray behind the scenes. She was awarded the OBE in 1967.

Nancy Balfour retired at just over sixty to devote herself to the cause of contemporary art, and to continue to follow her other passion, that of an international tourist and traveller: her recreations, self-defined in her *Who's Who* entry, were 'sightseeing, ancient and modern; viewing work by living artists'. She set up the Nancy Balfour charitable trust to support working artists. Her vocation was to support contemporary art, in which activity Nancy was both officially and unofficially involved: as a member, honorary secretary, chairman (1976–82), and president of the Contemporary Art Society, founded in 1910 by Roger Fry and other Bloomsbury luminaries to purchase and present contemporary works of art to public museums and galleries. She was an ardent collector. With independent means, she lived in a comfortable flat in Eaton Square, Westminster, London, surrounded by contemporary works of art, some major, but a great many in a minor key in terms of size, and sometimes of quality: charming, delightful, but inconsequential. 'I know what I like and that is why I buy—if I can afford it. As I live alone, I have no one to consult but myself.' She described herself as 'a compulsive, but perhaps not very discriminating collector'. She always bought work by living artists, and sometimes bought work purely as a gesture of support. She never bought in auctions, but deliberately bought from galleries as a gesture of support to the market which often took risks on the young unknowns, and occasionally from artists' studios, although she disliked having to approve or disapprove in front of the artist himself. She had an interest in contemporary decorative arts and served on the Crafts Council, where she was vice-chairman from 1983 to 1985. She was also a founder member of the British American Arts Association.

Those who worked with Nancy at times compared her to a very small terrier, nipping at their heels to make sure that they did what she saw not only as necessary, but as essential. In this context her irreverent nickname was Gnasher and little was beyond her to make sure the job was done: she was not above going through the desk of her administrator at the Contemporary Art Society. She preferred to work behind the scenes, not only chivvying, but bringing people together who would not otherwise have met for their mutual benefit.

Nancy also chaired SPACE, an organization dedicated to finding workable studio space for artists, often in schools and warehouses awaiting redevelopment; she was on the board of the Public Art Development Trust (1983–91), the moving force behind the arts committee of *The Economist*, encouraging temporary exhibitions of sculpture on its plazas in St James's and works of art on its walls, a tradition carried on by the Contemporary Art Society after her death. In old age she was still a determined city walker, visiting East End studios and West End galleries. She took no pleasure in country life, and was bemused when her niece became involved with the Ramblers Association. When she retired from *The Economist* she became a visiting fellow of the Kennedy Center for Government at Harvard University (1973–4).

Under Nancy's leadership the Contemporary Art Society pioneered specialist cultural travel for its members and set up a consultancy to advise businesses on corporate art collections, both innovations taken up in the wider art world. She was numerate, realistic, and practical, the least sentimental of characters: it was typical that not only should she leave, after personal bequests, her art collection to the Contemporary Art Society but that she left to the society's discretion what should be given to museums and galleries and what should be sold to benefit the society. She died at her home, 36E Eaton Square, Westminster, on 29 August 1997. She was unmarried.

Nancy was short of stature, extremely hard-working, indefatigably curious, and possessed of unusual tenacity and determination. She dressed elegantly in couture clothes tailored to her diminutive but full-busted figure and until the end of her life kept her neatly coiffed hair ash blonde. She was unusually robust: until her final illness she had been in hospital only once as an adult.

MARINA VAIZEY

Sources *The Guardian* (5 Sept 1997) • *The Economist* (6 Sept 1997) • *The Times* (11 Sept 1997) • *Daily Telegraph* (15 Sept 1997) • *The Independent* (17 Sept 1997) • *WWW* • personal knowledge (2004) • private information (2004) • d. cert.

Archives Tate collection, papers | SOUND BL NSA, oral history interview

Likenesses photograph, repro. in *The Guardian* • photograph, repro. in *The Times*

Wealth at death £4,450,148: probate, 1998, *CGPLA Eng. & Wales*

Balfour, Nisbet (1743–1823), army officer, was born at Dunbog, Fife, the son of Henry Balfour, laird of Dunbog, and his wife, Katherine Porterfield. He and his four brothers all entered the army, as had their father before them. The family expended much of its money on buying commissions; in February 1778 Nisbet explained that his progress in the service had caused him to go 'monstrously in debt' (Polwarth papers, Bedfordshire RO, L30/12/3). He became an ensign in the 4th or King's Own foot on 27 January 1761, and thereafter rose steadily within the regiment: when the American War of Independence began he was a captain, serving with his corps at Boston.

Balfour was wounded at the battle of Bunker Hill (17 June 1775) but recovered to take part in the fighting around New York in the summer and autumn of 1776. At the end of that campaign, promoted major in the army, he returned home with General Howe's dispatches. In January 1777, dining at Lord Grantham's, Balfour presented a distinctly pessimistic view of the course of the war across the Atlantic (Robinson papers, Bedfordshire RO, MS L29/214). He was sent back to America with instructions from the ministry to do all he could to encourage greater activity and less conciliation by the British commanders. His advice seems to have been ignored. Even so, early in 1778, despite the loss of Burgoyne's army at Saratoga the previous October, Balfour, newly promoted lieutenant-colonel of the Royal Welch Fusiliers, was confident that only a few more reinforcements were needed to extinguish the rebellion. He returned home again at the end of that year on sick leave, and took no further part in the war until he joined General Clinton's army before Charleston, South Carolina, in March 1780.

Balfour played a prominent role in the southern campaigns that followed. On the capture of Charleston in May, Clinton sailed back to New York and Earl Cornwallis took command of the British troops left to reclaim the rest of South Carolina. Balfour proved a loyal and conscientious subordinate to Cornwallis. He shared his chief's view that plunder had to be kept to a minimum if the local population was to be won over, and expressed sharp criticism of the ill conduct of some of the loyalists who had been armed by the British. His letters show a keen appreciation of the relationship between military operations and what he described as 'the fluctuating State of Politicks' in the southern states (Cornwallis papers, PRO, 30/11/109, fol. 49). Cornwallis clearly valued this awareness of the political dimension of the struggle, telling Balfour of his 'most implicit faith in your discretion & experience' (ibid., 30/11/78, fol. 3). Given his evident sensitivity to the problems encountered by the civilian population in a bitter internecine conflict, it was somewhat ironic that Balfour earned considerable notoriety when, as commandant of Charleston, he ordered the execution of a planter, Isaac Hayne, who had broken the terms of his parole and taken up arms again against the British.

After the war Balfour was promoted colonel and aide-de-camp to the king. In 1790, thanks to the influence of his brother-in-law, Robert Stewart of Castle Stewart in Wigtownshire, and on the interest of John Stewart, seventh earl of Galloway, Balfour became MP for Wigton Burghs, which he represented until 1796. From 1797 to 1802 he was MP for the scot and lot borough of Arundel, Sussex, after Sir George Thomas vacated the seat and offered the nomination to Pitt. He was a loyal supporter of Pitt's ministry. Meanwhile he had been promoted major-general on the outbreak of the war against revolutionary France (February 1793), and in 1794 he joined the duke of York's forces in Flanders. He never again saw active service, but became lieutenant-general in 1798 and general in 1803. He died, unmarried, at Dunbog on 10 October 1823.

H. M. Stephens, *rev.* Stephen Conway

Sources *DNB* • HoP, *Commons, 1790–1820* • Polwarth papers, Beds. & Luton ARS • Cornwallis papers, PRO • Robinson papers, Beds. & Luton ARS • L. Cong., manuscript division, various collections • I. D. Gruber, *The Howe brothers and the American Revolution* (1972) • P. Mackesy, *The war for America, 1775–83* (1993) • *Report on American manuscripts in the Royal Institution of Great Britain*, 4 vols., HMC, 59 (1904–9), vol. 2

Archives NAM, book of general orders issued at Colchester and Ipswich • PRO, corresp., dispatches, etc. while commanding at Charlestown, PRO 30/11 • PRO, corresp., PRO 30/55

Balfour, Robert (*b. c.*1555, *d.* in or after 1621), philosopher and classical scholar, was born at Tarrie in Forfarshire; that he matriculated at St Andrews University in 1571 suggests a date of birth about 1555. After graduating he taught at St Andrews, but subsequently travelled to France to continue his studies, as many Scots did in the sixteenth century. Having spent some time in Paris, where he may have taught as well as studied, he moved to Bordeaux, probably before 1580, to teach at that city's major educational institution, the Collège de Guyenne. He remained there for the rest of his life, initially holding the chair of philosophy and then one in mathematics, which had been specially endowed for him by the noted mathematician and student of hermeticism François Foix de la Candale. Balfour became principal of the Collège de Guyenne in 1602 and held this position until 1621. It is not known when he died.

As a teacher Balfour offered courses covering most of Aristotelian philosophy, as well as more general surveys of logic, ethics, and astronomy. His published commentaries on Aristotle's *Organon* (2 vols., 1618–20) and his edition of Cleomedes' astronomical treatise, *De motu circulari corporum caelestium* (1605), were undoubtedly derived from his teaching. His Aristotelian commentaries are notable for the rhetorical flair of their literary style and also for their energetic defence of moral philosophy as a guide to a useful and virtuous life. His edition of Cleomedes won the approval of Isaac Casaubon and Joseph Scaliger, and was so far respected by Cleomedes' next editor in 1820 that he reproduced its commentary. The prefaces to these works reveal Balfour's wide range of contacts among contemporary scholars in southern France, especially Toulouse, and his high standing in the Bordeaux community. They show vast erudition, as well as a strong conservatism, particularly in a predictable emphasis on Copernican cosmology as merely hypothetical. His Catholicism is also reflected in his edition of works by Gelasius and Theodoret relating to the early fourth-century Council of Nicaea (1599). Balfour was a minor figure, significant primarily as a representative of the long-standing cultural affinity between Scotland and France, one which persevered in spite of the divisions created by the Reformation. Within this tradition he managed to be an effective scholar, teacher, and university administrator.

Balfour's general course on philosophy, mathematics, and astronomy is preserved in manuscript as Bordeaux, Bibliothèque Municipale, MS 1558. There also survive letters which he wrote to Fédéric Morel, professor of Latin at the Collège Royal at Paris (Leiden, Bibliotheek der Rijksuniversiteit, MS 758 C 28). ROBERT B. TODD

Sources T. Dempster, *Historia ecclesiastica gentis Scotorum* (Bologna, 1627), 19 • D. Buchanan, *De scriptoribus Scotis libri duo*, ed. D. Irving, Bannatyne Club, 55 (1837), 129–30 • F. Michel, *Les écossais en France, les français en Écosse*, 2 vols. (1862), vol. 2, pp. 196–203 • E. Gaullieur, *Histoire du Collège de Guyenne* (1874), chap. 24 • A. I. Dunlop, ed., *Acta facultatis artium universitatis Sanctiandree, 1413–1588*, 1, Scottish History Society, 3rd ser., 54 (1964), 438, 441, 443 • R. B. Todd, 'Cleomedes', *Catalogus translationum et commentariorum*, 7 (1992), 1–11, esp. 9–11 • A. Broadie, 'Philosophy in Renaissance Scotland: loss and gain', *Humanism in Renaissance Scotland*, ed. J. MacQueen (1990), 75–96

Archives Bibliothèque Municipale, Bordeaux, MS 1558 • Bibliotheek der Rijksuniversiteit, Leiden, MS 758 C 28 • NL Scot., lectures on Aristotle

Balfour [*formerly* Arnot], **Robert, second Lord Balfour of Burleigh** (*d.* **1663**), politician, was the son of Sir Robert Arnot of Fernie (*d.* 1606), chamberlain of Fife, and his wife, Margaret Averie. In September 1606 he married Margaret (*d.* 1639), daughter of Michael Balfour, Lord Balfour of Burleigh, and Margaret, daughter of Lundie of Lundie. Apparently prior to the marriage he took his future father-in-law's surname and, in return for large sums paid over by the elder Robert Arnot, was made joint heir to Lord Balfour with Margaret. Balfour entered local affairs as a JP for Fife and Kinross in 1610 and on 8 July 1613 assumed his father's former position as chamberlain of Fife. He and his wife succeeded her father on 15 March 1619 and by a letter from James VI and I he became second Lord Balfour of Burleigh and as such sat in the parliaments of 1621, 1633, and 1639, and in the 1625 convention of estates. In 1627 he was appointed to the commission for surrenders and teinds, set up to implement Charles I's revocation scheme. He was also named to local government positions, to oversee the highways from Dunfermline to Falkland, and as a Fife member of commissions for warning beacons (1627) and to implement legislation against Jesuits and seminary priests (1629).

Although Burleigh lacked the obvious presbyterian-constitutionalist background of some Fife nobles, his allegiance to those causes quickly became apparent. At the Scottish parliament on 11 June 1640, in the absence of a royal commissioner, the estates appointed the radical Burleigh their president. He sat on the committee for provisioning the army (4 June 1640) and on the committee of estates. In the autumn of 1640 he was fitting out a regiment in Fife for Alexander Leslie's army in Newcastle. He served as a commissioner in London for the treaty of peace with England (1640–41) and in 1641 again held the office of president of parliament. The Scottish parliament appointed Burleigh *ad vitam aut culpam* to the privy council on 11 November 1641 and he was a constant member of the committee of estates from 1641 to 1647. He continued to support the covenanter military by serving on the committee for standing regiments (November 1641) and on the committees for levying and supplying the army raised for service in Ulster and for funding the army of the solemn league and covenant, raised for service in England (1643–4). On 28 February 1643 he lent £300 for provisioning the Ulster army. During the campaigns against Montrose he energetically supported the covenanter government. His military career, however, though enthusiastically embarked upon, met with signal failure. From April 1644 he was joint colonel of a regiment of Fife foot with his future son-in-law David Wemyss, Lord Elcho. The unit served in Argyll's spring campaign against the north-eastern royalists, and Burleigh took an active role in suppressing them. He served as president of the committee for the north from 16 April 1644. Following orders from the estates, he took command in Aberdeen after the covenanter defeat at Tippermuir. He addressed the inhabitants at Greyfriars Kirk on 26 August, appealing for men to defend the covenant, the Reformation, and their lives, women, children, and goods against the Irish and their highland allies. Montrose defeated him outside Aberdeen on 12 September 1644 when instead of using the burgh defences he marched his forces outside the burgh, then failed to exercise any control of his subordinates. After the battle he fled south. At Kilsyth, on 15 August 1645, he was one of the committee of estates who forced General William Baillie into a disastrous flank advance which resulted in Montrose's greatest victory. Burleigh's regiment ceased to exist some time after 30 January 1646.

As one of ten kirk party nobles, Burleigh unsuccessfully opposed the engagement to rescue the king from the English parliamentarians in 1648 and helped lead the Fife contingent in the Whiggamore raid that overthrew the engager regime in late September. In September and October 1648 he was an unofficial member of the committee of estates. In January 1649 Burleigh was one of only sixteen nobles present at parliament. The estates named him a colonel of foot for Fife, though he failed to act on the commission, and in the same year he became one of the commissioners of the treasury and exchequer. In 1650 he served as vice-president of parliament. On 28 June parliament appointed him to the committee set up to purge the army of former royalists and engagers, and on 3 July he received a commission as colonel of foot for the shires of Roxburgh, Selkirk, and Peebles. On 13 August he was one of the colonels who presented the anti-royalist West Kirk declaration to the committee of estates. Burleigh's radical sympathies led him to vote against condemning the western remonstrance (critical of Charles II and of alleged breaches of the covenants) in a meeting of the committee of estates in late November 1650. The only reference to activities of his last military command was an order of 24 December to garrison Lochleven Castle. On 31 March 1651 he began his final stint as president of parliament. He became protectorate JP for Fife in 1656. From August to

December 1660 he was the only radical noble who regularly attended the committee of estates meetings, and he remained active in politics, attending the 1661–3 parliaments despite the defeat of the covenanters at the Restoration.

Burleigh died at his home, Burleigh Castle, near Kinross, on 10 August 1663, and was buried at Orwell parish church on the 12th. His wife had died before him, at Edinburgh in June 1639, and was also buried at Orwell. They had one son, John *Balfour, third Lord Balfour of Burleigh, who married Isabel, daughter of Sir William Balfour of Pitcullo, lieutenant of the Tower, in 1649—which marriage his father tried to annul—and four daughters: Anna married David *Wemyss, second earl of Wemyss [*see under* Wemyss, David, fourth earl of Wemyss]; Margaret was the wife of Sir James Crawford of Kilbirnie; Isabel married Thomas Ruthven, first Lord Ruthven of Freeland; and Jean seems to have married a cousin, Arnot of Fernie.

EDWARD M. FURGOL

Sources *APS* • *Reg. PCS*, 1st ser. • *Reg. PCS*, 2nd ser. • *Scots peerage* • J. R. Young, *The Scottish parliament, 1639–1661: a political and constitutional analysis* (1996) • D. Stevenson, *Alasdair MacColla and the highland problem in the seventeenth century* (1980) • *The memoirs of Henry Guthry, late bishop*, ed. G. Crawford, 2nd edn (1748) • J. Spalding, *Memorialls of the trubles in Scotland and in England, AD 1624 – AD 1645*, ed. J. Stuart, 2 vols., Spalding Club, [21, 23] (1850–51) • R. Menteth, *The history of the troubles of Great Britain … 1630–1650*, trans. J. Ogilvie, 2nd edn (1738) • R. A. Bensen, 'South-west Fife and the Scottish revolution: the presbytery of Dunfermline, 1633–52', MLitt diss., U. Edin., 1978 • C. H. Firth, ed., *Scotland and the protectorate: letters and papers relating to the military government of Scotland from January 1654 to June 1659*, Scottish History Society, 31 (1899) • synod record of Fife, NA Scot., vol. 1 • presbytery record of Dunfermline, NA Scot., vol. 1

Archives NA Scot., Parliamentary Affairs MSS

Balfour, Robert, fifth Lord Balfour of Burleigh (*d.* **1757**), murderer and Jacobite sympathizer, was the son of Robert Balfour, fourth Lord Balfour of Burleigh (*d.* 1713), and Lady Margaret Melville, daughter of the first Earl Melville. Robert's attraction to a young woman of lesser social rank prompted his parents to send him on the grand tour in the hopes of breaking their attachment. Before leaving, however, Robert threatened the young woman that if she married in his absence, he would return and kill her husband. During his tour she married Henry Stenhouse, the schoolmaster at Inverkeithing, after acquainting him with the threat. Balfour returned in 1707, immediately enquiring after his lady-love. On 9 April 1707, at the news of her marriage, he and two attendants rode directly to the schoolhouse at Inverkeithing, where he called Stenhouse out and wounded him in the shoulder. Balfour returned quietly to the family home at Burleigh. On 21 April the schoolmaster died from his wound. Balfour was arrested, tried for murder before the high court of the judiciary in August 1709, and found guilty. Under sentence of death by beheading, Balfour escaped from prison ('the heart of Midlothian') by exchanging clothes with his sister, to whom he bore a strong resemblance. He lay low on family lands around Burleigh, perhaps hiding for a period in a large hollow ash tree associated with him in local legend.

Balfour became the fifth Lord Balfour of Burleigh on his father's death in 1713. He resurfaced in May 1714, drinking to the health of the Pretender (James Stuart) at a meeting of Jacobites at Lochmaben, and damning all those who would not participate. For his participation in the 1715 rising, he was attainted by act of parliament and his estates forfeited to the crown. When he died, without issue, in 1757, his claims passed to his sisters, Mary and Margaret, one of whose descendants, Alexander Bruce, succeeded in reversing the act of attainder in 1868.

MARGARET D. SANKEY

Sources W. Anderson, *The Scottish nation*, facs. edn (Bowie, MD, 1995) • *Debrett's Peerage* (1985) • P. Rae, *The history of the late rebellion* (1718) • C. K. Sharpe, *Criminal trials, illustrative of the tale entitled 'The heart of Mid-Lothian'* (1818)

Balfour, Robert Arthur, second Baron Riverdale (**1901–1998**). *See under* Balfour, Arthur, first Baron Riverdale (1873–1957).

Balfour, Thomas Graham (1813–1891), physician, the son of John Balfour, a merchant of Leith, and his wife, Helen, daughter of Thomas Buchanan of Ardoch, was born in Edinburgh on 18 March 1813. He was great-grandson of James Balfour, professor of moral philosophy at Edinburgh, and of Robert Whytt, physician. He graduated MD at Edinburgh in 1834, and in 1836 entered the Army Medical Service.

Soon after joining the service Balfour began work on the first four volumes of the *Statistics of the British Army*. From 1840 to 1848 he served as assistant surgeon in the Grenadier Guards. In 1848 he became surgeon to the Duke of York's Asylum for Soldiers' Orphans at Chelsea. In 1856 he married Georgina, daughter of George Prentice of Armagh; they had one son, Graham *Balfour (1858–1929), author and educationist. In 1857 he was appointed secretary to Sidney Herbert's committee on the sanitary state of the army, and in 1859 he became deputy inspector-general in charge of the new statistical branch of the army medical department. He was elected FRS on 3 June 1858 and in 1860 became a fellow of the Royal College of Physicians of London. Promoted to surgeon-general in 1873, he became principal medical officer at Netley and later at Gibraltar.

In 1876 Balfour was placed on half pay as surgeon-general. He was appointed honorary physician to the queen in 1887, and in the following year he became president of the Royal Statistical Society. Balfour died at his home, Coombe Lodge, Inner Park Road, Wimbledon Park, Surrey, on 17 January 1891.

Balfour is best-known for his reorganization of army medical statistics between 1857 and 1860 while serving in the new statistical branch of the Army Medical Service. His efforts yielded the *Statistical Report on the Health of the Army*, which he presented to parliament in 1860. A. R. Skelley considers this report to have contained such 'accurate and complete' medical statistics about the army that 'they became the most reliable of any army's in Europe' (Skelley, 44). Balfour's work in this area of military medical statistics also contributed to 'the realisation that the ill-health of the British people was mirrored in the physical condition of army recruits' (ibid.). Ultimately Skelley suggests that although Balfour is not as well known as Florence Nightingale and Sidney Herbert, he deserves consideration as an influential reformer of military medicine who showed contemporaries how this field could affect matters of public health.

NORMAN MOORE, *rev.* JEFFREY S. REZNICK

Sources A. R. Skelley, *The Victorian army at home: the recruitment and terms and conditions of the British regular, 1859–1899* (1977) • *Journal of the Royal Statistical Society*, 54 (1891), 575–6 • personal knowledge (1901) • *CGPLA Eng. & Wales* (1891)

Archives BL, corresp., Add. MS 50134 | BL, corresp. with Florence Nightingale, Add. MS 45772

Likenesses W. Strang, etching, *c.*1870–1879, NPG, Wellcome L.; repro. in R. Burgess, *Portraits of doctors and scientists in the Wellcome Institute, London* (1973) • D. Strang, etching (after W. Strang), NPG

Wealth at death £14,660 15*s.* in UK: probate, 11 Feb 1891, *CGPLA Eng. & Wales*

Balfour, Sir William (*d.* 1660), parliamentarian army officer, was the son of Colonel Henry Balfour (*d.* 1580), a member of the Balfour family of Pitcullo, Fife, and his wife, Christian Cant.

William Balfour followed his father's example by serving the Dutch in the Scottish brigade. By 19 February 1594 he had risen to lieutenant, and he was then advanced to the captaincy of Colonel Bartolt Balfour's company of 150 heavy infantry. Balfour seems to have returned to Britain at some point. On 15 April 1605 James VI and I supported a petition of Balfour's to the Dutch estates for a debt due to his father, describing him as 'notre serviteur domesticque' ('our household servant'); Balfour had by that point also acquired a knighthood. From March to November 1605 he served as a captain in Scott of Buccleuch's regiment in the Netherlands. In 1608 he petitioned the estates again for money owed to his father and Captain David Cant, his uncle, but he met with no success. He served as sergeant-major of the Scots regiment on the Juliers campaign in 1610. Between 1613 and 1615, with the assistance of King James, the elector palatine, and the Dutch ambassador to Britain, Balfour managed to secure the payment of 2000 guilders in cash and 600 guilders per annum for his father's, his uncle's, and his own arrears. Balfour served as a captain of horse arquebusiers from 1615 or 1616 to 1624. In April 1621, as a cavalry captain in Nijmegen, he petitioned for eleven months' pay incurred between November 1618 and September 1619, while his petition noted that he had been absent once on business in England. In 1622 the Spanish captured him at Emmerich.

In 1625 Charles I requested that the estates lend him Balfour to command a company of Carabiniers, but the Dutch refused. Two years later, on 18 August 1627, the king approved Balfour as the earl of Morton's choice as his lieutenant-colonel, and again wrote to the Dutch for his services. This time he was released and served on the Île de Ré expedition under the duke of Buckingham. In January 1628 he and Colonel John Dalbier received orders to raise 1000 horse from Friesland. However, the estates refused permission for levying in the United Provinces because of their own needs in the war with Spain. Balfour and Dalbier moved their efforts to Emden in north Germany. Buckingham's death in July led to the refusal of bills of exchange for the regiment; thus the English could not support the 1000-man regiment. The Dutch had no desire for the unit, but agreed to pay for its quartering before it disbanded. Meanwhile Balfour had resigned his commission with his long-time employers, who reluctantly released him with a gold chain worth 1000 guilders and the promise to keep him in mind for future services.

Balfour's first wife, Helen, daughter of Sir Archibald *Napier of Merchiston, died in December 1629, and at some later point he married a woman named Isabella (*d.* 1661). Balfour's concentration on serving Charles I in England during the personal rule proved to his advantage. The king appointed him a gentleman of the privy chamber, and he succeeded Sir Allen Apsley as lieutenant of the Tower of London on 18 October 1630 following the latter's death. In July 1631 the crown paid him for his recruiting efforts of three years earlier. From 24 September to 9 November Balfour went on a secret mission for the king observing French activities near Dunkirk. Balfour continued as a dedicated servant of the crown for some years. In 1633 with Sir William Parkhurst and Andrew Palmer he received a grant to make gold and silver money in the Tower for eleven years. That December the privy council named him one of the commissioners to investigate the complaints of the opponents of the soap monopoly. In January 1635 he was named to the commission examining the conduct of the keeper of the Fleet prison. In the following year he assisted with plague control in London and as a surveyor of the armoury's swords (which dragged on until 1641). His role as a royal jailer involved him in the seizure of the papers of William Prynne and with conducting Bishop John Williams of Lincoln to Lambeth in 1637. His support for the crown continued with appointments to the council of war in June 1638 and to boards investigating illegal duties charged in Bristol and the fortification of the Isles of Scilly. In May 1640 he mobilized the London militia and reinforced the Tower garrison with some of them.

The king's defeat in the second bishops' war seems to have wrought a change in Balfour's attitude. The arch-Scotophobe Clarendon later wrote,

> from the beginning of [the Long] Parliament (according to the natural custom of his country), [he] forgot all his obligations to the King, and made himself very gracious to those people whose glory it was to be thought enemies to the Court. (Clarendon, *Hist. rebellion*, 1.477)

Religious motivation, his presbyterianism, and anti-Catholicism probably played the largest part in his volte-face (in 1638 he struck a priest 'two or three sound Blows with his Battoon' who was trying to convert his wife; Radcliffe, 2.166). But latent Scottish nationalism may also have had something to do with his change. Balfour served as the earl of Strafford's gaoler and sat beside him daily during his trial in the spring of 1641. He refused entry to Captain Billingsley's band of would-be rescuers of the condemned earl on 2 May and a few days later he spurned Strafford's offer of £20,000 and a good match for his son for allowing him to escape. It was reported that Balfour voluntarily resigned the lieutenancy of the Tower on 22 December 1641 but it is likelier, given the king's confrontational attitude in the winter of 1641–2, that his parting was forced; his departure from a post so vital to the security of the capital alarmed both the House of Commons and inhabitants of London.

Balfour's departure from a position of public trust proved only temporary. In the spring of 1642 he was given command of a horse regiment destined for service in Ulster, a command which would have combined religious commitment and self-interest (one newsbook indeed suggested that he had resigned the lieutenancy so that he could go to protect his estates there against the Catholic rebels). However, the war in England intervened and the parliament rapidly secured the sexagenarian Balfour's services. On 7 August 1642 he was appointed lieutenant general of horse under the command of the earl of Bedford. In September he won a skirmish on the Severn. At Edgehill he commanded the reserve and performed a brilliant role in preventing a parliamentarian collapse. At the head of his and Stapleton's horse regiments he charged and broke Sir Nicholas Byron's foot brigade. Turning on Colonel Richard Fielding's foot brigade Balfour's command routed it. The cavalrymen then charged the royalist artillery, driving the gunners away and capturing some guns. However, Balfour lacked the equipment to spike the guns, so he had his men merely cut the guns' ropes. Before withdrawing Balfour attacked the guard protecting princes Charles and James.

In 1643 he missed the first battle of Newbury, having gone abroad to take the waters. In March 1644 Essex detached him to Sir William Waller's army with four regiments of horse and a regiment of dragoons (1500–2000 men). At the battle of Cheriton on 29 March Balfour assisted Waller in defeating Sir Ralph Hopton's royalist army. In the pursuit on 30 March he captured Elizabeth, Lady Hopton, and 200 royalists. Afterwards he rejoined Essex and marched with him into Cornwall, having taken Weymouth and Taunton in June 1644. When Essex's army was surrounded Balfour managed to break out with the cavalry. He linked up with Lieutenant-General John Middleton, commander of Waller's horse. At the second battle of Newbury he commanded the right wing of the parliamentarian horse. On 28 October Sir Archibald Johnston and John Crew MP reported that 'Sir W. Balfour used great diligence' in the battle (*CSP dom.*, *1644–5*, 76).

Essex reported Balfour ill on 7 November and requested a replacement. On 21 January 1645 the House of Commons ordered that Balfour receive 'fit recompense and acknowledgement of the faithful services done by him to the public' as he left the army owing to the self-denying ordinance (which forced foreigners to resign) (*JHC*, 4.26). Six days later the earl of Leven received orders to give Balfour's ten troops of horse who were serving in Ulster to the command of Lieutenant-Colonel George Munro. In mid-February Balfour undertook his last public service for parliament when he subdued a mutiny of three cavalry regiments (including his own) at Beaconsfield, Buckinghamshire. Suspicions about Balfour's loyalty to the English parliament arising from intercepted correspondence delayed the settlement of his arrears: the £1677 awarded him in November 1646 went unpaid until late 1655. On 3 July 1650, as Cromwell's invasion of Scotland loomed, the Scottish parliament put Balfour in command of 'strangers or native volunteiris' (*APS*, 6, part 2.600). Although he does not seem to have acted on the commission his allegiance was with the Scots. In April 1651 his wife was given four weeks to leave England. Balfour lived in obscurity in Westminster in the 1650s, and died there, having made his will on 16 July 1660; he was buried twelve days later in St Margaret's, Westminster.

Two of Balfour's sons had, like their father and grandfather, served in the Dutch army; both had been killed in the civil wars, one in Somerset and one in Ireland, so that only one son, Charles, outlived Balfour. Charles was eventually succeeded by his son, Charles William (*d.* 1739). Sir William had four daughters. Isabel (or Isabella) married John *Balfour, master of Burleigh (later third Lord Balfour of Burleigh), in London in 1649, a marriage which the young man's father tried to get annulled. Emilia (*d.* 1683) married Alexander *Stewart, fifth earl of Moray, in or before 1658. Susanna (or Susan) married Hugh *Hamilton of Ballygally, co. Tyrone, Baron de Deserf in the nobility of Sweden and first Lord Hamilton of Glenawly in the peerage of Ireland; after his death she married Henry Mervyn of Trillick, co. Tyrone. Balfour's fourth daughter, Lucy, married Blayney Townley, another Irish settler. Their son Harry became the heir of Charles William Balfour and founded the family of Balfour of Townley Hall, co. Louth.

EDWARD M. FURGOL

Sources J. Ferguson, ed., *Papers illustrating the history of the Scots brigade in the service of the United Netherlands, 1572–1782*, 1, Scottish History Society, 32 (1899) · *CSP dom.*, *1625–60* · GEC, *Peerage* · *Scots peerage*, 6.415–17 · *JHC*, 2–5 (1640–48) · *JHL*, 4–9 (1628–47) · Clarendon, *Hist. rebellion* · *APS*, *1648–60* · P. Young, *Edgehill, 1642* (1967) · J. Adair, *Cheriton, 1644* (1973) · *The letters and journals of Robert Baillie*, ed. D. Laing, 3 vols., Bannatyne Club, 73 (1841–2) · *Corrections and additions to the Dictionary of National Biography*, Institute of Historical Research (1966) · *DNB* · will, PRO, PROB 11/303, sig. 1 · G. Radcliffe, *The earl of Strafforde's letters and dispatches, with an essay towards his life*, ed. W. Knowler, 2 vols. (1739) · J. Spalding, *Memorialls of the trubles in Scotland and in England, AD 1624 – AD 1645*, ed. J. Stuart, 2 vols., Spalding Club, [21, 23] (1850–51) · *The diary of Mr John Lamont of Newton, 1649–1671*, ed. G. R. Kinloch, Maitland Club, 7 (1830)

Likenesses engraving, repro. in J. Ricraft, *A survey of Englands champions* (1647) · two line engravings, NPG

Wealth at death see will, PRO, PROB 11/303, sig. 1

Balfour, William (1784–1838), army officer, was born at Edinburgh on 16 July 1784. He was appointed ensign in the Hon. George Hanger's recruiting corps on 31 August 1798, and joined the 40th regiment on 25 July 1799, being promoted lieutenant on 8 August 1799. He served at The Helder, where he was commended by Sir John Moore. He served on the staff of Major-General Sir Brent Spencer in the Mediterranean, and was promoted captain on 22 September 1802. He was present at the capture of Copenhagen, where a horse was shot under him, and became a regimental major on 4 February 1808. He received a brevet lieutenant-colonelcy for service in the field with the 40th in the Peninsula and the south of France in 1813–14, having been present at the battles of Nivelle, Nive, Orthez, and Toulouse. He received the gold medal in command of his regiment at Nivelle. In 1810, at Dublin, he had married Charlotte Stanley Clarke, who died on 22 August 1825 at Launceston, Van Diemen's Land; they had five sons and three daughters.

After a few years on half pay Balfour became lieutenant-colonel of his former regiment, commanding it for several years in New South Wales, and he was afterwards in command of the 82nd foot in Mauritius. He retired from the army in 1832, having 'suffered much from bad health, the effect of a residence in a tropical climate' (*GM*, 661), and died in London on 10 February 1838.

H. M. CHICHESTER, *rev.* JAMES LUNT

Sources *Army List* • *GM*, 2nd ser., 9 (1838), 661 • PRO, Returns of officers, War Office, W.O. 25/801 • R. H. R. Smythies, *Historical records of the 40th (2nd Somersetshire) Regiment* (1894) • W. F. P. Napier, *History of the war in the Peninsula and in the south of France*, 3 vols. (1882)

Balgarnie, Florence (1856–1928), feminist and temperance campaigner, was born at 2 Belle Vue Terrace, Scarborough, Yorkshire, on 19 August 1856, the eldest of three daughters of the Revd Robert Balgarnie (1826–1899) and his wife, Martha Rooke. Her father, minister of the South Cliff Congregational Church in Scarborough, came from a Scottish background, arriving in Scarborough from Newbattle, Dalkeith. He was a well-known reformer, who wrote and spoke in favour of temperance and other causes. His wife was of Irish descent.

Florence Balgarnie was educated in England and Germany. She devoted most of her life to public affairs, never marrying. Until she was nearly thirty she resided in Scarborough, where she was an active Liberal and was elected in 1883 for a three-year term to the Scarborough school board. In Scarborough she was also a founder and secretary of the town's branch of the university extension scheme. An active feminist, in the early 1880s Balgarnie toured the northern cities speaking at meetings organized by the National Society for Women's Suffrage in favour of voting rights for women. She was also an ardent supporter of the anti-Contagious Diseases Acts movement.

In 1885 Balgarnie moved to 29 Parliament Street, London, and joined the newly founded Men and Women's Club, organized to bring together men and women to discuss social, political, and economic relationships between the sexes; in October 1888 she read a paper to the club on women's emancipation. In 1885 she also became secretary of the central committee of the National Society for Women's Suffrage, a position she held in this and its successor society (the Central National Society for Women's Suffrage) for a number of years. She resigned from her position in 1888 over the issue of married women and the franchise, but was persuaded by the committee to rescind her resignation. Florence Balgarnie held that all women, married and single, should get the vote on the same basis as men, and opposed the acceptance of any halfway measures such as the extension of the franchise to single women householders.

An active Liberal all her adult life, Balgarnie was an early member of the Women's Liberal Federation, serving on its executive committee in the 1890s and also on the federation's temperance committee. She was a leader in the federation's 'progressive party', a name given to members who successfully fought to have the Women's Liberal Federation adopt women's suffrage as part of the Liberal Association's official programme. She was also a leader in another successful fight to get the association to refuse its help for parliamentary candidates who would not support women's suffrage in the House of Commons. In the 1889 London county council elections she spoke and worked on behalf of the successful candidacies of Jane Cobden and Margaret, Lady Sandhurst. Florence Balgarnie lectured on women's suffrage to Liberal Association meetings throughout the country and also to groups abroad. True to her background in Scarborough Liberal circles, she was an outspoken supporter of the provincial associations, working to give them a greater voice in federation decisions. In the 1892 annual meeting of the Women's Liberal Federation she spoke in favour of holding future annual meetings in towns outside the capital.

Temperance was another reform which Florence Balgarnie actively promoted. She was a founding member of the British Women's Temperance Association, and played a prominent role in its work. She supported moral suasion methods to fight drunkenness but, not a fanatic, she eschewed extreme suppressive anti-drink measures. In keeping with her own personal views on women's role in public life, she became a leading supporter of president Lady Henry Somerset in her fight to adopt the feminist 'do everything' policy for the association in the early 1890s. At the bitter discordant annual meeting of the association in 1893, Florence Balgarnie publicly identified herself with the president. After winning the fight and reorganizing the association, Lady Henry Somerset rewarded her supporter by appointing her to the association's executive committee and making her head of a newly created department of politics and women's suffrage within the association.

Along with her commitment to women's suffrage, Florence Balgarnie was a great believer in the necessity of economic independence for women and she fought continuously for the betterment of working women. She was a founder of the Women's Trade Union Association, and between 1885 and 1888 she worked with Lady Aberdeen in a successful campaign to get the Home Office to appoint women inspectors of factories. She and her supporters were later victorious in their campaign for the appointment of matrons for police stations. Although not a prolific writer, she produced two pamphlets; the first, *A Plea for the Appointment of Police Matrons at Police Stations*, was published by the British Women's Temperance Association in 1894, and in 1899, with Louisa Twining, she wrote *Police Matrons* to raise awareness of the need for matrons in police courts and stations. At the 1891 annual meeting of the Women's Liberal Federation she proposed a resolution, passed unanimously, which called for the removal of customary and legal obstructions preventing women from working in the trades and professions. It also advanced the principle of equal pay for equal work. Florence Balgarnie was also the secretary of the London-based Anti-Lynching League, founded in 1894 after a visit to England by Ida Wells, an African American.

Balgarnie was regarded as one of the finest women speakers of her period. She made a number of international speaking tours, lecturing in India and the United States and speaking for temperance in New Zealand. Besides speaking on reform topics, she frequently celebrated the lives of notable women in history: Joan of Arc was one of her favourites, and she was also known for her public lectures on her fellow Yorkshirewoman Charlotte Brontë. In 1911 Balgarnie and some of the older women Liberal speakers supported the foundation of the Liberal Women's Speakers Club and taught classes in public speaking intended to train the younger members of the Women's Liberal Federation. Florence Balgarnie died at the Pensione Gozolli, 9 Piazza Indipendenza, in Florence on 25 March 1928, while on a tour of Italy, a country which she loved. She was buried in that city.

LILIAN LEWIS SHIMAN

Sources *Women's Penny Paper* (16 March 1889) • *Manchester Guardian* (30 March 1928) • *Manchester Guardian* (31 March 1928) • *Scarborough Evening News* (27 March 1928) • *Daily Post* (27 March 1928) • E. McLaren, *The history of the women's suffrage movement in the Women's Liberal Federation*, 2nd edn (1903) • L. Bland, *Banishing the beast: English feminism and sexual morality, 1885–1914* (1995) • review of Balgarnie's *A plea for the appointment of police matrons*, *Englishwoman's Review*, 25 (1894), 199 • *Englishwoman's Review*, 30 (1899), 71–3 • b. cert. • *CGPLA Eng. & Wales* (1928)

Likenesses engraving, *c*.1889, repro. in *Women's Penny Paper*

Wealth at death £8172 9*s*. 2*d*.: resworn probate, 15 June 1928, *CGPLA Eng. & Wales*

Balguy, Charles (1708–1767), physician, son of Henry Balguy of Newbold, Derbyshire, was born at Derwent Hall, Derbyshire, and was educated at Chesterfield grammar school and St John's College, Cambridge. He took the degree of MB in 1731 and MD in 1750. He practised in Peterborough, and was secretary of the literary club there. He contributed to the *Philosophical Transactions*, and in 1741 he published, anonymously, a translation of Boccaccio's *Decameron*. This was reprinted several times. He wrote some medical essays and particularly a treatise on the 'sweating sickness', entitled *De morbo miliari* (1758). He died at Peterborough on 28 February 1767 and was buried in the chancel of St John's Church, where there is a marble monument to his memory bearing the inscription 'a man of various and great learning'.

S. O. ADDY, *rev.* CLAIRE L. NUTT

Sources S. O. Addy, 'Charles Balguy', *Journal of the Derbyshire Archaeological and Natural History Society*, 6 (1884), 11 • Nichols, *Lit. anecdotes*, 6.4, 74 • Venn, *Alum. Cant.*

Likenesses marble effigy on a monument, St John's Church, Peterborough

Balguy, John (1686–1748), Church of England clergyman and moral philosopher, was born on 12 August 1686 at Sheffield, son of Thomas Balguy (*c*.1643–1696), master of the Sheffield Free School for over 30 years, and his wife, Sara Hathornwhite, whom he had married on 8 June 1682. He studied under his father, his father's successor (Charles Daubuz), and Mr Drake (probably a relation), and on 3 February 1702 he was admitted as sizar to St John's College, Cambridge, his father's old college, where his tutors were William Edmondson and Robert Lambert, who later became the master. Balguy confessed to wasting two years at Cambridge reading romances, but after encountering Livy he turned to more serious work. He graduated BA in 1706 and proceeded MA in 1726. After leaving Cambridge he taught for a while at his old school, and then in 1708 became private tutor to Joseph Banks, son of Mr Banks of Scofton, Nottinghamshire, and grandfather of Sir Joseph Banks the naturalist. In 1710 he was ordained deacon and in 1711 priest by John Sharp, archbishop of York; he then entered the family of Sir Henry Liddel, of Ravensworth Castle, co. Durham, who presented him to the livings of Lamesley and Tanfield. He married Sarah Broomhead (*bap.* 1686), daughter of Christopher and Sarah Broomhead of Sheffield, on 6 June 1715, and left Sir Henry's house for one nearby called Cox Close, Lamesley. They had one son, Thomas *Balguy (1716–1795), whose contribution to the *Biographia Britannica* provides the principal source of detailed information about his father's life.

For the first four years of his clerical career Balguy wrote a new sermon every week; he destroyed most of them (on one occasion burning 250) in order to encourage his son to follow his industrious example. His first publications were contributions to the Bangorian controversy: under the name of Sylvius he published three defences of Hoadly against Stebbing and Sherlock (1718–20). Sherlock, despite being severely treated by Balguy on this occasion, recommended him to Queen Caroline for promotion and was a great admirer of his later work. Hoadly persuaded Balguy to suppress another reply to Stebbing on the grounds that the booksellers and the public were losing interest in the controversy. He also persuaded him not to print a letter to Samuel Clarke, whom Balguy greatly admired: Hoadly and Clarke were both afraid of anything being published that would prejudice Clarke's interest, though the subject of the letter was not the Trinity but purely philosophical matters.

Balguy's most important publications in the fields of theology and moral philosophy were contributions to the deist controversy and the debate about the foundation of morals. He attacked Shaftesbury's *Inquiry Concerning Virtue*, despite his considerable admiration for the work, because of its dismissal of future rewards and punishments: 'to prescribe and preach up Virtue without a Future State, appears to me no otherwise than as a Sort of

Religious Knight-Errantry' (J. Balguy, *A Letter to a Deist, Concerning the Beauty and Excellency of Moral Virtue*, 1726, 15). He was always a strong supporter of Clarke, and in *A Second Letter to a Deist, concerning a Late Book Entitled, 'Christianity as Old as the Creation'* (1731) he took exception to what he saw as Tindal's gross misunderstanding of Clarke's supposed inconsistencies. In two important analyses of Hutcheson's moral sense theory, *The Foundation of Moral Goodness* (1728) and *The Second Part of the Foundation of Moral Goodness* (1729), the latter in the form of answers to a friend (Lord Darcy) who had defended Hutcheson, Balguy explored very effectively the problems of founding morality on instinct instead of reason: 'In short, acting according to *Instinct*, may be looked upon as the Infant State of *Virtue*; but acting according to *Reason*, its Maturity and Perfection' (p. 82). Balguy was described by Thomas Rutherforth, who disagreed with him, as 'the most candid, the clearest, and most judicious writer, that ever undertook the defence of this scheme of morality' (T. Rutherforth, *An Essay on the Nature and Obligations of Virtue*, 1744, 130), and he was cited approvingly by Richard Price, who used many of the same arguments in *A Review of the Principal Questions in Morals*.

Balguy's theological writings included *Divine Rectitude* (1730), in which he argued that the Deity's first spring of action was rectitude (his respondents, Bayes and Grove, thought it benevolence and wisdom respectively), and its sequel, *An Essay on Redemption* (1741), in which he explained the doctrine of the atonement in a manner similar to that later employed by John Taylor of Norwich. He published his chief works as *A Collection of Tracts Moral and Theological* (1734), with a long dedication to his patron, Hoadly; in addition there were three collections of sermons, two of them posthumous, the fullest being that published in two volumes by his son in 1790.

On 25 January 1728 Balguy was collated by Hoadly to a prebend in Salisbury, and through the friendship of Bishop Talbot obtained from the chapter of Durham (12 August 1729) the vicarage of Northallerton in Yorkshire, worth £270 per annum. He probably got to know Talbot through Rundle (later bishop of Derry), and he was acquainted with the future bishops Benson, Secker, and Butler. He had many friends among Presbyterians and Quakers, especially Lord Barrington and Philip Glover, and maintained a philosophical correspondence with the latter. He remained vicar of Northallerton until his death. His son writes that his remaining in this position was his own fault for neglecting ways of recommending himself to his superiors, adding that he declined many invitations from Blackburne (archbishop of York) and Chandler (bishop of Durham). He became an invalid and withdrew from company except at Harrogate, which he frequented every season, and where he died on 21 September 1748.

Isabel Rivers

Sources A. Kippis and others, eds., *Biographia Britannica, or, The lives of the most eminent persons who have flourished in Great Britain and Ireland*, 2nd edn, 1 (1778), 548–52 [information provided by John Balguy's son, Thomas] · J. E. B. Mayor, ed., *Admissions to the College of St John the Evangelist in the University of Cambridge*, pts 1–2: *Jan 1629/30 – July 1715* (1882–93), 160–61 · Nichols, *Lit. anecdotes*, 1.157; 3.138–9, 220n.; 8.157n. · H. D. Jones, *John Balguy: an English moralist of the 18th century* (1907) · *DNB* · *IGI*

Archives Yale U., Beinecke L., letters to his son Thomas

Balguy, Thomas (1716–1795), Church of England clergyman, was born on 27 September 1716 at Cox Close, Lamesley, co. Durham, the only child of John *Balguy (1686–1748), Church of England clergyman and moral philosopher, and his wife, Sarah Broomhead (*bap.* 1686). He was educated at the free school, Ripon, Yorkshire, under Mr Stephens, and on 28 May 1734 was admitted as pensioner to St John's College, Cambridge. He graduated BA in 1738, proceeded MA in 1741, and on 17 March 1741 was elected to a Platt Fellowship, which he held until 1748. He was ordained deacon (21 September 1740) and priest (21 December) by the bishop of Lincoln, and on 9 April 1741 he was collated rector of North Stoke, Lincolnshire, by Potter, archbishop of Canterbury, his father's right of presentation having lapsed. He was instituted rector of Hagworthingham, Lincolnshire, on 26 July 1746, having resigned North Stoke; he petitioned the archbishop of Canterbury and received dispensation on 21 November 1746 to hold the two livings together (worth respectively £95 and £55), and was reinstituted to North Stoke (once more in the gift of his father) on 16 December 1746.

From the early 1740s to 1760 Balguy was active in Cambridge. In 1744 he became assistant tutor to his friend William Samuel Powell (afterwards master of St John's), who had just been promoted principal tutor, and for 16 years he read lectures in moral philosophy and the evidences of natural and revealed religion in St John's. In 1743 he was deputy public orator under James Tunstall, who was acting as chaplain to Potter at Lambeth. In 1758 he took the degree of BD. His closest friends in Cambridge were Powell and Richard Hurd. When Powell died in 1775 Balguy edited his *Discourses on Various Subjects* (1776), with a brief life of Powell, and it was thought that he had a chance of succeeding him as master. His friendship with Hurd can be traced through Hurd's letters to him over a period of almost 50 years. Other members of his Cambridge circle were Thomas Gray and William Mason; Gray refers affectionately to Mason's former tutor as 'your Uncle Balguy' (*Works*, 2.574). Hurd introduced Balguy to Warburton, who valued his friendship and welcomed his criticisms: the long appendix added to volume 2 of the *Divine Legation* is indebted to some of Balguy's remarks. Samuel Parr regretted that Balguy did not write Warburton's biography.

Balguy said he owed all his clerical preferments to the favour and friendship of Bishop Hoadly, also his father's patron. He was for a time Hoadly's chaplain. In 1748 he was collated (31 May) and installed (16 July) to a prebend in Lincoln Cathedral; on 1 November 1757 he was collated to a prebend in Winchester Cathedral; and on 23 July 1759 Hoadly appointed him archdeacon of Winchester. In 1760 he gave up his connection with St John's and moved to Winchester, his cousin Sarah Drake joining him to keep house. On 19 September 1771 he was instituted vicar of Alton, Hampshire, on the presentation of the dean and chapter of Winchester, whereupon he ceded his two benefices in Lincolnshire; he held the vicarage of Alton, the archdeaconry of Winchester, and the two prebends until his death.

Balguy was greatly esteemed by churchmen like Warburton and Hurd, who were anxious to defend the established church from the attacks of dissenters, modernizers, and sceptics. He published little, but he kept these enemies firmly in view. He took a very conservative view of the need for subscription to the Thirty-Nine Articles, claiming in a sermon 'On church authority', preached at the consecration of Bishop Shipley of Llandaff and published by order of the archbishop of Canterbury (1769), that 'A religion founded on Reason willingly submits to human authority in all points not essential to the cause of Piety and Virtue' (T. Balguy, *Discourses*, 1.94). This was answered by Priestley in *Considerations on Church-Authority* (1769). Another sermon on the same subject, preached at the consecration of bishops Hurd of Lichfield and John Moore of Bangor and similarly published by order, was answered by John Disney in *Remarks on Dr Balguy's Sermon* (1775); Disney took particular exception to Balguy's argument that subjection to authority is the invariable duty of a Christian. On the publication of Hume's *Dialogues Concerning Natural Religion* (1779) Hurd set about persuading Balguy to 'obviate' Hume's 'destructive impiety' (Kilvert, 135–7). Balguy had long been interested in the subject of Hume's attack; as an undergraduate he published a Latin poem entitled 'Divina bonitas demonstrari potest a posteriori' ('The divine goodness is capable of proof from its effects'; see *GM*, 94/2, 1824, 596–8). In response to Hurd's urging he published *Divine Benevolence Asserted; and Vindicated from the Objections of Ancient and Modern Sceptics* (1781). Hume's name is not mentioned, but the context can readily be inferred: in the preface Balguy describes it as a specimen of a larger work on natural religion, 'why published at this time, will be too easily conjectured' (Balguy, *Divine Benevolence Asserted*, iii). It is interesting as an illustration of what he was lecturing on at St John's in the 1740s and 1750s (his arguments are mainly drawn from Cicero and Butler), but disappointing as an answer to Hume. An oddity of the work is his enthusiasm for Hutcheson, his father's *bête noire*. He never completed it.

At one stage Balguy must have been ambitious for high office: Gray refers to him in a doggerel poem to Mason as '*Balguy* with a Bishop in his belly!' (*Works*, 3.993). In 1781 George III, who thought him 'the first Man in point of reputation in the Republic of Letters of either University' (*Letters*, ed. Hurd, xxiii), offered him the see of Gloucester, but he refused on the grounds of ill health. In 1785 he published his *Discourses on Various Subjects* with a dedication to the king; they were reissued in 1822 with a second volume of unpublished manuscripts by his relation James Drake. Balguy died on 19 January 1795 at Winchester, and on 26 January was buried in the cathedral, where a tablet commemorates him as 'a strenuous and able defender of the Christian Religion and of the Church of England'.

ISABEL RIVERS

Sources R. F. Scott, ed., *Admissions to the College of St John the Evangelist in the University of Cambridge*, 3: *July 1715 – November 1767* (1903), 76, 451–2 · *The early letters of Bishop Richard Hurd, 1739–1762*, ed. S. Brewer (1995) [incl. biography of Balguy] · F. Kilvert, *Memoirs of the life and writings of the Right Rev. Richard Hurd* (1860) · T. Balguy, *Discourses on various subjects*, ed. J. Drake, 2 vols. (1822) · Nichols, *Lit. anecdotes*, 1.579; 3.220–21n.; 5.652; 8.157 · [W. Warburton], *Letters from a late eminent prelate to one of his friends*, ed. R. Hurd [1808] · A. W. Evans, *Warburton and the Warburtonians: a study in some eighteenth-century controversies* (1932) · *GM*, 1st ser., 65 (1795), 169, 252 · A. Kippis and others, eds., *Biographia Britannica, or, The lives of the most eminent persons who have flourished in Great Britain and Ireland*, 2nd edn, 1 (1778), 549 · *Correspondence of Thomas Gray*, ed. P. Toynbee and L. Whibley, 3 vols. (1935); repr. with additions by H. W. Starr (1971) · *DNB* · G. H. Blore, 'An archdeacon of the 18th century', *The Winchester Cathedral Record*, 20 (1951), 19–22 · S. Parr, ed., *Tracts by Warburton, and a Warburtonian* (1789), 183

Archives St John Cam., lecture notes, MS W.3 | NL Scot., letters to Lord Hailes

Likenesses oils, St John Cam.

Balint, Michael Maurice [*formerly* Mihaly Bergsmann] (**1896–1970**), psychoanalyst, was born on 3 December 1896 in Baross Street, Jozsefvaros, a residential section of Budapest, Hungary. He was the first of the two children of Ignac Bergsmann, a general medical practitioner. Both his parents were descendants of German Jewish families who had been fully assimilated Hungarians for only two or three generations. He later changed his name to Balint. At secondary school Balint became a voracious reader and haunted Budapest's public libraries. His younger sister by eighteen months, Emmi, studied mathematics and was at school with two other future psychoanalysts, Margaret Mahler and Alice Szekely-Kovacs; the latter became Balint's wife. As a young man Balint enjoyed skiing, ice-skated in Budapest's municipal park, rowed on the Danube, and was keen on boxing. His initial ambition was to be an engineer but his father disapproved and insisted, in 1913, that he enrol in medical school. He was conscripted into the army when the First World War started, serving first at the Russian front and then in the Italian Dolomites. He was sent home, however, following a serious injury to a thumb, caused while trying to dismantle a hand grenade. He returned to his medical studies two years later and graduated MD in 1920. In 1918 he married Alice, whose mother was Vilma Kovacs. Alice was an ex-patient, and then a pupil of Sandor Ferenczi; she later become a psychoanalyst, well known for her work on analytic supervision.

After reading Freud's *Totem and Taboo* Balint attended courses in psychoanalysis given in 1919 by Ferenczi and came under his influence. As the political situation in Budapest was still unsettled, and Balint's future uncertain, he decided to live in Berlin, where he worked as an assistant research biochemist in the laboratory of Otto Heinrich Warburg. Balint demonstrated his astounding energy and drive by pursuing his growing interest in psychoanalysis at the same time. Balint and his wife began their analytic training with Dr Hans Sachs and decided to study what was later called psychosomatic illness. This was the start of Balint's lifelong interest in relating psychoanalytic concepts to clinical medicine. He was soon working part time at the Berlin Institute of Psychoanalysis. In 1923 he also joined the staff of the First Medical University Clinic in Berlin's Charité Hospital. After

Michael Maurice Balint (**1896–1970**), by Dr Edward H. Stein

obtaining his PhD in chemistry and physics in 1924 Balint and his wife returned to Budapest, where their son Janos was born in March 1925. Balint spent two years as a research assistant in one of the departments of medicine at the University Hospital and both he and his wife went to Ferenczi for a further two years to complete their analyses. He became a full member of the Hungarian Psychoanalytical Society in 1926, was appointed a training analyst, and started in practice as a psychoanalyst at 12 Meszaros Street, Budapest, the headquarters of the Budapest Psychoanalytical Institute, where he and his wife also lived. Until the early part of 1926 Balint published papers on bacteriology and biochemistry. From then on he wrote on psychoanalytical subjects. The first of these were *Psychotherapy for General Practitioners* (1926) and *Psychotherapy and Psychogenesis of Physical Symptoms* (1926), which reflect the early development of his interest in the nature and content of the doctor–patient relationship. In 1930 Balint played an important part in establishing the Psychoanalytic Outpatient Clinic in Budapest at Meszaros Street, and in that year he was appointed vice-director of the Budapest Psychoanalytical Institute. Ferenczi was its director until his death in 1935, when Balint became its director, serving until 1939.

Increasing political unrest in Hungary during the years 1932–8, and the *Anschluss*, put Hungarian psychoanalysts in a very difficult situation. John Rickman, president of the International Psychoanalytic Association, advised all Jewish analysts to leave Hungary, and was instrumental in gaining entry into the United Kingdom for many of them, including Balint and his family early in 1939. They took up residence at 1 Mayfair Cottage in Fielden Park, Manchester, where, within a few months, Alice collapsed and died from rupture of an abdominal aneurysm, which they had both known she had. Balint continued to look after their son and in spite of his grief he also worked for, and obtained, the British qualifications which he needed in order to practise as a doctor in the United Kingdom. He was appointed consultant psychiatrist at the Manchester Northern Royal Hospital, and director of the North East Lancashire and the County Borough of Preston child guidance clinics.

Balint had a very difficult time until 31 July 1943, when he married Edna Henshaw, *née* Yates (*b.* 1903/4), a psychologist and former psychoanalyst, but this marriage broke down, and they separated in March 1947 and divorced in 1952. Early in 1945 he received the tragic news that his parents had committed suicide with lethal injections of morphine, when they were about to be arrested by the Hungarian Nazis, rather than face the certain fate of the gas chambers. Later the same year he moved with his son to live in London, first at New Grove House, Hampstead Grove, and after a short time at 7 Park Square West, Regent's Park. He worked as director of the Chislehurst Child Guidance Clinic from 1945 until he became a naturalized British subject in October 1947, after which he became a member of the British Psycho-Analytical Society, and started to practise as a psychoanalyst again. In 1948 Balint was awarded an MSc (Psychol.) by the University of Manchester for his medical sciences thesis on 'Individual differences of behaviour in early infancy', which was based on his researches into the patterns of infants' behaviour during feeding, and the mother–infant relationship.

In the same year Balint was invited to join the staff of the Tavistock Clinic, where he stayed until his retirement from the National Health Service in 1961. He was then invited to join the staff at the University College Hospital, London, where he continued his work with his training-*cum*-research groups for general practitioners, as well as participating in the scheme which had been started in 1958 for Balint-groups for medical students.

Balint considered and commented on almost every topic of psychoanalytic research. He left a remarkable legacy of several major concepts in psychoanalytic theory, the first of which must be his recognition of the importance of the mother–infant relationship for the individual's future ability to relate to others. This led him to the concepts of 'primary love' (1952) and the 'basic fault' (1968), while other contributions about the theory and techniques of psychoanalysis relate to regression and its use as a therapeutic agent.

In *Thrills and Regressions* (1959) Balint develops his belief that human emotions can be understood only in relation to an object, and he describes two very different types of human functioning. In the first of these, when personal security is threatened there is a need to hold on to something familiar and well known, something firm, a form of functioning which he called 'ocno philic'; while, in states of emergency, the other type of individuals, whom he called 'philo bats', set a distance between themselves and those familiar things which represent safety, and tend to be self-reliant, and to thrive on independent, thrill-acquiring activity. As extreme examples he cites acrobats, lion tamers, pilots, mountain climbers, and skiers.

Balint's eminence as a psychoanalyst was recognized by his election in 1968 to the presidency of the British Psycho-Analytical Society. During his presidency he initiated the popular biennial English-Speaking Conferences of the European Psycho-Analytical Federation. He had also been president of the medical section of the British Psychological Society.

As important as his work was in the advancement of psychoanalysis, Balint will also be remembered for his work in his other main interest. After only a short time at the Tavistock Clinic he had been invited to join Enid Flora Eicholtz, *née* Albu [*see below*], who was working for the Family Welfare Association developing techniques for treating people with marital difficulties, and then training social workers in their use. She became Balint's third wife on 2 January 1953. A seminar for training social workers was formed in 1948 and became the Family Discussion Bureau. Together they devised the case discussion seminar, a method of parallel therapy of the two marital partners by two separate therapists to help them deal with their problems. After further development and growing success it became the Institute of Marital Studies in 1968 (later the Tavistock Marital Studies Institute).

It was about 1948, possibly as a result of changes in medical practice brought about by the introduction of the National Health Service, that Balint returned to his earlier conviction that the essence of good medical practice lay in the doctor–patient relationship, and he sought to develop a better understanding of the emotional problems encountered by general practitioners in their everyday practice. So it was that Balint's timely invitation published in *The Lancet* (1952) for doctors to attend a discussion group seminar on psychological problems in general practice at the Tavistock Clinic was so attractive to so many. This led to the writing of his classic book, *The Doctor, his Patient and the Illness* (1957), which was translated into fourteen languages and proved to be extremely influential. Balint focused his attention on how the doctor's attitudes and approach had a vital impact on the patient's response and progress, so that he was able to show that

> the most frequently used drug in general practice was the doctor himself, i.e. it was not only the bottle of medicine or the box of pills that mattered, but the way the doctor gave them to his patient—in fact, the whole atmosphere in which the drug was given and taken. (Balint, 1)

It followed that as with any other drug, it was necessary to consider its pharmacology, its indications, dosage, limitations, the best ways of administering it, and its possible side-effects. Balint also demonstrated how doctors were limited by what he called their apostolic function, the ingrained attitudes and biases due to their training at medical school, in addition to the effects of their own upbringing and life experience.

Balint started seminar discussion groups with the Family Planning Association in 1952 for the treatment of psychosexual disorders. These were highly successful and the Institute of Psychosexual Studies developed from them. He was responsible also for setting up a workshop in 1955 for the development of brief focal psychotherapy with psychoanalysts from the Tavistock Clinic and the Cassel Hospital. Enid Balint reciprocated his earlier collaboration with her in her work with social workers and others, after his first few years organizing his training groups, and often joined him as co-leader.

Balint was the first doctor to undertake research into the psychological aspects of general practice in a highly scientific way. In devising his method for training doctors in recognizing possible underlying psychological aspects of their patients' illnesses he stated clearly and firmly that there was a great need for research in this area, and that teaching and research had mostly been in the hands of specialists of various kinds, but the research needed in this context could be done only in general practice. Balint-groups and societies were formed worldwide. In Switzerland the Foundation of Psychosomatic Medicine and Social Medicine has a keen interest in Balint's work. An International Balint Federation was also established.

For many years Michael and Enid Balint travelled a good deal to attend a variety of meetings and, frequently by invitation, to give lectures or lead groups. Although he was not known as a man who sought honours and awards he was happy with his appointment as visiting professor, and Enid's as associate professor, of the University of Cincinnati, Ohio, which they visited regularly from 1958 onwards. Balint's contribution to medicine was summed up by Lord Max Rosenheim, who wrote: 'By all reckoning, Michael Balint was a remarkable doctor and psychoanalyst, a man for all time, whose impact on general practice and on the understanding of the doctor–patient relationship has been felt all round the world' (Hopkins, 'In memoriam', vii). During the last few years of his life, Balint suffered the effects of diabetes and glaucoma, with resultant severe impairment of his vision, and, although very few people were aware of this, he depended very much on his wife's guidance for his mobility. Balint died on 31 December 1970 while being taken to Southmead Hospital, Bristol, and was cremated.

Balint's third wife, known after a later marriage as **Enid Flora Balint-Edmonds** [*née* Albu] (1903–1994), psychoanalyst and welfare worker, was born in London on 12 December 1903. She was educated at Hampstead high school and Cheltenham Ladies' College before entering the London School of Economics in 1922, and graduated BSc (Econ) in 1925, having specialized in public administration. On 25 March 1926 she married Robert N. Eicholtz, a professor of philology. She organized the Citizens' Advice Bureaux in London on behalf of the Family Welfare Association, helping to deal with the social and family dislocations which the civilian population suffered during and after the Second World War. In 1948 she began training in psychoanalysis under J. Rickman, and with a few of her colleagues set up the Family Discussion Bureau in order to train social workers who were needed for family counselling. She met Michael Balint in connection with this work; her first marriage having ended, they married on 2 January 1953 and thereafter worked closely together, co-authoring books and lecturing at universities and conferences abroad. After Balint's death she kept the movement alive and became honorary president of the International Balint Federation. She continued in private practice following her third marriage, in 1976, to Robert Humphrey Gordon Edmonds (*b.* 1920), a retired diplomat. She died on 30 July 1994, following a surgical operation, survived by Edmonds and two daughters from her first marriage. PHILIP HOPKINS

Sources M. Balint, *The doctor, his patient and the illness* (1957) • A. E. Haynal, *The technique at issue: controversies in psychoanalysis: from Freud and Ferenczi to Michael Balint* (1988) • I. Hermann, 'Souvenirs de Michael Balint, 1896–1971 [*sic*]', *Le Coq-Heron*, 85 (1974), 45–7 • H. Stewart, *Michael Balint: object relations pure and applied* (1996) • E. Balint-Edmonds, 'The doctor / patient relationship in the 1980s', *Journal of Balint Society*, 9 (1981), 12–18 • E. Balint-Edmonds, 'Michael Balint: the development of his idea on the use of the "drug" doctor', *Journal of Balint Society*, 12 (1984), 5–12 • E. Balint-Edmonds, 'Michael Balint in London', *Journal of Balint Society*, 14 (1986), 8–10 • private information (2004) • personal knowledge (2004) • P. Hopkins, interview with Dr Michael Balint on 27 Nov 1970, *London Doctor*, 2 (1971), 17–18 • P. Hopkins, 'In memoriam: interview with Dr Michael Balint on 27 Nov 1970', *First International Conference of the Balint Society* [London, 1972], ed. P. Hopkins (1972), 316–19 • P. Hopkins, 'Holistic medicine and the influence of Michael Balint', *Integrated medicine: the human approach*, ed. H. Maxwell (1976), 45–59 • *Fourth International Conference of the Balint Society* [London, 1978], ed. P. Hopkins (1979) • P. Hopkins, 'Personal memories of Michael Balint', *Journal of Balint Society*, 14 (1986), 14–18 • P. Hopkins, 'Michael Balint's early years in England' [forthcoming] [paper read at Michael Balint Centenary Congress, 1996, in Budapest] • P. Hopkins, 'Michael Balint: training and research', Michael Balint memorial lecture, *Journal of Balint Society*, 15 (1987), 4–13 • P. Hopkins, 'Michael Balint in England, 1939–1970' [forthcoming] [lecture in Budapest Congress, May 1996] • *Journal of Balint Society*, 1–24 (1971–96) • d. cert. • d. cert. [Enid Balint-Edmonds] • m. certs. [Edna Henshaw and Enid Eichholtz] • *The Times* (18 Aug 1994) • M. Moreau-Ricaud, 'Enid Balint-Edwards (1904–1994)', *International Association for the History of Psychoanalysis Journal*, 18 (winter 1994), 7–8

Archives priv. coll. | SOUND priv. coll., tape recording of interview, 27 Nov 1970 [published in *London Doctor*, 2 (1971), 17–18, and in *First International Conference of the Balint Society* [London, 1972], ed. P. Hopkins, 316–19]

Likenesses E. H. Stein, photograph, priv. coll. [*see illus.*] • several photographs, priv. coll.

Wealth at death £19,445: probate, 8 Nov 1971, *CGPLA Eng. & Wales* • £65,084—Enid Balint-Edmonds: probate, 28 Feb 1996, *CGPLA Eng. & Wales* (1996)

Baliol. *See* Balliol.

Baliol, Alexander de. *See* Balliol, Alexander de (*d.* 1310?).

Baliol, Bernard de, the elder. *See* Balliol, Bernard de (*d.* 1154x62).

Baliol, Bernard de, the younger. *See* Balliol, Bernard de (*d.* *c.*1190).

Baliol, Edward de. *See* Balliol, Edward (*b.* in or after 1281, *d.* 1364).

Baliol, Henry de. *See* Balliol, Henry de (*d.* 1246).

Baliol, John de. *See* Balliol, John de (*b.* before 1208, *d.* 1268); John (*c.*1248x50–1314).

Ball, Albert (1896–1917), airman, was born at 301 Lenton Boulevard, Nottingham, on 14 August 1896, the elder son and second of three surviving children of Sir Albert Ball (1863–1946), master plumber, land agent, and sometime mayor of Nottingham, and his first wife, Harriet Mary Page (*d.* 1931) of Derby. He was educated at Lenton church school, Grantham grammar school, Nottingham high school, and from January 1911 at Trent College, Long Eaton, Derbyshire, where he was regarded as a conscientious if shy boy with a natural aptitude for anything mechanical. On leaving school in December 1913 he bought an interest in an electrical engineering and brass-founding firm in Nottingham, but at the outbreak of war enlisted in the Nottinghamshire and Derby regiment.

Swiftly promoted sergeant, Ball was commissioned on 29 October 1914, and spent the winter in training but, anxious to get to France, transferred to the north midlands divisional cyclist company. Again frustrated in his desire to see active service, in June 1915 he began training privately as a pilot, and gained his Royal Aero Club certificate on 15 October. After applying to transfer to the Royal Flying Corps (RFC), he underwent further flying instruction and was awarded his pilot's brevet on 22 January 1916, before being officially transferred to the RFC on 29 January.

Briefly with 22 squadron at Gosport before being posted to France, Ball joined 13 squadron at Marieux on 18 February 1916, flying BE 2c aircraft on artillery reconnaissance and bombing raids. He performed his duties conscientiously but felt the burden of responsibility for his observer's life. Hence he was pleased to be allowed occasionally to fly one of two Bristol Scouts attached to the squadron. His skill and enthusiasm as a single-seat pilot attracted attention, and on 7 May he was posted to 11 squadron at Savy Aubigny, one flight of which was equipped with the Nieuport 16, then the best single-seat scout in RFC service. Ball became an enthusiastic proponent of the French fighter, and was to score the majority of his victories while flying Nieuports.

Ball's first success with 11 squadron, a German reconnaissance aircraft forced down, came on 16 May. Two further successes came on 29 May, and the single-mindedness with which he was approaching the task of engaging the enemy was shown on 1 June, when he circled over an enemy aerodrome at Douai, inviting combat and driving down two enemy aircraft which took off to engage him. His dedication showed also in the arrangements he made at Savy, where he built a small wooden shed close to the hangar in which his aircraft was housed. There he lived and sometimes ate, the better to tend his personal Nieuport and the quicker to take off should an opportunity for combat present itself. His dedication was recognized by the award, on 25 June, of the Military Cross.

When the bloody and unsuccessful battle of the Somme began on 1 July 1916, Ball was unknown outside 11 squadron. By its end, in November, he was the top-scoring RFC pilot, and famous. Yet his rise to pre-eminence was not straightforward. On 2 July he destroyed two enemy aircraft, but did not score again before, on 18 July, he was

Albert Ball (1896–1917), by E. N. Birkett, *c.*1915–16

posted to 8 squadron, flying BE 2cs. The transfer, which Ball strongly resented, resulted from a request for a few days' rest. His reaction was to fly additional sorties whenever possible, including a difficult night flight to land a spy behind enemy lines. His passionate commitment to his duties brought the desired result: on 15 August, promoted to lieutenant, he returned to 11 squadron.

In the next eleven days Ball destroyed four enemy aircraft, three of them on 22 August 1916: the first time that such a feat had been accomplished in the RFC. That day he had attacked single-handed four enemy formations, one seven strong and another five, before returning with his aircraft riddled with bullets. The award of the DSO, gazetted on 26 September, at the same time as a bar to the DSO, acknowledged his achievements. A second bar was to be gazetted on 25 November, following the award in September of the Russian order of St George, fourth class.

On 23 August 1916 Ball was transferred to 60 squadron, a scout unit, in which he fully came into his own. The commanding officer, Major R. R. Smith-Barry, recognized his talent and gave him a roving commission. This paid handsome dividends for 60 squadron and for Ball, who by the end of August had seventeen confirmed victories. A month later this had risen to thirty-one and the intensity with which he flew his mainly solo sorties can be seen from the fact that on four more occasions he had brought down three enemy aircraft in a day.

Promoted captain on 13 September 1916, Ball was, at his own request, posted to home establishment on 4 October. Yet it was not long before he was agitating, unsuccessfully, to return to France. After a period with 34 reserve squadron at Orfordness, he was sent on a course at the school of aerial gunnery, Hythe. Gunnery instruction he found particularly irksome, and it was with relief that on 2 January 1917 he was transferred to 7 wing at King's Lynn, Norfolk, as a fighting instructor.

Ball's frustration was exacerbated by the adulation to which he found himself continually subjected, adulation which his father tended to foster. Around Nottingham he took to wearing an old trench coat in order to avoid drawing attention to himself and to his medal ribbons, and his speech on 19 February 1917 accepting the freedom of the city of Nottingham was brief and modest in the extreme. As an antidote to his frustration Ball put a great deal of energy into promoting a single-seat fighter whose design he had instigated the previous year, and which the Austin Motor Company built. He persuaded the government to order two prototypes, but they were not completed until after Ball's death and attracted no production order.

On 25 February 1917 Ball was posted to the newly formed 56 squadron, with which he crossed to France on 7 April. From the first no. 56 was an élite unit, despite major teething problems with the engines and guns of the SE 5, which the squadron was the first to take into action. Ball himself took an immediate dislike to the type, and was permitted to retain a Nieuport for his use when on solo patrol, and it was on a Nieuport that he achieved his (and the squadron's) first victory, on 23 April, and his last, on 5 May.

Between these dates, flying the SE 5 (to which he gradually became reconciled), Ball scored another eleven victories, seven of them between 1 and 5 May. Two days later, on 7 May 1917, he made his last flight. Eleven machines went out in bad weather that evening and engaged a large German force. Ball was seen pursuing an opponent into thundercloud, and then, by German observers on the ground, emerging from the cloud base in a shallow inverted dive, with the propeller stationary, to crash near Annoeullin. His aircraft had sustained no battle damage and Ball's only injuries were sustained in the crash. Various explanations have been suggested, but the most likely is that advanced by Revell: that Ball became disoriented in the cloud, and the engine cut out when the aircraft was inverted. What is certain is that the German authorities erred in crediting Lothar von Richthofen, younger brother of the Red Baron, with Ball's death.

Ball, who died unmarried, was buried at Annoeullin by the Germans with full military honours on 9 May 1917. Just under one month later, on 8 June, the award of the Victoria Cross was gazetted; later the French government made him a chevalier of the Légion d'honneur. The Victoria Cross citation spoke of Ball's 'exceptional courage, determination, and skill'. These qualities he certainly possessed. But any assessment of Ball must take account also of aspects of his personality and fighting style which made him a legend in his lifetime.

Of medium height and build, Ball had a penetrating gaze and a shock of black hair, which he wore longer than was customary in the RFC. He was high-spirited and acquired a reputation for mild eccentricity, partly through such idiosyncrasies as flying without a helmet or goggles. By living in his hut and spending his spare time gardening, Ball also set himself somewhat (and literally) apart from his fellows. He was not a naturally gifted pilot but became highly skilled, and his fast reflexes, outstanding eyesight, and accuracy of shooting made him a formidable opponent. Devoutly religious, he trusted firmly in divine providence, yet there is no doubt that in attacking whatever the odds he was at times foolhardy, and that he was lucky to survive as long as he did. Nor is there any doubt that in the last weeks of his life he was exhausted. After his last successful combat, on 5 May, he wrote home: 'It is all trouble and it is getting on my mind. Am feeling very old just now' (Kiernan, 141).

Like James McCudden, who was awarded the Victoria Cross in 1918, Ball lavished a great deal of care on his aircraft, and like McCudden he felt no personal animosity towards his opponents. To his father he wrote in July 1916:

> I only scrap because it is my duty, but I do not think anything bad about the Hun. Nothing makes me feel more rotten than to see them go down, but you see it is either them or me, so I must do my duty best to make it a case of *them*. (Bowyer, 63)

And in his last letter to his father he wrote: 'I do get tired of always living to kill, and am really beginning to feel like a murderer' (ibid., 138).

Ball's victory tally of forty-four was soon surpassed, but his place in the pantheon of British military aviators is assured. More than any other individual he provided the inspiration which, after the appalling losses of 'Bloody April' 1916, raised and sustained the morale of the RFC and later the Royal Air Force. DAVID GUNBY

Sources C. Bowyer, *Albert Ball, V.C.* (1977) • R. H. Kiernan, *Captain Albert Ball* (1933) • A. Revell, *High in the empty blue: the history of 56 squadron RFC RAF, 1916–1919* (1995) • C. Shores and others, *Above the trenches: a complete record of the fighter aces and units of the British empire air forces, 1915–1920* (1990), 59–60 • T. B. Marson, *Scarlet and khaki* (1930) • *CGPLA Eng. & Wales* (1918)

Archives Castle Museum, Nottingham, medals and artefacts • IWM, artefacts • Royal Air Force Museum, Hendon, artefacts • Trent College, Long Eaton, artefacts | Notts. Arch., letters to his parents | FILM BFI NFTVA, documentary footage • BFI NFTVA, news footage | SOUND IWM SA, oral history interview

Likenesses A. A. Archer, carbon print, *c*.1915, NPG • E. N. Birkett, photograph, *c*.1915–1916, IWM [*see illus.*] • photographs, *c*.1916–1917, IWM • E. Newling, oils, 1919, Castle Museum, Nottingham; version, IWM • D. Davis, oils (after photograph?), Castle Museum, Nottingham • D. Davis, oils, Trent College, Long Eaton • H. Poole, bronze cast of statuette, NPG • H. Poole, statue on monument, Castle Museum grounds, Nottingham • photograph, repro. in P. G. Cooksley, *VCs of the First World War: the air VCs* (1996) • photographs, repro. in Revell, *High in the empty blue*

Wealth at death £5977 1*s*. 7*d*.: administration, 5 March 1918, *CGPLA Eng. & Wales*

Ball, Sir Alexander John (1756–1809), naval officer and politician in Malta, was born on 22 July 1756 at Ebworth Park, Painswick, Gloucestershire, the son of Robert Ball (1714/15–1766), high sheriff of that county, and Mary, *née* Dickinson. He attended Market House School in Stroud and entered the navy on completion of his education. From the late 1770s Ball served, initially as a lieutenant, on

Sir Alexander John Ball (1756–1809), by unknown engraver, pubd 1803

the North American and Newfoundland stations, and then in the West Indies in the flagships of Sir George Rodney. He was with Rodney in the *Formidable* at the battle of the Saints (1782), which secured British control of the West Indies. Ball received his commander's commission and thereafter served in other stations, including the Newfoundland for a second time. In 1783 in order to learn French he spent time on half pay in France which is where, at St Omer, he first came to the attention of Horatio Nelson.

Having returned to Gloucester in 1784, Ball remained on half pay until July 1790 when he was appointed to the frigate *Nemesis* (28 guns) in which he remained until moving to the *Cleopatra* (32 guns) in 1793 and serving on the Newfoundland station under Vice-Admiral Sir Richard King. In May 1798, two years after he had been appointed to the *Alexander* (74 guns) and after short stints off Brest and Cadiz, Ball was sent into the Mediterranean under Nelson's orders. Later that month, after sailing from Gibraltar, the *Alexander* came to the rescue of Nelson's flagship, *Vanguard*, which had been dismasted in a violent gale (21 May). It is clear from Nelson's dispatches that Ball's action may have saved the rear-admiral's life; certainly it earned Ball Nelson's lifelong friendship and also made possible the continuation of Nelson's command of the British fleet at a crucial time, two months before the battle of Abu Qir Bay on 1 August 1798.

Ball's association with Malta, for which he is now best known, began in October 1798 when he was ordered to the island to institute a naval blockade to support the islanders' recent insurrection against French rule. His involvement in Maltese affairs may be divided into three phases. The first dates from the start of the blockade which soon led to his coming ashore and his assumption of the presidency of the Maltese 'national congress' until the French capitulation in September 1800. In this role he acted as a go-between for the sometimes feuding Maltese leaders and military commanders. He also pleaded for reinforcements and ensured that foodstuffs, especially grain, reached islanders simultaneously engaged in anti-French resistance and afflicted with epidemic. However, when after a bitter two-year struggle the French surrendered they did so not to Ball, who was left out of negotiations, but to a newly arrived British army and naval officer. Ball, who had hoped to become the island's governor and who described himself as the 'father' of the Maltese, was rightly aggrieved at Britain's handling of the transfer and left the island in April 1801.

Ball's second period in Malta began in June 1802 when he returned to the island as the minister-plenipotentiary to the order of St John. Ball's return followed the signing of the treaty of Amiens with the French in which Malta was to be returned to the order and would thereafter remain neutral, her independence being guaranteed through the agreement of Britain, France, Austria, Spain, Russia, and Prussia. Ball, along with the Maltese leadership, remained highly doubtful as to whether the provisions of the treaty could be enforced and sceptical of the merits of restoring the order of St John. Ball was secretly advised to play for time and to delay welcoming back the order's grand master, a tactic which ended with Britain's decision to retain the island and their signing of the third coalition against Napoleon.

Ball's final, and longest, period of involvement in Maltese affairs centred on his work as the island's civil commissioner and *de facto* governor from 1803 until his death. If his powers in this office were considerable then so too were the problems he faced. Discontent quickly arose over the lack of financial assistance for members of the disbanded Maltese 'congresso', and was exacerbated by the arrival of large numbers of Sicilians, Albanians, Genoese, and Jewish Gibraltarians—prompting demonstrations in 1805. The situation was eased during the period of the continental blockade, with Malta prominent in the Mediterranean contraband trade. Ball's period of rule also witnessed the establishment of a civil service and banking and insurance systems, together with significant improvements to the island's infrastructure. One of his final initiatives was the appointment of the first Maltese bishop, Ferdinando Mattei, a move which confirmed British control while ensuring good relations with the Vatican and the Sicilian monarchy. Ball was not only a fine seaman and an efficient captain but (what was rarer in his profession) a man of wide culture, humanity, and judgement: qualities he fully displayed in his demanding position in Malta and for which he was praised by Samuel Taylor Coleridge, his one-time secretary on the island.

In 1800 Ball had been created a baronet following the British take-over of the island. In 1805 he was made a rear-admiral, though he did not hoist his flag. He died at Sant' Anton Palace, Attard, Malta, on 25 October 1809 and was buried on 31 October at Fort St Elmo, Valletta. He was survived by his wife, Mary, who died on 27 September 1832. Following his death the Maltese readily subscribed to a monument to Ball which still stands in Valletta's Lower Barracca Gardens. HENRY FRENDO

Sources *DNB* · H. Frendo, 'Reflections on the anti-French insurrection in Malta, 1798–1800', *Cahiers de la Méditerranée*, ed. F. Pomponi (1999) · H. Frendo, *Malta's quest for independence: reflections on the course of Maltese history* (1989) · H. Frendo, *Party politics in a fortress colony: the Maltese experience*, 2nd edn (1991) · W. Hardman, *A history of Malta during the period of the French and British occupations, 1798–1815*, ed. J. H. Rose (1909) · C. Testa, *The French in Malta, 1798–1800* (1998) · D. F. Allen, 'New light on Malta during the peace of Amiens, 1801–1803', *British Library Journal*, 20 (1994) · J. J. Cremona, *Human rights documentation in Malta* (1966) · M. Galea, *Sir Alexander John Ball and Malta* (1990) · D. Gregory, *Malta, Britain and the European powers, 1793–1815* (1996) · A. V. Laferla, *British Malta*, 2 vols. (1938–47), vol. 1 · J. W. Damer Powell, 'Sir Alexander Ball', *Blue Peter*, 15/156 (March 1935), 106

Archives BL, letters to Lord Nelson, Add. MSS 34903–34931 · BL, letters to Granville Penn, Add. MS 37268 · Herts. ALS, letters to William Leake · NL Scot., Minto MSS, corresp. with Hugh Elliot; corresp. with Francis Graham · NMM, letters to Sir William Hamilton; letters to Lord Nelson

Likenesses line engraving, pubd 1803, NPG [*see illus.*] · H. W. Pickersgill, oils (posthumous), NMM

Ball, Andrew (*d.* 1653), naval officer, is believed to have been a native of Bristol, but of his family and early life there is no certain account. The first official mention of his name is in early 1648 when he replaced Thomas Bedell as captain of the *Adventure*, an appointment which suggests he was already an experienced shipmaster. He was soon in action, capturing the Irish frigate *Angel*. When a large part of the parliamentarian fleet revolted to the king in the second civil war he supported parliament. He secured Holy Island, while Sir Arthur Hesilrige reported that 'Captain Ball doth great service at Berwick' (Powell and Timings, 326). He then joined the earl of Warwick's fleet in the Thames and later sailed to Goree in pursuit of the royalists. He was appointed commander at Walmer Castle, in the Downs, in 1648 and may at some time have served ashore in a military capacity; he would later be described as 'that noble and approved soldier' (Gardiner and Atkinson, 4.101). During 1649 he was employed in the channel, cruising off the Lizard or Land's End protecting commerce. Later in that year he was with Blake's squadron off Kinsale, and in 1650 sailed with Blake to Portugal in pursuit of Prince Rupert's squadron. In November 1650, still in the *Adventure*, he was selected to accompany Captain Penn to the Mediterranean, and continued absent on that voyage for nearly sixteen months, arriving in the Downs on 1 April 1652 just as the First Anglo-Dutch War was beginning. During the following summer he was engaged in fitting out the *Antelope*, a new ship only just launched, missing all the summer's action, but in September was sent to Copenhagen in command of a squadron of eighteen ships. The king of Denmark, in collusion with the Dutch, had embargoed twenty English ships in Danish harbours for allegedly failing to pay their sound dues, and it was hoped that the appearance of Ball's force would lead to a more conciliatory attitude. They sailed from Yarmouth on 9 September, and on the 20th anchored a few miles below Elsinore. Ball's negotiating position was weakened by instructions which prevented him from using force, as the king of Denmark was probably aware. They were still hoping that the ships might be released, when, on 30 September, they were caught in the open roadstead in a violent storm; the cables parted, the *Antelope* was hurled on shore, the other ships, more or less damaged, were swept out to sea. It was not until 2 October that they could get back and take up the survivors from the wreck. Further negotiations being pointless, given the weakened state of his ships, he set sail for England, and arrived in Bridlington Bay on 14 October, from where they went to Harwich and the Thames to refit. After the severe check which Blake received off Dungeness, on 30 November, Ball was appointed to the *Lion* (50 guns) in place of Captain Saltonstall, whose conduct in the battle had been called in question. In December 1652 and January 1653 he was occupied in refitting the *Lion*, and he joined the fleet off Queenborough at the beginning of February. There he was promoted to command General Blake's own ship, the *Triumph*. General Richard Deane, recently arrived from Scotland, may have been responsible for this signal honour. Like Ball, he came from the Bristol area, and both men seem to have been religious Independents; the like-minded Captain John Woolters referred to Ball as his 'dear brother in the fellowship of the Gospel' (Gardiner and Atkinson, 3.422). The fleet sailed down the channel to intercept the Dutch who were escorting home merchantmen from western France. The two fleets met off Portland on 18 February 1653. The fight lasted with great fury throughout the day, and during the whole time the enemy's chief efforts were directed against the *Triumph*, which suffered heavily in hull, in rigging, and in men. 'that precious soul Capt. Ball' being one of those killed (ibid., 4.172). In acknowledgement of his services, the state assigned a gratuity of £1000 to his widow; no mention is made of any children, but the Andrew Ball who commanded the *Orange Tree* in the Mediterranean, under Sir Thomas Allin, in 1668, and was then accidentally drowned, may have been a son.

J. K. LAUGHTON, *rev.* MICHAEL BAUMBER

Sources BL, Add. MS 9300 • BL, Add. MS 9305 • *JHL*, 10 (1647–8) • *The manuscripts of his grace the duke of Portland*, 10 vols., HMC, 29 (1891–1931), vol. 1 • S. R. Gardiner and C. T. Atkinson, eds., *Letters and papers relating to the First Dutch War, 1652–1654*, 1–4, Navy RS, 13, 17, 30, 37 (1899–1910) • *The letters of Robert Blake*, ed. J. R. Powell, Navy RS, 76 (1937) • G. Penn, *Memorials of … Sir William Penn*, 2 vols. (1833), vol. 1 • J. Charnock, ed., *Biographia navalis*, 1 (1794), 214–5 • *CSP dom.*, *1649–53* • J. R. Powell and E. K. Timings, eds., *Documents relating to the civil war, 1642–1648*, Navy RS, 105 (1963)

Ball, Anne Elizabeth (**1808–1872**). *See under* Ball, Robert (1802–1857).

Ball, Frances [*name in religion* Mary Teresa] (**1794–1861**), Roman Catholic nun, was the fifth and youngest child of John Ball of Dublin (*d.* 1804), a wealthy merchant, and his second wife, Mabel Clare Bennett (*d.* 1831). She was born on 9 January 1794 at 47 Eccles Street, Dublin, and baptized the same day. At the age of nine she was sent to England to be educated at the Bar Convent, a branch of the Institute of the Blessed Virgin Mary (IBVM), or the Sisters of Loreto, outside Micklegate Bar, York; she remained there until the death of her father. Then she returned to Dublin, where she met Daniel Murray, afterwards archbishop of Dublin, who became her close friend and spiritual director. She became active in the charitable circle of her eldest sister, Anna Maria *O'Brien, but about 1812, the conflicting demands of her social activities and her spiritual expectations led to a crisis, which convinced her that she was called to the religious life. Murray directed her to establish a female teaching order in Ireland and, after the opposition of her mother had been overcome, Frances Ball entered the Bar Convent as a novice on 11 June 1814.

Here Frances Ball spent seven years, preparing to return to Ireland to found a new branch of the IBVM. She received the white veil in September 1814, and was professed on 9 September 1816, when she took the name of Mary Teresa. While at the Bar Convent her preference seems to have been for the contemplative life: she found teaching a distraction from her devotions, and is said to have spoken of her projected return to Ireland as if she were to be sent to Russia. She remained at York for longer than had originally been envisaged by Murray, because several postulants who were to accompany her to open the Irish branch of the order died prematurely. In 1821, however, Murray purchased a suitable house at Rathfarnham, near Dublin, and Mother Frances Mary Teresa and two companions, Anne Therry and Eleanor Arthur, travelled to Dublin. They took up residence at Rathfarnham on 4 November 1822 with a dozen pupils.

The early days of the foundation were not easy, and were marked by the deaths of several hard-worked nuns. But as early as September 1823 Rathfarnham had two novices, and many friends, relatives, and pupils of the first members were professed there. In addition to the boarding-school for young ladies, Mother Frances Mary Teresa opened a poor school in an outbuilding; such dual establishments became characteristic of her foundations. She worked tirelessly, assisting with such mundane activities as wall-papering and fruit-picking, as well as composing a martyrology for use in the houses and designing the plans for the abbey church at Rathfarnham, the first stone of which was laid in 1838.

The first filiation of the Loreto at Rathfarnham was established at Navan in 1833; it was followed by the establishment of a boarding-school and a poor school in Harcourt Street, Dublin (later 53 St Stephen's Green), in 1833, and a Loreto house at 43 North Great George's Street in 1837. In 1842 Mother Frances Mary Teresa purchased property at Dalkey on the east coast of Ireland, where she established a health resort for the nuns and arranged for the construction of a swimming pool. In 1841 she was asked to found a sister house in Calcutta and, after some hesitation, she agreed. Seven sisters were sent out, and a school was opened in 1842; other filiations in India followed. In 1845 the mission in Canada opened in Toronto; several daughter houses were founded, including one at Niagara Falls in 1861. Meanwhile the order expanded in Ireland, with the establishment of houses at Gorey in Wexford (1843), Fermoy (1845), and elsewhere. Mother Frances Mary Teresa's last foundation was at Killarney in 1860.

In the October of that year Mother Frances Mary Teresa fell and fractured her hip, probably also incurring some internal injuries. She did not recover, and in May 1861 she went to Dalkey, where she died on the 19th. Her body was taken back to Rathfarnham Abbey and buried there.

THOMPSON COOPER, *rev.* ROSEMARY MITCHELL

Sources W. Hutch, *Mrs Ball: a biography* (1879) • H. J. Coleridge, *The life of Mother Frances Mary Teresa Ball* (1881) • *Joyful mother of children: Mother Frances Mary Teresa Ball* (1961)
Archives Rathfarnham Abbey, near Dublin
Likenesses J. P. Haverty, portrait, 1834, Rathfarnham Abbey, near Dublin

Ball, Francis Elrington (1863–1928), author and historian, born on 18 July 1863 at Portmarnock, co. Dublin, was the third son of John Thomas *Ball (1815–1898), lord chancellor of Ireland from 1875 to 1880, and his wife, Catherine (*d.* 1887), daughter of the Revd Charles Richard *Elrington (1787–1850), regius professor of divinity in the University of Dublin. For health reasons, he was educated by a private tutor, and was not sent to Trinity College, Dublin, although his father was vice-chancellor of the university.

Ball began his career working for the Unionist cause in Ireland. His distaste for speaking on the platform kept him in the background; but it became generally recognized that the organization of the Unionist Party in Ireland and many of its successes at the polls were largely due to his efforts. In 1897 he married Florence Eglantine (*d.* 1913), daughter of the Revd William Arthur Hamilton DD, rector of Taney, Dundrum, and canon of Christ Church, Dublin. After his marriage his house became a leading Dublin social centre. The couple had no children.

At the general election of 1900 Ball stood for South County Dublin as an independent Unionist, in opposition to Sir Horace Plunkett, the official Unionist candidate. Ball polled a respectable number of votes, but the result of the split was that the seat was gained by the nationalists.

Ball then decided to abandon politics for letters, and it is as a writer, and scholar, rather than as a politician, that he is remembered. In 1902 he collaborated on *The Calendar of the Manuscripts of the Marquess of Ormonde* for the Royal Commission on Historical Manuscripts, and later that year published the first part of his *A History of the County Dublin* (six parts, 1902–20). At the time it was the authoritative local history, and was republished in 1979 and 1993. In 1909 he edited C. Litton Falkiner's *Essays Relating to Ireland*, and wrote a memoir.

Ball had begun some preliminary work on Swift's letters with Falkiner before his death in 1908, and in 1910 he published volume one of *The Correspondence of Jonathan Swift, D.D.*, the sixth and last volume of which appeared in 1914. It was the first scholarly edition, painstakingly annotated, and it established his reputation as the greatest authority on Swift of his time, while also winning him respect as a historian. A new edition was published in 1971. As J. H. Bernard commented in his introduction to the first volume, 'a study of [the Correspondence] is indispensable to anyone who wishes to understand the intrigues of political parties during the first half of the eighteenth century' (Bernard, 'Introduction', xix). In recognition of Ball's achievement, the University of Dublin conferred upon him the honorary degree of LittD in 1911.

Ball's wife Florence died in 1913, and five years later, troubled by the advent of home rule, he left Dublin for London, where he divided his time between the British Museum and the Carlton Club. He became a member of the Royal Society of Antiquarians of Ireland, and turned from Swift to an entirely different subject, *The Judges in Ireland, 1221–1921*. His historiography reflected his political convictions: for Ball, Irish history was the history of the 'civilising influence' of the English on Ireland's native culture. He explains his Unionist project in his preface: his history of the Irish judges deals solely with 'the seven centuries during which the authority of England was absolute in their appointment' (*DNB*). Since much of Ball's information was gathered from documents which perished in the burning of the Irish Records Office in 1922, his work has become the primary authority. It was issued in the Lawbooks Recommended for Libraries series in 1927, and reprinted in 1993.

In the last two years of his life, Ball was working on a commentary on Swift's poetry. He returned to Dublin, where he died at the Fitzwilliam Nursing Home, Pembroke Street, on 7 January 1928. His work on Swift was in its final stages, and was published posthumously as *Swift's Verse: an Essay* in 1929, and reissued in 1977. *Notes and Queries* praised it as a 'solid and important work in the elucidation of Swift', adding that 'students of the period will know precisely what services Dr Ball's researches have rendered' (p. 125).

KATHERINE MULLIN

Sources *N&Q*, 156 (1929), 125–6 • J. H. Bernard, introduction and preface, in *The correspondence of Jonathan Swift*, ed. F. E. Ball, 1 (1910), v–x, xix–lvi; repr. (1971) • 'Ball, John Thomas', *DNB* • *Irish Times* (9 Jan 1928) • *CGPLA Eng. & Wales* (1928)
Archives Royal Society of Antiquaries of Ireland, Dublin, papers
Wealth at death £17,255 9*s.* 5*d.*: probate, 6 June 1928, *CGPLA Eng. & Wales*

Ball, Sir George Thomas Thalben- (1896–1987), organist, was born on 18 June 1896 in Sydney, Australia, the elder son (there were no daughters) of George Charles Ball, who had gone to live temporarily in Australia on business, and his wife, Mary Hannah Spear, daughter of a miller, of Newquay, Cornwall. The family returned to England in 1899 and settled in Muswell Hill, where the father kept a shop. Both his parents were amateur musicians and George became a member of the choir of St James's Church. The Thalben of George's surname, which he added by deed poll in 1924, although he used it from 1917, has some Cornish connection. After attending Highfield, a private school in Muswell Hill, he entered the Royal College of Music on an exhibition in 1911, and studied piano with Frits Hartvigson, Franklin Taylor, and Fanny Davies, organ with Sir Walter Parratt and F. A. Sewell, and composition and history with Sir Charles Stanford, Sir Hubert Parry, and Charles Wood. He quickly took part in ensemble and solo performances at the Royal College of Music, playing, among other works, Liszt's sonata in B minor and, with the orchestra conducted by Stanford, the solo part in Rakhmaninov's piano concerto no. 3 in D minor, the performance of which made a profound impression on his seniors and peers alike.

As an organist Thalben-Ball's energies were largely directed towards developing the music at the various churches where he held appointments: as organist of Whitefield's Tabernacle, Tottenham Court Road (1911); as organist and choir-master of Holy Trinity Church, Castelnau, Barnes (1914–16), and St James's, Sussex Gardens (1916–19); and as acting organist (from 1919) and organist (1923–81) of the Temple Church, near Fleet Street, London. His association with Sir Walford Davies, which led eventually to Thalben-Ball's appointment at the Temple Church, began with Saturday morning choir-training classes at the Royal College of Music, when he took part in conducting and accompanying the choir, and succeeded in getting Walford Davies to allow him to bring along his choristers from Barnes to take part. Thalben-Ball's work at the Temple was the cornerstone of his musical life. Throughout an association of more than sixty years he maintained a uniquely high standard of performance, and a musical style, traditional and in some ways limited, of extraordinary consistency. His achievement was all the more remarkable because the choir, for which the boys were drawn from the City of London School, had essentially to be re-established in the early 1950s following the ravages of the Second World War and the later rebuilding of the church. Thalben-Ball was helped, however, by a strong association of old choristers, which provided a continuing nucleus of singers.

The importance of church and choral music to Thalben-Ball makes his position as an organist somewhat paradoxical. Endowed with an exceptionally robust constitution, possessing impeccable technique and powers of co-ordination, showing concentration and alertness at all times, he became the outstanding British organ recitalist for more than half a century: he could knock spots off everyone else! Together with his seniors, Sir Walter Alcock and George Dorrington Cunningham, he inaugurated the Royal Albert Hall organ in 1924, and was the preferred choice for many opening recitals. He became curator-organist of the Albert Hall in 1934, and was a regular soloist at the Henry Wood Promenade Concerts for many years, making a great effect with Wood's transcriptions of Handel concertos for modern resources. After a recital at Birmingham town hall in 1948, following Cunningham's death, he was persuaded to take on the post of city organist in 1949, together with that of university organist. He always had reservations about this job, but none the less enjoyed the rail journeys from London, and performed a large repertory in more than a thousand recitals before his retirement in 1982.

With his many-sided work and musical interests, Thalben-Ball was never a specialist organist, and this fact helps to explain why his reputation is more that of an executant than an interpreter; his natural sympathies lay firmly within the period bounded by the standard concert repertory of his time, which excluded early music and, to a considerable extent, radical modern composition. His teaching was consistent with this outlook. He would work hard and long, even if somewhat spasmodically, with his pupils at the Royal College of Music, and yet a student often received the greatest enlightenment, not from explanation and discussion, but from persuading the master himself to get on the organ bench and demonstrate his way of doing things. He seemed most at home in music of the era from Mendelssohn to Elgar, and produced memorable accounts of the organ works of Liszt and Julius Reubke. As an accompanist he performed extraordinary feats in turning the organ into an orchestra, such as when playing for Kathleen Ferrier in *The Dream of Gerontius*.

Thalben-Ball was religious music adviser to the BBC from 1941, concerned with directing music for broadcast services and composing choral introits for them. This at first involved constant travel, as the department had been evacuated from London to Bedford. Even with the later commitments of Birmingham and the re-formed Temple Church choir, Thalben-Ball was able to keep his BBC connection until 1970. He was appointed CBE in 1967 and knighted in 1982. He was FRCO (1915), FRCM (1951), FRSCM (1956, diploma 1963), FRSA (1971), and honorary RAM (1973). He was president of the Royal College of Organists in 1948–50 and an honorary bencher of the Inner Temple (1959). He won the grand prix de Chartres (1973) and the EMI gold disc (1963, for Mendelssohn's 'Hear my prayer'). He had an honorary DMus and gold medal from Birmingham (1972).

Thalben-Ball was about 5 feet 6 inches in height, stockily built, with a small moustache and a ramrod-straight back. His dapper dress and turnout made him a man of the city. He married in 1926 a New Zealand artist, (Grace) Evelyn (1888–1961), daughter of Francis Chapman, a New Zealand wheat exporter. They had a son and a daughter. Evelyn died in 1961 and in 1968 Thalben-Ball married the organist Jennifer Lucy Bate, daughter of Horace Alfred Bate, organist of St James's, Muswell Hill. They had no children and the marriage was annulled in 1972. Thalben-Ball died at a nursing home in Wimbledon on 18 January 1987. He was buried at Highgate cemetery. JAMES DALTON, *rev.*

Sources J. Rennert, *George Thalben-Ball* (1979) • D. Lewer, *A spiritual song: the story of the Temple choir* (1961) • personal knowledge (1996) • private information (1996, 2004) [John Thalben-Ball, son] • *CGPLA Eng. & Wales* (1987)

Likenesses A. Fuller, portrait, oils, Royal College of Organists

Wealth at death £210,085: probate, 20 May 1987, *CGPLA Eng. & Wales*

Ball, Hannah (1734–1792), follower of Wesleyan Methodism and diarist, was born on 13 March 1734, probably in Buckinghamshire. Nothing is known of her family other than that she was one of a family of twelve children and that her mother died in 1779, aged seventy-nine. At the age of nine she went to live with an uncle in High Wycombe, before spending five years in Hertfordshire. In 1750 she resided with her brother, a widower, looking after his four children. Initially against the Methodists, she was influenced by reading the sermons of Thomas Walsh (*c*.1730–1759), a Wesleyan Methodist itinerant, and became attracted to their teaching. Over the years John Wesley and other Methodist preachers had visited High Wycombe, but it was probably on his visit in January 1765 that Hannah Ball first met him and was converted. She began to keep a diary in 1766, later published, along with some of her letters, as her memoirs in 1796. She was a regular correspondent of John Wesley, who on several occasions entrusted her with the delicate task of ensuring that some of his preachers were spiritually and pastorally adequate. In 1779 he seems to have encouraged and advised her about the building programme for a chapel at High Wycombe, which he opened on 11 November 1779. However, these letters and her diary contain little personal information, being chiefly concerned with her spiritual development. Her letter-book of 19 May to 6 December 1776, comprising about thirty letters, three written to John Wesley and the rest to women friends, concentrates on giving advice on spiritual growth and recounting her own religious experiences.

Hannah Ball was an assiduous visitor of the sick, both women and men, catering in particular for their spiritual, rather than physical, welfare. Her ministrations also extended to family and friends. John Wesley encouraged her to visit and counsel 'back-sliders' in the hope of bringing them back to faith. She also continued the Methodist tradition of prison visiting.

In August 1776 Hannah Ball travelled to London, spending nine days there during the Methodist conference. Here she attended fourteen preaching services, at six of which Wesley preached, and also holy communion services. She herself was involved in fourteen meetings, testifying and counselling. Some were band meetings, some class meetings, and others personal interviews. Hannah Ball was not preaching or exhorting in the formal sense, which was officially forbidden to women in Wesleyan Methodism, but nevertheless she was exercising a considerable and effective ministry and John Wesley encouraged her in her travels.

Hannah Ball is chiefly remembered as a precursor of the Sunday school movement. Robert Raikes (1725–1811) of Gloucester is credited with founding the first Sunday school in 1780; however, Hannah Ball had started a school in High Wycombe in 1769, meeting the children regularly each Sunday and Monday. She reported in a letter, dated 16 December 1770, to John Wesley that they were 'a wild little company, but seem willing to be instructed' (*Letters of the Rev. John Wesley*, 5.218). Samuel Wells, a Wesleyan Methodist preacher, supported her work. Her sister Ann continued the school after Hannah died, unmarried, at High Wycombe on 16 August 1792. E. DOROTHY GRAHAM

Sources *Memoirs of … Hannah Ball, extracted from her diary by J. Cole*, rev. edn (1839) • letters of Hannah Ball, JRL, Methodist Archives and Research Centre • *The works of John Wesley*, [another edn], 18–23, ed. F. Baker and others (1988–95) • *The works of John Wesley*, 25–6, ed. F. Baker and others (1980–82) • *The letters of the Rev. John Wesley*, ed. J. Telford, 5 (1931), 78, 218
Archives JRL, Methodist Archives and Research Centre, diary and letters

Ball, John (*d.* 1381), chaplain and leader of the peasants' revolt, was of obscure origins. He had been an itinerant radical preacher for nearly twenty years before the revolt. He described himself, in letters circulated during the rising, as 'seynte marye prist' and 'som tyme seynte marie prest of ȝork. and now of Colchestre' (Justice, 14), suggesting that he had at one time been a chantry priest in York and afterwards moved to Colchester. At least three men called John Ball are mentioned in Colchester records of the late fourteenth century, but none can be firmly identified with the rebel leader. A suggestion that he was the son of William and Joan Ball of Peldon, a few miles south of Colchester, born *c.*1329, appears to be without foundation.

John Ball (*d.* 1381), manuscript illumination [centre, on horseback, with (front, left) the rebel leader, Wat Tyler]

On 25 February 1364 Edward III issued a letter patent describing how he had granted Ball protection in response to a complaint by him that he feared injury from his enemies while pursuing his business. The king had heard, however, that Ball was instead wandering from place to place preaching articles contrary to the faith of the church, and withdrew the protection. Six months later Bishop Simon Sudbury of London requested Ball's arrest as an obdurate excommunicate. In 1366 the dean of Bocking was ordered to cite Ball to appear before Archbishop Simon Langham (*d.* 1376). Over the next fourteen years repeated attempts were made to silence Ball by excommunication and arrest, without effect. In April 1381 Sudbury, now archbishop of Canterbury, excommunicated Ball yet again, and on 29 April the sheriff of Kent was ordered to arrest him.

At the end of May 1381 attempts to enforce payment of the third poll tax led to riots in Essex, which spread to Kent. Knighton states that one of the first acts of the Kentish rebels was to free Ball from the archbishop's prison at Maidstone. In fact Ball would have been in the royal prison there, which was not stormed by the Kentish rebels under Wat Tyler until 11 June, when the rising was well advanced. Having already caused mayhem across northern Kent from Dartford to Canterbury, Tyler's men were by the time they attacked Maidstone gaol making a concerted move towards London. Froissart also antedates Ball's release from prison, wrongly stating that he was with Tyler at Canterbury. The claim in an Essex indictment that Ball was not in Maidstone at all, but was released by Essex rebels from the bishop of London's gaol at Bishop's Stortford on 11 June, is difficult to reconcile with the other evidence, and probably mistaken.

On 12 June the Kentish insurgents assembled on Blackheath and remained there until the following day. Ball preached to the rebels while they were at Blackheath, taking as his text the words:

Whanne Adam dalfe and Eve span,
Who was þanne a gentil man?

Although this couplet has become associated with Ball's name, it was a popular proverb which is recorded from at least the early fourteenth century. According to Walsingham, Ball used his text to demonstrate that 'all men were created equal by nature, and that servitude has been introduced by the unjust and evil oppression of men, against the will of God' (Walsingham, *Chronicon Angliae*, 321). Walsingham and others alleged that Ball was a follower of John Wyclif (*d*. 1384). This was not the case, but as R. B. Dobson has observed:

> In their understandable reaction from the deliberately propagated legend that John Ball was John Wycliffe's disciple, historians … have sometimes unduly discounted a not unimportant connection between these two ideologues—that the audience for their respective messages must certainly have sometimes overlapped. (Dobson, xxxvii)

During the morning of 13 June Richard II and his ministers attempted unsuccessfully to talk to the rebels at Rotherhithe. Following the failure of this meeting the rebels entered London where, among many acts of destruction and bloodshed, they burnt the Savoy Palace of John of Gaunt, duke of Lancaster, destroyed the headquarters of the hospitallers at Clerkenwell Priory, and executed Simon Sudbury, the archbishop of Canterbury, and Robert Hales, the treasurer of England and prior of the hospitallers. Ball's role in these events is not clear. The chroniclers mention him, if at all, only in general terms as a leader and chief counsellor of the rebels. After the killing of Wat Tyler during an interview with the king at Smithfield on 15 June Ball fled. He was eventually arrested at Coventry and was tried by Robert Tresilian (*d*. 1388) at St Albans on 12 July. The anti-Wycliffite compilation *Fasciculi zizaniorum* contains a confession supposedly made by Ball at this time, in which he states that he was an agent of Wyclif, but this document is a fabrication. Ball was hanged, drawn, and quartered at St Albans on 15 July 1381.

Knighton and Walsingham reproduce six letters in English urging on the rebels. Ball is named as the author of three of these, and it has usually been assumed that he wrote them all, but their language suggests that the other three are by different hands. These letters have been chiefly celebrated for their early mention of Piers Plowman. But they should also be valued, along with Ball's famous couplet and his reported preaching, for the unique insight they provide into the radical Christian egalitarianism that constituted much of the ideology of the rebels.

ANDREW PRESCOTT

Sources [T. Walsingham], *Chronicon Angliae, ab anno Domini 1328 usque ad annum 1388*, ed. E. M. Thompson, Rolls Series, 64 (1874) · *Oeuvres de Froissart*, ed. S. Luce and others, 10 (Paris, 1897) · *Chronicon Henrici Knighton, vel Cnitthon, monachi Leycestrensis*, ed. J. R. Lumby, 2 vols., Rolls Series, 92 (1889–95) · V. H. Galbraith, ed., *The Anonimalle chronicle, 1333 to 1381* (1927) · E. Powell and G. M. Trevelyan, eds., *The peasants' rising and the Lollards* (1899) · D. Wilkins, ed., *Concilia Magnae Britanniae et Hiberniae*, 3 (1737), 64–65, 152–153 · F. Logan, *Excommunication and the secular arm in medieval England* (1968) · M. Aston, 'Corpus Christi and Corpus Regni: heresy and the peasants' revolt', *Past and Present*, 143 (1994), 3–47 · *VCH Essex*, 9.24–25 · S. Justice, *Writing and rebellion: England in 1381* (1994) · [T. Netter], *Fasciculi zizaniorum magistri Johannis Wyclif cum tritico*, ed. W. W. Shirley, Rolls Series, 5 (1858) · R. B. Dobson, ed., *The peasants' revolt of 1381*, 2nd edn (1983) · B. Bird and D. Stephenson, 'Who was John Ball?', *Essex Archaeology and History*, 3rd ser., 8 (1976), 287–8 · PRO, Court of King's Bench, ancient indictments, KB 9/43, KB 145/3/6/1 · *Chancery records* (RC)

Likenesses manuscript illumination, BL, Royal MS 18 E.i, fol. 165v [*see illus.*]

Ball, John (1585–1640), Church of England clergyman and religious writer, was born at Cassington, Oxfordshire, in early October 1585, the son of William Ball and his wife, Agnes Mabet. Although in humble circumstances, his parents sent him to a private school in the neighbouring village of Yarnton. Such were his 'scholastical gifts' (Clarke, 152) that in his fifteenth year he obtained a place as a servitor at Brasenose College, Oxford, where he matriculated on 24 October 1600. He subsequently transferred to St Mary Hall and graduated BA on 24 January 1604.

Lacking the means to continue his university studies, however, Ball became tutor to the children of Lady Cholmondeley in Cheshire, a formative experience, since he now came into contact with a group of 'severe Puritans' (Clarke, 152) who made such a deep impression on him through their fervent prayers, fasting, and Bible readings that he felt increasingly called to the ministry. Determined to obtain Anglican ordination without subscription to the Thirty-Nine Articles, in 1610 he and his lifelong friend Julines Herring succeeded, owing to the compliance of an Irish bishop. Ball now settled at Whitmore, a chapel of ease in the parish of Stoke-on-Trent, Staffordshire, where he served as the curate for the next thirty years. His stipend was only £20 per annum, and although he also kept a school, at which he was apparently successful, he remained poor. He bore this with great fortitude, despite lacking even a house of his own when he first moved to Whitmore. For 'many years' (Clarke, 148) he lived at Whitmore Hall as a guest of the patron of the living, Edward Mainwaring, until the latter built a small cottage for him in the village. On 4 August 1612, at Whitmore Chapel, Ball married Ellen Buckenhall, with whom he had six sons and a daughter.

According to Simeon Ashe's dedication to Ball's *The Power of Godliness* (1657), the latter led an obscure if conscientious life in his parish, but eventually such were 'his high parts' and 'eminent piety' that he was 'owned, approved and honoured' throughout the land. Towards the end of his life Ball moved in fairly exalted circles, having contacts with puritan peers like Edward Montagu, Viscount Kimbolton, and Lord Saye and Sele. He is also known to have preached sermons before Lady Margaret Bromley at Sheriff Hales in Shropshire; to have attended a conference of puritan clergy in Warwick Castle at the invitation of Lord Brooke; and to have engaged in theological disputation at Fawsley, Northamptonshire, with a clerical colleague of a sectarian persuasion in the presence of Richard Knightley, John Pym, and others.

As a known nonconformist Ball suffered from 'prelatical persecution' (Clarke, 150) throughout his ministry; indeed, he was reputedly deprived of a living in Cheshire before securing that at Whitmore as well as suffering two periods of confinement, and in the late 1630s he seriously considered emigration to New England but was dissuaded by John Dod, a fellow clergyman. With the summoning of the Short Parliament in the spring of 1640 Ball travelled to London with his clerical associate Thomas Langley, to lobby 'some Parliament men' (ibid., 153) against the Laudian harassment of men of their religious ilk. But though Ball entertained hopes of 'further Reformation of things woefully out of order' (ibid.) in the established church, his hopes were dashed with the premature dissolution of that assembly and he was forced to return home with a heavy heart. Ball now fell seriously ill and after a 'languishing sicknesse' (ibid., 155) died at his house at Stoke Whitmore, Staffordshire, on 20 October 1640. He was buried in Whitmore Chapel. A man of 'a sweet, humble, peaceable spirit' (ibid., 154), Ball was eulogized by diverse contemporaries, but perhaps the most eloquent tribute came from Richard Baxter, who declared that Ball merited 'as high esteem and honour as the best bishop in England' (Wood, *Ath. Oxon.*, 2.671).

Ball was a prolific author, though few of his works saw the light of day before 1640. At least five of his manuscript treatises were published posthumously by his 'bosom friend' (Clarke, 152) and literary executor, Simeon Ashe. Of his eight major works, the most popular was the first, *A Short Treatise Containing All the Principal Grounds of Christian Religion*, which went through fourteen editions before 1632 and was even translated into Turkish. Its dialogic form epitomized Ball's 'plaine and naturall style' (preface). Ball's *Treatise of Faith* (1631) was commended to the reader by Richard Sibbes who thought its author 'deserved well of the church' (foreword). Undoubtedly the most substantive work was his *A Friendly Triall of the Grounds Tending to Separation* (1640). Written in the first instance 'for (the) satisfaction of Mr Richard Knightley' (Wood, *Ath. Oxon.*, 2.671), this expressed the disquiet felt by Ball for the growing sectarian tendencies within puritanism. By robustly championing the legitimacy of 'a stinted liturgy' and set forms of prayer in church services Ball incurred the wrath of his stricter brethren who accused him of 'deserting the non-conformist cause' (ibid.), a charge which surfaced again after the publication in 1642 of his refutation of the ideas of the separatist leader John Canne. Entitled *An Answer to Two Treatises of Mr John Can*, this sought to demonstrate that, for all its imperfections, nothing justified outright separation from the Church of England. *A Tryall of the New-Church Way in New England and in Old* (1644) was inspired by the theological controversies which arose in the wake of nine queries submitted by Ball on behalf of the English puritan clergy to their counterparts in the Bay Colony about 1637. In this dispute Ball took exception to those 'tenets' in New England puritanism which 'drew men to seperation' (p. 8) and again insisted that there were no possible grounds for deserting the English church whose institutional failings he attributed to 'human fraility' (p. 13). *Treatise of the Covenant of Grace* (1645), *The Power of Godliness* (1657), and *Treatise of Divine Meditation* (1660) were typical products of Ball's pen, possessing 'more of solidity than lustre, of use than show' (*Treatise of Divine Meditation*, second preface). Ball's religious outlook is difficult to categorize: paradoxically he was labelled by one contemporary 'the Presbyterians' Champion' and by another as belonging to the 'tribe' of Independents, a confusion caused by his own writings, a careful reading of which suggests that he was a 'non-separating Puritan' whose ideal church was a 'congregational presbytery' (Schneider, 171, 173, 179–180).

JOHN SUTTON

Sources S. Clarke, *The lives of thirty two English divines*, in *A general martyrologie*, 3rd edn (1677), 147–54 • Wood, *Ath. Oxon.*, new edn, 2.670–74 • R. Morrice, 'Ent'ring book', DWL, vol. 3 • Fuller, *Worthies* (1662), 2.339 • B. Brook, *The lives of the puritans*, 2 (1813), 440–44 • S. Ashe, foreword, in J. Ball, *The power of godliness* (1657) • S. Ashe, preface, in J. Ball, *A treatise of divine meditation* (1660) • parish register, Stoke Whitmore, 1558–1765, Staffs. RO, MS D3332/1/1 [marriage] • Foster, *Alum. Oxon.* • T. Webster, *Godly clergy in early Stuart England: the Caroline puritan movement, c.1620–1643* (1997) • A. Hughes, 'Thomas Dugard and his circle in the 1630s—a "parliamentary-puritan" connexion?', *HJ*, 29 (1986), 771–93 • T. Edwards, *Antapologia* (1644), 22 • *Reliquiae Baxterianae, or, Mr Richard Baxter's narrative of the most memorable passages of his life and times*, ed. M. Sylvester, 1 vol. in 3 pts (1696), pt 3, p. 19 • C. G. Schneider, 'Roots and branches: from principled conformity to the emergence of religious parties', *Puritanism: transatlantic perspectives on a seventeenth century Anglo-American faith*, ed. F. Bremer (1993)

Ball, John (1654–1745), Presbyterian minister, was born in November 1654, the eldest of five children of William Ball (1624–1670), presbyterian minister, who was ejected from Winsham, Somerset, in 1662, and his wife, Susanna. He studied with Henry Hickman (*d.* 1692) at his school at Dunthorp, near Bromsgrove, Worcestershire, and Ames Short (1617–1697) at Lyme Regis, Dorset, before conducting his own academy for conformists and nonconformists in Dorset. Following Monmouth's rebellion in 1685 he fled to the Netherlands as tutor to two young men, Colonel Henley and Colonel Trenchard, and studied medicine at Utrecht. He settled in Honiton some time before his ordination on 20 January 1696, and in 1705 he reunited the Presbyterians with the Baptists at the Bridge Meeting. He regularly attended the Exeter assembly from 1696, serving five times as moderator. He was fluent in French and Dutch and had facility in Greek and Hebrew, while 'Latin flow'd from him as Water in a Pipe' (Walrond, 16). He regularly preached from the Hebrew psalter.

Ball was one of the leaders of the orthodox dissenters in the dispute with James Peirce (1674–1726) in the Exeter controversy which occurred between 1716 and 1719, and he insisted all ministers make an orthodox declaration concerning the Trinity. He published *Arius Detected and Confuted* (1719), as part of the debate, to which Peirce replied in *Plain Christianity Defended* (1719). *An Answer to some Common Objections* (1727) evoked an eirenic response by Joseph Hallett (1691–1744), *The Reconciler* (1727). His last works were *The Importance of Right Apprehensions of God with Respect to Religion and Virtue* (1736) and a sermon preached in 1730, *Some Remarks on a New Way of Preaching* (1737). In the latter he defended revealed truth and rejected Locke's advocacy of reason. This provoked a response from Henry Grove in 1737.

Ball, who was married, died at Honiton on 6 May 1745 in his ninety-first year, supported by his granddaughter, a daughter of John Lavington (1690?–1759); he left his family well provided for. Walrond had stressed his disregard for money and his puritanism in dress and diet, which prompted a deist opponent to comment 'that Man is what a Minister should be' (Walrond, 19).

ALEXANDER GORDON, *rev.* DAVID KEEP

Sources J. Walrond, *The character of a good minister: a sermon occasioned by the death of the Reverend John Ball who departed this life May 6th 1745* (1745) • A. Brockett, ed., *The Exeter assembly: the minutes of the assemblies of the United Brethren of Devon and Cornwall, 1691–1717*, Devon and Cornwall RS, new ser., 6 (1963) • *Calamy rev.* • A. Brockett, *Nonconformity in Exeter, 1650–1875* (1962) • J. Murch, *A history of the Presbyterian and General Baptist churches in the west of England* (1835) • Moger transcript of the will of John Ball of Honiton, 1747, Devon RO

Wealth at death more than £300 cash; property; South Sea shares: typed transcript of will, Devon RO

Ball, John (1818–1889), glaciologist and politician, was born in Dublin on 20 August 1818, the eldest child of Nicholas *Ball (1791–1865), judge and politician, and his wife, Jane (*née* Sherlock) of Butlerstown Castle in co. Waterford. Until the age of eleven he received little formal education, but from his earliest years he displayed a precocious interest in science. In his seventh year he was taken to Switzerland, where he was deeply affected by the view of the Alps from the Jura. Indeed, he later wrote that 'for long years that scene remained impressed on my mind, whether asleep or awake, and perhaps nothing has had so great an influence on my entire life' (*DNB*). The following year he began to measure the heights of hills barometrically and to construct geological sections, and before his twelfth year he had completed the manuscript of what he termed his 'Elements of chemistry'.

Ball's parents were Roman Catholics, and in 1831 he was sent to St Mary's College at Oscott near Birmingham, whence he was admitted into Christ's College, Cambridge, on 23 June 1835. That summer he participated in the Dublin meeting of the British Association for the Advancement of Science (he attended many of the association's subsequent meetings), and in Cambridge, over the next four years, he joined the classes of John Stevens Henslow in botany, and Adam Sedgwick in geology. With Henslow's family the charming Irishman became extremely popular as a chess player, at the piano, and as a vocalist. Strangely, in 1839 he achieved no higher standing

John Ball (1818–1889), by unknown photographer

than that of forty-first and last wrangler, while his religious convictions prevented his being conferred with a degree. However, Roman Catholics had since 1793 been eligible to receive degrees in the University of Dublin, and on 8 February 1840 he therefore came on to the books of Trinity College, Dublin, 'from Cambridge', although in the event he never took a Dublin degree.

On 13 April 1840 Ball was elected a member of the Royal Irish Academy, and in Trinity term 1843 he was called to the Irish bar at the King's Inns. He never practised at the bar, and between 1840 and 1845 can have spent little time in Ireland. For much of that period he travelled in Europe, visiting the mountain regions (for which he felt a deep affinity), botanizing, and communing with kindred scientific spirits. During 1845 he was at Zermatt seeking to develop the glaciological studies pioneered by James David Forbes, but that was the year when a failure of the Irish potato crop marked the beginning of the great Irish famine, and Ball felt duty-bound to return to his distressed homeland.

In April 1846 Ball became an assistant with the commissioners for administering the laws for the relief of the poor in Ireland, but ill health brought on by overwork forced his resignation in November 1847. A period of continental travel restored his constitution, and he returned to Ireland during 1849 to assume the more senior office of second poor law commissioner, a post which remained his until 1 July 1852. His substantial pamphlet *What is to be done for Ireland?* drew attention to the 'utter ruin which is impending over entire provinces', and appeared in two editions (1847 and 1849).

While in the Dingle peninsula, co. Kerry, during 1846, Ball recognized that many of the landforms were analogous to features which he had seen being shaped by modern glacial processes within the Alps. Clearly, he reasoned, there must once have been glaciers in Ireland, and the paper on this subject which he presented to the Geological Society of Dublin on 14 November 1849 is the earliest published study of Pleistocene events within any region of Ireland.

In July 1848 Ball stood, without success, as a parliamentary candidate for Sligo borough, but on 26 July 1852 he was returned (by a majority of only two votes) as the member for Carlow County. In the Commons he spoke only briefly and somewhat infrequently, but he did make his mark, and in February 1855 the prime minister, Lord Palmerston, named him as assistant under-secretary of state in the colonial department. In this office he took the opportunity to further the cause of science in several ways. His energetic representations were largely responsible for ensuring the adequate financing of the expedition led by John Palliser for the exploration of western Canada, and he was instrumental in inducing the home government to support the efforts of Sir William Jackson Hooker towards the publication of colonial floras.

At the election on 11 April 1857 he was heavily defeated when he stood for Sligo County, and on 15 February in the following year he was again defeated when he contested Limerick City. His rejection in 1858 was attributed to an unpopularity among Limerick's Roman Catholic clergy arising from his friendship with such Italian liberals as Count Camillo Benso di Cavour and Quintino Sella. Although subsequently offered several parliamentary seats, he resolved henceforth, as a man of independent financial means, to devote himself exclusively to travel and to natural history.

Following the foundation of the Alpine Club in December 1857 he served as its first president (1858–60), and he edited *Peaks, Passes, and Glaciers*, the club's earliest publication (two editions in 1859). The three volumes of his *Alpine Guide* (first editions 1863, 1864, 1868) are classics among the literature of mountain travel. In 1856 he married Eliza Parolini, daughter of the naturalist and traveller Count Alberto Parolini (there were two sons of the marriage), and between 1861 and 1869 he lived much in Italy, where, on his wife's death about 1867, he inherited an estate near to Bassano and at the foot of the Venetian Alps. By 1863 he had crossed the main chain of the Alps forty-eight times by thirty-two different routes, being accompanied upon some of his journeys by his close friend William Edward Forster. In 1869 Ball married Julia O'Beirne, the youngest child of Francis and Winefred O'Beirne of Jamestown, co. Leitrim.

Ball was fluent in several European languages and published extensively in the periodical literature of science. In the company of Joseph Dalton Hooker he visited Morocco and the Atlas Mountains between April and June 1871, and their joint work descriptive of the excursion was published in 1878. Between March and August 1882 he sailed to the Caribbean, crossed the isthmus of Panama, and completed a circumnavigation of South America via the Strait of Magellan, his account of this journey being published in 1887. During the 1880s trouble with his throat caused him to winter abroad in places such as Algeria, Tunisia, and the Canary Islands.

While in the Engadine during the autumn of 1889 Ball was stricken with illness. He was taken home to London where, shortly after an operation and somewhat unexpectedly, he died at midnight on 21 October 1889 at his home, 10 Southwell Gardens, South Kensington. He was buried in the churchyard of St Thomas's at Walham Green on 25 October. Among his distinctions were the Italian order of SS Maurizio e Lazzaro (1865), fellowship of the Linnean Society (2 December 1856), fellowship of the Royal Society (4 June 1868), and honorary fellowship of Christ's College, Cambridge (3 October 1888).

GORDON L. HERRIES DAVIES

Sources *Proceedings* [Royal Geographical Society], new ser., 12 (1890), 99–108 · *Geological Magazine*, new ser., 3rd decade, 7 (1890), 47–8 · Boase, *Mod. Eng. biog.*, vol. 4 · Venn, *Alum. Cant.* · *Nature*, 40 (1889), 626 · J. D. H. [J. D. Hooker], *PRS*, 47 (1889–90), v–ix · F. S. Smythe, *British mountaineers* (1942) · R. L. Praeger, *Some Irish naturalists: a biographical note-book* (1949) · J. D. Hooker and J. Ball, *Journal of a tour in Marocco and the Great Atlas* (1878)

Archives RBG Kew, botanical papers | BL, letters to Sir Austen Layard, Add. MSS 38983–39119, *passim* · BL, corresp. with Lord Ripon, Add. MS 43545 · Bodl. Oxf., corresp. with Lord Kimberley · Harvard U., Arnold Arboretum, letters to Asa Grey · UCL, letters to Sir Francis Galton

Likenesses photograph, RBG Kew [*see illus.*] · portrait, repro. in *Alpine Journal*, 25/107 (Feb 1890)

Wealth at death £20,742 11*s*. 3*d*.: probate, 1889, *CGPLA Eng. & Wales*

Ball, John (1861–1940), golfer, was born on 24 December 1861 at Hoylake, Cheshire, the second son of John Ball (*d.* 1905) and his wife, Margaret Parry. The father was of yeoman farmer stock and the owner of the Royal Hotel at Hoylake, which became the headquarters of the Royal Liverpool Golf Club when the course was laid out in 1869. The boy was therefore brought up with golf on his doorstep, and his early promise was such that at the age of sixteen he entered for the open championship in 1878 and finished sixth.

Ball's career in big matches began in 1883, and he became widely known when the amateur championship was founded in 1885; but it was not until 1888 that he came into his own by beating J. E. Laidlay at Prestwick by five and four in the final of the amateur championship. He won the championship again at Hoylake in 1890, and in that same year—on what Dr Laidlaw Purves called 'a great day for golf'—he won the open championship at Prestwick with a score of 164; he beat all the professionals, a feat hitherto deemed impossible for an amateur. In 1892 he tied for second place in the open championship at Muirfield, which was won by another Hoylake amateur, Harold Hilton, and he also won the amateur championship for the third time at Sandwich. In 1894 he won it for the fourth time at Hoylake, and in 1899 won again at Prestwick.

After the Second South African War, when he served with the Denbighshire yeomanry, Ball's play showed no perceptible falling off; but it was not until 1907 that he won the amateur championship again, this time at St Andrews. In 1910 at Hoylake he won it for the seventh time, and in 1912 at Westward Ho! won for the eighth time, a record wholly without parallel. Of these matches the most memorable were that of 1894 at Hoylake with S. Mure Fergusson, in which Ball played a famous brassy shot over the cross bunkers to the Dun (then the seventeenth) hole and won by a hole, and the Prestwick final of 1899 against his great Scottish competitor F. G. Tait, when Ball won at the thirty-seventh hole. Having been at one time five down, Ball retrieved himself and stood one up with two to play: at the thirty-fifth hole both played historic recovery shots, Tait from a watery bunker and Ball from hard wet sand close to the boarded edge of the same hazard. Tait saved the match with a three at the home hole, but at the thirty-seventh Ball laid an iron shot about 8 feet from the hole and holed the putt for a winning three. In 1912 he beat Abe Mitchell, later a famous professional, at the thirty-eighth hole, but perhaps the finest golf he ever played in his later years was in the final of 1910, when he beat Collinson Charleton Aylmer by ten and nine.

Ball's lesser successes were innumerable: he was three times Irish open amateur champion (1893, 1894, and 1899); he won the St George's cup at Sandwich, then considered the amateur stroke play championship, four years running (1888–91); and he regularly played for England against Scotland from the first international match in 1902 until 1911.

Ball's style was eminently characteristic, with a peculiar underhand grip of the right hand, but the swing was a perfect model of grace and rhythm. He was a magnificent iron player and he set a new standard of accuracy in long iron shots right up to the flag. If he had a comparatively weak spot, it was on the green: he was inclined to miss short putts. As a match player he had the most indomitable spirit and seemed to revel in a close finish. No golfer has ever come close to his record of eight amateur championships plus an open championship, nor is ever likely to do so.

A quiet, reserved man, and always something of a puritan in golfing matters, Ball had a great dislike of publicity, but none the less a remarkable power for inspiring hero worship, especially at Hoylake. In his later years he parted with his interest in the Royal Hotel there, and went to live at Lygan-y-wern, near Holywell, Flintshire, with his unmarried sister Elizabeth and their housekeeper Nellie Williams, whom he married in July 1932, a development which severed Ball's remaining family ties. From Flintshire he made very occasional forays back to Hoylake, not least to witness the amateur championship of 1939, where the beautiful condition of the fairways ('damned croquet lawns') earned his particular scorn. One of the greatest and most romantic figures in the history of English golf, John Ball died at Lygan-y-wern on 2 December 1940. His wife survived him.

BERNARD DARWIN, *rev.* RICHARD FISHER

Sources J. Behrend, *John Ball of Hoylake: champion golfer* (1989) · B. Darwin, *Pack clouds away* (1941), 145–52 · G. B. Farrar, *The Royal Liverpool Golf Club, 1869–1932* (1933) · *Golf*, Badminton Library (1902) · personal knowledge (1949)

Archives Royal Liverpool Golf Club, Hoylake, MSS, publications, and other printed memorabilia

Likenesses F. A. Cooper, photograph, repro. in *Golf* · Elliott & Fry, photogravure photograph, NPG · R. E. Morrison, oils, Royal Liverpool Golf Club, Hoylake · photograph, repro. in Behrend, *John Ball*

Ball, John Thomas (1815–1898), judge, born in Dublin on 24 July 1815, was the eldest son of Major Benjamin Marcus Ball (1789–1841) and Elizabeth (1789–1838), daughter of Cuthbert Feltus of Hollybrook, co. Carlow. His father was an officer who served with distinction in the 40th regiment of foot during the peninsular campaign. He was educated at Dr Smith's school in Rutland Square, Dublin, and entered Trinity College in 1831 at an unusually early age. Ball won a classical scholarship in 1833 and in 1835 graduated as senior moderator and gold medallist in ethics and logic. In 1836 he graduated BA. While at Trinity, Ball made friends with Isaac Butt (1813–1879), Samuel O'Sullivan (1790–1851), Mortimer O'Sullivan (1791–1859), Joseph Sheridan le Fanu (1814–1873), and other eminent men of his generation; he was also a frequent contributor to the *Dublin University Magazine*, and was president of the college historical society in 1837. Ball's articles were mostly on historical and biographical subjects, but he also wrote verse. In 1844 he graduated LLD.

Ball had been called to the Irish bar in 1840. He quickly rose to an eminent position, and in 1854 he took silk. In 1852 he married Catherine Elrington (*d.* 1887), daughter of the Revd Charles Richard *Elrington, regius professor of divinity in the University of Dublin. They had three children, the youngest of whom, Francis Elrington *Ball, is noted for his authorship of *The Judges in Ireland, 1221–1921*. As a queen's counsel Ball's practice lay mainly in the ecclesiastical courts, and later in the Probate and Matrimonial Division, where his knowledge of civil law and his subtlety in argument led to his rapid promotion to a senior position. In 1862 the primate, Marcus Beresford, appointed him vicar-general of the province of Armagh. This appointment marked the beginning of Ball's active interest in the affairs of the Church of Ireland, of which he was a devout member. In 1863 he was elected a bencher of the King's Inns, and in 1865 he was made queen's advocate in Ireland.

In the same year Ball first entered politics and stood in the general election as an independent candidate for the University of Dublin. He was a proponent of legislation for ecclesiastical reform; his policy involved the admission of deficiencies within the church structure and he was defeated at the polls. In 1867 Ball was nominated as a member of the royal commission appointed by Disraeli to

John Thomas Ball (1815–1898), by unknown engraver, pubd 1875

inquire into the state of the Church of Ireland, and in the following year he became a member of the Conservative administration as solicitor-general for Ireland. Later in the same year he was promoted to the position of attorney-general for Ireland. In the meantime Gladstone's declarations had raised the issue of disestablishment in a direct form, and Ball's abilities and knowledge of ecclesiastical affairs meant that at the general election of 1868 he was returned to parliament as member for the university.

Ball played a leading role in opposing the Irish Church Act, a measure aimed at the disestablishment of all churches in Ireland. His speech on the second reading was a remarkable oratorical triumph, placing him in the front rank of parliamentary speakers and winning him the approbation of Disraeli. Ball's efforts were sustained throughout the long struggle over the details of the bill. Early in 1870, when the marquess of Salisbury was installed as chancellor of the University of Oxford, his services were acknowledged by the conferral of the honorary degree of DCL. Subsequently he helped to frame the future constitution of the disestablished Church of Ireland, not only devising and drafting that constitution but acting as assessor to the primate in the often stormy meetings of the general synod.

From 1869 to 1874 Ball remained a vigorous member of the Conservative opposition and took an active part in the debates on Gladstone's Irish Land Bill of 1870 and the Irish University Bill of 1873. His opposition to the Land Bill was confined to effective criticism of its details; but his objections to Gladstone's university scheme (involving the closure of some Irish third-level institutions and the opening of a new university) attacked the bill in principle. Ball's parliamentary activity was not confined solely to Irish questions; one of his finest speeches dealt with the Ballot Act and evinced his opposition to the extension of the franchise.

In 1874, on the formation of Disraeli's second administration, Ball's position and services made him a clear contender for the highest office in the law in Ireland; but the prime minister wished to keep him in the House of Commons so that he could work on the Irish Judicature Bill, and he was reappointed attorney-general. Therefore it was not until 1875 that he became lord chancellor of Ireland, where he remained until the fall of the Disraeli government in April 1880. During that time he earned a reputation as a judge whose appeals from the Probate Division were especially distinguished by legal learning, argumentative power, and literary form.

On his retirement from the chancellorship, Ball became less involved in public life, though in 1880 he accepted the nomination by Earl Cairns to the office of vice-chancellor of the University of Dublin. In 1881 he presided over the section of jurisprudence at the meeting of the social science congress at Dublin, and delivered an address on jurisprudence and the amendment of the law.

On the return of his party to office under Lord Salisbury in 1885, Ball did not feel that he was in strong enough health to resume the Irish chancellorship, and he spent his time in writing. In 1886 he published *The Reformed Church of Ireland*, a work in which he traced the history of the church from the Reformation to his own time. The book won praise from churchmen of the day for its even-handedness, and a second, enlarged edition appeared in 1890. In the year after his wife's death, Ball's work of church history was followed by his *Historical Review of the Legislative Systems Operative in Ireland from the Invasion of Henry the Second to the Union* (1888, second edn 1889), in which he sought

> to trace the succession of these systems to each other, the forms they respectively assumed, and their distinctive peculiarities, and at the same time to consider the controversies connected with the claim made by the English parliament to legislate for Ireland. (Author's preface)

The author's objective and balanced approach to contentious topics won him praise from Gladstone, Smith, and Lecky, who emphasized the judicial impartiality with which the book was written.

From 1890 old age confined Ball more to his home at Dundrum, co. Dublin. However, he retained until 1895 his office of vice-chancellor of the university. Subsequently his declining health compelled him gradually to divest himself of numerous honorary offices such as those of chancellor of the archdioceses of Armagh and Dublin, assessor to the general synod of the Church of Ireland, senator of the Royal University, and chairman of the board of intermediate education. He died at Dundrum on St Patrick's day, 17 March 1898, and was buried at Mount Jerome cemetery, Dublin.

Ball was remembered as an impressive orator and as one of the few nineteenth-century Irishmen who were able to persuade the Commons. A portrait of him was left to the hall of the King's Inns, Dublin; there is also a woodcut in the National Portrait Gallery, London, and a photograph, reproduced in W. Ball-Wright's *Records of the Anglo-Irish Families of Ball*. C. L. Falkiner, *rev.* Sinéad Agnew

Sources W. Ball-Wright, *Records of the Anglo-Irish families of Ball* (1887) · *Men of the time* (1884) · Boase, *Mod. Eng. biog.* · *The Times* (18 March 1898) · *Daily Express* [Dublin] (18 March 1898) · L. C. Sanders, *Celebrities of the century: being a dictionary of men and women of the nineteenth century* (1887) · J. Kirk, *Biographies of English Catholics in the eighteenth century*, ed. J. H. Pollen and E. Burton (1909) · A. T. C. Pratt, ed., *People of the period: being a collection of the biographies of upwards of* *six thousand living celebrities*, 2 vols. (1897) • 'Our portrait gallery, second series, no. 15', *Dublin University Magazine*, 85 (1875), 402–6 • Carlton Club list of members, 1836

Archives CUL, letters to the duke of Marlborough

Likenesses Cranfield, photograph, repro. in Ball-Wright, *Records of the Anglo-Irish families of Ball* • W. Osborne, oils, King's Inns, Dublin • wood-engraving, NPG; repro. in *ILN* (23 Jan 1875) [*see illus.*]

Ball, Sir (George) Joseph (1885–1961), intelligence officer and political administrator, was born at 24 Inkerman Street, Luton, Bedfordshire, on 21 September 1885, the son of George Ball, bookstall clerk, of Salisbury, and his wife, Sarah Ann Headey. He was educated at King's College School, Strand, and at King's College, London. After leaving college he worked as a civilian official in Scotland Yard, and he was called to the bar with first-class honours by Gray's Inn in 1913. He was a keen footballer, and played centre-half for the Casuals until prevented by injury. He was a good shot and an expert fly-fisher. On 16 April 1914 he married Gladys Emily, a school teacher, daughter of John Burch Penhorwood, with whom he had a daughter; after her death in 1918 he married, on 6 October 1919, her half-sister Mary Caroline Penhorwood (*d.* 1957), with whom he had two sons and one daughter.

On the outbreak of the First World War Ball joined MI5, and in 1919 he was appointed OBE. He remained in the service until 1927, when he was persuaded by J. C. C. Davidson, chairman of the Conservative Party, to join the party organization as director of publicity. Major Joseph Ball, as he then was, proved to be a notable asset, along with Sir Patrick Gower, also diverted by Davidson from government employment. Years later, in 1955, Davidson said of Ball:

> he is undoubtedly tough and has looked after his own interests … On the other hand he is steeped in the Service tradition, and has had as much experience as anyone I know in the seamy side of life and the handling of crooks. (*Memoirs of a Conservative*, 272)

One of Ball's successful clandestine efforts was to insert agents in the Labour Party headquarters and in Odham's Press, which did most of the party's printing. In this way he managed to secure both Labour reports of political feeling in the country and also advance 'pulls' of their leaflets and pamphlets; it was thus possible for the Conservatives to reply suspiciously instantaneously to their opponents' propaganda. Not surprisingly, Ball was closely involved in assisting Stanley Baldwin to deal with the parliamentary debate in 1928 on the affair of the Zinoviev letter, which had occurred four years earlier. Baldwin was able to emerge triumphantly. It is not known whether Ball played any part in the original episode.

In 1930, in the aftermath of the loss of the general election, Davidson created the Conservative Research Department and made Ball its director, under the chairmanship first (briefly) of Lord Eustace Percy and then of Neville Chamberlain, to whom Ball is said to have taught the art of fly-fishing. Chamberlain respected Ball's knowledge, discretion, and reliability, and later used him in 1938 as an intermediary with Count Grandi, Italian ambassador in London, in order to bypass the foreign secretary, Anthony Eden. Ball was appointed KBE in 1936.

Ball was a very able director. He did much to lay the foundations for the success of the Conservative Party's research department after the Second World War, and recruited for it many young people of high calibre, among others Henry Brooke and Frank Pakenham; the latter, however, later moved to the Labour Party. Ball retired in 1939. From 1940 to 1942, having reverted to his earlier profession as an intelligence officer, he served as deputy chairman of the security executive.

After the end of the war Ball entered the world of business, and became chairman of Henderson's Transvaal Estates and five subsidiary companies, and also of Lake View and Star. He was a director of Consolidated Goldfields of South Africa and of the Beaumont property trust. He was chairman of the Hampshire rivers catchment board (1947–53). He died at St Thomas's Home, Lambeth, London, on 10 July 1961.

Ball moved for most of his life in the shadow of events and was deeply averse to publicity of any sort. He gave very little away, and the formal accounts of his career, whether written by himself or others, are curt and uninformative. He was, however, a quintessential *éminence grise*, and his influence on affairs cannot be measured by the brevity of the printed references to him.

ROBERT BLAKE, *rev.*

Sources *The Times* (12 July 1961) • L. Chester, S. Fay, and H. Young, *The Zinoviev letter* (1967) • G. Bennett, *A most extraordinary and mysterious business: the Zinoviev letter of 1924* (1999) • J. Ramsden, *The age of Balfour and Baldwin, 1902–1940* (1978) • *Memoirs of a Conservative: J. C. C. Davidson's memoirs and papers, 1910–37*, ed. R. R. James (1969) • Burke, *Peerage* (1959) • b. cert. • m. certs. • *CGPLA Eng. & Wales* (1961)

Archives Bodl. Oxf., corresp. with third earl of Selborne • U. Leeds, Brotherton L., corresp. with Henry Drummond-Wolff

Wealth at death £59,906 12*s.* 9*d.*: probate, 7 Sept 1961, *CGPLA Eng. & Wales*

Ball, Mary (1812–1898). *See under* Ball, Robert (1802–1857).

Ball, Nathanael (*c.*1623–1681), clergyman and ejected minister, was born at Pitminster, near Taunton Dean, Somerset, and later attended the school there. From Pitminster he went to Cambridge University, matriculating as a sizar from King's College at Easter 1644. He cannot, therefore, be the Nathanael Ball of St Mary Hill registered as a student at Merchant Taylors' School in 1645. Ball graduated BA in 1648 (listed under the name Balls) and proceeded MA of Pembroke College in 1660. At Cambridge he built a high scholarly reputation, especially for his facility for languages; he is reputed to have spoken French almost as a native, and according to Calamy won the respect and affection of Tillotson, the future archbishop.

On 1 March 1650 Ball was approved as a minister by the Westminster assembly and in the same year the commission charged to survey church livings in Hertfordshire reported that the vicarage of Furneaux Pelham 'is worth £35 per annum, and that Nathanael Ball is minister and pays one fifth to the wife of Dr [Henry] Hancock', the sequestered incumbent (Urwick, 763). By 1652, Ball had settled at Barley in Hertfordshire, a vicarage earlier sequestered from Herbert Thorndike, and married Mary, daughter of Philip Parr, a neighbouring clergyman. Of their ten sons and three daughters, the first of five appearing in the Barley parish register is Nathaniel, on 17 December 1652. During the 1650s Ball is alleged to have helped in the preparation of Bishop Brian Walton's London polyglot Bible of 1657.

In 1660 Thorndike recovered his living, and Ball was ejected from Barley. For some time he continued to live in the parish but later that year he left for Royston, 'a market town of great profaneness and but little religion', apparently on the invitation of a group of its parishioners; here he 'set up a lecture on the market day, which was blessed with great success. The trade of wickedness was spoiled there …' (Calamy, *Abridgement*, 2.363). It seems probable that he acted as curate at Royston, resigning after the Act of Uniformity in 1662, but remaining for some time in the town and preaching when occasion arose. He then lived for more than seven years at Little Chishill, of which parish his brother-in-law, Robert Parr, became the rector in 1662. There he acted as an evangelist, preaching also at Epping, Bayford, and Cambridge. In 1668 he was reported at Hardwick, Cambridgeshire, and on 20 January and 1 July 1669 he took part with the presbyterian Stephen Scanderet and others in two public disputes (of which the second seems to have been extremely bad tempered) with the Quaker George Whitehead. In the same year Archbishop Sheldon was informed that Ball was a teacher to a conventicle at Thaxted. On the issuing of the declaration of indulgence of 1672, Ball was described as of Nether Chishill, but he was licensed (25 May) as a 'general Presbyterian teacher in any allowed place' (Davids, 598). By June 1672 he was living at premises at Epping, licensed in that month as a presbyterian meeting-place, and in August was himself licensed to teach there. Calamy records that Ball lived 'in a small cottage of forty shillings a year rent', stressing his great labours and poverty in his last years (Calamy, *Abridgement*, 2.365); he died of consumption on 8 September 1681, aged fifty-seven or fifty-eight, probably at Epping.

At his death Ball entrusted his manuscripts to the keeping of Thomas Gouge, of St Sepulchre's, London, on whose early death they passed to another ejected minister, John Faldo. In 1683, Faldo published Ball's *Spiritual Bondage and Freedom*, dedicated to Ball's friend 'the right honourable and truly virtuous the Lady Archer, of Coopersail, in Essex', who 'did so bountifully minister to the reverend author's subsistence in his greatest straits' (sig. A3). The epistle to the reader supplies information on which Calamy based much of his own account. It describes Ball's role in his house:

> When it was a convenient time for the whole house to meet together, he came from his study, and summoning them to duty, he expounded one or two chapters, and examined his children and servants what they did remember, encouraging the diligent, reproving the negligent; which being done he called on God for them, and with them …. Duty being ended, he retired shortly upon it into his study, where he commonly abode till dinner. At every meal he preached as it were a short sermon; and thanks being returned unto God, he hastened again into his study; allowing himself no recreation, but what arose from reading, praying and instructing others. (Ball, foreword)

As to his younger children, Ball 'would not indulge any of them in a sinful action. T'was his judgement that a father might wink at anything, saving sin against God. Therefore in his use of the rod he designed their good', explaining that neither he nor God took pleasure in the punishment, but 'that sin being bound up in the heart of the child, t'was the Lord's ordinance to drive it out, and therefore he always accompanied the rod with prayer, that … correction might be seconded with conversion, and crowned with universal reformation' (ibid.). In 1885 Alexander Gordon found it 'greatly to be deplored that his biblical and oriental manuscripts—the laborious occupation of a lifelong student—and his extensive correspondence are now lost. They are known to have been in existence in comparatively recent times' (*DNB*). STEPHEN WRIGHT

Sources N. Ball, *Spiritual bondage and freedom, or, A treatise …* (1683), foreword • Venn, *Alum. Cant.* • *Calamy rev.* • E. Calamy, ed., *An abridgement of Mr. Baxter's history of his life and times, with an account of the ministers, &c., who were ejected after the Restauration of King Charles II*, 2nd edn, 2 vols. (1713) • W. Urwick, *Nonconformity in Hertfordshire* (1884) • T. W. Davids, *Annals of evangelical nonconformity in Essex* (1863) • Mrs E. P. Hart, ed., *Merchant Taylors' School register, 1561–1934*, 2 vols. (1936) • R. Ludgater, G. Whitehead, and others, *The glory of Christ's light within expelling darkness* (1669)

Ball, Nicholas (1791–1865), judge and politician, was born in Dublin, the son of John Ball (1728–1804), silk mercer of Dublin, and his wife, Mabel Clare, *née* Bennett. Ball, a Catholic, was educated at Stonyhurst College, Lancashire, and at Trinity College, Dublin (1808–12), where his contemporaries included Richard Sheil and W. H. Curran. Ball was called to the Irish bar in 1814, and afterwards spent two winters in Rome with his contemporary Thomas Wyse. Both young men saw a good deal of Cardinal Gonsalvi, secretary of state, and these visits were the subject of much controversy. It was alleged that the young men had sought to influence and support a scheme for the appointment of Irish Catholic bishops, subject to the veto of the English government. At a time when religious tensions were running high over Catholic emancipation, the visits fuelled the fires of suspicion. Ball took silk in 1830, and was admitted a bencher of the King's Inns in 1836. Valued as an equity lawyer, he obtained a lucrative practice in the rolls court and in the court of chancery, where his reputation was that of an acute, clear, and ready advocate. In 1836 Ball was elected member of parliament for Clonmel; in 1837 he was appointed attorney-general and in 1838 privy councillor for Ireland. He disliked parliamentary life, and was famous for his 'devotion to supper and silence in debate' (Ball, 261). He was glad to take refuge in a judgeship of the common pleas (Ireland), to which he was preferred in 1839, and which he held until his death. He was the second Roman Catholic barrister promoted to a judgeship after the passing of the Emancipation Act.

In 1817 Ball married Jane Sherlock of Butlerstown Castle, co. Waterford. They had seven children, the eldest of whom, John *Ball (1818–1889), became under-secretary of state for the colonies under Lord Palmerston's administration. Their son Thomas was a captain in the Dublin militia, and Nicholas and Alex Francis followed their father into the law. Of the three daughters, Jane married, and Anna and Mary became nuns. Their mother died in 1863.

As a judge, Ball was renowned for his sense of humour in court and there are many anecdotes of his quips and his imitations of witnesses. Ball was a sound and able lawyer, as well as being a sincere Roman Catholic, Liberal in his politics, and committed to the cause of Catholic emancipation. He held the office of judge of the common pleas until his death; he died at his home, 85 St Stephen's Green, Dublin, in January 1865, and was buried in the family vault under the pro-cathedral of Dublin.

P. B. Austin, *rev.* Sinéad Agnew

Sources W. Ball-Wright, *Records of the Anglo-Irish families of Ball* (1887) • F. E. Ball, *The judges in Ireland, 1221–1921*, 2 vols. (1926) • Boase, *Mod. Eng. biog.* • R. B. Mosse, *The parliamentary guide* (1836) • *Freeman's Journal* [Dublin] (16 Jan 1865) • *Freeman's Journal* [Dublin] (20 Jan 1865) • *Daily Express* [Dublin] (16 Jan 1865) • *Daily Express* [Dublin] (19 Jan 1865) • *The Tablet* (21 Jan 1865)

Wealth at death under £35,000: probate, 2 Feb 1865, *CGPLA Ire.*

Ball, Sir Peter (*bap.* **1598**, *d.* **1680**), lawyer and antiquary, was the second-born (but eldest surviving) son of Giles Ball (*b.* 1573) of Mamhead, Devon, and his wife, Urith (*d.* 1644), daughter of Humphrey Copleston of Instow, Devon. He was baptized at Mamhead on 24 December 1598. After a brief sojourn at Oxford, where he matriculated in 1614, Ball was admitted to the Middle Temple from Lyon's Inn on 26 February 1616, and was called to the bar seven years later. Returned by the mayor and burgesses of Tiverton to Charles I's second parliament, Ball spoke up strongly for Buckingham's impeachment, and was named to the committee which drafted the general petition of grievances. In 1628, again representing Tiverton, Ball attacked the billeting of troops, proposed a bill rather than petition of right to confirm Magna Carta, and condemned Arminianism. This robust stance evidently commended him to the corporation of Exeter, where he was appointed one of the city's legal counsel in October 1628, and recorder in 1632. But Ball was noticeably silent in the final parliamentary session of 1629, and shortly thereafter began to receive modest crown preferment. In 1636 he became solicitor-general to Queen Henrietta Maria and an associate to the Middle Temple bench. In January 1640, as queen's attorney-general, Ball was appointed king's counsel at large, promotions which help explain both his prominence as an advocate for moderation in the Short Parliament, and his non-return for Tiverton in October of that year.

Ball's 1641 reading on Magna Carta's first chapter (on ecclesiastical jurisdiction and rights) gave him full membership of the Middle Temple's governing body where he remained active for the next thirty-five years. There seems no reason to doubt his later claim that 'relation of service' to the crown accounts for his civil war royalism (*Calendar of the … Committee for Compounding*, 1228). Knighted in 1643 and created DCL at Oxford the following year, Ball compounded for his delinquency in 1646, although his assessment was not fully discharged until 1650. He appears to have been back at the Middle Temple by November 1647, and in December 1649 forwarded to his fellow Middle Templar Bulstrode Whitelocke a brief and somewhat self-serving treatise on law reform and legal education which is now in the British Library (Whitelocke letters, Longleat, 10, fol. 80).

Ball's willingness to conform to the new dispensation later gained him Cromwell's protection after he petitioned the protector in 1656 against the likely effects of the anti-royalist decimation tax on himself, his wife, Ann (daughter of Sir William Cooke of Highnam, Gloucestershire), and their seventeen children, who included the astronomer William *Ball (*c.*1631–1690) and the physician Peter *Ball (*c.*1638–1675). But it cannot have helped his fortunes at the Restoration, when he was among those former royalist Devon gentry who were not reappointed as JPs for the county, a snub for which another Middle Temple near contemporary Edward Hyde must have been at least partly responsible. Ball did regain the recordership of Exeter, despite having been twice dismissed during the 1640s, and continued as the queen mother's chief law officer for the rest of her life, in which capacity he received a pension of £200 from 1665, besides his annual fee. Samuel Pepys, who was earlier impressed by Ball's 'civility' in his official capacity, noted in 1667 that 'old Sir P. Ball' was still capable of a competent forensic performance before the House of Lords (Pepys, 2.28; 8.27). In 1672 Ball was among those commissioned to oversee the dispersal of his late mistress's jointure lands, but in 1676 he resigned the recordership of Exeter on the grounds of age and infirmity. Buried at Mamhead on 4 September 1680, Ball was memorialized twenty years later as 'excellently well Skilled in Antiquities, and Wrote several Volumes therein; but with so ill an Hand, that they are not legible' (Prince, 112).

Wilfrid Prest

Sources 'Ball, Sir Peter', HoP, *Commons, 1604–29* [draft] • W. R. Prest, *The rise of the barristers: a social history of the English bar, 1590–1640*, 2nd edn (1991) • C. T. Martin, ed., *Minutes of parliament of the Middle Temple*, 4 vols. (1904–5), vols. 2–3 • J. Prince, *Danmonii orientales illustres, or, The worthies of Devon* (1701) • J. L. Vivian, ed., *The visitations of the county of Devon, comprising the herald's visitations of 1531, 1564, and 1620* (privately printed, Exeter, [1895]) • S. K. Roberts, *Recovery and restoration in an English county: Devon local administration, 1646–1670* (1985) • M. A. E. Green, ed., *Calendar of the proceedings of the committee for compounding … 1643–1660*, 5 vols., PRO (1889–92) • M. A. E. Green, ed., *Calendar of the proceedings of the committee for advance of money, 1642–1656*, 3 vols., PRO (1888) • *The Short Parliament (1640) diary of Sir Thomas Aston*, ed. J. D. Maltby, CS, 4th ser., 35 (1988) • *The autobiography and correspondence of Sir Simonds D'Ewes*, ed. J. O. Halliwell, 1 (1845), 252 • H. A. C. Sturgess, ed., *Register of admissions to the Honourable Society of the Middle Temple, from the fifteenth century to the year 1944*, 1 (1949), 104 • *Reg. Oxf.*, vol. 2/2 • GEC, *Peerage* • *Report on records of the city of Exeter*, HMC, 73 (1916) • *Report on the manuscripts of Allan George Finch*, 5 vols., HMC, 71 (1913–2003), vol. 2 • M. M. Rowe and A. M. Jackson, *Assizes and quarter sessions in Exeter* (1971) • N. R. R. Fisher, 'The queenes courte in her councell chamber at Westminster', *EngHR*, 108 (1993), 314–37, esp. 329 • Pepys, *Diary*, vol. 2–3, 8 • *IGI* • W. A. Shaw, *The knights of England*, 2 (1906), 216 • W. R. Prest, 'Law reform and legal education in interregnum England', *Historical Research*, 75 (2002), 112–22

Archives BL, Add. MS 32096, fols. 177–8 • Harvard U., law school, notes on reading, MS 138e

Ball, Peter (*c.*1638–1675), physician, was the third son and one of the seventeen children of Sir Peter *Ball (*bap.* 1598, *d.* 1680), lawyer, and his wife, Ann, daughter of Sir William Cooke, of Gloucestershire. The astronomer William *Ball was his elder brother. Peter was admitted to the Middle Temple, London, in 1652 and called to the bar in 1657. In 1659, at the age of twenty, he was entered as a medical student at Leiden, but proceeded to Padua, where he took the degree of doctor of philosophy and physic in 1660. To celebrate this feat, a series of laudatory verses entitled *Apollinare sacrum* (1660) was published in Padua.

Ball was admitted as an honorary fellow of the College of Physicians in London in December 1664. He was elected a fellow of the Royal Society in 1663, and was one of the council in 1664, 1666, and 1669. In 1667 he became a member of the committee charged with producing a catalogue of the library and manuscripts of Arundel House. While at his father's residence, Mamhead House in Devon, in October 1665, Ball, together with his brother William, made the observation of Saturn mentioned under William Ball. Ball died in July 1675; he was buried on the 20th of that month in the round of the Temple Church.

GORDON GOODWIN, *rev.* MICHAEL BEVAN

Sources J. Prince, *Danmonii orientales illustres, or, The worthies of Devon* (1701) • Munk, *Roll* • M. Hunter, *The Royal Society and its fellows, 1660–1700: the morphology of an early scientific institution*, 2nd edn (1994) • Temple Register • *The Athenaeum* (21 Aug 1880) • *The Athenaeum* (9 Oct 1880) • D. Bank and A. Esposito, eds., *British biographical index*, 4 vols. (1990)

Ball, Robert (1802–1857), naturalist, was born at Cobh, co. Cork, on 1 April 1802, the elder son of Robert Stawell Ball (1768–1841), a customs official, and Mary, *née* Green, of Youghal. His younger sisters were Anne Elizabeth Ball and Mary Ball [*see below*]; he also had a younger brother, Bent. He was educated at the notable Quaker school at Ballitore, co. Kildare, where James White encouraged his zoological studies. Leaving school at sixteen, Robert soon moved with his family to Youghal and, with his sisters, actively observed and recorded local flora and fauna. Having taken much interest in public and charitable institutions, he became a local magistrate about 1823. His desire to study medicine was precluded by family finances and he moved to Dublin, where, from 1827 to 1852, he was employed as assistant librarian and keeper of records in the under-secretary's office. In 1837 he married Amelia Gresley Hellicar of Bristol; among their seven children was Robert Stawell *Ball, astronomer. Although highly praised for his exemplary work in Dublin, Ball's interest in science was an obvious distraction, and in 1852 he was retired owing to the fact that he had 'devoted much attention to scientific pursuits, and that it was not expedient that public servants should be thus occupied' (*DNB*). Nevertheless, he received a pension of £800 per annum which allowed the family to live in moderate comfort.

Ball's spare time indeed had been devoted to natural history pursuits. His holidays were zoological expeditions, frequently with William Thompson of Belfast, to whose publications, especially *The Natural History of Ireland*, he added numerous details. Highly respected in Dublin's scientific life, Ball became a council member of the Royal Irish Academy and other societies and president of both the Geological Society of Ireland and Dublin University Zoological Association. As secretary of the Zoological Society of Ireland he put forward ingenious ideas which developed its exhibits, gardens, and programmes in innovative directions. He introduced the penny admission for the working classes and 'zoo breakfasts' for members in 1844. In the same year he was appointed director of Trinity College Museum to which his large natural history collection of mainly Irish specimens was donated; he was awarded an honorary LLD in 1850. Further appointments came as secretary of the Queen's University in Ireland (1851), secretary to the joint committee of lectures (1854), and assistant examiner to the civil service commission (1855). However, other accolades were to come in 1857 when he was proposed as a fellow of the Royal Society, as 'the Inventor or Improver of the Naturalists' Dredge. Distinguished for his acquaintance with the science of Practical Zoology, Eminent as a Promoter of Natural Science'. That same year he was appointed president elect of the British Association's natural history section for the Dublin meeting, but on 30 March 1857 he died, probably of a heart attack, at his home, 3 Granby Row, Rutland Square, Dublin, and both honours were denied him. He was buried at Mount Jerome cemetery, Dublin. In private life Ball's social qualities and honourable nature were highly esteemed, and he enlivened many a children's party. His scientific papers on Irish zoology, ranging from seals and cephalopods to fossil Irish elk, bear, and oxen remains, were published mainly in the *Proceedings* and *Transactions* of the Royal Irish Academy, the *Proceedings of the Zoological Society*, the *Annals of Natural History*, and the *Natural History Review*.

Anne Elizabeth Ball (1808–1872), algologist, and the elder of Robert Ball's sisters, was born at Cobh. In about 1818 she moved with the family to Youghal, and there, when she was in her early twenties, she started to collect and study marine algae. From 1837 she collected algae from around Dublin, where she had gone to live with her sister and father.

Anne Ball became a most successful algologist. As was then customary, her work was published by male naturalists such as William Henry Harvey, James Mackay, and others. As the elder sister she was conventionally cited in publications as Miss Ball, as distinct from her sister who was cited as Miss M. Ball. Although not a member of the Dublin scientific societies, Anne Ball benefited greatly from Robert's support and his friendship with many notable naturalists. William Harvey assisted and encouraged Anne and dedicated to her several new species that she had first collected, such as *Ballia callitricha* and *Cladophora balliana*. She contributed records of hydroids to William Thompson, published in volume four of *The Natural History of Ireland* (1856). Anne died at home in Belmont Avenue, Dublin, in 1872. She did not marry and her extant collections were later housed in the herbaria at University College, Cork, and at the Royal (later National) Botanic Gardens, Glasnevin, which acquired her drawings of seaweeds and fungi.

Mary Ball (1812–1898), zoologist, and younger sister of Robert Ball, was born at Cobh on 15 February 1812. She engaged in natural history pursuits from her youth. By the age of twenty-one she had an impressive cabinet of Irish butterflies and subsequently collected a wide range of insects, shells, and other marine invertebrates. Her perceptive observations were passed to her brother and his naturalist friends, including William Thompson, of Belfast, who named a mollusc, *Rissoa balliae*, after her in 1856. Through field and indoor studies she assembled information on insect habits and made the first record of stridulation in corixid water bugs, published by Robert Ball in 1845–6. Baron de Selys-Longchamps, the European authority on dragonflies, visited her collection and subsequently published her notable observations and records in 1846. Like her sister Mary Ball maintained a lifelong interest in gardening, but her natural history studies waned in the 1850s following the deaths of her brother, Thompson, and other close friends. Although in 1834 Thompson had rated Mary's among thirty notable Irish collections of shells and invertebrates, only a small part remains in the National Museum collections. She did not marry and survived Anne Ball by more than twenty years. She died on 17 July 1898 at the home the sisters had shared in Dublin. HELENA C. G. CHESNEY

Sources R. Patterson, 'Memoir of the late Robert Ball LLD, MRIA', *Natural History Review*, 5 (1858), 1–34 · J. Bronte Gatenby, 'The history of zoology and comparative anatomy in Trinity College, Dublin', *Irish Journal of Medical Science*, 432 (1961), 395–407 · G. E. Hutchinson, 'The harp that once… a note on the discovery of stridulation in the corixid water bugs', *Irish Naturalists' Journal*, 20 (1982), 457–66 · W. Thompson, *The natural history of Ireland*, ed. R. Patterson, 4 vols. (1849–56) · M. A. Wilson, 'Anne Elizabeth Ball of Youghal', *Irish Naturalists' Journal*, 11 (1954), 213–15 · J. Robertson, 'The stridulation of corixa', *Irish Naturalist*, 4 (1895), 319 · A. R. Nichols, 'The stridulation of corixa', *Irish Naturalist*, 4 (1895), 79 · H. M. Parkes, 'Some notes on the herbarium of University College, Cork', *Irish Naturalists' Journal*, 11 (1963), 102–6 · H. M. Parkes and M. J. P. Scannell, 'Anne E. Ball: two volumes of algae in the herbarium, National Botanic Gardens, Dublin', *Irish Naturalists' Journal*, 16 (1970), 369 · H. Ross, 'Mary Ball, naturalist', *Some people and places in Irish science and technology*, ed. C. Mollan, W. Davis, and B. Finucane (1985), 44–5

Archives NHM, corresp. with Sir Richard Owen and William Clift · Belfast, Ulster Museum, W. Thompson MSS

Likenesses A. Edouart, silhouette, 1834, NG Ire. · A. Edouart, silhouette, 1835 (with family), repro. in Hutchinson, 'The harp that once'; priv. coll. · T. H. Maguire, lithograph, BM, NPG; repro. in T. H. Maguire, *Portraits of honourary members of the Ipswich Museum* (1852) · G. Schroeder, portrait (Mary Ball), priv. coll. · G. Schroeder, portrait (Mary Ball), repro. in Hutchinson, 'The harp that once' · M. A. Wilson, silhouette (Anne Ball), repro. in Wilson, 'Anne Elizabeth Ball of Youghal' · pencil drawing, repro. in Patterson, 'Memoir of the late Robert Ball', fronstispiece · portrait (Mary Ball), repro. in Ross, *Some people and places* · silhouettes (Anne Ball; Mary Ball), repro. in Ross, *Some people and places*

Ball, Sir Robert Stawell (1840–1913), astronomer, was born on 1 July 1840 at 3 Granby Row, Dublin, the second of the seven children of Robert *Ball (1802–1857), a civil servant who was honorary secretary of the Dublin Royal Zoological Society, and his wife, Amelia Gresley Ball, *née* Hellicar (*d.* 1895). He received his early education at Dr John Lardner Burke's School in Dublin and then at Dr Brindley's school in Tarvin, near Chester, where he excelled in mathematics and science. Following the death of his father in 1857, he attended, first as a sizar and then as a scholar, Trinity College, Dublin, where physical concepts were being treated by methods of mathematical analysis that, owing their origin to the work of mathematicians in continental Europe, were relatively new to Britain and Ireland. As a young man Ball briefly met Sir William Rowan Hamilton (1805–1865), his famous predecessor as royal astronomer, who had spent the greater part of his life working in isolation in Dunsink Observatory.

Although a promising undergraduate student, Ball failed to gain a fellowship in Trinity College, Dublin. When the third earl of Rosse (1800–1867), at Birr Castle, sought a qualified tutor for his children (one of them, Charles A. Parsons, was later the inventor of the steam turbine), Ball, nominated by Johnstone Stoney, was accepted on the basis that he would also use the giant telescopes built there in the 1840s. He noted: 'I sometimes followed Herschel's example and remained observing from dusk to dawn' (*Reminiscences*, 68). After only two years at Birr, in 1867 Ball was appointed professor of applied mathematics and mechanics in the newly founded Royal College of Science in Dublin. He developed vivid physical demonstrations and laid the foundation of a successful style of lecturing that was to earn him fame in later years.

Seven years later, in 1874, Franz F. E. Brünnow resigned as royal astronomer of Ireland and Andrews' professor of astronomy in the University of Dublin (Trinity College), and Ball submitted an elaborate and successful seven-page printed application for the vacant post. After his appointment he was able, with the benefit of a succession of gifted assistants—R. Copeland, C. E. Burton, J. L. E. Dreyer, and A. A. Rambaut—to build successfully on the work of his predecessor and, over a period of eighteen years, to achieve a high standard of work at Dunsink Observatory. He used the visual micrometer on the 12 inch Grubb refractor for determining the annual parallax of stars, with limited success; he used the Pistor and Martin transit circle for meridian observations, including the setting-up of a time service for Dublin in conjunction with the Dublin Port and Docks Board; and he continued his own speciality in mathematics—*The Theory of Screws*—dealing with the kinematics of solid bodies and their general motion in three dimensions. This last work earned him the Cunningham medal of the Royal Irish Academy in 1879. Towards the end of his time at Dunsink he negotiated the installation of Isaac Roberts's gift of a 15 inch reflector, an instrument that was eventually used successfully by E. T. Whittaker and H. C. Plummer. He was friend and adviser to the Dublin telescope maker Sir Howard Grubb, his near contemporary, and was on the committee that supervised the construction of Grubb's 27 inch Vienna refractor of 1882. Besides these varied activities, Ball gradually established himself as a first-class popular lecturer and, in due course, as a widely known author of popular books on astronomy. He travelled extensively to fulfil lecture commissions in Britain and Ireland, and secured busy lecture tour engagements in the United States in 1884, 1887, and 1901–2. Between 28 October and 28 November 1901, at the age of sixty-one, he gave twenty-four lectures in the Boston area before going on to other cities. Wherever he travelled he benefited from his experiences, enhancing the attractive diversions he employed in his lectures. His most popular books went through many editions; in particular, *The Story of the Heavens* (1885) had a new edition as late as 1950 and continued to provide inspiration to keen enquirers into astronomy. From 1883 Ball suffered increasingly from defects in his right eye, which was eventually removed in 1897. He contributed several times to the Christmas lectures of the Royal Institution, and he was scientific adviser to the board of Irish lights (lighthouses and so on) from 1882 until his death in 1913.

In 1892 Ball was appointed Lowndean professor of astronomy at Cambridge and director of the university observatory, where, under his initiative, Grubb was employed in the construction of an unconventional *coudé* refractor—the Sheepshanks telescope. It was successfully used for determining the parallaxes of stars photographically, including work by H. N. Russell in his epochal discovery of the 'Hertzsprung–Russell diagram'. At Cambridge, as well as continuing his mathematical work and his popularization of astronomy, it is related that Ball was among those who warmly welcomed Ernest Rutherford when he first arrived from New Zealand.

As a mathematician Ball was competent, prolific, and capable of utilizing new ideas, but he might not quite qualify as 'one of the two or three greatest British mathematicians of his generation', so attributed by E. T. Whittaker (*Reminiscences*, 396). His many papers and his books on *The Theory of Screws* (1876, 1900, and a German account of 1889) were highly regarded as a contribution to a branch of mathematics that seems almost to have been peculiarly his own, since he never had a co-author in this prolific work. As a practical astronomer, Ball well understood physical principles, but his opinion sometimes betrayed lack of long-term vision. With astronomy becoming based on astrophysical notions, his intuition was good but limited by the concepts of the nineteenth century. As the source of the sun's heat, and recognizing the limitations of chemical fuels, he accepted contraction due to gravity, now plainly seen to be inadequate. On the other hand, for the origin of the ice ages he favoured an explanation in terms of the variation of the orbital elements of the earth, the Milankovich hypothesis. This variation has been recognized, since the 1980s, by examination of deep ice cores, to have a definite partial influence on periodic ice ages.

In his later years, requiring substantial fees for his lectures, which made him relatively wealthy, and working generally from a prepared script, Ball was able to combine effectively his Irish gifts as raconteur and his sound physical insight and mathematical competence. On reading his popular writings of today, such as *The Story of the Heavens*, and judging them by hindsight, his belief in scientific progress becomes evident, and he shows concern for possible exhaustion of the earth's resources. However, his writings were not prophetic: he limited himself to conventional mechanical and chemical concepts; he refers to chemical elements, but not to atoms. Also, in a penetrating discussion of the formation of the tails of comets, foreshadowing modern ideas quite well, he invokes the possibility of electrical repulsion, but he does not mention radiation pressure, which was already understood from Maxwell's theories of electromagnetism, and was indeed mentioned by Ball himself in a letter to G. F. Fitzgerald in October 1881.

Ball combined kindness and geniality with authority as a scientist in a wide range of subjects to a most unusual degree. With his wife, Frances Elizabeth Steele, whom he married in 1868, he had a family of four sons and two daughters. His many popular books, more than fifteen titles, have been enjoyed by several generations of enthusiastic readers and his fame in Ireland remains considerable more than 100 years after he left Dublin for Cambridge.

Ball was made a fellow of the Royal Society of London in 1873, served as royal astronomer of Ireland from 1874 to 1892, and was knighted in 1886. He was president of the Zoological Society of Ireland (1890–92), the Royal Astronomical Society (1897–9), the Mathematical Association of London (1899–1900), and Section A (Mathematics) of the British Association for the Advancement of Science (1886–7). He died at his home by the observatory on 25 November 1913 and was buried on 29 November in St Giles's churchyard in Cambridge. P. A. WAYMAN

Sources *Reminiscences and letters of Sir Robert Ball*, ed. W. V. Ball (1915) • P. A. Wayman, *Dunsink observatory, 1785–1985: a bicentennial history* (1987) • C. Mollan, W. Davis, and B. Finucane, eds., *Some people and places in Irish science and technology* (1985), 56 • F. W. D. and J. T. B., *PRS*, 91A (1915), xvii–xxi, esp. xx • E. B. K. [E. B. Knobel], *Monthly Notices of the Royal Astronomical Society*, 75 (1914–15), 230–36 • *DNB*

Archives Cambs. AS, family corresp. and papers, lecture notes, journal • CUL, lecture notes and notebook • MHS Oxf., corresp. • TCD, letters • U. Cam., Institute of Astronomy Library, corresp. and papers | Cambridge Observatory, MS items • CUL, letters to Sir George Stokes • Dunsink Observatory, Dublin, book collection • Dunsink Observatory, Dublin, pamphlets [reprints] • RAS, letters to Royal Astronomical Society

Likenesses R. Lehmann, chalk drawing, 1894, BM • W. & D. Downey, photograph, NPG; repro. in W. Downey and D. Downey, *The cabinet portrait gallery*, 2 (1891) • H. Furnies, pen-and-ink drawing, NPG • S. Purser, oils, TCD • Spy [L. Ward], caricature, NPG; repro. in *VF* (13 April 1905) • photograph, Dunsink Observatory, Dublin

Wealth at death £12,045 13*s*. 1*d*.: probate, 23 Dec 1913, *CGPLA Eng. & Wales*

Ball, (Walter William) Rouse (1850–1925), educationist and historian, was born at 81 New Bond Street, London, on 14 August 1850, the only son of Walter Frederick Ball, oilman, and his wife, Mary Anne Rouse. He went to University College School and then University College, London, where he gained the degree of MA and won a gold medal for mathematics. In 1870 Ball went up to Trinity College, Cambridge. He graduated BA in 1874, as second wrangler and first Smith's prizeman. He was elected a fellow of his college in 1875, and proceeded MA in 1877. In 1876 he was called to the bar (Inner Temple) and practised briefly as an equity draftsman and conveyancer. At the invitation of Trinity College he returned to Cambridge as a lecturer (from 1878) and tutor (from 1880) in mathematics, positions he occupied until 1905. He was, from 1891, also director of mathematical studies. On 1 September 1885 he married Alice Mary (1851/2–1919), daughter of William Snowdon Gaid.

From 1878, for the rest of his life, Ball devoted his principal energies and attention to Trinity College, its students, finances, boat club, and history. In addition to his teaching duties he gave particular attention to the university chess club (representing Cambridge in early matches against Oxford graduates), to the Trinity College boat club (of which he wrote a detailed history), and to the history of the college (of which he wrote several general and specialized histories). He also represented the university on the Cambridge borough council.

Ball wrote several histories and monographs about the history of mathematics. He also wrote the comprehensive *Mathematical Recreations* (2nd edn, 1892) which had reached its 13th edition by 1987 and which is probably the work for which he will be generally remembered. It deals with mathematical puzzles and problems, such as cryptanalysis, map colouring, and the calculation of the position of shuffled playing cards, as well as other imaginative mathematical problems associated with magic tricks. Ball's other popular mathematical publications relate to such diverse subjects as Chinese tangrams, indigenous Japanese mathematics, string figures, the mathematics of Pythagoras, early calculus, magic squares, mazes, and chess board problems, as well as scholarly articles on cubic curves and the number theories of Marin Mersenne.

In 1893 Ball wrote a seminal *Essay on Newton's 'Principia'* in which, following a suggestion in 1838 by Stephen Peter Rigaud, he was probably the first person to set forth a detailed plan explaining the need for a variorum edition of the work, which he hoped to carry forward himself. In fact, this would have been a massive undertaking even for a man of Ball's energy and abilities and it was a task ultimately completed only well into the twentieth century by teams of scholars (led by I. Bernard Cohen, Herbert W. Turnbull, and Derek T. Whiteside in their respective scholarly editions of the Newton papers). Nevertheless, Ball's plan was a notable exception in an age disinclined towards such projects and did lead to him reprinting what was, in his day, the fullest text of the correspondence between Newton and Robert Hooke and between Newton and Edmond Halley.

Ball was popular with his students and he spared no effort to extend them hospitality (even building a billiard room and squash racket court in his house for their use) and kept in touch with many of them for the rest of his life. He was equally close to his colleagues at Trinity College and counted among his close friends J. J. Thomson, the discoverer of the electron and fellow boat club enthusiast.

Ball died at his home, Elmside, 49 Grange Road, in Cambridge, on 4 April 1925. He was commemorated in Cambridge by a Rouse Ball lectureship in mathematics (established three years before his death), which has been awarded over the years to Albert Einstein (1932), Wolfgang Pauli (1949), and Paul Dirac (1969), among others. Since 1925 there have also been at Cambridge a Rouse Ball professorship of English law and a Rouse Ball professorship of mathematics, both endowed under the generous terms of Ball's will.

Rouse Ball made no significant original contribution to mathematics but his long and effective teaching career, his numerous and often reprinted mathematical works for a broad reading public, together with his total devotion to Trinity College, combine to provide strong evidence of a generous, energetic, and inquisitive man who gave his own utmost to his science and to friends and colleagues. GEOFFREY V. MORSON

Sources *The Times* (6 April 1925) · J. J. Thomson, *Cambridge Review* (24 April 1925), 341–2 · Venn, *Alum. Cant.* · *The Trinity Magazine* [magazine of Trinity College, Cambridge], 6 (June 1925), 53–4 · W. W. R. Ball, *Mathematical recreations and essays*, ed. H. S. M. Coxeter, 13th edn (1987) · W. W. R. Ball, *An essay on Newton's 'Principia'* (1893) · *Historical register of the University of Cambridge*, 11 vols. (1917–91) · *WWW* · H. M. Innes, ed., *Fellows of Trinity College, Cambridge* (1941) · J. R. M. Butler, *Henry Montagu Butler: master of Trinity College, Cambridge, 1886–1918* (1925) · D. E. Smith, *History of mathematics*, 2 vols. (1958) · I. B. Cohen, *Introduction to Newton's 'Principia'* (1971) · *The mathematical papers of Isaac Newton*, ed. D. T. Whiteside, 8 vols. (1967–80), vol. 1 · D. Gjertsen, *The Newton handbook* (1986) · W. W. Rouse Ball and J. A. Venn, eds., *Admissions to Trinity College, Cambridge*, 5 vols. (1911–16) · Trinity Cam., Ball MSS, *c*.1910–*c*.1923 · b. cert. · m. cert. · d. cert.

Archives Trinity Cam., photograph album and portrait collection

Likenesses photograph, *c*.1875, Trinity Cam.

Wealth at death £38,038 3*s*. 7*d*.: probate, 19 Aug 1925, *CGPLA Eng. & Wales*

Ball, Sidney (1857–1918), socialist and educational reformer, was born on 20 April 1857 at Perrott House, Bridge Street, Pershore, Worcestershire, the second of seven children of Edwin Ball (*d*. 1867), solicitor, and his wife, Mary Ann (*d*. 1899), daughter of Owen Ffoulkes, of Chester. He had three brothers and three sisters. Ball was educated at Wellington College (1870–75), where he was school captain, and then held a scholarship at Oriel College, Oxford (1875–9), where he obtained a second class in *literae humaniores*. The next three years were spent recovering from the disappointment of not gaining his expected first class, attending philosophy lectures at German universities, and studying political economy. In December 1882 Ball was elected to a lectureship in philosophy and a fellowship at St John's College, Oxford. Already known as a radical (he was a founder member of the university Palmerston Club and the university home-rule league), his position in what was then the most resolutely conservative college in Oxford was often uneasy. His alleged response to the college toast to 'church and king' was 'religion and the republic'. When Ball married

Oona Howard in 1891, the college declined, on a technicality, to renew his fellowship and for some years he taught for the college while excluded from its governing body. He was eventually re-elected to a fellowship in 1902, although he suffered the disappointment of failing to gain election as president of the college when a vacancy arose in 1909. From 1882 until his death he carried out his teaching and pastoral duties with an energy and kindness that won him the affection of generations of St John's undergraduates. His tutorial manner is evoked in the character of Mr Prendergast in W. W. Penn's novel *My Father's Son* (1912).

Ball was also an energetic university reformer, advocating, for example, the establishment of a school of English language and literature, the admission of women to full membership of the university, and the abolition of compulsory chapel. However it was his unceasing agitation for the systematic study of social problems at Oxford that made his mark on the university and earned him the title of 'Oxford's socialist don'.

Influenced by T. H. Green and Arnold Toynbee, Ball was one of the generation of dons moved by the social question. It was in a meeting at Ball's college rooms, on 17 November 1883, that Samuel Barnett outlined detailed plans for establishing a university settlement in the East End of London. The subsequent foundation of a settlement house, Toynbee Hall, convinced Ball that social problems should be studied systematically by Oxford students, and this meant promoting the study of the social sciences, especially political economy. Therefore in 1884 Ball established the Social Science Club, where undergraduates, graduates, townspeople, and workers met in his rooms to hear speakers lecture on social problems; later in 1886 he helped establish the Oxford Economic Society, which consisted of young graduates and dons interested in systematic research on economic questions. He was also active in the foundation of the *Economic Review* by the Christian Social Union, of which he was later a member.

In 1886 Ball joined the Fabian Society and he helped in 1895 to found the Oxford University Fabian Society. In 1907 he was elected to the Fabian Society's national executive committee, by which time he was widely acknowledged as the leading representative of socialist thought in the university. His article on 'The moral aspects of socialism', first published in the *International Journal of Ethics*, was reprinted as Fabian tract 72 (1896). He tried to balance a moderate socialism with a respect for personal liberty. He emphasized the duties of citizenship and social co-operation while maintaining an abiding interest in the development of individual character.

Ball was one of the earliest supporters of the Workers' Educational Association, founded in 1903, and was a member of the committee that drew up the influential report *Oxford and Working-Class Education* (1908). Among the report's recommendations was that working-class students, principally those from Ruskin College, of which Ball was an executive council member, should be admitted to the university diploma in economics (created in 1904). He had supported the agitation to establish a postgraduate school of economics at Oxford to encourage the study of economics and related subjects, for which Ball himself offered informal teaching in economic theory, history of economic theories, and socialism. After the 1908 report the number of students studying for the diploma increased dramatically, thereby greatly increasing the demand for lecturers in economics. His last attempt to promote the systematic study of social issues at Oxford was his assistance in founding Barnett House, which opened in 1914 as a centre for social research. Ball did not live to see the establishment of the undergraduate course in philosophy, politics, and economics, but there is no doubt that its emergence owed much to his earlier efforts, and the school is his continuing legacy to Oxford. Another is the designation of the Oxford research degree as 'DPhil', a compromise suggested by Ball in 1916 to avoid the German associations of 'PhD' and to distinguish the new credential from the more prestigious 'DLitt'. Ball died at his home, Willowgate, Boars Hill, Oxford, on 23 May 1918, and was survived by his wife and daughter. F. S. LEE

Sources O. H. Ball, *Sidney Ball: memories and impressions of 'an ideal don'* (1923) • A. Kadish, *The Oxford economists in the late nineteenth century* (1982) • A. Briggs, 'Social welfare, past and present', *Traditions of social policy*, ed. A. H. Halsey (1976) • A. Kadish, *Apostle Arnold: the life and death of Arnold Toynbee, 1852–1883* (1986) • C. V. Butler, *Barnett House, 1914 to 1964: a record for its friends* (privately printed [Oxford], [1964]) • W. Young and F. S. Lee, *Oxford economics and Oxford economists* (1993) • *Hist. U. Oxf.* 8: *20th cent.* • L. Macfarlane, 'Sidney Ball: Oxford's foremost Fabian', *Oxford Magazine*, 8th week, Michaelmas term (1997)

Archives Oriel College, Oxford, L. R. Phelps MSS

Likenesses Lafayette, photograph, 1909, repro. in Ball, *Sidney Ball*, facing p. 102 • S. Anderson, etching, 1913, repro. in Ball, *Sidney Ball*, frontispiece • portrait, Barnett House, Oxford

Wealth at death £8025 15s. 7d.: probate, 16 July 1918, *CGPLA Eng. & Wales*

Ball, Thomas (1590–1659), hagiographer and Church of England clergyman, was born at Alberbury, Shropshire, of unknown parents. In 1613 he was appointed usher of a Mr Puller's school at Epping, Essex, and it was his employer's letter of recommendation which introduced him to John Preston of Queens' College, Cambridge. Ball entered the college in 1615, graduated BA in 1622, and was one of the 'twelve disciples' (Ball, 86) who followed Preston to Emmanuel College when he became master. Proceeding to MA in 1625, Ball was elected a fellow, and ordained a priest at Peterborough on 19 May 1627. In 1628 Preston, on his deathbed, bequeathed to Ball his pupils—Lord Saye and Sele's brother and the sons of the earl of Warwick and Sir John Pickering. Ball wrote the life of his mentor, later included in Samuel Clarke's collection of godly lives, and collaborated with Richard Sibbes and Thomas Goodwin to produce a posthumous edition of Preston's sermons. On 11 November 1629 he acceded to a request from the corporation of Northampton to become vicar of its church of All Saints. With his first wife, Dorothy (*d.* 1631), he had a daughter, Elizabeth.

Ball was a prominent member of a self-consciously godly community centred on Northampton and an active organizer of local opposition to crown policies of the

1620s and 1630s. Through Preston he was associated with national opponents of the regime, especially Christopher Sherland, who described him as his 'reverend and pious friend' (PRO, PROB 11/161/10), and Lord Saye. On 5 June 1633 Ball married Sherland's widow, Jane, *née* Oglethorpe (*d.* 1635): Ruth was their only child. Ball regarded Preston and himself as guardians of a Calvinist orthodoxy which by 1626 had been abandoned by the crown in favour of an anti-Calvinist 'prelaticall' (Ball, 101) party—'several of the Bishops … were Arminians' (ibid., 123)—which sought to replace the authority of scripture with 'unwritten Traditions' (ibid., 124) while marginalizing orthodox Calvinists as treasonous puritans. His public opposition began in 1627 when he defaulted over payment of the forced loan at Northampton (before becoming vicar), and in 1633 he omitted to read the anti-sabbatarian Book of Sports. He was repeatedly harassed by the church courts for not administering the communion in the Laudian fashion—only to those who kneeled at the altar rails—and for not bowing at the mention of Jesus's name. In turn, godly backsliders who conformed were condemned by Ball and Saye. Despite pressure from the courts (which discouraged afternoon sermons) Ball preached twice on Sundays and invited an impressive range of visiting ministers to read the Thursday lecture in contravention of royal instructions of 1633. The next year he was suspended for preaching controversial doctrine. The Northampton pulpit was used to sound a clarion call against 'Idolatry' and its sponsors, the 'p[er]secutors of [Christ]ians' (Woodford's diary, 135), while Ball and Saye attended a public fast in support of Laudianism's opponents, Henry Burton, John Bastwick, and William Prynne. During the 1630s Ball also acted as the intermediary between Northamptonshire puritans and John Dury, who planned to establish a pan-protestant union against Catholicism; Ball worked with William Twisse on the project.

In November 1637 Ball married his third wife, Jane (*d.* 1660), the widow of a Mr Hatch. They had eight children, Thomas, Jane, Samuel, Nathaniel, Martha, Dorothy, Timothy, and Joseph. Ball canvassed for the godly candidate, Sir Gilbert Pickering (his former pupil), in the shire contest for the Short Parliament. He had omitted to pay the clerical tax to fund the bishops' wars, was prominent at the clerical conference at Kettering in August 1640 which supported the aims of the invading Scots, and refused to take the 'etcetera oath' legitimizing the new ecclesiastical canons.

During the civil war Ball acted as adviser to the local committee for plundered ministers, which was dominated by Pickering. In 1648 he subscribed to the Northamptonshire agreement with the London testimony in support of presbyterian church government and in 1656 published *Pastorum propugnaculum* in defence of a national ordained ministry against the attacks of the sectaries. He died at Northampton in 1659 and was buried in All Saints' Church on 21 June; the funeral oration was preached by the Presbyterian John Howes. J. FIELDING

Sources J. Howes, *Real comforts extracted from moral and spiritual principles presented in a sermon preached at the funeral of that reverend divine Mr Thomas Ball late minister of Gods word at Northampton upon the 21 day of June AD 1659 with a narrative of his life and death* (1660), 37–51 • T. Webster, *Godly clergy in early Stuart England: the Caroline puritan movement, c.1620–1643* (1997), 257–61 • T. Ball, *The life of the renowned Dr Preston*, ed. E. W. Harcourt (1885) • H. I. Longden, *Northamptonshire and Rutland clergy from 1500*, ed. P. I. King and others, 16 vols. in 6, Northamptonshire RS (1938–52), vol. 1, p. 169 • A. J. Fielding, 'Conformists, puritans and the church courts: the diocese of Peterborough, 1603–1642', PhD diss., U. Birm., 1989 • R. Woodford's diary, 1637–41, New College, Oxford, MS 9502, 11, 77, 135, 408 • will, PRO, PROB 11/161 [will of C. Sherland], sig. 10 • *DNB* • P. R. Brindle, 'Politics and society in Northamptonshire, 1649–1714', PhD diss., University of Leicester, 1983, 107, 142

Wealth at death £900, plus estates/lands: will, PRO, PROB 11/294, sig. 445

Ball, William (*c.*1631–1690), astronomer, was the son of Sir Peter *Ball (*bap.* 1598, *d.* 1680), a barrister of the Middle Temple, and his wife, Ann, daughter of Sir William Cooke of Highnam, Gloucestershire. He was the eldest of seventeen children in a legal and mercantile family of minor Devon gentry, whose estate was centred on the hamlet of Mamhead on the eastern escarpment of the Haldon hills. His father was knighted at Oxford in 1643 for his services to the king's cause, and was appointed attorney-general to Henrietta Maria, having served as her solicitor since at least 1636; he was then evicted from the Middle Temple and reportedly imprisoned, and his estate was sequestered. The whereabouts and fortune of his son and heir at this time are not known.

In 1646 William Ball was registered at the Middle Temple, a few months after commons and exercises were restored; there is no record of his subsequently being called to the bar. His family began to recover their fortunes somewhat in 1653. Ball first enters the historian's line of vision two years later, as one of a group of virtuosi who were actively engaged in observing the puzzling changes in the appearance of the planet Saturn. Their work was generally conducted around the observatories in the tower of Wadham College, Oxford, at Gresham College, in the City of London, and at Sir Paul Neile's residence at White Waltham. Ball's observations seem to have been conducted independently, though other astronomers were kept informed of his progress, in particular Christopher Wren (1632–1723) in Oxford and London, and Christiaan Huygens (1629–1695) at The Hague.

The location from which Ball made his observations is not recorded but it was probably in the vicinity of London rather than in Devon, as Wren writes that Ball's important observation of a faint shadowy belt on the surface of Saturn was shown to him 'immediately' upon its discovery in 1655 (*Œuvres complètes*, 3.422). The instrument with which Ball made this discovery is recorded: according to John Wallis it was a 12 foot telescope made in Rome by Eustachio Divini (1610–1685) (ibid., 2.305). Ball's observations played an important role in the formation of Wren's hypothesis that Saturn was surrounded by a thin elliptical 'corona' of uneven width, and they were also extensively used by Huygens in support of his theory that the planet was surrounded by a solid circular ring. Huygens's theory, made public in 1659, gained the broad acceptance of the astronomical community during the 1660s.

It is not known how Ball first became acquainted with the group of astronomers interested in Saturn. It is possible that he was associated with the displaced royalists who assembled at the London home of Charles Scarburgh between 1646 and 1649. Both Seth Ward, who was at the centre of the Wadham and Gresham astronomical groups in the 1650s, and the young Christopher Wren, of Ball's own generation, were among their number. Alternatively he may have come into contact with astronomy through attending lectures at Gresham College. Thomas Sprat, in a report replete with inaccuracies, writes that Ball was one of the virtuosi who met regularly at Gresham College during the 1650s (*History of the Royal Society*, 1667, 57).

In the Michaelmas term following the Restoration, Ball was one of the twelve virtuosi who met after Christopher Wren's Gresham lecture and discussed a 'designe of founding a Colledge for the promoting of Physico-Mathematicall Experimentall Learning' (*Record of the Royal Society*, 7), agreeing to formalize their proceedings to this end. Ball's 'chamber in the Temple' (ibid.) was initially designated as one of the society's meeting places and he was appointed its treasurer. This new society subsequently gained royal approval and support. Ball was nominated a member of the governing council of the Royal Society in its charters of 1662 and 1663, and his appointment as treasurer was confirmed in May 1663. At the first annual election in November 1663 he was elected to the council but not to the office of treasurer, which went to Abraham Hill. The detailed accounts that Ball drew up during his tenure as treasurer survive, and form the core of the society's earliest administrative records.

Ball continued as an active member of the Royal Society for another two years. He was a regular participant in a number of the committees responsible for arranging a collective experimental programme, and he had particular responsibility for experiments relating to magnetic phenomena. In the plague year of 1665 he withdrew to Mamhead, where he continued his astronomical observations intermittently. In September and October of that year he observed Saturn's ring in an elongated condition and indented towards its centre, so that it appeared to touch the planet on either side. The report of this observation reached London at the height of the plague, when the Royal Society was in recess. Sir Robert Moray thought that it 'will puzzle anew Mr Hugens his conceit of a circle' and saw it as evidence that Saturn's ring actually touched the planet's body, as it did in Wren's hypothesis (*Correspondence of Henry Oldenburg*, 2.608–9). The claim made by some nineteenth-century historians that Ball discovered the principal division in Saturn's ring in 1665 is, however, false.

Ball suffered from continual ill health, which he attributed to his having fallen 30 feet onto hard ground in 1660. Informing the secretary of the Royal Society in 1666 that 'I intend not to see London a great while if I can help itt' (*Correspondence of Henry Oldenburg*, 3.89), he denied lacking philosophical ambitions. Rather, 'my desires being as large as any but my body by soe long a disorder hath beene a great obstruction to that designe of pleasure' (ibid., 3.93). For a brief period in 1667 and 1668 he returned to London, where he married Mary Posthuma Hussey, daughter of Thomas Hussey of Honnington, Lincolnshire, at St Paul's in Covent Garden on 10 July 1668, after which he returned to Mamhead permanently. The Balls had five sons and one daughter, of whom four sons survived into adulthood. William Ball's engagement in managing the family's estate in Devon left him little time for scientific pursuits. He wrote to Huygens in 1675 that he was 'very unhappy wanting leisure from the troublesome incumbrances of a country life, usually esteemed retirement … having the care of much husbandry for my father as well as myselfe' (ibid., 11.223).

The Balls were a disappointed family, not having received the preferment they felt was their due on the return of the monarchy, as William Ball frankly recorded on the memorial that he erected to his father in Mamhead church. The improvements that were planned for the house and park at Mamhead had to wait until the eighteenth century. William Ball died in 1690, ten years after inheriting the estate, and was buried on 22 October in the round of the Temple Church, London.

JOSEPH GROSS

Sources *The correspondence of Henry Oldenburg*, ed. and trans. A. R. Hall and M. B. Hall, 1–3 (1965–6); 11 (1977) • *Œuvres complètes de Christiaan Huygens*, ed. Société Hollandaise des Sciences, 22 vols. (1888–1950), vols. 1–3 • R. Polwhele, *The history of Devonshire*, 3 vols. (1793–1806), vol. 2 • *The record of the Royal Society of London*, 4th edn (1940) • A. van Helden, 'Christopher Wren's *De corpore Saturni*', *Notes and Records of the Royal Society*, 23 (1968), 213–29 • M. Hunter, *The Royal Society and its fellows, 1660–1700: the morphology of an early scientific institution*, 2nd edn (1994) • J. Prince, *Danmonii orientales illustres, or, The worthies of Devon* (1701) • H. A. C. Sturgess, ed., *Register of admissions to the Honourable Society of the Middle Temple, from the fifteenth century to the year 1944*, 3 vols. (1949) • A. R. Ingpen, *The Middle Temple bench book* (1912) • J. Hutchinson, ed., *A catalogue of notable Middle Templars: with brief biographical notices* (1902) • A. van Helden, 'Saturn and his anses', *Journal for the History of Astronomy*, 5 (1974), 105–21 • A. Armitage, 'William Ball', *Notes and Records of the Royal Society*, 15 (1960), 162–72 • T. Birch, *The history of the Royal Society of London*, 4 vols. (1756–7); repr. with introduction by A. R. Hall (1968), vol. 1 • M. Hunter, *Establishing the new science: the experience of the early Royal Society* (1989) • S. Pumfrey, 'Ideas above his station: a social study of Hooke's curatorship of experiments', *History of Science*, 29 (1991), 1–44 • R. E. W. Maddison, 'The accompt of William Balle', *Notes and Records of the Royal Society*, 14 (1959–60), 174–83 • W. G. Hoskins, *Devon*, new edn (1972) • W. B. Wright, *Ball family records* (1908) • M. A. E. Green, ed., *Calendar of the proceedings of the committee for compounding … 1643–1660*, 2, PRO (1890) • *IGI*
Archives RS

Ball, William (*fl.* 1911–1913), suffrage activist and trade unionist, came from a working-class family, possibly based in the midlands. Little is known of his early years apart from his paid work after leaving school. After working initially as a gardener, he became a master tailor with his own business, moving into unskilled work when this failed. In 1911–12 he was living in Birmingham with his wife and five children and was a member of the Transport Workers' Federation.

Ball came to public attention in 1912 as a result of involvement in the Men's Political Union (MPU), one of several men's groups campaigning for women's suffrage.

As a working-class man, he was an anomaly in an organization whose members were predominantly from middle-class educated backgrounds. Ball was arrested in December 1911 after breaking Home Office windows in protest against the prison treatment of a fellow MPU member. On 22 December 1911 he was sentenced to two months' hard labour. Once in prison he went on hunger strike and refused to wear prison clothes. As a result he was forcibly fed twice a day for five weeks. By 25 January 1912 prison authorities recorded that he was 'restless and talking wildly' but was taking food voluntarily four days later (Holton, 'Manliness and militancy', 126). However, on 9 February 1912 he was declared insane and was released as a pauper into the care of a lunatic asylum, on the grounds that he had no family or friends to receive him. Ball's wife had been informed of his release only after the event, and was able to move him into private care only after some argument.

The issue of Ball's prison treatment and release into a lunatic asylum was taken up by members of the MPU, in particular by Hugh Franklin, who protested to his uncle Herbert Samuel, a member of the Liberal government. The MPU was concerned not only that Ball had been released before the end of his sentence, but also that he had been sent to an asylum without his family being informed. The haste and apparent secrecy surrounding this action, together with grave concerns about his health, raised questions about the mistreatment of Ball in prison and about the possible attempt to cover this up. A doctor examining William Ball after his release from prison found high levels of sugar in his urine and an ulcer on his throat, yet there was no reference to either condition in his prison notes, nor was any date given for the onset of the mental illness which was supposedly the reason for releasing him in the first place.

Bowing to pressure, the Home Office launched an inquiry into Ball's prison treatment, headed by Sir George Savage. The resulting white paper vindicated the prison authorities, maintaining that Ball was a man of 'feeble intellect', 'defective' in general knowledge, and 'illiterate'. It concluded that his mental breakdown had nothing to do with his treatment as a prisoner on hunger strike, but was the outcome of 'living in a state of emotional excitement because of his suffrage activities, or maybe the consequence of an accident he had suffered as a dock labourer' (Holton, 'Manliness and militancy', 126). Prison records reported that although Ball had co-operated with forcible feeding, he had shown some evidence of sensory and auditory hallucinations, believing he had experienced electrical torture. After his release Ball maintained that he had been tied down and given electric shocks while being force-fed.

The MPU and others challenged the report, arguing that Ball was a literate, skilled worker who had fallen on hard times, and that the industrial injury to which the report attempted to attribute his breakdown was a strain to his knee, not to his intellect. It is notable also that Ball conducted his own defence in court when arrested; this action certainly seems at odds with the Savage report's claims about his inferior intellect.

Ball was back in prison a year later after involvement in another protest. Although he went on hunger strike, he was released after two days when his fine was paid anonymously. Nothing is known of his life after these events. CATHERINE BLACKFORD

Sources S. Holton, 'Manliness and militancy: the political protest of male suffragists and the gendering of the "suffragette identity"', *The men's share? Masculinities, male support and women's suffrage in Britain, 1890–1920*, ed. A. V. John and C. Eustance (1997) · S. Holton, *Suffage days: stories from the women's suffrage movement* (1996) · A. John and C. Eustance, 'Shared histories—differing identities', *The men's share? Masculinities, male support and women's suffrage in Britain, 1890–1920*, ed. A. V. John and C. Eustance (1997) · B. Harrison, *Prudent revolutionaries: portraits of British feminists between the wars* (1987) · E. S. Pankhurst, *The suffragette movement: an intimate account of persons and ideals* (1931); repr. (1984)

Ball, William Platt (1844–1917), freethinker and author, was born on 28 November 1844 at 12 Regent Row, Birmingham, the son of Abraham Ball, copper plate printer, and his wife, Mary Platt. He was educated at the Birkbeck Institute, London, and was briefly a schoolteacher before resigning in protest against religious instruction. In 1866 he matriculated at the University of London. He subsequently made a unique use of his pedagogical skills, spending 1870–71 in Turkey teaching pyrotechny in the sultan's service. After a brush with death, upon the bursting of a mortar, he received the order of the Mejidiye, and returned to England.

Ball became a contributor to the *National Reformer* in 1878. His early articles, such as 'The ten commandments', 'Gentle Jesus, meek and mild', and 'Divine atrocities', began his campaign against the contradictions, unscientific falsehoods, and inhumanity of Christian scripture which culminated in *The Bible Handbook for Freethinkers and Inquiring Christians* (1888), which he co-edited with G. W. Foote. A self-proclaimed atheist, Ball was on the staff of Foote's *Freethinker* from 1881 to 1886 before retiring due to ill health. Having established himself as a contributor to the *National Reformer*, *The Freethinker*, and *Progress*, Ball continued to produce occasional articles for the free-thought press, but mainly lived off his savings. In later years he provided *The Freethinker* with weekly batches of newspaper cuttings, delivering his last batch the day before his death.

Among freethinkers Ball achieved notoriety in the early 1880s for his vehement opposition to Annie Besant's conversion to socialism. He first openly detected 'socialism in disguise' in Besant's weekly 'Daybreak' column in late 1884. After several journalistic skirmishes, he challenged her to debate 'creeping socialism' in early 1885. His *Mrs. Besant's Socialism: an Examination and an Exposure* (1886) was a strong denunciation of socialism and Besant, and an affirmation of individualism.

Contemporaries described Ball as possessing a 'quiet and unassuming nature' and being 'naturally of a genuine scientific cast of mind' (Cohen, 29). From his earliest anti-Christian writings, Ball wed his religious unbelief to his commitment to Darwinism. Convinced that overpopulation was the greatest problem facing the social reformer, and that natural selection was the only mechanism of evolutionary change, Ball espoused 'evolutional Malthusianism'. The axiom that 'people must proportion their families to their means and prospects' (*Progress*, 4 Nov 1884, 236) underpinned Ball's anti-Christian, anti-socialist, and scientific writings. It even surfaced in his poetry:

'Choose well your parents.' Yes, good friend,
The Ancestry whence you descend
Needs soundest choice; because your birth
Decides all else for you on earth.
(*Progress*, 6 May 1886, 226)

His own choice never to marry may have been his ultimate act of Malthusian, artificial selection.

In *Are the Effects of Use and Disuse Inherited?* (1890), Ball aligned himself with the neo-Darwinians in opposing the neo-Lamarckian belief that the effects of use and disuse were inherited. By 30 June 1891, of a print run of 1500, 560 copies had been sold and 117 presented free. T. H. Huxley informed him that 'the case could hardly be better stated' (Huxley, 267). F. H. Collins, in contrast, responded with his Spencerian pamphlet, *The Diminution of the Jaw in the Civilised Races, an Effect of Disuse* (1891). Convinced that Collins composed 'sad rubbish', Ball continued in his adherence to evolutional Malthusianism and the necessity of natural or artificial selection, and embarked on a grand project to produce a large book on the evolution of man from a sociological perspective. Although he claimed to have written two-thirds of it by 1895, the book was never published. The Weismann–Spencer controversy over the inheritance of acquired characters, however, motivated him to contribute two articles on the subject to *Natural Science* in 1893 and 1894.

In early 1917 Ball made his final Malthusian statement. In a suicide note, he explained: 'I am 72 years of age and the machine is breaking down in all directions' (*The Times*, 12 Jan 1917). By ending his life, he reasoned, he could leave a small bequest to his blind niece (Gladys Emily Thurston, daughter of his sister Mary Thurston) before he had spent it on his daily existence. He believed, moreover, that such economizing during wartime was an act of true patriotism. At his long-time residence at 72 Chisenhale Road, Bethnal Green, London, Ball died after taking cyanide of potassium on 8 January 1917. At an inquest three days later the coroner returned a verdict of 'suicide during temporary insanity'. As Ball had wished, his funeral was held without any ceremony and 'without—in the customary sense—mourners' (Cohen, 29). J. F. M. Clark

Sources [C. Cohen], 'Death of William Platt Ball', *The Freethinker* (14 Jan 1917), 29 • 'Patriotism and suicide', *The Times* (12 Jan 1917), 3 • J. M. Wheeler, *A biographical dictionary of freethinkers of all ages and nations* (1889) • ICL, Huxley MSS, vol. 10, fols. 217–25 • Oxf. U. Mus. NH, Hope and Arkell Libraries, Poulton MSS • L. Huxley, *Life and letters of Thomas Henry Huxley*, 2 (1900), 267–9 • E. Royle, *Radicals, secularists and republicans: popular freethought in Britain, 1866–1915* (1980) • A. Taylor, *Annie Besant: a biography* (1992) • M. Ridley, 'Coadaptation and the inadequacy of natural selection', *British Journal for the History of Science*, 15 (1982), 45–68 • F. B. Churchill, 'The Weismann–Spencer controversy over the inheritance of acquired characters', *Human implications of scientific advance: the 15th International Congress of the History of Science* [Edinburgh 1977], ed. E. G. Forbes (1978), 451–68 • Wills and administration register • b. cert.
Archives BL, Add. MS 42579, fol. 51 • ICL, Huxley MSS • Oxf. U. Mus. NH, Hope and Arkell Libraries, Poulton MSS
Wealth at death £755 16*s*. 9*d*.: wills and administration register

Ballance, Sir Charles Alfred (1856–1936), surgeon, was born at Taunton on 30 August 1856, the eldest son and second child of Charles Alfred Ballance, silk throwster, and his wife, Caroline Hendebourck, daughter of Samuel Hendebourck Pollard, of Taunton. He was educated first at Taunton College, then in Germany, and finally at St Thomas's Hospital, where he graduated MB (London) with first-class honours. He became aural surgeon at St Thomas's in 1885, and assistant surgeon to the West London Hospital. He was among the first to succeed in radical mastoid surgery. In 1882 he proceeded MS with a gold medal. In 1883 Ballance married Sophie Annie (*d.* 1926), only daughter of Alfred Smart, of Blackheath; they had one son and five daughters.

Ballance was elected assistant surgeon at St Thomas's in 1891, surgeon in 1900, and consulting surgeon in 1919; he was also surgeon with Victor Horsley at the National Hospital for the Paralysed and Epileptic, in Queen Square (1891–1908). During the First World War he was a consultant with the rank of colonel in the Army Medical Service in Malta, and he was appointed CB in 1916 and KCMG in 1918. He was president of the Medical Society of London in 1906, a member of the council of the Royal College of Surgeons in 1910 and its vice-president from 1920 to 1921, and the first president of the Society of British Neurological Surgeons in 1927. He was chief surgeon to the Metropolitan Police from 1912 to 1926.

Ballance approached surgical problems through physiological experiments on living animals, in the tradition of John Hunter. Some of his methods were superseded in his lifetime—for instance, his technique for ligation of large arteries. His work with Charles Sherrington, published in 1889 in the *Journal of Physiology*, on the formation of scar tissue, added significantly to contemporary knowledge. Ballance was a general surgeon who favoured aural and neurological surgery. In *Some Points in the Surgery of the Brain and its Membranes* (1907), he surveyed a field in which he had been an early practitioner, and his scholarly *Essays on the Surgery of the Temporal Bone* (2 vols., 1919) recorded his valuable contributions over thirty years. The repair of nerves was his chief interest. With James Purves-Stewart he wrote *The Healing of Nerves* (1901), and he applied their findings in the treatment of facial palsy. In 1919 he gave the Bradshaw lecture, on the surgery of the heart, to the Royal College of Surgeons. In the United States of America, in 1932, he studied the development of nerve grafts, and finally in London he developed a complicated cross-suture of divided nerves. In 1933 he gave the Lister memorial lecture and was awarded the Lister memorial medal. He received honorary degrees from the universities of Glasgow and Malta.

Ballance was a large and imposing figure. A slow, deliberate manner hid his cultivation and charm. He died a widower, at his home, 34 St John's Wood Court, London, on 8 February 1936. W. R. LE FANU, *rev.* B. A. BRYAN

Sources *The Times* (10 Feb 1936) · *BMJ* (15 Feb 1936), 339 · *The Lancet* (15 Feb 1936), 396 · *The Lancet* (22 Feb 1936), 450 · *WWW* · M. Rantch, *A century of surgery, 1880–1980* (1981), 318, 346, 351, 436 · *St Thomas's Hospital Gazette*, 35 (1935–6), 337–40 · personal knowledge (1949) · *CGPLA Eng. & Wales* (1936)

Likenesses photograph, repro. in *St Thomas's Hospital Gazette* · photograph, repro. in *The Lancet* (22 Feb 1936), 450

Wealth at death £15,734 8*s.* 10*d.*: resworn probate, 22 April 1936, *CGPLA Eng. & Wales*

Ballance, John (1839–1893), newspaper proprietor and premier of New Zealand, was born on 27 March 1839 at Ballypitmave, near Glenavy, co. Antrim, Ireland, the eldest of the eleven children of Samuel Ballance (1800–1879), a tenant farmer, and his wife, Mary McNiece, the daughter of Conway McNiece. He was educated at the local national school and Wilson's academy in Belfast. By the age of sixteen he was helping his father, an evangelical protestant who was active in local politics, to write his speeches. He left school early and took a job with a Belfast hardware firm. In 1857 he left Belfast for Birmingham to work as a travelling salesman, and enrolled in evening classes at the Birmingham and Midland Institute to study politics, biography, and history. He married Fanny Taylor, the daughter of a licensed victualler, at the church of St Peter and St Paul, Aston, on 17 June 1863. Not long afterwards, owing in part to Fanny's ill health, they decided to emigrate to New Zealand, where Fanny had a brother living in Wanganui. In April 1866 they left London on the *Ruahine* bound for Melbourne, and after a short stay continued to New Zealand on the *Albion*. They arrived at Wellington on 11 August, and a few days later travelled to Wanganui.

In Wanganui, Ballance opened a jewellery store as a temporary expedient, but it did not prosper. In 1867 he established the *Evening Herald* (later the *Wanganui Herald*) and its weekly edition, the *Weekly Herald* (later *The Yeoman*). An able and innovative journalist, he ran the paper with considerable success. During the war against Titokowaru in 1868–9, when Wanganui felt itself under immediate threat, the *Herald* was outspoken in criticizing the performance of the British forces and Titokowaru. Regarded by the authorities as a maverick troublemaker, Ballance spent a night in gaol after refusing to join the local militia, the compulsion having offended his liberal beliefs. However, he later saw limited action with the Wanganui cavalry volunteers, when he combined the roles of soldier and war correspondent. In March 1868 Fanny Ballance died, at the age of twenty-four. On 19 May 1870, in Wellington, Ballance married Ellen Anderson, the daughter of the Wellington merchant David Anderson and his wife, Ann Thompson. There were no children from either marriage, but in 1886 Ellen and John adopted Ellen's four-year-old niece.

Increasingly involved in Wanganui affairs, Ballance in 1875 narrowly won the Rangitikei parliamentary seat on a platform stressing abolition of the provincial system and

John Ballance (1839–1893), by Alfred Martin, 1875–89

support for state education. He joined George Grey's ministry in January 1878 as commissioner of customs, commissioner of stamp duties, and minister of education. Shortly afterwards he became colonial treasurer—high office for a politically inexperienced man. His budget of 6 August 1878 was arguably the most significant since Julius Vogel's public works announcement eight years earlier; he reformed the tariff and introduced a modest but symbolically important land tax. Ballance won the Wanganui seat in 1879 but two years later suffered his only electoral defeat. Out of parliament he continued to advocate closer land settlement, writing a series of articles (collected in 1887 as *A National Land Policy Based on the Principle of State Ownership*) on land reform and nationalization. A convinced secularist, he formed the Wanganui Freethought Association in 1883 and brought out the monthly *Freethought Review* (1883–5).

Returned at the 1884 general election by a sizable majority, Ballance joined the Stout–Vogel ministry and held the lands and immigration, native affairs, and defence portfolios. His important Land Act of 1885 aimed to place as many people as possible on the land by encouraging leasehold tenure and establishing government-assisted special settlement schemes. As native minister he pursued an enlightened, if somewhat paternalistic, policy aimed at protecting Maori land from private sale. The government was defeated in 1887, and two years later Ballance was elected leader of the opposition. A radical land policy was the dominant theme of his campaign at the December 1890 election, which took place against a background of strikes and economic depression. Liberals and their trade unions fared well at the polls, and in January 1891 Ballance formed the country's first Liberal government.

Having surrounded himself with talented cabinet colleagues, Ballance steered his government through two difficult years before his death in 1893, and in doing so laid the foundation for a long period of Liberal rule. A major problem was opposition to his legislation from the legislative council. The defeated premier, Harry Atkinson, had arranged for the appointment of seven councillors in an attempt to block the new government. The council subsequently rejected key measures passed in the lower house. Ballance failed to persuade the governor to redress Atkinson's actions by appointing Ballance nominees. The matter was passed to the Colonial Office in London, which in 1892 ruled in Ballance's favour, thus securing the passage of Liberal legislation and marking a major step in New Zealand's path to independence.

During his premiership Ballance established the Liberal Federation, the first attempt in New Zealand to form a nationwide party organization. As colonial treasurer he introduced land and income taxes to replace the property tax. Other legislation included the Land Act 1892 and the Land for Settlements Act 1892. The new taxes were much criticized at home and overseas, but critics were largely silenced when Ballance announced a record budget surplus in 1892. In his last months in office he supported moves to enfranchise women, a reform he had long advocated. In this he was strongly influenced by his wife, Ellen, who was prominent in the growing feminist movement in New Zealand and vice-president of the Women's Progressive Society.

Ballance was not charismatic, nor was he a great public speaker. He was kind, courteous, considerate, and honest, and attracted extraordinary loyalty among his cabinet. Many viewed his mild temperament as a sign of weakness. W. P. Reeves described him as 'absolutely the most unassuming and unpretentious' of all the successful men he had known. But, he added, 'as a Premier—and I say it emphatically—he knew how to be master in his own house' (*The Yeoman*, 10 June 1893).

Ballance died of cancer at Premier House, Wellington, on 27 April 1893. After a state funeral he was buried at Wanganui three days later. Death in office helped serve his positive popular reputation, although over the following long premiership of Richard Seddon, Ballance's major contribution to Liberalism tended to disappear from view. Ellen Ballance survived her husband and remained active in community organizations in Wanganui, where she died on 14 June 1935. TIM MCIVOR

Sources T. McIvor, *The rainmaker: a biography of John Ballance* (1989) · *New Zealand parliamentary debates* · R. Stout, 'Character sketch: the Hon. John Ballance', *Review of Reviews for Australasia* (May 1893) · *The Yeoman* (10 June 1893)
Archives NL NZ, Turnbull L.
Likenesses A. Martin, photograph, 1875–89, NL NZ, Turnbull L. [*see illus.*] · P. Tennyson Cole, oils, *c*.1892, Sargent Gallery, Wanganui, New Zealand · statue, 1897, Parliament Buildings, Wellington, New Zealand · photographs, NL NZ, Turnbull L.

Ballantine, James (1807/8–1877), stained-glass artist and writer, was born in Edinburgh, the son of James Ballantine, a brewer, and his wife, Margaret Anderson. He served an apprenticeship with David Roberts, then working as an Edinburgh house decorator and theatrical scenery painter, and also studied draughtsmanship at the Trustees' Academy in Edinburgh. His specialization in the neglected art of glass staining was almost certainly the result of time spent at an English studio—perhaps in Newcastle upon Tyne—and clearly gave him sufficient confidence in his mastery of the medium to set up his own company in Edinburgh in 1837 and publish *A Treatise on Painted Glass* in 1845. Despite advocating domestic use of stained glass and criticizing 'antiquing' of new glass, this work was conservative in approach and did not advocate any radical departures in terms of subject matter or technique.

Early successes included a number of windows for the House of Lords (1843), a set of armorial windows based on David Roberts's designs for the Scott monument, Edinburgh (1847), and an extensive scheme for St John's Episcopal Church, Edinburgh (1850s). The 1850s also brought controversy when Ballantine's scheme for Glasgow Cathedral was overruled by a committee which favoured the enamelled glass produced by the royal Bavarian glassworks in Munich. Pompously declaring the Munich glass superior to any native product, the committee ensured a national outcry and a consequent flurry of commissions to salve the injured pride of Ballantine. Notable later work included windows for Ibrox parish church, Glasgow (*c*.1863), the choir of St Giles's Cathedral, Edinburgh (1874–7), and Dunfermline Abbey (from 1873). The last two, based on designs by Robert Herdman and Joseph Noël Paton respectively, are of particular note and did much to vindicate the quality of indigenous glass staining.

In parallel with his business career, Ballantine enjoyed a considerable reputation as a poet and writer. Recognized as an authority on Robert Burns, he wrote songs and verses of his own which owe much to Burns's idiom. These appeared periodically in *The Scotsman* and were then collected and published from 1843 in a series of monthly parts as *The Gaberlunzie's Wallet*. Songs such as 'Bonnie Bonaly', 'Ilka Blade o'Grass', and 'Castles in the Air' were among the most popular songs of their time, but seem to have enjoyed no enduring success. Other notable publications include the *Miller of Deanhaugh* (1845) and *Lilias Lee* (1871), a tale in Spenserian verse. His *Life of David Roberts, R.A.* (1866) is a fulsome eulogy of the man whose brushes he had once cleaned and who set him on the path to become the chief revivalist of Scottish ecclesiastical stained glass. Ballantine died at Harrender Lodge, Edinburgh, on 18 December 1877, aged sixty-nine; he was survived by his wife, Henrietta, *née* Miller; his legacy was sustained by his son Alexander and grandson, James, both successful stained-glass artists. Another son, James, was a house painter. R. G. H. NICHOLSON

Sources *DNB* · M. Donnelly, *Scotland's stained glass* (1997) · T. Royle, *The mainstream companion to Scottish literature* (1993) · M. Harrison, *Victorian stained glass* (1980) · d. cert.
Archives Edinburgh Central Reference Library, MSS relating to glass manufacture and painting, literary MSS, and memoranda
Likenesses J. Fred, group portrait, ink and wash drawing, *c*.1840, Scot. NPG · D. O. Hill and R. Adamson, three calotypes, *c*.1850, Scot.

NPG • oils, *c.*1860–1865, Scot. NPG • D. O. Hill and R. Adamson, group portrait, NPG • D. O. Hill and R. Adamson, photographs, NPG • pencil, ink, and watercolour drawing, Scot. NPG

Wealth at death £10,244 9*s.* 11*d.*: probate, 31 Jan 1878, *CCI* • £1,961 9*s.* 7*d.*: eik additional estate, 21 March 1878, *CCI* • £20: eik additional inventory, 9 April 1901, *CCI*

Ballantine [Bannatyne], **William** (1617/18–1661), Roman Catholic priest, was probably born at North Berwick, Haddingtonshire, the second son of Thomas Ballantine (or Bannatyne; *b.* *c.*1574, *d.* in or before 1639), Church of Scotland minister, and Margaret Cockburn, his wife. From 1621 his father was minister of Douglas, Lanarkshire, where William had his schooling until in 1635 he matriculated at Edinburgh University. He did not graduate but travelled on the continent and became a Catholic in Paris. Having been a student at the Scots College there, he entered the Scots College, Rome, in 1641. He completed his studies with distinction, was ordained priest on 3 December 1645 and in March 1646 went to Paris to prepare for missionary work. After arriving in Scotland in January 1649, he quickly realized the need for some co-ordination among the secular priests, who were few in number and lacking in cohesion compared with the Jesuits. After only a short stay he went to Paris, where he conferred with five other secular priests. It was decided to petition the congregation of Propaganda in Rome to provide a superior and financial help, with William Leslie (one of them) acting as their Roman agent. Ballantine returned to Scotland in February 1650 and was appointed prefect of the Scottish secular priests on 13 October 1653. He lived with the marquess of Huntly.

About this time Ballantine journeyed to France and back. When he went again in the summer of 1656 he was arrested on his return to England in September and held in confinement in London for twenty-two months. He apparently established friendly relations with the secretary of state, John Thurloe, while Cromwell seemed interested in using his services and indeed paid for his journey to France when he was banished in July 1658.

Ballantine was then prefect of studies in the Scots College, Paris, and during this time he compiled a spiritual work, *A Preparation for Death* (1672, reprinted 1715) from the writings of a French Jesuit, Jean Suffren. In May 1660, having written a full report for Propaganda, he returned to Scotland and lived in Elgin with the widowed marchioness of Huntly. He fell ill in July 1661 and died, at Elgin, six weeks later on 2 September aged forty-three. After funeral rites in the house the body was taken in a torchlight procession to Elgin Cathedral and buried in the Huntly aisle. Quite remarkably, the Elgin magistrates and a large gathering attended the funeral.

Though described as tall and comely, Ballantine was apparently not robust and he never recovered from his confinement in London. He comes across as a spiritual man as well as being liked and respected. Although he made a number of notable converts while in Scotland, he realized that the greatest need was to build up an organized body of priests and accordingly he made journeys to Paris for business and sent students there. The editor of his book declared that 'his Memory ought to be in perpetual Benediction, amongst all good Catholicks of this Kingdom' (preface to W. Ballantine, *A Preparation for Death*, 1715, x).

MARK DILWORTH

Sources W. J. Anderson, 'William Ballantine, prefect of the Scottish mission, 1653–1661', *Innes Review*, 8 (1957), 19–20 and pl. 1–12 • J. Darragh, *The Catholic hierarchy of Scotland: a biographical list, 1653–1985* (1986), 2, 116 • J. F. S. Gordon, ed., *The Catholic church in Scotland* (1874), vi–xi, 519–21 • M. V. Hay, *The Blairs papers, 1603–1660* (1929) • J. Darragh, 'The imprisonment in London of Prefect Ballantine, 1656', *Innes Review*, 26 (1975), 121–3 • W. J. Anderson, 'Narratives of the Scottish Reformation: Prefect Ballantine's report, *circa* 1660', *Innes Review*, 8 (1957), 39–66, 99–129 • B. M. Halloran, *The Scots College, Paris, 1603–1792* (1997) • P. J. Anderson, ed., *Records of the Scots colleges at Douai, Rome, Madrid, Valladolid and Ratisbon*, New Spalding Club, 30 (1906), 111–13 • *Fasti Scot.*, new edn, 1.380, 2.231, 3.300, 8.34

Archives Bibliotheca Vallicelliana, Rome, report, R. 109 • Rome, reports/letters to Propaganda

Ballantine, William (1778/9–1852). *See under* Ballantine, William (1812–1887).

Ballantine, William (1812–1887), serjeant-at-law, was born in Howland Street, Tottenham Court Road, London, on 3 January 1812, the eldest son of **William Ballantine** (1778/9–1852). His father was called to the bar from the Inner Temple on 5 February 1813, was magistrate of the Thames police, had control of the river police force from 1821 to 1848, and died aged seventy-three at 89 Cadogan Place, Chelsea, London, on 14 December 1852. Ballantine was educated at St Paul's School, London, and at Ashburnham House, Blackheath. He was admitted to the Inner Temple on 28 May 1829, and was called to the bar on 6 June 1834, and occupied rooms in Inner Temple Lane. He joined the Middlesex sessions, where his father occasionally presided, and there he made the valuable acquaintance of John Huddleston. He subsequently joined the central criminal court, and for convenience chose the home circuit. As a young man Ballantine was an assiduous haunter of the old literary taverns in Covent Garden, and he later recorded a number of interesting reminiscences of literary figures from Harrison Ainsworth to Dickens and Trollope. On 4 December 1841 he married Eliza, daughter of Henry Gyles, of London.

The first case of importance in which Ballantine was engaged was a suit in the House of Lords in 1848 to annul the marriage of an heiress, Esther Field, on the grounds of coercion and fraud. Sir Fitzroy Kelly, Sir John Bayley, and other distinguished counsel were in favour of the bill. Ballantine alone opposed it, but his cross-examination was so able and searching that the earl of Devon, who was the chairman of the court, declined to move the further progress of the bill. A murder trial at Chelmsford assizes in 1847 was the first of many in which his client's life was involved, and the trial gave Ballantine his 'first lesson in the art of silent cross-examination'.

On 3 November 1856 Ballantine received the coif of a serjeant-at-law, but he had to wait until 1863 to obtain from Lord Westbury his patent of precedence, which was required to place serjeants on the same level as queen's counsel. In 1863 he was engaged in the Woolley arson case,

William Ballantine (1812–1887), by unknown photographer

and in the following year he received through the marchese d'Azeglio the thanks of the Sardinian government for his exertions on behalf of Pellizzioni, a Sardinian subject. During 1867, the last year in which the House of Commons enjoyed jurisdiction in the case of contested elections, he practised before parliamentary committees in work of this kind. In 1868 he lost an action in which he defended the *Daily Telegraph* on a charge of libel, against his frequent rival and opponent, Serjeant John Humffreys Parry. He was, however, specially appointed by the House of Commons in 1869 to prosecute the mayor of Cork for eulogizing the attempt of O'Farrell to assassinate the duke of Edinburgh (the action was subsequently dropped), and he was no less distinguished by the tact which he displayed in the Mordaunt divorce case of 1870, when the prince of Wales was subpoenaed in the court.

The three forensic performances with which Ballantine's name is mainly associated are his prosecution with Sir Robert Collier, the solicitor-general, of Franz Müller for the murder of Mr Briggs in 1864, in which the crown secured a conviction despite the brilliant defence of Serjeant Parry; his advocacy on behalf of the Tichborne claimant in his ejectment action in 1871; and his defence of Malhar Rao, the Maharaja Gaikwar of Baroda, arraigned for the crime of attempting to poison the British resident. The result in this case, which was tried at Baroda in February 1875, was an acquittal, but the British and native commissioners were divided as to the guilt of the Gaikwar, who was deposed on the grounds of incapacity and misconduct. Ballantine had extricated himself with skill from his position in the Tichborne case before matters became utterly desperate for his client, and in the trial of the Gaikwar his cross-examination of Colonel Robert Phayre was considered a masterpiece. His honorarium of £10,000 was among the largest paid to counsel at that time.

Ballantine was made an honorary bencher of the Inner Temple on 22 November 1878, and retired from active work as an advocate some three years later. *Some Experiences of a Barrister's Life*, which he published in 1882, was an amusing miscellany of gossip and reminiscence, literary and legal, which sold very well and remains of value, especially to literary historians. In November 1882 Ballantine went to America hoping—as it transpired wrongly—to make money by public readings; he recorded his experiences in *The Old World and the New* (1884). Ballantine died at Margate on 9 January 1887. His son, (William Henry) Walter Ballantine (1847–1911), was Liberal MP for Coventry from 1887 to 1895.

Ballantine moved easily in the hinterland between legal and theatrical society. He understood the criminal mind, and much of his success flowed from this. He was generally credited with being the original of Chaffanbrass in Anthony Trollope's *Orley Farm*. According to the *Law Times*, 'he died very poor indeed' and 'left behind him scarcely any lesson, even in his own poor biography, which the rising generation of lawyers could profitably learn' (*Law Times*, 15 Jan 1887).

THOMAS SECCOMBE, *rev.* H. C. G. MATTHEW

Sources Boase, *Mod. Eng. biog.* • *Men of the time* (1887) • *GM*, 2nd ser., 39 (1853), 101 • *The Times* (10 Jan 1887) • *Law Times* (15 Jan 1887) • *ILN* (22 Jan 1887)

Likenesses Faustin, caricature, chromolithograph, NPG • caricature, chromolithograph, NPG; repro. in *VF* (5 March 1870) • photographs, NPG [*see illus.*] • portrait, repro. in W. Ballantine, *The old world and the new* (1884)

Wealth at death 'very poor indeed': *Law Times* (15 Jan 1887)

Ballantrae. For this title name *see* Fergusson, Bernard Edward, Baron Ballantrae (1911–1980).

Ballantyne, James (1772–1833), printer and newspaper editor, was born at Kelso, Roxburghshire, Scotland, on 15 January 1772, the eldest child of John Ballantyne (1743–1817), general merchant, and Jean (1745?–1818), daughter of James Barclay, rector of Dalkeith high school, and his wife, Elizabeth. His early education was at Kelso grammar school, where in 1783 he first met Walter Scott, who briefly attended the school while staying at Kelso. From 1785 to 1786 Ballantyne attended Edinburgh University, and subsequently was apprenticed to a Kelso solicitor. He returned to Edinburgh University to complete his legal training, and renewed his acquaintance with Scott (both were members of the Teviotdale Club).

Ballantyne returned to Kelso in 1795 to practise as a lawyer. His first involvement with editing and printing came as a result of being asked in 1796 to be editor of a proposed anti-radical weekly newspaper, the *Kelso Mail*. The first number of the *Mail* appeared on 13 April 1797. Ballantyne embraced his new role, travelling to London to make literary and business contacts and to Glasgow to purchase new type. In 1799 Scott proposed that Ballantyne should undertake to print some of his ballads, and twelve copies of a

James Ballantyne (1772–1833), by John Ballantyne

small volume entitled *Apology for Tales of Terror* were prepared. Scott's recognition of Ballantyne's potential led him to recommend a move to Edinburgh, and to entrust him with the first two volumes of *The Minstrelsy of the Scottish Border*, published in 1802 under the Kelso imprint. These books demanded a complex layout and typography, which even at that early stage Ballantyne was able to provide.

In November 1802 Ballantyne moved to Edinburgh, and at Abbey Hill opened a shop with the designation 'The Border Press' and equipped with 'two presses and a proof one' (Lockhart, *Memoirs*, 1.378). In 1805 he moved to larger premises, at Paul's Work, and lived nearby, at 10 St John Street. When Scott's *The Lay of the Last Minstrel* was published to acclaim in January 1805 the quality of the printing was widely acknowledged. A consequent increase in orders meant a need for more capital, and Scott entered into a formal partnership with Ballantyne. The deed of co-partnery of 14 March 1805 noted the mutual advantages to be derived from the agreement and formalized the existing financial arrangement. For the move to Edinburgh Scott had advanced a loan of £500; in order to become an equal but secret partner this became a portion of his investment, with the addition of £1508. Ballantyne's contribution consisted of his property in the printing house, estimated at £2090. For managing the business he was to receive a third of the profits, with the remainder to be divided equally between the partners. Ballantyne became 'celebrated for his improvements in the art of printing' (*GM*, 94). In his negotiations with publishers Scott stipulated that his works were to be printed by James Ballantyne & Co. and that he depended on the printer's attentive eye for detail and careful corrections of his manuscripts and proofs. The connection with Ballantyne became even more important when in 1814 Scott began writing the Waverley novels and strove to keep secret his identity as their author.

The success of the printing company did not mean that it was always conducted in a financially prudent manner, and much of the continued expansion was based on borrowings against Scott's future publications. In 1809 another partnership was formed, to establish a bookseller's business under the care of Ballantyne's younger brother John *Ballantyne (1774–1821). James Ballantyne was to receive one fourth of the profits, and works issued by the company were to be printed by his firm. When the resulting dilution of capital funds put the printing business at risk the publishing concern was gradually wound up. In October 1815 Ballantyne's negotiations to marry Christian (*d.* 1829), daughter of the prosperous Carfrae farmer Robert Hogarth, required his release from partnership in the printing company and any responsibility for its liabilities. Scott became sole owner early in 1816 and Ballantyne was manager at a salary of £400. He married Christian on 1 February 1816. Their son, John Alexander, was born on 29 November 1816, followed by four daughters, one of whom, Mary Scott, died in infancy.

In April 1817, in partnership with Scott and with his brother-in-law George Hogarth, writer to the signet, Ballantyne acquired the *Edinburgh Weekly Journal*, for which he was to serve as editor and drama critic. His editorials were written in an engaging but prolix style. Their content became the subject of dispute between Scott and Ballantyne during the political unrest of 1819 and 1820. Scott particularly objected to the editorial position criticizing the magistrates' actions in the Peterloo affair. However, when Scott hinted at withdrawing from the journal Ballantyne modified his position. The disagreement did not have a lasting effect on their relationship, and in May 1822 Ballantyne was readmitted as a partner in the printing business; he remained a part-owner with Scott until 1826. When a financial crisis affecting the entire publishing industry resulted in the bankruptcy of Scott's publishers, Archibald Constable & Co., publisher and printer were entangled in a web of mutual obligations and bills. The resulting failure of James Ballantyne & Co. meant that Scott's affairs and those of the printing house were placed in the trust whose debts were eventually paid by Scott's heroic productivity over the final years of his life. Ballantyne reverted to his role as salaried manager of the company. Lockhart attributed the failure to Ballantyne's lack of expertise in financial management and to his excessive personal drawings from the company. This was not, however, Scott's opinion, and his high regard for Ballantyne and for his considerable abilities as a first-rate printer never diminished.

After the financial disaster of 1826 Ballantyne suffered a further blow: the death of his wife, on 17 February 1829. He experienced a severe and prolonged depression. Subsequently he and Scott again quarrelled about politics, this time over Ballantyne's support for the Reform Bill, and although the two continued to communicate about business matters they never resumed their former friendship. Both men were in declining health. Ballantyne, who had always been short and stout, became increasingly corpulent and pompous in later life; in recognition of this Scott called him Aldiborontiphoscophornio. After Scott died, in September 1832, a meeting of his creditors provided Ballantyne with a discharge from his obligation for the printing company's debts. On his sickbed Ballantyne wrote the poignant memorandum of his association with Scott that was later employed by Lockhart in his unfairly critical portrayal. Ballantyne died at his home, in Hill Street, Edinburgh, on 17 January 1833.

SHARON ANNE RAGAZ

Sources *The letters of Sir Walter Scott*, ed. H. J. C. Grierson and others, centenary edn, 12 vols. (1932–79) · J. G. Lockhart, *Memoirs of the life of Sir Walter Scott*, 7 vols. (1837–8) · J. Millgate, 'From Kelso to Edinburgh: the origins of the Scott–Ballantyne partnership', *Papers of the Bibliographical Society of America*, 92 (1998), 33–52 · E. Johnson, *Sir Walter Scott*, 2 vols. (1970) · J. C. Corson, *Notes and index to Sir Herbert Grierson's edition of the letters of Sir Walter Scott* (1979) · [W. L. Dobson and W. L. Carrie], *The Ballantyne Press and its founders, 1796–1908* (1909) · James Ballantyne, memorandum, 1832, NL Scot., MS 921, fols. 159–207 · J. Millgate, *Scott's last edition* (1987) · P. Garside, 'Scott as a political journalist', *Review of English Studies*, 148 (1986), 503–17 · *A refutation of the misstatements and calumnies contained in Mr. Lockhart's life of Sir Walter Scott respecting the Messrs. Ballantyne*, Ballantyne Trustees (1838) · J. G. Lockhart, *The Ballantyne humbug handled in a letter to Sir Adam Ferguson* (1839) · *A reply to Mr. Lockhart's pamphlet entitled 'The Ballantyne humbug handled'*, Ballantyne Trustees (1839) · J. Sutherland, *The life of Walter Scott: a critical biography* (1995) · W. Scott, letters to J. Ballantyne, NL Scot., Walpole MSS · bap. reg. Scot. · m. reg. Scot. · *GM*, 1st ser., 103 (1833), 94

Archives NL Scot., corresp. and papers | NA Scot., letters to Waldie family · NL Scot., corresp. with Blackwoods · NL Scot., corresp., mainly with Robert Lundie · NL Scot., corresp. with Sir Walter Scott · NL Scot., Walpole collection · Signet Library, Edinburgh, Douglas papers

Likenesses T. Faed, group portrait, 1849 (*Sir Walter Scott and his friends at Abbotsford*), Scot. NPG · J. Ballantyne, pen-and-ink drawing, Scot. NPG · J. Ballantyne, pencil and wash drawing, NG Scot. [*see illus.*] · portrait, Abbotsford House, near Melrose

Wealth at death £5692 14*s*. 3*d*.: NA Scot., SC 70/488 [1833]

Ballantyne, James Robert (1813–1864), orientalist, was born on 13 December 1813 in Kelso, Roxburghshire, the eldest son of Alexander Thomson Ballantyne (1776–1847), newspaper owner, editor, and printer in Edinburgh, and his wife, (Anne) Randall Grant (*c.* 1786–1855). Alexander Ballantyne was a younger brother of James Ballantyne (1772–1833), Sir Walter Scott's publisher. One of James Robert's brothers was the author Robert Michael *Ballantyne.

Ballantyne was educated at Kelso grammar school, Edinburgh (New) Academy (1824–7), and Edinburgh College, where he began to study oriental languages. He continued this at the East India College, Haileybury (1829–32), under his uncle, Major James Michael, professor of Hindu literature, and Francis Johnson, professor of Sanskrit. Ballantyne published his first book, *A Grammar of the Hindustani Language*, in 1838, and the following year he was appointed to teach Hindi and Sanskrit at the Scottish Naval and Military Academy, Edinburgh. In 1844 he married his first wife, Violet Robertson. The next year he was made an LLD by Glasgow University.

Meanwhile, the government of the North-Western Provinces of India had decided to add English literature and science to the Sanskrit syllabus of the Government College, Benares. On the recommendation of Horace Hayman Wilson, Boden professor of Sanskrit at Oxford and librarian to the East India Company, the company's court of directors appointed Ballantyne principal of the college in 1845 to supervise the reorganization. As principal (from 1856 also professor of moral philosophy), his task was to bring the Sanskrit students to appreciate European thought and ways without losing the influence among their countrymen which was based on their mastery of the traditional learning of India. His tact, broad-mindedness, and genuine respect for the best in Hindu thought enabled him to succeed by winning their trust; he described his methods and approach to Indian traditions in the introductions to his *Synopsis of Science in Sanskrit and English* (1852) and *The Bible for the Pandits* (1860). These were the two most notable of a number of works, designed primarily for his Benares pupils, in which he aimed to adapt the Sanskrit philosophical vocabulary so that it could express European concepts, and which also included a version (1852) of Francis Bacon's *Novum organum*.

Ballantyne published several English translations of Hindu philosophy (especially the aphorisms of the Nyaya, Sankhya, and Vedanta schools) and of Indian linguistics (notably the *Mahabhashya* (1856), Patanjali's 'great commentary' on the classic grammar of Panini), besides European-style grammars of Sanskrit, Hindi, Maratha, and Persian. These were intended to make Indian thought more accessible to Europeans, whom he hoped to dissuade from their tendency to scorn or distrust Indian achievements.

In 1854 Ballantyne married his second wife, Annabella Georgiana Monck-Mason, who survived him; the couple had several children. Ballantyne's health, however, began to fail in India, and in 1861 he resigned from the college and returned to Britain. He served as librarian to the India Office until his death on 16 February 1864, at his London home, 14 Bessborough Street, Pimlico.

R. S. SIMPSON

Sources *Journal of the Royal Asiatic Society of Great Britain and Ireland*, new ser., 1 (1865), v–vii · *The Athenaeum* (12 March 1864), 373 · [T. Henderson and P. F. Hamilton-Grierson], eds., *The Edinburgh Academy register* (1914), 9 · J. R. Ballantyne, *A synopsis of science*, 2nd edn (1856), i–xxxi · L. C. Sanders, *Celebrities of the century: being a dictionary of men and women of the nineteenth century* (1887) · Allibone, *Dict.* · Boase, *Mod. Eng. biog.* · W. I. Addison, *A roll of graduates of the University of Glasgow from 31st December 1727 to 31st December 1897* (1898)

Archives BL OIOC, MS collection | BL OIOC, letters to Horace Wilson, MS Eur. E 301

Wealth at death under £3000: probate, 3 May 1864, *CGPLA Eng. & Wales*

Ballantyne, John (1774–1821), publisher and literary agent, was born at Kelso, Roxburghshire, Scotland, on 13

John Ballantyne (1774–1821), by unknown artist, *c.*1810

May 1774, the second of three children of John Ballantyne (1743–1817), general merchant, and Jean (1745?–1818), daughter of James Barclay, rector of Dalkeith high school, and his wife, Elizabeth. The younger brother of James *Ballantyne (1772–1833), he was educated at Kelso grammar school, which Walter Scott attended in 1783. He went to London in 1794 and worked as a clerk in the banking firm of Messrs Currie. On returning to Kelso in 1795 he became a partner in his father's business. In June 1797 he married Hermione Parker (*d.* 1854), stepdaughter of the Revd William Rutherford, assistant minister at Kelso. Soon afterwards the partnership with his father was dissolved, but Ballantyne carried on the business until, as a consequence of financial difficulties, he moved to Edinburgh in January 1805. There he was employed in James Ballantyne's printing business, as a clerk at £200 per year. Small, slight, and dark-haired, he was a talented storyteller, mimic, and singer. His cheerful optimism and good humour led to Scott's enduring affection for a man he called Jocund Johnnie (*Letters of Sir Walter Scott*, 7.127) and Rigdumfunnidos.

When, in January 1809, it was decided to establish a publishing house with Scott as secret partner John Ballantyne was appointed manager, at a salary of £300 and one-fourth of the profits. In preparation he went to London to meet John Murray and made arrangements to be the Edinburgh publisher of the *Quarterly Review*. John Ballantyne & Co. was established on Hanover Street, Edinburgh, in March 1809 and later held the designation 'bookseller to the regent'. Ballantyne's two-volume novel, *The Widow's Lodgings*, was probably written at the beginning of his career as a publisher; the second edition is dated 1813. According to James Ballantyne he also contributed ballads for the *Edinburgh Annual Register*, which the company began issuing in 1810. Though the publishing house enjoyed some initial success it was hampered by lack of capital. The *Register* project lost money from the beginning, and the company's financial problems were further exacerbated when Ballantyne impulsively bought up stock that later proved unsaleable. By 1813 it was apparent that the business could not continue, and Scott re-entered negotiations with Archibald Constable & Co. The stock was gradually sold off at reduced rates, with Constable taking the bulk of it, and the partnership was finally dissolved on 1 February 1816.

Though Scott's letters to Ballantyne during this period reflect a sense of exasperation his continued regard is evident from his decision to hire him as literary agent. This arrangement proved financially advantageous for Ballantyne, since it came to include a share in the profits from the Waverley novels. Ballantyne made the Hanover Street premises into a saleroom for literature and art, and his lively character and sociability ensured him success in his capacity as auctioneer. In 1816 he purchased Trinity Grove, at 70 Trinity Road, on the Firth of Forth. The house had earlier belonged to the bookseller William Creech; renamed Harmony Hall, it became the site of lavish parties attended by theatrical, musical, and literary people. From 4 January to 12 July 1817 Ballantyne published a weekly periodical, *The Sale-Room*, which was designed to draw attention to the auction house. In November 1820 he proposed a series of reprinted novels, to be entitled Ballantyne's Novelists' Library, and Scott agreed to provide prefatory biographical essays. The first volume was published by Hurst & Co. in February 1821.

Ballantyne's health began to decline in 1819, and in December 1820 he retired. He moved back to Roxburghshire—to Kirklands, near Earlston—and in April 1821 took Walton Hall, at Kelso, with a view to settling there. However, in early June, when he was at his brother's Edinburgh residence—10 St John Street—he became acutely ill. On the morning of 16 June 1821 he died, probably of tuberculosis. Though Lockhart was severely critical of Ballantyne, he recorded that on attending the burial at Canongate churchyard, on 20 June, Scott turned away to say 'I feel as if there would be less sunshine for me from this day forth' (Lockhart, *Memoirs*, 5.76). Scott was a trustee of the will, by whose terms he was designated to receive £2000. In the event Ballantyne had died almost penniless, and the executors had difficulty finding any money for his widow. His mistress, Hermione Robertson, of Friars, near Kelso, may possibly have received her £100. Scott continued to contribute additional biographies to the Novelists' Library project, for the benefit of Ballantyne's widow. SHARON ANNE RAGAZ

Sources *The letters of Sir Walter Scott*, ed. H. J. C. Grierson and others, centenary edn, 12 vols. (1932–79) • J. G. Lockhart, *Memoirs of the life of Sir Walter Scott*, 7 vols. (1837–8) • [W. L. Dobson and W. L. Carrie], *The Ballantyne Press and its founders, 1796–1908* (1909) • E. Johnson, *Sir Walter Scott*, 2 vols. (1970) • J. C. Corson, *Notes and index to Sir Herbert Grierson's edition of the letters of Sir Walter Scott* (1979) • *A refutation of the misstatements and calumnies contained in Mr.*

Lockhart's life of Sir Walter Scott respecting the Messrs. Ballantyne, Ballantyne Trustees (1838) • J. G. Lockhart, *The Ballantyne humbug handled in a letter to Sir Adam Ferguson* (1839) • *A reply to Mr. Lockhart's pamphlet entitled 'The Ballantyne humbug handled'*, Ballantyne Trustees (1839) • T. Constable, *Archibald Constable and his literary correspondents*, 3 vols. (1873) • J. Sutherland, *The life of Walter Scott: a critical biography* (1995) • bap. reg. Scot. • bur. reg. Scot.

Archives NL Scot., diary and papers • NL Scot., journal [copy] | NL Scot., corresp. with Sir Walter Scott • NL Scot., Walpole collection • Signet Library, Edinburgh, Douglas papers

Likenesses oils, *c*.1810, Scot. NPG [*see illus.*] • J. Ballantyne, oils?, Scot. NPG • pencil, ink, and watercolour drawing, Scot. NPG

Wealth at death died almost penniless: NA Scot., RD5, pp. 504, 506

Ballantyne, John (1778–1830), United Secession minister, was born in the parish of Kinghorn in Fife on 8 May 1778. After being educated in the village school at Lochgelly, he entered the University of Edinburgh in 1795, and joined the Burgher branch of the Secession church, although his parents belonged to the established Church of Scotland. He taught at schools in Lochgelly and Colinsburgh before being ordained minister of Stonehaven in Kincardineshire in 1805. In 1824 he published *A Comparison of Established and Dissenting Churches, by a Dissenter*. In 1830 this pamphlet, which had failed to excite notice, was republished with additions during the voluntary church controversy of the period. Ballantyne's partisanship in the controversy is said to have injured the reception of his *Examination of the Human Mind*, the first part of which appeared in 1828; two further parts were planned, but never appeared. The failure, however, may be accounted for without the influence of party spirit: the *Examination* was a substantially unoriginal work, drawing largely on the work of Thomas Reid (1710–1796) and Dugald Stewart (1753–1828), although offering some criticism of Thomas Brown (1778–1820). Ballantyne apparently managed to pay for publication out of his own savings, handing over £200 which he had received from a patron. Reputedly suffering from indigestion brought on by overwork, Ballantyne died on 5 November 1830 at Stonehaven. He was buried in the parish church of Fetteresso, where a marble monument was erected to his memory.

[Anon.], *rev.* Rosemary Mitchell

Sources Anderson, *Scot. nat.* • J. McKerrow, *History of the Secession church*, 2 vols. (1839), 913–16 • J. McCosh, *The Scottish philosophy: biographical, expository, critical, from Hutcheson to Hamilton* (1875), 388–92

Ballantyne, John (1815–1897), portrait painter, was born on 25 April 1815 in Kelso, Roxburghshire, one of ten children of Alexander (Sandy) Thomson Ballantyne (1776–1847), newspaper editor and manager, and his wife, (Anne) Randall Scott Grant (*d.* 1855). His parents were both Scottish; his father is primarily remembered for having copied for press some of Sir Walter Scott's early Waverley novels. John Ballantyne was educated at the Edinburgh Academy and received his artistic training at the Trustees' Academy in Edinburgh under William Allan and Thomas Duncan. He then travelled to Paris, Rome, and London to complete his student education. After returning to Edinburgh in 1839, he established himself as a portraitist,

John Ballantyne (1815–1897), by John Pettie, 1880

though he also painted historical genre subjects and still lifes. He regularly exhibited at the Royal Scottish Academy (1831–83) and the Royal Academy (1835–83) and was elected an associate member of the Royal Scottish Academy in 1841. He became a full member in 1860.

From the 1840s until the early 1860s Ballantyne played a significant role in Edinburgh's art world. He was a founder member and president of the Smashers, a sketching club established in 1848 by the city's younger artists. By 1845 Robert Scott Lauder, new head of the Trustees' Academy, had appointed Ballantyne as preceptor of life classes, where he taught draughtsmanship until he moved to London in 1863. As Lauder's chief assistant he assisted with the successful restoration of the falling reputation of the academy, teaching some of the most significant artists of the next generation, including William McTaggart, William Quiller Orchardson, and John Pettie. Some of his theories about art were expressed in his published 1856 pamphlet, *What is Pre-Raphaelitism?*, in which he linked the artistic principles and working practices of the movement to his own techniques.

Despite Ballantyne's active participation in Edinburgh's art world, he was by the 1860s in serious financial difficulty. While he had been in some demand in the 1850s as a portraitist, he had fallen out of vogue by the next decade.

His career was not aided by his personality, for the frail, thin, bearded man was very ill at ease promoting himself. His financial pressures mounted, for he had a family to support—he had married his second cousin, Christina (Teenie) Hogarth, about 1845 and they had had three children, Randal, Dot, and Edith. From this point until his death his brother Robert Michael *Ballantyne (1825–1894), the highly successful writer of books for boys, contributed considerable sums in support of John and his family.

Attempting to seek more sympathetic patronage, Ballantyne and his family moved to London in 1863. Here he took in pupils to generate income and revived friendships with the many former Edinburgh colleagues who had already moved there. These artists re-established their sketching group, renaming it the Auld Lang Syne Club. Most importantly, Ballantyne and his brother Robert formulated a plan to enable him to establish his reputation and make money by painting portraits of famous London artists at work in their respective studios. At least seventeen of this series were completed, including those of William Powell Frith, Sir Francis Grant, William Holman Hunt, Sir Edwin Landseer, John Millais, and David Roberts. Landseer proved an especially troublesome subject, as he belatedly decided that he would not give permission for the painting of him completing the Trafalgar Square lions for the Nelson memorial to be exhibited in 1865 or to be reproduced and sold as chromolithographs because he was not yet ready to unveil these sculptures to the public. Although Ballantyne's paintings received a good press when exhibited, they apparently made little money. They are nevertheless his most important and most frequently exhibited works today. Highly significant as the first visual records of Victorian artists portrayed at work in their studios, they provide the only or finest records of what these large and often impressive rooms actually looked like, and they eloquently capture a sense of how each artist worked. While his other rather mediocre works are virtually unknown today, the artist series is very widely reproduced and admired. Some of the finest examples are in the collections of the National Portrait Gallery, London, and the Scottish National Portrait Gallery, Edinburgh.

This project proved to be Ballantyne's final major effort. By the late 1860s his eyesight began to fail, and his productivity dropped to a handful of works annually. In 1869 he took the position of curator at the Royal Academy of Arts but was forced to resign due to further ill health. He then retired to Seend, near Melksham in Wiltshire, where by the mid-1880s he had ceased painting altogether. The impoverished artist lived on a small pension and aid from his brother until his death at Seend on 12 May 1897. He was survived by his wife. JOSEPH F. LAMB

Sources E. Quayle, *Ballantyne the brave: a Victorian writer and his family* (1967) • L. Darbyshire, '"The Studios of Celebrated Painters": a series of portraits by John Ballantyne RSA', MA diss., Courtauld Inst., 1996 • L. Darbyshire, '"The Studios of Celebrated Painters": a series of portraits by John Ballantyne', *Apollo*, 147 (May 1998), 21–7 • R. Ormond, 'Artists in their studios', *Christie's Review of the Season* (1979), 72–4 • P. J. M. McEwan, *Dictionary of Scottish art and architecture* (1994) • Maulstick, 'Our streets and studios', *Building News*, 12 (1865), 895–6 • *Art Journal*, 26 (1864), 122 • d. cert.

Archives NL Scot. • NPG • Royal Scot. Acad. • Scot. NPG

Likenesses J. Pettie, portrait, 1880, Royal Scot. Acad. [*see illus.*] • J. Faed, ink and wash (with Thomas Faed and Wm Fettes-Douglas), Scot. NPG • photograph, repro. in Quayle, *Ballantyne the brave*

Wealth at death £247 19*s*. 5*d*.: probate, 30 Aug 1897, *CGPLA Eng. & Wales*

Ballantyne, Robert Michael (1825–1894), author, was born on 24 April 1825 at 25 Ann Street, Edinburgh, the ninth of ten children of Alexander Thomson Ballantyne (1776–1847), newspaper editor and printer, and his wife, Anne, known by her second name, Randall (*c*.1786–1855), daughter of Dr Robert Grant and his wife, Mary. Ballantyne's father transcribed the manuscripts of Walter Scott's novels to preserve the author's anonymity when they were printed at the Ballantyne press of Ballantyne's uncle, James Ballantyne (1772–1833), and the family's fortunes fell with Scott's financial crisis in 1826. Ballantyne's only formal schooling was a brief period (1835–7) at Edinburgh Academy, his education being completed by his mother and sisters in the bosom of a musical and artistic family. His eldest brother, James Robert *Ballantyne (1813–1864), attended East India College, Haileybury, on a scholarship and subsequently edited and translated many works of oriental religion and philosophy; his other brother, John *Ballantyne (1815–1897), an artist, painted the portrait of him which is in the National Portrait Gallery.

At sixteen Robert Ballantyne, the youngest son, signed on for five years with the Hudson's Bay Company, which he served in Rupert's Land and Canada (the modern Canadian provinces of Manitoba, Ontario, and Quebec), travelling extensively by canoe and sleigh and trading with Indians for furs, experiences he described in a journal and in letters home. On return to Edinburgh he took employment as a clerk and only at the suggestion of a family friend revised his journal and letters for publication, with his own illustrations, as *Hudson's Bay, or, Every-Day Life in the Wilds of North America* (1848). Some years later, again at the suggestion of another (the publisher William Nelson), Ballantyne used his knowledge of Canada to provide the setting for a story for boys, *Snowflakes and Sunbeams, or, The Young Fur Traders* (1856), establishing a pattern for his career as author of boys' adventures set in authentic backgrounds. When he had exhausted his personal experience, he turned to published accounts of travel as sources, most successfully with *The Coral Island: a Tale of the Pacific Ocean* (1858), which is the only one of his many tales still read and remembered. He set other works in places he had not visited, such as Brazil (*Martin Rattler*, 1858) and equatorial Africa (*The Gorilla Hunters*, 1861), but he preferred to write from experience. According to his own autobiographical account, a 'blunder' in *The Coral Island*, in which he described coconuts growing without husks, 'in the same form as that in which they are usually presented to

Robert Michael Ballantyne (1825–1894), by John Ballantyne, *c.*1855

us in grocers' windows', led him 'to visit—when possible—the scenes in which my stories were laid' (Ballantyne, 13, 15). Many of his later books were indeed based on personal research, which took him 12 miles off the Scottish coast to the Bell Rock for *The Lighthouse* (1865) and to the bottom of the Thames in a diving suit for *Under the Waves* (1876).

After the death of a sister in 1848 Ballantyne became a regular churchgoer and at twenty-four was elected an elder of the Free Church of Scotland, his firm faith pervading his writing as well as his life. His social conscience and commercial sense were successfully combined in works like *The Lifeboat* (1864) and *Fighting the Flames* (1867), which simultaneously inspired and thrilled, and in public lectures in which Ballantyne, well built and hirsute, singing in a fine baritone or shooting a stuffed eagle, publicized good causes and his own books. A Scottish lifeboat was gratefully named in his honour, but his principal achievement was his corpus of tales of manly boys in exotic locations, tales which opened to young readers the imperial prospect of a wide world to explore and exploit. Following the lead of Marryat and other previous writers, Ballantyne adapted the *Robinson Crusoe* model for Victorian boys and influenced subsequent Scottish writers such as R. L. Stevenson, who admired as a boy Ballantyne's works and their author, 'an exceedingly good-looking, dark, full-bearded man' (Stevenson, 226) he later acknowledged in the verses prefacing *Treasure Island* (1883). William Golding's *Lord of the Flies* (1954) was a twentieth-century reaction to this whole tradition, and to *The Coral Island* in particular.

Ballantyne's boy heroes were not distracted by girls and his own adventures in researching fire brigades and railway trains were not disrupted when he married on 31 July 1866 a minister's daughter, Jane Grant (*c.*1845–*c.*1924), with whom he had three sons and three daughters. Control of his copyrights and continuing success afforded Ballantyne the opportunity to move in 1873, for the health of his family, from Edinburgh to Europe, from where he returned to England for his children's education, settling at Harrow in 1879. The vertigo symptomatic of (undiagnosed) Ménière's disease began to trouble him in 1890 and when this worsened he was unable to complete his autobiography, which was published nevertheless, entitled *Personal Reminiscences*, in 1893. He travelled to Italy for an unsuccessful cure in October 1893, died at via del Corso 7, Rome, on 8 February 1894, and was buried there in the protestant cemetery. NEIL RENNIE

Sources R. M. Ballantyne, *Personal reminiscences in book-making* (1893) • E. Quayle, *Ballantyne the brave: a Victorian writer and his family* (1967) • E. Quayle, *R. M. Ballantyne: a bibliography of first editions* (1968) • [T. Henderson and P. F. Hamilton-Grierson], eds., *The Edinburgh Academy register* (1914) • R. L. Stevenson, 'Memoirs of himself', *The works of Robert Louis Stevenson* (1922–3), 26.205–37 • *BL cat.* [Robert Michael Ballantyne, James Robert Ballantyne]

Archives Edinburgh Central Reference Library, letters • NL Scot., corresp. and papers

Likenesses photographs, 1847–93, repro. in Quayle, *Ballantyne the brave* • J. Ballantyne, oils, *c.*1855, NPG [*see illus.*] • print, 1894 (after photograph by Fradelle and Young), NPG; repro. in *ILN* (17 Feb 1894) • photograph, repro. in Quayle, *R. M. Ballantyne*

Wealth at death £2404 6*s.* 4*d.*: probate, 23 May 1894, *CGPLA Eng. & Wales*

Ballantyne, Thomas (1806–1871), newspaper editor, was born in Paisley, where his first employment was as a weaver. He then became editor of the *Bolton Free Press*, and was active in promoting radical causes. He became closely associated with Richard Cobden and John Bright in their agitation against the corn laws, and in 1841 he published the *Corn Law Repealer's Handbook*. In 1841 he joined the staff of the *Manchester Guardian*, but his path to promotion was blocked by Russell Scott Taylor. Accordingly, in 1845 he joined Bright and two others to found the *Manchester Examiner* as a more radical paper than the *Guardian*; he edited it for nearly three years. After the fusion of the *Examiner* with the *Manchester Times* in 1848, he became editor of the *Liverpool Journal*, and later of the *Liverpool Mercury*. Subsequently he moved to London to edit *The Leader*, and was for a time associated with Charles Mackay in the editorial department of the *Illustrated London News*. He also started *The Statesman*, which he edited until its close, when he became editor of the *St James's Chronicle*.

In addition to this rather unsettled editorial career, Ballantyne wrote papers for various periodicals and published several books, including *Passages Selected from the Writings of Thomas Carlyle, with a Biographical Memoir* (1855), *Prophecy for 1855, Selected from Carlyle's Latter-Day Pamphlets* (1855), *Ideas, Opinions, and Facts* (1865), and *Essays in Mosaic* (1870). Carlyle recognized Ballantyne's skill as a compiler; he had, he wrote, 'a real talent for excerpting significant passages from books, magazines, newspapers (that contain *any* such), and for presenting them in lucid arrangement, and in their most interesting and readable form'. Ballantyne died at Tufnell Park, Holloway, London, on 30 August 1871. T. F. HENDERSON, *rev.* H. C. G. MATTHEW

Sources *Glasgow Daily Mail* (9 Sept 1871) • *Paisley Weekly Herald* (11 Sept 1871) • Boase, *Mod. Eng. biog.* • C. W. Sutton, *A list of Lancashire authors* (1876) • D. Ayerst, *Guardian: biography of a newspaper* (1971)

Ballard, Edward George (1791–1860), writer, was born on 29 April 1791 in Salisbury, Wiltshire, the only child of Edward Ballard, an alderman of Salisbury, and Elizabeth, daughter of George Fowles Benson, also of Salisbury; his parents were married on 18 August 1788. Because of early ill health his education was much neglected, though he was schooled a little in Salisbury, and in Pimlico when his parents moved to London. He obtained employment in the Stamp Office in 1809 and, upon resigning this appointment, entered the Excise Office, which he also left of his own accord in 1817 to apply himself vigorously to study. In 1817 he became a contributor to Wooller's *Reasoner*. In 1818 he married Mary Ann Shadgett, and wrote several criticisms and verses for the *Weekly Review*, then edited by his brother-in-law, William Shadgett. He also received a reader's ticket for the British Library in 1818, which he frequented. In 1820 his wife died, leaving him a widower with a son and a daughter. He contributed to the *Literary Chronicle* and the *Imperial Magazine* under the signature E. G. B., and to the *Literary Magnet* and the *World of Fashion* under the sign of Γ. In 1825 he published a volume entitled *A New Series of Original Poems*, and in 1829 another entitled *Microscopic Amusements*. He was exceedingly fond of research. Robert Benson, his cousin, and Henry Hatcher received considerable help from him in writing their *History of Salisbury* (1843), which formed part of Richard Colt Hoare's *Wiltshire*. He helped John Gough Nichols in the works undertaken for the Camden Society. For many years he was a member of the Russell Institute and later the Islington Literary and Scientific Association. In 1848 he brought out some parts of a continuation of John Strype's *Ecclesiastical Memorials* in a publication called *The Surplice*, but this paper and Ballard's scheme soon came to an end. He also occasionally contributed to the *Gentleman's Magazine* and *Notes and Queries*. Ballard died at Compton Terrace, Islington, London, on 14 February 1860. He was survived by his son, Edward Ballard MD, author of several medical works, and a daughter. He was buried in Brookwood cemetery, Woking, Surrey, on 18 February 1860.

WILLIAM HUNT, *rev.* REBECCA MILLS

Sources *GM*, 3rd ser., 8 (1860), 412–13 • *IGI* • Watt, *Bibl. Brit.*, 1.67
Archives Bodl. Oxf., notebook relating to Welsh history, papers relating to letters and memorials of female nobility of England • Shakespeare Birthplace Trust RO, Stratford upon Avon, historical notes and papers relating to Boston compiled for Pishey Thompson | Bodl. Oxf., letters to J. G. Nicholls
Likenesses Green, portrait

Ballard, George (1705/6–1755), antiquary, was baptized on 14 February 1706 at Chipping Campden, Gloucestershire, one of five sons and three daughters of Samuel Ballard (*bap.* 1663, *d.* 1710), a chandler, and his wife, Elizabeth Willis (*d.* 1744), a midwife. His father died, aged forty-six, in July 1710, when George was only four years old, but his mother lived for another thirty-four years, and died on 10 July 1744 at the age of seventy-three. Ballard was a sickly child, deemed unsuited for any trade which involved bodily strength. He was, as a consequence, apprenticed as a maker of female clothing and was thereafter referred to variously as a staymaker, tailor, habit-maker, or mantua-maker. Thomas Hearne, to whom Ballard was introduced in 1726 by Richard Graves, reported that his antiquarian interests were first aroused by 'the little historical twelve-penny pieces put out under the name of Richard Burton [Nathaniel Crouch], in which are abundance of pretty diverting delightfull stories, which have made the books to be in great vogue among the Vulgar' (*Remarks*, 11.219). Both Ballard and his elder sister, Elizabeth (who, like their mother, was a midwife), developed early in life an absorbing interest in coins and books, and Ballard, 'stealing a few hours from sleep, after the business of the day was over' (Walker, 2.93), taught himself Old English. He further recorded that before reaching the age of fourteen he had read many of the polemical writers on religion who 'gave me the greatest abhorrence to Popery' and 'almost as bad an opinion of the Dissenters' (ibid., 2.143–4). He subsequently learned Latin and, according to Hearne, was by 1729 spending much of his time travelling about on foot, collecting coins, and, forsaking his trade, living 'chiefly upon his mother' (*Remarks*, 10.118).

Ballard gradually built up a wide circle of correspondents including many of the foremost antiquaries of the day, and was admitted to read in the Bodleian Library on 9 December 1747. Three years later on the recommendation of the Revd William Talbot of Kineton, Warwickshire, and of Browne Willis, he was admitted to Magdalen College, Oxford, as one of the clerks on 1 November 1750 and was matriculated by the university on 15 December at the age of forty-four. Finances were provided by an annuity of £100 offered by Lord Chedworth and the members of his hunt at Chipping Campden, though this was reduced to £60 at Ballard's request.

Ballard wrote a historical account of Campden church in 1731 which was read to the Society of Antiquaries in 1771, but his principal literary work was his *Memoirs of Several Ladies of Great Britain, who have been Celebrated for their Writings or Skill in the Learned Languages, Arts and Sciences* (1752). The preface is dated at Magdalen College on 23 November 1752 and Edward Gibbon, who was there at that time, was one of the book's 400 subscribers, 143 of whom were women. The section of the work which covers the fifteenth and sixteenth centuries is dedicated to the wife of the Revd William Talbot 'as a small testimony of gratitude for extraordinary favours' conferred on Ballard by herself and her husband; the section covering later centuries is dedicated to Mrs Mary Delany, 'the truest judge and brightest pattern of all the accomplishments which adorn her sex'.

Perhaps because of the nature of his trade Ballard was acquainted with many women in the Chipping Campden area, and he is credited with rescuing his fellow Saxonist

Elizabeth Elstob from penury in Evesham by introducing her to another Gloucestershire acquaintance, Hester Chapone, who succeeded in raising an annuity for her.

Ballard never married. He died on 24 June 1755 owing, according to John Nichols (Nichols, *Lit. anecdotes*, 2.470), to 'too intense application to his studies', though William Talbot in a letter to John Loveday on 2 July reported that 'the stone' was the cause of his painful death (Markham, 395). He was buried at Chipping Campden on 27 June. Nichols gives the text of a memorial in Latin, but bearing the date 1740, said to be from a monument erected in the church there. No other evidence survives, however, that this monument ever existed. Under his will of April 1754 the Bodleian received coins, as well as manuscripts and correspondence (MSS Ballard 1–73) including forty-four volumes of letters chiefly addressed to Dr Arthur Charlett, master of University College, Oxford. Many of the letters were published by the Revd John Walker in *Letters Written by Eminent Persons in the Seventeenth and Eighteenth Centuries* (1813). DAVID VAISEY

Sources J. R. Bloxam, *A register of the presidents, fellows … of Saint Mary Magdalen College*, 8 vols. (1853–85), vol. 2, pp. 95–102 • *Remarks and collections of Thomas Hearne*, ed. C. E. Doble and others, 11 vols., OHS, 2, 7, 13, 34, 42–3, 48, 50, 65, 67, 72 (1885–1921), vols. 9–11 • [J. Walker and P. Bliss], eds., *Letters written by eminent persons in the seventeenth and eighteenth centuries*, 2 vols. (1813) • W. D. Macray, *Annals of the Bodleian Library, Oxford*, 2nd edn (1890), 254–6 • Nichols, *Lit. anecdotes*, 2.466–70; 4.123 • Foster, *Alum. Oxon.* • I. Bickerstaff [R. Steele] and others, *The Tatler, or, The lucubrations of Isaac Bickerstaff*, ed. J. Nichols, new edn, 6 vols. (1786), vol. 2, pp. 323–7; vol. 5, p. 397 • S. Markham, *John Loveday of Caversham, 1711–1789* (1984), 378, 394–5 • F. Madan, *A summary catalogue of Western manuscripts in the Bodleian Library at Oxford*, 3 (1895), nos. 10787–10858 • *DNB*

Archives Bodl. Oxf., corresp., literary papers, and collections • S. Antiquaries, Lond., transcripts of directions for illuminating MSS and of Orosius, Stowe MS 753 | BL, letters to Charles Lyttelton • Bodl. Oxf., MSS Browne Willis • Bodl. Oxf., MSS Rawlinson

Wealth at death see will, PRO, PROB 11/817, sig. 232; Macray, *Annals*, 255–6

Ballard, George (*fl.* 1807–1830), menagerie keeper and showman, is of unknown parentage and upbringing. He is almost certainly the 'Mr Baller' who exhibited 'wild beasts' at St James's fair, Bristol, in September 1807, paying £5 5*s.* for his standing (account book, Bristol RO, P/St. J/F/18, 9). His animals—as ferocious and unusual as could be obtained—were housed in cages carried on shuttered wagons which, for the purposes of exhibition, were drawn into a square to make a booth. Ballard appears to have toured mainly in the south of England, often showing his collection at country or suburban fairs. In 1810 he made his first appearance at one of England's largest pleasure fairs, Bartholomew fair, London, where he was a regular exhibitor for the next twenty years. In January 1814 Ballard's 'Grand Collection of Wild Beasts' was at the Castle Ditches, Norwich. An advertisement in the *Norfolk Chronicle* (1 January 1814) suggests a small but successful concern with several wagons containing a lion, a Bengal tiger, a leopard from Senegal, and a porcupine 'with a great number of other curiosities and scarce animals'. At St James's fair, Bristol, later in the same year, he paid no less than £36 15*s.* for his ground.

Ballard is now best-known for an incident that took place on 20 October 1816 outside The Hut (now The Pheasant), a coaching inn at Winterslow, Wiltshire. The menagerie's temporary halt *en route* for Salisbury fair coincided with the arrival of the Exeter–London mail coach. At this point Ballard's lioness broke out of her cage, escaped from the wagon, and leapt on the lead horse. Two passengers from the coach, a Mr Fowler and a Mr Perham, fled to the inn, leaving the coachman and the armed guard sitting on the box. Ballard and his keepers arrived in haste. There were calls from the inn to fire on the lioness, but the showman pleaded for the life of his valuable animal, described by Ballard as worth £500 and 'as tame as a rabbit if not irritated'. Ballard's Newfoundland dog eventually drove off the lioness. The horse was changed and the mail coach continued to London with the news, widely reported in the papers, that the lioness was still at large.

In addition to coverage in the London press the incident was commemorated in several pictures, the best-known being a painting by the coaching artist James Pollard reproduced as a print engraved by Robert Havell and inscribed 'Drawn from the information of Joseph Pike, Guard of the Mail at the time of the event'. Other images include an engraving from a painting by the animal artist Abraham Cooper (reproduced in the *Sporting Magazine*, January 1817) and a large painting by Matthew Wyatt exhibited at the Egyptian Hall, Piccadilly, in March 1819. The story also persisted through an unconfirmed report—presented in exaggerated form in Charles Harper's *The Exeter Road* (1899)—that one of the coach's passengers was so seriously affected by the encounter that he was confined for life in the Laverstock Asylum. The asylum's admission register (Wilts. & Swindon RO, A1/560/9) does indeed record the admission of one William Fowler, a sailcloth maker from Teignmouth, on 1 October 1819, though it is uncertain whether he was the person present.

Ballard managed the aftermath of the incident in typical showman fashion. He bought the horse—which was not seriously hurt but which bore the scars of its ordeal—and exhibited it, with his dog and lioness, at the next Bartholomew fair. The 'Exeter Mail lioness' was the main attraction of Ballard's show and was still on display when the author William Hone visited the menagerie in September 1825. In 1828 Ballard's 1*d.* show was said to have taken £89 during three busy days at Bartholomew fair, indicating more than 21,000 visitors. Even so, he was no longer keeping pace with the larger menageries of enterprising showmen such as Thomas Atkins and George Wombwell whose 6*d.* shows attracted about 40,000 and 68,000 visitors respectively. Two years later his menagerie at the fair was described as 'a rather meagre collection' (London, Guildhall Library, cutting MS 1514), and thereafter George Ballard's career merges with the shadows. MARK SORRELL

Sources *Sporting Magazine* (Oct 1816) • *Sporting Magazine* (Jan 1817) • account book, St James's fair, Bristol, Bristol RO, P/St.J/F/18 • GL, MS 95; MS 1514 • *Norfolk Chronicle and Norwich Gazette* (1 Jan 1814) • *Morning Post* (23 Oct 1816) • *The Courier* (4 Sept 1817) • *The Star*

(9 Sept 1828) • R. D. Altick, *The shows of London* (1978) • W. Hone, *The Every-day Book and Table Book*, 1 (1826–7) • *The Sun* (22 Oct 1816)

Ballard, George Alexander (1862–1948), naval officer, son of General John Archibald *Ballard (1829–1880), and his wife, the daughter of Robert Scott-Moncrieff, was born at Bombay on 7 March 1862. After a few months at the well-known naval crammer, Dr Burney's academy, at Gosport, Hampshire, he entered the training ship *Britannia* in January 1875. He first went to sea in January 1877 in the ironclads *Resistance* and then *Achilles*, in the channel and Mediterranean, and was present at the forcing of the Dardanelles in February 1878. In September 1878 he joined the corvette *Tourmaline*, part of the 'flying squadron' which made a 21-month voyage round the world. He returned in July 1882 as an acting sub-lieutenant. He then trained as a torpedo specialist, and in August 1883 was appointed to the experimental torpedo boat depot ship *Hecla*, a converted merchant ship, which was presently dispatched with troops to the Red Sea, where Ballard, with many of his shipmates, was landed to campaign with the army in the Sudan. In March 1884 he was promoted lieutenant in the field. After returning to sea he served briefly in several ships in the Mediterranean before joining the gunboat *Woodlark* at Rangoon in May 1885, and serving up-country in the Third Anglo-Burmese War, where he became General Prendergast's naval aide-de-camp, and took part in the storming of Mandalay. Between 1887 and 1895 he had appointments at home, in the Mediterranean, and on the China station, and in October 1895 he received his first command, the destroyer *Janus* at Sheerness. From her he moved in May 1896 to the torpedo gunboat *Renard*, and in December 1897 was promoted commander. The following year he married Mary Frances, daughter of James Paterson of Whitelee, Selkirk; they had two sons and one daughter, and his wife survived him.

After service as commander of the cruiser *Isis*, Ballard joined the naval intelligence division in February 1902, and in December 1903 was promoted captain. In 1906 he attended the senior officers' war course at Portsmouth, from which he moved in June 1906 to command the large cruisers *Terrible* and *Hampshire* (August 1907), followed by the battleships *Commonwealth* (December 1909) and *Britannia* (December 1910), all four in home waters. In practice he spent five months from December 1906 ashore at Portsmouth presiding over a secret committee charged by Sir John Fisher with reviewing plans for amphibious landings against Germany—which it dismissed as impossible. Ballard was judged 'a man of great intellectual power and character' (Hankey, 1.33), '100% the ablest officer of his rank and standing now in the Service' (Sir Charles Ottley, Esher MSS, quoted by Lambert, 265). Under Fisher he was used as an unofficial adviser, and when Winston Churchill took office in October 1911 he pressed for Ballard to be the next director of naval intelligence. He was considered too junior for this, but when the naval war staff was instituted in December Ballard became director of the operations division, where he remained until 1914. Rear-Admiral Troubridge, his new chief, did not take well to a subordinate with 'more brains in his little finger than Troubridge has in his great woolly head' (Major Grant-Duff of the imperial defence committee, Grant-Duff MSS, quoted by Lambert, 266), while Churchill likewise soon took against one who ruthlessly shot down his wilder schemes. Ballard's career was rescued by the approach of war. He was promoted commodore in May 1914 (rear-admiral in August) and admiral of patrols, commanding the defences of the east coast. As the Grand Fleet had now abandoned the southern North Sea, Ballard's flotillas were in the front line, and he was responsible for executing the strategy, based on submarines, minefields, and aircraft, that he himself had drawn up. His reputation may have suffered from the German raids of 1914 and 1916; certainly there was no vacancy in the naval war staff under Sir Henry Jackson for so clever and independent an officer, and he moved in September 1916 to the responsible but unglamorous position of admiral superintendent of Malta Dockyard. A vice-admiral in February 1919, he left Malta in September, and retired in June 1921. In March 1924 he became admiral on the retired list.

Ballard occupied his retirement in historical research, writing a substantial study, *The Influence of the Sea on the Political History of Japan* (1921), followed by *Rulers of the Indian Ocean* (1927). He also published a long series of illustrated articles in the *Mariner's Mirror* on the warships of the mid-Victorian navy, combining serious research, skilful draughtsmanship, and his own evocative memories. He died on 16 September 1948 at his home, Hill House, Downton, near Salisbury, Wiltshire.

N. A. M. Rodger

Sources *The Times* (18 Sept 1948), 4 • *The Times* (28 Sept 1948), 7 • *WWW, 1941–50* • Boase, *Mod. Eng. biog.* • A. J. Marder, *From the Dreadnought to Scapa Flow: the Royal Navy in the Fisher era, 1904–1919*, 5 vols. (1961–70) • A. J. Marder, *From the Dardanelles to Oran: studies of the Royal Navy in war and peace, 1915–1940* (1974) • S. W. Roskill, *Naval policy between the wars*, 2 vols. (1968–76) • Lord Hankey [M. Hankey], *The supreme command, 1914–1918*, 2 vols. (1961) • S. W. Roskill, *Hankey, man of secrets*, 3 vols. (1970–74) • Kelly, *Handbk* • N. A. Lambert, *Sir John Fisher's naval revolution* (1999)

Archives NMM, corresp. and papers, MS 80/200 • Royal Navy Museum, Portsmouth, memoirs

Wealth at death £7762 4*s*. 11*d*.: probate, 10 June 1949, *CGPLA Eng. & Wales*

Ballard, John (*d.* 1586), Roman Catholic priest, was the son of William Ballard of Wratting, probably in Cambridgeshire, since he was said to be of the Ely diocese. He was educated at Elmdon, Essex, and Cambridge University. After matriculation at St Catharine's College at Michaelmas 1569 he was admitted to Gonville and Caius College on 18 January 1570 and proceeded BA from King's College in 1574–5. He went to Rheims on 29 November 1579, was ordained priest at Châlons on 4 March 1581, and was sent to England on 29 March.

To protect his identity in England, Ballard used the aliases of Thompson, Turner, and Captain Foscue or Fortescue. At the Red Lion, Holborn, over Christmas 1582 he converted John Hambley. He also visited the Gatehouse prison at this time and befriended Anthony *Tyrrell, an association which was to lead him to notoriety and execution for involvement in the alleged Babington conspiracy against Elizabeth. Tyrrell escaped from the Gatehouse before 5 January 1582 and was in Ballard's company in several counties until 1584, when they left England for Rome, arriving on 7 September 1584. At Christmas 1584 they crossed together from Rouen to Southampton.

From now the story becomes complex. Catholics who were taken to be in sympathy with Spain were closely pursued by the government. English Catholic priests fell into various categories. The majority eschewed politics and avoided contact with a government which they suspected to be interested only in their extermination. On the continent some, especially the Jesuits, accepted the support of Spain to the point where they actively supported attempts at invasion from 1582 onwards. A small minority abandoned Catholicism and became undercover agents of the government, co-operating actively in the persecution of former brethren. Another group of priests, rather larger, became convinced as the 1580s advanced that any attempt at a forceful answer to their plight was doomed to failure. The only hope for papists was to throw themselves on the mercy of government, proving their loyalty to the regime by informing on their brethren. Ballard and Tyrrell belonged to this group. Theirs was a dangerous game since, while the government was prepared to use them, it was also prepared to destroy them if *raison d'état* demanded it.

The key man in the story of the 1586 Babington plot was a renegade cleric, Gilbert Gifford. He served Francis Walsingham, who held in his hand all the threads of a conspiracy which was supposed to have been hatched in Rome by Ballard and Tyrrell. They had gone there in 1584 with the express purpose of getting Pope Gregory XIII's approval for a plot to assassinate Elizabeth. Gregory might have been willing, but the Jesuit Alfonso Agazzari, rector of the English College, was not. While political theory since the days of John of Salisbury allowed tyrannicide as a last resort, the Jesuits, including Persons, rejected it as practical politics. In any case, the only 'evidence' was a confession made by Tyrrell which he afterwards repudiated as a fabrication: extracted from him no doubt under the threat of torture.

Tyrrell was arrested in London on 4 July 1586 and put in the Counter, Wood Street, where he made the confession implicating Ballard and other Catholics. In May 1586 Ballard went to Paris to contact Charles Paget, the Spanish ambassador, and other friends of Mary, queen of Scots. Hoping, no doubt, to become her regular channel of communication, he brought back with him letters for the queen. He was arrested on his return from France and sent to join Tyrrell in his prison on 4 August 1586. On 15 August he was put in the Tower and severely racked. Only a confession of guilt in a general way was obtained, no doubt for the good reason that he knew nothing himself of anything more specific that he was supposed to have done. The trial of Ballard, Babington, and five more took place on 13 and 14 September 1586. They were all found guilty. Fourteen were executed by hanging, drawing, and quartering at Tyburn; Ballard was the first of the first batch who died more barbarously on 20 September. The queen allegedly insisted on special cruelty, which, proving counter-productive, was mitigated for the second contingent. So ended the life of a man who

> came in a grey cloak laid on with gold lace, in velvet hose, a cut satin doublet, a fair hat of the newest fashion, the band being set with silver buttons; a man and a boy after him, and his name, Captain Fortescue. (*State trials*, 1.1150)

FRANCIS EDWARDS

Sources G. Anstruther, *The seminary priests*, 1 (1969) • J. H. Pollen, *Mary queen of Scots and the Babington plot*, Scottish History Society, 3rd ser., 3 (1922) • J. E. Paul, 'The queen's tragedy', Archives of the British Province of the Society of Jesus, London, 48/6/6 • L. Hicks, *An Elizabethan problem: some aspects of the careers of two exile-adventurers* (1964) • *CSP Scot.*, 1585–6, 584, 588; 1586–8 • J. Morris, ed., *The troubles of our Catholic forefathers related by themselves*, 2 (1875), 157–9, 337–47, 357–90 • T. F. Knox and others, eds., *The first and second diaries of the English College, Douay* (1878) • *State trials*, vol. 1 • R. Chantelauze, *Marie Stuart, son procès et son exécution* (1876)

Ballard, John Archibald (1829–1880), army officer, was born at Portbury, Somerset, on 20 June 1829, the son of George and Eliza Ballard of Portbury. He was educated at the East India Company's military college, Addiscombe, near Croydon, 1847–8, and in 1850 was commissioned into the Bengal Engineers. In the spring of 1854 he went on sick leave.

Attracted by news from the Danubian provinces, Ballard travelled to Bulgaria. At Omar Pasha's camp at Shumla, Omar invested him with the rank of lieutenant-colonel in the Turkish army, and deputed him to Silistria as a member of the council of war in that fortress, then besieged by the Russians. Before Ballard's arrival, on 13 June, two other British officers, Captain Butler of the Ceylon Rifles and Lieutenant Nasmyth of the Bombay artillery, had been aiding the garrison, but Butler had been killed and Nasmyth was called away to Omar's camp a few days after Ballard's arrival. During the remainder of the siege, which was raised by the Russians on 23 June, Ballard was the only British officer in the fortress, and it was mainly owing to his exertions, and his influence over the garrison, that the defence was successfully maintained.

At the attack and capture of the Russian position at Giurgevo, Ballard commanded the skirmishers and kept back the enemy until the Turks could entrench themselves. He received the thanks of the British government and, from the Turkish government, a gold medal and a sword of honour.

After serving with the Turkish troops at Eupatoria and in the expedition to Kerch, Ballard commanded a brigade in Omar Pasha's Transcaucasian campaign for the relief of Kars. At the battle of the Inguri River, Ballard and his brigade were for several hours hotly engaged with the Russians, and he was again notable for his coolness under fire. He was also concerned for the well-being of his troops.

Ballard returned to India in 1856, still a subaltern of engineers, but with the CB and order of the Mejidiye. He served as assistant quartermaster-general in the Persian campaign, and afterwards in the Indian mutiny with the Rajputana field force, taking part in the pursuit and rout of Tantia Topi's forces. His promotion was singularly rapid, advancing in 1858 from lieutenant to lieutenant-colonel. He was subsequently mint-master at Bombay. Having attained the rank of lieutenant-general, he retired in 1879. He received an Edinburgh honorary LLD in 1868. He married a daughter of Robert Scott-Moncrieff of Fossaway, Perth; Admiral George Alexander *Ballard (1862–1948) was their son. Ballard died suddenly on 2 April 1880 near Livadia, in Greece, when visiting the pass of Thermopylae. A. J. ARBUTHNOT, *rev.* JAMES LUNT

Sources A. W. Kinglake, *The invasion of the Crimea*, [new edn], 1 (1877) • *Hart's Army List* • *Royal Engineers Journal* • *Household Words* (27 Dec 1856) • J. W. Kaye and G. B. Malleson, *Kaye's and Malleson's History of the Indian mutiny of 1857–8*, new edn, 6 vols. (1897–8) • *The Times* (10 April 1880) • *CGPLA Eng. & Wales* (1880) • Kelly, *Handbk* (1879)

Archives NAM, diaries, letters, and memoirs

Wealth at death under £12,000: probate, 23 April 1880, *CGPLA Eng. & Wales*

Ballard, Philip Boswood (1865–1950), educationist, was born on 13 February 1865 at Tŷ Gwyn, Maesteg, Glamorgan, the second of four children of Evan Ballard, grocer, draper, and later manager of a tinplate works, and his wife, Mary, daughter of Philip Cook, a local doctor. Between the ages of five and seventeen, he attended the local British elementary school in Castle Street, Maesteg, under the tutelage of T. L. Roberts, who enjoyed a reputation for being the best schoolmaster in the area. He exerted a major influence upon Ballard's early education. For five years, Ballard was apprenticed to Roberts as a pupil teacher, obtaining a first-class position in the 1883 queen's scholarship examination. In 1884, Ballard entered Borough Road Training College, London, where after two years he was awarded his teacher's certificate, also in the first-class division. In later life, he took an active interest in his old college, meeting regularly for 'Old Bs' reunions and serving as chairman of the college committee.

In 1886 Ballard entered the service of the London school board as an assistant master at Settles Street Boys' School in the East End, where he remained for eight years. Teaching in crowded conditions, with classes of upwards of seventy-five boys, all of whom came from poor homes, was a challenging task for a young teacher. Yet he attributed his subsequent career success to the experience of these formative teaching years. In 1888 he enrolled for a part-time degree course at the University of London and, devoting all of his spare time to study, was awarded a first-class BA in 1891. In 1894, his teaching career took a new turn as he became involved with specialized instruction of pupil teachers and was promoted to an assistantship at the Chelsea Pupil Teacher Centre. With five years' experience of working with London pupil teachers behind him, he returned to south Wales as principal of the Tondu Pupil Teacher Centre in Glamorgan, meanwhile studying for his London MA, which he was awarded in 1903. He gained the Carpenter gold medal for mental and moral science.

In 1904 Ballard was appointed as an inspector of elementary schools under Glamorgan county council, but he left south Wales for good in 1906 to begin his long career as an inspector of schools with London county council (LCC). He married, on 27 March 1907, Florence Lucy Stone (*b.* 1880/81), a schoolmistress, daughter of Thomas Stone, a clerk. On 3 March 1915, then a widower, he married his second wife, Freda Mary (*b.* 1886/7), daughter of Frederick William Bartlett, an architect. They had one child—a daughter named Mary Bronwen.

Through his work as district inspector of London's elementary schools, Ballard became interested in educational psychology. Along with W. H. Winch, a fellow inspector of the LCC, and other key figures such as Charles Spearman, John Adams, Thomas Percy Nunn, and Cyril Burt, he was one of the leading pioneers of modern educational psychology in the British education system. On the basis of his ground-breaking work, published in 1913 as *Obliviscence and Reminiscence*, he was awarded an honorary doctorate by London University. He was inspired by Burt's meritocratic and progressive vision of educational opportunity suited to the intellectual needs of all children, and was responsible for popularizing much of Burt's work on mental testing and for introducing psychology to the LCC education department. He was a founder member of the British Psychological Society and a lifelong member of the editorial board of its journal the *British Journal of Educational Psychology*. He was also president of the Child Study Society and took a keen interest in the work of the Child Guidance Council. During the 1930s, working closely with Burt and Spearman, he was a member of the International Institute examinations inquiry which sought to publicize and promote a more scientific and objective approach to public examinations. He lectured widely on mental testing at various prestigious institutions including the London School of Economics, University College, and the London Institute of Education and became well known for his witty and inspiring style.

Ballard's writing for teachers on the subject of testing included a number of successful books of which *Mental Tests* (1920), *Group Tests of Intelligence* (1922), *The New Examiner* (1923), and *The Changing School* (1925) were the best-known. They demonstrated his passionate commitment to assisting the practical needs of serving teachers in schools. He firmly believed in the professional right of classroom teachers to advance the knowledge and practice of education and was keen to break down barriers between the academic and the practical in educational psychology.

Ballard's final career promotion, in 1928, was to a divisional inspectorship. He retired from the LCC on 30 April 1930, aged sixty-five. An official LCC report paid tribute to his work: 'Few men have had a more important or a more beneficial influence upon the teaching profession, and few inspectors have brought a more cultivated mind or more happy gifts of temperament to their official duties' (Hughes, 164). Throughout his retirement he continued to keep abreast of educational changes, writing books and making frequent topical contributions to the *Times Educational Supplement*. He had a remarkable capacity for hard work but was above all remembered for his generous and friendly counsel to teachers, his genial personality, and his good sense of humour. Ballard died at his home, Hazel Cottage, Chute, Pewsey, Wiltshire, on 1 November 1950. He was survived by his wife. WENDY ROBINSON

Sources P. B. Ballard, *Things I cannot forget* (1937) • A. G. Hughes, *British Journal of Educational Psychology*, 21 (1951), 163–6 • *WWW* • *The Times* (4 Nov 1950) • *Times Educational Supplement* (10 Nov 1950), 868 • *Journal of Education*, 82 (1950), 680–81 • P. B. Ballard, 'Forty years on: elementary school children in 1888', *Teachers World* (21 July 1926), 792–3 • will, proved, London, 6 Jan 1951 • b. cert. • m. certs. • d. cert. • *CGPLA Eng. & Wales* (1951) • A. Wooldridge, *Measuring the mind: education and psychology in England, c.1860–c.1990* (1994) • G. Sutherland and S. Sharp, *Ability, merit and measurement: mental testing and English education, 1880–1940* (1984)

Likenesses photograph, 1887, repro. in *Teachers World* (21 July 1926), 792–3 • photograph (after portrait by J. Cooper), repro. in *Teachers World* (28 July 1926), frontispiece • photograph, repro. in Ballard, *Things I cannot forget*, frontispiece

Wealth at death £15,329 15s. 9d.: probate, 6 Jan 1951, *CGPLA Eng. & Wales*

Ballard, Samuel James (1764?–1829), naval officer, was the son of Samuel Ballard—a subordinate officer in the navy, who had retired without promotion after the peace of 1763 and had engaged in business at Portsmouth—and his wife, whose maiden name was Flint. Samuel James Ballard entered the navy in December 1776, under the patronage of John Leveson-Gower, then captain of the *Valiant* in the Grand Fleet under Admiral Keppel during the summer of 1778. In October 1779 he was transferred to the *Shrewsbury* (Captain Mark Robinson), and in her was present when Sir George Rodney defeated the Spanish fleet off Cape St Vincent, on 16 January 1780. In the following July the *Shrewsbury* rejoined Rodney's flag in the West Indies, was present off Martinique on 29 April 1781, and led the van in the strategic defeat off the Chesapeake on 5 September 1781. On this fatal day the brunt of the fight fell on the *Shrewsbury*, of whose men fourteen were killed and fifty-two wounded, including Captain Robinson who lost a leg. The ship afterwards returned to the West Indies with Sir Samuel Hood, and was with him in the operations at St Kitts in January 1782, after which she had to be sent to Jamaica for repairs. On 10 February 1783, while still at Jamaica, Ballard was made a lieutenant by Admiral Rowley, and was actively employed in different ships during the ten years of peace. When war broke out again he was a lieutenant of the *Queen*, which carried Rear-Admiral Gardiner's flag through the last days of May and 1 June 1794. This great victory won for Ballard his commander's rank (5 July), and on 1 August 1795 he was further advanced to the rank of captain.

Early in 1796 Ballard was appointed to the frigate *Pearl*, and during the next two years was continuously and happily employed in convoying the trade for the Baltic or for Newfoundland and Quebec. In March 1798 he accompanied Commodore Cornwallis to the coast of Africa and to Barbados, from which station he returned in June of the following year. In October he carried out General Fox to Minorca, and remained attached to the Mediterranean Fleet for the next two years. The *Pearl* was paid off on 14 March 1802, after a commission of upwards of six years, during which time she had taken, destroyed, or recaptured about eighty vessels, privateers and merchantmen.

Captain Ballard then commanded a district of sea fencibles for more than seven years. It was not until October 1809 that he was appointed to the *Sceptre* (74 guns); he sailed shortly afterwards for the West Indies. Here he flew a commodore's broad pennant, and on 18 December 1809 commanded the squadron which captured the two heavily armed French frigates *Loire* and *Seine*, and destroyed the protecting batteries at Anse-la-Barque off Guadeloupe. At the capture of Guadeloupe in January and February 1810 he escorted one division of the army and commanded the naval brigade which, however, was not engaged. He returned to England with the *Sceptre* in the following September, and was for the next two years attached to the fleet in the channel and Bay of Biscay, but without being engaged in any active operations. His service at sea closed with the paying off of the *Sceptre* in January 1813, although in course of seniority he attained the rank of rear-admiral, on 4 June 1814, and of vice-admiral, on 27 May 1825.

Ballard married first his cousin Maria, only daughter of James Flint of Feversham; they had eight children of whom only a son and two daughters survived him. On 2 December 1822 he married Catharine, daughter of Sir Thomas Crawley Boevey, bt, of Flaxley Abbey, Gloucestershire. He resided for several years at Bath, and died at Exmouth on 11 October 1829.

J. K. LAUGHTON, *rev.* ANDREW LAMBERT

Sources J. Marshall, *Royal naval biography*, 2 (1835), 639–40 • *GM*, 1st ser., 99/2 (1829)

Ballard, Volant Vashon (1774?–1832), naval officer, a nephew of Admiral James Vashon, served as a midshipman with George Vancouver in his voyage to the north-west coast of America. Shortly after his return to England he was made a lieutenant, on 6 June 1795; and on 25 December 1798, while commanding the sloop *Hobart*, on the East India station, was posted into the frigate *Carysfort*. He subsequently commanded the frigate *Jason*, the *De Ruyter* (68 guns), and the *Beschermer* (50 guns), but without opportunity of distinction. In 1807, while commanding the 32-gun frigate *Blonde*, he cruised with great success against privateers, capturing seven in a few months. In 1809–10, still in the *Blonde*, he served under the command of his namesake, Commodore Ballard of the *Sceptre*, at the capture of the French frigates in Anse-la-Barque and the capture of Guadeloupe for which he was honourably mentioned by both the naval and the military commanders-in-chief. On 18 September 1811 he married Isabella Sarah, eldest daughter of James Crabb of Shidfield Lodge, Hampshire. He obtained his flag rank on 27 May 1825. He died at Bath on 12 October 1832, and was buried at the church of St Saviour, Walcot, Wiltshire.

J. K. LAUGHTON, *rev.* ANDREW LAMBERT

Sources D. Syrett and R. L. DiNardo, *The commissioned sea officers of the Royal Navy, 1660–1815*, rev. edn, Occasional Publications of the Navy RS, 1 (1994) • *GM*, 1st ser., 102/2 (1832), 644

Ballenden, William. *See* Ballantine, William (1617/18–1661).

Balleny, John (*b.* *c.*1770, *d.* in or after 1842), merchant navy officer and Antarctic discoverer, was born *c.*1770 but nothing is known about his early life and education. He may have been a Londoner, brought up in the Newcastle coal trade. From 1798, when he was living in the parish of St George-in-the-East, London, he is occasionally recorded in the coasting, home, and foreign trades as master of various vessels.

In 1838 Messrs C., H., and G. Enderby, of London, managing owners for a joint venture, sent the schooner *Eliza Scott* and the cutter *Sabrina* on a commercial voyage of discovery, hoping to find new lands and sealing grounds. At the last moment Balleny was brought out of retirement and appointed master of the *Eliza Scott*, which was not a good sea boat. Some scientific instruments were lent by the hydrographer John Washington for the making of barometrical observations. Balleny sailed from the Thames on 14 July 1838, sighted Amsterdam Island, and reached Chalky Bay, New Zealand, on 3 December. At Campbell Island on 7 January 1839 he met John Biscoe, who was on a similar search for land in the Antarctic.

At 11.30 a.m. on 9 February 1839, north of the Ross Sea, Balleny sighted land in lat. 66–7° S, long. 162–3° E. This was a group of five islands, which he called the Balleny Islands. Captain Freeman of the *Sabrina* landed briefly, but there was no suitable place for a party to land and explore further. The striking point was Balleny's accuracy in navigation, for after days of dead reckoning, his latitude and longitude were in error by no more than 5 miles, despite difficulties of navigation in those waters: this suggests that he was an experienced sailor.

Sailing westwards, on 2 March 1839, in lat. 64°58′ S, long. 121°08′–122°44 E, Balleny charted 'Sabrina Land', which does not in fact exist. He may have seen the continental ice cap, raised by mirage. The *Sabrina* was lost on 24 or 25 March 1839 but Balleny returned to Britain on 18 September, just as Captain James Clark Ross was leaving for Antarctic exploration. Balleny gave Ross a copy of his chart and extracts from his logbook. When Ross reached that area, he charted the islands as a separate group, the Russell Islands. Balleny's barometrical observations had had to be abandoned after difficulties with instruments. Neither was the voyage a commercial success. Profits from the sealskins he brought back covered no more than a fraction of the expedition's cost, although it seems likely that Charles Enderby, a keen geographer and the main organizer of the venture, never envisaged that it would bring commercial gain. However, its geographical results were notable. A report of Balleny's voyage was made to the Royal Geographical Society by Charles Enderby in 1839 and published in the society's journal in the same year.

In 1840–41 Balleny was master of the new barque *Taglioni* on its voyage to Calcutta, and in 1842 to Australia. He seems to have died about this date, for there is no further record of him.

A. G. E. JONES, *rev.* ELIZABETH BAIGENT

Sources A. G. E. Jones, 'New light on John Balleny', *GJ*, 135 (1969), 55–61 • A. G. E. Jones, 'Captain John Balleny and the Balleny Islands', *Fram*, 1/2 (1984), 497–505 • J. Balleny and C. Enderby, 'Discoveries in the Antarctic Ocean in February 1839', *Journal of the Royal Geographical Society*, 9 (1839), 517–28

Archives Admiralty Library, Taunton, Hydrographic Office, MSS • RGS, logbooks of the *Eliza Scott*

Ballin, Ada Sarah (1862–1906), magazine editor and proprietor, and writer on health, was born on 4 May 1862 at 47 Woburn Place, Bloomsbury, London, first of the three children of Isaac Ballin (*c.*1811–1897), merchant, and his wife, Annie, *née* Moss. She was brought up in a Jewish home and educated privately before attending University College, London, in 1878, the first year that women were allowed open entrance for degree courses. Although she did not take a degree and may not have stayed the full three years, her academic talents were not in doubt. She was awarded the Hollier scholarship in 1880 for Hebrew, and in 1880–81 the Fielden scholarship for French and German as well as the Heimann silver medal for German. She also studied under W. H. Corfield, professor of hygiene and public health, who stirred her interest in medical issues.

In 1881 Ballin published her first book, *A Hebrew Grammar with Exercises Selected from the Bible*, written with her younger brother, Francis Louis Ballin. Four years later she published *The Science of Dress in Theory and Practice*. Between 1880 and 1887 she lectured to the National Health Society, before turning to journalism full-time in 1887, in which year she founded her first and most successful publication, *Baby: the Mothers' Magazine*, an illustrated monthly. In addition she edited the health and beauty departments of the *Lady's Pictorial*, until 1894, and contributed to many other papers. Throughout the 1890s Ballin wrote and edited a series of sixpenny pamphlets in the Mothers' Guide series, which included: *How to Feed our Little Ones* (1895), *Bathing, Exercise and Rest* (1896), *Early Education* (1897), and *Children's Ailments* (1898).

By the time she married for the first time, on 21 September 1891, Mrs Ballin, as she continued to style herself, was already an authority on baby and child care, with a particular interest in dress. She stated in the first issue of *Baby*: 'Over 100,000 children die each year in England from preventable diseases, the chief causes of which are improper feeding and insufficient clothing'. Ballin favoured wool, not cotton or linen, and insisted that rational clothes for babies should cover every part of the body while leaving the arms free. Children trained to wear proper clothing, she argued, 'will not be likely when they grow up to endure voluntarily such sufferings and constraints as the corrupt fashion of the present day imposes upon their mothers and elder sisters'. Although not formally connected to the Rational Dress Society, Ballin's theories, many of which echoed Dr Jaeger's ideas, were broadly in line with the hygienic and rational, rather than the artistic and aesthetic, side of the movement. Her principal targets were tight lacing and the danger of poisonous dyes, but she believed the new bifurcated garment for women was unnecessary, and constantly emphasized that her goal was reform, not revolution.

Ballin's marriage to Alfred Thompson, a solicitor ten

years her senior, ended in divorce. They had one child, a daughter, Annie Isabella, born in 1892. On 25 April 1901 Ballin married Oscar George Daniel Berry, a clerk at the Royal National Lifeboat Institution, seven years her junior; this was presumably a matter of some concern to her as she falsified by four years her own age on the marriage certificate.

In December 1898 Ballin launched her second new journal, a monthly called *Womanhood*, aimed at the 'new woman' of the 1890s, whose intellectual and physical needs, she contended, were not yet being catered for. In the first issue she stated her aims boldly: to supply these highly educated women with a more solid literary diet than other papers, as well as offering them legal advice, articles of political interest, and information on personal health, beauty, and culture.

> I may say, without seeming egotistical, that I am the authority in the latter department as although very many papers give articles on the toilet and beauty and even answers to correspondents on these subjects, these are in the main drawn from former writings of my own. (Ballin, 'Introduction')

Many of the articles written by Ballin herself, a keen cyclist and dance enthusiast, were on the newly trumpeted importance of sport and exercise for women. Her writings reveal a wide-ranging knowledge of medical and cosmetic topics and she insisted that she was read by many medical students. Her advice was highly practical, her intention being to make women think for themselves, 'not in opposition to their male relations but in order to be able to be true helpmeets to them and not mere dolls to be looked at, admired and petted'. Her principal books were *Health and Beauty in Dress from Infancy to Old Age* (1892), *The Kindergarten System Explained* (1896), *Nursery Cookery* (1900), and *From Cradle to School* (1902).

For nearly twenty years Ballin worked as a counsellor, giving advice privately to mothers and nurses who consulted her at home. She also invented and marketed several products such as the Ballin baby bottle, the Ballin baby safety corselet, the Ballin hygienic layette, and Ballin's cold cure.

Ada Ballin died, aged forty-four, on 14 May 1906, after falling 60 feet from a first-floor balconied window at her home, 18 Somerset Street, Portman Square, London, and impaling herself on railings below. The coroner believed that, feeling faint, she had stepped outside the window to get some fresh air and then fallen. The inquest returned a verdict of accidental death. By her will, made at the time of her marriage to Berry, she bequeathed the management of her periodicals to her brother; *Playtime* and *Womanhood* both ceased publication after a year but *Baby* continued until 1915. ANNE M. SEBBA

Sources A. Ballin, 'Rational dress for children', *Baby: the Mothers' Magazine* (Dec 1887) • A. Ballin, 'Introduction', *Womanhood* (Dec 1898) • UCL • *The Times* (17 May 1906) • *Marylebone Gazette* (19 May 1906) • *Jewish World* (30 July 1880) • b. cert. • m. certs. • d. cert. • will, 7 Sept 1906 [London] • *CGPLA Eng. & Wales* (1906)

Likenesses photograph, repro. in A. Ballin, 'Introduction'

Wealth at death £1466 5s. 4d.: probate, 1906, *CGPLA Eng. & Wales*

Ballingall, Sir George (1780–1855), military surgeon and medical writer, was born on 2 May 1780 at Forglen, Banffshire, the son of the Revd Robert Ballingall, and his wife, a daughter of J. Simson of Edinshead. His education began at the Falkland parish school in Fife. Afterwards he attended the University of St Andrews, in which town he was also apprenticed to a Dr Melville, before moving on in 1803 to the University of Edinburgh, where he became an assistant to the anatomy lecturer John Barclay. Ballingall later compiled Barclay's lectures into a book (*Introductory Lectures to a Course of Anatomy, Delivered by the Late John Barclay*, 1827), and in 1813 honoured Barclay with the gift of a preserved skeleton of an elephant which was later displayed in the museum of the Royal College of Physicians of Edinburgh.

In 1806 Ballingall joined the 2nd battalion of the 1st Royals as an assistant surgeon; soon after he departed for India, where he remained until 1814. The duke of Kent was then colonel of the regiment, and he became one of Ballingall's principal patrons. Aside from volunteering to join the expedition to Java in 1811, Ballingall did not see much action in India. However, he had to contend with the high mortality and morbidity rates which beset British regiments there. Conditions in India confirmed his belief that most diseases and illnesses could be avoided or at least ameliorated through preventive measures. India itself was not inherently unhealthy; rather, it was the lifestyles of the European residents that were at fault. In 1815 Ballingall was promoted to full surgeon following his transfer to the 33rd foot, which corps comprised part of the army of occupation in Paris. In 1817, shortly after his return to Edinburgh, he married a daughter of his distant cousin, James Ballingall of Perth. He retired on half pay in 1818.

Ballingall next set up practice in Edinburgh. There he also began to write, beginning with *Practical Observations on Fever, Dysentery and Liver Complaints, as they occur amongst the European Troops in India* (1818), followed shortly by *Essay on Syphilis* (1820). He was appointed lecturer of military surgery at the University of Edinburgh in 1823, and despite considerable opposition from the medical community at Edinburgh, who wished to dispense with the chair altogether, or at least convert it to a professorship of general surgery (in 1823 Ballingall attracted only four pupils on top of the thirty-three from the services), he was appointed professor of military surgery in 1825. Ballingall quickly proved to be one of the more popular lecturers; in 1839 he had eighty students. This professorship, partly subsidized by the government, was then the only position in Britain which specifically addressed military medicine; a similar chair was established in Dublin in 1846.

Even after his appointment to the University of Edinburgh Ballingall continued to travel extensively on the continent, where he observed developments in military medicine and built up a network of medical and military contacts. Consequently, ideas and practices which were

Sir George Ballingall (1780–1855), by unknown engraver

developing in Europe featured in his lectures and writings. His lectures in Edinburgh formed the basis of his two best-known works: *Introductory Lectures to a Course of Military Surgery* (1830), and *Outlines of Military Surgery* (1833), which became a standard reference and instructional work for military and naval surgeons. He also wrote several pamphlets on military and medical matters, including *Remarks on Schools of Instruction for Military and Naval Surgeons* (1843), *On Schools of Naval and Military Surgery* (1844), *Extract of a Lecture on Corporal Punishment* (1847), and *Observations on the Site and Construction of Hospitals* (1851), as well as articles for the medical press, chiefly the *Edinburgh Medical Journal*.

Ballingall made no significant advances in medical theory. His early writings on diseases of hot climates were soon eclipsed by others, partly because his belief in the ability of Europeans to acclimatize to Indian conditions was becoming less popular as the century wore on. He was, however, an early critic of the extensive use of mercurials in treating venereal diseases and dysentery, and he made some headway in limiting army surgeons' use of mercury on venereal cases. His real importance lay in his efforts to persuade the army to take preventive medicine more seriously. Despite his title of professor of military surgery, most of his writings and lectures dealt with what he termed military hygiene. He stressed the need for sanitary reforms, and pressed for increased attention to the placing of barracks, diet, discipline (especially corporal punishment), and arrangements for wholesome leisure activities to counteract the 'ruinous consequences of excesses amongst the soldiery' (G. Ballingall, *Outlines of Military Surgery*, 1833, 41).

Contemporaries described Ballingall as tall and slender, and quiet and even-tempered. He was elected FRSE in 1820, and in 1830 he was knighted by William IV. Recurring bouts of bronchitis so incapacitated Ballingall in the last years of his life that he was forced to limit his lectures to the summer months. Complications arising from his bronchitis led to his death on 4 December 1855 at his country house of Altamont, Blairgowrie, Perthshire. Two sons and a daughter survived him: William, the eldest son, joined the Indian army; George, the second son, joined the medical service of the East India Company and eventually became professor of surgery at Grant Medical College in Bombay; and his daughter travelled to Bombay, where she married John Stuart. DOUGLAS M. PEERS

Sources G. A. Ballingall, 'Memoir of Sir George Ballingall', *Journal of the Royal Army Medical Corps*, 6 (1906), 59–63 • S. Devlin-Thorp, ed., *The Royal Society of Edinburgh: one hundred medical fellows elected, 1783–1844* (1982), vol. 3 of *Scotland's cultural heritage* (1981–4) • N. Cantlie, *A history of the army medical department*, 2 vols. (1974) • *Edinburgh Medical Journal*, 1 (1855–6), 668 • D. G. Crawford, *A history of the Indian medical service, 1600–1913*, 2 vols. (1914) • *GM*, 2nd ser., 45 (1856) • M. Harrison, '"The tender frame of man": disease, climate and racial difference in India and the West Indies, 1760–1860', *Bulletin of the History of Medicine*, 70 (1996), 68–93 • J. Irving, 'A concise view of the progress of military medical literature in this country', *Edinburgh Medical and Surgical Journal*, 65 (1846), 34–49 • C. Lawrence, 'The Edinburgh medical school and the end of the "Old Things", 1790–1830', *History of Universities*, 7 (1988), 259–86

Archives Wellcome L., corresp. and papers

Likenesses T. Lawrence, oils, Royal College of Physicians of Edinburgh • W. Stewart, engraving (after portrait by T. Lawrence), repro. in Devlin-Thorp, ed., *Royal Society of Edinburgh* • engraving, Wellcome L. [*see illus.*]

Ballinger, Sir John (1860–1933), librarian, was born in Pontnewynydd, Monmouthshire, on 12 May 1860, the younger son and second of four children of Henry Ballinger of Whitchurch, Herefordshire, a metallurgical engineer, and his wife, Jane Williams (1827–1896) of Llanrumney. His father died in 1866. He was educated at Canton School, Cardiff, and privately until 1875, when he was apprenticed at Cardiff Free Library. In 1880 Ballinger was appointed librarian at Doncaster. Before returning to Cardiff as chief librarian in 1884 he developed journalistic skills, contributing a series 'About books' to the *Doncaster Chronicle* between 1880 and 1884. In 1888 he married Amy, daughter of Captain David Boughton, master mariner, of Cardiff. They had two sons and a daughter.

Cardiff's policy of providing school libraries, inaugurated in 1899, and children's reading-halls in branch libraries, evidenced the practice of principles advocated by Ballinger in a stream of papers and pamphlets urging their educational function. Children's literature became an abiding interest. *Books for Village Libraries* (with Frank Burgoyne, 1895) and articles on library planning and administration, foreshadowing *The Rate Limit and the Future of Public Libraries* (1902) and *Library Politics: a Sequel* (1905), reinforced Ballinger's many dynamic contributions to the public libraries movement.

Although Ballinger knew little Welsh, he made a name as a bibliographer by publishing the monumental *Catalogue of Printed Literature in the Welsh Department of Cardiff Free Library* (1898), articles on Vicar Prichard of Llandovery (1899) and on the Trefeca printing press (1905), and *The Bible in Wales* (1906), all with the assistance of James Ifano Jones. Bibliography and acquisitions of valuable collections of Welsh books and manuscripts for Cardiff led to his appointment in 1908 as first librarian of the National Library of Wales at Aberystwyth, which was opened in 1909.

There Ballinger's reputation as an administrator and expository bibliographer increased with the publication of reports and papers on the library and its educational role, and with his contributions to the south Wales press, the journal of the Welsh Bibliographical Society, which he served as treasurer (1910–24), and *Y Cymmrodor*. He pioneered the historiographic use of ephemera in *Gleanings from a Printer's File* (1928). Assisted by William Llewellyn Davies and other Welsh scholars, he prepared new editions of *The History of the Gwydir Family* (1927), and *Basilikon Doron* (1604), and four seventeenth-century Welsh religious books for the University of Wales press board, on which he served from 1922 until 1930. He co-directed, then directed, the Library Association's summer schools at Aberystwyth from 1917 until 1929.

Ballinger was awarded an honorary MA by the University of Wales in 1909 and he was appointed CBE in 1920. He served as president of the Library Association (1922–3), was elected an honorary fellow of the association in 1929, and, just before he retired, was knighted in 1930. In 1932 the Honourable Society of Cymmrodorion awarded him its medal for services to Wales in the field of Celtic bibliography. In private an autocrat, Ballinger was popular with the public and its political representatives, whom he impressed with his authority, journalism, and the exhibitions he organized; but, sadly, his lack of humour and austere sense of mission alienated many of his associates and he intimidated his subordinates.

Until he died at Hawarden, Flintshire, where he lived, on 8 January 1933 Ballinger helped organize the St Deiniol's Library of Henry, Baron Gladstone of Hawarden. He was buried at St Deiniol's, Hawarden, and was survived by his wife. M. A. Bloomfield, *rev.*

Sources *Library Association Record*, 3rd ser., 3 (1933) • *DWB* • *Library History*, 3/1 (1973) • M. A. Bloomfield, 'Sir John Ballinger: an annotated bibliography', NL Wales, MSS XEX 1149 and EX 1150 • *The Times* (10 Jan 1933) • private information (2004) • *CGPLA Eng. & Wales* (1933) • *DNB*

Archives NL Wales, corresp. and papers • NL Wales, papers relating to library administration and historical research | NL Wales, corresp. with Sir Joseph Bradney • NL Wales, letters to John Glyn Davies • NL Wales, letters to Thomas Iorwerth Ellis and Annie Hughes Griffiths • NL Wales, letters to Sir Evan Vincent Evans • NL Wales, letters to William Haines • NL Wales, letters to Sir John Herbert Lewis • NL Wales, letters to Edward Owen • NL Wales, letters to Sir Daniel Lleufer Thomas

Likenesses W. Goscombe John, bronze plaque, exh. RA 1901, Cardiff Central Library • Culliford of Aberystwyth, photograph, repro. in *Library Association Record*, 24 (1922), facing p. 307 • J. M. Staniforth, cartoon, repro. in *Cardiff Evening Express* (1897)

Wealth at death £2012 9s. 7d.: probate, 28 April 1933, *CGPLA Eng. & Wales*

Ballinger, William George (1892–1974), trade unionist and politician, was born at 2 back 45 Gooch Street, Birmingham, on 21 September 1892, the first-born among the six children of Walter George Ballinger (1862–1907), a blacksmith, and his wife, Mary Minnie Johnson (1866–1927), a former actress. In 1901 the Ballingers moved to the Scottish industrial town of Motherwell, where they lived in a poverty-stricken working-class area. When Walter Ballinger died William had to end his formal education; thereafter he educated himself through adult education programmes such as the Scottish Labour College, the International People's College, Elsinore, Denmark, and the Workers' Educational Association. He had to find employment to provide for his family, and entered the blacksmithing section of the Railway Rolling Stock as an apprentice. Here, as a member the Amalgamated Engineering Union (AEU), he became a dedicated socialist. Although he eventually became a co-operative insurance agent, he remained an 'out of trade' member of the AEU.

In 1916 Ballinger joined the Independent Labour Party, and in 1917 he became president of the Motherwell no. 3 branch of the AEU. In 1921 he became secretary of the Motherwell and Wishaw trades and labour council. This was a thankless task. With a large immigrant population of Irish protestant and Catholic workers, Motherwell was politically volatile, and sectarian tension and violence were widespread. There was little working-class unity: the Conservative Party in Motherwell had extensive support among protestant workers associated with the Orange order. There were also differences between communists and the moderate wing of the labour movement.

Ballinger had no sympathy with communism and played a leading role in countering communist activities. He was, however, unable to prevent the communist-dominated United Front candidacy of Walton Newbold, a Marxist intellectual, for Motherwell. Newbold secured a sensational victory in the parliamentary election of 1922, but was defeated in 1923. In the general election of 1924 the moderates under Ballinger's leadership regained control of the Motherwell labour movement and secured the Revd James Barr, a respected United Free Church minister, as its candidate and eventual member of parliament. Ballinger was elected a Dalziel parish councillor (1922–5) and a Motherwell town councillor (1926–8). He was the unofficial leader of the Labour minority group on the council. By the late 1920s the uncompromising politics in this depressed community had made him a tough and abrasive politician.

Ballinger's position in Motherwell failed to satisfy his ambition, and in 1928 he applied for the position of adviser to the Industrial and Commercial Workers' Union (ICU), the largest black trade union in South Africa. In 1926 the novelist Winifred Holtby had visited South Africa. She was disturbed by the treatment of Africans by whites and feared that communists could exploit their grievances.

Like other white sympathizers she believed that the ICU leader Clements Kadalie required white guidance. With Kadalie's consent she and Arthur Creech Jones, national secretary of the administrative and clerical group of the Transport and General Workers' Union, recruited Ballinger for the task. Until her death Holtby remained a source of moral and financial support for Ballinger. Her admiration and respect for him is reflected in her last novel, *South Riding*. Joe Astell, a Scots trade unionist, is a fictionalized Ballinger.

On Ballinger's arrival in Cape Town on 16 July 1928 the South African government attempted to declare him a prohibited immigrant, eventually allowing him entry on a temporary permit. In Johannesburg he discovered that the ICU was breaking up because of financial and organizational problems and leadership disputes. He attempted to reorganize and rebuild the union, but the ICU was already in such a state of disintegration that it proved impossible to revive it. Although he was committed to the ICU, Ballinger's political moderation and abrasive personality alienated many of its members, and they made him the scapegoat for the union's collapse. For his efforts he was also attacked from both the left and the right. Conservative white South Africans saw him as a dangerous communist agitator and demanded his deportation, while the communists vilified him as a reformist right-wing collaborator of the capitalists.

After the demise of the ICU in the early 1930s Ballinger became a general trade-union adviser to blacks, and encouraged them to develop co-operatives to improve their position. He also set out to change the racial attitudes and prejudices of white South Africans. In 1934 he published a pamphlet, *Race and Economics in South Africa* (Hogarth Press), in which he analysed South African economics and politics and made recommendations to improve the position of blacks. With (Violet) Margaret Livingstone Hodgson (1894–1980), a history lecturer at the University of the Witwatersrand, whom he married on 12 September 1934, he published two other pamphlets: *Indirect Rule in Southern Africa: Basutoland* (1931) and *Britain in Southern Africa: Bechuanaland Protectorate* (1932). The pamphlets give an overview of the socio-economic and administrative conditions in the two British protectorates. His reputation as an expert on black labour conditions in southern Africa resulted in invitations to the international labour conferences of 1935 and 1936 in Geneva, where he was a technical adviser to the British workers' delegation.

In 1934 British supporters of Ballinger formed the Society of the Friends of Africa to assist him in his South African task. The society became a purely South African organization in 1940. By then, however, Ballinger's abrasive nature and his constant feuds with those with whom he was involved ensured that he had become a marginalized and peripheral figure among trade unionists and white liberals. In 1936 the Representation of Natives Act removed black voters from the common voters' roll in the Cape Province and placed them on a separate roll to elect three white representatives for the house of assembly. The black males could elect four white senators in all. In 1937 Ballinger stood for election to the senate. Although he was defeated, Margaret was elected as a native representative for the Eastern Cape in the house of assembly. Ballinger's main concern now became to assist her parliamentary career as an uncompromising opponent of racial oppression. She became the first president of the South African Liberal Party.

Ballinger was elected as a native representative in the senate in 1948 on a platform of full citizenship rights for the black population. His election led to judicial proceedings when his defeated pro-apartheid opponent claimed that his residence on a temporary permit prevented him from becoming a citizen. In a landmark court case the dispute was settled in his favour. Although Ballinger proved an uninspiring parliamentarian, he was a conscientious representative of his constituents and a dogged opponent of apartheid. A member of the Liberal Party, he was seen by many black nationalists as too moderate. His parliamentary career ended in 1960 when the National Party government abolished the system of native representation. He retired to Cape Town, where he died on 20 July 1974; he was cremated at Maitland crematorium, Cape Town, four days later. His marriage was childless.

Slightly built, with distinctive high-powered horn-rimmed spectacles, Ballinger was gruff and humourless. A courageous opponent of apartheid, he did his utmost to improve the position of the black population, but his abrasive personality and tactlessness harmed his reputation and work and alienated many people. Yet he contributed to the maintenance of the ideal of a democratic, non-racial South Africa. F. A. MOUTON

Sources F. A. Mouton, *Voices in the desert: Margaret and William Ballinger* (Pretoria, 1997) • F. A. Mouton, '"A rising councillor": the origins and making of William Ballinger, 1892–1928', *Kleio*, 25 (1993), 79–94 • F. A. Mouton, '"A cusser when crossed": the turbulent career of William Ballinger', *Kleio*, 27 (1995), 145–64 • P. L. Wickins, *The Industrial and Commercial Workers' Union of Africa* (1978) • H. Bradford, *A taste of freedom: the ICU in rural South Africa, 1924–1930* (1987) • M. Shaw, *The clear stream: a life of Winifred Holtby* (1999) • b. cert. • *The Labour who's who* (1927) • R. McKibbin, *The evolution of the labour party, 1910–1924* (1974) • d. cert., South African department of home affairs

Archives University of Cape Town Library, Cape Town, corresp. and papers relating to South Africa • University of the Witwatersrand, Johannesburg | Hull Central Library, corresp. with Winifred Holtby • University of the Witwatersrand, Johannesburg, Industrial and Commercial Workers' Union collection

Wealth at death R144,429: Muster of the supreme court, Cape Town, Estate of W G Ballinger (no. 4975/74)

Balliol [Baliol], **Alexander de** (*d.* **1310?**), nobleman and administrator, was the second son of Henry de *Balliol (*d.* 1246), chamberlain of Scotland, and his wife, Lora de Valognes (*d.* in or before 1272). Alexander, who was lord of Cavers in Roxburghshire, is clearly distinguishable from his namesake and contemporary, Alexander de Balliol, lord of Barnard Castle from 1271 to 1278 and third son of John de Balliol (*d.* 1268), who was cousin german to the subject of this memoir. Alexander de Balliol of Cavers was heir to his elder brother, Guy, who was killed while serving as standard-bearer for Simon de Montfort at the battle of Evesham on 4 August 1265. Since Alexander himself was also a baronial rebel, he was not allowed to succeed to his English estates until he returned to the king's peace, which he did in late 1266. He married, shortly after 7 November 1270, Isabel, heir to the barony of Chilham in Kent, which Alexander continued to hold 'by courtesy of England' after her death in 1292. His tenure of this barony, together with his mother's Valognes inheritance, which was particularly extensive in Hertfordshire and Essex, made Alexander a landowner of some consequence in south-eastern England.

Already holder of extensive estates in southern Scotland, Alexander de Balliol's Scottish interests were also enlarged by marriage. His wife was the widow of David of Strathbogie, earl of Atholl from 1264 until his death in 1270, when Alexander's stepson, John *Strathbogie, was probably still a minor. After a long period of difficulties, Alexander and Isabel eventually secured John's succession—he was first styled earl of Atholl early in 1284. Whatever the source and nature of the difficulties, Alexander's involvement in Scottish affairs increased noticeably following the accidental death of Alexander III, king of Scots, in 1286.

By early December 1287 Balliol was serving the guardians of the realm of Scotland as chamberlain, a post held by his father, his maternal grandfather, and great-grandfather before him. He continued in this office during the remaining period of the guardianship and for much of the reign of his second cousin, King *John, at least until early December 1295. Throughout his period of office, the fortunate chance survival of a series of letters of protection and attorney, together with numerous official writs and receipts, even the transcript of an exchequer account, not only testify to much intense activity on his part in Scotland, but also clearly demonstrate how this important and demanding office worked. His brother, William, a clerk and probably the rector of Kirkpatrick Durham (Kirkcudbrightshire), acted as his deputy or agent in 1288 and again in 1291–2. Clearly, Alexander was regarded as a key figure in Scottish government circles, being one of the twelve guardians elected at the Stirling parliament of July 1295 to take the direction of government out of King John's hands.

Enough is known of Balliol's later career to suggest that, although he was frequently employed in the service of the king of England, Edward I never regarded him as being above suspicion. His English and Scottish estates were temporarily forfeited in 1296–7 but were restored after Alexander's performance of military service in Flanders in 1297. He served with Edward on military campaign in Scotland, evidently being present on the English side at the battle of Falkirk (1298) and the siege of Caerlaverock (1300). His role as one of Edward's agents in southern Scotland was enhanced upon his appointment in 1302 as keeper of the forest of Selkirk and warden of the important garrison of the peel of Selkirk. However, in 1301 his eldest son, another Alexander, had been taken into English royal custody, probably as surety for his father's conduct, and in early February 1303 Balliol himself was arrested for alleged trespass. About six weeks later, upon delivery as hostage of another son, Thomas, he was released and had his lands restored; in the meantime, the peel of Selkirk had fallen to Edward's enemies.

After February 1304, when the submission of most Scots seemed to assure permanent success for Edward I, Alexander de Balliol began to petition him vigorously for the restitution of those Scottish lands and rights which had been confiscated (for instance his lands between the Mounth and the Forth), or for the granting of those which had been promised (such as Kirkpatrick Durham in Kirkcudbrightshire) or had come into the English king's gift (notably the lands of Richard Fraser and Alexander Menzies). The greater emphasis that Alexander placed latterly on his Scottish estates is also indicated indirectly by the fact that in November 1303 he sold the manor of Benington, the centre of his Hertfordshire estates, and other lands and rights elsewhere in Hertfordshire and Essex, the purchaser being John de Benstede (or Binsted), controller of the wardrobe under Edward I. The balance was tilted even further towards Scotland as a result of one of Alexander's last recorded acts, in March 1310, by which he resigned his courtesy tenure of the barony of Chilham. There is little doubt that the events in Scotland in 1306 threw Balliol firmly onto the English side, and there is record of his military involvement against Robert I between 1307 and 1309.

The final recorded reference to Alexander de Balliol occurs in April 1310, and he probably died in that year. His second son, Thomas, appeared in possession of the lordship of Cavers later in 1310, and was married in early 1313. His eldest son, Alexander, was evidently released by Edward II from almost nine years' imprisonment in March 1310, following his father's resignation of Chilham. His stepson, John Strathbogie, earl of Atholl, followed an entirely divergent political course, marrying into the Mar family and becoming a firm and militant adherent of the Brus family as early as 1290. The extent of Alexander de Balliol's progeny is otherwise uncertain, but may have included a third son, William, and a daughter, Margaret. There is no evidence to support the suggestion that he may have married more than once. G. P. Stell

Sources G. A. Moriarty, 'The Baliols in Picardy, England and Scotland', *New England Historical and Genealogical Register*, 106 (1952), 273–90, esp. 285–90 • G. P. Stell, 'The Balliol family and the Great Cause of 1291–2', *Essays on the nobility of medieval Scotland*, ed. K. J. Stringer (1985), 150–65, esp. 154 • *Chancery records* • PRO, esp. Ancient petitions, S18 • BL, Cotton MS Claud D.xiii • W. Fraser, ed., *Liber S. Marie de Dryburgh*, Bannatyne Club, 83 (1847) • J. H. Round, 'Comyn and Valoignes', *The Ancestor*, 11 (1904), 129–35 • J. A. C. Vincent, *The Genealogist*, 6 (1882), 1–7 • J. Bain, *The Genealogist*, new ser., 4 (1887), 141–3 • J. Bain, *N&Q*, 6th ser., 5 (1882), 61–2 • J. Greenstreet, *N&Q*, 6th ser., 5 (1882), 142–3 • J. A. C. Vincent, *N&Q*, 6th ser., 5 (1882), 290–91 • J. Bain, *N&Q*, 6th ser., 5 (1882), 389–90 • H. C. Andrews, *The Benstede family*, Walthamstow Antiquarian Society (1937), 13–17

Balliol, Bernard de (*d.* 1154x62), baron, was the leading member of the second generation of his family in England, having succeeded to the estates of his uncle Guy by 1130–33. He is referred to as 'senior' in the Durham *Liber vitae*. Guy de Balliol had been established in England in the

1090s by William II on lands partly carved out of the forfeited earldom of Northumbria and almost certainly in return for support rendered in William's campaigns on the eastern frontier of Normandy in 1091 and 1094. Of the several families of the Balliol name (or its derivative forms) in medieval Britain and France, Guy and his successors originated from Bailleul-en-Vimeu near Abbeville in the county of Ponthieu, outside the boundary of the duchy of Normandy, in an area which later became part of the *département* of the Somme. Their Picard associations remained strong throughout the eight generations of the family's history down to the death of Edward Balliol in 1364.

A somewhat less shadowy figure than his uncle, Bernard de Balliol was one of the two barons—the other was Robert (I) de Brus—sent from the English royal camp to negotiate with David I, king of Scots, before the battle of the Standard in 1138. Having failed to dissuade David from crossing the River Tees into Yorkshire, Balliol publicly renounced the personal oath of fealty he had sworn to David on an earlier occasion, possibly in 1135, while Brus retracted the homage he owed the king for lands held of him in Scotland. Unlike the Brus family the Balliols did not at that date have any possessions in the northern kingdom. As a continuing supporter of King Stephen, Bernard de Balliol shared in his defeat at Lincoln in 1141, and suffered depredations at the hands of William Cumin, the pretender and usurper of the see of Durham, from 1141 to 1144.

Four of Bernard de Balliol's charters provide the earliest evidence of the family's Picard origins. His name is commemorated in the castle and 'new town' of Barnard Castle (*Castrum Bernardi*), co. Durham, although a ringwork fortification probably already existed there before 1130 and the actual date of his eponymous foundation of the borough is not known. The eldest of at least four other brothers—Ralph, Ingram, Hugh, and Joscelin—Balliol himself had four sons and a daughter with his wife, Maud: Ingram, Guy, Eustace, Bernard, and Hawise. But the third generation of the family came to be represented in the male line in Britain by Bernard de *Balliol 'junior' (*d. c.*1190) alone. Ingram predeceased his father, who was succeeded, probably fairly briefly, for a period between 1152–3 and 1161 by his second son, Guy. G. P. Stell

Sources *A history of Northumberland*, Northumberland County History Committee, 15 vols. (1893–1940), vol. 6 · G. A. Moriarty, 'The Baliols in Picardy, England and Scotland', *New England Historical and Genealogical Register*, 106 (1952), 273–90 · G. P. Stell, 'The Balliol family and the Great Cause of 1291–2', *Essays on the nobility of medieval Scotland*, ed. K. J. Stringer (1985), 150–65 · L. C. Loyd, *The origins of some Anglo-Norman families*, ed. C. T. Clay and D. C. Douglas, Harleian Society, 103 (1951) · A. O. Anderson, ed., *Scottish annals from English chroniclers, AD 500 to 1286* (1908) · [A. H. Thompson], ed., *Liber vitae ecclesiae Dunelmensis*, SurtS, 136 (1923) · unpubd charter evidence

Balliol, Bernard de (*d. c.*1190), baron, referred to as 'junior' in the Durham *Liber vitae*, was probably the fourth son of Bernard de *Balliol 'senior', and succeeded his elder brother, Guy, in the early 1160s, certainly by 1167. He is best known for his part in the events surrounding the capture of William the Lion, king of Scots, at Alnwick in 1174, an action for which he was singled out for praise by some chroniclers. He was *vir nobilis atque magnanimus* ('an honorable and magnanimous man') according to William of Newburgh, and a *seur chevalier* ('trustworthy knight') to Jordan Fantosme, conventional terms of praise perhaps but sufficient to delineate a strength of character in this, one of the few ascertainable details of his public life.

Balliol's wife was Agnes de Picquigny, who was probably of the family of the *vidames* of that name, French royal officials and territorial lords of Picquigny, which was no great distance from Bailleul-en-Vimeu. There is, however, no evidence to connect her and her family with the Pinkenys, Domesday tenants on the honour of Huntingdon who also originated from Picquigny. Despite unfounded statements to the contrary, Bernard de Balliol had no children, certainly none that survived long enough to find their way into written record. His last datable act was a final concord with the bishop of Durham in the court of Richard I at Dover in early December 1189, and he was succeeded during 1190 by his cousin, Eustace de Helicourt, who assumed the Balliol patronymic and remarried in that year. His sons, also listed in the *Liber vitae*, were Hugh, Ingram (or Ingelram), Bernard, and Henry: Ingram and Henry de *Balliol established cadet branches in Scotland at Inverkeilor and Cavers respectively; Hugh, who had probably succeeded his father about 1209, and Bernard were conspicuous members of the group of northern English barons who were staunch supporters of King John. Hugh's own son, John de *Balliol, possibly even named after the king, acquired Scottish interests through marriage to Dervorguilla de *Balliol, and his grandson, *John (*c.*1248x50–1314), became king of Scots (1292–6). G. P. Stell

Sources *A history of Northumberland*, Northumberland County History Committee, 15 vols. (1893–1940), vol. 6 · G. A. Moriarty, 'The Baliols in Picardy, England and Scotland', *New England Historical and Genealogical Register*, 106 (1952), 273–90 · G. P. Stell, 'The Balliol family and the Great Cause of 1291–2', *Essays on the nobility of medieval Scotland*, ed. K. J. Stringer (1985), 150–65 · A. O. Anderson, ed., *Scottish annals from English chroniclers, AD 500 to 1286* (1908) · [A. H. Thompson], ed., *Liber vitae ecclesiae Dunelmensis*, SurtS, 136 (1923) · unpubd charter evidence

Balliol, Dervorguilla de, **lady of Galloway** (*d.* **1290**), noblewoman and benefactor, was a daughter of *Alan, lord of Galloway (*b.* before 1199, *d.* 1234), and his second wife, Margaret, eldest daughter of *David, earl of Huntingdon (*d.* 1219). Born some time after 1209, the date of her parents' marriage, her distinctive Gaelic name, Derbhforgaill, was probably derived from an Irish ancestor in the Galloway line, possibly from an aunt, and was in turn transmitted to a granddaughter through one of her own daughters. Although Dervorguilla was the lord of Galloway's third daughter, and the second of his marriage to Margaret, the fact that Margaret was herself an eldest daughter was adjudged to give Dervorguilla's son, *John, the stronger right to the vacant throne of Scotland over the claims of Robert (V) de Brus, son of Margaret's younger sister, Isabel. This was the outcome of the Great Cause of 1291–2, the culmination of a series of events in which Dervorguilla's connections transformed the fortunes of the Balliol family.

In 1233, at least five years after the death of her mother, and two years after the death of her uncle—the last of her father's legitimate male heirs—Dervorguilla married John de *Balliol (*b.* before 1208, *d.* 1268), lord of Barnard Castle in co. Durham. In the following year, on or about 2 February 1234, her father died, and Dervorguilla and her new husband inherited a third share of the Galloway lordship; they later took charge of her natural brother, Thomas of Galloway, imprisoning him in Barnard Castle. Following the death in 1237 of her maternal uncle John (le Scot), earl of Huntingdon and Chester, Dervorguilla and her elder sister, Christina (or Christiana), succeeded to their mother's right in the honour of Huntingdon and in Earl John's Scottish lands, mainly in eastern and north-eastern Scotland, and to various properties in eastern England granted in exchange for their claims upon the earldom of Chester which Earl John had inherited in 1232 through his mother, Maud, wife of David, earl of Huntingdon, and sister of Ranulf (III), earl of Chester; after 1237 the honour of Chester was retained in English royal hands. The deaths of Christina (in 1246) and Earl John's widow meant that Dervorguilla's share was substantially enlarged. Christina's death also meant that her share of her father's inheritance was divided between Dervorguilla and her eldest (half-)sister, Helen, wife of Roger de Quincy, earl of Winchester and constable of Scotland, Dervorguilla's evidently being the larger and more valuable share.

Between 1234 and 1246 Dervorguilla clearly brought a considerable accession of wealth to the Balliol family. Precise figures are lacking, but her Scottish lands alone probably came to be worth slightly less than £470 per annum. In her widowhood, after 1268, she retained much of her vast inheritance and dower in her own hands and was a considerable patron. An early fifteenth-century chronicler, Andrew Wyntoun, composed a lengthy panegyric entitled 'How Devorguil that Lady Spendyt hyr Tresoure Devotly', crediting her with the foundation of friaries in Dumfries and Wigtown. As in the case of the fifteenth-century bridge across the Nith at Dumfries that bears her name, her reputation for pious munificence has probably gone beyond authenticated record. None the less, she was the first and last member of the Balliol family to have both the incentive and the means to become the founder of a major monastery. In 1273 she endowed the Cistercian abbey of Dulce Cor or Sweetheart in eastern Galloway in fond memory of her husband, whose corpse was reburied there, and whose embalmed heart she kept in an ivory casket. On his behalf, she also brought together the endowments and formulated the statutes of Balliol College, Oxford, a house of scholars founded as an indirect result of transgressions committed by her husband against the bishop of Durham in 1255 (her name is commemorated there by the Dervorguilla Society).

Dervorguilla de Balliol died on 28 January 1290 and was buried in Sweetheart Abbey. She is known to have had at least eight children with John de Balliol, and she outlived all except the youngest of her four sons, Hugh, Alan, Alexander, and John, later King John. The names and sequence of her four daughters are uncertain but they were probably Margaret, Cecily, Ada, and Eleanor, in that order.

G. P. STELL

Sources *A history of Northumberland*, Northumberland County History Committee, 15 vols. (1893–1940), vol. 6, pp. 16–73, esp. 50–51 · G. P. Stell, 'The Balliol family and the Great Cause of 1291–2', *Essays on the nobility of medieval Scotland*, ed. K. J. Stringer (1985), 150–65 · A. O. Anderson, ed. and trans., *Early sources of Scottish history, AD 500 to 1286*, 2 vols. (1922) · A. O. Anderson, ed., *Scottish annals from English chroniclers, AD 500 to 1286* (1908) · *Johannis de Fordun Chronica gentis Scotorum / John of Fordun's Chronicle of the Scottish nation*, ed. W. F. Skene, trans. F. J. H. Skene, 2 vols. (1871–2) · A. O. Anderson and M. O. Anderson, eds., *The chronicle of Melrose* (1936) · H. E. Salter, ed., *The Oxford deeds of Balliol College*, OHS, 64 (1913) · Andrew of Wyntoun, *The orygynale cronykil of Scotland*, [rev. edn], ed. D. Laing, 3 vols. (1872–9) · W. Huyshe, *Dervorgilla, lady of Galloway and her abbey of the Sweet Heart* (1913) · *CIPM*, 2, no. 771

Likenesses seal, BL; Birch, *Seals*, 15,746 · statue (headless), Sweetheart Abbey, Galloway

Balliol, Edward (*b.* in or after **1281**, *d.* **1364**), claimant to the Scottish throne, was the eldest son of *John (John Balliol), king of Scots (*c.*1248x50–1314), and Isabel, daughter of John de Warenne, sixth earl of Surrey (*d.* 1304). He was probably born soon after their marriage, which took place before February 1281. He had a younger brother, Henry, who died in 1332.

Disinherited prince Little is known of Edward Balliol's early life. When in 1296 his father was forced to resign the throne of Scotland and was taken to England, Edward was taken with him; he was lodged at times in the household of the future Edward II and at times in the Tower. When, however, John was transferred in 1299 to papal custody in France, Edward was retained in England, though now in the care of his cousin John de Warenne, seventh earl of Surrey (*d.* 1347). He was still being held honourably in custody in 1310, when he was removed from his cousin's household to that of Thomas and Edmund, the brothers of Edward II. After his father's death he was allowed to take possession of the Balliol estates in France, and he appears to have stayed there, except for occasional visits to England. Although according to the Franco-Scottish treaty of 1295 he was to have married a niece of Philippe IV of France, nothing had come of this; nor was he ever to marry, probably because he never again enjoyed the secure status which alone could have commanded a bride of the rank to which he aspired.

It is possible that the obscure Soulis conspiracy against Robert I which was uncovered in 1320 was made on Balliol's behalf. Be that as it may, it is certain that in the late 1320s there were signs of interest being taken in England of the exile.

In 1325 Edward II's alienated queen, Isabella, and their son the future Edward III came to France, allegedly on diplomatic business. Already there were some nobles, notably Sir Henry de Beaumont, who had been 'disinherited' by the Scots for their failure to follow Robert I and who were anxious to recover the Scottish lands to which they

Edward Balliol (*b.* in or after 1281, *d.* 1364), regnal seal

had a claim. They joined in Isabella's and Mortimer's successful invasion of England in 1326, and supported the campaign made in response to the Scottish invasion of the north of England in July and August of 1327. Balliol may have been there: he was expected in England in the middle of July, when a safe conduct was issued for him. But after the Scots escaped from the English attempt to entrap them it became clear that Isabella and Mortimer were contemplating a final peace, which became a reality in 1328.

This suited neither Balliol nor the 'disinherited', and some of the latter, now back in France, became involved in the resistance to the queen and her lover. When the rule of Isabella and Mortimer was ended by the coup of 1330 and power was taken by the young Edward III, Balliol's prospects rose. Robert I had died in 1329, and Scotland was now governed by Thomas Randolph, earl of Moray, as regent for the infant David II. Several visits to England are recorded at this period; ultimately, though Edward III was not prepared to intervene directly, he was prepared to tolerate an invasion of Scotland by Balliol and the 'disinherited', who were now committed to an attempt to establish Balliol as king of Scots. This was launched just after the death of the Scottish regent on 20 July 1332. The invasion found the Scots in some disarray and resulted in a remarkable and decisive victory at the battle of Dupplin Moor on 11 August. Balliol was crowned at Perth on 24 September; styling himself king of Scots, he proceeded to try to establish his authority.

King of Scots At this stage Edward III had not finally decided upon his attitude towards the new king. If Balliol were king of Scots, Edward clearly assumed that he would hold Scotland as an English fief, and Balliol himself made proposals in November 1332 under which he was to do homage for Scotland and convey a large portion of the southern part of the country to direct English rule. He even suggested that he might marry Edward's sister Joan, who was still of an age to repudiate her marriage to David II. But Edward III also had in mind the possibility of taking direct control of Scotland himself, to which he believed he might be entitled, and this idea was put to a parliament at York, where it was coolly received. Events for the moment overtook any such schemes. After a successful skirmish at Roxburgh, in which the newly appointed guardian of Scotland, Sir Andrew Murray, was captured, Balliol retired to spend Christmas in what he thought of as security at Annan, near the ancestral Balliol lands in Galloway. Here he was surprised by a party headed by Sir Archibald Douglas and John Randolph, earl of Moray, and forced ignominiously to flee to England in total disarray. His brother Henry was killed in the fray.

Edward III was left with the choice of supporting the campaign in Scotland openly or of giving up any hopes he had of asserting his overlordship. Given his desire to make his own reputation after the failures of his father, there was no doubt which he would choose. His response was a full-scale invasion and siege of Berwick, originally taken by Edward I, but recovered by Robert I in 1318. This resulted in the crushing Scottish defeat at Halidon Hill on 19 July 1333 and the re-establishment of Balliol as king of Scots. He rapidly set about rewarding his supporters, who included some English nobles to whom he gave estates in Scotland. He also began to put together an administration, appointing William Bullock chamberlain and custodian of the castle of Cupar in Fife and at least one sheriff, Alan Lisle, who held office in Bute and Cowal. In the absence of records of its operations we have only scattered references to Balliol's officials, but it is clear that his government had great difficulty in functioning. He was able to hold a parliament at Holyrood in February 1334, in which he obtained confirmation of his arrangements with Edward III. This was followed by his formal performance of homage to the English king at Newcastle on 19 June; a week earlier he had ceded the sheriffdoms of Berwick, Roxburgh, Selkirk, Peebles, Dumfries, and the three parts of Lothian to Edward III. In the mean time the young David II and his queen had taken sanctuary in France, and they spent the next seven years at Château Gaillard in Normandy.

Gains and losses Despite Balliol's apparent success, his position remained uncertain. There were quarrels among the 'disinherited', whom he had restored to the estates they claimed in Scotland; and supporters of David II, particularly Robert the Steward in Ayrshire and Sir William Douglas in the south-west, were already mounting resistance. In August 1334 Balliol had to flee to Berwick, whence he sought further support from Edward III. It rapidly became clear that his regime could survive only with substantial English support, which for a time was forthcoming. Over Christmas 1334–5 Edward III joined Balliol in a campaign to recover control of Roxburgh. For the moment it achieved little else, but plans were in hand for a larger effort the next summer, including, at Balliol's suggestion, an attack on the western seaboard from Ireland.

This followed in June 1335. Balliol, now at Newcastle, advanced without opposition up the east coast while

Edward III, starting from Carlisle, marched through Nithsdale. The pincer movement was planned to close at Glasgow, which it did at the end of July. From there the two Edwards marched to Perth. In addition to Roxburgh and Lochmaben, garrisons were established at Stirling and Perth. The areas ceded in southern Scotland by the agreement of 1334 were taken into English control, and sheriffs established at Berwick, Edinburgh, and Dumfries. Many of those who had deserted Balliol the previous year returned to his allegiance, and even Robert the Steward is reported to have made his peace. The autumn of 1335 was the high water mark of Balliol's fortunes. Even so, he did not remain in Scotland. Instead he appointed one of the 'disinherited', David Strathbogie, titular earl of Atholl, as guardian on his behalf and, rather surprisingly in the circumstances, retired to spend the winter at Holy Island in Northumberland. Perhaps age was already taking its toll.

Resistance to Balliol continued, led chiefly by Sir Andrew Murray and Sir William Douglas, and on 30 November 1335 Murray defeated and killed Strathbogie at the battle of Culblean in south-west Aberdeenshire. This brought Edward III to Scotland in the autumn of 1336 on yet another campaign, in which he recovered and repaired Bothwell Castle in Lanarkshire, refortified Perth and left it with an English garrison, and sacked Aberdeen.

It was, however, to be Edward's last campaign in Scotland; his concerns now centred on France, and he left Scotland to others. Balliol's prospects consequently declined. In 1337 Andrew Murray campaigned successfully in Angus and Fife, recovering the castles of St Andrews and Leuchars, though not Cupar, and also recapturing and slighting Bothwell. English attempts to besiege Dunbar Castle in 1337 and 1338 failed. Balliol last appears at Perth in August 1338; thereafter he seems to have retired to the north of England, where in 1339 he was appointed commander of an English army against Scots who were invading the marches. Balliol's effective presence in Scotland had ended, and supporters of David II were left to get on with the task of removing the remaining English garrisons: Perth fell in 1339, Edinburgh in 1341, and Roxburgh and Stirling in 1342. In June 1341 David and his queen were able to return to their kingdom amid general rejoicing.

Decline, resignation, and death Balliol's impact on the history of Scotland after that time was limited. He stayed mainly in the north of England, receiving payment for his services from Edward III. In October 1339 a warrant was issued to pay the wages of 1264 men from Cumberland and Westmorland who were going to Scotland under the command of Balliol and others to raise the siege of Perth, but Perth had in fact surrendered on 17 August. Although at several points in the 1340s Balliol was appointed to command armies directed against the Scots, there is little evidence of his achievements. More is known about his impact on Galloway, where lay his ancestral lands. In August 1339 several important Galloway landowners had returned to the peace of Edward III, and Balliol, though unable to occupy his ancestral castle of Buittle at this point, seems to have been able to fortify Hestan Island off the coast of Kirkcudbrightshire. He left a garrison there under Duncan MacDowell, to which supplies were on several occasions ordered to be sent by Edward III. After the English victory at Nevilles Cross on 17 October 1346 Balliol again acted as commander of English armies reoccupying the south of Scotland; texts exist of documents granted by Balliol at Hestan Island in 1348 and at Buittle in 1352.

Balliol's usefulness to Edward III was declining. The latter came to recognize the desirability of reaching some arrangement with his captive, David II, if only terms could be agreed that suited Edward. To these negotiations, Balliol's insistence on his own rights in Scotland was an obstruction, and an obscure and partially coded memorandum, probably belonging to 1350, suggests that pressure was being brought on him to be more accommodating. By 1351 there was at least the prospect of an agreement between David and Edward III, and David was temporarily released to see if the Scots would agree to Edward's demands. At this point they would not, and David returned to captivity, but it was clear that Edward III was prepared to abandon any support for Balliol.

In 1356 Balliol was brought, on the plea of age and infirmity, to resign to Edward III all rights he had in the crown and kingdom of Scotland. He is said by Andrew Wyntoun to have called the Scotsmen 'ill and wicked', perhaps remembering his father's similar invective against his former subjects after he resigned the Scottish throne. In return for his surrender Balliol received an annuity of £2000, on which he lived in retirement at Wheatley, near Doncaster, in Yorkshire.

Edward Balliol has generally been dismissed by Scottish historians as of little significance, but he showed considerable persistence and on occasions, as in his tactical advice to Edward III in 1336, also revealed some military capacity. His pension continued to be paid until he died, probably at Wheatley, in January 1364. The exact day is uncertain, but it must have been between the 1st and 24th of the month. BRUCE WEBSTER

Sources *Johannis de Fordun Chronica gentis Scotorum / John of Fordun's Chronicle of the Scottish nation*, ed. W. F. Skene, trans. F. J. H. Skene, 1 (1871), 356–73 • Andrew of Wyntoun, *The orygynale cronykil of Scotland*, [rev. edn], 2, ed. D. Laing (1872), 382–457, 477–85 • W. Bower, *Scotichronicon*, ed. D. E. R. Watt and others, new edn, 9 vols. (1987–98), vol. 7, pp. 64–149, 270–89 • J. Stevenson, ed., *Chronicon de Lanercost, 1201–1346*, Bannatyne Club, 65 (1839), 267–97 • T. Grey, *Scalachronica: the reigns of Edward I, Edward II and Edward III*, trans. H. Maxwell (1907), 88–120 • *CDS*, vols. 3, 5 • R. Nicholson, *Edward III and the Scots: the formative years of a military career, 1327–1335* (1965) • R. Nicholson, *Scotland: the later middle ages* (1974), vol. 2 of *The Edinburgh history of Scotland*, ed. G. Donaldson (1965–75), 124–61 • B. Webster, 'Scotland without a king, 1329–1341', *Medieval Scotland: crown, lordship and community: essays presented to G. W. S. Barrow*, ed. A. Grant and K. J. Stringer (1993), 223–38 • E. W. M. Balfour-Melville, 'The death of Edward Balliol', *SHR*, 35 (1956), 82–3 • A. A. M. Duncan, '*Honi soit qui mal y pense*: David II and Edward III, 1346–52', *SHR*, 67 (1988), 113–41 • R. C. Reid, 'Edward de Balliol', *Transactions of the Dumfriesshire and Galloway Natural History and Antiquarian Society*, 3rd ser., 35 (1958), 38–63 [incl. 'acts' issued by Edward Balliol as king of Scots] • A. A. M. Duncan, 'The war of the Scots, 1306–23', *TRHS*, 6th ser., 2 (1992), 125–51 • GEC, *Peerage*

Archives texts of charters of Edward Balliol as king of Scots, incl. some originals
Likenesses regnal seal, BL; Birch, *Seals*, 14,809 [*see illus.*]
Wealth at death held no lands or tenements in Yorkshire: Balfour-Melville, 'The death of Edward Balliol'

Balliol [Baliol], **Henry de** (*d.* **1246**), nobleman and administrator, was the youngest brother of Hugh de Balliol (*d.* 1229) of Barnard Castle; together with another of his elder brothers, Ingelram or Ingram (*d. c.*1244), he was the first of his family to acquire lands and interests in Scotland. These interests came through marriage and drew him into Scottish royal service during the reign of Alexander II. He served as chamberlain of Scotland for two terms, from 1223 to 1230 and again from 1241 to his death in 1246, and occasionally acted as the king of Scots's representative or envoy to the English court. In 1237, for example, he was one of the sureties sworn to keep the terms of the treaty of York on behalf of Alexander II, and in 1244 was one of the four barons who swore by Alexander's soul to observe his promise of non-hostility to England. Henry's identity and career are, however, often confused with a Nottinghamshire baron of the same name, active in the reign of King John, and with his own nephew and nephew's son in the Inverkeilor–Urr branch of the family.

Balliol's wife, Lora, whom he had married by 1233, was eldest daughter and coheir of William de Valognes, through whom Henry succeeded to a share of the extensive Valognes estates in England and Scotland, including those subsequently inherited from Lora's cousin, Christiana, countess of Essex. His holdings came to be centred on the baronies of Benington (Hertfordshire) and Cavers (Roxburghshire). The office of chamberlain of Scotland may have been associated, though not strictly hereditably, with tenure of the lordship of Cavers, which had originally been Scottish royal demesne. William de Valognes, and his father, Philip, before him, had both been chamberlains, while Henry's second son, Alexander de *Balliol, later served in this capacity for the guardians and for his cousin, *John, king of Scots. Henry de Balliol died shortly before 15 October 1246 and, also like his Valognes predecessors, he received the signal honour of burial in the chapter house of Melrose Abbey, where certainly his daughter Ada, and possibly also his widow, who died before April 1272, were interred. In addition to Alexander and Ada, Henry's children included another daughter, Lora, who married Gilbert de Gaunt (or Gant), and two other sons. Guy de Balliol, his eldest son, was killed fighting on the baronial side at Evesham in 1265, and William de Balliol, his third son, became a clerk, later working as agent for his brother, Alexander, when the latter was chamberlain of Scotland. G. P. Stell

Sources G. A. Moriarty, 'The Baliols in Picardy, England and Scotland', *New England Historical and Genealogical Register*, 106 (1952), 273–90, esp. 285–90 • G. P. Stell, 'The Balliol family and the Great Cause of 1291–2', *Essays on the nobility of medieval Scotland*, ed. K. J. Stringer (1985), 150–65, esp. 154 • *Chancery records* • A. O. Anderson and M. O. Anderson, eds., *The chronicle of Melrose* (1936) • [C. Innes], ed., *Liber sancte Marie de Melros*, 2 vols., Bannatyne Club, 56 (1837) • H. Maule, *Registrum de Panmure*, ed. J. Stuart, 2 vols. (1874) • A. O. Anderson, ed. and trans., *Early sources of Scottish history*, AD *500 to 1286*, 2 vols. (1922) • J. H. Round, 'Comyn and Valoignes', *The Ancestor*, 11 (1904), 129–35 • J. A. C. Vincent, *The Genealogist*, 6 (1882), 1–7 • J. Bain, *The Genealogist*, new ser., 4 (1887), 141–3 • J. Bain, *N&Q*, 6th ser., 5 (1882), 61–2 • J. Greenstreet, *N&Q*, 6th ser., 5 (1882), 142–3 • J. A. C. Vincent, *N&Q*, 6th ser., 5 (1882), 290–91 • J. Bain, *N&Q*, 6th ser., 5 (1882), 389–90 • H. C. Andrews, *The Benstede family*, Walthamstow Antiquarian Society (1937), 13–17 • GEC, *Peerage*, 5.133n

Balliol [Baliol], **John de** (*b.* before **1208**, *d.* **1268**), magnate and benefactor, was the eldest son and heir of Hugh de Balliol (*d.* 1229), lord of Barnard Castle in co. Durham and of Bailleul-en-Vimeu in Picardy. Probably named after King John, to whom his father, exceptionally among the baronage of the north of England, had remained loyal, John was born some time before 1208, and succeeded to his patrimony on his father's death in 1229. Probably the single most decisive event in his long career, however, was his marriage in 1233 to Dervorguilla (*d.* 1290) [*see* Balliol, Dervorguilla de], third daughter of *Alan, lord of Galloway, and the second daughter of his second marriage, to Margaret, daughter of David, earl of Huntingdon (*d.* 1219). In 1234 Dervorguilla's father died, and she and John inherited a third share of the Galloway lordship. Further substantial inheritances followed upon the deaths of Dervorguilla's maternal uncle, John (le Scot), earl of Huntingdon and Chester, and his widow, Helen, in 1237 and *c.*1253 respectively, and of her own elder sister, Christina (or Christiana), in 1246. By the middle of the thirteenth century Dervorguilla had thus brought considerable material wealth to her husband; hence Matthew Paris's contemporary reference to John de Balliol as 'rich and powerful', and to the 'money which he had in abundance' (Paris, *Chron.*, 5.507, 528), a fact which did not escape Henry III's notice. This dramatic increase in wealth is particularly clearly expressed in the impressive architecture of mid- and later thirteenth-century date at Barnard Castle, the principal Balliol residence and stronghold in England, and at Buittle in Kirkcudbrightshire.

Judging by the frequency of his appearances in English government record from the mid-1240s onwards, this wealth also gave John de Balliol a platform for involvement in public life far beyond that of his predecessors. He was the first member of the family to be appointed as a sheriff, serving as sheriff of Cumberland and constable of Carlisle Castle between 1248 and 1255, and as sheriff of Nottingham and Derby between 1260 and 1264. In 1251 he assumed a prominent role on behalf of Henry III as joint protector of the young king of Scots, Alexander III, and his wife, Margaret, Henry's daughter; his role may have been largely nominal, however, and was certainly subordinate to that of his colleague, Robert de Ros (*d. c.*1270) of Wark and Sanquhar, with whom he was removed from office in 1255. Between 1258 and 1265, throughout the course of the barons' wars, Balliol was usually to be found among Henry III's select group of counsellors, temporarily suffering forfeiture in 1263 and the effects of the king's defeat at Lewes in 1264. His cross-border landed interests led to his becoming a trusted envoy to Scotland and to France, where, remarkably, he retained possession of the Balliol patrimony, principally because his lands lay in the counties of Vimeu and Ponthieu in Picardy, outside the duchy of Normandy and thus not confiscated by the king of France in 1204.

Notwithstanding his international responsibilities, it was a local problem which brought John de Balliol into conflict with his powerful neighbour, the bishop of Durham, and which led to his foundation of Balliol College, Oxford, the best-known memorial to the family name. The origins of the dispute lay in the homage and service for five and a quarter knights' fees held by the Balliols within the wapentake of Sadberge, especially their holdings in the vill of Long Newton. Sadberge, which incorporated part of the Balliol barony of Gainford, held in chief of the king since about 1093, had been purchased by Bishop Hugh du Puiset from Richard I, and since the last decade of the twelfth century had thus effectively become absorbed within the bishopric. In an agreement drawn up in 1231 John de Balliol acknowledged that the homage and service previously due to the king would be transferred to the bishop, but he evidently found difficulty in observing these terms.

A series of royal writs culminated in a letter of August 1255, in which Balliol was charged with the capture of the church of Long Newton, and with physical assault on the men of Bishop Walter Kirkham (*d.* 1260) by a group which included John's brothers Eustace and Jocelin; four of the bishop's men had been imprisoned at Barnard Castle. On this occasion agreement and redemption were secured. In an account in the *Chronicle of Lanercost*, John de Balliol is clearly identifiable as the anonymous baron of the bishopric of Durham who, having transgressed against the church, submitted himself to a public whipping by the bishop in front of the cathedral church door, and undertook to maintain scholars studying at Oxford. Some provision for the support of a house of scholars was made before his death in 1268, and further endowments were made in accordance with the terms of his will; these were brought together and the statutes of what became Balliol College were formulated in 1282 by his widow, Dervorguilla. The latter's uncommonly strong and romantic attachment to her husband was reflected in her foundation, in 1273, of the Cistercian abbey of Dulce Cor, or Sweetheart, in Galloway in memory of him. During her widowhood, she also had his embalmed heart set within an ivory casket always by her side, and, according to Andrew Wyntoun, she instructed that on her death it should be laid 'betwene hyr pappys twa' (Andrew of Wyntoun).

John de Balliol was the head of a family which was evidently both widely ramified and closely knit, acting in concert when occasion demanded, as the Long Newton episode in 1255 shows. The career of his second brother, Eustace, closely shadowed his own, including regular performance of royal service overseas, and a crucial period in office between 1261 and 1265 as sheriff of Cumberland and constable of Carlisle Castle. Married to an important Cumbrian heiress, Helewise of Levington, Eustace may also have been party to unrealized Balliol ambitions in north-western England, bridging the geographical gap between the lordships of Barnard Castle and Galloway. Of John's other brothers, Jocelin and Bernard were also in English royal service in the 1250s and early 1260s, and both benefited from John's marriage by acquiring lands in Scotland, in the Garioch and Berwickshire respectively. A fourth brother, Hugh, also appears fleetingly in Scotland, in Irvine on John's Cunningham estates in 1260, but is much more closely associated with the family's possessions in Picardy. John's only known sister was Ada, who married John Fitzrobert of Warkworth. One of their younger sons, Hugh de Eure or Iver, was executor, possibly principal executor, of John de Balliol's will, later serving as an envoy for his cousin, John, king of Scots.

John de Balliol died shortly before 27 October 1268. He and Dervorguilla had at least eight children. Three of their four sons survived to maturity and married within the social milieu of English earls and the English royal court—a measure of the family's considerably expanded horizons. Hugh (*d.* 1271), the eldest son, married Agnes de Valence, daughter of the earl of Pembroke and niece of King Henry III; Alexander (*d.* 1278), the third son, married Aliénor de Genoure, a kinswoman of Queen Eleanor; while John, the youngest son, later *John, king of Scots, married Isabel, second daughter of John de Warenne, earl of Surrey (*d.* 1304). The names and sequence of John and Dervorguilla's four daughters are uncertain, but they were probably Margaret, Cecily, Ada, and Eleanor, in that order. Margaret may have married into the Cumbrian family of Moulton; Cecily certainly married John de Burgh, grandson of the famous justiciar Hubert de Burgh (*d.* 1243); Ada married William de Lindsay, heir to the lordships of Kendal and Lamberton (Berwickshire); and Eleanor married John *Comyn (*d.* c.1302), lord of Badenoch, justiciar of Galloway, and one of the guardians of Scotland. Through her, one of the most powerful political figures in Scotland became brother-in-law to the future King John. G. P. STELL

Sources *A history of Northumberland*, Northumberland County History Committee, 15 vols. (1893–1940), vol. 6, pp. 16–73, esp. 50–51 · G. P. Stell, 'The Balliol family and the Great Cause of 1291–2', *Essays on the nobility of medieval Scotland*, ed. K. J. Stringer (1985), 150–65 · H. E. Salter, ed., *The Oxford deeds of Balliol College*, OHS, 64 (1913) · *Chancery records* · J. Stevenson, ed., *Chronicon de Lanercost, 1201–1346*, Bannatyne Club, 65 (1839) · Paris, *Chron.*, vol. 5 · *CIPM*, 1, no. 691 · Andrew of Wyntoun, *The orygynale cronykil of Scotland*, [rev. edn], ed. D. Laing, 3 vols. (1872–9)

Likenesses portrait, 17th cent., Balliol Oxf.

Wealth at death English holdings: *CIPM*

Balliol, John de. *See* John (*c.*1248x50–1314).

Ballon [Baalun], **John de** (*d.* **1235**), baron, came of a family that took its name from Ballon, Maine, France, and was established in Herefordshire, as lords of Much Marcle, during the reign of William II. John succeeded his father, Reginald de Ballon, when the latter died in 1203. Reginald had succeeded his brother William, and this seems to have given rise to litigation, since John is recorded in 1207 as owing 100 marks and a palfrey so that a fine made by his father over the family lands should be observed. John is also recorded as engaged in litigation concerning property in Wiltshire, where he held the manor of Great Cheverell, and Herefordshire between 1206 and 1212. Although he went to Ireland with King John in 1210, he later joined the baronial revolt against that ruler, with the result that in July 1216 his lands were given to Peter de Bosco; there is no obvious motive for Ballon's rebellion, but the fact that the Herefordshire antiquary W. H. Cooke names his wife as Joanna, daughter of William de Brouse, raises the possibility of a connection with William (III) de Briouze, ruined by the king in 1210.

However, by 22 June 1217 Ballon had come into Henry III's allegiance, and his estates were restored to him. He was in the king's army at the siege of Newark in 1218, and served on the Welsh march in 1223. On 11 February 1225 his name occurs as the last witness to the reissue of the charters, and four days later he was appointed to assess that year's fifteenth in Gloucestershire. Later in 1225 he was appointed one of the justices to hear assizes of novel disseisin and to deliver gaols in the same county. In 1228 he was summoned to serve on the Montgomery campaign; it is not known if he went, but in 1230 he paid 40 marks for scutage and for exemption from the expedition to Brittany. John de Ballon died in 1235, and was succeeded by the eldest of his three sons, another John, whose payment of a relief of £100 for succession to his father's lands shows that they were regarded as constituting a barony, notwithstanding their relatively insignificant extent. The elder John de Ballon, in an early instance of a practice that was later commonplace, had previously safeguarded the descent of some of his Herefordshire lands by conveying them to trustees, who subsequently reconveyed them to the heir. The Ballon family afterwards fell into obscurity, and its manor of Much Marcle was acquired by the Mortimers later in the thirteenth century.

HENRY SUMMERSON

Sources *Chancery records* • *Curia regis rolls preserved in the Public Record Office* (1922–), vols. 4, 6 • *Pipe rolls*, 5–13 John, 14 Henry III • D. M. Stenton, ed., *Pleas before the king or his justices, 1198–1212*, 3, SeldS, 83 (1967) • J. Duncumb and others, *Collections towards the history and antiquities of the county of Hereford*, 3 (1882), 3–4 • I. J. Sanders, *English baronies: a study of their origin and descent, 1086–1327* (1960) • J. C. Holt, *Magna Carta* (1965) • J. H. Round, 'The family of Ballon and the conquest of south Wales', *Studies in peerage and family history* (1901), 181–215

Ballon [Baalun], **Sir Roger de** (*d.* **1225**), landowner, was probably connected to the minor Herefordshire baronial family of Ballon, but the exact nature of the relationship is obscure. He appears to have been a minor landowner in Hampshire; if, as seems likely, he was related to the William de Ballon who occurs several times in the mid-thirteenth century as a witness to grants to Selborne Priory, then his interests may have lain in the north-east of that county. He is often recorded as active in Hampshire in a legal context—first, in 1200, as an attorney in a lawsuit over property at South Fontley, later several times as a knight of the grand assize. He became one of the county's coroners, and in 1220 headed a commission to try a homicide case at Winchester. In 1225 he was appointed in February to be an assessor of the fifteenth in Hampshire, in June to be one of the justices who were to take assizes and deliver gaols in that county. He was dead, apparently very recently, by 27 December 1225. HENRY SUMMERSON

Sources *Chancery records* • *Curia regis rolls preserved in the Public Record Office* (1922–), vols. 3, 8–9 • W. D. Macray, ed., *Calendar of charters and documents relating to Selborne and its priory*, 2 vols., Hampshire RS, 4, 9 (1891–4) • T. D. Hardy, ed., *Rotuli litterarum clausarum*, RC, 2 (1834), 91, 147

Ballow [Bellewe], **Henry** (1704?–1782), legal writer, was probably born on 3 May 1704 in the parish of St Martin-in-the-Fields, Westminster, the son of Henry Ballow and his wife, Dorothy. He was admitted a pensioner at Magdalene College, Cambridge, on 15 October 1720, and admitted to Lincoln's Inn on 27 January 1721. Ballow was called to the bar on 6 November 1728. By 9 July 1731 he held the post of deputy chamberlain of the exchequer, subsequently rising to be senior deputy chamberlain. He is said to have obtained his position in the exchequer, which relieved him of the necessity to practise, through the influence of the Townshends 'to whom he had been a kind of law tutor' (Hawkins, 244), but his father may himself have been deputy chamberlain of the exchequer between 1688 and 1713.

Ballow's legal learning was deep and extensive, and Samuel Johnson attributed his own knowledge of the law chiefly to Ballow's teaching, regarding him as a 'very able man' (Boswell, 2.294). Ballow's legal learning appears to have manifested itself in permanent form in *A Treatise upon Equity*, published anonymously in 1737, which appeared in 1793–4 with references and substantial notes by John Fonblanque, and reached its fifth edition in 1820. The treatise provided, in six short books, a systematic explanation of equity in terms of contract theory. The author regarded the specific enforcement of contracts as the core of equity, and his work represents for later generations the state of equity in the period between the times of the great lord chancellors Lord Nottingham and Lord Hardwicke. The treatise was founded upon the cases, the results of which it stated accurately, though the author cited very few authorities and gave no references to the cases, which rendered the book less valuable to the student than it might have been. Ballow's authorship, though generally accepted, is not certain. Fonblanque pointed out that if Ballow were the author he had produced the work while still of less than ten years' standing at the bar. Further doubt may arise from the apparent influence of Roman law training upon the book's method. However, Francis Hargrave's copy contains a note by Hargrave that the book was written by Mr Bellewe, and one of the manuscripts which passed to Lord Camden as Ballow's literary executor contained a large portion of the work, revised and corrected apparently for publication.

Beyond his legal learning, though possessed of 'vulgar manners', and described as 'a little deformed man' (Hawkins, 244), Ballow was said to be an accomplished Greek scholar and to have been famous for his knowledge of old philosophy. At one time he frequented Tom's Coffee House in Devereux Court, London, where his splenetic temper led him into a quarrel with the poet and physician Mark Akenside, whom Ballow envied for his eloquence and hated for his republican principles. Akenside's consequent challenge went unanswered, the difference being made up by friends, and the antagonists adhering to their respective resolutions that one would not fight in the morning and the other would not fight in the afternoon. Ballow died suddenly in Parliament Street, London, on 26 July 1782. He did not marry. N. G. JONES

Sources *GM*, 1st ser., 52 (1782), 406 • [H. Ballow], *A treatise of equity*, ed. J. Fonblanque, 2nd edn, 2 vols. (1799) • J. Hawkins, *The life of Samuel Johnson, LL.D.* (1787), 244 • Holdsworth, *Eng. law*, 12.191–3 • W. A. Shaw, ed., *Calendar of treasury books*, [33 vols. in 64], PRO (1904–69) • J. Boswell, *The life of Samuel Johnson*, ed. [E. Malone], 5th edn, 4 vols. (1807), vol. 2, p. 294 • St Martin-in-the-Fields, baptism register, 1704 • W. P. Baildon, ed., *The records of the Honorable Society of Lincoln's Inn: admissions*, 1 (1896), 388 • W. P. Baildon, ed., *The records of the Honorable Society of Lincoln's Inn: the black books*, 3 (1899), 288 • Venn, *Alum. Cant.* • W. H. Maxwell and L. F. Maxwell, eds., *English law to 1800*, 2nd edn (1955), vol. 1 of *A legal bibliography of the British Commonwealth of Nations* (1938–58), 256

Ballyann. For this title name *see* Kavanagh, Cahir Mac Art, baron of Ballyann (*d.* 1554?).

Balmain. For this title name *see* Ramsay, John, Lord Bothwell and Lord Balmain (*c.*1464–1513).

Balme, David Mowbray (1912–1989), university administrator and classical scholar, was born on 8 September 1912 at Carlisle, eldest of the four children of Harold Balme (1878–1953), a surgeon, and his wife, Hilda Carr (*d.* 1968). He spent his first ten years in China, while his father was professor of surgery at Cheeloo (Qilu) University. He was educated at Marlborough College and at Clare College, Cambridge (1931–4), where he gained first class honours in both parts of the classical tripos. He then embarked on research into ancient Greek philosophy and science, spending 1934–6 with Julius Stenzel at the University of Halle. This led in 1939 and 1940 to two trail-blazing articles on Greek science, and to a lifelong concern with the scientific works of Aristotle. On 29 December 1936 he married Beatrice Margaret Rice, and they had four sons and a daughter.

After two terms as a lecturer at Reading University, Balme returned to Cambridge in 1937, first winning a research fellowship at Clare, and then (1940) as a fellow of Jesus College. However, his academic progress was almost immediately interrupted by his call-up into the Royal Air Force. He qualified so well as a pilot that his initial employment was as a flying instructor. But he wanted a more active part in the war and was eventually allowed to convert to fly four-engined Lancaster bombers. With the newly commissioned Balme's arrival in 207 squadron at the end of March 1943 there began a remarkably illustrious wartime RAF career. By August, outstanding courage and determination had brought him an immediate DFC, exceptional promotion to squadron leader, and appointment as flight commander. Four months later, having completed thirty-one operations, many of them outstandingly successful, he was made DSO. Balme then served for a time in the Air Ministry, but by the end of the war he was again on active service as a wing commander commanding Lancaster squadrons.

By the end of 1945 Balme was back in Cambridge as tutor, soon senior tutor, at Jesus College. This experience combined with his scholarship and wartime leadership to make him an ideal candidate for recruitment to lead one of the university colleges then being set up to help in the post-war development of Britain's tropical colonies. Balme initially resisted this, but in 1948 he accepted a five-year contract to be the founding principal of the university college in the Gold Coast. There he set out to build a university institution of the very highest standard. To Balme this meant something which would in due course stand comparison with the University of Cambridge. He quickly sought to move away from the professor-dominated system of government originally provided for his college to a collegiate form in which all dons would have a voice, and he gave priority in the building programme to the construction of pleasant residences which were home to dons as well as students. He resisted any charge, whether from layman or academic, Ghanaian or Briton, that his institution was inappropriate for Africa, or that it was too expensive, and continued to pursue his goal with the same single-minded determination with which he had once conducted bombing raids into Germany and Italy. But as the colonial Gold Coast began to turn into the independent state of Ghana, so there was increased competition for development funds, and so less opportunity for Balme to mould his university as he thought best. After his first five years Balme was made a CMG in 1955, but he found a second five-year contract appreciably less attractive. Already a committed Christian, he was now received into the Roman Catholic church. He was disappointed by the refusal of his colleagues to accept his bold view that his college should become a full university, free from the guiding reins of London University with which it had set out, before it became open to the political whims of an independent Ghanaian state, so when in October 1957 a senior classics post became available at Queen Mary College, University of London, he decided the time had come to return to the teaching and research which had become increasingly squeezed out of his life.

In 1964 Balme was elected professor of classics at Queen Mary College, and he continued in this post until his retirement in 1978, building up a reputation as a formidable and much loved teacher, and producing publications relating to Aristotle's scientific works that won international renown. In addition to pioneering articles, these included annotated translations of *De partibus animalium I* and *De generatione animalium I* (1972), and the posthumous edition of and commentary on the *Historia animalium* (1991). In 1966 he made his home at Gumley in the Leicestershire countryside, where fox-hunting became a major enjoyment alongside his lifelong pursuit of music. There, on 23 February 1989, he died of a brain tumour; he was buried on 2 March in the local churchyard. He was survived by his wife. J. D. FAGE

Sources A. D. Dick, ed., *In memoriam: David Mowbray Balme* (privately printed, 1990) · A. Gotthelf, ed., *Aristotle on nature and living things: philosophical and historical studies presented to David M. Balme on his seventieth birthday* (1985) · personal knowledge (2004) · private information (2004) [Mrs B. M. Balme] · I. C. M. Maxwell, *Universities in partnership* (1980), 144–55 · *The Times* (27 Feb 1989) · *Daily Telegraph* (3 March 1989) · *The Independent* (8 March 1989) · *The Guardian* (14 March 1989) · *WWW*

Archives Bodl. RH, papers relating to University College of the Gold Coast / Ghana

Likenesses B. Enwonu, bust, *c*.1960, University of Ghana, Balme Library

Balme, Matthew (1813–1884), factory reformer, was born in Tong, Yorkshire, on 8 July 1813, the third son of Francis Balme (1742–1819), a yeoman farmer, and his wife, Elizabeth West (*d*. 1846), of Redhill Farm, Dudley Hill, Bradford. He was baptized at St James's Church, Tong, in the parish of Birstall, a month later, and maintained a close association with the Church of England throughout his life. After losing his father at the age of six he became the protégé of the Reverend George Stringer Bull, the evangelical curate of Bierley, near Bradford, who later described Balme affectionately as 'my old pupil at Bierley and afterwards my fellow labourer in the good work of youthful protection and instruction' (Ward, 'Balme', 226). On Bull's recommendation, he was appointed superintendent of the model factory school at Bowling, opened in October 1832 by John Wood, the leading Bradford tory evangelical worsted spinner, who had been instrumental in the conversion of Richard Oastler to the cause of factory reform in September 1830. Balme remained superintendent of Wood's school for fourteen years, and when Lord Ashley visited Bradford in 1844 he extolled the virtues of the school where '500 children, under thirteen years of age, are receiving daily the benefits and blessings of a bringing up in the fear and nurture of the Lord' (ibid., 221). On 27 February 1843 Balme married Mary (1815–1866), daughter of Joshua Milner, a Bradford tailor, with whom he had a daughter, Mary (1843–1932). He subsequently entered local government as registrar for the townships of Bolton, Eccleshill, and Idle, and also served as clerk to the Bolton local board, playing a prominent role in both its foundation in 1865 and its controversial dissolution in 1873, when it became incorporated into the expanding borough of Bradford.

Although the early historians of the factory movement Samuel K. Kydd and Philip Grant recognized his energetic contribution to the success of the movement, Matthew Balme has been described by J. T. Ward, a later historian of the movement, as perhaps the least remembered of the nineteenth-century factory reformers, notwithstanding his steadfast commitment to the campaign for factory regulation from 1831 until 1874. As Balme informed the National Association for the Promotion of Social Science meeting in Bradford in October 1859, 'from his own knowledge and recollection', he could testify to the sufferings of 'children of tender age … required to toil in factories' for excessive hours and experiencing 'cruelties of a revolting nature … often resulting in deformity, sometimes in death' (proceedings of Social Science Association meeting, Bradford, October 1859; Bradford Local Studies Library). As a schoolmaster he had first-hand acquaintance with the impact of the factory system on children, and supplied compelling factual evidence to the Bradford short-time committee, of which he became an early member, during Sadler's campaign for factory regulation in 1831. He became secretary of the Bradford committee in 1838, and of the West Riding committee in 1840. He was responsible for advising local committees throughout the county, correlating their reports and briefing the parliamentary leaders of the movement: Lord Ashley, with whom he maintained a warm personal correspondence for over forty years; John Fielden, who succeeded Ashley as parliamentary leader in 1846; and Lord John Manners, who led the parliamentary rearguard action in 1850 against the use of the relay system by manufacturers determined to circumvent the Ten Hours Act of 1847. He organized election canvassing, petitioning campaigns, and fund-raising drives. He also liaised with the Lancashire central committee, Richard Oastler (who was incarcerated in the Fleet debtors' prison in 1840–44), and other parliamentary supporters of the movement, including leading churchmen, notably C. T. Longley, bishop of Ripon, who vigorously supported the campaign for factory reform in the House of Lords.

In many respects Balme typified the tory Anglican involvement in the movement, asserting the Conservative paternalistic ethos against the dominant *laissez-faire* economic doctrines of the influential West Riding Liberal dissenting manufacturers. On 25 April 1863 he was presented with a testimonial recognizing his key contribution to the development of the factory movement, providing 'the connecting link between the more wealthy of its supporters and its less fortunate advocates among the working classes themselves' (W. Yorks. AS, Matthew Balme Collection, deed box 4, case 9, item 80c). After ailing for some months Balme became seriously ill early in August 1884, and died at his home, Blakehill Cottage, Idle, Yorkshire, on 26 August 1884. His obituary in the *Bradford Observer* (27 August 1884) recalled approvingly that

> on all occasions when attending the meetings of operatives he never omitted to warn the workers against any acts that would bring them into conflict with their employers and as frequently reminded them that it was only by mutual forbearance that satisfactory results could be arrived at.

A photograph of Balme in later life reveals a patriarchal profile, with a sympathetic demeanour, well-defined features, and long silvery-white hair, whiskers, and beard. He was buried in Calverley churchyard on 29 August 1884; a monument erected over his grave, paid for by the subscriptions of over 2000 factory operatives and a cluster of prominent public figures such as W. E. Forster and the earl of Shaftesbury, records that 'for upwards of fifty years he was a faithful and earnest advocate in promoting the physical, social and moral improvement of factory workers'. JOHN A. HARGREAVES

Sources J. T. Ward, 'Matthew Balme (1813–1884), factory reformer', *Bradford Antiquary*, new ser., 8 (1952–60) • J. T. Ward, *The factory movement, 1830–1855* (1962) • J. T. Ward, 'The factory movement, 1830–1850', PhD diss., U. Cam., 1956 • W. Robertshaw, 'The settlement of Ryecroft, in Tong', *Bradford Antiquary*, new ser., 6 (1933–9) • W. Cudworth, *Histories of Bolton and Bowling* (1891) • *Bradford Observer* (27 Aug 1884) • W. Yorks. AS, Bradford, Matthew Balme papers, Case 9, Box 4 • W. Cudworth, *A series of sketches round and about Bradford* (1876) • J. C. Gill, *Parson Bull of Byerley* (1963) • J. T. Ward, 'Slavery in Yorkshire: Bradford and factory reform', *Journal of the Bradford Textile Society* (1961), 41–52 • J. T. Ward, *Popular movements, c.1830–1850* (1970) • monument, parish church of St Wilfred, Calverley, Yorkshire

Archives W. Yorks. AS, Bradford, Bradford district archives, Matthew Balme collection

Likenesses photograph, *c.*1880, repro. in Gill, *Parson Bull*, facing p. 69

Wealth at death £189 7*s.* 5*d.*: probate, 23 Dec 1884, *CGPLA Eng. & Wales*

Balmer, George (1805–1846), landscape painter, was born at North Shields, Northumberland, on 3 November 1805, and baptized on 5 January 1806 at Tynemouth, Northumberland, the second son of George Balmer (*c.*1767–1829), house and ship painter, and Ann Reed (*d.* 1835), of Stannington, Northumberland. At the age of fourteen he decided to follow his father's trade and after serving an apprenticeship with the firm joined former Newcastle housepainter Thomas Coulson's decorating business in Edinburgh. Here he became acquainted with the work of fellow Coulson employee John Wilson Ewbank, and, inspired to try his own hand as a professional artist, returned to North Shields. In 1826 he sent his first work for exhibition, showing *A View of North Shields*, at the Northumberland Institution for the Promotion of the Fine Arts, Newcastle upon Tyne. He again exhibited at this institution in the following year, and showed no fewer than seven works at the first exhibition of Newcastle's newly opened Northern Academy, in 1828. He continued to exhibit at Newcastle for several years, and in 1830 sent his first work to the British Institution: *Fishing Lodge Near Inch Islay on the Tay—Moonlight*. In 1831 he moved from North Shields to Newcastle, and in this year showed at the town's exhibition of watercolours one of his best known works, *The Juicy Tree Bit*, and collaborated in the production of another, *The heroic exploit of Lord Collingwood, when captain of the Excellent at the Battle of Cape St Vincent* (Trinity House, Newcastle), with his close friend John Wilson Carmichael. As far as can be determined he remained at Newcastle until late in 1833, when he decided to move to London. In 1834 he sent his first work for exhibition at the Suffolk Street Gallery of the Society of British Artists, London, and also exhibited at Newcastle. He then set off on a tour of Holland, thereafter proceeding up the Rhine, and travelling through Switzerland, making several studies of the Alps *en route*. He next went to Paris, where he spent several months studying at the Louvre, and copied the work of Cuyp, Claude Lorrain, Paul Potter, and Ruisdael. Back in London by 1835 he called on his friend and fellow artist John Wykeham Archer, and announced his intention of practising there. He remained in London until 1842, during which period he continued to exhibit at the British Institution and the Suffolk Street Gallery showing scenes of the continent and north-east England; among the former were *Scene Near Dordrecht* and *Haarlem Mere—Moonlight*, and among the latter *Entrance to the Port of Sunderland* and *The Salmon Leap at Bywell*. Several of these works were bought by wealthy collectors, notably Harrison of Liverpool. In 1836 Balmer suggested to the engraver and publisher brothers Edward and William Finden a publication on *The Ports, Harbours, Watering-Places and Picturesque Scenery of Great Britain*. They accepted his proposal and many of his views of parts of north-eastern England appeared in a volume published in 1842. A short time after its publication Balmer inherited some property at Gateshead, co. Durham, and retired there without exhibiting again. He died at Bensham Grove, Bensham, Gateshead, on 10 April 1846 following an illness, and was buried in Jesmond old cemetery, Newcastle. He was predeceased by his wife, Mary Ann Cook (*d.* 1843), and survived by his only son, George. Balmer's reputation as a coastal painter was considerable in his day; his friend Archer observed in a long obituary in the *Art Union* of October 1846: 'My old friend was never so much in his element as when painting a stranded ship, an old lighthouse, or the rippling of the waves on a shingly coast'. MARSHALL HALL

Sources J. W. Archer, *Art Union*, 8 (1846), 280–81 • R. Welford, *Men of mark 'twixt Tyne and Tweed*, 3 vols. (1895) • M. Hall, *The artists of Northumbria*, 2nd edn (1982) • *DNB* • Wood, *Vic. painters*, 3rd edn • parish registers, Tynemouth • *Newcastle Courant* (20 June 1829) • monumental inscriptions of Jesmond old cemetery, Newcastle Central Library

Balmer, Robert (1787–1844), United Secession minister and theologian, was born at Ormiston Mains, in the parish of Eckford, Roxburghshire, on 22 November 1787, the eldest of four children of Thomas Balmer and Margaret Biggar (*d.* 1839). Sickly as a child, he later enjoyed tolerably good health apart from problems with his eyesight. His parents were both seceders although they adhered, quite amicably, to different congregations. His father, a land steward, died when Robert was about ten. He attended school, latterly at Morebattle and Kelso, before entering Edinburgh University in 1802. In 1806 he continued his studies at the Associate Synod Divinity Hall at Selkirk, under George Lawson (1749–1820), while also attending divinity classes at Edinburgh University. Thus qualified, he could have opted for the ministry of the established church, and the delay after completing his studies caused some to think that he was contemplating this course. However, he was eventually licensed in August 1812. Ordained minister at Berwick upon Tweed in March 1814, he remained with the congregation at Golden Square for the rest of his ministry. He married Jane, daughter of Alexander Scott of Aberdeen, in 1826.

In 1834 Balmer became professor of pastoral theology to the United Secession church, rapidly exchanging this chair for that of systematic theology. His duties required him to be absent from his congregation for two months each year. In 1840 he was awarded a DD by St Andrews University. A man of liberal instincts both in church and secular affairs, Balmer latterly came under attack from a fellow minister and controversialist, Andrew Marshall (1779–1854). In the course of the atonement controversy, occasioned by James Morison's suspension and deposition for arguing a universalist position, Marshall had formed the view that the church's professors were not only sympathetic to Morison but the very source of his views. Balmer's particular offence was to contribute a recommendatory preface to an unfortunately timed edition of Edward Polhill's *Essay on the Extent of the Death of Christ* (1842). Balmer patiently and reasonably explained his position to the satisfaction of his church, though he did not live to see the final resolution of the controversy. In 1843 he distinguished himself at a meeting in Edinburgh to mark the bicentenary of the Westminster assembly, at which he made a powerful speech on Christian union. Beset by a brief but painful illness, he died on 1 July 1844 at Berwick upon Tweed. His funeral there on 9 July attracted some 5000 mourners.

Scrupulous, thoughtful, and unsectarian, Balmer was a man of mild nature and modest bearing. An effective teacher rather than a brilliant scholar, 'His views … were more comprehensive than acute' (Henderson, 66), as one colleague put it. He published little in his lifetime, but a two-volume *Academical Lectures and Pulpit Discourses* (1845) appeared posthumously.

W. G. Blaikie, *rev.* Lionel Alexander Ritchie

Sources J. Henderson, 'Memoir', in R. Balmer, *Academical lectures and pulpit discourses* (1845) • J. Henderson and J. Brown, *Discourses delivered on the occasion of the death of the Rev Robert Balmer DD* (1844) • Chambers, *Scots.* (1835) • Anderson, *Scot. nat.* • W. Mackelvie, *Annals and statistics of the United Presbyterian church*, ed. W. Blair and D. Young (1873), 101 • I. Hamilton, *The erosion of Calvinist orthodoxy* (1990)

Likenesses F. Schenk, lithograph (after painting by M. Button), NPG • sketch, repro. in Anderson, *Scot N*

Balmerino. For this title name *see* Elphinstone, James, first Lord Balmerino (1557–1612); Elphinstone, John, second Lord Balmerino (*d.* 1649); Elphinstone, John, third Lord Balmerino and second Lord Coupar (1623–1704) [*see under* Elphinstone, John, second Lord Balmerino (*d.* 1649)]; Elphinstone, John, fourth Lord Balmerino and third Lord Coupar (1652–1736) [*see under* Elphinstone, John, second Lord Balmerino (*d.* 1649)]; Elphinstone, Arthur, sixth Lord Balmerino and fifth Lord Coupar (1688–1746).

Balmford, James (*b. c.*1556, *d.* after 1623), Church of England clergyman, is first recorded in 1594, the year in which he published *A Short and Plaine Dialogue Concerning the Unlawfulness of Playing at Cards*. This pamphlet of eight leaves is dedicated to his patrons, the mayor, aldermen, and burgesses of Newcastle upon Tyne; according to Hazlitt's *Hand-Book* the work also appeared as a broadside. In 1623 Balmford reprinted his *Dialogue*, prefacing it with an address to the reader, dated 14 September 1620, in which Balmford describes himself as 'a man of 64 yeares compleate', and adding to it a lengthy criticism of Thomas Gataker's *Of the Nature and Use of Lots* (1618), which was itself a response to Balmford's tract. Gataker quickly responded with *A Just Defence of … a Treatise Concerning the Nature and Use of Lots*, in which he followed contemporary practice by reproducing the whole of Balmford's work in his own, answering its objections point by point. Balmford's arguments rest on an analogy between cards and dice: that whereas lots depend wholly on chance, and are thus evil in that they are a denial of God's providence, cards depend somewhat on chance, and by analogy are somewhat evil. This is not to say that lots may not be used for the settling of controversies that otherwise could not be resolved—and for this biblical precedent is cited; but since they depend on chance, they, and by analogy cards, are strictly forbidden as a source of amusement.

By 1603 Balmford was rector of St Olave's, Southwark. In that year, which saw a major outbreak of plague, he published *A Short Dialogue Concerning the Plagues Infection*, dedicated to his parishioners; he also published two different editions of a catechism (1597 and 1607). He also published in 1607 *Carpenter's Chippes, or, Simple Tokens of Unfeined Good Will to the Christian Friends of J. B., the Poor Carpenter's Sonne*. Dedicated to Margaret Clifford, countess of Cumberland, it reproduces an earlier work by Balmford dedicated to the third earl of Huntingdon on the lawfulness of executing Catholic priests, not on religious grounds but for treason, in that they had sworn fealty to a foreign potentate, namely the pope, and for seditiously teaching disobedience to the queen. He makes a comparison between priests and Anabaptists, asserting that the latter are justly condemned for denying the divine prerogative of the magistrate and not for their denial of the incarnation, however impious that may be. And likewise priests are not executed for believing damnable things, like the efficacy of prayers to the saints, but for denying the sovereignty of Elizabeth, whom the pope has excommunicated and thus separated from any obedience owed her by her subjects. Also included in *Carpenter's Chippes* is a treatise on the proper observance of Sunday, *Three Positions Concerning the Lord's Day*, first published earlier in 1607. The dedications of *Carpenter's Chippes* and *A Short and Plaine Dialogue* may indicate that Balmford had northern connections. No reference to him has been found after 1623, and it is not known when he died. He may have been the father of the Church of England clergyman Samuel *Bamford (*d.* 1657).

Gary W. Jenkins

Sources Watt, *Bibl. Brit.* • W. C. Hazlitt, *Hand-book to the popular, poetical and dramatic literature of Great Britain* (1867) • *STC, 1475–1640* • *DNB*

Balmford, Samuel. *See* Bamford, Samuel (*d.* 1657).

Balmuto. For this title name *see* Boswell, Claud Irvine, Lord Balmuto (1743–1824).

Balmyle, Nicholas [Nicholas of St Andrews] (*d.* 1319/20), administrator and bishop of Dunblane, first appears on record, described as master, in 1259. Balmyle may be derived from one of two places in Perthshire. Neither his date of birth nor his place of study is known. He is rarely mentioned before the 1280s and 1290s, during which time he is variously recorded as official of the archdeacon of St

Andrews, vicar of Haddington, and, when he did homage to Edward I in 1296, parson of Calder-Comitis, Edinburghshire. In 1297, as the bishop's official, he was appointed by the chapter to administer the diocese during its vacancy following the death that year of Bishop William Fraser, and probably continued to do so until the new bishop, William Lamberton (*d.* 1328), returned from the continent in 1299.

In the latter part of 1292 Balmyle joined the auditors for John Balliol in the Great Cause, and in 1293 he attended the king's first parliament. By 31 January 1301 he had become chancellor of Scotland, perhaps through the influence of Bishop Lamberton, who was a guardian in 1299–1300. His appointment coincided with a change in the diplomatic and seal of acts of the government to re-emphasize the authority of King John: acts were again issued in John's name, not those of the guardians, and the obverse of the seal bore the king's name and title. In 1301 Balmyle was one of a delegation to Canterbury to discuss peace terms with English and French representatives; he may also have helped to draw up the brief for Baldred Bisset's diplomatic mission that year to Boniface VIII (*r.* 1294–1303), two members of which were known to him as St Andrews clerics. He may have remained chancellor until 1305.

When Balmyle was elected bishop of Dunblane, between January 1306 and December 1307, he was already a canon, perhaps appointed by Bishop Alpin, a former St Andrews cleric who had been auditor for King John and treasurer in his government. Robert I may have favoured the election of Balmyle as a patriot, but one of the electors, William Eaglesham, may have been acting on behalf of Lamberton, and would have known Balmyle from St Andrews. Balmyle was subsequently consecrated at the papal court at Poitiers by the bishop of Ostia.

Balmyle's career illustrates the influence of St Andrews clergy in Scottish affairs. His importance lies in the key role which he played in the patriotic cause during the struggle against the English crown. His support for King John continued after 1296, when he acted as chancellor and diplomat. With the guardian John Soulis (*d.* 1321) (perhaps appointed directly by the king) and Lamberton, he constituted a government which saw the national cause as bound up with the restoration of the rightful king, and hoped to achieve it by diplomacy with papal support. Like Lamberton, Balmyle may have found it difficult to change allegiance to Robert I: although he put his seal to ecclesiastical declarations of support for Robert (in 1310 and between 1314 and 1316) and may have attended the parliament of 1309, he witnessed only six royal acts before his death, which occurred between 8 February 1319 and 30 January 1320. He and the other bishops probably saw Robert as the only man who could secure and maintain independence. NORMAN F. SHEAD

Sources D. E. R. Watt, *A biographical dictionary of Scottish graduates to AD 1410* (1977) • G. W. S. Barrow, *Robert Bruce and the community of the realm of Scotland*, 3rd edn (1988) • G. W. S. Barrow, *The kingdom of the Scots: government, church and society from the eleventh to the fourteenth century* (1973) • J. Dowden, *The bishops of Scotland … prior to the Reformation*, ed. J. M. Thomson (1912), 201–2 • D. E. R. Watt, ed., *Fasti ecclesiae Scoticanae medii aevi ad annum 1638*, [2nd edn], Scottish RS, new ser., 1 (1969) • M. Ash, 'William Lamberton, bishop of St Andrews, 1297–1328', *The Scottish tradition*, ed. G. W. S. Barrow (1974), 44–55 • A. Theiner, *Vetera monumenta Hibernorum et Scotorum historiam illustrantia* (Rome, 1864), 179 • G. W. S. Barrow and others, eds., *Regesta regum Scottorum*, 5, ed. A. A. M. Duncan (1988) • *CDS*, vols. 2–3 • E. L. G. Stones and G. G. Simpson, eds., *Edward I and the throne of Scotland, 1290–1296*, 2 (1978), 85, 220

Balnaves, Henry (*d.* 1570), diplomat and religious reformer, is said by Calderwood to have come from Kirkcaldy and studied in Cologne. He returned to St Andrews, appearing on the rolls of St Salvator's College in 1527 as *magister*, the title by which he is usually designated, though where he received his MA degree is uncertain. He worked as a procurator in St Andrews for several years subsequently, his clients including David Beaton, then abbot of Arbroath. By 1537 he was an advocate in the court of session in Edinburgh, and on 29 July 1538 he was promoted as a lord of session. In the following year he bought Halhill, in Fife, with his wife, Christine Scheves. By 1539 Balnaves's friendship with John Melville of Raith had helped him to secure the position of clerk to the treasurer, Sir James Kirkcaldy of Grange. In January 1540 he first acted as a diplomat, going to Coldstream where he and Thomas Bellenden met with Sir William Evers to arrange mutual extraditions. At this meeting Bellenden raised the possibility that James V might follow Henry VIII's lead in ecclesiastical affairs; given Balnaves's reformist associations, he probably approved.

As treasurer's clerk, Balnaves was a regular attender at parliament in the late 1530s and early 1540s. After James's death in 1542, Balnaves and Kirkcaldy supported the second earl of Arran in his bid to become governor, 'as he apperit to be a trew gospeller' (*Memoirs of His Own Life*, 71); Arran in turn appointed Balnaves as secretary on 28 February 1543. In the following month Balnaves was among those who argued in parliament in favour of the act which allowed Bible reading in the vernacular, and shortly afterwards he went to England to negotiate a marriage treaty between the infant Mary, queen of Scots, and the future Edward VI. By November, however, Arran's English policy having changed, Balnaves had been removed from office and imprisoned in Blackness Castle, where he remained until the following spring. Cardinal Beaton, who instigated this purge, targeted his former advocate along with the fourth earl of Rothes and Patrick, Lord Gray, as 'he loved him worst of all' (*LP Henry VIII*, 18/2, no. 425). However, Balnaves was back in parliament by November 1544, and sitting in court by June 1545.

Whether or not Balnaves was aware of Henry VIII's plots against Beaton, he was not implicated when the cardinal was assassinated on 29 May 1546; in fact he continues to appear on privy council sederunts until 3 August, and was present when the murder was declared treasonous and a summons issued for the conspirators. By the middle of August, however, he was no longer appearing at council; during the autumn he entered St Andrews Castle, where the assassins were holding out, and in November he and Norman Lesley boarded an English ship under heavy fire.

After arriving in London, Balnaves and Lesley were awarded £100 and they briefed the English privy council. Balnaves offered to gain 'assurances' of support for English intervention from many Scottish nobles, and obtained promises of financial support for the castilians and a pension for himself. By 9 March 1547 he had returned to Scotland and he began compiling a list of assurances for Edward VI which was thought to contain 200 signatures. Having made another secret trip to England in April, Balnaves and others encouraged John Knox to preach, probably in May. At the end of July the castle fell to the French, and Balnaves, who had assisted in burning churches in St Andrews, was taken prisoner with the rest of the castilians.

Balnaves was imprisoned in the castle of Rouen, where, 'becaus he was judged learned … learned men war appointed to trawall with him', evidently concerning religious issues (*Works of John Knox*, 1.226). Perhaps in conjunction with these debates, Balnaves wrote a treatise in prison on justification by faith, *The Confession of Faith, Conteining how the Troubled Man should Seeke Refuge at his God*. This treatise displays Balnaves's theological understanding and biblical knowledge; it is a thorough exposition of the doctrine of justification by faith alone, and is based on a sweeping array of scriptural material. Balnaves was strongly influenced by Luther, and was clearly familiar with Luther's commentary on Galatians. He discusses vocation, in the sense of the call made to each Christian to lead a godly life, in Lutheran terms, and consequently follows the German reformer in conceding authority to the prince to restore true religion where it has become corrupted. Balnaves sent his treatise to Knox, who annotated it, added a précis, and sent it to Scotland; it was lost there, temporarily, and not published until 1584.

While in prison Balnaves was forfeited, but he was released by the early 1550s and remained in France until 1556, when Mary of Guise reversed his forfeiture. Back in Scotland, by 1559 Balnaves was again involved in secret diplomacy, between the Scottish reformist lords of the congregation and the English agents Ralph Sadler and James Croft at Berwick. Balnaves's primary goal was English funding for the lords, and in this he generally succeeded; he was also a signatory to the Anglo-Scottish treaty of Berwick on 27 February 1560. Following the establishment of the reformed kirk by parliament, Balnaves eventually returned to his old occupation, being readmitted to the bench in 1563. Later that year he was chosen by the general assembly to help revise the first Book of Discipline, a project which came to nothing.

Balnaves's final diplomatic commission came in autumn 1568, when he acted as an assistant to Regent Moray in the latter's bringing charges against Mary, queen of Scots, at conferences at York and Westminster. Balnaves was a regular attender at council in 1568 and 1569, and during this time he helped James Melville, his eventual heir, to meet the regent. Balnaves died in Leith in February 1570, leaving chattels valued at £333 11*s*. 2*d* Scots. He bequeathed most of his estate to Melville, but a few items to another long-term associate, Alexander Clerk. Respected for his learning and diplomatic skills, Balnaves occupied an important role in the promotion of the reformed kirk, both in securing English support and in advising the protestant nobles. Moreover, in his treatise he shows a grasp of basic protestant theology remarkable in a layman. MARTIN HOLT DOTTERWEICH

Sources *LP Henry VIII*, vols. 15–21 • *CSP for.*, 1553–62 • *The works of John Knox*, ed. D. Laing, 6 vols., Wodrow Society, 12 (1846–64), vol. 1, pp. 99, 102, 106, 114–16, 186, 226–7; vol. 2, pp. 38, 381; vol. 3, pp. 1–28, 403–542 • J. B. Paul and C. T. McInnes, eds., *Compota thesaurariorum regum Scotorum / Accounts of the lord high treasurer of Scotland*, 7–9, 12 (1907–70) • D. Calderwood, *The history of the Kirk of Scotland*, ed. T. Thomson and D. Laing, 8 vols., Wodrow Society, 7 (1842–9), vol. 1, pp. 158–9; vol. 2, p. 247 • *Memoirs of his own life by Sir James Melville of Halhill*, ed. T. Thomson, Bannatyne Club, 18 (1827), 71, 81, 205, 211 • R. K. Hannay, ed., *Acts of the lords of council in public affairs, 1501–1554* (1932), 471, 488 • *CSP Scot.*, 1547–63, 14 • M. H. B. Sanderson, *Cardinal of Scotland: David Beaton, c.1494–1546* (1986) • J. Kirk, *Patterns of reform: continuity and change in the Reformation kirk* (1989), 232–5 • H. Watt, 'Henry Balnaves and the Scottish Reformation', *Records of the Scottish Church History Society*, 5 (1933–5), 25–39 • J. M. Anderson, ed., *Early records of the University of St Andrews*, Scottish History Society, 3rd ser., 8 (1926), 225 • J. M. Thomson and others, eds., *Registrum magni sigilli regum Scotorum / The register of the great seal of Scotland*, 11 vols. (1882–1914), 1513–46, 450 • C. Edington, *Court and culture in Renaissance Scotland: Sir David Lindsay of the Mount* (1994) • *APS*, 1424–1567, 352–3, 355, 368, 384, 409, 446, 594 • *Reg. PCS*, 1st ser., 1.619, 623, 628, 639–40, 642, 673 • C. Rogers, *Three Scottish reformers* (1874) • M. Livingstone, D. Hay Fleming, and others, eds., *Registrum secreti sigilli regum Scotorum / The register of the privy seal of Scotland*, 3 (1936)

Wealth at death 'iij c.xxxiij.lib. xj.s. ij.d' [£333 11*s*. 2*d*. Scots]: *Works of John Knox*, ed. Laing, vol. 3, pp. 427–30

Balnea, Henry (*supp. fl.* **early 15th cent.**), supposed religious writer, was stated by Thomas Tanner (1674–1735) to be the author of the *Speculum spiritualium*, an anonymous early fifteenth-century devotional and mystical miscellany associated with the Bridgettines and Carthusians which survives in at least eleven manuscripts as well as in an early edition printed in Paris and published in London in 1510. Balnea's name appears to stem from a misreading of the contracted form of 'Henricus domus Cartusiensis de Bethleem' ('Henry of the Carthusian house of Bethlehem of Sheen'), with whom the *Speculum spiritualium* is associated in an ambiguous entry in the early sixteenth-century catalogue of the brothers' library of the Bridgettine abbey of Syon. There were two monks named Henry at Sheen in the early fifteenth century. Both were Germans, but although Tanner supposed its compiler to have been English, there is in fact nothing in the *Speculum spiritualium* to make this essential; indeed, many of its sources are foreign, and such as might have appealed to, or been brought to England by, monks from Germany. In any event, it is possible that the author of the catalogue was identifying 'Henricus' as the compiler not of the *Speculum spiritualium* but of the indexes to it.

W. N. M. BECKETT

Sources Tanner, *Bibl. Brit.-Hib.* • M. Bateson, A. I. Doyle, and V. Gillespie, eds., *Catalogue of the library of Syon Monastery, Isleworth*, [new edn] [forthcoming] • A. I. Doyle and V. Gillespie, eds., *Catalogue of* *the library of Syon Monastery, Isleworth* [forthcoming] • CUL, MS Dd.iv.54 • *A catalogue of the manuscripts preserved in the library of the University of Cambridge*, 1, ed. C. Hardwick (1856), vol. 1 • T. K. Abbot, *Catalogue of the manuscripts in the library of Trinity College, Dublin* (1900) • N. R. Ker, ed., *Medieval libraries of Great Britain: a list of surviving books*, 2nd edn, Royal Historical Society Guides and Handbooks, 3 (1964) • A. G. Watson, ed., *Medieval libraries of Great Britain: a list of surviving books ... supplement to the second edition*, Royal Historical Society Guides and Handbooks, 15 (1987) • A. I. Doyle, 'Publication by members of the religious orders', *Book production and publishing in Britain, 1375–1475*, ed. J. Griffiths and D. Pearsall (1989), 109–23 • A. I. Doyle, 'The European circulation of three Latin spiritual texts', *Latin and vernacular: studies in late-medieval texts and manuscripts*, ed. A. J. Minnis (1989), 129–50 • M. G. Sargent, *James Grenehalgh as textual critic*, 2 vols., Analecta Cartusiana, 85 (1984) • W. N. M. Beckett, 'Sheen Charterhouse from its foundation to its dissolution', DPhil diss., U. Oxf., 1992 • H. E. Allen, *Writings ascribed to Richard Rolle, hermit at Hampole, and materials for his biography* (1927) • E. M. Thompson, *The Carthusian order in England* (1930) • *Speculum Spiritualium* (1510)

Balogh, Thomas, Baron Balogh (1905–1985), political economist, was born in Budapest, Hungary, on 2 November 1905, the elder son and elder child of Emil Balogh, director of the transport board, Budapest, and his wife, Eva, daughter of Professor Bernard Levy, of Berlin and Budapest. He was educated in the city's Modelgymnasium, from which so many other distinguished émigré Hungarians graduated. After studying law and economics at the universities of Budapest and Berlin, he went in 1928 to America for two years as a Rockefeller fellow at Harvard University.

Balogh served in the research departments of the Banque de France, the Reichsbank, and the Federal Reserve before he went to England. J. M. Keynes, who once said he could hear more of what was going on from Balogh in an hour or two than he himself could pick up during several days in London, published his first article in the *Economic Journal* and helped him to his first job in England with the banking firm of O. T. Falk & Co. in 1932.

While a lecturer at University College, London, between 1934 and 1940, Balogh wrote for the National Institute of Economic and Social Research his *Studies in Financial Organization* (1947). He was naturalized in 1938. Against high-level opposition he went in 1939 to Balliol College, Oxford, as a lecturer. In 1945 he was elected to a fellowship, which he held until 1973, and in 1960 became a university reader. He was one of the founding members of the Institute of Statistics at Oxford.

In the 1950s Balogh turned his attention increasingly to the problems of the economically underdeveloped countries. As adviser to the Food and Agriculture Organization of the United Nations (1957–9) he used an afforestation project to design a series of ambitious development plans for the countries round the Mediterranean. Planting trees remained one of his hobbies. The demand of Dominic Mintoff (then prime minister of Malta) for integration with the United Kingdom appealed particularly to Balogh's economic philosophy, and he was deeply disappointed when the negotiations failed.

Harold Wilson worked with Balogh throughout the 1950s and early 1960s, and in particular on the preparation for the 1964 election. One of Balogh's lines of argument was that a Labour government would be heavily committed to a policy of faster growth, sustained by a strong incomes policy and supported by more state intervention in industry. He thought that the Treasury would not be capable of carrying out such a policy, and this led to the call for a separate ministry of expansion or planning. These ideas were the origin of the Department of Economic Affairs.

After Labour's victory in October 1964 Balogh was brought into the Cabinet Office as adviser on economic affairs, with special reference to external economic policy. Some of Balogh's greatest contributions in Whitehall stemmed more from his uncanny knowledge of everything that was going on than from contributions to committee work, where his criticisms, though scintillating, were too radical. When Wilson's government was defeated in June 1970 he retained his close personal contacts with Harold Wilson, spent more time in Oxford at both Balliol and Queen Elizabeth House, and returned to writing.

Balogh retired from his Oxford readership in 1973 and became a fellow emeritus of Balliol; he was a Leverhulme fellow in 1973–6. But he was about to enter a new career. In 1974 he was made a minister of state at the Department of Energy and, as a life peer, which he had been created in 1968, its spokesman in the House of Lords. The theme of his maiden speech was the need for a tougher incomes policy, while investment and innovation were carried out, and for stricter foreign-exchange controls. He played a key role in the creation of the British National Oil Corporation and was its deputy chairman from 1976 to 1978.

Balogh was awarded an honorary doctorate by his old university Budapest in 1979, and an honorary degree by York University, Toronto. He married in 1945 Penelope (*d.* 1975), daughter of the Revd Henry Bernard Tower, vicar of Swinbrook, Oxfordshire; she was the widow of Oliver Gatty. She became a distinguished psychotherapist, and they had two sons and a daughter (there was also a daughter from the previous marriage). This marriage was dissolved in 1970. In the same year Balogh married Catherine, daughter of Arthur Cole, barrister, Lincoln's Inn. She was a psychologist and prolific author, particularly of children's books, and previously the wife of (Charles) Anthony Storr, psychiatrist, with whom she had three daughters.

Balogh had a flamboyant mind and considerable moral courage. He was neither a systematic thinker nor a popular figure; indeed, he seemed to court hostility. To his friends he showed unbounded loyalty. He died on 20 January 1985 at his home, Flat 3, 12 Frognal Gardens, Hampstead, London.

Paul Streeten, *rev.*

Sources personal knowledge (1990) • private information (1990) • *The Times* (21 Jan 1985) • *CGPLA Eng. & Wales* (1985) • P. Streeten, 'In memory of Thomas Balogh', *World Development*, 15 (1985), 465–6 • P. Streeten, 'Thomas Balogh', *Unfashionable economies: essays in honour of Lord Balogh*, ed. P. Streeten (1970) • J. Morris, biography [forthcoming] • d. cert.

Archives Balliol Oxf., letters and papers | BLPES, corresp. with editors of the *Economic Journal* • HLRO, letters to David Lloyd George • King's AC Cam., letters to Richard Kahn • LPL, memoranda on economic aspects of post-war reconstruction | SOUND BL NSA, 'Personal view', xx (1822512.1)
Likenesses cartoons, Balliol Oxf. • portrait, Balliol Oxf.
Wealth at death £288,707: probate, 18 June 1985, *CGPLA Eng. & Wales*

Balsham, Adam of [Adam de Parvo Ponte] (**1100x02?–1157x69?**), logician, was born in Balsham, near Cambridge, on the estate of his father, whose family came from Beauvais in France. About 1120 he left England for Paris, at that time the goal of many young Englishmen who aimed to study the arts and theology. By 1132, the date of publication of his major work, the *Ars disserendi*, Adam, who cannot now have been much less than thirty, was established as the master of a school, teaching on the Petit Pont which links the Île de la Cité with the Left Bank. When after several years of studying in France the need to earn a living obliged John of Salisbury to take up teaching young noblemen, he felt the need for frequent revision courses; in this context he became closely acquainted with Adam of Balsham, whom he praises for his acute mind, his wide learning, and his outstanding knowledge of Aristotle. John passed on to Adam his own pupil, Guillaume de Soissons, who had devised an instrument to detect logical fallacies. Yet John's grateful appreciation of Adam's helpfulness did not prevent his strongly criticizing the latter's cynical principle of teaching, whereby (in John's eyes) he cultivated an unnecessarily complicated approach to logic in order to enhance his own reputation; moreover, John took care to stress that Adam had never been his own teacher. But the lifelong affection for Adam and his school shown by Alexander Neckam, a prominent scholar who was Adam's pupil three decades later, suggests that John's criticisms may not have been entirely fair.

Fragments of treatises by Adam of Balsham on transubstantiation and on the Trinity, presumably composed about 1145, have come to light. These theological writings may account for the fact that, about 1146, Adam became a canon of Paris Cathedral. As such he took part in the Paris synod of 1147, presided over by Pope Eugenius III, at which Bishop Gilbert of Poitiers defended himself against charges of heretical doctrines concerning the nature of God and the Trinity. Adam, along with Hugues de Champfleury, the king's chancellor, testified under oath that they had heard Gilbert utter the incriminating propositions. Bishop Otto of Freising, an admirer of Gilbert, expressed himself astonished that men so learned contented themselves with an oath instead of producing rational arguments. In 1148 Adam appeared again, with well-known masters, at the Council of Rheims, when Bernard of Clairvaux's accusations against Gilbert were fully discussed.

The *Ars disserendi* of Adam of Balsham claims to be the first systematic approach to logic produced in recent times, one which replaces the antiquated language of the current textbooks, their inaccurate translations, and their artificial terminology. It sets out to revive the art of discourse through discussion, rather than exposition. Novel in its approach and in its extensive use of Aristotle's *Topics*, and above all of his newly translated *Sophistical Refutations*, its acute examination of ambiguities and fallacies started the discussion of a subject that engaged philosophers during the next three centuries. The earliest known English logician, Adam was the first to stress the importance of careful attention to language as a safeguard against faulty thinking. Though disliked by many of his contemporaries, Adam of Balsham attracted many young students to his school. In his *Entheticus* John of Salisbury criticizes them for their disrespectful attitude towards older scholars and their boastful claim to originality. But as late as the beginning of the following century the school remained active, commanding the loyalty of masters like Gilles de Corbeil and, above all, Neckam, who more than fifty years after the event remembered Adam's correcting Thierry of Chartres's wrong reading of a passage in Aristotle's *Sophistical Refutations*. Neckam praises the teaching of the school, criticizing only its indulgence in logical casuistry.

Adam of Balsham also wrote a treatise of a different kind, *De utensilibus ad domum regendam* (sometimes from its opening words called *Phalae tolum*), composed after returning on a visit to his native village, which he had left twelve years before. It is his response to criticism by a friendly colleague, Master Anselm, who had reproached him for his vacuous prose. Adam displays a wealth of forgotten words, taken from ancient authors (mostly from Isidore of Seville, but also from Aulus Gellius and some glossaries), to show the appropriate terms for objects of everyday use. He does so by a detailed description of his family home: the courtyard, the stable with its horses, the house itself, an elaborate meal with his many relatives (followed by the appearance of lyre players and pipers), the collection of arms in a tower, the barns, the kitchen, the women's quarters with the clothes and ornaments they contained. Though he mixes facts with imagination, he provides a lively picture of an early twelfth-century English country house.

It is not known when Adam of Balsham died. The day of his death—6 August—but not the year is given by the obituary of the abbey of Notre-Dame-du-Val, in the diocese of Paris. Alexander Neckam, who arrived in France in 1175 at the age of seventeen, and entered the school of the Petit Pont shortly afterwards, refers to Adam's star as still shining in his own time. But his statement shows only that the memory of the school's founder remained alive. It does not provide information about the date of Adam's death, and is much more likely to refer to the life of the school, still flourishing when those of other famous masters had disappeared. In the absence of any conclusive evidence, the precise date of Adam's death must be left open, between the late 1150s and the late 1160s.

On the authority of Du Boulay's *Historia universitatis Parisiensis*, Adam of Balsham has been frequently confused with another Master *Adam, also a canon of Paris, who became bishop of St Asaph and died in 1181. This second

Adam is usually referred to as Adam the Welshman; the name under which Du Boulay confused the two men, Adam Angligena, was his own invention.

RAYMOND KLIBANSKY

Sources Adam [of Balsham], 'Ars disserendi', *Twelfth century logic: texts and studies*, ed. L. Minio-Paluello, 1 (1956), i–iii • Adam of Balsham, *De utensilibus ad domum regendam*, *Notices et extraits de quelques manuscrits latins de la Bibliothèque Nationale*, ed. B. Hauréau, 6 vols. (Paris, 1890–93), vol. 3 • *Ioannis Saresberiensis episcopi Carnotensis Metalogicon libri IIII*, ed. C. C. I. Webb (1929) • John of Salisbury, 'Entheticus', ed. R. E. Pepin, *Traditio*, 31 (1975) • L. Minio-Paluello, 'The *Ars disserendi* of Adam of Balsham Parvipontanus', *Mediaeval and Renaissance Studies*, 3 (1954) • *Ottonis et Rahewini gesta Friderici I imperatoris*, 3rd edn (Hanover, 1912), 75 • C. E. Du Boulay, *Historia universitatis Parisiensis*, 2 (Paris, 1665), 715 • R. W. Hunt, *The schools and the cloister: the life and writings of Alexander Nequam*, rev. M. Gibson (1984) • L. M. de Rijk, *Logica modernorum* (1962), 1.62–81, 545–609 • W. Kneale and M. Kneale, *The development of logic* (1975) • Egidius Corboliensis, *Viaticus*, ed. V. Rose (1907) • *Obituaires de la province de Sens: 1. diocèses de Sens et de Paris*, pt 1 (1902), 630 [cites Abbaye de Notre-Dame du Val] • T. Hunt, *Teaching and learning Latin in thirteenth-century England*, 1 (1991), 165–76

Balsham, Hugh of (*d.* 1286), bishop of Ely and benefactor, took his name from Balsham, Cambridgeshire, one of Ely Priory's manors. Nothing is known of his background, except that during the controversy aroused by his election as bishop it was alleged that he was of servile origins. He became a monk at Ely, and rose to be sub-prior of the monastery. Following the death of Bishop William of Kilkenny, on 21 September 1256, Balsham was elected bishop by the monks. Matthew Paris, characteristically anxious to speak up for monastic liberties and to present Henry III in a bad light, gives a misleading account of the controversy that followed, presenting the king and Archbishop Boniface of Canterbury as working together to thwart the Ely monks and persecute their chosen bishop. Ely was a wealthy see, commonly reserved for one of the king's leading administrators, and Henry was undeniably offended by the convent's action. But the monks themselves declared that they would not resort to litigation if the king objected to their choice. It was Archbishop Boniface who did most to stir up discord, when he tried to bring the election under his own jurisdiction by announcing that he would examine the bishop-elect's suitability. The king's proctors appealed to Rome against the archbishop's action, while the monks asked the pope to investigate Balsham's fitness for office and confirm his election. But Boniface ignored them, and proceeded to declare the election invalid—his purpose in doing so was to promote the career of the celebrated Franciscan theologian Adam Marsh, whom he provided to the see.

At Rome Pope Alexander IV (*r.* 1254–61), faced with the problem of defining the extent of his own jurisdiction, in an area where it had hitherto been imprecise, decided that any appeal would suffice to bring a disputed episcopal election before the curia; by making this decision Alexander was also ruling that Boniface's actions since the election had been invalid, and thereby secured Balsham in his see. He confirmed Balsham as bishop of Ely on 6 October 1257, and consecrated him on the 14th. Balsham promised that he would in future visit Rome every three years (a pledge from which he was released in 1278) and returned to England. His diocese had meanwhile been extortionately administered by royal agents, and although Henry III accepted the pope's action, and restored the temporalities on 15 January 1258, Balsham subsequently complained that during its vacancy the bishopric had suffered 'immense trespasses and damages' (*CPR*, *1258–66*, 48). It is arguable that he never truly recovered the king's goodwill; he accompanied Henry III to France in October 1259, but enjoyed none of those gifts of timber and venison that marked out those who stood within the magic circle of royal favour.

Between 1259 and 1262 Balsham seems to have been much abroad, perhaps in part because of his promise to make triennial visits to Rome. During the barons' wars his diocese suffered severely, especially after 1265, when the Isle of Ely was occupied by die-hard rebels; in September 1266 he was granted the money he owed for military service 'in aid of the recovery of the Isle of Ely and the pursuit and arrest of the king's enemies who hold out there and destroy the country' (*CPR*, *1258–66*, 675). Five years later Balsham's own losses were described as 'innumerable'. Even so, he was more than once suspected of a lukewarm attitude to the king's cause. In April 1264 it was ordered that his barony be confiscated because of his failure to send the knights he owed to the army mustered to oppose Llewelyn. In the following year he was summoned to Montfort's parliament, and probably attended, since he was subsequently prosecuted in king's bench for 'offences against the peace and other transgressions against the king' (Jacob, 293). He was only occasionally engaged in public affairs thereafter: in 1274 he was ordered to take steps for the defence of Ely, after rumours circulated of an impending attempt by unnamed enemies to occupy it, and he was present in parliament in November 1276 when the king and his councillors resolved to attack Llewelyn. In May of the latter year he was licensed to crenellate his manor of Fen Ditton, suggesting that he enjoyed easier relations with Edward I than with Henry III.

During the twenty-eight years of his episcopate Balsham proved to be an active and determined administrator. At least once he issued synodal statutes. Their chronology is rendered uncertain by the fact of their surviving among three basic recensions of Ely statutes, the earliest of them heavily dependent on statutes issued by Bishop Robert Grosseteste of Lincoln in or about 1239. Balsham was certainly responsible for the third recension, datable to between 1268 and 1276, and very possibly for the second, issued between 1254 and 1268. The relatively small number of statutes unquestionably his record Balsham as dealing with such issues as clerical ignorance and the promotion of the cult of St Etheldreda. In his dealings with his cathedral priory Balsham showed himself concerned to promote up-to-date administrative practices, through the injunctions he issued after a visitation in 1261. The convent had earlier entrusted the management of its finances to two monks, who were charged with submitting an annual account, but Balsham clearly found this inadequate, since he ordered that treasurers be appointed, who were to receive all manorial revenues, and who were henceforth to have overall control of the house's expenditure. He also implemented Archbishop Robert Kilwardby's decree concerning the customary gifts of candles made by the sacrist to all the inhabitants of Ely at Christmas. The growth of the town's population made this a serious burden on the convent's finances, and could no longer be tolerated.

Balsham was meticulous about ordaining vicarages in churches appropriated to religious houses in his diocese, such as the nunneries of Denny and Chatteris. He also licensed the foundation of a chapel at Brame, near Ely, on recently cleared land which would eventually form part of the sacrist's endowment. Direct gifts to the Ely monks included the churches of Foxton and Wisbech St Mary, intended to augment the resources of the monastery's almonry and refectory respectively, and a site for a brewery near the bishop's own fish pond, between the queen's chamber and the monastic bakery. The building of the queen's chamber itself seems to have been provided for in 1277, by a gift of money that was to be paid when the monks built their own stone house; it now survives as the house occupied by the headmaster of Ely School. Nor did Balsham neglect his own episcopal interests. Soon after his consecration he re-established his rights in his see's lodging in the Temple, London. To compensate for his grants to Ely Priory and others he acquired the manor of Tydd St Giles, north of Wisbech, and the advowsons of the churches of Bexwell in Norfolk and of Cherry Hinton and Conington in Cambridgeshire.

Balsham was closely involved in the development of the University of Cambridge. By the mid-thirteenth century there was a studium in the town headed by a chancellor, and functioning under the protection and direction of the bishop, many of whose clerks were masters in the schools. It is not surprising, therefore, that in 1276 a dispute about the statutes, and about the claim of the archdeacon of Ely to control the rector of the local grammar schools, should have been referred to Balsham's arbitration. But of greater long-term significance was the licence that Balsham obtained from Edward I in December 1280 for the foundation of a college of 'scholars of the bishop of Ely in Cambridge', modelled on Merton College, Oxford. The scholars were at first lodged in the hospital of St John, which was staffed by Augustinian canons, but the scholars and canons quarrelled, and on 31 March 1284 Balsham transferred the former to two hostels outside the town's Trumpington Gate, and appropriated to the scholars alone the church of St Peter (now Little St Mary's) previously held by the hospital, which was compensated elsewhere. From this grant the college took its name of Peterhouse. Balsham also appropriated to the college the church of Thriplow, and later in the year increased the value of the vicarage by 4 marks. Nevertheless the new college—Cambridge's first—was poor at first. It is likely that Balsham intended to make further endowments; as it was, on his deathbed he bequeathed £200 to Peterhouse, specifically to enable the scholars to build on their site. They are said to have used the bequest to build a new hall.

In the heat of the controversy over his election to Ely Balsham was described by Henry III as 'a man inadequate and entirely useless' (*Close Rolls*, 10.108–9). He may have been a somewhat colourless personality, though he showed a degree of humanity in granting the Ely monks permission to wear the copes appropriate to their order so as to protect themselves against the coldness of their church, but of his competence and concern for order there can be little doubt. When he made his will, in July 1279, he procured its sealing at the provincial council held at Reading in the same month. Balsham died at his manor of Dodington, in the Isle of Ely, on 13 June 1286, and was buried on the 24th before the high altar of the cathedral. A brass now in Balsham church is said to represent the bishop. DOROTHY M. OWEN

Sources W. Ullmann, 'The disputed election of Hugh Balsham, bishop of Ely', *Cambridge Historical Journal*, 9 (1947–9), 259–68 · F. M. Powicke, *King Henry III and the Lord Edward: the community of the realm in the thirteenth century*, 1 (1947), 260; 2 (1947), 556–7 · D. M. Owen, 'Two medieval parish books from the diocese of Ely', *Reading Medieval Studies*, 11 (1985), 121–32 · F. M. Powicke and C. R. Cheney, eds., *Councils and synods with other documents relating to the English church, 1205–1313*, 1 (1964), 515 · *Documents relating to the university and colleges of Cambridge*, Cambridge University Commission, 2 (1852), 1–4 · *VCH Cambridgeshire and the Isle of Ely*, 3.334–5 · Paris, *Chron.*, 5.635–6, 652 · S. J. A. Evans, ed., 'Ely chapter ordinances and visitation records, 1241–1515', *Camden miscellany, XVII*, CS, 3rd ser., 64 (1940), v–xx, 1–74 · [H. Wharton], ed., *Anglia sacra*, 1 (1691), 637 · J. Bentham, *The history and antiquities of the conventual and cathedral church of Ely*, ed. J. Bentham, 2nd edn (1812), 149–50 · *Chancery records* · *CEPR letters*, vol. 1 · *Ann. mon.*, vol. 3 · E. F. Jacob, *Studies in the period of baronial reform and rebellion, 1258–1267* (1925), 293 · D. R. Leader, *A history of the University of Cambridge*, 1: *The university to 1546*, ed. C. N. L. Brooke and others (1988) · C. Hall and R. Lovatt, 'The site and foundation of Peterhouse', *Proceedings of the Cambridge Antiquarian Society*, 78 (1989), 5–46 · R. A. L. Smith, *Collected papers* (1947) · *CPR, 1258–66* · *Close rolls of the reign of Henry III*, 10, PRO (1931)

Archives CUL, Ely dean and chapter cartularies and charters

Likenesses mezzotint, pubd 1714 (after J. Faber, senior), NPG · brass, probably Balsham church, Cambridgeshire

Balthere [St Balthere, Baldred, Balther] (*d.* **756**), hermit, is often confused with an earlier saint of the same name. The later and better-known Balthere was described by his near contemporary Alcuin, in his poem on the bishops, kings, and saints of York. The so-called York annals, which underlie the chronicle of Symeon of Durham of the late eleventh century, give 756 as the date of Balthere's death (there spelt Balther). Alcuin regarded the solitaries Balthere and Echa as examples of the most complete monastic dedication to poverty, chastity, and solitude, as associated with Northumbrians like Cuthbert and Drythelm. One story has it that by his prayers Balthere moved the Bass Rock into the Firth of Forth; his temporary residence on the rock may be at the base of this tradition. The hermit died at Tyninghame (near North Berwick) and another legend claims that Tyninghame, Auldhame, and nearby Preston all claimed his body after death and that it was miraculously multiplied by three so that each church gained possession of it. This story, also recounted of other Celtic saints, was probably invented to explain how each church could claim his relics. A simple division seems a more likely explanation. During the late eleventh century Alfred Westow of Durham, a notorious relic collector, claimed to have found the bodies of Balthere and Billfrith, the goldsmith who decorated the binding of the Lindisfarne gospels, and brought them both back to Durham, where their feast was celebrated on 6 March.

Alcuin praised the hermit Balthere as 'a mighty warrior who vanquished time and again the hosts of the air that waged war on him in countless shapes'. This language seems to echo the life of Antony by Athanasius and that of Guthlac by Felix. Alcuin also attributed to him the miracles of walking on water and of the deliverance from diabolical torments of a deacon who had touched a woman unchastely. Sparse as these details are, they represent esteem and respect on the part of one of the most articulate writers of his age.

Northumbrian saints such as Wilfrid, Bede, Cuthbert, and the hermit Balthere gained recognition through Alcuin. No such writer existed in the Glasgow area to record the life of **Baldred** (*d.* 608?), bishop, who was a follower of St Kentigern, and later writers falsely attributed details of the life of the hermit Balthere to that of the bishop Baldred. D. H. FARMER

Sources Alcuin, *The bishops, kings, and saints of York*, ed. and trans. P. Godman, OMT (1982) · D. A. Bullough, 'Hagiography as patriotism: Alcuin's 'York poem' and the early Northumbrian Vitae sanctorum', *Hagiographie, cultures et sociétés: IVe–XIIe siècles* (1980), 339–59 · Symeon of Durham, *Opera* · A. P. Forbes, *Kalendars of Scottish saints* (1872) · A. P. Forbes, ed., *Lives of S. Ninian and S. Kentigern* (1874) · 'De sanctis anachoretis Balthero … et Bibfrido', *Acta sanctorum: Martius*, 1 (Antwerp, 1668), 448–52 · D. D. C. P. Mould, *Scotland of the saints* (1952) · K. H. Jackson, 'The sources for the Life of St Kentigern', in N. K. Chadwick and others, *Studies in the early British church* (1958), 273–358 · *Butler's Lives of the saints*, rev. H. Thurston and D. Attwater, 2nd edn, 1 (1956), 502

Balthild [St Balthild, Balthilda] (*d.* *c.*680), queen of the Franks, consort of Clovis II of Neustria, was a Saxon, almost certainly born in England, probably in the early or mid-630s. She became a Frankish queen and founded the convent of Chelles, to which she retired during the last years of her life. There she was revered as a saint soon after her death. Her life, written before 690–91 by someone at Chelles (probably a nun) who had known her, is, despite the limitations of its genre, the main source of information about Balthild, and all citations below, unless otherwise indicated, are from it.

Queen, regent, nun Balthild was enslaved as a child and taken 'from across the sea' (hence she was of Anglo-Saxon rather than continental Saxon origin) to Francia, acquired by Erchinoald, mayor of the palace of the Merovingian kings, 'for a low price' in or soon after 641. She became Erchinoald's cup-bearer, and performed personal service for him and other lords including, presumably, his important visitors, 'taking off their boots and washing their feet'. The life's early chapters draw phrases from the biblical book of Esther to intimate Balthild's queenly destiny. Erchinoald, now a middle-aged widower, wanted to marry Balthild, but she successfully took evasive action: not only a wise virgin, she was *astuta*, shrewd (a new quality in a Merovingian saint). 'Divine providence had decided … that, since she had refused a king's follower, she would marry the king himself, and from her royal progeny would come forth'. King Clovis II (born 633, reigned 638–57) married Balthild as soon as he came of age, in 648. Clovis ruled the western Frankish kingdom of Neustria, since his father, Dagobert, had divided Francia, giving the eastern part, Austrasia, to his younger son, Sigibert III. As Clovis's queen, Balthild 'with watchful eagerness obeyed the king as her lord, was a mother to the princes, a daughter to the priests, and to the young men and youths the best kind of nurturer'. She interested herself particularly in alms-giving to the poor and in supporting monasteries. Her 'royal progeny' consisted of three sons: Chlothar (III), Theuderic (III), and Childeric (II). After Clovis II's death, Chlothar ruled Neustria 'with the excellent princes, Bishop Robert of Paris, Bishop Audoin of Rouen and Ebroin, the [new] mayor of the palace'. Ebroin was among the young men 'nurtured' by Balthild. The life fails to add that Balthild became regent for her young son (the early eighth-century *Liber historiae Francorum* reports this). Yet the life's account of Balthild's activities during Chlothar's minority presupposes her regency, and her attestations on royal documents between 657 and 664 constitute further firm evidence. When the Austrasian king Childebert died in 662, Balthild's youngest son, the seven-year-old Childeric, was 'received' by the Austrasians as their king 'by the arrangement of the Lady Balthild and through the advice of the leading men … With God guiding, and in accordance with the great faith of the Lady Balthild, [these] kingdoms kept the harmony of peace among themselves'. Balthild's opposite number in Austrasia was the dowager queen Chimnechild, whose daughter now became Childeric's child bride, this rare instance of Merovingian first-cousin marriage sealing the family compact engineered by the two married-in queens.

Within Neustria, says the life, Balthild put a stop to simony, and to infanticide; she founded monasteries, including Corbie; she refounded the convent of Chelles, which she staffed with nuns and an abbess, Bertila, 'summoned' from Jouarre, and endowed with 'fields and money'. Her lavish gifts to other churches included 'her own royal belt'. So generous was she that her husband 'gave her' an almoner of her own. Extending Clovis II's policy, she ordered bishops to confer privileges, which she herself supported with royal immunities (jurisdictional privilege): on the 'senior basilicas' of St Denis near Paris, and of St Germain, Paris; St Médard, Soissons; St Peter, Sens; St Aignan, Orleans; and St Martin, Tours, 'or wherever her precept reached'. Her influence secured an episcopal privilege for Corbie in 664. She forbade the enslavement of Christians and prohibited the export of any such slaves abroad; and she ransomed many captives, 'especially from her own people, men and also many girls'. Chlothar came of age in 665. Balthild was now 'permitted' by the Neustrian magnates to enter Chelles, where she continued her prayer and charitable work. 'She often suggested to [the abbess] that she should constantly visit the king and queen and the palace nobles in befitting honour with gifts'. At Chelles, her son Chlothar III was buried in 673. After her death, on 30 January, in the early 680s, Balthild was revered as the latest in a line of holy Frankish queens (in the life she is likened particularly to Radegund). Her relics, preserved to this day at Chelles, and rediscovered in 1983, reveal something of what Balthild looked like: unique data for an early medieval royal personage. Skeletal remains indicate that she was just over 5 feet tall. She was buried wrapped in a semicircular cloak, of almost 3 yards diameter, of yellow and pink silk. Her clothing included silk straps decorated with animal ornament, and one little brooch, five-eighths of an inch long. A plait of her hair survives among the clothing: she had been blonde, but had gone grey.

The Anglo-Saxon connection Two interestingly problematic features of Balthild's career involve the Anglo-Saxon connection. The first is that of Balthild's social origins. That she was a Saxon captive is plausible enough: the taking of captives, for sale or ransom, was rife in the early middle ages. To become a captive said nothing about one's original rank, however. The life's stress on Balthild's 'lowliness', as one of those 'poor', whom 'God raises from the dust and causes to sit with the princes of his people' (Psalm 112: 7–8), has generally been taken to mean that Balthild was low-born. An early ninth-century reviser of the life found this idea uncongenial and claimed instead that Balthild was, like virtually all other early medieval saints, of noble birth (later still she was alleged to have been of royal descent). Some Merovingian kings had taken low-born, even slave, women as wives, however, and it clearly was possible for a low-born queen (though there is no certain example of an ex-slave doing this) to attain effective power through her relation with her husband. The *Liber historiae Francorum* says that Balthild was *de genere Saxonorum*, but this means only that she belonged to that people, rather than to a noble, or ruling, family among them. Yet Balthild may have been of high birth. There is much evidence for seventh-century contacts, including intermarriage, between the Frankish élite and their Anglo-Saxon counterparts. Erchinoald, already related to the Merovingians via his kinswoman Berthetrude, who was King Dagobert's mother, allied himself with the Kentish royal family via his daughter's marriage to King Eadbald. The son of that marriage, Eorcenberht, was named in part for his maternal grandfather; and Eorcenberht's daughter Eorcengota was sent to be a nun at Faremoutiers. Eadbald's own sister Æthelburh had married the Northumbrian king Eadwine, and she subsequently (after Eadwine's death and her own flight from Northumbria) sent her own son and step-grandson to seek safety in Francia with her *amicus* (friend, perhaps kinsman) Dagobert. The ninth-century *Gesta* of the abbots of St Wandrille suggest that Balthild's royal marriage was arranged by Erchinoald, who remained mayor of the palace until his death in 658 or 659. Alternatively, the newly adult king himself chose to demand Balthild as his bride. In either case, the probable aim was to reinforce an existing network of Anglo-Saxon contacts; and this would make more sense on the assumption that Balthild herself was already well-connected. If the gold swivelling seal matrix, apparently from the bezel of a signet ring, found by metal detector at Postwick, near Norwich, with stylistic affinities to Frankish seventh-century seal rings and inscribed 'Baldehildis', is to be linked with Balthild, the case for the queen's original high status seems strengthened; but the date and associations of this perplexing object have not been determined conclusively.

A second problem turns on Balthild's political methods. While the life stresses her generosity towards, and hence good relations with, churchmen of all kinds, her support for monasteries and their 'cultic-liturgical business' (Ewig, 112–13) pitted her against entrenched episcopal interests. Merovingian rulers, reliant on bishops as key supporters of their authority in the regions, had traditionally intervened in local aristocratic politics to secure the election as bishops of men they could trust. Balthild, as queen, had made useful clerical friends at court, notably Eligius of Noyon (*d.* 660) and Audoin of Rouen, and as regent she secured the elections of Leudegar (Léger) and Erembert to the sees of Autun and Toulouse respectively. But not all bishops were enthusiastic about granting privileges which diminished their power and income. The claim that Balthild was sometimes driven to *un*traditional tactics is made in an Anglo-Saxon work, the life of Wilfrid by Stephen of Ripon (Eddius Stephanus): 'Balthild caused nine bishops to be put to death … She was just like the most impious queen Jezebel'. The case Stephen recounts is that of Aunemund of Lyons. That this is the *only* such case allegedly involving Balthild suggests Stephen's partisanship. His hero Wilfrid had received patronage early in his career from Aunemund, and Stephen depicts him as a witness and confessor of Aunemund's 'martyrdom'. The bishop's death seems, in fact, to have resulted from local factional conflict, though it is certainly true that Balthild used the vacancy at Lyons to appoint her almoner, Genesius. In writing up the episode, Stephen stressed Wilfrid's Englishness, yet made no reference to Balthild's. She could be seen as thoroughly at home in the Frankish political world. Paradoxically in view of her energetic monastic patronage, Stephen's criticism, repeated by Bede, later gave Balthild 'a bad name in her native country' (Levison, 10). Yet according to the early eighth-century life of Abbess Bertila, kings of Saxony sent to Balthild for teachers and monastic founders.

A queen's remains The ending of Balthild's regency was apparently precipitated by the hostility of Neustrian magnates, perhaps led by Ebroin, her former client and ally, to one of her probable appointees, Sigobrand, who replaced Robert as bishop of Paris in late 664 or early 665. His 'pride [*superbia*] among the Franks' provoked an 'insurrection' which resulted (justifiably, the author of the life thought) in the bishop's killing, but 'against [Balthild's] will'. Those responsible, afraid of the queen's revenge, 'allowed her suddenly to go to the convent' which she had founded. Clearly Balthild's 'retirement' was not entirely voluntary.

Her subsequent sanctity, Plummer observed, 'is not conclusive as to her character, very curious people finding their way in those days into the ranks of the saints' (notes to Bede, *Historia ecclesiastica*, 5.19, p. 322). Yet an extraordinary piece of evidence survives for Balthild's personal piety. Her so-called 'chasuble', preserved for centuries along with her other relics but detached from them since the sixteenth century, is now in the Musée de Chelles. It is the surviving front part of a two-piece tabard or apron. It consists of a piece of finely woven linen, about 46 inches by 33, decorated with embroidery: two concentric 'necklaces' around the neck of the garment, a large 'pectoral cross', and a large deep 'necklace' with pendant 'medallions'. All these depictions of jewels are closely paralleled in objects of late antique or early medieval date, including treasures that belonged to a Lombard queen. Yet the tabard's whole embroidered ensemble *represents* the riches of a queen's ceremonial dress in relatively cheap materials, not even using gold thread, but only coloured silks. According to his life, Eligius appeared three times to one of Balthild's courtiers (the date must be between 660 and 665), with an urgent message for the queen: 'out of reverence for Christ, she must take off the insignia of gold and the adornments of gems which till then she was in the habit of wearing when she attended religious services'. Balthild obeyed, keeping only one pair of gold bracelets, and presumably offering the rest of her personal jewellery to God (or the saint). This was exactly what her predecessor Radegund had done, and the life emphasizes the resemblance. Balthild, if the ninth-century account of her relics' translation can be believed, named her god-daughter after the sixth-century queen. Balthild's tabard, which she perhaps made herself before her retirement, and which she took with her to Chelles, by evoking (like a photographic negative) the days when she had been decked out like a Byzantine empress, attested the subsequent reality of her renunciation. Whether or not the sixteenth-century nuns of Chelles were right in believing that Balthild wore this tabard when she served the community at table, she, it seems, self-consciously lived out the part of a saintly queen. JANET L. NELSON

Sources P. Fouracre and R. A. Gerberding, 'Vita sanctae Balthildis, A', *Late Merovingian France: history and hagiography, 640–720* (1996), 97–132 • 'Vita sanctae Balthildis, A', *Fredegarii et aliorum chronica*, ed. B. Krusch, MGH Scriptores Rerum Merovingicarum, 2 (Hanover, 1888), 475–508 • 'Vita Eligii', *Passiones vitaeque sanctorum aevi Merovingici*, ed. B. Krusch, MGH Scriptores Rerum Merovingicarum, 4 (Hanover, 1902), 663–741 • 'Liber historiae Francorum', *Fredegarii et aliorum chronica*, ed. B. Krusch, MGH Scriptores Rerum Merovingicarum, 2 (Hanover, 1888), 215–328 • 'Continuator of Fredegar', *The fourth book of the chronicle of Fredegar: with its continuations*, ed. and trans. J. M. Wallace-Hadrill (1960) • E. Stephanus, *The life of Bishop Wilfrid*, ed. and trans. B. Colgrave (1927); pbk edn (1985) • Bede, *Historia ecclesiastica gentis Anglorum*, ed. C. Plummer, 3 vols. (1896) • Bede, *The ecclesiastical history of the English people*, ed. J. McClure and R. Collins (1994) [Eng. trans. of *Historiam ecclesiasticam gentis Anglorum*] • *Acta sanctorum: September*, 7 (Antwerp, 1768), 744–6 • *Gesta sanctorum patrum Fontanellensis coenobii*, ed. F. Lohier and J. Laporte (1936) • J. L. Nelson, 'Queens as Jezebels: Brunhild and Balthild in Merovingian history', *Medieval women*, ed. D. Baker, SCH, Subsidia, 1 (1978), 31–77; repr. in J. L. Nelson, *Politics and ritual in early medieval Europe* (1986), 1–48 • M. J. Couturier, *Sainte Bathilde, reine des Francs* (1909) • J. P. Laporte, 'La reine Balthilde ou l'ascension sociale d'une esclave', *La femme au moyen âge*, ed. M. Rouche and J. Heuclin (1990), 147–69 • I. Wood, *The Merovingian kingdoms* (1994) • E. Ewig, 'Das Privileg des Bischofs Berthefrid von Amiens für Corbie von 664 und die Klosterpolitik der Königin Balthild', *Francia*, 1 (1973), 63–114; repr. in *Spätantikes und fränkisches Gallien*, ed. H. Atsma, 2 (Munich, 1979) • W. Levison, *England and the continent in the eighth century* (1946) • H. Vierck, 'La chemise de Bathilde à Chelles et l'influence byzantine sur l'art de la cour mérovingienne au VIIe siècle', *Centenaire de l'abbé Cochet: actes du colloque international d'archéologie*, 3 (1978), 521–64 • J.-P. Laporte, *Le trésor des saints de Chelles* (Chelles, 1988) • L. Dupraz, *Le royaume des Francs et l'ascension politique des maires du palais au déclin du VIIe siècle* (1948) • F. Graus, *Volk, Herrscher und Heiliger im Reich der Merowinger: Studien zur Hagiographie der Merowingerzeit* (1965) • 'Recent Archaeology', *Norfolk Archaeology*, 43/3 (2000), 509–10

Balthrop, Robert (1522–1591), surgeon, was the son of Richard Balthrop (*d.* 1539) and his wife, Agnes (*d.* 1547), who was described as midwife to Queen Jane, mother of Edward VI. The family owned land and houses in Greenwich. From about 1537 to 1544 Balthrop was apprenticed to Nicholas Alcock (surgeon to Edward VI), who, at his death in 1550, bequeathed Balthrop his russet worsted gown trimmed with squirrel fur and velvet. Later the distinguished surgeon Thomas Vicary, who died in 1561, was also to leave him his best gown, as well as an embroidered velvet coat and a silver syringe. Balthrop was admitted to the freedom of the Barber–Surgeons' Company of London on 3 March 1545 and to the livery on 20 October 1552. He served as warden for the usual yearly term in 1560–61 and 1564–5, and was elected master in 1565 and 1573. When the company's examiners in surgery were increased from five to seven in 1570 he was named as one of them. About 1562 he was appointed sergeant-surgeon to Elizabeth I and held the office until his death. Though he apparently left no original writings on surgery his will mentions translations that he made and he is credited with helping John Banister in his work on the latter's *An Antidotarie Chyrurgicall* (1589).

From about 1559 Balthrop held the tenancy of a house in West Smithfield, next to St Bartholomew's Hospital on the site of the later medical school buildings, though there is no evidence that he practised in the hospital. He appears to have sublet the property to William Balthrop, probably his brother. On 12 January 1567 Balthrop married Dorothy, a daughter of Robert Lone of Sevenoaks, Kent, but they had no children. His will, made shortly before he died on 9 December 1591, refers to his house at Manfield Park, Taplow, Buckinghamshire, actually part of his wife's estate. At his death his lands and property in Greenwich passed to William and Richard Balthrop, the sons of his brother William. He also had a sister, Jacomine.

Balthrop's will shows that he had a considerable estate. His bequests of surgical instruments and equipment are of particular interest. To his servants and former servants he left three surgery chests, plaster boxes, salvatories, a precipitate box, syringes, catheters, and other items, as well as books on surgery and physic in English, French, and Latin, many of which are identified: they include Guidi's *Chirurgia*, Bartholomeus's *De proprietatibus rerum*, Cataneus's *De morbo Gallico*, and Valescus's *Practica*. To the

Barber-Surgeons' Company he left a book in Latin of the surgical writings of Joannes Tagaultius (*d.* *c.*1545) together with his own translation into English, as well as two works by Ambroise Paré (1510–1590) which he had translated for the use of his brethren practising surgery who did not understand Latin, for their daily use and reading. All other medicines, books, instruments, bottles, boxes, pots, and other surgical items not mentioned or retained by his wife were to be given to London's two hospitals for the sick and injured, St Bartholomew's and St Thomas's.

Balthrop was buried in St Bartholomew-the-Less, within the precincts of St Bartholomew's Hospital, on 12 December 1591. On the south wall of the church there is a handsome monument in his memory, with an effigy of him kneeling on a low stool and an inscription beginning:

> Heere Robert Balthrope lyes intombd, to Elizabeth our Queene
> Who Sergeant of the Surgeons sworne, neere thryte yeeres hathe beene.

ANDREW GRIFFIN

Sources S. Young, *The annals of the Barber–Surgeons of London: compiled from their records and other sources* (1890) • records of the Barber–Surgeons' Company, Barber–Surgeons' Hall, London • private information (2004) [R. Bartrop] • journals; ledgers, St Bartholomew's Hospital, London, St Bartholomew's Hospital archives, HA 1/1–3; HB 1/1–3 • parish registers (burials), 12 Dec 1591, St Bartholomew's Hospital, London, St Bartholomew's Hospital archives, SBL 10/1 • *IGI* • M. Pelling and C. Webster, 'Medical practitioners', *Health, medicine and mortality in the sixteenth century*, ed. C. Webster (1979), 165–235, esp. 176–7

Likenesses effigy on monument, St Bartholomew-the-Less, West Smithfield, London

Baltimore. For this title name *see* Calvert, George, first Baron Baltimore (1579/80–1632); Calvert, Cecil, second Baron Baltimore (1605–1675); Calvert, Benedict Leonard, fourth Baron Baltimore (1679–1715); Calvert, Charles, fifth Baron Baltimore (1699–1751); Calvert, Frederick, sixth Baron Baltimore (1732–1771).

Baltinglass. For this title name *see* Eustace, James, third Viscount Baltinglass (1530–1585).

Baltroddi, Walter of (*d.* **1270**), bishop of Caithness, succeeded to that see in 1261. His name probably derives from Baltroddi in Gowrie, Perthshire, now represented by Pitroddie, but his family affiliations are unknown. He was styled master by 1259, but it is not known which university he attended. He held an Aberdeen canonry and a Caithness canonry at the time of his election by the Caithness chapter. The papal mandate for his installation expressed some doubts about his legitimacy, but ordered three bishops to examine him, and promote and consecrate him if suitable. Nothing is known of his time as bishop, although his see would have been disturbed during the 1263–4 expedition to the north and west of Scotland by the king of Norway, Haakon IV Haakonsson, which affected Caithness, as did the Scottish king's response during the following years. There is a tradition in clan Mackay history that Iye Mor Mackay married a daughter of Bishop Walter, and thus acquired the twelve davachs (units of land) which formed the episcopal estate in Durness (the most north-westerly headland of the Scottish mainland, comprising, unusually, fertile limestone pasture). Bishop Baltroddi died in 1270, according to Walter Bower, who describes him as 'discreet in counsel and commendable in the holiness of his life' (Bower, 5.379). He was mentioned in 1275 as having been involved in disputes, as had his predecessors Gilbert and William, with the earl of Sutherland over lands and rights in south-east Sutherland. These presumably stemmed from the endowments of the cathedral church at Dornoch, founded by Bishop Gilbert earlier in the thirteenth century.

BARBARA E. CRAWFORD

Sources D. E. R. Watt, *A biographical dictionary of Scottish graduates to AD 1410* (1977) • A. Mackay, *The book of Mackay* (1906) • A. W. Johnston and A. Johnston, eds., *Caithness and Sutherland records*, Viking Club, 1 (1909) • W. Bower, *Scotichronicon*, ed. D. E. R. Watt and others, new edn, 9 vols. (1987–98), vol. 5

Baltzar, Thomas (*c.*1630–1663), violinist, was the eldest child of David Baltzar (*d.* 1647), town musician of Lübeck, and his wife, whom he married on 4 October 1630 but whose name is unknown. His father's family had been musicians for at least four generations. It is possible, as Tilmouth suggests, that he studied the violin with Gregor Zuber (a civic musician in Lübeck from 1641) and composition with Franz Tunder. The composer-violinist Nicolaus Bleyer taught Thomas Baltzar's younger brother Joachim in Lübeck, and (particularly given their shared interest in writing sets of divisions for solo violin) it seems likely that he also taught Thomas. To complicate matters further, a note (attributed to one Dreyer) in Samuel Hartlib's 'Ephemerides' of 1656 claims that 'Hee lived under that famous Musitian and Componist of Hamburg Schoppius [Johann Schop], who hath scarce his like in all Europe'. By 1653 Baltzar held a position at the Swedish court (and, in fact, it was probably here that he came under Schop's influence). There he must have met the English musicians who accompanied Bulstrode Whitelocke on his embassy to Sweden (1653–4). Baltzar left Stockholm, presumably after Queen Kristina's abdication in June 1654, and returned to Lübeck where, early in 1655, he was appointed *Ratslautenist*. Before long, however, he had moved to England, and it seems that it was his Swedish associations that took him there. Hartlib's 'Ephemerides' (1656) twice describes him as being in the service of Count Christer Bonde, the Swedish ambassador who arrived on 27 July 1655. Baltzar stayed on after the ambassador's departure thirteen months later and was listed among the instrumentalists who performed in *The Siege of Rhodes* (originally planned for September 1656 but possibly not presented until 1659). According to Anthony Wood, from the summer of 1658 Baltzar was 'entertained by Sir Anthony Cope of Hanwell House, Banbury, Bart., with whom he continued about two years' (Bodl. Oxf., MS Wood D.19(4)). In 1658 he played in both Cambridge (at Benjamin Rogers' MusB degree ceremony) and, on several occasions, in Oxford. In 1661 he became a member of the king's private musick at the very favourable salary of £110 per annum.

Several extended descriptions of his playing convey a

sense of the impact Baltzar made in England. John Evelyn recorded in his diary for 4 March 1656 that:

> This night I was invited by Mr. *Rog: L'Estrange* to heare the incomperable *Lubicer* on the Violin, his variety upon a few notes & plaine ground with that wonderfull dexterity, as was admirable, & though a very young man, yet so perfect & skillfull as there was nothing so crosse & perplext, which being by our Artists, brought to him, which he did not at first sight, with ravishing sweetenesse & improvements, play off, to the astonishment of our best Masters: In Summ, he plaid on that single Instrument a full Consort, so as the rest, flung-downe their Instruments, as acknowledging a victory.

Anthony Wood heard him in Oxford two years later and was similarly impressed by his dexterity:

> A. W. did then and there, to his very great astonishment, heare him play on the violin. He then saw him run his fingers to the end of the finger-board of the violin, and run them back insensibly, and all with alacrity and in very good tune, which he nor any in England saw the like before. (*Life and Times of Anthony Wood*, 1.257)

On this occasion John Wilson, the professor of music in Oxford (and described by Wood as the greatest judge of music that ever was) 'did, after his humoursome way, stoop downe to Baltzar's feet, to see whether he had a huff on, that is to say to see whether he was a devill or not, because he acted beyond the parts of man'.

Inevitably, Baltzar was compared with his English confrères. Evelyn pronounced that 'There were at that time as excellent in that profession as any were thought in Europ: *Paule Wheeler, Mr. Mell* and others, 'til this prodigie appeared & then they vanish'd'. Wood offered a more extended comparison:

> One Davis Mell was hitherto accounted the best in England for the violin but after Baltzar had shewed his parts, he by the generality [was] accounted better yet those that were proficient in music did acknowledge that Mell though he had not the ground or the command of his hand to run up and back the fingerboard yet he played sweeter far. (Bodl. Oxf., MS Wood D.19 (4))

Baltzar's surviving compositions are musically interesting and indicate a more advanced technique than Mell's. His 'divisions' (found in John Playford's *The Division Violin*, 1684) require the ability to move about the violin rapidly. Some of his other works reveal more of his virtuosity. Two movements in a C major suite for three violins (Bodl. Oxf., MSS mus. sch. D.241–3) have rapid semiquaver scale passages ascending to *e'''*, requiring the use of the fourth position (which to English observers in the 1650s might well have seemed as close 'to the end of the finger-board' as a violinist might safely go). His D major suite for two violins and continuo bass (Bodl. Oxf., MS mus. sch. D.102) is quite similar in this respect, while his solo violin pieces (Bodl. Oxf., MS mus. sch. F.573) demand facility in chord playing and string crossing. Baltzar wrote a number of pieces with *scordatura* (non-standard) tunings.

Baltzar was apparently a heavy drinker, and this (according to Wood) hastened his death on 24 July 1663. He was buried in the cloisters of Westminster Abbey.

PETER WALLS

Sources A. Ashbee, ed., *Records of English court music*, 9 vols. (1986–96) · A. Ashbee and D. Lasocki, eds., *A biographical dictionary of English court musicians, 1485–1714*, 2 vols. (1998) · B. Bellingham, 'The musical circle of Anthony Wood in Oxford during the Commonwealth and Restoration', *Journal of the Viola da Gamba Society of America*, 19 (1982), 6–70 · W. Davenant, *The siege of Rhodes: a critical edition*, ed. A.-M. Hedbäck (1973) · G. Dodd, *Thematic index of music for viols* (1980–) · Evelyn, *Diary* · M. Greengrass, M. Leslie, and T. Raylor, eds., *Samuel Hartlib and universal reformation: studies in intellectual communication* (1994) · *The Hartlib papers*, ed. J. Crawford and others (1995) [CD-ROM] · J. Hennings, *Musikgeschichte Lübecks*, 1 (Kassel, 1951) · Highfill, Burnim & Langhans, *BDA* · P. Holman, *Four and twenty fiddlers: the violin at the English court, 1540–1690*, new edn (1993) · P. Holman, 'Thomas Baltzar (?1631–1663), the "Incomperable *Lubicer* on the violin"', *Chelys*, 13 (1984), 3–38 · F. Madan and others, *A summary catalogue of Western manuscripts in the Bodleian Library at Oxford*, 7 vols. (1895–1953) · E. H. Meyer, *Der mehrstimmige Spielmusik des 17. Jahrhunderts in Nort- und Mitteleuropa* (Kassel, 1934) · *Roger North's The musicall grammarian, 1728*, ed. M. Chan and J. C. Kassler (1990) · A. Pirro, *Dietrich Buxtehude* (Paris, 1913) · M. Roberts, ed., *Swedish diplomats at Cromwell's court, 1655–1656: the missions of Peter Julius Coyet and Christer Bonde*, CS, 4th ser., 36 (1988) · J. D. Shute, 'Anthony A Wood and his manuscript Wood D 19 (4) at the Bodleian Library, Oxford: an annotated transcription', PhD diss., International Institute of Advanced Musical Studies, Clayton, Missouri, 1979 · R. Spalding, *The improbable puritan: a life of Bulstrode Whitelocke, 1605–1675* (1975) · I. Spink, *The seventeenth century* (1992) · M. Tilmouth, 'Baltzar, Thomas', *New Grove* · *The diary of Bulstrode Whitelocke, 1605–1675*, ed. R. Spalding, British Academy, Records of Social and Economic History, new ser., 13 (1990) · J. Wilson, *Roger North on music* (1959) · *The life and times of Anthony Wood*, ed. A. Clark, 5 vols., OHS, 19, 21, 26, 30, 40 (1891–1900)

Balvaird. For this title name *see* Murray, Andrew, first Lord Balvaird (*c*.1597–1644).

Baly, Monica Eileen (1914–1998), nurse and historian of nursing, was born on 24 May 1914 at 23 Shirley Park Road, Shirley, near Croydon, Surrey, the first of the two children, and the only daughter, of Albert Frank Baly (*d*. 1953), a clerk with Southern Railways, and Anne (or Annie) Elizabeth Marlow (*d*. 1961), his wife. Baly was educated at an Anglican convent, St Hilda's School for Girls, in west London, leaving at eighteen with a scholarship to Croydon Art School. She would have liked a university education, but there was insufficient money and she chose nursing as the next best thing. She started her nursing career at Brook Hospital, London, in 1932, training for two years as a fever nurse, and continuing with general nursing at the Middlesex Hospital, London, becoming a registered general nurse in 1937. She followed this with midwifery at the Middlesex and then worked on the staff there for a short time before joining the armed services.

Baly served with the Princess Mary's Royal Air Force Nursing Service from 1942 to 1946, spending three and a half years overseas in the Middle East and Italy. She worked as a theatre sister and was responsible for setting up a burns unit treating severely burnt airmen in Foggia, Italy, for which she was mentioned in dispatches (1944). Her last six months in the services were spent nursing typhoid patients in Cairo.

By 1946 Baly had come to realize that much ill health was caused by social conditions, and decided to train as a health visitor. After a short spell as a health visitor in Surrey she was seconded to the Foreign Office as chief

Monica Eileen Baly (1914–1998), by unknown photographer [detail]

nursing officer for displaced persons in the British zone in Germany. She started a public health programme with a British nurse in each region and persuaded the Foreign Office to allow her to set up a school of nursing in Hanover to train public health nurses. These courses helped to rehabilitate the profession of nursing in Germany after its compromising position during the Nazi years.

On her return to Britain in 1950 Baly joined the staff of the Royal College of Nursing, becoming one of the first area officers; she had responsibility for the south-western region and went to live in Bath, which remained her home for the rest of her life. The National Health Service was still settling down and she had the task of persuading the new hospital management committees that nurses needed better pay and conditions. She also had to convince nurses that they needed a professional organization, and during her twenty-four years with the college she was very successful in recruiting new members. Baly's belief in the professional status of nurses inspired her work and she was chosen to lead some of the college's most successful pay campaigns in the late 1960s and early 1970s.

When Baly retired from the college in 1974 she started a second career as a writer and historian of nursing. For some time she had been a lecturer and examiner for the diploma in nursing (University of London) and out of these lectures grew her first book, *Nursing and Social Change* (1973). She published several books on nursing, *Professional Responsibility* (1975), *Nursing* (Past-into-Present series, 1977), and *A New Approach to District Nursing* (1981), as well as completing an Open University degree in history in 1979. She was commissioned by the Nightingale Fund Council to write a history of the council; this became her PhD dissertation (University of London, 1984), and was published as *Florence Nightingale and the Nursing Legacy* (1986). There she exposed many of the myths which had grown up around Florence Nightingale and the nurses' training school at St Thomas's Hospital, London.

This research was the beginning of Baly's deep interest in Florence Nightingale, and thereafter she was regarded as an expert on Miss Nightingale, whose article she prepared for the *Oxford Dictionary of National Biography*. She founded and chaired the history of nursing society at the Royal College of Nursing, pioneering the first journal dedicated to new research in the history of nursing, which was influential in stimulating research at an international level. She continued writing and publishing books and journal articles up to her death, and her last book was published posthumously as *A History of Nursing at the Middlesex Hospital* (2000). In her will she left £10,000 to establish a scholarship in history of nursing. She was made a fellow of the Royal College of Nursing in 1986.

Baly was a good-looking woman, always elegant, and an accomplished cook. She was secretary of the Royal Crescent Society, Bath, where she lived for more than forty years, and was a guide for the museum at the Royal Crescent. She loved music, opera, and theatre and was a supporter of the Bath Festival and Bath Theatre Royal. She died at her home, 19 Royal Crescent, Bath, on 12 November 1998 and was cremated at Bath on 20 November; a thanksgiving service was held in Bath Abbey. She never married. SUSAN MCGANN

Sources Royal College of Nursing Archives, Edinburgh, Monica Baly papers • M. E. Baly, recorded interview, 1995, Royal College of Nursing Archives, Edinburgh, T100 • *The Guardian* (20 Nov 1998) • *The Independent* (18 Nov 1998) • *The Times* (20 Nov 1998) • M. Baly, 'Early recollections of an area officer', *History of Nursing Society Journal*, 4/1 (1992–3), 17–22 • b. cert. • personal knowledge (2004) • private information (2004)

Archives Royal College of Nursing Archives, Edinburgh, papers | SOUND Royal College of Nursing Archives, Edinburgh, recorded interview (1995), T100

Likenesses photograph, *c.*1970, repro. in *The Independent* • black and white photographs, Royal College of Nursing Archives, Edinburgh • photograph, News International Syndication, London [*see illus.*] • photograph, repro. in *The Guardian*

Wealth at death under £200,000—gross; under £100,000—net: probate, 4 Jan 1999, *CGPLA Eng. & Wales*

Baly, William (1814–1861), physician, was born and brought up in King's Lynn, Norfolk, the son of a bibliophile local businessman and his energetic intelligent wife. He attended King's Lynn grammar school and was apprenticed to a local general practitioner. In 1831 Baly began his medical studies at University College, London, and in 1832 he began pupillage at St Bartholomew's Hospital. In 1834 he passed the examinations of the Royal College of Surgeons and Apothecaries' Hall and he spent two years abroad studying at Paris, Heidelberg, and Berlin where he graduated MD in 1836. On return that same year he began general practice in London, first in Vigo Street, then in Devonshire Street, and finally in Brook Street. He was also for a short time medical officer to the St Pancras workhouse.

Between 1837 and 1842 Baly translated the work of the eminent German physiologist Johannes Müller (*Elements of Physiology*, 2 vols.) and thus evidenced a considerable intellectual and academic ability which would be amply displayed later in life in his published work on morbidity and disease in prisons ('On mortality in prisons', *Medico-Chirurgical Transactions*, 27, 1845), the physiology of motion, cholera (report commissioned by the Royal College of Physicians, 1854), and on dysentery (*Goulstonian Lectures*, 1847). Indeed Baly had a minute knowledge of dysentery and was the first to observe that dysenteric sloughs in the large intestine may be associated with the true ulcers of enteric fever in the small intestine. In 1841 Baly became lecturer on forensic medicine at St Bartholomew's Hospital and in 1846 was admitted a fellow of the Royal College of Physicians and in 1847 a fellow of the Royal Society. In 1854 he became assistant physician at St Bartholomew's and in 1855 lecturer on medicine there.

On the recommendation of Dr Latham, who had been employed as a consultant at Millbank penitentiary at the time of severe epidemic scurvy, diarrhoea, and dysentery in the 1820s leading to many deaths and the temporary abandonment of the prison, Baly was appointed in 1840 to visit and report on the health of prisoners at Millbank. This institution had been opened on the banks of the Thames in London in 1816 as the showcase prison of Europe for convicts and it held up to 1000 prisoners of both sexes and, as indicated, had subsequently gained a reputation for putting the health of prisoners at risk. In 1841 Baly was appointed permanent medical superintendent there on the resignation of the post holder. At that time the prison served as a depot for holding transportees until removal to Australia, and later became part of the system of home-based penal servitude for convicts which replaced transportation after 1850.

The governor (and chaplain) at this time was the Revd Daniel Nihill who was dedicated to the spiritual and moral reform of prisoners. However, it was clear to Baly that dysentery was epidemic there in 1842 and he engaged closely with this problem through the next two years, which saw Nihill replaced by the choleric disciplinarian Captain Groves who remained governor throughout the rest of Baly's time there. Baly arranged for more meat to be included in the diet but he was anxious to devise a multidimensional analysis of the high levels of dysentery, diarrhoea, and fever. Thus he emphasized that disease was imported through transfer from other prisons, that prisoners were languishing longer than previously in Millbank itself, that dysentery was prevalent in London generally, that prisoners were poorly fed and suffered from cold, that lack of ventilation and foul air led to spread of disease in the prison and its neighbourhood, and that inmates were generally vulnerable to all disease as a result of mental depression engendered by long-term imprisonment. At this time Groves's irascible disposition resulted in a public inquiry into alleged abuse of staff and prisoners at which Baly gave evidence in Groves's defence.

In 1848 the cholera epidemic reached Millbank leading to high mortality for that year of 5.8 per cent among prisoners rising to 9.3 per cent in 1849 of which half was due to cholera. Baly suggested, again on the theory of miasmic contagion, that the proximity to nearby foul-smelling manufactories and sewers and damp, foetid atmosphere from the very polluted River Thames were the main causes. However, he also began to wonder whether the custom in the prison, and of other nearby institutions having a high incidence of cholera, of drawing drinking water from the Thames was also implicated. Although he was not sure of this he pressed for an artesian well to supply the prison and in 1854 this was dug near Trafalgar Square and a direct supply piped to the prison. Cholera all but disappeared from the institution. Baly, none the less, believed contaminated water to be no more than a subsidiary, 'exciting' cause of the disease. In mid-July 1859 he retired to take the post of physician-extraordinary to Queen Victoria. He acted also as censor of the College of Physicians (1858–9) and sat as a crown representative on the General Medical Council.

On the evening of 28 January 1861 the 5.10 p.m. train from Waterloo to Portsmouth careered off the track on a bridge 20 yards from Epsom Junction onto the road below. William Baly was the only passenger to be killed although several others were severely injured. He was buried seven days later at Kensal Green cemetery near his home in Queen Anne Street, London. Baly never married and was survived by two sisters. He was a dedicated and humane pioneer of prison medical care who, moreover, contributed significantly to scientific medical knowledge and was greatly respected by the medical profession as a whole. The College of Physicians instituted a gold medal awarded biennially in his name, for distinction in physiology. BILL FORSYTHE

Sources *DNB* · S. McConville, *A history of English prison administration*, 1: 1750–1877 (1981) · *The Times* (30–31 Jan 1861) · *The Times* (4–5 Feb 1861) · J. Sim, *Medical power in prisons: the prison medical service in England, 1774–1989* (1990) · *The Lancet* (9 Feb 1861) · 'Appendix G. Report from Dr. Guy', J. Jebb, *Suggestions on an improved system of convict discipline* (1863) · Munk, *Roll* · annual reports, Millbank penitentiary, *Parl. papers* (1841–60)

Likenesses J. P. Knight, oils, exh. RA 1863, St Bartholomew's Hospital, London · wood-engraving (after photograph by Maull & Polyblank), NPG; repro. in *ILN* (9 Feb 1861)

Wealth at death £7000: probate, 12 March 1861, *CGPLA Eng. & Wales*

Bambridge, Thomas (*d.* 1741), prison warden, became briefly notorious for the regime of extreme cruelty he inflicted upon the prisoners under his charge. The details of his parentage and childhood are unknown. He practised as a London attorney and had chambers at the Inner Temple, though by 1722 he was in serious arrears of rent and was barred from access. It was possibly from this time that John Huggins, warden of the Fleet prison, employed him as one of his deputies.

The Fleet, like other prisons at the time, was a private enterprise and combined conditions of freedom with brutal restraint. Its inmates were mainly debtors, usually decent but economically unfortunate tradespeople who, as the law allowed, could be retained by their creditors in gaol until debts had been settled. In August 1728 Huggins, who had bought the wardenship from Edward Hyde, third earl of Clarendon, during the reign of Queen Anne, sold his patent to Bambridge and an associate named Dougal Cuthbert for £5000; and by the end of September Bambridge was acting as warden 'in his own right'. He was already a hardened accomplice in Huggins's harsh regime of extorting 'fees' from prisoners in return for petty benefits and privileges outside the prison walls but within its 'rules', while those who could not pay were thrown into pestilent dungeons. The wardenship of the Fleet prison was a guaranteed money-spinner and Bambridge could reckon on yearly profits in excess of £4600. Under his brief rule conditions became even more barbaric until the death of one of the prisoners, Robert Castell, an architect of some note, led to his public exposure as a social villain.

Castell was a friend of the philanthropically minded MP James Edward Oglethorpe, and had been visited several times by him in prison. Oglethorpe was enraged to hear of Castell's demise on 12 December 1728 in a smallpox-infected 'sponging house' where Bambridge had consigned him for failure to pay fees, so much so that on 25 February 1729 he raised the matter in parliament and a committee was appointed under his chairmanship to inquire into the state of the nation's gaols. The committee gave first priority to the Fleet, and after beginning its inspections on 27 February was dismayed when Bambridge contemptuously disregarded their instruction to remove iron shackles from one of the prisoners, Sir William Rich. Next day Oglethorpe notified the matter to the House of Commons and Bambridge was immediately ordered into custody. Oglethorpe's report to the house on 20 March catalogued the full extent of Bambridge's inhumanity. There was overwhelming evidence of Bambridge's arbitrary and unlawful conduct, and the house readily concurred that he was 'guilty of … the highest crimes and misdemeanours in the execution of his said office' (*JHC*, 21.282), whereupon he was committed to Newgate gaol and crown proceedings initiated against him. An act of parliament (2 Geo. II c. 32) divested him of the wardenship and incapacitated him from holding any other office. Oglethorpe's committee of MPs meanwhile continued their investigations of other London gaols amid huge applause from the public and the press for their humanitarian spirit.

The opposition newspaper *The Craftsman* published a satirical piece on 10 May elaborating at length upon the parallel between Bambridge and the prime minister, Sir Robert Walpole, as lovers of tyranny and arbitrary power. But when Bambridge was brought to trial at the Old Bailey on 22 May for Castell's murder he was acquitted. He was also acquitted of charges of theft from several Fleet prisoners early in December; and when tried once more at London's Guildhall in January 1730 on an 'appeal for murder' brought by Castell's widow, he again walked free. There was speculation, not least among Oglethorpe's parliamentary colleagues, that Bambridge's skin had been saved through the agency of highly placed friends in the judiciary. Bambridge largely disappears from view after this. In 1733 he began proceedings to regain possession of his chambers at the Inner Temple, and in 1735 commenced a bill of chancery in order to effect this. He appeared in person at the Temple to press his case in May 1741, but his arguments were rejected. His death was reported two months later, though whether it was suicide, as has been suggested, has not been verified.

A. A. HANHAM

Sources will, PROB 11/294 (mic. reel 713) • *JHC*, 21 (1727–32), 237–8, 247, 274–83, 384–7 • *State trials*, 17.383–462, 563–81 • F. A. Inderwick and R. A. Roberts, eds., *A calendar of the Inner Temple records*, 4 (1933), 80, 305, 428–9, 431, 463 • *London Magazine*, 10 (1741), 362 • A. Boyer, *The political state of Great Britain*, 37 (1729), 463–5 • *Country Journal, or, The Craftsman* (10 May 1729) • L. F. Church, *Oglethorpe: a study of philanthropy in England and Georgia* (1932), 11–12 • *Manuscripts of the earl of Egmont: diary of Viscount Percival, afterwards first earl of Egmont*, 3 vols., HMC, 63 (1920–23), vol. 1, pp. 46, 95 • *The parliamentary diary of Sir Edward Knatchbull, 1722–1730*, ed. A. N. Newman, CS, 3rd ser., 94 (1963), 88, 92

Likenesses studio of W. Hogarth, group portrait, oils, *c.*1729 (*Committy of the House of Commons (the gaols committee)*), NPG • R. Grave, line engraving, 1819, BM, NPG; repro. in J. Caulfield, *Portraits, memoirs, and characters of remarkable persons*, 4 vols. (1819–20)

Bambourgh. For this title name *see* Uhtred, earl of Bamburgh (*d.* 1016); Osulf, earl of Bamburgh (*d.* 1067).

Bamburgh, Odard of (*fl.* *c.*1115–*c.*1133), administrator, has been identified as a son of Liulf of Bamburgh, sheriff of Northumberland between *c.*1103 and 1116 (Round, *Genealogist*, 5.25–8), though the identification cannot be regarded as certain. An important royal servant in the north, Odard was sheriff of Northumberland by 2 February 1116, when he was one of the addressees in a writ of Henry I that ordered the restoration of lands belonging to Bishop Ranulf of Durham. Between 1115 and 1119 Henry's son, William, notified Odard that the king had granted him land for the service of three knights, and on 11 April 1121 Odard, described as sheriff of the Northumbrians, attended an assembly of northern magnates at Durham, at which they discussed Durham Priory's claim to Tynemouth. He was also one of the addressees in royal writs commanding that the monks of Tynemouth should have quiet possession of their lands (1120–33), and that they and the abbot of St Albans should have right of warren in their Northumberland lands (*c.*1116–*c.*1126). Between 1119 and 1124 he attested Earl David of Huntingdon's foundation charter for Selkirk Abbey. Between 1115 and 1127 Odard was notified by Henry I of his gift of property to Eustace fitz John, and between 1118 and 1128 himself attested a charter of Henry I in favour of William, son of Aluric of Corbridge. He was still sheriff of Northumberland in 1130, when he was pardoned 15*s.* for danegeld.

Odard was probably the father of William fitz Odard of Bamburgh, and of William's brothers, Adam, John, and Ernald; he may also have had a daughter named Gumilda. About 1133 Henry I granted to William fitz Odard of Bamburgh all the lands that his father had held in chief (lands named in a charter of King Stephen as situated in Bamburgh and Corbridge, 'Burnulfestona' and 'Chinewallia'), which suggests that Odard was dead by then. The shrievalty of Northumberland passed to Adam, and John acquired the lordship of Embleton in Northumberland and was the ancestor of the Viscount family.

Odard the sheriff of Northumberland may have been the same man as Odard the sheriff of Carlisle; under the Carlisle heading, the 1129/30 pipe roll records the debts of this Odard 'for the old farm of the pleas of Carlisle which belong to the shrievalty', for the same farm in the previous year (1128/9), and for the pleas of Walter Espec and Eustace fitz John. If the two Odards were one and the same, it would appear that Odard of Bamburgh held some authority over Carlisle or Cumberland generally. Another sheriff Odard, lord of Wigton in Cumberland, may or may not have been the same man as Odard the sheriff of Carlisle, and therefore may possibly be identifiable with Odard of Bamburgh. A much less likely identification is with yet another Odard, son of Hildred of Carlisle, the man who accounted for the farm of Carlisle in the 1129/30 pipe roll. PAUL DALTON

Sources J. A. Green, *English sheriffs to 1154* (1990) · J. A. Green, *The government of England under Henry I* (1986) · W. P. Hedley, *Northumberland families*, 2 vols., Society of Antiquaries of Newcastle upon Tyne, Record Series (1968–70) · W. P. Hedley, 'Odard *vicecomes*', *Transactions of the Cumberland and Westmorland Antiquarian and Archaeological Society*, new ser., 59 (1960), 41–50 · *Reg. RAN*, vols. 2–3 · J. Hunter, ed., *Magnum rotulum scaccarii, vel, Magnum rotulum pipae, anno tricesimo-primo regni Henrici primi*, RC (1833) · J. H. Round, 'Odard the sheriff [pt 1]', *The Genealogist*, new ser., 5 (1888), 25–8 · J. H. Round, 'Odard the sheriff [pt 2]', *The Genealogist*, new ser., 8 (1891–2), 200–04 · J. E. Prescott, *The register of the priory of Wetherhal* (1897) · Symeon of Durham, *Opera*

Bamford [Balmford], **Samuel** (*d.* **1657**), Church of England clergyman, was born in the parish of St Edmund, King and Martyr, Lombard Street, London, a first cousin of Lambert Osbaldeston (1594–1659). Since he mentions in his will that he was 'for divers yeares bredd upp' (PROB 11/267, fols. 343–4) in the parish of St Olave Southwark, he may have been the son of James *Balmford (*b.* *c.*1556, *d.* after 1623), vicar there in 1603. He was admitted a pensioner at Emmanuel College, Cambridge, on 24 April 1612, and was subsequently elected a scholar. He graduated BA early in 1616 and proceeded MA in 1619.

Very little is known of Bamford's career over the next thirty years. The bequest in his will of a 'faire silver and gilt cupp which the Queene of Bohemia was pleased to bestowe upon me' (PROB 11/267, fols. 343–4), suggests that he may have spent some time in her service, and the bequest of 'my narrative papers of English and forreine Eclesiasticall and Civill affaires' suggests that he had international interests. He married twice: his first wife's name is unknown; his second wife (who survived him) was Elizabeth, daughter of Nicholas *Byfield (1578/9–1622) and sister of Adoniram Byfield (*d.* 1658x60).

In 1652 Bamford became rector of the relatively poor London parish of St Alban, Wood Street, which had been a stronghold of presbyterianism in the 1640s. He gained a reputation among the godly for orthodoxy, humility, studiousness, and good teaching, and worked on 'many excellent pieces intended for the presse' (Balmford, A3). When he drew up his will on 17 March 1655 he had a library of Latin and English books, and was able to leave his only child, Elizabeth, not yet eighteen years old, a portion of £400. He died in 1657; his will was proved on 1 September by his widow and executor. Two years later 'Balmford's' only publication, *Habakkuk's Prayer Applyed to the Churches* (1659), two sermons preached before the provincial assembly of London, was printed for his brother-in-law Adoniram. Accompanied by testimonials to Bamford's character and talents from Thomas Parsons and Edmund Calamy, these mourn the current state of the divided church and exhort ministers not to falter in the quest for revival. VIVIENNE LARMINIE

Sources Venn, *Alum. Cant.* · PRO, PROB 11/267, fols. 343–4 [will] · S. Balmford, *Habbakuk's prayer applyed to the churches* (1659) · 'Balmford, James', *DNB* · Tai Liu, *Puritan London: a study of religion and society in the City parishes* (1986)

Wealth at death £400—bequest to daughter: will, PRO, PROB 11/267, fols. 343–4

Bamford, Samuel (1788–1872), radical, was born in Middleton, Lancashire, on 28 February 1788, one of five children of Daniel Bamford, a dissenting muslin weaver, part-time teacher, and later master of the Salford workhouse, and his wife, Hannah. After private tuition Bamford was sent to the Manchester grammar school, from which he was withdrawn by his father, who refused to let him study Latin. He learned weaving instead, and was then employed as a warehouseman in Manchester. Here he read Homer's *Iliad* and Milton's poems, which cultivated a lifelong taste for poetry as shown in his own compositions.

Bamford had an unsettled early adulthood: in 1802 he joined the local militia, but left to return to warehousing; he then became a farm worker near Prestwich, worked on a collier trading between Shields and London, and returned to warehousing before finally settling down as a weaver. He married in 1812.

The onset of Luddite unrest prompted Bamford's political consciousness, already given direction by the writings of Robert Burns and William Cobbett. A gifted organizer, Bamford helped found the Hamden Reform Club, Middleton, in 1816, and represented the club at a reform gathering in London that year. Despite his opposition to the Blanketeers, his reformist activities led him to be charged with treason in March 1817, although he was acquitted. He chronicled this in his *Account of the Arrest and Imprisonment of Samuel Bamford* (1817).

On 16 March 1819 Bamford led the Middleton contingent to St Peter's Fields, where they witnessed the Peterloo massacre. Bamford was charged later with treason, but although the evidence showed that his own conduct and that of his contingent were peaceful and orderly, he was sentenced to a year in Lincoln gaol for inciting a riot.

Upon his release Bamford returned to weaving, but writing took up an increasing amount of his time. In 1819 he published *The Weaver Boy, or, Miscellaneous Poetry*, but to little critical success. However, by 1826 he had discarded weaving to become Manchester correspondent for the *Morning Herald*, although he continued to hold a series of other jobs as well. By 1839 Bamford abandoned full-time journalism in order to devote himself to writing the autobiographical works *Passages in the Life of a Radical* (1840–44) and *Early Days* (1849), as well as *Homely Rhymes* (1843), *Walks in South Lancashire* (1844), and *Tawk o'seawth Lankeshur* (1850).

In the meantime, Bamford withdrew from the forefront of radical politics: his last radical tract was a poem on the acquittal of Queen Caroline entitled *The Queen's Triumph* (1820). Although he continued to support moderate reform, disillusionment—prompted in particular by the increasingly violent rhetoric of Chartism, but also by the petty antagonisms among the radical leadership and their condescension towards the working classes—drove him away. Indeed, he served as a special constable in Middleton during the Chartist agitation there, and became a member of the Anti-Corn Law League.

In 1846 a private subscription was raised to assist Bamford, and in 1851 he moved to London to take up the post of messenger in Somerset House. Here he published his *Life of Amos Ogden* (1853) and *The Dialect of South Lancashire* (1854). Unhappy with the city of London and his employment, Bamford returned to Manchester in 1858 and attempted to survive on the proceeds from public readings of his poetry. In 1864 a group of Manchester Liberals became aware of his near destitution and raised an annuity, which supported him until his death at Harpurhey, Lancashire, on 13 April 1872.

Bamford has been viewed as something of an apostate of radicalism owing to the popularity with which his memoirs were greeted by members of the middle classes, and in the light of his strong opposition to Feargus O'Connor's physical-force Chartism. This has led editors of his writings either to marginalize Bamford's intellectual consistency or to emphasize his increasing irrelevance to Victorian working-class agitation. Recently, however, his role has been reappraised.

Bamford can be seen as the voice of a class-conscious radicalism which was nevertheless compelled to oppose physical-force activism. He believed the 1830s and 1840s had demonstrated the capacity of parliament to reform itself in the face of moral pressure; furthermore, he was haunted by the spectre of the Peterloo massacre and remained convinced that the physical power of the state could always crush radical militancy. It was the confluence of these factors which gave Bamford's later life an appearance of political passivity. However, he remained a strong supporter of continued legal and political reforms, and of a self-disciplined and self-educated working-class movement independent of middle-class machinations. Consequently, his writings continue to be of great use to social historians of nineteenth-century Britain.

PETER SPENCE

Sources *Manchester Guardian* (April 1872) • *Manchester Examiner* (April 1872) • Boase, *Mod. Eng. biog.* • J. F. Smith, ed., *The admission register of the Manchester School, with some notes of the more distinguished scholars*, 3 vols. in 4 pts, Chetham Society, 69, 73, 93, 94 (1866–74) • M. Hewitt, 'Radicalism and the Victorian working class: the case of Samuel Bamford', *HJ*, 34 (1991), 873–92 • W. J. Baker, 'Bamford, Samuel', *BDMBR*, vol. 1 • W. H. Chaloner, introduction, *The autobiography of Samuel Bamford*, ed. W. H. Chaloner, new edn, 1 (1967) • *DNB* • *DLB*

Archives JRL, MS of Lancashire glossary • Man. CL, Manchester Archives and Local Studies, diaries | Man. CL, Manchester Archives and Local Studies, letters to John Harland

Likenesses print, repro. in Chaloner, ed., *The autobiography of Samuel Bamford*

Bamforth, James (1842–1911), photographer, was born on 4 March 1842 at Holmfirth, Yorkshire, the eldest of the twelve children of Joseph Bamforth (1818/19–1899), a decorative painter, and his wife, Mary Ann Moxon (1824/5–1891). After elementary education locally, James chose to follow his father's trade. 'Possessing the artistic instinct' (*Holme Valley Express*, 28 Oct 1911), he took up the study of photography in his youth. His early success and astute business acumen enabled him to purchase the studio of Holmfirth's leading photographer, William Fraser Ferguson, when Ferguson emigrated, and in 1870 to found a family business which achieved renown for its production of lantern slides, picture postcards, and early silent films. Bamforth photographed a series of carefully staged tableaux, using his friends, neighbours, and local children as life models, and his own painted canvas backgrounds and authentic foregrounds incorporating real moss, bracken, and boulders to illustrate sentimental, moral, or patriotic themes, well-known hymns, and popular songs and ballads, such as 'Goodbye Dolly Gray'. Indeed, he had such an extensive range of costumes and stage props that he boasted in 1905 of needing only 'an hour's notice to illustrate any song on the market' (*Caxton Magazine and British Stationer*, 1905–6, 3).

After 1902, when the Post Office first allowed messages to be written on the reverse of postcards, Bamforth moved to new purpose-built studios at Hillside, Station Road, Holmfirth, and produced his earliest views of abbeys, castles, and other famous landmarks. By 1905–6 Bamforths had established branches in London and New York, and in 1910 it became a limited company. Under Bamforth's direction the firm took 'special care … to avoid anything in any way even approaching vulgarity' (*Caxton Magazine and British Stationer*, 1905–6, 4). It was his son Edwin (1877–1939) who shifted the emphasis of the business towards the saucy seaside postcards which prompted George Orwell's famous observation in 1941: 'Who does not know … the penny or twopenny coloured postcards with their endless succession of fat women in tight bathing dresses and their crude drawing and unbearable colours?' (Green, 12).

James Bamforth began life model photography in his studio for the production of magic lantern slides in the early 1880s, soon acquiring a reputation as the 'King of the Lantern Slides'. These slides, with titles such as 'slaves of drink' or 'before and after taking the pledge', were mainly used to illustrate temperance lectures at Band of Hope meetings, cocoa and reading room events, and Sunday school occasions. By 1905–6 the firm had a stock of some 2 million slides and was producing some 600 new titles annually. Bamforth also used his artistic skills to illustrate edifying literature by the novelist and preacher Silas K. Hocking. In 1898 he produced his first cine films, staging his first public cinematograph show at Holmfirth Drill Hall on 15 March 1900 to raise money for the Second South African War, with footage of local volunteers leaving Halifax barracks. Subsequently Bamforths became the first firm in Britain to make cinematograph films for public exhibition on a commercial basis, and by 1915 the firm's list of some 126 films included the epic *Paula*, produced by Bertram Phillips.

In 1899 a local newspaper paid tribute to James Bamforth's versatility as 'a scene-painter, stage carpenter, stage manager, photographer, plumber, glazier and gasfitter and much more' (*Holme Valley Express*, 4 March 1899). A lifelong devoted churchman, he had been responsible for the redecoration in the 1870s of the chancel of Holmfirth parish church, where he worshipped regularly and sang for many years in the church choir. He was also a member of the Holmfirth District Choral Society, founded in 1882, and a regular concert-goer, invariably following performances from his own copy of the musical score. A staunch Conservative, he was a prominent supporter of tariff reform and intensely patriotic, serving for twenty years with the 32nd West Yorkshire volunteer company from its formation in 1860. The death of his wife, Martha Ann (1843/4–1894), with whom he had six children by 1881, was traumatic, causing a deterioration of his health; it was reported in 1899 that he was exhausted each September and needed to rest. Yet he was photographed six years later at the top of a ladder in his new studio, adding the finishing touches to a scenic background which he had painted on a wall-sized canvas in forty minutes for a visiting reporter. An earlier studio photographic portrait reveals a handsome, stylishly attired younger man with sparkling eyes, a smooth complexion, back-combed wavy hair, side-whiskers, and a neatly trimmed heavy beard and moustache. He died, 'one of Holmfirth's most honoured townsmen' (*Holme Valley Express*, 28 Oct 1911), on 26 October 1911 at Fern Bank, his residence in Holmfirth, and was buried in Holmfirth parish church burial-ground on 28 October 1911.

JOHN A. HARGREAVES

Sources *Holme Valley Express* (4–11 March 1899) • *Holme Valley Express* (28 Oct–4 Nov 1911) • *Caxton Magazine and British Stationer* (1905–6) • b. cert. • d. cert. • G. J. Mellor, *Movie makers and picture palaces: a century of cinema in Yorkshire, 1896–1996* (1996) • F. Alderson, *The comic postcard in English life* (1970) • B. Green, *I've lost my little Willie: a celebration of comic postcards* (1996) • E. Williams, *Holmfirth from forest to township* (1975) • F. G. Burley, *History trail of Holmfirth* (1980) • census returns, 1851, 1881 • *White's Clothing District* (1870) • *White's Clothing District* (1881) • *The Times* (28 Sept 2000) • *Daily Telegraph* (28 Sept 2000) • *The Independent* (7 Oct 2000)

Archives W. Yorks. AS, Kirklees, Robert W. Scherer Bamforth Postcard collection, postcards | FILM BFI NFTVA, copies of many early Bamforth films • BFI NFTVA, Pioneers of Yorkshire collection, 125 Bamforth silent films

Likenesses photograph, *c*.1905, W. Yorks. AS, Kirklees • photograph, *c*.1905, W. Yorks. AS, Kirklees; repro. in *Caxton Magazine & British Stationer*

Wealth at death £2185 18*s*.: probate, 30 Dec 1911, *CGPLA Eng. & Wales*

Bampfield, Sir Coplestone. *See* Bampfylde, Sir Coplestone, second baronet (1637/8–1692).

Bampfield, Francis (1614–1684), Seventh Day Baptist minister, was probably born at Poltimore, Devon, the third son of John Bampfield (*d. c*.1650), who served as sheriff of Devon, and his wife, Elizabeth, daughter of Thomas Drake of Buckland Monachorum, Devon; Thomas's brother was Sir Francis Drake. Intended for the ministry by his pious parents, Bampfield received his early education in godly families. In 1631, aged sixteen, he entered Wadham College, Oxford, as a commoner, matriculating on 16 May 1634 and graduating BA on 4 July 1635 and MA on 7 July 1638. Reflecting on his Oxford years in 1681 he wrote of 'that void space of his time' in which he had made little advancement in 'Scripture-Learning' (Bampfield, 2, 36) and mocked puritan students.

Bampfield was ordained deacon by Bishop Joseph Hall of Exeter, and priest by Bishop Robert Skinner of Bristol. Appointed rector of Rampisham, Dorset, on 25 July 1639, he used the income of nearly £100 p.a. to provide hospitality, assist the poor, and purchase bibles. He was appointed a prebendary of Exeter Cathedral on 15 May 1641. When civil war erupted Bampfield supported the royalists and consulted Dr Gilbert Ironside about the legality of paying taxes levied by parliament. An opponent of the solemn league and covenant, he drafted a statement explaining his position. In May 1645 he took a horse and weapons to royalist troops at Berry Pomeroy, Devon. As late as 1674, according to Richard Baxter, Bampfield was still speaking against the parliamentary cause. He used the Book of Common Prayer longer than any minister in Dorset, stopping only when compelled by troops. Bampfield had had a change of heart by January 1647, for on 19 January his father, with the Dorset committee's approval, presented him with the rectory of Wraxall. His parting gift to the parishioners at Rampisham was a new parsonage worth approximately £300. In his new living he supported himself on an annuity of £80 p.a. provided by his father, much of which Bampfield used for charitable purposes. When his congregation resisted his efforts to impose greater discipline he began to preach at Sherborne about 1653, following William Lyford's death. He was formally admitted as its vicar on 28 April 1657 in a service led by an Independent and a presbyterian minister and attended by 2000 people. Bampfield had the triers' approval, though he neither sought it nor appeared before them. Nor did he take the engagement, contrary to Edmund Calamy's claim. Indeed, for preaching against the engagement he was briefly imprisoned; he may have been the Bamfield released on a £1000 recognizance on 19 September 1659. Bampfield's assistant at Sherborne was Humphrey Philips, formerly chaplain to Bampfield's father and now a fellow of Magdalen College, Oxford.

At the Restoration Bampfield regained his prebend, but he declined an invitation to become rector of Trinity, Dorchester. On 1 November 1660 Baxter recommended him for a bishopric to Chancellor Hyde, but nothing came of this. About 1661, when Bampfield became very ill, he sought the anointing of the sick mentioned in James 5. After neighbouring clergy refused this ministration he anointed himself, claiming the authority of a secret voice, and subsequently recovered. About this time he voluntarily paid the exchequer £30 to compensate for augmentations from the royal revenue Philips had received as his assistant. The Sunday before St Bartholomew's day 1662 Bampfield preached a farewell sermon at Sherborne, from which he and Philips were shortly ejected; Bampfield also lost his prebend. The Book of Common Prayer to which he had once been so faithful was, he now opined, an 'unclean Constitution of humanely invented Worship' (Bampfield, 4). While conducting a service for a small group of neighbours in his home on 19 September 1662 Bampfield, with Philips and approximately twenty-five others, was arrested and detained for five days. Summoned before the deputy lieutenants Bampfield, insisting his activities were not seditious, was released after providing sureties and agreeing to appear at the next assizes. With Philips, Bampfield went to his brother Thomas *Bampfield's house at Dunkerton, near Bath, where they held more conventicles. For illegally preaching at Shaftesbury, Dorset, Bampfield and John Westley were arrested on 23 July 1663 and imprisoned in Dorchester. The two were fined 40 marks apiece, but this was reduced by half, with a provision to compound for 1 s. per pound. Although Westley was released after three months Bampfield remained in prison with other dissenting clergy—Peter Ince, Thomas Hallet, Josiah Banger, and John Sacheverell. About a year later Bampfield wrote to Charles II, denouncing sedition, promising not to oppose lawful authority, and affirming his willingness to suffer rather than cease preaching. After he had been incarcerated a year and a half, Bampfield and his associates were offered freedom if they provided security for good behaviour, but Bampfield refused because he deemed this tantamount to acknowledging guilt.

During the early part of his imprisonment Bampfield preached every day and twice on Sunday until the gaoler received orders to curtail him. In prison Bampfield gathered a congregation to whom he preached as much as sixteen times a week near the end of his confinement. About 1664, after concluding that all ministers in the Bible had known the scriptural languages, he resolved to acquire greater facility 'in the inner knowledg of the Hebrew Significations by the Holy Spirits Teachings' (Bampfield, 8). About a year later Bampfield concluded that both scripture and nature prescribed Saturday as the sabbath for Christians as well as Jews. When two ministers failed to dissuade him he began holding services on Saturday. Bampfield's conviction that Saturday was the proper day for Christians to worship and rest was intimately related to the millenarian outlook of the Seventh Day Baptists. The papal Antichrist, the little horn of the apocalyptic prophecy in Daniel 8, was adjudged responsible for denigrating the fourth commandment by altering the sabbath and urging respect for unscriptural holy days. Approximately a year later Bampfield had a vision in which he was seemingly transported to heaven, where he 'had a clear view of Christ in his Glorified Humanity' (Bampfield, 4). He recorded other visions, one of which he deemed the baptism of the Holy Spirit. Such experiences, including the marriage of his body, soul, and spirit to the Trinity, were essentially mystical. Bampfield's sabbatarian views elicited refutations from Baxter in *The Divine Appointment of the Lord's Day* (1671), and William Benn in *The Judgment of Mr. Francis Bampfield* (1672), which includes Bampfield's account of his position.

The earl of Arlington issued a warrant for Bampfield's release on 17 May 1672, and on 29 June he received a general licence to preach under the declaration of indulgence. During his imprisonment he had embraced the doctrine of believers' baptism, and he and a companion now went to Salisbury, where Bampfield was baptized in the Avon 'as by the Hand of Christ himself' (Bampfield, 17). While in gaol Bampfield had met Damaris Town (*d.* 1694), who provided relief to prisoners; her father, a doctor of divinity in Limerick, had lost his estate in the Irish rising. For a time she accompanied Bampfield on his preaching itineraries, and he finally married her on 23 September 1673 to avoid scandal. Because she had no dowry Bampfield was criticized for marrying beneath his station, but he retorted that he preferred grace to earthly riches. Later the same year he went to London, settling in Bethnal Green. Before founding his own church in 1674 he preached to Seventh Day Baptist congregations in Mill Yard and Bell Lane. In 1675 he preached to churches in Salisbury (where he was imprisoned for eighteen weeks), Hampshire, Dorset, Gloucestershire, and Berkshire. From Salisbury gaol he defended himself in *The Open Confessor and the Free Prisoner* (1675). After schism rent his congregation he organized the remnants into a new church on 5 March 1676. The following year he published two substantive volumes, the first of which, *All in One*, averred that proper teaching of the Bible was the way to perfect the arts and sciences. On this foundation he proposed erecting a new educational system, with lecturers in every county, teaching geared to students' abilities, instruction in Hebrew for all students, an end to traditional philosophy and astrology, and the study of scriptural geography. The second work, *Septima dies*, was an exposition of the works of creation, including a defence of the seventh day sabbath and an explication of covenant theology. During the Popish Plot scare Bampfield forwarded a prophecy from Elizabeth Hooker to the king, urging him to establish Christ's laws.

In 1681 Bampfield moved his expanding congregation to Pinners' Hall, Broad Street, a decision made by lot. After the move increasing numbers of young men and women joined the congregation. Bampfield founded several (unidentified) congregations in several counties, though his attempt to establish an association of sabbatarian churches in England, Wales, the Netherlands, and New England failed for unexplained reasons. In part Bampfield had wanted an association to train ministers, provide better education for children, relieve the indigent, and convert Jews. He offered a blueprint for his proposed educational reforms in *The House of Wisdom* (1681), in which he repeated his call for instruction in Hebrew and a curriculum shaped by scripture. The academy he envisioned in this work would provide instruction in a variety of subjects, accommodating students' interests and abilities. Pupils could study for the magistracy or ministry as well as for other occupations. Most of the instruction was utilitarian in nature, dealing with such subjects as husbandry, seamanship, the military arts, and artisanry. Due attention was accorded to geometry, medicine, and astronomy, but Bampfield insisted that Christ must be the principal subject of the curriculum, that the Bible must be the only authoritative book, and that all subjects should be studied in biblical words and phrases wherever possible. If teachers spoke Hebrew, Bampfield thought deaf people could learn to speak by observing the movements of the instructors' mouths and tongues. Such attention to education set Bampfield apart from most Seventh Day Baptists. In 1681 he also published his autobiography, *A Name, an After-one*, in which he compared himself to St Paul.

Bampfield again found himself in legal trouble when, on 13 February 1683, he was arrested while preaching at Pinners' Hall. He and some six of his congregation were taken before the lord mayor, who fined several of them £10 before releasing them. A week later Bampfield was rearrested and incarcerated in Newgate prison, where he remained after refusing to take the oath of allegiance. His refusal stemmed from principled opposition to oaths, not hostility to the regime in general; although he knew something about the Monmouth cabal's consideration of a proposed insurrection through his contact with the printer Francis Smith, he did not endorse such action. When he again rejected the oath at his trial in the Old Bailey on 17 March the judge directed the jury to find him guilty, and on 28 March his chattels were forfeited and he was sentenced to imprisonment for life or during the king's pleasure. Bampfield published an account of these events in *The Lords Free Prisoner* (1683). Before Lord Chief Justice Edmund Saunders and three other judges he again rejected the oath on 18 April. He remained steadfast in further appearances at the Old Bailey on 12 and 13 October, and twice in January 1684, which he recounted in *A Just Appeal from Lower Courts* (1683) and *A Continuation of a Former Just Appeal* (1684). While in prison he also wrote *The Holy Scripture* (1684), in which he reiterated his call for schools to educate pupils in Hebrew and biblically based arts and sciences. He was also in communication with radical printers; in May 1683 he received a letter from Francis Smith which he was asked to forward to Mr Culliford, a printer with ties to the plotter Robert Ferguson. Bampfield passed the letter to Jane Curtis who, with her husband, Langley, printed dissident material. Aged seventy, Bampfield died in Newgate prison on 16 February 1684 and was buried three days later in the Baptists' graveyard in Glasshouse Yard, near Aldersgate Street. His wife survived him. Many nonconformists of varying persuasions attended his funeral, and several elegies, including *Counsel for the Living* and *An Elegy on that Special Messenger* (both 1684) commemorated his life. His religious pilgrimage had been one of the most extensive in seventeenth-century England, taking him from the conformists to the Seventh Day Baptists.

Francis Bampfield's brother Thomas (*d.* 1693), recorder of Exeter and MP (1654–60; speaker in 1659), had embraced Seventh Day Baptist tenets by 1667, defending them in *A Reply to Doctor Wallis* (1693); he also wrote *An Enquiry whether the Lord Jesus Christ Made the World* (1692). The oldest brother, Sir John Bampfield (*c.*1610–1650), served in the Long Parliament and the parliamentary army. RICHARD L. GREAVES

Sources F. Bampfield, *A name, an after-one* (1681) • R. L. Greaves, *Saints and rebels: seven nonconformists in Stuart England* (1985), chap. 7 • B. W. Ball, *The seventh-day men: sabbatarians and sabbatarianism in England and Wales, 1600–1800* (1994) • PRO, State Papers 29/424/114 • *CSP dom.*, *1659–60*, 211; *1663–4*, 612; *1671–2*, 597; *1672*, 292; *1676–7*, 543; *Jan–June 1683*, 277–8 • *Calamy rev.* • *Reliquiae Baxterianae, or, Mr Richard Baxter's narrative of the most memorable passages of his life and times*, ed. M. Sylvester, 1 vol. in 3 pts (1696), pt 1, p. 432; pt 3, p. 150 • *The nonconformist's memorial … originally written by … Edmund Calamy*, ed. S. Palmer, [3rd edn], 2 (1802), 149–55 • *Calendar of the correspondence of Richard Baxter*, ed. N. H. Keeble and G. F. Nuttall, 2 (1991), 8–9 • Wood, *Ath. Oxon.*, new edn, 4.126–8 • T. Crosby, *The history of the English Baptists, from the Reformation to the beginning of the reign of King George I*, 4 vols. (1738–40), vol. 1, pp. 356–68
Archives PRO, autographed letter, State Papers 29/390/147

Bampfield, Joseph (1622–1685), army officer and spy, was probably born in Devon, one of a family long established in the west country, but his parentage and early life are obscure. There is no validity for the earl of Clarendon's later statement that he was an Irishman, although he may have been educated at Trinity College, Dublin, in the 1630s. He began his military career aged seventeen in 1639 as an ensign in Lord Astley's regiment in the expedition against the Scots known as the first bishops' war. In the second bishops' war he was a lieutenant and then captain in the regiment of Colonel Wentworth. By September 1642 he was a major in the royalist army commanded by the marquess of Hertford and fought at Yeovil on 7 September 1642, when he was taken prisoner. He had escaped by December 1642 and, still only nineteen, was commissioned a colonel by Charles I by 16 January 1643. About this time, certainly by 1 February 1643, he married Catherine (1622–1657), daughter of John Sydenham of Brympton, Somerset. The couple were estranged by 1645–1646 and had no children. Bampfield was involved in the royalist occupation of Malmesbury in April 1643 and played a prominent role in the sieges of Exeter and Dartmouth. Late in October 1643 he was part of Lord Hopton's army and with Sir Edward Ford was given the task of recapturing Arundel Castle in December. Having been given command of the castle Bampfield found himself besieged by Sir William Waller's forces and surrendered on 6 January 1644, attracting some criticism from the royalist side. He was again taken prisoner and remained in the Tower for some five months, until released on parole, when he immediately absconded to Oxford and rejoined the king's forces in the west. In autumn 1644 he was in action at Lyme and Taunton, but after a disorderly retreat from

Chard in December 1644 he was arrested and then dismissed from service by Hopton.

In the course of the following year, however, Bampfield gained the confidence of Charles I, who employed him as a courier, occasional adviser, and intelligence agent from late 1645 until access to the king's person was halted in 1648. He appears to have followed a pro-presbyterian line in his advice to the monarch. His greatest adventure of the latter years of the second civil war was contriving the escape of James, duke of York, from parliamentary hands in April 1648. Overcoming James's own scruples Bampfield engineered an escape from London on 20–21 April with the prince disguised in woman's clothes. The pair were assisted in the venture by Anne Murray (1623–1699) and landed at Zeeland on 22 April 1648. Bampfield had met Anne [*see* Halkett, Anne] in late 1647 or early 1648 and they had a lengthy affair from 1648 to 1653, although the details of their relationship remain obscure. In 1648 Bampfield was advised that his wife, whom he had not seen for some time, was dead and it is possible that he and Anne were privately married, bigamously, in Bampfield's case, in the Netherlands in winter 1648–9. Their relationship came to an end in March 1653 when Anne finally accepted that Bampfield's wife was still living.

Despite Bampfield's success in rescuing James his dabbling in court politics for the presbyterian interest damaged his standing at the exiled court and his attempts to make use of the duke of York's authority to improvise a naval expedition in summer 1648 to save the king were a failure. His subsequent comments that the king's children should have taken a lead in rescuing their father permanently lost him the friendship of the prince of Wales and he returned to England.

In the months following the death of Charles I Bampfield was in hiding in London, often in the company of Anne Murray. Arrested in December 1649 he was imprisoned in the Gatehouse but was able to escape with the help of friends that same month and fled to the Netherlands. On the boat over he was recognized by Sir Henry Newton, Anne's brother-in-law, and challenged to a duel for the offence he had caused the family by maintaining this liaison. Bampfield wounded Newton and was once more forced into hiding. Although Charles II refused to see him Bampfield followed him to Scotland in summer 1650 where he attempted to redeem himself by being very active in royal affairs, but 'was frequently agitated betwixt hope and despair' (*Bampfield's Apology*, 81).

Charles II received Bampfield at Paris in 1653, but the king's continued dislike of him was obvious and consequently, in spring or summer 1654, he entered the service of John Thurloe as an agent of the protectorate. He provided intelligence about the exiled court, conspiracies, and foreign affairs in the late 1650s, frequently returning to England, in the early years of his employment, to receive instruction from Thurloe. An attempt to enter military service again by raising a regiment of English and Scots troops to fight in the French army failed when Oliver Cromwell became suspicious of his motives, imprisoned him in March 1657 and then exiled him from Britain. He remained abroad until Cromwell's death in 1658, continuing to write intelligence reports for Thurloe, although without much encouragement. Shortly before the restoration of the king he returned to England, hoping that he would be included in the general pardon given out at Breda, but Charles II remained hostile and by May 1660 Bampfield was in the Tower.

Released on 30 July 1661 Bampfield left England for the Netherlands. He settled in Middelburg in Zeeland from 1661 to spring 1665, attending the English reformed church there and claiming he had been exiled because of his nonconformity. In October 1662 he was encouraged to act as an agent for the government of Charles II by Sir Allen Apsley and Sir Henry Bennet and for nearly two years he spied on the dissenters and other republican rebels located in the United Provinces and also supplied foreign intelligence to the British. His correspondence at this time was littered with pleas for money and pitiful expressions over his miserable condition, but his hopes for a pardon from Charles II and a return to good fortune remained unfulfilled. In spring 1664 he attracted the attention of John de Witt, the grand pensionary. Although warned that Bampfield had a reputation as a notorious rogue de Witt was intrigued by his 'very through knowledge of the Court of England and of our present disturbances' (*Bampfield's Apology*, 192) and recruited him in March 1665 as an agent for the Dutch government. Bampfield identified English spies in the Netherlands, reported on political opposition, and proffered advice, whether wanted or not, to de Witt on the current political situation in Europe. He became entangled in numerous conspiratorial schemes and had convoluted associations with William Scot, son of Thomas Scot the regicide, and Aphra Behn in 1665–6.

Bampfield volunteered for naval service in 1665 and by mid-October he had been given a major's commission to organize a troop of cavalry. The English government took revenge by attainting Bampfield for high treason in 1665, effectively preventing him from ever returning to England. For the remainder of the 1660s de Witt employed Bampfield in political negotiations relating to the role of the prince of Orange and as a military adviser. Despite his apparent value, de Witt kept Bampfield short of money and he had to wait until 19 March 1671 to become a colonel. With the approach of war he was sent to Cologne to recruit troops, returning to the Netherlands in February 1672 while his men were stationed in garrisons along the Rhine valley. In spring 1672 Bampfield was attached to the army assembling at Ijssel under the prince of Orange. During a French offensive at Zwolle, Bampfield apparently tried to rouse the local populace, but the town surrendered and Bampfield was blamed. His career in the Dutch army was finally ruined when his post at Ameide, south of the River Lek, was overrun in a French attack on 27 November. Rumours that he had betrayed the post to the French did not help his cause, nor did his former association with de Witt. Although Bampfield was exonerated by two courts martial and restored to his rank, William of Orange intervened and he was dismissed from the army.

Bampfield retired to Bergum in Friesland in 1674. At the end of September 1679 he moved to Leeuwarden. When in 1682 the earl of Argyll settled in Friesland, having fled England after involvement in treasonable activities, Bampfield once more became a potential source of intelligence to the English government and a somewhat desultory correspondence was carried on with the secretary of state, Sir Leoline Jenkins, from 1682 to 1684. In 1685 Bampfield published a pamphlet justifying his career, notably leaving out his activities as a spy. In it he noted that he had for 'a long time considered death … as the only end of my calamities which I could reasonably hope for and my most sure azile' (*Bampfield's Apology*, 37). He died in Leeuwarden in 1685 and was buried in the Netherlands.

ALAN MARSHALL

Sources *Colonel Joseph Bampfield's apology: written by himself, 1685*, ed. J. Loftis and P. H. Hardacre (1993) • *The memoirs of Anne, Lady Halkett and Ann, Lady Fanshawe*, ed. J. Loftis (1979) • *The life of James the Second, king of England*, ed. J. S. Clarke, 2 vols. (1816) • W. J. Cameron, *New light on Aphra Behn: an investigation into the facts and fictions surrounding her journey to Surinam in 1663 and her activities as a spy in Flanders in 1666* (Auckland, 1961) • R. Fruin, *De Oorlog van 1672* (Groningen, 1972) • C. H. Firth, 'Thomas Scot's account of his actions as intelligencer during the Commonwealth', *EngHR*, 12 (1897), 116–26 • Thurloe, *State papers* • H. H. Rowen, *John de Witt, grand pensionary of Holland, 1625–1675* (New Jersey, 1978) • *Brieven van Johan de Witt*, ed. R. Fruin and N. Japikse, 2 vols. (Amsterdam, 1919–22) • *Brieven van Johan de Witt*, ed. R. Fruin, G. W. Kernkemp, and N. Japikse, 4 vols. (Amsterdam, 1906–13) • Baron Vercken, *Reflexions du Colonel Bampfield sur les commentaires de Mr. Vercken touchent l'attacque des François sur les escluses d'Ameyden le 27 Novembre* (1672) • D. Underdown, *Royalist conspiracy in England, 1649–1660* (1960)
Archives BL, Add. MS 18982, fol. 118 • PRO, SP 84/167, 168, 169, 170 • PRO, SP 29/422, fol. 134

Bampfield, Thomas (1622/3–1693), speaker of the House of Commons, was a younger son of John Bampfield (*d.* *c.*1650) and Elizabeth, daughter of Thomas Drake. The Bampfields were one of Devon's leading gentry families, seated at Poltimore near Exeter. After attending Exeter College, Oxford, where he matriculated, aged seventeen, on 15 May 1640 but did not take a degree, Bampfield was admitted to the Middle Temple on 28 October 1642, and was called to the bar in 1649. Back in his native county he was made deputy recorder of Exeter in 1652, and succeeded Edmund Prideaux as recorder in 1654. He was first included in the Devon commission of the peace in 1653, and had been admitted to the quorum by 1656. He was a commissioner for ejecting scandalous ministers in the county from 1654, and this appointment accorded well with his presbyterian leanings. He provided £100 for the building of a wall in 1657 in Exeter Cathedral that separated presbyterian and Independent congregations, and as a county magistrate was an advocate of the so-called reformation of manners.

Elected to the first protectorate parliament on 12 July 1654 for Exeter, Bampfield took little or no part in this assembly, and may have been initially reluctant to take the Recognition, imposed by the government on MPs as a test of loyalty to the new constitution. He and another MP went to discuss their scruples with Lord Protector Oliver Cromwell before concluding that to accept the Recognition was justifiable. He was returned again to the second Cromwellian parliament, and this time played a major role both in committees and in debate on the floor of the house. He reported from the large and emotionally charged committee that examined James Nayler, the notorious Quaker, and urged repeatedly that the committee's verdict that Nayler was a blasphemer be accepted and acted upon by the house: 'If you set this aside, and do nothing in it, I shall say it is no more Nayler's sin, but set it upon your doors' (*Diary of Thomas Burton*, 1.33). On other matters before this parliament Bampfield demonstrated a country suspicion of the government, and was quick to detect any threat to the legislature by the executive.

In the parliament of Richard Cromwell, Bampfield was first appointed speaker on a temporary basis on 16 March 1659, and then on 15 April was elected speaker in his own right until the dissolution a week later. His severity in the chair was noted, as was his capacity to keep control of proceedings. It was probably his advocacy of parliament as a check on the government that recommended him as speaker, both to republicans as well as to Cromwellians. Later that year Bampfield presented to the revived Commonwealth government from the Devon gentry a petition calling for a free parliament, in effect recommending some kind of restored monarchy.

In 1660 Bampfield was elected to the Convention to represent both Exeter and Tiverton, but chose to sit for the former. He was a staunch supporter of a presbyterian church settlement, seeking to confirm ministers in their livings. He resisted the return of the Thirty-Nine Articles of the Church of England. He helped draft a petition to the king in favour of clemency for John Lambert and Sir Henry Vane, and moved that 'the King should be desired to marry and that it should be to a Protestant' (Cobbett, *Parl. hist.*, 4.119). Although he lost his recordership of Exeter while the Convention was still in being he did not respond by modifying his advocacy of presbyterian inspired solutions to issues of public drunkenness and profanity. He saw new legislation on the excise and the militia as deliberate revivals of the authoritarian government style of the mid-1650s, and opposed the revival of the dukedom of Norfolk as 'an act of grace to those of the popish religion' (Cobbett, *Parl. hist.*, 4.155).

The corporation of Exeter retained respect for Bampfield even after his loss of office, voting him a small reward for his efforts in parliament on their behalf, but he probably read the omens correctly in not standing again for parliament. He kept a place on the Devon bench until 1665, but thereafter only re-entered public life briefly. He was listed as a supporter of James II in the failed election of 1688, and made an appearance on the hustings at the Exeter by-election of June 1689, but did not press his own candidature. From 1687 he was the leading member of an Exeter committee to administer a fund for presbyterian ministers. He was buried at St Stephen's, Exeter, on 8 October 1693.

STEPHEN K. ROBERTS

Sources M. W. Helms and J. S. Crossette, 'Bampfield, Thomas', HoP, *Commons, 1660–90* • S. K. Roberts, *Recovery and restoration in an*

English county: Devon local administration, 1646–1670 (1985) • *Diary of Thomas Burton*, ed. J. T. Rutt, 4 vols. (1828) • T. Gray, ed., *Devon documents* (1996) • J. L. Vivian, ed., *The visitations of the county of Devon, comprising the herald's visitations of 1531, 1564, and 1620* (privately printed, Exeter, [1895]) • A. Brockett, *Nonconformity in Exeter, 1650–1875* (1962) • J. J. Alexander, 'Exeter members of parliament, pt 3', *Report and Transactions of the Devonshire Association*, 61 (1929), 193–215, esp. 196–7, 203–4, 212 • E. S. Chalk, 'Notes on the members for Tiverton (Devon), 1621–1832', *Report and Transactions of the Devonshire Association*, 67 (1935), 315–47, esp. 324–5 • C. T. Martin, ed., *Minutes of parliament of the Middle Temple*, 4 vols. (1904–5), vol. 2 • Foster, *Alum. Oxon.* • *Archaeologia*, 24 (1832), 139–40 • R. Izacke, *Remarkable antiquities of the city of Exeter* (1681) • Cobbett, *Parl. hist.*, 4.119, 155 • R. Polwhele, *The history of Devonshire*, 3 vols. (1793–1806), vol. 1, p. 308 • Som. ARS, Willoughby MSS, DD/WO Box 57 • parish register, Exeter, St Stephen's, 8 Oct 1693 [burial]

Bampfylde [Bampfield], **Sir Coplestone, second baronet (1637/8–1692)**, politician, was the eldest son of Sir John Bampfield (*c*.1590–1650) of Poltimore, Devon, and Gertrude (1611–1658), daughter and coheir of Amyas Coplestone of Warleigh House, Tamerton Foliot, Devon. Succeeding at the age of twelve to 'a fair estate, and a very plenteous fortune', he was entered at Corpus Christi College, Oxford. He changed the spelling of his surname, possibly to indicate rejection of the puritan and parliamentary sympathies of the older generation. At the university he distinguished himself by his 'very generous and splendid way of living' (Prince, 122, 125). His first wife, Margaret, daughter of John Bulkeley of Nether Burgate, Hampshire, whom he married in 1655, also came of presbyterian gentry stock, but Bampfylde was 'actuated even then with Principles of Loyalty to his Sovereign, though in Exile, and the Church, then under a Cloud' (ibid., 122). Nevertheless it was probably his uncle, Thomas *Bampfield, who secured Bampfylde's election for Tiverton to Richard Cromwell's parliament. Bampfylde played a leading part in promoting the Restoration in Devon: he presented to George Monck the petition for a free parliament and raised a troop of 120 gentlemen to disarm 'disaffected and seditious persons' (ibid., 123–4). As sheriff it fell to him to conduct the county election in 1661 at the head of his customary retinue, and his speech at the hustings exhorting the electorate to choose 'only those who were, and always had been, loyal subjects and good Christians' found its way into the government-controlled London press (*Mercurius Publicus*, 25 April 1661).

Bampfylde was returned for Devon at a contested by-election in 1671 when Sir Thomas Clifford, on behalf of the cabal, failed to secure the victory of a candidate more favourable to the dissenters. 'Much addicted to tippling' according to a hostile account, he was 'presented to the King by his pretended wife, Bett Roberts, in Pall Mall' (*English Historical Documents*, 8.239). In 1674 Bampfylde contracted a second marriage with Jane (*c*.1654), daughter of Sir Courtenay Pole of Shute, Devon, and a pillar of the new court party as reconstructed by Sir Thomas Osborne on firmly Anglican principles, but the Popish Plot and fears of French influence at court brought this ministry down, and Bampfylde did not sit in any of the three Exclusion parliaments that followed.

Bampfylde again represented Devon in James II's parliament. On grounds of declining health he handed over his militia command to his son Hugh at the time of the Monmouth rebellion. He gave the standard negative answers on the proposed repeal of the laws against Roman Catholicism and was dismissed from local office. In 1688 he sent his son to wait on William of Orange at Exeter 'as one come to preserve our laws and religion and maintain the established Government', but he could not accept the transfer of the crown to William and Mary, and 'so far declared against these Proceedings as to refuse Payment of any New made Rates and Taxes'. His son was killed in a riding accident in 1691 and it was during a visit to his widowed daughter-in-law and his infant grandson at Warleigh that Bampfylde died of gout on 9 February 1692, in his fifty-fifth year. 'On his death-bed he charged his family that they should always continue faithful to the Religion of the established Church of England and be sure to pay their Allegiance to the right heirs of the Crown' (Prince, 124). He died intestate, having lived for many years above his income, and was buried at Poltimore without any monument.

John Prince described Bampfylde as

> the goodliest person that ever mine Eyes beheld, exceeding by some inches six Foot in heigth … Of a manly and yet a charming Countenance, a ready wit and a good Judgment, and was of a truly large and generous Soul. (Prince, 125)

He cut no great figure in any of his three parliaments and shone only on the provincial stage, where his career illustrates the problems of conflicting loyalties to church and to crown. His three children, all with his first wife, predeceased him, but his grandson, the third baronet, sat in the Hanoverian parliament as a Jacobite. JOHN FERRIS

Sources J. Prince, *Danmonii orientales illustres, or, The worthies of Devon* (1701), 122–5 • J. L. Vivian, ed., *The visitations of the county of Devon, comprising the herald's visitations of 1531, 1564, and 1620* (privately printed, Exeter, [1895]) • HoP, *Commons, 1660–90* • GEC, *Baronetage*, 2.101 • T. Fowler, *The history of Corpus Christi College*, OHS, 25 (1893), 438 • *Mercurius Publicus* (25 April 1661) • *English historical documents*, 8, ed. A. Browning (1953), 239 • parish register, Fordingbridge, Hampshire, Society of Genealogists, 16 Nov 1655 [marriage] • A. Browning, *Thomas Osborne, earl of Danby and duke of Leeds, 1632–1712*, 3 (1951)

Likenesses portraits, priv. coll.

Wealth at death indebted: Prince, *Danmonii orientales illustres*

Bampfylde, Coplestone Warre (1720–1791), landscape painter and garden designer, was born on 28 February 1720 at Hestercombe House, Kingston, Taunton, great-grandson of Sir Coplestone *Bampfylde (1637/8–1692) and the eldest of nine children of John Bampfylde (1691–1750), MP for Exeter and Devon, and his second wife, Margaret (1694–1758), only daughter of Sir Francis Warre of Hestercombe and his second wife, Margaret, *née* Harbin. Bampfylde was educated at Kingston and then Tiverton before attending Winchester College from 1731 to 1738. He matriculated at St John's College, Oxford, on 27 February 1738 but did not graduate. Bampfylde's earliest recorded painting is a life-size equestrian self-portrait dated 1746 (exh. Lane Fine Art, London, 1995) jointly painted with Richard Phelps of Porlock, a student of Thomas Hudson.

An etching by Bampfylde of a pollarded tree is dated 1749 (exh. Christies, 1995) and his earliest dated watercolour is a view of Exeter (1750; Royal Albert Museum, Exeter).

Bampfylde's early pictures show the influence of George Lambert, whose paintings of Plymouth were redrawn by Bampfylde, engraved by James Mason and P. C. Canot, and published by Lambert in 1755 as *Views at Mount Edgcumbe*. In the same year he married Mary Knight (*d.* 1806) of Wolverley, near Kidderminster, by special licence; there were no children. The poet William Shenstone wrote in 1758 to the writer Richard Graves (1715–1804), 'Perhaps you may have heard of Mr Bampfylde who is very much at Bath, is there now with his lady, or has left the place but lately and whose fortune, person, figure and accomplishments can hardly leave him unnoticed in any place where he resides' (*Letters*, 481–2). In 1776 Bampfylde provided humorous illustrations for *An Election Ball* by his friend Christopher Anstey, author of *The New Bath Guide*. In 1776 Anstey published an *Epistola poetica familiaris* addressed by him to Bampfylde, in which were included Bampfylde's *An Election Ball* illustrations engraved by W. Hibbart. For various reasons the full set of illustrations was not finally printed in *An Election Ball* until the fifth edition in 1787. Bampfylde drew the frontispieces for *Columella, or, The Distressed Anchoret* (1779), which features the cascade at Hestercombe, and *Eugenius, or, Anecdotes of the Golden Vale* (1785), both by Richard Graves. He also designed the elaborate title cartouche for *Map of Somerset* by William Day and Charles Harcourt Masters (1782). In 1791, the year of his death, Bampfylde provided an illustration of Hestercombe for John Collinson's *History and Antiquities of Somerset* (1791), a view of Taunton Castle for Joshua Toulmin's *History of the Town of Taunton* (1791), and an aquatint of Oakhampton Castle, Devon, which was published by W. Hibbart.

Bampfylde made several painting tours including Hampshire (1765, 1770), the Peak District (1766, 1780), and the Lake District (1780). He exhibited at the Society of Artists in 1763 and 1766, the Free Society in 1783, and the Royal Academy, as an honorary exhibitor in 1771, 1772, 1774, and 1783. Many of Bampfylde's oil paintings are of idealized classical landscapes influenced by Salvator Rosa, whereas his watercolours encompass Italianate capriccios to extremely fine topographical views. Two watercolours of Stourhead (Stourhead House, Wiltshire) were engraved by F. Vivares (1777) and his painting *The Storm* (exh. RA, 1774) was engraved by P. P. Benazech and published in 1779.

Bampfylde had inherited Hestercombe in 1750 and started what was to become his most important achievement—the creation of a magnificent landscape garden. Much had already been achieved by 1761 when it was first recorded by his brother-in-law Edward Knight. Bampfylde continued adding to the garden throughout his life and in 1786 erected an urn to the sacred memory of his lifelong friends Henry Hoare of Stourhead and his neighbour Sir Charles Kemes Tynte of Halswell, both of whom also created landscape gardens. Water features are an important component of the design of Bampfylde's garden at Hestercombe, where he constructed the great cascade after 1762. He also designed the cascade at Stourhead (1765) and a penstock sluice for George III at Virginia Water (1788). A competent amateur architect, he submitted plans for the new Wardour Castle, Wiltshire, in 1770, and in 1772 he designed the Market House, Taunton, which still dominates the centre of the town. Bampfylde was commissioned in 1758 as major in the 1st Somerset militia, and became its colonel on 27 August 1767. He was still active in the militia as late as 1779 when he was recalled with his men to Plymouth as the French and Spanish fleets lay off the Lizard. Bampfylde died on 23 August 1791 at four o'clock in the morning, and was buried on 30 August at St Mary's Church, Kingston, in the Warre family tomb, where he was commemorated by a fine wall plaque erected by his nephew and heir, John Tyndale Warre.

PHILIP WHITE

Sources P. White, *A gentleman of fine taste: the watercolours of Coplestone Warre Bampfylde, 1720–1791* (1995) [exhibition catalogue, Christies, London] · Som. ARS, Hestercombe papers, SRO DD GC 68; SRO DD SAS C/795 · T. Hugo, *The history of Hestercombe* (1874) · HoP, *Commons, 1715–54* · HoP, *Commons, 1660–90* · *The letters of William Shenstone*, ed. M. Williams (1939), 481–2 · C. Anstey, *An election ball*, ed. G. Turner (1997) · W. J. W. Kerr, *Records of the 1st Somerset militia* (1930) · Colvin, *Archs.* · Graves, *Artists* · Worcs. RO, Knight family papers, 899: 310 BA 10470/2

Archives Som. ARS, corresp. with Christopher Anstey · Som. ARS, Hestercombe papers, SRO DD GC 68; SRO DD SAS C/795 · V&A, Bampfylde Album, Acc. No. E.-355-1949 · Worcs. RO, Knight family papers, 899: 310 BA 10470/2

Likenesses C. W. Bampfylde and R. Phelps, self-portrait, 1746 · M. Chamberlain, oils, *c.*1770, repro. in White, *Gentleman of fine taste*

Bampfylde, John Codrington Warwick (1754–1796), poet, was born on 27 August 1754, the second son of Sir Richard Warwick Bampfylde, baronet (1722–1776), of Poltimore, Devon, and his wife, Jane Codrington (*d.* 1789). He was educated at Trinity Hall, Cambridge (where he matriculated on 25 October 1771), and published *Sixteen Sonnets* in 1778. William Jackson, a well-known musician of Exeter, told Southey that Bampfylde lived as a youth in a farmhouse at Chudleigh and often used to walk to Exeter in order to read Jackson his poems.

Bampfylde went to London where he began to lead a dissipated life. His mother, Lady Bampfylde, sat for Sir Joshua Reynolds in 1777 and he was painted in a double portrait with George Huddesford entitled 'Portraits of Two Gentlemen' in 1778–9. In his *Popular Handbook to the National Gallery*, Cook compares the two men, saying of Bampfylde that he 'has more inspiration in his face, and a certain wild look which was not belied by his after-life' (Cook, 2.247). Bampfylde proposed to Miss Palmer, afterwards marchioness of Thomond, niece of Sir Joshua Reynolds, to whom the sonnets are dedicated. Sir Joshua, however, disapproved of the match, and refused to allow the poet in his house. As a consequence Bampfylde broke Sir Joshua's windows and was sent to Newgate. On coming to town soon after, Jackson found that the poet's mother had got him out of prison, but that he was almost destitute. Jackson rescued him, before returning to Exeter, but he soon had to be confined in a private madhouse. In 1796, after twenty years' confinement, he recovered his senses only to die of consumption in that year.

Bampfylde's poems consist of the sonnets mentioned above, with two short poems later published by Southey and one by Park. In *Specimens of Later English Poets* Southey called them 'some of the most original in our language' (p. 434). LESLIE STEPHEN, *rev.* S. C. BUSHELL

Sources E. Brydges, *Censura literaria: containing titles, abstracts, and opinions of old English books*, 2nd edn, 7 (1815), 309–11 • E. Brydges, *The autobiography, times, opinions, and contemporaries of Sir Egerton Brydges*, 2 (1834), 257–9 • R. Southey, *Specimens of the later English poets, with preliminary notices*, 3 vols. (1807), 3.434–7 • *The poems of John Bampfylde*, ed. R. Lonsdale (1988) [with introduction] • *The new Cambridge bibliography of English literature*, [2nd edn], 2, ed. G. Watson (1971) • Allibone, *Dict.* • L. Baillie and P. Sieveking, eds., *British biographical archive* (1984), fiche 62, frame 150 [microfiche] • Venn, *Alum. Cant.* • J. D. Gutteridge, 'Coleridge and Bampfylde: "To evening"', *N&Q*, 225 (1980), 502–3 • E. T. Cook, *A popular handbook to the National Gallery*, 8th edn, 2 (1912), 247

Likenesses J. Reynolds, oils, 1778 (with George Huddesford), Tate collection; *see illus. in* Huddesford, George (*bap.* 1749, *d.* 1809) • W. Biscombe Gardner, engraving (after J. Reynolds), repro. in *English Illustrated Magazine* (1890–91), 72

Bampton, John (*fl.* **1317–1341**), Carmelite friar and theologian, according to John Bale (quoting an untraced Leland reference) came from the west country. He may possibly be identified with the Carmelite of the same name who was ordained deacon at Winchester on 17 December 1317, and who was listed as from the Gloucester convent when he was licensed to hear confessions in the Worcester diocese in 1328. Bampton is known to have studied at Cambridge, where on 9 September 1337 he was licensed to hear confessions in the diocese of Ely. He was recorded as *magister* and a member of the Cambridge community on 21 December 1341, when he received a licence to hear confessions for a further two years. He studied and lectured on the works of Aristotle, and he wrote one philosophical work, *De veritate propositionum*, which consisted of eight *quaestiones*, and a possible second work, *Lecturas scholasticas in theologia*. Both are now lost. RICHARD COPSEY

Sources J. Bale, Bodl. Oxf., MS Bodley 73 (SC 27635), fol. 208 • J. Bale, BL, Harley MS 3838, fol. 177 • Emden, *Cam.* • Bale, *Cat.*, 2.46

Bampton, John (**1689–1751**), benefactor, was born in 1689; details of his place of birth, parentage, and upbringing are unknown. He was educated at Trinity College, Oxford, where he graduated BA (1709) and MA (1712). Having taken orders he was installed as a prebendary at Salisbury Cathedral on 7 May 1718, and on 5 May 1726 succeeded Thomas Wyatt to become canon of Salisbury, where he remained until his death on 2 June 1751. In his will Bampton bequeathed land to the University of Oxford for the endowment of eight annual lecture sermons to be delivered at St Mary's, Oxford, 'to confirm and establish the Christian Faith and to confute all schismatics and heretics'. The lectures were intended to instil undergraduates with a conservative Anglicanism by confirming the orthodoxy of the Trinity, defending the Christian faith as expressed in the apostles' and Nicene creeds, and, in the Oxford tradition, through emphasizing the authority of the scriptures and the church's early fathers. Lecturers were to be in holy orders and hold an MA from either Oxford or Cambridge; they were chosen by college heads only 'and by no others, in the room adjoining to the Printing-House'. The first Bampton lectures were given in 1780 by James Bandinal who spoke in defence of Christian revelation. True to Bampton's wishes, early lecturers spoke out against innovations in religious thought so that, as R. Greaves has put it, 'from these lectures alone it would be possible to construct a list of those dangers to the minds and souls of the junior members … chiefly enthusiasm and scepticism' (*Hist. U. Oxf.* 5: *18th-cent. Oxf.*, 5.419–20). The Bampton lectures remain an ongoing part of theological instruction at the university though, since 1895, the series has been given biennially. In 1952 a second series of sermons, the Sarum lectures, was founded from the Bampton fund for non-Anglican theologians, and in 1968 a Bampton fellowship was established to support research on subjects considered in the lectures.

PHILIP CARTER

Sources *Hist. U. Oxf.* 5: *18th-cent. Oxf.* • *Fasti Angl., 1541–1857*, [Salisbury] • N. Sykes, *Church and state in England in the XVIII century* (1934) • *A catalogue of all graduates … in the University of Oxford, between … 1659 and … 1850* (1851) • F. L. Cross and E. A. Livingstone, eds., *The Oxford dictionary of the Christian church*

Wealth at death estate sufficient to found Bampton lectures (inaugurated 1780)

Banastre, Alard (*fl.* **1166–1175**), administrator, was a landowner in Berkshire, probably at Finchampstead. William Achard's return to Henry II's inquest of 1166 into feudal subtenancies declared that Alard and John Banastre had been enfeoffed on his demesne by William's father in Henry I's time; Finchampstead appears in Henry I's grant to Robert Achard, and in 1220 an Alan and a Roger Banastre are recorded there. In 1166/7 Alard Banastre accounted in Berkshire for 40*s.* from the pleas of Alan de Neville, probably for a forest offence; the debt had been paid off by Michaelmas 1168. If this Alard was identical with the man enfeoffed under Henry I, he was of age in 1135. At Easter 1170 Alard Banastre became sheriff of Oxfordshire, and remained in office until Michaelmas 1175, that is, throughout the rebellion of 1173–4. In 1173 or 1174 he and the constable of Oxford assessed a tallage on the borough of Oxford. But in 1176 he was one of many who were amerced for forest offences as royal authority was reaffirmed following the rebellion; his amercement was the fairly substantial one of 40 marks, and may indicate why he had been removed from office in the previous year. Some offenders subsequently received pardons, but Banastre had paid in full by Michaelmas 1177, when 1 mark was also accounted for from him, 'for a false summons'.

Alard Banastre was the second lay witness to a deed of Jocelin de Bohun, bishop of Salisbury (*d.* 1184), concerning land in Sonning, Berkshire, between *c.*1165 and 1173. He is also recorded as sheriff. He was the first witness to an agreement made before him in Oxfordshire county court between Godfrey, abbot of Eynsham, and Walkelin Harang; and among the records of an agreement made before Alard and the county of Oxfordshire between

Abbot Henry and the monks of Winchcombe, and William Taillard and his heirs, there occurs a deed of Alard Banastre himself, confirming and testifying to the agreement made, and issued with the counsel and consent of the county. It is not known when he died.

JULIA BOORMAN

Sources *Pipe rolls* • *VCH Berkshire*, 3.241–3, 430 • H. Hall, ed., *The Red Book of the Exchequer*, 3 vols., Rolls Series, 99 (1896), vol. 1, p. 308 • D. Royce, ed., *Landboc, sive, Registrum monasterii beatae Mariae virginis et sancti Cenhelmi de Winchelcumba*, 1 (1892), 186–93; 2 (1903), 184–7 • H. C. M. Lyte and others, eds., *Liber feodorum: the book of fees*, 3 vols. (1920–31), vol. 1, pp. 304, vol. 2, pp. 845, 849, 855–6 • W. Lyon, *Chronicles of Finchampstead, in the county of Berkshire* (1895) • H. E. Salter, ed., *Eynsham cartulary*, 1, OHS, 49 (1907), 94–5 • W. H. Rich Jones, ed., *Vetus registrum sarisberiense alias dictum registrum S. Osmundi episcopi: the register of St Osmund*, 2 vols., Rolls Series, 78 (1883–4), vol. 1, p. 249 • B. R. Kemp, ed., *Reading Abbey cartularies*, 2, CS, 4th ser., 33 (1987), 253–7 • *Chancery records*

Banastre [Banaster], **Gilbert** (*d.* **1487**), composer and poet, is of obscure origins, but was possibly related to (or even the son of) Henry Banaster (*d.* 1456) of Southwark, a yeoman of Henry VI's household. His mother, Alice, was still alive when he made his will. A birth date not later than *c.*1425 is suggested by the rhyming translation by 'Gilbert Banester'—the earliest surviving in English—of Boccaccio's 'Tale of Guiscardo and Ghismonda', which is dated before 1450 (BL, Add. MS 12524).

Banastre was working in or near London by 1456, when he joined the city's fraternity of St Nicholas. He also seems to have been associated with Canterbury: the chronicle of John Stone, a monk of Christ Church Priory, preserves a poem attributed (if uncertainly) to Banastre, *Miraculum sancti Thome martyris* (1467) (Corpus Christi College, Cambridge, MS 417), and a manuscript believed to have been copied there contains his *Vox saecli justi judices* and *Alleluia: laudate pueri*, liturgical pieces for two and three voices which were probably written *c.*1460 (Pepys Library, Magdalene College, Cambridge, MS 1236, fols. 15*v*–17*v*, 101–101*v*).

Banastre became a lay clerk of Edward IV's household chapel, first being mentioned as such on 25 February 1469 when granted a corrody in Daventry Priory. He acquired corrodies at more than ten religious foundations to supplement his salary and traded them with other members of the household in order to improve his financial portfolio. In 1479 (having started in the post the previous Michaelmas) he was formally promoted to master of the choristers, with a further 40 marks per annum to instruct the boy choristers. Like his successors, he may have diversified from training in plainsong and polyphony to the production of dramatic interludes outside the chapel—one dated 1482 has been attributed to him.

Banastre's extant compositions are mostly modest in scale. Later than the Pepys Library pieces are a three-part secular carol, 'My Feerfull Dreme' (BL, Add. MS 5465, fols. 77*v*–82), and, most important, a five-part motet, *O Maria et Elizabeth*, one of the earlier works to be found in the Eton choirbook (Eton College, MS 178, fols. 71*v*–74). Its text combines a prayer for peace and loyalty to an unspecified monarch with a narrative of the visitation story; its likeliest context is the marriage of Henry VII and Elizabeth of York in January 1486 or Elizabeth's pregnancy later that year. The complexities of its rich polyphonic structure appear to have overstretched Banastre's compositional technique. 'My Feerfull Dreme', less adventurous but more accomplished, shares several characteristics with the larger motet: a combination of simple syllabic declamation and florid cadential melisma, syncopation of rhythmic patterns, and cross-quotation of melodic cells.

Banastre had settled at East Greenwich, Kent, where he expressed a wish to be buried, when he made his will on 18 August 1487. He was dead by 1 September, when his corrodies began to be redistributed. The will also shows that he had actively developed his landed concerns—besides his own house and a quantity of silver and gilt, he left eleven tenements and several plots of land within the parishes of East Greenwich and Kidbrooke. He was survived not only by his mother, but also by his brother, Roger, his wife, Johann (Joan; perhaps his second wife), and four daughters, Agnes, Margaret, Elizabeth, and Alice.

JONATHAN HALL and MAGNUS WILLIAMSON

Sources J. Caldwell, 'Banaster, Gilbert', *New Grove*, 2.104 • A. Ashbee and D. Lasocki, eds., *A biographical dictionary of English court musicians, 1485–1714*, 1 (1998), 61–2 • M. Williamson, 'Royal image-making and textual interplay in Gilbert Banaster's *O Maria et Elizabeth*', *Early Music History* [forthcoming] • PRO, C1, C81, PSO1 • will, PRO, PROB 11/8 [Milles 11] • Eton, MS 178 • CCC Cam., MS 417 • Magd. Cam., Pepys Library, MS 1236 • S. R. Charles, 'The provenance and the date of the Pepys MS 1236', *Musica Disciplina*, 16 (1962), 57–71 • R. Bowers, 'Cambridge, Magdalene College, MS Pepys 1236', *Cambridge music manuscripts, 900–1600*, ed. I. Fenlon (1982), 111–14 • BL, Add. MSS 5465, 12524; Harley MS 543 • H. Wright, ed., *Early English versions of the tales of Guiscardo and Ghismonda and Titus and Gisippus from the 'Decameron'*, EETS, old ser., 205 (1937) • Norfolk RO, DCN 41/86 • *CPR*, 1429–36, 183; 1476–85, 133 • *CClR*

Archives BL, Add. MS 5465 • Eton, MS 178 | BL, Add. MS 12524 • CCC Cam., MS 417 • Magd. Cam., Pepys Library, MS 1236

Wealth at death see will, PRO, PROB 11/8 [Milles 11]

Banbury. For this title name *see* individual entries under Banbury; *see also* Knollys, William, first earl of Banbury (*c.*1545–1632); Knollys, Nicholas, third earl of Banbury (1631–1674) [*see under* Knollys, William, first earl of Banbury (*c.*1545–1632)]; Knollys, Charles, styled fourth earl of Banbury (*bap.* 1662, *d.* 1740); Knollys, William, styled eighth earl of Banbury (*bap.* 1763, *d.* 1834) [*see under* Knollys, Charles, styled fourth earl of Banbury (*bap.* 1662, *d.* 1740)].

Banbury, Frederick George, **first Baron Banbury of Southam** (**1850–1936**), politician and stockbroker, was born in London on 2 December 1850, the eldest son of Frederick Banbury of Shirley House, Surrey, and his wife, Cecilia Laura, daughter of William Cox of Woodford Hall, Essex. He was educated at Winchester College and afterwards abroad. In 1872 he was elected a member of the stock exchange and from 1879 until his retirement in 1906 was head of the firm of Frederick Banbury & Sons, stockbrokers; the firm was known for arranging foreign loans. At the general election of 1892 he was elected as a Conservative for the Peckham division of Camberwell, and he retained that seat until heavily defeated in 1906. In June

1906 he was returned unopposed at a by-election for the City of London and retained his seat until he entered the House of Lords in January 1924 as Baron Banbury of Southam in Warwickshire. In 1903 he was created a baronet and he was sworn of the privy council in 1916.

Although Banbury never held ministerial office, he made for himself a unique position as an opponent of legislation which appeared to him unnecessary and of change which he did not regard as progress. This was facilitated by his ability to talk at any length at any moment on any subject; unembarrassed by other MPs' complaints, he talked out many a clause and many a bill. He declared that in his opinion there was too much legislation and he generally opposed bills proposed by private members. His opposition prevented trams being allowed to cross London's bridges. His long experience in the City made him an able critic of finance bills, on which he was an undoubted authority, and a ferociously effective member of the public accounts committee, of which he was for a time chairman, and during the 1905–15 Liberal government he energetically exposed corruption. He was a member of the select committee on the Marconi scandal (1912–13) and of that on national expenditure (1919–20). He earned esteem by his technical knowledge, and his criticism of his own party was seldom resented. A master of House of Commons procedure, he was dextrous in raising points of order.

> Punctual in his attendance, he came to be regarded in his corner of a back bench as the uncompromising champion of the old order … He was always most carefully dressed, and with his formal frock-coat and tall hat, and his slow dignified carriage he would walk to his seat and look round at the increasingly slipshod attire of his colleagues with sad disapproval. The advent of women members into the house he regarded as nothing short of an outrage. Banbury, in fact, became an institution. (*The Times*)

A. G. Gardiner thought him 'the sort of person that our public-school system turns out in troops' (Gardiner, 336).

Banbury was for many years a member, and in 1927–8 chairman, of the council of the Royal Society for the Prevention of Cruelty to Animals and was prominent in Our Dumb Friends League. He was a director of the Great Northern Railway from 1903 and its chairman from 1917, and he was a director of the London and Provincial Bank. He married in 1873 Elizabeth Rosa (*d.* 1930), daughter and coheir of Thomas Barbot Beale of Brettenham Park, Suffolk; they had one son, who was killed in action in 1914, and one daughter. Banbury died at Warneford Place, Highworth, Wiltshire, on 13 August 1936, and was succeeded as baron by his grandson, Charles William (1915–1981).

E. I. Carlyle, *rev.* H. C. G. Matthew

Sources *The Times* (14 Aug 1936) · *Financial Times* (14 Aug 1936) · J. Ramsden, *The age of Balfour and Baldwin, 1902–1940* (1978) · D. T. A. Kynaston and R. P. T. Davenport-Hines, 'Banbury, Frederick George, 1st Lord Banbury of Southam', *DBB* · A. G. Gardiner, *Pillars of society* (1913) · G. R. Searle, *Corruption in British politics, 1895–1930* (1987)

Archives U. Warwick Mod. RC, company registers | HLRO, corresp. with Andrew Bonar Law · PRO, Rail 236

Likenesses B. Stone, photograph, 1899, NPG · J. Collier, oils, 1923, National Railway Museum, York · E. T. Reed, pencil drawing, NPG · caricature, NPG; repro. in *VF* (16 April 1913) · photograph, repro. in Gardiner, *Pillars of society*

Wealth at death £281,608 5*s.* 6*d.*: probate, 26 Oct 1936, *CGPLA Eng. & Wales*

Bancroft, Edward (1744–1821), chemist and spy, was born at Westfield, Massachusetts, on 9 January 1744. His tutor was Silas Deane, later a member of the American congress. After a brief apprenticeship to a physician in Connecticut, Bancroft went to sea at the age of eighteen. In 1763 he was in Dutch Guiana, where he extended his education and practised medicine.

Bancroft moved to England in 1767 and studied at St Bartholomew's Hospital in London. He began his literary career with *An essay on the natural history of Guiana … with an account of the religion, manners, and customs of several tribes of its Indian inhabitants* (1769), and in the same year he published *Remarks on the Review of the Controversy between Great Britain and her Colonies*, a critical response to William Knox (1732–1810) and George Grenville, in which Bancroft defended the rights of British colonies. In 1770 he published the novel *Charles Wentworth*, through which he expressed his ideas as a freethinker. He befriended Benjamin Franklin and Joseph Priestley, and through them began working for the journal *Monthly Review*.

Bancroft was elected a fellow of the Royal Society on 20 May 1773, and at that time was described as MB. Subsequently he was awarded his MD by Aberdeen University.

At the outbreak of war with the American colonies, Bancroft acted as a spy for Franklin. He was accused of conspiring with others in an attempt to burn Portsmouth Dockyard. (James Aitken was later arrested and executed for his part in the conspiracy.) Bancroft avoided arrest by escaping to France, where, in 1776, he turned king's evidence, and provided the British government with information acquired from Silas Deane, then an American commissioner based in Europe. From December 1776 Bancroft received regular payments from the British for his spying activities, and the American government continued to pay him for similar services until 1783. Bancroft sometimes used the alias Edwards during the colonial wars.

About two years after arriving in England, Bancroft began to study dyeing and calico printing. He made a number of trips to the Americas to study native woods for use as dyestuffs, and around 1771 discovered a yellow colourant present in the inner bark of the American black oak (*Quercus velutina*). In 1775 the British parliament passed an act providing Bancroft with patent rights for its importation and use. In 1785 Bancroft gained extended patent rights for the dye, which in the relevant act was called quercitron, a name that has been in use ever since. Bancroft's monopoly over control of the dye in England expired in 1799, when an application to extend his rights by a further seven years failed to pass the House of Lords due to opposition from northern calico printers. Ironically, the price of the bark trebled within a year.

In 1794 Bancroft published in London his *Experimental Researches Concerning the Philosophy of Permanent Colours*. It was a blend of practice and theory in which he demonstrated his ability to apply chemical knowledge to dyeing and printing. In the introduction he defined terms that entered the industry's vocabulary, namely, substantive dyes (those that do not require mordants) and adjective dyes (those that do). He also adopted the new nomenclature of chemistry introduced by French chemists a few years earlier. His writings on chemistry and dyeing were influential. His theories of colours and of attachment of dyes to fabrics appealed to leading chemists, including Claude-Louis Berthollet and Jean-Henri Hassenfratz, and contributed towards the downfall of Newton's mechanical theory of light. The theoretical discussion and polemics, however, were not appreciated by most practising dyers and printers during the first half of the nineteenth century.

After 1800 Bancroft made further journeys to North and South America, but without great success, in part due to his ill health. His loss of income from the quercitron monopoly probably prevented publication of a revised edition of his book, and of a second volume (as promised in the 1794 edition), until 1813. A United States edition was published in 1814. The German translation of 1817–18 was reprinted as late as 1834. Bancroft lived in reduced circumstances, probably even before the second edition of his book was published. However, he continued with the study of chemistry and dyeing.

Bancroft was married to Penelope Fellows; Edward Nathaniel *Bancroft was their son. He died at his home in Margate on 8 September 1821. His quercitron was used as a colourant in the dyeing industry until the early 1900s.

ANTHONY S. TRAVIS

Sources A. S. MacNalty, 'Edward Bancroft, MD, FRS, and the War of American Independence', *Proceedings of the Royal Society of Medicine*, 38 (1944–5), 7–15 • G. T. Anderson and D. K. Anderson, 'Edward Bancroft: aberrant "practitioner of physick"', *Medical History*, 17 (1973), 356–67 • S. M. Edelstein, 'Historical notes on the wet processing industry, VI: the dual life of Edward Bancroft', *American Dyestuff Reporter*, 43 (1954), 712–13, 735 • A. E. Shapiro, *Fits, passions, paroxysms: physics, method and chemistry and Newton's theories of colored bodies and fits of easy reflection* (1993) • C. A. Browne, 'A sketch of the life and chemical theories of Dr. Edward Bancroft', *Journal of Chemical Education*, 14 (1937), 103–7 • *IGI*

Likenesses N. Branwhite, group portrait, stipple engraving, pubd 1801 (after S. Medley, 1800), BM [*see illus.*] • photograph (after portrait), RS

Bancroft, Edward Nathaniel (1772–1842), physician, son of Edward *Bancroft (1744–1821), American spy and writer on natural history, and Penelope Fellows, was born in London and received his schooling under Dr Charles Burney and Dr Samuel Parr. He was entered at St John's College, Cambridge, in 1789, and graduated BM in 1794. In 1795 he was appointed a physician to the forces. Bancroft served in the Windward Islands, in Portugal, in the Mediterranean, and with Abercromby's expedition to Egypt in 1801. On his return to England he proceeded MD at Cambridge, in 1804, and began to practise as a physician in London, retaining half-pay rank in the army. He joined the Royal College of Physicians in 1805, became a fellow in 1806 and in the same year was appointed to give the Goulstonian lectures, and was made a censor in 1808, at the comparatively early age of thirty-six.

At this time Bancroft wrote two polemical pamphlets: *A letter to the commissioners of military enquiry, containing animadversions on some parts of their fifth report* (1808) and *Exposure of misrepresentations by Dr McGrigor and Dr Jackson to the*

Edward Bancroft (1744–1821), by Nathan Branwhite, pubd 1801 (after Samuel Medley, 1800) [*Institutors of the Medical Society of London*; standing, far left]

commissioners of military enquiry (1808). Both publications addressed proposed changes in the army medical department, specifically in the distinctions between physician to the forces and regimental surgeon. Bancroft argued for the precedence of the former in the military-medical hierarchy, because 'for one officer or soldier who is likely to want the aid of a surgeon, 20 may be expected to want that of a physician' (Bancroft, *Letter*, 1808). His opponents in the controversy were two army medical officers holding Scottish degrees, James McGrigor (afterwards created baronet, and director-general of the army medical department) and Robert Jackson. McGrigor charged Bancroft with lack of accuracy and candour, and with partiality. Jackson accused him of being 'presumptuous in his professional rank, which he conceives to be superior to actual knowledge' (Jackson). Bancroft wanted the best physicians admitted to the military and he believed that they could be drawn from civilian circles, not simply from the lower ranks (of regimental surgeons) of the military-medical hierarchy. Civilian physicians, he argued, had more experience in medical matters generally, and were therefore better equipped to be admitted to the upper military-medical ranks than regimental surgeons.

During this year of great disagreement with colleagues, Bancroft was appointed a physician to St George's Hospital. In 1811, however, he gave up his practice in London owing to ill health, but not before publishing his most memorable and well-received work, *An essay on the disease called yellow fever, with observations concerning febrile contagion, typhus fever, dysentery, and the plague, partly delivered as the Gulstonian lectures before the College of Physicians in the years 1806 and 1807* (1811), a *Sequel* to which was published in 1817. Although Bancroft's *Essay* mistakenly associated the development of yellow fever with malarious conditions, this conclusion was none the less adopted by contemporaries largely because of the author's skill in explaining away entire sets of facts vouched for by authorities such as Sir John Pringle, Donald Marvo, and Sir Gilbert Blane.

In 1811, Bancroft resumed his full-pay rank as physician to the forces and proceeded to Jamaica. He remained there until his death on 18 September 1842 in Kingston. After his death the physicians and surgeons of Jamaica placed a mural tablet to Bancroft's memory in the cathedral church of Kingston, commemorating his 'acute and accurate reasoning' and his keen ability 'as a polemical writer' to 'form the facts or arguments of an antagonist against himself' (Munk, *Roll*, 1818, 68).

CHARLES CREIGHTON, *rev.* JEFFREY S. REZNICK

Sources Munk, *Roll* • E. N. Bancroft, *A letter to the commissioners of military enquiry, containing animadversions on some parts of their fifth report* (1808) • E. Bancroft, *Exposure of misrepresentations by Dr McGrigor and Dr Jackson to the commissioners of military enquiry* (1808) • J. McGrigor, *A letter to the commissioners of military enquiry* (1808) • J. McGrigor, *A reply to some animadversions of Dr Bancroft* (1808) • R. Jackson, *A letter to the commissioners of military enquiry with a refutation of errors and misrepresentations contained in a letter by Dr Bancroft* (1808) • C. Murchison, *A treatise on the continued fevers of Great Britain* (1862) • Venn, *Alum. Cant.* • *IGI*

Bancroft, George (*d.* 1573?), religious writer and Church of England clergyman, is first recorded in 1544, when he was presented by Giles Gore, esquire, to the Wiltshire rectory of Grittleton. On 14 October 1547, still incumbent of Grittleton and now also chaplain to William Parr, marquess of Northampton, he was dispensed to hold another benefice. In that same year he was presented to Nettleton by John Butler of Great Badminton. In 1548 he published, as a translation from the Latin, *The answere that the preachers of the gospel at Basile made for the defence of the true administration and use of the holy supper of Our Lord. Agaynst the abhomination of the popyshe masse.* It is dedicated to 'his singular good Master Silvester Butler', who, appearances notwithstanding, was his patron's wife, elsewhere impartially recorded as Silvester and Silvestra.

Bancroft's translation of his unidentified original constitutes a modest contribution to Reformation debate. His preface and the main text alike follow a strongly reformist line. Both mount a fierce attack on the Catholic mass as idolatrous and detestable and on the priests who administer it, denounced by Bancroft for their avarice—'whan they here of any riche manes death they flocke together lyke ravennes to a dead carren' (sig. Aiiiv); in the translation they are castigated for pride as well. In the latter English readers are instructed that the Lord's supper is an act of commemoration, rather than a renewal of Christ's sacrifice, that Catholic priests err when they 'denye that we are Justified by fayth only ascribinge part of our justificacion to good workes' (sig. Eiii), and that indeed 'there be no priestes nowe appointed of God to offer for synnes, but every christian man is ordeined of Christe to be a prieste' (sig. Fiiiiv). Such teaching was fully in accord with protestant doctrine as laid down by leading Swiss reformers, and now increasingly propagated in England.

The theological content of *The answere* seems likely to have appealed to Bancroft's patrons. Northampton was an evangelical, and so was Andrew Baynton, who in 1554 presented Bancroft to the living of Bromham. Bancroft was deprived of Grittleton and Nettleton in the same year, but presumably thanks to Baynton's protection he retained Bromham, and apparently also Yatton Keynell, where the advowson was shared by his former patron Giles Gore throughout Mary's reign. It must have helped him that Baynton does not seem to have flaunted his protestantism, whereas in 1557 Mrs Butler was pardoned her involvement in a conspiracy in the course of which she was said to have exclaimed, 'I wold the Kyng and Quene were in the sea in a botomles vessell' (*CPR, 1555–7*, 400–01). Bancroft resigned Yatton Keynell in 1560 but was at some point reinstated in Grittleton, holding that living and Bromham until he died, probably in 1573, when successors were presented to both benefices following Bancroft's death.

HENRY SUMMERSON

Sources G. Bancroft, *The answere that the preachers of the gospel at Basile made* (1548) [*RSTC* 1544] • T. Phillipps, *Institutiones clericorum in comitatu Wiltoniae*, 1 (1825) • D. S. Chambers, ed., *Faculty office registers, 1534–1549* (1966) • *CPR, 1555–7*

Bancroft, Ian Powell, Baron Bancroft (1922–1996), civil servant, was born at Risedale Maternity Home, Barrow in Furness, Lancashire, on 23 December 1922, the only son of Alfred Ernest Bancroft (*b.* 1886), a schoolmaster who later

Ian Powell Bancroft, Baron Bancroft (1922–1996), by unknown photographer, 1977

became an inspector of schools, and his wife, Lilian, *née* Stokes (*b.* 1889). He was educated at Coatham School, Cleveland, where he became head of school, and from where he won a scholarship to Balliol College, Oxford, to read English. Graduating with a second-class degree in 1942, he immediately joined the rifle brigade, serving with the 7th armoured division throughout the landings in Normandy and the advance through France and Germany. Demobilized with the rank of captain in 1945, he returned briefly to Balliol College for a year's further study.

Civil service career Bancroft joined the civil service in 1947 as one of the 'reconstruction' entrants and was posted to the Treasury, where he was quickly marked out as someone who had the potential to go very high in the service. He was soon made private secretary to Sir Henry Wilson Smith, a second secretary, and then assistant private secretary, first under William Armstrong and then under Louis Petch, to the chancellor of the exchequer, R. A. Butler. When Butler left the Treasury on becoming lord privy seal in December 1955, he took Bancroft with him as his private secretary; he later described Bancroft as 'the best Private Secretary I ever had' (*The Independent*). Before returning to the Treasury Bancroft served a spell in the Cabinet Office. Once back in the Treasury he was promoted to assistant secretary in the public expenditure divisions. In 1964 he became principal private secretary to the chancellor of the exchequer, first to Reginald Maudling and then, on the change of government, to James Callaghan. Meanwhile, on 28 June 1950 he had married Jean Hilda Patricia Swaine (*b.* 1925), daughter of David Richard Swaine, an inspector of schools. They had two sons and a daughter, and enjoyed a long and very happy marriage.

On leaving the private office in 1966 Bancroft was promoted to under-secretary in the establishment side of the Treasury. Following the recommendations of the Fulton commission on the civil service, this part of the Treasury was hived off in 1968 to become the major part of the newly created Civil Service Department, under William Armstrong as permanent secretary and head of the home civil service. Bancroft's duties there included responsibility for the machinery of government division of the Civil Service Department, which was involved in the many proposals to change the functions of departments and the boundaries between them in which successive prime ministers liked to indulge. One of the several major departmental changes in which he played an important part at this time was the proposed amalgamation of three departments—housing and local government, transport, and public building and works—to form the Department of the Environment. Once the decision to amalgamate was taken Bancroft was sent to the Department of the Environment to assist the process by being appointed its director-general of establishments on promotion to deputy secretary. He had the task of overseeing the merging of the central organizations of three departments with quite different structures, traditions, and priorities, into a single co-ordinating division. Such mergers inevitably affect adversely the career prospects of many individuals and can damage staff morale generally. Bancroft was helped by the fact that he was an outsider and not suspected of favouring one of the merging departments against the others. By 1972 he had helped his permanent secretary to create a well-integrated department which was functioning well and in which morale was high. He had as a result gained a reputation as an organizer and manager who was particularly good in the field of staff relations, and this strongly influenced the rest of his career.

Bancroft's success at the Department of the Environment led to his next step when, at the end of 1972, he was moved to customs and excise with the expectation that he would take over as head of that department when its permanent secretary, Sir Louis Petch, reached retiring age a few months later. There was, however, a change of plan as the Civil Service Department needed him back. Sir William Armstrong, its permanent secretary, was being used by the prime minister, Edward Heath, as his principal adviser on economic policy, in preference to relying on the Treasury. The main economic problem facing the government was how to reduce the level of unemployment, which was regarded as unacceptably high, yet at the same time contain the rising pressure in the economy on costs and prices. The government was attempting to deal with these problems by a strategy which combined a relatively expansionary fiscal policy with a tight control of public sector pay (and later of pay and prices generally). This involved actions which breached previous understandings about the principles governing civil service pay, and was not only producing unrest and low morale in the civil service generally but also a call for industrial action by some members of civil service unions. Armstrong did not have the time to deal with these civil service problems. A new post of second permanent secretary was therefore created in the Civil Service Department, and Bancroft was brought back to fill it on promotion. He made his primary objective the removal of some of the resentment and ill feeling among civil servants, by demonstrating that civil service managers were aware of the problems that the civil service unions were experiencing and by seeking through negotiation in the civil service Whitley councils to find ways of dealing with the more sensitive issues. While he was successful in improving relations between civil service managers and staff, this could not lead to any major change in the Heath government's policies, which became more rigid with the passing of legislation to enforce the control of prices and incomes. Even with some relaxation after the change of government in early 1974, the inherent conflict between central government economic strategies and the traditional way of negotiating public sector remuneration remained. The continuing problems of the economy at large meant that pay issues, low morale, and industrial unrest would overhang civil service management for many years and severely affect the last period of Bancroft's civil service career.

At the end of 1975 Bancroft went back to the Department of the Environment as its permanent secretary. It had already seemed likely that he would become the next head of the home civil service and that a spell as a departmental permanent secretary would provide him with valuable experience. In the Department of the Environment he had again to deal with issues that required sensitive handling. Relations between central and local government were deteriorating. The Layfield report on local government had pointed to the excessive dependence of local government on central government finance, and had recommended major changes in the financing arrangements in order to give local authorities more independence and responsibility. These proposals, while welcomed by local government bodies, were not in the circumstances of the time acceptable to central government. Local authorities were already increasingly overspending the public expenditure allocations agreed by ministers, and the government feared that this tendency would be augmented by greater independence. With public expenditure as a whole growing faster than central government wanted, the mood at the centre was for more rather than less control of local government spending, particularly in the context of general public expenditure cuts in 1976. Local authorities were therefore becoming both disappointed and resentful.

The general direction of policy towards local government fell to the Department of the Environment, although other Whitehall departments had degrees of responsibility for some services administered through local government bodies. Bancroft's experience of working with departments in the context of Treasury expenditure control was valuable in securing the co-ordination and cohesion of the approaches of central government to local government issues, and at the same time he quickly established good personal relationships with local government leaders. In most respects the amalgamation of departments into the Department of the Environment, which Bancroft had earlier done so much to bring about, had proved to be one of the more successful changes in the machinery of government.

The decision of the prime minister in 1976 to split the Department of the Environment and create a separate Department of Transport therefore came as a great shock to Bancroft, as it seemed to be about to destroy the work of many civil servants over several years. However, close and friendly co-operation between Bancroft and Peter Baldwin, who became permanent secretary of the Department of Transport, enabled a number of collaborative functions to be retained, especially the maintenance of common staff lists and a common staffing organization. Once again Bancroft's way of discussing issues with his colleagues and the staff associations concerned, and his sensitive handling of the staff most affected by the change, reduced the upset created by the reorganization.

Bancroft's experience and achievements made him a strong candidate to succeed Sir Douglas Allen as head of the home civil service when Allen retired at the end of 1977. But by then the continuing problems of morale and increasing militancy over pay issues in the civil service were having to be handled in a political environment which had become far more critical of all aspects of public administration. On appointment as head of the civil service Bancroft found that the economic situation and policies of the time gave very little room for manoeuvre. His problems increased with the change of government in 1979. The new prime minister, Margaret Thatcher, was determined to improve the efficiency of the civil service by bringing in private sector methods and by cutting staff numbers. She was very critical of what she regarded as the negative attitudes of senior civil servants when they were made to contemplate new ideas. Bancroft accepted that the civil service would have to be reduced substantially and that the Civil Service Department would have to play a key role in that reduction, but he felt that the management problems with which his senior colleagues would have to grapple as numbers were reduced and posts eliminated were insufficiently understood in no. 10. His attempt to persuade the prime minister that some of her criticisms of senior civil servants were unfair was seen as an example of the weakness which the prime minister believed permeated government departments generally and the Civil Service Department in particular. He persuaded the prime minister to give a dinner to permanent secretaries at which he hoped that a better understanding might be achieved, if problems could be discussed informally in a relaxed atmosphere. It proved to be a disaster. The explanation of difficulties merely persuaded the prime minister that very few of the permanent secretaries were 'one of us', and she ended the dinner unexpectedly early. From that moment Bancroft's position became increasingly untenable.

The prime minister's decision in November 1981 to abolish the Civil Service Department and divide its functions between the Treasury and the Cabinet Office brought to an abrupt end the concept of a separate department for civil service affairs which had been the major recommendation of the Fulton commission's report of 1969. Bancroft's distinguished career as a civil servant came to a premature and distressing end along with his department. It also permanently affected the balance of top civil service posts. The functions of the head of the civil service were initially divided between the secretary of the cabinet and the permanent secretary of the Treasury as joint heads of the service, but on the subsequent retirement of the then permanent secretary of the Treasury, Sir Douglas Wass, in 1983, the cabinet secretary became the head of the civil service. Bancroft was bitter about the decision to abolish his department but accepted it with dignity, and did what he could to ensure that his colleagues did not suffer unduly. In recognition of his public services, in 1982 he was offered and accepted a life peerage (he had already been made CB in 1971, KCB in 1975, and GCB in 1979). He became a cross-bencher.

Post-civil service career After leaving the civil service Bancroft took on a number of non-executive directorships, including the Rugby Group, Grindlays Bank, Bass, and Sun Life (of which he had a spell as deputy chairman). He was a visiting fellow of Nuffield College, Oxford, from 1973 to 1981, and chairman of the Royal Hospital and Home, Putney, from 1984 to 1988. Despite these commitments, however, he continued to devote attention to civil service affairs, and in speeches and lectures expressed his concern that the unity and integrity of the civil service was being endangered by over-rapid changes, the full consequences of which had not been adequately considered. He became a very effective speaker on these issues in the House of Lords, where his turn of phrase and keen wit injected a sharp sting into his criticism of government policies affecting the public services. Especially irate about the Conservative government's proposal in 1996 to privatize the recruitment and assessment agency of the civil service commission, he played a very persuasive role in the debate on that proposal in the House of Lords, which led to a government defeat in the relevant vote there and to the setting up of a select committee of the House of Lords to report on the public service. But by that time Bancroft was too ill to serve on that committee himself. He lived to see the special report of the select committee, which recommended that the recruitment and assessment agency should not be privatized, and the rejection of that recommendation by the government, which gave a contract to a private company. In February 1999 the Labour government announced that the selection stages of the fast stream recruitment process would be returned to direct civil service management when that contract expired in 2001; Bancroft would have been delighted.

Character As a civil servant Bancroft was conscientious and hard working, calm, and fully in control, taking care to plan and organize his work in co-operation with his colleagues, and an excellent team leader. He was well liked and highly regarded by all his staff and colleagues and by the ministers he served, especially valued for his support as a private secretary. He was always concerned about the well-being of those who worked with him and saw great virtues in the long-established traditions of the civil service, as typified in many of the senior officials under whom he had worked in his younger days. Having entered the civil service at a time when memories of wartime co-operation between government and both sides of industry were strong and there was a high degree of consensus on economic policy issues, he always looked for ways to find solutions to problems by securing agreement on policies after dispassionate analysis. The integrity of the service, the absence of corruption, and the outlawing of patronage were objectives he fought for and was prepared to defend against all proposals he regarded as damaging to them. He became head of the civil service when many of those traditions he valued were being questioned, and he greatly regretted his inability to persuade politicians that some of the proposed changes affecting the service could be severely damaging both to standards of service and to the integrity of government. Unlike many of his colleagues he appeared to enjoy being cross-examined by parliamentary committees about the work of his departments, seeing this as an opportunity to foster a better understanding of departmental objectives. By contrast, however, in the light of the difficulties he experienced, he was reluctant to be interviewed by the media while a civil servant, and warned his senior colleagues against undue exposure. But he no longer felt the need for such restraint after he had left the civil service, and he became a very effective participant and campaigner in various public causes. He died at Trinity Hospice, London, on 19 November 1996, of liver cancer, and was cremated on 25 November. He was survived by his wife and three children. DOUGLAS CROHAM

Sources personal knowledge (2004) • private information (2004) [Lady Bancroft] • *WWW* • *The Times* (21 Nov 1996) • *The Independent* (22 Nov 1996) • *Daily Telegraph* (21 Nov 1996) • b. cert. • m. cert. • J. Jones and S. Viney, eds., *The Balliol College register, 1930–1980*, 5th edn (privately printed, Oxford, 1983?)
Archives SOUND BL NSA, current affairs recording
Likenesses photograph, 1977, Hult. Arch.; repro. in *The Independent* [*see illus.*] • photograph, repro. in *The Times* • photograph, repro. in *Daily Telegraph*
Wealth at death under £180,000: probate, 27 Feb 1997, *CGPLA Eng. & Wales*

Bancroft, John (1574–1641), bishop of Oxford, was born at Asthall, Oxfordshire, between Burford and Minster Lovell in the Cotswolds. His father, Christopher, was brother of Richard *Bancroft (*d.* 1610), bishop of London and later archbishop of Canterbury, and through his paternal grandmother he was great-great-nephew of Hugh Curwen, the second bishop of Oxford. He was educated at Westminster School and as a Westminster student went up to Christ Church, Oxford, in 1592. There he took the degrees of BA on 16 June 1596 and MA on 21 May 1599. He was twenty-seven when his uncle presented him to the

John Bancroft (1574–1641), by unknown artist, *c.*1632–5

rectory of Finchley, Middlesex, vacant by the death of Richard Latewar. Seven years later he resigned it when his uncle, now archbishop, offered him Orpington in Kent (27 May 1608). Bancroft further increased his nephew's income by granting him two sinecures in Kent, those of Woodchurch (1609) and Biddenden (1610). On 23 October 1609 John Bancroft was presented with the prebend of Maplesbury in St Paul's Cathedral, on the elevation of Samuel Harsnett to the episcopate.

Having gained his BD degree on 9 July 1607, Bancroft was made DD on 25 June 1610 after successfully defending the conformist thesis 'major est auctoritas scripturae quam ecclesiae' ('the authority of scripture is greater than that of the church'). On 2 March 1610 he had been elected master of University College, Oxford, probably at the behest of his uncle, who as archbishop was the college's visitor. A tireless administrator, over the next twenty-three years Bancroft set the college on a sound financial basis, and in 1629 he was among those chosen to oversee the revision of the university's statutes. His mastership of University College ended on 23 August 1632, soon after he had been consecrated bishop of Oxford at the hands of Archbishop Abbot on 10 June.

That he owed his see to his friend William Laud, as William Prynne later alleged, is undoubtedly true, but if there is truth in Prynne's defamation of Bancroft as 'a corrupt, unpreaching popish prelate' (Prynne, 353), it is only in the charge of Bancroft's lack of preaching, for, singularly among those whom Charles I sanctioned to become his bishops, Bancroft had seemingly never served as a chaplain-in-ordinary and was absent, even as a bishop, from any royal pulpit; for Palm Sunday 1635 Archbishop Laud entered Bancroft's name as an alternative to his own in case he did not preach the Lent sermon at court, but in the event he did. The Short Parliament ceased sitting before Bancroft's designated Sunday duty on 24 May 1640 and he died before he could preach his turn during the Long Parliament.

Rather, Bancroft's appointment was the result of Laud's determination to build a new courtyard at his old Oxford college of St John's, and it is Bancroft's work in the building of Canterbury Quadrangle that has most contributed to the preservation of his memory in Oxford. He acted as both broker and chief fundraiser for his friend Laud. At 16 April 1636 the final account showed that, of the £3260 10*s.* 5*d.* raised for the quadrangle, £3170 had been remitted by Bancroft allowing, as William Juxon, president of St John's, had assured Laud, for the grander court, 'of the largest size that Art can allowe' (Juxon to Laud, 12 March 1632, PRO, SP 16/214/38), and the surviving receipts show regular and substantial payments for the new building. By the terms of his will Bancroft asked that the proceeds from selling half his books should go to Laud's other major project, the repair of St Paul's Cathedral.

In the diocese Bancroft was a noted upholder of the conformist position and may, like Laud himself, have imposed only the railing-in and eastward position of the holy table when enforcing Laud's metropolitical injunctions (Davies, 218). He sanctioned the remodelling of furnishings at his cathedral church, consecrating communion plate as well as ecclesiastical fixtures of a new pulpit, reading desk, and communion table there on 18 December 1636 after an ordination. Dean Fell commented that the form of words used was as 'pious and serious' (Bodl. Oxf., MS Rawl. D 399, fol. 280) as the form for consecrating churches drawn up by Lancelot Andrewes. Similar regard for propriety and correct usage led him to become embroiled in arguments over the repair of a spire at Witney in 1638, in the 1639 altercation between John Dowson and his parishioners at Maidenhead, and in vigorously demanding winter repairs at the decaying church at Churchill in 1639–40. Richard Gardiner, in *A Sermon Concerning the Epiphany* (1639), congratulated Bancroft on restoring altars to their primitive accustomed places in churches, and beyond the diocese he consecrated the chapel, 'newly built and recently embellished' (Nicolson, 28), at Sissinghurst on 15 September 1639.

Bancroft was concerned to prevent lax ordinations and in 1639 refused to ordain twenty men whom he regarded as unsuitable candidates: they were, however, later ordained in other dioceses. It was later alleged, in charges that might have been brought against him had he lived, that he required his examining chaplain, Edward Fulham, to ask all ordinands whether the order of bishops was a divine institution, bowing at the name of Jesus a pious ceremony, and 'whether a Minister may not with a safe conscience administer the sacrament to one not kneelinge?' (Bodl. Oxf., MS Rawl. D 353, fol. 159, articles 5, 6, 8). The more trenchant question, of theology rather than practice, was whether 'Christ did locally descend into hell' (ibid., 9).

Little more than a year into his episcopate at Oxford, Bancroft was being discussed as a possible successor to

Laud as bishop of London (E. Nicholas to Sir J. Pennington, 12 Aug 1633, PRO, SP 16/244/53), but he was to remain in the diocese until his death. By collating himself to the vicarage of Cuddesdon (reckoned to be worth £70 per annum), which was later annexed in perpetuity to his see by royal warrant, Bancroft was able to build a much needed palace for himself and his successors at Cuddesdon, 7 miles out of Oxford. Something of the scope of the property was glimpsed when Archbishop Laud, with his retinue of fifty mounted servants, stayed there in August 1636 *en route* for the royal celebrations that marked the completion of his Canterbury Quadrangle. Bancroft died in London on 11 February 1641 and his body was taken back to Cuddesdon and buried below the south transept wall of the parish church the next day, 'without any other monument then a plaine stone' (PRO, PROB 11/186/80). He never married. His new episcopal palace was soon demolished for fear of its falling into parliamentarian hands.

NICHOLAS W. S. CRANFIELD

Sources Foster, *Alum. Oxon.* • *Reg. Oxf.*, 2.10 • *The works of the most reverend father in God, William Laud*, ed. J. Bliss and W. Scott, 7 vols. (1847–60) • J. Davies, *The Caroline captivity of the church: Charles I and the remoulding of Anglicanism, 1625–1641* (1992) • PRO, SP 16/214/38; 16/244/53; 16/260/80; 16/269/89; 16/272/28; 16/273/48; 16/274/58; 16/277/62; 16/283/86; 16/289/47; 16/297/17; 16/300/65; 16/311/58; 16/318/34; 16/331/14; 16/350/24; 16/379/30; 16/385/91; 16/410/95; 16/432/92; 16/445/55 • R. Thompson, MS history, Bodl. Oxf., MS Tanner 147 • Bodl. Oxf., MS Rawl. D. 353, 399 • R. Gardiner, *A sermon concerning the Epiphany* (1639) • N. Nicolson, *Sissinghurst Castle* (1964) • W. Prynne, *Canterburies doome, or, The first part of a compleat history of the commitment, charge, tryall, condemnation, execution of William Laud, late arch-bishop of Canterbury* (1646) • PRO, LC 5/134 • PRO, PROB 11/186/80 • Wood, *Ath. Oxon.*

Likenesses oils, after 1632, Christ Church Oxf. • oils, *c.*1632–1635, University College, Oxford [*see illus.*]

Bancroft, John (1655–1696), playwright and surgeon, was born in London, perhaps in the Postern, on 3 June 1655, the son of John Bancroft (*bap.* 1614, *d.* 1705), sergeant carver to the lord mayor from 1660, and his second wife, Rebecka, *née* Cole (*bap.* 1631, *d.* 1711). He was apprenticed to the surgeon Richard Wiseman on 3 September 1669 and later practised in the fashionable Covent Garden area. Becoming 'infected by the Vicinity of the Wits with Poetry' (Gildon, 5), he wrote a blank-verse tragedy, *Sertorius*, which was staged at Drury Lane early in 1679 and published shortly afterwards as by 'John Bancroft, Gent.' It was not a success. His *King Edward the Third*, premièred late in 1690, was published anonymously in 1691. The actor William Mountfort signed the dedicatory letter, describing the play as 'a Present to me'. Mountfort doubtless prepared the play for the stage and oversaw the production; the epilogue stated that the author's payment was to go to 'the Player'. It fitted the political temper of the time and did well, Queen Mary and her maids of honour seeing it at Drury Lane on 4 February 1691. An anonymous adaptation, *The Fall of Mortimer*, was popular in 1731 as an anti-Walpole piece. The *Gentleman's Journal* for October 1692 (appearing in late November) announced: 'A new Play, by the Author of that call'd *Edward the Third*, which gave such universal satisfaction, hath been acted several times with applause' (p. 24). This was *Henry the Second*, which also appeared anonymously in 1693 with a dedication signed by Mountfort, who presumably again reworked the play where necessary. The play had strong acting roles for Thomas Betterton as the king, Elizabeth Barry as the jealous queen, and Anne Bracegirdle as the fair Rosamond. It opened on 8 November 1692 and was performed every day until at least 14 November, when the queen was present. Late in the evening of 9 December Mountfort was attacked by Captain Richard Hill and Lord Mohun, after their failed attempt at abducting Anne Bracegirdle. Bancroft, hurriedly summoned to Mountfort's house after midnight, found the actor 'very Desperately wounded' (Egerton MS 2623, fol. 47*v*) and stayed with him until four o'clock. He returned at eight, remaining until he was called to give evidence to the justices. Mountfort, who died that afternoon, told Bancroft that Hill, not Mohun, stabbed him. Bancroft was a witness at Mohun's trial, Hill having escaped.

John Bancroft married Diana King (1658–1709) of Ashby-de-la-Launde, Lincolnshire. Four of their children, three of whom died in infancy, were baptized at St Paul's, Covent Garden, between 1681 and 1692, and Bancroft was buried there on 1 September 1696.

OLIVE BALDWIN and THELMA WILSON

Sources [C. Gildon], *The lives and characters of the English dramatick poets … first begun by Mr Langbain* [1699] • A. S. Borgman, *The life and death of William Mountfort* (1935) • W. Van Lennep and others, eds., *The London stage, 1660–1800*, pt 1: *1660–1700* (1965) • A. H. Scouten, ed., *The London stage, 1660–1800*, pt 3: *1729–1747* (1961) • *Gentleman's Journal* (Oct 1692) • *The tryal of Charles Lord Mohun* (1693) • BL, Egerton MS 2623 • registers of apprentice bindings of the Barber-Surgeons' Company • D. C. R. Francombe and D. E. Coult, *Bancroft's School, 1737–1937* (1937) • K. R. Wing, *A history of Bancroft's School, 1737–1987* (1987) • parish register, St Dunstan-in-the-East, 8 June 1655 [baptism] • parish register, Covent Garden, St Paul's, 1 Sept 1696 [burial]

Bancroft [*née* Wilton], **Marie Effie**, **Lady Bancroft** (1839–1921), actress and theatre manager, was born on 12 January 1839, probably in Doncaster, the eldest of the six daughters of Robert Pleydell Wilton (1800–1873), a provincial actor, and his wife, Georgina Jane (1818–1866), the daughter of Samuel Faulkner, proprietor of the London *Morning Chronicle*.

Burlesque actress Marie Wilton was taught elocution by her mother and began performing at the age of six, playing the emperor of Lilliput in a pantomime, *Gulliver's Travels* (Manchester, 1846), followed by Fleance in *Macbeth* and Prince Arthur in *King John*. She won praise from both Macready and Charles Kemble for these Shakespearian roles. In 1856 Charles Dillon cast her in the important part of his son Henri in the long-running melodrama *Belphegor* by Charles Webb at the London Lyceum. By 1858 she was playing both boys and young girls in the burlesques of H. J. Byron at the Strand Theatre. Although modern commentators suggest that sexual titillation was the main appeal of cross-dressing in the Victorian theatre, there was a long tradition of actresses playing adolescent boys in serious drama, and, according to Charles Dickens, Wilton as Pippo in Byron's *The Maid and the Magpie* was 'so stupendously like a boy, and unlike a woman, that it is perfectly

Marie Effie Bancroft, Lady Bancroft (1839–1921), by Barraud, 1885 [with her husband, Squire Bancroft]

free from offence'. The training in both technique and characterization gained from playing *en travestie* stood Wilton in good stead throughout her career. Tom Robertson's description of the 'burlesque actress' in the *Illustrated Times* (1860) indicates the range of talents expected of such a performer:

> She can waltz, polk, dance a *pas seul* or a sailor's hornpipe, La Sylphide, or Genu-ine Transatlantic Cape Cod Skedaddle, with equal grace and spirit; and as for acting she can declaim à la Phelps or Fechter; is serious, droll; and must play farce, tragedy, opera, comedy, melodrama, pantomime, ballet, change her costume, fight a combat, make love, poison herself, die, and take one encore for a song and another for a dance, in the short space of ten minutes.

Clement Scott, a lifelong devotee, claimed that Wilton's 'genius' was matched only by that of the legendary burlesque actor Frederick Robson.

Management and marriage However, for both professional and social reasons, Wilton did not want to remain typecast in burlesque. In 1864 she planned a management partnership with Byron, performing some burlesques, but extending the repertory beyond that of the Strand Theatre. On 15 April 1865 she opened the refurbished Queen's Theatre, Tottenham Street, as the Prince of Wales's, to which she hoped to attract a 'respectable' audience from the residential districts of Bloomsbury, Regent's Park, and St John's Wood. She introduced upholstered stalls into the pit, which was carpeted, and flower vases into the boxes, giving it a 'bright and bonnie appearance' (Bancroft and Bancroft, *Recollections*). The first season relied on the light comedies and burlesques in which she had made her reputation, but the production of Tom Robertson's *Society* (11 November 1865) was such a success that it 'was destined to expel burlesque from the Prince of Wales's stage and to establish a new method in authorship, decoration and acting' (Archer, 5.25). For this play she hired two actors she had worked with in Liverpool the previous summer, neither of whom had been born into the profession. The first was John Hare, a clever mimic who specialized in playing old men. The other, whose professional attraction was his manner of confident sociability, was **Squire Bancroft** (1841–1926). He had been born Squire White Butterfield on 14 May 1841 in Rotherhithe, the son of Secundus Bancroft White Butterfield (*d.* 1846/7), an oil merchant, and his wife, Julia, the daughter of Thomas Anthony Wright. The death of his father when Squire was only five meant that he was not sent to public school, but was educated in private schools in London and France.

In search of a career, Bancroft went in 1860 to New York, where he saw E. A. Sothern create his famous caricature aristocrat, Lord Dundreary, in *Our American Cousin*. Sothern was not of a theatrical family, and his success may have inspired Bancroft to break with his own family to become an actor, starting in January 1861 at the Theatre Royal, Birmingham, under the name of Squire Bancroft. He played at several provincial theatres, notably at Liverpool with Mr and Mrs Alfred Wigan, exponents of restrained 'naturalistic' acting, where he first performed with Marie Wilton. Archer described him as 'an actor of limited range, but, within that range, of remarkable intelligence, refinement and power … Quiet humour, subdued feeling and unflagging intelligence are his distinguishing qualities—what he lacks in grace he makes up for in manliness'. He also identified him as a 'sound practical businessman' (Archer, 5.31–2). He and Marie Wilton were married on 28 December 1867, at St Stephen's, Avenue Road, Primrose Hill. She had performed her last burlesque, *Little Don Giovanni*, earlier that year, and Bancroft replaced Byron as joint manager of the theatre. They had one son, George Pleydell Bancroft, born in 1868.

Although Wilton had initiated the policies and set the tone at the Prince of Wales's, once she and Bancroft had married he took control of the commercial business, and increasingly the artistic policy as well. He later complimented his wife that she

> placed perfect confidence in my choice of plays, and accepted my opinion in all important matters, even when it chanced to be at variance with her own … She never once allowed her faith in me to be shaken by an occasional mistake. (Bancroft and Bancroft, *Recollections*, 125–6)

They were certainly a formidable team, combining her theatrical charm with his business acumen.

'Social drama' The success of Robertson's 'social drama' was confirmed by *Caste* (6 April 1867), the main attraction of which was the 'naturalism' of both staging and acting—solid doors with locks and handles, tea that came steaming out of the pot, and characters who 'looked and talked so like beings of everyday life that they were mistaken for such, and the audience had a curiosity to know how they were getting on after the fall of the curtain' (Bancroft and Bancroft, *Recollections*, 96). In fact the plots and sentiments of Robertson's 'cup-and-saucer' plays remained melodramatic, but they ideally suited the intimate size of the Prince of Wales's and the restrained playing of the company. However, the vivacious comic roles which Robertson provided for Wilton provided scope for her burlesque talents. William Archer wrote that the

> practical-humorous heroines—Mary Netley, Polly Eccles, Naomi Tighe—always fell to the lot of Mrs Bancroft, whose alert and expressive face, humid sparkling eyes, and small compact figure seemed to have been expressly designed for these characters. She possessed, too, the faculty of approaching the borderline of vulgarity without overstepping it—an essential gift for the actress who has to deal with Robertsonian pertness. (Archer, 5.31)

In 1871 Robertson died. He had directed his last new play for the Bancrofts—*MP* (23 April 1870), which ran for 150 performances—from his sickbed, and had attended the first night of their revival of *Ours* (26 November 1870), which ran for 230. These long runs enabled the Bancrofts to introduce several managerial innovations which were to become general in most London theatres. They abandoned the practice of performing several plays, with entr'acte entertainments, each night, relying instead on a single play for as long as it would sell. This shorter evening suited the 'carriage-trade' who wished to dine out as well as visit the theatre. In 1878, with the success of *Diplomacy* (from Sardou's *Dora*), they began to present afternoon matinées. Long runs and a relatively small company enabled the managers to improve actors' salaries—George Honey received £18 a week playing in *Caste* in 1867, but collected £60 for its revival in 1871—and Squire Bancroft was proud of their 'respectable' practice of delivering pay packets to the actors rather than have them queuing at the office.

With no more new plays from Robertson, the Bancrofts embarked on a policy of revivals—Bulwer-Lytton's *Money* (6 May 1872), Sheridan's *The School for Scandal* (4 April 1874), *The Merchant of Venice* (17 April 1875)—but the same production methods developed by Robertson were applied, providing settings of meticulous accuracy and acting of understated restraint. This suited the witty dialogue of Bulwer-Lytton and Sheridan, with Marie Bancroft creating 'a lady Teazle who is the fresh, genuine, impulsive maiden wedded to an old bachelor, and not the practiced actress, with all her airs and graces' (Scott, 1.580), but the Shakespeare production, although designed with advice from the artist and architect E. W. Godwin, was ill-served by the conversational tone of Charles Coghlan's Shylock. Ellen Terry's Portia, however, was highly praised—and inspired Henry Irving to recruit her for his Lyceum company.

It was only in later years, shortly before the couple acquired the Haymarket, that Squire Bancroft's own acting received genuine critical praise. After his performance of Triplet, the impoverished poet in Charles Reade's *Masks and Faces*, a critic remarked: 'it can no longer be said that this excellent actor is merely a "haw haw" swell' (*Dramatic Review*, 7 March 1875). Irving, a close social acquaintance, wanted him to act in Boucicault's *The Corsican Brothers* in 1880, and eventually persuaded him to play the Abbé Latour in the French Revolutionary melodrama *The Dead Heart* (28 September 1889). This was so successful, particularly the spectacular sabre duel (fought by two myopic actors without their glasses!) that Irving remarked to Bancroft, 'What a big name you might have made for yourself had you never come across those Robertson plays—what a pity—for your sake—for no actor can be remembered long who does not appear in classical drama' (Bancroft and Bancroft, *Recollections*, 333).

The Haymarket years The Prince of Wales's lease had expired in 1880, and the Bancrofts took over the much bigger Haymarket Theatre, where they introduced similar policies aimed at 'improving the tone' of the audiences. They replaced all the 3*s.* 6*d.* pit seats with 10*s.* orchestra stalls, thus banishing the poorer spectators to the upper gallery. On the opening night there was a vociferous protest of 'Where's the pit?', but the days of theatre riots were past and the embourgeoisement of this once rowdy patent theatre soon prevailed. Symptomatic of their theatrical aesthetic was the new design for the Haymarket proscenium arch. It was 'set all around in an immense gilded frame, like that of some magnificent picture' (H. James, *The Scenic Art*, 1949, 148). The naturalistic convention of the invisible 'fourth wall', behind which the actors performed apparently oblivious of their audience, was a logical development of the Bancroft style, and foreshadowed in the live theatre the circumscribed illusion of the cinema screen.

The financial acumen with which the Bancrofts exploited their theatres was such that, even having spent £10,000 renovating the Prince of Wales's and £20,000 refurbishing the Haymarket, they were able to retire in 1885, having made a personal profit over twenty years of management of £180,000. According to Arthur Pinero it was Bancroft's rule

> that expenses should not exceed one-third of the holding capacity of the theatre. If it held £1200 a week, he would not spend more than £400 on salaries and so on. He could well afford to play to houses which were not full every night. (Fyfe, 268)

Retirement and reputations However, neither Marie Wilton's popularity nor her skill had diminished with her retirement, and she returned to the stage, with her husband, under the management of their old colleague John Hare, in revivals of *Diplomacy* (1893) and *Money* (1894). She also appeared in Sardou's *Fedora*, with Mrs Patrick Campbell, under Herbert Beerbohm Tree at the Haymarket in 1895. Her final performance was for a charity benefit, featuring act II of Robertson's *Ours* (1896).

Squire Bancroft was certainly respected by his fellow actors, and, when no longer in the invidious position of manager, he was often asked to arbitrate theatrical disputes and to preside at gatherings such as the celebration of Irving's knighthood in 1895. When Bancroft was himself knighted in the 1897 diamond jubilee honours it was more for his professional pre-eminence than his artistic merits. He had always been socially influential as a member of the Athenaeum and the Garrick, at a time when few actors were accepted as members, and of the more informal Lambs, Kinsmen, and Irving's own Beefsteak dining clubs. After their retirement he and Marie regularly entertained members of 'polite society' at their home, 18 Berkeley Square, London. In 1882 Bancroft, Irving, and J. L. Toole had founded the Actors' Benevolent Fund, financed by West End managements, and in 1891 Bancroft supported the Actors' Association founded by Robert Courtneige and Frank Benson. In 1906 he became its president, but was opposed by several members who felt the association was dominated by actor-managers whose interests were incompatible with the association's increasingly trade union-like activities.

Indeed Bancroft, born into a family of entrepreneurs, had brought to the theatre a strong sense of capitalist professionalism. His own companies had been run as tight businesses, and many late Victorian and Edwardian West End managers had received their tutelage under the Bancrofts. In 1900 Beerbohm Tree invited him to join the council of his Academy of Dramatic Art (later RADA), where he endowed the Bancroft gold medal for the most outstanding student of the year.

Marie Wilton's career epitomized the general change in the London theatrical scene during the last thirty years of the nineteenth century. Brought up in the brash popular traditions of burlesque and melodrama, she contributed both as an actress and as a manager in partnership with her husband to a social transformation. They gave theatregoing a middle-class respectability, as the materialistic literalism of their productions appealed to middle-class audiences more than the raw emotions of mid-Victorian spectacular melodrama. They were not the only innovators, indeed several other husband and wife teams—the Wigans, the Kendals, and the Vezins—had championed domestic dramas set in respectable society, but the Bancrofts, having Tom Robertson as their house playwright and stage director and adopting commercial strategies appropriate to the changing market, won the acclaim of Clement Scott: 'The Bancrofts and the Bancrofts alone, must have the full credit for what has been justly called the renaissance of English dramatic art …'. Less extravagantly he recorded that

> their unselfishness is beyond question … she who could make a play, and has never marred one, again and again effaced herself when it was deemed necessary, and, with a rare generosity extended a helping hand to a younger generation … Apart from the nobility of it all, it proved a most remunerative plan … The Bancrofts [were] pioneers of what is now known as 'natural acting' … and earned the confidence of the learned and liberal professions. (Scott, 2.362–4)

Lady Bancroft remained a respected member of her profession, though in retirement she channelled her irrepressible energy into 'good works'—she was received into the Roman Catholic church in 1885—and into writing three plays and a novel, *The Shadow of Neeme* (1912). She died at the Burlington Hotel, Folkestone, on 22 May 1921. Sir Squire Bancroft survived her for five years, and died at his flat, A1, The Albany, Piccadilly, London, on 19 April 1926. GEORGE TAYLOR

Sources W. Archer, 'Mr & Mrs Bancroft', *Actors and actresses of Great Britain and the United States*, ed. B. Matthews and L. Sutton, 5 (1886) · M. Baker, *The rise of the Victorian actor* (1978) · [S. Bancroft and M. E. Bancroft], *Mr and Mrs Bancroft on and off the stage: written by themselves*, 2 vols. (1888) · M. E. Bancroft and S. Bancroft, *The Bancrofts: recollections of sixty years* (1909) · R. C. Buzecky, *The Bancrofts at the Prince of Wales's and Haymarket theatres* (1970) · J. Colman, *Players and playwrights I have known*, 2 vols. (1888) · A. Filon, *The English stage* (1897) · H. Fyfe, *Sir Arthur Pinero's plays and players* (1930) · C. E. Pascoe, ed., *The dramatic list*, 2nd edn (1880) · T. E. Pemberton, *The life and writings of T. W. Robertson* (1893) · T. E. Pemberton, *John Hare, comedian, 1865–1895* (1895) · M. Sanderson, *From Irving to Olivier: a social history of the acting profession, 1880–1983* (1984) · C. Scott, *The drama of yesterday and today*, 2 vols. (1899) · G. Taylor, *Players and performances in the Victorian theatre* (1989) · W. Tydeman, *Plays by Tom Robertson* (1982) · W. Tydeman, *The Bancrofts at the Prince of Wales's Theatre*, Theatre in Focus (1996)

Archives King's Cam., letters to Oscar Browning

Likenesses H. Watkins, albumen prints, 1856–9, NPG · Count Gleichen, bust, exh. RA 1880?, Garr. Club · Barraud, photograph, 1885, NPG [*see illus.*] · T. J. Barker, oils, NPG · Spy [L. Ward], lithograph, repro. in *VF* (1891) · Walery, photograph, NPG

Wealth at death £3596 10*s*. 4*d*.: administration, 26 Sept 1921, *CGPLA Eng. & Wales* · £174,535 4*s*. 11*d*.—Squire Bancroft: probate, 6 July 1926, *CGPLA Eng. & Wales*

Bancroft, Richard (*bap.* 1544, *d.* 1610), archbishop of Canterbury, was baptized at Prescot, Farnworth, Lancashire, on 12 September 1544. He was the second son of John Bancroft, gentleman, and his wife, Mary, daughter of James Curwen and niece of Hugh Curwen (*c.*1500–1568), archbishop of Dublin (1555–67) and bishop of Oxford (1567–8).

Education and early career Bancroft was educated locally at the grammar school in Farnworth. He was older than was usual for his generation when admitted to Cambridge, where he was elected scholar at Christ's College, graduating BA in 1567. Although his reputation was said to be higher on the sports field in boxing, wrestling, and quarterstaff, he was nevertheless chosen to greet Elizabeth during her first visit to Cambridge in 1564. He delivered an overweening encomium, lauding her shining example and praising her as a judge against the raging bulls of the pope.

Financial uncertainty may have delayed Bancroft's initial entry to university. In his final undergraduate year Archbishop Curwen granted him the prebendal stall of Malhidert in St Patrick's, Dublin. As he was not yet ordained this would assist him financially. With it came a royal licence to be absent from the university for six months. It is also possible that education in a newly reformed university may not have been an altogether appealing option for someone from a traditionalist background in the north-west. A fellow Lancastrian student, Laurence Chaderton, some eight years senior to Bancroft, came from a financially more secure background and yet did not enter Christ's until he was almost thirty.

For a time Bancroft may have been a close member of Chaderton's wide-flung network of patronage and acquaintance. The two remained lifelong, if unlikely, friends even when Bancroft removed to Jesus College as a tutor (he was never a fellow there). Later Bancroft regarded men like John Rainolds, William Whitaker, and Chaderton as respectable moderates, and in his

Richard Bancroft (*bap.* 1544, *d.* 1610), by unknown artist, *c.*1600

Daungerous Positions (1593) he deliberately omitted any mention of Chaderton's leading role in the conference movement. He retained broad sympathies for the moderate puritan position and with them opposed the Elizabethan university statutes of 1572.

Bancroft proceeded MA from Jesus in 1572, and two years later, at the age of thirty, he was ordained priest in the diocese of Ely by Bishop Richard Cox. Cox, who had supported the university statutes of 1572, was also visitor of Jesus. He made Bancroft one of his chaplains, in which post he probably served until Cox died in 1581. He later offered him a prebend at Ely (21 December 1575) and collated him to the rectory of Teversham, near Cambridge (24 March 1576). Later that year he was licensed as one of the twelve preachers in the university. 'By the appointment of Archbishop [Edmund] Grindal, he did once visite the Diocese of Peterborough', in the wake of the 'disorders' involving preachers in Northamptonshire in 1576 (CUL, Mm.1.47, fol. 332). This would appear to be the first time that he had acted as the bishop's proxy in matters of discipline. In 1580 or 1581 Bancroft entered the service of the lord chancellor, Sir Christopher Hatton, as a chaplain, 'for the most part in her Majesties Court, & was in good Reputation with him, & often employed in sundry maters of great Importance, for her Highnes service' (ibid.).

It was as one of the university select preachers, and not as an episcopal visitor, that Bancroft was sent to preach at the Bury St Edmunds assize in July 1583. Bury had recently become troubled by the sermons of Robert Browne, a kinsman of Lord Burghley, who had been released from his imprisonment for unauthorized preaching in Cambridge and had moved his centre of operations to the neighbouring diocese of Norwich. The choice of Bancroft as assize preacher was deliberate. Browne had earlier appeared before him, as the bishop's officer, to be reminded of the need for an episcopal licence when he had delivered his Cambridge homilies. Bancroft's new position in Hatton's household meant that he would be able to report back fully to the government on the presbyterian claims of the sectaries.

As Archbishop John Whitgift attested in 1597, it was while Bancroft was in Bury that:

> he detected to the Judges, the writings of a Poesie, about Her Majesties Armes, taken out of the Apocalyps, but apply'd to her Highness most falsely & seditiously. It had been sett up a quarter of a year, in a most publick place, without controulment. (CUL, Mm.1.47, fol. 332)

The libel, pinned to the royal achievement in one of the city churches, compared the queen, England's Deborah, to 'that woman Jezebel', of Revelation 2:20. Its discovery led to the arrest and subsequent death of two Brownists, John Copping and Elias Thacker, who had been distributing *A Treatise of Reformation without Tarrying for Anie* (1582) by Browne and books by Robert Harrison. Chief Justice Sir Edmund Anderson gave Bancroft a copy of Harrison's *Three Formes of Catechismes* (1583) by way of an honorarium. Bancroft dated the gift to the day of the death of Archbishop Grindal (6 July 1583).

Spokesman for conformity John Whitgift, who succeeded Grindal at Canterbury, immediately demanded clerical subscription to three articles, asserting that the queen had supreme authority in matters ecclesiastical, that the Thirty-Nine Articles of 1563 were agreeable to the word of God and that the Book of Common Prayer contained nothing contrary to scripture. He met forceful opposition in both parliament and the privy council, where Lord Burghley made explicit his concern that 'the Inquisitors of Spain use not so many questions to comprehend and to trap their preyes', concluding that 'this kind of proceeding is too much savouring of the Romish Inquisition' (J. Strype, *The Life and Acts of … John Whitgift*, 1718, new edn, 3 vols., 1822, 3.104–7).

Whitgift had, however, a further string to his bow. John Aylmer, bishop of London, who had been *de facto* primate during the years of Grindal's suspension, had done much to reinvigorate the ecclesiastical commission, which now operated as an independent 'court of high commission'. As such, part of its function was to pursue and discipline clerical nonconformists. Although both Whitgift and Aylmer remained at the head of its affairs, Bancroft rapidly became the more powerful figure behind the scenes. The high commission worked methodically to extirpate presbyterianism, to stifle subversive publications, and to suspend—although only selectively, in view of the privy council's continued propensity to challenge its decisions whenever its victims had friends at court—those leading sectaries who refused to subscribe to Whitgift's articles.

Bancroft was increasingly involved in developing an

anti-puritan rhetoric, and by the time that he was admitted DTh at Cambridge in April 1585 he had produced a series of investigative accounts of puritanism in which he wrote warmly in the defence of episcopacy and denounced the practices of gathered congregations. He condemned the heresies in Robert Browne's books, wrote of the 'Opinions and Dealings of the Precisians', and sought to exploit the inner weaknesses and rivalries of the fissiparous movement. Against William Turner he wrote his 'Discourse upon the bill and book exhibited in parliament by the puritans for a further reformation of the church principles' (PRO, SP 12/199/1).

Not that all Bancroft's energies were directed against the godly at home. In 1584 he joined Archbishop Adam Loftus of Dublin in a remonstrance to prevent Sir John Perrot alienating the endowment and church site of St Patrick's, Dublin, in order to found a university college. Loftus, who had succeeded Bancroft's great-uncle as archbishop in 1567, had been dean of St Patrick's from 1565 and may therefore have known him from that foundation. Perrot's plan was essentially based on the models of many Oxford and Cambridge colleges; Bancroft's second college, Jesus, had been reformed out of the former monastic foundation of St Radegund. The appeal was upheld and the plan for a college or university in Dublin was revised.

Not until 10 February 1586 did Bancroft receive his first major appointment, becoming treasurer of St Paul's Cathedral by royal prerogative. The same year Sir Christopher Hatton presented him to the rectory of Cottingham, Northamptonshire. Bancroft had earlier successfully sought the parsonage of St Andrew's, Holborn, in August 1584 through Hatton's intercession with Burghley. Accordingly he is gazetted as non-resident and double-beneficed in a contemporary list drafted for the lord mayor and aldermen by members of the London clerical conference. This document sought the support of the lay authorities in petitioning the queen to 'have consideration of the state of the Ministry of London, for speedy Reformation of it' (Peel, 2.96, 180). Following the death of Cox, Bancroft was also appointed to the commission of visitation for the diocese of Ely, which administered the see throughout its lengthy vacancy (1581–1600). On 19 July 1587 he was installed as a canon of Westminster.

Pulpiteer and polemicist On 23 June 1586 Star Chamber enacted an ordinance to restrain the printing of seditious propaganda: no volume might be printed without a licence from either the archbishop of Canterbury or the bishop of London. This established a form of censorship which went far beyond that imposed upon the Stationers' Company and was to remain in place until 1640–41. Its immediate effect was to foment a series of underground publications and from the summer of 1588 there appeared a series of lampoons and tracts, written by 'Martin Marprelate', whose identity has never been established. It was Bancroft who uncovered the location of the printing press, at Newtown near Manchester, and silenced it.

In his Paul's Cross sermon of 9 February 1589 Bancroft responded to many of the charges of Martin Marprelate. He claimed that episcopacy itself had existed as a form of ecclesiastical government since apostolic times. He further attacked the 'Arians, Donatists, Papists, Libertines, Anabaptists, the Familie of Love and sundrie other' heresies (R. Bancroft, *A Sermon Preached at Paules Crosse*, 1589, 3). Bancroft's agenda was threefold. The sermon was clearly directed at the parliamentary session that had begun the previous week, but at the same time it sought to underscore the essentially anti-establishment nature of the godly reform programme. For the first time it also took the battle of scholarship into Scotland. The general assembly of the kirk had agreed on 10 May 1586 that 'the name of a Bishop hath a speciall charge in the function annexed to it by the word' but that this was no different from an 'ordinary Pastor'. It further ruled that only the general assembly could admit any pastor to be bishop or minister as granted by the king. The Pauline style of *episkopos* was to be 'appointed to a speciall floke where he shall keepe his residence & serve the cure as another Minister' (BL, Sloane MS 271, fol. 73*r*). Bancroft's defence of episcopacy against this argument raised fundamental questions about church order and the essentials of faith and in conformist circles became a benchmark for a discussion of church polity for half a century, until the abolition of bishops in 1643.

Bancroft's homily had another intended target: those who exalted the word of God to the point that it became the sole authority that, by preaching and prophesyings, threatened the balance within a church that set greater store by the use of sacraments. He denounced those false prophets who

> would have the people to be alwaies seeking and searching: and these men (as well themselves as their followers) can never finde wherupon to rest. Now they are carried hither, now thither. They are alwaies learning (as the apostle saith) but do never attaine to the truth. (Bancroft, *A Sermon Preached at Paules Crosse*, 38)

For Bancroft, the ploughboy in the field, whom Erasmus hoped would have the scripture to hand, had become 'the pratling old woman, the doting old man, the brabling sophister'. All of them assume that they have obtained the truth when in fact 'they teare it in peeces, and take upon them to teach it before they have learned it' (ibid., 41).

With regard to Scottish affairs Bancroft greatly miscalculated and put his own future career in jeopardy. He had the temerity to criticize John Knox and falsely (albeit understandably) attributed to James VI a declaration about the church in Scotland which had in fact been drafted by Patrick Adamson, archbishop of St Andrews. A furious Burghley, who was keen to maintain discreet relations with the Scottish king, summoned Bancroft to account for himself and refused him leave to read his own carefully prepared defence that he had taken the precaution to bring with him. Burghley ordered him back to Hatton's residence in Ely Place to write a submission to the king. When, however, James himself pressed for a full public apology Burghley firmly demurred. North of the border the issue remained a live one; John Davidson chided Bancroft as late as September 1590 in *D. Bancrofts Rashness in Rayling*.

In 1592, after the death of Sir Christopher Hatton, Bancroft became one of Whitgift's household chaplains at Lambeth. The following year he 'did sett out two Books in defence of the State of the Church, & against the pretended Holy Discipline: which were liked and greatly commended, by the learnedest Men in the Realm' (CUL, Mm. 1.47, fol. 333). The first, *A Survay of the Pretended Holy Discipline*, was an extended form of remarks he had passed in his sermon of 1589. In it he traced the origins of the reform movement to Geneva under Calvin and its propagation in England to the work of Beza and the admonition of 1572. The work espoused a *jure divino* case for episcopacy, largely drawn from two recently published tracts: Hadrian Saravia's influential *Diverse Degrees of the Ministers of the Gospel* (1590) and Matthew Sutcliffe's *Treatise of Ecclesiastical Discipline* (1591). Bancroft undertook to explain why the Church of England retained hierarchical office as a sign of the true church and rejected the pattern of reformation demanded by the godly. He emphasized that episcopacy was both scriptural and historical, whereas 'the institution of this pretended Government cannot be shewed out of the Old Testament: and then by their own confessions ... it may not be urged out of the New' (R. Bancroft, *A Survay*, 1593, 69). Such claims advanced the bishops well beyond the status of ecclesiastical civil servants that had been Burghley's and the earl of Leicester's preferred model for the early Elizabethan episcopate.

Bancroft further advanced the cause of episcopal government and attacked puritanism in his next publication, *Daungerous Positions and Proceedings, Published and Practiced within this Iland of Brytaine, under the Pretence of Reformation, and for the Presbiterial Discipline* (1593), a work that was reprinted in 1640 as a clarion call against the Scottish sympathizers in the country. 'The devilish and traitorous practices of the seminary priests and jesuits' were as bad as 'the lewd and obstinate course held by our pretended reformers, the consistorian puritans', since both of them were 'labouring with all their might by railing, libelling and lying to steal away the people's hearts from their governors, to bring them to a dislike of the present state of our church' (R. Bancroft, *Daungerous Positions*, 2–3). By stressing the links between the conference movement and subversives, like William Hacket and Henry Coppinger, Bancroft wrote a scaremonger's handbook to political resistance and ensured that conformity, whether of puritans or of papists, would be judged in the light of allegiance to the crown. An act of parliament of 1593 (35 Eliz. I c. i) threatened sectaries with imprisonment for staying away from divine service and made conventicles unlawful. By then puritanism had already been driven underground; the Dedham conference had met for the last time in June 1589, Thomas Cartwright was imprisoned, and Henry Barrowe, John Greenwood, and John Penry had been put to death (under the act of 1581 that forbade seditious writings), although not before Penry's damaging tract, *A briefe discovery of the untruthes and slanders (against the true government of the church of Christ) contained in a sermon preached 8. of Februarie 1588 by D. Bancroft*, had appeared anonymously in Edinburgh.

Bishop of London As a theologian and church leader Whitgift was a thoroughgoing Calvinist. For all his outbursts he never regarded the likes of Cartwright and fellow members of the conference movement as more than disaffected brethren who needed to be brought to their senses. The logic of Bancroft's approach, however, recast not only exasperated radicals, who were moving towards semi-separatism, but also 'moderate puritans' as politically subversive. This effectively identified authority within the church with authority in the state.

Despite this difference in attitude Whitgift now canvassed Bancroft's elevation to the bishopric of London, which John Aylmer was willing to resign in his favour if his own translation to Worcester could be effected. The plan came to nothing, apparently because Bancroft would not agree to the pension from episcopal revenues that was Aylmer's price for his resignation. On his deathbed in 1594 Aylmer is said to have regretted that he had not written to Elizabeth to commend Bancroft as his successor.

It is unlikely that such a representation would have persuaded Elizabeth against more powerful patrons since Burghley, at this stage, preferred William Day, dean of Windsor, while the earl of Essex backed Richard Fletcher, bishop of Worcester. Whitgift, no doubt aware that Bancroft had little chance of promotion, in December 1595 added his voice to that of Essex and Bishop Fletcher was duly translated. Fletcher's unexpected death on 15 June 1596, coming soon after Day's appointment to Winchester, gave Whitgift a second chance. He wrote candidly that in the past fifteen or sixteen years (in other words since Bancroft himself had entered centre-stage politics in the household of the lord chancellor):

> 17: or 18: of his Juniors (few or none of them being of his experience) have been preferred, eleven to Deaneries, & the rest to Bishopricks. Of which number, some have been formerly inclin'd to Faction, & the most as neuters have expected the Issue, that so they might, as things should fall out, run with the time. (Strype, *Whitgift*, 2.386–8)

This remarkable assessment, which disparages many, strongly argues for Whitgift's support of Bancroft; when he thanked Robert Cecil for making the appointment possible, he claimed that Secretary Cecil would 'finde him a honest, true and faythfull man' (Hatfield House, MS 49, fol. 108). At the age of fifty-three Bancroft was elected on 21 April 1597, consecrated on 8 May, and enthroned on 5 June.

As a new diocesan bishop, Bancroft set out at once to implement locally the reforms that he and Whitgift had devised for the church at large. In the first instance he was determined to ensure the conformity of London ministers. Although there are no surviving subscription rolls for London in the period 1597–1604, Bancroft felt confident enough to assure Cecil on 2 April 1601 after four years in post, that 'all within my diocese have conformed themselves save Mr Egerton' (*Salisbury MSS*, 11.154). This somewhat pointed remark was prompted by antagonism as Stephen Egerton of Blackfriars owed the continuation of his ministry to Cecil's protection at the behest of William Fitzwilliam, a kinsman of Lady Burghley.

Bancroft's primary visitation articles of 1598, which were later reissued with minor amendments for the visitations of both 1601 and 1604, constitute a detailed and careful inquiry into the ministry. They became the model for many such episcopal articles in the Jacobean and Caroline church, being used, for instance, by Richard Neile at Coventry and Lichfield (1610), John Howson (Oxford, 1619–28), and Richard Corbet (1629). In them Bancroft ordered a dozen ministers in the diocese to bring confirmation candidates forward, either to himself or to his suffragan, John Sterne, bishop of Colchester. Here he was following Whitgift's directive of 1591 to ensure that 'bishoppings' were held regularly and that those coming forward for confirmation were suitably prepared in the faith. Despite Bancroft's claim at the Hampton Court conference that his chaplains ensured this and so prevented indiscriminate confirmation, Nicholas Ferrar remembered being confirmed twice by Bancroft during his visitation of 1598. Bishop Aylmer had ensured that London clergy had some vocational training and Bancroft retained this emphasis; the visitation call book for 1598 records that more than 100 clergy were interviewed by commissaries for their suitability as licensed preachers. Among his chaplains acting as a commissary for the visitation was Samuel Harsnett, whom he later preferred as archdeacon of Essex (1602) and bishop of Chichester (1609) and who served as one of his executors.

The Catholic threat If Bancroft's primary visitation gave him an opportunity to regulate the preaching ministry of the established church he also became involved in monitoring the activities of Romish priests resident in England. Cardinal Cajetan's appointment of George Blackwell to the office of archpriest with supreme authority over the English mission (7 March 1598) highlighted the divisions in the Catholic parties in the country. Bancroft's policy was to foment rivalry between secular priests in England and Jesuits abroad. Contemporaries believed that he was personally, and even solely, responsible for ensuring that 'the appellant priests have such liberty' (Anthony Rivers to Robert Persons, 3 March 1602, in H. Foley, *Records of the English Province of the Society of Jesus*, 7 vols., 1877–83, 1.22). All the main appellant leaders wrote to Bancroft at some time or other and he, with the cognizance of Cecil, whom he kept informed at every stage, offered them limited licences to ensure a degree of local control within the Catholic community. He also read widely, on both sides of the controversy.

One secular priest, William Watson, who had come from Rheims to England in June 1586, was living at Fulham Palace by September 1601. It was claimed then that he was, 'under the Bishop's elbow, by whose appointment he is placed there' (Dodd, 3.cxlvii). Bancroft assured Cecil on 18 August that he was 'very tractable to whet his pen against the jesuits' (*Salisbury MSS*, 11.350). But he was quick to disown him when Watson fell out with Rome and began to dabble in treason; in July 1603 he claimed he had not seen him since January. Watson had become involved in the so-called Bye plot to kidnap James I and impose toleration of Catholics; he was executed on 29 November that year. In the parliament of 1604 an action was brought against Bancroft alleging that he had committed treason in allowing the printing of appellant books; the bill was suppressed by the crown when Bancroft was being considered for the primacy.

This policy of limited toleration, intended to discredit the Jesuits, had been co-ordinated by Robert Cecil and the privy council. Bancroft was not yet a member of the council and needed an official letter from it to cover his clandestine activities throughout the controversy. Following the revelations of the Bye plot Bancroft may have acted scarcely a moment too soon to ensure that his conduct had the sanction of the crown. When at the Hampton Court conference John Rainolds of Corpus Christi College, Oxford, claimed that there were too many popish books in circulation, James VI and I defended Bancroft as having acted with official warrant. In fact, he was being employed on other government business too. For instance he was part of a diplomatic mission to Emden with Dr Christopher Perkins and Dr Richard Swale to resolve a dispute with Denmark and is said to have led pikemen against the London citizenry raised by the earl of Essex. Whitgift's failing health also thrust Bancroft centre stage in the church. As Thomas Fuller later averred, 'he was in effect Archbishop whilst Bishop' (Fuller, *Worthies*, 122).

The Hampton Court conference Whitgift was alarmed by the modest demands made in the millenary petition presented to the new king in his journey south for 'a uniformity of doctrine' and for 'no popish opinion to be any more taught and defended'. On 12 May 1603, a week after the new king had entered London, he wrote to the bishops requiring them to compile lists of all their clergy and preachers, with details of their academic qualifications, their licences (if any), and their place of residence. Detailed responses were not forthcoming, and at the end of the summer Whitgift was still trying to obtain answers. Those who saw the new reign as an opportunity for securing a new settlement of religion were more organized in achieving results from their own county-wide surveys. As a result the king issued a royal proclamation on 24 October 1603 (*CPR*, James I, 1/3) 'concerning such as seditiously seek reformation in church matters', intending to hold a public disputation on 1 November. The plague, however, was raging in London and when the conference met it was at Hampton Court, in sessions on 14, 16, and 18 January 1604.

Bancroft was one of nine bishops who, with Whitgift and James Montagu, dean of the Chapel Royal, represented the church hierarchy. The distinctly moderate puritan disputants were led by John Rainolds, who enjoyed good relations with Whitgift, and included Laurence Chaderton, a long-standing acquaintance of Bancroft. Among the several accounts of the proceedings, that of William Barlow, dean of Chester, is the lengthiest and as the officially commissioned version casts the bishops' contribution in the most favourable light, yet the Bancroft he praises with Thomas Bilson, bishop of Winchester, for his 'pains and dexteritie' (Cardwell, 168), emerges not just as a dominant but also as an impatient, hardline, and sometimes overbearing participant. While Whitgift left the detail of much of the debate to both Bancroft and Bilson, Bancroft was more combative than either. On the first day, in response to the king's opening oration discussing the alleged shortcomings of the church, it was Bancroft who asserted the apostolic institution of confirmation. Whitgift defended public absolution, but Bancroft defended private absolution too. Whitgift and the bishop of Worcester thought that the founding fathers of the English church had intended to suppress baptism by the laity, but had been compelled by circumstances to proceed obliquely; Bancroft asserted that there was no ambiguity, rather, they had intended to permit it as a necessity, since 'if [a child] die baptised, there is evident assurance that it is saved' (ibid., 175). When on the second day Bancroft intervened in Rainolds's exposition of the puritan case, advancing authorities to argue that those who spoke against bishops and the established liturgy should not be heard, the king excused his 'passion' but 'misliked his sudden interruption of D[r] Reinolds' (ibid., 180). Uncowed, Bancroft repeated this tactic later in the day. He defended himself vigorously against an accusation he sensed (probably correctly) was aimed at him of insufficiency in taking action against the publication of popish books, and moved three petitions indicative of his views on pastoral priorities: that attention should be given to the establishment of a praying ministry; that the reading of homilies should be promoted; that pulpits should not 'be made pasquils' (ibid., 192) for the airing of discontent. On the third day James, having apparently considered the case for change to the articles and prayer book and found it wanting, seems to have spoken in measured terms for the maintenance of the *status quo*. It was Bancroft who characteristically responded with a call for no concessions to nonconformists and for a strict time-limit on subscription. It was also Bancroft who 'ended all with a thanksgiving to God' (ibid., 212) and a prayer for the royal family.

On 31 January the king issued a writ of summons to the southern convocation to meet at St Paul's Cathedral on 20 March. In the interim Archbishop Whitgift died, on 29 February, and ten days later James issued a second writ, to Bancroft, as dean of the province of Canterbury, appointing him to preside in the convocation of clergy. When it met, convocation proceeded to adopt 141 constitutions and canons that Bancroft had drawn from the articles, injunctions, and synodical acts passed in the reigns of Edward VI and Elizabeth. Convocation approved them in April 1604 and James hoped to impose them unilaterally by letters patent on the province of York as well, but objections meant that they were not ratified by the northern province until 1606. Parliamentary sanction was technically supplied through citation of the Act for the Submission of the Clergy of 1534 (25 Henry VIII, c. 19) but parliament, meeting from 19 March, had in fact strenuously resisted them, even passing a resolution that no canon passed in the last decade could have any authority to impeach or hurt anyone's liberty. The canons enshrined, in canon 36, Whitgift's three articles of 1583. No fewer than 73 and no more than 83 ministers lost their benefices for their refusal to subscribe, of whom 7 later conformed and were reinstated.

Archbishop of Canterbury The appointment of Bancroft as successor to Whitgift was not without controversy. He was obviously a leading candidate, recognized as an astute bureaucrat and a talented polemicist, but the archbishop of York, Matthew Hutton, was thought by many to have the edge. In turn Hutton himself sought to advance either Bilson of Winchester or the great preaching prelate in the north, Tobie Matthew of Durham. Like Bancroft, both the bishop of Durham and Archbishop Hutton had entertained James VI and I on his arrival in England at the outset of his reign and had been among the first to preach before the new king. The rivalry of such candidates may explain why the *congé d'élire* for Bancroft's appointment was not granted until 6 October 1604. He was formally nominated on 9 October, elected on 17 November, and confirmed on 10 December by the bishops of Durham, Rochester, St David's, Chester, Chichester, and Ely.

Bancroft at once took up the king's business of ensuring conformity, and during the following six years some eighty ministers were deprived. In a circular to the bishops of 22 December 1604 he required them to remove those who refused to subscribe or would not accept ceremonial conformity. During the summer of 1605 Bancroft carried out a metropolitical visitation of ten dioceses where he set out to improve standards of preaching among the clergy and address other 'abuses' raised in parliament's criticism of the ministry. By so doing he may have addressed himself to issues facing the whole province at the cost of neglecting his own diocese; there is no evidence that he ever visited the diocese of Canterbury and in both 1607 and 1608 he sent Barlow, now bishop of Rochester, in his stead.

Bancroft was determined to address standards of preaching, non-residency, and catechizing among the clergy. In the letter of 28 May 1605 to his commissary in Bath and Wells which accompanied his articles of visitation he highlighted several of the canons of 1604. He specified canons 43, 44, 45, 46, 47, 59, and 74, 'all of them concerninge the increase of the preachinge of the word of God, the catechisinge and instructinge of the younger sort in the principles and grounds of Christian religion', as a way of countering charges of non-residency and scandal of an inattentive ministry, 'the defects wherof you knowe hath bynn often and so violentlie complayned of in parliament' (Fincham, *Visitation Articles*, 4, 5). Surprisingly, they made no requirements for confirmation. They did, however, provide (art. 33) 'for halfe an houre or more' for Sunday catechizing, and concerned themselves with the use of the sign of the cross at baptism (art. 21), and the reporting of recusancy (art. 37; (ibid., 9)). The articles necessarily embodied a tougher drive towards conformity and as a consequence a number of ministers lost their livings. However, it is not always possible to trace which presentments had arisen from which visitation, so that the overall effect of the metropolitical visitation should perhaps not be overemphasized. The articles of visitation themselves were not wholly original: Bancroft drew widely on those already used elsewhere. None the less, his became a model for articles widely used throughout the Church of England until the abolition of the hierarchy, including those of his successor, Abbot, and they were significantly more thoroughgoing than those of Whitgift's twenty-two articles.

Fighting on two fronts As bishop of London, with Whitgift's support Bancroft had followed a policy of divide and rule when dealing with recusants. But as primate he faced something of a resurgence in English Catholicism which required in response more than subtle support for seculars against the Jesuits. There had been rumours at James's accession that he would grant full toleration to recusants; Anne of Denmark's status as a Catholic convert, though not widely known, may have informed such expectations. If the Gunpowder Plot of November 1605 largely put paid to these hopes, James was still prepared to offer tolerance if not toleration, allowing that Catholics who remained quiet and secluded would not be harried. He explained to a furious House of Commons that not all those who professed the 'Romish religion' were disloyal subjects.

Although Bancroft too was concerned to mitigate violence and to uphold religion and the church without recourse to extreme measures, he was nevertheless implacable in his opposition to the papists. A number of high-profile defections to Rome, following the controversy over the oath of allegiance of 1606, led Bancroft to attack Catholics before the privy council in the years between 1607 and his death. When more than ten dozen suspected recusants failed to answer charges at the metropolitical visitation of Winchester diocese in 1607, they were summarily excommunicated. Having been elected in 1608 the first clerical chancellor of Oxford University since Mary's reign, Bancroft dismissed the appeal against suspension made by Humphrey Leech, a canon of Christ Church who had preached suspect sermons and denounced Calvin. Leech defected to Rome and Bancroft warned the university against publicly disputing matters contrary to the teachings of the church. In 1609 he ordered that every parish in the land should have a copy of Bishop John Jewel's *Apologie*, the classic defence of the Church of England as established under Elizabeth.

Meanwhile Bancroft was tangentially involved in King James's attempts to settle the Church of Scotland. He offered open hospitality to Andrew Melville, the head of Aberdeen University, and seven presbyterian colleagues when they were summoned to London by the king in the autumn of 1606, although this was refused. With the prince of Wales, fellow clergy, and leading laymen, Bancroft attended the meeting between James and the Scottish commissioners at Hampton Court. After the gathering had been treated to four sermons on order and obedience, on 6 October Bancroft tried privately to get the Scots to sign an agreed statement but to no avail. The latter remained in London under house arrest, and when in November Andrew Melville was hauled before the privy council for criticizing the St Michael's day service he had witnessed, his frustration led to an outburst in which he seized the sleeve of Bancroft's cassock, calling his vestments 'Romish ragis, and a pairt of the beastis mark' (A. R. MacDonald, *The Jacobean Kirk, 1567–1625*, 1998, 125).

There were later attempts to reconcile the Scots to episcopacy, most notably when George Downham, one of Bancroft's eight household chaplains, preached at James Montagu's consecration in April 1608. This sermon, and its defence in 1611, demonstrate how Bancroft used his authority over his household chaplains to preach conformity at the very heart of the system, at the consecration of the successors of the apostles. When published it caused a furore and one of the numerous treatises attacking it called upon the privy council 'not to depend upon the mouthes of Bishops and their Chaplains (who in this case are rather to be mistrusted of Godly wise men, as Achabs 400 *prophets* were of Jehosophat)' (*Informations, or, A Protestation, and a Treatise from Scotland*, 1608, sig. 2). The printing of Downham's sermon was clearly part of a carefully co-ordinated campaign intended to convince the Scots of the need for episcopacy so that although Bancroft, as primate of all England, could exercise no jurisdiction over the Scots, he could still provide his king with a theological armoury. When in 1610 three bishops were sent from Scotland to be consecrated in England, it was agreed that they should receive orders at the hands of the bishop of London and other bishops and not attend at Lambeth, lest there be any confusion over Bancroft's authority. Their orders were nevertheless the hard-won fruits of his exertions.

At the end of his life Bancroft was still fighting the twin menaces of public Catholicism and an inadequate ministry. On 21 July 1610 the Spanish ambassador, Alonso de Velasco, reported to Philip III the outcome of a recent heated meeting of the privy council at which the archbishop had denounced the earls of Northampton, Suffolk, and Worcester as Catholics, claiming that they frequently absented themselves from communion. However, Robert Cecil, earl of Salisbury, ensured that the king took no action against Suffolk and Worcester and so thwarted the archbishop. The two earls had both had very public roles at the creation of the prince of Wales on 4 June 1610, and Bancroft's blistering attack may have been partly designed to point up the danger of allowing Catholics to stand so close to the crown. He will also have known how Salisbury relied on Lady Suffolk as his go-between with successive Spanish ambassadors.

At the end of July 1610, following the year's first parliamentary session, Bancroft sent instructions to the dioceses in the king's name. The session had not been an easy one; a sermon by Bishop Samuel Harsnett, another of Bancroft's former chaplains, had aroused controversy, and Bancroft's patience had snapped over a bill on pluralities. The instructions show that he was still keen to remove the twin evils of non-residency and pluralism, although he had previously failed to obtain a parliamentary statute to restore impropriated tithes to vicars and curates as a way of funding parish clergy. They also show that he was concerned with standards of ecclesiastical administration, charging the bishops:

> to examine very narrowly the proceedinges of your chauncellors, commissaries, archdeacons and officials; for whilest we repose soe much truste in them as we doe, and they intend little (I meane espicially chauncellors, commissaries and officialls) but theire owne profitt, many true complaynts and mischiefes doe indeede thereof ensue. (Fincham, *Visitation Articles*, 1.95)

Bancroft may have placed too much blind trust in his bishops in this regard. Certainly the promiscuous ordinations by Bishop Sterne of Colchester had attracted criticism.

At the same time, ecclesiastical power was under attack from another quarter. In the first decade of the century common lawyers had increasingly urged that in matters ecclesiastical the high commission was subject to parliament (which had passed the statute of 1559 authorizing the commission), and that, therefore, parliament's authority in religious matters outweighed the king's. Furthermore, since Cowdrey's case in 1591 Bancroft had been under personal attack, above all from Edward Coke, who was successively solicitor-general (1592), attorney-general (1593), and chief justice of common pleas. In this context, following the Hampton Court conference disillusioned puritans had again resorted to the law to contest the authority of the high commission. When facing prosecution in the church courts, they would turn to common law courts for writs of prohibition. Since the commission compelled self-incrimination, by putting defendants on oath in order to interrogate them about their religious affiliations, Coke was able to argue that the oath taken *ex officio* tempted men to perjury and placed their souls at risk. He averred that only the common law or statute should ever require such extreme measures. Although by October 1605 Bancroft presented the king with a list of complaints (the *Articuli cleri*) in which he attacked the judges, the latter continued to issue writs of prohibition, while a series of ineffectual conferences was held over the next four years. In November 1608 James I sought to take the matter into his own hands, but he was attacked by Coke for meddling in matters that took lawyers years to learn. Although the king demanded that all cases in matters ecclesiastical be reported to him, as the fount of all justice, the judges disregarded the instruction, thereby weakening the sovereign's authority in the church, a central pillar of Whitgift's and Bancroft's drive for conformity. Bancroft witnessed one final indignity when his friend, the civilian John Cowell, was brought before the House of Commons at Coke's behest, and worsted.

Death and will Bancroft died at Lambeth Palace on 2 November 1610. As he had specified in his second will, dated 28 October, he was interred two days later without great ceremony in the chancel of the parish church of Lambeth. A single slab, inscribed with his name, marks the spot. There is no memorial sculpture. He provided that within a month of his death a memorial sermon should be preached in the church before his household, requesting it be given by either George Abbot, Samuel Harsnett, or by one of his eight household chaplains. His first will was popularly supposed to have left his entire estate to the church but, according to Thomas Fuller, he latterly thought better of it. As the first post-Reformation archbishop routinely to use a carriage, he bequeathed his best coach and four Dutch geldings to his successor, while his second coach and the team of English geldings went to his nephew Dr Newman. His will distributed £60 to the poor of Lambeth and Croydon, generously provided for his household staff, and further honoured his nephews and nieces with items of silver and his musical instruments. As well as giving four bishops (Barlow, Montagu, Neile, and Harsnett) each 'a round hoope ring of gold of a marke in weight with this inscription *Sic sanctorum communio*, two hands being joyned together within the round at the beginning of the inscription' (PRO, SP 14/57/115), he gave lesser gold rings to a handful of friends, including Sir Christopher Hatton and Sir George Paule. He gave his library in perpetuity to the archbishops of Canterbury, enjoining the king 'and his most Royal Successors, when they receave the homage of any Archbishop of Canterbury, first to procure him to enter Bonde to leave all the said Books to his Successors' (ibid.). This substantial donation formed the basis of the replacement library set up after Matthew Parker had alienated the earlier collections. It included William Camden's manuscripts, which had come to Bancroft as a result of a long-held friendship between the two men. At the interregnum parliament ordered that the library should be transferred to the University of Cambridge and only the persistence of Archbishop Gilbert Sheldon after the Restoration ensured that it was returned to Lambeth.

His collection of some 6065 volumes shows Bancroft to have been a lover of the classics—he owned copies of works by Seneca and Virgil, Aristotle, Homer, Horace, Martial, Ovid, Plato, Pliny, Plutarch, and Petronius among 531 volumes of *literae humaniores*. He also bequeathed 102 bibles, 294 volumes of patristic theology, and 659 volumes of biblical commentary, as well as 755 works of Catholic theology and of controversy. Patrick Young, who became keeper of the royal library in 1609 but had been acting keeper since 1597, complained a month after the archbishop's death that Bancroft had at least 500 books from the royal collection, many of which have remained at Lambeth since. This suggests that Bancroft, like many serious bibliophiles, was often not too scrupulous about matters of ownership. He could also be generous, and shortly before his death was considering contributing books to the young prince of Wales's library (BL, Add. MS 6094, fol. 174*r*).

Bancroft appointed both Harsnett and Abbot, men from very different wings of the church, to be the overseers of this will. He left the first a silver-gilt basin and ewer for his pains, and the latter, 'if it should not please God and his Majesty, that he may suceede me in the Archbishoprike', 100 marks to bestow as plate (PRO, SP 14/57/115). No trace of Abbot's funeral eulogy has been found, but his succession to Canterbury had been assured, even though some contemporaries still imagined that Lancelot Andrewes, Thomas Bilson, or Tobie Matthew might be appointed.

Bancroft's legacy It has been argued that Bancroft's single-mindedness reconstructed the Church of England after a period of Elizabethan neglect, but such an opinion misjudges the very real work undertaken by his predecessor, Whitgift, from whom he learned, and equally exaggerates the success of his own policies of insistence, whether upon clerical subscription, the imposition of the canons of 1604, or the enforcement of his visitation articles. All three derived from concerns and considerations of the church post-1588 when the Marprelate tracts seemed, alongside the Spanish Armada, to threaten a pincer movement against the Church of England. In a very real sense Bancroft's achievements derived from his faithful service to Whitgift and not from the period of his own occupancy of the chair of St Augustine. His years as a dogged ecclesiastical bloodhound brought the highest promotion, and his nomination of his successor was honoured, but his tenure of the primacy was little more than as a servant of the crown, even if he imbued that service with religious content. The king had made clear at Hampton Court that he could act independently of his bishops, and it may be that Bancroft was one of the few to appreciate the limitations that set him.

At Lambeth, Bancroft surrounded himself with a diverse but highly articulate group of chaplains, all of them of his own preferred academic mind. Several of them preached and wrote on matters close to his heart. Leonard Hutton defended the use of the cross in baptism in 1605; Thomas Rogers defended kneeling at communion in 1608; the same year Downham defended episcopacy. Bancroft astutely used their penmanship to infuse ceremonies that might otherwise have remained unpopular with a sense of God-given decency. At each stage his own persona remains discreetly in the background, but there can be no mistaking his presence among the ghost writers. The earl of Clarendon's opinion that Bancroft 'had almost rescued' the church 'out of the hands of the Calvinian party, and very much subdued the unruly spirit of the Non-conformists' may have been optimistic, but his contention that he 'understood the church excellently' stands better with the evidence (Clarendon, *Hist. rebellion* (Macray edn), 1.186). NICHOLAS W. S. CRANFIELD

Sources *Tracts ascribed to Richard Bancroft*, ed. A. Peel (1953) • A. Peel, ed., *The seconde parte of a register*, 2 vols. (1915) • Fuller, *Worthies* (1662) • A. Cox-Johnson, 'Lambeth Palace Library, 1610–1664', *Trans. Cambridge Bibl. Soc.*, 2 (1955), 105–26 • Venn, *Alum. Cant.* • S. R. Day, 'A life of Archbishop Richard Bancroft, 1544–1610', DPhil diss., U. Oxf., 1956 • S. B. Babbage, *Puritanism and Richard Bancroft* (1962) • G. Bray, ed., *The Anglican canons, 1529–1947* (1998) • E. Cardwell, *A history of the conferences and other proceedings connected with the revision of the Book of Common Prayer* (1840) • K. Fincham, ed., *Visitation articles and injunctions of the early Stuart church*, 2 vols. (1994–8), vol. 1 • F. Shriver, 'Hampton Court re-visited: James I and the puritans', *Journal of Ecclesiastical History*, 33 (1982), 48–71 • P. Collinson, 'The Jacobean religious settlement', *Before the English civil war*, ed. H. Tomlinson (1983), 27–51 • *Calendar of the manuscripts of the most hon. the marquis of Salisbury*, 11, HMC, 9 (1906) • will, LPL, Wharton MS 577, fol. 58 • will, PRO, SP 14/57/115 • *Dodd's Church history of England*, ed. M. A. Tierney, 5 vols. (1839–43)

Archives BL, corresp. and papers, Add. MSS 5496, 5813, 5831, 6094, 6177–6178 • CUL, letters and papers • Hatfield House, Hertfordshire, letters and papers • Inner Temple, London, letters and papers • LPL, letters and papers | NL Scot., corresp. relating to Scotland [copies]

Likenesses oils, *c.*1600, Knole, Kent [*see illus.*] • oils, *c.*1600–1610, LPL • oils, after 1604, NPG • attrib. J. van Belcamp, oils, *c.*1630–1640, Knole, Kent • N. Hilliard, miniature, AM Oxf. (stolen) • bust, Knowsley Hall, Lancashire • oils, Church commissioners, Millbank • oils, Trinity Cam. • oils, Jesus College, Cambridge • oils, Trinity Hall, Cambridge • oils, Radnor Castle • oils, New College, Oxford

Bancroft, Sir Squire (1841–1926). *See under* Bancroft, Marie Effie, Lady Bancroft (1839–1921).

Bancroft, Thomas (*fl.* 1613–1658), poet, was born at Swarkston, Derbyshire, and matriculated at St Catharine's College, Cambridge, at Easter 1613. Alluded to in contemporary records as the 'small poet', he was known to be living at Bradley, Derbyshire, in 1658. His published works are *The Glutton's Feaver* (1633), *Two Books of Epigrammes and Epitaphs* (1639), a romance in eight cantos entitled *The Heroical Lover* (1658), and a collection of twenty satires, *Times out of Tune* (1658). *The Glutton's Feaver*, written in the first person from the perspective of the repentant glutton, places him in a series of trials and punishments for his past error-strewn years; atonement follows, as the glutton is made to see his mistaken ways. The *Two Bookes of Epigrammes and Epitaphs* are similar in tone to *The Glutton's Feaver*, and in all the book contains 480 short pieces. Some lighter compositions are to members of the Knyveton family, one to Swarkston village, and another to the Trent River, yet most continue the ashen view of life seen in his earlier work. His epigram 'Of Human Life' is a model of his early pessimism:

> If life be but a thread, then why not
> Sharpe misery be th' needle, death the knot?
> (epigram 179, book 2)

The satires found in *Times out of Tune, Plaid upon However in XX Satyres* are against sectaries; the abuse of poetry; presumption; pride in apparel; lying; vanity; discord; weakness; falsehood in friendship; gluttony; excess in drinking; ambition; whoredom; voluptuousness; timidity; detraction; injustice; cruelty; and discontentedness. Given that they are written against largely abstract concepts, they lack the precision or venom of those by other authors targeted against individuals. If the subjects chosen seem to leave no aspect of unbuttoned human life to enjoy, the author was aware that whatever his disapprobation, human nature would still indulge. His most amiable work is *The Heroical Lover*, a romance in which the hero Antheon seeks his queen Fidelta. The poem shows little interest in love *per se*, and the plot is basically a means of exploring Bancroft's interests in geography and vulcanology. Each canto sees Antheon in another country, though the geographical progress defies common sense. Borrowing from *The Odyssey* each country provides Antheon with female temptation, which he stoically refuses, preferring to return to his quest to find Fidelta. Antheon is also equipped with the arts of war, able to lay siege or to attack, yet spends his journey somewhat restlessly. He travels first to Italy and the Roman campagna, and is tempted by a 'Lady of the Lake' before moving to

France. After a further temptation offered by a woman at court he goes to Spain, passing across the '*Pyrenean* hills', before he meets Sordezza, 'That Harpy-like, Hell-raking Sorceress'. A further canto is set in Greece, before his journey to Sicily: here 'Aetna' is described. The penultimate canto finds Antheon in Belgium, plied with alcohol and tobacco, which again he refuses, before his first meeting with Fidelta in a land called Eutopia (not far from Atlantis).

An encounter with Bancroft's lighter work, with its excitement over geography and volcanoes, represents an interesting supplement to a reading of the lengthy texts devoted to his main areas of interest with their various measures of disapprobation. NICHOLAS JAGGER

Sources T. Bancroft, *Heroical lover* (1658) · T. Bancroft, *Times out of tune* (1658) · Venn, *Alum. Cant.* · *DNB*

Bancroft, Thomas (1756–1811), Church of England clergyman and schoolmaster, was born in Deansgate, Manchester, son of Thomas Bancroft, a thread maker. He was educated at Manchester grammar school from the age of six and at Brasenose College, Oxford, whence he matriculated on 8 April 1778, aged twenty-two. He graduated BA in 1781 and was awarded his MA in 1784. After leaving Oxford he worked briefly as assistant master at Manchester grammar school under the headmaster, Charles Lawson, before being appointed headmaster of King Henry VIII School at Chester. Little is known of his headmastership apart from the assessment of the Cheshire antiquary George Ormerod, that 'the school attained a considerable degree of classical celebrity' under Bancroft's headship (Ormerod, 1.366n.). He published a collection of Greek, Latin, and English exercises, written partly by his pupils, at Chester in 1788 as *Prolusiones poeticae*, described in the dedication to the bishop of Chester as 'the literary first-fruits of the King's School, Chester' (T. Bancroft, *Prolusiones poeticae*, 1788, dedication). Bancroft became a minor canon of Chester Cathedral and was ordained deacon at Chester on 29 June 1783. He was ordained as a priest on 28 September 1783.

While headmaster of King Henry VIII School, Bancroft married Elizabeth, the daughter of a Mr Bennett, wine merchant and alderman of the city of Chester. Bennett was opposed to the marriage, and after Bancroft and his fiancée ran away to be married, Mr Bennett chased them, stabbed Bancroft in the leg with his sword, took his daughter back home, and forbade them to have any contact. However, they eloped a second time, and after they married Bennett disowned his daughter and they were never reconciled, though he did bequeath £1000 to each of their two daughters, Elizabeth (*bap.* 6 May 1789) and Ann (*bap.* 7 May 1783).

In 1793 Bancroft became vicar of Bolton, where he remained until his death in 1811. He became domestic chaplain to the first Viscount Castle-Stewart, chaplain to the Bolton Volunteers in 1798, and was appointed as king's preacher for Lancashire in 1807. He also served on the Bolton magistrate's bench.

Bancroft was an intellectual, a frustrated academic who had missed out on the opportunity of taking his doctorate at Oxford. He published translations of Latin and Greek works but the majority of his publications concerned matters of theology and Christian duty. He was a high-church tory, and a close associate of Colonel Ralph Fletcher, a founder member of the English Orange order, and he was not above using the pulpit for the purpose of political propaganda. His published sermons testify to his vehement antagonism to civil and religious dissent, and revolutionary politics, which he associated with heathenism. He believed in the notion of a chain of being, and that each individual was allocated to a station in life by God. He also believed that England and the English protestant constitution were superior to any other system of civil government or theological doctrine. Moreover, he believed that England had a special relationship with God and that divine providence had blessed England with prosperity and liberty. Political loyalism, therefore, was a religious act, and a fundamental part of Christian duty, for, as he argued, 'One irregular stone in the Fabric may prejudice the firmness, as well as destroy the symmetry of the whole' (T. Bancroft, *Christian Zeal and Civil Obedience Earnestly Recommended to the Friends of Piety and Good Government*, 1800). Yet Bancroft did not write for posterity and clearly had no desire for his political preaching to survive his death. In his will he directed that his sermons be destroyed to safeguard them against passing into the hands of others or being used by others.

Bancroft died on 5 February 1811 and was buried at Bolton parish church. A. J. GRITT

Sources Bolton biographical cuttings, Lancs. RO · will, 1811, Lancs. RO · Foster, *Alum. Oxon.* · *IGI* · G. Ormerod, *The history of the county palatine and city of Chester*, 3 vols. (1819) · J. F. Smith, ed., *The admission register of the Manchester School, with some notes of the more distinguished scholars*, 3 vols. in 4 pts, Chetham Society, 69, 73, 93, 94 (1866–74), vol. 1, pp. 103–6; vol. 3, p. 340

Wealth at death under £2000: will, 1811, Lancs. RO

Bancroft, William James (1871–1959), rugby player and cricketer, was born on 2 March 1871 in the Carmarthen Arms, Waterloo Street, Swansea, Glamorgan, the eldest of the eleven children of William Bancroft (1848–1906), cobbler and cricket professional, and his wife, Emma Jones. At two years of age William junior went to live with his grandfather in the groundsman's cottage in the southwest corner of St Helen's football and cricket field in Swansea (he attended St Helen's elementary school). He lived there until his marriage in 1892 to Harriet Florence Turner (*d.* 1934), with whom he had four daughters and three sons.

Reared in the atmosphere of the famous rugby ground, Bancroft came into regular contact with footballers and cricketers, and by the age of sixteen was playing rugby for the local Excelsiors. He soon progressed via the established Bryn-y-môr team to the senior Swansea side, for whom he played his first game against Newport on 5 October 1889. After only seventeen games with 'the whites' he won his first international cap, without a trial, when the player originally selected, Newport's Tom England, broke his leg and was forced to withdraw. Bancroft stepped in to make his début against Scotland at Cardiff Arms Park on 1 February 1890, and went on to win an uninterrupted sequence of thirty-three caps, a record for a Welsh full-back not broken until 1975, by J. P. R. Williams.

Known variously as Billy, Banky, or W. J., Bancroft captained the Swansea club in 1893–4 and for a further five seasons between 1896 and 1901 in a playing career that ended only in 1905 when he received a testimonial of £322 from his admirers. By then he was recognized as one of the leading Welsh sportsmen of his time. He captained Wales on eleven occasions and was the first Welsh player to be a member of two triple crown sides, those of 1893 and 1900. In 1893 on the occasion of England's first ever visit to Cardiff Arms Park, his combination of total self-confidence and assiduously practised goal-kicking enabled him to drop-kick a last-minute penalty goal virtually from the touchline to score a 12–11 victory and set Wales on the road to its first triple crown. He took every free kick, penalty, and conversion awarded to Wales between 1890 and 1901, scoring sixty points in all.

At 5 feet 5½ inches in height, and weighing little over 10 stones—albeit 'ten stones of fencing wire fitted with the electricity of life' according to the *Bristol Evening News* in January 1903 (Farmer, 71)—Bancroft was not best equipped to meet the stern defensive requirements of the full-back position. But he was sturdier than he looked, and this, allied to speed and 'a cock-sureness that terrified selectors and aggravated anxious spectators' (Owen), more than compensated. Reckoned to be the fastest man over 25 yards in the Swansea team, he possessed a change of pace, a sidestep, and a sharp eye for an opening. He also had a rare ability to kick long and accurately from the hand while running at speed; he was perhaps the first running full-back the game had seen, even if his running was aimed more at tiring the opposition than linking with his team-mates. His favourite ploy was to tease lumbering forwards into chasing him from one side of the field to the other until he eventually banged the ball into touch over their exhausted heads. Well groomed and dapper, even something of a dandy with his trim moustache and jaunty walk, he was the inevitable target of less fastidious opponents, and when the boisterous Ryan brothers eventually caught him in the Irish match at Cardiff in 1899, they threw him into the crowd, cracking a few of his ribs in the process.

Like his father, Bancroft played cricket as well as rugby for Swansea. Both his father and his grandfather were professional cricketers with the Swansea club, established in 1850, and Bancroft himself became in 1895 the first regular professional to be employed, at £2 a week to supplement his meagre income as a cobbler, by the recently founded (1889) Glamorgan County Cricket Club. His quick reflexes and sure catching at full-back in rugby owed a good deal to the safe hands of the cricketer who enjoyed fielding in suicide positions close to the wicket. A right-handed batsman, medium-paced bowler, and wicket-keeper, he was a fine all-rounder whose services were crucial to Glamorgan's survival in the minor counties' championship in the early 1900s. In a cricketing career of 230 matches between 1889 and 1914 he scored over 8000 runs, making his first-class début in June 1910 for the west of England at Cardiff, and playing for south Wales against the South African tourists at Swansea in June 1912. He retained his association with St Helen's after retiring by opening a sports shop close to the ground, and in the inter-war years acting as steward in the members' enclosure, invariably sitting at the bottom of the pavilion steps.

William's brother Jack Bancroft (1879–1942) followed him in playing cricket for Glamorgan from 1908 to 1922 and winning thirteen caps for Wales at full-back between 1908 and 1912, scoring 88 points. When the writer A. A. Thomson told a Welsh friend that as a boy he had 'seen and admired the great Bancroft' in 1912, he was told in return that 'maybe the man you saw was wonderful … but he was not the great Bancroft. He was merely the great Bancroft's little brother.' Thomson concluded that 'if W. J. was all that better than J. he must have had wings as well' (Thomson, 59). Bancroft died at the house of his eldest son, Reginald, Killeen, Higher Lane, Langland, Swansea, on 3 March 1959 and was buried at Oystermouth three days later. GARETH WILLIAMS

Sources D. Farmer, *The all whites: the life and times of Swansea RFC* (1995) • D. Smith and G. Williams, *Fields of praise: the official history of the Welsh Rugby Union, 1881–1981* • A. Hignell, *Centenary history of Glamorgan county cricket club* (1988) • J. B. G. Thomas, *Great rugger players* (1955) • W. J. T. Collins, *Rugby recollections* (1948) • W. Thomas, *A century of Welsh rugby players, 1880–1980* (1980) • A. A. Thomson, *Rugger my pleasure* (1955) • O. L. Owen, *The Times* (17 March 1959) • *South Wales Evening Post* (4 March 1959) • *South Wales Echo* (4 March 1959) • W. W. Price, 'Biographical index', NL Wales

Likenesses photograph, repro. in J. B. G. Thomas, *Illustrated history of Welsh rugby* (1980), 27 • photographs, repro. in Farmer, *The all whites*, 14, 44, 59

Banda, Hastings Kamuzu (*c.*1898–1997), president of Malawi, was born in a small village near the trading centre Kasungu in the British protectorate of Nyasaland, the son of Mphonongo Banda and his wife, Akupinganyama Phiri. (He later gave 1906 as his year of birth.) His parents were Chewa peasants who separated when he was about seven years old. He received his early education from African teachers of the Livingstonia Mission of the Free Church of Scotland at the local village school. In 1915 he left Nyasaland and, following the path trodden by a growing number of Nyasa labour migrants, sought employment in Hartley in Southern Rhodesia, where he worked for two years as a hospital cleaner. He then travelled to a mine outside Johannesburg, where he spent eight years, first as an underground miner and then as a clerk in the compound office.

Banda's intention in making the 1000 mile trek to South Africa was to obtain entrance to the Scottish-run Lovedale Institution in the eastern Cape. In the event, his religious contacts at the Witwatersrand deep mine were with black American members of the African Methodist Episcopal church, which he joined in 1922. In the following year he met the leader of the church, Bishop W. T. Vernon, who was so impressed by the young man that he agreed to sponsor his education in America. In 1925 Banda travelled

Hastings Kamuzu Banda (*c*.1898–1997), by Rex Coleman for Baron Studios, 1964

to Ohio, where he completed his high school education in the Wilberforce Institute, Xenia. From there he went to the universities of Indiana and Chicago, graduating in history and political science in 1931. In the same year he enrolled in Meharry Medical College in Nashville, Tennessee, from which he graduated as doctor of medicine in 1937.

Banda's American qualifications did not allow him to practise on British soil, so in 1938 he moved to Edinburgh, where he was admitted LRCP and LRCS in 1941, the year in which he also became an elder in the Church of Scotland. His intention at this time was to return to Nyasaland as a government or mission doctor, and to this end in late 1941 he took a course in tropical medicine in Liverpool. The colonial government, however, refused to employ him on the same terms as European doctors, with the result that he abandoned his plan to return and went into general practice, first in Liverpool and North Shields, and then, from 1945, in the north London suburb of Harlesden. It was in North Shields in 1944 that he met Mrs Merene Margaret Ellen French, *née* Robbins (*d*. 1976), the wife of William Henry French, a schoolmaster and wartime major; she became his partner, housekeeper, and receptionist for the next thirteen years.

Banda's achievement in building up a flourishing practice in Harlesden was a remarkable demonstration of his ability to transcend the racism of 1940s Britain. A dedicated doctor, impeccably dressed in a dark three-piece suit, he won the trust and respect of his patients (almost all of them white), just as he had done in Liverpool and North Shields. He read voraciously, particularly biographies and histories of ancient Greece and Rome, joined the Fabian Colonial Bureau (whose founder, Arthur Creech Jones, he had met at a conference in Leeds), and corresponded with other politicians interested in colonial freedom. He attended the Pan-African Congress in Manchester in 1945, and became a friend of and physician to Kwame Nkrumah.

Banda's consuming concern, however, remained the future of Nyasaland. His involvement in its politics went back to 1938, when he gave evidence to the Bledisloe commission, investigating the case for the amalgamation of Nyasaland and the Rhodesias. A year later he acted as adviser to Chief Mwase, from his own home district, on the latter's visit to London, and in 1944 he joined forces with a former Livingstonia missionary, Cullen Young, to edit a collection of essays by young Malawians, published in 1946 under the title *Our African Way of Life*.

With the founding in 1944 of the Nyasaland African Congress, Banda's involvement in politics increased. Appointed London representative, he took up its concerns with Creech Jones, now a minister at the Colonial Office, and with various members of parliament. But it was the emergence in 1949 of plans for the federation of Nyasaland with Northern and Southern Rhodesia that brought Banda into conflict with the British government. Convinced, not unreasonably, that this was a scheme designed to maintain white supremacy in central Africa, Banda wrote a pamphlet, *Federation in Central Africa* (1949), denouncing the proposals, and threw himself into the anti-federation campaign. For the next three years he masterminded the Congress's policy of bringing together chiefs and commoners in an alliance, only to suffer defeat in 1953 when federation was finally imposed. In the same year, disillusioned with British democracy, he went to live with Merene French in the Gold Coast, now moving towards independence under Nkrumah, where he set up his practice in the northern provincial capital of Kumasi. He remained there until 1958 when, after repeated requests from the young leaders of the newly resurgent Nyasaland African Congress, he agreed to become leader of the party. Meanwhile, in 1955 he was cited as co-respondent in the divorce of William and Merene French.

On his return to Nyasaland (without Merene French) on 6 July 1958, forty-three years after his departure, Banda set himself with exceptional energy and skill to create a monolithic nationalist party with himself as its undisputed leader. Giving speeches in English, still dressed in the three-piece suit and Homburg hat that he had worn on his rounds in north London, he appeared an incongruous figure to many observers. But through his organizational skills women and the young were incorporated into the movement in far larger numbers than before, and his position as president-general of Congress was consolidated. In a remarkable campaign, peasant grievances against government soil conservation schemes were equated with opposition to the hated federation, thus spreading political agitation deep into the countryside. As the campaign gained in popularity, disturbances broke out, leading the Nyasaland governor, Sir Robert Armitage, to declare a state of emergency on 3 March 1959. Banda was arrested along with over 1000 Congress leaders and taken to Gwelo gaol in Southern Rhodesia.

Banda remained in prison for over a year, during which time the British and Nyasaland governments debated his future. An anti-communist, firm in his admiration of British institutions, Banda at one level was precisely the type of politician to whom the British government wished to transfer power. However, his uncompromising opposition to federation made him appear a more dangerous opponent in some eyes than other, socially more radical, African leaders. His cause was strengthened by the publication in July 1959 of the Devlin report, which found no evidence of Banda's involvement in a murder plot, as alleged by British ministers, and which emphasized the almost universal opposition to federation now existing among Africans in Nyasaland. By October 1959 the new colonial secretary, Iain Macleod, had become convinced that without Banda no settlement in Nyasaland would be possible. Against the opposition of Armitage and the federal prime minister, Roy Welensky, Macleod released Banda on 1 April 1960 and invited him to the first of a series of constitutional talks in London.

Freed from prison, Banda asserted his control over the Nyasaland African Congress's successor, the Malawi Congress Party (MCP), becoming life president of the party in 1960 and the centre of an extravagant personality cult. An adept negotiator, he combined periodic volcanic rages with considerable charm in his dealings with successive British politicians. After the overwhelming success of the MCP in the elections of 1961, he was appointed minister of natural resources and local government, and then prime minister in August 1963. A year later, in July 1964, he led the country into independence as Malawi (a name chosen by Banda to commemorate the pre-colonial Maravi state).

The cabinet crisis that erupted a few weeks later marked the first serious challenge to Banda's authority and the beginning of a new style of regime. Requested to accept the principle of collective leadership by his young ministerial colleagues, Banda reacted by dismissing or forcing the resignation of six of them and by turning to his white-officered army and police force for support. New powers were granted to the paramilitary Young Pioneers, hundreds of opponents were detained, and a brief rebellion was crushed. Elected president of Malawi under the new republican constitution in 1966, and life president in 1971, Banda introduced a personal style of government that was exceptional even in Africa. Parliament and party were reduced to the role of ciphers and he ruled through a small group of shifting confidants. The most important of these were his new companion, Cecilia Tamanda Kadzamira, who had replaced Merene French on his return to Nyasaland, and Cecilia's uncle, John Tembo. For almost thirty years no criticism of the life president or the MCP was tolerated, and thousands of victims were jailed. But in his prime Banda also shrewdly created networks of collaborative alliance through the extensive provision of patronage to his political supporters. This was made possible through the dramatic growth in the 1970s of Press Holdings, his privately owned company, as one of the most powerful economic institutions in the country, with extensive interests in tobacco estates and retail trade as well as in two commercial banks.

For more than twenty years the severity of Banda's rule appeared to be balanced by the relative success of his pro-capitalist and pro-western policies. Money was squandered on the luxurious palaces he built in Blantyre and Lilongwe, but there was a sustained growth in export crops, notably tobacco, sugar, and tea. The anti-apartheid rhetoric of other African leaders was rejected. Instead, Banda in 1967 opened diplomatic links with South Africa and was rewarded by being supplied with a substantial South African loan to finance the building of a new capital at Lilongwe. In 1970 J. B. Vorster, the South African prime minister, visited Malawi; and in the following year Banda paid a much publicized state visit to South Africa.

Banda's decline dated from the late 1970s. By now aged over eighty and increasingly frail, he was confronted by severe food shortages and a worsening economic climate which the intervention of the World Bank in the early 1980s did little to alleviate. External protests grew, particularly after the government-directed murder in 1983 of four members of parliament, two of them senior ministers. Britain continued to provide support. But in 1992 western donors, in a change of policy, suspended aid, and Malawi's Roman Catholic bishops issued a pastoral letter condemning the abuse of human rights. Pressurized by a growing popular movement inside the country as well as from outside, Banda was forced to hold a referendum in June 1993, in which Malawians voted decisively for multi-party democracy. In the following May he and the MCP were defeated in Malawi's first democratic election. Placed under house arrest in 1995 for the murder of the four politicians twelve years earlier, he was acquitted for lack of evidence directly linking him and his immediate associates with the killings. He died of pneumonia at the Garden City Clinic, Johannesburg, South Africa, on 25 November 1997 and was given a full state funeral on 3 December at the capital he had founded at Lilongwe. He was survived by his 'official hostess', Cecilia Kadzamira.

JOHN MCCRACKEN

Sources P. Short, *Banda* (1974) • *The Guardian* (27 Nov 1997) • *Daily Telegraph* (27 Nov 1997) • *The Independent* (27 Nov 1997) • *The Times* (27 Nov 1997) • R. Pendlebury, 'The despot and his mistress', *Daily Mail* (20 Dec 1997) • T. D. Williams, *Malawi: the politics of despair* (1978) • R. I. Rotberg, *The rise of nationalism in central Africa: the making of Malawi and Zambia, 1873–1964* (1966) • J. L. Lwanda, *Kamuzu Banda of Malawi: a study in promise, power and paralysis* (1993) • C. McMaster, *Malawi: foreign policy and development* (1974) • T. Cullen, *Malawi: a turning point* (1994) • *Where silence rules: the suppression of dissent in Malawi*, Africa Watch (1990) • T. C. Young and H. K. Banda, preface, *Our African way of life*, ed. T. C. Young and H. K. Banda (1946), 15–28 • J. Kydd, 'Malawi in the 1970s: development policies and economic change', *Malawi: an alternative pattern of development*, Centre of African Studies, Edinburgh University (1985), 293–380 • L. Vail and L. White, 'Of chameleons and clowns: the case of Jack Mapanje', *Power and the* *praise song: southern African voices in history*, ed. L. Vail and L. White (1991), 278–318 • J. Kees van Donge, 'Kamuzu's legacy: the democratization of Malawi', *African Affairs*, 94 (1995), 227–57 • J. McCracken, 'Democracy and nationalism in historical perspective: the case of Malawi', *African Affairs*, 97 (1998), 231–49 • P. G. Forster, 'Culture, nationalism and the invention of tradition in Malawi', *Journal of Modern African Studies*, 32/3 (1994), 477–97 • *Daily Times* [Malawi], special issue (2 Dec 1997) • PRO, CO 525 • Bodl. RH, Devlin commission papers • National Archives of Malawi, Zomba • *The Nation* [Malawi] (27 Nov 1997) • certificate of decree absolute [William French, Merene French]

Archives Bodl. RH, corresp. with Arthur Creech Jones • Bodl. RH, Devlin commission papers • National Archives of Malawi, Zomba • PRO, series CO 525 and CO 7031 | FILM National Archives of Malawi, Zomba | SOUND BBC archives, London

Likenesses R. Coleman for Baron Studios, photograph, 1964, NPG [*see illus.*] • photograph, repro. in *Daily Times* [Malawi] • photographs, Hult. Arch.

Bandaranaike, Solomon West Ridgeway Dias (1899–1959), prime minister of Ceylon, was born on 8 January 1899 at the family home in Horagolla, Veyangoda, the only son of Sir Solomon Dias Bandaranaike (1862–1946) and his wife, Daisy Ezline, daughter of Sir Solomon Christoffel Obeyesekere. He was born into a family of wealth and influence in a society where those with high social status were expected to lead. His father had been an adviser to several British colonial governors and enjoyed easy access to the policy makers of the colonial administration. Unusually, the British governor was his godfather. As a child he had extensive contact with the British colonial leaders and their culture, which smoothed his transition to the environment at the prestigious St Thomas College in Colombo. The school prepared him for Christ Church, Oxford, where he obtained a second class in the classical honours moderations in 1921, and a third in jurisprudence in 1923. At first he felt uncomfortable in his Oxford surroundings and described his first year of university as a 'nightmare struggle'. However, in 1921 he joined the university debating society, the Oxford Union, and won great praise for his debating ability. In 1924 he ran for the presidency of the union and finished a poor third. He attributed his loss to prejudice among his fellow students and suffered a great hurt that probably affected his attitude towards the British throughout his public life.

Entry into politics Bandaranaike returned to Colombo to practise law in 1925, and ran for a seat on the Colombo municipal council in a by-election in 1927. By defeating A. E. Goonesinghe, the most influential trade union leader in the colony, Bandaranaike won recognition as an important leader of the anti-British forces, and later that year was elected secretary of the Ceylon National Congress (CNC). The CNC was at the forefront of Ceylonese agitation against the British for self-government and included all the influential political leaders of the period. In 1931 the Donoughmore constitution introduced a self-governing legislative council to the crown colony and adult suffrage. Bandaranaike was elected to it unopposed and remained a member of every legislature thereafter, until his death in 1959.

Throughout his life Bandaranaike, the privileged son of the Ceylonese élite, rebelled against authority: first

Solomon West Ridgeway Dias Bandaranaike (1899–1959), by Kenneth J. Somanade, 1959

against his father, and later, at Oxford, he challenged the authority of those who set the rules. After returning to Ceylon from England, his rebelliousness led him into new directions. He began to rebel against the British, initially by renouncing the Anglican religion of his parents, and later by challenging the colonial authority of the British. In 1937 he formed the Sinhala Maha Sangha (SMS) to represent Sinhalese Buddhist interests. His experiences at Oxford and while living under British rule had made him concerned about the impact of Europeans on the indigenous culture of Ceylon. The SMS was his attempt to protect his country's culture not only from the British, but also from the British-oriented Ceylonese élite. Although still a member of Don Stephen Senanayake's CNC, he was beginning the process of renouncing the Christian and British values espoused by the CNC leadership. The CNC was founded by members of the English-speaking Ceylonese élite. Many of its members were more comfortable in London than in Colombo, and had little in common with the vast majority of the population, who lived in rural areas and did not speak English. The SMS was the personal movement of its founder, Bandaranaike, and, unlike the CNC, it appealed to the Ceylonese peasants by championing their needs and culture.

Bandaranaike's rebelliousness did not extend to his marital relations. He accepted the traditional guidance of his family and allowed his father to arrange a marriage in 1940 to the much younger Sirimavo Ratwatte (1916–2000), the daughter of one of the most powerful families in the Kandyan hills of central Ceylon. The marriage, on 3 October 1940, united two of the most influential families in the country. Sirimavo was a dutiful wife, bearing him two daughters, Sunethra and Chandrika, and a son, Anura. Although she had been educated at St Bridget's Convent, neither she nor her husband could have envisaged that she would become the world's first female prime minister in 1960.

Independence and opposition British rule in Ceylon ended in 1948. Their departure unleashed a series of forces on which Bandaranaike would capitalize in his rise to power. As long as the British ruled, ethnic differences were kept in check; as soon as they left, the struggle for power began. Despite Ceylon's small size, it was an ethnically diverse society: two major languages were spoken, the Indo-Aryan Sinhala (the majority group, to which Bandaranaike belonged) and the Dravidian Tamil. The two groups also followed different religions, the Sinhalese being Buddhist, the Tamils Hindu. The Sinhalese believed that during British rule their culture and religion had been repressed, and that speakers of English had been given preferential treatment for colonial jobs and benefits. Bandaranaike based his political movement on their claims; his policies to promote Sinhalese Buddhism adversely affected the Tamil minority, who from the 1970s were driven to rebel against the government.

Bandaranaike's allegiance to the leadership of D. S. Senanayake and his United National Party (UNP), which had been formed by a merger between the CNC and his own SMS in 1947, began to weaken after the British withdrawal. Although he was the heir apparent to Senanayake as leader of the UNP, there were those within the party who wanted either Senanayake's cousin Sir John Kotelawala or his son Dudley to succeed him. Bandaranaike, who had served as minister of health and local government since 1947, finally led a revolt against Senanayake's leadership and crossed the floor of parliament to the opposition on 12 July 1951. He had hoped to lead a mass rebellion against Senanayake and his allies, but only five other members of parliament followed him to form the Sri Lanka Freedom Party (SLFP). This was not even enough for him to become leader of the opposition. His defection was precipitated by the UNP's rejection of his proposals to make Sinhala the sole national language and to promote Buddhism and the traditional ayurvedic system of medicine. English, spoken by a tiny minority of the population, was thus still to be used as a 'link language', uniting the two linguistic communities on the island. In his speech on that occasion he declared that 'I go, in the words of Abraham Lincoln "with malice towards none and with charity to all", not only in regard to those who have honoured me with their friendship, but even in regard to those who honoured me with their enmity.' In the elections the next year the SLFP won only nine seats out the fifty that they contested, and Bandaranaike became the leader of the opposition.

Coalition-building and government One of Bandaranaike's strongest qualities was his pragmatic ability as a compromiser and coalition builder. After his death he was quoted as once saying that 'the whole truth lies neither on one side, nor on the other. It is very often a rather puzzling compound of many things'. His defeat in the 1952 elections did not deter him. He immediately began to expand his political base by making alliances with others. By 1956 he had assembled an unlikely coalition of leftists, communists, and Sinhalese Buddhist nationalists into an electoral alliance that would transform Ceylonese politics. The SLFP would sweep the 1956 elections, propelling Bandaranaike into power. His own personality, coupled with the ideology of rural populism, held the coalition together for as long as Bandaranaike led it. Although the coalition constituents were united in their dislike of the conservative UNP, Bandaranaike offered them a complex populism that appealed to the leftist parties through its economic egalitarianism, and to the more conservative nationalist groups through its offer of empowerment for the rural Sinhalese peasant. Intense disagreements between conservatives, who sought to maintain the traditional hierarchical social and caste relations, and the leftists, who sought to replace hierarchy and deference with a meritocratic order, would destroy the coalition after Bandaranaike's death: they had little in common except his leadership. Because of Bandaranaike's efforts Ceylon would finally have a two-party system, but more importantly he opened the political system up to the poor and the lower classes, who were mobilized by his promises of change. He had found a wellspring of electoral support among the vast majority of the population, who did not speak English and lacked the educational and employment opportunities of those living in Colombo and the larger cities. The UNP had lost touch with the population, and Bandaranaike had forged a Sinhalese nationalist alliance which had appealed to the rural peasantry with his promise of 'Sinhala only'.

Bandaranaike saw himself as the leader of a new social order. He once described his role as

> both a nurse and a midwife. I am a nurse at a deathbed … I would like to see, as should be the case at every deathbed, that the death is reasonably peaceful and dignified … I am also, I feel, a midwife at a birth. I would like that birth to be auspicious and painless as far as possible.

He stressed the concept of fair play in his actions and political statements; his government would enact a series of policies which would redirect the political system of Ceylon. He created a welfare state that provided a minimum standard of living for all Ceylonese. He also began to restore the Sinhalese Buddhist culture to what Sinhalese nationalists believed was its rightful place in the society. The Sinhala language was made the national language, replacing English, and Buddhism was given more rights. Both of these actions angered non-Buddhist and non-Sinhala-speaking people, and led to severe rioting by Tamils in 1958.

Bandaranaike's three-year term of office (1956–9) was marked by many new legislative initiatives, but also by a delicate manoeuvring to keep the political forces he had unleashed under control. On one side were the leftists, who wanted more land reform and welfare policies. On the other were the Sinhalese Buddhist nationalists, who sought increased rights for their culture and religion while maintaining the economic and social status quo. The great compromiser had to keep his coalition together and also to make concessions to the angry Tamil minority, which was most severely affected by the pro-Sinhalese policies. In the end he would fail, not on broad political grounds, but on the petty personal issues that had crept into the political debate.

Assassination On 25 September 1959 the forces that Bandaranaike had worked so hard to keep under control destroyed him and his coalition. After an early-morning meeting with the new American ambassador at his home in Cinnamon Gardens, Colombo, Bandaranaike paused to greet some well-wishers and clients who had gathered on his verandah to greet him or to seek his help. He first turned to a Buddhist *bhikkhu* (monk) and gave the traditional greeting with a short bow and his hands clasped in front of him. The monk blessed him and left. A second monk stepped forward and Bandaranaike began to greet him in a similar manner. As Bandaranaike bowed, the monk pulled a gun from his robes and began shooting. Bandaranaike fell back into a chair, at first unaware of the severity of his wounds. He died twenty-four hours later. His assassin was wounded and arrested while trying to escape.

A Buddhist monk, the Venerable Mapitigama Buddharakkitha, had conspired with the assassin and several other former Bandaranaike supporters to kill the prime minister. The precipitating factor appears to have been an anonymous pamphlet which alleged that Buddharakkitha had been sexually involved with a female member of Bandaranaike's cabinet. When Bandaranaike refused to take action against the possible authors of the pamphlet, Buddharakkitha conspired to kill him. Although it was alleged that some members of Bandaranaike's cabinet, including Wijayananda Dahanayake, who became prime minister after Bandaranaike's death, may also have been involved in the plot, they were never charged with the conspiracy.

Bandaranaike, the man of wealthy origins who had turned his compassion to the poor of the country, displayed the same compassion in a statement made from his deathbed to a journalist. 'A foolish man dressed in the robes of a *bhikkhu* fired some shots at me in my bungalow this morning. I appeal to all concerned to show compassion to this man and not try to wreak vengeance on him … I appeal to all to be calm, patient and to do nothing that might cause trouble to the people.' A few hours later he died. His death shocked the nation. The mourning population stood in two 6 mile-long queues, with an average wait of seven hours, to file past his body as it lay in state. When the mourning was over, more than half a million people had paid him their respects.

Assessment and legacy Few leaders of any country have had such a profound effect on their country as Bandaranaike did on Ceylon (which only in 1972 officially adopted the name Sri Lanka by which the Sinhalese had always known it). His welfare policies raised the quality of life for the average Ceylonese so much that by the end of the twentieth century his country had health provisions and life expectancy comparable with Western countries, despite its poverty. Although later governments changed his policies, they left the basic elements of the welfare state in place.

The nationalist forces Bandaranaike unleashed spread into a civil war in the 1980s and forced a continuing debate about the role of Sinhalese Buddhist nationalism. However, his admirers point to his unfinished efforts to achieve a compromise with the leadership of the main Tamil party, the Federal Party. The legacy he left had a profound effect on Ceylonese politics. So too did his family's influence. His widow, Sirimavo, became the first elected female head of government in the world, serving from 1960 to 1965. She was re-elected as prime minister from 1970 to 1977 and again from 1994 until two months before her death, on 10 October 2000. Also in 1994 Bandaranaike's younger daughter, Chandrika Kumaratunga, was elected president of Sri Lanka. Kumaratunga charmed the nation with charisma similar to her father's. She rebelled against her mother's leadership of the SLFP and left the party for most of the 1980s before returning to lead it to electoral victory in the parliamentary and presidential elections of 1994. R. C. OBERST

Sources J. Manor, *The expedient utopian: Bandaranaike and Ceylon* (1989) • W. H. Wriggins, *Ceylon: dilemmas of a new nation* (1960) • *DNB*

Archives University of Peradeniya | FILM BFI NFTVA, current affairs footage • BFI NFTVA, documentary footage • BFI NFTVA, news footage

Likenesses group photograph, 27 June 1956 (*Commonwealth group*), Hult. Arch. • K. J. Somanade, photograph, 1959, Hult. Arch. [*see illus.*] • photograph, 17 Dec 1959 (of portrait on his tomb), Hult. Arch. • portrait, Oxford Union

Bandinel, Bulkeley (1781–1861), librarian, was born in Oxford on 21 February 1781, the third child of James Bandinel (*d.* 1804), fellow of Jesus College, and his wife, Margaret. His ancestors, originally from Italy, had moved to Jersey early in the seventeenth century. His father was the first of the family to settle in England. Educated at Winchester College and New College, Oxford, Bandinel proceeded from BA in 1805 to MA in 1807 and to BD and DD in 1823. He was ordained in 1805 and served as chaplain in the Royal Navy in 1808. He held the rectory of Haughton-le-Skerne, co. Durham, and the curacy of Wytham, Berkshire, until 1855. In 1815 he married Mary (*d.* 1875), daughter of John Phillips, of Culham, Berkshire; they had no children.

John Price, Bodley's librarian and Bandinel's godfather, appointed him under-librarian in 1810, and on Price's death three years later Bandinel was elected unopposed to his place. Within four months the Bodleian statutes were

Bulkeley Bandinel (**1781–1861**), by unknown photographer

altered to increase its staff, its annual grant, its opening hours, and its librarian's salary. Bandinel's long period in office was marked by the continuous expansion of the library's collections. A decision in the court of king's bench in 1814 confirming the copyright libraries' claim to all British publications left the increased grant available for the purchase of foreign and rare books and manuscripts. Bandinel prided himself on the speed with which he responded to items coming on the market, and through judicious purchases he significantly strengthened the holdings of incunables and early bibles. Extensive purchases of English material filled gaps in the library's holdings, for example seventeenth- and eighteenth-century plays and pre-1814 booksellers' catalogues in 1834 and, in 1837, over 19,000 pamphlets of the period 1660 to 1820. Bandinel made spectacular purchases of manuscripts both western and oriental, among them the collections of Canonici in 1817 and Oppenheimer in 1829 and selections from those of Saibante in 1820 and Ouseley in 1844.

Bandinel's energies were not confined to acquisition. As under-librarian he prepared the catalogue of the large Gough collection, which was published in 1814. As Bodley's librarian he set about the daunting task of producing a general catalogue of printed books to replace the existing one which, published in 1738 and containing many inaccuracies, was a woefully inadequate guide to the collections. Attempts made through Lord Grenville, chancellor of the university, to acquire a grant from the civil list to assist in this 'national object' came to nothing, and the work proceeded slowly. In 1837 Bandinel, eloquently pointing out that some 160,000 items had been added to the collections since 1813, asked for more staff. Three additional assistants were appointed and the catalogue was published in three volumes in 1843. A fourth volume, covering the accessions of 1835–47, appeared in 1851.

In the evidence presented to the 1850 royal commission of inquiry into the state of the university, there was much cause for congratulation for the librarian who had ruled the Bodleian for thirty-seven years. Bandinel could take pride in the richness of the collections, the courtesy of the staff, and the existence of published catalogues. His health was, however, failing and he took little part in the general overhaul which, in the Bodleian as elsewhere in the university, followed the publication of the commission's findings. His attendance at the library declined, but he clung to office, resisting change, while his governing body of curators turned increasingly to his subordinates. He was eventually persuaded to retire in September 1860. He died of angina after a severe attack of bronchitis at his Oxford home, 31 Beaumont Street, on 6 February 1861 and was buried six days later.

Outside the Bodleian, Bandinel's scholarly interests lay in editing. He served for many years as delegate of the university press. With John Caley and Henry Ellis he produced a lavish new edition of Dugdale's *Monasticon* (1817–30). Although hailed as an outstanding achievement in its day, its reputation has not survived the rigours of modern scrutiny. David Douglas, in his *English Scholars, 1660–1730* (rev. edn 1951, 38–40), dismisses it as 'almost entirely derivative'.

Contemporary accounts of Bandinel's character vary. His obituary in the *Gentleman's Magazine* described his endearing combination of universal courtesy and kindness. His gracious reception of Francis Douce when he visited the library in 1830 caused that great collector to alter his will in favour of the Bodleian. Yet he was clearly autocratic and did not suffer fools gladly. W. D. Macray, in his *Annals of the Bodleian*, admitted that Bandinel sometimes lacked 'the general courtesy which should be exhibited to all duly qualified readers alike' (Macray, 371 n). This verdict was endorsed by Professor Friedrich Max Müller, who in his *Autobiography* (Müller, 251), deplored Bandinel's rough treatment of his subordinates. Perhaps he had, as Sir Edmund Craster speculated in his *History of the Bodleian*, learned vigour of expression in the navy (Craster, 30). Macray, who served under him for twenty years, ended his account of Bandinel with the words 'all the staff trembled at Jupiter's nod'.

MARY CLAPINSON

Sources H. H. E. Craster, *History of the Bodleian Library, 1845–1945* (1952) • W. D. Macray, *Annals of the Bodleian Library, Oxford*, 2nd edn (1890) • F. M. Müller, *My autobiography: a fragment* (1901) • E. Edwards, *Memoirs of libraries* (1858) • *GM*, 3rd ser., 10 (1861), 465–6 • minutes of curators' meetings, 1793–1862, Bodl. Oxf., Library records d.12 • extracts from the diary of H. O. Coxe, Bodl. Oxf., MS library records d.1745 • parish register (baptisms), Oxford, St Peter-in-the-East, 20 March 1781 • *CGPLA Eng. & Wales* (1875) • *Oxford Chronicle and Berks and Bucks Gazette* (9 Feb 1861), 5 • parish register transcript (burials), Oxford, St Mary Magdalen, 12 Feb 1861

Archives Bodl. Oxf., antiquarian collections, bibliographical notebooks, corresp., and other papers • Bodl. Oxf., library records | BL, corresp. with Sir Frederic Madden, Egerton MSS 2837–2846, *passim* • BL, letters to Philip Bliss, Add. MSS 34568–34581, *passim* • Bodl. Oxf., corresp. with Sir Thomas Phillipps • E. Sussex RO, corresp. relating to H. E. H. Gage's debts while at Christ Church • U. Edin. L., corresp. with James Halliwell-Phillipps

Likenesses T. Kirkby, oils, 1825, Bodl. Oxf. • daguerreotype, 1860, Bodl. Oxf. • miniatures (with his wife), Bodl. Oxf.; repro. in Craster, *History of the Bodleian*, facing p. 30 • photograph, NPG [*see illus.*]

Wealth at death £16,000: probate, 2 March 1861, *CGPLA Eng. & Wales*

Bandinel, David (*d.* 1645), dean of Jersey, settled in Jersey with his English wife, Elizabeth Stallenge, towards the end of the reign of Elizabeth I. Of his earlier life nothing is known beyond his contemporaries' statement that he was Italian. In September 1601 he offered himself to the Calvinist colloquy in Jersey as a candidate for the ministry. He was accepted for the parish of St Brelade and installed there only two months later, so it appears that he had already trained for the ministry elsewhere. He remained there nearly twenty years, during which time his seven children, five sons and two daughters, were born. After St Brelade's he served St Mary's and then St Martin's.

The presbyterian form of church government was not destined to last much longer in the island. James I, on the understanding that this arrangement had been formally sanctioned by Elizabeth, confirmed it in the first year of his reign, but Sir John Peyton, appointed governor of the island by the king in 1603, was soon in conflict with the colloquy over the right of appointment to benefices. In 1614 there was still greater controversy over an appointment made by Peyton: the colloquy's objection in that case was related to the candidate's having received episcopal orders. In the same year delegations went to London, one representing each of the episcopal and presbyterian parties. Bandinel formed part of the delegation favouring the continuation of the presbyterian form of church government, though he accepted the office of dean when it was re-established.

When, on 15 April 1620, Bandinel was sworn into office, he was the first to hold it since John Paulet, who had been appointed under Henry VIII and served into Elizabeth's reign. One of Bandinel's first tasks as dean was to oversee the drawing up of the 'canons and constitutions ecclesiastical of the isle of Jersey'. An ecclesiastical court was established, which first met in September 1623, and Bandinel presided at its sittings.

Bandinel's appointment as dean was controversial: there was a heated dispute in the states on the occasion of his swearing in. Some of the rectors in the island objected strongly to what they saw as a non-scriptural innovation in church government. It is hard to determine whether there was much feeling against Bandinel personally, particularly since at least from the time of the contemporary account of island life in the 1640s contained in Jean Chevalier's *Journal* he was cast strongly as a troublesome foreigner allowed to hold too much power in the island—a view inspired almost entirely by his quarrel with the lieutenant-governor, Sir Philip de Carteret, and by his involvement in the parliamentary party in Jersey.

De Carteret was appointed by Charles I, and, although a zealous protestant, was always an ardent loyalist. He is said to have been a man of ability and integrity, but of austere manners, and he was accused by his enemies of absorbing all the more lucrative offices in the island. He and the governor, Sir Thomas Jermyn, were charged with having attempted to deprive the dean of part of his tithes, an act which roused Bandinel's animosity to the lieutenant-governor, which was in turn fostered by subsequent events.

During the civil war, Bandinel was among those leaders of the parliamentary party who kept back supplies from the besieged fortresses of Elizabeth Castle and Mont Orgueil, where the lieutenant-governor and his wife were confined. The hardships which he had to endure undermined de Carteret's health, and Bandinel revealed the extent of his bitterness in refusing all spiritual and material comforts to de Carteret in his final illness, keeping even his wife from him until the last moment. When on de Carteret's death in 1643 his son, Sir George Carteret, became lieutenant-governor in his place, he arrested Bandinel and his eldest son, Jacques, the rector of St Mary, on a charge of treason. The Bandinels were confined first in Elizabeth Castle and afterwards in Mont Orgueil, where, after more than twelve months' imprisonment, they formed a plan for escape. Having knotted together bed linen and other material, on the night of 10 February 1645 they forced their way through the grating of their cell and lowered themselves down the side of their prison. The son succeeded in reaching the end of the line but it was too short and he fell, seriously injured. The line broke under Bandinel's weight and he in turn fell, but from a greater height onto the rocks below, where he was discovered unconscious by a guard in the morning; he died later that day, 11 February. He was buried on 13 February in St Martin's churchyard. Elizabeth Bandinel survived her husband; Jacques Bandinel escaped for a time, but was recaptured and died in prison. HELEN M. E. EVANS

Sources *Journal de Jean Chevalier*, ed. J. A. Messervy, 9 parts (1906–14) • G. R. Balleine, *A biographical dictionary of Jersey*, [1] [1948] • minutes of the Jersey Calvinist colloquy, 1577–1614, CUL, MS Dd.11.43 • J. A. Messervy, ed., *Actes des états de l'Île de Jersey, 1597–1605* (1898) • J. A. Messervy, ed., *Actes des états de l'Île de Jersey, 1606–1651* (1899) • *Ordres du conseil et pièces analogues enregistrés a Jersey, 1536–1678*, 1 (1897) • J. A. Messervy, 'Listes des recteurs de l'Île de Jersey', *Annual Bulletin* [Société Jersiaise], 7 (1910–14), 5–29, 265–88 • J. A. Messervy, 'Listes des recteurs de l'Île de Jersey', *Annual Bulletin* [Société Jersiaise], 8 (1915–18), 81–110 • 'Mémoires de la famille La Cloche', *Annual Bulletin* [Société Jersiaise], 2 (1885–9), 461–507, esp. 462 • J. A. Messervy, 'Liste des doyens de l'Île de Jersey', *Annual Bulletin* [Société Jersiaise], 9 (1919–22)

Bandinel, James (1783–1849), civil servant, was the son of James Bandinel (*d.* 1804), fellow of Jesus College, Oxford, and his wife, Margaret. Bulkeley *Bandinel, Bodley's librarian, was his elder brother. James entered the Foreign Office as a clerk on 5 April 1799, became senior clerk in March 1822, and retired in December 1845 through ill health. About 1813 he married Marian Eliza, daughter of the Revd Robert Hunter (*d.* 1815), a Glaswegian who was rector of two parishes in Dorset. Bandinel was closely acquainted with Lady Arabella Harvey and Lord and Lady Rosebery. From 1824 until 1845 he was superintendent of the slave trade department, and as such bore considerable responsibility for the abolition of the slave trade. In 1842 he published a substantial work, *Some account of the trade in slaves from Africa as connected with Europe and America, especially with reference to the efforts made by the British government for its extinction*, and dedicated it to Lord Aberdeen, then foreign secretary (next year he asked Aberdeen for a living for his son). The book 'is an invaluable abstract of the Foreign Office slave trade papers' (Bethell, 6). Also in 1842 he was a member of a small commission to assess the role of the navy in the suppression of the slave trade; its report in 1844 led to increased naval action on the west coast of Africa. Bandinel latterly supported the use of force by the navy, arguing to the select committee on the Brazilian trade in 1847–8 for 'making redress by force of arms' when necessary (ibid., 307). He died of Asiatic cholera at his house in Berkeley Square, London, on 29 July 1849.

His son, **James Bandinel** (1814–1893), Church of England clergyman and theologian, graduated from Wadham College, Oxford, and worked under the supervision of William Palmer of Worcester, the high-church theologian, whose extreme views came to stand in the way of Bandinel's preferment. He published many theological works of a high-church sort. He held livings in Oxfordshire and Yorkshire. His marriage to his first cousin, Julia Le Mesurier of the Guernsey family, ended in separation, which caused a breach between the Bandinels, father and son. Of their children, James Julius Frederick Bandinel was a merchant's clerk in Newchwang (Yingkou), China, in the 1890s. H. C. G. MATTHEW

Sources *DNB* • *Annual Register* (1849) • J. M. Collinge, ed., *Office-holders in modern Britain*, 8: *Foreign office officials, 1782–1870* (1979) • L. Bethell, *The abolition of the Brazilian slave trade* (1970) • R. Anstry and P. F. H. Hair, *Liverpool, the African slave trade, and abolition* (1976) • report 25903 (Bandinel), NRA, priv. coll.

Archives Duke U., Perkins L., corresp. and papers | Shrops. RRC, corresp. with third Baron Berwick • U. Durham, letters to Viscount Ponsonby

Likenesses J. C. Horsley, lithograph, 1850, NPG • C. Baugniet, lithograph (after sketch), NPG • R. J. Lane, lithograph (after J. C. Horsley, 1850), NPG

Bandinel, James (1814–1893). *See under* Bandinel, James (1783–1849).

Bandon. For this title name *see* Bernard, Percy Ronald Gardner, fifth earl of Bandon (1904–1979).

Banerjea [Bandyopadhyay], **Sir Surendranath** (**1848–1925**), politician, the second child of Dr Durgacharan Banerjea, was born in Taltala, Calcutta, on 10 November 1848. Durgacharan, a disciple of David Hare, the philanthropist who helped him to get his medical education, was one of the most successful doctors in the city and a friend of the reformer Vidyasagar, whom he introduced to English education. The tension between the very orthodox Brahmanical family traditions and his father's modernist outlook was an important influence in the development of Surendranath's intellectual and social concerns. Educated at the Parental Academic Institution of Calcutta and Doveton College, Calcutta, after graduation he left for England in the company of R. C. Dutt and Bihari Lal Gupta to sit for the Indian Civil Service examination in 1869. All three were successful in the competition, but Banerjea's appointment was held up as there was doubt regarding his age; his appeal to court on this issue was successful and he was admitted to the service. He was appointed assistant magistrate in Sylhet in 1871, but he was suspended and dismissed in 1873 on grounds of negligence. His 'crime' was that he had signed an official document which listed a closed case as adjourned. The belief persisted that he was the victim of racism, having incurred the wrath of the local European officials by claiming equality of social status for himself and his wife, Chandidevi, a view indirectly supported by two lieutenant-governors of Bengal. Banerjea went to England to appeal against the decision but was unsuccessful. He joined the Middle Temple to seek qualification as a barrister, but the benchers refused to call him to the bar in view of his dismissal. He returned to Calcutta a disgraced official and was virtually ostracized by local society. Vidyasagar offered him a lectureship in English in

Sir Surendranath Banerjea [Bandyopadhyay] (**1848–1925**), by Johnston & Hoffmann

Metropolitan College, which he accepted in 1876. This was the beginning of a teaching career which was to last for thirty-seven years, in the course of which he also taught at Free Church College (later renamed Scottish Church College) and at City College (founded by the leaders of the Brahmo Samaj). He established a new college in 1882 which was later named Ripon College.

The first forum of Banerjea's political activity was the Calcutta Students' Association. Ananadamohan Basu, who was inspired by the activities of the Bombay students, was the co-founder of the organization. Banerjea's great fame as a speaker who could electrify his audiences began with his speeches to this association, on subjects such as 'The life of Mazzini', 'The rise of the Sikh power', 'Chaitanya', and 'Indian unity'. His purpose was to create a political consciousness and patriotic concern among the students. He held up as his ideal the self-dedication of the Italian nationalists Mazzini and Garibaldi, though he pleaded for constitutional agitation as practised in Britain rather than active, especially armed, resistance. He also underlined the message of radical social change in Chaitanya's teaching which indirectly challenged the caste system, the patriotic fervour of the Sikhs who had defeated the British, and the underlying unity of Indian society. His younger contemporaries bore witness to the consciousness-raising impact of Banerjea's speeches. His purpose, in his own words, was to create among the young men of his country 'a genuine, sober and rational interest in public affairs'. The effect of his propaganda went far beyond this restrained objective.

Banerjea felt the need for an institutional base for sustained constitutional agitation. The Indian Association established in 1876 was the product of this concern. Leaders of the Brahmo Samaj were among the enthusiastic sponsors of this organization: the individualistic ideal they upheld in their programme of social and religious reform had a political counterpart in this new initiative. As Bipin Pal, the extremist leader, pointed out, there had really been no serious effort to propagate democratic ideals in India until then. The older British Indian Association was a body restricted to and speaking for the landowners, and the more democratic Indian League enjoyed very little support. The Indian Association thus proved to be the first democratic forum for middle-class Indians. The Brahmoists' insistence on freedom of individual action had created conflicts within Indian society. Those who were attracted by their ideology but were hesitant to face conflict within the family circle could now express their love of freedom through actions which were risk-free. Banerjea's tours of the districts attracted large audiences of up to 30,000 people, and he concentrated on issues such as reduction of the salt tax, the need for trial by jury, freedom of the press, and the end to racial discrimination in the judicial system.

One of the first activities of the Indian Association was its campaign against the British decision to reduce further the age of entrance into the Indian Civil Service, which would have undermined the chances of Indians entering the service. Banerjea's lecture tours in this connection to many parts of India made him aware that there was already a homogeneous class of Indians educated in the same Western system and sharing the same aspirations. The possibility and need for an all-India political organization now became evident to him, as to many others. The Arms Act and the Vernacular Press Act passed by the viceroy, Lord Lytton, which took away the Indians' right to carry arms and restricted severely the freedom of the press, led to further agitations that cemented this new awareness. Meanwhile Banerjea had acquired a new instrument for his campaign, the ownership of a weekly paper, *The Bengalee*, which he started editing in 1879; it became a daily in 1900. An editorial he wrote criticizing a judge of the Calcutta high court whose action had offended Hindus led to a prosecution for contempt of court and a sentence of imprisonment in 1883, an incident which provoked great resentment throughout the country.

Now more keenly aware than ever of the need for sustained propaganda and agitation both in India and in England, Banerjea took the initiative in setting up a National Fund. His oratorical skills proved of great value in this effort while the British agitation against the Ilbert Bill (which was designed to bring Europeans in India under the jurisdiction of Indian magistrates) sharpened the sense of political bondage. The old British Indian Association and the more middle-class Indian Association now forgot their differences and merged into the National Conference, which paved the way for the founding of the Indian National Congress in 1885. Though he missed the first meeting of the new national organization Banerjea was involved in its activities from the very start, and was twice elected its president (in 1895 and in 1902). He also participated to great effect in the representative institutions of the period, as municipal chairman from 1885 onwards and as a member of the Bengal legislative council for eight years from 1893. In 1890 he went to England as a member of the mission sent by the Congress to plead for an increased measure of representation in the decision-making bodies. He visited England on two more occasions, to give evidence before the Welby commission in 1897 and as a representative of the Indian press at the imperial press conference in 1909.

Banerjea assumed a more confrontational role in the campaign against the partition of Bengal in 1905. He was arrested and fined on charges of leading a banned procession during a conference in the district town of Barisal. Yet as the tension between the moderates and the extremists within the Indian National Congress grew sharper Banerjea found himself firmly on the side of the moderates. On the passing of the Montagu-Chelmsford reforms of 1919 and Gandhi's decision to launch the non-co-operation movement the following year, he was among the leaders who left the Congress organization and co-operated with the reforms. He accepted a knighthood from the British in 1919 and joined the Bengal cabinet as minister for local self-government in 1921. His credibility as a nationalist leader suffered a serious blow through these actions, and he was defeated in the provincial election of 1923 by a young doctor sponsored by C. R. Das, Dr B. C. Roy. For a man who had once been hailed as the uncrowned king of Bengal and the father of national consciousness this was an intolerable humiliation. He died, a broken man, in Calcutta on 6 August 1925.

Despite the rejection he suffered in his last days, when the political situation had undergone a sea change, leaving men of his persuasion entirely isolated, Banerjea's great contribution to the growth of nationalist consciousness in India is universally recognized. His autobiography, *A Nation in Making* (1925), is a remarkable account of the emergence of that consciousness.

TAPAN RAYCHAUDHURI

Sources S. Banerjea, *A nation in making: being the reminiscences of fifty years in public life* (1925) • S. Sengupta and A. Basu, eds., *Samsada Banali caritabhidhana* (Calcutta, 1976) • M. Bagchee, *Rashtraguru Surendranatha* (Calcutta, [1963]) • S. P. Sen, ed., *Dictionary of national biography*, 4 vols. (1972–4), vol. 1 [India] • *The Bengalee* • *Speeches and writings of S. N. Banerjea*, ed. G. A. Natesan (1918) • *Amritabazar Patrika* (8 Aug 1925)
Archives BL OIOC • National Archives of India, New Delhi • West Bengal Archives, home department records, government of Bengal
Likenesses Johnston & Hoffmann, photograph, repro. in Banerjea, *A nation in making*, frontispiece [*see illus.*] • photograph, National Library of India, Calcutta • portrait, West Bengal assembly building, Calcutta, India • statue, Curzon Park, Calcutta, India

Banff. For this title name *see* Ogilvy, George, first Lord Banff (*d.* 1663).

Banham, (Peter) Reyner (1922–1988), architectural critic and historian, was born on 2 March 1922 in Norwich, the elder son (there were no daughters) of Percy Banham, gas engineer, and his wife, Violet Frances Maud Reyner. Reyner Banham (known to only his close friends as Peter) had a typical Norfolk upbringing in the nonconformist and Labour tradition, in which education was highly valued. His father's family had been Primitive Methodists, and an influential maternal uncle was Edwin George Gooch, a Labour MP. His parents were not well off, and he had a scholarship at the local public school, King Edward VI School in Norwich, whose teachers subsequently wanted him to go to Cambridge to read French. But Banham, whose interest in technology had been formed early, won a national scholarship to train as an engineer with the Bristol Aeroplane Company, with which he spent much of the war (1939–45). Back in Norwich he became involved with the Maddermarket Theatre, lecturing on art and writing arts reviews in the local Norwich paper. On 16 August 1946 he married Mary, a teacher at the local art school and daughter of John Mullett, a park-keeper in south London. They had a son and a daughter.

In 1949 Banham enrolled at the Courtauld Institute of Art in London. Having graduated BA in 1952 and begun a PhD, he joined the staff of the *Architectural Review*, where his doctoral supervisor, Nikolaus Pevsner, was an editor. Already Banham and his wife had instigated weekly open houses to discuss contemporary art and design, and he soon became a prominent member of the Independent Group of the Institute of Contemporary Art, whose fellow members were the leading figures of the post-war revolt against modernism in art and architecture. Its major outcomes were the new brutalism in architecture and pop art—of which Banham was the leading proselytizer and chronicler. His incisive writing in the influential *Architectural Review* established him as a major commentator on contemporary architecture and design. His reputation was confirmed by the publication of his doctoral thesis, *Theory and Design in the First Machine Age* (1960). This dazzling, densely argued, and meticulously researched work became the seminal reassessment of the history of the modern movement in architecture.

In 1964 Banham became a senior lecturer at the Bartlett school of architecture, University College, London. He became a reader in 1967 and in 1969 was given a personal chair in the history of architecture at the Bartlett. Meanwhile he had published *The New Brutalism* (1966), a history of the movement which he had espoused from the late 1950s onwards and which he felt had run its natural course. After *The Architecture of the Well-Tempered Environment* (1969), about architecture as determined by its mechanical services, he published three books, the most successful of which, especially among the locals, was *Los Angeles: the Architecture of Four Ecologies* (1971).

In 1976, tired of the post-1968 gloom which had settled on British architectural academic life, Banham took up the post of chairman of the department of design studies at the University of New York at Buffalo. This turned out to be a disappointment, and in 1980 he moved to a chair in art history at the University of California, Santa Cruz, where his wife became director of the Eloise Pickard Smith Gallery. A powerful figure in her own right, she was an essential part of Banham's life and career. They lived happily in a house overlooking the ocean at Santa Cruz, and Banham cycled up to the university, where he taught art history as well as architectural history. While at Santa Cruz he travelled widely, and in 1982 he published the lyrical *Scenes in America Deserta* about the great American deserts in whose thrall he had been since the early 1960s. He became honorary FRIBA in 1983 and was awarded an honorary DLitt by East Anglia University in 1986.

In 1987 he was appointed to the Sheldon H. Solow chair at the Institute of Fine Arts, New York University. Before he could take up this prestigious post it was found he had cancer. He returned to London for his final months and wrote the six essays which form the text of a book about his old friend and Archigram member, Ron Herron. Banham died on 19 March 1988 in University College Hospital, London, with this and the inaugural lecture, which he knew he could never deliver in person, just completed.

Banham was the towering architecture and design critic and polemicist of the post-war era. Tall, well built, a prodigious conversationalist, and, from the early 1960s onwards, patriarchally bearded, he had a penchant for string ties, silver belt-buckles, unexpected headgear, and the small-wheeled Moulton bicycle. His great gift was in looking at major issues from vantage points which nobody else had thought of occupying. Last in the line of the school of German art history which placed primary valuation on meticulousness in dealing with source material, Banham's point of departure from this tradition was only in the subjects to which he applied it. His position was that the design of a new refrigerator, automobile, or the latest film could and should be analysed with the same rigour and methodology as a painting by Piero della Francesca. SUTHERLAND LYALL, *rev.*

Sources *WWW* · personal knowledge (1996) · private information (1996, 2004) [Mary Banham, widow] · *CGPLA Eng. & Wales* (1988)
Archives Architectural Association slide collection, Rayner Banham collection · Architectural Association slide collection, Denis Crompton collection · Getty Foundation, art and architecture collection | SOUND BBC
Likenesses photograph, priv. coll.
Wealth at death £32,879: probate, 12 Oct 1988, *CGPLA Eng. & Wales*

Banim, John [*pseud.* Abel O'Hara] (**1798–1842**), novelist and playwright, was born in the city of Kilkenny, on 3 April 1798, the younger son of Michael Banim, a proprietor of a gun and tackle shop, and his wife, Joannah Carroll. His elder brother, **Michael Banim** [*pseud.* Barnes O'Hara] (1796–1874), was also born at Kilkenny, on 5 August 1796. The brothers were educated locally at Dr MacGrath's Catholic school, but an improvement in the family fortunes allowed John to be sent to St John's College, Kilkenny, where he gained an education more usually reserved for protestants. At sixteen, Michael began legal training, but financial troubles forced him to give up his studies to take over his father's business. Meanwhile, John had demonstrated a precocious talent for painting, and in 1813 he joined the drawing academy of the Royal Dublin Society, where he won the highest prize at the end of his first year. After graduating in 1816, he returned to Kilkenny to take up work as a drawing-master in a girls' boarding-school. There he fell in love with one of his pupils, the daughter of a protestant land agent, but her father on religious grounds refused him permission to marry her. She was removed from Kilkenny, and when she died several months later from tuberculosis, John believed she had died for love of him. His disappointment precipitated a period of depression from which his biographer Patrick Murray dates the first symptoms of the spinal disease that would eventually prove fatal.

In 1820 John Banim returned to Dublin, where he turned to journalism, contributing to the *Leinster Gazette*, the *Limerick Evening Post* under the pseudonym A Traveller, and various magazines. Hampered by debts, he travelled to London to advance in his profession, and there he was introduced to Richard Lalor Sheil, a playwright and politician influential in the campaign for Catholic emancipation. Banim's poem 'Ossian's Paradise', based on the legend of St Patrick's attempt to convert the pagan hero Ossian, was shown by Banim to Sir Walter Scott, who admired it; in 1821 it was published as *The Celt's Paradise*. Sheil also introduced Banim into theatrical circles, and although his first play, *Turgesius* (1820), remained unstaged, his second, *Damon and Pythias*, was performed at Covent Garden on 28 May 1821. The tragedy, using classical settings reflecting Banim's ascendancy education and with William Macready and Charles Kemble in the principal roles, was successful enough to allow Banim to return to Kilkenny and discharge his debts.

On 27 February 1822 John Banim married Ellen, the daughter of John Ruth, a Kilkenny farmer, and in March the couple travelled to London, where they set up home in Brompton, and Banim joined the staff of the newly formed *Literary Register*. While in Kilkenny, he had outlined to his brother Michael a plan for a series of national tales that the two would write in collaboration. Over the next two years the brothers worked upon a first volume, John being supported in London by the friendship of the Irish novelist Gerald Griffin, while Michael was gathering material in Ireland. The brothers adopted the pseudonyms Abel and Barnes O'Hara respectively, and were in constant communication over drafts of each other's fiction. An insight into the close collaborative nature of the Banims' writing practice can be gathered from John's letter to Michael at this time, in which he requests 'your severest criticism […] sit in judgement and send me all your opinions sincerely given' (quoted in Cronin, 46). Each brother freely edited the work of the other, deleting passages, adding new sections, and even reshaping the other's characters or plot.

John Banim's third play, *The Prodigal*, was accepted at Covent Garden in 1823 but was never performed. Frustrated, he published *Revelations of the Dead-Alive* (1824), a satire upon the London literary scene. Within a year the publication of John's *John Doe, or, Peep O'Day* and *The Fetches*, and Michael's *Crohoore of the Billhook* as *Tales from the O'Hara Family* made the Banims part of that scene. The *Tales* reflected the brothers' commitment to Daniel O'Connell's campaign for Catholic emancipation, and both *Crohoore* and *John Doe* endeavoured to explain the underlying causes of Whiteboy agrarian violence. *Crohoore*, which focused upon 'life in the cabin', was considered by many contemporary critics to be the best of the O'Hara tales. The *Edinburgh Review* remarked that 'It is pleasant after ages of bad romances in politics to find good politics in romances' (*EdinR*, 43, 1826, 172), while Gerald Griffin praised the Banims' 'excellent tact in seizing on all parts of national character which are capable of effect' (Griffin, 231).

Tact was essential to the Banims' success, as they published in London, and wrote in English at a time when 50 per cent of the Irish population spoke Gaelic. While John Banim might remark to his compatriots that his work was inspired by 'an indignant wish to soften the hearts of Ireland's oppressors' (Wolff, introduction to Murray, xlvi), to his English readers he described 'the uniform political tendency' of the *Tales* as 'for the formation of a good and affectionate feeling between England and Ireland' (Wolff, xlvii). As Michael Banim explained, it was necessary to 'insinuate through fiction the causes of Irish discontent, the conclusion to be arrived at by the reader' (Webb). All three of the first collection of tales endeavoured to attract English readers by placing an Englishman abroad figure at the centre of their narratives. The presentation of dialogue between Irish characters (rather than any more overt form of direct address to the reader), was also a preferred method of persuasion for hesitant English well-wishers.

Following the success of the *Tales*, Michael Banim spent several months in 1825 researching a second volume, through travel in the south of Ireland and correspondence with folklorists such as the bookseller Patrick Kennedy. In 1826 he travelled to London, partly to celebrate the birth of his niece, Mary, and partly to supply his brother with background information. John Banim's third novel, *The Boyne Water*, was a direct and controversial appeal for Catholic emancipation set in the 1690s during the battle of the Boyne; it concludes by insisting that the English had reneged upon the treaty of Limerick, which had expressed conciliatory intentions towards Catholics. Again, an English readership was encouraged to identify with the hero, Robert Evelyn, an Anglican Orangeman. With his sister he meets a Catholic brother and sister, Edmund and Eva McDonnell; the couples fall in love, but are driven apart by sectarian violence. Some of the novel's dialogue was written in Gaelic, with translations footnoted.

The Boyne Water was published in 1826, together with John Banim's *The Nowlans* and *Peter of the Castle* as the second volume of *Tales from the O'Hara Family*, dedicated to Thomas Moore, 'Ireland's True Son and First Poet'. *The Nowlans*, the first in a long line of Irish Catholic novels about 'spoiled priests', including George Moore's *The Lake* (1905) and Gerald O'Donovan's *Father Ralph* (1913), was especially favourably reviewed, and in 1895 W. B. Yeats admired the novel enough to include it in his list of thirty best Irish books. Reviewers commented that the O'Hara family 'borrowed largely from the storehouse of Sir Walter's machinery' (*Monthly Review*, 4th ser., Jan 1827, 131), and *The Boyne Water*, which stood for more than a century as the most widely acclaimed Irish historical novel, was favourably compared with Scott's *Waverley*.

In 1827 Michael Banim began work on *The Croppy*, which like *The Boyne Water* invited support for Catholic emancipation. *The Croppy* traced the cultural confusion of the 1820s to the 1798 rising, penetrating to the heart of the Wexford rising while retaining the Banim spirit of reconciliation. It appeared in a third volume of O'Hara tales, alongside John's *The Conformist*, about a Catholic victim of the penal laws who ousts his family from their hereditary holdings by turning protestant, and *The Last Baron*, encouraging Catholic secession from the materialism of Ulster. Both John Banim's novels were heavily revised in the wake of the Catholic Emancipation Act of 1828, and the volume was prefaced with the hope that English readers would not be offended, and was dedicated to Arthur, duke of Wellington.

Later in 1828 John Banim published another novel, *The Anglo-Irish in the Nineteenth Century*, where the hero, the absentee landlord George Blount, has his hatred and contempt for the 'uncivilised Irish' challenged by his love for a 'wild Irish girl' who initially masquerades as a sophisticated Frenchwoman. Banim's satire on the political divisions between social classes in Ireland appeared anonymously, and the contrast with the O'Hara tales was so pronounced that it was thought to have been written by Sydney Owenson's husband, Charles Morgan.

During the following year John Banim became severely ill and moved to Boulogne to convalesce. Financial hardship advanced with ill health, and the success of the O'Hara tales in America and their translation into French and German in 1830 was not enough to defray the increased expenses necessitated by medical care and the birth of two sons in 1831 and 1832. John worked on *The Smuggler*, his only novel set in England, and contributed several light pieces to the English Opera House, mostly adaptations of the first volume of O'Hara tales. These successes failed to prevent the Banims from declining into further poverty, and at the end of 1832 John Banim's wife, Ellen, visited John Sterling, the editor of *The Times* and a friend of her husband's. Sterling organized a relief fund in *The Times*, and Richard Lalor Sheil set up a similar subscription fund in Dublin to 'assert the eminence of an author who had reflected so much honour upon his country' (Murray, 226).

Although John Banim's financial distress was alleviated by these tributes to his reputation, his sufferings continued. In 1834 he became paralysed from the waist down and was pronounced incurable by his doctors, and later that year both his sons died. He became eager to leave France and return to Ireland, and his arrival in Dublin in July 1835 was greeted with much enthusiasm. Performances of his play *Damon and Pythias* and of his adaptations of the O'Hara tales were given for his benefit at the Dublin Theatre Royal. Shortly after his arrival in Kilkenny, John Banim was granted a civil-list pension of £150 per annum, with an extra £40 for his daughter. Although too ill to write, he managed to assist his brother with his stories *The Ghost Hunter and his Family* and *The Mayor of Windgap*, which appeared along with *The Smuggler* in a fourth O'Hara volume.

The Bit o'Writing appeared in 1838, and represented a collection of twenty stories including sketches by Michael Banim and selections from John Banim's contributions to periodical literature. The large sales of the collection combined with Michael's commercial success in the family business to make the brothers wealthy, and in 1840 Michael Banim married Catherine O'Dwyer, with whom he had two daughters, Mary and Mathilde. However, within a year of his marriage Michael's business collapsed due to the bankruptcy of a merchant, and he lost the greater proportion of his fortune.

In preparation for the next O'Hara volume, Michael Banim had researched the Kilkenny branch of the Whiteboys, the Whitefeet: a rural protest movement committed to the abolition of church tithes. Michael had interviewed Whitefeet leaders, and wished to write another novel as a companion to *Crohoore of the Billhook*, his earlier examination of Whiteboyism. Yet John Banim advised him 'we have given too much of the darker side of the Irish life: let us for the present treat of the amiable' (Murray, 240), and the brothers instead collaborated on a character study of a kindly priest who had been a friend since childhood. *Father Connell* (1842), although in parts sentimental, gave a grim picture of pre-famine rural poverty.

On 13 August 1842 John Banim died at Kilkenny of the progressive spinal illness that had afflicted him since his teens. He was diagnosed as suffering from spinal tuberculosis, although his symptoms also indicate multiple sclerosis. His wife, Ellen, and daughter, Mary, survived him, although Mary died a year later. Michael Banim had lived in his brother's shadow for most of his life, as John Banim was not only better known, but was also considered to be the possessor of 'the poetic vein', whereas Michael's talents were considered to rest more mundanely in the close observation of social background and peasant life. In 1852 Michael Banim published a short story, 'Clough Finn, or, The Stone of Destiny', in the *Dublin University Magazine*. Later that year he was appointed postmaster of Kilkenny, which distracted him from writing for another decade. In 1864 his final book, and the only one to bear his name, appeared; *The Town of the Cascades* was a temperance novel describing the disastrous effects of drink upon family life.

During the 1850s Michael Banim assisted Patrick Murray in writing a biography of his brother, and *The Life of John Banim* was published in 1857, running through ten editions in London and Dublin until 1869, and reprinted in facsimile by Robert Lee Wolff in 1978. In 1865 Banim wrote the introduction and notes for the collected works of the 'O'Haras', the first edition to be published in Dublin. Michael Banim became ill in 1873, and resigned as postmaster in order to retire to Booterstown on the coast of co. Dublin. A grant from the Royal Literary Fund did little to defray the financial hardship in which he spent his last years. He died at Booterstown on 30 August 1874, and his widow received a civil-list pension. His daughter Mary became a journalist for the *Weekly Freeman* and travel writer, best known for *Here and There Through Ireland* (1893), a nationalist account of a journey through post-famine Ireland.

The Banims gained a lasting posthumous reputation as nationalist novelists, and several of the novels were reprinted in the twentieth century. As Sir Charles Gavan Duffy remarked in 1891, 'Moore's Melodies, Griffin's and the Banims' novels have been a constant cordial to the sorely tried spirit of our people' (Gilligan, 81).

KATHERINE MULLIN

Sources P. J. Murray, *The life of John Banim* (1857) [ed. with an introduction by R. L. Wolff (1978)] • A. Brady and B. Cleeve, eds., *A dictionary of Irish writers* (1985) • M. D. Hawthorne, *John and Michael Banim: a study in the early development of the Anglo-Irish novel* (1975) • B. R. Friedman, 'Fabricating history, or, John Banim refights the Boyne', *Éire-Ireland*, 17/1 (1982), 39–56 • A. J. Webb, *A compendium of Irish biography* (1878) • L. C. Sanders, *Celebrities of the century: being a dictionary of men and women of the nineteenth century* (1887) • Ward, *Men of the reign* • J. F. Waller, ed., *The imperial dictionary of universal biography*, 3 vols. (1857–63) • *EdinR*, 43 (1826), 172, 365 • K. Lubbers, 'Author and audience in the early nineteenth century', *Literature and the changing Ireland*, ed. P. Connolly (1982), 25–36 • W. J. McCormack, 'A manuscript letter from Michael Banim', *Éire-Ireland*, 8/1 (1973), 95–6 • D. Gilligan, 'Natural indignation in the native voice: the fiction of the Banim brothers', *Anglo-Irish and Irish literature: aspects of language and culture*, ed. B. Bramsbäck and M. Groghan, 2 (1986), 77–91 • R. Welch, ed., *The Oxford companion to Irish literature* (1996) • J. Cronin, *The Anglo-Irish novel*, 1 (1980) • T. Flanagan, *The Irish novelists, 1800–1850* (1959) • D. Griffin, *The life of Gerald Griffin* (1857), 231

Archives BL, letters to Sir Robert Peel, Add. MSS 40413, fol. 317; 40419, fols. 55, 57 • NL Scot., letters to Sir Walter Scott

Likenesses E. Fitzpatrick, pen-and-ink drawing, repro. in Murray, *Life of John Banim*, frontispiece • G. F. Mulvany, oils, NG Ire. • T. C. Thompson, oils (Michael Banim), NG Ire. • lithograph, NG Ire.

Banim, Michael (1796–1874). *See under* Banim, John (1798–1842).

Banister [*formerly* Banester], **John** (1532/3–1599?), surgeon, was the son of John Banister and his wife, Margaret, daughter of Richard Lowth, of Sawtry, Huntingdon. He had a brother, Gabriel, and a sister, Elizabeth. Little else is known about his origins. After service at sea he went as surgeon with the earl of Warwick's army sent to relieve Le Havre in 1563. When Warwick was struck by a poisoned bullet on 29 July, Banester successfully treated him. It was probably during this campaign that he began a long friendship with William Clowes the elder. Some time after his return he studied medicine at Oxford and received a licence to practise on 30 June 1573. Meanwhile, on 12 February 1572, he had been admitted to the Barber–Surgeons' Company, enabling him to practise in London. On moving to London he changed his name from Banester to Banister. His description in the company's court minutes (B/1/1) as 'of Nottingham' confirms that he had not served a surgeon's apprenticeship in London.

A painting in Glasgow University Library (MS Hunter 364) shows Banister delivering a visceral lecture at the Barber–Surgeons' Hall, Monkwell Street, London. Four such lectures were given each year and all freemen and guests were invited to attend. Dated 1581, and giving Banister's age as forty-eight, the picture represents the method of teaching anatomy in the late sixteenth century. Before an audience of young surgeons he points to a skeleton beside which there is an opened medical text, while in front of him there is a body in the process of dissection. In 1582–3 Banister served as surgeon on the *Leicester*, one of four ships which took part in an expedition to China and the East Indies financed by a group of wealthy citizens with the support of the earl of Leicester. However, the voyage was unsuccessful. Banister lost forty-five of his patients and the ships got no further than the Atlantic so he learned nothing of tropical diseases. Two years later he went with the earl of Leicester's expedition to the Netherlands.

In 1593 Banister was licensed to practise medicine and surgery by the College of Physicians of London, in obedience to a letter from Queen Elizabeth. The letter referred to Banister's honesty and skill and noted that he had 'always jointlie used the art of Physick with Chirurgerie'. Being licensed to practise medicine as well as surgery was unusual at a time when the surgeon, who had learned his craft through apprenticeship, was considered subordinate to the university educated physician. The college had once censured him for illicit practice. It has been suggested that the queen's letter reflects attempts to further the union of medicine and surgery in late Tudor times, and also the College of Physicians' opposition to the idea. Banister's daughter Cicely married the surgeon John Read, who also opposed the separation of medicine from surgery.

Banister was a prolific writer. He wrote the epilogue to William Clowes's book on syphilis, *A Short and Profitable Treatise*, first published in 1579. His own works were *A needefull, new, & necessarie treatise of chyrurgerie, briefly comprehending the generall and particular curation of ulcers* (1575), which was dedicated to Thomas Stanhope, high sheriff of Nottingham, and was based largely on ancient and modern authors but including some of his own treatments; *The Historie of Man, Sucked from the Sappe of the most Approved Anathomistes* (1578), which includes a passing reference to his treatment of young children in Nottingham suffering from pleurisy; *Compendius Chirurgery, Gathered and Translated Especially out of Wecker* (1585), which includes many annotations to correct the errors of Johann Jacob Wecker and to supply new information; and *An Antidotarie Chyrurgicall* (1589). His collected works were published in 1633. Banister's books contain little original thinking and were less highly regarded than those of William Clowes, whose practical outlook he lacked. Compiled from the standard authorities their purpose was to bring to the fraternity of surgeons what Banister considered to be the theory and practice of the day. He was one of a group of medical practitioners who not only 'advocated chemical therapy but also projected themselves as allies of the Paracelsians' (Webster, 327). Banister's wife was named Joan; they had a daughter, Catherine, who married the physician Stephen Bradwell. In later years Banister lived in Silver Street, London, and was buried at St Olave, Silver Street, where a monument erected to his memory was destroyed, together with the church, in the great fire. He is possibly the 'Mr John Banister' who was buried there on 16 January 1599. ANDREW GRIFFIN

Sources S. Young, *The annals of the Barber–Surgeons of London: compiled from their records and other sources* (1890) • records of the Barber–Surgeons' Company, Barber–Surgeons' Hall, London • J. J. Keevil and others, *Medicine and the navy, 1200–1900*, 1: *1200–1649* (1957) • Munk, *Roll* • Foster, *Alum. Oxon.* • 'John Banester, 1533–1610', *British Journal of Surgery*, 5 (1917), 8–16 • D. Power, 'Notes on early portraits of John Banister, of William Harvey, and the Barber–Surgeons' visceral lecture in 1581', *Proceedings of the Royal Society of Medicine*, 6 (1912–13), 18–36 [section of the history of medicine] • M. Pelling and C. Webster, 'Medical practitioners', *Health, medicine and mortality in the sixteenth century*, ed. C. Webster (1979), 165–235 • C. Webster, 'Alchemical and Paracelsian medicine', *Health, medicine and mortality in the sixteenth century*, ed. C. Webster (1979), 301–31 • *DNB* • The anatomical tables of John Banester, U. Glas., MS Hunter 364 • private information (2004) [M. Cooke, A. H. Nelson]

Likenesses portrait (delivering the visceral lecture at Barber–Surgeons' Hall, London, 1581), U. Glas., MS Hunter 364

Banister, John (1624/5–1679), violinist and composer, was the son of a wait in St Giles-in-the-Fields, London. He played (alongside Thomas Baltzar) in William Davenant's *Siege of Rhodes* (scheduled for September 1656 but possibly not performed for another three years). Pepys heard him perform at the Mitre tavern at the beginning of 1660. By the end of the year he had been appointed to one of the new places in the court musical establishment. He was then, according to Anthony Wood, sent to France 'to see and learn the way of the French composition' (Bodl. Oxf., MS Wood D 19(4)). In April 1662 he was placed in charge of twelve violins (to be chosen by him from the band of twenty-four) who accompanied the king to Portsmouth to welcome the new queen, Catherine of Braganza.

In 1662 Banister was appointed to a place in the king's private music, filling a vacancy created by the death of Davis Mell in April. In July of the following year he was placed in charge of the select band of twelve violins, which was now to be constituted as a permanent ensemble. Not only was Banister given total artistic control, but he was also responsible for disbursing the £600 per annum allocated to the group; this was eventually to become the source of a grievance among the other players.

For the moment, however, Banister's career continued to flourish. In November 1663 he was elected as an assistant in the Corporation for Regulating the Art and Science of Musick, and in June 1664 he was made one of the wardens for the following year. An order of 9 May 1665 from the lord chamberlain gave him joint responsibility with George Hudson and Matthew Locke for 'composing, ordering and directing of all his Majesty's violins (in the absence of the Master of his Mats Musick)'.

But then things started going quite seriously wrong. Banister got into personal financial difficulties, and by 1665 was being importuned by creditors. This was a predicament shared by many of the king's musicians, since salary payments were well in arrears. In July 1665 Banister applied for the payment of the £600 allowance due to the select band, complaining that he had

> spent much tyme in soliciting ye payment of the said Augmentacon to his own Damage by the hindrance of yor Ma^{ts} service and finds that wthout the constant payment of the same allowance yor Ma^{ts} Comands cannot effectually bee obayed …

The following November the payment of some arrears was authorized in a warrant which noted that up to that date little more than a third of the money owing to the group had been paid over. A year later, on 7 November 1666, Banister and eleven other violinists (all but three of them members of his select group) signed another petition which emphasized the difficulties of their situation:

> That yor pet^{rs} … are in Arreare of their Sallaryes at the Trea[su]ry Chambers fower yeares and three quarters. And that severall of your Ma^{ies} pet^{rs} have had their houses and Goods burnt by the late Fire, which hath reduced them to great misery and want.

But on 14 March the following year an order was issued for the £600 allowance to be paid not to Banister, but to Louis Grabu (who had been sworn in as master of the musick four months earlier). By the end of the month Banister's colleagues in the select band had turned against him, submitting a lengthy 'Remonst[ran]ce against Mr Banister' in which they accused him of embezzlement and even blackmail; he

> ... demanded of the Company £20 a peice ... which if wee refused hee swore wee should be turn'd out of the Band. for saies he, I am to carry upp the names to morrow morning to the Councell Chamber, and they that will not doe this, their names shall be left out and others put in.

All of this coincides with reports of Banister's rather hot-headed and arrogant behaviour. Anthony Wood had the idea that Banister had been displaced by Grabu as the director of the select band 'for some saucy words spoken to His Majesty (viz. when he called for the Italian violins, he made answer that he had better have the English)' (Bodl. Oxf., MS Wood D 19(4)). And Pepys reported in his diary in February 1667 that 'they talk also how the King's viallin, Bannister, is mad that the King hath a Frenchman come to be chief of some part of the King's musique, at which the Duke of York made great mirth'. Worse was to come. In May Banister was arrested for abusing Grabu and several other musicians. He had become, it seems, a somewhat disaffected member of the king's music. Banister was twice married. Following the death of his first wife, Mary, he married on 14 January 1671 Mary Wood (*b.* 1620/21), a widow; the marriage licence, issued on 11 January 1671, stated his age to be forty-six.

Throughout this period, Banister had been heavily involved with theatrical music, particularly for the King's Company, managed by Thomas Killigrew. The company's theatre in Bridges Street (completed in 1663) introduced to England the placement of musicians in front of the stage (the area now known as the pit). An order from the lord chamberlain dated 20 December 1664 required members of Banister's select band to 'attend at his Majesty's theatre whenever Thomas Killigrew shall desire them'. Within a few months, the remaining members of the twenty-four violins were filling a similar role for the Duke's Company at its theatre in Lincoln's Inn Fields. This arrangement seems to have been doubly satisfactory to the court since it ensured both that the king and queen would be treated to excellent music when they visited the theatre and that these instrumentalists were getting some cash in hand at a time when their court salaries were hopelessly in arrears.

Banister's own involvement with the theatres was as composer as well as performer. In fact, he provided music for at least ten productions in the first decade of the Restoration period—more than any other composer. The first seems to have been Sir Robert Stapylton's *The Slighted Maid* (performed by the Duke's Company in February 1662), whose text records that 'the Instrumental, Vocal, and Recitative Musick, was composed by Mr Banister'. Banister's next theatrical compositions were songs to be sung between the acts of Katherine Phillips's *Pompey*, which was performed by Ogilby's Men in Dublin in 1663. The following year he wrote songs and instrumental music for *The Indian Queen* by John Dryden and Robert Howard. After his displacement as the leader of the select band in 1667, Banister's compositional output increased and his loyalties shifted towards the Duke's Company: he provided music for its productions of Dryden's *Sir Martin Mar-All* (1667), Dryden's adaptation of *The Tempest* (1667) (to which Pelham Humfrey also contributed), Davenant's *The Man's the Master* (March 1668), Thomas Shadwell's *The Royal Shepherdess* (1669), Aphra Behn's *The Forc'd Marriage* (1670), Samuel Tuke's *The Adventures of Five Hours* (a 1671 revival), John Crowne's *Juliana* (1671), William Wycherley's *The Gentleman Dancing Master* (1672), Shadwell's *Epsom Wells* (1672), and Davenant's *Circe* (1677). He contributed music for just two productions by the King's Company: Charles Sedley's *The Mulberry Garden* (1668) and Dryden's *The Conquest of Granada*, part 1 (1670).

Banister, needing to find a way out of his financial difficulties, became an innovator in other ways. Roger North gives a vivid account of his contribution to the development of the public concert in England:

> The next essay was of the elder Banister, who had a good theatricall vein and in composition had a lively style peculiar to himself. He procured a large room in Whitefryars, neer the Temple back gate, and made a large raised box for musitians, whose modesty required curtaines. The room was rounded with seats and small tables alehous fashion; 1s. was the price and call for what you pleased. There was very good musick, for Banister found means to procure the best hands in towne, and some voices to come and performe there, and there wanted no variety of humour, for Banister himself (inter alia) did wonders upon a flageolett to a thro base and the severall masters had their solos. This continued full one winter, and more I remember not. (Hereford Cathedral Library, MS R.II.xlii)

Banister's concerts began at the end of 1672 in his house in Whitefriars ('the Musick School'). At the beginning of 1675 they moved to Chandos Street, Covent Garden, and from November 1678 until his death in 1679 they were held in the Essex Buildings, near St Clement's Church in the Strand. Despite North's assertion that the audience could call out requests, these concerts must, from time to time at least, have been quite elaborately structured. A booklet by Banister entitled *Musick, or, A Parley of Instruments* provides a dramatic framework for one of the 1676 concerts, which included such items as a 'Symphony of Theorboes, Lutes, Harps, Harpsicons, Guittars, Pipes, Flutes, Flagellets, Cornets, Sackbutts, Hoboys, Rechords, Organs, and all sort of Wind Instruments ... with assistant Voices, and Violins'.

Banister's financial troubles continued to the end. In 1679 he was still petitioning to be paid six years' worth of salary arrears. In May he was given six months' leave from his court duties, and in July he obtained a passport for himself and his son to travel abroad. The trip was never made, and he died on 3 October. PETER WALLS

Sources A. Ashbee, ed., *Records of English court music*, 9 vols. (1986–96) • A. Ashbee and D. Lasocki, eds., *A biographical dictionary of English court musicians, 1485–1714*, 2 vols. (1998) • J. Banister and T. Low, *New ayres and dialogues composed for voices and viols ... together with lessons for viols or violins* (1678) • J. Banister, *Musick, or, A parley of instruments: the first part* (1676) • J. Buttery, 'The evolution of English opera between 1656 and 1695: a reinvestigation', PhD diss., U. Cam., 1967 • W. Davenant, *The siege of Rhodes: a critical edition*, ed.

A.-M. Hedbäck (1973) • A. Harbage, *Annals of English drama, 975–1700*, 2nd edn, ed. S. Schoenbaum (1964) • Highfill, Burnim & Langhans, *BDA* • P. Holman, *Four and twenty fiddlers: the violin at the English court, 1540–1690* (1993) • A. A. Luhring, 'The music of John Banister', PhD diss., Stanford University, 1966 • F. Madan, *A summary catalogue of Western manuscripts in the Bodleian Library at Oxford*, 8 vols. (1905) • *Roger North's The musicall grammarian, 1728*, ed. M. Chan and J. C. Kassler (1990) • Pepys, *Diary* • C. Price, *Music in the Restoration theatre* (Ann Arbor, 1979) • C. B. Schmidt, 'Newly identified manuscript sources for the music of Jean-Baptiste Lully', *Notes*, 43 (1987), 7–32 • E. B. Schnapper, ed., *The British union-catalogue of early music printed before the year 1801*, 2 vols. (1957) • J. D. Shute, 'Anthony A Wood and his manuscript Wood D 19 (4) at the Bodleian Library, Oxford: an annotated transcription', PhD diss., International Institute of Advanced Musical Studies, Clayton, Missouri, 1979 • I. Spink, ed., *The seventeenth century* (1992) • M. Tilmouth, 'A calendar of references to music in newspapers published in London and the provinces (1660–1719) [2 pts]', *Royal Musical Association Research Chronicle*, 1 (1961); 2 (1962) • W. Van Lennep and others, eds., *The London stage, 1660–1800*, pt 1: *1660–1700* (1965) • *Roger North on music*, ed. J. Wilson (1959) • *The life and times of Anthony Wood*, ed. A. Clark, 5 vols., OHS, 19, 21, 26, 30, 40 (1891–1900)

Banister, John (1650–1692), naturalist, was born in Twigworth, Gloucestershire, the son of John Banister, whose family were described as 'common folk'. In 1667 he enrolled at Magdalen College, Oxford, where he graduated BA in 1671 and proceeded MA in 1674. He remained at Magdalen, serving as a clerk and librarian from 1674 to 1676 and as a chaplain from 1676 to 1678. Banister became deeply interested in natural history during these years at Oxford, where he was probably influenced by William Browne and Professor Robert Morison, both ardent botanists. The extensive plant collections at the Oxford Physic Garden and herbaria from Africa, Europe, and the New World provided Banister with an opportunity to study much of the known flora of the day. By the time he sailed to North America in 1678 he was well qualified as a naturalist and, after brief sojourns in Barbados and Grenada, he arrived in Virginia, where he promptly began work on a 'natural history' of the colony. Little is known of Banister's private life. By 1687 he had married, his wife's name being given as Martha; their one son was named John.

Whether Banister went to America to work as a naturalist or to serve the Anglican church is uncertain, but it was not until 1689 that he received his appointment as a minister in Virginia. Meanwhile, by 1679, within a year of settling there, he was sending botanical specimens and species lists to correspondents in England, including Henry Compton, bishop of London, Martin Lister, Jacob Bobart the younger, and Morison. In 1680 he provided a lengthy catalogue of Virginia plants to John Ray, who published the list in volume two (1688) of the *Historia plantarum*, where he described Banister as 'eruditissimus vir et consummatissimus botanicus' ('a most learned man and most consummate botanist'). In 1690 Banister acquired 1735 acres of land near the Appomatox River in Charles City county, Virginia. He was a founder and trustee of the College of William and Mary in Williamsburg. His extensive library of natural history and religious books was acquired after his death by William Byrd of Virginia.

During the last decade of his life Banister shipped plants, insects, molluscs, and fossils to his associates in England, eventually providing more than 340 plant species, more than 100 insects, and many drawings of shells, plants, and insects. While collecting plants along the Roanoke River, Virginia, in May 1692, Banister was accidentally shot and killed by a member of his exploring party. After his death many of his specimens, drawings, and species catalogues were sent to England, where some went to Oxford and others passed into the possession of Sir Hans Sloane and eventually became part of the collections at the Natural History Museum in London.

Banister was the first university-trained naturalist to send specimens, illustrations, and natural history data from North America to England. Although he died without publishing any material under his own name, he contributed significantly to the progress of natural sciences through the published works of others. Extracts of his letters to Lister appeared in volume seventeen of the *Philosophical Transactions of the Royal Society* (1693), and some of his entomology records were printed by James Petiver in volume twenty-two of the *Philosophical Transactions* (1701) and in the *Monthly Miscellany, or, Memoirs for the Curious* (1707). Johann Frederick Gronovius used Banister's data extensively in the *Flora Virginica* (1739, 1743), while Carl Linnaeus relied heavily on Banister for his Virginia species descriptions in *Species plantarum* (1753). Linnaeus had obtained much of his information from Banister's drawings in Leonard Plukenet's *Phytographia* (1691–1705) and from Banister's data published in Ray's *Historia plantarum* (1686–1704) and in volume three of Morison's *Plantarum historiae* (1699). Additionally, Banister's data and writing were used without attribution by Robert Beverley in the *History and Present State of Virginia* (1705) and by John Oldmixon in his *British Empire in America* (1708).

James Britten, *rev.* Marcus B. Simpson jun.

Sources J. Ewan and N. Ewan, *John Banister and his natural history of Virginia* (1970) • Wood, *Ath. Oxon.* • J. R. Bloxam, *A register of the presidents, fellows … of Saint Mary Magdalen College*, 8 vols. (1853–85) • J. Ray, *Historia plantarum*, 2 (1688) • J. F. Gronovius, *Flora Virginica*, 2 vols. (Leiden, 1739–43) • R. Beverley, *The history and present state of Virginia* (1705) • L. Plukenet, *Phytographia* (1691–1705) • R. Morison, *Plantarum historiae* (1699) • J. Oldmixon, *The British empire in America*, 2 vols. (1708)

Archives BL, papers, Sloane MS 4002 • Bodl. Oxf., botanical notes on Virginia • NHM, department of botany • U. Oxf., school of botany | Bodl. Oxf., Sherard MSS • NHM, Sloane MSS

Banister, Richard (*c.*1570–1626), oculist, whose precise date and place of birth are unknown, was the son of Gabriel Banister. He was one of four brothers, two of whom died early, all apprenticed to surgeons or barber–surgeons. His grandfather was John Banister of Cobham, Surrey. He studied surgery under his uncle John *Banister (or Banester) and practised for fourteen years in Sleaford, Lincolnshire, during which time he was also trained in couching cataracts by various oculists, including the itinerant Henry Blackborne, Robert Hall of Worcester, Master Velder of Fennie-Stanton, Master Surflet of Lynne, and Master Barnabie of Peterborough. From these he learned 'much practice, but little Theorie', for which reason, by his own account, he read late at night the writings of 'Rasis, Mesue, Fernelius, Vesalius, and others'. Thereafter

Richard Banister (*c*.1570–1626), by unknown artist, *c*.1620

Banister was based in Stamford, 25 miles from Sleaford, travelling as requested to other towns, such as Norwich and even London. He practised primarily as an oculist, but also gave 'helpe of Hearing by the instrument, the cure of the Hare-lip, and the wry Necke'.

An incomplete and anonymous memoir preserved in the British Library (MS Sloane 3801), entitled 'Briefe discourse of ye chefeste oculistes', can confidently be assigned to Banister. It is an important source for the social role of early English oculists, as in it he comments on the prominent oculists of his day and on his own training. The names of many of these contemporary oculists are repeated in the preface to his *Breviary of the Eyes*, a collection of aphorisms, ocular therapies, and case histories compiled by Banister in 1621 while in Stamford; it was published the following year in London, as an essay preceding a reprint of an English translation (said by Banister to be long unavailable) of the *Traité des maladies de l'oeil qui sont en nombre de cent treize* by Jacques Guillemeau, originally published in Paris in 1585. The first printing of this English translation had appeared in London some time between 1586 and 1589 under the title *A Worthy Treatise of the Eyes*; the translator, given as A. H. (possibly A. Hunton of Nottinghamshire), had, like Guillemeau himself, dedicated the work to Banister's uncle, John Banister. It was bound in one volume with three other medical treatises. These same three treatises were included, along with the English translation of Guillemeau's book, in Banister's book, published in 1622 under the general title *A treatise of one hundred and thirteene diseases of the eyes, and eye-liddes, the second time published, with some profitable additions of certaine principles and experiments*. From the preface it is evident that Banister did not intend to claim credit for any but the first item, his *Breviary of the Eyes*, although later writers unjustly accused him of plagiarism.

Banister's *Breviary* contains, in addition to an exposé of 'proud quacksalving Mountebankes' and 'emptie empirickes', some interesting observations of medical practices of the day. In it he recognized hardness of the eye as an important diagnostic and prognostic sign, anticipating by a century and a quarter the work of J. Z. Platner. Banister also published *An Appendent Part of a Treatise of One Hundred and Thirteene Diseases of the Eyes*, which was intended to follow on the *Breviary*, published in 1622, but was in fact printed in London the year before. It consists of sixteen chapters devoted to the uses of a 'purging Ale' of his devising, with case histories attesting to its usefulness.

Of Banister's personal life very little is known, although he has provided many anecdotes about other oculists of his day. His first wife, Anne, died in 1624 in Stamford; they had three daughters, Frances (*d.* 1619), Brigett, and Susan, and four sons, Gabriel, Richard, John, and Francis. Banister died in April 1626 at the age of about 56 and was buried on 7 April 1626 at St Mary's churchyard in Stamford. He had been a benefactor of the church, having built a public library in the south choir to which he donated books, including the writings of Galen and others on medicine and surgery; he left an additional sum in his will for the continued increase and maintenance of the library. His personal library appears to have been substantial, for in his will he divided his collection of medical and Latin books, as well as his medical equipment, among his sons. To his two surviving daughters he left £50 each, large trunks, and all his English books, with the elder also receiving a cloak and gown belonging to his first wife, and the younger his medical bag and *lignum vitae*. His second wife, Elizabeth, was left the lands he owned in Stamford and in the county of Northampton.

EMILIE SAVAGE-SMITH

Sources R. R. James, 'The seventeenth century', *Studies in the history of ophthalmology in England prior to the year 1800*, ed. R. R. James (1933), 50–86 · A. Sorsby, 'A late sixteenth-century ophthalmic book in English', *British Journal of Ophthalmology*, 16 (1932), 345–55 · A. Sorsby, 'Hardness of the eye: an historical note', *British Journal of Ophthalmology*, 16 (1932), 292–5 · R. R. James and A. Sorsby, 'Richard Banister: additional facts in relation to the father of British ophthalmology', *British Journal of Ophthalmology*, 18 (1934), 156–9 · A. Sorsby and W. J. Bishop, 'A portrait of Richard Banister', *British Journal of Ophthalmology*, 32 (1948), 362–6 · R. Banister, 'Briefe discourse of ye chefeste oculists', BL, Sloane MSS, MS 3801 · A. Sorsby, 'Richard Banister and the beginnings of English ophthalmology', *Science, medicine and history*, ed. E. A. Underwood (1953), 42–55 · *DNB* · will, 4 April 1626, Lincs. Arch. [Lincoln consistory court], 1626, fol. 496 · parish records (burial), Stamford, St Mary's Church, 7 April 1626

Likenesses oils, 1620, RCP Lond. · oils, *c*.1620, RCS Eng. [*see illus.*]

Wealth at death see will (4 April 1626), Lincs. Arch., Lincoln consistory court, 1626, fol. 496

Banister, Thomas (*d.* 1571), merchant, of whose parentage or education nothing is known, married on 3 March 1549

Elisabeth Gamadge, a widow. He may have been member of parliament for Reigate in 1558 and was first warden of the Skinners' Company in 1563. In the 1550s he exported cloth to Danzig and Denmark, and imported raisins, Bilbao iron, and felts from Spain and figs from Portugal; he had agents in both countries. In 1558 he was a promoter of the third Guinea voyage, being part owner of the *Christopher Bennett*. He was a charter member of the Russia Company and was concerned in the commission for pressing men for its first voyage in 1553.

In 1568 Banister and Geoffrey Ducket accompanied Thomas Randolph, the ambassador to the tsar, to advise him on the affairs of the company, some of whose representatives had intrigued with the Dutch against its interests, and to develop trade with Persia through Russian territory. They sailed from Harwich and reached the site of Archangel on 2 August. They reported that they found 'the estate of the Company to stande varye evill'; if they had not come 'the holle trayde had been utterlye overthrowen'. They believed, however, that properly managed 'it will maynetene thirtie or fortie greate shippes, such as the lyke be not within the realme of merchants shipps', would give useful training to sailors, and would absorb 'all the Kerseyes maid within the realm' (Morgan and Coote, 258–9). Russia could supply cables, cordage, masts, sails, pitch, and tar, which would end English dependence on Danzig and Denmark. They were hopeful about trading in silk and spices through Russia, warning that this would conflict with the interests of Italians, Portuguese, and Flemings. They had decided to send James Bassendine (or Bassington) in a Russian boat to search for the north-east passage beyond Pechora. It is not known what, if anything, came of this.

On 3 July 1569 they embarked at Yaroslavl with some twelve English sailors and forty Russians in the *Thomas Bonaventure*, a specially built barque of 70 tons, to sail down the Volga. Some 40 miles above Astrakhan they were attacked with arrows by about three hundred Nogai Tartars. They fought for two hours. Banister was twice wounded, 11 of the party were killed, and 25 wounded; they learned afterwards from an escaped Russian captive that 120 Tartars had been killed and 60 or 80 wounded. They reached Astrakhan on 20 August, remaining to allow their wounded to recover. On 12 and 13 September an army of Ottomans, Crimean Tartars, Nogais, and Cherkes, estimated at over 120,000, attacked the town. The English shared in its defence until the besiegers withdrew because of the approach of winter and their fear of a relieving Russian force. The English sailed on 16 October on a stormy voyage to Bil'bilkent and went on to Shabran, where they spent a few days preparing for their journey, their provisions being depleted by the attacks of jackals. They spent the winter at Shemakha.

In April 1570 Banister wrote from Kashan and at some time visited Tehran, 'where never any English travelled before' (*CSP for.*, 1569–71, 221). They spent five or six months at Ardabil but found trade disappointing, 'the towne being more inhabited and frequented with gentlemen and noblemen than merchants' (Morgan and Coote, 425), and they witnessed religious riots. Shah Tahmasp summoned them to Qazvin; Ducket was ill but Banister responded, ingratiated himself with one of the shah's sons, and was favourably received. Tahmasp granted all his requests, demurring only at allowing the transit of horses for export to India. He bought 200 kerseys for ready money at a good price, and asked Banister for coins to send to Mecca because they had been gained honestly, whereas his own coins were the product of fraud and oppression. After six months Banister left for Tabriz, where he found Ducket fully recovered. He then went to Tiflis to recover debts and to Shemakha to organize the transport of the goods intended for England. Two hundred camels were loaded with the merchandise. Banister then went to Arrash to buy raw silk. He died there in July 1571, probably of malaria, as did another Russia merchant, Laurence Chapman, and five other Englishmen.

Banister's will, made before he left England, was proved in 1575. His wife, Elisabeth, had already died; she had a son, Roger, from a former marriage. Banister's mother, Ellen, was still living. He left six children, John, Phillip, Thomas, Mary, Grace, and Elisabeth. His property included a house and the lease of a garden adjacent to St Mary Axe, London. C. F. BECKINGHAM

Sources R. Hakluyt, *The principall navigations, voiages and discoveries of the English nation* (1589) • E. D. Morgan and C. H. Coote, eds., *Early voyages and travels to Russia and Persia*, 2 vols., Hakluyt Society, 72–3 (1886) • T. S. Willan, *The Muscovy merchants of 1555* (1953) • Records of the Skinners' Company • will, PRO, PROB 11/58, sig. 1 • *IGI* [index MS 9016 (H/S 3)] • Banister and Ducket's letters, S. P. (Foreign 1570), nos. 309, 813, 1685

Banister, Sir William (*bap.* **1653**, *d.* **1721**), judge, was baptized on 29 March 1653 at Turkdean, Gloucestershire, the son and heir of William Banister (1614/15–1685), gentleman, and his wife, Jane (1618/19–1707). He was admitted to Christ Church, Oxford, in 1669, and to the Middle Temple in 1672. In 1679 he was called to the bar. He married Elizabeth Edwards of Bristol, and they had two daughters. Little is known of his practice, save that in 1704 his chambers in Brick Court were destroyed by fire. Banister did not become a bencher of his inn, though in 1704 he was made a Welsh judge, as second justice on the Brecon circuit, and the following year he took the coif at the only general call of serjeants held under Queen Anne. In 1713 he was transferred to the Carmarthen circuit as chief justice, and later in the year Lord Chancellor Harcourt chose him to fill Sir Salathiel Lovell's place as a baron of the exchequer, whereupon he was knighted. His appointment gave dissatisfaction, however, and after the queen's death the following year the new lord chancellor, Lord Cowper, took the opportunity to revoke his patent on 14 October 1714. Banister died at his ancestral home at Turkdean on 17 January 1721. There is a memorial inscription to him in Turkdean church. J. H. BAKER

Sources Baker, *Serjeants* • Sainty, *Judges* • Foss, *Judges* • Foster, *Alum. Oxon.* • W. Musgrave, *Obituary prior to 1800*, ed. G. J. Armytage, 1, Harleian Society, 44 (1899) • R. Atkyns, *The ancient and present state of Glostershire*, 2 pts in 1 (1712) • *IGI* • R. Bigland, *Historical, monumental and genealogical collections, relative to the county of Gloucester*, 2 vols.

(1791–2) • W. R. Williams, *The history of the great sessions in Wales, 1542–1830* (privately printed, Brecon, 1899)

Bank [Banke], **Richard** (*d.* **1415**), justice, was probably the son of John Bank of Bank Newton in Gargrave, in the West Riding of Yorkshire. Bank seems likely to have distinguished himself during his legal training at one of the London inns of court, for his is the only name of a practising lawyer found in the moot cases of the period. He first appears in government records in 1388, when, as Richard Bank of Yorkshire, he is listed as one of a group of four men providing surety for the good behaviour of John Gargrave, previously imprisoned at Newgate 'upon suspicion of spying out the king's counsel' (*CClR, 1385–1389*, 597). In 1395 he was one of three commissioners appointed to inquire into expenditure on the paving of the road between Charing Cross and the New Temple Bar. He served as lord treasurer's remembrancer from 1397 to 1410, his career apparently undamaged by the deposition of Richard II and the succession of Henry IV, and he was one of a group of seven commissioners, headed by Sir William Rickhill, appointed in 1403 to inquire into the case of 'certain bondmen and tenants in bondage … who have leagued themselves together to refuse their due services' at Tottenham in Middlesex (*CPR, 1401–5*, 361). On 19 June 1410 Bank was named as one of the barons of the exchequer, and his appointment was renewed on 28 April 1413. He died, probably in London, in 1415, between 19 October, when he added a codicil to his will, and 2 December, when probate was granted. However, owing to a clerical oversight he continued to be paid his baron's salary until Michaelmas 1416.

It is likely that Bank's patron, possibly his mentor, had been Sir Robert Plessington, who was chief baron of the exchequer between 1380 and 1386. Plessington had lands in Wharfedale, Yorkshire, close to Bank's home; in May 1405 moreover, Bank was granted the wardship and marriage of Plessington's son, also Robert. Bank's will, dated 6 October 1415, records his receipt of 11 marks owed to the younger Robert, and also refers to some of the father's law books and two silver belts which had come into his possession. The closeness of the relationship is suggested by Bank's stipulation that the belts are to be sold and the proceeds distributed 'for his soul, my soul and the souls of all to whom Robert was indebted' (*Register of Henry Chichele*, 2.67).

Bank was married to Margaret, daughter of William Rivere, who predeceased him. There were three children of the marriage: William, Thomas, and Elizabeth. Two of his brothers are mentioned in his will: John Pierson (perhaps a half-brother) and Thomas Bank; the latter was also a lawyer, who is recorded as attorney in the exchequer for the duchy of Lancaster in 1399, and died as a baron of the exchequer in 1426. Richard Bank's main bequests were £100 to each of his children, four silver cups, and his armour, in addition to his books. In his will Bank stipulated that, should he die in London, he was to be buried next to his wife in the priory of St Bartholomew, Smithfield; Stow confirms that there was a memorial to them there. Bank's ties with Yorkshire were not forgotten; the codicil to his will left 100 marks for a chantry in the church of St Mary of Whixley, York, where his family also owned property. KATHLEEN E. GARAY

Sources E. F. Jacob, ed., *The register of Henry Chichele, archbishop of Canterbury, 1414–1443*, 2, CYS, 42 (1937), 66–9, 638 • S. E. Thorne and J. H. Baker, eds., *Readings and moots at the inns of court in the fifteenth century*, 2, SeldS, 105 (1990), xlvii, 42–3, 49, 53 • Sainty, *Judges*, 115–16 • *Chancery records* • W. Dugdale, 'Chronologie of the lord chancelors and keepers of the great seal', *Origines juridiciales, or, Historical memorials of the English laws* (1666), 57 • J. Stow, *A survay of London*, ed. A. M. [A. Munday], rev. edn (1618), 714 • T. D. Whitaker, *The history and antiquities of the deanery of Craven, in the county of York*, 3rd edn, ed. A. W. Morant (1878)

Wealth at death left £100 to each of three children; property in Alvythley; four silver cups, two silver belts, law books and a psalter: will, Jacob, ed., *The register of Henry Chichele*, 66–9

Bankes, George (**1787–1856**), politician and lawyer, was born on 1 December 1787, the third son of Henry *Bankes (1757–1834) of Kingston Lacy, Dorset, who represented Corfe Castle for nearly fifty years, and of Frances (1760/61–1823), daughter of William Woodley, governor of the Leeward Islands. He was a lineal descendant of Sir John Bankes, chief justice of the common pleas in the reign of Charles I. Bankes was educated at Westminster School (1795–1803). He attended Trinity Hall, Cambridge, in 1805, graduating LLB in 1812; he was a fellow there from 1814 to 1822. He studied law first at Lincoln's Inn and in 1815 at the Inner Temple, being called to the bar that year. Practising on the western circuit, he unexpectedly was offered the seat of Corfe Castle and joined his father as its second tory representative until 1823. He was again returned for Corfe Castle in 1826, and sat until 1832, when the family borough was united with that of Wareham. He was appointed one of the bankruptcy commissioners in 1822, and cursitor baron of the exchequer in 1824 (he was the last holder of this office, abolished on his death). In 1829, under the Wellington administration, he became chief secretary of the Board of Control, and in the next year a junior lord of the Treasury and one of the commissioners for the affairs of India. At the general election in 1841 he again entered parliament, being returned by the county of Dorset, for which he continued to sit until his death. He opposed repeal of the corn laws, arguing that the 'whole class' of tenants would be 'swept away' (Crosby, 140). During Derby's administration in 1852, Bankes held the office of judge-advocate-general and was sworn a privy councillor.

On 8 June 1822 he married Georgina Charlotte Nugent, whose supposed father was Admiral Sir Charles Edmund Nugent but whose real father was probably Ernest, duke of Cumberland. They had three sons and five daughters; six of the children died in childhood. On the death of his maverick elder brother, William John *Bankes, in 1855, Bankes succeeded to the family estates of Kingston Lacy and Studland in Dorset. He died at his London house in Old Palace Yard, Westminster, on 8 July 1856 and was buried at Studland, where a stained-glass window is dedicated to his memory. Bankes was the author of *The Story of Corfe Castle* *and of Many Who Have Lived There* (1853) (he was thrice mayor of Corfe Castle) and of *Brave Dame Mary*, a work of fiction founded on the *Story*.

G. V. BENSON, *rev.* H. C. G. MATTHEW

Sources HoP, *Commons* • *ILN* (12 July 1856) • T. L. Crosby, *English farmers and the politics of protection, 1815–1852* (1977) • V. Banks, *A Dorset heritage* (1953) • Burke, *Peerage*
Archives Niedersächsisches Hauptstaatsarchiv Hannover, letters to the duke of Cumberland

Bankes, Henry (1757–1834), politician and parliamentary diarist, was born on 19 December 1757; he was the second but only surviving son of Henry Bankes (*bap.* 1700, *d.* 1776), commissioner of customs, a member of the parliamentary dynasty descended from the royalist chief justice Sir John Bankes (1589–1644) and his second wife, Margaret, daughter of John Wynne, bishop of Bath and Wells. Having been educated at Westminster School (1767–73) he entered Trinity Hall, Cambridge, in 1773 and graduated BA (1778) and MA (1781). In September 1776 he succeeded to his father's extensive Dorset estates and to the country house of Kingston Lacy, Wimborne, which he commissioned Robert William Brettingham to remodel from 1784. On 18 August 1784 he married Frances (1760/61–1823), daughter of William Woodley (1728–1793), MP and governor of the Leeward Islands, and Frances Payne. They had five sons and two daughters; two of his sons and one of his daughters predeceased him.

From 1780 Bankes represented the rotten borough of Corfe Castle, of which he was the electoral patron; his father had held the seat from 1741 to 1762. In the Commons he opposed Britain's prosecution of the war against the American colonies, and from the mid-1780s he was a supporter of the administrations of William Pitt, a personal friend. But he always pursued a self-righteously independent course in financial matters, reprobating the cost of continental warfare, advocating reductions in peacetime expenditure, and urging the abolition of sinecures. At times a dangerous critic of government his influence peaked in 1812, when he at last secured an—albeit temporary—act to prevent the granting of offices in reversion (52 Geo. III c. xl). Initially a friend to Catholic relief he gave his last vote in its favour in 1812 and announced his change of heart in a printed speech on 25 February 1813. A procedural expert and an indefatigable committee man he was active, for example, on behalf of the British Museum, of which he was a trustee. With a house at 5 Old Palace Yard, Westminster, which was occasionally used for political meetings, he was well placed for the life of a busy politician, and indeed he had his own recognized seat on the cross benches in the chamber. His manuscript parliamentary journal, which he kept for most of his career, provides an almost daily account of proceedings in the Commons, with illuminating comments on the abilities of the principal speakers. His scholarly reputation was made by the appearance in 1818 of his only published work, *The Civil and Constitutional History of Rome from its Foundation to the Age of Augustus F.P.*

After several thwarted attempts to gain a county seat Bankes was finally elected for Dorset in February 1826. By that time a fierce critic of Catholic emancipation, he helped to lead the unsuccessful rearguard opposition of the ultra-tories against it in early 1829—for instance, by his *Speech … in Defence of the Protestant Constitution* on 30 March. An alarmist over parliamentary reform he was defeated in Dorset by his whig rival, John Calcraft, at the general election of 1831. He declined to offer himself for the vacancy caused by Calcraft's suicide in September but his fifty years' service in parliament were celebrated at a tory dinner in Dorchester on 26 July 1832. He was considered a dull but earnest parliamentarian, although Nathaniel Wraxall observed in 1818 that his 'talents compensated by their calm solidity for the want of brilliancy. His enunciation, slow, formal, precise, and not without some degree of embarrassment, was nevertheless always controlled by judgment, caution, and good sense' (*Historical and Posthumous Memoirs*, 4.80). He died at Tregothnan, near Truro, Cornwall, the home of his son-in-law Lord Falmouth, on 17 December 1834 and was buried at Wimborne Minster, Dorset, on 24 December. His estate was inherited by his elder surviving son, William John *Bankes (1786–1855), who, like his younger son George *Bankes (1787–1856), was also an MP. His third surviving son, Edward, became rector of Corfe Castle.

S. M. FARRELL

Sources Dorset RO, Bankes MS D/BKL [incl. parliamentary journal] • V. Bankes, *A Dorset heritage: the story of Kingston Lacy* (1953), 107–23 • *The diary and correspondence of Charles Abbot, Lord Colchester*, ed. Charles, Lord Colchester, 3 vols. (1861) • *The historical and the posthumous memoirs of Sir Nathaniel William Wraxall, 1772–1784*, ed. H. B. Wheatley, 5 vols. (1884), vol. 4, p. 80 • M. M. Drummond, 'Bankes, Henry', HoP, *Commons, 1754–90* • R. G. Thorne, 'Bankes, Henry', HoP, *Commons, 1790–1820* • *GM*, 2nd ser., 3 (1835), 323–4 • *Dorset County Chronicle* (25 Dec 1834) • Colvin, *Archs.*, 159 • *DNB*
Archives Dorset RO, corresp. and MSS, incl. MS parliamentary journal, D/BKL • priv. coll., MSS
Likenesses P. Batoni, two portraits, 1779–82, Kingston Lacy, Dorset
Wealth at death under £90,000 personalty: PRO, death duty registers, IR 26/1375/140

Bankes, Sir John (1589–1644), judge, was the son of John Bankes, a merchant of Keswick, Cumberland, and his wife, Jane Malton. He matriculated at Queen's College, Oxford, in February 1605. Having left without a degree, he began his legal studies at Gray's Inn in 1607. According to Nicholas Fuller, following his call to the bar in 1614 Bankes 'for some years … solicited suits for others', which suggests that he was more involved in the conduct of litigation, in which he obtained 'great practical experience' (Fuller, *Worthies*, 1.344), than with arguing technical points of law. Whatever the truth of this, it is likely that his early career centred on the north of England; from at least 1619, and throughout the 1620s, his professional opinion was frequently sought by Lord William Howard of Naworth.

Bankes was returned to parliament as a member for Wootton Basset in 1624, and in 1626 and 1628 he sat for Morpeth, almost certainly thanks to the influence of Lord Howard, whom Bankes had advised in his recent dispute with the town over the exercise of his seigneurial rights there. In the 1626 session, moreover, Bankes began to make his name as a parliamentarian, speaking regularly in debates that were also participated in by other notable lawyers such as William Noy, John Selden, and Edward Littleton. In 1628 he chaired two important committees of the house: that considering the king's claim to be entitled to take tonnage and poundage, and that dealing with the grievances of parliament. Bankes argued that the liberty of the subject should be protected by law from arrest by the king without cause being shown, and he was critical of the recent imposition by the crown of martial law and the billeting of soldiers on the country. Making the point on 16th April 1628 that 'the King's supply and the fundamental liberties go together' (Johnson, 2.481), he thought that recent royal commissions introducing martial law were contrary to the common law: subjects have their rights and the kings their prerogatives, '[y]et the ocean hath banks, and common law limits prerogative' (ibid.). Explaining the illegality of billeting of soldiers, he developed a historical approach, claiming that a search of the records revealed that there was no tenurial obligation to 'find such soldiers' (ibid., 2.363).

In 1630 Bankes gave the Lent reading at Gray's Inn on the Jacobean Statute of Limitations (21 James I c. 26). In 1631 he became a bencher, and from that date until 1635 also acted in the important capacity of treasurer of the society. Along with several of his former parliamentary colleagues, Bankes also received royal recognition and promotion. He was knighted in June 1631 and became attorney-general to the infant prince of Wales in July. In early 1632 he was appointed to a commission for inquiring into the evasion of customs duties by smugglers. It is also likely that he was working with Noy, now attorney-general, on developing the legal case behind the crown's attempts to increase revenue by launching commissions to inquire into the bounds of the royal forests and the extent to which royal privileges within them had been evaded. When Noy died in August 1634 Bankes was evidently preferred over Littleton and Selden as his replacement as attorney-general. Although one of the earl of Strafford's correspondents described Bankes as more judicious than Ellesmere, more eloquent than Bacon, and more learned than Noy himself, the earl's opinion was that he would prove to have 'something of the indifferent in him, betwixt the Sow's ear and the Silken Purse' (Radcliffe, 1.294). Nevertheless, now occupying an office that was probably worth approximately £10,000 p.a., Bankes made an impressive addition to his landed estate in 1635 by purchasing Corfe Castle on the Isle of Purbeck from Lady Elizabeth Hatton, the estranged widow of Sir Edward Coke.

Bankes appears to have been primarily an instrument rather than an initiator of royal policy that, during this period, was rapidly expanding the exploitation of the prerogative powers of the crown in order to raise money. Within weeks of his appointment he was busy searching for medieval precedents of royal levies of ship money. The extensive archive that has survived from his tenure as attorney-general shows that, in addition to commissions for enforcing the forest laws and for uncovering defective titles to land, he also drew up and was asked about the legality of letters patent, in which (in return for payment) the crown granted powers to groups of projectors that enabled them to regulate a wide range of trades, mainly in London, including coachmen, tobacco-pipe makers, glaziers and combmakers, distillers, musicians, and the brick and tile makers of Westminster. He also considered schemes for finding ways to license alehouse-keepers, brewers, and the owners of dovecotes, as well as plans to create commissions for enforcing the laws requiring the regular exercise of archery. Some observers thought that Bankes might lose his office in the wake of the outcry that followed the revelation that he had regularly permitted the illegal exportation of gold in return for a heavy fine, rather than initiating prosecutions in Star Chamber, as was prescribed in the proclamation prohibiting the practice. On this occasion, however, the king, evidently impressed by the income generated, promised his support, and there is little other evidence that Bankes himself profited directly by becoming involved in the many projects his paperwork launched.

As attorney-general Bankes was also responsible for initiating actions in Star Chamber in the king's name, and in this capacity he introduced the case against the religious dissidents Prynne, Bastwicke, and Burton, as well as that of Bishop John Williams. In May 1638 he examined John Lilburne for comments he uttered about the bishops while he was sitting in the pillory, and after the outbreak of war with Scotland in 1639 Bankes questioned a number of people who were reported to have made suspect political statements. In May 1638, when vigorously prosecuting the case against Thomas Harrison, a Northamptonshire vicar who had publicly called the judge Sir Richard Hutton a traitor because he had ruled against the legality of ship money, Bankes said that Harrison had cast an aspersion on his profession by claiming that all the clergymen in England thought the king had a right to command whatever he wanted; Harrison had failed to realize that the king's power was based on the law, and that the duty of judges was to determine to the best of their understanding what the law was. Bankes's own political views appear to have involved a strongly historical approach to the interpretation of the common law, combined with the belief that legally justified royal powers could be used both to profit the crown and to enforce social and economic regulation, which was arguably for the good of the Commonwealth. Commenting on a scheme for collecting a quarterage payment from all 'foreigners' resident in London, Bankes observed that it was 'free from the least touch of oppression or monopoly, but agreeable to the old Roman law called *Lex peregrinaria* and the modern rules of policy and sound government' (Bankes Papers, 6/16). Returning legislation that had been approved for passage by the Irish parliament, Bankes wrote to Wentworth in March 1635 commending the bills for making 'Ireland to be England in point of Government' (Radcliffe, 1.387). His three-day-long address that put the king's argument before the judges in the case of ship money (*R.* v. *Hampden*) in 1637 was largely historical in thrust. Citing an array of precedents, it illustrated the way in which early charters contained exceptions that allowed the king to raise money for the defence of the realm, and Bankes claimed that levies such as ship money had been collected in time of danger since before the Norman conquest. The writs themselves were based on many records, and were issued according to the laws and customs of England. He made it plain that he thought one of the reasons why kings could act in time of danger was that they had existed before parliaments. Royal power was inherent in the king's person, and in no way derived from the people, 'but [was] reserved unto the king when positive laws first began' (*State trials*, 3, col. 1017). The king was the sole judge of imminent danger and how the danger was to be prevented and avoided. Furthermore, having sat in parliament himself in 1628, he argued that the petition of right never intended that any prerogative power of the king should be diminished. Confirming the 'antient and old liberties' (ibid., col. 1056) of the subject, the debates surrounding its passage had never touched on the issue of ship money.

According to Clarendon, Bankes was concerned in late 1640 about investigations by the Long Parliament into some of the grants that had passed through his hands during his time as attorney-general. Hence he was relieved when made chief justice of the court of common pleas on 29 January 1641, following Edward Littleton's elevation to the lord keepership. On joining the king at York in the spring of 1642 he was sworn of the privy council, and thereafter appeared regularly at the side of Charles I, evidently becoming a voice in favour of moderation. When the king became dissatisfied with the prevarication of Lord Keeper Littleton, he resisted giving the great seal to Bankes largely on grounds that he was no less cautious. Bankes himself claimed to have earned the king's displeasure by not speaking out firmly enough against the legality of parliament's militia ordinance. Along with other peers and councillors he signed a declaration on 15 June 1642 that the king had no intention of making war on parliament, and he evidently maintained good relations with members of the parliamentary leadership. During the spring and early summer of 1642 he was in regular correspondence with, among others, the earl of Northumberland and Lord Saye and Sele in an attempt to find a peaceful solution to nation's problems, which he acknowledged involved fears on both sides. The alternative, civil war, would lead to the misery of the people, and, possibly, threaten the involvement of foreign powers.

When war did break out Bankes accompanied the king to Oxford, where he received an honorary DCL degree on 20 December 1642. Peace propositions presented by the two houses to the king in February 1643, which were concerned with the maintenance of the judiciary, called for Bankes to retain his position as chief justice of common pleas in the proposed settlement, but while keeping summer assizes on the western circuit in the same year, Bankes gave a charge that denounced the earls of Essex and Manchester as traitors. In May of the same year, parliamentary forces laid the first of two sieges on Corfe Castle, which was famously defended by Sir John's wife, the former Mary Hawtrey [*see* Bankes, Mary (*d.* 1661)], daughter of Ralph Hawtrey of Ruislip, Middlesex, whom he had married some years earlier.

Bankes's house in London was sequestered and sold by parliament in February 1644, and a resolution of the Commons on 22 July 1644 formally accused him of high treason. He died at Oxford on 28 December 1644 and was buried in Christ Church Cathedral, where there is a monument to his memory. His will, dated 20 September 1642, provided £200 in addition to £30 p.a. for the establishment of a workhouse for the poor in his native Keswick. He had a large number of children, and expressed the desire that 'whatever professions they or any of them shall undertake, they shall labour with all diligence to attaine the perfect knowledge thereof. And then with all industry and a good conscience towards God and man, practise the same' (PRO, PROB 11/642). CHRISTOPHER W. BROOKS

Sources [G. Ornsby], ed., *Selections of the household books of the Lord William Howard of Naworth Castle*, SurtS, 68 (1878), 114, 115, 200, 209, 259, 302 • *State trials*, vol. 3 • Bodl. Oxf., Bankes MSS • W. B. Bidwell and M. Jansson, eds., *Proceedings in parliament, 1626*, 4 vols. (1991–6) • R. C. Johnson and others, eds., *Proceedings in parliament, 1628*, 6 vols. (1977–83) • G. Bankes, *The story of Corfe Castle, and of many who have lived there* (1853) • G. Radcliffe, *The earl of Strafforde's letters and dispatches, with an essay towards his life*, ed. W. Knowler, 2 vols. (1739) • Fuller, *Worthies* (1840) • will, PRO, PROB 11/642 • P. E. Kopperman, *Sir Robert Heath, 1575–1649: window on an age* (1989) • Clarendon, *Hist. rebellion* • *CSP dom.*, 1629–31, 551; 1632, 253 • *JHC*, 2 (1640–42) • K. Sharpe, *The personal rule of Charles I* (1992)

Archives BL, reading of Bankes on statute of limitations, Hargrave MS 91 • Bodl. Oxf., papers relating to attorney-generalship; further papers | Dorset RO, Kingston Lacy papers

Likenesses oils, 1643, Sudbury Hall, Derbyshire • oils (after type by G. Jackson, *c.*1641), NPG

Wealth at death houses in London and Keswick as well as Corfe Castle: will, PRO, PROB 11/642

Bankes, Sir John Eldon (1854–1946), judge, was born on 17 April 1854 in London, the eldest son of John Scott Bankes (1826–1896) of Soughton Hall, Flintshire, and his first wife, Annie (1829–1876), daughter of Sir John *Jervis, chief justice of the common pleas. He was directly descended from Sir John Bankes, chief justice of the common pleas in 1641. His father's mother was the daughter of the lord chancellor, John Scott, first earl of Eldon.

Bankes was educated at Eton College, where he was president of the rowing club, and rowed for the school at Henley in 1872. From Eton he went on to University College, Oxford (1872), where he was secretary of the Oxford University boat club and president of Vincent's Club, having rowed for Oxford in 1875 when, after five successive defeats, they won the boat race by 10 lengths. After graduating with a second class in jurisprudence in 1876, he was called to the bar by the Inner Temple in 1878 and was a pupil of Richard Webster (later Viscount Alverstone). On 10 August 1882 he married Edith (1856–1931), daughter of Robert Peel Ethelston of Hinton Hall, Shropshire; they had two sons and two daughters.

Modest, unassuming, and courteous, good-looking and with a dry sense of humour, Bankes had a good practice on the common-law side and took silk in 1901, having become a bencher of his inn in 1899. He was unsuccessful as Unionist candidate for Flint in 1906, although a profile in *Vanity Fair* stated that had the women and children of the constituency enjoyed the suffrage, he would have won easily. In 1910 Lord Chancellor Loreburn appointed him a puisne judge and he was knighted; in 1915 he was promoted to the Court of Appeal and became a privy councillor.

As judge and lord justice, Bankes won a high reputation as a careful, clear-headed, and able lawyer. During his later years in the Court of Appeal, he acted as chairman of one of its branches, and in this capacity, often sitting with Sir T. E. Scrutton and Sir J. R. Atkin, he gave the first judgment in many important cases that illustrated his grasp of common-law principles. The prestige of this branch of the Court of Appeal under his chairmanship is evidenced by the small number of appeals made to the House of Lords from its unanimous decisions. Bankes retired in 1927 and was made a GCB in 1928.

Throughout his long life Bankes was a devoted churchman. He was at one time treasurer and later chairman of the London Diocesan Fund, served as chancellor of St Asaph diocese (1908–10), and with John Sankey and Atkin drafted the constitution of the disestablished Church in Wales. He was chairman of the representative body of the Church in Wales (1928–43). At the age of eighty-one he was appointed chairman of the royal commission on traffic in arms. He was chairman of Flintshire quarter sessions for thirty-three years, and was an alderman and chairman of Flintshire county council.

Treasurer of the Inner Temple in 1923, Bankes was an honorary LLD of Wales (1921) and Manchester (1923), an honorary fellow of University College, Oxford, and a fellow of Eton. A countryman at heart, he enjoyed managing the home farm and family estate of Soughton Hall, Northop, Flintshire, which he inherited from his father in 1894. Tall and athletic, he walked daily from his home in Eaton Square to the Temple, and at weekends during term was wont to take a train into the home counties and walk his preferred distance of 21 miles, carefully measured on a pedometer.

Bankes died aged ninety-two on 31 December 1946 at Soughton Hall. He was cremated on 4 January 1947, and his ashes were interred in the family vault at St Peter and St Eurgain, Northop, on the 7th. His son, Robert Wynne Bankes, was private secretary to successive lord chancellors (1919–29) and before his retirement in 1950 successively assistant secretary and secretary to the Institute of Chartered Accountants. The younger daughter, Margaret Annie, married Sir W. H. P. Lewis, her father's former pupil. P. A. Landon, *rev.* T. G. Watkin

Sources private information (1959, 2004) • *The Times* (2 Jan 1947) • *Law Reports: king's bench division* (1910–27) • Minutes of governing body and representative body of the Church in Wales, Representative Body Office, Cardiff • *VF* (29 March 1906)

Archives Flintshire RO, Hawarden • NL Wales | Representative Body Office, Cardiff, Representative Body of the Church in Wales MSS

Likenesses J. St H. Lander, oils, priv. coll.; repro. in *DNB*; copy, University College, Oxford; copy, Inner Temple, London • Spy [L. Ward], caricature, NPG; repro. in *VF* (29 March 1906) • W. Stoneman, photographs, NPG

Wealth at death £84,258 11*s.* 5*d.*: probate, 7 March 1947, *CGPLA Eng. & Wales*

Bankes [*née* Hawtrey], **Mary, Lady Bankes** (*d.* **1661**), royalist landholder, was the only daughter and an heir of Ralph Hawtrey (1570–1638) and his wife, Mary Altham (1578–1647). The Hawtreys claimed Norman descent and established themselves in Ruislip, Middlesex, in the sixteenth century. In 1618 she married Sir John *Bankes (1589–1644), a successful lawyer, knighted in 1634, and successively attorney-general and chief justice of the common pleas. Between 1621 and 1644 they had fourteen children. In 1635 Bankes bought Corfe Castle, Dorset, which henceforth became the family's seat.

With the outbreak of civil war Bankes accompanied the king to Oxford; he was impeached by parliament in 1643. Lady Bankes retired to Corfe Castle which, set on a steep hill and commanding the entrance to the Isle of Purbeck, was regarded as 'one of the impregnablest Forts of the Kingdome' (Ryves, 98). Parliamentarian soldiers first attempted to occupy it in 1643 under cover of a traditional May day stag hunt but, forewarned, she denied them entrance, and 'very wisely, and like her selfe' (ibid., 100), called in a guard. With her small force—reputedly only five men and her women servants—she repelled attempts to seize the castle's four cannon, and in the succeeding lull she built up supplies and called in a garrison of eighty royalist soldiers. On 23 June the castle was surrounded by Sir Walter Erle, a Dorset neighbour, with five or six hundred men, but bombardment and threats against the defenders, and promises of rewards to the parliamentarian soldiers, proved equally ineffective. When a storm was finally attempted Lady Bankes, her daughters, and women servants joined in the defence by dropping stones and hot embers over the walls onto the attackers. Erle's casualties were heavy, and on 4 August, after learning of the approach of relieving forces, he precipitately departed. Though an undistinguished affair, this first siege demonstrated Lady Bankes's resourcefulness and 'brave resolution' (ibid., 107).

On 28 December 1644 Sir John Bankes died suddenly in Oxford. As his executor Lady Bankes had to deal with the legal and financial problems associated with inheritance by minor children, as well as with the burdens of heavy tax assessments and punitive sequestration of the estate. A parliamentarian tax assessment of £300 on 8 January 1645 was followed by assessment at £1000 on 30 May. She did not pay, and on 22 September the committee for the advance of money ordered that she be taken to London in custody. On 1 October it ordered her committed to the Peterhouse in London, and on 6 October she agreed to pay the £1000 within fourteen days. Meanwhile she also faced the consequences of her husband's sequestration. A pass for her to go to London to compound had been issued on 16 July, and on 2 September she submitted the first of several petitions. On 10 September the Commons, before the sequestration committee had reached its decision, awarded £100 from the first profits of sale to the daughters of Captain Robert Turpin, executed after conviction by Sir John Bankes and other royalist judges. Lady Bankes petitioned again on 15 October on behalf of her ten minor children. She explained that the manor of Andleby, Lincolnshire, had been settled on her for life at the time of her marriage while Sir John had, in 1642, settled Dorset lands comprising most of the estate on her for the benefit of the younger children until the heir, John, now twenty, reached the age of twenty-four. As this settlement predated Sir John's sequestration, she urged either that the sequestration be removed or that she should be allowed to compound for it and for her son's wardship. She added that only a few years remained in which to raise portions and maintenance for the younger children. Finally, she asked that her £1000 assessment payment should be considered in the composition.

Lady Bankes and her advisers hoped to preserve the family's fortunes by appeals to law and compassion. These efforts were undercut by the fact that Corfe Castle continued to hold out and on 27 November 1645 the question was raised as to whether she should be allowed to compound before Corfe was reduced. In December Sir Thomas Fairfax turned serious attention to the castle. Lady Bankes rejected an opportunity to escape, but one defending colonel deserted in February 1646 while Lieutenant-Colonel Thomas Pitman offered to deliver the castle in return for future protection. He brought up 200 parliamentarians disguised as royalists, half of whom secured admission. Faced by renewed attack without and interlopers within, the defenders succumbed to 'stratagem and storm' (Sprigge, 334–5) and finally surrendered on 27 February 1646 after a siege of forty-eight days. The terms were generous if imperfectly observed, and the parliamentarian commander Colonel Bingham, a neighbour, returned the keys of the castle to Lady Bankes as a gesture of respect for her courage. On 5 March 1646 parliament voted that the castle be demolished. It was stripped of its rich contents and of its stone and timber, but the massive surviving ruins bear witness to the impossibility of total destruction. The keys were later enshrined in the family's new house at Kingston Lacy, Dorset.

On 4 February 1646 Lady Bankes's status as a delinquent royalist in her own right, independent of her husband, had been reasserted. In June, Dorset officials reminded London of her active defence of the castle and inquired 'whether your Lordships are not informed of any delinquency in her since her husband's decease' (Bankes, 307). In early 1647 her petitions were finally answered, the committee for compounding setting fines of £380 on her own estate, £1794 on her son John's, and £444 on that held by trustees for the younger children. After minor adjustments to these figures parliament formally pardoned her and discharged the sequestration in September 1647. In several cases between 1648 and 1650 she secured reductions on assessments. In the latter year her major responsibility for the estate ended when John Bankes turned twenty-four, but she, John, and the children's trustees again faced heavy taxes in 1651. She was also fined £350 for under-reporting the value of lands in Dorset, and was penalized for a similar offence in 1652. Thereafter she seems to have escaped serious financial scrutiny. In her financial dealings she displayed the same persistence and adroitness demonstrated in her defence of Corfe Castle, while benefiting from the services of family associates including Giles Green MP, co-trustee and tenant, her kinsman John Hawtrey, and her 'most affectionate servant' John Hunt. She sought to trace the dispersed contents of Corfe Castle; one agent's report in January 1647 recorded tapestries, carpets, and furniture that had found their way to a London broker and a Dutch merchant. Losses, meticulously chronicled, remained a persistent irritant in relations with Dorset neighbours such as Erle, Bingham, and humble but opportunist local people into whose hands Bankes goods had strayed. After John Bankes's death in 1656 his brother Ralph continued his mother's efforts to retrieve these goods, with little success.

Lady Bankes apparently spent her later years in London and at Damory Court, Dorset. She died without fuss and 'with great peace of mind' (Bankes, 245) on 11 April 1661. Her memorial, erected in St Martin's Church, Ruislip, by Ralph Bankes, declared that she 'had the honour to have borne with a constancy and courage above her sex a noble proporçon of the late calamities, and the happiness to have outlived them' (ibid., 245). A surviving copy of a contemporary miniature shows her as a determined widow. The circumstances of civil war forced her to turn that determination not only to the military action for which she attained a degree of fame but, like many other women who gained no such renown, to the preservation of the family fortunes. BARBARA DONAGAN

Sources [B. Ryves], *Mercurius rusticus* (1646), 98–107 · 'Autograph letters, vol. 1', MSS, Kingston Lacy, Dorset · M. A. E. Green, ed., *Calendar of the proceedings of the committee for compounding … 1643–1660*, PRO, 1–2 (1889–90) · M. A. E. Green, ed., *Calendar of the proceedings of the committee for advance of money, 1642–1656*, 3 vols., PRO (1888) · A. R. Bayley, *The great civil war in Dorset, 1642–1660* (1910) · G. Bankes, *The story of Corfe Castle* (1853) · National Trust, *Corfe Castle, Dorset* (1999) · National Trust, *Kingston Lacy, Dorset* (1998) · will, PRO, PROB 11/305, fols. 14–14v · *JHC*, 4 (1644–6), 462 · *JHC*, 5 (1646–8), 302, 311 · J. Sprigge, *Anglia rediviva* (1647)

Archives Dorset RO, MSS · Kingston Lacy, Dorset, letters | Bodl. Oxf., MSS Tanner

Likenesses Baron Marochetti, bronze sculpture, *c*.1853–1855 (after miniature by Bone), Kingston Lacy, Dorset · H. Bone, miniature, copy (after miniature by J. Hoskins), Kingston Lacy, Dorset

Wealth at death income from children's estate (where she acted as trustee); also what appear to be her own holdings; £800 on a bond owed to her; rents on tenement in London; other rents and moneys due; proceeds from sale of property to be used to make up full amounts for younger children's portions; any surplus to go to the four children 'undisposed of'; 'few jewels remaining' go to daughters, except bracelet to son Ralph, who is also to have a set of hangings; £10 to brother Edward Hawtrey: will, PRO, PROB 11/305, fols. 14–14v

Bankes, William John (1786–1855), traveller and antiquary, was born on 11 December 1786, second son of Henry *Bankes (1757–1834) of Kingston Lacy, Dorset, politician and author, and his wife, Frances (1760/61–1823), daughter of William Woodley, governor of the Leeward Islands, and the elder brother of George *Bankes. He was

William John Bankes (1786–1855), by Sir George Hayter, 1836

educated at Westminster School (1795–1801) before entering Trinity College, Cambridge, on 25 June 1803. In 1806, on the death of his elder brother, Henry, Bankes became heir to his father's estates and, with an income of £8000 a year, he led a life at Cambridge which earned him a reputation for extravagance and eccentricity which he was to keep, and indeed cultivate, throughout his life. At Cambridge he became a firm friend of Byron, who described him as the 'father of all mischief' in their fast set (*Byron's Letters and Journals*, 12 Oct 1820). Bankes graduated BA in 1808 and proceeded MA in 1811. In 1810 he was elected MP for Truro, where his prospective brother-in-law was the patron. He supported his father's efforts to abolish sinecures, but otherwise supported the administration. Despite his lifelong reputation as a brilliant conversationalist in private circles, he seems to have been a poor public speaker, and his parliamentary speeches were sometimes strangely delivered and incoherent.

Bankes, with Byron, was prominent in the London season of 1812 and, after having given up his parliamentary seat and having had his proposal of marriage to Annabella Milbanke, afterwards Lady Byron, refused, he set out, with letters of introduction from Byron, for the East. He followed Wellington's army through Portugal and Spain, buying treasures which now decorate the Spanish Room in the family home at Kingston Lacy. By September 1815 he reached Cairo, making preparations for a voyage up the Nile to see the antiquities in the company of the interpreter, attendant, and janizary Giovanni Finati, whose memoirs he later translated from the Italian, edited, and published as *Narrative of the Life and Adventures of Giovanni Finati* (2 vols., 1830). Bankes enjoyed the bizarre, daring, and exotic, but was also a serious scholar, making detailed sketches and notes of the monuments he passed and amassing a collection of Egyptian antiquities now at Kingston Lacy. He reached the Second Cataract and Wadi Halfa before returning to Cairo, having adopted eastern dress and grown a beard. In October 1818 he made his second and longer Nile journey in the company of Henry Salt, the British consul-general, Giovanni Belzoni, and three artists to help record their discoveries. Bankes's first attempt to remove an obelisk which he had discovered on the island of Philae on his earlier trip ended with the pillar's lying on the river bed, but it was finally rescued, brought to Kingston Lacy in 1821, and, with a pedestal and a base, which belongs to a quite different temple in Nubia, was erected in 1839 on the south lawn where it still stands. While in Egypt, Bankes spent a month at Abu Simbel, uncovering figures and systematically recording the interior. Bankes went on to Palestine, Syria, and Jordan in the company of James Silk Buckingham. He returned to Europe in 1819, meeting Byron in Italy in 1820. He arrived back in England in 1820, where he basked in society admiration and enjoyed the nickname from Byron the Nubian Discoverer. He wrote or inspired a review of Silk Buckingham's work on Palestine which appeared in the *Quarterly Review* (January 1822) and in a published letter repeated allegations that Buckingham had plagiarized drawings and some observations from his (Bankes's) notebook which he had mistakenly left with Buckingham. On 26 October 1826 Buckingham obtained £400 damages from Bankes for this libel, although some modern interpreters are less sure of the justice of his case (personal information).

While on his travels in 1815, on the death of his uncle Sir William Wynne, Bankes inherited Soughton Hall, Flintshire, and after 1834, when he succeeded to his father's estate, he commanded a considerable fortune. He made extensive changes to both Soughton and Kingston Lacy with the help of Charles Barry. He was tory MP for the University of Cambridge (1822–6) and for Marlborough (1829–32) before succeeding to his father's county seat and representing Dorset (1832–4).

Having already been the subject of gossip and a suit for criminal conversation with Lady Buckinghamshire (*née* Anne Pigot, married name Anne Hobart) in 1823, in 1833 he was charged with meeting a guardsman for 'unnatural purposes' in a public convenience between Westminster Abbey and St Margaret's Church. He was found not guilty after many people, including the duke of Wellington, had given character references, but the suggestion of impropriety and the detailed discussion of his personal habits undermined his public career. In 1841 another such charge drove him abroad and, having made over his estates to his brother George, he took up residence at Venice, from where he continued to direct in minute detail the furnishing of Kingston Lacy. Bankes died in Venice unmarried and childless on 15 April 1855. He was buried at the family vault at Wimborne Minster, Dorset.

Bankes's drawings at Kingston Lacy remain an important source for Egyptologists because they are detailed site plans, measured sections, elevations, and meticulous transcriptions, not artistic impressions, and because many of the objects he recorded have since been lost, destroyed, or moved from their original environment. The drawings from Nubia and the Sudan are particularly important as they are some of the earliest to be made of those regions. Bankes did many of the drawings and transcriptions himself; others in the collection are wholly or in part by others but were made under Bankes's direction by Finati and Louis Linant. His contribution to the decipherment of the hieroglyphic script, one of the purposes for which the collection of drawings was made, was significant, but his influence was greatly and unfortunately limited by his failure to publish any account of his travels other than his notes to Finati's *Narrative*. The first systematic study of his papers (Usick, 2002) shows the importance of his scholarship and quite how much has been lost since he visited Egypt and Nubia.

ELIZABETH BAIGENT

Sources P. Usick, *Adventures in Egypt and Nubia: the travels of William John Bankes (1786–1855)* (2002) • HoP, *Commons* • Burke, *Peerage* • Venn, *Alum. Cant.* • *The Times* (3 Dec 1833) • *The Times* (3 Sept 1841) • P. Usick, 'William John Bankes' collection of drawings of Egypt and Nubia', *Travellers in Egypt*, ed. P. Starkey and J. Starkey (1998), 51–60 • V. Bankes, *A Dorset heritage: the story of Kingston Lacy* (1953) • O. Garnett, 'Out of Egypt', *National Trust Magazine* (spring 1994), 36–7 • S. Rogers, *Table talk* (1856) • E. Iversen, *Obelisks in exile* (1968) • *Byron's letters and journals*, ed. L. A. Marchand, 1 (1973) • W. R. Dawson and E. P. Uphill, *Who was who in Egyptology*, 3rd edn, rev. M. L. Bierbrier (1995) • private information (2004)

Archives Dorset RO, archaeological drawings • National Trust, archaeological drawings and watercolours

Likenesses G. Sanders, miniature, 1812, Kingston Lacy, Dorset; repro. in Garnett, 'Out of Egypt', 37 • G. Hayter, portrait, 1836, Kingston Lacy, Dorset [*see illus.*] • G. Hayter, group portrait, oils (*The House of Commons, 1833*), NPG • portrait, Kingston Lacy, Dorset

Bankhead, Charles (*c.*1797–1870), diplomatist, was probably the son of Dr Charles Bankhead (*c.*1768–1859), personal physician to Lord Castlereagh. Bankhead began his diplomatic career as a clerk to The Hague from 5 July 1814 to 5 January 1815 and then worked at St Petersburg from June 1820 to December 1822 and again from December 1824 to June 1825. In 1826 he was transferred to Washington as secretary of legation. He served as chargé d'affaires for long periods during the 1830s while the British minister, Sir Charles Vaughan (1774–1849), was on leave of absence in Britain. He took part in the continuing negotiations over the north-eastern boundary dispute between Maine and Canada and was instrumental behind the scenes in resolving the crisis in 1835–6 between France and the United States over unpaid indemnities owed to the latter. He was relieved in 1836 by Henry Stephen Fox (1791–1848), who had been appointed minister-plenipotentiary.

Bankhead's next assignment was in 1838 as secretary of embassy in Constantinople; then in 1843 he was transferred to Mexico as minister-plenipotentiary. He arrived in March 1844 and was confronted by a deepening crisis in Mexican–American relations. Texas, formerly a province of Mexico, had overthrown Mexican rule and established an independent republic in 1836. Mexico had refused to conclude a treaty with Texas and for years Britain had tried to mediate a settlement between the two states as part of a wider strategy of maintaining Texan independence. Bankhead was instrumental in persuading Mexico to recognize Texas in 1845; however, when given the choice between annexation to the United States or independence, Texas opted for the former. This led directly to war between the United States and Mexico, and Bankhead was instructed to offer mediation by Britain, which was rejected by both parties. He was, however, able to facilitate communication between the adversaries during the conflict.

Bankhead was also active in promoting British commercial interests in Mexico, and at one time advocated an ambitious colonization scheme in California to prevent the province from falling under American control. He also believed that a European-sponsored monarchy would be a solution to Mexico's political instability. Neither suggestion, however, was followed up by the British government. Bankhead left Mexico on 19 October 1847 owing to illness and retired officially from the diplomatic service on 6 April 1851. He died at his home, 8 St James's Street, London, on 11 March 1870.

LELIA M. ROECKELL

Sources D. Pletcher, *The diplomacy of annexation: Texas, Oregon and the Mexican war* [1973] • W. Beckles, *Friendly relations: a narrative of Britain's ministers and ambassadors to America, 1791–1930* (1969) • C. R. Middleton, *The administration of British foreign policy, 1782–1846* (1977) • PRO, Foreign Office MSS, series 50 (Mexico) • BL, Aberdeen MSS, Add. MS 43126 • d. cert.

Archives All Souls Oxf., letters to Sir Charles Vaughan • BL, corresp. with Lord Aberdeen, Add. MSS 43126, 43170, 43238 • PRO, Foreign Office MSS, series 50 (Mexico) • U. Southampton L., corresp. with Lord Palmerston

Wealth at death under £700: resworn probate, Oct 1877, *CGPLA Eng. & Wales* (1870)

Bankhead, John (1738–1833), minister of the Presbyterian General Synod of Ulster, was born into a family that is thought to have come from Bank Head, Edinburghshire, and settled near Clough, co. Antrim. He is believed to have been educated at Glasgow University but his name is not in any college register. He was licensed by Ballymena presbytery before 29 June 1762 and called on 13 February 1763 to Ballycarry congregation, co. Antrim, which had been vacant since the death of James Cobham, on 22 February 1759. On 26 July 1763 Bankhead subscribed the confession of faith according to the following cautious formula: 'I believe the Westminster Confession to contain a system of the Christian doctrines, which doctrines I subscribe as the confession of my faith' (Witherow, *Memorials, 1731–1800*, 136). He was ordained minister on 16 August 1763 and remained all his life at Ballycarry, where the disadvantage of a salary of £45 was offset by the income from a grazing farm and the pleasure of his close friendship with the Edmonstone family of Redhall. He declined the call (and promise of a higher salary) from the richer congregation of Comber, co. Down, in July 1774. He married, first, Jane Martin, and following her death he married, in February

1812, Mary Magill, who survived him. He was father to twenty-two children.

In 1800 Bankhead served as moderator of synod. In 1786, however, he had published a catechism that hinted at his unease with doctrinally orthodox forms, for though the questions are those of the orthodox Westminster shorter catechism the answers are simply scriptural passages, printed without comment. In the second edition, published in 1825, some of the Westminster questions are omitted and others are altered. His assistant, William Glendy (1781/2–1853), who had been ordained on 30 July 1812, broke with orthodoxy and joined the Remonstrant Synod of Ulster in 1829, taking the Ballycarry congregation with him. Bankhead remained on the roll of the general synod, and so his denominational affiliation in his last years is unclear.

A convivial man and an excellent mimic, Bankhead was gently satirized in a poem by the Revd William Heron of Ballyclare, 'The Ulster Synod' (1817):

> In jovial mixture, and in dose enough
> Scattering bright wit, sound sense, and Dublin snuff
> To make you sneeze, or learn, or loudly laugh.
> (Witherow, *Memorials, 1731–1800*, 138)

He died at Ballycarry on 5 July 1833, aged ninety-five and six weeks short of his seventieth year as minister at Ballycarry. He was buried in the churchyard of Templepatrick. Of the nineteen of his children who survived into adulthood John and Charles (*d.* 1859) became physicians, James (*d.* 1824) was minister of Dromore, co. Down, and William (*d.* 1881) served as Unitarian minister at Brighton and Diss, Norfolk, before leaving the ministry.

Alexander Gordon, *rev.* S. J. Skedd

Sources *Belfast News-Letter* (12 July 1833) • *Christian Unitarian*, 1 (1862), 84 • *Christian Unitarian*, 2 (1863) • T. Witherow, *Historical and literary memorials of presbyterianism in Ireland, 1731–1800* (1880), 136–40 • *Records of the General Synod of Ulster, from 1691 to 1820*, 3 vols. (1890–98)

Bankin [Bankyn], **John** (*fl.* **1347–1387**), prior of the Augustinian convent, London, and religious controversialist, is said by John Bale to have been born in London, where he entered and was educated at the Augustinian convent. By 1347 he had moved to the convent in Oxford, although between 7 March 1347 and 14 November 1348 he was also licensed to hear confessions in Sarum diocese. While in Oxford, again according to Bale, he acquired the reputation of *supremae classis magister*. He completed his DTh at some time before 1382.

In 1371 Bankin and another Augustinian friar (perhaps Thomas Ashbourne) laid articles before parliament urging the use of clerical endowments to help finance the war in France. In making such a proposal they were voicing what seem to have been widely held ideas. When John Wyclif (*d.* 1384), himself a spectator at this parliament, argued such ideas later in the decade, therefore, Bankin was almost certainly one of his supporters: he may even have been one of the four friars produced by John of Gaunt, duke of Lancaster (*d.* 1399), to defend Wyclif at St Paul's Cathedral on 19 February 1377. If Bankin began by supporting Wyclif, however, he then changed his position, probably in response to the publication of Wyclif's *De eucharistia* in 1380. In May 1382 he was among those who condemned Wyclif's views at the council held at Blackfriars, London.

By 18 July 1387 Bankin had succeeded Ashbourne as prior of the London convent. As such he had to deal with the apostasies of at least two fellow Augustinians, Peter Pateshull and Robert Stokesley, alias York, who had abandoned the religious life and returned to the world. It is not known when he died. John Bale credits Bankin with three works, *Contra positiones Wiclevi*, *Determinationes variae*, and *Sermones ad populum*, none of which has survived, and also describes him as a popular preacher and able disputant. His *Contra positiones Wiclevi* suggests that he ultimately became an active anti-Wycliffite polemicist.

Christina von Nolcken

Sources Emden, *Oxf.* • A. Gwynn, *The English Austin friars in the time of Wyclif* (1940), 211–79 • V. H. Galbraith, 'Articles laid before the parliament of 1371', *EngHR*, 34 (1919), 579–82 • Bale, *Cat.*, 1.504–5 • M. Aston, 'Caim's castles', *Faith and fire: popular and unpopular religion, 1350–1600* (1993), 95–131, esp. 104–8 • *DNB* • K. B. McFarlane, *John Wycliffe and the beginnings of English nonconformity* (1952), 58–88 • H. B. Workman, *John Wyclif*, 2 vols. (1926), vol. 1, pp. 210–30; vol. 2, pp. 261–2 • A. Hudson, *The premature reformation: Wycliffite texts and Lollard history* (1988), 338 • P. Gradon, 'Langland and the ideology of dissent', *PBA*, 66 (1980), 179–205, esp. 186–8 • [T. Netter], *Fasciculi zizaniorum magistri Johannis Wyclif cum tritico*, ed. W. W. Shirley, Rolls Series, 5 (1858), 286 • Robert Wyvil register, Wilts. & Swindon RO, vol. 1, fol. 19 • *CPR, 1385–9*, 386

Banks, Benjamin (1727–1795), musical instrument maker, was born at Salisbury on 14 July 1727, the third of the five children of George Banks, master butcher, and his wife, Barbery Huttoft. In 1741 Banks commenced a seven-year apprenticeship with his uncle William Huttoft, musical instrument maker and retail music dealer of Salisbury. In fact Huttoft is not recorded as a stringed instrument maker and it seems probable that Banks spent some time in the workshops of London makers such as Peter Wamsley of Piccadilly (1715?–1751) or members of the Hill family, particularly Joseph Hill (1715–1784). There was also a later London connection with the Cahusac instrument retail business, for Banks's eldest daughter, Ann, married Thomas Cahusac in 1780. Banks used as his main London outlet the retail music firm of Longman and Broderip, whose instruments so labelled were made for them by others and may occasionally reveal Banks's signature or initials internally. Despite the attraction of London as a marketing base, Banks continued to maintain his workshop in Salisbury.

After two centuries Banks's reputation stands high, a number of authorities referring to the almost faultless workmanship, particularly in his copies made on the grand Amati model, after Nicolo Amati of Cremona. Banks himself is often referred to as 'the English Amati'. He also made instruments, supposedly mainly for the trade, on the highly arched Germanic Stainer model, which are less well regarded, and occasionally produced copies of Stradivari some decades before this became fashionable. Banks's sonorous cellos in particular remain highly prized by professional players and have long competed for favour with those of William (Royal) Forster of London (1739–1808), who enjoyed the patronage of the prince of Wales. Banks is thought to have produced violins, violas, and cellos in roughly even numbers, no doubt with the help of his sons. Examples of his work are to be found in the Salisbury and South Wiltshire Museum.

Banks married Ann Burtt in Salisbury on 8 August 1749 and they had nine children, two of whom, James and Henry, carried on the family business in Catherine Street, Salisbury, until that moved to Liverpool in 1811. Their output varies in standard. Banks died on 18 February 1795 and was buried with his wife at the church of St Thomas in Salisbury High Street. His tombstone bears the words 'Restored 1863 … in memory of the most eminent English maker of stringed musical instruments'.

Brian W. Harvey

Sources A. Cooper, *Benjamin Banks, the Salisbury violin maker* (1989) • W. M. Morris, *British violin makers: a biographical dictionary of British makers of stringed instruments*, 2nd edn (1920) • B. W. Harvey, *The violin family and its makers in the British Isles: an illustrated history and directory* (1995) • C. Beare, 'Banks, Benjamin', *The new Grove dictionary of musical instruments*, ed. S. Sadie (1984) • W. Henley, *Universal dictionary of violin and bow makers*, 1 vol. edn (1973) • C. Beare, 'Banks, Benjamin', *New Grove*

Likenesses C. Rosenberg, silhouette, *c.*1785–1790, Salisbury and South Wiltshire Museum; repro. in Cooper, *Benjamin Banks*

Banks, Sir Edward (1770–1835), builder and contractor, was born near Richmond, Yorkshire, on 4 January 1770; nothing is known of his parentage. As a young man he went to sea for two years. After returning to Yorkshire, in 1789 he became involved with the first of many construction projects, undertaking sea banking and draining in Holderness.

In 1791 Banks became contractor on the Leeds and Liverpool Canal, and in 1793 under the engineer John Rennie (1761–1821) worked on the Lancaster and Ulverston canals, rapidly extending his operations in 1795–7 to the Huddersfield (including the 3½ mile Marsden Tunnel), Peak Forest, and Ashton under Lyne canals. In 1800 he worked on several Derbyshire canals under William Jessop, as well as on tram roads and turnpikes, and began a carrying trade in coal and limestone, employing thirty barges. Jessop then engineered the Surrey iron railway (on which trucks were drawn by mules), which in 1803 Banks extended from Croydon to Merstham, where Colonel Hylton Jolliffe MP had an interest in lime works. Banks formed a partnership with Jolliffe, developing a considerable trade with London in building materials. Banks himself in 1810 surveyed the line of a canal to link Merstham with the proposed Grand Southern Canal to Portsmouth.

In 1807 the Revd William John Jolliffe (1774–1835) replaced his brother in the partnership, which rapidly became a major contractor—probably the largest of the day—for public works, principally of an engineering character, such as embanking Cardiff marshes (1808), erecting a lighthouse at Heligoland, and constructing Rennie's Howth harbour in Dublin Bay (1809–19). More conventional building such as the Croydon court house (1809) and prisoner-of-war accommodation at Princetown, Dartmoor (1809–10), was also undertaken. In 1822 they contracted for the canal and locks which created the port of Goole on the Humber, and also tendered unsuccessfully for Nash's new Royal Mews, Pimlico, which they later completed as assignees of Want and Richardson.

Rennie's knowledge of Banks's efficiency doubtless assisted in gaining the latter a footing in London's rapidly developing enclosed dock system. By submitting what Rennie described as very reasonable competitive tenders, and carrying out excellent work, including state-of-the-art coffer dam techniques, Banks undertook a number of important projects from his yard at Beaufort wharf, Strand. In 1811 Jolliffe and Banks reconstructed the Limehouse entrance to the West India Dock at their own estimate, work by another contractor having collapsed; in 1813 they made good failed piling for a dock at Chetney Hill lazaretto; in 1816 they excavated for the no. 2 rum warehouse at West India Dock; and in 1817 they built a new entrance for London docks, and contracted at a low price for similar work and river walls at Deptford Dockyard. Although theirs was not the lowest tender for a new river wall and wharf at the London custom house in 1817, Rennie recommended them because they had all the required materials in hand as well as pile engines and other machinery from work on Southwark Bridge, 'and from their great experience in works of this sort there is the best assurance of its being well and speedily executed' (Rennie, 9.70). In 1828 the partners built the saltpetre warehouse on the south side of the Blackwall basin, West India Dock, having previously in 1811 rebuilt the outer wing walls of its western Limehouse basin.

Rennie had established himself as the principal bridge builder in the capital, and Jolliffe and Banks became contractors for his granite Waterloo Bridge (1811–17), described by Canova as the noblest bridge in the world, under the new system of lump-sum contracts with a single firm; for the piling, masonry, and centering for Southwark Bridge (1814–19), the largest cast-iron bridge ever built, with a central span of 240 ft; and under the younger Rennie for the new thousand-foot granite London Bridge (1824–31), the smaller but socially conspicuous bridge over the Serpentine, Hyde Park (1821–4), and Staines Bridge which was also of granite. The stoneyard at Millwall was probably laid out specifically for the London Bridge contract, their bridge-building operations having led them to open a trade with Aberdeen (from where they also drew masons) for large blocks of granite, expending £155,000 by 1821. Later they drew supplies from Dartmoor. For building the arches of London Bridge they employed preframed centering ingeniously floated into position, a device sometimes credited to Banks rather than to Rennie.

Jolliffe and Banks were also, with Nicholson of Rochester, employed in a series of excavation, piling, and walling contracts for Rennie's vast Sheerness naval dockyard (1812–30), a £3 million work designed for 'the building and equipment of ships of war of the largest dimensions' (Westall and Owen, 167). Their 1815 contract for tonguing-

and-grooving sheet piling proved unremunerative so Rennie invented a machine, executed at their cost, which greatly reduced the expense and performed the work more efficiently. Because they already had on site steam-engines, mortar mills, lime-kilns, railways, and scaffolding, Rennie recommended employing them for a further large contract in 1817 if they would bring down their price to within £2000 of the lowest tender. They failed to do so and were replaced by another contractor, though they subsequently constructed the northern sector, an £850,000 contract. Close by, Banks founded Banks Town (later Sheerness-on-Sea) as a speculation, instituting a tri-weekly service from London by steamboat (built by Jolliffe, Banks & Co.). With Jolliffe, he was a founder of the General Steam Navigation Company (1824).

Another extensive enterprise undertaken by the partners in association with Rennie was the 3 mile Eau Brinck Cut on the Ouse at King's Lynn, 1817–21, to drain 300,000 acres of the Great, or Bedford, Level of the fens, where they executed £40,000 worth of works before receiving any return. This was a labour by which 'an immense value has been given to otherwise worthless swamps and wastes' (Smiles, 169). Similar works executed on the Nene (a new cut of over 5 miles, where they employed about 1300 men, 1827–31), Witham (1828), and Ancholme (1828) were engineered by Telford or the younger Rennie. The partnership was dissolved in 1834, the year before both Banks and Jolliffe died.

Banks lived in Adelphi Terrace, Westminster, and had country properties at Oxney Court, Dover, and Sheppey Court, both in Kent. In 1793 he married Nancy (*d.* 1815), daughter of John Franklin, with whom he had five sons and three daughters; in 1821 he married Amelia (*d.* 1836), daughter and coheir of Sir Abraham Pytches of Streatham, and sister of his partner's wife. One of his daughters married Jolliffe's son. There were no children from his second marriage.

Banks was knighted on 12 June 1822 for his skill and perseverance in building Waterloo and Southwark bridges, the first knighthood bestowed on an engineer (the elder Rennie having declined one in 1817). Obituaries remarked on his perseverance, integrity, piety, and benevolence. He died at his daughter's house at Tilgate, Sussex, on 5 July 1835. He was buried in a family grave at Chipstead, Surrey, the beauty of which spot he had observed when working on the Merstham tram road many years earlier.

M. H. Port

Sources S. Wells, *History of the drainage of the Great level of the fens, called Bedford level*, 1 (1830) • H. W. Dickinson, 'Jolliffe and Banks: contractors', *Transactions* [Newcomen Society], 12 (1931–2), 1–8 • A. W. Skempton, 'Engineering in the Port of London, 1808–1834', *Transactions* [Newcomen Society], 53 (1981–2), 73–96 • W. Westall and S. Owen, *A picturesque tour of the Thames* (1828) • will, PRO, Prob. 11/1849, fol. 410 • J. Rennie, reports, Inst. CE, vols. 6–10 • J. M. Crook and M. H. Port, eds., *The history of the king's works*, 6 (1973) • E. W. Brayley, J. Britton, and E. W. Brayley, jun., *A topographical history of Surrey*, 4 (1844), 305–7 • *The Times* (21 July 1835), 4e • *GM*, 2nd ser., 4 (1835), 444 • S. Smiles, *Lives of the engineers*, 2 (1861), 164
Archives Som. ARS, Jolliffe MSS, partnership papers
Likenesses W. Patten, oils, 1835, NPG • T. Smith, bust, *c.*1835, St Margaret's Church, Chipstead, Surrey • W. Patten or G. Patten, oils, Guildhall Art Gallery, London • portrait, priv. coll.

Banks, George Linnaeus (1821–1881), author and journalist, born at the Bull Ring, Birmingham, on 2 March 1821, was the son of John Banks, a seedsman. The father was an inflexible Methodist; he once took a copy of *Robinson Crusoe* from his son and thrust it into the fire. When a boy George was totally blind for seven months, and was eventually cured by a quack, who applied leeches to the soles of his feet. He was sent to work for an engraver, but his eyes proved too weak for this work; afterwards he went to a modeller, then, neglected by his father, bound himself apprentice to a cabinet-maker. His master's business failed, and Banks became, at the age of seventeen or eighteen, a contributor to newspapers and magazines, an amateur actor, and orator. He had a remarkable faculty for silhouette portraiture. He was an active radical, and from December 1846 a popular lecturer. One of his lyrics, 'What I Live For', was frequently quoted by platform and pulpit orators; it is believed that it first appeared in a Liverpool newspaper. During his residence in Liverpool he wrote a play called *The Swiss Father*, in which William Creswick took the leading part. He wrote a number of other plays, including *The Slave King* for the black actor Ira Aldridge. His songs, especially 'Dandy Jim of Caroline' (a 'negro melody'), 'The Minstrel King', and 'Warwickshire Will' were long popular. On 27 December 1846 Banks married Isabella [*see* Banks, Isabella Varley (1821–1897)], daughter of James Varley, a chemist, of Manchester; she was the author of a volume of poetry, *Ivy Leaves*, and several novels.

Between 1848 and 1864 Banks was editor of the *Harrogate Advertiser*, *Birmingham Mercury*, *Dublin Daily Express*, *Durham Chronicle*, *Sussex Mercury*, and *Windsor Royal Standard*. For a time he had some share, along with William Sawyer, in the *Brighton Excursionist*. He also published several volumes of poetry, including *Daisies in the Grass* (1865), which contained work by himself and his wife, and took part in the Shakespeare tercentenary. He was a characteristic Victorian autodidact, who flourished in the world of the radical intelligentsia. In his later years his mind clouded and he destroyed most of his papers, thus frustrating his wife's intention of writing his biography. He died of cancer of the penis and pneumonia on 3 May 1881 in Dalston, London, and was buried at Abney Park cemetery; his wife survived him.

W. E. A. Axon, *rev.* H. C. G. Matthew

Sources personal knowledge (1885) • Boase, *Mod. Eng. biog.*
Archives JRL, corresp., notebooks, and papers • State Library of New South Wales, Sydney, Dixson Wing, letters and papers
Likenesses R. & E. Taylor, woodcut (after photograph), NPG; repro. in *Illustrated Review* (25 Sept 1873), 261–3

Banks, Isabella Varley [*née* Isabella Varley; *known as* Mrs G. Linnaeus Banks] (1821–1897), public lecturer and writer, was born on 25 March 1821, at Oldham Street, Manchester, the daughter of James Varley, chemist (*d.* 1842), and his wife, Amelia Daniels. Her grandfather, James Varley the elder, of Bolton, discovered chloride of lime as a means of bleaching cotton. She was educated at Green Street School, Miss Hannah Spray's Ladies' day school, and the Revd John Weelden's academy. Her first literary effort, a poem entitled 'A Dying Girl to her Mother', was published in the *Manchester Guardian*, 12 April 1837, when she was just sixteen. From 1838 to 1848 she kept a school at Cheetham, near Manchester, and in 1842 became a member of the ladies' committee of the Anti-Corn Law League. The first of her three volumes of poetry, *Ivy Leaves: a Collection of Poetry*, was published in 1844. She was also skilled in needlework and knitting and produced a fancy-work pattern each month for forty-five years from 1850 to 1895; these were published in little quarterly volumes. A deep interest in the tradition of British literature prompted her participation in the London Shakespeare tercentenary (23 April 1864), where she baptized a memorial oak, presented by Queen Victoria and planted by the actor Samuel Phelps, with water from the River Avon, and delivered an address.

On 27 December 1846, Isabella Varley married George Linnaeus *Banks (1821–1881), a journalist and poet from Birmingham, and later assisted him in his work by contributing to the journals he edited. These included: the *Harrowgate Advertiser*, the *Birmingham Mercury*, the *Dublin Daily Express*, the *Durham Chronicle*, the *Sussex Mercury*, and the *Windsor Royal Standard*. As she accompanied him about the country to these various posts, she acquired the historical and dialectal background which she would later use in her novels. In 1865 she and her husband co-authored a collection of songs and poetry, *Daisies in the Grass*.

Mrs Banks's domestic life was difficult: she gave birth to eight children, five of whom predeceased her; she suffered more or less constantly from ill health; and her husband had a progressive drinking problem which eventually caused him several times to sell their household furniture to raise money for alcohol, and resulted in his near-suicidal depression in later life. When she was forty-three she turned to novel writing to support her family. Her first novel, *God's Providence House* (1865), was set in Chester and was well received by critics. Between 1865 and 1894 she published twelve novels, three volumes of poetry, and three volumes of stories, many of the titles running to multiple editions, which kept her name before the public almost continually during those years. She became known as the Lancaster Novelist because of the setting of her novels in such places as Yorkshire, Wiltshire, Durham, Birmingham, Chester, and Manchester. 'In every case the dialect is as carefully done as the rest of the details, the author having a special gift for reproducing in type the peculiarities of local pronunciation' (*Woman's Signal*, 22 Oct 1896).

Mrs Banks's most famous and enduring novel was *The Manchester Man* (1870) which went through eleven editions, five during her lifetime and six posthumously, the latest being 1991. It is set in Manchester at the beginning of the nineteenth century and gave the best available picture of the 'buildings, institutions, and personalities in the days of "Peterloo"' (*Woman's Signal*, 13 May 1897). Another of her books, *More than Coronets* (1881), which first appeared as a serial in the *Girl's Own Paper*, is of interest because one of the main characters, Hesba Stapleton, a physician, is based on her friend the noted journalist and feminist Florence Fenwick *Miller, who practised medicine briefly in the 1870s (*Woman's Signal*, 13 May 1897).

Mrs Banks was a firm supporter of women's rights and women's suffrage, saying that as long as 'women have to pay for the maintenance of governments, local and national, I consider that they have as clear a right to vote for proper representation as have their masculine relations' (*Woman's Signal*, 13 May 1897).

Despite the popularity of Mrs Banks's writing, finances were a continual problem for her. She received numerous grants from the Royal Literary Fund, and attracted the special attention of fellow novelist Anthony Trollope, who suggested that her 'reward in literary life had fallen short of [her] deserts' ('Anthony Trollope at the Royal Literary Fund', *Nineteenth-Century Fiction*, December 1982, 322). She also received a pension from the civil list in 1895. Among her contemporary literary friends were Charles Dickens, Victor Hugo, Mary Howitt, Elizabeth Gaskell, Mrs Henry Wood, Eliza Cook, and John Strange Winter (Henrietta Stannard).

Mrs G. Linnaeus Banks died on 4 May 1897 of heart failure, following influenza and bronchitis, at her home, 34 Fassett Square, Dalston, London.

ROSEMARY T. VAN ARSDEL

Sources *Woman's Signal* (22 Oct 1896) • *Woman's Signal* (13 May 1897) • E. L. Burney, *Mrs. G. Linnaeus Banks* (1969) • *ILN* (15 May 1897) • Boase, *Mod. Eng. biog.* • *WWW*, *1897–1915* • *BL cat.* • 'Mrs. G. Linnaeus Banks', *Manchester Faces and Places*, 4 (1892–3), 40–43 • *Manchester Guardian* (6 May 1897) • Blain, Clements & Grundy, *Feminist comp.* • *CGPLA Eng. & Wales* (1897) • d. cert. • *DNB*

Archives BL, letters relating to grant applications to Royal Literary Fund, loan no. 96 • JRL, letters, notebooks, and papers | JRL, letters to William Andrews • JRL, letters to William E. A. Axon • Man. CL, Manchester Archives and Local Studies, letters to Charles Sutton

Likenesses photograph, repro. in *Woman's Signal* (22 Oct 1896) • portrait, repro. in *Manchester Faces and Places*

Wealth at death £270 4s.: probate, 9 Nov 1897, *CGPLA Eng. & Wales*

Banks, Sir John, baronet (*bap.* **1627**, *d.* **1699**), merchant and financier, was baptized at the parish church of All Saints, Maidstone, Kent, on 19 August 1627. He was the eldest in the family of two sons and one daughter of Caleb Banks of Maidstone and his wife, Martha Dann, of Faversham. His father was a prosperous woollen draper and former mayor of Maidstone. In 1644 John Banks was admitted to Emmanuel College, Cambridge. By 1652 he had become a member of a syndicate engaged in victualling the navy. In 1654, building upon his father's connections with the London business world, he married Elizabeth, daughter of John Dethick, a leading London merchant who became lord mayor in 1655 and was knighted by Oliver Cromwell in 1656. Banks then moved ahead rapidly in trade and finance, becoming a shareholder in the East India Company and a member of the Levant Company. Despite his earlier links with the parliamentary cause (he was MP for Maidstone in 1654–9) he pursued a moderate royalist line at the Restoration and in 1662 was made a baronet.

During the 1660s Banks's trading ventures were overshadowed by involvement in naval finance. He advanced money, in ever-growing sums, especially during the second and third Anglo-Dutch wars, and showed great skill in securing repayment, in discounting operations, and in profiting from the high rates of interest which the government had to pay for ready cash. When the stop of the exchequer was forced upon the government in 1672 he received favourable treatment in the resulting settlement.

Banks did not resume his role as a major lender until after 1689 but meanwhile he had blossomed into a Kentish landowner and re-entered parliament. He invested his business gains in building up an estate, purchasing as a country seat the former Carmelite priory of Aylesford. He became a director of the East India Company in 1669 and served as its governor in 1672–4 and again in 1683. He was also a director of the Royal African Company and its sub-governor in 1674–6. In the course of the 1670s he bought a town house on the grandest side of Lincoln's Inn Fields, as well as spending lavishly on extensive rebuilding at Aylesford. He was re-elected to parliament in 1679 for Rochester, and sat for that borough until 1690; thereafter, until 1694, he represented Queenborough and finally Maidstone again in 1695–8.

Of Banks's five children, Martha (1658–1675) and John (1668–1669) died young. His eldest surviving daughter, Elizabeth, was married in May 1678, complete with a portion of £10,000, to Heneage Finch, who became solicitor-general in 1679–86; he was the second son of Heneage Finch (later first earl of Nottingham), the lord chancellor. Despite this association with one of the central families of the emerging tory party Banks soon showed himself willing to extend his financial activities to the post-Revolution whig governments. Throughout the 1690s he advanced substantial sums through various channels. His money-lending activities also included loans to members of the Finch family and their political connections. In 1693 his second daughter, Mary, was married to John Savile, of Methley, a member of an important Yorkshire tory family. The substantial portion of £18,000 doubtless reflected *inter alia* the disparity of age: Mary Banks was thirty, John Savile twenty-two.

Banks's concern with naval matters led to a friendship with Samuel Pepys. Like Pepys, he had interests wider than finance and administration. In 1668 he was elected a fellow of the Royal Society, becoming thereby one of the very few businessmen in that body. He served on the society's council in the 1670s; and in 1677, after consulting various fellows of the society, Banks appointed John Locke to act as tutor to his surviving son, Caleb (1659–1696), during the latter's stay in France in 1677–8.

Shrewd, methodical, and determined, Banks combined business acumen with political trimming. Although filling such conventional offices as JP and deputy lieutenant for Kent, he generally preferred profits to power. His few surviving letters show that he brooked no nonsense from the unbusinesslike; his domestic relationships indicate a generous regard for his family; and his record of successful money-making, from Cromwell to William III, suggests that he learned well the lesson that adaptability is one of the crucial conditions of business survival.

By 1698 Banks's health was failing and he died on 19 October 1699. His meticulously kept accounts reveal a landed income of about £5000 per annum and total assets at death worth about £180,000, a sum which if translated roughly into modern values would put him into the multi-millionaire category. His wife and his son Caleb having both died in 1696, the baronetcy became extinct, and most of his wealth passed to Elizabeth and Heneage Finch who, in 1714, was created earl of Aylesford. The only remaining visible signs of Banks's life are a set of almshouses in Maidstone, built in accordance with his will, and a massive baroque tomb in Aylesford church.

D. C. Coleman, *rev.*

Sources D. C. Coleman, *Sir John Banks, baronet and businessman* (1963) · B. D. Henning, 'Banks, Sir John', HoP, *Commons, 1660–90*, 1.590–91 · Pepys, *Diary*, vols. 5–9 · M. Hunter, *The Royal Society and its fellows, 1660–1700: the morphology of an early scientific institution* (1982) · will, PRO, PROB 11/452, sig. 166

Archives CKS, business and estate papers · GL, ledger | Bodl. Oxf., corresp. with J. Locke

Wealth at death approx. £180,000: *DNB*

Banks, John (1652/3–1706), playwright, was born in obscurity. Before embarking upon a career as a playwright, he enrolled at the New Inn court of chancery where he was trained in the law. However, following the success of Nathaniel Lee's *The Rival Queens* at Drury Lane in March 1677, Banks turned his attention to the stage. His first tragedy, *The Rival Kings*, was performed at Drury Lane in June 1677 and published shortly afterwards. In November 1678 a second tragedy, *The Destruction of Troy*, was acted at Dorset Garden, with the text of the play published the following January.

After the failure of his third play, *Cyrus the Great, or, The Tragedy of Love* (written in 1681), which was rejected by the actors, the playwright revised his style. Abandoning the bombastic language of his early tragedies, Banks produced a series of dramas based upon episodes drawn from English history. In May 1681 the company at Drury Lane staged *The Unhappy Favourite, or, The Earl of Essex*, which appeared with a prologue and epilogue by John Dryden. A further historical tragedy, *Vertue Betray'd, or, Anna Bullen*, was staged at Dorset Garden in March 1682. In 1684 the playwright's third attempt at exploring Tudor history, *The Island Queens, or, The Death of Mary, Queen of Scotland*, was banned from the stage, presumably on account of its contentious portrayal of the rivalry between Elizabeth I and her Catholic cousin. Although Banks's sympathetic portrayal of Mary Stuart met with the approval of the Catholic duke of York, the ban on the play remained in force, obliging Richard Bentley to publish a quarto text of the tragedy 'in Defence of the Author and the Play' in 1684. This failure of *The Island Queens* to reach the stage appears to have impoverished the playwright, Robert Gould noting in 1685 that Banks was now 'in Tatters' as a result of his 'bad Poetry' (Gould, 2.241).

Following the death of Charles II Banks resumed his legal career, and on 21 February 1691 he married Elizabeth Thompson (*c*.1662–1702) at St Paul's, Covent Garden. However, his name continued to be connected with the theatre. In 1694 Bentley published Banks's *The Innocent Usurper, or, The Death of the Lady Jane Gray*, a dramatization of the Tudor succession crisis of 1553. Although Banks claimed to have written the play ten years earlier, an attempt by the United Company to stage the play in the 1692–3 season was thwarted by the lord chamberlain, who noticed in Banks's tragedy a series of reflections upon the accession of William and Mary in 1689. In December 1695 the playwright's *Cyrus the Great* was finally produced at Drury Lane. However, the tragedy enjoyed only four performances, its run being cut short by the death of the actor William Smith. Following the death of his wife in May 1702, Banks began work on an adaptation of his earlier play, *The Island Queens*, striving to offer the censor a more sympathetic portrait of Elizabeth I. The resulting tragedy, *The Albion Queens*, proved popular with the Drury Lane audience, running for seven nights in March 1704, although the text of the play remained unpublished until the end of Queen Anne's reign. Despite this success, Banks again appears to have fallen into debt. He died in April 1706, owing money to two principal creditors. On 9 April 1706 he was buried at St James's Church, Westminster.

Although Banks's early heroic plays were soon forgotten, his historical tragedies, with their protracted scenes of sadness and distress, proved influential. In *Vertue Betray'd* and *The Albion Queens*, Banks pioneered the 'she-tragedy', a dramatic form peculiar to the late Restoration. This genre of tragedy, which abandoned the concept of poetic justice in favour of a persistent emphasis upon the suffering of an innocent heroine, was later popularized by Nicholas Rowe. CHARLES BRAYNE

Sources J. Banks, *The unhappy favourite, or, The earl of Essex* (1735); repr. with introduction by T. M. H. Blair (1939) • W. Van Lennep and others, eds., *The London stage, 1660–1800*, pt 1: *1660–1700* (1965) • G. J. Armytage, ed., *Allegations for marriage licences issued by the vicar-general of the archbishop of Canterbury, July 1687 to June 1694*, Harleian Society, 31 (1890) • R. Gould, 'The playhouse, a satyr', in R. Gould, *Works* (1709), vol. 2 • C. Brayne, 'Gender politics and constitutional politics in post-revolution English tragedy', DPhil diss., U. Oxf., 1999 • G. Langbaine, *An account of the English dramatick poets* (1691) • *The parish of St James, Westminster*, 1/2, Survey of London, 30 (1960)

Wealth at death appears to have died in debt: Banks, *Unhappy favourite*, 6

Banks, John (1709–1751), poet and biographer, was born at Sonning, Berkshire. After the death about 1715 of his father, John, his education was entrusted to his uncle, who placed him at a local private school run by Mr Belpene. Banks proved to be a bright and able scholar but was shortly afterwards withdrawn from the school, allegedly because his schoolmaster was jealous of his ability. A more plausible explanation would be that the uncle was unwilling or unable to continue to pay for his nephew's education. Banks was placed as an apprentice to a weaver in Reading but before he could complete his apprenticeship he broke his arm, which prevented him from working. He was saved from destitution by a timely legacy of £10 from a distant relation. He moved to London and set up a bookstall in Spitalfields.

Banks, impressed by the success of Stephen Duck's poem *The Thresher* and the patronage Duck received from Queen Caroline, was inspired to emulate him. He published in imitation in 1730 *The Weaver's Miscellany*, but this failed to produce the required effect. Even Banks admitted that it was a work of little distinction. Soon afterwards he gave up his bookstall and became an assistant at the bookshop of Mr Montague. He now found time to write poetry and sent a poem to Alexander Pope, who was sufficiently impressed to agree to subscribe to Banks's forthcoming publication, which appeared in 1738 entitled *Miscellaneous Works in Verse and Prose*. This not only enhanced Banks's reputation as a poet but enabled him to become a writer by profession. His next work, *A Life of Christ*, also proved popular with the public. His most renowned work was *A Short Critical Review of the Political Life of Oliver Cromwell* (1739), which, unlike previous biographies of Cromwell, was sympathetic towards its subject. This led to accusations by staunch tories that Banks was a subverter of the truth and an enemy of the monarchy. Nevertheless the book was well received by the public and by 1769 had reached a fifth edition. Further biographical works followed: in 1740 he wrote a biography of Peter the Great and in 1744, amid increasing fears of an imminent French invasion and a landing by James Stuart, the Pretender, published *The History of the Life and Reign of William III*. This did much to restore his reputation as a true patriot and dispel any lingering doubts that he entertained Jacobite sympathies. In the late 1740s Banks wrote for, and may have edited, the opposition essay newspapers, the *Old England Journal* and the *Westminster Journal*.

Towards the spring of 1751 Banks's health, which for long had been delicate, visibly deteriorated. He was diagnosed as suffering from a nervous disorder which ultimately proved fatal. He died at his home in Islington on 19 April 1751. FRANCIS ESPINASSE, *rev.* M. J. MERCER

Sources R. Shiels, *The lives of the poets of Great Britain and Ireland*, ed. T. Cibber, 5 (1753), 310 • Allibone, *Dict.* • *GM*, 1st ser., 21 (1751), 187 • A. Chalmers, ed., *The general biographical dictionary*, new edn, 3 (1812), 422

Banks, John Sherbrooke (*bap.* 1811, *d.* 1857), army officer in the East India Company, baptized at Naas, co. Kildare, Ireland, on 7 October 1811, was the son of Samuel Banks, physician in HM forces, of Burton upon Trent, and his wife, Lucinda. In 1828 he was nominated to a cadetship in the Bengal army by the Rt Hon. Charles Wynn, then president of the Board of Control. Arriving in India and commissioned ensign, both in December 1829, he was posted to the 33rd Bengal native infantry, of which he became quartermaster and interpreter in 1833. He was subsequently employed on civil duties in the Saugor and Nerbudda territory. He was promoted lieutenant in October 1835, captain in January 1846, and major in 1857. In 1842 he served in Afghanistan with General Pollock's army of retribution in the march upon Kabul, and shortly afterwards was appointed to a post in the military secretariat. In this office he was brought into contact with the governor-general, the marquess of Dalhousie, whose confidence he speedily acquired. Owing to the absence of the head of the department on sick leave, it devolved upon Banks to make the arrangements for the expedition which resulted in the conquest of Pegu. Shortly after the war in 1853, he accompanied Dalhousie on a visit to British Burma, and subsequently became a member of the governor-general's personal staff as military secretary. In July 1855 he was sent to Lucknow, to communicate to Sir James Outram, the resident, the governor-general's intentions on the annexation of Oudh. Banks married at Ootacamund on 13 October 1855 Elizabeth Hutchinson, youngest daughter of Major-General Robert Bryce Fearon.

When Dalhousie left India in 1856 Banks joined the Oudh commission as commissioner of Lucknow, and became the trusted adviser and friend of the chief commissioner, Sir Henry Lawrence, by whom, on his deathbed, he was nominated to succeed as chief commissioner, but whom he survived only a few weeks. During the defence of the Lucknow residency, on 21 July 1857, Banks was shot through the head and killed. Banks was a man of judgement and tact, able and industrious in his duties, a brave soldier, and an excellent linguist. His widow received a special pension from the India Office for her husband's services.

A. J. ARBUTHNOT, *rev.* JAMES FALKNER

Sources *Indian Army List* • *The Times* (15 Oct 1857) • *LondG* (1857) • G. MacMunn, *The Indian mutiny in perspective* (1931) • V. C. P. Hodson, *List of officers of the Bengal army, 1758–1834*, 4 (1947)

Banks, Sir John Thomas (1816–1908), physician, was born on 14 October 1816 in London, the second son of Percival Banks (1764–1848), surgeon, of Ennis, co. Clare, Ireland, and his wife, Mary, daughter of Captain Thomas Ramsay. Percival Banks studied medicine at Rheims and Paris and he served in the navy and army before returning to Ennis where his father, also named Percival, was a doctor. Percival junior became surgeon to the county infirmary and physician to the fever hospital. John Banks was educated at Erasmus Smith's Grammar School in Ennis. He began his medical studies in the Royal College of Surgeons in Ireland as a pupil of Sir Henry Marsh, professor of the practice of medicine. He obtained the licence of the college in 1836. He also studied arts and medicine at Trinity College, Dublin, where he began his studies in 1833. Four years later he graduated BA and MB and in 1843 he proceeded MD. His older brother Percival Weldon Banks also studied at Trinity College before going on to become a barrister and writer. He was best-known for his contributions to *Fraser's Magazine* which were written under the pseudonym Morgan Rattler.

In 1840 Banks was appointed lecturer on materia medica at the Park Street school of medicine, Dublin. Two years later he was appointed lecturer on the practice of medicine at the Carmichael school of medicine and the following year he was appointed physician to the Richmond, Whitworth, and Hardwicke hospitals, where he was a colleague of Sir Dominic Corrigan and Robert Adams. He held this last position until his death. He was an excellent teacher and he was greatly admired as an accomplished physician. He became a fellow of the King and Queen's College of Physicians in Ireland in 1844. Banks was appointed king's professor of the practice of medicine in the school of physic at Trinity College in 1849 and this post was linked to an appointment as physician to Sir Patrick Dun's Hospital. He resigned these appointments in 1868 but he was subsequently appointed consulting physician to the hospital. In 1851 he became assistant physician and in 1854 physician to the Richmond Lunatic Asylum. In his later years he was also consulting physician to the Royal City of Dublin Hospital. In 1880 he was elected regius professor of medicine at Trinity College, Dublin, and he held the post for eighteen years. Banks was president of the King and Queen's College of Physicians in Ireland between 1869 and 1871 and he was president of the Dublin Pathological Society in 1861. When the Royal Academy of Medicine in Ireland was founded in 1882 he was unanimously chosen to be its first president. He was president of the British Medical Association when it met in Dublin in 1887.

Banks had a major interest in medical education and he represented at first the Queen's University and then the Royal University (as it became) on the General Medical Council from 1880 to 1898. He pleaded for a high standard of education before entry to medical school and he stressed the importance of psychological and psychiatric studies for medical students. At that time psychiatric disorders, although commonly encountered in general practice, were largely excluded from undergraduate medical studies and Banks played a role in bringing about the inclusion of mental illness as a subject in the medical curriculum. He also urged the lengthening of the medical curriculum from four to five years. Banks was a handsome and dignified man whose ethical behaviour and professional conduct were always above reproach. These attributes made him the natural leader of his profession and a dominant figure in the social life of Dublin for many years. He was a noted conversationalist and he was admired for his princely hospitality. His busy social life was almost certainly an explanation for his comparatively modest research output. He was not a prolific writer on medical subjects. One of his more interesting contributions was his note on the writ 'De lunatico inquirendo' in relation to the mental stability of the ageing Jonathan Swift which was published in the *Dublin Journal of Medical Science* in 1868.

Banks married Alice (*d.* 1899), daughter of Captain Wood Wright of Golagh, co. Monaghan, in 1848. They had one daughter, Mary. In 1891 he served as high sheriff in Monaghan. He received an honorary LLD from the University of Glasgow and a DSc from the Royal University. He was physician-in-ordinary in Ireland to Queen Victoria and to Edward VII and in 1889 he was made KCB in recognition of his distinguished services to medicine. In 1906 he endowed a postgraduate scholarship in medicine at Trinity College, Dublin, which is still awarded by the university. A John Banks medal in bronze is also given to the successful candidate. Banks died on 16 July 1908 at his home, 45 Merrion Square, Dublin, and he was buried at Mount Jerome cemetery after a service in the chapel of Trinity College, Dublin. DAVIS COAKLEY

Sources *Medical Press* (29 July 1908) · *BMJ* (25 July 1908) · *Irish Times* (17 July 1908) · C. A. Cameron, *History of the Royal College of Surgeons in Ireland* (1886) · *DNB* · E. O'Brien, A. Crookshank, and G. Wolstenholme, *A portrait of Irish medicine* (1984) · T. P. C. Kirkpatrick, *History of the medical teaching in Trinity College, Dublin, and of the School of Physic in Ireland* (1912) · 'Percival Banks', *Dublin Quarterly Journal of Medical Science*, 5 (1848), 569–70

Likenesses S. Purser, oils, 1881, Royal College of Physicians, Dublin · O. Sheppard, portrait, bronze low-relief, 1906, TCD · Chancellor, photograph, repro. in *BMJ* · O. Sheppard, bronze medallion, NG Ire.

Wealth at death £18,300 18*s*. 1*d*.: Irish probate sealed in England, 6 Oct 1908, *CGPLA Eng. & Wales*

Banks, Sir Joseph, baronet (1743–1820), naturalist and patron of science, was born on 13 February 1743 at 30 Argyll Street, London, the first child and only son of William Banks (1719–1761), gentleman, of Revesby Abbey, Lincolnshire, previously named William Banks Hodgkinson, of Overton, Derbyshire, as heir to his maternal grandfather, William *Hodgkinson (1661/2–1731), merchant and landowner. Joseph's, mother was Sarah (1709–1804), eldest daughter of William Bate and his wife, Arabella.

Sir Joseph Banks, baronet (1743–1820), by Sir Joshua Reynolds, 1771–3

Education Banks was educated in a manner appropriate to his status as the heir to a landed fortune, being sent first to Harrow School (1752–6) and then to Eton College (1756–60). At Eton he was a fairly indifferent student as regards the traditional classical curriculum but, largely thanks to his own efforts, he there began his lifelong preoccupation with botany. His mother may also have played a part in his developing botanical interests: he was encouraged by a copy of Gerard's *Herbal* which he found in her dressing-room. At Oxford, where he matriculated at Christ Church as a gentleman commoner in 1760, he largely devoted himself to natural history rather than the predominantly classical course of studies. Such was his determination to receive botanical instruction that, at his own expense, he brought the Cambridge botanist Israel Lyons to give a set of lectures at Oxford in 1764, thereby filling the vacuum created by the reluctance of Oxford's professor of botany, Dr Sibthorp, to teach. Though there was little in the formal curriculum at Oxford which bore on his natural history interests, his time as an undergraduate helped to consolidate his love of the study of nature. He found other students who shared his enthusiasm and participated in informal societies devoted to such pursuits as botanizing and the study of geology.

After his father died in 1761, leaving him the Revesby estate in Lincolnshire, Banks had the financial means to follow any calling he chose and so devoted himself to the pursuit of natural history. Increasingly he divided his time between Oxford and London, where his mother's new house at 22 Paradise Row, Chelsea, gave him ready access to the Chelsea Physic Garden of the Society of Apothecaries, then the most important centre of botanical activity in the country. 1764, the year in which he came of age, was the last year he spent any length of time at Oxford which, like many of his social class, he left without taking a degree. Thereafter he immersed himself in the cultural world of the London élite, becoming both a fellow of the Royal Society and a fellow of the Society of Antiquaries in 1766 (he had previously become a member of the Society for the Encouragement of Arts, Manufactures, and Commerce in 1761). He also spent a great deal of time at the British Museum and there he came to know his close collaborator, Daniel Solander, who held the post of assistant librarian from 1765 until his death in 1788. Solander had trained under the great Linnaeus and, after coming to Britain in 1760, helped to disseminate his classificatory system. Through his friendship with Solander, which was cemented by their time together on the *Endeavour*, Banks was, then, indirectly a disciple of Linnaeus, with whom he exchanged cordial correspondence.

Expeditions Banks served his apprenticeship as a scientifically trained Linnaean naturalist—as opposed to an undiscriminating virtuoso gentleman collector—by accompanying his old Etonian friend, the naval officer and future MP and lord of the Admiralty, Constantine Phipps, on an expedition in 1766 to Labrador and Newfoundland. Though Banks was the sole naturalist on board, Solander assisted him in his choice of equipment and reference works, and later helped put his specimens from this voyage (now in the Natural History Museum, London) in order. Banks's journal (ed. A. M. Lysaght, 1971) indicates the close attention he paid to the full Linnaean domain of natural history which embraced not only the flora, fauna and minerals of an area but also its human population.

This expedition served as a virtual rehearsal for the great *Endeavour* voyage of 1768 to 1771 which lifted Banks from the ranks of gentlemen naturalists to become a figure of international scientific significance. He owed his position as a self-funded member of the *Endeavour* expedition to Lord Sandwich, first lord of the Admiralty and his close friend. Both were enthusiastic London clubmen as well as being fellow devotees of a free-living *demi-monde*. Thus, for example, David Hume reported the two fishing near Newbury in the company of 'two or three ladies of pleasure' (Carter, *Sir Joseph Banks*, 1988, 152).

The *Endeavour* expedition made it possible for Banks to explore a whole portion of the globe hitherto largely unexposed to European gaze. In doing so, he was ably assisted by the scientific party he had brought with him at his own expense. Along with Solander, there was another Swede, Herman Spöring, who served as secretary, together with two draughtsmen, Alexander Buchan, who specialized in landscapes, and Sydney Parkinson, who concentrated on natural history specimens. The chief goal of the voyage was to observe the transit of Venus at Tahiti where the *Endeavour* anchored on 13 April 1769; it remained there for three months, during which time Buchan died.

This lengthy stay gave Banks ample opportunity to study the flora and fauna of the island as well as to observe the character of its human society. He learned Tahitian and was fascinated by points of contrast with English society, being ready on occasions to admit the superiority of some aspects of Tahitian society, and that Europeans could benefit from a knowledge of some of the islanders' practical skills. He participated enthusiastically in local customs, even to the point of undergoing the painful operation of being tattooed. Like many of his shipmates, too, he formed liaisons with the Tahitian women and, in Enlightenment fashion, he later discoursed on the way in which Tahitian society was less oppressed by sexual taboos than was Europe. When the Tahitian Omai was brought to England in 1774, Banks became his patron, introducing him to the court and to élite society more generally.

Following his sealed Admiralty orders, Cook, captain of the *Endeavour*, next turned south to explore the largely unknown territories which earlier Dutch explorers had termed New Zealand and New Holland. Though six months were spent in circumnavigating and charting New Zealand, Banks had only limited opportunities to investigate its natural history since there were few landfalls. This was partly because of the warlike nature of the Maori people, whose cannibalism Banks regarded as undermining the proper position of man in the great chain of being. Australia offered more possibilities for natural history—as Cook's choice of the name Botany Bay for the area near the future city of Sydney indicates. However, Banks was disappointed not to have made more contact with the native peoples, and used the few opportunities that presented themselves (such as the enforced sojourn for repairs following the *Endeavour*'s encounter with the Great Barrier Reef in June 1770) to compile some record of their customs and languages. His lack of any conception of racial superiority is evident in his remarks about the Australian Aborigines in his *Endeavour* journal.

Because of the need for a thorough overhaul following the *Endeavour*'s near fatal grounding on the Great Barrier Reef, Cook called at Batavia on 9 October 1770. There his proud record of keeping his men safe from disease (and especially scurvy, the traditional scourge of long ocean voyages) was broken when thirty men died as a result of the Java fevers—among them Banks's associates, Parkinson and Spöring. Banks and Solander survived their own illness largely by leaving Batavia for the Javanese countryside. After a stay of over three months the depleted ship left Batavia and made its way back to Britain, landing at Deal on 12 June 1771.

Back in England, Banks received a rapturous welcome which overshadowed that of Cook himself. He was introduced to George III, beginning a long association which saw him become a close friend and the king's adviser on matters related to science or agriculture. The success of Cook's first great Pacific voyage prompted the organization of another in 1772, which Banks enthusiastically supported. This time he planned to take a much larger entourage including, it would seem, a valet who appears to have been a mistress in disguise. But the adulation that he had received on his return from the *Endeavour* expedition had blinded him to the limitations of his influence with the navy and his attempts to reorganize the expedition to accommodate this large party led to his former patron, Lord Sandwich, turning against him. Thus thwarted, Banks withdrew from the *Resolution* voyage in high dudgeon and employed the scientific party he had formed on a shorter voyage in 1772 to explore the geology and natural history of Iceland. This was the beginning of a lifelong association with that island and its people which led to his intervening on their behalf with the British government in 1810 to lessen the effects of the naval blockade of the island—a blockade which was really directed at Denmark, Iceland's ruler, which was then an ally of Napoleon.

President of the Royal Society, 1778–1820 The voyage to Iceland marked the end of Banks's overseas travel (apart from a short trip to the Netherlands in 1773). More and more he devoted his always considerable energies to furthering the cause of science. In 1773 his close association with the king led to his appointment as the virtual director of the Royal Botanic Gardens at Kew, an institution he transformed from a royal pleasure garden to a major scientific centre devoted to fostering botanical exchange around the globe—especially if such an exchange benefited England's larger imperial purposes. In the following year he served for the first time on the council of the Royal Society, thus beginning his steady rise within that body which culminated in his election as president in 1778.

Another indication of Banks's increasingly single-minded sense of purpose was his move in 1777 from bachelor quarters at New Burlington Street to a much larger establishment at 32 Soho Square which became a virtual research institute. He employed a series of naturalists (Solander, Dryander, and Robert Brown) to keep his ever-increasing collections in order. The transition from the youthful man about town to the gentleman assuming his social responsibilities was also marked by his marriage in 1779 to Dorothea Hugessen (1758–1828), a well-acred heiress. Marriage meant parting from his long-established mistress, Sarah Wells, but the leave-taking appears to have been a civilized one with, no doubt, a suitable financial arrangement. An earlier association with Harriet Blosset dated from just before he left on the *Endeavour* but though, according to the naturalist Daines Barrington, Banks admitted he gave Blosset 'the strongest reason to expect he would return her husband' (Barrington to Pennant, 24 Aug 1771, NL NZ, Turnbull L.), he broke off the connection on his return, paying some £5000 in compensation.

Banks's election as president of the Royal Society, followed by his marriage, marked the end of his life as a free-living youthful adventurer and his elevation to the position of a statesman of science. However, he took some time to establish his authority, despite the king's bestowal of a baronetcy in 1781, since he was seen by some in the society, and especially those who regarded themselves as custodians of the mathematical Newtonian tradition, as a gentleman virtuoso without respectable scientific credentials except in the less prestigious area of natural history. This, together with his cavalier manner in dealing with some of the office-bearers, especially his ousting of Charles Hutton as the society's foreign secretary, helps account for the disputes within the organization over his presidency in 1783–4. He survived these assaults, which were led chiefly by Bishop Samuel Horsley, editor of Newton's works, and thereafter he established an unprecedented sway within the society as its longest serving president, continually re-elected until his death.

During his long tenure Banks greatly strengthened the links between the Royal Society and the political establishment, helping to make science part of the natural concerns of the British state. The price for this was a reluctance on his part to elect low-born fellows or those suspected of political radicalism. Election depended very much on Banks's favour. However his continual re-election as president is an indication that the generally independent-minded fellows did not regard his firm hold on affairs as oppressive. Throughout his presidency he remained fiercely protective of the society: thus he opposed the foundation of the Geological Society in 1809 and the Astronomical Society in 1820, since he regarded the foundation of such new bodies as a challenge to its traditional dominance of the scientific estate.

His position was the hub around which Banks's ever-mounting scientific and political responsibilities revolved. As president of the Royal Society he was an *ex officio* member of the governing boards of the few institutions established by the British government to deal specifically with scientific affairs: the Royal Observatory, the board of longitude, and (from 1793) the board of agriculture. Moreover he considerably broadened the scope of his activities in order to link the possibilities of science more closely with the apparatus of the British state. The main bureaucratic agency through which he worked was the privy council committee on trade. There he had a firm ally in Charles Jenkinson (from 1786 to 1796 known as Lord Hawkesbury and then as the first earl of Liverpool) who was appointed the committee's first president in 1786. Like Banks, Jenkinson was something of a neo-mercantilist committed to ensuring as great as possible economic and strategic independence for Britain, and so greatly valued Banks's advice on the ways in which it might be possible to transfer economically valuable crops such as cotton and tea to areas of the globe under the British flag. Banks's work with the committee on trade and on coin ultimately led, in 1797, to his elevation to privy councillor.

Together with the privy council committee on trade, Banks provided scientific advice through a number of other bureaucratic channels including the Board of Control (for India), the Home Office, and the Admiralty. At the last he benefited from his association with that scientifically minded administrator, Sir Evan Nepean, with whom he closely worked when organizing expeditions such as the ill-fated *Bounty* expedition of 1787–9 and Flinders's circumnavigation of Australia on the *Investigator* expedition of 1801–3—expeditions which merged scientific purposes with Britain's larger imperial designs. The *Bounty* venture was well in accord with Banks's mercantilist goal of increasing Britain's economic self-sufficiency through the application of science to imperial policy, for its object was to transfer breadfruit from Tahiti to provide a cheap source of food for the slaves in the British West Indies. Banks's close supervision of the expedition extended to the appointment of his client, William Bligh, as captain both of the eventful *Bounty* expedition and of its successor, the *Providence*, which successfully brought the breadfruit to the West Indies in 1793. The focus for such ventures in imperial botany was the Royal Botanic Gardens at Kew, which, thanks to Banks's efforts, became the centre of a worldwide network of colonial botanical gardens often staffed by Kew-trained collectors.

Alongside his position as what his close friend, William Eden, Lord Auckland, facetiously described as HM minister of philosophic affairs, that is, a virtual minister for science, Banks also acted as an adviser to government on other imperial issues. In 1779 he strongly urged the House of Commons to consider establishing a penal settlement at Botany Bay using his own firsthand knowledge to argue that it could support a convict population. Thereafter he remained closely involved with Australian affairs, advising the British government on suitable appointments as governors and doing what he could to represent the infant colony's interest at a time when British politicians were preoccupied with the French wars.

Along with his promotion of Australian interests Banks was actively involved in promoting greater British involvement in the exploration of Africa. He was one of the founders of the African Society, which was established in 1788 with the goal of sponsoring expeditions to Africa and, in particular, charting the course of the Niger. The most celebrated of these were those led by the Scot Mungo Park (in 1795–9 and 1805–6), the German Friedrich Hornemann (1797–1801), and the Swiss Johann Burckhardt (1809–17). The last two owed their appointments to Banks's connections with the University of Göttingen which, as part of Hanover, was linked with the British crown.

Banks's associations with Göttingen are a reminder that, along with his determination to use science, wherever possible, to promote the interests of the British empire, he also retained an allegiance to a larger and cosmopolitan republic of letters. His attempt to keep open the channels of scientific communication with France led him to use his influence to recover for the French Republic a large natural history collection captured by the British navy in the course of the war with revolutionary France in 1795. This had been assembled by La Billardière, the botanist on the D'Entrecasteaux expedition sent in search of the lost expedition led by La Pérouse. It was partly in recognition of this service that Banks was chosen as a member of the National Institute of France in 1802 and his enthusiastic public letter acknowledging this honour and describing the French Institute as 'the first Literary Society in the World' led to accusations that he was unpatriotic and had slighted his own Royal Society and with it the king.

Last years With the descent into madness of his chief patron, George III, and the political eclipse of his close ally the earl of Liverpool, who resigned his last public office in 1802, Banks's role in public affairs declined in his last two decades. He did, however, continue to give advice on behalf of the Royal Society for such scientific expeditions as the 1818 Arctic expedition commanded by John Ross. Such activities, together with his own example in combining naval and scientific purposes, helped to forge the tradition of scientific exploration which, in the nineteenth century, produced such notable voyages as those undertaken by the *Beagle*, *Rattlesnake*, and *Commander*. Banks was also able to increase the sway of the Royal Society through securing, in 1818, a bill for changing the composition of the board of longitude to include more representation from the Royal Society.

In 1818 Banks was involved in a carriage accident which led to the death of his beloved sister, Sarah *Banks, who had lived with him most of his life and shared his love of collecting. Both, in their different ways, were examples of that cultural type, the virtuoso, who amassed large collections of the rare and the curious. But while Sarah built up a huge and miscellaneous collection of everything from coins to visiting cards, Banks brought to his collecting activities greater system and purpose, using the Linnaean and, subsequently, other systems of classification (notably that of Antoine de Jussieu) to give his private museum—which after his death became the core of the British Museum's natural history division (now the Natural History Museum, London)—a scientific purpose. His house-cum-research institute at Soho Square was open to serious naturalists of all nationalities and it also provided the setting for his celebrated scientific soirées which helped bring together major figures from the worlds of science and politics. The rather brash but eager young man who withdrew in pique from the second Cook voyage gave way to a more courteous but, none the less, determined advocate of science—a transformation captured in the contrast between his two best-known portraits, that by Joshua Reynolds painted in 1771–2 soon after his return from the *Endeavour* expedition (now in the National Portrait Gallery) and that painted by Thomas Phillips in 1815 as his official portrait as president of the Royal Society (still in the Royal Society). He was more at home in male than female company, and was, the painter, Joseph Farington, noted, 'rather coarse and heavy' (*Farington Diary*, ed. Greig, 1.136). Lord Glenbervie described him more fully as 'awkward in his person, but extremely well-bred, in the best mode of English breeding … one of the many instances to prove that the personal graces are far from essential to politeness' (*Diaries of Sylvester Douglas (Lord Glenbervie)*, ed. F. Bickley, 1928, 2.206).

Along with his position at the centre of scientific and political affairs in London, Banks also maintained close ties with his family seat at Revesby Abbey in Lincolnshire. Thence he returned every summer to supervise the improvement of his estates and to renew his ties with his fellow squires. In county politics he worked, where possible, to prevent political division but his fundamental conservatism is apparent in his hostility to any would-be Lincolnshire politician connected with the cause of reform. He also took the view that it was incumbent on him, as president of the Royal Society and as a loyal servant of the king, to be seen to be above the noisy din of party politics. Thus he would accept the honour of being made a knight in the Order of the Bath in 1795 only when it was apparent that it was a direct gift from the king rather than a recognition for service to any party. None the less, he would intervene—as unobtrusively as possible—in the political process when he felt the welfare of what he termed the country interest was at stake. Thus he played an important but discreet role in organizing the opposition to the Wool Bill of 1788 which favoured manufacturers at the expense of growers, and he was a spirited defender of the need for a system of corn laws. Indeed, his sympathies on the latter issue were widely enough known for his London house to be attacked during the corn laws riots of 1815.

Though a determined defender of the constitutional order in church and state—particularly when it came under threat in the age of the French revolution—Banks's own religious views hovered between an enlightened Christianity and deism. As an improving landlord he was hostile to the system of clerical tithes, and to clerical privilege more generally. Theological discussion he regarded as largely fruitless and he had an aversion to ritual forms of religion. Though prepared to encourage missionary activity to promote larger imperial designs he was doubtful of its worth: in his words he was 'little inclined to Conversions. The will of God will, no doubt, put + keep all mankind on the right way; + his mercy will most assuredly despise all Ceremonial and all mistaken Faith' (Gascoigne, *Joseph Banks*, 42). He was animated by a strong sense of public duty, which complemented his strictly hierarchical view of society. Hence the choice of the lizard for his seal, 'an animal said to be Endowed by nature with an instinctive love of mankind'. He hoped the choice would serve

> as a Perpetual Remembrance that man is never so well employd, as when he is Laboring for the advantage of the Public; without the Expectation, the hope or Even a wish to Derive advantage of any kind, from the Result of his Exertions. (ibid., 18)

Banks remained active to the end of his life despite increasingly severe gout. He died on Monday 19 June 1820 and was buried (at his own request) without any monument at the parish church of Heston near his Middlesex country house, Spring Grove in the village of Spring Grove, the site of a number of his botanical and horticultural experiments. When he died he had achieved a European-wide reputation as one who had fruitfully brought together the worlds of government and science. As the great French naturalist, Georges Cuvier, generously acknowledged in his *éloge* before the French Académie des Sciences, Banks's publications were few but his role as a statesman of science meant that 'his name will shine with lustre in the history of the sciences' (Cuvier, 3.49). However, Banks's fame soon faded since he was regarded as the embodiment of a scientific old regime which was being transformed by the reforms of the nineteenth century. Moreover, accident and the sheer mass and eventual scattering of his papers prevented the appearance of the massive biography which was his due. Not until the late twentieth century has his importance again been properly acknowledged as his papers have been reassembled by H. B. Carter and the historiography of science has become more sympathetic to the patrons as well as the practitioners of science. JOHN GASCOIGNE

Sources H. B. Carter, *Sir Joseph Banks, 1743–1820* (1988) • J. Gascoigne, *Joseph Banks and the English Enlightenment* (1994) • H. B. Carter, *Sir Joseph Banks (1743–1820): a guide to biographical and bibliographical sources*, St Paul's Bibliographies (1987) • J. Gascoigne, 'The scientist as patron and patriotic symbol: the changing reputation of Sir Joseph Banks', *Studies in scientific biography*, ed. M. Shortland and R. Yeo (1996), 243–65 • P. O'Brian, *Joseph Banks: a life* (1987) • *The Endeavour journal of Joseph Banks, 1768–1771*, ed. J. C. Beaglehole, 2 vols. (1962) • *The Farington diary*, ed. J. Greig, 8 vols. (1922–8) • G. Cuvier, 'Éloge historique de Sir Joseph Banks, lu le 2 Avril 1821', *Recueil des éloges historiques: lus dans les séances de l'Institut Royal de France*, 3 (1827), 49–92 • *Joseph Banks in Newfoundland and Labrador, 1766: his diary, manuscripts and collections*, ed. A. M. Lysaght (1971) • R. A. Rauschenberg, 'The journals of Joseph Banks's voyage up Great Britain's west coast to Iceland and to the Orkney isles, July to October, 1772', *Proceedings of the American Philosophical Society*, 117 (1973), 186–226 • *Sir Joseph Banks: a global perspective* [London 1993], ed. R. E. R. Banks and others (1994) • D. Mackay, *In the wake of Cook: exploration, science and empire, 1780–1801* (1985) • H. C. Cameron, *Sir Joseph Banks, KB, PRS: the autocrat of the philosophers* (1952) • H. B. Carter, *His majesty's Spanish flock: Sir Joseph Banks and the merinos of George III of England* (1964) • H. B. Carter, *The sheep and wool correspondence of Sir Joseph Banks, 1781–1820* (1979) • *The Banks letters*, ed. W. R. Dawson (1958) • J. Gascoigne, *Science in the service of empire: Joseph Banks, the British state and the uses of science in the age of revolution* (1998) • P. Fona, 'Presidential portraits: Joseph Banks in the National Library', *National Library of Australia News*, 9/3 (1998), 7–10 • will, PRO, PROB 11/1634, sig. 510

Archives American Philosophical Society Library, Philadelphia, corresp. • Auckland Public Library, notes on Cook's voyages • BL, corresp. and papers, Add. MSS 8094–8100, 8967–8968, 33977–33982, 43837, 52281 • BL, corresp. and papers relating to Lincolnshire estates, Add. MS 43837 • BL, corresp., notebook, and papers, Add. MSS 56297–56302 • California State Library, San Francisco, corresp. and papers • CKS, corresp., diaries, and papers • CUL, journals • Derby Local Studies, journal • FM Cam., corresp., minutes, and memoranda relating to the British Museum • ICL, corresp. relating to Derby's lead mining • Lincs. Arch., corresp., estate corresp., and papers; family and estate corresp. and papers; agricultural and estate papers; corresp. and papers relating to Lincolnshire militia • McGill University, Montreal, Blacker-Wood Library of Biology, journal and papers • Mitchell L., NSW, corresp. and papers • NHM, corresp., journal extracts, and papers • NL Aus., corresp. • NL NZ, Turnbull L., papers • NMM, journal of dockyard visitations • RBG Kew, corresp. and papers • Royal Geographical Society of Australia, Adelaide, journal, notes on Iceland [on deposit in State Library of South Australia] • RS, corresp. and papers • RSA, corresp. • RSA, corresp. • SOAS, papers relating to Pacific languages • State Library of New South Wales, Sydney, Dixson Wing, journal and papers • U. Reading L., corresp. and papers • University of Wisconsin, Madison, corresp. relating to Iceland • Wellcome L., corresp., journal, and papers • Yale U., Sterling Memorial Library, corresp. and papers • Yale U., Beinecke L., corresp. and papers | Birm. CA, corresp. with Matthew Boulton and M. R. Boulton • BL, letters to George Chalmers, etc., Add. MSS 22549, 22900–22901, 23669, 24727, 27937, 28545, 42072, 62114; Egerton MSS 2137, 2180 • BL, corresp. with R. F. Greville, Add. MS 42072 • BL, corresp. with William Hamilton, Add. MSS 34048; Egerton MS 2641 • BL, letter to Nikolaus Joseph Jacquin, Add. MS 62114 • BL, letters to earls of Liverpool, loan 72 • Bucks. RLSS, letters to duke and duchess of Somerset • Derbys. RO, letters to William Philip Perrin • Herefs. RO, corresp. with T. A. Knight • Hollandsche Maatschapij der Wetenschappen, letters to Martin Van Marum • Lincs. Arch., letters to Lord Brownlow • Lincs. Arch., letters to Sir Henry Hawley • Linn. Soc., corresp. with Sir James Smith • NA Scot., letters to Hope family • NL Scot., corresp. mainly with Sir John Leslie • NL Wales, letters to John Lloyd • NMM, letters to Matthew Flinders and his wife • PRO, Pitt MSS, letters to William Pitt, PRO 30/8 • RAS, corresp. with Sir William Herschel • Rothamsted Experimental Station Library, Harpenden, corresp. with Sir John Sinclair, Lord Liverpool, etc. • Selkirk Library, corresp. with Mungo Park

Likenesses J. Reynolds, oils, 1771–3, NPG [*see illus.*] • B. West, oils, *c.*1772, repro. in Carter, *Sir Joseph Banks*, frontispiece; priv. coll. • J. R. Smith, mezzotint, pubd 1773 (after B. West), BM • W. Parry, group portrait, oils, 1776 (with Omani and Dr Daniel Solander), Parham Park, West Sussex • J. Reynolds, group portrait, oils, 1777–9 (*The Society of Dilettanti*), Society of Dilettanti, Brooks's Club, London • A. S. Damer, bust, 1795, BM • J. Gillray, caricature, etching, pubd 1795, NPG • T. Lawrence, oils, 1806, NPG • T. Lawrence, oils, exh. RA 1806, BM • T. Phillips, oils, 1810, NPG • P. Turnerelli, marble bust, *c.*1814, RCP Lond. • T. Phillips, oils, 1815, RS • W. Wyon junior, bronze medal, 1816, Royal Mint, Tower Hill, London • F. Chantrey, bust, 1818, National Gallery, Melbourne, Australia • F. L. Chantrey, bust, 1818, RS • T. Phillips, oils, 1820, Royal Horticultural Society, London • F. Chantrey, bust, 1822, Linn. Soc. • F. Chantrey, marble statue, 1826, BM • attrib. J. Flaxman, medallions, Wedgwood Museum, Barlaston, Staffordshire • T. Hearne, pencil drawing, BM • T. Lawrence, pencil drawing, NPG • T. Philips, oils, Guildhall,

Boston, Lincolnshire • J. Sharples, pastel drawing, Bristol City Art Gallery • oils, repro. in Lysaght, ed., *Joseph Banks*; priv. coll.
Wealth at death under £40,000: PRO, IR 26/813, fols. 145v–147r

Banks, Leslie James (1890–1952), actor, was born on 9 June 1890 in West Derby, Liverpool, Lancashire, son of George Banks, general merchant, and his wife, Emily Dalby. He won a classical scholarship at Trinity College, Glenalmond, and then went on to Keble College, Oxford, again as a classical scholar. He made his first professional appearance on the stage in 1911 at the town hall, Brechin, as Old Gobbo in *The Merchant of Venice* with the company of Frank Benson. He remained with Benson until the following year, when he went on tour with George Dance's company in *The Hope* by Cecil Raleigh and Henry Hamilton, a racing melodrama from Drury Lane. He then joined H. V. Esmond and Eva Moore in a tour of the United States and Canada, making his first New York appearance in a small part in Esmond's comedy *Eliza Comes to Stay*. Returning to London he made his West End début at the Vaudeville in May 1914, in Esmond's *The Dangerous Age*.

The First World War cut short Banks's career just as it was beginning to show promise. He served in the Essex regiment, receiving a disfiguring wound in the face that might have driven a weaker character to seek some less public profession. Banks never allowed it to deter him and when he started acting again after the war he found that it did not handicap him. In 1915 Banks married Gwendoline Haldane, daughter of Edwin Thomas Unwin; they had three daughters. A month after the armistice he made a fresh start under Nigel Playfair at the Lyric, Hammersmith; from there he went to the Birmingham repertory theatre under Barry Jackson, and in 1919–20 he played leads in the repertory company of Lena Ashwell. A Shaw season at the Everyman, Hampstead, followed early in 1921, and in May of the same year he had his first important part in a successful West End play, as Archie Beal in *If* by Lord Dunsany at the Ambassadors.

In little more than two years Banks had established himself in the good opinion of most of the managements in London at a time when the disillusion consequent on the war had forced down the standard of public taste to a depressingly low level. Because he was so much in demand he was free to pick the plays in which he wanted to act, and to study the long list of parts he played is to realize what care he took to avoid claptrap or rubbish. To see Leslie Banks's name on a playbill or in a theatre programme was to be given a virtual guarantee that the play had merit. He was an actor of very wide range and as his services were constantly in demand in films as well as on the stage he was able to avoid being stereotyped. No better evidence of this need be asked for than the fact that in a season of repertory with John Gielgud's company at the Haymarket, from October 1944 to June 1945, he played Lord Porteous in W. Somerset Maugham's *The Circle*, Tattle in Congreve's *Love for Love*, Claudius in *Hamlet*, Bottom in *A Midsummer Night's Dream*, and Antonio Bologna in Webster's *The Duchess of Malfi*; he also played such disparate leading roles as those in *Goodbye Mr Chips* (1938) and *Life with Father* (1947). Among the many films in which he appeared were the Hitchcock productions *The Man Who Knew Too Much* (1934) and *Jamaica Inn* (1939). Banks belonged to that stalwart type of actor which, ranking as leading man rather than popular star, is able for that very reason to reach a pitch of distinction in his career that many stars miss.

One of the most variously talented and deeply respected figures on the British stage of his time, no man in private life ever looked or behaved less like the popular conception of an actor. Banks showed no trace of that exhibitionism, that desire to be noticed, which is the motivating force with many actors of every degree of distinction. 'He remained through all his success', said A. A. Milne, 'the man next door, a good neighbour and a good friend'. Yet the serene integrity of his nature did not interfere with his versatility as an artist. He was able to understand and play with sympathy a character with whom it seemed he could have nothing at all in common: as Gerald Coates in *Grand National Night* at the Apollo in 1946 the character's besetting fault, which brought him to ruin, was a streak of wild recklessness—it was unthinkable that Leslie Banks in his own person could ever yield to such weakness. He was also a successful producer, among his productions being Galsworthy's *The Eldest Son* (Everyman, 1928) and Norman MacOwan's *The Infinite Shoeblack* (1929). Banks was appointed CBE in 1950 and he died at his home, 27 South Terrace, Kensington, London, on 21 April 1952.

W. A. Darlington, *rev.* K. D. Reynolds

Sources J. Parker, ed., *Who's who in the theatre*, 6th edn (1930) • *The Times* (23 April 1952) • personal knowledge (1971) • private information (1971) • *WWW* • *CGPLA Eng. & Wales* (1952)
Likenesses W. R. Sickert, oils, 1937, Bradford City Art Gallery
Wealth at death £19,094 14s. 4d.: probate, 21 Aug 1952, *CGPLA Eng. & Wales*

Banks, Sir (William) Mitchell (1842–1904), surgeon, was born in Edinburgh on 1 November 1842, the son of Peter Spalding Banks, solicitor, and his wife, Ann Williamson. He received his early education at the Edinburgh Academy and then entered Edinburgh University, where in 1864 he graduated MD with honours and won the gold medal for his thesis on the Wolffian bodies. At the university he acted as prosector to Professor John Goodsir and at the local infirmary he acted as dresser and as house surgeon to James Syme. After graduating he was demonstrator of anatomy for a short time to Professor Allen Thomson, at the University of Glasgow. Afterwards he went to Paraguay, where he acted as surgeon for the republican government.

In 1864 Banks settled at Liverpool, and in 1874 he married Elizabeth Rathbone, daughter of John Elliott, a merchant of Liverpool; they had two sons. He began his career at Liverpool by joining the staff of the school of medicine at the infirmary, where he was first first demonstrator and then lecturer on anatomy. This latter post he retained—and he later became professor—when the infirmary school was merged with University College, Liverpool. He resigned his chair in 1894, when he became emeritus professor of anatomy. In addition Banks was pathologist and curator of the museum, and he succeeded Reginald Harrison as assistant surgeon to the Royal Infirmary at Liverpool in 1875. He was full surgeon there from 1877 until November 1902, when he was appointed consulting surgeon.

Banks was admitted FRCS (England) on 9 December 1869 without having taken the membership examinations. He served as a member of the college council from 1890 to 1896, and he was also the first representative of Victoria University, Manchester, on the General Medical Council. In 1885 he was one of the founders of the Liverpool Biological Association and was elected its first president; in 1890 he was president of the Medical Institution. In 1892 he was made JP of Liverpool, and in 1899 he was knighted and awarded an honorary LLD from the University of Edinburgh.

Banks deserves recognition both as a surgeon and as a great organizer. As a surgeon he was an early advocate of radical mastectomy in cases of breast cancer, and in the face of strenuous opposition he carried out extensive operations involving the removal of the axillary glands when most surgeons were content with the older practice of partial removal. He made this latter treatment the topic of his Lettsomian lectures at the Medical Society of London in 1900. As an organizer Banks was one of the team who built up the fortunes of the medical school at Liverpool. Having found it at a very low ebb he and his associates worked hard to raise its quality first to that of a top medical college and finally to that of a well-equipped medical faculty at a modern university. The plan involved the rebuilding of the infirmary, and Banks was a member of the medical deputation which visited many continental hospitals to study their design and equipment before the foundation stone of the Liverpool building was laid in 1887.

Banks died suddenly at the Karlsbad Hotel, Aachen, Germany, on 9 August 1904, while on his way home from Homburg, and was buried in the Smithdown Road cemetery, Liverpool. His wife survived him. The William Mitchell Banks lectureship at Liverpool University was founded and endowed by his fellow citizens in his memory in 1905. D'A. POWER, *rev.* CHRISTIAN KERSLAKE

Sources *The Lancet* (20 Aug 1904), 566–9 • *BMJ* (20 Aug 1904), 409–12 • *Liverpool Medico-Chirurgical Journal* (Jan 1904), 2 • D. de Moulin, *A short history of breast cancer* (1983) • b. cert. • *CGPLA Eng. & Wales* (1904)

Archives U. Lpool, copies of journals and papers

Likenesses portrait (after J. Collier, *c.*1894), repro. in *BMJ*

Wealth at death £24,097 9*s.* 2*d.*: probate, 28 Oct 1904, *CGPLA Eng. & Wales*

Banks, Sarah Sophia (1744–1818), collector of antiquarian items, was born on 28 October 1744 at 30 Argyll Street, London, the second child and only daughter of William Banks (1719–1761), gentleman, and his wife, Sarah Bate (1709–1804). While her brother, Sir Joseph *Banks, largely devoted his collecting to the realm of natural history, Sarah amassed antiquarian items which documented the social history of her age. Her extensive collections, now kept in the British Museum and British Library, encompassed coins and medals along with historically valuable ephemera such as broadsheets, newspaper clippings, visiting cards, engravings, advertisements, and playbills. Together with her omnivorous interest in the social world of élite society she also retained a strong interest in the folk culture of Lincolnshire (where the family seat of Revesby Abbey was located)—an interest evident in her painstaking collection of Lincolnshire dialect words, 'Glossaries in Lincolnshire dialect, 1779–1783' (BL, Add. MS 32640).

Sarah Sophia Banks (1744–1818), by John Russell, 1790

Though British élite culture offered few opportunities for women, the large number of visitors to her brother's residence in Soho Square, where she lived from shortly after his marriage in 1779 until her death, made it possible for Sarah to achieve some recognition in the scientific and scholarly circles in which her brother moved. She died, unmarried, on 27 September 1818, following a carriage accident. Her unusual status was acknowledged in a glowing obituary in the *Gentleman's Magazine*.

JOHN GASCOIGNE

Sources *GM*, 1st ser., 88/2 (1818), 472 • W. Matthews, 'The Lincolnshire dialect in the eighteenth century', *N&Q*, 169 (1935), 398–404 • copy of will, 21 Sept 1818, NHM • H. B. Carter, *Sir Joseph Banks, 1743–1820* (1988) • J. T. Smith, *A book for a rainy day, or, Recollections of the events of the last sixty-six years* (1845), 211–14

Archives BL, printed ephemera in nine volumes, LR.301.h.3–11 • BL, Add. MS 32640 • BL, corresp. and papers, Add. MSS 6300–6341, *passim* | CKS, copies of journals of Sir Joseph Banks • NHM, copies of journals of Sir Joseph Banks

Likenesses N. Hone, miniature, 1768, NG Ire. • J. Russell, pastel drawing, 1790, Knatchbull Portrait Collection [*see illus.*] • A. Kauffmann, oils, Knatchbull Portrait Collection; on loan to Maidstone county hall, Kent • process block print (after J. Russell), BM

Banks, Thomas (1735–1805), sculptor, was born on 22 December 1735 in Kennington, south London, and baptized in St Mary, Lambeth, on 18 January 1736, the eldest of the three sons of William Banks, later landscape gardener, land steward, and surveyor to the fourth duke of Beaufort at Badminton in Gloucestershire, and his wife, Mary.

Education Educated in Ross-on-Wye, Herefordshire, Banks first worked for his father, who was then supervising building works at Badminton under William Kent. According to the sculptor John Flaxman, Banks's father was an architect and taught his son the principles of the profession and how to draw. His younger brother Mark became an architect with the board of works. Aged fifteen or nineteen (the date is uncertain as until 1803 he believed he was born in 1739) Banks returned to London to be apprenticed to the mason and woodcarver William Barlow. He may have assisted Barlow with chimney-pieces for the Mansion House, London, and with wood-carving for the house of the Rt Hon. Henry Pelham in Arlington Street. Banks spent his evenings studying drawing and modelling in the studio of Peter Scheemakers in Vine Street, Piccadilly. Here he met the sculptor Joseph Nollekens, and both were able to study the clay and marble copies that Scheemakers had brought back from Italy.

On completing his seven-year apprenticeship, Banks enrolled for life classes at the St Martin's Lane Academy. His marriage on 31 August 1766 to Elizabeth Hooton (1748–1834) brought him a modest income from land in Mayfair. By 1769 the sculptor Richard Hayward probably employed Banks as his assistant in Piccadilly. Between 1763 and 1769 Banks earned considerable sums in prize money from the Society of Arts for ambitious sculptures of historical subjects. According to the only account of his life published while he was alive (*European Magazine*, 18, July–December 1790, 23), Banks decided to become a sculptor rather than remain a mason carver in response to premiums then on offer. In 1763 he was awarded a premium of 30 guineas for a bas-relief in Portland stone, *The Death of Epaminondas*. In 1765 he won a premium of 25 guineas for a marble relief, *The Ransoming of Hector*, and in 1769 he received a premium of 20 guineas for a life-size clay statue, *Prometheus and the Vulture*. The award of 20 guineas in 1766 for a *Design for Ornamental Furniture* confirmed his versatility and potential employment beyond sculpture. He also exhibited at this time with the Free Society of Artists, showing *The Ransoming of the Body of Hector* in 1767 (presumably the marble relief completed two years before) and models of *The Judgment of Paris* in 1768 and of *Perseus* in 1769. From 1769 to 1772 he is recorded living in New Bird Street, Oxford Road (on the north side of the present Oxford Street).

In 1769 Banks moved his allegiance to the new Royal Academy of Arts and on 30 June was admitted to the Royal Academy Schools. His younger brother Charles (*c*.1745–1795) also enrolled as a student that year; he won the gold medal in 1774 and became his brother's assistant. At the academy exhibition of 1769 Thomas Banks exhibited two models, *Aeneas and Anchises Escaping from Troy* and the same subject 'in another point in time' (as stated in the exhibition catalogue). In the first election for associateships of the Royal Academy, held that year, he was unsuccessful, yet he won the academy's gold medal for sculpture with the bas-relief *The Rape of Proserpine*. He also received £10 from the academy as the first instalment of a stipend to study in Rome. The first sculptor to receive the Rome scholarship, he did not depart until 1772. In 1771 he exhibited at the academy a portrait study in chalks of its first porter and model, John Malin (RA), probably after a death mask, together with a model for a monument showing *A Cherub Decorating an Urn*. In 1772 he showed a model for a sculpture of *Mercury, Argus and Io*.

Visits to Italy and St Petersburg Banks arrived in Rome with his wife on 22 September 1772. He may have intended to settle there in the hope of finding international patronage among the gentlemen on the grand tour for the historical and poetical subjects for which he had received prizes, but little employment, in London. His daughter, Lavinia, was born in Rome in 1774, and he remained a further four years after his academy stipend expired in 1775, returning to England only after protracted physical and mental illness caused by unreliable patrons, including Frederick Hervey, bishop of Derry, later fourth earl of Bristol. His reputation rests, essentially, on five surviving works from these years. Sir Joshua Reynolds 'pronounced him the first British sculptor who had produced works of classic grace, and said "his mind was ever dwelling on subjects worthy of an ancient Greek"' (Cunningham, 3.86).

Banks first sent back to the academy an oval marble relief, *Alcyone Discovering the Dead Body of her Husband Ceyx* (Leeds City Council, Lotherton Hall, Yorkshire), exhibited at the academy in 1775, and in 1778 he showed there a marble bust of a lady. Between these years he produced three marble reliefs: *Caractacus before Claudius* (priv. coll.); *The Death of Germanicus* (priv. coll.); and *Thetis and her Nymphs Rising from the Sea to Console Achilles for the Loss of Patroclus*, together with the terracotta statuette *Achilles Arming* (both V&A). These works illustrate the two great influences on Banks in Rome: the carving techniques of the Italians, discovered with the assistance of Giovanni Battista Capezzuoli, and the Romantic classicism of Henry Fuseli and the international circle in Rome that included George Romney, Nicolai Abildgaard, and the sculptor J. T. Sergel.

In 1779 Banks recovered from his illness sufficiently to visit Naples, and in May he returned to England with his family and Maria Hadfield (at whose marriage to Richard Cosway in 1781 he was a formal witness). In 1780 he showed at the academy his marble relief of *Caractacus before Claudius*, prior to installing it opposite Christophe Veyrier's *Darius before Alexander* in the entrance hall at Stowe, and a bust of the painter Benjamin West, Banks's neighbour in Newman Street. The following year he exhibited two other works begun in Rome and finished in London: a portrait of Princess Sophia of Gloucester as *Psyche Plucking the Golden Wool* and a statue of Cupid (formerly

Pavlovsk Palace, Russia). Lord Bristol had commissioned the latter in marble in early spring 1778 but left it in Banks's hands.

Still determined to find patronage for sculpture of poetical and historical subjects, Banks set out alone for St Petersburg in June 1781 with the statue of Cupid, hoping to sell it to Catherine the Great. In this he succeeded, and he also received commissions for a portrait of Catherine the Great and a bas-relief, *The Armed Neutrality*, emblematic of the current political standing of Russia, which did not favour Britain. He returned to London in 1782, to his family's surprise, probably as a result of the declining political climate. He may also have been prompted to come home by a commission for a monument to Thomas Newton, dean of St Paul's Cathedral, to stand in the cathedral, which he began immediately upon his return (formerly St Mary-le-Bow, Cheapside). Newton had encouraged a scheme, led by Reynolds, for decorating St Paul's, and it seems likely that Reynolds secured Banks the commission.

Church memorials Banks's ambitions for sculpture found some fulfilment in his church memorials, which, unlike those of contemporaries such as Bacon and Flaxman, are all individual designs and do not tend towards standardization. In 1783, through the architect George Dance, the East India Company commissioned Banks to produce the vast monument to Sir Eyre Coote, still in Westminster Abbey, completed in 1789. In this otherwise traditional sculpture, the life-size heroic nude figure of a *Mahratta Captive* (exh. RA, 1789) received particular praise. At the academy exhibition in 1784 Banks had shown a colossal sculpture, *Achilles Enraged for the Loss of Briseis* (British Institution vestibule 1805–68; RA entrance hall until 1899; presumed destroyed *c.*1920). This full-size plaster helped secure his election as an associate of the Royal Academy in November and as a Royal Academician three months later, in 1785. As his diploma piece he deposited the marble *Falling Titan* (RA), which his daughter later stated to be based on sketches Banks had made with Fuseli in Rome. In 1789 his high-relief *Shakspeare between the Dramatic Muse and the Genius of Painting* (New Place gardens, Stratford upon Avon), for the entrance façade of Boydell's Shakspeare Gallery in Pall Mall, London, received general acclaim. Banks's last known surviving work of a poetical nature is the portrait of Mrs Johnes and her infant daughter as *Thetis Dipping the Infant Achilles in the Styx* (1790; V&A). Thomas Johnes of Hafod in Cardiganshire commissioned it after he had withdrawn his order for a marble of the *Achilles Enraged*.

The most celebrated of Banks's church memorials is the recumbent effigy of Penelope Boothby (St Oswald's Church, Ashbourne, Derbyshire), the only child of Sir Brooke Boothby. When the model (Sir John Soane's Museum, London) of the six-year-old girl, apparently sleeping, was exhibited at the academy in 1793 it prompted Queen Charlotte and her daughters to burst into tears. Other important memorials include the reliefs commemorating Isaac Watts (1779) and William Woollett (1791) (both Westminster Abbey) and that to Mrs Petrie (1795; St Mary's, Lewisham). His monuments in St Paul's Cathedral to Captain Richard Burgess (1802) and Captain Westcott (1802–5) attracted criticism for their combination of portraiture with heroic nudity.

Later years Portrait busts by Banks are exceptional in their intellectual intensity. More than thirty-five are recorded, the most accessible and admired of which today are *Warren Hastings* (1790–91; marble, India Office Library; bronze, NPG) and *Dr Anthony Addington* (1791; marble, V&A). His last exhibited work, a bust of Oliver Cromwell (priv. coll.), was ordered to be withdrawn from the exhibition of 1803 to avoid embarrassment to the Royal Academy. Banks had been arrested on suspicion of treason in 1794 when the artist Joseph Farington noted in his diary (16 January 1794): 'Banks is a violent democrat' (Farington, *Diary*, 1.144). Farington's observation was made after noting Banks's failed attempt to be appointed librarian at the academy. His known political sympathies must have harmed his career. Since 1780 he had exhibited annually at the academy, missing only three years (1786, 1790, and 1801). Regularly elected a visitor to the Royal Academy Schools, he served on the academy council, exhibition hanging committee, and schools committee, as well as on the committee for monuments in St Paul's Cathedral, but he was not selected from a shortlist presented to George III for the keepership in 1803.

In the history of collecting old master drawings in Britain, Banks holds a significant position. For his time, he was unusual in the interest he took in the early Renaissance masters, including Parmigianino and Dürer. Drawings from his collection were later divided between Sir Thomas Lawrence and Banks's great-grandson, the painter Sir Edward Poynter. Partially paralysed by a stroke in 1803, Banks destroyed many of his terracottas that year. He died at his home, 5 Newman Street, London, on 2 February 1805 and was buried in the churchyard of St Mary's, Paddington. A tablet to his honour was the first erected to a sculptor in Westminster Abbey. Flaxman wrote a lecture on Banks immediately after his death, but he was denied permission to deliver it by the academy, who feared that the king would see it as a celebration of a democrat.

Posthumous reputation The nineteenth century regarded Banks as a founding father of the British school of art. This reputation endured through the prominence of his works and publications such as Cunningham's *Lives* (1830). Flaxman's 'Address on Banks' appeared in the second edition of his *Lectures on Sculpture* (1838), a volume presented to prizewinning students throughout the century. At a time when churches were the equivalent of today's museums and galleries of modern sculpture, Banks's monuments were seen in Westminster Abbey, St Paul's Cathedral, and local churches, particularly in London. His sculptures of poetical and historical subjects could be seen in the National Gallery, the British Institution, Sir John Soane's Museum, and the entrance halls of the Royal Academy and of country houses such as Stowe, Buckinghamshire, and Holkham Hall, Norfolk. The International Exhibition of 1862 included his four best-known works: *Falling Titan* and the three Achilles subjects mentioned above.

Today, despite the destruction of many London churches and the loss of most of his terracotta sketches, Banks is admired, with his contemporaries John Bacon and Joseph Nollekens, as the leading sculptor of the era of patriotic patronage that saw the founding of the Royal Academy. After the great generation of immigrant artists who had dominated sculpture in the second third of the eighteenth century (including Roubiliac, Rysbrack, and Scheemakers) Banks was the first native sculptor to answer the ambitions of his time. Despite his disappointments with his patrons, his best surviving works are distinguished by a commitment to the spirit of the antique while drawing on wider artistic sources, resulting in an originality that stretched the familiar vocabulary of the fashionable neo-classical style. JULIUS BRYANT

Sources C. F. Bell, ed., *Annals of Thomas Banks* (1938) • M. Whinney, *Sculpture in Britain, 1530–1830* (1964), 175–82 • N. L. Pressly, *The Fuseli circle in Rome* (New Haven, 1979), 48–53 • R. Gunnis, *Dictionary of British sculptors, 1660–1851* (1953); new edn (1968) • A. Cunningham, *The lives of the most eminent British painters, sculptors, and architects* (1830), vol. 3. pp. 82–121 • J. Flaxman, *Lectures on sculpture*, 2nd edn (1838) [for 'An address ... on the death of Thomas Banks'] • L. Stainton, 'A re-discovered bas-relief by Thomas Banks', *Burlington Magazine*, 116 (1974), 327–9 • J. Bryant, 'Mourning Achilles: a missing sculpture by Thomas Banks', *Burlington Magazine*, 125 (1983), 742–5 • J. Bryant, 'The church memorials of Thomas Banks', *Church Monuments*, 1 (1985), 49–64 • J. Bryant, 'Thomas Banks's anatomical crucifixion', *Apollo*, 133 (1991), 409–11 • will, PRO, PROB 11/1421, sig. 148 • letter from Lavinia Forster to George Cumberland, 3 Feb 1805, BL, Add. MS 36500, fol. 110

Archives BL, letters to George Cumberland, Add. MSS 36498–36500, *passim*

Likenesses J. Northcote, oils, 1777, priv. coll. • J. Condé, stipple, 1791 (after a bust by T. Banks), BM, NPG; repro. in *European Magazine* (1791) • J. Northcote, oils, 1792, RA • G. Dance, two chalk drawings, 1793–4, BM, RA • W. Blenkinsop, stipple, pubd 1802 (after J. Northcote), BM • J. Flaxman, chalks, 1804, FM Cam. • R. Cosway, pencil drawing, BM • W. C. Edwards, line engraving (after J. Flaxman), BM, NPG; repro. in Cunningham, *Lives* • H. Singleton, group portrait, oils (*Royal Academicians, 1793*), RA

Wealth at death left all to widow: will, PRO, PROB 11/1421, sig. 148

Banks, Thomas Christopher (1765–1854), genealogist, was the eldest child of Thomas Banks, a gentleman pensioner. He claimed a relationship to the Banks family of Whitley; on his mother's side, he claimed descent from the Nortons of Barbados. He studied law, and on the strength of his genealogical knowledge offered his services as an agent in cases of disputed inheritance. From 1813 to 1820 he practised at 5 Lyon's Inn, London, and subsequently he took an office, called the Dormant Peerage Office, in John Street, Pall Mall. Although he specialized in cases based on the weakest of claims (which he strengthened with largely fanciful pedigrees), some of his published works were well researched and accurate.

The Manual of the Nobility, his first publication, appeared in 1807. The same year he brought out the first volume of the *Dormant and Extinct Baronage of England*; a second volume followed in 1808, and a third in 1809. The work drew heavily on Sir William Dugdale's *Baronetage of England* (1675–6). In 1812 he published the first volume of a corresponding work on the *Peerage*, which was never completed. The same year he edited, in one volume, reprints of Sir William Dugdale's *Ancient Usage in Bearing ... Arms* (first published in 1682), Dugdale's *Discourse Touching the Office of Lord High Chancellor*, with additions, together with Sir William Segar's *Honores Anglicani* (1590). In 1825 he brought out *Stemmata Anglicana, or, A Miscellaneous Collection of Genealogy*. The second part contained an account of the ancient and extinct royal families of England, re-embodied from the *Extinct Peerage*. In 1837 this was republished as a fourth volume of the *Dormant and Extinct Baronage of England*, and continued down to January 1837, with corrections, appendices, and index.

In 1812 Banks published the first of his pamphlets in support of spurious claims to peerages under the title *An Analysis of the Genealogical History of the Family of Howard*. In 1815 the pamphlet was republished with the more exciting title *Ecce homo, the Mysterious Heir, or, Who is Mr Walter Howard? An Interesting Inquiry Addressed to the Duke of Norfolk*. A third edition appeared in 1816. In the same year another pamphlet appeared, entitled *The Detection of Infamy*, written anonymously by Banks on behalf of Thomas Drummond, of Biddick, claimant to the estates of the earl of Perth. During the next twenty-five years he continued to take on similar cases. In the late 1820s he undertook the case of Alexander Humphrys, who laid claim to the earldom of Stirling. He wrote several pamphlets in support of Humphrys's cause and travelled to North America (1826–8) and Ireland (1828–9) to search for evidence. Banks gave proof of his own personal faith in the claims of Humphrys by allowing the pretendant, in accordance with rights conferred on the first earl of Stirling by King James, to create him a baronet, and by accepting from him (in anticipation) a grant of 6000 acres of land in Nova Scotia. When the documents on which Humphrys founded his claims were discovered to be forgeries, Banks ceased to make use of his own title. While the Stirling case was still in progress, Banks published the imaginary discovery of another unrecognized claim to a peerage, under the title of a *Genealogical and historical account of the earldom of Salisbury, showing the descent of the Baron Audley of Heleigh from the William Longespé, earl of Salisbury, son of King Henry II by the celebrated fair Rosamond*. In 1844 he published, in two parts, *Baronia Anglica concentrata*.

Banks was a knight of the holy order of St John. During his later years he resided near Ripon, Yorkshire; he died at Greenwich, Kent, on 30 September 1854.

T. F. HENDERSON, *rev.* MICHAEL ERBEN

Sources *GM*, 2nd ser., 43 (1855), 206–8 • Boase, *Mod. Eng. biog.*

Archives BL, corresp. and genealogical papers, Add. MSS 24855, 27585, 33981–33982, 35649 • Cardiff Central Library, corresp., notes, and pedigrees • NHM, family corresp. [copies] • S. Antiquaries, Lond., drafts and papers relating to bastardy • Yale U., Beinecke L., MS essays ready for publication | BL, letters to Sir Joseph Banks, Add. MSS 33981–33982 • Bodl. Oxf., Montagu MSS • Bodl.

Oxf., letters to Sir Thomas Phillipps and others • Lincs. Arch., letters mainly to James Gunman and G. R. P. Jarvis

Banks, William [Richard] (*fl.* **1591–1637**), showman, the exhibitor of a famous performing horse called Morocco or Marocco, is hard to identify precisely. This is perhaps because of the kind of cultural phenomenon the horse and his trainer represent. It is the horse's activities that are described in detail in the literature of Banks's day. Banks, who may have been a native of Staffordshire, becomes the shadowy figure behind the performance, as an epigram in Thomas Bastard's *Chrestoleros* (1598) makes clear: '*Bankes* hath a horse of wondrous qualitie, For he can fight, and pisse, and daunce, and lie. And finde your purse, and tell what coyne ye have. *But Bankes*, who taught your horse to smel a knave?' (p. 62).

Banks's first recorded appearance with a horse was in Shrewsbury in 1591. According to *Tarlton's Jests* (1611), Banks originally served the earl of Essex, exhibiting his horse 'of strange qualities … at the Crosse Keyes in Gracious-streete' (Hazlitt, 217). He may be identified with William Banks, a vintner in Cheapside, London, in later years, who is said to have 'taught his Horse to dance, and shooed him with Silver' (*The Life and Death of Mrs. Mary Frith*, 1662, 75). This William Banks achieved his vintner status not through the company but by special royal licence from the king. In a record of May 1637, a mock bill of fare is preserved 'sent to Bankes the Vintner in Cheapside'. It itemizes delicacies from the animal kingdom such as 'a rhinoceros boyled in alligant; sixe tame lyons in greene sawce; a whole horse sowced after the Russian fashion' (Halliwell-Phillipps, 52; MS Ashmole 826). Mention is made of 'mine host Bankes' in James Shirley's *The Ball* as late as 1639 (H4*v*), which seems to support the celebratory horse trainer-turned-vintner idea. In German records of performances of the horse, however, the owner is named 'Reichardt [Richard] Banckes' rather than William (Schrickx, 138).

Tarlton's Jests tells of the horse's ability to single out persons named by his master, as does Richard Braithwaite's *Strappado for the Divell* (1615). Marocco's talent for counting out money is mentioned by Shakespeare in *Love's Labour's Lost* (1594–5?), by Joseph Hall in his *Virgidemiarvm … of Byting Satyres* (1598), and by Sir Kenelm Digby in *The Nature of Bodies* (1644).

At the end of 1595 a pamphlet was published called *Maroccus extaticus*, 'or Bankes Bay Horse in a Trance, a discourse set downe in a merry dialogue between Bankes and his beast, anatomizing some abuses and bad trickes of this age'. A woodcut included with the dialogue represents Banks in the act of opening his entertainment, the horse standing on his hind legs with a stick in his mouth, and there are dice on the ground. From the title-page it appears that Banks was then showing his horse at the Belsavage inn without Ludgate. About 1600 the horse was said to have performed his most famous feat—that of climbing to the top of St Paul's Cathedral. In *The Owles Almanacke* entry for 1617 (by 'Iocundary Merrie-braines', published 1618) it is stated that 'since the dancing horse stood on the top of Powles, whilst a number of asses stood braying, below—17 [years]' (p. 7). References to the event are to be found in many of Thomas Dekker's plays and tracts, in William Rowley's *A Search for Money* (1609), and elsewhere.

In 1601 Banks exhibited his horse at Paris, and the best account of Morocco's feats is given by a French eyewitness, Jean de Montlyard, in a note to a translation of *The Golden Ass* by Apuleius (*Les metamorphoses, ou, L'asne d'or*, 1602). According to this text a magistrate of Paris had suspected that his tricks were performed by magic, and for some time Banks was imprisoned and his horse impounded. When Banks demonstrated how he had instructed Morocco by signs, they were both released, and Banks was permitted to continue his performances. At Orléans, according to Thomas Morton, Morocco was again suspected of being a pupil of the devil. Banks, to counter the suspicion, 'commanded his horse to seeke out one in the preasse of the people who had a crucifixe on his hat'. This done, he 'bad him kneele downe unto it, & not this onely, but also to rise up againe and to kisse it' (*Direct Answer unto the Scandalous Exceptions of Theophilus Higgons*, 1609, 11). The same account describes how man and horse visited Frankfurt shortly after this adventure. More recent research has found records of performances before Henry Julius, duke of Brunswick-Wolfenbüttel, in April 1605, and this is where the name Reichardt is recorded.

Texts like Gervase Markham's *Cavelarice* (1607) continued to refer to Banks's tricks with his horse when the original Morocco would have been too old to perform, and was probably dead or retired. Playful allusions in Ben Jonson's *Epigrams* (1616) and in a marginal note to the mock romance of *Don Zara del Fogo*, by Basilius Musophilus, killed off horse and trainer by having them both burnt at Rome 'by the commandment of the pope' (Basilius Musophilus, *Don Zara del Fogo*, 1656, 114).

If it is not known what happened to the bay gelding, something is known of what happened to Banks after his initial equine success. In 1608 Henry, prince of Wales, temporarily employed Banks as a horse trainer, as did the duke of Buckingham, according to records of 1622–5. Curious allusions to Banks and his dancing horse are found in late publications written *c*.1635–40 (William Davenant's 'The Long Vacation' in *Wit and Drollery*, 1656, 84; and Thomas Killigrew's *The Parson's Wedding*, 1664, in *Comedies and Tragedies*, 86). An early Lancashire pedigree states that a 'daughter of … Banks, who kept the horse with the admirable tricks', married John Hyde of Urmeston, a member of an ancient county family (Hunter).

EVA GRIFFITH

Sources S. H. Atkins, 'Mr Banks and his horse', *N&Q*, 167 (1934), 39–44 • W. Schrickx, 'Richard Banks and his horse in Wolfenbüttel in 1605', *N&Q*, 277 (1982), 137–8 • A. Freeman, *Elizabeth's misfits: brief lives of English eccentrics, exploiters, rogues, and failures, 1580–1660* (1978), 123–9 • J. Bondeson, *The Feejee mermaid and other essays in natural and unnatural history* (1999), 1–18 • J. Hunter, *New illustrations of the life, studies and writings of Shakespeare*, 2 vols. (1845), vol. 1, p. 265 • *Tarlton's jests*, *Old English jest books*, ed. W. C. Hazlitt (1884) (1611), 2.217 • J. O. Halliwell-Phillipps, *Memoranda on 'Love's labour's lost', 'King John', 'Othello', and on 'Romeo and Juliet'* (1879), 52 • *DNB*

Likenesses woodcut, 1595, repro. in Bondeson, *Feejee mermaid*, 6

Banks, William Stott (1821–1872), antiquary, was born at Wakefield, Yorkshire, on 9 March 1821, the son of William Banks and his wife, Harriet Stott, and baptized on 15 April following at the Salem Independent Chapel. He was educated at the Lancasterian School there, and at the age of eleven began work in the office of John Berry, a local solicitor. He subsequently became a clerk in the office of Marsden and Ianson, solicitors and clerks to the West Riding justices, and remained with Ianson at the dissolution of the firm in 1844. He then took articles, was admitted an attorney in Hilary term 1851, and in 1853 became Ianson's partner. On the formation of the Wakefield borough commission in March 1870 he was elected clerk to the justices, an office that he retained until his death.

In 1865 Banks published a short but scholarly *List of Provincial Words in Use at Wakefield*, and in the following year the first of three volumes of *Walks in Yorkshire* (1866–71), which combined antiquarian and topographical notes and were highly regarded for their research. Banks died at his house in Northgate, Wakefield, on 25 December 1872, shortly after a visit to the continent, undertaken for health reasons. He was survived by his wife, Susannah.

Gordon Goodwin, *rev.* William Joseph Sheils

Sources *Yorkshire Archaeological and Topographical Journal*, 2 (1871–2), 459–60 • *Wakefield Free Press* (28 Dec 1872) • *Wakefield Free Press* (18 Jan 1873) • *N&Q*, 4th ser., 11 (1873), 132 • *CGPLA Eng. & Wales* (1873) • chapel register, PRO, RG 4/3705

Wealth at death under £4000: probate, 29 July 1873, *CGPLA Eng. & Wales*

Bankton. For this title name *see* McDouall, Andrew, Lord Bankton (1685–1760).

Bankwell, John de. *See* Banquell, Sir John (*d.* 1308).

Bankwell, Roger. *See* Baukwell, Roger (*d.* in or after 1350).

Bankyn, John. *See* Bankin, John (*fl.* 1347–1387).

Bannard, John (*fl.* 1402–1411), Augustinian friar and theologian, is first mentioned in exercises dated 1402 in the theological notebook of an unknown bachelor (now Oxford, Corpus Christi College, MS 280), as opponent to questions raised on the second book of Peter Lombard's *Sentences*; only the bachelor's replies are noted, but Bannard evidently defended the doctrine of the immaculate conception, and put forward a further thesis on angels and the earthly paradise. He must have already graduated bachelor or doctor of theology to play this role. He must have remained in Oxford for a further decade, as his name is mentioned in two documents of 1411 as chancellor or acting chancellor; some time after 31 May he signed the bursar's account at University College, and on 11 November he made an agreement on behalf of the university with the assessors for the tenth and fifteenth levied in the parish of St Mary Magdalen. Almost certainly he was acting as commissary only within a brief period, lasting from 9 September to 18 November, when the office of chancellor was under contention. There is no evidence for him after 1411.

Jeremy Catto

Sources CCC Oxf., MS 280, fols. 126v–127v, 129, 133 [*quaestiones*] • Bodl. Oxf., MS Wood D.2, fol. 299 [St Mary Magdalen church deed] • *Snappe's formulary and other records*, ed. H. E. Salter, OHS, 80 (1924), 333 • Emden, *Oxf.*, 1.102

Bannatyne, George (1545–1607/8), compiler of the Bannatyne manuscript, was born in Edinburgh on 22 December 1545, the seventh child and fourth (but second surviving) son of James Bannatyne of Kirktown of Newtyle (1512–1584) and Catherine Telfer (1522/3–1570). George had eleven brothers and eleven sisters. No offspring is known from his father's second marriage in 1573 to Jonet Cockburn, widow of James Wood, portioner of Bonnington (*d.* 1546) and, secondly, of David Forrester, merchant burgess of Edinburgh (*d.* 1572). In 1558 a George Ballenden matriculated at St Mary's College, St Andrews, where he also appears among the *baccalaurei* and *intrantes* of 1560–62, this time with the name spelt Ballandyne. This is most likely to be George Bellenden, half-brother of Sir John Bellenden, justice-clerk, who was studying in Paris in 1564. However, since scribes regularly mistook the name Bannatyne for Ballenden, the possibility cannot be entirely ruled out that this is in fact George Bannatyne; several of his brothers studied in St Andrews, their names likewise misspelt. Bannatyne was never styled *maister* in later life, but he may have obtained his master's licence without having been able to go through the required formal ceremonies because of the troubles of the Reformation, with his later career in business never requiring him to rectify this. However, it is more likely that he did not go to university altogether.

George's father, burgess of Edinburgh, was writer to the signet, keeper of the rolls, member of Edinburgh town council, searcher of English ships, and deputy justice-clerk. He was closely related to the poet John Bellenden and to Sir John and Sir Lewis Bellenden, consecutive justice-clerks. George Bannatyne was thus connected to the contemporary literary, legal, and political establishment, which is confirmed by the 'Memoriall buik' in which he faithfully copied the births, marriages, and deaths of loved ones.

These urban and legal circles with connections to church, court, and literature enabled Bannatyne to compile the Bannatyne manuscript, the most wide-ranging of the contemporary Scottish literary miscellanies, arranging some four hundred texts, many otherwise unknown, into five sections of religious, moral, merry, amatory, and narrative poetry, for an audience that wanted such texts for a range of didactic and leisure-time purposes. Opinions are divided as to whether he copied the manuscript at his family's estate of Newtyle in Angus (Forfarshire) or at their Edinburgh residence in the Cowgate; whether he did so in the last three months of 1568 or from 1565 to 1568; whether it was meant to be printed; and whether it was intended as a conceptually focused family miscellany, or even a coterie anthology.

The lack of evidence for any other cultural enterprise by Bannatyne suggests that ethical and utilitarian rather than aesthetic or nationalist impulses lie behind his compilation. Merging an appreciation of vernacular texts with socially conservative yet culturally open-minded tastes, his editing presents literature as both moral counsel and entertainment in a laicized society that, based on law and education, emphasizes civic responsibility. Such 'vernacular humanism' fits with Bannatyne's public profile as a reformer concerned with the *bonum commune* rather than with doctrinal issues; as a result, his protestant self-censorship was not rigorous and some Roman Catholic features of his copy-texts remained. In their attempt to combine the archaic dictates of courtly love with a more rational philosophy of love, the two eloquently conventional poems attributed to Bannatyne in the manuscript reflect a similar mindset.

In 1572 James Bannatyne gifted his son a tenement in Leith near Edinburgh, adjacent to property owned by William Fowler, elder brother of the poet of the same name and uncle to another poet, William Drummond of Hawthornden. George Bannatyne was also presented in 1582 with the income deriving from the chaplaincy of St Michael's altar in the parish church of Crieff, vacant by decease of John Bannatyne, his uncle. On 27 October 1587 he was made merchant and guild brother of Edinburgh; he was styled 'merchant' throughout his life, but his wealth derived mainly from numerous financial transactions, especially speculation with annual rents. At an uncertain date he married Isobel Mauchan (1545/6–1603), widow of the bailie William Nisbet and mother of Edward and Isobel Nisbet. They had three children, Jonet (1587–1631), James (1589–1598), and a stillborn daughter (1593). Jonet in 1603 became the second wife of George Foulis (1569–1633), second son of James Foulis of Colinton and master of the king's mint. Through this marriage the Bannatyne manuscript passed into the Foulis family; it is now in the National Library of Scotland. The best diplomatic version is that edited by W. Tod Ritchie, *The Bannatyne Manuscript* (Scottish Text Society, 1928–1934), which contains many transcripts of family documents. An excellent facsimile edition is provided by Denton Fox and William A. Ringler, in *The Bannatyne Manuscript* (1980).

In 1600 Bannatyne was appointed master of Trinity Hospital, just outside Edinburgh, for a year, an appointment which indicates that Bannatyne linked business acumen with charity. In 1606 he lived with his daughter's family in Dreghorn, a few miles south-west of Edinburgh. He was still alive on 10 September 1607 but had died by 5 April 1608, a document of that date stating that the deceased George Bannatyne had been searcher of customable skins, an office that had been held by several members of his family before him. His wife's testament—his own has not been preserved—suggests the couple enjoyed a comfortable lifestyle. THEO VAN HEIJNSBERGEN

Sources register of deeds, NA Scot., RD 1 • register of testaments, NA Scot., CC 8 • privy council register, NA Scot., PC 1 • register of the privy seal, NA Scot., PS 1 • register of sasines, NA Scot., RS 24 • J. H. Ballatyne, 'Mr Thomas Bellenden of Auchnoull (*c.*1490–1547)', MS, NA Scot. • W. Scott, ed., *Memorials of George Bannatyne. MDXLV–MDCVIII*, Bannatyne Club (1829) • M. Wood and R. K. Hannay, eds., *Extracts from the records of the burgh of Edinburgh*, AD *1589–1603*, [6] (1927) • D. Laing, ed., *Charters of the Hospital of Soltre, of Trinity College, Edinburgh, and other collegiate churches in Mid-Lothian*, Bannatyne Club (1861) • *The account book of Sir John Foulis of Ravelston, 1671–1707*, ed. A. W. C. Hallen, Scottish History Society, 16 (1894) • C. B. B. Watson, ed., *Roll of Edinburgh burgesses and guild-brethren, 1406–1700*, Scottish RS, 59 (1929) • A. I. Dunlop, ed., *Acta facultatis artium universitatis Sanctiandree, 1413–1588*, 2 vols., Scottish History Society, 3rd ser., 54–5 (1964) • *The poems of George Bannatyne, MDLXVIII*, ed. D. Laing, Bannatyne Club (1824) • E. Bennett, 'A new version of a Scottish poem', *Modern Language Review*, 33 (1938), 403 • J. Hughes and W. S. Ramson, eds., *Poetry of the Stewart court* (1982) • T. van Heijnsbergen, 'The interaction between literature and history in Queen Mary's Edinburgh: the Bannatyne manuscript and its prosopographical context', *The Renaissance in Scotland: studies in literature, religion, history, and culture offered to John Durkan*, ed. A. A. MacDonald and others (1994), 183–225 • A. A. MacDonald, 'The Bannatyne manuscript: a Marian anthology', *Innes Review*, 37 (1986), 36–47 • A. A. MacDonald, 'The printed book that never was: George Bannatyne's poetic anthology (1568)', *Boeken in de late Middeleeuwen*, ed. J. M. M. Hermans and K. van der Hoek (1994), 101–110 • G. Bannatyne, 'Memoriall buik', NL Scot., Foulis MSS

Archives NL Scot., MSS

Bannatyne, Richard (*d.* 1605), secretary to John Knox, may have originated in western Scotland, for his brother James was a merchant in Ayr around the time of Richard's death. There is no evidence to support suggestions that he belonged to the same family as his contemporary George Bannatyne, the collector of Scottish poetry. Richard Bannatyne became secretary to John *Knox, attracted to the latter's service primarily out of admiration for his integrity and ministry, not for 'worldlie commoditie' (Bannatyne, 94). He appeared frequently in the kirk's general assembly, and prior to the earl of Moray's assassination, on 21 January 1570, he twice carried messages from Knox to the countess, urging her to advise Moray not to return from Stirling to Edinburgh via Linlithgow (where his killer was waiting). When Knox was attacked in an anonymous handbill for his criticism of Queen Mary in 1571, Bannatyne, on his own initiative, attempted (unsuccessfully) to persuade the general assembly formally to endorse Knox's position, and was 'not a litill in choler that his just desyre was refuised' (Bannatyne, 95). When Knox went to St Andrews in July 1571, Bannatyne lived in the priory with him and his family. As a student at St Leonard's College, James Melville watched Bannatyne help the frail Knox to the church and into the pulpit each day. By now in failing health, Knox asked his wife and Bannatyne to read to him from John 17, Isaiah 53, a chapter of Ephesians, the Psalms, and Calvin's sermons in French. Three days after he had instructed Bannatyne to have his coffin made, the reformer died, on 24 November 1572, with his secretary at his side. Knox left the care of his wife and three small daughters to Bannatyne, asking that he 'be a husband, in my rowme' (Bannatyne, 288).

After Knox's death, Bannatyne petitioned the general assembly for financial assistance to enable him to preserve the reformer's manuscripts. In addition to giving him £40, the assembly instructed the Edinburgh church to appoint several scholars to assist him. It has been suggested that Bannatyne composed the fifth part of the *History of the Reformation within the Realm of Scotland*, covering the period 1564–7, possibly using Knox's notes, but this is doubtful. The two men's literary interdependence is more probably manifested in Bannatyne's *Memoriales of Transactions in Scotland*, covering the years 1569–73.

Having completed his work for the general assembly about 1575, Bannatyne became a clerk for the advocate Samuel Cockburn of Tempill, or Tempillhall. In that capacity Bannatyne almost certainly had contacts with his employer's relatives, Sir Robert Cockburn, lord privy seal, and Sir John Cockburn, lord justice clerk. In 1575 he published Henry Balnaves's treatise on justification by faith (written in 1548, and then revised with Knox's assistance), which he had found in Lady Alison Sandilands's papers. Bannatyne served Samuel Cockburn for nearly three decades, during which time he continued his ties with the Knox family. Bannatyne's will, dated 27 August 1605, appointed his brother James as joint executor along with Cockburn; his possessions were worth £1181 Scots. Bannatyne died on 4 September 1605. His importance derives primarily from his *Memoriales*, which presents Knox, the 'light of Scotland', in a flattering manner. The view that Knox was strongly anti-episcopalian, which some modern scholars have challenged, was shaped in part by Bannatyne and by David Calderwood, who relied extensively on the *Memoriales*. Although the *Memoriales* became an invaluable source, Bannatyne is sometimes vague or unreliable, as in his exaggerated claim that the king's forces exceeded 4000 when the siege of Edinburgh commenced in October 1571. Bannatyne's discovery and publication of Balnaves's influential treatise, with its proclamation of the religious character of ordinary occupations, its stress on the separation of the spiritual from the temporal office, and the limitations it urged for the prince's power over the church, likewise constituted an important service to the Scottish Reformation in its formative period.

RICHARD L. GREAVES

Sources R. Bannatyne, *Memoriales of transactions in Scotland, 1569–1573*, ed. [R. Pitcairn], Bannatyne Club, 51 (1836) • J. Ridley, *John Knox* (1968) • W. S. Reid, *Trumpeter of God: a biography of John Knox* (1974) • D. Calderwood, *The true history of the Church of Scotland, from the beginning of the Reformation, unto the end of the reigne of King James VI* (1678) • *The autobiography and diary of Mr James Melvill*, ed. R. Pitcairn, Wodrow Society (1842) • M. Lynch, *Edinburgh and the Reformation* (1981) • J. Row, *The historie of the Kirk of Scotland*, ed. B. Botfield, 2 pts in 1 vol., Maitland Club, 55 (1842)

Archives NL Scot., diary

Wealth at death £1181 Scots: Bannatyne, *Memoriales*, 364

Bannatyne, Sir William Macleod, Lord Bannatyne (1744–1833), judge, was born on 26 January 1744, perhaps in Edinburgh, the son of Roderick Macleod (*d.* 1784) of Sunbank, writer to the signet, and his first wife, Isabel (*fl.* 1736–1744), daughter of Hector Bannatyne of Kames. He was admitted as a member of the Faculty of Advocates on 22 January 1765. Through his mother he succeeded to the estate of Kames, in Bute, when he assumed the name Bannatyne, and he was appointed sheriff of Bute in February 1776. Although letters of 1802–3 show that he hoped to marry a Miss Brisbane, this suit was unsuccessful, and he never married.

Sir William Macleod Bannatyne, Lord Bannatyne (1744–1833), by Sir Henry Raeburn

Bannatyne was one of the political group which gathered around Henry Erskine, a Scottish branch of the opposition whig connection, which hindered his professional ambition in the alarmist 1790s. When he asked his patron, John Stuart, fourth earl of Bute, to try to secure a place on the bench for him in March 1795, Bute reported that Bannatyne's attendance at a dinner held in Edinburgh in honour of Charles James Fox's birthday in January that year had excluded him from consideration. Bannatyne argued strenuously and persistently that his political views were very moderate, and he was eventually allowed to take a gown at the court of session on 16 May 1799 as Lord Bannatyne, after the death of Lord Swinton. He remained courageously loyal to his old allies, however: in January 1796 he voted in support of Henry Erskine in the ballot which deposed Erskine as dean of the Faculty of Advocates in Edinburgh for having presided at a public meeting to oppose government policy. As a judge Bannatyne was generally regarded as impartial, sound, and clear, although a choleric William Adam in 1811 described him as one of a group of judges who were 'worse than Faggots in a Muster roll', from whose incapacity 'nothing is to be expected' (Adam, 'Memorandum'). He retired from the court of session in 1823 and was knighted on 22 December 1823, becoming Sir William Macleod Bannatyne. He was father of the Scottish bar when he died in 1833.

Bannatyne's interests and friendships extended from the professional and the political to the literary and the philanthropic. He was associated with Henry Mackenzie,

Robert Cullen, William Craig, and others in producing the Edinburgh periodicals *The Mirror* (1779) and its successor *The Lounger* (1785–7), which arose out of an informal essay club and which were modelled on *The Spectator*. Bannatyne himself wrote for five issues of *The Mirror* (nos. 6, 28, 46, 58, and 76) and two issues of *The Lounger* (nos. 13 and 39). The Bannatyne Club, of which he was a founder member, was established in 1823 for the purpose of publishing Scottish antiquarian papers. His colleague Sir Walter Scott edited an account of the life and manuscripts of the poetry collector George Bannatyne (1545–1607/8) for volume 35 and included some of Sir William's own verses as an appendix, which Scott privately described as 'sad trash' (*Letters of Sir Walter Scott*, 10.495). Reflecting his practical interest in the economy and culture of highland Scotland, Bannatyne was a founder member of the Highland Society of Scotland in 1784. He also maintained a strong personal connection with the highlands through the Macleod family, for whose senior members, such as General Norman Macleod (1754–1801), he sometimes acted as a trustee and legal adviser.

Bannatyne, clubbable, popular, and described by Cockburn as 'an honest merry old gentleman' (*Memorials … by Henry Cockburn*, 133), sacrificed the Kames estate to his enjoyment of Edinburgh culture and society, selling it about 1810 to James Hamilton, writer to the signet. He died on 30 November 1833 at his home, Whiteford House on the Canongate in Edinburgh.

EMMA VINCENT MACLEOD

Sources J. Kay, *A series of original portraits and caricature etchings … with biographical sketches and illustrative anecdotes*, ed. [H. Paton and others], new edn [3rd edn], 2 (1877), 370–71 • writs and papers relating to the Bannatyne family, Stirling central regional council archives, MacGregor of MacGregor MSS, PD 60, box G • W. Adam, 'Memorandum on the present state of the court of session in Scotland', 3 Oct 1811, priv. coll. • *The letters of Sir Walter Scott*, ed. H. J. C. Grierson and others, centenary edn, 12 vols. (1932–79), vol. 10, p. 495 • Anderson, *Scot. nat.* • *The Scotsman* (4 Dec 1833) • *GM*, 2nd ser., 1 (1834), 105 • *Memorials of his time, by Henry Cockburn* (1909); repr. with introduction by K. F. C. Miller (1974), 133 • *Journal of Henry Cockburn: being a continuation of the 'Memorials of his time', 1831–1854*, 2 (1874), 209 • F. J. Grant, ed., *The Faculty of Advocates in Scotland, 1532–1943*, Scottish RS, 145 (1944), 10 • *Register of the Society of Writers to Her Majesty's Signet* (1983), 207 • H. Paton, ed., *The register of marriages for the parish of Edinburgh, 1701–1750*, Scottish RS, old ser., 35 (1908), 351 • W. J. Couper, *The Edinburgh periodical press*, 2 (1908) • C. S. Terry, *A catalogue of the publications of Scottish historical and kindred clubs and societies, and of the volumes relative to Scottish history issued by His Majesty's Stationery Office, 1780–1909* (1909) • D. D. McElroy, *A century of Scottish clubs, 1700–1800*, 2 vols. (1969), vol. 1, pp. 142–7 • J. Grant, *Cassell's old and new Edinburgh*, 3 vols. [1880–83], vol. 2, p. 35 • membership lists, 'Register of the actings and proceedings of the general assembly of the Church of Scotland', NA Scot., CH1/1/63 ff.

Archives Bodl. Oxf., letters to Maria Edgeworth • Royal Highland and Agricultural Society of Scotland, corresp. relating to Gaelic matters | Stirling central regional council, archives, MacGregor of MacGregor MSS • Dunvegan, Skye, Macleod of Macleod MSS

Likenesses J. Kay, caricature, etching, 1799, NPG • J. Kay, oils, 1799, repro. in Kay, *Series of original portraits* • J. Kay, oils (*Last sitting of the Old Court of Session, 11 of July 1808*), repro. in Kay, *Series of original portraits* • H. Raeburn, oils, Polesden Lacey, Surrey [*see illus.*]

Wealth at death library (apparently valuable): Anderson, *ScottN*, 1.236

Banneker, Benjamin (1731–1806), astronomer and farmer in America, was born on 9 November 1731 in Baltimore county, Maryland, in what later became the community of Oella, the first of four children of Robert (*d.* 1759), a former slave from Guinea who had been given his freedom, and his mixed-race wife, Mary Banneky (*d.* after 1775). Having no family name, Robert took that of his wife, Banneky, which common usage eventually changed to Banneker. Mary was the eldest child of Molly Welsh, a Wessex dairy maid who had been arrested as a felon and transported to Maryland as an indentured servant. After serving her term and gaining freedom, she cultivated tobacco in Baltimore county and eventually was able to purchase two slaves from Africa to help her. Later she married one of them, named Bannka, who was the son of a Wolof tribal chief in the Senagambian region captured by slave traders and sold to Maryland tobacco planters.

Banneker received a minimum of formal schooling, not more than several weeks in winter in a one-room country schoolhouse. His grandmother, Molly, taught him to read and write by means of a bible she imported from England for the purpose. He developed a great love of reading, borrowing books where and when he could on his favourite subjects, history and poetry. From his boyhood he demonstrated a natural talent for mathematics, creating mathematical puzzles and solving those brought to him by others. A man of self-taught mechanical and mathematical skills, in his youth Banneker had constructed a successful wooden striking clock without, he claimed, previously having seen one. Carved from wood with his penknife, the clock drew the popular interest of people throughout the region. From his youth he cultivated tobacco on the family farm, first with his parents and then on his own until his failing health forced his retirement.

A factor that changed the life of the region as well as Banneker's life was the arrival in the neighbourhood about 1771 of the Ellicott brothers from Bucks county, Pennsylvania. They purchased large areas of land, on which they constructed mills and established an industrial centre which became Ellicott City. Banneker was intrigued by his new neighbours and their activities. One of them befriended him and lent him astronomical instruments and texts from which he taught himself to make observations and calculate ephemerides for almanacs. Early in February 1791 Andrew Ellicott was appointed by President George Washington to survey a 10 mile square in Maryland and Virginia for a federal territory in which would be established a national capital. Lacking other competent assistants, Ellicott selected Banneker to maintain the instruments and clock in the field tent. Banneker worked on the project for about four months before returning home. There he completed his calculations for the ephemeris of an almanac for the coming year 1792, and sold it to a Baltimore printer. This was the first of a series of almanacs bearing his name produced for the Maryland, Virginia, and Pennsylvania region.

Banneker sent a manuscript copy of his calculations for

1792 to the secretary of state, Thomas Jefferson, accompanied by a letter, in which he made a strong plea to the statesman to bring an end to the injustices experienced by his race, and urged recognition of the equality of black men with white. He likened the slavery of African Americans to the enslavement of the American colonies by the British crown and proposed justifying the correction of one state of oppression upon the basis of the other. It was a letter deliberately planned to evoke a statement of position from the statesman. Jefferson responded promptly, acknowledging Banneker's wish for the improvement of the black race and expressing his hope that a suitable system could be developed for doing so. Impressed with Banneker's ephemeris, Jefferson sent the manuscript calculations to the French statesman the marquis de Condorcet with a covering letter describing the circumstances that had brought it to his attention. He urged presentation of the ephemeris to the Académie Royale des Sciences as an example of the equal talents of the black race. His decision to send Banneker's manuscript to Condorcet demonstrated his intention to provide Banneker with the best possible exposure if his work deserved it. Due to the political instability in France, however, Jefferson's communication was never received by the academy.

Jefferson's reply to Banneker was published in the second Banneker almanac, for the year 1793, and the exchange of letters between Banneker and Jefferson was published in a separate pamphlet that received wide distribution. Although its publication brought public recognition to Banneker, it damaged Jefferson's candidacy for the presidency in the 1797 election, which he lost. The American abolitionist movement helped to promote Banneker's almanacs during the next six years and projected the hitherto unknown black tobacco planter into the public's gaze. At least twenty-eight editions of his almanacs for the period of six years were published. Banneker continued to make calculations for ephemerides until 1802, but no almanacs appeared after the one issued for 1797.

Banneker was described by his contemporaries as a heavy-set man of deep colour with long white hair and dignified mien. He was deeply religious, and attended religious meetings in the area but adopted no denomination. He was never married, depending on his married sisters for domestic support. He lived a quiet solitary life in retirement on his farm, tending his bees and orchards and pursuing his astronomical interests. He died quietly in his sleep on 9 October 1806 at his home after returning from a walk. He was buried in the family burial-ground on his farm. In recent years part of his tobacco farm became a public park with a museum and visitor centre commemorating the life and work of the amateur astronomer. His obituary in the *Federal Gazette* of Baltimore described him as 'a prominent instance to prove that a descendant of Africa is susceptible of as great mental improvement and deep knowledge into the mysteries of nature as that of any other nation'. Banneker has been recognized as the first African-American man of science.

SILVIO A. BEDINI

Sources S. Bedini, *The life of Benjamin Banneker* (1999) • *Banneker, the Afric-American astronomer: from the posthumous papers of Martha E. Tyson* (1884) • J. McHenry, 'Account of Benjamin Banneker, a free negro', *Universal Asylum* (1791), 300–01 • M. D. Conway, 'Benjamin Banneker, the negro astronomer', *Atlantic Monthly* (1863), 79–84 • *A sketch of the life of Benjamin Banneker, from notes taken in 1836*, ed. J. Saurin Norris (1854) • S. A. Bedini, 'The survey of the federal territory', *Washington History*, 3 (1991), 76–95 • W. D. Jordan, *White over black: American attitudes towards the negro, 1550–1812* (1968) • 'Letter from the famous self-taught astronomer, Benjamin Banneker, a black man, to Thomas Jefferson, esq., secretary of state', *Universal Asylum and Columbia Magazine*, 2 (1792), 222–34

Archives Maryland Historical Society, Baltimore, astronomical journal | Hist. Soc. Penn., abolitionist papers

Banner, Sir John Sutherland Harmood-, first baronet (1847–1927), accountant and steel maker, was born at Dingle Mount, Toxteth Park, Liverpool, on 8 September 1847, the second son of Harmood Walcot Banner (1814–1878), an accountant, and his wife, Margaret, *née* Sutherland. The family were prosperous members of the Lancashire business community: his paternal grandfather was involved in the founding of the Liverpool stock exchange; and his father left £160,000 when he died, the rewards from his accountancy business.

From 1856 to 1864 Harmood-Banner (as he was known during his adult life) was educated at Radley College and then joined his father's firm in 1865, becoming a partner in 1870. In 1875 he married Elizabeth (1850–1903), the daughter and coheir of the leading Wigan industrialist and MP, Thomas Knowles. They had four sons and two daughters. This marriage was an important influence on his later career, as his father-in-law chaired Pearson and Knowles, a coal and iron conglomerate based in Warrington. He joined the board of this company and became deputy chairman after Knowles's death in 1883.

Harmood-Banner's main career in the 1880s and 1890s was in accountancy. The work was varied and he advised several firms that were in financial difficulties. In 1912–13 he helped in the reconstruction of Samuel Allsopp & Son, brewers in Burton upon Trent. In 1916 Spiers and Ponds, the hotel owners, went into liquidation, and under Harmood-Banner's chairmanship new managers and directors had to be appointed. For many years he was also the auditor of the Bank of Liverpool and the Lancashire and Yorkshire Railway. In 1904–5 he was president of the Institute of Chartered Accountants. This career as an accountant evidently presented him with opportunities as an adviser and investor in a number of other, mainly Liverpool-based, businesses. These included insurance companies (such as the Liverpool Reversionary Company), speculative gold-mining ventures (notably the Spes Bona Mining Company in the Transvaal), similar operations in South America (for example, the Anglo-Chilian Nitrate and Railway Company), and property companies (Canadian City and Town Properties, formed in 1910, of which he was chairman). On 11 March 1908 he married, in Marylebone, London, his second wife, Ella Wilstone (1881/2–1954), a widow, daughter of John Ernest Herbert Linford.

Harmood-Banner combined his accountancy and advisory work with a political career, having followed his father into Liverpool city council in 1895. His civic career flourished: he was a justice of the peace and deputy lieutenant for Cheshire, mayor of Liverpool in 1912, and alderman two years later. In 1905 he was elected Unionist MP for Everton, launching a parliamentary career that was to last until 1924. A 'tory democrat', he denounced ritualism in the church, supported Ulster protestants, and based his support in Liverpool on sectarianism. In the House of Commons he became a spokesman for Lancashire businesses, particularly the liquor trade with which he had the closest links: in 1915 he served on a cabinet committee which reported on liquor trade restrictions; and between 1922 and 1926 he was chairman of Robert Cain & Sons, brewers in Liverpool.

With Harmood-Banner as its deputy chairman, Pearson and Knowles continued to expand. By 1907 it had acquired the wire making firm of Rylands, which gave the parent company the opportunity to supply its new subsidiary with semi-manufactured steel. This was to be done by the Partington Steel Company, formed in 1910 with a capital of £700,000 and built on a 90 acre site on the banks of the River Irlam near Warrington. With its 3000 ton capacity for the production of billets, rails, and joists, the Partington Company was fully operational by 1913. It has been described as the largest single investment in the steel industry during Edwardian times. Three new blast furnaces were added during the massive expansion of the First World War, a period which also saw Pearson and Knowles set record output levels. Like most steel firms, however, the group had overexpanded, and the post-war legacy was obsolescent plant, debt, and falling orders. By 1920 Pearson and Knowles had been sold to Armstrong Whitworth, at which time Harmood-Banner lost his seat on the board.

In his latter years Harmood-Banner still had several major interests. He was deputy chairman of British Insulated and Helsby Cables, and held directorships on the boards of several electric supply, telegraph, and oil companies, both in Britain and overseas. He was, for example, chairman of Black Sea Amalgamated Oilfields, which was part of the Anglo-Maikop group. In 1921 he became chairman of the Imperial and Finance Corporation, and in the same year joined the board of a London foreign-banking firm. He also served on several government committees, such as that on the luxuries tax in 1918, the royal commission on income tax in 1919, and the railway rates tribunal in 1921–2. He was knighted in 1913 and created a baronet in 1924.

Harmood-Banner retired due to ill health about 1925. He died on 24 February 1927 at his home, Ingmire Hall, Sedbergh, Yorkshire, after a highly successful and varied business career. His eldest son, Harmood Harmood-Banner, succeeded to the baronetcy. GEOFFREY TWEEDALE

Sources R. P. T. Davenport-Hines, 'Harmood-Banner, Sir John Sutherland', *DBB* • *The Times* (25 Feb 1927) • J. C. Carr and W. Taplin, *History of the British steel industry* (1962) • P. J. Waller, *Democracy and sectarianism: a political and social history of Liverpool, 1868–1939* (1981) • A. Offer, *Property and politics, 1870–1914* (1981) • *CGPLA Eng. & Wales* (1927) • *WWW* • b. cert. • m. cert. [John Sutherland Harmood-Banner and Ella Wilstone] • d. cert.

Wealth at death £449,279 10s. 11d.: probate, 11 May 1927, *CGPLA Eng. & Wales*

Bannerman [Bannermann], **Alexander** (*b.* **1730s**, *d.* in or after **1774**), printmaker, was probably born in Cambridge. Nothing is known of his youth or education and most of what is known of him has to be deduced from his work. Bannerman worked principally as a copper-engraver and specialized in reproductions of old master works, most of which were published by Alderman John Boydell. According to T. Mortimer's *The Universal Director* (1763) he was a 'History and Architecture Engraver', but his exhibits at the Society of Artists, between 1761 and 1774, suggest an interest in Dutch genre, for example *A Fiddler* after Ostade and religious scenes after eighteenth-century favourites such as Guido Reni and Spagnoletto. In 1762 he was lodging in Great Queen Street, London, with a fellow engraver, 'Mr Basire', but in 1766 he moved to Fountain Court in the Strand before returning to Cambridge in 1770.

In addition to the information provided in the exhibition catalogues of the Society of Artists, several comments in Horace Walpole's correspondence are also revealing. Bannerman's relationship with him began about 1762 when Walpole was preparing his *Anecdotes of Painting* for the press. Developed from George Vertue's manuscripts *Anecdotes* was the first ever history of British art and this fact must have ensured a large degree of exposure for Bannerman. He worked on this venture alongside engravers such as Thomas Chambars and Johann Sebastien Müller, producing thirty-two of the portrait heads that illustrated Walpole's first three volumes.

When he came to commission the illustrations for the fourth volume of *Anecdotes of Painting*, Walpole was keen to use Bannerman, 'though there will be a little trouble, as he does not reside in London' (Walpole, *Corr.*, 1.198). Despite his relocation to Cambridge, Walpole was happy to employ Bannerman because he could rely on the Revd William Cole to keep an eye on his progress. This was important to Walpole as he appears to have had little trust in Bannerman's rate of work, his accuracy, or his commitment. One can do little more than speculate upon the causes, but in March 1771 Walpole was 'very … angry with Bannerman, who shall do nothing for me' (ibid., 14.188). Consequently, he asked Thomas Gray, another of his emissaries, to take all outstanding work from Bannerman and 'deliver them to Mr Tyson's engraver' (ibid.). Apart from his submissions to the Society of Artists exhibitions of 1773 and 1774 nothing more is heard of Bannerman.

LUCY PELTZ

Sources Redgrave, *Artists* • Graves, *Soc. Artists* • Walpole, *Corr.* • Thieme & Becker, *Allgemeines Lexikon* • T. Mortimer, *The universal director* (1763) • private information (2004) [D. Alexander]

Bannerman, Anne (**1765–1829**), poet, was born on 31 October 1765 in Edinburgh, the daughter of William Bannerman, and his wife, Isobel Dick. Bannerman was a highly gifted poet, part of the Edinburgh poetic circle that also included John Leyden, Thomas Campbell, and Dr Robert

Anderson. Anderson, the editor of the *Edinburgh Magazine*, encouraged Bannerman's publications from the late 1790s, sending copies and praising her poetry to important literary figures of the day. Through the efforts of Anderson and Thomas Park (the antiquary and editor), Bannerman's poetry was read and admired by such literary men as James Currie (Burns's first biographer), Bishop Percy (editor of *Reliques of Ancient English Poetry*), and Joseph Cooper Walker (Irish writer on Italian tragedy and lifelong friend of Charlotte Smith). Bannerman was an old friend of John Leyden (Scott's co-editor of *The Minstrelsy of the Scottish Border*, 1802–3), whose best-known ballad, 'The Mermaid', appeared two years after Bannerman's own remarkable ode, 'The Mermaid', was published in her 1800 *Poems*. Leyden and Bannerman fell out shortly before he left Edinburgh for London, on his way to India, though after his death there in 1811 it was Bannerman who rescued many of his papers which had been abandoned by his executor.

Like most Romantic writers, Bannerman began her career by publishing in the periodicals, as Augusta, as B, and under her own name in the *Monthly Magazine*, the *Poetical Register*, and the *Edinburgh Magazine*. Her first volume, *Poems* (1800), was widely praised in reviews and correspondence, although it did not sell well. *Poems* contains a series of remarkable original odes, as well as a sonnet series translated from Petrarch, one series based on *The Sorrows of Werther*, and original sonnets. In her two sonnet series Bannerman expanded Joanna Baillie's theory of dramatic composition, elaborated in Baillie's 'Introductory discourse' to her *Plays … on the Passions* (1796), by applying it to the sonnet, explaining in *Poems* that 'an attempt has been made in the "Sonnets from Werter" [*sic*], to delineate the progress of a single passion … In this manner a *unity* may be communicated' (Bannerman, 220). A great admirer of Baillie, Bannerman sent her a presentation copy of *Poems*.

Bannerman's longer 1800 poems, such as 'The Genii' and 'Ode: the Spirit of the Air' were often singled out for praise in reviews, as evoking a sublime and visionary poetic identity, as the *Critical Review* noted: 'Anne Bannerman's Odes may be quoted as an irrefragable proof that the ardour, whatever be its gender, which gives birth to lofty thought and bold expression, may glow within a female *breast*' (*Critical Review*, 435). She may also have been the author of the anonymous verse *Epistle from the Marquis de Lafayette to General Washington*, also published in 1800.

Bannerman's second volume, *Tales of Superstition and Chivalry* (1802), published anonymously, comprised ten Gothic ballads and four engravings, the fourth of which, 'The Prophecy of Merlin', caused a small scandal because it featured a nude female figure, causing it to be withdrawn from the volume at the author's request, although some copies have survived. Unlike her positively reviewed 1800 volume, the *Tales* was frequently derided, with critics and fellow poets such as Anna Seward growing frustrated with her Gothic poetry's cultivation of the 'palpable obscure' (*Letters of Anna Seward*, 5.325). In 1802 she also translated several verse passages for Joseph Cooper Walker's *An Historical and Critical Essay on the Revival of the Drama in Italy* (1805), and declined his offer to translate longer works.

The death of her mother in 1803 and of her brother left Bannerman without any source of income, and she began to support herself through the charity of friends such as Anderson, Park, and Beattie. Anderson and Park obtained for her a new edition of her poems by subscription, hoping that she would be able to live off the interest. At first reluctant to publish by subscription, Bannerman soon agreed, though the volume, *Poems: a New Edition* (1807) sold poorly and had insufficient subscribers to grant her an annuity. The volume included most of the poems in the 1800 and 1802 volumes, with some revised and some new works, such as her poem 'To Miss Baillie'. Park was able to obtain £20 from the Royal Literary Fund for her in 1805, though an attempt to gain her a pension failed. With Anderson's help and insistence, in 1807 Bannerman accepted the position of governess for Lady Frances Beresford's daughter in Exeter for £60 per year. She visited Park in Hampstead during this time, and by the early 1810s was back in Scotland, existing at least partially through gifts from the Beresford family, and visiting the writer Anne Grant in 1824.

On 29 September 1829 Bannerman died an invalid and in debt in Portobello, near Edinburgh, with two of her poems appearing in *The Laurel* (1830) and *The Casket* (1829). After her death, Lady Frances Beresford and her family paid £22 toward Bannerman's debts and spoke fondly of her, though she urged a mutual friend to destroy all of Bannerman's letters. After her death, Walter Scott praised her poetry in his 'Essay on imitations of the ancient ballad' (1830), and noted her poetry's characteristic obscurity:

> Miss Anne Bannerman likewise should not be forgotten, whose *Tales of Superstition and Chivalry* appeared about 1802. They were perhaps too mystical and too abrupt; yet if it be the purpose of this kind of ballad poetry powerfully to excite the imagination, without pretending to satisfy it, few persons have succeeded better than this gifted lady, whose volume is peculiarly fit to be read in a lonely house by a decaying lamp. (Scott, 4.16–17)

Bannerman was the only female poet Scott included in this essay on Scottish ballads, and she remains significant for her Gothic ballads, as well as for her innovative sonnet series and her bold original odes. ADRIANA CRACIUN

Sources letters and literary matters addressed to R. Anderson, 1798–1826, NL Scot., MSS 22.4.10, 22.3.11 • papers of and relating to J. Leyden, NL Scot., MSS 971, 3380–3382 • J. Baillie to A. Bannerman, 9 June 1800, priv. coll. • Lady Beresford to Mrs Walker, priv. coll. • A. Bannerman, *Poems*, new edn (1807) • *The correspondence of Thomas Percy and Robert Anderson*, ed. W. E. K. Anderson (1988), vol. 9 of *The Percy letters*, ed. C. Brooks, D. N. Smith, and A. F. Falconer (1944–88) • W. Erskine to Cadell and Davies, 1799, NL Scot., MS 3112 • R. Leyden to A. Bannerman, 1818, NL Scot., MS 3381 • R. Anderson to J. C. Walker, U. Edin. L., MS La II.598 • W. Scott, 'Essay on imitations of the ancient ballad', *Sir Walter Scott's Minstrelsy of the Scottish border*, ed. T. F. Henderson, 4 (1902), 1–52 • *Letters of Anna Seward: written between the years 1784 and 1807*, ed. A. Constable, 5 (1811) • J. C. Walker, *An historical and critical essay on the revival of the drama in Italy* (1805) • *Archives of the Royal Literary Fund, 1790–1918*, microform (compiled by N. Cross, 1982), file 170 • review of Bannerman's *Poems* (1800), *Critical Review*, [new ser.], 31 (1801), 435–8 • *Memoir and correspondence of Mrs Grant of Laggan*, ed. J. P. Grant, 3 (1844), 67–8, 162, 167 • *Blackwood*, 27 (1830), 135

Archives BL, Evelyn MSS, A. Bannerman to Mr Hood, 1804, 4, vol. 1 • priv. coll. | NL Scot., letters and literary matters addressed to R. Anderson, MSS 22.4.10, 22.3.11 • NL Scot., Leyden MSS, MSS 971, 3380–3382

Wealth at death at least £22 in debt: Lady Beresford to Walker, priv. coll.

Bannerman [*née* Watson], **Helen Brodie Cowan** (**1862–1946**), children's writer, was born on 25 February 1862 at 35 Royal Terrace, Edinburgh. She was the eldest daughter and fourth child of seven children of Robert Boog Watson (1823–1910), minister of the Free Church of Scotland, and his wife Janet (1831–1912), daughter of Alexander Cowan of Moray House, Edinburgh, and Helen Brodie. Both Helen Watson's parents were Scottish, as was her husband William Burney Bannerman (1858–1924), a physician, the son of James *Bannerman (1807–1868) and (David) Anne Douglas (1819–1879). She lived in Madeira, where her father was minister at the Scottish church, from the age of two to the age of twelve. When the family returned to Edinburgh she was educated at Miss Oliphant's school. At a time when women were not admitted to Scottish universities she sat external examinations and was made an LLA (lady literate in arts) by St Andrews University in 1887.

After her marriage on 26 June 1889, Helen Bannerman went with her husband to India and lived there as the wife of an officer in the Indian Medical Service (IMS) until he retired as a major-general in 1918. They had four children in India: Janet Cowan Watson (1893–1976), Davie Anne Douglas (Day; 1896–1976), James Patrick (Pat; 1900–1955), and Robert Boog Watson (1902–1988).

The book for which Helen Bannerman is best known, *The Story of Little Black Sambo*, was written for her two daughters, to amuse them during a journey from the hill station of Kodaikanal to Madras. This involved being carried on a chair down the steep hillside, then travelling in a bullock cart, and finally going by train, with stops at rest houses and for meals along the way. It took two days and two nights—time to refine the story of the adventures of a little black boy who outwits several tigers until it became a classic of economy and drama. She illustrated the book herself in watercolour and bound it into a small volume, with a picture facing every page. A friend took it to London and sold it to a publisher—despite Helen's admonitions not to sell the copyright—for £5.

Little Black Sambo was published by Grant Richards in London in 1899 and became a runaway best-seller. It was published in the USA in 1900. American publishers rushed out copies of the book with, in later years, illustrations by a variety of artists, many of whom set their pictures in the deep south of the USA, associating the book with the American experience of slavery, and sowing the seeds for hatred of the book by black Americans in the years ahead.

Having effectively lost the copyright—though she had never agreed to its sale—Helen Bannerman made nothing more than the original £5 from her best-seller. She did, however, publish subsequent books, though none was such a success as her first. They were *The Story of Little Black Mingo* (1902), *The Story of Little Black Quibba* (1903), *The Story of Little Degchiehead* (1904), *Pat and the Spider* (1905), *The Story of the Teasing Monkey* (1906), *The Story of Little Black Quasha* (1908), *The Story of Little Black Bobtail* (1909), and *The Story of Sambo and the Twins* (1937). After her death her daughter Day gathered together some unfinished text and pictures, and completed them, and published *The Story of Little White Squibba* in 1966 under her mother's name.

Helen Brodie Cowan Bannerman (1862–1946), by unknown photographer

Helen Bannerman was a small, neat figure, with her fair hair in a bun, and blue eyes. She had a quick intelligence and enjoyed puns and verbal wit. She was no housekeeper but very much the intellectual. She was deeply Christian in her attitudes. She knew, at the end of her life, of the criticisms of her book *Little Black Sambo* as racist and found them hard to understand; the child is the hero of the story and in her pictures he and his parents are lovingly drawn. In her picture of the closing scene (used in subsequent British reprints), where Sambo and his parents celebrate his escape from the tigers by eating pancakes, she shows the family sitting at a table with a clean white cloth, using plates and forks. In the American Stoll and Edwards edition a debased Sambo, sitting by himself, shovels the food into his mouth off the bare wooden table. As her son Robert put it in a letter to *The Times* on 1 May 1972 when the book was under attack: 'My mother would not have published the book had she dreamt for a moment that even one small boy would have been made unhappy thereby'.

Helen and William Bannerman retired to Edinburgh in

1918; he died there in 1924. She suffered a stroke in 1939, after which she was bedridden. She lived with her daughter Day in her home at 11 Strathearn Place, Edinburgh, and died there of a fractured femur and cerebral thrombosis on 13 October 1946; she was cremated.

ELIZABETH HAY

Sources H. Bannerman and W. Bannerman, letters to their children, 1902–17, NL Scot. [17 vols.] • E. Hay, *Sambo sahib: the story of Helen Bannerman, author of Little black Sambo* (1981) • P. Yuill, *Little black Sambo: a closer look* (1976) • P. Yuill, 'Little black Sambo: the continuing controversy', *School Library Journal* (March 1976) • S. G. Lanes, *Down the rabbit hole* (1972) • b. cert. • d. cert. • private information (2004)

Archives NL Scot., letters [incl. watercolour illustrations] | SOUND BBC, Radio Four feature (6 April 1971) 'Far away, far away over the sea' (produced Elizabeth Smith) [includes interviews with Helen Bannerman's children and much original material]

Likenesses photograph, NL Scot. [*see illus.*] • portrait, repro. in Hay, *Sambo sahib*; priv. coll.

Wealth at death £3170 19*s*. 4*d*.: confirmation, 14 Feb 1947, *CCI*

Bannerman, Sir Henry Campbell- (1836–1908), prime minister, was born at Kelvinside, Glasgow, on 7 September 1836, the second son and the youngest of the six children of Sir James Campbell (1790–1876) and his wife, Janet, *née* Bannerman (*d.* 1873). His extra surname was acquired as a condition of inheriting his maternal uncle's estate in 1871. He did not like his 'horrid long name', preferring 'Campbell *tout court*', or, 'as an alternative, CB' (Spender, 1.62).

Sir Henry Campbell-Bannerman (1836–1908), by George Charles Beresford, 1902

Family background and education Campbell's forebears had been tenant farmers at Inchanoch, Menteith, since the seventeenth century. In 1803 his paternal grandfather, James McOran Campbell (1752–1831), sold the farm lease and followed his eldest son to Glasgow. There he founded a grocery business, but it failed. However, his second and fourth sons, James and William, succeeded in their various enterprises, founding in 1817 a flourishing warehouse and drapery business. The Campbells rapidly established themselves among Glasgow's leading commercial families. As tenacious and purposeful in politics as he was in business, James Campbell became the leader of Glasgow's Conservatives, was knighted in 1841, and served as lord provost from 1840 to 1843. Twice he stood unsuccessfully for parliament. His elder son, Sir James Alexander Campbell (1825–1908), was Conservative MP for the universities of Glasgow and Edinburgh (1880–1906).

The Campbells were kindly but strict parents. Despite their wealth they chose not to live ostentatiously. Their views on religion as on politics were strongly held, but differences of opinion were tolerated and were never allowed to disrupt family harmony. Concerned for their children's education, they valued knowledge of the world as highly as book learning and esteemed particularly travel and the acquisition of foreign languages. The young Campbell attended Glasgow high school from 1847 to 1850, but at the age of fourteen, with his brother and cousin, he journeyed through Europe for almost a year. On returning home he went first to Glasgow University (1851–3), then to Trinity College, Cambridge (1854–8), where he read mathematics and classics. He confined his social life to a small group of friends. Unusually for a future politician, he chose to play no part in the university's union. He neither impressed nor was impressed by Cambridge. His examination results (twenty-second senior optime in the mathematical tripos and a third class in the classical tripos) were disappointingly modest.

Marriage and changing political allegiance After university Campbell straightaway joined the family firm. He showed aptitude but was not particularly enthusiastic, and he acquired a reputation for indolence. He was made a partner in 1860. In that same year he met (Sarah) Charlotte (*d.* 1906), the rather plain, stout daughter of the late Major-General Sir Charles Bruce, and they married in September. The young couple were entirely devoted to each other. Cultivated, though not clever, Charlotte was an instinctively shrewd judge of character. She became closely associated with all her husband's plans, jealously guarding his interests and resenting the least supposed slight to his reputation. Her aspirations for his success compensated for his lack of ambition. Years later he told John Morley that Charlotte's contentment was more important to him than his life.

Campbell entered parliament in 1868 as an earnest, impatient radical, yet not until the late 1850s had he begun to question the Conservative principles in which he had been nurtured. The process had begun at Cambridge, prompted by reading Darwin and Spencer. But the deciding factor was his friendship with the radical and Chartist Daniel Lawson. When Campbell ought to have been engaged in his work, he was instead endlessly discussing and debating politics with his friend. His political metamorphosis was confirmed during a year-long correspondence with his brother-in-law, Henry Bruce, that embraced the gamut of contemporary political problems. At Westminster, the tyro politician soon modified his recently acquired beliefs, rejecting republicanism, while his strong faith in individualism turned him resolutely against *dirigisme*. Imperialism in any guise never held any appeal. His unswerving allegiance to those ideas that inspired Richard Cobden and W. E. Gladstone was as much instinctual as intellectual. He defined Liberalism, simply and pragmatically, as 'the politics of common sense' (Wilson, 230).

MP for Stirling Burghs and early ministerial appointments In 1865 dilatoriness cost Campbell the opportunity to contest a Glasgow constituency. Three years later, at a by-election in April 1868, he stood for Stirling Burghs as a radical opposing another Liberal of whig sympathies. Though he successfully rebutted the charge that his radicalism was mere opportunism and that he was really a tory in disguise, he narrowly lost. In November 1868, at the general election, against the same opponent but on a greatly enlarged electoral register, he triumphed. Campbell represented Stirling Burghs without interruption for the rest of his parliamentary career.

Both Campbell-Bannermans valued their creature comforts highly. In London they lived in a series of large, well-appointed houses at convenient, fashionable addresses. The weekends they spent at Gennings, a country property CB had inherited near Maidstone, Kent. In 1884 he bought Belmont Castle, at Meigle, Perthshire, after restoration and extension their much loved Scottish home. For forty years their annual routine scarcely changed. When parliament was in session they lived in London. When London became too oppressive they would spend a few days at Dover, at the Lord Warden Hotel. CB's favoured form of exercise was to sit for hours on the pier reading one of his beloved French novels. They always went to Paris for Easter. In June and July, which became established as the season for speech making in the country, they were in Scotland. Then from August to October they invariably travelled on the continent, with six weeks reserved for the 'cure' at Marienbad. Their European peregrination always ended in Paris. The autumn parliamentary session found them once more in London, and the year ended as it had begun, entertaining friends at Belmont.

From the first, CB enthusiastically embraced parliament's time-worn conventions. Theatricality, excitement, verbal dexterity, and repartee never fail to please the House of Commons, and CB was eager to oblige. He proved a rather dull dog, hopeless at extempore exchange, easily flustered if interrupted. His speeches were carefully prepared, succinct, persuasive, but, for the most part, read. Myopia obliged him to hold his notes close to his face. He rarely attracted the attention of his auditors, so consequently was discounted as, at best, a mediocre parliamentary performer. Nevertheless, after only three years, he was promoted from the back benches.

Edward Cardwell needed a financial secretary to secure economies at the War Office, and in November 1871 he chose CB for this key appointment. Courageous, determined, impervious to parliamentary criticism, Cardwell made the ideal ministerial mentor and exercised a powerful influence over his junior colleague's subsequent parliamentary career. A change of government in 1874 sent Cardwell to the Lords, and CB became Liberal spokesman on defence in the Commons. He did not make the most of his opportunity and entirely failed to impress the house. In April 1880, when the Liberals returned to power, he did not gain promotion but returned to the War Office, this time to serve under the less than inspiring Hugh Childers. The department was beset by difficulties: war in the Transvaal and, even more distracting, a struggle with the crown over the appointment of Garnet Wolseley as adjutant-general. CB was delivered from these problems when, in May 1882, he was transferred to the Admiralty. There his officials were surprised, then impressed, by his quiet authority and efficient dispatch of business. The unexpected, unintended 'reward' for his political acuity in helping to defuse a naval scare campaign was to be offered, in October 1884, 'the most disagreeable post in the public service' (Rosebery to CB, 26 Oct 1884, BL, Add. MS 41226, fol. 100), the Irish chief secretaryship.

Irish chief secretary and home rule Others had been offered the appointment and refused. CB accepted only because Charlotte pressed him to seize the opportunity. At Westminster the Irish nationalist MPs could scarcely contain their eagerness to rend this new secretary, whose previous small reputation suggested an easy victim. To their amazement, they found no weaknesses in his armour. He 'laughed at their vituperation and was jaunty under their cyclone of attack' (O'Connor, 26). While his duties were heavy and exacting, they were made easier by his excellent relationship with the viceroy, Spencer, who considered CB the ideal parliamentary spokesman. Though he was chief secretary for only seven months, until the fall of Gladstone's government in June 1885, this proved long enough for CB's reputation and status to be utterly transformed.

On the problem of Ireland's future, CB's general election address in November 1885 was ambivalent. The flight of the 'Hawarden kite' in December revealed that Gladstone favoured an Irish parliament. Until Salisbury's intransigence on the Union was declared CB clung to the possibility of compromise. Only after a period of further doubt and misgiving did he declare his support for Gladstone. He admitted on several occasions that his thinking had been inconsistent. The 'indispensable condition' that finally determined his support for home rule was that there should be 'an end to agitation' (CB to Sir H. James, 21 July 1886, BL, Add. MS 41232, fol. 300). But Gladstone's proposals, far from ending agitation, divided the Liberal Party and ensured its defeat in the Commons in June 1886 and its electoral rout in the country in July 1886. Despite this political shambles, CB spoke warmly and eloquently for home rule and expressed unqualified support and admiration for Gladstone. When the Liberals again took office, in 1892, their parliamentary majority was too small to secure home rule. Nevertheless, a bill that CB helped to draft was prepared. Though secretary of state for war, CB chose to ignore the declared concerns of the army and lightly dismissed Ulster's opposition as 'Ulsteria'. The bill was slain in the Lords. Public opposition to home rule was overwhelming. Gladstone capitulated, and Ireland's governance became a dormant issue at Westminster.

Cabinet minister: the War Office, 1886, 1892–1895 Campbell-Bannerman was forty-nine when, in February 1886, he entered the cabinet in Gladstone's third government as secretary of state for war. Gladstone would have preferred Childers but deferred to the queen, who insisted she wanted CB. The ministry was no sinecure, and even his first brief tenancy made CB aware of how much the queen interfered, listening to her soldiers rather than to her ministers. Once more in opposition CB proved effective and vigorous. In 1888 he joined somewhat reluctantly Hartington's commission of inquiry into the army's civil and professional administration. He opposed the proposed appointment of a chief of staff because his time at the War Office had impressed him with how senior officers constantly sought to interfere with the minister's decisions. He demonstrated the typical Liberal distrust of militarism and, as a devoted Cardwellian, argued there was no need of any further immediate military reform.

In August 1892 Campbell-Bannerman returned to the War Office, with a seat in the cabinet, in Gladstone's fourth administration, and he retained that office when Rosebery succeeded Gladstone as prime minister in 1894. As minister for war he proposed a series of changes embodying those among the recommendations of the Hartington commission that he approved. He was well aware that, for any reform to succeed, the queen's elderly cousin would have to resign as commander-in-chief. The problem was that George Cambridge was resolutely opposed to resigning. There could be no better testimony to CB's determination, patience, resource, and tact than that, in a mere six weeks, he persuaded the duke to resign, in June 1895. At this moment of triumph the opposition censured CB for compromising the nation's safety by providing insufficient small-arms ammunition and cordite. The charge was false, but CB's rebuttal was unconvincing, and the government was narrowly defeated on St John Brodrick's motion in the House of Commons on 21 June 1895. Had the government been so minded the vote could easily have been reversed. Instead they chose to depart, Rosebery loudly insisting that a cabinet without CB as his colleague was unthinkable. The award of a GCB acknowledged not only Rosebery's genuine appreciation of his worth, but also the queen's gratitude at CB's sensitive handling of her uncle's 'resignation'.

In opposition the Unionists had excoriated CB's military reforms as entirely inadequate. In government they were obliged to admit that their own proposals were very little different. CB had been a popular minister with soldiers and civilian advisers alike. Of the ministers with whom he had dealings, Wolseley thought CB much the most capable. CB insisted that his responsibilities were not to be shared or limited, though this never prompted any greater activity on his part or willingness to master the fine details of any brief. What he did demonstrate was the happy, priceless ability to eviscerate verbiage to expose the heart of any matter. Now when he spoke to parliament on defence it was as one thoroughly familiar with military matters. He robustly defended Cardwell's system in the army estimate debates of 1898, and in October 1899, expressing satisfaction with the army's mobilization, he boasted that Cardwell's reforms had entirely fulfilled their purpose and confounded the critics—a reflection that proved somewhat premature. He made nonsense of the military reforms proposed by Unionist secretaries of state, and his frequent assertion that conscription was 'impossible' pleased almost all kinds and conditions of Liberals.

Liberal leadership in the Commons In February 1894 *The Spectator* nominated CB as 'the dark horse in any future liberal leadership stakes' and as the 'only person capable of stilling the fierce conflicts' (*The Spectator*, 17 Feb 1894). Few would have agreed and many would have shared Esher's estimate that, 'compared with his colleagues', CB was 'very undistinguished' (*Journals and Letters*, 1.181). Far from coveting the party leadership, CB sought the speakership, as it offered an honourable escape from the wrangles of party politics and would allow more time for him to be with Charlotte, whose deteriorating health was a cause of much concern. His initiative startled and discomfited some colleagues, while others supposed he was not being serious. When he pressed his claim, Rosebery told him bluntly that his services could not be spared. CB fumed that his modest, legitimate request should be frustrated. A second appeal to Rosebery proved equally unavailing. Reluctantly CB acknowledged that, apparently, his unavoidable fate was to be a permanent party protagonist.

Following Gladstone's retirement the Liberals were in a hapless state, the parliamentary party riven by jealousy and discontent. Rosebery had every reason to appreciate CB's quiet loyalty. Possessing neither the character nor the will to face down the formidable obstacles confronting his leadership, Rosebery resigned in October 1896. Sir William Harcourt succeeded as Liberal leader in the Commons, but from the beginning his credibility was undermined by the general belief that, when it suited Rosebery, he would resume the leadership. By December 1898 Harcourt had endured enough. Unintentionally, John Morley forfeited his chance to succeed by too close association with Harcourt's resignation. Rosebery declined the reversion, so the choice was confined to the four remaining former cabinet ministers: Bryce, Fowler, Asquith, and CB. Somewhat surprisingly CB emerged as favourite. He was dismissed disparagingly by *The Times* as 'a temporary leader who will serve adequately enough as a warming pan until a more commanding figure emerges' (*The Times*, 17 Jan 1899). In February 1899, at the Reform Club, CB was unanimously confirmed as Liberal leader in the Commons. Not alone among commentators, J. A. Spender noted CB's anomalous position as the leader of a party 'whose men of greatest reputation' stood outside presenting a 'disturbing, inscrutable threat' (*Westminster Gazette*, 6 Feb 1899).

The Second South African War There were those Liberals who would have been happy had CB denounced the Liberal Imperialists as heretics, but in his public statements he strove not to offend Roseberyite sensibilities. These efforts to emphasize Liberal unity came to nothing when war in South Africa exacerbated and emphasized differences. CB never doubted that it was 'Joe's war', and that it had been Joseph Chamberlain's 'policy of bluff' that had fomented the conflict (CB to David Bannerman, 25 Oct 1899, BL, Add. MS 41246, fol. 73). But, as the leader of a national party in wartime, he believed it was not proper to express such views publicly. Nor did he wish to widen the breach with the Liberal Imperialists, despite their showing an almost indecent enthusiasm for the Unionist government's conduct. To pro-Boer Liberals, the issue was perfectly simple. There could be no future for Liberalism if it chose to acquiesce in what was 'morally detestable' (Channing to CB, 19 Nov 1899, Koss, *Pro-Boers*, xxvi).

To rumours of an imminent general election, CB had affected indifference. Military successes in the summer of 1900 tempted the government to seek a mandate from the country. CB, who was at Marienbad, did not return to England until five days after parliament's dissolution. For the Liberal Party, prospects could not have been blacker. Their organization was in hopeless disarray, they were short of money, and there was a jingo spirit abroad in the towns that it was assumed would favour the government. CB determined it would be best to husband their few resources. His unquenchable enthusiasm and optimism boosted morale, stilled panic, and rallied Liberals to fight in a common cause. The result of the election was not determined, as so many supposed, by jingo passions but by voter apathy. The Unionist majority scarcely increased, and CB's electoral strategy was completely vindicated. Wisely he discounted the unanimous approval of his leadership, warning friends that extremists in the party—he identified the Roseberyites as the most insidious and deadly—would magnify small differences into mighty schisms.

The government had assumed that the war was all but won when the Boers successfully adopted guerrilla tactics. The British army responded by burning Boer farms and interning Boer families. On 14 June 1901, at a dinner in London given by the National Reform Union, CB passionately condemned these tactics as 'methods of barbarism' (*The Times*, 15 July 1901). The extempore comment excited praise and derision in equal measure. It was no less than his heartfelt response to the bombastic policy that he considered unworthy and stupid. He blamed his political opponents, but they accused him of slandering British troops when for the past eighteen months he had consistently extolled the army's humanity, discipline, and generosity. No fewer than fifty Liberal Imperialist MPs demonstrated their disgust and dissatisfaction with CB's leadership by walking out of the Commons and refusing to support a radical motion condemning the concentration camps. The short-lived 'war to the knife and fork' (Lucy, 85) that followed provided the ludicrous spectacle of pro-Boer and imperialist Liberals attempting to dine and counter-dine each other out of existence. Just as suddenly they determined to kiss and make up, declaring unanimous belief in CB's leadership.

Rosebery still retained his powerful hold over the public imagination. 'I would like to bite him harder', CB confided to Ripon, 'but it would not do to outrun the general feeling' (CB to Ripon, 28 Nov 1901; Strong, 143). At Chesterfield, on 16 December 1901, Rosebery, seeking to recast Liberalism in his own image, implored Liberals to abandon obsolete policies and adopt a 'clean slate'. At last it seemed that Rosebery was to give up his self-imposed exile. But the psychological moment to strike came and went. CB delayed his response until 19 February 1902. Then, at Leicester, he thrilled his audience with a powerful avowal that, as a convinced, impenitent Liberal, *he* would never abandon a single tenet of his faith. When Rosebery was made president of the Liberal League, the breach between the two men was institutionalized. CB was contemptuously tolerant of a body whose *raison d'être* was to promote Rosebery. It failed hopelessly, and the earl was reduced to complaints in the press that he had effectively been excommunicated by CB. Reserved animosity between the two was briefly breached when, during the tariff reform controversy, Rosebery so far forgot himself as to call for Liberal unity. As on numerous previous occasions, CB extended a sceptical welcome to no avail.

Self-inflicted Liberal wounds were soothed by peace in South Africa, a process enhanced by a royal commission report that condemned the government's unpreparedness in 1899. Salisbury's resignation, and the succession as Unionist leader and prime minister by his nephew Arthur Balfour, signalled a significant turn of the tide of British opinion. Attention switched from foreign to domestic issues, from stale Liberal dissension to Unionist disagreements. Balfour's Education Act of 1902 did more than rouse nonconformist anger; miraculously it united Liberals in opposition. CB censured Balfour's measure as much because it denied democratic as religious rights. He was determined to retain nonconformist support and not repeat Gladstone's mistake of 1874. The immediate political advantage for the Liberals was a spate of spectacular and unexpected by-election victories. When Chamberlain, in May 1903, launched his tariff reform campaign, CB immediately condemned it root and branch, yet advised patience, not confrontation, as the better tactic, for it would allow time for Unionist differences to fester. It was his equally shrewd decision to concentrate the campaign for free trade in the country rather than at Westminster. The hapless Unionists damaged themselves further by approving Milner's scheme to employ indentured Chinese labourers in the Transvaal goldmines, an issue that excited a host of powerful prejudices in the minds of the electorate.

By the end of the parliamentary session in 1904, indifferent health, domestic anxiety, and political strain had reduced CB to utter exhaustion. Yet he returned from his customary long continental holiday apparently as vigorous and determined as ever. He told the Irish nationalists that immediate home rule was impractical and offered instead a gradualist policy of amelioration. To this, John Redmond, leader of the Irish party, somewhat surprisingly agreed, promising in addition that he would use his best efforts to secure the Irish vote for the Liberals, considered vital for electoral success. This was an extraordinary tribute to the trust and affection in which CB was held by the nationalists. With the concurrence of Asquith and Grey, CB publicly announced at Stirling, on 23 November 1905, his step-by-step policy, while reaffirming Liberal support for eventual Irish self-rule. This last provoked Rosebery to sever any remaining connection with CB. It was a disastrous miscalculation that left Rosebery politically isolated and powerless. At last CB was freed of his greatest political incubus. With courage, determination, principled politics, and shrewd tactics, the temporary incumbent of six years earlier had strengthened his hold on the Liberal leadership. Unionist hubris, incompetence, and division had eased CB's task, while death, disease, and finally political miscalculation had successively removed his rivals. But fortune rewarded his resolution only after many sore trials. He had never sacrificed his innate modesty, and with rare selflessness had invariably put his party before his own success. Only a truly gifted leader could have forged out of powerless, disaffected fragments a viable anti-Unionist coalition that embraced a motley collection of whigs, Gladstonian Liberals, radicals, progressives, Lib–Lab trade unionists, and ex-Unionist free-traders. Ever the political realist, CB did not allow euphoria to betray his hard-won success. Liberal homogeneity, he acknowledged, was more apparent than real. The party he led remained, at best, a fragile coalition.

Appointed premier, December 1905 Supposing that Rosebery's outburst signalled renewed Liberal strife, Balfour resigned as prime minister on 4 December 1905 without seeking a dissolution. Minority government had been a dilemma that many Liberals had anticipated with dread. It was not a prospect that held any fears for CB. On 5 December 1905 he happily accepted the king's commission and selected a cabinet that reflected every aspect of the Liberal coalition, rewarding old friends, acknowledging talent, indulging sentiment, and encouraging promise. Three of Rosebery's senior lieutenants, fearing the prospect of a 'little England' administration led by a man they supposed a weak, tired mediocrity, had earlier agreed among themselves to refuse office unless CB went to the Lords. This outrageous proposal would have made him prime minister in name only. CB successfully called their bluff. Despite their perfidy, he offered them three key cabinet posts: the exchequer, and the Foreign and War offices. Asquith's presence in a Liberal cabinet had always been indispensable, whereas Grey and Haldane were given high office partly to reassure the Roseberyites but mainly to enhance the chances of a Liberal victory at the impending general election, for the new government immediately dissolved parliament.

The speech with which CB launched the electoral campaign at the Albert Hall, on 21 December 1905, received the kind of rapturous acclaim that previously Gladstone alone had commanded. Unionist failings were highlighted. Although old-age pensions were not mentioned, the speech skilfully suggested long-held Liberal aspirations were about to be rewarded. CB firmly nailed free-trade colours to the Liberal mast, the better to promote party unity and induce Unionist discord. Balfour supposed that CB was the helpless hostage of wild revolutionaries, whereas the bulk of the party, CB very well knew, were of a decidedly cautious and centrist disposition. Consequently his speech was descriptive, not prescriptive, and instead of a programme he offered an electoral slogan redolent of the past: 'peace, retrenchment, and reform'. In the polling, which took place during January 1906, the Liberals swept to a landslide victory. CB's considerable contribution was rightly acknowledged, but the result largely reflected the electorate's dissatisfaction with the Unionists. When he met the new Commons, his assured and effective performances from the dispatch box—most notably his verbal lashing of Balfour's dialectical meanderings as 'foolery'—roused Liberals to a frenzy of enthusiasm. Deservedly he basked in their respect and affection, 'the great, outstanding personality of the new Ministry, dwarfing and submerging all the others' (O'Connor, 87). It was a fitting culmination to a remarkable parliamentary journey: from respectable obscurity to leadership; from obloquy to popularity, praise, and affectionate admiration.

House of Lords, South Africa, and women's suffrage To satisfy the nonconformists, the legislative priority consisted of two bills, on education and temperance. Also, to retain support from the Irish nationalists, legislation short of home rule was required. All these plans were thwarted by the opposition of the House of Lords. Liberal administrations customarily suffered at the hands of the upper house. CB on numerous previous occasions had condemned the absurdity of parliament's second chamber behaving as though it were an annexe of the Unionist Party. In 1894 he had advised the queen that one day the Lords' behaviour would inevitably lead to deadlock and constitutional chaos. Now the Lords, at Balfour's direct behest, were mutilating and destroying Liberal measures. CB angrily insisted that democracy would triumph and the will of the people prevail, yet counselled patience rather than confrontation. It is uncertain whether he desired that the Lords be given the opportunity to mend themselves, or thoroughly to alienate the electorate by their intemperate behaviour. Technically his tactics were wise, but his nonconformist supporters in particular grew frustrated and resentful. They supposed that their prime minister lacked the political will for a fight. Meanwhile, CB wisely rejected a proposal from a cabinet committee to reform the composition of the Lords. He recognized the priority was to resolve relations between the two houses. He persuaded cabinet colleagues to accept the suspensory veto, and introduced the measure on 24 June 1907 with arguably the most impressive speech he ever made to the Commons—all the more remarkable for its being made the day after he suffered a heart attack. The problem of the Lords was not solved in CB's lifetime, but he effectively determined his successor's path towards the 1911 Parliament Act.

During the Second South African War CB had declared publicly that the former Boer republics should be returned to self-government, and he never wavered from that belief. The Colonial Office did not share his opinion, but he rejected their advice, together with that of a cabinet committee. Virtually single-handed he persuaded his colleagues to return self-government to the Transvaal and the Orange River Colony. In August 1906 he was able to circumvent the Lords' veto by an order in council, thus giving South Africa what he could not give Ireland. His magnanimous act of statesmanship hastened the South African Act of Union of 1910 and secured friendship and trust from a generation of South African political leaders.

On constitutional issues CB's record was not entirely beyond reproach. He was a sympathetic but not enthusiastic supporter of votes for women. As party leader he not unreasonably refused to pledge Liberals on an issue peripheral to the main political debates and upon which they were divided. On 19 May 1906 he told a deputation led by Emily Davies that he considered their case conclusive and irrefutable, but he nevertheless counselled them to be patient and to continue lobbying—advice that encouraged the constitutionalists but enraged the militants. In 1906 and again in 1907 private members' bills for women's franchise were talked out of the house. CB's attitude has been well described as 'friendly but timid' (Rover, 122). His unspoken concern was that, if women were enfranchised, it might serve Unionist more than Liberal interests.

Progressivism and Labour In the public mind the radical prime minister was associated with the new Liberalism of C. F. G. Masterman and the *Daily News*. Many had hoped, though some dreaded, that the Liberals would introduce a vigorous programme of economic and social reforms. As opposition leader CB had frequently been urged to sponsor a disparate range of progressive measures. His election address had included the promise to modernize the poor law, alleviate unemployment, and improve conditions in the sweated industries. He was deeply and genuinely concerned about the plight of the poor and so had readily adopted the rhetoric of progressivism, but he was not a progressive. This was not, as Haldane suggested, because he was 'a dear old Tory ... determined to do little' (Wilson, 500). CB was old and set in his ways, and he remained what he had for so long been: a Gladstonian Liberal. In office, like Gladstone, he proved a better constitutional than social reformer. His attachment to orthodox Gladstonian economics prompted his desire to reduce public expenditure. This appeared to be at odds with the financial implications of any ambitious reform scheme. What mattered most to CB, however, was the knowledge that social reform divided Liberals, whereas party unity was his major concern.

Was the progressive anti-Unionist alliance that CB had helped to forge no more than a convenient electoral device? Labour and Liberal politicians traditionally adopted different views on how to improve working-class conditions. Judgements differed whether it was possible, even desirable, to create a single, progressive party sheltering Labour and Liberal views and uniting the radical vote. A party that sounded and acted so differently when street-corner evangelizing as socialist and debating at Westminster as Labour necessarily prompted ambivalence in the most sympathetic Liberal mind. CB never took Labour's taunts and propaganda seriously. He did not believe that socialism was about to replace Liberalism. He had been closely associated with the 1903 electoral pact between the Liberal chief whip, Herbert Gladstone, and Ramsay MacDonald on behalf of the Labour Representation Committee, which, while it ensured that Labour candidates would be unopposed by Liberals, had been designed to serve Liberal as much as Labour interests. He did not suppose that he had gullibly 'afforded room to the Socialist cuckoo in the Liberal nest' (Douglas, xii). Nor was he unduly concerned about Labour intervention in by-elections. For personal as much as political reasons he had appointed John Burns a minister.

That CB's sympathy for many Labour aspirations was genuine is well illustrated by his conduct over the Trade Disputes Bill (1906). Against his instincts, he had deferred to a majority cabinet decision that legislation to reverse the Taff Vale judgement should restore limited rights only to trade unions. To the consternation and amazement of colleagues, on the floor of the Commons he spoke, then voted, for a Labour-sponsored bill. Despite the formidable opposition of Liberal lawyers and senior colleagues, he succeeded in embodying the total immunity of the Labour bill into the government's legislation. Labour and Liberal differences concerning the treatment of trade unions were of long standing. CB had always tended to favour Labour's views, and fifteen years earlier he had been censured by Elgin for supporting striking railway workers. Although CB personally liked and got on well with most Labour leaders, his sympathy for their proposals never implied commitment. Arthur Ponsonby, CB's secretary and himself a Labour sympathizer, noted that the prime minister was always anxious that his administration should never be thought to be 'in the hands and at the mercy of Labour' (Ponsonby to Bryce, 24 May 1907; Harris and Hazlehurst, 377).

Despite trials and tribulations, CB's administration secured a number of important social reforms. What it achieved was consistent with traditional Liberal values, and because it did not challenge Unionist interests it was not destroyed in the Lords. There was legislation concerning factories, workshops, and mines and workmen's compensation. Perhaps most significantly, the groundwork was laid for major reforms later achieved under Asquith's leadership. The budget of 1907 trailed provision for the funding necessary for old-age pensions. Given CB's views on economics, it was no accident that part of the financial strategy to secure funding for pensions was to effect economy in the spending upon the armed forces.

Defence policy Most Liberals thought the army a waste of time and money. Radicals—the loudest, most scathing anti-militarists—neither liked nor trusted Haldane, the secretary of state for war, but supposed he would 'be compelled to abjure his heresies and support the democratic policies of his chief' (*Concord*, January 1906, 4). CB knew that Haldane was an incorrigible conspirator, but acknowledged he was also an able administrator, capable, as few others were, of undertaking required army reforms. Haldane assiduously cultivated the support of the prime minister, whom he had not supported when in opposition. It was given unstintingly. Both prime minister and secretary of state recognized that 'the inevitable result of failure' would be 'an agitation for compulsion'—that is, compulsory military service (Haldane to J. A. Spender, 26 Feb 1907; Koss, *Haldane*, 51). Haldane's restoration of the essential features of Edward Cardwell's system of army organization mollified CB. But he also saw, despite the opacity of Haldane's rhetoric, the minister's conceptual clarity, placing economy and voluntarism—both sound Liberal principles—at the heart of his proposals.

Disowning responsibility for increased costs in his department, Haldane happily and frequently emphasized that foreign and defence policies are complementary. Diplomatic apprehensions about Germany's hostile intent were immediately reflected in increased estimates for the Admiralty. The problem was exacerbated when the launch of the first Dreadnought battleship in 1906 transformed naval strategy, technology, and economy. Privately CB thought continued observance of the two-power naval building standard irrational. He proposed a cut in the capital shipbuilding programme with the caveat that, if the peace conference at The Hague in 1907 failed, the cut would be reversed. On the eve of the conference CB published in *The Nation* (March 1907) some anodyne proposals for armament cuts. They reflected his generous, trusting nature, but the Germans perversely saw it as a plot to secure permanent British naval supremacy. So CB's single foray into public diplomacy proved an abject failure. Naval 'economists' who had been elated by CB's proposals were now instead obliged to deplore a small rise in the 1908 naval estimates. CB was well aware that selfish departmental imperatives were driving ever upwards the estimates of the armed services. He was uneasy at the constant lobbying and squabbling for increased funding. Had the committee of imperial defence (CID) fulfilled its intended role, that would have helped resolve the difficulties. He changed his earlier opinion that the CID was a mischievous assembly, but he never fully exploited its potential.

Foreign policy Radicals, who were averse to the notion of continuity, wanted a progressive foreign policy distinct from that pursued by the Unionists. They dubbed CB's election address the 'league of peace' speech, emphasizing his opposition to aggression and support for disarmament; they thereby chose to ignore his equally clear statement that foreign policy would continue upon existing lines. In December 1905 a demoralized France, bullied in Morocco by Germany, wished to discover exactly what Britain would do if war broke out with Germany. Grey approved military and naval conversations between the military and naval staff of both countries. CB agreed though he had misgivings, as he recognized joint preparations for a war came uncomfortably close to an honourable undertaking. He did not inform certain senior cabinet colleagues about these arrangements because he expected their opposition. Knowledge of the conversations became general only after CB's death. Radicals argued either that he had not known of the talks or that he had been deliberately misled by Grey as to their significance. Grey, they maintained, was the willing accomplice—some even suggested cipher—of his anti-German permanent officials at the Foreign Office, or else he had been duped by French chauvinists. CB had supported Grey but, making no allowance for diplomatic or military initiative, had naïvely assumed, or hoped, that no further commitment was implied. This was the limited view he advertised to Clemenceau in April 1907. The French premier was shocked and angered by what Cambon, with unfailing diplomatic finesse, described as 'un petit malentendu' (Wilson, 544). When the two premiers next met, in January 1908, there was no repeat of the misunderstanding.

Many Liberals condemned negotiations with Russia, begun in July 1906, as politically unacceptable—a moral affront and a diplomatic disaster. CB considered these criticisms ill-informed. The tsar's ill-advised dissolution of the Russian parliament appeared to ruin any chance of a diplomatic agreement. CB, who that day was due to address the Interparliamentary Union, immediately added a postscript to his speech, 'La Douma est morte—Vive la Douma' (23 July 1907; Spender, pl. facing 2.264). His audience, which included Russian delegates, greeted his peroration with wild enthusiasm. It was a further example of CB's extraordinary ability exactly to capture a public mood or sentiment in a few simple, sincere words. At the end of August 1907 the Anglo-Russian agreement was signed, and CB was the first to congratulate Grey for 'a great achievement that … [would] make things easier in Europe' (CB to Grey, 3 Sept 1907; Trevelyan, 189). Those who condemned the agreement as designed to isolate Germany diplomatically later perversely argued that CB had opposed Grey's Russian policy.

Conduct of the cabinet and prime ministerial routine It was CB's policy never to interfere more than absolutely necessary in the affairs of any department of state, and this undoubtedly exaggerated the Foreign Office's already notorious independence. Never pretending to the part of a dynamic, innovative leader such as Gladstone, CB managed, facilitated, and mediated the work of his colleagues. He never sought to steal the limelight, for he lusted neither for prizes nor for personal glory. If the occasion required he never hesitated to demonstrate his authority, for he knew his own mind and was determined, but invariably tactful. Given the fragile unity of the Liberals, there was much to recommend his cautious, quietist approach. His emollient wisdom kept the cabinet 'peculiarly and happily free from personal differences and restlessness' (Grey, 1.67). Nevertheless, there were reservations about his style of managing the cabinet. Haldane likened it to 'a meeting of delegates'. He criticized CB for 'insufficient consultation … relying unduly upon the initiative of individual ministers'. Yet Haldane acknowledged that, once the prime minister's confidence was secured, 'there were few better chiefs to work for' (Haldane, 182, 217–18). Everyone who worked with CB had reason to appreciate his spontaneity, generosity, and kind-heartedness. What was not always realized was that although he readily forgave he did not so easily forget. His private secretary noted that CB was 'outwardly easy-going … inwardly … firm and resolute' (Hirst, 262). The suggestion by some critics that CB's *laissez-faire* attitude reflected indolence is incorrect: he was never lethargic or indifferent.

Trivial routine and lesser activities occupied CB's days as much as grave matters of state. As a Presbyterian, he professed not to know what a rural dean was, yet for someone who was a lifelong advocate of disestablishment he took inordinate pains over church preferments. 'You said I never acted on your advice', he wrote to his friend Archbishop Randall Davidson, 'But you will be lenient to my doubts and perplexities!' (CB to Davidson, 5 Nov 1907; Bell, 1239). Averse to high-churchmen, he sought to promote evangelicals, his intention bolstered by the opposition of a predominantly Anglo-Catholic bench of bishops in the Lords to the government's education bills. But, as he enquired with mock bemusement of Spence Watson, the Quaker president of the National Liberal Federation, 'What is a poor devil to do when all the new school of Church Liberals are Sacerdotalists and the Evangelicals of note, pronounced Tories?' (CB to Spence Watson, 13 July 1907; BL, Add. MS 41242, fol. 254).

CB was noted for his pawky sense of humour, and few subjects were as unfailing a source of amusement to him as the effrontery, exaggerated expectation, and obvious unsuitability of many who sought inclusion in the honours list. The party had been long out of power, and now the importunate faithful expected their reward. On occasion CB was overgenerous, but he was genuinely alarmed to discover the large sums routinely extracted from ambitious petitioners by the Liberal chief whip. Despite his disapproval, the time-dishonoured traffic continued unabated. He refused an earldom for Curzon on the grounds that it was absurd to recommend what the viceroy's own political friends had denied. This argument did not impress the king, who supported Curzon's claim.

Edward VII enjoyed his prime minister's company when taking the cure at Marienbad, but generally their relationship was fraught with niggling difficulties rooted in the king's antipathy to CB's political beliefs. The king disapproved of his behaviour during the Second South African War, particularly the 'methods of barbarism' speech, he deprecated CB writing about disarmament in a radical journal, he was horrified as much as amazed that he agreed with female enfranchisement, he was angered by CB's failure to curb the more extravagant language of young colleagues, and he blamed him for exacerbating the clashes between the Commons and the Lords. Edward was much exasperated, and not entirely without reason, by the meagreness of CB's cabinet letters. CB informed Knollys that he was sorry to have earned the king's displeasure but, characteristically, proffered no apology. He found that cabinet meetings were generally tedious and saw no reason why he should pretend otherwise merely to amuse the king. It was typical of their relationship that Edward discouraged CB, despite the prime minister's mortal illness, from returning too soon, so that he would not be incommoded by having to cut short his holiday at Biarritz.

Bereavement and death During CB's comparatively short time as prime minister his energy was eroded by illness, age, and grief. Much the most severe blow he suffered was the death of his beloved wife, on 30 August 1906, from which he never fully recovered, emotionally or physically. Charlotte's illness had grown increasingly painful and debilitating. Through every crisis CB nursed her with tender care and anxious devotion. He readily acknowledged to Knollys that the time and energy he gave unstintingly to his wife meant that he neglected his prime-ministerial duties. He knew this was not right, but he could do no other. Never were a couple more devoted than Henry and Charlotte: 'their hearts were as one' (from the lines of Tasso chosen by CB to be inscribed on his wife's memorial tablet in Meigle church).

Shortly after Charlotte's death, CB suffered the first of a series of progressively more serious and damaging heart attacks. Each time he appeared to have made a rapid and full recovery. He returned to Westminster, made speeches in the country, carried out his official duties, and even visited Paris and Biarritz. But these jaunts did not have the savour of earlier visits to the continent, and CB grew increasingly fatigued. His illness was kept from the public until a fourth attack, which was particularly sharp and debilitating, in late November 1907. Asquith, as crown prince, increasingly handled the reins of power, but CB did not formally resign office until 4 April 1908. He died on the morning of 22 April 1908 while still in residence at 10 Downing Street. Generous tributes were paid CB in parliament, and an impressive service was held at Westminster Abbey. Arthur Ponsonby was not so much impressed by the establishment's conventional obsequies at the death of a prime minister as he was by the intense reverence and sympathy etched on the faces of the silent masses in the streets mourning the passing of a much loved old man. As CB's coffin sped north for interment on 28 April next to Charlotte's in Meigle churchyard, groups of railwaymen stood bare-headed at the railway side, paying silent tribute to a good man.

CB in history In the debates between historians about Labour's rise to power and what George Dangerfield characterized as Liberal England's strange death, where the focus has been personality it has concentrated almost exclusively upon CB's successors as prime minister, Asquith and Lloyd George. The leader who, more than any other, made possible the Liberal decade of dominance has been relatively ignored. Yet CB has been fortunate in his two major biographers, J. A. Spender and John Wilson. Though not an intimate, Spender knew CB well and was thoroughly familiar with the contemporary political scene. CB's official life, published in 1923, is detailed, unvarnished, and straightforward. Radical and Labour critics complained that it insufficiently emphasized CB's supposedly distinctive views on peace, disarmament, and the conduct of foreign affairs. Ponsonby supposed Spender had fallen into error not only because of his Liberal Imperialist sympathies but also because he effectively ignored the memoir of CB that he (Ponsonby) had written. Despite their considerable value, especially on domestic issues during CB's premiership, Ponsonby's notes are not particularly reliable on military and diplomatic issues, as his memory was coloured by the events of the First World War. F. W. Hirst used the notes in writing an idealized portrait of CB that concludes with the assurance: 'he kept the faith to the end and was no way responsible for the European tragedy that came to pass six years after his death' (Hirst, 265). Wilson's biography, published in 1973, is worldly-wise in its judgements; scholarly and subtly nuanced, it does justice to CB as a man and a politician. It confirms the broad outlines of Spender's earlier work. Some reservation has been expressed that his account is stronger on character than interpretation. The torrents of monographs and articles analysing so many aspects of Victorian and Edwardian political life, as well as the further release of private papers, have, it is true, added considerable detail. Yet they do not suggest any need for major revision of the viewpoint taken in Wilson's balanced, persuasive portrait of Britain's first and only radical prime minister. A. J. A. MORRIS

Sources BL, Campbell-Bannerman papers • J. A. Spender, *The life of the Rt. Hon. Sir Henry Campbell-Bannerman, GCB*, 2 vols. (1923) • J. Wilson, *CB: the life of Sir Henry Campbell-Bannerman* (1973) • T. P. O'Connor, *Sir Henry Campbell-Bannerman* (1908) • *DNB* • J. F. Harris and C. Hazlehurst, 'Campbell-Bannerman as prime minister', *History*, 55 (1970), 360–83 • R. Strong, 'Campbell-Bannerman as an opposition leader, 1899–1905', PhD diss., Council for National Academic Awards, 1983 • H. W. Lucy, *The Balfourian parliament, 1900–1906* (1906) • *Journals and letters of Reginald, Viscount Esher*, ed. M. V. Brett and Oliver, Viscount Esher, 4 vols. (1934–8), vols. 1–2 • G. M. Trevelyan, *Grey of Fallodon* (1937) • Viscount Grey of Fallodon [E. Grey], *Twenty-five years, 1892–1916*, 2 vols. (1925) • R. B. Haldane, *Autobiography* (1929) • F. W. Hirst, *In the golden days* (1947) • E. Halévy, *The rule of democracy, 1905–1914* (1934) • S. E. Koss, *Lord Haldane: scapegoat for liberalism* (1969) • C. Rover, *Women's suffrage and party politics, 1866–1914* (1967) • R. Douglas, *History of the liberal party, 1895–1970* (1971) • S. E. Koss, *The pro-Boers* (1973) • G. K. A. Bell, *Randall Davidson, archbishop of Canterbury*, 2 vols. (1935) • R. A. Jones, *Arthur Ponsonby: the politics of life* (1989) • A. J. A. Morris, *Radicalism against war, 1906–14* (1972) • A. J. A. Morris, ed., *Edwardian radicalism, 1900–1914* (1974) • P. Stansky, *Ambitions and strategies* (1964) • H. C. G. Matthew, *The liberal imperialists* (1973) • A. K. Russell, *Liberal landslide: the general election of 1906* (1973) • W. S. Hamer, *The British army: civil–military relations, 1885–1905* (1970) • G. P. Gooch, *British diplomatic documents, 1898–1914* (1926–38)

Archives BL, corresp. and papers, Add. MSS 41206–41252, 52512–52521 • NL Scot., corresp. • NL Wales, letters | BL, corresp. with J. E. Burns, Add. MS 46282 • BL, letters to Sir Guy Fleetwood-Wilson, Add. MS 59846Q • BL, corresp. with Lord Gladstone, Add. MSS 45987–45988 • BL, corresp. with W. E. Gladstone, Add. MS 44117 • BL, corresp. with Lord Ripon, Add. MSS 43517–43518 • BL, corresp. with J. A. Spender, Add. MS 46388 • Bodl. Oxf., corresp. with Herbert Asquith • Bodl. Oxf., corresp. with Sir William Harcourt and Lewis Harcourt • Bodl. Oxf., letters to Lord Kimberley • Bodl. Oxf., corresp. with Lord Ponsonby • CAC Cam., corresp. with David Saunders • CAC Cam., corresp. with W. T. Stead • Cardiff Central Library, letters to Sir Hugh Owen • CKS, letters to Edward Stanhope • CUL, corresp. with Lord Hardinge • Glos. RO, letters to Sir Michael Hicks Beach • HLRO, letters to Herbert Samuel • Hove Central Library, Sussex, letters to Lord Wolseley and Lady Wolseley • King's AC Cam., letters to Oscar Browning • NL Ire., corresp. with John Redmond • NL Scot., letters to A. C. Cunningham • NL Scot., letters to Lord Kimberley • NL Scot., corresp. with Lord Rosebery • NRA Scotland, priv. coll., letters to Lord Aberdeen

Likenesses photograph, 1893, Hult. Arch. • B. Stone, photographs, 1897–8, NPG • G. C. Beresford, photograph, 1902, NPG [*see illus.*] • G. C. Beresford, photogravure, 1902, NPG • H. Speed, chalk drawing, 1907, NPG • Autotype Co., print (after J. H. F. Bacon), NPG • J. H. F. Bacon, portrait; formerly in the Reform Club, 1912 • J. C. Forbes, portrait; formerly in the National Liberal Club, London, 1912 • F. C. Gould, caricatures, ink drawings, NPG • F. C. Gould, watercolour drawing, NPG • J. Guthrie, oils, Scot. NPG • London Stereoscopic Co., photograph, NPG • P. R. Montford, bust, Westminster Abbey • B. Morgan, oils (after J. C. Forbes), National Liberal Club, London • F. Sargent, drawing, repro. in Wilson, *CB*, 144; priv. coll. • Spy [L. Ward], chromolithograph caricature, NPG; repro. in *VF* (10 Aug 1899) • portraits, repro. in Spender, *Life*

Wealth at death £54,908 10*s*. 6*d*.: probate, 2 Nov 1908, *CGPLA Eng. & Wales*

Bannerman, James (1807–1868), Free Church of Scotland minister and theologian, was born on 9 April 1807 in the manse of Cargill, Perthshire, the son of James Patrick Bannerman (*d*. 1807), minister of Cargill. He was educated at Perth Academy and, from 1822, Edinburgh University and Divinity Hall. He was licensed by the presbytery of Perth in January 1833 and, after assisting briefly at Dron, he became minister of Ormiston, in East Lothian, in the August of that year. On 2 April 1839 he married David Anne (*d*. 1879), the daughter of David Douglas, Lord Reston, a senator in the courts of justice. They had three sons and six daughters.

Bannerman played a leading part in the events leading up to the Disruption in 1843. In 1840 the general assembly appointed him as convenor of the committee charged with providing temporary ministers for the contested parishes of Strathbogie; in the same year, he published a *Letter to the Marquis of Tweedale on the Church Question*, a trenchant reply to speeches in support of patronage made at a meeting in Haddington. In 1841 he visited London in a delegation representing the non-intrusionist position to the government. Later he was also prominent in unsuccessful negotiations for the union of the presbyterian churches of Scotland and England. In 1849 he was appointed professor of apologetics and pastoral theology in the Free Church New College in Edinburgh, an office which he held until his death. In 1850 he received a DD from Princeton College, New Jersey.

Bannerman published several theological works: one of the most significant, *Inspiration: the Infallible Truth and Divine Authority of the Holy Scriptures* (1865), was criticized by the theologian A. B. Davidson (1831–1902) for calling forth 'no opposition and no assent' (Drummond and Bulloch, 263). Nevertheless, it sounded a cautious retreat from the fundamentalism of Free Church orthodoxy, as Bannerman dissociated himself from the theory of verbal inspiration and accepted translations (and even paraphrases) as equally valid with the Greek and Hebrew scriptural originals. Also important (but less original) was the posthumous *The Church of Christ* (1868), which was praised by Robert Rainy as 'a fresh statement of our fundamental principles' (Bannerman, 1.viii). Bannerman died in Edinburgh on 27 March 1868. ROSEMARY MITCHELL

Sources *Fasti Scot.*, 1.342–3 • J. A. Wylie, *Disruption worthies: a memorial of 1843*, ed. J. B. Gillies, new edn (1881), 15–22 • A. L. Drummond and J. Bulloch, *The church in Victorian Scotland, 1843–1874* (1975), 263–4 • D. D. Bannerman, 'Editor's preface', in J. Bannerman, *The church of Christ*, 2 vols. (1868), 1.v–ix

Archives NL Scot., papers

Wealth at death £28,775 8*s*. 3*d*.: inventory, 1868, Scotland • £35,085 6*s*. 10*d*.: corrective inventory, 2 Dec 1881, NA Scot., SC70/1/203/885 (1868)

Bannerman, John Macdonald, Baron Bannerman of Kildonan (1901–1969), politician and rugby player, was born at 71 Seymour Street, Crossmyloof, Glasgow, on 1 September 1901, the son of John Roderick Bannerman (*d.* 1938), who was originally from South Uist, and his wife, Mary Macdonald (*d.* 1914/15), whose family came from the Isle of Skye. His paternal great-grandfather's family had been evicted from the Strath of Kildonan during the highland clearances. He grew up in the highland community of Glasgow, where Gaelic was the native tongue, and to all intents and purposes he regarded himself as a highlander. His father had begun his working life as a telegraph boy, but after studying at evening classes rose through the clerical ranks of the General Post Office to become its superintendent in Glasgow, in charge of several hundred men. After the mother's death when he was thirteen, Bannerman's father, who had a great knowledge of Gaelic songs and literature and organized Gaelic cultural activities in Glasgow, was a major influence on him.

Bannerman was educated at Shawlands Academy until the age of thirteen and then at Glasgow high school, where he was captain of the rugby football fifteen (1919–20), before studying at Glasgow University; there he graduated MA and BSc in agriculture in 1926. He then spent three years on a scholarship as a postgraduate in agricultural economics, first at Balliol College, Oxford (1927–9), where he was a rugby blue, and then in the USA (1929–30), mainly at Cornell University.

During the 1920s Bannerman was a celebrated international rugby player. A second-row forward weighing nearly 13 stone, with 'sturdy legs and well muscled shoulders' (*Memoirs*, 57), he won thirty-seven consecutive caps between 1921 and 1929 and was on the winning side on twenty-five occasions. This included the golden period for Scottish rugby in the mid-1920s, when Scotland won the triple crown in 1925; in that season he played in the inaugural match at Murrayfield in which Scotland beat England for the first time since 1912. In all he made nine appearances in the Calcutta cup against England, captaining Scotland in 1929. Throughout his rugby career, in which he later became president of the Scottish Rugby Football Union, he was a strong proponent of the amateur ethos, believing strongly that the game should be primarily for players rather than spectators.

In 1930 Bannerman became farm manager, and then factor, to James Graham, sixth duke of Montrose, the father of his Oxford friend the marquess of Graham, with the responsibility of managing the Graham estates around Loch Lomond. On 8 October 1931 he married Jenny Murray (Ray) Mundell (*b.* 1906/7), the daughter of Walter Mundell of Dalchork near Lairg in Sutherland; they had two sons and two daughters. Bannerman and Montrose were close, and their politics blended. They were Scottish patriots, though not of the republican and separatist kind found in the nationalist organizations of the late 1920s. Both had a liberal outlook, even though the duke took the tory whip in the House of Lords until 1936. It was the duke's involvement with the Scottish Party (formed in 1932 as a right-wing devolutionist counterweight to the more left-wing and separatist National Party of Scotland) that brought Bannerman into active politics. As Montrose's right-hand man, he took part in the public meetings and negotiations that eventually led to the creation of the Scottish National Party in 1934, and campaigned for John MacCormick, the party's leading figure, at Inverness-shire at the general election of 1935.

Like the duke of Montrose, Bannerman grew disillusioned with nationalist politics in the 1930s as interminable arguments about policy and strategy, coupled with poor discipline and organization, blocked electoral progress. Both men ended up in the Liberal Party, Bannerman being adopted as prospective candidate for the Conservative-held seat of Argyll in 1938. When a by-election for the seat arose in 1940, Conservatives in Argyll held out the prospect that he might run as a National Liberal, but negotiations broke down and he decided not to contest the election. At the general election of 1945 he stood for Argyll as a Liberal but came a poor third behind the Conservatives and Labour, a result which was repeated when he stood for the combined Scottish universities at a by-election in 1946. He was unsuccessful in four contests for Inverness (1950, 1954, 1955, and 1959), though he pushed up the Liberal vote (in 1955 he cut the Conservative majority to below 1000) and established a credible Liberal presence in the constituency. He narrowly failed to win Paisley against Labour at a by-election in 1961, but was defeated by an increased margin when he stood for the same seat at the general election of 1964, his final electoral contest.

Bannerman was chairman of the Scottish Liberal Party between 1956 and 1965, presiding over a period of improved fortunes for the organization. He did much to reinforce a distinctive identity for the party north of the border. Following his lead, the party reaffirmed its commitment to Scottish home rule at a time when both the tories and Labour opposed devolution. He was also keen to promote rural issues and highlight the concerns of small-town Scotland. Stress was laid on the need to have good candidates familiar with the locality where they were standing. The strategy paid dividends as, during his period as chairman, the Liberal Party in Scotland increased the number of parliamentary seats which it contested from five to twenty-six, while the number of its MPs rose from one to five, and its membership was boosted. In 1965 he became joint president of the party.

Bannerman ceased to be the duke of Montrose's factor in 1952 in order to concentrate on his own farming interests. He was appointed OBE in 1952 for his services to the Festival of Britain. In 1957 he was elected rector of Aberdeen University. A member of the Forestry Commission from 1942 to 1957 and an active commentator on highland affairs (he was president of An Comunn Galdhealach, the highland association of Scotland), he helped to promote the Highlands and Islands Development Board, which was established in 1965. He broadcast Gaelic programmes on BBC Scotland, regularly appeared on the radio discussion programme *Matter of Opinion*, and took part in fireside ceilidhs on Scottish television.

In December 1967 Bannerman was created a life peer. He used his position in the House of Lords to promote Scottish home rule and the welfare of the highlands and rural communities. One controversial issue was his refusal to vote with the Liberal Party for the renewal of sanctions against Rhodesia, as his old Oxford friend, now the seventh duke of Montrose, was a member of Ian Smith's cabinet. He died at Tidworth, Hampshire, on 10 May 1969. RICHARD J. FINLAY

Sources *The Times* (12 May 1969) • *Bannerman: the memoirs of Lord Bannerman of Kildonan*, ed. J. Fowler (1972) • R. Michie, 'John Bannerman', *Dictionary of liberal biography*, ed. D. Brack and M. Baines (1998) • b. cert. • m. cert. • *WWW* • E. Lemon, ed., *The Balliol College register, 1916–1967*, 4th edn (privately printed, Oxford, 1969) • W. D. Rubinstein, ed., *The biographical dictionary of life peers* (New York, 1991) • F. W. S. Craig, *British parliamentary election results, 1918–1949*, rev. edn (1977) • F. W. S. Craig, *British parliamentary election results, 1950–1970* (1971) • R. J. Finlay, *Independent and free: Scottish politics and the origins of the Scottish national party, 1918–1945* (1994)

Likenesses G. Russell of Paisley, photograph, repro. in Fowler, ed., *Bannerman*, frontispiece • photographs, repro. in Fowler, ed., *Bannerman*

Bannerman, Patrick (1715–1798), Church of Scotland minister and writer on religious and civil liberties, was born at Inveravon, the son of James Bannerman (1670–1758), minister of Inveravon and then of Forglen, Banffshire, and his wife, Ann Cunningham (*d.* 1758), a minister's daughter. Educated at King's College, Aberdeen, between 1730 and 1733, he was licensed by the presbytery of Haddington on 17 April 1739, and ordained at St Madoes in Perthshire on 8 October 1741. He married Beatrix Goldie (*d.* 1792) on 29 June 1742; they had a son, Patrick, who became a merchant in Dunbar in Haddingtonshire. Bannerman was translated to Kinnoull, Perthshire, in 1746, and in 1760 moved to Saltoun, Haddingtonshire, where he spent the remainder of his career.

Bannerman was presented to Saltoun by that parish's patron and leading citizen, Andrew Fletcher, Lord Milton. Yet he soon established a reputation as an adherent to the popular party in the church (the party opposed to leaving the power of clerical calls to parish patrons over the objections of the elders and the congregation) as well as a staunch defender of civil and religious liberty. His first publication, *A Sermon upon Reformation and Revolution Principles* (1751), is a celebration of the civil and religious liberty enjoyed by a nation of Britons and protestants. In 1766 Bannerman introduced into the general assembly an important measure that became known as the 'schism overture', calling for an inquiry into the causes of the rapidly growing secessions from the church, which members of the popular party blamed principally upon the enforcement of patronage. His *Address to the People of Scotland, on Ecclesiastical and Civil Liberty* (1782) advanced the cause of the popular party in its opposition to ecclesiastical patronage not simply on religious grounds, but for the harm it did to piety and morals and, as a result, to virtue and commerce, by exalting rank and polish among clerical candidates over religious sentiment or the ability to instruct and influence the people. Bannerman's political radicalism showed through in that address: he claimed that the constitution of the Presbyterian church was inherently republican, whereas patronage smacked of arbitrary power, and he urged his fellow Scots to abandon their servile behaviour at a time when Britons in North America and Ireland were engaged in resisting arbitrary power through force of arms.

Bannerman also preached and wrote about philosophy and manners. In 1775 he published two volumes of *Religious correspondence, or, The dispensation of divine grace vindicated, from the extremes of libertine and fanatical principles*, dedicated to Mrs Fletcher of Saltoun. There he addressed such topics as the dangers of infidelity and enthusiasm and their detrimental effects upon manners, as well as the principles of common-sense philosophy. He also preached a funeral sermon upon the death of Lord Milton in 1766, and published a *Plan of Education for Rural Academies* in 1773. Bannerman died at Saltoun on 31 December 1798.

Bannerman typified a kind of minister that emerged in the Church of Scotland during the middle years of the eighteenth century, one who combined the polish and manners of a gentleman and an attachment to the new learning with a continuing devotion to Presbyterian orthodoxy and an opposition to the leadership of the church. In Bannerman's case, that opposition was voiced most explicitly in political terms: his antipathy to patronage derived from the same hostility towards an emphasis upon social hierarchy and an excessive subservience that he castigated in the political sphere.

NED C. LANDSMAN

Sources *Fasti Scot.*, new edn • N. C. Landsman, 'Liberty, piety and patronage: the social context of contested clerical calls in eighteenth-century Glasgow', *The Glasgow Enlightenment*, ed. A. Hook and R. B. Sher (1995), 214–26 • T. Somerville, *My own life and times, 1741–1814*, ed. W. Lee (1861) • J. R. McIntosh, *Church and theology in Enlightenment Scotland: the popular party, 1740–1800* (1998)

Archives NA Scot., Church of Scotland records

Bannermann, Alexander. *See* Bannerman, Alexander (*b.* 1730s, *d.* in or after 1774).

Bannister, Charles (*bap.* 1741, *d.* 1804), actor and singer, was baptized at some time between May and October 1741 in Newland, Gloucestershire, the son of John Bannister and his wife, Rebecca Powell. He was brought up in Deptford, where his father worked in the victualling office for the navy. He was fascinated by theatre from childhood, and played such roles as Romeo and Richard III in amateur productions. After being rejected by David Garrick, whose company he had applied to join, he acted on the Norwich–Ipswich circuit until Samuel Foote engaged him in April 1762 to join his company at the Haymarket Theatre in Foote's *Oratorial Lectures*, one of the latter's attempts to present drama but evade the constrictions of the Licensing Act. But Bannister was not a success and returned to the provinces, acting at Dublin in 1764, at Richmond, Surrey, in 1766, and at Norwich in 1766–7.

Bannister was finally invited to join Garrick at Drury Lane, and made his first appearance there as Merlin in Garrick's *Cymon* on 22 September 1767. William Hopkins, the prompter, noted that he 'was received with Applause,—is a tall Figure,—good Voice and sings well' (*BDA*). In October Bannister played Hopkins in Garrick's backstage farce *A Peep behind the Curtain*. From that season until 1783 he acted at Drury Lane in a wide range of roles, though he specialized in eccentric old men. He often played for Foote's Haymarket Theatre in the summers and sang at performances at Marylebone Gardens and Ranelagh as well. In 1783–4 he was at Covent Garden, where he doubled his salary to £12; he kept the rise when he returned to Drury Lane. For the next few years he oscillated between the two major companies, but his career was declining. He finally retired at the end of the season in 1799 while a member of Colman's company at the Haymarket.

Bannister's considerable reputation as a singer was built not only on his striking physique and his superb bass voice and accomplished falsetto range but also on his talents as a mimic. As an anonymous attack on him noted in *Momus* (1767):

> See B[annister] assume (unaw'd by shame)
> A mimic's vile and despicable name [...]
> A very monkey with a human name.

His imitations of other, better-known, singers were clearly extremely funny, but he was also known as a moving singer of sentimental songs. As a versatile actor he was most successful in dozens of dialect roles and playing caricatures of Italian singers. By the 1780s he was famous enough to be imitated himself by provincial comics. It was claimed that he could not read music and had to be taught songs by the pianist at Covent Garden. In 1782 he played Polly Peachum in a cross-dressed production of Gay's *The Beggar's Opera* so successfully that, it was said, a Mrs Fitzherbert laughed so much that she died from the after-effects three days later.

A clubbable man and at times a heavy drinker, well known for his practical jokes and careless with money, Bannister was much in demand at private gatherings and was a member of such groups as the Glee Club, the Anacreontic Society (a club for noblemen and professional singers), and the School of Garrick, a club he led for those who had acted with Garrick. He was painted by Zoffany and by others in a variety of his best-known roles, including as Polly Peachum.

It is not known when Bannister married his wife, Sarah, but they had three children: Charles (*d.* 1762), John *Bannister (1760–1836), even more successful as an actor than his father, and Jane (*fl.* 1783–1829). He died at the house in Suffolk Street, Charing Cross, London, where he had lived most of his life, on 19 October 1804, three days after a full house at Drury Lane for his benefit night. He was buried at St Martin-in-the-Fields, London, on 25 October. In 1808 his estate, worth a mere £200, was passed on to his son John, Sarah having died at some date in the interim.

PETER HOLLAND

Sources Highfill, Burnim & Langhans, *BDA* • J. Adolphus, *Memoirs of John Bannister, comedian*, 2 vols. (1839) • G. W. Stone, ed., *The London stage, 1660–1800*, pt 4: *1747–1776* (1962) • C. B. Hogan, ed., *The London stage, 1660–1800*, pt 5: *1776–1800* (1968)
Likenesses J. Sayer, portrait, 1781 • Miss Bannister, pencil drawing, Garr. Club • T. Pye or C. Pye, oils (as Steady in *The Quaker*), Garr. Club • Ridley, engraving, repro. in *European Magazine* (1804) • J. R. Smith, engraving (after J. Sayer, 1781) • J. B. Swendall, tinted pencil, Garr. Club • attrib. J. Zoffany, oils, Garr. Club • drawing, Garr. Club • prints, BM, NPG
Wealth at death £200: Highfill, Burnim & Langhans, *BDA*, 265

Bannister [*née* Harper], **Elizabeth** (**1757–1849**), actress and singer, was, according to the encomium in the *Thespian Magazine* (1793), the daughter of a Mrs Harpur, 'now a mantua-maker [dressmaker] at Bath', who, having made a marriage disapproved of by her family, educated her daughter perforce 'to her business' (Highfill, Burnim & Langhans, *BDA*); Elizabeth's maternal uncles were Francis Rundell, actor and theatre patentee, and the fantastically wealthy jeweller and goldsmith Philip *Rundell; another uncle was married to the cookery writer Maria Eliza *Rundell. She was first heard in public in 1777, singing at Marylebone Gardens, London, with her future father-in-law, Charles *Bannister, on the same programme. According to the *Thespian Magazine*, a Mr Paul ('a gentleman of musical taste'), impressed with her abilities, obtained an engagement for her at the Haymarket in 1778. Fiske refers to George Colman the elder's discovering Elizabeth Harper during the 1778 season; she 'stayed with him [at the Little Theatre] for five summers' (Fiske, 433). Her theatrical début was as Rosetta in Isaac Bickerstaff's *Love in a Village* at the Little Theatre on 22 May 1778, attracting favourable notice. Her early performances were not without their difficulties: the *Morning Chronicle* (11 September 1778) reported that

> from the blunder of some person whose business it was to have the guittar ready, she was much disconcerted when she was to sing the song, and was obliged, after sitting some time, to leave the stage while the instrument was put in tune behind the scenes. (Highfill, Burnim & Langhans, *BDA*)

The reviews of her first appearance as Polly in John Gay's *The Beggar's Opera* (8 June 1778) reflected not only her authentic dramatic qualities in the role—'Miss Harper's Polly was what Gay really intended' (ibid.)—but also the descriptions of her own character in the biographical sources: the *Gazette* of 9 June 1778 referred to her 'modesty mixed with a proper degree of female sensibility' and to

Elizabeth Bannister (1757–1849), by John Russell, 1799

the tasteful singing and naturalness of her portrayal (ibid.). Anthony Pasquin's poetic tribute to her in *The Children of Thespis*, part 2, characterized her as 'placid and mild … uninjur'd in fame by a strong competition' (Pasquin, 133); according to Pasquin:

> Celestial Decency led her along,
> Corrected her manners, and sweeten'd her song.
> (ibid.)

Her husband's biographer John Adolphus wrote of her 'sweetness of voice' (Adolphus, 1.278) and 'correctness of ear' (ibid., 1.279), further claiming that she had 'improved a voice of the first quality by an excellent musical education, close study, and unremitting practice' (ibid., 1.82). Her professionalism and skill on stage are suggested by Pasquin's comment that she 'oft prov'd the pilot that sav'd a burletta' (Pasquin, 133). Most of her roles were in comedy, including, besides those mentioned, Clara in *The Duenna* by Richard Brinsley Sheridan and Thomas Linley, Olivia in *Twelfth Night*, and Laura in *The Agreeable Surprise* by John O'Keefe and Samuel Arnold, although she played Ophelia in 1780. The *Morning Chronicle* referred to her engagement at the Pantheon for two years from 1778, 'at the salary of *One Thousand Pounds*' (Highfill, Burnim & Langhans, *BDA*), and she is known to have indeed commanded remuneration of this magnitude; in the early 1780s she was booked to perform at Covent Garden for the 'very high salary, for a debutante' (ibid.), of £12 per week; her first great success there was in the title role of *Rosina*, by Frances Brooke and William Shield. The *Thespian Magazine* (1793) mentioned a lottery prize of £1000 or £2000; added to her substantial earnings, this 'realized a genteel and independent fortune' (ibid.). Her reputation remained unsullied: 'in the whole of her career censure never attached to her' (Adolphus, 1.278), which, for a leading singer in the theatre, 'amounts to an eulogy' (ibid.).

On 26 January 1783 Elizabeth Harper married the actor and comedian John *Bannister (1760–1836). Bannister had been an acclaimed Hamlet and Prince Hal at Drury Lane, but his standing was threatened by the rise of John Philip Kemble; consequently 'his wife took him in hand and taught him to sing' (Fiske, 441). Their marriage was a very happy one. Their first London address was Bedford Street, Covent Garden, and by April 1783 they were at Great Russell Street; they continued to live at a succession of West End addresses. They had four daughters, Elizabeth (*bap.* 23 January 1784), Rosina (Rosenna; *bap.* 6 April 1785), Ann (*bap.* 17 February 1791), and Frances, and two sons, John (*bap.* 23 March 1787) and Charles. In 1792 Elizabeth retired from the stage, speaking a farewell address to her audience on 5 September at the Haymarket in order

> to fulfil her desire,
> And trim Friendship's lamp round her family fire
> (Pasquin, 154)

Possibly, as Adolphus suggests, the advent of Elizabeth Billington spurred John Bannister to encourage his wife's retirement. Adolphus, who knew the Bannister family through several generations and drew on John Bannister's diary for his biography, considered that John reared his family 'on strict religious principles', aided by Elizabeth, who 'after performing for so many years all the duties of a wife, a mother, and a friend, was still as unaffected … as gentle in disposition, as when she was Miss Harper. Time had made no inroads upon her temper' (Adolphus, 2.291).

Elizabeth accompanied her husband on his tour to Paris in 1827. She died at her house, 65 Gower Street, St Giles, Middlesex, on 15 January 1849, and was buried beside her husband in the Bannister family's vault in St Martin-in-the-Fields. SUSAN WOLLENBERG

Sources Highfill, Burnim & Langhans, *BDA* • J. Adolphus, *Memoirs of John Bannister, comedian*, 2 vols. (1839) • A. Pasquin [J. Williams], *The children of Thespis*, 13th edn (1792) • R. Fiske, *English theatre music in the eighteenth century*, 2nd edn (1986)

Likenesses engraving, pubd 1778 (as Rosetta in *Love in a village*), Harvard TC • R. Laurie, mezzotint, 1780 (after R. Dighton), NPG • J. Condé, portrait, 1793, Harvard TC; repro. in *Thespian Magazine* (Aug 1793) • J. Russell, pastel drawing, 1799, NPG [*see illus.*] • J. McGoffin, engraving, 1800–40 (as Mrs Page in *The merry wives of Windsor*; with Anne Crawford) • Thornthwaite, engraving (after Roberts), repro. in J. Bell, *Bell's British theatre*, 21 (1781) • portrait (with George Mattocks), repro. in W. Lowndes, *New English theatre* (1782) • prints, BM, NPG

Wealth at death £4000: Highfill, Burnim & Langhans, *BDA*

Bannister, James (1758/9–1836), circus proprietor, is of unknown parentage and upbringing. He was one of the earliest circus owners to take his show, Bannister's Equestrian Troupe, on tour. In 1804 they were at Stamford in Lincolnshire for the mid-Lent fair and soon afterwards performed at Grantham with Bannister's daughter, Miss S. Bannister [*see below*], on the tightrope and slack wire. Individually and also in partnership with his fellow equestrian performer, James West, Bannister toured the north of England and Scotland from about 1810; later displays of Bannister's Equestrian Company and Bannister's Olympic circus, an offshoot of Astley's Amphitheatre, appeared at Norwich (1813) and Newcastle and Hull (1815–16). During this period the company employed several prominent performers, among them the equestrians Mr Kemp, Henry Bryson, and James West, and the rider and rope dancer Henry Michael Hengler. In 1816 Bannister employed the artist and later Royal Academician David Roberts (1796–1864) as a scene-painter at his Nicholson Street circus in Edinburgh. Roberts toured with the circus from April 1816, stopping at Carlisle, Newcastle, Hull, and York; in January 1817 Bannister established a new circus and theatre company, the Pantheon, with the musician Montague Corri. Soon afterwards Roberts left the company when his employer was declared bankrupt. Bannister died, aged seventy-seven, on 6 November 1836 and was survived by his two daughters, both of whom worked with their father's companies.

Miss **S. Bannister** (*b.* 1787), equestrian performer and tightrope dancer, was with the equestrian troupe at Stamford in 1804 and in later tours of northern England and Scotland. After her father's business failed she worked at Astley's Amphitheatre, where she was principal equestrian on John Conway Philip Astley's death in October 1821. She remained at the amphitheatre under its new proprietor, William Davis, and was then described by the manager, Charles Dibdin, as possessing 'on the rope and on the horse much celebrity'. She married Edward Wilson; details of her date and place of death are unknown. James Bannister's second daughter, **Mary Bannister** (*d.* 1877), equestrian performer, worked at the Olympic circus in Leeds where, in 1818, she regularly introduced displays of swordsmanship while on horseback; in addition she advertised lessons in the art of riding to ladies by appointment. She later performed for several seasons at Covent Garden, London, and in pantomime with the celebrated tightrope dancer Thomas Wilson, whom she subsequently married before retiring from the circus in 1832. She died in Camberwell, London, on 20 November 1877 and was buried at Norwood cemetery.

JOHN M. TURNER

Sources J. M. Turner, *Victorian arena: the performers* (1995) · G. Speaight, *A history of the circus* (1980)

Bannister, John (1760–1836), actor, born at Deptford on 12 May 1760, was the son of the actor Charles *Bannister (*bap.* 1741, *d.* 1804) and his wife Sarah. In 1777 he became a student at the Royal Academy, where he had for associate and friend the caricaturist Thomas Rowlandson, but his theatrical bent led to his abandoning painting and adopting the stage as a profession. Before leaving the academy he called on David Garrick, who, two years previously, in 1776, had retired from the stage. Bannister's account of an interview which, though formidable, was not wholly discouraging, is preserved in the diary used by his biographer, J. Adolphus.

Bannister's first appearance took place at the Haymarket, for his father's benefit on 27 August 1778, as Dick in Murphy's farce *The Apprentice*. He recited on this occasion a prologue by Garrick, and wound up his share in the entertainment by giving imitations of well-known actors. The following season (1778–9) saw Bannister engaged with his father as a stock actor at Drury Lane; he made his début on 11 November 1778 in the character of Zaphna in James Miller's version of Voltaire's *Mahomet*, playing opposite Perdita Robinson. He had been coached intensively in this part by Garrick. He appeared, again in Voltaire, as Dorislas in a version by Aaron Hill of *Mérope*. In February 1779 at Covent Garden he played Achmet in Brown's tragedy *Barbarossa*. His only other appearance that season was for his benefit at Covent Garden in April 1779, when he acted the Prince of Wales in *1 Henry IV* and Shift in Samuel Foote's comedy *The Minor*, and gave his imitations. While Drury Lane was shut, Bannister joined Mattocks's company at Birmingham, playing such characters as Macduff, Orlando, Edgar Lothario in Nicholas Rowe's *The Fair Penitent*, and Simon Pure in Susannah Centlivre's *A Bold Stroke for a Wife*.

His first 'creation' of importance appears to have been Don Ferolo Whiskerandos in Sheridan's *The Critic*, which was produced at Drury Lane in October 1779, and in which he later played Sir Fretful Plagiary. An unremarkable appearance in *Hamlet* followed, and whatever capacity Bannister possessed in tragedy had shortly to yield to the growing fame of John Philip Kemble. Happier efforts were made in the comic roles of Charles Surface and Parolles.

On 26 January 1783 Bannister married Elizabeth Harper (1757–1849) [*see* Bannister, Elizabeth], an actress and singer at the Haymarket; the first of their family of four daughters and two sons was baptized the following January. By 1787 Bannister's social and professional position was established. His repertory continued to increase, with Brisk in Congreve's *The Double Dealer*, Sir David Dunder in Colman's *Ways and Means*, Ben in Congreve's *Love for Love*, Brass in *The Confederacy*, Scrub in Farquhar's *The Beaux' Stratagem*, Trappanti in Cibber's *She Would and She Would Not*, and Speed in *The Two Gentlemen of Verona* among the parts that prepared the way for his conspicuous success as Sir Anthony Absolute and Tony Lumpkin, characters in which he was received with pleasure to the end of his career. He retained, in the height of his success, his taste for painting, and Rowlandson, George Morland, and Gainsborough were his close friends. From this time forward his career was an unbroken triumph. The principal comic parts in the old drama fell to him, and his acceptance of a role in a new piece was considered a favourable augury. Bob Acres in *The Rivals*, Job Thornbury in *John Bull*, Marplot in *The Busybody*, Dr Ollapod in *The Poor Gentleman*, and Dr Pangloss in *The Heir-at-Law* were among his greatest performances; Mercutio was the only comic character of importance that seemed outside his range. In 1802–3 he succeeded Kemble as acting manager at Drury Lane.

In 1809 Bannister took a monologue entertainment with songs, entitled *Bannister's Budget*, on a tour of the provinces and Ireland; it opened in London in Lent 1810, and was a financial, popular, and critical success. On 1 June 1815 Bannister retired from the stage, at Drury Lane, playing Echo in Kenney's comedy *The World*, a character created by him and which afforded room for a display of his mimetic gifts, and Walter in Thomas Morton's *Children in the Wood*. His career had been connected with Drury Lane for thirty-seven years, but no less celebrated were his regular summer engagements at the Haymarket and his frequent and extensive provincial tours. He died at his house, 65 Gower Street, on 7 November 1836, at 2 a.m., and was buried on the 14th in the church of St Martin-in-the-Fields in a vault with his father.

An extremely sociable man and a practising Christian, Bannister counted aristocrats, painters, and writers among his friends, as well as members of his own profession; all acknowledged his charm, while his acting obtained the high praise of the acutest judges. Of the galaxy of comic actors which marked the close of the eighteenth and the beginning of the nineteenth century, he was one of the brightest stars.

JOSEPH KNIGHT, *rev.* NILANJANA BANERJI

Sources J. Adolphus, *Memoirs of John Bannister, comedian*, 2 vols. (1838) • Adams, *Drama* • Highfill, Burnim & Langhans, *BDA* • *The thespian dictionary, or, Dramatic biography of the eighteenth century* (1802) • *The thespian dictionary, or, Dramatic biography of the present age*, 2nd edn (1805) • T. Gilliland, *The dramatic mirror, containing the history of the stage from the earliest period, to the present time*, 2 vols. (1808) • Hall, *Dramatic ports.* • M. Kelly, *Reminiscences*, 2 vols. (1826) • Genest, *Eng. stage* • J. Doran, *'Their majesties' servants': annals of the English stage*, 2 vols. (1864) • L. Hunt, *Critical essays on the performers of the London theatres* (1807) • [J. Haslewood], *The secret history of the green rooms: containing authentic and entertaining memoirs of the actors and actresses in the three Theatres Royal*, new edn, 2 vols. (1795)

Likenesses T. Rowlandson, caricature, pen and wash drawing, 1783, Yale U. CBA • M. Brown, mezzotint, pubd 1787 (after J. R. Smith), BM, NPG • S. De Wilde, group portrait, exh. RA 1793, Garr. Club • S. De Wilde, mezzotint, pubd 1794 (after E. Bell), BM, NPG • S. De Wilde, mezzotint, pubd 1794 (after J. R. Smith), BM, NPG • S. De Wilde, oils, 1797 (with Suett), Garr. Club • J. Russell, pastel drawing, 1799, NPG • G. Dance, pencil drawing, 1800, NPG • J. Russell, pastel drawing, 1802, Garr. Club • J. Varley, pencil drawing, 1816, Garr. Club • Barrett, engraving (after painting by Riley), repro. in J. Parsons, *The minor theatre* (1794) • Bromley, engraving, repro. in J. Bell, *Bell's British theatre*, 8 (1791) • J. Chapman, engraving (after drawing by H. Moses), repro. in *British Drama*, 9 (1817) • G. Clint, mezzotint (after engraving?), NPG • J. Condé, engraving (after his drawing), Garr. Club • W. Greatbach, engraving (after G. Clint), repro. in Adolphus, *Memoirs* • T. Murray, mezzotint (after R. Williams), BM, NPG • Ridley, engraving (after painting by S. De Wilde), repro. in *European Magazine*, 59 (1811) • Ridley, engraving (after W. Beechey), repro. in *Monthly Mirror* (1797) • P. Roberts, engraving (after his painting), repro. in *European Magazine*, 28 (July 1795) • J. Rogers, engraving, repro. in *Oxberry's Dramatic Biography*, 4 (1826) • R. A. Russell, portrait, Garr. Club • Scriven, engraving (after painting by S. De Wilde), repro. in J. Cawthorne, ed., *Cawthorne's minor British theatre*, 6 vols. (1806) • R. Smith, engraving (after painting by S. De Wilde), repro. in J. Cawthorne, ed., *Cawthorne's minor British theatre*, 6 vols. (1806) • J. Zoffany, oils (as Scont in *The village lawyer*), Garr. Club • drawings, Garr. Club • portrait, repro. in *Lady's Magazine* (1817) • portrait, repro. in *Town and Country* (Dec 1788) • portrait, repro. in W. Oxberry, *New English drama* (1818–23) • prints, BM, NPG

Bannister, John (1816–1873), philologist, was born at York on 25 February 1816, the son of David Bannister (1788–1854) and his wife, Elizabeth Greensides (1789–1864). From 1839 he was educated at Trinity College, Dublin, where he studied classics and Hebrew (BA, 1844; MA, 1853; LLB and LLD, 1866). He was ordained priest in 1845, and served as curate of Longford, Derbyshire, from 1844 to 1845. From 1846 he was perpetual curate of Bridgehill, Duffield, Derbyshire, where on 16 August 1849 he married Patience Statham Newham (*b.* 1828, *d.* in or after December 1878). In 1857 he was appointed perpetual curate of St Day, Cornwall.

As a philologist Bannister's principal work was *A glossary of Cornish names, ancient and modern, local, familiar, personal, &c.: 20,000 Celtic and other names now or formerly in use in Cornwall; with derivations and significations, for the most part conjectural …* (1869–71). This work was brought out in seven parts. The supplement, which was to have formed three additional parts, was never published, owing to the death of the author. Bannister also published *Jews in Cornwall* (1867) and a number of articles in the *Journal* of the Royal Institute of Cornwall.

Bannister died at Gwennap, St Day, on 30 August 1873 and was buried in the churchyard at St Day on 4 or 5 September. He was survived by his wife who was living in Penzance in December 1878. Bannister's library, comprising some 2000 volumes of theology, philology, antiquities, and early typography, was bought by the British Museum. It included *Gerlever Cernouak, a Vocabulary of the Ancient Cornish Language* (Egerton MS 2328, fol. 4), *An English–Cornish Dictionary*, a copy of Johnson's *Dictionary*, interleaved with Cornish and other equivalents (Egerton MS 2329, fol. 5), *A Cornish Vocabulary*, being copious additions by Bannister to his printed work (Egerton MS 2330, fol. 6), and *Materials for a Glossary of Cornish Names* (Egerton MS 2331).

THOMPSON COOPER, *rev.* JOHN D. HAIGH

Sources Boase & Courtney, *Bibl. Corn.*, 1.10, 3.1047 • Catalogue of Egerton MSS, BL • Crockford (1860) • Burtchaell & Sadleir, *Alum. Dubl.*, 2nd edn • *The Athenaeum* (27 Sept 1873), 397

Wealth at death under £200: probate, 27 Oct 1873, *CGPLA Eng. & Wales*

Bannister, Mary (*d.* 1877). *See under* Bannister, James (1758/9–1836).

Bannister, S. (*b.* 1787). *See under* Bannister, James (1758/9–1836).

Bannister [*née* Stourton], **Sarah Jane** (1858–1942), educationist and local politician, was born on 5 August 1858 at Norton St Philip, Somerset, the daughter of John Stourton, a journeyman mason, and his wife, Harriet, *née* Moon. In 1879, after completing a course of teacher training at Tottenham College, Middlesex, she was appointed a resident lecturer by the college, where she remained for two years until her marriage. On 22 December 1881 she married Henry Bannister (1842/3–1925), fifteen years her senior, a widowed schoolmaster working for the London school board (LSB). In January 1882 Sarah Bannister was appointed by the LSB to teach physiology and domestic economy at the William Street and Sumner Road evening classes for pupil teachers. At the same time she was also appointed an inspector for the Bradford school board.

In 1884 Sarah Bannister and her husband Henry were chosen by the LSB to pilot a new scheme for training pupil teachers in central classes. Sarah Bannister was appointed headmistress of a centre for girls in a school room under the Lycett Memorial Chapel, Mile End Road, and Henry Bannister headmaster of a centre for boys based in the East End's famous university settlement, Toynbee Hall. As a result of their pioneering work, eleven, and subsequently twelve, new centres were established. Sarah Bannister remained London's only female centre principal at the Stepney centre for girls until it closed in 1908. During the early years of her headship at Stepney, she also found time to study for a part-time correspondence degree course with the University of St Andrews, and was subsequently awarded an LLA.

In January 1897 Sarah Bannister was invited to join the education department's departmental committee on the pupil-teacher system, chaired by Thomas Wetherherd Sharpe, senior chief inspector of schools, which was appointed to investigate the working of the pupil-teacher system and to recommend any improvements. She was one of three women (the others being Elizabeth Phillips Hughes and Lydia Manley of the Cambridge and Stockwell training college, respectively) on a committee of twelve, which consisted mainly of leading inspectors of schools, clergy, and training college principals. As well as giving her own evidence as a witness, she pursued a clear agenda in questioning other witnesses, contributing to nearly every session. The report of this committee, together with a number of other political and educational changes, contributed to the decline of the pupil-teacher system and the eventual closure of the pupil-teacher centres at the turn of the twentieth century under new government policy.

After the closure of the Stepney centre on 4 May 1908 Sarah Bannister was appointed principal of a new London county council (LCC) teacher training initiative, a non-residential day training college at Moorfields for 312 women. Moorfields was short-lived: as a war measure it was amalgamated in 1915 with other LCC colleges. For the remainder of her professional working life, until she retired from the LCC in 1919, she served as an assistant inspector of schools.

In 1918 Sarah Bannister was invited by the Hendon women citizens' council to offer herself for election to the then Hendon urban district council. She was duly elected and served without interruption until 1938, when she finally retired. When Hendon became a borough in 1932 she was one of the first aldermen to be elected and the only woman to receive that distinction. She served on almost every statutory committee of the council, as well as on many subcommittees. The bulk of her work, however, lay with the education committee and she was the prime mover in the founding of the Hendon Free Library. At one time she was the council's representative on the National Association of Education Committees and on the assessment committee for central Middlesex. She was also council representative on the garden suburb institute council, and on the governing body of the Henrietta Barnett School and the Hendon county school. To mark twenty years of service to the civic life of Hendon, she was presented with a portrait of herself in oils at a special ceremony in the town hall in March 1939. She died of cancer on 16 March 1942 at her home, 1 Hill Close, Hampstead Way, Golders Green, Hendon, attended by her only daughter, Winifred, and was cremated on 20 March 1942 at Golders Green crematorium. WENDY ROBINSON

Sources W. Robinson, '"Willing and able to teach": Sarah Jane Bannister and teacher training in transition, 1870–1918', *Practical visionaries: women, education and social progress, 1790–1930*, ed. P. Hirsch and M. Hilton (2000) • *Departmental committee on the pupil teacher system* (1898) • b. cert. • m. cert. • d. cert. • [H. Barnett], *Canon Barnett: his life, work, and friends*, 2nd edn, 1 (1919), 347 • London county council minutes, LMA, 1908, p. 400 • LMA, EO/TRA/4/14, 17 Nov 1908 • LMA, SBL 742, 16 May 1898 • LMA, SBL 734, 738, 739, 747 • LSB minutes of proceedings, LMA, 1884 • education minutes, LMA, 30 June 1915, p. 808 • education calendar, LMA, 1916–17 • *Times Education Supplement* (23 Feb 1935), 61

Archives Barnet Archives and Local Studies Centre, London, papers

Likenesses photograph, 1932, Barnet Archives and Local Studies Centre • oils, *c.*1938, Barnet Archives and Local Studies Centre • portrait, repro. in *Woman Teacher's World* (10 Jan 1912), cover

Wealth at death £419 2*s.* 9*d.*: probate, 2 June 1942, *CGPLA Eng. & Wales*

Bannister, Saxe (1790–1877), lawyer, son of John Bannister, was born at Bidlington House, Steyning, Sussex, on 27 June 1790, and attended schools at Lewes and Tonbridge and then Queen's College, Oxford (BA, 1813, MA, 1815). He volunteered for active service when Napoleon escaped from Elba and, with a captain's commission, was on the way to Belgium when the battle of Waterloo ended the war. He retired from the army on half pay, and was called to the bar at Lincoln's Inn.

In October 1823 Bannister was appointed attorney-general of New South Wales under the New South Wales Act of that year. With a guaranteed salary of £1200 he was also given the right of private practice as a barrister, and was sworn in at the first sitting of the NSW supreme court on 17 May 1824. Later that year he advised Governor Brisbane that he had no power to license or censor the press without special legislation, and that free persons accused of crime at the court of quarter sessions had to be tried by a civilian jury. He thus introduced such bodies and a free press into New South Wales.

However, Bannister's relationship with Governor Darling was tumultuous, Darling considering that though he was 'an upright, conscientious man, the apparent eccentricity of his mind and his want of experience in his profession prevented my depending on his counsel' (*Historical Records of Australia*, dispatch, 1 March 1829, 148). Chief Justice Forbes, like other officials, thought him at times mentally unbalanced.

Bannister's correspondence continually lamented that his salary was inadequate. In July 1825 he informed Lord Bathurst, the secretary of state, that unless it was more than doubled he could not stay in New South Wales. Bathurst refused to sanction any increase, and informed Darling that his majesty had no other alternative but to accept Bannister's resignation. Much aggrieved, Bannister sailed for England nine days later, but not before he became embroiled in a duel with Dr Wardell, editor of *The Australian*, from which both men emerged uninjured. On his return to England, Bannister vainly sought re-employment by the Colonial Office for the next seventeen years. In 1848 he accepted the position of gentleman bedel of the Royal College of Physicians at a salary of £50 a year in fees.

Bannister had a keen interest in philanthropic causes, and was concerned with the welfare of children, convicts, and especially Aborigines. He was instrumental in the establishment of the first infants' school in Sydney, and published numerous pamphlets dealing with the subjects of transportation and government policy towards indigenous people. His other written works covered a diverse range of topics including the constitution and laws of the United States, a description of the *Mappa mundi* in Hereford Cathedral (1849), and a biography of William Patterson, founder of the Bank of England (1857). He was a lucid and engaging writer whose works reveal an agile and learned mind.

On 16 September 1832 Bannister had married Mary Lambe (*b*. 1796), and he died on 16 September 1877 at Thornton Lodge, Thornton Heath, Croydon, Surrey, the home of Mrs Wyndham, their only child.

DEAN WILSON

Sources *AusDB* · J. M. Bennett, ed., *A history of the New South Wales bar* (1969) · Foster, *Alum. Oxon.* · *DNB* · [F. Watson], ed., *Historical records of Australia*, 1st ser., 11–14 (1917–22); 4th ser., 1 (1922)
Archives Mitchell L., NSW | Bodl. Oxf., corresp. with Sir Thomas Phillipps · Derbys. RO, letters to R. J. Wilmot Horton · UCL, letters to the Society for the Diffusion of Useful Knowledge · W. Sussex RO, letters to the dukes of Richmond
Likenesses B. R. Haydon, group portrait, oils, 1840 (*The Anti-Slavery Convention*), NPG

Bannon, Dorothy Edith (1885–1940), nurse, was born on 7 June 1885 at New Romney, Kent, the daughter of James Norman Bannon, a solicitor, and his wife, Kate Mann. She trained as a nurse at the Nightingale School of Nursing at St Thomas's Hospital, London, from 1913 to 1916. She was the first probationer to be awarded the medal for proficiency in the theory and practice of nursing by the Nightingale Training School, and was appointed a ward sister at St Thomas's Hospital on completion of her training. Her organizational and teaching skills were soon recognized, with the award in 1918 of a Cowdray scholarship by the College of Nursing to study on the newly inaugurated sister tutor course at King's College of Household and Social Science, Campden Hill, London. At the request of the dean of King's College, Bannon's scholarship was extended for a further year by the Nightingale Fund committee to enable her to study public health, which gave her an insight into the social context of nursing.

Bannon returned to St Thomas's Hospital in 1920 as night superintendent and in 1922 was appointed matron of St Mary's Hospital, Paddington. Within seven months of her arrival she established a preliminary training school for nurses to prepare new probationers for their entry onto the wards. With the aid of Mary Lane, the sister tutor, who had also been a student on the King's College course, Bannon supported the General Nursing Council's introduction of a new syllabus for training state-registered nurses, and loaned equipment and premises for the newly introduced state registration examinations. She was a strict disciplinarian, being very particular about correct nursing uniform. A believer in maintaining hierarchical discipline, she deliberately kept her successor as matron at St Mary's, Mary Milne, waiting for over half an hour because Milne had been her junior when training at St Thomas's. She also encouraged the foundation in 1922 of St Mary's Hospital Past and Present Nurses' League as a means of maintaining contact between current hospital staff and those who had trained at the hospital, and became its first president. A nursing badge awarded by the league was introduced as an inducement for staff to remain at the hospital for a year after completing their training.

Bannon resigned from St Mary's in 1928 to enter an Anglican convent. She soon returned to a wider sphere of influence with her appointment in October 1929 as the first matron-in-chief of the London county council hospital and school medical service. Her appointment coincided with the transfer, under the 1929 Local Government Act, to London county council of the hospital services formerly run by the twenty-five London boards of guardians and the Metropolitan Asylums Board. She was confronted with the task of co-ordinating and reorganizing the nursing in seventy-five hospitals, containing over 40,000 beds, all with differing initial standards of patient care. Under her remit came the differing nursing requirements of general, specialist, fever, children's, and isolation hospitals, tuberculosis sanatoria, mental deficiency institutes and asylums, and the London county council school nursing service. She was responsible for the direction, supervision, and training of the 11,000 nursing staff under her charge.

Bannon's managerial abilities and administrative precision came to the fore in the task of organizing what Sir Frederick Menzies, medical officer of health for London county council, described as 'one of the most efficient nursing services in the world' (Cope, 120). In dealing with the many committees set up to run a municipal hospital scheme, tact and discretion were essential in securing support for her aims of extending the standards of the voluntary hospital system to a municipal hospital service. Uniform standards were introduced for nursing in the London county council hospitals, though there were problems with the inheritance of many antiquated and inadequate buildings. Attempts were made to reduce overcrowding in wards, with the introduction of standardized space between beds, and to provide proper accommodation for special categories of patient, including maternity cases and sufferers from mental illness and venereal diseases.

Bannon remained a keen exponent of nurses' training and oversaw the organization of a training scheme for nurses within the public health department nursing service. Stress was laid on the availability to a probationer nurse of varied training, both general and specialized, within the London county council nursing service, whose hospitals were depicted as offering 'an entirely unique opportunity for rapid and substantial advancement to the nurses serving in them' (*Nursing as a Career*, 1938). Training facilities and accommodation were in reality no better than in the voluntary hospitals.

With the approach of the Second World War Bannon was involved with the organization of nursing within the Emergency Medical Service and the incorporation of London county council hospitals into the ten sectors into which London was divided. On the outbreak of war, hospital wards in central London were cleared to prepare for the expected air-raid casualties. This created a shortage of civilian hospital services during the 'phoney war' period. The school nursing service was severely disrupted by the evacuation of schoolchildren from London, and Bannon reassigned school nurses to other duties. She was made a CBE. At the height of her influence she contracted meningitis, and died, unmarried, at St Thomas's Hospital, London, on 1 February 1940. KEVIN BROWN

Sources *Nursing Times* (10 Feb 1940) • M. Milne, letters and notes on nursing to Sir Zachary Cope, 28 Aug 1954, St Mary's Hospital Archives, London, DP 7/2 • J. Sheldrake, 'The L.C.C. hospital service', *Politics and the people of London: the London county council, 1889–1965*, ed. A. Saint (1989), 187–98 • Z. Cope, *A hundred years of nursing* (1955) • matron's reports to the governors, 1922–8, St Mary's Hospital Archives, London, SM/NR 1/1/9 • private information (2004) • b. cert. • d. cert.

Likenesses photograph, repro. in Cope, *A hundred years of nursing*

Banquell [Bankwell], **Sir John** (*d.* **1308**), administrator, came of a family who had connections with the leather and fur trades in London. He married Cecily, sister of the prosperous wool merchant Laurence of Ludlow, before the autumn of 1285, by when he was a king's clerk, responsible for receiving recognizances of debts from the city's traders, while in May 1286 he was granted custody of the merchants' seal, under the law merchant. He also became active as a financier and moneylender. His rapid rise to prominence in London owed much to crown patronage, particularly after 1285, when Edward I took over the government of the capital and replaced the mayor and sheriffs with royal appointees. By November that year Banquell had been installed as common clerk of the city, the second known holder of the office. He probably relinquished the post soon afterwards on becoming an alderman, first for Cripplegate ward (1286–91) and later for Dowgate (1291–8). One of the most influential citizens, effectively a deputy to the wardens appointed by the crown, he was on several occasions appointed by the civic authorities to present the city's business in the king's council. In recognition of his services to the city he was granted a plot of land near the Guildhall which, by the late fourteenth century, had become the site of a cloth market known as Backwell, or Blackwell, Hall. The grant was completed in June 1293. Numerous other properties in London, as well as lands at Lee, Bromley, and other places in Kent, were acquired by Banquell and his wife.

Banquell remained a London alderman until April 1298, when control of the city's government was ceded back to the citizens. Despite this reversal his ties with the crown enabled him to develop his career into new areas. From 1297 onwards he became active as a justice and, probably in the early summer of 1299, he was appointed seneschal of Ponthieu, the French county inherited by the young Edward, prince of Wales, from his mother, Queen Eleanor. He held this post until 1305, becoming a member of the prince's council and receiving a knighthood. He was also sent on a number of diplomatic missions to France before the signing of a peace treaty with Philippe IV in May 1303 and was among those chosen to visit the pope at Lyons in October 1305 in connection with Edward's proposed marriage to Isabella of France. In March 1304 and April 1306 he was one of two commissioners appointed to meet with their French counterparts to inquire into the losses incurred by merchants on both sides following breaches of the truce.

Banquell had probably relinquished the post of seneschal by August 1305, when he was one of the justices of gaol delivery who tried and convicted William Wallace. Entrusted with the task of accompanying Cardinal Sabina, the papal pro-nuncio, on his visit to England between December 1306 and March 1307, he was later appointed a baron of the exchequer. He was summoned to Edward II's first parliament, to be held in March 1308, but died while attending the coronation, held at Westminster Abbey on 25 February. According to the London chronicles, he was crushed to death when a stone wall collapsed under the weight of the large crowds. He was buried in the Austin friary in London and was survived by his wife, Cecily (*d.* 1328) and their two sons, Thomas (*d.* 1333) and John. MATTHEW DAVIES

Sources G. A. Williams, *Medieval London: from commune to capital* (1963) • G. P. Cuttino, *English diplomatic administration, 1259–1339*, 2nd edn (1971) • H. Johnstone, 'The county of Ponthieu, 1279–1307', *EngHR*, 29 (1914), 435–52 • CLRO • PRO • W. Stubbs, ed., *Chronicles of the reigns of Edward I and Edward II*, 2 vols., Rolls Series, 76 (1882–3) • *Chancery records* • B. R. Masters, 'The town clerk', *Guildhall Miscellany*, 3 (1969–71), 55–74

Wealth at death see Calendar of patent rolls

Bansley, Charles (*fl.* *c.*1550), poet, is unknown except as the author of *A Treatyse Shewing and Declaring the Pryde and Abuse of Women now a Dayes*, a caustic and often bawdy rhyming satire attacking the love of dress in women. It begins with the line 'Bo pepe what have I spyed!' and concludes with a benediction of Edward VI. There can be no doubt of Bansley's religious opinions. The poem (written in fifty-nine four-line stances) castigates Catholic Rome as much as women's dress. Bansley even blames that city as the source of the feminine love for light raiment, declaring that:

> From Rome, from Rome, thys carkered pryde,
> from Rome it came doubtles:
> Away for shame wyth soch filthy baggage,
> As smels of papery and develyshnes!

The poem was printed by Thomas Raynold, (*c.*1550), which places it within a year of William Thomas's *An Argument wherein the Apparaile of Women is both Reproved and Defended* (1551), which had defended women against a vicious attack on female attire. Within the poem Bansley also refers to *The Scole House of Women*, a tract published by Edward Gosynhill in 1560, but probably circulating in manuscript before that date.

JAMES MEW, *rev.* CATHY SHRANK

Sources J. Ritson, *Bibliographia poetica* (1802) • Watt, *Bibl. Brit.* • W. C. Hazlitt, *Hand-book to the popular, poetical and dramatic literature of Great Britain* (1867) • W. T. Lowndes, *The bibliographer's manual of English literature*, ed. H. G. Bohn, [new edn], 6 vols. (1864) • Tanner, *Bibl. Brit.-Hib.* • J. P. Collier, *Bibliographical and critical account* (1841) • *STC, 1475–1640* • C. Bansley, *A treatyse shewing and declaring the pryde and abuse of women*, ed. J. P. Collier (1841) • *DNB*
Archives Hunt. L., works

Banting, Sir Frederick Grant (1891–1941), physician and medical researcher, was born near the town of Alliston, Ontario, Canada, on 14 November 1891, the fourth son and fifth and youngest child of William Thompson Banting (1849–1929), a farmer of Irish descent, and his wife, Margaret (1854–1940), daughter of Alexander Grant, a miller of Scottish ancestry in Alliston.

Banting was educated in local schools and in 1910 entered Victoria College at the University of Toronto. After having to repeat the first year of the arts programme, he decided to switch to medicine. On graduation in 1916 (officially the class of 1917), he was immediately granted a commission in the Royal Canadian Army Medical Corps. He served in England and France as a battalion medical officer, and was awarded the Military Cross for valour during an engagement at Cambrai in September 1918, during which he was seriously wounded by shrapnel. After the war Banting trained for a year in surgery at Toronto's Hospital for Sick Children, and when his staff appointment was not renewed, opened a practice in London, Ontario, as a physician and surgeon. With time on his hands, he accepted a post as a part-time demonstrator at the local University of Western Ontario.

After doing some preparatory reading one night for a talk on the pancreas, Banting speculated that researchers' failure to isolate the long-sought internal secretion of the pancreas might have been due to the destructive action of enzymes in the pancreas's external secretion. He jotted down an idea he hoped would eliminate that problem:

> Diabetus [*sic*]
> Ligate pancreatic ducts of dog. Keep dogs alive till acini degenerate leaving Islets.
> Try to isolate the internal secretion of these to relieve glycosurea [*sic*]

Banting presented his idea to the professor of physiology at the University of Toronto, J. J. R. Macleod, who, with surplus resources at hand, agreed to allow him to test his hypothesis. Banting began work in May 1921, assisted by a graduating student, Charles H. Best, and under the supervision of Macleod. Preliminary results in the summer of 1921 convinced Banting and Best that an active diabetic principle could be prepared from extracts of degenerated pancreas. The research was intensified that autumn and a trained biochemist, James Bertram Collip, was added to the team in December at Banting's request.

The first paper about the Toronto research, delivered by Banting, Best, and Macleod to the American Physiological Society in New Haven, Connecticut, in late December 1921, met with a cautious response. A clinical trial of extract of fresh beef pancreas, made by Banting and Best, on a fourteen-year old diabetic boy, Leonard Thompson, in Toronto General Hospital on 11 January 1922, was deemed a failure. But on 23 January 1922 injections of pancreatic extract, purified by a process developed by Collip, began working splendidly, eliminating the symptoms of Thompson's diabetes. Within a few months the medical world celebrated the Toronto group's breakthrough in isolating 'insulin' as a spectacularly effective replacement therapy in the treatment of diabetes.

Banting, who never understood the extent to which the emergence of insulin relied on a well-supported collaborative effort begun with his faulty idea, fought for and received acclaim as the primary discoverer. In 1923 the Ontario legislature created for him the first research professorship in a Canadian university. In the same year the parliament of Canada granted him a lifetime annuity of $7500. In 1923 the Nobel prize in medicine or physiology was awarded to Banting and Macleod. Banting immediately divided his share of the Nobel money with Best, as did Macleod with Collip. Banting's later honours included the Cameron prize (Edinburgh, 1927), the Flavelle medal of the Royal Society of Canada (1931), the Apothecaries' medal (London, 1936), and the F. N. G. Starr medal of the Canadian Medical Association (1936). He was elected to the Royal Society, London, in 1935, and became an honorary fellow or member of many British and foreign scientific societies. He was appointed KBE in 1934 in the last round of honours granted to Canadians.

Banting's later research on the adrenal cortex, cancer, and other problems was unproductive, and he gradually became aware of the considerable limits of his scientific expertise. But his prominence meant that the outbreak of war in 1939 found him occupying the leading place in Canadian medical science. As head of the Medical Research Committee of the National Research Council of Canada, he worked enthusiastically to stimulate research, including investigation of chemical-biological warfare. His department of medical research at the University of Toronto became a centre for research in aviation medicine.

Banting was twice married: in 1924 to Marion (*c.*1900–*c.*1945), daughter of William Robertson, physician, of Elora, Ontario; they were divorced in 1932. In 1939 he married Henrietta (1912–*c.*1976), daughter of Henry Tenny Ball, a customs officer, of Stanstead, Quebec. One son, William, came from the first marriage. Attempting to visit Britain for liaison and personal reasons, Banting died in a plane crash on 21 February 1941, south-west of Musgrave Harbour, Newfoundland. He was buried in Mount Pleasant cemetery, Toronto, on 3 March 1941.

Banting was a rough-hewn, hard-drinking, obstinate, intelligent, and democratic Canadian. In his later years he was the 'good old boy' and popular figurehead of Canadian medical research. In leisure hours he became one of Canada's most accomplished amateur painters, adopting the techniques and style of friends in the Group of Seven, Canada's national art movement.

Memorials to Banting and the discovery of insulin abound at the University of Toronto and in medals and lectureships sponsored by diabetes associations around the world. MICHAEL BLISS

Sources M. Bliss, *The discovery of insulin* (1982) • M. Bliss, *Banting: a biography* (1984) • M. Bliss, 'Re-writing medical history: Charles Best and the Banting and Best myth', *Journal of the History of Medicine and Allied Sciences*, 48 (1993), 253–74
Archives National Research Council, Ottawa • University of Toronto, Thomas Fisher Rare Book Library | University of Toronto, Thomas Fisher Rare Book Library, W. R. Feasby MSS, Best MSS, Collip MSS, Macleod MSS • University of Toronto, records of insulin committee, board of governors | FILM University of Toronto, Thomas Fisher Rare Book Library
Likenesses photographs, 1921–5, Hult. Arch. • C. Williamson, oils, 1925, Banting Institute, Toronto • F. Loring, bust, University of Toronto • portraits, University of Toronto

Banting, William (1796/7–1878), writer on diet, was a funeral director in St James's Street, London. He may have been the William Banting, son of Thomas Banting and his wife, Ann, who was baptized at St Martin-in-the-Fields, Westminster, in December 1796. On 20 January 1818 he married at St Mary, Newington, Surrey, Mary Ann Thurmott (1793–1862).

Banting was somewhat short (5 feet 5 inches), and as he got older suffered great personal distress from his increasing fatness. It was said that by the time he was sixty he found himself unable to stoop to tie his shoes, 'or attend to the little offices which humanity requires, without considerable pain and difficulty'. He was forced to go downstairs slowly backwards, to avoid the jar of increased weight on the ankle joints, and with every exertion 'puffed and blowed in a way that was very unseemly and disagreeable'. His doctors told him to take exercise, which he did; he walked long distances, rowed, and took up other sports. But all this only improved his appetite and added to his weight, and no other solution was offered. On 26 August 1862 at the age of sixty-five, he weighed 14 st 6 lb, an amount which he found unbearable. After further trying a course of fifty Turkish baths and 'gallons of physic' without any success, he happened to consult a surgeon, Mr William Harvey, for an increasing problem of deafness. Mr Harvey, believing that obesity was the source of the hearing problem, suggested that Banting cut out bread, butter, milk, sugar, beer, soup, potatoes, and beans, and in their place adopt a diet of mainly flesh meat, fish, and dry toast. The result of this treatment was a gradual reduction of 46 lb in weight, and better health at the end of several weeks than Banting had enjoyed for the previous twenty years.

The delight at being so much relieved by such simple means induced Banting to write and publish a pamphlet entitled *A Letter on Corpulence, Addressed to the Public* (1863), in which he singled out sugar and fats as the chief causes of obesity. Written in plain, sensible language, this tract became an overnight success. There were four editions by 1869, and it was successfully translated into French and German. 'To bant', or 'banting', became a popular phrase for adopting a slimming diet and continued in use well into the twentieth century; it remains the accepted word in some languages, such as Swedish. Thousands took up the Banting dietary principles, and thus threw the medical profession into great confusion over the right 'carbonaceous and nitrogenous qualities of food'—doctors were especially concerned at the exclusion of milk. As a *Times* leader commented: 'Whatever medical men may say, the chymistry of digestion is at present very little understood, and the reason amateurs are beginning to dogmatise upon it is that physicians have neglected a material part of their own science' (*The Times*, 19 Sept 1864). Certainly a great deal of research was undertaken in food chemistry in the last quarter of the century; and far greater attention was paid to diet in the patient's regimen after Banting.

Banting scrupulously donated the profits of his book to charity, and continued to take an interest in charitable hospitals until his death at his house in The Terrace, Kensington, London, on 16 March 1878, aged eighty-one. According to Banting's will, he had three daughters and two sons. ROBERT HARRISON, *rev.* VIRGINIA SMITH

Sources *The Times* (19 Sept 1864), 7a • 'William Banting, his system of diet', *The Times* (27 Sept 1864), 9f • *Blackwood*, 96 (1864), 607–17 • T. Tanner, *The practice of medicine*, 1 (1865), 148 • *Banting up-to-date* (1902) • will • private information (2004) [David Banting]
Wealth at death under £70,000: probate, 8 April 1878, *CGPLA Eng. & Wales*

Banting, William Westbrook (1857–1932), undertaker, was born on 8 November 1857 at 24 Ladbroke Square, Kensington, London, the third of seven children of William Banting (1826–1901) and his wife, Mary (1833–1906), daughter of Richard Thomas Pugh, gentleman. He was baptized on 10 June 1858 at the parish church of St John the Evangelist, Notting Hill.

Banting was the fourth generation of his family to conduct royal funerals and, with the obsequies of Queen Victoria and Edward VII, brought the art of fashionable funerals to a peak. More than any other, he established the concept of the funeral director as the one who oversaw the funeral panoply, while contracting out the associated trades of coffin- or cabinet-making, upholstery, embalming, furnishings, and transport.

Banting's great-grandfather Thomas and William France were appointed jointly as 'cabinet makers and upholsterers' to George III in 1811 (warrant dated 10 June). They had worked together from 1780 at 101 St Martin's Lane, spectacularly so in Nelson's funeral in 1806. From 1811 they undertook all royal funerals, depositing the royal remains in the vault beneath St George's Chapel, Windsor, which had recently succeeded Westminster Abbey as the royal tomb-house. A picture of George IV's ornate coffin can be seen in the Museum of London. At the accession of William IV, Thomas Banting alone was reappointed as upholsterer to the king (warrant dated 1 September 1830) and Bantings continued to hold the royal warrant to Queen Victoria, to Edward VII as prince of

Wales and as king, and to George V until 1928. Bantings' indispensability was evident as early as 1834 (see PRO, LC 2/62).

Banting's grandfather William *Banting made a name for himself from a pamphlet of 1863 on dieting. His famous funerals included the duke of Wellington and the Prince Consort Albert. At the time of Victoria's funeral, Banting's father sent him to Osborne House with the coffin and lead shell to smooth arrangements with the royal family and attendant bishop of Winchester. The whole funeral cost £594 8*s.* 3*d.*

Banting himself finally inherited the business in March 1901 when his father died. His elder brother had already died and his brother's son had not been allowed to enter 'trade'. His showrooms at the then 26 and 27 St James Street were soon embellished. In 1900 Banting conducted only sixteen funerals in the whole year; by 1903 it was double that number. Two ledgers survive (now priv. coll.) and reveal intimate details of aristocratic and royal funerals. On the news of Edward VII's death Banting was called from his home at 10 p.m. He had to visit Buckingham Palace three times before Queen Alexandra would allow him and his men to seal and remove the coffin. The ledger indicates the entry 'not done' and a fee for each visit, and the overall cost of £318 18*s.* 11*d.*

The First World War put an end to 'the gorgeousness of grief', at which Banting achieved a mastery often emulated but never matched. He did not marry. The business was destined to die with him, and royal warrant was never to be reissued. Banting died, 'a man of independent means', on 9 December 1932 at his home, 158 West Hill, Wandsworth, London, of 'anuria, pulmonary infarct and carcinoma of the bladder'. His will, dated only three days before his death, left his extensive property in Broadstairs, Thanet, in Kent, to his two younger brothers. Probate later valued his estate at just under £92,000. His funeral was held on 14 December at Kensal Green cemetery. After a service at 12 noon in the chapel, his body was deposited in a grave of his own making (no. 38565/128/PS) in a brick-lined vault for twelve members of his own family. He is thus buried, not only with his family but also among many former clients in this 'Valhalla of England'.

The hallmark of Banting funerals was grandeur and finery, 'the pomp of death'. Exhibitions and publications from the Victoria and Albert Museum at the close of the twentieth century revived interest in the style and chivalry of such funerals. If there is to be a re-evaluation of the English funeral, much of the inspiration will come from William Westbrook Banting. DAVID BANTING

Sources O. Bland, *The royal way of death* (1986) • J. Litten, *The English way of death: the common funeral since 1450* (1991) • N. Llewellyn, *The art of death: visual culture in the English death ritual, c. 1500–c. 1800* (1991) • Kensington registry (birth), 8 Nov 1857 • parish register, Notting Hill, St John the Evangelist, 10 June 1858 [baptism] • d. cert. • A. Barrister, 'Preface', in W. Banting, *The rational cure of obesity*, rev. edn (1902)

Archives priv. coll.

Wealth at death £91,812 8*s.* 10*d.*: probate, 10 Feb 1933, *CGPLA Eng. & Wales*

Bantock, Geoffrey Herman (1914–1997), educationist, was born at 22 Layton Avenue, Blackpool, on 12 October 1914, the only child of Herman Sutherland Bantock (1874–1965), musician, and his first wife, Annie, *née* Bailey (1885–1936). His father, a viola player, was a cousin of the composer Sir Granville Bantock. At Wallasey grammar school from 1924 to 1933 he gained distinctions in English and history, became head of school, and won borough and state scholarships to Cambridge. At Emmanuel College, Cambridge, he read history followed by English literature, was awarded an honorary senior exhibition in 1936, and completed his degree with an upper second in 1937. Like many contemporary students of English at Cambridge he was inspired by the reform of literary studies under the embattled F. R. Leavis and carried those ideals into the world of education, as a teacher at boys' grammar schools in Ealing and Ilford before his appointment in 1946 to a lectureship in English at the City of Leeds Training College. On 6 January 1950 he married one of his students at Leeds, who was to become a teacher, (Dorothy) Jean Pick (*b.* 1927), daughter of Robert Pick, master tailor.

While at Leeds, Bantock contributed to the journal *Scrutiny*, becoming its dominant voice on educational matters, and challenging concepts of planning, popularization, and freedom. These articles formed the core of his first book, *Freedom and Authority in Education: a Criticism of Modern Cultural and Educational Assumptions* (1952), which achieved what he described as 'a minor "succès de scandale"'. Meanwhile he had been appointed to a lectureship at University College, Leicester, in 1950, in an education department which was soon to become notable for its progressive outlook and its leadership of the national campaign for comprehensive secondary schools. Bantock, however, stood his ground in defence of selective grammar schools for the intellectual élite, and in opposition to progressivism. He was appointed reader in education in 1954, published a study of the novelist L. H. Myers (1956), and continued to write, for the educational press and for academic journals, philosophical critiques of progressivist educational thought and of modern educational methods. In his second major book, *Education in an Industrial Society* (1963), consolidating some of his previously published papers, he sought to define a differentiated curriculum appropriate to varying capacities. Against the background of a growing campaign for greater equality of opportunity in secondary schools this book was widely reviewed and generated considerable debate. In the following year he was promoted to the chair of education at Leicester. Bantock published further books and numerous articles in the later 1960s and 1970s.

Bantock's participation in educational campaigns from 1969 projected him into the fray of an impassioned public debate on educational policy. The *Critical Quarterly* had taken up the baton of cultural criticism laid down by *Scrutiny*, and, responding to a cultural crisis symbolized by the campus unrest of 1968, began to publish its polemical Black Papers on education, in which Bantock came to write regularly. His contributions over the years 1969 to 1977 included critiques of 'discovery methods' and of teacher education. In this connection he was also a founding sponsor in 1972 of the National Council for Education Standards, a pressure group led by university lecturers and independent school headmasters. In 1975 he retired from his university post to bring to fruition his major research project, intended from early in his career, a history of progressive education. This work appeared as the two-volume *Studies in the History of Educational Theory*, vol. 1: *Artifice and Nature, 1350–1765* (1980), and vol. 2: *The Minds and the Masses, 1760–1980* (1984). Volume 2 was awarded a prize by the standing conference on studies in education.

The Leavisian influence on education in post-war Britain was great, effected in part through a number of prominent educationists, of whom Bantock became perhaps the best known. Other professors of education who had been touched by Leavis included William Walsh and Boris Ford, and, of a younger generation, Brian Cox and A. E. Dyson, originators of the Black Papers. Although differing from this group in many particulars, Bantock shared with them a belief in the values of high culture conveyed supremely in literature, and accessible only to a small élite. He considered that in the humanities and especially in literature 'is to be found the morality appropriate to a modern, decision-making, sophisticated minority', set against the 'vulgarised cultural order of the industrial–bureaucratic state' (Bantock, *Education in an Industrial Society*, 1963, 227, 202). In the course of his writing he dealt critically with Rousseau for his 'child-centredness' and with Dewey for his egalitarianism. 'The equality we need is that which reverently accepts the essential nature and uniqueness of every human being; the hierarchy, one which recognises different levels of intelligence and sensitivity and recruits itself on this basis' (ibid., 224). He wrote appreciatively of Matthew Arnold and Cardinal Newman, but drew inspiration above all from D. H. Lawrence and T. S. Eliot. Eliot offered personal support, sympathizing strongly with Bantock's arguments and recommending the publication of his first book by Faber and Faber; he encouraged him to produce his second major book on education, and Bantock made fulsome acknowledgement in *Education and Values* (1965), published shortly after Eliot's death. Bantock also published *T. S. Eliot and Education* (1969); a further volume, *Education, Culture and the Emotions* (1967), was dedicated to Leavis, who had also supported Bantock in his academic career.

Bantock described himself as an educationist, resisting classification as either an English scholar or a philosopher of education. Sincere and tenacious in his views, he made contributions which lent academic authority to the Black Papers, but the debate unleashed a reaction in educational policy, aspects of which ran counter to his ideals. A quiet, retiring man, he was hurt by the opprobrium which his ideas attracted. He collected antiques and enjoyed drama, music, and dance, which he promoted as curriculum subjects. He died of lung cancer at his home, the Old Rectory, 1807 Melton Road, Rearsby, Leicestershire, on 1 September 1997, and was buried on 4 September at St Michael and All Angels Church, Rearsby. He was survived by his wife. PETER CUNNINGHAM

Sources *WWW* • *Daily Telegraph* (19 Sept 1997) • *The Times* (25 Sept 1997) • *The Guardian* (15 Oct 1997) • F. Mulhern, *The moment of scrutiny* (1979) • C. B. Cox, *The great betrayal* (1992) • R. Barrow, *An introduction to philosophy of education*, 3rd edn (1988) • private information (2004) • *CGPLA Eng. & Wales* (1998) • b. cert. • m. cert. • d. cert.
Archives priv. coll. | University of Manchester, C. B. Cox MSS
Likenesses P. Suschitzy, photographs, priv. coll. • oils, repro. in *Times Educational Supplement* (10 Nov 1967), p. 1065
Wealth at death £449,101: probate, 1998, *CGPLA Eng. & Wales*

Bantock, Sir Granville Ransome (1868–1946), composer and university professor, was born on 7 August 1868 at 44 Cornwall Road, Notting Hill, London, the eldest son of an eminent surgeon and gynaecologist, George Granville Bantock (1837–1913), and his wife, Sophia Elizabeth (Bessie) Ransome (1843–1909). George Bantock had been born in Sutherland, where his father became gamekeeper for the infamous second duke on his Dunrobin estate. Granville Bantock's mother, from an East Anglian entrepreneurial Quaker family, was a munificent and vivacious theatre-loving woman.

Bantock was educated privately in London. It was not until his mid-teens that he acquired the all-abiding musical intent that led him to clash with his father over a career in the Indian Civil Service. He was then sent to the London City and Guilds Institute to study chemical engineering, but was eventually permitted private lessons in harmony and counterpoint at Trinity College of Music and on 22 September 1888 entered the Royal Academy of Music, where his primary subjects were composition and harmony under Frederick Corder. Notwithstanding a flagrant musical naïvety, he was the first recipient of the Macfarren scholarship, and was eventually appointed sub-professor in harmony. On leaving, he was given the unprecedented privilege of a complete concert of his music.

On leaving the Royal Academy in 1893 Bantock founded the periodical *New Quarterly Musical Review*, which ran for three years. In 1893 he conducted a burlesque, *Bonnie Boy Blue*, around the country. He then began a more lasting association with the Gaiety Company, run by George Edwardes: first on two provincial tours with *A Gaiety Girl* by O. Hall and *In Town* by A. Russell and J. T. Tanner in 1894; then abroad, with dates in the USA and Australia into 1894–5—characteristically, he returned with multifarious mementos, including a monkey. Over the next few years he continued to work in musical comedy, and even produced a couple of 'hit' music hall songs. The following year he toured with Stanford's *Shamus O'Brien* around north-west England and Ireland.

Still unsuccessful at obtaining an academic appointment, Bantock organized two London concerts of works by himself and other young British composers—the first on 15 December 1896 to some furore. There followed a stint conducting incidental music for French plays at the Royalty Theatre, London, during May and into June 1897. Then at the beginning of June he took up an appointment as musical director at the Tower Gardens, New Brighton, Cheshire. This period proved to be a turning point in his life. First, on 9 March 1898, he married Helen Francesca Maude (1868–1961), daughter of Carl Adolph Herman

Schweitzer. Bantock's wife was a poet and artist and was to provide numerous texts for songs and vocal works. The couple set up home at Liscard: two sons, Angus and Raymond, were born during their stay on the Wirral. Second, Bantock quickly transformed the military band at New Brighton into an orchestra of national reputation with programmes to rival those of Dan Godfrey in Bournemouth and August Manns at the Crystal Palace. He not only performed major orchestral works, but also devoted whole concerts to contemporary, often British, composers (invariably with them as guest conductors). He formed his own local choral society and took up an appointment with the Runcorn Choral Society in September 1897. He now too began to mature as a composer, escaping the dominating influence of Wagner in particular. The first of six sets of *Songs of the East* was begun just weeks after his meeting with Helen in March 1896, and *Elegiac Poem* (1898) and *Helena Variations* (1899) were highlights amid continuing, more sprawling conceptions like *Christus* (1900).

In 1900, backed with prestigious recommendations, Bantock became principal of the Birmingham and Midland Institute School of Music. The midlands were to become his musical home for most of his remaining career: another son, Hamilton, and a daughter, Myrrha, were born soon after the family's move south. (There was also to be another son from a later love affair with the singer Denne Parker, and it is thought there were other extramarital liaisons.) He soon transformed the school into a vibrant musical centre, and also took up appointments with orchestral and choral societies in Liverpool, Wolverhampton, Birmingham, and Worcester. In 1908 Bantock replaced Elgar as Peyton professor of music at Birmingham University and began intertwining the teaching of the two establishments into one enterprising, broad-based system of education, with many prominent figures becoming associated with their work. Conspicuously active in the musical life of his adopted city, he was instrumental in the early establishment of a city orchestra. His involvement in the competitive festivals movement as a composer and arranger of test pieces and as a much travelled judge now also became a major aspect of his work. Though Bantock's personality possessed a strong streak of conservatism (he loathed jazz), this, like his later concern with brass bands, partly reflected his evolved political inclinations and commitment to the labour movement, which included work for the Workers' Educational Association and writing, at Keir Hardie's request, *Labour March* and other compositions for the Trades Union Congress.

Despite all his academic responsibilities, it was during his years in Birmingham that Bantock composed the body of work that constitutes the core of his reputation, including his best-known pieces, the tone-poem *Fifine at the Fair* (1911) and the overture *The Pierrot of the Minute* (1908). His music revealed an abiding fascination with world literature. This was manifest in orchestral works like *The Witch of Atlas* (1902) and *Dante and Beatrice* (1910), as well as in his many settings of poetry, of the Romantics in particular. From student days he had been drawn to the culture and philosophy of the East: *Omar Khayyam*, a setting of Edward FitzGerald's poem, is often regarded as his finest work. Its three parts were at first performed separately: the first at Birmingham (1906), the second at Cardiff (1907), and the final part at Birmingham again (1909). There were subsequently complete performances, notably at the Queen's Hall, London, and in Vienna.

Bantock also made fruitful use of oriental and Near Eastern literature, as in the charming if less ambitious string quartet *In a Chinese Mirror* (1933), and in his many settings of Chinese poets. Classical antiquity was the inspiration of some of his other excellent works, notably the *Pagan*

Sir Granville Ransome Bantock (1868–1946), by Herbert Lambert, pubd 1923

Symphony (1923–8) and *Sappho* (1906). Though fascinated by more arcane spiritualities, he turned to biblical material for his *Song of Songs* and the second of his three innovative choral 'symphonies', *Vanity of Vanities* (1913). He involved himself with English, Welsh, and Irish song, but his Scottish ancestral connection especially engendered a number of major scores. The most important of these were the enchanting *Hebridean Symphony* (1915) and the folk opera *The Seal-Woman* (1924), with a libretto by Marjory Kennedy-*Fraser.

Although Bantock's works had long been out of favour, he was knighted in 1930. He retired from Birmingham in 1934 and moved to London to continue work and touring for Trinity College. He recorded a set of 'mood' pieces plus a couple of more weighty works such as *Four Chinese Landscapes* (1936); the glory of his last years, the twenty-minute *Celtic Symphony* (1940), was also recorded on disc.

'GB', as he was known, was bearded and of broad bearing; a charismatic and much loved figure, genial and kindly, open-minded and full-hearted, energetic and enthusiastic, and known for his engaging sense of humour, eccentricities, and all-consuming fads. Cultured and linguistic, he corresponded with and befriended many of the most significant artistic figures of the period. He was conspicuously generous in his support of fellow composers at home and abroad. He was one of the first advocates of Sibelius, to whom he played host on his visits to England; and in gratitude, Sibelius dedicated his third symphony to Bantock and happily accepted the first presidency of the Bantock Society.

A prolific composer, noted for his commanding orchestration, Bantock left behind a wide-ranging *œuvre*, essentially Romantic, sometimes of grand conception, often expressly programmatic and inspired by poetic, heroic, and exotic themes. For some, his work was composed with an all-too-easy facility, lacking both self-critical restraint and an individual voice, and was too much steeped in late Victorian and Edwardian Romanticism to survive beyond its time. For others, he left behind a fascinating range of music, including works to rival even the best of his more illustrious compatriots. He arguably remains one of the most unfairly neglected figures in twentieth-century British music.

Bantock died in All Saints' Hospital in London on 16 October 1946, after a fall following a minor operation. His ashes were later scattered on Moelwyn above Coed-y-bleiddiau, where the family had spent so many happy holidays. In 1972 his daughter Myrrha published *Granville Bantock: a Personal Portrait*. VINCENT BUDD

Sources Worcs. County RO, St Helen's branch, Fish Street, Worcester, Bantock archive • V. Budd, *An introduction to the life and work of Sir Granville Bantock* (2000) • M. Bantock, *Granville Bantock: a personal portrait* (1972) • H. Orsmond Anderton, *Granville Bantock* (1915) • T. Bray, 'Granville Bantock: his life and music', PhD diss., U. Cam., 1972 • *Bantock Society Journal*, new ser. (1996–9) • *CGPLA Eng. & Wales* (1947) • b. cert. • m. cert. • d. cert. • P. J. Pirie, 'Bantock, Sir Granville', *New Grove* • private information (2004) [family]

Archives priv. coll., diaries, etc. • U. Birm. L., corresp. • Worcs. RO, corresp. and papers | BL, letters to his son Raymond; letters to Sir Henry Wood, Add. MS 69450; Add. MS 56419 • Bodl. Oxf., corresp. with Gilbert Murray • NL Scot., letters to William Wallace • U. Birm. L., letters to R. J. Buckley; letters to his son Raymond; corresp. with Ernst Newman • U. Edin. L., letters to Marjory Kennedy-Fraser | SOUND BBC WAC • BL NSA, 'Granville Bantock', M1370R C1 • BL NSA, performance recordings

Likenesses J. B. Munns, oils, 1920, Barber Institute of Fine Arts, Birmingham • H. Lambert, photogravure, pubd 1923, NPG [*see illus.*] • G. H. Holland, oils, 1933, NPG • G. C. Hudson, oils, 1934, U. Birm. • G. H. Holland, oils, 1957–8 (after his earlier portrait), Royal Academy of Music, London • W. Stoneman, photograph, NPG • portrait, Trinity College, London

Wealth at death £3562 2*s.* 5*d.*: probate, 6 Jan 1947, *CGPLA Eng. & Wales*

Banu, Halime (1770–1853). *See under* Indian visitors (*act. c.*1720–*c.*1810).

Banwell, Keith Deamer [Tex] (1918–1999), soldier, was born on 8 October 1918 at Pond Street, Wenden Lofts, Newport, Essex, the son of Frederick Deamer Banwell, then serving with the Australian Imperial Force, and his wife, Elsie, *née* Walters. His family moved to Australia when he was three, and when Keith returned to England fifteen years later he began his military life in the Coldstream Guards. Seeking an adventurous overseas posting, he soon transferred to the Royal Hampshire regiment and was enrolled in the 1st battalion which was serving on the north-west frontier of India.

In 1938 his battalion moved to Palestine, where it was engaged in counter-terrorist duties, and from there to Egypt, where it was joined by members of the French Foreign Legion. Banwell, nicknamed Tex, was soon appointed a physical training instructor and it was noted that though the Foreign Legion had a reputation for toughness, Banwell was tougher. When he heard that volunteers were required for an unspecified new force demanding the highest physical and military skills he applied. He was promptly enrolled in 52nd Middle East commando regiment, which planned to conduct harassing raids along the coastline of enemy-held territory; unfortunately a shortage of shipping suitable for such assignments restricted their activities, and Banwell realized that there were greater possibilities of action with the long range desert group (LRDG) which was making deep reconnaissance forays behind the German lines in the desert. The LRDG contained experienced desert explorers who travelled in trucks or jeeps, navigating by sun compasses, in specially adapted vehicles equipped with water condensers and devices for traversing soft sand, as well as a formidable supply of weapons. Although the LRDG was primarily for reconnaissance it was soon operating closely with the Special Air Service (SAS), which used similar vehicles to reach its targets (usually enemy airfields) deep in enemy territory. The LRDG put its expertise at the disposal of the SAS and was often at hand to extricate the latter when the SAS vehicles had been damaged during a raid.

Banwell was captured in a raid on Tobruk but managed to steal a German truck and escape; in a subsequent raid on Crete he was taken prisoner at Heraklion and was put under the personal supervision of Max Schmeling (world heavyweight boxing champion, 1930–32) who was serving with the German army. However, Banwell and a few of his comrades managed to slip away from their captors and acquire an assault landing craft. Unfortunately this austere craft ran out of fuel and drifted for nine days before reaching the north African coast. The privations of the journey resulted in twelve weeks in hospital for Banwell where it was noticed that he bore a resemblance to General (later Field Marshal) Montgomery. At the time there were numerous spies operating in the Middle East and in order to confuse the enemy about allied plans it was decided that Banwell should impersonate Montgomery and be sent on various trips around the region. He was sent to Cairo to meet Montgomery and given the appropriate clothing and badges, but as he was considerably taller than Montgomery he was told that he must on no account get out of the car.

After a while Banwell found this new role too boring and requested a transfer back to the infantry. He developed an interest in parachuting and joined the 10th battalion of the Parachute regiment, in which his arduous work schedule did not, however, prevent him from having many successes in regimental boxing and cross-country running. On 4 March 1944 he married Winifred Violet Sleet, with whom he had a son and two daughters.

In September 1944 Banwell flew into Arnhem, where the 1st airborne division attempted to capture the vital bridge but found that enemy troops in the area were too numerous and too well armed. The Dakota aircraft in which he was flying was carrying fifteen parachutists, six of whom were killed when it was hit by enemy fire. Banwell landed safely and fought throughout the ensuing battle until he was wounded and taken prisoner by the Germans. He escaped by jumping from a moving train as it was entering Germany and linked up with the Dutch resistance, for whom he became an instructor in weapons and explosives, as well as a leader in raids. On one of his forays, however, he was again captured by the Germans. They decided he had forfeited his military status by living with the Dutch resistance, court-martialled him, and sentenced him to death. He was told that if he disclosed the names of his Dutch resistance contacts he would be reprieved. When he refused to do this he was taken out and put before a firing squad which was given all the orders except the one to fire. He was then returned to his cell but was told that the next day he really would be shot. The following morning the ritual was repeated, but this time the squad fired blanks. As he still refused to talk, he was taken to Auschwitz concentration camp, kept in a 6 foot square cage and starved, reducing him to half his normal weight. When the allies approached he was moved to Fallingbostel, from where he was liberated by the Russians just in time.

After returning to England, Banwell rejoined 10th Parachute regiment, which had now been re-formed, but on one parachute jump he landed so badly that he was pronounced dead and was taken to a mortuary. Eventually an attendant noticed a flutter of one eyelid and successfully resuscitated him.

Banwell remained in the army for some years after the war, and then worked for the Post Office until his retirement. But he continued parachuting, made his 1000th jump at Arnhem on the fortieth anniversary of the battle, and jumped again on the fiftieth anniversary at the age of seventy-seven.

He was a member of the 10th battalion cross-country team which won the eastern command cup for six successive years, was a second Dan black belt at judo and held the record for the 10th battalion road walk from Birmingham to London. He marched from London to Brighton in ten and a half hours. He also marched from John o' Groats to Land's End in full army kit, wearing standard issue leather boots with no socks in them. He represented 10 para in the Westminster to Devizes canoe race five times. At the end of his army service he served in the special constabulary. He was awarded a British Empire Medal in 1969 and the Netherlands silver cross for services to Dutch resistance in 1992.

Tex Banwell died on 25 July 1999 at Chase Farm Hospital, Enfield, and was buried in north London on 3 August; he was survived by his second wife, Elsie.

PHILIP WARNER

Sources private information (2004) [family] • L. Heaps, *The grey goose at Arnhem* (1977) • M. James, *Born of the desert* (1945) • J. M. Strawson, *History of the SAS regiment* (1984) • *The Guardian* (30 Aug 1999) • *Daily Telegraph* (23 Aug 1999) • *London Evening Standard* (2 Aug 1999) • *The Mirror* (4 Aug 1999) • *New York Times* (24 Aug 1999) • b. cert. • m. cert. [Winifred Sleet] • d. cert.

Banyer, Henry (1690–1749), physician, was the nephew of Lawrence Banyer (*d.* 1720), apothecary of Wisbech, Cambridgeshire. He studied at St Thomas's Hospital, and practised as a surgeon and then as a physician (extra-licentiate of the Royal College of Physicians, 1736) at Wisbech. He translated with additions Joannes van Horne's *Micro-techne, or, A Methodical Introduction to the Art of Chirurgery* (1717), and wrote a *Pharmacopoeia* (4 edns, 1721–39). He was married and appears to have been prosperous. Banyer died in Wisbech in 1749: he was survived by his wife, who died in 1759. [ANON.], *rev.* JEAN LOUDON

Sources Munk, *Roll* • P. Cave, 'Richard Middleton Massey', *Annual Report* [Wisbech Society], 43 (1982), 13 • *VCH Cambridgeshire and the Isle of Ely*, vol. 4 • *GM*, 1st ser., 29 (1759), 606 [death notice of Mrs Banyer] • private information (2004) • A. Berman, 'Henry Banyer's hospital dispensatories', *Bulletin of the American Society of Hospital Pharmacists*, 13 (July–Aug 1956), 7 [this journal held only in Pharmaceutical Society Library, London]

Barak [Bairuk, Beruk, Beerack, Berak], **William** (1823?–1903), Australian Aboriginal leader, was born near the Yarra and Plenty rivers in south-east Australia, probably in 1823, the son of Jerrum Jerrum (Bebejern; *fl.* 1820–1830), and given the name Barak. He was brought up in the traditional fashion in the Wurundjeri clan, sub-group of the Woi-wurrung, and witnessed the meeting of his clan leaders with John Batman near Port Phillip in June 1835. As a result of the British settlement and the dislocation of Aboriginal life, Barak was not properly initiated, though at a ceremony in 1836 the tribal marks (keloids) were incised on his chest. In 1837 he went to George Langhorne's Anglican mission school about 2 miles from Melbourne, and attended it irregularly until it closed early in 1839. After five years of casual living, in January 1844 he joined Captain Henry Dana's native police corps, and was given the additional name of William. He was an excellent tracker and, like some of his fellows, partially adapted to Western ways. He served, with a couple of breaks, until the corps was disbanded in 1852, when he found that the elders of a Gippsland tribe had arranged for him to marry Lizzie (*d.* 1864), his first wife. They had three children, all of whom died in infancy.

During the 1850s Barak worked as a stockman for various settlers, was converted to Christianity, and ceased to be a heavy drinker. In 1860, when new reserve stations were established for the Aborigines, he settled at the Mohican station, Acheron, Victoria. Because it faced local opposition there, in 1863 the reserve was moved to Coranderrk, about 40 miles from Melbourne, near the River Yarra (and present-day Healesville)—much to Barak's delight, for this was in his former tribal territory. The following year there were sixty-seven Aborigines at the station, which soon became self-sufficient; Barak was active in horse breeding, bark-tanning, and growing vegetables and hops. His wife died in 1864 and in 1865 he married a Murray woman called Annie.

Barak became one of the station's leaders. For years the Aborigines had to fight the Aboriginal board's authoritarian paternalism and its desire to move the station further away and open the land for selection, but Barak led several deputations to Melbourne, won over the press, and in 1881 persuaded the premier, Graham Berry, to let Coranderrk stay where it was. That year his second wife and their son David died of consumption; on 7 June 1890 he married Sarah Wood, the sister of his first wife, but she too died only four years later.

Barak himself died on 15 August 1903, the last full-blood survivor of his tribe, intelligent, dignified, and highly respected. He was a talented painter in charcoal and ochre, and a few of his expressive works survive. He was a valuable source of information to writers and anthropologists about Aboriginal customs and beliefs, their 'dreaming', their music, their kinship patterns, and their property rules, and he twice visited Sale to help A. W. Howitt on his book *Native Tribes* (1904). In June 1934 the chancellor of Melbourne University unveiled a stone memorial in Healesville, which was moved to Barak's grave site at Coranderrk in 1955. A. G. L. SHAW

Sources S. W. Wiencke, *When the wattles bloom again: the life and times of William Barak* (1984) • 'Coranderrk Aboriginal Station: report of board of inquiry', *Votes and proceedings*, Victoria Legislative Assembly (1882–3), vol. 2 • M. Fels, *Good men and true: Aboriginal police* (1988) • M. F. Christie, *Aborigines in colonial Victoria* (1979) • D. Barwick, 'Coranderrk and Cumeroogunga', *Opportunity and response*, ed. T. S. Epstein and D. Penny (1972) • A. Massola, *Coranderrk: a history of the Aboriginal station* (1975) • P. Marcard, 'Barak, William', *AusDB*, vol. 3

Archives Healesville, Victoria, Frank Endacott collection

Likenesses J. Fuller, oils, 1885, State Library of Victoria, Melbourne, Australia, La Trobe coll.

Barantyn, Drew (*c.*1350–1415), goldsmith and mayor of London, was the younger son of Thomas Barantyn, lord of Chalgrove in Oxfordshire (he had an older brother, Thomas, who died in 1400). Barantyn's talents as a craftsman rather than his family connections were to be the key to his success in the world. He was apprenticed to Robert Oxenford in 1363, and became a freeman of the city of London and member of the Goldsmiths' Company in 1370, taking apprentices himself from 1379. He was twice warden of the company: in 1380 and 1385. Thereafter it was as a court supplier, financier, and one of the rulers of London that he was most prominent. Among Barantyn's many commissions for the royal household in the later years of Richard II's reign were two collars and a brooch set with rubies, pearls, and diamonds made 'for the king's own person' in 1393. In association with Hans Doubler, an immigrant goldsmith and diamond merchant, Barantyn established a reputation for work in precious stones.

Barantyn was introduced to court circles by Sir Nicholas Twyford. He worked for Twyford before establishing his own business, became one of his executors, and Twyford's patronage was a determining factor in his career. Twyford died in 1390, and Barantyn's first wife, Margery (*d. c.*1414), was Twyford's widow as well as being the granddaughter of Simon Burgh, another goldsmith. Barantyn followed his patron in pursuing a middle course through the turbulent politics of Richard II's reign. In the quarrel which erupted between Richard and the city of London in 1392 Barantyn, as a newly elected alderman, was one of those summoned to appear before the king and council on 25 June 1392 to answer for defaults in the government of the city. But he was confirmed in his aldermanry by the king on 22 July, and elected sheriff in the following year and mayor in 1398—appointments which, at a time when the city's liberties remained conditional upon royal favour, epitomize the career of one whose expertise in his craft commended him to the crown, but who had the confidence of his fellow citizens as well. That confidence was further expressed in Barantyn's election to the parliaments of 1395, 1397 (September), 1404 (January), 1410, 1413 (February), and 1413 (May), and as mayor once again in 1408.

On 7 May 1393 Barantyn was one of three leading goldsmiths to whom the king granted licence to alienate lands and rents held in mortmain, in aid of the implementation of the company's new charter. Behind the comparatively modest sum of 20 marks paid by the goldsmiths for this grant on 6 February 1393 lay an altogether more substantial exaction. In the same month, as the price of pardons to the Londoners, Richard II acknowledged the receipt of £10,000, a sum that was accompanied by gifts of jewels and plate to an equivalent amount. No doubt the alienations of Goldsmiths' property were intended to finance that company's share of the city's composition with the king. In the relationship between the crown and the wealthy London capitalists during this period, the patronage disposed of by the former was of paramount importance. Henry IV's charter of 1404, granting extended powers to the Goldsmiths, owed much to Barantyn's standing and influence with the king.

Even as Twyford's customers had included not only

Richard II but Edward, the Black Prince, and John of Gaunt, so Barantyn's association with Henry of Lancaster antedated the latter's accession to the throne. In 1394 Henry's new year gifts included two gold rings set with diamonds purchased from Barantyn. The mayor who headed the procession which welcomed Lancaster to the city on 1 September 1399 was well known to the duke; for the rest of Henry IV's life Barantyn was to serve him just as he had served Richard. Payments to him by the king in 1408 included £550 for a gold collar garnished with pearls, 1000 marks for a brooch, and £99 12*s*. for silver vessels given to the French ambassadors. The most outstanding of the jewels pledged by Henry V before Agincourt was 'the Michael', purchased from Barantyn in the previous reign. Loans by Barantyn to Henry IV varied from comparatively small amounts of £27 (1408) and 100 marks (1410) to £150 (1402) and £1500 (1410).

If Barantyn's skill as a craftsman and prestige as a retailer were the bases of his wealth, his marriage to Twyford's widow raised him to the top rank of London's property owners. To the estate acquired through this marriage Barantyn added further investments in land. In the city the most notable of his purchases was the Jewengarden, with adjacent shops and houses, in the parish of St Giles without Cripplegate, a property which, together with houses in Gutter Lane, he left to the Goldsmiths' Company in his will. In the lay subsidy of 1412 Barantyn's assessment of £55 16*s*. 11*d*. exceeded that of the wealthy mercer Richard Whittington (*d*. 1423), and even that of the Goldsmiths' Company itself. Outside London, Barantyn again added to Twyford's holdings, principally in Oxfordshire, Cambridgeshire, Suffolk, and Buckinghamshire. In his later years Barantyn's varied credit operations and commercial interests, including Mediterranean trade in cloth and wool, contributed to his working capital.

Barantyn died on 14 December 1415, survived by his second wife, Christine, whom he had married not long before. There were no children of either of his marriages. In his will he made provision for his burial in the church of St John Zachary, and for a chantry there for the souls of himself, his first wife, Margery, and Nicholas Twyford, the charges to be met from the property left to the Goldsmiths' Company. 100 marks were to be distributed to 'poor and needy men and women of the goldsmiths' craft in the city of London' to pray for his soul, an obligation which the goldsmiths' ordinances show to have been incumbent twice weekly upon the company's almsmen. Barantyn's bequests amounted to over £1000 and included legacies to his servants in both town and country, and also £60 for 'the poor kinsfolk of Nicholas Twyford' (PRO, PROB 11/2B, sig. 31). His widow's dower was confiscated by the crown in 1419 after she married John Manning, coroner of Wiltshire, without royal licence. Recovered by fine, the dower was the subject of extensive litigation when, after Manning's death, Christine married the heir to the greater part of Barantyn's estates, his nephew, Reynold Barantyn. LORNA E. M. WALKER

Sources Worshipful Company of Goldsmiths of London, MSS 1518, 1642, 1643, 2524 • will, PRO, PROB 11/2B, sig. 31 [C 138/20/43, C 139/34, E101, E136, E401, E403, E404] • HR, CLRO • HPL, CLRO • CLRO, published calendars • *Chancery records* • T. F. Reddaway, *The early history of the Goldsmiths' Company, 1327–1509*, ed. L. E. M. Walker (1975) • HoP, *Commons, 1386–1421* • F. Devon, ed. and trans., *Issues of the exchequer: being payments made out of his majesty's revenue, from King Henry III to King Henry VI inclusive*, RC (1837) • A. B. Beaven, ed., *The aldermen of the City of London, temp. Henry III–[1912]*, 2 vols. (1908–13) • C. M. Barron, 'The quarrel of Richard II with London, 1392–7', *The reign of Richard II: essays in honour of May McKisack*, ed. F. R. H. Du Boulay and C. M. Barron (1971), 173–201 • S. L. Thrupp, *The merchant class of medieval London, 1300–1500* (1948) • J. Stow, *A survey of London*, rev. edn (1603); repr. with introduction by C. L. Kingsford as *A survey of London*, 2 vols. (1908); repr. with addns (1971) • J. C. L. Stahlschmidt, ed., 'Lay subsidy temp. Henry IV: original documents', *Archaeological Journal*, 44 (1887), 56–82

Wealth at death Individual bequests totalling over £1000; property in London assessed at £38 p.a. in 1415; considerable revenues from property in the country: Stahlschmidt, ed., 'Lay subsidy'; PRO C 138/20/43; E 136/108/13; PROB 11/2B, sig. 31

Barbar, Thomas. *See* Barber, Thomas (*b*. *c*.1545, *d*. after 1603).

Barbauld [*née* Aikin], **Anna Letitia** [Anna Laetitia] (**1743–1825**), poet and essayist, was born on 20 June 1743 at Kibworth Harcourt, Leicestershire, elder child of the Revd John *Aikin (1713–1780), schoolmaster, and his wife Jane (1714–1785), daughter of the Revd John Jennings of Kibworth and his wife Anna Letitia Wingate. Both her parents were Presbyterian. She was educated by her mother, who taught her to read by the age of two but who also, fearing that a girl brought up in the presence of schoolboys would become a 'hoyden', strictly curbed her activity (LeBreton, 24–5). Later she persuaded her father to teach her Latin and some Greek, and she read avidly in his library. In 1758 her family moved to Warrington, Lancashire, where Mr Aikin served as tutor in languages, literature, and divinity at Warrington Academy. Among its tutors and students she made lifelong friends, notably Joseph Priestley (1733–1804), his wife Mary (1742–1796), and William Enfield (1741–1797).

Inspired by Warrington's intellectual atmosphere and encouraged by her brother John *Aikin (1747–1822), with whom she shared literary and scientific tastes, Anna Aikin began, around the mid-1760s, to write poems. The poems display her varied interests: zoology ('To Mrs. P[riestley], with some Drawings of Birds and Insects'), the new industrial infrastructure of Lancashire ('The Invitation', praising the duke of Bridgewater's canal), opposition politics ('Corsica', 1769, written for a subscription in aid of Corsican independence), humane treatment of animals ('The Mouse's Petition'), intense devotional experience ('An Address to the Deity'), and friendship, especially with women (poems to Mary Priestley, her cousin Elizabeth Belsham, and others). In style her poems range from burlesque ('The Groans of the Tankard') to sublime ('A Summer Evening's Meditation'); some are impishly humorous. Her *Poems* (1773) was a popular and critical success, reaching five editions by 1777 (with another in 1792) and winning the adulation of the *Monthly Review* ('a justness of thought, and vigour of imagination, inferior only to the works of Milton and Shakespeare') and the admiration of women readers—for instance, Mary Scott wrote in *The*

Female Advocate (1774): 'We feel thy feelings, glow with all thy fires, / Adopt thy thoughts, and pant with thy desires' (*Works*, xxxii). Her next publication, jointly with John Aikin, was *Miscellaneous Pieces in Prose* (1773), a collection of essays. One, 'On romances', an imitation of Samuel Johnson, earned his praise; another, 'Against inconsistency in our expectations', was admired for its ethical argument and stylistic elegance.

Although shy and awkward in manner, Anna Aikin 'possessed … great beauty, distinct traces of which she retained' into old age (Aikin, ix–x), and at Warrington she had several suitors. According to legend, one was Jean-Paul Marat, who is said to have served briefly as tutor in French at the academy (Rodgers, 43–4). On 26 May 1774 she married the Revd Rochemont Barbauld (1749–1808), an academy graduate, son of a Church of England clergyman descended from French Huguenot refugees. At Warrington Rochemont Barbauld converted to dissent; he later became a zealous Unitarian. Having no children of their own, in 1777 the Barbaulds adopted Charles Rochemont *Aikin (1775–1847), her brother's second son.

After their marriage the Barbaulds settled at Palgrave, Suffolk, where on 25 July 1774 they opened a school for boys. A great success, the school drew boys from as far as New York and the West Indies; during the Barbaulds' tenure an estimated 130 boys passed through it. Several achieved eminence in later years: examples are William Taylor (1765–1836), whose translations of German literature influenced the first generation of Romantic poets, and Thomas Denman (1779–1854), drafter of the Reform Act of 1832. The school also occasioned Barbauld's most influential books: *Lessons for Children* (4 vols., 1778–9), written to teach Charles to read, and *Hymns in Prose for Children* (1781), a primer in religion for her youngest pupils. Reprinted in England and America throughout the nineteenth century, and translated into other languages, they profoundly affected reading pedagogy among the middle classes; the name Mrs Barbauld became virtually synonymous with infant instruction. Equally popular was her brother's *Evenings at Home* (1792–6), of which she was widely thought the principal author although she wrote only fourteen of the pieces it comprised.

In 1785 the Barbaulds resigned from Palgrave School and travelled in France, meeting liberal aristocrats and, perhaps, a future leader of the French Revolution, Jean-Paul Rabaut de Saint-Étienne (1743–1793). In 1787 they settled in Hampstead, Middlesex, where they took pupils. Roused by Edmund Burke's attacks on the French Revolution and parliament's failure (March 1790) to repeal the Test and Corporation Acts, Barbauld returned to authorship with a powerful tract, *An Address to the Opposers of the Repeal of the Corporation and Test Acts* (1790), in which she hailed the French Revolution as sublime evidence of human improvement. In 1791 she responded to parliament's failure to abolish the slave trade with a Juvenalian verse satire, *An Epistle to William Wilberforce, esq. … on the Rejection of the Bill for Abolishing the Slave Trade*. In 1793 she denounced the British government's entry into war against France in a sermon, *Sins of Government, Sins of the Nation*. In the controversy over public worship, however, she argued eloquently for traditional practice (*Remarks on Mr. Gilbert Wakefield's Enquiry into the Expediency and Propriety of Public or Social Worship*, 1792). Although she associated with Unitarians and was claimed by them, it is doubtful that she shared all their beliefs. Her churchgoing habits were eclectic, her religious attitude was liberal, and she valued devotional spirit over doctrine.

Starting with essays and poems in her brother's *Monthly Magazine* (1796–1802), Barbauld began contributing to periodicals and taking commissions from booksellers. She wrote for the *Annual Review* (1803–9), edited by her nephew Arthur *Aikin (1773–1854), and provided prefaces to editions of Mark Akenside (1794), William Collins (1797), and Addison and Steele (1804). She was the first editor of the correspondence of Samuel Richardson (6 vols., 1804); subsequent scholars have criticized her editing, but her biography of Richardson remains valuable. Barbauld also wrote prefaces for a 50-volume collection, *The British Novelists* (1810), producing an important body of criticism of the novel and individual novelists. In 1809 she began to write for the *Monthly Review*, contributing some 340 reviews during six years. She also brought out a literary anthology for young women, *The Female Speaker* (1811). Her last separate publication and most ambitious work was *Eighteen Hundred and Eleven* (1812), a poem deploring Britain's participation in the seemingly endless, apparently disastrous war against Napoleonic France and foretelling Britain's economic decline while, however, asserting its cultural dominion over the coming American empire. This poem met with extreme hostility from the tory press (John Wilson Croker's abusive review in the *Quarterly*—formerly attributed to Robert Southey—is legendary); today, however, *Eighteen Hundred and Eleven* is considered a major poem of the Romantic era.

In 1802 the Barbaulds settled in Church Street, Stoke Newington, Middlesex. Their associates included the circle of radical intellectuals gathered around Joseph Johnson (1738–1809), Barbauld's publisher, and such literary figures as Joanna Baillie, George Dyer, Maria Edgeworth, William Godwin, and Henry Crabb Robinson. Barbauld, who took benevolent interest in young men, sought to mentor Samuel Taylor Coleridge; later he turned against her, and his ridicule injured her posthumous reputation. Her husband appears to have suffered from manic-depressive disorder; this affliction troubled their marriage until, in 1808, Rochemont grew violent and a separation became necessary. She remained at Stoke Newington after his death by suicide in 1808, but subsided into melancholy; the death of her beloved brother John in 1822 deeply affected her. Gradually she developed asthma (a family ailment) and she died of it at Stoke Newington, on 9 March 1825, and was buried with her brother in the graveyard of St Mary's parish church. Her niece Lucy *Aikin (1781–1864) edited her *Works* (1825), adding fifty-two poems to the fifty-five Barbauld had published, and a volume of teaching pieces and essays called *A Legacy for Young Ladies* (1826).

During the century after her death Barbauld came to be

remembered chiefly as a writer for children, as the author of one poem, 'Life', which Wordsworth had praised, and as the object of attacks by Coleridge and Charles Lamb on the basis of her didacticism. A dislike of the moral tale led E. Nesbit to place Barbauld among the unpleasant Book People in *Wet Magic* (1913). However, along with her sister writers, Barbauld benefited from feminist reappraisal after the 1970s and is now perceived as a leading writer of early Romanticism. WILLIAM MCCARTHY

Sources A. L. Barbauld, *The poems of Anna Letitia Barbauld*, ed. W. McCarthy and E. Kraft (1994) • B. Rodgers, *Georgian chronicle: Mrs Barbauld and her family* (1958) • A. L. LeBreton, *Memoir of Mrs. Barbauld, including letters and notices of her family and friends* (1874) • L. Aikin, 'Memoir', in *The works of Anna Lætitia Barbauld*, ed. L. Aikin, 1 (1825), viii–lxxii • W. McCarthy, 'The celebrated academy at Palgrave: a documentary history of Anna Letitia Barbauld's school', *Age of Johnson*, 8 (1997), 279–392 • C. Moore, 'The literary career of Anna Letitia Barbauld', PhD diss., University of North Carolina, 1969 • B. C. Nangle, *The Monthly Review, second series, 1790–1815: indexes of contributors and articles* (1955) • baptismal record, PRO, RG 4/678, fol. 7 • parish register, Warrington, St Elphin, NL Wales [marriage], 26 May 1774

Archives Hackney Archives, London, corresp. • Hackney Archives, London, Aikin-Barbauld MSS • Hornel Library, Broughton House, Kirkcudbright, Aikin-Barbauld MSS • priv. coll. • priv. coll. • Yale U., Beinecke L. | Lpool RO, Nicholson MSS • Lpool RO, Roscoe MSS • V&A, Forster collection • Warrington Library, Warrington

Likenesses R. Samuel, oils, *c.*1775, NPG • prints, pubd 1776–1822, BM, NPG • E. Armytage, fresco, 1869, University Hall, London; repro. in E. J. Morley, *The life and times of Henry Crabb Robinson* (1935) • stained-glass window, 1896, Harris Man. Oxf. • Allan & Ferguson, engraving (after silhouette, late in life, by S. Hoare), repro. in Aikin, ed., *The works of Anna Lætitia Barbauld* • T. Holloway, medallion, line engraving, BM, NPG; repro. in *European Magazine* (1785) • E. Walker, photogravure (after H. Meyer), NPG • Wedgwood jasper medallion (after J. Smith, 1775), Wedgwood Museum, Barlaston, Staffordshire

Wealth at death over £230 in cash; also value of house in Church Street, Stoke Newington: will, PRO, PROB 11/1696

Barbellion, W. N. P. *See* Cummings, Bruce Frederick (1889–1919).

Barber, (Charles) Chapman (**1801x4–1882**), barrister, was the first son of Chapman Barber, a solicitor of Chancery Lane, London (*d.* before 1829). He was educated at a school in Saffron Walden, Essex, before being admitted to St John's College, Cambridge, in 1824, graduating BA in 1833 and MA in 1836. He first entered Lincoln's Inn in May 1824, was recorded as having been readmitted five years later, and was called to the bar on 2 May 1833. He was a pupil of Lewis Duval, an eminent conveyancer. Barber never took silk, but acquired a high reputation as an equity draftsman. For nearly half a century he had an extensive practice at the junior bar, conducting his business from the late 1830s onwards from chambers at 11 New Square, Lincoln's Inn. On 24 September 1845 he married Harriet Frances Bambrick at the chapel of the British embassy in Paris (*IGI*).

In December 1850 Barber was appointed secretary to the commission set up to investigate reform of chancery court procedure, at a salary of £600; he was paid an additional £300 for the preparation of bills arising from the commission's first report of January 1852. His experience of chancery work was clearly invaluable for this role, and in this connection was later published *Mr Barber's Statement on the Practice and Procedure of the Court of Chancery in England* (1865). Barber's spell in the limelight, however, came during the affair of the Tichborne claimant, during which he was a junior counsel on the defendants' legal team. At the initial hearing in July 1867, held at the Law Institution, Chancery Lane, it was he who cross-examined the claimant on key points of his story, most notably on the means of his escape from the shipwreck that was supposed to have claimed the life of Sir Roger Tichborne. The general opinion of the common law bar was that Barber, as a chancery barrister, was not best fitted for this task. Sir Henry Hawkins, who went on to lead for the defence, felt that Barber's mild style of questioning had let the claimant off the hook, and made the hindsight-gifted assertion that 'had I been instructed I am perfectly sure I could have extinguished the case then and there' (*Reminiscences*, 1.310–11). But historians of the affair have defended Barber, who had never before undertaken a cross-examination, on the grounds that in the preliminary hearing, the aim was only to establish the key points of the claimant's story, and that in any event Hawkins had been on the spot to direct the junior counsel had he felt so inclined. Whatever his shortcomings as an inquisitor, Barber was retained by the defence for the 103-day civil trial in common pleas (*Tichborne* v. *Lushington*, 1872), during which his experience in the law of real property and settlement was called upon in connection with the descent of the Tichborne and Doughty estates, and by the crown for the 188-day criminal trial for perjury that followed (April 1873–February 1874). On the conclusion of this, Barber was appointed a county court judge for Hull and the East Riding, but resigned after only a month in the post to resume his practice at the bar.

Barber died on 5 February 1882 at his residence, 71 Cornwall Gardens, South Kensington, London. He was survived by his wife, the sole executor of his estate. At his death he was 'the father' of the junior equity bar, and was eulogized as 'one of the most skilful and experienced conveyancers of his day', whose advice and opinion were regularly sought by his junior colleagues (*The Times*, 11 Feb 1882). H. J. SPENCER

Sources F. H. Maugham, *The Tichborne case* (1936) • J. D. Woodruff, *The Tichborne claimant: a Victorian mystery* (1957) • *The Times* (11 Feb 1882) • *DNB* • *The reminiscences of Sir Henry Hawkins*, ed. R. Harris, 2 vols. (1904) • *IGI* • Venn, *Alum. Cant.* • Boase, *Mod. Eng. biog.* • J. M. Collinge, *Officials of royal commissions of enquiry, 1815–70* (1984) • W. P. Baildon, ed., *The records of the Honorable Society of Lincoln's Inn: admissions*, 2 (1896), 107, 132

Wealth at death £6283 3*s.* 10*d.*: probate, 18 March 1882, *CGPLA Eng. & Wales*

Barber, Charles (*bap.* **1784**, *d.* **1854**), landscape painter, was baptized on 28 January 1784 at St Martin, Birmingham, one of the sons of Joseph *Barber (1757–1811), landscape painter, and his wife, Elizabeth. Charles attended his father's art school, where he was a fellow pupil of the watercolour landscape painter David Cox (1783–1859), with whom he formed a long friendship. Barber was one of the founders of the first Society of Birmingham Artists in 1809, which developed into the Birmingham Academy of Arts. By 1818 he was working in Liverpool as a drawing-master and was exhibiting at the Liverpool Academy by 1822. He was intimately connected with the various associations established in Liverpool in his lifetime. He was among the earliest members and most frequent contributors of the Literary and Philosophical Society, and helped to found the Architectural and Archaeological Association. Thomas Rickman found much support and encouragement from him in his early studies of Gothic architecture, and for years his house was the centre of the intellectual society of Liverpool. He also maintained close contacts with the Birmingham Society of Arts, exhibiting nine works there from 1829 to 1851.

As a landscape painter Barber was a close observer of nature, and endeavoured to reproduce effects of mist and sunshine with accuracy. He exhibited three times in the Royal Academy, and was a regular contributor to local exhibitions. His painting *Dovedale, Derbyshire*, exhibited at the Royal Academy in 1829, is now in the Walker Art Gallery, Liverpool. In spite of a severe attack of paralysis, he continued to practise his art to the end, and his two best-known pictures, *Evening after Rain* (exh. RA, 1849) and *The Dawn of Day* (exh. RA, 1849), were exhibited in Trafalgar Square at the Royal Academy in 1849. He was elected president of the Liverpool Academy some years before his death in Liverpool in 1854. Birmingham City Art Gallery holds fifty-six of his paintings and forty-six drawings.

C. E. DAWKINS, *rev.* JOHN SUNDERLAND

Sources S. Morris and K. Morris, *A catalogue of Birmingham and west midland painters of the nineteenth century* (1974) • Graves, *RA exhibitors* • *IGI*

Barber, Christopher (1735/6–1810), portrait painter, of whose parents nothing is known, painted portraits in oil, watercolour, and crayon, and miniatures in watercolour on ivory. He exhibited at the Royal Academy between 1770 and 1808, at the Society of Artists (of which he was a member before being forced to resign in 1765) from 1763 to 1765, and at the Free Society of Artists between 1763 and 1769. He excelled in preparing his own pigments, which lent his portraits a characteristic brilliance of colour. An enthusiastic lover of music, he was well acquainted with the works of Handel and Purcell, while his convivial nature encouraged a large and warm circle of friends to grow around him. He exhibited from London addresses in St Martin's Lane, Clerkenwell, Marylebone, and the Strand, but by 1808 had moved to 29 Great Marylebone Street where he died on 8 March 1810. He was buried on 18 March in St Marylebone churchyard. Considered by his obituarist to be 'an excellent portrait painter' (*GM*, 293), Barber was a minor artist whose work is now little known.

C. E. DAWKINS, *rev.* V. REMINGTON

Sources *GM*, 1st ser., 80 (1810), 293 • D. Foskett, *Miniatures: dictionary and guide* (1987), 484 • B. S. Long, *British miniaturists* (1929), 13 • L. R. Schidlof, *The miniature in Europe in the 16th, 17th, 18th, and 19th centuries*, 1 (1964), 60 • B. Stewart and M. Cutten, *The dictionary of portrait painters in Britain up to 1920* (1997) • Graves, *RA exhibitors* • parish register (burial), 18 March 1810, London, St Marylebone

Likenesses self-portrait, exh. RA 1806

Barber, Edward (*d.* 1663), General Baptist preacher, was a son of William Barber (*d.* in or before 1611), yeoman of Sherborne, Somerset. In July 1611 he was apprenticed in London's Merchant Taylors' Company and gained his freedom in August 1620. Barber set up trade as a cloth drawer and by 1624 had married Mary (*d.* 1682) and was living in the London parish of St Benet Fink, where he resided for the remainder of his life. A number of his children were baptized in the parish and by his own account he was a conforming member of the established church for many years. However, in 1637 Barber and his wife were excommunicated from St Benet Fink, having been identified as Baptists.

In June 1639 Barber was summoned before the court of high commission for denying that infant baptism and the payment of tithes were God's ordinance. For this and his refusal to take the *ex officio* oath he was imprisoned in Newgate for eleven months. In 1641 the first of Barber's nine works was published, a petition, *To the Kings most Excellent Majesty, and the Honourable Court of Parliament*. This advanced the central principle of Barber's writing, namely a belief in religious liberty for all individuals on the grounds that only God had authority to judge in matters of faith. This, combined with the doctrine that God had endowed all men with the capacity for salvation, made any form of religious coercion abhorrent. Such views were typical of his sect, but Barber's second tract was far more original in its content. *A Small Treatise of Baptisme or Dipping*, published in late 1641, was the first work in England during the seventeenth century that favoured immersion as a form of baptism.

Alongside Thomas Nutt, a fellow General Baptist, Barber published *The Humble Request of Certain Christians* in September 1643. The authors called upon Londoners to join them in their petitions to the Westminster assembly and parliament commending Baptist doctrines as the word of God. However, their request generated little response. In Kent in 1644 Barber and Thomas Lambe, the prominent London General Baptist, debated issues of faith with the Particular Baptist leaders William Kiffin and Thomas Patient. This may have been part of a larger evangelical campaign, as in his 1645 tract, *A True Discovery of the Ministery of the Gospell*, Barber emphasized the importance of the role of the travelling apostle among the true churches of Christ. The same work attacked the established ministry with its lineage to Rome, arguing that a true minister required the gifts of God, not a university education, to perform his office. For, according to Barber, the minister of Christ was a baptized believer, a member of a true church who worked for a living to ensure that the gospel remained free.

Barber was almost certainly among the leading members of London's early General Baptist meetings and Thomas Edwards reported that in November 1645 he attended a congregation in a large house in Bishopsgate. Edwards's account also described Barber and one unnamed person laying their hands on some eighty people. The practice of laying on of hands on baptized believers at their reception into the church was to prove divisive among the General Baptists and this meeting may have been among the first to adopt the custom.

In August 1648 Barber's *A Declaration and Vindication* described how in July of that year a number of the parishioners of St Benet Fink invited him to the parish church to debate with the London minister, Edmund Calamy. After Calamy delivered a morning lecture Barber had attempted to speak but the congregation turned against him and became threatening. Fearing for his life, Barber was escorted home by a constable while Calamy and other ministers looked on.

Barber's tract of June 1649, *An Answer to the Essex Watchmens Watchword*, combined an attack on the established clergy and a plea for liberty of conscience with support for the Levellers' *Agreement of the People*. He emphasized that the Leveller programme, with its aim of destroying tyrants in both civil and ecclesiastical government, would guarantee not only individual political rights but a complete freedom of worship. Prior to this pamphlet Barber's writings were little concerned with secular matters and he had not been among the General Baptist supporters of the Levellers. But by 1649 dissatisfaction with the presbyterian church settlement and the lack of a true reformation may have led to his endorsement of the *Agreement* on the premise that he and the Levellers sought similar freedoms. Two years later, following the Levellers' demise, Barber turned to the officers of the New Model Army with a similar plea. His final work, *The Storming and Totall Routing of Tythes* (1651), praised the army grandees for releasing the people from their bondage under the prelates, but demanded a more thorough reformation within the state. He argued that tithes were a remnant of popery and only their abolition would heal the current distractions of the nation. Barber died in 1663 and was buried in the parish of St Benet Fink on 22 June.

P. R. S. Baker

Sources Greaves & Zaller, *BDBR*, 34–5 • W. K. Jordan, *The development of religious toleration in England*, 4 vols. (1932–40), vol. 3 • E. Barber, *A declaration and vindication of the carriage of Edward Barber* (1648) • churchwardens' accounts, St Benet Fink, London, 1610–1700, GL, MS 1303/1 • E. Barber, *A small treatise of baptisme, or, dipping* (1641) • E. Barber, *The storming and totall routing of tythes* (1651) • parish register, London, St Benet Fink, 1538–1720, GL, MS 4097 [baptism, marriage, burial] • Merchant Taylors' Company, apprentice binding books, vol. 6B, 1610–13, GL, microfilm 314, fol. 59 • Merchant Taylors' Company, court minute books, vol. 6A, 1619–30, GL, MF 327, fol. 87 • Merchant Taylors' Company, index to freemen, 1530–1929, GL, MF 324 • K. Lindley, *Popular politics and religion in civil war London* (1997) • *CSP dom.*

Barber, Francis (*c.*1745–1801), servant, was born a slave in Jamaica; his birth name and family are unknown. He was brought to England by Richard Bathurst, father to Johnson's friend of that name, who had him baptized and named Francis Barber, and sent him to a school in Barton in Teesdale, North Riding of Yorkshire. Freed by the terms of Bathurst's will, the boy was placed in Samuel Johnson's service upon the death of his wife in 1752, and remained with him until Johnson's death.

There were two occasions on which Francis left Johnson's household. The first was in October 1756, when he went to work for a Mr Farren, apothecary in Cheapside, for about two years. 'My boy is run away', Johnson complained (*Letters of Samuel Johnson*, 1.145), but the relationship was not completely fractured: the boy returned to visit Johnson regularly. Barber returned to Johnson but soon ran away again, this time to join the navy on 7 July 1758. From the Deptford tender *Golden Fleece*, he was transferred on 10 July to the *Princess Royal*, and on 18 December to the *Stag*, on fishery protection duty at Yarmouth. Influence with the Admiralty was secured, aided by Smollett, who described Barber as 'a sickly lad, of a delicate frame' (Boswell, *Life*, 1.349n.). Barber was discharged on 8 August 1760.

Barber performed his domestic duties diligently, though friends doubted Johnson's need for his service: 'Diogenes himself never wanted a servant less' (Hawkins, 326). Johnson used to buy food for Hodge, the cat, himself so that Frank's 'delicacy be not hurt, at seeing himself employed for the convenience of a quadruped' (Hill, 1.318). Certainly Johnson's devotion to Francis had the tenderness of a parent—he prayed with him, gave him continual moral guidance, and paid for him to attend the grammar school at Bishop's Stortford for five years from 1767. Johnson's affection emerges from his letters to the school: 'Do not imagine I shall forget or forsake you', he writes, and in another 'You can never be wise unless you love reading' (*Letters of Samuel Johnson*, 1.350).

Barber proved an attractive young man: 'Frank has carried the empire of Cupid farther than most men' said Johnson after returning from Lincolnshire in 1764, where the lad had so impressed the local girls that Mrs Piozzi asserted that one followed him back to London (Hill, 1.290–91). On 28 January 1773 he married Elizabeth Ball (*c.*1755–1816). They had five children. In 1783 the whole family came to live with Johnson at his house in Bolt Court, London.

Barber was a continuous presence in Johnson's life, accompanying him on many of his travels. On Johnson's death in 1784 he was the principal legatee, receiving an annuity of £70. The Barbers moved to Lichfield following their benefactor's advice that Francis remove himself from the temptations of London, but through extravagance they soon sank into poverty, and were reduced to selling gifts from Johnson to greedy collectors. For the last years of his life Barber kept a small village school in the nearby village of Burntwood. He died in Stafford Infirmary on 13 January 1801, and was buried on 28 January at St Mary's, Stafford.

William R. Jones

Sources A. L. Reade, *Johnsonian gleanings*, 2: *Francis Barber: the doctor's negro servant* (privately printed, London, 1912) • A. L. Reade, 'Francis Barber: some more material for his biography', *Johnsonian gleanings*, 8 (privately printed, London, 1937), 73–82 • J. Ingledew, 'Some new light on Francis Barber, Samuel Johnson's servant', *N&Q*, 229 (1984), 8–9 • Boswell, *Life* • *Johnsonian miscellanies*, ed. G. B. Hill, 2 vols. (1897) • J. Hawkins, *The life of Samuel Johnson, LL.D.* (1787) • *GM*, 1st ser., 71 (1801), 190 • *GM*, 1st ser., 63 (1793), 619–20 • *The letters of Samuel Johnson*, ed. B. Redford, 1 (1992)

Barber, John (*c.*1500–1549), clergyman and civil lawyer, is of obscure origins. He was a fellow of All Souls College, Oxford, from 1528 to 1538, having graduated as a bachelor of canon law (4 February 1525) and of civil law (19 February 1528). He became a member of the College of Advocates on 8 March 1532, and incepted as a doctor of civil law at Oxford on 17 February 1533. He was apparently ordained by 1524, and was admitted as vicar of St Giles', Oxford, on 7 December 1531, where he remained until November 1534. On 6 September 1537 he was collated to the living of Wrotham, Kent, to which was added the living of Charing, also in Kent, on 26 February 1545. In 1538 he became a canon and prebendary of the newly founded King Henry VIII College at Oxford, and he remained there until the college was dissolved on 10 May 1545. He continued to draw a pension on the foundation until 1547.

Barber was one of Archbishop Cranmer's chaplains and an official of the provincial court of Canterbury, but his special vocation was to advise the archbishop on civil law matters. In 1538 he was consulted by Cranmer on behalf of Henry VIII, on a subtle point of law touching the dowry of the duchess of Richmond, widow of the king's natural son; and on 18 August 1538 the archbishop asked Thomas Cromwell to appoint Barber to a royal commission to try and examine whether the blood of St Thomas of Canterbury was not 'a feigned thing and made of some red ochre, or of such like matter' (Jenkyns, 1.260–63). On 21 November 1538 Cranmer attempted to use his influence with Cromwell to obtain a prebendal stall at Christ Church, Oxford, for him, but he does not appear to have been successful, for Barber's name is not mentioned by Anthony Wood in his account of Christ Church. In this letter the archbishop speaks of Cromwell's knowledge of Barber's 'qualities and learning', and calls him 'an honest and meet man'. Barber also appeared as one of the proctors for Anne Boleyn at the annulment of her marriage on 17 May 1536.

In 1541 Cranmer appointed Barber to visit All Souls College a second time, as his deputy, because the 'compotations, ingurgitations, and enormous commessations' reported there had excited the archbishop's indignation (Strype, *Cranmer*, 1.131). His signature is appended to *A Declaration Made of the Functions and Divine Institution of Priests* (BL, Cotton MS Cleopatra E V, fol. 45) and to a Latin judgment on the rite of confirmation, both of which were framed to meet the demands of the post-Reformation church. In 1543 Barber repaid Cranmer's kindness to him by joining in a plot for the archbishop's ruin. On the authority of Ralph Morice, Cranmer's secretary, John Foxe mentions that the archbishop elicited a condemnation of a hypothetical case of treachery from Barber and Richard Thornden (Thornton), the suffragan bishop of Dover, and then produced their letters, showing that they were the guilty persons. According to Foxe, Cranmer magnanimously forgave them, but Strype says that Cranmer 'thought fit no more to trust them, and so discharged them of his service' (Strype, *Cranmer*, 1.173). Barber died at Wrotham in the spring of 1549 and was buried in the churchyard there. His will was dated 27 March of that year and was proved on 20 July. GERALD BRAY

Sources Emden, *Oxf.*, 4.23 • G. D. Squibb, *Doctors' Commons: a history of the College of Advocates and Doctors of Law* (1977), 146 • H. Jenkyns, *The remains of Thomas Cranmer, D.D., archbishop of Canterbury*, 4 vols. (1833), vol. 1, pp. 231–3; 260–63; 275–6 • J. Strype, *Ecclesiastical memorials*, 1/2 (1822), 350 • J. Strype, *Memorials of the most reverend father in God Thomas Cranmer*, new edn, 2 vols. (1812), vol. 1, p. 173 • *LP Henry VIII*, 13/2.370; 21/1.309; 21/2.443 • Bodl. Oxf., MSS dd All Souls College, b. 30 • chancellor's register, Oxf. UA, EEE, hyp/A/4, fol. 340v • D. Wilkins, ed., *Concilia Magnae Britanniae et Hiberniae*, 3 (1737), 803–4 • *The acts and monuments of John Foxe*, ed. S. R. Cattley, 8 vols. (1837–41), vol. 8, p. 29

Wealth at death insignificant, a few possessions: will, PRO, PROB 11/321, sig. 26

Barber, John (*bap.* 1675, *d.* 1741), printer and local politician, was born at Gray's Inn Lane, London, in the parish of St Andrew's, Holborn. He was baptized at St Andrew's on 11 April 1675. His father, Morgan Barber, had been a journeyman barber–surgeon to Benjamin Tomlinson, whose widow, Mary, he subsequently married; John was the only surviving child of the marriage. With the help of his godfather Elkanah Settle, the 'City Poet', John was sent to a school in Hampstead. On 6 May 1689 Settle apprenticed him to George Larkin, a printer in Bishopsgate. Barber served most of his time, however, with Mrs Hannah Clarke, a widow who continued her husband's printing business at Thames Street. Barber was freed of the Stationers' Company on 6 June 1696.

Barber became a manager for Mrs Clarke before setting up his own business in 1700. His business prospered, and in 1705 he became a liveryman of the Stationers' Company, but his rise to prominence in printing circles was attributable to his contacts with the tory party. The printer of *The Examiner*, he became a friend of Jonathan Swift and Henry St John, later first Viscount Bolingbroke, and the lover of Mrs Delarivier *Manley, with whom he lived from 1714 onwards. When the tories achieved power in 1710 Barber landed some lucrative contracts. In 1711 he became the official printer of the *London Gazette* and the South Sea Company. Two years later he obtained a reversion to the office of the queen's printer.

Although Barber found himself in the political wilderness with the tories' fall from power after the death of Queen Anne in 1714, he remained loyal to his friends and true to his tory principles. In 1715 he was called 'Tyrant' by the duke of Ormond in a letter to Swift, a nickname that proved enduring (Rivington, 71). In 1720 he speculated successfully in South Sea stock, making an apparent profit of £30,000, and this enabled him to purchase a coat of arms, an estate in East Sheen, and a town house at Queen Square, London, and to consider retiring from business. In the same year a former servant of Mrs Manley's, Sarah Dovekin or Duffkin (*bap.* 1699, *d.* 1758) replaced Manley in Barber's affections.

Barber's independent fortune also enabled him to focus his energies on civic politics. Already a common councilman for Queenhithe (since 1711) and a well-known opponent of the great whig financiers who dominated the City's upper court, he became alderman for the tory ward of Castle Baynard in 1722 and a leading City critic of Sir Robert Walpole. In 1722 he was implicated in the Atterbury plot (an attempt to restore James Stuart to the throne) following Barber's departure in April for Rome bearing £50,000 in bills of exchange. Never formally accused or punished for this, he was nevertheless unable to return to England until August 1724. Once back in London, he opposed the City Elections Act of 1725 and as sheriff (1729–30) facilitated the acquittal of Richard Franklin, the printer of *The Craftsman*, who had been prosecuted by the government for seditious libel. As lord mayor (1732–3) he co-ordinated the City's opposition to Walpole's Excise Bill in 1733, and vigorously defended the raucous jubilation that accompanied its withdrawal from the Commons.

Barber's defence of the City's political liberties and trading interests made him very popular in London circles. Even so, he was narrowly defeated in the City parliamentary election of 1734 and failed to make the opposition slate in 1740–41. On both occasions his tory-Jacobite past counted against him.

Barber's interest in City politics waned a little after 1738, but he was active in the controversial mayoral elections of 1740 when the whig-dominated court of aldermen sought to exclude Sir Robert Godschall from the chair. Barber died on 2 January 1741 at his home in Queen Square, London. The bulk of his estate went to his common-law wife, Dovekin. He had no children. NICHOLAS ROGERS, *rev.*

Sources C. A. Rivington, *'Tyrant': the story of John Barber, 1675 to 1741* (1989) · E. Curll, *An impartial history of the life, character, amours, travels and transactions of Mr John Barber* (1741) · *The life and character of John Barber* (1741) · city papers, CLRO · private information (2004) [E. Cruickshanks] · E. Cruickshanks, 'Lord North, Christopher Layer and the Atterbury plot: 1720–23', *The Jacobite challenge*, ed. E. Cruickshanks and J. Black (1988), 92–106 · F. Morgan, *A woman of no importance* (1986)

Barber, John (1734–1793), coalmaster and inventor, was born at Greasley Castle Farm, Nottinghamshire, and baptized at Greasley on 22 October 1734, the eldest son of Francis Barber (*d.* 1782), Nottinghamshire coalmaster, and his wife, Elizabeth Fletcher (*d.* 1787). His mother's father, John Fletcher (*d.* 1735), since 1712 of Stainsby House, Smalley, Horsley, Derbyshire, had made his fortune in the nearby collieries of Heanor, Smalley, and Denby and was sheriff of Derbyshire in 1731–2. The arms then granted him unusually show an array of mining equipment. On 13 October 1731 Francis Barber married Elizabeth Fletcher and the coalmining partnership of Barber and Fletcher was born. Francis and his brother-in-law, John Fletcher junior, soon proved aggressive coalmining entrepreneurs. Accused of monopolizing local coal sales by stopping up soughs and drowning competitors' workings, they in 'January 1740, offered to supply any persons with coals for 40 years to come at 2*s.* 6*d.* to 3*s.* a ton and to give security for the performance of the same' (Glover, 2.612).

From an early age John Barber was trained by his childless uncle, John Fletcher junior, as a coalmaster. When Fletcher died in January 1766 Barber inherited all his estates and took over his colliery business, including coalmines at Camp Hill, Nuneaton, where Barber lived from 1762. In April 1766 he married Martha (*bap.* 1735, *d.* 1814), daughter of George Goodwin (*d.* 1782), of Monyash, Derbyshire. Barber proved as entrepreneurial as Fletcher and in 1766 took out his first patent, for raising water, for instance from mines or ships. This showed a desire to break away from the ponderous beam of the steam engine to achieve more uniform motion via a water turbine. Another clause in this patent specified the application of the crank to the steam engine, an issue which became significant when the patent lapsed in 1780. James Pickard of Birmingham immediately took out a new patent, famously blocking James Watt's ability to use any such device.

In 1769 the Swede Johann Jacob Ferber (1743–1790) visited Derbyshire, reporting that one of the Newcomen steam engines at Stainsby coalmine 'was improved by the owner Mr Barber's specifications … in that the operation of steam from the … boiler, and the introduction of cold water, were sideways or horizontal, not … vertical' (Ferber, 40). Barber seems to have been one of the first to try to relieve the boiler and engine-house from vibrations caused when a large cylinder was slung from a beam above the boiler. That same year Barber and his father-in-law leased land to erect water-wheels to de-water lead mines at Matlock. Between 1771 and 1776 Barber worked fifteen mines here 'in some of which he expended very considerable sums … without having the good fortune to re-imburse himself' because of 'ill luck and ruinous expenses occasioned … by his own visionary schemes' (BL, Add. MS 6676, fols. 235–244).

In 1773 Barber's second patent was for a 'machine … to purify fossil-coal and extract metals from their ores and collect their particles when volatilised'. This, beautifully illustrated, also involved the recovery of that valuable by-product coal gas. In the 1770s Barber was a commissioner of the act enabling construction of the Erewash Canal, built to transport Nottinghamshire coal. In 1776 came his third patent, for machinery for draining mines, propelling vessels, and so on, via a reaction turbine mounted on top of a haystack boiler geared to a beam for pumping.

But on 9 December 1780 a commission of bankruptcy was issued against Barber. From March 1782 notices of the sales of his estates and mines filled the regional newspapers. The death of his aged father in 1782 was noticed in the same issue that announced the start of these sales. His assignees sold Stainsby House in 1783, and Barber now became an itinerant. The effect of his bankruptcy on his family can be gauged by the shilling he received from his mother's estate in 1788. Some of the collieries held in trust to him from her father had been quickly reassigned to her by December 1780, when Barber was living at Weddington Hall, Nuneaton. Here he planned a branch line from the Coventry Canal to his Nuneaton collieries.

By March 1789 Barber had moved to Drayton Hall, Leicestershire. In July 1790 he announced that he could now repay his debts. His inventive activities soon resumed. His most remarkable patent, filed from Attleborough House, Nuneaton, to which he had moved by October 1791, was to obtain and apply motive power. This,

his finest achievement, was based on much careful experimentation and his earlier work on coal gas. No mere paper exercise, it gave the first suggestion of any motor driven by explosion from inflammable gas (from coal, wood, or other materials) in air. It used the same methods later used by almost all who experimented with the internal combustion turbine. Barber here also predicted the pure jet engine which was to follow 140 years later. It has rightly been called 'world historic' (Bruce, 506).

Barber's final patent of 1792 concerned the smelting and purification of metallic ores. His will dated 18 February 1793 left all his patent rights, but less than £600, to his widow. He died on 17 June 1793 at Attleborough and was buried at Monyash church. The *Gentleman's Magazine*, hinting at the depths of the papyrophobic tragedy which had overtaken Barber's inventiveness, called him 'a man of universal knowledge', since 'by his death the world lost a sound philosopher, an eminent mineralogist, and a good mechanic who expended an ample fortune in benefiting mankind' (*GM*, 1st ser., 63/2, 1793, 960). His probate account showed that his debts still amounted in 1796 to nearly £5000 (Lichfield RO, B/C/5/1796: 8).

John's younger brothers, Robert (1737–1820) and Thomas (1738–1818), were by 1779 operating a worsted spinning mill in Derby then employing twenty hands. Their material was sent to Yorkshire for carpet manufacture. They took out seven textile-weaving patents, Robert between 1774 and 1805 and Thomas between 1774 and 1783, with many of which John must have been involved. Robert is described as another 'prolific inventor, far ahead of his time' (Reisfeld, 57). A Nottingham historian later reported that, like his elder brother, he had 'spent a fortune of £50,000 in mechanism, and in permitting knaves to impose on his credulity' (Blackner, 229). This was because his last 1805 patent had been much infringed, as soon as it was adopted, to supply Admiralty trousers and jackets. In September 1809 Robert was declared bankrupt, in a major bankruptcy enlarged in October. His problems apparently stemmed from lawsuits over his last patent. All his frames and patent rights were sold to a rival weaver, John Passman, in May 1810. Thomas became, in 1787, a founding partner of the later important Nottinghamshire and Yorkshire colliery company, Barber, Walker & Co., which survived until nationalization of the coal industry in 1947, having earlier provided much crucial inspiration for D. H. Lawrence's novels.

H. S. Torrens

Sources A. K. Bruce, 'John Barber and the gas turbine [2 pts]', *The Engineer* (29 Dec 1944), 506–8; (8 March 1946), 216–17 • H. S. Torrens, 'Early Warwickshire patent history', *Warwickshire History*, 6 (1984), 10–20 • G. C. M. Whitelock, *250 years in coal: the history of Barber, Walker & Co.* [n.d., 1955?] [privately published, Derby] • D. Lysons and S. Lysons, *Magna Britannia: being a concise topographical account of the several counties of Great Britain*, 5 (1817) • J. J. Ferber, *Versuch einer Oryktographie von Derbyshire in England* (1776) • pedigree of Barber and Fletcher families, c.1895, R. Barber and Sons, West Bridgford, Nottinghamshire • Barber patents, 1766–1805 • bankruptcies, *LondG* (5–9 Dec 1780), 3; (5 Sept 1809); as reported in *The Times* (7 Sept 1809), 4a • A. R. Griffin and C. P. Griffin, 'The role of coal owners' associations in the east midlands in the nineteenth century', *Renaissance and Modern Studies*, 17 (1973), 95–121 • D. Warriner and others, 'Ringing rake and Masson soughs', *Bulletin of the Peak District Mines Historical Society*, 8/2 (1981), 92–3 • R. S. Fitton, *The Arkwrights: spinners of fortune* (1989) • C. L. Cummins jun., *Internal fire* (1989) • private information (2004) [R. Flindall] • *Leicester and Nottingham Journal* (22 June 1782) • S. Glover, *History of the county of Derbyshire*, 2 vols. (1813) • parish register, Greasley, 22 Oct 1734, Notts. Arch. [baptism] • marriage allegation, 22 April 1766, Lichfield RO • *Coventry Mercury* (30 Sept 1793) • parish register, Monyash, Derbyshire (entered after 1 Dec 1793) [burial] • Adam Woolley MSS, BL, Add. MSS 6669–6670, 6676 • A. Reisfeld, *The history of warp knit arts and trades* (New York, 1999) • J. Blackner, *The history of Nottingham* (1815) • will, Lichfield RO, B/C/11–1793

Archives BL, Adam Woolley MSS, Add. MSS 6669–6670, 6676

Likenesses portrait, priv. coll.

Wealth at death under £600; 'all his patent rights' and estate to widow: will, 23 Sept 1793, Lichfield RO, B/C/11–1793

Barber, Joseph (1757–1811), landscape painter, was born at Newcastle upon Tyne, one of the six children of Joseph Barber, bookseller and copperplate printer, who resided at Amen Corner, and his wife, Eleanor. He settled at Birmingham, where he established a successful drawing school whose students included the watercolourist David Cox, and was locally well known as a painter of small, picturesque landscapes. He also painted some views of north Wales. Unknown in London, he never exhibited at the Royal Academy. A number of his rustic landscapes in watercolour are in the Birmingham Art Gallery, with others in the British Museum and the Victoria and Albert Museum, London; Dudley Art Gallery; Newport Art Gallery; and the Ulster Museum, Belfast. He died in Birmingham on 16 July 1811. With his wife, Elizabeth, he had two sons, Charles *Barber and **Joseph Vincent Barber** (1788–1838), both of whom were also painters. Joseph was taught by his father and lived for most of his life in Birmingham, where he was secretary of the Birmingham Academy of Arts in 1814 and a member of the Birmingham Society. He exhibited landscapes with figures at the Royal Academy in 1812, 1821, 1829, and 1830, and prepared some of the drawings for the *Graphic Illustrations of Warwickshire* (1829). His sister, Ann Matilda Barber, was the mother of Joseph Barber Lightfoot, who became a biblical scholar and bishop of Durham. He died at Rome. Examples of his work are in the Birmingham City Art Gallery.

C. E. Dawkins, *rev.* R. J. Lambert

Sources Waterhouse, *18c painters* • Bryan, *Painters* • M. H. Grant, *A dictionary of British landscape painters, from the 16th century to the early 20th century* (1952) • Mallalieu, *Watercolour artists* • *GM*, 1st ser., 81/2 (1811), 285 • R. Welford, *Men of mark 'twixt Tyne and Tweed*, 3 vols. (1895) • *IGI*

Archives Courtauld Inst., Witt Library

Barber, Joseph Vincent (1788–1838). *See under* Barber, Joseph (1757–1811).

Barber, Margaret Fairless [*pseud.* Michael Fairless] (**1869–1901**), religious writer, was born on 7 May 1869 at Castle Hill House, Rastrick, West Riding of Yorkshire, the youngest of three daughters of Fairless Barber (1835–1881), solicitor and archaeologist, and his wife, Maria Louisa, *née* Musgrave (1831–1890). Margaret, who called herself Marjorie from about the age of four, was at first educated at home by her mother and elder sisters. She read omnivorously, finishing the complete works of Dickens and much of Scott before she was twelve. When her father died in 1881 her mother was prostrated by the loss; unable to cope, she sent Margaret for a few months to relatives in Torquay, Devon, where she attended a local school. It was at this time that she began to suffer from the spinal condition that resulted in her tragically early death. With one of her sisters now married and the other away, her mother decided that the family house at Castle Hill was too large to manage and sought a home elsewhere, eventually settling in Bungay, Suffolk.

In 1884 Margaret went to London to train as a nurse at a small children's hospital, but regularly returned to Torquay, where she helped to nurse an ailing relative. In London she also worked for a brief period among the East End sick, notably in the slum district known as the Jago, and earned there the title 'the fighting sister'. Her mother died unexpectedly at the age of fifty-nine in 1890. From that time on Margaret lived a varied existence, staying at different places in England and visiting Germany, where she and a female friend lodged in an old tower by the Rhine. It was while she was there that problems with her sight began, requiring treatment in Wiesbaden. Her generally poor health also necessitated nursing from a sister of charity. Margaret recovered sufficiently to return to London and resume her philanthropic work. She was financially independent and had no immediate claims on any of her relatives. It was through one of her missions that she met the Dowsons, a family with great literary, artistic, and scientific interests. They offered her a home in their Georgian house by the Thames and effectively adopted her. This upset many of Margaret's relatives, but her eldest sister approved of the arrangement, relieved that Margaret would now receive the care and attention she constantly required.

Margaret's increasing weakness and frequent painful spells now obliged her to give up her charitable work, and she took up writing under the name of Michael Fairless. The surname was from her father, while the first name, retaining her original initial, was that of a childhood friend, Michael McDonnell (1882–1956), later chief justice of Palestine, who as a young boy had often spent his summer holidays with her family. Writing was physically difficult, and was done sitting in bed, or, if that was too tiring, lying down. When her right hand failed her, she changed to the left, and when growing weakness made writing altogether impossible, she dictated. Her first completed book was *The Gathering of Brother Hilarius* (1901), a religious romance centring on the black death, with Bungay serving as the goal of the blind friar's journey. But for some months Margaret had also been drafting pages for the work that brought her fame, *The Roadmender* (1902), a series of meditations on the road to heaven, of which she was the 'roadmender'. This extraordinarily popular book was reprinted thirty-one times in ten years.

Margaret Fairless Barber died on 24 August 1901 at Mock Bridge near Henfield, Sussex, in the farmhouse where the Dowsons spent their summers. She was buried at Ashurst, near Steyning. A complete edition of her works, including a selection of letters, was published in one volume in 1931, with *The Roadmender*'s dedication: 'To my mother: and to earth, my mother, whom I love'. Adrian Room

Sources W. S. Palmer [M. E. Dowson] and A. M. Haggard, *Michael Fairless: her life and writings* (1913) · M. E. Dowson, 'A biographical note', *The complete works of Michael Fairless* (1931) · The Tramp [A. H. Anderson], *The roadmender's country* (1924) · A. Wilde, 'A pilgrimage to the roadmender country: memories of Michael Fairless', *Sussex Daily News* (25 Feb 1938) · Blain, Clements & Grundy, *Feminist comp.* · b. cert.

Likenesses photograph, *c.*1900, repro. in *Complete works of Michael Fairless* · M. E. Dowson, drawing, 1901, repro. in Palmer and Haggard, *Michael Fairless* · M. E. Dowson, drawing (after photograph, *c.*1882), repro. in Palmer and Haggard, *Michael Fairless*

Barber, Mary (*c.*1685–1755), poet, is of unknown parentage. She married Rupert Barber (*d.* 1777?), a Dublin woollen draper, and lived in Werburgh Street, Dublin, from at least 1705 to at least 1724. In 1719 her husband acquired rights to property at Delville, north of Dublin, adjoining that of Patrick Delany, a friend of Swift and later chancellor of St Patrick's; by 1744, when Mrs Delany, formerly Mary Pendarves, came to Delville, Mary Barber and her family were neighbours. She had nine children, four of whom survived infancy: Constantine, born in 1714, later MD, professor of materia medica at Trinity College, Dublin, and president of the Royal College of Physicians; Mira, born in 1717; Rupert, born in 1719 and later known as an artist in miniature and an enamellist; and Lucius, born in 1720.

Barber admitted in the preface to her *Poems* (1734) that a woman should not enter into public debate and that she wrote poetry to educate her children, but almost a decade previously she had attracted the attention of Lord Carteret, the lord lieutenant of Ireland, and Lady Carteret with several poems, one of which, a petition on behalf of the widow of an army officer, is the earliest evidence of the social conscience which she demonstrated in her *Poems*. These poems also came to the attention of the poet Thomas Tickell, whom Carteret had appointed chief secretary in Ireland in 1724 and who was on favourable terms with Swift. Through her connection with the Carterets Barber entered Swift's circle, coming to know Delany, the poet and classical scholar Constantia Grierson, and Laetitia Pilkington. Swift praised Barber's work, including her in his 'triumfeminate' with Constantia Grierson and the literary critic Elizabeth Sican (Psyche).

In 1730 Barber visited England, with Swift's support, to raise subscriptions for a volume of her work. Against his advice she approached, and irritated, Alexander Pope, evidently expecting the encouragement she had readily obtained in the *senatus consultum* of her friends in Dublin, where Swift, in the chair, Constantia Grierson, Laetitia Pilkington, her husband Matthew, and Delany had discussed her verse. While Swift believed, as he wrote to Pope in 1731, that 'her Modesty and her Ambition' had been in conflict (*Correspondence*, 3.457), mystery surrounds an incident later in 1731 in which Swift's signature was forged on a letter to Queen Caroline in praise of Mary Barber. Swift denied any involvement in a letter to Pope and Mary Barber has never been cleared of suspicion.

Barber travelled between Ireland and England several times in the early 1730s, visiting London, Tunbridge Wells, and Bath. She contributed anonymously to *Tunbrigialia, or, Tunbridge Miscellanies, for the Year 1730*. In 1732 Swift attempted to assist her, without success, when he asked his friend John Barber, lord mayor of London, who was no relation, to secure a position for her husband. In 1734 she was arrested in England with Matthew Pilkington and others for possession of manuscript copies of some of Swift's political poems attacking Walpole's administration. Matthew Pilkington had informed against her. After an early release she lived for some years in Bath, possibly with her son Rupert. She obtained over 900 subscribers to her *Poems* (1734), including leading figures of the Irish and British establishments. Swift subscribed for ten copies. The Pilkingtons were conspicuously absent. Six poems by Constantia Grierson were published posthumously in this volume. Barber's son Constantine contributed five and Elizabeth Rowe one. One poem, 'Apollo's Edict', has since been published as Swift's and has inspired scholarly controversy. A second edition followed in 1735 and was reissued in 1736. Swift and Mary Barber wrote prefaces to the earl of Orrery, one of her most influential patrons.

In 1737 Swift gave Barber the manuscript of his *Complete Collection of Genteel and Ingenious Conversation* (1738) in response to her plea for support. She was unwell, having suffered considerably for some years from gout, for which she had been treated by Dr Richard Mead. She abandoned her idea of sailing to Georgia and returned to Ireland, where she lived near the Delanys at Delville, possibly with her son Rupert. She wrote very little after 1734, notably some verse on gout in the *Gentleman's Magazine* in 1737 and some minor pieces. She corresponded with her printer Samuel Richardson about *Pamela* in 1741, and indirectly with George Ballard in 1747 about Constantia Grierson. She was given significant representation in *Poems by Eminent Ladies* (1755).

Barber died on 14 June 1755, 'in an advanced Age' (*Dublin Journal*, 14/17 June 1755). A few months before, Mrs Delany, her friend from the early 1730s, wrote that 'Old Mr. Barber *is alive*, drinks his claret, smokes his pipe, and *cares not a pin for any of his family*'. He survived his wife by twenty-two years (Pilkington, 2.391).

Swift's praise of Barber as 'the best Poetess of both Kingdoms' (*Correspondence*, 4.186) was not universally accepted. Her most trenchant critic, Laetitia Pilkington, thought her work 'might … be seen in the Cheesemongers, Chandlers, Pastry-cooks, and Second-hand Booksellers Shops' (Pilkington, 2.383). Swift referred to her 'bashfulness' (*Correspondence*, 4.456) but that did not protect her from controversy. Her world of the friendships and social conscience of an early eighteenth-century Irishwoman has been generally neglected since her own time, but since the 1970s she has received individual scholarly and critical attention as a woman writer and a significant figure in Irish culture and eighteenth-century studies.

BRYAN COLEBORNE

Sources M. Barber, *Poems on several occasions* (1734) • *The poetry of Mary Barber ?1690–1757*, ed. B. Tucker (1992) • L. Pilkington, *Memoirs of Laetitia Pilkington*, ed. A. C. Elias, 2 vols. (1997) • A. C. Elias, 'A manuscript book of Constantia Grierson's', *Swift Studies*, 2 (1987), 33–56 • *The prose writings of Jonathan Swift*, ed. H. Davis and others, 14 vols. (1939–68) • *The poems of Jonathan Swift*, ed. H. Williams, 3 vols. (1937); 2nd edn (1958); repr. (1966) • *The correspondence of Jonathan Swift*, ed. H. Williams, 5 vols. (1963–5) • I. Ehrenpreis, *Swift: the man, his works and the age*, 3 vols. (1962–83) • P. Fagan, ed., *A Georgian celebration: Irish poets of the eighteenth century* (1989) • R. Lonsdale, ed., *Eighteenth-century women poets: an Oxford anthology* (1989) • R. Lonsdale, ed., *The new Oxford book of eighteenth-century verse* (1984) • O. W. Ferguson, 'The authorship of "Apollo's edict"', *Publications of the Modern Language Association of America*, 70 (1955), 433–40 • D. F. Foxon, ed., *English verse, 1701–1750: a catalogue of separately printed poems with notes on contemporary collected editions*, 2 vols. (1975) • B. Coleborne, ed., 'Anglo-Irish verse, 1675–1825', *The Field Day anthology of Irish writing*, ed. S. Deane, A. Carpenter, and J. Williams, 1 (1991), 395–499 • A. Carpenter, ed., *Verse in English from eighteenth-century Ireland* (1998) • M. A. Doody, *The daring muse: Augustan poetry reconsidered* (1985)

Barber, Mary (1911–1965), bacteriologist, was born in Derby on 3 April 1911, the third daughter of Hugh Barber, physician, and Ethel M. Howlett. She was educated at Alice Ottley School, Worcester, and the London School of Medicine for Women; she obtained the conjoint diploma in 1934 and graduated MB BS in 1936. She then became resident pathologist and A. M. Bird scholar in the pathology unit of the Royal Free Hospital, London. In 1938 she became assistant pathologist at the Archway Group Laboratory, and in 1940, the year she obtained her London MD degree, assistant pathologist at the Hammersmith Hospital in west London; in 1947 she was appointed lecturer in bacteriology there.

Barber had already published papers on various infections, but at the Hammersmith she began work on the topics that were to establish her reputation and engage her for the rest of her life: antibiotics and resistance to them; staphylococci; and hospital cross-infection. In 1947 she showed that penicillin resistance among staphylococci in the hospital was increasing, and she was the first to recognize that this resistance was due to the selection in the course of treatment of a small minority of cells capable of producing an enzyme which destroyed penicillin.

In 1948 Barber was appointed reader in bacteriology at St Thomas's Hospital, London, from where she conducted comprehensive studies of cross-infection and proposed a programme of preventive measures, notably an antibiotic prescribing policy that required the use of antibiotic combinations. She was invited back to the Hammersmith in 1958, as reader in clinical bacteriology, and there by dint of energy, enthusiasm, and force of personality she persuaded her notably individualistic colleagues to abide by her policies. They were rewarded by a substantial decline in the prevalence of antibiotic resistance and she was rewarded with the title of professor in 1963 and membership of the Royal College of Physicians in 1965.

Although Barber's work was rooted in the ward, it was underpinned by a grasp of microbial biochemistry and genetics that allowed her a warm communion with non-medical scientists. She was intensely interested in the development of a semi-synthetic penicillin active against penicillinase-producing staphylococci and was among the first to have new antibiotics made available to her for independent assessment. This led to an invitation to write a comprehensive account of antibiotics and their clinical use. She was joined by L. P. Garrod, and the book *Antibiotic and Chemotherapy* was published under their joint names in 1963.

Barber had strong views and became a fluent, forceful, and sometimes funny speaker. Wherever she attended meetings around the world she was instantly recognizable by her slight figure, glasses, straight hair held by a clip, cosmetic-free countenance, and functional clothes. She was a good teacher but was principally absorbed in her work at the bench, where associates recall equally vividly her sharp tongue and her kind heart.

Generous to her causes and those close to her Mary Barber never married and for most of her working life lived in a flat at 9 Canfield Gardens, London. From there she regularly escaped to her boat, moored on the east coast; she also enjoyed separate interests in politics and religion. Her political views were well to the left and some of her overseas visits were in pursuit of ideology rather than science. She was, however, no atheistic communist, but a pillar of the Anglican church. For years she was a churchwarden and generous benefactor of Holy Trinity Church, Dalston, where religion and politics were joined in her long-standing friend and Aldermaston co-marcher Canon S. G. Evans. They were together on 11 September 1965, driving to a meeting of the Campaign for Nuclear Disarmament, when they collided with a van at Osbournby crossroads in Lincolnshire: both were killed. A memorial service was held at All Souls, Langham Place, London. FRANCIS O'GRADY

Sources *The Journal of Pathology and Bacteriology*, 92 (1966), 603–10 · *BMJ* (18 Sept 1965), 707 · *The Lancet* (18 Sept 1965), 595–6 · R. Knox, *Nature*, 209 (1966), 559–60 · *Journal of Clinical Pathology*, 18 (1965), 697–8 · *The Times* (13 Sept 1965), 10a · *The Times* (15 Sept 1965), 6d · *The Times* (9 Oct 1965), 12b · *The Times* (12 Oct 1965), 13f · *The Times* (17 Oct 1965), 14b · d. cert. · *Medical Directory* (1940–65)
Archives Royal Free Hospital, London, MSS
Likenesses photograph, repro. in *Journal of Pathology and Bacteriology*, 603 · photograph, repro. in *Journal of Clinical Pathology*, 697
Wealth at death £7874: probate, 7 Feb 1966, *CGPLA Eng. & Wales*

Barber [*née* Bowker], **Mary Elizabeth** (**1818–1899**), poet and natural historian, was born at Manor Farm, South Newton, Wiltshire, on 5 January 1818, the ninth child and first daughter of Miles Bowker (1758–1839), woollen manufacturer and sheep farmer of Gateshead, and Anna Maria (*c*.1784–1868), daughter of Captain John Mitford, of Mitford Castle, Northumberland, and his wife, Dorothy Young. The Bowker family emigrated to South Africa as part of the British settler movement of 1820 and eventually comprised nine sons and two daughters. Mary was educated at home, acquiring her love of natural history from her father, and her observational skills from her older brothers who became renowned hunters. Interested in botany, in 1838 she began a correspondence with William Henry Harvey and Sir Joseph Dalton Hooker, which was to last for some thirty years, sending them many new plants and seeds, many of which Harvey named after her. On 19 December 1842 Mary married Frederick William Barber (1814–1892), a cousin of Dr W. G. Atherstone. Frederick described her to his brother as 'a plain simple minded, warm hearted, well informed affectionate girl.— a hater of towns and fashionable life, … slight and rather tall in person, gentle and lady like in manner, and universally beloved' (F. W. Barber, letter, 3 March 1844). They had two sons and a daughter.

From 1863 Mary wrote to Roland Trimen the entomologist, who introduced her to Charles Darwin. Darwin recommended publication of two of her papers by the Linnean Society and the Entomological Society of London. Hooker also helped publish her work. Her painting of *Brachystelma barberiae*, a new asclepiad, appeared in *Curtis's Botanical Magazine* in November 1866 with Hooker's comment 'an admirable coloured drawing, made by our accomplished correspondent Mrs. Barber, of The Highlands, Graham's Town'. Throughout her life she produced accurate paintings of many of the birds, butterflies, and plants that she found. One project was a complete series of the *Stapelia* succulents, two of which she had discovered.

In 1869 Mary's husband left her in charge of their farm to go diamond prospecting. Several articles on her experiences after she joined him in Kimberley were printed in the *Cape Monthly Magazine* between 1871 and 1881. In England an account of the cave cannibals of the Transgariep appeared in popular journals under the pseudonym of Mr Layland. Originally written by Mary Barber and her brother, it was given to Edgar Layard, curator of the South African Museum, who had promised to get it published for her while in London. It created a rift between her and Layard for some time.

Mary Barber became interested in the region's geology and archaeology, and was an early collector of prehistoric stone tools. Her acquaintances now included such well-known politicians, explorers, and scientists as two Cape governors Sir Henry Bartle Frere and Sir Henry Barkly, Cecil Rhodes, Sir Charles Warren, Edward J. Dunn, Emil Holub, and the hunter Frederick Courtney Selous, who claimed that her careful nursing saved his life in 1879. The South African Philosophical Society, founded in 1877, elected Mary a member in 1878, and published two of her most important papers. In Kimberley her sons had shown her bird paintings to Emil Holub, an associate of August von Pelzeln, custodian of the Austrian imperial collection of birds and mammals in Vienna. In 1882 Mary was elected a corresponding member of the Ornithologischer Verein in Wien. She was the first lady member of both societies.

By 1879 Mary's marriage was breaking down. Frederick decided to visit a brother in England and he stayed for ten years. Mary moved from Kimberley in 1881 to spend winters with her brother James Henry Bowker in Durban, Natal, and summers with her sons as they farmed ostriches or went gold prospecting. They discovered the goldfield at Barberton, and were among the founders of the Witwatersrand mines in Johannesburg, probably sinking the first deep shaft there. In 1886 her paper dealing with preservation of the insectivorous birds of the colony was read to the Eastern Province Literary and Scientific Society in Grahamstown. The economic aspects were of primary importance as the colony's fruit crops were suffering extensive insect damage. The paper was published in pamphlet form for general distribution.

In 1889 Mary and her sons travelled to England. She renewed acquaintance with her fellow artist Marianne North, visited Kew, and visited scientific friends throughout Europe. Back in South Africa her husband settled in Grahamstown, dying there in January 1892, while Mary moved between her brother in Durban, and her daughter Mrs Highlie Bailie, in Pietermaritzburg.

At the age of eighty Mary saw her poems published. The introduction to *The Erythrina Tree and other Verses* contained this tribute by Roland Trimen:

> through many vicissitudes of Kaffir Wars, adventures by flood and field, trekking to newly-settled lands, on quiet farmstead or in turbulent mining camp, wherever her lot for the time was cast, Mrs. Barber has always been distinguished by her equanimity, cheerful self-reliance, fine sense of humour and cool courage but more than all for her steady perseverance in the pursuit of natural history researches. (p. vii)

Mary Elizabeth Barber died at her daughter's house in Pietermaritzburg on 4 September 1899 and was buried in the Commercial Road cemetery nearby.

The herbaria at the Royal Botanic Gardens, Kew, and Trinity College, Dublin, both benefited from Mary's plant collecting. The Albany Museum, Grahamstown, South Africa, has her personal herbarium, butterfly collection, and many paintings. The Kew herbarium has some paintings, others are in the Linnean Society archives, and the Trimen correspondence is in the Royal Entomological Society of London. ALAN COHEN

Sources A. Cohen, 'Mary Elizabeth Barber: South Africa's first lady natural historian', *Archives of Natural History*, 27 (2000), 187–208 • F. W. Barber to Henry Barber, letter dated from Farm Glen Avon, 3 March 1844, Albany Museum, SM739 • M. E. Barber, *The Erythrina tree and other verses* (1898), vii • Desmond, *Botanists*, rev. edn, 43 • E. J. Dunn, 'Stone implements in South Africa', *Transactions of the South African Philosophical Society*, 1879–80, 2/1 (1881), 6–22 • M. Gunn and L. E. Codd, *Botanical exploration of southern Africa* (1981) • H. E. Hockley, *The story of the British settlers of 1820 in South Africa* (Cape Town, 1948) • E. Holub, *Seven years in South Africa* (1881) • I. Mitford-Barberton, *The Barbers of the Peak* (1934) • I. Mitford-Barberton, *Commandant Holden Bowker* (1970) • I. Mitford-Barberton and R. Mitford-Barberton, *The Bowkers of Tharfield* (1952) • I. Mitford-Barberton and V. White, *Some frontier families* (1968) • R. W. Murray, *The diamond field keepsake for 1873* (1873) • M. North, *Recollections of a happy life: being the autobiography of Marianne North*, ed. Mrs J. A. Symonds, 2 vols. (1892) • *The journals of Sophia Pigot*, ed. M. Rainer (1974) • S. Schönland, 'Biography of the late Mrs. F. W. Barber, and a list of her paintings in the Albany Museum', *Records of the Albany Museum*, 1 (1904), 95–108 • F. C. Selous, *A hunter's wanderings in Africa* (1881) • C. Thorpe, *Tharfield: an eastern Cape farm* (privately printed, 1977) • C. Warren, *On the veldt in the seventies* (1902) • A. F. Williams, *Some dreams come true; being a sheaf of stories leading up to the discovery of copper, diamonds and gold in southern Africa, and of the pioneers who took part in the excitement of those early days* (1948) • *DSAB* • *Men of the times: old colonists of the Cape Colony and Orange River Colony* (Johannesburg, 1906) • private information (2004)

Archives Albany Museum, Grahamstown, South Africa • Rhodes University, Grahamstown, South Africa, Cory Library, journal | priv. coll., family archive • RBG Kew, directors' letters • Royal Entomological Society, London, Trimen corresp.

Likenesses photograph, *c*.1860, Hunt Institute for Botanical Documentation, Pittsburgh, Pennsylvania • photograph, *c*.1885, priv. coll. • photographs, Albany Museum, Grahamstown, South Africa

Barber, Samuel (1737/8–1811), minister of the Presbyterian General Synod of Ulster, was the younger son of John Barber, a farmer near Killead, co. Antrim, and his wife, Sarah. He matriculated from the University of Glasgow in 1757 and graduated MA two years later. Having completed his 'trials' with the presbytery of Templepatrick he was ordained at Rathfriland, co. Down, on 3 May 1763, where he ministered for the rest of his life. He subscribed to the Westminster confession of faith, though he was an advanced Arian in his theology. In 1771 he married Elizabeth (*c*.1743–1833), daughter of the Revd Alexander Kennedy of Mourne; they had seven children.

Like many other Presbyterian clergymen Barber played a prominent role in the volunteer movement that spread throughout Ireland during the American War of Independence. He was a founder of the Rathfriland Volunteers (14 April 1779) and was soon chosen as captain of the company (24 June 1779). At the end of 1780 Lord Glerawly, a local nobleman, resigned, demanding the return of the weapons that he had originally supplied to the company. Barber organized a subscription list, and with the help of donations from volunteer companies in Belfast, Lisburn, and Newry the Rathfriland corps was rearmed. This episode is indicative of the social tensions that emerged in Ulster during these years as the 'independent interest' sought to challenge the electoral dominance of the larger landowners. In the County Down election of 1783 Barber supported the independent candidate, Robert Stewart, later Lord Londonderry, against Lord Kilwarlin, son of the earl of Hillsborough. It was reported that some years earlier Kilwarlin had refused to contribute to the rebuilding of the Rathfriland meeting-house, replying that he would sooner give money to pull it down. Accusations were exchanged between the two men until, on 24 August 1783, Kilwarlin appeared at Barber's meeting-house and launched a personal attack on the minister before his congregation.

Barber's credentials as a parliamentary reformer were established by his election as a delegate to the volunteer conventions held at Dungannon in 1782, 1783, and 1793. More unusually he was also an early advocate of Catholic relief. In October 1779 he preached a sermon to two volunteer companies, calling for protestant unity against the threat of invasion but praising the 'present generation' of Roman Catholics for behaving 'peaceably and quietly, though as a religious society they have been subjected to penal laws too shocking to enumerate' (S. Barber, *A Sermon Delivered … to the Castlewellan Rangers, and Rathfriland Volunteers*, 1779, 9). During the tithe controversy of 1787, which had been sparked off by the publication of *The Present State of the Church of Ireland* by Richard Woodward, bishop of Cloyne, Barber wrote two pamphlets condemning the principle of church establishments, the tithe system, and the penal laws against Roman Catholics. In 1791 he preached a sermon as moderator to the General Synod of Ulster on Revelation 18: 20. He took this opportunity to reiterate his belief in religious equality, now reinforced by a strong tinge of millenarianism. The reign of Antichrist, which Barber associated with the alliance of church and state, was traced back to the Council of Nicaea, and the French Revolution taken as an omen of its demise.

The nature of Barber's connection with the United Irish movement is not clear, though he certainly sympathized with its aims. In July 1792 he accompanied Wolfe Tone and Samuel Neilson on a mission to suppress sectarian disturbances between the Peep o'Day Boys (protestants) and The Defenders (Catholics) in the Rathfriland area. Both the informer Nicholas Mageean and the United Irishman Charles Hamilton Teeling state that Barber was involved in the preparations for the rising of 1798. He was arrested and imprisoned for several months during the summer of 1797. Following the outbreak of the rising he was convicted by court martial, on a charge of having uttered seditious words, and imprisoned a second time, from July 1798 to January 1799, though he maintained his innocence.

Barber died in Rathfriland on 5 September 1811, in his seventy-fourth year. He was said to be well over 6 feet tall.

I. R. McBride

Sources A. Morrow, 'The Revd Samuel Barber, A.M., and the Rathfriland volunteers', *Ulster Journal of Archaeology*, new ser., 14 (1908) · W. D. Bailie, 'The Revd Samuel Barber, 1738–1811: national volunteer and United Irishman', in J. L. M. Haire and others, *Challenge and conflict: essays in Irish Presbyterian history and doctrine* (1981), 72–95 · W. I. Addison, *A roll of graduates of the University of Glasgow from 31st December 1727 to 31st December 1897* (1898) · W. I. Addison, ed., *The matriculation albums of the University of Glasgow from 1728 to 1858* (1913) · *An historical account of the late election of knights of the shire for the county of Down, together with the petition to parliament complaining of an undue election and return for the said county … also, the several addresses, songs, squibs &c. which were published before and during the election* (1784) · T. Witherow, *Historical and literary memorials of presbyterianism in Ireland*, [2 vols.] (1879–80) · J. McConnell and others, eds., *Fasti of the Irish Presbyterian church, 1613–1840*, rev. S. G. McConnell, 2 vols. in 12 pts (1935–51) · W. T. W. Tone, *Life of Theobald Wolfe Tone*, ed. T. Bartlett (1998) · I. R. McBride, *Scripture politics: Ulster Presbyterians and Irish radicalism in the late eighteenth century* (1998) · C. H. Teeling, *Sequel to the history of the Irish rebellion of 1798* (1876); repr. (1972) · Presbyterian Historical Society of Ireland, Belfast, Barber MSS · Ulster Museum, Belfast, Barber MSS · *DNB* · *Belfast News-Letter* (10 Sept 1811)

Archives Presbyterian Historical Society of Ireland, Belfast, sermon and commonplace book · Ulster Museum, Belfast, corresp. and notes

Likenesses print, Presbyterian Historical Society of Ireland, Belfast

Barber [Barbar], **Thomas** (*b. c.*1545, *d.* after 1603), Church of England clergyman, hailed from Middlesex. Born to unknown parents, he matriculated as a pensioner of St John's College, Cambridge, on 8 November 1560, graduated BA in 1564, and was elected a fellow on 11 April 1565. Ordained deacon at Ely on 29 July 1565, he proceeded MA in 1567 and was one of the many who petitioned for Thomas Cartwright's restoration as Lady Margaret professor in 1570. He had moved to London by August 1574, for he was certainly the 'Barber' listed as curate of St Sepulchre during Edwin Sandys's episcopal visitation that month. In October 1575 he was presented to the vicarage of Stoke Newington, Middlesex, by John Dudley, esquire, a kinsman of the earl of Leicester. In a survey drawn up in December 1576 by Thomas Watts, archdeacon of Middlesex, Barber was described as resident, married, an MA learned in Latin and the scriptures, but licensed to preach only in St Sepulchre.

Some time after reaching the capital Barber joined the London clerical conference established in 1570 by John Field and Thomas Wilcox in the hope that further reform of the 1559 settlement, possibly along fully presbyterian lines, could be introduced by parliamentary means. Barber was consistently involved with its proceedings until its demise in 1590.

It was an impossible dream, but meanwhile Barber soldiered on in London on behalf of the reformist cause. On 11 April 1576 the vestry of St Helen, Bishopsgate, appointed him their evening lecturer on Wednesdays and Fridays at an annual salary of 20 marks. Although he had yet to be troubled for nonconformity, he relinquished the post in 1578, and had resigned Stoke Newington by July 1580.

Barber seems to have spent the rest of his life in the parish of St Botolph without Bishopsgate. A daughter, Dorcas, was baptized there on 10 January 1580, and six other children followed: Thomas (1582), Nehemia (1584), Rachel (1587), Prudence (1589), Bartholomew (1591), and Martha (1593). Identification is proven by the fact that in the 1591 entry Barber is described as 'preacher'.

By 1584, when he was lecturing both at St Mary Woolchurch and St Mary-le-Bow, Barber had become one of the London clergy whom John Whitgift, archbishop of Canterbury, was disposed to silence. Whitgift finally suspended him in June for his refusal to subscribe the three articles which he had introduced in November 1583 as his yardstick of conformity. Barber was nevertheless chosen as a member of the 'national synod' which Field convened to lobby sympathetic MPs during the parliament of 1584–5. After petitions on his behalf Whitgift offered to restore him in December 1587, but Barber still refused to satisfy the archbishop as to his future conformity. He never preached officially in London again.

Barber was one of those at whose activities a ban on unlicensed preachers in March 1589 was specifically aimed, and he was closely involved in the death throes of the conference movement. A delegate to the 'presbytery' at St John's College, Cambridge, in 1590 (as it was described by its opponents in the college, though defended as a routine clerical conference by those who attended it), he was also a member of the last general conference in London the same year. In September 1591 he was one of the nonconformist leaders who was interrogated in Star Chamber about the clandestine activities of the previous twenty years, and it is largely as a result of his evidence, and that of Thomas Edmunds, that so much is known about them. While Barber's part in unmasking his colleagues presumably distanced him from some of them, he was evidently not rejected by the godly community at large. The will of the London draper Thomas Eaton, in December 1599, mentions his 'good friends Thomas Barber and Stephen Egerton', who each received £20.

Barber is credited with *The Apocalypse or Revelation of St John, with a Methodicall Exposition upon every Chapter* (1596), a translation from the French of François du Jon's recent work. No copy of his *Dialogue between the Penitent Sinner and Sathan*, mentioned by older authorities, is known to survive. His wife, Prudence, was buried at St Botolph on 15 December 1595. Barber remarried, for a daughter, Mary, was baptized at St Botolph in 1604. There are no further references to him or his family in the London records, and he seems to have died intestate. BRETT USHER

Sources Venn, *Alum. Cant.*, 1/1.82 • GL, MS 9537/3, fol. 112*r* • exchequer, first fruits and tenths office, composition books, PRO, E334/9, fol. 58*r* • LPL, carte miscellanee XII/1, fols. 1*v*, 8*r* • A. W. C. Hallen, ed., *The registers of St Botolph, Bishopsgate, London*, 1 (1889), 100–57, 317 • A. Peel, ed., *The seconde parte of a register*, 2 vols. (1915) • R. G. Usher, ed., *The presbyterian movement in the reign of Queen Elizabeth, as illustrated by the minute book of the Dedham classis, 1582–1589*, CS, 3rd ser., 8 (1905) • P. S. Seaver, *The puritan lectureships: the politics of religious dissent, 1560–1662* (1970) • P. Collinson, *The Elizabethan puritan movement* (1967) • J. E. Cox, ed., *The annals of St Helen's, Bishopsgate, London* (1876) • will, PRO, PROB 11/95, sig. 1 [will of Thomas Eaton] • parish register, St Botolph without Bishopsgate, 15 Dec 1595 [burial] • parish register, St Botolph without Bishopsgate, 1604 [baptism]

Barberi, Domenico Giovanni Luigi [*name in religion* Dominic of the Mother of God] (**1792–1849**), Passionist priest, was born at Pallanzana, near Viterbo, then in the Papal States, on 22 June 1792. He was the youngest of the eight children, five boys and three girls, of Giuseppe Barberi (*d.* 1798), a small farmer, and Maria Antonia (*d.* 1803) *née* Pacelli. After the death of his mother he was brought up at Merlano by his uncle Bartolomeo Pacelli, who intended him to become a farmer and his heir, and to marry.

At the age of twenty Barberi decided to join the Congregation of Discalced Clerks of the Most Holy Cross and Passion, an order founded by St Paul of the Cross in the 1720s in devotion to the sufferings of Christ. In 1814, while he was a lay postulant at Sant' Angelo at Vetralla, a retreat house of the congregation, he received what he believed to be a divine call to undertake missionary work in England. Barberi was without formal education, but his superior noted his knowledge of the Vulgate, and he was clothed not as a lay novice but as a cleric at Santa Maria di Pugliano near Paliano on 14 November 1814. He made his vows on 15 November 1815 and was ordained priest on 1 March 1818. In 1821 he was appointed lector of scholastic philosophy at Vetralla. From 1826 he taught theology and philosophy at the Passionist house in Rome. Much of his writing dates from this period; his unpublished works in the Passionist archives run to 180 titles and 100 volumes, including sermons, devotional works, a tract against the revolutionaries of 1831, and an entire course of philosophy in 1557 pages.

In 1830 Barberi was asked to teach the Cornish convert ordinand Sir Harry Trelawney, who was visiting Italy, to say mass. Two other English converts to Catholicism, the Hon. George Spencer, who later became a Passionist, and

Domenico Giovanni Luigi Barberi (1792–1849), by unknown engraver

the Leicestershire squire Ambrose Phillipps De Lisle, who founded Mount St Bernard's Cistercian monastery, refired Barberi's dream of converting England; De Lisle, who was equally struck by meeting Barberi for the first time in 1828, later translated and published Barberi's *Lament of England* (1831), a threnody on the lost glories of the Catholic church in England in the style of Jeremiah. Barberi was appointed rector of a new foundation at Lucca in 1831, and in 1833 the general chapter of the order referred to its next meeting his plea for an English foundation; he was elected provincial for three years of the Passionist southern province of the Sorrowful Virgin. He became first consultor in 1836, and gave heroic service in Ceprano in the Campagna during the cholera epidemic of 1837, when he also completed a commentary on the Song of Solomon.

In 1838 De Lisle and Spencer began among the French clergy a campaign of prayer for the conversion of England. In 1839 the Passionist general chapter accepted for 'an opportune time' a memorial drawn up by Monsignor Charles Acton and presented by Barberi asking for an English Passionist foundation. Barberi was elected provincial again in 1839, but was then chosen to head a new Belgian foundation in the Château d'Ère; on 26 May 1840 he left Italy for ever.

Barberi first landed in England on 27 November 1840, after being offered Aston Hall, Staffordshire, by Bishop Walsh of the central district through his assistant Nicholas Wiseman, president of Oscott. Leaving the Belgian community in 1841, Barberi moved on 17 February 1842 into Aston Hall. A church was opened in nearby Stone in 1844, in the teeth of protestant opposition: Barberi was no beauty, short and stocky, with bushy eyebrows and piercing eyes, and his Passionist habit, with its emblem of a heart and cross, was a provocation in itself. Many Catholics were also repelled by this holy fool. His preaching in Britain, on scores of missions and retreats, his principal activity apart from his work as superior, combined fluency and wit with a poor command of English pronunciation, which both edified and amused, though the story that he told a convent of nuns: 'without face it is impossible to be shaved' is probably apocryphal. He also urged a congregation to become saints, 'but not canonized ones: it costs too much' (Wilson, 345). In 1841 he published 'To the professors of the University of Oxford' in response to a letter in *L'Univers* from John Dobrée Dalgairns, whom in 1845 he received into the church. He had no direct forewarning of the most famous action of his life: on 8 October 1845, dripping wet from a coach journey from Aston on his way to Belgium, he received John Henry Newman's submission to Rome at Littlemore. He admitted Newman to the church the next day.

At the request of the convert William Leigh, Barberi made another foundation in 1846 at Northfield House, Woodchester, where the new church was designed by Charles Hansom; the Dominicans succeeded the Passionists in 1850. The first London foundation of the order was established at Poplar House, Hampstead, in 1848. Barberi died of a heart attack at the Railway tavern, Reading, on 27 August 1849. His body was buried at Aston, but was taken to Cotton Hall in 1855 and later in the same year to his last foundation, St Anne's, Sutton, where it remained incorrupt until 1886. Spencer was buried beside him.

A mystic who experienced visions and had a wide reputation for sanctity, Barberi's life and its central enthusiasm, the conversion of England, touched the major figures of the early Victorian Catholic revival in England as well as many unknown Catholics in Staffordshire, London, and elsewhere. His posthumously published writings include *La divina paraninfa* (1860), *L'Anima fedele guidata da Jesu* (1877), *Excellence de Marie* (translated into French by Canon Francis Labis, 1899), *Il gemito della Colomba* (1954), and *Autobiography* (1959). He was beatified on 27 October 1963.

SHERIDAN GILLEY

Sources A. Wilson, *Blessed Dominic Barberi: supernaturalized Briton* (1967) • U. Young, *Life and letters of the Venerable Father Dominic (Barberi)* (1926) • *Dominic Barberi in England: a new series of letters*, ed. and trans. U. Young (1935) • D. Gwynn, *Father Dominic Barberi* (1947) • Pius Devine, *Life of the Very Rev. Father Dominic of the Mother of God* (1898)

Archives Archives of the Postolazione, Rome, MSS [100 volumes] • English Province of Passionate Fathers, corresp. and papers • Passionist general archives, Piazza dei SS Giovanni e Paolo, Rome

Likenesses 'Ducky' Doyle, drawing, repro. in Gwynn, *Father Dominic Barberi* • engraving, Birmingham Oratory [*see illus.*] • portrait, repro. in Young, *Life and letters*

Barbier, Jane (*fl.* 1711–1740), singer, was said by John Hawkins to be 'a native of England' (Hawkins, 5.156). A contralto, she made her first stage appearance with the opera company at the Queen's Theatre in the Italian pasticcio *Almahide* in November 1711, singing a role previously taken by the castrato Valentini. The charming nervousness of the young singer 'recommended her no less than her agreeable Voice, and just Performance' (*Spectator*).

Mrs Barbier remained with the company until June 1714, often playing the male roles which suited her voice and dark good looks. In revivals of Handel's *Rinaldo* she sang Eustachio and later the title role, and she created Dorinda in his *Pastor fido* and Arcane in *Teseo*. She sang in English as Telemachus in John Galliard's *Calypso and Telemachus* (17 May 1712), and Handel wrote for her in his ode for the birthday of Queen Anne of 1713. Mrs Barbier left the opera company and sang at Drury Lane from March 1715, creating the female leads in Johann Christoph Pepusch's English masques *Venus and Adonis* (12 March 1715), *Myrtillo* (5 November 1715), and *Apollo and Daphne* (12 January 1716). Pepusch's future wife, Margherita de l'Epine, took the leading male roles, but in *The Death of Dido* (17 April 1716) Barbier sang Aeneas to l'Epine's Dido. John Hughes described Mrs Barbier's character with affectionate amusement in 'The Hue and Cry' (1717), written when she suddenly left her parental home:

> Gay, scornful, sober, indiscreet,
> In whom all contradictions meet …
> Much want of judgment, none of pride,
> Modish her dress, her hoop full wide,
> Brown skin, her eyes of sable hue,
> Angel, when pleas'd, when vex'd, a shrew.
> (Hughes, 1.219–20)

Mrs Barbier joined John Rich's Lincoln's Inn Fields company in January 1717 to sing Turnus in a revival of the English adaptation of Giovanni Bononcini's *Camilla*. She sang entr'acte music in Italian and English, created Syrinx in John Galliard's one-act opera *Pan and Syrinx* (14 January 1718) and Decius in his *Decius and Paulina* (22 March 1718), and was Orontes in a revival of the English pasticcio *Thomyris*. In the 1719–20 season she made only one appearance, on 7 April. Then, on 6 August, *Applebee's Original Weekly Journal* reported: 'Mrs. Barbier, the famous Singer at the New Play-House, having gain'd above 5000l. by South Sea Stock, has sung her last Farewell to the Stage'. However, she returned to Lincoln's Inn Fields in April 1724 to assume her old repertory and create the roles of Proserpine, Venus, Ceres, and Perseus in Rich's phenomenally successful series of pantomime afterpieces. In March 1730 she announced the 'last Benefit Mrs. BARBIER will have in England, notwithstanding any Reports that have or may be to the contrary' (*Daily Journal*). She is next heard of in Dublin on 4 December 1731, singing Italian arias and the ballad 'Peggy Grieves Me' at the Crow Street music hall, when Mrs Pendarves commented: 'she sings well, with a bad voice' (*Autobiography … Mrs Delany*, 1.327). Back in London, Mrs Barbier took the leading male roles in John Christopher Smith's unsuccessful operas *Teraminta* (20 November 1732) and *Ulysses* (16 April 1733) and in Thomas Augustine Arne's *Rosamond* (7 March 1733). She then made a few appearances at Drury Lane in spring 1734, when Arne had become musical director there. John Boyle, fifth earl of Cork and Orrery, was to say of Barbier: 'She never could rest long in a place; her affectations increased with her years' (Hughes, 1.219).

According to the *Gentleman's Magazine*, 'Mrs Barbier, formerly a Noted Singer in the Opera's' died on 5 February 1737, but she reappeared on stage for two performances of her old role in *Pan and Syrinx* in December 1740, when she (or the piece) was hissed. It is likely that she was the Jane Barbier, spinster, buried at St Margaret's, Westminster, on 27 December 1757, who in her will left 50s. each to the debtors in Whitechapel prison, set out precautions to ensure that she was not buried alive, and requested white gloves and scarves for the pall-bearers and white plumes for the hearse and horses at her funeral.

OLIVE BALDWIN and THELMA WILSON

Sources E. L. Avery, ed., *The London stage, 1660–1800*, pt 2: 1700–1729 (1960) • A. H. Scouten, ed., *The London stage, 1660–1800*, pt 3: 1729–1747 (1961) • *The Spectator* (24 Nov 1711) • *Applebee's Original Weekly Journal* (6 Aug 1720) • *Daily Journal* (9 March 1730) • 'On Mrs Barbiere's first appearance on the stage at the rehearsal of Almahide', *Miscellaneous poems and translations by several hands* (1712) • J. Hughes and others, *The correspondence of John Hughes, esq., and several of his friends*, 2 vols. (1773), vol. 1 • O. E. Deutsch, *Dokumente zu Leben und Schaffen*, vol. 4 of (1985) *Händel-Handbuch*, ed. W. Eisel and M. Eisel (1978–85) • J. Milhous and R. D. Hume, eds., *Vice Chamberlain Coke's theatrical papers, 1706–1715* (1982) • J. Milhous and R. D. Hume, eds., *A register of English theatrical documents, 1660–1737*, 1 (1991) • *The autobiography and correspondence of Mary Granville, Mrs Delany*, ed. Lady Llanover, 1st ser., 1 (1861) • B. Boydell, *A Dublin musical calendar, 1700–1760* (Dublin, 1988) • T. J. Walsh, *Opera in Dublin, 1705–1797: the social scene* (1973) • J. Hawkins, *A general history of the science and practice of music*, 5 (1776) • Burney, *Hist. mus.*, vol. 4 • W. Dean and J. M. Knapp, *Handel's operas, 1704–1726* (1987) • D. Hunter, *Opera and song books published in England, 1703–1726* (1997) • *GM*, 1st ser., 7 (1737), 124 • will, proved, 9 Dec 1757, PRO, PROB 11/834, sig. 350 • parish register, St Margaret's, Westminster, 27 Dec 1757 [burial]

Wealth at death 50s. to each of the debtors in Whitechapel prison; £5 to the poor of her parish; 20 guineas to each of her two executors: will, proved 9 Dec 1757, PRO, PROB 11/834, sig. 350

Barbirolli, Sir John [*formerly* Giovanni Battista] (**1899–1970**), conductor and cellist, was born Giovanni Battista at 12 Southampton Row, London, on 2 December 1899, the elder son and second of the three children of an émigré Italian violinist, Lorenzo Barbirolli (1864–1928), and his Parisian wife, Louise Marie Ribeyrol (1870–1962). He began to play the violin when he was four, but a year later changed to the cello. He was educated at St Clement Danes Grammar School and, at the same time, from 1910, was a scholar at Trinity College of Music. He made his public début in a cello concerto in the Queen's Hall in 1911. The following year he won a scholarship to the Royal Academy of Music, which he attended from 1912 to 1916. He was elected an associate of the academy at the age of thirteen. From 1916 to 1918 he was a freelance cellist in London, playing in the Queen's Hall Orchestra, in opera under Sir Thomas Beecham, and in theatre and cinema orchestras.

Barbirolli served in the Suffolk regiment (1918–19), and on demobilization resumed his orchestral career, although he was gifted enough to be soloist in Sir Edward Elgar's cello concerto at Bournemouth in 1921. In 1924 he became the cellist in both the Music Society and Samuel Kutcher string quartets. However, his ambition since

Sir John Barbirolli (1899–1970), by Georges Maiteny

childhood had been to conduct, and later that year he formed his own string orchestra. He gradually attracted attention and in 1925 was invited to conduct for the British National Opera Company (BNOC); he made his début in Gounod's *Romeo and Juliet* in Newcastle upon Tyne in 1926.

When the BNOC foundered financially in 1929 Barbirolli was appointed conductor of the Covent Garden touring company and also conducted regularly at the Royal Opera House, Covent Garden, in the grand opera season. In 1933 he became conductor of the Scottish Orchestra, rejuvenating the playing and programmes and winning most favourable opinions. Even so, no one was prepared for the sensation in 1936 when the Philharmonic-Symphony Society of New York, having been forced by public protests to withdraw their invitation to Wilhelm Furtwängler to succeed Arturo Toscanini as its conductor, asked Barbirolli for the first ten weeks of the 1936–7 season. He conducted in Carnegie Hall for the first time on 5 November 1936 and a month later was offered a three-year contract.

The years in New York were both rewarding and scarring for Barbirolli. Working with a great orchestra, with whom he was always on excellent terms, and with the most talented of the world's soloists, matured him musically; but the handicap imposed upon him by having succeeded Toscanini, who was idolized in New York and for whom a rival orchestra was created, was almost insurmountable. The critics, whose power and influence in New York at that time were notorious, were savage in their attacks on Barbirolli's interpretations. Nevertheless, in 1940 his contract was renewed for a further two years.

The issue by the Barbirolli Society since his death of transfers to CD of recordings he made in New York proves that the orchestra played superbly for him and that the criticism of him was largely unjustified.

When in April 1943 Barbirolli was invited to become permanent conductor of the Hallé Orchestra at a time of crisis in its history, he accepted without hesitation. He arrived in Manchester to find that he had a month in which to recruit forty players to add to the thirty-five under contract. He scoured the country for talent—no easy task in 1943—and launched a virtually new orchestra, which was soon acclaimed as the best in the country. This period, when he re-created the orchestra, bound him emotionally and indissolubly to the Hallé, so that despite lucrative offers from elsewhere, and despite his own exasperation with its post-war financial problems, he could not be lured away. He was knighted in 1949 and was awarded the Royal Philharmonic Society's gold medal in 1950. In 1959 he accepted engagements in America and returned to a rapturous welcome from public and critics in New York. He was a regular guest conductor of most of the leading European orchestras, including the Vienna Philharmonic, with whom he recorded the Brahms symphonies. In 1961 he began a decade of association with the Berlin Philharmonic, by which he was much admired, and from 1961 to 1967 was conductor-in-chief of the Houston Symphony Orchestra. But the Hallé was still his principal concern and, after twenty-five years with it, in 1968 he was appointed conductor laureate for life. He was made a Companion of Honour in 1969.

On 18 June 1932 Barbirolli married Marjorie Parry, a soprano. The marriage was not a success and they were divorced in 1939, when Barbirolli married (5 July) a celebrated oboist, Evelyn Alice (*b.* 1911), the daughter of R. H. Rothwell, a tea dealer, of Wallingford, Berkshire. There were no children of either marriage. Barbirolli was a fellow of the Royal Academy of Music (1928) and an honorary freeman of Manchester, King's Lynn, and Houston, Texas. Honorary degrees were conferred on him by the universities of Manchester (1950), Dublin (1952), Sheffield (1957), London (1961), Leicester (1964), and Keele (1969). He received the Bruckner (1959) and Mahler (1965) medals and was decorated by the governments of Italy, Finland, and France. For some years Barbirolli suffered from heart disease, and he died at Huntsworth Mews, London, on 29 July 1970 after a day of rehearsal in preparation for concerts with the New Philharmonia Orchestra in Japan. His ashes were buried in Kensal Green cemetery.

Barbirolli was a complete musician. His magnetism as a conductor was exemplified by his ability to obtain quickly the special quality of sound which he liked from an orchestra. His aim was to lead players and listeners into the composer's world: this power of commitment was his strength, as his recordings testify. If concentration on broad lines and expressive phrasing meant some loss of rhythmical impulse, that was a weakness which was usually outweighed. In the music of Mahler, Elgar, Sibelius, Brahms, and Vaughan Williams he was at his greatest, combining power and poetry, but his excellent Haydn was underrated and it was most unfortunate that after 1936 he conducted comparatively little opera, although he returned to Covent Garden in the 1950s and was offered (but refused) the post of music director. He had a natural flair for opera, especially the works of Puccini and Verdi, and in the last years of his life recorded *Madama Butterfly* and *Otello* and conducted *Aida* in Rome to great acclaim. No one who saw him—dynamic, with a touch of arrogance in his demeanour on the rostrum, small of stature but big in every other way—would have guessed that after a concert he would often lapse into deep depression. He was prey to an insecurity which stemmed partly from experiences during his rise to fame, was partly the result of his years in New York, and was also due to his own genuine humility in the face of great music. But with his sardonic humour, his courage, and his gift for friendship he concealed these human failings from all but his intimates. His capacity for work was prodigious and he demanded most from himself. MICHAEL KENNEDY

Sources M. Kennedy, *Barbirolli, conductor laureate* (1971) • C. Reid, *John Barbirolli* (1971) • M. Kennedy, *The Hallé tradition* (1960) • *The Times* (30 July 1970)

Archives Royal Academy of Music, London, collection | NL Scot., letters to D. C. Parker | FILM BFI NFTVA, *Monitor*, BBC, 11 March 1965 • BFI NFTVA, current affairs footage • BFI NFTVA, documentary footage • BFI NFTVA, performance footage | SOUND BBC WAC • BL NSA, *Music Weekly*, BS177/01 • BL NSA, *Recollections*, xx (738207.1) • BL NSA, *Richard Baker compares notes*, B332/02 • BL NSA, *Talking about music* 123, 1LP0153281 S1 BD1 BBC TRANSC • BL NSA, *Talking about music* 308, 1LP025482 S2 BD1 BBC TRANSC • BL NSA, documentary recordings • BL NSA, oral history interview • BL NSA, performance recordings • BL NSA, recorded talk

Likenesses photographs, *c.*1933–1967, Hult. Arch. • W. Stoneman, photograph, 1952, NPG • A. John, drawing, 1959? • B. Hailstone, oils, 1964, NPG • B. Howard, sculpture, Royal Philharmonic Society; on loan to Royal Festival Hall, London • G. Maiteny, photograph, NPG [*see illus.*] • H. Riley, paintings, priv. coll.

Wealth at death £36,307: probate, 11 Dec 1970, *CGPLA Eng. & Wales*

Barbon, Nicholas (1637/1640–1698/9), builder and economist, was the son of the London leather merchant and sectarian politician Praisegod *Barbon (*c.*1598–1679/80), after whom the short-lived parliament of 1653 was nicknamed Barebone's Parliament. He was educated at the universities of Leiden and Utrecht, where he studied medicine, graduating MD at Utrecht in 1661. After returning to London he was admitted an honorary fellow of the College of Physicians in 1664 but soon gave up the practice of physic for more lucrative pursuits in the turbulent business world of his day.

A number of plans were put forward for building insurance in the aftermath of the great fire of 1666, with Barbon's 'Insurance office for houses' the first to become operative after the issue in 1680 of a prospectus offering to insure up to 5000 homes in the city. Barbon became a key player in the rebuilding of modern London. The expansion and merging of the cities of London and Westminster, the need for rebuilding in the wake of the great fire, along with the growing concentration of wealth and population in the capital, led to a property and building boom facilitated by some innovations in the terms of mortgages and ground rents pioneered by Barbon. He played a leading role in the redevelopment of the Strand, linking the two ancient cities, and in the district of Bloomsbury. In the late seventeenth and early eighteenth centuries London finally lost its medieval character and became an impressive modern city and world trading capital. Green fields were rapidly covered with modern housing and commercial architecture. Some interests opposed this recasting of the cityscape. Royal decrees and acts of parliament had been enacted between 1580 and 1602 prohibiting new building, and this policy was adopted under successive protectorate and Restoration parliaments, but Barbon bypassed or simply ignored the surviving legislation that had acted as a brake upon new construction. He was impervious to the conservatism of the crown and the majority of city dwellers, and this led to some bitterness and conflict, occasionally even violence. At times he was known to demolish homes and rebuild on the site without having first secured permission of the legal owner, and to face down any subsequent legal action.

In 1684 Barbon's workmen were involved in a stand-up fight against the lawyers of Gray's Inn, who were protesting over his plans to develop Red Lion Fields without official sanction. His skill as a builder lay, according to North, 'more in economising ground for advantage and the little contrivances of a family than the more noble aims of architecture, and all his aim was at profit' (North, 53). Poorly constructed vaults in his early buildings in Mincing Lane led to a disastrous collapse of foundations, but his reputation survived this setback. By these means he became a presiding influence upon the new architecture and land use of the city. His redevelopment of Red Lion Fields, the Temple, and the streets around what had been Essex House stand as his most noteworthy contributions to the rebuilding of London. He built his own grand home at Crane Court, Fleet Street, where he set up the centre for his dealings. He later acquired as a residence Osterley House on the Thames to the west of London.

His role as projector and speculator in the burgeoning economy of Restoration England aroused a good deal of hostile commentary in Barbon's own day and continues to contribute to a scurrilous reputation as a practised schemer and manipulator of men. North, who knew him personally and well, described him as a 'mob master', who knew amply 'the arts of leading, winding, or driving mankind in herds' (North, 53–4). There can be no doubt that at times his practices were deliberately dishonest. An intimidating, argumentative, and combative figure, he was all but impervious to personal slights—'he would be called rogue, knave, damned Barbon, or anything, without being moved' (ibid., 54)—and showed no signs of his father's religious enthusiasm. A fine and showy dresser, he lived in sumptuous style, partly in order to maintain social appearances and also to inspire confidence in his business schemes. A reckless speculator, known at times to overvalue his assets and the extent of his credit, some of his enterprises failed, leaving a trail of creditors and dissatisfied co-projectors making suit against him. At times he preferred to accrue debts in this manner and face drawn-out legal actions for recovery, sometimes setting one group of creditors against another, and deliberately delaying by complicating court actions, calculating this to be a cheaper means of obtaining credit than arranging conventional loans and paying interest. He was said to keep in his employ a team of clerks and lawyers specifically for these purposes. He was elected as member of parliament for Bramber in 1690 and 1695 after having bought a placeman's seat. He was thus able to claim parliamentary protection from prosecution and thereby frustrate some outstanding cases against him in the courts.

Barbon was also an innovator in economic theory. His early training as a physician was a factor in common with Sir William Petty and others of the seventeenth-century economists and political arithmeticians. He is considered by modern commentators to have propounded advanced views on free trade, the function of money, interest rates, and consumption. His *Discourse of Trade* (1690) argued that money had no intrinsic value. Rather it functioned symbolically as a means of facilitating exchange. He conducted debates with John Locke over the debasement of the coinage, and in favour of a legal reduction in the rate of interest in his *Discourse Concerning Coining the New Money Lighter* (1696). Barbon well understood that modern economic conduct was driven by desire and appearances as well as necessity:

> the use of most things being to supply the wants of the mind, and not the necessitys of the body; and those wants, most of them proceeding from imagination, the mind changeth; the things grow out of use, and so lose their value. (N. Barbon, *A Discourse of Trade*, 1690, 6)

The fashion for frivolous luxury goods might then have beneficial consequences. Excess itself would spur trade, prodigality was a vice that was prejudicial to individuals, but not to trade, whereas covetousness was prejudicial to both men and trade.

> Fashion, or the alteration of dress is a great promoter of trade because it occasions the expense of cloths before the old ones are worn out. It is the spirit and life of trade; it makes a circulation, and gives a value, by turns, to all sorts of commodities; keeps the great body of trade in motion. (ibid., 65)

He scorned the current classical nostalgia for the ancients in politics as neither Livy nor Machiavelli had taken due account of trade.

Barbon's economic theory was in many ways linked to and informed by his commercial activities. The roles of MP, builder, projector, and writer were all intertwined in practice. Among later schemes there was a plan for an orphans' bank and a plan to raise drinking water from the Thames. One of his last projects, the National Land Bank, aimed to raise funds secured on landed property and sought to compete with the newly established Bank of England. The bank received royal assent in 1696, but when Barbon was called upon in July of that year to provide financial support for overseas military operations, funds were found wanting and the bank folded soon after. Barbon wrote his will on 18 May 1698, giving instructions that his debts should be paid, especially that owing for his late wife's funeral. He probably died at Osterley House, Middlesex, later that year; his will was proved on 6 February 1699. R. D. SHELDON

Sources R. North, *The autobiography of the Hon. Roger North*, ed. A. Jessopp (1887) • N. Barbon, *Apology for the builder, or, A discourse showing the cause and effects of the increase of building* (1685) • N. Barbon, *Account of two insurance offices* (1684) • E. McKellar, *The birth of modern London* (1999) • N. Luttrell, *A brief historical relation of state affairs from September 1678 to April 1714*, 6 vols. (1857) • D. Vickers, 'Barbon, Nicholas', *The new Palgrave: a dictionary of economics*, ed. J. Eatwell, M. Milgate, and P. Newman (1987) • N. G. Brett-James, 'A speculative London builder of the 17th century, Dr Nicholas Barbon', *Transactions of the London and Middlesex Archaeological Society*, new ser., 6 (1933), 110–45 • *VCH Middlesex*, 3.109 • will, PRO, PROB 11/449, sig. 19

Barbon [Barebone], **Praisegod** (*c*.1598–1679/80), lay preacher and politician, first appears in 1623, when he was made free of the Company of Leathersellers in London; having served an eight- or nine-year apprenticeship, he was probably then aged about twenty-five. At an unknown date, but probably by 1632, Barbon joined the semi-separatist congregation founded in 1616 by Henry Jacob, and later led by John Lathrop and then, from 1637, by Henry Jessey. On 18 May 1640 this church was divided 'by mutual consent' with half of the original congregation following Jessey and the other half choosing Barbon. At this date Jessey is known to have been living in east London, in the liberty of the Tower, whereas Barbon's shop-cum-warehouse was outside the western wall of the city, so the division was probably a matter of geographical convenience.

By May 1632 Barbon had married Sarah, a member of Lathrop's church; they had at least one son, Nicholas *Barbon (1637/1640–1698/9). Praisegod was clearly doing well in his trade, for he was elected a warder of the yeomanry of the leather-sellers in 1630, and a liveryman in 1634. His premises, at the Lock and Key, at the lower end of Fleet Street near Fetter Lane, were spacious enough, for here on 19 December 1641 he preached before about 150 people, including (according to an outraged reporter) as many women as men. Perhaps Barbon was straining to make himself heard before such a crowd, but the noise of his oration attracted the attention of passers-by. Outside the Lock and Key, hostile crowds gathered. In the course of a long sermon directed against the bishops and the Book of Common Prayer, apprentices began smashing the windows and sought to break down the door. Eventually the constables arrived; some of Barbon's congregation were taken to the Bridewell prison, others to the Counters, and still others made their escape over the roof-tops, while the crowd was left to destroy his shop-sign.

Barbon's association with the Jessey church and its offshoots brought him into contact with groups more hostile to the Church of England. At the Lock and Key disturbance, a second preacher, the separatist leader John Green, was also arrested. The following month more than fifty persons, including many members or former members of Jessey's church, were rebaptized by immersion in London. Barbon strongly disagreed with these advocates of

Praisegod Barbon (*c*.1598–1679/80), by unknown engraver

believers' baptism, and within a few weeks he issued *A Discourse Tending to Prove the Baptism … to be the Ordinance of Jesus Christ*. No evidence has been discovered for the frequent assertion that Barbon himself was rebaptized; the claim that he was an 'anabaptist' probably derives from post-Restoration royalist diatribes. However, his *Discourse* and a second work issued in spring 1643, *A Reply to the Frivolous and Impertinent Answer of RB*, are important sources for the views and practices of the Baptists at this early stage in their development. Just like other controversialists, such as the separatist Samuel Chidley, Barbon defended baptisms received in the Church of England, though unlike Chidley he also defended the authenticity of the English church. However, Barbon stood for a broadly pluralistic outlook against the enthusiasts for the imposition of Anglican orthodoxy. God 'causeth much profit to come out of the variations of his servants, the truth is the more sought into and discovered, and cometh to shine forth more fully afterward' (Barbon, *Discourse*, A3r).

Barbon's adherence to semi-separatist views, in the tradition of Henry Jacob, enabled him to participate in the political life of the parish. He was involved over the next few years in a series of conflicts with the group of wealthy men who controlled the vestry of St Dunstan-in-the-West, and with Francis Kemp, the lawyer and (up to 1642) common councillor who acted for them. In 1643 Barbon was involved in an action against the parish officers in the court of king's bench; in 1645 he was chosen as a member of a committee for the establishment of a free school in the parish, but this too seems to have involved wrangles with the vestry. The following year there was controversy over the election by show of hands of a churchwarden. It seems that one source of tension was the high presbyterianism of the vicar, Anthony Perne, to whom Barbon and some other prominent parishioners were strongly opposed, and another was the exclusion of many householders from the franchise. Barbon was made third warder of the Leathersellers' Company in 1648, but it was only the following year, after the purge of presbyterians from the City government, that he was returned as common councilman for his parish of St Dunstan-in-the-West. Other radicals and separatists were becoming prominent in London politics at the same time. Barbon was re-elected as a common councilman for 1650–51, and served also on the committee of safety in 1651.

The peak of Barbon's political career, however, was in 1653, when he was selected, as one of the seven members for London, for the parliament which, probably even while it was sitting, attracted the sobriquet derived from his name. It seems that in July 1653 the London bookseller George Thomason picked up a list of the members of 'Barebones Parliament', in which those of moderate politics were distinguished from the rest. The combination of Barbon's pious first name, his unfortunate surname (lampooned as Rawbones by John Taylor even twelve years earlier), and his (relatively) humble social status were all open to ridicule. This combination was irresistible to opponents of the assembly, keen to belittle it. Barbon himself was a member of the committee which published on 12 July the enthusiastic and hopeful announcement in which the new body proclaimed itself the parliament of the Commonwealth, and he was shortly appointed to the committee for receiving petitions. Though never elected to the council of state, Barbon was in the second rank of the most active and influential members in the new house. He was one of the radicals who sat on the committee on tithes set up on 19 July, and was also one of the thirteen original members of the committee established on 19 August to consider a thoroughgoing reform of the law. In late July at Westminster large numbers of women demonstrated in support of John Lilburne, who was on trial having returned to London from exile without a pass. Possibly it was Barbon's reputation as a radical, and his long history of involvement with the semi-separatists, that led parliament to select him for the unrewarding task of placating Kathleen Chidley and the other leaders.

It is clear that while Barbon was more radical than some, he did not always vote with the radicals, and appeared more than once as a teller in divisions alongside a known moderate. Sometimes, however, his opposition to apparently radical innovations such as the bill for a high court of justice, defeated on 28 September, probably arose from the fear that the new instrument might be used against radicals as well as royalists. Among the more extreme members of parliament was the group of Fifth Monarchists. It may be suspected that Barbon shared their millennial aspirations, but he was uneasy about both their predictions and the insurrection to which many looked forward. In November 1654 members of ten London congregations signed a Fifth Monarchist declaration against what they took to be the most offensive features of the newly established protectorate. Though more than twenty members of his congregation set their names to this work, Barbon did not, and neither does he appear to have been involved in any of the later Fifth Monarchist plots against the Cromwellian regime.

Barbon was re-elected to the common council for the three years from 1657 to 1660, and after the restoration of the Rump Parliament he was named to the London militia committee under the act of 7 July 1659. In January 1660 he was one of the common councillors who opposed the proposal that the City should send its compliments to General George Monck. The following month he was appointed as controller of the commissioners for compounding at the generous salary of £300 p.a. Barbon was the chief promoter of a petition presented to parliament on 7 February in the name of the well affected of London and Westminster. This warned against the 'return of the justly-secluded members, or a Free Parliament, without due qualifications' (Davies, 279) and demanded that all office-holders, and members of either parliament or the council of state, should renounce both Charles Stuart and rule by any other single person. It probably helped provoke, during the next few weeks, the two attacks on his house by royalist crowds. The smashing of Barbon's windows marked both the beginning and the end of the interregnum.

In July, following the Restoration, there appeared a royalist tract, the *Picture of the Good Old Cause Drawn to the Life*, which reprinted the petition of 7 February and published also an engraving in which Barbon appears in gaunt and serious mien with cap and gown. On 5 September 1661 it was reported that he was a frequent visitor to both Vavasor Powell and Major John Bremen, then in the Fleet prison. These were dangerous connections, and Barbon was also named as one of those who frequented Nonsuch House in Bow Street, a republican meeting place. He was arrested on 25 November 1661 and charged with treason alongside James Harrington and Samuel Moyer. These and others were thought to have plotted the military seizure of London and restoration of the Long Parliament. On 27 July 1662, following a petition of his wife, Sarah, it was ordered that Barbon be freed from his close imprisonment in the Tower, since he was 'so ill that he must perish unless released' (*CSP dom., 1661–2*, 447). The fortunes of the Lock and Key did not improve. Barbon had taken out a new fourteen-year lease on the premises in 1656 at the very considerable rent of £40 p.a., but in 1666 it was one of the most westerly buildings to be engulfed in the great fire of London. The loss of his workplace must have caused Barbon acute difficulty. On 10 March 1667, in the court of judicature, he obtained a judgment against his landlords, a widow, Elizabeth Speght, and her son Paul Speght, which stipulated that in exchange for rebuilding the property, he should be entitled to a reduction in annual rent to £15, and that on these terms forty extra years should be added to the lease. On 5 January 1669, having completed the work, Barbon sold the rights and the lease to his son Nicholas, who proceeded to take out a mortgage for £300, probably to help his father recoup some of the considerable costs of reconstruction.

This experience did nothing to weaken Barbon's millenarian convictions. In *Good Things to Come* (1675) Barbon looked forward to the coming of Christ and his rule for a thousand years: 'his kingdom and reign shall be outward, and visible on earth … when he shall come the second time, in power and great glory' (p. 10). Barbon died about the end of 1679 and was buried on 5 January 1680 near the artillery ground, in the parish of St Andrew Holborn.

STEPHEN WRIGHT

Sources A. Woolrych, *Commonwealth to protectorate*, pbk edn (1986) · K. Lindley, *Popular politics and religion in civil war London* (1997) · C. Burrage, *The early English dissenters in the light of modern research, 1550–1641*, 2 vols. (1912) · M. Tolmie, *The triumph of the saints: the separate churches of London, 1616–1649* (1977) · *The discovery of a swarme of separatists, or, A leathersellers sermon* (1641) · B. S. Capp, *The Fifth Monarchy Men: a study in seventeenth-century English millenarianism* (1972) · court book, 1632–50, Leathersellers Hall, London · R. Brown, 'Praise-God Barbon and the fire of London', *N&Q*, 152 (1927), 453–5 · Tai Liu, 'Barebone, Praisegod', Greaves & Zaller, *BDBR* · G. Davies, *The restoration of Charles II, 1658–1660* (1955) · R. L. Greaves, *Deliver us from evil: the radical underground in Britain, 1660–1663* (1986) · *CSP dom.*, 1661–2 · *A declaration of several churches of Christ and godly people* (1654) · M. A. E. Green, ed., *Calendar of the proceedings of the committee for compounding … 1643–1660*, 5 vols., PRO (1889–92) · *N&Q*, 4th ser., 3 (1869), 215 [cited from the parish register] · C. H. Firth and R. S. Rait, eds., *Acts and ordinances of the interregnum, 1642–1660*, 3 vols. (1911) · [J. Taylor], *New preachers new* (1641)

Likenesses engraving, BL, 669 f25 (57) · line engraving, BM, NPG [*see illus.*]

Barbour, Sir David Miller (1841–1928), administrator in India and writer on monetary issues, was born at Omagh, co. Tyrone, Ireland, on 29 December 1841, the fifth child of Miller Barbour and his wife, Margaret Denny, into an established family of farmers and small landowners at Calkill, near Omagh. He was educated at Omagh Academy and Queen's College, Belfast, graduating in 1862 with a BA from the Queen's University of Ireland.

Barbour passed sixth in order of merit into the Indian Civil Service in 1862, taking first place in the examination in mathematics. He arrived in India in December 1863, and was posted to Bengal. He became under-secretary to the government of India in the finance department in 1872 and subsequently held the posts of accountant-general in the Punjab, Madras, and Bengal, then acted as secretary to the government of Bengal in the finance department and later in the revenue and general department. In 1880, following the Second Anglo-Afghan War and the British occupation of Kabul and Kandahar, he published a pamphlet under the initials D. B. entitled *Our Afghan Policy and the Occupation of Candahar* calling for a prompt withdrawal from Afghanistan. In 1882 Barbour was awarded the honorary degree of LLD by the Royal University of Ireland, which superseded the Queen's University in that year, and in 1883 he married Katherine Constance, daughter of Thomas Gribble, who had been connected with the wine trade in Portugal.

In 1882 Barbour also returned to the government of

Sir David Miller Barbour (1841–1928), by Walter Stoneman, 1917

India as secretary in the department of finance and commerce. For the next decade the financial and currency problems of India were the subject of intense international discussion and debate, as her economic history was dominated by the decline in the price of silver bullion against that of gold. This change in the relative prices of the two precious metals on which the world's currency systems depended had been precipitated by the abandonment of the silver standard by Germany and the United States, which led to a fall in the price of silver relative to gold, unseating the apparently stable ratio of 15½ to 1 that had been effective for most of the previous century. The result of these changes in India, where the silver rupee remained tied to the gold price of its silver-bullion content, was to devalue the currency sharply against sterling and to increase the exchange costs of the transfers that the government of India had to make to meet its considerable expenditure in Britain. This also increased the transfer costs of servicing private investment, which, coupled to the uncertainty of the exchange rate, may have deterred British capital from investing in India. While devaluation also had some small impact on the international prices of India's main exports of agricultural produce and imports of manufactured goods, the effect of this was masked by the global price fall in the period brought about by increased productivity, reduced shipping costs, and fluctuations in the world supply of monetary gold and other instruments of international liquidity.

Barbour feared that a continued fall in the price of silver against gold would lead to a depression in the Indian domestic economy, limiting the spread of commercialization and the use of money. Thus he argued consistently in favour of a return to bimetallism—the use of both precious metals at a stable exchange rate in international monetary transactions—and was one of the substantial minority (five out of twelve) of the royal commission on gold and silver in 1886 that argued in favour of such a system. However, he knew that bimetallism could only be re-established by virtually unanimous international agreement, and that it was very unlikely that such an agreement could ever be secured. The gold and silver commission reported in 1888 and on 22 November of that year Barbour became finance member of the governor-general's council. He was made KCSI on 1 January 1889.

The continued fall in the gold price of silver, and the failure of any international agreement to remedy the situation, made the financial position of the government of India extremely precarious in the early 1890s. As Barbour himself recognized, and pointed out in introducing the Indian budget for 1891–2, India was being forced onto the gold standard for lack of any alternative. To achieve this meant closing the Indian mints to the free coinage of silver, so that the token value of the rupee could rise above its bullion value, and this step was taken on 26 June 1893, when the mints were closed following the report of a special Indian currency committee chaired by Lord Herschell. Barbour resigned from the Indian Civil Service and left India in November 1893, but in 1898 he was appointed to the committee on Indian currency chaired by Sir Henry Fowler, which reported in 1899 with a recommendation that the exchange value of the rupee be formally stabilized at the rate of 15 rupees to the pound, with gold sovereigns being free to circulate in India at that rate, and that action be taken to build up the sterling and gold reserves of the government of India to establish international confidence in the currency. The effect of these measures was to establish a gold exchange system in India, by which silver rupees circulated as a token currency, supported in a fixed exchange rate with sterling by currency reserves in London, and an alliance between British financial institutions and the colonial authorities to manage the market in foreign exchange. Subsequently, Barbour acted as chairman of committees set up to consider the currency problems of the west African colonies and protectorates and the Straits Settlements, and recommended that a similar system to the one operating in India be introduced into these territories.

In the 1890s and 1900s Barbour served on a wide variety of committees and commissions of imperial importance, for which he was made KCMG in 1899. In 1894 he was a member of the royal commission on the financial relations between Great Britain and Ireland and wrote a minute of dissent distinguishing himself, as a keen Ulsterman, from the home-rule sentiments of the majority. In 1896 he was a member of the royal commission that reported on the economic condition and prospects of the British West Indies; in 1899 he reviewed the financial problems of Jamaica, urging much greater prudence in the colony's affairs; and in 1900 he reported on the financial situation of the newly conquered South African Boer republics of the Orange River and the Transvaal. In 1903–5 he served as chairman of the royal commission on London traffic; in 1906–9 he was a member of the royal commission on shipping rings, for which he wrote a minority report demanding action to ensure greater competition; and in 1907–8 he was a member of the committee on Indian finance and administration chaired by Lord Inchcape. Barbour also pursued a successful career in business, joining the board of the East Indian Railway Company in 1895, becoming deputy chairman in 1917, and chairman from 1919 to 1924. He was also a director of the Standard Bank of South Africa from 1901 until 1927.

Barbour's last intervention in the making of imperial financial and monetary policy came with the evidence he gave to the committee on Indian exchange and currency in 1919 (the Babbington-Smith committee), in which he was one of those who argued strongly that the fixed exchange rate system for the rupee, which had lapsed owing to the strains of wartime finance, and the rise in world silver prices coupled to the fall in the gold value of the pound sterling after 1918, should not be reimposed at a new rate until the disturbed and difficult conditions of the post-war world had become stabilized. This case was weakened, however, by the absence of any strong recommendation as to what a suitable future exchange rate or standard might be, and was ignored in the committee's final proposals for a gold-standard rupee at a new rate of 10 rupees to the gold pound. The subsequent failure of the Indian monetary authorities to implement this policy, and the dramatic decline of the rupee exchange rate to well below its pre-war parity, showed just how disturbed international conditions had become, and the rupee was not finally stabilized on a fixed exchange rate with sterling until 1927.

Barbour's lifelong interest in international monetary issues was demonstrated by the three books he published on the subject of bimetallism: *The Theory of Bimetallism* (1885), *The Standard of Value* (1912), which was an account of his tenure as finance member in India, and *The Influence of the Gold Supply on Profits and Prices* (1913). He died on 12 February 1928 at his home, Tiltwood, Crawley Down, Sussex, and was survived by his wife, three sons, and one daughter. B. R. TOMLINSON

Sources S. Ambirajan, *Political economy and monetary management: India, 1766–1914* (1984) • B. R. Tomlinson, *The political economy of the raj, 1914–1947* (1979) • *DNB* • *CGPLA Eng. & Wales* (1928)

Likenesses W. Stoneman, photograph, 1917, NPG [*see illus.*]

Wealth at death £70,503 2*s*. 3*d*.: resworn probate, 20 March 1928, *CGPLA Eng. & Wales*

Barbour, John (*c*.1330–1395), ecclesiastic and verse historian, was author of the Old or Middle Scots poem *The Bruce*. His birth is usually placed about 1325, as much to give him a toehold in Robert I's reign as for anything his career tells us, and a slightly later date seems likelier. The trade name he inherited suggests that his father was a barber, and John's first appearance, in 1356 resigning the precentorship of Dunkeld which he held for just a year, links his family to that see. *The Bruce* records the dash and bravery of William Sinclair, bishop of Dunkeld (*d.* 1337), and his following in repelling an English force in 1317; John may have grown up on the fringes of the bishop's household, his father barber to Bishop William and perhaps to his successors, for when John obtained the precentorship in 1355 he was evidently at the papal court at Avignon with the new bishop, previously precentor. His promotion may also have been earned by their diplomatic activity on behalf of the guardian, Robert Stewart: in 1354 David II had been about to return from captivity in England, but the unenthusiastic guardian allowed the ransom negotiations to lapse while negotiating for military assistance from France.

In 1356 Barbour was appointed to the archdeaconry of Aberdeen, presumably from the same Stewart patronage. But David II came home in November 1357 for an even larger ransom, at which prospect Barbour had sought leave to study at Oxford; he was the first Scot to be granted a safe conduct for that purpose in August 1357 and in September was his bishop's proctor at the council which discussed the king's release. He had further English safe conducts to leave Scotland during the years 1357–71, when David II was an active king, for study in England (1364), to visit St Denis (1365), and to study in France (1368), which he probably did in the following three years. That he had been to a university is almost certain because he is called on occasion master, but given the rarity of this description it is likely that he had not graduated and was not entitled to it.

After 1356 Barbour received no further advancement in his long life, certainly not the bishopric for which he was as well qualified as any of the bishops. Everything suggests that he was a known client of Robert Stewart, who in 1371 at last ascended the throne as Robert II. Barbour, it seems, wrote *The Bruce* for this royal patron, whose father, Walter, appears in a generous measure and light in its pages. When Barbour began to write is a matter of judgement, but the poem as it stands must have taken two or more years, perhaps as many as five or six. Composition started, therefore, about 1372 and detained him at or brought him to court, as a result of which he was employed in February 1373 as one of the auditors at the exchequer (worth £40 per annum), acting for the second time in that office two years later. The date 1375 marks the conclusion of the poem he planned and was followed by a change in his career, for he now appears in a north-eastern context: in 1378 the king granted him a pension of £1 annually from Aberdeen burgh's annual payment to the crown. This was paid until his death and (since the grant was perpetual, to assigns) from 1395 to his legatees, the cathedral chapter; in 1429 it was said to have been granted 'for the compilation of the book of the deeds of the late King Robert the Bruce' (Burnett and others, 4.457).

The poem of 1375, written in rhyming octosyllabic couplets, sketches the Bruce claim to the throne in 1292, but moves rapidly to the Edwardian occupation, presumably of 1304. After the killing of Sir John Comyn, cursorily described, it gives a vivid depiction of the battle of Methven on 19 June 1306 and an extended treatment of the early tribulations of Robert I and of Sir James Douglas. It skims over the years 1309–13, partly because there was a truce, but mainly, it would seem, because of lack of sources. The narrative resumes with the taking of Perth, Roxburgh, and Edinburgh, going on to a full account of the battle of Bannockburn and the king at the top in the revolution of Fortune's wheel; there follow, briefly, the return of the king's daughter, her marriage to Walter Stewart, and the birth of their child Robert, in the fifth year of whose reign, 1375, this poem is being written. It is the only year date in the whole poem, and surely marks the end of the original composition, over 8000 lines long. It is a 'romance' (Barbour's word) of chivalry, with emphasis on loyalty, bravery, and wisdom. It claims to be truthful, but Barbour has often been misled by his sources, as over the chronology of events leading to Bannockburn, and sometimes tailors the facts to create a better literary effect, as when Edward I condemns to death the prisoners taken at Kildrummy, an action wrongly placed for dramatic impact at the time of Edward's own death. It has nothing on romantic love, and women are rare in its pages. Its most famous passage is an encomium of freedom, which, it can reasonably be pointed out, in Barbour is enjoyed by men of nobility.

In the 1380s Barbour returned to court, serving as auditor again in 1383, 1384, and 1385; he had several one-off gifts of money from the king in 1382–6 and in 1388 an annual pension of £10 for life, this last suggesting that he had satisfactorily completed a literary work, but was not to be given a bishopric. The work was probably the continuation of *The Bruce*, in a further 5000 lines, up to the deaths of Sir James Douglas (1330) and Thomas Randolph, earl of Moray (1332). These sections show a less sure touch and lack the exempla from French romances which are a marked feature of the earlier part.

The division of the whole poem into twenty books is entirely modern. Barbour used a collection of tales of the king's adventures in 1306–8 and a narrative, perhaps put together about 1332 from some annals and personal recollections of the rest of the reign. But the main chivalrous character, of whom a vivid picture is given, is Douglas, and a literary life of him was surely known to Barbour. A highly coloured, minstrel-like narrative of Edward Bruce would explain the erratic account of the Irish campaigns, a tenth of the poem. There are those, however, who would credit Barbour with piecing much of the story together himself, from reminiscences collected by himself, on the grounds that he virtually never mentions written sources, but frequently says, 'I heard tell'.

What else did Barbour write? Before 1449 the chroniclers Wyntoun and Bower had ascribed to him *The Bruce* (sections and lines from which were silently borrowed by Wyntoun), *The Brut*, *The Stewartis Oryginalle*, and *The Stewartis Genealogy*. The last two are certainly identical, and if a mythical Trojan origin were suggested for the Stewarts, *The Brut* could be another title for the same. They surely confirm that Barbour devoted his literary talents pretty single-mindedly to one family, the Stewarts. And whether one or two works, they are lost. Although *The Bruce* survives in only two manuscripts, it was clearly influential upon all later Scottish historiography and pseudo-history, for Blind Hary took episodes from it shamelessly to attribute to Wallace. A number of other works were once said to have come from Barbour's pen: *The Buik of Alexander*, with many unattributed borrowings from *The Bruce*, but ascribed to 1438 in the manuscript of its text; sections of a translation of Guido delle Colonne's Latin history of the taking of Troy; and all or part of a translation of the legends of the saints. Cogent reasons have been given for rejecting all the ingenious hypotheses supporting these attributions.

His patron, Robert II, having died in 1390, Barbour was at Aberdeen in 1391–2, and probably until his death. Aberdeen Cathedral lists give the anniversary of his death on 13 and 14 March, and the transfer of his £1 pension shows that the year was 1395; it is likely that he was buried in the cathedral. A. A. M. DUNCAN

Sources D. E. R. Watt, *A biographical dictionary of Scottish graduates to AD 1410* (1977), 28–9 • J. Barbour, *The Bruce*, ed. W. W. Skeat, 2 vols., STS, 31–3 (1894) • J. Barbour, *The Bruce: selections for use in schools*, ed. W. M. Mackenzie (1909) • *Barbour's Bruce*, ed. M. P. McDiarmid and J. A. C. Stevenson, 3 vols., STS, 4th ser., 12–15 (1981–5) • J. Barbour, *The Bruce*, ed. A. A. M. Duncan (1997) • G. Burnett and others, eds., *The exchequer rolls of Scotland*, 1–4 (1878–80)

Barbour, John (**1849–1918**), clothing manufacturer, was born on 9 March 1849 at Bogue Farm, Dalry, Kirkcudbrightshire, formerly part of the Lochinvar estate, one of twin sons of James Barbour (*d.* in or after 1871), a prosperous farmer, and his wife, Agnes, *née* Milroy (*d.* in or before 1871); his brother's name was James. Both his parents were Scottish, with ancestry traceable to the fourteenth century. Rejecting a career in farming Barbour left the south-west of Scotland at twenty to seek a living in the world of business, and within a year he and a cousin had established themselves as travelling drapers based in Newcastle upon Tyne. On 10 October 1871, at the Free Church manse in Dalry, he married Margaret (*b.* 1850/51), daughter of John Haining, minister. She was born on the island of Gigha, near the Mull of Kintyre, and had known Barbour since childhood; they settled in Newcastle. They had ten children, two of whom eventually followed their father into the family business. Suffering from poor health, Margaret was confined to bed for much of her married life.

While in Newcastle, Barbour established a mercantile enterprise and opened a shop in partnership with two other drapers. By 1890 he had amassed sufficient capital to establish his own firm, and moved to South Shields, where he began a tailoring business, aiming to establish an enduring enterprise in the town. Within two years his business had both expanded and become specialized in marketing protective oilskins and waxed wet-weather wear. In this Barbour not only drew upon his particular experience and expertise but also had identified an untapped segment of the clothing market. In 1894 his business, trading as J. Barbour & Co.—rather misleadingly described as 'Tailors and Drapers'—operated from premises in the town's market place. From the outset the garments sold by the business were unique, and have remained so. Durable, expensive, and carefully handmade, mainly by outside contractors in the early years, Barbour's products quickly established a reputation among the local fishing and sailing community for their effective protective qualities. It was the mail-order business, which Barbour's son Malcolm created in 1908, that generated booming business in the years before the First World War. The early catalogues reveal the diversity of the company's products, which included fashionable garments for both men and women as well as protective sporting and working clothes.

Barbour died on 9 July 1918, in Linden Avenue, Darlington, survived by his wife. Gradually the firm moved more extensively into manufacture, most rapidly after his death. His two eldest sons, John and Malcolm, carried on the business, though during the depressed years of the 1920s it faltered, and John resigned. Malcolm, who in any case had been responsible for much of the enterprise's early expansion, took the business to a period of renewed success. The profitability of J. Barbour & Sons Ltd was sustained during the remainder of the twentieth century and into the next, under the leadership of successive generations of Barbours, as its traditional market among outdoor workers was supplemented by demand from the wealthier social groups for robust yet attractive outdoor country wear. The dark-green Barbour wax jacket with its characteristic large toothed metal zip—as well as a range of accoutrements—achieved symbolic status as it became standard garb for the rich at play.

KATRINA HONEYMAN

Sources 'A brief history of J. Barbour and Sons Ltd' [provided by the company] • www.barbour.com, 15 Nov 2001 • *Financial Times* (31 Dec 2001), 15 • bap. reg. Scot. • m. cert. • d. cert. • *CGPLA Eng. & Wales* (1918)

Wealth at death £17,169 9*s*. 0*d*.: probate, 17 Sept 1918, *CGPLA Eng. & Wales*

Barbour [*née* Rough], **Mary** (**1875–1958**), labour activist and politician, was born on 22 February 1875 in Kilbarchan, Renfrewshire, third of the seven children born to James Rough, carpet weaver, and his wife, Jane Gavin. After being educated locally, Mary left school at the age of fourteen. She began work as a thread twister in Elderslie, where the family had moved in 1887, and later became a carpet printer. On 28 August 1896 she married David Barbour from Johnstone and they settled in Govan Burgh near Glasgow where she became active in the Kinning Park co-operative guild, the first one established in Scotland.

Mary Barbour was also a member of the Independent Labour Party and socialist Sunday school, but her political career really began with the Glasgow rent strike during the First World War. In early 1914, as a result of steep rent increases by landlords, Andrew McBride, Independent Labour Party councillor, and Mary Laird, Women's Labour League president, formed the Glasgow Women's Housing Association. It was in Govan in June 1915, however, that the first signs of active resistance arose with the non-payment of rent increases by tenants, mainly housewives, and the formation of the South Govan Women's Housing Association under the strong and imaginative leadership of Mary Barbour.

As a working-class housewife with two sons and a husband who was an engineer in Fairfield's shipyards, Mary Barbour was actively involved in organizing tenement committees, helping the women to fight evictions, and drive out the sheriff's officers. The strike spread to other areas, culminating on 17 November 1915 in one of the biggest demonstrations seen in Glasgow when thousands of women—nicknamed 'Mrs Barbour's Army' by William Gallacher—accompanied by shipyard and engineering workers, converged on the sheriff's courts in the city centre. The resulting Rent Restrictions Act marked a turning point in Glasgow's housing history and benefited tenants nationwide, while the role played by Mary Barbour made her a popular legend in Govan. In June 1916, together with her friends Helen Crawfurd and Agnes Dollan of the Women's International League, Mary Barbour was instrumental in founding the Women's Peace Crusade in Glasgow and became a popular speaker at colourful rallies on Glasgow Green.

In 1920 Mary Barbour was one of three candidates for Fairfield ward, Govan. She polled 4701 votes, mainly from women, and was elected to Glasgow town council as their first Labour woman councillor. Mary Barbour advocated municipal banks, wash-houses, laundries, and baths, a pure milk supply free to schoolchildren, child welfare centres and play areas, home helps, pensions for mothers, and a campaign against consumption. From 1924 until 1927 she served as the first woman bailie on Glasgow corporation and was appointed one of Glasgow's first women magistrates, gaining distinction on children's panels. Her council work on eight committees, including housing and health, further developed her lifelong commitment to the welfare of women and children.

As a supporter of birth control for married women, Mary Barbour pioneered the first family planning centre—the Women's Welfare and Advisory Clinic—in Glasgow in 1925 and chaired its committee, raising funds to maintain its staff of women doctors and nurses.

After retiring from council work in 1931, Mary Barbour continued her activities on housing, welfare, and co-operative committees and in later years organized seaside outings for children of poor families. In 1953 she was a guest speaker in Glasgow at the inaugural meeting of the Scottish National Assembly of Women. David Barbour died in November 1957. Mary Barbour died aged eighty-three at the Southern General Hospital, Glasgow, on 2 April 1958; her funeral was held on 5 April at Craigton crematorium in Govan.

In appearance Mary Barbour was a woman of medium build with dark hair and a pleasant determined expression conveying strength of character. She admitted to having high ideals but these were allied to a practical nature and a forthright, honest approach which earned her the respect of colleagues. One of the group of pioneering Labour leaders on Clydeside, she was held in high regard and affection by her local community and worked tirelessly to see many of her objectives achieved, to the benefit of countless Scots women and their families.

AUDREY CANNING

Sources W. Gallacher, *Revolt on the Clyde: an autobiography* (1936), 52–8 • R. Horne, '1915: the great rents victory', *Scottish Marxist*, 2 (winter 1972), 19–26 • H. Crawfurd, autobiography (unpublished), Glasgow Caledonian University, Gallacher Memorial Library, Helen Crawfurd MSS, MSS 144–8 [also Marx Memorial Library, London] • J. Melling, *The rent strikes, 1890–1916* (1983) • *Govan Press* (22 Oct–5 Nov 1920) • *Govan Press* (25 March 1921) • *Govan Press* (11 April 1958) • private information (2004) • J. J. Smyth, 'Working class women in Glasgow during the First World War', diss., U. Glas., 1980 • P. Dollan, *History of Kinning Park Coop. Society* (1923), 116, 147 • Glasgow Corporation minutes, 1920–27, Mitchell L., Glas., Glasgow City Archives • Domesday Book, Mitchell L., Glas., Glasgow City Archives • Glasgow Women's Welfare and Advisory Clinic reports, 1934–5, Mitchell L., Glas. • *Red skirts on Clydeside*, documentary film, Scottish Film Institute, Glasgow • J. Blair, 'Mary Barbour, a fighter for Govan', *Shetland Life* (Dec 1968) • d. cert. • *Evening Times* [Glasgow]

Archives Glasgow Caledonian University, Gallacher Memorial Library • Mitchell L., Glas., Glasgow City Archives • Mitchell L., Glas. | FILM Scottish Film Institute, Glasgow, 'Red skirts on Clydeside' [documentary film]

Likenesses photograph, 1920 (in bailie's robes), Glasgow Caledonian University, Gallacher Memorial Library • group photograph, 1920–29 (*The four Marys*), City Chambers, Glasgow • group portrait, three photographs, 1940–58, Glasgow Caledonian University, Gallacher Memorial Library • photograph, Glasgow Caledonian University, Gallacher Memorial Library, election address, Fairfield 31st ward, Glasgow, 1920, cover

Barcaple. For this title name *see* Maitland, Edward Francis, Lord Barcaple (1808–1870).

Barclay, Alexander (*c*.1484–1552), poet and clergyman, was born at a place and date that are still obscure. John Bale, in the mid-sixteenth century, described him once as 'English', once as 'Scottish', and stated on a third occasion that 'some contend that he was a Scot, others an Englishman' (*Scriptorum illustrium Maioris Brytannie*, 1557–9, 723). Another early witness, William Bullein of Ely, writing in his *Dialogue Against the Fever Pestilence* (1564), believed that Barclay was 'born beyond the cold river of Tweed' and the belief is supported by six stanzas in praise of King James IV of Scotland, inserted by Barclay into his translation of *The Ship of Fools* (1509) where the context did not require them. On the other hand, Barclay's recorded life was spent wholly in England or continental Europe, and he had cousins living in London at the time of his death. His connection with Scotland, if it existed, was limited to parentage, birth, or childhood, or to a misunderstanding of origins in the far north of England, whose inhabitants were often confused with Scots by people from further south.

The date of Barclay's birth is usually given as 1475 or 1476, on the ground that he gives his age as thirty-eight in the prologue to his *Eclogues*, parts of which were written as early as 1513 or 1514, but it is not known when the prologue was composed. He does not appear in records until ordained priest in 1508, and the placing of his birth in the mid-1470s has given rise to speculation that he spent his young adulthood in a lengthy period of travel and study on the continent of Europe. He has also been credited with the anonymous English translation of Pierre Gringore's work *The Castle of Labour*, printed in Paris about 1503. There is as yet no direct evidence, however, about an early career spent on the continent or about his authorship of the translation, and it is more economical to place his birth close to 1484: the latest possible date, since the priesthood was not conferred until the age of twenty-four. His first known appointment was a relatively junior one, and although he states in the prologue to *The Ship of Fools* that he has been 'a scoler longe, and that in dyvers scoles', he also asks readers to pardon his youth (*Ship of Fools*, 1.3–4). He could easily have attended a series of schools, travelled abroad, and acquired the familiarity with French and German which he claims in *The Ship*, between the late 1490s and 1508.

Ottery and *The Ship of Fools* Barclay was evidently educated in Latin to a high standard (he later edited a Latin schoolbook and worked as a schoolmaster), but it is unclear whether this was followed by university study. He certainly did not gain a degree higher than that of BA until the 1530s, since only one reference before that decade calls him 'Master Barclay'. The first certainty in his life comes in March and April 1508, when he was ordained subdeacon, deacon, and priest at Exeter Cathedral to a title, or guarantee of support, provided by the collegiate church of Ottery St Mary in Devon. He had previously been living in the diocese of Lincoln, whose bishop issued letters dimissory allowing him to seek ordination elsewhere. Barclay entered the priesthood to qualify himself for employment in the church of Ottery, probably as chaplain (or clerk) of the lady chapel, a junior office responsible for teaching song to the choristers and young adult 'secondary clerks' of the college and for organizing the daily services in the chapel in honour of the Virgin Mary. His stay at Ottery was brief but notable for the production of his first major work, *The Ship of Fools*, the translation of Sebastian Brant's *Narrenschiff* (1494) into English verse. It was printed in London in December 1509 (when Barclay had left the college) by Richard Pynson, who published most of the author's subsequent works.

Barclay embellished his translation with copious additions. He dedicated it to Thomas Cornish, warden of the college and suffragan bishop in the diocese of Exeter, who may have been responsible for bringing him to Ottery, and included complimentary references to Henry VIII, Sir John Kirkham of Paignton, Devon, and John Bishop, rector of St Paul's Church, Exeter. The work enabled him to mount attacks on a range of contemporary social groups and practices: attacks which accord with traditions of social criticism going back to the fourteenth century, while reflecting some of the concerns of humanist writers in the early sixteenth. His targets included fond parents and ungrateful children, inconstant and evil women, all who wore extravagant clothes, pluralist clergy, ignorant gentlemen, avaricious merchants, corrupt lawyers and physicians, riotous servants, and sturdy undeserving beggars. He also took the opportunity to settle some private scores. The secondary clerks of the college were singled out for their unwillingness to learn, the neighbouring parish clergy for ignorance and worldliness, and a group of named men of Ottery (who appear to have been ordinary laity) for being frauds and thieves. The work shows a sympathy with humanist Latin, and criticizes those attached to the medieval grammar of Alexander of Ville-Dieu rather than to the works of Priscian and the Renaissance grammarian Giovanni Sulpizio.

Years in the Benedictine order By 1513 Barclay had become a Benedictine monk of Ely Cathedral priory, a considerable shift both geographically and vocationally. As he was sixteenth in seniority out of thirty monks in 1516, it is likely that he went there straight from Ottery about 1509. This alteration of direction seems to have embodied a genuine calling, since Barclay had hardly been a secular priest for long enough to feel disappointed at lack of advancement. It may have reflected an ambition to pursue a career as an author, and gave him a secure and comfortable environment in which to do so. His subsequent writings, all or most of which were undertaken at Ely, spanned a range of genres. Pre-eminent are his five verse *Eclogues*, the first major pastoral poems to be written in English. The first three, which discuss the miseries of courts and courtiers, were translated from works by Aeneas Sylvius Piccolomini (Pope Pius II). The fourth, on the behaviour of rich men to poets, and the fifth, a dispute between a citizen and a countryman, were based on poems by Mantuan (Baptista Spagnuoli). Barclay seems to have written the fourth, the easiest to date from mentions of current events, in 1513–14. The *Eclogues* were apparently first printed separately, the earliest surviving editions being approximately datable to 1518 (the fifth), 1521 (the fourth), 1523 (the first), and 1530 (the first three). They were the most successful of Barclay's writings in the sixteenth century, to judge from the number of reprints. Their appeal no doubt reflected their pleasant traditional pictures of landscapes, seasons, and rural life; their gentle criticisms of courts, towns, and neglect towards scholars; and their numerous references to places and people in England.

Barclay produced at least six other works during his time at Ely. *Alex. Barclay his Figure of our Mother Holy Church Oppressed by the French King*, a lost printed book in English recorded by the bibliographer Andrew Maunsell, may have dated from 1512 when Louis XII of France was campaigning in Italy, or 1515 when his successor, François I, was doing the same. *The Life of St George* in verse, also based on a work by Mantuan, was printed about 1515, and *The Mirror of Good Manners* in verse, translated from a Latin text of the humanist scholar Domenico Mancini, about 1518. Later, Barclay applied himself to more practical works in prose. His revision of an elementary school treatise on Latin words, *Vocabula* by John Stanbridge, was published in 1519 with further reprints in 1524 and 1526–7; his English translation of Sallust's *History of the Jugurthine War* about 1520; and his *Introductory to Write and to Pronounce French* in 1521. The last of these works, as Barclay admitted, drew on older guides to the French language produced for English people. John Palsgrave, who published a large-scale work on French in 1530, *L'esclarcissement de la langue francoyse*, paid tribute to Barclay in his preface as a 'studious clerke', but warned readers later on that he differed from Barclay on orthography and other matters, and caustically remarked 'I have sene an olde boke written in parchement in maner in all thynges like to his sayd *Introductory*, which by conjecture was nat unwritten this hundred yeres. I wot nat if he happened to fortune upon suche another' (*L'esclarcissement*, sig. A.iiiv). Bale also ascribes to Barclay lives of St Katherine and St Margaret, and later scholars have suggested other titles, without secure confirmation.

Barclay was a productive monastic writer on the scale of John Lydgate, whom he resembled in the variety of his output, the undertaking of translations, and the writing of verse in English. His works were dedicated to important people of the day, either for his own benefit or for that of Ely Cathedral. The principal person so honoured was Thomas Howard, duke of Norfolk, who is praised in the fourth eclogue and to whom *The Life of St George*, *The Jugurthine War*, and *The Introductory* were all addressed. *The Jugurthine War* was also offered to John Veysey, bishop of Exeter, and *The Mirror of Good Manners* to Sir Giles Alington, a courtier and knight of Cambridgeshire. Barclay appears to have had links with the royal court during his time at Ely, especially with the Chapel Royal—a fact which recalls his probable duties in the lady chapel at Ottery. Not only are his first three *Eclogues* moralizations on court life, but the second of them praises John Kyte, the subdean of the Chapel Royal; William Cornish, the master of its choristers; and William Crane, one of its gentleman singers. In April 1520 Sir Nicholas Vaux asked Thomas Wolsey to send Barclay to devise historical subjects and other themes to embellish the buildings planned for the English court at the Field of Cloth of Gold in Flanders. The *Eclogues* also include a commendation of John Colet, dean of St Paul's, London, and contain dismissive references to poets laureate which appear to allude to John Skelton, whose poem 'Philip Sparrow' is mentioned by name. Bale credited Barclay with a work *Contra Skeltonum*.

The impact of Barclay's writings can be judged partly from the observations of his contemporaries and partly from the editions of his works. Henry Bradshaw of Chester, a fellow Benedictine, linked him with Chaucer, Lydgate, and Skelton in 1513, and William Bullein with the same writers in 1564. Bale (followed by Raphael Holinshed) called him 'a notable rhetorician and poet', and William Forrest described him in 1569 as 'eloquent'. His only works to be reprinted in the sixteenth century, however, were the first three *Eclogues* about 1548 and about 1560, *The Jugurthine War* in 1557, and *The Ship of Fools* with the whole of the *Eclogues* in 1570, this last edition being an enterprise of the London printer John Cawood. Thereafter he attracted little notice in literary circles until his works began to be reprinted in the nineteenth century.

Years in the Franciscan order Barclay himself appears to have exhausted his literary ambitions by the 1520s. Between 1521 and 1528 he abandoned Ely to become a Franciscan friar, possibly at Canterbury, a house of the reformed or Observant branch of the Franciscan order. This was another unusual change of direction—monks and friars had different traditions, objectives, and ways of life—and signified a further large vocational adjustment on Barclay's part. He now ceased to write either poetry or practical works, and much of his time was probably given to the study of theology, a study which may have provided one motive for joining the friars, who were more committed to it than were monks. By 1538 he was styled 'doctor', doubtless of divinity, indicating that he had graduated in this study in a university outside England, since he is not recorded as taking a degree at either Oxford or Cambridge.

In October 1528 the German informer Hermann Rinck wrote to Cardinal Wolsey that various dissidents including 'William Roy, William Tyndale, Jerome Barlow, Alexander Barclay and their adherents … formerly Observants of the Order of St Francis but now apostates … ought to be arrested, punished, and delivered up on account of Lutheran heresy' (*LP Henry VIII*, 4/2.2083 (no. 4810)). The rest of these men were living in Germany, which makes it appear as if Barclay was based there too. Rinck's letter is a principal piece of evidence that Barclay joined the reformed or Observant branch of the Franciscan order rather than the original and larger Conventual branch, but the letter is not entirely accurate: Tyndale was not a friar. Another Observant friar, John West, who mentions that he was soon to meet Barclay about April 1529, accused him of calling Wolsey a 'tyrant' and other 'opprobrious and blasphemous words' (*LP Henry VIII*, 4/3.2406 (no. 5463)). It is not impossible that Barclay was attracted by aspects of Lutheranism at this time, but he did not voluntarily adhere to the Reformation until much later; on the contrary, he acquired a reputation in England during the late 1530s of being a religious conservative.

In 1534 the English Observant houses were closed because of their hostility to Henry VIII's claim of supremacy over the Church of England, and the surviving members were transferred to the mainstream Conventual houses. Barclay is likely to have returned to England by about this date, in view of the increasing separation of England from the Catholic church, and it is possible that he ended his career as a friar in or near London. The London chronicler Charles Wriothesley singled him out by name, under the year 1538, as one who refused to give up wearing his religious habit in public until he was compelled to do so. John Foxe the martyrologist later recounted a version of this story in which Thomas Cromwell personally threatened Barclay with hanging unless he changed his clothes. In the summer and autumn of 1538 Barclay carried out a number of private preaching engagements, including sermons at Thetford Priory, Norfolk; Barking, Suffolk, at Whitsuntide; and in the diocese of Exeter in October. Reports of his demeanour were duly transmitted to Cromwell. At Barking he had not spoken in favour of the king's supremacy or against the pope; at St Germans, Cornwall, he had made his conservatism known, albeit in a circumspect way; and in Cornwall and Devon he was doing 'much hurt' with 'open preaching and private communication' (*LP Henry VIII*, 13/2.222 (no. 571), 232 (no. 596), 272 (no. 709)). What action Cromwell took, if any, is not clear, because Barclay drops out of the records for the next eight years. As a friar, he did not receive a pension after the suppression of his order, and the only pointer to his whereabouts and support in the early 1540s is his will, which reveals a number of links with lay people in London.

Final years When Barclay reappears it is in yet another role, that of a beneficed clergyman and eventually a clerical pluralist, signifying that he had come to accept the English Reformation, at least as an accomplished fact, and had resolved to make a new career as a secular priest in the Church of England. In March 1546 William Bowerman, subdean of Wells Cathedral, presented Barclay to the vicarage of Wookey, Somerset, near Wells, with an income of £12 15*s*. 8*d*. He probably lived at one or other of these places for the next two years. In the summer of 1547 the headmaster of Wells Cathedral school, Richard Edon, fell ill and Barclay took his place, probably on a temporary basis, with a further salary of £13 6*s*. 8*d*. He was paid to run the school until Michaelmas or Christmas 1548, when he moved abruptly from Somerset to the other side of England to become vicar of Great Baddow, Essex, on the presentation of a local gentleman, John Pascall. The date of Barclay's admission to Great Baddow is traditionally given as 7 February 1547, but this is based on a mistake by the eighteenth-century historian Richard Newcourt; the correct year is 1549. Barclay went to stay at Great Baddow in January of that year and lodged with Pascall until April, paying him money to organize the rebuilding of the vicarage. This fact emerged in 1554 when Pascall sued Barclay's executors, claiming further unpaid costs of the project. Great Baddow was a more valuable benefice than Wookey, with an income of £18 6*s*. 8*d*., and since Barclay obtained permission to go on holding Wookey as well, his net income rose to a respectable £25, supposing that he paid a curate to serve his Somerset parish. In 1552 he was presented by the dean and chapter of Canterbury Cathedral to a third, even wealthier, living: the rectory of All Hallows, Lombard Street, London, with an income of £22 6*s*. 8*d*. This promotion involved his giving up one of his other two parishes, but he died at Croydon, Surrey, before he could do so, in June 1552, and was buried there on the tenth of the month.

Barclay's will was made on 25 July 1551, and proved on the day of his burial. Its monetary bequests amount to over £70 which, together with the mention of a sum of £80 owed to him by one Cuthbert Croke of Winchester, suggests that his career as a beneficed clergyman had already made him moderately wealthy. He left small sums to the poor of Great Baddow and Wookey, and the residue of his goods and chattels to the bedridden, maidens, widows, and other helpless people. Money for rings was given to thirteen other men and women, including Sir John Gates, Sir Henry Gates, Mr Cheke, and four London citizens. The chief beneficiaries of his will were members of his family: his cousins Parnell Atkinson and Joan Bowyer; Parnell's husband Thomas Atkinson, a London scrivener; and their four daughters. Atkinson was made executor, together with a gentleman named Thomas Edon, and the speedy probate of the will may explain why two other relatives, Michael and John Barclay, subsequently tried to contest its validity. Barclay asked those to whom he made bequests to pray to God for remission of his sins and mercy on his soul—phrases that look conservative, but his will by no means shows that he died a reluctant protestant. Cheke was probably John Cheke, tutor to Edward VI, and the Gates brothers were close associates of the duke of Northumberland, and deeply implicated in his attempt to exclude Mary Tudor from the throne in 1553. That Barclay made friends with such pillars of Edward's protestant regime provides a final twist to the convoluted story of his life.

NICHOLAS ORME

Sources *The eclogues of Alexander Barclay*, ed. B. White, EETS, original ser., 175 (1928) • A. Barclay, *The ship of fools*, ed. T. H. Jamieson, 2 vols. (1874) • A. Barclay, *The life of St George*, ed. W. Nelson, EETS, original ser., 230 (1955) • *STC, 1475–1640* • *LP Henry VIII*, 4/2.2083; 4/3.2406; 13/2.222, 232, 272 • N. Orme, *Education and society in medieval and Renaissance England* (1989) • will, PRO, PROB 11/35, fols. 130*r*–130*v* (17 Powell); PROB 11/36, fols. 73*v*–74*r* (11 Tashe) • H. Cooper, *Pastoral: medieval into Renaissance* (1977) • parish register, Croydon, 10 June 1552 [burial]

Wealth at death over £80: will, PRO

Barclay, Andrew Whyte (1817–1884), physician, was born on 21 July 1817 in Dysart, Fife, the son of Lieutenant John Barclay, a naval officer, and Henrietta Whyte. He was educated at the high school, Edinburgh, and began studying medicine at Edinburgh University in 1834. In 1836–7 he visited London and studied at the Westminster Hospital. He also visited Berlin and Paris before returning to Edinburgh, where he gained his MD in 1839. He then continued travelling and visited Germany, Switzerland, France, Italy, and Madeira. After his return to England he entered Gonville and Caius College, Cambridge, in 1842; he proceeded MD in 1852. He also studied at St George's Hospital, London, and was appointed medical registrar there, a post which he held for many years.

Barclay became the first medical officer of health for Chelsea in 1855. His *Progress of Preventive Medicine and Sanitary Measures* appeared in 1856. He was elected assistant physician to St George's Hospital in 1857, and he paid particular attention to the interests of the medical school, where he lectured on medicine. He served as physician from 1862 to 1882. He married the eldest daughter of a Dr Noble in 1864. Henry Noble Barclay (1866–1939) was their son.

At the Royal College of Physicians Barclay became a fellow in 1851, and he was examiner in medicine, councillor, censor, Lumleian lecturer, and Harveian orator (for 1881); he was elected treasurer in 1884. He was president of the Royal Medical and Chirurgical Society for the year 1881, and he contributed to the transactions of that society two papers on heart disease. Barclay was shrewd and cautious as a physician, and concise and polished as a writer. He wrote *A Manual of Medical Diagnosis* (1857), *On Medical Errors*, and *On Gout and Rheumatism in Relation to Diseases of the Heart* (1866).

Barclay retired to Stevenage, Hertfordshire, in 1882, and was also appointed consulting physician at St George's Hospital in London. He died on 28 April 1884 at Whitney Wood, Stevenage.

R. E. THOMPSON, *rev.* KAYE BAGSHAW

Sources *BMJ* (10 May 1884), 932–3 · *The Lancet* (10 May 1884), 872 · Munk, *Roll* · Venn, *Alum. Cant.* · parish register (birth), 21 July 1817, Dysart, Fife · *CGPLA Eng. & Wales* (1884)

Wealth at death £13,878 7*s.* 11*d.* in UK: probate, 30 May 1884, *CGPLA Eng. & Wales*

Barclay, David, of Ury (1610–1686). *See under* Barclay, Robert, of Ury (1648–1690).

Barclay, David (1682–1769), merchant, was born in Ury, Scotland, on 17 September 1682, the second son and second child in the family of three sons and four daughters of the Quaker apologist Robert *Barclay (1648–1690), of Ury, and his wife, Christian (*c.*1651–1724), daughter of Gilbert Molleson of Aberdeen. Barclay's father gave him 9000 Scottish merks (£500) to start on a mercantile career. He was apprenticed on 1 March 1698 to John Perry of London (*d.* 1718), a member of the Drapers' Company since 1686, as the eighth of Perry's sequence of eighteen apprentices. On completion of his articles on 3 April 1706, Barclay was admitted a freeman of the Drapers' Company; in 1720 he became a liveryman of that company. In 1746 he was elected to its court of assistants, serving until 1768. He was nominated renter-warden (the third of the four wardens of the company) in 1746, and in 1756 master, but on both occasions he paid a fine, as was customary for refusers, to avoid election.

Barclay began to deal in linens while still a freeman, being described in the company's records as 'linen-draper of Cheapside at the White Bear'. His cousin John Falconar was already an established Cheapside merchant. Barclay sold Scottish linens on commission, and dealt in Irish linens with his brother, John Barclay of Dublin. He gradually extended the range of his business by exporting German linens to Philadelphia on joint account with local merchants. Already by 1728 one of them was able to describe him as 'better Acquainted with our Trade than any Draper in London' (Price, 'The great Quaker business families', 391). By the time of his retirement in 1767, Barclay's firm was 'the first house in their business' (ibid.), owning ships, and trading to New York, Pennsylvania, the Chesapeake, and the West Indies. At his death, two years later, Barclay was reputedly worth over £100,000. He was an active member of the monthly, quarterly, and yearly meetings of the Society of Friends, of its meeting for sufferings, and of the latter's subcommittee for American affairs.

Barclay married, first, on 12 April 1707, Anne (*d.* 1720), daughter of James Taylor, citizen and glover of London; second, on 8 June 1723, Priscilla, daughter of John *Freame (1665–1745) of Lombard Street, a leading Quaker banker. Freame, who was the son of Robert Freame, clothier of Cirencester, was in a banking partnership from the 1690s with his brother-in-law Thomas Gould (*d.* 1728), son of Thomas Gould, a Quaker of Enfield. Freame married Thomas Gould's sister Priscilla, and Thomas Gould married Freame's sister Hannah, both events occurring in 1697. The banking partnership ended with Thomas Gould's death, Freame continuing alone, then in partnership with his son Joseph (*d.* 1766), at what later became 56 Lombard Street. In 1733 James Barclay, David Barclay's son by his first marriage, married Sally Freame, Priscilla Barclay's sister (thus his step-aunt) and joined the partnership, which became Freame and Barclay, until his death in 1766. Joseph Freame's own son John (*d.* 1770) was also a partner from 1759 (Freame, Barclay, and Freame). On Joseph Freame's death, the Barclay interest in the bank continued through the two sons of his sister Priscilla and David Barclay, David and John, who progressively withdrew from their father's linens trade because of the American war, which they strongly opposed. From 1776 the bank was Barclay, Bevan, and Bening, stabilizing as Barclay, Tritton, and Bevan from 1797. It can be seen from this that, although David Barclay senior was not the founder of Barclays Bank, as he has sometimes been named, his sons James, David, and John were important early partners in the bank, and the mercantile fortune he had built up was an important source of capital for it from the 1770s.

Barclay's house at the sign of the White Bear in Cheapside, opposite St Mary-le-Bow Church, was earlier used by Charles II in 1671, William and Mary in 1689, and Anne in 1702, to view the lord mayor's procession. This custom continued under David Barclay, who entertained there George I in 1714, George II in 1727, and the young George III and his new bride in 1761, the last occasion attracting widespread interest in the metropolitan press.

Barclay had two sons and four daughters from his first marriage, and two sons and six daughters from his second. Alexander, a child of his first marriage, was a collector of customs in Philadelphia; David *Barclay (1729–1809), banker and brewer, from his second marriage, was prominent in the Quaker anti-slavery movement. Barclay died on 18 March 1769 at Bush Hill, Winchmore Hill, Middlesex, a house inherited from his father-in-law John Freame.

P. G. M. DICKSON, *rev.*

Sources P. W. Matthews, *History of Barclays Bank Limited*, ed. A. W. Tuke (1926) · C. W. Barclay and others, eds., *A history of the Barclay family*, 3 vols. (1924–34) · M. Ackrill and L. Hannah, *Barclays: the business of banking, 1690–1996* (2001) · F. G. Hilton Price, *A handbook of London bankers* (1876); repr. (New York, 1970) · J. M. Price, *Capital and credit in British overseas trade: the view from the Chesapeake, 1700–1776* (1980) · J. M. Price, 'The great Quaker business families of eighteenth century London', *The world of William Penn*, ed. R. S. Dunn and M. M. Dunn (1986), 363–99 · Drapers' Hall, London, Drapers' Company records · digest registers of births, marriages, and burials, RS Friends, Lond.

Barclay, David (1729–1809), banker and brewer, was the younger son of David *Barclay (1682–1769), Quaker merchant, and his second wife, Priscilla, daughter of John Freame, banker, of Lombard Street. David and his brother

David Barclay (1729–1809), by Houghton

John became partners in their father's linen and merchant house in Cheapside.

Even before the death of his father in 1769, David Barclay had begun a strategic redirection of the family's efforts and resources. Perceiving more clearly than most the dangers inherent in the darkening American situation, the Barclay brothers first gave up their commission merchant business, and then gradually reduced their export trade to North America. By 1783 they had decided to wind up their old linen business. Through his mother, Barclay was to inherit a share in the Freame bank, the oldest surviving Quaker bank in London. In 1776 he became an active partner in this firm, now styled Barclay, Bevan, and Bening, which developed as the Lombard Street node of a network of Quaker country bankers, financing bridges and canals as well as trading enterprises. (After many changes of partners, with the Barclays, Bevans, and Trittons predominating, this firm became the nucleus of the corporate merger of 1896 which became Barclays Bank.) In 1781 Barclay and his nephews, Robert Barclay and Silvanus Bevan, bought the Anchor Brewery in Southwark from Mrs Hester Thrale. This became Barclay, Perkins & Co., one of the three great London breweries of the nineteenth century. The later partnership records of the bank suggest that he became a sleeping partner at some time in the 1780s.

Like his father, David Barclay was a conscientious and active Quaker, and a pacifist. He was a good friend of Benjamin Franklin and tried unsuccessfully in 1774–5 to mediate between Franklin and the government of Lord North to avoid the impending break with the American colonies. His philanthropies were many, and he used his influence to move English Quakers into a stronger stand against slavery—a difficult position for a retired West India merchant, whose bank financed slavers and slave owners, and had the non-Quaker Bevans, with less severe views on such matters, as partners. On a Jamaican cattle ranch acquired in settlement of some debts, he freed the slaves and transported them at his own expense to Philadelphia for resettlement, incurring a £3000 loss.

On 6 May 1749 Barclay married his first wife, Martha, daughter of John Hudson, of Thames Street, London, hop merchant. They had an only child, Agatha, who married (3 August 1773) Richard Gurney, a Quaker banker of Norwich. She was the mother of Hudson *Gurney, David Barclay's principal heir. In 1767 Barclay married his second wife, Rachel, daughter of Sampson *Lloyd (1699–1779), banker. In his will Barclay remembered numerous nephews and cousins, some of whose descendants were active in his bank and brewery until well into the twentieth century. He died at Walthamstow, Essex, on 30 May 1809. JACOB M. PRICE, *rev.* LESLIE HANNAH

Sources M. Ackrill and L. Hannah, *Barclays: the business of banking, 1690–1996* (2001) · C. W. Barclay and others, eds., *A history of the Barclay family*, 3 vols. (1924–34) · P. Mathias, *The brewing industry in England, 1700–1830* (1959) · P. W. Matthews, *History of Barclays Bank Limited*, ed. A. W. Tuke (1926) · R. S. Dunn and M. M. Dunn, eds., *The world of William Penn* (1986)

Archives Barclays Bank archives, London · Norfolk RO, personal and commercial corresp. and papers | Barclays Bank archives, London

Likenesses Houghton, portrait, NPG [*see illus.*]

Barclay, Sir George (*c.*1636–1710), army officer and Jacobite conspirator, was a Scot, but appears in no known Barclay family pedigree; perhaps his leadership of the assassination plot of 1696 made his relations hide the connection. A government propagandist then mentioned 'the Obscurity of Sir *George*'s Character, that he hath no great Interest in his own Country, and is not much known in *England*' (*Observations*, 7), although events that year proved that he had reliable relatives or friends—perhaps a wife—near London. A proclamation of 1696 described him as aged about sixty. A Catholic, he evidently spent most of his military career in foreign service. He wrote in 1688 to Charles Middleton, second earl of Middleton, his patron, recounting his battlefield experience and his zeal, known to James II and Middleton, in the worst of times—possibly referring to the Popish Plot. Barclay's first recorded British commissions were issued on 2 May 1685, when, already an experienced captain, he was appointed to command a fort to be built on Stirling Bridge (never completed), and as inspector of the Scottish army. He already had west highland contacts. On 28 November 1685 he became major of the English infantry regiment of his fellow Catholic Sir Edward Hales, and on 3 October 1686 its lieutenant-colonel; he commanded it until the revolution. He had been knighted by October 1688. In January 1689, when he, like other Jacobites, wished to follow James to France, he was seriously ill in London. He was allowed to remain there by William of Orange, who then gave him a pass to go to France.

Barclay was with James in Ireland in 1689, but in early

July that year he crossed with Brigadier-General Cannon and other officers to Mull to join Viscount Dundee (John Graham of Claverhouse) and the Jacobite highland rising, carrying a commission for a proposed dragoon regiment. At Killiecrankie on 27 July he helped command Sir Donald Macdonald of Sleat's clan regiment on the left flank—he was one of the few professional soldiers whom the highlanders admired. In September 1689 he was badly wounded and captured by raiding Williamites at Alexander Robertson of Struan's house in Atholl, but was exchanged that winter. In February 1690 he carried a letter from the clan chiefs to James in Ireland, asking the king to send his illegitimate son James Fitzjames, duke of Berwick, to command them. Barclay returned with money for the clans and was promoted brigadier-general in July 1690. That autumn he stayed with Macdonell of Glengarry and encouraged him to continue resistance.

By June 1691, however, Barclay, now a major-general, was convinced that the clans, lacking French help, could no longer hold out. He persuaded the hesitant Jacobite commander, Major-General Thomas Buchan, to enter into negotiations at Achallader with John Campbell, earl of Breadalbane, who acted as William's representative in the highlands. Barclay was chosen and then replaced as a messenger to ask James's permission for the clans to submit, but finally left on that mission in September, when no reply had been received. Without his support, Buchan was increasingly influenced by those opposed to the settlement, which virtually collapsed in November. That month Barclay finally joined Breadalbane's agent Duncan Menzies at St Germain. After a proposed French invasion of Scotland came to nothing, they persuaded James to sign a warrant releasing the clans on 12 December 1691 NS (2 December 1691 OS). A Dunkirk privateer would take them to Scotland; but they did not yet realize that William's revised deadline for the chiefs' submission, 1 January 1692, was in deadly earnest. They were captured off Dover on 12 December 1691 OS and taken to London. Barclay, on refusing to take the oaths to William, was prevented from carrying his news north. Menzies was allowed to do so on 15 December, and reached Edinburgh within a week; but snow delayed its dissemination among the clans. The chiefs rushed to submit in late December mainly because a winter campaign was imminent, not on account of James's permission; but had the messengers not been detained, the particular delay which prevented Alexander Macdonald of Glencoe from taking the oaths on time, and so led to the massacre of Glencoe, might not have occurred. Barclay felt sympathy for the clans; it is unknown whether the massacre affected his attitude to William.

Barclay was allowed to return to France in February 1692, and was involved in the Scottish side of the French invasion attempt that May. In 1692 he was appointed lieutenant of the second troop of James's guards. On 28 September 1693 NS he transferred to the first troop, of which Berwick was captain. During the summer they often served with the French army. In December 1693 Barclay and a Captain Francis Williamson were in England to obtain for the rival secretary to Middleton, John Drummond, earl of Melfort, opinions from various leading Jacobites that James should invade swiftly with a French army 30,000 strong. They carried back several propositions from lesser men for kidnapping William, which were disregarded.

In the winter of 1695–6 James at last prepared to lead a small French invasion. According to Berwick, who was in overall charge of the rising intended to support it, Barclay was appointed second-in-command to Sir John Fenwick in the leadership of 2000 Jacobite cavalry expected to assemble in London and the south-east. In November 1695 James instructed Barclay to cross secretly to London and organize the rising in conjunction with the leading Jacobites involved. Officers and troopers of James's guards would follow, and he should appoint them to stiffen the raw regiments in the rising. James's secretary of state, John Caryll, had Barclay paid £800 to buy horses for them. His commission, issued on 27 December 1695 NS, the day he set off, authorized James's subjects to rise and make war on William, and particularly to seize strongholds in England. To cover Barclay's absence from St Germain, he was rumoured to be undergoing a pox cure at Paris. For security reasons, the guardsmen who followed him over in pairs were simply told to receive their orders from him. He reached London about 27 December OS, but was almost recalled at once over a problem of seniority as a general—a confirmation that his mission was genuinely for the rising.

Barclay lived in London in disguise. His normal appearance was described in 1696 as tall, thin, hook-nosed, and ruddy-faced, with a crippled right hand. He changed lodgings several times, and secretly met and paid the Jacobite guardsmen who followed him in the piazza of Covent Garden. According to Barclay, Robert Charnock and Sir William Parkyns, both particularly active in preparing a rising, were the first to suggest to him an attack to assassinate William as a way of improving the invasion's chances. He responded eagerly, and showed Parkyns, a lawyer, his commission, probably to confirm that it could be interpreted as covering such attacks. Evidence of how unready most south-eastern Jacobites were to rise before the French landed, noted also by Berwick, evidently confirmed his determination, since he apparently never approached Fenwick. While keeping William's movements under observation, he received suggestions from various Jacobites of possible methods and places, besides alternative operations such as seizing the Tower. Barclay showed as much caution as such a plot allowed. He opposed, for instance, trusting George Porter, who, after capture, was to become the most damaging crown witness. Finally the conspirators, after several conferences, agreed to ambush William at Turnham Green as he returned from Saturday hunting at Richmond, with forty horsemen. Barclay with eight men would attack the king's coach and kill everyone inside, while the remainder in two parties fought the accompanying lifeguards. Barclay obtained nearly half the number of horsemen, ironically, from the officers and men of James's own lifeguards who had crossed. Several followed orders reluctantly, assuming that this was the mission for which James had told them to obey him, under a commission which, the leading conspirators claimed, specifically authorized it. There were no plans for securing the conspirators' safety afterwards, merely Barclay's assurance that James would land very soon. Berwick did not veto the scheme, under its thin cover of a kidnapping, but retired to France to avoid involvement.

Saturday 15 February was the day intended. Barclay gathered the guardsmen 'and declared, that these were his janissaries, and that he hoped they would bring him the garter' (*State trials*, 12.1326). However, the plot had been betrayed by two conspirators whom Barclay never met and one double agent whom he had kept from full knowledge, and William stayed at home. As no alarm was given, a further attempt was planned for 22 February, when the participants reassembled. This time, when William's preparations to hunt were cancelled, rumours of a plot spread, and the would-be assassins dispersed for good. A proclamation offered £1000 for Barclay's capture. The exposure of the plot and of James's apparent responsibility temporarily crushed Jacobitism, and strengthened William's government politically when economic factors were bringing it near total collapse. The executed plotters included Ambrose Rookwood, an officer in James's guards, and several others were imprisoned without trial for life by parliament's authority: obeying a military superior's orders was not accepted as justification.

Both the government ministers and his fellow Jacobites, misled by his false trails, assumed that Barclay had instantly fled back to France when the plot was exposed. In fact he remained in hiding in London, and by late March had organized regular payments to his imprisoned subordinates, which were exposed in late May. According to his son Alexander, he remained in England until September. There were later false sightings and alarms. It was only in July 1697 that he was authorized to revisit St Germain. On 4 August 1697 NS he completed at Paris a short account of his mission. The delay in his return apparently cooled any anger over his actions.

When Hans Willem Bentinck, first earl of Portland, entered Paris as ambassador in February 1698, he protested at finding Barclay and other would-be assassins appearing freely there and at St Germain. Louis XIV replied that Barclay had recently been paid off when his company was disbanded, and he did not know his whereabouts. Presumably to avoid further complaints and suspicions, he was afterwards sent to reside, receiving a French pension, at Bourges in Berry. On 22 April 1710 NS he wrote from Issoudun in Berry complaining that he had not received that year's pension, which he needed to supply his wife, who was then in England. Nothing further is known about her; nor about a former wife, except that she had bequeathed him the interest on £2000 sterling. He died at Issoudun shortly before 18 November 1710 NS, and the French government seized his papers. That perhaps provoked the ludicrous rumour that he had been 'the Man in the Iron Mask'. He left the Scots College, Paris, a bequest of 500 livres and an annuity of 300 livres, and asked for his heart to be buried there, but it is unclear whether the bequest was ever paid. Barclay's illegitimate son Alexander Barclay was interrogated in London in 1705 aged twenty-seven. Born in Britain, he studied at the Scots College before accompanying his father on his mission of 1695–6. He afterwards trained as a chemist and surgeon.

PAUL HOPKINS

Sources *State trials*, vols. 12–13 • *The life of James the Second, king of England*, ed. J. S. Clarke, 2 vols. (1816) • P. A. Hopkins, *Glencoe and the end of the highland war*, rev. edn (1998) • *CSP dom., 1696* • U. Nott. L., Portland MSS • D. Nairne, journal, NL Scot., MS 14266 • J. Macpherson, ed., *Original papers, containing the secret history of Great Britain*, 2 vols. (1775) • J. Garrett, *The triumphs of providence: the assassination plot, 1696* (1980) • Barclay's papers, Archives du Ministère des Affaires Étrangères, Paris, correspondence politique, Angleterre, 230, fols. 373–90 • Barclay's commission, 29 Sept 1693, Bodl. Oxf., MS Carte 256, fol. 22 • Barclay to Middleton, 22 April 1710, Bodl. Oxf., MS Carte 210, fol. 358 • E. Cruickshanks and E. Corp, eds., *The Stuart court in exile and the Jacobites* (1995) • C. Dalton, ed., *English army lists and commission registers, 1661–1714*, 6 vols. (1892–1904) • C. Dalton, ed., *The Scots army, 1661–1688* (1909) • Barclay to Middleton, 14 Oct 1688, BL, Add. MS 41805, fol. 57 • M. Smith, *Memoirs of secret service* (1699) • L. Barclay, *History of the Scottish Barclays*, rev. C. L. Barkley, rev. edn (Lovettsville, VA, 1995) • examination of Alexander Barclay, 14 Sept 1705, BL, Add. MS 70340 • *State papers and letters addressed to William Carstares*, ed. J. M'Cormick (1774) • *Inventaire sommaire des archives du department des affaires étrangères: correspondance politique*, 1 (Paris, 1903), 224 • *Report of the Deputy Keeper of the Public Records*, 39 (1878), appx, 808–9 • *Calendar of the manuscripts of the marquess of Ormonde*, new ser., 8 vols., HMC, 36 (1902–20), vol. 8 • J. Fitzjames [Duke of Berwick], *Memoirs of the marshal duke of Berwick*, 2 vols. (1779) • *Observations upon the papers which Mr Rookwood and Mr Lowick deliver'd to the sheriffs* (1696) • J. Noone, *The man behind the iron mask* (1988)

Archives Archives du Ministère des Affaires Étrangères, Paris, correspondance politique, Angleterre

Wealth at death probably very little; depended largely on French pension; 1704 will left Scots College, Paris, 500 livres and 300 livres annuity, unknown if paid: Cruickshanks and Corp, eds., *The Stuart court in exile*, 22; Bodl. Oxf., MS Carte 210, fol. 358

Barclay, Hugh (1799–1884), judge, was born on 18 January 1799 in the Gorbals, Glasgow, son of John Barclay, merchant, and Jean McKinlay. After serving his apprenticeship as a law agent he was admitted a member of the Faculty of Advocates in 1821. In 1829 he was appointed sheriff-substitute of Dunblane and in 1833 sheriff-substitute of Perthshire. He wrote *A digest of the law of Scotland, with special reference to the office and duties of the justice of the peace* (2 vols.; 2nd edn, 1852–3), a work which passed into several editions and proved very useful to legal practitioners. Besides editions of various other legal works, he also published on a range of miscellaneous legal matters, from the law of highways to the Scots law against profaning the sabbath. He was a frequent contributor to the *Journal of Jurisprudence* and other legal periodicals, and various of his papers, including 'Curiosities of the game laws' and 'Curiosities of legislation', were also published by him in a collected form.

Barclay was married to Margaret Buchanan, and they had at least one son and one daughter. For many years he was a prominent member of the general assembly of the

Church of Scotland, and, taking an active interest in ecclesiastical and philanthropic matters, he published *Thoughts on Sabbath Schools* (1855) and a few other small works of a similar kind. Barclay died at his residence at Early Bank, Craigie, near Perth, on 1 February 1884, having for several years been the oldest judge in Scotland. He was survived by his wife. T. F. HENDERSON, *rev.* ERIC METCALFE

Sources Irving, *Scots*. • *The Scotsman* (2 Feb 1884) • parish register (births and baptisms), Gorbals, Glasgow, 19 Jan 1799 • *CCI* (1884)

Wealth at death £4442 12*s*. 0*d*.: confirmation, 25 April 1884, *CCI*

Barclay, James (*fl.* **1763–1774**), Church of England clergyman and lexicographer, was for many years a curate at All Saints' Church, Edmonton, Middlesex, and a teacher at schools in Goodman's Fields and Tottenham. In 1763 he published *What is Meant by Coming to Christ*, the text of a sermon he had delivered in one of the London churches. His fame, however, rests on his *Complete and Universal English Dictionary*, first published in 1774; it was to pass through at least twenty-four reprints and editions by 1851. (The editions of 1813, 1841, and 1848 were revised by William Shorton, Henry W. Dewhurst, and Bernard Bolingbroke Woodward, respectively.)

Despite its title the work took account of only a selection of English vocabulary, including 'Difficult Words and Technical Terms in all Faculties and Professions'. The stress-point in words was marked, and words were noted which were apparently synonyms: Barclay was the first English lexicographer to attempt the latter. In addition, the reader was provided with information more usually to be found in an encyclopaedia than in a dictionary. Thus, there were articles on politics and society, both past and present (for example, a listing of important historical events, descriptions of major towns and cities in the world, and details of Britain's trading relationships with the rest of the world), and on religion (the denominations of the church) and literature (a listing of Greek, Roman, and English classics). Illustrations accompanied some of the entries. Barclay's interest in linguistic matters *per se* is evidenced by the inclusion of an article on the origin of language by the Frenchman Abbé Antoine Anselme (1652–1737), and by a series of articles on the history, grammar, pronunciation, and orthography of English, very probably by Barclay himself. The dictionary won immediate acceptance from the public, especially the lower classes, for whom it acted, until well into the Victorian age, as an important means of self-education.

Barclay's son James, who died on 13 June 1771 at the age of twenty-four, was the youthful author of *An Examination of Mr Kenrick's Review of Mr Johnson's Edition of Shakespeare* (1766). M. K. C. MACMAHON

Sources W. Robinson, *The history and antiquities of the parish of Edmonton, in the county of Middlesex* (1819) • R. C. Alston, *A bibliography of the English language from the invention of printing to the year 1800*, 5 (1966) • *Sermons by Robert Barclay … with a brief memoir* (1878) • S. Delvin, *A history of Winchmore Hill* (1987) • R. Barclay, *A genealogical account of the Barclays of Urie*, ed. H. Mill (1812) • Watt, *Bibl. Brit.* • ordinations and licensing in diocese of London, 1550–1842, GL, MSS 9535A, 9548, and 9549

Barclay, John (**1582–1621**), writer, was born on 28 January 1582 at Pont-à-Mousson, Lorraine, the son of William *Barclay (1546–1608) and his wife, Anne de Malleviller. His father was Scottish, and professor of civil law in the college recently founded in Pont-à-Mousson by the duke of Lorraine; his mother was native to Lorraine. Despite his place of birth and upbringing, and even though there is no record of his ever visiting Scotland, Barclay seems to have been proud of his Scottish ancestry and to have valued his allegiance to James VI and I. However, during Barclay's residence in England, state records consistently refer to him as French, and make little or no reference to his Scottish parentage.

Barclay was educated at the Jesuit school in Pont-à-Mousson until about 1602; he may also have tried the noviciate, but either because he was unsuited or because of his father's quarrel with the order and resignation from his post, in the end Barclay did not join. Instead, he developed an antipathy to Jesuit modes of education and recruitment, which he satirizes in his *Satyricon* (1605). At the age of nineteen Barclay had published his first work, *In P. Statii Papini Thebaidii libros III commentarii et in totidem sequentes notae* (Pont-à-Mousson, 1601) a commentary on Statius's *Thebaid*. It was the beginning of a distinguished literary career, which would bring him fame all over western Europe.

Barclay's movements between 1602 and 1606 are uncertain, although he may have attended his father in Paris. During this period, probably in 1605, he married Louise Debonnaire (*c*.1585–1652), the daughter of an army paymaster, with whom he had two daughters and a son. During the same time he published the first part of *Euphormionis lusinini satyricon* (Paris, 1605; reports of an earlier edition in London in 1603 seem to be unfounded), a Menippean satire modelled on Petronius's *Satyricon*. Barclay's choice of model was a first in Renaissance Latin writing and his version was as irreverent as the original. Barclay's *Satyricon* is the story of Euphormio, a citizen of an ideal realm who arrives in seventeenth-century Europe, and his adventures therein. Almost as soon as it was published, keys appeared to interpret the characters and locations depicted in it. Barclay did not produce any keys himself, only an apology for some of the associations (*Apologia pro se*, sometimes identified as the third part of the *Satyricon*, first published in Paris in 1610), and the interpretations of his satire are diverse. Of the references agreed by most authorities, two stand out: James VI as Neptune, a benevolent and powerful figure, and Acignius as the Jesuits. Although Euphormio is generally held to be a figure of Barclay, the extravagance of the character's adventures argue against a directly autobiographical reading. The second part of the *Satyricon*, containing further adventures of Euphormio, appeared in Paris in 1607. The work was very popular, the first part running to six and the second to five editions within Barclay's lifetime. Its popularity continued into the vernacular, and by the eighteenth century the *Satyricon* had been translated into French, German, and Dutch. Its attraction is a combination of speculation as to the correct interpretation of the figures within the narrative and delight in the comic misadventures of Euphormio. The work was Barclay's first great literary success, and its dedication to James VI and I doubtless helped his progress at the British court.

By 1606 the family was in England, where Barclay sought favour at the Jacobean court. He had already written *Regi Jacobo Primo, carmen gratulatorium* (Paris, 1603) to congratulate James on his accession to the English throne, and he continued his practice of literary flattery in a number of other works, such as *Sylvae* (1606), a collection of poems addressed to James and to some of his courtiers. Much of Barclay's quest for royal favour seems to have been channelled through Robert Cecil, earl of Salisbury, for there are records of Barclay sending laudatory verses to Salisbury in 1606 and of William Barclay writing to him on his son's behalf in 1607. Such approaches were evidently successful, for several times Barclay appears to have been paid a pension by Salisbury, who was later reimbursed by the king.

While at court Barclay took on a variety of literary tasks. He maintained his satirical edge in *Icon animorum* (1614), which sometimes appears as the fourth part of the *Satyricon*, but which in fact is a collection of sketches of the characters of nations. He also diversified by writing a directly political work, the *Series patefacti divinitus parricidii inter maximum regum regnumque Britanniae cogitati et instructi* (1605), a commentary on the Gunpowder Plot, and then undertook the editing and publishing of a work by his father, *De potestate papae* (1609), which argues for the pope's disqualification from secular power. Both of these were designed to appeal to James, and Barclay became involved in one of the king's own literary projects. On 27 April 1609 Barclay was rewarded for his translation work on the 'king's book' (*CSP dom., 1603–10*, 506); this book was presumably *Apologie for the Oath of Allegiance*, published first in 1607–8 and then in a revised version in 1609. A month later Barclay, together with the Scottish poet Robert Aytoun, received £300 for 'expenses on their journey with His Majestie's letters to divers foreign princes' (ibid., 514, 591). Among these letters seems to have been included a copy of the 'king's book', which Barclay carried to the magnates of Lorraine, Bavaria, and Savoy. On his return from this mission, Barclay continued to enjoy royal favour: not only did James award him a new pension of £200 in 1610, but later the same year he also intervened to ask the French king to suppress an attack made by Bellarmine on *De potestate papae*.

Despite these signs of royal favour Barclay left England for the papal court in 1615. In the preface to *Paranesis ad sectarios* (Rome, 1617), a piece of Catholic apologetics, he says he left England to allow his children to remain Catholic, and the English court may have become less welcoming to Roman Catholics during the 1610s. It is also possible that his place there was not financially secure, since a letter survives to Salisbury from Barclay in 1611, then in Paris, asking that his pension still be paid. His final departure from James's court was not without its scandal, for it was believed—wrongly—that he had written a book against James, such that could only have been composed by an intimate. The preface to *Paranesis* may have been written in part to defend himself, but it was not until 1618 that the true author of the book in question was revealed as a lecturer at the University of Louvain.

In Rome Barclay undertook his greatest work, the *Argenis*. It was published posthumously in Paris in 1621 and dedicated to Louis XIII of France, suggesting that even then Barclay was seeking a new sponsor. It is a romance written in Latin centred on Argenis, an ideal princess, with three suitors, one good, one bad, and one who is finally recognized as her long-lost brother. It is also an allegory of seventeenth-century Europe, and keys for its characters also survive, for example identifying Archombrotus and Poliarchus as figures of Henry IV, Hyanisbe of Elizabeth I, and Radirobanes of Philip II. In contrast to the *Satyricon*, however, there is no character that can be identified as a type of Barclay himself. Like the *Satyricon*, the *Argenis* was instantly popular: in London in May 1622, because of demand, the cost of a volume rose from 5*s*. to 14*s*. and James commanded Ben Jonson to translate it, although if a translation ever existed, it seems not to have been published. Other translations appeared, in many European vernaculars, and two sequels, by other hands, were also published.

Barclay died in Rome on 15 August 1621, a fortnight after he had fallen ill with a fever and only eighteen days after he had finished the *Argenis*. He was buried in the church of St Onofrio in Rome. His widow returned to France and died at Orléans in 1652. Although Barclay can be claimed as French and also as Scottish, his contribution to literature is very much international. Through his associations with the court of James VI, his place in British cultural history is assured, but his works, particularly the *Satyricon* and *Argenis*, were read all over Europe. Such works demonstrate clearly the accessibility and importance of Latin as a language of literature and culture in the seventeenth century; they also show that the response to classical literature continued to develop throughout the Renaissance.

NICOLA ROYAN

Sources *DNB* • D. A. Fleming, introduction, in J. Barclay, *Euphormionis lusinini satyricon*, trans. D. A. Fleming (Nieukoop, 1973), ix–xxxvi • *CSP dom., 1603–18* • *Calendar of the manuscripts of the most hon. the marquis of Salisbury*, 24 vols., HMC, 9 (1883–1976), vols. 18–22 • *CSP Venice, 1607–10* • J. Ijsewijn, *History and diffusion of neo-Latin literature, pt 1 of companion to neo-Latin studies* (Leuven, 1990), 32–40, 131–5, 168–9 • *Johannis Barclai Euphormionis lusinini satyricon*, ed. I. Des Jardins (Avignon, 1969) • P. Turner, introduction, in J. Barclay, *Euphormionis satyricon*, trans. P. Turner (1954) • A. Becker, *Johann Barclay, 1582–1621* (Berlin, 1903)

Archives Hatfield House, Hertfordshire, letters, Salisbury MSS • PRO, state papers

Likenesses F. Duquesnoy, marble bust, 1627–8, Convento di Sant' Onofrio, Rome; version, Museo Tassiano, Rome • C. Mellan, line engraving (after D. du Monstier), BM, NPG; repro. in J. Barclay, *L'Argenis* (Paris, 1623) • oils, University of Amsterdam

Barclay, John (1733–1798), Church of Scotland minister and founder of the Berean church, was born in Muthill, Perthshire, in March 1733, the son of Ludovick Barclay, a farmer and miller, and his wife, Martha MacInnes. He proceeded from the village school to the University of St Andrews, where he graduated MA in 1755. Thereafter he studied divinity at St Mary's College, St Andrews, and was strongly influenced by the teaching of Archibald Campbell, who taught that no knowledge of God was possible from creation through fallen reason. In his writings and preaching Barclay developed this precept into a firm affirmation that all knowledge of God comes directly from the scriptures.

After serving as a private tutor in the parish of Crieff, Barclay was licensed to preach by the presbytery of Auchterarder on 27 September 1759 and became assistant to the Revd James Jobson of Errol, a Marrow sympathizer. Despite deep disagreements between the two, Barclay remained in Errol until 1763, when he became assistant to the Revd Antony Dow at Fettercairn, where he lived until Dow's death in August 1772. In Fettercairn, Barclay gained a reputation as a preacher, and crowds, including many from neighbouring parishes, filled the church. Despite his youthful appearance 'his fervid manner, in prayer especially, impressed the minds of his audience … He had a most luxuriant fancy and a great taste for poetry' (Cameron, 201). While at Fettercairn he published *A Paraphrase of the Book of Psalms* (1766) and *Rejoice Forever* (1767), which contains 196 hymns based on scripture passages. Barclay set his hymns to popular tunes and wrote a large amount of verse. In both works he maintained that the psalms should be interpreted in such a way that Christ is the speaker in all first person passages. This view was questioned by the presbytery of Fordoun. In 1769 he addressed a letter to James Smith and Robert Ferrier, founders of the Old Scots Independents, on *The Eternal Generation of the Son of God*, in which he supported the orthodox doctrine, and in the same year he wrote *Without Faith, without God*, in which he attacked the whole system of Scottish education because it was founded on the premise of natural revelation: 'pretended reason murders faith' (Barclay, 126). With the publication of *The Assurance of Faith Vindicated* in 1771, Barclay's peculiar views were now in print: there is no natural revelation; God reveals himself in sovereign acts throughout scripture; the psalms must always be interpreted as referring to Christ; assurance is of the essence of faith, which is an intellectual act; the sin against the Holy Ghost is unbelief.

For the parishioners of Fettercairn Barclay was the natural successor to Dow in 1772. However, the presbytery, the synod, and finally the general assembly of May 1773 upheld the claim of a rival candidate, Robert Foote. Barclay had as his advocate at the general assembly James Boswell. He was also refused a certificate of character by the presbytery, and he separated himself from the Church of Scotland. A group of supporters in Edinburgh invited him to become their pastor, and he received ordination by a classis of the Presbyterian church at Newcastle upon Tyne. Meanwhile in Fettercairn the great majority of the parish seceded and built a meeting-house at Sauchieburn in the parish of Marykirk, where for several years James McRae, inducted by Barclay, had over one thousand hearers. This congregation, which sought fellowship with Congregational churches in Dundee and Newburgh (Fife), survived until 1854.

The name Berean (from Acts 17: 11) was probably chosen by Barclay himself for his followers, who were also known as Barclayans and Barclayites. Churches were founded in Glasgow, Edinburgh, Crieff, Montrose, Kirkcaldy, and other centres of independent church activity in Scotland. Between 1776 and 1778 Barclay was in London, where several churches, along with a debating society, were established; there was also a church for a time in Bristol. Barclay was a good classical scholar, well read in the theology of his day, 'a metaphysician rather than a prophet, an acute reasoner rather than an inspirational visionary' (Miller, 2.521). He made quite exclusive claims for his church, which by 1850 was a tiny remnant, rousing itself in Glasgow to a last effort by republishing an eight-volume collection of Barclay's *Works* in 1852.

The Berean churches were notable as small, exclusive, and close-knit fellowships. Apart from Barclay himself they did not attract many educated men, and pastors were chosen from the congregation, but appointed by Barclay or his successor. Worship was similar to that of the Glasites and Scotch Baptists, communion being celebrated monthly. Most Bereans maintained paedobaptism, but in Glasgow and Dundee Baptist Bereans are recorded. Despite their general adherence to Calvinist orthodoxy, their strong doctrine of assurance led to their being suspected of antinomianism, and 'Berean' became a term of abuse in the controversy surrounding John Macleod Campbell and Edward Irving in the 1830s. David Thom of the Scottish kirk in Liverpool became in the 1820s a strong advocate of Barclay's views. He was deposed from the ministry, began an independent cause and reached a somewhat 'advanced' theological position.

Barclay was married twice, without children, although further details are unknown. He received a 'small property' through his first wife, but struggled with poverty most of his life. He died on 29 July 1798 in the house of a friend and in the presence of his nephew John Barclay, a well-known Edinburgh physician. He was buried in the old Calton cemetery, Edinburgh. DEREK B. MURRAY

Sources *DNB* • N. R. Needham, 'Barclay, John', *DSCHT* • A. Miller, 'Barclay, John', *Encyclopedia of religion and ethics*, ed. J. Hastings, 13 vols. (1908–26), 2.521 • J. Barclay, *Essays on various subjects* (1776) • *Fasti Scot.*, new edn, 5.462 • A. C. Cameron, *The history of Fettercairn* (1899) • J. Brown, *Religious denominations of Glasgow* (1860) • H. Escott, *A history of Scottish Congregationalism* (1960) • J. Campbell, 'The Berean church, especially in Edinburgh', *Records of the Scottish Church History Society*, 6 (1936–8), 138–46

Barclay, John (1741–1823), marine officer, entered the corps in March 1755 as second lieutenant, and became first lieutenant in July 1756. He served throughout the Seven Years' War (1756–63), in the Mediterranean, at Belle Île (off the Britanny coast) in 1761, and on the coast of Africa; he was promoted captain in October 1762. He served with distinction through the American War of

Independence, particularly in 1777 in Lord Howe's operation on the Delaware River at the Red Bank, and in the mud forts; he was in command of the marines on board the *Augusta* (sixty-four guns), when she bombarded the forts, and was abandoned after catching fire (on 23 October 1777). For these services he was promoted brevet major in August 1777. He served at the first relief of Gibraltar. He was one of the commanding officers of marines in Rodney's victory at the battle of the Saints (off Dominica, 12 April 1782), and afterwards was promoted lieutenant-colonel by brevet in February 1783.

Barclay had no further active service at sea, but was for the next thirty years chiefly employed on the staff of the marines in England. He became major in the marines in December 1791, and lieutenant-colonel in the marines, and brevet colonel in 1794 (marine officers then held concurrent marine and army ranks). In May 1796 he became major-general, and in February 1798 second colonel commandant in the corps. As such he was much involved with the marines' organization, and made changes in their drill and uniform including, in 1805 when he was commandant of the Chatham division, the introduction of blue working jackets for the Royal Marine Artillery. In 1803 he became lieutenant-general (September) and colonel commandant of the marines (December), and in September 1806 he became resident colonel commandant. He was then practically commander-in-chief of the corps, and its good character indicated the quality of its organization. In the 1797 Spithead and Nore mutinies and in other mutinous manifestations, the marines proved reliable against mutiny among the sailors. In June 1813 Barclay became general (though still colonel in the marines), and in April 1814 he retired on full pay, after fifty-nine years' continuous employment. He was married and had children. He went to live at Taunton, Somerset, where he died on 12 November 1823.

Barclay's son Fletcher Barclay entered the 56th (West Essex) regiment as ensign in 1791, served in the West Indies, the Low Countries, and India, was promoted lieutenant-colonel in 1811, commanded his regiment, was promoted colonel in the army in 1825, and retired in 1831. H. M. Stephens, *rev.* Roger T. Stearn

Sources *GM*, 1st ser., 94/1 (1824), 83 • J. Philippart, ed., *The royal military calendar*, 3 vols. (1815–16) • C. Field, *Britain's sea soldiers: a history of the royal marines and their predecessors*, 2 vols. (1924), vol. 1 • *Army List* (1809) • *Army List* (1821) • *Army List* (1824) • *Army List* (1830) • *A list of the officers of his majesty's royal marine forces* (1816) • W. L. Clowes, *The Royal Navy: a history from the earliest times to the present*, 3 (1898); repr. (1996) • *Historical record of the fifty-sixth, or the west Essex regiment of foot* (1844) • J. Black, *Britain as a military power, 1688–1815* (1999) • S. Conway, *The War of American Independence, 1775–1783* (1995)

Barclay, John (1758–1826), anatomist, was born at Muthill, Perthshire, on 1 December 1758, the son of Lodowick Barclay, a farmer, and Margaret McIlwhannel. John Barclay (1733–1798), founder of the Berean confession in Edinburgh, was his uncle. In 1776 Barclay obtained a bursary in St Andrews University with the intention of entering the church. He was licensed as a minister and then became a tutor in Mr C. Campbell's household in 1781. While a tutor

John Barclay (1758–1826), by John Syme, 1816

he developed an interest in natural history and human anatomy. In 1789 he became the tutor of Sir James Campbell's two sons and accompanied them to Edinburgh University. In 1792 Barclay attended lectures on anatomy and, after a period of hesitation, decided to pursue his interests in anatomy and physiology by studying medicine. While a student he acted as the assistant to John Bell (1763–1820), a private anatomical lecturer. With the sponsorship of Sir James, Barclay graduated MD from Edinburgh University with the thesis '*De anima, seu principio vitali*' in 1796; he spent the following winter studying anatomy and surgery in London with Andrew Marshall of Holborn. He returned to Edinburgh in 1797 and began giving his own course of lectures on anatomy. He remained in Sir James's household until 1811, when he married Campbell's daughter Eleanora on 25 October that year.

When Barclay began lecturing, the Napoleonic Wars had created a demand both for surgeons and for anatomy courses to instruct them. The Royal College of Surgeons of Edinburgh had instituted a new degree for surgeons, and in 1804 Barclay's course was recognized as fulfilling its anatomy and surgery requirements. Barclay's lecture hall was well placed to attract students, next door to the Royal Medical Society (the chief student society) and across the street from Surgeons' Hall. Until 1825 he gave two sets of lectures a day, at 11 a.m. and 6 p.m. during the six-month winter session, and towards the end of his life he gave a summer course in comparative anatomy. He became a fellow of the Royal College of Physicians of Edinburgh in 1806. At one point the creation of a university chair in comparative anatomy was proposed, with Barclay as its first incumbent, but this was opposed by the medical faculty.

Several of Barclay's publications stemmed from his desire to fill lacunae in the literature available to his students: *Muscular Motions of the Human Body* (1808) and *A Description of the Arteries of the Human Body* (1812). He also provided references to *A series of engravings representing the bones of the human skeleton; with the skeletons of some of the lower animals* (1819), engraved by Edward Mitchell from the illustrations in M. Sue's edition of Alexander Monro's *Traité d'ostéologie* (Paris, 1759), on condition that the book be sold at a low price to students. Other publications, from his thesis through to his last work, *An Inquiry into the Opinions, Ancient and Modern, Concerning Life and Organization* (1822), reflect his firm belief in the existence of an organizing principle in living organisms which explained physiological functions. He also had a keen interest in the new science of chemistry, particularly its applications to physiology. Several of his books were dedicated to his friend Thomas Thomson, an Edinburgh private lecturer who became professor of chemistry at Glasgow University, and in *A new anatomical nomenclature relating to the terms which are expressive of position and aspect in the animal system* (1803) Barclay proposed a new nomenclature for anatomy inspired by that of A. Lavoisier in chemistry.

Barclay became ill in 1825, and his classes were taught by Robert Knox. He died on 21 August 1826.

LISA ROSNER

Sources G. Ballingall, 'Introductory lectures to a course of anatomy, delivered by the late John Barclay M.D., with a memoir of his life', *The Lancet* (16 Feb 1828), 726–9 • J. D. Comrie, *History of Scottish medicine*, 2nd edn, 2 (1932), 493–6 • S. C. Lawrence, *Charitable knowledge: hospital pupils and practitioners in eighteenth-century London* (1996) • *DNB* • parish register (birth), 1 Dec 1758, Muthill, Perthshire • parish register (marriage), 25 Oct 1811, Dunblane, Perthshire

Archives NL Scot., corresp. with George Combe

Likenesses J. Syme, oils, 1816, Scot. NPG [*see illus.*] • T. Hodgetts, mezzotint, 1820 (after J. Syme), Wellcome L. • J. Kay, caricature-etching, NPG • Lizars, line engraving (after J. Syme), Wellcome L.

Barclay, Joseph (1831–1881), bishop of Jerusalem, was born on 12 August 1831 near Strabane in co. Tyrone, Ireland, the son of John Barclay (*d.* 1845), gentleman, and his wife, Rebecca Brandon (*d.* 1874). His parents were of Scottish extraction, and he had two sisters. He was educated at a school in Strabane kept by a Presbyterian minister. Barclay went on to Trinity College, Dublin, and proceeded BA in 1854 and MA in 1857, but showed no particular powers of application or study. He was ordained deacon in the Church of Ireland in 1854 (and priest the following year), taking up a curacy at Bagnelstown, co. Carlow.

During this period Barclay began to take a great interest in the work of the London Society for the Promotion of Christianity among the Jews. The question of Jewish conversion was then agitating the religious world in England, and Barclay energetically supported the cause in his own neighbourhood, until in 1858 his enthusiasm led him to offer himself to the London Society as a missionary. He left Ireland, much regretted by his parishioners and friends, and after a few months' study in London was appointed to Constantinople. The mission there had been established in 1835, but no impression had been made on the 60,000 Jews calculated to inhabit the town. Barclay stayed in Constantinople until 1861, making missionary journeys to the Danubian provinces, Rhodes, and other nearer districts. He acquired a thorough knowledge of the Spanish dialect spoken by the Sephardic Jews, and diligently prosecuted his studies in Hebrew. In 1861 he was nominated incumbent of Christ Church, Jerusalem, a position requiring energy and tact to avoid getting entangled in local quarrels; these rivalries Barclay described as a 'fretting leprosy', neutralizing his best efforts.

In 1865 Barclay visited England and Ireland on private matters, received the degree of LLD from his university, and married on 21 December. His wife was Lucy Agnes (*d.* 1882), the third daughter of the Revd W. W. Andrew of Ketteringham, Norfolk. The couple had a large family. On his return he found it impossible, as a married man, to continue in his post unless his salary was increased, and the London Society's refusal compelled his resignation in 1870. He returned to England and filled for a time the curacies of Howe in Lincolnshire and St Margaret's, Westminster, until in 1873 he was presented to the living of Stapleford in the St Albans diocese. The comparative leisure thus afforded him enabled him to publish in 1878 a book containing his translations of extracts from the Talmud. He had worked on it for sixteen years and, according to his biographer, it faithfully reproduced 'the sententious interrogative and involved style of the Rabbis' (Courtenay, 403). Unfortunately, critical opinion was divided over its importance; and Jewish readers regarded it as marked by an animus against their nation and literature. In 1880 Barclay received the degree of DD from Dublin University.

In 1879 the see of Jerusalem became vacant, and Dr Barclay's experience and attainments marked him out as the only man likely to fill the post successfully. He was consecrated at St Paul's Cathedral in London on 25 July 1879. He was most enthusiastically welcomed to Jerusalem, and entered on his duties with his usual vigour, but his sudden death there, after a short illness, on 23 October 1881 put an end to the hopes of those who believed that at last some aims of the bishopric's founders were to be realized. Bishop Barclay's attainments were considerable. He preached in Spanish, French, and German; he was intimately acquainted with biblical and rabbinical Hebrew; he was diligently engaged at his death in perfecting his knowledge of Arabic; and he had acquired some knowledge of Turkish during his residence in Constantinople. The bishop's widow returned to England, but she died on 5 March 1882 when giving birth to their eighth child.

RONALD BAYNE, *rev.* ROBERT BROWN

Sources J. B. Courtenay, *Joseph Barclay: a missionary biography* (1883) • *CGPLA Eng. & Wales* (1882) • Boase, *Mod. Eng. biog.* • W. H. Hechler, *The Jerusalem bishopric* (1883) • T. D. Halsted, *Our missions:*

being a history of the principal missionary transactions of the London Society for Promoting Christianity amongst the Jews (1866) · m. cert.
Wealth at death £9567 15s. 11d.: probate, 21 July 1882, *CGPLA Eng. & Wales*

Barclay, Robert (1611/12–1682), Roman Catholic priest and college head, was born probably in Kincardineshire, the youngest of the four sons of David Barclay (1580–1660) of Mathers and Elizabeth Livingston, daughter of Sir John Livingston of Dunnipace. He graduated MA from Aberdeen University in 1633. After conversion to Roman Catholicism, Barclay studied at the Scots College, Paris, and the College of St Nicolas du Chardonnet. He was probably one of the group of students from the former who mustered at the Paris residence of John Clerk of Penicuik in 1638 to protest that Clerk had called them all beggars and poor men's sons. After ordination to the priesthood he taught in St Nicolas du Chardonnet for six years and became prefect of studies in the Scots College, Paris. In 1650 he was one of a group of Scottish priests involved in negotiations with the Congregatio de Propaganda Fide in Rome which led to the establishment of a prefecture apostolic in Scotland, and he was appointed agent in Paris for the secular clergy.

Barclay became principal of the Scots College, Paris, about 1655. He restored the discipline of the college, and provided it with a grand new building which was ready for use in 1665, and to which a chapel and north wing were added in 1672. In addition, he purchased several properties in Paris which yielded rents for the benefit of the college. Some critics said that he built for his own glory. The indications are that Barclay was a stern disciplinarian and that he was inclined to quarrel. He had many wrangles with the Jesuits in Paris, mainly on account of their attempts to wean his ecclesiastical students into their own order. By stringent measures, such as forbidding his students to visit the Jesuit college, he was often successful in dissuading students from taking such a course, but failed in the case of his own kinsman, John Strachan, who joined the Jesuits at Naples. The principal also failed to convert permanently to Catholicism his nephew and namesake who became the famous Quaker apologist. There were also tensions between Barclay and two priests who had been educated in Rome, William Leslie, the Scots agent in Rome, and Alexander Dunbar, prefect of the Scottish mission. Nevertheless Barclay was successful in producing fine priests, and his students included Thomas Placid Fleming, later abbot of Regensburg, Louis Innes, Thomas Innes, Richard Augustine Hay, and Robert Munro, the intrepid missionary martyr.

Barclay also helped to get Irish missionaries for the Scottish mission, and took part in the missionary conferences in Paris that were organized by the Vincentians. During Barclay's time the college in Paris became a pastoral training centre for Scottish priests who had been trained in Rome. Barclay also gave refuge to priests who were exiled from Scotland for religious reasons, including John Walker and William Ballantine, prefect apostolic of the Scottish mission, both of whom wrote religious works in their sojourn at the college. Robert Barclay died on 7 February 1682, and was buried in the college chapel.

Brian M. Halloran

Sources M. V. Hay, *The Blairs papers, 1603–1660* (1929) · C. W. Barclay and others, eds., *A history of the Barclay family*, 2, ed. H. F. Barclay (1933), 152, 191, 200 · B. M. Halloran, *The Scots College, Paris, 1603–1792* (1997) · R. Barclay, *A genealogical account of the Barclays of Urie*, ed. H. Mill (1812), 20, 49f. · B. M. Halloran, 'Spirited Scottish students: the Scots College Paris in 1639', *Innes Review*, 45 (1994), 171–7 · J. L. Carr, *Le Collège des Ecossais à Paris (1662–1962)* (1963), 12, 23 · Scottish Catholic Archives, Edinburgh, Blairs letters collection, letters · Scottish Catholic Archives, Edinburgh, colleges abroad collection, letters · Archivio Vaticano, Vatican City, archives of Propaganda Fide, Scozia, vol. 1, fol. 679*v* · P. J. Anderson, ed., *Roll of alumni in arts of the University and King's College of Aberdeen, 1596–1860* (1900), 10 · private information (2004)
Archives Archivio Vaticano, Vatican City, archives of Propaganda Fide, Scozia, SC vol. 1, fol. 670*v*, fol. 741*f* · Scottish Catholic Archives, Edinburgh, Blairs letters collection, letters · Scottish Catholic Archives, Edinburgh, colleges abroad collection, letters
Wealth at death unknown amount left to Scots College, Paris: Scottish Catholic Archives, Edinburgh BL, 1/74/8, L. Innes to W. Leslie, 18 Sept 1682

Barclay, Robert, of Ury (**1648–1690**), religious writer and colonial governor, was born at Gordonstown, Moray, on 23 December 1648, the eldest of the five children of **David Barclay of Ury** (1610–1686), soldier and politician, and Katherine Gordon (1620–1663), daughter of Sir Robert Gordon of Gordonstown. David Barclay was born in 1610 at Kirktownhill, Mearns, the son of David Barclay, the laird of Mathers (1580–1660), and Elizabeth Livingston. David Barclay of Mathers overspent at court and lost his estates to creditors, prompting his son David and grandson Robert to devote considerable energies to restoring the family fortunes. Following his education, possibly at local schools between about 1616 and 1626, David Barclay became a professional soldier; from 1626 he served in Germany, eventually rising to the rank of major under Gustavus Adolphus in the Thirty Years' War before returning to Scotland in 1638 on the eve of the civil wars. He served in covenanting armies for the next decade, becoming colonel of a horse regiment under General John (afterwards first earl of) Middleton. David Barclay and Katherine Gordon were married on 26 January 1648. She was third cousin to Charles I, and about the time of the wedding Barclay began to veer to the royalist side. Later in 1648 he purchased the ruinous estate of Ury (also Urie) near Stonehaven, 15 miles from Aberdeen, from William Keith, seventh Earl Marischal, but he would remain in Gordonstown until 1665. Barclay supported the Scottish engagement with the king, for which he was made to do penance when the kirk party returned to power, and seems not to have participated in resisting the English invasion of 1650. Marischal did resist, and after the conquest all properties associated with him were forfeited, including Ury. David Barclay ingratiated himself with the English, however, and was appointed trustee of lands forfeited by royalists. He used that position and his subsequent election to the Cromwellian parliaments of 1654 and 1656 to win back Ury for himself while protecting and promoting Marischal's interests.

Conversions David Barclay could see early on that his son Robert was 'very Ambitious of Knowledge' (Barclay, *Truth Triumphant*, 678). Robert later recalled that he was first schooled locally 'by the strictest Sort of Calvinists', but with the Cromwellian regime crumbling and the prospect of renewed civil war looming, in 1659 the ten-year-old was sent to Paris to be educated by his uncle and namesake, Robert Barclay, rector of the Scots Theological College (ibid.). Young Robert flourished in Paris, perfecting his French and Latin, honing his debating skills, and winning book prizes from his tutors. He also converted to Catholicism ('I became quickly defiled with the Pollutions thereof', he subsequently wrote), much to the horror of his mother (ibid.). As Katherine Gordon lay dying in March 1663 she begged her husband to bring Robert, not yet fifteen, back to Scotland and protestantism. The uncle offered to make Robert his heir if he would remain in Paris, but that summer he returned to Scotland with his father. Robert Barclay promptly renounced the Catholic church and would remain hostile to it (though not to individual Catholics) for the rest of his life. That early association, however, helped fuel conspiracy theories to the effect that Quakers in general, and Barclay in particular, were really papists in disguise.

In August 1665 David Barclay was committed to Edinburgh Castle at the behest of enemies resentful of his dealings during the interregnum. He shared a cell for a time with John Swinton, a fellow Scottish MP under Cromwell who had turned Quaker in 1657. David Barclay declared himself a Quaker in March 1666. Prison officials strove to keep Robert Barclay away from his father and Swinton, but their brief visits culminated in his own conversion to Quakerism early in the winter of 1666–7, about the time of his eighteenth birthday. His ability to articulate the Quaker experience was immediately apparent, and his first evangelizing trip took him to the north of Scotland with Swinton and George Keith in May 1667. Soon after, his father sent him to live at Ury, where he immediately established a weekly Quaker meeting. David Barclay was released from prison in 1669 and set about building a new manor house at Ury and (contrary to the terms of his release) an adjacent Quaker meeting-house.

In February 1670 Robert Barclay married Christian Molleson (*c.*1651–1724), daughter of Margaret Smith, one of Aberdeen's first Quaker converts, and Gilbert Molleson, a merchant and a magistrate on the town council that persecuted Quakers. The couple were married in her father's house (her mother having died the year before): it was the first Quaker wedding in Aberdeen and was attended by no minister, a throng of Quakers inside, and a mob of scandalized Aberdonians outside. The couple raised three sons and four daughters, and were considered exemplary parents. Their eldest son, also Robert Barclay (1672–1747), succeeded to Ury on the death of his father and married Elizabeth Brain, daughter of a London merchant, while the second son, David *Barclay (1682–1769), became a London merchant himself and grew rich in the American trade. All seven children were alive in 1740 for the fiftieth anniversary of their father's death.

Robert Barclay as author By the 1670s there were only a few hundred Quakers in Scotland, mainly in and around Aberdeen. Small numbers did not save them from persecution at the hands of the authorities; nor did it prevent Scottish Quakers, led by Robert Barclay, from having a disproportionately large impact on the 60,000-strong international Quaker movement. It was the need to combat persecution that drove Barclay to write the books that became the definitive statement of the Quaker faith for upwards of two centuries. Barclay was only thirty when the persecution of Scottish Quakers ended in 1679, but he published very little after that date.

In 1672 Barclay felt called by God to walk through the streets of Aberdeen in sackcloth as a call to repentance. By then, however, he had already started to publish Quaker tracts, and no further such spectacles were required of him. He was a charismatic speaker and a gifted controversialist in person and on paper, and his talents (and his gentry pedigree) quickly drew the attention of Quaker leaders in England. Indeed, Barclay soon emerged as a leader in the campaign to transform Quakerism from a loose, ecstatic movement into a tight, disciplined sect. The intensely personal, experiential nature of Quakerism militated against an official creed, but mainstream Quakers facing persecution needed a way to dissociate themselves from their more extreme members and from the wilder accusations of their enemies. To win toleration, the Quakers had to convince the authorities that they and their beliefs were tolerable. The Quaker counter-offensive was led on the literary front by Robert Barclay, his friend and mentor George Keith, and William Penn; and on the diplomatic front by Penn and Barclay.

Barclay and Keith, who was ten years older, worked closely together. Keith defected to the Church of England after Barclay died and claimed, correctly, that Barclay borrowed much from Keith's early work, including his cavalier way with patristic sources. Nevertheless, it was Barclay's work that was regarded as definitive by friend and foe alike, particularly his distinctive doctrine concerning inward and immediate revelation and the universal saving light. His most important works were all completed before he turned twenty-eight, beginning with the *Catechism and Confession of Faith* in 1673. This was followed by *Theses theologicae* in 1674, a fifteen-point statement of Quaker principles accompanied by Barclay's challenge to debate these with 'clergy, of what sort soever' (Barclay, *Truth Triumphant*, 259). This sparked lengthy correspondence with a number of continental clerics, and led in April 1675 to a rowdy public debate in Aberdeen between Barclay and Keith, on the one hand, and three overmatched postgraduate divinity students on the other. It was all grist for Barclay's mill while he was writing *An Apology for the True Christian Divinity*, an elaborate defence of the *Theses* completed in November 1675. The *Apology* was composed and first published in Latin in 1676. With a boldness that seems to have endeared him to the Stuart kings, Barclay opened the book with a plea for toleration addressed to

Charles II and written in direct and somewhat admonitory language much admired by Voltaire, among others. The *Apology* appeared in English in 1678, and has since been reprinted many times and in many languages. Robert Barclay's reputation among Quakers has waxed and waned, but the *Apology* remains the classic statement of Quaker principles, and few would dispute Leslie Stephen's judgement in the *Dictionary of National Biography* that the book is 'impressive in style; grave, logical, and often marked by the eloquence of lofty moral convictions'.

Barclay was not writing for posterity, however, but from an urgent need to win respect and tolerance for his people. In Restoration Scotland legislation directed against conventicling presbyterians also applied to Quaker men, who were arrested for attending their outlawed meetings and kept in prison when they refused to pay their fines or swear an oath to desist. Robert Barclay was imprisoned briefly in Montrose in 1672 but remained at liberty for the next four years. In addition to his writing, he continued to travel on Quaker business. He attended his first yearly meeting at London in 1673. In 1676 Barclay was again in London, just back from his first tour of Quaker outposts in the Netherlands and Germany, when he learned that his father and nearly every adult male Quaker in the north-east of Scotland had been imprisoned in the Aberdeen tolbooth. David Barclay, the old politician, advised his son to seek an audience with the duke of Lauderdale, but the duke proved unhelpful. In Germany Robert Barclay had met and befriended Elisabeth, princess palatine of the Rhine, and though she resisted the lure of Quakerism she asked her brother Prince Rupert to intercede with the king on behalf of the Aberdonian prisoners; however, Rupert did nothing. In Edinburgh, on his way back to Ury and certain imprisonment, Barclay made the Quaker case to the Scottish privy council, but again to no avail. He was imprisoned in Aberdeen from November 1676 to April 1677 with as many as forty other Quakers. When the overcrowding was at its worst, several élite prisoners, including the Barclays and George Keith, were moved to a disused chapel on the outskirts of town. The single tiny window made reading and writing difficult, but Robert Barclay and Keith kept up their voluminous writing and correspondence. Barclay's treatise *Universal Love* (1677) was composed in prison, as was a letter summarizing his most important ideas, published as 'The possibility and necessity of inward and immediate revelation' in *Truth Triumphant* (1692).

Colonial ambitions Robert Barclay, David Barclay, and George Keith were released in the spring of 1677, but most of the other Aberdeen Quakers remained in prison. David Barclay settled into vigorous old age at Ury, where he died of a fever about 10 October 1686 and was buried on 12 October. Robert Barclay attended the yearly meeting in London in 1677 and stayed on to lobby on behalf of his colleagues in Aberdeen. He had two hopeful meetings with the duke of York (afterwards James II) at which they discussed the Quaker prisoners and Penn's colonial plans. In July and August of 1677 Robert Barclay returned to the Netherlands and Germany on a celebrated missionary tour with Penn, Keith, and George Fox. Upon his return, he met with York again. Accepting the duke's sincerity but sensing his lassitude, Barclay urged him to speak firmly to Lauderdale on behalf of Quakers. York seemed to like Barclay despite his forwardness (according to Keith, Barclay—unlike Penn—would not bow, even for royals), but merely offered a letter granting him and his father immunity. Barclay considered attendance at court 'drugery', but his connection with the future king proved beneficial (*Reliquiae Barclaianae*, 68). The Aberdeen Quakers were finally set free in November 1679, coincident with the duke of York's arrival in Edinburgh, and Barclay grudgingly acknowledged that 'tho' not for several years, yet at last [the duke's] interposing proved very helpful' (ibid., 67–8).

Robert Barclay continued to preach and travel on behalf of Quakers, but no longer wrote for publication. He spent time with his family and saw to his financial affairs, which began to improve after Charles II restored Ury to the status of a free barony, complete with criminal and civil jurisdiction, in 1679. The final decade of his short life, however, was mainly spent promoting Quaker colonial enterprises and Scottish emigration. Fox and Penn counted on Barclay's ready access to the duke of York in Edinburgh to help steer Penn's colonial plans through the murky political waters of the early 1680s: as proprietor of New York, James had to be part of any agreement. Barclay attracted a circle of wealthy Scottish investors, but advised Penn that Pennsylvania land prices were too high: 'thou has land enough, so need not be a churl' (*Papers of William Penn*, 1.132). Barclay and the Scots preferred to invest in East and West New Jersey, and in 1682 the proprietors of East New Jersey, mainly Quakers and friends of the duke, appointed Barclay governor for life.

Robert Barclay accepted the governorship of East New Jersey on condition that he did not have to go there, but he was a tireless advocate for the colony. His brothers John and David emigrated, the latter dying on the way. Barclay worked hard to attract Scottish settlers, casting his promotional net as far as Belfast. He won the right to transport covenanters and religious prisoners, and probably wrote the unsigned broadsheets advertising the colony. His powers of personal persuasion were such that a young man visiting Aberdeen in 1684 was apparently so taken by Barclay's sales pitch that he immediately boarded and set sail for the New World, without telling his family. Upwards of 700 Scots, mainly from the north-east, moved to East New Jersey in the 1680s, but immigration slumped after 1690 with the fall of James II and the death of Barclay.

Laird of Ury since his father's death in 1686, Robert Barclay made his last trip to London in 1688 when he presented his eldest son, Robert, at court. His last visit to King James came just as William of Orange was expected in England. After James fled, Barclay retired to a quiet life at Ury. He died there of a fever on 3 October 1690, aged forty-one, and three days later was buried beside his father on the estate. As a final tribute from the Quaker leadership, his complete works were gathered and published in 1692 under the title *Truth Triumphant*. GORDON DESBRISAY

Sources R. Barclay, *A genealogical account of the Barclays of Urie … together with memoirs of the life of Colonel David Barclay of Urie, and his eldest son, the late Robert Barclay of Urie* (1740) • *Reliquiae Barclaianae: correspondence of Col. David Barclay and Robert Barclay of Urie and his son Robert* (1870) • R. Barclay, *Truth triumphant through the spiritual warfare: Christian labours and writings of … Robert Barclay* (1692) • R. Barclay, *An apology for the true Christian divinity, as the same is held forth and preached, by the people, called in scorn, Quakers* (1701) • D. E. Trueblood, *Robert Barclay* (1968) • 'A brieff account of the most material passages and occurrences that happened to friends of truth during that great and long tryall of sufferings and persecution at Aberdene', NA Scot., CH10/13/35 • W. F. Miller, 'Gleanings from the records of the yearly meeting of Aberdeen, 1672 to 1786', *Journal of the Friends' Historical Society*, 8 (1911), 40–46, 53–80, 113–22 • W. F. Miller, 'The record book of Friends of the monthly meeting at Urie', *Journal of the Friends' Historical Society*, 7 (1910), 91–8, 184–90 • M. C. Cadbury, *Robert Barclay: his life and work* (1912) • *Diary of Alexander Jaffray*, ed. J. Barclay, 3rd edn (1856) • G. DesBrisay, 'Quakers and the university: the Aberdeen debate of 1675', *History of Universities*, 13 (1994), 87–98 • G. DesBrisay, 'Catholics, Quakers, and religious persecution in Restoration Aberdeen', *Innes Review*, 47 (1996), 136–68 • A. P. F. Sell, 'Robert Barclay (1648–1690), the fathers and the inward, universal saving light: a tercentenary reappraisal', *Journal of the Friends' Historical Society*, 56 (1990–93), 210–26 • J. P. Wragge, *The faith of Robert Barclay* (1948) • G. P. Insh, *Scottish colonial schemes, 1620–1686* (1922) • N. C. Landsman, *Scotland and its first American colony* (1985) • *The papers of William Penn*, ed. M. M. Dunn, R. S. Dunn, and others, 1–3 (1981–6) • *The short journal and itinerary journals of George Fox*, ed. N. Penney (1925), 225–73 • W. C. Braithwaite, *The second period of Quakerism* (1919); 2nd edn, ed. H. J. Cadbury (1961) • *The Conway letters: the correspondence of Anne, Viscountess Conway, Henry More, and their friends, 1642–1684*, ed. M. H. Nicolson, rev. edn, ed. S. Hutton (1992) • P. J. Pinckney, 'The Scottish representation in the Cromwellian parliament of 1656', *SHR*, 46 (1967), 95–114 • E. M. Furgol, *A regimental history of the covenanting armies, 1639–1651* (1990) • E. W. Kirby, *George Keith (1638–1716)* (1942) • D. Barron, ed., *The court book of the barony of Urie in Kincardineshire, 1604–1747*, Scottish History Society (1892)

Archives RS Friends, Lond., MS account books and diary | NA Scot., Aberdeen Monthly Meeting and Quarterly Meeting minutes, CH10/3/1 • NA Scot., Aberdeen Monthly Meeting and Quarterly Meeting minutes, CH10/3/2

Barclay, Robert (1774–1811), army officer, entered the army as an ensign in the 38th regiment on 28 October 1789, and embarked with it for the East Indies, where he distinguished himself in most of the actions fought there in 1793. He was promoted lieutenant on 31 May 1793, and captain on 8 April 1795. Taken prisoner by the enemy, he suffered much in captivity, and in 1796 he returned to England. Though entitled to six months' leave, he hastened to rejoin his regiment, then in the West Indies.

Barclay's great qualities having become known to Lieutenant-General Sir John Moore, he was promoted major in the 52nd on 17 September 1803, and lieutenant-colonel on 29 May 1806. In 1808 he accompanied Moore on the expedition to Sweden, and afterwards to Portugal. He was mentioned in dispatches for his distinguished conduct at the action on the Coa on 24 June 1810. Afterwards he commanded a brigade and, while leading a charge on the French on the heights of Busaco, he received a gunshot wound below the left knee. Again he was mentioned in dispatches. His wound obliged him to leave the service, and he died from the effects of it on 11 May 1811.

A. S. BOLTON, *rev.* DAVID GATES

Sources W. S. Moorsom, ed., *Historical record of the fifty-second regiment (Oxfordshire light infantry), from the year 1755 to the year 1858* (1860), 122 • *The dispatches of … the duke of Wellington … from 1799 to 1818*, ed. J. Gurwood, new edn, 4: *Peninsula, 1790–1813* (1837), 184–306 • *Army List* (1791–1838)

Archives BL OIOC, home misc. series, corresp. relating to India • NL Scot., corresp. as military secretary

Barclay, Robert (1833–1876), Quaker and ecclesiastical historian, was born on 4 August 1833 at Croydon. He was the younger son of John Barclay (1797–1838), a descendant of the Quaker apologist Robert Barclay, and himself an expert on the early literature of the Society of Friends. After attending a preparatory school at Epping, he went to the Friends' school at Hitchin, run by Isaac Brown. His education was finished at Bruce Grove House, Tottenham. He attained a good knowledge of botany and chemistry, was fond of electrical experiments, and had skill as a watercolour artist. He married on 14 July 1857 Sarah Matilda, eldest daughter of Francis *Fry of Bristol, the bibliographer of the English Bible. They had nine children.

Trained for business at Bristol, Barclay bought, in 1855, a London manufacturing stationery concern (in Bucklersbury, afterwards in College Street and Maiden Lane), taking into partnership his brother-in-law, J. D. Fry, in 1867. In March 1860 he patented an 'indelible writing paper' for the prevention of forgery, the process of manufacturing which he described in a communication to the Society of Arts.

Both at home and abroad Barclay was interested in efforts for the evangelization of the masses; though not recorded as a minister of the Society of Friends, he preached in their meetings and missions. Thirty-six of his sermons, which were written, an uncommon thing with Friends, were published by his widow in 1878. In 1868 he delivered a lecture on the position of the Society of Friends in relation to the spread of the gospel during the previous sixty years, and was anxious to see the body regaining its position as an evangelical church. He was strongly in favour of the public reading of the Bible in Friends' meetings, and thought Richard Claridge's *Treatise of the Holy Scriptures* (1724) presented a more accurate view of the sentiments of the early Friends than their controversial writings. He was strongly opposed to the practice of birthright membership, introduced among Friends in 1737; his work *On Membership in the Society of Friends* (1873) was one of the most important contributions to the debate. His opinions on these points led to his undertaking the important series of investigations which culminated in *The Inner Life of the Religious Societies of the Commonwealth* (1876), in which he examined the internal constitution of the obscurer Commonwealth sects, the ramifications of which he traced with a diligence which caused his book to be highly regarded by contemporaries.

His presentation of the doctrinal aspects of primitive Quakerism was ably criticized from the standpoint of a quietist Friend in an *Examen* (1878) by Charles Evans of Philadelphia.

Barclay's health was undermined by his work, and before the last proof-sheets of his book had been finished the rupture of a blood-vessel in the brain caused his death on 11 November 1876 at his home, Hillside, Reigate, Surrey. He was buried in the Winchmore Hill burial-ground in Middlesex. In addition to editing his sermons, his widow published *The Self-Revealing Jehovah of the Old Testament the Christ of the New Testament* (1885).

ALEXANDER GORDON, *rev.* K. D. REYNOLDS

Sources *Sermons by Robert Barclay*, ed. S. M. Barclay (1878) · E. Isichei, *Victorian Quakers* (1970) · *Annual Monitor* (1877), 29 · Boase, *Mod. Eng. biog.* · *CGPLA Eng. & Wales* (1876)
Archives Wellcome L., corresp. with John Hodgkin
Likenesses oils, repro. in *Sermons*, ed. Barclay
Wealth at death under £40,000: probate, 24 Nov 1876, *CGPLA Eng. & Wales*

Barclay, Thomas (*c.*1570–1632), university teacher, was born in Aberdeen of unknown parents. He was sent to Bordeaux in the 1580s to study the Latin and Greek humanities and philosophy at the municipal Collège de Guyenne. This was one of the leading schools in France and had strong Scottish connections. George Buchanan had taught there earlier in the century, and one of Barclay's professors was the later principal, Robert Balfour. On leaving the college, Barclay probably studied law at the University of Bordeaux before gaining employment in the early 1590s as professor of rhetoric at the Toulouse Collège de l'Esquille, another municipal humanist powerhouse. He taught there for three or four years under the principal, Simon Tubeuf, then, in the middle of the decade, returned to the Collège de Guyenne as professor of philosophy. This time, though, he stayed no more than a year or two before being recalled to the Collège de l'Esquille in 1596 as principal on Tubeuf's death. Barclay presided there for twelve years and proved an effective administrator, persuading the municipality to double its annual subsidy and building up its boarding facilities by getting the councillors to outlaw private lodgings in the city with more than six pupils. He himself taught philosophy, and he had two other Scots on his teaching staff: his brother, Patrick, a Catholic priest, and Thomas Dempster. Barclay resigned as principal in 1608 and at some date in the next few years took up a chair of law at the University of Poitiers, where he lectured on Justinian's *Institutes*. In 1614–15 he represented the University of Poitiers at the royal court, but almost immediately gave up his professorship to move to a chair in the more prestigious law faculty at Toulouse. He held this position until his death at Toulouse in 1632, serving as the university's rector in 1621.

Barclay was married, possibly in 1600 when he paid a flying visit to Scotland, and had three children: Françoise (who became the wife of a financial official), Jean-Antoine, and Thomas (whose careers are unknown). He owned an expensive town house in Toulouse, purchased in November 1608, and a farm in the neighbouring countryside. Nothing is known about his abilities as a professor, but he must have been highly thought of by contemporaries to hold the posts he did. Toulouse was so keen to engage his services as a law professor that he was apparently appointed without having to demonstrate his learning alongside other candidates in a series of disputations, as was the custom. Barclay left no printed works, but a transcription of his course on the *Institutes*, given at Toulouse in 1619, survives (Bibliothèque Municipale, Toulouse, MS 429). He should not be confused with William Barclay (1546–1608), a contemporary Scottish law professor on the continent.

L. W. B. BROCKLISS

Sources T. Dempster, *Historia ecclesiastica gentis Scotorum* (Bologna, 1627), 124–5 · R. Corraze, 'L'Esquille, collège des capitouls', *Mémoires de l'Académie des Sciences, Inscriptions et Belles-Lettres de Toulouse*, 12th ser., 15 (1937), 155–228 · E. Gaullieur, *Histoire du Collège de Guyenne* (1874), 375–6 · P. Boissonnade, ed., *Histoire de l'université de Poitiers: passé et présent* (1932), 173–4 · G. Boyer and P. Thomas, eds., *L'université de Toulouse: son passé, son présent* (1929), 99–133
Archives Bibliothèque Municipale, Toulouse, Antoine de la Garrigue, 'Juris civilis institutiones, quas audivi in universitate Tholosana, sub doctissimo dd. du Barclay, juris professore, quae fuerunt 11 novembris die, anno 1619, inceptae', MS 429

Barclay, Thomas (1792–1873), university principal, was born at Unst, in Shetland, in June 1792, the youngest of the five sons of James Barclay (1745–1793), the minister of the parish, and his wife, Ursula, daughter of William Archibald, James Barclay's predecessor as minister. Educated at Lerwick Academy, Thomas headed the bursary competition in 1808 for a place at King's College in the University of Aberdeen, where he graduated MA in 1812. He remained in Aberdeen, completing his theological studies with a view to following his father into the church. He supported himself by teaching elocution, publishing in 1815 *The Academic Reciter, or, Select Classical Extracts in Prose and Poetry*. Barclay abandoned his chosen career in 1818 in favour of journalism with *The Times* in London. As a general and parliamentary reporter he covered many national events, including the Peterloo massacre, the Glasgow radical riots, and the trial of Queen Caroline. On 21 September 1820 he married Mary (*d.* 1881), daughter of Captain Charles Adamson of Kirkhill, with whom he had nine children.

Barclay was licensed by the presbytery of Lerwick in June 1821 and presented to the parish of Dunrossness in September 1822 by Lord Laurence Dundas. Five years later, again on Dundas's recommendation, he moved to the more prestigious charge of Lerwick, where he made a reputation as a preacher and a liberal. It was during his time here that Sir Henry Holland heard him preach and on the Monday went sailing with him. A storm got up, the helmsman panicked, and Barclay, taking over, steered the boat safely to shore. Holland was much impressed. Barclay was elected synod clerk of Zetland in 1831. He left Shetland in September 1843 for Peterculter, where he remained for just ten months before accepting the charge of Currie near Edinburgh. In 1849 the University of Aberdeen conferred upon him the degree of DD. These were difficult times for the Church of Scotland in the immediate aftermath of the Disruption. Barclay took a moderate

Thomas Barclay (1792–1873), by Thomas Annan, pubd 1871

liberal position, and became a close friend and supporter of Dr Robert Lee (1804–1868), minister of Greyfriars and, from 1847, professor of biblical criticism at Edinburgh University. He defended Lee's innovations in forms of worship and church architecture.

In 1858 Dr Duncan Macfarlane, principal of Glasgow University, died and Barclay was appointed his successor (13 February 1858), reputedly on the recommendation of Holland, who remembered their earlier encounter. This is unlikely and it is more probable that the professors, led by Alexander Hill, lobbied the chancellor, the fourth duke of Montrose, and the rector, Lord Lytton, for the appointment of a moderate, tolerant churchman. His scholarly interests included biblical learning and philology, more particularly in the languages of northern Europe. As principal his remarkable physical resemblance to John Knox immediately made him a popular figure with the students. His arrival in Glasgow coincided with profound changes in the organization of the university following the Universities of Scotland Act (1858), which transformed the powers of senates and established university courts and general councils representing graduates. The legislation caused a considerable storm in Glasgow, where the twelve professors of the old foundation were shorn of most of their privileges, particularly the patronage of the non-regius chairs, which passed to the court. The moderate reforms embodied in the act were to be implemented by commissioners, with whom Barclay was in constant contact—often travelling to London for the purpose.

The university occupied a cramped site in the old city centre surrounded by slums and industry. Most of Barclay's principalship was dominated by securing funds to obtain a fresh location in the west end of Glasgow and the construction of new buildings. These, built to the designs of George Gilbert Scott, were the largest public buildings undertaken in Victorian Britain after Barry's Palace of Westminster and cost more than £266,000, of which more than half was raised by donations. On 19 July 1870, when the structure was as complete as money would allow, Barclay led a symbolic procession of his colleagues through the city to view their new home. By this time his health had succumbed to the Glasgow smog and he was forced to spend time in Egypt during the winter to relieve chronic asthma. Barclay died at his official residence, The College, Gilmore Hill, Glasgow, on 23 February 1873 and was buried at Sighthill cemetery, Glasgow. His wife, two married daughters, and a son survived him. One biographer noted: 'With an energy derived from his old Norse descent, he combined love of liberty, which determined his attitude to the changes of his time, and he was ever found on the side of freedom in both Church and State'.

ARTHUR H. GRANT, *rev.* MICHAEL S. MOSS

Sources *Fasti Scot.* • *Edinburgh Courant* (24 Feb 1873) • *Glasgow Herald* (24 Feb 1873) • *Glasgow Herald* (1 March 1873) • *The Scotsman* (25 Feb 1873) • J. Caird, *In memoriam: a sermon preached before the University of Glasgow on the occasion of the death of the Very Rev. Thomas Barclay* (1873) • H. Holland, *Recollections of past life* (1872) • J. Coutts, *A history of the University of Glasgow* (1909) • *A historical sketch of the Glasgow Society of the sons of ministers of the Church of Scotland*, 5th edn (1910)

Archives U. Aberdeen • U. Glas.

Likenesses T. Annan, photograph, pubd 1871, NPG [*see illus.*] • portrait, repro. in T. Cannan, *Memoirs and portraits of the Old College* (1970)

Wealth at death £753 10*s.* 2*d.*: confirmation, 11 April 1873, NA Scot., SC 36/48/71/75–78

Barclay, Victor Robert [Bob] (**1911–1987**), musician and bandleader, was born at 45 Wellington Street, Greenock, Renfrewshire, on 10 July 1911, the elder son and eldest of three children of William Bartholomew Barclay, labourer and coalminer, and his wife, Janet Adamson, *née* Chrystal, factory worker. His father was of Caribbean, probably Jamaican, descent; his mother was Scottish. He grew up in Doncaster and in Liverpool where, aged twelve, he played euphonium in Dingle Temperance Band. He moved to Shipley, Yorkshire, and played with the brass band of Salt's (Saltaire) Ltd and others, before switching from euphonium to tuba, a change made on the advice of celebrated brass band conductor H. B. Hawley. He played tuba under Hawley at Bradford's City Band Club, but continued to make a living outside music, working as a panel beater and lorry driver and moving frequently. Invariably he joined a brass band wherever he settled, the most notable being the Brighouse and Rastrick. On 28 September 1935 he married, in Keighley, Ellen O'Hara (*b.* 1912/13), daughter of Bernard O'Hara, turner; they had two children, Molly (*b.* 1936) and Anthony (*b.* 1937). He drove petrol lorries during the Second World War and continued to work as a driver afterwards and to play with brass bands.

In 1947, at the old Leeds Rhythm Club, Barclay met several jazz musicians including the trumpeter Dick

Victor Robert Barclay (1911–1987), by Terry Cryer, c.1956

Hawdon. They decided to form a New Orleans group, first known as the Twin City Washboard Beaters, and although Barclay had not heard jazz until he was sixteen, he was included. From this nucleus the Yorkshire Jazz Band was formed in 1949, its main protagonists being Hawdon, trombonist Eddie O'Donnell, and clarinettist Alan Cooper, with Barclay as leader. They were invited to London where they created a sensation in traditional jazz circles and recorded for the Tempo label.

Barclay became a prominent member of Yorkshire's traditional jazz community and a popular figure with students and the denizens of Leeds's bohemian milieu. He opened a record recital club in 1950, then met Iris Isobel Price (*b.* 1922/3), a widow, and daughter of James Campbell, nurseryman. Barclay's first marriage having ended in divorce, they married on 24 August 1955; their daughter Cheryl was born the same year and a son, Simon, in 1963. A circle and a kind of mystique developed around Barclay during this period and for a while he and Iris provided accommodation for travelling musicians; the ambience of the building where he lived as caretaker was later captured by George Melly in *Owning-Up* (1965).

With a fluctuating personnel which included the guitarist Diz Disley and clarinettist Dennis Rayworth, the Yorkshire Jazz Band appeared regularly at Leeds's Metropole Hotel and Oasis Club and at pub venues across the county during the 1950s. Barclay remained the band's one constant feature and, with a shrewd eye for business opportunities, he started regular jazz club sessions in Boar Lane, Leeds. Following further London visits and a recording date for the progressive Esquire label, in 1956 he opened Studio 20, a popular late-night rendezvous, at New Briggate. There, known to some as Black Bob, he hosted proceedings and took charge of the cooking, serving up the occasional steak as well as vocals, for an audience of university students and others who came to hear the music and to rub shoulders with the cream of Britain's jazz musicians.

Although originally devoted to traditional jazz, and folk and skiffle from groups such as the Vipers, the club gradually began to feature modern jazz. This was unusual given the polarization that existed between jazz modernists and traditionalists of the period, but, in an inspired move, Barclay organized separate sessions for the two camps during which the 'opposition' could dance to a jukebox in an adjoining room. Eventually the club became known as a venue for the leading modernists such as Ronnie Scott, Tubby Hayes, and Joe Harriott. It attracted famous visitors too: from Shirley Bassey, Prince Ras Monolulu, and the Harlem Globetrotters to the American instrumentalists Louis Armstrong and Count Basie, and singers Jimmie Rushing, Big Bill Broonzy, and Brother John Sellers.

A short and heavy-set man with a bluff manner and strong Yorkshire accent, Barclay was one of the few black Britons to play traditional jazz. On his feature number *Big Chief Battleaxe* (1955), his musical approach stemmed from the revivalist West Coast school rather than the original New Orleans style, but he was capable of providing as much drive as any band required. With Studio 20 he created an environment for jazz that was unique outside London, and thus was a social innovator, regarded by his admirers as 'the father of traditional jazz in the North' (Eagle, 4).

Towards the end of his career Barclay preferred to play the double bass rather than tuba. He moved away from Leeds to live in Brontë country and the relative peace of a small house in Haworth, and, divorced from Iris in 1967, he married Mary Doris Rowlands (*b.* 1911/12), formerly Simpson, on 13 October 1977; she was the daughter of Michael Quinn, master builder. He continued to work as a lorry driver and was living in Keighley when he was hospitalized with a stroke in August 1982. He died on 15 February 1987 at Raikeswood Hospital, Skipton, North Yorkshire, from cerebral thrombosis and diabetes mellitus. He was survived by the children of his first two marriages.

VAL WILMER

Sources M. Webb, 'Yorkshire pioneer', *Melody Maker* (22 July 1972), 30 · J. Wilson, liner notes, *King tuba* (Esquire (S) 338) · V. Wilmer, 'Bob Barclay', *New Grove dictionary of jazz*, 2nd edn (2001) · J. Eagle, letter, *Jazz Journal International* (Aug 1982), 4 · G. Melly, *Owning-up* (1965), 40 · T. Cryer, *One in the eye* (1992) · private information (2004) · personal knowledge (2004) · b. cert. · m. certs. · d. cert.

Likenesses T. Cryer, photographs, c.1956, priv. coll. [*see illus.*]

Barclay, William [Guillaume] (**1546–1608**), civil lawyer, was born in Scotland. According to Sir Robert Sibbald he was descended from the Barclays of Collairnie in Fife; but according to a note attached to James Gordon's *History of*

William Barclay (1546–1608), by Karel van Mallery, pubd 1600

Scots Affairs (1841) he was a grandson of Patrick Barclay, baron of Gartly, Aberdeenshire. A birth date of 1546 appears on the inscription above his portrait kept in the museum at Nancy. He was educated at King's College, Aberdeen.

A devoted Catholic, close to Queen Mary, Barclay made the decisive choice of leaving his own country and the university in 1569 when the general assembly made it compulsory for all members of Aberdeen College to sign the confession of faith. He emigrated to France with the intention of studying law, which he did in Paris and in Bourges. There he exchanged the name William for Guillaume. The exact date of his arrival at Bourges is not known, but there is proof that he was already there in 1572, for he states in his *De regno* that he had François Hotman and Hugues Doneau as his professors before they left the university in August 1572. Barclay remained in Bourges until 1576. At first he was a student and then was appointed as lecturer in charge of reading the *Institutiones* in March 1575. According to Berriat Saint-Prix, he was taught in August 1575 by Cujas, who may also have been president of his doctorate. It is stated in the town accounts that for the year 1575 Barclay's income was £70. After he complained of the meagreness of his wages, he received an annual salary of £100 until the last day of March 1576. There is no evidence of his lectures, but Collot states that he adopted the 'historical method' following the lessons of Alciat, Baron, and Le Duaren.

On the invitation of his uncle, the Jesuit Edmund *Hay, rector of the recently founded University of Pont-à-Mousson, William Barclay left Bourges for Pont-à-Mousson. The duke of Lorraine appointed him professor of civil law and he started teaching during the academic year 1576/7; he was appointed doctor-regent at the end of the year. The duke made Barclay councillor of state and master of requests. In 1581 Barclay married Anne de Malleviller, a young lady of the Lorraine nobility. James VI sent Barclay letters patent for the wedding attesting his (Barclay's) good birth and nobility of the professor. A son was born, John *Barclay (1582–1621), the author of *Argenis*. Barclay was joined by Pierre Grégoire from Toulouse in 1582, and at the latter's death on 3 April 1598 he became dean of the faculty of law. None the less the insecurity of the Scot's position was evident two years before, for dissensions arose between him and the Jesuits who dominated the university. Barclay and Pierre Grégoire sided together in a quarrel regarding the status of the rector, but failed to maintain the independence of the faculty of law. A second cause of discord was the attitude of the Jesuits who soon endeavoured to attract John to their order, but the father stood firm. His strong personality, his integrity, and sense of responsibility forbade him to yield to influences offensive to him, and, having lost the favour of the duke of Lorraine, Barclay resigned his chair on 26 July 1603. He immediately left the duchy, after twenty-seven years of hard work.

In 1600 the editor Guillaume Chaudière had published in Paris Barclay's first important work, *De regno et regali potestate, adversus Buchananum, Brutum, Boucherium, et reliquos monarchomachos*. *De regno* is divided into six books and is furnished with a dedication to Henri IV. The first two books deal with a refutation of Buchanan's work *De jure regni apud Scotos* and are presented in the form of a dialogue. The third and fourth books are directed against Hubert Languet—in Barclay's opinion a heretic comparable with Machiavelli—who wrote *Vindiciae contra tyrannos* under the name Stephanus Junius Brutus. In the fifth book Barclay turns to Jean Boucher and his *De justa Henrici tertii abdicatione e Francorum regno*. The sixth and last book is a repetition of arguments, combined with references to Scottish and French history. *De regno* is neither a philosophical nor a theoretical treatise; its value is historical. Barclay's views are discussed in the *Civil Government* of Locke, who defines him as 'the great assertor of the power and sacredness of kings'.

After he left the duchy Barclay went to Paris and then to London, where James VI, who had just succeeded to the English crown, was attracting Catholics by his alleged sympathies with the Church of Rome. It is said that the king welcomed this defender of the divine right of kings, but his offer of preferment was on condition that he accept the Church of England, which he refused to do. Barclay returned to Paris at the end of 1603. The chair of civil law in the University of Angers had been vacant since 1599, and the town officials, well informed of the Scot's good reputation, sent a deputation to Barclay requesting him to accept the chair. In the town register of 5 February 1603 Barclay is described as 'l'un des grands personnages de ce temps'. He accepted the position but stipulated that he should have the first place in the faculty. On 15 January 1604 he signed the contract by which he was to teach at the University of Angers for five years. On 1 February 1605, by a special decree of the university and despite the strong opposition of his colleagues, he was appointed dean of the faculty of law. To the end he remained the magnificent Scottish professor who used to go to his lectures, accompanied by his son and two valets, clad in a superb garment and wearing a heavy gold chain around his neck, as can be seen in his portrait.

Barclay was dark-haired, and with a pointed beard and a long thin waxed moustache cut a dignified and austere figure. He died at Angers on 3 July 1608 and was buried in the church of the Cordeliers, which no longer exists. His second work, *Commentarii in titulos pandectarum de rebus creditis et de jurejurando*, was also published in Paris during his lifetime in 1605. His *De potestate papae* was published in London in 1609 and at Pont-à-Mousson in the same year with a preface by his son; further editions appeared in 1610, 1612, and 1617, as well as two French and two English translations which attest to the interest of the work. Barclay spent more than ten years writing the essay, which is directed against the power of the pope over the temporal power of kings. The controversy was so great that Cardinal Bellarmine published a treatise against Barclay's, asserting that the pope possessed supreme power over temporal matters. The publication of his posthumous work cast a light on what appeared obscure in the *De regno*. Barclay had a cosmopolitan point of view and his position as an exile gives his theory of the divine right of kings special value. MARIE-CLAUDE TUCKER

Sources M.-C. Bellot-Tucker, 'Maîtres et étudiants écossais à la faculté de droit de l'Université de Bourges aux XVIe et XVIIe siècles', PhD diss., University of Clermont-Ferrand, 1997 • C. Collot, *L'école doctrinale de droit public de Pont-à-Mousson (Pierre Grégoire et Guillaume Barclay) fin du XVIe siècle* (1965) • G. Mackenzie, *The lives and characters of the most eminent writers of the Scots nation*, 3 (1722), 468–78 • E. Dubois, *Guillaume Barclay, jurisconsulte écossais, 1546–1608* (1872) • *DNB* • G. Ménage, *Remarques sur la vie de Pierre Ayrault* (1675), 228–30 • D. B. Smith, 'William Barclay', *SHR*, 11 (1913–14), 136–63 • P. Taisand, *Les vies des plus célèbres jurisconsultes de toutes les nations* (1721), 56–7 • D. Irving, *Lives of Scotish writers*, 1 (1839), 210 • Chambers, *Scots*. (1855) • J. Berriat Saint-Prix, *Histoire du droit romain suivie de l'histoire de Cujas* (1821), 574 • Archives Municipales de Bourges, CC 351, fol. 31; BB 8, fol. 128; CC 352, fol. 45 • Archives Départementales de Meurthe et Moselle, B. 1171, fol. 165; D. 1, fol. 153 • registre de délibérations du corps de ville, 5 Dec 1603, Archives d'Angers, BB 51, fol. 1372° • Archives d'Angers, A A 5, fol. 147; B B 52, fols. 9, 19, 20, 21, 25, 26 • extrait des actes de l'état civil d'Angers Paroisse Saint-Mauville, Archives d'Angers, registre, GG 112, fol. 80v • J. Gordon, *History of Scots affairs from 1637–1641*, ed. J. Robertson and G. Grub, 3 vols., Spalding Club, 1, 3, 5 (1841)

Likenesses ink drawing, pubd 1666 (after engraving by L. Crasso), Scot. NPG • K. van Mallery, line engraving, BM, NPG; repro. in W. Barclay, *De regno* (1600) [*see illus.*] • pen-and-ink drawing (after engraving), NPG • portrait, Musée Historique Lorrain, Nancy, France

Barclay, William (*b*. *c*.**1570**, *d*. in or after **1627**), medical writer and Latin poet, was born at Cullen, Banffshire, one of at least three sons of Walter Barclay (*d*. 1587), the fiar of Towie, and his wife, Elizabeth, or Elspeth, Hay (*fl*. 1553–1601). In 1586 William Barclay entered the Catholic college at Pont-à-Mousson, in France, run by his namesake William Barclay (1546–1608) with whom he is sometimes confused. It is possible that he was back in Scotland by 1590, when he was named in legal documents arising from the murder of his father by William Meldrum.

In April 1593 Barclay entered the seminary at Douai, and continued from there to Louvain University, where he studied under Justus Lipsius. Lipsius was said to have considered Barclay among his favourite pupils, and according to the 1670 reprint of *Callirhoe*, Lipsius said 'that if he were dying he knew no person on earth he would leave his pen to but the doctor' (Leask, 3.4). Certainly, Barclay provided a Latin 'praemetia' to the 1599 Paris edition of Lipsius's Tacitus. By 1598 Barclay had moved to Paris, where he was teaching, and was preparing to return to Scotland as a priest (*Records of Scots Colleges*, 5).

Barclay's career in Scotland is difficult to distinguish owing to the presence of another namesake, an advocate who in time became procurator fiscal of Aberdeen: however, it is clear that it was William Barclay of Towie who was present at a mass being said at the house of William Naper in Edinburgh in March 1601. The house was raided, and Barclay was among those arrested. Barclay, who had previously taken an oath that he was not a Catholic, was declared infamous and sentenced to banishment. In May Patrick Barclay provided bail of 2000 marks to enable his brother to live quietly at home with his mother until the sentence took effect (*Reg. PCS*, 683), and Barclay returned to France, moving to Nantes. It has also been suggested that he raised a family in Sweden during this period as well, but the evidence for this is flimsy (Barclay, 2.229–30).

It is not clear when Barclay returned again to Scotland, but when he did, he went as a doctor. His best-known publications are English-language tracts on medicine published at Edinburgh. *Nepenthes, or, The Vertues of Tobacco* (1614) argues for the health-giving properties of tobacco. It is dedicated to Patrick Barclay, his brother Patrick's son. *Callirhoe, or, The Well of Spa* (1615) is a short report on the medical benefits to be gained from bathing in the spring at Aberdeen. In 1618 Barclay wrote a similar pamphlet about the Kingshorn well.

In addition, Barclay composed several pieces of occasional Latin verse, usefully anthologized in *Musa Latina Aberdonensis* (1910). A note accompanying one of them, 'Apobaterium, or Last Farewell to Aberdeen', published in Barclay's *Sylvae tres* (1619), implies that he was on the point of moving to England, evidence perhaps strengthened by the fact that his next work, *G. Barclayii Judicium* (1620)—an attack on the psalm translations of Eglisham—was printed in London. His fellow Catholic Thomas Dempster, writing in 1627, described Barclay as still alive and practising medicine in Scotland, but nothing is known of his career after this date. MATTHEW STEGGLE

Sources C. W. Barclay and others, eds., *A history of the Barclay family*, 3 vols. (1924–34) • W. K. Leask, ed., *Musa Latina Aberdonensis*, 3:

Poetae minores, New Spalding Club, 37 (1910), 3–20 • P. J. Anderson, ed., *Records of the Scots colleges at Douai, Rome, Madrid, Valladolid and Ratisbon*, New Spalding Club, 30 (1906) • *Reg. PCS*, 1st ser., vol. 6

Barclay, William (1603–1676), army officer in the Swedish service, was born in Siggot, Scotland. Although he was the son of the laird of Siggot, his parents' identity remains unknown beyond that. He entered Swedish military service some time during the Thirty Years' War (the exact date is unclear) and earned promotion to the rank of colonel. In 1646 he was listed as the colonel and chief of a cavalry squadron from Värmland and Dalarna.

Barclay may have returned to Scotland in 1642 for a short visit, and this was also when he first became involved in a lengthy battle to get a debt settled by the Swedish government. Barclay was to feature in a series of disputes after this, none of which harmed his standing in Swedish society. The following year a land donation was authorized for him and in 1645 the Riksråd (Swedish state council) ordered that Barclay's debt be settled. In 1645 he married Margareta Becker, the widow of another Scot in Swedish service, Patrick Kinnemond, who had been ennobled posthumously. They had four sons and one daughter. Soon Barclay found himself again in trouble with the Swedish authorities. He was convicted by a Swedish war tribunal of excessive plundering during the German campaigns and lost his colonelcy in 1648 as a result. However, this did not prove an obstacle to his ennoblement that same year. Barclay then served as major of the city militia in Stockholm in 1652 and actively sought admission to the house of nobility. Queen Kristina yielded to his entreaties by formally introducing him into the house in 1654, but she denied his requests for further land donations. Barclay's continued social power was again demonstrated two years later when the Stockholm town council chose him in preference to another officer for promotion to city colonel. Later that year he was also chosen to receive Queen Kristina as a city representative when she returned from Prussia. Before long Barclay became embroiled once more in a conflict with the Riksråd, on this occasion over a dispute with the master of court, whom he blamed for not undertaking his duties properly; and in the following year, Barclay, always controversial, upset the chief governor of Stockholm by raising a matter with the military college without discussing it first with the governor.

For all his various altercations, Barclay overcame these setbacks and remained in royal favour, being appointed a commissioner for conscription for the Swedish army in 1657. Later that year he was involved in yet another quarrel, this one between Stockholm's military defence corps and the burgesses of the city. Like many officers of the time, Barclay continued to seek his overdue wages. Although he was receiving at least 500 Swedish riksdaler a year from Stockholm city (another source gives the figure as 750 daler) his royal wages for earlier military service had still not been paid, and Barclay threatened resignation from the army unless they were. The situation was resolved by 1665 as he was then promoted major-general. Barclay died in Stockholm in 1676, but it appears that his estates were not passed on to his sons.

A. N. L. Grosjean

Sources G. Elgenstierna, *Den introducerade svenska adelns ättartavlor med tillägg och rättelser*, 9 vols. (1925–36), vol. 1 • 'Svenska Sändebuds till utländska Hof och deras Sändebud till Sverige', 1841, Riksarkivet, Stockholm • katalog öfver sköldebref, Riddarhusarkivet, Stockholm, Sweden • military muster rolls, 1646–9, Krigsarkivet, Stockholm • N. A. Kullberg, S. Bergh, and P. Sondén, eds., *Svenska riksrådets protokoll*, 18 vols. (Stockholm, 1878–1959) • S. Bergh and B. Taube, eds., *Sveriges ridderskaps och adels riksdags-protokoll*, 17 vols. (1871), 5 • J. Kleberg, *Krigskollegii historia biografiska anteckningar, 1630–1865* (1930) • T. A. Fischer [E. L. Fischer], *The Scots in Sweden* (1907)

Barclay, William (1797/8–1859), miniature painter, was born possibly in London and was also possibly the son of William Barclay (*fl.* 1764–1769), miniature painter, of Tottenham, Middlesex. He entered the Royal Academy Schools on 15 January 1820, aged twenty-two, under the title 'William Barclay Jnr'. He established himself as a miniature painter, practising in London and Paris throughout the period 1830 to 1859.

Barclay specialized in making copies of the works of the great Italian masters in the Musée du Louvre in Paris, as well as producing portrait miniatures on ivory in the style of, but considerably weaker than, Sir William Ross. A large full-length miniature in watercolour on ivory of Dom Pedro, duque do Bragança, and Dom Luís, duque do Pôrto, demonstrating this affinity with Ross, was acquired by Queen Victoria in 1843 (Royal Collection). Barclay's miniature of Mrs Bacon (1836) and two miniatures of unknown sitters are in the Victoria and Albert Museum, London. Two of these are signed 'Barclay' in his characteristic fashion. He exhibited portrait miniatures and some copies in watercolour at the Paris Salon between 1831 and 1859, as well as at the Royal Academy between 1832 and 1856. He died in 1859, possibly in Paris. A successful miniature painter of his time, Barclay has been classified by most recent commentators as a competent but second-rank artist.

V. Remington

Sources S. C. Hutchison, 'The Royal Academy Schools, 1768–1830', *Walpole Society*, 38 (1960–62), 123–91, esp. 172 • D. Foskett, *Miniatures: dictionary and guide* (1987), 422, 485 • B. S. Long, *British miniaturists* (1929), 14 • L. R. Schidlof, *The miniature in Europe in the 16th, 17th, 18th, and 19th centuries*, 1 (1964), 62 • Graves, *RA exhibitors* • Livrets du Salon, Paris, 1843 • Livrets du Salon, Paris, 1846 • Livrets du Salon, Paris, 1857 • G. Hall and others, *Summary catalogue of miniatures in the Victoria and Albert Museum* (1981) • *DNB* • G. C. Williamson, *The history of portrait miniatures*, 1 (1904), 206

Barclay, William (1907–1978), New Testament scholar, writer, and broadcaster, was born on 5 December 1907 in Wick, Caithness, the only child of William Dugald Barclay (1864–1936), a bank manager and lay evangelist, and his wife, Barbara Linton McLeish (1867–1932). In 1912 the family left for the industrial south-west when William Dugald was transferred to manage the Bank of Scotland's branch in Motherwell. There his son performed brilliantly at Dalziel high school, particularly in English literature, shared (with embryonic misgivings) his father's United Free

William Barclay (1907–1978), by unknown photographer

Church activities, and acquired an affection for Gilbert and Sullivan and Motherwell Football Club. He gained a first in classics (1929) and a BD degree 'with distinction' (1932) at Glasgow University, before a year's study at the University of Marburg.

In February 1933 Barclay was ordained and inducted to Trinity Church, Renfrew, whose members were largely involved in Clydeside shipyards and factories. On 30 June he married Catherine Barbara Gillespie (1905–1979), a college cook and domestic science graduate, the youngest daughter of the Revd James Hogg Gillespie (*d.* 1951) and his wife, Mary Muir Ferguson (*d.* 1944). Trinity quickly warmed to a caring pastor who with heavy Lanarkshire accent succeeded in his aim to make the obvious interesting. With 1939 came war, and this pacifist admirer of Winston Churchill worked tirelessly and imaginatively for a community beset by bombs, blackouts, and restrictions. His reputation grew also as guest speaker, supporter of organizations such as the YMCA, Boys' Brigade, and Sunday School Union, and writer of *New Testament Studies* (1937).

After fourteen fruitful but exhausting parish years, Barclay with his wife, son, and daughter moved to Glasgow on his appointment as New Testament lecturer at his alma mater. Although he was superbly equipped academically for the task, advancement to a professorial chair at the university was delayed until 1964, perhaps because of his direct style and sturdy individualism sometimes bordering on capriciousness (he totally ignored discussion of the Dead Sea scrolls, and seldom attended presbytery meetings).

A self-styled 'liberal evangelical', Barclay was reticent about the inspiration of scripture, sceptical about the virgin birth, and regarded miracles not so much historically but as symbolic of what Jesus can still do. He rejected substitutionary atonement as incompatible with the New Testament God of love. It was that love, he said in a BBC interview, that had stilled the storm in his own heart when in 1955 his daughter drowned in an accident at sea. An anonymous letter from Northern Ireland declared 'God killed your daughter … to save her from being corrupted by your heresies' (Rawlins, 204). That he raised Conservative hackles was seen too when the minister of a large central London church called him 'the most dangerous man in Christendom' (ibid., 281). He drew criticism also for smoking and for a changed attitude toward the teetotalism of his youth.

In 1953 the kirk enlisted Barclay as a stopgap writer for daily Bible readings 'until we can get someone useful to do them for us' (Rawlins, 163). No one emerged, and he continued the project; the 1959 edition of the *Daily Study Bible (New Testament)* sold more than 5 million copies. From that period came also *The Mind of St. Paul* (1958) and *Educational Ideas in the Ancient World* (1959)—and all this from one who, denying any claim to original thinking, regarded himself as a religious entrepreneur. His success as a communicator he attributed to a good memory, a disciplined mind (he never wrote a sermon after Thursday), a facility with words, and an ability to think in pictures rather than in theological abstractions. He disliked the pretentious, 'the cult of unintelligibility', and the closed mind, but rejected just as much the mind 'open at both ends'.

Like Friedrich von Hügel, Barclay urged students to have some non-religious interests, including watching television to keep them abreast of current talking points. That he himself walked the world with open eyes was seen in the couthie anecdotes used in a remarkably popular religious television series. His hobbies included stamp collecting and golf. Music he found a great tension-reliever whether it be the Scottish National Orchestra or the Beatles. Although he was deaf for more than forty years, he had a hearing aid that enabled him to conduct the Trinity College choir which travelled throughout Scotland. The singers facing him often saw tears in his eyes, for Barclay was an emotional man, as was confirmed in the autobiographical *Testament of Faith* (1975). He pursued a frenetic timetable, but students who sought his counsel found him relaxed and a good listener.

Although Barclay was sometimes charged with trying overmuch to be all things to all men, or with being a 'mere popularizer', he was a percipient raiser of discomforting questions. Did not character matter more than doctrine? Was it not blasphemy to blame God for Aberfan? There was impish coat-trailing too: a celibate ministry was undesirable in men, but married women pastors disrupted family life. Once he embarrassed the establishment by declining nomination as moderator of the general assembly. He was, however, proud to accept from Edinburgh University an honorary degree of DD, and in 1969 the queen made him a CBE.

After retirement in 1974 Barclay was briefly visiting professor of ethics at Strathclyde University, aided by his *Ethics in a Permissive Society* (1972), and he began work on the Old Testament part of his *Daily Study Bible*, but increasing ill health prevented its continuance. A long-time sufferer from emphysema and afflicted latterly by Parkinson's disease, William Barclay died in Mearnskirk Hospital, Glasgow, on 24 January 1978, and was cremated on 27 January at Woodside crematorium, Paisley.

Barclay's books, more than seventy in number, with translations in thirty languages, ranged over a wide field, and included *God's Plan for Man* (1950), *Bible and History* (1968), *The New Testament: a New Translation* (1969), and *Jesus of Nazareth* (1977). His writings and broadcasts spoke—and still speak—about Christianity to millions otherwise unreached. He wrote as he spoke and, like C. S. Lewis, he made righteousness readable. He proved that for the Christian communicator it is not enough to know the Lord's song in a strange land—he must also know how best to present it. J. D. DOUGLAS

Sources C. L. Rawlins, *William Barclay: the authorised biography* (1984) · R. D. Kernohan, ed., *William Barclay: the plain uncommon man* (1980) · J. Martin, *William Barclay* (1984) · personal knowledge (2004) · private information (2004) · *WWW*

Archives NL Scot., corresp. and papers | SOUND BL NSA, 'It takes all sorts', M3084 WC1

Likenesses photograph, repro. in Rawlins, *William Barclay* [*see illus.*]

Wealth at death £135,361.90: confirmation, 10 July 1978, *CCI*

Barcroft, George (*d.* 1610), Church of England clergyman and musician, is of unknown parentage. From 1565 to 1571 he was a chorister of Winchester Cathedral. He entered Trinity College, Cambridge, as a sizar on 12 December 1574, and graduated BA in 1578; during 1575–7 he was also a singing-man of the chapel choir. In 1578–9, despite his youth, he was admitted organist and master of the choristers of Ely Cathedral, and after a period of probation received formal appointment on 19 January 1583. In addition to his statutory duties of training the chorister boys and playing the organ at the three daily services, he undertook to take his part in the singing of the services and to train the boys in playing musical instruments. Having taken priest's orders on 30 August 1590, he was appointed in plurality to a minor canonry of the cathedral in 1592. Generous as was his aggregate annual stipend of £23 6*s.* 8*d.*, he had regular gratuities from an appreciative chapter, as well as remuneration for copying music for the choir to use.

Barcroft was a noteworthy pedagogue. Andrew Willett, canon of Ely, remembered him particularly for the distinction of two of his pupils, the instrumentalist Thomas Jordan (chorister in 1584–7) and the composer John Amner (1593); he could have added the composers William Stonard and Thomas Yarrow (both 1596–8). Three of Barcroft's compositions have survived, all in the simpler four-voice idiom characteristic of their day. The two short anthems to prayer book texts exhibit some grace and modest skill; the paired Te Deum and Benedictus are rather less distinguished. Barcroft received his last chapter gratuity 'in his sickness' during the spring of 1610, and vacated both his offices, doubtless by death, between March and June 1610. ROGER BOWERS

Sources I. Payne, *The provision and practice of sacred music at Cambridge colleges and selected cathedrals, c.1547–c.1646* (1993) · H. W. Shaw, *The succession of organists of the Chapel Royal and the cathedrals of England and Wales from c.1538* (1991), 99 · CUL, Ely cathedral archives [including Music MSS 4, 5, 18, 28] · A. Willet, *Harmony upon the first [and second] book of Samuel* (1614), Epistola dedicatoria · Venn, *Alum. Cant.*, 1/1.83 · W. W. Rouse Ball and J. A. Venn, eds., *Admissions to Trinity College, Cambridge*, 2 (1913), 100 · P. Phillips, *English sacred music, 1549–1649* (1991), 307, 311 · I. Payne, 'The musical establishment at Trinity College, Cambridge, 1546–1644', *Proceedings of the Cambridge Antiquarian Society*, 74 (1985), 53–69 · G. Barcroft, *Te Deum and Benedictus* (c.1900) · G. Barcroft, *Two anthems*, ed. A. Greening (1969)

Barcroft, Henry (1904–1998), circulatory physiologist, was born on 18 October 1904 at 92 Chesterton Road, Cambridge, the elder of two sons of the distinguished physiologist Sir Joseph *Barcroft (1872–1947), Cambridge professor, and his wife, Mary Agnetta (Minnie; 1875–1961), daughter of Sir Robert Ball, astronomer royal of Ireland and subsequently professor of astronomy and geometry at Cambridge. Thus Henry was primed and encouraged to become an academic himself. Apart from four years at boarding-school (Marlborough College, 1918–23) his early life was spent in Cambridge, where he entered King's College choir school as a non-choral day boy (1912–18) and continued as an undergraduate (1923–7) and then as a research student (1927–8) at King's College. He was deeply attached to his home and family and collaborated with his father to publish two papers while still an undergraduate. Having failed to gain a fellowship he left Cambridge and undertook clinical medical training at St Mary's Hospital, London (1928–32); on qualifying he was immediately appointed lecturer at University College, London (1932–5). In spite of a heavy teaching load (150 lectures a year, plus practical classes) he continued to work on blood flow in animals; he was, however, strongly attracted by the novel work being done on human circulation at University College Hospital, just across the road. On 17 February 1933 he married Bridget Mary (Biddy; 1907/8–1990), daughter of Arthur Stanley Ramsey, president of Magdalene College, Cambridge, and sister of Michael, the future archbishop of Canterbury. She had just qualified in medicine, to which she returned after bearing him three sons and a daughter; for twenty-five years she was medical officer to an infant welfare clinic serving the boroughs of Camden and Islington, London. She died in 1990 after a long illness, during which he looked after her devotedly.

At the age of thirty Barcroft was appointed Dunville professor of physiology at Queen's University, Belfast (1935–48). He then fulfilled the university's expectation that he would build up research in spite of being given practically no assistance and being required to give the medical students all their physiology lectures; he covered every relevant topic and lectured for six days a week at 9 a.m. In his research he deliberately switched from animal to human work and took on newly qualified clinicians for training in research leading to an MD, providing enthusiastic collaborators; subsequently some also made research their life's work. Together they skilfully exploited and developed the method of venous occlusion plethysmography to measure blood flow in the arms of human volunteers and willing patients, distinguishing between the flow to skin and the flow to deep tissues, especially and importantly to muscle. The work demonstrated that the sympathetic nervous system could both actively dilate and actively constrict the blood vessels to muscle—a finding essential to understanding the origin of high blood pressure. A striking finding was that human fainting is an active process, even when induced by emotion; it occurs when the blood-vessels to muscle are suddenly widened by nervous action, so that blood rushes into the muscles and blood pressure drops precipitately, thereby depriving the brain of blood and oxygen. This all justified Barcroft's election to the Royal Society in 1953 and was summarized in a seminal and readable monograph *Sympathetic Control of Human Blood Vessels* (1953, with H. J. C. Swan, a junior collaborator).

In 1948 Barcroft moved back to London and he spent the rest of his life there, first as professor of physiology at St Thomas's Hospital medical school (1948–71) and then in a long retirement. Once again he successfully built up a distinguished department from a low state and encouraged a wide range of research. He also took on other activities, becoming a Wellcome trustee, and gave several named lectures, even after retiring. He was a particularly kindly man, a characteristic stemming in part from his secure background, with both his eightieth and ninetieth birthdays marked by embarrassingly appreciative speeches from former colleagues. Though he received honorary degrees he was overtly less distinguished than his father and maternal grandfather, both of whom were knighted for their science, but his contribution should be equally enduring. He died at his home, 73 Erskine Hill, Hampstead, London, on 11 January 1998.

PETER B. C. MATTHEWS

Sources A. D. M. Greenfield and I. C. Roddie, *Memoirs FRS*, 46 (2000), 3–17 • *WW* (1996) • *Medical Directory* (2000) • F. J. W. Roughton, *Obits. FRS*, 6 (1948–9), 315–45 • A. D. M. Greenfield, 'Professor Henry Barcroft', *The Independent* (19 Jan 1998) • m. cert. • d. cert. • *CGPLA Eng. & Wales* (1998) • private information (2004) [Mrs S. Falk, daughter]

Archives Wellcome L., corresp.; MSS; notebooks

Likenesses photograph, 1993, repro. in Greenfield and Roddie, *Memoirs FRS* • photograph, repro. in *The Independent*

Wealth at death £362,253: probate, 27 April 1998, *CGPLA Eng. & Wales*

Barcroft, Sir Joseph (1872–1947), physiologist, was born on 26 July 1872 at The Glen, Newry, co. Down, Ireland, the second of the five children of Henry Barcroft (*d.* 1905), linen merchant and inventor, and his wife, Anna Richardson Malcolmson (1840–1924), daughter of David Malcolmson of Melview, Clonnel, co. Tipperary, and his wife, Sarah Nicholson. Barcroft, or J. B., as he was widely known, received his early schooling at home until the age of twelve, and then went to the Friends' school at Bootham, York. He then attended the Leys School in Cambridge. Several of his contemporaries at the school distinguished themselves in later life; among them was H. H. Dale. In his last year at school (1891), Barcroft astonished his friends by passing the BSc degree of London University; however, the effort apparently affected his health to such an extent that he then took a year off.

Sir Joseph Barcroft (1872–1947), by Lafayette, 1933

In 1893 Barcroft went up to King's College, Cambridge, and read for the natural sciences tripos, obtaining first-class honours in part one in 1896, and part two (physiology) in 1897. Among his contemporaries were E. Rutherford and H. H. Dale, both of whom became fellows, and later presidents, of the Royal Society. At a meeting of the Natural Sciences Club, Barcroft demonstrated what may have been the first X-ray photograph produced in England.

Barcroft began a research programme in the Cambridge Physiological Laboratory in 1897 and continued this, with occasional interruptions, throughout his entire life. His first project was on the effect of stimulation of the nerves to the submaxillary gland, and particularly the resulting oxygen uptake and carbon dioxide output in the gland. This work sparked his interest in blood gases and led to his development of a differential blood-gas manometer. Over the next few years he collaborated with J. S. Haldane on blood-gas analysis, with T. G. Brodie on the kidney, with E. H. Starling on the pancreas, and with W. E. Dixon on the heart. The focus of all these projects was the gaseous metabolism of these organs. Barcroft gained the Walsingham medal in 1899 and was awarded a prize fellowship and appointed lecturer at King's College. In 1904 he was made junior demonstrator in the physiological laboratory, and three years later he was promoted to senior demonstrator.

In 1903 Barcroft married Mary Agnetta (Minnie) Ball (1875–1961), daughter of the astronomer Sir Robert *Ball, who was a professorial fellow at King's College. They lived at 13 Grange Road, which became a popular meeting place for friends and visiting scientists from all over the world. They had two sons: Henry *Barcroft (1904–1998), who became a fellow of the Royal Society and professor of physiology at St Thomas's Hospital, London, and Robert Ball Barcroft, who became an army officer.

Barcroft's early work on blood gases was the beginning of a lifelong interest in haemoglobin, and particularly its combination with oxygen. Aspects which he studied included the effects of temperature, carbon dioxide pressure, acidity, salts, dialysis, diet, exercise, and high altitude. The last prompted him to participate in two high-altitude expeditions, one to Tenerife in 1910 and another to Monte Rosa in 1911. His studies on haemoglobin culminated in his classic book *The Respiratory Function of the Blood*, which was published in 1914. He was elected fellow of the Royal Society in 1910. During the same year he became assistant tutor at King's and also proctor of the university.

The outbreak of the First World War in 1914 posed a dilemma for Barcroft, as his family had been members of the Society of Friends since the seventeenth century. He resolved the issue by working on medical and physiological effects of gas poisoning, both at Cambridge and at the government's experimental station at Porton Down, Wiltshire. He claimed that as a civilian he could be much more assertive to the military top brass. C. G. Douglas, who was in the RAMC, recounts an anecdote concerning Barcroft's visit to an advanced dressing station near the French lines, which was within the range of the German guns. Barcroft insisted on standing prominently on a crossroads but no shells were fired, possibly because he was wearing his bowler hat, and this may have unsettled the gunners. During his time at Porton Barcroft took part in an enterprising experiment, when he exposed himself and a dog to hydrocyanic acid in a closed chamber. The animal nearly died, but Barcroft was unaffected, a dramatic demonstration of how different species vary in their response to toxic gases. He was appointed CBE in 1918 for his services during the war.

In 1919 Barcroft returned to Cambridge as reader, and developed his interest in high-altitude physiology, in particular the issue of whether the lungs actively secreted oxygen, as claimed by J. S. Haldane in Oxford, and earlier by Christian Bohr in Copenhagen. In 1911 Haldane had led an expedition to Pike's peak, Colorado, where strong evidence for oxygen secretion was apparently obtained. Barcroft tested this in a famous experiment in 1920, when he placed himself in a glass box for six days, while the oxygen concentration was gradually reduced until it was equivalent to the oxygen pressure at an altitude substantially above Pike's peak. Blood was drawn from his radial artery using the newly developed technique of arterial cannulation, and there was a dramatic moment when the first blood came out blue rather than red, indicating that oxygen secretion by the lungs was not occurring. Subsequent careful measurements confirmed this.

In 1921–2 Barcroft led a high-altitude expedition to Cerro de Pasco in Peru, in order to study pulmonary gas exchange, blood biochemistry, and several other topics. In the report of this, he commented on the extraordinary athletic ability of the permanent residents of Cerro, but added that they had 'impaired physical and mental powers' compared to sea-level dwellers. This remark incensed the Peruvian physician Carlos Monge, who subsequently embarked on an extensive study of the high-altitude dwellers. It could be argued that this influential Peruvian school owed its origin to Barcroft's report and possibly to this single unguarded statement. These high-altitude interests culminated in 'Lessons from high altitudes', the first part of the second edition of *The Respiratory Function of the Blood*, which was published in 1925 and became a classic. Barcroft became professor of physiology at Cambridge in the same year.

Another period in Barcroft's research began when he worked on the storage organs of the blood, particularly the spleen. Much of this research was done on dogs in which the organ had been exteriorized by operation, so that it could be directly inspected through a window. This was also a period when Barcroft organized a substantial extension of the Cambridge Physiological Laboratory, with the result that it became one of the most impressive physiological institutions in the country. He also paid several visits to the United States, and a series of lectures to the Harvard medical school was published in 1934 in his famous book, *Features in the Architecture of Physiological Functions*, which is remarkable for the breadth of its scholarship.

A final period of research, which included a short spell at Porton at the outbreak of the Second World War, occupied Barcroft's time between 1932 and 1947. His primary focus was now on foetal physiology, and he left an indelible impression on this field. The topics he investigated included blood volume, placental blood flow, the physiology of the foetal heart, both foetal and maternal haemoglobin, and metabolism and growth *in utero*. This work was brought together in Barcroft's last book, *Researches in Pre-Natal Life*, the first volume of which was published only a few weeks before his death.

Barcroft was knighted in 1935. He delivered the Croonian lecture on 'Foetal respiration' to the Royal Society in the same year, and the Linacre lecture at Cambridge in 1941 on 'Respiratory patterns at birth'. By this time he was head of the Agricultural Research Council unit in animal physiology at Cambridge. In 1943 he was awarded the Copley medal of the Royal Society; he had already won its royal medal in 1922. Barcroft, who loved sailing, riding, and golf, died suddenly in Barton Road, Cambridge, on 21 March 1947. He was cremated, following a service at King's College chapel, on 25 March. In 1952 Mount Barcroft, a peak in the White Mountains, California, was named in his honour. JOHN B. WEST

Sources K. J. Franklin, *Joseph Barcroft, 1872–1947* (1953) • F. J. W. Roughton, *Obits. FRS*, 6 (1948–9), 315–45 [incl. bibliography] • F. J. W. Roughton and J. C. Kendrew, eds., *Haemoglobin: a symposium based on a conference held at Cambridge in June 1948 in memory of Sir Joseph Barcroft* (1949) • K. S. Comline and others, eds., *Foetal and neonatal physiology: proceedings of the Sir Joseph Barcroft centenary symposium* (1973) • *DNB* • *CGPLA Eng. & Wales* (1947) • W. J. O'Connor, *British physiologists, 1885–1914* (1991)

Archives Medical Research Council, London, corresp. • U. Cam., department of physiology library, papers | CAC Cam., corresp. with A. V. Hill • Nuffield Oxf., corresp. with Lord Cherwell

Likenesses Lafayette, photograph, 1933, NPG [*see illus.*] • photograph, 1943, repro. in Franklin, *Joseph Barcroft*, frontispiece • photograph, Wellcome L.

Wealth at death £34,054 1*s.* 6*d.*: probate, 4 Sept 1947, *CGPLA Eng. & Wales*

Bard, Henry, first Viscount Bellomont [Bellamont] (**1615/16–1656**), royalist army officer and diplomat, came of an old-established Lincolnshire family, and was the younger son of George Bard (*d.* 1616), vicar of Staines, Middlesex, and his wife, Susan, daughter of John Dudley. A scholar at Eton College from about 1628, Bard was admitted to King's College, Cambridge, on 23 August 1633, where he became a fellow in 1636; he graduated BA in 1637 and proceeded MA in 1641. His restless and roving disposition led him to travel extensively, mainly on foot, in western Europe, Turkey, Palestine, Arabia, and Egypt, where he acquired (allegedly stole from a mosque) a handsome Koran, which he later (on 28 May 1644) presented to King's College. He sent a detailed account of his travels to a King's contemporary, Dr Charles Mason.

Bard returned to England about 1642, and on the outbreak of the civil war his reputation as a traveller and linguist secured him a colonel's commission, possibly through the influence of the queen, Henrietta Maria. He later told parliament 'that he had taken up arms neither for religion … nor for that mousetrap the laws, but to re-establish the king on his throne' (Bence-Jones, 187). He was knighted on 22 November 1643 and created an Oxford DCL the same year. Having gained the confidence of Prince Rupert, he was sent to Ireland, where he raised two regiments of foot. At Cheriton, Hampshire, on 29 March 1644, against orders, and 'with more youthful courage than soldier-like discretion' (Adair, 140), he impetuously charged the roundhead cavalry and his whole regiment was either killed or captured, Bard himself losing the use of an arm. After a brief imprisonment (April/May 1644) he was granted the reversion to the offices of governor of Guernsey and captain of Cornet Castle. He was created a baronet on 8 October 1644, joined the king at Oxford, and was given the command of a brigade. In 1645 he married Anne (*d.* in or before 1668), daughter of Sir William Gardiner of Peckham, Surrey; they had a son and three daughters.

Early in 1645 Bard was governor of Campden House, Gloucestershire; according to Clarendon he 'exercised an illimited tyranny over the whole country' (Porter, 30), ordering the constable of Kineton to be thrown into a pond. When the garrison was withdrawn in May he burnt the house to the ground to prevent its occupation by the enemy. After playing a distinguished role in the capture of Leicester on 30 May he commanded a division at Naseby with Sir George Lisle. Shortly afterwards he was appointed governor of Worcester, and on 1 November 1645 he threatened local constables who were late in paying their assessments with 'a troop of unsanctified horse (to) … fire your houses … hang up your bodies and scare your ghosts' (Whitelocke, 1.181). On 18 July 1645 Bard was raised to the Irish peerage as Baron Bard of Dromboy, co. Eastmeath, and Viscount Bellomont, co. Dublin (an attempt to latinize Ballymount). While sailing to Ireland in December 1646 he was captured by a parliamentarian vessel and brought back, a prisoner, to England. The following year he was released on condition he left the country—possibly through the good offices of his elder brother, Maximilian, a wealthy London mercer who provided horses for the parliamentarian army, and on whom Bellomont appears to have been financially dependent throughout his life.

Upon moving with his family to the exiled court of Charles II, where he became a Catholic, Bellomont was arrested on 12 May 1649 at The Hague and charged with the murder of Isaac Dorislaus, the Commonwealth's ambassador; the charge was soon dropped. In 1653 Bellomont was sent by the king as his envoy to Shah Abbas II of Persia, in the hope of raising money for the royalist cause from payment of an alleged debt owed to the English crown for naval aid in the capture of Hormoz (1622) and from diverting to royal use the East India Company's share of the customs at Gombroon. His journeys were, long afterwards, narrated by Niccolao Manucci, a Venetian boy befriended by Bellomont and allowed to accompany him. Travelling in disguise through Turkey and Armenia, they reached Tabriz early in September 1654. But though the shah was friendly (Bellomont named his youngest daughter Persiana) he proved dilatory over a pecuniary settlement. After more than a year at Esfahan, Bellomont left with calculated brusqueness, and on his own initiative proceeded to India to seek aid from the Mughal, Shah Jahan. He reached Surat in January 1656, but on 20 June he died, probably from heat apoplexy, at Hodal, between Agra and Delhi, where he was buried; fifteen months later his body was reburied at Agra, probably in the Roman Catholic cemetery. Anthony Wood alleged he had hoped to become grand master of the knights of Malta.

Bellomont left his family in straitened circumstances: his widow petitioned the king for a pension in the autumn of 1660 and she seems to have been aided by his old college. Of Bard's children, Charles Rupert, his son (1648–1667) and Charles II's godson, was killed fighting the

French on St Kitts; with his death the viscountcy became extinct. Frances, his eldest daughter (1646?–1708), was (*c*.1664–7) the mistress of Prince Rupert; their son, Dudley Bard (1666?–1686), was sent by Rupert to Eton College and died at the siege of Buda. Although a Catholic and Jacobite supporter, Frances later resided at the court of Hanover as a close friend of the Electress Sophia, Rupert's youngest sister.

Bellomont was more than the heavy-handed, licentious soldier depicted by Clarendon, and a picturesque, intrepid adventurer. Manucci says that he treated him like a son, and the Dutch East India Company's surgeon at Surat found him 'very well-informed, modest and courteous' (Bence-Jones, 192). A manuscript by John Hall (*c*.1660) at King's College calls him 'a man of a very personable body and of a stout and undaunted courage' (GEC, *Peerage*, 105), and even the waspish Wood, who says he always lived 'high', pronounced Bellomont 'a compact body of vanity and ambition, yet proper, robust and comely' (Wood, *Ath. Oxon.*, 4.62). BASIL MORGAN

Sources M. Bence-Jones, *The cavaliers* (1976), 185–92 · GEC, *Peerage*, new edn, vol. 2 · *GM*, 2nd ser., 7 (1837), 52–5 · N. Manucci, *Storia di Mogor*, ed. J. Irvine, 4 vols. (1907–8), 1.72–83 · P. Morrah, *Prince Rupert of the Rhine* (1976) · W. Foster, ed., *The English factories in India*, 9–10 (1915–21) · Wood, *Ath. Oxon.*, new edn, 4.66–7 · J. Adair, *Cheriton, 1644* (1973) · Venn, *Alum. Cant.*, 1/1 · W. Sterry, ed., *The Eton College register, 1441–1698* (1943) · A. A. Leigh, *King's College* (1899) · *CSP dom.*, *1660–61* · S. Porter, *Destruction in the English civil wars*, paperback (1997) · B. Whitelocke, *Memorials of English affairs*, new edn, 4 vols. (1853), vol. 1

Wealth at death financially dependent on elder brother; widow petitioned for financial assistance in 1660

Bard, Wilkie [*real name* William August Smith] (**1874–1944**), music-hall performer, was born on 19 March 1874 at 19 Alderley Street, Hulme, Manchester, son of William Herbert Smith, a bookkeeper, and his wife, Marie Stetzer. He was educated in Manchester, first worked there in a cotton spinner's warehouse, and became well known as a concert singer, performing at such local venues as the Slip Inn, the Falstaff, and Liston's Bar. He made his first professional appearance on 11 February 1895 at the Grand, Manchester, as a singer of coster songs (such as ''E ain't the bloke I took him for at all'), billed as Will Gebard (from a family name). Shortly afterwards he secured a twelve-week contract for the Moss and Thornton tour, a leading music-hall circuit.

Bard made his London début on 6 May 1895 at Collins Music-Hall, Islington—it seems he adopted his stage name of Wilkie Bard about this time. One of several reasons given is that his grotesque make-up resembled the accepted image of Shakespeare; it featured a high, bald forehead, with black spots above each eyebrow, and became so celebrated that P. G. Wodehouse, in his 1910 novel *Psmith in the City*, compared one of its female characters to him. Bard's earliest successes included 'All becos 'e's minding a 'ouse' and 'Our Dramatic Club', written by Frank Leo, who composed many of his most popular songs. His first pantomime engagement was at the Gaiety Theatre, Dublin (1899/1900), as the baron in *Little Red Riding Hood*. He soon became popular as a pantomime dame, with a distinctively mellifluous voice. He married Nellie Stratton (*c*.1875–1947), a fellow music-hall performer, in 1894 and they often appeared on stage together.

Bard formed a partnership with Will Evans, appearing in pantomime for several seasons at Drury Lane from 1908, reviving the harlequinade tradition with himself as Pantaloon and Evans as Clown. In 1912 Bard was selected to appear at the first royal command variety performance at London's Palace Theatre, performing his character study 'The Nightwatchman' but exceeding the time-limit allocated to his spot, to the consternation of the management. He recorded more than thirty songs between 1904 and 1936, including his most famous—'I want to sing in opera'—and such pantomime tongue-twisters as 'She sells sea shells on the sea shore', which established his reputation.

In 1913 Bard played the Palace Theatre, New York, but quit after a poor reception at his opening matinée. When *Variety*'s correspondent told him he shouldn't try to Americanize his act he reverted to his usual style and was an overwhelming box-office success. He could command up to £600 per week on tour in the USA and a top fee of £250 at home. According to pioneer agent George Foster, Bard 'had a grand sense of character burlesque … he always managed to make amusing observations of human eccentricities, and his method of working was all the more effective because it was quiet and never forced' (Foster, 93). The eminent music critic Neville Cardus described how Wilkie Bard, as a charwoman, came down the stage carrying a bucket of soapsuds and a cleaning cloth. On his knees he made a wide wet circle on the floor with the cloth, indicating the area to be cleaned; suddenly rising he would come before the footlights and announce by song, in a soft contralto voice, that 'I want to sing in opera', 'thus confiding in us a lofty but natural ambition' (Cardus, 29).

When music-hall waned Bard worked in newly popular revues, directing *The Whirl of the Town* at the London Palladium in 1915. In 1921 he spent most of the year touring South Africa, Australia, and New Zealand. He retired early but returned to the stage in Sir Oswald Stoll's *Veterans of Variety* at the London Coliseum in 1927, where he had been a favourite in earlier times. Two of Bard's most famous sketches, 'The Nightwatchman' and 'The Cleaner', were filmed by British Sound Film Productions in 1928 but are now believed to be lost. He also took part in Lew Lake's *Stars who Never Fail to Shine* tours from 1931 although, it seems, his mental health was beginning to decline. Bard broadcast for the BBC from its earliest days and radio producer Charles Brewer recalled how he would discuss a proposed broadcast in a quiet, dignified manner.

In 1939 Bard appeared in *Stars who Made the Holborn Empire Famous*, along with Ada Reeve, who recalled in her autobiography that he was by then a sick man. Nevertheless, he still appeared regularly in pantomime until his death on 5 May 1944 at his home, Glengarry, Trees Road, Hughenden, Buckinghamshire. His wife found him dead in an armchair after he had been listening to the nine o'clock news on radio: he had suffered a coronary thrombosis. He was buried in Highgate cemetery, Middlesex.

The *Times* obituarist recalled that 'the picture of him standing, hands folded in front of him, leaning slightly forward, with a tolerant, attentive gaze on his face under the domed bald forehead and the eyebrows painted out and replaced with the black dots', lingered vividly in the memory, as did 'the slightly muffled, fruity quality of his speech' (*The Times*). Wilkie Bard's name has entered music-hall mythology as rhyming slang: use of the Variety Artists' Federation (later part of Equity) membership card to gain performers free admittance to matinées has been referred to as 'getting in on the Wilkie'.

MICHAEL POINTON

Sources b. cert. • d. cert. • J. Parker, *Who's who in variety* (1916) • N. Cardus, *Full score* (1970) • C. Brewer, *The spice of variety* (1948) • A. Reeve, *Take it for a fact* (1954) • *The Times* (6 May 1944) • S. T. Felstead, *Stars who made the halls* (1946) • C. Pulling, *They were singing* (1952) • Green and Laurie, *Show biz from vaude to video* (1951) • H. Finck, *My melodious memories* (1937) • G. Foster, *The spice of life: sixty-five years in the glamour world* [1939] • private information (2004) • P. G. Wodehouse, *Psmith in the city* (1910) • H. C. Newton, *Idols of the halls* (1928)

Archives SOUND BBC Radio Sound Archives, 'These names made variety', 25/8/39 • BBC WAC

Likenesses portrait, 1908–9 (after poster in *Sunday Chronicle Pantomime Annual*, 1927–8), M. Pointon archive • portrait, 1909, repro. in W. David and G. Arthurs, *I can say truly rural* [1909], sheet music cover; M. Pointon archive • portrait, repro. in Felstead, *Stars who made the halls*

Bardd y Brenin. *See* Jones, Edward (1752–1824).

Barde, Walter (*fl.* **1360–1390**). *See under* Moneyers (*act.* *c.*1180–*c.*1500).

Bardelby, Robert (*d.* **1332/3**), administrator, was probably the son of Thomas, son of Walter Bardelby; his family took its name from Barlby, near Selby, in the West Riding of Yorkshire. Robert is first recorded in 1284, acting as attorney for a group of Yorkshiremen in king's bench. He may have acquired an ecclesiastical training as a means of rising in the service of the crown, for while in August 1286 Archbishop John Romanus of York described him as a clerk of legitimate birth and good character, holding no benefice in the diocese, in the same year he is also recorded as a chancery clerk, probably introduced by William Hamilton, who came from Brayton, a few miles from Barlby. In July 1291, by now a subdeacon, Bardelby was presented to his first benefice, Burghwallis, north of Doncaster. The means whereby he won promotion in chancery are usually undetectable, but his services were sufficiently valued for him to be excused attendance at the London hustings court in 1298, and an appearance before the archbishop of York in 1301, because he was engaged on the king's business. On 12 April 1302 he witnessed the charter whereby Roger (IV) Bigod, earl of Norfolk, made over nearly all his lands to Edward I, and by March 1303 he apparently stood first among the chancery clerks, after the chancellor and keeper of the rolls. He attended the Carlisle parliament of January–March 1307, and on 19 April took charge of the great seal immediately after the death of his friend the chancellor William Hamilton. Not surprisingly, he received rewards from the crown for his services, starting with the living of Sandhurst, Kent, in 1294, and culminating in the prebend of Dunnington in York Minster in October 1305. Others, too, saw him as a man worth cultivating—hence, no doubt, the yearly pension of 5 marks he came to receive from the templars.

The accession of Edward II did Bardelby's career no harm; indeed, it led to greater eminence. A feature of administrative practice during the reign is the number of occasions on which the great seal, nominally the responsibility of the chancellor, was entrusted to commissions of three or four chancery clerks. Between 12 May 1310 and 14 November 1321 Bardelby was a member of twenty-four such commissions. Twice he and colleagues had the custody of the seal for some six months, but more often they controlled its workings for only a few weeks, while on one occasion in June 1318 it was entrusted to them for just twenty-four hours. During these years Bardelby was several times named as a royal councillor; in March 1315, for instance, he was present at York for negotiations with envoys from the count of Flanders. He was a trier of petitions in parliament in 1315, 1316, and 1321, and an assessor of the fifteenth in London in 1316. A priest by 18 November 1311, he continued to add to his benefices, notably the Lincolnshire livings of Gedney and Boston (the latter in the face of some opposition) and a prebend in the collegiate church of South Malling, Sussex, all in 1311, and a prebend in the royal free chapel of Penkridge, Staffordshire, in 1314. And he added to his inheritance at and near Barlby. Perhaps he came to feel uneasy about his own acquisitiveness, for in 1316 he endowed a chantry for his soul in the London church of St Dunstan-in-the-West, Fleet Street (where he had property), and in February 1321 he founded another chantry, this time in Southwark Priory.

On 14 November 1321 Bardelby was licensed to leave court because of illness. This may have been a turning point in his career. He never had the custody of the great seal afterwards, and although he appears to have continued to act as a chancery clerk—he was present on 4 July 1325 when Henry Cliffe took oath as keeper of the chancery rolls—he was not promoted to a bishopric, unlike some of his colleagues. In August 1321 he had exchanged Dunnington for a prebend in Chichester Cathedral (perhaps Henfield), and thereafter he is increasingly to be found in the south of England, and especially Sussex, where he was several times appointed to commissions and inquests. In September 1328 he was reported to be dead, and his prebend in South Malling was given to another royal clerk. But he recovered, and even acted once more as a royal commissioner. In February 1332 he was licensed to endow Chichester Cathedral with a yearly rent of 20s. for the commemoration of his anniversary; licence was given in acknowledgement of 'laudable service in the Chancery in the reign of Edward I, Edward II and the present king, discharged at great cost to himself' (*CPR, 1330–34*, 254). Bardelby was still believed to be alive on 30 June 1332, but had probably died by 18 August 1333, when another incumbent was instituted at Gedney. As an ordained clerk he had neither wife nor children. But he attended to the interests of his nephews, acting as the guardian of one during his minority, obtaining a post in the Dublin exchequer for another. It is also possible that the Robert and Hugh Bardelby later recorded in royal service were his relations, introduced into government by him.

HENRY SUMMERSON

Sources *Chancery records* • *CIPM*, 7, no. 634 • F. H. Slingsby, ed., *Feet of fines for the county of York from 1272 to 1300*, Yorkshire Archaeological Society, 121 (1956) • M. Roper, ed., *Feet of fines for the county of York from 1300 to 1314*, Yorkshire Archaeological Society, 127 (1965) • *RotP*, 1.350, 357, 365 • F. Palgrave, ed., *The parliamentary writs and writs of military summons*, 2/3 (1834), 478–9 • H. G. Richardson and G. O. Sayles, eds., *Rotuli parliamentorum Anglie hactenus inediti, MCCLXXIX–MCCCLXXIII*, CS, 3rd ser., 51 (1935), 92 • F. W. Maitland, ed., *Records of the parliament holden at Westminster on the twenty-eighth day of February … 1305*, Rolls Series, 98 (1893) • *Fasti Angl., 1300–1541*, [York], 46 • *The register of John le Romeyn … 1286–1296*, ed. W. Brown, 1, SurtS, 123 (1913) • *The register of Thomas of Corbridge, lord archbishop of York, 1300–1304*, 1, ed. W. Brown, SurtS, 138 (1925) • *Registrum Roberti Winchelsey, Cantuariensis archiepiscopi, AD 1294–1313*, ed. R. Graham, 2 vols., CYS, 51–2 (1952–6), 53–4, 1209 • Tout, *Admin. hist.*, 6.7–10 • J. L. Grassi, 'Royal clerks from the archdiocese of York in the fourteenth century', *Northern History*, 5 (1970), 12–33 • *CPR, 1330–34*

Bardney, Richard (*fl.* 1485/6–1519), Benedictine monk and author, is probably to be identified with the *prior studentium* (the academic superior of a college or hostel) of that name recorded at Cambridge in 1485–6, and with the Richard Barney, also *prior studentium* and with the degree of BTh, whose name is entered in a copy of Raymond de Sebonde's *Theologia naturalis* (Strasbourg, 1486) with the date 1490 (Bodl. Oxf., MS Douce 158). Bardney was the author of verse lives of Robert Grosseteste and of Little St Hugh of Lincoln which in 1503 he dedicated to Bishop William Smith of Lincoln. He gave a copy to the library of St Stephen's collegiate church at Westminster, from where it passed to Sir Robert Cotton's collection, in which it constituted folios 43–69 of MS Otho C. xvi. The volume was utterly destroyed in the Ashburnham House fire of 1731, but substantial extracts from the life of Grosseteste were published in Henry Wharton's *Anglia sacra* (1691).

Wharton had a low opinion of Bardney's work; he shortened the life by weeding out what he described as 'grosser fables and inane flourishes' (Wharton, 2.xvii), and stated that he was only publishing the residue because he could find nothing better. For more than 250 years such scholars as noticed the life at all were equally dismissive; David Douglas spoke for the consensus when he described it as 'valueless'. But first J. C. Russell in 1944 and then R. W. Southern in 1986 gave cogent reasons for believing that although he contaminated it with fables Bardney had nevertheless faithfully transmitted the essentials of a much earlier source, perhaps a life of Grosseteste prepared to support efforts to secure his canonization between about 1260 and 1310. Although it is notably lacking in names and dates, his work has the particular value of providing a plausible account of Grosseteste's deeply obscure early years, with many details not found in any other source; for Southern it is 'the only substantial medieval biography of Grosseteste' (Southern, 75). Nothing certain is known of Bardney after 1503. He may have been the Richard Bardenay charged at Bishop Atwater's visitation of Bardney Abbey on 9 July 1519 with offences that included failing to get up for matins and leaving the monastery without permission. If so, he was probably dead by 12 May 1525, when his name does not appear in a list of the Bardney monks.

HENRY SUMMERSON

Sources [H. Wharton], ed., *Anglia sacra*, 2 (1691), xvii, 325–41 • Emden, *Cam.*, 36 • 'A report from the committee appointed to view the Cottonian Library', *Reports from Committees of the House of Commons*, 1 (1732), 443–536, esp. 478 • J. C. Russell, 'Richard of Bardney's account of Robert Grosseteste's early and middle life', *Medievalia et Humanistica*, 1st ser., 2 (1944), 45–54 • R. W. Southern, *Robert Grosseteste: the growth of an English mind in medieval Europe* (1986) • A. H. Thompson, ed., *Visitations in the diocese of Lincoln, 1517–1531*, 2, Lincoln RS, 35 (1944), 77–9 • R. de Sebonde, *Theologia naturalis*, 1486, Bodl. Oxf., MS Douce 158 • D. C. Douglas, *English scholars, 1660–1730*, 2nd edn (1951)

Bardolf. For this title name *see* individual entries under Bardolf; *see also* Phelip, William, Baron Bardolf (1383/4–1441).

Bardolf, Hugh (*d.* 1203), justice, was the son of Hugh Bardolf (*d.* *c.*1176), a Lincolnshire knight, and of Isabel, possibly of the Twist family of South Carlton, Lincolnshire. In 1200 he married Mabel de Limesy, daughter of Gerard de Limesy, and sister and coheir of John de Limesy (*d.* 1193), baron of Cavendish in Suffolk. Bardolf is first recorded in attendance on the royal court at Chinon on 5 April 1181, where he attested a charter as steward, a post which he retained until the end of Henry II's reign in 1189. He acted as a royal justice almost annually between *c.*1185 and 1203, more often as a justice in eyre than at Westminster; he sat as a justice following the king during John's early visits to England in 1200–01. He also acted as sheriff of Cornwall (1184–7), Wiltshire (1187–9), Somerset and Dorset (1188–9), Staffordshire, Warwickshire, and Leicestershire (1190–91), Yorkshire (1191–4), Westmorland (1191–9), Northumberland (1194–8), Cumberland (1198–9), Cornwall and Devon (1199–1200), and Nottinghamshire and Derbyshire (1200–03).

Bardolf set out with Richard I on his journey to the Holy Land and was one of Richard's sureties at Messina in November 1190, but returned to England soon afterwards, and was associated in the justiciarship with the bishops of Durham (Hugh du Puiset) and Ely (William Longchamp) while the king was on crusade. He was involved, with Walter de Coutances, in the commission that was to supplant Longchamp; accordingly, he was among those excommunicated by Longchamp, but was offered pardon if he would surrender Scarborough and his counties of Yorkshire and Westmorland. In 1193, as associate justiciar and sheriff of Yorkshire, he assisted the archbishop of York to fortify Doncaster for Richard, but refusing, as John's vassal, to besiege Tickhill, was denounced as a traitor, and on Richard's return, in March 1194, was dismissed from his Yorkshire post. He was at once, however, transferred to Northumberland, and ordered to take it over from the bishop of Durham, then, on the latter's resistance, to seize it (July 1194). At du Puiset's death, on 3 March 1195, the castles of Norham and Durham were surrendered to Bardolf, who, remaining faithful to Richard, retained his counties until John's accession in 1199. From John he received the counties of Nottingham and Derby and the custody of Tickhill Castle.

Bardolf continued to act as an itinerant justice and to sit in the royal court until his death some time before Michaelmas in 1203. He won some reputation as a legal expert, for he was one of the few justices to be mentioned by name in early texts of Glanville. He was also a financial expert, appearing from the rolls to have acted as a baron of the exchequer in all three reigns. He was escheator for the north of England, 1194–7, one of the keepers of the Jews, 1194–7, and responsible for the stannaries, 1199–1200. Bardolf held considerable property at his death, for his brother offered a £1000 fine for his inheritance; and William (III) de Briouze offered £1000 to marry his son to Hugh's widow. Hugh and his wife had no children, and Hugh's heir was his brother Robert Bardolf.

J. H. Round, *rev.* Ralph V. Turner

Sources C. Clay, 'Hugh Bardolf the justice and his family', *Lincolnshire History and Archaeology*, 1 (1961), 5–29 • R. V. Turner, *The English judiciary in the age of Glanvill and Bracton, c.1176–1239* (1985) • *Pipe rolls* • *Chancery records* (RC) • *Curia regis rolls preserved in the Public Record Office* (1922–) • D. M. Stenton, 'Development of the judiciary, 1100–1216', *Pleas before the king or his justices, 1198–1212*, ed. D. M. Stenton, 3, SeldS, 83 (1967), xlvii–ccxliv • R. W. Eyton, *Court, household, and itinerary of King Henry II* (1878) • L. Landon, *The itinerary of King Richard I*, PRSoc., new ser., 13 (1935) • A. Hughes, *List of sheriffs for England and Wales: from the earliest times to AD 1831*, PRO (1898); repr. (New York, 1963) • *Chronica magistri Rogeri de Hovedene*, ed. W. Stubbs, 4 vols., Rolls Series, 51 (1868–71)

Wealth at death fine of £1000 offered by brother on death: *Pipe rolls*, 5 John, 103

Bardolf, Thomas, fifth Baron Bardolf (1369–1408), landowner and rebel, was born at Birling, Kent, on 22 December 1369, the son of William, fourth Baron Bardolf (1349–1386), and his wife, Agnes (*d.* 1403), the daughter of Michael *Poynings, first Lord Poynings (*c.*1318–1369). His father died on 29 January 1386, and for the rest of his minority Thomas Bardolf seems to have been in the custody of his father-in-law, Ralph, Lord Cromwell, whose daughter Amice he had married by 8 July 1382. Their two daughters were both born at Cromwell's castle of Tattershall, Lincolnshire, in 1389 and 1390 respectively. In the latter year Thomas Bardolf made proof of age and had livery of his father's lands, which were centred upon Wormegay in Norfolk; however, these were much diminished by his mother's dower, and by joint settlements which gave her a life interest in other estates. On 7 September 1391 he was called to parliament for the first time, and thereafter received regular summonses. But he seems to have played little part in public affairs in England, and was appointed to very few commissions. Described by Walsingham as 'a man vigorous in arms, and in bodily shape and stature second to none in the realm' (*Johannis de Trokelowe*, 402), he preferred to occupy himself overseas. In May 1392 he was licensed to go abroad. He accompanied Richard II's expedition to Ireland of 1394–5. In 1396 he was licensed to travel abroad again, and in 1397 he went overseas on the king's service, presumably to Gascony. In 1399 he once more went with Richard II to Ireland, and was robbed in Wales on his return.

Initially Bardolf appears to have accepted the usurpation of Henry IV, and served in the expedition of 1400 to Scotland. For his part, Henry seems to have tried to gain Bardolf's support, appointing him to commissions in Norfolk, and summoning him to parliaments and councils. On 24 May 1400 he renewed for Bardolf the grant of 100 marks per annum made in 1319 by Edward II to Bardolf's great-grandfather Sir Roger Damory. But ultimately Bardolf was not to be won over to the Lancastrian cause. He may have retained Ricardian sympathies. The effect of his annuity was probably vitiated by the difficulties he experienced in obtaining his money, requiring repeated instructions to the exchequer and reissues of tallies. He is unlikely to have viewed with equanimity the new regime's use of the duchy of Lancaster estates in East Anglia to build up the crown's position there at the expense of local magnates like himself. And he evidently came under the influence of the earl of Northumberland. There may have been a connection between the Percys and the Bardolfs dating from the mid-fourteenth century, when Thomas Percy was bishop of Norwich—at his death in 1369 Bishop Percy bequeathed a cup engraved with the Bardolf arms. But the links later became closer; when Bardolf's mother died, on 12 June 1403, she appointed Northumberland and her son to be overseers of her will.

There is no evidence that Bardolf took part in the Percy revolt of 1403, but in 1405 he committed himself to treasonable courses. He opposed royal policy in councils held at London and St Albans, and one chronicle even makes him the instigator of the scheme of February that year for a tripartite division of England between Northumberland, Owain Glyn Dŵr, and Edmund (IV) Mortimer. When in May Henry IV summoned him to campaign in Wales, Bardolf slipped away secretly and made his way north, to join Northumberland. Like the earl, he failed to support Archbishop Scrope's rising, and, following its defeat, the two men fled to Scotland. When Bardolf was formally declared a traitor in the parliament of December 1406, it was claimed that it was on his advice that the earl of Northumberland had entered into treasonous negotiations with the Scots and French. By then, however, the Scots had proved untrustworthy allies, and in the summer of 1406, after receiving warning of a conspiracy to hand them over to Henry IV, Bardolf and Northumberland fled to Wales. There they had the support of Glyn Dŵr, and were able to raise a small force, but this was defeated by Edward Charlton, and they moved on again, to France and the Low Countries. Raising money by pawning their jewels, they visited Paris, but their hopes of French support were dashed by the opposition of the duke of Orléans, and they made their way to Bruges. By the end of 1407 they were back in Scotland.

According to John Hardyng, Bardolf and Northumberland were now 'with all thair hertes fayne Thaym to submytte unto the kynge agayne' (BL, MS Lansdowne 204, fol. 207*v*). But the conciliatory mood passed, and early in 1408 they invaded England with such men as they could gather, hoping to exploit the prevailing discontent with King Henry's government to arouse a rebellion. The

Scottish nobles, according to one account, waved them off with the words 'Go ahead, you have England with you' (*Eulogium historiarum*, 3.411). Words and events flattered to deceive. At first the invaders met with no resistance. When they reached Thirsk they presented themselves as liberators, and called upon those who desired freedom from oppressive government to join them. Some men did enlist, and thus reinforced Bardolf and Northumberland resumed their advance. But they found their way blocked by the sheriff of Yorkshire, Sir Thomas Rokeby, at the head of the county levies, and were finally brought to battle on 19 February on Bramham Moor, near Tadcaster, where their forces were routed. Northumberland was killed, and Bardolf, severely wounded, was captured, and died later that day. Bardolf's head was sent to Lincoln, while his quarters were displayed in London, York, Bishop's Lynn, and Shrewsbury. On 13 April 1408 his remains were delivered to his widow for burial. Bardolf's heirs were his two daughters, Anne, who married successively Sir William Clifford and Reginald, Lord Cobham, and Joan, who married Sir William *Phelip, who later styled himself Lord Bardolf. Many of their father's estates were at first distributed among the king's supporters, but most of them were later recovered. Bardolf's widow, secured in her dower, lived until 1 July 1421.

HENRY SUMMERSON

Sources Chancery, treaty rolls, PRO, C 76/76, 81, 82 • Exchequer, treasury of receipt, issue rolls, PRO, E 403/571, 578 • Exchequer, treasury of receipt, warrants for issues, PRO, E 404/16. 17 • *Chancery records* • GEC, *Peerage*, new edn, 1.419–20 • W. Dugdale, *The baronage of England*, 2 vols. (1675–6), vol. 1, pp. 682–3 • N. H. Nicolas, ed., *Proceedings and ordinances of the privy council of England*, 7 vols., RC, 26 (1834–7), vol. 1 • *RotP*, vol. 3 • *CIPM*, 16–19 • *Reports … touching the dignity of a peer of the realm*, House of Lords, 4 (1829) • John Hardyng's chronicle, BL, Lansdowne MS 204 • *The chronicle of John Hardyng*, ed. H. Ellis (1812) • *The chronicle of Adam Usk, 1377–1421*, ed. and trans. C. Given-Wilson, OMT (1997) • J. A. Giles, ed., *Incerti scriptoris chronicon Angliae de regnis trium regum Lancastrensium* (1848) • *Thomae Walsingham, quondam monachi S. Albani, historia Anglicana*, ed. H. T. Riley, 2 vols., pt 1 of *Chronica monasterii S. Albani*, Rolls Series, 28 (1863–4), vol. 2 • G. B. Stow, ed., *Historia vitae et regni Ricardi Secundi* (1977) • F. S. Haydon, ed., *Eulogium historiarum sive temporis*, 3 vols., Rolls Series, 9 (1858), vol. 3 • *Johannis de Trokelowe et Henrici de Blaneforde … chronica et annales*, ed. H. T. Riley, pt 3 of *Chronica monasterii S. Albani*, Rolls Series, 28 (1866) [Walsingham] • T. Walsingham, *The St Albans chronicle, 1406–1420*, ed. V. H. Galbraith (1937) • H. Castor, 'The duchy of Lancaster and the rule of East Anglia, 1399–1440: a prologue to the Paston letters', *Crown, government, and people in the fifteenth century*, ed. R. E. Archer (1995), 53–78

Bardolf, William (*b.* in or before **1206**, *d.* **1275/6**), baron, was the son and heir of Doun Bardolf of Shelford, Nottinghamshire, and Beatrice, daughter and heir of William de Warenne of Wormegay, Norfolk. He was a middle-ranking baron with a long career in royal service, who supported the baronial reformers in 1258, but took the side of the king when civil war broke out in 1264.

After the death of Doun in 1205, and of her second husband, Ralph (*c*.1210), Beatrice married Hubert de Burgh, earl of Kent, who became guardian of her son William Bardolf following her own death in 1214. Although Bardolf had livery of his inheritance in 1215, his stepfather contrived to keep control of the honour of Wormegay until his death in 1243. Bardolf was already married to Nichola, whose parentage is unknown, when he attended Henry III on his visit to France in 1230. He commanded the expedition which captured William de Marisco and other outlaws on Lundy island in 1242, served the king in Scotland and Wales in 1244, and accompanied Queen Eleanor to France in 1254. His rewards included grants of free warren, fairs and markets in his manors, and favourable terms for the payment of his debts to the king.

In the political crisis of 1258, however, Bardolf was one of the twelve chosen by the barons to reform the realm, and on 22 June he was appointed constable of Nottingham Castle under the terms of the provisions of Oxford. By March 1259 he had been elected to the parliamentary committee of twelve, and in 1261 he used his local influence to obstruct the work of the king's sheriff in Norfolk. He was one of the Montfortians who in December 1263 agreed to the arbitration of Louis IX on the quarrel with the king, but after the rebels were defeated at Northampton in April 1264 he joined the king and was captured at the battle of Lewes that May. He received only modest grants of the lands of rebels after the battle of Evesham in August 1265. When he died, shortly before 5 January 1276, he was succeeded by his son, also William Bardolf.

CLIVE H. KNOWLES

Sources *Chancery records* • R. F. Treharne, *The baronial plan of reform, 1258–1263* (1932) • R. F. Treharne and I. J. Sanders, eds., *Documents of the baronial movement of reform and rebellion, 1258–1267* (1973) • *Ann. mon.*, 4.146 • H. R. Luard, ed., *Flores historiarum*, 3 vols., Rolls Series, 95 (1890), vol. 2, p. 496 • I. J. Sanders, *English baronies: a study of their origin and descent, 1086–1327* (1960)

Wealth at death landed wealth: *CIPM*, 2, no. 190

Bardsley, Cuthbert Killick Norman (1907–1991), bishop of Coventry, was born on 28 March 1907 at Ulverston rectory, Ulverston, Lancashire, the youngest of the six children of the Revd Canon Norman Joseph Udall Bardsley (1869–1928), rector of Ulverston, and from 1907 to 1928 vicar of Lancaster, and his wife, Mabel Annie (1872–1939), daughter of William Killick, a Liverpool merchant. His father was from a line of twenty-eight clergy, including two bishops. His education at Summerfields preparatory school, Oxford, Eton College, and New College, Oxford (from where he graduated with a fourth-class degree in politics, philosophy, and economics in 1929), was unremarkable. But from his family heritage he received his large frame, large heart, immense enthusiasm; and, underlyingly, his acute instinct for the right creative spiritual initiative. It was this instinct which drew him at university to join Frank Buchman's Oxford Group, then to work full time with it (from 1935 to 1939), but later also to leave it. It also attracted him to a curacy with Tubby Clayton (Toc H), which first linked him with people at the workplace (1932–4).

The same instinct empowered Bardsley when he became rector of Woolwich on the eve of the blitz. There (1940–44) and also when he was summoned to be provost of Southwark (1944–7), all his gifts came into play, of cherishing people and convincing them that they mattered infinitely, of selecting good colleagues, forming a central worshipping group on which he could draw, preaching memorably with alliterative points and stories punched home with passion, producing grand central occasions at which he enjoyed performing, and getting alongside people in shelters or rubble as the bombs rained down, or supremely in factories where they worked. The cathedral expanded his mission. The central occasions were now lectures or concerts, or large-scale diocesan events. The outreach included nearby office workers. Post-war visits to the armed services in Europe, at the archbishop of Canterbury's instigation, to raise morale by rekindling faith, led to the summons to leave his vibrant cathedral to become suffragan bishop of Croydon (1947–56) and of the forces, to repeat and develop his success. He conveyed spiritual reality, combining evangelical and catholic, stressing sacraments *and* Bible, and this worked.

Bardsley was enthroned in Coventry in the ruins of the old cathedral in May 1956. He soon set about preparing for the new, 'a consecrated people for a consecrated Cathedral' (a phrase from one of the new cathedral team he boldly appointed in 1958). He visited every deanery and clergyman, orchestrated diocesan-wide prayer and study groups, led a mission, speaking to 20,000 people, and finally after a Cross of Nails from the ruins had been carried from parish to parish, bore it up to the new high altar on the eve of the consecration. The central point of his whole life and work was the consecration of Coventry's renewed cathedral, on 25 May 1962, in the presence of the queen and representatives of many nations. As Bardsley's towering figure, in a brilliant yellow cope and mitre, moved purposefully from one focal point to another, calling upon the spirit in his huge voice, 'Be here! Be here!', he caught the imagination of a widespread television audience.

In the following years Bardsley never lost this creative instinct. People might criticize his preaching for being stronger in style than in content, and some found his fervour uncongenial. His enthusiasm sometimes clouded his judgement. His sudden impulses tested his colleagues. But at the heart of his zest for dramatic occasions there was an utterly genuine humility, a depth of prayer and holiness. He was universally loved (people never forgot his parish visits). And these qualities, combined with that brilliant flair for spotting growth points, gave him his greatness.

Bardsley was involved in founding the University of Warwick, to which he gave its name. He inaugurated the Arthur Rank Centre, a Christian presence at the Royal Agricultural Show. He encouraged industrial mission. His influence was felt in many places, among business people, farmers, or as president of Coventry City Football Club. He engaged in many other initiatives, including the Lee Abbey movement, the ministry of healing, especially at Burrswood, the Church of England Men's Society, and countless missions. He married surprisingly and quite late (on 1 August 1972) but intensely happily Ellen Edith Mitchell (*b.* 1910), a former secretary and Warwickshire county councillor, a long-standing friend of his sister, and a pillar of the diocese.

Bardsley's retirement as bishop of Coventry in 1976 was the end not only of a great episcopate but of an era. Clergy were invited to come and choose a book from his library and one of the pictures painted by him. These latter were surely symbols of that phenomenal presence, which many years later still made its impress felt on the diocese, and they conveyed something of his essence. Lashings of paint and vibrant colour depicted scenes from a larger than life world, strong in the brush strokes, lacking in detail and complexity, but forever fresh and vivid. After a long, active retirement Bardsley died of cancer at his home, Grey Walls, Berkeley Road, Cirencester, Gloucestershire, on 9 January 1991. He was survived by his wife. His ashes were, fittingly, interred behind the high altar of Coventry Cathedral. SIMON BARRINGTON-WARD

Sources D. Coggan, *Cuthbert Bardsley: bishop, evangelist, pastor* (1989) · C. Bardsley, *Sundry times, sundry places* (1962) · C. Bardsley and W. Purcell, *Him we declare* (1963) · *The Times* (11 Jan 1991) · *The Independent* (11 Jan 1991) · *The Independent* (28 Jan 1991) · *WWW*, 1991–5 · personal knowledge (2004) · private information (2004)
Archives SOUND BL NSA, performance recordings
Likenesses photograph, repro. in *The Times* · photograph, repro. in *The Independent* (11 Jan 1991) · photographs, repro. in Coggan, *Cuthbert Bardsley*
Wealth at death £193,171: probate, 30 April 1991, *CGPLA Eng. & Wales*

Bardsley, Sir James Lomax (1801–1876), physician, the son of Edward and Elizabeth Bardsley, was born at George Street, Nottingham, on 7 July 1801. He studied medicine in Glasgow and Edinburgh, and at St Bartholomew's Hospital, London, where he was taught by the surgeon John Abernethy, who became a firm friend. He also spent some months studying in Paris. Bardsley graduated MD (Edinburgh) in 1823 with a thesis on rabies. Later that year he was elected honorary physician to the Manchester Royal Infirmary, following the resignation of his uncle, Samuel Argent *Bardsley (1764–1850), who had been honorary physician there since 1790.

James Lomax Bardsley, then only twenty-two years old, became the youngest man ever appointed to the honorary staff of the Manchester Royal Infirmary. From 1824 he became associated with Thomas Turner, who established the Pine Street school of medicine in Manchester. He lectured there on the principles and practice of physic, materia medica, and medical botany. These lectures, together with his *Hospital Facts and Observations* (1830), demonstrated the breadth of Bardsley's professional expertise and sound common sense. He also wrote articles on diabetes and hydrophobia for the *Cyclopaedia of Practical Medicine* (1833).

Bardsley was essentially a practical man concerned particularly to advance the professional standing of rank-and-file doctors. He was active in establishing the Provincial Medical and Surgical Association (PMSA) in 1832, and five years later he gave a 'Retrospective address' at its annual meeting in Cheltenham. He remained committed throughout his life to the PMSA, which later became the British Medical Association. He left a legacy of £500 to its

Sir James Lomax Bardsley (1801–1876), by unknown engraver (after D. Fabronius)

benevolent fund. He was president of the Manchester Medical Society in 1838, and from 1845 until 1848. He was also president of the Medico-Ethical Association in 1850, and president of the Manchester Institute for Diseases of the Ear.

In 1831 Bardsley married Elizabeth Shuttleworth, widow of R. H. Shuttleworth. Although he retained consulting rooms in his house in Chatham Street, which he had taken over from his uncle, the couple went to live in a large house at Greenheys, Manchester.

By the 1840s Bardsley had built up a large professional practice. In 1843 he resigned as honorary physician to the infirmary and was appointed consulting physician. He was deputy lieutenant for Lancashire and a justice of the peace. In 1853 his considerable reputation was recognized by the conferment of a knighthood. Bardsley was the first Manchester physician to receive such an honour.

Bardsley suffered from heart disease in the later years of his life, and he gradually reduced his professional work. He died on 10 July 1876 at his house, The Orchards, Greenheys, Manchester. STELLA BUTLER

Sources E. M. Brockbank, *Sketches of the lives and work of the honorary medical staff of the Manchester Infirmary: from its foundation in 1752 to 1830* (1904), 262–7 • *The Lancet* (22 July 1876), 137 • *BMJ* (22 July 1876), 130 • J. T. Slugg, *Reminiscences of Manchester 50 years ago* (1881) • *IGI* • *BMJ* (7 Oct 1876), 475

Archives JRL, Manchester collection

Likenesses E. Edwards, photograph, 1868, Wellcome L. • lithograph (after D. Fabronius), NPG [*see illus.*] • photograph, repro. in Brockbank, *Honorary staff of the Manchester Infirmary*

Wealth at death under £60,000: probate, 8 Aug 1876, *CGPLA Eng. & Wales*

Bardsley, John Wareing (1835–1904), bishop of Carlisle, was born at Keighley, Yorkshire, on 29 March 1835, the eldest son of the Revd James Bardsley (1805–1886) and Sarah Wareing. He had six brothers, all of whom were ordained. He was educated at Burnley and Manchester grammar schools, and entered Trinity College, Dublin, where he graduated BA in 1859 and MA in 1865. He was awarded a Lambeth DD in 1887. On 24 April 1862 he married Elizabeth (*b.* 1833), daughter of the Revd Benjamin Powell of Wigan; they had a family of two sons and three daughters.

Bardsley was ordained deacon in 1859 and priest in 1860. He was curate successively of St Anne's, Sale (1859–60), and of St Luke's, Liverpool (1860–61), before becoming the perpetual curate of St John's, Bootle (1864–71). Between 1861 and 1864 he was secretary of the Islington Protestant Institute, where he gained popularity as a lecturer and preacher. From 1871 to 1887 he was the perpetual curate of St Saviour's, Faulkner Square, Liverpool, and on J. C. Ryle's appointment as bishop of Liverpool, Bardsley became his domestic chaplain and archdeacon of Warrington. In 1886 he was offered, but refused, the living of Islington parish church, and became instead archdeacon of Liverpool. A popular archdeacon, he became known as an industrious organizer and a fluent preacher.

In 1887 Bardsley became bishop of Sodor and Man, where he developed the theological college. It had been re-established by his predecessor in 1878, and in 1889 Bardsley transferred it to Bishopscourt as Bishop Wilson's Theological School (closed in 1943). In 1892 he was translated to Carlisle, and in his enthronement sermon made clear his intention of not being the bishop of a party, and of being interested in mission rather than controversy. In the following year he formed a sustentation fund for the poor incumbents of the diocese and a retirement pension fund for older clergy. As a bishop he won a reputation as 'a firm administrator, a wise counsellor and above all, a faithful friend' (*Church and People*, 16, 1904–5, 151) and was much respected by his clergy. Bardsley was a lifelong total abstainer and his simplicity was shown in his use of 'Carlisle' and not 'Carliol' in his episcopal signature. Although a moderate evangelical himself, he was tolerant of Anglo-Catholic practice. He travelled in the Middle East, particularly to the Holy Land, and when in Egypt in 1898 had an attack of food poisoning from which he never fully recovered. He died of heart failure at his episcopal residence, Rose Castle, outside Carlisle, on 14 September 1904, and was buried at Raughton Head. From a memorial fund a monument was placed in Carlisle Cathedral and £1300 given to the Bishop Bardsley Memorial Clergy Pension Fund. A. F. MUNDEN

Sources *DNB* • C. M. L. Bouch, *Prelates and people of the lake counties: a history of the diocese of Carlisle, 1133–1933* (1948), 447–9 • *The Times* (15 Sept 1904) • *The Times* (19 Sept 1904) • *Liverpool Review* (27 Aug 1887) • *Carlisle Journal* (26 April 1892) • *Carlisle Journal* (16 Sept 1904)

Likenesses Bassano, photographs, 1897, NPG • photograph, NPG • portrait, Rose Castle, near Carlisle

Wealth at death £12,298 18*s*. 8*d*.: probate, 17 Oct 1904, *CGPLA Eng. & Wales*

Bardsley, Samuel Argent (1764–1850), physician, the son of James Bardsley and his wife, Felicia Stephana Browne, was born at Kelvedon, Essex, on 27 April 1764. In 1778 he entered into an apprenticeship with Benjamin Maddock, a surgeon apothecary of Nottingham. After completing the apprenticeship he studied medicine at London, Edinburgh, and Leiden, where he was a student from 1786 to 1789. He graduated MD and then practised for a short time at Doncaster, before moving to the Manchester Royal Infirmary in 1790 as honorary physician. His election to this post followed the introduction of new rules which enlarged the medical staff of the hospital.

Through his work at the infirmary, particularly with home patients, Bardsley became active in the 1790s in campaigns for the containment and treatment of fever. As an infirmary physician he became a member of the board of health established in 1795, and in the following year he published a paper outlining his concerns for the health of children employed in cotton mills. For the children, many of whom worked long hours, Bardsley advocated the benefits of cleanliness and ventilation, and in 1801 the board of health published his *Advice to the Poor*, which again stressed the value of cleanliness and fresh air. In 1807 Bardsley published *Medical Reports of Cases and Experiments*, which contained his observations on diabetes, rheumatism, and hydrophobia.

Bardsley played an active role in the Manchester Literary and Philosophical Society, acting as secretary from 1793 to 1796 and vice-president from 1797 to 1808. To this society he contributed the papers 'Party prejudice' (1798) and 'The use and abuse of popular sports and exercises' (1803). He later became involved in the Royal Institution (established 1816), attending many of the meetings and lectures even after his retirement from practice.

In August 1823 Bardsley wrote to the infirmary to resign his appointment as honorary physician, and in the same letter he recommended his nephew, James Lomax *Bardsley (1801–1876), as his successor; the latter was duly elected. After his resignation Samuel Bardsley continued to maintain an active interest in the affairs of the hospital. In 1827 he successfully opposed a proposal to increase the number of honorary infirmary posts. Two years later he became physician-extraordinary, a position he retained until his death.

Until 1827 Bardsley continued to practise from his rooms in Chatham Street, Manchester, where he had lived since 1794. He then gave up his rooms to his nephew and moved locally to a house at Ardwick Green. Bardsley died on 29 May 1850 at Fairlight, near Hastings, while on a visit to a friend. He was buried at St Saviour's Church, Upper Brook Street, Manchester. STELLA BUTLER

Sources E. M. Brockbank, *Sketches of the lives and work of the honorary medical staff of the Manchester Infirmary: from its foundation in 1752 to 1830* (1904), 163–9 • F. Renaud, *A short history of the rise and progress of the Manchester Royal Infirmary from the year 1752 to 1877* (1898) • R. A. Smith, *A century of science in Manchester* (1883) • J. V. Pickstone, *Medicine and industrial society* (1985), 50–51 • *Provincial Medical and Surgical Journal*, 14 (1850), 364 • P. J. Wallis and R. V. Wallis, *Eighteenth century medics*, 2nd edn (1988) • *IGI*

Archives JRL, Manchester collection

Likenesses J. Thomson, stipple, pubd 1848 (after C. A. Duval), NPG • engraving (after du Val), repro. in Brockbank, *Honorary staff of the Manchester Royal Infirmary*

Bardwell, Thomas (1704–1767), painter and writer, lived most of his life in East Anglia and was probably born there. Talley gives three possible ancestral sources: he was probably connected to the Bardwells associated with Woodton Hall in Norfolk, but there are also claims for the Bardwells of Southwold in Suffolk; there is a possibility that his parents were James Bardwell and Dorothy Hacon, who married at Ditchingham, Norfolk, on 26 November 1702 (Talley, 93–5).

Bardwell started in the 1720s as a decorative painter in Norfolk, and by 1732 had a thriving business in Bungay, employing at least one apprentice. In 1738 he handed over the decorative painting to his younger brother, Robert, in order to develop his career as a portraitist in oils. His first known dated painting is a conversation piece from 1736, the *Brewster Family* (Talley, no. 114, 15d). Thereafter he established a good local clientele and may also have worked in London; in 1740–41 he produced the portraits *John Campbell, Duke of Argyll*, and *David Garrick*, newly acclaimed as Richard III at Goodman's Fields (respectively NPG and Russell-Cotes Art Gallery, Bournemouth). In 1752 he journeyed to Scotland, via Yorkshire, painting a number of portraits and some decorative work. He was back in the south by the end of 1753 and from 1759 to the end of his life thrived as a portraitist in Norwich.

Bardwell was probably self-taught as an artist, though Talley speculates whether he might have come into contact with the Norfolk portraitists D. Heins and Thomas Page, and the London painters J.-B. Van Loo and Joseph Van Aken. Stylistically his work is in the manner of Thomas Hudson, London's most successful portraitist during the 1740s, but there are also compositional references to Van Dyck. In addition, many sitters wear the shiny 'Van Dyck' costume which was fashionable for portraiture at the time. Formats range from portrait busts to life-size full lengths. A notebook containing drawings after finished portraits has been confidently attributed to Bardwell by Ellen Miles.

By the early nineteenth century Bardwell was remembered more as a copyist of paintings than as a portraitist (*Dictionary of National Biography*, after Edwards), and he might be little known as a painter, had it not been for his book, *The Practice of Painting and Perspective Made Easy*. Published in London in 1756 after a royal licence, it was dedicated to the earl of Rochford, whose *Portrait with Horse and Groom* he had painted in 1741 (Brodick Castle, Arran). 'the Works of *Van Dyck* and *Rembrandt* are the surest Guides to Nature', wrote Bardwell in the introduction, while describing how the book arose from a private attempt to recapture the lost art of great colouring. 'It is out of these most excellent Masters, that I have established my Method: … From them I have learned the Virgin Teints, and finishing Secrets; tho' I have always applied them to practice from Nature.' He drew on many earlier authors, principally the French theorists Roger de Piles and C.-A. Du Fresnoy, but for all that it is an original thesis: the practical instructions, though presented in a traditional format, resulted from genuine study of seventeenth-century paintings in East Anglian collections, combining what he believed to be their technique with his own experience as a painter. Talley and Groen, and White, have established through analysis that he applied most of the methods to his own work. Despite a disastrous contemporary review, the book went into two pirated editions in 1795 and 1840. Edwards noted its impact on youthful painters in its day, though he doubted the validity of the section on perspective.

Bardwell died a widower on 9 September 1767 and was buried on 11 September in the church of St Mary at Bungay. Most of his paintings remain in private collections. Public collections not cited above include the Castle Museum, Norwich; the Ashmolean Museum, Oxford; and the Laing Art Gallery, Newcastle upon Tyne.

RICA JONES

Sources M. Kirby Talley, 'Thomas Bardwell of Bungay, artist and author, 1704–1767, with a checklist of works', *Walpole Society*, 46 (1976–8), 91–163 • M. Kirby Talley and K. Groen, 'Thomas Bardwell and his practice of painting: a comparative investigation between described and actual painting technique', *Studies in Conservation*, 20 (1975), 44–108 • R. White, 'An examination of Thomas Bardwell's portraits—the media', *Studies in Conservation*, 20 (1975), 109–13 • E. G. Miles, 'A notebook of portrait compositions by Thomas Bardwell', *Walpole Society*, 53 (1987), 181–92 • E. Edwards, *Anecdotes of painters* (1808); facs. edn (1970), 6–7 • Waterhouse, *18c painters*, 36–7 • Bénézit, *Dict.* • H. Belsey, 'Bardwell, Thomas', *The dictionary of art*, ed. J. Turner (1996) • *DNB* • parish register, Bungay, St Mary, Norfolk [burial]

Likenesses T. Bardwell, self-portrait, oils, 1765, The Guildhall, Thetford; repro. in Kirby Talley, 'Thomas Bardwell of Bungay, artist and author, 1704–1767', pl. 16B

Bareau, Paul Louis Jean (1901–2000), journalist, was born on 27 April 1901 in Antwerp, Belgium, the only son of Louis Bareau (*d.* 1925), commodity trader, and Elisa van Caneghem (*d.* 1909). His father dealt in exports from the Belgian Congo. Paul, who had a sister, was educated at the Athénée, Antwerp, until 1914. When Germany invaded Belgium at the start of the First World War, the family moved to London. Intensive English lessons allowed Paul to complete his schooling at Dulwich College and graduate from the London School of Economics (LSE) in 1925 with a bachelor of commerce degree. As an amateur boxer he won public school and university championships.

Bareau began his career in financial journalism in 1926 on the staff of *The Statist*, a business-oriented weekly, published in London since 1873. After three years he switched to the daily *Financial News* and formed a good relationship with its editor, Oscar Hobson (1886–1961). The financial press in the 1920s was growing in status and ambition; Bareau belonged to the new breed of columnists who could broaden coverage beyond straightforward market reporting to more general economic analysis. When Hobson moved to the *News Chronicle* as City editor in 1933, Bareau soon followed and became his deputy. In working for the last Liberal daily newspaper in London, he was faithful to his own political principles. He divorced his first wife, Kathleen Doreen Pauling, and married Katharine Dorothy Gibson (*b.* 1907/8), known as Kitty, on 15 September 1934; by 1942 they had two sons and two daughters.

The economic turmoil of the 1930s profoundly influenced Bareau's thinking. It did not turn him against free-market capitalism; on the contrary, he saw government intervention as an impediment to the revival of international trade and traced the vicious circle of protection, exchange controls, and competitive devaluation to the suspension of US dollar convertibility in 1933. His interest always focused especially on international monetary issues.

From 1944 to 1947 Bareau served as press officer of the British treasury delegation in Washington. He accompanied Lord Keynes to the Bretton Woods conference in July 1944 and the meeting of the governors of the International Monetary Fund in March 1946. He appraised the Bretton Woods system of fixed exchange parities with a margin of flexibility as a shining success: its breakdown after twenty-five years was attributable more to unwise national policies than to inherent defects.

When Bareau returned to the *News Chronicle* in 1947, he found his reporters spending less time with bankers and brokers and rather more with civil servants. Along with Harold Wincott (1906–1969) of the *Investor's Chronicle*, he argued vigorously against the Attlee government's tight regulation of the economy, explaining how the 'cheap money' policies of Hugh Dalton would stoke inflation. The LSE engaged him as lecturer on comparative banking (1947–51). In 1953, when Hobson retired, Bareau became the *News Chronicle* City editor. The interventionist drift of post-war economic orthodoxy incurred his scorn, and he joined the new free-market think-tank the Institute of Economic Affairs, which in 1958 published *The Future of the Sterling System*, his call for the abolition of exchange controls. He was long an advocate of British membership of the European Economic Community.

Bareau left the *News Chronicle* in 1958—it ceased publication in 1960—but continued to supply quantities of copy for *The Banker*, the *Daily Mirror*, *The Economist*, and other periodicals. BBC radio used him as an economics commentator. If his views were unchanged, he did not scruple to recycle old material. A sociable man, with a round face yet sharp features, he found relaxation at the piano. After 1961 he edited *The Statist*, swelling its circulation from 2000 to 20,000. Even so, it could not compete with *The Economist*; the International Publishing Corporation closed it down in 1967, but retained Bareau as an adviser to Mirror group newspapers. He was also employed part-time by Barclays Bank group, a life assurance institution, a building society, and two investment trusts. Well into his eighties he wrote occasional articles and participated in conferences and seminars, sometimes giving his affiliation as 'University of Fleet Street'.

In the 1960s Bareau criticized the pursuit of economic growth by means of fiscal and monetary policies: what was needed were supply-side reforms to raise productivity. British governments suffered from a pathological fear of rising unemployment, which led them to shield workers from the consequences of undeserved pay increases. He was appointed OBE in 1971 but despaired of the Heath government when it reflated in 1972–3. Though monetarism struck him as a naïve oversimplification, the basic thrust of Thatcherism naturally earned his approval. He remained troubled by freely floating exchange rates, however, and urged a return to some form of gold standard: if given unrestricted power to issue paper money, governments were sure to abuse it.

Paul Bareau lived long enough to see a general return to the kind of free-market economics that he had consistently championed. He died, aged ninety-eight, of bronchopneumonia at a care home, Crondall Lodge, Church Street, Crondall, Hampshire, on 18 March 2000. His second wife predeceased him. JASON TOMES

Sources *The Times* (31 March 2000) • *Daily Telegraph* (10 April 2000) • *Financial Times* (1 April 2000) • P. Bareau, *The disorder in world money: from Bretton Woods to SDRs* (1981) • R. Harris and A. Seldon, *Not from benevolence ... twenty years of economic dissent* (1977) • 'When money makes news and news makes money', *The Economist* (26 Dec 1987) • S. E. Koss, *The rise and fall of the political press in Britain*, 2 (1984) • m. cert. [Katharine Gibson] • d. cert. • P. Ellis and D. Williamson, eds., *Debrett's distinguished people of today*, 3rd edn (1990)
Likenesses photograph, repro. in *The Times* • photograph, repro. in *Daily Telegraph*

Barenger, James (1780–1831), animal painter, was born on 25 December 1780, the son of James Barenger (1745–1813) of Kentish Town, London, a painter and glazier who exhibited a number of watercolour drawings of insects at the Royal Academy (1793–9). It is likely that Barenger trained under his father; he may also have received instruction from his uncle M. S. Barenger, an engraver, William Woollett (an uncle on his mother's side), and Benjamin Thomas Pouncey, another relative. In 1807, at the age of twenty-seven, Barenger exhibited his first pictures at the Royal Academy: *Sheep from Nature* and *Famous Setter*, when he gave his address as Kentish Town. By 1812 he had moved to Camden Town.

Barenger gained a reputation as a painter of racehorses, deer, and dogs, as well as sporting scenes. He exhibited at the Royal Academy from 1807 until his death in 1831 and occasionally showed at the British Institution. Among his numerous patrons was the earl of Derby for whom he painted *Jonathan Griffin, Huntsman to the Earl of Derby's Staghounds* (1813; Tate collection), engraved by R. Woodman and published in 1823 under the title of *The Earl of Derby's Staghounds* with the names of the principal sitters lettered below. In 1819 Barenger painted for the earl of Derby *Jonathan Griffin, Huntsman of the Earl of Derby's Staghounds, on Spanker* (Paul Mellon collection, Virginia Museum of Fine Arts, Richmond, USA), which was also engraved. Other patrons included the duke of Grafton, the marquess of Londonderry, and the bloodstock auctioneer Richard Tattersall (1785–1859). From 1814 Barenger was said to be living near Tattersalls at Hyde Park Corner, and from 1815 onwards all his paintings were shown at Tattersalls. His works were popular with publishers of sporting literature. The eighth volume of *British Field Sports*, by William Henry Scott (1818), contains seventeen illustrations of his sporting subjects. Thomas McLean's *The Sporting Repository* (1822) includes five plates after Barenger, and *Annals of Sporting by Caleb Quizem, Esq. and his Various Correspondents* (1824) reproduces two engravings from his pictures by his uncle S. M. Barenger: *Topthorn, a Celebrated Hunter* (1824) and *Marengo, a White Charger* (of the horse that belonged to Napoleon).

Barenger's animal paintings included prize cattle such as *Durham Twin Steers* engraved by Charles Turner in 1817, and *The Famous Lincolnshire Ox* engraved in 1823. In *Evans and Ruffy's Farmers Journal* of 1811, Barenger was described as 'a well-established sporting and animal painter' and the review of the Smithfield show in 1811 recorded that 'Mr. James Barenger the artist exhibited most admirable portraits of a horse and a dog belonging to Mr Westcar' (*Evans and Ruffy's Farmers Journal*, 1811). Many of Barenger's works were engraved in a large size, such as the companion prints *Pheasants* and *British Feathered Game* (each 17½ x 14 in.) engraved by Charles Turner and published by Ackermann in 1810. Within the genre of animal painting, Barenger's subject range was wide, encompassing hunt scenes, horses, dogs, cattle, and game birds—one of his best-known works in this last category being a life-size canvas of a cockfight (30 x 25 in.). He apparently bred pointers and his portrait *Dol*, engraved by John Scott and reproduced in the *Sporting Magazine* (1826), is said to have been one of his own dogs. His own involvement in the sporting scene clearly contributed to his success as a painter. His paintings are characterized by a precise and accurate rendering of his subjects based on careful observation. Though a stiffness about his animals has been noted, this does not detract from the quality and charm of his work. There are few works by Barenger in British public collections but the Tate collection, the Walker Art Gallery, Liverpool, and the Harris Museum and Art Gallery, Port Sunlight, each holds one of his oil paintings. Barenger died in London on 1 October 1831 and was buried in St Pancras old churchyard. SARA SOWERBY

Sources S. Mitchell, *The dictionary of British equestrian artists* (1985) • W. Gilbey, *Animal painters of England*, 3 vols. (1900–11) • W. S. Sparrow, *British sporting artists: from Barlow to Herring* (1922) • G. L. Pendred, *An inventory of British sporting art in United Kingdom public collections* (1987) • J. Egerton, ed., *British sporting and animal paintings, 1655–1867* (1978) • J. Egerton, *British sporting paintings: the Paul Mellon collection in the Virginia Museum of Fine Arts* (1985) • E. Moncrieff and others, *Farm animal portraits* (1996) • Redgrave, *Artists* • S. H. Pavière, *A dictionary of British sporting painters* (1965) • J. C. Wood, *A dictionary of British animal painters* (1973) • M. A. Wingfield, *A dictionary of sporting artists, 1650–1990* (1992)

Baret, John (*d.* 1578), lexicographer, became a sizar at St John's College, Cambridge, at Easter 1551, but then moved to Trinity College. He took the degree of BA in 1554–5 and MA in 1558, and became a fellow of Trinity in 1560.

Baret's dictionary, *An Alvearie, or Triple Dictionarie, in Englyshe, Latin and French*, was published in 1574. The work was dedicated to William Cecil, Lord Burghley, and the Cambridge scholar and linguist Sir Thomas Smith, and Alexander Nowell may have assisted with its expense. Others, such as 'Maister Powle, & Maister Garth', also encouraged Baret to publish (*Alvearie*, preface). Dedicatory verses were supplied by Richard Mulcaster and Arthur Golding, among others. Baret's preface mentions that he had been abroad 'for language and learning', and had also been 'conversant about the Innes of Court', where some former pupils had gone (ibid.).

This was the third triple dictionary in English, the first having been published by John Veron in 1552 (Latin–English–French), and the second being John Higgins's revision of Richard Huloet's dictionary (English–Latin–French). Baret's dictionary also contained a modest number of Greek equivalents. In the preface he explains that he taught Latin in Cambridge 'about eyghteene yeres agone', that is, about 1555, since the preface is dated 2 February 1574 (*Alvearie*, preface). The dictionary, he claims, was compiled from his and his students' notes by inverting the order to English–Latin; it is actually largely based on Thomas Cooper's *Thesaurus*, as well as Robert Stephanus's *Dictionarium Latino-Gallicum*. Many other minor sources have been identified. Baret seems to have been teaching in London during work on the dictionary.

The term 'hard words' (words too learned or obscure for ordinary readers), the basis of early monolingual English lexicography, first appeared in the prefatory material of Baret's *Alvearie*. He thought it best to concentrate on these hard words rather than familiar ones. The work has indexes and numbers for cross-reference in the main dictionary, so that the reader can find the equivalent of any Latin or French word. Baret also supplies grammatical information, gives indications of stress, and discusses spelling reform.

In 1577, shortly before his death, Baret was admitted MD at Cambridge, though there is no known evidence that he actually practised; he is described as 'Doctor in physick' in his will (PRO, PROB 11/60, sig. 38, fol. 293*v*). Legitimizing an existing medical practice by taking an MD degree much later was, however, a common practice.

Baret died in 1578 at some point between 6 October, when he drew up his will, and 31 October, when the will was proved, but not before revising the dictionary for a new edition, published in 1580, which considerably expanded the work, adding material from new sources, and greatly supplementing the Greek material. A dedication in this edition laments the author's recent death, and an elegiac by Mulcaster also appeared. Other contributors included Abraham Fleming and Thomas Speght.

Baret left his estate to his brother, Richard, also his executor. There is no indication of its extent; the only other bequest was £20 to one Matthew Kenne in the event of his marriage to Baret's niece, Elizabeth. Neither wife nor children are mentioned. R. W. McConchie

Sources *DNB* • Venn, *Alum. Cant.* • De W. T. Starnes, *Renaissance dictionaries: English–Latin and Latin–English* (1954) • G. Stein, *The English dictionary before Cawdrey* (1985) • J. H. Sledd, 'Baret's *Alvearie*, an Elizabethan reference book', *Studies in Philology*, 43 (1946), 147–63 • C. M. Neale, *The early honours-lists (1498–9 to 1746–7) of the University of Cambridge* (1909) • will, PRO, PROB 11/60, sig. 38

Baretti, Giuseppe Marc'Antonio (1719–1789), writer, was born in Turin, Italy, on 24 April 1719, the eldest son of Luca Baretti (1688–1744) and Anna Caterina Tesio (*c.*1695–1735);

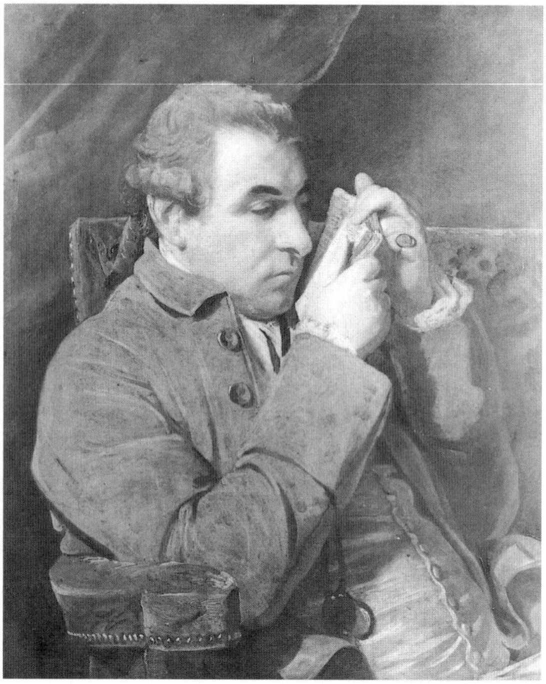

Giuseppe Marc'Antonio Baretti (1719–1789), by Sir Joshua Reynolds, 1773

he was baptized on the same day. His grandfather, Marc' Antonio (1656–1704), a physician from Rivalta Bormida, a small village now in the Piedmontese province of Alessandria, married Diana Maria Arcasio from the nearby town of Bistagno. They moved to Mombercelli in the province of Asti, where Luca Baretti was born on 17 October 1688. By 1692 Marc'Antonio had returned to his home town of Rivalta, where he became mayor. His son Luca studied architecture in Turin and was employed as bursar by the Turin Royal University. In 1716 Luca married Anna Caterina Tesio, a person of humble origins, and of this union four sons were born: Giuseppe, Filippo, Giovanni Battista, and Amedeo.

Early life As was common at the time, Giuseppe Baretti at a very young age was destined by his father for the priesthood, which would guarantee a livelihood and an education. When the boy resisted this plan it was thought that he might study to become an architect like his father, but the idea was abandoned owing to Giuseppe's extreme short-sightedness. A month after Baretti's mother died in May 1735, his father, Luca, married Genoveffa Astrua, who brought into the Baretti household Miglyna di Capriglio, her *cicisbeo* (or male companion of the kind then customarily kept by well-to-do women), as her attendant. Disgusted by what apparently turned out to be a *ménage à trois*, the young Baretti left the parental home following a quarrel and went to live with his uncle, Giambattista, at Guastalla, near Mantua, where he worked as a clerk for a local merchant. Employed in the same office was the poet Carlo Cantoni, who instilled in Baretti a love for Italian literature, especially burlesque poetry. Two years later, in

1737, Baretti returned to Turin, where for a year he attended some of the university lectures given by the professor of literature Girolamo Tagliazucchi, whom he regarded highly.

Literary activities in Italy The years 1738 and 1739 were spent in Venice, where Baretti made the acquaintance of the young Gasparo Gozzi, who was destined to become one of the chief literary figures of the period. In 1740 Baretti moved to Milan. Here he mixed with writers such as Passeroni, Tanzi, Bicetti, and Balestrieri, who soon after established the respected literary circle the Accademia dei Trasformati. While in Milan he studied Latin and made Italian translations of Ovid's *Remedia amoris* and *Amores*, which he published more than ten years later, in 1752 and 1754. The war of the Austrian Succession began in 1740, and after returning briefly to Turin in 1742 Baretti obtained employment in Cuneo, as keeper of the stores for the city's new fortification works. However, a few days before the French and Spanish armies laid siege to the town in September 1744, he returned to Milan, from where he travelled again to Venice. Here he joined another literary circle, the Accademia dei Granelleschi, and translated into blank verse the tragedies of Pierre Corneille; these translations were published in four volumes in 1747–8. It was in Venice that his polemical nature first gained notice when, following criticism made by a quarrelsome priest, Dr Biagio Schiavo, of a sonnet that Baretti had written previously, he published in response a *Lettera ad un suo amico*, in which he ridiculed Schiavo's character, literary ability, and physical appearance. On his return to Turin, Baretti found another pretext to be controversial, this time reaching a much wider audience. His dislike of both the relatively new science of archaeology and of Giuseppe Bartoli, the professor of literature who had succeeded Tagliazucchi at the University of Turin, led him to denounce Bartoli's study of an antique diptych owned by Cardinal Quirini. In 1750 Baretti published what he entitled his 'First prattle', *Primo cicalamento sopra le cinque lettere del signor Giuseppe Bartoli intorno al libro che avrà per titolo 'La vera spiegazione del dittico quiriniano'*, in which he mocked Bartoli and attacked archaeologists and antiquaries in general. Enraged archaeologists publicly denounced Baretti for criticizing a university professor who had been appointed by the king. Baretti was summoned before the president of the senate and the chancellor of the University of Turin, reprimanded, and ordered not to write any more *cicalamenti*. In the same year he published a collection of his poems, *Le piacevoli poesie*, which were burlesque and satirical in style in the manner of the sixteenth-century poet Francesco Berni. These poems, compiled over several years up to 1750, also included attacks on Bartoli, whose lack of literary ability he criticized, but Baretti avoided the wrath of the censors by tempering his language and not referring to Bartoli directly.

First period in England As early as 1747 in Turin, when he met Lord Charlemont during the latter's tour on the continent, Baretti had thought of travelling to England. No doubt the difficulty of living and of writing in his homeland, which he had deeply felt during the events of 1750, induced him to leave for England in January 1751. After arriving in London, he began studying English in a far more earnest fashion than he had done previously in Italy. He met another Italian from Turin, the violinist Felice Giardini, who obtained employment for him at the Italian opera for the next two years. Baretti was struck by the size of London and its contrasts, where the bustling, dirty streets were filled on the one hand with charming and attractive women, and on the other with countless beggars and petty criminals.

Two years after his arrival in London, Baretti was introduced to the writer Mrs Charlotte Lennox, who was anxious to learn Italian in order to read Italian works, and was willing to offer lessons in English in return. Baretti promptly agreed to become her tutor, and was introduced to Mrs Lennox's circle of artists and literary friends, who included Henry Fielding, Sir Joshua Reynolds (who later painted Baretti's portrait), David Garrick, and—most significantly for Baretti—Samuel Johnson. Baretti's presence in the group was appealing because of his familiarity with literary academies in Italy, and for his knowledge of French and Italian literature. Baretti, for his part, saw the circle as providing access to some of the most cultured people in London and a direct link to possible publishers of his own writings. Indeed, that year, 1753, was a prolific year for Baretti. He published two booklets, both written in French, dealing with current disputes at the opera. He produced an essay, *Remarks on the Italian Language and Writers*, which, given that he had not yet fully mastered English, was probably first drafted in French and then turned into English with the help of one of his new friends. In addition, no doubt encouraged to write on the subject of Italian poetry by his English friends, and as a means of making some money, he published a *Dissertation upon the Italian Poetry*, which included a censure of Voltaire. The vocabulary, syntax, and writing style used in the *Dissertation* clearly point to the involvement of Johnson, whom Baretti very much admired. In the years that followed, Baretti, not just because of his cultural ideals and the interest of his learned friends but also for mere pecuniary reasons, realized that one of his major roles in England was to be that of promoter of Italian language and literature, and a writer who could make contemporary Italian culture accessible to the English. In the same decade he published a bilingual collection of Italian prose and verse, entitled *An Introduction to the Italian Language* (1755), and *The Italian Library* (1757), which provided short commentaries on the lives and works of well-known Italian writers, as well as a brief history of the development of the Tuscan language.

Baretti's Italian and English dictionary Inspired by the success of Johnson's recently published English dictionary, in the latter part of the 1750s Baretti set about compiling an Italian and English bilingual dictionary for the use of both Italian- and English-speakers. He considered Johnson's dictionary an extraordinary achievement that could dispute the pre-eminence of lexicography with that of the

Florentine *Vocabolario degli Accademici della Crusca* (1612), a volume that had been compiled not by one person but by numerous academicians. He stipulated in an agreement with London booksellers that he would revise Ferdinando Altieri's previous Italian and English dictionary (1726–7) for £200, a considerable sum. Baretti published *A Dictionary of the English and Italian Languages* in 1760, in two volumes, with the addition of an Italian and English grammar and a dedicatory letter written by Samuel Johnson. In the preface Baretti made a virulent attack on Altieri, claiming that his predecessor's dictionary definitions awakened his 'risibility' and were evidence of his 'ignorance', and that Altieri himself 'had not the least spark of poetical fire in his soul'. One would have therefore expected Baretti to have carried out a radical revision of Altieri's previous work. The fact was, however, that the alterations and additions wrought by Baretti were, all in all, very minor. In the Italian word-list he inserted a modest selection of the additional vocabulary contained in the latest edition of the *Vocabolario della Crusca*, and on the English side he added some of the entries from Johnson's dictionary.

Despite representing only a minor revision, Baretti's dictionary marked the death knell for Altieri's twin volumes of three decades before. Baretti's work proved extremely successful, for its author financially as well, and may be considered the most important work he published during his first stay in England. The dictionary, as the standard reference work of its kind, went through numerous reprints and revisions, some long after his death, and the last as recently as 1928.

Return to Italy Flushed with the success of his dictionary, Baretti the same year took the opportunity to accompany to Italy a young aristocrat, Edward Southwell, whose intention it was to embark on the usual continental tour, travelling first through Portugal and Spain. Baretti planned to return to Italy definitively, in the expectation that there he would now achieve greater fame as an Italian writer than previously. Before his departure Johnson suggested he write a daily journal of his travels as the basis for a future publication, a request Johnson reiterated in his correspondence with Baretti while the latter was abroad. After visiting his brothers in Turin, Baretti travelled to Milan and then to Venice, where he parted from his companion Southwell, having completed his contract as his tour guide. On returning to Milan, he was introduced to the new governor, Count Firmian, who was a patron of the arts and letters, in the hope that the governor might provide him with patronage. He renewed his contacts with those who frequented the Accademia dei Trasformati, and made the acquaintance of the poet Giuseppe Parini.

In 1762 Baretti published the first of what were to be four volumes that recounted his recent journey to the continent, giving it the title *Lettere familiari ai suoi tre fratelli*. But following a complaint lodged with Count Firmian by the Portuguese minister in Milan, who believed that Baretti had unjustly criticized the hospitality of the Portuguese, Firmian ordered him to halt further publication. Baretti, having lost the opportunity both to obtain patronage and to publish his travel journal, moved to Venice, thinking that he might be able to complete the publication there. But the Venetian government was just as unsympathetic, and allowed him to publish the second volume in 1763 only after he had deleted any suggestion of criticism of Portugal. Although the two Italian volumes remained incomplete, they reflected Baretti's new-found maturity as a writer who demonstrated, somewhat like a modern journalist, that he was an acute observer of everyday life, able to provide vivid descriptions of the places that he had visited and the people whom he had met.

Baretti's despondency at the difficulties that he had encountered in Italy (which was evidently heightened by an ill-fated love affair about which Johnson wrote a letter of consolation in December 1762) was alleviated by his contacts with the renowned writers Carlo and Gasparo Gozzi, whose company he assiduously frequented while in Venice. That year, in Padua, Baretti submitted to the censors a request to publish a fortnightly journal *La Frusta Letteraria* ('The Literary Scourge') which aimed, like Addison's *Spectator* and Johnson's *Rambler*, to evaluate contemporary customs and literature, to review books, and to condemn, as necessary, examples of bad taste. The first issue appeared in October 1763. In subsequent issues Baretti attacked archaeologists, the Venetian playwright Carlo Goldoni, the Arcadians, Voltaire, Pietro Verri and the Milanese journal *Il Caffè*, and blank verse. The journal, as an independent and iconoclastic publication, did not bow to any public authority, and did not hesitate to be critical of the art and culture of its time or to censure otherwise untouchable writers who had achieved fame and respect. For this reason *La Frusta Letteraria* became the work for which Italians today most remember Baretti. His continued attack on writers, including the revered sixteenth-century Venetian Pietro Bembo, resulted in the journal's being suppressed by the Venetian authorities in 1765. Baretti fled Venice, and, after several months spent near Ancona, where he published his last issues of the journal (April–July 1765), he decided that he could no longer continue to write and publish in Italy.

Second period in England Baretti left Italy for England in August 1766 having made the decision to reside there permanently. In the literary environment of London, which he found much more congenial than the one he had just left, he renewed his acquaintance with his old friends, especially Samuel Johnson, who had kept up a correspondence with him during his absence in Italy. The circle had by now become the renowned Literary Club, where Baretti was introduced to Oliver Goldsmith, James Boswell, and Edmund Burke. Baretti's first publication in London was *An Account of the Manners and Customs of Italy* (1768), written as a reply to the inaccurate and superficial description of Italian customs and manners given in *Letters from Italy* by Samuel Sharp, published two years earlier. Unlike the negative view of Italy that he had portrayed in *La Frusta*, Baretti's *Account* provided a more favourable picture of Italian life and culture that appealed to his Italophile British friends. The book was so popular that a second edition followed in 1769, containing an answer to Sharp's criticism of the first edition. Baretti had now established his reputation as an English writer, so much so that in 1769 the king appointed him secretary for foreign correspondence to the Royal Academy of Painting, Sculpture and Architecture. In 1768 Baretti visited France and Spain to collect more material for what would be the English edition of his *Lettere familiari*, which he had not been able to complete in Italy.

In October 1769, while walking at the Haymarket, Baretti was struck a blow by a prostitute. Owing to the darkness and his bad eyesight he retaliated by striking her female companion. Three pimps appeared on the scene, and Baretti drew a fruit-knife that he carried and fatally wounded one of them. He was arrested and subsequently brought to trial for murder at the Old Bailey. His friends Topham Beauclerk, Sir Joshua Reynolds, Dr Johnson, Edmund Burke, David Garrick, Oliver Goldsmith, and others—'a constellation of genius', in Boswell's account—rallied to support him and testified at the trial to his good character (Boswell, 419). The jury acquitted him on the grounds of self-defence. Baretti felt more than ever now that justice and his real friends resided in England. He told his old friend Lord Charlemont that 'those I had about me did their part so well that they have made me an Englishman forever' (Collinson-Morley, 222).

In the following year Baretti published the definitive edition of his *Lettere familiari*, entitled *Journey from London to Genoa* (1770). The work, enlarged and now in English, achieved instant success: Johnson called it one of the best travel books ever written. Baretti was now at the height of his success. He decided to pay a visit to Italy to see his brothers and to enjoy the pleasure of appearing as a famous writer, but within a year, after visiting Turin, Genoa, and Florence, he returned to England to what he now called his 'nest', unhappy with the country of his birth, which he referred to as dull, and whose people he felt were ignorant. This was his last trip to Italy. In London he returned to writing, publishing in 1772 *An Introduction to the most Useful European Languages* and in 1773, in three volumes, *Tutte le opere di Niccolò Machiavelli*. His popular dictionary was reprinted in 1771.

Between 1773 and 1776 Baretti became the language tutor to Hetty (Queeney), the daughter of Henry Thrale, brewery proprietor, and his wife, Hester Thrale, to whom he was introduced by Johnson. During these three years Baretti chose to live on and off at their villa at Streatham, where the Thrales were accustomed to entertaining artists, writers, and distinguished professional people. In 1775 they arranged for Baretti and Johnson to travel with them for two months to France. Mr Thrale was so pleased with the French tour that they planned another trip, this time to Italy the following year, but were prevented from leaving owing to the death of their only son, Harry. In 1775 Baretti wrote and published a collection of dialogues, *Easy Phraseology for the Use of Young Ladies*, which had been originally intended for his pupil Hetty. The relationship between Baretti and Mrs Thrale, however, became so tense in 1776 that Baretti abruptly left the house and returned to London.

Last years Baretti's most important work of this period was the defence of Shakespeare that he published in 1777 in response to a letter written to the French Academy the year before by Voltaire, in which Voltaire denounced his countryman Pierre Letourneur for translating and publishing Shakespeare's plays. Baretti's *Discours sur Shakespeare et sur Monsieur de Voltaire* attacked Voltaire for his lack of appreciation of Shakespeare's artistic merit, and for his limited knowledge of the English language and therefore of Shakespeare's plays. Baretti's decision to write the work in French (a language Johnson felt that Baretti knew as fluently as English) meant that it was accessible to readers on the continent, including Italy, where the classical tradition held sway and Shakespeare's plays were still very little known. That year was also spent preparing a two-volume Spanish and English dictionary, which was published in London by Nourse in 1778. Baretti labelled it a second edition, since it was essentially a minor revision of the dictionary of Giral Delpino published in 1763. As was the case with his earlier Italian and English dictionary, the revision of the Spanish dictionary was mainly editorial—the expurgation of previous inconsistencies and inaccuracies—with additional vocabulary inserted primarily on the English side, where Baretti included words from Johnson's dictionary. The Spanish dictionary, too, was well received and was republished with revisions well into the nineteenth century.

In 1779 Baretti's output continued at the same pace. That year Nourse invited him to compile an anthology of Italian letters as a language text for students of Italian. Not satisfied with those written by earlier Italian writers, Baretti chose instead to resort to letters that he himself had previously sent, or pretended to have sent, to friends and acquaintances. The resulting *Scelta di lettere familiari fatta per uso degli studiosi di lingua italiana* provided students with a useful variety of topics, vocabulary, and writing styles, as well as a showcase for English readers of his opinions on Italian language, literature, and society, and of his own ability as a writer of Italian prose. Looking for another opportunity to earn some money, in the same year Baretti translated Horace's *Carmen seculare* for the French musician Philidor, who set it to music and performed it with some success at the Freemasons' Hall, but then disappeared with part of the takings. Baretti had few financial resources until 1782, when he managed to obtain a government pension of £80 annually, which, coupled with the income from his published writings, would thereafter provide him with just enough money to support himself.

Three years after her husband's death in 1781, Mrs Thrale created a scandal by marrying the singer Gabriele Mario Piozzi, who was her daughters' music teacher. Baretti's animosity towards Mrs Thrale reached its peak after Johnson's death, when she published two volumes of letters to and from Johnson, among which were passages that were offensive to Baretti. Enraged, Baretti decided to vent his anger in print, attacking Mrs Thrale in three 'Strictures' in the *European Magazine* between May and

August 1788, in which he made unsubstantiated allegations about her tyrannical behaviour and about Piozzi's background. Baretti's decision to vent his feelings in print only worsened the reputation that he had acquired in later life as combative and ill-natured. In 1789, pressed for money and with his pension three-quarters in arrears, he began revising his Italian dictionary in the hope of gaining some income, but he was taken ill with an attack of 'gout' (a contemporary term that could cover a range of maladies), and died, unmarried, in London on 5 May. He was buried in Marylebone on 9 May in a cemetery that was later cleared, so that today the site of his grave cannot be traced. His executors destroyed all the papers and manuscripts in his possession.

Baretti and Johnson Baretti claimed that Johnson was the best friend he ever had and the person to whom he was indebted for the best part of the knowledge that he had acquired. For his part, Johnson, who never managed to visit Italy, admired Baretti for his linguistic and conversational skills—praising his English, for example, for 'its purity and vigour'—his scholarship, and his knowledge of Italian culture (Boswell, 256). At the same time he was sensitive to Baretti's limitations, noting in 1768 that 'There are strong powers in his mind. He has not, indeed, many hooks; but with what hooks he has, he grapples very forcibly' (ibid., 395). Both writers had an overbearing and stubborn temperament; but each greatly respected the other. They enjoyed each other's company for nearly thirty years until, a year before Johnson's death, they quarrelled—not over a profound philosophical issue but about the outcome of a game of chess. Boswell's view of Baretti, however, captured some of the less attractive qualities of the Italian: in 1766 he described him as 'so wretchedly perverted to infidelity, that he treated the hopes of immortality with brutal levity' (ibid., 357).

Johnson's influence on Baretti's writings is indisputable. Johnson's presence can be found in many of Baretti's works, either explicitly, in the dedications and prefaces that he wrote for the Italian's publications, or implicitly, in the input of Johnson's ideas on language and literature, and in the kinds of works that Baretti chose to publish. To say, however, as Foscolo did, that Baretti simply aped Johnson, or to conclude, with a more recent scholar, that Baretti totally lacked originality (C. J. M. Lubbers-Van der Brugge, 1–3), does not do him justice. Rather, Baretti's long-term contact with Johnson confirms how much they had in common in terms of both temperament and literary tastes. The relationship assisted Baretti to mature intellectually, broadened his outlook on art and literature, introduced him to English writing and culture, and allowed him to make a living and achieve fame as an author, without having to resort to a Maecenas or patron; Johnson, similarly freed from the need for literary patronage, noted that Baretti had been the first author to receive 'copy-money' in Italy for his works (Boswell, 846). In England his publications helped to promote a renewed interest in Italian language and literature, including the works of Dante. In Italy his works encouraged the study of writings by English authors, especially Shakespeare. Of the eighteenth-century critics he is the Italian best remembered in the English-speaking world.

Desmond O'Connor

Sources L. Collinson-Morley, *Giuseppe Baretti, with an account of his literary friendships and feuds in Italy and in England in the days of Dr Johnson* (1909) • C. J. M. Lubbers-Van der Brugge, *Johnson and Baretti: some aspects of eighteenth-century literary life in England and Italy* (1951) • *Thraliana: the diary of Mrs. Hester Lynch Thrale (later Mrs. Piozzi), 1776–1809*, ed. K. C. Balderston, 2nd edn, 2 vols. (1951) • *The letters of Samuel Johnson*, ed. R. W. Chapman, 3 vols. (1952) [incl. letters from Mrs Thrale] • N. Jonard, *Giuseppe Baretti (1719–1789): l'homme et l'œuvre* (Clermont-Ferrand, 1963) • G. Baretti, *Prefazioni e polemiche*, ed. L. Piccioni, 2nd edn (Bari, 1933) • M. L. Astaldi, *Baretti* (Milan, 1977) • M. Cerruti and P. Trivero, eds., *Giuseppe Baretti: un piemontese in Europa* (Alessandria, 1993) • B. Anglani, *Il mestiere della metafora: Giuseppe Baretti intellettuale e scrittore* (Modena, 1997) • G. Baretti, *Epistolario*, ed. L. Piccioni, 2 vols. (Bari, 1936) • D. O'Connor, *A history of Italian and English bilingual dictionaries* (Florence, 1990) • D. Bucciarelli, 'Appunti per la storia di un problema critico: i rapporti tra Giuseppe Baretti e Samuel Johnson', *Italianistica* [Milan], 8/2 (1979), 319–32 • M. Fubini, 'Baretti, Giuseppe', *Dizionario biografico degli italiani* (Rome, 1964) • *DNB* • I. Crotti, *Il viaggio e la forma: Giuseppe Baretti e l'orizzonte dei generi letterari* (Modena, 1992) • M. Fubini, *Dal Muratori al Baretti*, 2 (Rome, 1975), 269–333 • *Giuseppe Baretti: scritti*, ed. E. Bonora (Turin, 1976) • J. L. Clifford, 'Johnson and foreign visitors to London: Baretti and others', *Eighteenth century studies presented to Arthur M. Wilson*, ed. P. Gay (1972), 97–115 • J. Boswell, *Life of Johnson*, ed. R. W. Chapman, rev. J. D. Fleeman, new edn (1970) • R. J. Steiner, *Two centuries of Spanish and English bilingual lexicography (1590–1800)* (1970) • J. Prior, *Life of Edmond Malone, editor of Shakespeare* (1860), 391

Archives BL, manuscript notes in English written in the margin of H. Lynch Piozzi, *Letters to and from the late Samuel Johnson* (1788)

Likenesses J. Reynolds, oils, 1773, priv. coll. [*see illus.*] • J. Watts, mezzotint, pubd 1780 (after J. Reynolds), BM, NPG • T. Banks, relief medallion, 1789, St Mary's parish church, Marylebone, London • oils (after J. Reynolds, 1773), NPG

Wealth at death died impoverished and without estate: Collinson-Morley, *Giuseppe Baretti*, 351–3

Barff, Samuel (1793?–1880), philhellene and banker, was probably born in England. In 1816 he established himself in Zante, Greece, where he became an important merchant and banker. He died there on 23 September 1880. He was probably married.

Barff's part in the struggle for Greek independence is evidenced in the papers of contemporary philhellenes such as Church and Blaquiere. Byron wrote to him early in 1824 after witnessing his untiring activities in the cause and his generous support of Englishmen then in difficulties in Greece. Barff offered his house on Zante to Byron should ill health compel the latter to leave Mesolonghi. Barff took part in negotiating the first western loans, especially in 1824 and 1825. When Greek rivalries made it uncertain to whom the funds should be given the money was frozen on Zante in Barff's care. He was foremost in urging his friend Richard Church (then in England) to accept the office of generalissimo of the Greek forces.

After the establishment of the Greek kingdom Barff joined George Finlay in supporting the project for setting up a bank in Greece and pressed for careful definitions of banking law. Throughout his life Barff kept himself informed on Greek political activities and pressed for governmental reform. For more than fifty years Barff, Hancock & Co. continued to provide indispensable banking services as Finlay's travel accounts and letter books show.

J. M. HUSSEY

Sources *The Times* (23 Sept 1880) • *Letters and journals of Lord Byron, with notices of his life*, ed. T. Moore, 2 vols. (1830) • S. Trikoupes, *Historia tes Hellenikes Epanastaseos* [History of the Greek revolution], 3rd edn, 4 vols. (Athens, 1888) • D. Dakin, *British and American philhellenes during the War of Greek Independence, 1821–1833* (1955) • *The journals and letters of George Finlay*, ed. J. M. Hussey, 2 vols. (1995)

Barfield, (Arthur) Owen (1898–1997), writer and philosopher, was born on 9 November 1898 at 6 Grosvenor Gardens, Muswell Hill, Middlesex, the youngest of the four children of Arthur Edward Barfield, a solicitor, and his wife, Elizabeth, *née* Shoults. It was a free-thinking family and so immune to all 'superstition' that Owen had hardly heard of Christianity until he went to school (Lewis, *Surprised by Joy*, 194). Highgate School enrolled him as a day pupil in 1906 (until that time he had been tutored at home by his mother, an ardent suffragette). There he received an ordinary classical education, with a strong emphasis on Latin and Greek grammar and literature.

Barfield won a classical scholarship to Wadham College, Oxford, but his undergraduate career was postponed by service in the First World War as a wireless officer with the Royal Engineers (1917–19). Eventually arriving at Wadham in the Michaelmas term of 1919, he transferred from 'Greats' to English language and literature. During his first term he met C. S. Lewis, an undergraduate at University College, whom he later described as 'the most unforgettable friend—part of the furniture of my existence' (*Owen Barfield on C. S. Lewis*, 3). For his own part, Lewis called Barfield the 'wisest and best of my unofficial teachers' in his dedication to Barfield in *The Allegory of Love*. They were both founding members of the Inklings, the Oxford group that also included J. R. R. Tolkien, Charles Williams, and Lord David Cecil. Barfield took a first in 1921 and then began a thesis for a BLitt degree (later published as *Poetic Diction: a Study in Meaning*).

On 11 April 1923 in St Cyprian's Church, Clarence Gate, off Glentworth Street, London, Barfield married Matilda Christian (Maud) Douie (1885–1980), a professional dancer who had worked with Gordon Craig. They adopted three children, Alexander, Geoffrey, and Lucy, to whom C. S. Lewis, her godfather, dedicated *The Lion, the Witch and the Wardrobe* (1950). In 1923 Barfield also became a follower of Rudolf Steiner, founder of the anthroposophical movement, who held the belief that the evolving of consciousness results from cosmic processes. While writing his thesis on poetic diction Barfield had reached the conclusion that Romanticism had never fulfilled itself. Later, in *Romanticism Comes of Age*, he declared: 'Anthroposophy included and transcended not only my own poor stammering theory of poetry as knowledge, but the whole Romantic philosophy. It was nothing less than Romanticism grown up' (*Romanticism*, 9). Lewis was dismayed by Barfield's interest in anthroposophy and the result was a philosophical debate between the two men, carried out mainly by letter, that became known as the 'great war'. It ended with the atheist Lewis's conversion to Christianity in 1931; Barfield, though remaining an anthroposophist to the end of his life, was baptized in St Saviour's Church, Uckfield, Sussex, on 25 June 1949.

In 1926 Barfield published *History in English Words*, many ideas from which were more fully developed in *Poetic Diction* (1928), perhaps his finest book. It influenced and was greatly admired by both Lewis and Tolkien. His work, concerned with how language and literature function in and upon consciousness, 'erects a structure of thought on the basis of a felt difference between what it calls "the Prosaic" and "the Poetic"', and 'reveals human consciousness as in a process of evolution' (*Poetic Diction*, 221). Barfield's ideas, influenced by Steiner, diverged from the view that human evolution proceeds haphazardly. Instead he proposed that all language proceeds from mythology, and an 'ancient unity' of meanings.

By the late 1920s Barfield's father needed Owen in the family law practice and so in 1929 he joined the London firm of Barfield and Barfield. He spent the next thirty years as a solicitor (for Lewis among others), during which period he had little time to write, though he did publish *Romanticism Comes of Age* (1944), and *Saving the Appearances: a Study in Idolatry* (1957), the latter reflecting his lifelong interest in the relation between science and religion. Language, for Barfield the 'storehouse of the imagination', remained his primary fascination. Nowhere was this more cogently stated than in his preface to the second edition of *Poetic Diction* (1952):

> Of all the devices for dragooning the human spirit, the least clumsy is to procure its abortion in the womb of language; and we should recognize … that those … who are driven by an impulse to reduce the specifically human to a mechanical or animal regularity, will continue to be increasingly irritated by the nature of the mother tongue and make it their point of attack. (p. 23)

A second life awaited Barfield when he retired from the law in 1959: he now wrote some of his best books, including *Worlds Apart* (1963), an analysis of modern intellectual fragmentation, *Unancestral Voice* (1965), *Speaker's Meaning* (1967), *What Coleridge Thought* (1971), *The Rediscovery of Meaning* (1979), and *History, Guilt and Habit* (1979). The self-effacing Barfield also became a visiting scholar in several American universities. The many admirers who were drawn to his home in Dartford, Kent, discovered for themselves, as Lewis had found, that Barfield 'cannot talk on any subject without illuminating it' (Lewis, 30 March 1962). He was small, lithe, and a keen walker (he and Lewis called themselves the 'cretaceous perambulators').

Maud Barfield died on 13 February 1980, and in 1986 Barfield moved into a retirement home, The Walhatch, Forest Row, Uckfield, Sussex. He died there of bronchopneumonia on 14 December 1997, his mind clear and bright to the end. Owen Barfield's funeral was held at the Forest Row Anthroposophical British Church and the Surrey and Sussex crematorium near Worth on 18 December 1997, after which his ashes were buried in the Forest Row cemetery.

WALTER HOOPER

Sources C. S. Lewis, *Surprised by joy: the shape of my early life* (1955) • O. Barfield, *Poetic diction: a study in meaning*, 3rd edn (1973), 221 • *Owen Barfield on C. S. Lewis*, ed. G. B. Tennyson (1989), 3 • C. S. Lewis, *The allegory of love: a study in medieval tradition* (1936), v • O. Barfield, *Romanticism comes of age* (1944) • letter from C. S. Lewis to Charles Huttar, 30 March 1962, Wheaton College, Wheaton, Illinois, Marion E. Wade Center

Archives Bodl. Oxf., papers | Wheaton College, Wheaton, Illinois, Marion E. Wade Center

Wealth at death £143,037: probate, 8 April 1998, *CGPLA Eng. & Wales*

Barford, William (*bap.* **1719**, *d.* **1792**), Church of England clergyman and classical scholar, was the son of the Revd Thomas Barford (*d.* 1765), rector of Chalbury, Dorset, where he was baptized on 2 September 1719. He was educated at Eton College (1730–38), and was a scholar at King's College, Cambridge, whence he graduated BA in 1743, MA in 1746, and DD in 1771. His first preferment was the vicarage of Milton, Cambridgeshire, in 1751. He became a tutor of the college, a proctor in 1761, and from 1762 to 1768 public orator, only resigning to stand for the Greek professorship, which he failed to obtain. Rector of Tilton, Northamptonshire, from 1764 to 1768, he became vicar of Fordingbridge, Hampshire, which is in the gift of King's College, in 1768. On 27 September 1764 he married Mary Hewer of Royston, Hertfordshire. In 1770 Sir John Cust, the speaker of the House of Commons, appointed him as his chaplain, but he served only one session before a new speaker, Sir Fletcher Norton, was elected and chose James King as his chaplain. Barford's friends were concerned that such a short tenure would not be rewarded by the customary preferment found for the chaplain. This incident established that the task was to be chaplain to the house, not merely to the speaker. 'The House is so much in possession of him that the Speaker cannot displace him without consulting the House' (Price, 31).

On 9 May 1770 it was moved an address be made to the king that Barford 'be favoured with the customary recompense for his service' (*GM*, 1793, 418). The fortuitous death that month of Francis Walwyn, a prebendary of Canterbury, provided a suitable vacancy to which he was installed in June. In 1773 he resigned Fordingbridge and accepted the rectory of Kimpton, Hertfordshire, and then in 1778 the dean and chapter of Canterbury living of All Hallows, Lombard Street, both of which he retained until his death. He became a fellow of Eton in 1784.

Barford's Latin dissertation on the first Pythian ode, first published in 1751, was included in Henry Huntingford's edition of the works of Pindar, which also contains a short biography and a bibliography of Barford's writings, including Latin and Greek verses and orations written while he was public orator. In his *New System of Mythology* Jacob Bryant pays tribute to Barford's talents and thanks him for his assistance. Barford died at Kimpton in November 1792, and was buried on 30 November in the church of Sts Peter and Paul, Kimpton. DONALD GRAY

Sources *JHC*, 32 (1768–70), 969 • *GM*, 1st ser., 62 (1792), 1155, 1218 • *GM*, 1st ser., 63 (1793), 418–19 • J. Price, shorthand diary, 1770, Canterbury Public Library, 31 • G. Hennessy, *Novum repertorium ecclesiasticum parochiale Londinense, or, London diocesan clergy succession from the earliest time to the year 1898* (1898), 79 • *Fasti Angl.* (Hardy), 1.55 • *City and court register* (1770), 68 • R. A. Austen-Leigh, ed., *Eton College lists, 1678–1790* (1907), 31, 240 • Archbishop of Canterbury's act books, LPL, 11.186, 187 • *DNB* • D. Gray, *Chaplain to Mr Speaker: the religious life of the House of Commons* (1991) • T. Harwood, *Alumni Etonenses, or, A catalogue of the provosts and fellows of Eton College and King's College, Cambridge, from the foundation in 1443 to the year 1797* (1797), 98 • Venn, *Alum. Cant.* • will, 31 Jan 1793, PRO, PROB 11/1227, sig. 10 • *IGI* • memorial, church of Sts Peter and Paul, Kimpton, Hertfordshire • parish registers, Kimpton, Sts Peter and Paul [burial]

Wealth at death bequeathed 20 shillings p.a. to be distributed among the poorest parishioners: will, PRO, PROB 11/1227, sig. 10

Bargany. For this title name *see* Hamilton, Sir John, later first Lord Bargany (*d.* 1658) [*see under* Hamilton, John, second Lord Bargany (*c.*1640–1693)]; Hamilton, John, second Lord Bargany (*c.*1640–1693).

Bargate [*married names* Proud, Keeffe], **Verity Eileen** (**1940–1981**), theatre producer and novelist, was born on 6 August 1940 in Exeter, the second child of Ronald Arthur Bargate, electrical shopkeeper and later sales manager in the London Metal Warehouse, and his wife, Eileen Dewes. Her childhood was disrupted by her parents' divorce in 1944, followed by her mother's departure to Australia, leaving Bargate and her elder brother Simon for four years in the care of their father. When her mother returned it was with a new husband, Clarke Taylor, a Royal Air Force doctor, who installed his new family in air force bases at Hornchurch, Essex, and Bicester, Oxfordshire, and dispatched his stepdaughter to a succession of boarding-schools and holiday homes. In later years she described her upbringing as that of a 'middle-class charity child' (private information).

On leaving school Bargate trained as a nurse at the Westminster Hospital, London, where she qualified as a state registered nurse and supplemented her income with private nursing. Although she was emotionally and physically unsuited to this profession (in which she came to rely on the 'pep pills' that sowed the seeds of her future intermittent spells of ill health), it was five years before she abandoned nursing and took a job with a media analysis firm in Paddington, London, where she remained until her meeting and subsequent marriage on 14 February 1970 to Frederick Proud, with whom she had two sons, Sam Valentine (*b.* 1971) and Thomas Orlando (*b.* 1973).

Proud was an aspirant director who had studied at the Rose Bruford College, and with Bargate he launched the Soho Theatre at an address in New Compton Street in 1969, as a somewhat late arrival on London's lunchtime theatre scene. With a policy of offering new and little-known work at low prices, it established itself as a home of good acting and arresting texts—which ranged from modern English and American plays to Sheridan and Cervantes. Reviewers got to know Bargate as the beautiful long-legged girl on the door. She had no theatrical experience but she knew about public relations work, and one reason for the theatre's success was her ability to win over the press with intelligence, good humour, and excellent home-cooked food. Even so, its position was precarious; and in 1971 it was obliged to quit its original premises for a temporary home at the King's Head Theatre in Upper

Street, Islington (to which it introduced lunchtime shows), before finding a more secure base in Riding House Street (behind Broadcasting House) in the following year, and changing its name to the Soho Poly.

Shortly after this move the marriage collapsed, leaving Bargate (from 1975) as the theatre's sole artistic director. She seldom directed shows herself; instead she emerged as a persistent and effective encourager of new talent. Policy for her meant 'putting on what I liked' (private information). This involved extending the lunchtime programme to full-length evening productions; opening the doors to women directors and designers; and concentrating exclusively on living writers with whom she worked as a catalyst and a midwife. Not all of them were full-time playwrights. The actor Bob Hoskins claims that she saved him from insanity by letting him present his one-man piece, *The Bystander*, as a therapeutic exercise. Among those whose careers advanced from the Poly to other stages were Hanif Kureishi, Tony Marchant, Micheline Wandor, Caryl Churchill, and Barrie Colin Keeffe (*b.* 1945), whose studies of alienated working-class youth spoke for a hitherto voiceless generation.

In Keeffe Bargate found a second partner who also persuaded her to embark on writing of her own; from this point her life underwent a powerful and subsequently fatal acceleration. Until now she had played the public role of a hopeful supporter of others, which had masked her spells of ill health and her private sense of oncoming calamity. She was convinced that, like her mother, she would die at the age of forty, and it was of great significance to her that her birthday fell on the same date as that of the bombing of Hiroshima. The dark side of her nature now found expression in her writing. With grim logic, her birth as a novelist coincided with the onset of cancer, and the remainder of her life became a neck-and-neck race between creativity and disease.

Of Bargate's three books, *No Mama No* was published in 1978, and *Children Crossing* in 1979. At the insistence of her publisher *Tit for Tat* (1981) was rewritten in its entirety, even though Bargate had one arm in a sling at the time. Her subjects were the lies and cruelties of the sexual contract, and the emotional wounds parents and children inflict on each other. Terrible things happen. A seaside holiday ends with the children dead under a juggernaut: mastectomy becomes an instrument of sexual revenge. But the narrative voice is irresistible, and connects the immediate events to a deep well of early pain.

Verity Bargate died in Greenwich Hospital, London, on 18 May 1981, two months after her marriage on 14 February to Keeffe and a month after the publication of her final book. Her ashes were scattered on the lake of Lewisham crematorium. Her memorials are her books, her theatre, and the annual Verity Bargate award for short plays.

IRVING WARDLE

Sources personal knowledge (2004) · private information (2004)
Archives FILM South Bank Show, devoted to her, transmitted 4/1981 · TV adaptation of her novel *No Mama No* transmitted by Thames TV 3/1979
Wealth at death £56,244: probate, 3 Sept 1982, *CGPLA Eng. & Wales*

Barger, George (1878–1939), chemist, was born in Manchester on 4 April 1878, the elder son of Gerrit Barger, a Dutch engineer, and his wife, Eleanor Higginbotham. He received his school education at Utrecht, and at the age of sixteen obtained a scholarship to University College, London, which he entered in 1896. After two years' study in London he proceeded in 1898 to King's College, Cambridge, with an entrance scholarship, and in 1901 gained a first class in part two of the natural sciences tripos in both chemistry and botany. On leaving Cambridge, where he had become friends with E. M. Forster, he was appointed demonstrator in botany under Leo Errera, of Brussels; and in 1903 he returned to England, to join the staff of the Wellcome Physiological Research Laboratories. In 1904 he married Florence Emily, the daughter of Alfred William Thomas, and they had two sons and one daughter. In that same year Henry Dale, whom Barger had known at Cambridge, joined the Wellcome laboratories, and the two men began a productive scientific partnership.

In 1909 Barger was appointed head of the department of chemistry at Goldsmiths' College, New Cross, London, and in 1913 became professor of chemistry at Royal Holloway College, Englefield Green, but retained a part-time, consulting connection with the Wellcome laboratories. In 1914 he joined the staff of the Medical Research Committee (later Medical Research Council); and in 1919 was appointed the first professor of chemistry in relation to medicine in the University of Edinburgh, where he remained until, in 1937, he accepted the regius chair of chemistry in the University of Glasgow, an appointment which he held for the rest of his life.

Barger's scientific work followed two main lines, namely, studies of alkaloids, and investigations of simpler nitrogenous compounds of biological importance: both arose from his studies of ergot initiated in the Wellcome laboratories. His main achievements in alkaloid chemistry were the isolation of ergotoxine from ergot; the elucidation of the constitutions of carpaine and physostigmine, and of a group of aporphine alkaloids; and an important contribution to the chemistry of yohimbine.

Barger's identification of tyramine as one of the compounds responsible for the biological activity of ergot extracts led to a series of studies of bases similarly derived from naturally occurring amino acids; among such bases isolated both from ergot and from mammalian tissues was histamine, a compound which later proved to be of the greatest physiological significance. In this field Barger's chemical expertise complemented the physiological skills of Dale. Together, the two men worked on a wide range of amines that mimicked the natural activity of the sympathetic nervous system. This led them to develop the significant concept of sympathomimetic amines, important for basic physiology and pharmacology, and for the later development of therapeutic compounds.

In the early part of work by others leading to the synthesis of thyroxine (by C. R. Harington), and of vitamin B1 (by A. R. Todd), Barger's contribution and continuing interest were considerable. His lifelong interest in ergot was expressed in *Ergot and Ergotism* (1931), a scholarly monograph covering all aspects of the subject; this was based on his Dohme lectures delivered in 1928 at Johns Hopkins University, Baltimore. In addition to many scientific papers, he published three other books on aspects of organic chemistry and its relationship to medicine.

Barger was an enthusiastic traveller, and his linguistic expertise enabled him to develop close scientific contacts in many countries, which he used to promote his ideal of free exchange between scientists of different nations. In his own work he was essentially an experimentalist and his scientific outlook was mechanistic. He was uncompromisingly honest and outspoken, not over-patient, but generous of himself to his friends and pupils.

Barger was a fellow of King's College, Cambridge, from 1904 to 1910 and was elected FRS in 1919, serving on its council from 1930 to 1932, and receiving the society's Davy medal in 1938. He was an active member of the Chemical Society for many years, serving on its council from 1913 to 1917, and becoming vice-president in the year in which he died, having been Longstaff medallist in 1936. He was Hanbury medallist of the Pharmaceutical Society (1934) in recognition of the importance of his work to pharmaceutical chemistry, and president of section B (Chemistry) of the British Association (1929). He received honorary degrees from the universities of Liverpool, Padua, Heidelberg, Utrecht, Michigan, and Lausanne. Barger died suddenly at Aeschi, Switzerland, on 6 January 1939, while on a lecture tour. C. R. HARINGTON, *rev.* E. M. TANSEY

Sources H. H. Dale, *Obits. FRS*, 3 (1939–41), 63–85 · C. R. Harington, *JCS* (1939), 715–21 · H. H. Dale, 'George Barger', *Nature*, 143 (1939), 107–8 · H. H. Dale, *The Lancet* (14 Jan 1939), 116–17 · A. J. Roche, 'Barger, George', *DSB*, 15.10–11 · *The Times* (7 Jan 1939) · private information (1949) · personal knowledge (1949) · G. K. Das and J. Beer, eds., *E. M. Forster: a human exploration* (1979), 171 · *CGPLA Eng. & Wales* (1939)

Archives Medical Research Council, London, corresp. and papers | Bodl. Oxf., corresp. with Society for Protection of Science and Learning · CAC Cam., corresp. with A. V. Hill · RS, Dale MSS · Wellcome L., letters to Sir Edward Mellanby

Likenesses P. K. P. Bolton, group photograph, 1905–6 (with Symons, Dale, Dowson, Suedmerson), Wellcome L. · W. Stoneman, photograph, 1921, NPG · F. Morley, portrait, 1923, priv. coll. · D. Young, photographs, Wellcome L. · group photograph, Wellcome L. · group photograph (with staff of Wellcome Physiological Research Laboratory), Wellcome L. · photograph, RS

Wealth at death £3201: confirmation, 29 March 1939, *CGPLA Eng. & Wales*

Bargery, George Percy (1876–1966), missionary and Hausa scholar, was born on 1 October 1876 at 7 Oxford Terrace, St James Road, Exeter, the son of George Thomas Bargery, commercial traveller, and his wife, Ellen Dawes. Educated in Exeter and at the University of London, he was ordained in the Church of England in 1900, and joined the Church Missionary Society, who sent him to Northern Nigeria. His first wife, Nina (*d.* 1932), whom he married in 1906, was with him in Nigeria until 1910 when she returned to Britain. His second marriage, on 11 April 1940, to Minnie Jane Martin, a retired headmistress aged sixty-five who had worked in Nigeria, lasted until her death in 1953. He had at least one son.

An early uncompleted medical training stood Bargery in good stead in his daily life in Nigeria. Lord Lugard's annual report on Northern Nigeria submitted to the British government for 1905–6 recognized Bargery's medical skills and his remarkable fortitude, saying of him:

> during an outbreak of sickness at Rimmo Mr Bargery saved the lives of over 80 persons, and the thanks of the Government were conveyed to this gentleman for having ridden on a bicycle 65 miles in one day to attend an officer of the West African Frontier Force. Having been overtaken by darkness, he spent the night in a tree in pouring rain. (Lugard, 469)

Bargery's major achievement, however—leading to his later appointment at the School of Oriental and African Studies (SOAS) in London—was the compilation of a dictionary of the Hausa language. This endeavour was entrusted to him by the governor of Nigeria, Sir Hugh Clifford, and he worked on it for some five years in the company of a group of Hausa scholars in Kano led by the intrepid Malam Mahmudu Koki. First published in 1934 after fourteen years of work, the dictionary remains an astonishing achievement, with 52,000 entries complete with tone patterns and detailed commentary upon meanings, synonyms, near-synonyms, dialectal variants, and specialized usages. In addition to a team of Hausa scholars, the colonial government of Nigeria seconded a gifted and trained linguist, Captain R. C. Abraham, to assist in the project over some two years. Neither Bargery nor his Hausa colleagues were trained linguists, and it is said that Bargery asked his new assistant to go through the trays of cards that had already been prepared and check for consistency. Alarmed at the growing pile of entries being rooted out, Bargery and his Hausa colleagues resolved their dilemma by returning after the day's work had been concluded, and all had retired to their various quarters, to reinsert by candlelight the items removed (private information).

After retirement from the Church Missionary Society, Bargery became a teacher and scholar of Hausa (1930–47) at SOAS; he was made reader in Hausa in 1937. He was awarded the degree of DLitt at the University of London in 1937, and was made an OBE in 1957. A close colleague described Bargery as 'intensely practical, forthright and down-to-earth, a stickler for order and punctuality, a hater of cant and humbug and on moral issues uncompromising' (Parsons, 490). His sense of humour was 'immense, earthy, and sometimes bordering on the macabre' (ibid.). He was a great storyteller, every tale being relived and dramatized, 'and he would end up with tears of laughter streaming down his mobile face, his deep-throated chuckles reverberating around the Common Room' (ibid.).

In retirement from SOAS Bargery accepted an invitation from the British and Foreign Bible Society to advise on a new translation of the Bible into Hausa, and from 1953 to 1959 he lived and worked in Kano, leaving at the age of eighty-two. He also continued to be a teacher and examiner of Hausa on Devonshire courses for the colonial service at Oxford and Cambridge. Progress in the service was dependent upon a growing mastery of local languages, a condition laid down by Lord Lugard in the early years of the colonial administration, and through his dictionary and other language materials, Bargery made an invaluable contribution to the efficiency of colonial administration.

Bargery died on 2 August 1966 at his home, Little Redlands, Cow Lane, Tring, Hertfordshire. His obituarist in the SOAS *Bulletin* praised his contribution to Hausa scholarship but also noted that he had been held in great affection by the many Nigerians who knew him:

> Bargery will be best remembered as a great lover of Nigeria, and of all peoples and things Nigerian—of the Tiv as much as of the Hausa … and all its other peoples too—Christian, Muslim, pagan alike. To him they were all 'brothers and sisters in God', and he accorded them that respect for their *mutunci* (human dignity) which so endeared him to them. (Parsons, 493)

GRAHAM FURNISS

Sources F. W. Parsons, *Bulletin of the School of Oriental and African Studies*, 30 (1967), 488–94 • F. Lugard, *Northern Nigeria: annual report, 1905–6* (1906) • *The Times* (4 Aug 1966) • private information (2004) • *CGPLA Eng. & Wales* (1966) • W. R. S. Miller, *Reflections of a pioneer* (1936) • b. cert. • d. cert. • m. cert. [Minnie Jane Martin] • d. cert. [Minnie Jane Bargery]
Archives SOAS, papers
Likenesses photograph, *c*.1960, repro. in Parsons, *Bulletin*, facing p. 489
Wealth at death £9140: probate, 26 Oct 1967, *CGPLA Eng. & Wales*

Bargrave, Isaac (*bap.* **1586**, *d.* **1643**), dean of Canterbury, was baptized at Bridge, Kent, on 12 June 1586, the sixth son of a yeoman farmer and tanner, Robert Bargrave (*c*.1540–1598), of Bridge, and Joan Gilbert, of Sandwich. He was educated at Cambridge, gaining his BA at Pembroke College in 1607 and proceeding to Clare College for his MA (1610). He was ordained deacon and priest at Peterborough on 10 May 1612 and in October of the same year became rector of Eythorne. However, he maintained his Cambridge connections and played the part of a Portuguese pander in George Ruggle's Latin comedy, *Ignoramus*, performed at the university before James I on 8 March 1615.

Between 1616 and 1618 Bargrave served as chaplain to his kinsman Sir Henry Wotton, the English ambassador in Venice, and became intimate with Paolo Sarpi, author of the *History of the Council of Trent*, who assured him that 'the Doctrine and Discipline of the Church of England were the most primitive of any in the World' ('Memoir', BL, MS Lansdowne 985, 9). On his return to England in 1618, bearing a letter of introduction from Wotton to the king, Bargrave's career prospered. One outcome of his stay in Italy was the publication in 1619 of his translation of Fulgenzio Micanzio's revealing description of the government of the Jesuit order; sixty years later this was to be revived by Titus Oates for anti-papal purposes.

In 1622 Bargrave received the degree of DD at Cambridge and was appointed a prebendary of Canterbury Cathedral, where his brother-in-law, John Boys, was dean. In the same year he was granted the living of St Margaret's, Westminster, and became chaplain to Prince Charles, an office which he retained after the prince ascended the throne in 1625. On the death of Boys, Bargrave was able to invoke the interest of the duke of Buckingham and succeeded to the deanery of Canterbury, to which he was formally admitted on 16 October 1625. He obtained the vicarage of Tenterden in 1626 and was presented to the benefice of Lydd by 'Abbot's collation' in September 1627; he held it for only a few weeks, since William Laud, then bishop of London, succeeded in quashing his admission.

Meanwhile, Bargrave's post at Westminster had earned him 'great esteem with the Parliament … who took the sacrament constantly at his hands' ('Memoir', BL, MS Lansdowne 985, 9). His sermons, of which several were published, displayed a marked independence. In 1623 he suffered royal displeasure for 'his sermon before Parliament … against Papery, Evil Counsellors, and Corruption' (ibid.). After Charles I's accession, however, he declared himself unflinchingly in favour of the divine right of kings, proclaiming in a sermon of 27 March 1627: 'No man hath learn'd to disobey his *King*, but he had learn'd before to disobey his *God*' (Bargrave, 20). As dean of Canterbury he gained a reputation for being 'learned and hospitable' (Walton). He introduced musical and liturgical innovations into the cathedral services, and also put on Latin plays at the deanery. However, his dedication to Anglicanism as a middle way between extremes, and his desire for influence among his Kentish neighbours, disadvantaged him with both sides as the conflict between royalists and puritans became increasingly polarized. Archbishop Laud took the side of the members of the cathedral chapter who complained of Bargrave's partiality in the distribution of patronage. In 1635 Laud also forced a conflict by insisting that the large congregation of French Huguenots worshipping in Canterbury should conform to the ritual of the Church of England. In this case, the dean and chapter combined with the mayor and corporation in resisting the change, but the archbishop could not be dissuaded.

Soon after the opening of the Long Parliament Bargrave faced criticism from its leaders. When the bill for the abolition of deans and chapters was introduced by Sir Edward Dering, a cousin of his wife, Bargrave increased his unpopularity there by going to the House of Commons on 12 May 1641 to present petitions against the bill from the University of Cambridge and from the almsmen, officers, and tenants of Canterbury Cathedral.

At the beginning of the civil war, in August 1642, Colonel Edwyn Sandys, one of the rare puritan sympathizers among the Kentish gentry, whom the dean had intervened to save from an indictment for rape in his early life, marched his troop to Canterbury and attacked the deanery. Bargrave was absent, but his wife and children were cruelly treated. On hearing that the dean was at Gravesend, Sandys proceeded there, arrested him, and sent him to the Fleet prison. After three weeks' imprisonment Bargrave was released without having been brought to trial. He returned to Canterbury broken in health, and died at the deanery early in January 1643. He was buried on 25 January 1643 alongside other deans of the period in the chapel of Our Lady Martyrdom in the cathedral. In 1679 a memorial was erected above the grave by his nephew John *Bargrave who was vice-dean at the time. The memorial consisted of a portrait of the dean, attributed to Cornelius Johnson, painted on copper, within an elegant marble cartouche that has been attributed to Wren's assistant, Edward Pierce. From Bargrave's marriage in 1618 to Elizabeth (1593–1667), daughter of John Dering, of Egerton, he had two sons and a daughter. Thomas, the eldest, married a niece of Sir Henry Wotton and was an executor of Sir Henry's will. His descendants continued to be lessees of Eastry Court, a former property of the cathedral, until the nineteenth century, when the male line died out. The second son, Robert *Bargrave (1628–1661), travelled widely in the Mediterranean and the Middle East.

Sidney Lee, *rev.* Stephen Bann

Sources 'Memoir of Dr Isaac Bargrave', BL, Lansdowne MS 985, 9 • E. Hasted, *The history and topographical survey of the county of Kent*, 2nd edn, 12 (1801), 17–19 • J. Philipott, 'The visitation of the county of Kent taken in the year 1619 [pt 1]', *Archaeologia Cantiana*, 4 (1861), 241–72 • Venn, *Alum. Cant.* • P. Collinson, 'The protestant cathedral, 1541–1660', *A history of Canterbury Cathedral, 598–1982*, ed. P. Collinson and others (1995), 154–203 • J. Bruce, ed., *Verney papers: notes of proceedings in the Long Parliament*, CS, 31 (1845) • S. Bann, *Under the sign: John Bargrave as collector, traveler and witness* (1994) • *Walker rev.* • J. Nichols, *The progresses, processions, and magnificent festivities of King James I, his royal consort, family and court*, 4 vols. (1828) • I. Bargrave, *A sermon preached before King Charles* (1627) • D. Gardiner, ed., *The Oxinden letters, 1607–1642* (1933) • I. Walton, *The lives of John Donne, Sir Henry Wotton, Richard Hooker, George Herbert, and Robert Sanderson*, [new edn] (1927), 139

Likenesses C. Johnson, oil on copper, *c.*1630, Canterbury Cathedral, Our Lady Martyrdom Chapel; repro. in J. Dart, *Antiquities of Canterbury* (1727), following p. 56 • J. Cole, line engraving (after medallion on monument), BM, NPG; repro. in J. Dart, *The history and antiquities of the cathedral church of Canterbury* (1726) • C. Johnson, oils, deanery, Canterbury; version, Clare College, Cambridge • relief medallion on monument (after C. Johnson), Canterbury Cathedral

Bargrave, John (*bap.* 1610, *d.* 1680), Church of England clergyman and collector of curiosities, was baptized at Nonington, Kent, on 18 November 1610. His father, also named John, was the elder brother of Isaac Bargrave and had increased the family fortune derived from tanneries in east Kent by his marriage to Jane Crouch, the daughter of a prosperous London haberdasher. A year after the birth of John, his second son, he received a grant of arms and soon afterwards retired from his profession as a mercenary soldier to build the country house of Bifrons, at Patrixbourne, near Canterbury. As a younger son, Bargrave was destined to follow his uncle into the church. He attended the King's School, Canterbury, between 1623 and 1626, and proceeded in 1629 to Peterhouse at Cambridge where Isaac's close friend Matthew Wren was master. He served as college librarian between 1634 and 1636 and was admitted as a fellow in 1637. By this stage Wren had been succeeded by John Cosin, at Archbishop Laud's special behest. In the polarization of political and religious views that preceded the outbreak of the civil war, Bargrave held to the churchmanship and royalist loyalties of his Kentish connections. His uncle, as dean of Canterbury, took a lead in defending universities and cathedral chapters against the Long Parliament in 1641, and helped to rally the Kentish gentry to the king's support in 1642. Bargrave himself was caught up in the reprisals, being ejected from his fellowship in 1644.

From 1645 until the Restoration, Bargrave chose to spend most of his time travelling on the continent. From time to time he had charge of young fellow travellers from among his Kentish and Cambridge connections. The first of these journeys, which took place in 1646–7, resulted in the first Italian guidebook published in the English language; it appeared under the name of his nephew John Raymond. The likelihood that Bargrave had a major part in this work is strengthened by the recent discovery of a manuscript journal of Bargrave's earlier French tour of 1645. Bargrave's periods of foreign residence, and particularly the four journeys to Rome that he undertook in 1647, 1650, 1655, and 1660, enabled him to collect numerous coins, curiosities, and small-scale antiquities. His subsequent comments in cataloguing them, together with his acute observations penned in the margins of a set of mounted prints of the College of Cardinals, provide innumerable piquant details about his life as a royalist exile.

With the Restoration Bargrave resumed his ecclesiastical career, though his longest foreign journey was still to come. In September 1662, simultaneously with his appointment as a canon of Canterbury, he took charge of a royal mission to ransom Christian slaves from the dey of Algiers; the mission, successfully concluded, allowed him to add a portrait of the dey and a mummified chameleon to his collection.

Bargrave's marriage in 1665 to Frances Osborne, *née* Wilde, a well-connected Kentish widow, was childless. Up to his death in Canterbury on 11 May 1680 he remained an active member of the cathedral chapter, compiling a survey of its revenues as receiver-general in 1675, and later serving as vice-dean. He was survived by his wife. Buried in Canterbury Cathedral, he had requested that the chains of one of the slaves whom he had redeemed be hung over his grave. His meticulously documented collection, housed originally in two cabinets and left to the dean and chapter in his will, has achieved a widespread reputation as the best preserved example of its kind in Britain.

Stephen Bann

Sources *Pope Alexander the Seventh and the College of Cardinals, by John Bargrave …; with a catalogue of Dr Bargrave's Museum*, ed. J. C. Robertson, CS, 92 (1867) • S. Bann, *Under the sign: John Bargrave as collector, traveler and witness* (1994) • D. Sturdy and M. Henig, *The gentle traveller: John Bargrave, canon of Canterbury and his collection* (1985) • J. Raymond, *An itinerary contayning a voyage made through Italy in the yeare 1646, and 1647* (1648) • J. Bargrave, 'A part of my journal of France 1645', Canterbury Cathedral Library, IRBY deposit, U11/8 • J. Harris, 'To oblivion and back: Dr Bargrave's Museum of Rarities', *Country Life*, 179 (1986), 278–80 • C. E. Woodruff, 'A seventeenth-century survey of the estates of the dean and chapter of Canterbury in east Kent', *Archaeologia Cantiana*, 38 (1926), 29–44 • Venn,

Alum. Cant., 1/1.84 • J. Philipott, 'The visitation of the county of Kent taken in the year 1619 [pt 1]', *Archaeologia Cantiana*, 4 (1861), 241–72, esp. 252 • A. Bernau, *Sixteenth-century marriages, 1538–1600* (1911) • P. H. Blake, 'The builder of Bifrons', *Archaeologia Cantiana*, 108 (1990), 270

Archives Canterbury Cathedral, IRBY deposit, U11/8 • Canterbury Cathedral, literary MSS, E 39

Likenesses M. Bolognini, oils, 1647, Canterbury Cathedral Library • assistant of G. B. Canini, oils, 1650, Canterbury Cathedral Library

Bargrave, Robert (1628–1661), merchant and diarist, was born in Kent, possibly at the family home, Eastry Court, Eastry, near Sandwich, on 25 March 1628, the second surviving son of Isaac *Bargrave (*bap.* 1586, *d.* 1643), dean of Canterbury, and his wife, Elizabeth (1593–1667), daughter of John Dering and his wife, Elizabeth Wotton. Bargrave was admitted pensioner of Clare College, Cambridge, on 23 March 1642 and then matriculated from Corpus Christi, Oxford, on 10 May 1643. Both *Alumni Cantabrigienses* and *Alumni Oxonienses* accept without question that he was the Robert Bargrave who had been admitted to Gray's Inn on 14 August 1640, at the unusually young age of twelve, along with his elder brother, Thomas. If this was so, then Tilmouth speculates that it may primarily have been to take part in the inn's dramatic entertainments (Tilmouth, 158).

Bargrave compiled a diary of four voyages undertaken between April 1647 and March 1656 as a merchant trading in the Levant and other Mediterranean locations (Bodl. Oxf., MS Rawl. C 799). The first account (April 1647 to September 1652) describes his journey by sea from England to Constantinople with the entourage of the new ambassador, Sir Thomas Bendish, and his experiences as a merchant in Turkey. The second account (September 1652 to March 1653) recounts his arduous travels home overland from Turkey to England. About 1653 Bargrave married Elizabeth Turner (*b.* 1632) of Canterbury. They had four children: Robert (1654–1659), Hester (*b.* 1658), Elizabeth (*b.* 1659?), and Isaac (1660–1663). Their two sons were commemorated in a pavement tablet at Canterbury Cathedral (removed in 1993 but reproduced in Cowper, 41). Bargrave's third voyage (November 1654 to February 1656) took him to Spain and then on to Venice; and his rapid progress home overland from Venice to England (February to March 1656) is described in the fourth account. Bargrave's diary records his extensive experiences of commercial and diplomatic affairs, as well as his encounters with émigré royalists, and his relatives John Bargrave and John Raymond, who together compiled the invaluable guidebook published under the latter's name as *An Itinerary … Made through Italy* (1648). Interspersed with these travel records are examples of Bargrave's own poetry, including a masque with musical settings and dance steps, and his general observations as a tourist. Another, now lost, manuscript of these travels was at Bargrave's childhood home, Eastry Court, until at least the mid-1830s.

After March 1656 Bargrave was employed as personal secretary to Heneage Finch, earl of Winchilsea. Through Winchilsea's influence, Robert was nominated as clerk of the castle court at Dover. He was then appointed by the Levant Company as secretary at Constantinople, following Winchilsea's appointment as ambassador there. This latter position was one of considerable influence, requiring Bargrave to serve as chancellor of the company's factory and also to deputize for Winchilsea if he was unable to perform his ambassadorial duties through absence, illness, or death. On 20 October 1660 Winchilsea sailed from the Downs on the *Plymouth*, under the command of Thomas Allin, with Bargrave and his new private secretary, Paul Rycaut. On route to Turkey, Winchilsea's party stopped at Lisbon and Algiers and several official documents concerning these visits (now in the PRO) were penned by Bargrave. The *Plymouth* arrived at Smyrna on 14 December and departed for Constantinople on 7 January 1661, leaving behind Bargrave who had been laid low by a severe fever. His death was reported on 9 February 1661 to Winchilsea by the English consul at Smyrna, Richard Baker: 'Your servant m^r Bargrave is dead & buried at Santa Venáranda whither wee all accompanied him; his wife most disconsolate & to be admired for her love & care of him' (Leics. RO, DG.7 Box 4982). His widow, Elizabeth, set out from Smyrna on 29 March for the return journey to England, accompanied by the retiring ambassador, Sir Thomas Bendish, with whom Bargrave had first travelled out to the Levant in 1647. MICHAEL G. BRENNAN

Sources *The travel diary of Robert Bargrave, Levant merchant, 1647–1656*, ed. M. G. Brennan, Hakluyt Society, 3rd ser., 3 (1999) • J. W. Stoye, *English travellers abroad, 1604–1667*, rev. edn (1989) • M. Tilmouth, 'Music on the travels of an English merchant, Robert Bargrave (1628–61)', *Music and Letters*, 53 (1972), 143–59 • BL, Sloane MS 1708, fol. 107 • *CSP dom.*, *1660–61*, 103 • Leics. RO, DG.7 Box 4982 [formerly HMC *Finch MSS*, 1.93] • Venn, *Alum. Cant.* • Foster, *Alum. Oxon.* • PRO, SP 71/1, pt ii, fols. 185, 195; SP 97/17, fols. 292–3, 295 • E. S. Curling, 'Journal of Robert Bargrave in Turkey', *GM*, 2nd ser., 6 (1836), 367–9, 604–8 • *GM*, 2nd ser., 7 (1837), 361–4 • *GM*, 2nd ser., 8 (1837), 22–4, 235–8 • S. P. Anderson, *An English consul in Turkey: Paul Rycaut at Smyrna, 1667–1678* (1989) • *The journals of Sir Thomas Allin, 1660–1678*, ed. R. C. Anderson, 2 vols., Navy RS, 79–80 (1939–40) • J. M. Cowper, ed., *The memorial inscriptions of the cathedral church of Canterbury* (1897)

Barham. For this title name *see* Middleton, Charles, first Baron Barham (1726–1813); Noel, Diana, *suo jure* Baroness Barham (1762–1823).

Barham, Charles Foster (1804–1884), physician, was born at Truro Vean, Cornwall, on 9 March 1804, the fourth son of Thomas Foster *Barham (1766–1844), a musician and writer of independent means, and his wife, Mary Ann, eldest daughter of the Revd Joshua Morton, of Blackheath, Kent. He was the brother of Francis Foster *Barham (1808–1871), Thomas Foster *Barham (1794–1869), and William Foster *Barham (1802–1845). He was educated privately at Penzance, at St Keverne, and at Bodmin, in Cornwall, between 1811 and 1819, and at Saffron Walden in 1819–20. He then went to Downing College, Cambridge, where he matriculated in October 1821. The following January he migrated to Queens' College, where he became a foundation scholar in May 1823. After studying medicine in Edinburgh, Paris, and Bologna, he took his MB degree at Cambridge in 1827, though he did not become MD until 1860. For four years he practised at Plymouth and at Tavistock

Dispensary, and in 1832 he moved to Truro and joined the staff of the Royal Cornwall Infirmary; he was appointed senior physician in 1838, and after resigning that post in 1873 he was elected consulting physician. On 28 September 1839 he married Caroline (*b.* 1811), second daughter of Clement Carlyon MD of Truro, Barham's superior at the infirmary.

After settling in Truro Barham joined the Royal Institution of Cornwall. He became its joint secretary in 1837, a post he held until he became its president in 1859, and over the years he contributed many articles to its report and journal. In 1856 he was sworn in as a magistrate for Truro and in 1858 he was appointed mayor. He was also consultant physician to the Truro Friendly Society, and he was president of the south-western branch of the British Medical Association for a number of years.

Barham was interested in antiquarian and scientific researches generally. The two subjects which had especial interest for him were the health of the miners who contributed to Cornwall's wealth, and the county's climate. Many of the papers written by him on these topics are listed in the first and third volumes of *Bibliotheca Cornubiensis* (1874, 1882). His *Report on the Sanitary State of the Labouring Classes in the Town of Truro* appeared in 1840. In 1842 he was a sub-commissioner on the children's employment commission, and he drew up reports on juvenile employment in mines and iron foundries in Cornwall. These were printed in the reports of the commission along with the evidence he had collected.

Barham died at his home, 11 Strangways Terrace, Truro, on 20 October 1884, survived by his wife, three sons, and four daughters. He was buried nearby, at Kenwyn, three days later. JUSTIN BROOKE

Sources *Royal Cornwall Gazette* (26 Oct 1884), 5 c.1–2 · Boase & Courtney, *Bibl. Corn.*, 1.10, 3.1048 · *Journal of the Royal Institution of Cornwall*, 8 (1883–5), 225 · *BMJ* (8 Nov 1884), 940–41

Likenesses T. Dunn, portrait, City Hall, Truro, Cornwall · H. Harvey, oils, Royal Institution of Cornwall, Truro, Cornwall

Wealth at death £8107 17*s.* 2*d.*: probate, 4 Nov 1884, *CGPLA Eng. & Wales*

Barham, Francis Foster [*known as* Alist Francis Barham] **(1808–1871)**, transcendentalist, was born on 31 May 1808 at Leskinnick, Penzance, Cornwall, the youngest of the five sons of Thomas Foster *Barham (1766–1844), musician and writer, and his wife, Mary Ann, daughter of the Revd Joshua Morton. His brothers included Charles Foster *Barham, Thomas Foster *Barham, and William Foster *Barham. A delicate child, often confined to the house by fever, he became a voracious reader of poetry and the Bible. 'From my earliest age', he later wrote, 'my mind was impressed by an intense love of the study of divinity' (Barham, *Alist: an Autobiography*, 5). In his youth he grew fit enough to ride, shoot, swim, sail, and keep animals. At Penzance grammar school, where discipline was famously severe, besides Greek, Latin, French, and mathematics he learned that 'asceticism begets energy and endurance' (Barham, *Memorial*, Introduction). Asceticism therefore became the guiding principle of his life.

While studying under his brother the Revd Henry Foster Barham of Epping Forest, Barham acquired a taste for collecting rare books. In 1826 he was articled for five years to a solicitor at Devonport, Plymouth. There, living alone and frugally, he read for eight to twelve hours a day. Offended by the 'detestable' style and phraseology of his law books, he turned to the lives of the saints and became particularly attached to Thomas à Kempis. After he qualified in 1831 he moved to London in order to practise as a member of one of the inns of court. Ill health prevented him from obtaining clients, and he decided to engage instead upon a literary career. He later recalled that 'as a solitary student in London, very retired, pale in countenance and toil worn in body, I seemed to exist for mind alone' (Barham, *Alist: an Autobiography*, 13). Two hundred pounds invested in the *New Monthly Magazine* procured him the joint editorship with John Abraham Heraud, the poet and dramatist. Finding the occupation 'unremunerative' (Barham, *Memorial*) he retired after less than a year, though he continued to contribute articles whose copyright he was careful to retain. Established in a comfortable boarding house in Camden Town, he dedicated all his time to reading in the British Museum: 'a great love of philology was born' (Barham, *Memorial*). Among the languages he mastered were Hebrew, Syriac, Arabic, Persian, Sanskrit, and Chinese; 'book opened book' his autobiography relates, and so he came to theosophy, freemasonry, alchemy, and occultism: 'I gave very long and earnest attention to collecting all the secret wisdom I could from this curious department of literature' (ibid., 11).

Prolonged study, loneliness, and lack of food—Barham lived for weeks on bread and water—intensified his belief in the importance of a spiritual life. His masters now were Philo; Dionysius, the pseudo-Areopagite; Tertullian; Origen; Fénélon; and William Law. They led him to a practical syncretism which strove to unite all the scattered truths of every religion without their errors—Barham was in no doubt he could identify the errors. After very long and arduous research he at last, about 1843, discovered the supreme central doctrine and gave it the name of Alism—A, Al, or Alah being the most ancient and universal title of the deity in Hebrew scripture. 'By Alism I meant that eternal Divinity, pure and universal which reconciled all divine truths to be found in scripture or nature, in theology, philosophy, science, or art' (Barham, *Memorial*, 12). This discovery justified Barham's fundamental optimism. He thought it would enable every living creature to attain the best possible condition according to its particular circumstances. 'Every man who labours for the advancement of piety, prosperity and peace, universal industry and generous recompense: he indeed is divine, he indeed is godlike' (*Alist: an Autobiography*, 19). Barham believed, moreover, that the transformation of society had already begun under the providential administration of Sir Robert Peel. After 1843 Barham began calling himself Alist Francis Barham. Later he dropped the title Alist, but he never resumed the use of his middle name, Foster (Barham, *Memorial*, iv).

During his fourteen years in London, Barham wrote and

edited many books, among which was a new edition of Jeremy Collier's *Ecclesiastical History of Great Britain*, on which he laboured from 1840 to 1844. He lectured to institutions and set up a literary agency near Gray's Inn to deal with authors' problems. He founded a Syncretic Society 'for the advancement of literature' (*Alist: an Autobiography*, 17), and a Society of Alists. He called for a return to enthusiasm, believing that, if the great religious revival heralded by his discovery of Alism were to succeed, the clergy must reform their present coldness and dullness. Among the preachers he most admired were Amos Bronson Alcott, Thomas Chalmers, and Edward Irving. He claimed to have put the Alist case to, among others, the mystic James Pierrepont Greaves, Scott, Carlyle, and Gladstone (Barham, *Alist: an Autobiography*, 9).

In 1844, aged thirty-six, having been a lifelong advocate of celibacy, he married Gertrude (*d.* 1869), daughter of the Revd Thomas Greenfield of Clifton, Bristol. The couple moved there, and for the next ten years Barham's time was principally occupied with the preparation of new translations of the Old and New Testament in chronological order, a herculean task which he was unable to complete. As a result of his labours he suffered from constant headaches, palpitations, and hallucinations. In 1854 he moved to Bath, where he and his wife lived at 8 St Mark's Place until she died on 23 December 1869. In the last eighteen months of his life he was befriended by a neighbour, Isaac Pitman, originator of the most widely used system of shorthand, and long a follower of Emmanuel Swedenborg. Barham died of a heart attack at his home in Bath on 9 February 1871, leaving manuscripts totalling 116 lb in weight, in very small handwriting and including treatises on ecclesiastical subjects, poems, plays, and propaganda for causes including pacifism, vegetarianism, and animal welfare. He also wrote on Swedenborg's works, and penned memoirs of James Pierrepont Greaves and Samuel Taylor Coleridge. These fell to Pitman, who published less than a tenth of the whole as an example of his new method of spelling in his *Phonetic Journal*.

Barham's prose was as lucid and precise as his vision of the world transformed by Alism. He was persuaded that Alah, God, the saints, prophets, and angels had an actual presence and communed with kindred intelligences, but he won few adherents for his ideas. ANNE TAYLOR

Sources F. F. Barham, *A memorial of Francis Barham*, ed. I. Pitman (1873) [mainly in phonetic script] • F. F. Barham, *The Alist or divine: a message to our times* (1840) • F. F. Barham, *The life and times of John Reuchlin, or Capnion* (1843) • F. F. Barham, *The Foster Barham genealogy* (1844) [privately printed] • *DNB* • [F. F. Barham], *Alist, an autobiography, or, An author's life in the nineteenth century* [1840]

Archives BL • DWL • Royal Literary and Scientific Institution, 18 Queen Square, Bath, MSS

Wealth at death under £3000: probate, 24 Feb 1871, *CGPLA Eng. & Wales*

Barham, Henry (1670?–1726), botanist, was descended from the Barhams of Barham Court in Kent. Little is known of his life beyond that conveyed in his letters to Sir Hans Sloane, which reveal that Barham's father, a physician, intended to give him a university education but died while his son was still young. His mother remarried soon afterwards, and the boy was apprenticed when he was about fourteen to a surgeon. He left this situation to become surgeon's mate in HMS *Vanguard*, from which he was promoted to be surgeon to another warship. Tiring of the monotony of his life, he went to Spain, then to Madras, arriving in Jamaica probably before the end of the century. According to his own account, he obtained a lucrative practice and was appointed surgeon-major over all regiments of horse in the island.

Barham stated that after he came to Jamaica he read widely, especially books on physical matters. Despite his irregular education, and his tendency to be led astray by fantastic and utopian ideas, he undoubtedly acquired a detailed knowledge of the flora and fauna of Jamaica. In 1715 he introduced the cultivation of logwood, later a common product. Barham was a prolific correspondent of Sir Hans Sloane, who transcribed many extracts from Barham's letters relating to the medicinal properties of plants into his own copy of his *Natural History of Jamaica*. Several specimens of Jamaican plant material went into Sloane's herbarium.

Sloane received in 1711 a treatise, 'Hortus Americanus', written by Barham; this was later published, in 1794, with a preface attributing it to Henry Barham MD (*d.* 1746), Barham's son. Nothing is known of Barham's wife who, according to a letter to Sloane, was still alive in 1725. Their son apparently practised as a physician in Jamaica from the beginning of the century, acquired much property on marriage, and returned to England in 1740 to settle at Staines, Middlesex.

About 1716 Barham returned to England and settled at Great Carter Lane in the City of London. He gave some eighty American plants to the Physic Garden at Chelsea, noting with regret that fewer than half were to be seen when he visited in 1718. He also devoted himself to the rearing of silkworms and the manufacture of silk, his treatise on this subject being read to the Royal Society and published in the *Philosophical Transactions* in 1719. He was elected fellow of the Royal Society in November 1717, and shortly after his arrival in England was made free of the Company of Surgeons, although his hopes of obtaining the diploma of MD were not fulfilled.

Barham promoted a scheme to mine silver in Jamaica, and applied in 1720 for the position of superintendent to a mining company formed to implement his proposals. He received the appointment on his own terms, having stated that his own business prospects were so good that he would not sacrifice them for less than £500 a year, but the enterprise was a complete failure and the one year's salary owed to him was never paid. He continued to reside in Jamaica until his death at Spanish Town in May 1726. Barham's 'History of Jamaica', which his son sent to Sloane in the hope that it might be published, remained in manuscript among Sloane's papers.

T. F. HENDERSON, *rev.* ANITA MCCONNELL

Sources J. Britten and J. E. Dandy, eds., *The Sloane herbarium* (1958), 87 · W. A. Feurtado, *Official and other personages of Jamaica from 1655 to 1790* (1896), 6 · BL, Sloane MS 4045, fol. 55
Archives BL, account of Jamaica, Sloane MS 3998 · BL, civil history of Jamaica, Add. MS 12422 | BL, letters to Sir Hans Sloane, Sloane MSS 4043, 4045–4048, 4078, *passim*
Likenesses G. Vertue, print, 1721, BM, NPG

Barham, Nicholas (*c*.1520–1577), serjeant-at-law, was born at Wadhurst, Sussex, the first son of Richard Barham of Wadhurst, and his wife, Alice Cradock. His was a branch of the Barham family of Teston House, Kent, which traced its descent from Robert of Barham who entered upon the estates of his kinsman Reginald Fitzurse, one of the murderers of Thomas Becket, upon the latter's flight into Ireland. Barham's legal training began at Barnard's Inn, which subsequently sued him for dues in 1546. He was admitted to Gray's Inn in 1540, where he is said to have been called to the bar in 1542. He became an ancient of the inn on 24 May 1552, and was Lent reader in 1558.

By 1561 Barham was counsellor to the town of Maidstone, Kent, and occupied the then conjoined offices of recorder and town clerk in succession to Henry Fisher, with whom he was returned to parliament for the borough in 1563. In 1562 Barham purchased the manor of Chillington, and Chillington Manor House in Maidstone, together with the chapel of St Faith, Maidstone, from the sons of Peter Maplesden, whose kinsman George had forfeited the manor and chapel for his part in Wyatt's rebellion. Barham's main residence, which he much improved, was the house called Digons in Knightrider Street, Maidstone, another property forfeited by George Maplesden. After Barham's death these properties were asserted to be concealed lands, upon which subject Peter Osborne wrote to Lord Burghley in July 1578 on behalf of Barham's widow, Mary (*d*. in or after 1585), daughter of John Holt of Cheshire, with whom he had two children, Margaret and Arthur; but the lands were still in the family's hands twenty years later when Arthur Barham sold them to Henry Hall. Barham built five pews for himself and his family in the south aisle of All Saints' Church, Maidstone, covenanting in return in 1570 to bear the cost of maintenance of a window in the aisle.

Barham was created serjeant-at-law in April 1567, joining Serjeants' Inn, Fleet Street, and was appointed queen's serjeant on 31 May of the same year. He was Sir James Dyer's principal companion as a justice of assize on the midland circuit from 1568 until his death, participating in the decision of *R.* v. *Saunders and Archer* (1573), a leading case on transferred malice in murder. At the bar, in addition to his common-law practice, Barham appeared frequently in the court of chancery. He argued the case of *Mines* ([1567] 1 Plowd. 313) for the crown, and was closely involved in the investigation of the Ridolfi plot and in the successful prosecutions arising from it: in January 1572 with the attorney-general and solicitor-general he conducted the prosecution before the lord high steward and his peers of Thomas Howard, duke of Norfolk, for treason, and in the following month with the attorney-general prosecuted Norfolk's servant Robert Higford in the court of queen's bench.

In 1573 Barham was appointed with two others to investigate and report upon a dispute between Richard Curtis, bishop of Chichester, and certain of the Sussex gentry. He was of counsel with Christopher Herenden in his attempt in the mid-1560s to upset a chancery decree against Herenden's late brother Walter in favour of Katharine, dowager duchess of Suffolk, and her husband, Richard Bertie, who had conveyed land to Walter Herenden in trust upon their flight into Poland in the face of the Marian persecution. But Barham appears to have had puritan sympathies, for he signed a petition about 1573 for John Strowde, a Kent minister who had been forbidden to preach by the archbishop. He died at Oxford on 25 July 1577 of gaol fever contracted at the trial of the recusant bookseller Roland Jenkes during the so-called 'black assizes', which fever killed also Sir Robert Bell, chief baron of the exchequer, and a large number of others.

N. G. Jones

Sources HoP, *Commons, 1558–1603*, vol. 1 · T. Benolt and R. Cooke, *The visitations of Kent taken in the years 1530–1 … and 1574*, ed. W. B. Bannerman, 1, Harleian Society, 74 (1923) · inquisition post mortem, PRO, C142/178/9 · inquisition post mortem, PRO, C142/189/94 (2) · K. S. Martin, ed., *Records of Maidstone* (1926) · W. H. Turner, ed., *Selections from the records of the city of Oxford* (1880) · Baker, *Serjeants* · J. M. Russell, *The history of Maidstone* (1881) · *A collection of state papers … left by William Cecill, Lord Burghley*, ed. W. Murdin, 2 (1759) · E. Hasted, *The history and topographical survey of the county of Kent*, 2nd edn, 4 (1798) · F. Hargrave, ed., *A complete collection of state-trials*, 4th edn, 11 vols. (1776–81) · S. Segar, 'A succession of readers extracted from severall ancient regesters with their coates armoriall in memorie thereof', *Gray's Inn: its history and associations, compiled from original and unpublished documents*, ed. W. R. Douthwaite (1886), 45–76 · Sainty, *King's counsel*

Barham, Richard Harris (1788–1845), writer and Church of England clergyman, was born on 6 December 1788 at 61 Burgate Street, Canterbury, the only (and illegitimate) son of Richard Harris Barham (*bap*. 1748, *d*. 1795), alderman, of Tappington Everard, Kent, and Elizabeth Fox (*fl*. 1788–1814), housekeeper. He was educated at St Paul's School (1800–07) and Brasenose College, Oxford (BA, 1811).

As a schoolboy Barham suffered a carriage accident which resulted in severe injury to his lower right arm and permanent disability. He first considered the law as a career, but withdrew after the briefest period of study. In 1813 he was ordained curate and in 1814 appointed to the parish of Westwell, Kent. Here he was married on 30 September 1814 to Caroline Smart (*d*. 1851), third daughter of Captain Smart of the Royal Engineers. Their marriage was happy, and they had seven children, four sons and three daughters, only three of whom outlived their father. In 1817 Barham moved to the living of Snargate and Warehorn, on Romney Marsh. In 1821 a chance encounter with an old schoolfriend prompted the offer of a minor canonry at St Paul's Cathedral. Barham moved his family to London, remaining vicar of Snargate until 1824, when he was appointed rector of St Mary Magdalen and St Gregory by Paul, and moved into Amen Corner in St Paul's Churchyard. Though he had already published some journalism

Richard Harris Barham (1788–1845), by Richard James Lane, 1842–3

and an unsuccessful novel, *Baldwin* (1820), moving into the capital's literary circles undoubtedly assisted his progress. He edited the *London Chronicle* in 1823, and contributed to several periodicals, including *John Bull*, the *Globe and Traveller*, the *Literary Gazette*, and *Blackwood's*. His friendship, from schooldays, with Richard Bentley led to a close association with *Bentley's Miscellany*. Bentley employed Barham at £10 a month as his adviser (in addition to paying £1 a page for his literary contributions), leading to Barham's role as peacemaker in disputes between Bentley and his successive editors, Dickens and Ainsworth.

Barham was a founder member in 1832 of the Garrick Club, where his sociable, tactful, and witty nature made him a popular figure. As Lord William Lennox recorded in his *Recollections* (1874), at the Garrick 'the literary man would find all that was agreeable and delightful in the society of the Reverend Richard Barham (Ingoldsby), Charles Dickens, William Makepeace Thackeray, Charles Reade' (Lennox, 162).

Conscientious in his clerical duties, both for St Paul's (where he was responsible for major improvements to the library) and for his parishes, Barham nevertheless found time to write, gaining popular repute through his *Ingoldsby Legends*, which began to appear in 1837 in *Bentley's Miscellany*. Under the guise of Thomas Ingoldsby of Tappington Everard in Kent, Barham 'discovered' old documents which provided the basis for his tales. In effect, most of these are reworkings of other narrative sources, from medieval chronicles to Kentish legends and Sir Walter Scott. The mixture of crime and the supernatural, in both verse and prose, is given a comic and grotesque dimension, immediately appealing to Barham's readers. The *Legends* went through three series in volume publication between 1840 and 1847. Many reprints were illustrated by artists such as Tenniel, Cruikshank, and Rackham. The work remained in print throughout the nineteenth century, and well into the twentieth. The People's Edition of 1881 had a printing of 100,000, of which 60,513 sold on publication day. Barham's verse is notable chiefly for its Byronic metrical and rhyming resourcefulness, and high-spirited energy. His knowledge of such areas as heraldry and witchcraft also lends a degree of authenticity to the *Legends*.

Barham's novel *My Cousin Nicholas* (1841) was first serialized in *Blackwood's*. In 1842 he was appointed divinity lecturer at St Paul's and exchanged his parish for that of St Augustine with St Faith's. Barham's interest in antiquities is reflected in his membership in 1843 of the recently formed British Archaeological Association. In the same year, when Bentley wished to dispense with his services, Barham resigned from *Bentley's Miscellany* (typically remaining on good terms with Bentley), moving to the *New Monthly Magazine* (under the editorship of another friend, Thomas Hood) for an enhanced payment. Here the remaining few Ingoldsby legends were published. However, Barham's last piece, the lyric 'As I laye a-thynkynge', was published in the *Miscellany*.

A throat infection in 1844 laid the foundation for a serious condition, resulting in Barham's death from ulceration of the larynx, at his home, the canonry house, Amen Corner, St Paul's Churchyard, London, on 17 June 1845. His funeral on 21 June was at his former church of St Mary Magdalene and St Gregory. There he was buried in the vault where four of his children had preceded him. When this church was destroyed by fire in 1886, the family remains were moved to Kensal Green cemetery, and the memorial tablet to Barham was transferred to the crypt at St Paul's.

Adult portraits of Barham reflect a plump and amiable personality. He was renowned in his day for his equable and genial temperament. He was 'scarcely esteemed second for his conversational powers to the Reverend Sydney Smith (his intimate friend)' according to his obituarist in the *Annual Register* (*Annual Register*, 1845, 283). It was Smith's residentiary house in Amen Corner that Barham had occupied for the last six years of his life.

ROSEMARY SCOTT

Sources W. G. Lane, *Richard Harris Barham* (1967) [incl. appx on 1st pubn of the pieces comprising the *Legends*] • *The life and letters of … Richard Harris Barham*, ed. R. H. D. Barham, 2 vols. (1870) [by his son Revd Richard Harris Dalton Barham] • T. Ingoldsby [R. H. Barham], *The Ingoldsby legends, or, Mirth and marvels*, ed. Mrs E. A. Bond, 88th edn, 3 vols. (1894) [incl. 'A bibliographical note on "The Ingoldsby Legends"' and memoir by Mrs E. A. Bond] • *Annual Register* (1845) • *The letters of Charles Dickens*, ed. M. House, G. Storey, and others, 1 (1965) • Foster, *Alum. Oxon.* • W. P. Lennox, *My recollections from 1806–1873*, 2 (1874) • R. B. Gardiner, ed., *The admission registers of St Paul's School, from 1748 to 1876* (1884)

Archives Harvard U., Houghton L., corresp., literary MSS, and papers | BL, letters as sponsor to the Royal Literary Fund, loan no.

96 • NL Scot., poems and letters to Blackwood's • NYPL, Berg collection

Likenesses oils, *c.*1794, Royal Museum, Canterbury • silhouette, *c.*1811 • oils, 1820, Corporation of Canterbury • oils, *c.*1822 • oils, *c.*1839 • R. H. D. Barham, pencil drawing, *c.*1840, NYPL • R. J. Lane, pencil drawing, 1842–3, NPG [*see illus.*] • C. Martin, drawing, 1845, BM • R. H. D. Barham, pen drawing, *c.*1847, Harvard U. • H. Griffiths, stipple (after R. H. D. Barham, *c.*1840), NPG; repro. in *Bentley's Miscellany* (1847) • etching (after G. Cruikshank), NPG; repro. in T. Ingoldsby, *The Ingoldsby legends*, 2 vols. (1870)

Barham, Thomas Foster (1766–1844), writer, was born on 8 October 1766 in Bedford, the third son of Joseph Foster, who in 1750 took the name of Barham by authority of a private act of parliament, and in accordance with the will of Henry Barham. He was educated at St John's College, Cambridge, where he matriculated in 1784 but did not graduate. After leaving the university he travelled on the continent. On his return he became associated with the mercantile house of Plummer & Co.; but ill health obliged him to leave London in 1806, and so he retired to the west of England, where he finally settled at Leskinnick, near Penzance, Cornwall. He married Mary Ann, the eldest daughter of the Revd Joshua Morton of Blackheath, on 7 October 1790, and had six children, including Charles Foster *Barham (1804–1884), Francis Foster *Barham (1808–1871), Thomas Foster *Barham (1794–1869), and William Foster *Barham (1802–1845). Barham's output included writings on theological topics, such as *Letter from a Trinitarian to a Unitarian* (1811), *Musical Meditations, Consisting of Original Compositions, Vocal and Instrumental* (1811, 2nd set 1815), and sacred poems and dramas, including *Abdallah, or, The Arabian Martyr* (1820) and *Colonel Gardiner* (1823). He also contributed various songs and adaptations, wrote a musical drama, *Lander Africanus* (1834), and edited and arranged Pergolesi's *Stabat mater* with English words in 1829. Barham died at Leskinnick on 25 February 1844.

THOMPSON COOPER, *rev.* DAVID J. GOLBY

Sources Brown & Stratton, *Brit. mus.* • Boase & Courtney, *Bibl. Corn.*, 1.12, 3.1049 • I. Pitman, *A memorial of Francis Barham* (1873) • Venn, *Alum. Cant.*

Barham, Thomas Foster (1794–1869), physician and classical scholar, was born at Hendon, Middlesex, on 10 September 1794, the eldest son of six children born to Thomas Foster *Barham (1766–1844) and his wife, Mary Ann Morton. Among his brothers, William Foster *Barham (1802–1845) was a writer, Charles Foster *Barham (1804–1884) was a physician, and Francis Foster *Barham (1808–1871) was the founder of Alism. Thomas Foster Barham entered Queens' College, Cambridge, in 1812, subsequently training at Guy's and St Thomas's hospitals in London; he took the Cambridge degree of MB in 1820 and in 1821 was made a licentiate of the Royal College of Physicians. He returned to Penzance, where his parents had settled, and took up a general practice and served as physician to the dispensary.

About 1830 Barham moved to Exeter and became physician to the Exeter Dispensary and to the West of England Institution for the Instruction and Employment of the Blind. He had from an early age been attached to Unitarianism; an effort to mediate Unitarian and orthodox views of the atonement appeared in the *Monthly Repository* in 1818 and 1819, and later he published several defences of Unitarianism. In Exeter he was an active supporter of George's Chapel, collaborating with its minister, Henry Acton (1797–1843), on a volume of forms of prayer for public worship (1846). Eventually he turned against all dogmatic theology, setting out his views in a pamphlet, *Christian Union in Churches without Dogmatism* (1840), rejecting any sectarian label at a time when James Martineau had scarcely begun his campaign against the Unitarian name.

On 2 July 1816 Barham married Sarah (1794–1837?), second daughter of Francis Garratt (*d.* 1808), a London tea dealer and member for Bridge ward of the court of common council of the City of London; they had a large family. His second marriage, on 14 December 1842, was to Margaret, daughter of Captain William Henryson RN of Stranraer. Independently wealthy, he gave up the practice of medicine and retired to a house he built at Highweek, near Newton Abbot. There he conducted religious services for himself, largely in accordance with the tenets of his old denomination, and devoted himself to scholarship and good works. He was persuaded by many of the arguments of the French socialist theorist Charles Fourier; while not accepting community of property, he lived simply, never employing servants for menial purposes, it is said (by J. T., *The Inquirer*, 20 March 1869), 'but treating them as equals, and sharing with them whatever was sufficient for natural wants and limited desires'. The fullest statement of his programme for social reform is *Philadelphia, or, The Claims of Humanity* (1858), which among other things advocated temperance, small farms, and cultivation of waste lands.

Barham's celebrated knowledge of Greek issued in an introduction to Greek grammar (1829), a book of Greek roots in English rhymes (1837) to help fix them in sense and memory, and *The Enkheiridion of Hehfaistiown, Concerning Meters and Poems* (1843), with an introductory essay, 'Prolegomena on rhythm and accent'. He contributed extensively to the proceedings of scientific societies in Cornwall and of the Devonshire Association for the Advancement of Science.

Barham died at Castle Dyke, Highweek, on 3 March 1869, and was buried in the churchyard there on 8 March. His last sermon, *The Prospect of Eternity*, on which he was working when he died, and his rendering of the first book of Homer's *Iliad* into English hexameters were published posthumously in 1869 and 1871.

R. K. WEBB

Sources *DNB* • *The Inquirer* (6 March 1869) • J. T., *The Inquirer* (20 March 1869) • Venn, *Alum. Cant.* • Boase & Courtney, *Bibl. Corn.*, 1.13–14, 3.1050 • *GM*, 1st ser., 86/2 (1816), 80 • *Report and Transactions of the Devonshire Association*, 3 (1869), 37–41 • d. cert. • m. cert. [Thomas Foster Barham and Margaret Henryson]

Archives Wellcome L., diary

Wealth at death under £14,000: resworn probate, Aug 1869, *CGPLA Eng. & Wales*

Barham, William Foster (1802–1845), writer, born at Marazion, Cornwall, on 22 October 1802, was the third son of Thomas Foster *Barham (1766–1844), writer, and Mary Ann, eldest daughter of the Revd Joshua Morton. Among his siblings were Thomas Foster *Barham (1794–1869), physician and classical scholar, Charles Foster *Barham (1804–1884), physician, and Francis Foster *Barham (1808–1871), the founder of Alism. He was educated in the grammar schools at Bodmin and Leeds, and was admitted to Queens' College, Cambridge, on 1 March 1820. On 24 February 1821 he migrated to Trinity College, Cambridge. He won the Porson prize in 1821 and 1822, and graduated BA in 1824 as twenty-second senior optime, second in the first class of the classical tripos, and second chancellor's medallist. He became a fellow of Trinity in 1825 and obtained his MA in 1827. He was the author of an unpublished poem, *Moskow* (*c.*1843). His Greek versions of portions of *Othello* and *Julius Caesar* are printed in a volume of *Translations which have Obtained the Porson Prize from 1817 to 1856* (2nd edn, 1857, 16–23). He also edited a travel book entitled *Descriptions of Niagara*, published in 1847. He died, unmarried, on 28 January 1845 and was buried at Penshurst, Kent. THOMPSON COOPER, *rev.* REBECCA MILLS

Sources F. F. Barham, ed., *The Foster Barham genealogy* (1844), 15, 17–18 · Venn, *Alum. Cant.*, 2/1.149 · Boase & Courtney, *Bibl. Corn.*, 3.1050 · H. R. Luard, ed., *Graduati Cantabrigienses*, 7th edn (1884), 26 · *N&Q*, 3rd ser., 3 (1863), 266, 399, 455 · J. Romilly, ed., *Graduati Cantabrigienses* (1846), 15 · J. Romilly, ed., *Graduati Cantabrigienses* (1856), 18 [T. F. Barham snr] · I. Pitman, ed., *A memorial of Francis Barham* (1873)

Baring, Alexander, first Baron Ashburton (1773–1848), merchant and banker, was born on 27 October 1773 (the frequently cited date of 1784 is incorrect) in Mincing Lane, London, the second child of the six sons and six daughters of Sir Francis *Baring (1740–1810), merchant and banker, and his wife, Harriet (1750–1804), daughter of William Herring of Croydon. Among his siblings were George *Baring (1781–1854) and Harriet *Wall (1768–1838). Part of his education was obtained at Hanau, Germany, and part as an apprentice in his father's firm of John and Francis Baring & Co. Sir Francis Baring was then one of London's leading merchants, well established in trade between the United States and Europe, influential in the affairs of the East India Company, and a respected adviser on commercial affairs to government ministers.

Early business experience, North America, and marriage In 1794 Alexander Baring was sent to work with Hope & Co., Barings' correspondents and leading merchants at Amsterdam, Europe's most important capital market. A long stay, undoubtedly leading to a partnership, was envisaged, but the French occupation of the city in 1795 forced the evacuation of Hopes to London. Baring was among the last to leave his post, fleeing by sea as French troops entered the city.

In late 1795 his father and the Hopes sent Baring to the United States to purchase land from Senator William Bingham, one of North America's wealthiest merchants. They sought a safe investment for their surplus funds outside war-torn Europe, and Baring, aged just twenty-two, was charged with appraising the investment and negotiating its purchase. He arrived in November, and in February 1796 he acquired 1,225,000 acres of land in Maine for £107,000, three-quarters for Hopes and the rest for

Alexander Baring, first Baron Ashburton (1773–1848), by Sir Thomas Lawrence, *c.*1810

Barings. With 'every circumstance weighed and every object worth attention … considered', he advised his principals, 'I have … closed this important bargain with the most *perfect* confidence of its being a most *lucrative* and *secure* investment' (ING Baring Archives, DEP3.5, doc.24). However, only a modest profit was made when the land was sold forty years later.

Baring remained in the United States until 1801, providing commercial intelligence for his father in London; 'a complete Jacobinical brouillon & I advise you to hold tight reigns with him' was his verdict on one client (ING Baring Archives, DEP3.5). Baring devoted part of his time to overseeing the management of Maine Lands, but he also traded as a merchant, believing that 'my *personal* credit here is higher than that of any commercial establishment in the country' (ibid., doc. 49). The United States' political stability, natural resources, and entrepreneurial spirit left him wholly convinced of its immense potential; 'I should make much more than all my prospects in Amsterdam ever promised in a much shorter period', he told his father in mid-1797 (ibid., DEP3.6).

Baring's links with Bingham were strengthened when on 23 August 1798 he married at Blackpoint, Philadelphia, the senator's elder daughter, Ann Louisa, and were strengthened again when his brother Henry married Bingham's other daughter, Maria, in 1802. Alexander Baring apparently received £20,000 by settlement and gifts as a result of his marriage and, following Bingham's death in 1804, his wife and sister-in-law shared three-fifths of the income from their father's $3 million estate, with their brother receiving the balance. This significantly added to Alexander Baring's wealth. He and his wife had five sons and four daughters.

Baring made his mark in influential circles. 'I am acquainted and constantly converse with the leading people who are of easy access here', he told his father six months after his arrival (ING Baring Archives DEP3.5, doc.27). One friendship struck up in 1796 was with Charles Maurice Talleyrand, foreign minister of France from 1797, with whom he agreed 'perfectly in his arguments'; he thought 'highly of his personal abilities but I should have some scruples in trusting to his integrity'. With careful calculation, he reckoned that 'he may perhaps be useful hereafter' (ibid., doc. 37). Other friendships were nurtured in government circles. By early 1797 Baring admitted to 'frequently conversing with men of influence in the finance department and with [Alexander] Hamilton, the late Secretary of the Treasury' and, 'by the direction of the President', was consulted on certain major government funding needs (ibid., doc. 42). In early 1799 he negotiated a proposed $5 million government loan with another secretary of the treasury, Oliver Wolcott; his clients left him unimpressed: 'You will perceive that our financiers of America as well as our politicians are quite novices' the 25-year-old told his father (ibid., DEP3.7, doc. 78).

Such comments revealed Baring's maturity: he was old before his years. As a young man he exuded *gravitas*, though his confidence bordered on arrogance. A thumbnail sketch in 1808 depicted him as 'a rather heavy looking young man with a hesitating manner but clear in his ideas and unassuming in his manners' (Hidy, 46).

In late 1801, having wound up his North American business on the pretext of having confidence in nobody to manage it for him, Baring returned home after an absence of six years. He pondered his future as a possible partner with Hopes but by late 1802 he had rejected the idea. His father's ambition for an alliance of Barings and Hopes, to form Europe's most powerful merchant bank under Alexander Baring's leadership, lay in ruins for want of a Baring partner of stature prepared to join Hopes in Amsterdam.

The 'Louisiana purchase' In early 1803 Barings and Hopes were appointed to arrange finance for the 'Louisiana purchase'. This 'operation of the utmost [financial] magnitude and importance, might stagger us in ordinary times and in the present would hardly attract the serious attention of any [financiers]' (ING Baring Archives, Northbrook MSS, A4, P. C. Labouchere to Francis Baring, 30 Jan 1803). One million square miles were to be purchased from French owners for $15 million. In April 1803 Baring, well briefed by his father, travelled to Paris to negotiate with the French and United States governments. 'We must … leave the decision to Alexander', wrote Sir Francis, 'who must be governed by circumstances, his own prudence and judgement' (ibid., F. Baring to P. C. Labouchere, 15 Feb 1803). In Paris Baring was instrumental in scaling down the initial French demand for 100 million francs to 80 million, and he then negotiated the purchase by Barings and Hopes from the French government of US government bonds worth $11.25 million, which had been handed to it as part of the consideration. This accomplished, Baring left for the United States in August to 'complete the agreement in a regular manner' (ibid., F. Baring to P. C. Labouchere, 21 April 1803), and to sell to American investors as many of the Louisiana bonds as was possible. The transaction underlined Baring's—now aged thirty—emergence as a leading international financier.

A partnership in Baring Brothers Sir Francis retired in December 1804, though he remained a significant source of advice and influence until his death in 1810; only in 1807 was the firm's title of Sir Francis Baring & Co. changed to Baring Brothers. He was impatient to go but his son's continued absence abroad had forced him to continue. In June 1804 Alexander Baring and his third brother, Henry, were admitted partners of Barings, joining their father, their eldest brother, Thomas, and Charles Wall. By 1809 Wall and Thomas had also left, and Alexander Baring was now the undisputed senior partner.

Although Baring accumulated wealth in the United States, his initial contribution to his firm's capital was modest. In June 1804 he and Henry were allocated £5000 each from profits which were credited to the capital account as their first contribution to the firm's resources. Thereafter Alexander's capital accumulated steadily so that in 1830, when he retired, he contributed at least £158,000 to the £392,000 total. Initially he received a quarter of the profits; this rose to five-eighths between 1810 and 1815, and then to two-thirds between 1816 and 1823; it then fell back to a quarter towards the end of his leadership. As profits frequently exceeded £50,000, his income was substantial. Like each of his three younger brothers, in 1810 he received £25,000 and $25,000 (about £5000) from his father's estate, the lion's share of which—about £450,000—passed to his eldest brother, Sir Thomas Baring.

In terms of capital, ability, and prestige, Baring dominated the firm, but he shied away from the routine work of managing the merchanting, the agency work, and trade finance. As Henry's contribution was always unremarkable, day-to-day management was placed in the hands of two senior clerks who were promoted to junior partners in 1809. Of much greater importance, in 1815 Baring brought in an outsider, Swinton C. Holland, an experienced merchant, to be his deputy and to take full charge of the company's routine affairs. Although diligent, Holland was over-cautious, inflexible, and unimaginative, and he tended to drive away good business.

Baring focused on government finance which, in the remaining years of the French wars, largely meant financing the British government's war effort by bidding for tranches of securities for resale to investors. In 1815, for example, Barings with another finance house marketed a £30 million debt to European investors, £9 million of which was remitted to Britain's allies to sustain their campaigns against France. In these large operations Baring became well known to Britain's political élite. Between 1805 and 1817 his influence was also extended through his directorship of the Bank of England.

Baring's reputation in North America came to exceed

his father's. Following the appointment of Baring Brothers in 1803 as London financial agents for the United States administration, numerous government commissions were received. During Britain's war with the United States from 1812 to 1814, Barings maintained the American government's credit in London, treading a careful course between loyalty to the British crown and service to a valued client. In the peace negotiations Baring, acting unofficially, brought together Castlereagh and the American negotiator, Albert Gallatin. Gallatin's son was convinced that Baring 'had done more than any other man in England to hasten the peace and had rendered very important financial assistance even when the war was going on' (H. Adams, *The Life of James Gallatin*, 1943, 522).

Financing French reparations In 1816 Baring was thrust centre-stage in financing reparations by France to the victorious allies. Initially, neither French bankers nor investors were prepared to lend to their government, so the latter mandated Barings and Hopes with the task of raising the funds. Baring negotiated with Louis XVIII's ministers, Richelieu and Corvetto; with the British prime minister, Lord Liverpool, and his ministers Castlereagh and Vansittart; with Wellington, who was then in Paris as British ambassador; and, initially, with G. T. Ouvrard, Napoleon's former financial adviser. In 1817 and 1818 Barings led *rentes* issues amounting to more than 500 million francs, mobilizing the resources of Europe's leading capitalists and making extraordinarily large profits—over £700,000, according to S. C. Holland. Baring was at the peak of his power. 'He has to a certain degree the command of the money market of the world and feels his power', reckoned Wellington in 1818, who found it 'not a very easy task to succeed in counteracting him' (*Supplementary Despatches*, 10.562–5). Richelieu supported this view, listing the six great European powers as Britain, France, Russia, Austria, Prussia, and Barings.

These loans coincided with Barings' development of a more broadly based business in securities, with large marketing positions being taken in Russian and Austrian government bonds. This was facilitated in 1813 when Baring achieved the ambition, unfulfilled by his father, of acquiring the Hope family's merchant banks in Amsterdam and London. These had now only a shadow of their former influence, but Baring was nevertheless prepared to pay £250,000 for the goodwill attached to their name. A strong alliance with Hopes provided a counterpoise to the growing power of the Rothschilds, based upon their network of European houses. Alexander Baring was the first Barings partner to confront Rothschilds' competition and he made dangerous enemies of them. 'He is quite a crook, this Baring', wrote Salomon Rothschild in 1817, 'we must certainly watch our step so far as he is concerned' (Rothschild Archives, T27/292).

Latin American securities In the early 1820s the dynamic feature of London's rapidly expanding capital market was the prominence of security issues for UK businesses and for newly formed Latin American republics. Baring avoided virtually all of them and escaped loss when most collapsed in the financial panic of 1825–6. The exception was an issue of £1 million 6 per cent Buenos Aires bonds in 1824. This was the first London issue of Argentinian securities and it heralded Barings' major commitment to that country later in the century. However, interest payments were suspended in 1828, badly sullying the firm's hitherto impeccable reputation among investors. Baring consolidated his firm's position in the United States by establishing the first market in Europe for state bonds and by financing the huge exchange operations of the Bank of the United States for which Barings had acted as London financial agent from 1817. But in the 1820s the going was harder in Europe where, in government finance, Rothschilds forced Barings into second place.

Retirement from the partnership An important explanation of this was Baring's growing uninterest in his business. Although only fifty-two, in 1825 he confessed that 'he regarded himself for sometime personally retired from commercial pursuits and had not been in London for the last three months' (*The Courier*, 15 Dec 1825). Under S. C. Holland's unremarkable management, the merchanting business also drifted and, when Holland died at his desk in 1827, crisis point was reached. Baring's response was quick and courageous. In 1828 he appointed three new partners as a preliminary to his retirement in 1830. These were his able but young and relatively inexperienced nephews Thomas and John Baring, sons of Sir Thomas Baring, and Joshua Bates, a well-known American merchant already working with John in the firm of Bates and Baring. The choice of Bates was inspired as, with outstanding ability, by the mid-1850s he had re-established Barings as London's most powerful merchant house.

After retirement Alexander Baring remained close to the business. The partners frequently consulted him on government loan business and for many years he left £100,000 capital in the company. He added greatly to this resource in the early days of the new partnership, and in 1846 he used it to write off Mexican and other debts due to Barings for which he had assumed responsibility on his withdrawal. Moreover, his second son, Francis, joined the partnership in 1823, albeit as a largely absentee member, maintaining the family influence and providing additional capital.

Political career An increasing preoccupation with politics was one reason for Baring's retirement. He entered the Commons in 1806 as member for Taunton and held that seat until 1826. He then sat for Callington (1826–31), for Thetford (1831–2), and, from 1833, for North Essex, until his elevation to the Lords in 1835. Initially he followed family tradition and sat as a whig, and he worked to remove restrictions from international trade. In 1805 he reckoned 'the most desirable system for trade … is to abstain from all restrictions, to leave it as free and uncircumscribed as possible and to desist from, or mitigate, all naval blockades' (ING Baring Archives, Northbrook MSS, A23). His views helped to frame Sir Robert Peel's own free-trade principles. In parliament his ability to see both sides of an argument was well known. The comment that 'he always gave his speech one way and voted another' (Ziegler, 59) was an exaggerated view of him. Nevertheless he enjoyed a formidable reputation as a leader among non-Ricardian economists and, as a practical man of business, he married the views of theoretical economists with the prejudices of country members.

Baring became progressively more conservative. His opposition to parliamentary reform was absolute and the whigs' support of it was the catalyst which propelled him to the tory benches, which earned him the title of 'See-saw Baring' (Ziegler, 59). In May 1832 he agreed to serve as chancellor of the exchequer in the abortive tory ministry which Wellington formed to block reform and, in opposing reform, he voted against his brother, his two sons, and his three nephews on the whig benches. He served in Sir Robert Peel's brief ministry, from 1834 to 1835, as president of the Board of Trade and master of the Royal Mint, and he was then raised to the peerage in 1835 as Baron Ashburton, reviving the title of his uncle John Dunning. Subsequently he opposed tory free-trade reform. 'To the entire removal of all protection from domestic industry', he advised Peel, 'I have an insuperable objection' (BL, Add. MS 40576, fol. 41).

In 1841 Baring came out of retirement and was dispatched to the United States as a British ambassador to negotiate with Daniel Webster, an old friend, for the settlement of the disputed boundary between the United States and Canada. Baring's high standing in the United States explained his appointment, but his critics reckoned the resulting Webster–Ashburton treaty of 1842 gave too much away. On his return Baring sought advancement to an earldom but was offered a viscountcy, which he declined.

Interests, property, and death Baring's other interests embraced land ownership and art collecting. In 1817 he acquired for £136,000 The Grange and its surrounding estate at Northington in Hampshire from the banker Henry Drummond, who had commissioned William Wilkins to transform it into one of Britain's finest neo-classical houses. In establishing this Hampshire presence Baring placed himself in direct competition with his elder brother, Sir Thomas Baring, the inheritor of Sir Francis Baring's estate 2 miles away at Stratton. Baring's land holdings extended far beyond Hampshire and rapidly outstripped those of his brother. As early as 1825 one commentator was convinced that Alexander Baring had spent £1 million on land and by the time of his death in 1848 his estates stretched across Hampshire, the Isle of Wight, Herefordshire, Somerset, Wiltshire, Suffolk, and Norfolk. From about 1805 his London home was at 25 Bruton Street and later he moved to 33 Portman Square. In 1821 he acquired Bath House, Piccadilly, and rebuilt it to create what Holland dubbed the 'Palazzo di Piccadilly'.

Baring collected magnificent pictures and furniture with which to fill The Grange and Bath House, buying from old English collections and from unlikely sources such as Charles Maurice Talleyrand, from whom a work by Van Dyck was acquired in 1831. On his death it passed, with most of his estate, to his eldest son, William Bingham, second Baron Ashburton [*see under* Baring, Harriet Mary], and then subsequently, through marriage, into the ownership of the marquesses of Northampton. His enthusiasm for art resulted in his appointment as a trustee of both the National Gallery and the British Museum.

Alexander Baring died on 12 May 1848 at Longleat House, Wiltshire, the home of his daughter the marchioness of Bath; he was buried at Northington. His wife survived him, but died later that year. JOHN ORBELL

Sources P. Ziegler, *The sixth great power: Barings, 1762–1929* (1988) • R. W. Hidy, *The house of Baring in American trade and finance: English merchant bankers at work, 1763–1861* (1949) • M. G. Buist, *At spes non fracta: Hope and Co., 1770–1815* (1974) • J. Orbell, *Baring Brothers & Co. Limited: a history to 1939* (privately printed, London, 1939) • J. E. Winston, 'How the Louisiana Purchase was financed', *Louisiana Historical Quarterly*, 12 (1929), 189–237 • *Supplementary despatches (correspondence) and memoranda of Field Marshal Arthur, duke of Wellington*, ed. A. R. Wellesley, second duke of Wellington, 15 vols. (1858–72), vol. 10, pp. 562–5 • NHM, Rothschild Archives, T27/292 • ING Barings, London, Barings archives • parish records (baptism), London, 25 Nov 1773 • d. cert.

Archives ING Barings, London, Barings archives, letters to Baring Brothers • NL Scot., corresp. and business papers | BL, corresp. with Lord Aberdeen, Add MSS 43127–43246 • BL, corresp. with Sir Robert Peel, Add. MSS 40404–40598 • Lpool RO, letters to Lord Stanley • NHM, Rothschild Archives, T27/292 • priv. coll., marquess of Northampton MSS • PRO NIre., corresp. with second earl of Caledon • UCL, letters to Lord Brougham

Likenesses T. Lawrence, portrait, *c.*1810, ING Barings, London [*see illus.*] • C. E. Wagstaff, mezzotint, pubd 1837 (after T. Lawrence), BM, NPG • G. Hayter, group portrait, oils (*The House of Commons, 1833*), NPG • G. P. A. Healy, oils, New York Historical Society • J. Partridge, group portrait, oils (*The fine arts commissioners, 1846*), NPG

Baring, (William) Bingham, second Baron Ashburton (1799–1864). *See under* Baring, Harriet Mary, Lady Ashburton (1805–1857).

Baring, Charles Thomas (1807–1879), bishop of Durham, was born on 11 January 1807, the fourth son of Sir Thomas Baring, second baronet (1772–1848), of the banking firm of Baring Brothers. His mother was Mary Ursula (*d.* 1846), daughter of Charles Sealy, a barrister of Calcutta. Francis Thornhill *Baring and Thomas *Baring were among his brothers. Charles Baring was privately educated, and entered Christ Church, Oxford, in 1825. At Oxford he greatly distinguished himself, and took a double first class in classics and mathematics in his final examination in 1829. In 1830 he married his cousin Mary Ursula (*d.* 1840), daughter of Colonel Charles Sealy of the East India Company, and took holy orders. At first he devoted himself to clerical work at St Ebbe's in Oxford, a noted centre for evangelicals, and then took the small living of Kingsworthy in Hampshire. In 1840 his wife died, and he married in 1846 Caroline (*d.* 1885), daughter of Thomas Read Kemp of Dale Park, Sussex. In 1847 he was appointed to the important benefice of All Saints', Marylebone, and became renowned as an earnest, simple preacher of the evangelical school. In 1850 he was made chaplain-in-ordinary to the queen, and was select preacher at Oxford. In 1855 he left London for the rectory of Limpsfield in Surrey, where, however, he did not long remain. In 1856 he was chosen to succeed J. H. Monk as bishop of Gloucester and Bristol. He entered with energy upon the duties of his episcopal office, but he did not stay at Gloucester long enough to make a decided mark, for in 1861 he was translated to the see of Durham, in succession to H. M. Villiers. Baring's name is chiefly associated with the work of church extension in the diocese of Durham. He found a district in which a manufacturing and mining population had increased with great rapidity, and had far outstripped the provision made for its spiritual welfare. A movement was already under way to remedy the deficiency. Baring's energetic leadership saw the formation of 102 new parishes, the building of 119 churches, and an increase of 186 in the number of parochial clergy. In his last charge to his clergy in 1878 he expressed his opinion that the limit of the formation of new districts had been reached, and that future progress should be made by erecting mission chapels.

Baring devoted himself largely to the work of his diocese. He rarely appeared in the House of Lords or spoke on any subjects which did not concern his immediate business. However, he opposed the declaration on *Essays and Reviews* (1860) and refused to sign an episcopal address on ritualism in 1875 on the grounds that it was insufficiently fierce in tone. Baring was a hard worker and initially opposed the division of his diocese, maintaining that he could manage it. However, in 1876 he admitted the necessity of dividing the see of Durham, and at his request provision was made in the act for the extension of the episcopate (1878) for the formation of a diocese of Newcastle.

Baring was a man of deep personal piety and of great kindliness. Though a wealthy man, he lived with great simplicity, and gave back to the diocese in donations for church purposes more than he received as the income of his see. His personal acts of charity, though done in secret, were very numerous. He was in theological opinions a strong evangelical, and in his public utterances did not disguise the fact. Those who did not agree with him complained that in the discharge of his official duties he followed too exclusively his own individual preferences. He took a more decided step than any other bishop by refusing to license curates to clergymen whose ritual he thought to be contrary to his interpretation of the prayer book. This gave rise to much controversy, but did not impair the respect in which he was personally held. In 1877 the chief laity of the county asked him to sit for his portrait, which they wished to present to Auckland Castle.

In 1878 Baring felt his health giving way and resigned on 2 February 1879, declining to draw on his pension. He died at Cecil House, Somerset Road, Wimbledon, Surrey, on 14 September 1879.

MANDELL CREIGHTON, *rev.* H. C. G. MATTHEW

Sources *The Durham diocesan calendar, clergy list and church almanack* (1880) • *The Times* (15 Sept 1879) • Burke, *Peerage* • J. S. Reynolds, *The evangelicals at Oxford, 1735–1871: a record of an unchronicled movement* (1953) • M. A. Crowther, *Church embattled: religious controversy in mid-Victorian England* (1970) • M. Hennell, *Sons of the prophets* (1979) • P. T. Marsh, *The Victorian church in decline: Archbishop Tait and the Church of England, 1868–1882* (1969) • d. cert.

Archives U. Durham L., corresp. | LPL, letters to A. C. Tait • U. Durham L., letters to third Earl Grey

Likenesses oils, 1885, deanery, Durham

Wealth at death under £120,000: probate, 5 Jan 1880, *CGPLA Eng. & Wales*

Baring, Edward Charles, first Baron Revelstoke (**1828–1897**), merchant banker, was born on 13 April 1828, the fifth son of Henry Baring (1776–1848), a merchant banker, and the second son of his second marriage, to Cecilia Anne (*d.* 1874), the daughter of Admiral Windham of Felbrigg in Norfolk. His grandfather was the merchant and founder of the house of Barings, Sir Francis *Baring (1740–1810), his father was a junior partner of Baring Brothers, and his brother was Evelyn *Baring, first earl of Cromer (1841–1917). He was educated at Rugby School. On 30 April 1861 he married Louisa Emily Charlotte (*d.* 1892), the daughter of John Crocker Bulteel, of Flete and Lyneham, Devon, from a Devon banking family. Of their seven sons and three daughters, the eldest surviving son, John *Baring (1863–1929), became Barings' senior partner while another son was the writer Maurice *Baring (1874–1945); two others died in infancy.

About 1850 Edward entered Barings as a clerk, and a year later he was sent 'with procuration' (Bates, diary, vol. 4, 16 Dec 1850) to their Liverpool house. On his return to London in 1854 he received power of signature with annual remuneration of £1000. Admission as a full partner followed two years later. 'He is sharp at a bargain', reckoned Joshua Bates, a senior partner who had little good to say of any of his juniors, 'but slovenly in keeping his accounts, inexact in his calculations and I doubt his judgements, expensive in habits but he likes business' (ibid., vol. 6, 1 Jan 1856). The other senior partner, Thomas *Baring (1799–1873), eventually agreed, but failed to curb Baring's influence, along with that of another junior, Russell Sturgis.

After Thomas Baring's death in 1873, Baring and Sturgis led Barings, and from 1883 Baring was undisputed leader. His share of the profits (and, if need be, the losses) rose steadily from 18/144ths in 1870 to 26/120ths in 1887, yet his capital contribution was modest. It stood at £50,000 in 1885, when total capital exceeded £2 million, but recovered to £220,000 by 1889. Barings, in most years, was highly profitable, but Baring did not plough back his profits; instead he withdrew them to fund an extravagant life—not least his acquisition of a 4000 acre estate and house at Membland, Noss Mayo, south Devon, and an opulent London house at 37 Charles Street, Mayfair. Everything was done with generosity and style; niggardliness was not in his character.

At Barings, Baring managed rapid growth in bond issuing, at a time when London's role as a supplier of international capital grew dramatically. Between 1873 and 1890 about eighty issues were handled, mostly for governments and railway companies in the United States, Canada, Argentina, and Russia, but also in many other countries besides. His management of trade finance, an important source of regular income, was at arm's length, while under his leadership Barings' work as merchants withered. He initiated issues for home businesses such as Whitbreads, the Manchester Ship Canal, and, not least, Guinness, which he floated with great profit but corresponding controversy. His other achievements included funding the completion of the Canadian Pacific Railway in 1885, after which the town of Revelstoke was named in his honour. In the same year his elevation as Baron Revelstoke recognized his importance as an international banker. The Bank of England appointed him a director from 1879 to 1891 and he was Lloyds' chairman from 1887 to 1892.

In the 1880s many of Barings' transactions were high risk and unprofitable. Bad debts written off in 1883 exceeded £150,000, and those the following year were more than £260,000. A huge bond issue for the Italian government almost brought ruin in 1882. Then in 1888 a £10 million issue for the Buenos Aires Water Supply and Drainage Company was inadequately underwritten and poorly taken up, causing a liquidity crisis at Barings in November 1890. In what was known as the Baring crisis, Barings' collapse and a major financial panic were avoided only by a Bank of England loan.

Revelstoke's judgement was held responsible. 'There is really no excuse for Ned', wrote his brother, 'he has been reckless … loosing his head from success, departing from all the old rules and traditions of the firm and doing things inconceivably foolish' (ING Barings, DEP 84). The price Revelstoke now paid was enormous. He retired disgraced, his wife died prematurely, and his assets were sold to meet his firm's debts. But his integrity and honour were never doubted. He died at 37 Charles Street on 17 July 1897, a broken man in straitened circumstances, but gratified that, under his son's leadership, Barings had paid its debts and was regaining much of its prestige.

John Orbell

Sources P. Ziegler, *The sixth great power: Barings, 1762–1929* (1988) • D. Kynaston, *The City of London*, 1 (1994) • J. Orbell, *Baring Brothers & Co. Limited: a history to 1939* (privately printed, London, 1985) • Boase, *Mod. Eng. biog.* • J. Bates, diary, ING Barings, London, Barings archives, DEP 74 • ING Barings, London, Barings archives • Burke, *Peerage* • d. cert.

Archives ING Barings, London, letters to Baring Bros.

Likenesses E. Boehm, statue, 1874, Barings plc, London • R. Lehmann, portrait, 1879, ING Barings, London • Lib, print cartoon, ING Barings, London • V. Noltz, drawing (as a child), ING Barings, London • photographs, ING Barings, London • portrait, ING Barings, London

Wealth at death £36,878 15*s.* 1*d.*: resworn probate, March 1898, *CGPLA Eng. & Wales* (1897)

Baring [*née* Vowler], **Elizabeth** (1702–1766), wool manufacturer and merchant, was born on 30 April 1702 in Exeter, the only daughter of John Vowler, grocer, and his wife, Elizabeth, the daughter of Thomas Townsend.

On 15 February 1728 Elizabeth married John Baring (1697–1748) who had arrived in Exeter from Germany at the age of twenty to learn the trade of serge-maker. Her dowry of £20,000 was a substantial amount, commensurate with her father's standing as one of the wealthiest merchants in Exeter. John was to be described later by his son as 'a man of exceeding good parts, of a most pleasant, excellent disposition' (Ziegler, 15). Together, John and Elizabeth Baring built up a thriving wool manufacturing and merchanting business. Their success enabled them to move, in 1736, from Palace Street, a crowded area near the South Gate in Exeter, to Larkbear House, a country house standing in 37 acres of land on the outskirts of the city. Growing prosperity was accompanied by a growing family. Elizabeth and John had nine children, though one was stillborn and three died in infancy.

In 1748 John Baring died, leaving Elizabeth with a young family of four sons and one daughter, but with an income sufficient for her to retire from business if she so wished. She decided otherwise, taking over the management of the business and expanding the profits, despite some serious setbacks such as a fire in 1763 which destroyed an uninsured new press house and in the process ruined goods worth £8000.

In order to secure the business she and her husband had built up, Elizabeth ensured that her sons received sound commercial educations. John (1730–1816), the eldest surviving son, travelled widely on the continent, gaining knowledge of markets and establishing connections before returning to Exeter in 1755 to take over the family business. Francis *Baring (1740–1810) and his younger brother Charles (1742–1829) were sent as apprentices to leading merchants in London, although Charles did not complete his apprenticeship, returning to Exeter in 1758 on the sudden death of his brother, Thomas. In 1755 at the age of fifteen, Francis began a seven-year apprenticeship with Samuel Touchet & Co., a leading Manchester and West Indian merchant business. Touchet, an old family friend, undertook to teach Francis all aspects of the business of a merchant, in return for £800. This was an onerous commitment for Elizabeth, but a far-sighted one. Elizabeth clearly took the education of her sons very seriously; Charles was to complain that he grew up 'under the Eye of a Mother, excellent in many respects, but very severe' (Ziegler, 17). Her features are recorded in a surviving portrait by Gainsborough.

Just over a month after his seven years were completed, Francis entered into an agreement with his elder brothers, John and Charles, to reorganize the family business and establish a London house. Two interlocking partnerships were formed on Christmas day 1762, one in Exeter, the other in London. John was to be head of both houses, but the west country business of John and Charles Baring & Co. was to be managed by Charles, while Francis was in charge of John and Francis Baring & Co. in London—from which was to emerge the merchant banking house of Barings.

Elizabeth had built up a considerable amount of confidence, experience, and knowledge through running the business and clearly felt reluctant to hand over to her sons. Almost right up to her death, she was advising Francis on the running of the London house. She wrote to him in March 1766 (one month before she died):

> As it was so long since I heard from you I imagined you had forgot you had a Mother. I am glad your business bears so promising an Aspect. I see you have begun in the Exchange

> way, as you say tis not a lucrative thing, advise you to be careful you do not run out of your depth. I am satisfied tis attended with risk and many houses called considerable abroad have often disappointed and sometimes absolutely ruined those who have placed Confidence in them, am sensible you may be drawn in to be answerable for large Sums before you are aware of it. (Ziegler, 20)

When Elizabeth died in April 1766 in Exeter, the value of the family business had almost doubled from £40,000 at the time of John Baring's death, to £70,000. She had also laid the foundations for future success; the family business had been restructured and a new branch opened in London, and two of her sons had been prepared for commercial, political, and social success. Her eldest son, John, felt she should be remembered particularly for 'her very extraordinary ability and great attention and usefulness to her family' (Orbell, 2). SERENA KELLY

Sources J. Orbell, *Baring Brothers & Co. Limited: a history to 1939* (privately printed, London, 1985) • P. Ziegler, *The sixth great power: Barings, 1762–1929* (1988) • W. G. Hoskins, *Industry, trade and people in Exeter, 1688–1800* (1935) • ING Barings, London, Barings archives, Northbrook MSS, G1.3
Archives ING Barings, London, Northbrook MSS
Likenesses T. Gainsborough, oils, ING Barings, London
Wealth at death £70,000: Orbell, *Baring Brothers*

Baring, Evelyn, first earl of Cromer (1841–1917), diplomatist and proconsul, was born on 26 February 1841 at Cromer Hall, Norfolk, the ninth son of Henry Baring (1776–1848), banker, and his second wife, Cecilia Anne, *née* Windham (*d.* 1874). He was a grandson of Sir Francis *Baring (1740–1810), who, with his brother John, had established Barings Bank in London. The families of both of Henry Baring's elder brothers, Thomas and Alexander, were established in the peerage under the titles of Northbrook and Ashburton. Evelyn Baring was thus born into a large, successful, and well-connected cousinhood. His elder brother Edward Charles *Baring (1828–1897), who became head of Barings Bank, entered the House of Lords as Lord Revelstoke in 1885. But as the youngest son of a father who died when he was seven, Evelyn was not marked out for a public career and it is interesting that he was not directed towards the family bank. Instead he was sent at the age of eleven to the Ordnance School at Carshalton, in preparation for a military career. At fourteen he entered the Royal Military Academy at Woolwich, but only after his mother had used her influence with Lord Raglan, the commander-in-chief, to overcome his rejection on grounds of poor eyesight. In 1858, at the age of seventeen, he was posted to Corfu, then a British protectorate, began learning Greek and Italian, and opened his long acquaintance with the eastern Mediterranean. After a short interval he returned to the island as an aide to the governor, Sir Henry Storks. Baring followed Storks to Malta and then to Jamaica for the inquiry into the insurrection there in 1865.

Early career Without the financial independence required for a sideways move towards a parliamentary or diplomatic career, Baring sought advancement in the army. He entered the Staff College in 1868 and passed out first in 1870. In the War Office topographical department (the forerunner of military intelligence) he studied the military capability of the Prussian, Russian, and Turkish armies. But perhaps the crucial influence on the direction of his subsequent official career was his role in supplying a brief for the abolition of the purchase system to which the Liberal government of 1868–74 was committed. The junior minister at the War Office whom Baring served so loyally, at some risk to his professional prospects, was his cousin Lord Northbrook. When the viceroy of India, Lord Mayo, was murdered in 1872, and Northbrook was rushed out to succeed him, Baring went with him as private secretary.

Evelyn Baring, first earl of Cromer (1841–1917), by John Singer Sargent, 1902

Baring's four years in India before Northbrook resigned in protest against Disraeli's Afghan policy were an important apprenticeship. As Northbrook's confidant, he saw at first hand the workings of an administrative system notoriously centralized and half drowned in paper. He was exposed to the powerful Anglo-Indian ideology of guardianship towards the rural cultivator, then at a vital stage in its formulation. And, with Northbrook's resignation, he had good reason to reflect upon the cross purposes of British and Indian interests in Asia and the difficulties of dealing with far-away ministers with very different political preoccupations. At the same time 'the Vice-Viceroy' (as he was revealingly nicknamed) had begun to display the brusque self-confidence and certainty in opinion which became his trademarks in later life. Professional laurels, close proximity to viceregal power, and a sense of embattled rectitude first in London, then in Simla, had transformed the easy-going youth posted out to Corfu nearly twenty years earlier.

First marriage, and Egypt Returning to Britain, Baring married, on 28 June 1876, Ethel Stanley (*d.* 16 Oct 1898), daughter and coheir of Sir Rowland Stanley Errington, eleventh baronet; they had two sons, Rowland Thomas *Baring (1877–1953) and Windham. Baring resumed work at the War Office and perhaps intended to settle in London. However, the financial crisis in Egypt brought an unexpected opportunity. In 1876 the ruler of Egypt (known as the khedive or viceroy) had set up a debt commission to reassure the largest foreign lenders, who were mainly British or French, and restore confidence in Egypt's public finances. He had sought the advice of G. J. Goschen, a former Liberal cabinet minister and a recognized expert on international finance. Goschen was asked to recommend a British member to the debt commission. At the suggestion of Sir Louis Mallet, a senior official at the India Office, he recommended Baring—though it is not unlikely that Baring's name added to his appeal from the khedive's point of view. Despite some private reservations Baring accepted the appointment. Once in Cairo he quickly discovered the ambiguous status of the commission's authority and the difficulties of co-operating with the Egyptian government.

The heart of the problem lay in the commission's determination to rein in the extravagance of the khedival court and to reduce public expenditure drastically to help meet the soaring debt charges already incurred. The commission proposed to take half the khedive's vast estates into public ownership, and to halve the army. A policy of savage deflation in 1878–9 aggravated the social effects of a rural famine. Isma'il, the khedive, with a throne to lose, pursued the dangerous tactic of encouraging local opposition to the commission while simultaneously posing as its champion abroad. When in April 1879 he dismissed his ministers and effectively repudiated the commission, Baring resigned and went home. But he was back almost immediately. Isma'il's erratic policy had finally united the great powers against him, and his nominal sovereign, the Ottoman sultan, formally dethroned him in June. Baring returned to Cairo as one of two controllers-general in the second phase of Egypt's financial crisis, the Anglo-French 'dual control' of 1879–82.

In India But not for long. The 'Midlothian election' of 1880 had swept the Conservatives from office, and a Liberal ministry appointed a Liberal viceroy to India: Lord Ripon. Baring's Indian experience, his Egyptian credentials as a zealous champion of sound finance, and his political connections with the Liberal Party—he had briefly thought of standing as a Liberal in East Norfolk—made him an obvious appointment to the post of finance member of the government of India. Like the viceroyalty itself, this post (the equivalent of the chancellorship of the exchequer) was usually filled by a nominee from home rather than by a British career administrator in the Indian Civil Service. The reasoning was plain enough. Indian financial policy was an imperial question: the cost of the 60,000 British troops in India and the interest payable on India's sterling loans were the first charges on Indian revenues. Moreover, the recurrent threat of a revenue tariff to prop up India's rickety finances was anathema to the British commercial interests (especially in cotton manufacture) vociferously represented in the House of Commons.

Baring's three-year term as finance member was not, however, an unqualified success. He maintained a regular correspondence with Sir Louis Mallet, the India Office financial expert and one of his patrons. As an outsider in the Anglo-Indian official hierarchy, Baring was contemptuous of its self-interested conservatism. An Indian reform bill was needed, he told Mallet on 19 February 1881:

> The natives must be admitted to a larger share in their own affairs … we cannot go on for long governing this huge country through the agency of seven men meeting twice a week around a green baize table and doing practically what they choose. (Mowat, 63)

Baring's preferred solution was to reinforce the influence of home opinion against the vested interest of local British officialdom, whom he dismissed as a 'clique of third-rate Englishmen', and to widen Indian participation in government beyond what he called the 'Baboos'.

Baring combined these traces of radical Liberalism with devotion to Gladstonian precepts in public finance. In his third budget he swept away the duties on imported cotton goods which offended free trade sentiment in Britain. But when he proposed to replace them by increased direct taxation, including an income tax, the viceroy grew restive. Baring, he complained, was a 'doctrinaire' with little sense of how to prepare the ground for his ideas. Faced with Ripon's opposition, Baring performed a rapid volte-face, abandoned the income tax, and now declared himself in favour of gradualist reform in local government. 'We shall not subvert the British Empire', he told Mallet with only a trace of irony, 'by allowing the Bengali Baboo to discuss his own schools and drains. Rather shall we afford a safety-valve if we turn his attention to these innocuous subjects' (Mowat, 83).

These three years in India might be seen as a watershed in Baring's public career and political attitudes. For all his energy, self-confidence, and moral rectitude in the face of Anglo-Indian mediocrity and inertia (as he doubtless saw it), he had made little impression on the system of Indian government. Instead he had earned the reputation of an arrogant doctrinaire. Not for the last time, he had avoided defeat by a timely U-turn. But perhaps the experience left its mark. The great characteristic of Baring's later career in Egypt was his flexibility in dealing with his superiors in London, and his careful avoidance of irretrievable positions. From being a doctrinaire, he became a *politique*, whose firmness of language rarely closed the door to compromise or retreat. His bruising encounter with the Anglo-Indian official machine may have persuaded him that wide discretion on a smaller stage was preferable to the niggling constraints and perpetual intrigue inseparable from grander authority. Finally, although the transition was gradual, and Baring himself, consciously or otherwise, veiled the change, his second tour in India marked a shift away from an enthusiastic radicalism in imperial attitudes towards a world-weary cynicism about the capacity of 'Eastern peoples' to attain the moral and intellectual qualities needed for self-government. It is ironic that for all his declared antipathy to the Anglo-Indian ethos, Baring gradually came to embody, certainly by the last years of his life, all the characteristic prejudices invoked to justify the indefinite prolongation of imperial rule. He was made KCSI in August 1883.

Consul-general In these circumstances the offer of the consulship-general in Cairo to Baring early in 1883 may have come as a relief to him, to the viceroy, and to his colleagues. The post was an oddity. Its humble designation reflected Egypt's formal international status as a viceroyalty of the Ottoman empire and not a sovereign state. In substance, however, the consul-general occupied a diplomatic post of acute political sensitivity and importance. Since 1880, when Baring had left for India, Egypt had passed through a double revolution. The attempt by Britain and France to maintain the so-called dual control over Egyptian finance, to restore Egyptian solvency and to ward off intervention by other powers, had finally collapsed in the nationalist revolt led by Arabi Pasha against the discredited authority of the khedive Tawfiq. In a confused situation that appeared to threaten the lives and property of the large (mainly Greek) foreign community, the financial interests of British, French, and other European bondholders, and Britain's strategic interest in the Suez Canal, the Gladstone government had decided on military intervention. In September 1882 a British force under Wolseley dispersed Arabi's army, revived the khedive's authority, and established Britain's 'temporary occupation' in Egypt. But when it came to deciding how British supremacy should be used and how long it should last, the Gladstone government was at sixes and sevens. Most ministers, including Gladstone himself, were determined not to be trapped into a permanent occupation, let alone annexation, fearing the financial, military, and diplomatic liabilities this would impose. On the other hand, they could hardly withdraw without making some provision for stable government in Egypt and for a financial recovery programme with better prospects than those which had repeatedly broken down between 1876 and 1882.

The initial reaction of the cabinet was to dispatch an envoy (Lord Dufferin) to draw up a comprehensive scheme of political reform which, once instituted, would permit early British withdrawal. Not surprisingly, a solution conceived in cabinet compromise had little relevance to local conditions, since Egyptian willingness to enact a 'British' scheme was unlikely to survive British departure. This was the circle which it was Baring's task to square: to uphold the commitment to an early withdrawal while simultaneously imposing on the Egyptian government the drastic administrative reforms required to reduce the public debt and pay off the foreign bondholders. All this had to be done without recourse to overt political control by annexation or by the creation of a protectorate, and without infringing the diplomatic interests and extraterritorial privileges of other European powers and communities in the country.

Even for an official of Baring's skill and experience, this was an exceptionally difficult hand to play, especially given the inconstancy of cabinet policy in London. His main advantage lay, perhaps, not in previous knowledge of Egypt and the financial expertise recently tested in India, but in the facility with which he adopted the ambivalent attitude required by London's policy. While he became increasingly convinced that reform in Egypt would be a long and arduous process, Baring was careful to speak the language of early and eager withdrawal. At the same time he grasped that while London would reject any commitment to an extended stay, it would accept the logic of forcefully supporting his own influence on the Egyptian government—the prerequisite, Baring insisted, for the very reforms that would liberate the Liberal cabinet from its 'bondage in Egypt'. 'I am really beginning to think', he told Northbrook on 23 December 1883, 'that the more power we assume temporarily, the better the chance of getting away in the end' (Mowat, 124). Thus the foreign secretary, Lord Granville, authorized the doctrine in 1884 that no Egyptian minister opposed to Baring's reforms could be allowed to stay in office. With infinite subtlety and reassuring rhetoric, Baring, with his unimpeachable Liberal credentials, drew his political masters steadily deeper into an effective political guarantee that there would be no withdrawal before the reform policy was complete. Precisely when, in Baring's own mind, the ides of March became the Greek calends is uncertain and perhaps unknowable. Perhaps it was only the arrival of Lord Salisbury in office in 1886 that encouraged him to resolve the ambiguities he had carefully cherished.

But before this more settled policy in London took shape Baring had passed through the political ordeal of the Sudan crisis, which culminated in the death of Gordon at Khartoum and Egypt's humiliating expulsion from its colony on the upper Nile. Egypt's own political upheavals after 1875 coincided with and contributed to the upsurge of Sudanese opposition to Egyptian control, which had been fastened on the region since the early nineteenth century. By 1883, the year of Baring's arrival as consul-general, the Mahdist revolt was in full spate. Baring, like the two governments he sought to guide, had to decide whether the Sudan should be retained and if so, how. There can be no doubt that this episode was the most painful and embarrassing of Baring's entire career. In later life he liked to stress that his own preference had been to concentrate on Egypt's financial recovery, which futile expenditure on the Sudanese struggle could only delay and perhaps wreck. But he also knew that to lose the Sudan would be a staggering blow to the khedival regime and threaten its partnership with Britain. Hence his advice to London, and even his attitude to the controversial matter of Gordon's appointment as governor-general with a mandate to save the Sudan, were marked by the vacillation and uncertainty which he liked to condemn in others. Having recommended the evacuation of the Sudan and opposed Gordon's dispatch, he changed his mind and enthusiastically endorsed Gordon's mission. When Gordon was besieged, Baring pressed the Gladstone government to send a relief expedition. Perhaps in reaction to his own involvement in an affair of such public horror and shame, Baring became deeply disillusioned (in a way later echoed in his protégé Milner) with the defects of party government and especially with Gladstone personally. He came to loathe what he saw as Gladstone's confident omniscience and the facility of speech which gave it full rein. There was scarcely a subject, he remarked later, which did not attract Gladstone's attention and on which he did not seem impelled 'to form decided opinions … and to let the world know what those opinions were', regardless of whether they were built on a foundation of knowledge (Zetland, 123). By contrast, the realism, irony, wit, and cynicism which were the trademarks of Salisbury's correspondence would have been welcome to Baring's own declared preference (if not invariable practice) for calling a spade a spade.

Egyptian reforms Indeed, between 1886 and 1892, with the assurance of firmer political support at home, Baring was able to dig the foundations of British control in Egypt rather more deeply. By 1889 the vacillation and uncertainty which had made the duration of the British presence so unpredictable began to clear away with the rise of the new doctrine of British predominance in the Nile valley. Baring's success in restoring Egyptian solvency contributed to the easing of the diplomatic pressure on London; simultaneously it reduced the necessity to negotiate with the other powers for a relaxation of the extra-territorial taxation privileges enjoyed by their subjects—long a source of rankling irritation among British officials. Baring could now set about turning the emergency regime of 1883–6 into something more robust. From the debris of successive experiments in foreign supervision, financial intervention, and dual control since 1875, he fashioned a system in which the form of an autonomous Egyptian government was carefully preserved. But its operations at every important level (including sub-provincial administration) were carefully shadowed by a phalanx of British inspectors and advisers who reported to the Egyptian ministers but also (no doubt in different terms) to him. In certain key departments, such as finance, officials were seconded from Britain to provide bureaucratic 'stiffening'; Milner served as under-secretary for finance between 1889 and 1892. The police and legal system were closely watched through the interior adviser, the judicial adviser, and the inspector-general of police. But the ultimate guarantee of British influence, apart from the British garrison of some 6000 men, was firm control of the Egyptian army. The old army which had revolted under Arabi's leadership was dispersed. The new army was organized along Indian lines with (some) British officers and a British *sirdar* or commander-in-chief. Here, it might be thought, was the best evidence that the 'temporary occupation' was indeed a 'veiled protectorate'.

But the keystone of this elaborate political edifice was the role of Baring himself. In keeping with the fundamental ambivalence running through his imperial thinking, Baring played two parts. On the one hand, as the diplomatic representative of the dominant European power in the eastern Mediterranean and on the Nile, his progresses through Cairo were of almost viceregal splendour: an elegant carriage accompanied by running grooms with white wands and flying sleeves. Baring himself was a large man of somewhat intimidating mien, and with a notoriously brusque manner: 'Well, is there anything else?' signalled the end of an interview. In Egypt, the Vice-Viceroy became 'the Lord' or 'al-Lurd'. On the other hand, he was at pains to conceal as far as possible the brutal fact of British control over the Egyptian government by insisting that he remain the 'whisper behind the throne', playing no public part in the conduct of Egypt's internal affairs. In reality, of course, Baring intended that the khedive and his ministers should know that he enjoyed the full confidence of the British government and that, in the last resort, he, and they, would not hesitate to remove ministers, or even a ruler, who defied their wishes. To sustain this conjuring trick of interventionist non-intervention required not only close surveillance of every move by the khedive or his ministers, but also a very firm grip upon the British officials in Egypt whose arrogance or exuberance periodically threatened an awkward political breakdown and perhaps even embarrassed disavowal in London.

From this can be seen, in the highly unusual political and diplomatic conditions prevailing in Egypt, the extent to which the successful functioning of the British occupation rested upon Baring's unique assemblage of personal talents and expertise. He had been by turns private secretary, staff officer, diplomat, and finance minister. He had excellent political contacts in London. He was a radical Liberal on the turn with a language to match. He had a forceful temperament and wide administrative experience. Above all, he had a shrewd sense of diplomatic and political realities and a commanding manner essential to his dealings not only with the Egyptian court but also with his own 'subordinates'—the British officials in Egypt. Perhaps it was the fact that he had built the occupation regime around himself, and exercised such full control over it, that explains both Baring's indispensability and his reluctance to accept more glamorous appointments with less real power.

Difficulties Even so, the system that Baring had constructed by 1892 was far from invulnerable. In 1893–4 it was plunged into crisis. The circumstances are revealing of the strengths and weaknesses of his regime. Two events signalled the onset of political turbulence. The first was the death in January 1892 of the khedive Tawfiq, placed and re-placed on the throne by the British in 1879 and 1882. Tawfiq was succeeded by Abbas II for whom Baring had initially felt considerable liking. But the change on the Egyptian throne was bound to have an unsettling effect on the triangle of Egyptian politics with its dynastic, landowning, and British components. The long struggle between the ruler and the landowning class for control of land, revenue, and administrative patronage was a political fact of great convenience to the British. But periodically the Egyptian parties sought to readjust the balance, usually by exploiting anti-foreign sentiment. This was Abbas's tactic. The second event may have encouraged him: the replacement of Salisbury by the fourth Gladstone ministry in 1892 and the possibility that Baring's political authority might be undermined by Liberal indecision in London.

Abbas's initial challenge alarmed Baring (who had been raised to the peerage on 20 June 1892 as Baron Cromer of Cromer), but had little success. He defied the unwritten rule of Anglo-Egyptian relations by appointing a new prime minister without consulting Cromer and chose a notorious Anglophobe. Cromer's reaction was predictably severe. He demanded from London permission if necessary to occupy government buildings in Cairo using the British garrison. As Abbas might have suspected, this request had a mixed reception in the Gladstone cabinet, where some ministers, including Sir William Harcourt, feared that Cromer would drag Britain into complications with the other powers. Rosebery, the foreign secretary, was forced to concede that Cromer's attitude was 'injudicious' (Rosebery to Queen Victoria, 18 Jan 1893, Crewe, 419); nevertheless, he secured authority to veto Abbas's choice and to reinforce the British garrison. Cromer had won the first round. But he was full of foreboding that 'this foolish boy' had smashed the old system whereby British influence was kept from public view and the proprieties of formal autonomy maintained.

Nor was it long before Abbas made a further attempt to roll back the frontiers of British control. Through a new prime minister, sanctioned by Cromer, he attacked the consul-general's eyes and ears. British advisers were denied information and access to the council of ministers. Resentment at the reforms imposed at British request on the courts and police was turned against the foreign power. 'Nine-tenths' of the official class was thoroughly hostile, Cromer warned Rosebery on 25 December 1893 (Mowat, 204). The legislative council, in which the landowning class was largely represented, took its cue and passed a motion calling for British withdrawal. But the climax of Abbas's campaign was his attempt to neutralize the mainspring of British control: the British garrison and British supervision of the Egyptian army. In January 1894, as a clear hint to the Egyptian officer corps, Abbas publicly criticized Kitchener, who was *sirdar*. This, however, was precisely the open challenge for which Cromer had been waiting. Kitchener resigned, but it was immediately clear that London would treat Abbas's move as a threat of direct confrontation. Abbas drew back, recanted, and Kitchener was reinstated. The crisis gradually subsided.

Thereafter Abbas showed no further inclination to subvert Cromer's authority. But Cromer himself was pessimistic about the survival of his system. He pressed Rosebery unsuccessfully to declare a British protectorate for ten to fifteen years. He gradually increased the number of British officials and established in 1902 a system for their regular recruitment into the Egyptian civil service. Gloomily, he forecast that Britain would have to choose between going 'forward'—annexation—or going 'back'—evacuation. His view of Egypt's own potential for political progress became harsher. Not unlike the Anglo-Indians he had despised fifteen years earlier, he came to regard the principal fault of 'oriental' politicians as their lack of moral character—a failing which could not be remedied by any known curriculum and which was always likely to recur when tested for. As the 'temporary occupation' took on some of the features of a more typical colonial regime, it increasingly drew its legitimacy, at least in the eyes of British opinion, from its claim to accomplish improving public works, especially in irrigation and drainage, and to uphold the interests of rural cultivators against the urban, commercial, and educated classes.

In large part, Cromer's extreme sensitivity to any symptom of political unrest in Egypt derived from the fear that it would encourage other European powers to reassert their extra-territorial rights and national interests—rights and interests for which the British claimed to act as a *de facto* trustee. Serious political unrest would set off not merely a crisis in Anglo-Egyptian relations, but also an international crisis which would test the nerve and resolution of a Liberal ministry at home to their limits. It was this same fear which dictated his often inconsistent approach to the problem of the Sudan, which had been only temporarily shelved by the Mahdist triumph of 1885 and the death of Gordon. Cromer's reluctance to embark on a reconquest is well known: he was fearful of the financial consequences of the effort, and of the political consequences of failure. But he was also acutely concerned with what was to happen when, as was generally expected, the Mahdist regime eventually collapsed. Already by 1889 he had signalled to Salisbury his nervousness that the growing Italian presence in north-east Africa might allow them to reach Khartoum before Britain could react to events on the upper Nile. Salisbury expressed agreement, but it is not clear how seriously he took the warnings of the importunate proconsul. A year later Cromer convinced himself that Mahdist power was about to disintegrate, and gained Salisbury's approval for a limited advance by the Egyptian army. It was a miscalculation, and the advance was halted. But it was the same sequence of pressure from Cromer and grudging agreement in London which led five years later to the establishment of the Anglo-Egyptian condominium in the Sudan.

On that occasion Cromer exploited Salisbury's willingness, partly for reasons of European diplomacy, to make a small gesture in support of Italian difficulties in Ethiopia. In March 1896 he persuaded Salisbury to enlarge the gesture by letting Kitchener invade the Sudan as far as Dongola. At first the omens were favourable: it seemed that Mahdist resistance would crumble quickly if the impetus of the advance was maintained. But a Mahdist counterattack belied his optimism. In the autumn of 1897 Cromer lost his nerve. The reconquest of Khartoum, he wrote, was 'beyond the military and financial resources of the Egyptian Government ... I tear my hair over the hurried decision of March 1896' (Sanderson, 261). Cromer now wanted to stand pat at Berber and opposed calling for British troops for which Egypt would have to pay and over whose disposition his own control would be limited. Circumstances forced his hand. By December 1897 Kitchener's position at Berber was so alarming that Cromer himself insisted that British reinforcements must be sought. From that moment on the argument for an advance to Khartoum became irresistible, since both strategic and financial reasons dictated the decisive use and swift withdrawal of the imperial contingent. On 2 September 1898, at Omdurman, Kitchener, with a mixed army of British and Egyptian troops, demolished the Mahdist state. The following month, on 16 October, Cromer's wife died.

For Cromer the British hand in the reconquest of the Sudan was a mixed blessing. It was a fixed point in his thinking that his system of covert supremacy in Egypt depended upon his own complete control over all the agencies of British influence. A British-ruled Sudan, with its own governor-general answerable to the colonial secretary in London, was anathema: not only would it undermine his influence in Cairo, but also it was certain to enrage a wide spectrum of Egyptian opinion. The eccentric regime invented for the Sudan in 1899 bore the marks of Cromer's will. It was not annexed but became a condominium—the Anglo-Egyptian Sudan—in which, technically, control was shared between the British and Egyptian governments. Its affairs, like those of Egypt, were supervised in London by the Foreign not the Colonial office. As if to hammer home the peculiar circumstances of its conquest, the British *sirdar* of the Egyptian army became *ex officio* the governor-general of Sudan, tying its administration securely into the network of British officials through whom the consul-general exerted his ubiquitous oversight. Thus British rule in the Sudan, like British influence in Egypt, was adapted to the Cromer 'system'.

Second marriage and last years in Egypt Cromer was to spend eight more years as consul-general. Having been made a viscount in January 1899, he was created earl of Cromer on 8 August 1901. In the same year he married on 22 October Lady Katherine Georgiana Louisa (1865–1933), daughter of John Alexander *Thynne, fourth marquess of Bath (1831–1896), and his wife, Frances. Their son (Charles) Evelyn *Baring (1903–1973) became a well-known colonial governor and in 1960 was created first Baron Howick of Glendale.

This was the period in which British predominance in the Nile valley was consolidated administratively and diplomatically. The successful negotiation of the Anglo-French entente in 1904, the details of which required constant reference to Cromer, marked the end of France's prolonged diplomatic campaign to evict the British from Egypt and, from Cromer's point of view, served to puncture any surviving illusion in Egypt politics that a foreign power would help restore its independence. But Cromer did not succeed in abolishing the extra-territorial privileges of the European powers—the great encumbrance which prevented the British from reshaping the political and financial regime in ways that might have widened their choice of local allies. Thus when Cromer retired in 1907 he bequeathed a system of influence which, in its essentials, was still precariously dependent upon the consul-general's ability to exercise a form of personal supremacy over the Egyptian ruler, the leading politicians, the ramifying network of British officialdom, and—not least—his superiors in London. Egypt's subsequent history showed how few of his successors could bend the bow of Ulysses. Indeed Cromer's own retirement took place under a cloud. The savage and disproportionate punishment meted out to the peasants involved in the notorious fracas at Dinshawai in July 1906, in the course of which a British officer had died, created a grim and bitter political atmosphere in Egypt and even aroused official misgivings in Britain. Cromer's insensitivity to this reaction suggests that in the last phase of his career in Egypt he drew his advisers and opinions from a narrow and perhaps sycophantic circle.

Publications and final years Cromer returned home in poor health and a depressed state, though the king had made him a member of the Order of Merit in 1906. Quite soon, however, the literary instincts which he had shown as a young staff officer were revived in a series of books and articles. In 1908 he published his apologia under the magnificent title of *Modern Egypt*, one of the classic works of Victorian imperialist writing. In *Ancient and Modern Imperialism* (1910) he combined his passions for classical literature and contemporary affairs. In his speeches in the House of Lords, and in the articles eventually collected in his *Political and Literary Essays* (published in three series in 1913, 1915, and 1916), he revisited the broader themes of imperial rule he had debated energetically with Sir Louis Mallet some thirty years before. Like many of his contemporaries, Cromer was now convinced that the future lay in great political conglomerates of which the British empire must be one: on those grounds he condemned as 'suicidal' any weakening of the Anglo-Irish union (Cromer, 'Speech at Unionist Free Trade Club, 2 June 1908', *Speeches*, 1.275). He was confident that non-Western societies could not withstand the stresses of Western influence and must succumb to Western domination. He rejected what he called 'excessive earth-hunger' but insisted that a 'sound but reasonable imperialist' should embrace Britain's 'manifest destiny' as an imperial power (Cromer, 'The government of subject races', *Political and Literary Essays*, 4–5; first published in January 1908). In what he called the 'government of subject races', Cromer believed that two requirements were paramount. The first was that imperial rule should be conducted according to the code of Christian morality, 'the one sure foundation on which the whole of our vast Imperial fabric can be built if it is to be durable' (ibid., 9). The second was to recognize that the 'self-interest of the subject race is the principal basis of the whole Imperial fabric' (ibid., 46), and that low taxation and careful attention to material conditions were the best means of countering demagogy. The success of this policy in Egypt, he claimed, had reduced Egyptian nationalism to a 'splutter' (Cromer, 'The French in Algeria', *Political and Literary Essays*, 253; first published in May 1913). It was the fusion of these two ideas which lent Cromer's imperialism its distinctive quality, for unlike Lord Salisbury or James Fitzjames Stephen, he resisted the grim conclusion that imperial authority must rest chiefly on force. If British rule avoided subservience to 'special interests' at home, he argued:

> though we can never create a patriotism akin to that based on affinity of race or community of language, we may perhaps foster some sort of cosmopolitan allegiance grounded on the respect always accorded to superior talents and unselfish conduct and on the gratitude derived from favours conferred and those to come. (Cromer, 'The government of subject races', *Political and Literary Essays*, 13)

Cromer's last public service was to assume in August 1916 the chairmanship of the wartime commission to inquire into the Dardanelles expedition. When announced in the House of Commons, his appointment was questioned by a number of members on the grounds of his failing health. Indeed he died before the report was published in February 1917, and the extent of his influence over its conclusions is hard to judge. Cromer died at his home, 36 Wimpole Street, Cavendish Square, London, on 29 January 1917, and was buried at Bounemouth cemetery, Hampshire, beside his first wife. A memorial tablet, designed by Sir W. Goscombe John, was placed in Westminster Abbey.

J. G. DARWIN

Sources marquess of Zetland, *Lord Cromer* (1932) • R. C. Mowat, 'Lord Cromer and his successors in Egypt', DPhil diss., U. Oxf., 1970 • earl of Cromer [E. Baring], *Political and literary essays, 1903–1913*, first ser. (1913) • G. N. Sanderson, *England, Europe and the upper Nile, 1882–1899* (1965) • earl of Cromer [E. Baring], *Speeches and miscellaneous writings, 1882–1911*, 2 vols. (1912) • earl of Cromer [E. Baring], *Modern Egypt*, 2 vols. (1908) • R. L. Tignor, *Modernization and British colonial rule in Egypt, 1882–1914* (1966) • R. O. A. Crewe-Milnes, *Lord Rosebery*, 2 vols. (1931) • R. Robinson and J. Gallagher, *Africa and the Victorians* (1961) • M. Shibeika, *British policy in the Sudan, 1882–1902* (1952) • *DNB*

Archives BL, drafts of *Modern Egypt* and papers, Add. MSS 44903–44911 • ING Barings, London, 'autograph' letter-books • LUL, corresp. and a typescript of the Greek poet Mosclius's *Europa* • priv. coll. • PRO, corresp. and papers, FO 633 | BL, letters to Lord D'Abernon, Add. MS 48929 • BL, letters to Sir Mansfeldt de Cardonnel Findlay, Add. MS 62124 • BL, corresp. with Lord Cecil, Add. MS 51072 • BL, corresp. with Macmillans, Add. MS 55246 • BL, corresp. with Lord Ripon, Add. MSS 43596–43599 • BL, corresp. to Cromer enclosed in corresp. of Sir Mansfeldt de Cardonnel Findlay, Add. MS 62124 • BL OIOC, corresp. with Sir Alfred Lyall, MS Eur. F 132 • BL OIOC, letters to Sir Richard Temple, MS Eur. F 86 • BLPES, corresp. with E. D. Morel • Bodl. Oxf., letters to Sir Henry Wentworth Acland • Bodl. Oxf., corresp. with Herbert Asquith • Bodl. Oxf., corresp. with Lord Kimberley • Bodl. Oxf., letters to Sir Horace Rumbold • Bodl. Oxf., corresp. with Lord Selborne • Bodl. RH, letters to Anti-Slavery Society • CAC Cam., corresp. with Lord Esher • CKS, letters to Edward Stanhope • CUL, corresp. with marquess of Crewe • CUL, corresp. with Lord Hardinge • Duke U., Perkins L., letters to Lady Talbot • Glos. RO, corresp. with Sir Michael Hicks-Beach • HLRO, letters to Herbert Samuel • ING Barings, London, corresp. with earl of Northbrook • LPL, corresp. with Bishop in Jerusalem • News Int. RO, corresp. with Moberley Bell • NL Scot., corresp. with Lord Rosebery • NRA Scotland, priv. coll., letters to duke of Argyll • PRO, corresp. with Lord Kitchener, PRO 30/57, WO 159 • Staffs. RO, letters to duke of Sutherland • U. Birm., corresp. with W. H. Dawson • U. Durham L., corresp. with khedive of Egypt • U. Durham L., corresp. with Sir Reginald Wingate • U. Leeds, Brotherton L., letters to Sir Edmund Gosse • W. Sussex RO, letters to Wilfrid Scawen Blunt

Likenesses Violet, duchess of Rutland, lithograph, 1898, NPG • J. S. Sargent, oils, 1902, NPG [*see illus.*] • G. C. Beresford, photograph, 1903, NPG • W. Strang, chalk drawing, 1908, Royal Collection • Bassano, photograph, NPG • G. C. Beresford, photograph, NPG • W. Goscombe John, medallion on memorial tablet, Westminster Abbey • London Stereoscopic Co., photographs, NPG • J. Russell & Sons, photograph, NPG • Spy [L. Ward], cartoon, chromolithograph, NPG; repro. in *VF* (2 Jan 1902)

Wealth at death £117,608 19*s*.: probate, 1917, *CGPLA Eng. & Wales*

Baring, (Charles) Evelyn, first Baron Howick of Glendale (1903–1973), colonial governor and Commonwealth diplomat, was born in Manchester Square, London, on 29 September 1903, the third son of Evelyn *Baring, first earl of Cromer (1841–1917), and his second wife, Lady Katherine Georgiana Louisa Thynne (1865–1933), daughter of the fourth marquess of Bath. He was educated at Winchester College and New College, Oxford, where he graduated with first-class honours in history in 1924.

Almost from birth Baring was destined—and from an early age saw himself as destined—for imperial service. While still a young boy he had visited his father, then consul-general in Egypt, in Cairo. He joined the Indian Civil Service in 1926, serving as an administrative officer in the United Provinces, first at Lucknow and later at Meerut. His work led him to his lasting interest in field administration, the problems of custom and religion, and the need for agricultural development. Indian service also took him in 1929 to South Africa as secretary to the Indian government's agent-general, and there Baring first came face to face with racial problems, which provided him with valuable experience for the future. In 1929 he returned to India for a tour of duty in the turbulent North-West Frontier Province, but in 1933 ill health forced him to return to Britain. Indifferent, at times poor, health was to dog him for the rest of his life; a damaged liver obliged him to become a teetotaller and he suffered frequent periods of exhaustion.

In Britain, Baring joined the family banking firm, working with trainee bankers. This experience of City of London life, which he did not particularly enjoy, was nevertheless subsequently to prove very useful, both in his governorship of Kenya and with the Commonwealth Development Corporation, providing him with some insight into and contacts with the world of finance. Later he left Barings to become a director of Sudan Plantations, concerned with cotton growing in Sudan, work that he found more congenial. On 24 April 1935 Baring married Lady Mary Cecil (Molly) Grey (1907–2002), elder daughter of the fifth Earl Grey. They had one son and two daughters.

Being unfit for military service Baring joined the staff of the Foreign Office after the outbreak of war in 1939, his duties being concerned with Egypt, in particular the Egyptian economy. In Whitehall his abilities were recognized and in 1942, while still only thirty-eight years old, he was offered the appointment of governor of Southern Rhodesia. The territory had been given full internal self-government in 1923, with government in the hands of the white resident community who elected their own prime minister and produced their own administrative officials. The role of the governor, although a London appointee, was therefore in practice limited to tactful diplomacy and example. The white community was seeking to entrench its privileged position; Baring's views were the reverse, essentially liberal, and it was greatly to his credit that he managed to develop a close and friendly relationship with the territory's prime minister, Sir Godfrey Huggins, despite their differing views on the best future for Southern Rhodesia. Here Baring urged co-operation with the two northern Colonial Office territories, Northern Rhodesia and Nyasaland, while Huggins remained cautious, fearing that an eventual amalgamation might prejudice Southern Rhodesia's white rule. In the day-to-day exercise of his governorship Baring took especial interest in African affairs, local customs and structures, African agriculture, and social development. These interests led to criticism from some among the white settler community, with whose blunt, at times rough, political voice Baring was always ill at ease.

In 1944 Baring was appointed high commissioner to the Union of South Africa, an appointment diplomatic in its aspect of relations with Pretoria, but also gubernatorial in that the high commissioner was, in practice, governor of the protectorates of Bechuanaland, Basutoland, and Swaziland. These territories had not been included in the Union of South Africa in 1910, but their incorporation had remained an aim of the union government. Baring's day-to-day diplomatic work with the union government remained smooth (and was facilitated by the visit of the royal family in 1947–8) while Field Marshal Smuts remained in power. With the victory of the Nationalist Party under Dr D. F. Malan in 1948 difficulties arose, Nationalist racial policy with its early apartheid legislation being sharply criticized in Britain, where the Labour Party had come to power in 1945.

In the Smuts period Baring passed on the British government's reservations over South Africa's desire to move towards an annexation of the League of Nation's mandate territory of South-West Africa, and, after some negotiation, he secured the supply of South African uranium for Britain's nuclear weaponry. The question of the three 'high commission' territories, however, was irreconcilable. At first Baring feared that the Churchill government might give the territories to Pretoria, despite clear local opposition. Later, especially after the return to power of the Nationalists, his fears centred on London's expressing such firm opposition to any transfer that the Commonwealth relationship with Pretoria would be damaged, possibly lost.

The issue was complicated by the marriage of the young Bechuanaland Bamangwato prince, Seretse Khama, to an English woman, at a time when one of the Malan government's early apartheid measures was to forbid mixed marriages. Opinion in the union, as expressed in the white media, was strident on the subject. Seretse's uncle Tshekedi, acting chief of the Bamangwato, also opposed the marriage but was soon faced with dwindling tribal support, Seretse himself becoming increasingly well regarded. Pretoria saw the issue as an added incentive for annexation. Baring's advice to a London where several changes of ministers added to the confusion was that British policy should be that of the lesser evil: Seretse should not succeed to the chieftainship, as British recognition would damage fatally relations with Pretoria and bring about conflict in Bamangwato society. Events were to prove him wrong on this, and the credit due to him for his rural development policies in the three territories has been overshadowed by criticism of his views on the Seretse issue.

In 1952, the year after his return from Pretoria, Baring received the most difficult and testing appointment of his career, the governorship of Kenya just at the moment of the outbreak of the Kikuyu Mau Mau uprising. The period of his governorship, 1952–9, saw first the containment and then the virtual extinction of Mau Mau; fundamental political change, despite the Mau Mau troubles; impressive economic development; and programmes prepared for a massive expansion of African agriculture. Supported by a Colonial Office in London as anxious as he to see a return to order and development, Baring played the lead role in the last three of these ongoing events. From the start Baring appreciated that lasting peace could be secured only with at least the acquiescence, if not the full support, of the majority of the colony's population. In order to secure this Baring's experience and personal interests led him to devote much of his time and energy to economic development, which he saw as essential for the success of political change. Successive constitutional changes in the colony followed, providing for ministerial participation in the government by members of all races and extension of African representation in the legislature. Such developments were not welcomed by many of the European settlers, with whom Baring often found it as difficult to deal as he had in Southern Rhodesia. By diplomacy and tactful argument, however, he was able to secure the co-operation of the more liberal settler spokesmen, notably Michael Blundell.

The colony's remarkable economic development, which owed much to specific government intervention, together with the ending of unequal racially based salary scales in the public services, served to create an emerging African middle class which could appreciate that real political change had begun and would accelerate, and among the African peoples generally, including the Kikuyu, the realization that violence was unnecessary and undesirable.

Perhaps singly the greatest achievement of Baring's entire career was in Kenya's African agriculture, where he secured funds from Britain and the World Bank for the Swynnerton Plan, a total revolution in African farming based on redistribution, consolidation, efficient farming, and the opening up of new areas for cash crops, all aimed at creating self-sufficient peasant family holdings with one or more cash crops. The development of this policy was facilitated by emergency legislation resulting from the Mau Mau uprising, which provided the government with powers for compulsory resettlement of Mau Mau detainees in areas of the government's choice and of agricultural potential. By 1959 a highly successful African farmer class was growing cash crops previously reserved for European farms.

Baring found the role of governor of a colony at a time of a violent and bloody uprising exceedingly difficult and uncongenial. He himself suffered periods of debilitating ill health. The white farmers and some of the military, police, and administration felt that he was too weak. Nevertheless he was convinced that Mau Mau had to be fought and suppressed. He firmly believed that Jomo Kenyatta had been its instigator, and that Kenyatta's trial, despite highly dubious witnesses and a controversial conviction, had been just. He held that, in governing a turbulent country, a strong and efficient secretariat and provincial administrative officers loyally supported by the governor were as important as the military and police. However, a number of senior Kenya administrative officers, faced with daily violence in their districts, were deliberately less than frank with him (and with his attorney-general and police commissioner) when continuing systematic excesses leading to torture and deaths were committed by their local security forces. In particular, these centred on locally recruited police and home guards, and in the huge, overcrowded, and insanitary detention camps through which some 70,000 Kikuyu were processed for rehabilitation. The most notorious example was the attempt to conceal from Baring the true facts of the Hola prison camp scandal, where eleven prisoners were killed by prison staff. Baring believed the initial story that he had been given and advised the Colonial Office that the prisoners had died from drinking poisoned water. Later, revelation of the real cause created a major political and parliamentary crisis in London. It can justly be argued that Baring, in his conviction that Mau Mau was evil and had to be suppressed, did not exercise a proper supervision of the administration, which he believed he had to support to the hilt. He also authorized the establishment of emergency courts for a wide variety of capital crimes, some relatively minor, in which procedures, on occasions mass trials, were more brutally arbitrary than just, with a very large number of death sentences imposed.

This necessary criticism of one aspect having been made, overall Baring's governorship of Kenya was one of the most important and outstandingly successful in the decades of decolonization, well summarized in his *Times* obituary: 'he found it a land of danger and left it a land of hope' (12 March 1973). And it was for him a personal pleasure that in the last days of his governorship he saved, at considerable risk to himself, an Indian girl from drowning off the Kenyan coast. For this gallantry he was awarded the queen's commendation for brave conduct.

In 1960 Baring became deputy chairman of the Commonwealth Development Corporation, succeeding as chairman later in the year. Here his wide experience and personal prestige enabled him to secure funds from the British government, the World Bank, and other European governments for a series of partnerships for development projects. Among them were the Kenya Tea Smallholders scheme and the Swaziland Usutu Forests, which he had helped to start earlier in his career. Other programmes included tobacco curing in Malawi, wattle tanning in Tanzania, oil palm in Sarawak and the Solomon Islands, together with help for smallholders, loans to public utilities, and assistance to manufacturing and processing industries in a number of countries—the range of the corporation's work being extended beyond the Commonwealth.

Baring was tall and distinguished in appearance, patrician—at times a little aloof—in style, and often a poor speaker. He was a very devout Christian. He possessed great strength of character and determination, at times ruthless but with his high intelligence ready to consider new ideas; ill health could, however, make him at times difficult to work with and slow to reach decisions. He was appointed KCMG in 1942, KCVO in 1947, GCMG in 1955, and KG in 1972. Baring received a hereditary barony in January 1960, taking the title of Lord Howick of Glendale. He had a passion for physical exercise, a characteristic that led to a fall while rock climbing and his death on 10 March 1973 in the Alnwick Hospital, Alnwick, Northumberland. He was buried in Howick churchyard, and was survived by his wife. ANTHONY CLAYTON

Sources C. Douglas-Home, *Evelyn Baring: the last proconsul* (1978) · *The Times* (12 March 1973) · *DNB* · Lord Howick and M. Perham, interview, 19–24 Nov 1971, Bodl. RH, MS Afr.s.1574 · D. A. Low and A. Smith, eds., *History of East Africa*, 3 (1976) · A. Clayton, *Counter-insurgency in Kenya, 1952–60* (Manhattan, Kansas, 1984) · M. Blundell, *So rough a wind* (1964) · Burke, *Peerage* (2000)

Archives Howick Grange, Howick, papers | BL, corresp. with P. V. Emrys-Evans, Add. MS 58244 · Bodl. RH, corresp. with M. Blundell · CUL, corresp. with Sir Peter Markham Scott

Likenesses photograph, repro. in Douglas-Home, *Evelyn Baring*, jacket

Wealth at death £249,880: probate, 5 July 1973, *CGPLA Eng. & Wales*

Baring, Sir Francis, first baronet (1740–1810), merchant and merchant banker, was born at Larkbear, Exeter, on 18 April 1740, third of the four surviving sons and one daughter of John Baring (1697–1748) and his wife, Elizabeth *Baring (1702–1766), daughter of John Vowler, a prosperous Exeter 'grocer' who dealt largely in sugar, spices, teas, and coffee. Despite being partially deaf from an early age, in 1762 Francis Baring established the London merchant house of Barings. He emerged as a powerful merchant banker and by the mid-1790s reckoned that his concerns had been 'more extensive and upon a larger scale than any merchant in this or any other country' (Barings archives, Northbrook MSS, A7).

Early life Baring's father, the son of a Lutheran pastor, emigrated from Bremen in 1717 and settled at Exeter, where he became a leading textile merchant and manufacturer, and a landowner; other than the bishop and the recorder, apparently he alone in Exeter kept a carriage. His premature death in 1748 resulted in Francis, aged eight, being brought up and strongly influenced by his mother. Her sound business head doubled her firm's worth and in 1762 she extended the business to London.

In preparation for this, in the early 1750s Francis was dispatched to London for education at Mr Fargue's French school at Hoxton and then at Mr Fuller's academy in Lothbury. Samuel Touchet, merchant of London, accepted him in 1755 for a seven-year apprenticeship, charging his mother a substantial premium of £800. Immediately upon his release, on Christmas day 1762 he joined his two surviving brothers in the interlocking partnerships of John and Francis Baring & Co. of London and John and Charles Baring & Co. of Exeter. Francis led the London concern and Charles the Exeter one, while John, a leading Exeter citizen and an MP from 1776, was a sleeping partner and the nominal head of both firms.

Initially the London business comprised the accounts and goodwill transferred to it from an old family friend, Nathaniel Paice, a London merchant who was retiring, but also much business came from John and Charles Baring & Co. and other Exeter merchants who required a London agent. Agency services for overseas merchants and trading speculations were soon added. But the firm lost money in eight of its first fourteen years, as Francis Baring learnt how to judge markets; having started out with £10,000 he reckoned that by 1777 his net worth stood at just £2500.

Notwithstanding these private reverses, the City of London quickly recognized Baring's special qualities and in 1771 the Royal Exchange Assurance, a giant public business, appointed him to its court. He underpinned his directorship, which continued until 1780, with a holding of £820 in the company's stock, no mean sum when his assets totalled £13,000. This appointment was important to hold; for the first time he was marked out from the throng of merchants populating the courts and alleys of the City.

On 12 May 1767, at Croydon, Baring married Harriet Herring (1750–1804). Over the years she contributed about £20,000 to the family coffers, received from her merchant father, William Herring of Croydon, and a cousin, Thomas, archbishop of Canterbury. Otherwise her early contributions were her frugality in managing a household accommodated above the business and, between 1768 and 1787, a capacity to bear six sons and six daughters, among them Harriet *Wall, religious controversialist. Later she emerged as a glittering social hostess, 'devoted to fashionable society' (Barings archives, DEP249), but this took its toll. Her health was 'irretrievably impaired by late hours and over-excitement' (ibid.), and she died comparatively young in 1804. In contrast her husband preferred 'the more tranquil enjoyment of a domestic circle' (*Public Characters*, 1805, 38). Harriet also introduced her husband to valuable business contacts. Harriet's sister Mary in 1766 married one of London's leading private bankers, Richard Stone of Martin & Co., with whom Francis Baring's firm had opened an account in 1764.

Independence from Exeter Baring's early business was constrained through the demands placed upon it by the much larger Exeter firm, which suffered under Charles Baring's speculations of a 'wild, strange, incoherent description' (Barings archives, Northbrook MSS, D1). The resulting conflict was only resolved in early 1777, when Baring took the initiative in dissolving the interlocking partnerships. Capital and management were now entirely separate, though Francis maintained strong family links with Exeter. Regularly he employed his wealth to rescue Charles from ruin and thus preserve the good name of his family; his motivation was an intense desire to see business and family prosper. Thus he was scandalized by Charles's 'almost monstrous management of the original and chief dependence of the Baring family' (ibid., D7).

Baring's brother John remained a sleeping partner until

Sir Francis Baring, first baronet (1740–1810), by Sir Thomas Lawrence, 1806–7 [left, with his brother John Baring (centre) and son-in-law Charles Wall (right)]

his retirement in late 1800. In 1781 two nominal partners were appointed, J. F. Mesturas, formerly a clerk, and Charles Wall, who in September 1790 married Baring's eldest daughter, Harriet. The two were soon afterwards promoted full partners. However, Mesturas withdrew in 1795 and was not replaced. Thus from 1777 until his retirement in 1804, Baring led the firm almost singlehandedly, for many years having Wall as his sole active partner.

The partnership capital grew steadily from £20,000 in 1777 to £70,000 in 1790, and to £400,000 in 1804. Baring came to contribute the major share, providing 12 per cent in 1777, 40 per cent in 1790, and 54 per cent in 1804. Annual profits rose to £40,000 in the 1790s and peaked, untypically, at over £200,000 in 1802; they were calculated after payment to partners at 4 per cent interest, sometimes 5 per cent, on their capital. Baring's share of the profits increased steadily from a quarter in the mid-1760s to a half from 1777 and to three-quarters from 1801. His total wealth, business as well as private, rose accordingly, from almost £5000 in 1763, to £64,000 in 1790, and to £500,000 in 1804.

Building a correspondent network Early on Baring's business profits were derived mostly from international trade, especially between Britain, the western European coast, the Iberian peninsula, Italy, the West Indies, and, from the 1770s, North America. They arose from trading on sole account or, more often, on joint account with other merchants; from acting as London agent for overseas merchants, buying and selling consignments, making and collecting payments, and arranging shipping and warehousing; and, in due course, from trade finance through making advances or, more frequently, accepting bills of exchange.

The success of this work was greatly influenced by the establishment of a powerful network of corresponding houses in the main international trading centres. These alliances with leading European and North American merchants were the keys to his success. Their establishment serves to underline Baring's outstanding personal qualities which seemingly effortlessly won him the confidence of older merchants. 'His great characteristics', wrote one contemporary, 'are method and dexterity in business, a sound judgement and a most excellent heart' (*Public Characters*, 1805, 38–9).

Hope & Co. of Amsterdam, the most powerful merchant bank in Europe's leading financial centre, was Baring's most valuable connection. Their association is said to have begun in the 1760s, when Hopes passed Baring some bills to negotiate and ended up 'exceedingly struck with the transaction which bespoke not only great zeal and activity, but what was still more important … either good credit or great resources … From that day Baring became one of their principal friends' (Barings archives, DEP249). The link was consolidated in other ways, in particular through the marriage in 1796 of Pierre César *Labouchère [*see under* Hope family], a leading figure at Hopes, to Baring's third daughter, Dorothy.

Vital connections were also established on the other side of the Atlantic. Baring was quicker than most to see the commercial potential of Britain's North American colonies, and his finance house quickly emerged as the European hub of a network of America's most powerful merchants. In 1774 his first American customer was the leading Philadelphia merchant trader, Willing, Morris & Co.; its influential partners included Robert Morris, a future financial architect of American independence from Britain, and Thomas Willing, a future president of the Bank of the United States. Through them Baring was introduced to Senator William Bingham, one of America's wealthiest men, a connection which gave rise to several lucrative transactions.

Government adviser Baring's work from 1782 as an adviser on commercial matters to cabinet ministers propelled him from relative obscurity to the inner circles of British political life, underlining how in these early years his influence was entirely disproportionate to the resources he commanded. The catalyst for this advancement was his Devon connections. His brother John was elected to parliament as a member for Exeter in 1776; more importantly, in 1780 his sister, Elizabeth, married another MP and fellow Devonian, John Dunning.

A rich and influential lawyer, Dunning was allied to Lord Shelburne, a powerful whig politician who held progressive views on political economy and whose borough of Calne Dunning represented in parliament. In July 1782, following Shelburne's promotion to prime minister and Dunning's appointment as chancellor of the duchy of Lancaster, Baring fulfilled the new prime minister's need 'to have recourse from time to time to mercantile advice' (Barings archives, Northbrook MSS, B1). Baring, by instinct a whig, became Shelburne's confidential adviser on commerce, or his 'handy City man', according to a discontented William Cobbett. Baring's ideas on political economy and commerce were well ahead of his time; in 1799 he rightly defended the Bank of England's decision (in 1797) to suspend specie payments as both correct and inevitable, in the face of hostile opposition from many of his peers.

Baring's knowledge of North American merchants and trade made him especially useful in the closing years of the American War of Independence when Shelburne, anxious for a liberal settlement, invited his comments on commercial aspects of the proposed peace treaty with the United States. Shelburne introduced Baring to Isaac Barré, his paymaster-general, and to such leading luminaries as William Pitt the younger, Henry Dundas, Jeremy Bentham, Edmund Burke, Sir Samuel Romilly, and lords Erskine, Camden, Sydney, and Melville. However, Baring's friendship with Lord Lansdowne (as Shelburne became in 1784), Dunning, and Barré ran particularly deep, and in 1787 he drew public attention to it by commissioning their triple portrait from Sir Joshua Reynolds. A private financial connection also existed. For six years from 1783 Baring loaned Lansdowne £5000, on security of a debt owing to Lansdowne. In 1805, on Lansdowne's death, Baring became a trustee of his estate, charged with the task of liquidating debts of £90,000.

Baring was not nearly as close to the tory leader William

Pitt, who followed Lansdowne as prime minister and who held office almost continuously until Baring's retirement from active business. Their views were far apart, and on Pitt's death Baring was quick to stress their lack of concurrence 'on any great political question for above 20 years, our political opinions and principles being different' (*The Times*, 6 Feb 1806). In particular he disagreed with Pitt's policy for the seemingly endless continuation of a wasteful war; they also suffered differences over government policy towards the East India Company. Baring's personal influence in government waned but his expert advice, always fairly delivered, continued to be provided on such matters as trade with Turkey, the importance of Gibraltar, and the funding of the national debt. As part of Pitt's cleansing of abuse from public office, in 1784 he appointed Baring a commissioner charged with investigating fees, gratuities, and prerequisites for holding certain offices.

The link with Lansdowne led Baring to the Commons in 1784 when, at a cost of £3000, he was elected MP for Grampound, Devon. He was ousted six years later, after which he stood unsuccessfully for Ilchester. Later he sat for Lansdowne's safe boroughs of Chipping Wycombe, Oxfordshire (1794–6 and 1802–6), and Calne, Wiltshire (1796–1802), which had formerly been represented by other Lansdowne favourites, Dunning and Barré. Notwithstanding his admission that 'my voice is so very unequal to the House of Commons' (Barings archives, Northbrook MSS, N4.4.295), his speeches were reckoned to be 'neat, flowing and perspicuous, aiming more by solidity of argument to arrest and convince his hearers, than by beautiful figures and impassioned eloquence to mislead the minds of men' (*Daily Advertiser, Oracle and True Briton*, 12 Oct 1805).

Both in private and from the benches, Baring advocated greater freedom of trade. 'Every regulation', he said, 'is a restriction, and as such contrary to that freedom which I have held to be the first principle of the well being of commerce', for good measure adding that

> a restriction, or regulation, may doubtless answer the particular purpose for which it is imposed, but as commerce is not a simple thing, but a thing of a thousand relations, what may be of profit in the particular, may be ruinous in general. (*Public Characters*, 1805, 34)

Government business in the 1780s There can be little doubt that Baring's firm benefited directly as well as indirectly from his political connections, in particular from Barré's almost limitless patronage as paymaster-general during the American War of Independence. In 1782 he advised Lansdowne that in 1781 and 1782 contractors' profits from supplying the army abroad represented over 13 per cent of the total value of transactions. Baring won the 1783 contract on the basis of 1 per cent commission, and, when war ended and the contract was terminated prematurely, he won contracts for the disposal of stores. Government savings were at least 10 per cent and Baring was personally rewarded in other ways. Between 1784 and 1786 he (and not his firm) received £7000 in commissions for undertaking government work and a further £4250 from interest on government money in his hands. Against this, in his private accounts he charged the £3000 expenses incurred in winning his Commons seat in 1784. Nevertheless, transactions for the government stretched his resources in these years. He apparently 'borrowed' stock from Martin & Co., his brother-in-law's firm, 'to enable me to negotiate the government business' (Barings archives, DEP193.40). Yet the returns on these risky adventures were clearly immense. During the war, when government expenditure soared, his firm also emerged as a contractor for marketing British government debt; it was believed to have made profits of £19,000.

The East India Company Francis Baring's other distraction from his firm was his directorship of the East India Company from 1779. By 1783 he led the City interest on the company's court, and in 1786 he was reckoned its most able member. His commitment was significant; he gave up each Wednesday and occasionally a Friday to its affairs. Notwithstanding his views on the liberalization of American trade, he promoted the company's monopoly and commercial independence 'with an ardour contrary to the usual moderation of his character' (*Public Characters*, 1805). He joined the East India Company when the British government was anxious to exert greater political control over it, recognizing the great territorial power that it had become. Baring actively fought off the far-reaching proposals of Lord North and Charles James Fox, believing that 'India is not a colony and God forbid that it ever should be' (Barings archives, Northbrook MSS, N4.5), but he worked with an old friend from the period of his apprenticeship and now a fellow director, Richard Atkinson, to modify and facilitate the acceptance of Pitt's India Act. In 1792 and 1793, as Pitt's preferred candidate, he was elected chairman and charged with the task of renegotiating the company's charter.

The experience of his chairmanship was both exhausting and distracting. His private accounts went unwritten for two years and in 1792, 'being obliged to travel for my health' (Barings archives, DEP193.40), he was utterly unprepared for the collapse in prices of British government securities which reduced his private capital of £20,000 by half. 'The more I work', he confided to Lansdowne, 'the greater the degree of jealousy and difficulty I have to encounter amongst the directors who are in general composed of either knaves or fools' (ibid., DEP193.17.1). Pitt rewarded Baring with a baronetcy on 29 May 1793, and he soldiered on as a director until his death in 1810, but increasingly he was disillusioned and absent from the court. As early as 1798 he had lost 'much of that consequence … which his superior knowledge, experience and abilities entitle him to' (C. H. Philips, *The East India Company, 1784–1834*, 1940, 164).

Transactions with Hope & Co. Throughout Baring's lifetime his good commercial intelligence, sound judgement, nimble-footedness, and instinct for speculative profit remained the hallmarks of his business style. Thousands of speculations detailed in his firm's ledgers attest to this, but his burgeoning business and rising confidence were graphically illustrated in 1787 when Hopes introduced him to speculation on a grand scale. The two houses set about controlling the entire European cochineal market by secretly buying up all available stocks, one quarter for Barings and the rest for Hopes. Correspondents from St Petersburg to Cadiz spent £450,000 but prices remained static and in 1788, with a huge loss anticipated, the partners of Barings agreed 'to forgo any participation of the profits of the trade for the last year' (Barings archives, DEP193.40).

The resumption of war in 1793 provided new challenges and opportunities. The evacuation of Hopes to London between 1795 and 1803, when Amsterdam was occupied by France, and the availability of their expertise, contacts, and capital to Barings were of immense assistance. The two houses embarked on bold transactions—invariably with a quarter for Barings and the rest for Hopes. Their first adventure was entirely private and aimed to secure a substantial part of their capital from the dangers of European revolutions and wars. In late 1795 Baring dispatched his 22-year-old son, Alexander, to Boston to negotiate and execute the purchase of more than 1 million acres of land in Maine for £107,000. The investment was introduced by the land's owner, Senator William Bingham, son-in-law of Barings' Philadelphia correspondent, Thomas Willing, and yet another friend of Lansdowne. Francis Baring undertook the initial appraisal and commitment to the investment, and the negotiations were left to his son Alexander, who afterwards remained in North America as Barings' representative and who consolidated his position by marrying Bingham's eldest daughter, Ann Louisa. The link was further strengthened through the marriage of Baring's third son, Henry, to Bingham's other daughter, Maria, in 1802. Both marriages brought considerable wealth to the Baring family.

Wartime finance British government expenditure, which grew to unprecedented levels during the European wars, created great opportunities for London merchant bankers such as Sir Francis Baring. After 1799 his firm headed the list of public debt contractors in twelve of the next fifteen years, supposedly giving rise to total profits of £190,000. For Baring, a key financier of the nation's war effort, it represented the pinnacle of his power and standing. Despite his retirement in 1804, he continued to appear as a contractor until his death because, as he explained, 'it was thought my name would be useful in the opinion of the publick' (Barings archives, Northbrook MSS, A21).

Britain's European allies needed funds and came to Baring who, with Hopes, now organized some of the first marketings of foreign bonds in London. Believing fervently that 'it may be desirable not to have the subject to discuss with our own Ministers, as you know very well how ignorant they are of foreign finance' (Barings archives, Northbrook MSS, A19), in 1801 he dispatched P. C. Labouchere of Hopes and his son George to negotiate a loan to the court of Lisbon. The resulting 'Portuguese diamond loan' of 13 million guilders was shared between Barings and Hopes on the usual 25:75 basis.

Of equal strategic importance was Baring's transmission of British government subsidies to allied governments to support their war efforts. This highly secret and sensitive work required expert knowledge of money transmission and a sound correspondent network; again it underlined the government's confidence in Baring. Opportunities for direct financing of the enemy were also presented to Baring, who knew he could hoodwink the government into consenting to them; 'but to have obtained that licence we must have presented a memorial so equivocal and in truth so unfounded that it would not suit us and therefore was abandoned' (Barings archives, DEP3.3.3, Francis Baring to Alexander Baring, 20 May 1799).

Baring applied a looser criterion in his choice of trading partners, however. Links with leading American merchants, such as the Codmans of Boston, Willing and Francis of Philadelphia, Robert Gilmour, and Robert Oliver & Brothers of Baltimore were now immensely important to Barings' business as its axis swung from continental European to transatlantic trade. In sustaining these extensive connections Baring undoubtedly facilitated, albeit passively, the breaching of Britain's continental blockade.

American finance Close connections with American merchants inevitably resulted in links with the United States government. Since the close of the American War of Independence, Baring had kept watch over the American government's finances in Europe. However, his first significant transaction for its account was the sale in 1795 of $800,000 worth of stock and the remittance of the proceeds in support of American negotiations with the north African Barbary powers. To secure the transaction Francis Baring admitted to acting with 'zeal, perhaps imprudence, in going beyond the letters of my orders' (New York Historical Society, Rufus King MSS, vol. 39, fol. 17), but the American ambassador in London commended his 'liberal and skilfull manner' and undertook to ensure that the government would 'entertain a proper sense of your Service in this Business' (ibid., vol. 51, fol. 461). Other business soon followed, including the sale of the government's shares in the Bank of the United States and the purchase of munitions from British manufactures for the government's account.

Considered to be an 'English house of the first reputation and solidity' (New York Historical Society, Rufus King MSS, vol. 55, fols. 378–9), Barings in 1803 was appointed London financial agent for the United States government, leaving Sir Francis Baring's influence in North American financial affairs unrivalled in London. At about this time, when a short interval of peace existed after the treaty of Amiens, Baring led his house, alongside Hopes, into its largest and most prestigious transaction yet. The French government wanted to sell 1 million square miles of the Territory of Louisiana, and the United States administration wanted to buy it; the purchase price was $15 million and Francis Baring was charged with finding it. He sent his son Alexander to Paris to negotiate with French and American representatives, and the eventual result was that on behalf of the French government Barings and

Hopes sold US government bonds worth $11.25 million. The business was of enormous size; 'my nerves are equal to the operation', Francis Baring reassured Hopes, but he added that 'we all tremble about the magnitude of the American account' (Barings archives, Northbrook MSS, A4). Later he confessed that 'what I suffered can never be described and it completely overpowered my nerves for the first and I hope last time' (ibid.).

The leading American house in London also acted as London banker for the Bank of the United States. Here again the close network of correspondents and friends which Baring so earnestly cultivated was vital. Thomas Willing, William Bingham's father-in-law and Barings' client at Philadelphia since 1774, was the bank's president and so its use of Baring's firm in making London payments, undertaking exchange transactions, and providing credits was seemingly inevitable.

Withdrawal from business Baring aimed to strengthen his links with Hopes even further, through his son joining their partnership, but Alexander Baring could not be persuaded to comply. Baring's ultimate goal was to establish a house under his control based on both Barings and Hopes, which would straddle the North Sea, dominate government finance in Europe, and provide an enormously powerful base for its American connections. Alexander's reluctance compelled him 'to abandon the colossal plan of one foot in England, the other in Holland' (Barings archives, DEP193.17.1, Baring to Shelburne, 9 Oct 1802). It was 'a sacrifice such as no head of a family ever made before', he confided to Lansdowne, 'but I must confess there is enough left for consolation' (ibid.).

In 1803 Baring began his withdrawal from business when he gave up his entitlement to a share of his firm's profits. Much of his capital remained on loan; by the time of his death in 1810 he still provided £70,000 or about 17 per cent of the firm's resources. He stood down as partner in 1804, handing the reins to Charles Wall, the 'principal manager' according to Farrington, and his three eldest sons, Thomas Baring, Alexander *Baring, and Henry Baring. In recognition of their assumption of leadership, in 1807 the nameplate of Sir Francis Baring & Co. was taken down and replaced by that of Baring Brothers.

Private wealth Baring's accumulation of great wealth allowed him to diversify his pursuits in gentlemanly living. In 1790 he began to acquire property at Beddington in Surrey, based around Camden House, and in 1796 he bought Manor House, Lee, a relatively modest country house about 6 miles from central London, from his old friend Joseph Plaice, for £20,000. Land in Buckinghamshire was soon added at a cost of £16,000 and by 1800 his total investment in country estates exceeded £60,000. Yet more ambitious plans for life as a country landowner were fertilized; from 1801 he acquired from the duke of Bedford land and a great house at Stratton in Hampshire to create 'the Kingdom of Stratton' (Barings archives, Northbrook MSS, A21). By 1803 his expenditure had reached £150,000, partly funded through the sale of his Buckinghamshire land. In 1802 he transferred his London home from above his business in Devonshire Square to Hill Street in the West End.

The architect George Dance was commissioned to remodel the house at Stratton, which was then filled with the finest furniture and best old masters. Baring's picture purchases had begun in 1795, when about £1500 was spent, and his expenditure grew apace after 1800; by 1808 he valued his acquisitions at £15,000. Dutch seventeenth-century masters were his particular passion but by 1804 he had 'done with all except the very superior'; now only works by Rembrandt, Rubens, or Van Dyck 'tempt me' but 'the first must not be too dark, nor the second indecent' (Barings archives, Northbrook MSS, A4.3). He was a patron of Sir Thomas Lawrence, whom he summoned to Stratton in 1806 to paint a magisterial triple portrait of Baring with his two senior partners as a memorial to his business achievement.

Otherwise, Baring's distractions from business were few. As chairman from 1803 to 1810 of the Patriotic Fund administered by Lloyds of London, he worked for the welfare of Britons wounded or bereaved during the French wars. The mercantile community sought his help as referee in settling disputes, and as a trustee he gave distinguished service in settling the affairs of the leading London merchants, Boyd, Benfield & Co., which had crashed in 1799. He held the presidency of the London Institution from 1805 until his death. As a pamphleteer his output was modest, with works on the Commutation Act in 1786, on the Bank of England in 1797, and on the affairs of Walter Boyd in 1801.

Baring died on 11 September 1810 at Lee and was buried in the family vault at Stratton, Micheldever, on 20 September. He was survived by five sons and five daughters. His eldest son, Thomas, succeeded to the baronetcy and country estates; Thomas's son Francis was to enter political life and in 1866 was created Baron Northbrook. His second son, Alexander, succeeded him as senior partner and was later created Baron Ashburton for his political services. The third son, Henry, was also a partner, albeit an unremarkable one, while the other surviving sons, George and William, never rose to prominence.

The size of Baring's estate underlines his achievement: £175,000 was distributed among his children other than Thomas, who inherited the balance; his capital remaining in Barings amounted to almost £70,000; his Hampshire and Lee estates were valued at £400,000; and his pictures, jewels, and furniture were worth almost £30,000.

In the twenty-five years since 1777, Baring had transformed his firm into London's most powerful merchant banking house; by about 1786 he reckoned that it was 'in a very flourishing situation, totally divested of moonshine' (Barings archives, DEP193.17.1, Baring to Shelburne, n.d.). By 1800 a network of influential correspondents stretched across Europe; agencies were held for leading Boston and Philadelphia merchants; leadership in marketing British government debt was undisputed; Baring was a respected adviser to senior politicians; his leadership in the East India Company had provided influence in trade east of Africa; and, not least, important commissions had been won from foreign governments. Francis Baring was Barings, and he dominated management, provided most of the capital, and received the lion's share of the profits.

After Baring's death tributes included one from Lord Lansdowne, son of his political friend, who reckoned Baring was a 'prince of merchants'. Another political ally, Lord Erskine, wrote: 'he was unquestionably the first merchant in Europe; first in knowledge and talents and first in character and opulence' (*GM*, 1st ser., 80, 1810, 293).

JOHN ORBELL

Sources P. Ziegler, *The sixth great power: Barings, 1762–1929* (1988) • R. W. Hidy, *The house of Baring in American trade and finance: English merchant bankers at work, 1763–1861* (1949) • M. G. Buist, *At spes non fracta: Hope and Co., 1770–1815* (1974) • J. Orbell, *Baring Brothers & Co. Limited: a history to 1939* (privately printed, London, 1985) • R. C. Alberts, *The golden voyage: the life and times of William Bingham, 1752–1804* (1969) • N. Baker, *Government and contractors: the British treasury and war suppliers, 1775–1783* (1971) • F. Baring, *The principle of the Commutation-Act established by facts* (1786) • F. Baring, *Observations on the establishment of the Bank of England* (1797) • F. Baring, *Further observations on the establishment of the Bank of England* (1797) • F. Baring, *Observations on the publication of Walter Boyd, esq., M.P.* (1801) • *Public characters of 1809–10* (1809), appx 12, p. 590 • 'Sir Francis Baring, Bart.', *Public characters of 1805* (1805), 30–39 • ING Barings, London, Barings archives

Archives BL OIOC, home misc. series, corresp. and papers relating to India • ING Barings, London, letters to Henry Dundas; letters to Lord Lansdowne | BL, letters to Lord Grenville, Add. MS 58977 • BL, corresp. with Warren Hastings, Add. MSS 29169–29192 • Bucks. RLSS, letters to Lord Hobart • priv. coll., corresp. with Lord Lansdowne and papers as trustee of his estate • RA, corresp. with Thomas Lawrence

Likenesses B. West, oils, 1804, ING Barings • T. Lawrence, drawing, *c*.1806, ING Barings • T. Lawrence, group portrait, oils, 1806–7 (with John Baring and Charles Wall), ING Barings, London [*see illus.*] • Evans, portrait, 1807 (after drawing by T. Lawrence), ING Barings • E. Pattry, watercolour, 1926, ING Barings • H. Bone, pencil drawing (after B. West), NPG • W. Evans, stipple (after T. Lawrence, 1807), NPG • P. Jean, watercolour miniature, ING Barings • studio of T. Lawrence, oils, ING Barings • C. Muss, oils on enamel (after T. Lawrence), NPG • J. Ward, group portrait, mezzotint (*The Baring family*; after T. Lawrence), BM, NPG

Wealth at death £606,000; also £70,000 in company holdings

Baring, Francis Thornhill, first Baron Northbrook (1796–1866), politician, was born at Calcutta on 20 April 1796, the eldest son of Sir Thomas Baring, second baronet (1772–1848), then in the East India Company's civil service, and his wife, Mary Ursula (*d*. 1846), daughter of Charles Sealy, barrister, of Calcutta. Thomas *Baring (1799–1873) and Charles *Baring (1807–1879), banker and bishop respectively, were his brothers. The elder Thomas Baring, son and successor of Francis, the first baronet and founder of Baring Brothers & Co., was himself to be a partner in the great banking house. Educated at Winchester College and Christ Church, Oxford (matriculating in 1814), Francis Thornhill Baring graduated with a double first in classics and mathematics in 1817, and was called to the bar at Lincoln's Inn in 1823. Heir to a substantial Hampshire estate and property in Kent, he did not enter the family business headed by his uncle Alexander, the first Lord Ashburton. On 7 April 1825 he married Jane (1804–1838), daughter of Captain Sir George Grey RN, first baronet, with whom he had five children. Marriage to a niece of Earl Grey, of

Francis Thornhill Baring, first Baron Northbrook (1796–1866), by Sir George Hayter, *c*.1833

Reform Bill fame, took him into the inner circle of whig politics.

From 1826 until his retirement in 1865 Baring sat as MP for Portsmouth, proud of the fact that his three elections to the unreformed parliament never cost him more than £25. He stood as a relatively advanced whig but supported Canning's brief ministry out of admiration for the man who had liberalized British foreign policy. He entertained no misgivings about parliamentary reform in 1831–2—'the mass of the English are eminently aristocratical', he opined—until ministers proposed to swamp the Lords' opposition by a large-scale creation of peers. A lord of the Treasury in Grey's government (1830–34), he acquiesced in the threat as 'the only course to avoid revolution' (*Journals*, 1.89–90). Promoted financial secretary to the Treasury (June–November 1834; 1835–9), he became chancellor of the exchequer and a privy councillor in August 1839 when Melbourne's hold on power was weakening: 'We have everything except a revenue and a majority', said Baring (ibid., 1.147). As chancellor, his finance was crippled by a principled aversion to an income tax; he borrowed and raised all indirect and assessed taxes before lowering selected import duties with free trade in view but out of his fiscal reach. In 1841 his politically inept proposal to cut the discriminatory tariff on foreign sugar produced by slave labour was defeated, and led to the government's fall on the resulting vote of confidence (27 August 1841).

Greville thought there was 'no stronger political partisan' than this disappointing chancellor (*Greville Memoirs*, 4.379). Baring was never comfortable with the former tory Palmerston, or with the methods of his foreign policy: the risks of war with France which they sometimes involved struck him as 'insanity' (ibid., 5.11). He refused the Treasury under Russell in 1846, staying out of the government, put off by the demands of his old post—'figures worked the brain as no other work did'—and by Palmerston's return to the Foreign Office over the objections of apprehensive colleagues. Baring also felt that with him the Greys and their connections would be decidedly over-represented in the cabinet (*Journals*, 1.234–5). His standing with the back-benchers made him a natural choice to chair the select committee which investigated the causes of the financial crisis of 1847, and his influence was apparent in the successful resistance to a higher income tax in Wood's budget of 1848. Russell was glad to have him back in the cabinet from January 1849 as first lord of the Admiralty.

Baring took over the Admiralty at a time of growing alarm, which he shared, about the attitude of the new Bonapartist regime in France: 'I have little doubt that their first attempt will be a dash at England' (*Later Correspondence of … Russell*, 2.89). On the other hand, anxious not to provoke the French, he refrained from concentrating the available strength in home waters, and kept the battle fleet out of their sight but not too far away. A modern authority has called this 'not an heroic … course, but … an intelligent attempt to relate British naval policy to the circumstances' (Bartlett, 284). The navy was at a critical stage in the transition from sail to steam. Baring and his Admiralty board were responsible for the domination of the fleet in the early 1850s by screw-assisted ships of the line and frigates. Baring's plans for a naval reserve to meet the acute problem of manning ships without reviving the press-gang bore fruit by the end of the decade. In the dockyards he could point to a considerable rise in productivity during his years at the Admiralty, but his well-meaning efforts to eliminate the political patronage for which dockyard administration was notorious met with little success.

After the fall of Russell's ministry in February 1852, and a brief interval of tory government, Baring was squeezed out of the Aberdeen coalition in December by Palmerston and the Peelites. Russell tried and failed to have so good a whig included. 'The grapes are sour', wrote Baring, 'I could not have got on well with Gladstone who is a Jesuit and more Peelite than … Peel' (*Journals*, 2.8–9). He voted against the increased income tax in Gladstone's historic budget of 1853, and sympathized with the opposition to the Crimean War, although, he remarked, 'Cobden and Bright have almost made it ridiculous' (ibid., 2.13). He twice declined a place in Palmerston's war ministry in February 1855, turning down the chancellorship of the duchy of Lancaster and, for the third and last time, the Treasury. Nevertheless, once it was clear that diplomacy could not stop the fighting, he proposed the form of words which committed a sceptical Commons to continuing the struggle (11 June 1855). The subsequent evolution of Liberalism left him behind. He was not asked to join the second Palmerston government in 1859, which he found too Peelite with a worrying radical element; as for the premier, 'we cannot call Palmerston a Whig, however old' (ibid., 2.128).

By his own admission, Baring spoke little in cabinet, and felt unequal to the Treasury in the new era of Peel's finance, and Gladstone's. If he were to return to that department, he told Palmerston in 1855, it would be like 'sending to sea an Admiral who knew nothing about steam' (*Journals*, 2.58–61). Fiscal conservatism, however, was arguably a virtue in him as the first chairman of the public accounts committee in 1861, appointed on Gladstone's motion. In these last years he retained, too, a lifelong interest in the suppression of slavery and the slave trade, clinging to an idealistic vision of the African future: 'Africa is to be reclaimed through Africans and I wish for no new European settlements' (ibid., 2.169). Politician, conscientious landlord, and man of wide culture, he was fortified by evangelical piety, and led family and household prayers with intense conviction. If he is usually remembered for a famous definition of whiggery in terms of property, caste, and constitutionalism, it was no more than 'a bit of fustian' to him beside ultimate realities (Southgate, 21; Mallet, 32–3).

Baring, who inherited his father's baronetcy and estates in 1848, remarried on 31 March 1841. His second wife was Lady Arabella Howard (*d.* 1884), daughter of Kenneth Alexander *Howard, first earl of Effingham; they had one son. After refusing a peerage in 1852 and again in 1857, Baring became Baron Northbrook (4 January 1866), on the recommendation of his old friend Russell, shortly after retiring from the Commons. He died at Stratton Park, Micheldever, his Hampshire seat, on 6 September 1866 and was buried at Micheldever parish church on 13 September. He was succeeded by his eldest son, Thomas George *Baring MP, later the first earl of Northbrook, whom he had groomed for what was to be a distinguished political career. DAVID STEELE

Sources *Journals and correspondence of Francis Thornhill Baring*, ed. Thomas George, earl of Northbrook [T. G. Baring] and F. H. Baring, 2 vols. (privately printed, Winchester, 1902–5) • P. Mandler, *Aristocratic government in the age of reform: whigs and liberals, 1830–1852* (1990) • D. Southgate, *The passing of the whigs, 1832–1886* (1962) • B. Mallet, *Thomas George, earl of Northbrook* (1908) • C. J. Bartlett, *Great Britain and sea power, 1815–1853* (1963) • S. Walpole, *The life of Lord John Russell*, 2 vols. (1889) • J. M. Prest, *Lord John Russell* (1972) • *The later correspondence of Lord John Russell, 1840–1878*, ed. G. P. Gooch, 2 vols. (1925) • *The Greville memoirs, 1814–1860*, ed. L. Strachey and R. Fulford, 8 vols. (1938) • ING Barings, London, Barings archives, Northbrook MSS • Boase, *Mod. Eng. biog.* • GEC, *Peerage*

Archives Hants. RO, travel journal • ING Barings, London, corresp., diaries, and papers | BL, corresp. with Charles Wood, Add. MS 49552, *passim* • Borth. Inst., corresp. with Lord Halifax • Borth. Inst., Hickleton MSS • Hants. RO, corresp., mainly with daughter Mary • ING Barings, London, letters to Thomas Baring • NL Scot., corresp. with Sir Thomas Cochrane • NL Scot., corresp. with Edmund Ellice • NMM, letters to Sir Charles Napier • NMM, letters to Sir Wallace Parker • PRO, corresp. with Lord John Russell, PRO 30/22 • PRO, corresp. with Lord Granville, PRO 30/29 • Royal

Arch., Melbourne MSS · U. Durham L., corresp. with third Earl Grey · U. Southampton L., Broadlands MSS · U. Southampton L., corresp. with Lord Palmerston · W. Sussex RO, letters to duke of Richmond

Likenesses G. Hayter, oils, *c*.1833, NPG [*see illus.*] · G. Hayter, group portrait, oils (*The House of Commons, 1833*), NPG · J. Phillip, group portrait, oils (*The House of Commons, 1860*), Palace of Westminster, London

Wealth at death under £16,000: probate, 9 Oct 1866, *CGPLA Eng. & Wales*

Baring, George (1781–1854), leader of the Western Schism and seceder from the Church of England, was born on 23 September 1781 in Mincing Lane, City of London, the fifth son of Sir Francis *Baring (1740–1810), the founder of Baring Brothers merchant bank and a whig MP, and his wife, Harriet (1750–1804), daughter and coheir of William Herring of Croydon, and cousin and heir of Thomas Herring, archbishop of Canterbury. George had four brothers, including Sir Thomas Baring (1772–1848), second baronet, and Alexander *Baring (1773–1848), first Baron Ashburton; he had five sisters, including Harriet *Wall (1768–1838). After a private education George married on 6 March 1806, in Calcutta (against his family's wishes), Harriet Rochfort Hadley D'Oyly, second daughter and fourth child of Sir John Hadley D'Oyly, sixth baronet (*d*. 1818) and MP, collector (chief administrative official) of Calcutta, and Diana, daughter of William Rochfort. They had four sons and eight daughters. As a young man Baring was employed as an agent for Baring Brothers, the oldest merchant bank in the City of London, undertaking special assignments for his father. Subsequently, while in the employ of the East India Company, he became involved in opium speculation at Canton (Guangzhou), losing a considerable fortune. Upon returning to England he apparently fell under the spiritual influence of his sister Harriet, being converted to 'serious religion'. He was ordained in September 1813 by John Fisher, bishop of Salisbury; in the following year he was appointed by his brother Alexander, MP for Taunton and patron of the living, vicar of Winterbourne Stoke, being instituted on 19 November 1814. He also served as curate of Durston under the well-known (but non-resident) evangelical Thomas Tregenna Biddulph.

In November 1815 Baring severed his connection with the Church of England and became the leader of the Western Schism, an evangelical secession from the established church which occurred in and around the west country. The doctrines advanced by the schismatics were complex and variable, sometimes including versions of heterodoxy on the doctrine of the Trinity. Particular redemption was held by each of the seceders, although not all went so far as to advance antinomianism—a charge commonly levelled at the entire movement. Baring then moved to Taunton, purchasing the nearby Walford House, where he installed his co-seceders, and the Octagon Chapel, a former Wesleyan stronghold in the town centre, which now became the spiritual headquarters of his religious connection. In January 1817 Baring purchased Northbrook House, near Exeter, in order to increase the schism's influence in and around the county of Devon, his ancestral home. At first, he served as minister to a small antinomian body which had recently seceded from South Street Baptist Chapel. On 16 August 1818 the schism's new chapel on Bartholomew Street, in Exeter, was dedicated. This structure, which could accommodate upwards of 1000 worshippers, cost Baring and his sister Harriet nearly £4000 to build. The Bartholomew Street Chapel became the centre of the schism's spiritual activity. Baring remained at Exeter as leader of the schism until the spring of 1819 when, owing to financial setbacks (and under pressure from his family), he suddenly abandoned England for the continent. Bartholomew Street Chapel was to be sold to the members of the congregation about 1835 and gave rise, in 1840, to a further secession by (Plymouth) Brethren. Baring lived at first in Baden-Baden, later settling in a villa in Florence. He apparently forsook all interest in religious affairs for the remainder of his life. So profligate was his lifestyle, however, that he was eventually forced to declare bankruptcy, his wealthy and powerful banking family coming to his financial assistance. He died on 4 October 1854 at Cumberland Villa, Shirley, near Southampton, having apparently returned to England from the continent some time after the death of his wife in Bologna in May 1833. Baring was a callow and somewhat volatile—albeit colourful—character who lived out most of his unpropitious life in the shadow of his illustrious family.

GRAYSON CARTER

Sources G. Carter, 'Evangelical seceders from the Church of England, *c*.1800–1850', DPhil diss., U. Oxf., 1990, 164–218 · S. Nicholson, *Select remains of the Revd John Mason* (1836) · P. Ziegler, *The sixth great power: Barings, 1762–1929* (1988) · J. Foster, ed., *Index ecclesiasticus, or, Alphabetical lists of all ecclesiastical dignitaries in England and Wales since the Reformation* (1890) · Burke, *Peerage* · A. Brockett, *Nonconformity in Exeter, 1650–1875* (1962), 165 · *Bristol Gazette* (4 Feb 1819) · *Salisbury and Winchester Journal*, 4 (13 Jan 1817) · *Woolmer's Exeter and Plymouth Gazette* (11 Jan 1817) · *The journal of the Hon. Henry Edward Fox*, ed. earl of Ilchester [G. S. Holland Fox-Strangways] (1946), 318–19 · *Hampshire Chronicle* (7 Oct 1854) · ING Barings, London, Barings archives · *GM*, 1st ser., 103/2 (1833), 94

Archives Devon RO, Bartholomew Street Chapel, minute book MSS · ING Barings, London, Barings archives

Baring, Harriet. *See* Wall, Harriet (1768–1838).

Baring [*née* Montagu], **Harriet Mary**, **Lady Ashburton** (1805–1857), literary hostess, eldest child of George John Montagu, sixth earl of Sandwich (1773–1818), and his wife, Lady Louisa Lowry-Corry (1781–1862), daughter of Armar Lowry-Corry, first earl of Belmore, was born on 14 May 1805. The early death of Lord Sandwich in 1818 left his widow with three small children, including the seven-year-old seventh earl, whose interests she managed during his minority. On 12 April 1823 Lady Harriet Montagu married William Bingham Baring, who succeeded as second Baron Ashburton in 1848; they had one son, who died at fifteen months. Profoundly aristocratic in her views, she had little time for her Baring connections, although she recognized the power that came from their banking fortune, commenting that 'The Barings are everywhere. They get everything. The only check upon them is, that they are all members of the Church of England; otherwise, there is no saying what they would do' (*I too am here*,

Harriet Mary Baring, Lady Ashburton (1805–1857), by Henry William Pickersgill

215). As Lady Harriet Baring, she established one of the foremost literary salons in the country, gathering around her such men of letters as Richard Monckton Milnes, A. H. Clough, Charles Buller, Sydney Smith, William Makepeace Thackeray, and, pre-eminently, Thomas Carlyle. To Carlyle, she was a 'glorious Queen', the 'lamp of my dark path'; unsurprisingly, Lady Harriet made a less favourable impression on Mrs Carlyle, who, after Lady Harriet's death, observed 'I sometimes think that [she] was an evil spirit. No malignant elf could have caused more misery' (Surtees, 55).

Witty, intelligent, and proud, Lady Ashburton (as she became in 1848) dominated the circle of literary men which gathered around her, at Bath House, Piccadilly, and The Grange, Alresford, Hampshire. She had little time for women or for the displays of sentiment which were expected of females. Her style of conversation was not universally pleasing. One guest noted that 'I do not mind being knocked down, but I can't stand being danced on afterwards' (*I too am here*, 215). Beauty played no part in Lady Ashburton's success. Lady Palmerston commented on her prominent nose and 'Redundancy of Chin' (Surtees, 55), while so biased an observer as Jane Welsh Carlyle wrote that 'She is immensely *large*—might easily have been one of the *ugliest* women living—but *is* almost beautiful—simply through the intelligence and cordiality of her expression' (*I too am here*, 218). Lady Ashburton died in Paris on 4 May 1857, while returning from Nice where she had been staying on account of her health. She was described in Monckton Milnes's *Monographs* (1873).

Lady Ashburton's husband, **(William) Bingham Baring**, second Baron Ashburton (1799–1864), was born in Philadelphia, USA, in June 1799, the eldest son of Alexander *Baring, first Baron Ashburton (1773–1848), and his wife, Ann Louisa Bingham (*d.* 1848), of Philadelphia. He enjoyed a moderately successful political career. Educated at Oriel College, Oxford, where he graduated BA in 1821 (MA 1836), he was MP for Thetford (1826–30), Callington (1830–31), Winchester (1832–7), North Staffordshire (1837–41), and Thetford again (1841–8), before succeeding to the peerage in 1848. He began as a whig, moving progressively towards the Conservative Party. He served as secretary to the Board of Control under Peel from 1841 until February 1845, and then as paymaster-general until July 1846. He was elected FRS in 1854, was made a commander of the Légion d'honneur in 1855, and was president of the Royal Geographical Society from 1860 to 1862. Deeply shy, his character contrasted dramatically with those of both his wives. The year after Harriet's death, Ashburton married, on 17 November 1858, Louisa Caroline (1827–1903), daughter and heir of James Alexander Stewart-Mackenzie [*see* Baring, Louisa Caroline]. The second Lady Ashburton was also a significant patron of the arts. Ashburton died at The Grange, Alresford, on 23 March 1864, leaving a daughter from his second marriage. K. D. Reynolds

Sources *I too am here: selections from the letters of Jane Welsh Carlyle*, ed. A. McQueen Simpson and M. McQueen Simpson (1977) • F. Kaplan, *Thomas Carlyle: a biography* (1983) • N. Clarke, *Ambitious heights: writing, friendship, love* (1990) • R. Monckton Milnes, *Monographs* (1873) • V. Surtees, *The Ludovisi goddess: the life of Louisa, Lady Ashburton* (1984) • GEC, *Peerage* • Foster, *Alum. Oxon.* • Boase, *Mod. Eng. biog.*

Archives NL Scot., corresp. and papers • priv. coll. | BL, corresp. with Lady Holland, Add. MS 51729 • BL, Peel MSS • NA Scot., Dundas MSS • NL Scot., Edward Ellice MSS • NRA Scotland, priv. coll., corresp. with earl of Wemyss • UCL, SDUK MSS

Likenesses F. Holl, lithograph, Thomas Carlyle's house, Cheyne Walk, London • H. W. Pickersgill, oils, unknown collection; copyprint, Witt Library, Courtauld Inst. [*see illus.*]

Wealth at death under £180,000—William Bingham Baring: probate, 1 June 1864, *CGPLA Eng. & Wales*

Baring, Henry Bingham (1804–1869), politician, was born on 4 March 1804 at York Place, London, the eldest son in the family of three sons and two daughters of Henry Baring (1777–1848), banker and gambler, and Maria Matilda, daughter of William Bingham of Philadelphia. He was educated at Christ Church, Oxford, matriculating on 18 January 1822 and taking his BA in 1825. He subsequently obtained a commission as major in the army and captain in the Life Guards, which he had resigned by 1833. Later he became a director of the family merchant bank, but appears not to have taken an active part. On 30 June 1827 he married Lady Augusta Brudenell (1809/10–1853), daughter of the sixth earl of Cardigan, with whom he had three sons and one surviving daughter. After standing unsuccessfully for Canterbury at the general election of 1830, Baring entered parliament the following year as the member for Callington, the Cornish pocket borough owned by his uncle Alexander *Baring (1773–1848), whose antipathy to the Grey ministry's parliamentary reform proposals he shared. In 1832 he was elected for Marlborough on the interest of the first marquess of Ailesbury (to whom he was connected through his wife), and continued to sit for the borough until 1868. He assisted in the management of the 1837 election for the Conservatives, showing himself diligent and decisive, though rough in manner, and on the recommendation of Granville Somerset to Peel, he was subsequently appointed as assistant whip. When his party came to power he was additionally made a junior lord of the Treasury, a post he held from September 1841 to July 1846. He supported the repeal of the corn laws, and after 1847 stood as a free-trade Conservative. From 1850 he was one of the Peelite MPs who usually followed Gladstone and Edward Cardwell. Though standing as a liberal Conservative in the 1857 general election, he indicated a willingness to support Palmerston. By then he had resigned from the Carlton Club and joined Brooks's: his successive London addresses were 13 Eaton Place (*c*.1832–1850), 23 Eaton Square (*c*.1851–1859), and finally 36 Wilton Place. Baring's first wife died in Switzerland in January 1853, and on 11 February of the following year, in Paris, he married a Russian lady, Marie de Martinoff (*d*. 1903), who (according to the diarist Charles Greville) had been his mistress for some time. They had no children. He died at Nice on 25 April 1869. NORMAN GASH

Sources N. Gash, 'The organization of the conservative party, 1832–1846 [pt 1]', *Parliamentary History*, 1 (1982), 137–59 • W. D. Jones and A. B. Erickson, *The Peelites, 1846–1857* (1972) • J. B. Conacher, *The Peelites and the party system* (1972) • *Parliamentary Pocket Companion* (1832–67) • Boase, *Mod. Eng. biog.* • Foster, *Alum. Oxon.* • Burke, *Peerage* (1853) • *Letters of Charles Greville and Henry Reeve, 1826–1865*, ed. A. H. Johnson (1924), 224 • census returns, 1841, 1851 • parish register, St Pancras Old Church • *London Directory* (1842–68) • *Army List* (1832–3) • R. W. Hidy, *The house of Baring in American trade and finance: English merchant bankers at work, 1763–1861* (1949) • parish register (baptism), St Marylebone parish, London, 6 Sept 1804 • H. J. Spencer, 'Baring, Henry Bingham', HoP, *Commons, 1820–32* [draft]
Archives BL, corresp. with Sir Robert Peel, Add. MSS 40351–40608, *passim*
Likenesses C. Silvy, photograph, 1860, NPG
Wealth at death under £60,000: probate, 31 May 1869, *CGPLA Eng. & Wales*

Baring, John, second Baron Revelstoke (1863–1929), merchant banker, was born on 7 September 1863 in Kingston upon Thames, the eldest child of the five surviving sons and three daughters of Edward Charles *Baring, later first Baron Revelstoke (1828–1897), and his wife, Louisa Emily Charlotte (*d*. 1892), daughter of John Crocker Bulteel of Lyneham, Devon. He was educated at Eton College and at Trinity College, Cambridge, where he excelled as an oarsman and horseman but did not take a degree.

Partnership at Barings and the crisis of 1890 Baring's father had from 1883 been senior partner in the merchant bank of Baring Brothers & Co., and John Baring joined the firm on leaving Cambridge. He served his apprenticeship as a clerk and from 1885 until 1887 he toured the world, during which he spent some time with the firm of Kidder Peabody in the United States. Power of procuration at Barings was given him in January 1889, and his admission as a full partner followed a year later. He was fluent in French and

John Baring, second Baron Revelstoke (1863–1929), by Vandyk

Spanish, having lived in Spain for six months, and he had a good grounding in Italian and German.

In 1890 Barings experienced a liquidity crisis and had to be rescued from collapse by a Bank of England loan which was guaranteed by the banking community. The City of London narrowly avoided catastrophe. Barings' chief embarrassment was a commitment, taken up in 1888 but unsupportable by late 1890, to raise £10 million for the Buenos Aires Water Supply and Drainage Company Ltd. In 1889 Barings' senior management had dispatched John Baring to Buenos Aires to investigate this company's difficulties; his discoveries shocked him and gave long notice of problems ahead.

In the face of what seemed to be inevitable liquidation, the junior partners, led by John and his older cousin Francis and buttressed by the assets of a retired partner, T. C. Baring, resolved to 'buckle to and make a fight of it' (Barings archives, DEP84). Bypassing their superiors they established a limited company, Baring Brothers & Co. Ltd, financed by shares to the value of £1 million taken up by relatives and City friends, and transferred to it the good business, leaving the bad debts with the old firm.

For the next fifteen years Baring, the firm's natural leader and chief workhorse, almost single-handedly rebuilt the business. He fully recovered its prestige, returned it to the private ownership of his family, and masterminded the orderly liquidation of the old bank whose debts were paid off and whose partners recovered some of their wealth. The achievement for a man not yet twenty-eight when the crisis broke was extraordinary, but the experience of ruin haunted him for the rest of his life, instilling in him a sense of excessive caution and a dread of being in debt. As a partner in the old business, the 1890 crisis had left him penniless and living off the generosity of relatives. His father died in 1897, and Baring was known thereafter, having inherited the barony, as Lord Revelstoke.

Head of Barings Following Francis Baring's retirement in 1901, Revelstoke became senior partner and remained Barings' autocratic head until his death. He gathered around him a partnership comprised mostly of relatives, so the business remained truly a family affair. However, he insisted on a deputy of outstanding ability. Gaspard Farrer (1860–1946), who worked 'cheek by jowl' (Barings archives, DEP193.74.14) with him from 1902, undoubtedly limited some of Revelstoke's autocratic excesses, and interpreted his actions to the junior staff. In 1925 Farrer was succeeded in this role by Edward Peacock.

Barings became extremely profitable, with declared profits increasing from £125,000 in 1891 to almost £600,000 in 1909, and to a £750,000 peak for the 1920s in 1924. From 1896 Barings was owned and controlled by a new partnership and Revelstoke gradually increased his interest in its profits until his death. Thus although his income was modest in the 1890s, he eventually accumulated enormous wealth, receiving over £100,000 for the first time in 1909, over £200,000 in 1915, and well over £100,000 in most years from then until his death. His endeavours to receive a greater share of the profits met with the outright opposition of his partners, led by Farrer who recognized the injustice to the junior employees.

Revelstoke was especially concerned with major transactions, such as bond issues during what was the heyday of London's capital market. But the environment was one of unprecedented competition from British and overseas banks, not least those in Paris, Berlin, and New York. He fought these competitors as ruthlessly as the next and withdrew only when profit was wanting or available at unacceptable risk. He moved with ease from one financial centre to the next, forming international syndicates of banks to underwrite bond issues and then taking a leading role in subsequent negotiations with the issuer. His clients were largely sovereign entities or giant corporations and his world was filled with presidents and finance ministers, ambassadors, and governors of national banks; the authority that he came to exercise meant that before 1914 many of them beat a path to his door. He moved around Europe by train, his secretaries furiously at work and his telegrams being sent and received at stations *en route*. His devoted assistant, Mr Hollings, organizer of this entourage, smoothed its progress through the largesse to be found in a bag of gold sovereigns. But Revelstoke himself eschewed flamboyance; he kept far from the public eye.

After 1902 Revelstoke resumed Barings' historical connection with Argentina, rehabilitating its credit in London through leadership of numerous bond issues, mostly for the government; likewise after 1900 he returned Barings to the financing of the imperial Russian government. However, issuing for the government and railways of Canada, so important before 1890, was lost permanently afterwards, whereas financing of American business was stronger than ever. Barings again focused on railway finance, via bond issues for transcontinental and regional lines; and here Revelstoke with Farrer pitted his wits against the likes of E. H. Harriman, J. J. Stillman, and J. P. Morgan.

Revelstoke had no great liking for Americans but he recognized fully the emerging strategic importance of their country to his firm's issuing and trade finance businesses. When younger he had visited the USA annually, and from 1891 until 1908 his brothers Cecil and Hugo led a sister house in New York. To strengthen his American business further, in 1904 and 1905 he negotiated with Pierpont Morgan for the merger of their respective businesses in New York and London. By far the most powerful transatlantic banking alliance would have been created, but each party's overriding desire to maintain undisputed dominance in their home city scuttled the plan.

Under Revelstoke's leadership Barings steered clear of close involvement in British industry until the 1920s. In 1911 Revelstoke admitted to having a 'horror of all industrial companies' (Barings archives, DPP2.2.14), but probably he had in mind equity issues for manufacturing business. He was happier issuing debentures for infrastructure projects, and here his clients included the Mersey Docks and Harbour Board and London United Tramways. Those industrial debentures he issued—largely for the armaments manufacturers Vickers, Sons and Maxim Ltd and William Beardmore & Co. Ltd—were handled under the name of a commercial bank, which was acting as little more than a receiving agent, as shown on the prospectus, in place of Barings. In turn the bank's own portfolio excluded securities in British industry.

Business appointments and government connections The increasing prominence of the Baring name, and Revelstoke's desire to draw attention to the rehabilitation of his house, resulted shortly after 1900, however, in a succession of business appointments. These included his trusteeship for the debenture holders of the Cunard Steamship Company Ltd; his membership in 1900 (and chairmanship a year later) of a royal commission to examine the workings of the port of London which recommended the formation of the Port of London Authority; and his mediation in 1904 and 1905 in a furious dispute between Cunard and International Maritime Marine over north Atlantic conference rates. Sometimes, when Revelstoke saw certain profit, his commitment to industry was significant; in 1907 he joined a small syndicate of London bankers to finance and guarantee the important Caucasus Copper Company Ltd.

The historical depth of Barings' links with the British government, coupled with the influence of relatives, meant that few London houses were closer to the political establishment. Revelstoke courted such connections assiduously and was closest to A. J. Balfour and Lord Lansdowne, both his clients, and to H. H. Asquith for whom, in 1906, he threw a dinner party to introduce the new chancellor of the exchequer to City leaders. After 1900 Barings, while never a tool of government, worked for the promotion of British influence overseas, especially in the eastern Mediterranean. Revelstoke was closely associated with the abortive Trans-Persia Railway, formed to link the railway systems of Europe and India. Along with Sir Ernest Cassel and Sir Alexander Henderson, he took a one-third interest in the unsuccessful National Bank of Turkey. He was especially close to Cassel, whom he treated with unaccustomed deference. In 1911 he advised the committee of imperial defence on the implications for the City of war with Germany.

A number of Revelstoke's other transactions had enormous political implications. In 1902 he managed one of the first external bond issues for the Japanese government, which paved the way in 1904 and 1905 to arranging huge sterling bond issues in London and New York, undertaken to finance Japan's war against Russia. In doing this, Barings' long-standing and continuing relationship with the Russian government seems to have caused Revelstoke few qualms. In 1912, with Foreign Office enthusiasm, Barings was recruited to strengthen that group of British banks co-operating with, yet also competing against, other national groups for a share in Chinese government external finance.

The First World War and afterwards During the First World War Revelstoke's chief preoccupation was the finance of allied governments in Europe; connections existed with those of Italy and Belgium but the needs of these administrations were dwarfed by those of Russia. Barings was London financial agent for the imperial government and Revelstoke now advised it on borrowing vast sums from the British government via the issue of Treasury bills, discounted at the Bank of England. His role was critical. As middleman he sat alongside Russian diplomatists at difficult Treasury meetings with Lloyd George, Reginald McKenna, and civil servants such as J. M. Keynes, arguing his client's cause and smoothing out difficulties. Sometimes he went to these meetings alone. He oversaw currency operations in support of the rouble and, from a distance, watched over the vast number of banking transactions required for Russia's munitions purchases. The business was immensely profitable.

Notwithstanding a potential conflict of interest, Revelstoke accompanied Lord Milner as minister-plenipotentiary and deputy head of the British mission to the allied conference at Petrograd in 1917. After the war he argued with the British government, steadfastly yet successfully, for the retention of frozen Russian government balances in Barings' books. Somewhat reluctantly he also arranged finance for the Omsk government resistance during the civil war that followed the Russian Revolution, via a syndicated advance secured on gold and provided by friends in London and New York.

After the war Revelstoke was less at ease in the City, where the international role of sterling was much reduced. Sovereign issues remained a staple activity of his business, but now they were invariably led jointly with old adversaries such as Rothschilds and Schroders, while seemingly everywhere the Americans had the upper hand. In 1929, as an elder statesman of British international capitalism, he joined Sir Josiah Stamp at Versailles as joint head of the British mission to the committee of experts—the so-called Young committee—reviewing the Dawes plan for German reparations. He was outraged by the tyranny of the Americans whose 'insolent wealth' arising out of Britain's 'loss of blood and treasure' made them 'the greatest profiteers that the World has ever seen' (Barings archives, 200011). He was highly important at these negotiations, petitioning forcibly for the establishment of the Bank for International Settlements, but he died before the committee's work was concluded.

While Revelstoke remained the undisputed head of his house in the 1920s, Edward Peacock, a Canadian recruited in 1924 as the future senior partner, steadily gained the initiative. Peacock differed culturally and temperamentally from Revelstoke and his appointment was as imaginative and courageous as it was brilliantly successful. Peacock gave the business vital new direction in the financing of British industry—an area where Revelstoke was distinctly out of place—which kept Barings at the forefront of London merchant banking. His appointment reflected Revelstoke's determination, strongly influenced by the 1890 crisis, to leave his house in capable hands.

Life beyond Barings Outside Barings, Revelstoke's business activities were largely restricted to his directorship of the Bank of England. He joined the court in 1898 and its influential committee of Treasury in 1915, and sat on both until his death. Because he 'could never forget the Baring Crisis' (Sayers, 643), he ruled himself out as governor or deputy governor. In 1917 and 1918 he headed the so-called Revelstoke committee, formed to investigate the management of the bank in the difficult circumstances of an open quarrel between the governor and several directors. Like so many others he fell under the spell of Montagu Norman and was unusually influenced by him.

The increasing complexity of investment decisions and of taxation meant that Revelstoke's expert advice was sought by family and friends on the management of their capital. From 1908 until his death he was an innovative receiver-general of the duchy of Cornwall, and from this base he became the trusted financial adviser and close friend of George V and Queen Mary. He was associated with several charitable institutions, in particular King Edward's Hospital Fund, of which he was treasurer from 1914 to 1929, and Guy's Hospital, where he chaired the finance committee. He was sworn of the privy council in 1902, appointed GCVO in 1911, and in 1926 was created by George V his lord lieutenant for Middlesex. He also received honours from France, Japan, and imperial Russia.

Revelstoke never married but enjoyed close friendships with a number of lady friends, the most enduring being with Lady Desborough (Ethel *Grenfell). His brief affair with Nancy Astor, before her marriage, was abruptly terminated by his questioning of her capacity to cope with the social requirements of being his wife. She labelled him a snob and she was right; when he sold his motor car to his sister he changed its upholstery lest it should be recognized as formerly his. He had natural hauteur and remoteness. His London home from 1903 was 3 Carlton House Terrace, where he entertained on a lavish scale, but always with great propriety. His nieces were sent dresses to wear for their visits while women, apparently, were discouraged from excesses lest their faces became flushed. His country home was Firbank, near Market Harborough, where he hunted with the Pytchley and the Fernie families. Each year he spent lengthy holidays at Aix les Bains.

Death and wealth Worn down by the Young committee negotiations, Revelstoke died of a heart attack at his Paris flat, 27 rue du Faubourg St Honoré, on 19 April 1929. He left unsettled net estate of over £2.5 million, of which almost £200,000 was bequeathed for the benefit of London's hospitals and a year's salary to each member of Barings' staff. His pictures were left to the National Gallery and the National Portrait Gallery. The barony passed to his brother Cecil. JOHN ORBELL

Sources P. Ziegler, *The sixth great power: Barings, 1762–1929* (1988) • J. Orbell, *Baring Brothers & Co. Limited: a history to 1939* (privately printed, London, 1939) • A. W. K., 'The late Lord Revelstoke: an appreciation', *Bankers' Magazine*, 127 (1929), 877–84 • 'The Right Honourable Lord Revelstoke', *Bankers' Magazine*, 69 (1900), 719 • J. Orbell, 'Baring, John', *DBB* • R. S. Sayers, *The Bank of England, 1891–1944*, 2 (1976), 643 • ING Barings, London, Barings archives

Archives ING Barings, London | CUL, corresp. with Lord Hardinge • Herts. ALS, letters to Lady Desborough, etc. • U. Reading L., corresp. with Nancy Astor

Likenesses J. S. Sargent, print, *c*.1920–1929, Barings plc, London • A. McEvoy, group portrait, 1926 (with his partners), Barings plc, London • A. McEvoy, portrait, 1926, Barings plc, London • A. Pollen, bust, Barings plc, London • Vandyk, photograph, NPG [*see illus.*] • photographs, Barings plc, London

Wealth at death £2,558,779: probate, 4 July 1929, *CGPLA Eng. & Wales*

Baring [*née* Stewart-Mackenzie]**, Louisa Caroline, Lady Ashburton (1827–1903)**, art collector and philanthropist, was born at Seaforth Lodge, Stornoway, Isle of Lewis, in the Outer Hebrides, on 5 March 1827, the third daughter and sixth child of James Alexander Stewart-Mackenzie (*d.* 1843), and Mary Frederica Elizabeth Stewart-*Mackenzie (1783–1862), eldest daughter of Francis Humberston *Mackenzie, Baron Seaforth and Mackenzie of Kintail, and widow of Sir Samuel *Hood. Many of her earliest years were spent on the grim moorland island inherited by her mother through the Seaforths, at Brahan Castle, Ross-shire, which remained her deeply loved home until her marriage. Several of her adolescent years were spent in Ceylon, where her father served as governor, and in Corfu, where he was appointed lord high commissioner in 1841. After his return, he died in 1843; Louisa Stewart-Mackenzie now lived at Brahan with her mother, who had been Walter Scott's prototype for Ellen in *The Lady of the Lake*.

At eighteen years old Louisa Stewart-Mackenzie was tall, with a superb posture; her brilliant dark eyes beneath firm brows were an inheritance from her Portuguese Sephardi paternal grandmother. So faithful were her strong, well-defined features to those of classical nobility that the art historian and critic Anna Jameson credited

Louisa Caroline Baring, Lady Ashburton (1827–1903), by Carlo, Baron Marochetti, 1861

her with a resemblance to the head of Juno in Rome, the 'Ludovisi goddess'. Yet, despite her attractions, a streak of pushiness, of ambition, was all too apparent; her emotions were uncontrolled, her capriciousness uncircumscribed, her restlessness inexhaustible. She was romantically inclined, and a readiness to fall in love flourished in conjunction with her eagerness for marriage. Ruskin, while giving her drawing lessons at Wallington Hall, Sir Walter Trevelyan's house in Northumberland, saw her as 'a romantic young lady—just on the edge of downhill' (V. Surtees, *Reflections of a Friendship*, 1979, 35). Her unreciprocated adoration for Sir William Maxwell-Stirling (in fact he scarcely knew her) took her nearly four years to conquer. Fervent female friendships were also a constant feature of her life. Letters eloquent of devotion to Florence Nightingale and Harriet Hosmer, the American sculptor in Rome, reflect her warmth of heart as well as her emotional effusiveness. Her most enduring and uncomplicated friendship was with Pauline, Lady Trevelyan, whom she first met in Corfu and loved dearly throughout her life. Louisa was hard-up and restless, with no suitors to hand other than Edwin Landseer (whom she was inclined to accept), when an invitation came from the highland shooting lodge, at Loch Luichart, of (William) Bingham *Baring, second Baron Ashburton (1799–1864) [*see under* Baring, Harriet Mary]. Lately left a widower at fifty-nine, extremely wealthy, and enfeebled by gout, he missed the stimulus of his magnificently brilliant and witty wife. Louisa Stewart-Mackenzie played her cards with dexterity and, with what Thomas Carlyle called 'a stroke of artful dodging', she married him and his material advantages at Bath House, Piccadilly, on 17 November 1858.

This happy marriage, fulfilled by the birth of a daughter, ended on 23 March 1864 with Lord Ashburton's death and, with it, the surrendering of Bath House and The Grange, a great neo-classical house in Hampshire. In her widowhood Lady Ashburton's manic collecting of magnificent paintings and modern sculpture gave an outlet for her 'locomotive energy'. No inventory of her art collection has been found: when she died her finances were in chaos and nearly everything was sold. However, it is known that she had sketches by Rubens, possibly Veronese cartoons, a Mantegna, a Rossetti watercolour, several watercolours by W. L. Leitch, many works by Harriet Hosmer, Edward Lear, G. F. Watts, and Marochetti, three sketches by Titian, and several examples of old master drawings. These works were housed in her multiplying residences: Seaforth Lodge, Devon, completed at the end of 1864, was followed by palatial Melchet Court, Hampshire, finished in 1868. Her final project, Kent House, Knightsbridge, was completed about 1873.

Socially ambitious, Lady Ashburton surrounded herself with well-known names. The Carlyles, Ruskin, the duke of Argyll, the Walter Trevelyans, Lear, W. W. Story, Robert Browning, Samuel Wilberforce (the bishop of Oxford), Lord Houghton, Millais, Professor John Tyndall, Charles Kingsley—all these and many more she gathered under her roof during her hectic career. In later life Carlyle was her great new objective, a pursuit apprehensively accepted by the aged widower. The epic controversy regarding her marriage proposal, probably made in August 1869, to Robert Browning and her fury at his rejection remains unresolved, though quite in character with her ambitions. Extravagance and an ever-changing scene were the stimulants of Lady Ashburton's final years; when her energies for building and art collecting began to flag, she devoted herself to philanthropy. In the last fifteen years of her life the mission to seamen in Canning Town, together with the Ashburton Home of Rest, played the largest part, but she supported many other charitable causes, including the Tower Hamlets mission, the Metropolitan Tabernacle at Islington, the Metropolitan Drinking Fountain and Cattle Trough Association, and the Holy Trinity Mission Fund, Bethnal Green; advocacy for temperance was integral to all. Distressed by her daughter's early death in 1902, Lady Ashburton died of cancer at Kent House, Knightsbridge, on 2 February 1903, the 'wandering meteor' being laid to rest in the soil of a highland glen.

VIRGINIA SURTEES

Sources NL Scot., Ashburton MSS [archive of the marquess of Northampton] • V. Surtees, *The Ludovisi goddess: the life of Louisa, Lady Ashburton* (1984) • NL Scot., Carlyle MSS • U. Newcastle, Pauline Trevelyan MSS • University of Kansas, Lawrence, Kenneth Spencer Research Library, Pauline Trevelyan MSS • GEC, *Peerage*

Archives NL Scot., corresp. and papers | NL Scot., Ashburton MSS • NL Scot., Carlyle MSS • U. Newcastle, Pauline Trevelyan MSS • University of Kansas, Lawrence, Kenneth Spencer Research Library, Pauline Trevelyan MSS

Likenesses C. Marochetti, marble bust, 1861, priv. coll. [*see illus.*] • E. Landseer, oils, priv. coll. • photograph (in old age), priv. coll.; repro. in Surtees, *Ludovisi goddess*

Wealth at death £285,588 9*s*. 1*d*.: probate, 1 July 1903, *CGPLA Eng. & Wales*

Baring, Maurice (1874–1945), poet and author, was born at 37 Church Street, Mayfair, London, on 27 April 1874, the fifth son of Edward Charles *Baring (1828–1897), who became first Baron Revelstoke, banker, and his wife, Louisa Emily Charlotte (*d*. 1892), daughter of John Crocker Bulteel, of Flete and Lyneham, Devon, and granddaughter of Charles *Grey, second Earl Grey. Evelyn Baring, first earl of Cromer, was his uncle. Baring was educated at Eton College and at Trinity College, Cambridge, but left the university without taking a degree. A genius for languages led him (1898) into the diplomatic service: he served as attaché in Paris, Copenhagen, and Rome, and also worked for a year at the Foreign Office in London. He resigned from the service in 1904. During his years spent *en poste* he formed several of the friendships which notably enriched his life, and many of the tastes, particularly in music and literature, which later composed the cultural background of his works. He went abroad again in 1904 as war correspondent for the *Morning Post* in Manchuria, and remained, after the end of the Russo-Japanese War, as special correspondent for the same newspaper in St Petersburg. During these years he learned Russian and developed an abiding sympathy for the Russian people which political changes could not disturb. It was about this time that Baring's lifelong friendship with G. K. Chesterton began, and it has been suggested that Baring was the model for Horne Fisher, the connecting character of the stories that compose *The Man Who Knew Too Much* (1922). In 1909 Baring went as correspondent to Constantinople and in 1912 he represented *The Times* in the Balkans. All this early period of Baring's life is admirably described in *The Puppet Show of Memory* (1922, repr. 1987) which remains a classic of autobiography. He there described the most important event of that period—his reception into the Roman Catholic church—as 'the only action in my life which I am quite certain I have never regretted'.

Baring had already published a number of books when war broke out in 1914. Two plays, *The Black Prince* (1902) and *Gaston de Foix* (1903), showed his double interest in history and the theatre, and also revealed a talent for the more traditional modes of verse. *Dead Letters* (1910) and *Diminutive Dramas* (1911) revealed a lightly satiric humour playing on historic themes. Baring had also published his war memoirs, *With the Russians in Manchuria* (1905), and an excellent short account of Russian literature, *Landmarks in Russian Literature* (1910). Here he displayed for the first time his remarkable gifts as a translator. In later years he selected the poems included in *The Oxford Book of Russian Verse* (1948). During the First World War he was attached to the Royal Flying Corps branch of the British expeditionary force, and for four years from August 1915 was 'mentor and guide' to Hugh (later Viscount) Trenchard. He became a staff officer of the Royal Air Force in 1918, and was also appointed OBE in that year. His experiences during the

Maurice Baring (1874–1945), by Howard Coster, 1934

First World War were recorded in *RFC HQ, 1914–1918* (1920; new edn 1968, repr. 1985). His letters to Lady Juliet Duff, 1915–18, were later published in *Dear Animated Bust* (1981). In 1925 Baring was given an honorary commission as wing commander in the Reserve of Air Force Officers; and in 1935 he was appointed officer of the Légion d'honneur. He also became a fellow of the Royal Society of Literature.

Several of Baring's closest friends were killed during the war: Raymond Asquith, Patrick Houston Shaw-Stewart, Auberon Herbert, eighth Baron Lucas, and the Grenfell brothers, Julian and Gerald William. The death in action of these men inspired him to some moving verse, which he published in 1919. Meanwhile he was preparing his first novel, *Passing By* (1921). This showed, in miniature, all the characteristics which were to make *C* (1924, repr. 1986), *Cat's Cradle* (1925), and *Daphne Adeane* (1926) representative and popular novels of the same decade. Later, in such books as *The Lonely Lady of Dulwich* (1934), Baring returned to the shorter form of the *nouvelle*; and in *Robert Peckham* (1930) and *In my End is my Beginning* (1931), in which the story of Mary Stuart is told from the point of view of each of her four ladies-in-waiting, he returned to history for his subject. He also published in 1933 a short biography of Sarah Bernhardt, whom he had known and ardently admired.

In 1936 Baring was already suffering from paralysis agitans; the last book he was able to write was perhaps his most popular. *Have you Anything to Declare?* (1936), an anthology of favourite quotations in several languages, with translation and comments, showed his character as well as his culture, and revealed how intimately the two were allied. In 1940 he left his house and carefully tended garden at Rottingdean, and was looked after thenceforward by friends in Scotland. His house was destroyed by enemy action. Baring died, unmarried, at Beaufort Castle, Beauly, Inverness-shire, on 14 December 1945.

Baring's novels have come to be regarded as:

> minor masterpieces in character study and social depiction. Limited as they are in subject and theme ... they can be appreciated for the accuracy with which they reproduce the world of the late Victorian élite, for the purity and simplicity of their style, and for the sensitivity and erudition which they display. (Irvine, 34.8)

ROBERT SPEAIGHT, *rev.* ANNETTE PEACH

Sources E. Letley, *Maurice Baring: a citizen of Europe* (1991) [incl. bibliography] • P. M. Irvine, 'Maurice Baring', *British novelists, 1890–1929: traditionalists*, ed. T. F. Stanley, DLitB, 34 (1985) • M. Baring, *The puppet show of memory* (1922); repr. (1987) • *The Times* (17 Dec 1945) • *The Times* (18 Dec 1945) • P. Horgan, *Maurice Baring reconsidered* (1969) • *TLS* (2 Oct 1970), 1130 • *Maurice Baring restored: selections from his work*, ed. P. Horgan (1970) • M. Baring, *RFC HQ, 1914–1918* (1920); new edn as *Flying corps headquarters, 1914–1918* (1968) • E. Smyth, *Maurice Baring* (1938) • L. Lovat, *Maurice Baring: a postscript* (1947) • *TLS* (6 March 1948) • L. Chaundy, *The writings of Maurice Baring* (1925) • personal knowledge (1959) • *Chesterton Review*, 19 (1988) [Maurice Baring special issue] • *Debrett's Peerage* • *CGPLA Eng. & Wales* (1946)

Archives A. P. Watt & Co., London • BL, corresp., Add. MS 73484, fols. 33, 36, 238–9 • Colby College Library, Waterville, Maine • Harvard U., Houghton L., corresp. and literary papers • NRA, corresp. and literary papers • Ransom HRC, diary | BL, letters to Lady Juliet Duff, Add. MS 57852 • BL, corresp. with G. K. Chesterton and family, Add. MS 73189, fols. 1–119 • BL, letters to Lytton Strachey and James Strachey, Add. MS 60656 • Girton Cam., letters to Eugene Strong • Herts. ALS, letters to Lady Desborough • NRA, priv. coll., letters to Edith Œnone Somerville • U. Leeds, Brotherton L., letters to Sir Edmund Gosse • U. Reading L., letters to Bodley Head Ltd • U. Texas, corresp. with John Lane

Likenesses C. Harris, print, 1929, NPG • W. Stoneman, photographs, 1931, NPG • J. Gunn, group portrait, oils, 1932, NPG; on loan • H. Coster, photographs, 1934, NPG [*see illus.*] • H. Leslie, silhouettes, NPG • photographs, repro. in Letley, *Maurice Baring*

Wealth at death £10,016 9*s*. 2*d*.: probate, 16 April 1946, *CGPLA Eng. & Wales*

Baring, (George) Rowland Stanley, third earl of Cromer (1918–1991), banker and diplomatist, was born on 28 July 1918, the only son and youngest of three children of Rowland Thomas *Baring, second earl of Cromer (1877–1953), courtier, and his wife, Lady Ruby Florence Mary (1886–1961), second daughter of Gilbert John Elliot-Murray-Kynynmound, fourth earl of Minto, viceroy of India. He was known by the courtesy title of Viscount Errington (his grandfather the first earl having died the year before his birth) until succeeding as third earl in 1953. He was educated at Eton College and at Trinity College, Cambridge, which he left after a year. His father was lord chamberlain (1922–38) and all his life he moved in court circles; he acted as page of honour to George V (who was his godfather) from 1931 to 1935, and to Queen Mary at the coronation in 1937. On 10 January 1942 he married the Hon. Esmé Mary Gabriel Harmsworth (*b.* 1922), younger daughter of Esmond Cecil *Harmsworth, second Viscount Rothermere. They had a daughter, Lana Mary Gabriel (*b.* 1943), and two sons, Evelyn Rowland Esmond (*b.* 1946) and Vivian John Rowland (*b.* 1950). Lady Cromer was later a lady-in-waiting and from 1967 lady of the bedchamber to Queen Elizabeth II.

After Cambridge, Errington acted as private secretary to the marquess of Willingdon, former proconsul, during his official goodwill visit to South America in 1938, and then, in October 1938, joined his family's merchant bank of Baring Brothers as a clerk. His career was cut short by the outbreak of war. He joined the Grenadier Guards in

1939 and (after accompanying the marquess of Willingdon to New Zealand in 1940) saw active service in north-west Europe. He was appointed MBE in 1945, and demobilized as a lieutenant-colonel in 1946.

Errington rejoined Barings in 1946 and for a year he worked in New York with Kidder Peabody and J. P. Morgan, among others. On his return in 1948 he was appointed a partner. He joined a partnership with several long-serving members, and for many years played a comparatively junior role in the firm's affairs. Nevertheless he took up directorships of public companies such as Royal Insurance and Daily Mail and General Trust, the latter being the family business of his father-in-law, Lord Rothermere. On succeeding as earl of Cromer, he found diversion in the House of Lords. He spoke on subjects ranging from the technical (no par value shares) to the general (the Suez crisis, when dressed in the full uniform of a lieutenant-colonel of the Grenadier Guards). In 1954 he joined a parliamentary delegation to Brazil. The connections he developed doubtless assisted his appointment (at the request of Sir Roger Makins, the British ambassador) in 1959 as economic minister and head of treasury and supply delegation at the British embassy in Washington, which he combined with the UK executive directorships of, among others, the International Monetary Fund and the World Bank.

In 1961 Harold Macmillan, who found Cromer 'very intelligent. He agrees with me' (H. Macmillan, *At the End of the Day*, 1973, 381), appointed him governor of the Bank of England, although Cromer was not Macmillan's first choice, Sir Oliver Franks having already declined the post. At forty-two, Cromer was the youngest governor since the eighteenth century. While a traditionalist, he was also a modernizer at a time when modernization was much needed by the City and the bank. He breathed new life into the bank, then at a low ebb following the Parker tribunal and the findings of the Radcliffe committee, by recruiting a generation of young and able managers. More generally, he helped to steer the City towards a dominating role in the emerging and immensely important Euro markets. A staunch defender of financial good order, his relationship with both Conservative and Labour governments was frequently difficult, as he pressed courageously for policies of economic probity to ensure low inflation and a sound currency. Macmillan and his chancellor, Selwyn Lloyd, came to find Cromer's warnings an irritant. Cromer's relations with prime minister Harold Wilson were more difficult still; they encountered bruising confrontation.

The Labour government elected in October 1964 aimed to carry through an ambitious programme of social welfare, but its inability to adapt this to the reality of what could be afforded led to a run on sterling in November. A 2 per cent rise in the interest rate failed to re-establish confidence, and the reserves were draining away. At the height of the crisis, Cromer demanded expenditure controls and the abandonment of Labour policies in order to restore confidence in sterling and head off a major international financial crisis. A defiant Wilson told him that the solution lay in the hands of the world's central banks and sent him off to raise from them $3 billion in credits. Cromer achieved this in a few hours of hectic telephoning, although he had anticipated the need and had already prepared his ground. Confidence was restored for the time being, which the next day enabled Wilson to rebut tory overtures for a national coalition government. While this credit-raising exercise won Cromer Wilson's admiration, in 1965 their relations grew worse as a succession of economic crises followed. Wilson's response to Cromer's continued pleas for moderation in expenditure was influenced by his belief that the governor was motivated in part by political considerations. On the eve of the 1966 general election, when Wilson sought to strengthen his precarious majority, he rejected an unpopular interest-rate rise proposed by Cromer to head off another crisis. Cromer warned him that the bank had a statutory right to act independently and, if overruled, it would say so publicly. 'In that case', the prime minister said, 'the history of the Bank of England, which had begun with Governor Houblon, would end with Governor Cromer' (*The Times*, 1 Jan 1997). It was hardly surprising that later in 1966 neither Cromer nor the chancellor wished for the governor's tenure of office to be renewed for a further five years. Cromer had continuously undermined his cause by public utterances and by an ability to antagonize the politicians; this underlined his attachment to a passing world of less politicized relationships. Labour leaders were later to establish easier relations with Cromer's successors, Leslie O'Brien and Gordon Richardson, and said so publicly.

In 1966 Cromer returned to Barings, where he was now senior partner both in terms of years of service and in his partnership share. But, devoted as he was to his family's bank, the somewhat humdrum existence it now offered him was an anticlimax, and at times he was out of step with its understated style. Outside Barings he sat as chairman of a committee of inquiry into the working of Lloyd's of London; had its report, which went unpublished for seventeen years, been acted on more fully, many of the market's later excesses might have been avoided. He became chairman of IBM (UK) Ltd and a director of Union Carbide Corporation of the USA, and joined a Board of Trade inquiry into export business generated by capital projects overseas. His implied criticism of Wilson's government continued. His public utterances—not least on the authoritative television programme *Panorama* on the eve of the June 1970 election, when he referred to the existence of 'a very much more difficult financial situation than the new government found in 1964'—were seized upon by the tories. It is reckoned these comments were a significant factor in tipping the scales in their favour.

Edward Heath, who knew Cromer well, rewarded him with the appointment from January 1971 as ambassador in Washington. Relations between the Heath government and President Nixon and his secretary of state, Henry Kissinger, were not close, but it is considered that Cromer did well in difficult circumstances. These were the years of British entry into the Common Market, and here Cromer's financial background well qualified him to explain Britain's position to the Americans. It was also the time of the Yom Kippur War, for which British support was tepid, and, not least, of Watergate.

On his return to London in March 1974 Cromer was still a comparatively young man, and he considered resuming his position at Barings; however, another generation of partners was now firmly in place and had embarked upon a process of overdue modernization. Instead Cromer became special adviser to the firm and resumed or took up afresh directorships of leading companies, including Shell Transport and Trading Company Ltd, IBM (UK) Ltd, P. & O. Steam Navigation Company, Imperial Group, and Compagnie Financière de Suez. He was made a privy councillor in 1966 and received numerous honours including appointment as GCMG in 1974 and KG in 1977. In 1980 he retired to Jersey but he returned to live in London in 1990. He died in London on 16 March 1991. He was survived by his wife and two sons (the elder of whom succeeded him as fourth earl of Cromer), his daughter having predeceased him in 1974. A memorial service was held at the guards' chapel, Wellington barracks, London, on 16 May 1991. JOHN ORBELL

Sources ING Barings, London, Barings archives, third earl of Cromer MSS, DEP243 · Bank of England archives · *The Times* (18 March 1991) · *The Times* (17 May 1991) · *Daily Telegraph* (18 March 1991) · *The Independent* (19 March 1991) · K. Middlemas, *Power, competition and the state*, 2 (1990) · H. Wilson, *The labour government, 1964–1970: a personal record* (1971) · J. Callaghan, *Time and chance* (1987) · P. Foot, *The politics of Harold Wilson* (1968) · D. Butler and M. Pinto-Duschinsky, *The British general election of 1970* (1971) · *The Times* (1 Jan 1997) · *WWW, 1991–5* · Burke, *Peerage*

Archives ING Barings, London, archive | Bank of England archives · CAC Cam., corresp. with Sir Edward Bullard · priv. coll., Cromer MSS · PRO

Likenesses E. Halliday, oils, 1968, Bank of England · photograph, repro. in *The Times* (18 March 1991) · photograph, repro. in *Daily Telegraph* · photograph, repro. in *The Independent* · photographs, Bank of England · photographs, ING Barings

Wealth at death £3,450,132: probate, 19 July 1991, *CGPLA Eng. & Wales*

Baring, Rowland Thomas, second earl of Cromer (**1877–1953**), courtier, was born on 29 November 1877 at Cairo. He was the elder son of Evelyn *Baring, later first earl of Cromer (1841–1917), diplomat, and his first wife, Ethel Stanley (*d.* 1898), second daughter of Sir Rowland Stanley Errington, eleventh baronet. A bad attack of typhoid contracted in Egypt in his boyhood affected his health all his life. He was educated at Eton College, where he made many friends, but left early by his father's wish, without particular distinction, in order to learn foreign languages. In 1900 he entered the diplomatic service, serving as third and second secretary between 1902 and 1906 at Cairo, Tehran, and St Petersburg. He then transferred to the Foreign Office and acted as private secretary to successive permanent under-secretaries of state between 1907 and 1911, when he resigned the service. On 4 April 1908 he married Lady Ruby Florence Mary Elliot (1886–1961), daughter of the fourth earl of Minto. They had a son and two daughters. His wife was of constant help to him in his career and his family life was ideal.

In 1913 Lord Errington, as he then was, became a managing director of Baring Brothers and, in a short time, acquired a useful knowledge of finance. In 1914 he joined the Grenadier Guards, serving as a lieutenant in the special reserve until 1920. In 1915–16 he was aide-de-camp to successive viceroys of India (Lord Hardinge of Penshurst and Lord Chelmsford). In 1916 he was appointed assistant private secretary and equerry to King George V. The prince of Wales wanted Cromer (as he had become on the death of his father in 1917) as his private secretary in 1918, but the king refused to release him from his duties. Cromer acted as chief of staff during the duke of Connaught's visit to India (1920–21), and returned there with the prince of Wales in the same capacity (1921–2). His relationship with the prince of Wales was not entirely smooth, as Cromer attempted to act as a restraining influence.

In 1922 Cromer was appointed lord chamberlain, an office which he held with distinction until 1938; it was under Ramsay MacDonald's Labour government in 1924 that the appointment was changed from a political one, made by the prime minister of the day, to a permanent one, made by the monarch. He continued in office under Edward VIII, although with some reluctance, as he considered that 'war was in effect declared [by the new king] against the old gang' (Ziegler, 258). In 1938 he became a permanent lord-in-waiting, serving both George VI and Elizabeth II. Apprehension about the status of the monarchy during the First World War, despite the devotion to duty of the king and queen, had been expressed in 1918, notably by Cromer himself and by Lord Esher. This disquiet was soon dissipated but Cromer never forgot the need for the monarchy to adjust itself to the post-war social revolution. By his tact and imperturbability and his liberal and shrewd interpretation of his diverse functions, he gave general satisfaction and very little cause for offence, according the same serious but always sympathetic attention to his social as to his political functions. Probably his work as censor of plays (one of the main duties of the lord chamberlain until 1968) interested him most. Cromer came to know a great deal about the theatre, and in this contentious field his tact and sympathy earned the respect and gratitude of dramatists and actors. In his administration and reformation of royal household affairs his business experience stood him in good stead. A sense of humour lightened the burden of his responsibilities, if on social occasions his determination to keep inviolable the confidences of his office sometimes kept it in check.

Cromer was of middle height and slim build. Never robust, he enjoyed shooting and riding but his favourite recreations were reading, family golf, and gardening. A chief virtue of his character was an endearing modesty, to which were added shrewd common sense, moral courage, and a far-sighted liberalism of outlook. He was devoted to children, and young people were always at ease in his company. He devoted much time and trouble to the Cheyne Hospital for children, and was president of the National Hospital for Chest Diseases. At various times he was a British government director of the Suez Canal Company and a director of the P. & O. and the British India steam navigation companies and various banking and insurance concerns. Cromer was not a rich man, and these City interests were of importance to him since the office of lord chamberlain carried no pension rights. In 1934–5 he was president of the MCC. He received many high British honours and a variety of foreign orders. He was sworn of the privy council in 1922 and rose to the rank of grand cross in the orders of the Bath, the Indian Empire, and in the Royal Victorian Order, and received the Royal Victorian Chain in 1935. Cromer died suddenly on 13 May 1953 at 20 Devonshire Place, London. He was survived by his wife and was succeeded by his only son, (George) Rowland Stanley *Baring (1918–1991), who was governor of the Bank of England from 1961 to 1966.

JOHN GORE, *rev.* K. D. REYNOLDS

Sources J. H. Wheeler-Bennett, *King George VI: his life and reign* (1958) • J. Gore, *King George V* (1941) • Duke of Windsor, *A king's story: the memoirs of HRH the duke of Windsor* (1951) • private information (1971) • Burke, *Peerage* (1967) • P. Ziegler, *King Edward VIII: the official biography* (1990) • K. Rose, *King George V* (1983) • GEC, *Peerage* • *The Times* (14 May 1953) • *CGPLA Eng. & Wales* (1953)

Archives BL, corresp. with Marie Stopes, Add. MS. 58541 • BL OIOC, letters to Lord Reading, MSS Eur. E 238, F 118 • Bodl. Oxf., corresp. with Rumbold • CUL, corresp. with Lord Hardinge • Tate collection, corresp. with Lord Clark in capacity of lord chamberlain • Wellcome L., corresp. with National Birthday Trust Fund | SOUND BL NSA, oral history interview

Likenesses W. Stoneman, two photographs, 1917–52, NPG • D. Wilding, photograph, 1940–49, NPG • P. A. de Laszlo, oils, 1971, priv. coll. • Powys Evans, caricature, repro. in *Saturday Review* (6 March 1926)

Wealth at death £52,988 16*s.* 3*d.*: probate, 14 July 1953, *CGPLA Eng. & Wales*

Baring, Thomas (1799–1873), banker and politician, was born on 7 September 1799 at Lee, near Lewisham, Kent, the second of the four sons and five daughters of Sir Thomas Baring (1772–1848), landowner, and his wife, Mary Ursula Sealy, daughter of Charles Sealy, a barrister at Calcutta. In 1799 Baring's father worked for John and Francis Baring & Co., later known as Baring Brothers, the eminent London merchant bankers, then led by its founder, Baring's grandfather Sir Francis *Baring (1740–1810). Subsequently Baring's father was admitted a partner, but he withdrew in 1810 on inheriting his father's baronetcy and estates at Stratton, Hampshire, and at Lee.

Education and early career Baring's childhood was spent at Manor House, Lee, and subsequently at Stratton, and his education included a brief period at nearby Winchester College. He may have spent time as an apprentice in Barings, which from 1804 until 1830 was under the leadership of his uncle, Alexander *Baring, later first Baron Ashburton (1773–1848). However in 1817 Alexander Baring blocked Sir Thomas Baring's suggestion that his son join Barings permanently. Instead Baring and his younger brother John were dispatched to Amsterdam to work with Hope & Co., leading merchant bankers, bond issuers, and financial advisers to governments. Barings enjoyed long links with Hopes, having often worked with them on joint business, and Alexander Baring had acquired control of their firm in 1813.

By 1819 Thomas Baring was 'so disgusted with the drudgery of the counting house at Amsterdam that', according

Thomas Baring (1799–1873), attrib. George Richmond, 1826

to his elder brother, Francis, 'he wanted to throw up commerce as a profession and take to the law' (*Journals and Correspondence*, 2.37). In 1820 he considered a career with the East India Company but his father and uncle dissuaded him. In 1824, however, they provided equally his contribution of 250,000 guilders to Hopes' capital on his admission to their partnership. His achievements at Hopes are largely unknown but during his partnership the firm was scarcely profitable. His father, in 1825, again suggested his admission as a Barings' partner but his uncle remained opposed. He wanted Baring to remain permanently in Amsterdam and Barings to be led by his immediate family. Sir Thomas then proposed lending Thomas and John £40,000 to establish their own London business, but it came to nothing.

A crisis of management succession at Barings changed Alexander Baring's mind in 1828. By then he wished to retire. His most able partner, S. C. Holland, had died suddenly in 1827, the competence of his junior partners was questioned, and Barings was in decline. In 1828 Alexander reorganized the business, establishing a new partnership which included Thomas, Thomas's brother John, and, not least, Joshua Bates, an experienced American merchant. Thomas withdrew his capital from Hopes.

In the early years of the new partnership Bates was senior to Baring in terms of experience and capital contribution, but in reality they were joint leaders, working in perfect harmony and forming the greatest partnership in Barings' history. By the 1850s Bates had reassured Baring that 'everybody considers you the master mind' as 'Head of the House', identifying himself as 'a good steady worker with long experience in all sorts of business, not over sharp but good natured' (ING Baring Archives, Northbrook MSS, NP 7.1.105).

After Alexander Baring's withdrawal in 1830, Bates and Baring revived the business, making it once more London's leading trade finance and merchanting house, though Rothschilds' leadership in government finance went unusurped. Initially Baring's contribution to his firm's £310,000 capital was modest, and it seems he also borrowed from his uncle. But he ploughed back his interest and profits consistently so that by 1863 he contributed £270,000 out of £770,000. In the year before his death he provided £610,000 out of £2.5 million.

While Bates managed merchanting and trade finance, Baring led the more complex and intellectually demanding sterling bond issues. London was now emerging as the leading international capital market catering for the needs of overseas sovereign and corporate borrowers. Their requirements were complicated, often involving the need to finance the construction of railways, the keystone of a modernizing economy. Baring had a flair for this business and by 1843 Bates recognized that 'he does this sort of correspondence to admiration—so much better than I can that I have made him take charge of that department' (Bates to Ward, 31 Jan 1843, Massachusetts Historical Society, Ward MSS).

Under Baring's leadership, bond issuing and dealing for the house account expanded. Whereas Bates reckoned Barings in 1831 was 'no longer a House concerned with foreign loans' (Bates to Ward, 13 Jan 1831, Massachusetts Historical Society, Ward MSS), in 1858 he could list the United States, Canada, Russia, Argentina, Norway, Austria, Chile, New Granada, Nova Scotia, New Brunswick, and Australia as countries for which Barings then acted as London financial agents and for which, to varying degrees, it provided long-term finance and banking services. Baring was largely responsible for building and maintaining these relationships, in particular those with the governments of the first four countries, by corresponding with their representatives, by receiving their deputations, and, in many instances, by visiting their countries. This work called for an establishment figure of keen intelligence, able to negotiate and communicate, to encourage and discourage clients as required, and to influence investors through a reputation for prudence and integrity. Baring had all these qualities, coupled with imagination and attention to detail. There is 'only one man [in London] to look to and consult, and to guide action in important financial matters', reckoned an American railway manager in 1853. 'Ask about anything and the reply is "What does Mr Thomas Baring say or think?"' (Hidy, 420).

Expanding influence and power Under Baring's management, the bank was appointed as London financial agents by the Russian government in the mid-1850s, and a string of sterling bond issues followed, confirming the firm's succession to Hopes as the government's most favoured overseas issuing house. However, this was the only significant continental sovereign account which Barings held consistently; elsewhere, especially in central Europe and Iberia, the Rothschilds proved unassailable. In North and South America, however, Barings retained the upper hand. In the 1830s the London agency for the government of Upper Canada was secured on joint account with Glyns Bank; this was followed by that for the dominion of Canada from 1867. The two houses nurtured Canadian credit through the private placement of government securities as opportunity allowed. Barings' role in Argentina was different. The Buenos Aires government's standing among bondholders had collapsed in 1828, following its suspension of interest payments on bonds Barings had issued in 1824. Under Baring's guidance, and in close co-operation with the bondholders' committee, a succession of emissaries was sent to Buenos Aires to negotiate a settlement which was finally achieved by George White, a Barings clerk, in 1857. Thereafter, Barings reasserted the Argentinian government's credit in London and handled two bond issues for it in the 1860s.

An entirely new area masterminded by Baring was the finance of railway construction, in particular for schemes in the United States, Canada, Russia, France, and Chile, but not in Britain. Railways consumed unprecedented amounts of capital on a scale which overwhelmed the savings and capital markets of most countries. Moreover, the standing of enterprises which promoted and managed the earliest railways was insufficient to attract London investors except, perhaps, on the most onerous terms. Initially many schemes were financed through bond issues guaranteed by local governments or through issues of government bonds, the proceeds of which were then lent on to the railway company. By the early 1850s Barings was issuing United States railroad bonds. 'Before bringing forward this new kind of bond here', cautioned Baring in 1852, 'it is indispensably necessary that the character of the security should be such as we can offer with credit to ourselves & safety to the public' (Hidy, 420).

Of major importance was the financing of the Grande Société des Chemins de Fer Russes and the Grand Trunk Railway Company of Canada, both of which were formed to build gigantic railway networks. Barings issued their securities and provided advances, while Thomas Baring gave credibility to them by sitting on their London boards. When bond prices collapsed, both turned out to be disasters for investors. Baring extricated himself with relative ease from the affairs of the Russian railway, but his involvement with Grand Trunk ran far deeper. He entered into acrimonious negotiations and successfully persuaded the company and Canadian government to stand by their obligations, and he bought for his own account a great deal of Grand Trunk stock to support the market price, rescuing some investors and, to an extent, sustaining the integrity of his house. By the time of his death he held Grand Trunk stock with a nominal value of £520,000 but with a market value of just £165,000.

After Bates's death in 1864, the leadership of Barings was wholly in Thomas Baring's hands, but his responsibilities had grown onerous. Like Bates he had little confidence in his junior partners, in particular Russell Sturgis and Edward Charles *Baring. Moreover the house's capital had collapsed from £1.4 million in 1862 to £627,000 in 1865, following Bates's death and the withdrawal of two other senior partners. In 1867 Baring responded to these problems with imagination and courage, though for a while the orderly liquidation of Barings must have seemed unavoidable. He merged Barings with Finlay, Hodgson & Co., bringing in new capital and management in the form of Kirkman D. Hodgson, a talented merchant and former Bank of England governor. However the manoeuvre failed to control the junior staff. Quickly they regained the initiative after Baring's death in 1873, and they eventually led Barings into a liquidity crisis and rescue by the Bank of England in 1890. Thomas Baring foresaw the problems and left Lady Northbrook in no doubt that 'the halcyon days of the Baring house are past' (Lady Northbrook to Lord Northbrook, 27 Nov 1873, ING Baring Archives, Northbrook MSS, NP 6.1.4). As early as 1849 Baring had admitted that 'half my pleasure is to work for a house which we intend to be perpetual' (ING Baring Archives, HC1.20.4); he must have died disillusioned.

Political career Baring was influential in political circles and, breaking with family tradition, he entered the Commons as a tory and sat in opposition to his father, several cousins, and, not least, his brother, Sir Francis Thornhill *Baring, later first Baron Northbrook, a whig chancellor of the exchequer from 1839 to 1841. He was elected member for Great Yarmouth, Norfolk, in 1835, but was defeated in 1837 and again in 1838 and 1841. As a protectionist in favour of 'regulated competition' (Disraeli, 87), he contested the City of London seat in 1843 but, in a celebrated by-election, was narrowly defeated by a candidate supported by the Anti-Corn Law League. From 1844 until his death he sat for Huntingdon, which frequently returned him uncontested. Sir Robert Peel, Lord Derby, and especially Benjamin Disraeli were close political friends, though Baring distanced himself from Peel on the issue of free trade. Peel proposed him as president of the Board of Trade in 1845, Disraeli wanted him as leader of the tories in the Commons in 1851, and Derby invited him to be chancellor of the exchequer in 1852 and 1858, but Baring declined all political office. In 1845 Bates rightly reckoned that 'the Bishopsgate house has too many temptations [for him] yet' (Bates to Ward, 3 Feb 1845, Massachusetts Historical Society, Ward MSS), but his effectiveness as a debater equipped him well as an MP. Peel commended 'his speaking in simple unaffected language on subjects thoroughly understood' (ING Baring Archives, Northbrook MSS, NP 7.1.115), while Disraeli in 1848 was certain he delivered 'one of the best speeches ever made in the House of Commons' (Disraeli, 526). In 1858 Baring declined Disraeli's offer of a peerage on the basis that such an honour would oblige him to withdraw from Barings.

In politics Baring followed a careful path to avoid a conflict of interests. As a banker to overseas governments, many sometimes hostile to Britain, he had to protect his clients' interests while at the same time serving those of his country. When the Russian government used Barings to evacuate its gold from London on the eve of the outbreak of the Crimean War, Palmerston labelled Baring the private agent of the emperor of Russia. The issues, however, were often far more subtle, as when during the same war Barings supported Russian credit by marketing sufficient Russian government bonds to cover interest payments due to London bondholders. Baring was also the recipient of British government commissions; in 1845–6 he spent £100,000 on overseas grain for use by the government in controlling home food prices at a time of scarcity. 'No one in our counting house', he told the government, 'has been entrusted with any particulars except my partner and myself' (Orbell, 35). Two years later Barings, with Rothschilds, was mandated to raise £8 million to fund expenditure to relieve the Irish famine. Nowhere is there a suggestion that Baring abused his position of privilege; indeed he declined to ask for a commission, either for the grain purchase or for the famine loan transactions.

Baring's influence in tory politics, coupled with his leading position in international finance, where he was rivalled only by James Rothschild of Paris, made him one of the most powerful figures in mid-Victorian Britain, though his unassumingness and self-mocking humour concealed it. His popularity in his circles was immense and he possessed an enormous capacity for work and a real sense of duty, but again he underplayed them. 'Three tumblers of water, a bath, walking between each, a segar, a sofa, the newspapers and a French novel [are] ample occupation for the day', he wrote from Aix-la-Chapelle to the dutiful Bates, hard at work at Barings, 'and I begin to think that my vocation is different from your's and that what I do best is nothing' (Orbell, 38).

Other activities and final years Baring devoted much time to other business and charitable activities. Like many of his contemporaries, he recognized a duty to serve the mercantile community's interests through the provision of expertise and capital to joint-stock companies, providing infrastructure upon which trade and industrial expansion were based. For example, he served on the boards of, and took modest shareholdings in, the East and West India Docks Company, the Royal Mail Steam Packet Company, and the West India Mail Company, of which he was chairman. From 1848 to 1867 he served on the Bank of England's court, being identified with the 'new probity', based upon service and duty, in place of the personal advantage sought by previous generations of the bank's directors. In the early 1850s he chaired the Commons' East India committee, considering the renewal of the East India Company's charter. From 1850 to 1869 Lloyds of London elected him its chairman, breaking with long tradition by not appointing an active underwriter in the post.

The institutions Baring supported included the Royal National Life Boat Institution, of which he was chairman from 1854, and the London Institution, where he was president. He was a royal commissioner for the 1851 exhibition, a trustee of the National Gallery, a commissioner of lieutenancy for the City of London, a neutrality law commissioner, and a fellow of the Royal Society and of the

Royal Geographical Society. He gave generously and privately to charitable works. From 1847 the annual bonuses paid to Barings' staff were made largely on his initiative; they were terminated in the year following his death.

Baring's accumulation of great wealth accelerated in 1853 when he inherited the estate of his cousin, Charles Baring Wall, which largely comprised 7000 acres based around Norman Court at Stockbridge in Hampshire, reckoned to be worth about £400,000. Baring added only modestly to the acreage but he filled the house with the finest pictures and furniture. 'The pictures and china are renowned; so is the cooking', noted a visitor, 'and with such wealth as is at our host's command, all the details are in perfection' (*Memoirs of Henry Reeve*, 2.154). Another visitor in the 1860s reckoned 'there could not be more luxury with less show' (*Letters of Henry Adams*, 1.465). His London homes were 40 Charles Street from 1828, 41 Upper Grosvenor Street from about 1851, and 4 Hamilton Place in 1873.

Baring's appetite for picture purchasing was prodigious. He collected several hundred works, the first being acquired in 1835 and the last in 1871, when expenditure exceeded £100,000. Dutch seventeenth-century pictures were his particular passion, and for £12,000 he purchased forty-two works from the collection of Baron Verstolk Van Soelen of The Hague in 1846. He spent a further £17,000 on seventy of his father's Italian and Spanish pictures, which he acquired from his brother, Lord Northbrook, in 1849.

Thomas Baring never married. He died of natural causes while convalescing at Fontmell Lodge, Bournemouth, on 18 November 1873, leaving an unsettled estate of under £1.5 million. His Norman Court property was left for life to his cousin William Baring, with remainder to William's son Francis. Thomas's brother Charles *Baring, bishop of Durham, along with his surviving sisters, each received substantial sums, while the balance was divided between his nephews, the second Baron Northbrook, F. H. Baring, and T. C. Baring, the last two being partners of Barings. His pictures passed to Lord Northbrook. To each member of Barings' staff he left a year's salary. JOHN ORBELL

Sources P. Ziegler, *The sixth great power: Barings, 1762–1929* (1988) • R. W. Hidy, *The house of Baring in American trade and finance: English merchant bankers at work, 1763–1861* (1949) • J. Orbell, *Baring Brothers & Co. Limited: a history to 1939* (privately printed, London, 1939) • D. Kynaston, *The City of London*, 1 (1994) • S. D. Chapman, *The rise of merchant banking* (1984) • ING Barings, London, Barings archives • Mass. Hist. Soc., Ward MSS • *Journals and correspondence of Francis Thornhill Baring*, ed. Thomas George, earl of Northbrook [T. G. Baring] and F. H. Baring, 2 (privately printed, Winchester, 1905) • B. Disraeli, *Lord George Bentinck: a political biography* (1852) • *Memoirs of Henry Reeve*, ed. J. Laughton (1898) • *The letters of Henry Adams*, ed. J. C. Levenson (1982) • d. cert.

Archives ING Barings, London, corresp. as a partner in Baring Bros.; business corresp. • ING Barings, London, political and private corresp. and papers | Bodl. Oxf., letters to Benjamin Disraeli • Borth. Inst., letters to Lord Halifax • Mass. Hist. Soc., Ward MSS

Likenesses attrib. G. Richmond, drawing, 1826, ING Barings, London [*see illus.*] • W. Holl, stipple (after G. Richmond), BM, NPG • Houston, oils, ING Barings, London • J. Linnell, oils, ING Barings, London • D. J. Pound, stipple and line (after photograph by J. and C. Watkins), NPG • G. Richmond, oils, ING Barings, London • oils, Hughenden Manor, Buckinghamshire

Wealth at death under £1,500,000: probate, 18 Dec 1873, *CGPLA Eng. & Wales*

Baring, Thomas George, first earl of Northbrook (1826–1904), politician and viceroy of India, was born at 16 Cumberland Street, London, on 22 January 1826, the eldest son of Sir Francis Thornhill *Baring, third baronet and later first Baron Northbrook (1796–1866), and his first wife, Jane (1804–1838), daughter of Captain Sir George Grey RN, first baronet. She was a niece of Earl Grey of the Great Reform Bill, and sister of the second Sir George Grey, an influential figure in mid-nineteenth-century whig cabinets, revered by his nephew. Thomas George Baring, so called to distinguish him from his tory uncle Thomas, united in his person the political traditions of the Greys and the wealth of the Barings, one of the greatest of City families. He was always true to his reforming whig origins, after as before he joined the Unionist secession from the Liberal Party in 1886, and his banking forebears' devotion to sound finance was natural to him.

A statesman in the making, 1826–1872 The elder Baring, a Wykehamist, had no kind memories of his old school and some doubts about his son's strength of character. After a little time at what later would have been called a preparatory school, the boy was entrusted to private tutors. Well taught and well read, he matriculated at Christ Church, Oxford, in 1843, taking a second in classics in 1846, a performance considered creditable to someone who gave the superficial impression of being typical of the scions of aristocracy at the House. His college friendships endured, and were the only close ones of his adult life. He was to sit in cabinet with two of those friends, Chichester Fortescue, later Lord Carlingford, and John Wodehouse, first earl of Kimberley—cultured, serious-minded young men like himself behind a conventional exterior. Baring's father, a former and future cabinet minister, encouraged him to enter politics, and arranged for a thorough grounding in his chosen career as an unpaid private secretary to a succession of ministers, to all of whom he was related. Between 1846 and 1857 he worked for an uncle, Henry Labouchere, when he was chief secretary for Ireland and then president of the Board of Trade; for another uncle, Sir George Grey, at the Home Office; and for Sir Charles Wood, a cousin, at the India board and the Admiralty. In an interval during this lengthy apprenticeship, he married on 6 September 1848 Elizabeth Harriet (1827–1867), the daughter of Henry Charles Sturt of Crichel, Dorset, and sister of two brothers in his Christ Church circle. They had three children. He read up political economy without much relish for its bleak imperatives and concluded that 'unfortunately free trade is true, and we must use all our efforts to give our manufacturers the power of underselling the world' (Mallet, 39).

At the invitation of two leading Quaker families with local influence, the Foxes and the Gurneys, Baring stood for Penryn and Falmouth at the general election of 1852, setting his face against the bribery for which the borough was well known, and lost. Returned in 1857, he was to look back nostalgically on the elections he fought there in the

Thomas George Baring, first earl of Northbrook (1826–1904), by Bassano

days of open voting: 'Strange taste, is it not?' (Mallet, 38). With his connections and experience he was at once given minor office, as civil lord of the Admiralty in the first Palmerston administration. In the second, following an interlude of tory government, he served as under-secretary in three departments: the India Office, 1859–61 and 1861–4, under Wood; the War Office, January to July 1861; and the Home Office, 1864–6, under Grey. He was particularly interested in War Office business, to which he came with nearly twenty years' service in the Hampshire yeomanry; from 1864 he commanded and met the bills for the troop based at Winchester. The military machine, he decided, was in need of 'extensive but judicious changes' (*Hansard* 3, 93, 16 July 1868, 1243). When he went back to the War Office in December 1868 as a peer and Cardwell's under-secretary, he was wholly in sympathy with his minister's far-reaching reforms and ably supported them. In a phrase that stung his opponents, he described the purchase system in the army, abolished in 1871 after a bitter struggle, as 'a spider's web of vested interests' (ibid., 207, 13 July 1871, 1550). Never a good speaker, he stuck closely to his departmental brief; but his quiet competence and authentic liberalism commended him to the premier, who early in 1872 rated him the under-secretary in the Lords best qualified for promotion to the cabinet (Gladstone to Argyll, 13 Feb 1872, Gladstone, *Diaries*, 8.110).

Northbrook, as he became on his father's death (6 September 1866), thought his political career had ended when he left the Commons, and was reconciled to the life, which he found quite satisfying, of a country gentleman with varied interests. The deaths of his wife, whom he never ceased to mourn, and of his younger son, a midshipman lost at sea three years later, intensified a deeply religious outlook, rooted in an eirenical Christianity. Politics became, and remained, a question of duty, if it had ever been anything else. He wrestled with his conscience and self-doubt when Gladstone, urged on by Wood, now Lord Halifax, preferred him to Lord Dufferin as viceroy of India. 'Not a case of duty', he told himself; 'No ambition for [the] office or feeling that I could do good in it' (Mallet, 53). But after telling Halifax that he did not wish the offer to be made, he accepted, succeeding Lord Mayo, assassinated in February 1872.

A Liberal viceroy, 1872–1876 Northbrook's first months in India confirmed him in a severely realistic view of the British position in the subcontinent: 'We are tolerated as being a less [*sic*] evil than what would be likely to follow us' (Northbrook to Gladstone, 9 Sept 1872, BL, Add. MS 44266). Against that background he attached great importance to reducing taxation of every kind and keeping it down. Before he left Britain he had discussed with Halifax the abolition of the unpopular income tax reintroduced by his predecessor, and carried it over the objections of half his council in India. Earlier that year, citing the political risks, he had vetoed a municipalities bill for Bengal in the light of Indian protests at the higher taxes it entailed. He was especially concerned about the most productive of Indian taxes, the land revenue assessed upon the ryots, the peasants: under-assessment was always preferable to over-assessment resulting in 'a discontented, and possibly a dangerous class' (Moulton, 46–7). In Bombay and Oudh the subordinate governments were induced to moderate their demands on the cultivator. He counted as one of his successes the battle with 'the Strachey School'—believers, like Sir John Strachey, a member of the viceroy's council and governor of the North-Western Provinces, in the economic virtues of forcing up the land revenue (Northbrook to Ripon, 8 Aug 1884, Northbrook MSS, MS Eur. C. 144/4). In one of his first letters to a presidency governor, another appointment from home, Northbrook remarked how little many high-ranking British civil servants in India appeared to know of the people, and advised him to elicit the views of district officers, and those of Indians 'wherever we can get them to speak freely'. He had come out fortified not only by the opinions of his enlightened whig circle, but by his time at the India Office, where the conservatism of Indian society and the dangers of exciting its fears were well understood after the rising of 1857: 'I shall therefore … legislate as little as possible', he decided from the outset (Northbrook to Lord Hobart, 19 May 1872, Northbrook MSS, MS Eur. C. 144/13). The mutiny was still fresh in British minds. When, later on, the question of increasing the size of the Indian army arose, he asked his friends at home to be careful in discussing it; everything they said was the subject of comment by Indian journalists, whose ability impressed him: 'It would not mend matters to tell our native troops that we never can trust them thoroughly after what has happened' (Northbrook to Lord Bessborough, 25 Jan 1875, Northbrook MSS, MS Eur. C. 144/23).

These anxieties did not have the usual effect of making Northbrook afraid to contemplate some of the changes that Westernization must inevitably bring. As his private secretary he had been involved in the preparation of Wood's education dispatch of 1854, and now saw the central problem of the not very distant future in the emergence of 'able men … with feelings and interests adverse to British rule … [and] a real desire … to show their independence and use their English education' (Northbrook to Maurice Drummond, 13 June 1875, Northbrook MSS, MS Eur. C. 144/23). They were, through their newspapers, creating an Indian public opinion of which an alien regime was compelled by its own liberal values to take note. Northbrook regarded this element more sympathetically than did many of his officials—'the Baboos are not … devoid of fun'—and defended the freedom of the Indian press against those who would have liked to restrict it (Northbrook to Argyll, 26 Sept 1872, Northbrook MSS, MS Eur. C. 144/9). A government with no representative institutions needed the newspaper criticisms even when they were 'more or less violent. … It is far more safe that these things should be said openly than that they should be said without the knowledge of government' (Moulton, 268–9). His internal and external policies for India were complementary. The determination to reduce both expenditure and the deficit he had inherited strengthened his opposition to the suggestions, increasingly being heard, that Russian expansion in central Asia should be countered by a corresponding British movement to secure India's north-western approaches. In his view Russia's advance made her more vulnerable, with over-extended lines of communication open to attack by local guerrillas financed and directed from India, relatively inexpensively. By the beginning of 1874, when the Liberals left office in Britain, India was on the way to a budgetary surplus and able to absorb the cost of averting mass starvation in the Bengal famine of that year.

Northbrook and the outgoing secretary of state, the duke of Argyll, worked well together. Lord Salisbury, the future tory premier who took over at the India Office, had held the post before, in 1866–7. He distrusted all bureaucracies—India's rather more than most—and was critical of the councils which the India Act of 1858 had given to the secretary of state in London and had continued for the viceroy in India. Salisbury reorganized the department, dominated his council, and sought by private correspondence with Northbrook to reverse a process by which the viceroy's councillors had acquired 'something of independent power' (Salisbury to Northbrook, 18 Dec 1874, Steele, 136). Northbrook, however, could not be persuaded to embrace the doctrine that a transient viceroy was alone deserving of the home government's full confidence. Through two years of argument on the point Northbrook insisted that his powers were properly exercised by the 'Governor-General *in Council*' (Northbrook to Salisbury, 3 March 1876, Salisbury MSS, HHM/3M/E12). This did not imply the viceroy's subjection to the council: he contrasted his control of its decisions with the independence that councillors had asserted under John Lawrence (1864–9).

Northbrook and Salisbury differed, the former realized, on 'some of the first principles of Indian administration' (Northbrook to Halifax, 2 Oct 1874, Northbrook MSS, MS Eur. C. 144/22). One of Salisbury's first actions at the India Office was to instruct the government of India in March 1874 to send legislative proposals home for approval prior to their introduction into the viceroy's council, sitting with additional members, European and Indian, in its law-making capacity. He followed this up with the India Councils Act of the same year, adding a public works member to Northbrook's council against his wishes. Salisbury's later Indian Legislation Bill, enabling the secretary of state to veto part of an Indian measure instead of having to sanction or disallow the whole, had to be withdrawn for lack of parliamentary time, and also because it was known that Northbrook's political friends were going to fight it. The viceroy did not dispute the authority of the secretary of state, with the cabinet and the House of Commons behind him, but argued that it should not take the form of dictation to 'men of Indian experience … in a position to give … advice with complete independence', that is, to councillors enjoying security of tenure under the act of 1858 (Northbrook to Salisbury, 20 Aug 1874, Salisbury MSS, HHM/3M/E12). Happy to work with those advisers, Northbrook did not want greater powers for himself.

By the time he left India Northbrook felt that '"Any stick is good enough to beat a dog with", and … I have the honour of being the dog' (Northbrook to Salisbury, 16 Aug 1875, Salisbury MSS, HHM/3M/E12). A cause of steadily worsening disagreement with Salisbury was policy towards Afghanistan, the buffer state in the path of Russian expansion. Viceroy and secretary of state both thought it would be unwise to advance into a fiercely Muslim and xenophobic country. Salisbury was much less influenced than Northbrook suspected by Sir Henry Rawlinson and Sir Bartle Frere, members of his council in London, who contended for a 'forward policy'. He believed it was enough that Britain and India should insist on a permanent diplomatic presence in Afghanistan—something considered impossible since the massacre of the British mission at Kabul in 1842 and the destruction of its supporting garrison. Northbrook adhered to Lawrence's school in frontier policy: neither British prestige nor the Russian threat required a resident envoy. 'Why the government were determined to meddle beats my comprehension', he reflected (Northbrook to Sir G. Clerk, 11 Feb 1876, Northbrook MSS, MS Eur. C. 144/23).

The same conviction that impelled Northbrook to resist 'a wrong thing' led to open conflict with Salisbury over the Indian cotton duties (Northbrook to Sir L. Mallet, 25 Feb 1876, Northbrook MSS, MS Eur. C. 144/23). For domestic and imperial reasons, Salisbury wished to end what Lancashire claimed was discrimination in favour of the infant Indian cotton industry. Northbrook and his council ignored Salisbury's statements to that effect and, more importantly, the directive of March 1874 when in August of the following year they passed new tariff legislation which preserved the duties with only minor changes and did so without first consulting the secretary of state. Salisbury did not disallow the legislation, as he was at first inclined to do. To have taken that step would have precipitated a crisis between the two governments and attracted parliamentary intervention. But he censured the government of India for its action. Northbrook represented that he had not been specifically ordered to begin doing away with the duties. While that was true, he had never seen any justification for relieving British exports of a light burden at the expense of Indian taxpayers. If Lancashire was really feeling the competition from Indian mills, overtrading with inferior goods was to blame (Northbrook to Mallet, 2 Oct, 29 Oct 1874, Northbrook MSS, MS Eur. C. 144/23). To the extent that the duties were protective he defended them by recalling that before the industrial revolution and free trade Britain had discriminated against Indian textiles. The sacrifice of Indian interests to Lancashire risked alienation of 'the best and most loyally disposed of the educated natives' (Northbrook to Salisbury, 29 Jan, 25 Feb 1876, Salisbury MSS, HHM/3M/E 12). In the event, the abolition of the duties carried through largely by Northbrook's successor, Lytton, did not inhibit the growth of the Indian industry.

Their differences obscured the much wider area of agreement between Salisbury and Northbrook. With the mutiny in mind they looked on Islam in India as the most worrying of potential threats to British rule; Mayo's assassin was a Muslim. Where the princely states were concerned, Northbrook was rather more careful than Salisbury of the princes' feelings and their rights, as in the cases of Baroda and Hyderabad's claim to Berar. In defence of the nizam of Hyderabad, he quoted Charles James Fox on the pervasive influence of British constitutionalism in India, even on 'the most absolute despotism'. Yet he persuaded Salisbury to excise the words 'the interests of the people' from his dispatch on Berar: used to justify withholding the territory from the nizam, they might be employed against the British (Northbrook to Salisbury, 30 Sept 1875, Steele, 132). That prudence was evident in his thinking on the delicate question of allowing a Westernized élite to enter the covenanted civil service in more than token numbers. While he disagreed with Salisbury's decision to lower the age limit for the competitive examination, to the assumed disadvantage of Indians, he also held that a change in the regulations was as yet unnecessary. If too many Indians did pass into the service, they might simply be barred from the examination: 'at any rate nothing should be done to encourage native candidates to compete' (Northbrook to Salisbury, 30 Sept 1875, Salisbury MSS, HHM/3M/E12). Consistently with these private views, Northbrook did not reverse the tory Mayo's educational policy, although he modified its application by Sir George Campbell as lieutenant-governor of Bengal. Too little had been spent on the beginnings of elementary education, and too much on secondary and higher education, often of doubtful quality; Northbrook did not care for the growing 'half-educated class' any more than Salisbury did. Like Salisbury again, he thought India's recent progress had been too rapid for comfort (Northbrook to Salisbury, 26 Feb, 12 Sept 1875, Salisbury MSS, HHM/3M/E12).

With hindsight, Northbrook was satisfied that the peasant masses had benefited from his policies, intended '"to give the land rest", as some of the natives phrased it': the Western-educated handful were, after all, only 'the froth of Indian society' (Northbrook to Lord Dufferin, 8 Sept 1884, 14 March 1885, Northbrook MSS, MS Eur. C. 144/5). It is, at first sight, surprising that this conservative fell out with a tory secretary of state. Northbrook failed to heed a friendly warning from a member of Salisbury's council that the telegraph 'tends much to reduce the viceroy to a puppet' (Sir E. Perry to Northbrook, 9 July 1875, Northbrook MSS, MS Eur. C. 144/23). He resented as interference the insistence of an unusually able and interested minister on being involved in Indian decision making from an early stage. He disliked, too, the tone of Salisbury's dispatches with their 'strong flavour of *Saturday Review* smart writing' (Northbrook to Lord Camperdown, 14 June 1875, Northbrook MSS, MS Eur. C. 144/5; Northbrook to Dufferin, 5 Aug 1885, Northbrook MSS, MS Eur. C. 144/5). The adviser closest to him and the moving spirit in his council's defiance of the secretary of state was not an Indian civilian but the law member, Arthur Hobhouse—a partisan Liberal who incited the viceroy to think Salisbury's behaviour arbitrary and unconstitutional. When Northbrook cut short his five-year term in India, it was supposed, Hobhouse told him, that he had been 'worried and bullied out of office' by Salisbury (Steele, 137). That was at least partly true; although Northbrook pleaded family reasons, interpreted to mean anxiety to take his son and heir away from an unsuitable attachment formed in India. He had not been a masterful viceroy but a competent administrator with clear ideas about what was desirable and possible. Official India respected him: educated Indians, to whom the future belonged, believed he was their friend.

Home politics, the navy, and public opinion, 1876–1885 If the earldom conferred (10 June 1876) by the tory government was in the nature of a routine promotion for a retiring viceroy, Northbrook's reputation stood high with his party when he returned home in May 1876. It rose higher when events justified his adherence to Lawrence's policy on the frontier. Under a new and weaker minister at the India Office, Lytton went further than Salisbury had envisaged: the disasters of 1879–80 were the outcome. Northbrook privately allowed that, in the circumstances, Salisbury 'was more sinned against than sinning' (Mallet, 145). Gladstone made the former viceroy first lord of the Admiralty after the Liberals' election victory in 1880, with the understanding that the cabinet would also draw on his Indian expertise. He gave Lord Hartington at the India Office and Lord Ripon, as Lytton's replacement, the benefit of his advice. He was staunchly Gladstonian about withdrawing the troops sent into Afghanistan: 'To me the moral aspect of the question is the one to which I attach the greatest weight. What right have we to annex Afghanistan?' He supported Ripon's resumption and extension of his own cautious liberalism in India, while counselling him 'not to forget … the lessons of the Mutiny' (Northbrook to Ripon, 22 Sept, 25 June 1880, BL, Add. MS 43570). When Ripon got into difficulties over the Ilbert Bill, Northbrook was equally mortified by the violent outcry from British expatriates at the prospect of having to appear before Indian magistrates. He championed the viceroy publicly, and in their correspondence suggested the compromise which saved 'the principle of … no race distinction in regard to … judges and magistrates … English or native', but narrowed its application (Northbrook to Ripon, 12 Aug 1882, BL, Add. MS 43572). The pragmatism was evident, more controversially, in his response to the pressures on him at the Admiralty.

With his naval connections, Northbrook always believed in the classical Liberal doctrine of 'keeping up our naval strength rather than playing at being a great military power' (Northbrook to Mallet, 31 May 1874, Northbrook MSS, MS Eur. C. 144/22). Yet he and his Admiralty board were famously indicted by W. T. Stead in the *Pall Mall Gazette* (September 1884) for their comparative neglect of the fleet. Writing half a century afterwards, the leading modern historian of the Victorian navy found Northbrook and his board guilty as charged of the gradual decline of the Royal Navy as a fighting force (Marder, 120). France and Germany between them had more first-class ironclads than Britain; Russia and Italy were expanding their navies. Amid gathering international tensions, the public took fright. The reaction to Stead's articles compelled Northbrook to announce a dramatic increase in spending on construction and ordnance. Defending himself against the criticisms, he pleaded that it was impossible for any British government 'to undertake large expenditure in advance of the general feeling of the people'. His estimates had been subject to Gladstone's political expectations of economy in the services (*Hansard* 3, 299, 14 July 1885, 624; Gladstone to Northbrook, 15 Dec 1880, Gladstone, *Diaries*, 9.643). Moreover, the record showed that Northbrook and his professional advisers had hesitated over the admittedly difficult decisions that quickening technological change imposed. His standing never recovered, though he was able to demonstrate that within the limits set by domestic political considerations he had worked with the first naval lord, Admiral Cooper Key, to protect the navy from obsolescence.

The Egyptian mission, 1884 Northbrook approved of a temporary British occupation of Egypt in 1882 to secure the Suez Canal and keep the French out. Like Gladstone, he considered the defeated nationalist leader, Arabi Pasha, to be a 'mere military adventurer' (Northbrook to Ripon, 16 June 1882, BL, Add. MS 43577). Although privately critical of the premier's slowness to agree to the Gordon relief expedition, he supported the decision to abandon the Egyptian Sudan to the Mahdi and his followers. A Northbrook mission was first suggested in April 1884 before the breakdown of the London conference of creditor nations called to strike a balance between the claims of their bondholders, the interests of the Egyptian government and people, and those of the occupying power (*Gladstone–Granville Correspondence*, 2.180 n.1). The idea and the man were acceptable to Gladstone, who wanted to withdraw from Egypt with the minimum of delay, and to Hartington, who headed the more imperially minded wing of the cabinet. Their mutual choice stipulated that he should be accompanied by his cousin, Evelyn Baring, the British agent and consul-general in Cairo, then on home leave. Baring, Northbrook's influential private secretary in India, had become a central figure in Britain's relations with Egypt and her effective ruler. Northbrook said afterwards that he could not have carried out his hurried task (September–October 1884) without the help of this 'Egyptian Whig', as Evelyn Baring described himself (E. Baring to Sir A. C. Lyall, 6 Nov 1879, Lyall MSS, MS Eur. F. 132/3G). Opposed to annexation, and sharing Gladstone's conviction that it would be an 'unnatural proceeding' to institute direct rule in what was, unlike India, a predominantly Muslim country, Northbrook had sided with the premier, and against Hartington, in preferring to see Egyptian neutrality secured by an international agreement that would permit the British to evacuate (Stanley, Derby diary, 7 May 1884, DER 920 (15); Northbrook to Ripon, 13 June 1884, Northbrook MSS, MS Eur. C. 144/4).

The most pressing problem in Egypt was financial: the London conference failed because France would not consent to a reduction in the interest paid to bondholders, the demand on which the British stood their ground. Northbrook was asked early in August to go out as a special commissioner and report urgently on the administration and finances. After their lengthy discussions before he left, Gladstone told him that he had accepted 'an impossible task and with the impossible no man can successfully contend'. The premier could discern no escape from the financial impasse. On his side, it is clear, Northbrook did not allude to thoughts about a possible solution which he knew would be unpalatable to Gladstone. Nothing could be done 'without making some sacrifice ourselves', by way of a large British loan; he enjoined his friend Sir Reginald Welby of the Treasury to keep this '*strictly and entirely* to yourself' (Gladstone to Northbrook, 29 Aug 1884, Baring archive, Northbrook MSS, NP6/4/2/11; Northbrook to Welby, 30 Aug 1884, Baring archive, Northbrook MSS). The danger arising from French resentment of the British presence in Egypt, and Bismarck's encouragement of France, weighed heavily with him. In the plan which took shape soon after his arrival in the country the continental powers were to be placated by the assurance that their bondholders would be paid in full. As Gladstone objected, these proposals meant that the British taxpayers were to underwrite the bondholders; it was, in his eyes, an unwarrantable surrender to international pressure. 'I have recommended a pusillanimous policy for Egypt', Northbrook admitted, 'because I know we could not hold our own at sea if there was to be a war' (Northbrook to E. Baring, 7 Nov 1884, Baring archive, Northbrook MSS, NP 6/4/2/3(2)). To Gladstone the British loan was at the same time a 'Jingo policy' that must strengthen the hands of those who wanted annexation, or at least an indefinite occupation (*Gladstone–Granville Correspondence*, 2.280). Northbrook reduced the figure for the loan from £15 million to £8 or £9 million, but Gladstone was immovable. On the day he asked his colleague to go to Egypt, he had promised the Commons not to commit Britain to any financial obligations there without consulting the house (*Hansard* 3, 291, 2 Aug 1884, 1528–9).

The disregard shown by the cabinet envoy for Gladstone's known position that 'Egypt … should … pay what and when she could' infuriated the latter. In one of his rare lapses into profanity, the premier complained that Northbrook had '"bitched" the whole concern from beginning to end' (Gladstone to Granville, 24 Sept 1884, *Gladstone–Granville Correspondence*, 2.266; Hamilton, 2.759). Gladstone had, it seems, conceived of the mission as a move in the campaign to get other creditor states to concede a reduction in the bondholders' interest. Northbrook's remaining proposals were overshadowed by the rejection of the loan and of a cut in the coupon. They included the substitution of British for Anglo-French administration of the railways and state lands, and more latitude for the Egyptian government in taxation. Coupled with a continuing British occupation for an unspecified period, they were designed to free Britain and Egypt from the legitimate intervention of the continental powers, and above all of France, based on Egyptian indebtedness. Their implementation would have made Evelyn Baring's indirect rule considerably easier and shortened his work of financial reconstruction. Gladstone simply refused to contemplate asking the Commons to sanction a guaranteed loan. With H. C. E. Childers, the chancellor of the exchequer, he set the Treasury to prepare an alternative solution and worked the press against Northbrook. Although all its peers favoured the Northbrook proposals, Hartington was the only member of the Commons in the cabinet to do so. 'I never had harder or more disheartening work in my life', wrote Northbrook just before he lost in December: 'Gladstone and Childers want to "burke" my recommendations altogether' (Northbrook to E. Baring, 27 Nov 1884, Baring archive, Northbrook MSS, NP 6/4/2/3(2); 'Financial memorandum, 1884–5', Baring archive, Northbrook MSS, NP 6/4/2/15). They succeeded: and his threatened resignation did not materialize. He had nothing to show for his efforts since August. Evelyn Baring's verdict stands: 'His mission was a failure' (Cromer, 2.371).

For the rest of the government's life Northbrook aligned himself with the cabinet critics of Gladstone's policy in Egypt and the Sudan, and was poised to resign more than once. The eventual solution to the problem of Egyptian finance, adopted by another London conference in March 1885, provided for an international guaranteed loan of £9 million, with no reduction of existing interest payments beyond a small face-saving Egyptian tax on the coupon for two years. The bondholders and France had prevailed. Northbrook consoled himself with the thought that he had contributed to the slow amelioration of the fellahin's lot by his brief visit and two reports, one financial and the other on the country's prospects generally: 'If we can say we have got rid of the courbash and corvée … we shall have done more for the people than all the dynasties' (memorandum, 29 Jan 1885, Baring archive, Northbrook MSS, NP 6/4/2/17).

A whig twilight, 1885–1904 Northbrook had been a distinctly liberal whig, supporting Gladstone's Irish land bills of 1880–82 with few of the misgivings that others felt. Nor does he appear to have had any serious qualms about Gladstone's handling of parliamentary reform in 1884. He made no secret, however, of his unhappiness with the way he had been treated over the Egyptian mission. Relieved to be out of office from June 1885, he declined Gladstone's offer of the viceroyalty of Ireland in the ministry formed in February 1886 to carry Irish home rule. He recognized the case for trying some form of home rule; he no longer had enough confidence in his party to join them in the experiment. From saying that he hoped the Liberals would be successful in a 'difficult and dangerous' enterprise, he moved quickly to private and public denunciation of Gladstone, 'the ablest, … the most eloquent and, I am afraid, the most conscientiously unscrupulous leader … in the history of English politics', whose failures of policy, Northbrook now discovered, made him 'more than any other man' responsible for the unrest in Ireland (Northbrook to Dufferin, 5 Feb, 30 July 1886, Northbrook MSS, MS Eur. C. 144/5; *Hansard* 3, 317, 6 July 1887, 902). Reflection had convinced him that there could only be one answer to 'the real question': was it right to hand Ireland over to 'Parnell & Co.' (memorandum, 11 Oct 1887, J. Chamberlain MSS, JC/8/4/3/22)? Yet Northbrook was never really at home in the Unionist alliance; he had no hesitation in turning down an invitation to enter Salisbury's cabinet in January 1887 with G. J. Goschen. Shortly before his death in 1904 he was one of those who came out against Unionism's shift away from free trade.

Something of an innocent in politics, Northbrook was deficient in its basic skills. 'I did not feel myself at liberty to give information to the newspapers', he told Gladstone's private secretary when he learned that the press was being worked against his Egyptian proposals ('Financial memorandum, 1884–5', Baring archive, Northbrook MSS, NP 6/4/2/15). While he had enjoyed electioneering in the past, and appeared regularly on Unionist platforms, he deplored the more heated atmosphere of the eighties: 'Oh, this constant extra-Parliamentary oratory, it is ruining us all', he lamented in 1885 (Mallet, 218). Northbrook was, perhaps, unfortunate in coming into conflict with two such formidable politicians as Salisbury and Gladstone. He was at his best in India, where the circumstances called for a period of consolidation. It has been unfairly said that he was 'frightened into inertia' (Gopal, 125). He understood better than some in his position the impact of Westernization and the nice judgements it demanded of liberal rulers. When he went to Egypt he secured the appointment to his staff of an Indian Muslim who could tell Egyptian notables of Northbrook's respect for the 'native raj' in the princely states and of his solicitude for the peasantry (Northbrook to Ripon, 8 Aug 1884, Northbrook MSS, MS Eur. C. 144/4). In his final report he strongly recommended lowering the land tax paid by the fellahin. His sympathy with a Westernized élite and his political insight led him to establish, and largely maintain, a club for Indian students in London which bore his name. He urged Salisbury, who was known to have doubts about the small concession to Indian opinion involved, not to drop what eventually became the Indian Councils Bill of 1892, saying characteristically, 'the Congress agitation … not altogether a comfortable thing … is not now dangerous' (Northbrook to Salisbury, 10 June 1890, Baring archive, Northbrook MSS, NP 6/4/1/4).

A. O. Hume, the British administrator who founded the Indian National Congress and endorsed Northbrook's caution in the seventies, nevertheless described him as 'feeble', but rich in private and public virtues (Gopal, 125). Physically strong, Northbrook filled much of his leisure with the traditional recreations of a wealthy countryman, besides yachting and continental travel, and was happiest fishing on the Itchen near his Hampshire home. Widely read, without being particularly intellectual, he sketched and painted in watercolours. He added to and cherished his impressive collection of old masters, mostly inherited from his uncle Thomas Baring on the latter's death in 1873, and was a generous patron and a friend of Edward Lear. In Lear's eyes, this reserved man was 'a luminous and amiable brick'—a glimpse of the humanity beneath a sometimes oppressive *gravitas*. A substantial share of his uncle's great fortune made him a much richer man. His income from urban landholdings on the southern edge of London and other non-agricultural investments enabled him to be a model landlord in town and country. In 1885 he was spending the gross rental of his 9000 acres in Hampshire on the upkeep of the estate (*Carlingford's Journal*, 144). His standing in that county was acknowledged by his appointment as lord lieutenant in 1892, followed by the chairmanship of the county council from 1894 to his death.

An unostentatious piety underlay the sense of duty that offset a lifelong want of self-confidence. When his friend Lord Ripon, a convert to Catholicism, replaced Lytton in India, Northbrook sent him a copy of the prayer he had used himself as viceroy. 'I am but a little child', it ran in words taken from 1 Kings 3: 7–9; 'Thy servant is in the midst of a great people … give … an understanding heart to judge … that I may discern between good and bad' (Northbrook to Ripon, 17 Feb 1884, BL, Add. MS 43570). His beliefs were not as simple as this might suggest; he read and reread the sermons of John Henry Newman, among others. His ideal of a churchman was A. P. Stanley, someone with 'broad liberal views' who did not 'push the dogmas of the Church of England to the detriment of the doctrines of Christianity' (Northbrook to Argyll, 21 March 1873, Northbrook MSS, MS Eur. C. 144/9). Christian divisions seemed insignificant to him beside the great religions of India. In his old age he compiled for the Indian mission field *The Teaching of Jesus Christ in his own Words* (1900); it had a huge circulation in English and in Indian languages. At home he used his chairmanship of the county council and of its education committee to select, personally, the Anglican, nonconformist, and Catholic members of a small *ad hoc* committee that devised an interdenominational syllabus for religious teaching subsequently taken up by several other counties as well.

Once the passions aroused by home rule in 1886 had begun to cool, Northbrook stepped easily into the part of elder statesman. He chaired a royal commission on the controversial question of mining royalties in 1890, and his views on Indian subjects were heard with respect. He died at his seat, Stratton Park, Hampshire, on 15 November 1904 and was buried four days later at Micheldever parish church, which he had restored. A privy councillor and GCSI (7 August 1869; 13 April 1876), FRS (8 January 1880), and the recipient of honorary doctorates from Oxford and Cambridge, he was succeeded by his elder and surviving son, Francis, Viscount Baring (*d.* 1929), a Liberal and then Unionist MP (1880–85 and 1886–92). DAVID STEELE

Sources ING Barings, London, Barings archives, Northbrook MSS · BL OIOC, Northbrook MSS, MS Eur. C. 144 · BL, Ripon MSS · BL, Gladstone MSS · Hatfield House Library, Salisbury MSS, HHM/3M · BL OIOC, Lyall MSS, MS Eur. F. 132 · Gladstone, *Diaries* · *The diary of Sir Edward Walter Hamilton, 1880–1885*, ed. D. W. R. Bahlman, 2 vols. (1972) · B. Mallet, *Thomas George, earl of Northbrook* (1908) · E. C. Moulton, *Lord Northbrook's Indian administration, 1872–1876* (1968) · S. Gopal, *British policy in India, 1858–1905* (1965) · E. D. Steele, 'Salisbury at the India Office', *Salisbury: the man and his policies*, ed. Lord Blake and H. Cecil (1987), 116–47 · A. J. Marder, *The anatomy of British sea power*, American edn (1940) · earl of Cromer [E. Baring], *Modern Egypt*, 2 vols. (1908) · P. H. Colomb, *Memoirs of Admiral the Right Honble. Sir Astley Cooper Key* (1898) · *Lord Carlingford's journal*, ed. A. B. Cooke and J. R. Vincent (1971) · *The political correspondence of Mr Gladstone and Lord Granville, 1876–1886*, ed. A. Ramm, 2 vols. (1962) · GEC, *Peerage* · U. Birm. L., Chamberlain MSS · E. Stanley, Derby diary, Lpool RO, Derby papers

Archives BL OIOC, corresp. relating to India, MS Eur. C. 144 · Duke U., Perkins L., corresp. and papers as first lord of the admiralty · ING Barings, London, political and private corresp. and papers, incl. diaries | BL, corresp. with Sir Henry Campbell-Bannerman, Add. MS 41232 · BL, corresp. with Sir Charles Dilke, Add. MS 43891 · BL, corresp. with W. E. Gladstone, Add. MSS 44266–44267 · BL, corresp. with Lord Halifax, Add. MSS 49554–49557, 49561, *passim* · BL, corresp. with Lord Ripon, Add. MSS 43570–43573 · BL OIOC, corresp. with Sir George Clerk, MS Eur. D. 538 · BL OIOC, letter to Sir Alfred Lyall, MS Eur. F. 132 · BL OIOC, corresp. with Sir Richard Temple, MS Eur. F. 86 · BL OIOC, corresp. with Sir Philip Wodehouse, MS Eur. D. 726 · Bodl. Oxf., corresp. with Sir Henry Burdett · Bodl. Oxf., corresp. with Sir William Harcourt and Lewis Harcourt · Bodl. Oxf., letters to Lord Kimberley · Borth. Inst., corresp. with Lord Halifax · Bucks. RLSS, corresp. with Lord Hobart · Chatsworth House, Derbyshire, letters to eighth duke of Devonshire · Hatfield House, Hertfordshire, Salisbury MSS, HHM/3M · Hove Central Library, Sussex, letters to Lord Wolseley · ING Barings, London, letters to Thomas Baring · LPL, letters to Lord Selborne · LPL, letters and papers to A. C. Tait · NL Scot., corresp., mainly with Lord Rosebery · NRA Scotland, Argyll MSS · NRA Scotland, priv. coll., letters to duke of Argyll · PRO, corresp. with Lord Cardwell, PRO 30/48 · PRO, corresp. with Lord Cromer, FO 633 · PRO, corresp. with Lord Granville, PRO 30/29 · U. Birm. L., corresp. with Joseph Chamberlain · U. Durham, letters to third Earl Grey

Likenesses A. S. Cope, oils, 1903, City Hall, Winchester · Bassano, photograph, NPG [*see illus.*] · E. Boehm, bronze statue, Calcutta · C. Hall, stipple (Grillion's Club series; after H. T. Wells), NPG · W. W. Ouless, oils, Calcutta · G. Richmond, watercolour, Netley

Castle, Hampshire • Spy [L. Ward], caricature, NPG; repro. in *VF* (9 Dec 1876) • T, caricature, NPG; repro. in *VF* (5 July 1882) • C. W. Walton, lithograph, NPG

Wealth at death £246,698 8*s.* 8*d.*: probate, 24 Dec 1904, *CGPLA Eng. & Wales*

Barinthus [St Barinthus, Barnitus, Barvitus] (*supp. fl.* **6th cent.**), legendary navigator, occurs in the *Navigatio sancti Brendani* and the various Latin and vernacular lives of St *Brendan of Clonfert (*d.* 573) [*see under* Connacht, saints of], where it is stated that his account of a journey, undertaken with a disciple called Mernoc, to the so-called 'Promised Land of the Saints' inspired Brendan to make his own 'navigation' in search of that island. These nautical associations no doubt underlie the claim by Geoffrey of Monmouth in his *Vita Merlini* that a 'Barinthus … to whom the waters and stars of the heavens were well known' (Geoffrey of Monmouth, 102) guided the ship carrying the wounded King Arthur after the battle of Camlan. Also, the *Vita sancti Davidis* by Rhigyfarch has a St Barre traversing the Irish Sea on a horse and encountering St Brendan *en route*. While it has been argued that this Barinthus is the vestige of some ancient pagan Celtic water-deity, his patronymic 'nepos Neil' ('descendant of Niall') suggests he is to be identified with the Cenél Conaill saint Bairrfhinn ua Néill, patron of Kilbarron (Cell Bairrfhinn, Donegal) and Drumcullen, Offaly, whose feast day is 21 May. According to the Irish saints' genealogies, Bairrfhinn was son of Muiredach mac Echdach of the Cenél Conaill (of the northern Uí Néill kin group) and Didnat ingen Mechair, but it is likely that he is ultimately one of the many manifestations of the 'wandering' cult of St *Findbarr [*see under* Ulster, saints of] which originated in north-east Ulster. In addition, there is also some late evidence of a Scottish cult of Barinthus: for example, a Barnitus (or, in a later variant, Barvitus), associate of St Brendan, was commemorated in Argyll on 5 (or 13) January and his relics were venerated at Dreghorn on 6 August.

DAVID E. THORNTON

Sources C. Selmer, ed., *Navigatio Sancti Brendani abbatis* (1959) • C. Plummer, ed., *Vitae sanctorum Hiberniae*, 1 (1910) • *Rhigyfarch's Life of St David*, ed. J. W. James (1967) • Geoffrey of Monmouth, *Vita Merlini / Life of Merlin*, ed. and trans. B. Clarke (1973) • P. Ó Riain, ed., *Corpus genealogiarum sanctorum Hiberniae* (Dublin, 1985) • *Félire húi Gormáin / The martyrology of Gorman*, ed. and trans. W. Stokes, HBS, 9 (1895) • R. I. Best and H. J. Lawlor, eds., *The martyrology of Tallaght*, HBS, 68 (1931) • *Félire Óengusso Céli Dé / The martyrology of Oengus the Culdee*, ed. and trans. W. Stokes, HBS, 29 (1905) • A. P. Forbes, *Kalendars of Scottish saints* (1872) • P. Ó Riain, 'St Finnbarr: a study of a cult', *Journal of the Cork Historical and Archaeological Society*, 2nd ser., 82 (1977), 63–82 • A. C. C. Brown, 'Barintus', *Revue Celtique*, 22 (1901), 339–44

Bark, Evelyn Elizabeth Patricia (1900–1993), charity worker, was born on 26 December 1900 at 18 Selwyn Road, Plaistow, West Ham, the first of four children of Frederick William Bark, commercial clerk, and his wife, Nellie Hephzibah, *née* Layton. Following an early childhood accident she was an invalid and educated at home until she regained mobility in her teens. She had a flair for languages, acquiring fluency in Swedish, Norwegian, Danish, Icelandic, French, and German. With verbatim speed shorthand also, she took employment with the Swedish Match Company, working in London, Stockholm, Hamburg briefly, and London again by 1939.

On the outbreak of the Second World War Bark trained as a British Red Cross Society (BRCS) volunteer and undertook hospital duties, while continuing full-time work at the Board of Trade. In 1944 she joined the foreign relations department of the BRCS, working on the 25-word postal message scheme which enabled civilians in Britain, France, and Germany to communicate with relatives anywhere via the central tracing agency of the International Committee of the Red Cross (ICRC) in Geneva. She also developed the Red Cross language card, enabling doctors and nurses to communicate with foreign patients. After the September 1944 liberation of Brussels she joined the BRCS commission in Europe, taking a list of enquiries for missing people in Belgium, typed on thin paper, weighing 11½ lb. Working in Belgium, Luxembourg, the Netherlands, and Germany she set up a tracing service for missing persons.

Bark entered Belsen concentration camp on the heels of five Red Cross relief teams in April 1945. With some 60,000 human bodies just alive, dying, or dead from brutal overcrowding, starvation, multiple disease, and typhus, the immediate task was to collect corpses, disinfect the survivors, and transfer the sick to an improvised hospital in neighbouring barracks. The Nazis had destroyed all records and Bark's Red Cross tracing service, helped by some internees, succeeded in the colossal task of identifying and registering over 35,000 survivors of twenty-two nationalities; gradually reunion of families and friends began. In April 1948, when Bark was promoted British Red Cross commissioner in Germany, her outstanding relief work among displaced persons and her organization of the German Bad Pyrmont Hospital and Rehabilitation Centre for disabled service and civilian war victims won the admiration of Red Cross colleagues, the army, and civilian relief authorities, and she was appointed OBE in 1952.

After withdrawal of the commission in September 1949 Bark became foreign relations and relief adviser (a title later changed to director, international affairs department) at BRCS headquarters in 1950, with operational responsibility for overseas disasters and emergencies assistance. She supported Angela, countess of Limerick, BRCS vice-chairman, at International Red Cross conferences and meetings of the League of Red Cross Societies throughout the period 1950–65. Her organizational ability, gift for friendship, and understanding of different cultures earned her a worldwide reputation. Her notable achievements include organizing the BRCS medical commission to Jordan, where the majority of a million Palestinian refugees had sought asylum in 1948; taking a Red Cross mission in 1950 to re-establish the Ethiopian Red Cross Society; and in 1953 visiting sheikhdoms in the Arabian Gulf to discuss creating national Red Crescent societies. In 1954–6 she accompanied Angela Limerick to the communist states of the Soviet Union, Poland, and China, and then Romania, Hungary, and Bulgaria. These visits, transcending political and ideological boundaries, strengthened Red Cross relationships and initiated closer co-operation in tracing and welfare enquiries. In 1956 the League of Red Cross Societies asked her to co-ordinate relief for Hungarian refugees in Austria and join the league's disaster relief advisory committee. Her unpublished second volume of memoirs, 'Yesterdays never die', included descriptions of her visits to Morocco to support the physiotherapist teams working among the oil paralysis victims in 1957 and to supervise relief after the Agadir earthquake in 1960; to Iran in 1962 to oversee relief expenditure in the areas devastated by earthquake, for which the first British television appeal had raised £400,000; and to Yemen in 1964 to monitor a British medical team working with the ICRC caring for civil war casualties.

The impact of Bark's dynamic personality was in inverse proportion to her stature: she referred to her height (5 feet) in her autobiography, *No Time to Kill* (1960), as no taller than Queen Victoria. Her outgoing personality, cosmopolitan lifestyle, and impish sense of humour made her a most amusing raconteur. The esteem and affection in which she was held was evident when she was the subject of Eamonn Andrews's television programme *This is Your Life* in 1963. Her achievements, courage, and compassion were recognized when she was appointed CMG in 1967 (the year after her retirement). She also was honoured by the Austrian government and received Red Cross decorations from ten countries. Bark led a full life in retirement until paralysed by a stroke in 1985. She died of heart failure on 6 June 1993 at Roselawn Nursing Home, 20 Westcote Road, Reading, Berkshire. She never married.

SYLVIA R. LIMERICK

Sources *The Independent* (24 June 1993) • *The Times* (26 June 1993) • E. Bark, *No time to kill* (1960) • E. Bark, 'Yesterdays never die', typescript, after 1970, BRCS archive • G. Djurovic, *The central tracing agency of the International Committee of the Red Cross: activities of the ICRC for the alleviation of the mental suffering of war victims* (Geneva, 1986) • W. R. F. Collins, 'Belsen camp: a preliminary report', *BMJ* (9 June 1945), 814–16 • *The relief of Belsen: eye witness accounts* (1991) • *WWW* • personal knowledge (2004) • private information (2004) • b. cert. • d. cert.

Archives British Red Cross Society Museum and Archives, London, unpublished MS, 'Yesterdays never die' | British Red Cross Society Museum and Archives, London

Likenesses photograph, 1956, repro. in *The Independent* • photograph, repro. in *The Times*

Wealth at death £2387: probate, 9 Sept 1993, *CGPLA Eng. & Wales*

Barke, James William (1905–1958), novelist, was born on 22 May 1905 at Torwoodlee, near Galashiels, Selkirkshire, the fourth child of James Bark (1862–1937), dairyman, and his wife, Jane (*b.* 1866), a dairymaid, daughter of Thomas Gibb, ploughman. The family moved in 1907 to Tulliallan, Fife, which Barke, remembering his happy rural childhood, considered to be in effect 'the land of my birth' (Barke, 279). In 1918 they moved again, to Glasgow. Barke was educated at Tulliallan parish school and Hamilton Crescent public school, Glasgow. He trained as an engineer and worked for a Glasgow shipbuilding and engineering firm, becoming manager of its brickworks, while beginning his writing career. His first novel, *The World his Pillow*, was published in 1933. The same year he married Agnes (Nan) Coats and they had two sons.

Barke listed his interests as 'Scotland, *piobaireachd* [bagpipe music] and anything controversial' (*Glasgow Herald*, 21 March 1958). A friend wrote: 'He was a man full of humanity, a very individual man. His novels are like him' (Allan). He was a committed socialist and his fourth novel, *Major Operation* (1936), argues the case for socialism at some length, while providing a striking impressionistic description of Glasgow in the depression years. *The Land of the Leal* (1939), considered his masterpiece, is a novel on an epic scale, the odyssey of a couple and their family in pursuit of work from their native Galloway to the Scottish borders, Fife, and Glasgow, echoing the experiences of Barke's parents.

After the Second World War, Barke resigned from his Glasgow job and moved to Ayrshire to work on an ambitious series of novels based on the life of Robert Burns. The Immortal Memory quintet, which appeared between 1946 and 1953, was extremely popular with readers, but was attacked by many Burnsians who deplored Barke's colourful rendering of the poet's life.

After an unsuccessful hotelkeeping venture in Ayrshire Barke returned to live in Glasgow in 1955. He had been in poor health for some years and died, following a heart attack, in Glasgow Royal Infirmary on 20 March 1958. A private cremation four days later was followed by committal at New Kilpatrick cemetery, Bearsden, where C. M. Grieve (the poet Hugh MacDiarmid) gave the funeral oration. Barke was survived by his wife.

MOIRA BURGESS

Sources Mitchell L., Glas., James Barke MSS • J. Barke, *The green hills far away* (1940) • *Glasgow Herald* (21 March 1958) • J. R. Allan, *Scotland's Magazine* (May 1958) • *CCI* (1958) • m. reg. Scot.

Archives Mitchell L., Glas., corresp., MSS, personal and family documents • Mitchell L., Glas., corresp. on proposed editions of Burns's works and *The merry muses of Caledonia* | Mitchell L., Glas., corresp. with John DeLancy Ferguson • NL Scot., letters to Neil Gunn

Likenesses photograph, repro. in *Glasgow Herald*

Wealth at death £924 0s. 2d.: confirmation, 5 Dec 1958, *CCI*

Barker, Andrew (*d.* 1577), merchant, of Bristol, was, in partnership with his brother John, later (1606–7) mayor of Bristol, for some years engaged in the often disputed trade with the Spanish in the Canary Islands. In 1570 one of his ships, the *Falcon*, was seized at Terceira, the cargo (worth £2600) confiscated, and her crew sent to the galleys. Barker returned home (1574), after some years' residence in Tenerife, and successfully sent two separate ships to the Canaries, which returned with wine and sugar. But in 1575, at Tenerife, the Inquisition captured the captain and crew of his ship the *Christopher*, and released them only on payment of fines which amounted to the value of the whole cargo (£1700). In reprisal Barker equipped two ships to recover his losses directly from the Spanish in the West Indies. He himself commanded the larger ship, the *Ragged Staff*, with Philip Roche as master, and the *Bear* was commanded by William Coxe. They sailed from Plymouth on

Whitsunday 1576 and after taking on board supplies in the Cape Verde Islands they crossed the Atlantic. Spanish sources suggest that Barker publicly announced the retaliatory nature of his voyage.

While sailing west from Trinidad along the South American mainland the expedition took several prizes. Off Veragua they captured a Spanish frigate with its crew and ordnance taken from John Oxenham's expedition. Hakluyt says the prisoners were put ashore, but the governor of Veragua alleged they were thrown overboard to drown. The leaking *Ragged Staff* was sunk and the frigate became the expedition's flagship. They captured and ransomed an important Spanish judge. But the officers quarrelled among themselves; Barker and Roche fought, and Coxe, heading a mutiny, turned Barker and his adherents on shore at La Guanaja in the Gulf of Honduras, where they were surprised by the Spaniards. In August 1577 Barker and a dozen others were killed, and Barker's head was sent as a trophy to the nearby town of Trujillo. Coxe took the survivors on board, broke open Barker's treasure chest, and shared out the contents. Having sacked the neighbouring island of Roatan, the company captured a pinnace, in which, together with a skiff and the captured Spanish frigate, they made for home. Disaster ensued. Off the west coast of Cuba the frigate capsized and most of the booty was lost. Coxe and the survivors laid low until spring 1578 in Central America, where they probably built the small vessel on which they reached the Isles of Scilly. The skiff was captured and its sailors hanged. Roche died, and in June 1578 Coxe and perhaps eighteen men reached home, carrying Oxenham's ordnance. But some were arrested at the suit of John Barker as accessories to his brother's death and responsible for the voyage's unsuccessful outcome. The main culprits received long sentences of imprisonment.

J. K. Laughton, *rev.* Basil Morgan

Sources I. A. Wright, ed., *Documents concerning English voyages to the Spanish main, 1569–1580*, Hakluyt Society, 2nd ser., 71 (1932) • *CSP dom., addenda, 1566–79*, 13 • *CSP Spain, 1568–79*, 508 • R. Hakluyt, *The principal navigations, voyages, traffiques and discoveries of the English nation*, 7, Hakluyt Society, extra ser., 7 (1904) • administration, PRO, PROB 6/2, fol. 208

Barker, Benjamin (1776–1838), landscape painter and drawing-master, was the son of Benjamin Barker (*c.*1720–1793), a former solicitor and minor artist, and his wife, Anne, and the younger brother of the painter Thomas *Barker (1767–1847), known as Barker of Bath. In the late 1770s the family moved from Trosnant, Pontypool, to Bristol and then in 1783 to Bath, where the young Benjamin established himself as a painter, teacher of drawing and painting, and restorer of pictures. As Benjamin West noted in 1807, drawing-masters in Bath made 'fortunes' in the first decade of the nineteenth century (*The Barkers of Bath*, 7). In 1801 Barker married Jane Hewlett (*d.* 1825), sister of the popular Bath flower painter and drawing-master James Hewlett (1768–1836). In 1814 Barker and Hewlett purchased a plot of land on Bathwick Hill, overlooking Bath, and Barker built Smallcombe Villa, where the antiquary John Britton 'spent many happy hours' enjoying Barker's 'hanging gardens, trout stream, woods, and paintings' (Britton, 225). Barker's most eminent visitor at the villa was Queen Charlotte, who came with the duke of Clarence and Princess Elizabeth in 1817. It was reported, perhaps unkindly, that the queen took more of an interest in Barker's famously well-equipped kitchen than in his paintings (Murch).

By 1800 Barker had made a sketching tour of north Wales and he made another about 1815. He also visited Yorkshire, Kent, Dorset, and Devon, making studies for the oil paintings and watercolours he exhibited in London and Bath. These were shown at the Royal Academy between 1800 and 1831, the British Institution from 1806 to 1838, and the Society of Painters in Water Colours between 1813 and 1820. In Bath in 1828, 1829, and 1830 Benjamin and his brother Thomas held joint exhibitions in the recently built Masonic Hall in York Street. Like Thomas, Benjamin Barker was a variable artist. At his best his small oils have an old-masterly richness of tone that approaches the work of John Crome; on other occasions he was, as Colonel Grant observed, 'commonplace' and sombre (Grant, 17). He rarely ventured beyond the genre of landscape but did paint *Adoration of the Child* for the rebuilt parish church of St Mary, Bathwick, in 1820 (*in situ*), and his last exhibited picture at the Royal Academy in 1831 was *A Battle, Flemish Costume*. A skilfully executed set of forty-eight aquatints by Theodore H. A. Fielding (1781–1851) after Barker, entitled *English Landscape Scenery*, met with success on publication in 1824, but thereafter Barker's career was in decline, and he was forced to sell Smallcombe Villa in 1833. He moved to live with his artist daughter Marianne in Totnes, Devon, where he died on 2 March 1838. A caricature sketch of Barker as a youth by the Bath art dealer and amateur artist Thomas Shew (*d.* 1839) may be the only surviving likeness of him (Victoria Art Gallery, Bath). In a sale conducted by Messrs Rainey in Bath on 27–28 February 1854, 'Valuable Paintings and Sketches in Oil, the Greater Part of which were the Genuine Property of the Late Benjamin Barker', were drawings and paintings by or attributed to Richard Wilson and Thomas Gainsborough as well as Thomas Barker (copy of the sale catalogue in Bath Central Library).

Susan Sloman

Sources *The Barkers of Bath* (1986) [exhibition catalogue, Victoria Art Gallery, Bath, 17 May–18 June 1986] • T. Fielding, *Benjamin Barker's English landscape scenery: … engravings by Theodore Fielding; from original paintings in oil by the late B. Barker, esq* (1843) [incl. 'Memoir of the artist' by Revd Edward Mangin] • M. Forsyth, 'Edward Davis: nineteenth-century Bath architect and pupil of Sir John Soane', *Bath History*, 7 (1998), 107–28 • M. H. Grant, *A dictionary of British landscape painters, from the 16th century to the early 20th century* (1952) • Graves, *RA exhibitors* • *Victoria Art Gallery concise catalogue of paintings and drawings* (1991) [Bath] • M. Holbrook, 'Painters in Bath in the eighteenth century', *Apollo*, 98 (1973), 375–84 • J. Murch, *Biographical sketches of Bath celebrities, ancient and modern* (1893), 199–200 • F. Shum, 'Reminiscences of the late Thomas Barker: a paper read at the Royal Literary and Scientific Institution on Friday, April 11, 1862', *Bath Chronicle* (17 April 1862) • J. Britton, *Auto-biography* (1850), 225

Likenesses T. Shew, caricature (as a young man), Victoria Art Gallery, Bath

Barker, Charles (1791–1859), advertising agent, was born on 22 October 1791 at Morton Hill, co. Durham, the first son of a non-practising attorney, Joseph Barker of Morton Hill, and Mary, daughter of the Revd John Hogarth of Kirknewton, Northumberland. Barker earned a reputation as the nation's leading advertising man in the early years of the nineteenth century by exploiting the unrivalled news coverage offered by *The Times*, then the foremost daily newspaper. Fortunately for him, the expansion of commerce and industry at this time was unprecedented. Demand for financial intelligence, even in summarized form, soared, with information published on market prices, fresh trade outlets, applications for shares in newly floated companies, and the frequency of failures. Described variously as 'newsagents', 'newspaper agents', or 'correspondents and advertising agents', from its claimed foundation in 1812 his firm had a very close link with the newspaper and represented its first foothold in the City.

In 1828 Barker married Harriet Corner (1804–1860). They lived at 31 Euston Square, Marylebone, where they raised at least two sons, Montague Cochrane Barker and Francis George Barker.

Outside London, the absence of daily newspapers permitted Barker to capitalize on a voracious appetite across the country for an express commercial news service to catch press days. To cater for this need, in or about 1815 he entered into a semi-private partnership with James William Lawson, the second son of the printer of *The Times*. Under the title of Lawson and Barker (later Charles Barker, and in 1860 Charles Barker & Sons), the enterprise formed, *inter alia*, the City advertising and publicity agency for *The Times*, which had no separate advertisement department nor 'City office' until 1821.

Operating under one roof a network of interrelated activities, a basically primitive press agency run by John Joseph, father of J. W. Lawson, was refined and upgraded. Known as 'London letters', standardized parliamentary and financial newsletters were syndicated to provincial, Scottish, and even continental journals. In its earlier days, the company's output was largely compiled—by agreement—from editorial material prepared by the newspaper's staff for self-publication, supplemented by a parliamentary reporter working for Barker. In addition to regular circulars, within a sliding scale of charges, special reports were provided on notable trials, such as those of Queen Caroline and the Cato Street conspirators (both in 1820). Subscribers could also receive copies of speeches from the throne on the opening of parliament. From December 1833 letters were signed only in the name of Charles Barker, arguing dissolution of the partnership that year, although the news service continued into the 1850s.

The location of Barker's first office is uncertain, though by 1826 it was established at 12 Birchin Lane, London EC3. Using Barker's agency, commercial and financial advertising expanded through the foreign loans announcements by merchant bankers, and Barker was not slow to profit from the rampant and speculative railway promotion of the 1830s and 1840s. Three years before his death in 1859, the business moved to 8 Birchin Lane, from where between 1867 and 1874 the firm published the *Joint Stock Company's Directory* (a forerunner of the *Stock Exchange Year Book*).

Enjoying so wide a flourish of valuable contacts, the firm gradually developed advertising as its principal activity. Despite his own description, Barker has been seen as more a 'space broker' than an advertising agent. He purchased blocks of advertising space in newspapers and magazines which were then resold to individual advertisers. His numerous non-commercial and political clients included London University, George Grote, the lavish spending Royal National Institution, and, for the 1832 election, Sir Edward Knatchbull and Sir William Geary.

In contrast to the advertising middlemen who preceded him, Barker enabled those who called on his services to deal with a single expert intermediary offering a full professional service. Thus the enduring concept of an advertising agency was born and a firm still bearing his name continued to flourish in the late twentieth century in London's West End. Charles Barker suffered from heart disease and dropsy in his later years and died at his home, 1 Upper Lansdowne Terrace, Kensington, London, on 23 March 1859. He was survived by his wife, who died the following year. GORDON PHILLIPS

Sources private information (2004) • T. R. Nevett, *Advertising in Britain: a history* (1982) • M. J. Baker, ed., *Macmillan dictionary of marketing and advertising*, 2nd edn (1990) • [S. Morison and others], *The history of The Times*, 1 (1935) • *Joint Stock Company's Directory* • baptism certificate, GL, GL 20065 • burial record, Kensal Green cemetery, GL, GL 20065 • b. cert. [Montague Cochrane Barker] • b. cert. [Francis George Barker] • d. cert.

Archives GL • History of Advertising Trust, Raveningham, Norwich

Likenesses cameo, GL, Charles Barker MSS

Wealth at death under £12,000: probate, 21 May 1859, *CGPLA Eng. & Wales*

Barker, Sir Christopher (*d.* 1550), herald, was one of three sons of William Barker of Stokesley, Yorkshire, and his wife, Jane, daughter of William Carlill or Carlisle of Newcastle; there were also half-brothers and a half-sister. Christopher Carlill (*d.* 1511), Norroy king of arms, was his uncle, and another Carlill uncle was a pursuivant.

Barker started his heraldic career in the private service of Sir Charles Brandon, being made Lisle pursuivant in 1513 soon after Brandon's creation as Viscount Lisle, and Suffolk herald in 1517 following Brandon's creation as duke of Suffolk; he is known to have been with Brandon in France in 1514 and 1515. On 1 November 1522 he entered royal service as Richmond herald. In 1525 he was attached to an embassy to Spain, for which his private notebook survives. Sir Richard Wingfield, one of the ambassadors, died in Toledo, and Barker helped solemnize the funeral. In 1529 he was at the peace talks leading to the treaty of Cambrai, and in 1530 he accompanied Thomas Boleyn, earl of Wiltshire, to Italy. In June 1536 Barker became Norroy king of arms, and was promoted swiftly to Garter king of arms on 15 July on the death of Thomas Wall. A herald accused of treason in 1538 brought up the rumour that Barker had given Cromwell a great reward to be made Norroy, but an earlier confidential assessment was that the new Garter was a 'much honester man than the last was' (*LP Henry VIII*, 12/1, no. 1039).

As Garter Barker helped organize and took part in domestic ceremonies like the baptism of Prince Edward and the funeral of Queen Jane Seymour in 1537, the arrival of Anne of Cleves in 1540, the proclamation of Henry VIII as king of Ireland in 1541, and the funeral of Henry and the coronation of Edward, at which he was made a knight of the Bath, in 1547. With Henry's return to war in the 1540s, Barker was sent abroad again. In 1543 he joined up with the imperial herald Toison d'Or at Calais with the intention of gaining an audience with François I, who, however, would not play ball. When Henry finally invaded France in person in 1544, Barker had a prominent place in front of the king's banner. Shortly before Henry's death Barker's evidence was crucial when Henry Howard, earl of Surrey, was condemned to death for quartering his arms with those of Edward the Confessor.

Barker seems usually to have been on relaxed terms with peers, soliciting wine or venison from them. In 1539 an agreement defining his position put an end for the time being to the squabbles between Garter and the provincial kings of arms, which had sucked in the other heralds. This peace, and Barker's contacts at court, were probably the reasons for the exemption from taxation granted to the heralds in 1549, which paved the way for their second charter of incorporation in 1555.

Barker's miniature portrait is to be found in the initials of some of his grants of arms. He married three times. His first wife was Margaret (*d.* 1521), widow of John Longe and previously of John Garret, and daughter of Robert Spechley of Worcestershire. His second wife was Ellen (*d.* after 1544), widow of Henry Rigby and daughter of Richard Dalton of Croston, Lancashire. With Ellen he had two sons who predeceased him; one of them, Justinian, died in Spain in 1543 as Rouge Croix pursuivant. A nephew, Laurence Dalton (*d.* 1561), became Norroy king of arms, and a Dalton kinsman, William Colbarne (*d.* 1567), mentioned in Barker's will, became York herald. Barker's third wife was Edith, widow of Robert Legge and previously of Robert Colwell, and daughter of John Boys of Nonington, Kent.

According to his will Barker had a 'mansion house' in Paternoster Row, London, where chapters of the heralds were sometimes held, and he had another substantial house in Wanstead, Essex. In 1521 he joined the Vintners' Company, of which he was master from 1540 to 1543. Recorded as lying sick at Christmas 1549, he died at Paternoster Row in London on 2 or 4 January 1550 and was buried in St Faith's under St Paul's; his widow survived him by about six months. His will lists considerable property in London and Essex, which eventually went to his nephew Edward. Heraldic miscellanies and other manuscripts compiled by him survive mainly at the College of Arms.

ROBERT YORKE

Sources M. Noble, *A history of the College of Arms* (1805), 137–42 • J. Anstis, ed., *The register of the most noble order of the Garter*, 1 (1724), 376–9 • officers of arms, Coll. Arms, vol. 1, fols. 226–9 • W. H. Godfrey, A. Wagner, and H. Stanford London, *The College of Arms, Queen Victoria Street* (1963) • *LP Henry VIII* • A. Wagner, *Heralds of England: a history of the office and College of Arms* (1967) • will, PRO, PROB 11/33, sig. 10 • will, PRO, PROB 11/33, sig. 20 [Edith, Lady Barker] • Coll. Arms, MS M.4, fol. 34 • L. Campbell and F. Steer, *A catalogue of manuscripts in the College of Arms collections*, 1 (1988) • A. Crawford, *A history of the Vintners' Company* (1977) • A. R. Wagner, *Heralds and heraldry in the middle ages*, 2nd edn (1956) • partition book, Coll. Arms, MS 1

Archives BL, Stowe MS 692 • BL, Harley MS 4632 • Coll. Arms, old partition book • Coll. Arms, MSS D.4 (additions), M.4, 6 *bis*, 13 *bis* (?part), and 16 *bis* (?additions); S. M. L. 19; Vincent 25 and 50 (?)

Likenesses Barker studio, portrait (in initial of grant of arms), PRO, SP 9/1(4), 1543 • J. Basire, engraving (after watercolour by Grimm, 1787), repro. in W. H. St. J. Hope, *Cowdray and Easebourne Priory in the county of Sussex* (1919), pl. XVI • S. H. Grimm, watercolour (after painting of coronation procession of Edward VI, now destroyed, 1785), S. Antiquaries, Lond.

Wealth at death owned property worth at least £140 p.a.; goods and plate worth at least £100: will, PRO, PROB 11/33, sig. 10

Barker, Christopher (1528/9–1599), printer, was born in Darr, Yorkshire, 3 miles west of Doncaster. The antiquary Roger Dodsworth reported that Barker was born in the vicarage house there, and Joseph Ames wrote in the mid-eighteenth century that he 'came of an ancient family, beinge, as I have heard, descended from Christopher Barker, knight, king at armes' (Ames, 357). Sir Christopher had also been a native of Yorkshire, and when he died in 1550 after long and influential service in the court of Henry VIII, his estate went to his nephew Edward Barker, who may have been the printer's father.

No record of Barker's early education survives, but in 1559 he was freed as a member of the London Drapers' Company by John Petyt, probably the brother or son of the printer Thomas Petyt. On 14 July 1563 he married widow Katherine Read of Islington, and the couple had at least two children, Robert (*b.* *c.*1568) and Margery. There is no evidence that Barker ever worked as a draper; instead, he entered the book trade, a field in which a number of freemen of the Drapers' Company played prominent roles. In 1569 he entered his first two books in the Stationers' register: *Morning and Evening Prayers* by Lady Elizabeth Tyrwhit (printed in 1574) and *Certen Prayers of Master Bullion* (of which no edition survives). On 28 March 1570 Barker signed a 21-year lease for part of the residence of the junior cardinal of St Paul's. This fronted on Pissing Alley in St Paul's Churchyard, the heart of the London book trade, and Barker used it as a bookshop under the sign of the Grasshopper.

In 1575 Barker published (but did not print) George Gascoigne's play *The Glass of Government*, with a punning device depicting a man stripping bark from a tree alongside the couplet:

> A Barker if ye will
> In name but not in skill.

Included among the front matter is a page of twenty-four moral precepts headed 'This worke is compiled upon these sentences following, set downe by mee C. B.' (sig.

A4r), suggesting that Barker exercised some editorial control. That same year he also published *The Book of Faulconrie or Hawking* by George Turberville and *The Noble Arte of Venerie or Hunting*, usually attributed to Turberville but actually translated by Gascoigne from J. de Fouilloux's *La venerie* (1573). For the latter volume Barker wrote a dedication to Henry Clinton, Queen Elizabeth's master of the hart hounds, in which he says that he had 'with some charge caused [this book] to be collected and translated out of sundry good authorities' and that 'my friend (the Translator)' had suggested dedicating it to Clinton (sig. B2r).

However, Barker's real interest as a publisher lay in the potentially lucrative royal printing patents. In December 1573 he was one of six stationers who paid £100 to be assignees of Francis Flower's royal patent to print books in Latin, Greek, and Hebrew. The most coveted patent was for the Bible, but the queen's printer Richard Jugge had an effective monopoly on English bibles as long as his patron Archbishop Matthew Parker was in power. Three weeks after Parker died on 17 May 1575, the Stationers' Company effectively ended Jugge's Bible monopoly and gave other stationers permission to print the officially sanctioned Bishops' Bible. At the same time Barker shrewdly went to the privy council and obtained a patent for the Geneva Bible, which had never been printed in England under Parker but which had been printed overseas by a fellow draper, Rowland Hall. However, Barker promised Jugge that he would not print anything 'hurtfull or prejudiciall' to Jugge's rights (Stationers' Company, liber A, fol. 27).

Barker quickly published an edition of the Geneva New Testament later in 1575, printed by Thomas Vautrollier since Barker had no press of his own yet. By early 1576 Barker had obtained a press and printed a new revision of the Geneva New Testament by Laurence Tomson, based on Theodore Beza's Latin translation. Tomson dedicated the translation to his employer, Sir Francis Walsingham, Elizabeth's secretary of state, and there is considerable evidence that Walsingham was Barker's patron as well. The Tomson New Testament contains a device prominently featuring the tiger's head from Walsingham's crest, which Barker was to use in many later books, and Walsingham's coat of arms also appears several times in the volume. Furthermore, in 1576 Barker leased a new shop in Paternoster Row at the sign of the Tiger's Head, where he sold his editions of the Tomson New Testament and the complete Geneva Bible. This property, which adjoined Barker's original shop on Pissing Alley, had previously been occupied by the draper–stationers Nicholas England and John Wight, and Barker occupied it until his retirement in 1588.

When Richard Jugge died in August 1577, the office of queen's printer went to Sir Thomas Wilkes. The following month Barker paid Wilkes a 'great somme' for the office, and was granted a patent which gave him exclusive rights to all English bibles, not just the Geneva Bible (Arber, *Regs. Stationers*, 1.115). Other printers objected because Barker was not a member of the Stationers' Company, but Barker successfully appealed to Walsingham and the privy council, who reaffirmed his patent against printers who were trying to violate it. On 4 June 1578 Barker was formally translated from the Drapers' Company into the Stationers' Company with the help of Walsingham, and three weeks later he was admitted to the livery of the company. That same year he printed two books by the martyrologist John Foxe which were dedicated to Walsingham (*De oliva evangelica* and *A Sermon Preached at the Christening of a Certain Jew*), and he subsequently printed many more books with ties to Walsingham. He also printed numerous propaganda pamphlets about alleged traitors captured by Walsingham's secret police, such as *A Discoverie of the Treasons Practised by F. Throckmorton* (1584).

Barker later wrote that he had invested £3000 to obtain his patent and print bibles, but this turned out to be a wise investment which made him a wealthy man. In 1579 he was granted a coat of arms (or, on a fess dancettee azure, three fleurs-de-lis of the field), and that same year he gave his home town of Darr a wooden pulpit carved with his arms and initials, which still exists there. He also donated a Bible (since lost, but described by Dodsworth in 1620) and gave money to improve the Darr church. Also in 1579, he began renting Bacon House near Foster Lane: this became the centre of his growing printing operations, and on 23 November 1585 he purchased it outright from Sir Nicholas Bacon. In 1583 Barker bought a country house in the estate of Southlea, Datchet, Buckinghamshire, conveniently close to the court at Windsor Castle. This property had previously belonged to the Benedictine priory of St Helens, but had been seized by Henry VIII at the dissolution of the monasteries.

Between 1578 and 1588 Barker played a prominent role in the affairs of the Stationers' Company, serving as lower warden in 1582–3 and upper warden in 1585–6. In late 1582, when dissatisfaction with royal patents was increasing among stationers, Barker wrote a lengthy report for Lord Burghley in which he detailed the history of the various patents. While ultimately defending the patent system, he complained that there were twenty-two printing houses in England when eight or ten would suffice, and that certain printers, particularly John Wolfe, were 'impugning and denying' the existing patents (Arber, *Regs. Stationers*, 1.144). A list taken in May 1583 shows that Barker had five presses, and another list three years later shows him with six, the most of any stationer. In January 1584, along with other patentees, Barker yielded several books to the company for the use of its poorer members.

In late 1587 Barker turned over day-to-day duties as queen's printer to his deputies, George Bishop and Ralph Newberry, and retired to his country house at Datchet. However, he successfully contrived to keep the lucrative position within his family, beginning a dynasty which would last (with some interruptions) for nearly a century. On 25 June 1589 his son Robert *Barker (*d.* 1646) was made a freeman of the Stationers' Company by patrimony, and on 8 August father and son were granted a lifetime patent as royal printers, including the right to print the Bible. In

July 1592 Robert was admitted into the livery of the Stationers' Company, and in 1593 he joined Bishop and Newberry as a deputy of his father. On 1 November 1594 Christopher Barker transferred control of Bacon House to Robert.

Barker spent the last decade of his life as patriarch of a growing extended family at Datchet. His son Robert had many children baptized there, beginning in 1590; two (Christopher and Robert) eventually became stationers, and another (Agatha) married the stationer John Legate. Barker's daughter Margery married Robert Constable and had two sons baptized at Datchet, Robert (*b.* 1590) and Francis (*b.* 1592); both were eventually apprenticed as stationers, and Francis became a well-known publisher of plays. Barker's sister Isabel also came to live at Datchet, and was buried there in 1596 next to Margery, who had also recently died. Barker himself died at Datchet on 29 November 1599 at the age of seventy, and was buried on the same day in the Datchet church. A memorial there says of him 'typographiam Anglicanam lateritiam invenit, marmoream reliquit' ('he found English printing like brickwork and left it like marble').

DAVID KATHMAN

Sources I. L. Lupton, *A history of the Geneva Bible*, 7 (1975), 44–65 · Arber, *Regs. Stationers* · *STC, 1475–1640* · J. Ames, *Typographical antiquities, being an historical account of printing in England* (1749), 357–62 · A. S. Herbert, *Historical catalogue of printed editions of the English Bible, 1525–1961* (1968) · C. G. Butterworth, *The literary lineage of the King James Bible, 1340–1611* (1941), 187–91 · R. Dodsworth, *Yorkshire church notes, 1619–1631*, ed. J. W. Clay (1904), 113 · P. W. M. Blayney, *The bookshops in Paul's Cross churchyard* (1990) · J. L. Chester and J. Foster, eds., *London marriage licences, 1521–1869* (1887), col. 76 · private information (2004) [P. W. M. Blayney] · liber A, Stationers' Company, London · monument, Datchet church, Buckinghamshire
Archives BL, petition to Lord Burghley, Lansdowne MS 48, art. 82, fols. 189–94

Barker, Cicely Mary (1895–1973), artist and writer, was born on 28 June 1895 at West Croydon, Surrey, the daughter of Walter Barker (1866–1912), a seed merchant, and his wife, Mary, *née* Oswald (1869–1960). Barker suffered from epilepsy and was a frail child, spending much of her youth housebound. She showed an early talent for drawing, encouraged by her father's talent for wood-carving, and, in 1908, enrolled in the Croydon Art Society. Her father's death in 1912 dealt a financial blow to the family. Her only sibling, Dorothy, opened a kindergarten in the Barker home, while Barker turned to drawing pictures, often using the kindergarten children as her models. From the 1920s she attended evening classes at Croydon Art School as both student and teacher. She was a devotee of the Pre-Raphaelites, particularly Edward Burne-Jones, and her work owes a debt to Beatrix Potter and Kate Greenaway.

Sir Arthur Conan Doyle's publication of *The Coming of Fairies* (1922) fed a public interest in fairies and Barker's interest in children and nature ensured that her talents were well in demand. Blackie's publication of *Flower Fairies of the Spring* (1923) was quickly followed by the other seasons. Barker's poetry was published in several magazines as well as being collected in *Old Rhymes for All Times* (1928), for which she did her own illustrations. The flowers in Barker's books are intricately drawn and botanically correct.

Barker was a devout Church of England Christian and her faith informed her works, whether religious or secular. She designed several memorial pieces, including the *Art of Great Tribulation* in the memorial chapel at Norbury Methodist Church and the reredos triptych *The Feeding of the Five Thousand* for the chapel at Llandoff House, Penarth (1929). *A Flower Fairy Alphabet* (1934) described a fairyland wherein Christian values are fundamental. Several books for children followed, the best-known being *The Lord of Rushie River* (1938), which details the adventures of a child who communicates with swans. During the Second World War Barker published *Flower Fairies of the Trees* (1940) and *Flower Fairies of the Garden* (1944). She also illustrated many texts, including R. L. Stevenson's *A Child's Garden of Verses* (1944).

Barker never married. She lived with her sister (*d.* 1954) and her mother (*d.* 1960) for most of her life. After their deaths, Barker's health deteriorated and she spent much of her time in nursing homes. She died at Storrington, Sussex, on 16 February 1973, and was buried there on 1 March. Her fairy books remain very popular and have been collected in many anthologies, while her flower and fairy paintings continue to be the focus of collectors.

STACY GILLIS

Sources S. Glyn-Jones, *Cicely Mary Barker: a Croydon artist* (1989) · J. Laing, *Cicely Mary Barker and her art* (1995) · B. Peppin and L. Micklethwaite, *Dictionary of British book illustrators: the twentieth century* (1983) · private information (2004) [family] · *CGPLA Eng. & Wales* (1973)
Archives priv. coll., papers
Likenesses photograph, priv. coll.
Wealth at death £26,006: probate, 31 May 1973, *CGPLA Eng. & Wales*

Barker, Collet (1784–1831), army officer and explorer, was born near Paradise Gardens, Hackney, Middlesex, on 31 December 1784, the son of William Barker (*c.*1748–1832), skinner and mercer of Newbury, Berkshire, and Sarah Collet (1755–1808), elder daughter of Samuel Collet, of an established family of Newbury merchants and manufacturers. Barker grew up in Newbury among his mother's family who were moderately wealthy dissenters. He was the eldest of his parents' seven children to survive.

Barker entered the army in January 1806 as an ensign in the 39th regiment. He was promoted lieutenant in 1809 and captain in 1825. He served in Sicily in 1807–11 and in the Peninsular War in Spain, in North America, and in France; subsequently he was stationed in Ireland, until in 1828 he sailed with his regiment for Australia. On his arrival in June he was appointed commandant of the settlement of Fort Wellington on Raffles Bay on the north coast, established in the hope of opening up trade with the Indian archipelago through the medium of the Malays. When Barker arrived on 13 September he found the convicts sent there full of complaints about the hostility of the Aborigines and the unhealthiness of the climate. Scurvy was very prevalent, but, by planting trees and vegetables, he restored the health of the community, and his just treatment of the Aborigines allayed their animosity. In the face of opposition he insisted on forbearance and humanity on the part of his men, and by trusting himself alone into the hands of the Aborigines and giving them other proofs of his goodwill he won great influence among them.

Unfortunately, before the news of Barker's success could reach the colonial government, it had ordered the abandonment of the settlement and Barker was appointed to the penal settlement at King George Sound on the south-west coast. He administered his new settlement with the same success as he had the first, but the penal station was closed, in March 1831, soon after his arrival. Governor Darling then appointed him resident in North Island, New Zealand, thinking him well suited to address problems with the Maori, but asked him, *en route* for Sydney, to search for a communication between Gulf St Vincent and Lake Alexandrina which Sturt had discovered the previous year. With three companions Barker examined the eastern coast of the gulf, ascended Mount Lofty, viewed the range to the east (named after him Mount Barker), and saw the plains upon which Adelaide was later established. On 21 April they found the Murray mouth and, since the others could not swim, Barker swam across alone to make some observations. But on 30 April he encountered some Aborigines at New Encounter Bay who speared him to death in revenge for ill treatment suffered at the hands of Europeans.

Barker was a successful administrator and explorer but he deserves chiefly to be remembered for his patient humanity towards Aborigines and for the success of his policy. Charles Sturt described him as honourable and just in private life, adding that he was 'in disposition, as he was in the close of his life, in many respects similar to Captain Cook' (Sturt, 1.243): like Captain Cook he suffered for the sins of others.

RONALD BAYNE, *rev.* ELIZABETH BAIGENT

Sources *Commandant of solitude: the journals of Captain Collet Barker, 1828–1831*, ed. D. J. Mulvaney and N. Green (1992) · A. Price, 'The work of Capt. Collet Barker in South Australia', *Proceedings of the Royal Geographical Society of Australasia, South Australian Branch*, 26 (1924–5), 52–66 · C. Sturt, *Two expeditions into the interior of southern Australia, during the years 1828, 1829, 1830 and 1831*, 2 vols. (1833) · private information (1885) · J. Back, 'Barker, Collet', *AusDB*, 1.57 and corrigenda · D. J. Mulvaney, *Search for Collet Barker of Raffles Bay* (1994) · [F. Watson], ed., *Historical records of Australia*, 3rd ser., 6 (1923)

Archives Dorset RO, copy journal · Mitchell L., NSW · State Archives of New South Wales, Sydney, journals

Wealth at death see will, Mulvaney, *Search for Collet Barker*

Barker, Edmund (*b.* 1720/21), physician, studied medicine at the University of Leiden, taking his doctor's degree in 1747, and set up as a physician in London. In the winter of 1749 Dr Johnson, as yet little known, established the Ivy Lane club, which met weekly at the King's Head in Ivy Lane near St Paul's; Barker was introduced to this conversational society by a fellow student, Samuel Dyer. Another member, Sir John Hawkins, in his *Life of Johnson* (1787), describes Barker as a dissenter by education, a Unitarian by religious profession, and a disciple of Lord Shaftesbury in philosophy. According to Hawkins, Barker was an acute reasoner on ethics, a deep metaphysician, an excellent classical scholar, and he read the Italian poets. He was, however, 'a thoughtless young man', and dressed in a 'full suit, brown tye-wig with a knot over one shoulder, and a long yellow-hilted sword … he was a caricature [and] succeeded ill in his profession' (Hawkins, 233–4). Hawkins says that Johnson so often snubbed Barker for his unitarianism that the latter's visits to the club became less and less frequent and that after leaving the Ivy Lane club, Barker went to practise at Trowbridge, Wiltshire. He returned to London two years later.

Barker became beadle and library-keeper to the College of Physicians from 1760 to 1771, at a salary of about £50 a year plus his board and lodging. He was a lay servant of the college, and was always referred to there as 'Mr'; the degree MD was never used in college records. Barker did his job well, and three months after he had left the college in 1771 he was given a Christmas present of coal, an unexpected present to give to a physician.

Edmund Barker translated from Latin into English L. Heister's *A Compendium of the Practice of Physic* (1757). He also translated from English into French the third part of George Edwards's *Gleanings of Natural History/Glanures de l'histoire naturelle* (1764), which is printed in parallel columns in both languages. Barker is described on the title page as *bibliothecaire* (librarian) and the author of the work, but not as MD. No obituary notice of him has been found in contemporary medical journals or in the *Gentleman's Magazine*.

J. M. SCOTT, *rev.* JEAN LOUDON

Sources A. S. Mason, 'Barker the odd bedell', *Journal of the Royal College of Physicians of London*, 31 (1997), 103–6 · R. W. Innes Smith, *English-speaking students of medicine at the University of Leyden* (1932) · J. Hawkins, *The life of Samuel Johnson, LL.D.* (1787) · annals, RCP Lond., vols. 11–14 · J. Boswell, *The life of Samuel Johnson*, 2 vols. (1791) · G. Edwards, *Gleanings of natural history*, 3 vols. (1758–64), vol. 3

Barker, Edmund Henry (1788–1839), classical scholar and editor, was born at Hollym vicarage, in the East Riding of Yorkshire, on 22 December 1788, the eldest son of Robert Barker (1750–1816), vicar of Hollym-with-Withernsea, and his wife, Ann, *née* Atkinson (*d.* 1829). After receiving his schooling at Beverley grammar school, he matriculated at Trinity College, Cambridge, on 25 September 1807 as a pensioner, and became a scholar of the college in the following year. In 1809 he gained the Chancellor's and Browne medals for Greek and Latin epigrams. Religious scruples may have prevented his taking a degree, but he did not in any case take the university examinations, which were largely mathematical. For several years (*c.*1810–1815) he lived in Samuel Parr's vicarage at Hatton, Warwickshire, where he acted as Parr's amanuensis and catalogued his library. While there Barker published a volume of essays, *Classical Recreations Interspersed with Biblical Criticisms* (1812). After Parr's death in 1825 he collected a mass of information and recollection about him which appeared in 1828 (*Parriana*, 2 vols.). A similarly sprawling collection on Richard Porson was published posthumously (*Literary Anecdotes and Contemporary Reminiscences of Professor Porson*, 2 vols., 1852). On 14 September 1814 Barker married Frances Sarah (*fl.* *c.*1790–1840), daughter of John Manley of the Inner Temple; they had been introduced by Parr, who officiated at their wedding in Thetford, Norfolk. Here they set up house, and here three children were born, of whom two, both daughters, survived.

Barker had already begun to contribute to the *Classical Journal* (1810–29) of Abraham Valpy, which he went on to edit. Later issues contained criticisms of his contributions, followed by triumphant refutations: both written by himself. This work led to his edition of Henri Estienne's *Thesaurus Graecus* (1816–28), also published by Valpy, which attracted more than 1000 subscribers. Both enterprises drew criticism from the Cambridge classical scholars J. H. Monk and C. J. Blomfield, who edited the rival *Museum Criticum* (1813–26). Blomfield's review of the *Thesaurus* (*Quarterly Review*, 22, 1820, 302–48) pointed out that Barker was inserting so much additional miscellaneous matter that its subscribers would have to wait fifty-five years for its completion. This led to the disappearance of Barker's name from the title-page and the curtailment of his contributions. His infuriated reply, *Aristarchus Anti-Blomfieldianus*, was in effect circulated by his opponent, being bound up, together with advertisements, with a later number of the *Quarterly Review*. In 1822 he issued an appeal for assistance for the cause of Greek independence, which he also supported by working for the establishment of county committees; in 1827–8 five pamphlets argued against the identification of Junius with Sir Philip Francis.

Barker's tendency to inflate his publications with masses of irrelevant information, evident in the *Thesaurus Graecus*, was also manifested in his editions of John Lempriere's *Classical Dictionary* (1828) and of Webster's *American Dictionary of the English Language* (1831–2). In both cases Barker initiated and pursued collaborations with American scholars: in the former case with Charles Anthon of Columbia University, in the latter with Noah Webster himself. The Lempriere grew over-large, as had the Greek thesaurus, and its second half was similarly, and incongruously, cut down. Comparing the original, Anthon's American edition, and Barker's re-editing of Anthon, a reviewer concluded that 'the original edition is the worst book we ever met with; … Mr Anthon's, with all its improvements, is bad enough; … Mr Barker's is considerably worse than Mr Anthon's' (*Quarterly Journal of Education*, 1, 1831, 321). As Barker was aware, Lempriere's original text was full of errors, but had the advantage of being out of copyright. Several of Barker's publications described him on their title-pages as O.T.N., a mysterious qualification which might have suggested an academic degree, rather like S.T.P. (Sanctae Theologiae Professor, that is, DD). In fact, it stood for 'Of Thetford, Norfolk'. His several editions of classical authors were notable for including explanatory matter in English, rather than in Latin, as was then usual. His works included a Greek–English dictionary, in which his co-editor was George Dunbar of the University of Edinburgh (1831), and the *editio princeps* of a Greek grammatical treatise ascribed to Arcadius (1820).

At first Barker's affairs prospered, helped by his wife's independent income, and he built up a large library. Soon, however, his eternal optimism and lack of judgement led him into debt. A lawsuit to establish his father's legitimacy, which had been doubted, was successful, but a subsequent claim to family estates at Potternewton failed. Barker's attempts to gain the posts of headmaster of Stamford School (1833) and professor of Latin (1827) and registrar (1838) of the University of London were all unsuccessful. In 1836 he petitioned the House of Commons, in vain, to be allowed to catalogue the classical books in the British Museum Library on a new plan of his own which combined chronological, author, and subject listings. In the previous year, having been forced to sell his library, he had left his wife and family and moved to lodgings in London. In May 1837, after some time in a sponging-shop, he was committed to the Fleet prison as a bankrupt. His appeals for money during his ten months there brought in several hundred pounds, but after his release he fell into the hands of swindlers and, incorrigibly gullible as ever, lost everything he had gained. On 21 March 1839 he was found dead in his Covent Garden lodgings, 12 Tavistock Row, where he had been living under a false name to evade his creditors. He was buried at St Andrew's, Holborn, on 26 March. The costs were borne by John Giles, who with other friends, including George Burges and Alexander Dyce, intended to erect an inscribed tablet over his grave; the fees due to the incumbent of the parish prevented this, and it remains unmarked. Dyce, however, tells us that it is 'about thirty feet in front of the north-wall of the church' (Dyce, 'Memoir', xlv).

Barker had talent as a classical scholar, but many of his scholarly enterprises were vitiated by his weakness of judgement. He could not bear to leave out anything he knew on a topic, and was prone to overload his publications with excursuses and appendices of great length. He once claimed that the three years he devoted to making the index to the *Thesaurus Graecus* were the happiest of his life. His financial judgement was little better. His correspondence with Anthon and Webster shows that he was well aware of the dangers of copyright and of competition; but he was continually throwing his own money—often more than he had—into risky ventures. In the end, his naïve optimism and gullibility combined to ruin him.

CHRISTOPHER STRAY

Sources [A. Dyce], 'Memoir of E. H. Barker', *Literary anecdotes*, 1 (1852), ix–xlvi · *DNB* · W. C. Boulter, 'Edmund Henry Barker', *N&Q*, 6th ser., 12 (1885), 442–5 · B. [George Burges], *GM*, 2nd ser., 11 (1839), 543–7 · *Reminiscences of Alexander Dyce*, ed. R. J. Schrader (1972), 139–43 · A. Blomfield, *A memoir of Charles James Blomfield, with selections from his correspondence*, 1 (1863), 27–36 · d. cert.

Archives Bodl. Oxf., corresp., MSS 1003–1006 · John Murray, London, archives, letters | BL, MSS, letters to S. Butler · BL, corresp. with J. Craddock, Add. MS 52285, *passim* · Col. U., letters to Charles Anthon · Linn. Soc., corresp. with Sir James E. Smith · NYPL, letters to Webster · Trinity Cam., letters to Dawson Turner · U. Cal., Berkeley, letters to M. J. Routh

Barker, Sir Ernest (1874–1960), political theorist, was born on 23 September 1874 at Heald Cottage, Woodley, Cheshire, the eldest of the seven children of George Barker, a

Sir Ernest Barker (1874–1960), by Elliott & Fry, 1939

miner turned farm labourer, and his wife, Elizabeth Pollitt. The family home was a small cottage on the farm of his maternal grandparents close to the Cheshire–Derbyshire border. He owed his academic success first and foremost to his mother, who was determined that her eldest child should become a scholar. But at the village school he was fortunate also in serving as a 'pacemaker' for the son of a local businessman who was working for a scholarship to the Manchester grammar school. In the event, Barker won the scholarship and began ascending one of few educational ladders to Oxford then available (first as classical scholar at Balliol in 1893, then as a Craven scholar in 1895, and as Jenkyns exhibitioner in 1897).

The firm, classical basis of Barker's education that had been laid at Manchester grammar school was well sustained at Oxford. But following firsts in classical moderations (1895) and in *literae humaniores* ('Greats') (1897), and undecided about his future, he read for the school of modern history. Under the guidance of the master of Balliol, A. L. Smith, he secured a first in 1898. Abandoning tentative thoughts of entering the civil service, Barker embarked upon a career of teaching and scholarship in which classics and history were never clearly demarcated. He combined a seven-year prize fellowship at Merton College, Oxford, from 1898 to 1905 with a lectureship in modern history at Wadham College from 1899 to 1909 and a tutorship for the non-collegiate students from 1899 to 1913. Although he was subsequently elected to fellowships in modern history at other Oxford colleges—St John's (1909–13) and New College (1913–20)—his classical learning continued to stimulate other scholarly interests. In this he was not untypical of contemporary Oxford dons. Indeed—as Barker himself commented in his autobiography, *Age and Youth*—'Greats' constituted 'something of a *lingua franca* and a common *esprit de corps*' across the different faculties (Barker, 17).

During this formative period of his life Barker married on 26 July 1900 Emily Isabel Salkeld (*d.* 1924), sister of a friend from Manchester grammar school and daughter of Richard Salkeld, the vicar of St Mark's, Dukinfield; there were two daughters and one son. The latter, Arthur Ernest Barker (1901–1989), was a foreign correspondent for *The Times* until joining the BBC in 1938. Barker's elder daughter, Margaret, married the painter John Mansbridge, son of the adult education pioneer Albert Mansbridge; his younger daughter, Elisabeth Barker (1910–1986), was a diplomatic correspondent for Reuters and writer on eastern European affairs. A research fund administered by the British Academy commemorates her achievements.

Development of his political thought Barker used ancient Greece as a sounding-board for his ideals of, and beliefs about, the modern world in his first book, *The Political Thought of Plato and Aristotle* (1906). This work analysed the writings of Plato and Aristotle from the perspective of a liberal concerned to uphold the twin values of personal liberty and government based upon the rule of law, while recognizing the integral role of society to the development of individuality. Here two streams of thought—those of whig liberalism and philosophical idealism—competed for Barker's political sympathies. However, he could neither accept the negative attitude towards the state that came to characterize a Liberal like Dicey with links to whiggism, nor embrace wholeheartedly the identity of state and society which characterized idealism in its less guarded moments. In his preface Barker acknowledged a substantial debt to T. H. Green, whose conception of the conformity of the ideal with the reality of the state was notoriously qualified. Green's understanding of the state as inherently less than perfect was important in shaping Barker's judgement of the respective merits of Plato and Aristotle's political ideas: while Plato was chided for the 'zeal' with which he pursued the notion of the state as the embodiment of reason and unity in society, Aristotle was praised for the more relaxed and flexible view that the state was merely 'the supreme association and the dominant end' (p. 228).

But further influences were at work too, not least a conception of English national character—a touchstone that was to become increasingly pronounced in Barker's political thought: he remarked that while there was 'something French in Plato's mind, something of that pushing of a principle to its logical extremes', in Aristotle's thought 'it hardly seems fanciful to detect more of an English spirit of compromise' (*The Political Thought of Plato and Aristotle*, 162). Also, when Barker emphasized Aristotle's awareness that the state co-existed with other communities, that a precondition of unity was diversity (ibid., 233), his receptiveness to the rising tide of pluralist thought is equally apparent. A deep impression had been made upon him by the legal historian F. W. Maitland, who introduced the pluralist ideas of the German jurist Otto von Gierke to an English readership in 1900. In 1897 he had heard Maitland deliver the Ford lectures, 'Township and borough', at Oxford, which he later recalled as a formative experience (Barker, 330).

This synthesis of the ideas of idealism, whiggism, and pluralism characterized and informed Barker's thought in the decades to come. It was never an entirely stable and coherent synthesis: the balance he attempted to strike between individuals, voluntary societies, and the state was uneven, and at various times in his life he tended to favour one at the expense of another. Early on in his career, he was strongly drawn towards pluralism, although even then his support was never unreserved. Later, however, his allegiances shifted more towards sovereign authority (see his preface to the American edition of *Church, State, and Education*, 1957). A critical factor here was the clear demonstration in the inter-war period that groups can develop malignant tendencies, belying the 'clubbable' side of associational life to which Maitland had warmed. When Barker turned to a translation of a further instalment of Gierke's *Genossenschaftsrecht*—published as *Natural Law and the Theory of Society* in 1934—his introduction was more sombre than Maitland's of some three decades earlier. Greatly disquieted by the 'upsurge' of groups in continental Europe, he warned of the dangers of the Romantic legacy in the theory of groups, a legacy whose full implications were currently being drawn out in Germany (*Natural Law and the Theory of Society*, xvii). But Romanticism was not only implicated in the ascendancy of racial exclusiveness in Germany: its spirit could also be detected in the dominance of nation in Italy and class in Russia (*Reflections on Government*, 1942, 160, 163). Barker defended the *regnum* with new zest against these tendencies, not least out of a deep concern for individual liberty and the never more evident threat posed to it by the assignment of 'real personality' to groups. He was drawn to the emphasis which Maitland gave to the associational instinct in British life, and also the stroke of genius by which the English system of equity had created trusts as diverse as churches, trade unions, Lloyd's Coffee House, the Jockey Club, and London clubs. The trust had allowed groups a considerable degree of latitude denied to them in Germany, where the odious 'concession' theory of groups prevailed under Roman law. However, Barker himself was wary of groups and their capacity to browbeat both members and non-members alike. While he gave all the groups and institutions to which he belonged his full commitment, he readily confessed in his autobiography to an entrenched aversion to 'Institutionalism' (Barker, 304).

Students and religion Barker's two decades as a member of the Oxford modern history faculty were fruitful for him as both a teacher and a writer. He taught students as diverse as Harold Laski—who became professor of political science at the London School of Economics in 1925—and the Christian sociologist Maurice Reckitt. He kept his distance from the political and religious views of both writers, while recognizing their talents and enjoying their acclaim. He also taught T. E. Lawrence and his brother Will. But he seems to have been most stimulated by the pupils he taught from the Roman Catholic religious orders, which were beginning to re-establish themselves at Oxford at the end of the nineteenth century. He seems to have particularly enjoyed the company of the Benedictines, and through his pupils he established lasting links with two major Benedictine schools in England: Ampleforth and Douai. He also taught pupils who became leading Catholic writers and journalists: for example, Christopher Dawson, Douglas Jerrold, and Douglas Woodruff. While he seems never to have considered becoming a Catholic himself, he did convert from the Congregationalism in which he had been brought up to Anglicanism just before he left Oxford in 1920. His Congregational background at the Hatherlow Chapel near his home had steeled him against the agnosticism which he found widespread at Balliol as an undergraduate (Barker, 301). But he did not conceive of his embrace of Anglicanism as a break with Congregationalism, nor as distancing himself from Catholic orders in England like the Benedictines (ibid., 53). Indeed, he valued organized religion in all its diversity, and in particular its capacity to enrich national life, not least English national life, and to be enriched in turn.

First World War: nationalism and patriotism For the most part, Barker carried on teaching at Oxford during the First World War, drawn away only temporarily in order to, among other duties, inspect factories and works committees in the north of England for the Ministry of Labour. But he was by no means a passive bystander: a master of crisp and direct as well as erudite prose, he wrote solemn and persuasive defences of Britain's role in the war for popular audiences. With other history dons at Oxford, he contributed to a book entitled *Why we Are at War* (1914) and also wrote a series of articles in *The Times* which were brought together in *Mothers and Sons in Wartime* (1915). He deplored what he regarded as 'the worship of power' in modern Germany, made evident in the actions of statesmen like Bismarck and in the ideas of philosophers such as Nietzsche and Treitschke alike. In other pamphlets he contrasted favourably British with German policy towards its constituent nations, noting in particular German repression of its linguistic minorities and British tolerance of the Irish language. Indeed, the war did much to crystallize his ideas on nationalism as a force for tyranny and instability. Far better, he argued in a journal article of 1919, to love one's neighbour than one's fellow national: neighbourliness was a 'quiet' virtue, yet 'deep and permeating' for all that ('Nationality', *History*, Oct 1919, 144). This was—in effect—a call for the elevation of patriotism over nationalism.

Translating this principle into the problem of Ireland, Barker supported home rule but not independence. He rejected moves to bestow dominion status on Ireland in 1921, proclaiming to A. D. Lindsay that he believed in 'the state rather than the nation' (Stapleton, *Englishness*, 97). None the less, while he stressed the priority of statehood over nationhood, and patriotism over nationalism, his unfailing loyalty to Britain was to the recognizably English symbols and institutions through which British identity was principally focused. This was not least because he conceived of England as a model of national inclusiveness—a cardinal theme of the Stevenson lectures he gave in Glasgow, which were published as *National Character and the Factors in its Formation* in 1927 (see esp. p. 194).

King's College, London The Stevenson lectures were the fruit of one of the few pieces of research Barker was able to undertake during his time as principal at King's College, London, from 1920 to 1927. He had not been able to resist the challenge of administration, an appetite for which had grown steadily upon him at Oxford. Also, he had developed London connections through his membership of the group formed around the periodical the *New Europe*—an offshoot of the Round Table movement—and spearheaded by such specialists in eastern European nationalism as R. W. Seton-Watson. At King's he enjoyed the stimulation of a notable academic community, and also forged ties with some of London's leading men of affairs. He did not feel at all disadvantaged by his working-class roots, as he was certain he would have done if he had become head of an Oxford college; in 1924 he was approached on several fronts concerning the forthcoming vacancy of the wardenship of New College (Barker to Julian Huxley, 8 Nov 1924, Huxley MSS, Rice University). In London he was also well placed to become involved in government. For example, he was recruited to the Hadow committee, which produced the report *The Education of the Adolescent* in 1927. Barker believed fervently in the importance of public provision for practical secondary education, this being in keeping with what he perceived as the active and 'practical' nature of 'the English genius'. He insisted, however, that an education in practical things could be a liberal education, and as chairman of the drafting committee he would have been responsible for emphasizing the need for parity between the two streams of grammar and secondary modern schools.

There were difficult times as well, particularly those which stretched Barker's capacity to deal with conflict. One such episode was the controversy over the Koraes chair in modern Greek, a post that had been funded partially by the Greek government but which threw the college into crisis as the first incumbent, Arnold Toynbee, denounced Greek atrocities in Anatolia. He was also greatly disconcerted by the short skirts of female students at King's (Catlin, 344–5). However, Barker was certainly not opposed to greater opportunities for women, despite cautioning against attempts to ground those opportunities in logic and individualism. (See his 'History and the position of women' in Z. Fairfield, ed., *Some Aspects of the Woman's Movement*, 1915, 44–6.) As principal he did all he could to secure employment for young women such as May Wedderburn Cannan whose lives had been devastated by the First World War (see Wedderburn Cannan, 172–5). His time at King's was overshadowed by the death of his first wife in 1924.

Cambridge It was with some sense of relief from the burdens of administrative office that Barker accepted in 1927 the offer of the newly established chair of political science at Cambridge, funded by the Rockefeller Foundation. It was only the third such chair in Britain. He had married again earlier that year, on 24 March. His new wife was Olivia Stuart Horner (1891–1976), daughter of John Stuart Horner, a Balliol man and director of an engineering firm; they had one son (Nicolas John; *b.* 1932) and one daughter (Sara Juliet; *b.* 1934). While his eleven-year tenure of the chair was not notable for its wealth of publication, he laid the foundations for the long and productive retirement which followed. He became a fellow of Peterhouse and member of the Cambridge history faculty, which he chaired in the last three years before his retirement. He was charged with teaching the two political science papers which had been instituted by Sir John Seeley in the historical tripos. It was on the basis of the lectures that he had given for these courses, as well as those which he delivered as a visiting lecturer at other universities, that he published two widely used texts in post-war political studies, *Reflections on Government* (1942) and *Principles of Social and Political Theory* (1951). These books and other writings were also inspired by his work for the National Council of Social Service, through which he became the chairman of a committee which sought to enhance the provision of community centres on the new housing estates of inter-war Britain. This task seemed ripe for the application of pluralist ideals of voluntary association and Aristotle's notion of the optimum conditions of the good social life. His tenure of the Cambridge chair, and the writings that arose out of it subsequently, was enriched too by the generous opportunities for travel abroad that it afforded. While he did not take full advantage of the one term off in every three to which he was entitled, he nevertheless travelled extensively in Europe, America, and India.

Critic of political extremism First-hand experience of the fascist turn in the politics of continental Europe made a particularly deep impression on Barker (Barker, 173). It helped to consolidate his ideas about the 'eruption of the group' and consequent 'militarization of the conception of the political' that constituted a unique contribution to political theory in the second quarter of the twentieth century (*Reflections on Government*, 142, 271). He was one of few people in Britain to appreciate the force of the 'friend–foe' analysis of politics of the Nazi political theorist Carl Schmitt. He easily straddled the institutional–theoretical divide in political science through his studies of extremist political systems in inter-war Europe. These he contrasted with the democratic and legal institutions of Britain, in particular, the characteristics of which acquired new poignancy when set against the disturbing features of continental politics. In this sense, Barker's own doubts and those of others, notably his earlier memoirist George Catlin (see the entry he wrote for the *Dictionary of National Biography*, and obituary in *PBA*), about his success in forging new paths for the discipline of politics were misplaced. Through deploying the traditional approaches of philosophy and history, he shed considerable light on contemporary political life.

Barker continued to assail Nazi, fascist, and Soviet dictatorship, and the ideologies which sustained them, throughout the 1930s. He exposed the evils of Nazism and Nazi propaganda—for example, reproducing a Nazi school history textbook covering the period 1914 to 1933 for the Friends of Europe publications in 1933. He contrasted modern dictatorship with the dictatorships of ancient Rome in a lecture at Chatham House in 1934 ('The prospects for democracy', published in *The Citizen's Choice*, 1937). And he made trenchant criticisms of Marxism in the editorial he wrote for *The Times* on the fiftieth anniversary of Marx's death (14 March 1933). Nevertheless, Barker vociferously supported Chamberlain on appeasement, defending his 'realism' against the 'Johnny Head-in-the-Air' attitude towards Germany of those—not least, fellow Liberals like Gilbert Murray—who protested (letter to *The Times*, 6 March 1939). Throughout the 1930s he grew increasingly disenchanted with the Liberal Party, which had hitherto provided his principal political anchorage, disliking its tendency towards what he called 'abstract intellectualism'. Indeed, so much was this the case that, like a fellow 'old' Liberal, G. M. Trevelyan, he gravitated towards the Conservative historian and activist Arthur Bryant. He never gave up on Liberalism, however, and became a trenchant critic of the 'progressivism' that issued in the post-war Labour government's penchant for planning (*Change and Continuity*, 1949).

Retirement Barker's retirement coincided with the outbreak of the Second World War. He was immediately recruited as director of studies for the courses in military and political studies which the War Office had established for selected officers, and which ran at Cambridge until 1941. As in the First World War, he also served his country through the pen, producing patriotic pamphlets for both the Ministry of Information at home and the British Council abroad. He worked closely with other scholars on more extended projects, editing, for example, *The Character of England* for Oxford University Press, which appeared in 1947. But he served the allied cause more widely through work which enhanced his European consciousness. He became chairman of the Books Commission established by the allied ministers of education in 1943. The commission's chief function was to provide a centre for the collection of books and periodicals and their dispersal to libraries in allied countries whose stock had been destroyed by bombing. For this work he was knighted in 1944.

Barker's new European horizons arising out of the war led to his editorship, with Paul Vaucher and George Clark, of *The European Inheritance* (1954). This work is significant in another respect. For despite Barker's concern to keep up his credentials as a 'publicist', which he had acquired at Oxford at the end of the nineteenth century (Barker, 183), he produced a steady stream of scholarly writings throughout his retirement. A sense of scholarly duty led him to accept an invitation to lecture on political science from an English point of view at the University of Cologne in the winter of 1947–8, a difficult although not unrewarding experience for a 73-year-old. The gratitude of the German government was made clear in the attendance of a representative of the German ambassador at the memorial service which was held for him at Peterhouse just after his death (see *The Times*, 27 Feb 1960, 12). The last four years of his life saw the publication of his histories of political thought through translated documents which spanned the Hellenic and patristic worlds and Byzantium, *From Alexander to Constantine* (1956) and *Social and Political Thought in Byzantium* (1957). He was also a founder member of the Political Studies Association of Great Britain (1950). His autobiography appeared in 1953.

Barker was elected a fellow of the British Academy in 1947. He was awarded the degree of DLitt at Oxford (1922) and (*ad eundem*) Cambridge (1928); honorary doctorates were conferred on him by the universities of Edinburgh, Harvard, Calcutta, Dalhousie (Canada), and Salonica. His foreign distinctions included membership of the order of the White Lion (Czechoslovakia) and the King Haakon VII liberty cross (Norway).

Tall and lanky in appearance, Barker never lost his broad Manchester accent. He was the subject of many anecdotes, nearly all of them affectionate and appreciative. He was a gifted and conscientious lecturer and tutor. Contemporaries remarked upon his frankness, naïve curiosity, acuteness, integrity, and sometimes unexpected perverseness (*The Times*, 13a). He was hailed, however, as an exemplary citizen–scholar for whom no service to the cause of greater intellectual and political understanding could be too much trouble. He died in the Evelyn Nursing Home, Cambridge, on 17 February 1960; he was cremated, and his ashes were buried on 25 March 1961 in St Botolph's churchyard, Cambridge.

Barker's posthumous reputation Barker's work plunged into a period of relative obscurity soon after his death. His ideas about democracy—particularly the centrality to it of discussion—enjoyed some prominence with the retreat from positivism in political science during the 1970s (Holden, 118). However, interest in his work on a more concerted and wide-ranging scale began to pick up in the 1990s. This interest was fuelled by the revival of pluralism and ideas of civil association as the statism and class polarization of the post-war decades began to recede. Barker's writings seemed to strike relevant chords here. As well as becoming the subject of a full-scale study (Stapleton, *Englishness*), Barker's interest in the relationship between church, state, and nationality was explored alongside that of other leading churchmen like William Temple (Grimley). In 1997 his contribution to pluralist thought received its most extended and nuanced exploration yet (Runciman). In addition, Barker began to attract attention as an exponent of civic nationalism more in keeping with the devolutionist times than the alternative 'ethnic' model (Kearney; Aughey). Furthermore, work on Barker has also featured in studies of intellectuals in the twentieth century (Jennings). The interest and sympathy that Barker has generated in the late twentieth and early twenty-first centuries draws much on his sense of the importance of diversity to unity in society and of community to individuality; the close integration of religion and culture; and the model he provided of the citizen-scholar. But he would have been the last to claim that he had resolved any of these antinomies. The basis of his thought lay in a conception of the irreducible nature of human personality and the overriding priority of individual liberty.

JULIA STAPLETON

Sources E. Barker, *Age and youth* (1953) · J. Stapleton, *Englishness and the study of politics: the social and political thought of Ernest Barker* (1994) · J. Stapleton, *Political intellectuals and public identities in Britain since 1850* (2001) · *The Times* (19 Feb 1960) · M. Grimley, 'Citizenship, community, and the Church of England: Anglican theories of the state, *c*.1926–1939', DPhil diss., U. Oxf., 1998 · D. Runciman, *Pluralism and the personality of the state* (1997) · H. Kearney, 'The importance of being British', *Political Quarterly*, 71/1 (2000), 15–25 · B. Holden, *The nature of democracy* (1974) · J. Jennings, 'Intellectuals and political culture', *European Legacy*, 5/6 (2000), 781–94 · G. E. G. Catlin, *PBA*, 46 (1960), 342–51 · M. Wedderburn Cannan, *Grey ghosts and voices* (1976) · U. Hull, Brynmor Jones L., Laski papers · M. B. Reckitt papers, U. Sussex · Burke, *Peerage* (1959) · I. Elliott, ed., *The Balliol College register, 1900–1950*, 3rd edn (privately printed, Oxford, 1953) · *DNB* · *CGPLA Eng. & Wales* (1960) · E. Barker, corresp., priv. coll. · *Church and state*, Church Assembly (1935), 75 · A. Aughey, *Nationalism, devolution and the challenge to the United Kingdom state* (2001) · b. cert.

Archives Peterhouse, Cambridge, papers, revised proofs of articles, unpublished article, notes for lectures, and notes on other topics | BL, corresp. with W. J. Ashley and reports on conferences, Add. MS 42250 · BLPES, letters to Sir William Beveridge · Bodl. Oxf., corresp. with Clement Attlee · Bodl. Oxf., corresp. with Lionel Curtis · Bodl. Oxf., letters to H. A. L. Fisher · Bodl. Oxf., letters to J. L. Hammond · Bodl. Oxf., letters to Francis Marvin · Bodl. Oxf., corresp. with Gilbert Murray · Bodl. Oxf., letters to J. L. Myres · Bodl. Oxf., letters to Lord Simon · Bodl. Oxf., letters to Alfred Zimmern · ICL, corresp. with Herbert Dingle · King's Lond., Bryant MSS · NL Scot., letters to the Haldane family · Rice University, Houston, Texas, Woodson Research Center, letters to Sir Julian Huxley | SOUND BL NSA, oral history interview

Likenesses Elliott & Fry, photograph, 1939, NPG [*see illus.*] · W. Stoneman, two photographs, 1944–54, NPG · Mrs Campbell Dodgson, drawing, priv. coll. · J. Mansbridge, drawing, priv. coll. · photograph, Peterhouse, Cambridge

Wealth at death £7745 5*s*. 7*d*.: probate, 24 May 1960, *CGPLA Eng. & Wales*

Barker, Francis (1771/2–1859), physician, was born in Waterford, the eldest of six children of William Barker (1731–1788), apothecary, and Elizabeth, daughter of the Revd William Acheson, of Duncormuck, co. Wexford. William Barker was sheriff of Waterford from 1759 to 1763.

Francis Barker entered Trinity College, Dublin, as a pensioner on 20 October 1788, aged sixteen, and graduated BA there in 1793. Two years later, he took his MD degree in Edinburgh, submitting a thesis entitled 'De animalium electricite'. In 1804 he married Emma (*d*. 1851), daughter of Revd Arthur Connolly, vicar of Donard, co. Wicklow. They had four daughters and one son, William (*b*. 1810), who lectured on chemistry at the Richmond school of medicine in Dublin and in 1850 was appointed to the chair of chemistry at the Royal College of Surgeons in Ireland. In 1805 Barker was admitted a licentiate of the King and Queen's College of Physicians in Ireland and was elected a fellow on 6 April 1807. In 1810 Trinity College granted him (*stip. con.*) the degrees of MB and MD.

Barker practised medicine, first in Waterford, later in Dublin, where, on 7 October 1801 he was appointed assistant lecturer to Dr Perceval, professor of chemistry at Trinity College. On 16 May 1808 he succeeded to the chair, a position he held until February 1850 when he was superannuated on an annual pension of £150, which he enjoyed until his death.

Barker was one of four editors of the *Dublin Medical and Physical Essays*, a quarterly medical journal that appeared for the first time in March 1807. The journal ceased publication in June 1808, after the sixth issue, possibly because of Barker's appointment as professor of chemistry at Trinity College.

Despite holding the Trinity chair for forty-two years, Barker was primarily a physician and only secondarily a chemist. He was probably best known for his work on fever. In 1799 he investigated the prevalence of the disease in Waterford for a committee which had assumed the task of establishing a fever hospital in the city. In his analysis, which was published in the *Reports of the Society for Promoting the Comforts of the Poor* (89–91, 106–7), Barker claimed that Waterford 'was never free from fever' and that the disease was responsible for much misery, 'often beggary and ruin', and many deaths. He added that the pauperizing effects of fever were exacerbated by the general 'dread of contagion', which deprived the fever-stricken of the charitable assistance they would ordinarily obtain from friends and neighbours.

In Dublin, Barker was appointed physician to the Fever Hospital and House of Recovery, Cork Street, where he served for many years, initially as physician, later as senior physician at an annual salary of £100. He published a lengthy medical report on the hospital's response to the fever epidemic in the years 1817–18 in volume two of the *Transactions of the Association of Fellows and Licentiates of the King and Queen's College of Physicians* (512–602). Barker observed that contagion was principally or solely responsible for the origin and diffusion of epidemic fever and that food shortages, or famine, and other social factors were contributory or concurrent causes only.

Barker's main work on fever, a detailed national survey of the 1817–19 fever epidemic, was a collaboration with John Cheyne entitled *An account of the rise, progress and decline of the fever lately epidemical in Ireland, together with communications from physicians in the provinces, and various official documents* (2 vols., 1821). Barker and Cheyne explained that their sense of duty and their habits of enquiry encouraged them to study the fever that was so prevalent in Dublin and elsewhere. Their aim was to present a record of the origin, diffusion, and decline of the epidemic fever in Ireland. Implicit in the undertaking was a hope that their work would contribute to a better understanding of the causation and prevention of epidemic fever. Their survey is a cornucopia of medical and social history, a unique reference work, valued by contemporaries but underutilized by modern historians.

Barker and Cheyne argued that the mortality of the 1817–19 fever outbreak was proportionally less than that of previous epidemics, a situation they attributed to private benevolence and government relief measures. In particular, they said, the establishment of fever hospitals in the wake of government legislation was of 'incalculable benefit' in stemming contagion. The act, 58 Geo. III, c. 47, which was passed on 30 May 1818, empowered county grand juries to levy funds for the erection and support of district fever hospitals. These were intended for one or more parishes or for baronies or half-baronies, and were funded by grand jury presentment and private subscriptions, the former not to exceed twice the latter. A corporation, consisting of *ex officio* members and subscribers of £20, or 1 guinea annually, could be appointed in each county, or county of a city, or county of a town, to build or hire houses for use as fever hospitals. Undoubtedly, the remedial and preventive steps that were taken helped to contain and eventually suppress the epidemic but the relative diminution in mortality over previous epidemics may have been due to a preponderance of relapsing fever rather than the more deadly typhus fever, or to the presence of a less virulent strain of the latter. Barker and Cheyne claimed that the benefits of isolating the infected in fever hospitals and the necessity for personal and domestic hygiene and disinfection had been further demonstrated during the epidemic and, they added, there was a greater awareness and understanding of the wretched existence of the poor. They believed that a spirit of benevolence had been fostered and that the different social classes had been drawn more closely together, which, they said, would improve the moral and physical condition of the Irish people and add 'to the resources and prosperity of the empire'.

By the time the report was published in 1821, official recognition and appointments had come Barker's way and his professional career had advanced significantly. In a very short time, he was commissioned to survey the fever epidemic in Munster, appointed a member of the central committee of health, and subsequently of the permanent General Board of Health, acting as salaried secretary of that body for more than thirty years. The function of the General Board of Health was to advise the government on epidemic disease and on public health generally. The immediate task was to conduct a national inquiry into the living conditions and living standards of the poor and their impact on the people's health. The board was also requested to investigate and report on the existing dispensaries and fever hospitals and to act as an advisory body on the country's medical charities.

Barker died on 8 October 1859 at Heytesbury Terrace, Wellington Road, Dublin. He was buried at Mount Jerome cemetery on 11 October. LAURENCE M. GEARY

Sources Royal College of Physicians of Ireland, Kildare Street, Dublin 2, Kirkpatrick Archive • T. P. C. Kirkpatrick, *An account of the Irish medical periodicals* (1916), 3–10 • *Medical Times and Gazette* (15 Oct 1859) • C. A. Cameron, *History of the Royal College of Surgeons in Ireland*, 2nd edn (1916) • [T. Bernard], ed., *The reports of the Society for Promoting the Comforts of the Poor*, 2 (1800) • H. F. Morris, 'The Barkers of Waterford', *Decies: Journal of the Old Waterford Society*, 17 (1981), 17–28 • E. M. Crawford, 'Typhus in nineteenth-century Ireland', *Medicine, disease and the state in Ireland, 1650–1940*, ed. E. Malcolm and G. Jones (1999), 121–37 • admission records, TCD • Mount Jerome cemetery records, Dublin

Likenesses J. J. Slattery, oils, Royal College of Physicians of Ireland

Wealth at death under £6000: probate, 4 Dec 1859, *CGPLA Ire.*

Barker, Frederic (1808–1882), Anglican bishop of Sydney, born at Baslow by Bakewell, Derbyshire, on 17 March 1808, was the grandson of William Barker, dean of Raphoe from 1757 to 1776, and the fifth son of the Revd John Barker (1762–1824), vicar of Baslow. He was educated at Grantham School and at Jesus College, Cambridge, where he took his BA degree in 1831 and proceeded MA in 1839. At Cambridge he was much influenced by Charles Simeon, the evangelical.

On 24 April 1831 Barker was appointed to the perpetual curacy of Upton, a small village in Cheshire, where he ministered until 28 September 1834, being ordained priest by Charles Sumner in April 1832; he spent a few months (4 October to 21 December 1834) in Ireland working for the Irish Home Mission Society. In the beginning of 1835 he was appointed to the perpetual curacy of St Mary's, Edgehill, Liverpool (in Sumner's diocese), a post he held for nineteen years. On 15 October 1840 he married Jane Sophia, daughter of John Harben and his wife, Janet, *née* Allan; Jane Barker was a strong evangelical who also had, through her father, connections with the poet Wordsworth and his circle (*AusDB*). In Liverpool, Barker published a number of anti-Roman tracts, including *Sermons on Romanism* (1840). On account of failing health, in 1854 Barker was induced to accept from the patron, the duke of Devonshire, the paternal vicarage of Baslow, which had fallen vacant by the death of his elder brother, the Revd Anthony Auriol Barker, on 21 December 1853.

Barker had been scarcely three months in residence at Baslow when he was selected by Archbishop Sumner in August 1854 to succeed William Grant Broughton as bishop of Sydney, New South Wales, an office carrying with it that of metropolitan of Australia. He was consecrated in 1854 at Lambeth on St Andrew's day, 30 November, and received the degree of DD *per literas regias*. He arrived in Sydney in May 1855. His predecessor had procured the establishment of the sees of Van Diemen's Land (Tasmania) in 1842, and of Adelaide, Melbourne, and Newcastle, all in 1847; and Barker in his lifetime founded the additional dioceses of Perth (1856), Brisbane (1859), Goulburn (1863), Grafton and Armidale (1866), Bathurst (1869), Ballarat (1875), and north Queensland (1878). Thus Barker's primacy, as first constituted, extended over twelve separate dioceses, in which, one after the other, the principle of constitutional government was developed in conformity with the precedent set by the dioceses of Victoria and Sydney. In addition to the diocesan synods he initiated, Barker succeeded, having visited Britain in 1870–72, in establishing a general synod for the exercise of certain legislative and administrative authority over the whole church in Australia and Tasmania. The formation of this general synod, which met on three occasions while Barker was in office, the last meeting taking place during

Frederic Barker (1808–1882), by John Hubert Newman, 1870s?

his absence in October 1881, was regarded as having perfected the constitution of the Australian church. Under this regime the diocese of Sydney continued more and more to prosper, and when state aid to religion was abolished in the colony, it was ordained by the legislature that Barker should continue to receive his government salary of £2000 a year.

Barker's work was arduous; and he paid three visits to England for the purpose of advancing the diocesan and provincial interests committed to his care. His first wife died in Sydney in 1876; on his third visit to England he married on 22 January 1878 his second wife, Mary Jane (*d.* 1910), the elder daughter of Edward and Mary Woods of London. He returned to Sydney in October 1878, but paid a fourth visit to Europe in 1881 in the hope of recovery from an attack of paralysis; after revisiting Derbyshire, he wintered on the Riviera in 1881–2. He died after four weeks' illness, at San Remo, Italy, on Thursday 6 April 1882, and was buried at Baslow on the 18th of the same month. He left no children.

Barker was an imposing evangelical (6 ft 5½ in. tall), and was known as 'the High Priest'. Although his influence waned in his latter years, he succeeded in achieving a strong evangelical presence in Australia as well as an effective diocesan structure.

ARTHUR H. GRANT, *rev.* H. C. G. MATTHEW

Sources *The Times* (7 April 1882) · *The Times* (19 April 1882) · *Church Times* (14 April 1882) · *Church Times* (21 April 1882) · *High Peak News* (22 April 1882) · *High Peak News* (29 April 1882) · K. J. Cable, 'Barker, Frederick', *AusDB*, vol. 3 · K. J. Cable, 'Mrs Barker and her diary', *Royal Australian Historical Society Journal and Proceedings*, 54 (1968–9), 67–105 · W. M. Cowper, ed., *Episcopate of the Right Reverend Frederic Barker* (1888)

Archives Mitchell L., NSW · Sydney diocesan archives | LPL, corresp. with A. C. Tait

Likenesses J. H. Newman, photograph, 1870–1879?, NL Aus. [*see illus.*] · wood-engraving, NPG; repro. in *ILN* (13 May 1882)

Wealth at death £3364 5*s.* 4*d.*: probate, 24 May 1882, *CGPLA Eng. & Wales*

Barker, George (1776–1845), lawyer, was born in 1776. Nothing is known of his early life, but he became prominent in political and cultural circles in Birmingham. He was a friend of the industrialists and inventors Mathew Boulton (1728–1809) and James Watt (1736–1819), and in 1811 he became engaged in a dispute with Welchman Whateley over the furnishing of Boulton's extravagant funeral.

Well known as a Conservative and churchman, Barker, with Whateley and J. F. Ledsam, led the campaign in 1838 against the incorporation of Birmingham, for which many leading citizens had petitioned. He and his associates argued that they represented the bulk of wealth and respectability locally and that they wished Birmingham to remain 'a town without a shackle' (Gill, 224). They drew up a counter-petition against incorporation, and two commissioners were sent to find the strength of the two sides among ratepayers. They were assisted by the Liberal William Scholefield and by Barker for the Conservatives. The report was confidential but Barker applied to know the result, which showed that there was much greater support for incorporation. Despite this, he continued to campaign against the charter, declaring that the growth of Birmingham in wealth and population was due 'to the very circumstances of the town not being incorporated'. His persistent opposition led Captain Dawson, one of the commissioners, to hope that the privy council would grant the charter and decline 'Mr Barker's interference' (Gill, 227). The charter was granted in October 1838; however, although the Conservatives continued to dispute it Barker was no longer foremost among them.

Barker remained active in Birmingham's Society of Arts, which he had helped found in 1821 for the cultivation of the fine arts, and he was the driving force behind the Birmingham Philosophical Society. He was associated with many charities, especially with the town's general hospital, for which he was an 'able and never-failing adviser', gratuitously conducting its legal business (*GM*). He was also prominent in the triennial music festivals which raised money for the hospital and influential in the building of the town hall to provide a venue for these festivals. A keen supporter of the railway connection between Birmingham and Liverpool, which opened in 1837, he was generally active in the public life of Birmingham. He was a street commissioner on the body which preceded the town council, and a governor of King Edward's School. Greatly interested in science, he was a distinguished botanist, and in 1839 he was elected a member of the Royal Society. Barker died on 6 December 1845 at his home, Springfield, Birmingham, and a Barker testimonial was set up to recognize his charitable work. Peter Hollins, a local artist, was commissioned to make a marble bust, which was put in the general hospital. CARL CHINN

Sources J. T. Bunce, *History of the corporation of Birmingham*, 1 (1878) • C. Gill, *Manor and borough to 1865* (1952), vol. 1 of *History of Birmingham* (1952–74) • *GM*, 2nd ser., 25 (1846), 324–5 • J. A. Langford, ed., *Modern Birmingham and its institutions: a chronicle of local events, from 1841–1871*, 2 vols. (1873–7) • W. Whateley, *A reply to a letter of Mr G. Barker, contained in documents relative to an investigation of the manner in which the funeral of the late M. Boulton was furnished* (1811) • *Report of proceedings connected with the Barker Testimonial, with a list of subscribers and statement of accounts* (1846)

Likenesses P. Hollins, marble bust, *c*.1846; formerly at General Hospital, Birmingham

Barker, George Granville (1913–1991), poet, was born on 26 February 1913 at 106 Forest Road, Loughton, Essex, the first son and fourth of the five children of George Barker (1879–1965) and his wife, Marion Frances, *née* Taaffe (1881–1953). His father, a former batman in the British army, had served under Kitchener; he had subsequently become a butler in a private household and was at the time of George's birth a temporary police constable; after a period as an insurance clerk he later became a much respected butler to Gray's Inn. His mother came from an old Catholic family in Drogheda, Ireland, where her father had been a pilot in the port. Because of insecure employment in the post-war years, the Barker family lived in relative poverty at a number of addresses around Chelsea and Fulham, where George attended Marlborough Road elementary school as well as taking instruction at the London Oratory.

Having acquired a love of verse but little else, Barker left school aged fourteen and briefly attended the Regent Street Polytechnic where, as a series of early notebooks attests, his determined purpose was already to be a professional writer. His chance came in 1932 when, encouraged by an elder sister, he sent the typescript of a recent journal, later published in fictionalized form as *Alanna Autumnal* (1933), to John Middleton Murry, editor of *The Adelphi*. Murry gave Barker reviewing work and an introduction to that Maecenas of 1930s poets Michael Roberts. At Roberts's suggestion he entered the bohemian circle which then frequented the Parton Street bookshop in Bloomsbury run by the generously disposed, though feckless, David Archer. By the age of twenty Barker was contributing to the *Twentieth Century*, a radical journal issued by the Promethean Society which had offices above the shop; in the same year Archer issued his *Thirty Preliminary Poems* at the Parton Press. On the strength of this success on 18 November 1933 Barker married his childhood sweetheart Jessie Winifred Theresa (Jessica) Woodward (1909–1989); they moved to a cottage overlooking the rugged coastline at Worth Matravers, Dorset, the first of several west country addresses.

It was while gazing down from the nearby St Aldhelm's Head that Barker had an idea for the vertiginous 'Daedalus', first item in successive *Collected Poems*; he sent the poem to Walter de la Mare; de la Mare forwarded it to T. S. Eliot at Faber and Faber, who promptly commissioned a

George Granville Barker (1913–1991), by John Deakin, *c*.1952

volume. His action was the making of Barker, who for several years came to rely on Eliot for advice and, to some extent, for financial assistance. Eliot soon organized a temporary and anonymous fund to support his protégé; he also proposed the contents and running order for *Poems* (1935), the volume that brought the young poet to the attention of W. B. Yeats. Yeats thought him the most promising of all the up-and-coming generation of British poets. Despite such praise, Barker spent the rest of the decade finding a consistent voice. A second volume of fiction, *Janus* (1935), and the long surrealistic poem *Calamiterror* (1937) did little to enhance his reputation. It was not until *Lament and Terror* (1940) was published shortly after the outbreak of war that Barker's individual blend of muscular rhythm, euphonious vowels, and medieval and Rilkean echoes attracted widespread respect.

By the time of its appearance, Barker and his wife had departed for Japan, where he had taken up a lectureship at the Imperial Tohoku University, Sendai, vacated by the British poet Ralph Hodgson. The appointment was not a success: Barker felt ill at ease as an academic and, more to the point, Japan was gradually being drawn into the ambit of the axis powers. Realizing the danger he was in, Barker wrote to Elizabeth *Smart (1913–1986), a Canadian writer who had been collecting his manuscripts since 1937. She arranged for passages for Barker and his wife to Vancouver, from where they joined her at an artists' commune near Big Sur in California. Barker's subsequent affair with Smart was to be the subject of her novel *By Grand Central Station I Sat Down and Wept* (1945). The book conveys her point of view of a relationship that, from Barker's own, was both rewarding and disruptive. By the time he left the United States to return to Britain in the summer of 1943, he had fathered a daughter with Smart and twins with his wife, whom he left behind in New York. He settled with Smart in the Cotswolds where their second child, a boy, was born; they were to have one more son and daughter. Barker was rejected for war work, made one more attempt to rebuild his marriage by revisiting New York in 1946, and then spent a wretched winter with Smart in Galway before fleeing to London in February 1947.

The 1950s were to be a creative decade for Barker, but his circumstances were no more settled than before. He continued to see Smart at her cottage at Tilty Mill, Essex, but in the meantime took up with the film-maker Betty (Cashenden) Cass (*b.* 1924?), with whom he travelled to Collioure in France, Zennor in Cornwall, and around Italy before renting a woodcutter's cottage near Haslemere. In Cornwall, Barker became the mentor and unofficial teacher of the younger poets John Heath-Stubbs (*b.* 1918) and David Wright (1920–1994) who had moved there to be near him; in Italy his companions were the raucous painterly duo Robert Colquhoun and Robert MacBryde. In England his social life consisted of crowded weekends at Tilty Mill, and regular forays to the pubs and clubs of Soho, where he swapped drinks and witticisms with the painter John Minton, the photographer John Deakin, and a host of young admirers.

As Barker's personality grew gregarious and florid, his work generally became more limpid. The lyrics of *Eros in Dogma* (1944) and *News of the World* (1950) demonstrate an increasing control and beauty of line. It was when he attempted more lurid effects—in the extended Villon-inspired ballade *The True Confession of George Barker* (1950) or *The Dead Seagull*, a novella of the same year intended as a riposte to Smart—that Barker lapsed into marginality. Eliot rejected the former; the latter remains a cult book. A dramatic turning point in Barker's life occurred in August 1957, when Cass left him for an alternative life (she was eventually to settle in San Francisco). He spent a year in Manhattan renewing former contacts and mixing with Allen Ginsberg and the beats. After a short interlude back in London, he then took up residence in Rome with Dede Farrelly, former wife of his friend the American writer and critic John Farrelly; with her he had three sons. Rome was to inspire *The View from a Blind I* (1962), among his most atmospheric volumes of verse, as well as the second, slightly disappointing, part of the *True Confession* (1964). After the first had been voted joint winner of the Guinness prize, Barker revisited London where at Smart's Westbourne Terrace flat in March 1963 he met the young Scottish writer Elizabeth Langlands (*b.* 1940), always known as Elspeth. Their long relationship and eventual marriage was to provide Barker with the most stable environment that he had ever known. With Elspeth he was to have five children; in 1967 they moved to Bintry House, a National Trust property in north Norfolk where—with the exception of semesters spent teaching at Buffalo, Wisconsin, and Florida—he spent the rest of his life, producing a volume of verse every few years, of which the most distinguished are *In Memory of David Archer* (1973) and *Villa stellar* (1978).

Three tendencies are especially marked in Barker's later work: a vocal delight in rural and family life; an increasing assurance in the composition of elegies through which he lamented the gradual demise of his generation; and strenuous meditation on his own lapsed Catholicism. All of these elements come together in what many consider to be his masterpiece: *Anno Domini* (1983), a rhetorical prayer to the absent God of post-Christian Europe at once fervent, humorous, and informal. A *Collected Poems* was issued in 1987, replacing an earlier edition of 1957.

From his Irish mother Barker inherited a direct blue gaze, above which was set that noble ridge of bone known as the 'bar of Michelangelo'. Tall and darkly handsome in youth, he early learned to stoop. In middle age, devoted to cars and roguish headgear, he reminded his friend the artist Bruce Bernard of 'a Bohemian motorist' (Fraser, 232). In his very last years, even if using a wheelchair, he resembled some suave erudite pirate.

After suffering from emphysema for some years Barker died at Bintry House on 27 October 1991. He was buried on 2 November in Itteringham churchyard, just a few yards from his last home.

The volume *Street Ballads* (1992) was published posthumously as was a *Selected Poems* (1995). As to Barker's place in twentieth-century British verse, opinions are still divided. When he wrote with discipline he was without doubt one of the most plangent and witty voices in modern literature; idiosyncrasy and excess, however, mar his weaker work. In *Calamiterror*, Barker described himself as a 'minor bird on the bough'. It was a typically risky pun, but also a self-estimate with which even his most ardent supporter would probably now concur. ROBERT FRASER

Sources R. Fraser, *The chameleon poet: a life of George Barker* (2001) · J. Heath-Stubbs and M. Green, *Homage to George Barker on his sixtieth birthday* (1973) · *The Times* (29 Oct 1991) · *The Independent* (29 Oct 1991) · R. Sullivan, *By heart: Elizabeth Smart, a life* (1991) · J. Heath-Stubbs, *Hindsights* (1993) · personal knowledge (2004) · private information (2004) · special supplement, 'George Barker at seventy', *Poetry Nation Review* [R. Fraser, ed.], 31, vol. 9/no. 5 (Feb–May 1983)

Archives BL, literary and personal papers · BL, notebooks, Add. MSS 71696–71699 · Col. U., Rare Book and Manuscript Library, corresp. and literary papers · Harvard U., Houghton L., poetical notebook · Ransom HRC, corresp. and literary papers · U. Leeds, MSS · U. Texas, MSS · University of Victoria, corresp. and literary papers | National Library of Canada, Elizabeth Smart papers · NYPL, Berg collection, MSS | FILM BFI NFTVA, South Bank Show, 'George Barker', January 1988 | SOUND BL NSA, interview with Robert Fraser, NSA 6537 NR

Likenesses J. Deakin, bromide print, *c.*1952, NPG [*see illus.*] · P. Swift, oils, repro. in Heath-Stubbs and Green, *Homage*

Barker, Sir George Robert (1817–1861), army officer, was the youngest son of John Barker, deputy storekeeper-general. After attending the Royal Military Academy, Woolwich, he was appointed second lieutenant in the Royal Artillery in 1834. In the Crimea, where he served from the outset of the campaign, initially as a captain, he soon attracted the favourable notice of Sir Colin Campbell, to whose division he was attached. He commanded a battery at Alma and Inkerman, the artillery in the Kerch expedition, and the batteries of the left attack at the fall of Sevastopol.

Barker returned to England a colonel, and during the mutiny was sent to India with a Royal Artillery force. Under Colin Campbell he served, with the local rank of brigadier-general, in command of the artillery at the siege and capture of Lucknow. Subsequently, at the head of a mixed brigade, he defeated the mutineers at Jammu, and captured the stronghold of Birwah, for which services he was made KCB. After the mutiny he was involved in the difficult task of incorporating the East India Company's artillery with the Royal Artillery. His promising career was cut short by his death at Simla on 27 July 1861. He was survived by his wife, Mary Anne (1817–1861), daughter of Walter George Stewart of Jamaica [*see* Barker, Mary Anne]; they had married in Jamaica in 1852 and had two sons, John Stewart (*b.* 1853) and Walter George (*b.* 1857).

H. M. CHICHESTER, *rev.* JAMES LUNT

Sources *Army List* • *LondG* (1854–6) • *Official catalogue of the Museum of Artillery in the Rotunda, Woolwich* (1906) • J. W. Kaye and G. B. Malleson, *Kaye's and Malleson's History of the Indian mutiny of 1857–8*, 6 vols. (1888–9) • F. C. M. Maude and J. W. Sherer, *Memories of the mutiny*, 3rd edn, 2 vols. (1894) • *GM*, 3rd ser., 11 (1861), 453 • Boase, *Mod. Eng. biog.* • *CGPLA Eng. & Wales* (1862)

Archives BL OIOC, George Hutchinson MSS, MS Eur. E 241

Wealth at death £5000: probate, 10 July 1862, *CGPLA Eng. & Wales*

Harley Granville Granville-Barker (1877–1946), by John Singer Sargent, 1900

Barker, Harley Granville Granville- (1877–1946), theatre director and playwright, was born (without the hyphenated surname) in Kensington, London, on 25 November 1877, the only son and elder child of Albert James Barker, a dilettante architect and property developer, and his wife, Mary Elisabeth Bozzi Granville, an entertainer celebrated for her bird imitations, who largely supported her family by her work. Barker was a playwright by the age of seventeen, was running a theatre by the age of twenty-seven, and had retired from the theatre by the time he was forty.

Barker had little or no education, but by an early age had acquired a thorough knowledge of Dickens and Shakespeare. A precocious child, by the age of thirteen he was assisting at his mother's recitals and even, on occasions, standing in for her. By the age of fourteen he was acting professionally in Harrogate and he made his first London appearance at the Comedy Theatre a year later. A tour with the actor–manager Ben Greet in 1895 brought him to the notice of William Poel for whom he played Richard II in 1899. Poel had a profound influence on Barker, with his passionate hatred of the commercial theatre—its long runs, its lack of rehearsal time, its superficiality—and a passionate love of Shakespeare. In an age of scenic excess and decoration, rewriting, bowdlerization, and indiscriminate cutting, Poel had embarked on a mission to return Shakespeare to his original text and to the bare Elizabethan stage. Barker learned from him the importance of verse speaking and respect for what Shakespeare wrote.

Barker became a socialist and a member of the Fabian Society, many of whose members were in the Stage Society—a group of enthusiasts who presented matinées and play-readings of unperformed plays. This led to his friendship with Bernard Shaw, his most important professional relationship. The first recorded connection between Shaw and Barker is the Stage Society performance of *Candida* in 1900, in which Barker played Marchbanks. Shaw did not approve the casting. 'I have often seen Granville Barker act and I cannot remember him in the least', he wrote, but he revised his memory later: 'I withdrew my observations concerning G. B., whom I certainly never saw before' (Kennedy, 10). There was a myth that Barker was the natural son of Shaw: they looked alike, each was a redhead and the dates added up. Shaw gave the younger man 'the tender interest and straight-from-the-shoulder-dealing of a son' (ibid., 62), said a friend. Barker, as Jack Tanner in *Man and Superman*, made himself up as Shaw, complete with beard and swept-back hair: he looked so like the playwright that it seemed a coded signal. Whatever the truth, Barker was certainly someone whom Shaw could, in his awkward way, cherish and admire, educate and castigate: a surrogate son.

Barker was almost 5 feet 11 inches in height, with a slight, wiry build, and looked extraordinarily youthful until well past middle age. He had a strong, sensitive face, warm brown eyes, a thin mouth, which became hard in his later days, and he parted his thick hair in the middle and threw it back rakishly. According to Lewis Casson, he 'had a curiously flabby handshake' (*DNB*), and, according to John Gielgud, he 'was a sort of young genius and wore sandals and ate nuts' (private information).

For the Stage Society, Barker directed and acted in a

number of premières of plays including Shaw's *Candida* and *Mrs Warren's Profession*. In 1902 he also presented his own play *The Marrying of Anne Leete*, a play of fantastic vision and precocity. Until then, dialogue in English plays was clean and linear. Maurice Maeterlinck—a favourite of the turn-of-the-century avant-garde—had shown that something different could be tried: a feathery, hushed, fragmented tone. Barker took the hint, but used as his tools the debris of ordinary speech: interruptions, overlaps, repetitions, *non sequiturs*, pauses. His play *The Voysey Inheritance*, which he wrote a few years later while acting, directing, and running a theatre, was his best play: a complex web of family relationships, a fervent, but never unambiguous indictment of a world dominated by the mutually dependent obsessions of greed, class, and self-deception. It is a virtuoso display of stagecraft: the writer-director showing that he could handle twelve speaking characters on stage at one time, the actor that he could deal with the most ambitious and unexpected modulations of thought and feeling.

Barker committed himself wholeheartedly to raising the standards of the then largely mindless and unambitious English theatre. He conceived plans for a theatre in which the conditions would be appropriate for serious theatre to flourish; with William Archer, a critic and the first translator of Ibsen's plays into English, he wrote in 1903 *A Scheme and Estimates for a National Theatre*, which was not published until 1907. Barker and Archer's scheme covered everything from staff and choice of plays to wages, royalties, and pension funds. A committee was formed to raise the necessary money; state aid was assumed to be out of the question. At the same time, Barker hatched a more immediately realizable plan. He wrote to Archer:

> Do you think there is anything in this idea? To take the Court Theatre for six months or a year and to run there a stock season of the uncommercial Drama: Hauptmann—Sudermann—Ibsen—Maeterlinck—Schnitzler—Shaw—Brieux etc … I would stake everything on plays and acting—not attempt 'productions'. (Kennedy, 18)

A businessman called Leigh had rented the Court Theatre (now the Royal Court) as a showcase for his young and attractive wife and needed a director for *Two Gentlemen of Verona*. Archer suggested Barker, who accepted on condition that he could revive *Candida* (not starring Mrs Leigh) for six matinées. The performances were so successful that in partnership with the manager of the Court Theatre, John E. Vedrenne, and in close association with Shaw, he embarked upon an extraordinarily productive period of work, which lasted at that theatre until 1907.

The seasons at the Court made Barker's name as a director and Shaw's as a dramatist, and became a landmark in the history of the British theatre. A new standard of intelligence and social criticism was brought into the theatre, and in both plays and acting there was an intense regard for truth to life rather than for meretricious theatrical effect. The second production of the season, *John Bull's other Island*, about Irish home rule, became so famous that it led to a special performance for Edward VII, who laughed so much that he broke the chair which Vedrenne had hired at some expense. Not for the last time, the Royal Court staged a radical work, only to see it become a smart success. In the three Vedrenne–Barker seasons just under 1000 performances were presented of thirty-two plays by seventeen authors. The writers included Ibsen, Maeterlinck, Galsworthy, Masefield, Yeats, and Hauptmann. Euripides had three productions at the Court: his quirky scepticism and feminist perspective were very much in the spirit of Barker's regime. But Shaw was the star and treated Barker to a stream of advice and exhortations; no fewer than 701 performances were of plays from his bursting portfolio of unperformed and under-exploited titles, which included *You Never can Tell* and *Man and Superman*. Lillah *McCarthy (1875–1960) joined the company in 1905 to act in these plays, and in 1906 she and Barker were married.

In 1907 Barker upped the stakes with a move to the much larger Savoy Theatre in the West End. But the expansion didn't work. Some of the cutting edge had gone, and the audience noticed. Shaw wrote:

> I learn with disgust and horror that you played the National Anthem and made the audience stand up on Monday … Have you any notion of the extent to which your sworn supporters are republicans or aristocratic souls with a loathing for public demonstrations? (*Bernard Shaw's Letters to Granville Barker*, ed. C. B. Purdom, 1956, 104)

The theatre's capacity was too large; money grew tight; the management split; worst of all, Barker's new play, *Waste*, intended as the season's centrepiece, was banned by the lord chamberlain. In 1910 Charles Frohman mounted a season of repertory at the Duke of York's Theatre, with Barker and Dion Boucicault sharing the productions. Barker had a great success, as director, with Galsworthy's *Justice*, and with his own play *The Madras House*, but the venture proved to be financially unworkable and failed within a few months. The plans for building a national theatre were maturing, and in 1912, in optimistic expectation of its fruition, Barker presented two plays by Shakespeare at the Savoy, and ushered in a style of production that still approximates to our ideas of the best in contemporary Shakespearian production: the determination to maximize the power of the text through the actor, allied to the desire to make the staging as expressive as possible through the use of space, scenery, lighting, and costume. Barker's production of *A Midsummer Night's Dream* embodied his ideas. His not-altogether-human fairies were slightly sinister adults rather than coy children, and they moved in a formally choreographed fashion against a forest of flowing purple and green draperies. They were gold from head to foot, shimmering like oriental statues, galaxies away from the traditional gauzy pantomime conventions of Victorian tradition. Further Shakespeare productions proved impracticable, but Barker had a great success with *The Great Adventure*, a comedy by Arnold Bennett in 1913, and in the same year directed a season which included Shaw's *Androcles and the Lion* and *The Doctor's Dilemma*. By this time Barker had developed a considerable reputation in Europe as well as Britain and as the putative director of the national theatre, which—backers permitting—was intended to be built in time for the tercentenary of Shakespeare's birth on 23 April 1916.

The First World War intervened and all hopes were demolished. In response to the war, Barker presented Hardy's *Dynasts* in his own adaptation. It was a *succès d'estime*, but the public wanted escapism and the production was a financial disaster. He went to New York in 1915 to direct *Androcles and the Lion*, *The Doctor's Dilemma*, and *A Midsummer Night's Dream* and fell wildly in love—'in the Italian manner' as Shaw said—with Helen Huntington, who, as Helen Gates, was an American poet and novelist of some distinction and the wife of one of his wealthy backers. His marriage fell apart. Neither partner was prepared to grant a divorce, and Barker escaped the strain by working first for the Red Cross in France, and then enlisting, later working for military intelligence.

Eventually the divorces went through, and on 31 July 1918 Barker married, acquired a hyphen in his surname, moved first to Devon to play the part of a country squire, and then to France to a life of seclusion. His wife (who died in 1950) had received a large divorce settlement but, while Barker was able to live in luxury, she insisted on almost complete severance from his work and his friends in the theatre, and above all from Shaw, whom she detested. It was mutual: Shaw thought that Granville-Barker had buried himself alive on her account. The truth was that Granville-Barker had decided to withdraw from the theatre years before: 'On the personal count I made up my mind … to give up acting when I was 30 and producing when I was 40' (Kennedy, 199). He was weary with management, with artistic compromise, with the lack of a context in which to work seriously, and was bitterly depressed by the war. Shaw could never reconcile himself to the loss of his surrogate son; it was, as his biographer Hesketh Pearson said, 'The only important matter about which he asked me to be reticent' (Holroyd, 3.369).

Granville-Barker's remaining work for the theatre was mainly professorial and literary, although almost surreptitiously he did a certain amount of directing of his own plays and translations. His last acknowledged stage production was Maeterlinck's *The Betrothal* in 1921. He wrote two plays in retirement, *His Majesty* and *The Secret Life*, which were not publicly performed until over forty years after his death. Out of his self-exile came one major work, assembled over many years: *The Prefaces to Shakespeare* (1927–45). His *Prefaces* have a practical aim: 'I want to see Shakespeare made fully effective on the English stage. That is the best sort of help I can lend.' They are the best primer for directors and actors working on the plays of Shakespeare.

Granville-Barker can be thought of as the real founder of the National Theatre, and as a writer who, unlike all his contemporaries, learned from Chekhov rather than Ibsen and rivalled both of them. He was also the first modern British director who invariably used all his gifts selflessly in the service of the dramatist to express the full potential of a play. Harcourt Williams, an actor, said:

> Roughly, one might say that Barker worked from the inside to the outside. He had an exceptional instinct for what was theatrically effective, but never got it by theatrical means. It had to be won by mental clarity and emotional truth—in fact the very opposite to the method of most producers.
> (H. Williams, *Old Vic Saga*, 1949, 163)

He knew the burrs and nettles of the actor's life, and he knew the sensitivity they engendered. He was a perfectionist but not a dictator: his productions were a seamless blend of word, gesture, and staging. As an actor he was gifted and forceful but, according to Lewis Casson, 'he had too much critical intelligence to be really successful' (*DNB*).

In 1930 Granville-Barker was appointed to the Clark lectureship at Trinity College, Cambridge, and in 1937 he was Romanes lecturer at Oxford. He received honorary degrees from Edinburgh in 1930, and from Oxford and Reading in 1937, in which year he became director of the British Institute in Paris where he had been living for some time. He resigned from the British Institute in 1939, and when Paris fell, he went to the USA, where he was a visiting professor at Yale and Harvard. He continued to take some interest in the British theatre and in 1940 returned to advise on John Gielgud's production of *King Lear* at the Old Vic, on condition that his name did not appear. Gielgud said:

> He was absolute genius to me … he was like a wonderful conductor of an orchestra, he knew exactly what not to bother with … he told me after a run-through of *Lear* that I was an ash and what was required was an oak. (private information)

He returned from the USA in failing health in 1945 and to Paris in 1946, where he died on 31 August and was buried in the cemetery of Père Lachaise. He had no children.

RICHARD EYRE

Sources D. Kennedy, *Granville Barker and the dream of theatre* (1985) · C. B. Purdom, *Harley Granville Barker: man of the theatre, dramatist, and scholar* (1955) · M. Holroyd, *Bernard Shaw*, 5 vols. (1988–92) · *DNB* · private information [J. Gielgud] · *CGPLA Eng. & Wales* (1947)

Archives BL, prompt copies of plays, Add. MS 65156 · Harvard U., Houghton Library, corresp. and papers · Ransom HRC, letters and MSS | BL, corresp. with William Archer, Add. MS 45290 · BL, corresp. with the Society of Authors, Add. MS 56660 · BL, corresp. with the League of Dramatists, Add. MS 56853 · BL, letters to George Bernard Shaw, Add. MS 50534 · BLPES, letters to the Fabian Society · BLPES, letters to Edward Pease · Bodl. Oxf., corresp. with Gilbert Murray · British Theatre Association Library, London, corresp. with William Archer · JRL, letters to the *Manchester Guardian* · King's AC Cam., letters and postcards to G. H. W. Rylands · NL Scot., corresp. with John Dover Wilson · U. Birm. L., letters to John Ramsay Allardyce Nicoll · U. Mich., Harlan Hatcher Graduate Library, letters to George Harrison · Vaughan Williams Memorial Library, London, corresp. with Cecil Sharp | SOUND BL NSA, documentary recording; performance recording

Likenesses J. S. Sargent, chalk drawing, 1900, NPG [*see illus.*] · A. L. Coburn, photograph, 1906, NPG · E. Kapp, drawing, 1913, U. Birm. · G. C. Beresford, photograph, 1918, NPG · M. Beerbohm, caricature, 1923, U. Cal., Los Angeles · M. Beerbohm, pencil caricature, 1923, Garr. Club · J. E. Blanche, portrait, 1930, NPG · W. Stoneman, photograph, 1931, NPG · C. Billing, bronze bust, British

Drama League • K. Kennet, bronze bust, Royal Shakespeare Theatre, Stratford • D. McFall, bust (posthumous), British Drama League • K. Scott, bronze bust; stolen from the Royal National Theatre, 1989 • K. Scott, statuette, Garr. Club • W. Strang, etching, NPG; repro. in W. Strang, *William Strang: Catalogue of his etched work, 1882–1912* (1912)

Wealth at death £10,395 6*s.* 8*d.*—in England: administration with will, 6 March 1947, *CGPLA Eng. & Wales*

Barker, Henry Aston (1774–1856), panorama proprietor and painter, younger son of Robert *Barker (1739–1806), the panorama painter, and his wife, Catherine, *née* Aston (1744–1842), was born in Glasgow. At the age of twelve he was set to work by his father to take the outlines of the city of Edinburgh from the top of Calton Hill for the world's first 360 degree show panorama. A few years later he would make drawings for such a panorama of London from the roof of the Albion mills. He arrived in London in 1788, and soon afterwards enrolled as a student at the Royal Academy Schools. His fellow students included J. M. W. Turner and Robert Ker Porter.

On 25 May 1793 Robert Barker opened the first purpose-built building for the display of 360 degree panoramas in Leicester Square. Appropriately it was called the Panorama. There H. A. Barker worked as Robert Barker's chief assistant, painting panoramas of cities and naval and military victories. He was responsible for making the drawings for most of the panoramas exhibited, and in order to do so was obliged to travel widely. In 1799, for instance, he went to Turkey to make drawings for two panoramas of Constantinople. On the way he visited Palermo, and called on Sir William Hamilton, then British ambassador to the court of Naples. Hamilton introduced him to Nelson who 'took me by the hand and said he was indebted to me for keeping up the fame of victory in the Battle of the Nile for a year longer than it would have lasted in the public estimation' (Corner, 10).

Constantinople from the Tower of Galatea was exhibited in Leicester Square, 1801–2, and *Constantinople from the Tower of Leander* in 1801–3. The Galatea view would be reproduced in 1813 as an eight-sheet aquatint. In 1801 Barker went to Copenhagen to make drawings for a panorama of the battle of Copenhagen, and while there was again received by Nelson who provided him this time with a written testimonial. In May 1802, during the peace of Amiens, he went to Paris and made drawings for two panoramas of that city. On this occasion he was introduced to Napoleon. The original drawings for H. A. Barker's *View of Paris between the Pont Neuf, the Louvre, the Mint, and Quatre Nations* are preserved in the Victoria and Albert Museum. The actual painting of the panoramas was carried out in a wooden rotunda erected behind Robert Barker's house at 14 West Square, St George's Fields. From 1828 they were painted in a brick rotunda at the back of Wilmot Place, Rochester Road, Camden Town.

Barker married Harriet Maria Bligh (1782–1856), daughter of Captain (later Rear Admiral) William Bligh of HMS *Bounty*, in 1802, and they moved into 13 West Square, next door to Robert Barker. In 1802 Barker's elder brother, Thomas Edward, in partnership with Ramsay Richard Reinagle but without his father's approval, left Leicester Square and opened a rival panorama in the Strand near Surrey Street. Father and son were never reconciled, and T. E. Barker was excluded from his father's will. Robert died on 8 April 1806 and bequeathed his panorama business to H. A. Barker, but also, according to Corner, 'certain encumbrances' which were made good as a result of his subsequent success. In 1816 Barker and John Burford bought out the Strand panorama, and proceeded to manage this second rotunda, regularly supplying it with panoramas. A number of the panoramas from this and the Leicester Square establishments went on tour, visiting Birmingham, Liverpool, Dublin, and Edinburgh, and various cities in the United States.

Whenever possible, Barker's panoramas dealt with matters of the moment. Following the abdication of Napoleon, Barker travelled to Elba to make drawings, and while there renewed his acquaintance with the former emperor. After the battle of Waterloo he travelled to the field of battle and also visited Paris in order to interview officers and glean further information. The resulting panorama was sensationally popular, making £10,000. H. A. Barker's last panorama—*The Coronation Procession of George IV*—was also a success. Early in 1824, on the strength of *Waterloo*'s success, and at the age of forty-eight, Barker retired, transferring the management of both rotundas to John and Robert *Burford.

In retirement, Barker lived firstly at Cheam in Surrey, then Bristol, and then Willsbridge, near Bristol. For the last thirty years of his life he lived at Bitton, near Bristol, where he died on 19 July 1856 and where he was buried.

The artists who assisted Barker in painting his panoramas in the main are unknown, though we know they included John and Robert Burford. J. A. Atkinson was employed to paint figures on *The Plains of Vittoria* panorama, and John Burnet to paint figures on *Waterloo*. A complete list of the paintings exhibited at the Leicester Square and Strand Panoramas appears in Wilcox.

Ralph Hyde

Sources G. R. Corner, *The panorama, with memoirs of its inventor, Robert Barker, and his son, the late Henry Aston Barker* (1857) • *GM*, 3rd ser., 1 (1856), 509–18 • S. B. Wilcox, 'The panorama and related exhibitions in London', MLitt diss., U. Edin., 1976 • R. D. Altick, *The shows of London* (1978) • S. Oetterman, *The panorama: a history of a mass medium* (1997) • R. Hyde, *Panoramania! the art and entertainment of the 'all embracing' view* (1988–9) [exhibition catalogue, Barbican Art Gallery, 3 Nov 1988 – 15 Jan 1989] • descriptive booklets sold at the exhibitions, 1801–24, GL • descriptive booklets sold at the exhibitions, 1801–24, BM

Archives NL Scot., journals, sketchbooks, and papers

Barker, Sir Herbert Atkinson (1869–1950), bone-setter, was born at Southport on 21 April 1869, the only son of Thomas Wildman Barker, solicitor, who became coroner for south-west Lancashire, and his wife, Agnes Atkinson; both parents died while Barker was a schoolboy. After leaving the grammar school at Kirkby Lonsdale and following a short visit to Canada, Barker was apprenticed to his cousin, John Atkinson, a bone-setter, of Park Lane, London, who himself had been taught by the famous Robert Howard Hutton. Atkinson was highly successful, enjoying the patronage of many aristocratic and wealthy patients.

Sir Herbert Atkinson Barker (1869–1950), by Augustus John, 1916

In 1889 Barker set up in practice on his own, first in Manchester, then in London, and later in Glasgow. In Manchester he was very successful, helped by referrals from the distinguished surgeon Walter Whitehead. He returned to London again in 1905 and managed at his second attempt to establish himself there. In 1907 he married Jane Ethel Walker, daughter of William Wilson Walker JP. There were no children.

Barker was a controversial figure. He fell foul of members of the medical establishment who were concerned about his lack of formal medical qualifications and who wanted to stop him practising. However, he also had many influential friends, including leading journalists, and a number of newspaper articles appeared in support of 'manipulative surgery', as he styled his bone-setting practices. An article, 'What is a quack?', published in *The Times* in 1912, argued that Barker did cure patients, many of whom had failed to obtain relief from qualified doctors. Both W. T. Stead, editor of the *Review of Reviews*, and R. D. Blumenfeld, editor of the *Daily Express*, wrote robust articles supporting Barker and his claims for recognition as a respectable practitioner. Barker also enjoyed the confidence of his patients, many of whom were public figures. The controversy over his practice reached its height after 1911 when the General Medical Council took action against Dr F. W. Axham for acting as anaesthetist for the unqualified Barker; Axham was removed from the professional register. This case aroused further public support for Barker, who also gained sympathy in 1917 when the refusal of his offer to treat soldiers was discussed in parliament. The government eventually conceded that individuals might consult an unqualified person but only on their own responsibility. By this time many eminent people, including leading medical practitioners, were anxious that Barker's skill should receive appropriate recognition. In 1920 the archbishop of Canterbury was asked to exercise his special powers and award Barker the degree of MD, Lambeth. However, this would not have 'qualified' him because it was not a degree recognized by the General Medical Council for registration. Finally, Barker was knighted in 1922. Following his retirement from regular practice soon afterwards, he spent much of his time on the continent and in the Channel Islands.

The animosity of the medical profession gradually died down. In 1936 Lord Moynihan suggested to the British Orthopaedic Association that Barker should be invited to demonstrate his techniques. A special meeting was held at St Thomas's Hospital, London, and the cases were later reported by Walter Rowley Bristow, a leading orthopaedic surgeon, in *The Lancet*, on 27 February 1937. Later, films were made at St Thomas's of Barker at work. Although he was never accepted as a conventional orthopaedic surgeon, he was held in great respect by many practitioners who were working hard during the 1920s and 1930s to establish orthopaedics as a speciality of high status. Bristow and many of his colleagues in the British Orthopaedic Association came to recognize the value of Barker's manipulative techniques and had great sympathy with his emphasis on treating patients 'holistically'. In 1941 Barker was elected manipulative surgeon to Noble's Hospital in the Isle of Man.

There had been many bone-setters before Barker, but none so eminent. His name became a household word, due in part to the reporting of his squabble with the medical profession, though this antagonism had been aroused, in part at least, because of the considerable professional reputation he had achieved. The secret of Barker's remarkable success was that in spite of being unqualified he had a gift for healing. He also had a strong personality, believing firmly in himself, and exuding confidence. He willed his patients back to normal life and did not cease treating them until they were cured. Long experience taught him which patients were unlikely to respond to his methods, and his medical friends (of whom he had many) were inundated with patients, mostly incurable, referred by him.

Barker died in the Royal Infirmary, Lancaster, on 21 July 1950; his wife survived him. STELLA BUTLER

Sources H. A. Barker, *Leaves from my life* (1927) · *BMJ* (29 July 1950), 260–61 · *The Lancet* (29 July 1950), 180 · W. Waugh, *A history of the British Orthopaedic Association* (1993), 32–3

Archives RCS Eng., papers | CAC Cam., letters to W. T. Stead · JRL, letters to the *Manchester Guardian*

Likenesses A. John, oils, 1916, NPG [*see illus.*] · J. Lavery, portrait, 1959, priv. coll. · Elf, caricature, Hentschel-colourtype, repro. in *VF* (18 Dec 1909) · A. John, portrait, Tate collection

Wealth at death £52,066 7*s*. 9*d*.—in England: administration with will, 14 June 1951, *CGPLA Eng. & Wales*

Barker, Hugh (1565–1632), civil lawyer, was the second of six sons of Robert Barker of Culworth, Northamptonshire, and his wife, Mary Danvers. The family was related to William of Wykeham, so it was natural that Barker should be educated at Wykeham's foundations, Winchester College and New College, Oxford. He graduated BCL in 1592, and subsequently became commissary of the dean of Chichester and master of Chichester Free School. Among his pupils was John Selden, and it was Barker who laid the foundations of the great legal scholar's education. His brother Anthony became Selden's tutor at Oxford.

In 1605 Barker received the degree of DCL in recognition of three dissertations on legacies. He became a full member of Doctors' Commons in 1607, and thereafter was an active practitioner in the London courts. Between 1608 and 1632 he was a member of the court of delegates, which heard appeals from the ecclesiastical courts. In 1618 he succeeded to the posts of official of the archdeacon of Oxford and chancellor of the diocese of Oxford, to which he held the reversion. He married, probably on 5 June 1620, Mary, daughter of Richard Pyott, a London alderman.

The early 1620s saw a drive against judicial corruption, and at about this time a number of charges of malpractice, chiefly misappropriation of commutation money and claiming unauthorized fees, were brought against Barker and two of his colleagues. His accuser was Humphrey Jones, the register of his court, who appears to have had a grudge against him. The case was eventually heard in the Star Chamber. The court found that Barker had been too casual in handling official moneys, but that the evidence was not reliable enough to convict him. It was doubtless because of this that in 1624 the bishop of Oxford made an unsuccessful attempt to dismiss him from office. This episode did not hinder his career, and in the following year he was appointed to the court of high commission and in 1625 became a proctor in convocation. During the 1620s he was included in a number of commissions relating to maritime affairs, and also became treasurer, and later president, of Doctors' Commons. He may briefly have held the senior judicial post of dean of arches, from about April 1632 until his death in the following autumn, although it is usually stated that Sir Henry Marten held the post continuously from 1624 to 1633. Barker was buried in the chapel of New College, Oxford, with a monument commemorating his successful career. His will shows that he was in comfortable financial circumstances, and that his heir was his daughter, Mary, his only recorded child.

SHEILA DOYLE

Sources B. P. Levack, *The civil lawyers in England, 1603–1641* (1973), 191–3, 208–9 • Dr Barker's case, 2 Rolle 384 • Doctor Barker & l'Evesq d'Oxon, 2 Rolle 306 • J. Selden, autobiographical fragment, Lincoln's Inn, London, Hale MS 12, item 42 • G. D. Squibb, *Doctors' Commons: a history of the College of Advocates and Doctors of Law* (1977), 117, 168 • *Hist. U. Oxf.* 4: *17th-cent. Oxf.*, 566 • A. Wood, *The history and antiquities of the colleges and halls in the University of Oxford*, ed. J. Gutch (1786), 200 • *CSP dom.*, *1631–3*, 402; *1633–4*, 330, 401–2 • note of Barker's succession to the posts of Anthony Blincowe, Oxford diocesan records, II.1.d. [as described in typed handlist in Oxfordshire Archives], fol. 191 • will, PRO, PROB 11/162/102

Archives Bodl. Oxf., letters and papers, and of his widow and daughter

Likenesses N. Stone, relief bust, 1632, New College chapel, Oxford

Wealth at death £200 in legacies; lands in Piddington, Oxfordshire, and elsewhere: will, PRO, PROB 11/162/102

Barker, James (1772–1838), naval officer, son of James Barker, shipowner at Rotherhithe, was born on 2 March 1772, and was entered on the books of the sloop *Beaver* as early as 13 June 1780. He afterwards, while still a boy, was on the *Prudent* in the West Indies, and was present in the engagement at St Kitts on 25 and 26 January 1782. In 1794 he was serving on the *Russell* (74 guns), and was present at the battle of 1 June. He was then transferred to the *Jupiter*, carrying the broad pennant of Commodore J. W. Payne; in the following spring he was on the royal yacht when Princess Caroline of Brunswick was brought over, a service that gained him promotion to lieutenant on 13 April 1795. He was afterwards appointed to the *Orion* (Captain Sir James Saumarez), and in her was present at the victories of L'Orient, Cape St Vincent, and the Nile; the latter gave him commander's rank on 8 October 1798. Later he commanded the hired ship *Moriston* in the Bristol Channel and on the coast of Cornwall, and was made post captain on 12 August 1812. He had no further employment in the navy and settled in the neighbourhood of Bristol. He died at Seymour Villa, near Bristol, on 4 May 1838. Barker had an undistinguished career lacking merit, promotions, and significant command experience.

J. K. LAUGHTON, *rev.* ANDREW LAMBERT

Sources D. Syrett and R. L. DiNardo, *The commissioned sea officers of the Royal Navy, 1660–1815*, rev. edn, Occasional Publications of the Navy RS, 1 (1994) • *GM*, 2nd ser., 10 (1838), 103 • J. Marshall, *Royal naval biography*, suppl. 3 (1829)

Barker, Jane (*bap.* 1652, *d.* 1732), poet and novelist, was baptized on 17 May 1652 in Blatherwycke, Northamptonshire, the second of three surviving children of Thomas Barker (*d.* 1681) and Anne, *née* Connock (*d.* 1685?). Thomas, whose family origins are uncertain, may have had a court position during the reign of Charles I as a member of the staff of the keeper of the great seal, for the notice of Jane's death in the St Germain parish register indicates he had been 'Secretaire du grand sceau d'Angleterre' (*Galesia Trilogy*, ed. Wilson, xviii). From 1662 he leased the manor at Wilsthorp, Lincolnshire (near Stamford), from the earl of Exeter, bequeathing the leasehold to Jane. On her mother's side the Connocks (or Connochs) were an old Cornish gentry family that produced a number of army officers, including Jane's 'cosen' Colonel William Connock, named by the Old Pretender to the Jacobite baronetage in 1732. William Connock was a cousin of Richard Lower, the physiologist. Anne appears to have come from an unlanded and possibly Roman Catholic branch of the family.

Jane grew up in Wilsthorp and was largely self-educated, studying Latin and medicine under the tutelage of her brother Edward (1650–1675), an MA of Christ

Church, Oxford, and exchanging verse with other amateur poets, including a group of scholars at St John's College, Cambridge. She moved to London some time after her father's death in 1681 and converted to Catholicism probably during the reign of James II. In a verse autobiography which survives in two manuscripts, she characterizes herself as Fidelia, and the political and theological reasons for her conversion are given in a powerful Drydenesque polemic (*DNB*). By June 1689 she had followed the Stuart court into exile at St Germain-en-Laye. In 1704 she returned to England to take up management of the Wilsthorp estate; by the 1710s she had the care of two young grandnieces and in 1717 was involved in a legal dispute over their custody with her niece Mary Staton (*née* Barker). She returned to France in 1727, taking up residence at the Chancellerie in St Germain. She died there in 1732, a spinster, and was buried on 29 March.

Unheralded in her own time, Barker is one of the most significant figures to emerge in the feminist recovery of early modern women writers. Over a writing career spanning nearly half a century she wrote friendship epistles, odes, satires on affairs of state, religious dialogues from a Catholic perspective, poetry on medical themes, a Jacobite heroic romance entitled *Exilius, or, The Banished Roman* (1715), and *The Christian Pilgrimage* (1718), a translation of a Lenten devotional manual by Fénelon. Her most important printed work is a trilogy of partly autobiographical prose fictions—*The amours of Bosvil and Galesia* (1713), *A Patch-Work Screen for the Ladies* (1723), and *The Lining of the Patch Work Screen* (1726)—which tell the story of a woman who slips free of the moorings of ordinary female destiny to 'espouse' instead 'a Book' (*Galesia Trilogy*, ed. Wilson, 15). The trilogy is remarkable for its psychological subtlety, acute analysis of the difficult position of a learned woman, and sympathetic rendering of the female single life. An unauthorized printing of some of her early coterie verse appeared as part 1 of *Poetical Recreations* (1688). A corrected version of this verse appears in the three-part Magdalen manuscript, which includes occasional verse written at St Germain as well as a sequence of pro-Stuart verses presented to the future Pretender in 1701, 'Poems Refering to the Times' (Magdalen College, Oxford, MS 343), another copy of which is in the British Library (Add. MS 21621). Barker remained committed to the Stuart cause all her life. A 1718 letter in the British Library shows her supplying information about a proposed invasion to the exiled Jacobite leader, the duke of Ormond (MS Stowe 232, fol. 93). Among the Stuart papers in the Royal Archives at Windsor Castle is a contribution to the Jacobite effort to canonize James II, a letter of 1730 (?) testifying to the healing powers of the blood of 'our holy king' (SP 208/129).

Although Barker is now recognized as one of the most innovative of the early novelists, her significance resides as much in the shape of her career as in the merits of her fictions. As a coterie and then court poet turned market place novelist, she exemplifies the emergence of female literary professionalism, her long and diverse writing life illustrating the shift from an amateur, court-centred manuscript-based literary system to the market-driven culture of print. She is an important Jacobite imaginative writer as well. Her verse-history 'Poems Refering to the Times' is a key Jacobite poetic text of the 1690s, while the later novels offer a sustained Catholic–Jacobite response to the declining fortunes of the Stuarts during the early Hanoverian period. KATHRYN R. KING

Sources K. R. King, 'Jane Barker and her life (1652–1732): the documentary record', *Eighteenth-Century Life*, 21 (1997), 16–38 • *The Galesia trilogy and selected manuscript poems of Jane Barker*, ed. C. S. Wilson (1997) • *DNB* • Archives municipales de Saint-Germain-en-Laye, Registre GG99, 45*r* • parish register, Blatherwycke, 1621–89, Northants. RO, 34 P/1 [baptism]

Archives BL, Stowe 232 • Royal Arch., Stuart papers 208/129

Barker, John (*fl. c.*1471–1482), logician, is first recorded as a king's scholar at Eton College about 1471, who subsequently entered King's College in 1474, was elected a fellow in 1477, and graduated MA in 1479. His Etonian connection may indicate that he was from the south of England. King's College had a system of internal lectures in which senior members taught their juniors. Barker taught logic to 'sophisters' (second-year undergraduates) using his own text, the *Scutum inexpugnabile*. No copy survives, but it was probably an introduction to Aristotelian logic and modal grammar. Brian Rowe, who came up to King's in 1499, wrote a commendatory preface for it in the early 1500s, indicating that it was then still in use in the college. Barker left King's in 1482, approximately the year John Fisher and John Colet came to Cambridge, and later joined the Franciscans. The date and place of his death are unknown. DAMIAN R. LEADER

Sources A. Allen, 'Skeleton Collegii Regalis Cantab.', King's Cam., 147–8 • S. M. Leathes, ed., *Grace book A* (1897) • F. L. Clarke, year lists of members of the foundation, King's Cam., fols. 259–314 • Emden, *Cam.* • W. Sterry, ed., *The Eton College register, 1441–1698* (1943)

Barker, John (*c.*1600–1653), naval officer and shipmaster, was possibly related to the John Barker of Ratcliffe, Middlesex, shipmaster and captain of the *Golden Cock* who in 1629, aged forty-five, appeared before the admiralty court in connection with illegally seizing, and selling, a ship belonging to the Levant Company, for which he was imprisoned (PRO, HCA 13/48, fol. 385). Nothing is known of his parents. In 1633 John Barker, a 'shipmaster of Ratcliffe … aged about 33' and the master of the *Marmaduke* of London, appeared before the admiralty court to give evidence about a voyage he had made to the Amazon River in 1631, possibly with supplies for the short-lived Guiana Company (PRO, HCA 13/50, fol. 472*v*). Barker was an associate of Maurice Thomson and other leading American traders, almost all of whom became parliamentarians, and in December 1640 he joined in a petition to parliament calling for support for English traders in the Americas against Spain (Brenner, 327n). In 1643 he commanded the hired merchant ship *John and Barbary* in parliament's summer guard. In December 1643 John Barker of Ratcliffe—'about 43 years'—was a witness in a case about the sale of the *Fortune of Hamburg*, renamed the *Mary of London*, to a Deptford resident (PRO, HCA 13/58, fol. 703). In 1646 he was captain of the *Lewis*, a merchant ship fitted for sea and held in reserve for naval service in any emergency, and in 1650 he commanded the *Great Lewis* (perhaps the same vessel) for parliament.

In April 1652 Barker hired to the state his ship *Prosperous of London*, 600 tons and 44 guns, as a man-of-war for six months at £565 a month, remaining as her captain. He was not present at Blake's engagement off Folkestone on 19 May 1652 as he was among the ships fitting out, but he was probably part of Blake's fleet on his cruise to the northward when he captured the Dutch herring fleet. In September, Barker was part of the small squadron commanded by Andrew Ball sent to Denmark, and narrowly escaped being lost in a storm at the same time as Ball's *Antelope* was wrecked. Barker returned with the fleet to England in October 1652 having taken thirteen or fourteen prizes as they returned. Ordered to refit, he missed the battle of Dungeness on 30 November 1652. After the defeat the navy was remodelled, but Barker was one of the captains in commission in a list drawn up at the end of December 1652.

Barker drew up his will on 11 February 1653 while off Harwich. He described himself as a 'Ratcliffe mariner and at the present the commander of the good ship *Prosperous*'. Barker:

> knowing that I and all men were borne to die, and that nothing is more Certain than death, but the place where and when as uncertain I therefore do with all humility both of soul and body, in and through Christ Jesus bequeath my body to the Grave and my Soul to the God that gave it me.

He left his 'well beloved wife and … yoke fellow' Elizabeth a house with a brew house and malthouse in Manningtree, Essex, two houses in Deptford, and shares in both the *Prosperous*, and the *Richard and Benjamin*, commanded by his son-in-law John Sherwin, as well as several small monetary bequests. He finished with a prayer: 'And so Almighty God our most loving Creator be pleased of his infinite Mercy to send us in his good time A Joyful meeting in this World or in the World to come at his good Pleasure Amen' (will, PRO, PROB 11/229, fol. 204). The *Prosperous* was part of Blake's Red squadron at the battle of Portland on 18 February 1653 (PRO, ADM 7/549). The vessel was in the thick of the battle and during it was engaged simultaneously by several Dutch ships led by De Ruyter. Barker behaved 'with singular dexterity and courage' but the ship was boarded by the Dutch, and after a brilliant defence, Barker and a great number of the crew were killed, the rest were wounded or overpowered, and the heavily damaged ship was captured. Her men were hastily transferred to De Ruyter's own ship, and a prize crew put on board the *Prosperous*. Captain Vesey of the frigate *Merlin* retook the *Prosperous* before nightfall, though the crew remained prisoners. Barker's widow was given a £400 gratuity, while the command of the *Prosperous* was given to Barker's son William, who had been master of the ship and badly wounded in the battle.

J. K. LAUGHTON, *rev.* PETER LE FEVRE

Sources PRO, high court of admiralty, HCA 13/48, 50, 58 • will, PRO, PROB 11/229, fol. 204 • PRO, admiralty papers, ADM 7/549 • *CSP dom.*, 1651–2 • R. Brenner, *Merchants and revolution: commercial change, political conflict, and London's overseas traders, 1550–1653* (1993) • J. R. Powell and E. K. Timings, eds., *Documents relating to the civil war, 1642–1648*, Navy RS, 105 (1963), 71, 246

Barker, John (1682–1762), Presbyterian minister, was born probably at Colchester, Essex. His parents are not known, but he is thought to have been related to Matthew Barker (1619–1698), minister of St Leonard Eastcheap, London, who was ejected in 1662. Apart from prior education at a grammar school, details of Barker's early life are unknown before he entered Timothy Jollie's academy at Attercliffe, Yorkshire, about 1699 to prepare for the ministry. Following the completion of his course he went to London to be licensed by the Presbyterians to preach. He commenced preaching at Finchingfield and Castle Hedington, Essex, about 1704, moving to a ministry in Colchester in 1707. In 1709 he became assistant preacher to Dr Benjamin Grosvenor at Crosby Square, London, then one of the foremost Presbyterian congregations in the capital.

In 1714 Barker moved to the congregation at Mare Street, Hackney, as minister on the death of Matthew Henry. This was a recognition of his growing importance as a preacher, and he restored what had become a flagging congregation. 'His preaching, which was mostly then without notes was so serious and striking as could not fail to interest his hearers' (Wilson, 2.40). However, his arrival caused a split in the congregation, the seceders forming the Gravel Pit Chapel in Hackney. The majority stayed with Barker, whose preaching was highly acceptable and theologically orthodox. In his early years at Hackney he married Bathshua Gledhill of Wakefield, Yorkshire, who died a few years later in September 1719. Barker did not court theological dispute, though at this time he was probably a Calvinist. He sided with the orthodox subscribers in the Salters' Hall debate, following which he delivered a series of addresses on the supreme and absolute divinity of Jesus Christ.

By the early 1730s Barker was recognized as one of the leading Presbyterian preachers and leaders in the London area. About this time he married a widow, Mrs Lamb of Lamb's Lane, Hackney, who also predeceased him. She brought a large fortune, so that he was relieved of financial concerns for the rest of his life. He continued in the ministry at Hackney until he suddenly resigned in 1738. This almost certainly arose out of the resignation of Philip Gibbs in 1737, who had been appointed Barker's co-pastor in 1729. Gibbs had moved to an advanced theological position that proved to be entirely unacceptable to a mainly Calvinistic congregation. Barker, while never approaching an anti-Trinitarian position, 'deviated, it would seem, from the strict letter of Calvinism' (Pike, 400) and did not see how he could continue to serve the congregation. He retired to Epsom, and then in his sixtieth year became morning preacher at Salters' Hall in 1741. He moved back to London to live in 1744, moving out to Walthamstow the following year. It is said that while he 'was not much concerned with his brethren in their temporal concerns' (Wilson, 2.54), he was an assiduous preacher and visitor to his flock. In 1748 his mother died 'at a great age' (ibid., 2.48).

Barker comes alive as a personality through his correspondence with Philip Doddridge, a close friend. They wrote about many things to each other, ranging from theology to the buying of horses. Doddridge had a very high regard for Barker as a preacher. He wrote to his wife, Mary, that he had heard Barker deliver 'an incomparable Sermon' (Nuttall, 31 July 1750, 335, no. 1637). He informed his daughter Polly that he could 'scarce forbear calling him the Prince of Preachers' (ibid., 3 Feb 1751, 349, no. 1697). Barker saw Doddridge and his academy as vitally important to the Presbyterian interest: 'Had not you supllyd our Presbyterian Churches for many Years past what would have become of Us' (ibid., 5 June 1750, 331, no. 1619). However, it is Barker's last known letter to Doddridge that is oft quoted and is a masterpiece of its kind. It rendered the dying Doddridge to tears. 'Consent and choose to stay with us a while longer—My dear Friend—if it please God ... Stay—O Stay & strengthen our hands whose shadows grow long ... Do'nt take leave abruptly ... who shall instruct our youth ...?' (ibid., 5 Aug 1751, 361, no. 1769).

Barker's published works, mainly sermons and tracts, do not suggest a light or humorous personality, but he did communicate to Doddridge the warmth of his feeling in several areas. He saw dissent in decline because it

> is not like itself: I hardly know it. It used to be famous for faith holiness and Love ... Now I hear prayers and sermons I neither relish nor understand. Evangelical Truth & Duty are quite old fashioned things ... One's ears are so dinnd with Reason. (Nuttall, 9 Oct 1744, 205, no. 1009)

'Some charge our fathers with having put believing in place of doing, I wish we may not put giving in place of believing' (ibid., 9 March 1743, 175, no. 869). As to Methodism, he concluded 'I have no expectation but that Methodism like any other enthusiasm will promote infidelity' (ibid., 4 Nov 1743, 186, no. 926). Like Doddridge he had a strong affection for his (much smaller) family.

> Our little Girl I may not improperly call the Musicke of our Family as she sung me this Morning a Hymn of Dr Watts set to a tune of her own making; and when she had done, said, O grandpappa Heaven is a fine place! (ibid., 7 Dec 1749, 317, no. 1555)

Barker continued at Salters' Hall until the spring of 1762, when he resigned. He died at Clapham on 31 May 1762, and was buried in Hackney churchyard in a family tomb.

ALAN RUSTON

Sources W. Wilson, *The history and antiquities of the dissenting churches and meeting houses in London, Westminster and Southwark*, 4 vols. (1808–14), vol. 1, p. 353; vol. 2, pp. 39–54 • *Calendar of the correspondence of Philip Doddridge*, ed. G. F. Nuttall, HMC, JP 26 (1979) • W. Harris, *Funeral sermon for Mrs. B. Barker* (1719) • C. E. Surman, index to dissenting ministers, DWL, card B.377 • W. D. Jeremy, *The Presbyterian Fund and Dr Daniel Williams's Trust* (1885), 127–8 • *DNB* • T. W. Davids, *Annals of evangelical nonconformity in Essex* (1863), 395, 501 • G. H. Pike, *Ancient meeting-houses, or, Memorial pictures of nonconformity in old London* (1870), 399–402 • will, PRO, PROB 11/876, fol. 236 • 'The Attercliffe Academy', *Transactions of the Congregational Historical Society*, 4 (1909–10), 333–42 • J. H. Colligan, *Eighteenth century nonconformity* (1915), 48, 54 • D. Coomer, *English dissent under the early Hanoverians* (1946), 47, 88, 110

Archives DWL, letters to P. Doddridge • United Reformed Church History Society, London, letters to P. Doddridge

Wealth at death see will, 1761, PRO, PROB 11/876, fol. 236

Barker, John (1708–1749), physician, son of John Barker of Derbyshire, was born on 18 April 1708. He was educated at St Thomas's Hospital, London, and at Wadham College, Oxford, where he matriculated in March 1728 and graduated BA in 1731, MA and MB in 1737, and DM in 1743.

Barker practised medicine in Salisbury for nine years from 1737 to 1746. He became involved in a public dispute with a fellow Salisbury physician, Henry Hele (1688–1778), over the nature and treatment of an epidemic fever which swept Salisbury, London, and various west-country towns between 1741 and 1742. Barker was fiercely opposed to the practice of venesection—the repeated bleeding of the patient—a method relied upon by Hele in the treatment of fever cases. When in consultation over a patient the two disagreed about the appropriate treatment, and the alleged failure of Barker's method in the case was made public, thereby damaging his reputation in the locality.

Barker published a defence of his views, entitled *An Inquiry into the Nature, Cause and Cure of the Epidemic Fever*, in 1742. An exchange of letters between the two doctors in the *Salisbury Journal* followed, with Hele implying that the youth and inexperience of Barker had led to his misunderstanding of the nature and treatment of the epidemic fever. In March 1743 Barker published a further defence of his views, incorporating within it the correspondence between the two men and the patient they both had treated.

Three years later, in 1746, Barker became a member of the Royal College of Physicians and moved to London to take up the post of physician to the Westminster Hospital. In September the following year he was appointed physician to the forces in the Low Countries and in 1748 he served as physician to the general hospital at Oosterhuit, during the campaign in the Netherlands. Barker died at Ipswich on 31 January 1749 and was buried in St Stephen's Church, Ipswich, where there is a tablet commemorating his name.

P. B. AUSTIN, *rev.* CLAIRE E. J. HERRICK

Sources B. W. Alexander, 'The epidemic fever (1741–42)', *Salisbury Medical Bulletin*, 11 (1971), 24–9 • A. Peterkin and W. Johnston, *Commissioned officers in the medical services of the British army, 1660–1960*, 1 (1968), 20 • Munk, *Roll* • Foster, *Alum. Oxon.* • S. C. Lawrence, *Charitable knowledge: hospital pupils and practitioners in eighteenth-century London* (1996)

Archives Sheff. Arch., corresp.

Barker, John (1771–1849), diplomatist and horticulturist, was born at Smyrna on 9 March 1771. His father, William Barker, of The Hall, Bakewell, Derbyshire, was on his way from Florida to India, when ill health caused him to settle at Smyrna. John Barker was educated in England, and at the age of eighteen joined the banking house of Peter Thellusson, in Philpot Lane, London, where he became confidential clerk and cashier. About 1797 he went to the Porte as private secretary to John Spencer Smith, British ambassador there. On 9 April 1799 he was commissioned by patent as pro-consul at Aleppo, and agent *ad interim* for the Levant and the East India companies. He was regularly appointed agent for the East India Company over the next thirty-three years.

Barker became full consul for the Levant Company on 18

November 1803; he introduced vaccination into Syria in the same year. In March 1807 he fled from Aleppo, because of tension between England and the Porte, and, having previously entrusted his wife and children to him, took refuge with the prince of the Druses in Lebanon. He managed to carry on his duties from Haris and transmitted information between Britain and India. His diligence allowed news of the suspension of the peace of Amiens and of the landing of Napoleon at Cannes to be forwarded to India with remarkable speed, preventing the surrender of Pondicherry to the French. When peace between England and Turkey was declared, Barker returned to Aleppo, making a splendid public entry on 2 June 1809.

In 1818 Barker travelled on leave to London via Marseilles, returning on 25 October 1820, and in 1825 was appointed British consul at Alexandria, arriving on 25 October 1826. He acted as consul-general in Egypt from 1827 and served formally in the post from November 1829 until 31 May 1833, when he left Egypt for his villa at Suediah, near Antioch.

At Suediah, Barker planted a garden, known throughout the East, where he grew all the fruits of the West, introduced many new species into Syria, and supplied new varieties to England, the most famous being the Stanwick nectarine, for which he received a medal from the Horticultural Society of London. He sent agents all over the Orient to collect cuttings of the best fruit trees and in 1844 visited England to introduce some of these exotic trees. He worked to improve silk and cotton culture, and promoted other enterprises in Syria. 'A perfect gentleman', according to Neale, 'an accomplished scholar, a sagacious thinker, a philosopher, and philanthropist.' He died of apoplexy at a summer house at Betias, on Mount Rhosus, on 5 October 1849 (*Syria and Egypt*, 2.285). He was buried beside the Armenian church at Betias, where a marble monument from Genoa was left to his memory. Among his children was the orientalist William Burckhardt *Barker. ARTHUR H. GRANT, *rev.* LYNN MILNE

Sources *Syria and Egypt under the last five sultans of Turkey: being experiences … of Mr Consul-General Barker*, ed. E. B. B. Barker, 2 vols. (1876) • F. A. Neale, *Eight years in Syria, Palestine and Asia Minor, from 1842–1850* (1851)
Archives BL, letters to Lord Wellesley, Add. MS 13793 • Bodl. Oxf., letters to Michael Bruce • Bodl. Oxf., corresp. with Lady Stanhope • Herefs. RO, corresp. with Sir Harford Jones • NL Scot., letters to Robert Liston

Barker, Sir John (1840–1914), department store owner, was born at Loose, Kent, on 6 April 1840, the son of Joseph Barker, a carpenter and brewer, and his wife, Ann Sells. He was educated privately and in 1853 began a three-year apprenticeship to a draper in Maidstone. Further experience in drapery shops followed in Folkestone and Dover until 1858, when he moved to London to join Messrs Spencer, Turner, and Boldero, a firm of furnishers and drapers in Marylebone.

After a few years in London, Barker was offered a position at William Whiteley's new emporium in Westbourne Grove. He proved a gifted salesman and was promoted to department manager with an annual salary of £300. Within a year he succeeded in doubling sales at the store and his salary was similarly doubled. He had hoped for a partnership, but Whiteley was reluctant to relinquish sole control. He did, however, offer Barker £1000 a year in compensation.

Meanwhile on 7 January 1865 Barker had married 28-year-old Sarah Waspe, daughter of William Waspe, 'gentleman', of Tuddenham, Suffolk, the ceremony being held at St Matthew's parish church, Bayswater. They had a daughter, Ann Sarah, and a son, John. The latter died young in a riding accident in 1914.

In 1870 Barker left Whiteleys to open a small drapery shop in Kensington High Street, and this was the germ from which sprang the famous department store Barkers of Kensington. His partner, James Whitehead, was already a wealthy merchant and provided capital and credit without interfering in the running of the business. As managing partner Barker drew an annual salary of £250 and lived over the shop with his family. As part owner, he was now able to exploit the modes of retailing that had proved so successful at Whiteleys. By dealing directly with manufacturers and selling for cash he was able to keep prices down and realize a rapid turnover.

Barker had long envisaged a vast store that, unlike most shops of the day, would carry diverse stock. To this end he bought up new premises whenever he could and by 1880 was trading in fifteen shops in Kensington High Street and Ball Street, selling not only drapery goods but also groceries, furnishings, and ironmongery. In 1893 he acquired Whitehead's share in the business. The business now boasted sixty departments and a staff of 1400. Barker continued to expand and in 1907 acquired Ponting Brothers, a fashion store specializing in art needlework in Kensington High Street that was in liquidation. Business continued to boom and in 1908 Barker was awarded a baronetcy in Edward VII's birthday honours list.

John Barker's interests were not restricted to retailing. In the 1890s he had bought a 300-acre estate in Bishop's Stortford which he farmed using the latest methods. He was a breeder of livestock and was famed for his polo ponies and flock of Syrian sheep. He also embarked on a political career, and in 1889 was one of the first aldermen to be elected to the new London county council. He was president of Hammersmith Liberal Association, councillor for Chelsea Liberal Association, and founder president of Bishop's Stortford District Liberal Association. He contested Maidstone three times, in 1888, 1898, and 1900, and although elected on the third attempt was unseated on petition by the Conservatives. From 1906 to 1910 he sat as MP for Penrhyn and Falmouth. He was also a member of the Reform and National Liberal clubs, and after the Second South African War was a prominent supporter of the Territorial Movement.

John Barker died of cerebral thrombosis and heart failure on 16 December 1914 at his home, The Grange, Bishop's Stortford, leaving no heir. ADRIAN ROOM

Sources A. Turton, 'Barker, Sir John', *DBB* • D. W. Peel, *A garden in the sky: the story of Barkers of Kensington, 1870–1957* (1960) • *Herts. and*

Essex Observer (19 Dec 1914) · *The Times* (17 Dec 1914) · b. cert. · m. cert. · d. cert.
Likenesses cartoon, repro. in *VF* (*c*.1908)
Wealth at death £239,145 8*s*. 6*d*.: probate, 12 March 1915, *CGPLA Eng. & Wales*

Barker, Joseph (1806–1875), Methodist minister and politico-religious controversialist, was born on 11 May 1806 at Bramley, near Leeds. His ancestors, originally of Keighley, had been settled in this area for several generations as farmers and manufacturers. The identity of his parents has not been discovered, though it is known that his father was employed in woollen manufacture and served for some time in the militia, and that Joseph was the fifth child and the fourth son in a family of eleven. Barker's autobiographical works, written late in life, emphasize the great deprivation and hardships of his childhood: he remarked that long hours at the spinning jenny resulted in physical disability and general weakness, but did afford him the opportunity to read as he worked. His early education was obtained largely through Sunday school; his parents were devout Wesleyan Methodists, and in 1822 he joined the church, though admitting that 'my determination to yield was not quite full' (*Life*, 40–41). He was involved in regular prayer meetings and became an occasional preacher. He furthered his education during this time with the help of Joseph Sutcliffe, a Wesleyan travelling preacher, who assisted him with his reading and grammar. Joseph Hill, a schoolmaster at Bramley and a local preacher, instructed him in Latin and Greek. When his family's financial circumstances improved, he was sent to the Methodist school run by James Sigston in Leeds.

About a year after joining the Wesleyans, Barker was encouraged to preach more regularly and 'put on the plan' as a home missionary and exhorter, and later as a local preacher in spite of questions about his views on the atonement. He proved popular, but was unable to offer himself as a travelling preacher because he was unwilling to serve abroad (those wishing to become travelling preachers were required to indicate a willingness to be sent anywhere by the conference). However, a much larger issue was the requirement to subscribe to the doctrine of the eternal sonship as taught by Richard Watson and Jabez Bunting, in opposition to Adam Clarke. This was a test to which Barker could not bring himself to subscribe. Reflection on these questions led Barker to scrutinize other aspects of the Wesleyan communion. He began to feel that the old connexion was wrong on other issues as well, and looked to the preachers of the Methodist New Connexion. He proclaimed that her 'doctrines were almost all expressed in Scripture language, and plainly designed to allow of considerable variety of opinion' (*Life*, 106).

Barker joined the ministry of the Methodist New Connexion and went to Nottingham to assist John Henshaw, who was ill, and then to Liverpool as a supply preacher. Barker was appointed as a travelling preacher on trial to the Hanley circuit in Staffordshire, from 1829 to 1830, and

Joseph Barker (1806–1875), by John Cochran, pubd 1880

to the Halifax circuit in Yorkshire from 1830 to 1831. During the latter appointment, in 1830 he married Francis Salt of Betley, in Staffordshire. They had at least two sons and a daughter. Conference rules forbade a travelling preacher to marry while on probation, and as a penalty Barker lost one year of his probationary term. In addition to this, a disciplinary migration sent him to Blyth, in the Newcastle upon Tyne circuit (1831–2), from whence he proceeded to Durham for service in the Sunderland circuit for six months (1832–3). In Newcastle, he benefited greatly from the vast library of Dr Tomlinson of St Nicholas's Church. One effect of his reading was a resolution to be free of the restrictions the connexion had placed upon him.

Despite his tremendous popularity, Barker feared that he would have difficulty being received into full connexion: while his abilities and labour were deemed satisfactory, a number of questions arose about his theological opinions, but he was none the less admitted into full connexion in 1833 and appointed to the Sheffield circuit. Here he became involved in various educational enterprises for young people and ministers, and also entered into the controversy with 'unbelievers' in the area, offering a course of public lectures and publishing *The Character and Tendency of Christianity* (1833). These activities further strengthened his resolve to become 'an evangelical or a theological reformer' (*Life*, 175–6). He became a teetotaller while in Sheffield and quickly became a zealous lecturer on the topic of abstinence both in Sheffield and afterwards in the Chester circuit (1835–7). The further radicalization of Barker's views was evident from his decision to give up tobacco, tea, and coffee for a time in 1835. From Chester, Barker moved to the Mossley circuit in 1837. There he began a weekly periodical called the *Christian*

Investigator and Evangelical Reformer, which explored a range of issues including temperance, marriage, trade, and education. The freedom of expression which Barker sought soon brought him difficulties. He held unorthodox opinions on child baptism and the Lord's Supper; his views were deemed by some to be heretical. At the conference of 1839 he was moved to Gateshead, a comparatively new circuit. It was here that he became a prominent lecturer against Owenite socialism. He published a number of pamphlets, tracts, and sermons on this subject in addition to materials in the *Evangelical Reformer*.

In the final issue of the *Reformer* (1840) Barker restated some of the theological views which had created controversy, and his case was brought before the conference of the Methodist New Connexion. Meeting at Halifax in 1841, it expelled Barker on the ground that he 'had denied the divine appointment of baptism, and refused to administer the ordinance' (*Life*, 260). His expulsion was followed by a loss to the connexion of '29 societies and 4,348 members', among them a congregation in Newcastle upon Tyne, of which Barker became the pastor. He was determined to model his new church as closely as possible on New Testament principles, but later admitted to the impracticable nature of such plans and to the gradual dispersal of his followers, who were known as Barkerites. In his chapel Barker delivered many lectures and encouraged free discussion on a range of topics. He also worked as a printer, and in addition to other publications began to issue a periodical called *The Christian*. During this period his views were in a state of flux, first inclining towards Quakerism, and afterwards to Unitarianism. In 1845 he preached in Unitarian chapels both in London and elsewhere. The Unitarians enabled him to start a printing establishment on a larger scale at Wortley, a suburb of Leeds: on 6 July 1846 Dr John Bowring presented him with a steam printing press, purchased at a cost of some £600 with money specially raised for the purpose. Some months previously Barker had issued a 'proposal for a new library of three hundred volumes, the cheapest collection of works ever published' (ibid., 285). He issued books on a range of theological, philosophical, and ethical topics which were bound in cloth and priced at between 1*s.* and 1*s.* 3*d.* each.

By 1846 Barker's political interests had become more radical. He advocated republicanism for England, repeal of the Act of Union for Ireland, and the nationalization of land. These views were presented in a weekly periodical called *The People*, which sought to 'wage unsparing war with every thing that stands in the way of the people's rights, the people's liberties, the people's improvement, and the people's prosperity' (*The People*, 1/1, 1846). At the height of its popularity it sold more than 20,000 copies each week. In 1847 Barker went on a six months' tour in America and became interested in various emigration schemes for the working classes. Back in England he was a delegate to the Chartist convention in 1848. He professed to be a peaceful advocate of the Charter, but found himself arrested for seditious libel along with a number of other political agitators following the Liverpool summer assizes of 1848. While on bail Barker went to Bolton, where he was elected MP for the borough at a by-election by popular acclaim, though he never sat in parliament. He also offered himself as a candidate for the town council of Leeds as a representative of the Holbeck ward and was elected by a considerable majority.

The charges against Barker were dropped at the winter assizes, and he made another trip to the United States in 1849. His impression of the States was so favourable that he determined to leave England with his family and settle there. In 1851 they moved to Knox county, Ohio—a location not too distant from Barker's brothers. Immediately he thrust his energies into the anti-slavery movement, travelling to many meetings in the north-eastern states from 1852 to 1854. The influence of the abolitionists William Lloyd Garrison and Henry C. Wright helped to accelerate Barker's growing religious scepticism. The belief that the Bible sanctioned slavery led him to become a deist, and his lectures became marked by a strong secularist anti-slavery agenda. He was effectively driven from rural Ohio by other settlers who found his trenchant secularism and radical opinions intolerable. In 1854 Barker returned to England, where his interest in the labour movement was reawakened. He believed that he must advance the case of the slaves and the English and Irish workers in tandem. During his lecture tour he encountered further difficulties as a result of his religious opinions, and returned to Ohio in the spring of 1855. After one or two temporary relocations, he eventually settled in Nebraska in 1856. In the summer of 1857 he began a long tour in Philadelphia, where he lectured every Sunday for eight months. After spending a few weeks with his family in Nebraska, he returned to Philadelphia in August 1858 to undertake another eight-month course of lectures, but completed only two months of the engagement. Having concluded that 'war with Christianity was not the way to promote the virtue and happiness of mankind' (*Life*, 341), he resolved to return to England, where he thought he might be able to distance himself from men of extreme views on religion and politics and feel free to pursue whatever path he believed to be true. Accordingly, he sailed from Boston on 11 January 1860, and his wife and children followed him in August of the same year.

In April 1860 Barker agreed to become one of the editors of the *National Reformer*, a secularist paper. He insisted on complete control over half of the paper, but soon found himself in conflict with his co-editor, Charles Bradlaugh. A turning point seems to have come when Barker was sent for review a secularist book which, in his view, undermined marriage and licensed extramarital sexual indulgence. He resigned the post in August 1861 and immediately began his own paper, *Barker's Review of Politics, Literature, Religion, and Morals, and Journal of Education, Science and Co-operation*. Around this time he was 'overpowered and reconverted by re-reading the Scriptures' (*Life*, 346–7), and began to retrace his steps back to Methodism via Unitarianism. In 1862 he became lecturer to a congregation of an eclectic kind of 'unbelievers' at Burnley, where he lived and laboured for more than a year, enforcing the precepts of morality and often taking occasion to speak favourably of the Bible and Christianity. As Barker returned to the fold, he considered seeking ordination in the Church of England, having dropped his objections to the state church. However, he recognized that his past and age were against him. He was formally reconciled to his old religious belief, and afterwards preached, at their invitation, to the Methodist reformers of Wolverhampton. After accepting like invitations from the Primitive Methodists of Bilston and Tunstall, he joined their community as a local preacher, and held the office until 1868. He was profoundly affected by the death of his wife in 1871, by which time his own health was failing. He returned to the United States, where he spent the winters in Philadelphia lecturing and printing Christian tracts and sermons. In the summers he joined his family in Nebraska. He died of dropsy and jaundice in Omaha on 15 September 1875, and was buried there. A few days before his death he solemnly declared that he died 'in the firm and full belief of Jesus Christ, and in the faith and love of His religion as revealed in His life and works, as described in the New Testament' (ibid., 385). EILEEN GROTH LYON

Sources *The life of Joseph Barker, written by himself, edited by his nephew* (1880) • J. Barker, diary, 1865–75, Nebraska State Historical Society, Lincoln, Nebraska, Barker collection • *The Christian* (1844–8) • *The People* (1848–9) • E. Royle, 'Barker, Joseph', *BDMBR*, vol. 2 • B. Fladeland, *Abolitionists and working class problems in the age of industrialization* (1984), chap. 7 • *DNB* • W. Baggaly, *A digest of the minutes … of the Methodist New Connexion* (1862) • O. A. Beckerlegge, 'Barker, Joseph', *The Blackwell dictionary of evangelical biography, 1730–1860*, ed. D. M. Lewis (1995) • *IGI*
Archives JRL, Methodist Archives and Research Centre, corresp. relating to expulsion from Methodist New Connexion • Nebraska State Historical Society, Lincoln, Nebraska, papers
Likenesses J. Cochran, engraving, repro. in *The life of Joseph Barker* [*see illus.*]

Barker, Dame **Lilian Charlotte** (1874–1955), prison administrator, was born on 21 February 1874 in Islington, the fifth of seven children and youngest daughter of James Barker, tobacconist, and his wife, Caroline Williams. Educated at the local elementary school, she was trained at Whitelands College, Chelsea, and began her career as a teacher in elementary schools under the London county council. After a break of seven years to nurse her invalid mother she resumed her teaching. Her success at teaching both boys and girls revealed her exceptional ability, and led to her appointment in 1913 as principal of the council's Women's Institute, which from 1914 was in Cosway Street, Marylebone.

The outbreak of war interrupted Barker's career and in 1915 she was appointed the first commandant of the women's legion cookery section in which she did valuable work in training cooks for the army. Later in 1915 she became lady superintendent at Woolwich arsenal, where her talent for dealing with people first found full scope. She was responsible eventually for the welfare of some 30,000 women in an organization where women had never before been employed. She set up canteens, first-aid posts, cloakrooms, and rest rooms. She organized outside recreation, sick visiting, convalescent and holiday homes, and the care of unmarried mothers and their babies; for all this she raised the necessary private funds. Output soared. She subdued strikers by oratory and her public presence, telling one mass meeting that anyone who limited output betrayed husbands and sweethearts at the front. Barker rejected 'ladies' as supervisors, preferring any woman with managerial experience. She was appointed CBE in 1917.

In 1919 Barker joined the training department of the Ministry of Labour, and in 1920 became executive officer of the central committee on women's training and employment to administer £600,000 for training and supporting women who had suffered from the economic effects of the war. In 1923 she became governor of the Borstal Institution for Girls at Aylesbury. Borstal training for girls had little public recognition, and the prison commissioners were fortunate to attract her services. She took a considerable drop in salary, but saw that the post was important, and took it when the commissioners assured her that she would have a free hand.

Up to that time Aylesbury, which housed about 100 of the worst female offenders between the ages of sixteen and twenty-one, had been run on lines which differed little from a contemporary conventional prison regime, and the results were not encouraging. Lilian Barker brought a new spirit. She used the insights of her experience at Woolwich, arguing that the will to lead a good and useful life is never manifest in the unhappy and unfulfilled, and at once set to work to humanize the treatment of 'her girls'. Print dresses replaced the old prison clothes, cells were transformed into pleasantly furnished rooms with comfortable beds, meals became appetizing, and organized games and a swimming pool were introduced. Even more important was her own personal influence.

Short and stocky, with iron-grey hair cut short under a pork-pie hat, and almost always dressed in a tweed suit of severe cut, Barker's somewhat mannish appearance was reinforced by a deep voice and a manner which could be very direct and even brusque. Both munitions workers and borstal residents speculated that she was a man. She was a devout Christian but common sense was more her text than scripture.

Contemporaries reported that Barker's laugh was full and infectious, her humour dry but penetrating; her bright eyes could flash with fun as well as anger. Her nightly talks to her girls over a cigarette were one of the secrets of her success. She was, however, a disciplinarian in her own way. Her punishments were imaginative if unconventional and aimed to fit the crime: the girl who in a fit of temper tore her blankets into strips was made to sew them up and sleep under the resulting covering. It was not long before Lilian Barker won the respect and affection of her difficult charges, yet there was never any doubt at Aylesbury that discipline was maintained. She continued to receive a voluminous fan mail from her old girls long after they had left, and took an interest in their weddings and their children. She herself never married.

In 1935 Lilian Barker was invited to become the first woman assistant commissioner of prisons. Although it cost her much to leave Aylesbury, she responded at once to this call to wider service. She became responsible for all women's prisons in England and Wales, and, by arrangement with the prison department there, also in Scotland. Under her guidance improvements were made in the clothing and feeding of women prisoners, and she was immersed in plans for creating a new prison for women outside London when the outbreak of war in 1939 brought this and other developments in which she was interested to an end. She retired in 1943 and was appointed DBE in 1944. She continued to live at her cottage at Wendover Dean and to maintain a lively interest in affairs until her death on 21 May 1955 while on holiday at Trouts Hotel, Hallsands, Devon. HAROLD SCOTT, *rev.* D. THOM

Sources employment section, IWM, women's work collection [Barker's evidence to the war cabinet committee on women in industry] • H. Bentwick, *If I forget thee: some chapters of autobiography, 1912–1920* (1973) • *The Times* (23 May 1955) • *The Observer* (29 May 1955) • 'Report of the commissioners of prisons', *Parl. papers* (1955), vol. 27, Cmd 9547 • E. Gore, *The better fight: the story of Dame Lilian Barker* (1965) • private information (1971) • personal knowledge (1971) • *WWW* • *CGPLA Eng. & Wales* (1955)

Likenesses photographs, IWM

Wealth at death £1857 15*s.* 10*d.*: probate, 19 Aug 1955, *CGPLA Eng. & Wales*

Barker, Lucette Elizabeth (1816–1905), painter, was born in Thirkelby, Yorkshire, and baptized there on 29 July 1816, the daughter of Thomas Barker and his wife, Jane Flower (*d.* 1858). Her father was the vicar in Thirkelby, and she was the eldest of four sisters, two of whom also became artists: Leila Florentina Catherine Barker (1825–1903) and Octavia Constance Barker (married name Kingsley; 1826–1917) painted still-life and botanical and flower studies in watercolour. Another sister, Laura Wilson Barker (1817–1905), became a composer. Lucette was taught to draw by her father, who also paid for lessons and encouraged visits to private collections and London exhibitions. However, he was determined that his daughters would not work for their living. The writer Margaret Gatty wrote of meeting Lucette and her family in 1846: 'Her designs are exquisitely beautiful—she is in short such a tremendous genius … The Father won't let them print or publish anything!' (Cherry, 132). Barker's early work included a book illustration of 1851, the frontispiece engraved by C. Simms for *The Fairy Godmothers and other Tales* by Margaret Gatty (1851). Despite her father's opposition, between 1853 and 1874 Lucette Barker exhibited twenty-one paintings: four at the Royal Academy, one at the British Institution, and sixteen at various other exhibitions. At the Royal Academy she exhibited portraits such as *Ellen, Daughter of R. Westmacott, Esq., R.A.* (in 1853) as well as two animal pictures, *Dogs' Heads* (in 1855) and *A Pet Terrier* (in 1856). At the British Institution she exhibited in 1853 a painting of a scene from Shakespeare's *Othello* entitled *Desdemona and Emilia.*

In 1855 Lucette Barker's sister Laura married the art critic for *The Times* and *The Graphic*, Tom *Taylor; he was also a playwright and later became editor of *Punch*. Taylor was supportive both financially and professionally of the Barker sisters while providing links to the London art world. During this period Lucette Barker, who remained unmarried, moved south to London and joined the Taylors at Eagle Lodge, Brompton. There she moved in the fashionable artistic circles associated with Little Holland House and made portrait sketches of its residents, the artist G. F. Watts and his wife, the actress Ellen Terry. After their mother's death on 20 March 1858 the sisters travelled to Italy, where Lucette produced a series of sketches and watercolours of people, architecture, and landscapes, later compiled into a presentation album (priv. coll.). In 1858 the Taylors moved to a new home, Lavender Sweep, Wandsworth, which became a meeting place and haven for artists, musicians, and actors including Ellen Terry. Lucette Barker filled presentation albums and sketchbooks with drawings of women friends and kin; when she met Margaret Gatty she presented her with a large chalk self-portrait as a token of friendship. Family albums also contain Lucette's watercolour studies of her sister Laura with her young son Wycliffe painted during the 1850s and 1860s (for example, those repro. in Cherry, pls. 16 and 24: *Laura Taylor and her Son Wycliffe*, 1859, priv. coll., and *Lavender Sweep, Wycliffe and 'Lieb Nurse'*, *c.*1864, priv. coll.). Her depictions of women and children engaged in domestic routines in comfortable interiors form part of a nineteenth-century genre available to women artists and celebrate the Victorian ideal of motherhood. Although it seems that she ceased to exhibit after the 1870s (perhaps as a result of the death of Tom Taylor in 1880), she continued to paint watercolour portraits and botanical and garden scenes until 1900. Following Taylor's death, Lucette and her sister Laura lived together at Porch House, Coleshill, Amersham, Buckinghamshire. Lucette Barker died there at the age of eighty-eight on 21 January 1905.

MEAGHAN E. CLARKE

Sources D. Cherry, *Painting women: Victorian women artists* (1993) • Graves, *Brit. Inst.* • Graves, *RA exhibitors* • Wood, *Vic. painters*, 3rd edn • Graves, *Artists* • C. Maxwell, *Mrs Gatty and Mrs Ewing* (1949) • E. Terry, *The story of my life* (1908) • *IGI* • d. cert.

Likenesses photographs, priv. coll.

Barker, Lucy Elizabeth Drummond Sale- [*née* Lucy Elizabeth Drummond Davies] (**1841–1892**), children's writer, was born in London, the third child of Francis Henry Davies (1791–1863), registrar of the court of chancery, and of his wife, Lady Lucy Clementina *Davies (1795–1879), author, only sister of George Drummond, fifth earl of Perth and sixth duke of Melfort in the peerage of France. On 25 August 1858 Lucy Davies married Lieutenant-Colonel James John Villiers (*b.* 1823/4), who died in command of the 74th highlanders at Belasse, India, on 10 May 1862, aged thirty-eight. Three years later, on 10 August 1865, she married John Sale-Barker (*d.* 1884), barrister, of Cadogan Place, Chelsea, London.

Lucy Sale-Barker began her literary career with occasional articles for the *Dublin University* and *St James's* magazines, and about 1872 began to write regularly for children. Between 1874 and 1888 she published more than forty volumes for juvenile readers with titles such as *Little Bright Eyes' Picture Book* and *Little Golden Locks' Story Book*. Many of the stories she had composed for her own children. She edited *Little Wide-Awake*, a magazine for children, from its commencement in 1874 until her death, and wrote the verses for Kate Greenaway's popular *Birthday Book for Children* (1880). Lucy Sale-Barker died on 4 May 1892 at her home, Inglenook, 93 Lennard Road, Penge, London.

ELIZABETH LEE, *rev.* VICTORIA MILLAR

Sources *The Times* (9 May 1892), 6 • F. Hays, *Women of the day: a biographical dictionary of notable contemporaries* (1885) • *GM*, 3rd ser., 13 (1862) • Burke, *Peerage* [Perth] • *BL cat.* • Allibone, *Dict.* • Boase, *Mod. Eng. biog.* • d. cert.

Wealth at death £146 7*s.* 6*d.*: probate, 16 Sept 1892, *CGPLA Eng. & Wales*

Barker [*née* Stewart], **Mary Anne**, **Lady Barker** [*other married name* Mary Anne Broome, Lady Broome] (**1831–1911**), journalist and writer, was born on 29 May 1831 in Spanish Town, Jamaica, the daughter of Walter George Stewart (*d.* 1864), last island secretary of Jamaica, and Susan Hewitt (*d.* 1856), daughter of the prosperous landowner William Hewitt. She had two brothers and two sisters. She was sent to England to be educated, thus becoming well travelled at an early age as she returned frequently for holidays. She also spent time in Paris learning French. In 1852 in Spanish Town she married Captain George Robert *Barker (1817–1861), an officer in the Royal Artillery, who was promoted to colonel in the Crimea and to brigadier-general in the Indian mutiny of 1859, when he was appointed KGB, she thereby becoming Lady Barker. They had two sons: John Stewart (*b.* 1853) and Walter George (*b.* 1857), later Lieutenant-Colonel Walter George Crole-Wyndham of the Royal Artillery (he changed his name after inheriting property from an aunt). In 1860 she and the children joined her husband in Bengal, but eight months later, in July 1861, he died in Simla. She returned to England, where she lived quietly.

On 21 June 1865 at Prees, Shropshire, Lady Barker married Frederick Napier *Broome (1842–1896), eldest son of the rector of Kenley, Shropshire, and at the time of their marriage a sheep farmer in New Zealand. She left her sons in England to be educated and sailed with Broome to life on a 9700-acre sheep ranch on the banks of the Selwyn River, South Island, which they named Broomielaw. Their first son, Hopton Napier, died on 12 March 1866, aged two months. Henceforth, Mary Anne's literary career was inextricably entwined with her husband's professional life.

During the voyage out and the three years she spent in the colony, Lady Barker, as she was known, was busy observing and reacting to her new home, storing material which formed the basis for her later writing. The Broomes sold their interest in the ranch in 1868 and left New Zealand for good, partly because of a devastating snowstorm which killed 4000 of their 7000 sheep, and partly because of a lack of single-minded attention to sheep-raising on the part of Broome, who favoured pig-hunting and writing poetry.

Back in London, both Broomes turned to journalism and authorship to earn a living. Their work appeared in the *Cornhill Magazine* and *Macmillan's Magazine*; Frederick became a special correspondent for *The Times*, where Mary Anne reviewed novels. She edited the monthly *Evening Hours: a Family Magazine* from 1874 to 1877. Encouraged by her friends Alexander Macmillan and George Grove, Mary Anne published *Station Life in New Zealand* (1870) describing her colonial life and based partly on letters written home to her younger sister, Jessie Stewart. Her lively and engaging style and refreshing sense of humour ensured its success: the book went through four editions, and numerous reprintings, between 1870 and 1887. It was also translated into French and German.

Over the next five years Mary Anne's writing career flourished: she published several more volumes of colonial experiences, including *Station Amusements in New Zealand* (1873); five books of children's stories, the best-known being *A Christmas Cake in Four Quarters* (1871); and, in 1874, *First Principles of Cookery*, which resulted in her appointment as first lady superintendent of a new National School of Cookery. She gave birth to two sons, Guy Saville (1870), and Louis Egerton (1874).

Over the next twenty-one years Broome's colonial appointments took them to Natal where he was colonial secretary (1875–7) and where Mary Anne wrote *A Year's Housekeeping in South Africa* (1877); to Mauritus, where he was colonial secretary and then lieutenant-governor (1877–80); to Western Australia, where he was governor (1882–90); and to Trinidad, where he was governor (1890–95). From Australia, Mary Anne published *Letters to Guy* (1884) for her son, who was at school in England, describing their life in a pioneer, newly developing colony. During the 1880s she also edited several travel books by Lady Anna Brassey, including the final one, *The Last Voyage* (1888). On 3 July 1884, Broome was appointed KCMG, and Lady Barker became Lady Broome.

Because of Mary Anne's active involvement in Australian public life, her writing career was curtailed. She travelled widely in the colony with her husband, presided at entertainments, and championed education for the young; she was described at this time as 'a fine, tall woman, with well-marked features and a somewhat decided manner' (Hasluck in *Remembered with Affection*, 8).

After five years as governor of Trinidad, Sir Frederick returned with Lady Broome to London, where he died in 1896, leaving his wife in straitened circumstances. She petitioned the government of Western Australia and was awarded a modest annuity of £150 in 1897, which allowed her to live comfortably in Eaton Terrace, London. She turned again to journalism and published a series of articles in the *Cornhill Magazine* in 1899 and 1900 and in *The Boudoir* in 1903. Some were later collected in her final work, *Colonial Memories* (1904). Lady Broome died at her home at 42 Eaton Terrace, London, on 7 March 1911 of heart disease.

Barker was 'at once an excellent writer, witty, extraordinarily informed … her botanical and ornithological knowledge, extensive' (Kidman, vii). Her final work is valuable for its autobiographical details, as social history, and 'as a picture of colonial expansion in Victorian times' (Hasluck in *Remembered with Affection*, 25).

ROSEMARY T. VAN ARSDEL

Sources A. Hasluck, introduction, *Remembered with affection* (1963) [new edn of Lady Broome, *Letters to Guy* (1885)] · C. Hankin, 'Barker, Mary Anne', *DNZB* · M. A. Broome, *Colonial memories* (1904) · F. Kidman, introduction, *Station life in New Zealand* (Boston, 1987) · G. H. Scholefield, ed., *A dictionary of New Zealand biography*, 2 vols. (1940), vol. 1, pp. 39–40 · A. Hasluck, 'Lady Broome', *Historical Studies: Australia and New Zealand*, 27 (Nov 1956), 291–302 · B. Gilderdale, *The seven lives of Lady Barker: author of 'Station life in New Zealand'* (1996) · *BL cat.* · *A bibliographical catalogue of Macmillan and Co.'s publications from 1843 to 1889* (1891) · J. Shattock, ed., *The Cambridge bibliography of English literature*, 3rd edn, 4 (1999) · *Wellesley index*, vol. 5, p. 105 · F. Hays, *Women of the day: a biographical dictionary of notable contemporaries* (1885) · Blain, Clements & Grundy, *Feminist comp.* · *The Waterloo directory of English newspapers and periodicals, 1800–1900*, 3 (1997), 1803

Likenesses J. S. Barker, portrait, repro. in Gilderdale, *The seven lives of Lady Barker* · photograph, NL NZ, Turnbull L.; repro. in Kidman, *Station life*, cover · photograph, repro. in *Christchurch Weekly Press* (29 March 1911)

Wealth at death £3202 8*s*. 5*d*.: probate, 31 March 1911, *CGPLA Eng. & Wales*

Barker, Matthew (**1619–1698**), Independent minister, was born in Cransley, Northamptonshire, of unknown parents. He was groomed for the ministry from an early age and matriculated from Trinity College, Cambridge, in 1634, graduating BA in 1638 and proceeding MA in 1641. Upon leaving university Barker was a schoolmaster in Banbury, Oxfordshire, until the outbreak of the civil war, when he was elected as the preacher to the London parish of St James Garlickhythe. In 1646 he moved to Mortlake in Surrey, where he preached to the London citizens who resided there in the summer months.

Barker was an avid parliamentarian and was invited to preach a sermon before the House of Commons on 25 October 1648. Though a congregationalist in the debate on church government and prominent among the Independent ministers in London, he was no controversialist. Despite his belief in congregationalism he did not entirely reject the parochial structure of the English church. Barker's return to London was due to the favour of the new republic. On 19 March 1650 he was presented under the great seal to the formerly presbyterian parish of St Leonard Eastcheap. He seems to have been well liked by his parishioners, although Nehemiah Wallington, one of the presbyterian ruling elders of the parish, wrote to Barker criticizing him for being too mild in his sermons on the doctrine of assurance. Barker's moderation earned him favour during the protectorate of Oliver Cromwell when he was made an assistant to the London commission in 1654. In 1659 he joined Joseph Caryl in carrying a letter written by John Owen in the name of the congregational churches to General Monck. The following year parliament appointed him as one of the commissioners for the approbation of ministers.

In 1662, after the restoration of the monarchy and the institution of the Act of Uniformity, Barker chose to follow many of his brethren into nonconformity. Calamy noted that Barker's decision was 'because he was not able to satisfy himself in some things required respecting conformity' (Calamy, 145). In 1663 he had gathered a congregation and was living in Soper Lane, Broad Street. Barker often joined his congregation with those of his former Restoration friends Joseph Caryl and George Cokayne. He also preached at the nonconformist gatherings known as the morning exercises. He accepted the indulgence of 1672 and on 29 May was licensed as a congregationalist at St James's, Duke Place. He was also elected to administer to the congregation of the Miles Lane meeting-house in Cannon Street.

After the revolution of 1688 Barker put his efforts into promoting unity among the nonconformists. Calamy remembered that 'he discovered a peculiar pleasure in conversing with younger ministers … chearfully encouraging them in the work they had undertaken' (Calamy, 144). To this end he published a collection entitled *Flores intellectuales* which gathered together advice to young scholars entering the ministry. Barker was one of the managers of, and contributors to, the Common Fund set up to assist nonconformists and was the last congregationalist minister to leave the ill-fated Happy Union between the congregationalists and the presbyterians. He was also one of the first 'messengers' appointed by the Congregational Fund Board in December 1695. His main published work was a volume of practical divinity, *Natural Theology*. In this book Barker sought to demonstrate the existence of God from nature and to suggest how this knowledge could be put to use by the believer. He died on 25 March 1698 at the parish of St Giles Cripplegate, London, and asked in his will that he be buried either in the parish of St Clement Eastcheap, near his congregation, or next to the grave of his wife, Elizabeth Cotton, *née* Sheafe, at College Hill. He was survived by one daughter; Elizabeth. E. C. Vernon

Sources *The nonconformist's memorial … originally written by … Edmund Calamy*, ed. S. Palmer, 2nd edn, 2 vols. (1777) · *Calamy rev.* · Congregational History Society Transactions, vol. 5 · M. Barker, *Flores intellectuales* (1691) · M. Barker, *Natural theology* (1674) · BL, Sloane MS 922 · M. Barker, *A Christian standing and moving* (1650) · *JHC*, 6 (1648–51)

Barker, Matthew Henry [*pseud.* the Old Sailor] (**1790–1846**), sailor and writer, was born at Deptford, London, where his father had attained some distinction as a dissenting minister. At sixteen he joined an East Indiaman. Afterwards he served in the Royal Navy, where, as he was without influence, he never rose beyond the rank of master's mate on the gun-brig *The Flamar*. After retiring from the service in 1813, he commanded a hired armed schooner, the *True Briton*, and was employed under Lord Keith in carrying dispatches to the English squadrons on the southern coasts of France and Spain. On one occasion he fell into the enemy's hands and was detained for some months as a prisoner of war. In 1825 he became editor of a West India newspaper and was afterwards employed, from 1827 to 1838, in a similar capacity at Nottingham. For some astronomical discoveries he was presented with a telescope by the Royal Astronomical Society.

Under the pseudonym the Old Sailor, Barker wrote a number of lively and spirited sea tales, very popular in their day. These included such works as *Land and Sea Tales* (1836); *Topsail-Sheet Blocks, or, The Naval Foundling* (1838), which ran into several editions; *The Naval Club, or, Reminiscences of Service* (1843); and *The Victory, or, The Wardroom Mess* (1844). He was naval editor of the *United Service Gazette* and a frequent contributor to the *Literary Gazette*, the *Pictorial Times*, and *Bentley's Miscellany*, the last at the time under the editorship of Charles Dickens, who came to value the consistent quality of the contributions of 'the old Sailor'. Barker was a friend of George Cruikshank, who illustrated seven of his works. One of the most attractive of these was the reprint of a series of sketches originally published in the *Literary Gazette* as 'The Life of a Man-of-War's Man'. The volume edition was called *Greenwich Hospital* (1826) and was a great success with the public, going into an almost immediate reissue. Two other of his works illustrated by Cruikshank were *Tough Years* (1835), which he dedicated to Captain Marryat, and *Nights at Sea* (1852). He was also a chief contributor to Cruikshank's *Omnibus*.

Barker felt that his publishers were less than generous with him, and the situation became worse as his sea tales fell out of fashion. He was married, but had increasing difficulty in supporting his family. He died, in poverty, on 29 June 1846. A. H. BULLEN, *rev.* REBECCA MILLS

Sources Ward, *Men of the reign*, 48 • *Pictorial Times* (July 1846) • R. L. Patten, ed., *George Cruikshank: a revaluation* (1992) • R. L. Patten, *George Cruikshank's life, times, and art*, 2 vols. (1992–6) • *The letters of Charles Dickens*, ed. M. House, G. Storey, and others, 1 (1965) • private information (1885) [R. G. Barker]
Archives BL, letters, as sponsor, to Royal Literary Fund, loan 96 • Bristol RO, letters and papers
Wealth at death died in poverty

Barker, Nicholas John (1933–1997), naval officer, was born in Sliema, Malta, on 19 May 1933, the son of Lieutenant-Commander John Frederick Barker (*c.*1906–1940), naval officer, and his wife, Jillian, *née* Paget (*d.* 1943), artist. His father was killed in action off Norway in June 1940 while in command of the destroyer *Ardent*, valiantly trying to protect the aircraft-carrier *Glorious* from the German battle cruisers *Scharnhorst* and *Gneisenau*. His mother (who was descended from Henry William Paget, first marquess of Anglesey, who led the cavalry at the battle of Waterloo) also died young, and Barker was brought up by his grandfather, also a naval captain. He was educated at Canford School, Dorset, and joined the navy as a national serviceman in 1951.

Barker was selected for a permanent commission in the Royal Navy in 1953, and served in the frigates *Termagant*, *Chichester*, and *Loch Fyne*. In 1957 he married Elizabeth Venetia Redman (*b.* 1935). There were two sons and two daughters of the marriage. Barker had his first command, the fishery protection vessel *Squirrel*, in 1963. He later commanded the minesweeper *Brereton* and the frigates *Jupiter* and *Nubian*. He was deputy commodore, contract built ships, from 1973 to 1975 and then stood by the frigate *Arrow*, the eighth ship of her name in the navy, building on the Clyde. (He was himself baptized in the ship's bell on board the previous *Arrow* in Malta when she was commanded by his father.) He commissioned her in 1976 and commanded her at the Spithead silver jubilee review in 1977. He then had appointments at HMS *Ganges*, the boys'

Nicholas John Barker (1933–1997), by Mark Pepper

training establishment at Shotley, Harwich; at HMS *Osprey*, the naval base at Portland; and in the naval secretary's department in the Admiralty.

Barker was appointed in command of the Antarctic patrol and Falkland Islands guardship *Endurance* in May 1980. This was a much more important command than it appeared. Although armed only with two 20 mm guns and two Wasp helicopters, *Endurance* was the sole regular bearer of the white ensign south of the equator and had great symbolic significance for the Falkland Islanders, being highly visible evidence that they were still British and still mattered to the United Kingdom. Thus *Endurance*'s captain had to be a diplomat as well as a sailor, acutely sensitive to the special political, historical, scientific, and navigational aspects of the Antarctic. To this multiple challenge Barker rose superbly.

With his knowledge of Antarctica, Barker was only too well aware of the catastrophic political effect on the whole region of the announcement in John Nott's 1981 defence review that *Endurance* was to be scrapped without relief, to save money. With Lord Shackleton he began a campaign to try and save the ship—until he was ordered to desist. The order came, he was told, from 10 Downing Street. *Endurance*'s removal convinced the Argentine junta that the United Kingdom was no longer interested in the Falkland Islands. When *Endurance* visited the southernmost Argentine port of Ushuaia in January 1982 Barker was told he was in 'the Malvinas war zone'. When he asked who the enemy was, the answer was: 'You' (Barker, *Beyond Endurance*, 113–14). Barker passed these and other warnings on, but Whitehall assumed they were merely his further attempts to save his ship. He was again ignored. But he was fully vindicated in March 1982 when Argentine 'scrap dealers' and marines landed illicitly on South Georgia and raised their national flag.

After the main Argentine invasion on April 2, *Endurance*'s first concern was to avoid the Argentine navy by hugging the coast of South Georgia, 'hiding behind a rock by day, pretending to be an iceberg', Barker said, 'not easy for a red-painted ship' (Barker, *Beyond Endurance*, 171). When he telephoned naval headquarters at Northwood to clarify the rules of engagement he was told 'to phone back after two o'clock as the particular staff officer was at lunch' (*Daily Telegraph*, 8 April 1997). Later in April, once the British had concerted their response to the Argentine invasion, *Endurance* took part in operation Paraquat, the operation to recapture South Georgia, which Barker said was 'in military terms, a monumental cock-up' (Barker, *Beyond Endurance*, 183), although it was ultimately successful. *Endurance*'s helicopters joined in harrying the Argentine submarine *Santa Fe* (whose captain was a friend of Barker's) with missiles until it ran itself aground. *Endurance*'s final operation, in June, was Operation Keyhole, the reoccupation of Thule, in the South Sandwich Islands, where the Argentinians had also installed a garrison. Following the war *Endurance* remained in the south Atlantic longer than almost any other ship—Whitehall's punishment, her sailors believed, for her captain's indiscretions. When she eventually returned it was public knowledge, having been broadcast on radio and television, that Whitehall had ignored Barker's warnings long before the invasion. Barker was met by two Ministry of Defence 'minders', who warned him: 'Your future in the Navy depends more upon Friday's press conference than anything you have ever done' (Barker, *Beyond Endurance*, 223). Barker was admirably noncommittal. He was appointed CBE in October 1982.

After *Endurance*, Barker spent a year on a defence fellowship at Churchill College, Cambridge, and from 1984 to 1986 commanded the fishery protection squadron. By then, he was not optimistic about promotion to flag rank. He was given command of the frigate *Sheffield* but commanded her for only a few weeks after she was commissioned in June 1988 before retiring. His first marriage was dissolved in 1989, and on 4 March 1989 he married Jennifer Jane Doggett, *née* Cayley (*b*. 1934), daughter of Commander Richard Douglas Cayley, naval officer, who was killed in action in January 1943 while in command of HM Submarine P 311; she was the former wife of Squadron Leader Arthur Christopher Doggett. In retirement Barker gave his time generously to the sea cadets and the Royal British Legion, and was honorary colonel of the Royal Marine reserve unit on Tyneside. He was a freeman of the City of London, a younger brother of Trinity House, a fellow of the Royal Geographical Society and of the British Institute of Management, and a member of the Nautical Institute. He managed the Sea Safety Centre and North East Marine Service in Sunderland. He was gazetted deputy lieutenant of Tyne and Wear in March 1997. He wrote 'The Falklands: a common denominator' in 1984; *Red Ice*, a thriller set in the south Atlantic, in 1987; and *Beyond Endurance: an Epic of Whitehall and the South Atlantic Conflict*, his account of his relationship with the Ministry of Defence and his views on the Falklands War, in 1997.

With his bluff, open features and a twinkle in his eye, Nick Barker was a handsome man with a swashbuckling disregard of rules and regulations which was bound to annoy bureaucrats. But he always took the greatest pains to look after his sailors, and they loved him in return. He was never bitter about his experience in *Endurance*. He gave as one of his recreations 'championing lost causes'. He returned to the Falklands for a BBC television programme in 1992. 'It was such an unnecessary war', he said. 'Once again, the armed forces had to save the politicians' necks' (*Daily Telegraph*, 8 April 1997). He died of prostate cancer at Low Farnham Farmhouse, Morpeth, Northumberland, on 7 April 1997, and was buried five days later at Holystone churchyard. He was survived by his second wife, Jennifer, and by the four children of his first marriage. JOHN WINTON

Sources N. Barker, *Beyond Endurance: an epic of Whitehall and the south Atlantic conflict* (1997) • N. Barker, 'The Falklands: a common denominator', typescript, 1984 • N. Shearman, dir., 'War stories: Captain Nick Barker', 1992 [television programme, BBC Bristol for BBC 2] • R. Perkins, *Operation Paraquat: the battle for South Georgia* (1986) • D. Brown, *The Royal Navy and the Falklands War* (1987) • M. Middlebrook, *Operation Corporate: the story of the Falklands War, 1982* (1985) • A. Lockett, N. Munro, and D. Wells, eds., *H.M.S. Endurance, 1981–82 deployment: a season of conflict* (1983) • G. Cox, extracts from letters home written on board *Endurance* during the Falklands conflict in typescript and manuscript, MarchxJune 1982, priv. coll. • *Daily Telegraph* (8 April 1997) • *The Times* (8 April 1997) • *The Independent* (9 April 1997) • *Navy List* • Burke, *Peerage* • private information (2004) • personal knowledge (2004)

Archives CAC Cam., naval and personal corresp. and papers, incl. papers relating to command of HMS *Endurance* during Falklands War

Likenesses M. Pepper, photograph, News International Syndication, London [*see illus.*] • photograph, repro. in *Daily Telegraph* • photograph, repro. in *The Independent*

Wealth at death £306,764: probate, 29 Aug 1997, *CGPLA Eng. & Wales*

Barker, Robert (*c*.1568–1646). *See under* Authorized Version of the Bible, translators of the (*act*. 1604–1611).

Barker, Sir Robert, baronet (*c*.1732–1789), army officer in the East India Company, only son of Robert Barker MD (*d*. 1745), of Hammersmith, Middlesex, and his wife, Hannah Whitehead, was born about 1732 in the parish of St Anne's, Soho, London. Barker was to become the first distinguished artillery officer of the East India Company's army. He probably first went to India about 1749. In 1756–7, as a captain, with the reappointment of engineer, he accompanied Clive to Calcutta in command of a contingent of royal and company artillery. After the capture of Fort William from Siraj ud-Daula, Barker submitted a proposal for the rebuilding of the Calcutta fortifications. He commanded the artillery at the capture of Chandernagore and at the battle of Plassey (23 June 1757), which marked Siraj ud-Daula's final defeat. Barker returned to Madras in 1758. By 1762 he had attained the rank of major and, again in command of the artillery, he accompanied the expedition sent from Madras under Colonel Draper to capture Manila, in the Philippines, from the Spanish during the Seven Years' War. He received the highest praise for his services from Draper, who recommended him to the king for a brevet commission in the royal army. He seems to have returned to England with Draper, for on 16

April 1764 he was knighted, when Draper was made a KB, but he returned to India in 1764 with the local rank of colonel in the king's army. In 1765 he became colonel of infantry in the company's service, commanding one of the new brigades Clive had created in Bengal. Clive said of him at this time that he 'is universally beloved and respected, [and] makes a most excellent officer' (Clive to John Walsh, 1 Dec 1765, BL OIOC, MS Eur. D 546, III–VII).

Barker was now stationed at Allahabad in Oudh, where his brigade helped to protect the company's ally the nawab-wazir of Oudh, Shuja ud-Daula. In his spare time Barker dabbled in science, submitting to the Royal Society, of which he had been elected a fellow, a number of papers which were published in the *Philosophical Transactions*. More lucratively, he was also exploiting his privileged position in Oudh to engage in trade, the profits from which, when added to the substantial prize money he had received at Plassey and Manila, made him a wealthy man. In 1768 he was commissioned to try to mediate between the nawab-wazir and the wandering Mughal emperor. By 1772, now a brigadier-general and commander-in-chief of the Bengal army, he had become so involved in 'country' politics that he took initiatives far beyond his instructions, to commit the company as guarantor to the treaty of Fyzabad between Shuja ud-Daula and the Rohillas, who controlled a strategically vital tract of territory on the east side of the Ganges, against the threatening Marathas. Then, without reference to Calcutta, he ordered a brigade further up country to confront a possible Maratha invasion. He was rebuked by Governor Cartier for going too far, and Warren Hastings, when he took over as governor the following year, travelled up to Oudh to negotiate in person with Shuja ud-Daula, shutting Barker out because, as he said, the nawab-wazir had to be disabused of the idea that the military ruled at Calcutta. In his chagrin at this rebuke, and angry at what he considered unwarranted civilian interference in army dispositions and administration, Barker resigned in July 1773 and returned to England. Despite their differences, the Calcutta council still wrote home fulsomely to the directors that they believed Barker

> to be possessed of many virtues which qualified him in an especial manner for Command in a Service like this, a Courage approved in the Course of many Years' Trial, a thorough practical Knowledge of his profession and great gentleness of Manners. (Calcutta council to court of directors, 30 Dec 1773, BL OIOC, MS E 4/4/32, p. 207)

Barker became MP for Wallingford in 1774, but seems never to have spoken in parliament. In March 1781 he was rewarded with a baronetcy for his consistent vote with the government. He had not sought re-election in 1780, and on 4 November of that year he married Anne (*d*. 1805/6), only child of Brabazon Hallowes of Galpwell, Bolsover, Derbyshire. They had no children, and lived at the seat he had bought for himself at Busbridge, Godalming, Surrey. He commissioned at least two pictures (1775 and 1781) from Tilly Kettle, which hung at Busbridge, one of himself concluding the treaty of Fyzabad, the other of the nawab-wazir of Oudh reviewing the English brigade. On 14 September 1786 Barker gave important evidence on the Rohilla War to the House of Commons. He died at Busbridge House on 14 September 1789, and was buried on the 28th at Hammersmith, Middlesex. The baronetcy became extinct. H. M. STEPHENS, *rev.* G. J. BRYANT

Sources BL OIOC • R. Clive, letter to J. Walsh, 1 Dec 1765, BL OIOC, MS Eur. D 546, III–VII • Calcutta council, letter to HEIC court of directors, 30 Dec 1773, BL OIOC, MS E 4/4/32 • F. W. Stubbs, ed., *History of the organization, equipment, and war services of the regiment of Bengal artillery*, 3 vols. (1877–95) • K. Feiling, *Warren Hastings* (1954) • G. Forrest, *The life of Lord Clive*, 2 vols. (1918) • A. M. Davies, *Warren Hastings* (1935) • H. H. Dodwell, *Dupleix and Clive: the beginning of empire* (1920); repr. (1967) • E. W. C. Sandes, *The military engineer in India*, 2 vols. (1933–5) • GEC, *Baronetage*, 5.210

Archives BL OIOC, home misc. series, corresp. relating to India • RS, observations on heat and cold made at Allahabad | BL, corresp. with Warren Hastings, Add. MSS 29117, 29133–29134, 29192, *passim* • BL OIOC, India Office records • NL Wales, Clive MSS

Likenesses T. Kettle, oils, 1775, Victoria Memorial, Calcutta; repro. in M. Archer, *India and British portraiture, 1770–1825* (1979)

Barker, Robert (1739–1806), inventor of the panorama, was born in Kells, co. Meath. Little is known about his early life. He married Catherine Aston (1744–1842), the daughter of an eminent Dublin physician, and they had three children—a daughter, later Mrs Lightfoot, Thomas Edward, and Henry Aston *Barker (1774–1856), who was born in Glasgow. Barker was engaged in an unknown business in Dublin; when that failed he took up portrait painting. The family moved to Scotland, and by 1786 Barker was listed in an Edinburgh directory as living on the High Street. His income came from painting portraits and teaching perspective.

In the mid-1780s, while walking on Calton Hill, it occurred to Barker to record the city using a square frame fixed to one spot. By drawing the scene within it, and then rotating and drawing the next section, and then the next, and so on, the entire 360 degree view would eventually be recorded. Drawings, presumably using this method, were made by the twelve-year-old Henry Aston. The outlines were then transferred to paper pasted on linen. However, Barker discovered that, when arranged in a circle, the horizontal lines of these drawings appeared curved. A system had to be devised to make them appear straight. In 1787 Barker took out a patent for 'an entire new Contrivance or apparatus called "La Nature à Coup d'Oeil" for displaying Views of Nature at large' (PRO, C66/3837, no. 12, transcribed in *Repertory*). The patent described a circular building in which light was admitted exclusively from the top. Inside, an enclosure prevented observers going too near the painting and a shade above the enclosure prevented them from seeing the top of the painting and also served to obscure the light source; an obstruction of some sort prevented the bottom of the painting from being exposed to view. A door would have interrupted the continuity of the scene, and so the enclosure or viewing platform was accessed from below. The object was to confine the visitor's visual field entirely to the endless painted image, and effectively to screen off all references to the physical surroundings. This way the eye could be fooled;

after a few minutes the visitor would imagine that he or she was viewing reality rather than a mere painted canvas.

Having surmounted the main difficulties, Barker produced what must have been a model. This he took to London and showed to Sir Joshua Reynolds, who pronounced the idea impracticable. Undeterred, and with financial backing from Francis Charteris, Lord Elcho, Barker then produced a larger version of the image, painting it in watercolour on paper pasted onto canvas, and then formed into a circle measuring 25 feet in diameter. The guard room of Holyrood Palace in Edinburgh served as his studio. In January 1788 the painting went on display at Archers' Hall and Barker announced his intention of taking it to London in the spring. Evidently the show was successful, for in March it was transferred to the assembly rooms in George Street, Edinburgh, and it was subsequently exhibited in Glasgow. It was not until November that Barker, with Henry Aston, moved to London. Their novel painting of Edinburgh went on show at 28 Haymarket on 14 March 1789. A six-sheet reproduction of the painting, aquatinted by J. Wells, was published in 1790.

Barker saw his invention as a radical breakthrough in landscape painting. Despite Edinburgh having being drawn 'with the idea of general effect' and on too small a scale to be totally effective, it did demonstrate the invention's potential. In the winter of 1790–91 Barker embarked on a second and larger 360 degree painting, this time of London. For this he sent Henry Aston to draw the view from the roof of the Albion mills on the south side of Blackfriars Bridge. From June 1792 the resulting image was exhibited in a building at the back of his residence at 28 Castle Street. 'This view', Henry Aston recalled later:

> was very successful. Even Sir Joshua Reynolds came to see it, and gratified my father much, when taking him by the hand he said, 'I find I was in error in supposing your invention could never succeed, for the present exhibition proves it is capable of producing effects, and representing nature in a manner superior to the limited scale of pictures in general.' (Corner, 6)

Classically educated friends of Barker concocted a new word for his invention—'panorama', meaning all-embracing view—and it was this word which, from June 1792, was used in all publicity. A six-sheet reproduction of the London panorama, etched by Henry Aston Barker and aquatinted by Frederick Birnie, was published in October 1792. In the same year Robert Barker acquired a site in Leicester Place and Cranbourne Street, and on it erected a rotunda built according to the 1787 patent. The building, designed by the Scottish architect Robert Mitchell, was named the Panorama. It accommodated two panorama paintings simultaneously, one 90 feet in diameter in a 'large circle' at ground level, the other 50 feet in diameter in an 'upper circle' supported by a central column. The rotunda opened on 25 May 1793 exhibiting in the large circle a view of the Grand Fleet at Spithead.

When the Panorama, Leicester Square, was first projected, a joint-stock company was formed to enable Barker to carry out his scheme, and in this enterprise Lord Elcho took a prominent part; but the enterprise proved so profitable that Barker was soon able to purchase all the shares and make the property his own. He painted several more panoramic views, of British cities such as Bath, Brighton, and Windsor, and naval triumphs including *The Glorious First of June* and *The Battle of the Nile*. By 1803 the panoramas were being painted by Henry Aston alone.

After Barker's patent expired in 1801, 360 degree panoramas by rival artists were painted and exhibited in London, including Thomas Girtin's *Eidometropolis*. A number of panoramas by Barker and his rivals toured the larger provincial towns. Barker died on 8 April 1806 at his house at 14 West Square, St George's Fields, London, and was buried at St Mary, Lambeth, London. For several decades after his death, panoramic entertainments flourished not only in Britain, but on the continent and in the United States. The phenomenon was energetically revived in the 1880s and 1890s. ROBERT HARRISON, *rev.* RALPH HYDE

Sources G. R. Corner, *The panorama, with memoirs of its inventor, Robert Barker, and his son, the late Henry Aston Barker* (1857) • S. B. Wilcox, 'The panorama and related exhibitions in London', MLitt diss., U. Edin., 1976 • R. D. Altick, *The shows of London* (1978) • S. Oettermann, *The panorama: a history of a mass medium* (1997) • R. Hyde, *Panoramania! the art and entertainment of the 'all embracing' view* (1988–9) [exhibition catalogue, Barbican Art Gallery, 3 Nov 1988 – 15 Jan 1989] • H. J. Pragnell, *The London panoramas of Robert Barker and Thomas Girtin* (1968) • descriptive booklets sold at the panorama exhibitions, 1801–6, GL • descriptive booklets sold at the panorama exhibitions, 1801–6, BM • *Repertory of arts and manufactures, consisting of original communications, specifications of patent inventions, and selections of useful practical papers* (1796), 4.165–7 • gravestone of Catherine Barker, Bitton, near Bristol

Likenesses J. Singleton, stipple and aquatint engraving, pubd 1802 (after C. Ralph), NPG • J. Flight, mezzotint (after C. Allingham), BM, NPG • miniature, oils, V&A

Barker, Samuel (1686–1759), Hebraist, is of unknown parentage and upbringing; he was a relation of William Higgs Barker (1743/4–1816), the Hebraist and schoolmaster. He owned property near Lyndon, in Rutland. He married Sarah, only daughter of the natural philosopher and theologian William *Whiston, in whose memoirs (2nd edn, 1753) he is mentioned; the couple's son, Thomas *Barker (1722–1809) wrote on theological and meteorological subjects. Samuel Barker published a Hebrew grammar, on which he was long engaged. He was the author of a letter dated 7 November 1723 to Joseph Wasse, rector of Aynho, Northamptonshire, printed by Nichols, concerning a passage in the Sigean inscription. Barker died in 1759, after which was published a collection of several learned tracts under the title, *Poesis vetus Hebraica restituta: accedunt quaedam de carminibus Anacreonticis, de accentibus Graecis, de scriptura veteri Ionica, de literis consonantibus et vocalibus, et de pronunciatione linguae Hebraicae* (1761).

JAMES MEW, *rev.* PHILIP CARTER

Sources Nichols, *Lit. anecdotes*, 9.680 • Watt, *Bibl. Brit.* • will, PRO, PROB 11/850, fols. 96*v*–97*v*

Barker, Dame Sara Elizabeth (1904–1973), political agent, was born on 15 February 1904 in Siddall, near Halifax, Yorkshire, the daughter of George Barker, grocer, and his wife, Ethel Brier.

Dame Sara Elizabeth Barker (1904–1973), by Brian Worth

Sara Barker was educated at Siddall elementary school before going on at the age of eleven to Halifax Technical College. There she studied a commercial course, leaving to join an engineering firm as an accounting clerk at the age of seventeen. For many years after she left school she attended evening classes run by the Workers' Educational Association, studying English literature, economics, and social sciences three nights a week. She regarded these classes as the most valuable part of her education.

Sara Barker's father, George Barker, whom she acknowledged as the most important political influence on her life, had been a lifelong worker for the Independent Labour Party and died while in office as mayor of Halifax. Sara Barker herself entered politics at an early age and one of her first recollections of working for the Labour Party was going from door to door collecting subscriptions. At sixteen, while still at college, she was secretary of the women's section of the Halifax Labour Party. In this way began her steady rise to the top of the administration of the Labour Party.

In 1935, when she was thirty-one, Sara Barker was the only woman among 135 applicants for the post of secretary and agent to the Halifax Labour Party. Her application was successful and she held the post until 1942, when she was appointed the Labour Party's organizer for women in Yorkshire. In 1952 she took over the post of assistant national agent of the Labour Party based at the party's headquarters, holding the job until 1960, when she was promoted to senior assistant national agent and chief officer for women. Two years later she became the first woman national agent of the Labour Party. The post of national agent was the second in command of the party machine and Sara Barker's main responsibility was to ensure that the constituency parties worked effectively.

Interviewed after her appointment as senior assistant national agent and chief officer for women, Sara Barker felt that her main tasks were to increase the number of women in the Labour Party, to expand the educational work directed towards women, and to bring women more into the general organization of the Labour Party. She aimed to set up more small discussion groups where women could meet together informally. She believed the Labour Party would benefit from increased participation by women as 'Women have always brought sound common sense to the Labour Party' (*The Guardian*). Sara Barker was a gifted administrator who had a firm grasp of the intricacies of the networks of party organization. In 1946 she published a pamphlet *How the Labour Party Works* and she also edited the journal *Labour Organiser*. She had no ambitions to enter the House of Commons as an MP.

The Labour Party played a central role in Sara Barker's life and she firmly believed that 'An organisation like ours is more than just a machine. It represents the fundamental belief of individuals in a cause' (*The Guardian*). Her interests outside the Labour Party included reading, particularly rereading the classics she had been introduced to during WEA classes, music, and walking. She never married. She lived at 4 Chevin Edge Crescent, Exley, Halifax, until she joined the Labour Party headquarters in London, when she moved to a converted almshouse in Stepney, east London. She was made a dame in 1970.

Sara Barker was quiet-voiced and reticent, but authoritative and someone who was happiest discussing facts rather than theory. She was the first woman to be appointed to a job of comparable importance in a major political party in Britain. She died on 19 September 1973.

SERENA KELLY

Sources *WWW* · *The Guardian* (23 Jan 1961), 6 · *Daily Telegraph* (18 April 1962) · *Daily Herald* (19 April 1962), 8 · *CGPLA Eng. & Wales* (1973)

Archives Labour History Archive and Study Centre, Manchester, national agents' MSS

Likenesses B. Worth, photograph, People's History Museum, Manchester [*see illus.*] · photograph, repro. in *The Guardian*

Wealth at death £7480: probate, 10 Dec 1973, *CGPLA Eng. & Wales*

Barker, Thomas (*fl.* 1651), writer on angling, was born in Bracemeol, Shrewsbury; his parents are unknown. He became a freeman and burgess, but made a living as an angling tutor and guide for members of the gentry and aristocracy, developing strong links with early tackle makers in London, where he eventually moved. He seems to have made no great fortune from this.

Barker's importance lies in his writings on angling, distilling his experience for a wider audience. He is claimed to have helped Izaak Walton to write *The Compleat Angler*; his advice on fly-fishing was modified by Walton on page 108 of the 1653 edition. His own *The Art of Angling*, first published in 1651 and dedicated to Lord Montague, who followed the sport, includes biblical texts, Latin tags, and doggerel verse to bolster his claims that fishing far surpasses all other recreations in promoting health and pleasure. The text offers much hard practical advice on fish species, tackle and bait, together with recipes, including pike with stewed oysters, and employs a successful formula for angling writing which has been much copied subsequently. His book went through several editions, being retitled *Barker's Delight* in 1657, and was republished as having more than antiquarian interest in the early nineteenth century. He was much praised by late Victorian angling writers who, however, deplored his 'heresy' of recommending salmon roe as a bait.

Barker does not seem to have married, since in old age he settled in the almshouses known as Henry VII's Gift, adjoining Westminster Abbey gatehouse, which were designated for the use of bachelors. The date of his death is unknown. J. R. LOWERSON

Sources *DNB* · T. Barker, *The art of angling: wherein are discovered many rare secrets, very necessary to be knowne by all that delight in that recreation* (1653) · *N&Q*, 2nd ser., 3 (1857), 288 · T. Westwood and T. Satchell, *Bibliotheca piscatoria* (1883), 21–3 · M. E. C. Walcott, *The memorials of Westminster* (1849), 280

Barker, Thomas (1722–1809), theologian and meteorologist, was born at Lyndon, Rutland, the son of Samuel *Barker (1686–1759), a Hebrew scholar, and his wife, Sarah, the daughter of the natural philosopher and theologian William *Whiston. He spent his life at Lyndon, where his family had property; Barker himself was interested in farming and beekeeping. He published three tracts in controversial theology, *A Treatise on the Duty of Baptism* (1771), *On Prophecies Relating to the Messiah* (1780), and *On the Nature and Circumstances of the Demoniacks in the Gospels* (1783). The views that he expressed in these works were considered unorthodox.

From the age of about eleven Barker began to keep a weather diary, and between 1771 and 1798 he forwarded to the Royal Society an almost annual register of his meteorological observations at Lyndon, most of which were published in the *Philosophical Transactions*. These diaries chronicled the 'little ice age' when winter temperatures were far lower than they are now, and are considered a useful resource for climate historians. He also wrote on the comet of 1682 and on other astronomical matters. His main scientific work was his *An Account of the Discoveries Concerning Comets* (1757). It was specially remarked of Barker that, though he lived to the age of eighty-eight, he had from infancy subsisted entirely on a vegetable diet. He died at his house at Lyndon on 29 December 1809.

R. E. ANDERSON, *rev.* JOSEPH GROSS

Sources *A new catalogue of living English authors: with complete lists of their publications, and biographical and critical memoirs* (1799) · Nichols, *Lit. anecdotes*, vol. 3 · RS · H. C. Englefield, *On the determination of the orbits of comets* (1793)

Archives Harvard U., Houghton L., notebook · Meteorological Office, London, meteorological journal · RS

Barker, Thomas (1767–1847), painter and lithographer, known as Barker of Bath, was born at Trosnant, Pontypool, in 1767, the son of a former solicitor and minor artist, Benjamin Barker (*c*.1720–1793) and his wife, Anne. He attended Shepton Mallet grammar school. In 1783 the family settled in Bath and Barker's artistic promise was quickly recognized. In 1793, when Barker was only twenty-six years old, Sir Edward Harington published in Bath *Schizzo on the genius of man: in which … the merit of Mr. Thomas Barker, the celebrated young painter of Bath, is particularly considered* to rebut claims that Barker was simply an imitator of Gainsborough.

Thomas Barker (1767–1847), self-portrait, 1789 [right, with his preceptor, Charles Spackman]

Barker never received any formal training but learned by copying paintings in the possession of his patron, the Bath businessman Charles Spackman (1749–1822). His *Self-Portrait with his Preceptor Charles Spackman* (Victoria Art Gallery, Bath) of 1789 is one of his most accomplished works and shows Barker painting a landscape in the style of Gainsborough. In the same year he painted the *Woodman in a Storm* (1789; Tate collection) in imitation of Gainsborough's famous *Woodman* (des.) that had been exhibited at Schomberg House, London, that spring. Barker's subsequent *Old Woodman* (1789–90; Torfaen Museum Trust, Pontypool) established his reputation while he set off on a grand tour financed by Spackman, travelling to Rome in 1790 with the young Bath printmaker Charles Hibbart (1765–1819), son of the etcher William Hibbart. Soon after Barker's return at the end of 1793 he took over Benjamin Vandergucht's large exhibition rooms in Lower Brook Street, London. He exhibited occasionally at the Royal Academy between 1791 and 1829 and regularly at the British Institution between 1807 and 1847.

Paintings such as the *Old Woodman* and the *Old Man with Staff* (Yale U. CBA) capture the spirit of the 1790s, when, in the light of the French Revolution, images of the virtuous British labourer assumed a special significance. Despite the popularity of these works, Barker was unable to sustain a London career and from 1800 lived and worked exclusively in Bath. In 1803 he married Priscilla Jones and commissioned an imposing picture gallery, later known as Doric House, from the young architect Joseph Michael Gandy. The gallery, dramatically situated on Sion Hill, above the city of Bath, opened to the public in 1805.

Barker was an enthusiastic pioneer in the new art of

lithography, contributing to the first set of lithographs published in Britain in 1803, and in 1813 he produced his own series of forty *Rustic Figures*, printed in Bath by D. J. Redman. Many of the original stones, still bearing Barker's drawings, have survived (Victoria Art Gallery, Bath). In the same year the first British treatise on lithography, Henry Bankes's *Lithography, or, The Art of Making Drawings on Stone* was published by Redman in Bath, including landscape illustrations almost certainly by Barker. A year later Barker again collaborated with Redman to produce a set of thirty-two lithographs entitled *Landscape Scenery*. His last major project was the *Massacre at Chios*, a fresco painted in 1825–6 inside the principal east elevation of Doric House, on a 30 foot long blank wall that must have served as the main hanging space for canvases twenty years earlier. This he hoped might revive his flagging reputation; the subject was perhaps inspired by Eugène Delacroix's famous painting of 1824, but was also in some respects an appropriate choice for the overtly Grecian architectural style of Doric House. An admission ticket for viewing the fresco shows that entrance daily between 11 and 5 o'clock cost 1s. (BM, department of prints and drawings). Barker's brother Benjamin Barker (1776–1838) was also an artist in Bath and four of Thomas and Priscilla Barker's eight children became artists, Thomas Jones and John Joseph being the most successful. In the long term Barker's technical skills were not supported by a clear sense of direction and his life ended in poverty. He died, surrounded by pawnbrokers' tickets, on 11 December 1847 at Doric House and was buried at All Saints, Weston, near Bath, on 18 December. SUSAN SLOMAN

Sources *The Barkers of Bath* (1986) [exhibition catalogue, Victoria Art Gallery, Bath, 17 May–18 June 1986] • [E. Harington], *Schizzo on the genius of man: in which … the merit of Mr Thomas Barker, the celebrated young painter of Bath, is particularly considered* (1793) • F. Shum, 'Reminiscences of the late Thomas Barker: a paper read at the Royal Literary and Scientific Institution on Friday, April 11, 1862', *Bath Chronicle* (17 April 1862) • M. Holbrook, 'Painters in Bath in the eighteenth century', *Apollo*, 98 (1973), 375–84 • M. Twyman, 'Thomas Barker's lithographic stones', *Journal of the Printing Historical Society*, 12 (1977–8), 1–32 • C. Young, 'Thomas Barker's *Interior of a mill* and the rustic figure', *Bulletin* [Allen Memorial Art Museum], 42 (1984–5), 25–35 • J. Hayes, *The landscape paintings of Thomas Gainsborough*, 2 vols. (1970) • C. Payne, *Toil and plenty: images of the agricultural landscape in England, 1780–1890* (1993) [exhibition catalogue, U. Nott. Art Gallery, 7 Oct – 14 Nov 1993; Yale U. CBA, 15 Jan – 13 March 1994] • J. Hayes, introduction, *Barker of Bath: an exhibition of paintings and drawings by Thomas Barker, 1769–1847* (1962) [exhibition catalogue, Victoria Art Gallery, Bath, 7 – 30 June 1962] • P. Tayler and A. Babbidge, *Benjamin and Thomas Barker, artists of Pontypool* (1982) [exhibition catalogue] • P. Bate, 'Thomas Barker of Bath [pt 1]', *The Connoisseur*, 10 (1904), 107–12 • P. Bate, 'Thomas Barker of Bath [pt 2]', *The Connoisseur*, 11 (1905), 76–81 • S. Sloman, 'Barker and Gainsborough', *Bath Museum News*, 24 (spring 1992), 5 • S. Smiles, 'Dressed to till: representational strategies in the depiction of the rural labor c.1790–1830', *Prospects for the nation: recent essays in British landscape, 1750–1880*, ed. M. Rosenthal, C. Payne, and S. Wilcox (1997)

Likenesses T. Barker, self-portrait, oils, 1789 (with Charles Spackman), Victoria Art Gallery, Bath [*see illus.*] • T. Barker, self-portrait, oils, *c.*1790, Tate collection; on loan to No. 1 Royal Crescent, Bath • T. Barker, self-portrait, oils, *c.*1793–1794, Holburne Museum of Art, Bath • T. Barker, self-portrait, oils, *c.*1810 (with Thomas Shew), NMG Wales • T. Barker, self-portrait, oil on copper, *c.*1820, Victoria Art Gallery, Bath

Wealth at death died in poverty; awarded £100 government pension in 1846

Barker, Thomas (1838–1907), mathematician, was born on 9 September 1838, the son of Thomas Barker, farmer, of Murcar, Balgonie, near Aberdeen, and of his wife, Margaret Knowles. Three other children died in infancy. He attended the grammar school, Aberdeen, and King's College, Aberdeen, graduating in 1857 with great distinction in mathematics. He entered Trinity College, Cambridge, as minor scholar and sub-sizar in 1858, became foundation scholar in 1860, and Sheepshanks astronomical exhibitioner in 1861. He was coached for the mathematical tripos by Routh, and came out senior wrangler and first Smith's prizeman in 1862. He was elected a fellow of Trinity, and was assistant tutor until 1865, when he was appointed professor of pure mathematics in the Owens College, Manchester. He held this post for twenty years, during which the college expanded, gained prestige, and became the nucleus of the Victoria University in Manchester. While doing his share of committee work, Barker kept a low profile within the university administration.

Mathematically, Barker turned his back on Cambridge methods and interests. He had a severely critical mind which restrained him from publishing much and inclined him to follow De Morgan and Boole; like them he was interested in certain fundamental aspects of mathematics. In this respect he was ahead of his time, presaging the introduction of 'rigour' into mathematics. In his teaching he endeavoured to set forth the processes of mathematical reasoning as a connected system from their foundation. His lectures consequently had a reputation for being 'unintelligible to all but the elect' (Wilkinson, 51) but on these few he made a deep impression. His success as a teacher is attested to by a number of distinguished pupils on whom he exercised a great and possibly a determining influence. These include John Hopkinson, J. H. Poynting, A. Schuster, Sir Joseph John Thomson, A. E. Steinthal, and J. W. Capstick.

Barker lived a simple life, was unmarried, and fortunate in his investments enabling him to retire in 1885 and devote his time to studying mosses, on which he was an authority. He maintained a lifelong friendship with J. Stirling, another former senior wrangler. Barker lived first at Whaley Bridge, Derbyshire, and afterwards at Buxton, where he died at his home, Woodlea, Lightwood Road, Fairfield, on 20 November 1907. He was buried in the Manchester southern cemetery. In his will he provided for the foundation of a professorship of cryptogamic botany at Manchester University, and for the endowment of bursaries for poor students in mathematics and botany.

HORACE LAMB, *rev.* ISOBEL FALCONER

Sources H. Lamb, 'The late Professor Barker', *Manchester Guardian* (23 Nov 1907) • H. Lamb, 'The late Professor Barker', *Manchester University Magazine* (Dec 1907) • J. J. Thomson, *Recollections and reflections* (1936) • *The Times* (22 Nov 1907) [will] • S. Wilkinson, 'Some college friendships', *Record of the Owens College jubilee* (1902), 51 • J. Thompson, *The Owens College: its foundation and growth* (1886) • R. H. Kargon, *Science in Victorian Manchester* (1977) • d. cert. • bap. cert.

Wealth at death £46,833 4*s*.: probate, 4 Dec 1907, *CGPLA Eng. & Wales*

Barker, Thomas Jones (1813–1882), war and portrait painter, was born on 19 April 1813 at Bath, Somerset, the eldest son and fifth child of Thomas *Barker (1767–1847) of Bath, painter and lithographer, and his wife, Priscilla, *née* Jones. Educated at Heckingham College, he was taught to paint by his father. From 1834 he studied in Paris under the military painter (Émile-Jean) Horace Vernet, and remained in his studio for several years. From 1835 Barker exhibited at the Paris Salon and in the French provinces, winning gold and other medals. He painted several pictures for King Louis Philippe, including *La mort de Louis XIV* (destroyed at the sack of the Palais Royal in the 1848 revolution) and was appointed to the Légion d'honneur. His outstanding work was the famous *La fiancée de la Mort* (1838–9; Victoria Art Gallery, Bath), painted for Louis Philippe's daughter Princess Marie and after her death bought back by Barker.

In 1845 Barker returned to England. Thenceforth he lived in London at various places, including three successive addresses in Gloucester Road, Regent's Park. He exhibited at the Royal Academy—a total of twenty-nine paintings from 1845 to 1876—at the British Institution between 1844 and 1867, the Society (later Royal Society) of British Artists between 1846 and 1874, and elsewhere. A traditional rather than innovative artist, he became a successful painter of portraits and varied historical, literary, religious, genre, hunting, and war scenes. His paintings, like Vernet's, often included horses in movement. His portraits included *Benjamin Disraeli* (1862; Royal Collection), acquired by Queen Victoria, *Lady Bancroft* (NPG), and *Dr John Snow* (exh. RA, 1847; priv. coll.; a modern copy is at the Royal College of Anaesthetists), the anaesthetist and epimediologist, who was the Barker family's general practitioner.

Barker was best-known as a painter of war scenes, including battle scenes, of which he was one of his generation's leading painters. He painted scenes of the Napoleonic wars, including *The Meeting of Wellington and Blucher at La Belle Alliance* (1851), painted for Alderman F. G. Moon, and *Wellington at Sorauren* (exh. RA, 1853; priv. coll.), bought by the second duke of Wellington. During the Crimean War he may possibly have visited the Crimea and made sketches, and during and after the war he painted scenes from it. These included *The Passage of the Alma* (1857; priv. coll.), *The Allied Generals with their Officers of their Respective Staffs before Sebastopol* (exh. German Gallery, Bond Street, London, 1856; priv. coll.), using Roger Fenton's photographs, and *Major General Williams and his Staff Leaving Kars* (exh. Lloyd Brothers, Auction Mart, London, 1857; NAM). He painted scenes of the Indian mutiny, including *The Relief of Lucknow* (1859; NPG), using Egron Lundgren's sketches made in India during the mutiny. In the 1860s Barker and George Jones were the only painters regularly exhibiting battle paintings at the Royal Academy. In 1870 during the Franco-Prussian War Barker returned to France, and he subsequently painted scenes of the war, including *Riderless War-Horses after the Battle of Sedan* (exh. RA, 1873; Maidstone Museum and Art Gallery). In the 1870s he painted more Crimean War scenes, including the last painting he exhibited at the Royal Academy, *The Return through the Valley of Death* (exh. RA, 1876) and *Taking the Russian Guns at Balaclava* (exh. Borgen's Danish Gallery, London, 1877; Staff College, Camberley). He portrayed, as had his French master, glorified patriotic scenes. His battle scenes were dramatic, with close-packed charging horsemen, waving swords, clouds of smoke, and dead soldiers but no agony.

Crucial to Barker's popular and commercial success were his principal patrons, the print publishers, notably Agnew & Sons of Manchester. A number of his military paintings, including *The Allied Generals … before Sebastopol* and *General Williams … Leaving Kars*, were commissioned, exhibited, toured and reproduced as engravings by publishers. The engravings sold well and were very profitable: those of *Allied Generals … before Sebastopol* grossed over £10,000. *The Secret of England's Greatness* (*c*.1862; NPG), showing Queen Victoria presenting a Bible to an unidentified African, toured northern England and Ulster. It was credited, arguably implausibly, with reversing republicanism in northern England, and was copied on Ulster Orange lodge banners. Though popular in its day, subsequently it was virtually forgotten. Following its purchase by the National Portrait Gallery in 1974, it became a favourite late twentieth-century icon of Victorianism, much reproduced in books, and Barker's best-known work.

Opinions of Barker's works varied. Contemporary critics did not favour them, and he was not elected to the Royal Academy. In 1858 *The Athenaeum*, reviewing his large panoramic painting *The Horse Race Down the Corso during the Carnival*, criticized his 'gaudy, lean, showy style of rather flimsy Art' (Hichberger, 57) and in 1861 it criticized his 'vapid sentimentalities' (Harrington, 172). However, James Dafforne in 1878 in the *Art Journal* was eulogistic, praising him as 'the *Horace Vernet* of England, our principal battle painter … master of the battle-field among our artists' (Dafforne, 69, 72). Latterly his battle pictures were overshadowed by those of Elizabeth Thompson, later Lady Butler. In ignoring him she and others who wrote about her exaggerated her originality and role as pioneer of Victorian battle painting.

Barker had married apparently in or before the 1840s Sarah Isaacs Irvine and they had at least one child; she survived him. He died on 27 March 1882 at his home, Avon House, 32 Steeles Road, Haverstock Hill, north-west London. Barker left £4127 19*s*. 5*d*. (probate value). Although he seems to have influenced such later Victorian painters as John Charlton and Ernest Crofts, after his death Barker's reputation, like Vernet's in England, soon evaporated. After the First World War many of his paintings were lost or destroyed, and in the Edwardian and inter-war periods they fetched very low prices. However, with the later twentieth-century revived appreciation of Victorian art,

Barker's reputation and prices increased. His works are displayed at the National Portrait Gallery, National Army Museum, and Victoria Art Gallery, Bath.

ROGER T. STEARN

Sources J. Dafforne, 'The works of Thomas Jones Barker', *Art Journal*, new ser., 17 (1878), 69–72 • *The Times* (29 March 1882) • P. Bishop and V. Burnell, *The Barkers of Bath* (1986) • P. Harrington, *British artists and war: the face of battle in paintings and prints, 1700–1914* (1993) • J. W. M. Hichberger, *Images of the army: the military in British art, 1815–1914* (1988) • J. Turner, ed., *The dictionary of art*, 34 vols. (1996) • Boase, *Mod. Eng. biog.* • Graves, *RA exhibitors* • Bryan, *Painters* • Bénézit, *Dict.* • P. Usherwood and J. Spencer-Smith, *Lady Butler: battle artist, 1846–1933* (1987) • R. T. Stearn, 'War images and image makers in the Victorian era: aspects of the British visual and written portrayal of war, *c*.1866–1906', PhD diss., U. Lond., 1987 • A. Munich, *Queen Victoria's secrets* (1996) • O. Millar, *The Victorian pictures in the collection of her majesty the queen*, 2 vols. (1992) • J. Marsh, 'Quest for the queen's secrets', *The Guardian* (27 Jan 2001), Saturday review, p.3 • *ILN* (5 May 1855), 430 • D. Zuck, 'Snow, Empson and the Barkers of Bath', *Anaesthesia*, 56/3 (March 2001), 227–30 • R. H. Ellis, ed., *The case books of Dr. John Snow* (1994) • M. P. Lalumia, *Realism and politics in Victorian art of the Crimean War* (1984) • E. Butler, *An autobiography* (1922)

Likenesses T. J. Barker, self-portrait (in middle age), Victoria Art Gallery, Bath; repro. in Bishop and Burnell, *Barkers of Bath*

Wealth at death £4127 19*s*. 5*d*.: probate, 11 May 1882, *CGPLA Eng. & Wales*

Barker, Thomas Richard (1799–1870), Congregational minister, born in London on 30 November 1799, was educated at Christ's Hospital (1807–16); he hoped to go on to Cambridge and to be ordained in the Church of England, but his parents, who were strict and conscientious nonconformists, refused their consent. After a time he decided to become an Independent minister, and entered Homerton College in 1821. He married in the same or the following year, thereby cutting short his college course. His wife died in 1833, and Barker later remarried.

In 1822 Barker became pastor of a village church at Alresford, Hampshire, and two years later he moved to Harpenden, near St Albans, where he remained for nine years, acting as pastor and teacher. In 1833 he moved to Uxbridge, and in 1838, at the recommendation of Dr J. Pye Smith, was appointed tutor in classics and Hebrew at the Congregational college then being established at Birmingham, Spring Hill College. Here in the following year he was joined by Henry Rogers, distinguished as a writer of Christian apologetics. Barker was provided with quarters in the college, and was responsible for the maintenance of its discipline, a duty which he discharged for more than thirty years with great efficiency: he always showed good sense, tact, and consideration, and was highly respected both by his colleagues and by ministers of other denominations in Birmingham and throughout the midlands.

During his life Barker had an aversion to speaking of death, remarkable in his time; his own death, however, was perfectly painless. After one day's illness he died on 23 November 1870 at his home, Larches Villa, Stratford Road, Birmingham. He was buried on 29 November in the Birmingham general cemetery. He was survived by his second wife, Susanah, two daughters, and three sons, of whom one, the Revd Philip C. Barker, became professor of mathematics at Rotherham Congregational college, Sheffield.

J. M. RIGG, *rev.* J. M. V. QUINN

Sources *Congregational Year Book* (1871) • *CGPLA Eng. & Wales* (1871)

Wealth at death under £4000: probate, 17 Jan 1871, *CGPLA Eng. & Wales*

Barker, William (*fl.* 1540–1576), translator and member of parliament, was humbly born but through the patronage of Anne Boleyn was educated at St John's College, Cambridge, graduating MA in 1540. A Roman Catholic, Barker left for Italy, probably in 1549, and travelled widely throughout the peninsula collecting Latin epitaphs (his *Epitaphia et inscriptiones lugubres, a Guglielmo Bercher, cum in Italia, animi causa, peregrinetur, collecta* was printed in London in 1554). He settled for a substantial period in Tuscany where he translated Xenophon's *Cyropaideia* (1554) and popular works from the Italian, such as Giovanni Battista Gelli's *I caprici del Bottaio* and Lodovico Domenichi's *La nobilità delle donne*. Barker's translation of Gelli, *The Fearfull Fancies of the Florentine Cooper*, was first printed in England in 1568; but *A Dyssputacion off the Nobylyte of Wymen*, his reworking of Domenichi's 1549 text which he altered to contain considerable autobiographical and specifically English material, remained in manuscript until 1904–5.

Barker returned to England soon after Mary I's accession. Furnished with excellent education and literary and linguistic skills, and accustomed to aristocratic company in Italy, but poor and of humble birth, his only option was service to a great noble: as he later remarked, 'hard fortune drove me to serve'. Barker entered the household of the duke of Norfolk as his secretary soon after 1554. Through Norfolk's patronage Barker was returned as MP for Yarmouth in 1558, 1559, and 1571, and for Bramber in 1563. The duke also used Barker as administrator of some of his estates by 1568, reflecting the trust he had achieved in the Howard circle.

As a known Roman Catholic, Barker was apprehended in 1569 with Norfolk for complicity in the conspiracies of that year, but was released. However, in 1571 Barker brought Roberto Ridolfi to Howard House to discuss a plot in favour of Mary, queen of Scots, and the restoration of the Catholic religion. When arrested, Norfolk denied the accusation. But Barker, fearful of torture, confessed and betrayed his master, resulting in the duke's famous comment about believing an 'Italianated Englishman'. Norfolk was condemned to death, as was his secretary. Barker's sentence, however, was not carried out. He spent two years in the Tower before receiving a pardon in May 1574; even his property was returned within two months, probably as recompense for turning crown's evidence. Barker appears last in a suit in the court of requests in February 1576.

KENNETH R. BARTLETT

Sources HoP, *Commons, 1558–1603* • G. B. Parks, 'William Barker, Tudor translator', *Papers of the Bibliographical Society of America*, 51 (1957), 126–40 • *A collection of state papers … left by William Cecill, Lord Burghley*, ed. W. Murdin, 2 (1759), 87–129 • K. R. Bartlett, 'William Barker', *Sixteenth-century British nondramatic writers: first series*, ed. D. A. Richardson, DLitB, 132 (1993), 48–52 • K. R. Bartlett, 'The creation of an Englishman Italified: William Barker in Italy, 1551–

1554', *Bollettino del Centro Interuniversitario di Ricerche sul 'Viaggio in Italia'*, 20 (1989), 209–17 • Venn, *Alum. Cant.*

Barker, Sir William (1909–1992), diplomatist and Russian scholar, was born on 19 July 1909 at 3 Plank Lane, Leigh, Lancashire, the eldest of the three children of Alfred Barker, master baker and later licensed victualler, and his wife, Annie, formerly Arden (*née* Atherton). He was educated at Leigh grammar school; Liverpool University, where he took first-class honours in Russian studies; and Charles University, Prague, where he obtained a doctorate for a dissertation on 'the influence of Lord Byron on the poet, dramatist, and journalist J. V. Frič (1829–1890)'. The thesis was supervised by Professor Vilém Mathesius and Professor Jiři Horák. Barker taught for a number of years at the English grammar school in Prague, but returned shortly before the Second World War to take up a post in adult education in Durham. On 19 August 1939 he married Margaret (*b.* 1911), a graduate teacher, daughter of Thomas Beirne, coalminer. They had a daughter and a son.

On the outbreak of war Barker joined the intelligence corps and was at first posted to the Bletchley Park codebreaking centre; but following the fall of France he was transferred to serve as a liaison officer with the Czechoslovak forces in Britain. In April 1943 he was seconded to the Foreign Office, and two years later he returned to Prague as first secretary in the British embassy when it was reopened at the end of the war. From 1947 to 1951 he served in Moscow, where, as head of the embassy's 'Russian secretariat', he made his mark as an expert interpreter of Soviet politics. Postings followed to Oslo (1951–4), Boston, Massachusetts (as consul-general, 1954–5), Washington DC (1955–60), and Moscow again (1960–63) as minister. Thereafter he held a fellowship at Harvard University Centre for International Affairs (1963–4); and was assistant under-secretary of state in the Foreign Office (1965–6) and ambassador to Czechoslovakia (1966–8). After retirement from the diplomatic service in December 1968 he was appointed Bowes professor of Russian at Liverpool University, a post he held from 1969 to 1976.

As a Slavonic linguist Barker was one of only a handful to emerge in Britain between the wars (remarkably, another was his own school contemporary G. H. Bolsover, later director of London University school of Slavonic and East European studies). By temperament a thinker rather than a man of action, he would probably have devoted his life to education had it not been for the war. His versatility however was attested by the fact that, though entering the Foreign Office at the relatively late age of thirty-four, he attained the highest rank in the service. His subsequent return to his alma mater, though personally gratifying, left insufficient time to consolidate his earlier scholarly promise.

Barker's two areas of expertise—linguistic and cultural studies and political analysis—complemented each other perfectly. This was well illustrated by his contact with and reaction to the Soviet leader Nikita Khrushchov. In April 1956 Barker was summoned from Washington to act as principal interpreter with Khrushchov and Bulganin during their celebrated visit to Britain. This experience gave him valuable insight into the Soviet leader's personality. He referred to it when delivering his inaugural lecture, 'N. S. Khrushchev: an assessment', at Liverpool on 4 December 1969: in this he offered a severely critical appraisal of Khrushchov as a state and party leader, concluding, however, with a typically humane comment: 'But you can't help liking the man!'.

The USSR was the state whose politics were the most important subject of Barker's attention as diplomat and academic; but Czechoslovakia was the Slav country which he first encountered and in which he lived for longest. When he returned there in October 1966 as ambassador, his pre-war experience and wartime and post-war contacts with Czechs and Slovaks stood him in good stead. Nevertheless, the Warsaw pact countries' invasion in August 1968 presented this mild-mannered, meticulous man with the toughest challenge of his career: how to organize the assembly, protection, sustenance, and repatriation of hundreds of British subjects who were caught in Prague. With the aid of the embassy staff and his immediate family he succeeded in this magnificently.

Bill Barker was a modest, kindly, and gracious but intellectually rigorous person, devoted to his family, and a distinguished servant of his country. He was appointed OBE in 1949, CMG in 1958, and KCMG in 1967. He was also awarded the Czechoslovak order of the White Lion. He died from a cerebral thrombosis on 8 January 1992 at his home, 19 Moors Way, Woodbridge, Suffolk. He was survived by his wife and their two children.

MARCUS WHEELER

Sources *The Times* (13 Jan 1992) • *The Independent* (27 Jan 1992) • *WWW* • PRO, PREM 11/1626 • PRO, FO 371/1228/9 • personal knowledge (2004) • private information (2004) • b. cert. • m. cert. • d. cert.

Archives CAC Cam., corresp. and papers relating to Soviet Union and Czechoslovakia

Likenesses photograph, repro. in *The Times*

Barker, William Burckhardt (1810/11–1856), orientalist, was the son of John *Barker (1771–1849), who was consul in Aleppo, Syria, at the time of his son's birth. From both his parents he inherited a remarkable linguistic aptitude. He was the godson of Johann Ludwig Burckhardt, who, about the time of Barker's birth, was for several months the guest of his father. He was brought to England in 1819, and educated there. From early boyhood he studied oriental languages, and became as familiar with Arabic, Turkish, and Persian as he was with the chief languages of Europe.

After his return to Syria, Barker undertook a journey to the scarcely known sources of the Orontes or Asi River, no account of which had, until the communication of his 'Notes' to the Royal Geographical Society of London in 1836, ever been published. Barker returned on 22 August 1835 to his father's residence at Suediah, near the mouth of the Orontes, about 15 miles from Antioch, and during part of the succeeding winter played chess almost every evening with Ibrahim Pasha, then resident at Antioch. Barker was for many years resident at Tarsus, Turkey, in an official capacity. In the list of members of the Syro-

Egyptian Society of London for 1847–8 he is designated, probably by mistake, as 'H. B. M. Consul, Tarsus'. While there he accumulated materials for his elaborate work, which was finally edited by William Francis Ainsworth, the geographer and traveller in Asia Minor, under the title of *Lares and penates, or, Cilicia and its governors* (1853). The book was a history of Celicia, a region of Anatolia, and a description of images of their household gods which he discovered and removed to England. He had earlier published a volume of translations into the 'Principal European and Oriental languages' of a speech by Prince Albert. Barker's other works included: *Turkish Tales in English; A Practical Grammar of the Turkish Language; with Dialogues and Vocabulary* (with Arthur Bleeck, 1854); *A Reading Book of the Turkish Language* (1854); and the *Baitâl Pachísí, or, Twenty-five tales of a demon*, a new edition of the Hindí text (1855). This last work had both free and literal English translations and was edited by the Hindustani scholar E. B. Eastwick, to whom it was dedicated. Barker for some time taught Arabic, Turkish, Persian, and Hindustani at Eton College, and he dedicated his Turkish grammar to E. C. Hawtrey, the provost.

During the Crimean War Barker placed his knowledge of oriental languages and people at the disposal of the British government. While in the Crimea in 1855 he published *Odessa and its Inhabitants*, a light work which none the less tried to question the motives of the Turks and present Russia in a good light, and *A Short Historical Account of the Crimea*. The former work alleges to be autobiographical, by 'An English prisoner in Russia', but it is not known whether Barker was in fact imprisoned. He died of cholera on 28 January 1856 at Sinope on the Black Sea, aged forty-five, while employed as chief superintendent of the land transport depot there. His collaborator, Arthur Bleeck, was similarly employed there.

ARTHUR H. GRANT, *rev.* ELIZABETH BAIGENT

Sources W. F. Ainsworth, 'Introduction', in W. B. Barker, *Lares and penates, or, Cilicia and its governors* (1853) • *Syria and Egypt under the last five sultans of Turkey: being experiences … of Mr Consul-General Barker*, ed. E. B. B. Barker, 2 vols. (1876) • *The Times* (20 Feb 1856)

Archives BL, corresp. with J. Lee, Add. MSS 47490–47491 [partly copies] • BL, corresp. with Lord Palmerston, Add. MSS 48451–48452, 48505

Barker, William Higgs (1743/4–1816), Hebraist and headmaster, was the son of George Barker, tailor, of Great Russell Street, London, and a relation of the Hebraist Samuel Barker (1686–1759). He was admitted on the foundation of St Paul's School on 10 May 1756, aged twelve. He became Pauline exhibitioner at Trinity College, Cambridge, in 1761, and then Perry exhibitioner (1764–7); he graduated BA in 1765. He was also a fellow of Dulwich College in Surrey between 1766 and 1767. Barker took holy orders and was rector of Bleddfa, Radnorshire, from 1793, and vicar of St Peter's, Carmarthen, from 1796; he held both positions until his death. On 22 July 1767 he was elected headmaster of Queen Elizabeth's Grammar School, Carmarthen, where he continued to teach until 1815. He published, first, a small work, *Grammar of the Hebrew Language Adapted to the Use of Schools, with Biblical Examples* (1774), and later a *Hebrew and English Lexicon* (1812). Barker died in 1816.

JAMES MEW, *rev.* PHILIP CARTER

Sources Venn, *Alum. Cant.* • *GM*, 1st ser., 44 (1774), 434 • *GM*, 1st ser., 86/1 (1816), 636 • R. B. Gardiner, ed., *The admission registers of St Paul's School, from 1748 to 1876* (1884) • J. Nichols, *Memoirs of the late John Bowyer Nichols* (1863) • W. Spurrell, *Carmarthen and its neighbourhood* (1860)

Barkham, John (1571/2–1642), antiquary and historian, was born in the parish of St Mary-the-Moor, Exeter, the eldest son of Lawrence Barkham of St Leonard's, Devon, and his wife, Joan, daughter of Edward Bridgman of Exeter. Having matriculated aged fifteen at Exeter College, Oxford, in December 1587 he was in August of the following year admitted scholar of Corpus Christi College, Oxford, where he graduated BA in February 1591, proceeded MA in 1594, and became a fellow in 1596. In 1603 he took the degree of BD, advancing to the degree of DD in 1615.

Barkham served as chaplain to Richard Bancroft, archbishop of Canterbury, an office which he also held under his successor, George Abbot. In June 1608 he was collated to the rectory of Finchley, Middlesex; in October 1610 to the prebend of Brownswold in St Paul's Cathedral; in March 1615 to the rectory of Packlesham, Essex; in the May following to the rectory of Lackington, in the same county; and in December 1616 to the rectory and deanery of Bocking, also in Essex. In 1615 he resigned the rectory of Finchley, and in 1617 that of Packlesham.

Barkham had the reputation of being an accomplished linguist, an able divine, and an antiquary and historian of great erudition, but he published comparatively little, and this more for the benefit of others than himself. Contemporaries also noted his great hospitality to the poor, and to younger scholars. John Speed acknowledged Barkham's assistance in providing material for *The History of Great Britaine* (1611). Barkham contributed the life of King John in that work, and was probably also the author of the life of Henry II. The latter had previously been written by Edmund Bolton, Speed's research assistant, but Bolton's Catholicism led him to too charitable a view of Archbishop Thomas a Becket, and Barkham was called upon to provide a replacement life. As with other parts of the *History*, Speed heavily edited and rewrote materials he was given, so it is difficult to tell precisely where Barkham's contribution stopped and Speed's began. The same is also true of Barkham's alleged contribution, a year earlier, to John Guillim's *A Display of Heraldrie* (1610), which was probably in the form of notes and rough materials; there is no evidence to support Wood's contention that Barkham was the principal author of Guillim's work. In 1625 Barkham published, with a preface, the posthumous volume of Richard Crakanthorpe, *Defensio ecclesiae Anglicanae contra M. Antonii de dominus injurias*.

Barkham also had a keen interest in ancient Greek and modern coins, and assembled a collection of each. The Greek coins he gave to Archbishop William Laud about 1634, and Laud presented them to the Bodleian Library; they are now in the Ashmolean Museum, and Barkham's manuscript catalogue describing them is in the Lambeth Palace Library. At about the same time Barkham was probably the donor to his former college, Corpus Christi, of a smaller collection of modern coins, none dated later than 1570. He died at Bocking on 25 March 1642 and was buried in the chancel of the church there. He was survived by his wife, Anne, daughter of Robert Rogers of Dartford, Kent, by his son, George, and by two brothers, Ezekiel and Steven. T. F. HENDERSON, *rev.* D. R. WOOLF

Sources Fuller, *Worthies* (1662) • P. K. [P. King], *The surfeit to A.B.C.* (1656) • J. Speed, *The history of Great Britaine* (1611) • J. G. Milne, 'A Bocking dean and his coins', *Essex Review*, 42 (1933), 122–4 • D. R. Woolf, *The idea of history in early Stuart England* (1990) • D. Lloyd, *Memoires of the lives … of those … personages that suffered … for the protestant religion* (1668) • J. Hutchins, *The history and antiquities of the county of Dorset*, 3rd edn, ed. W. Shipp and J. W. Hodson, 4 (1874), 10; facs. edn (1973) • Foster, *Alum. Oxon.* • Wood, *Ath. Oxon.*, new edn, 3.35–7 • PRO, PROB 11/190, fol. 92
Archives LPL, MS
Wealth at death bequests of £220 to widow; £10 to local poor; £10 to 'Powles buildings': will, PRO, PROB 11/190, fol. 92

Barking, Adam of (*fl.* *c.*1176–*c.*1200), Benedictine monk and religious poet, was, according to John Leland, a monk of Sherborne, Dorset. Leland's account can be partly verified: he credits Adam with a poem *De serie sex aetatum*, which can be identified with one in Cambridge, Corpus Christi College, MS 277; quite late in the poem the author names himself Adam. The manuscript is the poet's autograph and shows his alterations; he began it as a vindication of Christianity but changed it, adding a new prologue, into an epic on the six ages of the world. After about 15,000 lines of rhyming hexameters he left it unfinished in the fourth age. An incomplete poem on the vanity of the world (*Quid mundus quid opes*) is extant in Longleat MS 27. Leland also credits him with a commentary on the gospels (unidentified) and a work *De natura divina et humana*. If the 'Johanni canonico Severiano' (to whom Leland says Adam dedicated the gospel commentary) was John of Salisbury, the work should probably be dated before 1176, when John became bishop of Chartres. The manuscript of the six ages was written *c.*1200. The accounts by John Bale and later biographers seem to have been spun from John Leland's wool. A. G. RIGG

Sources *Commentarii de scriptoribus Britannicis, auctore Joanne Lelando*, ed. A. Hall, 1 (1709), 232 • A. G. Rigg, *A history of Anglo-Latin literature, 1066–1422* (1992), 133–5 • M. R. James, *A descriptive catalogue of the manuscripts in the library of Corpus Christi College, Cambridge*, 2 (1912), pt 1, pp. 40–41 • Bale, *Cat.*, 263
Archives CCC Cam., MS 277 • Longleat House, Wiltshire, Longleat MS 27

Barking, Clemence of (*fl.* 1163–*c.*1200), Benedictine nun and hagiographer, of Barking Abbey, was responsible for an Anglo-Norman life of St Catherine of Alexandria which is the only life of this saint known to have been written by a woman in medieval Britain. Of Clemence's own life as much or as little is known as of that of her famous contemporary Marie de France (*fl.* 1154–1189): both women name themselves in their texts, and this, together with the texts themselves, is the basis for knowledge of them. The earliest extant manuscript of Clemence's *La vie de Sainte Catherine* dates from *c.*1200. A learned woman at Barking Abbey in this period is likely to have been from noble or at least gentry stock, and although unprofessed women sometimes spent time in such convents, Clemence, on her own testimony, was a nun. She chose a virgin martyr and patron saint of female learning as the subject of the life for which she claimed authorship, and the *Vie de Sainte Catherine* emphasizes the superiority of the saint's life as bride of Christ to that of the married life of the emperor Maxentius's wife (whom Catherine converts).

Learning among the women of Barking is witnessed in the seventh century and from the tenth century to the dissolution, making the abbey perhaps the longest-lived, albeit not continuously recorded, institutional centre of literary culture for women in British history. Clemence's Latin, like that of some other women at Barking in the twelfth century, seems to have been good: her life of Catherine is a skilful translation from the most ornate and learned of the Latin lives of St Catherine (the longer, so-called 'vulgate' version). The translation was probably made for a double audience: Clemence names herself as the translator and says that her poem was undertaken 'for love of Barking' (Clemence of Barking, verses 2690–2), but within the poem she also addresses the audience as *segnurs* (ibid., verse 1159). This suggests that in addition to the nuns of Barking and, perhaps, other conventual audiences, Clemence had a court audience in mind. As one of the old Benedictine royal nunneries, Barking was a cultivated and aristocratic milieu which remained closely connected with the Anglo-Norman court. An Anglo-Norman verse life of Edward the Confessor, underlining both his virgin sanctity and the legitimacy of the Anglo-Norman succession, was produced by an anonymous nun of Barking between 1163 and 1189. Clemence has been thought, though not proven, to have been its composer.

La vie de Sainte Catherine is written in accomplished Anglo-Norman octosyllabics, and draws on liturgical, devotional, and romance registers in elaborating its source material. The poem alludes extensively to the Anglo-Norman *Tristan* as part of its comparison of courtly and marital love with the love experienced by the celibate woman as a bride of Christ. It may also owe something to Anselm's thought on God's nature and power.

An elegant and powerful hagiography, the poem is of particular value as a twelfth-century woman writer's account of the emotional and intellectual value of a life vowed to virginity. In addition to extended treatment of Catherine's debate with fifty pagan philosophers, the life contains much narratorial commentary and reflection. Like all medieval women and medieval laymen, enclosed nuns were forbidden preaching (and many other forms of public speaking such as university *disputatio*), but Clemence used the hagiographic legend as a vehicle for addressing the concerns of her own community and of the society in which she lived.

The manuscript evidence suggests that her voice, in so far as it is represented by her *Vie de Sainte Catherine*, did not go unheard. While some Anglo-Norman hagiography survives only in a single holograph, Clemence's text is extant in three manuscripts (two insular, one continental), and it is also quoted in a large insular preaching compilation of the late thirteenth or fourteenth century. The life also has echoes and analogies in other Anglo-Norman hagiographic works, though the significance of these textual connections is not yet fully established. The possibilities of mutual influence between Clemence and the other named women writers of post-conquest Britain—Marie de France; Marie, who may have been a nun of Chatteris, author of the Anglo-Norman life of St Æthelthryth; the Marie who wrote the *Espurgatoire Seint Patrice*; and the writer of the Barking *Edouard*, if this was not Clemence herself—also have yet to be fully investigated.

JOCELYN WOGAN-BROWNE

Sources Clemence of Barking, *The life of St Catherine*, ed. W. MacBain, Anglo-Norman Texts, 18 (1964) • Clemence of Barking and anon., *Virgin lives and holy deaths: two exemplary biographies for Anglo-Norman women*, trans. J. Wogan-Browne and G. S. Burgess (1996) • E. C. Fawtier-Jones, 'Les vies de Sainte Catherine d'Alexandrie en ancien français', *Romania*, 56 (1930), 80–104 • D. Robertson, 'Writing in the textual community: Clemence of Barking's *Life of St Catherine*', *French Forum*, 21 (1996), 5–28 • C. Batt, 'Clemence of Barking's transformations of *courtoisie* in *La vie de Sainte Catherine d'Alexandrie*', *New Comparisons*, 12 (1991), 102–23 • W. MacBain, 'The literary apprenticeship of Clemence of Barking', *Journal of the Australasian Universities Language and Literature Association*, 9 (1958), 3–22 • *VCH Essex*, 2.115–22 • S. K. Elkins, *Holy women of twelfth-century England* (1988), 147–9 • J. Wogan-Browne, '"Clerc u lai, muïne u dame": women and Anglo-Norman hagiography in the twelfth and thirteenth centuries', *Women and literature in Britain, 1150–1200*, ed. C. M. Meale (1993), 61–85 • D. Robertson, *The medieval saints' lives: spiritual renewal and old French literature* (1995) [appx on Paris, Bibliothèque Nationale, MS fonds fr. 23112]

Archives Bibliothèque Nationale, Paris, *Vie de Sainte Catherine d'Alexandrie*, MS nouv. acq. fr. 4503, fols. 43*r*–74*r* • Bibliothèque Nationale, Paris, fr. 23112, fols. 317*v*–334*v* • BL, Add. MS 70813, fols. 246*r*–265*v* • Trinity Cam., MS B. 14. 39, fol. 80*v* b

Barking, Richard of (*d.* 1246), abbot of Westminster and royal counsellor, was presumably a native of Barking in Essex. His mother, Lucy, was commemorated by an obit celebration at Westminster, and can probably be identified as Lucy, widow of Richard of Barking, who gave the abbey land at Westminster during the reign of King John. At the time of his election as abbot Richard was serving as prior of Westminster, and he was almost certainly the prior who in November 1220 received the gold spurs used at the coronation of Henry III, to be put towards the work of the abbey's recently founded lady chapel. His election as abbot followed the death of his predecessor, William du Hommet, on 20 April 1222, and had taken place by 30 April that year, when the king ordered the restoration of the abbey's temporalities. However, objections appear to have been raised, since in July 1222 the pope appointed judges delegate to investigate the circumstances of Richard's promotion. Shortly afterwards, following what had been intended as a friendly wrestling match, a violent dispute erupted between the abbot's men and the citizens of London, perhaps reflecting the fact that Abbot William had recently obtained confirmation of the wide-ranging immunity claimed by Westminster Abbey from the jurisdiction of the bishops of London. Abbot Richard and his household were besieged in the house of the royal counsellor Philip d'Aubigny (*d.* 1236), and the rioting was only ended after violent reprisals carried out against the Londoners by the justiciar Hubert de Burgh (*d.* 1243). The ceremonial blessing of Richard as abbot was delayed until 18 September 1222 and was carried out by Peter des Roches, bishop of Winchester (*d.* 1237), again reflecting Westminster's newly won independence from the bishops of London.

As abbot Richard of Barking greatly increased the wealth of his house, acquiring major liberties from the crown, together with land and rents valued by the chronicler Matthew Paris at 300 marks a year. It was under Richard that Westminster obtained a pre-eminent place in the affections of Henry III, receiving a stream of royal benefactions intended to transform the abbey into a mausoleum for Henry and his family. In 1246 the king decreed that his own body was to be buried at Westminster after his death. Richard himself gave the monks relics of saints Felix and Vitalis, and a pair of decorated tapestries intended to foster the cult of St Edward the Confessor. In 1245, towards the end of his life, the east end of the abbey was demolished as the first stage in a lavish programme of rebuilding. His relations with the Westminster monks were placed on a firmer footing in 1225, with an ordinance intended to regulate the division of property and jurisdiction between abbot and convent; however the monks were later to complain that the settlement was biased heavily against them, forcing at least two later revisions to the original award.

As a close familiar of the king Richard of Barking was sent as envoy to the court of France in 1225, and again, probably to Poitou, in 1240. Between 1242 and 1244 he appeared at the royal exchequer, where he audited accounts and witnessed writs on the memoranda roll. However, the claim made by the fifteenth-century chronicler John Flete, that he served as royal treasurer, appears to be unfounded. He was regularly appointed to act as papal judge-delegate, although in 1232 he was briefly suspended from office and forced to travel to Rome, after resisting a general visitation of Benedictine houses ordered by the pope. In 1245 he was excused attendance at the papal Council of Lyons because of his official duties during the king's campaign against the Welsh. He died on 23 November or 1 December 1246 and was buried in the lady chapel of Westminster Abbey, having earlier ordained an extensive obit celebration to be held by the Westminster monks. His acquisition of new liberties and lands for the abbey was not without its cost, and Richard of Barking is said to have burdened his successor with debts of 1700 marks.

NICHOLAS VINCENT

Sources *Ann. mon.* • Paris, *Chron.* • Exchequer memoranda rolls, E159, king's remembrancer, E368, lord treasurer's remembrancer • E. H. Pearce, *The monks of Westminster* (1916) • B. F. Harvey, ed., *Documents illustrating the rule of Walter de Wenlok abbot of Westminster, 1283–1307*, CS, 4th ser., 2 (1965) • E. Mason, J. Bray, and D. J. Murphy, eds., *Westminster Abbey charters, 1066–c.1214*, London RS, 25 (1988) • N. Vincent, ed., *Winchester, 1205–1238*, English Episcopal Acta, 9

(1994) • H. R. Luard, ed., *Flores historiarum*, 3 vols., Rolls Series, 95 (1890) • T. Madox, *The history and antiquities of the exchequer of the kings of England*, 2nd edn, 2 vols. (1769) • P. Binski, 'Abbot Berkyng's tapestries and Matthew Paris's *Life of St Edward the Confessor*', *Archaeologia*, 109 (1991), 85–100 • *Chancery records*

Barkla, Charles Glover (1877–1944), physicist, was born at Albert Road, Widnes, Lancashire, on 7 June 1877, second son of John Martin Barkla, a Cornishman and secretary of the Atlas Chemical Company. His mother, Sarah Glover, came from Prescot. Barkla attended the Liverpool Mechanics' Institution until 1895 when he won Bibby and county council scholarships to University College, Liverpool. He studied mathematics, and subsequently experimental physics under Oliver Lodge, obtaining a first-class BSc in 1899. He helped found the University Physical Society, becoming its first president. Barkla proceeded, with an 1851 Exhibition scholarship, to the Cavendish Laboratory, Cambridge, to study under J. J. Thomson the propagation of electric waves along thin wires. In his second year he transferred from Trinity to King's College, where he joined the chapel choir under A. H. Mann; Barkla had a magnificent bass voice, which attracted large audiences.

In the spring of 1902, feeling isolated from the mainstream of Cavendish research and at Thomson's suggestion, Barkla began studying secondary rays scattered from gases exposed to X-rays. He was much influenced by G. G. Stokes's theory, adopted by Thomson, that X-rays were pulses of electromagnetic radiation. Barkla conceived a great admiration for Thomson, recalling that 'I felt that the papers that I wrote were for him to read: the appreciation of others was of quite secondary importance. His interest and his publications on and around the subject were then my greatest inspiration' (Barkla to Rayleigh, 20 Dec 1940, priv. coll.). Nevertheless, poor facilities and a lack of intellectual privacy prompted Barkla to leave the Cavendish later in 1902.

Barkla was awarded a Cambridge BA research degree in 1903, having already taken up the Oliver Lodge fellowship at Liverpool. In 1904 Liverpool University made him a DSc. In 1907, following his appointment to a special lectureship, Barkla married Mary Esther, daughter of John Thomas Cowell JP of the Isle of Man. They had three sons and one daughter. Barkla was tall, well built, and conservative in dress, with a friendly manner, especially with children. He always preferred living in rural surroundings. A staunch Methodist, he saw scientific investigation as 'a part of the quest for God, the Creator' (*DNB*).

Barkla's finding that X-rays were scattered by the electrons within atoms was published in the *Philosophical Magazine* in 1903 (6th ser., 5, 685–98). Thomson incorporated this conclusion within his scattering formula, which Barkla in turn used to obtain two major results. The first was his demonstration that the number of electrons in an atom was comparable with the atomic weight (published in *Philosophical Magazine*, 6th ser., 7, 1904, 543–60), which dealt a significant blow to the view that matter was composed entirely of electrons, and indicated that most of the atom's mass must reside in the positive portion. The second result came from his realization that scattered X-rays should be polarized. In 1904 he tried scattering low energy X-rays from carbon. Encouraged by the results, he undertook a double scattering experiment suggested by his colleague L. R. Wilberforce. His unambiguous demonstration that X-rays could be polarized succeeded where every experimentalist since Röntgen had failed, and reinforced the supposition that X-rays were transverse electromagnetic waves; the experiment appeared in *Proceedings of the Royal Society*, 77A (1906), 247–55.

In 1907–8 Barkla became embroiled in a controversy with W. H. Bragg over whether gamma and X-rays were waves or particles, which was finally resolved only in the 1920s with appreciation of their dual nature. Barkla predicted that for unpolarized X-rays twice as much radiation should be scattered forward as at right angles to the incident ray. His experimental confirmation was regarded as strong evidence for the wave nature of X-rays. Barkla found that contrary to light element scattering, radiation scattered from heavy elements such as iron was both unpolarized and of significantly lower energy than the incident rays. It appeared to have an energy characteristic of the emitting element. Working with A. L. Hughes, C. A. Sadler, and J. Nicol, he confirmed the homogeneity of the characteristic radiation and distinguished two groups of homogeneous X-rays from each heavy element. He interpreted these as two series of X-ray spectral lines, 'denoted by the letters K and L … as it is highly probable that series of radiations both more absorbable and more penetrating exist' (C. G. Barkla, 'The spectra of the fluorescent Röntgen radiations', *Philosophical Magazine*, 6th ser., 22, 1911, 406). The importance of this interpretation was widely recognized when H. G. Moseley demonstrated the relation between X-ray spectra and atomic number.

In 1909 Barkla was appointed Wheatstone professor of physics at King's College, London. He continued to live in the country, at Northwood, Middlesex. He was elected a fellow of the Royal Society in 1912. With his students he continued working on characteristic X-rays, investigated the ionization of gases and used new values of the relevant constants to recalculate the number of electrons per atom. He found this to be about half the atomic weight, predating by a year the realization of the significance of the atomic number by E. Rutherford, N. Bohr, and H. G. Moseley.

In 1912 W. Friedrich and P. Knipping's demonstration of X-ray diffraction was of great significance to Barkla, for it exploited characteristic X-radiation and appeared conclusive evidence for the wave nature of X-rays. Barkla immediately began experiments on X-ray diffraction, collaborating with G. H. Martyn. These were interrupted by Barkla's move to Edinburgh University, where he was appointed professor of natural philosophy in the summer of 1913, soon moving his family to the Hermitage of Braid. He became well known for his singing, and served as a member of the faculty of music, establishing a close friendship with D. F. Tovey, professor of music.

Barkla took a prominent part in instituting honours degrees in pure science at Edinburgh and in developing the honours school of physics, modelling his leadership style on that of Thomson at the Cavendish. Among other work on the behaviour of electrons, he and A. E. M. M. Dallas obtained results which foreshadowed the discovery of the Auger effect in 1925 (*Philosophical Magazine*, 5th ser., 47, 1924, 1–23). In 1916 he gave the Bakerian lecture; he was awarded the Hughes medal of the Royal Society in 1917, and he received the 1917 Nobel prize for his discovery of characteristic X-radiation. In 1918 he decided against applying for the Cavendish professorship at Cambridge, despite Thomson's encouragement.

After moving to Edinburgh Barkla began searching for a J-series of characteristic radiations, foreshadowed by his work in 1911. In 1916 he and J. G. Dunlop found evidence, when scattering heterogeneous X-rays, for a series of energetic X-rays from the light elements. His first suggestion that these represented transitions from an electron shell inside the K shell proved untenable as atomic theory developed. Barkla then proposed a radically new idea, the J phenomenon. Through his suggestion that the characteristics of a heterogeneous X-ray beam depended on the beam as a whole rather than being the sum of the characteristics of its constituent wavelengths as was generally assumed, Barkla hoped to arrive at a fundamental physical picture underlying the mathematical formalism of quantum theory. While most physicists ignored his results, a few apparent refutations implied that Barkla was a crank. Reassessment in the 1970s suggested that Barkla's results remained unexplained by quantum theory and that although his interpretation may have been mistaken, his questioning of fundamental assumptions was valid, expressed in his view that: 'It is to the apparent violations of known laws and not to further confirmation under very precise and specialized conditions that we must look for advance in knowledge' (*Nature*, 131, 1933, 166).

Barkla ceased publishing after 1933 but continued investigating the J phenomenon, relying extensively on his personal assistant, W. H. Stevens. In 1943 he wrote, 'I hope for a solution before I retire in five years! That would be worth many years of toil' (Barkla to Russ, 5 Jan 1943, priv. coll.). Twenty-one months later Barkla died relatively suddenly at his home, Braidwood, 23 Corrennie Gardens, Edinburgh, on 23 October 1944, his health undermined by the death of his youngest son in service at Carthage the previous year. His wife and three children survived him.

Isobel Falconer

Sources H. S. Allen, *Obits. FRS*, 5 (1945–8), 341–66 • B. Wynne, 'C. G. Barkla and the J phenomenon: a case study in the treatment of deviance in physics', *Social Studies of Science*, 6 (1976), 307–47 • private information (1959) • R. J. Stephenson, 'The scientific career of Charles Glover Barkla', *American Journal of Physics*, 35 (1967), 140–52 • *DNB* • B. Wynne, 'C. G. Barkla and the J phenomenon', *Physics Education*, 14 (1979), 52–5 • priv. coll. • b. cert. • d. cert. • *CCI* (1945) • election certificate, RS

Archives priv. coll., corresp. and papers | CUL, letters to Lord Rutherford • Ransom HRC, letters to Sir Owen Richardson

Likenesses W. Stoneman, photograph, 1926, NPG • D. Foggie, pencil drawing, 1934, U. Edin. • photograph, repro. in Allen, *Obits. FRS* (1947), facing p. 341

Wealth at death £14,107: confirmation, 4 Jan 1945, *CCI*

Barkly, Arthur Cecil Stuart (1843–1890). *See under* Barkly, Sir Henry (1815–1898).

Barkly, Sir Henry (1815–1898), colonial governor, was born on 24 February 1815 at Highbury, Middlesex, the only surviving son of Aeneas Barkly (1768–1836), formerly of Kirkton Farm, Cromarty, Scotland, and his wife, Susannah Louisa, *née* ffrith, the orphan daughter of a Jamaican planter. He was educated at Bruce Castle School, Tottenham, where the emphasis of the curriculum left him with a lifelong interest in statistics and the natural sciences.

In 1832 Barkly entered his father's West Indian business in London, and on the latter's death in August 1836 he inherited both financial obligations towards his two sisters and a failing estate in British Guiana. Nevertheless, on 18 October 1840, at Aldenham, Hertfordshire, Barkly—tall and distinguished—married Elizabeth Helen Timmins of Hillfield. On 26 April 1845 he was returned at a by-election as MP for Leominster. As such, he ably but independently supported Sir Robert Peel on colonial issues. The latter's fall left him without prospects, so in December 1848 he gratefully accepted from his former Liberal opponents an offer of the governorship of British Guiana.

Here, in the words of the secretary of state, Lord Grey, Barkly's 'remarkable skill and ability' widened the franchise of the electoral college of *kiezers* ('choosers') and overcame the planter clique's refusal to concede supplies in the court of policy. With his appreciation of the economic problems of British Guiana and of the West Indies more generally, Barkly also supported introducing indentured labourers from Asia. A planter himself, he proved adept at wooing the colonists of this and later colonial governments.

On 18 July 1853 Barkly was knighted KCB and in August 1853 he became governor of Jamaica. Here he attempted to supplant the deadlocked and debt-ridden representative institutions with a form of responsible government, according to Colonial Office instructions. But even his remarkable talents were overstretched in driving the machinery of this so-called responsible government, where cohesive parties were lacking, where the governor retained considerable executive power, and where the franchise remained absurdly narrow. He tried valiantly to widen the franchise and to articulate legislative and executive action, but left after his short term on 6 May 1856 without fully resolving Jamaica's constitutional dilemma of an executive responsible mainly to the governor confronting a capricious and unrepresentative assembly. Henceforth he was convinced that responsible government could rest only on the solid foundation of organized and popular parties in colonial legislatures.

In December 1856 Barkly arrived in Victoria, Australia, with the task of working the newly introduced responsible government. The auspices were hardly favourable. At Eureka stockade gold-diggers and soldiers had recently

Sir Henry Barkly (1815–1898), by unknown photographer

clashed, and land tenure was a problem where pastoral squatting was still a way of life. With such unpliant human instruments as John O'Shannassy and Charles Gavan Duffy to hand, but with his usual tact and constitutional correctitude, Barkly nevertheless succeeded in reconciling the vibrant infant democracy to the limited executive authority that the governor still wielded. Growing mellower too, he aligned himself with colonial endeavours such as the Burke and Wills exploratory expedition and with the library, university, and learned societies. On 2 June 1864 he was elected fellow of the Royal Society and in 1870 of the Royal Geographical Society.

Lady Barkly died at Melbourne on 17 April 1857; their union had produced four sons and a daughter. On 21 July 1860 Barkly married Anne Maria, the daughter of Sir Thomas Pratt, who survived him. All his sons from his first marriage predeceased him.

On 1 September 1863 Barkly arrived as governor of Mauritius. Here he faced the frustrations of overcoming deficits on railway construction, rebuilding after a devastating hurricane, devising measures for a malaria epidemic, and trying to work an anomalous variant of the system of crown colony government, in which unofficial nominees outweighed officials in the legislative council. Nevertheless, it was typical of Barkly that he should sacrifice his hard-earned leave to cope with the consequences of the hurricane. Predictably, he was hardly relieved when on 19 August 1870 he was appointed to another semi-bankrupt colony, the Cape.

Here Barkly's three main problems were the future of the disputed yet diamondiferous Griqualand West, the introduction of responsible government under Colonial Office pressure, and co-operating with Lord Carnarvon's scheme of South African confederation.

In 1871, as high commissioner with perceived extraterritorial authority, Barkly took a short cut in proclaiming British sovereignty over Griqualand West without following instructions to secure the Cape's clear agreement to incorporate it. Instead, the annoyed secretary of state had to create a small but separate crown colony in 1872. While Barkly's unauthorized scheme had at least been based on the Keate award, which indirectly favoured an imperial claim to Griqualand West, and on experience of handling the digger population of Victoria, he had lost much of his former support in the Colonial Office in London. Nor was this really restored by his protracted, though eventually successful, campaign of 1871–2 to establish responsible government under J. C. Molteno. Nevertheless he was awarded the GCMG on 9 March 1874. But, as Molteno was a colonial 'westerner', the eastern Cape remained bitterly unreconciled to the new dispensation.

These divisions were exacerbated when Lord Carnarvon, as secretary of state, attempted through his private emissary, J. A. Froude, to promote South African confederation in 1875. Because Molteno perceived this scheme as favouring eastern Cape separatism, and because Froude himself proceeded to encourage the easterners, the responsible ministry based in the west obstructed Carnarvon's plan. Barkly was left on the horns of a dilemma. In communicating the negative standpoint of his colonial premier, Molteno, he drew Carnarvon's hostility, which was further fed by the 'black flag' revolt in Griqualand West in June 1875. Although he concluded a guarded truce with Carnarvon in 1876, Barkly was only too pleased to escape his embarrassments when he retired on 21 March 1877. In his latter years he held several London directorships. Still in what he believed to be straitened circumstances from West Indian losses and family obligations, he died of cardiac failure at his home, 1 Bina Gardens, South Kensington, London, on 20 October 1898 and was buried in Brompton cemetery.

As one of the most experienced of imperial officials in handling responsibly governed colonies, Barkly had found himself obliged at the end of a distinguished and successful career to introduce and work the system of a colonial executive in the divided and unfavourable human environment of the Cape, with consequent problems that all but overcame him.

Barkly's eldest son, **Arthur Cecil Stuart Barkly** (1843–1890), colonial governor, was educated at Harrow School. From the 6th Carabiniers he went on to be, successively, private secretary to his father at Mauritius and the Cape, resident magistrate in Basutoland (1877), chief commissioner of the Seychelles, lieutenant-governor of the Falkland Islands (1886), and the last British governor of Heligoland (1888–90). He died at Stapleton Park, near Pontefract, Yorkshire, on 27 September 1890, survived by his wife, Fanny, *née* Hatchard. JOHN BENYON

Sources M. MacMillan, *Sir Henry Barkly* (1970) • A. Wilmot, *The life and times of Sir Richard Southey* (1904) • W. E. G. Solomon, *Saul Solomon* (1948) • C. F. Goodfellow, *Great Britain and South African confederation, 1870–1881* (1966) • J. A. Benyon, *Proconsul and paramountcy in South Africa: the high commission, British supremacy and the subcontinent, 1806–1910* (1980) • *DNB* • B. A. Knox, 'Barkly, Sir Henry', *AusDB*, vol. 3 • A. F. Hattersley, 'Barkly, Sir Henry', *DSAB*

Archives NL Scot., family and personal papers • RBG Kew, papers relating to Stapeliae | Bodl. Oxf., letters to Lord Kimberley • National Library of South Africa, Cape Town, Merriman MSS • National Library of South Africa, Cape Town, Molteno MSS • PRO, corresp. with Lord Carnarvon, PRO 30/6 • U. Durham L., corresp. with third Earl Grey

Likenesses E. Roworth, oils, Cultural History Museum, Cape Town, South Africa • W. H. Schröder, cartoon, Mendelssohn Library, Cape Town, South Africa • Spy [L. Ward], caricature, chromolithograph, NPG; repro. in *VF* (9 July 1887) • C. Summers, marble bust, State Library of Victoria, Melbourne, Australia • photograph, NPG [*see illus.*] • photographs, repro. in MacMillan, *Sir Henry Barkly* • photographs, priv. coll.

Wealth at death £12,842 0s. 2d.: probate, 1 Feb 1899, *CGPLA Eng. & Wales* • £1277 7s. 10d.—Arthur Cecil Stuart Barkly: resworn probate, Dec 1890, *CGPLA Eng. & Wales*

Barksdale, Clement (1609–1687), Church of England clergyman and author, was born on 23 November 1609, St Clement's day, at Winchcombe, Gloucestershire, the son of John Barksdale. He was educated at the grammar school in Abingdon, Berkshire, and matriculated at Merton College, Oxford, in February 1626. However, shortly after this he transferred to Gloucester Hall (later Worcester College), and graduated BA in October 1629 and proceeded MA in 1632. After being ordained Barksdale acted for a short time in 1637 as chaplain of Lincoln College at All Saints' Church, Oxford. Later in the same year he moved to Hereford, where he was appointed master of the free school. In 1641 he was made vicar choral and rector of St Nicholas in the city. A firm royalist, he remained in his position as rector until the parliamentary forces occupied Hereford in 1646. At this time the Chandos family, who employed Barksdale as a chaplain, enabled him to take shelter in Sudeley Castle, not far from his birthplace.

Subsequently Barksdale moved to Hawling, in the Cotswolds, where he taught at a private school and was rector in 1650. Although there is no record of when he was married it is likely to have been by about 1650. His son Charlton, born in 1651 or 1652, matriculated at Magdalen College in 1667 and was made rector of Hawling in 1676; another son, Charles, matriculated at Wadham College in 1668. While in Hawling, Barksdale set up fraternal meetings with other clergymen for theological discussion, and in November 1653 he engaged in a public disputation at Winchcombe with the Independent Carnsew Helme. The published account, *The Disputation at Winchcombe* (1653), records Barksdale's defence of the Anglican prayer book, articles, catechism, and mixed communion.

While at Hawling, Barksdale embarked on an ambitious programme of writing and translating. In the course of his career he published over thirty books, including translations, collections of biographies and sayings, a volume of his own poetry, several of his own sermons, and a few other short books. His literary output was scorned by Anthony Wood, who characterized him as 'a good Disputant, a great admirer of Hugo Grotius, a frequent Preacher, but very conceited and vain, a great pretender to Poetry, and a Writer and Translater of several little Tracts, most of which are meer Scribbles' (Wood, 2.811–14). Yet Wood's cursory dismissal of Barksdale does him an injustice. Although his books contain little of his own writing, his translations and collections were deliberately designed to foster the development of a moderate, latitudinarian Anglicanism. Rather than being a mere scribbler Barksdale was a man with a clear sense of mission. He wanted to introduce his readers to the less dogmatic figures within the Reformed tradition; men like Sebastian Castellio, Richard Hooker, Hugo Grotius, and Henry Hammond. His theological project is evident even in his book of poems, *Nympha libethris, or, The Cotswold Muse* (1651), which includes verses in praise of Grotius, Hammond, Jeremy Taylor, George Herbert, and the Arminian Independent John Goodwin for his book on the doctrine of justification. Barksdale's *Memorials of Worthy Persons*, published in five volumes between 1661 and 1670, also endeavoured to familiarize the reading public with distinguished moderate divines.

Yet Barksdale's greatest significance lay in his work as a translator of Grotius. As Hugh Trevor-Roper suggests, Barksdale's translations illustrate 'the renewal of interest in Grotius and his English disciples' (Trevor-Roper, 223). Between the early 1650s and the mid-1670s Barksdale translated many of the Dutchman's writings, including major works like *De jure belli ac pacis* and *De veritate religionis Christianae*. He also helped to popularize Grotius by translating a biography in 1652, and producing a collection entitled *Annotationum selectarum* (1675) of his 'judgements' on such diverse subjects as predestination, Socinus, the pope, Servetus, 'Calvin's impatience', the sacraments, and saints. To Barksdale, Grotius was 'the wisest Scholar of his time', the 'Moderator 'twixt the State and Church', and the one who taught men:

> how to reconcile
> This and that Church in mild Cassanders stile.

As if to drive home the point, he also translated Catholic authors like the Jesuit Scrottus. As a writer and translator Barksdale laboured to fashion Anglicanism in the image of Grotius: tolerant, ecumenical, rational, and learned.

On 24 May 1660 Barksdale preached at Winchcombe a sermon subsequently published as *The King's Return*, and that year he was appointed rector of Naunton and Stow on the Wold, Gloucestershire. He retained this position and continued writing and translating until his death at Naunton on about 6 January 1687. He was buried at Naunton. JOHN COFFEY

Sources Wood, *Ath. Oxon.*, 2nd edn, 2.811–14 • Foster, *Alum. Oxon.* • T. Corser, *Collectanea Anglo-poetica, or, A … catalogue of a … collection of*

early English poetry, 11 vols., Chetham Society (1860–83) • H. Trevor-Roper, *Catholics, Anglicans and puritans: seventeenth-century essays* (1987), 223 • *Walker rev.*, 191–2

Barkstead, John [created Sir John Barkstead under the protectorate] (*d.* **1662**), major-general and regicide, was probably the son of Michael Barkstead, a London goldsmith, and his wife, Anne, daughter of John Downing. His grandfather had lived at Lichfield in Staffordshire and his family was originally from Germany. Barkstead's brother, Michael, was also a goldsmith, and before the civil war Barkstead himself was probably also active in the business in London, for he was later lampooned by his critics for having sold thimbles and bodkins. He was a congregationalist in his religious beliefs.

At the start of the first civil war Barkstead took up arms for parliament as a captain of foot in Colonel Venn's regiment within the earl of Essex's army. According to the republican Edmund Ludlow he fought because he was 'sensible of the invasions which had been made upon the liberties of the nation' (*Memoirs of Edmund Ludlow*, 2.322). In July 1644 he was appointed governor of Reading, a post he held until January 1647. Later in 1647 he was given command of a New Model Army regiment of foot, previously under Richard Fortescue. In the spring of 1648 he was involved in the suppression of royalist disturbances in London and later that year he commanded his regiment at the siege of Colchester.

In December 1648 Barkstead was named as one of the commissioners for Charles I's trial: he attended every session except one [*see also* Regicides]. At his own execution fourteen years later he claimed that he was named as a commissioner without his knowledge and that, as one of the judges, he had acted 'without any malice' (*Speeches Discourses and Prayers*, 15). During 1649 he served as governor of Great Yarmouth in Norfolk and in April 1650 his regiment was appointed to guard parliament and the City of London. In August 1652 he was appointed lieutenant of the Tower of London, a position he retained until 1659. In his speech at the opening of the second protectorate parliament in 1656 Cromwell praised Barkstead's efficiency in that capacity, commenting that 'there never was any design on foot but we could hear of it out of the Tower' (*Writings and Speeches*, 4.266). Barkstead's enemies, however, were very critical of him. In the anonymous pamphlet *Invisible John Made Visible, or, A Grand Pimp of Tyranny Portrayed* (1659) he was denounced as 'the most indefatigable drudge in the nation to the late tyrant', and accused of acting cruelly and insolently to prisoners and of amassing a large fortune by charging extortionate fees from them, behaviour which, the author claimed, 'stincks in the nostrils of both good and bad'.

In 1654 Barkstead was elected to the first protectorate parliament for Colchester and the following year he was appointed major-general for Middlesex and Westminster. He also acted as deputy major-general for London under Philip Skippon. His association was the smallest of twelve created, but also probably the most populous. Again he was efficient and uncompromising in carrying out his new duties. He liaised closely with Cromwell's secretary of state, John Thurloe, to maintain the security of London and also took steps to clamp down on immorality and ungodliness in the capital and the surrounding area. He arrested prostitutes, confiscated the horses of those found riding on Sundays, supervised the closure of the bear garden in Bankside, and suppressed traditional Shrove Tuesday celebrations.

Barkstead was knighted by Cromwell for his services in January 1656 and later that year sat in the second protectorate parliament for Middlesex. He also sat in Richard Cromwell's parliament, where he came under attack for his behaviour as lieutenant of the Tower, and in June 1659 the recalled Rump dismissed him from this post. At the Restoration, Barkstead escaped to Germany but in 1661 he travelled to the Netherlands, where, along with John Okey and Miles Corbet, he was arrested by the English ambassador, Sir George Downing, and sent back to England. Following a brief trial Barkstead was executed at Tyburn on 19 April 1662. He died professing his belief in the rightness of his actions and his commitment to congregationalism. His scaffold speeches were later published in *The Speeches, Discourses and Prayers of John Barkstead, John Okey, and Miles Corbet* (1662). CHRISTOPHER DURSTON

Sources Thurloe state papers, Bodl. Oxf., MS Rawl. A • C. H. Firth and G. Davies, *The regimental history of Cromwell's army*, 2 vols. (1940) • PRO, Interregnum state papers, SP 18–28 • *Invisible John made visible, or, A grand pimp of tyranny portrayed* (1659) • *The speeches, discourses and prayers of John Barkstead, John Okey, and Miles Corbet* (1662) • *Memoirs of Edmund Ludlow*, ed. C. H. Firth, 2 vols. (1888) • *DNB* • *The writings and speeches of Oliver Cromwell*, ed. W. C. Abbott and C. D. Crane, 4 vols. (1937–47) • Thurloe, *State papers*
Archives Bodl. Oxf., Thurloe state papers, MS Rawl.
Likenesses line engraving, pubd 1810, BM, NPG • T. Athow, wash drawing, AM Oxf. • oils, DWL

Barksted [Backsted, Baxter], **William** (*fl.* **1607–1630**), actor and poet, whose date and place of birth are unknown, was the author of two narrative poems which also provide our earliest knowledge of his life. *Mirrha the Mother of Adonis, or, Lustes Prodegies* was published in 1607, and *Hiren, or, The Faire Greeke* in 1611, but presumably written before *Mirrha* because the author, in two separate dedications, one to the earl of Oxford, the other to the countess of Derby, describes *Hiren* as 'The bashfull utterance of a maiden Muse' and protests that he was 'never guilty of that crime before'. The last stanza of *Mirrha* is a tribute to Shakespeare:

> His song was worthie merrit (*Shakespeare* hee)
> sung the faire blossome, thou [Barksted's muse] the
> withered tree

The two poems are written in imitation of Shakespeare's *Venus and Adonis* and *Lucrece* respectively, suggesting that Barksted had taken the older poet-actor and playwright as a model for his career in the theatre, trying in the first place to secure patronage by exhibiting his poetic gifts.

The two works must be very youthful productions; on the title-page of the second Barksted is described as 'one of the servants of his Majesties REVELS', that is a member of the company that acted at the Whitefriars in 1607 and 1608 under the unauthorized name of Children of the

King's Revels, cashing in on the disappearance in the previous year of the Children of the Queen's Revels at the Blackfriars, a theatre that was taken over shortly after by the King's Men. It is likely that Barksted had started as a boy actor with the Queen's Revels and had moved on with his fellow 'children' to the short-lived King's Revels. The reference on the title-page of *Hiren* in 1611 may indicate that the copy for the printer had been prepared some years before, when the company was still active.

The Whitefriars was taken over in 1609 by the new Children of the Queen's Revels, and Barksted was one of them: in the 1616 folio of Ben Jonson's *Works* the name 'Will. Barksted' appears among the 'principall Comoedians' in the play *Epicene* 'first acted, in the yeer 1609 By the Children of her majesties Revells' and in the 1679 edition of the collection entitled *Fifty Comedies and Tragedies* by Beaumont and Fletcher, 'Will. Barckstead' figures among the players in *The Coxcomb*, acted at the Whitefriars in the 1609–10 season. By this time the word 'children' to designate theatre companies was a mere convention: Nathaniel Field, for instance, whose name appears with that of Barksted in both lists of actors, was born in 1587. It can be assumed that Barksted also was then in his early twenties, and in fact two years later he was one of the members of an adult company, the Lady Elizabeth's Men, who on 29 August 1611 subscribed a document for a loan from the theatre manager Philip Henslowe.

As well as acting, Barksted tried his hand at playwriting. When in 1608 John Marston was arrested for a second time and was forced to abandon playwriting, the draft of his *The Insatiate Countess* must have been completed by other hands. The title-page of the first quarto of 1613 presents the play as 'Acted at White-Fryers. Written by John Marston', but Marston's name is cut out from half the extant copies of the edition and in 1944 a further copy was discovered with a cancel title-page: 'The Insatiate Countesse. A Tragedie, as it was sundry times Acted at the White-Friers, by the Children of the Revels. Written By Lewis Machin, and William Bacster'. This suggests that Barksted completed the draft for performance by his company, in collaboration with a fellow writer. Lewis Machin is known for having added the comic scenes to Gervase Markham's *The Dumb Knight* performed by the Children of the King's Revels and published in 1608. His 'Three Eglogs, The First is of Menalcas and Daphnis: The other Two is of Apollo and Hyacinth', was appended to Barksted's *Mirrha*, testifying to the close friendship between the two young men.

Barksted's name appears spelt Baxter in a complaint against Henslowe in 1615, and again, as Backsted, when after Henslowe's death in 1616 the debts of the Lady Elizabeth's Men were remitted by Henslowe's successors, but does not figure in a further document of the players the following year; it appears that by then he had joined the recently revived Prince Charles's Company, active until 1625 at the Red Bull, but mostly travelling in the provinces.

A clue to Barksted's later life is provided by an anecdote reported by John Taylor, the Water Poet, in *Taylors Wit and Mirth* (1629), of 'Will. Backstead the Plaier' (Bentley, 2.358), and by 'A Prologue to a Playe to the Cuntry People' entered after May 1630 under the name of 'Wm Backstead, Comedian' by the poor knight of Windsor Nicholas Burghe in his commonplace book (now MS Ashmole 38 in the Bodleian Library). The latter is an all purpose verse prologue for a travelling company, possibly suggested to Barksted by his experience with Prince Charles's Men. The fact that in the third quarto of *The Insatiate Countess* (1631) the title-page bearing Marston's name had to be replaced by a cancel stating that the play was 'By William Barksteed' implies that he had lodged a complaint against the attribution to Marston. But he died before 1638, when the Water Poet reported in *Taylors Feast* another anecdote about 'Will. Baxted, a late well knowne fine Comedian' (Bentley, 2.358). GIORGIO MELCHIORI

Sources G. Melchiori, 'Attore drammaturgo e repertorio in una compagnia di ragazzi', *Le Forme del teatro*, 2 (1981), 101–37 • A. B. Grosart, ed., *Occasional issues of unique or very rare books*, 3 (1876) • W. Barksted, *Mirrha the mother of Adonis, or, Lustes prodegies … whereunto are added certain eglogs, By L. M.* (1607) [unique copy in Bodl., Oxf.] • W. Barksted, *Hiren, or, The faire Greeke* (1611) • L. Machin and W. Bacster [W. Barksted], *The insatiate countesse* (1613) [unique copy in Folger] • W. Barksteed [W. Barksted], *The insatiate countesse* (1631) [unique copy in Hunt. L.] • G. Melchiori, 'Introduction', in J. Marston and others, *The insatiate countess*, ed. G. Melchiori (1984), 1–17 • 'A prologue to a playe to the cuntry people', Bodl. Oxf., MS Ashmole 38, fol. 145, art. 198 • W. C. Hazlitt, *Hand-book to the popular, poetical and dramatic literature of Great Britain* (1867) • *Taylors wit and mirth, Shakespeare jest books*, ed. W. C. Hazlitt, 3 vols. (1864), vol. 2 • *Taylors feast* (1638) • W. W. Greg, *Henslowe papers: being documents supplementary to Henslowe's diary* (1907) • G. Langbaine, *An account of the English dramatick poets* (1691) • H. N. Hillebrand, 'The Children of the King's Revels at Whitefriars', *Journal of English and German Philology*, 21 (1922), 318–34 • H. N. Hillebrand, *The child actors*, 2 vols. (1926) • E. Nungezer, *A dictionary of actors* (1929) • E. K. Chambers, *The Elizabethan stage*, 4 vols. (1923), vols. 2–3 • G. E. Bentley, *The Jacobean and Caroline stage*, 7 vols. (1941–68), vol. 2 • A. Gurr, *The Shakespearian playing companies* (1996), esp. 394–415

Barkworth [*alias* Lambert], **Mark** (*bap.* **1570**, *d.* **1601**), Benedictine monk and martyr, was baptized at Searby, Lincolnshire, in April 1570. Nothing is known of his parents. Searby church records seem to indicate that his brother George was baptized in March 1576. When he was young a woman gifted with prophecy told Barkworth he would die on the scaffold. This so upset his parents that he left home and studied for a time at Oxford. There is no record of him in the records of Oxford University, so he did not graduate there.

Barkworth 'was brought up a Protestant, but going abroad, when twenty-two … he was converted to the Catholic faith at Douay, in Flanders, by a Flemish Jesuit' (Gillow, *Lit. biog. hist.*, 1.129–30). He matriculated at the English College, Douai, on 5 October 1594. He then went to St Alban's College, Valladolid, in Spain, on 28 December 1596, and was a student there until 1599. While there he applied to join the Benedictine order, but was advised to spend time as a missionary first. He was granted permission, if in danger of death, to profess himself a member of that order. He was ordained a priest in 1599 and left for England in July. He stopped *en route* as a novice at Irache. In England he used the alias Lambert. He was arrested and sent to Bridewell. After repeated examinations he was tried at the Old Bailey, charged with being a priest. On being examined by the lord chief justice he did not admit to being a priest, though did not deny it. 'The Recorder, without further ceremony, neither taking the depositions of witnesses, having the confession of the accused, nor waiting for the verdict of the jury, pronounced sentence … as in cases of high treason' (Gillow, *Lit. biog. hist.*, 1.130).

On 27 February 1601 Barkworth was hanged, drawn, and quartered at Tyburn. On the gallows he professed to be 'a monk of the Order of St Benet, as likewise St Augustine had been, who was sent by St. Gregory … to bear the same faith to our island for which he was to die' (Foley, 416–19). Dressed in the habit of a Benedictine monk, he died with Roger Filcock and Ann Line, convicted of harbouring Filcock. Barkworth has been described as 'a man in stature tall and well proportioned, showing strength, the hair of his head brown, his beard yellow, somewhat heavy eyed' (Anstruther, 1.21). He was buried near Tyburn, though his body was later retrieved. There is a portrait of him at St Alban's College, Valladolid. Barkworth was one of the 136 martyrs beatified by the pope in 1929.

Antony Charles Ryan

Sources G. Anstruther, *The seminary priests 1: Elizabethan, 1558–1603* [1966], 21–2 • M. E. Williams, *St Alban's College, Valladolid: four centuries of English Catholic presence in Spain* (1986) • Gillow, *Lit. biog. hist.* • D. A. Bellenger, ed., *English and Welsh priests, 1558–1800* (1984), 36 • T. B. Snow, *Obit book of the English Benedictines from 1600 to 1912*, rev. H. N. Birt (privately printed, Edinburgh, 1913), 252 • J. Stow and E. Howes, *The annales, or, Generall chronicle of England … unto the ende of the present yeere, 1614* (1615), 794 • H. Foley, ed., *Records of the English province of the Society of Jesus*, 1 (1877), 416–19 • C. Dodd [H. Tootell], *The church history of England, from the year 1500, to the year 1688*, 3 vols. (1737–42) • *Calendar of the manuscripts of the most hon. the marquis of Salisbury*, 11, HMC, 9 (1906), 270 • *Report on the manuscripts of the earl of Ancaster*, HMC, 66 (1907), 363–4 • T. F. Knox and others, eds., *The first and second diaries of the English College, Douay* (1878), 282 • *The manuscripts of his grace the duke of Rutland*, 4 vols., HMC, 24 (1888–1905), vol. 1, p. 369

Likenesses oils, 1620?, St Alban's College, Valladolid, Spain

Barlas, John Evelyn [*pseud.* Evelyn Douglas] **(1860–1914)**, poet and anarchist-communist, was born in Rangoon, Burma, on 13 July 1860, the third and only surviving son of John Barlas (1826–1861), a merchant in the East Indies, and his wife, Elizabeth Anne (1835–1878), the daughter of William Davis, a civil servant of the mint in Calcutta. Barlas was a direct descendant of the fifteenth-century Scots heroine Kate Douglas, who was known as Barlass, and also a distant relative of George Gilfillan on his mother's side. Barlas was barely a year old when his father died suddenly of apoplexy, and his mother took him back to Glasgow. By 1874, however, mother and son were living at 8 Belsize Crescent, London. Barlas first briefly attended St John's Wood School and then, in December 1874, entered the Merchant Taylors' School, where he stayed for three years, winning the Sir James Tyler English history prize for 1875. After his mother's death in 1878, Barlas took rooms in Great Russell Street, London, to study by himself. His earnest study of Marxist literature at the same time led to his conversion to socialism. He then went up as a commoner to New College, Oxford, where he matriculated on 16 October 1879.

Barlas was conspicuous at Oxford for his uncompromisingly radical views, for his extremely handsome and athletic personality, and for his histrionic talents. He was self-respecting and independent-minded in thought and action, and, although he characterized himself as 'one of those horrid proud people', in a letter of 1885 to André Raffalovich, he was a humane person and a gentleman. He was thought to be an aristocrat in those days, possessing some £20,000, with which he often assisted friends in need. Robert Harborough Sherard, his contemporary at New College and a lifelong friend, admits that he himself was saved by Barlas from death by starvation on more than one occasion. It was while Barlas was still an undergraduate that, on 25 June 1881, his early and romantic marriage took place, by special licence, to the beautiful Rangoon-born Eveline Honoria Nelson Davies (1861–1934), a great-grandniece of Admiral Lord Nelson and fourth daughter of Horatio Nelson Davies, assistant commissioner at Thayetmyo, Burma. According to an unsubstantiated rumour, Barlas had literally carried away his future wife from a ship at Southampton bound for Burma, to which country she had been summoned by her father. Their first child, Evelyn Adelaide Isabella, was born in May 1882. In the same year he also entered the Middle Temple to become a barrister, but after keeping only four terms abandoned the idea of a legal career.

Having obtained his BA (a second class in *literae humaniores*) in 1884, Barlas went to Ireland, as professor of languages—he was widely read in classical literature and in Hebrew, French, German, and Greek—to St Stanislaus Roman Catholic College at Rahan, Tullamore. Here life was tranquil and he continued to write verse, a passion that had begun in 1876 while on a summer holiday in Yarmouth. However, in June 1885, three-year-old Evelyn died, and he and his wife returned to England, where Barlas obtained the post of assistant classical master at the local grammar school in Chelmsford, Essex, where he was regarded as a brilliant and inspiring teacher. He also made his presence felt in a different way, when he started a socialist society in Chelmsford, and was often seen distributing anarchist literature and preaching the socialist creed in public places, sporting a red ribbon in his buttonhole. He still found time to write poems or sonnets every day. In November their son Ernest Douglas Montague was born in his maternal grandparents' home in Lee, Kent.

Barlas left Chelmsford in December 1886, and apparently went to Crieff—by now his family home. The months he spent in Perthshire were enlivened by his friendship with a fellow Scottish poet, John Davidson, the music critic and composer Frank Leibich, and E. T. Peberdy—all of whom were teachers at the local Morrison's academy. His sixth book, *Bird-Notes* (1887) was dedicated to Peberdy and Davidson in memory of 'Happy days in the Highlands gladdened by the two best things in life—Music and Literature'. It is not known exactly when Barlas arrived in Egham, Surrey, where briefly he coached students in the army examination, but he was to remain at Vine Cottage, in nearby Englefield Green, until mid-1891. It was while he was there that a correspondence began with the poet John Gray, later Canon Gray, which continued until the end of 1892 and which saw the regular exchange of letters and their latest poems in manuscript.

As a socialist and supporter of the working classes, Barlas toured the country after leaving Chelmsford, preaching socialism, and offering help in getting up demonstrations in support of striking workers. Reputedly, Barlas was a good speaker and an able organizer. He was one of the demonstrators at Trafalgar Square on 'bloody Sunday', 13 November 1887, and received a severe blow to the head from a police truncheon and fell unconscious, bleeding profusely, at the feet of fellow-demonstrator Eleanor Marx. The blow caused permanent damage—lifelong bouts of delirium and depression, and it was during one such bout of depression that, on the morning of 31 December 1891, Barlas fired a number of revolver shots near the Speaker's Green, at the House of Commons, announcing himself as an anarchist whose action had been to show his contempt for parliamentary democracy. He was promptly taken into custody by the police and a fortnight later his friends Oscar Wilde and H. H. Champion of the Social Democratic Federation stood surety for him, when Barlas was bound over to keep the peace. However, his mental state deteriorated and by September 1892 he was an inmate of James Murray's Royal Asylum, Perth. In March 1893 he was discharged, cured, but about a year later he was admitted to Gartnavel Royal Asylum near Glasgow, where he died twenty years later. According to a letter written to R. H. Sherard on 18 July 1914, during this period he wrote twenty-three dramas, twenty volumes of lyrics, an unspecified number of novels, and other writings. The present whereabouts of these manuscripts, however, as well as that of an unpublished autobiography, which A. J. A. Symons had seen about 1930, remain a mystery.

Of Barlas's eight known volumes of verses and dramas, seven appeared under the pseudonym Evelyn Douglas, and *Holy of Holies: Confessions of an Anarchist* (1887) was published anonymously. His first two volumes were issued through Trübner & Co., London, but the rest of his works were printed at provincial presses in Chelmsford and Dundee, at his own expense and mostly for private circulation. They were reviewed neither widely nor well. However, in 1895 George Meredith praised Barlas's sonnets for their 'nobility of sentiment' and maintained that they placed him in 'a high rank among the poets of his time'. The first major writer to appreciate Barlas's work in print was the humanitarian and socialist author Henry S. Salt, contributing 'The poetry of John Barlas' to *The Yellow Book* (vol. 11, October 1896, 79–90). It appears that Salt knew Barlas from the early days of the Social Democratic Federation, either personally or through his writings, since he included a selection of Barlas's poems in *Songs of Freedom*, an anthology he edited in 1893. Barlas's correspondence with Salt (some seventy letters) led Salt to declare that Barlas was also a thinker. He also visited Barlas at Gartnavel Asylum and, in 1925, edited a selection of his poems. Remembering Barlas in an autobiographical volume, Salt called him 'the Keats of the Socialist movement' (Salt). Other admirers of Barlas's work include Oscar Wilde; the American writer Hamlin Garland; the poet Ralph Hodgson; and Ramsay MacDonald, the future prime minister.

The most remarkable feature of Barlas's work is the conspicuous absence of his socialist and anarchist beliefs, which he so fervently preached in public life. Love—of natural beauty, of a woman, of liberty and intellectual freedom—and a notion of universal brotherhood are his chief themes. He possessed a fresh lyrical gift, an intense imagination, and original thought, with a masterly flair for painting word pictures. His shorter poems are delicate and simple, written with an effortless ease and admirable skill. His longer and descriptive poems are picturesque and fascinating.

Barlas died on 15 August 1914, of valvular disease of the heart. He was buried four days later in Glasgow necropolis. His widow died in 1934, and his only son, Ernest, died in 1952, after a successful career as a solicitor. His grandson, Richard Douglas, who died in 1982, retired as senior clerk in the House of Commons, having been knighted in recognition of his services to that very parliamentary democracy for which his grandfather had such great contempt. GUTALA KRISHNAMURTI

Sources D. Lowe, *John Barlas: sweet singer and socialist* (1915) · R. H. Sherard, *My friends the French* (1909) · H. S. Salt, *Company I have kept* (1930) · *The Times* (1 Jan 1892) · *Pall Mall Gazette* (7 Jan 1892) · *Pall Mall Gazette* (12 Jan 1892) · *National Reformer* (25 Dec 1892–9 April 1893) · *Wyvern Review* (17 Jan–3 April 1896) · *Yellow Book*, 11 (Oct 1896) · *Humane Review* (Oct 1902) · *Bookman's Journal and Print Collector* (Feb 1922) · A. J. A. Symons, note, U. Cal., Los Angeles, William Andrews Clark Memorial Library · F. Liebich, reminiscences of J. Davidson, U. Cal., Los Angeles, William Andrews Clark Memorial Library · private information (2004) [John Barlas] · missionary records, BL OIOC, N/I, 98, fol. 42; 44, fol. 75

Archives Mitchell L., Glas., poems and corresp. · NRA, corresp. and literary papers | NL Scot., letters to John Gray and André Raffalovich · U. Reading L., letters to R. H. Sherard

Likenesses photograph, repro. in Lowe, *John Barlas*, cover

Wealth at death £860 19*s*. 3*d*.: English probate endorsed in Scotland, 15 Dec 1914, *CCI*

Barley, Maurice Willmore (1909–1991), archaeologist and local historian, was born at 52 Lindum Avenue, Lincoln, on 19 August 1909, the son of Levi Baldwin Barley (1885–1971), a worker in a local engineering firm, and his wife, Alice, *née* Willmore (1886–1968). Both parents were working class. However, his was the sort of Edwardian working-class background in which education played an important part. It included attendance at university extension lectures and tutorial classes of the Workers' Educational Association. Nor were the arts neglected, particularly music. Both his father and his mother were Methodists but there was very little in Barley's early education to leave much of a trace of religious observance. After Lincoln School he went to Reading University, where he studied history and graduated in 1932. While at university he met Diana Morgan (*b.* 1910); they fell in love and were married on 13 April 1934. Diana Morgan was very much of a

Maurice Willmore Barley (1909–1991), by Simon I. Hill

middle-class background. Her father, Arthur Eustace Morgan, was an English scholar, professor of English at Sheffield University and later principal of the University College of Hull. Her mother, May Melhuish, came from another solid middle-class family. For fifty-eight years Maurice and Diana had a happy married life, based on shared values and interests; and with two sons and a daughter they formed a closely knit family.

Barley's first academic appointment was at Hull, where he was active in adult education, teaching extension courses and tutorial classes in the East and North ridings of Yorkshire and in Lincolnshire. Both town and college, as well as the surrounding countryside, were propitious for an early interest in local history, including not only the history of the localities themselves but the lives of ordinary people over the ages and the development of their housing, and the architecture in the rural and smaller urban areas. The war caused an exodus from the college as from many other universities, and in 1940 Barley was recruited into the Ministry of Information southern regional office in Reading, where he stayed until 1946. In the latter year he became a lecturer at Nottingham University, which was to remain his academic anchor for the rest of his life. At Nottingham he was again very much involved in adult education. This gave him the opportunity to extend his interests in local history into another area, Nottinghamshire. He advanced in his academic career until in 1971 he became professor of archaeology and developed the archaeology department at the university. He retired in 1974 but continued to be active in his chosen fields until his death.

Barley produced a substantial body of work which had the distinction of being strictly scholarly and yet accessible to the ordinary reader interested in local history and in archaeology. His work was embodied in a large number of articles, books, and lectures to learned societies. His earliest major work, *Lincolnshire and the Fens* (1952), has remained a classic. He became more and more interested in buildings and human dwellings as one of the most important indications of the history of the locality he was studying. In 1971 he published *The House and Home*, a review of 900 years of home planning and furnishing. In 1980 he gave a lecture which was published as *Houses and History* in 1986. In 1985 he contributed an important article, 'Rural buildings in England', for the *Cambridge Agrarian History of England and Wales*. Although the bulk of his work was concerned with England he also studied local history elsewhere, taking the opportunity of visits to study developments in Spain, Germany, and Italy. His final work, finished just before his death, was a sensitive yet scholarly autobiography and family history called *The Chiefest Grain*, published posthumously by the University of Nottingham in 1993.

Barley, in addition to his academic achievements, had many outside interests and high positions, particularly in the Council for British Archaeology, of which he was secretary from 1954 to 1964 and president from 1964 to 1967. He was vice-president of the Society of Antiquaries from 1965 to 1968, a member of the Royal Commission on Historical Monuments from 1966 to 1976, and chairman of the York Archaeological Trust from 1972 to 1990 (overseeing the creation of the Jorvik Viking Centre). His great merit was to have furthered the study of local history, then in its infancy, including housing and building, an achievement which will for ever remain to his credit. His style was limpid, direct, and without affectation. It reflected very much his character. He died of cancer at his home, 60 Park Road, Chilwell, Nottingham, on 23 June 1991 and was buried on 28 June; he was survived by his wife and three children. The Barley Centre, York (a living history centre, set in restored medieval buildings), was named after him.

Eric Roll

Sources personal knowledge (2004) • private information (2004) [D. Barley] • M. Barley, *The chiefest grain* (1993) • *WWW*, 1991–5 • *The Times* (26 June 1991) • *The Independent* (28 June 1991)

Archives Bodl. Oxf., typescript survey with photography of farmhouses and cottages in Lincolnshire and Nottinghamshire • Notts. Arch., MS maps of open field recontructions drawn up with others • S. Antiquaries, Lond., corresp. and papers relating to British topological collections • U. Nott. L., corresp., papers • U. Reading L., notes relating to Matthew Parker

Likenesses S. I. Hill, photograph, repro. in *The Times* • S. I. Hill, photograph, York Archaeological Trust [*see illus.*]

Barling, Sir (Harry) Gilbert, baronet (1855–1940), surgeon and academic administrator, the fourth son of William Barling (*d.* 1896), farmer and veterinary surgeon, of Newnham-on-Severn, Gloucestershire, and his wife, Eliza Sharpe, was born at Newnham-on-Severn on 30 April 1855. Barling was educated at a boarding-school at Weston, near Bath. The agricultural depression prevented him from succeeding his father as a farmer, and the family lacked the money necessary to fund his medical training. When almost sixteen, Barling was therefore apprenticed to a chemist in Manchester, where he learned little of value and was used by his principal as a drudge and errand-boy. Nevertheless, he qualified as a chemist and passed the matriculation examination of London University.

In 1874 Barling became a student at St Bartholomew's Hospital, London, where lack of funds compelled him to take part-time employment. Finding that this occupied too much of his time, he began to coach younger students. One of his pupils was the son of a Birmingham surgeon, who so much appreciated the kindness shown to his son that he promised to help Barling if the opportunity ever arose. Shortly after graduating MB from London in 1879, Barling made use of this contact and managed to obtain the appointment of resident pathologist at the General Hospital, Birmingham. On 21 October 1885 he married Katharine Jaffray (*d.* 1920), second daughter of Henry Edmunds, bank manager at Edgbaston; they had two daughters.

Elected FRCS in 1881, Barling was appointed assistant surgeon at Birmingham in 1885, and full surgeon in 1891, a position which he occupied until his retirement in 1915, when he was appointed consulting surgeon. While an assistant surgeon, Barling drew up a scheme for rebuilding the hospital which was accepted and used in the construction of the new General Hospital, opened in 1897.

Barling's association with the University of Birmingham was as important as that with the General Hospital. In 1885 he was appointed demonstrator of anatomy at Queen's College, where the medical school was based until its transfer to Mason College, the precursor of the university. He was the first holder of the chair of pathology, to which he was appointed in 1886, and in 1893 he was made professor of surgery. After seven years' tenure of the deanship of the medical faculty, he resigned it in 1912, and the following year was elected vice-chancellor (a title changed to pro-chancellor in 1927); he held this office for twenty years, during which time under his guidance the university research departments in mental diseases and cancer were founded. As a result of his financial skill and ability to influence generous donors, the university, when he retired, was free from debt, and had a greatly increased income, despite the great developments in staffing and in buildings which had taken place during his tenure of office.

Apart from the period between October 1916 and August 1917, when he was consulting surgeon in France, Barling was consulting surgeon to the southern command of the British army during the First World War. For these services he was twice mentioned in dispatches, was appointed CB in 1917 and CBE in 1919, and in the latter year was created a baronet.

Barling took a leading part in the early negotiations for the union of the two voluntary teaching hospitals in Birmingham—Queen's and the General—into one body, the United Hospital, and he was also chairman of the committee which launched the Hospitals Centre Scheme. This scheme planned the building of a hospital teaching centre and a new medical school in close proximity to the main university buildings at Edgbaston. Unfortunately, in 1926, a serious illness forced Barling's retirement from the committee, but he lived to see the first part of the scheme completed and the opening of a large new general hospital, the Queen Elizabeth Hospital, as well as a well-equipped medical school. Although Barling retired from the active staff in 1915 he maintained an interest in the General Hospital and was its president for four years (1924–7).

Barling was a hard worker and talented administrator, teacher, and speaker. His record of hospital, university, and other public service was recognized in 1935 by the presentation of the gold medal of the Birmingham Civic Society; the university conferred upon him the honorary degree of LLD in 1937. Barling died at his home, 6 Manor Road, Edgbaston, Birmingham, on 27 April 1940.

L. G. PARSONS, *rev.* JEFFREY S. REZNICK

Sources *The Times* (29 April 1940) • *BMJ* (4 May 1940), 748 • *The Lancet* (18 May 1940), 947–8 • Burke, *Peerage* • *WWW* • D'A. Power and W. R. Le Fanu, *Lives of the fellows of the Royal College of Surgeons of England, 1930–1951* (1953)

Archives U. Birm., letters | U. Birm., letters to Oliver Lodge

Likenesses E. F. Harper, oils, 1915, General Hospital, Birmingham • G. F. Watt, oils, 1924, U. Birm. • W. Stoneman, photograph, 1931, NPG • portrait, 1940?, repro. in *BMJ*

Wealth at death £51,240 4*s*. 4*d*.: probate, 29 June 1940, *CGPLA Eng. & Wales*

Barling, John (1804–1883), Unitarian minister, was born on 11 August 1804 at Weymouth to John and Edith Barling; he was the eldest of eight children recorded in the registers of the St Nicholas Street Independent Chapel. He was educated for the ministry at Homerton College, London, where the theological tutor was the formidable John Pye Smith, and settled as a Congregationalist minister at the Square Chapel, Halifax, in 1829. On 30 November 1831 he married Elizabeth (1810?–1857), elder daughter of Riley Kitson, wine and spirit merchant in the town, and through her acquired considerable property; one child died early, and four sons survived.

In 1834 Barling resigned his charge, his opinions having become Unitarian, and he joined the congregation at Northgate-End Chapel. After some years' residence in the south of England, he returned to Halifax, lecturing at Northgate-End Chapel in 1849 on the atonement. He occasionally assisted the minister, William (III) Turner, and on Turner's death at the end of 1853 Barling was chosen as his successor. He expressed some concern (in a letter of 28 February 1854) that his earlier orthodox connection might cause hostility, but he assured the congregation that he had made a great sacrifice for the cause of truth and, with God on his side, he would fear nothing. In June 1855, pleading the state of his health, he asked for a co-pastor; Russell Lant Carpenter was appointed, and Barling turned over to Carpenter the whole of his stipend. After his wife's death in September 1857 he did not again enter the pulpit and on 12 January 1858 resigned, noting that his inability to find satisfaction on certain religious questions required that he abstain from ministerial duties. On 16 January 1862 he married Emma, daughter of Abraham Ellis, a stone contractor; she survived him.

Barling had a mind of metaphysical power and a spirit never embittered by controversy, as is suggested by the respect in which he was held by both the congregations which he had served. His principal theological work was *A review of trinitarianism, chiefly as it appears in the writings of Bull, Waterland, Sherlock, Howe, Newman, Coleridge, Wallis, and*

Wardlaw (1847), which was praised by Charles Wicksteed for the acuteness and irresistible logic with which he demonstrated the disagreements on the subject among the principal authorities, who thus cancelled each other out. Wicksteed's favourable judgement is the more remarkable because Barling held firmly to the older school of Unitarianism, which relied on scripture and on natural religion founded on the argument from design, while Wicksteed was a leader of the newer school, which sought religious assurance within the individual soul. Barling told Carpenter towards the end of his life that he feared that Unitarianism was abandoning reason for feeling, whereas true religion must rest on both. He left manuscripts on idealism and scepticism and on final causes.

After his resignation Barling settled at Belle Grange, Windermere, which gave him the opportunity to experiment with the propulsion of vessels. He moved to Leeds, where he died at his home, 94 Belle Vue Road, on 20 August 1883. He was buried with his first wife and their dead child in the general cemetery, Leeds, on 23 August.

R. K. Webb

Sources *The Inquirer* (1 Sept 1883) • R. L. Carpenter, *The Inquirer* (15 Sept 1883) [letter] • Northgate-End Chapel, Halifax, vestry and congregational minutes, 1811–72, W. Yorks. AS, Calderdale, Calderdale District Archives, esp. letters from John Barling, 28 Feb 1854 and 12 Jan 1858 • register, St Nicholas Street Independent Chapel, Weymouth • *An index to the archbishop of York's marriage bonds and allegations* (1986) • 'Mr. Barling on the atonement', *Christian Reformer, or, Unitarian Magazine and Review*, new ser., 5 (1849), 385–97, 513–25 • m. cert. [John Barling and Emma Ellis] • *CGPLA Eng. & Wales* (1883) • d. cert.

Archives W. Yorks. AS, Calderdale, Calderdale District Archives, Northgate-End Chapel vestry and congregational minutes

Wealth at death £4268 10s.: resworn probate, 14 Dec 1883, *CGPLA Eng. & Wales*

Barlow. For this title name *see* Rawlings, Margaret Lilian [Margaret Lilian Barlow, Lady Barlow] (1906–1996).

Barlow, Sir (James) Alan Noel, second baronet (1881–1968), civil servant, was born in London on 25 December 1881, the eldest of the five children of Sir Thomas *Barlow (1845–1945), who was created baronet in 1901, physician to the royal family, and his wife, Ada Helen (1843–1928), daughter of Patrick Dalmahoy, writer to the signet, of Edinburgh. He was educated at Marlborough College and Corpus Christi College, Oxford, of which he was a scholar and later an honorary fellow, and took a first in *literae humaniores* in 1904.

In 1906 Barlow was appointed to a clerkship in the House of Commons but a year later Sir Robert Morant, displaying his characteristic ability to spot men of talent, selected him as a junior examiner in the Board of Education. Here he rose to be private secretary to the parliamentary secretary in 1914, but not before he had married, on 6 April 1911, Emma Nora (*d.* 1989), the daughter of Sir Horace Darwin; they had six children. His wife was the granddaughter of Charles Darwin, whose *Beagle* diaries and autobiography she edited in 1933 and 1958 respectively, and it was she who fostered in Barlow an interest in science. Given his own strong artistic instincts this laid the

Sir (James) Alan Noel Barlow, second baronet (1881–1968), by Walter Stoneman, 1941

basis for success in his later career—a success not unhindered by his own family connections and his wife's relationship through marriage to Sir Edward Bridges, the future cabinet secretary and head of the civil service.

In 1915 Barlow was transferred to the Ministry of Munitions as private secretary to Christopher Addison in his capacity first of parliamentary secretary and then of minister. In 1917 Barlow was promoted to deputy controller of labour supply and a year later to controller of the labour department. He became well versed in the problems of industrial relations, and so after the war it was natural that he should join the newly founded and much overstretched Ministry of Labour, where he was initially responsible for demobilization and training before securing in 1924 a major promotion to principal assistant secretary in charge of the industrial relations department.

After 1929 Barlow's main responsibility reverted to training and it was in this area that he left his principal mark. His decisiveness and executive drive established a core of efficient and well-respected government training centres which could be, and were, rapidly expanded in war. His sensitivity to the antipathy of both the Treasury and the labour movement, however, allied to his own instinct (as a descendant of a family of Manchester cotton spinners) that industry should train its own workforce, meant that government in peacetime did little to remedy the country's chronic lack of skilled manpower.

In 1933 Barlow was selected, at the surprisingly late age of fifty-one, to be principal private secretary to the prime minister, Ramsay MacDonald. The appointment was not a success. The two men were temperamentally unsuited, and his brother, Sir Thomas Dalmahoy *Barlow, as a leading member of the Lancashire chamber of commerce, became embroiled in a major political row over the doctoring (to the government's advantage) of the chamber's evidence to the parliamentary committee on Indian constitutional reform. Barlow was transferred in 1934 to the Treasury, as under-secretary in charge of the supply divisions and thus public expenditure, a responsibility he retained when promoted to third secretary in 1939 and second secretary in 1942. During the war he also assumed responsibility for, and thereby became a member of an interlocking range of committees concerned with, the machinery of government.

At the Treasury Barlow's influence was largely covert, although it has been claimed that he was one of the six most creative reformers to leave a lasting mark on the modern civil service (Chapman and Greenaway, 217). He shared the traditional Treasury distaste for public expenditure. The one major exception was educational expenditure, to which he was generally sympathetic, and he famously chaired the committee whose 1946 report, 'Scientific man-power' (*Parl. papers*, 1945–6, 14, Cmd 6824), called for the doubling of scientific graduates and the establishment of a new technological university—an unfulfilled ambition which caused resignations from the Conservative cabinet in 1953. He must also share the blame for failing permanently to adapt Whitehall to the greater interventionist role of post-war government in economic and social policy, and thus for what has been called '*the* greatest lost opportunity in the history of British public administration' (Hennessy, 120). In the short term, however, his range of contacts—not least in the scientific world—ensured the flexibility of the wartime service, just as his contacts with the artistic world ensured that its interests were not wholly neglected by government in peace.

Barlow's contacts were consolidated and much of his work discharged in a range of London clubs, most notably the Savile and the Athenaeum, where he was well known as 'a man of the world, of the dining and card tables, of conversation and of appropriate silences' (Meynell, 238). This urbanity was somewhat at odds with his initial appearance, for as Austin Strutt noted 'with his heavy and lined face he could, peering through his glasses, appear a forbidding person' (*DNB*). Hugh Dalton even called him 'desiccated and sinister' (Pimlott, 700). To those who knew him, however, he was warm, sympathetic, even-tempered, and humorous, albeit ever ready to offer direct and forceful advice to whomever, and at whatever level, it was required. He was appointed CBE (1918), CB (1928), KBE (1938), KCB (1942), GCB (1947), and succeeded his father as second baronet in 1945.

Barlow retired from the Treasury in 1948. His economic and scientific interests were reflected by his membership of the Iron and Steel Board from 1946 to 1948 and his continuing membership of the Advisory Council on Scientific Policy. His academic contacts were maintained as a member of the court of the University of London between 1949 and 1956. Above all, however, his artistic interests were recognized by his appointment between 1948 and 1955 as a trustee of the National Gallery (where he served as chairman from 1949 to 1951) and as president of the Oriental Ceramic Society. He had himself an exceptional collection of Islamic pottery and Chinese ceramics, which he had started at the age of eighteen and from which he made many donations to the Ashmolean, Fitzwilliam, Victoria and Albert, and British museums as well as to the University of Sussex. Together with his love of old books and modern printing he also became interested in archaeology, particularly in his home county of Buckinghamshire. Here, as well as being a keen gardener, he farmed several hundred acres near Wendover; and it was at his farm, Boswells, that he died on 28 February 1968.

RODNEY LOWE

Sources *DNB* • *The Times* (29 Feb 1968) • J. M. Lee, *Reviewing the machinery of government, 1942–1952* (privately printed, London, 1977) • F. Meynell, *My lives* (1971) • R. A. Chapman and J. R. Greenaway, *The dynamics of administrative reform* (1980) • *The Second World War diary of Hugh Dalton, 1940–1945*, ed. B. Pimlott (1986) • P. Hennessy, *Whitehall* (1989) • M. Gilbert, *Winston S. Churchill*, 5: *1922–1939* (1976) • Burke, *Peerage* (1999) • *CGPLA Eng. & Wales* (1968)

Archives Wellcome L., family corresp. and papers

Likenesses W. Stoneman, photograph, 1941, NPG [*see illus.*]

Wealth at death £146,584: probate, 12 Aug 1968, *CGPLA Eng. & Wales*

Barlow, Sir (Clement) Anderson Montague-, baronet (1868–1951). *See under* Barlow, William Hagger (1833–1908).

Barlow, Edward [St Edward Barlow; *name in religion* Ambrose] (*bap.* **1585**, *d.* **1641**), Benedictine monk, was born at Barlow Hall, Manchester, and baptized on 30 November 1585 at Didsbury, Lancashire. He was the son of Sir Alexander Barlow (1558–1620) and his wife, Mary Brereton, of the ancient family of Barlow Hall, and a younger brother of the Benedictine monk William (Rudesind) *Barlow (1584–1656). He received his education at Douai University and the English colleges at Douai and Valladolid. Afterwards he was professed in the order of St Benedict at St Gregory's, Douai, on 5 January 1616. Sent on the English mission he exercised his priestly ministry in south-east Lancashire for about twenty years. At length he was finally arrested on Easter Sunday, 25 April 1641, at Morleys Hall, Leigh, tried, and condemned as a Catholic priest on 7 September 1641 before Chief Justice Heath. He was executed at Lancaster Castle on 10 September 1641 and was canonized by Pope Paul VI on 25 October 1970.

THOMPSON COOPER, *rev.* G. BRADLEY

Sources J. Stonor, *Blessed Ambrose Barlow* (1961) • B. Camm, 'The skull of Wardley Hall', *Forgotten shrines: an account of some old Catholic halls and families in England* (1910), 202–46 • B. Camm, *Nine martyr monks* (1931) • R. Challoner, *Memoirs of missionary priests*, ed. J. H. Pollen, rev. edn (1924) • T. B. Snow, *Obit book of the English Benedictines from 1600 to 1912*, rev. H. N. Birt (privately printed, Edinburgh, 1913) • Gillow, *Lit. biog. hist.*, 1.134 • J. A. Myerscough, *A procession of Lancashire martyrs and confessors* (1958), 160–72 • J. E. Bamber, 'The skull at Wardley Hall', *Recusant History*, 16 (1982–3), 61–77 • F. O.

Blundell, *Old Catholic Lancashire*, 2 (1938), 16–24 • A. Allanson, *Biography of English Benedictines* (1999)
Likenesses portrait, repro. in Camm, 'The skull of Wardley Hall', 230 • portrait, repro. in Blundell, *Old Catholic Lancashire*, 28

Barlow, Edward. *See* Booth, Edward (1638–1719).

Barlow, Edward (1642–1706?), mariner, was born at Prestwich, Manchester, on 6 March 1642, one of the six children of George Barlow (*c*.1599–*c*.1686), husbandman, and his wife, Ann (*d*. 1692). Disliking his apprenticeship as a 'whitester' (that is, in the bleaching trade), he went to London in 1657 to live with an uncle who had a friend in the Navy Office, a connection that in 1659 procured Barlow a place as apprentice to the chief master's mate of the *Naseby* (100 guns). He was aboard her when she carried Charles II back from Holland at the Restoration, being paid off in March 1661. He remained an apprentice aboard the warships *Augustine* and *Martin Galley* in 1661–2, serving in the Mediterranean, and made his first merchant voyage in 1662–4, visiting Lisbon, Barcelona, and Brazil. He served as a seaman for the whole of the Second Anglo-Dutch War (1664–7) aboard the third-rate *Monck*, fighting in all the major engagements. On his return from a merchant voyage to the Canaries in 1667–8 he was pressed aboard the frigate *Yarmouth* in May 1668, serving aboard her for a year. In 1670–71 he made his first voyage to the East Indies, sailing to Bombay, Surat, and Malabar aboard the *Experiment*. Sailing in the same ship from Gravesend on 27 September 1671 and visiting Bantam and Taiwan, Barlow was captured by the Dutch in the autumn of 1672: his ship knew nothing of the outbreak of war, and found itself outnumbered eight to one. It was during his time as a prisoner of war in Batavia that Barlow taught himself to write and began the journal which constitutes his great claim to fame. Lavishly illustrated with pictures of his ships and the places he visited, the journal provides a lively narrative of Barlow's life, and is justly regarded as probably the most important first-hand account of seafaring in the seventeenth century. Fiercely patriotic and intensely curious about all he saw, Barlow was also an outspoken critic of shipowners, the naval authorities, and indeed all landsmen, who in his view either ignored or abused the common seamen. Barlow possessed more than a hint of puritan self-righteousness, constantly bemoaning the hardships of the seaman's life and the general wickedness of the times he lived in.

Barlow was transported back to Europe as a prisoner in 1674, arriving at Hellevoetsluis in September after an eight-month voyage. He signed on the *Florentine* as gunner for a voyage to Bergen in May 1675, but the ship was wrecked on the Goodwin Sands on 23 August; Barlow, who was always inclined to the superstitious, attributed this in part to Norwegian witches with whom the crew had quarrelled at Bergen. Barlow served in a number of other merchantmen in 1675–82, voyaging to the Mediterranean and Jamaica and eventually becoming chief mate. In one of his rare sojourns ashore he married Mary Symons at Deal on 21 January 1678. He sailed to the East Indies again in November 1682 as chief mate of the *Delight*, and apart from two six-month interludes in England, he remained in the east until 1690. From February to October 1691 he returned to the Royal Navy as a volunteer aboard the *Royal Sovereign*. In March 1692 he sailed again for the east as chief mate of the *Sampson*, returning to England in November 1694, and made further East Indies voyages as chief mate in the *Sceptre* (1695–8), the *Wentworth* (to Macao, 1699–1701), and the *Fleet Frigate* (to Canton, 1702–3). After he returned from the last of these voyages, Barlow took passage in the frigate *Kingfisher* as a passenger from St Helena to England, and his journal ends with his return home in December 1703. It was long assumed that he retired from the sea at that time, but in June 1705 Barlow finally achieved his life's ambition of becoming a captain, gaining the command of the East Indiaman *Liampo* for a voyage to Mocha in the Red Sea. She sailed from Portsmouth on 7 January 1706, but was lost off Mozambique. Barlow's will, made on 18 November 1705, was proved on 9 April 1708. By it, he left his goods to his wife, Mary, although he also mentions two surviving children, Edward and Ann. The journal, fortunately, had not gone with him on the *Liampo*, and was purchased from the earl of Hardwicke by Basil Lubbock, who published it in abridged form in 1934. Lubbock speculated that the journal might have been sold to the Hardwickes by one of Barlow's descendants, but whatever its provenance, its publication immediately assured Barlow's posthumous fame. The manuscript itself was subsequently deposited at the National Maritime Museum. J. D. Davies

Sources *Barlow's journal*, ed. B. Lubbock, 2 vols. (1934) • will, PRO, PROB 11/500, fols. 284v–285 • W. Salisbury, 'Captain Edward Barlow, of *Barlow's journal*', *Mariner's Mirror*, 52 (1966), 313–14 • A. G. Course, *A seventeenth century mariner* (1965) • East India Company court minutes, BL, B43, B44 • A. Farringdon, *A catalogue of East India Company ships' journals and logs, 1600–1834* (1999), 382 • A. Farringdon, *A biographical index of East India Company maritime service officers, 1600–1834* (1999), 44
Archives NMM, journal | BL, East India Company court minutes, B43, B44
Likenesses self-portrait, drawing, repro. in Lubbock, ed., *Barlow's journal*, vol. 1
Wealth at death bequests of silver goods, incl. tankard, two cups, a salver, a supper dish, six spoons, a pottinger, four small teaspoons, and a small dram cup: will, PRO, PROB 11/500, fols. 284v–285

Barlow, Elizabeth (*d*. 1518). *See under* Barlow, William (*d*. 1568).

Barlow, Francis (*d*. 1704), painter and etcher, was said by George Vertue to have come from Lincolnshire and to have been apprenticed in London to the portrait painter William Shepherd. His earliest dated work is a drawing of 1648 depicting David slaying the lion (British Museum). He was made free of the Painter–Stainers' Company on 4 March 1650.

In 1653 Richard Symons recorded a conversation with Barlow about the colours used in portraits, landscapes, and natural history paintings; at the time he was living near The Drum in Drury Lane and charging £8 for a painting of fish. On 19 February 1656 John Evelyn recorded in his diary that he had visited Barlow, and referred to him as 'the famous Paynter of fowle Beastes & Birds' (Evelyn, 3.166–7). Surviving paintings of natural history subjects include six large oils at Clandon Park, Surrey (originally painted for Denzil Onslow at Pyrford Manor, Surrey), and a pair of overdoors of 1673 at Ham House, Surrey, painted for the duke of Lauderdale. Portraits in oil of General Monck (which Barlow also etched) and an unknown boy with a groom are in the Tyrwhitt-Drake collection.

In the 1650s and early 1660s, and between 1685 and 1694, Barlow designed sets of natural history plates, which were etched by Wenceslaus Hollar, Richard Gaywood, Jan Griffier, and Francis Place. These prints continued to be published well into the following century and were an important source for artists and craftsmen of succeeding generations. Barlow's finest etchings are the plates for Edward Benlowes's *Theophila* (1652) and for an edition of *Aesop's Fables* which he published himself in 1666 (a second edition with additional plates, bringing the total to 143, appeared in 1687). There are preliminary drawings in the British Museum. Barlow's address was given on the original title-page of *Aesop's Fables*, dated 1665, as 'the Golden Eagle in New-Street, near Shoo-lane'; the house was burnt in the great fire but the copper plates for the volume survived.

Barlow's propaganda prints supporting the whig cause during the Popish Plot of 1679 and afterwards were among the earliest satirical prints published in England. They included a very popular series of playing cards illustrating events from the time of the Rump Parliament (1648–53) to the alleged Warming Pan Plot of 1688; preliminary drawings are held in the British Museum. According to Vertue, Barlow was left a considerable sum by a friend but died poor in 1704. He was buried at St Margaret's, Westminster, on 11 August 1704. SHEILA O'CONNELL

Sources E. Hodnett, *Francis Barlow: first master of English book illustration* (1978) • P. Hofer, 'Francis Barlow's Aesop', *Harvard Library Bulletin*, 2 (1948), 279–95 • A. Griffiths and R. A. Gerard, *The print in Stuart Britain, 1603–1689* (1998), 140–42, 167–9, 248 [exhibition catalogue, BM, 8 May – 20 Sept 1998] • E. Croft-Murray and P. H. Hulton, eds., *Catalogue of British drawings*, 2 vols. (1960) • Vertue, *Note books*, 2.135–6 • R. Symons, notebooks, BL, Egerton MS 1636 • Evelyn, *Diary*

Wealth at death died poor: Vertue, *Note books*

Barlow, Sir George Hilaro, first baronet (1763–1846), acting governor-general of Bengal, was born on 20 January 1763, the third of four sons of William Barlow (*d.* 1798), mercer of King Street, Covent Garden, and of Hilaire, *née* Butcher (*d.* 1774). His brother was Sir Robert *Barlow, and he had two sisters. Barlow was made a writer in the Bengal service of the East India Company in 1778. His first important appointment was as assistant to Thomas Law, collector of Gaya, in Bihar. Law was a man of wide-ranging intellect who experimented with new systems of revenue management and tried to introduce new manufactures. Barlow fully shared in these interests. His work came to the notice of the governor-general, Lord Cornwallis, who described him as 'master of the languages of the country and equally conversant in the revenue and commercial business; he has an active benevolence, an earnestness to relieve the distressed and to promote the happiness of mankind rarely to be met with' (*Brief Sketch of the Services of Sir G. H. Barlow*, 12).

Sir George Hilaro Barlow, first baronet (1763–1846), by unknown artist, *c.*1840

Barlow was commissioned in 1787 to inquire into trade from Bengal westward to Oudh and Benares. His reports were both highly informative and strongly influenced by a commitment to free trade. They won further golden opinions from Cornwallis, who in 1788 made him sub-secretary to the supreme council with responsibility for revenue matters and later for judicial administration as well. He remained in the secretariat, becoming the chief secretary in 1796, until he was promoted to the supreme council in 1801. During that period he was very closely concerned with the devising and implementing of the permanent settlement of the Bengal revenue enacted by Cornwallis in 1793. He was given responsibility for drafting the judicial regulations, known as the Cornwallis code. Barlow's correspondence with Cornwallis shows his total commitment to the principles embodied in the permanent settlement: security of property and government accountable to law. Cornwallis was generous enough to say that his 'system' had been based on 'adopting and patronizing your suggestions' (*Observations on Lt. Col. Malcolm's Publication*, 142).

As councillor, Barlow became the colleague of a

governor-general of a very different disposition, the Marquess Wellesley, whose opinion of him was as high as Cornwallis's had been: 'His judgement, discretion, temper, morals, and integrity, are universally acknowledged ... I never met with a man of more worth in any part of the world' (Ingram, 73). Barlow identified himself as enthusiastically with Wellesley's expansionist policy towards Indian states as he had done with Cornwallis's ostensibly pacific administration. In 1803 the government rewarded his services with a baronetcy.

Cornwallis returned to India to replace Wellesley in 1805 and to reverse his policies. He died shortly after his arrival and the task of making peace and retrenching expenditure passed to Barlow as acting governor-general from October 1805 to July 1807. Peace and economy were not to the liking of many in India. Barlow's treaties with the Maratha leaders Holkar and Sindhia were condemned by those who had been fighting the war as betrayals of the company's allies. There is much evidence that, policies apart, Barlow was not a popular figure as acting governor-general. He was commonly regarded as remote and aloof. His successor, Lord Minto, noted his 'constitutional coldness and apathy of temper' (*Minto in India*, 24–5). Whether he was confirmed as governor-general did not, however, depend on any assessment of his qualities, but on the insistence of the government on its right to make its own choice of a British political figure. Minto replaced Barlow in 1807, bringing with him the insignia of the Bath, as 'an honourable mark' of the King's 'approbation' of Barlow.

Shortly after his supersession, Barlow was given the governorship of Madras, which he filled from 1807 to 1813. His major concern there was again revenue administration. In the Madras presidency the Bengal model of the permanent settlement had been challenged by an alternative system of settlements with individual cultivators, known as ryotwar. In 1808 the Madras government decided that settlements with villages should replace ryotwar. This decision had only been partially implemented when orders from Britain authorized a return to ryotwar.

Barlow's administrative work at Madras was overshadowed by controversies set off by what amounted to mutiny by most of the European officers in the East India Company's Madras army in 1809. The officers objected to economies in allowances enforced on them and to what they took to be the civilian government's disregard for their rights and status. Barlow took strong action to quell disaffection, suspending individuals, insisting on pledges of obedience, and threatening the officers with the use of the royal regiments and even of their own Indian soldiers. Fighting broke out at one of the garrisons and lives were lost. The intense dislike which Barlow's personality evoked and some tactical errors on his part may have made the crisis more acute, but the governor seems to have coped with resolution with an officer corps that would only accept authority on its own terms.

Barlow was initially commended in Britain, but attacks on him in the court of directors of the company and in the House of Commons led to his recall in 1812. He had become too closely associated with the powerful chairman of the company, Charles Grant, whose opponents struck at him through Barlow, while some opposition MPs seem to have regarded the Madras officers as victims of oppression. Barlow was made GCB in 1815 as some compensation. He was clearly a man of great intellectual capacity and administrative ability, but he was thought to lack the social status appropriate for the highest offices and his personal qualities did not endear him to those who served under him, much as he was admired by those who worked closely with him.

Barlow lived out the rest of his life in a long and reasonably affluent retirement. He appears to have remitted to Britain accumulated savings in India of nearly £100,000. He had married Elizabeth, daughter of Burton Smith, in Calcutta on 16 April 1789 and had fifteen children. In 1815 he discovered that one of them had in fact been fathered by George Pratt Barlow, a young kinsman whom he had admitted to his household in India in 1803. The marriage was dissolved by act of parliament in 1816. From 1829 he lived with his daughters in a rented house at Farnham in Surrey. He died, aged eighty-three, on 18 December 1846, 'coming down stairs to breakfast' (Charles Barlow to Robert Barlow, 18 Dec 1846, MS Eur. F. 176/41). By then little of his fortune was left to be inherited by his son Robert Barlow (1797–1857) as the second baronet.

P. J. MARSHALL

Sources *A brief sketch of the services of Sir G. H. Barlow bart. and K.B., governor of Madras* (1811) • *Observations on Lt. Col. Malcolm's publication ... relative to the disturbances in the Madras army* (1812) • A. Cardew, *The white mutiny: a forgotten episode in the history of the Indian army* (1929) • A. T. Embree, *Charles Grant and the British rule in India* (1962) • *Correspondence of Charles, first Marquis Cornwallis*, ed. C. Ross, 3 vols. (1859) • *The despatches, minutes and correspondence of the Marquess Wellesley ... during his administration in India*, ed. M. Martin, 5 vols. (1836–40) • 'Select committee on the affairs of the East India Company: fifth report', *Parl. papers* (1812), vol. 7, no. 377 • C. H. Philips, *The East India Company, 1784–1834* (1940); repr. with minor corrections (1961) • *Lord Minto in India: life and letters of Gilbert Elliot, first earl of Minto, from 1807 to 1814*, ed. E. E. E. Elliot-Murray-Kynynmound (1880) • *Memoirs of William Hickey*, ed. A. Spencer, 4 (1925), 322–3 • N. Mukherjee, *The ryotwari system in Madras, 1792–1827* (1962) • E. Ingram, ed., *Two views of British India* (1970), 72–3 • BL OIOC, MSS Eur. F 176/30, 176/40, 176/41

Archives BL, corresp. and papers relating to India, Add. MSS 13578, 13719–13722, 13813 • BL OIOC, Home misc. series, corresp. and papers relating to India • BL OIOC, personal and family papers, MS Eur. F 176 • Cleveland Public Library, letters | BL, corresp. with Lord Wellesley, Add. MSS 13710, 13712, 13719–13722, 13758, 37281, 37284, 37311, *passim* • Duke U., Perkins L., corresp. and papers • NL Scot., corresp. with first earl of Minto • NL Scot., Elliot-Murray-Kynynmound MSS • PRO, Cornwallis MSS

Likenesses B. Thorvaldsen, bust, 1828, Thorvaldsen Museum, Copenhagen • oils, *c*.1840, NPG [*see illus.*] • G. Watson, oils, Government House, Madras

Wealth at death £6400 in consols; £3600 in plate and other items: letters of Frances Barlow, 20 Jan 1847, and Charles Barlow, 29 Jan 1847, BL OIOC, MS Eur. F 176/41

Barlow, Hannah Bolton (1851–1916), ceramicist, was born on 2 November 1851 at Church End House, Little Hadham, Hertfordshire, the seventh of nine children of Benjamin Irlam Barlow (1813–1866), bank manager, and his Quaker wife, Hannah Bolton (1816–1882). As she grew up in rural Hertfordshire and Essex, Hannah Barlow acquired a love of nature, particularly animals, which inspired her art. After attending Lambeth School of Art and Design in London in 1868, she was briefly employed at Minton's art pottery studio in Kensington Gore. In 1871 she joined the Doulton art pottery in Lambeth founded by the industrialist Sir Henry Doulton. Hannah's work in the sgraffito technique, incised drawing, either directly on to the clay body or through applied slip (liquid clay), was instrumental in the success of Doulton ware, relief-decorated saltglazed stoneware pottery. Her etched designs featured, more usually in a reserved frieze or panel, on vases, jugs, and bowls. Collaborators sometimes included her siblings also employed by Doulton: Arthur (1845–1879), whose early death cut short a promising future, and her younger sisters, Florence, who specialized in *pâte-sur-pâte* painting of birds, and Lucy, a relief border decorator. While her sketchbooks (now in the Sir Henry Doulton Gallery, Stoke-on-Trent) include humorous anthropomorphic compositions, Hannah's ceramic subjects are naturalistic and unsentimental, mainly of domestic livestock and pets and occasionally wild animals. Human figures feature rarely. John Sparkes, the Lambeth School of Art's principal, wrote:

> She possesses a certain Japanese facility of representing the largest amount of fact in the fewest lines, all correct, and all embodying in a high degree the essential character of her subject. (Sparkes)

Sometimes she painted on other Doulton ceramic wares: Faience, Crown Lambeth, and Carrara, and in *pâte-sur-pâte*. Occasionally she decorated plaques and tiles and more rarely modelled in high relief.

A prolific artist, whose style changed little during her long employment, Hannah Barlow produced an estimated 1000 unique pieces annually until her retirement as head of studio in 1913. From 1871–2 her work was shown at major national and international exhibitions, winning many awards. Her watercolour paintings were included in 'Studio Notes', the Doulton art pottery's manuscript in-house magazine, during the 1880s, when the Royal Academy also exhibited a number of her high-relief terracotta animal sculptures. Hannah was famed for her unusual menagerie which included a tame fox, Simon, and a 'black mountain sheep answering to the euphonious name of Lady Gwen Morris' ('Lady artists: Miss Hannah Bolton Barlow', 215). A terracotta panel of Sir Henry Doulton and his artists, modelled *c.*1876 by George Tinworth (1843–1913) above the old Doulton art pottery on Lambeth High Street, includes Hannah and her pet cat.

Employment by Doulton & Co. offered career possibilities for 'respectable' middle-class women in Victorian times. As a successful artist and designer, signing her own work, Hannah Barlow represents one of the earliest female contributors to the British pottery industry. Her ceramic designs for Doulton exemplify the radical arts and crafts movement's advocacy of a return to individual craftsmanship in manufacture. Ruskin, on visiting the Lambeth pottery, selected a jug by Hannah 'with all the little piggies scurrying around under the handle' (Gosse, 85). Examples of her work are held in museum ceramic collections worldwide including the Sir Henry Doulton Gallery, Stoke-on-Trent; the Victoria and Albert Museum, London; Powerhouse Museum, Sydney, Australia; National Museum of Tokyo, Japan; and the Smithsonian Institution, Washington.

Hannah Barlow died, unmarried, on 15 November 1916 at 46 Binfield Road, Clapham, London, and was buried in Norwood cemetery in south London on 20 November.

JULIE MCKEOWN

Sources P. Rose, *Hannah Barlow: a Doulton artist* (1985) [exhibition catalogue, Christies, 6–10 Aug 1985] · D. Eyles, *The Doulton Lambeth wares* (1975) · H. Barlow, *Memoir of Arthur Bolton Barlow by his mother* (1879) · E. Gosse, *Sir Henry Doulton: the man of business as a man of imagination*, ed. D. Eyles (1970) · C. Buckley, 'A private space in a public sphere', *Potters and paintresses: women designers in the pottery industry, 1870–1955* (1990), 50–69 · 'Lady artists: Miss Hannah Bolton Barlow', *The Lady* (24 March 1887), 215–16 · *The Times* (18 Nov 1916) · *The Times* (23 Nov 1916) · J. Sparkes, 'On some recent inventions and applications of Lambeth stoneware, terracotta, and other pottery for internal and external decorations', *Journal of the Society of Arts*, 22 (1873–4), 557–68 · G. W. Rhead and F. A. Rhead, *Staffordshire pots and pottery* (1906), 351, 355–6 · *The Harriman Judd collection British art pottery*, pt 1 (2001) [sale catalogue, Sothebys, New York, 22 Jan 2001] · Minet Library, Lambeth, cemetery records · b. cert. · d. cert.

Archives Lambeth Archives, London, assorted MSS, records · Royal Doulton, Burslem, Stoke-on-Trent, Sir Henry Doulton Gallery, pottery collection, sketchbooks, and associated records

Likenesses G. Tinworth, portrait, high relief terracotta panel, *c.*1876, old Doulton art pottery headquarters, Lambeth High Street, London · photograph, *c.*1880, Minet Library, Knatchbull Road, Lambeth, London; repro. in commemorative volumes presented to Henry Doulton by lady artists · photograph, *c.*1887, Royal Doulton, Burslem, Stoke-on-Trent, Sir Henry Doulton Gallery · photograph, *c.*1913, Royal Doulton, Burslem, Stoke-on-Trent, Sir Henry Doulton Gallery · J. Piltone?, engraving, repro. in 'Lady artists: Miss Hannah Bolton Barlow', p. 215 · double portrait, engraving (with sister Florence, in their studio), repro. in 'The worktable, women's industries, pottery work and china painting', *The Queen: The Lady's Newspaper* (1 Oct 1887)

Wealth at death £8463 10s. 7d.: probate, 23 Dec 1916, *CGPLA Eng. & Wales*

Barlow, Harold Everard Monteagle (1899–1989), university professor, was born on 15 November 1899 at 45 Balfour Road, Islington, London, the second child in the family of four sons and two daughters of Leonard Barlow, professional electrical engineer, and his wife, Katharine Monteagle, of Glasgow. After attending Wallington grammar school, Surrey, he entered the Finsbury Technical College, London, at the age of fifteen, and in June 1917 obtained the college certificate in electrical engineering. He then wanted to follow his elder brother Leonard into the Royal Flying Corps, but he was persuaded to make better use of his training in experimental work with the signal school at Portsmouth, as a sub-lieutenant in the Royal Naval Volunteer Reserve (1917–19). After the war he studied electrical engineering at University College, London (UCL), graduating with first-class honours in 1920. Research under Professor Sir Ambrose Fleming led to a PhD three years later. He then joined his father's electrical engineering consulting firm but was not altogether happy with the work. When Fleming offered him an assistant lectureship,

Harold Everard Monteagle Barlow (1899–1989), by Elliott & Fry, 1950

he gladly returned to UCL in 1925. He soon became an excellent all-round academic, producing a substantial research output, seeming equally at home in power and communications. His research included a fundamental experimental study of Ohm's law at high-current densities. He also invented a valve ammeter and a protective system for fluorescent tubes. In 1931 he married Janet Hastings, daughter of the Revd Hastings Eastwood, minister at Christ Church (Presbyterian), Wallington, Surrey; the marriage was a very happy one. They had three sons and a daughter.

With war again threatening, the Air Ministry was selecting suitable academics to be told the secrets of radar. Barlow, by now a reader, was a natural choice, and when war broke out in 1939 he was deeply involved. He eventually became superintendent of the radio department at the Royal Aircraft Establishment (1943–5), with a staff of about 800. During this time he realized that microwave techniques, essential to radar, could also be important in civil applications.

On his return to UCL after the war as professor of electrical engineering (1945–50) and Pender professor (1950–67), Barlow built up a strong research school in microwaves, and an undergraduate course with a firm foundation of electromagnetic theory. His principal research interest now was in the use of millimetre-wave waveguides for telecommunications, and he was influential in persuading the Post Office to initiate a major programme of research and development in this area, to which UCL made considerable contributions. He was a strong advocate of the use of guided waves wherever possible, so releasing frequency bands for mobile services, for which free-wave communication was imperative. He was also very active in surface-wave research, and in the application of electromagnetic forces and the Hall effect to the measurement of microwave power.

Barlow was a regular and always welcome participant in scientific conferences, especially those of the International Union of Radio Science, from which in 1969 he received the Dellinger gold medal. His other honours included election as a fellow of the Royal Society (1961), honorary doctorates of the universities of Heriot-Watt (1971) and Sheffield (1973), foreign membership of the Polish Academy of Sciences (1966), foreign associateship of the US National Academy of Engineering (1979), the Microwave Career award of the (American) Institute of Electrical and Electronics Engineers (1985), and a royal medal of the Royal Society (1988).

Barlow retired from the UCL Pender chair in 1967 but remained in the department as an honorary research fellow. Optical fibres were then emerging as an alternative to waveguides for telecommunications. It was characteristic of Barlow that, once convinced of the superiority of optical fibres, he switched his own research in that direction. He had a delightful personality, with a characteristic and infectious laugh, frequently heard in the laboratory. He was interested in everything that was going on in the department and retained this interest to the end of his life. In his last few years illness prevented him from going up to London to his beloved University College, but it did not stop him working on optical fibres.

Barlow was of average height and build, with clear blue eyes, a healthy complexion, and a ready smile. He had a forward-looking attitude, an enthusiasm for research, and a zest for life. His own modest comment on his career was: 'Finally, I regard such success as I have been able to achieve as largely dependent upon my good fortune in having a happy home and a healthy life.' He died at his home, Penrith, 13 Hookfield, Epsom, Surrey, on 20 April 1989 after a long and painful period of suffering, first with arthritis, and later also cancer. ALEX CULLEN, *rev.*

Sources A. L. Cullen, *Memoirs FRS*, 36 (1990), 17–42 • personal knowledge (1996) • *CGPLA Eng. & Wales* (1989)
Archives CAC Cam., papers on development of radar and microwaves
Likenesses Elliott & Fry, photograph, 1950, NPG [*see illus.*]
Wealth at death £283,069: probate, 28 July 1989, *CGPLA Eng. & Wales*

Barlow, Henry Clark (1806–1876), literary scholar, was born in Churchyard Row, Newington Butts, Surrey, on 12 May 1806, the only child of Henry Barlow (1783–1858), revenue officer, and Sophia, *née* Clark (*d.* 1864), youngest daughter of Thomas Clark, solicitor. Barlow was educated at Gravesend and Hall Place, Bexley, before being articled in 1822 to George Smith, an architect and surveyor, of Mercers' Hall, and soon became a student of the Royal Academy. In 1827, however, in consequence of an accidental wound in the nerve of the right thumb, he relinquished the profession, and devoted two years to 'private study, to supply the deficiencies of a neglected education' (*Brief Memoir*, 10). In 1829 he was in Paris attending the public lectures in the Jardin des Plantes and at the Collège de France. After a preliminary course of classical study at Dollar Academy, he matriculated at Edinburgh as a medical student in November 1831 and took the degree of MD on 3 August 1837. He returned to Paris, where he devoted himself not only to medical and scientific studies, but also to artistic criticism.

In 1840 and 1841 Barlow travelled around the continent before settling for nearly five years in Italy. It was at Pisa, during the winter of 1844–5, that Barlow became acquainted with Dante's writing and found a focus for his considerable energies. In 1846, after revisiting England, he returned to Florence. In October 1847 he made 'a pilgrimage to Ravenna, the Mecca of all Dantophilists'. In 1848 he extended his travels to Athens and Constantinople, returning by way of the Danube through Hungary and Austria. In 1849 he resided for some time in Berlin, Dresden, and Prague. In 1850, from Newington Butts, he published a slight paper on Dante entitled *La divina commedia: Remarks on the Reading of the 59th Verse of the 5th Canto of the 'Inferno'*. While he was a poet and a prolific critic and essayist on numerous topics, Barlow's whole life seems to have been devoted to the study of Dante. In 1852 he studied the 'Codici' of Dante in the various libraries in Paris and afterwards collated over 150 other manuscripts in Italy, Germany, Denmark, and England. *Letteratura Dantesca: Remarks on the Reading of the 114th Verse of the 7th Canto of the Paradise of the 'Divina commedia'* was published in 1857. Two years later *Francesca da Rimini, her Lament and Vindication; with a Brief Notice of the Malatesti* (1859), which anticipated the late-nineteenth century cult of Francesca as a wronged heroine, appeared. In 1862 Barlow published *Il gran rifiuto, what it was, who made it, and how fatal to Dante Allighieri, a Dissertation on Verses 58 to 63 of the 3rd Canto of the 'Inferno', Il Conte Ugolino e l'Arcivescovo Ruggieri: a Sketch from the Pisan Chronicles*, and a fragment of English history entitled *The Young King and Bertrand de Born*. In 1864 Barlow published the final result of his laborious work on the *Divina commedia, Critical, Historical, and Philosophical Contributions to the Study of the 'Divina commedia'*. Barlow took a prominent part in the celebration of the sixth centenary of Dante's birth at Florence in 1865 and described the festival in his *Sixth Centenary Festivals of Dante Allighieri in Florence and at Ravenna* (1866). The king of Italy bestowed on Barlow the title of *cavaliere* of the order of SS Maurizio e Lazzaro.

Barlow was also a fellow or member of many learned societies in England, Italy, and Germany and contributed some fifty articles to *The Athenaeum* on 'subjects in reference to Dante and Italy'. He was a constant correspondent of the *Morning Post*. After the Dante commemoration he spent his time both in studious seclusion and studious travel at home and abroad. He died, unmarried, while on a foreign tour, at Salzburg on Wednesday 8 November 1876. He left an endowment to the Geological Society for the furtherance of geological science.

Perhaps Barlow's greatest contribution to Dante studies was his endowment of a lecture series at University College, London. Lecturers in the late nineteenth and early twentieth centuries included the eminent Dantists Edward Moore and E. G. Gardner, and, after the Second World War, Kenelm Foster, Maria Corti, and Robert Hollander. ARTHUR H. GRANT, *rev.* ALISON MILBANK

Sources H. C. Barlow, *Henry Barlow: a memoir in memoriam* (1859) • *The Athenaeum* (11 Nov 1876) • *The Athenaeum* (18 Nov 1876) • *The Academy* (2 Dec 1876) • *Athenaeum Index*, website • M. Caesar, *Dante: the critical heritage* (1989) • *A brief memoir of Henry Clark Barlow* (1868) • *BL cat.* • *National union catalog*, Library of Congress

Archives UCL, corresp., diaries, notebooks, and MSS | BM, letters to F. Madden

Likenesses C. C. Vogel, drawing, Staatliche Kunstsammlungen, Dresden

Wealth at death under £7000: resworn probate, April 1878, *CGPLA Eng. & Wales* (1877)

Barlow, James (1767–1839), obstetric surgeon, was born at Croichley Fold Farm, Hawkshaw, Lancashire, the son of William Barlow (*d.* 1815) and his wife, Catherine Taylor (*d.* 1768); they also had a daughter, Catherine, and an elder son, John. He was a descendant of the Barlows and the Taylors of Turton, though he claimed to be the descendant of Sir Alexander Barlow. The *Palatine Note-Book* for 1884 mentions that Barlow discovered and acquired a portrait of Sir Alexander painted in 1616. After training at Manchester he may have attended St Bartholomew's Hospital since he later dedicated his major publication to three well-known teachers at the hospital. About 1790 Barlow, a Roman Catholic, began to practise in Chorley, Lancashire. In 1793 he was called to see Jane Foster in Blackrod, where he performed a caesarean section on Wednesday, 27 November 1793. This was the first such operation in Britain where the mother survived. In this particular case the patient lived a long life, dying at the age of seventy-six in October 1829. During this operation Barlow's assistant, a local general practitioner, fainted and Barlow had to rely on a female attendant to assist in the procedure. Barlow went on to perform a further three such operations in his career. Barlow's triumph was referred to during a debate in 1798 between two well-known Manchester doctors, John Hull and William Simmons. Hull, although a champion of the caesarean section, attempted to minimize the importance of Barlow's achievement, claiming that Barlow only removed the foetus from the peritoneum. Hull's remarks may have been motivated by the fact that Barlow's estranged wife, Elizabeth Winstanley, was Hull's sister-in-law.

After the breakdown of his marriage (which lasted only a matter of months), Barlow established himself in practice at Blackburn in 1795. He never married again but in 1812 adopted a son, James Barlow Stewardson Sturdy, who later became the mayor of Blackburn. Barlow inherited £12,000 cash and significant valuable property on the death of his father in 1815. He also built up a lucrative practice.

Barlow was the first to suture the uterus after caesarean section. He strongly advocated the use of callipers for pelvimetry, and described various degrees of pelvic deformity and gave indications of the mode of delivery in each case; he designed and described the sound, a polished solid steel instrument. Barlow published *Essays on Surgery and Midwifery: with Practical Observation and Select Cases* in 1822, and *An Address to Medical and Surgical Pupils on the Studies and Duties of their Profession* in 1839. Barlow died at his home, Spring House, Blackburn, on 20 August 1839 and was buried in Blackburn parish church; no tombstone exists. Some manuscript material of Barlow's exists at Blackburn Library and two of his portraits and a miniature at Blackburn Art Gallery. Copies of the portraits are also held at the Royal College of Obstetricians and Gynaecologists, London. NASIM H. NAQVI

Sources G. C. Miller, 'Blackburn worthies', *Blackburn Times* (1959) • N. H. Naqvi, 'James Barlow, 1767–1839: operator of the first successful caesarean section in England', *British Journal of Obstetrics and Gynaecology*, 92 (1985), 468–72 • J. A. McQuay, 'A Blackburn surgeon: James Barlow', *The Practitioner*, 195 (1965), 103–8 • J. Hull, *A defence of the Caesarean operation with observations on embryulcia and the section of the symphysis pubis* [1798] • *Palatine Note-Book*, 4 (1884) • private information (2004)
Archives Blackburn Central Library
Likenesses miniature, Blackburn Art Gallery • portraits, Blackburn Art Gallery; copies, Royal College of Obstetricians and Gynaecologists, London
Wealth at death £9000: will, Lancs. RO

Barlow, Jane (1857–1917), poet and writer, was born on 17 April 1857 at Clontarf, Dublin, the eldest daughter of the Revd James William Barlow (*d*. 1913), later vice-provost of Trinity College, Dublin, and his wife, Mary Louisa (*d*. 1893/4). Barlow was educated at home and was said to have been 'frail in body and slight in build' (*Irish Book Lover*, 141).

Using the pseudonyms Antares Skorpios and Felix Ryark, Barlow was a frequent contributor to the *Dublin University Review* from 1866. Her first poem was published in the *Dublin University Magazine* in 1886. However, it was through her stories that she gained popularity. *Bogland Studies* appeared in 1892 and contained narrative poems making abundant use of the supposed dialect of the peasantry, including words such as 'begorrah', 'musha', and 'bedad'. *Irish Idylls* was also published in 1892. Set in the fictional Connemara village of Lisconnel, the tales deal with the peasantry in a sentimental way. Lady Augusta Gregory was attracted by Barlow's account of peasant life and declared that *Irish Idylls* was 'one of my sermon books' (*Diaries*, xx).

Barlow lived quietly in Raheny, near Dublin, for most of her adult life. She never married. In February 1893 Douglas Hyde described her as 'the great "incognita"' (Daly, 160). Hill walking was her main pastime. A friend of a number of Irish literary figures of the period, Barlow knew William Butler Yeats and Katherine Tynan, who first met her in 1893 at an afternoon party hosted by the artist Sarah Purser. Tynan noted Barlow's shyness and observed that she found it difficult to speak to anyone (Tynan, *Middle Years*, 74). Tynan and Barlow became good friends and corresponded for over twenty years. Purser, who maintained a weekly correspondence with Barlow for some time, painted a portrait of her in 1894. She also illustrated a number of Barlow's stories and painted portraits of her mother and father.

Barlow's novels were usually critical of the Irish landowning class. *Kerrigan's Quality* (1894) describes the effect of the famine and evictions from the viewpoint of a returned Irish-Australian emigrant. In 1895 William Butler Yeats chose *Irish Idylls* as one of his 'Best Irish Books', praising Barlow's mastery of the 'circumstances of peasant life' but regretting that she seemed 'to shrink from its roughness and its tumult' (*W. B. Yeats: Uncollected Prose*, 370). *Strangers at Lisconnel*, a second series of stories, was published in 1895. Further collections followed: *Maureen's Fairing* (1895), *Mrs Martin's Company* (1896), and *A Creel of Irish Stories* (1897). Barlow's work was much admired in America, where her books went into many editions. In her novel *Flaws* (1911) she gives a satirical view of middle- and upper-class Anglicized protestants in the south of Ireland, depicting them as full of petty jealousies and snobbishness.

Although Barlow subscribed to the foundation of the Abbey Theatre, her one play, *A Bunch of Lavender* (1911), which was produced there, was a notable failure. She continued to write and publish until ten days before her death. Her last sketch, 'Rescues', appeared in the *Saturday Review* in April 1917. Jane Barlow died on 17 April 1917 at St Valerie, Bray, co. Wicklow. Her last novel, *In Mio's Country*, was published posthumously in 1917. MARIA LUDDY

Sources A. U. Colman, *A dictionary of nineteenth-century Irish women poets* (1996) • *Irish Book Lover*, 8 (1916–17), 141–2 • J. O'Grady, *The life and work of Sarah Purser* (1996) • *Irish Times* (18 April 1917) • D. Daly, *The young Douglas Hyde* (1974) • *W. B. Yeats: uncollected prose*, ed. J. P. Frayne, 1 (1970) • *Lady Gregory's diaries, 1892–1902*, ed. J. Pethica (1996) • K. Tynan, *The middle years* (1916) • K. Tynan, *The years of the shadow* (1919) • S. J. Kunitz and H. Haycraft, eds., *Twentieth century authors: a biographical dictionary of modern literature* (1942) • *IGI* • *CGPLA Ire.* (1917)
Archives BL, letters to A. R. Wallace • JRL, corresp. files of Katherine Tynan and family • NL Ire., F. S. Bourke collection, Sarah Purser corresp. • TCD, letters to Seumas O'Sullivan
Likenesses S. Purser, oils, 1894, Hugh Lane Municipal Gallery of Art, Dublin
Wealth at death £8122 19*s*. 2*d*.: administration, 22 June 1917, *CGPLA Ire.*

Barlow, Joel (1754–1812), poet and diplomatist, was born on 24 March 1754 at Redding, Connecticut, the fourth child of Samuel Barlow, farmer, and his second wife, Esther Hull. For several generations the Barlow family maintained a reputation as respectable farmers in America, and Joel was to benefit from a good education which progressed from Moor's Indian Charity School at Hanover, New Hampshire, and Dartmouth College in 1773, to Yale University the following year. Within twelve months he had published his first poem, though a copy does not exist, and in 1776 he joined the Connecticut militia to take part in the battle of Long Island. Following his graduation on 9 September 1778 Barlow was employed briefly as a schoolteacher, but he returned to Yale to complete a master's degree before becoming a chaplain in 1780 of the 3rd Massachusetts brigade. Preaching, too, was only temporary and, following his marriage to Ruth Baldwin (*d*. 1818) on 26 January 1781, with whom he remained until his death, Barlow moved to Hartford, Connecticut, to pursue his literary ambitions. The result was the publication of *A Poem, Spoken at the Public Commencement of Yale College* (1781) and *An Elegy on the Late Honorable Titus Hosmer, Esq.* (1782).

In 1784 Barlow joined Elisha Babcock in editing the *American Mercury*, an association which gave Barlow the chance to publish an edition of *Doctor Watts' Imitation of the Psalms of David* (1785). This partnership, however, was to dissolve by December 1785 and Barlow began studying law, leading to his admission to the bar in April 1786. With his career momentarily settled, Barlow's literary reputation began to flourish with his satirical 'Anarchiad' (published in twelve instalments between October 1786 and September 1787 in the *New Haven Gazette and Connecticut Magazine*) and the publication of *An Oration, Delivered at the North Church of Hartford* (1787). It was, however, the release of his long-awaited poem *The Vision of Columbus* (1787) which seemed to justify a reference in 1788 to Barlow as 'the Poet Laureate of all America' (Ford, 26).

In spite of his rising reputation as a poet, Barlow was less successful as a lawyer, and on 25 May 1788 he departed for France as an agent selling land for a group known as Scioto Associates. Following a brief trip to England, Barlow returned to Paris in time to witness the fall of the Bastille and to establish a company in partnership with William Playfair, a Scottish scientist, called La Compagnie du Scioto. This venture soon came to an end and Barlow was left debt-ridden and seeking refuge in England in 1790. One month before joining the London Society for Constitutional Information in March 1792, Barlow contributed to the prevailing pamphlet debate on the French Revolution through the first part of his radical *Advice to the Privileged Orders* (1792). He followed this with a satirical attack on English conservatism in a poem called *The Conspiracy of Kings* (1792) and compiled *A Letter to the National Convention of France* (1792), which eventually saw him bestowed the dubious honour of French citizenship in February 1793.

With the spurious growth of his radical reputation came the real threat of prosecution in late 1792, at which time Barlow decided to move to France, from where he completed the second part of his *Advice to the Privileged Orders* (1793). As a delegate of the Society for Constitutional Information, he travelled with John Frost to deliver a congratulatory address to the National Convention on 28 November 1792. Barlow then involved himself in French politics, unsuccessfully campaigning for election to the convention from Savoy and urging the inhabitants in the nearby Italian region of Piedmont, through a pamphlet originally published in French and Italian and translated as *A Letter, Addressed to the People of Piedmont* (1793), to welcome French forces. From politics Barlow turned his attention to personal ventures and left for Hamburg in the spring of 1794, where he stayed for a year amassing a fortune as an importer. On his return to Paris, Barlow was appointed consul to Algiers, and until 1805 he remained in Europe pursuing his business and political interests and compiling such works as the poem *Hasty Puddy* (1796), *The Political Writings of Joel Barlow* (1796), and *Letters from Paris, to the Citizens of the United States of America* (1800), and translating Brissot's *Nouveau voyage* as *The Commerce of America with Europe* (1794) and Volney's original work as *Ruins* (1802).

By August 1805 Barlow had returned to America, settling first in Washington and then, in 1807, moving to a mansion situated on the banks of Rock Creek between Georgetown and Washington. His arrival in the United States coincided with his ideas for establishing an institute of education that emphasized both research and teaching, set out in a *Prospectus of a National Institution to be Established in the United States* (1805). It was, however, the publication of *The Columbiad* (1807), a revised edition of his earlier epic poem *The Vision of Columbus*, which was the highlight of Barlow's literary efforts in his final years. Indeed, following the release of this work he spent most of his time between 1807 and 1811 working unofficially as an adviser to Thomas Jefferson and James Madison, his sporadic attention to prose and verse in these years exemplified by such productions as *Letter to Henry Gregoire* (1809) and *A Review of Robert Smith's Address to the People of the United States* (1811). Barlow also had intentions of publishing a two-volume collection of his writings in 1811, but he was appointed as an envoy to France to negotiate trade relations with Napoleon. For over twelve months the French showed little interest in American offers, but in October 1812 Barlow was invited to Vilna, Poland, to finalize a treaty arrangement. As a result he was caught in Napoleon's retreat from Russia, and despite reaching Warsaw safely Barlow died on 24 December 1812 of pneumonia in the village of Zarnowiec, near Cracow. His body remains buried in an obscure grave in Poland.

MICHAEL T. DAVIS

Sources A. L. Ford, *Joel Barlow* (1971) • J. Woodress, *A Yankee's odyssey: the life of Joel Barlow* (1958) • V. C. Miller, *Joel Barlow: revolutionist, London, 1791–2* (1932) • C. B. Todd, *Life and letters of Joel Barlow* (1886) • M. C. Tyler, *Three men of letters* (1895) • R. F. Durden, 'Joel Barlow in the French Revolution', *William and Mary Quarterly*, 8 (1951), 327–54 • M. B. McGuire, 'Barlow, man of freedom', *Personalist*, 42 (1961), 203–6 • J. L. Blau, 'Joel Barlow, enlightened religionist', *Journal of the History of Ideas*, 10 (1949), 430–44 • M. R. Adams, 'Joel Barlow, political romanticist', *American Literature*, 9 (1973), 113–52 • *The works of Joel Barlow*, ed. W. K. Bottorff and A. L. Ford, 2 vols. (1970)

Likenesses J. A. Houdon, sculpture, New York Historical Society

Wealth at death $290,540—in cash deposits, corporate stocks, and land: Adams, 'Joel Barlow, political romanticist'

Barlow, John (*fl.* 1517–1552). *See under* Barlow, William (*d.* 1568).

Barlow, Margaret Lilian, Lady Barlow. *See* Rawlings, Margaret Lilian (1906–1996).

Barlow, Peter (1776–1862), mathematician and physicist, was born in the parish of St Simon, Norwich, in October 1776. Details of his early life are sparse. He was educated at a local foundation school before starting work in trade; later he became a schoolmaster, and, having by his own exertions attained considerable scientific knowledge, he became a regular correspondent of the *Ladies' Diary*, then under the management of Dr Charles Hutton, professor of mathematics at the Royal Military Academy, Woolwich.

Peter Barlow (1776–1862), by Samuel Cousins (after Sir William Boxall, exh. RA 1853)

Barlow first attracted attention as a mathematician. On Hutton's advice he sought, and after a severe competitive examination obtained in 1801, the post of assistant mathematical master, from which he was subsequently advanced to that of professor, in the Royal Military Academy. His first book, *An Elementary Investigation of the Theory of Numbers*, was published in 1811, followed in 1814 by *A New Mathematical and Philosophical Dictionary*. In the same year he published his *New Mathematical Tables*, giving the factors, squares, cubes, square and cube roots, reciprocals, and hyperbolic logarithms of all numbers from 1 to 10,000, together with the first ten powers of numbers under 100, and the fourth and fifth of all from 100 to 1000. His *Essay on the Strength of Timber and other Materials* (1817, 6th edn, 1867), compiled the results of numerous experiments in Woolwich Dockyard, providing much-needed data for engineering calculations. The experiments on the resistance of iron which formed the basis of the design for the Menai suspension bridge were submitted by Telford to his examination, and were printed as an appendix to the third edition of his *Essay* (1826). His services to the profession led to his admission, in 1820, as an honorary member of the Institution of Civil Engineers. Barlow was also much occupied with experiments designed to afford practical data for steam locomotion. He sat on railway commissions in 1836, 1839, 1842, and 1845, and two reports addressed by him in 1835 to the directors of the London and Birmingham Company on the best forms of railway equipment were regarded as of the highest authority.

In 1819, with a view to devising a remedy for the large deviations of the compass due to the increasing quantities of iron used in the construction and fittings of ships, Barlow undertook the first experimental investigation ever attempted of the phenomena of induced magnetism. By observing the deflections of a magnetic needle near an iron globe, he established that magnetic intensity depends on the extent of surface rather than of mass. This was shown by Poisson in 1824 to be mathematically deducible from Coulomb's law of magnetic action. In his *Essay on Magnetic Attractions* (1820), Barlow detailed his experiments, and described a simple method of correcting ships' compasses by fixing a small iron plate in such a position as to compensate for all other local attractions. After successful trial in various latitudes, it was adopted by the Admiralty, although the method proved inadequate in ships built wholly of iron. He received a grant of £500 from the board of longitude as well as presents from the chief naval boards, a gold watch and chain from the Tsar Alexander on the introduction of the device into the Russian navy in 1824, and the gold medal of the Society of Arts in 1821. He was elected a member of the Imperial Academy of Brussels and a corresponding member of the French Académie des Sciences. In 1823 he became a fellow of the Royal Society and he was elected onto its council in 1824. He was also a member of the Astronomical Society and was active in its administration.

Barlow was one of several English experimenters during the 1820s, including Michael Faraday and William Sturgeon, to further develop Hans Christian Oersted's discovery of electromagnetism in 1820. One of his particular contributions was Barlow's wheel, in which a serrated copper disc suspended between the poles of a magnet rotated when an electric current was passed through it. This instrument became a standard demonstration device in the following decades. Some of his results were published in a revised edition of his 1820 *Essay* (1823), which also included one of the first efforts by an Englishman to produce a comprehensive mathematical theory of magnetism. In 1831 he published the results of an experiment displaying the similarity between the magnetic action of the earth and of a wooden globe coiled round with a current-carrying copper wire. This too became a well-known demonstration device, being on show for example at the Adelaide Gallery of Practical Science in London. This kind of experiment, demonstrating the analogy between natural and laboratory phenomena, was common during the period. Barlow also experimented on the transmission of electricity over long distances, concluding that telegraphy by such a method was impracticable.

Barlow's optical experiments, which began about 1827, arose from efforts to reduce lens aberration in telescopes. Since suitable flint glass was difficult to find, Barlow found a substitute in disulphide of carbon, a perfectly colourless liquid, with about the same refractive, and more than twice the dispersive, power of flint glass. He constructed two telescopes, of respectively 3 and 6 inches aperture, in which the corrections both for colour and curvature were effected by a concavo-convex lens composed of this substance enclosed in glass, of half the diameter of the plate-lens, and fixed at a distance within it of half its focal length. Aided by a grant from the board of longitude, he shortly afterwards advanced to an aperture of 7.8 inches (surpassing that of any refractor then in England), and was willing with some further improvements to attempt one of 2 feet. A committee appointed by the Royal Society in 1831 to report upon the practicability of this daring scheme advised a preliminary trial on a smaller scale, and a 'fluid-lens' telescope of 8 inches aperture and the extremely short focal length of 8¾ feet (one of the leading advantages of the new principle) was in 1832 executed by Dollond from Barlow's designs. The success of this trial was not, however, sufficient to warrant the prosecution of the larger design. The 'Barlow lens' later used for increasing the power of any eyepiece was a negative achromatic combination of flint and crown glass, suggested by Barlow, and applied by Dollond in 1833. It was first employed by Dawes in the measurement of minute double stars.

Barlow resigned his post in the Woolwich Academy in 1847, his public services being recognized by the continuance of full pay. He was married but his wife's name is not known. Two sons, Peter William *Barlow and William Henry *Barlow, were civil engineers. Barlow retained the powers of his mind and the cheerfulness of his disposition until his death, on 1 March 1862, at his home, 13 Maryon Road, Charlton, Kent.

A. M. CLERKE, *rev.* IWAN RHYS MORUS

Sources D. Gooding, 'Experiment and concept-formation in electromagnetic science and technology in England, 1820–1830', *History and Technology*, 2 (1985), 151–76 • *PICE*, 22 (1862–3), 615–18 • *Monthly Notices of the Royal Astronomical Society*, 23 (1862–3), 127 • *CGPLA Eng. & Wales* (1862)

Archives Inst. CE, corresp. and report on London Bridge project | RS, corresp. with Sir John Herschel • RS, letters to Sir John Lubbock • UCL, letters to T. J. Hussey

Likenesses Miss Turner, lithograph, 1835 (after T. Fielding), BM, NPG • S. Cousins, mezzotint (after W. Boxall, exh. RA 1853), BM, NPG [*see illus.*]

Wealth at death under £3000: probate, 26 April 1862, *CGPLA Eng. & Wales*

Barlow, Peter William (1809–1885), civil engineer, was born at Woolwich on 1 February 1809, the elder son of Professor Peter *Barlow (1776–1862), mathematician. His mother's name is unknown. His younger brother was William Henry *Barlow (1812–1902). After an education at private schools he followed his early ambition of a career in civil engineering by becoming a pupil of Henry Robinson Palmer (1795–1844), a founder member of the Institution of Civil Engineers (ICE), who proposed him as an associate member in January 1826. Palmer at that time was heavily involved in extensions to the London docks, and Barlow worked on this and the Liverpool and Birmingham Canal.

From 1832 Palmer surveyed proposals for a railway between London and Dover, and Barlow assisted him. William Cubitt (1791–1863) replaced Palmer, now in poor health, as the engineer for the South Eastern Railway after it received parliamentary approval. He appointed Barlow

Peter William Barlow (1809–1885), by Maull & Polyblank

one of the four resident engineers for the construction of the line, initially on the Tonbridge District. While these works progressed Barlow married Bethia Crawford Caffin, on 5 July 1836. They had two daughters, and one son, also called Peter William Barlow, who became a builder.

Cubitt resigned as engineer of the railway in 1844 when a conflict of interest arose over proposals for a north Kent line, and was replaced by Robert Stephenson (1803–1859) and George Parker Bidder (1806–1878). Barlow supervised the construction of the north Kent scheme, and in 1847 became engineer-in-chief to the South Eastern Company. He had already acted as engineer-in-chief for the Tunbridge Wells branch, which involved him in experiments on the atmospheric railway system with a view to its introduction on the branch. His critical conclusions were reported to the ICE in 1845 in a paper entitled 'The comparative advantages of the atmospheric railway system' (*PICE*, 4, 1845, 114–50). While engineer to the South Eastern Company he was responsible for the Tunbridge Wells to Hastings, Ashford and Hastings, and Reading, Guildford, and Reigate lines. When his brother, William, experienced problems with rolling his 'Barlow' rail, Barlow became interested in alternative systems of railway track, and began to investigate his own system of cast-iron sleepers and iron diagonal ties for permanent way. He introduced this in May 1850, and extended it to 61 miles of track. A subsequent investigation of this system concluded that it had unduly engrossed his attention to the exclusion of the company's affairs. Having failed to convince the company of the value of the system, Barlow resigned on 10 July 1851.

In the 1850s Barlow worked on the Newtown and Oswestry, Londonderry and Enniskillen, and Londonderry and Coleraine railways. While investigating the possibility of a link between the Enniskillen and Coleraine lines across the Foyle at Londonderry, Barlow became interested in the design of long span bridges. In 1858 he made use of large scale models to demonstrate that, by stiffening suspension bridges with relatively light parallel girders extending from pier to pier, less material was required than for a more conventional parallel girder. While pursuing these studies Barlow visited the USA and in his *Observations on the Niagara Railway Suspension Bridge* (1860) concluded that a suitably stiffened suspension bridge was best for long spans and proposed bridges across the Mersey and East River, New York.

On his return Barlow became engineer for Lambeth Bridge, London, which was opened in 1862. His design comprised a wire suspension bridge with its vertical hangers stiffened by diagonal ties. At the time the bridge was commended for its economy in design; but in retrospect its chief interest lies in Barlow's claim that it was sufficiently stiffened to withstand the heaviest gale. This was one of the last references to wind as a factor in suspension bridge design before the Tacoma Narrows Bridge failure of 1940.

Barlow's most lasting contribution to the development of civil engineering was his tunnelling shield. The Lambeth Bridge piers comprised cast iron cylinders driven into the clay beneath the river bed. Barlow realized that this principle could also be applied to driving cylinders horizontally through suitable ground. Since the completion of the Thames Tunnel in 1843 there had been little progress in the use of tunnelling shields. In 1864 Barlow took out a patent (no. 2207) which described a shield comprising a wrought iron or steel cylinder, fitted at the front with cutting plates, which would be jacked forward. The system involved the use of cast-iron linings and cement joints. In 1868 the patent was modified to include a diaphragm with a door, which would help facilitate the application of compressed air to tunnelling.

The first successful application of Barlow's invention was the Tower subway driven beneath the Thames near the Tower of London in 1869 to serve a cable railway. The tunnel was soon converted to pedestrian use. Barlow was engineer for the project, and his assistant, James Henry Greathead, who had joined his staff in 1864, helped design the shield and supervised the construction. The success of the construction method paved the way for the development of tube railways over the next thirty years.

Barlow largely retired after the completion of the Tower subway, although he designed a bridge across the Lea, and reported on a proposal for an underwater tunnel at Rio de Janeiro. His sight was severely damaged by cataracts in 1881, which an operation only partially remedied. He was an active member of the Institution of Civil Engineers, becoming a member in 1845, and contributing several papers. He was elected FRS in the same year, contributing several papers to its *Philosophical Transactions* and *Proceedings*. He also presented papers to the British Association and the Franklin Institute, and was the author of several pamphlets. Barlow died at his home, 56 Lansdowne Road, Notting Hill, London, on 20 May 1885.

MIKE CHRIMES

Sources *PICE*, 81 (1884–5), 321–3 • *PRS*, 38 (1884–5), xxxix–xl • *The Engineer*, 59 (1885), 422 • d. cert.
Archives Inst. CE, membership records, published MSS, etc. • LMA • PRO, railway records • RS
Likenesses Maull & Polyblank, photograph, Sci. Mus. [*see illus.*]
Wealth at death £1486 8*s*. 5*d*.: probate, 5 Aug 1885, *CGPLA Eng. & Wales*

Barlow, Ralph (1573/4–1631), dean of Wells, was the son of Henry Barlow of Cheshire. He matriculated from Oriel College, Oxford, in 1594 and as chaplain of New College graduated BA in 1596 and proceeded MA in 1599, BD (as from Corpus Christi College) in 1606, and DD in 1610. In 1603 he was one of a number of fellows of Corpus questioned for their puritan sympathies, but thereafter his conformity was never in doubt. His earliest preferments were to the livings of Woodmansterne, Surrey (1601), Radnage, Buckinghamshire (1606), and Farthingstone, Northamptonshire (1609). About that time he became chaplain to Bishop William Barlow of Lincoln, his namesake and possible relative, who in 1609 collated him to a canonry at Lincoln and to the archdeaconry of Winchester. The following year he became incumbent at Yaverland on the Isle of Wight, in the gift of William Stirropp, diocesan registrar at Lincoln, and acquired a new patron, Bishop Thomas Bilson of Winchester, who presented him to livings at Fawley (1610) and Chilbolton (1613), both in Hampshire, and Knoll Magna in Wiltshire (1613).

Such favour was probably the result of Barlow's marriage, before 1613, to Dorothy Wolrege (1595–1620), great-niece of Bishop Bilson; the couple had five children before Dorothy's death in 1620. Shortly afterwards Barlow married Christian Marsh, a widow with children, and though the union produced one son, Henry, it was a troubled relationship which in Barlow's view caused him needless expense and endless trouble in pursuing lawsuits in the court of wards and meeting bills, so that in his will he left his widow a small legacy, dependent on her good behaviour.

In September 1621 Barlow was presented to the deanery of Wells by the crown. Later, in 1627, as a royal chaplain-in-ordinary, he became vicar of Cheddar, Somerset, on the instructions of Charles I, who subsequently dispensed him from residence at the deanery. Barlow was an active evangelical, describing himself in his will as a preacher of thirty-two years standing, and on one occasion preached at five out of eight sessions at his archidiaconal visitation. He was associated at Winchester and Wells with a circle of preachers, most notably Arthur Lake, his fellow archdeacon at Winchester and later bishop of Bath and Wells. In his will of 1631 Barlow reproduced the long preamble to Lake's will, and asked to be buried close to the bishop's grave in Wells Cathedral. On his death on 20 July 1631 Barlow left £1800 to be divided among his six children, and a copy of the sermons of bishops Arthur Lake and Lancelot Andrewes, both published in 1629, to his overseers. He was buried at Wells Cathedral on 27 July.

KENNETH FINCHAM

Sources will, PRO, PROB 11/160, sig. 123 • W. H. Challen, 'Thomas Bilson, bishop of Winchester, his family and their Hampshire, Sussex and other connections', *Papers and Proceedings of the Hampshire Field Club and Archaeological Society*, 19 (1955–7), 35–46, 253–75 • T. Bilson, bishop's register, 1597–1616, Hants. RO, Winchester diocesan records, 21M65.A1/29 • K. Fincham, *Prelate as pastor: the episcopate of James I* (1990) • P. Collinson, *The religion of protestants* (1982) • J. W. Legg, ed., *English order for consecrating churches in the seventeenth century* (1911) • Lincs. Arch., LT • Lincs. Arch., D2 • *Calendar of the manuscripts of the dean and chapter of Wells*, 2, HMC, 12 (1914) • *Hist. U. Oxf.* 4: *17th-cent. Oxf.*, 574 • *Reg. Oxf.*, 2/3.197 • BL, Sloane MS 856 • T. Phillipps, ed., *Institutiones clericorum in comitatu Wiltoniae*, 2 vols. (1825) • matriculation register, Oriel College, Oxford

Archives Hants. RO, Winchester diocesan records • Lincs. Arch., LT, D2

Wealth at death considerable moveable wealth: will, PRO, PROB 11/160, sig. 123

Barlow, Sir Robert (1757–1843), naval officer, was born in London on 25 December 1757, the eldest son of William Barlow (*d.* 1798) of Bath, a mercer in King Street, Covent Garden, and Hilaire (*d.* 1774), daughter of Robert Butcher of Walthamstow. Barlow's brother was Sir George Hilaro *Barlow. On 6 November 1778 he was promoted lieutenant of the *Courageux* with Lord Mulgrave, and he continued in her in the Grand Fleet until the peace in 1783, taking part in the capture of La Minerve on 4 January 1781, and the relief of Gibraltar in October 1782. In 1785 he married Elizabeth (*d.* 1817), daughter of William Garrett of Worting in Hampshire. The couple had a large family; one of their daughters married George, sixth Viscount Torrington and another married William, first Earl Nelson.

From 1786 to 1789 Barlow commanded the revenue cutter *Barracouta*, and on 22 November 1790 he was promoted to command the brig *Childers*, which was employed on the same service on the coast of Cornwall during 1791–2. On 2 January 1793 he was sent to reconnoitre Brest. This the French would not allow, and fired on the brig. As the two countries were still at peace Barlow hoisted his colours, and all the batteries within range opened on him. The brig succeeded in getting out, one shot only—of 48 lb—striking, and doing no particular damage. War was declared on 2 February, and on 15 February Barlow, still in the *Childers*, being off Gravelines, captured the privateer *Patriote*, the first armed vessel taken by a British ship in the French Revolutionary War. He was promoted captain on 24 May, and in the following year he commanded the frigate *Pegasus*, which was attached to the fleet under Lord Howe as a signal repeating ship for the centre squadron, and took part in the action of 1 June. Lord Howe was so pleased with his work that he persuaded the king to intervene with the Admiralty to have him moved into the larger frigate *Aquilon*. In December 1795 Barlow was appointed to the frigate *Phoebe* (44 guns), in which, on 21 December 1797, he captured the *Néréide* (36 guns) 180 miles west of Ushant, and on 19 February 1801, near the Strait of Gibraltar, the frigate *Africaine* (44 guns). The French ship was lumbered up by military stores and 400 soldiers destined for the army in Egypt, in addition to her complement of 315 men. The two-hour action was conducted at very close range, and on the French ship the slaughter was terrible. Her loss was returned as 200 killed and 143 wounded; that of the *Phoebe* as one killed and twelve wounded. The numbers were certified by the captain of the *Africaine*. This action was his last as a frigate captain, a service he had performed with as much success and skill as any officer in the navy.

On 16 June 1801 Barlow was knighted, and shortly afterwards he was appointed to the *Triumph* (74 guns), in the Mediterranean, which he brought to England, and paid off at the end of 1804. In 1805–6 he was flag-captain to Lord Keith, then commander-in-chief in the Downs, and on 20 June 1806 he was appointed deputy controller of the navy, from which office he was moved in December 1808 to that of commissioner at Chatham Dockyard. On 20 May 1820 he was nominated a KCB, and on his retirement from Chatham on 24 January 1823 he was put on the superannuated list with the rank of rear-admiral. In this administrative phase of his career Barlow proved to be in every way as effective as he had been while at sea. On 12 November 1840, at the age of almost eighty-three, he was restored to the active list with the rank of admiral of the white, and on 23 February 1842 he was made a GCB. He died at the archbishop's palace at Canterbury on 11 May 1843.

J. K. LAUGHTON, *rev.* ANDREW LAMBERT

Sources J. Barrow, *The life of Richard, Earl Howe* (1838) • J. M. Collinge, *Navy Board officials, 1660–1832* (1978) • A. B. Sainsbury, *The Royal Navy day by day* (1992) • *The Keith papers*, 2, ed. C. Lloyd, Navy RS, 90 (1950)

Archives BL OIOC, letters to Sir George Barlow, etc., MS Eur. F 176

Barlow, Roger (*d.* 1558). *See under* Barlow, William (*d.* 1568).

Barlow, Thomas (1493–1558). *See under* Barlow, William (*d.* 1568).

Barlow, Thomas (1608/9–1691), bishop of Lincoln, was born at Long-Gill, Orton, Westmorland, the son of Richard Barlow (*d.* 1637). He was educated under William Pickering at Appleby grammar school. He matriculated as a servitor from the Queen's College, Oxford, on 1 July 1625 aged sixteen, and later became a taberdar. He graduated BA on 24 July 1630, proceeded MA on 27 June 1633, and was elected a fellow of Queen's the same year.

Early career Barlow's college and the university remained the centre of his life for the next forty years or more. He established enduring friendships and connections and laid the foundations of an encyclopaedic knowledge of the philosophical and theological learning then current in Oxford. In 1635 he was appointed the university reader in metaphysics and in this capacity delivered lectures, later published as *Exercitationes aliquot de metaphysicae de Deo* (1637, but appended to a 1638 publication). Barlow's reputation was as a teacher of philosophy, logic, and casuistry; his pupils included John Owen. Some sense of Barlow's intellectual formation and of his likely legacy to his pupils can be gained from the many annotated reading

Thomas Barlow (1608/9–1691), by unknown artist, *c.*1672–5

lists which he prepared. The best-known of these dates from the 1650s and, although his suggestions are more exhaustive than some, it offers a typical range of seventeenth-century reading—including ethical compendia, works by the schoolmen, and works of natural philosophy by authors such as Gassendi, Descartes, and Bacon. Barlow also prepared a guide to mastering the rudiments of the civil or canon law in so far as it was needed by a minister.

Barlow leaned not only towards the scholastics, but also towards a high Calvinist theology which was increasingly unfashionable in 1630s Oxford. This did not however prevent him—on his own evidence—from being invited to Lord Falkland's house at Great Tew and from advising both Falkland and William Chillingworth on their antipapal writings at the end of the 1630s. Indeed, to judge from the presentation volumes that Barlow received from authors throughout his long life, he was able to maintain friendships with a diverse range of people. As he later wrote when refuting a piece by his old acquaintance Thomas Hobbes, 'It is the positions of that Authour which I severely (may be) but truely confute; not his person … soe say I, of Mr Hobs and truth; I love Both, but truth better. Nor is this any breach of friendship' (*Correspondence of Thomas Hobbes*, 2.787).

Civil war and interregnum Barlow's life during the civil war is not well documented, but he seems to have been in royalist Oxford pursuing his academic and clerical duties. After the defeat of the king parliament sent a visitation to the university to purge it of unsuitable elements. In May 1648 he told the visitors that he was not yet satisfied 'how I can without violence to my conscience submitt to this Visitation' (Burrows, 74, 89) and his name consequently appeared in a list of those expelled from the university. Yet he remained undisturbed. Barlow's retention of his fellowship was perhaps less surprising than some later maintained. Although he may have benefited from the protection of friends like John Owen and John Selden, the explanation of his conformity is more likely to be found in the influence of Gerard Langbaine, provost of Queen's, who practised, along with John Wilkins of Wadham, 'a skilful and often unobtrusive policy of minimal tactical concession' to the demands of the intruded authorities. Queen's was a college with a pronounced royalist reputation and character: it had an unusually high number of fellows who survived the purge of 1648; and it was a college 'resorted to by all that were cavaliers or of the King's party'—little wonder then that so many later tories were bred there during the interregnum (Worden in *Hist. U. Oxf.* 4: *17th-cent. Oxf.*, 760–61, 767). A rather poor attempt at satire, *Pegasus, or, The flying horse from Oxford, bringing the proceedings of the visitors and other Bedlamites* (1648), is often attributed to Barlow.

Barlow's residual loyalty to both king and Church of England is attested by his subscription to a secret collection raised in 1654 by Francis Mansell and Leoline Jenkins for the distressed bishops in exile. Barlow corresponded with two of the church's leading lights, Henry Hammond and Robert Sanderson, about the most effective way of defending the Church of England. In June 1655 he wrote to Hammond about his interpretation of scripture in the debate on the distinction between *presbyteros* and *episcopos* and expressed a concern that Hammond had conceded too much to the presbyterians. His letters to Sanderson in 1656 and 1657 expressed his concern at the innovative teachings of Jeremy Taylor on original sin. In reply Sanderson urged him to write about original sin and to answer 'all the objections of the old Pelagians, or late Socinians' but to do so without naming Taylor or dividing the episcopalian party (*Works of Robert Sanderson*, 6.381). Obviously there may have been some coolness between those like Hammond and Taylor who had been ejected and Barlow who had complied with the new authorities, but this was complicated by their theological differences since Barlow remained a staunch Calvinist and an outspoken opponent of Arminianism (indeed he later explicitly blamed Hammond for the spread of that dangerous doctrine). Meanwhile the Calvinist puritans around Barlow in interregnum Oxford admired his theology: Louis du Moulin believed that Barlow 'did keep this university of Oxon from being poyson'd with Pelagianism, Socinianism, popery etc' during the 1640s and 1650s (Wood, *Ath. Oxon.*, 3.1058). But this did not mean that they regarded him as one of their number.

As ever in the university the claims of scholarship could be balanced against those of political affiliation. In 1652 Barlow was appointed as the keeper of the Bodleian Library. In this post he opposed 'both on statute and on principle the lax habit of lending books, which had been the cause of serious losses' to the library (*DNB*). Barlow and the library formed an impressive academic resource. He prepared a paper for the debate on the readmission of the Jews 'at the request of a person of quality'. He gave Anthony Wood an 'assisting hand' and showed him 'fatherly favours' (*Life and Times of Anthony Wood*, xxiii, lix); he helped Thomas Fuller with information about the university for his *Church History*; he patronized the outstanding young Hebraist Thomas Smith; and he was on hand to welcome scholars, even Catholic ones like Sancta Clara, who visited the library. It was during Barlow's tenure of office that the library received one of its most notable accessions: in 1659 the library of John Selden (*d.* 1654)—8000 printed volumes and a rich collection of manuscripts—arrived at the Bodleian.

From 1656 Barlow was assisted by the pushy young Henry Stubbe who exploited his superior's reputation in his successful attempt to establish a correspondence with Hobbes. It was through Stubbe that Hobbes sent Barlow a copy of *De corpore*, and Barlow's letter of thanks dated 23 December 1656 has survived. In this letter Barlow records that he has read Hobbes's works as they appeared. Despite Hobbes's suspicion of the universities Barlow expressed the hope that they might be 'seminaries of all good letters, in which the youth of this nation may (upon just principles) be taught religion and piety towards God, and obedience and duty to their governors' (*Correspondence of Thomas Hobbes*, 2.420–21).

On 23 July 1657 Barlow gained the degree of BD. On Gerard Langbaine's death in 1658 the fellows of the Queen's College moved swiftly to thwart any external interference and elected Barlow as his successor. Obadiah Walker congratulated Barlow with the comment that they have 'their father [eldest fellow] to their Provost, under whose experienced government they may assure themselves of all happiness that they are capable of. 'Tis no wonder that everyone without reluctancy cheerfully concurred in that election' (*Correspondence of Thomas Hobbes*, 2.786).

Restoration At the Restoration, Barlow, as a respected intellectual and an undisputed supporter of both monarchy and the Church of England, could have anticipated influence on the settlement of religion. Moreover his perspective as a convinced Calvinist and as someone who had found a *modus vivendi* with the religious pluralism of the interregnum was possibly more in tune with the presbyterian sentiments which seemed likely to prevail in 1660. At the request of his friend Robert Boyle, Barlow wrote a manuscript 'Case of a toleration in matters of religion', which he described as 'adversaria (tumultuously put together)' (Barlow, *Several Cases of Conscience*, 1692, 93). In this tract he discussed whether a state could tolerate false religions and scrupulously refrained from any simple conclusion. He held that no state could tolerate a religion which was destructive of the state or of true religion and that the authorities could compel those of other religions to hear arguments and sermons for the truth. But in the end belief had to be voluntary. Others, like Edward Stillingfleet, were not only composing but even publishing speculative discussions about religious toleration in the uncertain months surrounding the Restoration. Interesting although Barlow's arguments were, they were soon left behind by events and were published only after his death.

Barlow had work to do in Oxford at the Restoration. He served as a commissioner for restoring members of the university ejected in 1648. He is reported to have helped John Owen and interceded for him when harassed for preaching in his own house. After the expulsion of Henry Wilkinson from the Lady Margaret professorship of divinity Barlow was appointed in his place and relinquished his position at the Bodleian. On 1 September 1660 he took the degree of DD by royal mandate as part of a group honoured, comments Wood, 'as loyalists, yet none of them suffered for their loyalty in the times of rebellion and usurpation' (Wood, *Ath. Oxon.*: *Fasti*, 2.238). On 25 September he was formally elected as Lady Margaret professor and collated to the prebendal stall at Worcester which was annexed to the chair. In 1661 he was nominated to succeed Barton Holyday as archdeacon of Oxford, but a dispute with Thomas Lamplugh over the appointment delayed Barlow's instalment until 13 June 1664.

Religious settlement As the national religious settlement took shape Barlow's views were sought. In the summer of 1661 he was asked to contribute his suggestions for revision of the Book of Common Prayer. His final report asserted 'the whole booke to be the best liturgy in the world, especially the communion service, it beeinge allmost impossible that any office penn'd by men (not divinely inspired) should breathe more piety, or contain more truth and decency' (Queen's College, Oxford, MS 279). However this did not mean that it was beyond improvement in areas such as the offices of baptism, confirmation, commination, and burial. Barlow's Calvinism logically created a difficulty for him over the baptism service. He had already expressed his unease over infant baptism to the baptist theologian John Tombes. In this report he once again asserted that baptism was not necessary to salvation and that the liturgy's claim that the baptized infant was really regenerated but then might eternally perish was nonsense.

The religious policies of the early 1660s seem to have caused Barlow no dismay. Neither his experience of the interregnum nor his Calvinist theology seem to have disposed him to generosity towards the nonconformists. In the winter of 1667–8 two initiatives were launched apparently from elements within the court to improve the position of the dissenters. One plan was for a 'comprehension' or widening of the terms of communion of the Church of England so that the moderate ministers excluded in 1662 might once again exercise their ministry within the national church. The other plan was for an 'indulgence', or toleration, of those, principally the Independents, who did not aspire to rejoin the established church. Neither of these schemes actually led to any bill being offered to parliament. A long-standing canard has associated Thomas Barlow with these negotiations. As he did with many other public events, Barlow collected the publications surrounding these schemes. He bound seventeen pamphlets connected with the proposals together and annotated them with what information he had been able to gather from his various sources in London. The resulting volume in the Bodleian (B.14.15.Linc) is the best source for the negotiations of 1667–8, but it implies nothing at all about Barlow's approval of these schemes, never mind any involvement on his part. At several points the annotations are clearly transcriptions of others' reports and Barlow sums up the whole volume as concerning the presbyterian endeavours in court and parliament which having received countenance from the king led to a 'boldness an[d] insolence both of Papists, Presbyterians and fanatiques'. Fortunately (from his perspective) parliament stepped in and obtained a proclamation from the king for enforcing the laws against conventicles. As Barlow wrote in a private letter of 8 January 1669:

> the Presbyterians and all non-Conformists desire and indeavour the dissolution of this, and the Call of another Parliament, hopinge to chuse such members as may give a Toleration (if not a greater incouragement or establishment) of their sect and way, and also (to ease the people of Taxes) give the kinge the Church Lands to raise money out of the churches ruines; and soe robb God, and invert the pious donations of their Ancestors.

He continues, 'I hope you and I shall not live to see that day'. He was confident that the present parliament would never be so sacrilegious, and if another parliament were to attempt it, 'I am persuaded his sacred Majesty (on whose head may the Crowne florish) will never consent' (Bodl. Oxf., MS Eng. lett. C. 328, fol. 509).

University duties absorbed Barlow's time and energies. Yet he saw his primary role as the defence and maintenance of the protestant religion within the university and beyond: so he is to be heard arguing at the university act in 1661 that Socianian teachings were destructive of church and state and that the Church of Rome was idolatrous. He was suspicious of the new science, fearing especially that its atomism would pave the way for atheism: 'I am troubled to see the scepticism (to say no worse) which now securely reigns in our miserable nation' (*Genuine Remains*, 155). His correspondence reveals a stream of requests from parish ministers and others for advice on 'cases of conscience' or moral problems. And of course as a teacher he was required to inculcate true religion and obedience among the students of the university and of his college in particular. In 1670 he assured Sir John Lowther that his grandson would be instructed in religion as well as literature and that he himself would:

> at convenient times (privately) read over the grounds of divinity to him, that soe he may have a better understandinge and comprehension of the reason of that religion, which alone is, or can be a just foundation of true comfort here, and of our hopes of a better life hereafter. (*Hist. U. Oxf.* 4: *17th-cent. Oxf.*, 312)

Barlow won back errant members of the Church of England like William Wycherley who temporarily converted to Rome while travelling abroad, and welcomed new adherents, such as Anthony Horneck, the German student who found a niche as a chaplain at Queen's before taking up a ministry in the English church. Yet it was undeniable that the theological tide had turned at the Restoration and Barlow increasingly found himself at odds with the new theological orthodoxies.

Barlow was distressed by any suggestion of a softening in the Church of England's implacable line against Roman Catholicism: he reacted badly to any hint of a concession to Catholic views on Lent or images or the real presence; above all he bitterly resented any questioning of the propositions that the pope was Antichrist and the Roman church was idolatrous. These two dogmas were, he claimed, to be found in the Church of England's homilies and (before its revision in 1662) in the liturgy for 5 November where 'Papists are call'd a Babylonish and Anti-Christian sect. And the Pope is call'd AntiChrist by all our old Divines, and the Question, An Papa sit Antichristus? Was ever held affirmative in both the Universities, till about the year 1628 or 1630'. Movement away from this position had been harmful: 'What benefit has accrued to our Religion or Church since we have been more kind to Rome I know not: but what damage both have sustained, all (who have eyes and will use them) may easily see' (MS marginalia, p. 306 of Peter Heylyn, *Cyprianus Anglicus*, 1668, Bodl. Oxf., N N 118 Th).

The other great shibboleth of the Church of England for Barlow was orthodox reformed theology. When Anglican authors presumptuously criticized the tenets of Calvinism, Barlow could barely contain his rage: in the margins of one attack on the Synod of Dort, he wrote, 'did not the Church of England, and all her obedient sons till 1626 or 1628 (both the universities) approve the doctrine of that synod?' (MS marginalia, p. 7 of John Goodman, *A Serious and Compassionate Inquiry*, 1674, Bodl. Oxf., 8° A 43 Linc). George Bull's *Harmonia apostolica* (1670), an attempt to reconcile St Paul on faith with St James on works, provoked a series of Latin lectures in the university from Professor Barlow between 1673 and 1676 in which he intermittently attacked Bull while comprehensively asserting an unmitigated belief in salvation by faith alone. Barlow also encouraged Thomas Tully of St Edmund Hall to reply to Bull in print and he is believed to have used his office as pro-vice-chancellor to question a fellow of All Souls for preaching Arminianism.

Bishop of Lincoln In the summer of 1675 Barlow gained the bishopric of Lincoln thanks to the lobbying of the two secretaries of state, Sir Joseph Williamson and Henry Coventry, both part of the network of Queen's men, and in the face of overt hostility from the ageing Archbishop Gilbert Sheldon. On 27 June Barlow was consecrated by Bishop George Morley of Winchester in the chapel at Ely House, Holborn, the palace of Bishop Peter Gunning of Ely, and 'after it, succeeded a magnificent feast, where were the Duke of Ormonde, Earl of Lauderdale, the Lord Treasurer, Lord Keeper etc' (Evelyn, 4.66–7). Although Sheldon and some other churchmen looked askance at Bishop Barlow, many contemporaries, such as John Evelyn, seem to have regarded this as a suitable climax to a career devoted to learning. Shortly after his consecration the new bishop wrote to Dean Honywood of Lincoln that he had 'seene and love the place, and like it as the fittest place of my abode … but for some reasons', he had to reside at the bishop's palace at Buckden, Huntingdonshire, 'till I can make better accommodation at Lincoln for my abode there' (Lincoln chapter muniments; quoted in *DNB*). In fact Barlow was slow to leave Oxford: he performed ordinations in the Queen's College chapel in 1677 and retained his archdeaconry of Oxford *in commendam* until 1677; Wood noted that in July 1678 Barlow had still not visited either Lincoln or Buckden. This omission eventually became a matter of public concern.

Barlow's episcopal responsibilities did not distract him from his constant concern to maintain orthodoxy. He was consulted by the earl of Anglesey about Hobbes's history of heresy and retorted with the fierce rebuttal of the tract and with professions of friendship for its author (1676). In the autumn of 1678 Bishop Barlow, like several other bishops, was prepared to vote with the country lords in pursuit of the truth about the Popish Plot and the nefarious activities of the Lord Treasurer, the earl of Danby. He was an enthusiastic proponent of the Test Act (1678) and was outraged by Bishop Gunning's denial in the House of Lords that the Church of Rome was idolatrous. In *Popery or, The Principles and Position of the Church of Rome Very Dangerous to All* (1678) and *Brutum fulmen* (1680), Barlow produced vitriolic attacks on the papacy and its pretensions, especially its claims to be able to depose princes, and thorough demonstrations that 'the pope is the great Antichrist, the man of sin, and the son of perdition'. In 1682 he answered the inquiry 'whether the Turk or pope be the greater antichrist' by affirming the latter, and in 1684 he once again proved that the pope was Antichrist in a letter to the earl of Anglesey. In 1683 he became embroiled in a dispute between the parishioners of Moulton in Lincolnshire and their minister Mr Tallents. The parishioners had whitewashed over the scripture sentences on the church walls and set up various images including pictures of St Paul above the royal arms, St Peter above the decalogue, and a dove symbolizing the Holy Ghost. Clearly finding this 'popish', Barlow sided with the incumbent and denounced both the new images and the erasure of the scripture texts as unlawful, but eventually lost the case in the court of arches in January 1685.

After 1681 the years of so-called tory reaction saw the weight of persecution shift from papists to protestant dissenters. Barlow was adamant that 'the execution of our laws (ecclesiastical and civil) against nonconformists' was not persecution (MS marginalia on title-page of Samuel Bolde, *A Sermon Against Persecution*, 1682, Bodl. Oxf., C 8 20 Linc). He had no compunction in instructing his diocesan clergy to publish the order of the Bedfordshire quarter sessions in 1684 that the laws against nonconformists be enforced to the letter. Perhaps coincidentally, in May 1684 Barlow wrote at length to Archbishop William Sancroft to defend himself against the calumny that he favoured presbyterians or dissenters (Bodl. Oxf., MS Tanner 32, fol. 54).

The bishop and the politics of 1685 to 1691 Barlow joined with the Church of England in welcoming the accession of James II, preferring to trust the king's promises for the security of the protestant church than contemplate any breach of loyalty. He was, after all, a convinced believer in the supremacy of the king in ecclesiastical affairs. Barlow himself was under a cloud because of his continuing failure to visit his diocese. In 1686 Archbishop Sancroft ordered a metropolitical visitation of the diocese of Lincoln by Bishop Thomas White of Peterborough. White was to concentrate on such matters as the state of the churches and to hold confirmations. Barlow dutifully accepted the primate's decision, but defensively claimed that his accusers were motivated by dislike of his adherence to the doctrine and religion of the Church of England. In response to the chiding of the marquess of Halifax, Barlow offered an elaborate apology, citing the example of his predecessors, his own age and infirmities, and the convenient location of Buckden, but he also promised that as soon as God gave him the ability he would visit Lincoln. A very similar letter to Sancroft dated 27 October 1686 also heaped abuse on Archdeacon Cawley of Lincoln, who had published an attack on his absentee bishop (Bodl. Oxf., MS Tanner 30, fol. 131).

Ageing, defensive, and out of sympathy with the tenor of his times, Barlow must have found the reign of James II difficult. He sought to balance his duty of obedience to his sovereign with the defence of the protestant Church of England. He did not believe that others in the Church of England were as devoted to its protestant heritage. He later claimed that Sancroft and his circle would not license his discussion of popish idolatry in his tract *Reasons why a Protestant should not Turn Papist*: 'a fifth reason concerning the gross idolatry of the Church of Rome in the adoration of the cross and eucharist' did not appear because 'my lord of Cant[erbury] and his chaplaine Dr Batterly refus'd to licence anno 1687, when the reste was licenc'd' (Queen's College, MS 215). His own loyalty was tested by the 1687 declaration of indulgence. He was one of the four bishops who did thank the king for the declaration's safeguards for the Church of England, and he got 600 of his clergy to sign an address of thanks. A letter defending his stance was later published in his *Genuine Remains*. Barlow sent James's second declaration to his clergy, but a circumspect letter to one of his clergy dated 29 May 1688 reveals the casuistical method at work. The same authority that requires the bishop to disseminate copies of the declaration requires the clergy to read them, explains Barlow: 'but whether you should, or should not read them, is a question of that difficulty, in the circumstance we now are, that you can't expect that I should so hastily answer it'. He observes that the London clergy had generally refused, yet he would not seek to persuade or dissuade:

> but leave it to your prudence and conscience, whether you will or will not read it; only this I shall advise, that, after serious consideration, you find that you cannot read it, but *reluctante vel dubitante conscientia*, in that case, to read it will be your sin, and you to blame for doing it. (Stoughton, 4. 147)

Any seventeenth-century clergyman would recognize the careful casuistry of this letter, its respect for the inviolable individual conscience, and its assertion that any doubt renders an action unconscionable.

So avowed an anti-papist as Barlow was easily able to accommodate himself to the providential removal of James II by his protestant nephew William. He voted for the notion that James had abdicated and the throne was vacant; he took the oaths of allegiance to William and Mary; and he was happy to replace those of his clergy who lost their livings for their refusal to take the new oaths. The Toleration Act was a much less welcome consequence of the revolution for Barlow. It was 'against the expresse law of God, of nature, and all' to grant freedom to those who had 'ruin'd church and state, and murder'd their kinge' (*Hist. U. Oxf.* 4: *17th-cent. Oxf.*, 884).

Barlow died unmarried at Buckden on 8 October 1691. At the last 'he did commend his soul unto God and his body to the earth to be decently interred and without pompe, having his coffin covered with a black cloth instead of a pall' (Bodl. Oxf., MS Eng. C 3190). He was buried as he requested in the same grave as a predecessor, Bishop William Barlow (*d.* 1613), in the chancel of the parish church.

Reputation Thomas Barlow's reputation as a timeserver is unfortunate and undeserved. He has been the victim of Anthony Wood's hostility, but also of his own longevity, reluctance to publish, and refusal to move with the theological times. Although hindsight can isolate certain aberrations, Barlow's principles were remarkably consistent across a very long lifetime: he was a believer in the authority of the monarch, a staunch anti-papist, and a full-blown Calvinist. His royalism was evident in the 1640s and did not subsequently waver despite the strains imposed by the rule of James II. Barlow steadfastly refused to change his mind about the Church of Rome even as all about him seemed to: he was convinced that the Church of Rome was formally idolatrous and therefore fundamentally in error. He clung, too, to his conviction that the pope was Antichrist as, he claimed, the majority of English divines had maintained from the Reformation to the end of James I's reign. Calvinism was the sheet anchor of his Christianity. He never ceased to teach the fundamental truths of justification by faith alone, absolute double decree predestination, the irresistibility of grace, and the perseverance of the saints. He repeatedly claimed that he stood fast by the Church of England while others deviated or innovated; but he also traced all the ills of the church to that one moment in the late 1620s when William Laud and his acolytes, including the young Gilbert Sheldon, betrayed the fundamentals of the Calvinist orthodoxy of the English church. In many ways he was fighting the battles of the 1620s and 1630s all his life. Not only did Barlow believe that he was a standing reproach to those who shifted with the times, but other sober serious individuals also seem to have been convinced of his integrity. Robert Boyle trusted him and consulted him in cases of conscience; Edward Harley and the earl of Anglesey valued his advice; and Bishop George Morley remained a friend.

Thomas Barlow's significance is manifold. He was an archetypal Calvinist clergyman of the Jacobean kind who survived long after his values and theology had ceased to be fashionable within the Church of England. One value that he did transmit to a later generation was antipopery. But Barlow's career and life also represent the interaction of university, church, and politics which was such a feature of seventeenth-century England. His was an academic cast of mind, hungry for books and controversy, caring of his pupils and surprisingly cordial in person towards those whose beliefs he detested. He was at the heart of an Oxford-centred network which was deeply influential in the administration and politics of Restoration England. A survivor, rather than a 'trimmer', who demonstrates the complexity of intellectual affiliations in seventeenth-century England, Barlow left a legacy which also includes the library he left to the Bodleian, the copious annotations in many of those books, and his manuscripts at the Queen's College. His friend and admirer, the earl of Anglesey, should have the last word:

> I never think of this bishop nor of his incomparable knowledge both in theology and church history and in the ecclesiastical law without applying to him in my thoughts the character that Cicero gave Crassus: *non unus e multis, sed unus inter omnes prope singularis*['not one among many but virtually unique']. (*Memoirs of … Anglesey*, 20)

JOHN SPURR

Sources Bodl. Oxf., MSS Tanner; MS Eng. lett. C. 328; MS Eng. C. 3190 • Queen's College, Oxford, Barlow MSS • BL, Harley MSS 3784–3785, 6942, 7377 • *The genuine remains of Dr Thomas Barlow* (1693) • *The works of Robert Sanderson*, ed. W. Jacobson, 6 vols. (1854) • *The correspondence of Thomas Hobbes*, ed. N. Malcolm, 2 vols. (1994) • *Memoirs of the right honourable Arthur, earl of Anglesey*, ed. P. Pett (1693) • M. Burrows, ed., *The register of the visitors of the University of Oxford, from AD 1647 to AD 1658*, CS, new ser., 29 (1881) • N. Pocock, ed., 'Illustrations of the state of the church during the great rebellion', *The Theologian and Ecclesiastic*, 6–15 (1848–54) • J. Stoughton, *The history of religion in Ireland*, revised edn, 6 vols. (1881) • R. S. Bosher, *The making of the Restoration settlement: the influence of the Laudians, 1649–1662*, rev. edn (1957) • R. Nelson, *The life of Dr George Bull* (1713) • M. Goldie, 'Danby, the bishops, and the whigs', *The politics of religion in Restoration England*, ed. T. Harris, P. Seaward, and M. Goldie (1990), 75–106 • I. M. Green, *The re-establishment of the Church of England, 1660–1663* (1978) • J. R. Jacob, *Henry Stubbe, radical protestantism and the early Enlightenment* (1983) • J. W. Packer, *The transformation of Anglicanism, 1643–1660, with special reference to Henry Hammond* (1969) • P. Seaward, *The Cavalier Parliament and the reconstruction of the old regime, 1661–1667* (1989) • N. Sykes, *From Sheldon to Secker: aspects of English church history, 1660–1768* (1959) • J. Spurr, *The Restoration Church of England, 1646–1689* (1991) • Pepys, *Diary* • M. Goldie, 'Sir Peter Pett, sceptical toryism and the science of toleration in the 1680s', *Persecution and toleration*, ed. W. J. Sheils, SCH, 21 (1984), 247–74 • *Calendar of the correspondence of Richard Baxter*, ed. N. H. Keeble and G. F. Nuttall, 2 vols. (1991) • *Calamy rev.* • *Walker rev.* • *Hist. U. Oxf.* 4: *17th-cent. Oxf.* • *The life and times of Anthony Wood*, ed. A. Clark, 5 vols., OHS, 19, 21, 26, 30, 40 (1891–1900) • Wood, *Ath. Oxon.*, new edn, 4.333–41 • Wood, *Ath. Oxon.: Fasti*, new edn • Foster, *Alum. Oxon.* • W. Kennett, *A register and chronicle ecclesiastical and civil* (1728) • *Fasti Angl.* (Hardy) • Evelyn, *Diary*

Archives Bodl. Oxf., corresp. and MSS • Inner Temple, London, letters • Queen's College, Oxford, notes | Bodl. Oxf., corresp. with Sancroft, etc.

Likenesses oils, *c.*1672–1675, Bodl. Oxf. [*see illus.*] • D. Loggan, line engraving, BM, NPG • R. White, line engraving (after Henne), BM, NPG; repro. in T. Barlow, *Several miscellaneous and weighty cases of conscience* (1692) • oils, Queen's College, Oxford

Barlow, Thomas (*c.*1669–1730), builder and estate surveyor, played a significant part in the expansion of the

West End of London which took place in the first three decades of the eighteenth century. Nothing is known about his origins and early life. In a deposition sworn in April 1721 he gave his age as about fifty-two, which would suggest that he was born in the late 1660s, and he was probably the Thomas Barlow who married Ann Kinsey at St Giles Cripplegate on 18 November 1689. His first wife's name was certainly Ann, and by the late 1690s they were living in Maiden Lane, Covent Garden, where they had numerous children, only one of whom, a son, Richard, born in 1709, survived infancy. Ann Barlow died in 1713, and on 14 August 1715 at St Martin-in-the-Fields Barlow married Bridget Scarlett as his second wife.

Barlow worked as a carpenter in Covent Garden, undertaking substantial repairs to the roof of St Paul's Church in 1714–15 and erecting a flagpole in the piazza to celebrate the accession of George I in 1714. He played a prominent part in the life of the parish, acting as churchwarden in 1712–14. He also undertook speculative house building, both in Covent Garden and elsewhere. In 1701 he was building in Albemarle Street, and shortly afterwards erected a large house in New Bond Street for the duke of Grafton. He built other houses in this area, including one in New Bond Street in which he and his second wife lived after moving from Maiden Lane. Barlow Place, off Bruton Street, is named after him. He was also building in Queen Square, Holborn, in 1709–11.

In 1715 Barlow appeared in a new capacity as agent for Lord Scarbrough, the landowner, in negotiations over the site of the future church of St George, Hanover Square. He may thus have been responsible for the layout of the Hanover Square area. He undoubtedly built several of the large, Germanic style houses in Hanover Square and St George Street. Letters from him about the fitting out of one of the latter for its first occupant, Earl Cowper, are preserved in the Hertfordshire Record Office (Herts. ALS).

On 10 August 1720 Barlow, who had by then a well-established reputation as a master builder, was given his most important commission when Sir Richard Grosvenor appointed him to oversee the development of his family's hundred-acre estate in Mayfair. The work was to be carried out according to 'a Scheme or Plann of the Said Intended Building … Drawn by the said Barlow' (Grosvenor archives, Eaton Hall, fourth baronet's personal MSS). With such a large area at his disposal Barlow could plan on a lavish scale, and his grid of wide, straight streets centred on Grosvenor Square, which itself covers some 8 acres and is the largest square in London apart from Lincoln's Inn Fields, is an outstanding example of early Georgian town planning.

Barlow took a long lease of a large area in the south-east corner of the estate, doubtless to encourage other builders to follow suit, and erected the first building on the estate, the Mount Coffee House in Grosvenor Street (now demolished), where much of his business was apparently conducted. In general, however, he built little on the estate, concentrating instead on his duties as estate surveyor in drawing up building agreements and arranging for leases to be granted to other builders.

Barlow was one of the founder directors of the Westminster Fire Office, a commissioner of sewers for Westminster, and one of the initial members of the select vestry of the new parish of St George, Hanover Square. When he died on 17 January 1730 he was described as 'a very noted Master-Builder' (*Daily Post*, 22 Jan 1730). His funeral took place on 21 January at St Paul's, Covent Garden, where his first wife and several of his children were buried. He was said to have left a leasehold estate worth £600 per annum in ground rents, £500 in improved rents, and £400 in rack rents, besides a personal estate of upwards of £1000. His widow, Bridget, died in 1733, and his son, Richard, in 1740, 'haveing greatly wasted and outrun his fortune' (PRO, C12/2201/2). VICTOR BELCHER

Sources F. H. W. Sheppard, ed., *The Grosvenor estate in Mayfair*, 2 vols., Survey of London, 39–40 (1977–80) • B. H. Johnson, 'On the early development of the sites of the buildings in Hanover Square and St George Street, Westminster', English Heritage, Survey of London [typescript] • W. H. Hunt, ed., *The registers of St Paul's Church, Covent Garden, London*, 1–4, Harleian Society, register section, 33–6 (1906–8) • will, PRO, PROB 11/635, q. 26 • Chancery case: Barlow v. Hodson, PRO, C12/2201/2 • Herts. ALS, Panshanger MSS, D/EP/T4209–4228J • Grosvenor estate records, City Westm. AC • Grosvenor family archives, Eaton Hall, Cheshire • *IGI* • *Daily Post* [London] (22 Jan 1730) • Middlesex deeds register, 1730, LMA, vol. 2, no. 145
Archives Herts. ALS, Panshanger MSS, letters, D/EP/T4209–4228J
Wealth at death £1500 p.a. leasehold estate; also more than £1000 personal estate: Chancery suit, PRO, C12/2201/2

Barlow, Sir Thomas, first baronet (1845–1945), physician, was born at Brantwood Fold, Edgworth, near Bolton, Lancashire, on 4 September 1845; he was the eldest of seven children of James Barlow (1821–1887) of Greenthorne, Edgworth, who established the cotton mills of Barlow and Jones at Edgworth and Bolton, and his wife, Alice (*d.* 1888), daughter of James Barnes, also of Edgworth. Barlow's early scientific interests led to thoughts of a medical career despite his father's wish that he join the family business. After four years at Owens College, Manchester, where he read natural sciences, Barlow graduated BSc (London) in 1867. There was, however, no good clinical training available in Manchester at that time, and the following year he entered University College, London, as a medical student. Having qualified in 1870 he was appointed house physician to Sir William Jenner at University College Hospital. Jenner's rigorous clinical method, particularly regarding post-mortem examination, was an important influence on Barlow's development as a clinician and medical researcher. He passed his second MB and BS in 1873, both with first-class honours, and was awarded his MD the following year.

In 1874 Barlow was appointed medical registrar at the Hospital for Sick Children, Great Ormond Street, London, and was elected assistant physician the following year. In 1885 he was promoted full physician, from which position he retired in 1899. He was also, successively, assistant physician at Charing Cross Hospital (1875–7) and of the London Hospital (1877–80) before returning to University College Hospital in 1880 as assistant physician; there he served as full physician from 1885 until his retirement in 1910, when he became consulting physician. He held the

Sir Thomas Barlow, first baronet (1845–1945), by Catharine Dodgson, 1936

Holme chair of clinical medicine from 1895 to 1907. He was also, from 1884 to 1888, on the staff of the London Fever Hospital.

On 30 December 1880 Barlow married Ada Helen (1843–1928), daughter of Patrick Dalmahoy, writer to the signet, of Edinburgh. She was a former ward sister at the Great Ormond Street Hospital; they had three sons and two daughters, the younger of whom died in infancy. The eldest son was Sir (James) Alan Noel *Barlow (1881–1968); the second was Sir Thomas Dalmahoy *Barlow (1883–1964); and the third, Patrick Basil (1884–1917), died on the western front during the First World War.

Barlow is best known for his original researches on scurvy in infants and young children. Although the disease in infants had been described by Francis Glisson in the seventeenth century, its subsequent decline in Britain led to some confusion among clinicians confronted by an increasing number of cases of rickets in the second half of the nineteenth century. The increase was associated with the adoption of artificial infant feeds, especially among the middle classes. Until Barlow's research was published the pseudo-scorbutic symptoms in such cases were generally viewed as conditions of acute rickets. Barlow's isolation of scurvy from rickets as a definite and separate disease—although often concomitant in the same child—was a triumph of deductive reasoning; outside the British Isles infantile scurvy is still commonly termed Barlow's disease. In March 1883 Barlow published his first findings on infantile scurvy, and its post-mortem appearances in three fatal cases, in a paper entitled 'On cases described as "acute rickets" … the scurvy being an essential and the rickets a variable element', which appeared in *Medico-Chirurgical Transactions*. For his Bradshaw lecture of 1894, entitled 'Infantile scurvy and its relation to rickets', Barlow added thirty-three more cases from his own personal experience.

In other diseases of children Barlow also made major contributions, notably in the study of meningitis and rheumatic illness. In 1878, in association with S. J. Gee, he published an article 'Cervical opisthotonos of infants' in *St Bartholomew's Hospital Reports* (vol. 14), which was an important contribution to the differentiation of tuberculous from simple meningitis; an account of the former was included in volume 7 of T. C. Allbutt's *System of Medicine* (1899, vol. 7). In volume 7 Barlow also published, with D. B. Lees, 'Simple meningitis in children', which elaborated further the distinction between forms of the disease. In 1881, with Francis Warner, Barlow presented to the International Medical Congress a paper on the subcutaneous tendinous nodules associated with acute rheumatism in children, establishing their relation to cardiac disease (published in *Transactions of the International Congress of Medicine, London, 1881*, 4.116–28). 'Rheumatism and its allies in childhood' was printed in the *British Medical Journal* (1883, 2.509–14). Barlow's other research interests were mainly in the neurological area. He translated Maurice Raynaud's papers 'Local asphyxia' and 'Symmetrical gangrene of the extremities' from the French, and published a number of cases of the condition known as Raynaud's disease. He contributed an article on the latter to volume 6 of Allbutt's *System of Medicine*, together with another on erythromelalgia, a related condition mainly affecting the feet. In 1906 Barlow addressed the Neurological Society, of which he was president, on nervous complications of acute febrile diseases, his paper later appearing in *Brain* (23.303–31).

Most of Barlow's important research was accomplished by the age of forty. After the mid-1880s his attention was increasingly focused on private practice. Resident first in Bloomsbury and, from 1887, at 10 Wimpole Street, he ministered to an ever more elevated circle of private patients, including the dukes of Grafton and Rutland, lords Selborne and Salisbury, and Randall Davidson, archbishop of Canterbury. In 1896 he was appointed physician to the royal household and, from 1899 to 1901, he was physician-extraordinary to Queen Victoria, being present at her deathbed. He continued to hold court appointments under Edward VII and also under George V. In 1901 he was created a baronet and, later the same year, was appointed KCVO.

Barlow's Wesleyan upbringing influenced his whole life. Until middle age he was an active Methodist, and at King's Cross chapel he was a leader in the weekly Bible class; later he attended Church of England services. He was a lifelong teetotaller and, from 1923 to 1930, he was president of the National Temperance League. Barlow's later life was laden with honours. He was elected FRS in 1909 and president of the Royal College of Physicians the following year, serving until 1914. In 1913 he presided at the Seventeenth International Medical Congress, held in

London. In retirement Barlow spent more time at his country home, Boswells, near Wendover in Buckinghamshire. He continued to travel, at home and abroad, accompanied by his surviving daughter, Helen (1887–1975), who never married. He died at 10 Wimpole Street on 12 January 1945, aged ninety-nine.

Barlow was short and stout, with a carefully trimmed beard, and he always wore spectacles. Throughout his life he retained traces of a Lancashire accent. His avuncular appearance matched his character, which was modest and humane. RICHARD ASPIN

Sources H. Barlow and A. Barlow, eds., *Sir Thomas Barlow, bt.* (1965) • R. K. Aspin, 'The papers of Sir Thomas Barlow', *Medical History*, 37 (1993), 333–40 • R. J. Godlee, 'Sir Thomas Barlow, Bart., F.R.S.', *University College Hospital Magazine*, 1 (1910), 1–6 • A. Barlow, 'Sir Thomas Barlow, 1845–1945', *Great Ormond Street Hospital Journal*, 10 (1955–6), 59–65 • K. J. Carpenter, *The history of scurvy and vitamin C* (1986) • E. M. R. Lomax, *Small and special: the development of hospitals for children in Victorian Britain* (1996) • Munk, *Roll* • *The Times* (15 Jan 1945) • *Manchester Guardian* (16 Jan 1945) • *BMJ* (20 Jan 1945), 99–100 • *The Lancet* (27 Jan 1945) • *National Temperance Quarterly* [supplement] (Jan 1945) • *University College Hospital Magazine* (March–April 1945) • T. R. Elliot, *Obits. FRS*, 5 (1945–8), 159–67 • *CGPLA Eng. & Wales* (1945)

Archives Great Ormond Street Hospital for Sick Children, London • Wellcome L., personal and professional corresp. and papers

Likenesses photograph, *c.*1900, University College Library • W. Stoneman, photograph, 1923, NPG • O. Birley, oils, *c.*1935, University College Medical School, London • C. Dodgson, chalk drawing, 1936, Athenaeum, London [*see illus.*] • C. Dodgson, chalk drawing, 1936, RCP Lond. • H. Salomon, oils, 1960, Wellcome L. • Spy [L. Ward], caricature, NPG; repro. in *VF* (12 April 1906)

Wealth at death £231,878 14*s.* 5*d.*: probate, 5 May 1945, *CGPLA Eng. & Wales*

Barlow, Sir Thomas [Tommy] **Dalmahoy** (1883–1964), industrialist and banker, was born in London on 23 February 1883, the second son in the family of three sons and two daughters of Sir Thomas *Barlow (1845–1945), physician-extraordinary to Queen Victoria and kings Edward VII and George V, and his wife, Ada Helen (1843–1928), daughter of Patrick Dalmahoy, writer to the signet, of Edinburgh. Thomas's elder brother was Sir (James) Alan Noel *Barlow (1881–1968).

Thomas was educated at Marlborough College (1897–1900) and Trinity College, Cambridge, and then entered the century-old family textile business, Barlow and Jones Ltd, of Bolton and Manchester, where he became one of the most prominent figures in the cotton-spinning and weaving industry. In 1911 he married Esther Sophia (*d.* 1956), daughter of Henry Gaselee, barrister-at-law; they had one son and two daughters. He also became a distinguished banker, joining the board of the District Bank in 1922 and becoming its chairman in 1947.

The interests of Lancashire industry were close to Barlow's heart. He became chairman of the Lancashire Industrial Development Council, and from 1931 to 1933 was president of the Manchester chamber of commerce. This experience fitted him for the wartime post of director-general of civilian clothing, which he held from 1941 to 1945. Shortly after the outbreak of war he went to work at

Sir Thomas Dalmahoy Barlow (1883–1964), by Walter Stoneman, 1934

the Board of Trade when Sir Cecil Weir and Alix Kilroy (later Meynell) were setting up the control of factory and storage premises. Their work involved closing factories not required by the war effort or for essential civilian production, thus releasing both employees for essential work and premises, which could be used for the replacement of factories which had been bombed. Such buildings could also be used for storage, particularly of American materials sent to Britain before the United States entered the war. Barlow was controller of factory premises, and indeed cleared one of his own factories of spinning and weaving machinery. As director-general of civilian clothing, Barlow had to cope with thousands of small businesses. Despite his outspoken and forthright manner and his vigorously held opinions, Barlow won the affection and co-operation of these businesses. Having gained their confidence, he was able to control them with a firm hand. He was an unassuming and courteous man, of great integrity and transparent honesty, with the strongest sense of public service. If he found in wartime that not everyone lived up to his high standards, he had no hesitation in telling them so, whoever they might be.

Barlow cannot have relished spending the whole week in London, but he had a strong sense of duty and must have known that he was at the top of a very short list of people who could do this job. Perhaps what finally decided him to accept was the thought that he would be able to wear his oldest clothes in London, thus demonstrating publicly his resolve not to buy a new suit until the end of the war. For among his many remarkable qualities masochism held an honoured place. He was known to catch a late, slow train, in order to avoid a public dinner in Manchester or a cocktail party in London. People were apt to wonder at his dislike of the latter curious form of entertaining which, it was argued, was entirely suited to his temperament, but was certainly not to his taste. For he was an excellent judge of food and wine, especially Moselle, and liked to invite a couple of friends to a small dinner at his house at Strand on the Green, Chiswick. He would carefully choose a simple dinner to match the qualities of the wines, on which his running commentary was an education. Perhaps, if the next morning were Saturday, he would catch a train to Manchester, where his wife had promised to meet him and escort him to a British restaurant, just completed in a disused factory. She was a great public worker and felt it was essential for him, a well-known personality, not only to visit such an institution, but to be seen to lunch there and, if possible, enjoy the novel experience.

Despite his robust views, Barlow was tolerant of those who disagreed with him. From disagreement there often developed respect and friendship. His annual statements to the District Bank shareholders, until his retirement in 1960, had the typical Barlow stamp of outspoken practicality, sound industrial and trade experience, and an understanding of financial affairs. His financial knowledge led him to be appointed a member of the Capital Issues Committee in post-war years.

Barlow's practical knowledge went hand in hand with artistic appreciation. He was a member of the Council for the Encouragement of Art in Industry. It was natural that Tommy Barlow, as he was known to everyone, should be called in for the preliminary discussions of the project to establish its successor, the council of industrial design, and that he should emerge as the chairman. In the early days of the council his valuable, down-to-earth comments were accepted by the well-known manufacturers who were invited to sit on the council but had not the advantage of his wide interests. It was certainly unfortunate that in 1947 he was reluctantly forced to give up the chairmanship on the strong advice of his doctors to avoid so much travelling. It was typical of him that almost immediately he took on the chairmanship of the District Bank in Manchester where, as a consolation, he was known to walk about with a book of Greek poems in his pocket. With his deep interest in the arts and his rare wish to influence his great textile business, he had started up before the war a small subsidiary, Helios, inside Barlow and Jones, to produce the finest individual weaving, and for this purpose had appointed a distinguished Swiss designer, Marianne Straub. Barlow also became a member of the council of the Royal College of Art.

Barlow's interest in beautiful things originated in his youth. He became a successful collector of early books and manuscripts, and gathered, over a period of forty years, a fine collection of Dürer woodcuts, engravings, and illustrated books. This collection was sold in 1956 to the National Gallery of Victoria, in Melbourne, to which Barlow had previously given important items. Barlow also lent pictures to the Art Treasures Centenary Exhibition (1957) of the Manchester City Art Gallery, of which he was for some years chairman of the council. He was created KBE in 1934 and GBE in 1946. Barlow died at his London home, 49, Strand on the Green, Chiswick, on 22 November 1964, from bronchial pneumonia.

GORDON RUSSELL, *rev.*

Sources *The Times* (24 Nov 1964), 14e · *The Times* (27 Nov 1964), 16d · *The Times* (8 Dec 1964), 14b · *The Times* (12 Dec 1964), 10c · personal knowledge (1981) · d. cert. · *CGPLA Eng. & Wales* (1965)
Archives Wellcome L., corresp. with members of his family
Likenesses W. Stoneman, photograph, 1934, NPG [*see illus.*] · portrait, repro. in *The Times* (24 Nov 1964)
Wealth at death £69,505: probate, 5 May 1965, *CGPLA Eng. & Wales*

Barlow, Thomas Oldham (1824–1889), engraver and etcher, was born on 4 August 1824 in Oldham, Lancashire, and baptized there at St Mary's Church on 8 August, the youngest child of Henry Barlow (1781–1851), an ironmonger, and his wife, Sarah Oldham (1783–1836), who lived in the High Street. Having attended the town's old grammar school, he was articled in 1839 to Messrs Stephenson and Royston, an engraving firm in Manchester, and received further training at the newly established Manchester School of Design. In 1846 he won a prize of 5 guineas offered for an original design for a muslin print: his drawing was entitled *Cullings from Nature*. That same year he settled in London, and in 1847 was living in Ebury Street. By 1851 he had moved to 9 Camden Square, and from 1873 he resided at Auburn Lodge, Victoria Road, Kensington. He married Ellen (1821–1908), the daughter of James Cocks of Oldham, on 25 August 1851, and they had two daughters, Lucy Jane and Mary Anna; their three sons died as infants. Barlow enjoyed a happy family life, spending his spare time travelling (especially in France and Germany), collecting porcelain and paintings, and joining in family outings (often to musical concerts).

Barlow's first independent work was a line engraving, *Courtship* (1848), after a painting by John Phillip. The two men became extremely close friends, despite the fact that, through ill health, Phillip spent much time in Spain. Barlow became best known for his reproductions of Phillip's paintings, especially those with a Spanish theme, including *Doña Pepita* (exh. RA, 1858) and *La gloria* (exh. RA, 1877). He also reproduced some of Phillip's other work: his history scenes, such as *The House of Commons* (1860; exh. RA, 1866); genre scenes, for instance *A Highland Breakfast* (exh. RA, 1879, as *Breakfast in the Highlands*); and portraits, notably exhibiting in 1859 a full length portrait of the prince consort in highland dress (1858; Aberdeen Town House), which Phillip had been commissioned to paint for the city of Aberdeen. In addition he assisted in the organization of a show of Phillip's work at the London International Exhibition of 1873, by lending pictures (including one of himself of 1856) and writing a catalogue. (He rendered a similar service to Thomas Creswick on the same occasion.) When Phillip died in 1867 Barlow acted as his executor.

Another artist whose work Barlow helped to popularize was John Everett Millais. Recognizing Millais's youthful talent, Barlow engraved *The Huguenot* (1856), and thereafter reproduced some of Millais's genre scenes, for instance *Awake* and *Sleeping* (exh. RA, 1868 and 1869 respectively), and portraits of public figures (painted for Messrs Agnew), including W. E. Gladstone, J. H. Newman, and Alfred Tennyson. Millais twice portrayed Barlow: once in the painting entitled *A Ruling Passion* (exh. RA, 1885; Glasgow Art Gallery and Museum), when Barlow acted as a model for the figure of the celebrated ornithologist John Gould (1804–1881); and once in a straightforward portrait, which shows Barlow bearded and bespectacled (exh. RA, 1886; Oldham Art Gallery and Museum).

Barlow also devoted energy to the reproduction of J. M. W. Turner's paintings. In 1856 Barlow engraved *The Wreck of the Minotaur* and *The Vintage at Macon*, both of which the earl of Yarborough had lent to the Art Treasures Exhibition. The proceeds from the sale of these engravings benefited the Artists' General Benevolent Institution. At the time of his death, Barlow was working on a mezzotint version of *The Vintage at Macon*; this was published in 1890 (exh. RA, 1890).

Barlow reproduced the works of other artists, among them animal scenes after R. Ansdell and E. Landseer and portraits by J. Sant, P. Westcott, and J. P. Knight. Although he produced few engravings specifically for books, some of his engravings did appear as book illustrations, for instance in Benet Woodcroft's *A Series of Portraits of Inventors* (1862) and in Tennyson's *Vivien* (1868), the latter with designs by Gustav Doré. By 1894 he had registered more than fifty plates at the Printsellers' Association, all published by such leading firms as H. Graves and T. Agnew. Often Barlow exhibited his engravings: the first one was *The Wanderer*, which he showed at the gallery of the Society of British Artists in 1849; thereafter he exhibited exclusively at the Royal Academy. His début was in 1851 with a drawing of *Highland Bridge*, and by 1890 he had shown more than forty engravings there. The high quality of his work was duly recognized by the academy. On 28 January 1873 he was elected an associate engraver; three years later he became an associate of the Royal Academy, and finally, on 5 May 1881, when Samuel Cousins retired, he was elected Royal Academician—only the fourth engraver to have been so honoured. His diploma picture was *Prayer in Spain* (exh. RA, 1873), after Phillip. Other public bodies recognized his talents as well: in 1873 he was elected an honorary member of the Manchester Academy of Fine Arts; he was a member (and long-standing secretary) of the Etching Club, and by invitation of the art department he was appointed, shortly before Richard James Lane's death in 1872, director of the etching class at South Kensington. He worked generally in a mixed manner, in the tradition of Samuel Cousins, a technique which was being increasingly abandoned in his day. A contemporary remarked that his 'perceptions of the value of colour and line were as exquisite as they were strong and exact' (*The Athenaeum*, 901–2). Barlow died at his home, Auburn Lodge, on Christmas eve 1889, after a short illness, and was buried in Brompton cemetery. A sale of his engravings took place at Christies on 24 March 1890. Proof impressions of Barlow's prints are in the Victoria and Albert Museum. SUSANNA AVERY-QUASH

Sources H. Thornber, 'Memoir of Thomas Oldham Barlow, R.A. and a catalogue of his engravings', *Manchester Quarterly*, 10 (April 1891), 131–41 • *The Athenaeum* (28 Dec 1889), 901–2 • *Art Journal*, new ser., 10 (1890), 94–5 • *ILN* (4 Jan 1890) • *The Times* (28 Dec 1889) • *ILN* (22 Feb 1890), 252 • *ILN* (15 Feb 1873), 157–8 • G. W. Friend, ed., *An alphabetical list of engravings declared at the office of the Printsellers' Association, London*, 2 vols. (1892) • *Engraved Brit. ports.* • Graves, *RA exhibitors* • R. K. Engen, *Dictionary of Victorian engravers, print publishers and their works* (1979) • *DNB* • Bryan, *Painters* (1903–5) • J. H. Slater, *Engravings and their value*, rev. F. W. Maxwell-Barbour, 6th edn (1929), 124 • Thieme & Becker, *Allgemeines Lexikon* • *CGPLA Eng. & Wales* (1890) • *IGI* • Barlow diaries and notebooks, V&A

Archives NL Ire., collection of material relating to him • Princeton University, New Jersey, corresp. • V&A NAL, diaries and notebooks

Likenesses J. Phillip, oils, 1856 • D. W. Wynfield, photographs, *c.*1862–1864, NPG • W. W. Ouless, oils, 1882, Aberdeen Art Gallery • J. Millais, oils, exh. RA 1886, Oldham Art Gallery and Museum; repro. in *Manchester Quarterly* (1886) • R. W. Robinson, photograph, *c.*1891, NPG; repro. in *Members and associates of the Royal Academy of Arts, 1891* (1891) • Elliott & Fry, photograph, repro. in *ILN* (15 Feb 1873) • A. F. Mackenzie, photograph, repro. in M. B. Huish, *The year's art* (1888) • photograph, repro. in F. G. Stephens, ed., *Artists at home* (1884) • various photographs, V&A, Barlow MSS • woodcut, BM

Wealth at death £14,942 16*s.* 6*d.*: resworn probate, Nov 1890, *CGPLA Eng. & Wales*

Barlow, Thomas Worthington (1824–1856), antiquary and naturalist, was born in Cheshire on 9 February 1824, the only son of William Worthington Barlow (1782–1846), a surgeon of Cranage, Cheshire, and his wife, Lucy, daughter of the Revd Thomas Hodges, vicar of Bromfield, Shropshire. Educated for the legal profession, he became a member of Gray's Inn in May 1843, and was called to the bar on 14 June 1848. In April 1848 he was elected a fellow of the Linnean Society, and he was also an early member of the Wernerian Club. He afterwards lived at Manchester, where he practised as a special pleader and conveyancer. On 24 November 1846 he married Hannah, daughter of William Green Kearsley of Manchester. They had two sons.

In 1853 Barlow started an antiquarian miscellany, the *Cheshire and Lancashire Historical Collector*, which ran until August 1855. He also wrote several works of history and natural history, including *Cheshire: its Historical and Literary Associations* (1852), a *Sketch of the History of the Church at Holmes Chapel, Cheshire* (1853), and *A Chart of British Ornithology* (1847).

In April 1856 Barlow was appointed queen's advocate for Sierra Leone, but less than four months after arriving in the colony he died at Freetown on 10 August 1856, aged thirty-two.

GORDON GOODWIN, *rev.* SIMON HARRISON

Sources *GM*, 3rd ser., 1 (1856), 656 • Boase, *Mod. Eng. biog.* • T. W. Barlow, 'Notes illustrative of the history of the chapelry of Holmes Chapel, my native place', Ches. & Chester ALSS, D4486/1
Archives Ches. & Chester ALSS

Barlow, William (*d.* 1568), bishop of Chichester, was probably the second son of John Barlow and his wife, Christian, daughter and heir of Henry Barley of Albury, Hertfordshire, and a descendant of the Essex–Hertfordshire branch of the landed family of Barlow, deprived of its possessions after being involved in Perkin Warbeck's revolt of 1497. He had a cousin, also William, who studied law at Cambridge and became archdeacon of Northampton. Barlow himself became an Augustinian canon at St Osyth's, Essex, and at Oxford, where he probably graduated DTh. After being a canon at Bicknacre, then Blackmore, and later prior of Tiptree (1509) and Little Leighs (1515–24), he became rector of Great Cressingham (1525) and prior of Bromehill (1525) until its dissolution by Wolsey in 1528, for which he received compensation of 40s.

Barlow's career from 1528 to 1534 is obscure. He is possibly to be identified with Friar Jerome Barlow, author of *The Burial of the Mass, a Dialogue between the Gentleman and the Husbandman*, and other anti-papist pamphlets prohibited by the bishops. The author of these recanted and published *A Dialogue … of these Lutheran Factions and many of their Abuses*, an anti-Lutheran pamphlet (in the second edition of 1553 authorship is attributed to William Barlow); or else, more probably, he served during the years 1528–34 as a diplomat engaged in negotiations over Henry VIII's divorce. In 1528 one William Barlow, 'king's chaplain', received the living of Wotton, Lincolnshire, and later the rectory of Sundridge, Kent. He became a favourite at court and was attached to an embassy in France and Rome in January 1530. The Barlow mentioned in the contemporary state papers may be either William or his brother John. Through Anne Boleyn's patronage he became prior of Haverfordwest, Pembrokeshire, in 1534. Letters written by him to Thomas Cromwell in 1535 show him to be already a fervent reformer. His zeal provoked furious opposition from the clergy of the neighbourhood. They ill-treated his servants and threatened him with violence and persecution. He complained to Cromwell of their blindness and ignorance, averring that 'no diocese is so without hope of reformation' (Wright, 79). In 1535 he was removed from hostile Pembrokeshire to the rich priory of Bisham, Berkshire, and was sent on three occasions between October 1535 and June 1536, once with Lord William Howard, on embassy to Scotland, with the intention of persuading James V to embrace Reformation doctrine. Although unsuccessful, these overtures produced lively exchanges.

While thus engaged Barlow was elected bishop of St Asaph on 16 January 1536; but before leaving Scotland he was translated to St David's without having exercised any episcopal functions and probably without being consecrated. On a short visit to London he was confirmed bishop of St David's in Bow church (21 April 1536). He returned to Scotland and there is no record of his consecration in Cranmer's registers. It is supposed that he was consecrated on 16 June 1536 after returning from Scotland; and he certainly sat in parliament and took possession of his see about this time. The issue of his own consecration assumes importance because of the controversies surrounding the consecration of Archbishop Matthew Parker in 1559, when Barlow was one of the bishops participating. In July 1537 he surrendered to the royal commissioners his priory of Bisham, hitherto held by him *in commendam*.

From 1536 to 1548 Barlow remained at St David's, where he was involved in heated quarrels with his clergy. He gave early notice of his plans: to move his cathedral from St David's to Carmarthen; to endow grammar schools and protestant preaching; and to enforce increased authority over his chapter. The latter, in 1537, dispatched a series of articles to the president of the council in the marches of Wales, accusing Barlow of holding that confession was inexpedient, that reverence of the saints was pure idolatry, that purgatory was an invention of the pope in order to make money, that only three sacraments were valid, and that the king could make any layman a bishop. Barlow mounted campaigns against relics, pilgrimages, veneration of saints (especially David), and similar customs. He established the practice, also adopted by his successors, of living at Abergwili near Carmarthen, but the accusation long held against him of stripping the lead from the roof of the superb episcopal palace at St David's has been shown to be unfounded. He was, however, responsible for alienating to Richard Devereux the manor of Lamphey, the most valuable of the bishop's possessions, in return for inadequate compensation. In January 1541 he founded in the buildings of the former Dominican friary at Brecon a grammar school and a college of preachers known as Christ College. Besides his diocesan activities, Barlow took part in general ecclesiastical politics. He signed the ten articles of July 1536 and shared in composing 'The institution of a Christian man' (1537). He opposed the Six Articles Act of 1539 but, unlike other like-minded bishops, managed to retain his see throughout Henry VIII's reign—thanks, presumably, to his steady support of Archbishop Cranmer. About this time Barlow was married to Agatha Wellesbourne (*d.* 1593).

Early in Edward VI's reign Barlow commended himself to the duke of Somerset by preaching against images, but deeply offended Bishop Gardiner. In February 1548 he was translated to the bishopric of Bath and Wells. On 20 May 1548 he sold to the duke seven manors together with the palace at Wells and certain other estates and profits of jurisdiction belonging to the see for, it is said, £2000, of which he appears to have received only £400. He is also reputed to have alienated valuable estates to the crown, receiving a few advowsons in exchange. The surrender to the crown was, however, simply for the purpose of a regrant. The king allowed the bishop and his successors to keep the advowsons at a yearly rent, gave back the estates granted to the crown on 20 May, and in consideration of the impoverishment of the see, permanently reduced the first-fruits. Bath Place and the Minories went to Somerset's brother, Lord Seymour. Barlow was lodged in the deanery. He deprived Dean Goodman for annexing the prebend of Wiveliscombe. In retaliation the dean tried to prove Barlow guilty of *praemunire*, the deanery being a royal donative. Barlow had to accept the king's pardon, but the dean's deprivation stood.

Barlow was committed to the Tower on 16 September 1553. Having twice unsuccessfully tried to escape, he recanted before Gardiner in January 1555 and fled to Emden, where he was minister of an English congregation. From there he went to Wesel and thence to Poland as part of the duchess of Suffolk's household.

The accession of Elizabeth brought Barlow back to England. He assisted in the consecration of Parker on 17 December 1559, and on 18 December was made bishop of Chichester, receiving also a prebend of Westminster in 1560. As bishop he complained of the lack of reliable preachers to spread protestant doctrine in his largely Catholic diocese, and quarrelled with the citizens of Chichester. He died on 13 August 1568 and was buried in Chichester Cathedral. He left a widow, who died in extreme old age, two sons, including William *Barlow (1544–1625), and five daughters, among them Frances *Matthew (1550/51–1629), all of whom were married to bishops.

William Barlow belonged to a distinguished generation in his family. His elder brother, **Roger Barlow** (*d.* 1558), the founder of the family of Barlow of Slebech, Pembrokeshire, is recorded in 1526 as an English merchant in the service of Spain, and as partner with two companions, Robert and Nicholas Thorne, sharing the risks of a venture to South America with Sebastian Cabot, of which Barlow left a permanent record in his *Briefe Summe of Geographie* (published by the Hakluyt Society in 1932). He returned to Lisbon in 1528 and made contact with Sir Thomas Boleyn. Having settled in Bristol he married Julyan, daughter and heir of Roger Daws of that city. He was living in Pembrokeshire by 1535, and in 1538 held a lease of the preceptory of Slebech from the order of St John. In August 1540 he was a commissioner of sewers for the Teifi and Tywi rivers. In 1543 he became a justice of the peace for Pembrokeshire and was employed by the privy council in relation to a Spanish ship driven ashore. In 1546 he and his brother Thomas bought the lands of Slebech, the Augustinian priory of Haverfordwest, and the Dominican friary there for £705 6*s.* 3*d.* In 1549 he became a vice-admiral of the Pembrokeshire coast. Roger Barlow died at Slebech in 1558—his will was proved on 20 May.

William Barlow had two younger brothers. **John Barlow** (*fl.* 1517–1552) studied at Oxford, and was admitted BA on 13 November 1517 and MA in 1521; he became a fellow of Merton College in 1520. From 1521 to 1527 he held the Essex livings of South Benfleet, Great Bentley, and Hawkeswell. Some time between 1525 and 1528 he was appointed chaplain to Sir Thomas Boleyn. He was a member of Anne Boleyn's household and much employed in Henry VIII's Great Matter. He was created dean of the college at Westbury-on-Trym in 1530, and subsequently became a prebendary successively of Peterborough (1541, resigned 1543) and Bristol (1544), and dean of Worcester (1544). He actively supported his brother in St David's diocese and was appointed a justice of the peace in Pembrokeshire in 1543. He is last recorded as dean on 24 September 1552, and had been deprived by April 1554; it is not known when he died. His younger brother **Thomas Barlow** (1493–1558) likewise became a cleric. He held the living of Abberton, Essex, from 1519 to 1541 and was also parson of Catfield, Norfolk. He resided with John Barlow at Westbury, and shared with Roger Barlow in the purchase of monastic lands at Slebech and Haverfordwest. He became prebendary of Mathry, St David's, in 1542 and of Nantcwnlle, Brecknockshire, and died possessed of both in 1558. His will was proved on 6 December 1558.

William Barlow also had a sister, **Elizabeth Barlow** (*d.* 1518), who was old enough to have become a lady-in-waiting to Margaret Tudor by 1503, when she accompanied her to Scotland for her marriage to James IV. By 1507 Elizabeth had married Alexander, first Lord Elphinstone, with whom she had a son, also Alexander, born in 1510. Her husband having been killed at Flodden in 1513, Elizabeth was married again in 1515, her new husband being John, sixth Lord Forbes (*d.* 1547). She died early in September 1518. GLANMOR WILLIAMS

Sources *DNB* • *DWB* • *LP Henry VIII* • Cooper, *Ath. Cantab.*, 1.276–80, 556 • T. Wright, ed., *Three chapters of letters relating to the suppression of monasteries*, CS, 26 (1843) • M. Barlow, *Barlow family records* (1922) • E. G. Rupp, *Studies in the making of the English protestant tradition* (1949) • R. Barlow, *A briefe summe of geographie*, ed. E. G. R. Taylor, Hakluyt Society, 2nd ser., 69 (1932) • E. Yardley, *Menevia sacra*, ed. F. Green (1927) • G. Williams, *Welsh Reformation essays* (1967) • G. Williams, *Wales and the Reformation* (1997) • F. Green, 'The Barlows of Slebech', *West Wales Historical Records*, 3 (1913) • B. G. Charles, 'The records of Slebech', *National Library of Wales Journal*, 5 (1947–8), 179–85 • GEC, *Peerage*, 5.57 • Emden, *Oxf.*, 4.26–7 • *Fasti Angl., 1541–1857*, [Chichester] • *Fasti Angl., 1541–1857*, [Ely] • *Fasti Angl., 1541–1857*, [Bristol] • R. B. Manning, *Religion and society in Elizabethan Sussex* (1969)

Barlow, William (1544–1625), Church of England clergyman and natural philosopher, was one of two sons and five daughters born to William *Barlow (*d.* 1568), then bishop of St David's, and his wife, Agatha Wellesbourne (*d.* 1593), a former nun. Barlow was educated at Balliol College, Oxford, and graduated BA in 1565. About 1573 he was ordained and in 1581 he was made a prebendary of Winchester and rector of nearby Easton. Each of Barlow's five sisters (who included Frances *Matthew) married bishops, ecclesiastical connections which were to his benefit—in 1588 he was transferred to a prebendal stall at Lichfield, which he resigned the following year on being appointed treasurer of that cathedral body. He became a prebendary of Southwell in 1614 and of York in 1617, and in 1615 archdeacon of Salisbury.

Barlow had left Oxford with a passion for mathematics and he was stimulated by the accounts of seafarers returned from distant lands to examine both the art of navigation and the design and construction of navigational instruments. He soon saw that mariners' compasses were defective in construction and, carelessly used, a danger rather than an aid to those who relied on them. In 1597 he published *The Navigator's Supply*, dedicated to

Robert Devereux, second earl of Essex, in which he described improved forms of the compass and his new inventions: the 'traveller's jewel', the pantometer, the hemisphere, and the traverse board. With the help of engravings made by the renowned London instrument maker Charles Whitwell, who could supply such instruments, Barlow explained in precise detail how compasses and their gimballed boxes ought to be made; his most important contributions were his advice to make the needle from steel, rather than iron, and to 'stroke' the needle with the lodestone, from the centre to the tips, which imparted a greater and more retentive magnetic force than the customary rubbing to and fro. His azimuth compass was a considerable improvement on those of Robert Norman and William Borough, and compasses to his design continued to be made into the nineteenth century; he was also the first to advise enclosing the dip circle within a glazed frame. The traveller's jewel was essentially an equinoctial sundial which enabled the traveller to find the time at any latitude in the world, the pantometer a surveying instrument which could measure both horizontal and vertical angles, of terrestrial or celestial objects; Barlow claimed that it was as efficient as Thomas Digges's theodolite of 1571. The hemisphere was a portable skeleton globe on whose graduated brass circles and plates problems of time, altitude, declination, and latitude could be solved, and resembled that described by Marcel Coignet in 1581. The traverse board likewise owed much to Cyprian Lucar's surveyor's plane table of 1590, with paper clamped by a scaled frame, but adapted for navigation, with ruler and protractor, enabling the ship's speed and headings to be plotted on the paper and her course subsequently transferred to the chart. His book included a brief explanation of the new Mercator and other map projections then in use. Barlow urged mathematicians and craftsmen to confer: 'idle knowledge without practise, and ignorant practise without knowledge, serve unto small purpose' (*Navigator's Supply*, unpaginated). He also urged young seamen to study mathematics, and hoped that public lectures could be set up in London, a situation which came to pass with the establishment of Gresham College in 1598.

Barlow was for seven years chaplain and tutor to Henry, prince of Wales (1594–1612), for whom an elaborate equinoctial dial, with inclining needle, and other instruments, were made by Barlow's Winchester craftsman. Barlow's interest in magnetism generally led him to exchange ideas with William Gilbert (1540–1603), whose *De magnete* (1600) treated the subject at length but was in Latin and therefore accessible only to the educated minority. Their one point of disagreement was over the earth itself, Gilbert taking the Copernican view that the earth rotated on its axis, whereas Barlow held to the church's teaching of a stationary earth. Barlow composed his treatise on magnetism in English (the *Oxford English Dictionary* credits him with the first use of the word), and about 1609 gave a copy to Sir Thomas Challenor, chamberlain to Prince Henry. Challenor mislaid this, and a second copy, which he had promised to see into print, so after his death in 1615 Barlow himself arranged for its publication, as *Magnetical Advertisements Concerning the Nature and Property of the Loadstone* (1616; repr. 1968). It was dedicated to Dudley Digges (1583–1639), known for his interest in magnetism, who had for many years urged Barlow to publish on this subject.

This publication brought Barlow into conflict with Mark Ridley, formerly physician to the tsar of Russia, who had published his own *Magnetical Bodies and Motions* in 1613. The two men then engaged in a pamphlet war: Ridley accused Barlow of plagiarizing *Magnetical Bodies*; Barlow accused Ridley of having surreptitiously gained access to his manuscript when it was in Challenor's hands; and Ridley then claimed that Barlow had simply copied from *De magnete*, although Barlow had annexed in *Advertisements* a letter which he had received from Gilbert referring to their shared ideas, and praising Barlow's scientific achievements. Barlow never married; his mother probably lived with him at Easton, where she was buried in 1593. He died on 25 May 1625 and was buried in the chancel of Easton church. ANITA MCCONNELL

Sources D. W. Waters, *The art of navigation in England in Elizabethan and early Stuart times* (1958) • G. D. Barlow, ed., *Published matter and records relating to the families of the name of Barlow* (1911) • R. C. Strong, *Henry, prince of Wales, and England's lost Renaissance* (1986) • Wood, *Ath. Oxon.*, new edn, 2.375 • P. F. Mottelay, *Bibliographical history of electricity and magnetism* (1922) • *VCH Staffordshire*, 3.171 • *N&Q*, 6th ser., 8 (1883), 33–4

Barlow, William (*d.* 1613), bishop of Lincoln, was by his own testimony born in London; but he was seemingly descended from a family long settled at Barlow Moor near Manchester, whose arms were placed on his tomb. His father's identity is unknown, but Barlow named his mother in his will as Alice Feild. He matriculated pensioner of St John's College, Cambridge, at Michaelmas 1580, graduating BA in early 1584 and MA in 1587. In 1590 he became a fellow of Trinity Hall, as which he took the degree of BTh in 1594. In 1599 he proceeded DTh, which he incorporated at Oxford on 7 August 1601.

Early career Barlow's first patron had been Richard Cosin, of whose life and death he published an account in 1598 (STC 1460). He was then taken up by Archbishop Whitgift, whose chaplain he became. He held this post when he preached at Paul's Cross on 8 August 1596 in celebration of the earl of Essex's victory at Cadiz. On 26 May 1597 Whitgift collated him to the rectory of St Dunstan-in-the-East, London. On 27 July he was, on Whitgift's recommendation, nominated for the next vacant canonry of Westminster. Also in 1597 he became rector of Orpington, Kent. Whitgift several times proposed Barlow for a chaplaincy to the queen, and was disappointed to see others preferred whom he considered less worthy.

Barlow had achieved a royal chaplaincy by 1 March 1601 when he again occupied the Paul's Cross pulpit, this time to present the official explanation of Essex's rebellion and execution. Barlow had been one of the three clergy who had attended the earl on the morning of his execution (25 February) and had heard his confession. Robert Cecil drafted specific guidelines for the Paul's Cross sermon next Sunday, which Barlow assiduously followed. He laid particular stress on the danger to the queen, while telling the Londoners that this was no mere palace coup, but a threat to their own security (STC 1454). He was criticized for breaking the seal of the confession (which he denied to have been confidential) and for spitefully turning on the man he praised in 1596 because the earlier sermon elicited no reward. Barlow also found himself shunned at court, since the queen did not want his presence to remind her of the lost favourite. His oleaginous pulpit manner was nevertheless much admired by Elizabeth, as by her successor, and it lubricated his passage to preferment well enough.

On 18 June 1601 Barlow was collated to the prebend of Chiswick in St Paul's Cathedral. On 27 June the queen arranged for him to be presented to the next vacant canonry of Canterbury in the crown's gift. Meanwhile on 4 August a vacancy had occurred at Westminster Abbey, allowing the reversionary grant of 1597 to be activated. Barlow was possessed of his stall there by 3 December when he was elected treasurer; this post he held until 1605, and from 1605 to 1607 he was subdean. At the opening of convocation on 30 October 1601 he gave a sermon which his opponents (by punning his name) called the 'Barley Loaf' (Harington, 148).

The Hampton Court conference On 13 February 1602, the very day on which Alexander Nowell died, Barlow wrote to Cecil asking to succeed to the deanery of St Paul's, complaining of the 'vile returns' of his Westminster Abbey stall, where he expected otherwise to remain a 'poor monk' (*Salisbury MSS*, 12, 52). This suit was unsuccessful, but by 8 May Barlow had been chosen dean of Chester, as which he was installed on 12 June. This office (perhaps reflecting his origins in the north-west) had little claim on his attention; its chief importance was that it gave him status to attend the Hampton Court conference of 14–18 January 1604. Barlow was commissioned to write the official account of these proceedings, in which the hierarchy confronted its puritan critics, with the king in the chair. Publication was delayed by Whitgift's death (29 February). On 12 May Barlow invited Cecil to accept the dedication, but the latter prudently asked to see the text first, and then avoided Barlow until the book had gone to press. Bancroft, the king's secretary (Sir Thomas Lake), and the king himself allegedly approved Barlow's draft, which appeared on 25 May as *The Summe and Substance of the Conference* (1604; STC 1456). It was immediately criticized for misrepresentation; in particular, for making the king side comprehensively with the bishops. James's strictures on the state of the church, recalled by others, were absent from Barlow's account. He had foreseen controversy, explaining that he did not claim to give a verbatim report, 'but … an extract, wherein is the substance of the whole' (sig. A3).

The extent to which Barlow's summary does indeed convey the substance remains central to the historiography of the conference. His report was long accepted as authentic, though differing interpretations were drawn from it. It has since been shown how he shaped his account for dramatic as well as polemical purpose. It is Barlow who gives James his famous line 'No bishop, no king', and who had him, riled by the advocacy of presbyterianism, bring the second day's session to a close with the words 'I shall make them conforme themselves, or I wil harrie them out of the land, or else doe worse' (Barlow, *Conference*, 82, 83). Other testimony confirms that while the king made a spirited retort, he did not end the day on this bitter note. To an extent the truthfulness of Barlow's version is of less consequence than the impact that it made. This lent powerful support to the view that the Stuart monarchy and the puritans were from this moment destined to collide.

Bishop of Rochester and Lincoln For the most substantive product of the conference, the Authorized Version of the Bible, Barlow had a share in translating the epistles from Romans to Jude. His efforts as publicist earned him the bishopric of Rochester, to which he was elected on 23 May 1606. He was consecrated at Lambeth on 30 June and enthroned by proxy in Rochester Cathedral on 25 July. With this promotion he vacated his deanery and (by 23 June 1606) his London rectory; he retained his canonries *in commendam*. He had hoped to keep both rectories; that of Orpington was already leased and without cure. He later boasted that he never held cure of souls in plurality.

Barlow conducted his primary visitation in 1605; the articles (which were published) included the recommendation that the clergy should study for seven hours each day (*Articles*, 1605; STC 10321). On 10 November 1605 he was once more put up as government spokesman at Paul's Cross, condemning the gunpowder treason revealed five days before (*The Sermon Preached at Paules Crosse*, 1606; STC 1455). A vacancy occurred in the chapter at Canterbury on 7 January 1606, to which Barlow succeeded by virtue of his grant of 1601. In September 1606 he was among those summoned to Hampton Court to preach to a delegation of Scots, part of the king's plan to impose an episcopal form of church government on Scotland. Barlow's sermon on 21 September defended episcopacy, on the grounds that the Holy Ghost distinguished ecclesiastics 'with equal concord but unequal dignitie' (*One of the Foure Sermons*; 1606, STC 1451, sig. B2*v*). One of the Scottish visitors acknowledged it a 'well-joyned sermone' but noted that it was 'fynely compactit in a lytle buik' which the preacher needed for a prompt (*Autobiography and Diary of … Melvill*, 653).

In 1607 and the following year Barlow acted as surrogate for Archbishop Bancroft in visiting the diocese of Canterbury. On 21 May 1608 he was elected bishop of Lincoln, being enthroned by proxy on 21 July following and in person on 1 September 1609. On translation he resigned his canonries of Canterbury and St Paul's, but retained that of Westminster (which provided a useful house). Courtier though he was, he devoted himself diligently to his vast diocese, coming to London for no more than a month each year. He deprecatingly referred to himself as a 'country retired bishop' (*Salisbury MSS*, 21, 134). He conducted a prolonged suit for reduction of his first-fruits (as previously he had done at Rochester). In 1609 he was again employed as an official propagandist, responding to Robert Persons with his *Answer to a Catholike English-Man* (1609; STC 1446). In the parliament of 1610 Barlow argued strongly against proposed lay involvement in enacting canons, alleging the royal supremacy was thereby compromised. He particularly defended the right of convocation to regulate non-residence among the clergy. He was the only bishop to enforce royal instructions of May 1611 against nonconformists.

Diocesan activities Barlow's churchmanship was eclectic. At Cambridge in 1599 he had expressed views for and against the prevailing Calvinist orthodoxy. He maintained friendships among the puritan clergy, and promoted not a few. He reinstated some who had earlier been deprived; most notably he restored Arthur Hildersham, who had been too radical to be acceptable as a delegate to Hampton Court, to his Leicestershire rectory. The king ordered Archbishop Abbot to reprimand Barlow, who in consequence had to explain to Lord Hastings, Hildersham's cousin, that he could no longer protect a man of whom he could say 'in truth I love him' (*Hastings MSS*, 2.54).

Barlow did not, however, love drunks or absentees. In his second triennial visitation of Lincoln diocese in 1611 he strove to correct these failings in his clergy. He encouraged them to study, and ordered non-preachers to hire curates for a minimum annual wage of 20 marks. Conversely he secured the dismissal of the headmaster of Eton College, Richard Langley, for being overqualified. He judged it an 'apostemated ulcer' that this doctor of divinity should be hired to teach schoolboys while neglecting the people of the two livings he held (Lyte, 209). Barlow, for all his tolerance to favoured nonconformists, did prosecute others; he suppressed three lectureships and prohibited the founding of another. His energies in the visitation of 1611 cost him, he claimed, his health and his voice. But prelates are not only pastors, and he was obliged to delegate his visitation to commissaries in September when he was ordered by the privy council to look to his military duties.

Barlow was never entirely associated with the Arminian party. Although, like Lancelot Andrewes, he abominated excessive preaching, he employed a chaplain, Robert Johnson, who dedicated to him a sermon in which sermonizing was extolled. Barlow was at odds with Richard Neile, to whom he alluded as 'one at his Majesties elbow, who watcheth mee for no good turne nor will' (Fincham, 46). Barlow did not belong to the circle of prominent Arminians whom Neile gathered round him at Durham House. He was, however, suspected of promoting Catholic practices; the Venetian ambassador reported that at a court sermon in Lent 1611 he 'praised very expressly auricular confession, invocation and fasting' (*CSP Venice, 1610–13*, p. 127). The allusion to invocation of the saints is likely to have been the ambassador's misunderstanding.

Death and legacies Barlow died at his palace at Buckden, Huntingdonshire, on 7 September 1613, and was buried in the parish church there. His tomb, defaced during the civil war, was restored by his namesake Thomas Barlow who succeeded to the see in 1675. William Barlow left his widow, Joan, £2000, and £1000 apiece to his daughters Alice and Jane. To his sister Katherine, wife of Thomas Johnson, fishmonger of London, he left £150, of which £100 was to pass to their son William. This boy was also to have such of the bishop's books as were not otherwise bequeathed, on condition of his becoming a scholar. If the daughters died before marriage their portions were to go to St John's College, Cambridge, for endowing scholarships and fellowships named after Barlow and the Fishmongers' Company. Since both daughters did marry, the educational foundation was not effective. Certain books were left to Trinity Hall, and his best plate to the Fishmongers (on condition that they used it as the grace cup for their feasts; otherwise to St John's with similar proviso). The Fishmongers' Company was appointed to oversee much of the estate, including £100 given to Whitgift's Hospital at Croydon. Barlow's *Summe and Substance of the Conference* was reprinted in 1840 as part of Edward Cardwell's *History of Conferences*. Facsimile editions were published in 1965 and 1975. C. S. Knighton

Sources *Fasti Angl.* (Hardy), 1.24–5; 2.24–5 • *Fasti Angl., 1541–1857*, [St Paul's, London], 28 • *Fasti Angl., 1541–1857*, [Canterbury], 28, 51 • *Fasti Angl., 1541–1857*, [Ely], 82–3 • Venn, *Alum. Cant.* • T. Baker, *History of the college of St John the Evangelist, Cambridge*, ed. J. E. B. Mayor, 1 (1869), 256–7, 667 • *CSP Venice, 1610–13*, 127, no. 193 • *Report on the manuscripts of the late Reginald Rawdon Hastings*, 4 vols., HMC, 78 (1928–47), vol. 2, p. 54 • *Calendar of the manuscripts of the most hon. the marquis of Salisbury*, 11, HMC, 9 (1906), 53, 178, 232; 12 (1910), 52; 16 (1933), 95, 242; 17 (1938), 580; 21 (1970), 134 • *CSP dom., 1595–7*, 475; *1598–1601*, 594–5, 598–9; *1601–3*, 114, 188; *1603–10*, 217, 229, 426, 506, 508, 515, 577, 609 • S. B. Babbage, *Puritanism and Richard Bancroft* (1962), 70, 185, 320n. • N. Tyacke, *Anti-Calvinists: the rise of English Arminianism, c.1590–1640* (1987) • *The autobiography and diary of Mr James Melvill*, ed. R. Pitcairn, Wodrow Society (1842), 653, 679 • *Diary of John Manningham*, ed. J. Bruce, CS, old ser., 99 (1868), 51 • P. Collinson, *Godly people: essays on English protestantism and puritanism* (1983), 483, 557, n. 77 • P. Collinson, *The religion of protestants* (1982), 11–12, 14–15, 28–9, 44 • K. Fincham, *Prelate as pastor: the episcopate of James I* (1990) • J. Harington, *A briefe view of the state of the Church of England* (1653), 147–8 • LPL, Reg. Whitgift, ii, fol. 344v • LPL, Reg. Bancroft, fol. 270v • CUL, MS Gg.1.29, p. (from front) 21; fols. (from rear) 41, 109–11 • H. C. Maxwell Lyte, *A history of Eton College, 1440–1898*, 3rd edn (1899), 209–11 • E. R. Foster, ed., *Proceedings in parliament, 1610*, 1 (1966), 75–6, 102, 135, 226, 230 • M. H. Curtis, 'Hampton Court conference and its aftermath', *History*, new ser., 46 (1961), 1–16 • F. Shriver, 'Hampton Court re-visited: James I and the puritans', *Journal of Ecclesiastical History*, 33 (1982), 48–71 • P. Collinson, 'The Jacobean religious settlement: the Hampton Court conference', *Before the English civil war*, ed. H. C. Tomlinson (1983), 27–51, 188–92 • C. S. Knighton, ed., *Acts of the dean and chapter of Westminster*, 2 (1999), 199, 201, 206, 211, 214, 220 • will, PRO, PROB 11/122, sig. 109

Archives CKS, episcopal registers: Rochester, DRb/Ar • Lincs. Arch., Lincoln, Add. Reg. 3, fols. 1–20

Wealth at death over £4500: will, PRO, PROB 11/122, fols. 349v–351

Barlow, William [*name in religion* Rudesind] (1584–1656), Benedictine monk, was born at Barlow Hall, Manchester, the son of Sir Alexander Barlow (1558–1620) and his wife, Mary Brereton, of Barlow Hall, and was elder brother of Edward (Ambrose) *Barlow (*bap.* 1585, *d.* 1641), also a Benedictine monk. William was educated at the English College, Douai (1602–5), and the University of Salamanca

(1606–11), professed in the order of St Benedict in 1606, and ordained priest in 1608. He became superior of St Gregory's Priory at Douai in 1614–20 and 1625–9, president of the English Benedictine congregation 1621–9, and professor of theology at St Vedast College, Douai, for forty years. He opposed Richard Smith, bishop of Chalcedon and vicar apostolic of England in his claim of ordinary jurisdiction, especially against the regulars, and expressed their concern to preserve their exemption. He published a collection of letters on this question, *Epistola R. A. P. praesidis generalis et regimini totius congregationis Anglicanae ordinis sancti Benedicti* at Douai in 1627. He died at St Gregory's Priory, Douai on 19 September 1656.

THOMPSON COOPER, *rev.* G. BRADLEY

Sources T. B. Snow, *Obit book of the English Benedictines from 1600 to 1912*, rev. H. N. Birt (privately printed, Edinburgh, 1913) • Gillow, *Lit. biog. hist.*, 1.136 • M. Lunn, 'William Rudesind Barlow, OSB, 1585–1656', *Downside Review*, 86 (1968), 139–54, 234–49 • M. Lunn, 'Benedictine opposition to Bishop Richard Smith, 1625–29', *Recusant History*, 11 (1971–2), 1–20 • D. Lunn, *The English Benedictines, 1540–1688* (1980) • P. Hughes, *Rome and the Counter-Reformation in England* (1942)

Archives archives of the archbishop of Westminster, London, corresp.

Barlow, William Hagger (1833–1908), dean of Peterborough, born at Matlock on 5 May 1833, was the younger son (of five children) of Henry Barlow, curate in charge of Dethick, near Matlock, and afterwards vicar of Pittsmoor, Sheffield, and his wife, Elizabeth, only daughter of John Hagger, of Sheffield. William, sent first to the grammar school and then to the collegiate school at Sheffield, won a school exhibition and a scholarship in classics at St John's College, Cambridge, where he matriculated in October 1853. He took honours in four triposes—a rare achievement (sixteenth junior optime and third in second class, classical tripos, 1857; second in first class, moral sciences tripos, and second class in theological examinations, 1858). He also won the Carus Greek Testament (bachelors') prize, 1858. He proceeded MA in 1860 and BD in 1875. Incorporated MA of Oxford through Christ Church (1874), he proceeded BD and DD there in 1895.

Barlow was ordained deacon on 30 May 1858 and priest on 10 June 1859, serving the curacy of St James, Bristol. When the new ecclesiastical district of St Bartholomew was formed out of this poor parish and a church built in 1861, he was the first vicar (1861–73). On 15 August 1861 he married Eliza Mary, eldest daughter of Edward Pote Williams of Upton Park, Slough (she died on 4 October 1905). She played an important part in his parish missions. After a brief incumbency of St Ebbe's, Oxford (1873–5), he was appointed in 1875 by the committee of the Church Missionary Society principal of their college in Upper Street, Islington, London, for the training of missionaries. Barlow quickly succeeded in improving the numbers and course of training. In 1883 he helped to collect £18,000 for the enlargement of the society's headquarters in Salisbury Square.

In 1882 Barlow was appointed vicar of St James, Clapham, London, and in 1887 was promoted by the trustees at the wish of the evangelical leaders to the vicarage of Islington, the 'blue ribbon' of their patronage. Barlow's tenure of this important benefice greatly strengthened his influence as an evangelical leader. He was a rural dean and was made trustee of the Peache, the Aston, and the Sellwood Church patronage trusts, which governed about 200 English and Welsh benefices. He became one of the chief founts of patronage in the Church of England of his day. The annual Islington clerical meeting, founded in a small way at the vicarage by Bishop Daniel Wilson in 1827, greatly expanded after Barlow took over its management in 1888, and it became the rallying point of the evangelicals. From 1887 to 1894 he was official chairman of the Islington vestry, and when the Local Government Act of 1894 took away the right of the vicar, the vestry continued to elect him to the chair from 1895 to 1899, entitling him to be JP for London.

Barlow, who was made a prebendary in St Paul's Cathedral by Bishop Mandell Creighton in 1898, accepted in May 1901 Lord Salisbury's offer of the deanery of Peterborough. Though a convinced evangelical, he attempted no changes in the manner of service at the cathedral, contenting himself with taking the north-end position at holy communion. He raised money for repairs in the north transept and the clerestory of the choir.

While actively engaged in the management of the chief evangelical, missionary, and educational institutions, Barlow was a member of Bishop Creighton's round-table conference at Fulham Palace on the holy communion (1900); served on the prayer-book revision committee of the lower house of Canterbury convocation which was appointed on 15 February 1907; was examining chaplain (1883–1900) to J. C. Ryle, bishop of Liverpool; and was select preacher at both Oxford and Cambridge. He was one of the promoters of Ridley Hall, Cambridge, and was on its council until 1908. He mainly owed his wide influence to his shrewd advice, his knowledge of men, and his ability to draw out opinions from others without parading his own. He died at the deanery, Peterborough, on 10 May 1908, and was buried beside his wife on the south side of the cathedral.

The Barlows had three sons and three daughters. The eldest son, Henry Theodore Edward Barlow (1862–1906), was honorary canon of Carlisle and rector of Lawford, Essex. The second son, **Sir (Clement) Anderson Montague-Barlow**, baronet (1868–1951), was educated at Repton School and King's College, Cambridge (where he obtained a first class in law), and became a barrister. He was on London county council, 1907–10, and was Conservative MP for South Salford, 1910–23. He raised the Salford brigade of Lancashire Fusiliers in 1914 and was knighted in 1918. He was a delegate at the international labour conferences, 1920–21, and, after being parliamentary secretary to the Ministry of Labour, 1920–22, was its minister, 1922–4, being sworn of the privy council in 1922. He chaired the royal commission on location of industry, 1937–40. Throughout his life he was an active Anglican layman and chaired the house of laity of the church assembly in 1945–6. He was created a baronet in 1924 and adopted the name of Montague in 1946.

Barlow published several works, including *Church and Reform* (1902) and *Barlow Family Records* (2 vols., 1932–5), and many commentaries on statutes, including those on education (1902), old-age pensions (1908), dock legislation (1910), and war pensions (1918). In 1934 he married Doris Louise, *née* Reed, formerly an administrator in the WRAF. Montague-Barlow died on 31 May 1951 and, being childless, his title became extinct.

E. H. PEARCE, *rev.* H. C. G. MATTHEW

Sources M. Barlow, *Life of W. H. Barlow* (1910) · C. A. Montague-Barlow, *Barlow family records*, 2 vols. (1932–5) · A. W. Greenup, *William Hagger Barlow* (1908) · *The Times* (11 May 1908) · *TLS* (17 Nov 1910), 447 · E. Stock, *The history of the Church Missionary Society: its environment, its men and its work*, 3 (1899) · *WWW* · *Record* (15 May 1908) · *Dod's Parliamentary Companion*

Likenesses Mayall & Co., photograph, repro. in Barlow, *Life*, frontispiece · oils, deanery, Peterborough · oils, repro. in Barlow, *Life*

Wealth at death £27,573 7s.: probate, 9 Oct 1908, *CGPLA Eng. & Wales*

Barlow, William Henry (1812–1902), civil engineer, was born on 10 May 1812 at Woolwich, London, the younger son of Peter *Barlow (1776–1862), mathematician and physicist, of the Royal Military Academy. His elder brother was Peter William *Barlow (1809–1885). Following private schooling, at the age of sixteen he studied civil engineering with his father for a year. He then began three years' engineering pupillage, initially in the machinery department at Woolwich Dockyard, and subsequently at London docks under the civil engineer Henry Robinson Palmer (1795–1844). In the spring of 1832, when he was still only twenty, he went to Constantinople on behalf of the firm of Maudslay, Sons and Field to install equipment for recasting and reboring Turkish ordnance.

Barlow remained in Turkey for six years, erecting a large structure to house the boring equipment, and reporting for the Turkish government on the lighthouses at the mouth of the Bosphorus. This work led to his first scientific papers, 'Experiments made at Constantinople on Drummond's light' (*Philosophical Magazine*, 8, 1836, 238–42) and 'The adaptation of different modes of illuminating lighthouses as depending on their situations and the object contemplated in their erection' (*PTRS*, 127, 1837, 211–16). There was to be a steady stream of papers for the remainder of Barlow's career. For his work in Turkey Barlow was made a member of the Nishan Iftikhar.

On his return to England in 1838 Barlow was appointed assistant to G. W. Buck on the Manchester and Birmingham Railway. On its completion in 1842 he became resident engineer on the Midland Counties Railway on the section between Rugby and Derby, retaining a similar position on the Midland Railway when it was incorporated in 1844. Barlow's links with this ambitious company were to enable him to emerge as one of the most important civil engineers of the nineteenth century. The Midland rapidly expanded its network and Barlow became its chief engineer. He developed the wrought-iron saddleback rail (patent 12438, 1849), which became known as the Barlow rail and was widely used, particularly on the Great Western Railway. He described this in his paper on the construction of the permanent way of railways (*PICE*, 9, 1849, 387). Barlow had been elected a member of the Institution of Civil Engineers (ICE) on 1 April 1845, contributing his first paper, also concerned with permanent way, the same year.

William Henry Barlow (1812–1902), by John Collier, 1880

In 1857 Barlow removed from Derby to 19 Great George Street, Westminster, setting up as a consulting engineer; and it was in subsequent years that he undertook his most significant projects. As consultant to the Midland Railway Company he was responsible for the southern section of its extension from Bedford to London (1862–9). This work included the 240 ft span St Pancras Station roof, the largest in the world at the time of its construction, and a structure that was pioneering in its abandonment of crescent trusses or other external bracing as a means of stiffening the arch ribs. Barlow was helped in its design by R. M. Ordish (1824–1868). It was one of the triumphs of Victorian structural engineering.

Barlow was involved as a consultant with a number of other outstanding structures. He had helped Sir Joseph Paxton with his calculations of the strengths of columns and girders for the Great Exhibition building. Following the demolition of the Hungerford suspension bridge in 1861 Barlow was appointed with John Hawkshaw (1811–1891) as joint engineer for a scheme to complete I. K. Brunel's proposed Clifton suspension bridge, which with a span of 702 ft was the largest in the country at the time. Barlow described the bridge in his paper to the ICE (*PICE*, 26, 1867, 243).

Following the failure of the Tay Bridge in December 1879 Barlow was appointed to the Board of Trade's commission of inquiry, one of the results of which was to recommend an investigation of wind pressure on railway structures. Barlow was appointed to the consequent Board of Trade committee which recommended inclusion of an allowance (of 56 lb per square foot) for wind pressure for the first time in the Board of Trade requirements for railway structures. The North British Railway Company appointed Barlow the engineer for the replacement Tay Bridge, the construction of which was entrusted to Barlow's second son, Crawford Peter Barlow (*d.* 1920), who was his partner from 1874.

In the wake of the Tay Bridge failure work had been suspended on the proposed Forth railway bridge, and Barlow, as consultant to the Midland Railway, was asked, along with John Fowler (1817–1898) and Thomas Elliott Harrison (1808–1888), the engineers to the other railway companies involved, to report on a suitable design for the crossing. Barlow was also consulted about Dufferin Bridge over the Ganges at Benares in 1880, and the Hawkesbury river bridge in New South Wales in 1885.

Alongside his design work Barlow pursued a series of scientific investigations. While in charge of the Midland's electric telegraph system he observed spontaneous deflections of the needles of the telegraph instruments and the effects of magnetic storms, and concluded that there were electric currents on the earth's surface (*Notices and Abstracts of Communications to the British Association for the Advancement of Science*, 1848, 2.21–2; *PTRS*, 139, 1849, 61–72). In the 1870s he became interested in recording the sound of the human voice, developing the logograph, which recorded sound waves graphically (*PRS*, 22, 1874, 277–86; Royal Dublin Society, *Scientific Proceedings*, 2, 1880, 153–72).

Barlow also investigated a range of structural problems typically faced by the engineers of the day. His first report, 'The existence, practically, of the line of equal horizontal thrust in arches, and the mode of determining it by geometrical construction' (*PICE*, 5, 1846, 162), was sceptically received by engineers such as Robert Stephenson as being of little practical assistance in design. It was, however, theoretically sound. In 1857 Barlow comprehensively revised G. W. Buck's classic work, *Oblique Bridges*, first published in 1839.

In recognition of this scientific research, Barlow was elected a fellow of the Royal Society on 6 June 1850. He also served as president of the ICE in 1879–80, and in his presidential address stressed the importance of study and experimental research, referring to his father's experiments on beams. He had himself undertaken work in this field in the 1850s, writing several papers on what he described as the 'resistance of flexure' (*PTRS*, 145, 1855, 225–42; *PTRS*, 147, 1857, 463–8). This work included an investigation into continuous girders, which led to his patent 908 of 1859, which described girders continuous over piers, where they had their greatest depth. This was, in essence, the principle followed in the Forth railway bridge design. His final paper on beams was published in 1870 (*PRS*, 18, 1869–70, 345–7).

From 1858, when he had begun testing steel at Woolwich arsenal, Barlow supported its use by engineers. He was a member of the committee of civil engineers formed in 1868 to conduct further tests. Following his presidential address to the mechanical section of the British Association in 1873 urging the adoption of steel he was appointed to a Board of Trade committee of inquiry. In 1877 this recommended for the first time a safe level of working stress for the use of steel in railway structures.

Barlow married Selina Crawford Caffin, the daughter of W. Caffin who worked in Woolwich arsenal, but the date is unknown. Of their four sons and two daughters only Crawford became a civil engineer. He and his father worked as W. H. Barlow & Son from 2 Old Palace Yard, Westminster, until 1891 when they removed to 53 Victoria Street. They both retired in August 1896. Barlow's own health had been in decline for a number of years and in 1888 he had been obliged to withdraw from the ordnance committee, of which he had been one of the original civil members, owing to ill health. Widely respected in his profession, he was an honorary member of the Société des Ingénieurs Civils de France, and a member of the Institution of Mechanical Engineers and the Society of Arts. Barlow died of exhaustion, following a fracture of the femur, at his house, High Combe, Old Charlton, Kent, on 12 November 1902. MIKE CHRIMES

Sources *PICE*, 151 (1902–3), 388–400 · *DNB* · *Engineering* (21 Nov 1902), 680–81 · d. cert. · *WWW*

Archives NA Scot., railway records · PRO, railway records · RS · University of Bristol, records of Clifton Suspension Bridge Trust | Inst. CE, corresp. wih Frederick Swanwick

Likenesses J. Collier, oils, 1880, Inst. CE [*see illus.*]

Wealth at death £68,014 17*s.* 11*d.*: probate, 5 Dec 1902, *CGPLA Eng. & Wales*

Barlowe, Jerome (*fl.* 1528–1529), Franciscan friar and writer, is an obscure figure. The one incontrovertible record of Barlowe is that he was sighted on the road north from Attleborough to Bishop's Lynn in June 1529. Cardinal Wolsey's agents exacted this information as they made enquiries in East Anglia for Barlowe and his companion William Roy. Having lost the trail in Yarmouth, they met a man from Lincolnshire at Langley Abbey who claimed to have spotted the fugitives. Roy hid his face and went off the road; Barlowe, 'who had a red head' (*LP Henry VIII*, 4/3, 5667), was more forward and asked the way to Lynn. Afterwards, Roy and Barlowe were reported to have caught a ship in Lynn for Newcastle, where, the agents told Wolsey, they intended to continue the pursuit.

Roy and Barlowe were the prime suspects for the production of *Rede me and be Nott Wrothe*, a truculent satire against Wolsey, written in octosyllabics interspersed with rhyme royals, and published anonymously, without printer's mark, in Strasbourg in 1528. The printer, Johann Schott (active 1500–44) published nothing in English except this and another work by Roy in the same year. Questioned on oath by Wolsey's representative Hermann Rinck, Schott confessed to printing 1000 copies each of the two English books, but said he had received no payment from Roy and Barlowe. Wolsey's men searched for the collaborators in various centres of book production, Strasbourg itself, Frankfurt, Antwerp, and lastly Cologne, where Roy and Barlowe were expecting (it was said) to collect the money. The attribution of *Rede me and be Nott Wrothe* was repeated by Thomas More in 1530 and has largely been taken as read since.

Tyndale in the *Parable of the Wicked Mammon* (1528) provides the fullest surviving account of Barlowe. He identifies him, like Roy, as a lapsed observant friar of the Franciscan convent at Greenwich. Barlowe (Tyndale says) had arrived in Strasbourg from Worms in 1527, professing his new baptism and promising to give up the friar's life of idleness. According to Tyndale, Roy 'gate [Barlowe] to him and sett him a werke to make rimes' (Tyndale, sig. A3*r*). It is possible, therefore, on Tyndale's evidence, to see Barlowe as the proper author and poet of *Rede me*.

The tract, written as a dialogue, contains topical references to the murder of Richard Hunne and the burning of Tyndale's New Testament by the bishop of London. Much of the dialogue is given over to a scurrilous anti-clerical attack on Wolsey, but what made it scandalous to More was the reference to the mass as dead and buried.

Jerome Barlowe has sometimes been confused (including in the *Dictionary of National Biography*) with William Barlow. It is conceivable that it was Jerome and not William who wrote an anti-protestant work called the *Lutheran Factions*, and recanted to Henry VIII in 1533. It is also conceivable that William, not Jerome, participated in the production of *Rede me*, since the recantation refers to 'the Treatyse of the Buryall of the Masse' (BL, Cotton MS Cleo E IV, fol. 121). Scholarship is divided on these questions.

BRIAN CUMMINGS

Sources D. H. Parker, ed., *Rede me and be nott wrothe* (1992) • W. Tyndale, *A parable of the wicked Mammon* (1528) • *LP Henry VIII*, 4/2, nos. 4693, 4810; 4/3, nos. 5462, 5667 • T. More, *The supplycacyon of soulys* (1530) • S. H. Scott, *Supplément au tome II du 'Répertoire bibliographique strasbourgeois jusque vers 1530' de Charles Schmidt* (Strasbourg, 1910), vi–vii, 14 • A. M. McLean, '"A noughtye and a false lyeng boke": William Barlow and the *Lutheran factions*', *Renaissance Quarterly*, 31 (1978), 173–85 • E. G. Rupp, *Studies in the making of the English protestant tradition (mainly in the reign of Henry VIII)* (1947)

Barmby [*née* Watkins], **Catherine Isabella** [*pseud.* Kate] (**1816/17–1853**), utopian socialist and writer on women's emancipation, was the daughter of Bridstock Watkins, a government officer. Little is known of her early life, but like most women of lower-middle class backgrounds she seems to have had some education, certainly enough to assist her in becoming an effective writer and lecturer.

Catherine Watkins first appeared on the public scene in 1835, when she wrote a series of articles for the Owenite socialist newspaper, the *New Moral World*, under the pen-name Kate. These articles, ranging in topics from women's restricted employment opportunities to the invidious effects of private property on family life, typified Owenite feminist concerns at the time. One article (6 February 1836), however, struck a premonitory note. Entitled 'The religion of the millennium', it offered a vision of a socialist faith founded on 'moral purity and moral liberty' and involving 'an unremitting love and practice of the truth'. The gently chiliastic tone of this piece was unremarkable in a movement in which a quasi-religious sense of destiny flourished. But in Catherine Watkins's case it pointed towards much greater things to come.

Millennialism, a literal belief in the imminent second coming of Christ, was widespread in early nineteenth-century Britain, and many Owenite radicals were touched by it. Robert Owen himself, it has been persuasively argued, was a millennialist for whom faith in socialism formed part of a wider pattern of eschatological belief, and many of his adherents shared this viewpoint. Among them was a young man named Goodwyn Barmby, who in the early 1840s began promoting a form of romantic chiliasm in which socialism and poetry served as the twin foundations of the New Jerusalem. 'The reign of the critic is over, the rule of the poet commences', an early Barmby article announced. 'All Messias [*sic*] will be acknowledged' (*The Promethean, or, Communitarian Apostle*, 1842).

(John) Goodwyn *Barmby (1820–1881) was the son of a Suffolk solicitor. He had been intended for a Church of England career, but on his father's death abandoned this plan for more radical ambitions. He was both a Chartist and an Owenite, and by 1840—when he and Catherine met—already had a reputation in left-wing journalism both in England and abroad. A sectarian man, intensely visionary and highly moralistic, Barmby was impatient with the imperfectly purist tone of the Owenite movement, and in 1841 he formed the Central Communist Propaganda Society, which soon became the Communist Church. In the same year, on 4 October, he and Catherine were married. 'I announce love to be the sacred bond of marriage', Goodwyn wrote at the time. 'I declare that two only at the same time can feel that particular love that is completed in marriage. I affirm that divorce begins when love ends' (*Educational Circular*, 1/1, 1841).

The Communist Church survived for eight years. The size achieved by the sect over this period is difficult to judge, but it seems likely that it remained very small, and probably drew most of its support from other Owenites with similar millennialist outlooks and sectarian dispositions. Certainly both it and its sister organizations (the White Quakers of Dublin and the Ham Common Concordium in Richmond) were composed of wonderfully inventive characters, committed to a range of enthusiasms which included not only various New Age prophecies but also vegetarianism, hydrotherapy, long hair and sandal wearing, and something called 'philanthropic philology'. Over the years Goodwyn became an increasingly Christ-like figure, with blonde hair to his shoulders, while Catherine acted as his adoring admirer, writing poems in his praise and serving as his co-worker in all their projects. Together the young couple travelled the streets of London in the early 1840s with a hooded cart from which they dispensed communist tracts and harangued startled passers-by. The final state of 'communization' was about to arrive, Goodwyn promised his audiences, and its probable site would be Syria, that 'earthly paradise'.

When the Barmbys finally did establish their utopia, however, it was in a small house in Hanwell, Middlesex, a place well known for its lunatic asylum. They lived there for a year, in some disarray, until the birth of their son, Moreville (or Morrville) Watkyns Barmby, on 27 April 1844 led to the experiment being abruptly abandoned. Thereafter the church concentrated on profession rather than practice, until its dissolution in 1849.

Catherine Barmby's role is difficult to assess. She seems to have served more as Goodwyn's auxiliary than as a leader in her own right, and certainly the bulk of communist propaganda was her husband's. Yet the influence of her feminist outlook was very clear, particularly in communist support (possibly the first from any organization) for female enfranchisement. In 1841 the Barmbys issued a 'Declaration of electoral reform' which demanded that the People's Charter be amended to include the vote for women, and in 1843 Catherine Barmby published a tract, *The Demand for the Emancipation of Women, Politically and Socially*, which set out the enfranchisement case. This tract and other articles written by her in the same period offered many of the arguments which would later feature in the women's suffrage struggle—but with a millennialist-communist twist. Catherine Barmby, in common with other Owenite feminists, insisted that full equality for women was possible only in a society organized on collectivist principles; but beyond this, she also evoked the figure of a female Messiah, a free woman, whose advent would free all humanity from the chains of sex-based oppression. Behind this last idea lay a number of influences: the eschatological preachings of the Devon 'female Christ', Joanna Southcott; the doctrines of the French Saint Simonians, who in the early 1830s eagerly awaited the arrival of a woman Messiah, *La mère*, whose coming would introduce socialism; and finally, Goodwyn himself, who in 1841 evolved a concept of the woman-man-power, a divinity foreshadowed by all earlier female prophets, whose arrival 'will socialise our planet and establish true communism amid our globe' (*New Moral World*, 1 May 1841). A similar chiliastic note was struck even more strongly by Catherine in the same year:

> The mission of woman is discovered by Communism: will she hesitate to perform it? The grass is growing, sorrow is accumulating—waves are rushing, the world is warring—life and death, soul and body, are in the conflict, the saviour is in the hearts of the redeemed, the prophet is the inspired out, WOMAN LEARN THY MISSION? DO IT? AND FEAR NOT?—the world is saved. (*Educational Circular*, 1/2 1841)

The free woman, at least in Catherine Barmby's divine version, failed to appear, and by 1848 the communist faith was crumbling. Catherine Barmby had a second child, a daughter named Maria Julia, in 1846, and after the demise of the Communist Church went on working as a feminist journalist, writing articles for progressive periodicals and even attempting to set up an independent feminist journal. But her health was poor, and she died of asthma and consumption on 26 December 1853 at Bridge Hill, Topsham, Devon. Goodwyn Barmby, who became a Unitarian minister, remarried in 1861; his second wife, Ada Shepherd, was also a feminist. He died in 1881.

BARBARA TAYLOR

Sources A. L. Mortin and J. Saville, 'Barmby, John Goodwyn and Barmby, Catherine Isabella', *DLB*, vol. 6 • B. Taylor, *Eve and the new Jerusalem: socialism and feminism in the nineteenth century* (1983) • W. H. G. Armytage, *Heavens below: utopian experiments in England, 1560–1960* (1961) • C. Barmby, *The demand for the emancipation of women, politically and socially*, New Tracts for the Times (1843) • Society of Friends, *Some account of the progress of truth as it is in Jesus* (1843) • *Educational Circular* (1841–2) • *Communist Chronicle, or, Promethean Magazine*, 1 (1843) • *New Moral World* (1835–45) • *The apostle and chronicle of the Communist Church* (1848) • m. cert. • d. cert.

Barmby, (John) Goodwyn (1820–1881), Chartist and socialist, was born at Yoxford in Suffolk and was baptized on 12 November 1820. His father, John, a solicitor, married to Julia, died when he was fourteen years old. Goodwyn—he never used his first Christian name—had no formal school education but read widely. He eschewed the professions and followed a career of social and political radicalism, reputedly addressing small audiences of agricultural labourers when aged sixteen.

Barmby claimed credit for founding the East Suffolk and Yarmouth Chartist council in September 1839. In December he was elected delegate to the Chartist convention and in 1840 and 1841 he was re-elected, though alienated from political radicalism by this time. Already a correspondent of the Owenites' *New Moral World* (writing on language reform and Charles Fourier), in 1840 he visited Paris with a letter of introduction from Owen. There he studied French social organization and claimed by this to have originated the English term 'communism'. He married at Marylebone on 4 October 1841 Catherine Isabella Watkins (1816/17–1853), who, under the signature of Kate, contributed to the *New Moral World* [*see* Barmby, Catherine]. They had a son, Moreville, and a daughter. On 13 October 1841 Barmby founded the Communist Propaganda Society and designated 1841 Year 1 of the new communist calendar. The Universal Communitarian Association followed, promoted by the monthly *Educational Circular and Communist Apostle*. In 1842 he founded and almost single-handedly wrote the monthly *Promethean, or, Communitarian Apostle*, which also promoted rational marriage and universal suffrage, and lectured at the 'communist temple' at Marylebone Circus, Marylebone, Middlesex. Out of this activity and through his contact with James Pierrepont Greaves (with whom he published the *New Age, or, Concordian Gazette*, the journal of Greaves's own Ham Common community), Barmby established the Moreville Communitorium at Hanwell in 1842. The following year he issued his *Communist Miscellany*, a series of tracts written by himself and his wife, and founded the weekly *Communist Chronicle*, which also supported the German communist Wilhelm Weitling.

Thomas Frost described Barmby at this time as 'a young man of gentlemanly manners and soft persuasive voice, wearing his light brown hair parted in the middle after the fashion of the Concordist brethren, and a collar and necktie à la Byron' (Frost, 57).

With the Communitorium renamed the Communist Church by 1844, Barmby began his move towards sectarianism; he conducted a propaganda tour in the north and midlands in the winter of 1845–6 and forged links with the Dublin sect of White Quakers. In 1845 he combined with Frost to revive the *Communist Chronicle*, for which he translated some of Reybaud's 'Sketches of French socialists', and wrote a philosophical romance entitled *The Book of Platonopolis*, which sought to fuse utopian fiction and modern science. However, Frost soon tired of Barmby's sectarianism and separated from him in 1846, to establish the *Communist Journal*.

Frost's competition with Barmby destroyed both journals but Barmby continued to proselytize in *Howitt's Journal*, and contributed to the *People's Journal*, *Tait's Magazine*, *Chambers's Journal*, and other periodicals. In 1847 he lectured at the Farringdon Hall, Poplar, London, and in July he convened a meeting at the John Street Institute in support of the Icarian settlements in Texas.

It was probably to his friendship with W. J. Fox MP that Barmby owed his introduction to Unitarianism, following his post-1848 disillusionment with communism. After his return from revolutionary Paris, where he had gone in 1848 as *Howitt's* representative and as the envoy of the Communist Church, he was successively minister at Southampton, Topsham, Lympstone, Lancaster, and Wakefield. He was one of the best-known ministers in the West Riding of Yorkshire and held his post in Wakefield for twenty-one years from 1858, founding and leading the Wakefield congregation which included the industrialist Henry Briggs. He was also secretary of the West Riding Unitarian mission. On 20 July 1861 Barmby married his second wife, Ada Marianne Shepherd, daughter of the governor of Wakefield gaol, with whom he had a daughter.

Barmby always retained his liberal political convictions, and was closely involved in the Wakefield Liberal Association from 1859: he chaired its North Westgate ward committee that year and the full town committee in 1860. In 1867 he organized a large public meeting there in support of parliamentary reform and joined the National Association for Women's Suffrage. Barmby was a member of the council of Mazzini's International League and also supported Polish, Italian, and Hungarian freedom.

Barmby wrote several volumes of pastoral poetry: *The Poetry of Home and Childhood* (1853), *Scenes of Spring* (1860), and *The Return of the Swallow* (1864). His devotional works included *Aids to Devotion* (1865), the *Wakefield Band of Faith Messenger* (1871–9), committed to the advance of theological liberalism, and a large number of hymns and tracts.

In 1879 Barmby's health deteriorated. He retired to Yoxford but continued to hold intensely devotional private services. He died there on 18 October 1881, and was buried at the cemetery of Framlingham, Suffolk. His second wife survived him. MATTHEW LEE

Sources *DLB* • A. L. Morton, *The English utopia* (1952), 132–8 • W. H. G. Armytage, *Heavens below: utopian experiments in England, 1560–1960* (1961), 196–207 • W. H. G. Armytage, 'The journalistic activities of J. Goodwyn Barmby between 1841 and 1848', *N&Q*, 201 (1956), 166–9 • *The Inquirer* (29 Oct 1881), 721 • W. Blazeby, *Unitarian Herald* (9 Nov 1881), 358 • G. J. Holyoake, *The history of co-operation*, 1 (1875), 228–30 • T. Frost, *Forty years' recollections* (1880) • *DNB* • *CGPLA Eng. & Wales* (1881)

Archives Co-operative Union, Holyoake House, Manchester, G. J. Holyoake MSS, letters • Co-operative Union, Holyoake House, Manchester, Robert Owen MSS, letters • Ipswich Public Library, Glyde MSS

Wealth at death £1219 0s. 2d.: probate, 18 Nov 1881, *CGPLA Eng. & Wales*

Barna, Victor [*formerly* Gyözö Viktor Braun] (**1911–1972**), table tennis player, was born into a Jewish family in Budapest on 24 August 1911. The son of a master printer, Richard Braun, he was the third of five children. He showed a talent for football but found his true vocation when a boyhood friend, Laszlo Bellak, was given a table tennis set for his thirteenth birthday. The boys played daily and such was Barna's aptitude for the game that he was junior champion of Hungary at the age of sixteen. In 1929 he won the men's doubles in the world championships inaugurated two years earlier by the International Table Tennis Federation.

Barna was singles world champion in 1930, 1932, 1933, 1934, and 1935. In the men's doubles he won seven consecutive times between 1929 and 1935. In 1932 and 1935 he added two mixed doubles titles to his collection. In 1935 he broke his playing arm during a motoring accident in France, necessitating the insertion of a platinum plate and four screws, but came back in 1939 to win the men's doubles again, the last of his world titles. He also helped Hungary to victory in the men's world team championship, the Swaythling cup, seven times.

Barna had studied chemistry and was employed by a pharmaceuticals firm in Hungary, but political unrest in central Europe led to his emigration to France in 1932. He then settled in Britain and adopted British citizenship in July 1947. Encouraged by Bill Pope, honorary secretary of the English Table Tennis Association, he won a record twenty English open titles; five singles, seven men's doubles, and eight mixed doubles. He also won the open championships of America, France, Hungary, Germany, and Austria.

Displays of Barna's talents, notably his prodigious backhand, the legendary 'Barna flick', were not confined to cramped sports halls; between championships he would bring the game to wider audiences by playing exhibition matches in ice rinks, circus tents, and leading theatres, including the London Palladium. On these tours he would be accompanied by Richard Bergmann of Austria, Bohumil Vana of Czechoslovakia, and his old friend Laszlo Bellak, by now known as the 'clown prince' of the game. He was employed as a promotional agent by a manufacturer of table tennis equipment.

Barna married his childhood sweetheart, Zsuzsanne (Suzette) Arany (*b.* 1917/18), daughter of Elemer Arany, a clerk, at Holborn register office on 27 April 1939. Bill Pope was the best man. At the outbreak of war the couple were in the USA. Victor refused the offer of American citizenship but returned to Britain after Pope sent him a telegram on Christmas day 1939 asking him to play charity matches for the Red Cross sports fund. Throughout the war he played in exhibition matches at a time when the game enjoyed considerable popularity as a recreation in air raid posts and barracks.

In 1947 the English Table Tennis Association controversially selected the newly naturalized Barna for the England Swaythling cup team. He helped his adopted country to a 5–4 victory over, inevitably, Hungary. After retirement from playing, Barna remained a part of the sport he loved by writing a regular column for *Table Tennis* magazine. He died, from a heart attack, in hospital in Lima, Peru, on 28 February 1972, while on a promotional tour at the time for the Dunlop Sports Company, who had employed him since 1946. TONY RENNICK

Sources P. Reid, *Victor Barna* (1974) • *The Times* (1 March 1972) • *Table Tennis* (Jan 1939) • *Table Tennis* (Feb 1939) • P. Matthews, I. Buchanan, and W. Mallon, *The Guinness international who's who of sport* (1993) • m. cert. • *CGPLA Eng. & Wales* (1972)
Archives FILM BFI NFTVA, news footage
Likenesses photographs, repro. in Reid, *Victor Barna*
Wealth at death £38,364: probate, 13 June 1972, *CGPLA Eng. & Wales*

Barnaby, Francis (*b.* 1573, *d.* in or after 1621), Roman Catholic priest, was born in the parish of Cawthorne, Yorkshire, on 21 May 1573 to Thomas Barnaby of Barnby basin and his wife, Beatrice Burdett. According to his own account he was educated at Oxford University and the inns of court, and arrived at Rheims on 13 January 1593. From there he was sent to Rome where he was admitted to the English College on 14 March 1593 and ordained on 30 November 1598. He returned to England the following year and was imprisoned in the Marshalsea by June 1599, but it appears that he was there chiefly to report to the government on his fellow priests. Along with other prisoners he was sent to Framlingham in 1601, by which time he was a strong advocate of the appellants' cause in their row with the Jesuits over loyalty to the regime. He was given leave to go to Rome with Christopher Bagshawe to prosecute the appellants' cause there in 1601, but after a disruptive stay at Douai he did not continue his journey, returning to England by way of Paris early in 1602. He was prisoner in the Clink by 11 April, but was given much freedom, being in constant touch with Bagshawe in Paris, with Bancroft, bishop of London, as a go-between. He was among those appellants who signed the memorial of allegiance in January 1603, and was given permission to cross to Paris where he also signed the memorial to Clement VIII on 3 May 1603. He travelled between the Clink, which was more or less his home, and Paris for the next year, and was probably in Paris when Bagshawe drew up the articles for peace and concord among English Catholic clergy in August 1603 in which it was suggested that Persons, Garnet, and other leading Jesuits be removed from England and the archpriest be deposed. It was in that year that he collaborated with William Clark in publishing a tract against Persons, *A Reply unto a Certain Libel Lately Set Forth by Fr Persons*, arguing the appellants' case. Back in prison in November 1603 Barnaby revealed details of the Bye plot, for which two of his fellow priests were executed, to the government, and in 1604 was granted a special pardon by the archbishop of Canterbury. In that year he was said to be active in Yorkshire, visiting his family home in the company of Anthony Champney, but nothing further is known of his activities until he turned up in Ireland as chaplain to Mabel Browne, a relative of the Catholic peer Viscount Montague, as a signatory to the oath of allegiance in Dublin in 1612. Described in 1599 as 'of personage tall and slender, fair complexion with a fresh colour, his hair reddish; no beard' (*Salisbury MSS*, 9.200), his last appearance in the record finds him back at his family home in Barnby on 8 February 1621 writing to the archbishops of York and Canterbury with details of the activities of Catholic priests, an act consistent with his previous commitment to allegiance, but one which tarnished his reputation with his co-religionists at the time and subsequently. WILLIAM JOSEPH SHEILS

Sources G. Anstruther, *The seminary priests*, 2 (1975) • *Calendar of the manuscripts of the most hon. the marquis of Salisbury*, 9, HMC, 9 (1902) • A. Kenny, ed., *The responsa scholarum of the English College, Rome*, 2 vols., Catholic RS, 54–5 (1962–3)

Barnaby, Sir Nathaniel (1829–1915), naval architect, the eldest son of Nathaniel Barnaby, inspector of shipwrights at Sheerness Dockyard, and his wife, Anna (*née* Fowler), was born at Chatham on 25 February 1829. At the age of fourteen, Barnaby became a shipwright apprentice at Sheerness, and in 1848 he won a scholarship at the Portsmouth central school of mathematics and naval construction. On leaving there in 1852 he was appointed draughtsman in the royal dockyard at Woolwich; in 1854 he became overseer of the *Viper* and *Wrangler*, ships being built in the Thames for the Crimean War. Later in 1854 he was appointed to the naval construction department of the Admiralty, where he assisted with the designs for the last wooden sailing line-of-battle ships and for the *Warrior*, the first British armoured battleship. He married in 1855 Sarah (*d.* 1910), daughter of John Webber of Birmingham; they had one son and two daughters.

When Sir Edward James *Reed, who had married Barnaby's sister Rosetta, became chief constructor of the navy in 1863, he made Barnaby head of his staff, and as such Barnaby worked on most of Reed's designs, including that of the *Monarch*, Reed's fully rigged seagoing turret ship.

Meanwhile the first lord, Hugh Childers, was forcing through the rival design of the *Captain* over the objections of Reed and Sir S. Robinson, the controller of the navy. In July 1870 Reed resigned, and Childers tried unsuccessfully to persuade Laird, builder of the *Captain*, to replace him. After the *Captain* sank on 7 September, Childers, whose son drowned aboard her, blamed Robinson, Reed, and their staff. Although he could not avoid appointing Barnaby, the obvious internal candidate to replace Reed, as a public mark of lack of confidence he was denied his brother-in-law's title and appointed only as 'president of the council of construction'. He later became chief naval architect in 1872 and director of naval construction in 1875.

The loss of the *Captain* aroused intense distrust in new warship designs, especially of turret ships, and Barnaby at once had to cope with the first of several outside committees of inquiry to be appointed during his term of office. The immediate focus of concern was the new turret ships

Devastation and *Thunderer*, then being built to Reed's design. As mastless ironclads mounting their main armament in two turrets fore and aft of the central superstructure, they can now be seen as the prototypes of twenty-five years of steady development, and Barnaby was able to persuade the committee of the essential soundness of the design, as well as suggesting improvements to its immediate successor, the *Dreadnought*.

Barnaby's first important design for a battleship was that for the *Inflexible*, laid down in 1874. She had moderate sail power, and a one-calibre armament of four 16 inch 80 ton muzzle-loading guns, two in each of two turrets placed in echelon in a central citadel 110 feet long, protected with armour 24 inches thick. The ends of the vessel were without side armour but were fitted internally with belts of cork upon strong under-water decks. By this time Reed, embittered by his ejection from the Admiralty, had adopted the truculent and unmeasured opposition to all Admiralty designs that he maintained for the next twenty years with all the weight that his professional reputation and a seat in the Commons gave him. His essential point was that all large warships should be unsinkable, and that any sacrifice of armour for some other purpose, such as carrying guns, was unacceptable. Accordingly he attacked the *Inflexible's* unarmoured ends, but another committee of inquiry rejected his strictures, and four similar but smaller vessels—*Ajax*, *Agamemnon*, *Colossus*, and *Edinburgh*—followed, the last in 1879.

Barnaby's next design was that for the *Collingwood*, laid down in 1880. She and five similar vessels—the *Admiral* class—varied somewhat in gun power, and were without sail. They carried breech-loading guns in barbettes, and a belt of 18 inch armour over nearly half the length of the ship.

Barnaby designed various other armoured vessels, including the cruisers *Impérieuse*, *Warspite*, *Shannon*, *Nelson*, and *Northampton*, and some notable unarmoured designs. The cruisers *Iris* and *Mercury*, laid down in 1875 and 1876, were the first vessels for the Royal Navy built entirely of steel, which Barnaby advocated and introduced. He designed the cruisers *Rover* and *Bacchante*, and the *Mersey* class and the *Comus* class, while the *Leander* class, the navy's first protected cruisers, were designed under his supervision. He also designed the *Vesuvius*, the first British vessel fitted with a tube for discharging torpedoes under water; the torpedo-ram *Polyphemus*, armed with under-water torpedo tubes; and the *Rattlesnake*, the forerunner of the destroyer.

As a naval architect, Barnaby was a brilliant technician, responsible for many important innovations, but he had the misfortune to work in an era of weak and confused naval thinking, under boards of Admiralty more willing to specify design details than to consider what sort of ships the navy required, and for what purposes. He was not the man to supply their deficiencies. His own ideas of naval warfare were at best unrealistic, at worst completely fanciful, and many of his designs lacked such practical qualities as seakeeping, speed, range, and the ability to steer straight. When Lord George Hamilton became first lord in 1885, and immediately discovered that the new cruisers of the *Orlando* class were completing seriously overweight because of muddle and irresponsibility in the Admiralty, in which Barnaby was greatly implicated, he resolved to seek a new director of naval construction. Barnaby himself, still close to his sister and a near neighbour of the Reeds, was so wearied by his brother-in-law's constant attacks that he was not unwilling to resign.

Barnaby was one of the founders of the Institution of Naval Architects; he presented many papers, and took an active part in discussing those relating to warship design. As a debater he was skilful and convincing. The foundation of the Royal Corps of Naval Constructors was largely due to him, and he became its first head.

Barnaby was made CB in 1876 and KCB in 1885; he also received several foreign decorations. He devoted much time to the Sunday school of the Baptist chapel at Lee, Kent, and wrote several hymns for it. He died at his home, Moray House, Belmont Hill, Lee, on 15 June 1915, and was buried in St Margaret's churchyard at Lee.

PHILIP WATTS, *rev.* N. A. M. RODGER

Sources D. K. Brown, *A century of naval construction: the history of the Royal Corps of Naval Constructors, 1883–1983* (1983) • N. A. M. Rodger, 'The dark ages of the admiralty, 1869–1885: change and decay, 1874–1880', *Mariner's Mirror*, 62 (1976), 33–46 • N. A. M. Rodger, 'British belted cruisers', *Mariner's Mirror*, 63 (1977), 23–36 • D. K. Brown, 'The age of uncertainty, 1863–1878', *Steam, steel and shellfire: the steam warship, 1815–1905*, ed. R. Gardiner and A. D. Lambert (1992), 75–94 • O. Parkes, *British battleships, 'Warrior' 1860 to 'Vanguard' 1950: a history of design, construction, and armament*, rev. edn [1966] • *CGPLA Eng. & Wales* (1915)

Archives NMM, Admiralty MSS • PRO, Admiralty MSS

Likenesses photograph, Royal Corps of Naval Constructors?; repro. in Brown, *A century of naval construction*, 47

Wealth at death £8080 13*s.* 5*d.*: probate, 23 July 1915, *CGPLA Eng. & Wales*

Barnacle, Nora Joseph. *See* Joyce, Nora Joseph (1884–1951).

Barnard, Sir Andrew Francis (1773–1855), army officer, was born at Fahan, co. Donegal. He was the son of the Revd Henry Barnard, of Bovagh, co. Londonderry (second son of William *Barnard, bishop of Derry, and brother of Thomas Barnard, bishop of Limerick), and his second wife, Sarah (*née* Robertson) of Bannbrook, co. Londonderry. He entered the army as ensign in the 90th regiment in August 1794, and was promoted lieutenant in the 81st in September and captain in November 1794. He served in St Domingo from April to August 1795, and on 2 December was transferred to the 55th. He took part in the expedition to the West Indies under Sir Ralph Abercromby, and was at the capture of Morne Fortuné.

In 1799 Barnard served in the expedition to The Helder. Later that year, on 19 December, he was gazetted lieutenant and captain in the 1st regiment of foot guards (major 1 January 1805). He embarked with the 1st brigade of guards for Sicily in 1806, and returned to England in September 1807. On 28 January 1808 he became lieutenant-colonel in the army, and in July embarked for Canada, having been appointed inspecting field officer of militia there. He was gazetted into the 1st Royals on 18 December, and returned to England in August 1809. On 29 March 1810 he exchanged into the 95th (later the Rifle brigade), with which his name was henceforth linked. He was appointed to command the recently raised 3rd battalion, and on 11 July 1810 he embarked with the headquarters and two companies in the frigate *Mercury*; on 29 July he landed at Cadiz, then besieged by Marshal Victor. He commanded his battalion at the battle of Barrosa, in which he was wounded twice, once severely; and he was at the sieges of Ciudad Rodrigo and Badajoz, and the battles of Salamanca and Vitoria. Soon after the capture of Badajoz he was transferred to the 1st battalion. After becoming a colonel on 4 June 1813 he was at the storming of San Sebastian, the passage of the Nivelle, where he was shot through the lung, and the battles of Orthes and Toulouse.

On 16 February 1814 Barnard was appointed to command the 2nd or light brigade (the 43rd, 52nd, and 1st battalion 95th) of the celebrated light division. For his Peninsular services he received a gold cross and four clasps, and was made KCB in January 1815.

On the resumption of war in 1815 Barnard embarked with six companies of the 1st battalion of the 95th and arrived at Brussels on 12 May. He was at Quatre Bras, was slightly wounded at Waterloo, and was awarded the Russian order of St George and the Austrian order of Maria Theresa. Wellington had so high an opinion of his services that he appointed him commander of the British division occupying Paris. In 1821 George IV appointed him a groom of the bedchamber, and on 13 June 1828 the king promoted him equerry. On 4 June 1830 he was gazetted one of three 'commissioners for affixing his majesty's signature to instruments requiring the same' (*London Gazette*, 4 June 1830). On the accession of William IV he became clerk-marshal in the royal household, and from 1837 to 1849 he was clerk-marshal to Adelaide, the queen dowager.

Barnard became major-general on 12 August 1819, colonel of the rifle brigade on 25 August 1822, and lieutenant-general on 10 January 1837. On 26 November 1849 Wellington appointed him lieutenant-governor of the Royal Hospital, Chelsea (salary £400 p.a.), and on 11 November 1851 he became a general. In 1842 he was awarded an honorary MA by Cambridge University. He was made KH in 1819, GCH in 1833, and GCB in 1840.

Barnard died, apparently unmarried, at the Royal Hospital, Chelsea, on 17 January 1855. Before his funeral pensioners who had served under him in the Peninsula obtained permission to see his remains. After they had left the coffin was found covered with laurel leaves, for each man, unobserved, had brought in one and laid it on the body of his venerated chief. He was buried on 22 January in the burial-ground of the hospital. He left most of his property to his nephew, Major-General Henry William *Barnard (1798–1857).

A. S. Bolton, *rev.* Roger T. Stearn

Sources *GM*, 2nd ser., 43 (1855), 309 • *Hart's Army List* (1854) • W. Cope, *The history of the rifle brigade* (1877) • W. F. P. Napier, *History of the war in the Peninsula and in the south of France*, 6 vols. (1828–40) • D. Gates, *The Spanish ulcer: a history of the Peninsular War* (1986) • R. Muir, *Britain and the defeat of Napoleon, 1807–1815* (1996) • A. J. Guy, ed., *The road to Waterloo: the British army and the struggle against revolutionary and Napoleonic France, 1793–1815* (1990) • Boase, *Mod. Eng. biog.*

Archives priv. coll., papers | BL, corresp. with Sir George Thomas Smart, Add. MS 41771 • Bodl. Oxf., letters to Sir William Napier • PRO NIre., letters to Sarah Robinson • U. Southampton L., letters to first duke of Wellington

Likenesses Count D'Orsay, pencil-and-chalk drawing, NPG • G. Jones, oils, NPG • W. Salter, group portrait, oils (*Waterloo banquet at Apsley House*), Wellington Museum, Apsley House, London • W. Salter, oil sketch (*for Waterloo banquet*), NPG • wood-engraving (after J. P. Knight), NPG; repro. in *ILN* (1852)

Barnard [*née* Lindsay], **Lady Anne** (1750–1825), writer, was born at Balcarres, Fife, on 8 December 1750, the eldest of eleven children born to James Lindsay, fifth earl of Balcarres (1691–1768), and Anne, daughter of Sir Robert Dalrymple, of Castleton. The family recovered from the fourth earl's Jacobite involvements but survived in reduced circumstances.

In Edinburgh in the 1770s Anne Lindsay found herself among leading intellectuals and writers of the day, and met the lawyer and politician Henry Dundas. She maintained a lifelong but complicated friendship with him. In 1781 she moved to London to live with her widowed sister Margaret Fordyce. She re-met Dundas, who had risen to high office in several ministries in the 1780s and had made an expedient marriage. The sisters played hostess to leading figures of the day, including Pitt, Burke, Sheridan, and William Windham, who, like Dundas, was to be secretary of war and colonies. Thereafter both played a part in Lindsay's emotional and material fortune. She was confidante and intermediary for Mrs Fitzherbert and the prince of Wales. She provided the political soirées that Dundas used to lobby for Pitt's elevation to the highest office, but she also found herself beguiled by a fickle Windham, who led her to believe that he intended to marry her. To complicate matters Dundas's wife died and he, having become increasingly attached to Lindsay, proposed marriage. This encouraged her to confront Windham in Paris, observing events at the height of the terror. Acknowledging that Windham had no intention of marrying her, she returned to London resigned to accepting Dundas's offer. Dundas, however, affronted by her approach to Windham, soon married someone else. Lindsay now took an unexpected step. Having failed to advance her own fortune and pursuits by attaching herself to a powerful man she reversed her course and on 31 October 1793 married Andrew Barnard (*d.* 1807), the impecunious son of the bishop of Limerick. Since he was without means or position and twelve years her junior she had previously rejected his suit. Now, aged forty three, she determined to call in the political and emotional debts that she believed were owed to her in order to further her husband's career. Urging Dundas to find him a position, she wrote: '*You owe me some Happiness,—in Truth you do*—pay me by making me the means of serving a man who has rebuilt in a considerable degree what tumbled to its foundation' (*Letters*, 15).

Dundas agreed to provide patronage but his delay

forced Anne Barnard to initiate a desperate and humiliating correspondence in which she reminded him of his promises and obligations to her. Dundas, after dispensing hurtful rebukes, offered Barnard the colonial secretaryship in the recently captured Cape of Good Hope. At first the prospect of office in an unimportant remote colony distressed her, but without anything else Barnard took up the post in 1797. Thereafter Anne Barnard strove to ensure that the office carried sufficient status within the colony's hierarchy. Dundas did not expect her to travel with her husband but, fearing that separation might weaken their relationship and convinced that she could offer valuable political and emotional support, she insisted on doing so. In the event she occupied positions of social and political importance in the colony. Because the governor, Earl Macartney, travelled without his wife Anne Barnard became his hostess in the new colony. Moreover Dundas commissioned her to keep a journal that was to be a report on the colony's potential value to Britain. Dundas was asking her to be, she wrote, 'an intelligent politician' (*Cape Journals*, 293).

Anne Barnard believed that her role was to '*bring the Nations together* on terms of good will' (*Cape Journals*, 178). The British administration had the support of only a part of the Cape's notables. Anne Barnard entered into the spirit of her task with enthusiasm but not without cynicism. '[A] little parade,' she wrote to Wellesley, 'suits the Dutch and procures respect from their stupid heads' (Streak, 41). But she ensured that the governor's household welcomed not only the Cape's élite but also the hostile up-country settlers. Her journals are an important, readable record of colonial social life and Cape Dutch political perspectives. They also contain insights into the behaviour of the British merchant community, garrison, and administration.

Anne Barnard had no illusions about settlers' treatment of Khoi-Khoi (Hottentot). She saw that landowners had reduced them to the status of a landless labouring population vulnerable to the deceptions and repression of the Afrikaner farmers. In supporting arguments for a permanent British occupation of the Cape she claimed that British rule would improve the treatment of non-European peoples by introducing them to British 'civilization' and 'religion'. While herself benefiting from the existence of slavery, she was not blind to the fact that some incoming British merchants took part in, or gave assistance to, the slave trade, and she wrote to Dundas to report officials and merchants who did so. She thought treatment of slaves less brutal in the Cape than in the Caribbean.

By 1801 Britain had agreed to restore the Cape to the Netherlands, and the Barnards returned to England, where Dundas's fortunes had declined calamitously, but Anne Barnard remained loyal to her old friend until his death, in 1811. With Windham in office she turned to him for patronage, reminding him of his obligations to her. Windham's patronage saw Andrew Barnard returned to the Cape in 1807, when British control was restored. In that same year he died, while he and Anne were apart. She had grown deeply attached to Barnard as time passed, noting that she had not had 'one moment of regret' and only 'heart felt satisfaction' in her decision to marry him. An even tenor of 'peace, gentleness and constant good humour, mutual consideration and tender affection,' she wrote, 'has subsisted between us' (*Cape Journals*, 232, 234).

After her husband's death Anne Barnard withdrew from public life, emerging only to write to Sir Walter Scott to acknowledge that she was the anonymous author of the famous ballad 'Auld Robin Gray'. Scott had quoted lines from it in 'The Pirate' (1823), which encouraged Barnard to reveal to him the history of her poem. She took the title from the name of an old shepherd at Balcarres, and longed to provide new words to an old Scottish melody, the original lines of which, 'The bridegroom greits as the sun gaes down', were felt to be 'far from choice' by Lindsay (Tytler and Watson, 23). Her poem was composed in 1771 in an effort to assuage her 'melancholy' at her sister's absence and 'amuse' herself 'by attempting a few poetical trifles' (Barnard, *Auld Robin Gray*, 1825, 2). What she completed was a 'little history of virtuous distress in humble life' (ibid., 4). The heroine, Jenny, believing her lover, Jamie, dead at sea and facing the illnesses of her parents as well as the theft of their cow, their only source of livelihood, marries auld Robin Gray. Jamie returns 'a week but only four' after the wedding, but Jenny stays faithful to her husband. A continuation of the tale, written later, was considered by many critics to be 'a grievous blunder' (Tytler and Watson, 99). It was argued that by making Robin Gray the thief who stole the cow and thus the 'treacherous villain of the tragedy', Lindsay detracted 'from the perfect innocence of the victims' (ibid.).

Various people claimed authorship of the ballad but Anne Lindsay resolutely maintained her anonymity: 'its popularity from the highest to the lowest … gave me pleasure while I hugged myself in my obscurity' (Barnard, *Auld Robin Gray*, 1825, 5). Only five years after its composition, in 1776, it was printed in David Herd's *Ancient and Modern Scottish Songs, Heroic Ballads, &c.* Another version appeared in *Select Scottish Songs, Ancient and Modern* (1810), edited by R. H. Cromek, which 'attained great notoriety' (Barnard, *Auld Robin Gray*, 1938, 19), but neither were like the original text. Barnard's authorship was recognized publicly when Scott published the poem in a thin quarto volume for the Bannatyne Club in 1825—'the first authentic edition'—of which only sixty-five copies were made.

Charles Kirkpatrick Sharpe said:

> Lady Anne Barnard's face was pretty and replete with vivacity; her figure light and elegant; her conversation lively; and, like the rest of the family, peculiarly agreeable. Though she had wit, she never said ill-natured things to show it; she gave herself no airs either as a woman of rank or as the Authoress of Auld Robin Gray. (Barnard, *Auld Robin Gray*, 1938, 6)

In addition to her writing Anne Barnard was an able watercolourist, and her work added to her record of Cape life. She died, aged seventy-four, at her home in Berkeley Square, London, on 6 May 1825.

A. B. GROSART, *rev.* STANLEY TRAPIDO

Sources Lord Lindsay [A. W. C. Lindsay, earl of Crawford], *Lives of the Lindsays*, [new edn], 3 vols. (1849) • A. Barnard, *South Africa a century ago: letters written from the Cape of Good Hope (1797–1801)*, ed. W. H. Wilkins • D. Fairbridge, *Lady Anne Barnard at the Cape of Good Hope, 1797–1802* (1924) • *Barnard letters, 1778–1824, selected from a mass of family papers: mainly the correspondence of Sir Andrew Francis Barnard, Lady Anne Barnard* (1928) • C. Matheson, *The life of Henry Dundas, first Viscount Melville, 1742–1811* (1933) • *The letters of Lady Anne Barnard written to Henry Dundas from the Cape and elsewhere, 1793–1803, together with her journal of a tour into the interior and certain other letters*, ed. A. M. Lewin Robinson (Cape Town, 1973) • M. Streak, *The Afrikaner as viewed by the English* (Cape Town, 1974) • H. B. Giliomee, *Die Kaap tydens die eerste Britse Bewind, 1795–1903* (Cape Town, 1975) • M. Boucher and N. Penn, *Britain at the Cape, 1795 to 1803* (Johannesburg, 1992) • *The Cape journals of Lady Anne Barnard, 1797–1798*, ed. A. M. Lewin Robinson, M. Lenta, and D. Driver, Van Reibeeck Society, 2nd ser., 24 (Cape Town, 1994) • *The Cape diaries of Lady Anne Barnard, 1799–1800*, ed. M. Lenta and others, 2 vols., Van Reibeeck Society, 2nd ser., 29–30 (Cape Town, 1999) • A. Barnard, *'Auld Robin Gray': a ballad* (1825) [introduction by Sir Walter Scott] • A. Barnard, *'Auld Robin Gray': a ballad*, ed. J. L. Weir (1938) • S. Tytler and J. L. Watson, *The songstresses of Scotland* (1871) • *IGI*

Archives NA Scot., letters and poems • NL Scot., letters, papers, literary MSS, and journals | BL, letters to duke of Wellington • Bodl. Oxf., corresp. with Sir James Blond Burges • Bodl. Oxf., letters to Lady Byron and her parents • Bodl. Oxf., letters to Sir Ralph Noel and Lady Judith Noel • Mount Stuart Trust, Isle of Bute, letters to Lady Loudon • NL Scot., corresp. with Sir Walter Scott • U. Southampton L., corresp. with duchess of Wellington

Likenesses wash drawing, Scot. NPG

Barnard [*née* Pye], **Charlotte Alington** [*pseud.* Claribel] (**1830–1869**), balladeer and poet, only child of Henry Alington Pye (1799–1883), a lawyer and speculator, and his wife, Charlotte Mary Yerburgh (*d.* 1847), was born at The Cedars, St Mary's Lane, Louth, Lincolnshire, on 23 December 1830. From about 1840 she attended a girls' school in Louth, run by Elizabeth Leak. On 18 March 1854 she married Charles Cary Barnard, a Church of England clergyman, and about four years after her marriage began to compose and publish, under the pseudonym Claribel, songs which for a time were extraordinarily popular. She had relatively little professional training in music, although she did take voice lessons from Euphrosyne Parepa and Charlotte Sainton-Dolby, two of the singers who popularized her ballads, and late in her life she studied composition. Between 1858 and 1869 she composed about 100 ballads, writing the words for most of them herself, although she also set to music poems by writers such as Tennyson and Charlotte Brontë. 'Janet's Choice', which she published at her own expense in 1859 and which was in its twentieth edition by 1865, was perhaps her most successful song.

Despite her popular success Barnard was attacked by the musical press; *The Orchestra*, in a denunciation of what it saw as tawdry popular ballads, dismissed the genre as 'Claribel-ware' and described one of Barnard's poems as the product of 'a hack Pegasus yoked to a CAB' (172.250). Some of this hostility might have arisen because her success in selling her ballads placed Barnard at the centre of the contemporary debate about royalties in music publishing. In addition to her songs Barnard published *Fireside Thoughts: Ballads* (1865), a collection of poetry and brief essays; another collection, printed for private circulation in 1870 as *Verses and Songs*, was expanded and published as *Thoughts, Verses, and Songs* in 1875. In 1868 Barnard followed her bankrupt father to Brussels, and she died at Wellington Crescent, Dover on 30 January 1869, on a brief return trip to England to visit her husband. She was buried in St James's cemetery, Dover.

W. B. Squire, *rev.* Pam Perkins

Sources P. Smith and M. Godsmark, *The story of Claribel* (1965) • 'Royalties and "Claribel"', *The Orchestra* (12 Jan 1867) • J. A. Sadie and R. Samuel, eds., *The new Grove dictionary of women composers* (1994)

Likenesses drawing, *c.*1834, repro. in Smith and Godsmark, *Story of Claribel* • photograph, 1861, repro. in Smith and Godsmark, *Story of Claribel* (1965) • watercolour, repro. in Smith and Godsmark, *Story of Claribel* (1965)

Barnard, Edward (**1717–1781**), headmaster and college head, the second son of George Barnard (1688/9–1760), rector of Knebworth (1737–60) and vicar of Luton (1745–60), and his wife, Dorothy, was born at Harpenden, Hertfordshire, and baptized there on 10 June 1717. He was educated at Eton (1732–5), where he was a scholar, but he was not elected to King's College, Cambridge; instead he entered St John's College, Cambridge, in 1735 and graduated BA in 1739, MA in 1742, BD in 1750, and DD in 1756. Ordained deacon (Lincoln) in 1741 and priest (Ely) in 1745, he was a fellow of St John's from 1744 to 1756. Since he had not been at King's he was not eligible to be assistant master at Eton but by 1752 he had returned to Eton as tutor to Henry Townshend, the son of Charles Townshend (1701–1780), and later to other boys. In 1754, when John Sumner retired as headmaster and it was expected that the lower master would succeed, Barnard at first persuaded the duke of Newcastle and Mr Townshend to lobby the fellows for the post of lower master for himself; but his prospects improved and in fact he was appointed headmaster, subsequently justifying his promotion.

Under Barnard the number of boys at Eton grew from approximately 350 to 550; Horace Walpole, in a letter of 1762 to Horace Mann, wrote that Barnard was 'the Pitt of masters, and has raised the school to the most flourishing state it ever knew' (Walpole, *Corr.*, 22.84). A large number of those whom he educated were aristocrats, of whom Charles James Fox was perhaps the most famous. Barnard was a good mimic with a fine voice and wit. He taught the sixth form effectively and included in the curriculum the Greek plays that evidently appealed to his theatrical taste; his pupil George Hardinge reflected that as an actor he might have rivalled Garrick, had he been less ugly. He could rule boys by the power of his tongue, sometimes aided by ridicule, and in so doing he reduced the amount of flogging; but he seems not to have been always fair, and discipline remained rough. Yet he had the reputation of spotting and bringing out talents in the young. Many favoured boys presented portraits of themselves on leaving, thus forming the nucleus of Eton's fine collection.

In October 1765, on the death of Dr Sleech, Barnard was appointed provost of Eton by George III, who admired him. His contribution as provost was far less successful, beginning with the choice of Dr John Foster as headmaster, whom he did not subsequently support. His second headmaster, Dr Jonathan Davies, was a happier choice. Barnard liked to dominate and Hardinge described him as 'an over-grown spoiled child'. While headmaster he had married Susannah Haggatt of Richmond on 26 August 1760 but she died young, leaving him with a son, Edward (*bap.* 1763), whom he chose to educate privately rather than at Eton. He had always sought his own preferment; in 1752 he was appointed rector of St Paul's Cray in Kent, in 1756 vicar of Ospringe in Kent, and in 1760 a canon of Windsor and chaplain to George III.

Barnard died of a stroke at Eton on 2 December 1781; the circumstances of his death were described by Jacob Bryant, the antiquary, who had saved him from drowning while both were boys at Eton and who had remained one of his many friends. Barnard was buried beside his wife at Harpenden. By his success in attracting boys to the school, by his occupancy of the rewarding position as provost, and by his pluralism he had become a very rich man. He had not been in every way admirable and he had not improved the institutions of Eton which he ruled by the force of his personality rather than by sound arrangements. But he was without doubt the most vivid figure in eighteenth-century Eton. TIM CARD

Sources Nichols, *Lit. anecdotes*, vol. 8 • *Etoniana*, 12 (1911), 192; 18 (1915), 279; 19 (1915), 298; 22 (1918), 341–4; 59 (1935), 140; 87 (1941), 584; 111 (1952) • *Nugae Etonenses* (c.1766) • H. C. Maxwell Lyte, *A history of Eton College, 1440–1910*, 4th edn (1911) • Venn, *Alum. Cant.* • *DNB* • *IGI*

Archives BL, corresp. with duke of Newcastle, Add. MSS 32956–32982

Likenesses oils, Eton

Wealth at death very wealthy; £13,000 to son

Barnard, Edward William (1791–1828), Church of England clergyman and writer, was born on 16 March 1791, the third son of Henry Boldero Barnard (1755–1815) of Cave Castle, Brough, Yorkshire, and his wife, Sarah (*d.* 1832), daughter of Roger Gee of Bishop Burton. He was educated at Harrow School and Trinity College, Cambridge. He graduated BA in 1813 and MA in 1817, but took no honours, owing to his dislike of mathematics. In 1814 he was ordained deacon, and in 1815 priest. After serving a curacy at Brantingham, Yorkshire (1815–17), he became vicar of South Cave in 1817 and then of Brantingham Thorp in 1822. On 25 April 1821 he married Philadelphia Frances Esther, daughter of Francis *Wrangham (1769–1842), archdeacon of the East Riding. They had one son and two daughters.

In 1817 Barnard published, anonymously, *Poems, Founded upon the Poems of Meleager*, which was re-edited in 1818 under the title of *Trifles, Imitative of the Chaster Style of Meleager*. The 1818 version was dedicated to the poet Thomas Moore (1779–1852), who had read the poems in manuscript and praised them for their elegance. Barnard's next publication, *The Protestant Beadsman* (1822), was described in *Notes and Queries* as a 'delightful little volume'; it commemorated the saints and martyrs of the English church in biographical notices and hymns.

At the time of his premature death, on 10 January 1828 at Dee Bank, Chester, Barnard was collecting materials for an elaborate life of the Italian Renaissance poet Marc-Antonio Flaminio, which was to accompany a translation of some of his poems. Such translations as were ready for publication were edited for private circulation, with some of Barnard's original poems and a short memoir, by Wrangham, under the title *Fifty Select Poems of Marc-Antonio Flaminio* (1829). Barnard had also planned a history of the English church, and collected many materials for the work. Barnard's widow married the Revd C. W. W. Eyton (*d.* 1870), rector of Ashton Clinton, Buckingham, in 1848.

RONALD BAYNE, *rev.* MARI G. ELLIS

Sources Venn, *Alum. Cant.* • Burke, *Gen. GB* • F. Wrangham, 'Memoir', *Fifty select poems of Marc-Antonio Flaminio, imitated by the late Reverend Edward William Barnard*, ed. F. Wrangham (1829) • *GM*, 1st ser., 98/1 (1828), 187 • *N&Q*, 4, 251, 290 • *N&Q*, 9th ser., 12 (1903), 13 • *N&Q*, 10 (1849), 119 • W. T. Lowndes, *The bibliographer's manual of English literature* (1867), vol. 1, p. 116 • *Journal of Thomas Moore*, ed. P. Quennell (1964)

Barnard, Frederick (1846–1896), illustrator and painter, was born in Angel Street, St Martin's-le-Grand, London, on 26 May 1846, the youngest child of Edward Barnard, a manufacturing silversmith. He studied first at Heatherley's Art School in Newman Street, London, and later under the painter Léon Bonnat in Paris. His earliest publication was a set of twenty charcoal drawings entitled The People of Paris, and he became a very popular artist in black and white, chiefly excelling in the delineation of street folk. As early as 1863 he had contributed to *Punch*, and for two years he was cartoonist to *Fun*. He was a fine interpreter of Charles Dickens's works; he illustrated nine of the twenty volumes of the Household Edition of Dickens (Chapman and Hall, 1871–9), which are characterized by vivid portrayals and strong draughtsmanship. The best are perhaps *Barnaby Rudge* and *Bleak House*, the former showing his grasp of period subjects, the latter of modern ones in the newer style of the 'sixties'. His style is typified by loose but vigorous penwork. In 1870 he married Alice Faraday, a niece of the chemist Michael Faraday.

Between 1879 and 1884 Barnard issued three series of Character Sketches from Dickens. He also illustrated novels by Justin Macarthy, H. E. Norris, and others, and much of his work appeared in *Good Words*, *Once a Week*, and the *Illustrated London News* (1863–96). A fine edition of Bunyan's *The Pilgrim's Progress*, mainly illustrated by Barnard, appeared in 1880. He collaborated with G. R. Sims in his *How the Poor Live* (1883), and during 1886 and 1887 he worked in the United States for Harper Brothers. Among his last productions was a series of parallel characters drawn from Shakespeare and Dickens, which appeared in Harry Furniss's weekly journal, *Lika Joko*, in 1894 and 1895. He painted a few oil pictures, which he exhibited from time to time at the Royal Academy and which were brought together at the exhibition at the Royal Institute of Painters in Water Colours, 'English humorists in art', in 1889. Of these the best are *My First Pantomime* and *My Last*

Pantomime (formerly Sir Henry Irving collection; exh. RA, 1879; ex Christies, 13 March 1992), *The Jury—'Pilgrim's Progress'*, *Saturday Night in the East End*, and *The Crowd before the Guards' Band, St James's Park*. Barnard was accidentally suffocated in a fire at a friend's house at Wimbledon, Surrey, on 27 September 1896. Examples of his illustrations are in the print room of the Victoria and Albert Museum, London. F. M. O'DONOGHUE, *rev.* SIMON HOUFE

Sources M. H. Spielmann, *The history of 'Punch'* (1895), 518–9 · [G. Dalziel and E. Dalziel], *The brothers Dalziel: a record of fifty years' work … 1840–1890* (1901); repr. as *The brothers Dalziel: a record of work* (1978), 338–9 · H. Furniss, *The confessions of a caricaturist*, 2 vols. (1901), 118–20 · *Victorian pictures, drawings and watercolours* [Christies, London, sales catalogue, 13/3/1992] · S. Houfe, *The dictionary of 19th century British book illustrators and caricaturists*, rev. edn (1996), 53–4 · C. G. Harper, *English pen artists of today* (1892) · *Scenes and characters from the works of Charles Dickens* (1908) [illustrations by F. Barnard] · private information (1901) · C. J. Jackson, *English goldsmiths and their marks* (1921) · *The Year's Art* (1887)

Likenesses F. Barnard, self-caricature, repro. in Spielmann, *History of 'Punch'*, 518 · H. Furniss, pen-and-ink caricature, NPG · wood-engraving, BM, NPG; repro. in *ILN* (14 May 1892)

Barnard, Sir Frederick Augusta (1743–1830), librarian, was the son of John Barnard (*d.* 1773), page of the backstairs to Frederick, prince of Wales, and to the prince's wife, Augusta (after whom Frederick was named), who may have been his godparents. The erroneous belief, which originated with the obituary of Barnard in the *Gentleman's Magazine*, that he was the illegitimate son of Frederick, prince of Wales, almost certainly arose from a confusion with Fitz Frederick (who died in infancy), son of the prince of Wales and Anne Vane, daughter of Lord Barnard. Barnard started in royal service as page of the backstairs to George III in 1760; by 1765 he was a member of the staff of the royal library, then newly housed in the octagon at the Queen's House.

The old royal library had been given to the British Museum by George II in 1757. George III employed Barnard as chief agent in his lifelong endeavour to build up a new collection, which later came to be known as the King's Library. Though still very young, Barnard rapidly established himself as a man of account and was responsible for introducing Samuel Johnson to the king in 1768. Shortly afterwards, in a lengthy and famous letter, subsequently printed in the King's Library catalogue, but denied by Barnard to Boswell, Johnson proffered invaluable advice to Barnard on book purchase. Barnard's association with the Johnson circle may have dated from this time. Between 1768 and 1771 Barnard, on a salary of £200 p.a. and with a purchasing allowance of £2000 p.a., travelled in Europe, buying books, visiting many of the principal cities—Paris, Vienna, Rome, Strasbourg, Dresden, Berlin, Amsterdam, Brussels—and taking advantage of the recent dispersal of many Jesuit libraries.

In 1774 Barnard succeeded Richard Dalton as royal librarian, a position he was to hold for half a century. He followed the king's wishes in building up a genuinely working library, albeit one well stocked with rarities, and including a magnificent topographical and cartographical collection, manuscripts, coins and medals, and drawings. It was a library collected (in Barnard's own words included in the printed catalogue):

> upon such a comprehensive and liberal design of embracing every species of Knowledge, that the Possessor of it can call to his aid upon any subject, all the Learning and Wisdom which the mind of man has hitherto communicated to the world. (*Bibliothecae Regiae catalogus*, 1820–29, 1.viii–ix)

By 1823, when George IV presented his father's library to the nation for deposit at the British Museum, the collection comprised over 65,000 volumes, 19,000 pamphlets, and the king's topographical collection of some 50,000 maps and charts. Barnard had doubts about the transfer of the military plans, charts, topography, and geography collections, and succeeded in reserving the king's maritime collection, the larger part of which was given to the museum only in 1844. In 1973 the King's Library passed into the care of the newly established British Library and was transferred in 1998 to the new British Library building at St Pancras. His portrait by John Knight, presented to the British Museum in 1926, hangs adjacent to the glass tower housing the King's Library.

Barnard became FSA in 1789 and FRS in 1790 when his proposers included a number of notable members of the Johnson circle such as R. P. Joddrell and John Paradise. He was largely responsible for compiling the catalogue of the King's Library, based on the twelve-volume manuscript catalogue, which was published in five volumes between 1820 and 1829 as *Bibliothecae Regiae catalogus*. He also checked and revised the catalogue of medals in 1814.

In October 1796 Barnard married Catherine (*d.* 1837), daughter of John Byde; they had one son, George (*d.* 1817), and at least one daughter, who died young. Barnard retired from the royal library in 1828, having overseen the transfer of it and its staff to the British Museum. In the same year he was made a knight commander of the Royal Guelphic Order. He died on 27 January 1830 at his house in St James's Palace. E. M. PAINTIN

Sources E. Edwards, *Memoirs of libraries*, 2 vols. (1859) · E. Edwards, *Lives of the founders of the British Museum* (1870) · E. M. Paintin, *The King's Library* (1989) · J. Brooke, 'The library of King George III', *Yale University Gazette*, 52 (1977), 33–45 · *GM*, 1st ser., 100/1 (1830), 571 · P. R. Harris, *A history of the British Museum Library, 1753–1973* (1998) · E. Miller, *That noble cabinet: a history of the British Museum* (1973) · *The letters of Samuel Johnson*, ed. R. W. Chapman, 1 (1952) · J. C. Sainty and R. Bucholz, eds., *Officials of the royal household, 1660–1837*, 1: *Department of the lord chamberlain and associated offices* (1997) · J. C. Sainty and R. O. Bucholz, eds., *Officials of the royal household, 1660–1837*, 2: *Departments of the lord steward and the master of the horse* (1998) · Royal Arch. · BM

Likenesses J. Knight, mezzotint (after S. W. Reynolds), BM · J. Knight, portrait, BL

Wealth at death see will, PRO, PROB 11/1767

Barnard, Sir Henry William (1798–1857), army officer, was probably born in September 1798 at Wedbury, Oxfordshire, the son of Revd. William Barnard of Water Stratford, Buckinghamshire, and his wife, the daughter of Moore Disney of Churchtown, co. Waterford; he was the great-grandson of William *Barnard (1696/7–1768), bishop of Derry. After attending Westminster School, he entered the Royal Military College, Sandhurst, when his family were living at Bighton, near Alresford, in Hampshire. He left Sandhurst on 24 June 1814, having been commissioned ensign and lieutenant in the 1st (later Grenadier) guards on 9 June. During the allied occupation of France (1815–8) Barnard apparently first served on the staff of his uncle Colonel Sir Andrew *Barnard in Paris, then with his regiment at Cambrai. He became a captain in the army (15 August 1822), and lieutenant and captain in the Grenadier Guards (29 August 1822), advancing to captain and lieutenant-colonel (17 May 1831). During these years he served for some time on the staff of Major-General Sir John Keane in Jamaica before returning to England. Barnard married on 17 January 1828 Isabella Letitia, second daughter of Brigadier-General James Catlin Craufurd; they had children and she survived her husband.

Barnard was on duty with the 2nd battalion during the coronation of Queen Victoria on 20 June 1837, and when it was reviewed by the duke of Wellington in Hyde Park on 21 March 1838, dining that evening with other regimental officers at Apsley House. In April 1838 he sailed with the battalion from Portsmouth for service in Canada, returning with it to London in November 1842. He then held a number of posts in England, being appointed adjutant-general to the northern and midland district on 15 February 1847, and later to the staff of the Monmouthshire and south Wales district. Barnard became a brevet colonel (9 November 1846), and went on half pay as lieutenant-colonel (1 June 1849). Initially, he commanded a brigade of Lieutenant-General Sir Richard England's division in the Crimea in 1854–5, having been promoted major-general on 20 June 1854. Following the death of Field Marshal Lord Raglan, the army commander, in June 1855, Barnard replaced Raglan's successor (Lieutenant-General Sir James Simpson) as chief of staff, and after the fall of Sevastopol commanded the 2nd division. He became local lieutenant-general on 30 July 1855 and CB on 27 September, when he was also financially rewarded for 'distinguished services'. He was appointed KCB on 3 May 1856, and became a commander of the Légion d'honneur (third class) and commander of the military order of Savoy (first class). He briefly commanded the division at Shorncliffe and Dover before being sent to Bengal, where he fretted to the governor-general (Lord Canning) about inactivity in an administrative post: 'Cannot you find some more tough job for me?' (Leasor, 143).

Towards the end of April 1857 Barnard reached Ambala to take over the Sirhind division, as rumours of disaffection among sepoys spread. On 10 May news came of the outbreak of the Indian mutiny in Meerut and Delhi and immediately Barnard sent word to the commander-in-chief, General the Hon. George Anson, at Simla. When Anson died of cholera a fortnight later, Barnard took charge of the field force ordered to relieve Delhi, pressing on rapidly, despite extreme heat. To conserve energy, the men rested by day and travelled by night. One participant wrote: 'Along the road came the heavy roll of the guns, mixed with the jingling of bits, and the clanking of the steel scabbards of the cavalry. The infantry marched on behind with a dull deep tread' while the baggage train 'toiled along for miles in the rear' (Forrest, 1.40). At Alipur, 10 miles from Delhi, on 5 June, Barnard halted to await a brigade from Meerut. Three days later, after this and his siege train had concentrated, he defeated a rebel force at Badli-ki-sarai and that evening took possession of an extended ridge overlooking the north-west of the city. Barnard simply reported to army headquarters: 'The object of the day having been then effected, the force was at once placed in position before Delhi' (ibid., 1.47). In acting so decisively, however, he had secured lines of communication for reinforcements and supplies, and immensely raised morale by recapturing the cantonments from which British troops had been driven a month previously.

On 10 June the acting commander-in-chief, Major-General Thomas Reed, arrived to supersede him, but soon fell ill, and direction of the siege devolved on Barnard. He displayed admirable concern for those under his command: a feverish staff officer, Lieutenant William Hodson, woke to 'find the kind old man by my bedside, covering me carefully up from the draught' (Leasor, 140). He entertained his staff at his own expense and, on his deathbed, was concerned to ensure that the chief engineer would not be blamed if an agreed operation failed. Colonel Keith Young, judge-advocate-general of the Bengal army, acknowledged that Barnard was 'kind hearted and brave', but queried his professional ability for delaying an assault on the rebel stronghold: 'He was no more fit for his present post than he was to be Pope of Rome' (ibid., 140). Despite repulsing enemy forays and himself sending parties successfully to destroy rebel batteries, postponement of a planned attack on 13 June and repeated delays in its subsequent execution suggested irresolution. In fact, with a maximum 4500 men and 44 guns, Barnard had to devise very carefully a means of overcoming an estimated 30,000 rebels with 174 guns behind the formidable defences of a city protected by a dry ditch and substantial ramparts with bastions at irregular intervals, and further strengthened by the River Jumna as an eastern barrier. Nevertheless, Brigadier Archdale Wilson, commanding the Meerut troops, supported Young: 'Fearful indecision and want of firmness … made him [Barnard] unfit for his position' (ibid., 181). And the civil officer with Wilson, Hervey Greathed, observed cuttingly that 'a Crimean education is not the best for this service' (ibid.). Barnard was a convenient scapegoat to cloak over-optimism represented by Greathed's assertion that 'we seem to have Delhi by the nose' (Forrest, 1.40) and the governor-general's dispatch of 4 July announcing that it had already fallen.

Barnard fell ill with cholera on 4 July 1857, before arrival of the reinforcements which might have allowed him to silence his critics, and died the following day. Fearing an enemy attack, his last words in delirium were allegedly 'strengthen the right' (Forrest, 1.61). In spite of the damning strictures of his detractors, he had laid the foundation for the eventual relief of Delhi and, by his swift advance and initial military successes, had gone far towards restoring British prestige in the area. Barnard was buried on 6 July 1857 in the Rajpur cemetery of the cantonment outside Delhi, his wooden coffin accompanied by an escort of lancers. Whatever the judgement about his performance under extreme conditions in a country which he had only recently reached and in which he had never previously served, Barnard's earlier distinguished career should not be overlooked. JOHN SWEETMAN

Sources *Army List* • A. C. Robertson, *Historical record of the king's Liverpool regiment of foot* (1883) • F. W. Hamilton, *The origin and history of the first or grenadier guards*, 3 (1874) • G. W. Forrest, ed., *Selections from the letters, despatches and other state papers preserved in the military department of the government of India, 1857–1858*, 4 vols. (1893–1912), vol. 1 • J. Leasor, *The Red Fort* (1956) • Fortescue, *Brit. army*, vol. 13 • *Despatches and papers relative to the campaign in Turkey, Asia Minor and the Crimea, 1854–6* • A. W. Palmer, *The banner of battle: the story of the Crimean War* (1987) • H. O. Mansfield, *Charles Ashe Windham: a Norfolk soldier* (1973) • Royal Military Academy, Sandhurst • Boase, *Mod. Eng. biog.* • *GM*, 3rd ser., 2 (1857), 340–41 • P. J. O. Taylor, ed., *A companion to the 'Indian mutiny' of 1857* (1996)
Archives HMC, Barnard file 1990 • priv. coll. | NAM, corresp. with William Codrington

Barnard, Howard Clive (1884–1985), educational historian, was born on 7 June 1884 at 11 King Edward Street in the heart of the City of London, the only child of Howard Barnard, journalist, and his wife, Sarah Ann Haggis. During the eighteenth century his ancestors established a firm of silversmiths in the City of London, and so became associated with the Goldsmiths' Company. Barnard was sixth in a direct line going back to about 1760 to become 'by patrimony' a member of this company and a freeman of the City. He was educated at University College School, London, when it was still in Gower Street, and at Brasenose College, Oxford, where he was a senior Hulme scholar. After taking third classes in both classical honour moderations (1905) and *literae humaniores* (1907) he was awarded a post-graduate scholarship for a further four years of study. This enabled him to pursue his interest in geography at the London School of Economics and to become a wandering scholar for a year, primarily at the universities of Heidelberg and Caen, where he perfected his German and French. Back at Oxford, he took a diploma in education with distinction and completed a BLitt thesis, 'The educational theory and practice of the Port-Royalists', which was published two years later by the Cambridge University Press as *The Little Schools of Port-Royal* (1913). At twenty-nine, he had embarked on what was to be a prolific literary career. Meanwhile, he married in 1910 Edith Gwendolen (*d.* 1956), daughter of John Wish, a civil servant. They had a son and a daughter.

Barnard's career as a schoolmaster got under way in 1911. At Manchester grammar school, Chatham House School in Ramsgate, and Bradford grammar school, he served as assistant master, being variously responsible for teaching German, English, and geography. Then in 1925 he moved to the headmastership of Gillingham grammar school, Kent, guiding it through a rapid expansion during his twelve years there. In 1937, at a time when it was unusual for a practising teacher to take up a professorship, he moved to the chair of education at Reading; but by then his distinction as a scholar ran parallel with his distinction as teacher and headmaster.

As scholar and historian, Barnard had been given stimulus and encouragement by his association with King's College, London, where, by a liberal interpretation of the term, he considered himself a part-time 'advanced student'. It was through his connection with King's College, and in particular with professors John Dover Wilson and J. W. Adamson, with both of whom he struck up a close friendship, that he became an MA (education) and DLitt of London University.

In 1918 Barnard brought out *The Port-Royalists in Education*, and in 1922 *The French Tradition in Education*, which remains a classic. It covers the period from the Renaissance to the eve of the French Revolution, exploring in detail the work of educationists and educational institutions, and impresses by its range and depth alike. Four further books, *Madame de Maintenon and Saint-Cyr* (1934), *Girls at School under the Ancien régime* (1954), *Fénelon on Education* (1966), and *Education and the French Revolution* (1969), testify to his unflagging interest in French education and became standard works on the subject. Other notable books are *Principles and Practice of Geography Teaching* (1933), *A Short History of English Education, from 1760 to 1944* (1974), a textbook well known to generations of students, and a splendid autobiographical account of his Victorian childhood, *Were those the Days?* (1970).

Ease of scholarship and an enviable limpidity of style characterized both his writing and lecturing, and Barnard was warmly admired by students and colleagues alike. By nature he was modest, detached, slightly impersonal. He lived to be the 'grand old man' of the university, but typically denied that there was any merit in being old.

For more than thirty years after his retirement Barnard regularly returned to the university to play the organ in the great hall. In the same hall, Reading University conferred an honorary DLitt on him in 1974; and it was there that family, students, friends, and colleagues held a commemorative service shortly after he died in a nursing home near Godalming, Surrey, on 12 September 1985 at the revered age of 101. RAYMOND WILSON, *rev.*

Sources H. C. Barnard, *Were those the days?* (1970) [autobiography] • P. Gordon, 'Present in the past', *Times Educational Supplement* (1 June 1984) • *The Times* (20 Sept 1985), 3a • *WWW* • R. Wilson, 'One hundred years, teacher and scholar', *Comparative Education* (20 March 1984) • personal knowledge (1990) • private information (1990) • *CGPLA Eng. & Wales* (1986)
Wealth at death £165,373: probate, 7 Jan 1986, *CGPLA Eng. & Wales*

Barnard, John (*b. c.*1591), music editor and composer, was between 1618 and 1622 a lay clerk at Canterbury Cathedral, where he was also employed to teach the cathedral choristers to play the viol. When he married Marie Martin there on 7 October 1619 his age was given as 'about 28'. A son, John, was baptized in the cathedral on 18 September 1621. By 1637 Barnard had moved to London, where he competed unsuccessfully for the post of master at St

Paul's Cathedral song school. In the same year he became a minor canon of St Paul's Cathedral.

Barnard's reputation rests principally on his role as the compiler of *The First Book of Selected Church Musick*, an anthology of English church music which was published in ten partbooks in 1641 for the use of cathedrals and collegiate church choirs. This was the only collection of English liturgical music printed in England between John Day's *Certaine Notes* (1565) and the civil war. No complete set survives in any library, although thirty-eight individual books (including copies of all ten partbooks) exist. A book of organ accompaniments is necessary for the performance of many of the compositions, but it is unlikely that one was ever printed, due to the complexity of setting keyboard music in moveable type. Barnard devoted his *First Book* to sixty-six compositions by nineteen deceased composers. According to the preface he intended to issue a further collection of music by living composers if his first collection was well received.

Between about 1625 and 1638 Barnard assembled (and may himself partly have copied) a manuscript collection of church music. This served as printer's copy for some of the pieces which later appeared in the 1641 collection, and is preserved in the library of the Royal College of Music, London (MSS 1045–1051; three of the original ten partbooks are lost). Barnard's manuscripts are the unique source of no fewer than fifty of the 174 compositions which they contain. The music is by forty-four identified composers, of whom six (Barnard himself, William Cobbold, Thomas Hunt, John Mace, John Oker or Okeover, and William West) are not otherwise represented in pre-Restoration liturgical sources. The manuscripts also contain six anonymous pieces. Barnard's manuscripts contain his own 'Preces and Responses for 27 March and 5 November' (the anniversaries of the monarch's accession and the Gunpowder Plot). John Barnard may also be the composer of a three-voice catch, 'Ah. Woe is me!', by a Mr Barnard, which was printed in 1663 in John Hilton's *Catch that Catch Can*. Nothing is known either of Barnard's later career or of the date of his death. JOHN MOREHEN

Sources J. Morehen, 'Barnard, John', *New Grove* • J. B. Clark, 'Adrian Batten and John Barnard: colleagues and collaborators', *Musica Disciplina*, 22 (1968), 207–28 • J. Morehen, 'The sources of English cathedral music, *c*.1617–c1644', PhD diss., U. Cam., 1969, 244–30 • R. T. Daniel and P. le Huray, *The sources of English church music, 1549–1660* (1972) • R. Hovenden, ed., *The register booke of christeninges, marriages, and burialls within the precinct of the cathedrall and metropoliticall church of Christe of Canterburie*, Harleian Society, register section, 2 (1878), 4, 55

Barnard, John (*bap.* **1628**, *d.* **1683**), biographer, was baptized on 10 November 1628 at Caistor, Lincolnshire, one of ten children of John Barnard (*d.* 1663), JP and attorney, and his wife, Isabell (*bap.* 1605, *d.* in or after 1670), daughter of James Wright of Bradley in the same county. The Barnards were a gentry family of some standing in Lincolnshire and owned property at Caistor and Laceby, outside Grimsby. Barnard was reputedly educated at Caistor grammar school, and then at Queens' College, Cambridge, where he was admitted a pensioner on 22 February 1645. He entered Oxford in 1648 upon the preferment of the board of visitors, was granted a BA on 15 April, and on 29 September was made a fellow of Lincoln College. He proceeded MA in 1651, and thereafter became a preacher in and around Oxford. In 1656 Barnard became rector of Waddington, near Lincoln. He purchased the perpetual advowson and that of Gedney on the Wash.

During the interregnum the young Barnard was probably a moderate royalist. A friend of the clergyman Peter *Heylyn, on 13 April 1657 he married the latter's daughter Lettice, or Letitia, at Abingdon, and probably mingled with royalist refugees at Heylyn's home nearby. However, like many discreet royalists, Barnard found it necessary to co-operate with the authorities in order to retain first his fellowship and later his livings. He belonged to the more 'precise' or godly wing of the royalist party that demanded the rigorous purge of profane and idle clergy as a precondition of the divine blessing of the Church of England. To this end he celebrated the role of Oliver Cromwell as a providential scourge in his *Censura cleri: against scandalous ministers not fit to be restored to the church's livings in prudence, piety and fame* (1660), which argued against the restoration of some notorious clergy ejected in 1654–5, and called for a priesthood distinguished by chastity and sanctity. Barnard regretted publishing the pamphlet, however, presumably because its constructive criticism of the church was misinterpreted as an endorsement of the discipline and rigour of some nonconformist practice and called into question Barnard's loyalty.

Barnard conformed at the Restoration, and in 1669 was granted the degrees of BD and DD. On 13 April 1672 he was made prebendary of Asgarby at Lincoln. He is best known for his *Theologo-historicus: a true life of the most revered divine and excellent historian, Peter Heylyn, D.D., sub-dean of Windsor* (1683). The work is both an answer to criticisms levelled at Heylyn by Richard Baxter, and a reply to a biography by George Vernon, rector of Burton, Gloucestershire, *The Life of the Learned and Reverend Dr Peter Heylyn* (1682). Barnard accuses Vernon of having damaged Heylyn's reputation by reprinting unsubstantiated rumours concerning his subject, and of plagiarism of Barnard's notes that had been entrusted to the Heylyn family. Barnard may have also written a catechism for the use of his parish, and a manuscript tract against Socinianism, which was never printed. He died on 17 August 1683 at Newark *en route* for a spa (presumably at Buxton), and was buried on 19 August in his own church of Waddington. He left at least one surviving child, a son John *Barnard (*b.* 1660/61, *d.* in or after 1713). GEOFFREY BROWELL

Sources *DNB* • Foster, *Alum. Oxon.* • Venn, *Alum. Cant.* • *Fasti Angl.* (Hardy), 2.103 • A. R. Maddison, ed., *Lincolnshire pedigrees*, 1, Harleian Society, 50 (1902), 87–8 • A. E. Preston, *The church and parish of St Nicholas, Abingdon: the early grammar school, to end of sixteenth century*, OHS, 99 (1935) • Wood, *Ath. Oxon.*, new edn, 4.96–7 • A. Kippis and others, eds., *Biographia Britannica, or, The lives of the most eminent persons who have flourished in Great Britain and Ireland*, 2nd edn, 1 (1778), 607–8 • parish register, Waddington, Lincolnshire [microfilm] • J. Barnard, *Theologo-historicus: a true life of the most revered divine and excellent historian, Peter Heylyn, D.D., sub-dean of Windsor* (1683)

Barnard, John [*known as* John Augustine Bernard] (*b.* **1660/61**, *d.* in or after **1713**), Roman Catholic convert and author, was the son of John *Barnard (*d.* 1683), rector of Waddington, Lincolnshire, and his wife, Lettice, daughter of Peter *Heylyn. Having matriculated from Lincoln College, Oxford, on 17 November 1676, aged fifteen, he graduated BA in 1680 and was elected a fellow of Brasenose College on 24 June 1681. He proceeded MA in 1683 and was ordained priest in December 1684.

In December the following year, after James II's accession, Barnard, as related by Anthony Wood, 'took all occasions to talk … in behalf of popery' soon becoming a Roman Catholic and styling himself John Augustine Bernard. 'Protected by the king' in May 1686, he was, alongside his mentor, Obadiah Walker, and two younger Catholic fellows of University College, 'dispenc'd from going to common prayer, [and] receiving the sacrament'. The group provoked disproportionate concern. On 1 January 1687 the king commanded that Bernard should succeed John Halton, of Queen's College, as moral philosophy lecturer. He was duly elected and admitted on 28 March. The university ignored another mandate, for him to be created DCL. In 1688 he contributed verses to the university's congratulatory volume on Prince James's birth. Following an appeal from the Catholic sheriff of Oxfordshire, Bernard volunteered to fight for James against William of Orange. He left Oxford in October, resigning his fellowship soon after and the moral philosophy lectureship on 5 January 1689. Later he was in Ireland and, 'taken notice of' by King James, 'wrote some little things that were there printed', but in September 1690 he appeared at Chester, 'very poor and bare'. Reconciled to the Church of England, he was 'maintain'd with dole for some time by the bishop of Chester' (Wood, *Ath. Oxon.*, 3rd edn, 4.610), and later he moved to London.

On 2 February 1694 Barnard wrote to his 'Dear Friend' Anthony Wood praising the *Athenae* and *Fasti Oxonienses* but objecting to the account given of his religion, which he admitted he could not clearly define himself. In the preceding year he had published an enlarged version of Edmund Bohun's *Geographical Dictionary*, enlisting the help of 'the ingenious Mr [Edmond] Hally' with the tables, and was now working on a 'History of the rise, progress, & growth, of [the] Com[m]on Law of England' (MS Wood F. 49, fol. 5*r*). About this no more was heard, but another edition of the dictionary by him, enlarged and continued to 1694, appeared in 1695. In 1695 he translated as *The Political Last Testament of Monsieur John Baptist Colbert* a work by Gatien de Courtilz de Sandras entitled *La vie de Jean-Baptiste Colbert*, prefacing it with a life of the subject. In a dedication to Lord Aston he revealed that he had been a short while in France. In 1698, as 'John Bernard, A.M.', he published in translation *The Lives of the Roman Emperors*, dedicated, as 'a Mark of my entire Fidelity and Affection to Your most Sacred Person and Government', to William III, 'the Constantine of this Age'. The abject protestation gained him no preferment.

Eventually, through his godfather, Bishop James Gardiner of Lincoln, Barnard was instituted to the Lincolnshire rectory of Ludford Parva on 30 July 1701 and presented to the nearby vicarage of Kelstern on 27 April 1702, but by 1708 financial embarrassment and hot pursuit by creditors had seemingly deranged his mind. In a series of letters to the bishop of Lincoln, William Wake, and to the archbishops, between March and July of that year (MS Rawl. A. 275, fols. 2*r*–37*r*), he made demands culminating in £100 to clear his debts, an annual pension of £100 and a Lambeth doctorate in law. He also subscribed to forty-one supposedly unanswerable 'positions': if his demands were met he would continue to conform outwardly; if not the 'positions' would be made public. Subsequently printed in a pamphlet, these upheld the Latin mass and transubstantiation, attacked the Book of Common Prayer and Book of Homilies, ridiculed the Thirty-Nine Articles, and questioned the efficacy of preaching, while insisting on the doctrine and discipline of the first six Christian centuries (Bodl. Oxf., pamph. 277 (17)). Sequestrated and excommunicated, Barnard began instead to issue 'positions' against the Catholic church from the end of 1709, and was back at Kelstern by 1713. After this nothing is known of Barnard, and even the date of his death is unrecorded. A. J. Hegarty

Sources Wood, *Ath. Oxon.*, new edn, 4.610 • Wood, *Ath. Oxon.: Fasti* (1820), 372 • Bodl. Oxf., MS Wood F. 49, fol. 5*r* • Bodl. Oxf., MS Rawl. A. 275, fols. 2*r*–37*r* • Bodl. Oxf., pamph. 277 (17) • Foster, *Alum. Oxon.* • R. A. Beddard, 'James II and the Catholic challenge', *Hist. U. Oxf. 4: 17th-cent. Oxf.*, 907–54 • E. Bohun, *A geographical dictionary … enlarged by Mr Bernard* (1693) • J. Bernard, *The lives of the Roman emperors*, 2 vols. (1698) • G. de Courtilz de Sandras, *The political last testament of Monsieur John Baptist Colbert*, trans. J. A. Bernard (1695) • *DNB* • private information (2004) [J. Lock]

Archives Bodl. Oxf., letters, MS Rawl. A. 275, fols. 2*r*–37*r* | Bodl. Oxf., letters to Anthony Wood, MS Wood F. 49, fol. 5*r* • Christ Church Oxf., Wake papers, corresp. with William Wake, vol. 4, fols. 205–339

Barnard, Sir John (*c.*1685–1764), politician, was born of Quaker parentage about 1685 at Reading, presumably in or near his maternal grandfather's estate of Play Hatch. Brought up in London, where his father was a prosperous wine merchant, and educated at a Quaker school in Wandsworth, he joined the family firm at the tender age of fifteen because of his father's failing health. He took over the active running of the business, and before long had extended his commercial activities into the field of marine insurance, which then became his chief occupation. On 5 October 1708 he married Jane (*d.* 1738), the younger daughter of John Godschall, a Turkey merchant. A serious-minded young man, and a voracious reader, Barnard had by this time persuaded himself out of his inherited principles in religion; in 1703 he had been baptized into the Church of England, supposedly by Bishop Compton of London, in the private chapel at Fulham Palace. He became a devoutly evangelical churchman, of a latitudinarian bent, who preferred clergymen to be 'Tories in the Church and Whigs in the state, not high-flying Tories but moderate ones who were for preserving the Church doctrines without violence and persecution, men at the same time who would exert themselves against popery' (HoP, *Commons*, 1.435). Thus, as an MP he opposed

Sir John Barnard (*c*.1685–1764), by Jacques-Antoine Dassier, 1744

the repeal of the Test Act and the general naturalization of foreign protestants and Jews, and promoted measures for moral reformation, in particular the regulation of theatres. His churchmanship also made him acceptable to surviving tory interests in the City, and when he stood for parliament for the first time, in the bitterly contested general election of 1722, he was included in the tory as well as the whig list for the London constituency, and was returned as an independent.

Barnard's political principles, however, were essentially those of a traditional 'country' whig. In the City he consistently advocated the rights of ordinary liverymen in common hall against the engrossing oligarchy of the court of aldermen, appearing in the role of a 'tribune of the plebeians' (a phrase coined by Hervey, 1.168). On economic questions he represented the interests of small merchants and manufacturers, always giving prime consideration in debates on taxation to the effects of proposed duties on trade, and making repeated attempts to curb the over-mighty power of high finance. In 1733 he introduced a bill to prevent 'the infamous practice of stock-jobbing' (something he had himself been falsely accused of in an election squib in 1722). Had the measure not been emasculated by a series of government-inspired amendments it would have prevented the development of the stock exchange. Concern over the influence of the 'moneyed interest' also induced Barnard to promote various schemes to reduce the size of the national debt or the rate of interest paid on it. More generally, he set himself up as an enemy to the corruption of those surrounding Robert Walpole. Although allegedly a dull speaker, more at home with figures on a balance sheet than figures of speech (Walpole, *Memoirs*, 1.45–6), he was none the less a persistent thorn in Walpole's side, active in the House of Commons in the gaols inquiry of 1729 and the Charitable Corporation affair two years later, and reaching an apogee of eloquence in the debates on the Excise Bill in 1733, when he took centre stage, fortified by the coincidence of his own private interest, as a wine merchant, with what he saw as the public interest, and memorably refuting Walpole's slur on the protesting 'multitudes' in the City as 'sturdy beggars'.

Barnard's popularity in the City, which had brought him an unopposed election as alderman for Dowgate ward in 1728, the honour of presenting the corporation's loyal address in 1732 (when he was knighted), and a triumphant re-election to parliament in 1734, survived a potential setback in 1737, when his scheme to reduce the interest on the national debt was thwarted only by Walpole's intervention. So incensed were investors in anticipation of the reduction that a mob burnt the former 'darling of the City' in effigy (*Egmont Diary*, 2.396), and 'a combination of merchants' threatened to withdraw their insurance business from him (Hervey, 3.726). However, not only did he continue to trade; he recovered his reputation to be elected lord mayor in 1737 (having served as sheriff two years before), and would have been chosen again in March 1741 had he not refused nomination on health grounds. The offer was in order to break a deadlock caused by the repeated refusal of the aldermen to accept the election of his brother-in-law, Sir Robert Godschall. Barnard was now at the height of his reputation, his bust placed alongside those of other patriot luminaries in the 'temple of British worthies' erected by Lord Cobham at Stowe. In 1740 he was made president of Christ's Hospital and published the only work which can confidently be attributed to him: *A present for an apprentice, or, A sure guide to gain both esteem and estate, by a late lord mayor of London*, a compendium of practical hints on everyday subjects, which he imbued with strong Christian moralizing. In the general election the following year pleas of ill health were again brushed aside, and he was returned for the City at the head of the poll.

When Walpole fell, Barnard retained his independence, refusing office for himself (though accepting a place for his son). According to Walpole, however, he 'attached himself' to Lord Granville (*Memoirs*, 1.45–6). Certainly after the dismissal of Granville he compared the new ministers unfavourably with the old, and once more launched into opposition, though with a discrimination that disdained the violence of faction. During the Jacobite rising of 1745 he rallied loyal opinion in London, and thereafter moderated his hostility to administration, flattered by Henry Pelham's 'complaisance' towards him. There was considerable advantage to Pelham in winning over a man who was still the acknowledged leader of opinion in London, the subject of so much public veneration that in 1747 a statue of him was erected outside the Royal Exchange. In 1749 Pelham even adopted a pet scheme of Barnard's to reduce interest on the national debt. Ironically, this was the point at which Barnard's political star began to wane. The resentment of investors ate into his hitherto invincible popularity, and his reputation as an expert on financial affairs suffered a blow. Although Pelham continued to make a show of consulting him, the ministry returned to dependence on the charmed circle of financial magnates. Old age was also sapping Barnard's political strength, and his position in the City was being undermined by the rise of William Beckford, to whom he conceded ground in 1756 by a further political misjudgement in opposing the corporation's address on the loss of Minorca. In 1757 Barnard was at last offered a chance to put into practice his long-held ideas about government finance, when the chancellor of the exchequer in the Pitt–Devonshire administration, H. B. Legge, sought his co-operation in the raising of supply. But Barnard's scheme, for a lottery and annuities based on an 'open' subscription of small investors instead of the usual 'closed' subscriptions dominated by the great bankers, failed to attract sufficient funds, and with the resignation of Pitt and Legge the duke of Devonshire turned again to Barnard's *bête noire*, the representatives of the 'moneyed interest', to bale out government.

Barnard resigned his alderman's place a year later, and gave up his seat in parliament at the 1761 election. In declining health, he lived in secluded retirement in Clapham, Surrey, until his death there on 29 August 1764. He was buried in Mortlake, Surrey, on 4 September. His fortune passed to his only son, John *Barnard (1709–1784), who spent some of it in collecting pictures, but was otherwise renowned as a miser. Of his two daughters, one married the banker and London alderman Sir Thomas Hankey; the other married Hon. Henry Temple, the younger son of the first Viscount Palmerston, and in due course became the mother of the second viscount.

D. W. Hayton

Sources H. Venn, *Memoirs of the late Sir John Barnard, knight, and alderman of the city of London* (1776) • H. R. Fox Bourne, *English merchants: memoirs in illustration of the progress of British commerce*, new edn, 2 vols. (1886), 282–97 • L. Namier, 'Barnard, Sir John', HoP, *Commons* • L. S. Sutherland, *Politics and finance in the eighteenth century*, ed. A. N. Newman (1984), 41–113, 387–413 • A. J. Henderson, *London and the national government, 1721–1742* (1945) • Walpole, *Corr.* • H. Walpole, *Memoirs of the reign of King George the Second*, ed. Lord Holland, 2nd edn, 3 vols. (1847) • *Manuscripts of the earl of Egmont: diary of Viscount Percival, afterwards first earl of Egmont*, 3 vols., HMC, 63 (1920–23) • W. Coxe, *Memoirs of the life and administration of Sir Robert Walpole, earl of Orford*, 3 vols. (1798) • John, Lord Hervey, *Some materials towards memoirs of the reign of King George II*, ed. R. Sedgwick, 3 vols. (1931) • N. Rogers, *Whigs and cities: popular politics in the age of Walpole and Pitt* (1989)

Likenesses P. Schecmakers, marble statue, 1737, Royal Exchange, London • J. Faber junior, mezzotint, pubd 1739 (after A. Ramsay), BM, NPG • J.-A. Dassier, bronze medal, 1744, NPG [*see illus.*] • J. Macardell, mezzotint, pubd 1754 (after A. Ramsay), BM, NPG • J.-A. Dassier, copper medal, BM • J. Kirk, medal, BM • M. Rysbrack, bust, Temple of British Worthies, Stowe, Buckinghamshire

Barnard, John, the younger (1704/5–1784), shipbuilder, was born in Ipswich, the son of John Barnard the elder (1665–1717), shipbuilder of the borough of Ipswich, and his wife, Mary (1666–1733). He probably attended the academy for dissenters in Ipswich. In 1723 he was apprenticed to Edmund Gooday, shipbuilder and burgher of the borough. On 14 October 1728 he married Annie Notcutt (1705–1751).

The Barnard family shipbuilding business was located at Wix Bishop, a hamlet in the parish of St Clement's on the upper reaches of the River Orwell. By 1739 the younger John Barnard was recognized as the leading shipbuilder on the river, not only contracting for local owners but also obtaining Navy Board contracts for men-of-war. In October he contracted to build the frigate *Biddeford* (20 guns) which was launched on 15 June 1740. A further contract was received for the *Hampshire* (50 guns). She was built at John's Ness, an isolated hard some 2 miles downstream of St Clement's, and was launched on 13 November 1741. A contract for the *Granado*, a bomb-vessel, was received on 14 September 1741; she was launched on 22 January 1742.

The restricted facilities and the tidal flows in the vicinity of the St Clement's yard weighed heavily against Barnard's ability to exploit fully the close association he had established with the Navy Board. In 1742, therefore, he elected to rent the King's Yard, Harwich, which had been rentable on a care and maintenance basis since 1713. He remained a tenant of the yard until 1781.

During his tenancy Barnard built some twenty-nine vessels for the Navy Board ranging from sloops to 74-gun ships, the workhorses of the fleet. The first vessels he was contracted to build in the King's Yard were warships to counter the increasing attacks by French privateers on British shipping. War was eventually declared between Britain and France on 2 March 1744. The treaty of Aix-la-Chapelle brought an uneasy peace from 1748 until the outbreak of the Seven Years' War in 1756. Barnard built eleven naval vessels in the King's Yard in the years of conflict. On 7 March 1759 he married his second wife, Sarah Dardey (1732–1802).

An incident far removed from the ravages of war occurred on 6 September 1761. Princess Charlotte of Mecklenburg, bride-to-be of George III, landed at Harwich. John Barnard, as tenant of the King's Yard, headed the reception committee formally handing her ashore. His grandson Edward George Barnard MP claimed that for this small service he was offered a knighthood, an honour which he declined, stating that he would much prefer an order for a new ship. In the year 1766 he was appointed high sheriff of Suffolk.

In the six years prior to the outbreak of the American War of Independence only four vessels had been built in the yard, one of which was a sloop. Between 1776 and 1783 Barnard built a further seven vessels, one again being a sloop.

Despite holding extensive property in Suffolk and Essex Barnard was unexpectedly declared bankrupt in 1781. He died on 8 October 1784 in his eightieth year at the home of his son William in Deptford, Kent, and was buried in the family vault at the dissenters' chapel, Tacket Street, Ipswich. William, also a shipbuilder, had moved with William Dudman from Ipswich to the River Thames in 1763, where, in partnership with Henry Adams of Beaulieu, Hampshire, they leased an extensive yard from the Evelyn estates at Grove Street, Deptford. Following Dudman's death in 1772 William Barnard continued to prosper and leased a further yard at Deptford Green, building on his own account both for the Navy Board and for the shipping interests of the East India Company.

John E. Barnard

Sources Suffolk RO, C/5/14/C • PRO, ADM 66/2557; ADM 106/916; ADM 106/926; ADM 106/2208

Archives PRO, ADM • Suffolk RO, Ipswich, C/5/14/C

Wealth at death declared bankrupt in 1781: PRO, ADM 106/2208

Barnard, John (1709–1784), collector of prints and drawings, was born in London and was baptized on 25 August

1709 at St Laurence Pountney, the eldest of the three children and only son of Sir John *Barnard of Greenwood (*c*.1685–1764), MP for the City of London, and Jane (*d*. 1738), daughter of John Godschall, a London merchant trading with Turkey.

Barnard, who inherited a large fortune from his father, for fifty years devoted himself to the formation of a collection of prints, drawings, and paintings, becoming one of the foremost connoisseurs of his day. The earliest printed account of his collection dates from 1761: it lists sixty-five pictures and records that he also had a collection of 'about twelve thousand prints, engraved and etched by the most celebrated masters of the three last centuries … They are contained in about 50 large volumes, besides above 60 volumes in sculpture and architecture' (Dodsley and Dodsley, 292). His collection of prints included works of Italian, French, Flemish, German, and Dutch artists, and was distinguished by a nearly complete representation of the work of Marcantonio Raimondi, Wenceslaus Hollar, Rembrandt, Van Dyck, and Rubens.

Barnard's collection of drawings was also very fine and sheets with a provenance from his collection are usually of the highest calibre, both in quality and in the state of preservation. Several of his Rembrandt drawings were said to have a provenance from the Six collection in Amsterdam, and other purchases were made from distinguished contemporary sales such as those of the earl of Arundel, Sir Peter Lely, Lord Somers, Richard Mead, and Sir Uvedale Price. The sculptor Joseph Nollekens was reputed to have been removed from Barnard's will for not sufficiently admiring Barnard's Italian drawings.

Barnard established himself in Berkeley Square, London, with many prominent contemporaries as neighbours. His sister Sarah had married Alderman Sir Thomas Hankey; his younger sister, Jane, was the mother of the second Viscount Palmerston, a patron of Joseph Nollekens. His wife was previously the mistress of John Wilkes. Her infidelity continued after her marriage, which produced one daughter who died young. Barnard had originally bequeathed his prints, drawings, and books to John Wilkes. This bequest was revoked because of a cooling in the friendship, brought about by the continuing closeness between his wife and Wilkes.

Barnard died at Berkeley Square in 1784. His drawings were sold first by Greenwood, auctioneer of Leicester Square, on 16 February 1787 and seven days following. His prints were sold next by Harry Phillips, auctioneer of New Bond Street, on 16 April 1798 and twenty-five days following. He left his pictures to his nephew, Thomas Hankey of Bedford Square; these were sold at Christies on 7–8 June 1799. His pictures are distinguished by having his monogram in black letters with an inventory number at the back. CHARLES SEBAG-MONTEFIORE, *rev.*

Sources R. Dodsley and J. Dodsley, *London and its environs described*, 1 (1761) • T. Martyn, *The English connoisseur*, 1 (1766), 1–11 • F. Lugt, *Les marques de collections de dessins et d'estampes* (Amsterdam, 1921)

Barnard, Joseph Edwin (1868–1949), hatter and microscopist, was born on 7 December 1868 at 321 Vauxhall Bridge Road, Pimlico, London, the son of Walter Barnard, hatter, and his wife, Elizabeth Phillips Jacob. He was educated at the City of London School, leaving at the age of sixteen as head boy. He entered his father's firm, with premises at 97 Jermyn Street, London, later becoming its proprietor. This business gave him the time and money to pursue his hobby of microscopy to a highly professional level.

In his own private laboratory Barnard worked with ultraviolet radiation at the ultimate resolution of the optical microscope. From 1899 he undertook photomicrographic work at the Jenner (later Lister) Institute of Preventive Medicine. He became honorary lecturer in microscopy at King's College, London, in 1909, a position he held for sixteen years. His book *Practical Photo-Micrography* (1911) remained the standard English textbook on the subject for over thirty years. In 1916 he was co-opted on to the trench fever committee of the War Office, and attempted to discover the causal organism of the fever. In 1920 he became honorary director of the department of applied optics, National Institute for Medical Research; he retired during the Second World War.

Barnard was elected a fellow of the Royal Microscopical Society in 1895, and served three times as its president (1918–19, 1928–9, and 1938–45). He was awarded an honorary fellowship in 1948. In 1911 he was a founder member of the Photomicrographic Society, whose Barnard medal he endowed. He was elected a fellow of the Institute of Physics in 1923, and of the Royal Society in 1924. On 23 March 1894 he married Amelia Muir Cunningham Burge (1867/8–1923), daughter of William Mark Burge, hatter; they had no children. On 18 August 1924 he married Daisy (*b*. 1892/3), daughter of Frederick William Russell Fisher, sheet metal worker. They had one son and one daughter.

Barnard's achievement was to develop the ultraviolet microscope (invented in Germany in 1903) for the study of viruses. In the course of twenty-five years of persistent pioneering work, he was responsible for novel design features, such as the duplex condenser (1924), objective changer (1926), and cone condenser (1930), the last allowing for the first time ultraviolet, dark-ground photographs of viruses. He collaborated with his friend Conrad Beck, the optical manufacturer, in applying these improvements to a production model, and the Beck–Barnard instrument, the first really efficient ultraviolet microscope, was placed on the market in 1929. As a result of his work, a number of viruses causing disease in plants, animals (he worked on foot-and-mouth disease), and humans were first observed. In 1925 he received national press publicity for discoveries concerning malignant growths.

In addition to his business, and his devotion to microscopy, Barnard found time for other interests. He was musical, and had an organ in his house; he enjoyed travel, motoring over much of the continent; and he was a keen photographer. He died at 19 Grimwade Avenue, Addiscombe, Surrey, on 25 October 1949.

G. L'E. TURNER, *rev.*

Sources J. A. Murray, *Obits. FRS*, 7 (1950–51), 3–8 • *Journal of the Royal Microscopical Society*, 3rd ser., 71 (1951), 104–13 • G. L'E. Turner,

God bless the microscope! (1989) • b. cert. • m. cert., 1894 • m. cert., 1924 • *CGPLA Eng. & Wales* (1950)

Archives University of Pennsylvania, Gilchrist family papers

Likenesses photograph, repro. in Murray, *Obits. FRS*, facing p. 3 • photograph, RS • photographic negative, RS

Wealth at death £60,908 5*s*. 7*d*.: probate, 4 March 1950, *CGPLA Eng. & Wales*

Barnard, Thomas (*bap.* **1727**, *d.* **1806**), bishop of Limerick, was born in Surrey and baptized at Esher, Surrey, on 22 February 1727, the elder son of Dr William *Barnard (1696/7–1768), bishop of Derry, and Anne Stone (*d.* 1782), sister of the Irish primate George Stone. He was educated at Westminster School and at Trinity College, Dublin, where he was admitted on 24 October 1744. He graduated BA in 1748 and proceeded MA from Cambridge University in 1749. On his collation to the archdeaconry of Derry on 3 June 1761 he was awarded the degree of DD by Trinity College, Dublin. After being instituted as dean of Derry on 2 June 1769, he was consecrated bishop of Killaloe and Kilfenora on 20 February 1780, and was translated to the united sees of Limerick, Ardfert, and Aghadoe by patent dated 12 September 1794. He married Anne (*d.* 1803), daughter of William Browne of Browne's Hill, co. Carlow. She was the niece of Bishop Robert Clayton of Clogher and inherited most of his fortune on his death in 1758. Mary Delany wrote of their marriage that Miss Browne:

> is to have one of the prettiest sort of young men in Dublin—modest, sensible, sober, a clergyman with a living between seven and eight hundred a year … Is it not strange he should desperately fall in love with one who is in every respect his opposite? (*Autobiography … Mrs Delany*, 3.221)

Following Anne's death Barnard married, on 30 August 1803, Jane, the twenty-two-year-old daughter of John Ross-Lewin of Fort Fergus, co. Clare; she died shortly afterwards.

Barnard was elected a fellow of the Royal Society on 29 May 1783 and was a member of many literary societies, including the Literary Club to which Garrick, Johnson, Burke, and Goldsmith also belonged. In conjunction with the president of the Royal Society, Sir Joseph Banks, he drew up the rules for the Royal Irish Academy (RIA), which was founded in 1785 and of which he was an original member. He served on the antiquaries committee of the RIA and owned a fine collection of pictures at his house in Henrietta Street, Dublin. Following the Act of Union, for which he voted, and the abolition of the Irish parliament, he longed to live in London and expressed a wish that he could resign his Limerick bishopric 'for a small pension, to end my days out of this barbarous country' (Powell, 130). He died on 7 June 1806 in Wimbledon in the house of his only son, Andrew Barnard, husband of Lady Anne *Barnard (*née* Lindsay). He was buried in Westminster Abbey. THOMPSON COOPER, *rev.* J. FALVEY

Sources A. Powell, ed., *Barnard letters, 1778–1824* (1928) • T. Ó Raifeartaigh, *The Royal Irish Academy: a bicentennial history, 1785–1985* (1985) • R. Cumberland, *Memoirs of Richard Cumberland written by himself*, 2 vols. (1806–7) • J. Falvey, 'The Church of Ireland episcopate in the eighteenth century', MA diss., University College, Cork, 1995 • *The autobiography and correspondence of Mary Granville, Mrs Delany*, ed. Lady Llanover, 1st ser., 3 vols. (1861) • *Report on the manuscripts of Mrs Stopford-Sackville*, 2, HMC, 49 (1910) • Venn, *Alum. Cant.*

Archives JRL, letters to Sir James Calwell; letters to Charles Wesley • Royal Irish Acad., MS 12, N.3 • Yale U., Beinecke L., corresp. with James Boswell

Likenesses W. Daniell, soft-ground etching, pubd 1812 (after G. Dance, 1793), BM, NPG

Barnard, William (1696/7–1768), Church of Ireland bishop of Derry, was born at Clapham, Surrey, the son of John Barnard, a lawyer. He entered Westminster School in 1713, and, aged twenty, was elected in 1717 to a scholarship at Trinity College, Cambridge. He graduated BA (1721), MA (1724), and DD (1740). He became a minor fellow of Trinity on 1 October 1723 and a major fellow on 7 July 1724. On 11 July 1726 Barnard was collated to the rectory of Esher, Surrey, and so became acquainted with the duke of Newcastle, who appointed him his chaplain. He was appointed chaplain to George II in 1728, and held the same office at Chelsea College. In January 1729 he was presented to the vicarage of St Bride's, Fleet Street, London, which he held until 1747. On 4 October 1732 he was installed prebendary of Westminster, and on 26 April 1743 became dean of Rochester. On 14 May 1744 Barnard was appointed bishop of Raphoe and on 3 March 1747 was translated to Derry, where he proved to be a generous benefactor. In 1752 he published a sermon 'preached before the Incorporated Society for Promoting English Protestant Schools in Ireland'. He was married to Anne (*d.* 1782), a sister of George Stone, archbishop of Armagh; the couple's elder son, Thomas *Barnard, was baptized in 1727, and later became bishop of Limerick; their second son, Henry, a Church of Ireland clergyman, was father of Sir Andrew Francis Barnard, army officer, and grandfather of Sir Henry William Barnard, army officer. William Barnard returned to England from Londonderry on account of ill health. He died on 10 January 1768 at Great Queen Street, Westminster, and was buried in the north aisle of Westminster Abbey. His wife survived him. THOMPSON COOPER, *rev.* PHILIP CARTER

Sources Venn, *Alum. Cant.* • H. Cotton, *Fasti ecclesiae Hibernicae*, 1–2 (1845–8) • *GM*, 1st ser., 2 (1732), 980 • *GM*, 1st ser., 38 (1768), 47 • will, PRO, PROB 11/935, fols. 335*v*–336*r*

Archives BL, corresp. with duke of Newcastle, Add. MSS 32689–33068, *passim*

Barnard, William (*bap.* **1774**, *d.* **1849**), engraver, was baptized on 7 August 1774 in the church of Holy Trinity Minories, London, the son of James Barnard and his wife, Mary. According to John Chaloner Smith, his first signed mezzotint was published in 1798, and throughout his career he specialized in reproductive mezzotint portraits of noble and military subjects. As exemplified by his *Alexander Davison Esqr* (1804), his engraving was executed in a 'solid and bold manner' (Smith, 1.7), and most of his prints conformed to the traditional compositional format of half-length, three-quarters profile, with an internal oval or squared border. Several of his plates do deviate from this standard: of the four portraits of Lord Nelson that he executed after Lemuel-Francis Abbott, his *Admiral Lord Nelson* (1799) is striking as a complex, full-length image which positioned Nelson on a rocky, coastal outcrop with a sea battle raging in the background. From the comparatively crude mezzotint of *Robert Orchard Grocer & Tea Dealer* (1803), which was effectively an advertising puff for that merchant, we can discern that Barnard also worked at the cheaper end of the print market—at least for individual clients. Two of his most renowned mezzotints were lavish, outsize folio prints after George Morland's *Winter* and *Summer*, which were often sold hand coloured.

Little else is known of the life of William Barnard except that he held the post of keeper of the British Institution after 1829. The correspondence of Thomas Uwins (1782–1857) records that Barnard, as keeper, had responsibility for hanging exhibitions and distributing the revenue from the sale of work; consequently he must have had some impact upon the reputation and fortunes of a number of contemporary artists. He died on 11 November 1849. LUCY PELTZ

Sources Bryan, *Painters* (1903–5) · *By-laws of the British Institution for Promoting the Fine Arts in the United Kingdom, established the 4th of June, 1805, under the patronage of His Majesty* (1805) · C. Le Blanc, *Manuel de l'amateur d'estampes*, 4 vols. (Paris, 1854–89) · minutes of the British Institution, 7 vols., 1805–70, MS, V&A NAL, RC V 11–17 · Redgrave, *Artists* · J. C. Smith, *British mezzotinto portraits*, 4 vols. in 5 (1878–84) · S. Uwins, *A memoir of Thomas Uwins*, 2 vols. (1858); repr. in 1 vol. (1978) · *IGI*

Barnardiston [*née* Banks], **Katherine, Lady Barnardiston** (*d*. **1633**), patron of puritanism, was born in the parish of St Michael-le-Querne, Paternoster Row, in the city of London, one of seven children of Thomas Banks (*c*.1538–*c*.1598), barber-surgeon, and his wife, Joan. Her first husband was girdler Bartholomew Soame, son of Thomas Soame. He died young in 1596, at which time they were living in the parish of St Mary Colechurch in the city. In 1599 Katherine married Thomas, the eldest son of Sir Thomas Barnardiston of Kedington in Suffolk. The couple moved to the mansion of Witham Place in the parish of Witham in Essex, together with Thomas's children from his first marriage, one of whom was Nathaniel (later Sir Nathaniel) *Barnardiston (1588–1653); Katherine lived there for the rest of her life. Her husband was knighted in 1603 but died in 1610, before his father. A year or two later, about 1612, Katherine married again. Her third husband was William Towse (*c*.1551–1634), a lawyer who had been treasurer of the Inner Temple before being made serjeant-at-law in 1614. She retained her name and title from her second marriage. As far as is known Katherine had no children of her own, but she kept in close touch with her relatives, the Bankses, Soames, and Barnardistons of London and East Anglia, many of whom were very influential, particularly in the puritan cause. They included masters of London companies, lord mayors of London, members of parliament, and wealthy lords of manors in Essex and Suffolk.

Like a number of early seventeenth-century women, Lady Barnardiston used her wealth and contacts to promote godly puritanism. For instance, evidence suggests that she helped several clergymen during her thirty years in Witham; the most notable was Thomas Weld. She almost certainly played a part in his appointment as vicar in the neighbouring parish of Terling. In contrast, she gave support to a campaign in the church courts against the alleged immorality of Francis Wright, who was the vicar in her own parish of Witham. One of the many interesting aspects of this episode is the co-operation between Dame Katherine and her lower-ranking fellow parishioners.

Lady Barnardiston died at Witham Place in 1633. Her lengthy and remarkable will, drawn up on 25 February that year and proved on 19 March, has a fervent religious preamble written in her own hand. She asked that the renowned vicar of Finchingfield, Stephen Marshall, should preach at her funeral, and she provided him with £200 to be distributed in religious works. He gave £150 of it to John Dury, the protestant ecumenicalist. Her bequests included about £7700 in specific gifts of money, together with other unquantified sums, jewellery, plate, furnishings, and a Suffolk manor. Among the nearly ninety beneficiaries were individuals of all ranks, and also many charitable causes, both in Witham and elsewhere. She asked to be buried in the parish of St Michael-le-Querne, but it is unclear whether this wish was implemented; a monument to her was erected at Kedington. Her husband survived her, but died the following year. JANET GYFORD

Sources J. Gyford, *Public spirit: dissent in Witham and Essex, 1500–1700* (1999), 72–4, 99–102, 163–6 · will, PRO, PROB 11/163, fols. 205–211*v* · J. Gyford, *Witham, 1500–1700: making a living* (1996), 182–5 · will of Bartholomew Soame, PRO, PROB 11/87, fol. 46 · will of Sir Thomas Barnardiston, PRO, PROB 11/116, fol. 104

Likenesses monument, *c*.1633, Kedington church, Suffolk; repro. in Gyford, *Witham*, 184 · drawing (after monument), repro. in Gyford, *Public spirit*, 101 · photographs (after monument), priv. coll. · portrait (after monument), Essex RO, Chelmsford

Wealth at death monetary bequests totalled approx. £7700: will, PRO, PROB 11/163, fols. 205–211*v*

Barnardiston, Sir Nathaniel (**1588–1653**), politician and ecclesiastical patron, was born at Kedington, Suffolk, the eldest son of Sir Thomas Barnardiston (*d*. 1610), and his first wife, Mary (*d*. in or before 1599), daughter of Sir Richard *Knightley of Fawsley, Northamptonshire. One of the oldest families in Suffolk, the Barnardistons traced their ancestors to the reign of Richard I, and in the early seventeenth century they possessed substantial estates, some of which had been owned by the earls of Clare, in the south-western part of the county, around Barnardiston (Barnston) and Kedington. Barnardiston deemed his father a godly man, and his father's second wife, Katherine (*d*. 1633), was a notable patron of puritan ministers [*see* Barnardiston, Katherine]; his grandfather, also Sir Thomas, had studied under John Calvin at Geneva. Barnardiston underwent a spiritual rebirth while in school and thereafter maintained a lifelong preference for puritan views. Following his father's death, on 29 July 1610, he inherited his estate.

On 18 May 1613 Barnardiston married at St Pancras,

Soper Lane, London, Jane, eldest daughter of Sir Stephen Soame, alderman and former mayor of London and the owner of estates at Thurlow, Suffolk. In addition to obtaining a sizable jointure and useful ties to an influential mercantile family, Barnardiston broadened his county associations, for two of his wife's sisters married Suffolk gentlemen with puritan interests, Sir John Wentworth of Somerleyton and Sir Calthrop Parker of Erwarton, whose son, Sir Philip, later represented Suffolk in the Long Parliament. The Barnardistons had two daughters, Anne and Jane, and seven sons, Thomas *Barnardiston (*c.*1618–1669) and Samuel *Barnardiston (1620–1707), both knighted, Nathaniel, Pelatiah, William, and Arthur who all engaged in trade to the East Indies, and John.

On 15 December 1618 Barnardiston was knighted and the following year he inherited additional lands when his grandfather died, increasing his annual income to more than £3500, possibly the largest in Suffolk. The Barnardistons controlled the appointments to four livings in the Church of England: at Kedington, Barnardiston, and Great Wratting in Suffolk, and at Great Coates in Lincolnshire. He and four like-minded allies, Sir William Spring, Sir William Soame, Sir John Wentworth, and Sir Philip Parker, provided advowsons for eight puritan ministers. In 1623 Barnardiston offered Samuel Fairclough the living at Barnardiston with the promise that he would receive a better one when it became available, and he arranged for Fairclough to take up his post in June without first appearing before Samuel Harsnett, bishop of Norwich, and subscribing the three articles, including one affirming that the Book of Common Prayer contained nothing contrary to the word of God. Previously Fairclough had been cited before Harsnett for nonconformity while lecturing at King's Lynn, Norfolk. When the benefice at Kedington, worth £200 per annum, became available following Abraham Gibson's death in 1629, Barnardiston apparently asked the parishioners at Barnardiston for their approval before offering Kedington to Fairclough. Again he arranged for Fairclough to assume his new position without appearing before the bishop to swear the oath of canonical obedience and subscribe the articles, on the grounds that a fall from his horse prevented him from riding any distance. To replace Fairclough, Barnardiston obtained the services of John Westley, lecturer at Haverhill, Suffolk. Barnardiston also patronized Christopher Burrell, Fairclough's brother-in-law, to whom he presented the rectory of Great Wratting in 1630. When Burrell was ejected by Richard Mountague, bishop of Norwich, Barnardiston replaced him with John Owen, Fairclough's assistant at Kedington. Fairclough himself was almost ejected by Bishop Matthew Wren in 1636 for refusing to read the Book of Sports. Barnardiston had ties as well with Stephen Marshall, to whom his wife gave £200 in 1637, about the time Marshall encouraged Barnardiston to support the work of Samuel Hartlib. Other puritan ministers of his acquaintance included Thomas Hooker, John Cotton, Thomas Weld, Nathaniel Ward, and John Wilson, to all of whom he sent his regards via the younger John Winthrop in 1636. He almost certainly invested in the Massachusetts Bay Company.

Appointed high sheriff and deputy lieutenant in 1624, Barnardiston, who also served as a justice of the peace for many years, took his under-sheriffs and bailiffs to lectures by puritan clergy. Following his election to parliament as MP for Sudbury in 1625 he served on a committee to draft a bill to prevent drunkenness in alehouses and inns, and the following year, with the support of John Winthrop, he was again returned to parliament for Sudbury. Appointed by the king as a commissioner for the forced loan in Suffolk, Barnardiston initially refused to take the oath or lend £20, whereupon the privy council summoned him in December 1626. When he and two other Suffolk gentlemen acknowledged their error and agreed to lend the money, the council quickly sent copies of their submissions to other commissioners, but Barnardiston soon recanted on grounds of conscience. For this he was imprisoned by the council in February 1627, initially in the gatehouse at Westminster and then in Lincolnshire. He was released early the following year, at least partly because of the intervention of Sir Simonds D'Ewes. In 1628 he was again elected to parliament, this time for the county, although the low turnout at the final poll suggests that freeholders in the Ipswich area were not enthusiastic about him. However, he was successful in supporting Spring for the other shire seat after Sir Edward Coke opted to sit for Buckinghamshire rather than Suffolk. In the Commons he helped Sir Robert Harley prepare a bill to punish cattle-drovers, carriers, and others who violated the sabbath.

In the election for the Short Parliament of 1640 lesser officials in Suffolk, secretly supported by unidentified powerful men, attempted to adjourn the shire court from Ipswich to Beccles, where Sir William Playters, whose brother was a Laudian minister, probably would have defeated Barnardiston, but the effort failed, Playters withdrew, and Barnardiston and Parker, his wife's nephew, were returned without opposition. Barnardiston set out for this parliament with a sense of mission, believing that failure to enact reforms would endanger the church and kingdom. Another attempt to defeat Barnardiston was made in the election to the Long Parliament, this time by Henry North, who had the support of Laudian clergy and those Suffolk gentry who preferred neutrality in the contest between king and parliament. Barnardiston and Parker won, but the former failed to secure the election to the Ipswich seat of Brampton Gurdon, a connection by marriage of his brother Arthur. Again Barnardiston hoped for great things from parliament, fearing what would happen if 'the rootes of all our mischiefes' were not excised (BL, Harley MS 384, fol. 66). His connections in the Long Parliament also included his cousins Richard Knightley and Sir Oliver and Sir Samuel Luke, his brother-in-law Thomas Soame, and D'Ewes, who was married to one of his cousins.

Barnardiston was a supporter of John Pym, though he played only a modest role in the Long Parliament, serving on lesser committees, including one concerned with the reformation of ecclesiastical courts. He was undoubtedly responsible for the invitation Fairclough received to preach to the House of Commons on 4 April 1641. In that sermon, published as *The Troublers Troubled* and dedicated to his patron, Fairclough called for the punishment of contemporary Achans (such as the earl of Strafford). On 31 January 1642 Barnardiston submitted a petition from Suffolk gentry protesting the blocking of reform bills in the House of Lords by bishops and Catholic peers, whose expulsion the petitioners sought. In June he pledged two horses and agreed to continue his loan of £500 to defend parliament. At the county level he supported the parliamentary cause, in part by bringing charges against Frederick Gibb, minister at Boxted, who refused to read a declaration from parliament. In the aftermath of rioting in the Stour valley in August he was influential the following month in implementing the militia ordinance in Suffolk and promulgating the Commons' prohibition of riotous assemblies. Moreover, the committee of MPs and local gentry he headed raised money for parliament. The cumulative effect of these actions brought Suffolk into the parliamentary camp with minimal opposition. The following year Barnardiston took the covenant, and on 11 November 1644 he presented another petition from Suffolk to the Commons, this time urging it to settle the church's polity, discipline, and worship as proposed by the Westminster assembly. The committee of both kingdoms required his appearance in May 1644 and May 1645, and in the latter year he was responsible for ensuring that Landguard Fort was garrisoned by trustworthy men. In May 1645 he successfully petitioned the Commons for repayment of the (now) £700 he had subscribed plus an additional loan of £500 towards the suppression of the Irish rising.

Although he could find no particular ecclesiastical polity clearly established in scripture, Barnardiston considered himself a presbyterian. As he told Winthrop, he loved pious Independents such as those who supported the governor in New England, but not those in England who championed religious toleration. Sectaries should be curtailed and presbyterian discipline employed to restore order. He took an active part in establishing presbyterian classes in Suffolk, and he and his son Thomas were members of the Suffolk presbytery.

Barnardiston continued to cultivate connections with other MPs, and in 1648 his son Nathaniel married a daughter of Nathaniel Bacon, who had been elected to sit for Cambridge University three years before. However, although he was not excluded in Pride's Purge, Barnardiston ceased to attend, either owing to ill health or because he disapproved of what had transpired. By mid-1649 he may have wanted to return, for in July his case was referred to a committee chaired by Cornelius Holland to determine whether he should be readmitted, but he never was. Retiring to Kedington, he spent substantial time in religious exercises and read Richard Baxter's *The Saints Everlasting Rest*. As his health deteriorated, he moved to Hackney and summoned Fairclough to discuss spiritual matters. After his death at Hackney on 25 July 1653, he was buried at Kedington on 26 August, with thousands reportedly in attendance. Fairclough's funeral sermon, published as *The Saints Worthinesse and the Worlds Worthlessnesse* (1653), lauded him as the father of his country for having defended its rights and liberties. His friends, including Christopher Burrell, published a volume of elegies, *Suffolks Tears* (1653). In his will Barnardiston left £40 for a vault in the Kedington parish church, but after the Restoration the family erected an alabaster monument with effigies of him and his wife, who was buried there on 15 September 1669. He died a wealthy man, with an annual income of nearly £4000 in the 1650s. A devout believer, he prepared a week or two before taking communion, observed the sabbath assiduously, shunned excessive mirth and frivolous speech, and maintained a household likened by Fairclough to a spiritual church because of the daily Bible reading, prayer, and psalm singing. He was manifestly a dominant force in the religious and political life of Suffolk from the late 1620s to 1648.

RICHARD L. GREAVES

Sources K. W. Shipps, 'Lay patronage of East Anglian puritan clerics in pre-revolutionary England', PhD diss., Yale U., 1971 · *Winthrop papers*, Massachusetts Historical Society, 1–4 (1929–44) · *DNB* · Keeler, *Long Parliament* · A. Everitt, *Suffolk and the Great Rebellion, 1640–1660*, Suffolk Records Society, 3 (1960) · R. P. Cust, *The forced loan and English politics, 1626–1628* (1987) · *JHC*, 2 (1640–42), 128, 543; 4 (1644–6), 133 · W. H. Coates, A. Steele Young, and V. F. Snow, eds., *The private journals of the Long Parliament*, 3 vols. (1982–92) · *CSP dom.*, *1625–6*, 178; *1644*, 175; *1644–5*, 513, 527, 624 · J. T. Cliffe, *Puritans in conflict: the puritan gentry during and after the civil wars* (1988) · M. Jansson and W. B. Bidwell, eds., *Proceedings in parliament, 1625* (1987) · *Sixth report*, HMC, 5 (1877–8), 59 · F. K. Lenthall, 'List of the names of the members of the House of Commons that advanced horse, money and plate …', *N&Q*, 12 (1855), 338, 358–60 · PRO, PROB 11/232, fol. 376 · *IGI* [register of St Pancras, Soper Lane, London]

Archives BL, Add. MS 15520, fol. 65 · BL, Add. MS 16537, fols. 359, 379 · BL, Add. MS 19116, fol. 537 · BL, Harley MSS 158; 160, fols. 29, 153; 165, fols. 5–8; 384, fols. 60–68 · Bodl. Oxf., MS Tanner 67, fol. 174 · PRO, State Papers, 16/95/35 · University of Sheffield, Hartlib MS 7/40/1A

Likenesses F. H. Van Hove, line engraving, BM, NPG; repro. in S. Clark, *The lives of sundry eminent persons* (1683)

Wealth at death see will, PRO, PROB 11/232, fol. 376

Barnardiston, Sir Samuel (1620–1707), politician, was born on 23 June 1620, the third son of Sir Nathaniel *Barnardiston (1588–1653) and his wife, Jane Soame (*d.* 1669). He was twice married, first to Thomasine (*d.* 1654), daughter of Joseph Brand of Edwardstone, Suffolk, and second to Mary, daughter of Sir Abraham Reynoldson, lord mayor of London and widow of Richard Onslow. He had no children by either marriage. Like many third sons he was encouraged to pursue a career in England's expanding overseas trade, and did so during the 1640s primarily in association with the Levant company. He acted as agent for the company and in the process amassed a considerable fortune. His wealth eventually allowed him to purchase a large estate at Brightwell near Ipswich in Suffolk and to build an impressive house, Brightwell Hall, which remained a neighbourhood fixture until it was pulled down in 1753.

The earliest expression of Barnardiston's political inclinations occurred during late 1641 when he took an active part in the famous apprentice riots which followed Charles I's appointment of the cavalier Colonel Thomas Lunsford to the lieutenancy of the Tower. The riots were intended to protest against Charles I's implicit threat to use military force to support his government and Barnardiston's involvement seems to reflect (quite apart from natural youthful exuberance) his genuine opposition to the king's heavy-handed methods. In one account of the affair the queen is said to have spied Barnardiston standing out among the closely cropped apprentice boys and exclaimed 'see what a handsome young Roundhead is there!', thereby giving birth to the epithet which came to denote future opponents of the Caroline regime (Rapin, 4.403). Whether or not the story was true Barnardiston's own political enthusiasms appear seriously to have waned in the immediate aftermath. He took no active part in the civil wars which followed and appears to have remained uninvolved in national politics during the interregnum, preferring instead to concentrate his time on local family business in Suffolk. Indeed, it was during these years that he seems successfully to have pursued his fortune in trade. In 1649 and 1650 he can be found acting as the agent for the Levant Company in Smyrna, Turkey.

The accumulation of wealth and property may have tempered his earlier interest in political activism. Barnardiston did not in fact enter political life again until the Restoration and only after he had been rewarded by Charles II for his 'irreproachable loyalty' with a knighthood (1660) and subsequently a baronetcy (1663). Over the course of the next forty years, however, he would develop a distinct profile and a formidable reputation as a leading figure in the intersecting worlds of London and Westminster. Initially, his reputation derived from his close association with the East India Company. A member of the company's board beginning in 1661, he assumed the position of deputy governor from 1668 to 1670. In that capacity he took responsibility for defending the company's interests in a famous law suit, *Skinner* v. *East India Company* in 1668, a case which created an extended constitutional crisis between the two houses of parliament. The defendant in the case, an English merchant named Thomas Skinner, appealed to the House of Lords in 1667 seeking redress against the East India Company. He had had his ship and goods seized by the company ten years before, ostensibly for trading in violation of the company's charter. In actual fact Skinner had begun his business in India long before the company's monopoly had been renewed by the lord protector, and understandably felt that their seizure was both illegal and unjust. Accordingly, on his return to England he sought redress from the king, and, beginning in 1661, a committee of the privy council had attempted to arbitrate a settlement. Their failure to do so led the king to refer the matter to the House of Lords in January 1667.

The Lords took up the case on the basis of Skinner's petition. The company, led by Barnardiston, demurred, refusing to acknowledge the Lords' jurisdiction to hear Skinner's complaint in the first instance. Their arguments failed, however, and the Lords proceeded to hear the case and eventually awarded the defendant damages of £5000 (29 April 1668). Barnardiston and the company responded by petitioning the House of Commons in protest, alleging that the Lords' actions violated 'the laws and statutes of this nation and the custom of Parliament'. They claimed that the upper house had done the company 'grievous harm' and had 'set a precedent of ill consequence to all the Commons of England hereafter' (*State trials*, 6.726–7). The Commons took up their petition and elected to challenge the Lords' proceedings, thereby precipitating a major constitutional crisis which would last, through two prorogations, until February 1670. Barnardiston himself was fined £300 and imprisoned by the upper house, first for his refusal to abide by their original judgment for Skinner and then for his part in drafting the subsequent petition to the Commons, an act which the Lords condemned as libellous (8 May 1668). He remained in prison until 10 August when he was mysteriously released, without either making submission to the upper house or paying his fine. In all probability the release was effected by the king as a means of defusing the crisis. If so, the effort failed. When parliament reassembled in October 1669 Barnardiston was immediately invited by the Commons to testify about his ordeal and in the aftermath the lower house voted to condemn the Lords' proceedings against him, thereby further inflaming the crisis. The quarrel was finally resolved in February 1670 when the king demanded that the dispute be permanently put to rest and all record of the proceedings in both houses be erased from their respective journals.

In a by-election in 1673 Barnardiston himself entered the House of Commons as member for Suffolk, though again the proceedings were plagued by controversy. The election appears to have been heavily contested between Barnardiston and Lord Huntingtower. Barnardiston won by over seventy votes, but his support was drawn in large measure from the commonality and, in particular, from dissenters, sectaries, and 'factious persons of every sort', while his opponent drew from the traditional county gentry and 'the church and loyal people' (Watson, 1.393). Claiming that Barnardiston was in league with the 'rabble', the county sheriff, Sir William Soame, an alleged supporter of Lord Huntingtower, raised doubts about the eligibility of some of his supporters and rather than declare his victory sent a double return to the House of Commons, leaving MPs to decide the final victor. A Commons committee eventually found in favour of Barnardiston and he was accordingly seated, while Soame was fined for failing to follow prescribed procedure.

The matter did not end there, however. Barnardiston felt he had been personally maligned and his honour impugned by the sheriff's suggestions and he sued Soame in the king's bench in November 1674. The case quickly took on a life of its own, largely because it reflected growing popular concerns about the nature of the electoral process. The key issue for the king's bench jury was whether Sheriff Soame had sent in the double return with malicious intent, thereby causing the plaintiff undue distress and financial hardship. The jury decided that he had, and awarded Barnardiston £800 in damages. The attorney-general, Sir Francis North, immediately moved to arrest the judgment, claiming, *inter alia*, that the validity of an election return was only determinable by the House of Commons, not by action at common law, and that, in any event, the office being contested was not for profit and the plaintiff's failure to secure it did not warrant financial damages. The court disagreed and the award was confirmed.

Soame then appealed their decision to the court of exchequer chamber. Eight of the twelve common law justices reviewed the case and, rather unusually, voted six to two to reverse the lower court judgment for Barnardiston. The decision itself was perhaps less important than the wide-ranging discussion which it seems to have provoked among the judges. At least as embodied in the contrary opinions of Sir Robert Atkins, justice of common pleas, and Sir Francis North (newly promoted to chief justice of common pleas), those discussions revealed important disagreements on the bench about the current state of common law jurisprudence, about the role and responsibilities of county sheriffs, and about the very nature of the electoral process—all issues reflecting the broadening philosophical differences which would give rise to political parties. In practical terms the judges' decision confirmed the House of Commons' jurisdiction over both the legality of election returns and the conduct of returning officers. Barnardiston, however, remained dissatisfied, and in 1689 appealed the exchequer chamber decision to the House of Lords. By this stage Sheriff Soame had died so his wife was named as defendant. The Lords reviewed the case during May and June 1689, but ultimately decided to reaffirm the exchequer chamber decision. Importantly perhaps their decree was not unanimous. Several lords entered a dissent on grounds that the decision denied Barnardiston his right to proper relief at common law, something these lords felt represented a notable failure of justice.

The long and contentious proceedings, to say nothing of his doggedness, helped create Barnardiston's political profile as an outspoken and dedicated whig. In the early stages of his career he formed a close association with the earl of Shaftesbury, and was an active participant in the political opposition in parliament in 1675, personally delivering in the (ultimately unsuccessful) articles of impeachment against the earl of Danby. A dedicated puritan by upbringing and persuasion, Barnardiston had little time for the established Church of England and even less for what he perceived to be the invidious influence of Catholics. He was elected to the Exclusion Parliaments of 1679 and 1681 and actively supported the cause. In November 1681 he served as jury foreman for the Middlesex grand jury impanelled to review the charge of high treason against the earl of Shaftesbury, and his careful handling of evidence and witnesses doubtless contributed to the failure of the indictment. Barnardiston himself came under similar scrutiny in 1684 in the wake of the Rye House plot. In letters to close personal associates, including Sir Philip Skippon, he expressed support for whig leaders William Lord Russell and Algernon Sidney, while making vaguely disparaging remarks about government figures such as the infamous jurist Sir George Jeffreys. The letters were made public and Barnardiston was indicted for seditious libel in February 1684. The content of the letters could hardly be described as seditious—Jeffreys himself was only alluded to rather than mentioned directly and was simply said to have 'grown very humble'—but this was a political trial and the requirements of law were studiously ignored. Jeffreys himself presided over the case, despite his direct personal involvement, and he saw to it that the jury returned a guilty verdict. Barnardiston was fined £10,000 and, when he refused to pay the fine, was imprisoned. He remained in prison for the next four years, until June 1688, when he was released after paying £6000 and giving bond for the remainder. Almost immediately he appealed the judgment to the House of Lords. They reviewed the proceedings in May 1689 and reversed Jeffrey's verdict, providing him with vindication, if not much solace for the substantial losses to his business interests he had incurred in the interim.

Barnardiston remained an active member of the House of Commons throughout the reign of William and Mary. He was elected to the Williamite parliaments of 1690, 1695, 1698, and 1701, and in 1690 was appointed to the all important commission for public accounts, which was made responsible for oversight of public expenditure. In 1697 he appears to have run afoul of the lower house by disobeying instructions to attend a conference with the House of Lords regarding the importation of East India silk. Why this would have represented a problem for him is not clear. He had severed his long-standing personal and financial ties with the East India Company in 1691 after a bitter quarrel, apparently born of political differences, with the then tory governor, Sir Josiah Child. He continued to serve in the House of Commons until his retirement in 1702 at the age of eighty-two. He died five years later, on 8 November 1707, at his house in Bloomsbury Square, London. Since Barnardiston had no heirs his title and estate passed in quick succession to his three nephews: first to Samuel, son of his eldest brother Nathaniel, who died shortly thereafter on 3 January 1710; subsequently to his youngest brother Pelatiah, who died two years later on 4 May 1712, and finally to Nathaniel, son of Pelatiah, who died on 21 September 1712, rendering the baronetcy extinct.

JAMES S. HART JR

Sources *DNB* • *CSP dom.*, *1649–50*, *1661–3*, *1672–3* • *State trials*, 6.1063–92 • *JHC*, 10 (1688–93) • *JHL*, 12 (1666–75) • J. Hatsell, ed., *Precedents of proceedings in the House of Commons*, 4th edn, 2 (1818), 369–84 • P. Watson, 'Barnardiston, Sir Samuel', HoP, *Commons*, *1660–90* • *The parliamentary or constitutional history of England*, 2nd edn, 24 vols. (1751–62), vol. 4, pp. 422–3, 431–4 • J. T. Cliffe, *The puritan gentry besieged*, *1650–1700* (1993), 150, 178, 185, 198, 207 • K. H. D. Haley, *The* *first earl of Shaftesbury* (1968), 200, 234, 400, 405, 461, 675, 677–8, 680 • J. S. Hart, *Justice upon petition: the House of Lords and the reformation of justice, 1621–1675* (1991), 242–50 • M. Knights, *Politics and opinion in crisis, 1678–1681* (1994), 124n., 234 • J. Britton, E. W. Brayley, and others, *The beauties of England and Wales, or, Delineations topographical, historical, and descriptive, of each county*, [18 vols.] (1801–16) • P. Rapin de Thoyras, *The history of England*, ed. and trans. N. Tindal, 4 (1725–31), 403

Likenesses R. White, line engraving, 1700, BM, NPG

Barnardiston, Sir Thomas, first baronet (*c*.1618–1669), politician, was the eldest son of Sir Nathaniel *Barnardiston (1588–1653), and his wife, Jane Soame (*d*. 1669). His father was the hugely wealthy leader of the puritan oligarchy which dominated early Stuart Suffolk. Thomas matriculated as a fellow-commoner from St Catharine's College, Cambridge, during Michaelmas term 1633 and was admitted to Gray's Inn on 1 May 1635. He was knighted by Charles I on 4 July 1641, and married Ann (1624–1671), daughter of Sir William Armine of Osgodby, Lincolnshire, in or before 1643.

Sir Thomas and his father were leading members of the parliamentarian civil-war government of Suffolk, and were appointed to the committee of the eastern counties' association. On 31 July 1643 Oliver Cromwell addressed a letter to Sir Thomas and his neighbours, in which he spoke of them as his 'noble Friends' and urged them in very forcible terms to raise 2000 foot soldiers (*Writings and Speeches*, 1.244). In 1645 Barnardiston became recruiter MP for Bury St Edmunds in place of a member disabled as a royalist; he brought a regiment of foot to the assistance of the parliamentarian forces at Colchester in 1648, was sent to quell a rising at Bury, and kept both houses apprised of the grave difficulties facing 'us that act for the Parliamentary Interest' that summer (*JHL*, 10, 1647–8, 301–2). He was perhaps the Thomas Barnardiston appointed by parliament in 1649 as comptroller of the mint, although it seems unlikely, he and his father having withdrawn from parliament at the purge in December 1648, then failing to secure readmission the following July. Sir Thomas was MP for Suffolk in Cromwell's parliaments of 1654 and 1656, and in Richard Cromwell's parliament of 1659. He was in 1654 one of the commissioners for ejecting scandalous, ignorant, and insufficient ministers and schoolmasters from Suffolk. On 20 November 1655 he headed the list of those who signed a declaration to secure the peace of the Commonwealth in the eastern counties, and great importance was attached to his signature by the major-general of the eastern counties.

Barnardiston adapted well to the new political exigencies of the Restoration. He was elected MP for Sudbury, Suffolk, in 1661 on a double return, but was unseated on 7 February 1662. He received a baronetcy from the king on 7 April 1663 'for the antiquity of the family and the virtues of his ancestors' (*DNB*), although clearly also on the interest of Viscount Andover, whose right of nomination was intended as compensation for being denied a diplomatic posting abroad. Barnardiston died intestate on 4 October 1669, and was buried at Keddington in Suffolk on the 14th. His wife survived him and their eldest son, Thomas, succeeded to the baronetcy. He was twice returned to parliament for Great Grimsby (1685 and 1689), and three times for Sudbury (1690, 1695, and 1698); he died in 1698. The baronetcy became extinct in 1745.

SIDNEY LEE, *rev*. SEAN KELSEY

Sources GEC, *Baronetage*, 3.272–3 • Venn, *Alum. Cant.*, 1/1.92 • J. Foster, *The register of admissions to Gray's Inn, 1521–1889, together with the register of marriages in Gray's Inn chapel, 1695–1754* (privately printed, London, 1889), vol. 1, p. 207 • W. A. Shaw, *The knights of England*, 2 (1906), 209 • *Members of parliament: return to two orders of the honorable the House of Commons*, House of Commons, 1 (1878), 494, 502, 505, 510, 529 • *CSP dom.*, 1648–9, 65–7; 1663–4, 96 • *JHL*, 10 (1647–8), 301–2 • *JHC*, 6 (1648–51), 268 • C. H. Firth and R. S. Rait, eds., *Acts and ordinances of the interregnum, 1642–1660*, 3 vols. (1911), vol. 1, pp. 94, 115, 150, 168, 234, 242, 293, 537, 624, 639, 853, 975, 1093, 1209; vol. 2, pp. 43, 478, 675, 975, 1080, 1379, 1431, 1435, 1443 • Thurloe, *State papers*, 4.225 • A. M. Everitt, *Suffolk and the great rebellion*, Suffolk RS, 3 (1960), 17, 18, 19, 26n., 27, 36, 52, 60, 72, 76, 77, 79, 88 • D. Underdown, *Pride's Purge: politics in the puritan revolution* (1971), 286n., 367 • HoP, *Commons, 1660–90*, 1.597–8 • *The writings and speeches of Oliver Cromwell*, ed. W. C. Abbott and C. D. Crane, 1 (1937), 244 • admon, PRO, PROB 6/44, fol. 134r

Likenesses R. Page, stipple, BM, NPG; repro. in *The lives of eminent and remarkable characters … in Essex, Suffolk, and Norfolk* (1820)

Wealth at death see administration, PRO, PROB 6/44, fol. 134r

Barnardiston, Thomas (1706–1752), law reporter, was born at Bury St Edmunds, Suffolk, the eldest child and only surviving son of Thomas Barnardiston (*b*. 1677) of Wyverstone and Bury St Edmunds, Suffolk, and his wife, Mary (*c*.1671–1728), daughter of Sir George Downing, first baronet (1623–1684), and his wife, Frances. Barnardiston's mother was aunt of Sir George Downing, third baronet (1684–1749), founder of Downing College, Cambridge, under whose will Barnardiston had an interest in remainder.

Educated at King Edward VI's Grammar School, Bury St Edmunds, Barnardiston was admitted a pensioner at Clare College, Cambridge, on 10 January 1722. Leaving Cambridge without a degree, he was admitted to the Middle Temple on 29 January 1724. He was called to the bar on 6 February 1730, and created serjeant-at-law at the last 'general' or 'public' call of serjeants in June 1736. His patrons upon creation were John Hervey, first earl of Bristol, who had close connections with Bury St Edmunds, and Charles Howard, sixth earl of Carlisle. On 9 August 1737 Barnardiston was elected recorder of the borough of Dunwich, Suffolk. He held the office until 9 August 1750, when he was dismissed on the ground of failure to attend borough assemblies or courts, and replaced by Sir Jacob Garrard Downing.

In 1742 he published a volume of reports of cases heard in the court of chancery between 1740 and 1741 during Lord Hardwicke's lord chancellorship, and in 1744 published two volumes of reports of cases heard in the court of king's bench in the period 1726–34. Barnardiston's reputation for accuracy as a reporter was not high. In *Zouch d. Woolston* v. *Woolston* (1761) Lord Mansfield forbade the citing of a report from Barnardiston's chancery volume, on the ground that such citation would be misleading to students who might read the report. Mansfield regarded it as marvellous to those who knew Barnardiston's manner of taking notes that he 'should so often stumble upon what was right', though 'there was not one case in his book, which was so throughout'. Similarly, Lord Lyndhurst once reminded counsel who cited a case from Barnardiston's chancery reports that it was said of the reporter that 'he was accustomed to slumber over his note-book, and the wags in the rear took the opportunity of scribbling nonsense in it' (Wallace, 424). But on the other side Lord Eldon said of the chancery volume that 'in that book are reports of very great authority' (*Duffield* v. *Elwes*, 1827), and comparisons of individual reports with manuscript notes and the official record of the court have shown Barnardiston's reporting of those cases to have been accurate. Lord Kenyon held a low opinion of the king's bench reports, regarding Barnardiston as 'a bad reporter' (*R.* v. *Stone*, 1801). Yet Lord Erskine once accepted a case cited from the king's bench reports as 'a precise authority' (*Nelthorpe* v. *Law*, 1807), and in *Salt* v. *Salt* (1798) Lord Kenyon himself, finding that Barnardiston's report of *Squire* v. *Archer* (1731) agreed with Strange's report of the same case, decided the case before him accordingly. Barnardiston died on 14 October 1752, and was buried at Chelsea parish church on 20 October 1752. He never married. His will records a bequest of his manuscripts to the Middle Temple. N. G. Jones

Sources A. R. Maddison, ed., *Lincolnshire pedigrees*, 1, Harleian Society, 50 (1902) • baptism register, St James, Bury St Edmunds RO • *GM*, 1st ser., 22 (1752), 478 • H. A. C. Sturgess, ed., *Register of admissions to the Honourable Society of the Middle Temple, from the fifteenth century to the year 1944*, 1 (1949), 294 • Venn, *Alum. Cant.*, 1/1.92 • J. W. Wallace, *The reporters*, 4th edn (1882), 423–6, 514 • Holdsworth, *Eng. law*, 12.138 • W. H. Maxwell and L. F. Maxwell, eds., *English law to 1800*, 2nd edn (1955), vol. 1 of *A legal bibliography of the British Commonwealth of Nations* (1938–58), 292, 345 • S. H. A. H. [S. H. A. Hervey], *Biographical list of boys educated at King Edward VI Free Grammar School, Bury St Edmunds, from 1550 to 1900* (1908), 16 • S. French, *The history of Downing College, Cambridge* (1978) • borough of Dunwich assembly minute book, 1694–1790, Suffolk RO, Ipswich, EE 6: 1144/14 • Baker, *Serjeants*, 456 • will of Thomas Barnardiston, PRO, PROB 11/797/325 • *Report on manuscripts in various collections*, 8 vols., HMC, 55 (1901–14), vol. 7 • *IGI*
Archives Middle Temple, London
Likenesses G. Bickham jun., line engraving, BM, NPG

Barnardo, Thomas John (1845–1905), philanthropist and founder of Dr Barnardo's Homes, was born on 4 July 1845 at 4 Dame Street, Dublin, the fourth of five children of John Michaelis Barnardo (1800–1874), a Prussian subject and furrier, and his second wife, Abigail, daughter of Philip O'Brien and his wife, Elizabeth *née* Drinkwater. John Barnardo had arrived in Dublin in 1823 and in 1827 married Elizabeth O'Brien, elder sister of Abigail. She died in childbirth in 1836 leaving five children. John Barnardo married Abigail at the German church in London in 1837 and was naturalized a British subject in 1860.

Thomas Barnardo's birth was difficult and he was not expected to survive. A delicate child, he was baptized at St Andrew's Church, Dublin. His mother was more or less an invalid, and it was due to the care of his half-sister Sophie, who nursed him through several severe illnesses, that he grew into a lively, strong-willed, intelligent boy. He went first to a school kept by the Revd Mr Andrews and subsequently followed his two elder brothers to the School for Collegiate and General Education, 112 St Stephen's Green, Dublin, run by the Revd William Dundas. Dundas was a bully and Barnardo retained unhappy memories of his school days. Unlike his elder brothers he did not go on to Trinity College, but was apprenticed at fourteen to a wine merchant. Dissatisfied with his life, he reluctantly allowed himself to be taken to revivalist evangelical meetings by his mother and two brothers. When, in 1862, as he himself put it, he was brought to Christ, Barnardo's life was changed. His natural arrogance and assertiveness found a new base, and his newly acquired conviction that his life was to be a channel for God's work gave him a sense of purpose, albeit ill-defined.

Thomas John Barnardo (1845–1905), by Stepney Causeway Studios, in or before 1905

To mark his changed life Barnardo went through a ceremony of believer's baptism in the Baptist Chapel in Abbey Street, and shortly after joined the open Plymouth Brethren and worshipped at Merrion Hall. Barnardo took up Sunday school teaching, joined the YMCA, and went visiting and preaching with Swift's Alley Mission. Barnardo was small, only 5 feet 3 inches, and his weak eyes meant he always had to wear spectacles; serious and with an earnest assertiveness, he was a somewhat conspicuous figure. With his restless energy, he found his life in Dublin unfulfilling.

Listening to Hudson Taylor's account of his work with

the China Inland Mission, Barnardo was fired with ambition to go to China. Against his father's wishes he left for London in 1866, and lodged at 30 Coburn Street with several other potential candidates. It was Barnardo's inexperience as well as his unwillingness to accept the necessity of 'headship and government' in the China mission that decided the leaders to delay consideration of his candidacy. There had been an outbreak of cholera in the East End and Barnardo visited and prayed with many of the sick. To gain experience while he waited Barnardo enrolled as a student at the London Hospital in 1867, and at the same time started teaching at the Ernest Street ragged school as well as preaching in the streets. Wishing to be his own master he appealed for funds for rooms where he could both teach and preach, and in 1868 acquired two cottages in Hope Place. Established as the East End Juvenile Mission this was the true beginning of Barnardo's work.

The discovery of Jim Jarvis, a homeless child, and the realization of the scale of child destitution and homelessness in the East End of London changed the focus of Barnardo's work. Originally concerned for the children's spiritual welfare, he saw the equal need to care for their material and physical well-being. Barnardo, always practical, set up a wood-chopping brigade and other trades to give the boys a means of earning a living, and those thought unlikely to prosper were sent to Canada under the auspices of Miss Annie McPherson, Scottish philanthropist and orphan-emigrator. Barnardo had the gift of telling a good story, boundless self-confidence, and a burning sense of mission. He was both appealing for funds and writing stories in *The Revival*, later known as *The Christian*. His stories provided him with a modest income; his appeals, coupled with the sale of photographs and help from wealthy evangelicals, enabled him to buy his first home for boys in Stepney in 1870–71.

Barnardo, an ardent advocate of the temperance movement, bought a notorious public house, the Edinburgh Castle in Limehouse, east London, in 1872 and transformed it into the British Working Men's Coffee Palace. Barnardo had never finished his studies at the London Hospital, but appropriated the title of 'doctor' and ordered that he should henceforth be known by that title. His decision to open another coffee house in the Mile End Road, however, brought him into conflict with another evangelist, Frederick Charrington, a member of the brewing family, who regarded the Mile End Road as his province.

Barnardo married Sarah Louise (Syrie) Elmslie on 17 June 1873 at Spurgeon's Metropolitan Tabernacle, London, in a Baptist service. The Elmslies lived in modest comfort in Richmond, and Barnardo had met Syrie through their joint interest in ragged-school work. Her father did not approve of the marriage, but a wealthy supporter, John Sands, gave the young couple a wedding present, Mossford Lodge, Barkingside, Essex, which enabled Barnardo to provide a home for girls as well as boys. The couple lived in the house, the girls all together in the coach house. It proved impossible to manage sixty girls under one roof, and Syrie's organizational powers in no way matched those of her husband. The experiment was not a success. Undaunted, Barnardo began to appeal for funds to build thirty cottages in the grounds.

The cottage-home system originated on the continent, and Barnardo, understanding its advantages, campaigned vigorously for a girls' village home. Funds for the first cottage were given as a memorial to a dead child, a popular idea, and in 1876 the first fourteen cottages were opened by Lord Cairns, the lord chancellor. It was at this time that the slogan 'No destitute boy ever refused admission' was changed to 'No destitute child ever refused admittance', a policy that would lead to repeated financial crises for the organization. Barnardo had acquired a magazine, the *Children's Treasury*, in 1874, for which he wrote and which was financially successful. He set up an editorial office at 279 Strand, London. His work in the East End was increasing and it was acknowledged that his mission was the largest and the fastest growing. With his flair for publicity, his entrepreneurial instincts—he set up a photographic studio and sold 'before' and 'after' photos of children he rescued—and his fundraising ever more successful, his organizational skills and capacity for work were exceptional.

A pattern to Barnardo's life was now emerging. In his haste to expand he worked phenomenally long hours, but he paid the price in terms of illness. The stress under which he worked led to bouts of nervous exhaustion, insomnia, and depression which could last for weeks. He suffered from bronchial trouble and, for the last ten years of his life, from angina and increasing deafness. In his almost messianic drive to succour destitute children the organization was seldom out of debt, a fact which alienated many of his Brethren friends, as they believed in the precept 'owe no man anything'. It was sometimes difficult to disentangle Barnardo's own financial situation from that of the homes, but by 1874 Mossford Lodge had become too expensive to maintain as a private residence and the Barnardos moved to Newbury House, Bow Street, Hackney.

Always sure of the righteousness of his cause, Barnardo broadcast the fact that he alone controlled the organization's funds, which had risen to over £23,000 by 1875. His outstanding success blinded him to the dangers such overconfidence breeds. Less successful rivals, in particular Frederick Charrington and George Reynolds, an obscure Baptist minister, spread rumours about Barnardo's financial probity, the treatment of the children, and his right to the title of doctor, and finally made allegations about his personal life. Asserting his doctorate Barnardo produced a letter from the University of Geissen, later shown to be forged. Unwisely he sanctioned the publication of two letters, signed 'A Clerical Junius', in the *East London Observer* on 28 August and 4 September 1875 attacking Charrington in vitriolic terms. Reynolds responded, and with the secret connivance of the Charity Organization Society (COS) published a pamphlet, *Dr Barnardo's Homes: Startling Revelations*. The publication gave the COS a reason to become publicly involved. One of the COS's functions was to investigate bogus charities and send warning letters to subscribers, and they blacklisted Barnardo's Homes. Barnardo took out a writ against Reynolds.

The evangelical community was appalled, as both sides had supporters. Although it was a bitter blow to Barnardo his trustees insisted that managerial responsibility be vested in them, and henceforth he was to be the director, appointed by them and able by them to be dismissed. They called in accountants, but the damage was done and funds started to fall. Barnardo himself went to Edinburgh and at the end of four months had obtained his licenciate from the Royal College of Surgeons. The trustees made Barnardo withdraw his writ against Reynolds and pushed Reynolds to agree to arbitration. They made application to the court of the exchequer and appointed the Hon. Alfred Thesiger to defend Barnardo, assisted by two juniors. The COS, which was covertly backing Reynolds, contributed to his defence, while Lord Cairns headed Barnardo's defence fund.

The opposition of the COS was based on its belief that indiscriminate charity was undermining the poor law, and under the leadership of C. S. Loch it never relaxed its efforts to discredit Barnardo both before and after the award was made. The arbitration was not exhaustive because Barnardo refused to reveal the name of the writer of the Clerical Junius letters. He admitted that he was closely associated with their production and accepted moral responsibility for them, but his refusal to name the writer was seen by many as a device to protect himself. As a result Reynolds refused to continue with his cross-examination, but the judges made an award none the less.

The arbitration had developed into a confrontation between those who sincerely disapproved of unorganized religious philanthropic endeavour and those who feared the threat to Barnardo's work represented a threat which could affect the whole Christian philanthropic movement. The award was generally favourable to Barnardo and the homes were crucially recognized as worthy of public confidence. Barnardo was criticized for his refusal to answer Reynolds and the use of artistic fiction in his photographs. He never sold photographs after 1877 and discontinued the use of the 'before' and 'after' photographs.

The arbitration, a turning point in Barnardo's life, was skated over in his official memoirs, edited by his wife and James Marchant in 1907. The case left Barnardo exhausted mentally and physically, and both director and the homes encumbered by debt. He had become a public figure, but doubts about his personal integrity lingered on. The homes now became known as Dr Barnardo's Homes and the title East End Juvenile Mission fell into disuse. Much against his will a committee of management was set up to bring about a measure of control. Cairns became president, a finance subcommittee was set up, and a visiting rota of trustees was established. To add to Barnardo's distress, owing to a business failure in 1883 he was forced to ask for an annual stipend, which was immediately granted. The arbitration also precipitated Barnardo's withdrawal from Brethrenism. He regarded his return to the Anglican fold as a private matter, fearing that if it became public he might lose supporters. The decision left him isolated and lonely.

Barnardo now had three children, William Stuart (*b.* 1874), Herbert (*b.* 1876), and Gwendoline (1879–1955), known as Syrie [*see* Maugham, (Gwendoline Maud) Syrie], who married Henry Wellcome in 1901 and, secondly, Somerset Maugham in 1917. The family had moved to The Cedars, Banbury Road, Hackney, in 1879 where Kenward (*b.* 1881), Tom (*b.* 1882), who died as a baby, Cyril (*b.* 1884), and Marjorie (*b.* 1890), who suffered from a lifelong disability, were born. Both Herbert and Kenward died young of diphtheria.

Barnardo increasingly viewed his fundraising campaign as a form of ministry. Public confidence began to return, but despite the growth of the Girls' Village Home and the acquisition of more properties by gift and purchase, Barnardo saw emigration as the only way in which he could keep to his 'ever open door' policy and meet the ever-increasing demands on the homes. In 1882 the first party of boys left for Canada, followed by a party of girls in 1883. Barnardo acquired a receiving home for girls and acquired by purchase and grant land and buildings for an industrial farm in Manitoba. Emigration became a key policy, and by 1905 more than 11,000 children had been sent overseas, mainly to Canada. Encouraged by the idea that emigration was advantageous to the child and the empire, Barnardo was supported both by the public and the state. He visited Canada five times, the last in 1900 in failing health when disquiet was already being voiced in Canada about the effects of emigration both for children and on the Canadian population.

In 1888 Barnardo became embroiled in a series of court cases involving three mothers, backed by the Roman Catholic church, who demanded that their children be restored to their custody. Barnardo's response was typically high-handed: two children were sent overseas and Barnardo applied to the courts to support his claim to keep the third child, arguing that what he called 'philanthropic abduction' was justified in certain cases. Barnardo took the case to appeal, incurring much hostile public criticism. Although he did not win the case, it was during this period that the Custody of Children Act of 1891 was passed. Barnardo's influence can be seen in that for the first time parental rights were subordinated to the overriding consideration of the welfare of the child, the principle at the heart of his argument.

By the end of 1880s the committee, unable to control the dynamic and driven director, who had now added a hospital for sick children and a boarding-out scheme to his work, became so alarmed at debts amounting to nearly £200,000, for which they were personally liable, that they demanded that Barnardo curtail his work. He had opened seven regional centres with the 'ever open door' slogan, which increased the number of admissions, and although he had appointed five lecturers to share the burden of fundraising and created the Young Helpers League, more loans and mortgages had had to be taken out.

Barnardo fought back, but, alienated from his committee and friends, unable to accept criticism, unable to delegate, and with his stubborn intransigence increasing his sense of isolation, he was nevertheless forced to retrench. However his passion for the cause of destitute children, his deep religious belief, and his powerful personality won him many supporters, a devoted and loyal staff, and the respect and gratitude of many of his children.

Barnardo was by then personally prosperous, and the family moved to a large house, Ardmore, Buckhurst Hill, Essex, before moving finally to St Leonard's Lodge, Surbiton. His appearance was described as being 'short and round, his complexion florid, his cheeks puffy and his eyes somewhat fierce. Even his moustache was martial' (*The Star*, 21 Sept 1905). Despite royal patronage and twice yearly packed meetings at the Albert Hall, where Barnardo was able to indulge his taste for drama and showmanship, the financial situation of the homes during the 1890s showed little improvement. In 1899 it was decided to apply for a certificate of incorporation, and to give the work a national character an impossibly clumsy title was chosen, The National Incorporated Association for the Reclamation of Destitute Waif Children, otherwise known as Dr Barnardo's Homes. The trustees, no longer personally liable, seemed to have abandoned all attempts to curb Barnardo's expansionist plans after that.

In response to need, more regional receiving homes, together with more orphanages, industrial homes, and homes for sick and blind children, were opened; Watts Naval Training School, the gift of E. H. Watts, trained boys for the navy and merchant service. By the time of Barnardo's death in 1905 total liabilities amounted to £249,000, and in spite of a national memorial appeal it was several years before all liabilities could be met. He was not the first to send children overseas or to use the boarding-out system for small children, but his close personal attention to detail, his thoroughness, and the scale of his work made his methods an example to others. He recognized from the start that it was not enough to rescue children from destitution but essential to train them to enable them to earn a living. He fervently believed that it was an essential part of his mission to ensure that they were brought up according to protestant evangelical principles.

Barnardo died at his home, St Leonard's Lodge, on 19 September 1905 from a heart attack, having returned too ill to complete a further course of treatment at Nauheim in Germany, where he had been on several previous occasions. Barnardo's body lay in state at the Edinburgh Castle for three days, and was then taken through streets lined with mourners to Liverpool Street Station. From Barkingside the cortège went to the Girls' Village Home, and Barnardo was interred on 4 October at a spot he had chosen himself. An imposing memorial by Sir George Frampton RA marks Barnardo's tomb. He stands out as a most successful philanthropist and a social reformer. Both through his work and his writings he publicized and tried to meet the needs of destitute children long before the state actively sought to deal with the issue.

GILLIAN WAGNER

Sources *The memoirs of Dr Barnardo*, ed. Mrs Barnardo and J. Marchant (1907) • G. Wagner, *Barnardo* (1979) • T. J. Barnardo, ed., *Night and Day*, 27 vols. (1877–1900) • T. J. Barnardo, ed., *Night and Day*, 27 vols. (1902–5) • T. J. Barnardo, *Rescue the perishing* (1876) • T. J. Barnardo, *Something attempted, something done* (1888) • J. Batt, *Dr Barnardo, foster father of nobody's children* (1904) • A. R. Newman, *Barnardo as I knew him* (1914) • J. W. Bready, *Dr Barnardo: physician, pioneer, prophet* (1930) • A. E. Williams, *Barnardo of Stepney* (1943) • N. Wymer, *Father of nobody's children* (1966) • G. Wagner, 'Dr Barnardo and the Charity Organisation Society', PhD diss., U. Lond., 1977 • J. Parr, *Labouring children* (1979) • S. Ryder and A. Fulwood, 'Reminiscences', Barnardo's, Ilford, Barnardo archive • G. Reynolds, *Dr Barnardo's Homes: startling revelations* (1875) • *East London Observer* (8 Sept 1877) [supplement] • *East London Observer* (15 Sept 1877) [supplement] • *The Barnardo investigation: report of the last two days' proceedings, 5–6 September 1877*, Charity Organisation Society (1877) • G. Wagner, *Children of the empire* (1982) • *Law reports: queen's bench division*, 23 (1889), 310–16 • *Law reports: queen's bench division*, 24 (1890), 283–302 • *Law reports: appeal cases* (1891), 388–400 • *Law reports: appeal cases* (1892), 326–341 • copy of C. S. Loch's diary, 1876–92, LUL • *The Revival* (1867–72) • *The Christian* (1872–1905) • private information (2004) • naturalization certificate • m. cert. • *The Times* (21 Sept 1905) • *Morning Post* (21 Sept 1905) • *The Record* (21 Sept 1905) • *Pall Mall Gazette* (21 Sept 1905) • *Manchester Evening Chronicle* (21 Sept 1905) • *English Churchman* (21 Sept 1905) • *The Star* (21 Sept 1905) • *Local Government Journal* (28 Sept 1905) • *London Opinion* (29 Sept 1905) • *London Leader* (29 Sept 1905)

Archives Barnardo's, Ilford, Essex, Barnardo Archive • Redbridge Central Library, Ilford, sermon notes • U. Lpool L., corresp. and sermon notes, Ref. D239, 281, 443 | FILM Barnardo's photographic archive, London, cine film of funeral

Likenesses Stepney Causeway Studios, photograph, in or before 1905, NPG [*see illus.*] • G. Frampton, effigy, 1907, Barnardo's, Tanners Lane, Barkingside, Ilford, Essex • F. Hager, black and white engraving • E. Parnelle, chalk sketch, Hove • A. R. Taylor, oils, Barnardo Archive • photographs, Barnardo Photographic Archive • photographs, Dr Barnardo's, Head Office, London

Wealth at death £13,485 5*s*. 10*d*.: probate, 14 Nov 1905, *CGPLA Eng. & Wales*

Barnato, Barnett Isaacs [Barney] (**1852–1897**), diamond merchant and financier, born on 5 July 1852 at Aldgate, London, was the second son of the five children of Isaac Isaacs, shopkeeper, and Leah Isaacs (said to be related to the master of the rolls, Sir George Jessel). Barnato's grandfather was a rabbi of the Jewish synagogue in Aldgate. For most of his early life Barnato lived with his elder brother, Harry (Henry), and three sisters over the shop. Both boys were given an elementary education under Moses Angel in the Jews' Free School, Bell Lane, Spitalfields, along with their cousin David Harris, leaving at the age of fourteen. Their elder sister Kate married Joel Joel, landlord of the King of Prussia public house. Barnato worked along with Harry at the pub, in their father's shop, and in the music-halls as Harry's straight man, assuming the name of Barnato by which both of the brothers came to be known.

In 1872 the Barnato brothers were drawn to the Kimberley diamond diggings by tales of easy wealth recounted by David Harris. Barnato followed Harry out to South Africa in July 1873 on the *Anglian*, allegedly with forty boxes of cigars and meagre savings, making his way by bullock

Barnett Isaacs Barnato (1852–1897), by Warren

wagon to Kimberley. There he learned the elements of diamond dealing from his cousins David Harris and Louis Cohen, and applied his natural quick-wittedness to buying from the diggers as a small-scale broker and selling to merchant shippers' representatives. Barnett (or Barney as he became universally known) formed a partnership with Harry—Barnato Brothers, 'dealers in diamonds and brokers in mining property'. As the number of dealers declined after 1875 with the formation of companies which sold direct to merchants, the successful survivors of Kimberley's cut-throat diamond trade were forced to diversify into mining. In 1876 the Barnatos bought for £150,000 a small block of claims in the Kimberley mine which produced profitably enough to enable them to venture into claims in De Beers and Dutoitspan mines. In the same year Barnato was elected to a seat on Kimberley municipal council, amid allegations of bribery. An assiduous councillor, Barnato treated meetings as theatrical occasions and harangued audiences with the verve and abandon of a man who just as frequently played in Kimberley's stage shows and survived its boxing matches. In the mid-1870s he took Fanny Bees, barmaid and actress, as a mistress, marrying her some years later, on 19 November 1892, at the Chelsea register office, London.

On his return to England in 1880 Barnato set up the London branch of Barnato Brothers at Austin Friars, leaving Harry to handle that end of the business. Back in Kimberley the same year, the prospering councillor followed in the steps of J. B. Robinson as mayor of Kimberley, thus keeping control of the municipality in the hands of mine owners and diamond merchants. At the same time Barnato Brothers speculated heavily in shares during the wave of company promotions (1880–81), and emerged with a stake in seven diamond mining companies in the Kimberley, De Beers, and Dutoitspan mines. Their most serious promotion centred on the Barnato Diamond Mining Company Kimberley Mine Limited (Barnato DMC), registered on 24 April 1881 with a capital of £115,000 and the bulk of shares owned by Barney and Harry. Barnato DMC paid big dividends but then failed to produce as claims were covered with fallen ground and debts accumulated.

None of this dampened Barnato's style in the 1880s. He laid out a racecourse, entertained lavishly, and rode in an open carriage with silver harness and outriders. But he found it difficult to shake off rumours and accusations of illicit diamond dealing which made him socially unacceptable to many, and he took refuge in the close-knit group of relatives who had followed the two brothers to Kimberley—Kate's daughter Ruth Joel, and Kate's sons Woolf, Isaac (Jack), and Solomon (Solly) Barnato Joel. Unfortunately there was substance to the charge of dealing in stolen diamonds among the Barnato-Joels; this came to light through the prosecution of Barney's nephew Isaac, who fled Kimberley for England in 1884. It is now established that Barnato tried to influence the course of justice by bribery and intimidation which did his reputation with the banks no good and kept him out of the Kimberley Club.

This willingness to take big risks by cutting legal corners is explained by the way in which Barnato DMC, as an investment in claims, was kept financially solvent only by the diamond dealing side of Barnato's business until it resumed mining in 1885. An additional technique to secure the diamond base lay in using directorships and investments in other diamond companies to control production in the Kimberley mine, beginning with an amalgamation of Barnato DMC and Standard Diamond Mining Company in March 1887, followed by Standard's absorption into Kimberley Central DMC. Share transactions based on inside knowledge more than compensated for earlier setbacks and loss of money in Barnato's gold ventures at Barberton and Pilgrim's Rest in 1885. The mergers, moreover, deployed the financial strength of Barnato Brothers in the business it knew best through consolidation of claims and companies, in much the same way that Rhodes was proceeding in the De Beers mine. The operation also brought Woolf Joel onto the board of Kimberley Central DMC and placed other representatives of Barnatos on the local and London sections of Kimberley Central's board. In short, this manoeuvring made Barnato Brothers into one of the biggest shareholders in the core company of the mine. As final amalgamation of companies in the De Beers and Kimberley mines accelerated, Kimberley Central acquired the Compagnie Française des Mines de Diamant du Cap (the French Company) in competition with De Beers, but at the price of a large stake in

Kimberley Central for De Beers DMC. By October 1887 Barnato had agreed with Cecil Rhodes, then chairman of De Beers, to amalgamation arrangements between the two mines, and by January 1888 Rhodes had secured transfer of Barnato's shares in return for a quota of diamond sales to Barnato Brothers, personal profit from the sale of Kimberley Central shares, the promise of a life governorship in the new De Beers Consolidated Mines Limited of 1888, and electoral support which took Barnato triumphantly into the Cape assembly on 14 November 1888 as a member for Kimberley, and into the Kimberley Club which had for so long kept him out.

Barnato made little of his parliamentary opportunities, though re-elected in 1894 as a De Beers backed candidate, and concentrated on his influential position as board director of a monopoly producer which sold to his firm of diamond merchants. After the amalgamation it was Barnato rather than Rhodes who chaired the first annual general meeting of De Beers in July 1889 and who announced the company's policies on regulation of supply. He could be relied upon to support sales through the London syndicate, but was ambiguous about Rhodes's more expansive imperial schemes, siding openly with board opponents, while writing privately in 1890 in praise of 'grand patriotic undertakings' in Ndebele. For a period in 1892 and 1893 Barnato, acting for Barnato Brothers, contracted directly with Rhodes on monthly quantities and prices, until both the syndicate and the London board of De Beers enforced longer-term arrangements. Only occasionally thereafter was Barnato allowed onto the Kimberley diamond committee of De Beers, and like other merchants he did not vote when contracts with the syndicate were confirmed, although Barnato Brothers retained the second largest annual quota of De Beers diamonds until the 1920s. He was closely associated, too, with the sale of British South Africa Company shares through De Beers, investing £30,000 of his own money. But he kept clear of Rhodes's (Consolidated) Gold Fields venture in favour of his own flotations of the New Primrose, the New Croesus, the Roodepoort and Glencairn, and Main Reef goldmining companies in the investment boom of 1888 and 1889.

Like other diamond men, Barnato gradually transferred his business activities to the Rand. He set up the Johannesburg Waterworks Company in 1887 and profited from a monopoly of supply. Elected a member of the stock exchange, he acquired control of its premises, brawled physically on its floor, and rebuilt it through his Johannesburg Estates Company. Barnato rode out the subsequent slump in 1889 to construct the Barnato Building, and amalgamated his Rand holdings into the Johannesburg Consolidated Investment Company Limited, arguably his most enduring financial monument, just as the Barnato Bank, Mining, and Estates Company, set up in London in 1894 to promote doubtful stocks, was his most questionable creation. Barnato made his money on the Rand mainly by setting up mining companies with little working capital and massive amounts of vendor shares in the hands of promoters during the long bull market before 1895; while prices rose much of this paper profit ended up in his bank. During the crash at the end of September 1895 he desperately spent some £3 million to hold up falling share values, but the bank had to be liquidated by sale of assets to Johannesburg Consolidated Investment in the following year.

Barnato survived dangerously and prospered visibly in the 1890s, with an estate at Barnato Park, Johannesburg, and a house in the Berea district which cost him £500,000 to construct. In London he entertained lavishly, shared a racing manager with the prince of Wales, and built on a site in Park Lane purchased from the duke of Westminster. By 1895 he was reckoned to be worth £4 million and stood fifth in the league of Johannesburg Randlords. Deeply mistrusted and resented by the City, his actions to save the 'Kaffir' market were rewarded, however, by admission to the London Carlton Club and by a banquet given in his honour by the lord mayor, Sir Joseph Renals, at Mansion House, on 7 November 1895, just as the political crisis in the Transvaal became more acute.

Barnato was not a member of the Transvaal National Union or of any other reform movement for extension of the franchise to foreigners in President Kruger's republic. Indeed he had a cautious sympathy for the Afrikaners' dilemma, and he was certainly not a trusted confidant of any of the conspirators behind the Jameson raid of January 1896, after he tried to obtain the services of the mining engineer John Hays Hammond in 1893 for a high salary, but lost him to Rhodes. Following the raid and the trial and conviction of the ringleaders, Barnato intervened with Kruger for commutation of their sentences (but probably would not have carried out any threat to close mines), and he generously put up £20,000 bail for Hays Hammond. After their release from Pretoria, Barnato hosted a banquet in honour of the reformers and sent two carved ornamental lions to Kruger as a gesture of reconciliation. They are still to be seen at an entrance to the old Pretoria residency.

After the financial and political crisis of 1895 Barnato alternated between bouts of depression and optimism, drank heavily, and made his last serious investments in property (later to become site of the Carlton Hotel, Johannesburg), but never won back the confidence of his creditors and shareholders abroad. Increasingly there were signs of mental instability, alcoholism, and paranoia. Persuaded to sail to England on the mail steamer *Scot* in June 1897 to attend the celebrations for Queen Victoria's diamond jubilee, Barnato, weakened by mental and physical ill health, jumped overboard, south of Madeira, on 14 June. His body was recovered and brought to Southampton where the coroner gave a verdict of suicide. Barnato was buried amid a certain amount of pomp in the Jewish cemetery in Willesden, attended by the lord mayor and Alfred Beit among other dignitaries. The market in 'Kaffir' shares trembled briefly, the Johannesburg stock exchange closed for a day, and the Cape parliament adjourned as a mark of respect for one who was admired and envied rather than respected, and whose reputation accumulated legends, as much as his career prospered from unscrupulous practices. Yet within the circle of family

Barney could be loving, and he was loved by his wife, by his cousins and nephews, and by his three children, Leah Primrose, Isaac Henry, and Wolf Barnato. Barnato Street in Berea, Johannesburg, is named after him; he paid for the original Barnato wing of Johannesburg General Hospital, and he served on the committee which founded the Johannesburg Public Library.

Short, strong, ready with his fists, from the time of his arrival in South Africa Barnato fought and cheated his way to the top with all the pugnacity of an East End Londoner on the make. He learned fast, keeping close to his own relatives and acquiring financial and manipulative skills rather than a deep knowledge of the diamond or gold industries. He read little, had little understanding of politics, and displayed a certain gross contempt for the mannered protocols of the Cape parliament, while indulging his vanity in exhibitions of his wealth. Historical research has treated Barnato less kindly than his early biographers and admirers, but he was not untypical of other pioneer businessmen in his methods, though he was certainly more brash than most in his success. By a mixture of luck, legal and illegal handling of goods, and foresight in securing claims he and his brother founded one of the best diamond dealerships in Kimberley and London. It remained a cornerstone of the international diamond market until the 1930s, while the Johannesburg Consolidated Investment Company ('Johnnies'), which began as a dubious and speculative trust, was transformed by Barnato's successors into one of the largest investment houses within the group system of South African mining.

COLIN NEWBURY

Sources S. Jackson, *The great Barnato* (1970) • B. Roberts, *The diamond magnates* (1972) • L. Cohen, *Reminiscences of Kimberley* (1911) • G. Wheatcroft, *The Randlords: the men who made South Africa* (1985) • G. A. Leyds, *A history of Johannesburg* (1964) • C. Newbury, *The diamond ring: business, politics and precious stones in South Africa, 1867–1947* (1989) • R. V. Turrell, *Capital and labour on the Kimberley diamond fields, 1871–1890* (1987) • L. Herrman, *A history of the Jews in South Africa, from the earliest times to 1895* (Johannesburg, 1935) • *DNB* • *CGPLA Eng. & Wales* (1897)

Archives Bodl. RH • De Beers, Kimberley, South Africa, archives of the Barnato Diamond Mining Company • Johannesburg Consolidated Investment Company Ltd, Johannesburg • Standard Bank Archive, Johannesburg

Likenesses H. Furniss, pen-and-ink caricature, NPG • Warren, photograph, repro. in H. Raymond, *B. I. Barnato* (1897) [*see illus.*] • oils?, Johannesburg Consolidated Investment Company Ltd, South Africa • portraits, McGregor Memorial Museum, Kimberley, South Africa • portraits, De Beers, Kimberley, South Africa

Wealth at death £963,865 8*s*. 6*d*.: probate, 4 Oct 1897, *CGPLA Eng. & Wales*

Barnbarroch. For this title name *see* Vaus, Sir Patrick, Lord Barnbarroch (*d*. 1597).

Barnby, Sir Joseph (1838–1896), composer and conductor, was born on 12 August 1838 at Swinegate, York, the youngest child in the family of fifteen children of Thomas Barnby, a shoemaker and organist, and his wife Barbara, *née* Robinson. At the age of seven he became a chorister at York Minster, as six of his brothers had been before him. He began to teach music at the age of ten, and was assistant organist and choirmaster at York Minster when he was only twelve. In 1854 he entered the Royal Academy of Music, and during his three years there he lived in the cloisters of Westminster Abbey with his brother Robert, a lay clerk. In 1856 he was narrowly defeated by Arthur Sullivan in the competition for the first Mendelssohn scholarship.

After holding the post of organist of Mitcham church for a short time, Barnby returned to York and taught music for four years. He then settled in London, and held posts of organist and choirmaster in several churches before in 1863 being appointed organist of St Andrew's, Wells Street, where Benjamin Webb, a Tractarian, was vicar. At St Andrew's, Barnby introduced full choral services on the lines of cathedral services, with a large surpliced choir. He adapted music from Catholic masses for use in the church, and Webb translated the texts. At the service of dedication for the new church building in 1866 a harp was used for the first time in an Anglican service, in a performance of Gounod's *Messe solennelle*.

From 1871 to 1886 Barnby was organist and choirmaster of St Anne's, Dean Street, Soho. Here he had a surpliced choir of sixty-four, including thirty-two boy trebles, whom he drilled every day, and for special services the choir was increased to seventy or eighty. The services, nicknamed the 'Sunday opera', attracted large congregations. Barnby was the first to perform Bach's St John passion in London, and from 1873 he gave annual Lenten performances.

In 1861 Barnby became an adviser to the music publishers Novello, Ewer & Co. He started 'Mr Barnby's choir' in 1867 under the auspices of Novello, and began giving oratorio concerts in St James's Hall the following year, reviving such works as Handel's *Jephtha*, Beethoven's *Missa solemnis*, and Bach's St Matthew passion. At the end of 1872 the choir was amalgamated with the Albert Hall Choral Society (later the Royal Choral Society), founded and conducted by Gounod. Barnby became conductor in 1873 and directed it until the end of his life. In 1884 he conducted the choir in a concert performance of Wagner's *Parsifal*, the first time the opera was heard in England; another important occasion was the first church performance in England of Bach's St Matthew passion, in Westminster Abbey on Maundy Thursday, 6 April 1871. Barnby also conducted the daily concerts organized by Novello in the Royal Albert Hall (1874–5) and the London Musical Society, which concentrated from 1878 to 1886 on performing neglected works, notably Dvořák's *Stabat mater* (1883). At the end of his life Barnby conducted the Cardiff musical festivals of 1892 and 1895.

As a composer, Barnby was particularly influenced by Gounod, Mendelssohn, and Spohr. His compositions, mainly vocal and choral, were extremely popular at the time, but their Victorian sentimentality was less appealing to later generations. His religious music includes an oratorio, *Rebekah* (1870), and 'The Lord is King' (Psalm 97, 1883). He wrote anthems, cathedral services (often used at St Paul's Cathedral), and many hymn tunes, such as 'For all the saints' and 'Cloisters'. He edited four hymnbooks, among them *The Hymnary* (1872), and was one of the musical editors of the *Cathedral Psalter* (1878). He also wrote partsongs, the most famous of which was his setting of Tennyson's 'Sweet and low' (1863).

In 1875 Barnby became precentor of Eton College, and in the seventeen years he spent there, instead of confining himself to the chapel services, he developed the post into that of director of music. He put on concerts and choral performances for the whole school, organized music lessons, and built up a department of eight assistants. He also wrote music for two of the Eton school songs. In 1892 he left Eton to become principal of the Guildhall School of Music. He was knighted in the same year.

In 1878 Barnby married Edith Mary, the daughter of Lieutenant-Colonel Silverthorne of Sussex. They had two sons and one daughter. He died suddenly at his home, 9 St George's Square, Belgravia, London, on 28 January 1896. The funeral service was held in St Paul's Cathedral, and he was buried in Norwood cemetery.

ANNE PIMLOTT BAKER

Sources N. Temperley, *The music of the English parish church*, 1 (1979) • E. H. Fellowes, *English cathedral music from Edward VI to Edward VII* (1941) • J. S. Curwen, *Studies in worship music* (1880), 179–83 • 'Mr Joseph Barnby', *Musical Herald* (May 1892) • *New Grove* • D. Baptie, *Sketches of the English glee composers: historical, biographical and critical (from about 1735–1866)* [1896] • M. B. Foster, *Anthems and anthem composers* (1901), 162–3 • *Musical Herald* (March 1896) • *MT*, 37 (1896), 80–81 • H. Barty-King, *GSMD: a hundred years' performance* (1980) • b. cert. • d. cert. • *Leading men of London: a collection of biographical sketches* (1895) • Burke, *Peerage*

Likenesses S. Goetze, oils, 1894, Corporation of London • W. & D. Downey, woodbury type photograph, NPG; repro. in W. Downey and D. Downey, *The cabinet portrait gallery*, 4 (1893) • Elliott & Fry, engraving (after photograph), repro. in *Musical Herald* (1 May 1892) • H. Hampton, bronze bust, Royal Albert Hall, London • attrib. J. W. Knowles, oils, City of York Art Gallery • Melhuish & Gale, photograph, repro. in *Musical Herald* • Spy [L. Ward], caricature, chromolithograph, NPG; repro. in *VF* (1 Nov 1894) • Window & Grove, photograph, repro. in Foster, *Anthems and anthem composers*, facing p. 197 • portrait, Guildhall School of Music and Drama, London

Wealth at death £4272 17*s*. 8*d*.: probate, 5 March 1896, *CGPLA Eng. & Wales*

Barne, Sir George (*c*.1500–1558), merchant and local politician, was the son of George Barne, grocer, of London, though the family seems also to have had connections in Wells, Somerset. His sister may have been the mother of Nicholas *Culverwell (*d*. 1569) [*see under* Culverwell family (*per*. *c*.1545–*c*.1640)], who later served as his apprentice. He was a member of the Haberdashers' Company, and prospered from various sectors of English commerce, both traditional and novel. He exported cloth and imported wine from Spain, and he was a leading figure in new enterprises. With William Garrard he was a 'principal doer' in promoting the first voyage to Muscovy of 1553, a founder and active member of the Russia Company, and a promoter of voyages to west Africa in 1553 and 1554.

Barne also took a full part in City politics. He was alderman from 1542 and lord mayor in 1552–3, when the crown passed precariously from Edward VI to Mary. He was knighted on 11 April 1553 and was one of the City fathers signing the letters patent of Edward which made Lady Jane Grey queen. Though consequently treated with some suspicion by the Marian regime, there is no evidence that he had strong protestant convictions: his loyalties were to the City and those who, like himself, were members of its élite.

Barne married Alice Brooke (*d*. 1559) of Shropshire, with whom he had at least three sons and two daughters, all of them involved directly or by marriage in London commerce. His heir, George, married William Garrard's daughter, Anne, and was subsequently governor of the Russia Company, mayor in 1586–7, and MP. Of his daughters, Anne married, first, Alexander Carleill, another Muscovy merchant, and, second, Sir Francis *Walsingham; and Elizabeth married John Rivers, lord mayor in 1573–4. Barne died on 18 February 1558. He and his wife were both buried at St Bartholomew by the Exchange, London. At the time of his death he had property in London, Southwark, and Hertfordshire.

PAUL SLACK, *rev.*

Sources T. S. Willan, *The Muscovy merchants of 1555* (1953) • J. G. Nichols, ed., *The chronicle of Queen Jane, and of two years of Queen Mary*, CS, old ser., 48 (1850) • will, PRO, PROB 11/40, sig. 13 • *The diary of Henry Machyn, citizen and merchant-taylor of London, from AD 1550 to AD 1563*, ed. J. G. Nichols, CS, 42 (1848)

Barnes, Alfred John (1887–1974), politician, was born on 17 July 1887 at 3 Gordon Terrace, Plaistow, West Ham, London, the youngest of seven children of William Barnes, a docker and coffee-house keeper, and his wife, Lucinda Margaret Smith. At the age of eight he lost a leg in a fairground accident. He was educated at the Star Road Boys' School, an elementary school between Manor Road and Barking Road, Canning Town, at the Northampton Institute from 1905, and at the London County Council School of Arts and Crafts. After serving his apprenticeship he became a skilled designer and worker in precious metals. He established his own silversmith's business, which he relinquished in 1922 when it was earning him an income in excess of the £400 a year he was paid on his election to parliament.

The grim poverty of the majority of inhabitants of east London was graphically described by the author Jack London in his book *The People of the Abyss* (1902), but Barnes learned about conditions of employment in the nearby docks from his father who, though he became a foreman, had joined the strike of 1889 for the dockers 'tanner'. His craft training had generated in him a search for realistic solutions to the problems he confronted, and from an early age he sought to improve the living conditions of the people of east London through co-operation and political action. In 1908 he joined the Stratford Co-operative Society and the Independent Labour Party (ILP).

Barnes was an industrious and reliable person who gained widespread respect for his integrity of character. These qualities ensured his quick promotion. Already by 1910 he was secretary of the East London Federation of the ILP. He was elected to the management committee of the Stratford Co-operative Society in 1914 and became its president in 1915. In 1920 he played a major part in the founding of the London Co-operative Society, and served as its first president from 1920 to 1923. He was also a council member of the National Union of Gold, Silver, and

Allied Trades. On 5 March 1921 Barnes married Leila Phoebe Real (*b.* 1900/01), whom he met through his silversmith business; she was the daughter of Charles Real, an engraver of Pitsea, Essex. There were three daughters of the marriage.

The circumstances of the First World War gave Barnes the opportunity to achieve one of his aims—the establishment of a Co-operative Party with representatives at Westminster and on local councils. Co-operative congresses as early as 1897 had voted in favour of such an organization, but the hesitation of societies whose members were adherents of the Liberal Party delayed the implementation of the resolution. By 1917, however, co-operators were in 'revolt from one end of the country to another' (A. J. Barnes, *The Political Aspects of Co-Operation*, 1922, 14) because of the unfair treatment received from the coalition government and its subordinate authorities as regards taxation (of dividends); allocation of supplies; representation on wartime fuel and food committees; and unjust decisions from military tribunals which exempted many owners and managers of small businesses from military service but denied similar concessions to managers of co-operatives. At the Swansea Co-operative Congress early in 1917 Barnes seconded a resolution calling for the establishment of a Co-operative Party. This won nearly unanimous support. At the 1918 general election the party fielded ten candidates, but only one was elected. He was elected to the Co-operative Party's national committee in 1920, and was its chairman from 1924 to 1945.

At the general election of November 1922 Barnes was elected as MP for East Ham South, one of four Co-operative Labour candidates to be returned to parliament. On the opposition benches at Westminster they were swamped by 138 MPs who were elected on the straight Labour Party ticket. Barnes, again always the realist, recognized that the situation had changed. At the Cheltenham congress of the Co-operative Party in 1927 he supported the continued existence of the party but acknowledged that its future lay in general support for the Labour Party, of which it became, in effect, a wing.

Barnes won steadily increasing, if unspectacular, recognition from his colleagues in the Parliamentary Labour Party because of his pleasant manner and transparent sincerity. Between his election to the Commons in 1922 and the loss of his seat at East Ham South in the general election débâcle of Labour of 27 October 1931, he was appointed parliamentary private secretary to William Graham at the exchequer (1922–4), Labour whip (1925–30), and junior lord of the Treasury from 11 June 1929 to 23 October 1930.

In the general election of November 1935 Barnes regained his seat at East Ham South and retained it until his voluntary retirement in 1955. Although he followed the Labour Party line in domestic politics, in the late 1930s co-operative society and party members, led by Barnes and Sydney Elliott, editor of the Co-operative Press Sunday newspaper, *Reynolds News*, took an independent position. They favoured the creation of an anti-aggression 'peace pact' of all peace-loving members of the League of Nations to resist fascist states that violated the sovereignty of other countries. At a big peace demonstration in London's Hyde Park on 19 September 1937 Barnes declared that the National Government was loading Britain with the burden of armaments, without a realization of the road by which peace could be secured. Elliott's proposed United Peace Alliance was, however, defeated when put to the vote at the Co-operative Congress in June 1938. He held no ministerial office during the Second World War, but remained active in the co-operative movement. He was a founder of the People's Entertainment Society and, in conjunction with Stafford Cripps, the Anglo-Chinese Development Society.

Barnes is chiefly remembered for his piloting through parliament of the Transport Bill, one of the major projects of nationalization of the post-war Attlee Labour government. He was appointed minister of war transport on 3 August 1945 and, when the department changed its name, minister of transport in 1946. The aim of the Transport Act, 1947, was to bring inland transport under comprehensive control through the British Transport Commission. This had supervision of the six executives for the six different forms of publicly owned transport, of which the railway executive was the most important. Barnes had little difficulty in gaining approval for the nationalization of the railways, as both Lloyd George and Churchill had advocated it as early as 1918. He had less success with his plans for the control of road freight haulage through the road haulage executive. On 12 March 1947, in a memorandum to the cabinet, he reported that: 'No feature of the Transport Bill raises so much opposition as the proposal to limit "C" licence holders [those who used their own vehicles for moving their own freight] to a distance of forty miles from their base', and that a deputation of hauliers he had interviewed were 'taking root and branch opposition to this part of the Bill' (PRO, CAB 128/9). Barnes removed the 40 mile limit from the bill; but in doing so he roused the ire of his own back-benchers, who saw the concession as undermining the transport integration objectives of the legislation.

For the management of the new undertakings established under the Transport Act, 1947, parliament adopted the policies of Herbert Morrison, lord president of the council. These took the form of the 'corporatism' exemplified by Morrison's London Passenger Transport Act, 1933, rather than of the 'mutualism' (workers' and transport users' participation) advocated by the Co-operative Party. In his *Socialisation and Transport* (1933) Morrison had urged that members of publicly owned boards should be appointed by the minister responsible 'primarily on suitable grounds of competence' (*Socialisation and Transport*, 157) as by these means 'Parliamentary action against a Board would be reduced to the minimum—which is much to be desired' (ibid., 174). However, adopting the Morrisonian approach left Barnes to confront back-bench opinion that it perpetuated the purely 'commodity' status of labour and denied workers a sense of involvement in the industry and the enjoyment of their full citizenship rights.

After his Transport Bill had passed through all its stages Barnes supported cautious consolidation of the public ownership measures so far achieved. He was one of the members of the cabinet who, on 7 August 1947, favoured the postponement of the introduction of the Steel Bill to the session 1948–9. He knew that the workforce in the steel industry was less committed to public ownership than were those employed in the coalmines or on the railways. On the other hand Barnes's more left-wing colleagues believed that 'he who controlled the citadel of steel would control shipbuilding, the motor industry—in effect British industry as a whole'. In the event, to placate the left the Iron and Steel Bill, which became law at the end of 1949, was a compromise measure which Barnes loyally supported.

In the general election of 25 October 1951 Barnes retained his seat with a large majority, but nationally the Conservatives secured a narrow majority and returned to power. The Churchill government rushed through the Transport Act, 1953, which provided for the return to private ownership of the road transport assets of the road haulage executive. The former minister of transport, who held that office for a longer period of time than any of his predecessors, was powerless to prevent the undermining of an important part of his main legislative achievement. He was now sixty-five and in the ensuing months felt that he was less needed in the Commons than he had been. He decided to retire from parliament at the end of the 1954–5 session.

In the 1930s Alfred Barnes's main hobby was caravanning with his wife and daughters. They toured the Essex coast until they found a site at Walton on the Naze, where he bought 2 acres of land as a parking place. On his retirement in 1955 he bought the adjacent Eastcliff Hotel, and more land on which he developed a holiday caravan site. The rooms of the hotel were converted into flats, one for his wife and himself and one each for two of his daughters. The third daughter lived in the USA with her American husband. In 1957 he was elected as independent—as all the councillors in that area were elected—to the Frinton and Walton urban district council. He died in his flat overlooking the North Sea, at Brenalwood, Hall Lane, Walton on the Naze, on 26 November 1974.

Philip S. Bagwell

Sources *The Times* (27 Nov 1974) · *DNB* · S. V. Bracher, *The Herald book of labour members* (1923) · *The Labour who's who* (1927) · b. cert. · m. cert. · B. Smith and G. Ostergaard, *Constitutional relations between the labour and co-operative parties*, Hansard Society (1960) · T. F. Carbery, *Consumers in politics: a history and general review of the co-operative party* (1969) · W. H. Brown, *A century of London cooperation* (1928) · K. O. Morgan, *Labour in power, 1945–1951* (1984) · H. A. Clegg, *Industrial democracy and nationalisation* (1951) · M. Sissons and P. French, eds., *Age of austerity* (1963) · *Cooperative News* (25 Sept 1937) · minutes of the socialisation of industries committee, 8 March and 9 May 1946, PRO, Cabinet MSS, CAB 134/687 · cabinet conclusions, 13 March 1947, PRO, Cabinet MSS, CAB 128/9 · cabinet conclusions, 22 Feb 1951, PRO, Cabinet MSS, CAB 128/19 · minutes of the cabinet emergencies committee, 12, 23, 28 June 1948, PRO, Cabinet MSS, CAB 134/175 · *CGPLA Eng. & Wales* (1975) · interview with A. J. Barnes, *Essex County Standard* (6 March 1959) · *WWW*, *1971–80*

Archives FILM BFI NFTVA, news footage · IWM FVA, actuality footage · priv. coll., video of co-operative party film, *The people's cinema*, vol. 2. [peace march from the Thames Embankment to Hyde Park, Alfred Barnes shown speaking, 19 Sept 1937]

Likenesses portrait, 1923, repro. in Bracher, *Herald book* · photograph, 1945, Hult. Arch. · portrait, 1951, repro. in *Express and Star* (2 Dec 1952) · portrait, 1958, repro. in Barnes, *Essex County Standard* · portrait, repro. in *ILN* (11 Aug 1945), front page · portrait, repro. in *The Times House of Commons* (1950), p. 105

Wealth at death £150,823: probate, 10 Sept 1975, *CGPLA Eng. & Wales*

Barnes, Ambrose (1627–1710), local politician, was born in the second half of 1627, the son of Thomas Barnes of Startforth in the North Riding of Yorkshire and his wife, probably named Anne, who was the daughter of Matthew Stodart of Barnard Castle. Barnes was educated at the local grammar school, where he distinguished himself by his good temper and application to his studies, and also by his success in the cockfighting ring, though he later disavowed the sport. In 1646, aged eighteen, he was bound apprentice to William Blackett, merchant adventurer, and a year later he was set over to Samuel Rawling, a draper and merchant. Barnes was stricken with the plague during one of its visitations to Newcastle, but survived. While still an apprentice he spent some time in Hamburg and possibly Königsberg, probably engaged in exporting English woollens and coal to northern Europe. A contemporary memoir comments upon his impressive command of the complexities of trade between the various northern European states.

Ambrose Barnes was tall, well-made, and of a sanguine complexion and grave, yet 'sweet and pleasant', aspect (Welford, 1.194). He began trading on his own account while still an apprentice, and in 1655 obtained release eighteen months early from his indentures. In that same year he married Mary (*d.* 1675), daughter of Thomas Butler, a merchant, and his wife, Mary Butler, the granddaughter on her mother's side of John Clavering, twice mayor of Newcastle. Ambrose and Mary Barnes had seven children, five of whom lived to adulthood. Barnes had been early drawn to the reformed religion and he oversaw an ostentatiously puritan household, in which was found close attention to prayer, strict sabbatarianism, a dislike of luxury, and a warm and enduring sympathy for Cromwellian republicanism and Independency.

Equipped by birth, marriage, occupation, and political and religious convictions for borough leadership, Ambrose Barnes moved swiftly into the town élite. In 1657 he was elected an alderman of Newcastle and, like other puritan magistrates in the Commonwealth period, worked to banish masquerades and plays, drunkenness, duelling, political corruption, and vagrancy as well as to regulate public charities, the coal-trade, and the quality of foodstuffs. He was tipped for the mayoralty but political events overtook him: as his contemporary biographer put it, 'if Monk and his Bishops come in, Alderman Barnes must go out' (Longstaffe, 105). Fearing royalist reprisals, Barnes resigned from office on 7 September 1659, shut up shop, called in his debts and contemplated emigrating to Hamburg, Danzig, New England, or Surinam. However, in the end he stayed in England and took the oath of supremacy and allegiance in October 1660. He was imprisoned for a time in Tynemouth Castle on suspicion of having designs against the new government, and he spent some years under virtual house arrest, adroitly evading writs and warrants and periodically paying fines for attending or holding secret conventicles. Rumour in the late 1660s had it that at one such meeting at Barnes's home the assembly sang a traitorous psalm in which it was predicted that 'God would put a Sword into the hands of the Saints to execute his Judgement upon the King and bind the Nobles in Bands of Iron'. Barnes himself in 1669, in a letter to the nonconformist divine Elkanah Wales, traced the rumour to his local bishop and called it 'a most vile forgery' (BL, Stowe MS 745, fol. 31). Notwithstanding his own difficulties, Barnes supported a number of ejected ministers financially; he knew Simeon Ashe, Richard Baxter, Edmund Calamy, and Richard Gilpin, who lived for a time in his home.

Barnes was appalled by Charles II's moral excesses as well as by his religious 'persecutions', and during the exclusion crisis he was imprisoned for a time as a 'great fanatick' (Bodl. Oxf., MS Rawl. D 850, fol. 141). The accession of James II brought easier times: Barnes favoured James II in his policy of religious toleration towards dissenters and was favoured by him in return. During this period he served a second term as alderman, and there are suggestions that James II wanted him for his next parliament. But in spite of this partial accommodation Barnes was too imbued with revolutionary spirit truly to prosper in any monarchical regime. He approved, at least initially, of William III's revolution, but was bitterly disappointed at what he saw as its timid and prevaricating character and its failure to effect real moral reform or bring full religious toleration for dissenters. Whiggery too offended him because of that party's 'degeneracy and contempt of religion', its support of stockjobbery, which he felt diverted funds from trade, and its ready embrace of political corruption 'whilst pretences were kept up for a free government' (Longstaffe, 186). His own shattered hopes and sense of political marginality were poured into writing a plan, heavily indebted to the republican theorist James Harrington, which proposed to reorganize England into a loose alliance of free city states, along the lines of the republics of Geneva or Venice, to be governed by men of merit, and devoted to trade and the fostering of good order and morality. Kings had no place there: 'The people have never been more fond of kings than their manners have been corrupted to the height, nor have ever more distasted them than when their spirits were bravest and most refined' (ibid., 213). There is, however, no evidence that this work was known outside a small circle during his own time, and the writings themselves perished in a fire at the Literary and Philosophical Society of Newcastle upon Tyne in 1893. Only brief extracts survive.

Mary Barnes died on 12 June 1675; Ambrose did not marry again. In later life he suffered from fading eyesight and from reverses in trade, including the 'breaking' of one of his sons-in-law and losses in lead-mining. Even so, until two months before his death in his early eighties he continued to ride out in the depths of winter to Cumberland to pay his miners. He died at Newcastle on 23 May 1710, reportedly in full assurance of his salvation, and was buried in St Nicholas's Church in the same city.

MARGARET R. HUNT

Sources *Memoirs of the life of Mr Ambrose Barnes*, ed. [W. H. D. Longstaffe], SurtS, 50 (1867) • R. Welford, *Men of mark 'twixt Tyne and Tweed*, 1 (1895) • M. R. Hunt, *The middling sort: commerce, gender and the family in England, 1680–1780* (1996) • A. Barnes to E. Wales, 12 Jan 1669, BL, Stowe MS 745, fol. 31 • I. Basire to [unknown], 1684?, Bodl. Oxf., MS Rawl. D. 850, fol. 141 • J. Hunter's extracts from Barnes's writings, 1811, BL, Add. MS 24607, fols. 75–6

Barnes [*née* Cappuccio], **Annie** (*c.*1887–1982), socialist and suffragist, probably born in Stepney, was the eldest of the twelve children of Lorenzo Cappuccio (*c.*1868–1935) and his wife, Antonietta (*c.*1865–1910). Her birth was unregistered, as were those of all her siblings until that of her youngest sister in 1909. It is likely that her father was an immigrant from Italy, although Annie Barnes makes no mention of an Italian heritage in her memoir. She mentions that her mother came from south London; there is no record of her parents having married in England. By the time she was born her father owned a shop in Stepney selling fruit, his name listed in the 1908 Post Office directory as Lawrence Cappacaus. She was educated at the Ben Jonson School in Stepney, an experience that she thoroughly enjoyed until forced to leave in 1902 when her mother became ill. From then until her marriage she worked at home, serving in the shop and looking after her siblings and her mother, until the latter's death.

About 1912 Annie Cappuccio became involved in the East London Federation of Suffragettes, the branch of the women's suffrage campaign conducted in the East End of London by Sylvia Pankhurst. Responsible as she was for the care of her family, she was clear that she could not take part in any militant activities that might lead to imprisonment but was happy to volunteer for less risky escapades. She willingly delivered copies of Sylvia Pankhurst's *Women's Dreadnought* in her neighbourhood and on one occasion scattered suffrage leaflets from the top of the Monument in the City of London. In her memoir (Barnes, 18, 60) she makes clear that her political and social awareness, her later success in local politics, and her quick repartee, were all nurtured by her association with the suffragette movement.

On 1 April 1919 Annie married Albert Barnes (*c.*1885–1958), a sawyer. Her father, denied his housekeeper and little interested in his remaining children, immediately remarried, but his new wife proved a cruel stepmother. Annie and Albert Barnes took over care of her younger brothers and sisters; they had no children of their own. Before the First World War Annie had joined the Independent Labour Party at Sylvia Pankhurst's behest but did not, in 1919, follow her into the Communist Party, joining instead the Stepney Labour Party and becoming secretary of its women's section. Later she was a member of the Mile End Labour Party. Annie Barnes was also active in the Women's Co-operative Guild, founding a local branch in

1929; she was, like her mother, an informal worker for the good of the poor of the area. She kept in touch with Sylvia Pankhurst, although shocked by the latter's unmarried motherhood, and on occasion housed Italian refugees sent to her by Sylvia.

In 1934 Annie Barnes was elected a Labour Party councillor in Stepney and immediately chose to serve on the housing and public health committees. Even with her lifetime experience of East End living she was shocked by the housing conditions endured by some of Wapping's inhabitants, and worked hard to provide them with adequate homes. Over the years she was a member of many different committees, as well as being three times vice-chairman of the public health committee. She was also a member of a board of school managers. She remained a councillor until 1937 and was re-elected again between 1941 and 1949. In 1938 she joined the committee of the Charity Organization Society, despite that society's reputation for high-handed philanthropy; knowing how obnoxious to the poor was the thought of 'charity', she was responsible for the society's name being changed to the Family Welfare Association. During the Second World War the Barnes's house in Stepney was bombed and they lost all their possessions. Now homeless, the couple were invited to live in Toynbee Hall in Whitechapel until, in 1949, they moved for a time to Pitsea in Essex, before returning to East Ham where Annie Barnes died, in the Memorial Hospital, on 22 February 1982 of bronchopneumonia and acute renal failure. In death her Italian roots were again obscured, her maiden name being rendered on her death certificate as Cutbush.

ELIZABETH CRAWFORD

Sources A. Barnes, *Tough Annie: from suffragette to Stepney councillor* (1980) [in conversation with Kate Harding and Caroline Gibbs] • m. cert. • d. cert. • *CGPLA Eng. & Wales* (1982) • A. Barnes and B. Harrison, interviews, 27 Nov 1974, 18 Dec 1974, Women's Library, London
Archives SOUND Women's Library, London, A. Barnes and B. Harrison, 27 Nov 1974, 18 Dec 1974
Likenesses photographs, *c*.1905–1979, repro. in Barnes, *Tough Annie*
Wealth at death under £25,000: probate, 22 March 1982, *CGPLA Eng. & Wales*

Barnes [Barns], **Arthur** (**1828–1908**), acrobat, was born at Birchall Street, Birmingham, the son of Henry Barns, an iron-founder, and his wife, Jane, *née* Williams. He was first noted performing with Edwin Hughes's circus for the 1845–6 season, then with William Cooke's circus in 1846, and with Pablo Fanque's circus from 1846 to 1849. In Copenhagen on 4 July 1848 he married Alexine Pettoletti, an equestrian performer and member of a famous Danish circus family, with whom he had two daughters, Annie (*b.* 1863) and Jessie (1872–1876).

Barnes became famous for his consecutive somersaults, thrown from a spring-board. He recounted that for a long time he could do only twenty or thirty, but that by constant practice he eventually managed fifty. In 1850 he achieved eighty-seven consecutive somersaults in a trial with William Cooke's circus at Gainsborough. In 1854 he visited America, where he eclipsed all his competitors, then returned the following year to perform with Hengler's circus at Liverpool. In 1857 he visited Denmark, and the next year performed in Denmark, Portugal, Spain, and France. He travelled throughout Britain with all the big circus companies of the day, including those of Wallett, Hernandez and Stone, Newsome, Frowde, and Sanger. In January 1864 at the Royal Agricultural Hall, Islington, London, it was claimed that Barnes had 'accomplished the unprecedented feat of throwing nearly 100 consecutive somersaults' (Morley, 55).

Barnes retired about 1867 to Sparkhill, near Solihull, where he purchased considerable property in Baker Street and lived comfortably on the rental income. His first wife having died, he married Catherine Edgington on 10 November 1875, and had two further children, Alexine Mary (*b.* 1877) and Arthur Henry (*b.* 1880). He died on 1 July 1908 at 36 Baker Street, Sparkhill, after forty years in retirement.

JOHN M. TURNER

Sources *The Era* (9 June 1850) • *The Era* (3 April 1853) • *The Era* (27 Sept 1857) • C. Keith, *Circus life and amusements* (1879) • private information (2004) • H. Morley, *The journal of a London playgoer from 1851 to 1866* (1866) • d. cert.
Wealth at death £819: probate, 6 Nov 1908, *CGPLA Eng. & Wales*

Barnes, Barnabe (*bap.* **1571**, *d.* **1609**), poet and playwright, was baptized at St Michael le Belfry, York, on 6 March 1571, the third son of Dr Richard *Barnes (1532?–1587), bishop of Durham, and his wife, Fridismunda Gifford (*d.* 1581). He matriculated at Brasenose College, Oxford, in 1586, but did not complete his degree. When Richard Barnes died he left one-third of his estate to his second wife, Jane Jerrard, a Huguenot, with the remaining two-thirds to be divided equally among his six children (*Injunctions*, xv). Barnabe appears to have lived on the income from his father's bequest. In August 1591 Barnabe joined the earl of Essex's expedition to Normandy; he returned at the end of two months when Essex's commission expired. Barnes published four works, and his reputation rests principally on the first of them, *Parthenophil and Parthenophe* (1593), a sequence of poems in the Petrarchan manner. The others are *A Divine Centurie of Spirituall Sonnets* (1595), *Foure Bookes of Offices* (1606), a prose work on the four cardinal virtues, ostensibly for the benefit of princes (it was dedicated to King James), and *The Divil's Charter* (1607), an anti-papal drama. While Barnes was resident in London with the printer John Wolfe he made the acquaintance of Gabriel Harvey, on whose behalf he wrote commendatory verses to *Pierce's Supererogation* (1593). He thus became a party to Harvey's quarrel with Thomas Nash, who attacked Barnes in *Have with You to Saffron-Walden* (1596), accusing Barnes of cowardice in France, petty thievery at court, and foppishness: 'getting him a strange payre of *Babilonian* britches, with a codpisse as big as a *Bolognian* sawcedge' (T. Nash, *Works*, ed. R. B. McKerrow, 5 vols., 1958, 3.109). Beneath the stalking horse of Nash's satirical exaggeration is an accurate perception of Barnes's irresistible attraction to Italian fashion. Though he decries Machiavelli's *The Prince* as 'that puddle of princely policies' in *Foure Bookes of Offices* (sig. A), Barnes owned Wolfe's Italian editions of both *Il principe* and *Discorsi sopra Livio*, and he quotes Italian from the former while drawing on the latter in *The Divil's Charter*. He uses a wider variation of Italian verse forms in *Parthenophil and Parthenophe* than any previous English sonneteer, and in *The Divil's Charter* he followed the fashion newly introduced by John Marston of drawing on recent Italian history: the play is based principally on Guicciardini's history of early sixteenth-century Italy, and the presenter is named 'Guicchiardine'.

Barnes's fascination with things Italian extended to life, as well as art. In 1598 he was accused in Star Chamber of dabbling in exotic forms of poisoning in the new Italian manner, offering his intended victim, John Browne, first 'a limonde which he had taynted and venomed with some subtyll poyson' (Eccles, 177) and then a flagon of wine which he had laced with mercury sublimate. Browne testified that he passed the lemon to another, but he drank the wine and 'fownde a great inflamacion torture and distemperature in his bodye' (ibid., 178). Fortunately for Barnes, Browne survived the attack, and powerful friends in the north must have intervened, for Barnes was not reapprehended after his escape from the Marshalsea. The likelihood is that Barnes undertook the assassination attempt at the behest of Lord Euer, whom Elizabeth had appointed as warden of the middle marches in 1595, though Attorney-General Edward Coke, who prosecuted Barnes in Star Chamber, did not make the connection (ibid., 192–211).

Parthenophil and Parthenophe is unique not only in the variety of its verse forms but in its ending, which involves a surprising consummation. Parthenophil, the virgin-lover of the title (a clear allusion to Sidney's Astrophil) has a dream in 'Sestine 5', the final poem, in which he uses black magic to compel the presence of the unattainable Parthenophe, riding naked on a goat, so that he can rape her. Since Parthenophe means virgin Barnes's dream seems unavoidably political, and the stance of frustrated expectation, occasioned by an unyielding and unapproachable female, seems appropriate to one of Essex's party in the early 1590s. Despite the piety of the *Spirituall Sonnets* and the moralism of *Foure Bookes of Offices* Barnes's ambivalent fascination with black magic appears again in *The Divil's Charter*, where he has Pope Alexander VI sell his soul to the devil in frank imitation of Marlowe's Dr Faustus; the play was performed at court by the King's Men on Candlemas (2 February) 1607. Also evident in Barnes's last work is a Machiavellian fascination with power, for the play turns on the ability to intimidate, and the pope is most powerful because his means of intimidation are the most sophisticated. When the devil forces him to grovel and beg for mercy, the pope finds himself in the unenviable position of those who have begged him for mercy throughout the play, and the outcome is inevitable. Whether Barnes's God is anything more than the most successful intimidator of all is an open question, for the devil acknowledges God's superior power. The ultimate godfather of *The Divil's Charter* may thus be God the Father. There is no record that Barnes ever married or fathered any children. He died at the age of thirty-eight of unknown causes. His burial is recorded in the registry of St Mary le Bow, Durham, in December 1609. He apparently left no will and his material worth at death is unknown.

John D. Cox

Sources M. Eccles, 'Barnabe Barnes', *Thomas Lodge and other Elizabethans*, ed. C. J. Sisson (1933), 166–241 · N. W. Bawcutt, 'Barnabe Barnes's ownership of Machiavelli's *Discorsi*', *N&Q*, 227 (1982), 411 · *The injunctions and other ecclesiastical proceedings of Richard Barnes, bishop of Durham*, ed. [J. Raine], SurtS, 22 (1850), xv · M. H. Dodds, 'Barnabe Barnes', *Archaeologia Aeliana*, 4th ser., 24 (1946), 1–59 · T. P. Roche, jun., *Petrarch and the English sonnet sequences* (1989) · J. N. Nelson, 'Lust and black magic in Barnabe Barnes's *Parthenophil and Parthenophe*', *Sixteenth Century Journal*, 25 (1994), 595–608 · J. D. Cox, 'Stage devilry in two King's Men plays of 1606', *Modern Language Review*, 93 (1998), 934–47 · L. A. Montrose, '"Shaping fantasies": figurations of gender and power in Elizabethan culture', *Representing the English Renaissance*, ed. S. Greenblatt (1988), 31–64

Barnes, Sir Denis Charles (1914–1992), civil servant and industrial relations expert, was born on 15 December 1914 at 4 Station Road, Openshaw, Manchester, the second son and fifth of six children of Frederick Charles Barnes (*c*.1870–*c*.1920), a school attendance officer for the local education committee, and his wife, Martha Lilley, *née* Berry (1876–*c*.1920). His parents were self-educated, avid users of public libraries, and keen to see their children educated. From this lower-middle-class metropolitan background, Barnes attended Plymouth Grove elementary school, Manchester, and won scholarships to Hulme grammar school, Manchester, and Merton College, Oxford, where he graduated with first-class honours in modern history in 1936 and a second-class degree in philosophy, politics, and economics in 1937. He went straight from Oxford into the civil service, joining the Ministry of Labour. On 29 April 1938 he married Patricia Abercrombie (*b*. 1917), a novelist and the daughter of Lieutenant-Colonel Charles Murray Abercrombie. They met at a party in London. After their marriage they lived in flats in Battersea and then at 170 Gloucester Place, London, acquiring a rural retreat at Serridge Lodge in the Forest of Dean in the 1960s. There were no children of the marriage.

Barnes spent his entire career in the home civil service, except for a year touring the USA and two years on secondment to the Foreign Office. He served as private secretary to the minister of labour, George Isaac, in 1945–7, and then progressed steadily within the ministry, becoming deputy secretary in 1963 and succeeding Sir James Dunnett as permanent secretary in 1966. The ministry was renamed the Department of Employment and Productivity in 1968 and the Department of Employment in 1970; Barnes remained permanent secretary until the end of 1973. He was made CB in 1964 and KCB in 1967.

Barnes was not an archetypal civil servant. Though possessing one of the best brains of his generation, he was more of a fixer than a paper-based policy analyst; he was very outward looking, and latterly spent much time offering advice lying on a ministry sofa. He did not treat his headquarters at 8 St James's Square as an ivory tower, instead forging very active personal links with the press (especially the corps of industrial correspondents), with industrial leaders, and with members of the TUC general council, including successive general secretaries. Defeatist and pessimistic about Britain's post-war, post-empire role, in private he would counsel orderly retreat in terms of global influence and industrial clout, and, at times, in the face of trade-union power.

Growing impatient with voluntary negotiation in the early 1960s, Barnes sought to improve workers' protection by a burst of legislation on contracts of employment, redundancy payments, and industrial training. He also favoured the establishment of the Donovan royal commission on trades unions and employers' associations (1965–8). Scarred by the Wilson government's failure to support the attempt of his minister Barbara Castle to implement the Donovan commission's findings by regulating unions' access to industrial action through the white paper *In Place of Strife* (1969), Barnes underwent something of a personal U-turn in his views in 1970, concluding that though statutory intervention was logically necessary, both to regulate strikes and to control pay inflation, no British government would see it through.

At his best when keeping his finger on the pulse of major industrial disputes, Barnes used the infamous back door to 8 St James's Square both to listen to and to advise a string of employers and trade-union leaders, and the occasional independent arbitrator. Immensely influential, this talent was widely recognized in Whitehall and he often visited no. 10 to give personal advice to prime ministers Wilson and Heath. Wilson went so far as to describe him as 'the best Permanent Secretary in Whitehall' (B. Castle, *The Castle Diaries, 1964–76*, 1990, 215). His influence probably peaked in 1972, which saw the first miners' strike settled by the Wilberforce inquiry and a prolonged search by the Heath administration for a voluntary pact on pay. Barnes viewed a pact as akin to the philosopher's stone and he fell out of favour when in November 1972 the Heath administration changed tack and a statutory pay, prices, and dividend freeze was introduced. As permanent secretary he permitted radical restructuring of his department, creating executive agencies including the Health and Safety Executive, the Training Services Agency (TSA), the Employment Services Agency (ESA), and the Advisory, Conciliation and Arbitration Service (ACAS).

In 1973 it was decided that the TSA and the ESA should be overseen by the tripartite Manpower Services Commission, and Barnes became the commission's first chairman, in 1974. Unemployment had reached a post-war peak of 1 million in early 1972. Barnes encouraged large-scale vocational training and job creation schemes, and saw the benchmark—100,000 trainees—achieved. He established a degree of independence from the department, which positioned the commission well for the subsequent development of extensive youth training schemes; these eventually *de facto* extended the formal period of education and training for most young people in Britain to the age of eighteen. He retired from the Manpower Services Commission in 1976, settling with his wife at Wittersham, Kent. He was president of the Manpower Society from 1976, and a director of Glynwed Ltd and the General Accident, Fire and Life Assurance Corporation.

Idiosyncratic, cynical, and sometimes destructively witty, Barnes inspired huge loyalty from the small circle of colleagues he allowed close. As a modern historian he looked back with pleasure at the lasting achievements of the Manpower Services Commission, and with amazement at Margaret Thatcher's changes to the industrial relations landscape he had thought unattainable. Perhaps to keep the dark arts of conciliation veiled, his own book (written with Eileen Reid), *Government and Trade Unions* (1980), was bland, uninformative, and pessimistic, and was described at the time by Geoffrey Goodman writing in the *Daily Mirror* (3 June 1980) as a Wagnerian account of frustration and failure. As a social reformer Barnes made permanent gains in worker protection and vocational training, but in industrial relations his caution and fear of revolution may have delayed reform. He was christened into the Church of England, but was not a practising member. He died following an allergic reaction to a bee sting at his home, the Old Inn, 30 The Street, Wittersham, Kent, on 6 May 1992, and was buried in Wittersham churchyard about five days later. He was survived by his wife.

IAN A. JOHNSTON

Sources D. Price, *Office of hope: history of the employment service* (2000) · *Daily Mirror* (3 June 1980) · *The Independent* (16 May 1992) · *The Times* (11 May 1992) · *The Times* (16 May 1992) · *WWW, 1991–5* · private information (2004) · personal knowledge (2004) · b. cert. · m. cert. · d. cert.

Archives priv. coll., family tree and private MSS

Likenesses photograph, repro. in *The Times* · photograph, repro. in *The Independent*

Wealth at death £56,634: probate, 20 Aug 1992, *CGPLA Eng. & Wales*

Barnes, Djuna Chappell (1892–1982), writer and artist, was born on 12 June 1892 in a log cabin on Storm King Mountain, Cornwall-on-Hudson, New York state, USA. She was the daughter of an American father, Wald Harold Barnes (1865–1934), and an English mother, Elizabeth Chappell (1862–1945), both of whom were caretakers of the estate of Wald's brother at the time of her birth. Djuna described her father as a 'cabinet maker, a painter, a novelist, a poet, a musician who played five instruments, a composer who wrote librettos for his own operas, a man who could never stay put' (Herring, 25). He was also an advocate of free love, and his mistress Fanny Faulkner joined the household when Djuna was five. Djuna later accused her father of arranging for a neighbour to take her virginity. The large family—which consisted of her elder brother, Thurn, younger brothers, Zendon, Saxon, and Shangar, and several half-siblings—was presided over by her grandmother Zadel Barnes, a journalist and theosophist, who knew Speranza Wilde and Eleanor Marx. Djuna was exceptionally close to her grandmother, perhaps incestuously so, and would always turn to her when in difficulty.

About 1895 the family moved to a farm in New York state. The children were educated mainly at home, and encouraged to write. Djuna was also encouraged by Zadel to 'marry' Fanny Faulkner's 52-year-old brother Percy in summer 1910, but it is not certain that an official ceremony took place. They lived in Bridgeport but Djuna left after two months, and returned to the farm. She nursed a lifelong resentment: 'father and his bastard children and mistresses had thrown me off marriage and babies' (Herring, 33).

Difficult years followed her parents' divorce in 1912. Djuna felt bound to help support her mother and brothers. She attended the Pratt Institute in Brooklyn from 1912 to 1913, and excelled in pictorial composition, but left to become a freelance journalist. She contributed short stories, Beardsley-esque drawings, theatrical reviews, interviews, and news reports for almost every English-language newspaper in New York; Carl Van Vechten at the *New York Press* called her his 'favourite genius' (Herring, 76). From 1914 to 1916 she was engaged to the bon vivant Ernst (Putzi) Hanfstaengl (1887–1975), later chief minister of the foreign press for Hitler. Ultimately, however, he refused to marry her because she was not German.

Barnes's first major publication was *A Book of Repulsive Women* (1915), a satire on women's sexual roles, which she called 'a disgusting little item', and of which she later burnt as many copies as she could find (O'Neal, 98). This book also contained illustrations—from 1915 to 1916 she studied at the Art Students' League of New York. From 1916 she lived in Greenwich Village among painters, artists, and writers, and with her new lover, the drama critic Courtenay Lemon (1883–1933), known for his socialist views. She was closely associated with the Provincetown Players, the theatre collective that launched Eugene O'Neill, and they influenced the dramatic pieces she wrote for the *New York Morning Telegraph*. These were not meant to be acted, but read as dialogue, and they show the emergence of her distinctive style: epigrams and striking imagery, with flashes of bitter wit. The best of her early work, including the short story 'A Night among the Horses' and the play *Three from the Earth*, was published in Margaret Anderson's and Jane Heap's *Little Review* between 1918 and 1922.

Barnes began a long association with Paris in 1921 with a journalistic assignment for *McCall's*. In the following year she interviewed James Joyce for an article that appeared in *Vanity Fair*. They became friends and Joyce sent Barnes a copy of the proof sheets of *Ulysses*. Inspired by his stylistic virtuosity, she began to move away from the Wildean formalism of her early work. A collection of her short stories, *A Book*, appeared in 1923, and was later republished as *A Night among the Horses* (1929). About this time Barnes became part of the expatriate group which included Man Ray, Hemingway, Yeats, Gertrude Stein, and Mina Loy. Her striking beauty—auburn hair and angular features—along with her famous black cape, her haughty manner, and cruel, 'wisecracking tongue' (McAlmon, 34), made her a legendary character. She featured in almost every literary memoir of Paris at this time. She was also part of Natalie Clifford Barney's lesbian circle, immortalized in her wickedly satirical *Ladies Almanack* (published privately and pseudonymously, under the name 'a Lady of Fashion', in 1928). That same year she produced *Ryder*, a novel based on an extended family much like her own. It had a Chaucerian bawdiness, with her own scatological illustrations, and dazzled with its array of styles and voices.

Barnes's time in Paris was dominated by her relationship with the American artist Thelma Ellen Wood (1901–1970). When Thelma's promiscuity and drunkenness ended the affair in 1928, Barnes started work on her novel *Nightwood*. It is a highly charged work, linguistically complex, and riven with pain and loss. It centres on the anguished narratives of Matthew O'Connor, a transvestite gynaecologist, and Nora Flood, who is in love with the enigmatic and boyish woman Robin Vote. Barnes's friend Emily Coleman saw 'a new suffering, a new intensity' in the work: 'There has been nothing written of such intense jealousy before' (Fuchs, 31). It has one of the most shattering endings in modern literature. It took years for Barnes to find a publisher, until Coleman pressured T. S. Eliot at Faber and Faber to accept it. Eliot, who wrote the preface, thought it was like an Elizabethan tragedy for its 'quality of horror and doom' (preface, Faber edn, 1985).

During the 1930s Barnes was restless: she was in New York and Tangier with the writer Charles Henri Ford, eighteen years her junior, but she felt that after Thelma Wood there was 'no room for any other "terrible attraction"' (Guirl-Stearley, 114). In summer 1932 and 1933 she stayed with her benefactor Peggy Guggenheim and her entourage at Hayford Hall in Devon, where, despite the almost incessant drinking and sexual high jinks, she wrote and reworked much of *Nightwood*. Pregnant after a fling with the French painter Jean Oberlé, she had an abortion in Paris in June 1933, performed by Dan Mahoney, the model for *Nightwood's* Matthew O'Connor. She worked for the Works Progress Administration to compile a guide to New York, and then, with *Nightwood* finally settled at Faber, Barnes spent much of 1936–7 in London and Paris, where her drinking got steadily worse. *Nightwood* was published to mixed reviews in October 1937: her friend Edwin Muir hailed it 'an undeniable work of genius' (*The Listener*, 28 Oct 1936), but Philip Rahv denounced its 'minute shudders of decadence' (*New Masses*, 4 May 1937).

Ill and depressed, Barnes returned to New York in October 1939, and was sent to a sanatorium by her family in the following year. She produced no new work in the 1940s primarily because of her alcoholism, which did not abate until the early 1950s. In September 1940 she moved to a one-roomed apartment at 5 Patchin Place, Greenwich Village, where, apart from a final voyage to Europe in 1950, she spent the rest of her life. She became, as she described in a rare interview, 'a form of Trappist' (*New York Times Book Review*, 24 May 1971). Her play *The Antiphon* (1958), about hatred between mother and daughter, was set in her mother's birthplace in Oakham, Rutland. It was a poisonous revenge on her family. The *New York Times Book Review* (20 April 1958) pronounced it 'scarcely a play', adding that 'one cannot imagine it on any stage'. It was performed in Stockholm in 1961. A clutch of poems and *Spillway* (1962), a further collection of stories, followed.

As her public life diminished, Barnes's status grew. Critical interest increased in the 1960s and 1970s, despite her attempts to block any enquiries (she ascribed her desire to protect her privacy to her 'English blood'). Increasingly cantankerous, she refused to allow critics to quote from her work, but her elegance and wit remained until the end. After an attempted suicide with pills in the late 1970s, she said she woke up feeling better than she had for years. She died of natural causes at 5 Patchin Place on 19 June 1982. She was cremated, and her ashes were scattered at Storm King Mountain. A collection of poems, *Creatures in an Alphabet*, appeared after her death. No longer the 'most famous unknown in the world' (Kaever, 5), Barnes is now considered one of the most significant writers of the first half of the twentieth century. CLARE L. TAYLOR

Sources P. Herring, *Djuna: the life of Djuna Barnes* (1995) · G. C. Guirl-Stearley, ed., 'The letters of Djuna Barnes and Emily Holmes Coleman (1935–1936)', *Missouri Review*, 22/3 (1999) · H. O'Neal, *Life is painful, nasty and short … in my case it has only been painful and nasty* (1990) · M. L. Broe, *Silence and power: a reevaluation of Djuna Barnes* (1991) · R. McAlmon, *Being geniuses together: 1920–1930* (1968) · M. Fuchs, 'The triadic association of Emily Holmes Coleman, T. S. Eliot, and Djuna Barnes', *ANQ: a Quarterly Journal of Short Articles, Notes and Reviews*, 12/4 (autumn 1999) · R. Giroux, '"The most famous unknown in the world"—remembering Djuna Barnes', *New York Times Book Review* (1 Dec 1985) · P. Guggenheim, *Out of this century* (1946) · K. Kaever, *Nachtwachen der Djuna Barnes* (1985)
Archives University of Maryland Libraries, papers
Likenesses photographs, University of Maryland Libraries, special collections, papers of Djuna Barnes

Barnes, Sir Edward (1776–1838), army officer, of Beechhill Park, near Barnet, began his career as an ensign in the 47th regiment on 8 November 1792, became a lieutenant in the army on 8 May 1793, and was promoted into the 86th regiment on 30 October. He became a captain in the 99th regiment on 11 February 1793, a major in the 79th regiment on 17 February 1800, a lieutenant-colonel in the 46th regiment on 23 April 1807, a colonel in the army on 25 July 1810, and a major-general on 4 June 1813. He was lieutenant-governor of Dominica (1808–12), and was appointed lieutenant-governor of Antigua in December 1813, although he did not take up the appointment.

Barnes served on the staff in the Peninsula from 1812, and commanded a brigade at the battles of Vitoria, Pyrenees, Nivelle, Nive, and Orthez, receiving a gold cross and three clasps. He also served in the campaign of 1815 in the Netherlands and France as adjutant-general, and was severely wounded at Waterloo. For this campaign he received the Austrian order of Maria Theresa and the Russian order of St Anne, first class. He had previously, on the enlargement of the Order of the Bath, been nominated KCB. He was colonel 4th garrison battalion 1815–16, and was appointed colonel of the 99th regiment on 24 October 1816; he was appointed to the staff in Ceylon in 1819. From 1820 to 1822 he was colonel 1st battalion rifle brigade. On 25 August 1822 he was made colonel of the 78th regiment, and became a lieutenant-general on 27 May 1825. From January 1824 until October 1831 he was governor of Ceylon. On 24 February 1831 he was made GCB, and on 7 June became commander-in-chief in India, which appointment he held until May 1833 with the local rank of

Sir Edward Barnes (1776–1838), by George Dawe, *c.*1818

general. On 14 October 1834 he became colonel of the 31st regiment.

In July 1834, on the death of the Rt Hon. Michael Angelo Taylor, Barnes contested Sudbury as a Conservative. The number of votes being equal, the mayor or returning officer claimed the privilege of selecting Barnes. A petition was in progress when the general election of 1835 ensued, at which Barnes failed to retain his seat, although at the next election (1837) he won it back at the head of the poll. He died in Piccadilly, London, on 19 March 1838, at the age of sixty-two.

A. S. BOLTON, *rev.* JAMES FALKNER

Sources *Army List* · *GM*, 2nd ser., 10 (1838), 214 · W. F. P. Napier, *History of the war in the Peninsula and in the south of France*, 3rd edn, 6 vols. (1832–40) · C. W. C. Oman, *A history of the Peninsular War*, 7 (1930)
Archives BL, register of dispatches, Add. MSS 19454–19455 · U. Southampton L., note book as adjutant-general of British army in France | U. Nott. L., corresp. with Lord William Bentinck, PwJF 334–408 · U. Southampton L., departmental letter-books as adjutant-general to duke of Wellington
Likenesses T. Heaphy, watercolour drawings, 1813–14, NPG · G. Dawe, oils, *c.*1818, Wellington Museum, Apsley House, London [*see illus.*] · J. Wood, oils, *c.*1825, Army & Navy Club · W. Salter, oils, 1834–7, NPG · H. Weekes, statue, 1846, Colombo, Sri Lanka · W. Salter, group portrait, oils (*Waterloo banquet at Apsley House*), Wellington Museum, Apsley House, London · mezzotint (after J. Wood)

Barnes, Ernest William (1874–1953), bishop of Birmingham, was born on 1 April 1874 in Altrincham, Cheshire, the eldest of the four sons of John Starkie Barnes (1843–1922) and his wife, Jane Elizabeth Kerry (1850–1938), of Charlbury, Oxfordshire. The fact of his having been born

Ernest William Barnes (1874–1953), by unknown photographer

on April fool's day delighted his many antagonists in later life. An elementary schoolteacher, J. S. Barnes was appointed headmaster of a school in Birmingham, so his son's boyhood was spent in the city which later knew him as its bishop. Educated at King Edward's School (the school of B. F. Westcott, J. B. Lightfoot, and E. W. Benson), Barnes went up to Cambridge as a scholar of Trinity College in 1893 and in 1896 was bracketed second wrangler. In 1897 he became president of the union and was placed in the first division of the first class in part two of the mathematical tripos. In the following year he was first Smith's prizeman and was elected a fellow of his college, becoming assistant lecturer in 1902, junior dean (1906–8), and tutor from 1908 to 1915. In 1909 he was elected a fellow of the Royal Society.

Barnes's relations with his Cambridge colleagues were not always harmonious. A shy man conscious of unusual powers, he could be arrogant in controversy and did not shrink from declaring his views. In particular, the strong pacifist principles of which the outbreak of war in 1914 found him an ardent champion failed to endear him to the more bellicose of his colleagues at Trinity, who deprived his friend Bertrand Russell of his fellowship because of his pacifism. It is said that Barnes, whose father was a Baptist, was a professed atheist when he first went up to Cambridge but as an undergraduate experienced conversion to Christianity. In 1902 he was made deacon and in 1903 he was ordained priest. In 1915–19 he was master of the Temple; in 1918 he was made canon of Westminster; and in 1924 Ramsay MacDonald, in the first act of episcopal patronage by a Labour government, nominated him bishop of Birmingham. In 1916 Barnes married Adelaide Caroline Theresa (1881–1963), daughter of Sir Adolphus *Ward, master of Peterhouse, Cambridge; there were two sons of the marriage, which was a very happy one.

A broad churchman, whose training at Cambridge had been primarily mathematical, Barnes conceived it to be his mission and duty to urge the need to substitute a world outlook based on the natural sciences for the traditionally scriptural outlook characteristic of Christian theology. He preached what came to be known as 'gorilla' sermons, supporting the evolutionary theory of man's biological descent from some creature akin to the apes. He opposed all forms of the doctrine of the real presence of Christ in the eucharist, which he saw as a hangover from pagan mystery religion. The essence of Christianity, as he understood and practised it, lay in a personal discipleship of the Jesus of the gospels, and in accepting an ethic based on the sermon on the mount. His congregation at the Temple during his mastership he believed to consist of 'wistful agnostics' in need of the spiritual diet of somewhat self-conscious modernism which he provided.

It was probably during this period that Barnes's best work as a preacher was done. There was a challenging incisiveness about his utterances, and an evident, if somewhat naïve, intellectual honesty, which his congregation of able lawyers could appreciate; nor at this stage does controversy of a public kind appear to have arisen, although at the Temple, as in Cambridge, there were those who shook their heads at Barnes's pacifism. The canonry of Westminster gave him a wider audience, and by the time of his appointment to Birmingham he had already become something of a controversial figure. His opinions were by now well known. His gorilla sermons were generally held to be unnecessary since the theory of evolution had long ceased to be a matter of dispute among educated churchmen. But his attacks upon the doctrine of the real presence caused pain and distress to many and were widely resented.

The Birmingham diocese to which he went in 1924 was largely Anglo-Catholic in tone, and there were plenty of parishes in which the accustomed usages were not such as the bishop approved. Barnes, who had no prior experience of parish life, was shocked to discover that the reservation of the sacrament was common in Birmingham churches. In 1925 trouble threatened because he refused to institute a patron's nominee to a vacant benefice (St Mark's, Washwood Heath), unless he agreed in advance to discontinue the practice of reservation which had been customary in the parish. The incumbent designate preferred to withdraw; the next candidate gave the assurance, although it went beyond anything the bishop was legally entitled to demand. Fifteen other Birmingham incumbents refused to accept his prohibition on the reservation of the sacrament; Barnes treated them as rebels, refusing to license curates for them, or to allow them support from diocesan funds.

In September 1927 the bishop preached a vigorous gorilla sermon in Westminster Abbey, and in Birmingham a fortnight later he delivered an address on sacramental teaching which contained a provocative onslaught on the doctrine of the real presence. A public protest was made ten days later in St Paul's Cathedral, where the bishop was about to preach, by a London incumbent who appeared with a large body of laymen. Denouncing the bishop as a heretic, he demanded that the bishop of London should inhibit Barnes from preaching in his diocese and that the archbishop of the province should arrange for his trial. The bishop took the unusual course of addressing an open letter to Archbishop Davidson in which he complained of the disturbance and, defending his position, remarked that no one should drive him to Tennessee or to Rome. The archbishop published a courteous reply, assuring the bishop that no one in England desired to lead or drive him to either, dismissing the evolutionary sermons as of little importance, but criticizing as needlessly wounding what the bishop had said about sacramentalism. Before the end of the year the bishop published, in reply to his critics, a book giving a positive account of his beliefs, with the title *Should Such a Faith Offend?*, which caused the controversy to die down for a time.

In 1929 the bishop once again refused to institute to a benefice the nominee of the patrons unless promises were made which went beyond those required by law. The patrons of this parish (St Aidan's, Small Heath) included the bishop of Truro, W. H. Frere, and the controversy went on for eighteen months. In the end the patrons obtained from a judge of the High Court a writ of mandamus directed to the archbishop of Canterbury enjoining him to license a fit person to the benefice. Archbishop Lang admitted the patrons' original nominee. Barnes was also a leading campaigner against prayer book revision in 1927–8, opposing the new book's latitude on the question of reservation.

The Second World War saw Barnes involved in a controversy with the makers of cement. At a public meeting in Birmingham in November 1940 about providing air raid shelters, he had attacked the Cement Makers' Federation as a ring of monopolists holding up the supply of cement at a time of great public need in the interests of their own private profit. The bishop was sued for slander. He did not appear in court, although he was represented by counsel. The cement companies were awarded £1600 damages. It was an index of the respect, and even affection, in which Barnes was held by this time that the money was raised by lay friends in the diocese. In a speech in the House of Lords in June 1941 the bishop returned undaunted to the attack, maintaining that a cement ring did exist, that it was contrary to the public interest, and that big business was using libel and slander actions to suppress criticism.

In 1947 Barnes entered the lists as a theological author. His book *The Rise of Christianity* aroused fierce opposition for his denial of miracles and his disparaging treatment of St Paul. Barnes's grasp of New Testament criticism was slight, confused, and outdated, and even his fellow modernists were embarrassed by the book. The outraged orthodox demanded his condemnation. Under great pressure to take action of some kind, but unwilling to prosecute, Archbishop Fisher, in a presidential address to convocation, after expressing deep appreciation of the bishop's Christian character and of the sincerity of his aims, delivered a strong and damaging criticism of his book and of certain of its presuppositions, and cautioned readers against accepting its claim to be an adequate and impartial setting forth of the truth. While declaring that he 'would have no trial in this matter', he went on to say: 'If his views were mine, I should not feel that I could still hold episcopal office in the church'. The hint was ignored by Barnes who made a defiant personal statement in the House of Bishops. Action parallel with that of the archbishop of Canterbury having been taken also in York convocation by Archbishop Garbett, the matter was allowed to drop.

The furore made the book a best-seller, and it was serialised in the *Sunday Pictorial*. But its long-term impact was negligible; Roger Lloyd described it as 'a theological dead-end' (Lloyd, 481). Nevertheless, many modernists felt that Barnes had gravely damaged their cause. For his part, Barnes always denied that he was a modernist, insisting instead that he was an evangelical.

Barnes also made controversial public interventions on other questions. He supported divorce law reform and the ordination of women, while his belief in eugenics led him to criticize Commonwealth immigration to Birmingham in the early 1950s, as he believed that immigrants would dilute the national stock.

The external record of recurring crises and controversies by which his tenure of the see of Birmingham was marked exhibits Barnes as a very unusual type of prelate: a stormy petrel of the episcopate. Yet there is another side to the story. Thorny and unbending in controversy, and indifferent to the exasperation roused by his utterances, he was none the less personally charming and manifestly a man of the highest character and purpose. He had made initial mistakes, but in the later phases of his episcopate he mellowed appreciably. He had either worn down opposition or had reached a tacit *modus vivendi* with his opponents. His was a complicated and many-sided character; he could be shy and awkward, but he was inwardly eager for friendship and capable of great personal kindness. The story is told that a young Anglo-Catholic curate who went to tea with him returned from the encounter remarking: 'I do not know whether I agree with him, but I know he is a saint'. By all but a few of the laity of his diocese he was held in the highest honour and admired as a man of inflexible courage. The administrative side of a bishop's work was admittedly not congenial to him, but during his time at Birmingham a considerable number of new churches were built and consecrated, and new parishes were formed to meet changing conditions. He resigned his see in May 1953 and died on 29 November of the same year at his home at Hurstpierpoint in Sussex. His ashes were interred in Birmingham Cathedral.

The best contemporary sketch of Barnes came from Hensley Henson:

> Tall, pallid with much study, with stooping shoulders, and a voice at once challenging and melancholy, he commands attention as well by his manner as by his opinions, which are almost insolently oppugnant to the general mind. He is a good man, but clearly a fanatic, and in a more disciplined age, could not possibly have avoided the stake. (Henson, 272)

Though he escaped the stake, Barnes suffered the punishment of ostracism by his fellow bishops, and became increasingly lonely and paranoid at the end of his life. One of his sons, Sir John Barnes, wrote a sympathetic biography, *Ahead of his Age* (1979), which went some way towards restoring Barnes's reputation as a serious thinker and church leader. Barnes was a fellow of King's College, London (1919) and Gifford lecturer at Aberdeen (1926–8); he received the honorary degrees of DD from Aberdeen (1925) and Edinburgh (1927), and LLD from Glasgow (1926). A. E. J. RAWLINSON, *rev.* MATTHEW GRIMLEY

Sources J. Barnes, *Ahead of his age: Bishop Barnes of Birmingham* (1979) · A. M. G. Stephenson, *The rise and decline of English modernism* (1984) · A. Vidler, *Scenes from a clerical life* (1971) · H. H. Henson, *Retrospect of an unimportant life*, 2: *1920–1939* (1943) · R. Lloyd, *The Church of England, 1900–1965* (1966) · A. Hastings, *A history of English Christianity, 1920–90* (1991) · A. Vidler, *Magic and religion* (1930) · *The Times* (30 Nov 1953) · personal knowledge (2004) · private information (2004) · G. K. A. Bell, *Randall Davidson, archbishop of Canterbury*, 2 vols. (1935) · *CGPLA Eng. & Wales* (1954)

Archives LPL, corresp. relating to dispute with crown over appointment to St Jude's, Birmingham · U. Birm. L., corresp., papers, and engagement diaries

Likenesses W. Stoneman, photograph, 1918, NPG · photograph, *c.*1924, NPG · E. Kapp, charcoal drawing, 1930, Barber Institute of Fine Arts, Birmingham · D. Wynne, bronze sculpture, 1954, Birmingham Cathedral · photograph, NPG [*see illus.*]

Wealth at death £21,899 19*s.* 6*d.*: probate, 24 Feb 1954, *CGPLA Eng. & Wales*

Barnes, Frederick Jester (1885–1938), singer, was born on 31 May 1885 at 219 Great Lister Street, Saltley, Birmingham, the only child of Thomas William Barnes (1860/61–1913), butcher, and his wife, Mary Alice Jester (*d.* 1899/1900). The family moved across to 214 Great Lister Street in 1887, when his father bought a bigger shop. Fred attended Ashted Row elementary school, Saltley, and boarded at Beechfield College, Malvern (*c.*1896–9). Pressed to join the family business, he recoiled from the slaughterhouse and determined to become a music-hall performer. He had been fascinated from the age of ten by Vesta Tilley, the male impersonator. In 1901 he auditioned for a pantomime at the Alexandra Theatre, Birmingham.

Fred Barnes made his début as a soloist at the Gaiety Theatre, Birmingham, in March 1906, and caught the eye of the songster George Lashwood, who helped him polish his act. After touring with a troupe called the Eight Lancashire Lads, he played in April 1907 at the Empress Theatre in Brixton, London, where his rendition of 'Raise your Hat to the Lady' was good enough to secure him George Foster as an agent. The song which made his name, however, was 'The Black, Black Sheep of the Family' (or 'The Scapegrace'), written and composed (unusually) by himself. Signed up in 1908 by the impresario Oswald Stoll, Barnes became a star of the major London music-halls: the Coliseum, Alhambra, Canterbury, Tivoli, and Oxford. There was a pantomime every Christmas and a pierrot show each summer. The first of six records came out in 1911. In three years his weekly earnings increased from £4 to £100.

Frederick Jester Barnes (1885–1938), by Dobson Studios, *c.*1920

Fred Barnes was categorized as a light comedian and character vocalist. Handsome, with blue eyes and wavy hair, he normally appeared as a debonair man-about-town in white tie and tails, with monocle and cane. His baritone voice was agreeable rather than outstanding; he owed his success primarily to his charm. Both on stage and off, he liked to please. His devotees were predominantly older women. There was something almost dainty about his dancing, and he wore a pink and white make-up more common among female artistes. Some people may have detected a double meaning in the sentimental lyric of his signature song:

> It's a queer, queer world we live in
> And Dame Nature plays a funny game—
> Some get all the sunshine,
> Others get all the shame.
> (Barnes, 1)

Fred seemed quite unabashed when audiences greeted him with cries of 'Hello, Freda!' In the profession, his homosexuality was an open secret—and rumours spread.

Barnes's father, Tom, committed suicide on 10 August 1913 with a butcher's knife. Fred, who inherited £10,000, reacted to this by becoming wildly hedonistic. He spent extravagantly on motor cars and clothes and entertained a crowd of fair-weather friends at his grandiose apartment near Regent's Park. There was no dividing line between publicity stunts (selling £1 notes for 2*d*. each and staging a hoax wedding) and sheer exhibitionism. He walked about London in white plus fours and pink stockings, with a marmoset perched on his shoulder. At night he picked up male prostitutes in his Rolls Royce.

Barnes wanted to join the army in 1914 but was rejected on account of a 'nervous condition' (possibly a euphemism for his sexual orientation). His career continued to flourish with hit numbers such as 'Alexander's Ragtime Band', 'Boys in Khaki, Boys in Blue', 'Samoa! Samoa! Some More!', and 'Give me the Moonlight, Give me the Girl'. He starred in revue at the London Palladium and toured Great Britain, Australia, and South Africa.

On the evening of 19 October 1924 Fred Barnes was arrested for drunken and negligent driving in the Carriage Road in Hyde Park, London, after he had knocked down a motorcyclist. He tried to bribe the police officer (since he had a half-naked sailor in the car) and ended up spending a month in Pentonville prison. Released in February 1925, he found his fans forgiving. There appeared to be some truth in the title of his song 'The Worse you are the More the Ladies Like You'. Barnes did face a ban on his attendance at the royal tournament, the annual military tattoo at Olympia; his ejection from the gymnastics display became a regular event.

It was not scandal but drink that destroyed Fred Barnes. Despite introducing popular new melodies, such as 'If you Knew Susie' and 'On Mother Kelly's Doorstep', in the late 1920s, he saw his diary of engagements shrink. Theatre managers could no longer rely upon him. Moss Empires and the Gulliver Syndicate paid Barnes off with £6000 in 1929. He sank the money into a loss-making variety show of his own devising. During 1931–2 he sobered up enough to take part in *Stars who Never Failed to Shine*—a nostalgic revue whose stalwarts were a generation older than himself—before alcoholic excess made him almost unemployable. A series of autobiographical articles in *Thompson's Weekly News* (January–April 1932) explained 'How Success Ruined Me'. Having squandered his wealth, he existed on handouts from former colleagues and performed in Essex pubs with a pet chicken. Terminal tuberculosis was diagnosed. On 23 October 1938 John Senior (the theatrical manager who was his lover from 1929) found Barnes lying dead on the floor of their lodgings in St Ann's Road, Southend-on-Sea, Essex, with his nose next to a gas ring. Barnes was buried in the churchyard of St Saviour's, Saltley, Birmingham. JASON TOMES

Sources T. Barker, 'Fred Barnes', *Music Hall*, 30 (1984) • P. Bailey, *Three queer lives* (2001) • H. Daley, *This small cloud* (1986) • N. Jacob, *Our Marie* (1936) • F. Barnes, *The scapegrace* (1909)

Likenesses Dobson Studios, photograph, *c*.1920, Theatre Museum, London [*see illus.*] • G. Whitelaw, sketch, repro. in Barker, 'Fred Barnes', cover • photographs, repro. in Bailey, *Three queer lives*

Barnes, George Nicoll (1859–1940), trade unionist and politician, was born on 2 January 1859 at Lochee, Forfarshire, the second of five sons of James Barnes, a skilled engineer and mill manager from Yorkshire, and his wife, Catherine Adam Langlands. The family moved back to England and settled at Ponders End in Middlesex, where his father managed a jute mill in which George himself began working at the age of eleven, after attending a church school at Enfield Highway. He then spent two years as an engineering apprentice, first at Powis James of Lambeth then at Parker's foundry, Dundee. After finishing his apprenticeship he worked for two years at the Vickers shipyard in Barrow before returning once again to the London area, where he experienced unemployment during the slump of 1879. He had a number of short-term jobs before settling for eight years at Lucas and Airds in Fulham. In 1882 he married Jessie, daughter of Thomas Langlands, with whom he had two sons and a daughter.

During his time in London Barnes became an active member of the Amalgamated Society of Engineers, a committed member of the co-operative movement, and a keen if moderate socialist, which led him to join the Independent Labour Party (ILP) on its foundation in 1893. Within the engineers' union he was a significant figure in the network of young London socialists who were influenced initially by figures on the far left, but who moved decisively back into the Labour mainstream during the 1890s. He succeeded John Burns on the national executive in 1889, organized Tom Mann's unsuccessful campaign to become the national secretary in 1891, and was eventually elected to that post himself in 1896 after four years as assistant secretary. For the next twelve years he therefore held a key post in the craft-union world, but it was to be a period of turmoil for the engineers since, while the industry was expanding and the employers were becoming increasingly united and aggressive, the union retained a high level of district autonomy which drew it into bitter and costly industrial disputes.

Thus in the summer of 1897 the London district's insistence on pressing for the eight-hour day resulted in a lengthy national lock-out without support from other unions, leading inevitably to a costly defeat for the engineers even if the principles of recognition and collective bargaining were maintained. Then in the course of the next decade Barnes found himself caught between the restrictive terms of settlement which had been imposed after the national defeat in 1898 and a resurgence of district pressure for improved conditions when local labour markets were buoyant. It became increasingly difficult to maintain the integrity of the union's decision-making processes in the face of district committees' refusals to follow the policies of the national executive, and Barnes resigned in frustration in 1908.

As an enthusiastic socialist Barnes had long been a champion of increased political representation for labour: he stood (unsuccessfully) as an ILP parliamentary candidate for Rochdale as early as 1895 and was the Amalgamated Society of Engineers delegate at the conference in London, on 27 February 1900, which founded the Labour Representation Committee (LRC). Standing for the ILP against both Conservative and Liberal opponents, he was elected for Glasgow Blackfriars (later Gorbals) at the 1906 general election, and was among the twenty-nine MPs elected under LRC auspices. He continued to hold the seat largely on the basis of the Irish nationalist vote until his retirement in 1922. No doubt the alternative attractions of an enhanced political career influenced his decision to resign his trade-union post. He went on to become one of the major spokesmen for the Labour position on such key Liberal welfare reforms as old age pensions and national insurance, having studied industrial welfare provision in Germany, Denmark, Sweden, and the USA (the latter as a member of the Mosely industrial commission in 1902). For a brief period in 1910 he served as chairman of the Parliamentary Labour Party.

Barnes was therefore well placed to continue as a leading Labour spokesman during the mobilization of national resources to fight the First World War. As well as helping to recruit skilled engineers for war work, visiting Canada for the purpose, he sat on a government committee on war pensions, chaired (1916) a government committee on savings, and was appointed as the first minister of pensions in the coalition government of December 1916, in which post he improved both the level and the system of administration of service pensions. In August 1917 he succeeded Arthur Henderson in the war cabinet as minister without portfolio representing the interests of organized labour, in which role he was responsible for a major sympathetic government inquiry into industrial unrest in 1917.

However, this role once again placed Barnes between two conflicting forces as the Labour Party began to move away from the coalition government over the speed and the methods of reaching a peace settlement with Germany. He took the view that he had been mandated to serve as a Labour representative in the government until a peace treaty was concluded, resigning from the Labour Party in order to remain in the cabinet. Consequently he faced increasing criticism from some of his erstwhile colleagues as well as an unsuccessful challenge for his parliamentary seat from an official Labour Party candidate (John Maclean) in the 1918 general election. Barnes, however, had not changed his political views and, as British labour's only representative at the Paris peace conference, he began to use his status to press for international machinery to promote the rights of working people. With the assistance of civil servants from the Ministry of Labour he drafted a set of proposals which, following further consultations with the leadership of the Labour Party and extensive discussions within the Commission for World Labour, eventually became the basis of part 13, or the labour chapter, of the treaty of Versailles. This covered such issues as minimum employment conditions for women and young people, industrial safety, and the right of combination, though Barnes himself saw such general commitments as less important than the establishment of an organization to promote specific reforms: the International Labour Office in Geneva and regular conferences of the International Labour Organization.

Seeing this as the culmination of his earlier choice between his party and the government, and aware that he had become physically very run down, Barnes resigned his ministerial post early in 1920, at which point he was made a Companion of Honour. However, he still attended the first assembly of the League of Nations later that year as one of the three British delegates, as well as remaining a back-bench supporter of the coalition government until his retirement from politics when the Labour Party announced that it would again field a candidate against him in the general election of 1922. As it was clear that the tide would turn strongly towards the official Labour candidates throughout Glasgow, and as he had no wish to serve in any other party, he decided to withdraw from his seat.

Barnes had a long and active retirement, continuing to support the International Labour Organization, serving as chairman of the Co-operative Printing Society, and publishing several books, including his autobiography, *From Workshop to War Cabinet* (1923), and a *History of the International Labour Office* (1926). He was a pleasant-looking, mild-mannered man, but little is known about his private life; one of his sons was killed during the First World War. He died on 2 April 1940 at his home, 76 Herne Hill, London, and was buried in Fulham cemetery.

ALASTAIR J. REID

Sources 'Barnes, George Nicoll', *DLB*, vol. 6 • *DNB* • G. N. Barnes, *From workshop to war cabinet* (1924) • J. Zeitlin, 'Engineers and compositors: a comparison', *Divisions of labour: skilled workers and technological change in nineteenth-century England*, ed. R. Harrison and J. Zeitlin (1985), 185–250 • H. A. Clegg, A. Fox, and A. F. Thompson, *A history of British trade unions since 1889*, 1–2 (1964–85)

Archives BLPES, corresp. with the Independent Labour Party • Labour History Archive and Study Centre, Manchester, papers • priv. coll., corresp. | HLRO, corresp. with J. C. C. Davidson incl. notes on the war • HLRO, corresp. with David Lloyd George

Likenesses B. Stone, photograph, 1907, Birmingham Reference Library • W. Stoneman, photograph, before 1917, NPG • W. Orpen, oils, 1919, City Art Gallery, Bradford • photograph, *c.*1924, repro. in Barnes, *From workshop to war cabinet*, frontispiece • M. Urquhart, oils, *c.*1934, International Labour Office, Geneva, Switzerland • J. Guthrie, group portrait, oils (*Statesmen of World War I*), NPG • J. Guthrie, oils (study for *Statesmen of World War I*), Scot. NPG • J. Russell & Sons, photograph, NPG

Wealth at death £3129 18*s.* 5*d.*: probate, 7 June 1940, *CGPLA Eng. & Wales*

Barnes, Sir George Reginald (1904–1960), radio and television director and college head, was born in Byfleet, Surrey, on 13 September 1904, the son of Sir Hugh Shakespear *Barnes (1853–1940), lieutenant-governor of Burma, and his second wife, Edith Helen, sister of Sir Kenneth Barnes, principal of the Royal Academy of Dramatic Art, and the actresses Irene and Violet Vanbrugh. Educated at the Royal Naval College at Osborne and Dartmouth, he was ultimately rejected for the navy because of his eyesight. But his interest in naval affairs never diminished, however varied and strong his other interests. With Commander J. H. Owen he published in 1932–8 four volumes of the private papers of the fourth earl of Sandwich and he

Sir George Reginald Barnes (1904–1960), by Howard Coster, 1954

always cherished the dream of finding time to write a study of the British navy in the early nineteenth century.

From Dartmouth, Barnes went to King's College, Cambridge, where he obtained a second class in part one of the historical tripos (1924) and a first in part two (1925). There was some expectation that he would try for the Foreign Office but the pull of the navy proved too strong and he returned to Dartmouth for three years (1927–30) as an assistant master. In 1927 Barnes married Dorothy Anne, daughter of Henry Bond, master of Trinity Hall, Cambridge (1919–29); they had one son. In 1930 he went as assistant secretary to the Cambridge University Press where he developed 'a fine taste and a good judgement in the economics as well as the aesthetics of the trade', and revised the *Hand-List of Cambridge Books*, extending it to 1800.

In 1935 Barnes joined the British Broadcasting Corporation, where his strong social conscience gave an educational impetus to his work. He believed that public taste needed guiding: that it should be led, not followed. Coupled with this belief was his sense of responsibility towards listener minorities and the complex needs of each individual listener. In 1941 he was appointed director of talks in succession to Sir Richard Maconachie, under whom he had worked since Maconachie joined the corporation in 1937; in 1945 he became Maconachie's assistant controller of talks. In that year he made his first visit to the United States, from which he returned with his horizons widened and with a final access of assurance which never deserted him.

When the Third Programme was established in 1946 Barnes was the obvious choice to give the idea practical form. He aimed at the highest standards in both programme and performance: 'We shall live or die by the amount we are prepared to experiment … We will experiment with new forms of radio, new writers, new performers, and new presentations' (private information). His own lifelong devotion to music found scope which he described as 'vast and even thrilling' in the Third Programme's long-term plan to give the finest available performances of music of every style and epoch, with special emphasis on rarely heard works of interest and beauty. Comparably large in conception was the great series of programmes entitled *Ideas and Beliefs of the Victorians* (1948).

In 1948 Barnes joined the BBC's board of management as director of the spoken word and in October 1950 he was appointed to the newly created post of director of television. The BBC's five-year plan to expand and develop its television service, giving priority to 'coverage', had been under way for a year. New transmitters were opened at Sutton Coldfield (1949) and Holme Moss (1951) and the Lime Grove Studios were taken over early in 1950. But the service was still based on Alexandra Palace and 'for two nightmare years', as Barnes later recorded in the *BBC Quarterly*, 'every piece of scenery and every property for the half-dozen different productions each day had to be transported twenty-four miles' (Barnes, 66). It was not until 1954 that concentration at Shepherd's Bush was achieved.

The enormous increase in range that BBC television obtained during the six years of Barnes's directorship is reflected in an increase in licences from 343,882 (1950) to 5,739,593 (1956). Among the many new ventures were the first experimental schools television programmes (May 1952); the televising of the coronation of Elizabeth II (June 1953); the first large-scale Eurovision link-up of eight countries (June 1954); the inauguration of a daily *News and Newsreel* (July 1954); and ceaseless experiment with colour television (the first colour television outside broadcast, transmitted on closed circuit to the children's hospital, Great Ormond Street, was of the coronation). In October 1953 on a visit to Lime Grove Studios the queen knighted Barnes with a sword which had been smuggled in from Buckingham Palace.

In 1955 the Independent Television Authority began commercial television. In the previous year Barnes had stressed the necessity of a second channel for the BBC to provide a planned alternative programme in order to cater for the varying tastes of its public; in 1956 he emphasized the need to maintain high standards and avoid the exclusive pursuit of mass popularity:

> The audience figures that are being bandied about in the fine shouting-war that is going on are not a criterion of excellence. To seek success in popularity alone is a trivial use of a great invention. Mass without mind always comes a cropper … (private information)

In 1956 Barnes became principal of the University College of North Staffordshire, which had been unfortunate in the death of its first two principals (Lord Lindsay of

Birker and Sir John Lennard-Jones) within a few years of their appointment. A similar fate was to strike Barnes, who died at Keele on 22 September 1960, after no more than four years of stimulating service to the new foundation. A memorial fund was devoted to the development and teaching of music in the university which Barnes had done much to improve. His concern was ever with quality, whether in music, the visual arts, or human relationships. From a wide circle of friends he entertained at Keele distinguished writers, politicians, painters, and scholars, whose visits greatly enriched the life of a small and relatively isolated university; and by his own diligence in accepting public engagements he sought in his turn to make Keele more widely known. A frail-looking man, he possessed great resilience and inner strength, nourished by his deep concern for the life of the chapel. His naval training imbued him with a sense of service and he devoted all his energy and practical idealism to the furtherance of the things of the mind and of the spirit that he valued.

At one time or another Barnes served on many bodies concerned with the interests he had at heart. They included the council of the Royal College of Art, the British Film Institute, the Standing Commission on Museums and Galleries, the Council of Industrial Design, the Wedgwood Society (formed early in 1955 with Barnes as first chairman), the British Pottery Manufacturers' Federation, and the committee appointed in January 1958 by the Gulbenkian Foundation to inquire into the needs of the arts in Britain. He received the honorary degree of DCL from Durham in 1956. LAURENCE GILLIAM, *rev.*

Sources *The Times* (23 Sept 1960) • A. Briggs, *The history of broadcasting in the United Kingdom*, 4 vols. (1961–79) • *WWW* • G. Barnes, 'Reflections on television', *BBC Quarterly*, 9/2 (summer 1954), 65–9 • *CGPLA Eng. & Wales* (1960) • personal knowledge (1971) • private information (1971)

Archives King's Cam., corresp. and papers • NMM, corresp. and papers relating to naval history | Bodl. Oxf., corresp. with Graham Pollard, etc. • CAC Cam., corresp. with Sir W. J. Haley • NL Wales, corresp. with Welsh National Opera

Likenesses H. Coster, photograph, 1954, NPG [*see illus.*]

Wealth at death £24,357 16*s*. 7*d*.: probate, 30 Nov 1960, *CGPLA Eng. & Wales*

Barnes, Sir Hugh Shakespear (1853–1940), administrator in India and banker, was born in Shahjahanpur, India, the son of James Ralph Barnes of the Indian Civil Service. His mother was sister of Sir Rivers Thompson (1827–1890), sometime governor of Bengal.

Barnes was a member of one of those families mentioned by Kipling in 'The Tomb of his Ancestors' in *The Day's Work* as serving India 'generation after generation'. His great-grandfather on his maternal side was George Nisbet Thompson, private secretary to Warren Hastings; his father was brother of George Carnac Barnes CB, who served in the Indian mutiny as commissioner of the Cis-Sutlej states and was foreign secretary in Lord Canning's government.

Educated at Malvern College, in 1871 Barnes came top of the list in the competitive Indian Civil Service examination. He joined the Indian Civil Service in Allahabad in 1874 and in less than two years had been selected by Sir John Strachey, then finance member of Lord Lytton's government, to be his private secretary. He married twice, first, in 1878, Winifred, daughter of Sir John Strachey; she died in Calcutta in 1892, leaving a son and a daughter, and second, in 1894, his cousin, Edith Helen, daughter of the Revd Reginald Henry Barnes, with whom he had two sons, including the radio and television director Sir George Reginald *Barnes.

A distinguished career in the Indian Civil Service, during which Barnes was revenue commissioner for Baluchistan under Sir Robert Sandeman, administrator and reformer, culminated in his being appointed foreign secretary to the government of India in 1900, president of the central committee for the Delhi durbar in 1903, and lieutenant-governor of Burma in the same year. He was created KCVO for his work for the Delhi durbar, and was credited with his KCSI earlier that year. For his service in Baluchistan—consolidating Sandeman's work, raising the standards of administration, and conciliating in the affairs of the chiefs—a bronze statue of Sir Hugh was unveiled in Quetta in 1904.

During his time as lieutenant-governor of Burma, Barnes recognized that communications were an imperative for the material advance of a country so rich in natural resources. He formulated a number of development projects, and impressed on the government of India the necessity of increasing the allocation for public works in Burma.

In 1905, on his appointment to the Council of India in Whitehall, Barnes resigned from Burma. While he was a member of the council, he was able to use his experience of India to criticize constructively the Morley–Minto reforms, which, among other improvements, broadened the basis of Indian government and allowed Indians to sit on the central legislative council.

In 1913, before his term was due to end, Barnes resigned from the council in order to take up work in the City. He was already on the board of the Anglo-Persian Oil Company (APOC), to which he was appointed in 1909; he now joined the boards of the Burmah Oil Company and the Imperial Bank of Persia. He became chairman of the bank in 1916, and served until 1937, and remained on the boards of both the bank and APOC, at that time the two most important institutions in Persia, until his death. He was also chairman of Tankers Ltd and of the Scottish-American Oil Transport Company, as well as director of many associated undertakings, and of the Anglo-Malay Rubber and Royal Insurance companies. On account of these directorships, and his chairmanship of the Imperial Bank, he became an important figure in the City. He used his considerable influence whenever required, notably in retaining Britain's commitment to Mesopotamia in 1920. Given his large interests in middle eastern oil and banking, this was not surprising.

Sir Hugh Barnes died at his residence, 19 Sheffield Terrace, London, on 15 February 1940, aged eighty-six. He was survived by his second wife and his four children.

FRANCES BOSTOCK

Sources *The Times* (16 Feb 1940) • *WWW* • G. Jones, *The history of the British Bank of the Middle East*, 1: *Banking and empire in Iran* (1986) • R. W. Ferrier, *The history of the British Petroleum Company*, 1: *The developing years, 1901–1932* (1982) • m. cert. • d. cert. • R. Kipling, 'The tomb of his ancestors', *The day's work*, 'Outward bound' edn (1899), 116–66

Archives Bodl. Oxf., official corresp. and papers | BL OIOC, letters to Lady Strachey • CUL, corresp. with Lord Hardinge

Likenesses bronze statue, 1904; last known in Quetta, India • photograph, repro. in *The Times*

Wealth at death £39,010 18s. 11d.: probate, 25 April 1940, *CGPLA Eng. & Wales*

Barnes, John (*c*.1581–1661), Benedictine monk and religious controversialist, was probably born in Norfolk 'of parents of humble condition', and studied at Cambridge (McCann and Connolly, 203). Having converted to Catholicism he entered the English College, Douai, on 18 November 1601 and was sent as a seminarian to Spain on 2 October 1603, being admitted to the English College, Valladolid, on 20 October. He left to become a Benedictine, taking the habit at San Benito, Valladolid, on 12 March 1604, and being professed on 21 March 1605. He seems to have been at St Gregory's Priory, Douai, in 1607 and in Spain again in 1608. Juan Alfonso Curiel, the distinguished Spanish divine who taught him, detected the Benedictine's propensity for controversy by calling him 'by the name of John Huss, because of a spirit of contradiction which was always observed in him' (Wood, *Ath. Oxon.*, 2.500). The next decade Barnes was engaged in teaching theology at the English monasteries at Dieulouard and (from 1611) St Malo, and at Marchiennes College in Douai, where the English Benedictines provided a lecturer.

In 1619 three distinct groups of English Benedictine monks—those in the Spanish congregation, those in the Cassinese congregation, and those who had been affiliated to the old English congregation by Sigebert Buckley—formed a reconstituted congregation which was recognized by the papal brief *Ex incumbenti*; however, it was a union born in controversy and papal approval did not settle the matter. Following the amalgamation Barnes joined Francis Walgrave at Chelles near Paris; Rudesind Barlow, writing in 1623, said that the two 'always be a-brawling and a-scolding' (Weldon, 136). In 1620 or 1621 Barnes and Walgrave attached themselves to the Cluniac congregation, of which Walgrave claimed to be the English superior. Barnes defended this move, arguing that before the dissolution of the monasteries in England there had been no such thing as a Benedictine congregation there apart from that represented by the alien priories of Cluny. He expounded these views in a book, *Examen trophaeorum congregationis praetensae Anglicanae* (Rheims, 1622), a spirited critique of Edward Maihew's *Trophea* of the same year which set forth the historical claims of the English Benedictine congregation. In its turn Barnes's volume was answered by the work compiled by Augustine Baker, put into Latin by Leander Jones and prepared for publication by Clement Reyner, *Apostolatus Benedictinorum in Anglia* (Douai, 1626). In correspondence with Baker, John Selden considered that Barnes's work 'had bin written by some drunken Dutchman' and that

> he conceived it dishonourable, yea and prejudiciall, not only to the Black Monks of England, but also to the nation itselfe, that so many and so great monasteries, as were of the order in England, should have belonged and owed subjection to any forrein Order or Congregation. (McCann and Connolly, 111)

Barnes's subsequent career was unsettled: he returned briefly to St Gregory's, Douai, spent some time in Oxford at the Bodleian Library in 1627, and published further works of controversy, including the *Dissertatio contra aequivocationes* (1625), an anti-Jesuit work on equivocation published in Paris despite its condemnation by the holy office on 23 December 1624. Arrested in Paris in 1627 Barnes was taken 'like a four-footed brute' and 'in a barbarous manner tied to a horse and hurried away into Flanders' whence he was removed to Rome and placed in the prison of the Inquisition (J. Barnes, *Catholico-Romanus pacificus*, 1680, preface). He was later transferred to an asylum for the insane behind the church of St Paul-the-Less, where he died in the latter part of 1661. 'If he was in his wits', wrote Leander Normington, 'he was a heretic, but they gave him Christian burial because they accounted him rather a madman' (Weldon, 139).

Barnes's Cluniac apology, which was historically tenuous, is explained to some degree by the difficult position in which he and his colleague Walgrave were placed as members of a pro-Spanish congregation in a France dominated by anti-Spanish sentiments. His historical researches, built on *voyages littéraires* characteristic of the monks of his generation, represented an onslaught on the newly re-established English congregation whose members replied to Barnes with vigour and never forgave him. His other writings reflect a sharp intelligence, if a lack of prudence, in their ability to attract an increasing number of enemies. He sought some accommodation with the Church of England and, in the words of Weldon, the Benedictine chronicler, 'to mince the Catholic truths that the Protestants might digest them without choking, and so likewise to prepare the Protestants errors that Catholic stomachs might not loathe them' (Weldon, 138). The most important of Barnes's ecumenical works was the *Catholico-Romanus pacificus*, first published in Oxford in 1680 from manuscripts supplied by Archbishop Sancroft, Lord Anglesey, and Edward Stillingfleet.

Dominic Aidan Bellenger

Sources A. Allanson, *Biography of the English Benedictines* (1999) • F. Madan, *Oxford literature, 1651–1680* (1931), vol. 3 of *Oxford books: a bibliography of printed works* (1895–1931); repr. (1964) • *DNB* • A. F. Allison and D. M. Rogers, eds., *The contemporary printed literature of the English Counter-Reformation between 1558 and 1640*, 1 (1989) • Y. Chaussy, *Les bénédictins anglais réfugiés en France au XVIIe siècle (1611–1669)* (Paris, 1967) • D. Lunn, *The English Benedictines, 1540–1688* (1980) • B. Weldon, *Chronological notes … of the English congregation of the order of St Benedict* (1881) • J. McCann and H. Connolly, eds., *Memorials of Father Augustine Baker and other documents relating to the English Benedictines*, Catholic RS, 33 (1933) • Wood, *Ath. Oxon.*, new edn, 2.500–02 • E. H. Burton and T. L. Williams, eds., *The Douay College diaries, third, fourth and fifth, 1598–1654*, 1, Catholic RS, 10 (1911) • E. Henson, ed., *The registers of the English College at Valladolid, 1589–1862*, Catholic RS, 30 (1930)

Barnes, John Gorell, first Baron Gorell (1848–1913), judge, was born at Anfield Cottage, Walton on the Hill, near Liverpool, on 16 May 1848, of a Derbyshire family. He was the eldest child of Henry Barnes, a shipowner in Liverpool, and Georgiana, *née* Smith, the daughter of the rector of Staveley, Derbyshire, who had also been a fellow and dean of Trinity College, Cambridge. His great-grandfather Edward Gorell was a member of the religious sect founded by John Glas, but his father and uncles eventually left the sect to become Anglicans. Barnes was educated at various private schools around Liverpool before being sent, after his father's sudden death on 15 February 1865, to Peterhouse, Cambridge, the college of the mathematician Edward John Routh who was related to the Barnes family by marriage. He was classed as a senior optime in his BA examination in January 1868. Cambridge had a big influence on his life and he was made an honorary LLD in 1898 and an honorary fellow of Peterhouse in 1899.

After a short period in his father's old shipowning firm, Barnes joined a firm of solicitors in Liverpool. He was never admitted and a few years later took his firm's advice to go to the bar. He joined the Inner Temple in 1873, and after reading in equity chambers became a pupil in October 1874 of James Charles Mathew, then the leading commercial junior in the Temple and later Court of Appeal judge. He worked there until Mathew was promoted to judge in 1881. Called to the bar in 1876, Barnes succeeded to Mathew's great junior practice. He gradually added a substantial Admiralty practice and much mercantile work on the northern circuit. He appeared regularly in the Court of Appeal, the House of Lords, and the privy council. In 1881 he married Mary Humpston (*d.* 1918), eldest daughter of Thomas Mitchell of West Arthurlee, Renfrewshire; they had two sons and a daughter.

After seven years of hard work, Barnes became queen's counsel in 1888 in an attempt to reduce his workload. He made an immediate mark as a weighty, industrious, and popular leader and in June 1892 was unexpectedly made a judge of the Probate, Divorce, and Admiralty Division in succession to Sir Francis Henry Jeune, afterwards Lord St Helier, who had just succeeded Sir Charles Parker Butt as president. In February 1905 Barnes succeeded Jeune, remaining president until February 1909, when he was raised to the peerage as Baron Gorell of Brampton, near Chesterfield. As president, he sat in the Court of Appeal and on the judicial committee of the privy council, and from July 1909 to July 1912 he sat regularly in the House of Lords.

Gorell found time and energy for much extra-judicial work. He was a member of a committee appointed by the lord chancellor to consider improvements in the High Court. He was chairman of the county courts committee which reported in 1909 and laid the basis for some of the proposals of the royal commission on divorce. In 1909 he also acted as an arbitrator in a dispute between the Great Eastern Railway Company and its employees. In the same year he was chairman of the copyright committee, whose report led to the Copyright Act of 1911.

Following a strong speech which Gorell made in the House of Lords in which he said that the law which he had administered as a judge for sixteen years needed radical amendment, a royal commission on divorce and matrimonial causes was established in 1909 and Gorell was appointed chairman. The majority report (signed on 30 January 1912) recommended an extension of the grounds for divorce to include desertion, cruelty, incurable insanity, habitual drunkenness, and penal servitude for life in commutation of a death sentence. The minority report, meanwhile, rejected any extension of the grounds for divorce. There was, however, agreement on a large number of reforms in law and procedure, including far-reaching proposals relating to nullity of marriage, presumption of death for purposes of remarriage, equality of the sexes for divorce purposes, and restraints on the publication of reports of divorce cases.

The commission came to an end in November 1913. By then Lord Gorell's health was rapidly breaking down. He died at Menton in France on 22 April 1913 and was buried on the 28th in Brampton churchyard, near Chesterfield, beside his grandfather John Gorell Barnes.

Gorell had a brief, rapid, and smoothly successful career at the bar. The judgments he made as a judge of first instance were rarely reversed. To him can be credited, in part at least, the foundation of the commercial court, since it was an idea he developed jointly with Sir James Charles Mathew. Soon after his appointment to the Probate, Divorce, and Admiralty Division, he announced that he was prepared to take cases raising points of insurance law, and so attracted commercial solicitors. The establishment of the commercial court from 1 March 1895 under Mathew was a successful development of Gorell's experiment (see *Weekly Notes*, 2 March 1895).

Gorell combined enthusiasm for his work with an unusual capacity for mastering complicated facts. He was particularly adept at exposing the principle underlying any particular set of circumstances. Many of his judgments made distinct contributions to the growth of English law, while his work on the divorce commission revealed his liberal and reformist tendencies. Throughout his life he retained some of the theological severity which had been so pronounced in his parents and grandparents.

Gorell was succeeded by his elder son, Henry Gorell Barnes, second Baron Gorell, a barrister of promise, who was killed in action at Ypres in January 1917, and was succeeded as third baron by his younger brother, Ronald Gorell Barnes.

J. E. G. de Montmorency, *rev.* Hugh Mooney

Sources J. E. G. de Montmorency, *John Gorell Barnes, first Lord Gorell: a memoir* (1920) • *Law Times* (26 April 1913), 613, 632 • *Solicitors' Journal*, 57 (1912–13), 456 • B. Aspinall, *Law Magazine*, 5th ser., 38 (1912–13), 460–62 • private information (2004) • *CGPLA Eng. & Wales* (1913)

Likenesses W. Llewellyn, oils, exh. RA 1896, Gov. Art Coll. • A. Airey, oils, Peterhouse, Cambridge • Spy [L. Ward], repro. in *VF*, 25 (1893), pl. 34 • portrait, repro. in *ILN*, 106 (1892), 683

Wealth at death £69,448 0s. 0d.: probate, 15 May 1913, *CGPLA Eng. & Wales*

Barnes, John Henry (1850–1925), actor, was born at Watlington, Oxfordshire, on 26 February 1850, the son of John Barnes, a miller and farmer, and his wife, Mildred (*née* Smith). His interest in acting was awakened by the sermons of J. C. M. Bellew, whom he considered to be 'the very best reader and elocutionist that I have ever heard' (Barnes, 5). Barnes's father would not hear of him going into the theatre, but after his father's death in 1868 Barnes made his first public appearance as a reader at the Westbourne Hall, Bayswater, on 22 October 1870. His stage début took place on the auspicious first night of Henry Irving's production of *The Bells* at the Lyceum Theatre, on 25 November 1871, when he appeared as Irving's double. Although he began his career with the rising star of the London theatre, Barnes later gained wide experience in the provinces, where he worked with several notable managers: Edward Saker in Liverpool, Mrs Wyndham in Edinburgh, and Charles Calvert in Manchester. While at the Theatre Royal in Manchester he played alongside the veteran Samuel Phelps—thus began 'my worship of Samuel Phelps' (Barnes, 67).

Generally known as Handsome Jack Barnes, throughout his career Barnes partnered a succession of celebrated leading ladies, who were glad to avail themselves of his attractive stage presence but were reassured that their own performances would not be eclipsed. He accompanied Adelaide Neilson to America in 1874; supported Geneviève Ward at the Lyceum in 1879; and partnered Madame Ristori at Drury Lane in 1882 (including Macbeth to her Lady Macbeth) and Mary Anderson at the Lyceum in 1883 and thereafter on the ill-fated American tour which ended with her retirement from the stage. His association with Ellen Terry stretched from Bassanio to her Portia in Irving's revival of *The Merchant of Venice* (Lyceum, 1 November 1879) to Sir Howard Hallam to her Lady Cicely Waynflete in Shaw's *Captain Brassbound's Conversion* for the Vedrenne–Barker management (Court Theatre, 20 March 1906).

Barnes belonged to a generation of actors whose careers bridged the Atlantic Ocean. As early as 1875 he took his own company to Canada, and scarcely had he disembarked in England on 3 June 1891 than he set sail again for New York on 16 September and remained in America for several years. In 1905 he worked there for Charles Frohman.

During Barnes's lengthy career his chosen profession changed beyond recognition. Like Johnston Forbes-Robertson, also an admirer of Phelps, Barnes provided continuity with the past. He appeared as Polonius to Forbes-Robertson's Hamlet at the Lyceum Theatre (11 September 1897), when his performance was not admired by Shaw. Barnes and Forbes-Robertson were reunited in their *Hamlet* roles for the latter's farewell season at Drury Lane (22 March 1913), shortly after which the two veterans shared the 'curious experience of being filmed for moving pictures in *Hamlet*', produced by Cecil Hepworth, at Walton-on-Thames (Barnes, 307). Appropriately, Barnes's last West End performance, at the Shaftesbury Theatre (17 April 1923), was as Lester Montague in *Merton of the Movies* by George S. Kaufman and Marc Connelly.

Though never a star in his own right, Barnes was a highly respected member of his profession: he was a founder member of the Green Room Club; worshipful master of the Drury Lane freemasons' lodge (1901); an advocate of and later instructor at the (Royal) Academy of Dramatic Art; and the recipient of a complimentary benefit matinée at the Palace Theatre (17 March 1922). Apart from his memoirs, *Forty Years on the Stage* (originally published serially in *The Stage* from October 1913), he wrote what he termed 'serious verse' and articles in the *Nineteenth Century*. He died at his home, Wyndham House, Shoot-up Hill, Cricklewood, on 10 November 1925, leaving a widow, Mary L. Barnes. RICHARD FOULKES

Sources J. H. Barnes, *Forty years on the stage* (1914) • *Era Almanack and Annual* (1896) • J. Parker, ed., *The green room book, or, Who's who on the stage* (1909) • J. Parker, ed., *Who's who in the theatre*, 5th edn (1925) • C. E. Pascoe, ed., *The dramatic list* (1879); repr. (1971) • D. Mullin, ed., *Victorian actors and actresses in review: a dictionary of contemporary views of representative British and American actors and actresses, 1837–1901* (1983) • G. B. Shaw, *Our theatres in the nineties*, rev. edn, 3 vols. (1932); repr. (1954) • *The Stage* (12 Nov 1925) • R. Manvell, *Shakespeare and the film* (1971) • J. P. Wearing, *The London stage, 1890–1899: a calendar of plays and players*, 2 vols. (1976) • J. P. Wearing, *The London stage, 1900–1909: a calendar of plays and players*, 2 vols. (1981) • J. P. Wearing, *The London stage, 1910–1919: a calendar of plays and players*, 2 vols. (1982) • J. P. Wearing, *The London stage, 1920–1929: a calendar of plays and players*, 3 vols. (1984) • b. cert. • d. cert.
Archives FILM presumed BFI, *Hamlet*, directed by Cecil Hepworth, 1913
Likenesses photographs, repro. in Barnes, *Forty years on the stage*

Barnes, John Morrison (1913–1975), toxicologist, was born in Sheffield at midnight on 11–12 January 1913, the elder son and elder child of Alfred Edward Barnes, later professor of medicine in the University of Sheffield, and his wife, Janet (Jessie) Morrison. Barnes's younger brother, (Harry) Jefferson Barnes (*d.* 1979) was knighted on retirement from the Glasgow School of Art. John Barnes, after education at Repton School, went to Trinity Hall, Cambridge, in 1930; he was awarded a scholarship in 1932, and took first classes in both parts of the natural sciences tripos (1932 and 1933), specializing in pathology in part two. In 1933 he entered Sheffield medical school, gaining conjoint and Cambridge qualifications in 1936—MB, BChir, MRCS, LRCP.

After a residency in Sheffield, Barnes took a house surgeonship at the Wingfield–Morris Orthopaedic Hospital in Oxford, which led to a Nuffield research fellowship in orthopaedics (1938–42). This was an important step, for it led to training under H. W. Florey in the Sir William Dunn School of Pathology, in research on the lymphocyte, and then to work with Josep A. Trueta on wound drainage and arterial spasm, and to Barnes's becoming honorary director of the Medical Research Council (MRC) burns unit at Oxford. His war service in the Royal Army Medical Corps was as a specialist pathologist in the biology section of the chemical warfare experimental station at Porton Camp, conducting research under the direction of Paul Fildes and D. W. W. Henderson. By 1947 he had been trained in experimental pathology, and had worked on shock, and on the toxicity of venoms, bacterial toxins, and the tannic acid used in the treatment of burns.

The MRC, during the secretaryship of Sir Edward Mellanby, decided in 1947 to establish a toxicology unit to undertake research in the general field of toxicology as it applied to chemical hazards in industry and agriculture. This was in response to the increasing number of enquiries from industry about the safety or otherwise of new chemical substances. Barnes was appointed the first director. The unit was initially housed at Porton, but with the need for expansion moved in 1950 to Carshalton. At the time of his appointment, toxicology hardly existed as a discipline, but was seen as a series of routine investigations into *ad hoc* problems, which was of little scientific interest. It was Barnes's life work to reveal its scientific potential, and to establish the value of analysing the general mechanisms by which bodily injury may be brought about as the best basis for rational decisions about control procedures. The study began with work on liver damage caused by beryllium, and on an insecticide and a weedkiller which were both widely used. It was followed by studies on DDT, tin compounds, dinitrophenol, the nitrosamines, the Senecio alkaloids, the groundnut fungal product aflatoxin, lead, dieldrin, mercury, and neuropathies and other damage due to industrial solvents. To such work was added fundamental research, usually of a biochemical type, on general mechanisms.

At the same time there was continuing service on MRC committees—those on toxicology (of which he was secretary for thirteen years), food adulterants, fungicides and insecticides, detergents, lung cancer, non-explosive anaesthetics, cancer of the tropics, and occupational health. The topics reflected the growing attention paid to toxicology both medically and politically, which owed much to Barnes's leadership in showing how to tackle extremely varied problems with scientific rigour. In turn this led to much other advisory work, especially for the World Health Organization, for which the toxicology unit became a reference centre.

In 1941 Barnes married Ruth Eleanor, daughter of the Revd Edward Joseph Northcote-Green, of Oxford. There were three children: the eldest, Andrew Nicholas, trained in chemistry; the second, Stephen Edward, became a consultant paediatrician in Salisbury; and the youngest, Rachel Elizabeth, married R. E. McGavin. Barnes was appointed CBE in 1962. He died on 24 September 1975 in the Atkinson Morley Hospital, Wimbledon.

Barnes combined great steadiness of character and a dry humour with extreme modesty and a detestation of pretentiousness of any kind. He concealed his own achievements and resisted being proposed for the Royal Society. A very hard worker, he listed his recreations as 'none'. He could seem rather austere and formidable, and yet those who came to know him, or better still to work with him, found him sensitive and supportive. He had a very good eye for new talent, enjoyed bringing on younger investigators, and never took his share of appreciation for their achievements. After his death British toxicology had advanced enough to justify the formation of a British Toxicology Society, which was largely due to the initiative of his colleagues and pupils. One of their early actions, after a well-supported appeal, was to establish the John Barnes lecture in his memory. W. D. M. PATON, *rev.*

Sources personal knowledge (1986) · private information (1986) · *CGPLA Eng. & Wales* (1976)
Archives Wellcome L., corresp. with Sir Ernst Chain
Wealth at death £46,189: probate, 4 Feb 1976, *CGPLA Eng. & Wales*

Barnes, Dame (Alice) Josephine Mary Taylor (1912–1999), obstetrician and gynaecologist, was born in Cliff Road, Sheringham, Norfolk, on 18 August 1912, the first of five children of Walter Wharton Barnes, a Methodist minister from Addingham, Yorkshire, and his wife, Alice Mary, formerly Ibbetson, of York, a fellow of the Royal College of Organists and student of Parry and Stanford. Her background had strong Methodist influences. In response to a Pauline vision her father had trained for the ministry and as a preacher the poetic rhetoric of his early years had drawn thousands to his congregation. He had been a chaplain among the carnage of the Somme. The Taylor line of her mother's ancestry had Methodist links back to Wesley, begun in the time of Francis and Jane Mortimer Taylor, who in eighteenth-century Langton on the York wolds had begun a dynasty. They had sixteen children in sixteen years and a hundred grandchildren following, among them John Francis Taylor (1818–1902), a captain of Victorian commerce in Yorkshire and one of York's principal lay Methodists. Taylor traditions, Taylor genes, and Taylor money were principal influences shaping the young Josephine Barnes.

Josephine Barnes's schooling followed the path of her father's ministry: Exeter, Scarborough, and Oxford, with an uncomfortable early teenage year at Queenswood School, Clapham, in London, as a boarder. Rescue came with a transfer to Oxford High School for Girls and the self-directed learning of Rosalind Haig Brown's flagship. Here, between 1925 and 1930, she grew the independence for which she was notorious, rejected Methodism, found science, and decided on medicine as a career. Too uncompromising to be a monitor, she compensated by winning the school's Ida Benson prize and gaining respect on the hockey field. She also dragged herself through early studies in chemistry and zoology for which the school was not prepared, and in leisure hours read three novels a week, undertook assistant organist duties at Yarnton parish church, and built a friendship with the composer and organist William Harris. Almost by accident she gained the last place at Oxford's Lady Margaret Hall in 1930, but she rose through prelims and voraciously read herself ahead of preclinical contemporaries, fired by Sir Charles Sherrington and John Eccles in physiology, Gavin de Beer in zoology, Rudolph Peters in biochemistry, and Alice Carleton in anatomy, who guided early advances in dissecting and sent her headlong into primary fellowship of the Royal College of Surgeons of England, early, at twenty-two. To this achievement her Taylor tenacity added three hockey blues and first-class honours in physiology.

Dame (Alice) Josephine Mary Taylor Barnes (1912–1999), by Nick Sinclair, 1995

Distinction for Barnes in clinical medicine was not long in following, beginning with a notable share in the medals at University College Hospital (UCH) medical school in London, where she transferred for clinical studies in 1934 as a Goldschmid scholar. Few hospitals in history had a greater array of clinical expertise. Her tutors included Thomas Lewis, Wilfred Trotter, Max Rosenheim, Harold Himsworth, Julian Taylor, Roy Marshall, and Francis James (F. J.) Browne, the principal architect of modern hospitalized maternity care, whose teaching and methods drew her to obstetrics and gynaecology at a time when the mysteries of the female reproductive tract were translating into hormones. With an intensity of commitment uncomfortable to many contemporaries, Barnes emerged from training in 1937 a formidable competitor in what was still an essentially male-dominated profession. But her UCH student years were not 'all work and no play'. Hockey and musical interests had their place, especially singing in Charles Kennedy Scott's London Philharmonic Choir, occasionally under the direction of Sir Thomas Beecham, once under the baton of Wilhelm Furtwängler.

Advancing surgical and medical qualifications, with a balance relevant to future advancement in obstetrics and gynaecology, was the preoccupation of Barnes's house appointment years at the King Edward VII Hospital, Windsor, and UCH in London. She also made influential detours into general practice in Cambridge, and the treatment of tuberculosis at the Mundesley Sanatorium in Norfolk, assisting Sydney Vere Pearson, pioneer of the artificial pneumothorax. The effects of tuberculosis on pregnancy had been the subject of a first research project at UCH. Barnes returned there in 1939 to begin specializing in obstetrics and gynaecology, but the outbreak of war saw her diverted to lesser hospitals, bracing war-depleted clinical teams. She had volunteered for military service, but found herself referred back to the home front, on which she served in 1940 at two of the capital's blitz-disrupted women's hospitals, Queen Charlotte's and the Samaritan Hospital for Women, where she helped at night with emergency midwifery services under the blackouts and the bombing.

Oxford provided modest respite in 1941. The temptation to work with James Chassar Moir, whose ergometrine would save a million women's lives in childbirth, was not resisted. As his professorial assistant at the Radcliffe Infirmary, Barnes ran a wartime maternity annexe coping with the increasing demands on services by south coast evacuees. When they began declining she returned, in 1942, to UCH as an obstetrics registrar, by which time she had consultant qualifications in medicine (MRCP, 1939), surgery (FRCS, 1939), and obstetrics and gynaecology (MRCOG, 1941), and an Oxford research degree (DM, 1941) for a thesis entitled 'Tuberculosis and pregnancy'. Adding marriage and motherhood to these qualifications, without any loss of clinical momentum, reflected the relentless efficiency characterizing a career in which ambition and caring keenly co-existed. Barnes married Harold Brian Seymour Warren (1914–1996), a junior colleague, on 28 November 1942, soon after her return to UCH and before he began serving with the Grenadier Guards as medical officer with its 1st battalion. The first of their three children arrived in 1943, by which time she had already added to her stringent clinical commitments by leading investigations validating the use of pethidine in obstetrics. Reducing the risks and pains of pregnancy and childbirth dominated her ambitions, in an age which seemed too slow in advancing female health and family planning.

With an advancing reputation as a clinical teacher, after the war Barnes was appointed deputy academic head of the obstetrics unit at UCH, in 1947. A series of student texts was to amplify her influence: *The Care of the Expectant Mother* (1954), *Lecture Notes on Gynaecology* (1966), which went through eight editions, and *The Scientific Foundations of Obstetrics and Gynaecology* (1970), which she co-edited through three editions. She continued at UCH until 1953, simultaneously combining other duties in London as a consultant at the Elizabeth Garrett Anderson Hospital (where she went on to serve for thirty years), and as a specialist surgeon at the Marie Curie Hospital. Added to this were commitments to the city's volunteer maternity 'flying squad' set up to assist women in back-street emergencies, commonly the result of illegal abortion. She continued in this role for eleven years, increasingly a campaigner for legalized abortion and advisory strategies on birth control for the nation. She served for the rest of her life on committees working for advances in maternity care and women's welfare, beginning with membership of the joint committee on social and economic aspects of childbirth established by the Royal College of Obstetricians and Gynaecologists and the Population Investigation Committee in 1946. Their surveys led to *Maternity in Great Britain* (1948), a blueprint for obstetrics care within the new National Health Service, by which time Barnes had also begun spreading her interests to the post-war development of her speciality in Europe. She became a contributing member of the French Gynaecological Society (1945) and the Royal Belgian Society of Obstetricians and Gynaecologists (1949), an early European, convinced of the values of international collaboration.

By the 1950s Barnes's career developments were increasingly contrasting with a lack of further recognition at UCH, where her promotion to the consultant staff seemed barred, following F. J. Browne's departure. With few consultant appointments being awarded to women, there was compensation in 1954 when Barnes secured the first staff appointment accorded to a woman by the Charing Cross Hospital, London, where she served until 1977 and was increasingly revered by a generation of patients benefiting from her surgical precision and clinical judgement, as well as by student cohorts seeing her operate. Always she made the first incision with the incisiveness of Beecham beginning a Schubert symphony; her procedures were paced with the same authority and her lists were always on time, tightly focused—her 'Taylor inheritance'. Professional causes were served with the same relentless effectiveness, and she brought characteristic strengths of leadership to the boards of the Royal College of Obstetricians and Gynaecologists, the Medical Defence Union, the Medical Women's Federation, the obstetrics section of the Royal Society of Medicine, the National Association of Family Planning Doctors, the Association of Physiotherapists in Obstetrics and Gynaecology, the Union Professionelle Internationale de Gynécologie et d'Obstétrique, and the National Association of Family Planning Nurses. Her sterling contributions to the British Medical Association established her its first woman president, in 1979.

However, Barnes regarded having a hand in three of the leading medical inquiries of her generation as the greatest privilege: the royal commission on medical education (Todd committee, 1965–8), the committee on the working of the Abortion Act (Lane committee, 1971–3), and the DHSS inquiry into human fertilization and embryology (Warnock committee, 1981–4). In 1974 she was appointed DBE in recognition of her public service and contributions to improvements in women's health. The citation could have honoured, also, her contributions to medicine and education on a wider international scale, but by this time the achievements of her own children had begun registering greater satisfaction.

Following her retirement from the National Health Service in 1977 Barnes continued for more than a decade in the private practice she had developed over thirty years at Wimpole Street in central London. She was uncompromising in regarding private medicine, like the public schools to which she had sent her children, as defending standards rather than being divisive, and as providing models to be emulated. The last chapters of her life continued the unfailing support for the organizations and causes of her career, and her great loves of choral music and travel. A roving ambassador of better midwifery care, she journeyed widely and generally alone. Her marriage had ended in 1964. She died at St George's Nursing Home, 61 St George's Square, Westminster, on 28 December 1999. Safer midwifery and a twentieth-century revolution in women's welfare had been the principal beneficiaries of her career. MAX BLYTHE

Sources 'Dame Josephine Barnes in interview with Sir Gordon Wolstenholme', 28 June 1989, Oxford Brookes University, Medical Sciences Video-Archive, Tape MSVA 044 • M. Blythe, *One woman's medicine: Dame Josephine Barnes, the early years, 1912–1955* [forthcoming] • oral history collection of Professor Max Blythe: 80 hours of recollections recorded between 1993–1999 and entitled 'Dame Josephine Barnes interviews', Medintel, Oxford, 1–32 • *The Times* (29 Dec 1999), 19a–f • A. Neustatter, *The Guardian* (29 Dec 1999), 16a–e • D. I. Williams, *The Independent* (4 Jan 2000), 6a–d • b. cert. • m. cert. • d. cert.

Archives FILM Oxford Brookes University, Medical Sciences Video-Archive, 'Dame Josephine Barnes in interview with Sir Gordon Wolstenholme', Tape MSVA 044

Likenesses N. Sinclair, photograph, 1995, NPG [*see illus.*]

Wealth at death £748,681—net: probate, 30 March 2000, *CGPLA Eng. & Wales*

Barnes, Joshua (1654–1712), Greek scholar and antiquary, was born on 10 January 1654, the son of Edward Barnes, a tailor from St Stephen, Coleman Street parish, London; he was baptized at St Giles Cripplegate on 22 January. He was educated at Christ's Hospital and admitted a servitor of Emmanuel College, Cambridge, on 11 December 1671. He graduated BA in 1675, was elected to a fellowship in 1678, and proceeded MA in 1679. He received a BD degree in 1686.

Early publications To the young Barnes, or perhaps in the first instance to his teachers, it was evident that his way ahead lay in the church. From adolescence onward, Barnes declared himself early and often on the side of God and the Stuarts; he published at the age of fifteen a volume of *Sacred Poems*, and the following year a poetic *Life of Oliver Cromwell the Tyrant*, both in English. At Emmanuel, Barnes learned that the study of Greek was the medium for pursuing such interests on an erudite level. The Oxford University Press, reviving a project of Archbishop Laud's, was busily issuing Greek patristic editions, while in Cambridge, Henry More, Ralph Cudworth, and Thomas Gale were demonstrating that the Hebrew Bible's moral and historical truths were well known to the ancient Greeks. The scholarly study of Greek poetry on a purely literary plane carried royalist and cavalier shadings—here Thomas Stanley and Edward Sherburne were pre-eminent. In Cambridge the reading and writing of classical Greek poetry could also figure as marks of a nearly truculent piety, as in the redoubtable productions of James Duport. From the 1630s Duport specialized in turning biblical narratives into Homeric poetry in Greek, including, for example, the book of Job and the Psalms. In another publication (*Homeri gnomologia*, 1660) Duport seemed to present Homer as the actual historical fulcrum

Joshua Barnes (1654–1712), by unknown artist

between the ancient Hebrews and the Greeks, extracting morally worthy passages from the Homeric poems and compiling parallels to them from both scripture and later Greek writings.

Barnes too leapt into the project of connecting classical and biblical antiquity, beginning with *Gerania* (1675), an English prose account of an expedition to visit the 'blameless pygmies' mentioned in Homer's *Iliad*. Their harmonious community resembled Francis Bacon's New Atlantis, but its laws had been established by Homer himself, a wandering sage versed in Greek, Persian, and Hebrew philosophy, as well as Christianity *avant la lettre*. Barnes turned next to the emulation of Duport's sacred poetry in Greek, a genre which, even more than the other forms of scholarly writing at his disposal, allowed Barnes to expound his ideas in a way alternately rigorous and nebulous as he found convenient. In 1679 he published his *Aulikokatoptron, sive, Estherae historia* ('A Mirror of Courtiers, or, The History of Esther'), a 1600-line rendition of the book of Esther into Homeric hexameters, complete with a commentary by Barnes in Greek (modelled, he observed, on the Homeric annotations attributed to Didymus). Like the *Paradise Lost* of Barnes's fellow Cambridge scholar John Milton, this biblical epic assumed that its readers knew Homer and Virgil intimately, while also commenting indirectly on its own project of adapting a narrative from the Hebrew Bible in a Christianizing and classicizing fashion. Barnes introduced, for example, a blind magus who sang at Persian feasts like the bards in Homer: one of his songs narrated the world's creation in terms that, Barnes argued, could have commanded the assent of Hesiod, Moses, or even Muhammad (Barnes silently drew his knowledge of the Koran from Hugo Grotius's *De veritate religionis Christianae*). Again, when the Hebrew narrative called for letters to be sent to the Persian provinces ordering the death of the Jews, Barnes referred to these letters as '*sēmata*' ('signs'; p. 71): this neatly alluded to Bellerophon in the *Iliad* (vi. 168), whose execution was ordered on a tablet bearing 'signs' that may or may not have been alphabetic, and which are the only instance of writing in the Homeric poems. Finally, a prophetic scene in which the ill-fated Haman wept at the story of Phaethon's death may have been inspired by the player scene in *Hamlet*, though Barnes's annotation explained Haman's gloomy foresight exclusively out of Platonic doctrine (p. 114). If Barnes left some literary points for his readers to discover independently, however, he assiduously documented the cultural and material habits he attributed to his Persian actors, drawing most frequently on the sixteenth-century antiquarian Caelius Rhodiginus, but also freely citing Josephus and ancient classical authors (translated, when necessary, from Latin into the Greek of Barnes's commentary). The political precepts promised in Barnes's title consisted largely of strictures against powerful women (Queen Vashti) and powerful courtiers (Haman); a few pointed passages aimed to make even clearer that Barnes's criticisms applied only to contemporary court underlings, not the Stuarts themselves. When the loyal Persian official Mardochius learns with horror of a plot against the king, Barnes's annotation reads:

> Everyone who loves God also loves his king, because the king, as Menander puts it, is *the living image of God*. From whence we also see how grave was the recent trespass of our countrymen who, on the pretense of piety, most impiously beheaded the most pious King Charles. (p. 49)

Here, as often in this text, Barnes managed to unite classical Greek, the Hebrew Bible, and the Stuarts in a rich if precarious compound.

Antiquarian and editor At the close of the Esther poem, Barnes announced that he would shortly turn to purely English subjects: he planned to publish poems on the Black Prince and on 'King Charles'—presumably the First—with the encouragement of Joseph Beaumont, the Cambridge divinity professor (p. 163; BL, Add. MS 23101, fol. 14*r*). In fact, though Barnes completed a *Franciad* on the Black Prince, his eventual publication was a prose *History of Edward III* (1688). This book represented a radical shift in Barnes's methods toward the antiquarian study of English history as cultivated especially in contemporary Oxford. The history's tendency was unmistakably to glorify the dashing figures of Edward III and the Black Prince, with their grandiose territorial ambitions and military exploits on the continent. In private, it appears, Barnes also thought of himself as the descendant of an ancient, aristocratic, and eminently English tradition. In preparing a memorandum about his ancestry, he paid special attention to one Juliana Barnes, 'a Learned Lady, that wrote about the Art of Cookery, also of *Hunting & Fishing*' (*Remarks*, 1.277). He later announced to Thomas Hearne a plan to edit Oppian's *Halieutica*, an ancient Greek treatise on the hunt.

Shortly after the *History* of Edward III appeared, the accession of William and Mary made Barnes's adulation for the Stuarts seem suddenly far less wise, though it probably continued undiminished. With approximately fifty others, Barnes petitioned for an explanation of the loyalty oath the new monarchs required, or to be excused from swearing it. Barnes must eventually have taken the oath, but like many another English university scholar at this moment, he rapidly came to see the virtues of the textual edition as a medium of publication. This previously under-exploited genre now offered the possibility of unambiguously demonstrating one's erudition and industry without requiring sustained argument about anything, particularly remote or recent history. In his Euripides (1694), Anacreon (1705), and Homer (1711), Barnes took standard sixteenth-century editions by Pier Vettori and Henri Estienne as his starting points. He rarely emended his texts, but commented often on their poetic metre and regularly reported the readings of the few English manuscripts he consulted. Like most contemporary classical editors in England, Barnes evidently saw the tasks of publishing ancient texts and studying manuscripts as complementary but not immediately interdependent projects.

On a broader level, none the less, Barnes's taste for paradoxical argument persisted in his Greek editions. For example, Barnes insisted against Richard Bentley that the letters attributed to Euripides were authentic, and he revealed his allegiance in the 'battle of the books' even more clearly when he sent Sir William Temple a copy of the *History* of Edward III in early 1693. Against William Baxter, Barnes argued that the poems of Anacreon contained no hint of immorality, much less paederasty—a bold claim when applied to drinking songs celebrating the beauty of youths named Bathyllus ('Mr Deep') and Megistes ('Mr Big'). Apropos Homer, Barnes composed an essay in Greek verse showing that the moral and political precepts of the *Iliad* and *Odyssey* were ultimately derived from Solomon, a theory that recalled Barnes's youthful *Gerania* and Esther version more than it answered contemporary taste. When Barnes hinted at his ideas to Thomas Hearne, who was then trying to lure Barnes to print his Homer at the Oxford University Press, the alarmed Hearne had the press's director, John Hudson, personally inform Barnes that 'your friends here are not for Prolegomena' (Bodl. Oxf., MS Rawl. lett. 24/27a). Left to his own devices, however, Barnes remained indomitable, and the survival of Barnes the fearless cultural commentator alongside Barnes the restrained textual editor was spectacularly apparent from his *Anacreon Christianus* ('The Christian Anacreon'), published in 1705 as a companion to his edition proper. Using the technique formally known as 'parody', Barnes rewrote Anacreon's poems into models of impeccably pious devotion. The famous first lines of Anacreon—'I want to tell of the sons of Atreus, I want to sing of Cadmus, but the strings of my lyre hold only love'—became in Barnes's hands 'I want to tell of the flesh, I want to sing of the world, but the strings of my lyre hold only Christ'. In the 1670s poetic exploits like these would have seemed respectable if mildly old-fashioned; by the first decade of the eighteenth century they were wilfully perverse at best.

Final years Barnes's intellectual preoccupations throughout his life were three: Greek poetry, biblical history and theology, and English political life of the present and past. He addressed these topics—generally more than one at a time—in original poems in several languages, his *History* of Edward III, and his series of Greek textual editions. In the rapidly changing intellectual landscape of his time, Barnes too changed course more than once, yet never enough to qualify as a follower of scholarly fashions, let alone a maker of them. In his youth he carried the air of the faintly obsolescent; in maturity he seemed every year more intent on showing contemporaries that he had been born too late.

Barnes never acquired secure patronage outside the university, and at some periods he apparently supplemented his income by selling sermons for others to deliver. Despite his gaining the professorship of Greek in 1695, Cambridge grew inhospitable to him as the university's political climate inclined toward William and Mary. By 1699, when Richard Bentley orchestrated a series of classical editions to be printed at the Cambridge University Press and published by Jacob Tonson, Bentley conspicuously declined to invite a contribution from Barnes. Instead, Barnes found friends and scholarly collaborators in Oxford—where his BD degree was incorporated in July 1706—including Edward Bernard, Edward Leedes, Thomas Baker, and the overtly Jacobite Francis Cherry, Henry Dodwell, and Thomas Hearne. Hearne supplied Barnes with Homer collations, and they corresponded regularly until Barnes's death.

In 1700 Barnes married a Mrs Mason, a widow with some property, living at Hemingford, near St Ives, Huntingdonshire. She took an intellectual interest in his work, but her resources did not enable Barnes to print books without funds from other parties any more than he had probably done in the past. His subscription scheme for publishing his Homer produced endless practical difficulty and left Mrs Barnes with many unsold copies after his death. This came, probably at Hemingford, on 3 August 1712, of a 'consumptive Cough', and he was buried at Hemingford, where Mrs Barnes placed a monument (*Remarks*, 3.429). Among Hearne's papers is a list of Barnes's unpublished works, of which many, including several series of lectures, are in the library of Emmanuel College.

KRISTINE L. HAUGEN

Sources *Remarks and collections of Thomas Hearne*, ed. C. E. Doble and others, 11 vols., OHS, 2, 7, 13, 34, 42–3, 48, 50, 65, 67, 72 (1885–1921), vols. 1–4 · *DNB* · 'Joshua Barnes', *Biographia Britannica, or, The lives of the most eminent persons who have flourished in Great Britain and Ireland*, ed. A. Kippis and others, 2nd edn, 1 (1778), 616–19 · J. M. Levine, *The battle of the books: history and literature in the Augustan age* (1991), chaps. 2, 5 · D. McKitterick, *A history of Cambridge University Press*, 2 vols. (1992–8) · M. Feingold, 'Reversal of fortunes: the displacement of cultural hegemony from the Netherlands to England in the seventeenth and early eighteenth centuries', *The world of William and Mary: Anglo-Dutch perspectives on the revolution of 1688–89*, ed. D. Hoak and M. Feingold (1996), 234–61 · J. Gascoigne, *Cambridge in the age of the Enlightenment* (1989) · S. Bendall, C. Brooke, and P. Collinson, *A history of Emmanuel College, Cambridge* (2000) • M. R. James, *The western manuscripts in the library of Emmanuel College: a descriptive catalogue* (1904) • K. L. Haugen, 'Richard Bentley: scholarship and criticism in eighteenth-century England', PhD diss., Princeton University, 2001 • BL, Add. MS 23101, fol. 14*r* • Bodl. Oxf., MS Eng. hist. G. 115(R) • Bodl. Oxf., MSS Rawl. letters 23, 24/27a, 25, 34–36, 40/3, 40/5, 40/12, 75 • parish register, London, St Giles Cripplegate, 22 Jan 1654, GL [baptism]

Archives BL, poems and papers, Add. MSS 5832, 6222, 6269, 6911 • Bodl. Oxf., corresp. and papers, MSS Rawl. letters 40, 75; Auct S 15 • Emmanuel College, Cambridge, MSS | Bodl. Oxf., corresp. with T. Hearne, MSS Rawl. letters 24, 35

Likenesses G. White, line engraving, BM, NPG; repro. in J. Barnes, ed., *Anacreon Teius* (1705) • engraving, repro. in J. Barnes, ed., *Homeri Ilias et Odyssea* (1711) • oils, Emmanuel College, Cambridge [*see illus.*]

Barnes, Sir Kenneth Ralph (1878–1957), college head, was the youngest child of the Revd Reginald Henry Barnes (*d.* 1889), vicar of Heavitree, Devon, and prebendary of Exeter Cathedral, and his wife, Frances Mary Emily, *née* Nation. He was born at the vicarage on 11 September 1878, and grew up within a close, richly talented family of six. Two of his sisters became the celebrated West End actresses Violet *Vanbrugh and Irene *Vanbrugh; another sister, Angela, became a professional musician; and his brother Reginald a distinguished and much decorated officer of hussars. In 1885 ill health obliged his father to relinquish his parish, and the entire family moved to west London, enabling young Kenneth to acquire a taste for theatre by seeing spectacular pantomime at Drury Lane, Buffalo Bill's Wild West show at Earls Court, and, at the Lyceum, what he later called the 'hypnotic' acting of Henry Irving.

Barnes was educated at Westminster School (1891–5) and, from January 1897, at Christ Church, Oxford, where he was a member of the Oxford University Dramatic Society (OUDS), and did just enough work to gain an indifferent pass degree in 1899. He led a comfortable middle-class existence—notwithstanding his father's death when he was eleven and his mother's subsequent remarriage—and indulged a penchant for foreign travel with tours of France, the Low Countries, and Germany (where he came under the operatic spell of Wagner) and a six-month visit to India. Footloose on leaving university, he was offered a clerkship at the Land Registry, a secure but undemanding post which allowed him to reside in London with ample leisure to enjoy membership of the Garrick Club, cricket at Lord's, and free passes at any theatre for the asking. He resigned after a few years in order to become a freelance writer and journalist, earnestly drafting plays, contributing dramatic criticism to *The Times* and other newspapers, and making an English adaptation of Paul Hervieu's Parisian success *Connais-toi* (ultimately produced as *Glass Houses* at the Globe in 1910) for his brother-in-law, the actor–manager Arthur Bourchier.

On the strength of these modest accomplishments and a recommendation from his other theatrical brother-in-law, Dion Boucicault the younger, Barnes was invited in September 1909 to take charge of the school of acting which had been founded by Sir Herbert Beerbohm Tree at His Majesty's five years earlier but which was now languishing for want of effective management. Expected by many to preside over its demise, he contrived to breathe new life into it. By regularizing audition procedures, maximizing fee income, and introducing progress-related student scholarships, he soon restored the venture's artistic and economic health, and then acquired the house and garden adjacent to its Gower Street premises to provide room for future expansion and the construction of a theatre for public performances fronting on Malet Street. In 1913 Barnes oversaw the incorporation of the Academy of Dramatic Art as a limited liability company. Further initiatives were interrupted by the outbreak of war, when, as an ex-territorial officer, he volunteered for duty. In 1915 he was commissioned in the Hampshire regiment, with which he served in India, the Middle East, and, after the armistice, in Siberia in support of the White Russian counter-revolution. Fortunate enough to escape armed combat, he devoted his energies to organizing garrison concert parties and dramatic performances, among them short plays of his own and an 'allegorical masque' on the theme of war—morale-boosting exercises for which he was mentioned in dispatches.

Barnes returned home in December 1919 to find the academy undersubscribed and again in financial difficulties. He set about remedying the situation, while raising additional money to complete the theatre, which had been left unfinished in 1914, and which was eventually opened by the Prince of Wales in May 1921. Other significant achievements under his administration between the wars included the award of a royal charter in 1920 and the acquisition by the newly dignified Royal Academy of Dramatic Art (RADA) of protective privileges already enjoyed by London's chartered music colleges—namely the allocation of an annual grant-in-aid from the Treasury, the ratification of charitable status (with consequential remission of income tax), and, most contentiously, the legal recognition of acting as a 'fine art' for the purposes of exemption from payment of the general rate. In 1923 Barnes collaborated with the Central School of Speech and Drama in launching a university diploma in dramatic art under the aegis of London University.

Barnes's next imperative was to fund the demolition of his existing, and inadequate, teaching accommodation and its replacement by a customized new building, opened in November 1931 by the duchess of York. She agreed to become the academy's patron and maintained a continuing interest in its welfare both as queen and as queen mother. In 1938 Barnes initiated a tradition of Shakespearian performances by his students to audiences of London schoolchildren. In the same year, at the instance of George Bernard Shaw, a firm friend and generous benefactor, he was knighted for services to the stage. During the Second World War, while acting as general secretary to the Entertainments National Service Association (ENSA), he resolutely kept the academy open, despite the destruction of its theatre in an air raid in April 1941. Thanks to his establishment of a post-war rebuilding fund—swelled by the proceeds from all-star matinées in the West End and donations he solicited from friends and colleagues—a new, better equipped theatre was completed in December 1954, the academy's jubilee year. It was named the Vanbrugh Theatre in memory of his actress sisters, who had done much to ensure the survival of the entire undertaking.

Barnes's dedication to the affairs of RADA left little room for outside activities, though he served on the Council for the Encouragement of Music and the Arts (CEMA) and several committees connected with the theatre, and had two further plays performed: *Undercurrents* by a club of RADA alumni in 1921 and *The Letter of the Law* at the Fulham Grand in 1924. On 12 December 1925 he married Daphne Graham (*b*. 1903), daughter of Sir Richard James Graham, fourth baronet; she had been a student of his, and acted professionally as Mary Sheridan. After his retirement in August 1955 at the age of seventy-six, a bronze bust of Barnes by Clemence Dane was installed in the entrance hall at Gower Street, and he had time to complete an illuminating autobiography, published posthumously in 1958 under the title of *Welcome, Good Friends*, before dying at his home, Spring Tide, Kingston Gorse, Sussex, on 16 October 1957. He was buried six days later at St Mary's, Hurley, near Maidenhead, Berkshire. He was survived by his wife, but was predeceased by their son Michael, whose untimely death at twenty-five had been a grievous loss.

Barnes clearly saw the development of RADA as his life's work, pursuing it with exemplary single-mindedness, tenacity, and commitment to his students' spiritual as well as professional well-being. The disadvantage of his relative lack of theatrical experience was offset by a sustaining religious faith and his profound belief in acting as a vocation rather than simply a career. His ready access to people of influence within the aristocracy, his university circle, and the theatre itself enabled him to advance the academy's cause and to give it a high public profile. These influential contacts, while attracting allegations that he was running a finishing school for the socially privileged and ignoring genuine, raw talent, helped the academy to overcome the opposition it had initially encountered from the acting profession. Barnes thus left behind an institution sturdy enough to meet the demands of more radical successors and of a changing theatrical climate.

DONALD ROY

Sources K. Barnes, *Welcome, good friends* (1958) · *Who was who in the theatre, 1912–1976*, 1 (1978) · *WWW, 1961–70* · *The Times* (18 Oct 1957) · *The Times* (25 Oct 1957) · *The Times* (29 Oct 1957) · P. Hartnoll, ed., *The Oxford companion to the theatre*, 3rd edn (1967) · S. D'Amico, ed., *Enciclopedia dello spettacolo*, 1 (Rome, 1954) · *Old Westminsters*
Archives FILM BFI NFTVA, documentary footage | SOUND BL NSA, performance recording
Likenesses W. Stoneman, two photographs, 1943–54, NPG · C. Dane, bronze bust, 1956, Royal Academy of Dramatic Art, London · photograph, repro. in *The Times* (18 Oct 1957) · photographs, repro. in Barnes, *Welcome, good friends*
Wealth at death £8274 15*s*. 2*d*.: probate, 19 Feb 1958, *CGPLA Eng. & Wales*

Barnes, Leonard John (1895–1977), writer and campaigner against colonialism, was born on 21 July 1895 in London, the only son of John Albert Barnes, a senior Colonial Office civil servant, and his wife, Kate Oakeshott. He attended Colet Court preparatory school and then St Paul's School, London. In 1914 he won an open scholarship at University College, Oxford, to read Greats, but his studies were delayed for five years by the outbreak of the First World War. He joined the King's Royal Rifle Corps (60th), serving on the western front and rising to the rank of captain. He was wounded three times—the last injury necessitating almost a year in hospital—and was awarded the Military Cross with bar. By the end of the war he had served a total of twenty-four months of front-line duty; very few infantry officers survived so long.

Resuming his interrupted academic work in 1919, Barnes gained a first in Greats, and was then the top scoring candidate in the higher civil service examinations. Few such 'high-flying' civil service entrants opted for the Colonial Office; but Barnes, following family tradition, chose to do so. In less than four years there, his responsibilities ranged very widely, from West Indian affairs to acting as liaison officer with Jan Christian Smuts's South African delegation at the 1923 Imperial Conference. None the less, he grew increasingly dissatisfied, partly because acquaintances such as Hugh Dalton, T. E. Lawrence, and above all Norman Leys were imparting to him their doubts about the morality of colonial rule, but perhaps more on account of a general restlessness which Barnes attributed to his traumatic war experiences. He resigned early in 1925 and went to South Africa with a wartime friend, Eric Gibb. Barnes and Gibb took up a 2000 acre cotton farm in Zululand under the South African government ex-servicemen's settlement scheme.

Barnes gradually came to doubt the morality of this work too, not least because he discovered that the land he and Gibbs farmed had previously been a black reserve and was thus, he felt, in effect stolen. Abandoning the partnership, he began a career in journalism, working for the *Cape Times*, the *Natal Witness*, and the Johannesburg *Star*. His articles became increasingly critical of South African racial policies and attitudes, and he started to work closely with opposition political activists, both white and black. From the journalism grew also two hard-hitting books, *Caliban in Africa* (1930) and *The New Boer War* (1932), warning that unless white people in South Africa changed their world view and political course, violent racial strife was eventually inevitable. He doubted, indeed, that such change could possibly come in time—partly because, he insisted, the supposedly more liberal English-speaking white inhabitants were in reality no less racist than the Afrikaners.

Late in 1932 Barnes returned to Britain, soon becoming active in the Labour Party. He joined its advisory committee on imperial questions, working closely with a group of other former South African residents including Julius Lewin and W. M. MacMillan, and stood unsuccessfully as Labour candidate for Derby in the 1935 election. In 1938, with Lewin, Norman Leys, and Frank Horrabin, he founded and edited the strongly anti-colonial monthly magazine *Empire*. Meanwhile Barnes took up an academic career, becoming lecturer in education at Liverpool University and warden of Rankin Hall, a hall of residence there. Most importantly, he continued the flow of polemical but closely researched books he had begun in South Africa, now widening the focus from a critique of South African racial policies to an assault on Britain's whole colonial record. *The Duty of Empire* (1935), *The Future of Colonies* (1936), *Empire or Democracy?* (1939), and *Soviet Light on the Colonies* (1944), taken together, formed the most substantial and perhaps most influential analysis of empire ever produced by any British left-wing critic of colonialism. The last two, published respectively as a Left Book Club edition and a Penguin Special, also reached a wide readership. Barnes's views became steadily more radical, as the very titles of the books may suggest, shifting from the 1935 plea to inject new moral meaning into the 'trusteeship' ideal to the 1944 suggestion that the USSR offered a positive role model for the future of Britain's colonies. This last view was, however, very much a product of the wartime Anglo-Soviet alliance; after 1945 Barnes was again to express a strongly anti-communist stance.

Alongside his anti-colonial writing, his academic duties, and his Labour Party work, Barnes continued to engage in a strikingly wide range of other activities. He published a volume of poems about his First World War experiences, *Youth at Arms* (1933), and a heavily autobiographical novel, *Zulu Paraclete* (1935). In 1945–8 he directed surveys on youth and community work for King George's Jubilee Trust. He acted as adviser for Malaya on both higher and primary education, serving on the Carr-Saunders commission investigating the former, and in 1950 himself chairing a commission on the latter.

In 1948 Barnes became secretary-director of Oxford University's delegacy for social training at Barnett House. From then until his retirement in 1962 he was the prime mover in achieving university acceptance that sociology, social psychology (by which he became increasingly fascinated), and social work were not only legitimate but also important fields of academic study, an acceptance symbolized by Barnett House's 'promotion' under Barnes's directorship from the status of delegacy to that of full department. At the same time he devoted enormous time and energy to restoring his sixteenth-century house outside Oxford, Water Eaton Manor. In 1961 he published a remarkable epic poem entitled *The Homecoming*. Spanning the whole sweep of human history, the poem traced humanity's, and Barnes's own, search for spiritual meaning

> the majesty
> Of universal pattern

amid the chaos of acquisitive materialism and the threat of nuclear annihilation.

On retiring from Oxford, Barnes plunged back into African affairs. Under the auspices of the United Nations Economic Commission for Africa, he travelled throughout the continent from 1964 to 1969, producing four reports for the commission on the newly independent states' social progress. His thinking on these themes found expression also in two further books, *African Renaissance* (1969) and *Africa in Eclipse* (1971). The sharply contrasting titles again told much of the story: Barnes's bright hopes for what Africa could achieve if only able to pursue genuinely autonomous development, set against his darker perceptions of an impending crisis that was not only African but also global. In his last years Barnes also wrote a very extensive, three-volume autobiography, 'Radical destination', of which Anthony McAdam edited an abridged version entitled 'Let them scratch'. Sadly, both variants of this remarkable work remain unpublished.

Barnes was twice married. In 1928 in South Africa he married Beatrice Davis of Pietermaritzburg, Natal. She died in 1943, and in the same year he married Margaret (Peggy) Blackburn from Kendal, Westmorland, who survived him. There were no children from either marriage. Barnes died in Oxford on 10 March 1977, aged eighty-one.

STEPHEN HOWE

Sources J. Saville, 'Barnes, Leonard John', *DLB*, vol. 8 • A. McAdam, 'Leonard Barnes and South Africa', *Social Dynamics*, 3 (1977), 2 • J. Lewin, 'Leonard Barnes, the man and his books', *African Affairs*, 74 (1975), 297 • *The Times* (14 March 1977) • *Oxford Times* (19 March 1977) • R. Symonds, *Oxford and empire: the last lost cause?* (1986) • S. Howe, *Anticolonialism in British politics* (1993), 131–4 • P. S. Gupta, *Imperialism and the British labour movement, 1914–1964* (1975) • *CGPLA Eng. & Wales* (1977)

Archives SOAS, corresp. and literary papers | Bodl. RH, corresp. with R. Hinden • Bodl. RH, corresp. with F. S. Livie-Noble

Wealth at death £9036: probate, 14 July 1977, *CGPLA Eng. & Wales*

Barnes, Richard (1532?–1587), bishop of Durham, was the seventh son of John Barnes of Bold, near Warrington, Lancashire, and Agnes Saunderson.

Education and early career Admitted on 3 February 1552 to Brasenose College, Oxford, on 28 April Barnes was appointed a fellow by authority of the king's council. He graduated BA on 1 February 1554, proceeded MA on 10 March 1557, and was probably ordained during Mary's reign. However, he embraced the church settlement of 1559 with some enthusiasm and soon married. His wife was Fridismunda or Fredesmund Gifford (*d.* 1581), daughter of Ralph Gifford of Claydon, Buckinghamshire, and sister of Roger *Gifford (*d.* 1597), later the queen's physician. Their eldest child, Emmanuel, was probably born in 1561.

On 12 July 1561 Barnes was appointed a prebendary of York and also chancellor and divinity reader. A loyal supporter of Archbishop Thomas Young, he soon added the rectories of Stonegrave and Stokesley to his list of preferments and was named suffragan bishop of Nottingham in 1567. In 1569 the earl of Sussex, lord president of the council in the north, commended his learning, zeal, orthodoxy, and liberality, but added that in his Wednesday and Friday lectures on the Apocalypse some thought him overvehement. Nevertheless, when the see of Carlisle fell vacant in 1570, following the death of Bishop John Best, Sir Thomas Gargrave and Sir Henry Gate wrote to Secretary of State William Cecil recommending Barnes's promotion. Their support may not have been entirely without reservation, but Barnes was elected bishop of Carlisle on 25 June and confirmed on 7 August. He wrote to Cecil on 27 October expressing his view that the people of Carlisle diocese seemed more tractable than those of Yorkshire and that if he received support from the secular power he would offer 'as faithful, painful (and if God will) effectual travail as ever poor bishop did perform within his cure' (Bouch, 206). In expectation of these good offices he was permitted to retain his chancellor's stall at York for a year and his two rectories for life, though he later exchanged Stokesley for Romaldkirk.

Bishop of Carlisle Barnes's main task at Carlisle was to contend with the aftermath of the rebellion of 1569. In June 1569 there had been a serious riot in Westward Forest, Cumberland, prompted by enclosures undertaken by Thomas Hussey, steward to the earl of Northumberland. Following the suppression of the rebellion, the unhappy impact of these enclosures was still affecting the tenants, yet by 1572 the bishop had managed to initiate an inquiry to alleviate the difficulties of these 'miserable wretches' (*CSP dom., addenda*, 1566–79, 367). More important was Barnes's role in gathering intelligence about the activities of Catholic sympathizers in the north-west. In 1570, for example, he passed on to Sussex a report from Lancashire where 'all things savoured of open rebellion' (ibid., 321–2) and in 1572 he was co-operating with Lord Scrope in the examination of Catholics with contacts in Scotland and the Low Countries. His visitation of the diocese in 1571 was a thorough investigation in which he continued his onslaught on 'relics and monuments of superstition and idolatry' (Bouch, 206). A surviving set of injunctions to the parish of Crosthwaite demonstrates a concern for proper furnishings; the implementation of three annual communions; and the abolition of festivals and practices which smacked of Catholicism. Moreover, between 1571 and 1576 seven clergy were deprived for failure to subscribe to the articles and, after a hiatus in the 1560s, Barnes took it upon himself to ordain no fewer than seventy deacons and fifty-six priests during the same period. Barnes established his reputation as a loyal and hard-working servant of the state and following the death of James Pilkington he was nominated bishop of Durham. Elected on 5 April, he received the royal assent on 29 April and was enthroned on 19 May 1577. He waited nearly three more years before he was created DTh, on 12 February 1580.

Appointment to Durham and clash with Archbishop Grindal Barnes's appointment to Durham, for which he thanked Cecil, now Lord Burghley, as his 'singular good lord and patron' (BL, Lansdowne MS 24, 17, fol. 36), was marred somewhat by bad feeling between Barnes and the archbishop of Canterbury, Edmund Grindal, recently suspended from his functions for his refusal to suppress prophesyings in the southern province. The precise cause of their animosity is not clear, but it probably stemmed from Barnes's work as commissary to Grindal during the latter's years as archbishop of York. Barnes had visited the diocese of Chester in 1572 and evidence of the commissary's 'venality and extortion' at that juncture may have come to light (Collinson, 194). On 25 April 1577 Grindal wrote to Dean Matthew Hutton at York informing him that:

> if I had any special credit when Durham and Carlisle were bestowed some had not sped so well … but blame yourself and Sir Thomas Gargrave; you two commended him, to be rid of him, and now Simon is as good as Peter.
> (*Correspondence of Dr Matthew Hutton*, 57)

The person referred to in this cryptic note is probably Barnes, though it is impossible to be certain. Barnes appears to have struck back by failing to visit Grindal at Lambeth and making some disparaging remarks about him, and on 2 February 1578 he was obliged to write to Burghley to explain himself, stating that the archbishop's prophesyings were 'savouring overmuch of anabaptismy' and that 'his own wilfulness and undutifulness be the just cause of his troubles' (BL, Lansdowne MS 25, fols. 161–2).

Barnes was Grindal's only outspoken opponent among the bishops, and the incident was a prelude to what was to be a highly controversial episcopate. As early as 23 March 1577 Barnes promised Burghley that he would not be 'unmindful to accomplish your lordship's behests … if I may be well backed at the beginning' (BL, Lansdowne MS 24, 17, fol. 36). What Burghley's 'behests' were is not clear, but they probably related to the disturbed state of Durham diocese under Bishop Pilkington and Dean William Whittingham. There had been suggestions of flagrant nonconformity; disruption on the cathedral estates; and a marked failure to grant leases of church lands to the crown and courtiers. Barnes was probably sent in to sort out a troublesome diocese and relaunch it on a sound pathway towards orthodoxy.

Cleansing the 'Augean stables': confrontation and faction In the summer of 1577 Edwin Sandys, newly appointed archbishop of York, included Durham diocese in the plans for his first metropolitan visitation and nominated Barnes as his deputy to carry out the task. Durham's traditional exemption was championed by Dean Whittingham who met the bishop at the door of the cathedral's chapter house on 8 August and denied his right to visit. The incident provoked a crisis. Barnes excommunicated Whittingham and his supporters; Sandys summoned them before the high commission; and the dean and chapter responded by taking their case before the court of delegates. Because the two bishops saw the frustration of their visitation as 'a disgrace offered them and such as could not be laid aside without a revenge' (M. A. E. Green, ed., 'Life of Mr William Whittingham, dean of Durham', *The Camden Miscellany*, 6, CS, 1871, 28), a 'plot' was hatched to remove Dean Whittingham. It embraced Sandys and Barnes; an anti-Whittingham faction in the Durham chapter headed by Ralph Lever; and Thomas Wilson, secretary of state, who had designs on the deanery. During the winter of 1577–8 Barnes undertook a (legitimate) visitation of the cathedral as bishop of Durham and on 11 February 1578 wrote to Burghley about 'that Augiae Stabulum, the church of Durham … whose stink is grievous in the nose of God and of men and which to purge far passeth Hercules' labours' (BL, Lansdowne MS 25, fols. 161–2). In May a commission was issued for a royal visitation of the cathedral which met for two sessions during October and November. Though Lever had submitted comprehensive articles against the dean accusing him of maladministration, most of the discussion hinged on the question of his ordination, and the effectiveness of the investigation was jeopardized by wrangling between two of the commissioners, Sandys and Hutton, from which Barnes, to his credit, stood aloof. Whittingham's death on 10 June 1579 temporarily put a halt to the proceedings and the new dean, Thomas Wilson, succeeded in patching up a compromise in the visitational conflict with York.

The plan had been for Barnes, Wilson, and Lever to control between them the cathedral and diocese, but the alliance soon came under pressure. Lever disapproved strongly of Barnes's disparaging attitude to Whittingham's ordination and the bishop soon concluded that Lever was too unpopular to be an effective vice-dean for the non-resident Wilson. Wilson and Barnes agreed on Robert Bellamy as a more suitable deputy and, once installed, Bellamy began to pursue the allegations of corruption, not investigated in 1578, with some relish. When Lever himself came under the spotlight for misappropriation of funds in 1575 he fell into alliance with Whittingham's former friends and the process of alienation from Barnes and Bellamy was complete.

Following a petition from Bellamy, Barnes was ordered by the queen to visit the cathedral again because of 'very great disorders' there (Marcombe, 'Dean and chapter', 262). The visitation commenced on 21 November 1580 and comprised a catalogue of accusations and counter-accusations between the supporters of Bellamy and Lever, Barnes himself being accused of attempting to exert unlawful influence on the chapter. When it was clear that the bishop's intervention had solved nothing, Lever directed a complaint against Bellamy to the privy council who, in March 1582, decided to revive the royal commission of 1578 and refer all of the complaints to it. The visitation provided an opportunity for Lever to unleash his full catalogue of grievances against Barnes, concluding 'there never was a preacher so misused by a bishop as your orator hath been by the Bishop of Durham' (BL, Lansdowne MS 36, fols. 53–4). When no result was forthcoming, Lever mounted a fresh attack on Barnes, taking advantage of disputes that the bishop was engaged in with his tenants in Allertonshire and Weardale. In the spring of 1583 the tenants, stirred up by Lever, complained to the privy council of Barnes's maladministration; and in September, Lever made his own complaint accusing Bellamy of 'evil government' (Marcombe, 'Dean and chapter', 265) in the cathedral and Barnes of denying him justice in his suits before the palatinate courts. Though there is no record of any ruling by the privy council, Barnes wrote to his officers on 30 September 1583 ordering them to support Lever and see that he received justice. This action seems to have calmed the situation. Lever, who was possibly mentally unbalanced, died in March 1585, freeing the bishop from eight years of turmoil which, as he rightly observed, had an extremely damaging effect on popular perceptions of the clergy. It probably also adversely affected the bishop's ability to concentrate on more important matters, such as the pursuit of seminary priests and recusants which was a growing problem in the 1580s.

In his administration of the diocese Barnes needed to remove Pilkington's more determined officers, such as Robert Swift and Francis Bunny, before he could run things in the way he wished. Further evidence of opposition to the Pilkington faction came when Barnes refused to allow the payments from the palatinate lands given to support Rivington School, a dispute which was settled in 1578 by the mediation of the earl of Huntingdon, lord president of the council of the north. More serious was the action he commenced against Bishop Pilkington's widow for dilapidations, the allegation being that Pilkington had allowed many of his residences to fall into decay and had deliberately plundered some of them for building materials. The suit was still not resolved by the time of Barnes's death, Mrs Pilkington wisely stating that 'a charitable course as my Lord's predecessors hath taken before had been far better' (PRO, SP 12/120, fol. 73).

Pastor, steward, and family man If Barnes's judgements of his colleagues and their actions were sometimes overharsh, he was indisputably an active and energetic bishop. He visited his diocese four times (in 1577, 1578, 1581, and 1584) and was planning a fifth visitation at the time of his death. His *Monitions* directed to the clergy and churchwardens in October 1577, placing emphasis on the ending of superstitious practice and conformity to the prayer book and Thirty-Nine Articles, emphasized the standards he expected. Following the example of Archbishop Sandys, education held a high place on his agenda and the twice-yearly general synods (which covered the whole diocese) and general chapters (which were directed at specific deaneries) were designed to establish conformity and encourage the reception of protestantism by clergy and laity alike. At general synods it was customary to set the clergy an educational task, such as a commentary on one of the gospels, which was to be presented at the next synod as proof of their 'progress in learning and studying of the scriptures' (Raine, *Ecclesiastical Proceedings*, 70). Moreover, at the general synod of September 1578 the bishop allocated a series of sermons to each of the thirty leading preachers in the diocese to preach 'of their benevolent good wills in assisting him in his great cure and parish' (ibid., 81). As a result, in a region generally considered to be devoid of preaching, 303 sermons a year were generated; the bishop led the way, pledging 23 sermons—more than anyone else.

If Barnes attracted a degree of admiration by his willingness to lead by example in the matter of preaching, his attitude to the alienation of lands to the crown and courtiers was much less respected. He has been described as 'sycophantic' and his land transactions have been condemned as 'dubious' (Heal, 230, 255, 295). On 14 August 1577 he wrote to Burghley granting the keepership of Birtley Woods to his servant, Thomas Speede, 'notwithstanding the same wood is within half a furlong of my house and the office of keeper thereof a needless charge' (Durham Cathedral Library, Surtees MS 45). Wolsingham Park, Coundon Grange, Craike, and Howden were among the choice episcopal properties leased to the queen for long periods. But most important was the 'grand lease' of the Gateshead and Whickham coalmines first granted in 1578 and eventually assigned to Henry Anderson and William Selby, aldermen of Newcastle. It took the most valuable coal producing lands in the north-east out of the hands of the diocese and placed them under the control of an oligarchical group of Newcastle capitalists known as the Hostmen. Whittingham and his supporters in the chapter did their best to resist this policy, but after Barnes's death Dean Tobie Matthew commented gloomily that 'the spoil of this bishopric is now very great' (BL, Lansdowne MS 66, fol. 220).

Despite his many real achievements, Barnes's administration attracted an unenviable reputation for corruption. His brother John, chancellor of Durham and his right-hand man in diocesan affairs, was commonly held to blame for its shortcomings. His son Emmanuel also became a prebendary of the cathedral in 1585. The bishop's posthumous reputation has been further blighted by his conflict with Bernard Gilpin, 'the Apostle of the North' and rector of Houghton-le-Spring, over visitation fees and other issues. With Barnes himself present among the congregation, Gilpin condemned what he perceived as the venality of Barnes's regime in a sermon at Chester-le-Street. Barnes judiciously avoided further confrontation by acknowledging that Gilpin was 'fitter to be bishop of Durham than myself to be parson of this church of yours' (Marcombe, 'Bernard Gilpin', 36–8), an act of contrition that may well have caused Gilpin a small pang of remorse.

Bishop Barnes liked to live in some style. He received a grant of arms in 1571, spent large sums of money on spices, and bought a pair of cygnets to adorn one of his moats. On coming to Durham in 1577 he commenced an ongoing series of repairs at Auckland, Stockton, and Durham Castle, spending in all in excess of £1000. Stockton, a house for which he had a particular affection, was full of things he had made himself, including an uncomplimentary painting of the pope depicted as an old sow. Richard Eades, who travelled north with Dean Matthew in 1583, visited Barnes at Stockton and although he was impressed by the scale of the welcome he received, he was less enamoured of the bishop and his family. In all the bishop had nine children—Emmanuel, Walter, Elizabeth, John, Barnabe *Barnes (*bap.* 1571, *d.* 1609), Mary, Timothy, Margaret, and Anne. Fridismunda Barnes died on 8 April 1581 and was buried at St Andrew's, Auckland, with a memorial brass, possibly to his own design, commissioned from a York goldsmith. On 28 March 1582, in the chapel at Durham Castle, Barnes married Jane Dillicotes, 'a French woman' (G. J. Armytage, ed., *Registers of Durham Cathedral, 1609–1896*, Harleian Soc., 23, 1897, 82), who survived her husband and subsequently married Leonard *Pilkington (1527–1599). Bishop Barnes made his will on 23 August 1587, emphasizing his belief in the Thirty-Nine Articles and requesting burial in the cathedral 'in such decent manner of funeral as to my place and calling appurtaineth' (Raine, *Ecclesiastical Proceedings*, xiv–xvi). He died, probably at Durham, on the following day at the age of fifty-five and was buried in the choir of the cathedral on 7 September following a sermon by Dean Matthew. A Latin epitaph was placed over his grave.

DAVID MARCOMBE

Sources Foster, *Alum. Oxon.* • D. Marcombe, 'The dean and chapter of Durham, 1558–1603', PhD diss., U. Durham, 1973 • *The injunctions and other ecclesiastical proceedings of Richard Barnes, bishop of Durham*, ed. [J. Raine], SurtS, 22 (1850) • *CSP dom.*, 1547–90, with addenda, 1566–79 • *APC*, 1577–8, 1581–2 • F. Heal, *Of prelates and princes: a study of the economic and social position of the Tudor episcopate* (1980) • BL, Lansdowne MSS 24, 25, 36, 66 • D. Marcombe, 'Bernard Gilpin: anatomy of an Elizabethan legend', *Northern History*, 16 (1980) • H. Gee, 'A sixteenth century journey to Durham', *Archaeologia Aeliana*, 3rd ser., 13 (1916) • PRO, SP 12/120; 159; 162; 173 • P. Collinson, *Archbishop Grindal, 1519–1583: the struggle for a reformed church* (1979) • C. M. L. Bouch, *Prelates and people of the lake counties: a history of the diocese of Carlisle, 1133–1933* (1948) • *Brasenose College register, 1509–1909* (1909), vol. 1, pp. 14–15 • *The correspondence of Dr Matthew Hutton, archbishop of York*, ed. [J. Raine], SurtS, 17 (1843) • G. E. Aylmer and R. Cant, *A history of York Minster* (1977) • W. Hutchinson, *The history and antiquities of the county palatine of Durham*, [2nd edn], 2 vols. (1823) • Borth. Inst., R VII, G/2569 • J. Raine, *Auckland Castle* (1852) • J. G. Waller, 'Notes on some brasses in the counties of Northumberland and Durham', *Archaeologia Aeliana*, new ser., 15 (1892)

Barnes, Robert (*c.*1495–1540), religious reformer, was a native of Bishop's Lynn, Norfolk; his parentage is unknown.

Early career as humanist and reformer According to John Bale, Barnes entered the house of the Austin friars in Cambridge while still a boy. Some time about 1517 he travelled to the University of Louvain, where he studied under Erasmus and developed humanist sympathies. On his return to Cambridge, in 1521 or slightly later, he became prior of the Austin friars there and initiated a series of reforms which centred on the introduction into the curriculum of such classical Latin authors as Terence, Plautus, and Cicero, and the replacement of scholastic authors with a course on the letters of St Paul. The absence of Greek authors from this programme would seem to indicate the limits of his own humanist education at this point. Nevertheless, Barnes's developing reputation as a humanist reformer led him to play a prominent role in the meetings of young intellectuals which were then taking place at the White Horse inn. These were not in essence early gatherings of protestants, since conservatives like Stephen Gardiner were also present, but they did reflect the growing interest in the new ideas that were then arriving from the continent.

In 1522–3 Barnes was incorporated BTh in the university, followed in 1523 by the award of a DTh. Then on Christmas eve 1525 he preached a sermon in St Edward's Church, Cambridge, in which he attacked the corruption of the clergy in general and that of Cardinal Wolsey in particular, and effectively launched himself on a reforming career. Barnes himself is the principal source for this address and for the actions against him which followed it, in two treatises both under the title *A Supplication*, the first in 1531 and the second in 1534. Theologically, the sermon does not appear to have been radical in any way, and the key protestant doctrine of justification by faith is conspicuous only by its absence. Rather it seems to have been typical of the Erasmian genre of a criticism of clerical abuses, and it was this, not Barnes's protestantism, which offended the authorities.

As a result of complaints about his sermon, Barnes was arrested by Wolsey's serjeant-at-arms on 5 February 1526. Taken to London, he appeared before Wolsey but, thanks to the qualified support of his former associate at the White Horse inn, Stephen Gardiner, and also that of Wolsey's secretary Edward Fox, he received a fair hearing and, by the standards of the time, relatively lenient treatment during the trial itself. Nevertheless on 11 February he was made to do public penance by carrying a faggot to Paul's Cross and then abjuring his perceived heresies (though it is very doubtful whether the sermon contained any ideas which were, strictly speaking, heretical). Barnes was then imprisoned in the Fleet to wait upon Wolsey's pleasure, and when he was released he was not permitted to return to Cambridge but placed under effective house arrest in the Austin Friary in London. While thus confined Barnes apparently established the London house as a centre for the sale and distribution of Tyndale's New Testament. This incident, attested by John Tyball, a Lollard from Steeple Bumpstead, points to an established relationship between Barnes and the Lollard underground, but there is no other extant evidence which would allow firmer conjectures about its nature. When in 1528 this activity came to the attention of the bishop of London, Cuthbert Tunstall, Barnes was swiftly moved to the Austin House in Northampton, where he was kept under close guard.

Wittenberg Barnes now staged an elaborate escape to rid himself of the unwanted attention from the authorities. Leaving a suicide note for Wolsey, a pile of clothes on the river-bank, and a letter to the mayor of Northampton instructing him to search for his body because there was a further letter to the cardinal secreted on his person, Barnes disguised himself as a pauper and fled to London, whence he sailed to Antwerp before travelling on to Wittenberg. There he became a good friend of Martin Luther, and though he devoted most of his time to study, in 1530 he published (under the Latin name Antonius Anglus) a book in the style of a medieval sentence collection dealing with various theological commonplaces from a vigorously protestant perspective, asserting nineteen points including justification by faith alone, the moral impotence of humanity outside of Christ, and the identification of the keys of the church with the word of God. Barnes's *Sentenciae ex doctoribus collectae, quas papistae valde impudenter hodie damnant* was printed by Joseph Clug, and contains a preface by Johann Bugenhagen (Pomeranus), with whom Barnes lodged. A second edition was published by Clug under Barnes's real name in 1536.

In the summer of 1531, while still at Wittenberg, Barnes was commissioned to ascertain Luther's opinion on the divorce proceedings between Henry VIII and Katherine of Aragon. Luther's response was unfavourable to the king, but Barnes's commission clearly opened a way for him to return to England as a man who could be useful as a diplomat. This possibility was reinforced in 1531 by the publication of the first edition of *A Supplication*, a work which was essentially an apology for his theology, framed as a direct, and somewhat sycophantic, appeal to Henry VIII. A copy of the work was sent to Henry by Stephen Vaughan, Cromwell's agent in the Low Countries, in a dispatch of 14 November 1531. Vaughan was so impressed by the Lutheran political philosophy of kingship which the work espoused (as opposed to its protestant theology) that he pleaded with Cromwell to grant the exile a hearing.

Royal agent Barnes's adulatory praise for Henry, his assertion of royal prerogatives, and above all his close relationship with Luther and the Wittenberg establishment, made him potentially very useful to the king, and so late in 1531 Barnes returned home with royal approval, as the imperial ambassador, Eustace Chapuys, noted in a letter to Charles V on 21 December, although Sir Thomas More was not at all pleased by his reappearance. Little is known about this stay in England except that Barnes probably had an interview with the king and certainly aroused the anger of More. He returned to the continent in 1532, where he lived in Hamburg and engaged in correspondence with More, defending himself (much to Sir Thomas's delight) against charges of sacramentarianism, an issue on which his position effectively separated him from the largely reformed thrust of much of the theology of such other English reformers as William Tyndale and John Frith. Barnes always maintained the real presence of Christ's humanity in the eucharistic elements, while Tyndale and Frith repudiated this, preferring more Zwinglian and Oecolampadian constructions respectively.

It is possible that Barnes was again in England in October 1533, and he was certainly back in London in the summer of 1534 with an embassy from the cities of Lübeck and Hamburg. In November of the latter year he published a second (and much revised) edition of *A Supplication*, printed by John Byddell, designed to capitalize on the anti-papal stance of current English policy. He also added a whole new section on the unfairness of the proceedings against him in 1526, while drastically abbreviating the amount of text devoted to the theological discussion which had formed the main body of the earlier edition. One extra section was added here, however, on the subject of clerical marriage. This was based upon the *Sentenciae* of 1530.

That the tide of change was now running in Barnes's favour was demonstrated in no uncertain fashion by the execution of Thomas More on 6 July 1535, an event which effectively signalled that Barnes, a favourite target of More's writing, could now enjoy much greater freedom of operation in England. From now on Barnes's career would be inextricably intertwined with the fortunes of Cromwellian domestic and foreign policy. In July 1535, as a royal chaplain, he was dispatched to Wittenberg for the purpose of persuading Melanchthon to abandon a planned trip to France and to come instead to England. Having at least induced Melanchthon to abandon his French expedition, Barnes then met up with Johann Friedrich, the elector of Saxony, opening the way for a formal embassy, headed by Edward Fox (now bishop of Hereford) and Nicholas Heath, which arrived in the following December. Barnes was disappointed, however, by his failure to secure an opportunity to debate the royal supremacy with the Catholic controversialist Cochlaeus—his letters to Cromwell indicate that this was one of Barnes's ambitions.

Early in 1536 Barnes published at Wittenberg his *magnum opus*, *Vitae Romanorum pontificum, quos papas vocamus, diligenter at fideliter collectae per D Doctorem R Barns*, a polemical piece designed to expose the immorality that underlay the history of the papacy. The work was dedicated to Henry VIII and contained a preface by Luther himself. The dedication did little, however, to ease Barnes's acute financial difficulties which were caused by the failure of the government to pay him either appropriately or sufficiently for his services rendered. Then, with the fall of Anne Boleyn in May 1536, it became necessary for him to lie low and he wrote to Melanchthon advising him to stay away from England. Indeed, he broke silence only in November of that year, whereupon he was promptly arrested by Sir John Gostwick, the bursar who had paid him so badly for his services, and sent to the Tower. But his release was soon secured by Cromwell, and he once again became the bane of theological conservatives through his outspoken preaching against the papacy and in favour of justification by faith. Indeed, Barnes's stature as a reformer is shown by the esteem in which his preaching was held by Hugh Latimer, who twice in 1537 praised it in letters to Cromwell, and by the fact that Humphrey Monmouth, a prominent London merchant and long-time friend and sponsor of reformers, bequeathed him £10 and a gown in his will, and asked that he should preach at his funeral.

Evangelical activist In 1538 Barnes continued both to preach and to act as an agent for Cromwell. Then in June an embassy arrived from Germany and Barnes once again resumed his diplomatic duties. The embassy established little, however, other than the fact that Henry's political approaches to the Germans were not to be paralleled by similar theological flirtations. Indeed, Henry himself was less than warm towards Barnes, suspecting his theological sympathies, and, when Cranmer requested in August that Barnes be given the deanery of Tamworth College in Staffordshire, Cromwell did not pursue the offer on the grounds that it was too dangerous to show such favour at this point. Instead Barnes was appointed in October to a commission charged with seeking out and examining Anabaptists. At this point he was involved in the prosecution and subsequent execution (22 November 1538) of an old associate from his Cambridge days, one John Lambert, who held sacramentarian views which were anathema to the Lutheran Barnes. The incident underlines the ambivalence of the relationship between Barnes and the broad movement of English reformers, and was chronicled by Foxe (who was clearly embarrassed by it) only in his account of the life of Lambert; he omitted it from his life of Barnes. The central issue was that of the eucharist: was Christ's humanity physically present in the elements? Like Luther, Barnes appears to have regarded this as a non-negotiable Christian doctrine, a position which divided him from many other English protestants of the time.

Early in 1539 Barnes was granted full diplomatic status and made his final trip to Europe to help in the negotiations between Henry and the duke of Cleves which were to culminate in Henry's ill-fated marriage to the duke's sister Anne. Barnes himself was not sent as an envoy to the duke but was employed rather to reinforce the negotiations by securing the goodwill of other northern princes and to test the ground for further alliances. Of these, his dealings with Christian III of Denmark bore fruit in a positive exchange of letters between the two kings. Nevertheless, the passing of the Act of Six Articles that summer effectively ended the likelihood of theological rapprochement between Henry and the protestant powers and dramatically undermined Barnes's own status as royal envoy. Indeed, a letter from Cruciger in Leipzig indicates that in July, Barnes had been frightened to return home, for fear of a climate of opinion that was becoming increasingly hostile to reform. None the less Barnes did return to England in August. He appears to have played no further part in the negotiations with Cleves, but in the autumn Cromwell arranged for him to be appointed to the prebend of Llanboidy in St David's Cathedral.

Protestant martyr The last months of Barnes's life were characterized by a series of bizarre twists that ultimately led to his death. First, Gardiner attacked Cromwell in council by declaring it to be a disgrace that he had employed Barnes, a known heretic, to conduct the king's business as ambassador. For this outburst Gardiner was put out of the privy council. A letter written by a protestant sympathizer on 24 February 1540 makes it clear that Barnes was at this time once more engaged upon his preaching ministry and quite possibly organizing others to do the same. It was almost certainly this activity that led to his appointment, with William Jerome and Thomas Garrard, as a Lenten preacher at Paul's Cross. On the first Sunday, however (14 February), Barnes had to give way to Gardiner, who used the opportunity to attack the doctrine of justification by faith; when Barnes took it upon himself to use the same pulpit to reply to the bishop a fortnight later (28 February), and that in his typically direct and personal manner, it was inevitable that Gardiner would take up the matter with the king. On the following Friday (5 March), Barnes was summoned to face Gardiner in Henry's presence. The next day Barnes broke down before Gardiner and begged him for forgiveness, but his repentance was somewhat short-lived: inspired by the preaching of Jerome and Garrard over the next few weeks, he returned, as it were, to the protestant fold, an act which again brought him, along with the two other Lenten preachers, before the king. All three were instructed to preach sermons of public recantation on the first three days of Easter week. Barnes did so on the Tuesday (30 March) in a bizarre ritual where he once again begged Gardiner for forgiveness before straightaway withdrawing his recantation. The result was that Barnes, along with his two fellow protagonists, was arrested and committed to the Tower by command of the privy council on 3 April.

The following months saw the return to the council of the three leading conservative bishops, Gardiner, Tunstall, and John Clerk of Bath and Wells; then, with the arrest of Cromwell on 10 June, the fate of Barnes and company was effectively sealed. On 22 July the three men were attainted as heretics, a procedure which denied them the chance to defend themselves in court, and sentenced to burn at Smithfield; their heresies were not specified. Finally, on 30 July 1540, Barnes, Garrard, and Jerome were taken to Smithfield, where they were burnt at the same time that three Catholics, Thomas Abell, Edward Powell, and Richard Fetherstone, were hanged, drawn, and quartered for treason. According to Foxe, when he was at the stake Barnes made a last profession of his protestant faith which made a great impression on the crowd; shortly afterwards it was published in German at Wittenberg (*Bekantus des Glaubens: die Robertus Barns, der heiligen Schrift Doctor (inn Deudshem Lande D Antonius genent) zu Lunden inn Engelland gethan hat*, 1540). Martin Luther, who supplied a preface, was visibly shaken when he heard the news of his friend's fate. CARL R. TRUEMAN

Sources R. Barnes, *A supplicatyon made by Robert Barnes* (1531) • R. Barnes, *A supplicacion made by Robert Barnes* (1534) • J. Foxe, *The book of martyrs*, ed. W. Bramley-Moore, new edn (1875) • *LP Henry VIII*, vols. 4–15 • Venn, *Alum. Cant.*, 1/1.93 • J. Strype, *Ecclesiastical memorials*, 3 vols. (1822) • Bale, *Cat.* • C. Wriothesley, *A chronicle of England during the reigns of the Tudors from AD 1485 to 1559*, ed. W. D. Hamilton, 1, CS, new ser., 11 (1875) • W. A. Clebsch, *England's earliest protestants, 1520–1535* (1964) • S. Brigden, *London and the Reformation* (1989) • J. P. Lusardi, 'The career of Robert Barnes', in St Thomas More, *The confutation of Tyndale's answer*, ed. L. A. Schuster and others, 3 vols. (1973), vol. 8/3 of *The Yale edition of the complete works of St Thomas More*, 1365–1415 • C. R. Trueman, *Luther's legacy: salvation and English reformers, 1525–1556* (1994) • C. R. Trueman, '"The Saxons be sore on the affirmative": Robert Barnes on the Lord's supper', *The Bible, the Reformation and the church*, ed. W. P. Stephens (1995), 290–307

Barnes, Robert (1817–1907), obstetric physician, was born in Norwich on 4 September 1817, the second of the six children of Philip Barnes (1791–1874), an architect and one of the founders of the Royal Botanic Society of London, and his wife, Harriet Futter, daughter of a Norfolk squire. His father claimed to be a descendant of Robert Barnes (*c*.1495–1540), the sixteenth-century heretic. After education at Bruges from 1826 to 1830 and at home, where one of his tutors was Robert Borrow, author of *The Bible in Spain*, at the age of fifteen Barnes began his medical training as an apprentice in Norwich to Richard Griffin, the founder of an association of Poor Law medical officers. When Barnes's family moved to London he continued his medical studies at University College, the Windmill Street School, and at St George's Hospital. After qualifying MRCS in 1842, he went to Paris, where he pursued his interest in mental illness. On his return to London a year later he applied without success for the post of resident physician at Bethlem Hospital; he thus settled in general practice in

Robert Barnes (1817–1907), by John Horsburgh, 1889

Notting Hill, supplementing his income by means of literary work for *The Lancet*. In 1848 he graduated MD (Lond.), and he became LRCP in 1853 and FRCP in 1859.

Barnes's ambition, however, was to be a medical teacher. After holding minor posts in London as obstetric surgeon to the Western General Dispensary and as lecturer on midwifery at the Great Windmill Street School of Medicine and on forensic medicine at Dermott's School, on 1 April 1859 he was elected assistant obstetric physician, and on 14 July 1863 obstetric physician to the London Hospital. He was also appointed physician to the Seamen's Hospital, the East London Hospital for Children, and the Royal Maternity Hospital. In April 1862 Barnes was invited to fill the post of lecturer on midwifery at St Thomas's Hospital, and on 24 April 1865 he was elected obstetric physician to that hospital. He was dean of St Thomas's medical school when he left in 1875 to take up a post as obstetric physician at St George's Hospital; in 1885 he was elected consulting obstetric physician there. He was also physician to the Chelsea Hospital for Women.

Barnes was actively involved in medical politics. He took a prominent part in the foundation of the Obstetrical Society of London in 1859 and was president in 1865–6. In 1876, as one of the examiners for the midwifery licence of the Royal College of Surgeons, he refused to examine Sophia Jex-Blake and her friends, who were trying to gain access to medicine by exploiting a loophole in the regulations for the licence. In 1884 a dispute with the council of the Obstetrical Society of London led him to found the British

Gynaecological Society, of which he was honorary president until his death. A pioneer of operative gynaecology, Barnes strenuously advocated the right of obstetricians to perform ovariotomy and other major gynaecological operations, but the Obstetrical Society of London had no sympathy for his cause. Ovariotomy was a controversial procedure and older obstetricians, notably James Matthews Duncan, a rival of Barnes both in debates and in practice, firmly believed that such operations were beyond the scope of obstetrics. The cause Barnes advocated eventually gained the day, and he lived to see the two societies united and merged into the Royal Society of Medicine (1907).

A leading teacher and gynaecologist, Barnes was censor at the Royal College of Physicians (1877–8) and he had the rare distinction of receiving the honorary fellowship of the Royal College of Surgeons in 1883; he was also honorary fellow of the Medical Society of London (1893) and of the Royal Medical and Chirurgical Society (1905). He delivered the Lettsomiam lectures at the Medical Society of London in 1858 and the Lumleian lectures 'On convulsive diseases in women' at the Royal College of Surgeons in 1873. He was one of the first to take an interest in the histopathology of the female reproductive system, and gave his name to an obstetric instrument and to a curve of the pelvis. Besides writing an official report on scurvy at the Seamen's Hospital (1864) and contributing many papers to the *Transactions of the Obstetrical Society of London* and to the *British Gynaecological Journal*, Barnes was the author of standard works on obstetrics and gynaecology. His collected *Lectures on Obstetric Operations, Including the Treatment of Haemorrhages* (1870) established his fame and were translated into French. *A Clinical History of the Medical and Surgical Diseases of Women* (1873), a classic in the literature of obstetric medicine, was followed by *A System of Obstetric Medicine and Surgery* (2 vols., 1884), written with his son, Fancourt Barnes.

Barnes was twice married, first to Eliza Fawkener, daughter of a London solicitor; second, in 1880, to Alice Maria, daughter of Captain W. G. Hughes, of Carmarthenshire, deputy lieutenant and JP for that county. With his first wife he had one son, R. S. Fancourt Barnes, a loyal supporter and collaborator, and two daughters; with his second wife he had one son and one daughter.

Barnes was an energetic man with a reputation for bellicosity. He forcefully defended his opinions, and in the process he made many enemies. Intellectually and physically vigorous to the end, he impressed his contemporaries by learning Spanish at the age of eighty-five, and by rowing out to sea and bathing from the boat daily until he was eighty-nine. He was a director of the Prudential Assurance Company (1848–9; 1884–1907), accumulated a large fortune, and gave generously to medical institutions. He died at his home, Bernersmede, in Eastbourne on 12 May 1907, of cerebral thrombosis, and was buried at Eastbourne on 16 May. ORNELLA MOSCUCCI

Sources *BMJ* (18 May 1907), 1221–2 • *The Lancet* (25 May 1907), 1465–9 • *DNB* • Munk, *Roll* • *CGPLA Eng. & Wales* (1907)

Archives Royal College of Obstetricians and Gynaecologists, London, casebook; notebooks, casebooks, reports • Wellcome L., certificates

Likenesses Barraud and Jerrard, photograph, 1873, Wellcome L. • J. Horsburgh, oils, 1889, Wellcome L. [*see illus.*] • Barraud, photograph, Wellcome L. • photograph, repro. in *The Lancet*, 1467

Wealth at death £183,074 16*s*. 5*d*.: probate, 11 July 1907, *CGPLA Eng. & Wales*

Barnes, Rowley. *See* Detrosier, Rowland (1800?–1834).

Barnes, Sydney Francis (1873–1967), cricketer, was born on 19 April 1873 at Cross Street, Smethwick, Staffordshire, the second son of the five children of Richard Barnes, a metal tester and later foreman shipper, who worked in Birmingham for the Muntz Metal Company for sixty-three years, and his wife, Ann Wood. He made four appearances for Warwickshire (1894–6) but was, from the start, reluctant to play on the day-to-day basis expected at first-class county level. Nor could any county offer him the financial return which he could achieve from Saturday afternoon cricket and a job during the week.

An association with Rishton (1895–9) in the Lancashire league, for whom he took 411 wickets in Saturday afternoon games, typified Barnes's cricketing allegiance to the leagues throughout his career. Nevertheless, he agreed to play two matches for Lancashire in 1899 while declining to join the staff. Instead, he joined Burnley (1900–01). At the end of 1901 the Lancashire captain, A. C. MacLaren, persuaded him to play against Leicestershire in the last match of the season. Barnes took six for 99 in the match (besides making 32 with the bat). On the strength of this performance and of his reputation as a bowler, MacLaren offered him a place in the team he was taking to Australia in less than a month's time.

Barnes justified his surprise selection by adding nineteen wickets in the first two tests to the mere thirteen he had taken in first-class cricket up to that point. MacLaren, however, overbowled him, and he broke down with a knee injury after bowling seven overs in the third test and did not play again on the tour. But he had done enough to top the England bowling averages for the series. With some reluctance—and a certain obligation imposed by MacLaren—he played as a professional for Lancashire in 1902 and 1903. His injury still troubled him but in two seasons he took 213 wickets. His relations with the county committee were never easy, and he parted company on three counts: there was no guarantee of winter employment; the terms offered were no better than those made to any other professional; and there was no promise of a future benefit in the match of his choice.

Barnes married Alice Maud, daughter of Charles Pearce, jeweller, and divorced wife of George Taylor, on 25 May 1903. They had one son. Having parted company with Lancashire, Barnes returned in 1904 to the comparative obscurity of league cricket. *Wisden* caustically remarked that had he 'possessed enthusiasm for the game … he might have made a great name for himself' (*Wisden*, 1904, 63). The point was missed. Barnes was ahead of his generation in his genuine concern for the financial security of the professional cricketer. League cricket and regular

Sydney Francis Barnes (1873–1967), by unknown photographer, c.1910

employment gave him what county cricket could not. As for the 'great name', the years to come established him, in the view of the critics—especially Australian ones—as the best bowler in the world.

Barnes bowled medium-pace off an accelerated run. He was capable of swinging the ball one way and breaking it the other in an era when one ball had to suffice for a whole innings. Pelham Warner wrote in 1909, when Barnes had shown his skills at the highest level, that he kept a perfect length, was deceptive in flight with a leg-break 'not only accurate but very quick off the pitch [and had] every attribute of a great bowler' (*Wisden*, 1910, 161). 'His greatness', wrote Neville Cardus, 'was directed by a subtle reserve power of destruction. The prehensile fingers, curving the ball gloatingly, were directed by one of the sharpest of all cricket intelligences' (Cardus, 153).

After leaving Lancashire, Barnes played for various clubs in seven different leagues from 1904 to 1940—including the First World War and with the single exception of 1939. In 1940, at the age of sixty-seven, he took twenty-eight wickets (at an average of 8·28). He also began an association with Staffordshire (1904–14, 1924–35), for whom he took 1441 wickets (8·15) in the minor counties' championship. His numerous successes included fourteen wickets for 13 runs against Cheshire (in one day) in 1909, fourteen for 29 against All-India in 1911, seventeen for 59 against Monmouthshire in 1912 and—as late as 1932 at the age of fifty-nine—thirteen for 50 against Lancashire. Throughout these years he took 4069 wickets (6·08) in league and club cricket.

Yet it is in his performances in test cricket that Barnes's stature must be measured. Like some meteor suddenly descending with awesome power, he went on to appear for England in a further twenty-three test matches up to 1914. He returned to Australia both in 1907–8 and in 1911–12, and helped England to a one-wicket win at Melbourne in 1908 by taking five for 102 and making a crucial 38 not out. On the same ground on 30 December 1911 he opened the test match, in dramatic fashion, by dismissing Australia's top four batsmen in five overs for one run. Against the South Africans, during the triangular tournament of 1912, he took thirty-four wickets for 282 in three tests, and finished his test career against the same opponents in 1913–14 by taking forty-nine wickets (10·93) in the series, including seventeen for 159 at Johannesburg, a test match record which stood until 1956. He was invited to tour Australia for a fourth time, in 1920–21, at the age of forty-seven, but he declined as he was not allowed to take his family with him as part of his remuneration. In test cricket he took 189 wickets (average 16·43) in twenty-seven matches. He was the last man to play test cricket regularly who did not have a first-class county affiliation.

Barnes made other occasional forays into the first-class game. He made his highest score of 93 for MCC against Western Australia in 1908. There were matches at home for MCC, the Players (against the Gentlemen), the minor counties, and Wales. In 1929 he was again the scourge of the South Africans. Against them, for the minor counties, he took eight for 41 in thirty-two consecutive overs. A month later, again versus the South Africans, playing for Wales (for which he had a brief residential qualification) he had a match analysis of ten for 90: at one point he had taken six for 8. His record in first-class cricket (1894–1930) was 719 wickets (average 17·09) together with 1573 runs (12·78). In all cricket it has been estimated he took 6229 wickets (8·33). At lower levels, he was a useful batsman and made several centuries.

Before 1914 Barnes earned his regular living as the clerk in a Staffordshire colliery. He was over forty when the First World War broke out. Too old to serve, he continued as a clerk and as a league cricketer (for Saltaire in the Bradford league). Thereafter he worked in the legal department of Staffordshire county council well into extreme old age. He was a calligrapher of rare quality and inscribed illuminated documents. In 1957 he presented Elizabeth II with a scroll of his own work describing the visit of Elizabeth I to Stafford.

Barnes was thus the epitome of a self-made Victorian, but without the deference to his superiors displayed by many another working-class man (including professional cricketers). The establishment found him hard to handle, while his fellow county cricketers failed to realize that he was taking a stance for their own future economic and social status. His taciturn manner, authoritative tone, and gaunt appearance did not make for easy relations with fellow cricketers; popularity and acceptance came only with the dignity and mellowness of age. Yet Pelham Warner saw him as a man who responded to kindness and the courtesies of life and he believed (in 1948) that there had 'been no greater bowler in the history of the game' (Duckworth, 202). The claim that Barnes was the best bowler of his generation gains credibility from the fact that all his contemporaries said so. The idea that he was the greatest bowler of all time must be tested against such statistics as length of service, aggregate of wickets, and test career. *Wisden* in 2000 conducted a voting survey of the greatest cricketers of the twentieth century. Of those who were strictly bowlers, Barnes was placed fourth (*Wisden*, 2000, 17).

Barnes was, in 1949, among the first list of professional cricketers made honorary members of the Marylebone Cricket Club, and four years later a testimonial match took place at Stafford in which many test cricketers participated. Barnes, who had just turned eighty, bowled two overs. Ten years later, at the age of ninety, he was elected president of the Warwickshire Old County Cricketers' Association. Age had conferred its accolades on the doughty nineteenth-century defender of players' rights. In his later years he was a firm friend of Pelham Warner, his exact contemporary and his antithesis in social background. They would be seen together watching cricket at Lord's. Barnes died at his home, 59 Moss Street, Chadsmoor, Cannock, Staffordshire, on 26 December 1967.

GERALD M. D. HOWAT

Sources W. S. White, *Sydney Barnes* (1935) • L. B. Duckworth, *S. F. Barnes: master bowler* (1967) • *Wisden* (1895–1968) • A. Searle, *S. F. Barnes: his life and times* (1997) • b. cert. • m. cert. • N. Cardus, *The Playfair Cardus* (1963) • *CGPLA Eng. & Wales* (1968)
Likenesses photograph, *c.*1910, Hult. Arch. [*see illus.*] • photograph, 1953, NPG
Wealth at death £3788: probate, 31 Jan 1968, *CGPLA Eng. & Wales*

Barnes, Thomas (1747–1810), Presbyterian minister and reformer, was born on 1 February 1747 at Warrington, the son of William Barnes and Elizabeth, daughter of the Revd Thomas Blinston, Presbyterian minister at Wigan. His father died when he was only three. He was educated at the grammar school in Warrington, before being sent in 1761 to the well-known dissenters' boarding-school conducted by the Revd Philip Holland of Bolton. He then studied at Warrington Academy (1764–8), and entered the ministry at Cockey Moor (Ainsworth, near Bolton) in 1768, serving for twelve years with considerable success, his congregation more than doubling in size. He was ordained in 1769. In September 1770 he married Elizabeth (1744x6–1814), daughter of John Mills, a member of his congregation.

In 1780 Barnes became co-minister, with the Revd Ralph Harrison, at Cross Street Chapel, Manchester, where he remained until his death. Cross Street was perhaps the wealthiest and most influential congregation in the north of England. Barnes proved to be an effective and popular preacher, cleverly concealing a deformed arm in his gown while preaching. From 1782 he voluntarily undertook a course of Sunday evening lectures every winter, which in later years drew an audience of 2000 people of different denominations. In doctrine Barnes was an Arian, denying the full divinity of Christ, and was, in Joseph Priestley's opinion, hostile to unitarianism. He was said to have been more orthodox than Harrison. Nevertheless, in 1792 he signed the petition to parliament for the repeal of the penal laws against Unitarians. In 1789 a number of members withdrew from Cross Street to establish a Unitarian congregation in Mosley Street, but his successor in 1810 was a Unitarian, suggesting that the leading members of Cross Street had moved beyond his doctrinal position by that date. His influence among English presbyterians was, however, considerable. According to the historian Alexander Gordon (*Heads of English Unitarian History*, 1895, 50), 'in Lancashire, Arianism held the field till the death of Thomas Barnes'.

With his close friend Thomas Percival (1740–1804), Barnes was a leading figure in all the main intellectual and reform movements of late eighteenth-century Manchester. He was a member of the first Manchester committee for the abolition of the slave trade in 1787, and chaired the public meeting held in Manchester on 15 May 1789 to renew the application to parliament for the repeal of the Test and Corporation Acts. He helped found the Manchester Literary and Philosophical Society in 1781, serving as a vice-president until 1785 and as joint secretary from 1785 to 1787. At his suggestion the College of Arts and Sciences was established in 1783, a short-lived attempt to provide a liberal education for the sons of businessmen. In 1784, at Percival's prompting, he received an honorary DD degree from Edinburgh University. In 1786, with Percival, Harrison, and other members of the Cross Street congregation, he was a leading promoter of a new dissenting academy at Manchester to replace Warrington Academy, which had closed in 1783. He was the first theological tutor (and therefore principal). It is clear that Barnes did not find his office easy, as the college—like all institutions supported by reformers—experienced great difficulties in the period following the French Revolution. He offered his resignation in 1792, but was persuaded to continue until 1798. It was alleged subsequently that Barnes resigned because of difficulties over student discipline, but at the time he gave as his reasons the health of his wife and the incompatibility of conducting the academy and fulfilling his pastoral duties. He then interested himself with the Manchester Infirmary and Fever House. In the final years of his life Barnes appears to have distanced himself from his earlier enthusiasm for reform. In 1803 he subscribed the handsome sum of £21 to the loyalist Manchester General Defence Fund in support of the Manchester and Salford Volunteers. Barnes wrote much but published little, only two sermons and his papers to the Philosophical Society. He died on 27 June 1810 at Ferneysides, Little Lever, near Bolton, and was buried on 2 July at Cross Street Chapel. His reputation with contemporaries rested on his outstanding ministerial talents, but it was his commitment to reform and his part in establishing the Literary and Philosophical Society and the Manchester Academy that historians have recognized. DAVID L. WYKES

Sources J. Bealey, *A funeral discourse, which was preached upon the death of the Rev. Thomas Barnes, D.D.* (1810) • J. Yates, *A funeral discourse occasioned by the death of the Rev. Dr Barnes* (1810) • *GM*, 1st ser., 80 (1810), 105–8 • *Monthly Repository*, 1st ser., 5 (1810), 408–12 • E. Baines and W. R. Whatton, *The history of the county palatine and duchy of Lancaster*, 3 (1836), 693; rev. edn, ed. J. Harland and B. Herford, 2 (1870), 240 • T. Baker, *Memorials of a dissenting chapel* (1884), 47–8, 145–7 [incl. complete work list] • B. Smith, ed., *Truth, liberty, religion: essays celebrating two hundred years of Manchester College* (1986) • F. Nicholson, 'The Literary and Philosophical Society, 1781–1851', *Manchester Memoirs*, 68 (1924), 99, 108, 113, 140 • minutes, Manchester Academy committee, 1781–1851, Harris Man. Oxf. • J. Priestley, letter to Theophilus Lindsey, 3 April 1789, DWL, MS 18.18

Likenesses E. Scriven, stipple, pubd 1811 (after J. Allen), BM, NPG

Barnes, Thomas (1785–1841), newspaper editor and essayist, was born in Southwark, London, on 11 September 1785, the eldest son of John Barnes (*b.* 1753), a solicitor practising in Clifford's Inn, Bloomsbury, and Tenterden, Kent, and his wife, Mary, *née* Anderson. His mother died when he was young, and he was initially raised by his grandmother with his brother, John (*b.* 1787), before entering his father's old school, Christ's Hospital, on 18 March 1796. At Christ's he was fortunate in two of his contemporaries, Leigh Hunt, who later employed him on *The Examiner*, and Thomas Mitchell, a celebrated academic. In Hunt's opinion, as a scholar Barnes was on a par with Mitchell, and, with Hunt, Barnes acquired a lifelong interest in Dante and other great Italian writers.

In 1804 Barnes went up to Pembroke College, Cambridge, as an exhibitioner and there excelled in Latin. He was an all-round sportsman of note, matching his cricket, boxing, and swimming with his classical studies. He took his degree in 1808 at the head of the senior optimes, the best degree by any Pembroke man between 1806 and 1810. On coming down Barnes hesitated between an academic career—a possible fellowship at Cambridge—and the law, but doubtless under family influence he opted for the latter, entering the Inner Temple in 1809. There he worked seriously for two years, but an all-pervading curiosity about politics tempted him from what appeared to him a life of drudgery. He had acquired an unconventional and relaxed view of life both at Cambridge and in London, and enjoyed the West End and its entertainments. He was, in the words of Denis Le Marchant, a 'complete voluptuary' both in mind and body (*History of 'The Times'*, 1.198); and dissipation took its toll on his Grecian good looks and fine physique, as did asthma and chronic rheumatism.

A spell of poverty, illness, and part-time work followed those early years of bohemianism, but another career was beckoning. Barnes became friendly with Barron Field, the theatre critic for *The Times*, who introduced him to its editor, John Walter (1776–1847), as a likely recruit to journalism. Barnes reported on law cases, the theatre, and politics with increasing frequency, and on Field's retirement succeeded him as the regular drama critic. He quickly rose in Walter's esteem and in January 1811 was appointed to the parliamentary staff. He was very much a product of his time, and with Leigh Hunt, Charles Lamb, Benjamin Haydon, William Hazlitt, and others he drank deeply of intellectual stimulation, literature, and brandy in water. A series of sketches by him of leading members of parliament is disparagingly referred to in the *Dictionary of National Biography* article on Barnes (1885) as juvenilia 'meagre in matter', but Edmund Blunden's centenary reappraisal of Barnes as a littérateur in the *TLS* (10 May 1941) set him firmly in context. These 'hasty sketches', later published as *Parliamentary Portraits* (1815), are in fact especially noteworthy, and show a powerful mind in full career. Assisting Leigh Hunt in *The Reflector* and the weekly *Examiner* between 1813 and 1814 Barnes reached his dramatic peak. He wrote strongly and incisively in the florid style of the time, the fifteen 'Portraits of authors' contributed under the pseudonym of Strada to *The Champion* being particularly noteworthy. His theatrical criticism revealed a particular sensitivity to the female mind, highlighted by his one surviving poem, 'Sapphic Verses', in Latin, whose 'utmost aim is prettiness' (published in *The Reflector*, 1811, 443).

Barnes was now ready 'to do for journalism what Beethoven did for music' (*London Mercury*, February 1935, 381) when in the autumn of 1817 he was made editor in succession to Dr John Stoddart, whose violently pro-tory leading articles he had been revising for some time. Plump and thick-set, Barnes looked older than his thirty-two years, and was of a liberal spirit and persuasion. He took a financial stake in the paper in 1819, and remained editor until his death twenty-two years later. During his editorship he justified the observation, attributed to the duke of Wellington by Charles Greville: 'Why, Barnes is the most powerful man in the country' (*History of 'The Times'*, 1.262).

On Barnes's appointment the paper was beginning to reap the advantages of Walter's rejection of bribes and subsidies. To report the news without interference was one thing; to comment freely upon it quite different. A fair judge of his own physical and intellectual resources under pressure, Barnes's strength lay in his knowledge of the people, in particular the middle classes, whose support he set out to win. The mainstreams of his policy were a staunch patriotism and a genuine compassion for the poor and the persecuted. The Peterloo massacre of August 1819 found Barnes in no mood to kowtow to any home secretary, and the general line of the paper thereafter was one of support for the whig opposition in parliament.

As editor, Barnes subordinated his personality to the public image of *The Times*. His view was that anonymous journalism was the only kind that would be read seriously. This anonymity was not abandoned on the paper until 10 January 1967, when the first staff byline appeared. Of Barnes's rivals, William Cobbett was sharpest in his resentment of 'the mighty and mysterious WE!' (*History of 'The Times'*, 1.193), for his journals *The Statesman* and *Political Register* were increasingly outclassed by the national daily's intelligence gathering. Barnes enjoyed power, 'but it was sweeter to him for its secrecy' (ibid., 1.205), and he vigorously opposed Thomas Spring Rice, chancellor of the exchequer in Lord Melbourne's second government, who urged that all journalists' names and addresses should be compulsorily registered.

Walter had fought strenuously for financial independence and freedom to procure overseas news. Barnes extended the scope of this freedom. He was quick to appreciate the opportunity for an independent newspaper to give expression and guidance to freshly awakened opinion, and swiftly appointed correspondents throughout the country. His innate liberal instincts led him to friendship with Henry Brougham, counsel for Queen Caroline, whose populist part the paper took in her trial before the House of Lords in 1820. Contact between the two men had increased after the death of Lord Liverpool in 1827, and Brougham provided much of the material upon which Barnes based his leaders thereafter. When Brougham became lord chancellor in 1830, Barnes had no compunction about requesting a government place for his barrister brother, John (Aspinall, 174).

In 1828 Barnes took a holiday in Ireland, and was so influenced by what he saw that thereafter *The Times* pressed for legislative concessions, such as Catholic emancipation, as an alternative to coercive policies. The visit removed from his mind a great deal of prejudice and false impression: 'I feel an interest for Ireland and its people which will render the support of its cause no longer a task but a cordial service' (*History of 'The Times'*, 1.278). Landlordism was attacked as a sin against justice and law, and Barnes was to rail passionately against racial bigotry.

The expansion of *The Times*'s format in 1825 was an outward sign of Barnes's increasing influence as a medium in the struggle for Catholic emancipation and parliamentary reform. By 1830 his paper was nicknamed The Thunderer (or The Turnabout to its foes), and it had become a mighty organ as 'the great, principal, and powerful advocate for Reform' (Robert Peel speaking in the House of Commons, *Hansard* 3, 22 March 1832). His greatest hour came in 1834 when the backstairs diplomacy of the incoming 'liberalized tory' administration under Sir Robert Peel pirouetted around the attitude likely to be taken by Barnes to the retrogressive duke of Wellington and others of his ilk. Spurred by his opposition to the whig new poor law, the paper took a progressive tory stance thereafter. Lord Brougham's concomitant fall from favour was illustrated on 21 March 1840, when Barnes ran the longest ever book review in *The Times*, thirteen columns (20,000 words) of invective, which carefully filleted Brougham's *Oration of Demosthenes upon the Crown*. Barnes had a steam-hammer touch when required, and though a friend of many powerful literary figures he was not seduced by them, and books received scant coverage. In one review he wrote: 'We are not in the habit of noticing the novels which are issuing in an almost continuing stream … we have little time for amusing ourselves with any romance except the extravagant romance of political life' (*History of 'The Times'*, 1.336). Space, however, was given to reviews by Thackeray between 1837 and 1840, and Barnes can take credit for the development of the 'Letters to the editor' page. The commissioned 'Runnymede' epistles on public affairs from 1836 to 1839 by Benjamin Disraeli, and the background correspondence between editor and contributor preserved at Hughenden Manor, reveal a mutual admiration and a delight in the chastisement they meted out to vanity and pretentiousness.

Henry Crabb Robinson's diary for 1820 refers to a rare trip abroad by Barnes with a travelling companion noted as a 'well-bred woman' (Hudson, 42). In fact, Barnes never married, but Mrs Dinah Mary Mondet, *née* Dunn (1792–1852), did the honours 'of his household' at 49 Nelson Square, Southwark (1821–36), and 25 Soho Square, London (1836 onwards), and was treated with remarkable respect by society, often being referred to as Mrs Barnes. Though blessed neither with children nor by the church they lived happily together for over twenty years, and Barnes in his will left her all his property. She died on 26 December 1852, eleven years after his own death on 7 May 1841 at 25 Soho Square, which *The Times* scarcely noticed: still cloaked in anonymity, his obituary ran to just twenty words. Other journals such as *Herepath's Railway and Commercial Journal* (15 May 1841) were more generous, but all were keenly aware that in the wings, awaiting his turn, was the 23-year-old John Thadeus Delane, the greatest journalist of Victoria's heyday.

Alongside Dinah Mondet and her mother, Barnes is at rest in Kensal Green cemetery. His original headstone, with its effusively phrased epitaph, has been lost, and replaced with a simple inscription by the newspaper he loved. Another memento, a plaque engraved for *The Times* by Eric Gill and designed for the Soho Square residence, was also untraceable at the end of the twentieth century.

GORDON PHILLIPS

Sources D. Hudson, *Thomas Barnes of 'The Times'* (1943) • [S. Morison and others], *The history of The Times*, 1 (1935) • E. Blunden, 'Thomas Barnes (1785–1841): literary diversions of an editor', *TLS* (10 May 1941), 226 • *DNB* • W. D. Bowman, *The story of 'The Times'* (1931) • P. Howard, *We thundered out* (1985) • O. Woods and J. Bishop, *The story of 'The Times'* (1983) • [T. Barnes], *Parliamentary portraits, or, Sketches of the public character of some of the most distinguished speakers of the House of Commons* (1815) • *The Age* [London] (9 May 1841) • *The Athenaeum* (8 May 1841), 370 • *The Examiner* (9 May 1841) • *Herepath's Railway and Commercial Journal* (15 May 1841) • *The Standard* (10 May 1841) • S. E. Koss, *The rise and fall of the political press in Britain*, 1 (1981) • A. Aspinall, *Politics and the press, c.1780–1850* (1949)

Archives Bodl. Oxf., letters to Benjamin Disraeli • News Int. RO, papers | BL, corresp. with J. C. Hobhouse, Add. MSS 36457–36458, 36464–36445, 36467, *passim* • Hughenden Manor, Buckinghamshire, Hughenden MSS, Barnes–Disraeli corresp. • priv. coll., letters to Denis Le Merchant

Likenesses G. Hayter, miniature, *c.*1820, NPG • W. Newton, miniature, 1832, Times Newspapers Ltd, London; repro. in *The history of 'The Times', 1785–1841* (1935), frontispiece • W. Newton, miniature on ivory, 1832, NPG • sketch, 1837 • G. Hayter, group portrait, oils (*The trial of Queen Caroline, 1820*), NPG

Barnes, Sir Thomas James (1888–1964), lawyer and public official, was born on 21 March 1888 at Wilmslow, Cheshire, the only son of Thomas Barnes and his wife, Esther Mary Pither. His father was a clerk attached to the Chancery Division of the High Court of Justice. After education at Mercers' School, Barnes was articled for five years to Robert John Ball, a partner in the firm of H. C. Coote and Ball, solicitors in the City of London, which specialized in shipping matters. He was admitted a solicitor in 1911. He did not take out a practising certificate, but just before his admission he followed his father into the Lord Chancellor's Department. He joined as a temporary clerk and later became a principal clerk in the Chancery registrars' office. Shortly after the outbreak of war in 1914 he joined the Royal Naval Volunteer Reserve. He became a chief petty officer in 1915 and sub-lieutenant in 1916, serving in the Dover patrol. His ship was blown up in 1916 and as a result of this experience he developed a lasting form of neurosis and was discharged in May 1917. In the following month he was lent by the Lord Chancellor's Department to the Ministry of Shipping legal adviser's department and within two years he had become the legal adviser. In 1920 he was appointed solicitor to the Board of Trade at the early age of thirty-two.

In 1934 Barnes was appointed procurator-general and Treasury solicitor, a position which he retained for nearly twenty years. He was the first solicitor ever to be appointed to these offices and he proved to be the outstanding government lawyer of his generation. During his time there was an enormous increase in the work of his office. At the beginning of the war new departments were set up for which the Treasury solicitor acted; many of them remained for the rest of his term of office.

As a general rule Barnes was content to let his staff get on with their allotted work with the minimum of supervision. He did, however, take personal and active charge over a number of matters of special importance and difficulty. He directed a number of inquiries under the Tribunals of Inquiry (Evidence) Act, 1921, the best-known being the budget leak in 1936 and the Lynskey tribunal in 1948. During the war he was particularly successful in settling difficult problems of compensation arising from the requisitioning of land and other property by the armed forces and government departments. Towards the end of the war he was actively concerned in the arrangements for setting up the Nuremberg tribunal to try the major war criminals.

Barnes had always been a formidable champion of the crown's position in the courts, but after the war he played a leading part in the Crown Proceedings Act, 1947, which made the crown liable to all the ordinary forms of action. The proposals for this reform had languished for twenty years or more, but he realized that the time had arrived for a big step forward, and he threw himself wholeheartedly into preparing the legislation, and later into making it work smoothly.

While Treasury solicitor, Barnes served on a number of important committees, including the Evershed committee on Supreme Court practice and procedure (1947–53). To all these problems he brought a lively intelligence. He worked very quickly and had an astonishing resourcefulness in solving intractable problems. He never dwelt on difficulties, but turned his acute and practical mind to the task of finding a solution. He had a real talent for negotiation. He always disclaimed an academic knowledge of the law, but he had an extremely tenacious memory and acquired a fund of legal wisdom and experience which was always available and to the point. It was a delight to work with him. He was always accessible and informal. If a colleague brought him a problem, he would listen intently, pick up the problem quickly, and then make some helpful suggestions, often referring to a precedent in the office or to some decided case which on examination proved to be exactly apposite. It was all done quickly and decisively and with charm and humour. He generously encouraged others. He had a good political sense and his advice was essentially practical. All these qualities endeared him to the ministers and departmental officials for whom he worked, and to his own staff.

Barnes retired in 1953 and became a part-time director of the Prudential Assurance Company. But the work did not appeal to him and he soon resigned. In 1954 he joined the Monopolies and Restrictive Practices Commission and remained a member until the end of 1959, when he retired on the grounds of ill health. While Treasury solicitor he had frequently been called on to advise on ecclesiastical matters. After his retirement, right up to the time of his death, he took a leading part in revising the canon law of the Church of England.

Barnes's main recreation was golf, which he much enjoyed. He had been brought up at Sunningdale, and for most of his life he was a leading member of Sunningdale and Swinley Forest golf clubs. Between the wars he played to a single-figure handicap, and was a difficult man to beat.

On 24 May 1924 Barnes married Elsie Margaret Clover, a widow, daughter of John Alexander, formerly chief clerk of Bow Street police court; they had no children. He was knighted in 1927, appointed KCB in 1938, and promoted GCB in 1948. He died at St Bartholomew's Hospital, London, on 4 February 1964 and his widow later in the same year. ROBERT SPEED, *rev.*

Sources *The Times* (6 Feb 1964) • private information (1981) • personal knowledge (1981)

Wealth at death £42,501: probate, 22 April 1964, *CGPLA Eng. & Wales*

Barnes, William (1801–1886), poet and philologist, was born on 22 February 1801, in a cob and thatch cottage, Rushay Farm, on Bagber Common, near Sturminster Newton, Dorset, the sixth of seven children of John Barnes (*bap.* 1762, *d.* 1846), and his wife, Grace, *née* Scott (*bap.* 1760, *d.* 1816). His father was of a farming family much reduced in circumstances, and was himself increasingly dependent on wage labour. His mother had been brought up with three sisters by her young widowed mother and in May 1789 marked with a cross the marriage register at Lydlinch church (later the subject of one of William's notable poems). His siblings were John, William, Charles, James, Anne, and Henry, he being given the same name as an older brother who died young (1791–1800).

William Barnes's education began in the village dame-school and continued at the Church of England endowed school in Sturminster Newton until he was thirteen. Through his abilities, especially his handwriting, Barnes was selected by Thomas Dashwood to join his solicitor's practice as an engrossing clerk in 1814. As a schoolboy and

William Barnes (1801–1886), by George Stuckey, *c.*1870

after he spent much time, perhaps living there for a time, at Pentridge Farm with his father's sister Ann and her husband Charles Rabbetts (or Roberts), the originals of his much loved aunt and uncle in several of his early poems.

How happy uncle us'd to be
O' zummer time, when aunt an' he
O' Zunday evenens, eärm in eärm,
Did walk about their tiny farm,
While birds did zing an' gnats did zwarm,
Drough grass a'most above their knees,
An' roun' by hedges an' by trees
Wi' leafy boughs a-swayen.
('Uncle an' Aunt', *Poems of Rural Life in the Dorset Dialect*, 1844)

Indeed, much of his rural poetry looked back to the good times of his youth, when agriculture was prosperous. The Rabbetts were adversely affected by the enclosure of the Bagber commons and even more so by the agricultural recession after the Napoleonic wars, Barnes being much affected by their distress on losing their farm.

Barnes himself was driven by a determination to better himself and even to reverse the family's pattern of decline. Thomas Hardy later observed of him, 'A more notable example of self-help has seldom been recorded' ('The Rev-William Barnes, B.D.', *The Athenaeum*, 16 Oct 1886, 501–2). It was very revealing that in 1847, in an affluent period of his life, Barnes derived great pleasure from buying two fields at Bagber, which he rented to a farmer. In owning land again he kept faith with his forefathers.

In 1818, after the death of Dashwood and his aunt and uncle's loss of their farm, Barnes moved to Dorchester where he worked for another solicitor, Thomas Coombs. He shared lodgings over Hazard's pastry shop in High West Street with William Gilbert Carey. Carey later informed Barnes in 1823 that his former teacher in Mere had died, leaving a vacancy, an opportunity which Barnes took up. In Dorchester, Barnes worked hard on self-improvement, engaging in music, engraving, learning languages, writing poetry, and classical reading. In 1822 he published *Orra: a Lapland Tale*, a poem illustrated by his own engravings.

Barnes's life was transformed in 1818 when he saw a girl alight from a stagecoach at the King's Arms Hotel. She was Julia Miles (1805–1852), then thirteen (not sixteen as suggested by his daughter's biography), the daughter of James Camfield Miles, a supervisor of the excise. Barnes's desire to prove he would be a suitable husband for her led him to embark on his career as a schoolmaster. She was the focus of much of his finest poetry, from a small collection, *Poetical Pieces*, which he had printed in 1820, to the verse written after her death. 'The Wife A-Lost' begins

Since I noo mwore do zee your feäce,
Up steäirs or down below,
I'll zit me in the lwonesome pleäce,
Where flat-bough'd beech do grow;
Below the beeches' bough, my love,
Where you did never come,
An' I don't look to meet ye now,
As I do look at hwome.
(*Hwomely Rhymes*, 1858)

Barnes taught in Mere from 1823 to 1835 with mixed financial success. Between 1823 and 1825 he taught on his own in the old schoolroom in the Market House, achieving a precarious livelihood. After his marriage on 9 July 1827, with Julia's organizing ability behind it, their relocated school at Chantry House flourished. There the school was mixed sex and partly boarding, with Julia teaching the girls and managing the domestic side. Barnes himself, already a polymath, expanded his teaching beyond reading, writing, arithmetic, grammar, geography, Latin, music, and drawing to a range of classical, modern European, and oriental languages. In these years he wrote on a broad range of topics for the *Dorset County Chronicle*, the *Gentleman's Magazine*, and *Hone's Yearbook*. He also published two mathematical booklets in 1834 and 1835, encouraged by his acquaintanceship with Major-General Henry Shrapnel, one of several scholarly gentlemen from whom he learned much. From early in 1834 he began writing the poems which were published as *Poems of Rural Life in the Dorset Dialect* (1844). In addition to developing the school and his scholarly and craft endeavours, he and Julia enjoyed music and their garden and began a family with Laura Liebe (1829–1918), Julia Eliza (1832–1915), and Julius (1834–1837).

At his wife's prompting, Barnes moved to Dorchester in 1835 to achieve greater success and social standing as a schoolmaster. He established a boys' school in Durngate, for boarders and day pupils. The prospectus for the school declared that Barnes would prepare pupils for commercial, mathematical, or learned professions, naval or military colleges, or universities, and, in listing his expertise, he included mention of his 'papers on classical and general learning which he published in periodicals and otherwise'. After two years in which he worked strenuously to master sufficient of his broad curriculum to teach and inspire the interest of his pupils, the school was relocated at Norman's House, South Street. From 1837, with Julia and her mother efficiently running the domestic side of the school, the family prospered. Barnes entered for a part-time degree of bachelor of divinity at St John's College, Cambridge, requiring a minimum of ten years' enrolment. He resumed his writing for the *Gentleman's Magazine* and published several educational booklets. He and Julia expanded their musical and other social interests and their family grew with the births of Lucy (1837–1902) [*see* Baxter, Lucy], Isabel (*b.* 1838), William Miles (1840–1916), and Egbert (1843–1877).

The mid-1840s brought Barnes success wider than solely as a schoolmaster. *Poems in the Dorset Dialect* (1844) was well received, reaching a fifth edition by 1866. It was followed by *Poems, Partly of Rural Life (in National English)* in 1846, *Hwomely Rhymes: a Second Collection of Dorset Poems* in 1850, *Third Collection of Poems in Dorset Dialect* in 1863, and *Poems of Rural Life in Common English* in 1868. On 28 February 1847 Barnes was ordained at Salisbury Cathedral with responsibility for the donative living of Whitcombe, offered to Barnes by Colonel Dawson Damer of Came House. Also, in October 1845, Barnes became one of the first joint secretaries (1845–58) of the Dorset County Museum which was formed in anticipation of the impact of the projected South-Western Railway on Dorchester and the surrounding area. This office reflected his standing by this time among the local scholarly society. This period was the apex of Barnes's life, not least because of the reputation as a poet that his 1844 collection secured him.

In the summer of 1847 Barnes entered his last phase as a schoolmaster. He relocated his school in the house of the late Mr Hawkins at 40 South Street, which he purchased for £700. His hopes for the new venture were dashed by the death from breast cancer of his wife, Julia, on 21 June 1852, compounded a year later by the death of her mother, the effective domestic manager of the school. His school declined while praise for his poetry increased. In April 1861 Palmerston's government awarded him a civil-list pension of £70 a year. Barnes was rescued financially in 1862 when Captain Seymour Dawson Damer offered him the living of Winterborne Came. Barnes closed down his school just when renewed success might have come, as a pupil, T. W. Hooper Tolbort, topped the list of the Indian Civil Service examination—but by this time Barnes was pleased to become rector with an income of £200 per annum.

In his last phase as a schoolteacher Barnes continued to write and to lecture. He wrote articles for *Macmillan's Magazine* and *Fraser's Magazine* as well as for the *Retrospective Review* and *The Reader*. Some of these essays and several of his small books, such as *Notes on Ancient Britain and the Britons* (1858), *Views of Labour and Gold* (1859), and *Early England and the Saxon English* (1869) stemmed from lectures. He had given lectures to the Weymouth and Sturminster Newton literary and scientific institutes (in November 1851 and January 1852) before Julia's death. As Trevor Hearl's research has shown, from the time of the foundation of the Dorchester Working Men's Mutual Improvement Society in late 1855 he gave nearly 200 lectures or readings to similar bodies over twenty-five years, most of which were either on history or of poetry. From 1856 to 1870 he gave between eight and twenty lectures each year between October and March. These were often extremely effective and well-attended occasions (for which he was paid only travel expenses). He retired from lecturing in 1880.

While rector of Winterborne Came, Barnes continued to research into philology. In 1854 he had published *A Philological Grammar*, with the subtitle indicating that it compared English with 'more than sixty languages'. Thereafter, he published *TIW, or, A View of the Roots and Stems of the English as a Teutonic Tongue* (1862), *A Grammar and Glossary of the Dorset Dialect* (1863), *An Outline of English Speech-Craft* (1878), and *An Outline of Rede-Craft (Logic) with English Wording* (1880). Barnes's philological work was marked by encyclopaedic reading and a rather eccentric and lonely campaign to de-Latinize and to Saxonize the English language. Barnes's philology, as Valerie Shepherd has argued, was rooted in notions of linguistic purity, and to return to purity involved discovering the language's roots. This belief reinforced his interest in the Dorset dialect which, though unfashionable among some well-to-do, he felt had its own roots in an Anglo-Saxon dialect. However, his efforts to substitute words such as 'breath-sounds' for 'vowels' predictably were as ill-fated as Cnut's alleged attempts to turn back the tide.

The philological books were not the only ones to combine heroic feats of learning with a mix of common sense and some eccentricity. This was very much the case with *Views of Labour and Gold* which, as Alan Chedzoy has observed, displays an approach whereby clear definitions of economic concepts are deemed to explain economic matters and where analysis gives way to a rag-bag of information and views. Barnes's prose writings were often infused with Christian kindness, critical views of capitalism and industrialization, and much harking back to earlier rural golden ages and to Saxon and earlier times.

As a rector Barnes exhibited piety and benevolence as well as an eccentric, old-fashioned style of dress. He was assiduous in carrying out his duties, and secured the help of two of his daughters in visiting parishioners. His health crumbled from January 1884 and he died in the rectory on 7 October 1886. Thomas Hardy, who attended Barnes's funeral on 11 October 1886, at the Winterborne Came churchyard, commemorated it with a notable poem, 'The Last Signal'.

Barnes was a very kindly man, highly considerate of others and in later life deemed 'the perfection of old-world courtesy'. He was scholarly to a fault: much of his mid-life financial success was due to his wife and mother-in-law. After their deaths he cultivated an image of a scholar of a bygone age, in his buckled shoes and knee-breeches, eccentric capes, and hats. He came near to being a 'jack of all trades and master of none'. Yet, at his best as a schoolteacher he commanded his pupils' interest and admiration. He was also the writer of much enduring verse.

Much of Barnes's finest verse is that written in dialect, which he wrote after and before writing poetry in standard English. The dialect verse more often has music and colour, a good portion of the verse in standard English appearing flat in comparison. His best verse, whether or not in dialect, combined considerable technical skill with an eye for images which acutely revealed much about the countryside and its people. For the Victorians, in a rapidly urbanizing and industrializing society, Barnes's skilful and attractive rustic verse had a particularly powerful appeal.

During his lifetime, Barnes's poetry received national recognition. His admirers included Matthew Arnold, Robert Browning, Edmund Gosse, Gerard Manley Hopkins, Francis Palgrave, Coventry Patmore, Sir Arthur Quiller Couch, and Alfred Tennyson as well as Thomas Hardy. For Hardy, Barnes provided the stimulus of a local skilled practitioner of poetry, and Hardy learned much from Barnes. 'His ingenious internal rhymes, his subtle juxtaposition of kindred lippings and vowel-sounds, show a fastidiousness in word-selection' (preface to *Select Poems*). Hardy demonstrated his ability to emulate and go beyond Barnes in his poem on Barnes's funeral, 'The Last Signal: a Memory of William Barnes'. In Barnes's later years many literary figures made a pilgrimage to Came rectory to visit him. Since his death there has been substantial interest in his work, with selections of his poetry edited by such literary figures as Thomas Hardy, Geoffrey Grigson, Robert Nye, and Andrew Motion. Barnes is known to generations by his poem 'Linden Lea', set to music by Ralph Vaughan Williams. Interest in his poetry was given firm foundations in 1962 with the superb, scholarly two-volume edition of his poems edited by Dr Bernard Jones and published by the Southern Illinois University Press. Like Hardy he is honoured in Dorchester with a statue, and there have been two William Barnes societies, the second flourishing from 1983. By the end of the twentieth century, Barnes had apparently secured a place among the widely accepted poets of English literature.

CHRIS WRIGLEY

Sources L. Baxter, *The life of William Barnes, poet and philologist* (1887) • G. Dugdale, *William Barnes of Dorset* (1953) • T. W. Hearl, *William Barnes the schoolmaster* (1966) • A. Chedzoy, *William Barnes: a life of the Dorset poet* (1985) • *The poems of William Barnes*, ed. B. Jones, 2 vols. (1962) • T. W. Hearl, 'William Barnes' family circle', *Proceedings of the William Barnes Society*, 1 (1983–8) • D. Ashdown, 'Researching William Barnes', *Proceedings of the William Barnes Society*, 1 (1983–8) • I. Jones, 'Some notes on William Barnes' family in Sturminster Newton', *Proceedings of the William Barnes Society*, 1 (1983–8) • T. Hearl, 'William Barnes and working men's institutes', *Proceedings of the William Barnes Society*, 2 (1989–92) • C. Wrigley, ed., *William Barnes: the Dorset poet* (1984) • C. Wrigley, 'William Barnes and the social problem', *Proceedings of the Dorset Natural History and Archaeological Society*, 99 (1977) • P. Keane, 'Prophet in the wilderness: Rev. William Barnes as an adult educator', *Proceedings of the Dorset Natural History and Archaeological Society*, 100 (1978) • C. Lindgren, 'Images of William Barnes', *William Barnes 1801–1886: a handbook*, ed. B. Jones (1986) • A. Chedzoy, 'William Barnes: antiquarian', *Notes and Queries for Somerset and Dorset*, 32 (1986–90), 479–82 • W. T. Levy, *William Barnes: the man and the poems* (1960) • E. M. Forster, 'William Barnes', *Two cheers for democracy* (1951) • *Select poems of William Barnes*, ed. T. Hardy (1908) • *Selected poems of William Barnes*, ed. G. Grigson (1950) • P. Larkin, 'The poetry of William Barnes', *Required writing* (1983) • V. Shepherd, *The poems of William Barnes* (1998) • Dorset County Museum, Dorchester, William Barnes MSS • L. Keen, *William Barnes: the Somerset engravings* (1989) • F. Austin and B. Jones, *The language and craft of William Barnes, English poet and philologist (1801–1886)* (2002)

Archives Dorset County Museum, Dorchester, autobiography, drawings, letters, and papers • Hunt. L., letters • St John Cam., autobiographical notes | BL, letters to Macmillan & Co., Add MSS 55253–55255

Likenesses attrib. Barnes, watercolour drawing, *c*.1815, Dorset County Museum, Dorchester • J. Thorne, oils, *c*.1845, Dorset County Museum, Dorchester • G. Stuckey, oils, *c*.1870, NPG [*see illus.*] • J. Leslie, two watercolour drawings, *c*.1884, Dorset County Museum, Dorchester • C. E. Barnes, oils (as an old man), Dorset County Museum, Dorchester • W. Barnes, self-portrait, oils, Dorset County Museum, Dorchester • E. R. Mullins, statue, St Peter's Church, Dorchester; model, Dorset County Museum, Dorchester • oils, Dorset County Museum, Dorchester • photograph (as an old man), Dorset County Museum, Dorchester • watercolour drawing (as a young man), Dorset County Museum, Dorchester

Wealth at death £922 10*s*. 5*d*.: probate, 19 Nov 1886, *CGPLA Eng. & Wales*

Barnes, William Emery (1859–1939), Church of England clergyman and biblical scholar, was born in London on 26 May 1859, the younger son of Samuel Emery Barnes, wine merchant, of London, and his wife, Charlotte Ann Noss. He was educated at Islington proprietary school and in 1877 went to Peterhouse, Cambridge; he gained a first class in the 1881 theological tripos, as well as the Jeremie prize (Septuagint), the Crosse scholarship (divinity), and the Tyrwhitt scholarship (Hebrew); he became BD (1891), and DD (1897). In 1883 he was ordained to a curacy at St John's Church, Waterloo Road, Lambeth, in London, and he returned to Cambridge in 1885 as lecturer in Hebrew at Clare College. Afterwards he was lecturer in Hebrew and divinity at Peterhouse, as well as a fellow, from 1889; he was college chaplain from 1885 to 1904, Hulsean professor of divinity at Cambridge from 1901 to 1934, and dean of Peterhouse from 1920 to 1921. In 1934 he retired to live at Canterbury, continuing, however, as warden of the Central Society of Sacred Study for the diocese of Canterbury, taking classes and giving occasional lectures. He married on 27 March 1890 Georgina de Horne (1847/8–1917), daughter of Alexander Bevington, underwriter of Lloyd's. They had no children.

Barnes was a fine scholar in Hebrew, rabbinic, and Syriac, and he had a working knowledge of several other languages. When pressed in his latter years to begin the study of Persian, he replied that he already kept seven languages going and could not add another. His most substantial contributions were in Syriac. After the death of R. L. Bensly, Barnes edited his unfinished *Fourth Book of Maccabees and Kindred Documents in Syriac* (1895), writing the general introduction and translating four of the six documents included. He published an *apparatus criticus* to the Peshitta text of Chronicles (in 1897); an edition of Samuel Lee's Syriac Pentateuch (in collaboration, in 1914); and an edition of the Peshitta text of the Psalms (1904). For younger students he produced editions of Chronicles

(1899), Kings (1908), and Haggai, Zechariah, and Malachi (1917) in the Cambridge Bible.

As joint editor with C. H. Turner of the *Journal of Theological Studies* at its inception in 1899, Barnes set a high standard and thereafter contributed to it various articles, notes, and reviews. He remained joint editor (from 1902 with Henry Austin Wilson) until 1903.

Always averse to controversy and unwilling to commit himself, Barnes accepted the new learning of his time and the new approach to the literary and historical study of the Old Testament, but used it very cautiously. Much of the new literature he regarded as 'wild' and he disliked intensely the way some scholars cut texts about; but he evaluated their arguments before rejecting them. With his strong conservative and devotional tendencies and his respect for tradition he was happiest in drawing out the moral and spiritual values of the books on which he commented, as he did in his edition of the Psalms for the Westminster Commentaries (1931).

Bishop Arthur Mesac Knight, a younger contemporary of Barnes at school, remembered him then as 'a trim and somewhat prim little figure, precise, careful, but with strength of character … and he had his own opinions'. This remained true of Barnes all through his later life. Gentle, quiet, sincere, kindly, and mildly humorous, he was a good friend to many different people and enjoyed gathering with them at luxurious lunches in Peterhouse. As a teacher he was painstaking and straightforward, anxious not to be above the heads of his pupils.

Of small stature and slight physique, Barnes was keenly interested in warfare. In his early days he joined the university rifle volunteers (later the OTC), when it had little support, and almost to the end of his time in Cambridge he went to the butts to fire. Military history, strategy, and tactics were his hobby, and in discussions of them in the combination room he sometimes corrected the master of his college, Field Marshal Lord Birdwood. He also favoured the revision of English spelling, on which he wrote to *The Times* and other papers, and he liked to make excursions into other fields of study, with something of his own to illustrate the subject. While visiting Exeter to lecture, he died there, at Mowbray House, on 17 August 1939.

J. F. BETHUNE-BAKER, *rev.* ROGER T. STEARN

Sources *The Times* (19 Aug 1939) · private information (1949) · personal knowledge (1949) · *WWW, 1941–50* · Venn, *Alum. Cant.* · H. Strachan, *History of Cambridge University officers training corps* (1976) · m. cert. · *CGPLA Eng. & Wales* (1939)
Archives NL Scot., corresp. with publishers
Likenesses F. Alliot, clay medallion, 1911, Divinity School, Cambridge · W. Rothenstein, drawing, 1933, Peterhouse, Cambridge
Wealth at death £12,051 2s. 2d.: probate, 31 Oct 1939, *CGPLA Eng. & Wales*

Barnet, John (*d.* **1373**), bishop of Ely, is first mentioned as prebendary of Chamberlainwood in St Paul's Cathedral, London, in 1346. He was ordained priest in the diocese of Winchester in 1348 and became rector of Westwell, Kent, in 1348 and also of East Dereham, Norfolk, in 1350, as well as holding canonries at Norton, co. Durham, and Lichfield Cathedral. Throughout the 1350s he maintained close links with the diocese of London, serving as vicar-general of Bishop Michael Northburgh (*d.* 1361) in 1354 and, after a possible unsuccessful election as dean of St Paul's in 1353, becoming archdeacon of London in 1356. As BCL, probably of Oxford, he was well equipped for a career in royal diplomacy, and had presumably been working in this capacity for some time before receiving personal summonses to great councils (from 1352) and parliaments (from 1355). He took an active part in the Anglo-French negotiations at Calais in 1360 and was leading diplomatic missions by 1361–2.

Barnet's appointment, by papal provision, as bishop of Worcester on 10 January 1362 was clearly approved by Edward III, who in February 1363 made him treasurer, a post he held until January 1369. It was unusual for one with no previous experience in royal finance to be put in charge of the main financial office of state, and Barnet's custodianship was not altogether successful: there was a serious scandal in the exchequer in 1365, when a clerk was alleged to have been embezzling funds. On the other hand, Barnet may have been responsible for the innovative financial statements, attempting to set out revenue and expenses, which were drawn up in the exchequer for the year 1363/4. He certainly retained the king's favour, and was translated first to the bishopric of Bath and Wells on 24 November 1363, and then to the wealthy bishopric of Ely on 14 December 1366. He retired from royal service after the resumption of war with France in 1369, and died at Hatfield, Hertfordshire, on 7 June 1373. His will was proved on 13 June. He was buried on the south side of the high altar at Ely, where the grey marble base of his tomb still survives.

W. M. ORMROD

Sources Emden, *Oxf.* · *Fasti Angl., 1300–1541* · W. M. Ormrod, *The reign of Edward III* (1990) · Tout, *Admin. hist.* · J. R. L. Highfield, 'The English hierarchy in the reign of Edward III', *TRHS*, 5th ser., 6 (1956), 115–38

Barnetson, William Denholm, Baron Barnetson (**1917–1981**), newspaper proprietor and television executive, was born in Edinburgh on 21 March 1917, the eldest child in the family of three sons and one daughter of William Barnetson, estate agent, of London and Edinburgh, and his wife, Ella Grigor, daughter of Dr Moir, medical practitioner, of Buccleuch Place, Edinburgh. He was educated at the Royal High School, Edinburgh, and at Edinburgh University. Study there was interrupted by the nineteen-year-old Barnetson's decision to become a freelance correspondent reporting on the Spanish Civil War. From Spain he returned to university and then in the space of one week in July 1940 he married Joan Fairley, daughter of William Fairley Davidson, publican, of Edinburgh, and Agustina Bjarnarson of Iceland, took his MA degree, and began service in the army.

Throughout the Second World War Barnetson served in anti-aircraft command, and reached the rank of major. As the war came to an end he was seconded for special duty on the reorganization of West German newspaper and book publishing in the British zone. He was responsible for helping to launch *Die Welt* and for choosing as a suitable person to be its subsequent publisher an ambitious young German—Axel Springer, who was to become one of West Germany's most influential newspaper proprietors. After returning to Edinburgh he joined the *Edinburgh Evening News* and from 1948 to 1961 was successively leader-writer, editor, and general manager—combining these duties with extramural lecturing at the university, and speaking and debating on radio and television.

It was Barnetson's habit to go into his office early each morning to thump out his leaders, articles, and speeches on his own typewriter—a habit he never forsook. On one such occasion, there walked into the deserted office a passenger, fresh from the night sleeper from King's Cross, who announced himself as Harley Drayton. This was the financier who already ruled a formidable commercial empire and was about to expand his interests in publishing. In Barnetson, Drayton recognized a man of integrity, a working journalist capable of moving into the management of a newspaper empire. A famous partnership had been born.

In 1962 Barnetson was made a director of United Newspapers. In the next four years he drew up a strategic plan for the morning, evening, and weekly provincial papers United already owned in Preston, Leeds, Doncaster, Northampton, and elsewhere. On Drayton's death in 1966 Barnetson succeeded him as chairman and, within three years, doubled the size of United by the acquisition of Yorkshire Post Newspapers, as well as acquiring *Punch* magazine. He recognized the value to his companies of good contacts with the professional and commercial worlds, and in the 1970s the Bill Barnetson lunches at the Savoy, attended by royalty, archbishops, cabinet ministers, diplomats, financiers, academics, and fellow newspapermen became an established part of the London social scene.

Meanwhile his interests and his directorships continued to grow. From 1976 he was deputy chairman of British Electric Traction; he sat on the boards of Hill Samuel, Trusthouse Forte, Argus Press, and the Press Association. From 1973 he was a member of the *Times* Trust; when Atlantic Richfield acquired *The Observer* in 1976 he became chairman, and from 1979 he was an influential chairman of Thames Television. At one time, reference books listed forty-two organizations with which he was associated.

One of his outstanding contributions to the newspaper world was achieved in the years 1968–79 when he was chairman of Reuters. During this time the agency's turnover rose from £6 million to £73 million and the foundations were laid for Reuters's technological development from a simple news agency into the worldwide business and economic information service that catered for almost every financial market in the world. Reuters brought out to the full the visionary, the shrewd manager, and the leader in Barnetson.

Amid all this activity he found time to spend weekends with his wife and family of one son and three daughters, at their home, Broom, in Crowborough, Sussex, where he could enjoy his books and his gardening. But there were increasing demands on his energies: the Open University, Press Council, English National Opera, Queen's Silver Jubilee Appeal, and St Bride's Church in Fleet Street received his personal support and encouragement. And through it all, the thumping of the typewriter keys and the puffing at a king-size briar pipe went on. Ceaseless activity seemed to suit him. For a somewhat bulky person he was surprisingly light of step, and this lent a pronounced sense of cheerful urgency to his movements. His working philosophy in dealing with all his many interests was simple: 'I leave the man on the spot to get on with the job. But he must know that I am available here all the time' (private information). Barnetson was knighted in 1972 and made a life peer in 1975. He died in Westminster Hospital on 12 March 1981. EDWARD PICKERING, *rev.*

Sources *The Times* (13 March 1981) · *Daily Telegraph* (13 March 1981) · G. Schofield, *The men that carry the news: a history of United Newspapers Ltd* (1975) · personal knowledge (1990) · *WWW* · *CGPLA Eng. & Wales* (1981) · private information (1990)

Wealth at death £483,898: administration, 22 May 1981, *CGPLA Eng. & Wales*

Barnett, Curtis (*d.* 1746), naval officer, was reputedly the son of Benjamin Barnett, a first lieutenant in the *Stirling Castle*, who was drowned when that vessel foundered in the great storm of 27 November 1703. Very little is known of Barnett's early career and connections, other than that he served in the Mediterranean in Sir George Byng's squadron during 1718. On 4 December 1718 Byng made Barnett lieutenant of the *Loo*. On 1 May 1723 he was made second lieutenant of the *Nottingham*, but on 19 November 1725 he became third lieutenant on this ship. Earlier in the year (13 May) he married Elizabeth, daughter of Benjamin Rosewell; the couple had two sons, Benjamin and Charles.

On 1 February 1726 Barnett was appointed third lieutenant in the *Torbay*, Sir Charles Wager's flagship in the Baltic cruise of that year. During this cruise Barnett appears to have served on the personal staff of the admiral. On 16 July 1728 he was appointed first lieutenant in the *Canterbury* and on 1 July 1730 master and commander of the sloop *Spence* on the coast of Ireland. On 26 January 1731 he became captain of the frigate *Bideford*, which was fitting out for the Mediterranean as part of the fleet under Sir Charles Wager. In October he was at Leghorn, and was sent by Sir Charles with dispatches for the king of Spain, then at Seville.

On 24 November 1731, during his return through the straits, Barnett encountered a French merchant ship, which fired at the *Bideford*, taking her for a Barbary corsair, and was forced to apologize after a short action. Barnett continued in the *Bideford* on the Mediterranean station for three years, returning home in August 1734. On 26 August he was commissioned captain of the *Nottingham* (60 guns) which served as guardship in the Downs. He moved to the *Dragon* (60 guns) in mid-1737 and continued in the channel for some time after the declaration of war with Spain in 1739 before being sent in October 1740 to join Admiral Nicholas Haddock off Cadiz.

In July 1741 Barnett was detached with the *Folkestone* and *Feversham* to cruise in the straits; on the night of 25 July he

Curtis Barnett (*d.* 1746), by John Ellys, *c.*1743–4

chased and came up with three French men-of-war, the *Borée* (60 guns), *Aquilon* (40 guns), and *Flore* (26 guns) homeward bound from the West Indies. Barnett hailed the *Aquilon*; she replied they were French from Martinique, but Barnett suspected that they were Spaniards. After repeated warnings, he fired into the *Aquilon*; she replied with a broadside, and a sharp action began. The *Folkestone* only was in company; but about daybreak the *Feversham* came up, when the Frenchmen brought to, and hoisted their colours. Barnett sent a boat on board the *Borée*, to explain the exchange had been precipitated by the captain of the *Aquilon*. After some discussion the ships separated.

Early in 1742 Vice-Admiral Haddock was compelled by ill health to hand over command of the fleet to Rear-Admiral Richard Lestock. A difference of opinion between Lestock and Barnett gave rise to a correspondence (Charnock, 4.212–21), which is of interest in the light of Lestock's subsequent behaviour at the battle off Toulon on 11 February 1744. It would appear that in manoeuvring the fleet, the *Dragon* and some of the other ships had not got into their station as quickly as Lestock had wished, and on 14 April 1742 he reprimanded their respective captains. Barnett questioned the validity of Lestock's criticism which led to his being accused by the rear-admiral of incompetent and unpatriotic conduct.

A few months later the *Dragon* returned to England. In March 1743 Barnett was appointed to the *Prince Frederick* for channel service, and was with the fleet under Sir John Norris when the French appeared off Dungeness on 24 February 1744. A few weeks later he was appointed to the *Deptford* (50 guns), and made commodore of a small squadron ordered to the East Indies to attack French trade. With this he put to sea on 1 May 1744, and on 26 May he anchored at Porto Praya in the Cape Verde Islands. There was already in the bay a Spanish privateer, which at first Barnett had no intention of disturbing out of respect for the neutrality of Portugal; but after being informed that this privateer had taken and burnt some British vessels he sent his boats on board and took possession of her and her prizes. He restored the prizes to their former owners, and sold the privateer to the Portuguese for 1200 dollars. After they had passed St Paul Island the squadron was divided, part of it making for the Strait of Malacca. Barnett, in the *Deptford*, with the *Preston*, went through the Strait of Sunda to Batavia, and thence for a cruise in the Strait of Banca, where, on 25 January 1745, they encountered, and after some resistance captured, three large French East-Indiamen, richly laden from China. The governor of Batavia readily bought the three ships for £92,000 which was at once shared out among the companies of the *Deptford* and the *Preston*.

This success effectively saw an end to the war in the Indian seas, and Barnett spent 1745 cruising in the Bay of Bengal, between Ceylon and the mouths of the River Ganges. On 2 May 1746, a few weeks before the appearance of a French squadron on the station, Barnett died, after a short illness, on board the *Harwich* at Fort St David, Madras.

J. K. Laughton, *rev.* Richard Harding

Sources PRO, ADM 1/1476–1479 · PRO, ADM 1/160 · PRO, ADM 6/13–15 · PRO, ADM 36/3606 · J. Charnock, ed., *Biographia navalis*, 6 vols. (1794–8) · PRO, PROB 11/755, sig. 171
Archives NMM, official letter-book · PRO, ADM MSS
Likenesses J. Ellys, oils, *c.*1743–1744, NMM [*see illus.*]
Wealth at death property: will, PRO, PROB 11/755, sig. 171

Barnett, Sir Denis Hensley Fulton (1906–1992), air force officer, was born in Dunedin, New Zealand, on 11 February 1906, son of Sir Louis Edward Barnett CMG (*d.* 1946), a surgeon, and his wife, Mabel Violet, *née* Fulton. He was educated at Christ's College, Christchurch, New Zealand, and Clare College, Cambridge, where he graduated BA in 1929, proceeding MA in 1935.

At Cambridge, Barnett learnt to fly with the university air squadron and was commissioned into the RAF officer reserve. He received a permanent commission in the RAF in 1929, rising to the rank of flight lieutenant by 1934. In these early years he had periods as an instructor and had some experience of what was then the fledgeling art of army co-operation. By the late 1930s, however, he was committed to bombers, and in 1938 was placed in command of 84 squadron, which operated antiquated Vickers Vincent biplanes from Shaybah, Iraq. On 22 April 1939 Barnett married Pamela (*b.* 1918/19), daughter of the late Sir Allen John Grant, engineer, at Christchurch, Sheffield. They had a son and two daughters.

Throughout the Second World War Barnett served with Bomber Command. With the fall of France in 1940 he was given command of 40 squadron of Blenheim bombers and ordered to attack German shipping in the channel ports where amphibious forces were being assembled for an invasion of Britain. These planes lacked any real punch in terms of bomb load, were lightly armed, and had a low top speed which made them easy prey to enemy fighters.

Faced with a difficult and dangerous task, Barnett and his crews nevertheless made a series of courageous raids whose nuisance value, if not material destruction, was considerable. His leadership in these operations earned him the DFC in 1940.

Barnett was promoted to group captain in 1941 and for the remainder of the war commanded bomber stations and a bomber group, subsequently occupying the posts of deputy director, bomber operations, Air Ministry (1944), and senior air staff officer, Bomber Command headquarters (1945). Promoted to air commodore in 1945, he served as director of air operations, Air Ministry, until 1946 before joining the air staff in India (1946–7). Periods of service with the Staff College, Camberley (1948), and central bomber establishment followed.

With the Malayan emergency of the early 1950s Barnett once more found himself organizing bombing operations with outdated aircraft, in this case the Avro Lincoln, a lumbering, piston-driven, four-engine bomber that made little impact against an enemy hiding in thick jungle. By contrast, at the time of the Suez crisis Barnett, who had risen to the rank of air vice-marshal in 1953, was placed in command of allied air task force, Near East, where an all-jet bomber force was at his disposal. When the Anglo-French offensive began on 31 October 1956, Valiant and Canberra bombers, together with the Royal Navy's carrier-borne aircraft, virtually annihilated the Egyptian air force on the ground within forty-eight hours. This action paved the way for the invasion which went ahead untroubled by Egyptian air attacks: a result that was a tribute to Barnett's ability to organize and utilize the precise capabilities of aircraft available to him.

Thereafter Barnett's career flourished. Promoted to air marshal in 1959 and air chief marshal in 1962, he held the posts of commandant, RAF staff college, Bracknell (1956); air secretary, Air Ministry (1957–9); air officer commanding-in-chief, RAF transport command (1959–62); and air officer commanding-in-chief, RAF Near East (1962–4). In this last and final position, he was responsible for British forces in Cyprus and the administration of the sovereign base areas.

In retirement Barnett was a full-time member of the Atomic Energy Commission with special responsibility for weapons research and development (1965–72). A quiet man who enjoyed fishing in his spare time, his leadership was thoughtful rather than fiery. Yet beneath a modest exterior was a person of great personal bravery with a capacity for outstanding tactical analysis. Barnett was made CBE (1945), CB (1956), KCB (1957), and GCB (1964). In addition, he was appointed commander, US Legion of Merit (1954) and awarded the French Légion d'honneur (commandeur) and Croix de Guerre (1958).

Barnett died at his home, River House, Rushall, Pewsey, Wiltshire, of coronary thrombosis on 31 December 1992. He was survived by his wife and children.

Brian Wimborne

Sources *Who's who in New Zealand* (1971) • *WW* (1990) • *The Times* (13 Jan 1993) • *WWW*, 1991–5 • *Debrett's handbook: distinguished people in British life* [n.d.] • *The Times* (13 June 1964) • *Debrett's People of today* (1991) • m. cert. • d. cert.

Archives IWM, papers

Wealth at death £100,100: probate, 1993, *CGPLA Eng. & Wales*

Barnett, Dame (Mary) Henrietta (1905–1985), air force officer, was born at Glasnevin, Barnes Close, in Winchester on 16 February 1905, the youngest child and second daughter of Colonel George Henry Barnett CMG DSO, and gentleman-at-arms, of the 60th rifles, and his wife, Mary Dorothea, *née* Baker. She was educated at Heathfield School, Ascot, Berkshire (where she was known as Molly) from September 1918 to July 1922. Perhaps inspired by her father, she started what was to become her military career in 1938 as a volunteer in the no. 45 county of Oxford company of the Auxiliary Territorial Service, before transferring to the Women's Auxiliary Air Force (WAAF) after its establishment on 28 June 1939. She quickly rose through the ranks, serving during the early part of the war at RAF Upper Heyford in Oxfordshire and at RAF Feltwell in Norfolk, and then, in the testing conditions of the London blitz, as officer-in-charge of WAAF at the Air Ministry. Having served on home bases throughout the war, a posting in the summer of 1945 took her to the different, but in many ways equally challenging, environment of the headquarters of the Mediterranean allied air forces. Here she was staff officer responsible for all WAAF personnel working in the RAF Mediterranean and Middle East command, which included bases in Algiers and Cyprus. Although based in the grounds of Caserta Palace in Italy, in a converted Nissen hut that she nicknamed the Mushroom, Barnett travelled widely throughout the command, resolving welfare and other problems with tact and diplomacy, inspecting existing WAAF quarters, and assessing the feasibility of posting WAAF still further afield.

On her return to Britain in October 1947 she served first as WAAF staff officer at headquarters Flying Training Command, and then from October 1948 as WAAF inspector, a job that again involved considerable travelling, although this time confined to bases within home commands. The immediate post-war years were a time of transition for the WAAF, from a wartime to a peacetime force, and also from an auxiliary and temporary adjunct to the RAF to a permanent, enlisted service. This latter change was a complex one involving considerable and lengthy negotiations and, although the requisite legislation was enacted in March 1948, it was to be almost another year before the permanent service was properly established. When the Women's Royal Air Force finally came into being on 1 February 1949 it was with Barnett as one of its two deputy directors, with responsibility for the selection, promotion, and career and personal problems of WRAF officers.

From June 1950 she served for two and a half years as WRAF staff officer for home command until, on 1 November 1952, she became the only female station commander in the RAF on her appointment as commanding officer of Hawkinge in Kent. Hawkinge was primarily the WRAF officer-training centre—the female equivalent of RAF Cranwell—but it was home not only to up to 200 WRAF, but also to 70 members of an RAF glider unit. This was suitable preparation for command on a rather larger scale, and on 1 August 1956 she was appointed director of the WRAF with the acting rank of air commandant.

During her time as director of the WRAF she sought particularly to promote the expansion of the service, and as part of her recruitment campaign she oversaw the introduction of a scheme of local service enlistment to the force, and the increase of WRAF rates of pay from 75 per cent to 85 per cent of the corresponding rates for the RAF. Her wartime experience of overseas service stood her in good stead in her role as ambassador for the service abroad, and she visited units in the Middle East, the Far East, Singapore, Malaya, Malta, Denmark, Gibraltar, and the NATO base at Fontainebleau, Paris. At home she enthusiastically led the WRAF in raising funds for the restoration of St Clement Danes Church on the Strand, London, which was reconsecrated as the official RAF church by the bishop of London on 19 October 1958, and in 1959 she oversaw the celebrations to mark the tenth anniversary of the integration of both the WRAF and the Princess Mary's Royal Air Force Nursing Service into the RAF. Tall and slim, she combined the requisite immaculateness in uniform with a homely and approachable appearance. She was appointed OBE in 1950, CBE in 1956, and DBE in 1958, and as director of the WRAF she was aide-de-camp to the queen.

In March 1960 Dame Henrietta Barnett retired to a cottage in Woodstock, Oxfordshire, where, as well as maintaining her links with the WRAF as a member and sometime chairman of the executive committee of the WRAF Officers' Association, she involved herself in local affairs, serving as mayor of Woodstock from 1968 to 1969, and she continued to enjoy the country pursuits of fishing and hunting; as commanding officer of Hawkinge she had entertained the local hunt. She died of a heart attack at her home, Hoggrove House, 24 Park Street, Woodstock, on 11 September 1985. TESSA STONE

Sources King's Lond., Liddell Hart C., M. H. Barnett MSS, GB99 KCLMA Barnett, M. H. • b. cert. • d. cert. • *The Times* (18 Aug 1941) • *The Times* (27 Oct 1952) • *The Times* (16 Jan 1956) • *The Times* (13 March 1956) • *The Times* (26 July 1956) • *The Times* (26 Feb 1960) • Heathfield School register, Heathfield School, Ascot • K. B. Beauman, *Partners in blue: the story of women's service with the Royal Air Force* (1971) • *The Times* (13 Sept 1985) • B. E. Escott, *Women in air force blue: the story of women in the Royal Air Force from 1918 to the present day* (1989) • F. Peake, *Pure chance* (1993) • RAF Museum, Hendon, London, department of research and information services, MF 13/1

Archives King's Lond., Liddell Hart C., papers, files GB99 KCLMA Barnett, M. H.

Wealth at death £238,269: probate, 5 Nov 1985, *CGPLA Eng. & Wales*

Barnett [*née* Rowland], **Dame Henrietta Octavia Weston** (**1851–1936**), social reformer, was born in Clapham, Surrey, on 4 May 1851, the daughter of Alexander William Rowland (*d.* 1869), whose family fortune derived from Rowland's Macassar Oil Company, and Henrietta Monica Margaretta Ditges (*d.* 1851). Her mother died shortly after giving birth to Henrietta, who was raised in comfort by her father. Her formal education consisted of several

Dame Henrietta Octavia Weston Barnett (1851–1936), by Elliott & Fry, *c.*1905 [with her husband, Canon Samuel Augustus Barnett]

terms spent at a boarding-school in Dover run by the Haddon sisters, disciples and sisters-in-law of the controversial aural surgeon and social and moral philosopher James Hinton. Given Hinton's and the Haddons' commitment to social altruism it is not surprising that Henrietta first demonstrated compassionate interest in the lives of poor children during her student days. Upon the death of her father in 1869 she devoted herself to helping the housing and charity reformer Octavia Hill conduct her philanthropic labours in the parish of St Mary's, Bryanston Square, Marylebone. Hill introduced her to Samuel Augustus *Barnett (1844–1913), a fellow worker and curate at St Mary's. They were an unlikely pair: she was, as her friend Beatrice Webb described her, 'pretty, witty and well-to-do' (B. Webb, *My Apprenticeship*, New York edn, 1926, 204); he was awkward in appearance and manners. But their shared passion for helping the poor convinced her that the 'gift' of Samuel's love 'was too holy to refuse' (H. Barnett, *Canon Barnett*, 1.53). On 28 January 1873 they married, and embarked on their remarkable collaboration as social reformers, and husband and wife, in the impoverished parish of St Jude's, Whitechapel, in east London. Beatrice Webb saw the Barnetts as 'an early example of a new type of human personality, in after years not uncommon; a double-star-personality, the light of the one being indistinguishable from that of the other' (Webb, 182).

From the outset Henrietta Barnett was her husband's equal partner in all their celebrated initiatives. She quickly threw herself into parish work on behalf of women and children, and gathered a circle of devoted women workers around her. In 1875 she was the first nominated woman guardian, and in the next year began her long association with the poor law district schools at Forest Gate, as a school manager. Despite her rescue work with female prostitutes and her belief that women should have the parliamentary franchise she was associated with neither the campaign for the repeal of the Contagious Diseases Acts nor the movement for female suffrage. She preferred to use her formidable creative energies and skills as an organizer more directly towards improving the lives of the London poor. She was a co-founder in 1876 of the Metropolitan Association for the Befriending of Young Servants and long-time leader of its Whitechapel branch. Her experiment, in 1877, of sending slum children for restorative country holidays grew into the Children's Country Holiday Fund (1884). She played a leading role in the departmental committee appointed to inquire into 'the condition of Poor Law Children', which led her and her sister Alice's husband, Dr Ernest Hart, to form in 1896 the State Children's Association, with Henrietta Barnett as honorary secretary.

In 1884 Henrietta and Samuel led the movement to establish the University Settlement in east London, better known as Toynbee Hall, in memory of their recently deceased friend the Oxford economic historian Arnold Toynbee. Settlements, as first envisioned by the Barnetts, were residential colonies of university men in the slums intended to serve both as centres of education, recreation, and community life for the local poor and as outposts for social work, social scientific investigation, and cross-class friendships between élites and their poor neighbours. A paper that Henrietta delivered on settlement work to the Cambridge Ladies' Discussion Society in the Lent term of 1887 led to the proposal to found the first women's settlement: the Women's University Settlement in Southwark. An important female presence at all-male Toynbee Hall and an outspoken advocate for the worldwide growth of the settlement movement, she also expanded her innovative parish work during these years. As Toynbee Hall demanded more of Samuel's time he confessed in 1886 that Henrietta had become 'Church as well as home curate' (Samuel Barnett to Frank Barnett, Easter 1886, Barnett papers, LMA, F/Bar/132). To the chagrin of more conventional churchmen and women she and Samuel organized free musical concerts and oratorios on Sundays, as well as the renowned Whitechapel Picture Exhibition of fine art held each year, about Easter, in St Jude's schoolrooms. The latter developed into the Whitechapel Art Gallery, of which Henrietta remained a trustee from its founding in 1901 until her death. At nearly seventy-two she took up painting, and her pictures were hung in several Royal Academy exhibitions.

In 1903 Henrietta Barnett embarked on her last and most ambitious project, which dominated the final decades of her life: rescuing 80 acres of Hampstead Heath for public enjoyment and creating the Hampstead Garden Suburb. She had long recognized that Toynbee Hall, with its transient and all-male population, was an 'artificial protest' (Barnett and Barnett, 338) against social divisions that could not serve as a society-wide model for those essential links between private domestic and public political life. Collaborating with the pioneer socialist architects of the Letchworth Garden City, Raymond Unwin and Barry Parker, she created a blueprint for a new kind of organic community consisting of young and old, able-bodied and infirm, rich and poor, married and unmarried. While the largest homes of wealthy residents were placed far from the modest cottages designed for artisans Henrietta hoped that residents of the suburb would be bound together by shared religious, social, educational, and recreational spaces. To this end she successfully advocated the erection of an Anglican church and a nonconformist chapel, along with a purpose-built clubhouse for artisans and their families; the institute, designed by Edwin Lutyens, served as the suburb's focal point for educational, cultural, and civic activity. Henrietta balanced her unwavering commitment to the mutual advantages of relationships between the classes with a staunch belief in the ineradicability of class differences. Autocratic and forceful in her dealings with others, her personality was tinged with élitist discomfort about the impact of the 'democratic microbe' (H. Barnett, 'Thrift in the home', *Charity Organisation Review* (June 1907), 307) on British society, and intolerance of her Jewish neighbours in Whitechapel. During her later years she vigorously supported two institutions: Barnett House at Oxford (1914), named in memory of Samuel, which remains the centre for social work and social policy education at the university; and the Dame Henrietta Barnett School (the foundation stone of which was laid on 23 October 1918), a single-sex, voluntary-aided school in Hampstead that emerged out of the educational programmes for girls at the institute.

Henrietta Barnett's many publications spanned fifty years and encompassed topics ranging from domestic economy (*The Making of the Home*, 1885) and human physiology (*The Making of the Body*, 1894) to social questions (*Practicable Socialism*, 1888; *Practicable Socialism, New Series*, 1915, and *Towards Social Reform*, 1909, all three written jointly with Samuel Barnett). She also wrote *Matters that Matter* (1930), a collection of quasi-autobiographical essays on various topics, and her most enduring monument to her partnership with Samuel: the two volume *Canon Barnett: his Life, Work, and Friends* (1918).

Henrietta Barnett valued highly motherhood and women's distinct moral gifts as peacemakers capable of defusing class war. Having no children of her own she was legal guardian of both her badly brain-damaged elder sister, Fanny, who shared her home for fifty-eight years, and of Dorothy Woods, the Barnetts' beloved adopted ward. From the 1890s Marion Paterson (whom Henrietta had first met in 1876) was her constant assistant, nurse, secretary, confidante, and companion. After Samuel's death, in

1913, her friendship and dependence upon Marion deepened, and it was Marion who received and responded to letters of condolence when Henrietta died, in their Hampstead home, on 10 June 1936. Henrietta had been appointed CBE in 1917 and DBE in 1924. SETH KOVEN

Sources [H. Barnett], *Canon Barnett: his life, work, and friends*, 2 vols. (1918) · H. Barnett, *Matters that matter* (1930) · S. Koven, 'Henrietta Barnett: the (auto) biography of a late Victorian marriage', *After the Victorians: private conscience and public duty in modern Britain*, ed. S. Pederson and P. Mandler (1994) · Hampstead Garden Suburb Trust, Henrietta Barnett papers · Swarthmore College, Philadelphia, Pennsylvania, Friends Historical Library, Jane Addams papers · Octavia Hill and Henrietta Barnett correspondence, BLPES, Coll. misc. 0512 · K. M. Slack, *Henrietta's dream: a chronicle of the Hampstead Garden Suburb, 1905–1982* (1982) · LMA, Toynbee Hall papers · LMA, Barnett papers · B. Webb, *My apprenticeship* (1926) · S. A. Barnett and H. Barnett, *Towards social reform* (1909) · *DNB*

Archives Hampstead Garden Suburb Trust, MSS · LMA, corresp. and papers · LMA, quasi-autobiography and papers | Birm. CA, letters to Elizabeth Cadbury and George Cadbury · BLPES, corresp. with Octavia Hill · Bodl. Oxf., letters to Francis Marvin and Edith Marvin · LMA, corresp. relating to Toynbee Hall · LMA, corresp. with various artists and literary figures · Swarthmore College, Philadelphia, Pennsylvania, Friends Historical Library, corresp. with Jane Addams · University of Illinois, Chicago, corresp. with Jane Addams

Likenesses Elliott & Fry, photograph, *c.*1905, NPG [*see illus.*] · H. von Herkomer, double portrait, 1908 (with Samuel Barnett), Toynbee Hall, Hampstead Garden Suburb · attrib. O. Edis, photograph, *c.*1932, NPG · Lafayette, photograph, 1932, NPG · J. Opffer, sanguine drawing, 1933, NPG

Wealth at death £34,749 17*s.* 2*d.*: probate, 6 July 1936, *CGPLA Eng. & Wales* · £34,749—gross: *The Times* (9 July 1936) · £32,289—net: *The Times* (9 July 1936)

Barnett, John (1802–1890), composer, born at Bedford on 15 July 1802 (some sources say 1 July), was the eldest son of a German Jewish diamond merchant, Bernhard Beer, and a Hungarian mother, who died during his early childhood. His father adopted the surname Barnett after taking up residence in England. The composer Giacomo Meyerbeer (Jakob Liebmann Meyer Beer) was a second cousin. According to Diehl, Barnett 'when a tiny boy sang like a bird' (Diehl, 298). A few years later he possessed a fine alto voice, and about 1812 he was articled to Samuel James Arnold, the proprietor of the Lyceum Theatre, where he made his stage début as Dick in *The Shipwreck* on 22 July 1813. Shortly afterwards he appeared at Drury Lane in the winter pantomime, where he sang 'The Death of Abercrombie'. He continued to sing on the London stage until his voice broke about 1818. His early vocal studies were with Charles Edward Horn and a Mr Price, the chorus master of the Lyceum; his abilities as a keyboard player were fostered by Pérez (organist of the Spanish embassy in London), Ferdinand Ries, and Frédéric Kalkbrenner; and his training in the techniques of composition was undertaken by William Horsley. By the age of eighteen Barnett had already composed and published a number of successful vocal works, including, in 1820, a 'grand scena', *The Groves of Pomona*, which was performed by the celebrated tenor John Braham. Among other unpublished works, written before he reached the age of twenty-five, were two piano sonatas, a violin sonata, two overtures, two masses, and a sacred cantata, *Abraham on the Altar of his Son*. His

John Barnett (1802–1890), by Charles Baugniet, 1845

early efforts attracted critical encouragement in the *Quarterly Musical Magazine and Review*, where his talent for the higher branches of his art was recognized. From about 1825 he began contributing occasional pieces to plays and musical entertainments at the Lyceum, the Adelphi, and Drury Lane.

In 1828, in partnership with the dramatist W. T. Moncrieff, Barnett opened a music shop in Regent Street. Nevertheless, he continued to expend a considerable portion of his energies on contributing incidental music to the slight theatrical pieces that were the staple fare of the English theatres at that time, including Moncrieff's burletta *Monsieur Mallet* in 1829. At the same time, in striking contrast, he completed an oratorio, *The Omnipresence of the Deity*, which, though printed, does not seem to have been publicly performed, and published his *Elements of Singing*. He also became involved in the then thriving business of adapting celebrated foreign operas to suit English taste when, in 1830, he helped to put together a version of Meyerbeer's *Robert le diable* as *Robert the Devil*, including music of his own, for production at Covent Garden. Some of his shorter vocal pieces achieved considerable success during these years, particularly 'The Light Guitar', which was performed by Lucia Vestris. His larger stage works at that time included *The Deuce is in her* (1830), *The Picturesque* (1831), *Win her and Wear her* (1832), and the operetta *The Convent, or, The Pet of the Petticoats*, produced at Sadler's Wells in 1832. This last was so well received that it was later performed in the larger London theatres. Barnett's appointment by Vestris as music director at the Olympic Theatre in 1832 resulted in his contribution to or composition and compilation of many such burlesques and farces; these contained individual numbers that he afterwards considered good enough to incorporate into later works.

Although such routine labours were necessary to gain recognition and sustain a position in the London theatres at that period, Barnett cherished ambitions to compose something of greater musical substance. His opportunity came when in 1834 Samuel Arnold planned to reopen the Lyceum Theatre (rebuilt after its destruction by fire in 1830) as the English Opera House, with the intention of presenting full-scale English operas. The Royal Lyceum and English Opera House opened on 14 July with Loder's *Nourjahad*, and this was followed on 25 August by Barnett's *The Mountain Sylph*. Barnett's genuine commitment to Arnold's aim is indicated by his dedication of the vocal score to his old master, 'for the spirit, zeal, and enthusiasm which he has shewn in the production of Native Operas, and in cherishing native talent'. *The Mountain Sylph* was highly successful with the public, enjoying an initial run of 100 nights and being periodically revived throughout the century; it was even distinguished by having its plot satirized in Gilbert's *Iolanthe*. The impression created by the style and seriousness of purpose of *The Mountain Sylph* (which was deeply indebted to German models) on other British musicians who aspired to emulate these earnest musical qualities was, nevertheless, considerable. Some twenty-five years later G. A. Macfarren claimed that 'its production opened a new period for music in this country, from which is to be dated the establishment of an English dramatic school, which, if not yet accomplished, has made many notable advances' (*Imperial Dictionary of Universal Biography*). Barnett's future reputation as a composer of significance rested largely on this one work; he failed to continue in the direction indicated by *The Mountain Sylph*.

In the same year as *The Mountain Sylph* Barnett published his collection of songs entitled *Lyric Illustrations of the Modern Poets*. His next theatrical contribution was the music for a burletta, *Monsieur Jacques*, with a text by Morris Barnett (no relation), produced at the St James's Theatre in January 1836. He then visited Paris, where he hoped to secure a production of his new four-act opera, *Fair Rosamond*, composed to a libretto by C. Z. Barnett (his brother) and F. Shannon; but at the invitation of Alfred Bunn the opera was brought out at Drury Lane on 28 February 1837. *Fair Rosamond* was not particularly successful; it is much longer than *The Mountain Sylph*, but indicates far less concern with musical continuity or with the correspondence of musical form and dramatic situation, and it is stylistically much more eclectic. At about this time Barnett was among a group of musicians, including Henry Bishop, who petitioned William IV for support and secured the promise of a patent for the establishment of English opera in London; but the scheme came to nothing when the king died shortly afterwards.

Barnett followed *Fair Rosamond* with two much slighter contributions to the theatre, the two-act musical romance *Blanche of Jersey* and the musical entertainment *The Little Laundress*, both given at the Lyceum in 1837. In the same year, on 9 May, at St George's, Hanover Square, he married Eliza Lindley (*bap.* 1814?), the daughter of the cellist Robert *Lindley. Together they travelled to Frankfurt, where Barnett studied Vogler's principles of composition with Schnyder von Wartensee and composed a symphony and a string quartet. In 1838 he returned to London for the production of his only other stage work to receive a public performance, the two-act serio-comic opera *Farinelli* (again with a libretto by his brother), which opened at Drury Lane on 8 February 1839. However, this opera, too, had only a limited success. In the same year he attempted to set up a permanent English opera house at the St James's Theatre, in partnership with Morris Barnett, but the project collapsed after only a week. The following year he made a final unsuccessful attempt to set up an English opera house, this time at the Prince's Theatre. Although Barnett completed two more operas, *Kathleen* in 1840 and *Queen Mab* in 1841, neither of which appears ever to have been staged, and abandoned another, *Marie*, in 1845, the failure of his efforts to establish English opera on a permanent footing effectively marked the end of his association with the London theatre, for early in 1841 he moved to Cheltenham. The causes of his withdrawal or exclusion from the London stage are complex, but they seem to have been connected partly with his comfortable financial circumstances, which made it easier for him to retire to the provinces, and partly with his natural tendency to contentiousness. He had fallen out with Arnold after a public dispute about a financial agreement, and he quarrelled with the impresarios Bunn and Mapleson. As early as 1832 he had been engaged in controversy in the press over the perceived failure of the Philharmonic Society to encourage English music, and he continued to involve himself in similar correspondence.

In Cheltenham Barnett built up a successful practice as a singing teacher and gave further rein to his trenchant views in a pamphlet, *Systems and Singing Masters* (1842), which was a direct attack on Mainzer's and Hullah's methods of vocal tuition, and he promoted his own methods of teaching in his *School for the Voice* (1844). During these years he remained very active as a composer of songs, part-songs, and instrumental music, and he continued to engage in polemical disputations in the press. For the sake of his children's education he and his family lived for several years in Germany and Italy. His daughters Rosamunda and Clara Doria studied singing and piano at the Leipzig conservatory, whence in 1860 it was reported that they had enjoyed extraordinary acclaim for their performances at the Gewandhaus. His son Domenico was later to teach piano at Cheltenham Ladies' College. About 1870 Barnett returned to live permanently in the Cheltenham area and purchased a substantial country house, Cotteswold, at Leckhampton, Gloucestershire, where he died on 16/17 April 1890, survived by his wife. He was buried at Leckhampton. Clive Brown

Sources *Quarterly Musical Magazine and Review*, 3–10 (1821–8) · *Musical World* (12 Aug 1836), 139–40 · review of *Fair Rosamond*,

Musical World (3 March 1837), 172–3 • review of *Fair Rosamond*, *Musical World* (10 March 1837), 188–9 • review of *Farinelli*, *Musical World* (21 Feb 1839), 117–18 • *Musical World* (3 Dec 1840), 349–52 • *Musical World* (10 Dec 1840), 365–7 • *Musical World* (17 Dec 1840), 393–4 • *Musical World* (5 May 1860), 287 • A. Bunn, *The stage: both before and behind the curtain*, 3 vols. (1840), vol. 1, pp. 138–40 • G. A. Macfarren, 'Barnett, John', *The imperial dictionary of universal biography*, ed. J. F. Waller, new edn (1877–84) • A. M. Diehl, *Musical memories* (1897) • N. Temperley, 'Barnett, John', *New Grove* • *IGI* • *CGPLA Eng. & Wales* (1890)

Likenesses C. Baugniet, oils, *c*.1839, NPG • C. Baugniet, lithograph, 1845, BM, NPG [*see illus.*] • S. Paget, oils, priv. coll. • engraving, repro. in A. Mayhew, *A jorum of Punch, with those who helped to brew it* (1895)

Wealth at death £12,391 15*s*. 9*d*.: resworn probate, Aug 1890, *CGPLA Eng. & Wales*

Barnett, John Francis (1837–1916), composer and pianist, born in London on 16 October 1837, was the son of a singing teacher, Joseph Alfred Barnett (the younger brother of the composer John *Barnett), and his wife, *née* Hudson. He showed an early talent for music and began to study the piano at the age of six. In 1848 he commenced piano lessons with Henry Wylde and the following year won the king's scholarship to the Royal Academy of Music. Before entering the academy he studied organ with George Cooper and acted as organist, first at the Roman Catholic church in Warwick Street and then at St Aloysius, Clarendon Square, where his father was choirmaster. He took up his scholarship in 1852 or 1853, and in the same year played Mendelssohn's D minor piano concerto at a New Philharmonic Society concert under Spohr's conductorship. In 1857, having completed his studies at the academy, Barnett travelled to Germany, intending to perform as a solo pianist; in Leipzig, however, he enrolled at the conservatory and studied counterpoint under Moritz Hauptmann and E. F. Richter, composition under Julius Rietz, and piano under Ignaz Moscheles and Louis Plaidy. Towards the end of this period his op. 1, a *caprice brillante* for piano, was published by Kistner. Shortly before returning to England he performed Mendelssohn's D minor concerto at a Gewandhaus concert on 22 March 1860.

The following month Barnett appeared with great success in London as the soloist in Beethoven's fifth piano concerto at a New Philharmonic Society concert. A contemporary reviewer remarked that he had spent the last couple of years, 'as we are enabled to judge from his playing on Monday evening, studying and practising with zeal and determination' (*Musical World*, 256). During the next few years he composed a succession of characteristic piano pieces, among them *Three Sketches*, op. 2, and *Return of Spring*, op. 7. His op. 8, published about 1863, however, was a string quartet in D minor, and it was a symphony in A minor (unpublished), performed at the Musical Society of London on 15 June 1864 and repeated at the Crystal Palace Saturday concerts, which drew attention to Barnett's merits as a composer. This led to his first commission, a cantata for the 1867 Birmingham festival. The success of the resulting composition, *The Ancient Mariner*, for which he arranged his own text from Coleridge's poem, led to further commissions. The rapid proliferation of choral societies throughout Britain created a steady demand for such works, and during the following decades Barnett composed *Paradise and the Peri* (1870), *The Raising of Lazarus* (1873), *The Good Shepherd* (1876), *The Building of the Ship* (1880), *The Wishing Bell* (1893), and *The Eve of St Agnes* (1913), as well as a number of smaller choral works. Other compositions included a piano concerto, a number of descriptive pieces for orchestra, a few chamber works, and many piano pieces and songs. In 1883 he completed Schubert's E major symphony from the autograph sketch belonging to Sir George Grove; he described the process in *Proceedings of the Musical Association* (17, 1890–91, 177). His *Musical Reminiscences and Impressions*, published in 1906, gives a valuable account of the musicians and music-making of his time.

Barnett was a fellow of the Royal Academy of Music. He was among the professors at the National Training School for Music from 1876 to 1882, and joined the staff of its successor, the Royal College of Music, in 1883. He also taught at the Guildhall School of Music from its establishment in 1880. During these years he continued to perform publicly as a pianist and occasionally appeared as a conductor. On 4 September 1875 he married Alice Dora Booth, the daughter of the artist Lorenzo John Booth, with whom he had several children. She died in 1882, and on 25 July 1891 he married Mary Millicent Tussaud, the daughter of Joseph Tussaud. Barnett died at 56 Acacia Road, St John's Wood, London, on 24 November 1916. CLIVE BROWN

Sources J. F. Barnett, *Musical reminiscences and impressions* (1906) • 'New Philharmonic concerts', *Musical World* (21 April 1860), 256 • E. F. Rimbault, 'Barnett, John Francis', Grove, *Dict. mus.* • m. certs. • d. cert.

Archives BL, letters to Richard Peyton, Add. MS 60391

Likenesses photographs, *c*.1867–*c*.1905, repro. in Barnett, *Musical reminiscences* • Barrauds Ltd, photograph, *c*.1885, repro. in Barnett, *Musical reminiscences*, p. 240

Wealth at death £853 12*s*. 6*d*.: resworn administration, 1917, *CGPLA Eng. & Wales*

Barnett, Lionel David (1871–1960), orientalist, was born in Liverpool on 21 October 1871, the eldest son of Baron Barnett, banker, and his wife, Adelaide Cowan. He was educated at the high school, institute, and University College, Liverpool. He went up to Trinity College, Cambridge, in 1892 and was elected a scholar in 1893. He was Sir William Browne's medallist (Greek ode, 1893, 1894, 1896; Greek epigram, 1893); gained a first class (division 1) in part one of the classical tripos in 1894 and was elected Craven scholar the same year. In 1896 he was awarded a first class, with special distinction in language, in part two of the classical tripos, together with the chancellor's medal. He was appointed Craven student in 1897 and in 1900 the University of Manchester conferred on him the degree of LittD. He studied Sanskrit at Cambridge and Halle. In 1901 he married Blanche Esther (*d*. 1955), daughter of the Revd B. Berliner, minister of the St John's Wood synagogue. They had a daughter and a son.

In 1899 Barnett joined the staff of the British Museum as assistant keeper in the department of oriental printed books and manuscripts, and after only nine years was promoted keeper of the department in succession to Sir Robert Douglas. To the duties of this post, its functions officially defined as 'to conserve, augment and catalogue the collections', he brought a remarkable threefold equipment of fine scholarship, administrative ability, and business acumen which resulted in the museum's store of oriental manuscripts and books being enormously enriched during his twenty-eight years of office. The vast range of his erudition in the cultures of both East and West was probably unique in the museum's history. He compiled a monumental series of no fewer than ten descriptive catalogues of oriental printed books in the Indo-Aryan and Dravidian languages, covering Sanskrit, Pali, Prakrit, Kannada, Badaga, Kurg, Tamil, Telugu, Burmese, Hindi, Bihari, Pahari, Panjabi, Saurashtra, and other languages, large quarto volumes containing in all some 8000 columns of text.

Library administration and bibliography on this massive scale were only a part of Barnett's many-sided activity. From 1906 to 1917 he held the professorship of Sanskrit at University College, London. When the university's School of Oriental Studies was founded he was included on its staff from 1917 as lecturer in Sanskrit; he was also lecturer in ancient Indian history and epigraphy (1922–48) and librarian (1940–47). When he retired from the school in 1948 a special volume of its *Bulletin* was published in his honour. He was elected FBA in 1936 and appointed CB in 1937. A prominent figure in the Royal Asiatic Society, he was at various times a member of council and vice-president, its honorary librarian from 1939 onwards, and was awarded its gold medal in 1950.

The Greek and Latin classics were Barnett's first love and throughout life his prodigious memory was stored with them. For the benefit of the young student and the cultured lay public he published between 1900 and 1904 a succession of useful volumes, some translated from the German, on classical history and literature. Thereafter the works he produced, as separate books or as monographs in learned periodicals, dealt almost entirely with Indological subjects. In addition to his translations, editions, and secondary studies of classical Indian texts in Sanskrit, Prakrit, and other languages, he also published a number of accessible and successful works aimed at informing a wider readership in Indian history, religion, and culture; these included several volumes in the series called The Wisdom of the East, some of which can still be profitably read by students. His numerous articles and book reviews in learned journals embraced Indian history, epigraphy, folklore, drama, philology, and Tibetan as well as Indian texts. He published translations of Spanish documents relating to the history of the Jewish community of which he was a faithful and active member, holding several of its honorary offices.

Barnett's encyclopaedic learning was carried with effortless ease and with never a trace of ostentation. His natural humility and his countless unobtrusive kindnesses, especially towards younger scholars, drew to him the affection of a host of friends. Although little given to outdoor recreation he enjoyed constant good health, until suddenly in 1932 his eyesight gave way under the intense strain of years, one eye becoming permanently useless and the sight of the other impaired. This grievous blow did not deter him, after a brief convalescence, from pressing on with fruitful academic work both in the study and in the lecture room. In 1948 when he retired from his university duties he might reasonably have sought an easier life after half a century of ceaseless industry, but hearing that his old department at the British Museum from which he had retired in 1936 was in sore straits for staff, he offered his services as an assistant keeper and for the last twelve years of his life the museum once more profited from his vast knowledge and experience. A fortnight before his death in London on 28 January 1960, the Asiatic Society of Bengal awarded him the Sir William Jones gold medal. His son, Richard David Barnett (1909–1986), was keeper of the department of western Asiatic antiquities in the British Museum from 1955 to 1974.

A. S. FULTON, *rev.* J. B. KATZ

Sources E. M. White, 'Bibliography of the published writings of Dr L. D. Barnett', *Bulletin of the School of Oriental and African Studies*, 12 (1947–8), 497–523 · A. L. Basham, 'Lionel David Barnett', *PBA*, 46 (1960), 333–9 · *The Times* (29 Jan 1960) · personal knowledge (1971) · private information (1971) · *CGPLA Eng. & Wales* (1960)
Archives Bodl. Oxf., corresp. with Sir Aurel Stein
Likenesses W. Stoneman, photograph, 1937, NPG · photograph, repro. in Basham, 'Lionel David Barnett', 333
Wealth at death £4944 19*s*. 10*d*.: probate, 22 March 1960, *CGPLA Eng. & Wales*

Barnett, Morris (1800–1856), actor and playwright, was of Jewish descent. He trained as a musician, and the earlier part of his life was spent in Paris. Having resolved to earn his living as an actor, he went as a comedian to Brighton and then to Bath. In 1833 he was engaged by Alfred Bunn for the Drury Lane Theatre, when he had his first great success in the part of Tom Drops in Douglas Jerrold's comedy *The Schoolfellows*. In 1837 he performed at the St James's Theatre the title role in *Monsieur Jacques*, a musical drama which he had adapted from a French piece. The show was the talk of the town, and the humour of Barnett's broken English was hugely appreciated.

After a period of concentration on literary work, Barnett reappeared in 1843 on the stage of the Princess's Theatre, where his Old Guard, in the piece of that name, attracted general attention. He then joined the literary staff of the *Morning Post* and *The Era* and was the music critic of those papers for nearly seven years. In September 1854 he decided to go to America, and before his departure gave a series of farewell performances at the Adelphi Theatre. The transatlantic trip was not successful. Severe ill health disabled him from professional work, and eventually led to his death, in Montreal, Canada, on 18 March 1856.

As an actor, Barnett had particular gifts for comedy and mimicry. His dramatic works included comedy, domestic drama, and opera, though his reputation was built on the comedies *Monsieur Jacques* and *The Serious Family*, also adapted from the French.

THOMPSON COOPER, *rev.* JOHN WELLS

Sources *GM*, 2nd ser., 45 (1856), 541–2 · *The Era* (13 April 1856) [town edn] · Adams, *Drama* · *The life and adventures of George Augustus Sala*, 3rd edn, 1 (1895), 64–8 · *BL cat.*
Archives BL, corresp., Add. MS 43382
Likenesses Saxony & Co., engraving, 1854, Harvard TC · J. Brandard, lithograph (as Monsieur Jacques), BM, NPG · W. T. Page, engraving (after J. Brandard), Harvard TC · four prints, Harvard TC

Barnett, Samuel Augustus (1844–1913), Church of England clergyman and social reformer, the elder son of Francis Augustus Barnett (*d.* 27 Dec 1883) and his wife, Mary Gilmore (*d.* 6 Nov 1880) of Bristol, was born at 5 Portland Square, Bristol, on 8 February 1844. His father was a wealthy manufacturer of iron bedsteads; his mother came from a long-established Bristol merchant family engaged chiefly in overseas shipping. Educated at home, Barnett went in June 1862 to Wadham College, Oxford. Undistinguished as a student (second class in law and modern history 1865, BA 1865, MA 1869), he subsequently was revered by generations of university men for bringing them in direct and living contact with the problems of the urban poor: Barnett House, founded at Oxford University in 1914 to promote the study of social problems, stands as testimony to this legacy. Barnett claimed that a journey to the United States in 1867 eradicated the last traces of his inherited tory prejudices. When he returned to England in December 1867 to be a curate at St Mary's, Bryanston Square, London, under William Henry Fremantle (later dean of Ripon), he struck contemporaries as a rather ordinary young man, distinguished more by his scraggly beard, balding pate, and dishevelled appearance than by any great promise.

Barnett's abilities as a worker on behalf of the Marylebone poor became quickly evident during his curacy under Fremantle. During these years (1867–73) he shared Fremantle's zeal both for church reform, which brought Barnett into contact with men like Arnold Toynbee, and for reforming the organization of charity in London. The latter led to the founding of the Society for Repressing Mendicity and Organising Charity (better known as the Charity Organization Society or COS) in 1869. Through the COS Barnett came under the influence of the housing reformer Octavia Hill, who in turn introduced him to one of her young workers, his future wife, Henrietta Octavia Weston Rowland [*see* Barnett, Dame Henrietta Octavia Weston].

Married on 28 January 1873, Samuel and Henrietta shared and inspired one another's work for the next forty years. Shortly after their marriage they went to St Jude's, Whitechapel, a notoriously poor and lawless parish in east London, where their imposition of COS principles, including the curtailment of outdoor relief, dismayed the poor but established their reputations as formidable reformers. Convinced of the benefits of direct one-to-one relations between rich and poor, the Barnetts none the less began in the early 1880s to distance themselves from the rigid opposition of the central office of the COS to all forms of state-funded assistance outside the new poor law (1834 and later legislation). They forged an alternative vision of social politics, 'practicable socialism', which combined a reverence for individual initiative and self-improvement with municipal and state support intended to address specific material needs. They also often found themselves in disfavour with traditional Anglicans who distrusted their innovations in Sunday worship, such as oratorios and picture exhibitions. Imbued with the aesthetic theories of John Ruskin, Barnett insisted that 'pictures … could take the place of parables' (Barnett to Bishop Jackson, 3 April 1882, Fulham MSS, vol. 2) as moral teachers to the poor. Under the Barnetts' aegis, the annual picture exhibitions held in the St Jude's schoolrooms grew into the Whitechapel Art Gallery, which was opened in 1901. Barnett further alienated some Anglicans of varied persuasions in 1884 when, on a non-denominational basis, he launched the scheme on which his fame most securely rests, Toynbee Hall, the university settlement in Whitechapel. Octavia Hill, his erstwhile mentor, was so disturbed by what she viewed as Barnett's lax churchmanship that she supported a rival plan undertaken on an explicitly religious basis by the high-church party of Keble College, the Oxford House settlement in Bethnal Green. Barnett's connections with Whitechapel lasted throughout his life, though he resigned St Jude's in 1893 to serve as a canon of Bristol, by which title he is best-known to posterity. In 1895 he was a select preacher at Oxford, and at Cambridge in 1889 and 1905; from 1906 to 1913 he was canon, and finally subdean, of Westminster.

While Barnett's fame rests mostly on his accomplishments as a secular social reformer, he was actuated by deep religious convictions informed by the teachings of the Christian socialist F. D. Maurice. His friend Beatrice Webb credited Barnett with importantly shaping the 'rediscovery' of poverty in the 1880s and social reform in late Victorian England by his insistence that 'the sense of sin has been the starting-point of progress' (Webb, 174). During his first decade at St Jude's, Barnett developed an extensive network of clubs and classes to address not only the spiritual but the intellectual and recreative needs of his parishioners. The unpopularity of these ventures encouraged him to think of an alternative non-parochial institutional framework for his work. Barnett capitalized on the anxieties unleashed by the sensational pamphlet about slum life *The Bitter Cry of Outcast London* (1883). He announced a plan to establish what he called a settlement, a residential colony of university men, committed to no particular religious creed, who would live among the poor as friends, neighbours, social-scientific observers, and practical social workers. From 1884 to 1906 he served as warden of Toynbee Hall, which attracted distinguished visitors and many imitators worldwide.

A man of abiding humility and optimism, Barnett believed in the potential goodness and educability of all people regardless of their life station. He was closely associated with university extension in east London, the Oxford Day Training College, pupil-teacher centres, and the Workers' Educational Association. There were few movements for social, cultural, or moral improvement of the poor in which Barnett did not take a prominent part. While *Punch* gently mocked his cultural philanthropy,

Barnett was also actively involved in many initiatives to improve the economic and material conditions of the poor, including slum clearance and housing reform (he was a leading promoter of the Artisans' Dwelling Act of 1875), old-age pensions, and labour farm colonies. He died at 69 Kings Esplanade, Hove, Sussex, on 17 June 1913; the funeral service on 21 June was, at Barnett's own instructions, held at St Jude's, but there is a memorial to him in Westminster Abbey; his remains were cremated. Predeceased by his adopted ward, Dorothy Woods, he had no children.

M. Clemenceau remarked in 1884 that Barnett was one of the 'three really great men' (Barnett, 2.45) he had met in England. While Barnett was an effective speaker and a pithy, aphoristic writer, his 'greatness' lay in his personality. His public and private persona were marked by a singular lack of vanity in his own achievements and a keenly tolerant sympathy for others which enabled him to discover what was best in those he counselled and help them to make it effective. His impact on twentieth-century Britain is most apparent in the work of the men whose lives he influenced during their residence at Toynbee Hall, including Robert Morant, Hubert Llewellyn-Smith, R. H. Tawney, William Beveridge, and Clement Attlee. Barnett's most important published works include *Practicable Socialism* (co-authored with Henrietta Barnett in 1888), *Religion and Progress* (1907), *Religion and Politics* (1911), *Worship and Work* (1913), and *Vision and Service* (1917), the two last-named published posthumously and edited by Henrietta Barnett. SETH KOVEN

Sources [H. Barnett], *Canon Barnett: his life, work, and friends*, 2 vols. (1918) • LMA, Barnett MSS • LMA, Toynbee Hall MSS • LPL, Barnett MSS • S. Koven, 'Culture and poverty: the London settlement house movement, 1870–1914', PhD diss., Harvard U., 1987 • E. K. Abel, 'Canon Barnett and the first thirty years of Toynbee Hall', PhD diss., U. Lond., 1969 • S. Meacham, *Toynbee Hall and social reform: the search for community* (1987) • A. Briggs and A. Macartney, *Toynbee Hall, the first hundred years* (1984) • B. Webb, *My apprenticeship* (1926) • Foster, *Alum. Oxon.* • *CGPLA Eng. & Wales* (1913) • LPL, Fulham MSS

Archives LMA, Toynbee Hall MSS, corresp. with various artists and literary figures; letters and papers • LPL, corresp. and papers relating to National Church Reform Union | BLPES, corresp. with William Beveridge • HLRO, letters to Herbert Samuel • King's AC Cam., letters to Oscar Browning • Swarthmore College, Swarthmore, Pennsylvania, Friends Historical Library, letters to Jane Addams

Likenesses G. F. Watts, oils, 1887, NPG • Elliott & Fry, photograph, *c.*1905, NPG; *see illus. in* Barnett, Dame Henrietta Octavia Weston (1851–1936) • F. Dodd, chalk drawing, 1906–13, NPG • H. von Herkomer, double portrait, oils, 1908 (with Henrietta Barnett) • F. Dodd, etching, BM • G. Frampton, sculpture, Westminster Abbey, London

Wealth at death £10,580 4*s.* 10*d.*: probate, 7 Oct 1913, *CGPLA Eng. & Wales*

Barnewall, Anthony (1721–1739), army officer in the Austrian service, was the sixth child and youngest son of John Barnewall, styled eleventh Baron Trimleston (1672–1746), and his wife, Mary (or Margaret; *d.* 1771), the daughter of Sir John Barnewall, kt, of Ballybrittan, King's county. His uncle Matthias Barnewall, tenth Baron Trimleston, served with James II's army in Ireland and was promoted to colonel of a regiment of foot after the battle of the Boyne. Later he joined the French service as a lieutenant with the duke of Berwick's 1st troop of Horse Guards. He died in the successful charge of his regiment against the Germans at Roumont in Flanders on 8 September 1692. His peerage and estates were forfeited though the latter were recovered by Anthony's father, John, before 9 May 1695. The protestant ascendancy induced many younger sons of the Catholic aristocracy in Ireland to seek military service abroad, and in 1738 at the age of seventeen, Anthony joined General Hamilton's regiment of cuirassiers in the Austrian service. 'His good sense, humility, good nature, and truly honest worthy principles, gained him the love and esteem of all who had the least acquaintance with him' (Lodge, 5.43). He served in all the major actions against the Turks, and he fell a victim to his headlong bravery in the stubborn battle of Krotzka in September 1739, when the Austrians were defeated by the Turks. Barnewall had been promoted to the rank of lieutenant only the day before. His regiment was one of the first that charged the enemy, and, the captain and cornet being killed at the first onset, Barnewall took command and led a series of charges. Having been repulsed twice, he turned to his men with the words, 'Come on, my brave fellows! we shall certainly do the work now' (ibid.), and for the third time he led his men forward. However, he was surrounded and fell, covered with wounds.

ROBERT HARRISON, *rev.* JONATHAN SPAIN

Sources Burke, *Peerage* (1970) • GEC, *Peerage* • J. G. Simms, 'The Irish on the continent, 1691–1800', *A new history of Ireland*, ed. T. W. Moody and others, 4: *Eighteenth-century Ireland, 1691–1800* (1986), 629–56, esp. 640 • J. Lodge, *The peerage of Ireland*, rev. M. Archdall, rev. edn, 5 (1789), 43

Barnewall, John, **third Baron Trimleston** (1470–1538), administrator, was the son and heir of Christopher Barnewall, second Baron Trimleston, and his first wife, Elizabeth, daughter of Sir Thomas Plunket of Rathmore, co. Meath. In 1504 John was the king's attorney and was appointed the king's serjeant-at-law. Early in Henry VIII's reign he was appointed second justice of the king's bench. In 1520 he presided at the negotiation of a truce between the earls of Ormond and Desmond at Waterford. Between 1524 and 1529 he served as under-treasurer. He married four times; his first wife was Janet or Genet, daughter of John Bellew of Bellewstown, co. Meath, and his second was Margaret, daughter of Patrick Fitzleons. His son and heir, Patrick Barnewall, fourth Baron Trimleston, was the only son from his first marriage. He and his second wife had four sons and two daughters. The names of his third and fourth wives are unknown and there were no children from these marriages.

Trimleston was appointed lord chancellor of Ireland on 16 August 1534, and in November attended Lord Deputy Skeffington at the defeat of Thomas, Lord Offaly, at Trim, co. Meath. In March 1535 he participated in the siege and capture of Maynooth Castle. In May he was required to answer allegations that he instructed a sergeant to surrender Dublin Castle to Lord Offaly. In August he delivered the great seal to John Alen and was summoned to the court. Upon his return he resumed his position as chancellor which he held uninterrupted until his death. In June 1536 he campaigned to vindicate Lord Deputy Grey from calumnious reports circulated about him, and in July and August he accompanied Grey on a campaign in Limerick against O'Brien and Fitzjohn of Desmond. In 1537 he was praised as being 'wise in council' (*LP Henry VIII*, vol. 12, pt 1, no. 1066). In May and June that year he campaigned against Brian O'Connor in Offaly and in summer was dispatched by Grey to negotiate with O'Neill near Dundalk. Along with his nephew, Patrick Barnewall, he was opposed to the bill for the suppression of the monasteries tabled in the Reformation Parliament. Trimleston died on 25 July 1538 and was described by Robert Cowley as having been 'ever a Geraldine' (*State Papers, Henry VIII*, 3.64).

Mary Ann Lyons

Sources *LP Henry VIII*, 7, no. 1068; 8, no. 755; 10, no. 266; 12; 13/2, nos. 40, 66–7, 152, 196, 216 • *State papers published under … Henry VIII*, 11 vols. (1830–52), 2.19, 35, 206, 223–4, 268, 353, 435, 471, 524; 3.17, 19, 37–9, 64, 68, 71, 96, 98, 257 • J. S. Brewer and W. Bullen, eds., *Calendar of the Carew manuscripts*, 1: 1515–1574, PRO (1867), 66 • *CSP Ire.*, 1509–73, 19–20, 44, 509 • J. Morrin, ed., *Calendar of the patent and close rolls of chancery in Ireland, of the reigns of Henry VIII, Edward VI, Mary, and Elizabeth*, 1 (1861), 13 • J. Lodge, *The peerage of Ireland*, rev. M. Archdall, rev. edn, 5 (1789), 35–7 • S. G. Ellis, *Reform and revival: English government in Ireland, 1470–1534*, Royal Historical Society Studies in History, 47 (1986), 40, 45, 101, 190, 220, 222, 224 • T. W. Moody and others, eds., *A new history of Ireland*, 9: *Maps, genealogies, lists* (1984), 509, 514, 518, 523 • R. Lascelles, ed., *Liber munerum publicorum Hiberniae … or, The establishments of Ireland*, 2 vols. [1824–30], pts 1–2, pp. 13, 32; pt 3, p. 52 • GEC, *Peerage*, new edn, vol. 12/2 • J. O'Hart, *Irish pedigrees, or, The origin and stem of the Irish nation*, American edn, 1 (New York, 1915), 363 • J. L. J. Hughes, ed., *Patentee officers in Ireland, 1173–1826, including high sheriffs, 1661–1684 and 1761–1816*, IMC (1960), 7

Barnewall, Nicholas, first Viscount Barnewall of Kingsland (1592–1663), politician, was the eldest son of Sir Patrick *Barnewall (*d.* 1622) of Turvey, Gracedieu, and Fieldstown, co. Dublin, and Mary, daughter of Sir Nicholas *Bagenal, knight marshal of Ireland. By 1600 he was at Douai College in the Spanish Netherlands and entered Gray's Inn, London, on 15 August 1611. In 1617 he married Brigid (*d.* in or after 1661), widow of Rory O'Donnell, earl of Tyrconnell, and eldest daughter of Henry Fitzgerald, earl of Kildare, and Frances, second daughter of Charles Howard, earl of Nottingham. They had five sons and four daughters. As well as enjoying a substantial inheritance in the pale where he lived at Drimnagh, co. Dublin, he held over 2000 acres in Roscommon. After 1625 he was one of the principal Catholic spokesmen, sitting as MP for Dublin county in the parliaments of 1634–5 and 1640–41 where he was a prominent opponent of the government. From November 1640 to August 1641 he was in London as a member of the Irish House of Commons committee charged with pressing for constitutional reform.

When rebellion erupted in Ireland in November 1641 Barnewall was appointed governor of Dublin county with commission to raise 300 men to fight the rebels. Soon afterwards he travelled to London with the government's permission. Virtually all his relatives and political associates joined the rebellion and his sympathies clearly lay with the insurgents. None the less he never broke with the crown and his castle at Ballyloge, Roscommon, acted as a sanctuary for local protestants. The fact that the bulk of his lands were concentrated around Dublin and were vulnerable to government troops weighed heavily upon him. He may also have acted as an unofficial envoy for the moderate Catholics, being able both to lobby on their behalf and to provide them with intelligence from London.

Barnewall later settled in Wales before returning to Ireland in March 1644, where the Catholic confederates allowed him to draw rents from his lands in their territory. Generally he kept out of confederate politics but he was strongly royalist. He was said to be close to the queen, and his eldest son, Patrick, served as a colonel in the royalist army during the English civil war. Knighted at some point in the 1640s Barnewall was created baron of Turvey and Viscount Barnewall of Kingsland on 29 June 1646.

Following the Cromwellian conquest Barnewall's estates in Leinster were confiscated, although he retained his Roscommon lands, and he was imprisoned for a period in June 1654. He travelled to London in late 1656 to petition for restoration to his estates. The government conditionally exempted him but he failed to meet the prescribed conditions and forfeited his lands. In May 1660 he was in London as an agent for the Irish Catholics, awaiting the arrival of the newly restored Charles II. By the time of his death at Turvey, co. Dublin, on 20 August 1663 he had fully recovered his estates. He was buried at Lusk, co. Dublin, on 3 September. His third son, Henry, succeeded to the titles.

Terry Clavin

Sources *CSP Ire.*, 1625–32, 246; 1647–60, 540, 609–11; 1660–62, 59 • *CSP dom.*, 1598–1601, 496 • GEC, *Peerage*, 1.427–8 • J. Lodge, *The peerage of Ireland*, rev. M. Archdall, rev. edn, 5 (1789), 48–50 • *Report on the manuscripts of the earl of Egmont*, 2 vols. in 3, HMC, 63 (1905–9), vol. 1, pp. 310, 334, 542 • *Calendar of the manuscripts of the marquess of Ormonde*, new ser., 8 vols., HMC, 36 (1902–20), vol. 2, p. 83 • *Calendar of the Clarendon state papers preserved in the Bodleian Library*, 3: 1655–1657, ed. W. D. Macray (1876), 182, 219, 223 • Bodl. Oxf., MS Clarendon 30, fol. 626 • L. J. Arnold, *The Restoration land settlement in county Dublin, 1660–1688* (1993), 38, 113, 123 • M. Perceval-Maxwell, *The outbreak of the Irish rebellion of 1641* (1994), 75, 140–41 • B. McGrath, 'A biographical dictionary of the membership of the Irish House of Commons, 1640–41', 2 vols., PhD diss., TCD, 1997, 52–4

Barnewall, Nicholas, third Viscount Barnewall of Kingsland (1668–1725), politician and army officer, was born on 15 April 1668, probably at the family seat, Turvey, in the parish of Donabate, co. Dublin, the son of Henry Barnewall, second Viscount Barnewall of Kingsland (*d.* 1688), and his wife, Mary (1648–1680), daughter of Richard Nugent, second earl of Westmeath. The family were landlords of a modest estate of about 5000 acres in north co. Dublin and in various parts of co. Meath. Owing to his father's illness and incapacity Nicholas was put in the guardianship of his maternal uncle Thomas *Nugent, later Baron Nugent of Riverston (*d.* 1715), a distinguished lawyer who became Irish chief justice and who also married Barnewall's half-sister. He was educated most probably by private tutors.

While Barnewall was still under age his guardian arranged a match for him with Mary Hamilton (*d.* 1736), who was born in France, the third and youngest daughter of Sir George Hamilton, Count Hamilton, an army general in France, and Frances Jennings, who married, secondly, Richard Talbot, duke of Tyrconnell, James II's lord deputy in Ireland. Barnewall succeeded to the title and an estate worth £3500 a year on the death of his father on 1 June 1688, having married Mary Hamilton on 15 May. Around the same time he joined Tyrconnell's remodelled and Catholic-dominated Irish army as a captain in Lord Limerick's dragoons. He took his seat in the Irish House of Lords in the parliament summoned by James II in Dublin in May 1689. For his part on the Jacobite side in the subsequent war he was outlawed. However, under the treaty of Limerick which ended the conflict he was in a position to have his outlawry reversed and to be restored to his estates.

Barnewall was summoned to William III's first Irish parliament in 1692. While he could agree to take the oath of allegiance to the king, he refused, as a Catholic, to take the further oath denying the pope's spiritual authority and to make the declaration against transubstantiation and accordingly was prevented from taking his seat in the House of Lords. When the bill to prevent the further growth of popery, the most rigorous and far-reaching of the penal statutes, was going through the Irish parliament in 1703–4 Barnewall together with other Catholic gentry succeeded in having the case against the bill argued by counsel at the bar of both houses. But the eloquence of eminent counsel simply fell on deaf ears.

Barnewall next figures in lists issued in 1705 and 1714 of Catholic nobility and gentry licensed to carry arms. This was a derogation on the penal statute which prevented Catholics from carrying arms. On the summoning of a new parliament in 1715 following the accession of George I, Barnewall and some other Catholic peers were summoned before the Irish House of Lords, but they again refused to take any oath other than the oath of allegiance and had to withdraw.

Barnewall died on 14 June 1725, probably at Turvey, and was buried on 16 June at Lusk churchyard, co. Dublin, near the family seat at Turvey. An elegy by 'R. V.' written on his death and published in Dublin in 1725, emphasized his kind treatment of his tenants. He was survived by his wife, who died at Turvey on 15 February 1736 and was buried with him, and their son Henry Benedict Barnewall, fourth Viscount Barnewall of Kingsland (1708–1774).

PATRICK FAGAN

Sources J. Lodge, *The peerage of Ireland*, rev. M. Archdall, rev. edn, 5 (1789), 48 · GEC, *Peerage*, new edn · R. C. Simington, *The civil survey*, 10 vols. (1931–61), vols. 5, 7 · *Calendar of the manuscripts of the marquess of Ormonde*, new ser., 8 vols., HMC, 36 (1902–20), vol. 2, p. 475 · *Journals of the House of Lords of the kingdom of Ireland*, 8 vols. (1783–1800), vol. 2 · *DNB* · C. C. Trench, *Grace's card: Irish Catholic landlords, 1690–1800* (1997)

Wealth at death landed estate valued at approx. £3500 p.a.: GEC, *Peerage*, 1, col. 428

Barnewall, Sir Patrick (*d.* 1622), landowner, was the eldest son of Sir Christopher Barnewall of Turvey, Gracedieu, and Fieldstown, and Marion, daughter of Patrick Sherle (Cherle) of Shallon, co. Meath. The grandson of Sir Patrick Barnewall, solicitor-general of Ireland, he inherited in 1575 the greatest patrimony in the pale comprising extensive holdings in Dublin, co. Louth, and co. Meath, including former monastic lands. None the less his family remained staunchly Catholic and Patrick's education in Spanish territory, probably the Spanish Netherlands, drew official distrust. He may also have had some legal training at the inns of court in London, but does not appear to have practised law. Strongly suspected of involvement in the pro-Catholic Baltinglass revolt of 1580 he was implicated in the importation of Catholic literature in 1581 and allowed his houses to be used to celebrate mass. His decision in 1582 to take an English wife, Mary, daughter of Sir Nicholas *Bagenal (*d.* 1590/91), knight marshal of Ireland, momentarily reassured the authorities of his loyalty and he was knighted in Dublin on 28 February 1588. However, generally he had an acrimonious relationship with the Dublin administration, particularly with Lord Chancellor Loftus.

For a period Barnewall was brother-in-law to Hugh O'Neill, earl of Tyrone, who eloped with his wife's sister from his house at Turvey, co. Dublin, in October 1591. In late 1593 he campaigned with royal troops alongside Tyrone in co. Monaghan. Within a year the earl's decision to go into rebellion made this association deeply embarrassing. Although Barnewall remained loyal to the crown during the campaign against Tyrone (1594–1603), sending military advice and intelligence to London, his criticism of the government's conduct of the war earned him a summons to court in April 1597. In June 1600 he was one of the agents sent to London to complain against the abuses committed by the royal army billeted on the pale. This mission marks his emergence as one of the chief spokesmen for the Old English Catholics. While he was warmly received by the queen his attempts to be given a command in the army and made a member of the Irish privy council were rebuffed.

After 1603 peace allowed Barnewall to buy land in co. Longford where he had a house at Ballyleg. Conversely it also meant that the government no longer needed to humour Old English sensibilities. In November 1605 a proclamation was issued ordering sixteen prominent Dublin Catholics to attend protestant church services or face prosecution in the court of castle chamber. Barnewall and his supporters framed a petition signed by the most influential of the pale gentry arguing, correctly, that such proceedings were illegal. When brought before Lord Deputy Chichester his defiance infuriated the governor, who imprisoned him in Dublin Castle on 2 December. The controversy developed into a crucial trial of strength between the Catholics and the government. When the king ordered that Barnewall be sent to London, supporters organized collections on his behalf in Munster and the pale. Upon arriving in London in May 1606 he was sent to the Tower but this was purely to save face for Chichester, who was ordered to end his anti-recusancy measures. He was released in December, returning proud and unrepentant to Dublin in March 1607.

In May 1613 Barnewall was summoned to London to prevent him from sitting in the upcoming Irish parliament. The pretext was a private letter of his, which had fallen into official hands, alleging that the parliament was to be packed with government supporters. In the event the Catholic MPs boycotted parliament and sent a delegation to London in July to which Barnewall, already there, was added. On 23 July he apologized before the king, retracting the allegations in his letter. He played a minor role in the ensuing negotiations and appears to have been under house arrest in London until shortly after July 1614. He died on 11 January 1622 and was buried at Lusk, co. Dublin. He had four daughters and one son, his successor, Nicholas *Barnewall, first Viscount Barnewall of Kingsland.

TERRY CLAVIN

Sources *CSP Ire.*, *1574–97*; *1600–01*; *1603–8*; *1611–14* • *CSP dom.*, *1598–1601*, 496 • *APC*, *1595–6*, 117; *1597*, 21; *1598–9*, 509, 516; *1613–14*, 27, 152, 499 • J. Lodge, *The peerage of Ireland*, rev. M. Archdall, rev. edn, 5 (1789), 46–8 • J. Kingston, 'Catholic families of the Pale', *Reportorium Novum*, 1/2 (1956), 336–41 • J. McCavitt, *Sir Arthur Chichester* (1998), 113, 117–19, 122–3, 131, 133, 228–9 • W. Medcalfe, *A book of knights* (1885), 208 • J. Morrin, ed., *Calendar of the patent and close rolls of chancery in Ireland, of the reigns of Henry VIII, Edward VI, Mary, and Elizabeth*, 2 (1862), 34, 100, 117 • *Calendar of the manuscripts of the most hon. the marquis of Salisbury*, 24 vols., HMC, 9 (1883–1976), vol. 18, pp. 361–2; vol. 24, pp. 97–8 • D. Creegan, 'Irish recusant lawyers in politics in the reign of James I', *Irish Jurist*, new ser., 5 (1970), 306–20 • H. Pawlisch, *Sir John Davies and the conquest of Ireland* (1985), 110–13

Barnewall, Richard Vaughan (1779/80–1842), barrister, was the fourth son of Robert Barnewall of London, merchant, and Sophia, daughter of Captain Silvester Barnewall (uncle of Robert Barnewall). His father was said to have been lineally descended from Sir Nicholas Barnewall, created in 1461 chief justice of the common pleas in Ireland. The baronies of Trimleston and Kingsland were held by different members of the family. A Roman Catholic throughout his life, Barnewall began his education at Stonyhurst College in 1794, and completed it at the University of Edinburgh. He was called to the bar at the Inner Temple in 1806, having previously studied in the chambers of Richard Blick, a prominent special pleader. For some years he practised at the Surrey sessions and on the home circuit.

In 1817 Barnewall turned his attention to reporting in the court of king's bench, a task which occupied him until his retirement in 1834. In this work he was successively associated with Edward Hall Alderson, afterwards baron of the exchequer, between 1817 and 1822; Sir Cresswell Cresswell, afterwards justice of the common pleas, between 1822 and 1830; and John Leycester Adolphus, between 1830 and 1834. The reports, which cover the period 1818–34, are notable for the care and accuracy with which they record judicial decisions.

In 1834, having succeeded to some property on the death of his relative, the baroness de Montesquieu, Barnewall retired from active life; he received a silver vase from the bar, and a testimonial from the bench in recognition of his achievement. Barnewall, who never married, died at his chambers at 13 King's Bench Walk in the Temple on 29 January 1842. He was buried in Paddington churchyard.

J. M. RIGG, *rev.* JONATHAN HARRIS

Sources *Annual Register* (1842), 247–8 • *GM*, 2nd ser., 17 (1842), 331–2 • *Stonyhurst Magazine*, 20/285 (Feb 1930), 447 • Burke, *Peerage* • B. Burke, *A genealogical history of the dormant, abeyant, forfeited and extinct peerages of the British empire*, new edn (1883), 23–4 • J. Lodge, *The peerage of Ireland*, 2 (1754), 45–55 • C. R. Dodd, *The annual biography: being lives of eminent or remarkable persons, who have died within the year MDCCCXLII* (1843), 34–7

Barnewall, Robert, styled twelfth Baron Trimleston (*c.*1704–1779), landowner and Roman Catholic activist, was the eldest son of John Barnewall, styled eleventh Baron Trimleston (1672–1746), and his wife, Mary, or Margaret (*d.* 1771), daughter and heir of Sir John Barnewall. Descended from an Anglo-Norman family whose estates in the counties of Meath and Dublin had been extensive, the Barnewalls had by the mid-seventeenth century begun to suffer the consequences of being prominent Roman Catholics. In 1652 the eighth Baron Trimleston was attainted and the family had its lands restored only by the Act of Settlement. The estates were again placed in jeopardy when Robert's uncle, the tenth baron, fought on the side of James II, eventually being killed in 1692. His successor, Robert's father, managed by application to the court of claims to rescue part of the estate. Robert, as a member of a proscribed religion, inherited a title which had no legal recognition; but this seems not to have dampened his aristocratic demeanour or way of life. One of three brothers, Robert was educated privately and spent much of his earlier life travelling abroad, occupying himself with the study of botany and physic. He married three times: first Margaret (*d.* *c.*1740), daughter of James Rochfort, of Laragh, co. Kildare, and later, in or before 1757, Elizabeth, daughter of John Colt, of Brightlingsea, and Elizabeth Man, of Tooting. His third wife was Anne (*d.* 1831), the fifth daughter of William Hervey, a merchant from London, and Elizabeth Barfoot.

By the time he returned to Ireland to succeed to the title in 1746, Barnewall was middle-aged. Visitors to the ancestral home, Trimleston Castle, remembered him for his hospitality, his style and superb taste, and for his generosity to the local poor whose ailments he treated without charge. During his time at Trimleston an aviary and a notable greenhouse graced the estate. Much of the anti-Catholic legislation of the period was aimed at excluding Catholics from political power. Consequently such Catholic political activity as prevailed was directed primarily towards securing relief from those legal strictures. Until the mid-eighteenth century most tentative Catholic political gestures had been spearheaded by the remnants of the Roman Catholic gentry, a mantle of leadership which Trimleston believed he had inherited. One effect of the penal legislation, however, was to direct Catholic professional ambitions into commerce, and by the 1750s this had led to the growth of a strong Catholic merchant class—wealthy, politically ambitious, and rivalling the more traditional landed power base of the gentry class.

When in 1759 the Catholic merchants formed a representative committee to advance their aims, Trimleston led a general refusal by the gentry to participate, and proceeded to negotiate with the ruling ascendancy in person and largely without reference to the committee. His proposal to government in 1762 that Catholics be enlisted for military service came to nothing. Within a year he suffered the ultimate embarrassment when his son and heir, Thomas, conformed to the established church. Trimleston retired from politics only to re-emerge in 1775 in a further attempt to wrest control of the committee from its elected leaders. In June of that year he led a body of some sixty eminent merchants and tradesmen in a mass subscription to a contentious oath of allegiance which had already caused divisions in the Catholic community. Trimleston's action helped to resolve the controversy and soon the oath, a matter essential to those who hoped to benefit from future relief legislation, was being widely accepted by the Catholic laity. Trimleston, in all probability to the fury of the merchants who had largely guided the committee since the early 1760s, slid smoothly into the position of leader and principal spokesman. His method had not been altogether dissimilar from that used by him in 1762.

The committee which had taken place at the outset of the American War of Independence clearly had led to no resolution or agreement as to tactics at this critical juncture. Trimleston had seized the advantage created by the obvious policy vacuum. With a sizeable following, he revived his 1762 suggestion to government that the king's war effort might be swelled by Catholics. By this time, however, the intensity of Catholic pro-establishment fervour (the American revolutionaries had condemned the pro-Catholic Quebec Act of 1774) was such that it had aroused protestant resentment in Dublin, with consequent political difficulties for the government. Trimleston orchestrated the scaling-down of the enthusiasm so skilfully that he won the praise of the government and yet kept the trust of his followers in the committee whose financial support was ever essential. The likelihood that Trimleston was the leading light even among the committee's 'gentry' members is suggested by the fact that when he relinquished the leadership his place was retaken by the merchants he had once displaced. His last apparent act as leader was the placing of his name at the head of the signatories to the Catholic address of loyalty to the new viceroy in 1777. Age and growing infirmity doubtless prevented him from playing a significant part in the agitation for the Catholic relief measure of 1778. He died in Dublin on 6 December 1779, and was buried at Trimleston. Trimleston appears to have had four children, two of whom died very young; the surviving two sons were the heir, Thomas, and Mathias, both of whom conformed to the established church. GERARD O'BRIEN

Sources M. McGeehin, 'The activities and personnel of the general committee of the Catholics of Ireland, 1767–84', MA diss., University College Dublin, 1952 • *Eighth report*, 1, HMC, 7 (1907–9), x • M. O'Conor, *The history of the Irish Catholics from the settlement in 1691, with a view of the state of Ireland from the invasion of Henry II to the revolution* (1813) • T. Wyse, *Historical sketch of the late Catholic Association of Ireland*, 2 vols. (1829), vol. 1 • Burke, *Peerage* (1938) • R. Pococke, *A tour in Ireland in 1752*, ed. G. T. Stokes (1891) • J. O'Keeffe, *Recollections of the life of John O'Keeffe, written by himself*, 2 vols. (1826) • R. L. Edgeworth and M. Edgeworth, *Memoirs of Richard Lovell Edgeworth*, 2 vols. (1820) • C. Maxwell, *Country and town in Ireland under the Georges* (1940) • *The letters of Charles O'Conor of Belanagare*, ed. C. C. Ward and R. E. Ward, 2 vols. (1980) • GEC, *Peerage* • T. Bartlett, *The fall and rise of the Irish nation: the Catholic question, 1690–1830* (1992)

Archives Royal Irish Acad., O'Conor MSS

PICTURE CREDITS

Awdry, Wilbert Vere (1911–1997)—© News International Newspapers Ltd

Ayer, Sir Alfred Jules [Freddie] (1910–1989)—© National Portrait Gallery, London

Aylmer, Sir Felix (1889–1979)—Garrick Club / the art archive

Ayrton, Acton Smee (1816–1886)—© National Portrait Gallery, London

Ayrton, Michael (1921–1975)—© Estate of Michael Ayrton; collection National Portrait Gallery, London

Ayrton, William Edward (1847–1908)—© National Portrait Gallery, London

Ayscough, Samuel (1745–1804)—© National Portrait Gallery, London

Ayscue, Sir George (*c*.1615–1672)—© National Maritime Museum, London, Greenwich Hospital Collection

Ayton, Sir Robert (1570–1638)—© Dean and Chapter of Westminster

Aytoun, William Edmonstoune (1813–1865)—Scottish National Portrait Gallery

Ayub Khan, Mohammad (1907–1974)—© reserved

Azariah, Vedanayagam Samuel (1874–1945)—© National Portrait Gallery, London

Azikiwe, Nnamdi [Zik] (1904–1996)—© News International Newspapers Ltd

Babbage, Charles (1791–1871)—© National Portrait Gallery, London

Babington, Gervase (1549/50–1610)—© National Portrait Gallery, London

Bach, Johann Christian (1735–1782)—© National Portrait Gallery, London

Bache, Samuel (1804–1876)—© National Portrait Gallery, London

Back, Sir George (1796–1878)—Howarth-Loomes Collection; photograph National Portrait Gallery, London

Backhouse, Robert Ormston (1854–1940)—Royal Horticultural Society, Lindley Library; photograph National Portrait Gallery, London

Backhouse, Sir Roger Roland Charles (1878–1939)—© National Portrait Gallery, London

Backwell, Edward (*c*.1619–1683)—© Copyright The British Museum

Bacon, Alice Martha, Baroness Bacon (1909–1993)—© Jorge Lewinski; collection National Portrait Gallery, London

Bacon [Cooke], Anne, Lady Bacon (*c*.1528–1610)—reproduced by permission of the Earl of Verulam. Photograph: Photographic Survey, Courtauld Institute of Art, London

Bacon, Francis, Viscount St Alban (1561–1626)—© The Royal Society

Bacon, Francis (1909–1992)—© John Hedgecoe; collection National Portrait Gallery, London

Bacon, Francis Thomas (1904–1992)—© National Portrait Gallery, London

Bacon, Sir Nathaniel (1585–1627)—reproduced by permission of the Earl of Verulam. Photograph: Photographic Survey, Courtauld Institute of Art, London

Bacon, Sir Nicholas (1510–1579)—© National Portrait Gallery, London

Bacon, Sir Reginald Hugh Spencer (1863–1947)—© private collection; photograph The Imperial War Museum, London

Baddeley, Hermione Youlanda Ruby Clinton (1906–1986)—© National Portrait Gallery, London

Baddeley, Sophia (1745?–1786)—Garrick Club; the art archive

Badel, Alan Fernand (1923–1982)—© Vivienne; collection National Portrait Gallery, London

Bader, Sir Douglas Robert Steuart (1910–1982)—© National Portrait Gallery, London

Baen, Jan de (1633–1702)—Collection Museum Bredius, The Hague

Bagehot, Walter (1826–1877)—© National Portrait Gallery, London

Bagford, John (1650/51–1716)—© National Portrait Gallery, London

Bagot, Lewis (1740–1802)—Christ Church, Oxford

Bagot, Richard (1782–1854)—The Dean and Chapter of Canterbury, photograph Mike Waterman

Bagot, Sir William (*d*. 1407)—reproduced by courtesy of H. M. Stutchfield, F.S.A., Hon. Secretary of the Monumental Brass Society

Bailey, Sir Donald Coleman (1901–1985)—© National Portrait Gallery, London

Bailey, Sir Harold Walter (1899–1996)—© reserved / The President and Fellows of Queens' College, Cambridge

Bailey, John (1644–1697)—courtesy of the Massachusetts Historical Society

Bailey, Philip James (1816–1902)—© National Portrait Gallery, London

Baillie, Alexander Dundas Ross Cochrane-Wishart-, first Baron Lamington (1816–1890)—© National Portrait Gallery, London

Baillie, George, of Jerviswood (1664–1738)—in a private Scottish collection

Baillie, Lady Grisell (1822–1891)—© National Portrait Gallery, London

Baillie, Dame Isobel (1895–1983)—© National Portrait Gallery, London

Baillie, Joanna (1762–1851)—© Copyright The British Museum

Baillie, Matthew (1761–1823)—by permission of the Royal College of Physicians, London

Baillie, Robert, of Jerviswood (*d*. 1684)—in a private Scottish collection

Baillie, Thomas (*c*.1725–1802)—© National Maritime Museum, London, Greenwich Hospital Collection

Baily, Francis (1774–1844)—© National Portrait Gallery, London

Bain, Alexander (1810–1877)—Science & Society Picture Library

Bain, Alexander (1818–1903)—© National Portrait Gallery, London

Baines, Edward (1774–1848)—© National Portrait Gallery, London

Baines, Peter [Augustine] (1786–1843)—© National Portrait Gallery, London

Baines, Thomas (1806–1881)—© National Portrait Gallery, London

Baines, (John) Thomas (1820–1875)—The Royal Geographical Society, London

Baird, Sir David, first baronet (1757–1829)—© National Portrait Gallery, London

Baird, John Logie (1888–1946)—© National Portrait Gallery, London

Bairnsfather, (Charles) Bruce (1887–1959)—Getty Images – Hulton Archive

Baker, David (1575–1641)—© National Portrait Gallery, London

Baker, Florence Barbara Maria, Lady Baker (1841–1916)—© National Portrait Gallery, London

Baker, Sir Geoffrey Harding (1912–1980)—© National Portrait Gallery, London

Baker, Sir George, first baronet (*bap.* 1723, *d.* 1809)—by permission of the Royal College of Physicians, London

Baker, Henry (1698–1774)—© National Portrait Gallery, London

Baker, Henry Frederick (1866–1956)—© National Portrait Gallery, London

Baker, Sir Herbert (1862–1946)—© National Portrait Gallery, London

Baker, Kenneth (1921–1999)—© News International Newspapers Ltd

Baker, Philip John Noel-, Baron Noel-Baker (1889–1982)—© National Portrait Gallery, London

Baker, Sir Samuel White (1821–1893)—© National Portrait Gallery, London

Baker, Sir (William) Stanley (1928–1976)—© Cornel Lucas; collection National Portrait Gallery, London

Baker, Valentine [Baker Pasha] (1827–1887)—© National Portrait Gallery, London

Bakewell, Robert (1725–1795)—© National Portrait Gallery, London

Balchen, Sir John (1670–1744)—© National Maritime Museum, London, Greenwich Hospital Collection

Balcon, Sir Michael Elias (1896–1977)—© National Portrait Gallery, London

Baldred (*fl. c*.823–827)—© Copyright The British Museum

Baldwin [of Forde] (*c*.1125–1190)—Master and Fellows of Corpus Christi College, Cambridge

Baldwin, Alfred (1841–1908)—© National Portrait Gallery, London

Baldwin, George (1744–1826)—© National Portrait Gallery, London

Baldwin, Richard (*c*.1666–1758)—by kind permission of the Board of Trinity College Dublin

Baldwin, Robert (1804–1858)—© National Portrait Gallery, London

Baldwin, Stanley, first Earl Baldwin of Bewdley (1867–1947)—© National Portrait Gallery, London

Balfe, Michael William (1808–1870)—© National Portrait Gallery, London

Balfour, Arthur, first Baron Riverdale (1873–1957)—© reserved; collection National Portrait Gallery, London

Balfour, Arthur James, first earl of Balfour (1848–1930)—© National Portrait Gallery, London

Balfour, Lady Evelyn Barbara (1898–1990)—© National Portrait Gallery, London

Balfour, Lady Frances (1858–1931)—© National Portrait Gallery, London

Balfour, George William (1823–1903)—Royal College of Physicians of Edinburgh

Balfour, Henry (1863–1939)—© National Portrait Gallery, London

Balfour, Sir James, of Denmiln and Kinnaird, first baronet (1603/4–1657)—Scottish National Portrait Gallery

Balfour, John Hutton (1808–1884)—© National Portrait Gallery, London

Balint, Michael Maurice (1896–1970)—private collection

Ball, Albert (1896–1917)—The Imperial War Museum, London

Ball, Sir Alexander John (1756–1809)—© National Portrait Gallery, London

Ball, John (*d*. 1381)—The British Library

Ball, John (1818–1889)—© Royal Botanic Gardens, Kew: reproduced by kind permission of the Director and the Board of Trustees

Ball, John Thomas (1815–1898)—© National Portrait Gallery, London

Ballance, John (1839–1893)—Alexander Turnbull Library, National Library of New Zealand, Te Puna Matauranga o Aotearoa / Tesla Studios Collection (G-70344-1/2)

Ballantine, William (1812–1887)—© National Portrait Gallery, London

Ballantyne, James (1772–1833)—National Gallery of Scotland

Ballantyne, John (1774–1821)—Scottish National Portrait Gallery

Ballantyne, John (1815–1897)—in the collection of the Royal Scottish Academy

Ballantyne, Robert Michael (1825–1894)—© National Portrait Gallery, London

Ballingall, Sir George (1780–1855)—Wellcome Library, London

Balliol, Edward (*b*. in or after 1281, *d*. 1364)—The British Library

Baly, Monica Eileen (1914–1998)—© reserved / News International Syndication; photograph National Portrait Gallery, London

Bancroft, Edward (1744–1821)—© Copyright The British Museum

Bancroft, Ian Powell, Baron Bancroft (1922–1996)—Getty Images – Hulton Archive

Bancroft, John (1574–1641)—University College, Oxford; photograph: The

Paul Mellon Centre for Studies in British Art

Bancroft, Marie Effie, Lady Bancroft (1839–1921)—© National Portrait Gallery, London

Bancroft, Richard (*bap.* 1544, *d.* 1610)—private collection. Photograph: Photographic Survey, Courtauld Institute of Art, London

Banda, Hastings Kamuzu (*c.*1898–1997)—© National Portrait Gallery, London

Bandaranaike, Solomon West Ridgeway Dias (1899–1959)—Getty Images - Kenneth J. Somanade

Bandinel, Bulkeley (1781–1861)—© National Portrait Gallery, London

Banerjea [Bandyopadhyay], Sir Surendranath (1848–1925)—© reserved

Banister, Richard (*c.*1570–1626)—reproduced by kind permission of the President and Council of the Royal College of Surgeons of London

Bankes, William John (1786–1855)—Kingston Lacy, The Bankes Collection (The National Trust). Photograph: Photographic Survey, Courtauld Institute of Art, London

Banks, Sir Joseph, baronet (1743–1820)—© National Portrait Gallery, London

Banks, Sarah Sophia (1744–1818)—The Knatchbull Portrait Collection. Photograph: Photographic Survey, Courtauld Institute of Art, London

Bannatyne, Sir William Macleod, Lord Bannatyne (1744–1833)—Polesden Lacey (The National Trust) / NTPL / John Hammond

Bannerman, Helen Brodie Cowan (1862–1946)—by kind permission of Mrs Anne Fisher

Bannerman, Sir Henry Campbell- (1836–1908)—© National Portrait Gallery, London

Bannister, Elizabeth (1757–1849)—© National Portrait Gallery, London

Bantock, Sir Granville Ransome (1868–1946)—© Jenny Letton, administered by Composer Prints Ltd.; collection National Portrait Gallery, London

Barberi, Domenico Giovanni Luigi (1792–1849)—The Fathers of the Birmingham Oratory

Barbirolli, Sir John (1899–1970)—© National Portrait Gallery, London

Barbon, Praisegod (*c.*1598–1679/80)—© National Portrait Gallery, London

Barbour, Sir David Miller (1841–1928)—© National Portrait Gallery, London

Barclay, David (1729–1809)—© National Portrait Gallery, London

Barclay, John (1758–1826)—Scottish National Portrait Gallery

Barclay, Thomas (1792–1873)—© National Portrait Gallery, London

Barclay, Victor Robert (1911–1987)—© Terry Cryer; Val Wilmer Collection

Barclay, William (1546–1608)—© National Portrait Gallery, London

Barclay, William (1907–1978)—Paternoster Press / Authentic Media; photograph National Portrait Gallery, London

Barcroft, Sir Joseph (1872–1947)—© National Portrait Gallery, London

Bardsley, Sir James Lomax (1801–1876)—© National Portrait Gallery, London

Baretti, Giuseppe Marc'Antonio (1719–1789)—© reserved

Barham, Richard Harris (1788–1845)—© National Portrait Gallery, London

Baring, Alexander, first Baron Ashburton (1773–1848)—ING Bank, NV, London Branch

Baring, Evelyn, first earl of Cromer (1841–1917)—© National Portrait Gallery, London

Baring, Sir Francis, first baronet (1740–1810)—private collection. Photograph: Photographic Survey, Courtauld Institute of Art, London

Baring, Francis Thornhill, first Baron Northbrook (1796–1866)—© National Portrait Gallery, London

Baring, Harriet Mary, Lady Ashburton (1805–1857)—photograph © National Portrait Gallery, London

Baring, John, second Baron Revelstoke (1863–1929)—© National Portrait Gallery, London

Baring, Louisa Caroline, Lady Ashburton (1827–1903)—property of the Marquess of Northampton; Beedle & Cooper

Baring, Maurice (1874–1945)—© National Portrait Gallery, London

Baring, Thomas (1799–1873)—ING Bank, NV (London Branch). Photograph: Photographic Survey, Courtauld Institute of Art, London

Baring, Thomas George, first earl of Northbrook (1826–1904)—© National Portrait Gallery, London

Barker, Sir Ernest (1874–1960)—© National Portrait Gallery, London

Barker, Frederic (1808–1882)—by permission of the National Library of Australia PIC/5476

Barker, George Granville (1913–1991)—© The John Deakin Collection; collection National Portrait Gallery, London

Barker, Harley Granville Granville- (1877–1946)—© National Portrait Gallery, London

Barker, Sir Herbert Atkinson (1869–1950)—© National Portrait Gallery, London

Barker, Joseph (1806–1875)—© National Portrait Gallery, London

Barker, Nicholas John (1933–1997)—© News International Newspapers Ltd

Barker, Dame Sara Elizabeth (1904–1973)—by permission of the People's History Museum

Barker, Thomas (1767–1847)—Victoria Art Gallery, Bath, and North East Somerset Council; Bridgeman Art Library

Barkly, Sir Henry (1815–1898)—© National Portrait Gallery, London

Barley, Maurice Willmore (1909–1991)—York Archaeological Trust for Excavation and Research Ltd; photograph by Simon I. Hill

Barlow, Sir (James) Alan Noel, second baronet (1881–1968)—© National Portrait Gallery, London

Barlow, Sir George Hilaro, first baronet (1763–1846)—© National Portrait Gallery, London

Barlow, Harold Everard Monteagle (1899–1989)—© National Portrait Gallery, London

Barlow, Peter (1776–1862)—© National Portrait Gallery, London

Barlow, Peter William (1809–1885)—Science & Society Picture Library

Barlow, Thomas (1608/9–1691)—© Bodleian Library, University of Oxford

Barlow, Sir Thomas, first baronet (1845–1945)—from the collection of the Athenaeum, London

Barlow, Sir Thomas Dalmahoy (1883–1964)—© National Portrait Gallery, London

Barlow, William Henry (1812–1902)—courtesy of the Institution of Civil Engineers Archives

Barnard, Sir John (*c.*1685–1764)—© National Portrait Gallery, London

Barnardo, Thomas John (1845–1905)—© National Portrait Gallery, London

Barnato, Barnett Isaacs (1852–1897)—© National Portrait Gallery, London

Barnes, Sir Edward (1776–1838)—V&A Images, The Victoria and Albert Museum

Barnes, Ernest William (1874–1953)—© National Portrait Gallery, London

Barnes, Frederick Jester (1885–1938)—V&A Images, The Victoria and Albert Museum

Barnes, Sir George Reginald (1904–1960)—© National Portrait Gallery, London

Barnes, Dame (Alice) Josephine Mary Taylor (1912–1999)—© Nick Sinclair; collection National Portrait Gallery, London

Barnes, Joshua (1654–1712)—Emmanuel College, Cambridge; photograph National Portrait Gallery, London

Barnes, Robert (1817–1907)—Wellcome Library, London

Barnes, Sydney Francis (1873–1967)—Getty Images - Hulton Archive

Barnes, William (1801–1886)—© National Portrait Gallery, London

Barnett, Curtis (*d.* 1746)—© National Maritime Museum, London

Barnett, Dame Henrietta Octavia Weston (1851–1936)—© National Portrait Gallery, London

Barnett, John (1802–1890)—© National Portrait Gallery, London